THE
GOOD
PUB
GUIDE

2017

D0976665

WYCHWOOD BREWERY
HOBGOBLIN
SINCE ★ 1983

I'm bringing taste to the nation with my Legendary Ruby & my Guilt Edged Golden Beer. So...

WYCH bREW arE YOU?

f hobgoblin beer @hobgoblin_beer

www.wychwood.co.uk

The Good Pub Guide 2017

Edited by Fiona Stapley

Associate Editor: Patrick Stapley
Managing Editor: Fiona Wright
Editorial Assistant: Sofia Hilton Rendall

Founded by Alisdair Aird in 1982

EBURY PRESS
LONDON

Please send reports on pubs to:

The Good Pub Guide
FREEPOST RTJR-ZCYZ-RJZT, Perrymans Lane, Etchingham TN19 7DN

or **feedback@goodguides.com**

or visit our website: **www.thegoodpubguide.co.uk**

If you would like to advertise in the next edition of *The Good Pub Guide*,
please email **goodpubguide@tbs-ltd.co.uk**

10 9 8 7 6 5 4 3 2 1

Published in 2016 by Ebury Press, an imprint of Ebury Publishing

Ebury Press, an imprint of Ebury Publishing
20 Vauxhall Bridge Road,
London, SW1V 2SA

Text © Ebury Publishing 2016
Maps © PerroGraphics 2016
Fiona Stapley has asserted her right to be identified as the author of this Work
in accordance with the Copyright, Designs and Patents Act 1988

www.eburypublishing.co.uk

Penguin
Random House
UK

Penguin Random House is committed to a sustainable future for
our business, our readers and our planet. This book is made from
Forest Stewardship Council® certified paper.

MIX
Paper from
responsible sources
FSC® C018179
www.fsc.org

To buy books by your favourite authors and register for offers,
visit www.penguin.co.uk

Typeset from authors' files by Jerry Goldie Graphic Design
Project manager and copy editor Cath Phillips
Proofreader Tamsin Shelton

Printed and bound in the UK by Clays Ltd, St Ives plc

ISBN 9781785033223

Contents

FIND YOUR MOUNTAIN

CONSISTENT GROWTH
CONSISTENTLY AWARD-WINNING

THIS UNIQUELY REFRESHING SESSION BEER, PACKED WITH FLAVOUR, HAS PICKED UP AWARDS FROM OUR PEERS AND RAVE REVIEWS FROM OUR CUSTOMERS EVER SINCE IT WAS LAUNCHED.

AND NOW, WITH A DYNAMIC NEW DESIGN AND RENEWED AMBITION, IT WILL CLIMB TO EVEN HEADIER HEIGHTS.

- MULTI AWARD-WINNING GOLDEN BEER
- #2 GOLDEN ALE FOR VALUE IN THE ON-TRADE*
- 2ND BEST SELLING GOLDEN CASK ALE*

SEARCH 'WAINWRIGHTGOLDENBEER' **f** 🐦 WWW.WAINWRIGHTGOLDENBEER.CO.UK

#FINDYOURMOUNTAIN

*CGA BRAND INDEX DATA 3/10/2015.

Introduction & The Good Pub Guide Awards 2017

Being social animals, we like meeting up with friends and enjoy mingling with other people in a relaxed and congenial atmosphere – and a good, well run pub is just the place to do this. But how do we feel if, in the background, there is constant music? Piped music, canned music, muzak, lift music, airport music – call it what you will, it's there. After badly behaved children in pubs, background music is the main source of complaints from our readers, and has been ever since we started the *Good Pub Guide* 35 years ago. It's such an issue that we have always asked every Main Entry pub since 1983 whether or not they have it, and then clearly state this in each review.

The sound of silence (or not)

Although today's sound systems are significantly better than the dreadful tinny noise we used to endure some years ago and the playlist companies have got more discerning in their choice of music, there are still bitter complaints from our readers. For example: 'At best, it's bad manners foisting a random choice of music on you that you have not chosen and do not want to hear; at worst, it interferes with people's hearing' and 'Somewhere in the past, someone has persuaded publicans that canned music relaxes customers and encourages them to spend more – people go to pubs to meet their friends, be sociable, have a drink or a meal and discuss the problems of the world.'

We asked some of our top licensees (many of whom own several pubs) for their thoughts on this thorny subject. They're at the top of their profession, having been at the helm of some of the best pubs in the country for many years, and they know the industry better than anyone else.

Not surprisingly, they have strong views. Many own country pubs that tend to be in lovely, centuries-old buildings, rich in character and heritage, and into which they've put enormous thought when it comes to décor and furnishings. The atmosphere is immediately informal and relaxing – often, the only sound you'll hear is the murmur of voices, laughter and the clinking of glasses. But while this is just what some of them aim for, an equal number feel that background music plays a large and positive part in their business. They don't use standard playlists and either rely on their own careful judgement or employ someone to help choose music for different times of day and to suit customers of differing ages. Their music systems tend to be zoned, so they can decide when and where to play it and at what volume. And if the pub is buzzing, they'll turn off the music altogether.

Some licensees run both country and town pubs and treat them quite differently when it comes to background music. They may avoid piped music in their country places, but use it in their urban venues. The buildings here can be grand, the customer base is different and the atmosphere more upbeat. As one explained: 'One of the immediate ways of setting the tone in a large town building is to have background music, which definitely gets round that awful feeling we've all experienced of being one of the first guests there. That hushed atmosphere and those whispered conversations do not make for an easy-going evening.'

But for members of the public who loathe background music in any shape or form, this is of little comfort – or interest. And while there may be publicans who have music that's been so individually chosen and reproduced so well that they feel it works subtly as a perfect part of the whole environment, there are thousands more that just use standard playlists (often left in the hands of young staff) on the assumption that it 'enhances the customer experience'.

In the end, it comes down to the question we've been asking for years. Do good pubs need piped music and do the majority of good pubs' customers want it? And hand on heart – of all the thousands of pubs we have visited over the many years of producing the *Good Pub Guide*, it's pretty rare (though it does happen) for us to feel our pub experience has been heightened by what is being played through speakers above our heads. Members of Pipedown (the organisation that campaigns for the freedom from all piped music in public places) are obviously fiercely against it – and we know we'll continue to receive vehement complaints on the subject. In all the decades of writing and editing the *Guide*, we can only remember one case of very mild disappointment (barely a complaint) from a reader about a pub because there *wasn't* background music.

The return of 'Mother's ruin'

For anyone involved in the UK gin industry, these are exciting times. According to the Wine and Spirit Trade Association (WSTA), sales of gin in the UK exceeded £900 million in 2015, are expected to reach £1 billion in 2016 and be worth £1.31 billion by 2020.

Gin was rather in the doldrums in the 1980s and '90s, when it was deemed to be a Home Counties older person's tipple. But that all changed seven years ago.

In the mid 18th century, London was swept by a gin craze, with small distilleries producing ten million gallons a year. Not surprisingly, this led to chronic health and crime problems (as depicted in Hogarth's *Gin Lane* illustrations) and gin production was restricted, with licences given only to industrial-scale distilleries. In 2009, after a two-year battle, would-be distiller Sipsmith successfully challenged HMRC's ban on boutique production and became the first company in London to be issued a licence since 1820. The gin revival had begun.

The number of distilleries licensed by Revenue & Customs rose to 233 by the end of 2015, with 49 new openings in that year alone. Numbers are still growing steadily with artisan outfits springing up across the UK that use increasingly exotic botanicals. All gins include juniper, but now ingredients encompass orange or lemon peel, dill, rose, angelica, cardamom, cinnamon, coriander and lemongrass – even liquorice, hops and honey. Each distiller has their own secret gin recipe to bring out the fruit or spice elements, and as a result, bartenders love using and experimenting with gin. They often choose unusual glass shapes for different gins, while garnishes can range from the usual lemon to watermelon, mint and other herbs, cucumber, pink grapefruit, apple, rhubarb and even samphire.

All this has piqued the interest of a younger crowd who are curious about the different styles and flavours. In the past 12 months, 42% of

British 18-34 year olds have drunk gin compared to 27% of those aged over 45. Nationwide, there are gin festivals, numerous 'Top Ten Gin' surveys by newspapers and magazines and, on 10 June 2017, World Gin Day will be holding its ninth event.

If you know little about gin, even wandering down the aisles of an average supermarket will open your eyes. If you want to learn more, many distilleries offer tours. You can see Sipsmith's three copper stills, Patience, Prudence and Constance (www.sipsmith.com); visit Bombay Sapphire's Laverstock Mill with its stunning contemporary glasshouses containing their botanicals (www.bombaysapphire.com); and tour Chase Distillery on the family farm in Herefordshire (http://chasedistillery.co.uk). You can even make your own gin at Adnams Copper House Distillery (www.tours.adnams.co.uk). But perhaps the most surprising place to find a distillery is in the Nicholas Culpeper pub at Gatwick Airport's North Terminal – the world's first airport gin distillery. It's before security, so you don't need a plane ticket to try it or to buy a bottle to take home.

This year while compiling the *Guide*, we found pubs throughout the UK offering an ever increasing number of interesting craft gins – but our winner has to be the **Cholmondeley Arms**, Cholmondeley, Cheshire, which stocks an incredible 366 different gins.

Drinks: the search for fair prices and top quality

Our national survey of beer prices shows a huge 87p-a-pint difference in the price of a pint of ale between Herefordshire, the cheapest area, and London, the most expensive. The average price for a pint of beer in Britain is now £3.47. How does your area rank? Here are the details, in average price order:

Bargain beer
Herefordshire, Yorkshire, Derbyshire, Cumbria, Worcestershire

Fair-priced beer
Wales, Cheshire, Northumbria, Lancashire, Shropshire, Northamptonshire, Leicestershire & Rutland, Dorset

Average-priced beer
Cornwall, Devon, Lincolnshire, Somerset, Nottinghamshire, Scotland, Gloucestershire, Wiltshire, Essex, Staffordshire, Bedfordshire, Cambridgeshire, Warwickshire, Suffolk, Norfolk, Hampshire

Expensive beer
Oxfordshire, Buckinghamshire, Isle of Wight, Hertfordshire, Sussex, Berkshire, Kent

Rip-off beer
Surrey, London

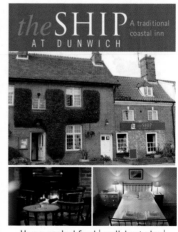

In what is the finest example of a Victorian tower brewery in the country and using water from deep wells underneath the building to brew their ales, Hook Norton in the Cotswold Hills started brewing commercially in 1856. An independent and passionate family business, they produce award-winning Hooky, Hooky Mild, Old Hooky, Lion and 14 seasonal beers which you'll find in their 38 pubs in and around Gloucestershire, Northamptonshire, Oxfordshire and Warwickshire. They still deliver the barrels to pubs within five miles of the brewery by shire horse-drawn drays. You can visit the brewery and join a two-hour tour – see www.hooky.co.uk. For their multi-award-winning beers, **Hook Norton** is our **Brewery of the Year 2017**.

This year's Top Ten Beer Pubs are spread all over the country and include the **Bhurtpore** at Aston and **Mill** in Chester (Cheshire), **Beer Hall at Hawkshead Brewery** in Staveley (Cumbria), **Tom Cobley** in Spreyton (Devon), **Fat Cat** in Norwich (Norfolk), **Malt Shovel** in Northampton (Northamptonshire), **Halfway House** in Pitney (Somerset), **Fat Cat** in Ipswich (Suffolk), **Nags Head** in Malvern (Worcestershire) and **Kelham Island** in Sheffield (Yorkshire). It would be pretty hard to beat knowledgeable and enthusiastic Colin Keatley's collection of 32 well kept ales, so the **Fat Cat** in Norwich is **Beer Pub of the Year 2017**.

You typically save yourself 48p a pint if you drink at one of the own-brew pubs in this edition. Our Top Ten Own-Brew pubs are the **Brewery Tap** in Peterborough (Cambridgeshire), **Brown Horse** in Winster and **Watermill** at Ings (Cumbria), **Old Poets Corner** at Ashover (Derbyshire), **Church Inn** at Uppermill (Lancashire), **Grainstore** in Oakham (Leicestershire & Rutland), **Dipton Mill Inn** at Diptonmill and **Ship** at Newton-by-the-Sea (Northumbria), **Gribble** at Oving (Sussex) and **Weighbridge Brewhouse** in Swindon (Wiltshire). For its ten excellent Watermill ales, the **Watermill** at Ings is our **Own-Brew Pub of the Year 2017**.

Wine in many pubs is now extraordinarily good with several even having their own little wine shop on the pub premises. Our Top Ten Wine Pubs are the **Old Bridge Hotel** in Huntingdon (Cambridgeshire), **Drunken Duck** near Hawkshead (Cumbria), **Nobody Inn** at Doddiscombsleigh (Devon), **Inn at Whitewell** at Whitewell (Lancashire), **George of Stamford** in Stamford (Leicestershire & Rutland), **Woods** in Dulverton (Somerset), **Crown** at Stoke-by-Nayland (Suffolk), **The Inn West End** at West End (Surrey), **Crown** at Roecliffe (Yorkshire) and **Griffin** at Felinfach (Wales). The exceptionally knowledgeable Patrick Groves reckons he could put 1,000 wines on his bar – and so **Woods** in Dulverton is our **Wine Pub of the Year 2017**.

You can be sure to find a fantastic range of malt whiskies in our Top Ten Whisky list: **Bhurtpore** in Aston (Cheshire), **Nobody Inn** at Doddiscombsleigh (Devon), **Bow Bar** in Edinburgh, **Bon Accord** in

BREWERY TOURS & VISITOR CENTRE

The Brewery Visitor Centre is a FREE self-guided exhibition which gives you an insight into the history and heritage of Wadworth & Co Ltd, as well as our traditional skills and crafts.

Open all year round from 9am - 5pm Monday to Saturday we offer award-winning tours at 11am & 2pm daily*. Tours include a visit to the Victorian Tower Brewery alongside our modern Brew House, our Sign Studio where all the pub signs are hand painted in the traditional way, plus a visit to our Shire Horses who deliver our beer locally - all finishing in The Harness Room Bar for a tutored beer tasting!

Brewery
Tours from
£9.00pp

*Advanced booking advised (fee applie

WADWORTH

Glasgow and **Sligachan Hotel** on the Isle of Skye (Scotland), **Acorn** in Evershot (Dorset), **Red Fox** in Thornton Hough and **Worsley Old Hall** in Worsley (Lancashire), **Black Jug** in Horsham (Sussex) and **Pack Horse** at Widdop (Yorkshire). The **Sligachan Hotel** on Skye, set amid stunning scenery and with a choice of over 400 whiskies, is **Whisky Pub of the Year 2017**.

Tim Bird and Mary McLaughlin founded Cheshire Cat Pubs and Bars (http://cheshirecatpubsandbars.co.uk) in 2008. Both have worked in the pub and restaurant trade for most of their lives (Tim was a former MD of Brunning & Price) and the pubs they own were all rescued from closure or near closure. They include the Cholmondeley Arms in Cholmondeley, Bulls Head, Church Inn and Roebuck (about to open as we went to press) all in Mobberley and Three Greyhounds Inn at Allostock (all to be found in Cheshire), as well as the Red Lion in Weymouth (Dorset) and Fitzherbert Arms on Lord Stafford's Estate in Swynnerton (Staffordshire). Each pub has a strong sense of individuality with interesting décor, a fine choice of drinks (80 malt whiskies in one, 80 rums in another and – as mentioned in our gin section earlier – 366 gins in the Cholmondeley Arms), rewarding food and an easy-going, gently civilised atmosphere. **Cheshire Cat Pubs & Bars** is our **Pub Group of the Year 2017**.

·PIPERS·
CRISP CO
— MADE BY FARMERS —

Great Crisps, Great Beer, Great Pub

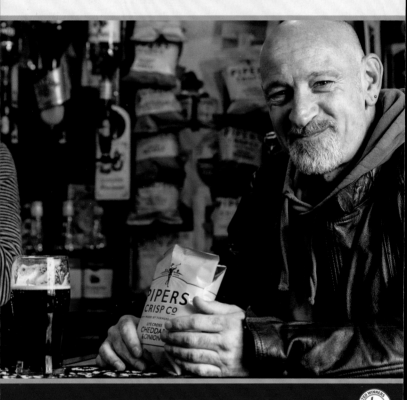

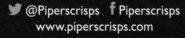

Town and country

Thanks to the dedication of landlords and landladies, there are still plenty of quite unspoilt and unpretentious pubs all around the country. Our Top Ten Unspoilt Pubs are the **White Lion** in Barthomley (Cheshire), **Barley Mow** at Kirk Ireton and **Olde Gate** in Brassington (Derbyshire), **Digby Tap** in Sherborne and **Square & Compasses** at Worth Matravers (Dorset), **Harrow** in Steep (Hampshire), **Three Horseshoes** in Warham (Norfolk), **Crown** in Churchill (Somerset), **White Horse** near Petersfield (Sussex) and **Birch Hall** at Beck Hole (Yorkshire). Built using timbers salvaged from Armada wrecks, the **Olde Gate** in Brassington is **Unspoilt Pub of the Year**.

Country pubs are just what many of our readers look for at weekends – particularly if they're away from home. With this in mind, our Top Ten Country Pubs are the **Crown & Garter** in Inkpen (Berkshire), **White Horse** in Hedgerley (Buckinghamshire), **Pheasant** in Burwardsley (Cheshire), **Rugglestone** near Widecombe (Devon), **Royal Oak** at Fritham (Hampshire), **Cottage of Content** in Carey (Herefordshire), **English Partridge** at Bighton (Sussex), **Malet Arms** at Newton Tony (Wiltshire), **Harp** at Old Radnor (Wales), and **Fleece** at Bretforton (Worcestershire). In a peaceful spot and once three labourers' cottages, the medieval **Cottage of Content** in Carey is our **Country Pub of the Year 2017**.

The Cock

Old Uckfield Road (A26), Near Ringmer, BN8 5RX

Food served 7 days a week lunchtime and evening and all day Sunday.

Large Garden and Sun Terrace
Log Fire in Winter
Roasts served all day Sunday
Open all day on Bank Holidays
Vegetarian Menu always available (5 choices)
Real Ales incl. Harveys and other locally sourced micro breweries
Home Cooked Food – something for every taste, diet and budget!

tel: 01273 812040
www.cockpub.co.uk

The Highlands Inn

Eastbourne Road, Ridgewood, Uckfield, TN22 5SP

Food served 7 days a week lunchtime and evening and all day Sunday until 6.30pm

Sports Bar showing all BT and Sky Sports fixtures with special Sports Bar menu
Formal Restaurant area with seating for 120 covers and separate Restaurant Bar Area
Real Ales incl. Harveys and other locally source micro breweries
Extensive selection of wines by the glass
Large Sun Trap Garden with al fresco Dining

tel: 01825 762989
www.highlandsinn.co.uk

If you're in a town or city, there's no place better than a good, well run pub to rest weary feet. Our Top Ten Town Pubs are the **Old Harkers Arms** in Chester (Cheshire), **Old Spot** in Dursley (Gloucestershire), **Wykeham Arms** in Winchester (Hampshire), **Wharf** in Manchester (Lancashire), **Bank House** in King's Lynn (Norfolk), **Perch** in Oxford (Oxfordshire), **Old Green Tree** in Bath (Somerset), **Old Joint Stock** in Birmingham (Warwickshire), **Kays Bar** in Edinburgh (Scotland) and **Olde Mitre** in central London. The stylish and handsome (it was Barclays bank's first opening) **Bank House** in King's Lynn, with its many bars for both eating and drinking and quayside seats, is **Town Pub of the Year 2017**.

One third of the Main Entries now holds one of our Stay Awards. The places mentioned here would make any weekend away very special: **New Inn** at Cerne Abbas (Dorset), **Kings Head** in Bledington (Gloucestershire), **Mill** at Gordleton at Hordle (Hampshire), **Bridge Inn** at Michaelchurch Escley (Herefordshire), **Inn at Whitewell** at Whitewell (Lancashire), **Lord Crewe Arms** at Blanchland (Northumbria), **Luttrell Arms** in Dunster (Somerset), **Red Lion** in East Chisenbury (Wiltshire), and **Angel** at Hetton and **Blue Lion** at East Witton (Yorkshire). Continuing enthusiasm from our readers and with open fires in some rooms, the elegant old manor house that is the **Inn at Whitewell** at Whitewell is our **Inn of the Year 2017**.

Food for thought

A total of 84 pubs in this edition hold one of our Value Awards, which means they have several interesting main dishes around the £10 mark – not easy to do given the rising costs of all raw materials. Our Top Ten Value pubs are the **Drake Manor** in Buckland Monachorum (Devon), **Digby Tap** in Sherborne (Dorset), **Red Lion** in Preston (Hertfordshire), **Church Inn** at Uppermill (Lancashire), **Queens Head** in Kirkby la Thorpe (Lincolnshire), **Old Castle** in Bridgnorth (Shropshire), **Halfway House** in Pitney (Somerset), **Bell** in Middleton (Suffolk), **Lamb** in Marlborough (Wiltshire) and **Crown & Trumpet** in Broadway (Worcestershire). For their interesting and very fair value lunchtime meals, the **Queens Head** in Kirkby la Thorpe is our **Value Pub of the Year 2017**.

Imaginative food using the best local, seasonal produce and cooked by chefs at the top of their game can be found in the **Pointer** at Brill (Buckinghamshire), **Cock** in Hemingford Grey (Cambridgeshire), **Treby Arms** in Sparkwell (Devon), **Wellington Arms** in Baughurst (Hampshire), **Stagg** at Titley (Herefordshire), **Assheton Arms** at Downham (Lancashire), **Red Lion** at East Chisenbury (Wiltshire), **Pipe & Glass** in South Dalton (Yorkshire), **Burts Hotel** in Melrose (Scotland) and **Griffin** in Felinfach (Wales). Britt and Guy Manning,

both stunning chefs, own and run the **Red Lion** at East Chisenbury – our **Dining Pub of the Year 2017**.

As ever, we're delighted with our new entries this year which range from unspoilt gems to smart dining pubs and are spread throughout the country. These include the **Winning Post** at Maidens Green (Berkshire), **Crown & Punchbowl** in Horningsea (Cambridgeshire), **Olde Gate** in Brassington (Derbyshire), **Victoria** in Salcombe (Devon), **Lion** in Winchcombe (Gloucestershire), **Verulam Arms** in St Albans (Hertfordshire), **Blacksmiths** in Clayworth (Nottinghamshire), **Fitzherbert Arms** in Swynnerton (Staffordshire), **White Hart** at South Harting (Sussex) and **Howard Arms** in Ilmington (Warwickshire). A historic former coaching inn, the restful and stylish **Lion** in Winchcombe is our **New Pub of the Year 2017**.

Whether you run a simple tavern or a stylish dining pub, the only way that place is going to be a roaring success is down to the hands-on landlord or landlady whose enthusiasm and sheer hard work bring it all together. Our Top Ten Licensees are **Philip and Lauren Davison** of the Fox in Peasemore (Berkshire), **Mary Short** of the Barley Mow in Kirk Ireton (Derbyshire), **Simon and Sally Jackson** of the Horse & Groom at Upper Oddington and **Kathryn Horton** of the Ostrich in Newland (Gloucestershire), **Tim Gray** of the Yew Tree in Lower Wield

(Hampshire), **Norman and Janet Whittall** of the Three Horseshoes at Little Cowarne (Herefordshire), **Patrick Groves** of Woods in Dulverton (Somerset), **Rob and Liz Allcock** of the Longs Arms in South Wraxall (Wiltshire), the **Mainey family** of the Crown in Roecliffe (Yorkshire) and **Judith Fish** of the Applecross Inn at Applecross (Scotland). Looking after her remote pub in its breathtaking position and offering a genuine welcome to her customers, who come from all over the world, **Judith Fish** of the Applecross Inn is our **Landlady of the Year 2017**.

The best of the best
There are so many wonderful pubs in Britain that to pick the absolute best is not an easy task – but high praise and enthusiasm on all aspects of certain pubs from our many readers helps enormously. Some, though, shine out so brightly that they easily make our Top Ten Pubs – listed below in county order. A 300-year-old inn with all the character that goes with great age but with inventive food, lovely service, cosy bedrooms and a lush garden, the **Horse Guards** in Tillington (Sussex) is our **Pub of the Year 2017**.

TOP TEN PUBS 2017
(in county order)

Bell in Horndon-on-the-Hill (Essex)

Horse & Groom in Bourton-on-the-Hill (Gloucestershire)

Wykeham Arms in Winchester (Hampshire)

Inn at Whitewell in Whitewell (Lancashire)

Rose & Crown in Snettisham (Norfolk)

Woods at Dulverton (Somerset)

Horse Guards in Tillington (Sussex)

Compasses in Chicksgrove (Wiltshire)

Blue Lion in East Witton (Yorkshire)

Pipe & Glass in South Dalton (Yorkshire)

Discover an Individual Inn...
...Individually Different

Individual Inns - Publican Awards Best Accommodation Operator 2014
Wheatsheaf Inn - Cumbrian Life - Food and Drink Pub 2015 & finalist 2016
Masons Arms - North West Pub of the Year 2012
Tempest Arms - UK Pub of the Year 2011

Exploring London's edgelands

By **Euan Ferguson**

Sometimes, even the most hardened of Londoners feel the city closing in. The traffic seems heavier, the buildings loom taller, the crowds get busier. We don't have to travel far for respite, though: towards the city's boundaries is a cornucopia of hills, fields, forests, lakes and even beaches, where without too much imagination we can feel as if we're somewhere far away from the heart of the metropolis.

And when we get out into those bucolic surroundings, there's no shortage of fine pubs. If you're heading into the outer boroughs for a stroll, a perambulation or a full-on hike, you won't have to look far to find a welcome halfway stop-off or an inn at which to finish. A walk in London's outskirts can be, in its own way, as restorative as a trip to the countryside proper, and all you really need to get there is an Oyster travelcard (or, occasionally, a car, if you have a responsible non-drinker on board).

The easiest way to travel is by tube. In the east, the Hainault loop of the Central line brings passengers tantalisingly close to London's edgelands, and those disembarking at Grange Hill station face only a short walk to Hainault Forest Country Park. A surviving pocket of the Forest of Essex, it's an evocatively ancient place and has a boating lake and a farm zoo. In Chigwell you'll find the **Two Brewers** (57 Lambourne Road, IG7 6ET), a cosy place with a real fire that services drinkers as much as diners – three cask ales, including one from a local brewery, are on tap.

One of London's great walks is to follow the Lea Valley from Limehouse all the way up to Waltham Abbey. This historic market town is outside the M25 so technically is in the county of Essex, but it's so close that it seems churlish to ignore it. The journey starts at Limehouse Basin by the Thames, and over a day's stroll the waterway slowly changes from a busy, urban, ex-industrial thoroughfare to a riparian idyll surrounded by nature, especially when it snakes through the Lea Valley Regional Park. You'll pass several great pubs on the way – if temptation takes over, there's the one-off **Palm Tree** in Mile End (see Also Worth a Visit London) or the **Anchor & Hope** (15 High Hill Ferry, E5 9HG) on the water in Clapton. If you hold out you can sit in the sun at the front of the timber-framed **Welsh Harp** in Waltham Abbey's Market Square, from where it's not too far to Waltham Cross station and a train back to the city.

For most Londoners, Cockfosters is the place where their Piccadilly line train ends up long after they've got off it. But staying on to the terminus will take you to the heart of Metroland, where everything is much greener: right next to Cockfosters station is Trent Country Park, which has miles of peaceful woodland walks, lakes, animals and a scheduled Ancient Monument in Camlet Moat. Mere metres away is the **Cock Inn** (Chalk Lane, EN4 9HU), a handsome 20th-century pub (with a big car park). Recently refurbished, it's now as much an eating destination as a drinking one, and roomy enough for everyone.

On the other side of London, as the capital peters out into the Colne Valley National Park then the Chilterns, the Metropolitan line offers fine opportunities for rambling and relaxing. Northmoor Hill, Horseshoe Bay, New Year's Green... They sound like far-flung parts of rural Britain, but all are in this area, which has countless walks around rolling escarpments, golf courses and commons. Not far from Eastcote tube is **The Case Is Altered** (see Also Worth a Visit London), a 17th-century pub

overlooking a cricket ground. There's good food and a few real ales, and if you're after some sedate exploration, historic Eastcote House has a walled garden and a wild meadow.

If you're heading westwards into Colne Valley, a good place to end a walk is the **Old Orchard** (see Main Entries London) in Harefield, which is maybe the closest thing London has to a proper country pub. The views it offers are stunning, so empty of human activity you'd think you were 200 miles from the city centre, not just 20. It's a pub with the generous sort of dimensions allowed by such a location, and also has a big green garden and a terrace. It's great for food too. Such splendid isolation means that explorers without their own transport may have to factor in getting back to a train station – it's about two-and-a-half miles to Denham.

A different train into the western suburbs will take you to Thames Ditton, and to two pubs that are worth visiting even without a walk in mind. The **Mute Swan** (see Main Entries London) and **Ye Olde Swan** (Summer Road, Thames Ditton KT7 0QQ) are a 20-minute walk apart and each have their own charms. The silent one is smart, foodie and well heeled (reflecting its location opposite Hampton Court Palace; the ancient one is pubbier, cosier and older – some parts date from the 13th century. Ye Olde Swan backs on to the Thames on a particularly pretty curve, while the Mute Swan is handy for a drink after sightseeing at Henry VIII's old pad. If you'd like some light exercise, both these anatine taverns are ideal for a loop round Bushy Park, London's second biggest royal park, with its vast open spaces, water gardens and ponds.

Further round the M25 is Chislehurst and its fascinating man-made caves. If you've never been out here, it's well worth it – they were originally hollowed out centuries ago for their chalk, but have been since used as an air raid shelter and for growing mushrooms. Above ground, there are pleasant walks around nearby Foots Cray Meadows and Scadbury Park Nature Reserve. The latter is a mile or so from the stately **Crown Inn** (see Also Worth a Visit London) in Chislehurst, which has tip-top beers from the Kentish brewer Shepherd Neame and even a few bedrooms, should your trip out of the city centre spill over into the next day.

Euan Ferguson is a freelance writer and was the principal bars and pubs writer for Time Out London for six years. He's the author of *Drink London: The 100 Best Bars and Pubs* (Frances Lincoln, 2014) and *Craft Brew: 50 Homebrew Recipes from the World's Best Craft Breweries* (Frances Lincoln, 2016).
Favourite pub Wenlock Arms, Hoxton, London N1.

Hotting up

By **Neil Rankin**

While craft beer is trending, our love for ale seems to be waning: this once-proud nation of beer guzzlers is being slowly driven out by picpoul de pinet quaffers. Germany drinks roughly double the amount of beer per head compared to the UK, while in the Czech Republic they drink almost three times as much. But even if you're not from Germany, the Czech Republic or, like me, are one of the few remaining Brits who still enjoys drinking the stuff, you'll enjoy this recipe – where you cook with it instead.

Porter and scotch bonnet chilli con carne

INGREDIENTS

500g cubed chuck steak

500ml chicken stock

1 onion, sliced

200g chopped tomatoes

1 bottle Pressure Drop Stokey Brown porter

handful of coriander, roughly chopped

2 tbsp chilli paste, made from:
  1 tbsp coriander seeds
  $1/2$ tbsp cumin seeds
  1 tbsp dried oregano
  1 tbsp cracked black pepper
  1 tbsp chopped dried ancho chilli
  1 jalapeño chilli
  $1/2$ tbsp cayenne pepper
  2 scotch bonnet chillies
  1 tbsp minced garlic
  1 tbsp soft light brown sugar

Serves: 3-4
Preparation time: 15 minutes
Cooking time: $2^1/_2$ hours

This recipe is similar to a Texan-style chilli. Ancho chilli is not vital, but scotch bonnets are integral to this recipe, as they carry so much more flavour than a standard chilli. If you're not a hot-food person, reduce the amount you use.

- Start with the chilli paste. Mix all the ingredients together with a pestle or a blender. Get a saucepan hot on the stove and brown the beef chunks by putting them in a few at a time. Don't worry too much about getting every side dark. Leave for a while on one side to get maximum colour, then remove and start a new batch.

- Once browned, add the stock until the meat is fully covered. Place a lid on top, leaving a small air hole, and simmer for 2 hours. Don't pull the meat apart, or it will lose texture.

- Once cooked, drain the meat and put it to one side. Pour the remaining stock into a container.

- Fry the onion in the same saucepan with a little oil until it begins to colour; then add the chilli paste and cook for another minute. Add the tomatoes, the remaining stock and the beer, and reduce by at least half. Put the meat back into the pan and cook until you have a good consistency. Season to taste with salt and add the chopped coriander.

- Serve with warm flour tortillas with a little sour cream, or top with sour cream and some puffy crisps.

Neil Rankin started his career in Michelin-level fine dining before discovering his love for meat and fire while working for BBQ guru Adam Perry Lang. Neil went on to open Pitt Cue Company, relaunch John Salt, and then open two Smokehouse restaurants with Noble Inns (all in London). He is now embarking on his first solo project (opening in central London later in 2016) and has just published a meat bible called *Low and Slow – How to cook meat* (Ebury, 2016).
Favourite pub Drapers Arms, 44 Barnsbury Street, London N1.

The In-Cider Scoop

By **Gabe Cook**

Yｏu need to have been living on a desert island for the last ten years not to notice the incredible renaissance that cider has undergone, both globally and here in the UK. Catalysed by the so-called Magner's effect, cider (once derided as the tipple du jour for the park bench regular) quickly became the 'new' alternative to beer and wine, and the fastest-growing alcoholic drink sector in the country.

However, in recent years, it's the introduction of fruit to cider that has become increasingly popular. These varieties tend to be tooth-achingly sweet and highly aromatised, veering far too close to the alcopops of the 1990s or the pre-mixed products you can buy these days, and ever more removed from the indigenous traditions, heritage and culture of cider making.

Thankfully, there are hundreds of artisan producers of apple cider (or as I like to call it, 'cider'), producing a dazzling array of the stuff, many from old orchards that have been around for centuries. These producers, among them Oliver's, Perry's and Newton Court, make ciders that exude class and quality. These are complex, rich and textured liquids that explode on the palate. The range of styles is enormous: still to sparkling, bone-dry to naturally sweet, minimal intervention to full *methode traditionelle* (like champagne) – it's incredible.

These guys have a deep knowledge of cider apple varieties (these apples are definitely not for eating). Containing high levels of tannin, these can have the same level of influence over a cider's flavour as the choice of grape variety does over a wine.

Good producers harness the flavours of their apples to produce some truly incredible ciders. As well as playing with different yeast strains, varying the maturation time, using different types of maturation vessel such as steel tanks or casks, and controlling the sweetness, it's a whole new level of technical expertise.

Cider, done properly, is unique and versatile, and should be celebrated with pride as our true indigenous drink. Here are five of my absolute favourites to help you on the way.

Know your apples

Henney's Dry Brisk though this cider may be, there's a pleasingly gentle, spicy undertone that perfectly balances this clean dry tipple. Easily available in most supermarkets, this is a rock solid go-to cider.

Sheppy's Goldfinch Made from a blend of classic Somerset cider apples, this lightly sparkling cider is brilliant with food. It has a great, mouth-puckering dryness, so try it with strong cheese or game dishes.

Pilton Cider Using apples from Glastonbury Festival's Worthy Farm, Pilton cider is made by producing partially fermented cider, which is then finished in the bottle. The end result is rich, semi-sweet and naturally sparkling, packed with ripe apple flavours.

New Forest Traditional Farmhouse This Dorset-based family firm run Borough Market's only cider stall, which is testament to its quality. Medium-dry, it has gentle, earthy aromas, and makes you feel like you're in a hay barn. Complex, but not challenging.

Once Upon a Tree, Kingston Red Streak Kingston Black and Somerset Redstreak apple varieties have been combined to make a bold, elegant drink. Made by a winemaker-turned-cider maker, this still drink is packed with smoke and spice.

Gabe Cook hails from the heart of cider country and has cider running through his veins. He has worked for cider makers of all sizes, from small farm producers to the world's biggest, in the UK and in New Zealand. A passionate advocate for cider, he champions the virtues of the fermented apple under his guise of The Ciderologist (www.theciderologist.com).
Favourite pub Crown Inn, Woolhope, Herefordshire.

Pubs for dog-lovers

By **Sasha Wilkins**

Growing up in the English countryside and spending a lot of time in pubs means I can't think of going out for a drink without a dog at my feet (or, shhh, sometimes on my lap). Sadly, in London, where I now live with two miniature dachshunds and the occasional visiting blue whippet, it's hard to find restaurants and bars that do welcome dogs. So, thank goodness that the majority of pubs in the city remain an oasis for dog-lovers. Some lovely pubs not only welcome dogs but go the extra mile, offering crispy pigs' ears and bowls of water – the Spaniards Inn, hard by London's Hampstead Heath, even has a dog-washing facility. Here are five of my favourite dog-friendly pubs, in London and beyond:

Gipsy Queen, London NW5

If a London pub 25 minutes from Oxford Circus can be called off the beaten path, then this is it. Somewhere in the no-man's land between Belsize Park and Kentish Town is this fantastic newish pub with a big sunny open room and generously sized tables. It has a serious chef (Tom Humphries, who can turn his hand to everything from the perfect Sunday roast to an epic cheese toastie at the bar and some thoughtful vegetarian options), a lovely secret beer garden and a welcome-to-all dog policy, whether you're eating, drinking or sitting at the bar. Happily, it's a short walk (or even shorter drive) from Parliament Hill Fields, where you can take the hounds to walk off all that delicious food. *166 Malden Road, London NW5 4BS. (020) 3092 0598, www.thegipsyqueennw5.co.uk.*

Greyhound, Stockbridge, Hampshire

Maybe the clue is in the name, but this pub with rooms is a really dog-friendly spot, welcoming four-legged friends in the bar, eating areas and upstairs. That's handy because the food is absolutely delicious, possibly the best we ate in a pub last year, the wine list is excellent and, if you stay overnight in one of the seven perfectly appointed ensuite bedrooms, you can make the most of the next day's epic breakfast. Make sure you snaffle the Cadbury's chocolate bars left as a welcome on the bed before your dog does. *31 High Street, Stockbridge, SO20 6EY. (01264) 810833, www.thegreyhoundonthetest.co.uk. See Also Worth a Visit, Hampshire.*

Royal Oak, Eydon, Northamptonshire

Curling up on a chair beside a fire in an inglenook fireplace with a dog next to your feet and a pint of Hook Norton in your hand is one of life's great pleasures. And this lovely old Northamptonshire ironstone building, parts of which date back 300 years, delivers in every respect. It has everything you could want in a traditional country pub, from uneven flagstone floors to low beamed ceilings and, of course, lots of dogs. As an added bonus, the Sunday lunch is a well priced delight, though vegetarians should probably give it a miss.

6 Lime Avenue, Eyedon, NN11 3PG. (01327) 263167, www.theroyaloakateydon.co.uk. See Also Worth a Visit, Northamptonshire.

Wheatsheaf, Northleach, Gloucestershire

While I'm strongly in favour of this beautiful rambling Gloucestershire pub's excellent (and award-winning) food, fine selection of real ales, spacious and dog-friendly ground-floor bedrooms, and pigs' ears in a jar behind the bar, the lovely terraced garden is the standout. It has both intimate shaded nooks for meals à deux, and communal tables for long slow summer lunches with families and friends. My sausage dogs absolutely love the place.

West End, Northleach, GL54 3EZ. (01451) 860244, www.cotswoldswheatsheaf.com. See Main Entries, Gloucestershire.

Globe, Rye, Sussex

There are lots of things to love about this charming pub. Not least, that they serve food through the afternoon (which in itself deserves a medal) and a range of excellent beers from local brewers. On a cold blustery day in January after a long walk on the beach, I was delighted by its low ceilings, homely atmosphere, lovely staff and absolutely delicious modern pub food, sourced with pride almost entirely from local farmers, fishmongers, bakers, grocers and butchers. They deserve a special shout-out for the generous board of Kentish and Sussex cheeses. The three dogs were in heaven, basking in front of the log fire like fat baby seals.

10 Military Road, Rye, TN31 7NX. (01797) 225220, www.globeinnmarshrye.com. See Also Worth a Visit, Sussex.

Writer, cook, broadcaster and sausage-dog owner, **Sasha Wilkins** is probably best known as the founder of the multi-award-winning website LibertyLondonGirl.com.
Favourite pub Gipsy Queen, 166 Malden Road, London NW5.

What is a Good Pub?

We hear about possible new entries in this *Guide* from our many thousands of correspondents who keep us in touch with pubs they visit – by post, by email at feedback@goodguides.com or via our website, www.thegoodpubguide.co.uk. These might be places they visit regularly (and it's their continued approval that reassures us about keeping a pub as a full entry for another year) or pubs they have discovered on their travels and that perhaps we know nothing about. And it's from these new discoveries that we make up a shortlist, to be considered for possible inclusion as new Main Entries.

What marks a pub out for special attention could be an out of the ordinary choice of drinks – a wide range of real ales (perhaps even brewed by the pub), several hundred whiskies, a remarkable wine list, interesting spirits from small distillers or proper farm ciders and perries. It could be delicious food (often outclassing many restaurants in the area) or even remarkable value meals. Maybe as a place to stay it's pretty special, with lovely bedrooms and obliging service. Or the building itself might be stunning (from golden-stone Georgian houses to part of centuries-old monasteries or extravagant Victorian gin-palaces) or in a stunning setting, amid beautiful countryside or situated by water.

Above all, what makes a good pub is its atmosphere. You should feel at home and genuinely welcomed by the landlord or landlady – it's their influence that can make or break a pub. It follows from this that a lot of ordinary local pubs, perfectly good in their own right, don't earn a place in the *Guide*. What makes them attractive to their regulars could make strangers feel a bit left out.

Another point is that there's not necessarily any link between charm and luxury. A basic unspoilt tavern may be worth travelling miles for, while a too smartly refurbished dining pub may not be worth crossing the street for.

The pubs featured as Main Entries do pay a fee, which helps to cover the *Guide*'s production costs. But no pub can gain an entry simply by paying this fee. Only pubs that have been inspected anonymously, and approved by us, are invited to join.

Using the *Guide*

The Counties

England has been split alphabetically into counties. Each chapter starts by picking out the pubs that are currently doing best in the area, or are specially attractive for one reason or another.

The county boundaries we use are those for the administrative counties (not the old traditional counties, which were changed back in 1976). We have left the new unitary authorities within the counties that they formed part of until their creation in the most recent local government reorganisation. Metropolitan areas have been included in the counties around them – for example, Merseyside in Lancashire. And occasionally we have grouped counties together – for example, Rutland with Leicestershire, and Durham with Northumberland to make Northumbria. If in doubt, check the Contents pages.

Scotland, Wales and London have each been covered in single chapters. Pubs are listed alphabetically (except in London, which is split into Central, East, North, South and West), under the name of the town or village where they are. If the village is so small that you might not find it on a road map, we've listed it under the name of the nearest sizeable village or town. The maps use the same town and village names, and additionally include a few big cities that don't have any listed pubs – for orientation.

We list pubs in their true county, not their postal county. Just once or twice, when the village itself is in one county but the pub is just over the border in the next-door county, we have used the village county, not the pub one.

Stars ★

Really outstanding pubs are awarded a star, and in one case two: these are the aristocrats among pubs. The stars do NOT signify extra luxury or specially good food – in fact, some of the pubs that appeal most distinctively and strongly are decidedly basic in terms of food and surroundings. The detailed description of each pub shows what its particular appeal is, and this is what the stars refer to.

Food Award 🍽

Pubs where food is really outstanding.

Stay Award 🛏

Pubs that are good as places to stay at (obviously, you can't expect the same level of luxury at £60 a head as you'd get for £100 a head). Pubs with bedrooms are marked on the maps as a square.

Wine Award ♀

Pubs with particularly enjoyable wines by the glass – often a good range.

Beer Award ◀

Pubs where the quality of the beer is quite exceptional, or pubs that keep a particularly interesting range of beers in good condition.

Value Award £

This distinguishes pubs that offer really good value food. In all the award-winning pubs, you will find an interesting choice at around £10.

Recommenders

At the end of each Main Entry we include the names of readers who have recently recommended that pub (unless they've asked us not to use their names).

Important note: the description of the pub and the comments on it are our own and not the recommenders'.

Also Worth a Visit

The Also Worth a Visit section at the end of each county chapter includes brief descriptions of pubs that have been recommended by readers in the year before the *Guide* goes to print and that we feel are worthy of inclusion – many of them, indeed, as good in their way as the featured pubs (these are picked out by a star). We have inspected and approved nearly half of these ourselves. All the others are recommended by our reader-reporters. The descriptions of these other pubs, written by us, usually reflect the experience of several different people.

The pubs in Also Worth a Visit may become featured entries in future editions. So do please help us know which are hot prospects for our inspection programme (and which are not!), by reporting on them. There are report forms at the back of the *Guide*, or you can email us at feedback@goodguides.com, or write to us at

The Good Pub Guide, FREEPOST RTJR-ZCYZ-RJZT,
Perrymans Lane, Etchingham TN19 7DN.

Locating Pubs

To help readers who use digital mapping systems we include a postcode for every pub. Pubs outside London are given a British Grid four-figure map reference. Where a pub is exceptionally difficult to find, we include a six-figure reference in the directions. The Map number (Main Entries only) refers to the maps at the back of the *Guide*.

Motorway Pubs

If a pub is within four or five miles of a motorway junction we give special directions for finding it from the motorway. The Special

Interest Lists at the end of the book include a list of these pubs, motorway by motorway.

Prices and Other Factual Details

The *Guide* went to press during the summer of 2016, after each pub was sent a checking sheet to get up-to-date food, drink and bedroom prices and other factual information. By the summer of 2017 prices are bound to have increased, but if you find a significantly different price please let us know.

Breweries or independent chains to which pubs are 'tied' are named at the beginning of the italic-print rubric after each Main Entry. That generally means the pub has to get most if not all its drinks from that brewery or chain. If the brewery is not an independent one but just part of a combine, we name the combine in brackets. When the pub is tied, we have spelled out whether the landlord is a tenant, has the pub on a lease, or is a manager. Tenants and leaseholders of breweries generally have considerably greater freedom to do things their own way, and in particular are allowed to buy drinks including a beer from sources other than their tied brewery.

Free houses are pubs not tied to a brewery. In theory they can shop around, but in practice many free houses have loans from the big brewers, on terms that bind them to sell those breweries' beers. So don't be too surprised to find that so-called free houses may be stocking a range of beers restricted to those from a single brewery.

Real ale is used by us to mean beer that has been maturing naturally in its cask. We do not count as real ale beer that has been pasteurised or filtered to remove its natural yeasts.

Other drinks. We've also looked out particularly for pubs doing enterprising non-alcoholic drinks (including good tea or coffee), interesting spirits (especially malt whiskies), country wines, freshly squeezed juices and good farm ciders.

Bar food usually refers to what is sold in the bar; we do not describe menus that are restricted to a separate restaurant. If we know that a pub serves sandwiches, we say so – if you don't see them mentioned, assume you can't get them. Food listed is an example of the sort of thing you'd find served in the bar on a normal day.

Children. If we don't mention children at all, assume that they are not welcome. All but one or two pubs allow children in their garden if they have one. 'Children welcome' means the pub has told us that it lets them in with no special restrictions. In other cases, we report exactly what arrangements pubs say they make for children. However, we have to note that in readers' experience some pubs make restrictions that they haven't told us about (children only if eating, for example). If you come across this, please let us know, so that we can clarify with the pub concerned for the next edition. The absence of any reference to children in an Also Worth a Visit entry means we don't know either way. Children's Certificates exist, but in practice children are allowed into some part of most pubs in this *Guide* (there is no legal restriction on the movement of children over 14 in any pub). Children under 16 cannot have alcoholic drinks. Children aged 16 and 17 can drink beer, wine or cider with a meal if it is bought by an adult and they are accompanied by an adult.

Dogs. If Main Entry licensees have told us they allow dogs in their pub or bedrooms, we say so; absence of reference to dogs means dogs are not welcome. If you take a dog into a pub you should have it on a lead. We also mention in the text any pub dogs or cats (or indeed other animals) that we've come across ourselves, or heard about from readers.

Parking. If we know there is a problem with parking, we say so; otherwise assume there is a car park.

Credit cards. We say if a pub does not accept them; some that do may put a surcharge on credit card bills, to cover charges made by the card company. We also say if we know that a pub tries to retain customers' credit cards while they are eating. This is a reprehensible practice, and if a pub tries it on you, please tell them that all banks and card companies frown on it – and please let us know the pub's name, so that we can warn readers in future editions.

Telephone numbers are given for all pubs that are not ex-directory.

Opening hours are for summer; we say if we know of differences in winter, or on particular days of the week. In the country, many pubs may open rather later and close earlier than their details show (if you come across this, please let us know – with details). Pubs are allowed to stay open all day if licensed to do so. However, outside cities many pubs in England and Wales close during the afternoon. We'd be grateful to hear of any differences from the hours we quote.

Bedroom prices normally include full english breakfasts (if available), VAT and any automatic service charge. If we give just one price, it is the total price for two people sharing a double or twin-bedded room for one night. Prices before the '/' are for single occupancy, prices after it for double.

Meal times. Bar food is commonly served from 12-2 and 7-9, at least from Monday to Saturday. We spell out the times if they are significantly different. To be sure of a table it's best to book before you go. Sunday hours vary considerably from pub to pub, so it's advisable to check before you leave.

Disabled access. Deliberately, we do not ask pubs about this, as their answers would not give a reliable picture of how easy access is. Instead, we depend on readers' direct experience. If you are able to give us help about this, we would be particularly grateful for your reports.

Electronic Route Planning

Microsoft® AutoRoute™, a route-finding software package, shows the location of pubs in *The Good Pub Guide* on detailed maps and includes our text entries for those pubs on screen.

Our website (www.thegoodpubguide.co.uk) includes every pub in the *Guide*.

iPhone and iPad

You can search and read *The Good Pub Guide* both on our website (www.thegoodpubguide.co.uk) and as a download on your smartphone or iPad. They contain all the pubs in this *Guide*. You can also write reviews and let us know about undiscovered gems.

There are apps available for iPhone and iPad – and the *Guide* can be downloaded as an eBook to your reader.

Changes during the year – please tell us

Changes are inevitable during the course of the year. Landlords change, and so do their policies. We hope that you will find everything just as we say, but if not please let us know. You can find out how by referring to the Report Forms section at the end of the *Guide*.

43

Editors' acknowledgements

We could not produce the *Guide* without the huge help we have from the many thousands of readers who report to us on the pubs they visit, often in great detail. Particular thanks to these greatly valued correspondents: Chris and Angela Buckell, Tony and Wendy Hobden, Clive and Fran Dutson, George Atkinson, Michael and Jenny Back, Michael Doswell, Gordon and Margaret Ormondroyd, John Pritchard, Richard Tilbrook, Brian and Anna Marsden, R K Phillips, Roger and Donna Huggins, Steve Whalley, Tracey and Stephen Groves, Simon and Mandy King, Gerry and Rosemary Dobson, Paul Humphreys, Susan and John Douglas, John Wooll, Ian Herdman, Peter Meister, Liz Bell, Ann and Colin Hunt, Michael Butler, John Beeken, Simon Collett-Jones, Tony and Jill Radnor, Sara Fulton and Roger Baker, Brian Glozier, Neil and Angela Huxter, David Jackman, Edward Mirzoeff, Roy Hoing, Sheila Topham, Taff Thomas, B and M Kendall, Mrs Margo Finlay and Jörg Kasprowski, Phil and Jane Hodson, Richard and Penny Gibbs, Comus and Sarah Elliott, Mike and Mary Carter, Guy Vowles, Ian Phillips, Richard Kennell, John and Sylvia Harrop, Dave Braisted, Derek and Sylvia Stephenson, Ross Balaam, Theocsbrian, John Evans, Christian Mole, R T and J C Moggridge, Dr J Barrie Jones, Giles and Annie Francis, Dr W I C Clark, John and Eleanor Holdsworth, Phil and Jane Villiers, John Evans, Stephen Woad, Tina and David Woods-Taylor, Bob and Margaret Holder, Ian Malone, Jeremy King, R L Borthwick, Brian and Jacky Wilson, Tony Scott, Roy and Gill Payne, David Stewart, S G N Bennett, Chris and Dorothy Stock, Martin Day, Dennis and Doreen Haward, David Lamb, Mike and Eleanor Anderson, David Fowler, Val and Alan Green, Nigel Espley, Adam Bellinger, Peter Randell, M G Hart, Paul Rampton and Julie Harding, Paul A Moore, Nigel Espley, Richard Mason, Charles North, Pat and Stewart Gordon, John Saul, W K Wood, Mr and Mrs P R Thomas, David and Judy Robison, Allan Lloyd and family, John Poulter, Ron Corbett, Martin and Alison Stainsby, Pat and Tony Martin, Barry Collett, Katharine Cowherd, Hilary Forrest, Dr J J H Gilkes, Richard Cox, Piotr Chodzko-Zajko, Hugh Roberts, Tim Brogan, David and Sally Frost, Alan Johnson, Peter and Anne Hollindale, Ian and Rose Lock, Robert W Buckle, Mrs P Sumner, Paul Baxter, Peter Andrews, Mr and Mrs Richard Osborne, Stephen Funnell, S Holder, Mr and Mrs D J Nash, Janet and Peter Race, Marianne and Peter Stevens, David Thorpe, Michael Sargent, Christopher Maxse, Adam Simmonds, Dr D J and Mrs S C Walker, Dr and Mrs J D Abell, Helen McLagan, Nigel and Sue Foster, Mike Kavaney, Hilary De Lyon and Martin Webster, Jestyn Phillips, Andy Dolan, Susan and Jeremy Arthern, Chris and Pauline Sexton, Jenny and Brian Seller, Andy and Sallie James, John Hills, Tony Tollitt, Alan and Angela Scouller, Margaret and Peter Staples, Derek Stafford, David and Stella Martin, Mrs Julie Thomas, Ray White, Pat and Graham Williamson, Liz and Brian Barnard, Steve Lowton, Lynda and Trevor Smith, Mrs Elaine Bickley, Gavin Markwick, Dr Peter Crawshaw, Tony and Rachel Schendel, Bill Adie, Roger and Anne Newbury, Eddie Edwards, Richard Stanfield, JPC, Alistair Holdoway, Nigel and Jean Eames, Stuart Reeves, Miss A E Dare, Mrs Zara Elliott, Lee and Liz Potter, Robert Wivell, David and Betty Gittins, Kevin Booker and Julia Atkins, Alan Cowell, V Brogden, Bill Gulliver and Harry Thomson, Mike and Margaret Banks, Dr Tony Whitehead, Dr and Mrs A K Clarke, Malcolm and Pauline Pellatt, Peter Emmerson, Ian and Barbara Rankin, Simon Cleasby, Simon Rodway, Steve and Liz Tilley, Mrs Maureen Pye, Helen and Brian Edgeley, Tom McLean, Peter Smith and Judith Brown, Quentin and Carol Williamson, Dr Michael Smith, MDN, Robert Lester, Mr and Mrs J Watkins, Noel and Judy Garner, David and Catharine Boston, Alistair Forsyth, Revd Michael Vockins, Denis and Margaret Kilner, Mrs J Ekins-Daukes, R and S Bentley, Phil and Helen Holt, P and J Shapley, Revd R P Tickle, Mr Yeldahn, Ian and Amanda Seamark, R W Batho, Roger and Pauline Pearce, Mrs P R Sykes, Adrian Johnson, David Delaney, Robert Kennedy, M A Borthwick, Roger White, Bernard Stradling MBE, J R Wildon, Ted George, Peter and Adriana Gill, Jamie and Sue May.

Thanks, too, to all those who helped us at The Book Service for their cheerful dedication: Maria Tegerdine, Michele Csaforda, Carol Bryant, Kerry Rusch, Miles Hooton, Danielle Isaac and Duncan Wilson. And particularly to John Holliday of Trade Wind Technology, who built and looks after our all-important database.

Fiona Stapley

ENGLAND

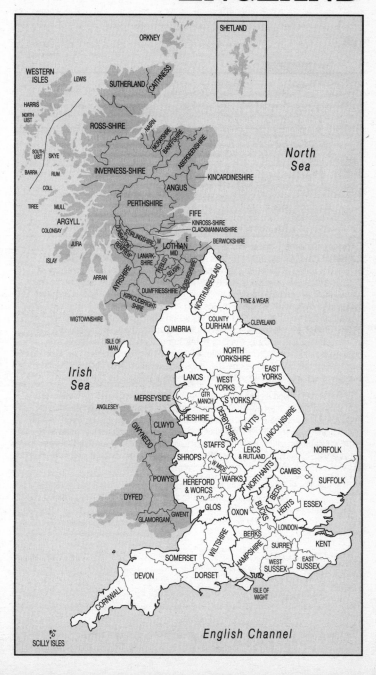

Bedfordshire

KEY ★ Star Pub 🍽 Top Quality Food 🍺 Great Beer
🍷 Good Wines £ Bargain Meals 🛏 Good Bedrooms 🍴 Serves Food

AMPTHILL TL0338 Map 5

Prince of Wales

(01525) 840504 – www.princeofwales-ampthill.com
Bedford Street (B540 N from central crossroads); MK45 2NB

Civilised and with neat décor and up-to-date food; bedrooms

Service is notably good – as is the food, so it's not a surprise to find lots of chatty customers in this attractive red-brick place. Set on two levels, it's more of an open-plan bar-brasserie than a straightforward pub, with comfortable, stylish furnishings and modern prints on mainly cream walls (dark green and maroon accents at either end). The slightly sunken flagstoned area with wooden tables and chairs and a log fire in the exposed brick fireplace leads to a partly ply-panelled dining room with dark leather dining chairs set around a mixed batch of sturdy tables, and there are plenty of church candles and big burgundy leather armchairs and sofas at low tables on bare boards; background music. Charles Wells Bombardier and Eagle on handpump, plenty of wines by the glass and good coffee. The nicely planted two-level lawn has picnic-sets, with more on a terrace by the car park.

🍴 Flavoursome food includes lunchtime sandwiches, baked baby camembert with onion chutney, tiger prawn skewers in chilli, garlic and lime with avocado purée, sausages of the week with mash, cheddar and sun-dried tomato quiche, bourbon and coke-marinated spare ribs with coleslaw and southern fries, salmon en croûte with white wine and dill sauce, and puddings such as crème brûlée of the day and chocolate brownie with chocolate fudge sauce; Thursday is steak night. *Benchmark main dish: daily special fish dish £18.00. Two-course evening meal £19.00.*

Wells & Youngs ~ Lease Richard and Neia Heathorn ~ Real ale ~ Open 11-11 (midnight Fri, Sat); 12-5 (8 in summer) Sun ~ Bar food 12-2.30 (3 weekends), 6.30-9, 7-9.30 Fri, Sat; not Sun evening ~ Restaurant ~ Children welcome ~ Dogs allowed in bar and bedrooms ~ Wi-fi ~ Bedrooms: £55/£70 *Recommended by Edward May, Richard Kennell, Susan and Jeremy Arthern*

BEDFORD TL0550 Map 5

Park 🍷

(01234) 273929 – www.theparkbedford.co.uk
Corner of Kimbolton Road (B660) and Park Avenue, out past Bedford Hospital; MK40 2PA

Civilised and individual oasis – a great asset for the town

There's always a wide mix of customers here popping in and out all day and the atmosphere is chatty and bustling. Appealing décor has thoughtful touches, and you can choose where to sit according to your mood: a more or less conventional bar with heavy beams, panelled dado and leaded lights in big windows, a light and airy conservatory sitting room with easy chairs well spread on a carpet, and an extensive series of softly lit rambling dining areas, carpeted or flagstoned. Charles Wells Bombardier Burning Gold and Eagle and Courage Directors on handpump, inventive bar nibbles and an excellent choice of wines by the glass; background music. The sheltered brick-paved terrace has good timber furniture, some under canopies, and attractive shrub plantings.

As well as weekend breakfasts (8-10.30am Sat; 9-11am Sun), the well thought-of food includes lunchtime sandwiches, salmon, crayfish and sweet potato fishcake with chive yoghurt, poached duck egg and gruyère bonbons with roasted garlic and parsley butter, sharing boards, a risotto of the day, beef liver with red onion gravy, chargrilled lemon chicken with quinoa, lentil and feta salad, hake with lemon roasted shallots, creamed leeks and smoked bacon, and puddings such as dark chocolate brownie and white chocolate ice-cream and st clement's cheesecake with chantilly cream; they also have a two- and three-course weekday set menu. *Benchmark main dish: sea trout fillet with smoked salmon scotch egg, courgette spaghetti, deep-fried capers £15.50. Two-course evening meal £21.00.*

Little Gems Country Dining Pubs ~ Manager Steve Cook ~ Real ale ~ Open 8am-11.30pm; 9am-11.30pm Sat; 9am-11pm Sun ~ Bar food 12-3, 6-10; 12-10 Sat; 12-8 Sun ~ Restaurant ~ Children in one bar and restaurant ~ Dogs allowed in bar ~ Wi-fi *Recommended by Harvey Brown, Ruth May, Tony Smaithe, Charles Todd*

FLITTON
White Hart ♀

TL0535   Map 5

(01525) 862022 – www.whitehartflitton.co.uk
Village signed off A507; MK45 5EJ

Simply furnished and friendly village pub with bar and dining area, real ales, interesting food and seats in the garden

The rewarding food is one of the big draws to this friendly village pub, but they do keep B&T Golden Fox and Shefford Bitter on handpump and 20 wines – as well as champagne and prosecco – by the glass. The minimally decorated front bar has dark leather tub chairs around low tables, contemporary leather and chrome seats at pedestal tables, and Farrow & Ball painted walls; TV. Steps lead down to a good-sized, simply furnished back dining area with red plush seats and banquettes on dark wooden floorboards. The nice garden has neat shrub borders, and teak seats and tables on a terrace shaded by cedars and weeping willows. A 13th-c church is next door.

As well as daily fresh fish and renowned steaks, the smashing food includes crayfish, prawn and apple cocktail, panko-crusted baby brie with cranberry sauce, artichoke, spring onion and pine nut pie, ham, egg and chips, cajun-spiced swordfish with avocado, mango and chilli salsa, chicken breast with pancetta, mushroom and blue cheese sauce, chargrilled lamb chops, and puddings such as treacle sponge and custard and espresso pannacotta with chocolate sauce; they also offer a two- and three-course set menu (not Sunday). *Benchmark main dish: aberdeen angus steaks with a choice of sauces £15.55. Two-course evening meal £20.00.*

Free house ~ Licensees Phil and Clare Hale ~ Real ale ~ Open 12-2.30, 6-midnight; 12-3, 6-1am Sat; 12-5 Sun; closed Sun evening, Mon ~ Bar food 12-2, 6.30-9 (9.30 Fri, Sat); 12-2.30 Sun ~ Restaurant ~ Children welcome ~ Dogs allowed in bar ~ Wi-fi *Recommended by Alison and Michael Harper, Colin Humphreys, Diane Abbott*

IRELAND
Black Horse 🖈 ♟ 🍷 🛏

TL1341 Map 5

(01462) 811398 – www.blackhorseireland.com

Off A600 Shefford–Bedford; SG17 5QL

Bedfordshire Dining Pub of the Year

Contemporary décor in old building, impressive food, good wine list, and lovely garden with attractive terraces; bedrooms

Our readers enjoy staying in the comfortable and well equipped chalet-style bedrooms that are found just across a courtyard in a separate building; continental breakfasts are included and taken in your room. The warm and relaxing bar has inglenook fireplaces, beams in low ceilings and timbering and they serve Adnams Bitter, Fullers London Pride and Sharps Doom Bar on handpump, 28 wines by the glass, a dozen malt whiskies, Weston's cider and good coffee from the long green-slate bar counter; staff are courteous and helpful. There are leather armchairs and comfortable wall seating, a mix of elegant wooden and high-backed leather dining chairs around attractive tables on polished oak boards or sandstone flooring, original artwork and fresh flowers; background music. French windows open from the restaurant on to various terraces with individual furnishings and pretty flowering pots and beds. The Birch at Woburn is under the same ownership.

 Excellent food using the best local, seasonal produce includes sandwiches, moules marinière, local estate venison and mushroom terrine with fruit chutney, pasta with chicken, chorizo, rocket and porcini oil, pie of the day, ratatouille crumble, burgers with toppings, beetroot slaw and fries, confit duck leg with braised puy lentils, truffle-infused mash and orange jus, and puddings such as soufflé of the day and dark chocolate and lavender pot; they also offer a two- and three-course set weekday menu (not Friday evening). *Benchmark main dish: griddled bass fillet £14.95. Two-course evening meal £23.00.*

Free house ~ Licensee Darren Campbell ~ Real ale ~ Open 12-3, 6-11; 11.30-11 Sat; 12-6 Sun ~ Bar food 12-2.30, 6-9.30; 12-6 Sun ~ Restaurant ~ Children welcome ~ Wi-fi ~ Bedrooms: /£79.95 *Recommended by Caroline Prescott, Ruth May, Jack and Hilary Burton*

OAKLEY
Bedford Arms 🍷

TL0053 Map 5

(01234) 822280 – www.bedfordarmsoakley.co.uk

High Street; MK43 7RH

Nice old village inn with real ales, wines by the glass, fish and other popular food in two dining rooms and seats in the garden

The daily fresh fish dishes in this updated 16th-c pub are quite special and they're certainly what our readers mention most in their reports. Each of the interconnected rooms has different contemporary décor. The pubbiest part has straightforward wooden furniture on bare boards, flower prints on the walls, daily papers, a decorative woodburning stove with a flat-screen TV above it, and Charles Wells Bombardier Burning Gold and Eagle and Courage Directors on handpump and 30 wines by the glass; darts. The four cosy, individually decorated rooms leading off the main bar are the nicest places for a drink and chat. One has a large circular pine table (just right for a private party), another has farmhouse chairs and a cushioned pew beside a small fireplace, the third has ladder-back chairs and shiny tables on ancient floor tiles and the last is very much Victorian in style. The stone-floored dining rooms have tartan-covered seating or wicker chairs, while the light, airy conservatory overlooks the pretty garden where there are seats for warm-weather meals.

As well as the fish dishes displayed on a board and gluten-free choices, they also serve lunchtime sandwiches, white crab and smoked salmon tagliatelle, baked fig stuffed with walnuts, camembert, honey and parma ham with avocado and red berry dressing, home-cooked ham and eggs, vegetable pancake with tomato and cheese sauce, a pie of the day, lamb rump with mint hollandaise and fried capers, and puddings. *Benchmark main dish: beer-battered fish and chips £12.95. Two-course evening meal £22.50.*

Wells & Youngs ~ Tenants Tim and Yvonne Walker ~ Real ale ~ Open 12-11 (10.30 Sun) ~ Bar food 12-2.30, 6.15-9.30; 12-4 Sun ~ Restaurant ~ Children welcome ~ Dogs allowed in bar ~ Wi-fi *Recommended by Michael Butler, Michael Sargent*

RAVENSDEN TL0754 Map 5

Horse & Jockey

(01234) 772319 – www.horseandjockey.info

Village signed off B660 N of Bedford; pub at Church End, off village road; MK44 2RR

Contemporary comfort, with enjoyable food and good range of drinks

Both drinkers and diners receive a genuine welcome in this friendly place. It's carefully run by enthusiastic licensees and the pleasantly modern interior has a quiet colour scheme of olive greys and dark red, careful lighting, leather easy chairs in the bar, a wall of meticulously arranged old local photographs and maybe copies of *Country Life* and daily papers; background music and board games. Adnams Ghost Ship and Southwold and Black Sheep Holy Grail on handpump and 20 wines by the glass served by charming staff. The bright dining room has nice chunky tables and high-backed seats, well lit prints and a contemporary etched glass screen; it overlooks a sheltered terrace with smart, up-to-date tables and chairs under cocktail parasols on decking and a few picnic-sets on the grass beside. The handsome medieval church with churchyard is further off.

From a thoughtful menu, the interesting food includes duck chorizo, potato, caramelised onions, bacon and parmesan topped with a poached duck egg, pigeon and foie gras terrine with pickles, wild mushroom, pea and mascarpone risotto, beef and pheasant pie, smoked haddock florentine, confit duck leg with potato purée and braised red cabbage, and puddings such as cappuccino crème brûlée with cinnamon ice-cream and banana, fig and date sticky toffee pudding with crème anglaise; they may offer a two- and three-course set lunch menu. *Benchmark main dish: catalan fish stew £17.00. Two-course evening meal £20.00.*

Free house ~ Licensees Darron and Sarah Smith ~ Real ale ~ Open 12-3, 6-11 (midnight Sat); 12-8 Sun ~ Bar food 12-2, 7-9; 12-6 Sun ~ Restaurant ~ Children welcome ~ Dogs allowed in bar ~ Wi-fi *Recommended by S Holder, Harvey Brown, Michael Sargent, Dennis and Doreen Haward*

WOBURN SP9433 Map 4

Birch

(01525) 290295 – www.birchwoburn.com

3.5 miles from M1 junction 13; follow Woburn signs via A507 and A4012, right in village then A5130 (Newport Road); MK17 9HX

Well run dining establishment with focus on imaginative food, good wines and attentive service

The several individually and elegantly furnished linked rooms in this edge-of-town pub have contemporary décor and furnishings. The upper dining area has high-backed leather or wooden dining chairs around tables on stripped and polished floorboards, while the lower part is in a light and airy conservatory with a pitched glazed roof, ceramic floor tiles, light coloured furnishings and original artwork and fresh flowers; background music. The bustling bar is similarly furnished and has a few high bar stools against the sleek, smart counter where they serve Adnams Bitter and Sharps Doom Bar on handpump, 15 good wines by the glass, a dozen malt whiskies and quite a few teas and coffees; background music. There are tables out on a sheltered deck, and in summer the front of the pub has masses of flowering hanging baskets and tubs. This is sister pub to the Black Horse at Ireland.

 From a seasonally changing menu, the good food includes lunchtime ciabattas, garlic mushrooms with a poached egg on chargrilled granary bread, cod brandade with pickled cucumber, steak burger with toppings and fries, free-range chicken leg stuffed with white pudding and smoked bacon with leek and sweetcorn fritters, duck breast with raspberry and beetroot purée, hake on caramelised onion risotto, and puddings such as pear and ginger crumble and black forest eton mess; they also may offer a two- or three-course set lunch. *Benchmark main dish: griddled bass fillet £14.95. Two-course evening meal £22.75.*

Free house ~ Licensee Mark Campbell ~ Real ale ~ Open 12-3, 6-11; 12-6 Sun ~ Bar food 12-2.30, 6.15-9.30; 12-5.30 Sun ~ Restaurant ~ Children welcome
Recommended by Tim and Sarah Smythe-Brown

WOOTTON   TL0046   Map
Legstraps
(01234) 854112 – www.thelegstraps.co.uk
Keeley Lane; MK43 9HR

Bustling village pub with a nice range of food from open kitchen, local ales and wines by the glass

There's a good mix in this village pub between drinkers and diners and the kind, efficient staff welcome everyone. The low-ceilinged bar has an elegant feel with contemporary and comfortable upholstered chairs around all size of tables, big flagstones, a woodburning stove in a brick fireplace with a leather sofa and box wall seats to either side, and leather-topped stools against the pale planked counter. They keep Fullers London Pride and Sharps Doom Bar on handpump, good wines by the glass and quite a few gins. The dining rooms have bold paintwork, similar furnishings to the bar, polished bare boards and flower prints on one end wall with paper butterflies on another.

From the open kitchen, the well thought-of food includes crayfish cocktail with saffron aioli, soft-boiled scotch egg with tarragon emulsion, cumberland sausage with bubble and squeak and red wine jus, beer-battered fish of the day with triple-cooked chips, burger with toppings, pickles and chips, aubergine bake, shorthorn beef rib with red cabbage slaw and skinny fries, and puddings such as chocolate mousse and seasonal fruit fool; they also offer a two- and three-course set lunch. *Benchmark main dish: fish of the day £13.50. Two-course evening meal £19.50.*

Free house ~ Licensee Ian Craig ~ Real ale ~ Open 12-3, 5.30-11; 12-midnight Fri, Sat; 12-7 Sun; closed Mon ~ Bar food 12-2, 6-9 (9.30 Fri, Sat) ~ Restaurant ~ Children welcome ~ Dogs allowed in bar ~ Wi-fi *Recommended by Ben and Diane Bowie, Tim and Sarah Smythe-Brown, S Holder*

Also Worth a Visit in Bedfordshire

Besides the fully inspected pubs, you might like to try these pubs that have been recommended to us and described by readers. Do tell us what you think of them: feedback@goodguides.com

AMPTHILL   TL0337
Albion (01525) 634857
Dunstable Street; MK45 2JT Drinkers' pub with up to 12 well kept ales including local B&T and Everards, real ciders and a perry, friendly knowledgeable staff, no food apart from lunchtime rolls; traditional music night second Sat of month; dogs welcome, paved beer garden, open all day. *(Tony Smaithe)*

BEDFORD   TL0550
d'Parys (01234) 340248
De Parys Avenue; MK40 2UA Dining pub in former red-brick Victorian hotel; contemporary revamp keeping original features such as parquet floors, stained glass, period fireplaces and sweeping staircase, open-plan drinking area with long wooden tables and benches, some leather button-back sofas, Charles Wells ales and plenty of wines by the glass, cocktails, popular food including weekday set lunch, separate counter serving coffee, ice-cream and sweets, friendly helpful staff; children welcome, outside seating, 14 stylish bedrooms, open (and food) all day. *(Ben and Diana Bowie)*

BEDFORD   TL0549
Embankment (01234) 261332
The Embankment; MK40 3PD Revamped mock-Tudor hotel (Peach group) adjacent to the river; airy L-shaped front bar with mix of modern furniture on wood floor, pretty blue-tiled fireplace, Charles Wells ales and several wines by the glass, good choice of food from sandwiches and deli boards up, cheerful helpful service, restaurant; background music; children welcome, seats out on front terrace looking across to Great Ouse, 20 bedrooms (best ones with river views), good breakfast, open (and food) all day. *(Ruth May)*

BEDFORD   TL0450
Wellington Arms (01234) 308033
Wellington Street; MK40 2JX Friendly no-frills backstreet corner local with a dozen well kept ales including Adnams and B&T, real cider/perry and good range of continental beers, lots of breweriana; some live music, no mobile phones; seats in backyard, open all day from midday. *(S Holder)*

BIDDENHAM   TL0249
Three Tuns (01234) 354847
Off A428; MK40 4BD Refurbished part-thatched village dining pub with bar, lounge and new restaurant extension, good

varied menu from traditional favourites and chargrills up, plenty of wines by the glass including champagne, well kept Greene King ales, efficient friendly service; spacious garden with picnic-sets, more contemporary furniture on terrace and decked area, open all day (till 6pm Sun). *(Colin Humphreys)*

BLETSOE   TL0157
★ Falcon (01234) 781222
Rushden Road (A6 N of Bedford); MK44 1QN Refurbished 17th-c building with comfortable opened-up bar, low beams and joists, seating from cushioned wall/window seats to high-backed settles, woodburner in double-aspect fireplace, snug with sofas and old pews, panelled dining room, enjoyable food from pub standards up (plenty of gluten-free choices), Charles Wells ales and a guest, decent choice of wines by the glass and good coffee, efficient friendly service; unobtrusive background music, daily papers; decked and paved terrace in lovely big garden down to the Great Ouse, open (and food) all day. *(Ruth May)*

BOLNHURST   TL0858
★ Plough (01234) 376274
Kimbolton Road; MK44 2EX Stylishly converted Tudor building with thriving atmosphere, charming professional staff and top notch food (must book Sat night), Adnams and a couple of interesting guests, good carefully annotated wine list (including organic vintages) with over a dozen by the glass, home-made summer lemonade and tomato juice, airy dining extension, log fires; children welcome, dogs in bar, attractive tree-shaded garden with decking overlooking pond, remains of old moat, closed Sun evening, Mon and for two weeks over Christmas. *(Hugo Jeune, Michael Sargent, Peter Andrews)*

BROOM   TL1743
Cock (01767) 314411
High Street; from A1 opposite Biggleswade turn-off, follow 'Old Warden 3, Aerodrome 2' signpost, first left signed Broom; SG18 9NA Unspoilt 19th-c village-green pub, four changing ales tapped from casks by cellar steps off central corridor (no counter), Potton Press cider, enjoyable traditional home-made food such as steak and kidney pudding, good value two-course lunch deal, original latch doors linking one quietly cosy little room to the next (four in all), low ceilings, stripped panelling, farmhouse tables and chairs on old tiles, open fires, games room with bar skittles and darts; children and dogs welcome (resident

jack russell), picnic-sets on terrace by back lawn, camping field, open all day, no food Sun evening. *(Tony Smaithe)*

CLOPHILL   TL0838
Stone Jug (01525) 860526
N on A6 from A507 roundabout, after 200 metres, second turn on right into backstreet; MK45 4BY Secluded old stone-built local (originally three cottages), cosy and welcoming with traditional old-fashioned atmosphere, well kept B&T, Otter, St Austell and a couple of guests, popular good value pubby lunchtime food (not Sun, Mon), various rooms around L-shaped bar, darts in small games extension; background music; children and dogs welcome, roadside picnic-sets and pretty little back terrace, open all day Fri-Sun. *(Charles Todd)*

GREAT BARFORD   TL1351
Anchor (01234) 870364
High Street; off A421; MK44 3LF Open-plan pub by medieval arched bridge and church, good sensibly priced food from snacks up, Charles Wells ales and guests kept well, river views from main bar, back restaurant where children allowed; background music; picnic-sets in front looking across to Great Ouse, three bedrooms, open (and food) all day weekends. *(Ruth May)*

HENLOW   TL1738
Crown (01462) 812433
High Street; SG16 6BS Nicely updated beamed dining pub with good choice of popular food including children's menu, several wines by the glass, well kept Caledonian Flying Scotsman, Courage Directors and a guest, smiley helpful staff, woodburners (one in inglenook); quiet background music, free wi-fi, daily newspapers; terrace and small garden, five good bedrooms in converted stables, open (and food) all day. *(Dr W I C Clark)*

HENLOW   TL1738
★ Engineers Arms (01462) 812284
A6001 S of Biggleswade; High Street; SG16 6AA Traditional 19th-c village pub, up to a dozen changing ales plus good choice of ciders/perries, bottled belgian beers and wines by the glass, helpful knowledgeable staff, limited range of good value snacks, comfortable carpeted front room with old local photographs, bric-a-brac collections and good open fire, smaller tiled inner area and another comfortable carpeted one; beer/cider/country wine festivals, monthly live music, disco and quiz nights; sports TVs, juke box and silenced fruit machine; dogs allowed in bar, plenty of outside seating, open all day (till 1am Fri, Sat). *(Charles Todd)*

HOUGHTON CONQUEST   TL0441
★ Knife & Cleaver (01234) 930789
Between B530 (old A418) and A6,

S of Bedford; MK45 3LA Refurbished and extended 17th-c village dining pub opposite church, good variety of well liked food from separate bar and restaurant menus, extensive choice of wines by the glass including champagne, Charles Wells ales and a guest, friendly staff; free wi-fi; children welcome, no dogs inside, nine chalet bedrooms arranged around courtyard and garden, good breakfast, free charging of electric cars for guests, open all day from 7am (8am weekends), till 8pm Sun. *(Colin Humphreys)*

HUSBORNE CRAWLEY   SP9635
White Horse (01525) 280565
Mill Road, just off A507; MK43 0XE Open-plan village pub arranged around central servery, a couple of real ales and good reasonably priced home-made food (vegetarians and special diets well catered for), friendly attentive staff, beams, wood and quarry-tiled floors, some stripped brickwork and woodburner; children welcome, tables outside, lovely hanging baskets, open (and food) all day, till 8pm (6pm) Sun. *(Ruth May)*

LITTLE GRANSDEN   TL2755
Chequers (01767) 677348
Main Road; SG19 3DW Village local in same family for over 60 years and retaining 1950s feel; simple bar with coal fire, darts and framed historical information about the pub, step down to cosy snug with another fire and bench seats, comfortable back lounge with fish tank, interesting range of own-brewed Son of Sid ales, no food apart from good fish and chips Fri evening (must book); open all day Fri, Sat. *(Tony Smaithe)*

MAULDEN   TL0538
Dog & Badger (01525) 860237
Clophill Road E of village, towards A6/A507 junction; MK45 2AD Attractive neatly kept bow-windowed cottage, enjoyable well priced food (booking advised weekends) including sharing boards, pizzas and grills, set lunch Mon-Sat and other deals, beams and exposed brickwork, high stools on bare boards by carved wooden counter serving Charles Wells ales and guests, mix of dining chairs around wooden tables, double-sided fireplace, steps down to two carpeted areas and restaurant; background music, sports TV; children welcome, tables and smokers' shelter in front, garden behind with sturdy play area, open all day Fri-Sun. *(Ruth May)*

MILTON BRYAN   SP9730
Red Lion (01525) 210044
Toddington Road, off B528 S of Woburn; MK17 9HS Refurbished red-brick village pub under newish management; Greene King ales and a guest, several wines by the glass, cocktails and good range of gins (Fever Tree tonic), well liked food from bar snacks and sharing boards up, lunchtime/early evening set menu and other deals, good friendly service, central bar with dining areas either

side, beams and open fire; quiz first Thurs of month; children and dogs welcome, nice big garden with pretty views, open all day Sat, till 7pm Sun, closed Mon. *(George Atkinson, Richard Kennell)*

NORTHILL TL1446
★ **Crown** (01767) 627337
Ickwell Road; off B658 W of Biggleswade; SG18 9AA Prettily situated village pub; cosy flagstoned bar with copper-topped counter, heavy low beams and bay window seats, woodburner here and in restaurant with modern furniture on light wood floor, steps up to another dining area with exposed brick and high ceiling, good brasserie-style food (not Sun evening) including lunchtime baguettes/panini, Greene King and guests, plenty of wines by the glass, good friendly service; soft background music; children welcome, no dogs inside, tables out at front and on sheltered side terrace, more in big back garden with play area, open all day Fri-Sun. *(Ben and Diane Bowie)*

ODELL SP9657
Bell (01234) 910850
Off A6 S of Rushden, via Sharnbrook; High Street; MK43 7AS Popular thatched village pub continuing well under new licensees, several low-beamed rooms around central servery, good reasonably priced home-made food (not Sun evening), well kept Greene King and guests, fine range of gins, friendly helpful young staff, log fire and woodburner in inglenook; children and dogs welcome, big garden backing on to river, handy for Harrold-Odell Country Park, open all day. *(Revd R P Tickle)*

OLD WARDEN TL1343
Hare & Hounds (01767) 627225
Village signposted off A600 S of Bedford and B658 W of Biggleswade; SG18 9HQ Popular family-run dining pub with four cosy refurbished rooms, tweed upholstered chairs at light wood tables on stripped wood, tiled or carpeted floors, log fire in one room, inglenook woodburner in another, prints and old photographs including aircraft in the Shuttleworth Collection (just up the road), very well liked food using local ingredients (some from own allotment), good value set lunch Tues-Fri, two Charles Wells ales and a guest, several wines by the glass, friendly attentive service; background music; children welcome, garden stretching up to pine woods behind, nice thatched village and good local walks, open all day, no food Sun evening. *(John Saul)*

POTTON TL2249
Old Coach House (01767) 260221
Village Square; SG19 2NP Comfortably refurbished 18th-c coaching inn, well kept ales such as Charles Wells and good range of wines by the glass, cocktails, popular food including good burgers in bar or restaurant, afternoon teas, friendly helpful staff; background music; children and dogs welcome, seats out at front and in courtyard, 11 bedrooms, open all day. *(David Stewart)*

RISELEY TL0462
Fox & Hounds (01234) 709714
Off A6 from Sharnbrook/Bletsoe roundabout; High Street, just E of Gold Street; MK44 1DT Modernised village pub dating from the 16th c; low beams, stripped boards and imposing stone fireplace, Wells Bombardier and Eagle, steaks cut to weight and other food, separate dining room; children and dogs (in bar) welcome, seats out in front and in back garden with terrace, open (and food) all day. *(Michael Sargent)*

SALFORD SP9339
Swan (01908) 281008
Not far from M1 junction 13 – left off A5140; MK17 8BD Popular Edwardian country dining pub (Peach group), well liked food from sandwiches and deli boards to dry-aged steaks, Sharps Doom Bar and a guest, good range of wines, gins and cocktails, friendly accommodating staff, updated interior with drinking area to right of central servery, sofas and leather chairs on wood floor, restaurant to left with modern country cottage feel and window view into kitchen; background music; children welcome, dogs in bar, seats out on decking, kitchen garden and own smokehouse, open (and food) all day. *(Ben and Diana Bowie)*

SOULDROP SP9861
Bedford Arms (01234) 781384
Village signposted off A6 Rushden–Bedford; High Street; MK44 1EY Village pub dating from the 17th c under new management; cosy low-beamed bar with snug and alcove, Black Sheep, Greene King IPA and three guests, several wines by the glass, tasty well priced pubby food, cottagey dining area with more low beams, broad floorboards and woodburner in central fireplace, roomy mansard-ceilinged part with sofas by big inglenook, local art for sale; open mike night first Sun of month, table skittles, shove-ha'penny and darts; children and dogs (in bar) welcome, garden tables, open all day Fri-Sun, closed Mon. *(Ruth May)*

STEPPINGLEY TL0135
French Horn (01525) 720122
Off A507 just N of Flitwick; Church End; MK45 5AU Comfortable dining pub next to church, linked rooms with stippled beams, standing posts and wall timbers, two inglenooks (one with woodburner), eclectic mix of chesterfields, leather armchairs, cushioned antique dining chairs and other new and old furniture on flagstones or bare boards, Greene King IPA and a changing guest, good range of wines by the glass and malt whiskies, well liked freshly made food (all day weekends) served by friendly staff,

elegant dining room; background music, TV, free wi-fi; children and dogs (in bar) welcome, seats outside overlooking small green, open all day (till 1am Sat). *(Isobel Mackinlay, Caroline Prescott, Mrs Margo Finlay, Jörg Kasprowski)*

STOTFOLD   TL2136
Fox & Duck (01462) 732434
Arlesey Road; SG5 4HE Welcoming roadside pub-restaurant with light modern interior, good food from varied menu including weekday set deal, Greene King IPA, a guest ale and plenty of wines by the glass, friendly accommodating staff, separate coffee lounge; free wi-fi; children welcome, big enclosed garden with play area, closed Sun evening, Mon, otherwise open all day. *(Rupert Hennen)*

STUDHAM   TL0215
Red Lion (01582) 872530
Church Road; LU6 2QA Character community pub with nice staff and jovial hands-on landlord; public bar and eating areas filled with pictures and bits and pieces collected over many years, house plants, wood flooring, carpeting and old red and black tiles, open fire, ales such as Adnams, Fullers, Greene King and Timothy Taylors, enjoyable pubby food (not evenings Sun, Mon, Tues); background music; children and dogs welcome, green picnic-sets in front under pretty window boxes, more on side grass, play house, open all day Fri-Sun. *(Tony Smaithe)*

SUTTON   TL2247
★ John o' Gaunt (01767) 260377
Off B1040 Biggleswade–Potton; SG19 2NE Friendly bustling village pub just up from 14th-c packhorse bridge and ford; beams and timbering, red-painted or pretty papered walls, local artwork for sale, refurbished flagstoned bar with leather seats and sofas around ships tables, open fire and hood skittles, Adnams and Woodfordes ales, local cider and 12 wines by the glass, good food cooked by landlord-chef, dining rooms with mix of furniture on bare boards, woodburner; background music, free wi-fi; children and dogs (in bar) welcome, seats in sheltered garden, pétanque, closed Sun evening, Mon. *(David Stewart, Margaret and Roy Randle)*

TILSWORTH   SP9824
Anchor (01525) 211404
Just off A5 NW of Dunstable; LU7 9PU Comfortably modernised 19th-c red-brick village pub under new management, good food from *MasterChef* finalist, three real ales including Greene King IPA, friendly attentive

service, dining conservatory; children welcome, picnic-sets in large garden, closed Mon, otherwise open all day. *(Ben and Diana Bowie)*

TOTTERNHOE   SP9721
Cross Keys (01525) 220434
Off A505 W of A5; Castle Hill Road; LU6 2DA Restored thatched and timbered two-bar pub below remains of a motte and bailey fort, low beams and cosy furnishings, good straightforward food (not Sun, Mon evenings), well kept ales including Adnams Broadside and Greene King IPA, dining room; big-screen TV; children and dogs (in bar) welcome, good views from attractive big garden, open all day Thurs-Sun. *(Colin Humphreys)*

TURVEY   SP9352
★ Three Fyshes (01234) 881463
A428 NW of Bedford; Bridge Street, W end of village; MK43 8ER Well maintained early 17th-c beamed village pub, big inglenook with woodburner, mix of easy and upright chairs around tables on tiles or ancient flagstones, good well priced home-made food served by cheery attentive staff, Marstons Pedigree, Sharps Doom Bar and a couple of guests, decent choice of wines, carpeted side restaurant; background music; children and dogs (in bar) welcome, charming garden with decking overlooking bridge and mill on the Great Ouse (note the flood marks), car park further along the street, open all day. *(George Atkinson)*

WESTONING   SP0332
Chequers (01525) 712967
Park Road (A5120 N of M1 junction 12); MK45 5LA Refurbished thatched village pub with enjoyable food including good value set lunch and other deals, Adnams and Greene King ales, good choice of wines by the glass and various teas/coffees, helpful friendly service, low-beamed front bar, good-sized stables restaurant; free wi-fi; children and dogs (in bar) welcome, courtyard tables, open all day from 9am (10am weekends) for breakfast. *(Tony Smaithe)*

WOBURN   SP9433
Bell (01525) 290280
Bedford Street; MK17 9QJ Small beamed bar area, longer bare-boards dining lounge up steps, pleasant décor and furnishings, decent good value food including set menu, friendly helpful service, Greene King ales and good choice of wines by the glass; background music, games; children welcome, back terrace, hotel part across busy road, handy for Woburn Abbey/Safari Park, open (and food) all day. *(Ruth May)*

Berkshire

BRAY

SU9079 Map 2

Crown

(01628) 621936 – www.thecrownatbray.co.uk
1.75 miles from M4 junction 9; A308 towards Windsor, then left at Bray signpost on to B3028; High Street; SL6 2AH

Ancient low-beamed pub with knocked-through rooms, enjoyable food, real ales and plenty of outside seating

The main emphasis here is on dining (not surprising given that the owner is Heston Blumenthal), but there's also a little bar area with high stools around an equally high table, simple tables and chairs beside an open fire and regulars who drop in for a chat and a drink: Courage Best and Directors and a couple of changing guest beers on handpump and around 18 wines by the glass. The snug rooms have some panelling, heavy old beams – some so low you may have to mind your head – plenty of timbers at elbow height where walls have been knocked through, a second log fire and neatly upholstered dining chairs and cushioned settles; board games. The covered and heated courtyard has modern slatted chairs and tables and there are plenty of picnic-sets in the large, enclosed back garden.

The highly regarded food includes lunchtime sandwiches, potted rabbit with sweet and sour onions, mussels with garlic, apple and cider, roasted butternut squash risotto, pork, leek and black pepper sausages with onion gravy, confit duck leg with blackberry sauce and braised red cabbage, stone bass fillet with spinach, tomato, shallot and rocket, and puddings such as sherry trifle and white chocolate bread and butter pudding with vanilla ice-cream. *Benchmark main dish: beer-battered fish and chips £16.50. Two-course evening meal £23.45.*

Scottish Courage ~ Lease David Hyde ~ Real ale ~ Open 11.30-11; 11.30-10.30 Sun ~ Bar food 12-2.30 (3 Sat), 6-9.30 (10 Fri, Sat); 12-8 Sun ~ Children welcome ~ Dogs allowed in bar ~ Wi-fi *Recommended by Mike Swan, Phoebe Peacock, Simon Collett-Jones*

BRAY

SU9079 Map 2

Hinds Head

(01628) 626151 – www.hindsheadbray.com
High Street; car park opposite (exit rather tricky); SL6 2AB

First class food in top gastropub, traditional surroundings, fine wines and real ales

The thoroughly traditional L-shaped bar in this handsome old place has dark beams and panelling, polished oak parquet, blazing log fires, red-cushioned built-in wall seats and studded leather carving chairs around small round tables, and latticed windows. High chairs line the counter where they keep beers from local breweries such as Oakham Green Devil IPA, Rebellion IPA and Roasted Nuts and Windsor & Eton Canberra on handpump, 14 wines by the glass from an extensive list, 18 malt whiskies and a dozen specialist gins and whiskies with interesting ways of serving them. This is Heston Blumenthal's second pub in the village.

Imaginative food includes crab (soup and sandwich), venison carpaccio with horseradish, turnip, shallot and caper dressing, goats cheese royale with artichoke, baby onions and butternut squash velouté, duck with beetroot, barley, turnips and duck sauce, fillet of cod with wilted chard, and onion, borage and mussel broth, bone-in sirloin of veal with cabbage, onion and sauce 'reform', oxtail and kidney pudding, and puddings such as hot chocolate wine with millionaire shortbread and rhubarb trifle; there's also a special set weekday menu. *Benchmark main dish: chicken, ham and leek pie £17.95. Two-course evening meal £25.90.*

Free house ~ Licensee Nabiel El-Nakib ~ Real ale ~ Open 11.30 (12 Mon)-11; 12-6.30 Sun ~ Bar food 12-2.30, 6.15-9.15 (9.30 Fri, Sat); 12-3.30 Sun ~ Restaurant ~ Children welcome ~ Dogs allowed in bar ~ Wi-fi *Recommended by Colin McLachlan, Andrew Stone, Valerie Sayer, Simon Day, Lindy Andrews, Edward Mirzoeff*

CHIEVELEY
SU4574 Map 2

Crab & Boar ⊙ ♀ ⇌

(01635) 247550 – www.crabandboar.com

North Heath, W of village; RG20 8UE

Stylish inn with a welcoming atmosphere, good drinks choice, imaginative food and charming staff; seats outside; well equipped bedrooms

The interconnected bars and dining rooms here have a friendly yet gently civilised atmosphere and you'll be genuinely welcomed by courteous staff. The L-shaped bar is light and airy at one end, with tall green leather chairs lining a high shelf, a couple of unusual, equally high tables with garden planter bases, a contemporary chandelier and stools lining the shabby-chic counter where they keep Ringwood Razorback and West Berkshire Mr Chubbs on handpump and good wines by the glass. The other end is cosier, with leather armchairs and sofas facing one another across a low table (set with chess pieces) in front of a woodburning stove in a large fireplace. The first room leading off here is really an extension of the bar, with beams and timbering, tartan-upholstered stall seating and leather banquettes, and framed race tickets on the walls. Dining rooms, linked by timbering and steps, are decorated with old fishing reels, a large boar's head, photos and prints, with an eclectic mix of attractive chairs and tables on bare floorboards or carpet; an end room is just right for a private party. The garden has elegant metal or teak tables and chairs on gravel and grass; there's also a fountain and an outside bar. The comfortable, well equipped bedrooms have fine country views and private courtyards and four have their own hot tub.

Particularly good food includes vodka-cured salmon with cucumber, dill and potato bread, fallow deer tartare with pickled shallots, bubble and squeak with wild mushrooms and mustard, rump and shoulder of lamb with artichoke, cavolo nero and anchovy, crab thermidor with boar jerky, fries and slaw, spatchcock chicken with seasonal greens and gravy, and puddings such as blood orange and almond tart and buttermilk pannacotta with nutmeg shortbread. *Benchmark main dish: slow-cooked pork with black pudding and hispi cabbage £17.00. Two-course evening meal £25.00.*

Free house ~ Licensee Sarah Deakin ~ Real ale ~ Open 12-11 ~ Bar food 12-2.30, 6-9.30 ~
Restaurant ~ Children welcome ~ Dogs allowed in bar ~ Wi-fi ~ Bedrooms: /£110
Recommended by Caroline Prescott, Emma Scofield, Sandra Morgan

HARE HATCH

Horse & Groom ♀ ◧

SU8077 Map 2

(0118) 940 3136 – www.brunningandprice.co.uk/horseandgroom
A4 Bath Road W of Maidenhead; RG10 9SB

Spreading pub with attractively furnished, timbered rooms, enjoyable food and seats outside

Well trained, courteous staff in this handsome old coaching inn warmly welcome all customers and offer a splendid range of drinks including a good changing range of 15 wines by the glass, Brakspears Bitter and Oxford Gold, Ringwood Fortyniner and Wychwood Hobgoblin on handpump, Weston's farm cider, 20 gins and 40 malt whiskies. There are plenty of signs of great age in the interconnected rooms – and much of interest too: beams and timbering, a pleasing variety of well spread individual tables and chairs on mahogany-stained boards, oriental rugs and some carpet to soften the acoustics, and open fires in attractive tiled fireplaces. Also, a profusion of mainly old or antique prints and mirrors, book-lined shelves, house plants and daily papers. A sheltered back garden has picnic-sets and the front terrace has teak tables and chairs under parasols.

High quality food from an interesting menu includes lunchtime sandwiches, chicken and ham terrine with piccalilli, char siu pork belly with pak choi and pickled ginger salad, aubergine, cauliflower and chickpea tagine with apricot and pine nut couscous and yoghurt dressing, burger with toppings, coleslaw and chips, bass fillets with bombay potatoes, spiced dhal and onion bhaji, lamb rump with rolled lamb belly, potato terrine and charred gem and lettuce sauce, and puddings such as lemon tart with passion-fruit coulis and sticky toffee pudding with toffee sauce. *Benchmark main dish: braised lamb shoulder with dauphinoise potatoes £18.95. Two-course evening meal £20.00.*

Brunning & Price ~ Manager Josh Nicholson ~ Real ale ~ Open 11.30-11 ~ Bar food 12-10
(9 Sun) ~ Well behaved children welcome ~ Dogs allowed in bar ~ Wi-fi
Recommended by D J and P M Taylor, Ian Herdman, Simon Rodway

INKPEN

Crown & Garter ⓧ ⇔

SU3764 Map 2

(01488) 668325 – www.crownandgarter.co.uk
Inkpen Common: Inkpen signposted with Kintbury off A4; in Kintbury turn left into Inkpen Road, then keep on into Inkpen Common; RG17 9QR

Carefully run country pub with modern touches blending with original features, enjoyable food and seats outside; bedrooms

For somewhere that feels so remote, this is a substantial and rather fine old brick inn. There's a spreading bar area with wooden stools against the counter where they serve West Berkshire Good Old Boy and Ramsbury Gold on handpump and ten wines by the glass. Leading off here is a snug area with a leather armchair and sofa by an open fire in a raised brick fireplace. Throughout, an assortment of upholstered dining chairs are grouped around simple tables on pale floorboards, with armchairs here and there, cushioned wall seating, mirrors and modern artwork on contemporary paintwork and wallpaper that depicts bookcases (in the smart restaurant) and old suitcases. The front terrace has seats and tables under parasols. The comfortable bedrooms are in a separate single-storey L-shaped building around an attractive garden. There's a separate bakery and coffee shop (which becomes a private dining space in the evening). Disabled access.

 Good british cooking using the best local ingredients includes all-day bar snacks plus lunchtime sandwiches, pigeon pastrami with radish and watercress salad on sourdough toast, poached trout with wilted sorrel and charred skin in trout broth, spiralised spiced root vegetable pasta with roasted peanuts, rocket and burnt butter, minted lamb burger with rosemary fries, redcurrant sauce and coleslaw, ham and mushroom pie, steak of the day with peppercorn sauce, and puddings such as salted caramel and white chocolate tart with milk chocolate ice-cream and rhubarb queen of puddings. *Benchmark main dish: beer-battered fish and chips £14.50. Two-course evening meal £20.00.*

Free house ~ Licensee Romilla Arber ~ Real ale ~ Open 8.30am-11pm; 8.30-6 Sun ~ Bar food 12-2 (2.30 Sun), 6.30-9 ~ Restaurant ~ Children welcome ~ Dogs allowed in bar ~ Wi-fi ~ Bedrooms: £110/£130 *Recommended by David and Judy Robison, Tom Stone, Mark Hamill*

INKPEN
SU3564 Map 2

Swan

(01488) 668326 – www.theswaninn-organics.co.uk

Lower Inkpen; coming from A338 in Hungerford, take Park Street (first left after railway bridge); RG17 9DX

Extended country pub with rambling rooms, traditional décor, real ales and plenty of seats outside; comfortable bedrooms

Owned by local, organic beef farmers (you can buy their produce and ready-made meals and groceries in the interesting farm shop next door) this much extended pub is a handy place after a walk. The rambling beamed rooms have cosy corners, traditional pubby furniture, eclectic bric-a-brac and three log fires, and there's a flagstoned games area plus a cosy restaurant. Butts Jester and Traditional and a changing summer guest on handpump, several wines by the glass and maybe home-made sloe gin; darts, shut the box and board games. The bedrooms are quiet and comfortable. There are picnic-sets on tiered front terraces overlooking a footpath.

Using their own produce, the tasty food includes sandwiches, home-cured bresaola, trio of smoked fish with horseradish cream, ricotta and spinach cannelloni, organic burgers with cheese and chips, steak and kidney pudding, chicken stuffed with brie and basil wrapped in parma ham with dauphinoise potatoes, and puddings such as fruit crumble and lemon cheesecake with lemon sorbet. *Benchmark main dish: home-reared roast beef (Sunday) £14.95. Two-course evening meal £19.00.*

Free house ~ Licensees Mary and Bernard Harris ~ Real ale ~ Open 12-2.30, 6.30-11; 12-11 Sat; 12-4 Sun; closed Mon, Tues, evening Sun ~ Bar food 12-2 (3 weekends), 7-9 ~ Restaurant ~ Children welcome ~ Wi-fi ~ Bedrooms: £70/£90
Recommended by Chris and Angela Buckell, Peter Brix, Charlie Parker

KINTBURY
SU3866 Map 2

Dundas Arms ♀ ⇤

(01488) 658263 – www.dundasarms.co.uk

Village signposted off A4 Newbury–Hungerford about a mile W of Halfway; Station Road – pub just over hump-back canal bridge, at start of village itself; RG17 9UT

Carefully updated inn with relaxed informal bar, good two-level restaurant, and lovely waterside garden; comfortable bedrooms

What makes this handsome pub special is its waterside setting, standing between the River Kennet and the Kennet & Avon Canal, surrounded by lots of ducks and banks of spring daffodils. As well as picnic-sets on decking, the large, pretty back garden (with water on each side) has plenty of well spaced tables on grass among shrubs and trees. The big windows of the smart two-level restaurant overlook this scene. At the other end is a smallish bar, taking its relaxed informal mood from the cheerful helpful staff. Here, there are sporting prints above a high oak dado, neat little cushioned arts-and-crafts chairs around a few stripped or polished tables on broad floorboards, and high chairs by the counter (decorated with highly polished old penny pieces), which serves Tutts Clump farm cider from handpump as well as Ramsbury Gold, Ringwood Razorback and a guest from West Berkshire brewery, and 14 wines by the glass. Between the bar and restaurant is a cosy, tartan-carpeted sitting room with wing chairs and a splendid leather and mahogany settee, daily papers, a good winter log fire flanked by glass-fronted bookcases, and big silhouette portraits on topiary-print wallpaper. Pleasant nearby walks.

From a well judged menu, food includes lunchtime sandwiches, gin- and juniper-cured salmon with lemon mayonnaise, chicken liver and cider pâté, moules frites, artichoke, leek and walnut hotpot, crab cakes with lemon and basil vinaigrette, chicken with herb butter, confit garlic and fries, spiced lamb belly with couscous and mint yoghurt, and puddings such as chocolate and berry cheesecake and eton mess. *Benchmark main dish: steak burger with fried egg and fries £14.00. Two-course evening meal £22.00.*

Free house ~ Licensee Emily Carr ~ Real ale ~ Open 11-11 (midnight Sat) ~ Bar food 12-2.45, 6-8.45; 12-3, 6-8 Sun ~ Restaurant ~ Children welcome ~ Dogs allowed in bar and bedrooms ~ Wi-fi ~ Bedrooms: /£140 *Recommended by Harvey Brown, Neil Allen, Tony Hobden*

MAIDENS GREEN
Winning Post 🛏

SU9072   Map 2

(01344) 882242 – www.winningpostwinkfield.co.uk
Signs to Winkfield Plain W of Winkfield off A330, then first right; SL4 4SW

18th-c inn with beams and timbering in character rooms, good food and drinks choice, friendly feel and seats in garden; bedrooms

Although this inn was deservedly packed on our Sunday lunchtime visit, we were genuinely welcomed by both the staff and the chatty locals crowding around the bar (several with dogs – ours got a treat). It's gently civilised but easy-going, with beamed open-plan rooms connected by timbering (some with leather crash pads). The main bar area has leather and wood tub chairs around a table in one window, a long cushioned settle in another, big flagstones and stools by the bar where efficient staff keep Upham Punter and Tipster on handpump and good wines by the glass. An end room, also with flagstones, has more tub chairs, wall seating and contemporary paintwork on planked walls; TV. The dining rooms are to the left of the bar: one long room has huge horse photos taking up whole walls, there are tartan banquettes, cushioned dining chairs around wooden tables on bare boards, a woodburning stove, hanging lanterns and bowler hat lights. A room to the back of the inn called the Winning Enclosure has horse-racing wall photos and a large raised fireplace. The partly covered terrace has good quality seats and tables and a rather smart conical smokers' hut. Quiet bedrooms, handy for Ascot and Henley, face the garden.

As well as rather good breakfasts (for non-residents too), the highly rated food includes potted crab and crayfish, crispy duck salad with pomegranate, flatbread croutons and roast garlic dressing, sharing platters, grilled artichokes with bulgar wheat, tomato, feta, olives and sorrel pesto, rack of lamb with feta, black olives, cherry tomatoes, spinach and dauphinoise potatoes, 6oz fillet of beef with braised ox cheek, carrots and spinach, and puddings such as honey and lavender crème brûlée and rhubarb and custard soufflé. *Benchmark main dish: burger with toppings and chips £13.50. Two-course evening meal £22.00.*

Upham ~ Manager Gregory Loison ~ Real ale ~ Open 11am-11.30pm (10.30 Sun) ~ Bar food 12-9.30; 12-4, 7-9 Sun ~ Restaurant ~ Children welcome ~ Dogs allowed in bar and bedrooms ~ Wi-fi ~ Bedrooms: £110/£130 *Recommended by Sarah Roberts, Millie and Peter Downing, Tom Stone*

NEWBURY
SU4767 Map 2

Newbury 🌟 ♀ 🍺

(01635) 49000 – www.thenewburypub.co.uk
Bartholomew Street; RG14 5HB

Lively pub with thoughtful choice of drinks, good food and plenty of bar and dining space

Once found, you're sure to go back to this cheerful, stylish town pub. The bar has an assortment of wooden dining chairs around sturdy farmhouse and other solid tables on bare boards, comfortable leather sofas, big paintings on pale painted walls and church candles. They keep a fantastic choice of drinks: a beer named for them (from Greene King), Timothy Taylors Landlord, Upham Punter and Tipster and a guest beer on handpump, a farm cider, 20 malt whiskies, around 23 wines by the glass, an extensive cocktail list and a fine range of coffees and teas (including tea grown in Cornwall). There is also an upstairs cocktail bar that leads out on to a roof terrace with an electric folding canopy roof. Light and airy, the dining rooms have wall benches and church chairs around more rustic tables on more bare boards, local artwork and shelves full of cookery books. The downstairs courtyard holds a smoker, which is put to great use.

 Rewarding food using carefully sourced local produce includes lunchtime open sandwiches, chicken liver parfait with apricot and vanilla chutney, gin- and earl grey-cured sea trout with gin and cucumber gel, pizzas from their italian pizza oven, quinoa and feta burger with harissa mayonnaise, duck egg with black pudding, potatoes, onions, spinach and pine nuts, slow-cooked lamb belly with garlic crumb and roasted vegetables, duck breast with mushroom fricassée, and puddings such as Guinness cake with chocolate and ale sauce and malt ice-cream and apple and boozy sultana crumble; they also offer weekend breakfasts (11am-1pm). *Benchmark main dish: 6oz rump steak with skinny fries and a choice of sauces £15.00. Two-course evening meal £20.00.*

Free house ~ Licensee Peter Lumber ~ Real ale ~ Open 12-11 (midnight Fri, 2am Sat, 10 Sun) ~ Bar food 12-3 (4 Sat), 6-10; 12-4 Sun ~ Restaurant ~ Children welcome ~ Dogs allowed in bar ~ Wi-fi *Recommended by Ian Herdman, Lionel Smith, Mary Joyce*

PANGBOURNE
SU6376 Map 2

Elephant

(0118) 984 2244 – www.elephanthotel.co.uk
Church Road; RG8 7AR

Plenty of elephant detail in bar and dining rooms, fair choice of ales and food and seats in sizeable garden; bedrooms

This bustling place is in a Thames Valley village, not far from the river. It's a handsome building and throughout the bars, dining room and seating areas there are indeed numerous elephants of all sizes – mainly indian in style and of painted wood – on mantelpieces, on shelves, in a cabinet and a huge one on wheels in the reception hall; the gantry above the bar is inlaid with wooden panels painted with Babar escapades. The main bar has simple wooden furniture, some leather banquettes, bare boards, a log fire with a large mirror above it and West Berkshire Good Old Boy and Mrs Chubbs and Sharps Doom Bar on handpump, 16 wines by the glass and two farm ciders; TV, background music and skittle alley. Two seating areas have comfortable sofas and armchairs and rugs on floorboards, while the dining room has plenty of tables and chairs on more rugs. In the big back garden are rattan-style sofas on flagstones, and picnic-sets on the lawn. Bedrooms are individually styled with bold colours and fine fabrics.

Tasty food includes sandwiches, potted duck liver parfait with red onion marmalade, southern fried chicken wings with spicy barbecue dip, mushroom, spinach and goats cheese omelette, cheese burger with slaw and spiced fries, honey-glazed gressingham duck breast with chambord sauce, celeriac purée and thyme-potato fondant, venison steak with redcurrant jus and sweet potato and beetroot gratin, and puddings such as banana tarte tatin with toffee sauce and spiced chai tea with honey-roasted pumpkin pannacotta. *Benchmark main dish: pork three ways with honey and mustard sauce £16.50. Two-course evening meal £20.00.*

Bluebelt Hospitality ~ Lease Dominic Bishop ~ Real ale ~ Open 11-11 (midnight Sat) ~ Bar food 12-2.30, 6-9.30; 12-9.30 weekends ~ Restaurant ~ Children welcome ~ Dogs allowed in bar and bedrooms ~ Wi-fi ~ Bedrooms: £110/£130 *Recommended by Sophie Ellison, Barbara Brown, Charles Welch*

PEASEMORE
Fox

SU4577 Map 2

(01635) 248480 – www.foxatpeasemore.co.uk
4 miles from M4 junction 13, via Chieveley: keep on through Chieveley to Peasemore, turning left into Hillgreen Lane at small sign to Fox Inn; village also signposted from B4494 Newbury–Wantage; RG20 7JN

Friendly downland pub on top form under its expert licensees

After a walk around the lovely surrounding countryside, this bustling, cheerful pub is just the place to head for – and you can be sure of a genuine welcome from the first class licensees. The long bare-boards bar has strategically placed high-backed settles (comfort guaranteed by plenty of colourful cushions), a warm woodburning stove in a stripped-brick chimney breast and, for real sybarites, two luxuriously carpeted end areas, one with velour tub armchairs. Friendly, efficient, black-clad staff serve Ridgeside Black Night, West Berkshire Good Old Boy and a changing guest on handpump, 15 wines by the glass and summer farm cider; background music. This is downland horse-training country, and picnic-table sets at the front look out to the rolling fields beyond the quiet country lane – on a clear day as far as the Hampshire border hills some 20 miles south; there are more on a smallish sheltered back terrace.

Enjoyable food includes lunchtime ciabatta sandwiches and omelettes, crispy fried brie with berry compote, charcuterie platter, goats cheese, mushroom and mediterranean vegetable tart on provençal sauce, home-made fishcakes, lambs liver and bacon with caramelised onion gravy, chicken breast wrapped in bacon on red wine sauce, and puddings such as crème brûlée and chocolate mousse. *Benchmark main dish: beef wellington £19.50. Two-course evening meal £19.50.*

Free house ~ Licensees Philip and Lauren Davison ~ Real ale ~ Open 12-2.30, 6-11; 12-11 Sat; 12-6 Sun; closed Mon, Tues ~ Bar food 12-2, 6-9; 12-3, 5.30-9 Sat; 12-4 Sun ~

Restaurant ~ Children welcome ~ Dogs allowed in bar ~ Wi-fi *Recommended by Harvey Brown, Ian Herdman, Sarah Roberts, Mrs P Sumner*

RUSCOMBE   SU7976   Map 2
Royal Oak 🏵🍺

(0118) 934 5190 – www.burattas.co.uk
Ruscombe Lane (B3024 just E of Twyford); RG10 9JN

Wide choice of popular food at welcoming pub with interesting furnishings and paintings, and local beer and wine

Known locally as Buratta's, this deservedly busy place is run by charming, hands-on licensees. The bars are open-plan and carpeted and cleverly laid out so that each area is fairly snug, but it still maintains an overall feel of a lot of people enjoying themselves. A good variety of furniture runs from dark oak tables to big chunky pine ones with mixed seating to match; the two sofas facing each other are popular. Contrasting with the old exposed ceiling joists, mostly unframed modern paintings and prints decorate the walls, which are painted in cream, white and soft green. Binghams (the brewery is just across the road) Space Hoppy IPA and Twyford Tipple and Fullers London Pride on handpump, 15 wines by the glass (they stock wines from the Stanlake Park vineyard in the village), several malt whiskies and attentive service. Picnic-sets are ranged around a venerable central hawthorn in the garden behind (where there are ducks and chickens); summer barbecues. The pub is on the Henley Arts Trail. Do visit the landlady's antiques and collectables shop, which is open during pub hours.

 Consistently good food includes sandwiches and panini, red thai chicken and prawn noodles, chicken liver pâté with red onion marmalade, ham and egg, a vegetarian sharing platter, stilton and bacon burger with chips, lamb kidneys with bacon and red wine sauce, venison with redcurrant and rosemary sauce, steak with peppercorn sauce, and puddings. *Benchmark main dish: chicken strips with mushrooms and shallots in brandy and mustard sauce £13.00. Two-course evening meal £22.00.*

Enterprise ~ Lease Jenny and Stefano Buratta ~ Real ale ~ Open 12-3, 6-11; 12-4 Sun; closed Sun and Mon evenings ~ Bar food 12-2.30, 6-9.30; 12-3 Sun ~ Restaurant ~ Children welcome ~ Dogs welcome ~ Wi-fi *Recommended by Bill Gulliver and Harry Thomson, Emma Scofield, Paul Humphreys*

SHEFFORD WOODLANDS   SU3673   Map 2
Pheasant

(01488) 648284 – www.thepheasant-inn.co.uk
Under 0.5 miles from M4 junction 14 – A338 towards Wantage, first left on B4000; RG17 7AA

Bustling bars, a separate dining room, highly thought-of food and beer and seats outside; bedrooms

Good, enjoyable food and a warm welcome consistently attract happy customers here. The various interconnecting bar rooms have a mix of elegant wooden dining chairs and settles around all sorts of tables, big mirrors here and there, plenty of horse-related prints, photos and paintings (including a huge mural) – the owners are keen racegoers – and a warm fire in a little brick fireplace. One snug little room, with log-end wallpaper, has armchairs, a cushioned chesterfield and a flat-screen TV. A beer named for the pub (from Marstons), Marstons Pedigree, Ramsbury Gold and Ringwood Best on handpump and quite a few good wines by the glass. There's also a separate dining room; background music. Seats in the garden have attractive views. The comfortable modern bedrooms (recently refurbished) are in a separate extension and breakfasts are good.

Rewarding food (breakfasts from 7.30 to 10.30am) includes sandwiches, ham hock terrine with piccalilli, whipped goats cheese with baby beetroot and dressed rocket, burger with chorizo jam, coleslaw and skinny fries, leek and potato gratin with toasted walnuts, roast baby carrots and candied olives, slow-roast pork belly with creamed leeks, apple purée and red wine jus, half roast chicken with herb fondant potato, wild mushroom and tarragon velouté, and puddings such as banoffi pot with chantilly cream and caramelised banana and spiced orange cake with plum sauce and vanilla ice-cream. *Benchmark main dish: beer-battered fish and chips £14.00. Two-course evening meal £21.00.*

Upham ~ Tenant Jack Greenall ~ Real ale ~ Open 11-11; 12-10.30 Sun ~ Bar food 12-3, 6-9.30; 12-5, 6-9 Sun ~ Children welcome ~ Dogs allowed in bar ~ Wi-fi ~ Bedrooms: /£110 *Recommended by Katharine Cowherd, Michael Sargent, B and M Kendall, Guy Vowles, Simon Rodway*

SONNING
Bull 🛏

SU7575   Map 2

(0118) 969 3901 – www.bullinnsonning.co.uk
Off B478, by church; village signed off A4 E of Reading; RG4 6UP

Pretty timbered inn in attractive spot, plenty of character in old-fashioned bars, friendly staff and good food; bedrooms

As this is a fine black and white timbered 16th-c inn near the River Thames, there are always plenty of customers; it probably looks its best in early summer when the wisteria is flowering and the courtyard is full of bright flower tubs. Inside, the two old-fashioned bar rooms have low ceilings and heavy beams, cosy alcoves, leather armchairs and sofas, cushioned antique settles and low wooden chairs on bare boards, and open fireplaces. Fullers HSB, Honey Dew, London Pride, Oliver's Island and a couple of guests on handpump served by helpful staff, 16 good wines by the glass, cocktails and a farm cider. The dining room has a mix of wooden chairs and tables, rugs on parquet flooring and shelves of books; TV. The bedrooms are comfortable and well equipped. If you bear left through the ivy-clad churchyard opposite, then turn left along the bank of the river, you come to a very pretty lock. The Thames Valley Park is close by.

Inventive food includes lunchtime sandwiches, chicken liver and Armagnac parfait with fig chutney, popcorn-dusted tiger prawn skewers with smoked aioli, beer and ale sausages with onion gravy, yellow fin tuna loin with dauphinoise potatoes and red wine jus, vegetables and shiitake mushrooms in miso and ginger broth with glass noodles, pak choi, beansprouts, spring onions and chilli, calves liver with bacon, mushroom and madeira sauce, and puddings such as rose water pannacotta with macerated rhubarb and chocolate brownie with hot chocolate sauce. *Benchmark main dish: pie of the day £15.50. Two-course evening meal £20.00.*

Fullers ~ Manager Christine Mason ~ Real ale ~ Open 10am-11pm (midnight Sat); 12-10.30 Sun ~ Bar food 10-9.30 ~ Restaurant ~ Children welcome ~ Dogs allowed in bar ~ Wi-fi ~ Tribute acts monthly ~ Bedrooms: /£105 *Recommended by Simon Collett-Jones, Roy Hoing, Susan and John Douglas, Allan Lloyd and family*

Please tell us if the décor, atmosphere, food or drink at a pub is different from our description. We rely on readers' reports to keep us up to date: feedback@goodguides.com, or (no stamp needed) The Good Pub Guide, FREEPOST RTJR-ZCYZ-RJZT, Perrymans Lane, Etchingham TN19 7DN.

SWALLOWFIELD

SU7364   Map 2

George & Dragon ⭐ ♀

(0118) 988 4432 – www.georgeanddragonswallowfield.co.uk

Church Road, towards Farley Hill; RG7 1TJ

Busy country pub with enjoyable bar food, real ales, friendly service and seats outside

The long-serving licensees here care for both their pub and their customers – and it shows. It's a comfortable, easy-going place and the various interconnected rooms have plenty of character: beams (some quite low) and standing timbers, a happy mix of nice old dining chairs and settles around individual wooden tables, rugs on flagstones, lit candles, a big log fire and country prints on red or bare brick walls; background music. Ringwood Best, Sharps Doom Bar and Upham Punter on handpump, quite a few wines by the glass and several gins and whiskies. There are picnic-sets on gravel or paving in the garden and the website has details of an enjoyable four-mile walk that starts and ends at the pub.

Proper country cooking includes lunchtime ciabattas, barbecue pork ribs with red cabbage and peanut coleslaw, chicken liver and white truffle oil parfait with tomato chutney, beer-battered fish and chips, venison sausages and game faggot with roast red onion gravy, corn-fed chicken with mushroom and chestnut stuffing and carrot and swede mash, monkfish with creamed leeks, sweet potato, parma ham and chardonnay sauce, and puddings such as lemon posset and dark chocolate mousse with black cherry compote. *Benchmark main dish: half shoulder of lamb with rosemary sauce £15.95. Two-course evening meal £25.00.*

Free house ~ Licensee Paul Dailey ~ Real ale ~ Open 12-11 (10 Sun) ~ Bar food 12-2.30, 7-9.30; 12-3, 7-9 Sun ~ Restaurant ~ Children welcome lunchtime only ~ Dogs allowed in bar ~ Wi-fi *Recommended by Simon Collett-Jones, Tony and Jill Radnor, Mark Hamill*

UPPER BASILDON

SU5976   Map 2

Red Lion ♀ 🍺

(01491) 671234 – www.theredlionupperbasildon.co.uk

Off A329 NW of Pangbourne; Aldworth Road; RG8 8NG

Laid-back country pub with friendly family atmosphere, popular food and a good choice of drinks

Handy after a walk for either a drink or a meal, this is a popular pub with plenty of customers. There's pale blue-grey paintwork throughout (even on the beams), and the bars have chapel chairs, a few pews and miscellaneous stripped tables on bare floorboards, and a green leather chesterfield and armchair; maybe hops on timbering and little plants on each table. Courage Directors, Sharps Doom Bar, Upham Punter and West Berkshire Good Old Boy on handpump, a dozen wines from an extensive list and a farm cider. Beyond a double-sided woodburning stove, a pitched-ceiling area has much the same furniture on cord carpet, though a big cut-glass chandelier and large mirror give it a slightly more formal dining feel. Maybe daily papers including the *Racing Post*, occasional background music and regular (usually jazz-related) live music. There are sturdy picnic-sets in the sizeable enclosed garden and summer barbecues and hog roasts.

🍴 Quite a choice of tasty food includes lunchtime sandwiches, smoked salmon and prawn cocktail, pork and madeira terrine with tomato and chilli jam, sharing platters, beer-battered haddock and chips, pork and leek sausages with onion gravy, barbecue ribs, coleslaw and potato wedges, lamb rump with white bean, garlic and thyme casserole and red wine gravy, pork chop with bubble and squeak croquettes, cabbage and smoked bacon and cider jus, and puddings such as dark chocolate mousse and apple and red berry crumble. *Benchmark main dish: seafood platter £18.50. Two-course evening meal £21.00.*

Enterprise ~ Lease Alison Green ~ Real ale ~ Open 11-3, 5-11; 11-11 Sat; 11-10.30 Sun ~ Bar food 12-2.30, 6-9 (9.30 Fri, Sat); 12-3.30, 6-7.30 Sun ~ Restaurant ~ Children welcome ~ Dogs allowed in bar ~ Wi-fi *Recommended by Belinda Stamp, Neil Allen, Angela Marlow, Nick Sharpe*

WHITE WALTHAM
Beehive

SU8477 Map 2

(01628) 822877 ~ www.thebeehivewhitewaltham.co.uk
Waltham Road (B3024 W of Maidenhead); SL6 3SH

● ●

Berkshire Dining Pub of the Year

Attractive village pub with welcoming staff and enjoyable food and drinks choice; seats in garden with table service

After refurbishments, the garden has been extended and updating of some facilities inside the pub has made quite a difference. The atmosphere remains bustling and friendly, helped along by the hospitable landlord and his friendly staff. To the right of the entrance are several comfortably spacious areas with leather chairs around sturdy tables, while to the left is a neat bar brightened up by cheerful scatter cushions on built-in wall seats and captain's chairs. Rebellion IPA, Sharps Doom Bar and Hook Norton Old Hooky on handpump, 20 wines by the glass from a good list and farm cider; background music. An airy dining room has glass doors opening on to the front terrace where teak seats and picnic-sets take in the rather fine view. The bigger back garden has plenty of seats and tables, and the village cricket field is opposite. Disabled access and facilities.

Imaginative food cooked by the landlord includes sandwiches, pickled mackerel with horseradish cream, dorset snails with garlic butter and gorgonzola, risotto of wild mushrooms, mozzarella, radicchio and parmesan, local rabbit and bacon pie, lemon sole with brown shrimps, cucumber and lemon butter sauce, peppered venison haunch with sauce poivrade, lamb cutlet and shoulder with ratatouille, and puddings such as rhubarb trifle and steamed treacle pudding with butterscotch sauce. *Benchmark main dish: fish and chips £14.50. Two-course evening meal £25.00.*

Enterprise ~ Lease Dominic Chapman ~ Real ale ~ Open 12-2.30, 5-11; 12-11 Sat; 12-8 Sun ~ Bar food 12-2.30, 6-9.30 (10 Fri, Sat); 12-4 Sun ~ Restaurant ~ Children welcome ~ Dogs allowed in bar ~ Wi-fi *Recommended by Dr Simon Innes, Charlie Parker, Simon Collett-Jones*

WOOLHAMPTON
Rowbarge

SU5766 Map 2

(0118) 971 2213 ~ www.brunningandprice.co.uk/rowbarge
Station Road; RG7 5SH

Canalside pub with plenty of interest in rambling rooms, six real ales, good bistro-style food and lots of outside seating

In warm weather you can make the most of the setting here, with wooden chairs and tables on a decked terrace and picnic-sets among trees by the Kennet & Avon Canal. Six rambling rooms with beams and timbering are connected by open doorways and knocked-through walls. The décor is gently themed to represent the nearby canal with hundreds of prints and photographs (some of rowing and boats) and oars on the walls, as well as old glass and stone bottles in nooks and crannies, big house plants and fresh flowers, plenty of candles and several open fires; the many large mirrors create an impression of even more space. Throughout there are antique dining chairs around various nice old tables, settles, built-in cushioned wall seating, armchairs, a group of high stools around a huge wooden barrel table, and rugs on polished boards, stone tiles or carpeting. Friendly, helpful staff serve Phoenix Brunning & Price Original plus guests such as Butts Blackguard Porter, Grand Union Best, Itchen Valley Hampshire Rose, Ramsbury Red Velvet and Tring Side Pocket for a Toad on handpump, 20 wines by the glass, 30 gins and 65 malt whiskies; background music and board games.

 Attractively presented brasserie-style food includes sandwiches, king prawn tempura with mango, chilli and coriander salsa, herb-crusted lamb with pea and mint pannacotta, mussels with leeks, bacon and cider, butternut squash and feta salad with wild rice and toasted walnuts, pork and leek sausages with onion gravy, duo of pheasant with roasted root vegetables, teriyaki bass with crispy wasabi rice balls and chilli, soy and sesame dressing, and puddings such as green tea jelly with blueberry compote and lemon sorbet and dark chocolate brownie with chocolate sauce. *Benchmark main dish: fish pie £13.95. Two-course evening meal £20.00.*

Brunning & Price ~ Manager Stephen Butt ~ Real ale ~ Open 11-11 (10.30 Sun) ~ Bar food 12-10 (9.30 Sun) ~ Restaurant ~ Children welcome ~ Dogs allowed in bar ~ Wi-fi
Recommended by Mrs P Sumner, Tony Hobden, John Preddy

YATTENDON
Royal Oak 🌟 ⌑ 🛏

SU5574 Map 2

(01635) 201325 – www.royaloakyattendon.co.uk
The Square; B4009 NE from Newbury; right at Hampstead Norreys, village signed on left; RG18 0UG

Civilised old inn with beamed and panelled rooms, imaginative food and seats in pretty garden; bedrooms

Although there is quite an emphasis on the good food here, you're more than welcome to drop in for a drink, and with the West Berkshire brewery actually in the village, the Good Old Boy, Maggs Mild and Mr Chubbs on handpump are on tip top form; the 12 wines by the glass are well chosen. The charming bar rooms have beams and panelling, an appealing mix of wooden dining chairs around interesting tables, some half-panelled wall seating, rugs on quarry tiles or wooden floorboards, plenty of prints on brick, cream or red walls, lovely flower arrangements and four log fires. Under the trellising in the walled back garden are wicker armchairs and tables and there are picnic-sets under parasols at the front. This is a comfortable place to stay and the light, attractive bedrooms overlook the garden or village square; breakfasts are good; boules. The pub is only ten minutes from Newbury Racecourse and gets pretty busy on race days.

 First class food includes sandwiches, hot buttered crab on toast, chicken livers in port and madeira jus, roast beetroot, quinoa and rocket with cranberries and sunflower seeds, chicken kiev, king prawn and chorizo tagliatelle, venison with artichoke purée and juniper jus, baked cod with smoked bacon and cheddar sauce, and puddings such as apple and pear crumble and chocolate and almond pudding with chocolate sauce; they also offer a two- and three-course set lunch. *Benchmark main dish: rib-eye steak with pepper sauce £25.00. Two-course evening meal £26.00.*

Free house ~ Licensee Rob McGill ~ Real ale ~ Open 11-11; 12-10.30 Sun ~ Bar food 12-2.30 (3 weekends), 6.30-9.30 (9 Sun) ~ Children welcome ~ Dogs welcome ~ Wi-fi ~ Bedrooms: /£100 *Recommended by Colin McLachlan, Alistair Forsyth, David and Stella Martin*

Also Worth a Visit in Berkshire

Besides the fully inspected pubs, you might like to try these pubs that have been recommended to us and described by readers. Do tell us what you think of them: feedback@goodguides.com

ALDWORTH SU5579
★**Bell** (01635) 578272
A329 Reading–Wallingford; left on to B4009 at Streatley; RG8 9SE Unspoilt and unchanging (in same family for over 250 years), simply furnished panelled rooms, beams in ochre ceiling, ancient one-handed clock, woodburner, glass-panelled hatch serving well kept Arkells, West Berkshire and a monthly guest, Upton cider, nice house wines, maybe winter mulled wine, good value rolls, ploughman's and winter soup, traditional pub games, no mobile phones or credit cards; can get busy weekends; well behaved children and dogs welcome, seats in quiet, cottagey garden by village cricket ground, animals in paddock behind pub, maybe Christmas mummers and summer morris, closed Mon (open lunchtime bank holidays). *(Valerie Sayer)*

ALDWORTH SU5579
Four Points (01635) 578367
B4009 towards Hampstead Norreys; RG8 9RL Attractive 17th-c thatched roadside pub with low beams, standing timbers and panelling, nice fire in bar with more formal seating area to the left and restaurant at back, good value home-made food (all day weekends) from baguettes up, bargain OAP lunch deal Mon-Weds, local Two Cocks and Wadworths 6X, friendly helpful young staff; children and dogs (in bar) welcome, garden over road with play area. *(Sarah Roberts)*

ARBORFIELD CROSS SU7667
Bull (0118) 976 2244
On roundabout; RG2 9QD Light open-plan dining pub with most tables set for their good popular food (need to book), extensive menu including some french dishes, well priced house wines, efficient friendly service; children welcome, picnic-sets in garden with play area, open all day Fri-Sun, closed Mon. *(John Pritchard)*

ASHMORE GREEN SU4969
Sun in the Wood (01635) 42377
B4009 (Shaw Road) off A339, right to Kiln Road, left to Stoney Lane; RG18 9HF Refurbished and extended 19th-c dining pub; enjoyable food (not Sun evening) from stone-baked pizzas and pub favourites up, Thurs grill night, Wadworths

ales and several wines by the glass, spacious interior with light open feel; background music, quiz nights; children welcome, dogs in bar, decked terrace and woodside garden, open all day. *(John Pritchard)*

ASTON SU7884
★**Flower Pot** (01491) 574721
Off A4130 Henley–Maidenhead at top of Remenham Hill; RG9 3DG Roomy red-brick country pub with nice local feel, snug traditional bar and airy back dining area, lots of stuffed fish and other taxidermy, roaring log fire, four well kept ales such as Brakspears and Ringwood, enjoyable food (not Sun evening) from baguettes to fish and game, quick friendly service; vocal parrot; very busy with walkers and families at weekends, dogs allowed in some parts, country views from big orchard garden, side field with poultry, Thames nearby, three bedrooms, open all day weekends. *(Edward Mirzoeff)*

BARKHAM SU7866
Bull (0118) 976 2816
Barkham Road; RG41 4TL Traditional pub run by friendly thai family, opened-up carpeted interior with dining area to one end, half a dozen ales such as Gales, Otter, St Austell and Timothy Taylors, popular food including good south-east asian choices; Mon quiz: open all day (till 7pm Sun). *(John Pritchard)*

BEECH HILL SU6964
Elm Tree (0118) 988 3505
3.3 miles from M4 junction 11: A33 towards Basingstoke, turning off into Beech Hill Road after about 2 miles; RG7 2AZ Five rooms, one with blazing fire, and nice rural views especially from more modern barn-style restaurant and conservatory, good food (not Sun evening) from lunchtime sandwiches and pub standards up, prompt friendly service, well kept ales such as Ringwood and Sharps, good choice of wines by the glass; children and dogs welcome, tables on heated front deck with palms, open all day. *(Robert Watt)*

BEENHAM SU5868
Six Bells (0118) 971 3368
The Green; RG7 5NX Comfortable red-brick Victorian village pub with good food

---

Post Office address codings confusingly give the impression that some pubs are in Berkshire, when they're really in Buckinghamshire, Oxfordshire or Hampshire (which is where we list them).

including imaginative additions to standard pub menu, West Berkshire Good Old Boy and a couple of guests, friendly owners and staff, large bar area with armchairs and winter fires, dining conservatory; board games; children welcome at lunchtime, four bedrooms, open all day Fri-Sun, closed Mon lunchtime. *(John Pritchard, Richard Tilbrook, Tony Hobden)*

CHARVIL SU7776
Lands End (0118) 934 0700
Lands End Lane/Whistley Mill Lane near Old River ford; RG10 OUE Welcoming 1930s Tudor-style pub with reasonably priced food from good baguettes to blackboard specials, well kept Brakspears and a dozen wines by the glass, efficient accommodating staff, open-plan bar with log fire, separate restaurant, various stuffed fish (good fishing nearby); children welcome, sizeable garden with terrace picnic-sets. *(Paul Humphreys)*

CHEAPSIDE SU9469
Thatched Tavern (01344) 620874
Off A332/A329, then off B383 at Village Hall sign; SL5 7QG Civilised dining pub with a good deal of character and plenty of room for just a drink; up-to-date often ambitious food (can be pricey) along with more traditional choices, good range of wines by the glass, Fullers London Pride, a beer named for the pub and a guest ale, Weston's cider, big inglenook log fire, low beams and polished flagstones in cottagey core, three smart dining rooms off; children welcome, dogs in bar, tables on terrace and attractive sheltered back lawn, handy for Virginia Water, open all day weekends and busy on Ascot race days. *(Dr Simon Innes)*

CHIEVELEY SU4773
★Olde Red Lion (01635) 248379
Handy for M4 junction 13 via A34 N-bound; Green Lane; RG20 8XB Attractive village pub with friendly landlord and helpful staff, three well kept Arkells beers, nice varied choice of generously served food from good sandwiches and baguettes up, reasonable prices, low-beamed carpeted L-shaped bar with panelling and hunting prints, log fire, extended back restaurant; background music, games machine, TV; wheelchair accessible throughout, small garden, five bedrooms in separate old building, open all day weekends. *(Mrs P Sumner)*

COMPTON SU5180
Swan (01635) 579400
High Street; RG20 6NJ Modernised village inn near Newbury Racecourse; flagstoned bar with cushioned wall seating, bucket chairs and some high tables, a couple of Greene King ales, well liked bar and restaurant food (service charge added), two dining rooms with dark tables on wood floor, log fire, also

room with sofas and piano; background music, TV, free wi-fi; children and dogs (in some parts) welcome, picnic-sets in big garden, six bedrooms, open all day. *(Charlie Parker)*

COOKHAM SU8985
★Bel & the Dragon (01628) 521263
High Street (B4447); SL6 9SQ Smartly updated 15th-c inn; heavy beams, log fires and simple country furnishings in two-room front bar and dining area, hand-painted cartoons on pastel walls, more modern bistro-style back restaurant, emphasis on good food (separate bar and restaurant menus) including weekend brunch, Rebellion IPA and a local guest, plenty of wines by the glass from extensive list, cocktails; children welcome, dogs in bar, well tended garden with tables on paved terrace, five bedrooms, Stanley Spencer Gallery almost opposite, open all day. *(Theocsbrian)*

COOKHAM SU8885
★White Oak (01628) 523043
The Pound (B4447); SL6 9QE Bustling red-brick pub with emphasis on landlord-chef's good interesting food, large back eating area and several other parts set for dining, front bar with Greene King IPA and good choice of wines by the glass, friendly efficient service; free wi-fi; children welcome, sturdy wooden furniture on sheltered back terrace and steps up to white wirework tables on grass, closed Sun evening, otherwise open all day. *(Simon Collett-Jones)*

COOKHAM DEAN SU8785
★Chequers (01628) 481232
Dean Lane; follow signpost Cookham Dean, Marlow; SL6 9BQ Cosy refurbished red-brick dining pub with good imaginative food from visible kitchen including set lunch deal (Mon-Sat), welcoming efficient service, busy little flagstoned bar with Rebellion ales and good wines by the glass, area on the left with stove in big brick fireplace, back conservatory overlooking sloping lawn, winter log fires; background music; children welcome, picnic-sets under parasols on front grass, open all day Sat, till 6pm Sun. *(Harvey Brown, Gus Swan)*

COOKHAM DEAN SU8785
★Jolly Farmer (01628) 482905
Church Road, off Hills Lane; SL6 9PD 18th-c pub owned by village consortium; unspoilt linked rooms with open fires, five well kept ales including Brakspears and Rebellion, good choice of wines by the glass and popular food with some italian influences, pleasant attentive service, good-sized more modern eating area and small dining room; occasional live music; well behaved children and dogs welcome, tables out in front and on side terrace, garden with big play area, open all day. *(Paul Humphreys, Simon Collett-Jones, Simon Rodway)*

COOKHAM DEAN
SU8785
Uncle Toms Cabin (01628) 483339
Off A308 Maidenhead–Marlow;
Hills Lane, towards Cookham Rise
and Cookham; SL6 9NT Welcoming
small-roomed local with simple sensitively
modernised interior, four well kept
mainstream ales and plenty of wines by the
glass, good food cooked by owner-chef, low
beams (and doorways), wood floors and sage-
green panelling, gleaming horsebrasses, open
fire; children in eating areas, dogs in bar,
seats out at front and in sheltered sloping
back garden, peaceful country setting, closes
at 9pm Sun and Mon. *(R K Phillips)*

CRAZIES HILL
SU7980
Horns (0118) 940 6041
Warren Row Road off A4 towards
Cockpole Green, then follow Crazies
Hill signs; RG10 8LY Refurbished 16th-c
beamed village pub under welcoming
enthusiastic new licensees; enjoyable food
from lunchtime sandwiches/baguettes and
traditional favourites up, Brakspears ales in
top condition and good choice of wines by
the glass, friendly helpful service, four rooms
including raftered barn restaurant; children
welcome, dogs in bar (resident black lab),
big garden with play area, open all day
Fri, Sat, till 7pm Sun, closed Mon. *(Paul*
Humphreys, Simon Collett-Jones)

DATCHET
SU9877
Royal Stag (01753) 584231
Not far from M4 junction 5; The Green;
SL3 9JH Ancient beamed pub next to
church overlooking green, well kept Fullers
London Pride and three Windsor & Eton ales,
enjoyable food including good Sun roasts,
friendly staff; Tues quiz; seats outside, open
(and food) all day. *(Miles Green)*

DONNINGTON
SU4770
Fox & Hounds (01635) 40540
Old Oxford Road; RG14 3AP Popular
refurbished family-owned pub (they also run
a local butchers – meat raffle every other
Sun), well kept beers including Fullers
and Sharps, decent wine range and good
food from pub favourites to grills, friendly
attentive young staff; children and dogs
welcome, tables out in front, handy for M4
(junction 13) and A34, closed Mon, otherwise
open all day. *(Ian Herdman)*

EAST GARSTON
SU3676
★Queens Arms (01488) 648757
3.5 miles from M4 junction 14; A338
and village signposted Gt Shefford;
RG17 7ET Friendly inn at the heart of
racehorse-training country; opened-up
bar with antique prints (many jockeys),
wheelbacks around well spaced tables on
bare boards, Ramsbury and Sharps Doom Bar,
plenty of wines by the glass and fair choice
of whiskies, lighter dining area with more

prints, good fairly traditional food (not Sun
evening); background music, TV for racing,
newspapers including *Racing Post*, free wi-fi;
children and dogs (in bar) welcome, seats
on sheltered terrace, spacious attractively
decorated bedrooms, fly fishing and shooting
can be arranged, good surrounding downland
walks, open all day. *(Richard Tilbrook, Mr and*
Mrs P R Thomas)

EAST ILSLEY
SU4981
★Crown & Horns (01635) 281545
Just off A34, about 5 miles N of M4
junction 13; Compton Road; RG20 7LH
Civilised brick and tile pub in horse-training
country, rambling beamed rooms, log fires,
enjoyable home-made food from sandwiches,
pizzas and pub favourites up including good
Sun lunch, five real ales, friendly efficient
staff; background music; children, dogs
and muddy boots welcome, tables in pretty
courtyard, modern bedroom extension,
open all day, busy on Newbury race days.
(Lindy Andrews)

FRILSHAM
SU5573
Pot Kiln (01635) 201366
From Yattendon take turning S, opposite
church, follow first Frilsham signpost,
but just after crossing motorway
go straight on towards Bucklebury
ignoring Frilsham signposted right;
pub on right after about half a mile;
RG18 0XX Recently redecorated red-brick
country dining pub; small bare-boards
bar with woodburner, four West Berkshire
ales including Brick Kiln named for the
pub, several wines by the glass and maybe
a couple of ciders, various dining areas
with wooden tables and chairs, signature
local game and other food from ciabattas
up; free wi-fi; children and dogs welcome,
unobstructed views from seats in big suntrap
garden with pizza oven, walks in nearby
woods, open all day Sat, till 9.30pm Sun.
(Dr Simon Innes, Luke Morgan)

GREAT SHEFFORD
SU3875
Swan (01488) 648271
2 miles from M4 junction 14, A338
towards Wantage (Newbury Road);
RG17 7DS Bay-windowed, low-ceilinged
18th-c pub backing on to River Lambourn;
enjoyable food from traditional favourites
and pizzas up, deals including half-price
main dishes Thurs evening, ales such as
Sharps Doom Bar and West Berkshire,
friendly helpful staff, easy chairs in bar area,
nice river-view dining room; background
music, quiz second Weds of month; children
and dogs welcome, tables on attractive
waterside lawn and terrace. *(Valerie Sayer)*

HENLEY
SU7682
★Little Angel (01491) 411008
Remenham Lane (A4130, just over
bridge E of Henley); RG9 2LS Civilised
dining pub, more or less open-plan but with

distinct modernised seating areas, bare boards throughout, little bar with leather cube stools, tub and farmhouse chairs, other parts with mix of dining tables and chairs, artwork on Farrow & Ball paintwork, contemporary food (all day weekends) from sharing plates up, Brakspears ales and several wines by the glass including champagne, pleasant attentive service, airy conservatory; background music; well behaved children allowed, dogs in bar, tables on sheltered floodlit back terrace looking over to cricket pitch, open all day. *(Roy Hoing, Simon Rodway)*

HOLYPORT   SU8977
George (01628) 628317
1.5 miles from M4 junction 8/9, via A308(M)/A330; The Green; SL6 2JL
Attractive 16th-c pub on picturesque village green with duck pond, colourful history and plenty of old-world charm, open-plan low-beamed interior, cosy and dimly lit, with nice fireplace, good food from pub favourites up, well kept Fullers London Pride and a couple of Rebellion ales, nice wines from sound list, friendly helpful service; background music, quiz first Mon of month; children and dogs (in bar) welcome, picnic-sets on pretty terrace, closed Sun evening, Mon. *(Paul Humphreys)*

HUNGERFORD   SU3368
Hungerford Arms (01488) 682154
High Street; street parking opposite; RG17 0NB Former Plume & Feathers renamed under new owners – refurbishment planned as we went to press; open-plan interior stretching back from the smallish bow-windowed façade, bare boards and some low beams, open fire at the back, three real ales including Greene King and a beer badged for the pub from island servery, well liked food; children welcome, small sheltered back courtyard, open all day. *(Mike and Mary Carter, Colin McLachlan, Paul Lucas)*

HUNGERFORD   SU3368
John o' Gaunt (01488) 683535
Bridge Street (A338); RG17 0EG
Welcoming 16th-c town pub with refurbished bare-boards interior, enjoyable generously served food from lunchtime sandwiches/ wraps to good Sun roasts, six well kept mainly local ales including own microbrews (tasting trays available), good bottled range too and local cider, efficient cheerful service from uniformed staff; children and dogs welcome, small sheltered garden, open all day, food all day Sun. *(Tony Hobden, Anthony Jones)*

HUNGERFORD NEWTOWN SU3571
Tally Ho (01488) 682312
A338 just S of M4 junction 14; RG17 0PP
Traditional red-brick beamed pub owned and restored by the local community, friendly and welcoming, with good food (not Sun evening) from baguettes to specials and popular Sun

lunch, well kept local ales such as Butts, Ramsbury, Two Cocks and West Berkshire, log fire; occasional music and quiz nights, free wi-fi; children welcome, picnic-sets out in front, open all day. *(Jim and Lynne Allen, Dr and Mrs R E S Tanner)*

HURLEY   SU8281
Dew Drop (01628) 315662
Small yellow sign to pub off A4130 just W; SL6 6RB Old flint and brick pub tucked away in nice woodland setting, shortish choice of food including good lunchtime sandwiches, Brakspears and a guest ale, log fire; children and dogs welcome, pleasant views from back garden, good local walks, open all day Sat, till 6pm Sun, closed Mon. *(Paul Humphreys)*

HURST   SU7973
★**Castle** (0118) 934 0034
Church Hill; RG10 0SJ Popular old dining pub still owned by the church opposite; very good well presented food (not Sun evening, Mon) from fairly priced varied menu including daily specials, well kept Binghams and local guests such as West Berkshire, plenty of nice wines by the glass, efficient friendly staff, bar with restaurant on left, snug to the right, beams, wood floors and old brick nogging, some visible wattle and daub, roaring fire; children and dogs (in bar) welcome, garden picnic-sets, open all day weekends, closed Mon lunchtime. *(John Pritchard, Paul Humphreys)*

HURST   SU8074
Green Man (0118) 934 2599
Off A321 just outside village; RG10 0BP
Partly 17th-c pub with enjoyable food from sandwiches, sharing plates and pub favourites up, a couple of Brakspears ales and a guest, several wines by the glass, friendly service, bar with dark beams and standing timbers, cosy alcoves, wall seats and built-in settles, hot little fire in one fireplace, old iron stove in another, dining area with modern sturdy wooden tables and high-backed chairs on solid oak floor; children and dogs welcome, sheltered terrace, picnic-sets under spreading oak trees in large garden with play area, open all day, food all day weekends. *(Paul Humphreys)*

KNOWL HILL   SU8178
★**Bird in Hand** (01628) 826622
A4, handy for M4 junction 8/9; RG10 9UP Relaxed, civilised and roomy, with cosy alcoves, heavy beams, panelling and splendid log fire in tartan-carpeted main area, wide choice of popular home-made food (special diets catered for) from baguettes up, four well kept mainly local ales and good choice of other drinks, efficient service, much older side bar, smart restaurant; soft background music, regular events including music and quiz nights, free wi-fi; tables on

front terrace and in neat garden, summer weekend barbecues, 22 bedrooms (some in separate block), open (and food) all day. *(Paul Humphreys, Susan and John Douglas)*

KNOWL HILL   SU8279
New Inn (01628) 822552
Bath Road (A4); RG10 9UU Revamped family-run roadside inn, nice bright interior with black-painted beams, popular italian-based menu (also tapas), good choice of wines, ales such as Binghams, Rebellion and Wychwood, friendly helpful service; children welcome, verandah above lawned garden, nine bedrooms, open (and food) all day. *(Valerie Sayer)*

LAMBOURN   SU3175
Hare (01488) 71386
aka Hare & Hounds; Lambourn Woodlands, well S of Lambourn itself (B4000/Hilldrop Lane); RG17 7SD Rambling 17th-c beamed restaurant-pub with well liked fairly priced food from lunctime sandwiches/baguettes to good Sun roasts, several small linked rooms including a proper bar with ales such as Ramsbury Gold and Sharps Cornish Coaster, friendly efficient service; background music, TV; children welcome, dogs in one part, garden behind, open all day (till 8pm Sun). *(Michael Sargent)*

LAMBOURN   SU3180
Malt Shovel (01488) 670006
Upper Lambourn; signed from B4000; RG17 8QN Refurbished under new management, but décor and customers still reflecting racing-stables surroundings; tartan-carpeted beamed bar with woodburner, well kept Ramsbury and West Berkshire, nine wines by the glass and enjoyable good value home-made food (all day weekends), friendly service; modern sports bar with pool, TVs for racing, weekend live music; children and dogs welcome, garden with new play area, five bedrooms, open all day. *(Sandra Morgan)*

LITTLEWICK GREEN   SU8379
Cricketers (01628) 822888
Not far from M4 junction 9; A404(M) then left on to A4 – village signed on left; Coronation Road; SL6 3RA Welcoming old-fashioned village pub in charming spot opposite cricket green (can get crowded); three well kept Badger ales and good choice of wines by the glass, enjoyable pub food (not Sun evening) from lunchtime sandwiches and baguettes to specials, traditional interior with three linked rooms, wood and quarry-tiled floors, huge clock above woodburner in brick fireplace; background music, TV, fortnightly quiz Tues; children and dogs (they have their own) welcome, pretty hanging baskets and a few tables out in front behind picket fence, open all day weekends (weekdays too if busy). *(Paul Humphreys)*

MAIDENHEAD   SU8582
Pinkneys Arms (01628) 630268
Lee Lane, just off A308 N; SL6 6NU Refurbished dining pub with good food (not Mon) from pubby choices and pizzas up (some choices expensive), well kept ales (mainly Rebellion) and decent wines, friendly efficient service ; outside gents', barn function room; children and dogs welcome, big garden, closed Mon lunchtime, otherwise open all day from midday. *(Paul Baxter)*

MARSH BENHAM   SU4267
Red House (01635) 582017
Off A4 W of Newbury; RG20 8LY Attractive thatched dining pub with good fairly traditional food with a twist from french chef-owner including set menu choices (Mon-Sat till 6.30pm) and specials, well kept West Berkshire and a guest, lots of wines by the glass, roomy flagstoned/wood floor bar with woodburner, refurbished restaurant, good friendly service; background music; children and dogs welcome, terrace and long lawns sloping to water meadows and the River Kennet, open (and food) all day. *(Tony Hobden, Ian Herdman)*

MIDGHAM   SU5566
Coach & Horses (0118) 971 3384
Bath Road (N side); RG7 5UX Comfortable main-road pub with good choice of food from baguettes up including lunchtime offers, cheerful efficient service, Fullers London Pride and West Berkshire Good Old Boy, flagstoned bar with sofa by brick fireplace, steps up to small half-panelled carpeted dining area with country-style furniture, second dining room; children welcome, garden behind, closed Sun evening, Mon. *(John Pritchard)*

MORTIMER   SU6564
Horse & Groom (0118) 933 2813
The Street; RG7 3RD Double-fronted Victorian pub facing common, reliable well cooked food from pub favourites up including good daily specials and seasonal game (they list local suppliers), two or three real ales and decent wines by the glass, open fire; Thurs quiz; children welcome, picnic-sets on side lawn, parking opposite. *(Dr and Mrs R E S Tanner)*

NEWBURY   SU4767
Lock Stock & Barrel
(01635) 580550 *Northbrook Street; RG14 1AA* Popular modern pub standing out for its canalside setting; refurbished interior with low ceiling, light wood or slate flooring and painted panelling, lots of windows overlooking canal, varied choice of enjoyable sensibly priced food all day from sandwiches up, well kept Fullers/Gales beers, efficient friendly staff; occasional live music, free wi-fi; children welcome, outside

seating including suntrap AstroTurf roof terrace looking over a series of locks towards handsome church, open till midnight Fri, Sat. *(Phil and Jane Villiers)*

OAKLEY GREEN   SU9276

★ **Greene Oak** (01753) 864294

Off A308 Windsor–Maidenhead at Twyford (B3024) signpost; Dedworth Road; SL4 5UW Several eating areas with variety of dining chairs, wall banquettes and tables from country kitchen-style to more formal, bare boards or flagstones, good modern cooking (not cheap) including excellent Sun roasts, dedicated drinkers' area to the right serving Greene King IPA and a couple of guests such as Trumans and Windsor & Eton, plenty of wines by the glass, friendly helpful staff; background music, free wi-fi; children welcome (menu for them), dogs in bar, sizeable terrace behind with decked area, handy for Legoland and Ascot (racegoers' champagne breakfast/dinner), open all day (till 7pm Sun). *(Simon Collett-Jones)*

PALEY STREET   SU8676

★ **Royal Oak** (01628) 620541

B3024 W; SL6 3JN Attractively modernised and extended 17th-c restauranty pub owned by Sir Michael Parkinson and son Nick; highly regarded british cooking (not cheap) and most here to eat, set lunch menu Mon-Sat, good service, dining room split by brick pillars and timbering with mix of well spaced wooden tables and leather chairs on bare boards or flagstones, smallish informal beamed bar with woodburner, leather sofas and cricketing prints, Fullers London Pride and wide choice of wines by the glass including champagne; background jazz; children welcome (no pushchairs in restaurant), seats outside among troughs of herbs, closed Sun. *(Sarah Roberts)*

READING   SU7173

★ **Alehouse** (0118) 950 8119

Broad Street; RG1 2BH Cheerful no-frills drinkers' pub with nine well kept quickly changing ales and a three craft kegs, also lots of different bottled beers, farm ciders and perry; small bare-boards bar with raised seating area, hundreds of pump clips on walls and ceiling, corridor to several appealing panelled rooms, some little more than alcoves, no food; background music, TV; open all day. *(Dr Simon Innes)*

READING   SU7272

Jolly Anglers (0118) 376 7823

Kennetside; RG1 3EA Simple two-room pub on River Kennet towpath, originally built for workers at the former Huntley & Palmers biscuit factory; four or more well kept changing ales and up to ten ciders/perries, good value home-made food including vegetarian/vegan choices, friendly landlord and staff, wood floors, original fireplaces,

darts and other pub games, piano; open mike night Mon; resident dogs (others welcome), picnic-sets in back garden up steep steps, open (and food) all day. *(Sarah Roberts)*

READING   SU7174

Moderation (0118) 375 0767

Caversham Road; RG1 8BB Modernised airy Victorian pub with enjoyable reasonably priced food including good thai/indonesian choices, pleasant prompt service, three well kept changing ales, some eastern influences to the décor; background music; seats out at front and in enclosed garden behind, open all day. *(Lindy Andrews)*

READING   SU7073

Nags Head 07765 880137

Russell Street; RG1 7XD Fairly basic mock-Tudor drinkers' pub just outside town centre attracting good mix of customers, a dozen well kept changing ales and 14 ciders, baguettes and pies, open fire, darts and cribbage; background and occasional live music, TV for major sporting events (busy on Reading FC match days); beer garden, open all day. *(John Pritchard)*

READING   SU7173

★ **Sweeney & Todd** (0118) 958 6466

Castle Street; RG1 7RD Pie shop with popular bar/restaurant behind (little changed in 30 years); warren of private period-feel alcoves and other areas on various levels, enjoyable home-made food all day including their range of good value pies, cheery service, small bar with four well kept ales such as Adnams and Hook Norton, Weston's cider and decent wines; children welcome in restaurant area, open all day (closed Sun evening and bank holidays). *(John Pritchard, Chris and Pauline Sexton)*

SHINFIELD   SU7367

★ **Magpie & Parrot** (0118) 988 4130

2.6 miles from M4 junction 11, via B3270; A327 just SE of Shinfield on Arborfield Road; RG2 9EA Unusual homely little roadside cottage with two cosy spic and span bars, warm fire and lots of bric-a-brac (miniature and historic bottles, stuffed birds, dozens of model cars, veteran AA badges and automotive instruments) Fullers London Pride and local guests from small corner counter, weekday lunchtime snacks and evening fish and chips (Thurs, Fri), hospitable landlady; no credit cards or mobile phones; pub dog (others welcome), seats on back terrace and marquee on immaculate lawn, open 12-7.30, closed Sun evening. *(Charlie Parker)*

SHURLOCK ROW   SU8374

★ **Shurlock Inn** (0118) 934 9094

Just off B3018 SE of Twyford; The Street; RG10 0PS Cosy village-owned pub with good food (all day Sun) from pubby choices up, four ales including West Berkshire Mr

Chubb and one from Rebellion, nice house wines, log fire in double-sided fireplace dividing bar and larger dining room, new oak flooring, panelling and one or two old beams; background music, weekend papers, free wi-fi; children welcome, dogs in bar, black metal furniture on side and back terraces, garden with picnic-sets under parasols and fenced play area, open all day Fri, Sat, till 9pm Sun. *(Dr Simon Innes)*

SULHAMSTEAD SU6269
Spring (0118) 930 3440
Bath Road (A4); RG7 5HP Old barn conversion with spacious bar and balustraded upstairs dining area under rafters, good variety of popular food from interesting sandwiches up, three real ales including Fullers and West Berkshire, nice range of wines by the glass, friendly efficient staff; children welcome, plenty of seats outside, open all day. *(Charlie Parker)*

SUNNINGHILL SU9367
Carpenters Arms (01344) 622763
Upper Village Road; SL5 7AQ Restauranty village pub run by french team, good authentic french country cooking, not cheap but they do offer a reasonably priced set lunch (Mon-Sat), nice wines, Sharps Doom Bar; no children in the evening, terrace tables, open all day and best to book. *(Alastair and Sheree Hepburn)*

SUNNINGHILL SU9367
Dog & Partridge (01344) 623204
Upper Village Road; SL5 7AQ Bright contemporary décor with emphasis on good freshly made food (all day Sun till 7pm), friendly helpful staff, Fullers, Sharps and Windsor & Eton, good range of wines; background music; children and dogs welcome, disabled facilities, part covered courtyard garden with pond and fountain, closed Mon, otherwise open all day. *(Lindy Andrews)*

THEALE SU6471
Bull (0118) 930 3478
High Street; RG7 5AH Modernised and extended old red-brick inn; large bar with tiled floor and dark half-panelling, carpeted dining area behind with banquettes, enjoyable good value food from pub favourites up delivered by dumb-waiter from upstairs kitchen, three or four well kept Wadworths ales; background and some live music, quiz nights; children and dogs (on leads) welcome, seats outside, open (and food) all day. *(John Pritchard)*

THEALE SU6471
Fox & Hounds (0118) 930 2295
2 miles from M4 junction 12; follow A4 W, then first left signed for station, over two roundabouts, then over narrow canal bridge to Sheffield Bottom; RG7 4BE Large neatly kept dining pub with well priced

pubby food (not Sun evening) from baguettes to specials, five well kept Wadworths ales, Weston's cider, decent wines and coffee, L-shaped bar with dividers, traditional mix of furniture on carpet or bare boards including area with modern sofas and low tables, two open fires; pool and darts, Sun quiz; children and dogs welcome, outside seating at front and sides, lakeside bird reserve opposite, open all day Fri-Sun. *(John Pritchard, Tony Hobden)*

THREE MILE CROSS SU7167
Swan (0118) 988 3674
A33 just S of M4 junction 11; Basingstoke Road; RG7 1AT Smallish traditional pub built in the 17th c and later a posting house, four well kept ales including Loddon and Timothy Taylors, enjoyable fairly standard home-made food at reasonable prices, friendly efficient staff, two beamed bars, inglenook with hanging black pots, old prints and some impressive stuffed fish; large well arranged outside seating area behind (also home to wolfhound Mr Niall, the London Irish RFC mascot), near Madejski Stadium and very busy on match days, open all day weekdays, closed Sun evening. *(John Pritchard)*

WALTHAM ST LAWRENCE SU8376
★ Bell (0118) 934 1788
B3024 E of Twyford; The Street; RG10 0JJ Welcoming 14th-c village local with well preserved beamed and timbered interior, good home-made blackboard food (not Sun evening) from bar snacks including own pork pies up, friendly service, five well kept mainly local beers, up to eight real ciders and plenty of wines by the glass, also good choice of whiskies, two compact connecting rooms, another larger one off entrance hall, warming log fires, daily papers; children and dogs welcome, pretty back garden with extended terrace and shady trees, open all day weekends. *(Paul Humphreys, Simon Collett-Jones)*

WARGRAVE SU7878
Bull (0843) 289 1773
Off A321 Henley-Twyford; High Street; RG10 8DE Low-beamed 15th-c brick coaching inn run well by hospitable landlady; main bar with inglenook log fire, two dining areas (one up steps for families), enjoyable traditional home-made food from baguettes up, Brakspears ales and a guest, friendly helpful staff; background music, free wi-fi; well behaved dogs welcome, walled garden with pond, four bedrooms, open all day weekends. *(Simon Collett-Jones)*

WARGRAVE SU7878
St George & Dragon
(0118) 940 5021 *High Street; RG10 8HY* Large smartly updated dining pub with decking overlooking Thames (they ask for a credit card if you eat outside), good range of

well presented food including some unusual dishes and fixed-price menu (weekdays till 6pm), central fire giving cosy feel; open (and food) all day. *(Mr and Mrs C R Douglas, Roy Hoing)*

WEST ILSLEY   SU4782
Harrow (01635) 281260
Signed off A34 at E Ilsley slip road; RG20 7AR Appealing and welcoming family-run country pub in peaceful spot overlooking cricket pitch and pond, Victorian prints in deep-coloured knocked-through bar, some antique furnishings, log fire, good choice of enjoyable sensibly priced home-made food (not Sun or Mon evenings), well kept Greene King ales and nice selection of wines by the glass, afternoon teas; children in eating areas, dogs allowed in bar, big garden with picnic-sets, more seats on pleasant terrace, handy for Ridgeway walkers, may close early Sun evening if quiet. *(Tom Stone)*

WINDSOR   SU9676
Carpenters Arms (01753) 863739
Market Street; SL4 1PB Nicholsons pub rambling around central servery with good choice of well kept ales and several wines by the glass, reasonably priced pubby food from sandwiches up including range of pies, friendly helpful service, sturdy pub furnishings and Victorian-style décor with two pretty fireplaces, family areas up a few steps, also downstairs beside former tunnel entrance with suits of armour; background music, no dogs; tables out on cobbled pedestrian alley opposite castle, no nearby parking, handy for Legoland bus stop, open (and food) all day. *(Simon Collett-Jones, David M Smith)*

WINDSOR   SU9676
Two Brewers (01753) 855426
Park Street; SL4 1LB In the shadow of Windsor Castle with three cosy unchanging bare-boards rooms, well kept ales such as Fullers London Pride, St Austell Tribute and Sharps Doom Bar, good choice of wines by the glass, enjoyable freshly made food (not

Fri-Sun evenings) from shortish mid-priced menu, friendly efficient service, thriving old-fashioned pub atmosphere, beams and open fire, enamel signs and posters on walls; background music, daily papers; no children inside, dogs welcome, tables and attractive hanging baskets out by pretty Georgian street next to Windsor Park's Long Walk, open all day. *(Nigel and Sue Foster, Simon Rodway)*

WINDSOR   SU9576
Vansittart Arms (01753) 865988
Vansittart Road; SL4 5DD Friendly three-room Victorian local with cosy corners and open fires, well kept Fullers/Gales beers, big helpings of enjoyable good value home-made food (all day weekends); background music, sports TV, pool, newspapers and free wi-fi; children and dogs welcome, good-sized beer garden, open all day. *(Donald Allsopp)*

WINTERBOURNE   SU4572
Winterbourne Arms (01635) 248200
3.7 miles from M4 junction 13; at A34 turn into Chieveley Services and follow Donnington signs to Arlington Lane, then follow Winterbourne signs; RG20 8BB Refurbished old pub with enjoyable food including blackboard specials, beers such as Ramsbury Gold and good choice of wines, big windows give peaceful rural views, winter log fire; children welcome, seats in big landscaped side garden, pretty village with lovely surrounding walks, closed Sun evening. *(Martin Day)*

WRAYSBURY   TQ0074
Perseverance (01784) 482375
High Street; TW19 5DB Welcoming old beamed village pub, enjoyable good value home-made food from sandwiches up, three well kept ales including Otter and decent choice of wines by the glass, good selection of gins too, friendly helpful staff, log fires (one in inglenook); Thurs quiz, live music Sun afternoon and first/third Tues of month, darts; children (till 9pm) and dogs welcome, nice back garden with pizza oven, open all day (till 9.30pm Sun). *(Lindy Andrews)*

Buckinghamshire

KEY ★ Star Pub | 🍽 Top Quality Food | 🍺 Great Beer

🍷 Good Wines | £ Bargain Meals | 🛏 Good Bedrooms | 🍴 Serves Food

---

ADSTOCK
Old Thatched Inn 🍽 🍺

SP7330 Map 4

(01296) 712584 – www.theoldthatchedinn.co.uk
Main Street, off A413; MK18 2JN

Pretty thatched dining pub with keen landlord, friendly staff, five real ales and good food

An enthusiastic landlord runs this attractive thatched dining pub surrounded by rolling farmland. The small front bar area has low beams, sofas on flagstones, high bar chairs and an open fire and they keep Fullers London Pride, Sharps Doom Bar, Thwaites Wainwright, Timothy Taylors Boltmaker and Tring Side Pocket for a Toad on handpump, 14 wines by the glass, a dozen malt whiskies and four ciders; courteous service. A dining area leads off with more beams and a mix of pale wooden dining chairs around miscellaneous tables on a stripped wooden floor; background music. There's also a modern conservatory restaurant at the back with well spaced tables on bare boards. The sheltered terrace has tables and chairs under a gazebo. This is an attractive village.

🍽 First class food includes sandwiches, ham hock fritters with mustard dressing and pickles, garlic and rosemary baked camembert with onion jam, beetroot and goats cheese tart with fig and balsamic jam, honey and pear cider sausages with red wine gravy, beer-battered haddock and chips, slow-cooked pork belly with cider-poached pear, roasted root vegetables and red wine jus, roasted salmon fillet with creamed leeks, and puddings such as sticky toffee pudding with caramel sauce and seasonal eton mess; they also offer a two- and three-course set lunch. *Benchmark main dish: duck breast with faggot, savoury cabbage and swede mash £17.50. Two-course evening meal £23.50.*

Free house ~ Licensee Andrew Judge ~ Real ale ~ Open 12-11 (midnight Sat, 10.30 Sun) ~ Bar food 12-2.30, 6-9.30 (5-9 Sat); 12-8 Sun ~ Restaurant ~ Well behaved children welcome ~ Dogs allowed in bar ~ Wi-fi *Recommended by Graham and Carol Parker, George Atkinson, Mike and Mary Carter, Tim and Sarah Smythe-Brown*

AYLESBURY
Kings Head 🍺

SP8113 Map 4

(01296) 718812 – www.farmersbar.co.uk
Kings Head Passage (off Bourbon Street), also entrance off Temple Street; no nearby parking except for disabled; HP20 2RW

Handsome town centre pub with civilised atmosphere, good local ales (used in the food too) and friendly service

Hidden away behind the shops and offices in a modern town centre, it's quite a surprise to come across a rather special 15th-c building, part of which is a pub. There's the Farmers Bar – as well as the tourist information office and conference rooms. Three timeless rooms have been restored with careful and unpretentious simplicity: stripped boards, cream walls with minimal decoration, gentle lighting, a variety of seating which includes upholstered sofas and armchairs, cushioned high-backed settles and some simple modern pale dining tables and chairs dotted around. Most of the bar tables are of round glass, supported on low cask tops. The neat corner bar has Chiltern Ale, Beechwood Bitter and Black (this is the brewery tap for Chiltern) and a guest like Otley Milk Stout on handpump, 11 wines by the glass, a farm cider and some interesting bottled beers. Service is friendly and there's no background music or machines. The atmospheric medieval cobbled courtyard has teak seats and tables, some beneath a pillared roof; summer barbecues and live events. The place is owned by the National Trust. Disabled access and facilities.

Lunchtime-only food includes sandwiches, whisky-infused scotch egg, baked potatoes, a pie of the day, ham and free-range eggs, venison and wild mushroom wellington, and puddings such as chocolate fudge cake and bread and butter pudding. *Benchmark main dish: beer-battered haddock and chips £12.50. Two-course evening meal £15.00.*

Chiltern ~ Manager George Jenkinson ~ Real ale ~ Open 11-11; 12-10.30 Sun ~ Bar food 12-2 (12-3 weekends); not evenings ~ Children welcome away from bar ~ Wi-fi
Recommended by Graham and Carol Parker, John Poulter

BOVINGDON GREEN
Royal Oak ⭐ ♀

SU8386 Map 2

(01628) 488611 – www.royaloakmarlow.co.uk
0.75 miles N of Marlow, on back road to Frieth signposted off West Street (A4155) in centre; SL7 2JF

Civilised dining pub with nice little bar, a fine choice of wines by the glass, real ales and imaginative food

It's the modern british food that most customers are here to enjoy, but they do keep Rebellion IPA on handpump, alongside changing guests such as Timothy Taylors Landlord and Woodfordes Wherry, 24 wines by the glass (plus pudding wines), several gins and farm cider. The low-beamed cosy snug, closest to the car park, has three small tables and a woodburning stove in an exposed brick fireplace (with a big pile of logs beside it). Several other attractively decorated areas open off the central bar with half-panelled walls variously painted in pale blue, green or cream (though the dining room ones are red). Throughout, there's a mix of church chairs, stripped wooden tables and chunky wall seats, with rugs on the partly wooden, partly flagstoned floors, co-ordinated cushions and curtains, and a very bright, airy feel. Thoughtful extra touches enhance the tone: a bowl of olives on the bar, carefully laid-out newspapers and fresh flowers or candles on the tables. Board games and background music. A sunny terrace with good solid tables leads to an appealing garden with pétanque, ping pong, badminton and swing ball; there's also a smaller side garden and a kitchen herb garden.

 Creative food championing local produce includes smoked haddock scotch egg with bombay-spiced aioli, bubble and squeak with oak-smoked bacon, free-range poached egg and hollandaise, roasted cauliflower cheese with gruyère, macaroni and piccalilli salad, free-range chicken breast with caramelised shallot tart, goats cheese, butternut squash and toasted hazelnuts, crispy pink peppercorn squid with chorizo risotto and padrón peppers, and puddings such as salted chocolate mousse

délice with orange curd and apricot sorbet and rhubarb crème brûlée with ginger cookie. *Benchmark main dish: slow-cooked short rib of beef in ale with horseradish mash £16.75. Two-course evening meal £22.00.*

Salisbury Pubs ~ Manager James Molier ~ Real ale ~ Open 11-11; 12-10.30 Sun ~ Bar food 12-2.30, 6.30-9.30; 12.3, 6-10 Fri, Sat; 12-9 Sun ~ Restaurant ~ Children welcome ~ Dogs welcome ~ Wi-fi *Recommended by Brian Glozier, Alistair Forsyth, Peter, Tracey and Stephen Groves, Ben and Diane Bowie*

BRILL SP6514 Map 4
Pheasant
(01844) 239370 – www.thepheasant.co.uk
Windmill Street; off B4011 Bicester–Long Crendon; HP18 9TG

Long-reaching views, a bustling bar with local ales, attentive staff and tasty food; bedrooms

There are plenty of seats and tables on the decked area and in the garden here, offering marvellous views over the windmill opposite (one of the oldest post windmills still in working order) and into the distance across five counties. Inside, it's more or less open-plan, with a raftered bar area, leather tub seats in front of a woodburner, and Chiltern Beechwood, Vale Brill Gold and a guest from Skinners on handpump and a dozen wines by the glass served by charming, attentive staff. Dining areas have high-backed leather or dark wooden chairs, attractively framed prints and books on shelves; background music. Bedrooms are comfortable and two are in the former bakehouse; good walks from the door. Roald Dahl used to drink here, and some of the tales the locals told him were worked into his short stories.

Enjoyable food includes lunchtime sandwiches, mussels of the week, chicken liver and truffle parfait with pickled mushrooms, local sausages with confit onions, seafood risotto, cajun chicken breast burger with coleslaw and fries, steak in ale pie, prawn curry, and puddings such as apple crumble and dark chocolate mousse; they also offer a Monday-Thursday takeaway menu and Thursday is gourmet burger night. *Benchmark main dish: scallops thermidor £18.00. Two-course evening meal £20.00.*

Free house ~ Licensee Marilyn Glover ~ Real ale ~ Open 12-11 (midnight Fri, Sat) ~ Bar food 12-9; 12-2.30, 6-9 winter; 12-9 winter Sat; 12-5 winter Sun ~ Children welcome ~ Dogs allowed in bar ~ Wi-fi ~ Bedrooms: £75/£95 *Recommended by Neil and Angela Huxter, David Jackman, John and Hilary Murphy*

BRILL SP6513 Map 4
Pointer ⭑◉ �
(01844) 238339 – www.thepointerbrill.co.uk
Church Street; HP18 9RT

Buckinghamshire Dining Pub of the Year

Carefully restored pub in a pretty village with rewarding food, local ales and interesting furnishings

Next to the church and by the village green, this handsome place is very stylishly furnished: low beams, windsor chairs, elegant armchairs and sofas with brocaded cushions, open fires or woodburners in brick fireplaces and animal-hide stools by the counter. A beer named for the pub (from the XT Brewing Company), Vale Best Bitter and Brill Gold (brewed in the village) and Rebellion Zebedee on handpump, a dozen fair-priced wines by the glass, a gin and a whisky menu and friendly, attentive staff. The airy and attractive restaurant has antique Ercol chairs around pale oak tables, cushioned window seats, rafters in a high vaulted ceiling and an open kitchen. French windows open on to the sizeable garden. Do visit their deli next door where you can buy their own produce and freshly baked bread (open Wednesday, Thursday and Friday afternoons and Saturday morning). Tolkien is said to have based the village of Bree in *The Lord of the Rings* on this pretty village.

Using meat from their own farm and other first class local, seasonal produce, the delicious food includes fallow deer dressed in douglas fir oil with kohlrabi, pumpkin seeds and pickled mushrooms, goats cheese and fig salad with fig jam, candied walnuts and sherry and walnut dressed leaves, mushroom risotto with crispy brie bonbons, veal pie with artichokes, pickled white cabbage and sauternes sauce, duck breast with duck fat carrots, orange and cardamom gravy, red mullet linguine with wild garlic and clam broth and sea herbs, and puddings such as treacle tart with bergamot and yoghurt and dark chocolate bar with passion-fruit sorbet and bitter chocolate snap; they also offer a two- and three-course set lunch. *Benchmark main dish: rare-breed sirloin and brisket with mushrooms, lovage and dripping chips £26.00. Two-course evening meal £25.00.*

Free house ~ Licensees David and Fiona Howden ~ Real ale ~ Open 12-11 (midnight Sat); 12-10 Sun; closed Mon ~ Bar food 12-2.30, 6.30-9 (10 Fri, Sat); 12.30-5 Sun ~ Restaurant ~ Children welcome ~ Dogs allowed in bar ~ Wi-fi *Recommended by Alfie Bayliss, Phoebe Peacock, Belinda Stamp*

BUTLERS CROSS
Russell Arms ♀ ◄

SP8407   Map 4

(01296) 624411 – www.therussellarms.co.uk
Off A4010 S of Aylesbury, at Nash Lee roundabout; or off A413 in Wendover, passing station; Chalkshire Road; HP17 0TS

Attractive old place with good food and local ales, friendly landlord and staff, and seats in sunny garden

Recently refurbished, this is an 18th-c beamed pub (and former coaching inn and servants' quarters for nearby Chequers, the prime minister's country retreat). The simply furnished bar has stools and chairs around polished tables on new pale floorboards, higher stools against the counter and well kept Chiltern Beechwood, St Austell Tribute and Tring Side Pocket for a Toad on handpump, 24 wines by the glass and artisan gins served by welcoming staff; background music and board games. The two dining areas have an open fire with logs piled high to either side of it and a woodburner in an inglenook, an eclectic collection of wheelback, mate's and elegant high-backed and cushioned chairs around scrubbed tables on bare boards, some panelling, tartan curtains and fresh flowers. One wall has a blown-up photo of Chequers with smaller photos of past prime ministers. French windows lead to a suntrap terrace with teak furniture and there are steps up to the garden with picnic-sets. The pub is well placed for Chilterns walks.

Championing local produce, the fine quality food includes ham hock terrine with pickles and mustard mayonnaise, citrus-cured salmon with cucumber, capers, avocado and crispy shallots, pearl barley risotto with peas, broad beans and asparagus, local sausages with mash and gravy, confit duck leg with duck vinaigrette and spring greens, fish pie, and puddings such as rhubarb tart with rhubarb ice-cream and carrot cake with mango and passion-fruit sorbet. *Benchmark main dish: gnocchi with wild mushrooms, cheese and truffle oil £14.95. Two-course evening meal £22.00.*

Free house ~ Licensee James Penlington ~ Real ale ~ Open 10am-11pm; 12-10.30 Sun; closed Mon ~ Bar food 12-2.30, 6.30-9; 12-4 Sun ~ Restaurant ~ Children welcome ~ Dogs allowed in bar ~ Wi-fi *Recommended by Julian Thorpe, Valerie Sayer*

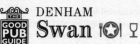

DENHAM

TQ0487 Map 3

Swan 🏅◑ ♀

(01895) 832085 – www.swaninndenham.co.uk

Village signed from M25 junction 16; UB9 5BH

Double-fronted dining pub in quiet village with interesting furnishings, log fires, fine choice of drinks and large garden

In a quiet and lovely village, this is a handsome Georgian pub that cleverly manages to appeal to both diners and drinkers. The stylishly furnished bars have a nice mix of antique and old-fashioned chairs and solid tables, rich heavily draped curtains, log fires, newspapers and fresh flowers. Friendly staff serve Rebellion IPA and a guest such as Caledonian Flying Scotsman on handpump, over 20 wines by the glass (plus pudding wines) and a good choice of vodkas and liqueurs; background music. In warm weather, the extensive back garden is a big draw (it's also floodlit at night) and there are seats and tables on a sheltered terrace, with more on a spacious lawn. It can get busy at weekends, when parking may be tricky. The wisteria is lovely in May.

 Rewarding food includes linguine with squid, crab, saffron, chilli and tomato, breaded lamb breast with caramelised onion purée, baby onions and black pudding, asparagus and pea risotto with truffle oil, steak burger with toppings, spicy sauce and sweet potato chips, moroccan poussin and apricot tagine with tabbouleh, hake fillet with chargrilled asparagus, chorizo potato cake and red pepper dressing, and puddings such as carrot and walnut cake with orange and cream cheese ice-cream and baked alaska with banana bread, banana ice-cream and toffee sauce. *Benchmark main dish: bubble and squeak topped with bacon, a poached egg and hollandaise £11.75. Two-course evening meal £23.50.*

Little Gems Country Dining Pubs ~ Manager Mark Littlewood ~ Real ale ~ Open 11.30-11.30; 12-11 Sun ~ Bar food 12-2.30, 6-9 (9.30 Fri); 12-9.30 Sat; 12-8 Sun ~ Restaurant ~ Children welcome ~ Dogs allowed in bar ~ Wi-fi *Recommended by David Jackman, Taff Thomas, Edward Mirzoeff, Nigel and Sue Foster*

EASINGTON

SP6810 Map 4

Mole & Chicken 🏅◑ ♀ 🛏

(01844) 208387 – www.themoleandchicken.co.uk

From B4011 in Long Crendon follow Chearsley, Waddesdon signpost into Carters Lane opposite indian restaurant, then turn left into Chilton Road; HP18 9EY

Fine country views, an inviting interior, real ales and enjoyable food and drink; nice bedrooms

In warm weather try to bag a table on the raised terrace and decked area behind this creeper-clad dining pub – the views over Buckinghamshire and Oxfordshire are lovely. The opened-up interior is arranged so that the different parts seem quite snug and self-contained without being cut off from the relaxed and sociable atmosphere. The heavily beamed bar curves around the serving counter in a sort of S-shape, and there are cream-cushioned farmhouse chairs around oak and pine tables on flagstones or tiles, a couple of dark leather sofas, church candles and good winter log fires. Vale Best Bitter and XT Four on handpump, several wines by the glass and quite a few malt whiskies; background music. This is a civilised place to stay in cosy and comfortable bedrooms, and the breakfasts are good too.

 As well as breakfasts for non-residents (7.30-9.30am weekdays, 8-10am weekends), the tempting food includes deep-fried squid with butternut squash, aioli, rocket, lime and chilli, crispy duck, green bean, mango and cashew nut salad, asparagus ravioli with shaved fennel and dill cream, beer-battered fish and chips, corn-fed chicken with haggis mash, creamed cabbage and bacon and wild mushroom jus, rump of lamb with charred lettuce, champ, wild garlic, peas and bacon, and puddings such as peach and macadamia nut pavlova with raspberry ripple ice-cream and warm chocolate fondant with honeycomb ice-cream. *Benchmark main dish: beef short rib with truffle and parmesan chips and celeriac purée £19.50. Two-course evening meal £24.00.*

Free house ~ Licensee Steve Bush ~ Real ale ~ Open 7.30am (8am weekends)-11pm ~ Bar food 12-2.30, 6.30-9.30; 12-3.30, 6-9 Sun ~ Children welcome ~ Wi-fi ~ Bedrooms: £95/£125
Recommended by Alfie Bayliss, Jo Garnett, Tim and Sarah Smythe-Brown

FINGEST   SU7791   Map 2

Chequers

(01491) 638335 – www.chequersfingest.com
Off B482 Marlow–Stokenchurch; RG9 6QD

Friendly, spotlessly kept old pub with big garden, real ales and interesting food

This is good walking country with quiet pastures sloping up to beechwoods, and you can walk from here to other pubs in this chapter. The unaffected public bar has real country charm, and other neatly kept old-fashioned rooms are warm, cosy and traditional, with large open fires, horsebrasses, pewter tankards and pub team photographs on the walls. Brakspears Bitter and Ringwood Boondoggle on handpump alongside quite a few wines by the glass, several malt whiskies and farm cider; board games and a house cat and dog. French doors from the smart back dining extension open to a terrace (plenty of picnic-sets), which leads to the big, beautifully tended garden with fine views over the Hambleden Valley. This 15th-c, white-shuttered brick and flint pub is in a charming spot opposite a unique twin-roofed Norman church tower – probably the nave of the original church.

Popular food includes lunchtime sandwiches, omelette arnold bennett, king prawn pil pil, pork and leek sausages with mash and onion rings, roasted red pepper and feta linguine, burger with toppings and fries, cod fillet with creamed leeks and pancetta, steaks with a choice of sauces, and puddings. *Benchmark main dish: beer-battered haddock and chips £12.95. Two-course evening meal £20.00.*

Brakspears ~ Tenants Jaxon and Emma Keedwell ~ Real ale ~ Open 12-3, 5.30-11; 12-11.15 Sat; 12-10.30 Sun; closed Mon ~ Bar food 12-2 (3 Sat, 4 Sun), 7-9 (9.30 Fri, Sat) ~ Restaurant ~ Children welcome ~ Dogs allowed in bar ~ Wi-fi *Recommended by Isobel Mackinlay, Simon Collett-Jones, Edward and William Johnston*

FORTY GREEN   SU9291   Map 2

Royal Standard of England 🍺

(01494) 673382 – www.rsoe.co.uk
3.5 miles from M40 junction 2, via A40 to Beaconsfield, then follow sign to Forty Green, off B474 0.75 miles N of New Beaconsfield; keep going through village; HP9 1XT

Full of history and character, with fascinating antiques in rambling rooms and good choice of drinks and food

Until after the Battle of Worcester in 1651 (when Charles I hid in the high rafters of what is now its food bar), this ancient pub used to be called the Ship. It's been trading for nearly 900 years and the leaflet documenting the pub's history is really interesting. The rambling rooms have some fine old features to look out for: huge black ship's timbers, lovely worn floors, carved oak panelling, roaring winter fires with handsomely decorated iron firebacks and cluttered mantelpieces – there's also a massive settle apparently built to fit the curved transom of an Elizabethan ship. Nooks and crannies are filled with a collection of antiques, including rifles, powder-flasks and bugles, ancient pewter and pottery tankards, lots of tarnished brass and copper, needlework samplers and richly coloured stained glass. Chiltern Ale and Elgoods Windsor Knot plus four changing guests on handpump, a carefully annotated list of bottled beers and malt whiskies, farm ciders, perry, somerset brandy and around a dozen wines by the glass. You can sit outside in a neatly hedged front rose garden or under the shade of a tree; look out for the red gargoyle on the wall facing the car park. The inn is used regularly for filming television programmes such as *Midsomer Murders*.

Honest, hearty food includes lunchtime sandwiches and baguettes, gin and beetroot-cured salmon with horseradish and beetroot purée, charcuterie plate, local sausages with onion gravy, chicken caesar salad, vegetable curry, steak and kidney pudding, fish pie, lamb shoulder with sautéed potatoes, lambs liver and bacon, and puddings such as crème brûlée and hot chocolate fondant. *Benchmark main dish: beer-battered fish and chips £14.00. Two-course evening meal £20.00.*

Free house ~ Licensee Matthew O'Keeffe ~ Real ale ~ Open 11am-11.30pm; 12-10.30 Sun ~ Bar food 12-10 ~ Children welcome ~ Dogs welcome ~ Wi-fi *Recommended by Roy Hoing, Paul Humphreys, James Allsopp, Julie Braeburn*

FULMER
Black Horse 🍴★ ♀

SU9985 Map 2

(01753) 663183 – www.theblackhorsefulmer.com
Village signposted off A40 in Gerrards Cross, W of junction with A413; Windmill Road; SL3 6HD

Appealingly reworked dining pub, friendly and relaxed, with enjoyable up-to-date food, exemplary service and pleasant garden; bedrooms

There's always a good mix of customers popping in and out of this extended 17th-c pub as it's helpfully open all day. It's a charming and thoughtfully run country pub with a lot of character: there's a proper bar in the middle and two cosy areas to the left with low black beams, rugs on bare boards, settles and other solid pub furniture and several open log fires. Greene King IPA and London Glory and a monthly guest ale on handpump, 21 wines by the glass and 20 malt whiskies; staff are friendly and efficient even when pushed. Background music, TV. The main area on the right is set for dining and leads to the good-sized suntrap back terrace where there's a summer barbecue bar. The two bedrooms are stylish and well equipped. This is a charming conservation village and the pub is next to the church.

Appealing food includes breakfast (8.30-11am), sandwiches (until 6pm), beetroot and vodka-cured salmon with fennel slaw and dill crème fraîche, prawn, crab and avocado cocktail, croque monsieur with skinny fries, wild mushroom and spinach risotto with truffle oil, indonesian chicken curry with crispy shallots, spiced lamb faggots with greens, pork belly with champ, black pudding and apple sauce, salmon en croûte with parsley sauce, and puddings such as triple chocolate brownie with cherry ice-cream and vanilla pannacotta with pineapple sorbet. *Benchmark main dish: beer-battered haddock and chips £14.50. Two-course evening meal £19.50.*

Greene King ~ Lease Matt Birchall ~ Real ale ~ Open 11am-midnight; 12-10.30 Sun ~ Bar food 8.30am-9.30pm (10 Fri, Sat); 12-7 Sun ~ Restaurant ~ Children welcome ~ Dogs allowed in bar ~ Wi-fi ~ Quiz Mon 8pm Sept-Apr ~ Bedrooms: /£130
Recommended by Julian Thorpe, Luke Morgan, Sally Wright

GREAT MISSENDEN

SP9000 Map 4

Nags Head

(01494) 862200 – www.nagsheadbucks.com

Old London Road, E – beyond Abbey; HP16 0DG

Well run and pretty inn with beamed bars, an open fire, a good range of drinks and modern cooking; bedrooms

If you stay here, the beamed bedrooms are well equipped and comfortable, and the breakfasts are very good. It was built as three small cottages in the 15th c and is now a quietly civilised dining pub. There's a low-beamed area on the left, a loftier part on the right, a mix of small pews, dining chairs and tables on carpet, Quentin Blake prints on cream walls and a log fire in a handsome fireplace. Rebellion IPA and a couple of guests such as Malt IPA and Vale Red Kite on handpump from the unusual bar counter (the windows behind face the road), 26 wines by the glass from an extensive list and half a dozen vintage Armagnacs. There's an outside dining area beneath a pergola and seats on the extensive back lawn. Roald Dahl used this as his local and the Roald Dahl Museum & Story Centre is just a stroll away.

Attractively presented food includes buttered shrimps on toasted focaccia, mushroom feuilletée with calvados cream, wild boar and apple sausages with chive mash and red wine gravy, lamb and mint burger with crème fraîche and skinny chips, red deer fillet and pulled muntjac with cranberry jus, a vegetarian dish of the day, slow-cooked suckling pig cheeks in ale with smoked bacon and mushrooms, and puddings such as bourbon vanilla crème brûlée and pear and forest fruit bread and butter pudding. *Benchmark main dish: beer-battered fish and chips £14.95. Two-course evening meal £25.00.*

Free house ~ Licensee Adam Michaels ~ Real ale ~ Open 11-11 (midnight Sat); 11-10.30 Sun ~ Bar food 12-2.30, 6.30-9.30; 12-7 Sun ~ Restaurant ~ Children welcome ~ Dogs allowed in bar ~ Wi-fi ~ Bedrooms: £75/£95 *Recommended by Toby Jones, Martin Day, Mr and Mrs J Watkins*

HAMBLEDEN

SU7886 Map 2

Stag & Huntsman

(01491) 571227 – www.thestagandhuntsman.co.uk

Off A4155 Henley–Marlow; RG9 6RP

Friendly inn with nice bar, plenty of dining space and good food, welcoming staff and country garden; bedrooms

You'll be sure to find cheerful, chatty regulars in this handsome pub that's set on the far edge of one of the prettiest Chilterns villages. Visitors are made welcome too, and the little bar has a thriving atmosphere, stools against the counter, built-in cushioned wall seating, simple tables and chairs and bare floorboards. Rebellion IPA, Sharps Doom Bar and a couple of guest beers on handpump and several wines by the glass, served by warmly, friendly staff. There's also a sizeable open-plan room with armchairs beside a woodburning stove in a brick fireplace, and a sofa and stools around a polished chest on more boards; this leads into the dining room with all sorts of wooden or high-backed red leather dining chairs around a variety of wooden tables, and hunting prints and other pictures on floral wallpaper. Darts and background music. The bedrooms are warm and comfortable and the breakfasts good. There are seats in the country garden.

Pleasing food includes breakfasts (8-10am), chicken liver parfait with port jelly, smoked fish with capers, red onion and celery and lemon dressing, quinoa salad with feta, pomegranate, mint, almond and lime dressing, beer-battered fish and chips, saffron risotto with roasted peppers, spring onions and cherry tomatoes, gammon with eggs and pineapple sauce, sausages with onion gravy and mash, and puddings such as chocolate brownie and bakewell tart. *Benchmark main dish: local steaks with a choice of sauces £19.95. Two-course evening meal £19.00.*

Free house ~ Licensee Claire Hollis ~ Real ale ~ Open 11-11 ~ Bar food 12-2.30, 6-9.30; 12-3, 6-9 Sun ~ Restaurant ~ Children welcome ~ Dogs allowed in bar ~ Wi-fi ~ Bedrooms: /£100
Recommended by Susan and John Douglas, Lindy Andrews, James Allsopp

HEDGERLEY   SU9687 Map 2
White Horse ★ ◀ £
(01753) 643225
2.4 miles from M40 junction 2; at exit roundabout take Slough turn-off following alongside M40; after 1.5 miles turn right at T junction into Village Lane; SL2 3UY

Old-fashioned drinkers' pub with lots of beers, home-made lunchtime food and a cheery mix of customers

A fine range of real ales in this charming, convivial country gem might include Rebellion IPA and up to seven daily changing guests, sourced from all over the country and tapped straight from casks kept in a room behind the tiny hatch counter. Their Easter, May, Spring and August bank holiday beer festivals (they can get through about 130 beers during the May event) are highlights of the local calendar. This marvellous range of drinks extends to craft ales in cans or bottles, three farm ciders, eight wines by the glass, 15 malt whiskies and winter mulled wine. The cottagey main bar has plenty of unspoilt character with beams, brasses and exposed brickwork, low wooden tables, standing timbers, jugs, ballcocks and other bric-a-brac, a log fire, and a good few leaflets and notices about village events. A little flagstoned public bar on the left has darts, shove-ha'penny and board games. A canopied extension leads out to the garden where there are tables, occasional barbecues and lots of hanging baskets; a few tables in front of the building overlook the quiet road. Good walks nearby, and the pub is handy for the Church Wood RSPB reserve and popular with walkers and cyclists; it's often crowded at weekends.

Lunchtime-only bar food includes good sandwiches, a salad bar with home-cooked quiches and cold meats, changing hot dishes such as soup, sausage or lamb casseroles, and proper puddings such as plum sponge and bread and butter pudding. *Benchmark main dish: pie of the day £7.50.*

Free house ~ Licensees Doris Hobbs and Kevin Brooker ~ Real ale ~ Open 11-2.30, 5-11; 11-11 Sat; 12-10.30 Sun ~ Bar food 12-2 (2.30 weekends) ~ Children allowed in canopied extension area ~ Dogs allowed in bar ~ Wi-fi *Recommended by Simon Collett-Jones, Alistair Forsyth, Gus Swan, Roy Hoing, Tracey and Stephen Groves, Dave Braisted*

LEY HILL   SP9901 Map 4
Swan ◀
(01494) 783075 – www.swanleyhill.com
Village signposted off A416 in Chesham; HP5 1UT

Charming, old-fashioned pub with friendly licensees, chatty customers, four real ales and quite a choice of popular food

There's a chatty and relaxed atmosphere here and the friendly, hands-on licensee keeps everything spic and span – not easy given the antiquity of the place. With plenty of original features and a lot of character, the main bar is cosily old-fashioned with black beams (mind your head) and standing timbers, an ancient range, a log fire, a nice mix of old furniture and a collection of vintage local photographs. St Austell Tribute, Timothy Taylors Landlord and Tring Side Pocket for a Toad on handpump and several wines by the glass. The dining section is light and airy with a raftered ceiling, cream walls, red and gold curtains and all sorts of old tables and chairs on timber floors. The pub looks its best in summer with picnic-sets among tubs of flowers and hanging baskets at the front, and more seats, benches and tables under parasols in the bigger back garden (where they offer full dining service). It's worth wandering over to the common opposite (where there's a cricket pitch and a nine-hole golf course) and then to look back and admire the pretty 16th-c timbered building.

Pleasing food includes lunchtime sandwiches (not Sunday), crab cakes with sweet chilli dip, black pudding with sautéed potatoes, bacon and free-range poached egg, vegetarian tagliatelle, steak and kidney pie, chicken with rösti potato and creamy mushroom sauce, sea bream fillet with parsley and lemon dressing, and puddings such as dark and white chocolate fondant and sticky toffee pudding with toffee sauce. *Benchmark main dish: slow-cooked pork belly with fondant potato, apple purée and red wine jus £14.75. Two-course evening meal £21.00.*

Free house ~ Licensee Nigel Byatt ~ Real ale ~ Open 12-2.45, 5.30-11; 12-4 Sun; closed Sun evening, Mon ~ Bar food 12-2.30, 6-9; 12-2.45 Sun ~ Restaurant ~ Children welcome until 9pm
Recommended by Alistair Forsyth, Carol and Barry Craddock

LITTLE MARLOW
SU8787   Map 2
Queens Head 🏵️
(01628) 482927 – www.marlowslittlesecret.co.uk
Village signposted off A4155 E of Marlow near Kings Head; bear right into Pound Lane cul-de-sac; SL7 3SR

Charmingly tucked-away country pub with good food and ales, friendly staff and appealing garden

On a summer's day, the garden in front of this pretty tiled cottage is a decided plus, though not large: sheltered and neatly planted, it has teak tables and quite closely arranged picnic-sets, and white-painted metal furniture in a little wickerwork bower. The friendly, unpretentious main bar has simple but comfortable furniture on polished boards and leads back to a sizeable squarish carpeted dining extension with good solid tables. Throughout are old local photographs on cream or maroon walls, panelled dados painted brown or sage, and lighted candles. On the right is a small, quite separate, low-ceilinged public bar with Fullers London Pride, Rebellion IPA and Sharps Doom Bar on handpump, several wines by the glass, quite a range of whiskies and good coffee; neatly dressed efficient staff and unobtrusive background music.

Much enjoyed food includes sandwiches, chicken, parma ham and tomato terrine with chutney, crispy peppered squid with cucumber and fennel, roasted halloumi and sweet potato filo roll with spiced tomato jam, braised beef shin with butternut squash purée, duck fat potatoes and port jus, gurnard fillet with butter bean patty and broccoli and corn salsa, lamb wellington with dauphinoise potatoes, and puddings such as pecan tart with bourbon ice-cream and rhubarb and honey cheesecake. *Benchmark main dish: beer-battered fish and chips £10.95. Two-course evening meal £20.00.*

Punch ~ Lease Daniel O'Sullivan ~ Real ale ~ Open 11-11; 11-10.30 Sun ~ Bar food 12-2, 7-9 ~ Restaurant ~ Children welcome ~ Wi-fi *Recommended by Alistair Forsyth, Peter Andrews, Gus Swan, Steve and Liz Tilley*

LITTLE MISSENDEN

SU9298 Map 4

Crown 🍺 £

(01494) 862571 – www.the-crown-little-missenden.co.uk

Crown Lane, SE end of village, which is signposted off A413 W of Amersham;
HP7 0RD

Long-serving licensees and pubby feel in little country cottage,
with several real ales and straightforward food; attractive garden

The bustling bars of this traditional brick cottage (run for over 90 years by the same friendly family) are more spacious than they might first appear and immaculately kept. There are old red floor tiles on the left, oak parquet on the right, built-in wall seats, studded red leatherette chairs and a few small tables and a winter fire. Otter Bitter, St Austell Tribute, West Berkshire Good Old Boy and Youngs Bitter on handpump or tapped from the cask, farm cider, summer Pimms and several malt whiskies; darts and board games. The large attractive sheltered garden behind has picnic-sets and other tables, and there are also seats out in front. Bedrooms are in a converted barn (continental breakfasts in your room only). Dogs may be allowed in if well behaved. No children. The interesting church in the pretty village is well worth a visit.

Honest lunchtime-only food (not Sunday) includes their famous bucks bite, sandwiches, baked potatoes, pasty with beans, salads with home-cooked meats, and smoked haddock and spring onion fishcakes with sweet chilli dip. *Benchmark main dish: steak in ale pie £8.75.*

Free house ~ Licensees Trevor and Carolyn How ~ Real ale ~ Open 11-2.30, 6-11; 12-3, 7-10.30 Sun ~ Bar food 12-2; not Sun ~ Wi-fi ~ Bedrooms: /£85 *Recommended by Edward May, Roy Hoing, William Slade*

LONG CRENDON

SP6908 Map 4

Eight Bells 🍺 £

(01844) 208244 – www.8bellspub.com

High Street, off B4011 N of Thame; car park entrance off Chearsley Road,
not 'Village roads only'; HP18 9AL

Good beers and sensibly priced seasonal food in nicely traditional
village pub with charming garden

Luckily, nothing changes here – which is just how our readers like it. The small bare-boards bar on the left has Ringwood Best, XT Four, Thwaites Wainwright and a changing guest ale on handpump or tapped from the cask, 16 wines by the glass and three farm ciders; service is cheerful. A bigger low-ceilinged room on the right has a log fire, daily papers and a pleasantly haphazard mix of tables and simple seats on ancient red and black tiles; one snug little hidey-hole with just three tables is devoted to the local morris men – frequent visitors. Board games, TV and background music. The small back garden is a joy in summer when there are well spaced picnic-sets among a colourful variety of shrubs and flowers; aunt sally. The interesting old village is known to many from TV's *Midsomer Murders*.

Good value food includes sandwiches, salt beef hash with a free-range egg and mustard dressing, chilli beef with crispy onions, pizzas with extra toppings, beer-battered fish and chips, chestnut and pearl barley bourguignon, duck leg ragoût with tagliatelle and crispy skin, and puddings such as apple and blackberry eton mess and chocolate and salted caramel tart. *Benchmark main dish: steak burger with sauce and chips £13.00. Two-course evening meal £20.00.*

Free house ~ Licensee Paul Mitchell ~ Real ale ~ Open 12-11; 12-10 Sun ~ Bar food 12-9;
12-4 Sun ~ Restaurant ~ Children welcome ~ Dogs welcome ~ Wi-fi ~ Live music last Sun
of month *Recommended by Brian Glozier, Martin Jones, Peter Brix, Ian Duncan*

MILTON KEYNES   SP8939   Map 4
Swan ♀

(01908) 665240 – www.theswan-mkvillage.co.uk
Broughton Road, Milton Keynes village; MK10 9AH

**Well thought-out rooms with open fires in inglenooks, enjoyable food
and drink and seats outside**

Original features mix well with contemporary furnishings in this pretty
thatched pub and the beamed main bar area has plush armchairs to each
side of an inglenook fireplace, several high tables and chairs dotted about, a
cushioned wall banquette with scatter cushions, and wooden dining chairs
and chunky tables on flagstones. Youngs Bitter and Wells Bombardier plus
guests like Black Sheep Holy Grail and Courage Directors on handpump, 30
wines by the glass, good coffees and courteous service. Leading off to the
left is a cosy room with a gas stove, more cushioned banquettes and similar
tables and chairs on parquet flooring, bookcase-effect wallpaper and photos
of the pub. The spreading, partly beamed restaurant, with views of the open
kitchen, has all manner of wooden and pretty fabric-covered dining chairs,
cushioned settles and wall seats and a few curved banquettes (creating snug,
private areas) on floorboards, and a woodburning stove. Doors open on to an
outside dining area overlooking the garden, where there are seats and
picnic-sets on grass.

Good food includes lunchtime sandwiches, chicken liver parfait with madeira
jelly, oak smoked salmon with maple and grain mustard dressing, sharing boards,
caesar salad with tuna, risotto of the day, chicken, jerusalem artichoke purée, wild
mushroom and tomato fricassée, plum tomato tarte tatin with goats cheese fritters
and balsamic glaze, guinea fowl with crushed sweet potato and warm bacon jam, and
puddings such as white chocolate and cherry cheesecake with jam and chocolate sauce
and a sundae of the day; they also offer a two- and three-course set weekday menu (12-3,
6-6.45). *Benchmark main dish: pie of the day £13.95. Two-course evening meal £20.50.*

Little Gems Country Dining Pubs ~ Manager Grant Owen ~ Real ale ~ Open 11-11
(midnight Fri, Sat); 12-10.30 Sun ~ Bar food 12-3, 6-9.30; 12-10 Fri, Sat; 12-8 Sun ~
Restaurant ~ Children welcome but must be well behaved ~ Dogs allowed in bar ~
Wi-fi *Recommended by Valerie Sayer, Beth Aldridge, Ben and Diane Bowie, Michael Butler*

PENN   SU9093   Map 4
Old Queens Head 🍴 ♀

(01494) 813371 – www.oldqueensheadpenn.co.uk
Hammersley Lane/Church Road, off B474 between Penn and Tylers Green; HP10 8EY

**Stylishly updated pub with highly enjoyable food, a good choice
of drinks and walks nearby**

The open-plan rooms in this smart pub have lots of different areas to
sit in, all with different aspects, and are decorated in a stylish mix of
contemporary and chintz. There are well spaced tables, a modicum of old
prints and comfortably varied seating on flagstones or broad dark boards.
Stairs lead up to an attractive (and popular) two-level dining room, partly
carpeted, with stripped rafters. The active bar side has Greene King Old
Speckled Hen and Ruddles County and a guest like Belhaven IPA on
handpump, over 20 wines by the glass (plus pudding wines), a dozen gins and

a good choice of liqueurs; the turntable-top bar stools let you swivel to face the log fire in the big nearby fireplace. Daily papers and background music. The sunny terrace overlooks St Margaret's church and there are picnic-sets on the sheltered L-shaped lawn. Walkers and their dogs head here after visiting the ancient beechwoods of Common or Penn Woods; dogs might be offered a biscuit.

Rewarding food includes potted crayfish with dill butter, devilled free-range duck livers on toasted brioche with bacon, black pudding and HP jus, chargrilled asparagus, aubergine and courgette quinoa salad with crispy halloumi croutons and basil oil, salmon with braised puy lentils, parmentier potatoes and red wine sauce, jamaican mutton curry, corn-fed chicken breast with chorizo and cheddar croquettes and slow-roast tomato sauce, and puddings such as rhubarb and custard knickerbocker glory and steamed treacle sponge with clotted cream custard; the first Monday of the month is fish and chip night, and Tuesday evenings are for speciality sausages. *Benchmark main dish: bubble and squeak cake with bacon, a poached egg and hollandaise £11.75. Two-course evening meal £20.00.*

Little Gems Country Dining Pubs ~ Manager Tina Brown ~ Real ale ~ Open 11.30-11.30 ~ Bar food 12-2.30, 6.30-9.30; 9.30-3, 6.30-10 Fri, Sat (snacks all afternoon); 12-9 Sun ~ Restaurant ~ Children welcome ~ Dogs allowed in bar ~ Wi-fi *Recommended by Peter Brix, Phoebe Peacock, Sandra and Nigel Brown*

PRESTWOOD
Polecat 🍴 ♀

SP8799   Map 4

(01494) 862253 ~ www.thepolecatinn.co.uk
170 Wycombe Road (A4128 N of High Wycombe); HP16 0HJ

Enjoyable food, real ales and a chatty atmosphere in several smallish civilised rooms; attractive sizeable garden

Civilised but easy-going, this is an enjoyable pub with plenty of customers. Several smallish rooms opening off the low-ceilinged bar have an assortment of tables and chairs, various stuffed birds, stuffed white polecats in one big cabinet, small country pictures, rugs on bare boards or red tiles, and a couple of leather wing chairs by a good open fire. Malt Golden Ale and Prestwoods Best, Rebellion IPA and Zebedee and a guest beer on handpump, 30 wines by the glass, quite a few gins and home-made cordials. The garden is most attractive with lots of spring bulbs, colourful summer hanging baskets and tubs and plenty of herbaceous plants; there are picnic-sets under parasols on neat grass out in front beneath a big fairy-lit pear tree, more on a large well kept lawn at the back and a large children's play area.

Good food includes sandwiches, chicken liver and pistachio pâté with apricot chutney, twice-baked stilton soufflé, smoked haddock and spinach fishcakes, greek spinach and feta pie with tomato and basil sauce, a trio of local sausages with onion gravy and bubble and squeak, chicken curry, short rib of beef with barbecue sauce and sweet potato fries with slaw, and puddings such as profiteroles with chocolate sauce and sticky toffee pudding with butterscotch sauce. *Benchmark main dish: pie of the day £12.00. Two-course evening meal £18.00.*

Free house ~ Licensee Philip Whitehouse ~ Real ale ~ Open 11.30-11; 12-6 Sun; 11.30-3, 6.30-11 winter ~ Bar food 12-9; 12-3 Sun ~ Restaurant ~ Children welcome ~ Dogs allowed in bar ~ Wi-fi *Recommended by Tracey and Stephen Groves, Peter and Jan Humphreys, William Slade*

Half pints: by law, a pub should not charge more for half a pint than half the price of a full pint, unless it shows that half-pint price on its price list.

STOKE MANDEVILLE

SP8310 Map 4

Bell ⭐🍴 ♀

(01296) 612434 – www.bellstokemandeville.co.uk

Lower Road; HP22 5XA

Friendly landlord and staff, a fine choice of drinks, interesting food and seats outside

Run with enthusiasm by a friendly landlord, this extended red-brick Victorian pub is popular for both food and drinks. The interconnected bar and dining areas have an easy-going atmosphere, flagstones or polished pine floorboards and prints, drawings and maps of local interest and hunting prints on the walls above a dark blue dado; background music and board games. High stools line the counter where they keep Wells Bombardier, Youngs Bitter and a guest ale on handpump and 20 wines (including sweet wines) by the glass; there are some equally high stools and tables opposite. Throughout are high-backed cushioned wooden and farmhouse chairs, wall settles with scatter cushions, and rustic benches around a medley of tables, some painted beams and a woodburning stove; a snug alcove has just one table surrounded by cushioned wall seats. The little side terrace has picnic-sets and there are more on grass beside a weeping birch.

 Top-quality food includes sandwiches, ham hock terrine with apple crisps and grain mustard dressing, cajun spiced squid with red pepper dip, sharing boards, pearl barley, squash, marrow and pea risotto, sausages of the day with onion gravy, venison steak with red wine jus and fondant potato, sea bream with roast mediterranean vegetables and pesto, and puddings such as blueberry crème brûlée and bread and butter pudding. *Benchmark main dish: bubble and squeak with smoked bacon, poached egg and hollandaise £11.25. Two-course evening meal £22.00.*

Distinct Pub Company ~ Lease James Penlington ~ Real ale ~ Open 10am-11pm (10.30pm Sun) ~ Bar food 12-9.30 (8.30 Sun) ~ Restaurant ~ Children welcome ~ Dogs allowed in bar ~ Wi-fi *Recommended by Ruth May, David Longhurst*

THE LEE

SP8904 Map 4

Old Swan

(01494) 837239 – www.theoldswanpub.co.uk

Swan Bottom, back road 0.75 miles N of The Lee; HP16 9NU

Country pub with character bars and dining areas, friendly service, real ales, highly thought-of food and seats in big garden

As there are good surrounding walks and cycling routes, you'll find plenty of cheerful customers in this friendly 16th-c pub. The attractively furnished linked rooms have heavy beams, flagstones and old quarry tiles, high-backed antique settles and window seats with scatter cushions, little plush stools and straightforward dining chairs around wooden tables and a log fire in an inglenook cooking range. High bar stools line the counter where they keep Chiltern Ale, Sharps Doom Bar and a guest such as Rebellion Waterloo on handpump and several wines by the glass. The big, spreading back garden has picnic-sets and contemporary seating around rustic tables; children's play area.

🍴 Elaborate food includes butternut squash cannelloni with caraway-infused goats curd and pickled beetroot, mackerel fillets with blood orange salsa and smoked horseradish, wild garlic and spinach pearl barley ragoût with truffle-infused black pepper ricotta and vegetable crisps, bubble and squeak with fried duck egg and hollandaise sauce, a pie of the day, chicken ballotine with puff pastry vegetable terrine, wild mushrooms and redcurrant jus, and puddings such as passion-fruit soufflé with passion-fruit ice-cream and dark chocolate ganache with toffee banana loaf, peanut butter mousse and salted caramel. *Benchmark main dish: 7oz rump steak with skinny fries and pepper sauce £12.50. Two-course evening meal £22.50.*

Free house ~ Licensees Phil and Jane Joel ~ Real ale ~ Open 12-3, 6-9; 12-11 Fri, Sat; 12-7 Sun; closed Mon lunchtime ~ Bar food 12-2.30, 7-9; 12-2.30, 6.30-9 Fri, Sat; 12-3 Sun; not Sun evening, Mon ~ Restaurant ~ Children welcome ~ Dogs allowed in bar ~ Wi-fi
Recommended by Emma Scofield, Peter Pilbeam, Mr and Mrs J Watkins, Richard Kennell

Also Worth a Visit in Buckinghamshire

Besides the fully inspected pubs, you might like to try these pubs that have been recommended to us and described by readers. Do tell us what you think of them: feedback@goodguides.com

AMERSHAM   SU9597
Elephant & Castle (01494) 726410
High Street; HP7 0DT
Modernised twin-gabled low-beamed local, good value tasty food from sandwiches to full meals including weekday set menu (lunchtime/early evening), three well kept ales such as Hook Norton Old Hooky from U-shaped counter, quick friendly service, woodburner in large brick fireplace, conservatory; background and some live music; garden behind, children welcome, open all day. *(Quentin and Carol Williamson)*

ASHERIDGE   SP9404
Blue Ball (01494) 758305
Braziers End; HP5 2UX Small open-plan country pub with light airy décor, ample helpings of enjoyable good value food cooked to order, well kept Courage Directors, Fullers London Pride and Youngs Bitter, Weston's cider, friendly landlady and staff; children (till 6pm) and dogs welcome, large well maintained back garden, good Chilterns walking country, open all day, no food Sun or Mon evenings. *(R Anderson, Mrs P Sumner, Roy Hoing)*

ASTON CLINTON   SP8811
Bell (01296) 632777
London Road; HP22 5HP Comfortably refurbished old Mitchells & Butlers village pub-restaurant; good choice of sensibly priced food from sandwiches and sharing boards up, Fullers London Pride, Sharps Doom Bar and a guest, plenty of wines by the glass including champagne, friendly efficient service; tables out under trees, 11 Innkeepers Lodge bedrooms, open (and food) all day from 8am. *(John Poulter)*

BEACONSFIELD   SU9490
Royal Saracens (01494) 674119
1 mile from M40 junction 2; London End (A40); HP9 2JH Former coaching inn with striking timbered façade and well updated open-plan interior, comfortable chairs around light wood tables, massive beams and timbers in one corner, log fires, welcoming young staff, wide choice of enjoyable food including shared dishes and fixed-price weekday menu till 6pm, busy at weekends when best to book, well kept ales such as Fullers London Pride and Sharps Doom Bar, craft kegs and plenty of wines by the glass, large back restaurant; attractive sheltered courtyard, open (and food) all day. *(Julian Thorpe)*

BOURNE END   SU8987
Bounty (01628) 520056
Cock Marsh, actually across the river along the Cookham towpath, but shortest walk – still about 0.25 miles – is from Bourne End, over the railway bridge; SL8 5RG Welcoming take-us-as-you-find-us pub tucked away in outstanding setting on bank of the Thames and accessible only by foot or boat; collection of flags on ceiling and jumble of other bits and pieces, well kept Rebellion ales from boat counter, basic standard food including children's meals, back dining area, darts and bar billiards; background music inside and out; dirty dogs and muddy walkers welcome, picnic-sets with parasols on front terrace, play area to right, open all day in summer (may be boat trips), just weekends in winter and closes early if quiet. *(Luke Morgan)*

BRADENHAM   SU8297
Red Lion (01494) 562212
A4010, by Walters Ash turn-off; HP14 4HF Welcoming NT-owned pub with small simple bar and good-sized low-beamed dining room, two or three well kept Rebellion ales, enjoyable home-made food from good baguettes to daily specials, efficient service; children, walkers and dogs welcome, picnic-sets on terrace and lawn, pretty village green nearby, closed Sun evening, Mon. *(David Lamb, Ross Balaam)*

BUCKINGHAM   SP6933
Villiers (01280) 822444
Castle Street; MK18 1BS Pub part of this large comfortable hotel with own courtyard

entrance; big inglenook log fire, panelling and stripped masonry in flagstoned bar, beers from Hook Norton and Black Sheep, reliably good food from shortish menu (also set menu choices), competent friendly staff, sofas and armchairs in more formal front lounges, restaurant with two large tropical fish tanks; children welcome till 9pm, no dogs, terrace tables, open all day. *(Julian Thorpe)*

CADSDEN   SP8204

Plough (01844) 343302

Cadsden Road; HP27 0NB Extended former 16th-c coaching inn with airy open-plan bar/dining area, clean and bright, with well spaced pine tables on flagstones, exposed brick and some faux beams, very popular with families and Chilterns ramblers, ales including Greene King, Rebellion and a Marstons house beer, enjoyable home-made food with main courses in two sizes, cherry pie festival first Sun in Aug, friendly service; lots of tables in delightful quiet front and back gardens, some woodland seating, pretty spot on Ridgeway path (shoe covers for walkers), close to Chequers and visited by prime ministers (most recently David Cameron with Chinese President Xi), bedrooms, open all day weekends (no food Sun evening). *(Charlie Parker)*

CHALFONT ST GILES   SU9895

★ **Ivy House** (01494) 872184

A413 S; HP8 4RS Old brick and flint beamed coaching inn, enjoyable home-cooked food served by friendly young staff, well kept Fullers ales, decent wines by the glass and over 30 whiskies, L-shaped bar where dogs allowed, log fire, lighter flagstoned dining extension; quiz first Thurs of month, free wi-fi; children welcome, some seats out under covered front part by road, pleasant terrace and sloping garden, five comfortable bedrooms, good hearty breakfast, open all day (food all day weekends, till 7pm Sun). *(V Brogden, Tracey and Stephen Groves, Mr and Mrs J Watkins)*

CHALFONT ST GILES   SU9893

Milton's Head (01494) 872961

Deanway; HP8 4JL Popular little pub-restaurant with good mainly italian food cooked by sardinian landlord, also pizza menu and traditional Sun roasts, reasonable prices and best to book, nice italian wines and coffee too, no real ales but Peroni on draught; children and dogs welcome, small side terrace, handy for John Milton's Cottage, closed Sun evening, Mon. *(Miles Green)*

CHEARSLEY   SP7110

Bell (01844) 208077

The Green; HP18 0DJ Cosy traditional thatched and beamed pub on attractive village green, Fullers beers and good wines by the glass, enjoyable sensibly priced home-made food (not Sun or Mon evenings), efficient friendly service, inglenook with

big woodburner; quiz (first Sun of month), bingo (first Tues); children in eating area, dogs welcome, plenty of tables in spacious back garden with heated terrace and play area. *(Julie Braeburn)*

CHENIES   TQ0198

Bedford Arms (01923) 283301

2 miles from M25 junction 18; A404 towards Amersham, then village signposted on right; Chesham Road; WD3 6EQ Popular country-house hotel with bright modernised front bar, good food here or in more formal oak-panelled restaurant, friendly efficient staff, Fullers London Pride, Tring Side Pocket for a Toad and a guest, decent choice of wines by the glass; tables on attractive front terrace and in lovely garden behind with mature oaks, 18 bedrooms, enjoyable walks, open all day. *(Richard Kennell, Brian Glozier)*

CHENIES   TQ0298

★ **Red Lion** (01923) 282722

2 miles from M25 junction 18; A404 towards Amersham, then village signposted on right; Chesham Road; WD3 6ED The welcoming long-serving landlord at this popular village pub is retiring, so things may change; L-shaped bar with comfortable built-in wall benches and other seats, old photographs of the village and traction engines, small back snug and neat dining extension with more modern décor, well kept Rebellion, Vale, Wadworths and a guest, ten wines by the glass, popular food including good lamb pie, friendly attentive service; no under-14s, dogs welcome in bar, pretty hanging baskets and window boxes, picnic-sets on small side terrace, good local walks, open (and food) all day weekends. *(John Evans, Richard Kennell, Roy Hoing)*

CHESHAM   SP9501

Queens Head (01494) 778690

Church Street; HP5 1JD Popular well run Fullers corner pub, two traditional beamed bars with scrubbed tables and log fires, their ales and a guest kept well, good thai food along with modest range of pub staples, restaurant, friendly staff and chatty locals; sports TV; children welcome, tables in small courtyard used by smokers, next to little River Chess, open all day. *(William Slade)*

COLESHILL   SU9594

★ **Harte & Magpies** (01494) 726754

E of village on A355 Amersham–Beaconsfield, by junction with Magpie Lane; HP7 0LU This popular roadside pub was changing hands as we went to press – reports please; open-plan interior with rambling collection of pews and high-backed booths making for plenty of snug corners, maybe patriotic antique prints and candles in bottles, Chiltern and Rebellion ales, tasty food; picnic-sets on terrace with wisteria-draped tree, big informal sloping garden, play area, good nearby walks, has opened all day. *(Edward May, Charlie Parker)*

COLNBROOK
TQ0277
Ostrich (01753) 682628
1.25 miles from M4 junction 5 via A4/ B3378, then 'village only' road; High Street; SL3 0JZ Spectacular timbered Elizabethan building (with even longer gruesome history – tales of over 60 murders!); contemporary interior with comfortable sofas on stripped wood and a rather startling red plastic/stainless steel bar counter, three well kept ales (one badged for them) and good choice of wines by the glass including champagne, enjoyable sensibly priced food from sandwiches and pub favourites up, good value set lunch Mon-Sat, efficient friendly service, attractive restaurant with open fire; soft background music, comedy and live music nights upstairs; children welcome, open all day Sun. *(Charlie Parker)*

CUDDINGTON
SP7311
★ ## Crown (01844) 292222
Spurt Street; off A418 Thame–Aylesbury; HP18 0BB Thatched cottage with chatty mix of customers and nice atmosphere, comfortable pubby furnishings including cushioned settles in two low-beamed linked rooms, big inglenook log fire, well kept Fullers and guests, around 20 wines by the glass and good reasonably priced home-cooked food (not Sun evening), competent friendly service, carpeted two-room back dining area with country kitchen chairs around mix of tables; children welcome; neat side terrace with modern garden furniture and planters, picnic-sets in front. *(Mike Kavaney, Mr and Mrs J Watkins)*

DENHAM
TQ0487
Green Man (01895) 832760
Village Road; UB9 5BH Welcoming 18th-c red-brick village pub, refurbished beamed bar with flagstones and log fire, well kept Fullers, Greene King and Rebellion, popular pubby food from sandwiches and baguettes up, cheerful efficient service, conservatory dining extension; Thurs quiz, free wi-fi; children and dogs welcome, sunny back terrace and garden, open all day. *(Taff Thomas)*

DINTON
SP7610
Seven Stars (01296) 749000
Signed off A418 Aylesbury–Thame; near Gibraltar turn-off; Stars Lane; HP17 8UL Pretty 17th-c community-owned pub run by french landlady and popular locally; inglenook bar, beamed lounge and

dining room, a couple of well kept ales (usually Vale) and plenty of wines by the glass, good food cooked to order from pub staples up including some french dishes (coq au vin recommended), friendly service; tables in sheltered garden with terrace, pleasant village, open all day weekends. *(David Lamb, Mr and Mrs J Watkins)*

DORNEY
SU9279
Palmer Arms (01628) 666612
2.7 miles from M4 junction 7, via B3026; Village Road; SL4 6QW Modernised and extended dining pub in attractive conservation village, good popular food (best to book) from snacks and pub favourites to more restauranty dishes, friendly efficient service, Greene King ales, lots of wines by the glass (interesting list) and good coffee, open fires in civilised front bar and back dining room; background music, daily newspapers; children and dogs (in certain areas) welcome, disabled facilities, terrace overlooking mediterranean-feel garden, enclosed play area, nice riverside walks nearby, open (and food) all day. *(I D Barnett)*

DORNEY
SU9279
Pineapple (01628) 662353
Lake End Road: 2.4 miles from M4 junction 7; left on A4 then left on B3026; SL4 6QS Nicely old-fashioned pub handy for Dorney Court (where the first english pineapple was grown in 1661); shiny low Anaglypta ceilings, black-panelled dados, leather chairs around sturdy country tables (one very long, another in big bow window), woodburner and pretty little fireplace, china pineapples and other decorations on shelves in one of three cottagey carpeted linked rooms on left, well kept Black Sheep, Fullers London Pride and a beer named for the pub (actually Marstons EPA), over 1,000 varieties of sandwiches in five different fresh breads, roasts on Sun; background music, games machine; children and dogs welcome, rustic seats on roadside verandah, round picnic-sets in garden, fairy-lit decking under oak tree, some motorway noise, open (and food) all day. *(James Allsopp)*

EMBERTON
SP8849
Bell & Bear (01234) 711565
Off A509 Olney–Newport Pagnell; High Street; MK46 5DH Old stone-built village pub with good interesting food cooked by landlord-chef including set lunch and tapas-style bar menu (Weds-Sat), four well kept changing ales, craft beers, real cider and good selection of other drinks, friendly efficient staff, bar with log fire and hood skittles, restaurant; well behaved

---

children and dogs (in bar) welcome, garden tables, open all day Fri-Sun, closed Mon lunchtime, no food Sun evening, Mon, Tues lunchtime. *(Ben and Diana Bowie)*

FLACKWELL HEATH　　　　SU8889

Crooked Billet　(01628) 521216

Off A404; Sheepridge Lane; SL7 3SG
Steps up to cosily old-fashioned unspoilt 16th-c pub, Brakspears and Charles Wells ales, reasonably priced traditional lunchtime food, charming landlord and friendly staff, eating area spread pleasantly through alcoves, low black beams and good open fire; lovely cottagey garden with nice views (beyond road), walks nearby. *(Susan and John Douglas)*

FRIETH　　　　　　　　SU7990

Prince Albert　(01494) 881683

Off B482 SW of High Wycombe; RG9 6PY
Friendly cottagey Chilterns local with low black beams and joists, high-backed settles, big black stove in inglenook and log fire in larger area on right, decent lunchtime food from sandwiches up (also Fri and Sat evenings – they ask you to book on Sat), well kept Brakspears and guests; quiz every other Tues, folk night last Weds of month; children and dogs welcome, nicely planted informal side garden with views of woods and fields, good walks, open all day. *(Sandra and Nigel Brown)*

GAWCOTT　　　　　　　SP6831

Crown　(01280) 822322

Hillesden Road; MK18 4JF Welcoming black-beamed village pub, good value popular food including carvery Weds and Sun, well kept ales such as Sharps Doom Bar from herringbone brick counter, restaurant area; background music, Sky TV, pool; children welcome, long back garden with swings, open all day (no food Sun evening, Mon). *(Julie Braeburn)*

GERRARDS CROSS　　　　TQ0089

★Three Oaks　(01753) 899016

Austenwood Lane, just NW of junction with Kingsway (B416); SL9 8NL
Civilised and relaxed dining pub facing Austenwood Common, welcoming neatly dressed staff, two-room front bar with fireside bookshelves, tartan wing armchairs, sturdy wall settles and comfortable banquettes, well kept Fullers, Rebellion and several wines by the glass, dining part with three linked rooms, popular highly regarded food including short set menu; soft background music, free wi-fi; children welcome, sturdy wooden tables on flagstoned side terrace, open all day. *(Sandra and Nigel Brown)*

GREAT HAMPDEN　　　　SP8401

★Hampden Arms　(01494) 488255

W of Great Missenden, off A4128; HP16 9RQ Friendly village pub opposite cricket pitch, good mix of locals and visitors, comfortably furnished rooms (back one more rustic with big woodburner), well kept Rebellion IPA and a couple of guests, Addlestone's cider and several wines by the glass from small corner bar, enjoyable reasonably priced pubby food including one or two greek dishes, cheerful efficient service; children and dogs welcome, seats in tree-sheltered garden, good Hampden Common walks, open all day weekends. *(David Lamb, Ross Balaam)*

GREAT KINGSHILL　　　　SU8798

★Red Lion　(01494) 711262

A4128 N of High Wycombe; HP15 6EB
Welcoming village pub with contemporary décor and relaxed informal atmosphere, well cooked brasserie-style food including fixed-price menu (Tues-Sat lunchtime, Tues-Thurs early evening), local beers and good value wine list, 'lobby' and cosy little flagstoned bar with leather tub chairs by log fire, spacious candlelit dining room; well behaved children welcome, closed Sun evening, Mon. *(William Slade)*

GREAT MISSENDEN　　　　SP8901

★Cross Keys　(01494) 865373

High Street; HP16 0AU Friendly and relaxed village pub dating from the 16th c, unspoilt beamed bar divided by standing timbers, traditional furnishings including high-backed settle, log-effect gas fire in huge fireplace, well kept Fullers ales and often an unusual guest, enjoyable fairly priced food (not Sun evening) from sandwiches and pizzas up, cheerful helpful staff, spacious beamed restaurant; free wi-fi; children and dogs welcome, picnic-sets on back terrace, open all day (till 1am Thurs-Sat). *(Sandra and Nigel Brown)*

GROVE　　　　　　　　SP9122

★Grove Lock　(01525) 380940

Pub signed off B488, on left just S of A505 roundabout (S of Leighton Buzzard); LU7 0QU Overlooking Grand Union Canal and usefully open all day; open plan with lofty high-raftered pitched roof in bar, squashy brown leather sofas on oak boards, eclectic mix of tables and chairs including butcher's block tables by bar, big open-standing log fire, steps down to original lock-keeper's cottage (now three-room restaurant area), enjoyable food from sandwiches to daily specials, Fullers ales and lots of wines by the glass; background music, free wi-fi; children welcome, seats on canopied deck and waterside lawn by Lock 28. *(James Allsopp)*

HADDENHAM　　　　　　SP7408

Green Dragon　(01844) 292331

Village signposted off A418 and A4129, E/NE of Thame; then follow Church End signs into Churchway; HP17 8AA
Shuttered 18th-c village dining pub under new management; open-plan modernised

interior with two log fires, well kept ales such as Black Sheep, Hook Norton and Tring, several wines by the glass and good interesting food (not Sun evening) from chargrilled sandwiches up, good value set lunch deal including a glass of wine, friendly service; children and muddy boots welcome, sheltered terrace and appealing garden, closed Mon, otherwise open all day. *(Sandra and Nigel Brown)*

HUGHENDEN VALLEY   SU8697
★ **Harrow** (01494) 564105
Warrendene Road, off A4128 N of High Wycombe; HP14 4LX Small cheerful brick and flint roadside cottage surrounded by Chilterns walks; traditionally furnished with tiled-floor bar on left, black beams and joists, woodburner in big fireplace, pewter mugs, country pictures and wall seats, similar but bigger right-hand bar with sizeable dining tables on brick floor, carpeted back dining room, tasty pub food (not Sun evening) from sandwiches up including meal deal Mon-Weds, Courage Best, Fullers London Pride and Shepherd Neame Spitfire, friendly attentive staff; Tues quiz; children and dogs welcome (there's a pub dog), disabled access, plenty of picnic-sets in front with more on back lawn, play area, open all day. *(Simon Collett-Jones)*

HYDE HEATH   SU9300
Plough (01494) 774408
Off B485 Great Missenden–Chesham; HP6 5RW Small prettily placed pub with traditional bare-boards bar and carpeted dining extension, good value traditional food including walkers' menu, Fullers London Pride, St Austell Tribute and a local beer, real fires; background music, TV; bikers welcome, picnic-sets on green opposite, open all day Fri-Sun. *(Charlie Parker)*

ICKFORD   SP6407
Rising Sun (01844) 339238
E of Thame; Worminghall Road; HP18 9JD Pretty thatched local with cosy low-beamed bar, friendly staff and regulars, Adnams, Black Sheep, Hook Norton and a weekly guest, enjoyable reasonably priced home-made food, log fire; children, walkers and dogs welcome, pleasant garden with picnic-sets and play area, handy for Waterperry Gardens, open all day weekends. *(Luke Morgan)*

IVINGHOE ASTON   SP9518
Village Swan (01525) 220544
Aston; signed from B489 NE of Ivinghoe; LU7 9DP Village-owned pub managed by welcoming dutch couple; traditional beamed interior with open fire, enjoyable home-made food from varied menu including some dutch dishes, three real ales and nice wines by the glass; quiz first Mon of month, free wi-fi; children, walkers and dogs welcome, covered outside area and garden, handy for

Ivinghoe Beacon and Icknield Way, open all day weekends, closed Mon and weekday lunchtimes. *(Ian Duncan)*

LACEY GREEN   SP8200
Black Horse (01844) 345195
Main Road; HP27 0QU Friendly mix of customers in this two-bar beamed country local, popular good value home-made food (not Sun evening, Mon) from baguettes up, breakfast from 9am Tues-Sat, four real ales including Brakspears, nice choice of wines by the glass, quotations written on walls, inglenook woodburner; darts, sports TV; children welcome, picnic-sets in garden with play area and aunt sally, closed Mon lunchtime, open all day Thurs-Sun. *(Sandra and Nigel Brown)*

LACEY GREEN   SP8100
Whip (01844) 344060
Pink Road; HP27 0PG Cheery hilltop local welcoming walkers, mix of simple traditional furnishings in smallish front bar and larger downstairs dining area, popular good value food from sandwiches to daily specials (booking advised weekends), six interesting well kept/priced ales and a couple of proper ciders, beer festivals (May and Sept) with live jazz, good landlord and friendly helpful service; TV, fruit machine; tables in mature sheltered garden looking up to windmill, open all day. *(Luke Morgan)*

LITTLE HORWOOD   SP7930
Shoulder of Mutton (01296) 713703
Church Street; back road a mile S of A421 Buckingham–Bletchley; MK17 0PF Partly thatched and timbered 15th-c village pub, friendly and hospitable, with good choice of well liked food cooked by landlady, Sharps Doom Bar, Youngs Bitter and a guest, rambling beamed bar, woodburner in huge inglenook, french windows to decked area and pleasant garden; some live music, sports TV, free wi-fi; children, walkers and dogs welcome, closed Mon lunchtime, open all day Fri-Sun. *(Charlie Parker)*

LITTLE KINGSHILL   SU8999
Full Moon (01494) 862397
Hare Lane; HP16 0EE Picturesque brick and flint village pub with popular well presented food from sandwiches and burgers up, Tues steak night, well kept Adnams, Fullers London Pride, Charles Wells and a guest, nice wines, friendly helpful service from busy staff, traditional beamed and quarry-tiled bar with open fire, bigger dining room; Thurs quiz; children and dogs welcome, round picnic-sets out at front, lawned garden with swings, good walks. *(Julian Thorpe)*

LITTLE MARLOW   SU8788
★ **Kings Head** (01628) 484407
Church Road; A4155 about 2 miles E of Marlow; SL7 3RZ Long, flower-covered

local with open-plan bar, low beams, captain's chairs and other traditional seating around dark wood tables, cricketing memorabilia (pitch opposite), log fire, up to half a dozen well kept ales such as Fullers and Rebellion, popular reasonably priced pubby food from baguettes up (booking advised weekends), free bar nibbles Sun, friendly long-serving staff, gingham-clothed tables in attractive dining room; big walled garden behind with modern terrace furniture, near the Thames and plenty of nice walks, open all day. *(Paul Humphreys, Roy Hoing, Ross Balaam)*

LITTLE MISSENDEN   SU9298
★ **Red Lion** (01494) 862876
Off A413 Amersham–Great Missenden; HP7 0QZ Unchanging pretty 15th-c cottage with long-serving landlord; small black-beamed bar, plain seats around elm pub tables, piano squashed into big inglenook beside black kitchen range packed with copper pots, kettles and rack of old guns, little country dining room with pheasant décor, well kept Hook Norton Lion, Skinners Betty Stogs and Tring Side Pocket for a Toad, fair-priced wines, enjoyable inexpensive pubby food and good friendly service; live music Tues and Sat; children welcome, dogs in bar, picnic-sets out in front and on grass behind wall, back garden with little bridge over River Misbourne, some fancy waterfowl, bedrooms, stables farm shop, open all day Fri-Sun. *(Roy Hoing)*

LITTLEWORTH COMMON   SP9386
Blackwood Arms (01753) 645672
3 miles S of M40 junction 2; Common Lane; SL1 8PP Traditional little 19th-c brick pub tucked away in lovely spot on edge of beechwoods (features in the film *My Week with Marilyn*), sturdy mix of furniture on bare boards, roaring log fire, enjoyable home-made food (not Sun evening) from open sandwiches up, well kept Brakspears and guests, interesting selection of wines, friendly accommodating staff; free wi-fi; children and dogs welcome, hitching rail for horses, nice garden and good local walks, closed Mon, otherwise open all day (till 7.30pm Sun). *(Alistair Forsyth)*

LUDGERSHALL   SP6617
Bull & Butcher (01844) 238094
Off A41 Aylesbury–Bicester; bear left to The Green; HP18 9NZ Nicely old-fashioned welcoming country pub facing village green, bar with low beams in ochre ceiling, wall bench and simple pub furniture on dark tiles or flagstones, inglenook log fire, back dining room, Black Sheep and Hook Norton Hooky, enjoyable well priced food

from sandwiches up; aunt sally and dominoes teams, occasional Sun quiz; children and dogs welcome, picnic-sets on pleasant front terrace, play area on green, circular walks from the door, open all day Sun, closed Mon and lunchtime Tues. *(David Lamb)*

MAIDS MORETON   SP7035
Wheatsheaf (01280) 822903
Main Street, just off A413 Towcester–Buckingham; MK18 1QR Attractive 17th-c thatched local, well kept ales such as Tring, Sharps and Skinners, good fairly pubby food, friendly service, spotless low-beamed bar with bare boards and tiled floors, two inglenooks, conservatory restaurant; seats on front terrace, hatch service for pleasant enclosed back garden, closed Mon, otherwise open all day. *(Julian Thorpe)*

MARLOW   SU8586
Coach
West Street; SL7 2LS Sister dining pub to Tom Kerridge's Hand & Flowers (see below), very well liked food (tapas-style helpings, no bookings) from open kitchen with rotisserie, bar area serving four changing ales from pewter-topped counter; silent TVs; open all day from 8am for breakfast. *(Sandra and Nigel Brown)*

MARLOW   SU8486
★ **Hand & Flowers** (01628) 482277
West Street (A4155); SL7 2BP Restaurant rather than pub owned by celebrity chef Tom Kerridge; nice informal atmosphere in three linked beamed rooms all set for dining, high-backed leather-seated chairs and brown suede wall seats around chunky tables, bare boards or flagstones, fresh flowers and candles, first class food (not cheap and must book long in advance), professional service, extension with stools at counter for dining and drinking plus more set tables, Greene King, Rebellion and a beer named for the pub, lots of wines by the glass from good list and specialist gins; children welcome, comfortable character bedrooms, Thames walks nearby, closed Sun evening. *(Gerry Price, Susan and John Douglas)*

MARLOW   SU8586
Two Brewers (01628) 484140
St Peter Street, first right off Station Road from double roundabout; SL7 1NQ Popular 18th-c red-brick beamed pub renovated after major fire; enjoyable freshly made food from lunchtime sandwiches up, friendly if not always quick service, Brakspears, Fullers and Rebellion ales, over 20 wines by the glass including champagne, various dining areas including upstairs room and cellar restaurant; children welcome,

---

'Children welcome' means the pub says it lets children inside without any special restriction; some may impose an evening time limit earlier than 9pm – please tell us if you find this.

dogs in some parts, seats outside, open all day (food all day Sat, till 4pm Sun). *(Julian Thorpe)*

MARSWORTH SP9114
Red Lion (01296) 668366
Vicarage Road; off B489 Dunstable–Aylesbury; HP23 4LU Partly thatched 18th-c pub close to impressive flight of locks on Grand Union Canal; plain public bar on right with quarry tiles, straightforward furniture and small coal fire, Fullers London Pride and good selection of guests, traditional food at low prices, friendly service, raised ceiling area with red leather stools and sofas, multi-level lounge to left with comfortable sofas in one part and various knick-knacks, two-roomed games area (bar billiards, darts and juke box); children and dogs welcome, picnic-sets out in front, back terrace with heated smokers' gazebo, steps up to sizeable garden, more seats on village green opposite with old stocks. *(Susan and John Douglas)*

MILTON KEYNES SP8737
Olde Swan (01908) 679489
Newport Road, Woughton on the Green; MK6 3BS Spacious and picturesque timber-framed Chef & Brewer overlooking village green; refurbished beamed interior with good log fires and nice nooks and corners, their usual wide menu, Greene King ales and good wine choice; children welcome, plenty of seating in large garden, footpaths to nearby lakes, open (and food) all day. *(Martin and Alison Stainsby)*

NEWPORT PAGNELL SP8743
Cannon (01908) 211495
High Street; MK16 8AQ Friendly little bay-windowed drinkers' pub with interesting military theme, four well kept reasonably priced ales, carpeted half-panelled interior with gas woodburner in central fireplace, live music and comedy nights in room behind; TV, juke box; seats out in small backyard, open all day. *(Sally Wright)*

NEWTON LONGVILLE SP8431
Crooked Billet (01908) 373936
Off A421 S of Milton Keynes; Westbrook End; MK17 0DF Brick and thatch pub with good food (not Sun evening) from pub standards to more restauranty dishes, set lunch menu Mon-Sat, afternoon teas, a beer badged for them along with Greene King Abbot and two guests, plenty of wines by the glass, modernised pubby bar, log fire in dining area; well behaved children welcome, no dogs, tables out on lawn, open all day. *(Ben and Diane Bowie)*

OAKLEY SP6312
Chandos Arms (01844) 238296
The Turnpike; brown sign to pub off B4011 Thame–Bicester; HP18 9QB 16th-c part-thatched village pub with two smallish rooms, low black beams some stripped stone, padded country kitchen chairs on wood floor, inglenook woodburner, Greene King IPA and Sharps Doom Bar, sensibly priced food (not Sun or Mon evening) including specials, separate dining room; background music, games machine, TV, darts; picnic-sets on front terrace, shut Mon lunchtime, otherwise open all day. *(David Lamb)*

OLNEY SP8851
★Swan (01234) 711111
High Street S; MK46 4AA Cosy little pub under same owners as the Rose & Crown at Yardley Hastings (see Northamptonshire); beamed and timbered linked rooms, good reasonably priced food from sandwiches and british tapas to interesting blackboard choices, at least three well kept changing ales and plenty of wines by the glass from good list, quick friendly service, rather close-set pine tables, cheery log fires, small back bistro dining room (booking advised); courtyard tables, open (and food) all day. *(Gerry and Rosemary Dobson)*

OVING SP7821
Black Boy (01296) 641258
Off A413 N of Aylesbury; HP22 4HN Extended 16th-c brick and timbered pub now under same ownership as the Eight Bells at Long Crendon (see Main Entries); low heavy beams, log fire in enormous inglenook, steps up to snug stripped-stone area, three changing ales (often Ringwood and XT) and good choice of wines by the glass, enjoyable food from baguettes and pizzas up, good friendly service, modern carpeted dining room with picture windows; children and dogs welcome, tables on spacious sloping lawns and terrace, expansive Vale of Aylesbury views, open (and food) all day, till 6pm (4pm food) Sun. *(Sandra and Nigel Brown)*

PENN SU9093
★Red Lion (01494) 813107
Elm Road, B474; HP10 8LF Bustling 16th-c pub opposite village duck pond (sister to the Royal Standard of England at Forty Green – see Main Entries); various bar rooms and mix of furniture including cushioned mate's chairs, settles and rustic tables with candlesticks, homely sofas and armchairs, rugs on ancient parquet or old quarry tiles, fantastic collection of British Empire prints and paintings, windowsills and mantelpieces crammed with Staffordshire dogs, plates and old bottles, hop-strung beams, woodburner in big fireplace, Chiltern, Windsor & Eton and a guest, real cider, good choice of wines by the glass, well liked home-made pubby food; TV for major sporting events only, shove-ha'penny, board games; children and dogs welcome, seats on front terrace and small side garden, open all day; still for sale as we went to press so things may change. *(Tracey and Stephen Groves, Roy Hoing)*

PENN STREET
SU9295

★ **Hit or Miss** (01494) 713109

Off A404 SW of Amersham, keep on towards Winchmore Hill; HP7 0PX Welcoming traditional village pub; heavily beamed main bar with leather sofas and armchairs on parquet flooring, horsebrasses, open fire, two carpeted rooms with interesting cricket and chair-making memorabilia, more sofas, wheelback and other dining chairs around pine tables, good interesting food (highish prices) including daily specials, Badger ales; background music, free wi-fi; children and dogs (in certain areas) welcome, picnic-sets on terrace overlooking own cricket pitch, parking over the road, open all day.
(D R Stevenson, Roy Hoing)

PENN STREET
SU9295

Squirrel (01494) 711291

Off A404 SW of Amersham, opposite the Common; HP7 0PX Friendly sister pub to nearby Hit or Miss (see above), open-plan bar with flagstones, log fire and mix of furniture including comfortable sofas, reasonably priced home-made pubby food from baguettes up (not Sun evening, Mon), good children's meals too, up to five well kept ales such as Rebellion, Tring, Vale and XT, Weston's cider, bric-a-brac and cricketing memorabilia, sweets in traditional glass jars; live acoustic music Fri, open mike last Sun of month, monthly quiz; dogs welcome, covered outside deck with sofas and logburner, good play area in big garden with village cricket view, lovely walks, closed Mon lunchtime, otherwise open all day. *(Ross Balaam)*

POUNDON
SP6425

Sow & Pigs (01869) 277728

Main Street; OX27 9BA Small beamed village local with L-shaped bar, pubby furniture on carpet or tiled floor, inglenook log fire, Brakspears ales and maybe a Marstons-related guest, good well priced home-made food (not Sun evening, Mon, Tues) from shortish menu; children and dogs welcome, tables in good-sized back garden, open all day Fri and Sat, till 6pm Sun, from 5pm other days. *(Tim and Sarah Smythe-Brown)*

PRINCES RISBOROUGH
SP8104

Red Lion (01844) 344476

Whiteleaf, off A4010; OS Sheet 165 map reference 817043; HP27 0LL Comfortably worn-in 17th-c family-owned pub in charming village, Sharps Doom Bar and a couple of guests, decent pubby food at reasonable prices, flowers on tables, log fire; traditional games; children, walkers and dogs welcome (no muddy boots – covers provided), seats in garden behind, extensive views over to Oxfordshire, four bedrooms, open all day weekends, closed Mon. *(Edward Mirzoeff)*

SEER GREEN
SU9691

★ **Jolly Cricketers** (01494) 676308

Chalfont Road, opposite the church; HP9 2YG Bustling red-brick Victorian pub with two parquet-floored bar rooms, woodburner in each, cushioned window seats, farmhouse and antique-style dining chairs around bare wood or painted tables, old cricketing photos, prints and bats, Rebellion IPA, Vale VPA and three guests, 16 good wines by the glass and 20 malt whiskies, maybe home-made sloe gin and blackberry vodka, good interesting food served by pleasant helpful staff, separate restaurant; background and monthly live music, quiz last Sun of month, TV, free wi-fi, board games; dogs and muddy boots in main bar, handsome wisteria at front, picnic-sets on back terrace, open all day (till midnight Fri, Sat), food all day Sun till 7pm.
(Roger and Donna Huggins, John Evans)

SKIRMETT
SU7790

★ **Frog** (01491) 638996

From A4155 NE of Henley take Hambleden turn and keep on; or from B482 Stokenchurch–Marlow take Turville turn and keep on; RG9 6TG Pretty pub in Chilterns countryside; nice public bar with log fire, prints on walls, cushioned sofa and leather-seated stools on main floor, high chairs by counter, Rebellion IPA, Gales Seafarer and a changing guest, 18 wines by the glass including champagne, 24 malt whiskies, two dining rooms in different styles – one light and airy with country kitchen furniture, the other more formal with dark red walls, smarter furniture and candlelight, good interesting food (not always cheap) from baguettes and deli boards up, friendly attentive staff; background music; children welcome, dogs in bar (their black lab is Belle), side gate to lovely garden with unusual five-sided tables, attractive valley views and farmland walks, Chiltern Valley Winery & Brewery nearby, three comfortable bedrooms, closed Sun evening Oct-May.
(Paul Humphreys, Richard Kennell)

STOKE GOLDINGTON
SP8348

★ **Lamb** (01908) 551233

High Street (B526 Newport Pagnell–Northampton); MK16 8NR Chatty village pub with friendly helpful licensees, up to five ales including Tring, real ciders and good range of wines, enjoyable generous home-made food (all day Sat, not Sun evening) from baguettes to good value Sun roasts, lounge with log fire and sheep decorations, two small pleasant dining rooms, darts and table skittles in public bar; may be soft background music, TV; children and dogs welcome, terrace and sheltered garden behind with play equipment, bedrooms in adjacent cottage, closed Mon lunchtime, otherwise open all day (till 7pm Sun).
(James Allsopp)

STOKE MANDEVILLE SP8310
Woolpack (01296) 615970
Risborough Road (A4010 S of Aylesbury); HP22 5UP Thatched Mitchells & Butlers pub with boldly decorated contemporary interior, Brakspears Oxford Gold, Sharps Doom Bar and a guest, several wines by the glass, cocktails, good choice of food including set weekday menu (till 6pm), amiable service and relaxed atmosphere; well behaved children allowed, seats in back garden and on the heated front terrace, open (and food) all day. *(Julian Thorpe)*

THE LEE SP8904
★Cock & Rabbit (01494) 837540
Back roads 2.5 miles N of Great Missenden, E of A413; HP16 9LZ Overlooking village green and run by same friendly italian family for over 25 years; much emphasis on their good italian cooking, also lunchtime baps and Weds evening pasta deal, Greene King, Sharps and a beer named for the pub, plush-seated lounge, cosy dining room and larger restaurant; children welcome, dogs in bar, seats outside on verandah, terraces and lawn, good walks, open all day weekends. *(Luke Morgan)*

TURVILLE SU7691
★Bull & Butcher (01491) 638283
Valley road off A4155 Henley–Marlow at Mill End, past Hambleden and Skirmett; RG9 6QU Popular 16th-c black and white pub in pretty village (famous as film and TV setting); two traditional low-beamed rooms with inglenooks, wall settles in tiled-floor bar, deep well incorporated into glass-topped table, Brakspears ales kept well and decent wines by the glass, enjoyable good value home-cooked food, friendly staff; background music (live last Fri of month); children and dogs welcome, seats by fruit trees in attractive garden, good walks (Chiltern Way runs through village), open all day weekends and can get very busy. *(Brian Glozier, Ross Balaam, Guy Vowles)*

WADDESDON SP7316
Long Dog (01296) 651320
High Street; HP18 0JF Renovated village pub with good food from open-view kitchen including english tapas, friendly accommodating service, well kept ales and nice choice of wines by the glass, bar area with open fire; background music, live jazz every other Tues; children and dogs welcome, tables out front and back, very handy for Waddesdon Manor (NT), open (and food) all day. *(R K Phillips)*

WEEDON SP8118
Five Elms (01296) 641439
Stockaway; HP22 4NL Welcoming cottagey thatched pub with two small bars, low beams and log fires, ample helpings of good traditional food cooked by landlord (best to book), well kept XT Four and good reasonably priced wines, old photographs and prints, separate compact dining room; games such as shove-ha'penny; a few picnic-sets out in front, pretty village, closed Sun evening and lunchtimes Mon, Tues. *(Amaya Arias-Garcia)*

WENDOVER SP8607
Firecrest (01296) 628041
London Road (A413 about 2 miles S); HP22 6QG Spacious roadside Vintage Inn, their usual food including Weds pie night, two or three mainstream ales and several wines by the glass, friendly welcoming staff, civilised eating areas, old fireplace, pictures on stripped brickwork; background music, children welcome, picnic-sets in small back garden, disabled parking, open (and food) all day. *(David Lamb)*

WENDOVER SP8609
Village Gate (01296) 623884
Aylesbury Road (B4009); HP22 6BA Country dining pub with interconnecting rooms, contemporary paintwork and furnishings, bar with woodburner in brick fireplace, ales such as St Austell, Rebellion and Tring, good choice of well liked food from bar snacks and sharing boards to restaurant dishes, other rooms laid for eating with high-backed plush, wooden or leather dining chairs around mix of tables on oak boarding (some carpeting and stone tiling too), one part with high-raftered ceiling; children welcome, outside seating including roped-off deck, long-reaching country views, open all day, no food Sun evening. *(Sandra and Nigel Brown)*

WEST WYCOMBE SU8394
George & Dragon (01494) 535340
High Street; A40 W of High Wycombe; HP14 3AB Rambling hotel bar in preserved NT Tudor village, massive beams and sloping walls, big log fire, three well kept Rebellion ales along with St Austell Tribute, good range of wines and well liked food including fixed-price menus (can eat in bar or restaurant), prompt friendly service; children and dogs welcome, tables in nice garden, 11 bedrooms (magnificent oak staircase), handy for West Wycombe Park (NT) and the Hell-Fire Caves, open (and food) all day, meals till 6pm Sun. *(Tim and Sarah Smythe-Brown)*

WESTON UNDERWOOD SP8650
Cowpers Oak (01234) 711382
Signed off A509 in Olney; High Street; MK46 5JS Wisteria-clad beamed village pub, enjoyable home-cooked food (special diets catered for) from bar snacks up, well kept Hopping Mad, Woodfordes Wherry and a couple of guests, several wines by the glass, friendly helpful staff, nice mix of old-fashioned furnishings including pews, painted panelling and some stripped stone, two open fires, restaurant behind;

background music, Mon quiz; children and dogs welcome, small suntrap front terrace, more tables on back decking and in big orchard garden, fenced play area, open all day weekends (till 9pm Sun). *(Luke Morgan)*

WINSLOW   SP7627
Bell (01296) 714091
Market Square; MK18 3AB Fine old coaching inn, comfortable and atmospheric, with reasonably priced food in beamed bar and carvery restaurant, Greene King ales, friendly welcoming staff, snug with historical photos and log fire; courtyard tables, 39 bedrooms (some with four-posters), open all day. *(Dr W I C Clark)*

WOOBURN COMMON   SU9187
★**Chequers** (01628) 529575
From A4094 at Bourne End roundabout, right for Wooburn, then straight over next roundabout into Kiln Lane; OS Sheet 175 map reference 910870; HP10 0JQ Bustling hotel with friendly low-beamed main bar, second bar to the left and smart restaurant – complete refurbishment planned as we went to press, news please; good range of well liked food from sandwiches, wraps and some pubby choices up, Rebellion, St Austell and a dozen wines by the glass from good list, fair range of whiskies and brandies too; background music, TV, free wi-fi; children and dogs (in bar) welcome, spacious garden set away from the road, comfortable bedrooms, open (and food) all day. *(Caroline Prescott, Charlie May, David Greene, Tracey and Stephen Groves)*

WORMINGHALL   SP6308
Clifden Arms (01844) 338429
Clifden Road; HP18 9JR Beamed and timbered thatched dining pub in attractive village, good varied menu from baguettes, sharing boards and pizzas up (booking advised weekends), ales such as Fullers, Ringwood and Sharps, friendly helpful staff; big-screen sports TV, quiz nights; children and dogs (in bar) welcome, nice garden with play equipment, self-catering apartments in converted barn, open all day Fri-Sun (no food Sun evening), closed Mon. *(William Slade)*

Post Office address codings confusingly give the impression that some pubs are in Buckinghamshire, when they're really in Bedfordshire or Berkshire (which is where we list them).

Cambridgeshire

BALSHAM   TL5850 Map 5

Black Bull 🎯 🍺 🛏

(01223) 893844 – www.blackbull-balsham.co.uk
*Village signposted off A11 SW of Newmarket, and off A1307 in Linton; High Street;
CB21 4DJ*

**Pretty thatched pub with bedroom extension – a good all-rounder –
enjoyable food too**

Both locals and visitors are welcomed into this thatched 17th-c inn by
the friendly landlord. The beamed bar spreads around a central servery
where they keep their own-label Red & Black Ale (from Nethergate) plus
Adnams Ghost Ship, Crafty Beers Sauvignon Blonde Golden Ale and
Woodfordes Wherry on handpump, 22 wines by the glass from a good list,
15 malt whiskies, draught lager and interesting juices. Dividers and standing
timbers break up the space, which has an open fire (and leather sofas in
front of it), floorboards and low black beams in the front part; furniture
includes small leatherette-seated dining chairs. A restaurant extension (in a
listed barn) has a high-raftered oak panelled roof and a network of standing
posts and steel ties. The front terrace has teak tables and chairs by a long
pleasantly old-fashioned verandah and there are more seats in a small
sheltered back garden. Smart, comfortable bedrooms are in a neat single-
storey extension. This pub has the same good owners as the Red Lion at
Hinxton.

🎯 Well regarded food includes sandwiches, twice-baked cheese soufflé, beetroot-
cured salmon with filo pastry, salmon roe and horseradish cream, mushroom
and courgette cannelloni, proper pies, gammon with free-range eggs, pineapple and
coleslaw, pheasant breast and leg with salsify, celeriac and curry sauce, a daily fish
special, and puddings such as tiramisu and lemon meringue tart. *Benchmark main
dish: beef with mussel and black bean dumplings, soy, honey and thyme reduction
£15.00. Two-course evening meal £22.00.*

Free house ~ Licensee Alex Clarke ~ Real ale ~ Open 7.30am (8.30am weekends)-11pm
(10.30pm Sun) ~ Bar food 12-2, 6.30-9; 12-2.30, 6.30-9.30 Fri, Sat; 12-3, 6.30-8.30 Sun ~
Restaurant ~ Well behaved children welcome ~ Dogs allowed in bar ~ Wi-fi ~ Bedrooms:
£90/£120 *Recommended by Neil Allen, Carol and Barry Craddock, William Slade*

'Children welcome' means the pub says it lets children inside without any special
restriction. If it allows them in, but to restricted areas such as an eating area or family
room, we specify this. Some pubs may impose an evening time limit. We do not mention
limits after 9pm as we assume children are home by then.

BRANDON CREEK
TL6091   Map 5

Ship

(01353) 676228 – www.theshipbrandoncreek.co.uk

A10 Ely–Downham Market; PE38 0PP

Fine riverside spot with plenty of outside seating, cosy snug and busy bar, four ales, good wines by the glass and well liked food

With up to five real ales and a thoughtful menu, this 17th-c waterside pub does get packed at peak times. It's a friendly place and the carefully modernised bar at the centre of the building has massive stone masonry in the sunken former forge area, a big log fire at one end and a woodburning stove at the other, interesting old fenland photographs and prints, and paintings by local artists. Adnams Southwold, plus a couple of guests such as Cottage Try Me and Two Rivers Hares Hopping on handpump, 14 wines by the glass and farm cider; board games and background music. There's a cosy snug on the left with another open fire and a restaurant overlooking both the Great Ouse and the Little Ouse rivers; seats on the terrace and in the riverside garden make the most of the position. They have moorings for visiting boats.

Good food using seasonal ingredients includes sandwiches, deep-fried breadcrumbed brie with bacon and tomato jam, creamy garlic mushrooms, local sausages with mash and gravy, seafood crumble, spinach and wild mushroom lasagne, chicken curry with onion bhaji, pork belly with apple and sage stuffing, and puddings. *Benchmark main dish: steak burger with toppings and chips £11.95. Two-course evening meal £18.00.*

Free house ~ Licensee Mark Thomas ~ Real ale ~ Open 12-11 ~ Bar food 12-3, 6-9; 12-9 Sat; 12-8 Sun ~ Restaurant ~ Children welcome ~ Dogs allowed in bar ~ Wi-fi ~ Live music Fri evening *Recommended by Carol and Barry Craddock, Dr Simon Innes, Brian and Sally Wakeham*

CAMBRIDGE
TL4459   Map 5

Punter

(01223) 3633221 – www.thepuntercambridge.com

Pound Hill, on corner of A1303 ring road; CB3 0AE

Good enterprising food in relaxed and interestingly furnished surroundings

As a former coaching inn, the rambling and informal linked rooms here have quite a bit of character. There are paintings, antique prints and a pleasing choice of seating on old dark floorboards – pews, elderly dining chairs and Lloyd Loom easy chairs. One prized corner is down a few steps, behind a wooden railing. The scrubbed tables feature candles in bottles or assorted candlesticks, and staff are quick and friendly. Adnams Ghost Ship, an ale named for the pub from Oakham, Sharps Doom Bar and a guest ale from the local Turpins Brewery on handpump and decent wines by the glass; board games and background jazz music. The flagstoned and mainly covered former coachyard has tables and picnic-table sets; beyond is a raftered barn bar, similar in style, with more pictures on papered walls, a large rug on dark flagstones and a big-screen TV. This is sister pub to the Punter in Oxford.

Food is good and interesting and as well as their bargain £5 lunch, includes salmon home-cured with beetroot and juniper with grapefruit, ham hock terrine with gooseberry and apricot compote, burger with toppings and chips, plaice fillet with spiced tomato, aubergine and garlic mash with saffron chive cream, beef bourguignon, guinea fowl with thyme-roasted root vegetables and burgundy sauce, and puddings. *Benchmark main dish: halloumi and vegetable tagine with couscous and yoghurt £11.00. Two-course evening meal £18.00.*

Punch ~ Lease Sarah Lee ~ Real ale ~ Open 12-midnight (11.30 Sun) ~ Bar food 12-3, 5-9; 12-10 Fri, Sat; 12-9 Sun ~ Children welcome ~ Dogs welcome ~ Wi-fi
Recommended by Lindy Andrews, Isobel Mackinlay, Mrs Margo Finlay, Jörg Kasprowski, David Thorpe, Ivor Smith

 DUXFORD   TL4746   Map 5
John Barleycorn
(01223) 832699 – www.johnbarleycorn.co.uk
Handy for M11 junction 10; right at first roundabout, then left at main village junction; CB22 4PP

Pretty pub with friendly staff, attractive beamed interior, enjoyable food and seats outside; bedrooms

This comfortable early 17th-century inn looks very much like a perfect English country pub with its low thatched roof and shuttered windows. It has a lot of character and the standing timbers and brick pillars create alcoves and different drinking and dining areas: hops on heavy beams and nice old floor tiles, log fires, all manner of seating from rustic blue-painted cushioned settles through white-painted and plain wooden dining chairs to some rather fine antique farmhouse chairs and quite a mix of wooden tables. There's also a lot to look at, including china plates, copper pans, old clocks, a butterchurn, a large stuffed fish and plenty of pictures on blue or pale yellow walls. Greene King Abbot and IPA and guests such as Harviestoun Bitter & Twisted and Joules Slumbering Monk on handpump and ten wines by the glass; background music. There are blue-painted picnic-sets beside pretty hanging baskets on the front terrace and more picnic-sets among flowering tubs and shrubs in the back garden. This is a comfortable place to stay and the bedrooms are in a converted barn. The pub was used by the young airmen of Douglas Bader's Duxford Wing during World War II. The Air Museum is close by.

Good quality food includes sandwiches, fried chicken livers in creamy mustard sauce, deep-fried crumbed brie with grape chutney, sharing boards, steak burger with toppings, chips and coleslaw, crispy duck with couscous, spring onion, cucumber and hoi sin sauce, a pie of the day, wild mushroom risotto, garlic and mint marinated lamb steak with skin-on chips, bass fillets with lime and chilli noodles and vegetable stir-fry, and puddings. *Benchmark main dish: venison with lyonnaise potatoes and wild mushroom sauce £17.95. Two-course evening meal £21.00.*

Greene King ~ Tenant Nicholas Kersey ~ Real ale ~ Open 11-11 (10.30 Sun) ~ Bar food 11-3, 5-9.30; 12-3, 5-8.30 Sun ~ Children welcome ~ Dogs allowed in bar ~ Wi-fi ~ Bedrooms: /£79.50 *Recommended by Lindy Andrews, Charlie May, David Jackman*

ELTON   TL0894   Map 5
Crown ⭐ ♀ ⇔
(01832) 280232 – www.thecrowninn.org
Off B671 S of Wansford (A1/A47), and village signposted off A605 Peterborough– Oundle; Duck Street; PE8 6RQ

Pretty pub with interesting food, several real ales, well chosen wines and a friendly atmosphere; stylish bedrooms

If you stay at this lovely golden-stone and thatched pub, the bedrooms are smart, comfortable and well equipped and the breakfasts especially good.

Softly lit, the beamed bar has leather and antique dining chairs around a nice mix of chunky tables on bare boards, an open fire in a stone fireplace and good pictures and pubby ornaments on pastel walls. The beamed main dining area has fresh flowers and candles and similar tables and chairs on stripped wooden flooring, and there's a dining extension too. High bar chairs against the counter are popular with locals, and they keep a house beer (from Kings Cliffe Brewery), Greene King IPA and Oakham JHB on handpump, well chosen wines by the glass and farm cider; board games, background music and TV. There are tables outside on the front terrace, and Elton Mill and Lock are nearby. This is a charming village. To find the pub, follow the brown sign towards Nassington.

 Cooked by the landlord using local produce, the tempting food includes sandwiches, gin-cured salmon with cucumber, fennel, mustard and dill dressing, oxtail ragoût with linguine and parmesan, omelettes, white bean and root vegetable cassoulet with goats cheese fritters, lamb shank with leek and potato mash and rosemary and mint sauce, beer-battered haddock and chips, duck with boulangère potatoes and cherry sauce, and puddings such as apple strudel with cinnamon ice-cream and dark chocolate and orange sponge with chocolate sauce and white chocolate mousse. *Benchmark main dish: slow-cooked free-range pork with bacon hash brown, cauliflower and gruyère gratin, apple and cider purée £16.95. Two-course evening meal £25.00.*

Free house ~ Licensee Marcus Lamb ~ Real ale ~ Open 12-11 ~ Bar food 12-2 (4 bank holidays), 6.30-9 ~ Restaurant ~ Children welcome ~ Dogs allowed in bar ~ Wi-fi ~ Bedrooms: £75/£125 *Recommended by Peter and Jean Hoare, Barry Collett, James Landor*

FEN DRAYTON
TL3468 Map 5

Three Tuns

(01954) 230242 – www.the3tuns.co.uk

Eastbound on A14, take first exit after Fenstanton, signed Fen Drayton and follow to pub; westbound on A14, exit at junction 27 and follow signs to village on Cambridge Road; High Street; CB24 4JS

Lovely old pub with traditional furnishings in bar and dining room, real ales, tasty food and seats in garden

There's a happy mix of people drinking and dining at this pretty thatched village pub and log fires in each room help create a warm and relaxed atmosphere, all helped along by the friendly licensees. The three rooms are more or less open-plan with heavy-set moulded Tudor beams and timbers, a mix of burgundy cushioned stools, nice old dining chairs and settles in the friendly bar and wooden dining chairs and tables on red-patterned carpet in the dining room; framed prints of the pub too. Greene King IPA and Old Speckled Hen and a couple of guests such as Timothy Taylors Landlord and Titanic Best Bitter on handpump and a dozen wines by the glass. A well tended lawn at the back has seats and tables, a covered dining area and a play area for children.

Popular food includes lunchtime sandwiches and wraps, deep-fried whitebait with tartare sauce, lamb samosas with mint and yoghurt dressing, honey-roast ham with egg or pineapple, a pie of the day, leek and cheese tart, cod loin with pea pesto, a curry of the day, and puddings such as cherry bakewell tart and sticky toffee pudding with ice-cream; the last Monday of the month is curry night, there's an OAP lunch menu (Monday-Friday) and takeaway choices (Monday-Thursday 6-9pm). *Benchmark main dish: sizzling chicken taco £11.50. Two-course evening meal £17.50.*

Greene King ~ Tenants Mr and Mrs Baretto ~ Real ale ~ Open 12-3, 6-11; 12-11 summer Fri, Sat; 12-4 Sun ~ Bar food 12-2, 6-9 (9.30 Fri, Sat); 12-2 Sun ~ Restaurant ~ Children welcome ~ Dogs allowed in bar ~ Wi-fi *Recommended by George Atkinson, Ivor Smith, Gordon and Margaret Ormondroyd*

GRANTCHESTER
Rupert Brooke 🏅 ♈

TL4455 Map

(01223) 841875 – www.therupertbrooke.com

Broadway; junction Coton Road with Cambridge–Trumpington Road; CB3 9NQ

Plenty of space for drinking and dining in airy, refurbished dining pub with modern food and local ales

Smartly refurbished, this is a stylish place at the end of the high street with an emphasis on dining – though they do keep Woodfordes Wherry and a guest from Milton on handpump and several wines by the glass, served by courteous staff. The contemporary wood-clad extension has huge windows, elegant wooden or leather dining chairs around polished tables on floorboards and leads back to a bar area where there are sofas in a cosy nook by the stairs. The two-level restaurant looks into the open kitchen and has mushroom-coloured button-back wall banquettes, pendant lights and photographs of Rupert Brooke as a child. Stairs lead upstairs to a club room with direct access to a roof terrace.

 Good, interesting food using local, seasonal produce includes scallops with glazed pork belly, sweetcorn and bacon popcorn, chicken thigh terrine with black trumpet mushrooms, charred leeks and jerusalem artichoke crisps, rare-breed burger with cheese and fries, duck breast with duck leg samosa, red cabbage purée, foie gras yoghurt and dauphinoise potatoes, spinach and garlic cannelloni with blue cheese velouté and cep soil, slow-roast lamb rump with crispy shoulder and moroccan-spiced chickpeas, and puddings such as coffee parfait with coffee reduction, mocha butter with spiced crumb and praline ice-cream and chocolate mousse with chocolate soil, cinnamon whipped cream and thyme. *Benchmark main dish: lemon sole with buttered prawns, silverskin onions and bisque sauce £16.00. Two-course evening meal £23.00.*

Free house ~ Licensee David Harrison ~ Real ale ~ Open 12-11; 12-7 Sun ~ Bar food 12-3, 6.30-9; 12-5 Sun ~ Restaurant ~ Children welcome ~ Dogs allowed in bar ~ Wi-fi
Recommended by Paul Scofield, Sally Wright, Hilary and Neil Christopher

GREAT WILBRAHAM
Carpenters Arms 🏅 ♈ 🍺

TL5558 Map 5

(01223) 882093 – www.carpentersarmsgastropub.co.uk

Off A14 or A11 SW of Newmarket, following The Wilbrahams signposts; High Street; CB21 5JD

Inviting village pub with traditional bar, good food in both the bar and in back restaurant; nice garden

They brew their own ale here – Crafty Beers Carpenters Cask, Mild Mannered and Sauvignon Blonde Golden Ale on handpump – and have a carefully chosen wine list (strong on the Roussillon region). The low-ceilinged village bar on the right is properly pubby with bar billiards, a woodburning stove in a big inglenook, copper pots and iron tools, and cushioned pews and simple seats around solid pub tables on floor tiles; background music, darts and board games. Service is spot-on: thoughtful, helpful and cheerful. On the left, a small cosy carpeted dining area has another big stone fireplace and overflowing bookshelves; this leads through to a sitting area with comfortable sofas and plenty of magazines. The light and airy extended main dining room has country kitchen chairs around chunky tables. A huge honeysuckle swathes the tree in the pretty back courtyard, and, further on, an attractive homely garden, with fruit and vegetables, has circular picnic-sets shaded by tall trees.

 Making everything in-house using local ingredients, the particularly good food cooked by the landlady includes sandwiches, smoked salmon with home-made blinis, crème fraîche and beetroot, terrine with chutney, mushroom, pine nut and truffle risotto, wild boar and apple burger with apple sauce, beef in ale pie, chicken stuffed with mushrooms and bacon with mushroom and brandy sauce, and puddings such as a crumble of the day and catalan cream with caramelised sugar topping. *Benchmark main dish: confit duck leg cassoulet £16.00. Two-course evening meal £22.00.*

Free house ~ Licensees Rick and Heather Hurley ~ Real ale ~ Open 11.30-3, 6.30-11; 11.30-3 Sun; closed Sun evening, Mon, Tues ~ Bar food 12-2, 7-9; 12-3 Sun ~ Restaurant ~ Children welcome ~ Wi-fi *Recommended by Michael Butler, Mike and Mary Carter, Ivor Smith, Brian and Sally Wakeham*

HEMINGFORD ABBOTS TL2870 Map 5
Axe & Compass

(01480) 463605 – www.axeandcompass.co.uk
High Street; village signposted off A14 W of Cambridge; PE28 9AH

Thatched pub with several linked rooms, a good range of drinks and food served by friendly staff and seats outside

This is a charming village and the partly 15th-c pub is very much its hub. The interconnected rooms have plenty of space and a cheerful mix of customers; the simple, beamed public bar has mate's chairs and stools around wooden tables on lovely ancient floor tiles, and an open two-way fireplace (not in use) into the snug next door where there's a woodburning stove. The main room has more beams and standing timbers, tweed tartan-patterned chairs and armchairs and cushioned wall seating around nice old tables on wood floors, local photographs and stools against the counter where they serve Adnams Lighthouse, Sharps Doom Bar and Woodfordes Reedlighter on handpump, 12 wines by the glass and local cider; there's a second woodburner in a small brick fireplace. Background music and board games. The long dining room has more photos on green walls and high-backed dark leather dining and other chairs around pale wooden tables. The garden, between the pretty thatched pub and the tall-spired church, has a fenced-off area with play equipment, contemporary seats and tables on the terrace and picnic-sets on grass; walks along the river. Disabled facilities.

Fairly priced food includes sandwiches, crab cakes with spiced potatoes, mango, aioli and apricot and red pepper chutney, crispy chilli beef strips in sweet chilli, sesame, coriander and soy sauce, sharing boards, mushroom, a pie of the day, pork steak with mustard mash, roast tomatoes and apple chutney, salmon fillet with sweet potato, lemon and squash hash and olive tapenade, and puddings such as warm chocolate brownie with mocha sauce and earl grey crème brûlée. *Benchmark main dish: burger with toppings, pickles, coleslaw and skin-on chips £10.00. Two-course evening meal £18.00.*

Enterprise ~ Lease Emma Tester ~ Real ale ~ Open 12-11 (10 Mon winter) ~ Bar food 12-2.30 6-9; 12-9 Sat; 12-4 Sun; maybe longer hours on summer weekends ~ Restaurant ~ Well behaved children welcome ~ Dogs allowed in bar ~ Wi-fi ~ Live music first Fri of month; quiz Tues *Recommended by D W Stokes, Sarah Nancollas, Mrs Margo Finlay, Jörg Kasprowski*

The 🍺 symbol shows pubs that keep their beer unusually well, have a particularly good range or brew their own.

HEMINGFORD GREY

TL2970 Map 5

Cock ⭐ ♀ ◀

(01480) 463609 – www.cambscuisine.com/the-cock-hemingford

Village signposted off A14 eastbound, and (via A1096 St Ives road) westbound; High Street; PE28 9BJ

••
Cambridgeshire Dining Pub of the Year

Imaginative food in pretty pub with extensive wine list, four interesting beers, a bustling atmosphere and a smart restaurant

---

We're not surprised that this is such a favourite with many of our readers as it's run with great care and attention to detail. The bar rooms have white-painted or dark beams and lots of contemporary pale yellow and cream paintwork, fresh flowers and church candles, artworks here and there, and throughout a really attractive mix of old wooden dining chairs, settles and tables. They've sensibly kept the traditional public bar (on the left) for drinkers only: it has an open woodburning stove on a raised hearth, bar stools, wall seats and a carver, and steps that lead down to more seating. Brewsters Hophead and Great Oakley Wagtail with guests such as Elgoods Cambridge Bitter and Nene Valley Dark Horse on handpump, 19 wines by the glass mainly from the Languedoc-Roussillon region, and Cromwell cider (made in the village); they hold a beer festival every August Bank Holiday weekend. In marked contrast, the stylishly rustic restaurant on the right – you must book to be sure of a table – is set for dining, with flowers on each table, pale wooden floorboards and another woodburning stove. There are seats and tables among stone troughs and flowers on the terrace and in the neat garden, and pretty hanging baskets. This is a delightful village on the River Ouse. This is sister pub to the Crown & Punchbowl at Horningsea and Tickell Arms in Whittlesford.

 Delicious food includes lunchtime sandwiches (not Sunday), potted rabbit with beetroot chutney, seared scallops with pancetta, baby gem and pea fricassée, shellfish bisque and orange oil, pea and mint risotto with crispy broad beans, parmesan and pea shoots, beef and chilli meatballs with tagliatelle and tomato sauce, venison with potato terrine, parsnip purée and port sauce, bass with garlic and rosemary rösti, caramelised apple purée and salsa verde, and puddings such as elderflower and blueberry jelly with honeycomb and white chocolate and vanilla pannacotta with passion-fruit gel, meringue and passion-fruit sorbet; they also offer a two- and three-course set weekday lunch. *Benchmark main dish: home-made sausages, choice of mash and sauce £12.50. Two-course evening meal £18.30.*

Free house ~ Licensees Oliver Thain and Richard Bradley ~ Real ale ~ Open 11.30-3, 6 (5 Fri)-11; 11.30-11 Sat; 12-10.30 Sun ~ Bar food 12-2.30, 6.30-9; 12-2.30, 6-9.30 Fri, Sat; 12-2.45, 6.30-8.30 Sun ~ Restaurant ~ No children after 6pm ~ Dogs allowed in bar ~ Wi-fi
Recommended by Mrs Margo Finlay, Jörg Kasprowski, Hilary De Lyon and Martin Webster, William Slade, Ivor Smith

---

HINXTON

TL4945 Map 5

Red Lion ⭐ ♀ ◀ ⇌

(01799) 530601 – www.redlionhinxton.co.uk

2 miles off M11 junction 9 northbound; take first exit off A11, A1301 N, then left turn into village – High Street; a little further from junction 10, via A505 E and A1301 S; CB10 1QY

16th-c pub with friendly staff, interesting bar food, real ales and a big landscaped garden; comfortable bedrooms

This pink-washed inn is handy for the Imperial War Museum at Duxford and for the M11. The low-beamed bar has oak chairs and tables on bare boards, two leather chesterfield sofas, an open fire and an old wall clock and a relaxed, friendly atmosphere. Their own-label Red & Black Ale (from the local Nethergate Brewery) plus Adnams Ghost Ship, Woodfordes Wherry and a guest such as Crafty Beers Sauvignon Blonde Golden Ale on handpump, 22 wines by the glass, 15 malt whiskies and first class service.

An informal dining area has high-backed settles, and the smart restaurant (with oak rafters and traditional dry peg construction) is decorated with various pictures and assorted clocks. Outside, there are teak tables and chairs on a terrace, picnic-sets on grass, a dovecote and views of the village church; another terrace by the porch has a huge parasol for sunny days. Well equipped, pretty bedrooms are in a separate flint and brick building. They also own the Black Bull in Balsham just up the road.

Good food includes sandwiches and ciabattas, scallops with butternut squash caponata, chicken and ham terrine with caper mayonnaise, pearl barley risotto with walnut, lemon and feta, honey and mustard glazed gammon with free-range eggs, steak in ale pie, home-smoked tomato and seafood linguine, free-range chicken with bubble and squeak and pink peppercorn and mushroom jus, and puddings such as passion-fruit posset and sticky toffee pudding with butterscotch sauce. *Benchmark main dish: local venison with dauphinoise potatoes and black cherry jus £17.00. Two-course evening meal £22.00.*

Free house ~ Licensee Alex Clarke ~ Real ale ~ Open 7.30am (8.30am weekends)-11pm (10.30pm Sun) ~ Bar food 12-2, 6.30-9; 12-2.30, 6-9.30 Fri, Sat; 12-8.30 Sun ~ Restaurant ~ Well behaved children welcome ~ Dogs allowed in bar ~ Wi-fi ~ Bedrooms: £95/£125
Recommended by Paul Scofield, Julian Thorpe, Rona Mackinlay

HORNINGSEA
TL4962   Map 5
Crown & Punchbowl 🌟 ♀ 🛏

(01223) 860643 – www.cambscuisine.com/
the-crown-and-punchbowl *Just NE of Cambridge; CB25 9JG*

Impressive food and thoughtful drinks choice in carefully refurbished old inn; seats outside; bedrooms

Given the track record of the other pubs in this little group, we know this will be a winner. It's a 17th-c former coaching inn that's been transformed and extended without losing original features or character. The beamed bar has a woodburning stove in a brick fireplace, leather banquettes and rustic old chairs, stripped boards, terracotta walls and an attractively carved counter where they serve freshly carved ham and home-made pickles. Behind the bar they keep Brewsters Hophead, Milton Pegasus and a changing guest tapped from the cask and 20 wines by the glass (with a focus on the Languedoc-Roussillon region), home-made punches (alcoholic and non-alcoholic), lavender lemonade and local cider. The timbered dining room has leather cushioned chairs around wooden tables on pale boards, wall panelling and candlelight. Another conservatory-style room has large windows and ceramic light fittings (a nod to the village's history as a centre for Roman pottery). There are rustic seats out the front, while the five guest bedrooms upstairs are well dressed, light and comfortable. This is sister pub to the Cock at Hemingford Grey and Tickell Arms in Whittlesford.

The menu is modern british and european, prepared using the best local, seasonal produce and daily fresh fish: duck parcel with sweet and sour cucumber and sweet soy and ginger dressing, smoked lamb scrumpets with roasted and spiced aubergine dip, pea and mint risotto with watercress, radish and pine nut salad, home-made sausages of the day with onion gravy, guinea fowl breast stuffed with truffle mousse, carrot purée and red wine sauce, hake fillet with white bean and bacon cassoulet, braised hispi cabbage and parsley and olive crumb, and puddings such as dark chocolate tart with basil cream and mango and thyme and lavender pannacotta with pineapple and candied lemon; they also offer a two- and three-course set menu (weekday lunchtimes and Sunday-Thursday evenings). *Benchmark main dish: guinea fowl with truffle mousse, carrot purée and red wine sauce £17.50. Two-course evening meal £22.00.*

Free house ~ Licensees Oliver Thain and Richard Bradley ~ Real ale ~ Open 12-3, 6 (5 Fri)-11; 12-11 Sat; 12-10.30 Sun ~ Bar food 12-2.30, 6.30-9 (9.30 Fri, Sat); 12-3, 6.30-8.30 Sun ~ Restaurant ~ Children welcome ~ Dogs allowed in bar ~ Wi-fi ~ Bedrooms: /£140
Recommended by Belinda Stamp, Caroline Prescott, Lindy Andrews, David Stewart

HUNTINGDON — TL2471 Map 5
Old Bridge Hotel
(01480) 424300 – www.huntsbridge.com
1 High Street; ring road just off B1044 entering from easternmost A14 slip road; PE29 3TQ

Proper bar in Georgian hotel with a splendid range of drinks, first class service and excellent food; fine bedrooms

While the civilised hotel side clearly dominates here, there's a wide mix of customers who very much enjoy the traditional pubby bar. This has a log fire, comfortable sofas and low wooden tables on polished floorboards, and Adnams Southwold and Nene Valley Blond Session Ale on handpump. They also have an exceptional wine list (up to 36 by the glass in the bar) and a wine shop where you can taste a selection of wines before you buy. Food is available in the big airy Terrace (an indoor room, but with beautifully painted verdant murals suggesting the open air) or in the slightly more formal panelled restaurant. There are seats and tables on the terrace by the Great Ouse, and they have their own landing stage. This is a special place to stay in luxurious bedrooms, some of which overlook the river.

Some sort of excellent food is available all day: hot and cold sandwiches, potted mackerel with capers, pickles and griddled bread, baked ricotta with pomegranate and pistachio salad, porcini mushroom risotto with seared and fried greens and parmesan, fishcake with poached egg, spinach and hollandaise, calves liver with shallot and pancetta sauce, lobster burger with roast gem, chilli and avocado and skinny chips, and puddings such as rum sponge with caramelised pineapple and coconut ice-cream and rhubarb crème brûlée with an orange biscuit; they also offer a two- and three-course set lunch (not Sunday). *Benchmark main dish: slow-cooked pork belly with bubble and squeak, crackling and apple sauce £18.95. Two-course evening meal £25.00.*

Huntsbridge ~ Licensee John Hoskins ~ Real ale ~ Open 11-11 ~ Bar food 12-2, 6.30-9.30; light snacks 11-10 ~ Restaurant ~ Children welcome ~ Dogs allowed in bar ~ Wi-fi ~ Bedrooms: £95/£188 *Recommended by Isobel Mackinlay, Lindy Andrews, Michael Sargent, Mike and Mary Carter*

KEYSTON — TL0475 Map 5
Pheasant
(01832) 710241 – www.thepheasant-keyston.co.uk
Just off A14 SE of Thrapston; brown sign to pub down village loop road, off B663; PE28 0RE

Smart but friendly country dining pub with appealing décor and attractive garden

This neatly kept, thatched white building has come a long way since it was the village smithy – it's now a civilised dining pub with attentive, neat staff and first class food. The main bar has pitched rafters high above, with lower dark beams in side areas, and the central serving area has padded stools along the leather-quilted counter and dark flagstones, with hop bines above the handpumps for Adnams Southwold, Brewsters Hop A Doodle Doo and Digfield Chiffchaff, and a tempting array of 14 wines by the glass. Nearby are armchairs, a chesterfield, quite a throne of a seat carved in 17th-c style, other comfortable seats around low tables, and a log fire in a lofty fireplace. The rest of the pub is mostly red-carpeted with dining chairs around a variety of polished tables, large sporting prints, some hunting-scene wallpaper and lighted candles and tea-lights. The attractively planted and well kept garden behind has tables on lawn and terrace, and there are picnic-sets in front. This is a quiet farming hamlet.

Excellent food cooked by the landlord includes sandwiches, crab with gnocchi, samphire, chilli, ginger, spring onion and mint, free-range chicken, duck and wild mushroom terrine with truffle mayonnaise, free-range sausages with confit swede, braised cabbage and red wine and rosemary sauce, beetroot and feta tart with pesto and toasted hazelnuts, skate with chickpeas, samphire and chermoula, wok-fried chicken with coriander, bean sprouts, pak choi, pickled ginger and asian dressing, and puddings such as quince sorbet and bread and butter pudding. *Benchmark main dish: chargrilled and braised beef with mushroom pommes purée and sauce bourguignon £18.95. Two-course evening meal £23.00.*

Free house ~ Licensee Simon Cadge ~ Real ale ~ Open 12-3, 6-11; 12-11 Sat; 12-5 Sun; closed Sun evening, Mon ~ Bar food 12-2 (2.30 Fri, Sat), 6.30-9.30; 12-3.30 Sun ~ Restaurant ~ Children welcome ~ Dogs allowed in bar ~ Wi-fi *Recommended by Michael Sargent, Geoffrey Sutton, Katherine Matthews*

KIMBOLTON
TL0967 Map 5

New Sun ⭐ ♀

(01480) 860052 – www.newsuninn.co.uk

High Street; PE28 0HA

Interesting bars and rooms, tapas menu plus other good food, and a pleasant back garden

This pleasant old pub fits in well with the village's delightfully harmonious high street and is usefully open all day. The cosiest room is perhaps the low-beamed front lounge with standing timbers and exposed brickwork, a couple of comfortable armchairs and a sofa beside a log fire, and books on shelves. This leads into a narrower locals' bar with Charles Wells Bombardier and Eagle and a weekly changing guest on handpump, 17 wines by the glass (including champagne and pudding wines) and a dozen gins; background music, board games, piano and quiz machine. The traditionally furnished dining room opens off here. An airy conservatory with high-backed leather dining chairs has doors leading to the terrace where there are smart seats and tables under giant umbrellas. Note that some of the nearby parking spaces have a 30-minute limit.

Much enjoyed food includes sandwiches, plenty of tapas (such as spanish meats with manchego, fried squid with aioli and pork belly nuggets with quince paste), smoked salmon with parsnip and chilli slaw, squash, sage and garlic risotto, chicken stuffed with stilton and apricot in serrano ham with tomato and basil cream, breadcrumbed pork cutlet with caper butter and sautéed potatoes, smoked haddock fishcake with poached egg, spinach and grain mustard sauce, and puddings such as Malteser cheesecake and a seasonal fruit crumble. *Benchmark main dish: steak and kidney pudding £11.75. Two-course evening meal £18.00.*

Wells & Youngs ~ Lease Stephen and Elaine Rogers ~ Real ale ~ Open 11.30-11;
12-10.30 Sun ~ Bar food 12-2.15 (2.30 Sun), 7-9.30; not Sun or Mon evenings ~ Restaurant ~
Well behaved children welcome away from bar ~ Dogs allowed in bar ~ Wi-fi
Recommended by Mike and Mary Carter, Carol and Barry Craddock, Richard Kennell

PETERBOROUGH   TL1899 Map 5
Brewery Tap 🍺 £

(01733) 358500 – www.thebrewery-tap.com
Opposite Queensgate car park; PE1 2AA

**Fantastic range of real ales including their own brews, popular thai
food and a lively, friendly atmosphere**

The own-brewed Oakham Ales (housed in a striking modern conversion of
an old labour exchange) and thai food may seem an unusual combination
– but it obviously works. The open-plan contemporary interior has an
expanse of light wood and stone floors and blue-painted iron pillars holding
up a steel-corded mezzanine level. It's stylishly lit by a giant suspended steel
ring with bulbs running around the rim and steel-meshed wall lights. A band
of chequered floor tiles traces the path of the long sculpted pale wood bar
counter, which is boldly backed by an impressive display of bottles in a
ceiling-high wall of wooden cubes. There's also a comfortable downstairs
area, a big-screen TV for sporting events, background music and regular live
bands and comedy nights. A two-storey glass wall divides the bar from the
brewery, giving fascinating views of the two-barrel brew plan from which
they produce their own Oakham Bishops Farewell, Black Hole Porter, Citra,
Inferno, JHB and seasonal ales; also, up to eight guests, quite a few whiskies
and several wines by the glass. It gets very busy in the evening.

The incredibly popular thai food includes set menus and specials, as well as
tom yum soup, chicken, beef, pork, prawn, duck and vegetable curries, stir-fried
crispy chilli beef, talay pad cha (prawns, squid and mussels with crushed garlic, chilli
and ginger), various noodle dishes, all sorts of salads and stir-fries and five kinds of
rice. *Benchmark main dish: pad thai noodles £7.50. Two-course evening meal £20.00.*

Own brew ~ Licensee Jessica Loock ~ Real ale ~ Open 12-11 (1am Fri, 2am Sat); 12-10.30
Sun ~ Bar food 12-2.30, 5.30-10.30; 12-10.30 Fri, Sat; 12-3.30, 5.30-9.30 Sun ~ Restaurant ~
Children welcome during food service times only ~ Dogs allowed in bar ~ Wi-fi ~ Live music
nights Fri-Sun *Recommended by Martin Jones, Neil Allen, Alison and Michael Harper*

REACH   TL5666 Map 5
Dyke's End 🍺

(01638) 743816 – www.dykesend.co.uk
*From B1102 follow signpost to Swaffham Prior and Upware; village signposted;
CB25 0JD*

**Candlelit rooms in former farmhouse, with enjoyable food
and own-brewed beer**

This looks every inch the classic English pub, situated next to the
church in a charming village-green setting, and it remains proud of
its old-fashioned values such as no background music, games machines,
food sachets or paper napkins. The simply decorated ochre-walled bar
has stripped heavy pine tables and pale kitchen chairs on dark boards. In
a panelled section on the left are a few rather smarter dining tables with
candles, and on the right there's a step down to a red-carpeted part with the
small red-walled servery and sensibly placed darts at the back; board games.
Adnams Southwold, Timothy Taylors Landlord and a couple of changing

guest beers on handpump alongside a decent wine list, and Old Rosie cider. There are picnic-sets under parasols on the front grass.

Honest food includes lunchtime sandwiches, caribbean-spiced beef dumplings with mango salsa, ham hock terrine with piccalilli, ham and egg, local sausages with onion gravy, beer-battered haddock and chips, calves liver and bacon, steak frites with mustard vinaigrette, and puddings such as lemon crème brûlée and sticky toffee pudding with butterscotch sauce. *Benchmark main dish: rib-eye steak with horseradish butter and chips £21.00. Two-course evening meal £25.00.*

Free house ~ Licensee George Gibson ~ Real ale ~ Open 12-2.30, 6-11; 12-11 Sat; 12-10.30 Sun; closed Mon ~ Bar food 12-1.45, 6.45-8.45; not Sun evening, Mon ~ Restaurant ~ Children allowed but must be well behaved ~ Dogs welcome ~ Wi-fi *Recommended by Hilary and Neil Christopher, Andrew Stone, Ivor Smith*

STILTON   TL1689   Map 5

Bell ♀ 🛏

(01733) 241066 – www.thebellstilton.co.uk
High Street; village signposted from A1 S of Peterborough; PE7 3RA

Fine coaching inn with character bars, popular food, thoughtful drinks choice and seats in a pretty courtyard; bedrooms

A lovely example of a 17th-c coaching inn on the Great North Road between London and York, this is an elegant and civilised hotel. Our readers tend to head for the neatly kept right-hand bar which has a great deal of character: bow windows, sturdy upright wooden seats on flagstone floors, a big log fire in a handsome stone fireplace, partly stripped walls with big prints of sailing and winter coaching scenes, and a giant pair of blacksmith's bellows. This room has been newly opened-up with the bistro to create a bar-cum-dining area with a bustling, chatty atmosphere. A beer named for the pub from Digfield, Greene King IPA and Old Speckled Hen and Oakham Bishops Farewell on handpump, quite a few malt whiskies and around a dozen wines by the glass; service is helpful and welcoming. Other rooms include a residents' bar and a restaurant; background music and TV. Through the fine coach arch is a very pretty sheltered courtyard with tables, and a well that dates from Roman times. The bedrooms mix old-world charm with modern facilities and three are on the ground floor.

From a well judged menu, food includes sandwiches, treacle-cooked pork with a slow-cooked egg and brown sauce, smoked haddock with bayleaf custard, crispy potato and curry, steak burger with harissa relish, stilton, coleslaw and chips, jerusalem artichoke risotto with king oyster mushroom and truffle, pork with black pudding and sage béarnaise, and puddings such as chocolate mousse with spiced banana compote and hazelnut brittle and steamed treacle sponge with custard. *Benchmark main dish: slow-cooked beef with mash and mustard sauce £14.95. Two-course evening meal £21.90.*

Free house ~ Licensee Liam McGivern ~ Real ale ~ Open 12-2.30, 6-11; 12-midnight Sat; 12-10.30 Sun ~ Bar food 12-2.15 (2.30 Sat), 6-9.30; 12-3, 6-9 Sun ~ Restaurant ~ Children welcome ~ Wi-fi ~ Bedrooms: £85/£110 *Recommended by Gus Swan, Emma Scofield, Margaret and Peter Staples, B and M Kendall, Mr and Mrs P R Thomas, David Stewart, Richard Kennell*

Real ale to us means beer that has matured naturally in its cask – not pressurised or filtered. We name all real ales stocked. We usually name ales preserved under a light blanket of carbon dioxide too, though purists – pointing out that this stops the natural yeasts developing – would disagree (most people, including us, can't tell the difference!).

SUTTON GAULT

Anchor 🏮 ♉ 🛏

TL4279 Map 5

(01353) 778537 – www.anchor-inn-restaurant.co.uk

Bury Lane off High Street (B1381); CB6 2BD

Charming candlelit inn with beamed rooms, exellent food, real ales and a thoughtful wine list; bedrooms

Most customers come to this tucked-away old inn for the lovely food, but this is more than a restaurant. Space for drinks may be limited at weekends, but at other times you can pop in for a pint of Morlands Old Hoppy Hen and Nethergate Azzanewt on handpump or one of the dozen or so wines by the glass. The four heavily timbered rooms are stylishly simple, with two log fires, antique settles and wooden dining chairs around scrubbed pine tables set with candles and nicely spaced on gently undulating floors. Service is helpful and friendly. There are seats outside and you can walk along the high embankment where bird-watching is good. Bedrooms are comfortable and well equipped and overlook the river, and breakfasts are very good.

 Inventive food includes scallops with olive purée, creamed razor clams and samphire, confit pork belly with black pudding, jerusalem artichoke purée, apple and sage, halloumi, avocado, fig and braised fennel salad with croutons and tzatziki dressing, chicken with crispy new potatoes, asparagus and pea purée, redcurrant jus and wild garlic mash, tuna steak and quail egg niçoise salad, beef fillet with mushroom-stuffed tomato, triple-cooked chips and peppercorn sauce, and puddings such as strawberry and rhubarb crème brûlée and broken banoffi pie on grilled pound cake with coconut ice-cream and banana chips. They also offer a weekday two- and three-course set lunch. *Benchmark main dish: venison steak with potato rösti, crispy butternut squash and madeira jus £18.95. Two-course evening meal £22.50.*

Free house ~ Licensee Becky Harper ~ Real ale ~ Open 12-11 ~ Bar food 12-2, 7-9; 12-2.30, 6-9.30 Sat; 12-2.30, 6.30-8.30 Sun ~ Restaurant ~ Children welcome ~ Wi-fi ~ Bedrooms: £59.50/£79.50 *Recommended by Colin and Daniel Gibbs, Charlie Parker, Millie and Peter Downing*

UFFORD

White Hart 🍺 🛏

TF0904 Map 5

(01780) 740250 – www.whitehartufford.co.uk

Main Street; S on to Ufford Road off B1443 at Bainton, then right; PE9 3BH

Lots of interest in bustling pub, bar and dining rooms, good food and extensive garden; bedrooms

Until the middle of the last century, this 17th-c stone pub was actually a farm – it's now a comfortable and friendly inn with plenty of drinking and dining space. The bar has an easy-going atmosphere, farm tools and chamber pots, scatter cushions on leather benches, some nice old chairs and tables, a woodburning stove, exposed stone walls and stools against the counter where they serve Fullers London Pride, Oakham JHB and a guest beer such as Grainstore Red Kite on handpump, 21 wines by the glass and 11 gins. There's also an elegant beamed restaurant and an airy Orangery. At the back, the three acres of gardens include a sunken dining area with plenty of chairs and tables and picnic-sets on the grass, steps up to various quiet corners, and lovely flowers and shrubs. Four of the comfortable bedrooms are in the pub, two are in a converted cart shed and four more are in the Old Brewery.

🍴 Flavoursome dishes include sandwiches, local game terrine with spiced date purée, salmon and crayfish salad, trio of local sausages with onion gravy, roast vegetable wellington with parsnip purée, chicken breast with tarragon cream sauce, bass with lyonnaise potatoes and celeriac purée, lamb shank with mint jus, and puddings such as pineapple and coconut upside-down cake with passion-fruit sorbet and chocolate brownie with honeycomb ice-cream; they also offer a two- and three-course set lunch. *Benchmark main dish: local pheasant with carrot purée, savoury bread and butter pudding and blackberry jus £13.95. Two-course evening meal £21.00.*

Free house ~ Licensee Sue Olver ~ Real ale ~ Open 10am-11pm (midnight Sat); 10-9 Sun ~ Bar food 12-2.30 (3 Sat), 6-9; 12-4 Sun ~ Restaurant ~ Children welcome ~ Dogs allowed in bar and bedrooms ~ Wi-fi ~ Bedrooms: /£80 *Recommended by Jack and Hilary Burton, John Sargeant, Daniel King*

WHITTLESFORD   TL4648   Map 5
Tickell Arms 🏵 ♟

(01223) 833025 – www.cambscuisine.com/the-tickell-whittlesford
2.4 miles from M11 junction 10: A505 towards Newmarket, then second turn left signposted Whittlesford; keep on into North Road; CB22 4NZ

Light and refreshing dining pub with good enterprising food and pretty garden

Although the main emphasis is on the dining area (through an ornate glazed partition), there is a proper L-shaped bar here with floor tiles and – under bowler-hatted lampshades over the counter – Brewsters Hophead, Elgoods Cambridge Bitter, Milton Pegasus and Nethergate Old Growler on handpump, 20 fairly priced wines by the glass including champagne, and farm cider. Also, three porcelain handpumps from the era of the legendarily autocratic regime of the Wagner-loving former owner Kim Tickell; these are now orphaned and decorate a high 'counter' that's suspended between a pair of ornate cast-iron pillars and lined with bentwood bar stools. Staff are neatly dressed and friendly. Tables in the dining room vary from sturdy to massive, with leather-cushioned bentwood and other dining chairs and one dark pew, and fresh minimalist décor in palest buff. This opens into an even lighter limestone-floored conservatory area, partly divided by a very high-backed ribbed-leather banquette. The side terrace has comfortable tables, and the secluded garden beyond has pergolas and a pond. This is sister pub to the Cock in Hemingford Grey and the Crown & Punchbowl at Horningsea.

Accomplished food using the best local produce includes sandwiches, ham hock terrine with parsnip and wholegrain mustard purée, fried duck egg with bacon jam, black pudding, maple syrup and brioche toast, sage and parmesan gnocchi with sage and hazelnut crumble, chicken with melted leeks, baked celeriac and red wine sauce, cod loin with parsley risotto, smoked bacon and charred leeks, and puddings such as vanilla pannacotta with mascarpone rice pudding and spiced pear syrup and chocolate and almond brownie with cherry sorbet; they also offer a two- and three-course set menu (not weekend lunchtimes, or Fri or Sat evenings). *Benchmark main dish: pork fillet and roasted belly with cauliflower cheese purée and port sauce £17.00. Two-course evening meal £22.00.*

Free house ~ Licensees Oliver Thain, Richard Bradley, Max Freeman ~ Real ale ~ Open 12-2.30, 6-11; 12-11 Sat; 12-10.30 Sun ~ Bar food 12-2.30, 6.30-9 (9.30 Fri); 12-3, 6-9.30 Sat; 12-3, 6-8 Sun ~ Restaurant ~ Children must be over 10 in pub and over 5 in evening restaurant ~ Dogs allowed in bar ~ Wi-fi *Recommended by Hilary and Neil Christopher, Alison and Michael Harper, Revd R P Tickle, Mrs Margo Finlay, Jörg Kasprowski*

The details at the end of each featured entry start by saying whether the pub is a free house, or if it belongs to a brewery or pub group (which we name).

Also Worth a Visit in Cambridgeshire

Besides the fully inspected pubs, you might like to try these pubs that have been recommended to us and described by readers. Do tell us what you think of them: feedback@goodguides.com

ABBOTS RIPTON TL2377
Abbots Elm (01487) 773773
B1090; PE28 2PA Open-plan thatched dining pub reconstructed after major fire; well liked food from snacks and bar meals to interesting restaurant dishes, extensive choice of wines by the glass including champagne, three well kept ales, good service; children and dogs welcome, three bedrooms, open all day Sat, till 5pm Sun. *(Julian Thorpe)*

ABINGTON PIGOTTS TL3044
Pig & Abbot (01763) 853515
High Street; SG8 0SD Welcoming Queen Anne local with two small traditional bars and restaurant, good choice of enjoyable home-cooked food at reasonable prices, friendly efficient staff, well kept Adnams Southwold, Fullers London Pride and guests, beams and log fires; children and dogs welcome, side and back terraces, pretty village with good surrounding walks, open all day weekends – very busy then. *(Andrew Stone)*

BARRINGTON TL3849
Royal Oak (01223) 870791
Turn off A10 about 3.7 miles SW of M11 junction 11, in Foxton; West Green; CB22 7RZ Rambling thatched Tudor pub with tables out overlooking classic village green, heavy low beams and timbers, mixed furnishings, a beer named for the pub from Greene King along with Adnams, Woodfordes and a local guest, Aspall's and Thatcher's cider, enjoyable food from pub favourites up, good wine list, friendly helpful service, airy dining conservatory; background music, free wi-fi; children welcome, classic car club meeting first Fri of month. *(Sally Wright)*

BOURN TL3256
★**Willow Tree** (01954) 719775
High Street, just off B1046 W of Cambridge; CB23 2SQ Light and airy dining pub with relaxed informal atmosphere despite the cut-glass chandeliers, sprinkling of Louis XVI furniture and profusion of silver-plated candlesticks; accomplished restaurant-style cooking (all day Sun till 8pm), Woodfordes and a local guest, several wines by the glass and inventive cocktails, friendly efficient staff; live jazz Sun evening; children welcome, smart tables and chairs on back deck, grassed area beyond car park with fruit trees, huge weeping willow and tipi, open all day. *(James Landor)*

BOXWORTH TL3464
Golden Ball (01954) 267397
High Street; CB23 4LY Attractive partly thatched 16th-c village pub with pitched-roof bar, restaurant and small conservatory, emphasis on good fairly priced food (all day Sun till 7pm) from baguettes through pubby choices and grills to blackboard specials, well kept Charles Wells ales, good wine and whisky choice; children welcome, nice garden and heated terrace, pastures behind, 11 quiet bedrooms in adjacent block, open all day. *(Rona Mackinlay)*

BRAMPTON TL2170
Black Bull (01480) 457201
Church Road; PE28 4PF 16th-c and later with updated low-ceilinged interior, stripped-wood floor and inglenook woodburner in split-level main bar, enjoyable well priced pubby food including good home-made pies, four real ales, friendly efficient staff; free wi-fi; children welcome, dogs in bar (home-made treats for them), garden with play area, open (and food) all day, till 9pm (4pm) Sun. *(Beth Aldridge)*

BRINKLEY TL6254
Red Lion (01638) 508707
High Street; CB8 0RA Old country pub under newish management, beams and inglenook log fire, enjoyable food (not Sun evening) from fairly pubby menu, Sun brunch, Adnams and a couple of guests, friendly service; children and dogs (in bar) welcome, garden tables, closed Sun evening, Mon, Tues. *(David Stewart)*

BROUGHTON TL2877
★**Crown** (01487) 824428
Off A141 opposite RAF Wyton; Bridge Road; PE28 3AY Attractively tucked-away mansard-roofed dining pub opposite church; fresh airy décor with country pine tables and chairs on stone floors, some leather bucket seats and sofa, good well presented food (not Sun evening) from lunchtime sandwiches up, friendly service, real ales such as Mauldons, restaurant; background music; children and dogs welcome, disabled access and facilities, tables out on big stretch of grass behind, open all day Sun till 8pm, may close Mon and Tues evenings in winter. *(Julian Thorpe)*

BUCKDEN TL1967
★**George** (01480) 812300
High Street; PE19 5XA Handsome and stylish Georgian-faced hotel with bustling informal bar, fine fan beamwork, leather and

chrome chairs, log fire, Adnams Southwold and a changing guest from chrome-topped counter, lots of wines including champagne by the glass, teas and coffees, popular brasserie with good modern food served by helpful enthusiastic young staff, also bar meals; background music; children and dogs welcome, tables under large parasols on pretty sheltered terrace with box hedging, charming bedrooms, smallish car park (free street parking), open all day. *(Richard Kennell, Michael Sargent)*

BUCKDEN   TL1967
Lion (01480) 810313
High Street; PE19 5XA Partly 15th-c coaching inn with dark beams and big inglenook log fire in airy bow-windowed entrance bar, enjoyable food from lunchtime sandwiches up, Adnams Southwold and guests, local Draycott bottled beers and good choice of wines by the glass, friendly service, panelled back restaurant beyond latticed window partition; free wi-fi; children welcome, back courtyard, 14 bedrooms, open all day and handy for A1; changing hands as we went to press, so may be changes. *(William Slade)*

CAMBRIDGE   TL4458
Anchor (01223) 353554
Silver Street; CB3 9EL Pub-restaurant in beautiful riverside position by punting station, popular with tourists and can get very busy; fine river views from upper dining room and suntrap terrace, five well kept beers and plenty of wines by the glass, good variety of food (fairly priced for the area), friendly service; live jazz Thurs; children and dogs welcome, open (and food) all day. *(Brian and Sally Wakeham)*

CAMBRIDGE   TL4658
★ **Cambridge Blue** (01223) 471680
85 Gwydir Street; CB1 2LG Friendly little backstreet local with a dozen or more interesting ales (some tapped from the cask – regular festivals), six craft kegs, 200 bottled beers and 35 whiskies, enjoyable well priced food including seasonal specials, all home-made (even the ketchup), attractive conservatory and extended bar area with lots of breweriana and old advertising signs; free wi-fi; children and dogs welcome, seats in back garden bordering cemetery, open (and food) all day and can get very busy weekends. *(Brian and Sally Wakeham)*

CAMBRIDGE   TL4558
Cambridge Brew House
(01223) 855185 *King Street; CB1 1LH* Contemporary open-plan pub visibly brewing its own beers (plenty of guest ales/craft beers on tap too), enjoyable food from open kitchen including british tapas, sharing boards and own-smoked meats and fish, weekend brunch, friendly staff, sports TV in upstairs bar; open (and food) all day. *(William Slade)*

CAMBRIDGE   TL4459
Castle (01223) 353194
Castle Street; CB3 0AJ Adnams range and interesting guest beers in big airy bare-boards bar, other pleasantly simple rooms including snug and quieter upstairs area, good value pub food from sandwiches and snacks to blackboard specials, efficient friendly young staff; background music, free wi-fi; children and dogs welcome, picnic-sets in good walled back courtyard, open all day. *(Simon Watkins, John Marsh)*

CAMBRIDGE   TL4658
Clarendon Arms (01223) 778272
Clarendon Street; CB1 1JX Welcoming backstreet corner local; flagstones and bare boards, standard well used furniture, lots of pictures including local scenes, step down to back bar, enjoyable home-made food (not Sun evening, Mon lunchtime) from snacks to Sun roasts, Greene King ales and a good locally distilled gin, friendly helpful service; children and dogs welcome, wheelchair access possible with assistance, seats in sunny back courtyard, open all day. *(Julian Thorpe)*

CAMBRIDGE   TL4657
Devonshire Arms (01223) 316610
Devonshire Road; CB1 2BH Popular and welcoming Milton-tied pub with two cheerful chatty linked bars, their well kept ales and guests, real cider, also great choice of bottled beers, decent wines and a dozen malts, low-priced food (not Sun evening) from sandwiches and pizzas to steaks, creaky wood floors, mix of furniture including long narrow refectory tables, architectural prints and steam engine pictures, woodburner in back bar; wheelchair access, handy for the station, open all day. *(William Slade)*

CAMBRIDGE   TL4458
★ **Eagle** (01223) 505020
Benet Street; CB2 3QN Once the city's most important coaching inn; rambling rooms with two medieval mullioned windows and the remains of possibly medieval wall paintings, two fireplaces dating from around 1600, lovely worn wooden floors and plenty of pine panelling, dark red ceiling left unpainted since World War II to preserve signatures of british and american airmen made with Zippo lighters, candle smoke and lipstick, well kept Greene King ales including

---

Post Office address codings confusingly give the impression that some pubs are in Cambridgeshire, when they're really in Bedfordshire, Lincolnshire, Norfolk or Northamptonshire (which is where we list them).

Eagle DNA (Crick and Watson announced the discovery of DNA's structure here in 1953) and two guests, decent choice of enjoyable food served efficiently considering the crowds; children welcome, disabled facilities, heavy wooden seats in attractive cobbled and galleried courtyard, open all day. *(Michael Butler, Barry Collett, John Wooll, Ivor Smith)*

CAMBRIDGE TL4558
Elm Tree (01223) 502632
Orchard Street; CB1 1JT Traditional one-bar backstreet drinkers' pub with welcoming atmosphere, ten well kept ales including B&T and Charles Wells, good range of continental bottled beers, local ciders/perries usually poured from the barrel, friendly knowledgeable staff, no food, nice unspoilt interior with breweriana, some live music; wheelchair access, a few tables out at side, open all day. *(Brian and Sally Wakeham)*

CAMBRIDGE TL4559
Fort St George (01223) 354327
Midsummer Common; CB4 1HA Picturesque old pub (reached by foot only) in charming waterside position overlooking ducks, swans, punts and boathouses; extended around old-fashioned Tudor core, good value bar food including traditional Sun lunch, well kept Greene King ales and decent wines by the glass, oars on beams, historic boating photographs, open fire; free wi-fi; children and dogs welcome, wheelchair access via side door, lots of tables outside, open (and food) all day. *(Simon Watkins, Ivor Smith)*

CAMBRIDGE TL4558
★**Free Press** (01223) 368337
Prospect Row; CB1 1DU Unspoilt little backstreet pub with interesting décor including old newspaper pages and printing memorabilia (was printshop for a local paper); Greene King IPA, Abbot and Mild plus regularly changing guests, good range of wines by the glass, 25 malt whiskies and lots of gins and rums, tasty good value food including evening set menu (Mon-Weds), friendly staff, log fire; TV for major sports events, board games; children and dogs (in bar) welcome, wheelchair access, small sheltered paved garden behind, open all day Fri, Sat. *(David Thorpe)*

CAMBRIDGE TL4657
★**Kingston Arms** (01223) 319414
Kingston Street; CB1 2NU Victorian backstreet pub with ten well kept interesting ales, over 50 bottled beers, a couple of real ciders and good choice of wines by the glass, enjoyable freshly prepared food (all day weekends) including some real bargains, companionably big plain tables and basic seating, thriving chatty atmosphere; free wi-fi; children and dogs welcome, back beer garden (heated and partly covered), open all day Fri-Sun. *(William Slade)*

CAMBRIDGE TL4557
Live & Let Live (01223) 460261
Mawson Road; CB1 2EA Popular backstreet pub, friendly and relaxed, five well kept ales including Oakham, proper cider and over 120 rums, snacky food, panelled interior with sturdy varnished tables on bare boards, some steam railway and brewery memorabilia, old gas light fittings, cribbage and dominoes; dogs welcome, disabled access awkward but possible. *(Jack and Hilary Burton)*

CAMBRIDGE TL4458
Mill (01223) 311829
Mill Lane; CB2 1RX Fairly compact old pub in picturesque spot overlooking mill pond (punt hire); seven mainly local ales and proper cider from plank-topped servery, reasonably priced food such as burgers, opened-up bar with bare boards, quarry tiles and some exposed brickwork, mix of old and new furniture including pews and banquettes, snug panelled back room; radiogram playing vinyl, Mon quiz, sports TV, free wi-fi; children welcome, open (and food) all day. *(Brian and Sally Wakeham, Richard Tilbrook)*

CAMBRIDGE TL4458
Mitre (01223) 358403
Bridge Street, opposite St John's College; CB2 1UF Popular Nicholsons pub close to the river and well placed for visiting the colleges; spacious rambling bar on several levels, good selection of well kept ales, farm cider and reasonably priced wines by the glass, their usual good value food including fixed-price menu, efficient friendly service; background music, free wi-fi; children welcome, disabled access, open (and food) all day. *(Revd R P Tickle, R T and J C Moggridge)*

CAMBRIDGE TL4559
Old Spring (01223) 357228
Ferry Path; car park on Chesterton Road; CB4 1HB Extended Victorian pub, roomy and airy, with enjoyable home-made food from traditional choices up, friendly efficient service, well kept Greene King IPA, Abbot and four guests, plenty of wines by the glass and good coffee, mix of seating including sofas on bare boards, two log fires, conservatory; background music; well behaved children welcome, dogs outside only, disabled facilities, seats out in front and on large heated back terrace, open all day, food all day Sun. *(Simon Watkins, Ivor Smith)*

CAMBRIDGE TL4458
Pint Shop (01223) 352293
Peas Hill; CB2 3PN Revamped former university offices on two floors; front bar with restaurant behind, parquet floors and grey-painted walls, simple furnishings and pendant lighting, 16 craft/cask beers from smaller brewers listed on blackboard, good selection of wines and around 60 gins,

unusual food from bar snacks up cooked on charcoal grill, set menu options Mon-Fri, local artwork for sale, further dining room upstairs; ground floor wheelchair access/facilities, handy for the Cambridge Arts Theatre and Corn Exchange, open all day. *(R Anderson)*

CASTOR TL1298

★ **Prince of Wales Feathers**

(01733) 380222 *Off A47; PE5 7AL* Friendly stone-built local with half a dozen well kept ales including Castor, craft beers and proper cider/perry, good value food cooked by landlady (not weekend evenings), open-plan interior with dining area to the left; Sat live music, Sun quiz, Sky TV, pool (free Thurs); children and dogs welcome, disabled facilities, attractive front terrace and another at the back with large smokers' shelter, open all day, till late weekends. *(Beth Aldridge)*

CATWORTH TL0873

Racehorse (01832) 710123

B660, S of A14; PE28 0PF Welcoming 19th-c village pub with enjoyable food from sandwiches/panini and sharing boards up, three well kept changing ales and good choice of wines, whiskies and gins, cheerful helpful service, smallish bar connecting to more spacious dining areas, log fire, delicatessen/coffee shop; some live music, pool, TV; children and dogs welcome, café-style tables outside, five bedrooms in converted stables, closed Sun evening, otherwise open all day (till 10pm Mon-Thurs). *(Michael Sargent)*

CONINGTON TL3266

White Swan (01954) 267251

Signed off A14 (was A604) Cambridge–Huntingdon; Elsworth Road; CB23 4LN Quietly placed 18th-c red-brick country pub under newish management; well kept Adnams and guests tapped from the cask, nine wines by the glass, good freshly made imaginative food (not evenings Sun-Tues, limited lunch menu Mon, Tues), friendly efficient service, traditional bar with tiled floor and log fire, restaurant extension, some old photographs and local artwork; children and dogs welcome, big front garden with play area, open all day. *(David Stewart)*

DUXFORD TL4745

Plough (01223) 833170

St Peters Street; CB22 4RP Popular early 18th-c thatched pub, clean bright and friendly, with enjoyable home-made food from shortish reasonably priced menu, Adnams, Everards and guests kept well, woodburner in brick fireplace; children welcome, handy for

IWM Duxford, open all day (no food Sun or Mon evenings). *(Jack and Hilary Burton)*

ELLINGTON TL1671

Mermaid (01480) 891106

High Street; PE28 0AB Popular village dining pub restored under present management (parts date to the 14th c); highly praised imaginative food (not Sun evening) from owner-chef including interesting tapas menu, a couple of Greene King ales and a guest from brick counter, several wines by the glass from good list, friendly attentive young staff, beams (some hiding coins left by US airmen), country furniture, woodburner, smallish dining rooms; background music (turned off on request); garden overlooking church, no proper car park, open all day weekends, closed Mon. *(Michael Sargent, Roy Shutz, Mike and Mary Carter)*

ELSWORTH TL3163

George & Dragon (01954) 267236

Off A14 NW of Cambridge, via Boxworth, or off A428; CB23 8JQ Neatly kept dining pub in same group as the Eaton Oak at St Neots and Rose at Stapleford; pleasant panelled main bar with fishy theme opening on left to slightly elevated dining area, woodburner, garden room overlooking attractive terraces, more formal restaurant on right, wide choice of popular food including deals, Greene King ales, a guest beer and decent range of wines, service friendly but can suffer at busy times; steps down to lavatories, free wi-fi; children welcome, dogs in bar, open (and food) all day Sun. *(Michael and Jenny Back)*

ELSWORTH TL3163

Poacher (01954) 267722

Brockley Road; CB23 4JS Restored 17th-c thatched and beamed corner local under new management; well kept Woodfordes Wherry, St Austell Tribute and a couple of guests from tiny servery, good reasonably priced pubby food (not Sun evening), friendly service, painted pine furniture on bare boards or tiles, open fire; background and some live music, monthly quiz, TV; children and dogs welcome, picnic-sets in back garden, good walks, open all day weekends. *(David Stewart)*

ELTISLEY TL2759

Eltisley (01480) 880308

The Green; village signposted off A428 Cambridge–St Neots; PE19 6TG Village-green inn with all sorts of rambling areas, grey-painted walls and beams, bare boards and flagstones, leatherette wall seats, curved high-backed settles and easy chairs by cast-iron stove in massive central chimneypiece,

Charles Wells ales and decent wines by the glass, food from sandwiches up, cosy low-beamed library down some steps, more formal raftered dining room; background music; children and dogs welcome, canopied deck in sheltered back area, six stylish bedrooms in separate block, open all day Sat, closed Sun evening, Mon. *(Michael Butler)*

ELTON   TL0893
Black Horse   (01832) 280591
Overend; B671 off A605 W of Peterborough and A1(M); PE8 6RU
Honey-stone beamed dining pub under new management; opened-up modernised interior, enjoyable food cooked by owner-chef, friendly attentive staff, four real ales including Digfield and Greene King, decent wines; children welcome, dogs in bar, terrace and garden with views across to Elton Hall park and village church, closed Sun evening, Mon, otherwise open all day. *(John Preddy)*

ELY   TL5479
Cutter   (01353) 662713
Annesdale, off Station Road (or walk S along Riverside Walk from Maltings); CB7 4BN Beautifully placed modernised riverside pub with bar, dining lounge and restaurant, good choice of enjoyable promptly served food, well kept Adnams, Sharps, Woodfordes and a guest from boat-shaped counter, nice wines by the glass, decent coffee, good views from window seats and terrace; children welcome, no dogs inside, moorings, open all day from 9am. *(Ian and Amanda Seamark)*

ELY   TL5480
Lamb   (01353) 663574
Brook Street (Lynn Road); CB7 4EJ
Good choice of food in popular hotel's panelled lounge bar or restaurant, friendly welcoming staff, Greene King and plenty of wines by the glass, decent coffee; children and dogs welcome, close to cathedral, 31 clean comfortable bedrooms, good breakfast (for non-residents too). *(John Wooll, Ian and Amanda Seamark)*

ETTON   TF1406
Golden Pheasant   (01733) 252387
Just off B1443 N of Peterborough, signed from near N end of A15 bypass; PE6 7DA Former Georgian farmhouse (a pub since 1964), spacious bare-boards bar with open fire, five real ales such as Adnams, Greene King and Grainstore from central counter, decent choice of wines and spirits, good food (all day Sat, not Sun night) including competitively priced weekday set menu (lunchtime/early evening), prompt cheerful service, back panelled restaurant; some live music; children and dogs welcome, big tree-sheltered garden with play area, table tennis and table football in marquee, vintage car meetings, on Green Wheel cycle

route, open all day Fri-Sun, closed Mon lunchtime. *(Howard and Margaret Buchanan)*

FEN DITTON   TL4860
Ancient Shepherds   (01223) 293280
Off B1047 at Green End, The River signpost, just NE of Cambridge; CB5 8ST Beamed 16th-c pub (originally three cottages) under newish tenancy; comfortable central lounge, heavy drapes, big leather sofas and armchairs, coal fire, comic fox and policeman prints plus steeplechasing and equestrian ones, step down to small pubby bar with another coal fire, Greene King IPA, Woodfordes Wherry and guest, eight wines by the glass, good traditional food including blackboard specials, separate restaurant; children and dogs (in bar) welcome, not suitable for wheelchairs, seats under trees in garden behind, closed Sun evening. *(Mrs Carolyn Dixon)*

FOWLMERE   TL4245
★ Chequers   (01763) 208558
High Street (B1368); SG8 7SR Popular 16th-c coaching inn with two comfortable downstairs rooms, long cushioned wall seats, dining chairs around dark tables, inglenook log fire, good traditional food served by friendly staff, Greene King, two guests and plenty of wines by the glass, attractive upstairs beamed and timbered dining room with interesting moulded plasterwork above one fireplace, spacious conservatory; children and dogs (in bar) welcome, terrace and garden with tables under parasols, four bedrooms planned, closed Sun evening, Mon, otherwise open all day. *(Richard Kennell)*

GRANTCHESTER   TL4355
★ Blue Ball   (01223) 846004
Broadway; CB3 9NQ Character bare-boards free house rebuilt 1900 on site of much older pub (cellars still remain), sensitive renovation by new licensees (there's a list of previous publicans back to 1767), changing real ales including Adnams, Elgoods and Woodfordes and ciders, good log fire, cards and traditional games including shut the box and ring the bull, newspapers and lots of books; children and dogs welcome, tables on small terrace with lovely views to Grantchester Meadows, good heated smokers' shelter, new bedrooms, nice village, open all day. *(Andrew Stone, Julian Thorpe)*

GREAT ABINGTON   TL5348
Three Tuns   (01223) 891467
Off A1307 Cambridge-Haverhill, and A11; CB21 6AB Peacefully set 16th-c beamed village pub, low-backed settles on stripped-wood floors, open fires, good authentic thai food (traditional roast on Sun), three well kept changing ales, welcoming landlord and friendly efficient staff; garden picnic-sets, nine well appointed bedrooms in modern block, open all day weekends. *(Mrs Margo Finlay, Jörg Kasprowski)*

GREAT CHISHILL   TL4239
★**Pheasant** (01763) 838535
*Follow Heydon signpost from B1039 in
village; SG8 8SR* Popular old split-level
flagstoned pub with beams, timbering, open
fires and some elaborately carved (though
modern) seats and settles, good freshly made
food (not Sun evening) using local produce,
welcoming friendly staff, two or three ales
including one for the pub from Nethergate,
good choice of wines by the glass, small
dining room (best to book); darts, cribbage,
dominoes; no under-14s inside, dogs allowed,
charming secluded back garden with small
play area, open all day weekends. *(Carol and
Barry Craddock)*

GREAT GRANSDEN   TL2655
Crown & Cushion (01767) 677214
*Off B1046 Cambridge–St Neots; West
Street; SG19 3AT* Small thatched and
beamed local in pretty village, two or three
well kept ales such as Adnams and Oakham,
authentic indonesian cooking from landlady
(Fri evening, Sat, Sun), friendly staff,
woodburner in big fireplace; live music; small
garden, open all day weekends, closed Mon
and lunchtimes Tues-Fri. *(Millie and Peter
Downing)*

HARDWICK   TL3758
Blue Lion (01954) 210328
*Signed off A428 (was A45) W of
Cambridge; Main Street; CB23 7QU*
Attractive 18th-c split-level dining pub, good
food from landlord-chef in bar and extended
dining area with conservatory, Greene King
IPA and guests, friendly efficient young
staff, beams and timbers, leather armchairs
by copper-canopied inglenook; children
welcome, pretty little front garden, more
seats on decking and lawn with play area,
handy for Wimpole Way walks, open all day
(food all day weekends). *(Andrew Stone)*

HEYDON   TL4339
★**King William IV** (01763) 838773
*Off A505 W of M11 junction 10;
SG8 8PW* Rambling dimly lit rooms with
fascinating rustic jumble (ploughshares,
yokes, iron tools, cowbells and so forth) along
with copperware and china in nooks and
crannies, some tables suspended by chains
from beams, central log fire, Fullers, Greene
King and Timothy Taylors, good varied choice
of well presented food including proper
home-made pies, helpful staff; background
music; children and dogs (in bar) welcome,
teak furniture on heated terrace and in
pretty garden, four bedrooms in separate
building, open all day weekends. *(Mrs Margo
Finlay, Jörg Kasprowski)*

HISTON   TL4363
★**Red Lion** (01223) 564437
*High Street, off Station Road; 3.7 miles
from M11 junction 1; CB24 9JD*
Impressive choice of draught and bottled
beers along with traditional cider/perry
(festivals Easter/early Sept), ceiling joists in
L-shaped main bar packed with hundreds of
beer mats and pump clips among hop bines
and whisky-water jugs, fine collection of
old brewery advertisements too, enjoyable
traditional food (all day Sat, not Mon, Fri,
Sun evenings), cheerful efficient service,
log fires, comfortable brocaded wall seats,
matching mate's chairs and pubby tables,
extended bar on left (well behaved children
allowed here) with darts, TV and huge
collection of beer bottles; mobile phones
discouraged, no dogs inside; disabled access/
facilities, picnic-sets in neat garden, limited
parking, open all day. *(Julian Thorpe)*

LITTLE WILBRAHAM   TL5458
★**Hole in the Wall** (01223) 812282
*High Street; A1303 Newmarket Road to
Stow cum Quy off A14, then left at The
Wilbrahams signpost, then right at Little
Wilbrahams signpost; CB1 5JY* Tucked-
away pub-restaurant with cosy carpeted
ochre-walled bar on right, log fire in big brick
fireplace, 16th-c beams and timbers, snug
little window seats and other mixed seating
around scrubbed kitchen tables, similar
middle room with fire in open range, rather
plusher main dining room with another fire,
highly regarded inventive cooking including
evening tasting menu (set lunch is more
affordable), excellent service, Fellows ales
and guests, ten wines by the glass and some
unusual soft drinks; well behaved children
allowed, dogs in bar, neat side garden with
good teak furniture and small verandah,
interesting walk to nearby unspoilt Little
Wilbraham Fen, closed Sun evening, all day
Mon and two weeks Jan. *(James Landor)*

MADINGLEY   TL3960
Three Horseshoes (01954) 210221
*High Street; off A1303 W of Cambridge;
CB23 8AB* Civilised thatched restaurany
pub – most customers come here for the
inventive italian-influenced food (not cheap
and they add a service charge); there is,
though, a small pleasantly relaxed bar, with
simple wooden furniture on bare boards
and open fire (can be a crush at peak
times), two real ales and plenty of wines
by the glass from excellent list, friendly
service, pretty dining conservatory; children
welcome, picnic-sets under parasols in sunny
garden. *(Andrew Stone)*

NEWTON   TL4349
★**Queens Head** (01223) 870436
*2.5 miles from M11 junction 11; A10
towards Royston, then left on to B1368;
CB22 7PG* Lovely traditional unchanging
pub run by same welcoming family for many
years – lots of loyal customers; peaceful bow-
windowed main bar with crooked beams in
low ceiling, bare wooden benches and seats
built into cream walls, curved high-backed

settle, paintings and big log fire, Adnams ales tapped from the cask, farm cider and simple food such as soup and sandwiches, small carpeted saloon, traditional games including table skittles, shove-ha'penny and nine men's morris; no credit cards; children on best behaviour allowed in games room only, dogs welcome, seats out in front by vine trellis. *(Sarah Flynn, Ivor Smith)*

OFFORD D'ARCY   TL2166
Horseshoe (01480) 810293
High Street; PE19 5RH Extended former 17th-c coaching house with two bars and restaurant, emphasis on good food including popular Sun carvery, friendly helpful service, up to five changing ales and well chosen wines, beams and inglenooks; children welcome, lawned garden with play area, open all day Fri-Sun. *(Rona Mackinlay)*

ORWELL   TL3650
Chequers (01223) 207840
Town Green Road; SG8 5QL Village dining pub with good food (not Sun evening) including popular themed nights, well kept ales such as Lacons and Sharps Doom Bar, decent choice of wines by the glass, pleasant helpful staff; children and dogs (in bar) welcome, disabled facilities, open all day Fri and Sat, till 8pm Sun, closed Mon. *(Julian Thorpe)*

PAMPISFORD   TL4948
★Chequers (01223) 833220
2.6 miles from M11 junction 10: A505 E, then village and pub signed off; Town Lane; CB22 4ER Traditional neatly kept old pub with friendly licensees, low beams and comfortable old-fashioned furnishings, booth seating on pale ceramic tiles in cream-walled main area, low step down to bare-boards part with dark pink walls, Greene King IPA, Woodfordes Wherry and two guests, good fairly priced food including themed nights, Sun carvery and OAP lunch Weds, good friendly service; TV, free wi-fi; children and dogs welcome (their collie is Snoopy), picnic-sets in prettily planted small garden lit by black streetlamps, parking may be tricky, open all day (till 4pm Sun). *(Roy Hoing)*

PETERBOROUGH   TL1998
★Charters (01733) 315700
Town Bridge, S side; PE1 1FP Interesting conversion of dutch grain barge moored on River Nene; sizeable timbered bar on lower deck with up to a dozen real ales including Oakham (regular beer festivals), restaurant above serving good value south-east asian food, lots of wooden tables and pews; background music, live bands (Fri and Sat after 10.30pm, Sun from 3.30pm); children welcome till 9pm, dogs in bar, huge riverside

garden (gets packed in fine weather), open all day (till midnight Fri, Sat). *(Barry Collett)*

PETERBOROUGH   TL1897
Coalheavers Arms (01733) 565664
Park Street, Woodston; PE2 9BH Friendly old-fashioned 19th-c flagstoned local, well kept Milton and guests, traditional cider and good range of continental imports and malt whiskies, basic snacks; Sun quiz, near football ground and busy on match days; pleasant garden, open all day Fri-Sun, closed lunchtime Mon-Weds. *(Brian and Sally Wakeham)*

PETERBOROUGH   TL1898
Drapers Arms (01733) 847570
Cowgate; PE1 1LZ Roomy open-plan Wetherspoons in converted 19th-c draper's, fine ale range, low-priced food all day, prompt friendly service; can get very busy Fri, Sat evenings; children welcome, open from 8am. *(Andrew Stone)*

SHEPRETH   TL3947
Plough (01763) 290348
Signed just off A10 S of Cambridge; High Street; SG8 5PP Extensively refurbished red-brick village pub, decent-sized bar area with vinyl record and Spitfire theme (IWM Duxford nearby), well kept ales including Elgoods and a house beer from Calverley, good selection of other drinks, enjoyable reasonably priced food from snacks to good Sun lunch, pleasant young staff, upstairs rooms displaying local artwork; background and some live music, free wi-fi; children welcome, garden with covered terrace, open (and food) all day weekends. *(Ian and Amanda Seamark)*

SPALDWICK   TL1372
George (01480) 890293
Just off A14 W of Huntingdon; PE28 0TD Former 17th-c village coaching inn, sofas in beamed bar, larger dining area including raftered part, nice food (till 7pm Sun) from good value bar snacks up, Timothy Taylors Landlord, Woodfordes Wherry and a guest, decent wines by the glass, friendly if not always speedy service; children and dogs (in bar) welcome, seats out behind under parasols, open all day Fri-Sun. *(Rona Mackinlay)*

ST NEOTS   TL1761
Eaton Oak (01480) 219555
Just off A1, Great North Road/Crosshall Road; PE19 7DB Under same ownership as the George & Dragon at Elsworth and Rose at Stapleford; wide choice of popular food including grills, fresh fish and very good value early evening deal for two (Mon-Thurs), Charles Wells ales and a guest, good friendly service, plenty of nooks and crannies in

older part, two front snugs, light airy dining area and conservatory; free wi-fi; children and dogs (in bar) welcome, disabled access and loos, tables out under parasols, hanging baskets and tubs of flowers, smokers' shelter, nine bedrooms, open all day (breakfast for non-residents). *(Michael and Jenny Back)*

STAPLEFORD   TL4651
Rose   (01223) 843349

London Road; M11 junction 11; CB22 5DG Comfortable sister pub to the Eaton Oak at St Neots and George & Dragon at Elsworth, emphasis on dining and can get very busy, wide choice of popular reasonably priced food including weekday early-bird deal, friendly uniformed staff, Courage Directors, Youngs Best and Wells Bombardier, small low-ceilinged lounge with inglenook woodburner, roomy split-level dining area; steps up to lavatories, faint background music; picnic-sets on back grass, open (and food) all day Sun. *(Rona Mackinlay)*

STOW CUM QUY   TL5260
White Swan   (01223) 811821

Off A14 E of Cambridge, via B1102; CB25 9AB Cosy 17th-c beamed village pub-restaurant; well kept ales such as Adnams, Nethergate, Oakham and Tring, Weston's cider, several wines by the glass from good list, local English Spirits range and nice selection of malt whiskies, good home-made food from bar snacks and pubby choices to more ambitious restaurant dishes, big fireplace, friendly chatty atmosphere; children and dogs welcome, wheelchair access through side door (ramps provided), terrace picnic-sets, handy for Anglesey Abbey (NT), open all day, no food Sun evening. *(John Pritchard)*

STRETHAM   TL5072
Lazy Otter   (01353) 649780

Elford Closes, off A10 S of Stretham roundabout; CB6 3LU Big rambling pub on Great Ouse next to residential/holiday lodge park, good river views from restaurant and sizeable garden with play area, popular reasonably priced food, up to five well kept changing ales and good choice of wines, clean and nicely furnished, warm fire; children and dogs (in bar) welcome, three bedrooms, moorings, open all day. *(James Landor)*

THORNEY   TL2799
★ **Dog in a Doublet**   (01733) 202256

B1040 towards Thorney; PE6 0RW Friendly dining pub across road from River Nene; really good food from pubby choices to upmarket restaurant dishes (some produce from own farm), interesting range of snacks too, well kept ales and good wines by the glass, deli counter, restaurant; children and dogs (in bar) welcome, handy for Hereward Way walks, four bedrooms and camping, open all day Fri-Sun, closed Mon and Tues lunchtimes. *(Janek Skutela, Rona Mackinlay)*

THRIPLOW   TL4346
Green Man   (01763) 208855

3 miles from M11 junction 10; A505 towards Royston, then first right; Lower Street; SG8 7RJ Welcoming little roadside pub owned by the village, good food from shortish daily changing menu along with blackboard tapas, four well kept ales and decent wines by the glass, efficient friendly service, free lift home for local evening diners (must book); quiz nights; children welcome, picnic-sets on small grassy triangle in front, two circular walks from the pub, closed Mon, otherwise open (and food) all day, till 7pm (6pm food) Sun. *(Millie and Peter Downing)*

TILBROOK   TL0769
White Horse   (01480) 860764

High Street (B645); PE28 0JP Welcoming and relaxed 18th-c pub at edge of village; low-beamed bar with interesting local prints and horsebrasses, dining conservatory, Charles Wells ales and several wines by the glass, enjoyable reasonably priced food (not Sun evening, Mon) including children's choices and daily specials, good range of coffees, friendly attentive service; pub games including table skittles, popular live music first Mon of month, free wi-fi; big garden with play equipment, goats, chickens and ducks, closed Mon lunchtime, otherwise open all day. *(John Allman)*

WARESLEY   TL2454
Duncombe Arms   (01767) 650265

Eltisley Road (B1040, 5 miles S of A428); SG19 3BS Comfortable and welcoming old pub under new management; long main bar with fire at one end, popular food (not Sun evening, Mon) cooked by landlord-chef from bar snacks and sandwiches up, Greene King ales, prompt cheerful service, back room and restaurant; children welcome, picnic-sets in shrub-sheltered garden, open all day weekends. *(Margaret and Roy Randle, Richard Kennell)*

WHITTLESFORD   TL4648
Bees in the Wall   (01223) 834289

North Road; handy for M11 junction 10 and IWM Duxford; CB22 4NZ Village-edge local with comfortably worn-in split-level timbered lounge, polished tables and country prints, small tiled public bar with old wall settles, darts, decent good value food from shortish menu, well kept Adnams Lighthouse and one or two guests, open fires; background and live music including folk club second Tues of month, small TV for major sporting events; children welcome, no dogs, picnic-sets in big paddock-style garden with terrace, bees still in the wall (here since the 1950s), closed all day Mon, lunchtimes Tues-Thurs (and Sat in winter), no food Sun evening or Tues. *(Brian and Sally Wakeham)*

Cheshire

ALDFORD   SJ4259   Map 7

Grosvenor Arms ★ 🍽️ 🍷 🍺

(01244) 620228 – www.brunningandprice.co.uk/grosvenorarms
B5130 Chester–Wrexham; CH3 6HJ

Spacious place with impressive range of drinks, wide-ranging imaginative menu, good service, suntrap terrace and garden

Part of the Grosvenor Estate and by the village green, this is a large brick and half-timbered pub with a good mix of customers of all ages. The various rooms have plenty of interest and individuality and a buoyantly chatty atmosphere – and staff are well trained and attentive. Spacious cream-painted areas are sectioned by big knocked-through arches with a variety of floor finishes (wood, quarry tiles, flagstones, black and white tiles), and the richly coloured turkish rugs look well against these natural materials. Good solid pieces of traditional furniture, plenty of pictures and attractive lighting keep it all intimate. A handsomely boarded panelled room has tall bookshelves lining one wall; good selection of board games. Phoenix Brunning & Price Original, Weetwood Eastgate and guests such as New Plassey Midnight Mild, Sharps Doom Bar and Thwaites Lancaster Bomber are served from a fine-looking bar counter and they offer 20 wines by the glass, over 80 whiskies, 30 gins and distinctive soft drinks such as peach and elderflower cordial and Willington Fruit Farm pressed apple juice. Lovely on summer evenings, the airy terracotta-floored conservatory has lots of gigantic low-hanging flowering baskets and chunky pale wood garden furniture. It opens out to a large elegant suntrap terrace and a neat lawn with picnic-sets.

 Up-to-date food is very good and includes sandwiches, venison, pancetta and shallot meatballs in juniper sauce, king prawn and chorizo salad with roasted cherry tomatoes, squash, aubergine and lentil curry with sultana rice and onion bhaji, steak and haggis burger with coleslaw, apple and whisky chutney and chips, french seafood stew with rouille, moroccan chicken salad with almond, apricot and pomegranate couscous, yoghurt and harissa, and puddings such as crème brûlée and chocolate and mocha pavlova with macadamia brittle. *Benchmark main dish: malaysian fish curry with coconut rice and pak choi £17.00. Two-course evening meal £22.00.*

Brunning & Price ~ Manager Tracey Owen ~ Real ale ~ Open 11-11; 12-10.30 Sun ~ Bar food 12-9 (10 Fri, Sat) ~ Children welcome ~ Dogs allowed in bar ~ Wi-fi
Recommended by Clive Watkin, John and Mary Warner, W K Wood, Aiden, Nick Sharpe

ALLOSTOCK   SJ7271 Map 7

Three Greyhounds Inn 🏅 ♀

(01565) 723455 – www.thethreegreyhoundsinn.co.uk

4.7 miles from M6 junction 18: A54 E then forking left on B5803 into Holmes Chapel,
left at roundabout on to A50 for 2 miles, then left on to B5082 towards Northwich;
Holmes Chapel Road; WA16 9JY

Relaxing, civilised and welcoming, with enjoyable food
and drink all day

The rooms are interconnected by open doorways and décor throughout
is restful: thick rugs on quarry tiles or bare boards, candles and soft
lighting, dark grey walls (or interesting woven wooden ones made from
old brandy barrels) hung with modern black-on-white prints. There's an
appealing variety of wooden dining chairs, cushioned wall seats, little stools
and plenty of plump purple scatter cushions around all sorts of tables – do
note the one made from giant bellows. A smashing choice of drinks includes
12 interesting wines by the glass, 50 brandies, a farm cider and Caledonian
Byley Bomber and Weetwood Three Greyhounds (named for the pub) plus
quickly changing guests such as Caledonian Deuchars IPA, Dunham Massey
Little Bollington Bitter and Tatton Red Red Rye on handpump; unobtrusive
background music. Above the old farm barns is a restored private dining and
party room called the Old Dog House. The big side lawn has picnic-table sets
under parasols, with more tables on a decked side verandah with a Perspex
roof. Shakerley Mere nature reserve is just across the road. The pub is owned
by Tim Bird and Mary McLaughlin.

 Imaginative food includes sandwiches, potted rabbit with pickled rhubarb,
yorkshire pudding stuffed with devilled lambs kidneys and apple jam, sharing
plates, halloumi and portobello mushroom burger with red onion marmalade, beer-
battered haddock and chips, chicken, coconut and tamarind curry with walnut and
coriander rice, crispy lamb chop and feta salad with pickled grapes, rosemary and red
wine dressing, and puddings such as milk chocolate cheesecake with malt ice-cream
and hot cross bun bread and butter puddings with vanilla ice-cream. *Benchmark main
dish: chicken, ham, leek and tarragon pie £13.50. Two-course evening meal £20.00.*

Free house ~ Licensee James Griffiths ~ Real ale ~ Open 12-11 (midnight Sat); 12-10.30
Sun ~ Bar food 12-9.15 (9.30 Sat, 8.45 Sun) ~ Children welcome until 7pm ~ Dogs allowed
in bar ~ Wi-fi ~ Live music every second Fri *Recommended by Nick Sharpe, John and Mary
Warner, Dr and Mrs A K Clarke, Brian and Sally Wakeham*

ASTBURY   SJ8461 Map 7

Egerton Arms £ 🛏

(01260) 273946 – www.egertonarms.co.uk

Village signposted off A34 S of Congleton; CW12 4RQ

Cheery pub with popular bar food, four real ales and large garden;
nice bedrooms

In a pretty spot opposite the village church, this popular 16th-c pub is handy
for Little Moreton Hall (National Trust). It's a warmly friendly place with
a hands-on landlord and landlady, and a bustling atmosphere. The cream-
painted rooms are decorated with newspaper cuttings relating to 'Grace' (the
landlady's name), the odd piece of armour, shelves of books and quite a few
mementoes of the Sandow Brothers (one of whom was the landlady's father)
who performed as 'the World's Strongest Youths'. In summer, dried flowers
replace the fire in the big fireplace; background music, games machine and
TV. Robinsons Dizzy Blonde, Double Hop, Unicorn and a guest beer on

handpump, nine wines by the glass, 15 malt whiskies and alcoholic winter warmers. There are picnic-sets on a terrace with more on grass and a gazebo and children's play area.

🍴 Fair priced, tasty food includes sandwiches and baps, duck and orange terrine, breaded prawns in chilli jam, stilton and vegetable crumble, steak and mushroom in ale pudding, salmon with ginger and lime butter, burger with toppings and chips, a choice of roasts, and puddings such as mandarin and chocolate sundae and raspberry bakewell tart. *Benchmark main dish: chilli con carne £10.95. Two-course evening meal £16.00.*

Robinsons ~ Tenants Allen and Grace Smith ~ Real ale ~ Open 11.30-11 (10.30 Sun) ~ Bar food 11.30-2, 6-9; 12-8 Sun ~ Restaurant ~ Children welcome ~ Wi-fi ~ Bedrooms: £60/£70
Recommended by Anne Taylor, Paul Matthews, Lionel Smith

ASTON
Bhurtpore ★ ♀ 🍷 £
SJ6146 Map 7

(01270) 780917 – www.bhurtpore.co.uk
Off A530 SW of Nantwich; in village follow Wrenbury signpost; CW5 8DQ

Fantastic range of drinks (especially real ales) in warm-hearted pub with some unusual artefacts; big garden

Enthusiastic customers come here on a regular basis to try the ever-changing range of around 11 real ales sourced from all over the country. Examples include Abbeydale A Chocwork Orange, Acorn Drop Kick, Burton Bridge Spring Ale, Cheshire Brewhouse TRYPA, Copper Dragon Golden Pippin, Hobsons Shropshire Stout, Ossett Citra, Rat Bohemian Ratsody, Salopian Lemon Dream, Three Tuns Clerics Cure and a changing guest from Derby. They also stock dozens of unusual bottled beers and fruit beers, a great many bottled ciders and perries and farm cider, over 100 different whiskies, 43 gins, 20 vodkas, carefully selected soft drinks and 14 wines from a good list; summer beer festival. The pub name commemorates the siege of Bhurtpore (a town in India) during which local landowner Sir Stapleton Cotton (later Viscount Combermere) was commander-in-chief. The connection with India also explains some of the quirky artefacts in the carpeted lounge bar – look out for the sunglasses-wearing turbanned figure behind the counter; also good local period photographs and some attractive furniture in the comfortable public bar; board games, pool, TV and games machine. Weekends tend to be pretty busy.

🍴 As well as their popular half a dozen curries, the tasty food includes sandwiches, pigeon breast with redcurrant sauce, smoked haddock pancake with leek and cheese sauce, salmon fillet with spinach cream in a pastry case with white wine sauce, venison haunch with pancetta, mushrooms and rosemary potatoes, chicken in stilton and smoked bacon sauce, and puddings such as salted caramel cheesecake and raspberry crème brûlée. *Benchmark main dish: steak and kidney in ale pie £10.75. Two-course evening meal £16.00.*

Free house ~ Licensee Simon George ~ Real ale ~ Open 12-11.30 (midnight Fri, Sat); 12-11 Sun ~ Bar food 12-2, 5.30-9.30 (8.30 Mon); 12-9.30 Fri, Sat; 12-8.30 Sun ~ Restaurant ~ Children welcome ~ Dogs allowed in bar ~ Wi-fi *Recommended by Nick Sharpe, Jo Garnett, Andrew Vincent, Thomas Green*

A star symbol after the name of a pub shows exceptional character and appeal. It doesn't mean extra comfort. And it's nothing to do with exceptional food quality, for which there's a separate star-on-a-plate symbol. Even quite a basic pub can win a star, if it's individual enough.

BARTHOMLEY

SJ7752 Map 7

White Lion £

(01270) 882242 – www.whitelionbarthomley.co.uk

M6 junction 16, B5078 N towards Alsager, then Barthomley signed on left; CW2 5PG

Timeless 17th-c thatched village tavern with classic period interior, up to half a dozen real ales and good value lunchtime food

---

This charming black and white tavern is very much part of the local community and popular with a good mix of people – it's also one of the most attractive buildings in a pretty village. The bar has a blazing open fire, heavy oak beams dating from Stuart times, attractively moulded black panelling, Cheshire prints on the walls, latticed windows and uneven wobbly old tables. Up some steps, a second room has another welcoming open fire, more oak panelling, a high-backed winged settle and a paraffin lamp hinged to the wall; shove-ha'penny; local societies make good use of a third room. Banks's Bitter, Jennings Cocker Hoop and Sneck Lifter, Marstons Burton Bitter and Pedigree and Sunbeam Best Bitter on handpump served by genuinely friendly staff. The gents' are across an open courtyard. In summer, seats on cobbles outside offer nice village views and the early 15th-c red sandstone church of St Bertoline (where you can learn about the Barthomley massacre) is worth a visit.

Fine value, lunchtime-only food includes sandwiches and baguettes, cottage pie, hotpots, sausage and mash with onion gravy, a changing pasta dish, and puddings such as fruit crumble and bread and butter pudding. *Benchmark main dish: steak in ale pie £7.95.*

Marstons ~ Tenant Peter Butler ~ Real ale ~ Open 11.30-11 (10.30 Sun) ~ Bar food 12-2 Mon, Tues; 12-3 Weds-Sun ~ Children welcome away from bar counter ~ Dogs allowed in bar ~ Wi-fi *Recommended by Dr W I C Clark, Nick Sharpe, Charlie May, Mike Swan*

BOSTOCK GREEN

SJ6769 Map 7

Hayhurst Arms ♀ 🍺

(01606) 541810 – www.brunningandprice.co.uk/hayhurstarms

London Road, Bostock Green; CW10 9JP

Interesting pub with a marvellous choice of drinks, a wide choice of rewarding food, friendly staff and seats outside

---

Cleverly renovated to incorporate the former stables and coach house, this is a handsome pub with lots to look at inside. The long main bar is divided into different dining areas by elegant support pillars, and it's light and airy throughout: big windows, house plants, bookshelves, standard lamps, metal chandeliers and prints, old photographs and paintings arranged frame-to-frame above wooden dados. The varied dark wooden dining chairs are grouped around tables of all sizes on rugs, quarry tiles, wide floorboards and carpet, and three open fireplaces have big mirrors above, with hefty leather armchairs to the sides. A couple of cosier rooms lead off; background music and board games. Phoenix Brunning & Price Original and Weetwood Eastgate Ale, with guests such as Cwrw lal Limestone Cowboy, Mobberley Maori and Sandstone Desert Dragon, Mild and Onyx on handpump, 25 wines by the glass, 70 malt whiskies and 25 gins; staff are efficient and courteous. The outside terrace has good quality tables and chairs under parasols, and the village green opposite has swings and a play tractor.

From a creative menu, the fine food includes sandwiches, air-dried beef with pickled radishes and mustard mayonnaise, parmesan and herb gnocchi with shallot purée, wild mushroom and leek quiche, lime and lemongrass chicken thighs with thai curry sauce, steak in ale pudding, bass fillets with roasted fennel and gazpacho sauce, shredded duck leg confit with pickled candied beetroot and bulgar wheat, and puddings such as treacle tart with liquorice and blackcurrant ice-cream and blackberry and apple fool. *Benchmark main dish: steak burger with toppings and chips £12.45. Two-course evening meal £20.00.*

Brunning & Price ~ Manager Christopher Beswick ~ Real ale ~ Open 11-11 (10.30 Sun) ~ Bar food 12-10 (9.30 Sun) ~ Children welcome ~ Dogs allowed in bar ~ Wi-fi
Recommended by Peter Pilbeam, Lindy Andrews, Katherine Matthews, Barbara Brown

BUNBURY
Dysart Arms 🍴⭐ ♀ 🍺

SJ5658   Map 7

(01829) 260183 – www.brunningandprice.co.uk/dysart
Bowes Gate Road; village signposted off A51 NW of Nantwich; and from A49 S of Tarporley – coming in this way on northernmost village access road, bear left in village centre; CW6 9PH

Civilised chatty dining pub with thoughtfully laid-out rooms, enjoyable food and a lovely garden with pretty views

Although the interior has been opened up here, the neatly kept rooms still retain a cottagey feel as they ramble around the pleasantly lit central bar. Cream walls keep it light, clean and airy, with deep venetian-red ceilings adding cosiness. Each room (some with good winter fires) is nicely furnished with an appealing variety of well spaced sturdy wooden tables and chairs, a couple of tall filled bookcases and just the right amount of carefully chosen bric-a-brac, properly lit pictures and plants. Flooring ranges from red and black tiles to stripped boards and some carpet. Phoenix Brunning & Price Original and Weetwood Best Bitter with guests such as Copper Dragon Best Bitter and Ossett Elizabeth Rose on handpump alongside a good selection of 17 wines by the glass and around 20 malts; background music and board games. There are sturdy wooden tables on the terrace and picnic-sets on the lawn in the neatly kept and slightly elevated garden, and the views of the splendid church at the end of this pretty village and the distant Peckforton Hills beyond are lovely.

 Appealing food includes sandwiches, thai crab cakes with pickled ginger and chilli jam, spiced falafel with mint, chilli and cucumber salad and coriander yoghurt, indonesian fish curry with spiced potato cake and coconut king prawn gado-gado, thyme-roast chicken breast with creamed cabbage and bacon and caramelised shallots, minted lamb rump on braised gem with broad bean, and feta salad and wild garlic dressing, and puddings such as pear and frangipane tart with cinnamon ice-cream and warm chocolate and mascarpone cake with peanut butter ice-cream and fruit jellies. *Benchmark main dish: fish pie £13.95. Two-course evening meal £20.00.*

Brunning & Price ~ Manager Kate John ~ Real ale ~ Open 11.30-11; 12-10.30 Sun ~ Bar food 12-9.30 (9 Sun) ~ Children welcome ~ Dogs allowed in bar ~ Wi-fi
Recommended by Edward May, Emma Scofield, Mary Joyce, Tony Smaithe

BURLEYDAM
Combermere Arms 🍴⭐ 🍺

SJ6042   Map 7

(01948) 871223 – www.brunningandprice.co.uk/combermere
A525 Whitchurch–Audlem; SY13 4AT

Roomy and attractive beamed pub successfully mixing a good drinking side with imaginative all-day food

There are plenty of nooks and crannies in this partly 16th-c pub that's been cleverly extended without losing its character. The many rambling yet intimate-feeling rooms are attractive and understated and filled with all sorts of antique cushioned dining chairs around dark wood tables, rugs on wood (some old, some new oak) and stone floors, prints hung frame-to-frame on cream walls, bookshelves, deep red ceilings, panelling and open fires. Phoenix Brunning & Price Original and Weetwood Cheshire Cat Blonde Ale and guests such as Acorn Barnsley Bitter, Copper Dragon Golden Pippin, Sharps Doom Bar and Timothy Taylors Boltmaker on handpump, 100 malt whiskies, 20 wines by the glass from an extensive list and three farm ciders; board games and background music. Outside there are good solid wood tables and picnic-sets in a pretty, well tended garden.

 Good, brasserie-style food includes sandwiches, shropshire blue fritter with apple and celery salad and beetroot relish, potted salmon and smoked mackerel with caper butter and pickled vegetables, cauliflower, chickpea and apricot tagine with lemon and coriander couscous, pork and black pudding sausages with onion gravy, tempura king prawns with pineapple, water melon, coconut and toasted cashew salad, seared duck with duck croquette and clementine purée, and puddings such as sticky toffee pudding with toffee sauce and crème brûlée. *Benchmark main dish: crispy beef salad £12.95. Two-course evening meal £20.00.*

Brunning & Price ~ Manager Lisa Hares ~ Real ale ~ Open 11-11 ~ Bar food 12-10 (9 Sun) ~ Children welcome ~ Dogs allowed in bar ~ Wi-fi *Recommended by John and Mary Warner, Dr Simon Innes, Dr and Mrs A K Clarke*

BURWARDSLEY
Pheasant ★ 🌟 ⚲ 🛏

SJ5256 Map 7

(01829) 770434 – www.thepheasantinn.co.uk

Higher Burwardsley; signposted from Tattenhall (which itself is signposted off A41 S of Chester) and from Harthill (reached by turning off A534 Nantwich–Holt at the Copper Mine); follow pub's signpost up hill from Post Office; OS Sheet 117 map reference 523566; CH3 9PF

Cheshire Dining Pub of the Year

Fantastic views and enjoyable food at this clever conversion of an old heavily beamed inn; good bedrooms

The comfortable, character bedrooms here are in the main building or ivy-clad stable wing and make a great base for exploring the area. The attractive low-beamed interior is airy and modern-feeling in parts, and the various separate areas have nice old chairs spread spaciously on wooden floors and a log fire in a huge see-through fireplace. Local Weetwood Best and Eastgate plus guests such as Cheshire Brew Brothers Chester Gold and Weetwood Cheshire Cat Blonde Ale on handpump, 13 wines by the glass, ten malt whiskies and local farm cider served by friendly, helpful staff; quiet background music and daily newspapers. From picnic-sets on the terrace, you can enjoy one of the county's most magnificent views right across the Cheshire plains; on a clear day with the telescope you can see as far as the pier head and cathedrals in Liverpool. There are some lovely surrounding walks and the scenic Sandstone Trail along the Peckforton Hills is nearby. Sister pubs are the Fishpool in Delamere and Bears Paw in Warmingham.

Interesting food includes sandwiches (until 6pm), smoked guinea fowl, ham hock and leek terrine with piccalilli, smoked haddock and chive fishcake with creamed leeks and horseradish mayonnaise, sharing boards, a pie of the day, vegetable burger with toppings and chips, chicken kiev with parmesan and truffle gnocchi, crispy skin and cabbage and smoked pancetta, pork tenderloin with carbonnade sauce, five-spice glazed pak choi and honey and sesame dressing, and puddings such as treacle tart with candied orange and pistachio ice-cream and dark chocolate brownie with griottine cherries and amaretto ice-cream. *Benchmark main dish: pheasant with smoked bacon, butternut squash gratin, chestnuts, blackberry jam and sage fritters £14.50. Two-course evening meal £22.00.*

Free house ~ Licensee Andrew Nelson ~ Real ale ~ Open 11-11 (10.30 Sun) ~ Bar food 12-9.30 (10 Fri, Sat; 9 Sun) ~ Restaurant ~ Children welcome ~ Dogs welcome ~ Wi-fi ~ Bedrooms: £100/£110 *Recommended by Hilary and Neil Christopher, R T and J C Moggridge, Toby Jones, Peter Harrison*

CHESTER
Albion ★ ⬤ £
SJ4066 Map 7

(01244) 340345 – www.albioninnchester.co.uk
Albion Street; CH1 1RQ

Strongly traditional pub with comfortable Edwardian décor and captivating World War I memorabilia; pubby food and good drinks

For over 40 years, the charming licensees here have amassed an absorbing collection of World War I memorabilia; in fact, this is an officially listed site of four war memorials to soldiers from the Cheshire Regiment. It's a genuinely friendly, old-fashioned pub and the peaceful rooms are filled with big engravings of men leaving for war and similarly moving prints of wounded veterans, as well as flags, advertisements and so on. There are also leatherette and hoop-backed chairs around cast-iron-framed tables, lamps, an open fire in the Edwardian fireplace and dark floral William Morris wallpaper (designed on the first day of World War I). You might even be lucky enough to hear the vintage 1928 Steck pianola being played; there's an attractive side dining room too. Big Rock Harvest Pale Ale, Moorhouses Pride of Pendle and Weetwood Cheshire Cat Blonde Ale on handpump, new world wines, fresh orange juice, organic bottled cider and fruit juice, over 25 malt whiskies and a good selection of rums and gins. Bedrooms are small but comfortable and furnished in keeping with the pub's style (free parking for residents and a bottle of house wine if dining). An attractive way to reach the place is along the city wall, coming down at Newgate/Wolfsgate and walking along Park Street. No children. Please note: if the pub is quiet they may close early, so it's best to ring ahead and check.

The generously served 'trench rations' include club and doorstep sandwiches, corned beef hash with pickled red cabbage, fish pie with cheese topping, boiled gammon and pease pudding with parsley sauce, haggis and tatties, and lambs liver, bacon and onions with cider gravy. *Benchmark main dish: cottage pie £9.90. Two-course evening meal £15.00.*

Punch ~ Lease Mike and Christina Mercer ~ Real ale ~ No credit cards ~ Open 12-3, 5 (6 Sat)-11; 12-2.30 Sun ~ Bar food 12-2, 5-8 (8.30 Sat) ~ Restaurant ~ Dogs allowed in bar ~ Bedrooms: £80/£90 *Recommended by Dr J Barrie Jones, John Beeken*

CHESTER
Architect ⭐ ♀ ⬤
SJ4066 Map 7

(01244) 353070 – www.brunningandprice.co.uk/architect
Nicholas Street (A5268); CH1 2NX

Busy pub by the racecourse with interesting furnishings and décor, attentive staff, a good choice of drinks and super food

This lively establishment is almost two separate places connected by a glass passage. The pubbiest part, with a more bustling feel, is the garden room where they serve Phoenix Brunning & Price Original and Weetwood Eastgate alongside guests such as Barngates Pale, Cheshire Brewhouse Cheshire Set, Peerless Pale, Salopian Hop Twister and Titanic Plum Porter on handpump, 18 wines by the glass, 74 whiskies and farm cider. Throughout there are elegant antique dining chairs around a mix of nice old tables on rugs or bare floorboards, hundreds of interesting paintings and prints on green, cream or yellow walls, house plants and flowers on windowsills and mantelpieces, and lots of bookcases. Also, open fires, armchairs in front of a woodburning stove or tucked into cosy nooks, candelabra and big mirrors, and a friendly, easy-going atmosphere; background music and board games. Big windows and french doors look over the terrace, where there are plenty of good quality wooden seats and tables under parasols. There are views over Roodee Racecourse (binoculars are provided).

Very good, interesting food includes sandwiches, cured salmon with fennel salad and beetroot pannacotta, baked camembert with candied walnuts and spiced carrot and apricot compote, wild mushroom tortellini with sage butter, honey-roast ham with free-range eggs, steak in ale pudding, bass fillet with crab and chilli butter, golden beetroot and samphire, and puddings such as rhubarb jelly with set vanilla cream and chocolate tart with candied orange peel and clotted cream. *Benchmark main dish: braised lamb shoulder with dauphinoise potatoes and gravy £17.75. Two-course evening meal £22.00.*

Brunning & Price ~ Manager Natalie Shaw ~ Real ale ~ Open 10.30am-11pm; 10.30-10.30 Sun ~ Bar food 12-10 (9.30 Sun) ~ Children welcome ~ Dogs allowed in bar ~ Wi-fi
Recommended by Edward Mirzoeff, Peter Pilbeam, Martinthehills, Sophie Ellison

CHESTER

Mill 🍺 £

SJ4166 Map 7

(01244) 350035 – www.millhotel.com
Milton Street; CH1 3NF

Big hotel with huge range of real ales, good value food and cheery service in sizeable bar; bedrooms

It's quite a surprise to find this modern, canalside hotel carries at least ten (and up to 16) real ales on handpump and they get through more than 2,000 guest ales a year. Weetwood Best and Mill Premium (brewed for them by Coach House) are available all the time, with guests such as Castle Rock Harvest Pale, Cheshire Brewhouse Cheshire Pride, Coach House Premium Bitter, Greene King Old Speckled Hen, Oakham JHB, Titanic Atlantic Red and Raspberry Wheat, and Yorkshire Brewing Pilots Pride Bitter; also, a dozen wines by the glass, two farm ciders and 20 malt whiskies. You'll find a real mix of customers in the neatly kept bar which has some exposed brickwork and supporting pillars, local photographs on cream-papered walls, contemporary seats around marble-topped tables on light wooden flooring, and helpful, friendly staff. One comfortable area is reminiscent of a bar on a cruise liner; quiet background music and unobtrusively placed big-screen sports TV. Converted from an old mill, the hotel straddles either side of the Shropshire Union Canal, with a glassed-in bridge connecting the two sections. The bedrooms are comfortable and rather smart.

There are several different menus, but the bar food includes sandwiches, chicken caesar salad, steak burger with coleslaw and home-made chips, vegetarian lasagne and steak and mushroom in ale pie; more elaborate dishes include smoked salmon with a toasted muffin, poached egg and hollandaise, breadcrumbed chicken stuffed with brie, leek and pine nuts in creamy tarragon sauce, and baked cod in creamy spinach sauce topped with a scallop; puddings include raspberry crème brûlée and lemon sponge pudding. *Benchmark main dish: beer-battered fish and chips £7.50. Two-course evening meal £18.00.*

Free house ~ Licensee Gordon Vickers ~ Real ale ~ Open 10am-midnight (11pm Sun) ~ Bar food 11.30-11; 12-10 Sun ~ Restaurant ~ Children welcome ~ Wi-fi ~ Live jazz Mon ~ Bedrooms: £74/£98 *Recommended by Peter Brix, John Harris, John Wooll*

CHESTER
Old Harkers Arms ♀ ◖

SJ4166 Map 7

(01244) 344525 – www.brunningandprice.co.uk/harkers
Russell Street, down steps off City Road where it crosses canal; CH3 5AL

Well run canalside building with a lively atmosphere, fantastic range of drinks and extremely good food

You can watch boats on the Shropshire Union Canal next to this cleverly converted warehouse from the tall windows that run the length of the main bar. The striking industrial interior with its high ceilings is divided into user-friendly spaces by brick pillars. Walls are covered with old prints hung frame-to-frame, there's a wall of bookshelves above a leather banquette at one end, the mixed dark wood furniture is set out in intimate groups on stripped-wood floors and attractive lamps lend some cosiness; board games. Cheerful staff serve Phoenix Brunning & Price Original and Weetwood Cheshire Cat Blonde Ale with guests such as Acorn Blonde, Titanic Plum Porter and Woodfordes Norfolk Nog on handpump, 120 malt whiskies, 20 wines from a well described list and six farm ciders.

Appealing food includes sandwiches, potted sea trout with pickled cucumber salad, spiced chickpea and beetroot spring roll with mint yoghurt and sweet chilli sauce, sausages with onion gravy, steak burger with toppings, coleslaw and chips, vietnamese noodle salad with tofu, grilled papaya, peanuts and lime and chilli dressing, duck breast with honey and mustard carrots and blackberry sauce, and puddings such as crème brûlée and salted caramel tart with caramelised banana and pistachio praline cream. *Benchmark main dish: steak in ale pudding £13.95. Two-course evening meal £19.95.*

Brunning & Price ~ Manager Paul Jeffery ~ Real ale ~ Open 10.30am-11pm; 12-10.30 Sun ~ Bar food 12-9.30 ~ Children welcome but no babies, toddlers or pushchairs ~ Dogs allowed in bar ~ Wi-fi *Recommended by Dr Kevan Tucker, Simon Collett-Jones, John Beeken, Jeremy Snaithe*

CHOLMONDELEY
Cholmondeley Arms ✪ ♀ 🛏

SJ5550 Map 7

(01829) 720300 – www.cholmondeleyarms.co.uk
Bickley Moss; A49 5.5 miles N of Whitchurch; SY14 8HN

Former schoolhouse with a decent range of real ales and wines, well presented food and sizeable garden; bedrooms

This interestingly converted schoolhouse has bar rooms with lofty ceilings and tall Victorian windows plus huge old radiators and school paraphernalia (hockey sticks, tennis rackets, trunks and so forth). There's a lot of individuality such as armchairs by the fire with a massive stag's head above, big mirrors, all sorts of dining chairs and tables, warmly coloured rugs on bare boards, fresh flowers and church candles; background music. Cholmondeley Best (from Weetwood) and three guests such as Big Shed

Engineers Best, Coach House Gunpowder Strong Mild, Wincle Sir Philip and York Pure Gold on handpump, 15 wines by the glass and an amazing range of 366 gins. There's plenty of seating on the sizeable lawn, which drifts off into open countryside, with more in front overlooking the quiet road. The bedrooms are in the old headmaster's house opposite and named after real and fictional teachers; the pictures dotted about actually did belong to former headmasters. Cholmondeley Castle Gardens are nearby. The pub is owned by Tim Bird and Mary McLaughlin, who also own the Three Greyhounds in Allostock, Bulls Head and Church Inn in Mobberley (all in Cheshire), Fitzherbert Arms in Swynnerton (Staffordshire) and the Red Lion in Weymouth (Dorset).

 Highly rewarding food includes lunchtime sandwiches, field mushrooms with white wine, cream and shallots, potted ham hock with tarragon butter, apple and radish salad and piccalilli dressing, asparagus, broad bean and feta tart with caramelised shallot salad, chicken breast stuffed with red pepper and air-dried ham with sweetcorn and butternut squash chowder, spiced hake fillet with roasted sweet potato, aubergine and spinach and mango and coriander cream sauce, and puddings such as dark chocolate cheesecake with cherry and port compote and sticky toffee pudding with rum and raisin ice-cream. *Benchmark main dish: steak and kidney pie £13.95. Two-course evening meal £19.00.*

Free house ~ Licensee Jessica Turner ~ Real ale ~ Open 12-11 (11.30 Fri, Sat) ~ Bar food 12-9.30 (9.45 Fri, Sat) ~ No under-10s after 7pm ~ Dogs welcome ~ Wi-fi ~ Bedrooms: £85/£100 *Recommended by Ray and Winifred Halliday, Dr and Mrs A K Clarke, Peter Harrison, R T and J C Moggridge, Roger and Anne Newbury*

COTEBROOK
SJ5765 Map 7
Fox & Barrel 🅰️ ♟
(01829) 760529 ~ www.foxandbarrel.co.uk
A49 NE of Tarporley; CW6 9DZ

Attractive building with stylishly airy décor, an enterprising menu and good wines

Food here is excellent and, of course, many customers are here to dine, but they do have high chairs against the bar counter and cushioned benches and settles where drinkers feel quite at home. Friendly staff serve Caledonian Deuchars IPA, Weetwood Eastgate and a couple of guests such as Black Sheep Golden Sheep and Wincle Lord Lucan on handpump; they also have 16 wines by the glass from a good list. A big log fire dominates the bar while a larger uncluttered beamed dining area has attractive rugs and an eclectic mix of period tables on polished floorboards, with extensive wall panelling hung with framed old prints. The front terrace has plenty of smart tables and chairs under parasols; at the back, there are picnic-sets on grass and some nice old fruit trees. There's a big new car park at the front.

 The confidently cooked food includes sandwiches, crispy chicken wings with dhal, spiced onions and yoghurt, home-cured salmon with whipped avocado, crayfish and tomato, chickpea, spinach and aubergine moussaka, pheasant suet pudding, omelette arnold bennett, cornish sole with brown shrimp butter, slow-roast pork belly with home-made black pudding, apple and potato confit, and puddings such as crème brûlée with raspberry confit and chocolate, cherry and almond mousse. *Benchmark main dish: beer-battered fish and chips £13.95. Two-course evening meal £21.00.*

Free house ~ Licensee Gary Kidd ~ Real ale ~ Open 12-11 (10.30 Sun) ~ Bar food 12-9.30 (9 Sun) ~ Children welcome ~ Dogs allowed in bar ~ Wi-fi *Recommended by Hilary Forrest, John Harris, Charles Fraser, Andrew Vincent*

DELAMERE
Fishpool ♀ ◀

SJ5667 Map 7

(01606) 883277 – www.thefishpoolinn.co.uk
Junction A54/B5152 Chester Road/Fishpool Road, a mile W of A49; CW8 2HP

Something for everyone in extensively interestingly laid-out pub, with a good range of food and drinks served all day

Cleverly and stylishly laid out, this place has plenty of snug, cosy areas leading off a big, cheerful open section with unusual and varied furnishings and décor. A lofty central area, partly skylit – and full of contented diners – has a row of booths facing the long bar counter, and numerous other tables with banquettes or overstuffed small armchairs on pale floorboards laid with rugs; then comes a conservatory overlooking picnic-sets on a flagstone terrace, and a lawn beyond. Off on two sides are many rooms with much lower ceilings, some with heavy dark beams, some with bright polychrome tile or intricate parquet flooring: William Morris wallpaper here, dusky paintwork or neat bookshelves there, sofas, armchairs, a fire in an old-fashioned open range, lots of old prints and some intriguing objects including carved or painted animal skulls; background music. Weetwood Best, Cheshire Cat and Eastgate plus guests such as Wincle Nimrod and Wibbly Wallaby on handpump, 13 wines by the glass, ten malt whiskies and farm cider; unobtrusive background music; upstairs lavatories. Sister pubs are the Pheasant in Burwardsley and the Bears Paw in Warmingham.

Enjoyable food includes sandwiches, crayfish, crab and smoked salmon cocktail, tandoori-spiced lamb koftas with harissa-spiced couscous and tzatziki, sweet potato and blue cheese pithivier with tomato ragoût, roast duck with stir-fried vegetables and plum sauce, lamb, apricot and mint burger with chips and coriander crème fraîche, corn-fed chicken with pancetta, baby onions and wild mushrooms and bordelaise jus, and puddings such as white chocolate and raspberry cheesecake with ginger ice-cream and clementine and whisky brûlée. *Benchmark main dish: pie of the day £13.25. Two-course evening meal £21.00.*

Free house ~ Licensee Andrew Nelson ~ Real ale ~ Open 11-11 ~ Bar food 12-9.30 (10 Fri, Sat); 12-9 Sun ~ Restaurant ~ Children welcome ~ Dogs allowed in bar ~ Wi-fi
Recommended by Lindy Andrews, R T and J C Moggridge, Miles Green, Caroline Sullivan

EATON
Plough 🛏

SJ8765 Map 7

(01260) 280207 – www.theploughinncheshire.com
A536 Congleton–Macclesfield; CW12 2NH

Neat and cosy village pub with up to four interesting beers, bar food, and big attractive garden; good bedrooms

The outside areas behind this friendly village pub really come into their own in warm weather. The big tree-filled garden offers fine views of the fringes of the Peak District, with picnic-sets on a lawn and seats and tables set for dining on a covered decked terrace with heaters. The carefully converted traditional bar has plenty of beams and exposed brickwork, a couple of snug little alcoves, comfortable armchairs and cushioned wooden wall seats on red patterned carpets, long red curtains, leaded windows and a woodburning stove in a big stone fireplace. Storm Desert Storm and Wells Bombardier plus a couple of guest beers such as Cheshire Brewhouse Cheshire Gap and Shepherd Neame Bishops Finger on handpump, ten wines by the glass from a decent list and 20 malt whiskies served by friendly, attentive staff; background music, board games and occasional TV. Moved here piece by piece from its original home in Wales, the heavily raftered barn at the back makes a striking restaurant. The appealingly designed bedrooms are in a converted stable block. Dogs are allowed at the management's discretion.

 Popular food includes sandwiches, confit tuna loin with fennel, radish and broad bean salad and lemon and tarragon dressing, wild mushroom and goats cheese linguine, beer-battered haddock with triple-cooked chips, thai red prawn curry with coconut rice and chopped peanuts, gammon with free-range eggs and pineapple chutney, and puddings such as sherry trifle and white chocolate and raspberry brioche bread and butter pudding; they also offer a two- and three-course set menu. *Benchmark main dish: steak in ale pie £12.95. Two-course evening meal £19.00.*

Free house ~ Licensee Nathan Jordan ~ Real ale ~ Open 12-11 (midnight Sat); 12-10 Sun ~ Bar food 12-9 (8 Sun) ~ Restaurant ~ Children welcome ~ Wi-fi ~ Bedrooms: £60/$75
Recommended by Caroline Prescott, John and Mary Warner, Mark Morgan, Patricia Hawkins

KETTLESHULME

SJ9879   Map 7

Swan 🍴

(01663) 732943
B5470 Macclesfield–Chapel-en-le-Frith, a mile W of Whaley Bridge; SK23 7QU

Charming 16th-c pub with enjoyable food, good beer and an attractive garden

Our readers enjoy their visits to this pretty white cottage very much and return on a regular basis. The interior is snug and cosy, with latticed windows, very low dark beams hung with big copper jugs and kettles, timbered walls, antique coaching and other prints and maps, ancient oak settles on a turkish carpet and log fires; the dining room has an open kitchen. Marstons Bitter on handpump with a couple of guest beers from breweries such as Phoenix and Whim, and 12 wines by the glass served by courteous, friendly staff. The front terrace has teak tables, another two-level terrace has further tables and steamer benches under parasols, and there's a sizeable streamside garden. The pub is handy for walks in the relatively unfrequented north-west part of the Peak District National Park.

🌟 Well thought-of food includes sandwiches, moules marinière, a daily vegetarian risotto, sausages with onion gravy, beef and stilton pudding, red thai chicken with lemongrass and lime leaves, langoustines with fennel and Pernod, steaks from their Josper oven, and puddings such as chocolate brownie and sticky toffee pudding. *Benchmark main dish: daily changing fish dishes £15.00. Two-course evening meal £21.00.*

Free house ~ Licensee Robert Cloughley ~ Real ale ~ Open 12-11 (midnight Sat); 12-10.30 Sun; closed Mon lunchtime ~ Bar food 12-9; 12-4 Sun; no food Mon ~ Restaurant ~ Children welcome ~ Dogs allowed in bar ~ Wi-fi *Recommended by David Heath, Alan Smith, Mary Joyce*

MACCLESFIELD

SJ9271   Map 7

Sutton Hall

(01260) 253211 – www.brunningandprice.co.uk/suttonhall
Leaving Macclesfield southwards on A523, turn left into Byrons Lane signposted Langley, Wincle, then just before canal viaduct fork right into Bullocks Lane; OS Sheet 118 map reference 925715; SK11 0HE

Historic building set in attractive grounds, with a fine range of drinks and well trained, courteous staff

Nearly 500 years ago, this was a manor house. It's now a busy pub and some of the remaining original features have been carefully restored to blend cleverly with up-to-date touches; the hall at the heart of the building is especially noteworthy – in particular the entrance space. There's a charming series of rooms (a bar, a library with books on shelves and a raised open fire and dining areas) divided by tall oak timbers: antique oak panelling, warmly coloured rugs on broad flagstones, bare boards and tiles, lots of pictures placed frame-to-frame, and two more fires. Background music and board games. The atmosphere is nicely relaxed and a good range of drinks includes Phoenix Brunning & Price Original plus Beartown Bearly Literate, Conwy Riptide, Weetwood Eastgate and Wincle Lord Lucan on handpump, 18 wines by the glass from an extensive list, 65 malt whiskies and 30 gins; service is attentive and friendly. The pretty gardens have spaciously laid-out tables (some on their own little terraces), sloping lawns and fine mature trees.

Modern, brasserie-style food includes sandwiches, thai-style potted fish with mango and ginger relish, wild mushrooms with poached egg and truffle oil on a brioche croute, crispy duck salad with hoisin, watermelon and chilli cashews, steak in ale pudding, baby squid and king prawns with chorizo, garlic and spicy chickpea salad, venison haunch with red wine jus, rosemary and garlic chicken with wild mushrooms, bacon, spinach and pasta, and puddings such as crème brûlée and rhubarb and custard tart with ginger mascarpone. *Benchmark main dish: beer-battered haddock and chips £12.95. Two-course evening meal £18.50.*

Brunning & Price ~ Manager Syd Foster ~ Real ale ~ Open 11-11 (10.30 Sun) ~ Bar food 12-10 (9.30 Sun) ~ Restaurant ~ Children welcome ~ Dogs allowed in bar ~ Wi-fi
Recommended by Hilary Forrest, Edward May, Jack and Hilary Burton, Brian and Sally Wakeham

MARTON
SJ8568 Map 7

Davenport Arms 🍺 £

(01260) 224269 – www.thedavenportarms.co.uk
A34 N of Congleton; SK11 9HF

Handsome pub with welcoming bar, comfortable restaurant, good food and drink, and good-sized sheltered garden

This former 18th-c farmhouse has two linked front bar rooms with a good traditional feel. There are comfortably cushioned wall settles, wing armchairs and other hand-picked furnishings on patterned carpet, a woodburning stove, a ticking clock, old prints on the cream walls and colourful jugs hanging from sturdy beams. You can eat (or just have a drink or coffee), and there's also a pleasantly light and airy more formal dining area behind; background music. Courage Directors, Theakstons Black Bull and a couple of guests such as Front Row Sin Bin and Storm Beauforts Ale on handpump, ten wines by the glass and friendly, helpful staff. Outside is a terrace with metal garden furniture, a fairy-lit arbour and a timber shelter, well spaced picnic-sets and a set of swings in the garden beyond, and a substantial separate play area. They take caravans but you must book. Do visit the 14th-c timbered church opposite.

Tasty food includes lunchtime baguettes and ciabattas, home-made giant black pudding scotch egg with grain mustard mayonnaise, baked mini camembert with red onion marmalade, chargrilled mediterranean vegetables with pasta and red pesto sauce, gammon with egg or pineapple, beer-battered fresh haddock and chips, a pie of the day, honey duck breast on gnocchi with teriyaki dipping sauce, and puddings; Tuesday is curry night. *Benchmark main dish: spare ribs in sticky barbecue sauce with coleslaw and chips £15.95. Two-course evening meal £19.00.*

Free house ~ Licensees Ron Dalton and Sara Griffith ~ Real ale ~ Open 12-2.30, 6-11; 12-11 Sat, Sun; closed Mon lunchtime except bank holidays ~ Bar food 12-2.30, 6-9; 12-9 Sat; 12-8 Sun ~ Restaurant ~ Children welcome but not in restaurant after 8pm ~ Wi-fi
Recommended by Jo Garnett, Mungo Shipley, Diane Abbott

MOBBERLEY

SJ7879   Map 7

Bulls Head 🍴 ♀ 🍺

(01565) 873395 – www.thebullsheadpub.co.uk
Mill Lane; WA16 7HX

Terrific all-rounder with interesting food and drink and plenty of pubby character

They hold live music twice a month in this particularly well run, friendly pub plus quiz evenings and themed food events – it's worth checking their website regularly. There's always a good mix of both locals and visitors and the whole place has been kept nice and pubby with just a touch of modernity. A fine range of drinks includes Wincle White Bull (named for the pub) and Weetwood Bulls Head Bitter, Cheshire Cat Blonde Ale and Mobberley Wobbly Ale on handpump, 15 wines by the glass, around 80 whiskies and local gins. Several rooms are furnished quite traditionally, with an unpretentious mix of wooden tables, cushioned wall seats and chairs on fine old quarry tiles, black and pale grey walls contrasting well with warming red lampshades, and pink bare-brick walls and pale stripped-timber detailing; also, lots of mirrors, hops, candles, open fires, background music and board games. Dogs get a warm welcome (they're allowed in the snug) with friendly staff dispensing doggie biscuits from a huge jar, and they keep popular walk leaflets; seats outside in the big garden. The pub is owned by Tim Bird and Mary McLaughlin, who also own three other Cheshire pubs – the Three Greyhounds in Allostock, Cholmondeley Arms in Cholmondeley, Church Inn (in this village) – as well as the Fitzherbert Arms in Swynnerton (Staffordshire) and the Red Lion in Weymouth (Dorset).

 Highly rated food includes sandwiches, seafood crockpot in creamy dill and white wine sauce, coronation chicken salad with mango and roasted red pepper, vegetables in ale pie topped with sweet potato mash, slow-roasted lamb shank in port and redcurrant with honey-roasted vegetables, beer-battered haddock and chips, chicken, smoked bacon and butter bean casserole with chervil and buttermilk dumplings, and puddings such as chocolate brownie with chocolate sauce and white chocolate ice-cream and apple and black cherry crumble with cinnamon ice-cream. *Benchmark main dish: steak in ale pie £13.95. Two-course evening meal £19.00.*

Free house ~ Licensee Barry Lawlor ~ Real ale ~ Open 12-10.30 (11 Weds-Sat); 12-10.30 Sun ~ Bar food 12-9.15 (9.45 Fri, Sat); 12-8.45 Sun ~ Children welcome but no under-10s after 7pm ~ Dogs allowed in bar ~ Wi-fi ~ Live music twice a month *Recommended by Dr and Mrs A K Clarke, Peter Brix, Lindy Andrews, Steve Whalley, Simon Day*

MOBBERLEY

SJ7980   Map 7

Church Inn ★ 🍴 ♀ 🍺

(01565) 873178 – www.churchinnmobberley.co.uk
Brown sign to pub off B5085 on Wilmslow side of village; Church Lane; WA16 7RD

Nicely traditional, friendly country pub with bags of character; good food and drink

The small, snug interconnected rooms in this pretty brick building have all manner of nice old tables and chairs on wide floorboards, low ceilings, plenty of candlelight and friendly young staff; it's best to book in advance to be sure of a table. The décor in soothing greys and dark green, with some oak-leaf wallpaper, is perked up by a collection of stuffed grouse and their relatives, and a huge variety of pictures; background music. Beartown Best Bitter, Mallorys Mobberley Best (George Mallory, lost near Everest's summit in 1924, is remembered in the church with a stained-glass window) and Tatton Church Ale-Alujah and Gold on handpump, and unusual and rewarding wines, with 16 by the glass; wine tastings can be booked in the upstairs private dining room. They give out a detailed leaflet describing a good four-mile circular walk from the pub, passing sister pub the Bulls Head en route. Dogs are welcomed in the bar with not just a tub of snacks on the counter, but maybe even the offer of a meaty 'beer'. The sunny garden snakes down to an old bowling green with lovely pastoral views and a side courtyard has sturdy tables and benches. The village church is opposite. The pub is owned by Tim Bird and Mary McLaughlin, who also own the Three Greyhounds in Allostock, Cholmondeley Arms at Cholmondeley, Bulls Head in this village (all Cheshire), Fitzherbert Arms in Swynnerton (Staffordshire) and the Red Lion in Weymouth (Dorset).

 Using local seasonal produce, the good, interesting food includes lunchtime sandwiches (not Sunday), smoked and poached salmon fishcake with pickled fennel and cucumber salad, horseradish and dill cream, chicken liver parfait with red onion marmalade, sharing boards, cottage pie, feta, roast courgette and pear salad with black olive dressing, steak and marrow burger with toppings and chips, slow-cooked lamb shoulder with watermelon and mixed root vegetables, and puddings such as ginger sponge with toffee sauce and stem ginger ice-cream and tiramisu cheesecake. *Benchmark main dish: slow-cooked pork belly with black pudding and creamed savoy cabbage £15.95. Two-course evening meal £23.00.*

Free house ~ Licensee Simon Umpleby ~ Real ale ~ Open 12-11 (10.30 Sun) ~ Bar food 12-9.15 ~ Children welcome but no under-10s after 6pm ~ Dogs allowed in bar ~ Wi-fi
Recommended by Belinda Stamp, Dr and Mrs A K Clarke, Peter Andrews, Julie Braeburn, Ben and Diane Bowie

MOTTRAM ST ANDREW
Bulls Head 🌟 ♀ 🍺
SJ8878   Map 7

(01625) 828111 – www.brunningandprice.co.uk/bullshead
A538 Prestbury–Wilmslow; Wilmslow Road/Priest Lane; E side of village; SK10 4QH

Superb country dining pub, a thoughtful range of drinks and interesting food, plenty of character and well trained staff

Consistently well run, this is a highly enjoyable pub that our readers regularly return to. There is a bustling bar but perhaps the main emphasis is on the dining areas at the far end. Four levels stack up alongside or above one another, each with a distinctive décor and style, from the informality of a sunken area with rugs on a tiled floor, through a comfortable library/dining room, to another with an upstairs conservatory feel and the last, with higher windows and more of a special-occasion atmosphere. The rest of the pub has an appealing and abundant mix of old prints and pictures, comfortable seating in great variety, a coal fire in one room, a blazing woodburning stove in a two-way fireplace dividing two other rooms and an antique black kitchen range in yet another. Phoenix Brunning & Price Original and Wincle Sir Philip with guests such as Moorhouses White Witch, Pennine Real Blonde and Timothy Taylors Landlord on handpump, around 20 wines by the glass, 50 malt whiskies, 20 gins and several ciders, and an attractive separate tea and coffee station with pretty blue and white china cups, teapots and jugs. Also, background music, daily papers and board games. The lawn has plenty of picnic-sets beneath cocktail parasols.

Excellent food includes sandwiches, pork and chorizo meatballs with arrabiata sauce, scallops with black pudding and apple bonbons, pea purée and lemon oil, spiced black bean burger with chilli pineapple salsa and sweet potato fries, malaysian chicken curry, steak and mushroom in ale pudding, steak burger with toppings, coleslaw and chips, sea bream with crab and dill potato cake and clam salsa verde, and puddings such as sticky toffee pudding with toffee sauce and hot belgian waffle with chocolate sauce. *Benchmark main dish: roast pork belly, braised cheek, fillet and black pudding hash cake with creamed cabbage £16.95. Two-course evening meal £21.00.*

Brunning & Price ~ Manager Andrew Coverley ~ Real ale ~ Open 10.30am-11pm; 12-10.30 Sun ~ Bar food 12-10 (9.30 Sun) ~ Children welcome ~ Dogs allowed in bar ~ Wi-fi
Recommended by Brian and Anna Marsden, W K Wood, Michael Butler, Peter Barrett

NETHER ALDERLEY   SJ8576   Map 7
Wizard

(01625) 584000 – www.ainscoughs.co.uk
B5087 Macclesfield Road, opposite Artists Lane; SK10 4UB

Bustling pub with interesting food, real ales, a friendly welcome and relaxed atmosphere

After a walk along Alderley Edge, head to this enjoyable pub for refreshment. The various rooms, connected by open doorways, are cleverly done up in a mix of modern rustic and traditional styles. There are beams and open fires, antique dining chairs (some prettily cushioned) and settles around all sorts of tables, rugs on pale floorboards, prints and paintings on contemporary paintwork and decorative items ranging from a grandfather clock to staffordshire dogs and modern lampshades. Thwaites Wainwright and a guest from Storm plus Jennings Red Rascal and Wells Bombardier on handpump and quite a few wines by the glass; background music and board games. There are plenty of seats in the sizeable back garden. The pub is part of the Ainscoughs group.

 Offering traditional staples plus seasonal specials, the food includes sandwiches, crispy salt and pepper squid with harissa mayonnaise, local venison and pork scotch egg with redcurrant sauce and pickled cabbage, a curry of the day, cheese pie with triple-cooked chips, beer-battered haddock and chips, maple-glazed pork belly with creamy cider sauce, salmon fillets in a creamy white wine sauce with roasted cherry tomatoes, and puddings such as toffee apple crumble and lemon millefeuille. *Benchmark main dish: steak in ale puddings £15.95. Two-course evening meal £19.00.*

Free house ~ Licensee Stacey Wood ~ Real ale ~ Open 12-10 (12-9 Sun) ~ Bar food 12-2.30, 6-9; 12-9 Sat; 12-8 Sun ~ Children welcome ~ Dogs allowed in bar ~ Wi-fi
Recommended by Anne and Ben Smith, John Harris, Edward and William Johnston, Sandra King

SANDBACH   SJ7560   Map 7
Old Hall ♀ ◖

(01270) 758170 – www.brunningandprice.co.uk/oldhall
1.2 miles from M6 junction 17: A534 – ignore first turn into town and take the second – if you reach the roundabout double back; CW11 1AL

Glorious hall-house with impressive original features, plenty of drinking and dining space, six real ales and imaginative food

This glorious 17th-c manor house is a masterpiece of timbering and fine carved gable-ends. There are many lovely original architectural features, particularly in the room to the left of the entrance hall, which is much as it has been for centuries, with a Jacobean fireplace, oak panelling and priest's hole. This leads into the Oak Room, divided by standing timbers into two dining areas with heavy beams, oak flooring and reclaimed panelling. Other rooms in the original building have hefty beams and oak boards, three open fires and a woodburning stove; the cosy snugs are carpeted. The Garden Room is big and bright, with reclaimed quarry tiling and exposed A-frame oak timbering, and opens on to a suntrap back terrace with teak tables and chairs among flowering tubs. Throughout, the walls are covered with countless interesting prints, there's an appealing collection of antique dining chairs and tables of all sizes, and plenty of rugs, bookcases and plants. From the handsome bar counter, efficient and friendly staff serve Phoenix Brunning & Price Original, Redwillow Feckless and Three Tuns XXX with guests such as Bollington White Nancy, Cheshire Brewhouse Blues Breaker and Titanic Black Ice on handpump, 16 good wines by the glass, 50 malt whiskies, 20 gins and farm cider; board games. There are picnic-sets in front of the building beside rose bushes and clipped box hedging.

 As well as weekend brunches (9-midday), the contemporary brasserie dishes include sandwiches, braised pig cheek with port sauce, chicken liver pâté with plum and ginger chutney, coq au vin, cauliflower, aubergine and dhal with red onion and coriander bhaji, lamb and mint pudding with onion gravy, smoked haddock and salmon fishcakes with tomato salad, duck with duck croquette and clementine purée, and puddings such as pecan pie with cinnamon ice-cream and chocolate and salted caramel tart and raspberry sorbet. *Benchmark main dish: crispy beef salad with satay sauce, pickled ginger and lotus root crisps £13.75. Two-course evening meal £20.00.*

Brunning & Price ~ Manager Chris Button ~ Real ale ~ Open 10.30am-11pm; 9am-11pm Sat; 9am-10.30pm Sun ~ Bar food 12-10 (9.30 Sun) ~ Restaurant ~ Children welcome ~ Dogs allowed in bar ~ Wi-fi ~ Live music last Fri of the month *Recommended by Tracey and Stephen Groves, Mike and Margaret Banks, Jeremy Snaithe, Alf Wright*

SPURSTOW
Yew Tree ★ ⬤ ♀ ◧

SJ5657 Map 7

(01829) 260274 – www.theyewtreebunbury.com
Off A49 S of Tarporley; follow Bunbury 1, Haughton 2 signpost into Long Lane; CW6 9RD

Plenty of individuality, smashing food and drinks and an easy-going atmosphere

An eclectic mix of customers enjoy this entertaining pub which creates a cheerful, informal atmosphere – all helped along by the friendly staff. Throughout, there are prettily cushioned dining chairs and built-in wall seats around all sorts of tables on bare boards, beams and timbering, walls hung with lots of prints and big vases of flowers. Some quirky and individual touches include Timorous Beasties' giant bees papered on to the bar ceiling, a stag's head looming out of the wall above a log fire, a magnificent hunting tapestry and a strange angled nook with tartan wallpaper; the doors to the loos are quite a puzzle – which of the many knobs and handles actually work?! Simple chairs line the bar counter where they keep Acorn Barnsley Gold and Calypso IPA, Stonehouse Station Bitter, Tatton Red Red Rye and Wincle Sir Philip on handpump, 40 malt whiskies, 15 wines by the glass from an interesting list and 20 gins; background music. A terrace outside has teak tables under parasols, with more on the lawn.

 Using first class local, seasonal produce, the excellent food includes sandwiches, king prawns with mango and chilli salsa, potted goosnargh duck with rhubarb compote, local sausages with onion gravy, a pie of the day, wild mushroom fricassée with goats cheese arancini, roast cod loin with prosciutto-wrapped gem and butter sauce, chicken escalope with anchovy butter and fried egg, and puddings such as chocolate and salted caramel tart and blackberry crème brûlée. *Benchmark main dish: stone bass with samphire and cockle butter £14.50. Two-course evening meal £20.00.*

Free house ~ Licensees Jon and Lindsay Cox ~ Real ale ~ Open 12-11 (10.30 Sun) ~ Bar food 12-9.30 (10 Fri, Sat; 9 Sun) ~ Well behaved children welcome ~ Dogs welcome ~ Wi-fi ~ Live music last Fri of month *Recommended by Paul Scofield, Sally Wright, Anne Taylor, Sally and David Champion*

 SWETTENHAM   SJ7967   Map 7
Swettenham Arms
(01477) 571284 – www.swettenhamarms.co.uk
Off A54 Congleton–Holmes Chapel or A535 Chelford–Holmes Chapel; CW12 2LF

Big old country pub in a fine setting with shining brasses, five real ales and tempting food

For over 20 years, the hard-working and welcoming licensees have kept this former nunnery rather special – our readers love it. The three interlinked dark beamed areas are still nicely traditional with individual furnishings on bare floorboards or a sweep of fitted turkey carpet, a polished copper bar, three woodburning stoves, plenty of shiny brasses and a variety of old prints – military, hunting, old ships, reproduction Old Masters and so forth. Friendly efficient staff serve Black Sheep Best, Hydes Original Bitter, Sharps Doom Bar and Weetwood Cheshire Cat Blonde Ale on handpump, 12 wines by the glass, 20 malt whiskies and farm cider; background music. Outside behind, there are tables on a lawn that merges into a lovely sunflower and lavender meadow; croquet. There are walks in the pretty surrounding countryside and Quinta Arboretum is close by. Do visit the interesting village church which dates in part from the 13th c.

Highly enjoyable food includes sandwiches, hand-dived scallops and salmon st jacques, asparagus and mushroom linguine, local beef, lamb or pork roasts with trimmings, chicken with spinach and mushroom mousseline and café au lait sauce, bass with pak choi, egg noodles and thai chilli broth, steak with onion rings and chips, and puddings such as orange tiramisu and coconut pannacotta with passion-fruit and pineapple compote. *Benchmark main dish: steak and mushroom in ale pie £13.00. Two-course evening meal £20.00.*

Free house ~ Licensees Jim and Frances Cunningham ~ Real ale ~ No credit cards ~ Open 12-11; 12-3, 6-11 winter ~ Bar food 12-9; closed 3-6pm winter ~ Restaurant ~ Children welcome ~ Dogs allowed in bar ~ Wi-fi *Recommended by Robert Wivell, Hilary Forrest, Mike and Margaret Banks, George Sanderson, Charles Fraser*

 THELWALL   SJ6587   Map 7
Little Manor
(01925) 212070 – www.brunningandprice.co.uk/littlemanor
Bell Lane; WA4 2SX

Restored manor house with plenty of room, lots of interest, well kept ales and tasty bistro-style food; seats outside

Linked by open doorways and standing timbers, the six beamed rooms in this big, handsome 17th-c house are crammed with things to look at; there are plenty of nooks and crannies too. Flooring ranges from rugs on bare boards through carpeting to some fine old black and white tiles, and there's an appealing variety of antique dining chairs around small, large, circular or square tables, as well as leather armchairs by open fires (note the lovely carved wooden one); background music. Lighting is from metal chandeliers, wall lights and standard lamps, and the décor includes hundreds of intriguing prints and photos, books on shelves and lots of old glass and stone bottles on windowsills and mantelpieces; plenty of fresh flowers and house plants too. Phoenix Brunning & Price Original, Coach House Cromwells Best Bitter and Tatton Blonde and five quickly changing guest beers on handpump, around 15 wines by the glass, 27 gins and 60 whiskies; the young staff are consistently helpful. In fine weather you can sit at the chunky teak chairs and tables on the terrace; some are under a heated shelter.

From a seasonally aware menu, food includes sandwiches, crab salad with pineapple, coconut and cashews, chickpea and carrot scotch egg with tzatziki and sweet chilli sauce, goats cheese and red onion quiche with sun-dried tomato, olive and caper salad, steak burger with toppings, coleslaw and chips, chicken, ham and leek pie, pork and leek sausages with onion gravy, and puddings such as lemon tart with mixed berry compote and double chocolate brownie with chocolate sauce and pistachio ice-cream. *Benchmark main dish: fish pie £13.95. Two-course evening meal £20.00.*

Brunning & Price ~ Manager Jill Dowling ~ Real ale ~ Open 10.30-11; 12-10.30 Sun ~ Bar food 12-10 (9 Sun) ~ Children welcome ~ Dogs allowed in bar ~ Wi-fi
Recommended by Alistair Forsyth, Brian and Anna Marsden, Michael Butler

WARMINGHAM
SJ7161   Map 7

Bears Paw 🍺 🛏

(01270) 526317 – www.thebearspaw.co.uk
School Lane; CW11 3QN

Nicely maintained place with enjoyable food, half a dozen real ales and seats outside; bedrooms

There's a maze of linked rooms with plenty of individual character here, but we especially like the two little sitting rooms with panelling, fashionable wallpaper, bookshelves and slouchy leather furniture with plumped-up cushions comfortably arranged by woodburning stoves in magnificent fireplaces; stripped wood flooring and a dado keep it all informal. An eclectic mix of old wooden tables and some nice old carved chairs are well spaced throughout the dining areas, with lofty windows providing a light and airy feel and lots of big pot plants adding freshness. There are stools at the long bar counter where cheerful, efficient staff serve Weetwood Best and Eastgate plus guests such as Cheshire Brew Brothers Chester Gold, Milestone Crusader, Mobberley 1924 and Timothy Taylors Landlord on handpump, ten wines by the glass, quite a few malt whiskies and local cider; background music. A small front garden by the car park has seats and tables. The well equipped bedrooms are comfortable and the breakfasts very good indeed. This is sister pub to the Pheasant in Burwardsley and the Fishpool at Delamere.

Rewarding food includes sandwiches (until 6pm), venison hash cake with fried egg, pear, crisp pancetta and red wine purée, goats cheese crotin with baked balsamic fig and beetroot three-ways, sharing boards, smoked cheese and vegetable burger with sweet potato fries, chicken wrapped in parma ham stuffed with cheese and spinach with caramelised onion purée and confit wing bonbon, cumin-roasted lamb rump with harissa couscous, confit tomato and raita, and puddings such as white chocolate pannacotta with orange salad and apple, pear and almond crumble with crème anglaise. *Benchmark main dish: steak in ale pie £13.50. Two-course evening meal £22.00.*

Free house ~ Licensee Andrew Nelson ~ Real ale ~ Open 11-11 (10.30 Sun) ~ Bar food 12-9.30 (10 Fri, Sat; 9 Sun) ~ Restaurant ~ Children welcome ~ Dogs allowed in bar and bedrooms ~ Wi-fi ~ Bedrooms: $105/$115   *Recommended by William and Ann Reid, Susan Allen, Susan Jackman, Rona Mackinlay*

WHITELEY GREEN
Windmill ♀ ◖

SJ9278 Map 7

(01625) 574222 – www.thewindmill.info

Brown sign to pub off A523 Macclesfield–Poynton, just N of Prestbury; Hole House Lane; SK10 5SJ

Extensive relaxed country dining bar with big sheltered garden and enjoyable food

Most of this pub is given over to dining tables, mainly in a pleasantly informal, painted base/stripped top style, on bare boards. But the interior spreads around a big bar counter, its handpumps serving Sharps Doom Bar and local guests such as Storm Bosley Cloud, Weetwood Best and Wincle Lord Lucan; also, a dozen wines by the glass served by friendly and helpful staff. One area has several leather sofas and fabric-upholstered easy chairs; another by a log fire in a huge brick fireplace has more easy chairs and a suede sofa. Background music, daily papers and cribbage. The pub is up a long quiet lane in deepest leafy Cheshire countryside, and its spreading lawns, surrounded by a belt of young trees, provide plenty of room for well spaced tables and picnic sets, and even a maze to baffle children. Middlewood Way (a sort of linear country park) and Macclesfield Canal (Bridge 25) are just a stroll away.

Tasty, well presented food includes sandwiches, potted ham hock with apple and pear coleslaw, tempura king prawns with red pepper and chilli dip, cheese pie and spiced roasted cauliflower with mustard cream sauce, steak and onion pudding with sticky red cabbage and rich gravy, chicken wrapped in air-dried ham with chorizo stuffing and courgette and almond salad with pesto, steaks with a choice of sauce, and puddings such as peanut butter and chocolate torte with peanut brittle and clotted cream ice-cream and lemon meringue and rhubarb slice with raspberry sorbet. *Benchmark main dish: beer-battered fish and chips £13.00. Two-course evening meal £17.00.*

Mitchells & Butlers ~ Lease Peter and Jane Nixon ~ Real ale ~ Open 12-11 (10.30 Sun) ~ Bar food 12-2.30, 5-9.30; 12-9.30 Sat; 12-8 Sun ~ Children welcome ~ Dogs allowed in bar ~ Wi-fi ~ Live acoustic music second Fri and live bands last Fri of month
Recommended by John Wooll, R W Batho, Harvey Brown, Belinda Stamp

Also Worth a Visit in Cheshire

Besides the fully inspected pubs, you might like to try these pubs that have been recommended to us and described by readers. Do tell us what you think of them: feedback@goodguides.com

---

ALLGREAVE SU9767

Rose & Crown (01260) 227232
A54 Congleton–Buxton; SK11 0BJ
Welcoming 18th-c roadside pub in remote upland spot with good Dane Valley views and walks; refurbished beamed rooms, wood floors and log fires, good local food from bar and restaurant menus including daily specials, half a dozen well kept ales such as Jennings and Wincle from new wood-clad servery; children and dogs welcome, lawned garden taking in the views, three bedrooms. *(Julie Braeburn)*

ALPRAHAM SJ5759

Travellers Rest (01829) 260523
A51 Nantwich–Chester; CW6 9JA
Timeless four-room country local in same family for three generations, friendly chatty atmosphere, well kept Tetleys and Weetwood, no food, leatherette, wicker and Formica, some flock wallpaper, fine old brewery mirrors, darts and dominoes; may be nesting swallows in outside gents'; dogs welcome, back bowling green, 'Hat Day' last Sun before Christmas with locals sporting unusual headgear, eggs for sale, closed weekday lunchtimes. *(Tony Smaithe)*

ASHLEY   SJ7784

Greyhound   (0161) 871 7765

3 miles S of Altrincham; Cow Lane;
WA15 0QR Refurbished and extended red-
brick Lees pub, their well kept ales, decent
wines and good choice of tasty reasonably
priced food, greyhound-theme décor and
some old photos of nearby Tatton Park (NT),
wood floors, central woodburner; fortnightly
quiz Tues, darts; children and dogs welcome,
seats out on lawn and terrace, handy for the
station, open (and food) all day. *(Gemma*
Clayton, Hilary Forrest)

BARBRIDGE   SJ6156

Barbridge Inn   (01270) 528327

Just off A51 N of Nantwich; CW5 6AY
Spacious open-plan family dining pub by
lively marina at junction of Shropshire Union
and Middlewich canals, enjoyable good value
food from sandwiches to steaks served by
friendly staff, own Woodlands beers (brewed
nearby), conservatory; background music, no
dogs inside; waterside garden with enclosed
play area, moorings, open (and food) all day.
(Giles and Annie Francis, Roger and Anne Newbury)

BARTON   SJ4454

★**Cock o' Barton**   (01829) 782277

Barton Road (A534 E of Farndon);
SY14 7HU Stylish contemporary décor in
bright open skylit bar, good choice of well
liked up-to-date food, cocktails and plenty
of wines by the glass, ales such as Spitting
Feathers and Stonehouse, Fri happy hour till
7pm, neat courteous staff, beamed restaurant
areas; background music; children welcome
(free main course for them on Sun), tables in
sunken heated inner courtyard with canopies
and modern water feature, picnic-sets on
back lawn, 14 new bedrooms, closed Mon,
otherwise open (and food) all day. *(Sally and*
David Champion)

BIRKENHEAD   SJ3386

Refreshment Rooms

(0151) 644 5893 *Bedford Road E;*
CH42 1LS Bow-fronted former 19th-c
refreshment rooms for the Mersey ferry;
three rooms with interesting collection of
old photographs and other memorabilia,
good selection of mainly local ales such as
Liverpool Organic, Peerless and a house beer
from Lees (HMS Conway), Rosie's welsh
cider and a couple of interesting lagers,
good competitively priced home-made food
including OAP deal (Mon-Weds) and other
set menus, friendly prompt service; quiz
Weds, live music last Fri of month, pool;
children and dogs welcome, beer garden
at back with play area, open (and food)
all day. *(Diane Abbott)*

BOLLINGTON   SJ9377

Church House   (01625) 574014

Church Street; SK10 5PY Welcoming
village pub with good reasonably priced
home-made food including OAP menu,
efficient friendly service, well kept Adnams,
Thwaites and a guest, nice open fire, separate
dining room; quiz second Sun of month;
children and clean dogs welcome, good place
to start or end a walk, four comfortable well
priced bedrooms, open all day weekends
(food all day Sun). *(Brian and Sally Wakeham)*

BOLLINGTON   SJ9477

Poachers   (01625) 572086

Mill Lane; SK10 5BU Stone-built village
local prettily set in good walking area,
comfortable and welcoming, with enjoyable
pubby food (all day Sun, not Mon) including
bargain lunches, well kept Storm, Weetwood
and three guests such as local Happy Valley,
efficient friendly service, log fire and wood
stove; charity quiz last Sun of month;
children and dogs welcome, sunny back
garden, open all day weekends, closed Mon
lunchtime. *(Maureen Wood)*

BOLLINGTON   SJ9377

Vale   (01625) 575147

Adlington Road; SK10 5JT Friendly tap
for Bollington Brewery in three converted
19th-c cottages, their full range and a couple
of guests (tasters offered), real ciders,
enjoyable food (all day weekends) including
range of locally made pies and daily specials,
helpful efficient service, interesting photos,
newspapers and books, roaring fire; picnic-
sets out behind overlooking cricket pitch,
near Middlewood Way and Macclesfield
Canal, open all day Fri-Sun. *(John Wooll)*

BRERETON GREEN   SJ7764

Bears Head   (01477) 544732

Handy for M6 junction 17; set back off
A50 S of Holmes Chapel; CW11 1RS
Beautiful 17th-c black and white timbered
Vintage Inn with civilised linked rooms, low
beams, log fires and old-fashioned furniture
on flagstones or bare boards, enjoyable well
prepared food served by friendly staff, Sharps
Doom Bar, Thwaites Wainwright and a guest;
25 bedrooms in modern Innkeepers Lodge,
open (and food) all day. *(Charles Todd)*

BROOMEDGE   SJ7086

Jolly Thresher   (01925) 752265

Higher Lane; WA13 0RN Spacious
well appointed dining pub with enjoyable
sensibly priced food including good value
set lunch, well kept Hydes ales, lots of
wines by the glass and good choice of other
drinks, restaurant and dining conservatory;
background music, free wi-fi; children and
dogs welcome, tables on paved terrace and
lawn, open (and food) all day. *(Hilary Forrest)*

BURTONWOOD   SJ5692

Fiddle i'th' Bag   (01925) 225442

3 miles from M62 junction 9, signposted
from A49 towards Newton-le-Willows;
WA5 4BT Eccentric place (not to everyone's
taste) crammed with bric-a-brac and

memorabilia, three well kept changing ales and enjoyable uncomplicated home-made food (cash only), friendly staff; may be nostalgic background music; children welcome, open all day weekends. *(Caroline Sullivan)*

CHELFORD   SJ8175

★**Egerton Arms** (01625) 861366
A537 Macclesfield–Knutsford; SK11 9BB
Cheerful rambling old village pub, beams and nice mix of furniture including carved settles, wooden porter's chair by grandfather clock, Copper Dragon, Wells Bombardier and local guests, several wines by the glass, good food and service, restaurant, steps down to little raftered games area with pool and darts; background music (live jazz last Fri of month), sports TV; children and dogs welcome, picnic-sets on canopied deck, more on grass and toddlers' play area, adjoining deli, open (and food) all day. *(John Wooll)*

CHESTER   SJ4065

★**Bear & Billet** (01244) 351002
Lower Bridge Street; CH1 1RU Handsome 17th-c timber and lattice-windowed Okells pub (an inn since the 18th c); their beers and three changing guests, belgian and american imports and nice range of wines by the glass, reasonably priced home-made pubby food including range of burgers and various deals, efficient friendly service, beamed bar with wood floor and panelling, open fire, scenes of old Chester in back dining part, further rooms above; Sun quiz and upstairs folk club, sports TVs; children and dogs welcome, courtyard seating, open (and food) all day), kitchen closes 7pm Sun. *(John Beeken)*

CHESTER   SJ4066

Boathouse (01244) 328709
The Groves, off Grosvenor Park Road; on Dee 5 mins from centre; CH1 1SD
Modernised pub on site of 17th-c boat house by River Dee, great views, enjoyable well priced pubby food from sandwiches and sharing plates up, Lees ales and decent choice of wines by the glass, friendly helpful staff; Weds quiz, free wi-fi; children welcome, dogs outside only, disabled access/facilities, tables and painted beach huts on paved terrace overlooking water, little bridge to floating seating area, open (and food) all day. *(Miles Green)*

CHESTER   SJ4065

★**Brewery Tap** (01244) 340999
Lower Bridge Street; CH1 1RU Tap for Spitting Feathers Brewery in interesting Jacobean building with 18th-c brick façade, steps up to lofty barrel-vaulted bar (former great hall) serving a couple of their well kept ales, five guest beers, a local cider and good choice of wines, hearty home-made food using local suppliers including produce from Spitting Feathers farm (rare-breed

pork), pews and other rustic furniture on flagstones, tapestries on walls, large carved red-sandstone fireplace, also smaller plainer room; children and dogs welcome, no wheelchair access, open (and food) all day. *(Roger and Anne Newbury)*

CHESTER   SJ4166

Cellar (01244) 318950
City Road; CH1 3AE Laid-back Canal Quarter bar with well kept changing ales, craft beers and interesting selection of imports, decent wines and cocktails too, Mon happy hour 5-8pm, limited snacky food, basement bar for private functions; live music Fri and Sat from 10pm (can get packed), sports TV; closed Mon lunchtime, otherwise open all day till late. *(Caroline Sullivan)*

CHESTER   SJ4066

Coach House (01244) 351900
Northgate Street; CH1 2HQ Updated 19th-c coaching inn by town hall and cathedral; comfortable lounge with central bar, well kept Thwaites ales and guests, good choice of bottled beers and wines by the glass, enjoyable reasonably priced home-made food from semi-open kitchen, afternoon teas, prompt friendly service; children and dogs welcome, tables out in front, eight bedrooms, open all day from 9am for breakfast. *(Robert W Buckle)*

CHESTER   SJ4065

Cross Keys (01244) 344460
Duke Street/Lower Bridge Street; CH1 1RU Small Victorian corner pub with ornate interior, dark panelling, etched mirrors and stained-glass windows, button-back leather wall benches and cast-iron tables on bare boards, open fire, well kept Joules ales and a guest, sensibly priced pubby food (not Mon, Tues), friendly service, upstairs function room; free wi-fi; no dogs inside, seats out in front, closed Mon and lunchtime Tues, otherwise open all day. *(Dr Kevan Tucker)*

CHESTER   SJ4066

Olde Boot (01244) 314540
Eastgate Row N; CH1 1LQ Lovely 17th-c Rows building, heavy beams, dark woodwork, oak flooring and flagstones, old kitchen range in lounge beyond, settles and oak panelling in upper area, well kept/priced Sam Smiths; cheerful service and bustling atmosphere; no children. *(Edward Mirzoeff)*

CHESTER   SJ4066

Pied Bull (01244) 325829
Upper Northgate Street; CH1 2HQ
Old beamed and panelled coaching inn with roomy open-plan carpeted bar, good own-brewed ales (brewery tours) along with guests, enjoyable fairly priced traditional food from sandwiches and baked potatoes up, friendly staff and

locals, imposing stone fireplace with tapestry above, divided inner dining area; background music; children welcome, handsome Jacobean stairs to 13 bedrooms, open (and food) all day. *(Miles Green)*

CHESTER SJ4066
Telfords Warehouse (01244) 390090
Tower Wharf, behind Northgate Street near railway; CH1 4EZ Well kept interesting ales in large converted canal building, fairly priced up-to-date food including good sandwich menu, friendly efficient young staff, bare boards, exposed brickwork and high pitched ceiling, big wall of windows overlooking the water, some old enamel signs and massive iron winding gear in bar, steps up to heavily beamed area with sofas, artwork and restaurant; late-night live music, bouncers on the door; tables out by canal, open all day (till late Weds-Sun). *(Edward Mirzoeff)*

CHURCH MINSHULL SJ6660
Badger (01270) 522348
B5074 Winsford–Nantwich; handy for Shropshire Union Canal, Middlewich branch; CW5 6DY Refurbished 18th-c coaching inn in pretty village next to church, good imaginative food from sharing boards up (pub favourite too), well kept ales such as Tatton, Titanic and Weetwood, Thatcher's cider, interesting range of wines and several malt whiskies, friendly helpful staff, bar and spacious lounge leading to back conservatory; children and dogs (in tap room) welcome, five bedrooms, good breakfast, open (and food) all day. *(Valerie Sayer)*

COMBERBACH SJ6477
Spinner & Bergamot
(01606) 891307 *Warrington Road; CW9 6AY* Comfortable 18th-c beamed village pub named after two racehorses, good home-made food (smaller helpings available for some main courses), well kept Robinsons ales and nice choice of wines, friendly attentive service, pitched-ceiling timber dining extension, two-room carpeted lounge and tiled-floor public bar where dogs allowed, log fires, some Manchester United memorabilia; unobtrusive background music, sports TV, Mon quiz; children welcome, small verandah, picnic-sets on sloping lawn, bowling green, open all day (food all day Sun). *(Julie Braeburn)*

CONGLETON SJ8659
Horseshoe (01260) 272205
Fence Lane, Newbold Astbury, between A34 and A527 S; CW12 3NL Former 18th-c coaching inn set in peaceful countryside; three small carpeted rooms with decorative plates, copper and brass and other knick-knacks (some on delft shelves), mix of seating including plush banquettes and iron-base tables, log fire, well kept predominantly Robinsons ales, popular hearty home-made food at reasonable prices, daily specials, friendly staff and locals; children welcome, no dogs, rustic garden furniture, adventure play area with tractor, good walks. *(Diane Abbott)*

CONGLETON SJ8762
Queens Head (01260) 272546
Park Lane (set down from flyover); CW12 3DE Friendly local by Macclesfield Canal, quaint dark interior with open fire, up to eight well kept ales, a real cider and good selection of malt whiskies, reasonably priced hearty pub food (not Sun evening), table skittles, darts and pool (free Sun); sports TV, quiz Mon, poker Tues; children and dogs welcome, steps up from towpath to nice garden with play area and boules, three bedrooms, useful for station, open all day. *(Tony Smaithe)*

COTEBROOK SJ5765
Alvanley Arms (01829) 760200
A49/B5152 N of Tarporley; CW6 9DS Welcoming newly refurbished roadside coaching inn, 17th-c behind its flower-decked Georgian façade, with beamed rooms and big open fire, Robinsons ales, several wines by the glass and good choice of other drinks, well liked reasonably priced food from sandwiches up, friendly efficient service; background music, free wi-fi; children welcome, disabled access, garden with new deck and large pond, pleasant walks, seven comfortable bedrooms. *(Malcolm and Pauline Pellatt)*

CREWE SJ7055
Borough Arms (01270) 748189
Earle Street; CW1 2BG Own microbrewery and lots of changing guest ales, good choice of continental beers too, friendly staff and regulars, two small rooms off central bar and downstairs lounge; occasional sports TV; picnic-sets on back terrace and lawn, open all day Fri-Sun, closed lunchtime other days. *(Charles Todd)*

DISLEY SJ9784
White Horse (01663) 762397
Up side road by Rams Head Hotel; SK12 2BB Proper straightforward pub popular with locals, four Robinsons ales and tasty well priced food (all day weekends), good friendly service; free wi-fi; children welcome, no dogs inside, handy for Lyme Park (NT), open all day. *(John Wooll)*

DISLEY SJ9784
White Lion (01663) 762800
Buxton Road (A6); SK12 2HA Welcoming pub at east end of village, nine well kept changing ales and enjoyable food (not Mon) including good home-made pies, friendly efficient staff; dogs welcome in one part (food for them too), closed Mon lunchtime, otherwise open all day. *(Brian and Anna Marsden)*

FADDILEY
SJ5852

★ Thatch (01270) 524223
A534 Wrexham–Nantwich; CW5 8JE
Attractive, thatched, low-beamed and
timbered dining pub carefully extended
from medieval core, open fires, raised room
to right of bar, back barn-style dining room
(children allowed here), well kept ales such
as Salopian and Timothy Taylors, good choice
of enjoyable popular food (booking advised
weekends), friendly helpful service, relaxing
atmosphere; soft background music, free
wi-fi; charming country garden with play
area, open all day weekends, closed all day
Mon and Tues lunchtimes. *(Brian and Sally
Wakeham)*

FRODSHAM
SJ5276

Travellers Rest (01928) 735125
B5152 Frodsham–Kingsley; WA6 6SL
Popular family-run roadside dining pub
with good food from sandwiches and pub
favourites up, well kept Black Sheep and two
guests, good selection of wines, attentive
cheerful service; free wi-fi; children welcome,
disabled access, superb views across Weaver
Valley, open all day (food till 6pm Sun).
(Tony Smaithe)

FULLERS MOOR
SJ4954

Sandstone (01829) 782333
A534; CH3 9JH Light and airy dining pub
with wide choice of good sensibly priced
fresh food from sandwiches and snacks up,
four well kept ales including Stonehouse
and own Sandstone (brewed in Wrexham),
friendly efficient staff, woodburner, dining
conservatory; Tues quiz; children and dogs
(in bar) welcome, spacious garden with
lovely views, handy for Sandstone Trail, open
(and food) all day weekends. *(Diane Abbott)*

GAWSWORTH
SJ8869

★ Harrington Arms (01260) 223325
*Off A536; Congleton Road/Church Lane;
SK11 9RJ* This unspoilt three-storey
building is still part of a working farm; low
17th-c beams, tiled and flagstoned floors,
snug corners and open fires, counter in
narrow space on right serving Robinsons ales,
a guest beer and good selection of wines and
whiskies, several unpretentious rooms off
with old settles and eclectic mix of tables and
chairs, lots of pictures on red or pale painted
walls, well liked hearty food from hot and
cold sandwiches to daily specials, friendly
relaxed atmosphere; background music (live
Fri), free wi-fi; children and dogs (in bar)
welcome, benches out on small front cobbled
area, more seats in garden overlooking fields,
lane leads to one of Cheshire's prettiest villages,
open all day weekends. *(Michael Butler)*

GOOSTREY
SJ7770

Crown (01477) 532128
Off A50 and A535; CW4 8PE Extended
and opened-up 18th-c red-brick village
pub, beams and open fires, good choice
of enjoyable food with some main courses
available in smaller sizes, five well kept
ales and plenty of wines by the glass,
friendly efficient service; Tues quiz; children
welcome, close to Jodrell Bank, open (and
food) all day. *(Tony Smaithe)*

GRAPPENHALL
SJ6386

★ Parr Arms (01925) 212120
*Near M6 junction 20 – A50 towards
Warrington, left after 1.5 miles; Church
Lane; WA4 3EP* Renovated black-beamed
pub in picture-postcard setting with picnic-
sets out on cobbles by church, more tables on
small canopied back terrace, good reasonably
priced food from ciabattas and sharing plates
to blackboard specials, friendly helpful
service, well kept Robinsons from central bar,
log fires; children and dogs welcome, open
(and food) all day. *(Hilary Forrest)*

GREAT BUDWORTH
SJ6677

George & Dragon (01606) 892650
*Signed off A559 NE of Northwich;
High Street opposite church; CW9 6HF*
Characterful building dating from 1722
(front part is 19th-c) in delightful village;
Lees ales kept well and plenty of wines by
the glass, welcoming friendly young staff,
good choice of enjoyable reasonably priced
home-made food from lunchtime sandwiches
and baguettes to specials, dark panelled
bar with log fire, grandfather clock and
leather button-back banquettes, back area
more restauranty with wood floors and
exposed brickwork, tables around central
woodburner, some stuffed animals and
hunting memorabilia; children and dogs
(in bar) welcome, open (and food) all day.
(Charles Todd)

HOLLINS GREEN
SJ6991

Black Swan (0161) 222 4444
*Just off A57 Manchester–Warrington,
3 miles from M6 junction 21; WA3 6LA*
Extended 17th-c coaching inn with enjoyable
fairly traditional food cooked to order, half
a dozen changing ales and good choice
of wines, friendly service; events such as
live music, poker and quiz nights, monthly
farmers' market; children welcome, sizeable
garden with terrace, duck pond and play
area, 14 bedrooms, local walks (leaflets
available), open (and food) all day.
(Julie Braeburn)

KERRIDGE
SJ9276

Lord Clyde (01625) 562123
Clarke Lane, off A523; SK10 5AH
Converted from two mid 19th-c stone
cottages, main emphasis on food but can just
pop in for a drink, first class creative cooking
from chef-owner (must book) including
tasting menus, also lunchtime sandwiches
and ploughman's, well kept ales such as
Greene King, Thwaites and Weetwood,
efficient friendly service; background music;

dogs in bar, good local walks, open all day Fri-Sun, closed Mon lunchtime (no food Sat lunchtime, Sun, Mon lunchtime). *(Brian and Sally Wakeham)*

KNUTSFORD   SJ7578
Lord Eldon (01565) 652261
Tatton Street, off A50 at White Bear roundabout; WA16 6AD Traditional red-brick former coaching inn with four comfortable rooms (much bigger inside than it looks), friendly staff and locals, beams, brasses, old pictures and large open fire, well kept Tetleys and a couple of guests, no food; music and quiz nights, darts; dogs welcome, back garden but no car park, handy for Tatton Park (NT), open all day. *(Sally and David Champion)*

KNUTSFORD   SJ7578
Rose & Crown (01565) 652366
King Street; WA16 6DT Beamed and panelled 17th-c inn with bar and Chophouse restaurant, well liked food including good value set menu (weekdays till 7pm), Mobberley ales, a beer badged for the pub (Chopper) and guests, plenty of wines by the glass including champagne, good personable service; children welcome, terrace tables, nine bedrooms, open (and food) all day. *(Tony Smaithe)*

LACH DENNIS   SJ7072
Duke of Portland (01606) 46264
Holmes Chapel Road (B5082, off A556 SE of Northwich); CW9 7SY Modernised village pub under new management – reports please; fairly pubby food from sandwiches and baked potatoes up, friendly service, four Marstons-related ales from handsomely carved counter, main dining area with lofty ceiling; background and some live music; children welcome, terrace with lovely country views, open (and food) all day. *(Peter Brix, Nick Sharpe)*

LANGLEY   SJ9569
★**Hanging Gate** (01260) 400756
Meg Lane, Higher Sutton; SK11 0NG Remote old place close to the moors with wonderful distant views to Liverpool Cathedral and even Snowdonia – now under same ownership as the Lord Clyde at Kerridge and refurbished; cosy low-beamed rooms on different levels, log fires, very good well presented food from short but interesting menu (all day Sun, not Mon evening), Hydes, a guest beer and nice choice of wines, friendly attentive service; background music, free wi-fi; children and dogs welcome, picnic-sets out on new deck taking in the view, good circular walk, open all day weekends. *(Sandra and Nigel Brown)*

LANGLEY   SJ9471
★**Leather's Smithy** (01260) 252313
Off A523 S of Macclesfield; OS Sheet 118 map reference 952715; SK11 0NE

Isolated stone-built pub in fine walking country next to reservoir; well kept Theakstons and two or three guests, lots of whiskies, good food from sandwiches to blackboard specials, efficient friendly service, beams and log fire, flagstoned bar, carpeted dining areas, interesting local prints and photographs; unobtrusive background music; children welcome, no dogs inside but muddy boots allowed in bar, picnic-sets in garden behind and on grass opposite, lovely views, open all day weekends (till 8pm Sun). *(Rona Mackinlay)*

LITTLE BOLLINGTON   SJ7387
★**Swan with Two Nicks**
(0161) 928 2914 *2 miles from M56 junction 7 – A56 towards Lymm, then first right at Stamford Arms into Park Lane; use A556 to get back on to M56 westbound; WA14 4TJ* Extended village pub full of beams, brass, copper and bric-a-brac, some antique settles and roaring log fire, good choice of enjoyable generously served food from baguettes up, popular Sun lunch (best to book), half a dozen well kept ales including a house beer from Coach House, decent wines and coffee, efficient service; children and dogs welcome, tables outside, attractive hamlet by Dunham Massey (NT) deer park, walks by Bridgewater Canal, open (and food) all day. *(Hilary Forrest, Brian and Anna Marsden, Dr D J and Mrs S C Walker, Tony Hobden)*

LITTLE BUDWORTH   SJ5867
Cabbage Hall (01829) 760292
Forest Road (A49); CW6 9ES Restauranty pub (part of the Pesto chain) specialising in good tapas-style (piattini) italian food, drinkers catered for in comfortable bar with ales such as Weetwood and decent wines by the glass, efficient friendly staff; children welcome, garden tables, open (and food) all day. *(Tony Smaithe)*

LITTLE BUDWORTH   SJ5965
Egerton Arms (01829) 760424
Pinfold Lane; CW6 9BS Welcoming 18th-c family-run country free house, enjoyable home-made food including wood-fired pizzas and range of burgers, six well kept local beers, good selection of bottled beers and interesting cocktails; weekend live music; children and dogs welcome, seats out in front and in garden behind overlooking cricket pitch, walks from the door, handy for Oulton Park racetrack, closed Mon, otherwise open all day (from 3pm Tues, Weds in winter). *(Paul Scofield)*

LITTLE LEIGH   SJ6076
Holly Bush (01606) 853196
A49 just S of A533; CW8 4QY Ancient thatched and timbered pub with good choice of enjoyable well priced food including several vegetarian options, charming helpful staff, Tetleys and a couple of mainstream

guests, bar with open fire, restaurant extension; children welcome, no dogs inside, wheelchair access, courtyard tables and garden with play area, 14 bedrooms in converted back barn, open all day weekends (food all day Sun). *(Lindy Andrews)*

LOWER PEOVER   SJ7474
★ **Bells of Peover** (01565) 722269
Just off B5081; The Cobbles; handy for M6 junction 17; WA16 9PZ New manager for this lovely old wisteria-clad dining pub in quiet hamlet; modern furnishings contrasting original panelling, beams and open fires, extremely good food including weekday set lunch and Fri steak night, helpful friendly staff, Robinsons ales and several wines by the glass; background music, free wi-fi; children welcome, no dogs inside, seats on front terrace overlooking fine black and white 14th-c church, spacious side lawn (beyond the old coachyard) spreading down through trees and rose pergolas to little stream, open (and food) all day. *(Anne Taylor, Valerie Sayer)*

LOWER WHITLEY   SJ6178
Chetwode Arms (01925) 730203
Just off A49, handy for M56 junction 10; Street Lane; WA4 4EN Rambling low-beamed dining pub dating from the 17th c, good food including range of exotic meats cooked on a hot stone, early-bird deal (before 7pm), welcoming efficient service, solid furnishings all clean and polished, small front bar with warm open fire, four real ales including Adnams, good wines by the glass; well behaved children allowed but best to ask first, limited wheelchair access, bowling green, closed lunchtimes opening at 5pm (3-9pm Sun). *(Lindy Andrews)*

LOWER WITHINGTON   SJ8268
Black Swan (01477) 571770
Trap Street; SK11 9EQ Neatly kept pub up for sale as we went to press; cottagey rooms with chesterfield sofas, wooden and prettily upholstered chairs around scrubbed pine and painted tables, floral lampshades and some cheerful wallpaper, antlers, decorative plates and open fires, Jennings Cumberland and guests, a dozen wines by the glass, good food including sandwiches from fairly pubby menu; free wi-fi; children and dogs (in bar) welcome, green-painted picnic-sets and other seats on side terrace, summer pizza oven, one-hour dog walk in fields opposite, open all day, food all day Sat, till 6pm Sun. *(Hilary Forrest, Sally Wright)*

LYMM   SJ7087
Barn Owl (01925) 752020
Agden Wharf, Warrington Lane (just off B5159 E); WA13 0SW Comfortably extended popular pub in nice setting by Bridgewater Canal, Thwaites ales and three guests, decent wines by the glass, reasonable choice of good value all-day pub food including OAP deals and Sun carvery, efficient service even when busy, friendly atmosphere; children and dogs welcome, disabled facilities, may be canal trips, moorings (space for one narrowboat). *(Miles Green)*

LYMM   SJ6886
Church Green (01925) 752068
Higher Lane; WA13 0AP Dining pub owned by celebrity chef Aiden Byrne, food can be very good (and pricey) in restaurant or smaller bar area, Caledonian and a guest beer, carefully chosen wines; background music; children welcome, disabled access/facilities, pretty garden including heated side deck, open all day (breakfast at weekends). *(Sally and David Champion)*

MACCLESFIELD   SJ9173
Snow Goose (01625) 619299
Sunderland Street; SK11 6HN Quirky laid-back bar with feel of an alpine ski lodge, well kept ales such as Storm and Wincle, several craft beers and good range of wines, unusual food from daily changing menu, bare-boards interior on three levels, woodburners, local artwork for sale, piano; background and live music, poetry/storytelling evenings, board games; children and dogs welcome, balcony overlooking back garden, closed Mon otherwise open all day, can get very busy. *(Adam Bellinger)*

MOBBERLEY   SJ8179
Plough & Flail (01565) 873537
Off B5085 Knutsford–Alderley Edge; at E end of village turn into Moss Lane, then left into Paddock Hill Lane (look out for small green signs to pub); WA16 7DB Extensive family dining pub tucked down narrow lanes; low-beamed bar with chunky cushioned chairs and stripped tables, flagstones and panelled dado, Lees ales and good choice of wines by the glass, wood-floored side area with low sofas, enjoyable food (Sun till 8pm) including daily specials, comfortable airy dining room and conservatory; background music, free wi-fi; teak tables on heated terraces, picnic-sets on neat lawns, play area, open (and food) all day. *(Mike and Margaret Banks)*

MOBBERLEY   SJ7879
Roebuck (01565) 873322
Mill Lane; down hill from sharp bend on B5085 at E edge of 30mph limit; WA16 7HX Scheduled to reopen shortly after we went to press (same owners as the

---

We include some hotels with a good bar that offers facilities comparable to those of a pub.

nearby Bulls Head and Church Inn – see Mobberley Main Entries); refurbished auberge-style interior with old shutters, reclaimed radiators and glass cabinets (all imported from france), bistro food from croque madame to venison bourguignon, craft ales, old-world wines and proper old-fashioned aperitifs; children welcome, enclosed garden, six rustic-style bedrooms, maybe honey for breakfast from own bees; reports please. *(Valerie Sayer)*

MOULDSWORTH   SJ5170
Goshawk (01928) 740900
Station Road (B5393); CH3 8AJ Comfortable Woodward & Falconer family dining pub (former station hotel); mix of furniture in extensive series of rooms including small 'library' area, masses of pictures, double-aspect log fire, good popular food from sandwiches to restauranty dishes, cheerful attentive uniformed staff, half a dozen well kept ales such as Montys, Weetwood and Woodland plus a couple of house beers brewed by Conwy, nice wines by the glass; background music; dogs allowed in bar, disabled facilities, good spot near Delamere Forest with big outdoor seating including play area and bowling green, open all day. *(Sandra and Nigel Brown)*

NANTWICH   SJ6452
★ Black Lion (01270) 628711
Welsh Row; CW5 5ED Cosy old black and white pub with plenty of character, beams, timbered brickwork, bare boards and stone floors, open fire, good food (not Sun evening, Mon) from short but varied menu, three well kept Weetwood ales and three regularly changing guests, good service, upstairs rooms with old wooden tables and leather sofas on undulating floors; covered outside seating area, open all day weekends, closed Mon lunchtime. *(Lindy Andrews)*

NANTWICH   SJ6552
Vine (01270) 619055
Hospital Street; CW5 5RP Black and white fronted pub dating from the 17th c, modernised interior stretching far back with steps and quiet corners, woodburner, four well kept ales including Hydes, popular good value food (Sun till 6pm) from fairly pubby menu including sandwiches and sharing plates, friendly staff and locals, raised seating areas; background music, sports TVs, darts; children and dogs welcome, small sunny outside seating area behind, open all day. *(Diane Abbott)*

NESTON   SJ2976
Harp (0151) 336 6980
Quayside, SW of Little Neston; keep on along track at end of Marshlands Road; CH64 0TB Tucked-away little two-room country local with well kept ales including Timothy Taylors, decent choice of bottled beers, wines and some good malt whiskies,

enjoyable simple pub food, woodburner in pretty fireplace, pale quarry tiles and simple furnishings, interesting old photographs, hatch servery to lounge; children and dogs allowed, garden behind, picnic-sets up on front grassy bank facing Dee Marshes and Wales, glorious sunsets with wild calls of wading birds, good walks, open all day. *(Edward and William Johnston)*

PARKGATE   SJ2778
Boathouse (0151) 336 4187
Village signed off A540; CH64 6RN Popular black and white timbered pub (Woodward & Falconer) with attractively refurbished linked rooms, wide choice of good food (booking advised) from snacks up, cheerful attentive staff, well kept changing ales including a couple of house beers from Conwy, several wines by the glass, big conservatory with great views to Wales over silted Dee estuary (RSPB reserve), may be egrets and kestrels. *(Julian Slade)*

PARKGATE   SJ2778
Ship (0151) 336 3931
The Parade; CH64 6SA Far-reaching estuary views from hotel's bow-windowed bar, well kept Brimstage, Marstons Pedigree and guests, several wines by the glass, over 50 whiskies and interesting range of gins, good reasonably priced home-cooked food including daily specials and popular Sun roasts, afternoon tea, good friendly service, log fire; Weds quiz night; children welcome, no dogs inside, a few tables out at front and to the side, 25 bedrooms, open all day. *(Brian and Sally Wakeham)*

PEOVER HEATH   SJ7973
★ Dog (01625) 861421
Wellbank Lane; the pub is often listed under Over Peover instead; WA16 8UP Nicely renovated traditional country pub with intimate rooms (sister pub to the Ship at Styal), good variety of well liked generously served food (all day weekends), five ales including Weetwood, decent choice of wines by the glass and malt whiskies, friendly efficient staff; children welcome, dogs in tap room, picnic-sets out at front and in pretty back garden, can walk from here to the Jodrell Bank Discovery Centre and Arboretum, six bedrooms, open (and food) all day. *(Mr and Mrs R Shardlow)*

POYNTON   SJ9483
Boars Head (01625) 876676
Shrigley Road N, Higher Poynton, off A523; SK12 1TE Welcoming red-brick Victorian country pub with enjoyable good value home-made food including speciality pies, four well kept ales such as Black Sheep and Jennings, warm woodburner; walkers and dogs welcome, next to Middlewood Way and close to Macclesfield Canal moorings, also handy for Lyme Park (NT), open all day weekends. *(Charles Todd)*

POYNTON
SJ9283
Cask Tavern (01625) 875157
Park Lane; SK12 1RE Busy Bollington pub with five of their well kept ales and a guest, craft beers, real ciders and several wines by the glass including draught prosecco, friendly staff, some snacky food; dogs allowed, open all day Fri-Sun, from 4pm other days. *(Brian and Anna Marsden)*

PRESTBURY
SJ8976
Legh Arms (01625) 829130
A538, village centre; SK10 4DG
Beamed inn with divided-up bar and lounge areas, Robinsons ales and decent wines by the glass, enjoyable bar food from sandwiches up, more elaborate restaurant choices, soft furnishings, ladderback chairs around solid dark tables, brocaded bucket seats, stylish french prints and italian engravings, cosy panelled back part with narrow offshoot, open fire; background music, daily papers; children and dogs welcome, seats on heated terrace, bedrooms, good breakfast, open all day. *(Sally and David Champion)*

SHOCKLACH
SJ4349
Bull (01829) 250335
Off B5069 W of Malpas; SY14 7BL
Welcoming 19th-c village dining pub, beams, bare boards and flagstones, some hand-painted floor tiles in one part, open fire, good food (all day weekends, not Mon) from lunchtime sandwiches and pub favourites up, a beer named for the pub from Marstons and up to three guests, decent house wines, garden room; background music, folk/acoustic night second Tues of month, quiz second Mon; children and dogs (in bar) welcome, picnic-sets on back terrace, open all day (from 4pm Mon). *(Jill Sparrow)*

STOAK
SJ4273
★ Bunbury Arms (01244) 301665
Little Stanney Lane; a mile from M53 junction 10, A5117 W then first left; CH2 4HW Big but cosy beamed lounge with antique furniture, pictures and books, small snug, wide choice of enjoyable fairly priced food (all day Sun) from sandwiches and wraps to interesting specials including fresh fish, three good changing ales, extensive wine list, open fires; Mon quiz, board games; garden tables (some motorway noise), short walk for Shropshire Canal users (Bridge 136 or 138), also handy for Cheshire Oaks shopping outlet, open all day. *(Lindy Andrews)*

STYAL
SJ8383
Ship (01625) 444888
B5166 near Ringway Airport; SK9 4JE
Refurbished 17th-c beamed pub under same ownership as the Dog at Peover Heath, good food from extensive menu and well kept ales including Dunham Massey and Weetwood, plenty of wines by the glass, friendly helpful service, some stripped brickwork and painted panelling, log fire; children welcome, seats out at front and on back terrace, attractive NT village with good walks on the doorstep, open (and food) all day. *(Mike and Wena Stevenson)*

SUTTON
SJ9273
Sutton Gamekeeper (01260) 252000
Hollin Lane; SK11 0HL Attractively updated beamed village pub (was the Lamb); good freshly made food from short but interestingly varied menu, Dunham Massey, Wincle and a guest, good friendly service, warm open fire; children welcome, well behaved dogs in bar, metal furniture in fenced garden behind, closed Mon, otherwise open all day till 10pm, food all day weekends (till 7pm Sun). *(Sandra and Brian Brown)*

TARPORLEY
SJ5562
Swan (01829) 733838
High Street, off A49; CW6 0AG
Elegant Georgian fronted inn (building actually dates from the 16th c) with rambling linked areas, beams and open fires, good food from sandwiches and snacks through pub favourites up, some main dishes available in smaller helpings, Weetwood ales and a couple of guests, lots of wines by the glass, efficient friendly staff; children and dogs (in bar) welcome, tables outside, 16 charming bedrooms, open (and food) all day. *(Malcolm and Pauline Pellatt)*

WESTON
SJ7352
White Lion (01270) 587011
Not far from M6 junction 16, via A500; CW2 5NA Renovated 17th-c black and white dining inn, low-beamed lounge bar with slate floor, standing timbers and inglenook woodburner, popular food here or in restaurant, three well kept ales including Salopian Shropshire Gold, cocktail bar; background music; children in eating areas, dogs in bar, lovely garden with bowling green (not owned by the pub), 17 comfortable bedrooms, open all day. *(Diana Abbott)*

WHITEGATE
SJ6268
Plough (01606) 889455
Beauty Bank, Foxwist Green; OS Sheet 118 map reference 624684; off A556 just W of Northwich, or A54 W of Winsford; CW8 2BP Comfortable country pub with bar and extended dining area, wide choice of good home-made food (best to book) from panini and baked potatoes up, cheerful efficient service, four well kept Robinsons ales and plenty of wines by the glass; background music, free wi-fi; no under-14s inside, well behaved dogs allowed in tap room, disabled access, picnic-sets out at front and in back garden, colourful window boxes and hanging baskets, popular walks nearby, open (and food) all day. *(Brian and Sally Wakeham)*

WILDBOARCLOUGH   SJ9868
Crag   (01260) 227239
Village signed from A54; bear left at fork, then left at T-junction; SK11 0BD
Old stone-built pub in charming little sheltered valley below moors (good walk up Shutlingsloe for great views), enjoyable generously served home-made food including Sun carvery, three well kept local beers, friendly staff, plates on delft shelving, various stuffed animals, open fires; walkers welcome, terrace with covered smokers' shelter.
(Tony Smaithe)

WILLINGTON   SJ5367
★Boot   (01829) 751375
Boothsdale, off A54 at Kelsall; CW6 0NH
Attractive hillside dining pub in row of converted cottages, views over Cheshire plain to Wales, popular food from pub staples to daily specials, local Weetwood ales and decent choice of wines and malt whiskies, friendly staff, small opened-up unpretentiously furnished rooms, lots of original features, woodburner, extension with french windows overlooking garden; well behaved children welcome (no pushchairs or highchairs), dogs outside only, picnic-sets on raised suntrap terrace, good walks, open all day. *(Lindy Andrews)*

WILMSLOW   SJ8481
Anthology   (01625) 533194
A stroll from train station; SK9 1HE
Large popular beamed pub (former Swan) refurbished under new owners; five mainstream ales, plenty of bottled beers and extensive wine and cocktail lists, good choice of sensibly priced food including tapas (Mon-Thurs), friendly service, contemporary décor with one or two quirky touches, rugs on wood floors and eclectic mix of furniture including banquette and booth seating, log fires; background music (live Thurs, from 4pm Sun), TVs, free wi-fi; small garden with teak furniture, pergola and fire pit, open (and food) all day, till 1am Fri, Sat.
(Adam Bellinger)

WINCLE   SJ9665
★Ship   (01260) 227217
Village signposted off A54 Congleton–Buxton; SK11 0QE Friendly 16th-c stone-built country pub; bare-boards bar leading to carpeted dining room, old stables area with flagstones, beams, woodburner and open fire, good generously served food (not Sun evening) from varied menu, three Lees ales and several wines by the glass, quick attentive service; children and dogs welcome, tables in small side garden, good Dane Valley walks, open all day. *(Thomas Green)*

WRENBURY   SJ5947
★Dusty Miller   (01270) 780537
Cholmondeley Road; village signed from A530 Nantwich–Whitchurch; CW5 8HG
Converted 19th-c corn mill with fine canal views from gravel terrace and series of tall glazed arches in bar, spacious modern feel, comfortably furnished with tapestried banquettes, oak settles and wheelback chairs around rustic tables, quarry-tiled area by bar with oak settle and refectory table, old lift hoist up under the rafters, Robinsons beers, farm cider and good generously served food (all day weekends), good friendly service; background music, free wi-fi; children and dogs welcome, disabled access/facilities, farm shop, closed Mon, otherwise open all day.
(Giles and Annie Francis)

Post Office address codings give the impression that some pubs are in Cheshire, when they're really in Derbyshire (and therefore included under that chapter) or in Greater Manchester (see the Lancashire chapter).

Cornwall

KEY ★ Star Pub 🌟 Top Quality Food 🍺 Great Beer
♀ Good Wines £ Bargain Meals 🛏 Good Bedrooms 🍴 Serves Food

BLISLAND
SX1073 Map 1
Blisland Inn 🍺 £
(01208) 850739 ~ www.bodminmoor.co.uk
Village signposted off A30 and B3266 NE of Bodmin; PL30 4JF

A fine choice of real ales, beer-related memorabilia, friendly staff, pubby food and seats outside

The genuinely welcoming landlord in this traditional, old-fashioned pub keeps around six real ales tapped from the cask or on handpump: two named for the pub by Sharps – Blisland Special and Bulldog – as well as quickly changing beers from west country breweries such as Atlantic, Bude, Otter, Padstow, Skinners and St Austell; also, farm cider, fruit wines and real apple juice. Service is good. Every inch of the beams and ceiling is covered with beer badges (or their particularly wide-ranging collection of mugs), and the walls are filled with beer-related posters and the like. The carpeted lounge has several barometers on the walls, toby jugs on beams and a few standing timbers, while the family room has pool, table skittles, euchre, cribbage and dominoes; background music. Plenty of picnic-sets outside. The popular Camel Trail cycle path is close by – though the hill up to Blisland is pretty steep. As with many pubs in this area, the approach by car involves negotiating several single-track roads.

🍴 Honest, home-cooked food includes baps, good soup, whitebait, ham and eggs, sausage and mash, leek and mushroom bake, chicken and ham pie, and puddings such as apple crumble and sticky toffee pudding. *Benchmark main dish: steak in ale pie £9.00. Two-course evening meal £15.50.*

Free house ~ Licensees Gary and Margaret Marshall ~ Real ale ~ Open 11.30-11.30 (midnight Sat); 12-10.30 Sun ~ Bar food 12-2, 6.30-9; not Sun evening ~ Restaurant ~ Children in family room only ~ Dogs welcome ~ Regular live music *Recommended by R J Herd, Susan Jackman, Mr Yeldahn*

BOSCASTLE
SX0991 Map 1
Cobweb
(01840) 250278 ~ http://cobwebinn.com
B3263, just E of harbour; PL35 0HE

Plenty of interest in cheerful pub, several real ales and friendly staff

This bustling pub is very near the tiny steeply cut harbour and pretty village. The two interesting bars have quite a mix of seats (from settles and carved chairs to more pubby furniture), heavy beams hung with hundreds of bottles and jugs, lots of pictures of bygone years and cosy log fires. They keep four real ales such as St Austell Proper Job and Tribute, Sharps Doom Bar and a guest beer on handpump and a local cider, and the atmosphere is cheerful and bustling, especially at peak times; games machine, darts and pool. The restaurant is upstairs. There are picnic-sets and benches outside (some under cover); dogs must be on a lead. A self-catering apartment is for rent.

Reasonably priced, traditional food includes sandwiches, crispy whitebait with citrus dip, chicken liver pâté, cornish pasty, beef, chicken or vegetarian burgers with coleslaw and chips, local sausages with mustard mash and caramelised onion gravy, gammon with pineapple, egg and home-made onion rings, curry of the day, and puddings. *Benchmark main dish: steak in ale pie £10.25. Two-course evening meal £16.00.*

Free house ~ Licensee Adrian Bright ~ Real ale ~ Open 10.30am–11pm (midnight Sat); 12-10.30 Sun ~ Bar food 11.30-2.30, 6-9.30 ~ Restaurant ~ Children welcome ~ Dogs allowed in bar *Recommended by Roy and Lindsey Fentiman, Susan Jackman, John Sargeant*

CONSTANTINE

SW7328   Map 1

Trengilly Wartha ♀ ⇤

(01326) 340332 – www.trengilly.co.uk

Nancenoy; A3083 S of Helston, signposted Gweek near RNAS Culdrose, then fork right after Gweek; OS Sheet 204 map reference 731282; TR11 5RP

Well run inn surrounded by big gardens with a friendly welcome for all, an easy-going atmosphere and popular food and drink; bedrooms

To make the most of this lovely area and explore all the surrounding walks, it makes sense to stay in the comfortable, cottagey bedrooms here; their breakfasts are very highly regarded. You'll get a warm welcome from the courteous licensees and their charming staff, and the long, low-beamed main bar has a sociable feel (especially in the evening, which is when the locals drop in). There are all sorts of tables and chairs, a woodburning stove, cricket team photos on the walls, Greene King Abbot, Penzance Potion No 9 and a guest from Skinners on handpump, up to 20 wines by the glass, 50 malt whiskies and quite a choice of gins and rums. Leading off the bar is the conservatory family room and there's also a cosy bistro. The six acres of gardens are well worth a wander and offer plenty of seats and picnic-sets under large parasols.

Rewarding food using the best local produce includes sandwiches, crab pot with chilli and spring onion, chicken liver pâté with home-made chutney, wild mushroom stroganoff, local mussels in wine, garlic and cream, beef and mushroom in ale pie, burger with Jack Daniels barbecue sauce, cajun chicken on spiced potatoes in rich tomato sauce, lamb shank in red wine and rosemary, and puddings. *Benchmark main dish: changing local fish dish £11.95. Two-course evening meal £21.00.*

Free house ~ Licensees Will and Lisa Lea ~ Real ale ~ Open 11-3, 6-11 ~ Bar food 12-2, 7-9 ~ Restaurant ~ Children welcome away from bar area ~ Dogs allowed in bar and bedrooms ~ Wi-fi ~ Live music Weds, Sun evenings ~ Bedrooms: £75/£84 *Recommended by Chris and Angela Buckell, Maureen Wood, Colin McLachlan, Dave Braisted*

People named as recommenders after the full entries have told us that the pub should be included. But they have not written the report – we have, after anonymous on-the-spot inspection.

DEVORAN
SW7938 Map 1

Old Quay

(01872) 863142 – www.theoldquayinn.co.uk

Devoran from new Carnon Cross roundabout A39 Truro–Falmouth, left on old road, right at mini roundabout; TR3 6NE

Light and airy bar rooms in friendly pub with four real ales, good wine and imaginative food and seats on pretty back terraces; bedrooms

Our readers really enjoy their visits to this bustling, cheerful pub and you'll get a warm welcome from both the staff and friendly locals. The roomy bar has an interesting 'woodburner' set halfway up one wall, a cushioned window seat, wall settles and a few bar stools around just three tables on stripped boards, and bar chairs by the counter. Bass, Exmoor Gold, Otter Bitter and Skinners Porthleven on handpump and good wines by the glass; you can buy their own jams and chutneys. Off to the left is an airy room with pictures by local artists (for sale), built-in cushioned wall seating, plush stools and a couple of big tables on the dark slate floor. To the other side of the bar is another light room with more settles and farmhouse chairs, attractive blue and white striped cushions and more sailing photographs; darts and board games. As well as benches outside at the front looking down through the trees to the water, there's a series of snug little back terraces with picnic-sets and chairs and tables. Nearby parking is limited unless you arrive early. There is wheelchair access through a side door. The pub is next to the coast-to-coast Portreath to Devoran Mineral Tramway cycle path.

 Interesting food includes sandwiches, ham and pea risotto, prawn cocktail, roast butternut squash with pistachio pesto and goats cheese, local mussels in white wine, cream and garlic, three-egg omelettes, chicken curry, slow-roast pork belly with smoky leek gratin, red wine jus and crispy sage, fish pie, flatiron steak with basil butter and dauphinoise potatoes, and puddings such as coconut and lime brûlée and chocolate and orange bread and butter pudding. *Benchmark main dish: burger with toppings, onion rings and chips £12.00. Two-course evening meal £17.00.*

Punch ~ Tenants John and Hannah Calland ~ Real ale ~ Open 11-11 ~ Bar food 12-3, 6-9 ~ Restaurant ~ Children welcome ~ Dogs allowed in bar ~ Wi-fi ~ Quiz Tues evening winter ~ Bedrooms: £58.50/£75 *Recommended by David Crook, Richard Tilbrook, Colin McLachlan, Chris and Angela Buckell, Julie Braeburn*

GURNARDS HEAD
SW4337 Map 1

Gurnards Head Hotel

(01736) 796928 – www.gurnardshead.co.uk

B3306 Zennor–St Just; TR26 3DE

Interesting inn with lots of wines by the glass, good inventive food and fine surrounding walks; comfortable bedrooms

There are glorious walks in rugged National Trust countryside all around this civilised but easy-going inn and the Atlantic is just 500 metres away. The bar rooms are painted in bold, strong colours and there are paintings by local artists, books on shelves, fresh flowers, open fires and all manner of wooden dining chairs and tables and sofas on stripped boards or rugs. St Austell Tribute and guests from local breweries such as Cornish Crown, Rebel and Skinners on handpump, 14 wines by the glass or carafe and a couple of ciders; background music, darts and board games. The large back garden has plenty of seats. Bedrooms are comfortable and have views of the rugged moors or the sea. This is under the same ownership as the Old Coastguard in Mousehole (also in Cornwall) and the Griffin at Felinfach (Wales).

Creative food from a short, interesting menu includes foraged nettle and mint gazpacho with lemon sour cream, local monkfish with pancetta, baby gem and charred tomatoes, tomato tart with basil pesto, courgettes and goats cheese, corn-fed chicken breast with fondant potatoes, broad beans, greens and madeira jus, ray wing with crushed potatoes, chard, samphire and shrimp butter, duck breast with green beans, passion fruit and shallots, and puddings such as treacle tart with raspberry compote and brownie with maple and pecan ice-cream; they may offer a two- and three-course set menu. *Benchmark main dish: pork belly, pak choi, cauliflower, coriander and miso jus £16.95. Two-course evening meal £22.50.*

Free house ~ Licensees Charles and Edmund Inkin ~ Real ale ~ Open 10am-11pm ~ Bar food 12-2.30, 6 (6.30 winter)-9.30 ~ Restaurant ~ Children welcome ~ Dogs allowed in bar and bedrooms ~ Wi-fi ~ Bedrooms: £95/£115 *Recommended by Sally Melling, Tony Smaithe, Peter Brix, John Preddy, William Slade*

HELFORD
Shipwrights Arms

SW7526 Map 1

(01326) 231235 – www.shipwrightshelford.co.uk
Off B3293 SE of Helston, via Mawgan; TR12 6JX

17th-c waterside inn with seats on terraces, cheerfully decorated bars, friendly service and tasty food

The terraces that drop down from this thatched pub to the water's edge give a lovely view of the beautiful wooded creek (at its best at high tide); seats on various levels make the most of this. Inside, there's quite a nautical theme, with navigation lamps, models of ships, paintings of fishing boats, drawings of fish and shellfish and even the odd figurehead; plenty of blue paintwork and blue patterned wallpaper add to the seaside feel. Painted high-backed dining chairs with attractive seats, leather wall banquettes and scatter cushions on window seats are grouped around wooden tables of varying sizes. Stools line the counter where they keep Harbour Light and Amber and St Austell Tribute on handpump, several wines by the glass and good rums; a winter open fire. There are good surrounding walks – including a long-distance coast path that goes right past the door.

Tasty food includes ham hock terrine with chutney, thai monkfish arancini balls with lemongrass and ginger dip, goats cheese with roasted pepper and tomato sauce and new potatoes, beer-battered fish and chips, beef curry, duck confit with braised red cabbage and creamed herby potatoes, steak with peppercorn sauce and chips, and puddings such as sticky toffee pudding with clotted cream and vanilla pannacotta with mixed berry coulis. *Benchmark main dish: whole grilled mackerel with sweet tomato ratatouille £12.50. Two-course evening meal £19.50.*

Free house ~ Licensees David and Vicky Harford ~ Real ale ~ Open 11-11 ~ Bar food 12-9 ~ Restaurant ~ Children welcome ~ Dogs welcome ~ Wi-fi ~ Live jazz Sun lunchtime *Recommended by Alfie Bayliss, Harvey Brown, Colin McLachlan, Helena and Trevor Fraser*

HELSTON
Halzephron

SW6522 Map 1

(01326) 240406 – www.halzephron-inn.co.uk
Gunwalloe, village about 4 miles S but not marked on many road maps; look for brown sign on A3083 alongside perimeter fence of RNAS Culdrose; TR12 7QB

Bustling pub in lovely spot with tasty bar food, local beers and good nearby walks; bedrooms

Well known as a smugglers' haunt, this busy inn is just 300 metres from Gunwalloe fishing cove. The neatly kept bar and dining areas have an informal, friendly atmosphere, some fishing memorabilia, comfortable seating, a warm winter fire in a woodburning stove, Sharps Doom Bar and guests such as St Austell Proper Job and Skinners Porthleven on handpump, nine wines by the glass, 41 malt whiskies and summer farm cider. The dining gallery seats up to 30 people; darts and board games. Picnic-sets outside look across National Trust fields and countryside. Church Cove with its sandy beach is nearby and there are lovely coastal walks in both directions.

 Well liked food includes sandwiches, creamy garlic mushrooms, local mussels in white wine, garlic and cream, lambs liver with crispy bacon in onion sauce, roast vegetable pasta with goats cheese and red pesto, steak in ale pie, beer-battered cod and chips, gammon with fresh pineapple, duck breast with red wine and plum sauce on red cabbage, and puddings. *Benchmark main dish: chicken stuffed with fresh crab in creamy dill sauce £14.50. Two-course evening meal £18.50.*

Free house ~ Licensee Claire Murray ~ Real ale ~ Open 11-11 ~ Bar food 12-2.30 (3 Sun), 6-9 ~ Restaurant ~ Children welcome ~ Dogs allowed in bar ~ Wi-fi ~ Bedrooms: £55/£94
Recommended by Toby Jones, Martin Jones, Robert Watt, Barbara Brown, Ian Duncan, Jane and Kai Horsburgh

LANLIVERY
SX0759 Map 1
Crown 🛏
(01208) 872707 – www.thecrowninncornwall.co.uk
Signposted off A390 Lostwithiel–St Austell (tricky to find from other directions); PL30 5BT

Chatty atmosphere in nice old pub, with traditional rooms and well liked food and drink; bedrooms

This pretty white-painted longhouse has been serving travellers walking the Saints Way since the building was constructed in the 12th c – and today, it still caters to both locals and visitors. The main bar has a log fire in a huge fireplace, traditional settles on big flagstones, church and other wooden chairs around all sorts of tables, old yachting photographs and beams in boarded ceilings. Sharps Doom Bar, Skinners Betty Stogs and a changing guest such as Arbor Spring Fever on handpump and several wines by the glass. A couple of other rooms are similarly furnished (including a dining conservatory) and there's another open fire; darts. The porch has a huge well with a glass top and the quiet, pretty garden has picnic-sets. Bedrooms (in separate buildings) are comfortable and overlook the garden; breakfasts are good. The Eden Project is a ten-minute drive away.

Food includes sandwiches, fresh crab tian, chicken liver parfait with chutney, mixed bean hotpot, hake on crushed potatoes with heritage beetroot, chicken on pea purée with basil oil, scallops with bacon and garlic butter, slow-braised lamb, and puddings such as toffee and hazelnut meringue and sticky toffee pudding. *Benchmark main dish: slow-roasted pork belly with apple and sage mash and ginger beer glaze £12.50. Two-course evening meal £18.00.*

Free house ~ Licensee Nigel Wakeham ~ Real ale ~ Open 11.30-11; 12-10.30 Sun ~ Bar food 12-2.30, 6-9 ~ Restaurant ~ Children welcome away from bar ~ Dogs allowed in bar and bedrooms ~ Wi-fi ~ Bedrooms: /£70 *Recommended by Wendy Breese, R T and J C Moggridge, Barry Collett*

Please keep sending us reports. We rely on readers for news of new discoveries, and particularly for news of changes – however slight – at the fully described pubs: feedback@goodguides.com, or (no stamp needed) The Good Pub Guide, FREEPOST RTJR-ZCYZ-RJZT, Perrymans Lane, Etchingham TN19 7DN.

LOSTWITHIEL

SX1059 Map 1

Globe ♀ ◖

(01208) 872501 – www.globeinn.com

North Street (close to medieval bridge); PL22 0EG

Traditional local with interesting food and drink, friendly staff and suntrap back courtyard

Good, enjoyable food and a friendly atmosphere continue to draw in customers here. The unassuming bar, which is long and narrow, has a mix of pubby tables and seats, local photographs on pale green plank panelling at one end and nice, mainly local prints (for sale) on canary yellow walls above a coal-effect stove at the snug inner end; there's also a small red-walled front alcove. The ornately carved bar counter, with comfortable chrome and leatherette stools, dispenses Sharps Doom Bar, Skinners Betty Stogs and a guest such as Tintagel Arthurs Ale on handpump, 11 reasonably priced wines by the glass, 20 malt whiskies and two local ciders; background music, darts, board games and TV. The sheltered back courtyard is not large but has some attractive and unusual plants, and is a real suntrap (with an extendable awning and outside heaters). You can park in several of the nearby streets or the (free) town car park. The 13th-c church is worth a look and the ancient river bridge, a few metres away, is lovely.

 The highly thought-of food includes moules marinière, chicken liver pâté, vegetarian roast with mushroom, red onion and port sauce, gammon with fresh pineapple, pie of the day, chilli con carne, fresh fish of the day, slow-cooked local lamb with gravy and creamy mash, and puddings such as banoffi pie and bread and butter pudding. *Benchmark main dish: seafood chowder £11.95. Two-course evening meal £20.00.*

Free house ~ Licensee William Erwin ~ Real ale ~ Open 12-11 (midnight Fri, Sat) ~ Bar food 12-2, 6.30-9 ~ Restaurant ~ Children welcome but no pushchairs in restaurant ~ Dogs allowed in bar ~ Wi-fi ~ Live music Fri, quiz Sun ~ Bedrooms: /£75 *Recommended by John Marsh, R K Phillips, Dennis and Doreen Haward, Daphne and Robert Staples*

MORWENSTOW

SS2015 Map 1

Bush 🛏

(01288) 331242 – www.thebushinnmorwenstow.com

Signed off A39 N of Kilkhampton; Crosstown; EX23 9SR

Ancient pub in fine spot, character bar, several dining rooms and outside dining huts and well liked food; bedrooms

One of the oldest pubs in Britain, this homely little place was once a monastic resting house on the pilgrim route between Spain and Wales. The character bar has traditional pubby furniture on big flagstones, a woodburner in a large stone fireplace, horse tack and copper knick-knacks, St Austell HSD and Tribute and a guest such as Dartmoor Legend on handpump, eight wines by the glass, several whiskies and farm cider; background music, darts and board games. One beamed dining room has tall pale wooden dining chairs and tables on bare boards, small prints on cream-painted walls, fresh flowers and another woodburning stove; a second has big windows overlooking the picnic-sets and heated dining huts. The neat bedrooms have lovely views and breakfasts are served until 11am; the courtyard room allows dogs. There are marvellous surrounding walks and good nearby surfing beaches too.

🍴 Good food includes sandwiches, cornish pasty with chutney, fishcakes with coriander, chilli and apricot chutney, sharing platters, spinach and ricotta cannelloni, a pie of the day, home-cooked honey roast ham with free-range eggs, slow-cooked lamb with greek salad, and puddings such as chocolate brownie with chocolate sauce and lemon crunch. *Benchmark main dish: burger with toppings and chips £10.00. Two-course evening meal £15.00.*

Free house ~ Licensees Colin and Gill Fletcher ~ Real ale ~ Open 12-12 (10 Mon winter) ~ Bar food 12-9 ~ Restaurant ~ Children welcome ~ Dogs allowed in bar and bedrooms ~ Wi-fi ~ Live music every other weekend ~ Bedrooms: £65/£90 *Recommended by David Crook, Sally Wright, Susan Busbridge*

MOUSEHOLE
SW4726 Map 1

Old Coastguard 🏅 ♀ 🛏

(01736) 731222 – www.oldcoastguardhotel.co.uk
The Parade (edge of village, Newlyn coast road); TR19 6PR

Lovely position for carefully refurbished inn with an easy-going atmosphere, good choice of wines and first rate food; bedrooms with sea views

The garden here is rather special with its tropical palms and dracaena and a path that leads down to rock pools; seats on the terrace look over the sea to St Michael's Mount and the Lizard. The bar rooms have boldly coloured walls hung with paintings of sailing boats and local scenes, stripped floorboards and an atmosphere of informal but civilised comfort. The Upper Deck houses the bar and the restaurant, with a nice mix of antique dining chairs around oak and distressed pine tables, lamps on big barrel tables and chairs to either side of the log fire, topped by a vast bressumer beam. Harbour Amber, Rebel Sail Ale and St Austell Tribute on handpump, 14 wines by the glass or carafe, a farm cider and a good choice of soft drinks. The Lower Deck has glass windows running the length of the building, several deep sofas and armchairs and shelves of books and games; background music. The comfortable bedrooms look over the water. This is sister pub to the Gurnards Head (also Cornwall) and the Griffin at Felinfach (Wales).

As well as breakfasts (8-10am), the impressive food includes pheasant sausage with puy lentils and pickled onions, grilled mackerel fillet with chorizo, apple salad and aioli, blonde ray with celeriac, apple, pancetta, crème fraîche and crisp potatoes, shallot tarte tatin with salt-baked celeriac and trompette mushrooms, pork loin with beetroot, mustard cream and crispy capers, beef rump with horseradish and red wine jus, and puddings such as marmalade iced parfait with dark chocolate and lemon posset with plums and bay fritter. *Benchmark main dish: bouillabaisse £16.00. Two-course evening meal £22.00.*

Free house ~ Licensees Charles and Edmund Inkin ~ Real ale ~ Open 8am-11.30pm ~ Bar food 12.30 (12 Sun)-2.30, 6.30-9 ~ Restaurant ~ Children welcome ~ Dogs allowed in bar and bedrooms ~ Wi-fi ~ Occasional live music Sun ~ Bedrooms: £100/£135
Recommended by Martin Jones, Toby Jones, Peter Andrews, John Sargeant, R T and J C Moggridge

MOUSEHOLE
SW4626 Map 1

Ship 🛏

(01736) 731234 – www.shipinnmousehole.co.uk
Harbourside; TR19 6QX

Busy little pub in pretty village with character bars, real ales and fair-priced food; bedrooms

This is a friendly harbourside local at the heart of a lovely village. The opened-up main bar has black beams and panelling, built-in wooden wall benches and stools around low tables, sailors' fancy ropework, granite flagstones and a cosy open fire. St Austell Cornish Best, HSD and Tribute on handpump, several wines by the glass and maybe background music. The bedrooms are above the pub or in the cottage next door and some overlook the water. It's best to park at the top of the village and walk down (traffic can be a bit of a nightmare in summer). The elaborate harbour lights at Christmas are well worth a visit.

Pubby food includes lunchtime sandwiches, seafood pâté with spiced chutney, half a pint of prawns with aioli, basket meals, edamame, chickpea, red onion and apple salad with lime and ginger dressing, vegetarian linguine, burger with toppings, onion rings and chips, local crab salad with lemon mayonnaise, and puddings. *Benchmark main dish: beer-battered fish and chips £12.50. Two-course evening meal £18.00.*

St Austell ~ Manager Melanie Matthews ~ Real ale ~ Open 11-11; 11-10.30 Sun ~ Bar food 12-2.30, 6-8.30 ~ Restaurant ~ Children welcome ~ Dogs allowed in bar and bedrooms ~ Wi-fi ~ Bedrooms: /£120 *Recommended by Charlie May, Toby Jones, Colin McLachlan, Alan Johnson, Andrew Stone*

MYLOR BRIDGE
Pandora ♀

SW8137 Map 1

(01326) 372678 – www.pandorainn.com

Restronguet Passage: from A39 in Penryn, take turning signposted Mylor Church, Mylor Bridge, Flushing and go straight through Mylor Bridge following Restronguet Passage signs; or from A39 further N, at or near Perranarworthal, take turning signposted Mylor, Restronguet, then follow Restronguet Weir signs, but turn left downhill at Restronguet Passage sign; TR11 5ST

Beautifully placed waterside inn with lots of atmosphere in beamed and flagstoned rooms, and all-day food

You must get to this medieval pub early to bag a seat outside as the idyllic position draws in the crowds on a sunny day, and the seats at the front and on the long floating jetty are snapped up when the doors open. Inside, there's a back cabin bar with pale farmhouse chairs, high-backed settles and a model galleon in a big glass cabinet. Several other rambling, interconnecting rooms have low beams, beautifully polished big flagstones, cosy alcoves, cushioned built-in wall seats and pubby tables and chairs, three large log fires in high hearths (to protect them against tidal floods) and maps, yacht pictures, oars and ships' wheels; church candles help with the lighting. St Austell HSD, Proper Job, Trelawny and Tribute on handpump, 17 wines by the glass and 18 malt whiskies served by friendly, efficient staff. Upstairs, the attractive dining room has exposed oak vaulting, dark tables and chairs on pale oak flooring and large brass bells and lanterns. Because of the pub's popularity, parking is extremely difficult at peak times; wheelchair access.

Some sort of food is offered all day: sandwiches (until 5pm), local scallops with leek purée and parmesan, ham hock terrine with home-made piccalilli, halloumi burger with portobello mushroom and sweet pepper chutney, mussels in cider, cream, ginger, honey and spring onion, lambs liver with carrot and blue cheese bubble and squeak, beer-battered fish of the day and chips, and puddings such as baked alaska and chocolate fondant with orange ganache. *Benchmark main dish: fish pie £13.00. Two-course evening meal £20.00.*

St Austell ~ Tenant John Milan ~ Real ale ~ Open 10.30am-11pm ~ Bar food 10.30-9.30 ~ Restaurant ~ Children welcome away from bar area ~ Dogs allowed in bar ~ Wi-fi *Recommended by Chris and Angela Buckell, David Eberlin, John Marsh, Mr and Mrs J Watkins, Richard Tilbrook*

PENZANCE SW4730 Map 1
Turks Head

(01736) 363093 – www.turksheadpenzance.co.uk

At top of main street, by big domed building turn left down Chapel Street; TR18 4AF

Cheerful pub with a good, bustling atmosphere and popular food and beer

There's always a lively mix of both regulars and visitors in this well run town pub and a friendly welcome is offered to all. The bar has old flatirons, jugs and so forth hanging from the beams, pottery above the wood-effect panelling, wall seats and tables and a couple of elbow-rests around central pillars; background music and board games. Sharps Doom Bar, Skinners Betty Stogs and guests such as Greene King Abbot and Wadworths 6X on handpump, a dozen wines by the glass and 12 malt whiskies. The suntrap back garden has big urns of flowers. There's been a Turks Head here for over 700 years – though most of the original building was destroyed by a Spanish raiding party in the 16th c.

 Reliably good food includes lunchtime sandwiches, pork, ham and smoked bacon terrine with chutney, whipped goats cheese with red onion marmalade, five bean, spinach and sweet potato lasagne, home-pickled beetroot and orange vinagrette, sausages of the day with pumpkin mash, caramelised onion and apple and red wine gravy, coq au vin, beer-battered fish of the day, steak burger with toppings and chips, and puddings. *Benchmark main dish: seafood pie £13.50. Two-course evening meal £15.00.*

Punch ~ Lease Jonathan and Helen Gibbard ~ Real ale ~ Open 11.30am-midnight; 12-11 Sun ~ Bar food 12-2.30, 6-10 ~ Restaurant ~ Children welcome ~ Dogs allowed in bar ~ Wi-fi
Recommended by Andrew Stone, Alan Johnson, Thomas Green

PERRANUTHNOE SW5329 Map 1
Victoria 🏵

(01736) 710309 – www.victoriainn-penzance.co.uk

Signed off A394 Penzance–Helston; TR20 9NP

Carefully furnished inn with interesting food, a friendly welcome, local beers and seats in pretty garden; bedrooms

The imaginative food is the main draw to this enthusiastically run, busy inn, but they do keep Sharps Doom Bar and guests from Cornish Crown and Skinners on handpump and over ten wines by the glass. The L-shaped bar has various cosy corners, exposed joists, a woodburning stove and an attractive array of dining chairs around wooden tables on oak flooring. The restaurant is separate; background music and board games. The pub spaniel is called Monty. The pretty tiered garden has seats and tables, and the bedrooms are light and airy. The inn is a minute from the South West Coast Path and just over a mile from the beaches of Mount's Bay.

Highly enjoyable food includes local scallops with hog's pudding, capers, apple and celeriac, shredded ham hock with cauliflower purée, spiced pineapple salsa and organic duck egg, moules marinière, roasted artichoke and pea tagliatelle with truffle oil, lemon zest, parmesan and crème friache, local plaice with leeks, cucumber, brown shrimps and dill and lemon butter sauce, garlic and thyme pork cutlet with apple butter and creamed potato, and puddings. *Benchmark main dish: pork belly with root vegetable mash, black pudding and rosemary jus £16.00. Two-course evening meal £21.00.*

Free house ~ Licensee Nik Boyle ~ Real ale ~ Open 12-11.30; 12-6 Sun ~ Bar food 12-2, 6-9; not Sun evening ~ Restaurant ~ Children welcome ~ Dogs allowed in bar ~ Wi-fi ~

Bedrooms: /£75 *Recommended by Ross Balaam, Charlie Parker, Christopher Mannings, Nigel Reed, Tom and Ruth Rees*

PHILLEIGH
Roseland

SW8739 Map 1

(01872) 580254 – www.roselandinn.co.uk
Between A3078 and B3289, NE of St Mawes just E of King Harry Ferry; TR2 5NB

Character bars and back dining room in attractive pub, local ales, good food and seats on the attractive front terrace

This 16th-c pub is just a mile from the King Harry Ferry and Trelissick Garden (National Trust) is just across the river. The two character bar rooms (one with flagstones, the other carpeted) have farmhouse and other dining chairs and built-in red cushioned seats, a woodburning stove, old photographs, brass spoons and horsebrasses, and some giant beetles and butterflies in glass cases. The tiny lower area is liked by regulars and there's a back restaurant too. Skinners Betty Stogs, Sharps Doom Bar and a guest beer on handpump and several decent wines by the glass; staff are friendly and helpful. There are seats out on a pretty paved front courtyard.

Popular food includes sandwiches, crab risotto, creamy peppercorn duck rillette with onion marmalade, local sausages and mash, mackerel niçoise, pork belly with pak choi stir-fry and sesame noodles, bass fillet with sunblush tomato, green bean and caper salad, and puddings such as salted caramel chocolate torte and lemon possett. *Benchmark main dish: slow-roast lamb shoulder with rosemary mash and mint jus £14.95. Two-course evening meal £20.50.*

Punch ~ Tenant Philip Heslip ~ Real ale ~ Open 11-3, 5.30-11; 11-11 Sat; 11-10.30 Sun ~ Bar food 12-2.30, 6-9 ~ Restaurant ~ Children welcome ~ Dogs allowed in bar ~ Wi-fi ~ Folk night first Weds of month *Recommended by R and S Bentley, Edward May, Phil and Jane Villiers*

POLKERRIS
Rashleigh

SX0952 Map 1

(01726) 813991 – www.therashleighinnpolkerris.co.uk
Signposted off A3082 Fowey–St Austell; PL24 2TL

Lovely beachside spot, with heaters on sizeable sun terrace, five real ales and quite a choice of food

The front terrace here has outside heaters, so you can make the most of the wonderful views towards the far side of St Austell and Mevagissey bays, even in cooler weather. The cosy bar has comfortably cushioned chairs around dark wooden tables at the front, and similar furnishings, local photographs and a winter log fire at the back. Otter Bitter, Skinners Betty Stogs, Timothy Taylors Landlord and a guest from Padstow or Rebel on handpump, several wines by the glass, two farm ciders and organic soft drinks. All the tables in the restaurant have a sea view. A fine beach with a restored jetty is just a few steps away and the local section of the South West Coast Path is renowned for its striking scenery. There's plenty of parking in either the pub's own car park or the large village one.

Good food includes sandwiches, baked whole camembert with cranberry sauce, smoked haddock and leek fishcakes with sweet chilli sauce, red onion and rocket curry with turmeric rice, local sausages with red onion gravy, burger with toppings, coleslaw and chips, a fresh fish dish of the day, steak in ale pie, and puddings such as crème brûlée and treacle tart. *Benchmark main dish: beer-battered cod and chips £9.95. Two-course evening meal £15.00.*

Free house ~ Licensees Jon and Samantha Spode ~ Real ale ~ Open 11-11 ~ Bar food 12-3, 6-9 ~ Restaurant ~ Children welcome ~ Dogs allowed in bar *Recommended by R K Phillips, Peter Brix, Sarah Roberts, Sally and David Champion*

POLPERRO
SX2050 Map 1

Blue Peter 🍺 £

(01503) 272743 ~ www.thebluepeter.co.uk
Quay Road; PL13 2QZ

Friendly pub overlooking harbour with a good mix of customers, fishing paraphernalia, real ales and carefully prepared food

The cosy low-beamed bar in this chatty little harbourside pub has a relaxed atmosphere, traditional furnishings that include a small winged settle and a polished pew, wooden flooring, fishing regalia, photographs and pictures by local artists, lots of candles and a solid wood bar counter. St Austell Tribute and guests from local breweries such as Bays, Cornish Crown and Harbour on handpump served by the friendly, long-serving licensees. One window seat looks down on the harbour, while another looks out past rocks to the sea; families must use the upstairs room. Background music and board games. There are a few seats outside on the terrace and more in an amphitheatre-style area upstairs. The pub gets crowded at peak times. Usefully, they have a cash machine (there's no bank in the village).

 Reasonably priced, tasty food includes sandwiches (the crab is good), chicken liver pâté with chutney, fishcakes with sweet chilli dip, a pie of the day, home-cooked ham and free-range eggs, pasta dish of the day, pork and apple burger with chips, seafood platter, local steaks, and puddings such as white chocolate pot and toffee apple crumble. *Benchmark main dish: beer-battered fish and chips £11.00. Two-course evening meal £17.00.*

Free house ~ Licensees Steve and Caroline Steadman ~ Real ale ~ Open 11-11; 12-11 Sun ~ Bar food 12-3, 6-9; all day in summer peak season ~ Restaurant ~ Children in upstairs family room only ~ Dogs allowed in bar ~ Wi-fi ~ Live music Fri and Sat evenings in summer *Recommended by Barry Collett, Edward May, Ian Herdman, Steve and Liz Tilley, Eddie Edwards*

PORT ISAAC
SX0080 Map 1

Port Gaverne Inn 🛏️

(01208) 880244 ~ www.portgavernehotel.co.uk
Port Gaverne signposted from Port Isaac and from B3314 E of Pendoggett; PL29 3SQ

Bustling small hotel with a proper bar and real ales, well liked food in several dining areas and seats in the garden; bedrooms

This civilised, early 17th-c inn is in a lovely spot just back from the sea and is surrounded by splendid clifftop walks. The bar is full of lively chat – especially in the evenings – and there are low beams, flagstones and carpeting, some exposed stone and a big log fire; the lounge has some interesting old local photographs. You can eat in the bar or in the 'Captain's Cabin' – a little room where everything is shrunk to scale (old oak chest, model sailing ship, even the prints on the white stone walls). St Austell Proper Job and Tribute, Skinners Betty Stogs and Timothy Taylors Landlord on handpump, a decent choice of wines and several whiskies. There are seats and tables under parasols at the front, with more in the terraced garden. The individually furnished and comfortable bedrooms have much character and although the stairs up to most of them are fairly steep, staff will carry your luggage.

Reliably good food includes sandwiches (until 6pm), salt and pepper squid with chilli and lime, sticky chicken wings with honey and soy, wild mushroom risotto with mozzarella, local sausages with onion gravy, steak burger with toppings, jalapeno mayonnaise and fries, grilled dover sole with seaweed and samphire butter, glazed ox cheek with roast garlic mash, onion compote and chanterelle mushrooms, and puddings such as dark chocolate cheesecake with caramel popcorn and passion-fruit and mango sorbet and rhubarb crumble with stem ginger ice-cream. *Benchmark main dish: fish pie £16.00. Two-course evening meal £21.50.*

Free house ~ Licensee Jackie Barnard ~ Real ale ~ Open 11-11 ~ Bar food 12-2, 7-9 ~ Restaurant ~ Children welcome ~ Dogs welcome ~ Wi-fi ~ Bedrooms: £95/£150
Recommended by Mrs A W Johns, Colin McLachlan, Sandra Hollies, Ian Duncan

PORTHLEVEN
Ship

SW6225   Map 1

(01326) 564204 – www.theshipinncornwall.co.uk
Mount Pleasant Road (harbour) off B3304; TR13 9JS

Friendly harbourside pub with fantastic views, pubby furnishings, real ales and tasty food and seats on terrace

In kind weather there are tables in the terraced garden here that make the most of the fine sea view, and the harbour is interestingly floodlit at night. Both the bustling bar and candlelit dining room share this view and there are open fires in stone fireplaces, quite a mix of chairs and tables on flagstones or bare boards, beer mats and brasses on the ceiling and walls, and various lamps and pennants. Sharps Cornish Coaster and Doom Bar, Skinners Porthleven and Rebel Gold on handpump; background music. They also have a cosy, traditionally furnished and separate function room. Seats in the terraced garden look over the water.

 Well liked food includes sandwiches, toasted focaccia with toppings, sharing platters, vegetable tart with herbed roast potatoes, spare ribs and fries, chicken and leek pie, burgers with onion rings and fries, crab salad with lemon mayonnaise, and puddings such as treacle tart and apple crumble. *Benchmark main dish: fish pie £11.95. Two-course evening meal £16.00.*

Free house ~ Licensee Oliver Waite ~ Real ale ~ Open 11am-midnight ~ Bar food 12-2.30, 6-9 ~ Well behaved children welcome ~ Dogs welcome ~ Wi-fi ~ Live music monthly
Recommended by Clifford Blakemore, Alan Johnson, Ray White, Jack and Hilary Burton

PORTHTOWAN
Blue

SW6948   Map 1

(01209) 890329 – www.blue-bar.co.uk
Beach Road, East Cliff; car park (fee in season) advised; TR4 8AW

Informal, busy bar by a stunning beach with modern food and wide choice of drinks

Of course, this isn't a traditional pub – it's a bustling bar with a wide mix of cheerful customers who've come hungry and thirsty straight off the wonderful beach next door. They all pile in here throughout the day and the atmosphere is easy and informal; big picture windows look across the terrace to the huge expanse of sand and sea. The front bays have built-in pine seats, while the rest of the large room has wicker and white chairs around pale tables on grey-painted floorboards, cream or orange walls, several bar stools and plenty of standing space around the counter; ceiling fans, some big ferny plants and fairly quiet background music. St Austell Tribute, Sharps Doom Bar and a guest from Skinners on handpump, several wines by the glass, cocktails and shots, and all kinds of coffees, hot chocolates and teas.

❚❚ Some sort of food is usefully served all day from 10am: brunch (until 11.45am), various fajitas, sharing platters, malaysian laksa curry, chicken katsu, mussels in white wine, cream and garlic, steaks, and puddings such as waffles and sticky toffee pudding. *Benchmark main dish: burger with toppings, coleslaw and rustic chips £8.75. Two-course evening meal £16.00.*

Free house ~ Licensees Tara Roberts and Luke Morris ~ Real ale ~ Open 10am-11pm (midnight Fri, Sat); 10am-10.30pm Sun ~ Bar food 10-9 ~ Children welcome ~ Dogs welcome ~ Wi-fi ~ Live music Sat evening *Recommended by Tom and Jill Jones, Colin Humphreys, Claire Adams, Nigel Havers*

 ROCK   SW9375   Map 1

Mariners ⭐ ♀

(01208) 863679 – www.themarinersrock.com

Rock Road; PL27 6LD

Modern pub with huge glass windows taking in the estuary views, highly popular food, three real ales and wines by the glass, friendly service and seats on front terrace

To make the most of the lovely view over the Camel estuary there's a front terrace here with lots of seats and tables (people often sit on the wall too), a much coveted small terrace leading from the first-floor restaurant, and huge windows and folding glass doors; it gets packed in warm weather. The bar is light and spacious with contemporary metal chairs and wall seats around pale wooden-topped tables on slate flooring; walls are partly bare stone and partly painted and hung with old black and white photos, modern prints and blackboards listing food and drink items. There's an open kitchen. Atlantic Ale, Sharps Doom Bar and a guest beer on handpump and good wines by the glass; background music and TV. The upstairs restaurant is similarly furnished and, if anything, the views are even better from here.

⭐ Robust, seasonal cooking includes lunchtime focaccia rolls, mussels in wheat beer with chilli and orange zest, potted rabbit with pickled red cabbage and dates, charred cauliflower with spinach, potato, saffron and dukkah, cod with seaweed dumplings and lime butter, faggots and smoked mash, lamb chop curry, grey mullet with braised fennel, cabbage roll and smoked paprika sauce, and puddings such as chocolate and stout cake with honeycomb, blood orange and orange curd and baked custard with rhubarb and gingerbread. *Benchmark main dish: 8oz local rump steak with béarnaise sauce and chips £19.50. Two-course evening meal £23.00.*

Free house ~ Licensee Nathan Outlaw ~ Real ale ~ Open 11am-midnight ~ Bar food 12-9; 12-4.30, 6-9 Sun ~ Children welcome ~ Dogs welcome ~ Wi-fi *Recommended by James Allsopp, Ben and Diane Bowie, Tim and Sarah Smythe-Brown*

 ST IVES   SW5441   Map 1

Queens 🛏

(01736) 796468 – www.queenshotelstives.com

High Street; TR26 1RR

Bustling inn just back from the harbour with a spacious bar, open fire, real ales and tasty food; bedrooms

Plenty of regulars and visitors crowd into the spreading bar here to enjoy the local ales and popular food. This open-plan bar has a relaxed atmosphere, all sorts of wooden chairs around scrubbed tables on bare floorboards, tartan banquettes on either side of the Victorian fireplace, a wall of barometers above a leather chesterfield sofa and some brown leather armchairs; fresh flowers and candles on tables and on the mantelpiece above the open fire. Red-painted bar chairs line the white marble-topped counter where they serve St Austell Cornish Best, HSD, Proper Job and Tribute on handpump, 15 wines by the glass, a good choice of gins and rums and farm cider; background music, board games and TV for sports events. The attractive bedrooms are airy and simply furnished with cornish artwork on the walls and some period furniture. The window boxes and hanging baskets are quite a sight in summer.

Pleasing food includes lunchtime sandwiches, mussels with white wine and cream, cured meat salad with olives and capers, mixed vegetable, wild mushroom and parmesan risotto, honey-roast ham with free-range egg and crispy capers, beef stew with dumplings, bass with crab and mussel sauce, and puddings such as dark chocolate and pistachio tart with rum and raisin ice-cream and apple and raisin crumble with vanilla ice-cream. *Benchmark main dish: braised lamb shoulder with dauphinoise potatoes and red wine jus £14.00. Two-course evening meal £19.50.*

St Austell ~ Tenant Neythan Hayes ~ Real ale ~ Open 11-11 (10.30 winter) ~ Bar food 12-2.30, 6-9; 12-9 (6 winter) ~ Children welcome ~ Dogs allowed in bar ~ Wi-fi ~ Bedrooms: £69/£79 *Recommended by Hilary and Neil Christopher, Peter Brix, Alan Johnson*

ST MAWGAN
Falcon

SW8765 Map 1

(01637) 860225 – www.thefalconinnstmawgan.co.uk
NE of Newquay, off B3276 or A3059; TR8 4EP

Friendly inn with compact, simply furnished bar and dining room, four ales, good food and seats in garden; bedrooms

The hub of the village, this 16th-c pub is a genuinly welcoming place to both loyal regulars and holidaymakers. The bar has a big fireplace with stone bottles to either side (a log fire in winter and fresh flowers in summer), farmhouse chairs and cushioned wheelbacks around an assortment of tables on patterned carpet, antique coaching prints and falcon pictures, and Colchester No 1, Sharps Perfect Storm, Tintagel Harbour Special and a changing guest on handpump; good wines by the glass. The compact stone-floored dining room has similar furnishings. Plenty of picnic-sets (some painted blue) in the pretty garden, a wishing well, and a cobbled front courtyard, too. Bedrooms are comfortable.

Good food includes lunchtime sandwiches, pâté of the day with piccalilli, smoked salmon and prawn salad, cornish pasty, ham and eggs, rare-breed pork sausages with spring onion and smoked cheese mash and real ale gravy, spinach, wild garlic and mushroom lasagne, chicken korma, lamb burger with smoked chipotle and onion relish, coleslaw and chips, and puddings. *Benchmark main dish: beer-battered haddock and chips £11.50. Two-course evening meal £19.00.*

St Austell ~ Managers David Carbis and Sarah Lawrence ~ Real ale ~ Open 11-3, 5.30-11 (midnight Fri); 11am-midnight Sat; 12-11 Sun ~ Bar food 12-2.30, 6-9.30 ~ Restaurant ~ Children welcome away from the bar ~ Dogs allowed in bar ~ Wi-fi ~ Bedrooms: £53/£94 *Recommended by Robert Watt, Donald Allsopp, Ruth May*

ST MERRYN SW8874 Map 1

Cornish Arms

(01841) 532700 – www.rickstein.com/eat-with-us/the-cornish-arms

Churchtown (B3276 towards Padstow); PL28 8ND

Bustling pub with lots of cheerful customers, bar and dining rooms, real ales, good pubby food, friendly service and seats outside

Holidaymakers crowd into this busy roadside pub during peak season – locals enjoy it more during less busy months. It's well run and friendly, and the main door leads into a sizeable informal area with a pool table and plenty of cushioned wall seating; to the left, a light, airy dining room overlooks the terrace. There's an unusual modern upright woodburner (with tightly packed logs on each side), photographs of the sea and former games teams, and pale wooden dining chairs around tables on quarry tiles. This leads to two more linked rooms with ceiling joists; the first has pubby furniture on huge flagstones, while the end room has more cushioned wall seating, contemporary seats and tables and parquet flooring. There's also a new dining room to the back. St Austell Proper Job, Trelawny and Tribute on handpump, 17 wines by the glass, a farm cider, friendly service, background music, board games and TV; they hold a beer and mussel festival every March. The window boxes are pretty and there are picnic-sets on a side terrace – with more on grass.

Pubby favourites plus daily specials include sandwiches, half pint of prawns, moules marinière, tomato and blue cheese tart, scampi in a basket, ham and free-range eggs, lamb curry, burger with toppings and chips, local pork sausages with mash and onion gravy, and puddings such as sunken chocolate cake and sticky toffee pudding. *Benchmark main dish: beer-battered fish and chips £13.50. Two-course evening meal £19.30.*

St Austell ~ Tenant Siebe Richards ~ Real ale ~ Open 11.30-11 ~ Bar food 12-2.30, 5.30-8.30; 12-8 Sun ~ Children welcome ~ Dogs welcome ~ Wi-fi ~ Quiz Sun winter
Recommended by Chris and Val Ramstedt, Katherine Matthews

ST TUDY SX0676 Map 1

St Tudy Inn

(01208) 850656 – www.sttudyinn.com

Off A391 near Wadebridge; PL30 3NN

Refurbished pub with several bars and dining rooms, good wines by the glass, enjoyable food and seats outside

Of course, most customers are here to enjoy the marvellous food cooked by the landlady, but they do keep a good choice of drinks such as Sharps Doom Bar and a beer named for the pub on handpump, 25 wines by the glass and a couple of ciders. It's a welcoming and attractive place and the main bar has a leather armchair beside a log fire in a raised fireplace (fairy lights on the bressumer beam), beer-cask seats, chairs and cushioned window seats by a mix of tables on floor slates, and stools against the wooden counter. The dining rooms are relaxed and informal with dark farmhouse, wheelback and elegant wooden chairs and tables on bare boards or rugs, a second fireplace, fresh flowers and candlelight; background music. There are picnic-sets under parasols at the front and more seats in the garden.

Interesting modern food includes scallops with garlic and thyme, pear, walnut, dandelion and blue cheese salad, baked aubergines with tomatoes, tarragon and crème fraîche, whole bream with rosemary butter and caramelised red onions, lamb with chilli, coriander, spice mix and sweet potato purée, guinea fowl with parsley sauce, and puddings such as chocolate mousse with baked quince and almond tart with raspberries. *Benchmark main dish: chicken with tarragon, cream and sunblush tomaotes £13.50. Two-course evening meal £22.00.*

Free house ~ Licensee Emily Scott ~ Real ale ~ Open 11am-midnight; 11-5 Sun; closed Mon ~ Bar food 12-2.30, 6.30-9; not Sun evening ~ Restaurant ~ Children welcome ~ Dogs allowed in bar ~ Wi-fi *Recommended by Caroline Prescott, Lindy Andrews, R T and J C Moggridge*

 TREBURLEY   SX3477 Map 1
Springer Spaniel
(01579) 370424 – www.thespringerspaniel.co.uk
A388 Callington–Launceston; PL15 9NS

Cornwall Dining Pub of the Year

Cosy, friendly pub with highly popular, first class food, friendly staff and a genuine welcome for all

Food is king here (the owner is a former *MasterChef* winner), but this is no restaurant, it's a proper pub with locals and their dogs (they keep a jar of dog biscuits) and a friendly, easy-going atmosphere. The small beamed bar has antlers and a few copper pans on an exposed stone wall above a woodburning stove, books on shelves, pictures of springer spaniels, a rather fine high-backed settle and other country kitchen chairs and tables and old parquet flooring. A little dining room has more bookcases, candles and similar tables and chairs, and stairs lead up to the main restaurant; a second woodburner is set into a slate wall with a stag's head above it. Dartmoor Jail Ale and St Austells Tribute on handpump and ten good wines by the glass (including sparkling); background music. Outside in the small enclosed, paved garden are picnic-sets. This is sister pub to the Treby Arms in Sparkwell (Devon).

First class food using the best local produce includes pigeon wellington with mushroom purée and sage and onion croquette, duck liver parfait with sesame crips and onion purée, macaroni cheese with tomato foam, burger with barbecued pulled ox cheek, onion rings and triple-cooked chips, white wine-battered fish and chips with chip shop treats, cocoa venison with textures of parsnip and chocolate jus, brill with caper mash and butter, and puddings such as lemon parfait with fennel meringue, lime and cardamom gel and shortbread and rhubarb compote with custard. *Benchmark main dish: glazed short ribs with pickled vegetables and chips £20.00. Two-course evening meal £28.00.*

Free house ~ Licensees Anton and Clare Piotrowski ~ Real ale ~ Open 12-11 ~ Bar food 12-3, 6-9; snacks all day weekends and peak season ~ Restaurant ~ Children welcome ~ Dogs allowed in bar *Recommended by Isobel Mackinlay, Edward May, Sarah Roberts, Tony Smaithe*

 TREVAUNANCE COVE   SW7251 Map 1
Driftwood Spars
(01872) 552428 – www.driftwoodspars.com
Off B3285 in St Agnes; Quay Road; TR5 0RT

Friendly inn with plenty of history, own microbrewery, a wide range of other drinks and popular food, and beach nearby; bedrooms

This is a smashing all-rounder and our readers always enjoy their visits. It's a well run pub in a fine spot close to a dramatic cove and beach and is usefully open all day. The bars are timbered with massive ships' spars (the masts of great sailing ships, many of which were wrecked along this coast), and furnishings include dark wooden farmhouse and tub chairs and settles around tables of different sizes, padded stools by the counter, old ship prints, lots of nautical and wreck memorabilia and woodburning stoves. It's said that an old smugglers' tunnel leads from behind the bar up through the cliff. Seven real ales on handpump might include their own Driftwood Alfie's Revenge, Bawden Rocks, Forest Blond and Lou's Brew with guests such as Cornish Crown Golden Crown, Sharps Doom Bar and Tintagel Gwaf Tan; they hold two beer festivals a year. Also, 25 malt whiskies, ten rums, seven gins and several wines by the glass; table football and pool. The modern dining room overlooks the cove and service is friendly and helpful. There are pretty summer hanging baskets and seats in the garden. The bedrooms are attractive, comfortable and have views of the coast.

Quite a choice of food includes sandwiches, melts and wraps, baked local brie studded with garlic and rosemary with ale and red onion jam, potted game with ale-pickled shallots, chargrilled polenta with spicy bean cassoulet and smoked garlic oil, sausage and mash with ale and red onion gravy, slow-roast pork belly with black pudding fritter, apple compote and gravy, corn-fed chicken in mushroom and tarragon sauce, hake with salsa verde, and puddings such as crumble of the day and chocolate fondant with ale and morello cherry ice-cream. *Benchmark main dish: mussels in beer and fennel £13.00. Two-course evening meal £20.00.*

Own brew ~ Licensee Louise Treseder ~ Real ale ~ Open 11-11 (midnight Sat; 10 Sun) ~ Bar food 12-2.30, 6-9 ~ Restaurant ~ Well behaved children welcome away from main bar ~ Dogs welcome ~ Wi-fi ~ Live music some weekends (phone to check) ~ Bedrooms: £64/£90
Recommended by Edward May, Simon Day, Charles Todd, Mr Yeldahn

WADEBRIDGE
SW9972   Map 1

Ship ♀

(01208) 813845 – www.shipinnwadebridge.co.uk
Gonvena Hill, towards Polzeath; PL27 6DF

One of the oldest pubs in town, with beams and open fires, carefully refurbished bars, real ales and good, seasonally changing food

This 16th-c pub was once owned by a shipbuilding family, so it makes sense that it has plenty of nautical memorabilia on the rough white-washed walls. Seating in the bar area ranges from leather button-back wall banquettes to all sorts of wooden dining chairs, stools and window seats topped with scatter cushions plus flagstone or bare-board flooring, books on shelves, church candles and open fires; background music. High chairs line the counter where attentive staff serve Padstow Pride and Sharps Atlantic and Doom Bar on handpump and 12 wines by the glass (they hold a wine club on the first Tuesday of the month). There are two dining areas, one with high rafters and brass ship lights. The small, sunny decked terrace outside has seats and chairs.

Good food includes lunchtime open sandwiches, ham hock terrine with fried quail egg and piccalilli, smoked mackerel with beetroot and horseradish, several burgers with toppings, coleslaw and fries, gammon with duck eggs, lamb rump with mint, peas and elderflower, local mussels with onion, fennel and cider, and puddings such as eton mess and lemon posset; it's burger night on Tuesday, vegetarian specials on Wednesday and surf and turf evening on Thursday. *Benchmark main dish: beer-battered fish and chips £11.95. Two-course evening meal £20.00.*

Punch ~ Tenants Rupert and Sarah Wilson ~ Real ale ~ Open 12-2.30, 5-11; 12-10 Sun ~ Bar food 12-2 (3 Sun), 5-9 (9.30 Fri, Sat); no food Sun evening except peak season ~ Children welcome ~ Dogs allowed in bar ~ Wi-fi ~ Folk club last Tues of month
Recommended by Jacqui Stevens, Lindy Andrews, R T and J C Moggridge

WAINHOUSE CORNER
Old Wainhouse

SX1895 Map 1

(01840) 230711 – www.oldwainhouseinn.co.uk

A39; EX23 0BA

Cheerful pub, open all day with friendly staff and a good mix of customers, plenty of seating spaces, real ales and tasty food; bedrooms

As this is the only pub on a 20-mile stretch of the A39 and also close to the South West Coast Path, it gets busy at peak times – best to book a table in advance. The main bar has an easy-going, cheerful atmosphere, an attractive built-in settle, stripped rustic farmhouse chairs and dining chairs around a mix of tables on enormous old flagstones, a large woodburner with stone bottles on the mantelpiece above it, and beams hung with scythes, saws, a horse collar and other tack, spiles, copper pans and brass plates; do note the lovely photograph of a man driving a pig across a bridge. Off here is a simpler room with similar furniture, a pool table and background music. The dining room to the left of the main door has elegant high-backed dining chairs around pale wooden tables, another woodburner and more horse tack. Sharps Cornish Coaster and Doom Bar on handpump and friendly service. Outside, a grass area to one side of the building has picnic-sets. The simply furnished but comfortable bedrooms are light and airy and look out towards the sea.

Tasty food using local meat, game and fish includes chicken liver parfait with onion jam, spiced aubergine bruschetta with soft-boiled egg and chive oil, beer-battered pollock and chips, red wine and blue cheese risotto with walnuts, tarragon-stuffed chicken breast wrapped in parma ham with jerusalem artichoke purée and red wine sauce, john dory with parsley brown butter, capers and garlic, and puddings such as crème brûlée and apple and cherry crumble with clotted cream. *Benchmark main dish: 10oz sirloin steak with home-made fries and béarnaise sauce £16.50. Two-course evening meal £19.50.*

Enterprise ~ Lease Bryony Self ~ Real ale ~ Open 10am-midnight ~ Bar food 10-9 ~ Restaurant ~ Children welcome ~ Dogs welcome ~ Wi-fi ~ Live music first Sun of month ~ Bedrooms: £47.50/£95 *Recommended by Peter Brix, Dr Simon Innes, George Sanderson, Maddie Purvis*

Also Worth a Visit in Cornwall

Besides the fully inspected pubs, you might like to try these pubs that have been recommended to us and described by readers. Do tell us what you think of them: feedback@goodguides.com

ALTARNUN SX2280
Kings Head (01566) 86241
Five Lanes; PL15 7RX Old mansard-roofed beamed village pub, Greene King Abbot and guests such as Dartmoor and local Penpont, Weston's cider, generous reasonably priced pubby food from sandwiches and baguettes up including popular Sun carvery, carpeted lounge set for dining with big log fire, slate floor restaurant and public bar with another fire, ghost of former landlady Peggy Bray; background music, TV, pool; children and dogs welcome, picnic-sets on front terrace and in small raised garden, refurbished bedrooms, open all day and handy for A30. *(Sarah Roberts)*

ALTARNUN SX2083
★**Rising Sun** (01566) 86636
NW; village signed off A39 just W of A395 junction; PL15 7SN Tucked-away 16th-c pub with traditionally furnished L-shaped main bar, low beams, slate flagstones and coal fires, good choice of food including excellent local seafood, Penpont, Skinners and guests, traditional cider, good friendly service; background music, pool; dogs and well behaved children allowed in bar but not restaurant, seats on suntrap terrace and in garden, pétanque, camping field, nice village with beautiful church, open all day weekends. *(Barry Collett)*

BODINNICK
SX1352
Old Ferry (01726) 870237
Across the water from Fowey; coming by road, to avoid the ferry queue, turn left as you go downhill – car park on left before pub; PL23 1LX Old inn just up from the river with lovely views from terrace, dining room and some of its 12 comfortable bedrooms; traditional bar with nautical memorabilia, old photographs and woodburner, back room hewn into the rock, well kept Sharps ales and at least one guest, nice wines, good food from lunchtime sandwiches up including daily specials and children's menu, friendly french landlord and helpful staff; free wi-fi; good circular walks, lane by pub in front of ferry slipway is extremely steep and parking limited, open (and food) all day. *(Giles Smith and Sandra Kiely)*

BOSCASTLE
SX0990
★ Napoleon (01840) 250204
High Street, top of village; PL35 0BD Welcoming 16th-c thick-walled white cottage at top of steep quaint village (fine views halfway up); cosy rooms on different levels, slate floors, oak beams and log fires, interesting Napoleon prints and lots of knick-knacks, good food from daily changing menu in bar areas or small evening restaurant, well kept St Austell tapped from casks, decent wines and coffee, traditional games; background music (live Fri, sing-along Tues), sports TV, free wi-fi; children and dogs welcome, small covered terrace and large sheltered garden, open all day. *(Barbara Brown, Patricia Hawkins, Colin Humphreys)*

BOSCASTLE
SX0991
Wellington (01840) 250202
Harbour; PL35 0AQ Old hotel's long beamed and carpeted bar, good fairly priced food from varied menu, ales such as Skinners and St Austell kept well, nice coffee and cream teas, roaring log fire, upstairs gallery area and separate evening restaurant with set menu (not cheap); children and dogs (in bar) welcome, big secluded garden, comfortable bedrooms, open all day. *(James Allsopp)*

BOTALLACK
SW3632
★ Queens Arms (01736) 788318
B3306; TR19 7QG Honest old pub with good home-made food including local seafood, meat sourced within 3 miles, well kept Sharps and Skinners, good friendly service, log fires (one in unusual granite inglenook), dark wood furniture, tin mining and other old local photographs on stripped-stone walls, family extension; dogs welcome, tables out in front and pleasant back garden, wonderful clifftop walks nearby, lodge accommodation, open all day. *(William Slade)*

BREAGE
SW6128
Queens Arms (01326) 564229
3 miles W of Helston just off A394; TR13 9PD Village corner pub refurbished under friendly new management; long part-carpeted bar with plush banquettes and woodburner at each end, up to seven well kept ales, enjoyable home-made pubby food (all day Sun) including daily specials, small restaurant with another woodburner, games part with pool and darts; background and live music, quiz nights, sports TV, free wi-fi; children and dogs welcome, seats outside under cover, barbecue and play areas, two refurbished bedrooms, caravan pitches, medieval wall paintings in church opposite, open all day. *(Daphne and Robert Staples)*

CADGWITH
SW7214
★ Cadgwith Cove Inn (01326) 290513
Down very narrow lane off A3083 S of Helston; no nearby parking; TR12 7JX Friendly little pub in fishing cove with lovely walks in either direction; simply furnished front rooms with bench seating on parquet, log fire, local photos and nautical memorabilia, big back bar with huge fish mural, Otter Bitter, Sharps Doom Bar, Skinners Betty Stogs and a guest from Atlantic, popular food including local fish/seafood (can be expensive); background music, folk night Tues, local singers Fri, TV, darts and board games; children and dogs welcome, front terrace overlooking old fishermen's sheds, comfortable bedrooms with sea views, coastal walks, open all day. *(David Eberlin, Barry Collett, Piotr Chodzko-Zajko, R T and J C Moggridge)*

CALSTOCK
SX4368
★ Tamar (01822) 832487
The Quay; PL18 9QA Cheerful and relaxed 17th-c local opposite the Tamar with its imposing viaduct; dark stripped stone, flagstones, tiles and bare boards, pool room with woodburner, more modern back dining room, good generous straightforward food and summer cream teas, well kept Sharps Doom Bar and other cornish ales, good service from friendly landlord and cheery young staff, reasonable prices; some live music; children away from bar and well behaved dogs welcome, nicely furnished terrace, heated smokers' shelter, hilly walk or ferry to Cotehele (NT). *(Sally and David Champion)*

CHAPEL AMBLE
SW9975
Maltsters Arms (01208) 812473
Off A39 NE of Wadebridge; PL27 6EU Country pub-restaurant with good food including Sun lunchtime carvery, friendly accommodating staff, St Austell Tribute and Sharps Doom Bar, Weston's cider, log fire, beams, painted half-panelling, stripped stone and some slate flagstones, modern back extension; music and quiz nights; children welcome, seats outside. *(Tony Smaithe)*

CHARLESTOWN   SX0351
Harbourside Inn (01726) 67955
Part of Pier House Hotel; PL25 3NJ
Glass-fronted warehouse conversion
alongside hotel, great spot looking over
classic little harbour and its historic sailing
ships, half a dozen ales including Bass,
Sharps and Skinners, enjoyable pubby food
from good sandwiches up, friendly efficient
service; live music Sat night, two sports
TVs, pool; interesting film-set conservation
village with shipwreck museum, good
walks, parking away from pub. *(Stanley and
Annie Matthews)*

CHARLESTOWN   SX0351
Rashleigh Arms (01726) 73635
Quay Road; PL25 3NX Modernised early
19th-c pub with nautical touches, public
bar, lounge and dining area, well kept St
Austell range, good wine choice and coffee,
enjoyable fairly priced food all day including
popular Sun carvery, friendly obliging service;
background music, fortnightly live bands Fri,
trad jazz second Sun of month, free wi-fi;
children welcome, dogs in bar, disabled
facilities, front terrace and garden with
picnic-sets, eight bedrooms (some with sea
views), seven more in nearby Georgian house,
Grade II listed car park (site of old coal
storage yards), attractive harbour with tall
ships. *(Ian McIntosh)*

COMFORD   SW7339
Fox & Hounds (01209) 820251
Comford; A393/B3298; TR16 6AX
Attractive rambling low-beamed pub;
stripped stone and painted panelling,
high-backed settles and cottagey chairs
on flagstones, some comfortable leather
seating too, three woodburners, well liked
freshly made food from interesting varied
menu including daily specials, St Austell
ales, good friendly service; background
music, newspapers, darts and board games;
children and dogs (in bar) welcome, disabled
facilities, nice floral displays in front, picnic-
sets in back garden, open all day weekends,
closed Mon. *(James McIntosh)*

COVERACK   SW7818
Paris (01326) 280258
The Cove; TR12 6SX Comfortable
Edwardian seaside inn above harbour in
beautiful fishing village; carpeted L-shaped
bar with well kept St Austell ales and
Healey's cider, large relaxed dining room
with white tablecloths and spectacular bay
views, wide choice of interesting if not always
cheap food including good fresh fish, Sun
lunchtime carvery, helpful cheery service,
model of namesake ship (wrecked nearby
in 1899); popular Weds quiz, pool; children
welcome, more sea views from garden and
four bedrooms, limited parking. *(Tom and
Jill Jones)*

CRACKINGTON HAVEN   SX1496
Coombe Barton (01840) 230345
Off A39 Bude–Camelford; EX23 0JG
Much extended old inn in beautiful
setting overlooking splendid sandy bay –
recent change of management and some
refurbishment; good fairly priced food from
shortish menu, three rotating cornish ales
and decent wine choice, friendly helpful
service; background and live music, quiz and
comedy nights, big-screen sports TV, darts
and pool; children welcome, dogs in bar, side
terrace with plenty of tables, fine cliff walks,
roomy bedrooms, open all day. *(Theocsbrian)*

CRAFTHOLE   SX3654
★ Finnygook (01503) 230338
*B3247, off A374 Torpoint road;
PL11 3BQ* 15th-c coaching inn with beams
and joists in smart bar, long wall pews and
carved cushioned dining chairs around
wooden tables on bare boards, central log
fire, high chairs and tables near counter
serving St Austell Tribute and a couple of
guests, decent choice of wines by the glass,
ten malt whiskies and a real cider, dining
room with fine views and unusual log-effect
gas fire, dining library, enjoyable food from
pub favourites up including daily specials,
friendly attentive service; occasional live
music Fri, quiz last Weds of month, free
wi-fi; children and dogs welcome, good
surrounding walks, bedrooms, open all
day. *(Sharon and John Hancock)*

CROWS NEST   SX2669
Crows Nest (01579) 345930
*Signed off B3264 N of Liskeard; OS Sheet
201 map reference 263692; PL14 5JQ*
Welcoming old-fashioned 17th-c pub with
good traditional food and well kept St Austell
ales, attractive furnishings under bowed
beams, big log fire, chatty locals; children
and dogs welcome, picnic-sets on terrace by
quiet lane, handy for Bodmin Moor walks,
open all day weekends. *(Helena and Trevor
Fraser)*

CUBERT   SW7857
★ Smugglers Den (01637) 830209
Off A3075 S of Newquay; TR8 5PY
Big open-plan 16th-c thatched pub tucked
away in small hamlet; good locally sourced
food and up to four beers (May pie and ale
festival), several wines by the glass, friendly
staff, neat ranks of tables, dim lighting,
stripped stone and heavy beam and plank
ceilings, west country pictures and seafaring
memorabilia, steps down to part with huge
inglenook, another step to big side dining
room, also a little snug area with woodburner
and leather armchairs; background music;
children and dogs welcome, occasional live
music, small front courtyard and terrace
(both newly decked) with nice country
views, sloping lawn and play area, camping
opposite, open all day. *(Tony Smaithe)*

DULOE SX2358

Plough (01503) 262556

B3254 N of Looe; PL14 4PN Popular
restaurant-y pub with three country-chic
linked dining rooms all with woodburners,
dark polished slate floors, a mix of pews and
other seats, good fairly priced locally sourced
food (must book weekends) including
some imaginative dishes, also lunchtime
sandwiches and snacks, reasonably priced
wines, well kept St Austell, Sharps and
summer guests, friendly service; unobtrusive
background music; children and dogs
welcome, picnic-sets out by road. *(Michael
and Jenny Virtue)*

EDMONTON SW9672

★ Quarryman (01208) 816444

*Off A39 just W of Wadebridge bypass;
PL27 7JA* Welcoming busy family-run pub
adjoining small separately owned holiday
courtyard complex; three-room beamed bar
with interesting decorations including old
sporting memorabilia, fairly pubby food from
shortish menu with good individual dishes
such as sizzling steaks and portuguese fish
stew, quick friendly service, well kept Otter,
Skinners and two guests, seven wines by
the glass, no mobile phones or background
music; well behaved children and dogs
allowed, disabled access (but upstairs
lavatories), picnic-sets in front and courtyard
behind, self-catering apartment, open all day.
(Robert Shipley)

FALMOUTH SW8132

5 Degrees West (01326) 311288

*Grove Place, by harbourside car park;
TR11 4AU* Modern split-level open-plan bar
with mixed furnishings including squashy
sofas and low tables on stripped wood floors,
log fire in driftwood-effect fireplace, local
artwork, enjoyable food from snacks to grills,
five real ales, nine ciders and good choice of
other drinks, back dining area; background
music (live Thurs, Fri), quiz Mon, free
wi-fi; children and dogs welcome, disabled
facilities, seats out at front and on attractive
sheltered back terrace, open (and food)
all day. *(Robert Watt)*

FALMOUTH SW8032

Beerwolf (01326) 618474

*Bells Court (opposite Marks & Spencer);
TR11 3AZ* Stairs up to intriguing old pub-
cum-bookshop hidden down little alley in
centre of town, good selection of well kept
changing beers and ciders, decent coffee, no
food but can bring your own, friendly staff
and laid-back atmosphere, eclectic mix of
furniture on bare boards, raftered ceilings;
table tennis and table football, free wi-fi;
children welcome, a few picnic-sets outside,

open all day. *(Giles and Annie Francis, Comus
and Sarah Elliott, Guy Vowles)*

FALMOUTH SW8033

Boathouse (01326) 315425

Trevethan Hill/Webber Hill; TR11 2AG
Two-level pub with buoyant local atmosphere,
four beers featuring some smaller cornish
brewers such as Black Rock, Penpont and
Rebel, good range of other drinks, enjoyable
home-made food including fresh fish/seafood;
background and live music; children and dogs
welcome, tables outside, upper deck with
awning and fantastic harbour views, open
all day. *(Tony Smaithe)*

FALMOUTH SW8132

★ Chain Locker (01326) 311085

Custom House Quay; TR11 3HH Busy
old-fashioned place in fine spot by inner
harbour with window tables and lots more
seats outside, good selection of Sharps and
Skinners ales, surprisingly good food from
sandwiches and baguettes to local fish,
nooks and crannies, bare boards and masses
of nautical bric-a-brac; background music,
darts alley, games machine; well behaved
children and dogs welcome, self-catering
accommodation, pay parking close by, open
all day. *(Mick and Moira Brummell, Richard
Tilbrook, Phil and Jane Villiers)*

FALMOUTH SW8132

Front (01326) 212168

Custom House Quay; TR11 3JT
Welcoming bare-boards drinkers' pub with
good changing selection of well kept ales,
some tapped from the cask, also foreign beers
and ciders/perries, friendly knowledgeable
staff, no food but can bring your own (fish
and chip shop above), good mix of customers;
seats outside, open all day. *(William Slade)*

FALMOUTH SW8032

Seven Stars (01326) 312111

The Moor (centre); TR11 3QA Quirky
17th-c local, unchanging, unsmart and not
to everyone's taste; friendly atmosphere
with chatty regulars, up to six well kept ales
tapped from the cask including Bass, Sharps
and Skinners, big key ring collection, quiet
back snug; no food, gimmicks or mobile
phones; dogs welcome, corridor hatch
serving roadside courtyard, open all day.
(Sarah Roberts)

FLUSHING SW8033

Royal Standard (01326) 374250

*Off A393 at Penryn (or foot-ferry from
Falmouth); Street Peters Hill; TR11 5TP*
Just back from the waterfront, bistro-bar feel
with enjoyable fairly priced blackboard food
including good spanish fish stew and Weds
curry night, local ales and decent wines by

If we know a pub has an outdoor play area for children, we mention it.

the glass, good coffee, friendly helpful staff; background and live music; children and dogs welcome, café-style furniture on small front terrace, garden behind with harbour views, open all day. *(Richard Tilbrook, Laura Smyth)*

FLUSHING   SW8033
Seven Stars   (01326) 374373
Trefusis Road; TR11 5TY Old-style waterside pub with welcoming local atmosphere, good selection of well kept ales (third of a pint tasters available), pubby food including Mon evening fish and chips, coal fire, separate dining room; darts and pool; children and dogs welcome, pavement picnic-sets, great views of Falmouth with foot-ferry across, open all day. *(Richard Tilbrook)*

FOWEY   SX1251
Galleon   (01726) 833014
Fore Street; from centre follow car-ferry signs; PL23 1AQ Superb spot by harbour and estuary, good beer range (local/national) and decent choice of wines, well liked food from extensive reasonably priced menu, slate-floor bar with modern décor, lots of solid pine and exposed stone, lofty river view dining area; live bands Fri night, jazz Sun lunchtime, projector TV, pool, free wi-fi; children welcome, disabled facilities, attractive waterside terrace and sheltered courtyard, seven bedrooms (two with estuary view), open all day. *(Ann and Mike Bolton, Ian Herdman)*

FOWEY   SX1251
★ King of Prussia   (01726) 833694
Town Quay; PL23 1AT Handsome quayside building with roomy neatly kept upstairs bar, bay windows looking over harbour to Polruan, nice choice of enjoyable food from crab sandwiches and tapas boards up, St Austell ales and sensibly priced wines, friendly helpful staff, side restaurant; background music, pool, free wi-fi; children and dogs welcome, partly enclosed outside seating area, six pleasant bedrooms (all with views), open all day. *(Ann and Mike Bolton, Alan Johnson)*

FOWEY   SX1251
Lugger   (01726) 833435
Fore Street; PL23 1AH Centrally placed St Austell pub with up to three of their ales in top condition, spotless front bar with nautical memorabilia, small back dining area, good mix of locals and visitors (can get busy), generous helpings of enjoyable good value food including local fish, friendly helpful staff; children welcome, pavement tables, open all day. *(Ann and Mike Bolton, Ian Herdman)*

FOWEY   SX1251
★ Ship   (01726) 832230
Trafalgar Square; PL23 1AZ Bustling old pub with open fire in bare-boards bar, maritime prints, nauticalia

and other bits and pieces, St Austell ales and good wines by the glass, steps up to dining room with big stained-glass window, well liked interesting food along with pub favourites and sandwiches, friendly helpful service; background and live music; children and dogs welcome, bedrooms (some oak-panelled), open all day. *(Nick Lawless, Alan Johnson, Ian Herdman)*

GERRANS   SW8735
Royal Standard   (01872) 580271
The Square; TR2 5EB Friendly little local (less touristy than nearby Plume of Feathers in Portscatho), narrow doorways linking carpeted rooms, up to three well kept cornish ales, Sharps cider and Skinners lager, short choice of well chosen wines, enjoyable pub food from sandwiches to local fish, old photographs on white plaster or black boarded walls, brass shell cases and kitchen utensils, woodburner, lakeland terrier called Millie; children welcome away from bar, disabled access, sunny beer garden, opposite interesting 15th-c church (rebuilt in 19th c after fire), self-catering apartment. *(Chris and Angela Buckell)*

GOLANT   SX1254
Fishermans Arms   (01726) 832453
Fore Street (B3269); PL23 1LN Partly flagstoned small waterside local with lovely views across River Fowey from front bar and terrace, good value generous pubby food and up to four well kept west country ales, friendly service, log fire, interesting old photographs; fortnightly quiz Tues; children and dogs welcome, pleasant garden, open all day in summer (all day Fri-Sun, closed Mon in winter). *(Simon and Alex Knight)*

GORRAN CHURCHTOWN   SW9942
Barley Sheaf   (01726) 843330
Follow Gorran Haven signs from Mevagissey; PL26 6HN Built in 1837 by local farmer and now owned and extensively refurbished by his great- (x3) grandson; enjoyable home-made food including popular Sun lunch, well kept Sharps Doom Bar and guests, local cider, friendly staff, upstairs overspill dining room; Tues quiz and some live music; children and dogs welcome, well tended sunny beer garden, open all day summer. *(Helena and Trevor Fraser)*

GRAMPOUND   SW9348
Dolphin   (01726) 882435
A390 St Austell–Truro; TR2 4RR Friendly St Austell pub with their well kept ales and decent choice of wines, good generous pub food (not Mon), two-level bar with black beams and some panelling, polished wood or carpeted floors, pubby furniture with a few high-backed settles, pictures of old Grampound, woodburner; Tues quiz, darts (they have the UK's first blind team), pool, TV; children welcome, dogs in bar, wheelchair access from car park, beer

garden, good smokery opposite, handy for Trewithen Gardens, open all day weekends, closed Mon lunchtime. (Tony Smaithe)

GUNNISLAKE   SX4371
Tavistock (01822) 832217
Fore Street; PL18 9BN Traditional old family-run inn with welcoming helpful landlord and staff, well kept St Austell Tribute and Sharps Doom Bar, enjoyable food from sandwiches to blackboard specials, carpeted bar with lots of decorative plates, old local pictures, horsebrasses on beams, separate restaurant, woodburners; free wi-fi, TV; dogs welcome, open (and food) all day. (Hugh Roberts)

HARROWBARROW   SX4069
Cross House (01579) 350482
Off A390 E of Callington; School Road – towards Metherell; PL17 8BQ Substantial stone building (former farmhouse) with spreading carpeted bar, some booth seating, cushioned wall seats and stools around pub tables, hearty helpings of enjoyable reasonably priced home-made food, well kept St Austell ales and nice wines by the glass, good friendly service, open fire and woodburner, darts area, restaurant; monthly quiz, free wi-fi; children and dogs (in bar) welcome, disabled facilities, plenty of picnic-sets on good-sized lawn, play area, handy for Cotehele (NT), open all day. (William Slade)

HELFORD PASSAGE   SW7626
★Ferryboat (01326) 250625
Signed from B3291; TR11 5LB Busy old pub in lovely position by sandy beach (can book seats on terrace in advance); bar with farmhouse and blue-painted kitchen chairs, built-in cushioned wall seats and stripped tables on grey slates, woodburner, St Austell Proper Job, Tribute and a guest, proper cider and a dozen wines by the glass, good food including local fish/seafood, friendly service, arched doorway to games room with pool and darts; live bands Fri and Sun, free wi-fi; children and dogs (in bar) welcome, summer ferry from Helford village across the water, can also hire small boats and arrange fishing trips, walk down from car park is quite steep, open all day. (Richard Tilbrook, Andrew Stone, Anne and Ben Smith)

HELSTON   SW6527
★Blue Anchor (01326) 562821
Coinagehall Street; TR13 8EL Many (not all) love this no-nonsense, highly individual, 15th-c thatched pub; quaint rooms off corridor, flagstones, stripped stone, low beams and well worn furniture, family room, traditional games and skittle alley, ancient back brewhouse still producing distinctive and very strong Spingo IPA, Middle and seasonals such as Bragget with honey and herbs, no food but can bring your own (good pasty shop nearby), friendly local atmosphere; regular live music, Mon quiz;

back garden with own bar, four bedrooms in house next door, big breakfast, open all day. (Ray White, Peter Johnson)

HESSENFORD   SX3057
Copley Arms (01503) 240209
A387 Looe–Torpoint; PL11 3HJ Friendly 17th-c village pub with slightly old-fashioned feel, popular with families and passing tourists, with focus on enjoyable reasonably priced food from sandwiches to grills in linked carpeted areas, well kept St Austell ales and nice choice of wines, variety of teas and coffee, log fires, tables in cosy booths, one part with sofas and easy chairs, big family room; background and some live music, Thurs quiz; dogs allowed in one area, a few roadside picnic-sets by small River Seaton, fenced play area, five bedrooms, open all day. (Dennis and Doreen Haward)

HOLYWELL   SW7658
St Pirans (01637) 830205
Holywell Road; TR8 5PP Great location backing on to dunes and popular with holidaymakers, friendly helpful staff, well kept ales such as St Austell and Sharps, decent wines, enjoyable food from sandwiches and pub favourites up, cream teas; children and dogs welcome, tables on large back terrace, open all day, but closed out of season and Mon in April. (Barbara Brown)

HOLYWELL   SW7658
Treguth (01637) 830248
Signed from Cubert, SW of Newquay; TR8 5PP Ancient whitewashed stone and thatch pub near big beach, cosy low-beamed carpeted bar with big stone fireplace, larger dining room at back, three real ales and popular food cooked by landlord-chef, friendly service; regular live music, Weds quiz, pool; children and dogs welcome, handy for campsites and popular with holidaymakers, open all day weekends. (Robert Shipley)

KINGSAND   SX4350
Devonport (01752) 822869
The Cleave; PL10 1NF Lovely bay views from front bar, well kept changing local ales and good food including local fish/seafood, nice sandwiches and afternoon teas too, friendly efficient service even at busy times, light airy modern décor, warming log fire; children and dogs welcome, tables out by sea wall, closed Tues during term time. (Steve and Liz Tilley)

LANIVET   SX0364
Lanivet Inn (01208) 831212
Truro Road; PL30 5ET Welcoming old stone pub with long L-shaped bar, woodburner in dining end, generous helpings of popular good value food (best to book) from sandwiches and wraps to daily specials, St Austell ales, friendly efficient service; background and live music, fortnightly quiz

Tues, pool, darts and TV; children and dogs (in bar) welcome, seats out in front and in fenced garden, handy for Saints Way trail, unusual pub sign recalling days when village supplied bamboo to London Zoo's pandas, open all day weekends. *(James Allsopp)*

LELANT
SW5436

Watermill (01736) 757912

Lelant Downs; A3074 S; TR27 6LQ Mill-conversion family dining pub; working waterwheel behind with gearing in dark-beamed central bar opening into brighter airy front extension, upstairs evening (and Sun lunchtime) restaurant, Sharps Doom Bar, Skinners Betty Stogs and a guest, enjoyable food served by friendly staff; live music Fri, quiz night Weds, free wi-fi; dogs welcome, good-sized pretty streamside garden, open all day. *(Alan Johnson)*

LERRYN
SX1356

Ship (01208) 872374

Signed off A390 in Lostwithiel; Fore Street; PL22 0PT Lovely spot especially when tide's in; local ales, traditional ciders and good wine and whisky choice, sensibly priced food served by cheerful staff, huge woodburner, attractive dining conservatory, games room with pool, library/internet café area; children welcome, dogs on leads (they have two black labs), picnic-sets and play area outside, near famous stepping stones and three well signed waterside walks, five bedrooms in adjoining building and self-catering cottage, open all day Fri-Sun and school holidays. *(Nick Lawless)*

LIZARD
SW7012

Top House (01326) 290974

A3083; TR12 7NQ Neat clean pub with friendly staff and regulars, enjoyable local food from sandwiches and snacks up including fresh fish, children's meals and cream teas, well kept cornish ales, lots of good local sea pictures, fine shipwreck relics and serpentine craftwork (note the handpumps), warm log fire; folk music Mon; dogs on leads welcome in bar, disabled access, sheltered terrace, eight bedrooms in adjoining building (three with sea views), good coastal walks, open all day in summer, all day weekends in winter. *(Stanley and Annie Matthews)*

LIZARD
SW7012

Witchball (01326) 290662

Lighthouse Road; TR12 7NJ Small friendly beamed pub popular with locals, good food including fresh fish and seafood, Sun carvery, well kept ales such as Chough, St Austell and Skinners, cornish cider,

cheerful helpful staff; Sat quiz; children and dogs welcome, front terrace, open all day summer, closed winter lunchtimes Mon-Wed. *(Tom and Jill Jones)*

LONGROCK
SW4931

Mexico (01736) 710625

Riverside; old coast road Penzance–Marazion; TR20 8JD New owners and refurbishment for this open-plan pub with connections to the old Wheal Mexico mine; massive stone walls, painted ceiling joists and some half-panelling, mix of furniture on bare boards including leather sofa and bucket chairs by woodburner, well kept cornish ales, good food (not Sun evening) from pub favourites up (licensees are both chefs), friendly service, dining extension; children and dogs welcome, closed Mon, otherwise open all day. *(Helena and Trevor Fraser)*

LOSTWITHIEL
SX1059

Earl of Chatham (01208) 872269

Grenville Road; PL22 0EP Traditional 16th-c split-level pub, beams, bare stone walls and open woodburner, generous helpings of enjoyable home-made food including popular Sun lunch (need to book), St Austell ales and nice choice of wines, friendly staff; children and dogs welcome, terrace picnic-sets, bedrooms, open all day. *(PL)*

LOSTWITHIEL
SX1059

Royal Oak (01208) 872552

Duke Street; PL22 0AG Welcoming old town pub doing well under present licensees; St Austell Tribute, Sharps Doom Bar and guests, traditional cider and several wines by the glass, good generously served pub food including Sun carvery, amiable helpful staff, bar, lounge and restaurant, open fires; background and live music (Fri); children welcome, dogs in bar (theirs is Radar), terrace picnic-sets under large willow, six comfortable clean bedrooms, open all day. *(Peter Foot)*

MARAZION
SW5130

★ **Godolphin Arms** (01736) 888510

West End; TR17 0EN Revamped former coaching inn with wonderful views across to St Michael's Mount; light contemporary décor and modern furnishings, good food from sandwiches and sharing plates up, St Austell and Skinners ales, lots of wines by the glass and good coffee, helpful friendly staff; children welcome, beachside terrace, ten stylish bedrooms (most with sea view, some with balconies), good breakfast, open all day from 8am. *(Phil and Jane Villiers)*

A star symbol before the name of a pub shows exceptional character and appeal. It doesn't mean extra comfort. Even quite a basic pub can win a star, if it's individual enough.

MARAZION
SW5130
Kings Arms (01736) 710291
The Square; TR17 0AP Old one-bar pub
in small square, comfortable, cosy and
welcoming with warm woodburner, good well
presented food (best to book) including local
fish from regularly changing menu, well kept
St Austell ales, friendly helpful staff; children
and dogs welcome, sunny picnic-sets out in
front, open all day. *(Alan Johnson)*

MAWGAN
SW7025
Ship (01326) 221240
*Churchfield, signed off Higher Lane;
TR12 6AD* Former 18th-c courthouse in
nice setting near Helford river on the Lizard
peninsula; high-ceiling bare-boards bar with
woodburner in stone fireplace, end snug,
raised eating area, emphasis on good food
including local fish/seafood and seasonal
game, well kept ales and decent wine list,
cheerful helpful young staff; well behaved
children and dogs welcome, garden with
picnic-sets, closed lunchtimes and all day
Sun, Mon. *(Clifford Blakemore)*

MAWNAN SMITH
SW7728
Red Lion (01326) 250026
*W of Falmouth, off former B3291
Penryn–Gweek; The Square; TR11 5EP*
Old thatched and beamed pub with cosy
series of dimly lit lived-in rooms including
raftered bar, enjoyable food from open-view
kitchen, good fresh fish and other daily
specials, friendly helpful service, plenty
of wines by the glass and three well kept
ales including one named for the pub, good
coffee, daily papers, woodburner in huge
stone fireplace, dark woodwork, country
and marine pictures, plates and bric-a-brac;
Tues quiz, background music, TV; children
(away from bar) and dogs welcome, disabled
access, picnic-sets outside, handy for
Glendurgan (NT) and Trebah Gardens, open
all day. *(Maureen Wood)*

MENHENIOT
SX2862
Golden Lion (01209) 860332
Top of village by reservoir; TR16 6NW
Tucked-away little stone pub in nice
spot by Stithians Reservoir; beamed bar
and snug, woodburner, St Austell ales
and good selection of wines by the glass,
enjoyable generous food (all day weekends)
from pub favourites up, friendly staff,
restaurant with lake view; folk night third
Sat of month; children and dogs welcome,
wheelchair access using ramps, disabled
loo, attractive garden with heated shelter,
good walks, camping, open (and food) all day
weekends. *(Mick and Moira Brummell)*

METHERELL
SX4069
Carpenters Arms (01579) 351148
*Follow Honicombe sign from St Anns
Chapel just W of Gunnislake A390;
Lower Metherell; PL17 8BJ* Steps up to

heavily black-beamed village local, huge
polished flagstones and massive stone walls
in cosy bar, carpeted lounge/dining area,
three well kept ales such as St Austell,
Sharps and Timothy Taylors Landlord,
good reasonably priced food (not Mon or
lunchtimes apart from Sun) cooked by
landlord including themed nights, friendly
staff and regulars; live music, free wi-fi;
children and dogs welcome, front terrace,
farmers' market and brunch first Sat of
month, handy for Cotehele (NT), open all day
Fri-Sun, from 2pm other days. *(Tim and Sarah
Smythe-Brown)*

MEVAGISSEY
SX0144
★ Fountain (01726) 842320
*Cliff Street, down alley by Post Office;
PL26 6QH* Popular low-beamed fishermen's
pub, slate floor, some stripped stone and
a welcoming coal fire, old local pictures,
piano, well kept St Austell ales, good food
at reasonable prices including local fish/
seafood (particularly good fish stew),
friendly staff, back bar with glass-topped pit,
small upstairs evening restaurant; children
and dogs welcome, pretty frontage with
picnic-sets, two bedrooms, open all day in
summer. *(Robert Shipley)*

MEVAGISSEY
SX0144
Kings Arms (01726) 843904
Fore Street; PL26 6UQ Small welcoming
local (tucked away behind the harbour)
under newish management; good varied
choice of ales and other drinks from
slabby-topped wooden counter, good
freshly prepared food using local suppliers
including home-smoked fish and own-
baked bread; acoustic open mike night first
Mon of month; opening times can vary.
(Claire Bethel)

MEVAGISSEY
SX0144
Ship (01726) 843324
Fore Street, near harbour; PL26 6UQ
16th-c pub with interesting alcove areas in
big open-plan bar, low beams and flagstones,
nautical décor, woodburner, fairly priced
pubby food including good fresh fish, small
helpings available, well kept St Austell ales,
cheery uniformed staff; background and
some live music, games machines, pool;
dogs allowed, children welcome in two
front rooms, five bedrooms, open all day.
(William Slade)

MINIONS
SX2671
Cheesewring (01579) 362321
Overlooking the Hurlers; PL14 5LE
Homely village pub (claims to be the
highest in Cornwall) useful for Bodmin
Moor walks, well kept ales including Sharps
Doom Bar and good choice of reasonably
priced home-made food, lots of brass and
ornaments, woodburner, friendly staff;
children and dogs welcome, bedrooms,
open all day. *(Dr Simon Innes)*

MITCHELL
SW8554
★**Plume of Feathers**
(01872) 510387/511125 *Off A30
Bodmin–Redruth, by A3076 junction;
take southwards road then first right;
TR8 5AX* 16th-c coaching inn with several
linked bar and dining rooms, appealing
contemporary décor with local artwork on
pastel walls, stripped beams and standing
timbers, painted dados and two open fires,
good food from varied menu including pub
standards, Sharps, Skinners and St Austell,
seveal wines by the glass, impressive
dining conservatory; background music;
children (away from bar) and dogs welcome,
picnic-sets under parasols in well planted
garden areas, comfortable stable-conversion
bedrooms, open all day from 8am. *(Maureen
Wood, Chris and Val Ramstedt)*

MITHIAN
SW7450
★**Miners Arms** (01872) 552375
Off B3285 E of St Agnes; TR5 0QF
Cosy stone-built pub with traditional
small rooms and passages, pubby furnishings
and open fires, fine old wall painting of
Elizabeth I in back bar, popular good value
food, Sharps and Skinners ales kept well,
friendly helpful staff; background music,
board games; children welcome, dogs in
some rooms, seats on sheltered front cobbled
forecourt, back terrace and in garden, open
all day. *(Maddie Purvis)*

NEWLYN
SW4629
★**Tolcarne** (01736) 363074
Tolcarne Place; TR18 5PR Traditional
17th-c quayside pub with very good food
cooked by chef-landlord, much emphasis on
local fish/seafood (menu changes daily) and
booking advised, friendly efficient service,
St Austell Tribute, Skinners Betty Stogs
and maybe a local microbrew; live jazz Sun
lunchtime; children and dogs welcome,
terrace (harbour wall cuts off view), good
parking. *(Martin and Anne Muers)*

NEWLYN EAST
SW8256
Pheasant (01872) 510237
Churchtown; TR8 5LJ Traditional village
pub in quiet backstreet, friendly and busy,
with enjoyable reasonably priced pubby food
including popular Sun carvery, Dartmoor
and Sharps ales, good service; not far from
Trerice House and Gardens (NT). *(Stanley
and Annie Matthews, Peter Andrews)*

NEWQUAY
SW8061
Fort (01637) 875700
Fore Street; TR7 1HA Massive recently
built pub in magnificent setting high above
surfing beach and small harbour; decent food
from sandwiches, hot baguettes and baked
potatoes up, full St Austell range, friendly
staff coping well at busy times, open-plan
areas divided by balustrades and surviving
fragments of former harbourmaster's house,

good solid furnishings from country kitchen
to button-back settees, soft lighting, games
part with two pool tables, excellent indoor
children's play area; great views from long
glass-walled side section and sizeable garden
with multi-level terrace and further play
areas, open (and food) all day. *(Adrian
Johnson, Alan Johnson)*

NEWQUAY
SW8061
Lewinnick Lodge (01637) 878117
*Pentire headland, off Pentire Road;
TR7 1QD* Modern flint-walled bar-
restaurant built into bluff above the sea
– big picture windows for the terrific views;
light and airy bar with wicker seating,
spreading dining areas with contemporary
furnishings on light oak flooring, three or
four well kept ales and several wines by the
glass, popular bistro-style food from shortish
menu, good service and pleasant relaxed
atmosphere even when busy; children and
dogs welcome, modern seats and tables
on terraces making most of the stunning
Atlantic views, ten bedrooms, open all day;
same management as the Plume of Feathers
in Mitchell. *(Mr and Mrs J Watkins)*

NORTH HILL
SX2776
Racehorse (01566) 786916
*North Hill, off B3254 Launceston–
Liskeard; PL15 7PG* New management for
this comfortably reworked beamed dining
inn (once the village school); bar, lounge and
restaurant, good well presented food from
short interesting menu, four cornish ales,
friendly attentive service; free wi-fi; children
welcome, country views from decking, three
bedrooms. *(Dr Simon Innes)*

PADSTOW
SW9175
★**Golden Lion** (01841) 532797
Lanadwell Street; PL28 8AN Old inn
dating from the 14th c, cheerful black-
beamed locals' bar and high-raftered back
lounge with plush banquettes, Sharps
Doom Bar, Padstow Windjammer and
Tintagel Castle Gold, reasonably priced
simple bar lunches including good crab
sandwiches, evening steaks and fresh fish,
friendly staff, coal fire and woodburner;
pool in family area, background music,
sports TV; dogs welcome, colourful floral
displays at front, terrace tables, three
good bedrooms, open all day (no food Sun
evening). *(Peter Kirkman)*

PADSTOW
SW9175
Harbour Inn (01841) 533148
Strand Street; PL28 8BU Attractive
old-school pub just back from the harbour
and a quieter alternative; long room with
nautical bric-a-brac, front area with comfy
sofas, woodburner, well kept St Austell ales
and enjoyable generously served pub food
including specials, good coffee, friendly
helpful staff; children and dogs welcome,
open all day. *(Sally and David Champion)*

PADSTOW
SW9175

London (01841) 532554
Llanadwell Street; PL28 8AN Intimate proper fishermen's local with lots of pictures and nautical memorabilia, mix of tables, chairs and built-in benches, friendly ex-merchant navy landlord, half a dozen well kept St Austell ales and decent choice of malt whiskies, good value bar food including fresh local fish, back dining area (arrive early for a table), two log fires; background and some live music; children and dogs welcome, four reasonably priced bedrooms named after boats, open all day. *(David Delaney)*

PADSTOW
SW9275

Old Custom House (01841) 532359
South Quay; PL28 8BL Large, bright and airy open-plan seaside bar, comfortable and well divided, with rustic décor and cosy corners, beams, exposed brickwork and bare boards, raised section, big family area and conservatory, good food choice from baguettes up, four St Austell ales, efficient service (they swipe your card if running a tab), adjoining seafood restaurant; background and live music, TV; good spot by harbour with attractive sea-view bedrooms, open all day and can get very busy. *(Adrian Johnson)*

PELYNT
SX2054

★ Jubilee (01503) 220312
B3359 NW of Looe; PL13 2JZ Popular early 17th-c beamed inn with wide range of good locally sourced home-made food (best to book in season), well kept St Austell ales and decent wines by the glass, friendly helpful young staff, spotless interior with interesting Queen Victoria mementoes (pub renamed in 1897 to celebrate her diamond jubilee), some handsome antique furnishings, log fire in big stone fireplace, separate bar with darts, pool and games machine; children and dogs welcome, disabled facilities, large terrace, 11 comfortable bedrooms, open all day weekends. *(Helena and Trevor Fraser)*

PENDOGGETT
SX0279

Cornish Arms (01208) 880263
B3314; PL30 3HH Welcoming old beamed coaching inn with traditional oak settles on front bar's polished slate floor, good range of St Austell ales, decent wines by the glass and enjoyable food, friendly efficient service, comfortably spaced tables in small carpeted dining room, proper back locals' bar with woodburner and games; provision for children, dogs welcome in bars, disabled access, terrace with distant sea view, bedrooms, open all day. *(Tony Smaithe)*

PENELEWEY
SW8140

Punch Bowl & Ladle (01872) 862237
B3289; TR3 6QY Thatched dining pub with good home-made food from sandwiches up, helpful chatty service, four St Austell ales, Healey's cider and good wine and whisky selection, black beams, some white-painted stone walls and oak panelling, rustic bric-a-brac and big sofas, steps down to lounge/dining area, restaurant; soft background music, free wi-fi; children (away from bar) and dogs welcome, wheelchair access (not from small side terrace), handy for Trelissick Garden (NT), open all day. *(Chris and Angela Buckell, PL)*

PENZANCE
SW4730

Admiral Benbow (01736) 363448
Chapel Street; TR18 4AF Wonderfully quirky pub, full of atmosphere and packed with interesting nautical paraphernalia, friendly helpful staff, good value above-average food including local fish, well kept cornish ales, cosy corners, fire, downstairs restaurant in captain's cabin style, upper floor with pool table, pleasant view from back room; children and dogs welcome, open all day in summer. *(James Allsopp)*

PENZANCE
SW4730

Crown (01736) 351070
Victoria Square, Bread Street; TR18 2EP Friendly little backstreet corner local with neat bar and snug dining room, own Cornish Crown beers plus a guest, several wines by the glass, no food but can bring your own; Mon acoustic music, Tues quiz, board games (beat the landlady at Snatch for a free pint); children and dogs welcome, seats outside, open all day. *(Patricia Hawkins)*

PENZANCE
SW4729

★ Dolphin (01736) 364106
Quay Street, opposite harbour after swing-bridge; TR18 4BD Well run old pub with enjoyable good value food including fresh fish, up to four well kept St Austell ales and good wines by the glass, roomy bar on different levels, nautical memorabilia and three resident ghosts; pool, juke box; children and dogs welcome, pavement picnic-sets, three comfortable bedrooms with sea/harbour views, no car park (public one not far away), handy for Scillies ferry, open (and food) all day. *(Helena and Trevor Fraser)*

PERRANARWORTHAL
SW7738

Norway (01872) 864241
A39 Truro–Penryn; TR3 7NU Large beamed pub with half a dozen linked areas, good choice of food including daily specials and carvery (Fri and Sat evenings, all day Sun, Tues lunchtime), St Austell ales and several wines by the glass, cream teas, good friendly service, open fires, panelling and mix of furniture on slate flagstones, restaurant; background music, free wi-fi; children and dogs welcome, tables outside, four bedrooms, open (and food) all day. *(Tony Smaithe)*

PERRANWELL STATION
SW7739

Royal Oak (01872) 863175
Village signposted off A393 Redruth–

Falmouth and A39 Falmouth–Truro; TR3 7PX Traditional old village pub, chatty and relaxed, with carpeted black-beamed bar, paintings by local artists, snug room behind with candlelit tables, big fireplace, St Austell Proper Job, Sharps Doom Bar, Skinners Lushingtons and a guest, proper cider and several wines by glass, hearty helpings of enjoyable home-cooked food including specials, good friendly service; free wi-fi; children and dogs (in bar) welcome, picnic-sets out at front, more seats in back garden, good surrounding walks, open all day weekends. *(Tom and Jill Jones, John Marsh, Chris and Angela Buckell)*

PILLATON   SX3664

★**Weary Friar** (01579) 350238

Off Callington–Landrake back road; PL12 6QS Tucked-away welcoming 12th-c inn, good generously served food from wide-ranging menu in bar and restaurant (best to book), friendly efficient staff, well kept St Austell and Sharps, farm cider, knocked-together carpeted rooms, dark beams, copper and brass, log fires in stone fireplaces; children welcome, no dogs inside, tables out in front and behind, church next door (Tues evening bell-ringing), 14 bedrooms, open all day. *(Ted George)*

POLGOOTH   SW9950

Polgooth Inn (01726) 74089

Well signed off A390 W of St Austell; Ricketts Lane; PL26 7DA Welcoming spacious country pub, separate servery for good generous food from sandwiches to daily specials, children's helpings and reasonable prices, well kept St Austell ales and good choice of wines by the glass, eating area around sizeable bar with woodburner, good big family room, live music; fills quickly in summer (handy for nearby caravan parks), no booking after 6.30pm and can be a wait for a table; dogs welcome, steps up to play area, tables out on terrace and grass, Sun summer barbecues, pretty countryside, open all day. *(William Slade)*

POLPERRO   SX2051

Crumplehorn Mill (01503) 272348

Top of village near main car park; PL13 2RJ Converted mill and farmhouse keeping beams, flagstones and some stripped stone, snug lower bar leading to long main room with cosy end eating area, well kept cornish ales, wide choice of enjoyable good value food from snacks to blackboard specials (booking advised), friendly speedy service, log fire; children and dogs welcome, outside seating and working mill wheel, bedrooms and self-catering apartments, open all day. *(Barry Collett, Eddie Edwards)*

POLPERRO   SX2050

Three Pilchards (01503) 272233

Quay Road; PL13 2QZ Small low-beamed local behind fish quay, generous helpings

of reasonably priced food from baguettes to good fresh fish, well kept St Austell Tribute and up to four guests, obliging service even when busy, lots of black woodwork, dim lighting, simple furnishings, open fire in big stone fireplace; children and dogs welcome, picnic-sets on terrace up steep steps, open all day. *(Barry Collett, Dennis and Doreen Haward)*

POLRUAN   SX1250

★**Lugger** (01726) 870007

The Quay; back roads off A390 in Lostwithiel, or foot-ferry from Fowey; PL23 1PA Popular and friendly waterside pub; steps up to cosy beamed bar with open fire and woodburner, well kept St Austell ales, good freshly cooked food from bar snacks to daily specials including local fish/seafood, Sun carvery, restaurant on upper level; quiz and live music nights; children, dogs and muddy boots welcome, not suitable for wheelchairs, good local walks, limited parking, open all day. *(Nick Lawless, Jane and Kai Horsburgh)*

PORT ISAAC   SW9980

★**Golden Lion** (01208) 880336

Fore Street; PL29 3RB Popular well positioned 18th-c pub retaining friendly local atmosphere in simply furnished old rooms; bar and snug with open fire, window seats and balcony tables looking down on rocky harbour and lifeboat slip far below, upstairs restaurant, enjoyable food including good local fish, well kept St Austell ales; background music, darts; children and dogs welcome, dramatic cliff walks, open all day. *(Adrian Johnson)*

PORTHALLOW   SW7923

Five Pilchards (01326) 280256

SE of Helston; B3293 to Street Keverne, then village signed; TR12 6PP Sturdy old-fashioned stone-built local in secluded cove right by shingle beach, lots of salvaged nautical gear, interesting shipwreck memorabilia and model boats, woodburner, cornish ales and enjoyable reasonably priced food including local fish, friendly chatty staff, conservatory; children and dogs welcome, seats out in sheltered yard, sea-view bedrooms, open all day Sun (in winter closed Mon lunchtime and all day Tues). *(Robert Shipley)*

PORTHLEVEN   SW6325

Atlantic (01326) 562439

Peverell Terrace; TR13 9DZ Friendly buzzy pub in great setting up above the harbour, good value tasty food including bargain OAP deal, ales such as Skinners and St Austell from boat-shaped counter, Weston's cider, big open-plan lounge with well spaced seating and cosier alcoves, good log fire in granite fireplace, dining room with trompe l'oeil murals; darts; children and dogs welcome, lovely bay views from raised front terrace, open all day. *(Sally and David Champion)*

PORTHLEVEN
SW6225

Harbour Inn (01326) 573876
Commercial Road; TR13 9JB Large neatly kept pub-hotel in outstanding harbourside setting; expansive lounge and bar with dining area off, big public bar, well kept St Austell ales and good range of pubby food, carvery Wed lunchtime and Sun, well organised friendly service; unobtrusive background music (live Sat), Thurs quiz, free wi-fi; children welcome, picnic-sets on spacious quayside terrace, 15 well equipped bedrooms (some with harbour view), good breakfast, open all day. *(James Allsopp)*

PORTLOE
SW9339

★ **Ship** (01872) 501356
At top of village; TR2 5RA Cheerful traditional pub in charming fishing village; L-shaped bar with tankards hanging from beams, nautical bric-a-brac, local memorabilia and an amazing beer bottle collection, straightforward dark pubby chairs and tables on red carpet, roaring log fire, St Austell ales, cider/perry and six wines by the glass, popular good value pubby food; background music, free wi-fi; children and dogs (in bar) welcome, sloping streamside garden across road, clean comfortable bedrooms, beach close by. *(Chris and Angela Buckell, Barry Collett, Keith Sturgess, Eddie Edwards)*

PORTSCATHO
SW8735

Plume of Feathers (01872) 580321
The Square; TR2 5HW Largely stripped-stone coastal village pub with sea-related bric-a-brac and pictures in two comfortable linked areas, also small side bar and separate restaurant, St Austell ales and enjoyable reasonably priced pubby food; background music, free wi-fi; children, dogs and muddy boots welcome, disabled access (steps to restaurant and gents'), picnic-sets out under awning, lovely coast walks, open all day in summer (and other times if busy). *(Richard Tilbrook, Comus and Sarah Elliott, Chris and Angela Buckell, Mr and Mrs J Watkins)*

ROSUDGEON
SW5529

Falmouth Packet (01736) 762240
A394; TR20 9QE Comfortably modernised old pub with bare-stone walls, slate/carpeted floors and open fire, good food using local produce (booking advised), own pickles, relishes etc for sale, well kept Penzance ales and guests, family run with good friendly service, conservatory; children and dogs welcome, picnic-sets out at front and on paved back terrace, self-catering cottage, open all day Fri, till 7pm Sun. *(Robert Shipley)*

RUAN LANIHORNE
SW8942

★ **Kings Head** (01872) 501263
Village signed off A3078 St Mawes Road; TR2 5NX Country pub in quiet hamlet

---

with interesting church nearby; relaxed small bar with log fire, Skinners and a guest, maybe farm cider, well liked food especially local fish, dining area to the right divided in two, lots of china cups hanging from ceiling joists, cabinet filled with old bottles, hunting prints and cartoons, separate restaurant to the left; background music; well behaved children allowed in dining areas, dogs in bar only, terrace across road and nice lower beer garden, walks along Fal estuary, in winter closed Sun evening and Mon. *(R and S Bentley, Barry Collett, R K Phillips)*

SCORRIER
SW7244

Fox & Hounds (01209) 820205
Set back from B3298, off A30 just outside Redruth; TR16 5BS Long well divided bar (eating area to the right) with woodburners at each end, half-panelling, stripped stonework and painted beams, emphasis on good home-cooked food including fresh fish/shellfish (best to book), local Keltek ales, friendly accommodating staff; background music, quiz nights; children and dogs welcome, picnic-sets on front terrace, handy for Portreath–Devoran cycle trail, open all day Fri, Sat and summer Sun. *(George Sullivan)*

ST DOMINICK
SX4067

Who'd Have Thought It
(01579) 350214 *Off A388 S of Callington; PL12 6TG* Large comfortable country pub refurbished under new management; popular reasonably priced home-made food (booking advised) from lunchtime sandwiches up, gluten-free and vegan choices, well kept St Austell ales and good value wine list, friendly competent service, superb Tamar views especially from conservatory, beams and open fire; live music and quiz nights; children and dogs (in bar) welcome, garden tables, handy for Cotehele (NT), open all day weekends. *(John Evans, Ted George)*

ST ISSEY
SW9271

Ring o' Bells (01841) 540251
A389 Wadebridge–Padstow; Churchtown; PL27 7QA Traditional slate-clad 18th-c village pub with open fire at one end of beamed bar, pool the other, well kept Courage Best, Sharps Doom Bar and a guest, good choice of wines and whiskies, friendly service, enjoyable sensibly priced local food (own vegetables and pork) in long narrow side dining room; live folk first Sat of month; children and dogs welcome, decked courtyard, pretty hanging baskets and tubs, four bedrooms, car park across road, open all day weekends and can get packed in summer. *(Helena and Trevor Fraser)*

ST IVES
SW5140

Lifeboat (01736) 794123
Wharf Road; TR26 1LF Thriving family-friendly beamed quayside pub, wide choice

of good value generously served pubby food, well kept St Austell ales, spacious interior with harbour-view tables and cosier corners, nautical theme including lifeboat pictures, friendly helpful staff; Sept music festival, sports TV, fruit machine; no dogs, disabled access/facilities, open (and food) all day. *(Barry Collett)*

ST IVES SW5441
Pedn Olva (01736) 796222
The Warren; TR26 2EA Hotel not pub, but has well kept reasonably priced St Austell ales in roomy bar, fine views of sea and Porthminster beach (especially from tables on roof terrace), all-day bar food and separate restaurant, good service; comfortable bedrooms. *(Alan Johnson)*

ST IVES SW5140
★**Sloop** (01736) 796584
The Wharf; TR26 1LP Popular low-beamed, panelled and flagstoned harbourside inn, bright St Ives School pictures and attractive portrait drawings in front bar, booth seating in back bar, good choice of food from sandwiches and baguettes to lots of fresh local fish, quick friendly service even though busy, well kept ales such as Greene King Old Speckled Hen and Sharps Doom Bar, good coffee, upstairs evening restaurant; background and live music, TV; children in eating area, beach view from roof terrace and seats out on cobbles, bedrooms, open all day (breakfast from 9am), handy for Tate gallery. *(Stanley and Annie Matthews, Alan Johnson)*

ST IVES SW5140
Union (01736) 796486
Fore Street; TR26 1AB Popular and friendly low-beamed local, roomy but cosy, with good value food from sandwiches to local fish, well kept Sharps Doom Bar and Weston's Old Rosie cider, decent wines and coffee, small hot fire, leather sofas on carpet, dark woodwork and masses of ship photographs; background music; dogs welcome. *(Alan Johnson)*

ST JUST IN PENWITH SW3731
Kings Arms (01736) 788545
Market Square; TR19 7HF Friendly pub with three separate carpeted areas, granite walls, beamed and boarded ceilings, open fire and woodburner, shortish menu of good home-made food (not Sun evening), helpful caring service, well kept St Austell ales; background music (live Sun), Weds quiz, TV; children and dogs welcome, tables out in front. *(Alan Johnson)*

ST JUST IN PENWITH SW3731
★**Star** (01736) 788767
Fore Street; TR19 7LL Low-beamed two-room local with friendly landlord and relaxed informal atmosphere, five well kept St Austell ales, no food (bring your own

lunchtime sandwiches or pasties), dimly lit main bar with dark walls covered in flags and photographs, coal fire; nostalgic juke box, live celtic music Mon, open mike Thurs, darts and euchre; tables in attractive backyard with smokers' shelter, open all day. *(Alan Johnson)*

ST KEW SX0276
★**St Kew Inn** (01208) 841259
Village signposted from A39 NE of Wadebridge; PL30 3HB Popular 15th-c pub with neat beamed bar, stone walls, winged high-backed settles and more traditional furniture on tartan carpeting, all sorts of jugs dotted about, roaring log fire in stone fireplace, three dining areas, St Austell beers from cask and handpump, good choice of well liked food (not Sun evening in winter), friendly attentive service; live music every other Fri; children away from bar and dogs welcome, pretty flowering tubs and baskets outside, picnic-sets in garden over road, open all day in summer. *(Mrs Edna Jones)*

ST MAWES SW8433
★**Rising Sun** (01326) 270233
The Square; TR2 5DJ Light and airy pub across road from harbour wall; bar on right with end woodburner and sea-view bow window, rugs on stripped wood, a few dining tables, sizeable carpeted left-hand bar and wood-floored conservatory, well prepared tasty food from local fish to good steaks, well kept St Austell ales and nice wines by the glass, friendly young staff, buzzy atmosphere; background music; awkward wheelchair access, picnic-sets on sunny front terrace, comfortable bedrooms, open all day. *(Tom and Jill Jones, John Marsh, Stanley and Annie Matthews, R K Phillips, Comus and Sarah Elliott, Phil and Jane Villiers)*

ST MAWES SW8533
St Mawes Hotel (01326) 270170
Marine Parade; TR2 5DN Refurbished harbourside hotel's relaxed bar, enjoyable food from small plates and pizzas up, a couple of real ales, nice wines and good italian coffee, upstairs restaurant, friendly helpful young staff; children welcome, a few tables out in front, good if not cheap bedrooms (lovely sea views), open all day. *(Guy Vowles)*

ST MAWES SW8433
Victory (01326) 270324
Victory Hill; TR2 5DQ Popular pub tucked up from the harbour; slate-floored locals' bar on left, carpeted dining area to the right, more formal upstairs restaurant with balcony, well kept Otter, Sharps and Skinners, good food including plenty of local fish, log fires, friendly staff; background music; children welcome, no wheelchair access, one or two picnic-sets outside, two good value bedrooms, open all day. *(Barry Collett)*

ST MINVER
SW9677
Four Ways (01208) 862384
Churchtown; PL27 6QH Friendly 17th-c
village inn run by the same family for almost
a century; slate-floored bar with oak beams
and open fire, St Austell Tribute and a guest,
reasonably priced home-made food;
summer live music Fri, pool; small enclosed
outside seating area, nine bedrooms.
(Adrian Johnson)

STITHIANS
SW7640
Cornish Arms (01872) 863445
*Frogpool, not shown on many road maps
but is NE of A393, ie opposite side to
Stithians itself; TR4 8RP* Traditional
18th-c village pub run by welcoming brother
and sister team (he cooks); long beamed bar
with fires either end, cosy snug, good value
tasty food (not Mon) from sandwiches and
four types of ploughman's to daily specials,
local ales and ciders; pool (free Tues),
euchre; well behaved children and dogs
welcome, closed Mon lunchtime.
(John Marsh)

TIDEFORD
SX3459
Rod & Line (01752) 851323
Church Road; PL12 5HW Small old-
fashioned rustic local set back from road up
steps, friendly lively atmosphere, Greene
King Abbot and St Austell Tribute kept
well, nice food including good fresh fish/
seafood from blackboard menu (order at
bar), angling theme with rods etc, low-bowed
ceiling, settles, good log fire; children and
dogs welcome, tables outside, open all day.
(Mark Mincher-Lockett)

TINTAGEL
SX0588
Olde Malthouse (01840) 770461
Fore Street; PL34 0DA Recently restored
14th-c beamed pub with inglenook bar
and restaurant, good generously served
home-made food (booking advised) from
ciabattas up, well kept local ales including
Tintagel, friendly helpful service; some live
music, free wi-fi; children and dogs welcome,
tables on roadside terrace, seven refurbished
bedrooms, good walks, open all day in
summer, closed Sun and lunchtimes (apart
from Sat) in winter. *(Piotr Chodzko-Zajko)*

TOWAN CROSS
SW4078
Victory (01209) 890359
Off B3277; TR4 8BN Comfortable roadside
local with enjoyable good value food, four
real ales including Skinners, helpful staff;
pool, euchre and Tues quiz; children and dogs
welcome, beer garden, camping, handy for
good uncrowded beaches, open all day.
(John Marsh)

TREBARWITH
SX0586
Mill House (01840) 770200
*Signed off B3263 and B3314 SE of
Tintagel; PL34 0HD* Former 18th-c corn
mill wonderfully set in own steep woods
above the sea; bar with white-painted beams,
Delabole flagstones and mix of furniture
including comfortable sofas, light and airy
restaurant with pitched ceiling, enjoyable bar
food and more upmarket evening restaurant
menu, friendly staff, up to four local ales,
decent wines by the glass and good coffee;
background and live music; children and
dogs welcome, sunny terrace and streamside
garden, eight bedrooms, open all day.
(Tony Smaithe)

TREBARWITH
SX0585
Port William (01840) 770230
Trebarwith Strand; PL34 0HB Lovely
seaside setting with glorious views and
sunsets, waterside picnic-sets across
road and on covered terrace, maritime
memorabilia and log fires inside, enjoyable
food from sandwiches and baked potatoes to
daily specials (they may ask to swipe a card
before you eat), St Austell ales; background
music; children and dogs welcome, eight well
equipped comfortable bedrooms, open all day.
(George Sullivan)

TREEN
SW3923
★Logan Rock (01736) 810495
*Just off B3315 Penzance–Lands End;
TR19 6LG* Cosy traditional low-beamed bar
with good log fire, well kept St Austell ales
and tasty food from sandwiches and pasties
to daily specials, good vegetarian options
too, small back snug with excellent cricket
memorabilia (welcoming landlady eminent in
county's cricket association), family room (no
under-14s in bar); dogs welcome on leads,
pretty split-level garden behind with covered
area, good coast walks including to Logan
Rock itself, handy for Minack Theatre, open
all day in season and can get very busy.
(Ana Figueiredo)

TREGADILLETT
SX2983
★Eliot Arms (01566) 772051
*Village signposted off A30 at junction
with A395, W end of Launceston bypass;
PL15 7EU* Creeper-covered with series of
small rooms, interesting collections including
72 antique clocks, 700 snuffs and hundreds of
horsebrasses, also barometers, old prints and
shelves of books/china, fine mix of furniture
on Delabole slate from high-backed settles
and chaises longues to more modern seats,
open fires, well kept St Austell Tribute,
Wadworths 6X and a guest, ample helpings
of enjoyable good value food, friendly staff;
background music, darts, games machine;
children and dogs welcome, outside seating
front and back, lovely hanging baskets and
tubs, two bedrooms, open all day. *(Barbara
Brown, Colin Humphreys, Sarah Roberts)*

TREGONY
SW9244
Kings Arms (01872) 530202
Fore Street (B3287); TR2 5RW Light and
airy 16th-c coaching inn, long traditional

main bar and two beamed and panelled front dining areas, St Austell ales, Healey's cider/perry and nice wines, enjoyable reasonably priced pub food using local produce, tea and coffee, prompt service and friendly chatty atmosphere, two fireplaces, one with huge cornish range, pubby furniture on carpet or flagstones, old team photographs, back games room; dogs very welcome and well behaved children, disabled access, tables in pleasant suntrap garden, charming village. *(James Allsopp)*

TREMATON   SX3960
Crooked Inn (01752) 848177
Off A38 just W of Saltash; PL12 4RZ
Friendly family-run inn down long drive; open-plan bar with lower lounge leading to conservatory (lovely views), beams, straightforward furnishings and log fire, cornish ales and decent wines by the glass, good choice of popular freshly made food from sandwiches to daily specials, helpful service; children and dogs welcome, terrace overlooking garden and valley, play area, roaming ducks and other animals, 15 bedrooms, open all day. *(John Evans)*

TRURO   SW8244
★ Old Ale House (01872) 271122
Quay Street; TR1 2HD City-centre tap for Skinners brewery, five of their ales (samples offered) plus guests, some from casks behind bar, west country ciders and several wines by the glass including country ones, tasty food from snacks and sharing plates up, good cheerful service, dimly lit beamed bar with engaging mix of furnishings, sawdust on the floor, beer mats on walls and ceiling, some interesting 1920s bric-a-brac, life-size cutout of Betty Stogs, daily newspapers and free monkey nuts, upstairs room with table football; juke box; children (away from bar) and dogs welcome, open all day.
(Alan Johnson)

TRURO   SW8244
White Hart (01872) 277294
New Bridge Street (aka Crab & Ale House); TR1 2AA Compact old city-centre pub with nautical theme, friendly staff and locals, five well kept ales including Greene King IPA, St Austell Tribute and Sharps Doom Bar, good reasonably priced pub food; background music, disco Sat, quiz Thurs; children and dogs welcome, open all day. *(Alan Johnson)*

TYWARDREATH   SX0854
New Inn (01726) 813901
Off A3082; Fore Street; PL24 2QP
Welcoming 18th-c local in nice village setting, St Austell ales and guests including Bass tapped from the cask, good food (not Tues)

in back restaurant and conservatory, friendly relaxed atmosphere; some live music; children and dogs welcome, large secluded garden behind with play area, open all day. *(Dr Simon Innes)*

VERYAN   SW9139
New Inn (01872) 501362
Village signed off A3078; TR2 5QA
Comfortable and homely one-bar beamed local; good value food from sandwiches up (can get busy in evening so worth booking), St Austell ales, Healey's cider and decent wines by the glass, friendly attentive service, inglenook woodburner, polished brass and old pictures; background music; dogs and well behaved children welcome, wheelchair access with help, secluded beer garden behind, two bedrooms, interesting partly thatched village not far from nice beach, nearby parking unlikely in summer.
(R K Phillips, Peter J and Avril Hanson)

WATERGATE BAY   SW8464
Beach Hut (01637) 860877
B3276 coast road N of Newquay; TR8 4AA Great views from bustling modern beach bar with customers of all ages, surfing photographs on planked walls, cushioned wicker and cane armchairs around green and orange tables, weathered stripped-wood floor, unusual sloping bleached-board ceiling, big windows and doors opening to glass-fronted deck with retractable roof looking across sand to the sea, simpler end room, three real ales including Skinners, decent wines by the glass and lots of coffees and teas, enjoyable modern food served by friendly young staff; background music; dogs welcome in bar, easy wheelchair access, open 9am-11pm, 10.30am-5pm in winter. *(Chris and Val Ramstedt)*

WENDRON   SW6731
New Inn (01326) 572683
B3297; TR13 0EA Friendly little 18th-c granite-built country pub, three well kept changing ales and enjoyable reasonably priced home-cooked food; children and dogs welcome, garden behind with valley views. *(William Slade)*

ZELAH   SW8151
Hawkins Arms (01872) 540339
A30; TR4 9HU Homely 18th-c stone-built beamed local, well kept ales such as Skinners Lushingtons and Tintagel Castle Gold, tasty well presented home-made food from sandwiches to blackboard specials, nice coffee, friendly staff, copper and brass in bar and dining room, woodburner in stone fireplace; children and dogs welcome, back and side terraces, well equipped three-bedroom static caravan for hire. *(John Sargeant)*

There are report forms at the back of the book.

ZENNOR   SW4538
★**Tinners Arms** (01736) 796927
B3306 W of St Ives; TR26 3BY Friendly
welcome and good food from ploughman's
with three cornish cheeses to fresh local fish,
long unspoilt bar with flagstones, granite,
stripped pine and real fires each end, back
dining room, well kept St Austell and Sharps
ales, farm cider, sensibly priced wines and
decent coffee, efficient service even when
busy, nice mix of locals and visitors; Thurs
folk night; children, muddy boots and dogs
welcome, tables in small suntrap courtyard,
lovely windswept setting near coast path and
church with 15th-c carved mermaid bench,
bedrooms in building next door, open all day.
(John Marsh, Malcolm and Pauline Pellatt)

ISLES OF SCILLY

ST AGNES   SV8808
★**Turks Head** (01720) 422434
The Quay; TR22 0PL One of the UK's
most beautifully placed pubs, idyllic sea
and island views from garden terrace, can
get very busy on fine days, good food from
pasties to popular fresh seafood (best to get
there early), well kept ales such as Skinners
Betty Stogs, proper cider, friendly licensees
and good cheerful service; children and dogs
welcome, closed in winter, otherwise open
all day. *(Stephen Shepherd)*

ST MARTIN'S   SV9116
Seven Stones (01720) 423777
*Lower Town above Lawrence's Flats;
TR25 0QW* Stunning location and sea and
islands views from this long single-storey
stone building (the island's only pub);
refurbishment under present welcoming
management and enjoyable food from
sandwiches to local fish, well kept St Austell,
Sharps and Skinners, five wines by the glass;
film and live music nights; children and
dogs welcome, lots of terrace tables some on
decking, lovely walks, open all day in summer
(Weds, Fri and Sat evenings, all day Sun till
early evening in winter). *(Thomas Green)*

ST MARY'S   SV9010
Atlantic Inn (01720) 422323
*The Strand; next to but independent
from Atlantic Hotel; TR21 0HY* Spreading
and hospitable dark bar with well kept St
Austell ales, pubby food including children's
menu, sea-view restaurant, low beams,
hanging boat and other nauticalia, mix of
locals and tourists – busy evenings, quieter
on sunny lunchtimes; background and live
music, pool, darts, games machines, free
wi-fi; nice raised verandah with wide views
over harbour, good bedrooms in adjacent
hotel. *(Stephen Shepherd)*

ST MARY'S   SV9010
Mermaid (01720) 422701
The Bank; TR21 0HY Splendid picture-
window views across town beach and
harbour from back restaurant extension,
unpretentious dimly lit bar with lots of
seafaring relics and ceiling flags, stone
floor and rough timber, woodburner, steps
down to second bar with tiled floor, boat
counter and another woodburner, large
helpings of enjoyable well priced food
including children's choices, Sun carvery,
well kept Ales of Scilly, Sharps and Skinners;
background music, pool; dogs welcome in
bar, packed Weds and Fri when the gigs race,
open all day. *(Thomas Green)*

ST MARY'S   SV9110
Old Town Inn (01720) 422301
Old Town; TR21 0NN Nice local feel in
welcoming light bar and big back dining
area, wood floors and panelling, good freshly
made food (not Mon-Weds in winter) from
daily changing menu, up to four well kept
ales including Sharps Doom Bar and a beer
badged for the pub, great range of ciders (35
in summer); live music including monthly
folk club, cinema in back function room,
pool and darts; children and dogs welcome,
wheelchair access, tables in garden behind,
three courtyard bedrooms, handy for airport,
open all day in season (from 5pm weekdays,
all day weekends in winter). *(Thomas Green,
Daphne and Robert Staples)*

TRESCO   SV8815
★**New Inn** (01720) 423006
New Grimsby; TR24 0QG Handy for
ferries and close to the famous gardens; main
bar with comfortable old sofas, banquettes,
planked partition seating and farmhouse
tables and chairs, a few standing timbers,
boat pictures, collection of old telescopes
and large model yacht, pavilion extension
with cheerful yellow walls and plenty of seats
on blue-painted floors, Ales of Scilly and
Skinners, a dozen good wines by the glass,
quite a choice of spirits and several coffees,
enjoyable food including daily specials;
background music, board games, darts and
pool; children and dogs (in bar) welcome,
seats on flower-filled sea-view terrace,
bedrooms, open all day in summer. *(Bernard
Stradling, R J Herd)*

Cumbria

 AMBLESIDE   NY3704   Map 9

Golden Rule

(015394) 32257 – www.goldenrule-ambleside.co.uk

Smithy Brow; follow Kirkstone Pass signpost from A591 on N side of town; LA22 9AS

Simple town local with a cosy, relaxed atmosphere and real ales

This no-frills town local doesn't change at all – which is just how its regular customers like it. The bar area has built-in wall seats around cast-iron-framed tables (one with a local map set into its top), horsebrasses on black beams, assorted pictures on the walls, a welcoming winter fire and a relaxed atmosphere. Robinsons Dizzy Blonde, Double Hop, Hartleys Cumbria Way and XBand White Label Blonde Rye on handpump and Weston's cider; they also offer various teas and good coffee all day. A brass measuring rule hangs above the bar (hence the pub's name). There's also a back room with TV (not much used), a room on the left with darts and a games machine, and another room, down a couple of steps on the right, with lots of seating. The backyard has benches and a covered heated area, and the window boxes are especially colourful. There's no car park.

⑪ The scotch eggs and pies (if they have them) run out fast, so don't assume you will get something to eat.

Robinsons ~ Tenant John Lockley ~ Real ale ~ Open 11am-midnight ~ Children welcome away from bar before 9pm ~ Dogs welcome ~ Wi-fi *Recommended by Carol and Barry Craddock, Anne Taylor, Ruth May*

 AMBLESIDE   NY3703   Map 9

Wateredge Inn ♀ 🛏

(015394) 32332 – www.wateredgehotel.co.uk

Borrans Road, off A591; LA22 0EP

Family-run inn by lake with plenty of room both inside and out, six ales on handpump and enjoyable all-day food; comfortable bedrooms

The sizeable garden here is right by Lake Windermere and in warm weather the picnic-sets get snapped up pretty quickly. Many of the stylish, comfortable bedrooms share this lovely view – as do seats by the big windows in the bar. This modernised bar (originally two 17th-c cottages) has a wide mix of customers, an easy-going, bustling atmosphere, leather tub chairs around wooden tables on flagstones and several different areas leading off with similar furniture, exposed stone or wood-panelled walls and interesting old photographs and paintings. A cosy and much favoured room has beams and timbering, sofas, armchairs and an open fire. The six real ales on handpump served by friendly, cheerful staff come from breweries such as Barngates, Cumberland, Jennings, Theakstons, Tirril and Watermill and they offer 17 wines by the glass, and quite a choice of coffees. Background music and TV. They have their own moorings.

All-day, popular food includes sandwiches, sticky pork back ribs with sweet chilli glaze, prawn cocktail, tempura haddock and chips, chicken curry, home sweet-cured bacon chop with free-range egg and caramelised pineapple, pasta with butternut squash, smoked cheese and creamy green peas, cumberland sausage with red wine and onion gravy, fish pie, and puddings such as caramelised lemon tart with damson ice-cream and chocolate mousse with orange chantilly cream. *Benchmark main dish: lamb hotpot £13.95. Two-course evening meal £19.00.*

Free house ~ Licensee Derek Cowap ~ Real ale ~ Open 10am (10.30am Sun)-11pm ~ Bar food 12-9 ~ Children welcome ~ Dogs allowed in bar ~ Wi-fi ~ Live music Fri, Sat ~ Bedrooms: £60/£125 *Recommended by John Oates, Tina and David Woods-Taylor, Bernard Stradling, Denis and Margaret Kilner*

BASSENTHWAITE LAKE
NY1930 Map 9

Pheasant ★ 🍴⭐ ♀ 🛏

(017687) 76234 – www.the-pheasant.co.uk
Follow Pheasant Inn sign at N end of dual carriageway stretch of A66 by Bassenthwaite Lake; CA13 9YE

Delightful, old-fashioned bar in smart hotel, with enjoyable bar food and a fine range of drinks; bedrooms

A t the heart of this civilised and smart hotel is a charming little bar of proper character used by chatty locals. Nicely old-fashioned, it has mellow polished walls, cushioned oak settles, rush-seat chairs and library seats, and hunting prints and photographs. Black Sheep Bitter, Coniston Bluebird and Hawkshead Bitter on handpump, a dozen good wines by the glass, over 60 malt whiskies and several gins and vodkas all served by friendly, knowledgeable staff. There's a front bistro, a formal back restaurant overlooking the garden and several comfortable lounges with log fires, beautiful flower arrangements, fine parquet flooring, antiques and plants. The garden has seats and tables and is surrounded by attractive woodland. Bedrooms are well equipped and comfortable and two are pet-friendly. There are plenty of walks in all directions.

Very good food can be eaten in the bar, bistro or lounges at lunchtime, and in the bistro and restaurant only in the evening: black pudding on brioche croûte with roasted red pepper, poached egg and hollandaise, smoked haddock fishcake with pickled cucumber, chilli and tomato salsa and tartare cream sauce, cumberland sausages with onion gravy, a pie of the day, bass fillet with asian-style broth, king prawns and noodles with pak choi and chilli, and puddings such as dark chocolate brownie with salted caramel ice-cream and vanilla crème brûlée; they also offer a two- and three-course set menu (6-7pm Sun-Fri). *Benchmark main dish: slow-cooked pork belly with black pudding crumbs and cider jus £14.50. Two-course evening meal £23.00.*

Free house ~ Licensee Matthew Wylie ~ Real ale ~ Open 11.30-11 ~ Bar food 12-2.30, 6-9 ~ Restaurant ~ Children welcome but must be over 8 in bedrooms ~ Dogs allowed in bar and bedrooms ~ Wi-fi ~ Bedrooms: £105/£120 *Recommended by Robert Wivell, Martin Day, Tina and David Woods-Taylor, Pat and Stewart Gordon, Gordon and Margaret Ormondroyd, Edward Mirzoeff*

We say if we know a pub allows dogs.

BOWLAND BRIDGE
Hare & Hounds 🌟 ♀ 🛏

SD4189 Map 9

(015395) 68333 – www.hareandhoundsbowlandbridge.co.uk
Signed from A5074; LA11 6NN

17th-c inn in quiet spot with a friendly, cheerful landlady, real ales, popular food and fine views; good bedrooms

Just three miles from Lake Windermere and with fine valley views, this is a genuinely friendly place that our readers enjoy greatly. The little bar has a log fire, daily papers to read and high chairs by the wooden counter where they serve Hare of the Dog (named for the pub by Tirril) and guests such as Coniston Bluebird and Thwaites Best on handpump, a farm cider from half a mile away and a dozen wines by the glass. Leading off here, other rooms are appealingly furnished with a mix of interesting dining chairs around all sorts of tables on black slate or old pine-boarded floors, numerous hunting prints on painted or stripped-stone walls, a candlelit moroccan-style lantern in a fireplace with neatly stacked logs to one side, and a relaxed atmosphere; background music and board games. The collie is called Murphy. There are teak tables and chairs under parasols on the front terrace, with more seats in the spacious side garden. The comfortable bedrooms make a good base for exploring the area.

 Interesting food includes sandwiches (until 6pm), beer-battered haggis fritters with wholegrain mustard sauce, Morecambe Bay potted shrimps, spicy bean, chickpea and tomato tagine with moroccan couscous, lamb hotpot, burger of the day with toppings, pickles and relish, bass on vegetable ratatouille with basil pesto cream, and puddings such as peanut, chocolate and caramel torte and sticky toffee pudding with butterscotch sauce. *Benchmark main dish: steak in ale pie £12.95. Two-course evening meal £20.00.*

Free house ~ Licensee Kerry Parsons ~ Real ale ~ Open 12-11 (10.30 Sun) ~ Bar food 12-2, 6-9; all day weekends ~ Children welcome ~ Dogs allowed in bar and bedrooms ~ Wi-fi ~ Bedrooms: £95/£135 *Recommended by Jacqui Stevens, Caroline Prescott, Simon Cleasby*

BOWNESS-ON-WINDERMERE
Hole in t' Wall 🍺

SD4096 Map 9

(015394) 43488 – www.robinsonsbrewery.com/newhallinn
Fallbarrow Road, off St Martins Parade; LA23 3DH

Lively and unchanging town local with popular ales and friendly staff

There's a lot to look at in the character bar here and a cheerful mix of both locals and visitors – all welcomed by the friendly licensees. It's the town's oldest pub and the split-level rooms have beams, stripped stone and flagstones, lots of country knick-knacks and old pictures, and a splendid log fire beneath a vast slate mantelpiece; the upper room has some noteworthy plasterwork. Robinsons Dizzy Blonde, Hartleys XB and Unicorn plus a couple of guest beers on handpump and 20 malt whiskies; juke box in the bottom bar. The small flagstoned front courtyard has sheltered picnic-sets and outdoor heaters.

🍴 Bar food includes pâté of the day, scampi and chips, a daily curry, fish pie, and puddings such as chocolate sponge and sticky toffee pudding. *Benchmark main dish: beef in ale pie £11.30. Two-course evening meal £18.00.*

Robinsons ~ Tenant Susan Burnet ~ Real ale ~ Open 11-11; 11-11.30 Fri, Sat; 12-11 Sun ~ Bar food 12-2.30, 6-8.30; 12-8 Fri, Sat; 12-5 Sun ~ Children welcome ~ Live music Fri
Recommended by I D Barnett, Simon Cleasby, Alf Wright, Sally Wright

BRIGSTEER
Wheatsheaf ♀

SD4889 Map 9

(015395) 68938 – www.thewheatsheafbrigsteer.co.uk

Off Brigsteer Brow; LA8 8AN

Bustling pub with interestingly furnished and decorated rooms, a good choice of food and drink, and seats outside; luxury bunkhouse bedrooms

'A perfect place for a pint or a tasty meal,' says one reader who comes here on a regular basis; many other customers agree. The various rooms have an easy-going, friendly feel and there's plenty of character throughout. The bar has a two-way log fire, carved wooden stools against the counter and Bowness Bay Swan Blonde, Hawkshead Bitter, Thwaites Wainwright and a changing guest beer on handpump, 16 wines by the glass and eight malt whiskies. There's an appealing variety of cushioned dining chairs, carved and boxed settles and window seats set around an array of tables on either flagstones or floorboards, walls with pale-painted woodwork or wallpaper hung with animal and bird sketches, cartoons or interesting clock faces, and the lighting is both old-fashioned and contemporary. Outside there are seats and tables along the front of the building and picnic-sets on raised terracing. Their luxury bunkhouse (half a mile up the road) has five ensuite rooms and fine country views; breakfasts are hearty.

 Tasty seasonal food includes potted duck in orange and thyme butter with prune and port compote, haddock and chorizo fishcake with lemon mayonnaise, sharing plates, cumberland sausages with apple and grain mustard mash and caramelised red onion gravy, pizzas, beer-battered haddock and chips, cider-braised pork belly with sage mash, black pudding, parsnip purée and mustard sauce, butternut squash and sage ravioli with basil and pine nut pesto, and puddings such as lemon posset with raspberry coulis and sticky ginger pudding with toffee sauce. *Benchmark main dish: pie of the day £12.95. Two-course evening meal £19.00.*

Individual Inns ~ Managers Nicki Higgs and Tom Roberts ~ Real ale ~ Open 10am-11pm ~ Bar food 12-3, 5.30-9; snacks 3-5.30; 12-7.30 Sun ~ Restaurant ~ Children welcome ~ Dogs allowed in bar ~ Wi-fi ~ Bedrooms: /£70 *Recommended by Hugh Roberts, Gordon and Margaret Ormondroyd, Ray and Winifred Halliday, Peter Andrews, Michael Doswell*

BROUGHTON MILLS
Blacksmiths Arms ⭐🍴

SD2190 Map 9

(01229) 716824 – www.theblacksmithsarms.com

Off A593 N of Broughton-in-Furness; LA20 6AX

Friendly little pub with rewarding food, local beers and open fires; fine nearby walks

After a day on the fells, this charming little 18th-c pub is just the place to head for. The four small bars have warm log fires, beams, a relaxed, friendly atmosphere and are simply but attractively decorated with straightforward chairs and tables on ancient slate floors. Three real ales from breweries such as Cross Bay, Strands and Tirril on handpump, ten wines by the glass and summer farm cider; darts, board games and dominoes. The hanging baskets and tubs of flowers in front of the building are very pretty in summer, and there are seats and tables under parasols on the back terrace.

🌟 Food is reliably good and includes lunchtime sandwiches, warm salad of shredded duck confit with hoisin sauce, baked goats cheese with red onion, walnut and sun-dried tomato salad and balsamic glaze, beer-battered hake and chips, wild mushroom, parmesan and cream risotto, burger with toppings and chips, pork tenderloin wrapped in pancetta with chorizo and chickpea casserole, and puddings such as dark chocolate brownie with chocolate sauce and lime and ginger crème brûlée; they also offer a two-course set lunch. *Benchmark main dish: slow-cooked lamb shoulder in honey and mint with dauphinoise potatoes £13.95. Two-course evening meal £18.50.*

Free house ~ Licensees Mike and Sophie Lane ~ Real ale ~ Open 12-2.30, 5-11; 12-11 Sat, Sun; closed Mon lunchtime ~ Bar food 12-2, 6-9; not Mon ~ Restaurant ~ Children welcome ~ Dogs welcome *Recommended by Jo Garnett, Simon Cleasby, Peter Meister, Lindy Andrews,*

CARLETON NY5329 Map 9

Cross Keys

(01768) 865588 – www.thecrosskeyspenrith.co.uk

A686, off A66 roundabout at Penrith; CA11 8TP

Friendly refurbished pub with several connected seating areas, real ales and popular food

This well run pub is at its busiest at lunchtime when walkers, cyclists and others crowd in for refreshment. The beamed main bar has a friendly feel, pubby tables and chairs on light wooden floorboards, modern metal wall lights and pictures on bare stone walls, and Tirril 1823 and a guest such as Shepherd Neame Spitfire on handpump. Steps lead down to a small area with high bar stools around a high drinking table and then upstairs to the restaurant: a light, airy room with big windows, large wrought-iron candelabras hanging from the vaulted ceiling, solid pale wooden tables and chairs and doors to a verandah. At the far end of the main bar are yet another couple of small connected bar rooms with darts, games machine, pool, juke box and dominoes; TV and background music. There are fell views from the garden. This is under the same ownership as the Highland Drove in Great Salkeld.

Robustly flavoured food includes sandwiches, chicken liver pâté with chutney, deep-fried garlic and rosemary brie wedges with redcurrant sauce, sharing platters, burgers with toppings and fries, butternut squash ravioli with thyme, rosemary and beetroot sauce, gammon with pineapple and egg, chicken with black pudding mash and wholegrain mustard sauce, harissa cod with vegetable couscous and tomato and red pepper stew, and puddings such as chocolate brownie with chocolate sauce and vanilla crème brûlée. *Benchmark main dish: steak in ale pie £11.50. Two-course evening meal £16.00.*

Free house ~ Licensee Paul Newton ~ Real ale ~ Open 12-2.30, 5-1am; 12-2am Sat; 12-1am Sun ~ Bar food 12-2.30, 6-9 (8.30 Sun); 12-2.30, 5.30-9 Fri, Sat ~ Restaurant ~ Children welcome ~ Dogs allowed in bar ~ Wi-fi *Recommended by Lindy Andrews, Tracey and Stephen Groves, Peter Andrews*

CARTMEL FELL SD4189 Map 9

Masons Arms

(015395) 68486 – www.masonsarmsstrawberrybank.co.uk

Strawberry Bank, a few miles S of Windermere between A592 and A5074; perhaps the simplest way to find the pub is to go uphill W from Bowland Bridge (which is signposted off A5074) towards Newby Bridge and keep right, then left at the staggered crossroads – it's then on your right, below Gummer's How; OS Sheet 97 map reference 413895; LA11 6NW

Stunning views, beamed bar with plenty of character, interesting food and a good choice of ales and wines; self-catering cottages and apartments

It pays to get to this extremely popular and well run pub early on weekday lunchtimes as tables fill up quickly and they don't take bookings then. The stunning views – from both inside and the rustic benches and tables on the heated and covered terraces outside – look down over the Winster Valley to the woods below Whitbarrow Scar. The main bar has plenty of character, with low black beams in the bowed ceiling, and country chairs and plain wooden tables on polished flagstones. A small lounge has oak tables and settles to match its fine Jacobean panelling. There's also a plain little room beyond the serving counter with pictures and a fire in an open range, a family room with the atmosphere of an old parlour, and an upstairs dining room; background music and board games. Bowness Bay Swan Blonde, Cumbrian Legendary Loweswater Gold, Hawkshead Bitter and Thwaites Wainwright on handpump, quite a few foreign bottled beers, 12 wines by the glass, ten malt whiskies and farm cider; service is friendly and helpful. The self-catering cottages and apartments are stylish and comfortable and share the same fine outlook.

 Rewarding food includes sandwiches (till 6pm weekends), black pudding with poached egg and crispy bacon on creamy mash with wholegrain mustard sauce, confit chicken leg with roasted garlic and chorizo bean stew, rabbit casserole, wild boar and damson burger with baked beans and smoked pancetta in tomato sauce and fries, vegetable shepherd's pie with sweet potato and cheese topping, plaice with garlic butter and herby roast new potatoes, and puddings such as toffee and banana sundae with salted caramel ice-cream and vanilla and blackcurrant vodka crème brûlée. *Benchmark main dish: pie of the day £12.95. Two-course evening meal £18.50.*

Individual Inns ~ Managers John and Diane Taylor ~ Real ale ~ Open 11.30-11; 12-10.30 Sun ~ Bar food 12-2.30, 6-9; 12-9 weekends ~ Restaurant ~ Children welcome ~ Dogs allowed in bedrooms ~ Wi-fi *Recommended by Gordon and Margaret Ormondroyd, Christian Mole, Edward and William Johnston, Sandra King*

CLIFTON
NY5326 Map 9

George & Dragon 🎯 🍷 🛏️

(01768) 865381 – www.georgeanddragonclifton.co.uk
A6; near M6 junction 40; CA10 2ER

Cumbria Dining Pub of the Year

Former coaching inn with attractive bars and sizeable restaurant, local ales, well chosen wines, imaginative food and seats outside; smart bedrooms

A top class all-rounder, this carefully restored 18th-c inn appeals to a wide range of customers. The relaxed reception room has bright rugs on flagstones, leather chairs around a low table in front of an open fire, a table in a private nook to one side of the reception desk (just right for a group of six) and a comfortable bed for visiting dogs. Through wrought-iron gates is the main bar area with more cheerful rugs on flagstones, assorted wooden farmhouse chairs and tables, grey panelling topped with yellow-painted walls, photographs of the Lowther Estate and of the family with hunting dogs, various sheep and fell pictures and some high bar stools by the panelled bar counter. Cumberland Corby Blonde, Hawkshead Bitter and a changing guest beer on handpump, 20 wines by the glass from a well chosen list and interesting local liqueurs. Another room is similarly furnished; background music and TV. The sizeable restaurant to the left of the entrance consists of four open-plan rooms: plenty of old pews and church chairs around tables set for dining, a woodburning stove and a contemporary open kitchen. Outside, there are tables in a decoratively paved front area and a high-walled enclosed courtyard. Bedrooms are stylish and comfortable and the breakfasts excellent.

 Accomplished cooking using produce from the Lowther Estate (of which this inn is part) includes lunchtime sandwiches, steamed clams with garlic, lime and chilli dressing, braised pig cheeks with dry cider, apple, peas, pancetta and oregano, bubble and squeak with wild garlic and fried duck egg, moroccan-spiced lamb burger with cucumber and mint yoghurt, corn-fed guinea fowl with tarragon sauce and thyme-roasted new potatoes, venison haunch with wild mushroom risotto, parsnip crisps and red wine reduction, and puddings such as ginger and pear sponge with pear custard and iced blueberry and white chocolate parfait with blueberry compote. *Benchmark main dish: chargrilled Estate burger with spiced tomato chutney and chips £13.00. Two-course evening meal £23.00.*

Free house ~ Licensee Charles Lowther ~ Real ale ~ Open 12-11 ~ Bar food 12-2.30, 6-9 ~ Restaurant ~ Children welcome ~ Dogs allowed in bar and bedrooms ~ Wi-fi ~ Live music every two months (best to phone) ~ Bedrooms: £85/£95 *Recommended by Robert Wivell, Dave Braisted, Lee and Liz Potter, Douglas Power, Geoffrey Sutton, Simon Cleasby*

CONISTON
Sun 🍺 🛏

SD3098 Map 9

(015394) 41248 – www.thesunconiston.com
Signed left off A593 at the bridge; LA21 8HQ

Extended old pub in fine spot with a lively bar, plenty of dining space, real ales, well liked food and seats outside; comfortable bedrooms

This 16th-c inn's position is splendid, surrounded by dramatic bare fells, and our readers like its cheerful bar best. There are beams and timbers, exposed stone walls, flagstones and a Victorian-style range. Also, cask seats, old settles and cast-iron-framed tables, quite a few Donald Campbell photographs (this was his HQ during his final attempt on the world water-speed record) and a good mix of customers – often with their dogs. A fine range of up to eight real ales on handpump might include Barngates Cracker Ale, Coniston Bluebird Bitter, Cumbrian Legendary Loweswater Gold, Ulverston Lonesome Pine and guests such as Fell YOLO, Cumbrian Legendary Esthwaite and Hardknott Continuum; the friendly staff also keep eight wines by the glass and 20 malt whiskies. Above the bar is another room with extra seating for families and larger groups, and there's also a sizeable side lounge that leads into the dining conservatory; pool, darts, and TV. The bedrooms are quiet and comfortable and their fine mountain views are shared by the seats and tables on the terrace and in the big tree-sheltered garden.

Bar food includes sandwiches, crayfish salad with dill and chive mayonnaise, ham hock terrine with piccalilli, lamb and black pudding hotpot, roast vegetable and cheese pasta with pecorino, steak in ale pie, slow-roast pork in cider, apple and honey with raisin and cinnamon red cabbage, and puddings such as chocolate tart and apple pie. *Benchmark main dish: cumberland sausage with mash and onion gravy £12.50. Two-course evening meal £17.50.*

Free house ~ Licensee Alan Piper ~ Real ale ~ Open 11-11 ~ Bar food 12-3, 5.30-8.30 ~ Restaurant ~ Children welcome ~ Dogs allowed in bar and bedrooms ~ Wi-fi ~ Bedrooms: £55/£84 *Recommended by Caroline Prescott, Paul Scofield*

The star-on-a-plate award, 🌟, distinguishes pubs where the food is of exceptional quality. The knife-and-fork symbol just means the pub serves food.

CROSTHWAITE
SD4491 Map 9

Punch Bowl 🏵️ ♈ 🛏️

(015395) 68237 – www.the-punchbowl.co.uk

Village signed off A5074 SE of Windermere; LA8 8HR

Smart dining pub with a proper bar and other elegant rooms, real ales, a fine wine list, impressive food and friendly staff; stylish bedrooms

The lovely bedrooms in this civilised inn are well equipped and breakfasts are very good. There's a relaxed and nicely uncluttered feel throughout, and the public bar has rafters, a couple of eye-catching rugs on flagstones, bar stools by the slate-topped counter, Barngates Tag Lag and Bowness Bay Swan Blonde on handpump, 16 wines and two sparkling wines by the glass, 15 malt whiskies and local damson gin. To the right are two linked carpeted and beamed rooms with well spaced country pine furniture of varying sizes, including a big refectory table, and walls that are painted in restrained neutral tones with an attractive assortment of prints; winter log fire, woodburning stove, lots of fresh flowers and daily papers. On the left, the wooden-floored restaurant area (also light, airy and attractive) has comfortable high-backed leather dining chairs; background music. Tables and seats on a terrace are stepped into the hillside and overlook the pretty Lyth Valley.

 Excellent food includes dressed white crab with brown crab mousse, passion fruit and fennel, steak tartare with bloody mary dressing, celeriac rösti with walnuts, pickled apple and slow-cooked egg yolk, barbecue pulled pork with potato cake, fried duck egg and damson ketchup, lamb rump with pea fricassée, feta and mint, brill and king prawn linguine with ginger, pink grapefruit and samphire, and puddings such as chocolate mousse with pineapple, yoghurt, rum and raisin ice-cream and salted caramel tart with damsons and crème fraîche. *Benchmark main dish: cod loin, mussels, leeks and bacon in cider £16.50. Two-course evening meal £22.00.*

Free house ~ Licensee Richard Rose ~ Real ale ~ Open 12-11 ~ Bar food 12-8.45; 12-4, 5.30-8.45 weekends ~ Restaurant ~ Children welcome ~ Dogs allowed in bar ~ Wi-fi ~ Bedrooms: £95/£130 *Recommended by Colin McLachlan, J R Wildon, Simon Cleasby, Lionel Smith, Daniel King, Anne Taylor*

ELTERWATER
NY3204 Map 9

Britannia 🍺 🛏️

(015394) 37210 – www.thebritanniainn.com

Off B5343; LA22 9HP

Much loved inn surrounded by wonderful walks and scenery, with up to seven real ales and well liked food; bedrooms

No matter how busy this very friendly and unpretentious little pub is (and it does get packed at peak times), staff remain helpful and friendly; there are walks of every gradient right from the front door and the scenery is spectacular. The little front bar has beams and a couple of window seats that look across to Elterwater through the trees, while the small back bar is traditionally furnished: thick slate walls, winter coal fires, oak benches, settles, windsor chairs and a big old rocking chair. A couple of beers are named for the pub – Britannia Special (from Coniston) and Britannia Gold (from Eden) – plus Coniston Bluebird Bitter, Cumberland Corby Amber and Blonde and three guest beers on handpump, and 12 malt whiskies. The lounge is comfortable, and there's also a hall and dining room. Plenty of seats outside, and visiting dancers (morris and step and garland) in summer. Bedrooms are warm and charming.

The inn usefully serves some sort of enjoyable food all day, including lunchtime sandwiches, crumbed brie with red onion marmalade, smoked salmon, haddock and mackerel fishcakes with garlic mayonnaise, steak and mushroom in ale pie, wild and button mushroom stroganoff, burger with toppings and chips, bass fillet with roasted mediterranean vegetables and basil oil, and puddings such as a brûlée of the day and home-made profiteroles with dark chocolate sauce. *Benchmark main dish: braised lamb shoulder in mint and spices with red wine gravy £15.50. Two-course evening meal £22.00.*

Free house ~ Licensee Andrew Parker ~ Real ale ~ Open 10.30am-11pm ~ Bar food 12-5, 6-9 ~ Restaurant ~ Children welcome ~ Dogs allowed in bar and bedrooms ~ Wi-fi ~ Bedrooms: £95/£105 *Recommended by Carol and Barry Craddock, Anne and Ben Smith, Peter Meister, Tina and David Woods-Taylor, Brian and Anna Marsden, Bernard Stradling*

GREAT SALKELD   NY5536   Map 10
Highland Drove 🌟

(01768) 898349 – www.highlanddroveinnpenrith.co.uk
B6412, off A686 NE of Penrith; CA11 9NA

Bustling place with cheerful customers, good food and fair choice of drinks, and fine views from the upstairs verandah; bedrooms

A father and son team continue to run this enjoyable pub with enthusiasm and friendliness. The spotlessly kept, chatty main bar has sandstone flooring, stone walls, cushioned wheelback chairs around a mix of tables and an open fire in a raised stone fireplace. The downstairs eating area has more cushioned dining chairs around wooden tables on pale wooden floorboards, stone walls and ceiling joists, and a two-way fire in a raised stone fireplace that separates this room from the coffee lounge with its comfortable leather chairs and sofas. There's also an upstairs restaurant – it's best to book to be sure of a table. A beer named for the pub from Eden, Theakstons Lightfoot Bitter and a guest ale on handpump, a dozen wines by the glass and 28 malt whiskies; background music, darts, pool and dominoes. The lovely views over the Eden Valley and the Pennines are best enjoyed from seats on the upstairs verandah; there are also seats on the back terrace. This is under the same ownership as the Cross Keys in Carleton.

Tasty, highly popular food includes sandwiches, twice-baked cheese soufflé, crayfish and prawn cocktail, sharing platters, beer-battered haddock and chips, steak in ale pie, cumberland sausages with mash and onion gravy, chicken in rosemary, lemon and garlic on cherry tomato and courgette pasta with mustard cream sauce, double barnsley lamb chop with parsley mash and mint and redcurrant sauce, and puddings. *Benchmark main dish: nile perch with stir-fried vegetables in thai curry sauce £13.50. Two-course evening meal £17.00.*

Free house ~ Licensees Donald and Paul Newton ~ Real ale ~ Open 12-3, 6-1am; 12-1am Sat; 12-midnight Sun; closed Mon lunchtime ~ Bar food 12-2, 6-9 (8.30 Sun) ~ Restaurant ~ Children welcome ~ Dogs allowed in bar ~ Wi-fi ~ Bedrooms: £50/£80 *Recommended by Dave Arthur, Mr and Mrs Richard Osborne, Dave Sutton*

HAWKSHEAD   NY3501   Map 9
Drunken Duck 🌟 ♀ 🍷 🛏

(015394) 36347 – www.drunkenduckinn.co.uk
Barngates; the pub is signposted from B5286 Hawkshead–Ambleside, opposite the Outgate Inn and from north first right after the wooded caravan site; LA22 0NG

Stylish little bar, several restaurant areas, own-brewed beers and bar meals as well as innovative restaurant choices; stunning views and lovely bedrooms

The own-brewed ales in the smart little bar attract walkers at lunchtime (which is when this civilised inn is at its most informal). From their Barngates brewery they offer Cat Nap, Chesters Strong & Ugly, Cracker Ale, Pride of Westmorland, Red Bull Terrier and Tag Lag on handpump and a new own-brew lager called Vienna – as well as 16 wines by the glass from a fine list, 25 malt whiskies and 16 gins. There's an easy-going atmosphere, leather bar stools by the slate-topped counter, leather club chairs, beams and oak floorboards, photographs, coaching prints and hunting pictures on the walls, and horsebrasses and some kentish hop bines as decoration. The three restaurant areas are elegant, and the beautifully furnished bedrooms get booked up months in advance; some have their own balcony and overlook the garden and tarn. Sit at the wooden tables and benches on grass opposite the building for spectacular views across the fells; the numerous spring and summer bulbs are lovely.

Imaginative food using the best local produce includes at lunchtime sandwiches, smoked haricot and leek chowder with poached egg, a meze board, peanut curry and beef stew with dumplings and red cabbage; evening choices include duck scotch egg with plum ketchup, crispy chicken thigh with buckwheat waffle and oyster mushroom, spiced cauliflower with lentil dhal and onion pakora, stone bass with swiss chard and haricot beans, halibut with carrot, kale and walnut, and puddings such as chocolate malt mousse with kendal mint ice-cream and apple tarte tatin with walnut ice-cream. *Benchmark main dish: cod with smoked brisket, charred leeks and mash £22.00. Two-course evening meal £27.00.*

Own brew ~ Licensee Steph Barton ~ Real ale ~ Open 11.30-11; 12-10.30 Sun ~ Bar food 12-4, 6.30-9 ~ Restaurant ~ Children welcome ~ Dogs allowed in bar ~ Wi-fi ~ Bedrooms: £78.75/£105 *Recommended by Colin McLachlan, Carol and Barry Craddock, Bernard Stradling, Malcolm and Pauline Pellatt, Peter Meister*

INGS   SD4498 Map 9
Watermill 🍺 🛏
(01539) 821309 – www.lakelandpub.co.uk
Just off A591 E of Windermere; LA8 9PY

Busy, cleverly converted pub with fantastic range of real ales including own brews, and well liked food; bedrooms

Following flooding, this bustling pub (cleverly converted from a wood mill and joiner's shop) has had a gentle refurbishment – but this in no way detracts from its character. The chatty bar has beams, black leather, wheelback and kitchen or mate's dining chairs around solid tables on tartan carpet and a woodburning stove in a stone fireplace. Another room has lots of nice old posters on rough plastered walls, and the interconnected dining rooms, similarly furnished, have flagstones and exposed and painted stone walls; several open fires, darts and board games. They keep up to 16 beers on handpump and their own brews include Watermill A Bit'er Ruff, Blackbeard, Collie Wobbles, Dogth Vader, Golden Retriever, Isle of Dogs, Windermere Blonde, Ruff Justice, Shih Tzu and W'ruff Night and there are guests such as Coniston Bluebird, Cumbrian Legendary Loweswater Gold and Theakstons Old Peculier. Also, scrumpy cider, a huge choice of foreign bottled beers and 40 malt whiskies. There are seats in the gardens and lots to do nearby. Dogs may get free biscuits and water. Readers enjoy staying here.

Some sort of good, popular food is served all day: sandwiches (until 4.30), black pudding with crispy pancetta, poached egg and mustard and honey drizzle, mussels in white wine and cream, chicken curry, goats cheese, beetroot and shallot tarte tatin with orange, walnut and dill-dressed salad, beer-battered haddock and chips, burger with toppings and chips, sweet-cured bacon chop with duck egg and pineapple, and puddings such as chocolate fudge cake and crème brûlée. *Benchmark main dish: steak in ale pie £10.95. Two-course evening meal £17.50.*

Own brew ~ Licensee Brian Coulthwaite ~ Real ale ~ Open 11-11 (10.30 Sun) ~ Bar food 12-9 ~ Children welcome ~ Dogs allowed in bar and bedrooms ~ Wi-fi ~ Storytelling first Tues, folk music third Tues of month ~ Bedrooms: £49/£89 *Recommended by Dennis Jones, Denis and Margaret Kilner, Rona Mackinlay, Douglas Power*

LANGDALE

NY2806 Map 9

Old Dungeon Ghyll 🍺 £

(015394) 37272 – www.odg.co.uk

B5343; LA22 9JY

Straightforward place in lovely position with real ales, traditional food and fine surrounding walks; bedrooms

The whole feel of this dramatically set inn is basic but cosy – and once all the fell walkers and climbers crowd in, full of boisterous atmosphere. There's no need to remove boots or muddy trousers: you can sit on seats in old cattle stalls by the big warming fire and enjoy the fine choice of six real ales on handpump: Jennings Cumberland, Theakston Old Peculier, Yates Best Bitter and quickly changing guests such as Cumbrian Legendary Esthwaite, Irwell Works Copper Plate Bitter and Pennine Best Bitter. Farm cider and several malt whiskies. It's a good place to stay, with warm bedrooms and highly rated breakfasts. It may get lively on a Saturday night (there's a popular National Trust campsite opposite).

Honest food includes their own bread and cakes, lunchtime sandwiches, pâté of the day, prawn cocktail, beer-battered fish and chips, a pie of the day, spicy chilli con carne, vegetable goulash, gammon and free-range eggs, and puddings. *Benchmark main dish: cumberland sausage with onion gravy and apple sauce £10.95. Two-course evening meal £16.50.*

Free house ~ Licensee Neil Walmsley ~ Real ale ~ Open 11-11; 12-10.30 Sun ~ Bar food 12-2, 6-9 ~ Restaurant ~ Children welcome ~ Dogs allowed in bar and bedrooms ~ Wi-fi ~ Bedrooms: £58/£116 *Recommended by Hilary and Neil Christopher, Peter Meister, Charles Todd, Julie Braeburn*

LEVENS

SD4987 Map 9

Strickland Arms 🍷 🍺

(015395) 61010 – www.thestricklandarms.com

4 miles from M6 junction 36, via A590; just off A590, by Sizergh Castle gates; LA8 8DZ

Friendly, open-plan pub with popular food, local ales and a fine setting; seats outside

As this particularly well run pub is by the entrance to Sizergh Castle (owned by the National Trust and open from April to October, Sunday to Thursday afternoons), it's advisable to book a table in advance. The bar on the right has oriental rugs on flagstones, a log fire, Bowness Bay Swan Blonde, Cross Bay Halo, Lancaster Amber, Old School Junior and Thwaites Wainwright on handpump, several malt whiskies and nine wines by the glass. On the left are polished boards and another log fire, and throughout there's a nice mix of sturdy country furniture, candles on tables, hunting scenes and other old prints on the walls, curtains in heavy fabric and some staffordshire china ornaments. Two of the dining rooms are upstairs; background music and board games. The flagstoned front terrace has plenty of seats; disabled access and facilities. The pub is part of the Ainscoughs group.

Good country cooking includes salmon and cod fishcake with micro salad and ginger and lemon dressing, chicken livers with shallots, madeira and charred bread, vegetarian cottage pie, organic steak burger with relish, pickles and chips, chicken in wild mushroom sauce with creamed potatoes, lancashire hotpot, fish pie, and puddings such as chocolate fudge brownie with honeycomb and strawberry and vanilla pannacotta. *Benchmark main dish: steak in ale pie £12.50. Two-course evening meal £18.50.*

Free house ~ Licensee Nicola Harrison ~ Real ale ~ Open 12-11 (10.30 Sun) ~ Bar food 12-2.30, 6-9; 12-9 Sat; 12-8 Sun ~ Children welcome ~ Dogs welcome ~ Wi-fi
Recommended by Richard Cox, Ray and Winifred Halliday, Rob Anderson, Mary Joyce, Andrew Vincent

LITTLE LANGDALE
NY3103 Map 9

Three Shires 🍺 🛏

(015394) 37215 – www.threeshiresinn.co.uk
From A593 3 miles W of Ambleside take small road signposted The Langdales, Wrynose Pass; then bear left at first fork; LA22 9NZ

Fine valley views from seats on the terrace, local ales, quite a choice of food and comfortable bedrooms

The view from seats on the terrace down over the valley to the partly wooded hills below is stunning; there are more seats on a neat lawn behind the car park, backed by a small oak wood, and award-winning summer hanging baskets. Our readers enjoy this reliably well run and friendly inn very much. The comfortably extended back bar has green Lakeland stone and homely red patterned wallpaper, stripped timbers and a stripped beam-and-joist ceiling, antique oak carved settles, country kitchen chairs and stools on big dark slate flagstones and cumbrian photographs. The four real ales on handpump come from local breweries such as Bowness Bay, Coniston, Cumbrian Legendary and Hawkshead, and they also have over 50 malt whiskies and a decent wine list. The front restaurant has chunky leather dining chairs around solid tables on wood flooring, wine bottle prints on dark red walls and fresh flowers; a snug leads off here, and the residents' lounge now has leather sofas and an open fire. Darts, TV and board games. The three shires are the historical counties of Cumberland, Westmorland and Lancashire, which meet at the top of nearby Wrynose Pass.

Rewarding food includes lunchtime sandwiches, black pudding fritters with apple chutney, local smoked venison slices with salad and balsamic glaze, minted lamb burger with onion rings, apricot chutney and chips, spinach, chickpea and sweet potato curry, beef in Guinness pie, pheasant on leeks and wild mushrooms with honey, thyme and grain mustard cream sauce, bass with orange beurre blanc and burnt orange salad, and puddings such as caramel pannacotta with caramel sauce and fruit cake fritter with brandy custard. *Benchmark main dish: local lamb rump with red wine and redcurrant sauce £15.95. Two-course evening meal £22.00.*

Free house ~ Licensee Ian Stephenson ~ Real ale ~ Open 11-10.30 (11 Fri, Sat); 12-10.30 Sun; closed 3 weeks Jan ~ Bar food 12-2, 6-8.45; snacks in afternoon ~ Restaurant ~ Children welcome ~ Dogs allowed in bar ~ Wi-fi ~ Bedrooms: /£118 *Recommended by Tina and David Woods-Taylor, Brian and Anna Marsden, Barry Collett, John Evans, Tracey and Stephen Groves, Christian Mole*

Please keep sending us reports. We rely on readers for news of new discoveries, and particularly for news of changes – however slight – at the fully described pubs: feedback@goodguides.com, or (no stamp needed) The Good Pub Guide, FREEPOST RTJR-ZCYZ-RJZT, Perrymans Lane, Etchingham TN19 7DN.

LOWESWATER
Kirkstile Inn

NY1421 Map 9

(01900) 85219 – www.kirkstile.com

From B5289 follow signs to Loweswater Lake; OS Sheet 89 map reference 140210; CA13 0RU

Lovely spot for this well run, popular inn with busy bar, own-brewed beers, good food and friendly welcome; bedrooms

---

This friendly little pub is surrounded by marvellous walks of all levels, and many readers make the most of them by staying overnight in the comfortable bedrooms; breakfasts are especially good. Downstairs, the bustling main bar has a cosy atmosphere, thanks to the roaring log fire, low beams and carpeting, comfortably cushioned small settles and pews, partly stripped stone walls, board games and a slate shove-ha'penny board. As well as their own-brewed Cumbrian Legendary Esthwaite, Langdale and Loweswater Gold, they often keep a guest such as Watermill Collie Wobbles on handpump, as well as nine wines by the glass and 20 malt whiskies. The stunning views of the peaks can be enjoyed from picnic-sets on the lawn, from the very attractive covered verandah in front of the building and from the bow windows in one of the rooms off the bar; if you're lucky, you might spot a red squirrel. Dogs are allowed only in the bar and not during evening food service.

Well liked food includes lunchtime sandwiches, duck egg wrapped in cumberland sausage and black pudding with fennel and orange salad and hoisin dressing, tiger prawns in ale batter with mango and red pepper salsa, wild mushroom risotto, salmon fillet with parsley and white wine cream sauce, chicken, ham and leek pudding, slow-roasted lamb with rosemary and redcurrant jus, and puddings such as fruit crumble of the day and dark chocolate brownie with cranberry and white chocolate sauce. *Benchmark main dish: steak in ale pie £11.50. Two-course evening meal £19.00.*

Own brew ~ Licensee Roger Humphreys ~ Real ale ~ Open 11-11 ~ Bar food 12-2, 6-9; light meals and tea in afternoon ~ Restaurant ~ Children welcome ~ Dogs allowed in bar ~ Bedrooms: £63.50/£103 *Recommended by Martin Day, Tracey and Stephen Groves, Mike and Eleanor Anderson, Dr Peter Crawshaw*

LUPTON
Plough 𝅮 ⌂

SO5581 Map 7

(015395) 67700 – www.theploughatlupton.co.uk

A65, near M6 junction 36; LA6 1PJ

Stylish inn with open-plan smart rooms, a good choice of drinks, interesting food and seats outside; fine bedrooms

---

If you want a break from the M6, this historic 18th-c inn is just the place. There are spreading open-plan bars with beams, a nice mix of antique dining chairs and tables, comfortable leather sofas and armchairs in front of a large woodburning stove, hunting prints and cartoons on grey-painted walls, rugs on wooden floors, fresh flowers and daily papers; background music. High bar stools sit beside the granite-topped counter, where neatly dressed, friendly staff serve Bowness Bay Swan Blonde, Kirkby Lonsdale Monumental, Thwaites Wainwright and a couple of guests on handpump, ten wines by the glass, ten gins and local vodka; board games. There are rustic wooden tables and chairs under parasols behind a white picket fence, with more in the back garden. Bedrooms are cosy, attractive and comfortable.

As well as lunchtime sandwiches and sharing boards, the wide choice of food includes seared duck livers in brandy cream sauce on toasted brioche, salad of whipped goats cheese, parma ham and baby beetroot, wild boar and damson sausages with caramelised onion mash and red wine sauce, chargrilled halloumi salad with orange, mint, toasted walnuts, beetroot and diced potatoes, burger with toppings, pickles and chips, sage-roasted chicken with confit garlic and wild mushrooms, and puddings such as chilled chocolate fondant with honeycomb and peanut butter ice-cream and vanilla crème brûlée with gin and tonic sorbet. *Benchmark main dish: maple-glazed duck breast with carrot purée, dauphinoise potatoes and duck confit samosa £16.75. Two-course evening meal £19.00.*

Free house ~ Licensee Paul Spencer ~ Real ale ~ Open 11-11; 12-11 Sun ~ Bar food 12-9 ~ Restaurant ~ Children welcome ~ Dogs allowed in bar and bedrooms ~ Wi-fi ~ Bedrooms: £85/£120 *Recommended by Charles North, Hugh Roberts, Pat and Stewart Gordon, Michael Doswell, Alistair Forsyth, Lee and Liz Potter*

 NEAR SAWREY   SD3795   Map 9

Tower Bank Arms 🍺 🛏

(015394) 36334 – www.towerbankarms.com
B5285 towards the Windermere ferry; LA22 0LF

Well run pub with several real ales, well regarded bar food and a friendly welcome; nice bedrooms

Immortalised in *The Tale of Jemima Puddle-Duck*, this friendly, busy pub backs on to Beatrix Potter's farm. The low-beamed main bar has plenty of rustic charm, with a rough slate floor, game and fowl pictures, a grandfather clock, a log fire and fresh flowers; there's also a separate restaurant. Barngates Cracker Ale and Tag Lag, Cumbrian Legendary Langdale and Loweswater Gold and Hawkshead Bitter and Brodie's Prime on handpump, nine wines by the glass, 15 malt whiskies and four farm ciders; board games and darts. There are pleasant views of the wooded Claife Heights from seats in the extended garden. The pretty bedrooms have a country outlook; good breakfasts are served.

🍴 Good quality food includes lunchtime sandwiches, crayfish cocktail, roasted fig and pine nut salad with orange and pomegranate dressing, ham and eggs, cumberland sausage with apple and sage mash and caramelised red onion gravy, ratatouille topped with sweet potato mash with tempura vegetables, chicken with tomato and coconut sauce and fondant potato, pork fillet with black pudding mash and white wine sauce, and puddings such as sticky toffee pudding and raspberry eton mess. *Benchmark main dish: beef in ale stew £12.75. Two-course evening meal £18.50.*

Free house ~ Licensee Anthony Hutton ~ Real ale ~ Open 11.30-11; 12-10.30 Sun; closed winter Mon, 1 week early Dec, 1 week Jan ~ Bar food 12-2, 6-9 (8 Sun, winter Mon-Thurs and bank holidays) ~ Restaurant ~ Children welcome ~ Dogs allowed in bar and bedrooms ~ Wi-fi ~ Bedrooms: /£97 *Recommended by Mike Swan, Belinda Stamp, David Travis, Beth Aldridge*

 NEWBY BRIDGE   SD3686   Map 9

Swan 🛏

(015395) 31681 – www.swanhotel.com
Just off A590; LA12 8NB

Bustling bar in riverside hotel, a fine choice of drinks, bold fabrics and décor and seats on a waterside terrace; comfortable bedrooms

Beside a five-arch bridge on the banks of the River Leven at the southern tip of Lake Windermere, this family-run, extended coaching inn has been offering hospitality to travellers since the 17th c. Its heart remains the bar, where you'll find locals, hotel guests and boating folk all mingling happily. There are low ceilings, cheerful floral print upholstered dining chairs around scrubbed tables on bare floorboards, window seats, a log fire in a little iron fireplace, pictures and railway posters on the pink walls, and stools at the long bar counter. Jennings Cumberland, Cumbrian Legendary Loweswater Gold and a changing guest beer on handpump, served by smart, friendly staff; background music. Towards the back is another log fire with a sofa and upholstered pouffes around a low table, and a similarly furnished further room; the front snug is cosy. Original features mix well with the bold fabrics and wallpaper, fresh flowers, nice old pieces of china and modern artwork – it's all been done with a great deal of thought and care. In the main hotel off to the left is a sizeable restaurant. Plenty of pretty iron-work tables and chairs line the riverside terrace. The contemporary bedrooms are comfortable and well equipped, and some overlook the river.

As well as breakfasts, sandwiches and afternoon teas, the interesting food includes black pudding and cheese hash browns with caramelised pear and cumberland dressing, black onion and sesame seed-crusted chicken goujons with wasabi mayonnaise, greek feta filo pie with roasted beetroot and garlic purée, confit pork belly with welsh rarebit mash, courgette and red pepper pesto salad, cod with chorizo, slow-roasted tomatoes, potatoes and pesto, and puddings such as peanut butter fudge sundae and plum and blackberry ripple brûlée. *Benchmark main dish: beer-battered fish and chips £13.95. Two-course evening meal £22.00.*

Free house ~ Licensee Lindsay Knaggs ~ Real ale ~ Open 10am-11pm (midnight Sat) ~ Bar food 10-9.30 ~ Restaurant ~ Children welcome until 7pm ~ Dogs allowed in bar ~ Wi-fi ~ Bedrooms: /£129 *Recommended by Caroline Sullivan, Margaret McDonald, Peter Barrett*

RAVENSTONEDALE   NY7203 Map 10
Black Swan 🌟 🛏

(015396) 23204 – www.blackswanhotel.com
Just off A685 SW of Kirkby Stephen; CA17 4NG

Bustling hotel with thriving bar, several real ales, enjoyable food and good surrounding walks; comfortable bedrooms

To guarantee a table, it's best to book in advance as this smart, neatly kept Victorian hotel is so well regarded. The popular U-shaped bar has quite a few original period features, stripped-stone walls, plush stools by the counter, a comfortable tweed banquette, various dining chairs and little stools around a mix of tables and fresh flowers; you can eat here or in two separate restaurants. Friendly, helpful staff serve Black Sheep Bitter and Timothy Taylors Boltmaker and two local guest ales on handpump, eight wines by the glass, more than 30 malt whiskies and a good choice of fruit juices and pressés; background music, TV, darts, board games, newspapers and magazines. There are picnic-sets in the tree-sheltered streamside garden across the road and lots of good walks from the door; they have leaflets describing some routes. The bedrooms are individually decorated (some have disabled access, others are dog-friendly) and breakfasts are generous. They also run the village store, which has café seating outside.

The thoughtful menu using local ingredients includes lunchtime sandwiches, local black pudding with crispy egg and mustard mayonnaise, scallops with pancetta, curried celeriac and apple salad and cauliflower purée, butternut squash, coconut and peanut curry, steak in ale pie, gammon with scotch egg and pineapple, corn-fed free-range chicken stuffed with wild mushrooms, rosemary and garlic and red wine sauce, salmon and clams with creamy saffron sauce, and puddings such as vanilla and blood orange pannacotta and champagne sorbet and chocolate fondant with caramel peanut butter sauce. *Benchmark main dish: lamb trio (belly, loin and kidney) with fondant potato, artichoke purée and rosemary jus £17.75. Two-course evening meal £20.00.*

Free house ~ Licensee Louise Dinnes ~ Real ale ~ Open 7.30am-midnight (1am Sat) ~ Bar food 12-9 ~ Restaurant ~ Children welcome ~ Dogs allowed in bar and bedrooms ~ Wi-fi ~ Bedrooms: £75/£85 *Recommended by Sandra Hollies, John and Mary Warner, Beth Aldridge*

RAVENSTONEDALE   NY7204   Map 10

Kings Head 🍺 🛏

(015396) 23050 – www.kings-head.com
Pub visible from A685 W of Kirkby Stephen; CA17 4NH

Riverside inn with beamed bar and adjacent dining room, attractive furnishings, three real ales and interesting food; comfortable bedrooms

Nicely opened up inside, this is a civilised but easy-going inn by a bridge over the River Lune. The beamed bar rooms have lovely big flagstones, assorted rugs, a wing chair by a log fire in a raised fireplace, an attractive array of fine wooden chairs and cushioned settles around various tables, a few prints on grey-painted walls and an old yoke above a double-sided woodburner and bread oven. Jennings Cumberland, Tirril Old Faithful and a changing guest on handpump and eight wines by the glass, served by friendly staff; background music and a games room with darts and local photographs. The dining room is similarly furnished, but with some upholstered chairs on stone floors, tartan curtains, fresh flowers and a few prints. Bedrooms are comfortable and breakfasts hearty. There are picnic-sets by the river in a fenced-off area, and plenty of good surrounding walks.

 Well thought-of food includes lunchtime sandwiches, local air-dried ham with gin and apple granita and melon salad, cheese and onion soufflé with chive cream sauce, lentil and nut cutlets with creamy tomato sauce, irish beef burger with onion rings, coleslaw and chips, cumberland sausages with onion gravy and parsnip crisps, tandoori lamb rump with chickpea and potato curry, and puddings such as warm chocolate dip with marshmallows and strawberries and coconut pannacotta with pineapple granola and raspberry sorbet. *Benchmark main dish: bass fillet thai-style with coconut prawns £16.75. Two-course evening meal £22.00.*

Free house ~ Licensee Leigh O'Donoghue ~ Real ale ~ Open 12-11 (10.30 Sun) ~ Bar food 12-9 ~ Restaurant ~ Children welcome ~ Dogs allowed in bar ~ Wi-fi ~ Bedrooms: £75/£98
Recommended by Carol and Barry Craddock, Rob Anderson, John Evans

STAVELEY   SD4798   Map 10

Beer Hall at Hawkshead Brewery 🍺

(01539) 825260 – www.hawksheadbrewery.co.uk
Staveley Mill Yard, Back Lane; LA8 9LR

Hawkshead Brewery showcase plus a huge choice of bottled beers, brewery memorabilia and knowledgeable staff

They keep the full range of Hawkshead Brewery ales here and from the 14 handpumps there might be Bitter, Brodie's Prime, Cumbrian Five Hop, Dry Stone Stout, Lakeland Gold, Lakeland Lager, Red, Windermere Pale and seasonal beers; regular beer festivals. Also, 40 bottled beers and 56 whiskies with an emphasis on independent producers. It's a spacious and modern glass-fronted building and the main bar is on two levels with the lower level dominated by the stainless-steel fermenting vessels. There are high-backed chairs around light wooden tables, benches beside long tables, nice dark leather sofas around low tables (all on oak floorboards) and a couple of walls are almost entirely covered with artistic photos of barley, hops and the brewing process. You can buy T-shirts, branded glasses and polypins and there are brewery tours. Parking can be tricky at peak times.

A choice of tapas-style dishes includes scotch egg and piccalilli, thai-spiced sausages, sweetcorn and coriander fritters with apricot chutney, and breaded whitebait and tartare sauce, plus more substantial choices such as mixed game casserole, beer-battered haddock and chips, cheese, onion and potato pie with damson chutney, pork pie topped with chicken and stuffing, and puddings such as cherry bakewell tart and sticky toffee pudding with caramel sauce. *Benchmark main dish: yorkshire pudding filled with braised beef and horseradish £6.50. Two-course evening meal £15.00.*

Own brew ~ Licensee Chris Ramwell ~ Real ale ~ Open 12-6 Mon-Thurs; 12-11 Fri, Sat; 12-8 Sun ~ Bar food 12-3; 12-8.30 Fri, Sat; 12-6 Sun ~ Children welcome ~ Dogs allowed in bar ~ Wi-fi ~ Live music Sun from 5pm *Recommended by Dennis Jones, John Poulter, David Travis, Douglas Power*

STAVELEY
Eagle & Child ♦ £ ⇘

SD4797 Map 9

(01539) 821320 – www.eaglechildinn.co.uk
Kendal Road; just off A591 Windermere–Kendal; LA8 9LP

Welcoming inn with warming log fires, a good range of local beers and enjoyable food; bedrooms

After a walk along the Dales Way, head here for lunch – though you might find lots of people with the same thought, so it's best to book ahead. The L-shaped flagstoned main area of the bar has a log fire beneath an impressive mantelbeam and plenty of separate parts furnished with pews, banquettes, bow window seats and high-backed dining chairs around polished dark tables. Also, police truncheons and walking sticks, some nice photographs and interesting prints, a delft shelf of bric-a-brac, a few farm tools and another log fire. Cumberland Legendary Loweswater Gold, Yates Bitter and guests from Barngates, Hawkshead and Ulverston on handpump, several wines by the glass, 20 malt whiskies and farm cider; background music, darts and board games. An upstairs barn-themed dining room has its own bar for functions. The bedrooms are comfortable and the breakfasts very generous. There are picnic-sets under cocktail parasols in a sheltered garden by the River Kent, with more on a good-sized back terrace and a second garden behind. This is a lovely spot with more walks that fan out from the recreation ground just across the road.

As well as their Monday-Saturday lunchtime Fiver deal, the highly regarded food includes deep-fried brie with own-made cumberland sauce, thai-style salmon fishcakes with sweet chilli and basil dip, malaysian vegetable curry, chicken wrapped in smoked bacon in barbecue sauce with cheese topping, steak in ale pie, local cumberland sausages with red wine and caramelised onion gravy, beer-battered haddock and chips, and puddings such as apple crumble and hot chocolate fudge cake. *Benchmark main dish: moroccan lamb £11.95. Two-course evening meal £18.00.*

Free house ~ Licensees Richard and Denise Coleman ~ Real ale ~ Open 11-11; 12-10.30 Sun ~ Bar food 12-2.30, 6-9; 12-9 weekends ~ Restaurant ~ Children welcome ~ Dogs allowed in bar ~ Wi-fi ~ Bedrooms: /£85 *Recommended by Tina and David Woods-Taylor, Julie Braeburn, Alf Wright, Sandra King*

STONETHWAITE

NY2513 Map 9

Langstrath

(017687) 77239 – www.thelangstrath.com

Off B5289 S of Derwentwater; CA12 5XG

Nice little place in a lovely spot, popular food with a modern twist, real ales and good wines, and seats outside; bedrooms

Walking from this friendly and civilised small inn is very popular as both the Cumbrian Way and the Coast to Coast path are close by. The neat, simple bar – at its pubbiest at lunchtime – has a welcoming log fire in a big stone fireplace, rustic tables, plain chairs and cushioned wall seats, and walking cartoons and attractive Lakeland mountain photographs on its textured white walls. Jennings Cumberland Ale and Cocker Hoop, Keswick Gold and Theakstons Old Peculier on handpump, 30 malt whiskies and several wines by the glass; background music and board games. The restaurant has fine views. Outside, a big sycamore shelters several picnic-sets with views up to Eagle Crag. The comfortable, warm bedrooms are just right as a base for a walking holiday and there's a cosy residents' lounge too (in what was the original 16th-c cottage).

Traditional food with a modern twist includes lunchtime sandwiches, pheasant, duck, chicken and pistachio terrine, feta, ricotta and spinach lasagne, chicken strips in wild boar, salami, leek, white wine and parmesan sauce with wild rice, cumberland sausage on wholegrain mustard mash with rich onion gravy, a fresh fish dish of the day, slow-roast local lamb with red wine gravy, pork schnitzel with bubble and squeak and leek and pancetta cream sauce, and puddings such as crumble of the day and chocolate brownie. *Benchmark main dish: steak and kidney pie £14.75. Two-course evening meal £20.50.*

Free house ~ Licensees Guy and Jacqui Frazer-Hollins ~ Real ale ~ Open 12-10.30; closed Mon, all Dec, Jan ~ Bar food 12-4, 6-9 ~ Restaurant ~ Children welcome but must be over 10 in bedrooms ~ Dogs allowed in bar ~ Wi-fi ~ Bedrooms: £75/£110 *Recommended by John Jenkins, Tracey and Stephen Groves, Pat and Stewart Gordon, Helena and Trevor Fraser, Martin Day*

TALKIN

NY5457 Map 10

Blacksmiths Arms

(016977) 3452 – www.blacksmithstalkin.co.uk

Village signposted from B6413 S of Brampton; CA8 1LE

Neatly kept and welcoming with tasty bar food, several real ales and fine nearby walks; bedrooms

Right by the green in a pretty village and extended from an early blacksmiths, this is a friendly, family-run inn. Several neatly kept, traditionally furnished bars include a warm lounge on the right with a log fire, upholstered banquettes and wheelback chairs around dark wooden tables on patterned red carpeting, and country prints and other pictures on the walls. The restaurant is to the left and there's also a long lounge opposite the bar, with a step up to another room at the back. Black Sheep Bitter, Coniston Bluebird and Yates Bitter and Golden Bitter on handpump, 20 wines by the glass, 30 malt whiskies and local gin and vodka; background music, darts and board games. There are a couple of picnic-sets outside the front door with more in the back garden. The cottagey bedrooms are comfortable, and there are good walks in the attractive surrounding countryside.

Traditional, honest food includes sandwiches, deep-fried brie with cranberry sauce, prawn cocktail, mushroom stroganoff, chicken curry, liver and bacon casserole, barnsley lamb chop with onion rings and potatoes, specials such as smoked haddock pasta and rump steak on haggis with a creamy peppercorn sauce, and puddings. *Benchmark main dish: steak and kidney pie £8.95. Two-course evening meal £14.00.*

Free house ~ Licensees Donald and Anne Jackson ~ Real ale ~ Open 12-midnight ~ Bar food 12-2, 6-9; 12-9 Sun ~ Restaurant ~ Children welcome ~ Wi-fi ~ Bedrooms: £60/£80
Recommended by Carol and Barry Craddock, Alf Wright, Comus and Sarah Elliott

TIRRIL   NY5026   Map 10

Queens Head

(01768) 863219 – www.queensheadinn.co.uk
B5320, not far from M6 junction 40; CA10 2JF

Dating from 1719 with two bars, real ales, speciality pies and seats outside; bedrooms

William Wordsworth once owned this early 18th-c pub and the oldest parts of the main bar have original flagstones and floorboards, low beams and black panelling, and there are nice little tables and chairs on either side of the inglenook fireplace (always lit in winter). Another bar to the right of the entrance has pews and chairs around sizeable tables on a wooden floor, and candles in the fireplace, while the back locals' bar has heavy beams and a pool table; there are three dining rooms too. Robinsons Hartleys Cumbria Way, Dizzy Blonde and Unicorn on handpump and several wines by the glass. Outside there are picnic-sets at the front, and modern chairs and tables under cover on the back terrace. The hard-working licensees also run the Pie Mill (you can eat their pies here) and the village shop. The pub is very close to several interesting places including Dalemain at Dacre, and Ullswater is nearby.

 Food includes up to eight pies, plus sandwiches, creamy garlic mushrooms, vegetable lasagne, honey-roast ham and egg, a curry of the day, slow-roast lamb shoulder in redcurrant gravy, steaks with trimmings and chips, and puddings such as a fruit pie of the day and sticky toffee pudding. *Benchmark main dish: pie of the day £10.50. Two-course evening meal £16.00.*

Robinsons ~ Tenants Margaret and Jim Hodge ~ Real ale ~ Open 11-11; 11-11.30 Sat; 12-10 Sun ~ Bar food 12-2.30, 5-8.30 ~ Restaurant ~ Children welcome ~ Dogs allowed in bar and bedrooms ~ Wi-fi ~ Bedrooms: £50/£80 *Recommended by Graham and Elizabeth Hargreaves, Tina and David Woods-Taylor, Martin Day, Alastair and Sheree Hepburn, Ivor Smith*

ULVERSTON   SD3177   Map 7

Bay Horse ♀ ⇐

(01229) 583972 – www.thebayhorsehotel.co.uk
Canal Foot signposted off A590, then wend your way past the huge Glaxo factory; LA12 9EL

Civilised waterside hotel with lunchtime bar food, three real ales and a fine choice of wines; smart bedrooms

Our readers enjoy staying here with many coming back regularly, and the bedrooms have french windows that open out on to a panoramic view of the Leven estuary (the bird life is wonderful); breakfasts are excellent. The bar is at its most informal at lunchtime and has a relaxed atmosphere – despite its smart furnishings: cushioned teak dining chairs, paisley-patterned built-in wall banquettes, glossy hardwood traditional tables, a huge stone horse's head, black beams and props, and lots of horsebrasses. Magazines are dotted about, there's an open fire in the handsomely marbled, grey slate fireplace and decently reproduced background music; board games. Jennings Cocker Hoop and Cumberland on handpump, 16 wines by the glass (including champagne and prosecco) from a carefully chosen, interesting list and several malt whiskies. The conservatory restaurant has lovely views over Morecambe Bay and there are seats outside on the terrace.

Enjoyable food includes sandwiches, deep-fried chilli prawns with sweet and sour sauce, chicken liver pâté with cranberry and ginger purée, steak and kidney pie, bobotie (spicy minced lamb with tomato, apricot and savoury egg custard), gammon with free-range egg and pineapple, crab and salmon fishcakes with white wine and herb sauce, and puddings such as lemon and passion-fruit cheesecake and coffee cream profiteroles with hot chocolate sauce. In the evening, the emphasis is on the restaurant with one sitting (at 7.30pm) and light snacks only available in the bar. *Benchmark main dish: aberdeen angus steak £23.00. Two-course evening meal £25.00.*

Free house ~ Licensee Robert Lyons ~ Real ale ~ Open 11-11; 12-10.30 Sun ~ Bar food 12-2, 7.30-8.30 ~ Restaurant ~ Children welcome at lunchtime and must be over 9 in bedrooms ~ Dogs allowed in bar and bedrooms ~ Wi-fi ~ Bedrooms: £95/£120 *Recommended by W K Wood, John Poulter, John and Sylvia Harrop, Simon Cleasby*

WINSTER
Brown Horse 🍺 🛏

SD4193 Map 9

(015394) 43443 – www.thebrownhorseinn.co.uk
A5074 S of Windermere; LA23 3NR

Traditional coaching inn, recently refurbished, with character bar and dining room, own-brewed ales, good food and seats outside; bedrooms

As well as an extraordinary list of 107 gins from all over the world, this refurbished 19th-c coaching inn brews its own Winster Valley ales: Best Bitter, Cartmel Chaser, Dark Horse, Hurdler, Lakes Blonde, Lakes Lager and Old School. Also, several wines by the glass and quite a few malt whiskies. The chatty beamed and flagstoned bar has church pews, a lovely tall settle and mate's chairs around a mix of tables, while the candlelit dining room has a medley of painted and antique chairs and tables, old skis, carpet beaters, hunting horns and antlers. The gents' is upstairs. There are seats outside among flowering tubs, with more on a raised terrace. The bedrooms are thoughtfully furnished and they also have three self-catering properties. This is a pretty valley with good walks.

Well thought-of food includes lunchtime sandwiches, prawn and crayfish cocktail, gravadlax with horseradish cream, platters, steak burger with toppings and fries, tagliatelle with tomatoes, spinach and mushrooms, corn-fed chicken with truffled potato purée, leeks, wild mushrooms and lancashire haggis, rillette of ham hock with caramelised pineapple, crispy egg and chips, a daily fresh fish dish, and puddings such as lemon and ricotta cheesecake with lemon curd ice-cream and chocolate fondant with bitter chocolate sorbet and salted caramel. *Benchmark main dish: steak in ale pie £12.95. Two-course evening meal £19.00.*

Free house ~ Licensees Karen and Steve Edmondson ~ Real ale ~ Open 11-11 ~ Bar food 12-2, 6-9 ~ Restaurant ~ Children welcome ~ Dogs allowed in bar ~ Wi-fi ~ Bedrooms: /£110 *Recommended by R T and J C Moggridge, Tim and Sarah Smythe-Brown, William Slade*

We checked prices with the pubs as we went to press in summer 2016. They should hold until around spring 2017.

WITHERSLACK
SD4482 Map 10

Derby Arms 🏅 🍺 🛏️

(015395) 52207 – www.ainscoughs.co.uk

Just off A590; LA11 6RH

Bustling country inn with half a dozen ales, good wines, particularly good food and a genuine welcome; reasonably priced bedrooms

Friendly, courteous staff here serve a fine range of drinks: up to six real ales on handpump such as Bowness Bay Swan Blonde, Chadwicks Kirkland Blonde Ale, Cumbrian Legendary Esthwaite, Fell Nectar, Thwaites Wainwright and a guest, plus 11 wines by the glass and 22 malt whiskies. The main bar has lots of sporting prints on pale grey walls, elegant old dining chairs and tables on large rugs over floorboards, some hops above the bar counter, an open fire and an easy-going atmosphere. A larger room to the right is similarly furnished (with the addition of some cushioned pews) and has local castle prints, a cumbrian scene above another open fire, and alcoves in the back wall full of nice bristol blue glass, ornate plates and staffordshire dogs and figurines. Large windows lighten up the rooms, helped at night by candles in brass candlesticks; background music, TV and pool. There are two additional rooms – one with dark red walls, a red velvet sofa, more sporting prints and a handsome mirror over the fireplace. Bedrooms are comfortable and fairly priced and there's plenty to do nearby – Sizergh Castle (National Trust), Levens Hall and good walks around the Southern Lakes and Dales. This is part of the Ainscoughs group.

 Highly rated food includes organic beef from their own farm plus lunchtime sandwiches (till 5pm at weekends), Morecambe Bay potted shrimps, goats cheese bonbons with beetroot purée and raspberry coulis, leek and sweet potato crumble with ginger and chestnuts in a creamy sauce, burger with toppings, pickles and chips, steak in ale pie, corn-fed chicken with wild mushroom and tarragon sauce, and puddings such as apple crumble and lemon posset; they also offer a two-course lunch menu. *Benchmark main dish: beer-battered haddock and chips £11.95. Two-course evening meal £16.95.*

Free house ~ Licensee Barry Thomas ~ Real ale ~ Open 12-11 (midnight Sat) ~ Bar food 12-2, 6-9.30; all day weekends ~ Children welcome ~ Dogs allowed in bar and bedrooms ~ Wi-fi ~ Live music Fri, Sat ~ Bedrooms: /$80 *Recommended by Belinda Stamp, Toby Jones, John and Sylvia Harrop, Hugh Roberts*

YANWATH
NY5128 Map 9

Gate Inn 🏅 ♟

(01768) 862386 – www.yanwathgate.co.uk

2.25 miles from M6 junction 40; A66 towards Brough, then right on A6, right on B5320, then follow village signpost; CA10 2LF

Emphasis on imaginative food but with local beers and thoughtfully chosen wines, a pubby atmosphere and a warm welcome from helpful staff

Plenty of locals do drop in for a drink and a chat, but most customers are here for the excellent food. It remains a civilised and immaculately kept 17th-c pub and the cosy bar of charming antiquity has country pine and dark wood furniture, lots of brasses on beams, church candles on all tables and a woodburning stove in an attractive stone inglenook. Barngates Pale, Hesket Newmarket Red Pike and Yates Bitter on handpump, a dozen or so good wines by the glass, 12 malt whiskies and Weston's Old Rosie cider; staff are courteous and helpful. The restaurant has been refurbished and has oak floors, panelled oak walls and heavy beams; background music. There are new seats on the terrace and in the garden.

🎖 From a seasonally aware menu, the particularly good, frequently changing food includes open sandwiches, partridge and cranberry terrine with chutney, swordfish ceviche with lemongrass, ginger and coriander, rack of lamb with mustard mash, root vegetables and port gravy, moroccan vegetarian tagine with spicy lemon harissa and coriander couscous, wild bass fillet with tiger prawn and chorizo risotto, and puddings such as orange and vanilla-infused pannacotta with candied nuts and sticky date pudding with butterscotch sauce; they also offer a two- and three-course set menu. *Benchmark main dish: venison haunch with celeriac purée, dauphinoise potatoes and bramble sauce £18.00. Two-course evening meal £23.00.*

Free house ~ Licensees Simon Prior and Caryl Varty ~ Real ale ~ Open 12-midnight ~ Bar food 12-2.30, 6-9 ~ Restaurant ~ Well behaved children welcome ~ Dogs allowed in bar ~ Wi-fi *Recommended by Dave Braisted, Tina and David Woods-Taylor*

Also Worth a Visit in Cumbria

Besides the fully inspected pubs, you might like to try these pubs that have been recommended to us and described by readers. Do tell us what you think of them: feedback@goodguides.com

ALLITHWAITE   SD3876
Pheasant (015395) 32239
B5277; LA11 7RQ Welcoming family-run pub on village outskirts, enjoyable freshly cooked traditional food including good Sun roasts, reasonable prices and deals, friendly helpful service, Thwaites Original and four other local beers, traditional bar with log fire, two dining areas off; Thurs quiz; children welcome (not in conservatory), dogs in bar, outside tables on deck with Humphrey Head and Morecambe Bay views, open (and food) all day. *(GSB, Mike Stokes, Peter Andrews)*

ALSTON   NY7146
Angel (01434) 381363
Front Street; CA9 3HU Simple 17th-c inn on steep cobbled street of this charming small Pennine market town, mainly local ales and generously served food including daily specials, reasonable prices, timbers, traditional furnishings and open fires, friendly local atmosphere; children and dogs welcome, tables in sheltered back garden, four bedrooms. *(Douglas Power)*

AMBLESIDE   NY4008
★ Kirkstone Pass Inn (015394) 33888
A592 N of Troutbeck; LA22 9LQ Historic inn (Lakeland's highest pub) set in wonderful rugged scenery; flagstones, stripped stone and dark beams, lots of old photographs and bric-a-brac, open fires, good value pubby food and changing cumbrian ales, hot drinks, daily papers; soft background music; well behaved children and dogs welcome, tables outside with incredible views to Windermere, bedrooms, bunkhouse and camping field, open all day

in summer (till 6pm Sun), phone for winter hours. *(Daniel King)*

APPLEBY   NY6819
★ Royal Oak (01768) 351463
B6542/Bongate; CA16 6UN Attractive old beamed and timbered coaching inn on edge of town, popular generously served food including early-bird and OAP deals, Black Sheep and one or two local guests, friendly efficient young staff, log fire in panelled bar, lounge with easy chairs and carved settle, traditional snug, restaurant; background music, TV; children and dogs welcome (menus for both), terrace tables, 11 bedrooms and self-catering cottage, good breakfast, open all day from 8am. *(Charles Todd)*

ARMATHWAITE   NY5045
★ Fox & Pheasant (016974) 72162
E of village, over bridge; CA4 9PY Well run friendly old coaching inn with lovely River Eden views, well kept Robinsons ales and decent wines by the glass, good freshly made food including daily specials, log fire in main beamed and flagstoned bar, converted stables dining area with exposed stone walls and woodburner, also a small more formal Victorian dining room; children and dogs welcome, picnic-sets outside, five comfortable bedrooms. *(Alf Wright)*

ASKHAM   NY5123
Punch Bowl (01931) 712443
4.5 miles from M6 junction 40; CA10 2PF Attractive 18th-c village pub on edge of green opposite Askham Hall; spacious beamed main bar, locals' bar, snug lounge and dining room, open fires, well kept Hawkshead and guests, decent choice

of enjoyable food (all day weekends) from pub standards up, friendly staff; children and dogs welcome, picnic-sets out in front and on small raised terrace, six bedrooms, open all day. *(Dave Sutton)*

BAMPTON GRANGE · NY5218
★ Crown & Mitre (01931) 713225
Opposite church; CA10 2QR
Old inn set in attractive country hamlet (*Withnail and I* was filmed around here); opened-up bar with comfortable modern décor and nice log fire, separate dining room, popular good quality home-made food from pub favourites up, three well kept ales (two in winter) such as Eden, Hesket Newmarket and Keswick, friendly staff; children and dogs welcome, good walks from the door, eight bedrooms, open all day in summer, from 5pm (1pm weekends) winter. *(Tina and David Woods-Taylor, Simon Cleasby)*

BARBON · SD6282
Barbon Inn (015242) 76233
Off A683 Kirkby Lonsdale–Sedbergh; LA6 2LJ Charmingly set 17th-c fell-foot village inn, comfortable old world interior, log fires (one in an old range), some sofas, armchairs and antique carved settles, a couple of local ales and nice selection of wines, good food from bar meals up, restaurant, friendly staff and regulars; children and dogs welcome, wheelchair access (ladies' loo is upstairs), sheltered pretty garden, good walks, ten bedrooms. *(John Poulter)*

BASSENTHWAITE · NY2332
Sun (017687) 76439
Off A591 N of Keswick; CA12 4QP
White-rendered 17th-c village pub; rambling bar with low black beams, blazing winter fires in two stone fireplaces, built-in wall seats and heavy wooden tables, two Jennings ales and a guest, generous food served by friendly staff, cosy dining room; children and dogs welcome, terrace with views of the fells and Skiddaw, open all day weekends, from 4pm other days. *(Daniel King)*

BEETHAM · SD4979
Wheatsheaf (015395) 62123
Village (and inn) signed off A6 S of Milnthorpe; LA7 7AL Striking old building with fine black and white timbered cornerpiece, handily positioned on the old road to the Lake District; traditionally furnished rooms, opened-up lounge with exposed beams and joists, main bar (behind on the right) with open fire, two upstairs dining rooms, residents' lounge, ales such as local Cross Bay and Thwaites Wainwright, several wines by the glass and quite a few malt whiskies, decent choice of food including deals, friendly service; children welcome, dogs in bar, plenty of surrounding walks, pretty 14th-c church opposite, five bedrooms, open all day. *(S G N Bennett)*

BOOT · NY1701
Boot Inn (019467) 23711
Aka Burnmoor; signed just off the Wrynose/Hardknott Pass road; CA19 1TG Beamed country inn with Robinsons ales, decent wines and enjoyable home-made food, friendly helpful staff, blazing log fire in bar, conservatory; children and dogs welcome, garden with play area, lovely surroundings and walks, nine bedrooms, open (and food) all day. *(Sandra and Nigel Brown)*

BOOT · NY1701
★ Brook House (019467) 23288
From Ambleside, W of Hardknott Pass; CA19 1TG Good views and walks from this friendly family-run inn, wide choice of enjoyable often interesting food from sandwiches up, half a dozen well kept ales such as Barngates, Cumbrian Legendary, Hawkshead and Yates, Weston's cider/perry, decent wines and over 180 whiskies, relaxed comfortable raftered bar with woodburner and stuffed animals, smaller plush snug, peaceful separate restaurant; children and dogs welcome, tables on flagstoned terrace, eight reasonably priced bedrooms, good breakfast (for nearby campers too), mountain weather reports, excellent drying room, handy for Eskdale miniature railway terminus, open all day. *(Alf Wright)*

BOOT · NY1901
Woolpack (019467) 23230
Bleabeck, midway between Boot and Hardknott Pass; CA19 1TH Last pub before the Hardknott Pass; warm welcoming atmosphere with main walkers' bar and more contemporary café-bar, also an evening restaurant (Fri, Sat), good home-made food including wood-fired pizzas, pies, steaks and daily specials, up to eight well kept ales, real cider and vast range of vodkas and gins, Apr sausage and cider festival, June beer festival; pool room, some live music; children and dogs welcome, mountain-view garden with play area, eight bedrooms, open (and food) all day. *(Sandra King)*

BOUTH · SD3285
★ White Hart (01229) 861229
Village signed off A590 near Haverthwaite; LA12 8JB Cheerful bustling old inn with Lakeland feel, six changing ales and 25 malt whiskies, popular generously served food using locally sourced ingredients (all day Sun) including children's menu, good friendly service, sloping ceilings and floors, old local photographs, farm tools and stuffed animals, collection of long-stemmed clay pipes, two woodburners; background music; no dogs at mealtimes, seats outside and fine surrounding walks, playground opposite, five comfortable bedrooms, open all day. *(Ruth May, Lee and Liz Potter)*

BOWNESS-ON-WINDERMERE SD4096

Royal Oak (015394) 43970

Brantfell Road; LA23 3EG Handy for steamer pier, interconnecting bar, dining room and big games room, old photographs and bric-a-brac, open fire, well kept ales such as Coniston, Jennings, Timothy Taylors and Tetleys, generous reasonably priced pub food from baguettes to specials, friendly efficient service; pool, darts, juke box and TV; children and dogs welcome, tables out in front, eight bedrooms, open (and food) all day. *(Douglas Power)*

BRAITHWAITE NY2324

Middle Ruddings (017687) 78436

Middle Ruddings, road running parallel with A66; CA12 5RY Welcoming family-run country inn, good food in bar or carpeted dining conservatory (no mobile phones) with fine Skiddaw views, friendly attentive service, three well kept changing local ales, good choice of bottled beers and ciders, afternoon teas; children and dogs welcome, garden with terrace picnic-sets, 14 bedrooms, good breakfast, open all day, no food weekday lunchtimes. *(David Heath, Edward Mirzoeff)*

BRAITHWAITE NY2323

Royal Oak (017687) 78533

B5292 at top of village; CA12 5SY Busy village pub with warm welcoming atmosphere, four well kept Jennings ales and hearty helpings of well priced traditional food (smaller servings available), prompt helpful service, beamed bar and restaurant; background music, TV, board games; children welcome, no dogs at mealtimes, ten bedrooms, open all day. *(Martin Day, Tina and David Woods-Taylor)*

BROUGHTON-IN-FURNESS SD2187

Manor Arms (01229) 716286

The Square; LA20 6HY End-of-terrace drinkers' pub on quiet sloping square, up to eight well priced changing ales and good choice of ciders, flagstones and nice bow-window seat in front bar, coal fire in big stone fireplace, old photographs and chiming clocks, limited food such as toasties; pool, free wi-fi; children and dogs allowed, bedrooms, open all day. *(Dr Peter Crawshaw)*

BUTTERMERE NY1716

Bridge Hotel (017687) 70252

Just off B5289 SW of Keswick; CA13 9UZ Welcoming and popular with walkers, hotel-like in feel but with two traditional comfortable beamed bars (dogs allowed in one), four well kept cumbrian ales and good food, more upmarket menu in evening dining room; free wi-fi; children welcome, fell views from flagstoned terrace, 21 bedrooms and six self-catering apartments, open (and food) all day. *(I D Barnett)*

CARLISLE NY4056

Kings Head (01228) 533797

Fisher Street (pedestrianised); CA3 8RF Refurbished 17th-c split-level pub, lots of beams (some painted), wood and stone floors, friendly bustling atmosphere, well kept Yates Bitter and guests, low-priced pubby lunchtime food from sandwiches and baked potatoes up, cheerful quick service, upstairs dining room; background and summer live music (in courtyard), TV; no children or dogs, historical plaque outside explaining why Carlisle is not in the Domesday Book, open all day. *(Dave Braisted, Pat and Graham Williamson, Comus and Sarah Elliott)*

CARTMEL SD3778

Cavendish Arms (015395) 36240

Cavendish Street, off the Square; LA11 6QA Former coaching inn with simply furnished open-plan beamed bar, roaring log fire (even on cooler summer evenings), three or four ales featuring a house beer from Cumberland, several wines by the glass and good range of gins, decent coffee, friendly attentive staff, ample helpings of enjoyable food from shortish menu including lunchtime sandwiches, restaurant; children welcome, dogs in bar, tables out in front and behind by stream, nice village with notable priory church, good walks, ten bedrooms – three more above their shop in the square, open (and food) all day. *(Sandra and Nigel Brown)*

CARTMEL SD3778

★ Kings Arms (015395) 33246

The Square; LA11 6QB Bustling 18th-c pub close to the priory; cosy beamed rooms with flagstones and bare boards, log fires, nice mix of furniture including some comfortable sofas, Hawkshead ales and a guest, popular food from sandwiches to daily specials, friendly staff; live weekend bands (pub open till 1am then), free wi-fi; children and dogs welcome, seats outside facing the lovely square, open (and food) all day. *(Gordon and Margaret Ormondroyd, Simon Cleasby)*

CARTMEL SD3778

★ Royal Oak (015395) 36259

The Square; LA11 6QB Low-beamed flagstoned inn under same management as the Kings Arms (above) next door; long rustic tables, settles, leather easy chairs and big log fire, cosy nooks, good value all-day food including traditional choices, home-made

---

We mention bottled beers and spirits only if there is something unusual about them – imported belgian real ales, say, or dozens of malt whiskies; so do please let us know about them in your reports.

pizzas, pasta and grills, well kept local ales such as Coniston, Cumbrian Legendary, Watermill and Unsworth's Yard, good choice of wines, welcoming helpful staff; background and weekend live music, two sports TVs, free wi-fi; children and dogs welcome, some seats out in square, nice big riverside garden behind with heated terrace, four refurbished bedrooms, self-catering cottage, open all day (till 1am Fri, Sat). *(Simon Cleasby, Ruth May)*

CASTERTON   SD6379

★ **Pheasant** (015242) 71230

A683; LA6 2RX Welcoming 18th-c family-run inn with neatly refurbished beamed rooms, good interesting food alongside traditional favourites, three well kept changing local ales and several malt whiskies, friendly helpful staff, arched and panelled restaurant; background music, free wi-fi; children and dogs welcome, a few roadside seats, more in pleasant garden with Vale of Lune views, near church with notable Pre-Raphaelite stained glass and paintings, ten bedrooms, closed Mon lunchtime, otherwise open all day. *(Denis and Margaret Kilner)*

CASTLE CARROCK   NY5455
Duke of Cumberland

(01228) 670341 *Geltsdale Road; CA8 9LU* Popular village-green pub under friendly family ownership, upholstered wall benches and mix of pubby furniture on slate floor, coal fire, dining area with old farmhouse tables and chairs, a couple of well kept local ales, enjoyable nicely presented pub food at reasonable prices; children welcome, no dogs inside, open all day. *(Daniel King)*

CHAPEL STILE   NY3205
Wainwrights (015394) 38088

B5343; LA22 9JH Popular white-rendered former farmhouse, half a dozen ales including Jennings and plenty of wines by the glass, enjoyable well priced pubby food from good sandwiches up, friendly helpful service, roomy new-feeling bar welcoming walkers and dogs, slate floor and good log fire, other spreading carpeted areas with beams, some half-panelling, cushioned settles and mix of dining chairs around wooden tables, old kitchen range; background music, TV and games machines, Weds quiz; children welcome, terrace picnic-sets, fine views, open (and food) all day. *(Charles Todd)*

COCKERMOUTH   NY1230
Castle Bar (01900) 829904

Market Place; CA13 9NQ Busy 16th-c pub on three floors, beams, timbers and other original features mixing with modern furnishings, five well kept local beers such as Cumbrian Legendary and Jennings (cheaper 4-7pm Mon-Fri, all day Sun), Weston's cider, enjoyable home-made food including good value Sun roasts in upstairs dining room

or in any of the three ground-floor areas, efficient service from friendly young staff; sports TV; children and dogs (downstairs) welcome, seats on back tiered terrace, open all day. *(Mike and Eleanor Anderson)*

COCKERMOUTH   NY1231
Trout (01900) 823591

Crown Street; CA13 0EJ Busy comfortably modernised old hotel with well liked food in bar, restaurant or bistro, local ales including Jennings and decent wines by the glass; gardens down to river, 49 bedrooms, open all day; reopening after we went to press following flood damage. *(Robert Wivell, John Jenkins)*

CONISTON   SD3097
Black Bull (015394) 41335/41668

Yewdale Road (A593); LA21 8DU Bustling 17th-c beamed inn brewing its own good Coniston beers; back area (liked by walkers and their dogs) with slate floor, more comfortable carpeted front part with log fire and Donald Campbell memorabilia, enjoyable food including daily specials, friendly helpful staff, lounge with Old Man of Coniston big toe (large piece of stone in the wall), restaurant; they may ask for a credit card if you run a tab; children welcome, plenty of seats in former coachyard, 15 bedrooms, open (and food) all day from 8am, parking not easy at peak times. *(Douglas Power)*

CROOK   SD4695
Sun (01539) 821351

B5284 Kendal–Bowness; LA8 8LA End-of-terrace roadside country pub refurbished under present welcoming management; low-beamed bar with dining areas off, stone, wood and carpeted floors, log fires, a house beer from Theakstons and a couple of guests, enjoyable traditional food from sandwiches up including early-bird and OAP deals Mon-Fri; children (games for them) and dogs (in certain areas) welcome, seats out at front by road, open all day Fri-Sun. *(Sandra King)*

DENT   SD7086
George & Dragon (015396) 25256

Main Street; LA10 5QL Two-bar corner pub in cobbled street, the Dent Brewery tap, with their full range kept well plus real cider and perry, old panelling, partitioned tables and open fires, enjoyable food from snacks up, friendly engaging young staff, steps down to restaurant, games room with pool and juke box; sports TV, free wi-fi; children, walkers and dogs welcome, ten bedrooms, lovely village, open all day. *(Alf Wright)*

DENT   SD7086
Sun (015396) 25208

Main Street; LA10 5QL Old-fashioned local with five well kept changing ales including Kirkby Lonsdale, generous helpings of tasty pub food, traditional beamed and flagstoned bar with coal fire; live acoustic music, darts and dominoes; children, dogs and muddy boots welcome, four bedrooms, open all day (food all day weekends). *(Chilliski)*

DUFTON NY6825
Stag (017683) 51608
Village signed from A66 at Appleby; CA16 6DB Traditional little 18th-c pub by pretty village's green; friendly licensees and regulars, good reasonably priced home-made food using local ingredients, interesting choice of well kept regularly changing beers, two log fires, one in splendid early Victorian kitchen range in main bar, room off to the left, dining room; fortnightly quiz Thurs, darts; children, walkers and dogs welcome, tables out at front and in back garden with lovely hill views, handy for Pennine Way, self-catering cottage, open all day weekends, closed Mon and Tues lunchtimes. *(Alan and Eileen Ormrod)*

ENNERDALE BRIDGE NY0716
Fox & Hounds (01946) 861373
High Street; CA23 3AR Popular community-owned village pub, clean beamed interior with woodburners, up to five well kept cumbrian ales including local Ennerdale, tasty reasonably priced home-made food, friendly staff; children and dogs welcome, picnic-sets in streamside garden, three spacious bedrooms, handy for walkers on Coast to Coast path, open all day (winter hours may vary). *(Dave Sutton)*

ENNERDALE BRIDGE NY0615
Shepherds Arms (01946) 861249
Off A5086 E of Egremont; CA23 3AR Friendly well placed walkers' inn by car-free dale, bar with log fire and woodburner, up to five local beers and good generously served home-made food, can provide packed lunches, panelled dining room and conservatory; free wi-fi; children welcome, seats outside by beck, eight bedrooms, good breakfast. *(Michael Byrne)*

ESKDALE GREEN NY1200
Bower House (01946) 723244
0.5 miles W of Eskdale Green; CA19 1TD Comfortably modernised 17th-c stone-built inn extended around beamed core, four regional ales including one named for the pub, usual food in bar and biggish dining room, log fires, friendly atmosphere; free wi-fi; children and dogs welcome, sheltered garden with play area, charming spot by cricket field with great view of Muncaster Fell, good walks, bedrooms (some in converted barn), open all day, food all day weekends. *(Sandra King)*

FAR SAWREY SD3795
Cuckoo Brow (015394) 43425
B5285 N of village; LA22 0LQ Renovated 300-year-old coaching inn, opened-up bar with wood floors and central woodburner, steps down to former stables with tables in stalls, harnesses on rough white walls, even water troughs and mangers, well kept Coniston, Cumbrian Legendary and a couple of local guests, good hearty food served by friendly helpful staff; background music; children, walkers and dogs welcome, seats on nice front lawn, lovely setting, 14 bedrooms, open (and food) all day. *(John and Louise Gittins)*

FAUGH NY5054
String of Horses (01228) 670297
S of village, on left as you go downhill; CA8 9EG Welcoming 17th-c coaching inn with cosy communicating beamed rooms, log fires, oak panelling and some interesting carved furniture, tasty traditional food alongside latin american/mexican dishes, well kept local beers and nice house wines, restaurant; background music, sports TV, free wi-fi; children welcome, no dogs, a few picnic-sets out in front, 11 comfortable bedrooms, good breakfast, closed lunchtimes and all day Mon. *(Sandra and Nigel Brown)*

FOXFIELD SD2085
★ Prince of Wales (01229) 716238
Opposite station; LA20 6BX Cheery bare-boards pub with half a dozen good changing ales including bargain beers brewed here and at their associated Tigertops Brewery, bottled imports and real cider too, huge helpings of enjoyable home-made food (lots of unusual pasties), good friendly service and character landlord, hot coal fire, pub games including bar billiards, daily papers and beer-related reading matter; some live music; children and dogs welcome, four reasonably priced bedrooms, open all day Fri-Sun, from 2.45pm Wed, Thurs, closed Mon, Tues. *(Edward and William Johnston)*

GOSFORTH NY0703
Gosforth Hall (019467) 25322
Off A595 and unclassified road to Wasdale; CA20 1AZ Friendly well run Jacobean inn with interesting history, beamed and carpeted bar (popular with locals), fine plaster coat of arms above woodburner, lounge/reception area with huge fireplace, ales such as Hawkshead, Keswick and Yates, enjoyable home-made food including good range of pies, restaurant; TV; nice big side garden, 22 bedrooms (some in new extension), open all day. *(Dave Sutton)*

GRASMERE NY3406
Travellers Rest (015394) 35604
A591 just N; LA22 9RR Welcoming 16th-c roadside coaching inn with attractive creeper-clad exterior, unmodernised linked rooms, settles, padded benches and other pubby furniture on flagstone or wood floors, local pictures and open fires, well kept Jennings ales and enjoyable reasonably priced food, good friendly service;

background music; children and dogs welcome, seats outside with fell views, nine bedrooms, open (and food) all day. *(Gordon and Margaret Ormondroyd)*

GREAT URSWICK   SD2674
General Burgoyne (01229) 586394
Church Road; LA12 0SZ Flagstoned early 17th-c village pub under friendly new management, four cosy rambling rooms with beams and log fires (look for the skull in a cupboard), three Robinsons ales and a guest, big helpings of traditional home-made food including a few daily specials, afternoon teas, side dining conservatory; occasional live music, fortnightly quiz (Sat) and poker (Tues); children and dogs welcome, picnic-sets out at front, open all day weekends, closed Mon. *(Charles Todd)*

GREYSTOKE   NY4430
Boot & Shoe (01768) 483343
By village green, off B5288; CA11 0TP Cosy two-bar 17th-c inn by green in pretty 'Tarzan' village; low ceilings, exposed brickwork and dark wood, good generously served traditional food including blackboard specials, well kept Black Sheep and local microbrews, bustling friendly atmosphere; live music; children and dogs welcome, seats at front and in back garden, on national cycle route, bedrooms, open all day. *(Ruth May)*

HARTSOP   NY4011
Brotherswater Inn (01768) 482239
A592; CA11 0NZ Walkers' and campers' pub in magnificent setting at the bottom of Kirkstone Pass, ales such as Jennings and Thwaites, good choice of malt whiskies and generous helpings of enjoyable reasonably priced food, friendly staff; free wi-fi; dogs welcome, beautiful fells views from picture windows and terrace tables, six bedrooms, bunkhouse and campsite, open all day (from 8am for breakfast). *(Tracey and Stephen Groves)*

HAWKSHEAD   SD3598
Kings Arms (015394) 36372
The Square; LA22 0NZ Old inn with low ceilings, traditional pubby furnishings and log fire, well stocked bar serving local ales such as Cumbrian Legendary and Hawkshead, good variety of enjoyable food from lunchtime sandwiches to daily specials, quick service, side dining area; background music, free wi-fi; children and dogs welcome, terrace overlooking central square of this lovely Elizabethan village, bedrooms, self-catering cottages nearby, free fishing permits for residents, open all day till midnight. *(WAH)*

HAWKSHEAD   SD3598
Queens Head (015394) 36271
Main Street; LA22 0NS Timbered pub in charming village, low-ceilinged bar with heavy bowed black beams, red plush wall seats and stools around hefty traditional tables, decorative plates on panelled walls, open fire, snug little room off, several eating areas, Robinsons ales and a guest, good wine and whisky choice, enjoyable bar food and more elaborate evening meals, friendly helpful staff; unobtrusive background music, TV, darts; children and dogs welcome, seats outside and pretty window boxes, 13 bedrooms, open all day. *(Jeff, Peter Meister)*

HAWKSHEAD   SD3598
Red Lion (015394) 36213
Main Street; LA22 0NS Friendly old inn with good selection of well kept local ales including Hawkshead, enjoyable traditional home-made food, original panelling and good log fire; dogs very welcome (menu for them), eight bedrooms (some sloping floors), open all day. *(Daniel King)*

HESKET NEWMARKET   NY3438
Old Crown (016974) 78288
Village signed off B5299 in Caldbeck; CA7 8JG Straightforward cooperative-owned local in attractive village, small bar with bric-a-brac, mountaineering kit and pictures, woodburner, own good Hesket Newmarket beers (can book brewery tours), generous helpings of freshly made pub food (not Mon), reasonable prices and friendly service, dining room and garden room; folk night first Sun of month, juke box, pool and board games; children and dogs welcome, lovely walking country away from Lake District crowds (near Cumbria Way), open all day Fri-Sun, closed lunchtimes other days; changing hands after we went to press, so could be changes. *(Alastair and Sheree Hepburn)*

KENDAL   SD5192
Riflemans Arms (01539) 241470
Greenside; LA9 4LD Old-fashioned local in village-green setting on edge of town, friendly regulars and staff, Greene King Abbot and guests, no food; Thurs folk night, Sun quiz, pool and darts; children and dogs welcome, closed weekday lunchtimes, open all day weekends. *(Hugh Roberts)*

KESWICK   NY2623
Dog & Gun (017687) 73463
Lake Road; off top end of Market Square; CA12 5BT Smartly refurbished beamed town pub, button-back leather banquettes, stools and small round tables on light wood flooring, collection of striking mountain photographs, reasonably priced hearty food including signature goulash, friendly helpful staff, half a dozen or so well kept ales (several from Keswick) including house Woof & Bang, log fire; children (till 9.30pm) and dogs welcome, open (and food) all day, can get very busy in season. *(Tracey and Stephen Groves, Margaret and Peter Staples)*

KESWICK
NY2623
George (017687) 72076
St Johns Street; CA12 5AZ Handsome
17th-c coaching inn with open-plan main
bar and attractive traditional dark-panelled
side room, old-fashioned settles and
modern banquettes under black beams,
log fires, four Jennings ales and a couple
of guests kept well, plenty of wines by the
glass, generous home-made food including
signature cow pie, friendly helpful service,
restaurant; background music, daily
papers, Tues quiz; children welcome in
eating areas, dogs in bar, 13 bedrooms,
open all day. *(Daniel King)*

KESWICK
NY2421
Swinside Inn (017687) 78253
Newlands Valley, just SW; CA12 5UE
Friendly pub in peaceful valley setting;
carpeted low-beamed bar with upholstered
settles and chairs around substantial tables,
open fire, well kept Caledonian, Theakstons
and a couple of guests, decent choice of
reasonably priced pubby food, stripped-floor
area beyond with woodburner, pool in back
games part; background and occasional
live music, TV, free wi-fi; children and dogs
welcome, tables in garden and on upper and
lower terraces giving fine views across to the
high crags and fells around Rosedale Pike, six
bedrooms, big breakfast, open all day. *(CIJH,
Tina and David Woods-Taylor)*

KIRKBY LONSDALE
SD6178
Orange Tree (01524) 271716
Fairbank B6254; LA6 2BD Family-run inn
acting as tap for Kirkby Lonsdale brewery,
well kept guest beers too and good choice of
wines, carpeted beamed bar with sporting
cartoons and old range, enjoyable good value
food in back dining room, friendly staff;
background music, pool and darts; children
and dogs welcome, comfortable bedrooms
(some in building next door), open all day.
(Charles Todd)

KIRKBY LONSDALE
SD6178
★Sun (015242) 71965
Market Street (B6254); LA6 2AU
Cheerful and busy 17th-c inn striking good
balance between pub and restaurant;
unusual-looking building with upper floors
supported by three sturdy pillars above
pavement, attractive rambling beamed bar
with flagstones and stripped oak boards,
pews, armchairs and cosy window seats, big
landscapes and country pictures on cream
walls, two log fires, comfortable back lounge
and modern dining room, good contemporary
food (booking advised), well kept
Hawkshead, Thwaites and a guest, friendly

helpful service; background music; children
and dogs welcome, nice bedrooms, no car
park, open all day from 9am, closed Mon till
3pm. *(Alf Wright)*

KIRKOSWALD
NY5641
Fetherston Arms (01768) 898284
The Square; CA10 1DQ Busy old stone
inn with cosy bar and various dining
areas, enjoyable food at reasonable prices
including good home-made pies, interesting
range of well kept changing beers, friendly
helpful staff; bedrooms, nice Eden Valley
village. *(Dave Sutton)*

LANGDALE
NY2906
Sticklebarn (015394) 37356
By car park for Stickle Ghyll; LA22 9JU
Glorious views from this roomy and busy
Langdale Valley walkers'/climbers' bar
owned and run by the NT; up to five well
kept changing ales and a real cider, shortish
choice of traditional home-made food (some
meat from next-door farm), mountaineering
photographs, two woodburners; background
music (live Sat in season); children, dogs
and boots welcome, big terrace with inner
verandah, outside pizza oven and firepit,
open (and food) all day, shuts winter at 6pm
(9pm weekends). *(Douglas Power)*

LEVENS
SD4885
Hare & Hounds (015395) 60004
Off A590; LA8 8PN Welcoming
freshened-up old village pub handy for
Sizergh Castle (NT), five well kept changing
local ales and good home-made pub food
including burgers and pizzas, partly panelled
low-beamed lounge bar, front tap room with
open fire and further seating down steps,
newly opened barn dining room; Weds winter
quiz; children, walkers and dogs welcome,
disabled loo, good views from front terrace,
four refurbished bedrooms, open (and food)
all day. *(Mr and Mrs Richard Osborne)*

LORTON
NY1526
★Wheatsheaf (01900) 85199
*B5289 Buttermere–Cockermouth;
CA13 9UW* Friendly local atmosphere
in neatly furnished bar with two log fires
and vibrant purple walls, affable hard-
working landlord, Jennings ales and regular
changing guests, several good value wines,
popular home-made food (all day Sun) from
sandwiches up, curry night Weds (quiz then
too), fresh fish Thurs and Fri evenings,
smallish restaurant (best to book), good
friendly service; children and dogs welcome;
tables out behind and campsite, open all
day weekends, closed lunchtimes Tues, Weds
(Mon-Thurs lunchtimes in winter). *(Pat and
Stewart Gordon)*

Though we don't usually mention it in the text, most pubs will now make
coffee or tea – it's always worth asking.

LOW HESKET   NY4646
Rose & Crown (01697) 473346
A6 Carlisle-Penrith; CA4 0HG Welcoming former 18th-c coaching inn, enjoyable home-made food including several vegetarian dishes and gluten-free choices, Jennings Bitter and guests, good service, dining room with railway memorabilia and central oak tree; children welcome, closed lunchtimes apart from Sun, no food Mon. *(Daniel King)*

LOWICK GREEN   SD3084
Farmers Arms (01229) 861853
Just off A5092 SE of village; LA12 8DT Stable bar with heavy black beams, huge slate flagstones and log fire, cosy corners, some interesting furniture and pictures in plusher hotel lounge/dining area, tasty reasonably priced pubby food (all day Fri-Sun) from sandwiches and basket meals up, Thwaites Wainwright, Fullers London Pride and three guests, decent choice of wines by the glass, good friendly service; background music, TV, pool and darts, free wi-fi; children and dogs welcome, ten comfortable bedrooms, good breakfast, closed Mon lunchtime, otherwise open all day. *(Charles Todd)*

MUNGRISDALE   NY3630
★**Mill Inn** (017687) 79632
Off A66 Penrith–Keswick, 1 mile W of A5091 Ullswater turn-off; CA11 0XR Part 17th-c pub in fine setting below fells with wonderful surrounding walks; neatly kept bar with old millstone built into counter, traditional dark wood furnishings, hunting pictures and log fire in stone fireplace, Robinsons, Hartleys and a guest beer, locally sourced food can be very good, separate dining room; darts, winter pool, dominoes; children and dogs welcome, seats in garden by river, six bedrooms, open all day. *(WAH, John Oates, Martin Day, Tina and David Woods-Taylor)*

NETHER WASDALE   NY1204
★**Strands** (01946) 726237
SW of Wast Water; CA20 1ET Lovely spot below the remote high fells around Wast Water, own-brew beers and popular good value food from changing menu, well cared-for high-beamed main bar with woodburner, smaller public bar with pool, separate dining room, pleasant staff and relaxed friendly atmosphere; background music, maybe a local folk group; children and dogs welcome, neat garden with terrace and belvedere, 14 bedrooms, good breakfast, open all day. *(Alf Wright)*

NEWBIGGIN   NY5649
Blue Bell (01768) 896615
B6413; CA8 9DH Tiny L-shaped one-room village pub, friendly and unpretentious, with a changing local ale and enjoyable pubby food cooked by landlady, fireplace on right

with woodburner; darts and pool, maybe storytelling last Thurs of month; children welcome, good Eden Valley walks, closed weekday lunchtimes. *(Ruth May)*

PENRITH   NY5130
Moo Bar (01768) 606637
King Street; CA11 7AY Bare-boards bar with ever-changing range of six local ales, craft beers and over 100 bottled imports, friendly knowledgeable staff and good mix of customers, no food, upstairs 'Udder Room' with sofas and sports TV, Mon folk night; well behaved dogs welcome, open all day. *(Douglas Power)*

PENRUDDOCK   NY4227
Herdwick (01768) 483007
Off A66 Penrith–Keswick; CA11 0QU 18th-c inn under newish management; well kept Jennings ales and an occasional guest from curved servery, decent wines and enjoyable food from baguettes up including OAP offer and other deals, friendly efficient service, carpeted bar with good log fire, dining room with upper gallery, upstairs games room (pool and darts); free wi-fi; children and dogs welcome (they have three friendly dogs), seats out at back, five bedrooms, hearty breakfast. *(Daniel King)*

POOLEY BRIDGE   NY4724
Sun (017684) 86205
Centre of village (B5320); CA10 2NN Friendly roadside local in row of whitewashed cottages, well kept Jennings and guests, decent choice of enjoyable fairly traditional food, two bars with steps between (dogs allowed in lower one), restaurant; children welcome, picnic-sets in garden with play fort, nine reasonably priced comfortable bedrooms. *(Alf Wright)*

RAVENSTONEDALE   NY7401
Fat Lamb (015396) 23242
Crossbank; A683 Sedbergh–Kirkby Stephen; CA17 4LL Isolated inn surrounded by great scenery and lovely walks; pews in comfortable beamed bar with fire in traditional black inglenook range, interesting local photographs and bird plates, propeller from 1930s biplane over servery, good choice of enjoyable food from sharing boards to daily specials, can eat in bar or separate dining room (less character), well kept Black Sheep, decent wines and around 60 malt whiskies, friendly helpful staff; background music; children and dogs welcome, disabled facilities, tables out by nature reserve pastures, 12 bedrooms, open all day. *(Sandra and Nigel Brown)*

ROSTHWAITE   NY2514
Scafell (017687) 77208
B5289 S of Keswick; CA12 5XB 19th-c hotel's big tile-floored back bar useful for walkers, weather forecast board and blazing log fire, up to five well kept local ales in

season, enjoyable food from sandwiches up, afternoon teas, also cocktail bar/sun lounge and dining room, friendly helpful staff; background music, pool; children and dogs welcome, tables out overlooking beck, 23 bedrooms, open all day. *(Ruth May)*

RULEHOLME   NY5060
Golden Fleece (01228) 573686
Signed off A689; CA6 4NF Hospitable whitewashed inn with series of softly lit linked rooms, good interesting food, a couple of local ales and good range of wines by the glass, friendly attentive service; children welcome, seven comfortable well equipped bedrooms, hearty cumbrian breakfast, handy for Hadrian's Wall and Carlisle Airport, open all day in summer, closed weekday lunchtimes in winter. *(Michael Doswell)*

RYDAL   NY3606
Glen Rothay Hotel (015394) 34500
A591 Ambleside–Grasmere; LA22 9LR Attractive small 17th-c country hotel with up to five well kept changing local ales in back Badger Bar, good choice of enjoyable locally sourced food from sandwiches up, beamed and panelled dining lounge with open fire, restaurant, helpful friendly staff; unusual loos cut into the rock; children, walkers and dogs welcome, tables in pretty garden (resident badgers are fed at dusk), eight comfortable bedrooms, good breakfast, open all day. *(Edward and William Johnston)*

SANDFORD   NY7316
Sandford Arms (01768) 351121
Village and pub signposted just off A66 W of Brough; CA16 6NR Neatly modernised former 18th-c farmhouse in peaceful village, good food (all day weekends Apr-Oct) from chef-landlord, friendly helpful service, L-shaped part-carpeted main bar with stripped beams and stonework, well kept ales including a house beer from Tirril, comfortable raised and balustraded eating area, more formal dining room and second flagstoned bar, woodburner; background music; children and dogs welcome, seats in front garden and covered courtyard, four bedrooms, closed Tues and lunchtime Weds. *(Ruth May)*

SANTON BRIDGE   NY1101
Bridge Inn (01946) 726221
Off A595 at Holmrook or Gosforth; CA19 1UX Old inn set in charming riverside spot with fell views, bustling beamed and timbered bar, some booths around stripped-pine tables, log fire, Jennings and guests, good food from well balanced menu including blackboard specials, Sun carvery, friendly helpful staff, separate dining room

and small reception hall with open fire and daily papers; background music, free wi-fi; children and dogs (in bar) welcome, seats outside by quiet road, plenty of walks, 16 bedrooms, open (and food) all day, breakfast for non-residents. *(Sandra and Nigel Brown)*

SATTERTHWAITE   SD3392
Eagles Head (01229) 860237
S edge of village; LA12 8LN Nice little pub prettily placed on edge of beautiful Grizedale Forest (visitor centre nearby); low black beams and comfortable furnishings, various odds and ends including antlers, horsebrasses, decorative plates and earthenware, old tiled floor, woodburner, four ales such as Barngates, Coniston, Cumbrian Legendary and Hawkshead, popular pubby food from shortish menu including good home-made pies, friendly welcoming staff; occasional live music, local artwork for sale; children, dogs and muddy boots welcome, picnic-sets in attractive tree-shaded courtyard garden, open all day summer, closed Mon in winter, food all day weekends. *(Glenwys and Alan Lawrence)*

SCALES   NY3426
White Horse (017687) 79883
A66 W of Penrith; CA12 4SY Traditional Lakeland pub, log fire in flagstoned beamed bar, little snug and another room with black range, three real ales such as Cross Bay, Cumberland and Tirril, good pubby food (all day weekends); board games, free wi-fi; children and dogs welcome, picnic-sets out in front, lovely setting below Blencathra, bunkhouse, open all day. *(Alf Wright)*

SEATHWAITE   SD2295
★ Newfield Inn (01229) 716208
Duddon Valley, near Ulpha (not Seathwaite in Borrowdale); LA20 6ED Friendly 16th-c cottage with good local atmosphere in slate-floored bar, wooden tables and chairs, interesting pictures, woodburner, three changing local beers and good straightforward food, comfortable side room, games room; children and dogs welcome, tables in nice garden with hill views and play area, good walks, two self-catering apartments, open all day. *(Dr Peter Crawshaw)*

SEDBERGH   SD6592
Red Lion (015396) 20433
Finkle Street (A683); LA10 5BZ Cheerful little beamed local opposite church, down to earth and comfortable, with good value generous home-made food (meat from next-door butcher) including blackboard specials and nice fruit pies, well kept Jennings and other Marstons-related beers, good open fire;

Real ale may be served from handpumps, electric pumps (not just the on-off switches used for keg beer) or – common in Scotland – tall taps called founts (pronounced 'fonts') where a separate pump pushes the beer up under air pressure.

quiz and music nights, sports TV, free wi-fi; children welcome, no dogs, open all day weekends when it can get very busy, closed Mon. *(John Evans, Derek Stafford)*

THRELKELD NY3225

★ **Horse & Farrier** (017687) 79688

A66 Penrith–Keswick; CA12 4SQ
Popular well run 17th-c inn at the foot of Blencathra; linked mainly carpeted rooms (some flagstones), mix of furniture from comfortably padded seats to pubby chairs and wall settles, candlelit tables, beams and open fires, good varied choice of nicely presented local food (booking advised), Jennings and guests kept well, efficient service, partly stripped-stone restaurant; children welcome, dogs allowed in one part of bar, disabled facilities, a few picnic-sets outside and fine views towards Helvellyn range, walks from the back door, bedrooms, open all day. *(Martin Day, Margaret and Peter Staples, Tina and David Woods-Taylor)*

THRELKELD NY3225

Salutation (017687) 79614

Old Main Road, bypassed by A66 W of Penrith; CA12 4SQ Friendly modernised former 17th-c coaching inn; two or three changing ales and good range of ciders and wines by the glass, enjoyable sensibly priced pubby food (not Mon, Tues), low beams and open fire, raftered restaurant with high-backed leather chairs at light wood tables, games area with pool, darts and TV; background music, free wi-fi; dogs welcome, views from pleasant outside area, five bedrooms and self-catering cottage, sister pub to nearby Horse & Farrier (above), open (and food) all day weekends. *(Dr Peter Crawshaw)*

TORVER SD2894

Church House (01539) 449159

A593/A5084 S of Coniston; LA21 8AZ
Friendly 14th-c coach house refurbished under new owners; pubby bar with heavy beams (some painted), straightforward tables and chairs on slate flooring, Lakeland bric-a-brac and big log fire in sizeable stone fireplace, enjoyable home-made food (all day weekends) from sandwiches and sharing platters up, four changing ales and seven wines by the glass from barrel-fronted counter, comfortable lounge, separate dining room; occasional live music; children and dogs (in bar) welcome, lawned garden, four bedrooms, standing for five caravans, good nearby walks to Lake Coniston, open all day. *(Sandra and Nigel Brown)*

TORVER SD2894

Wilson Arms (015394) 41237

A593; LA21 8BB Old family-run roadside inn with adjoining deli; beams, nice log fire and one or two modern touches, well kept Cumbrian ales and good locally sourced food cooked to order in bar or dining room, friendly service; free wi-fi; children and dogs welcome, hill views (including Old Man of Coniston) from tables in large garden, area with pigs, goats and ducks, seven bedrooms and three holiday cottages, open (and food) all day. *(Charles Todd)*

TROUTBECK NY4103

Mortal Man (015394) 33193

A592 N of Windermere; Upper Road; LA23 1PL Beamed and partly panelled bar with cosy room off, log fires, well kept local ales including a house beer from Hawkshead, several wines by the glass and well liked food in bar and picture-window restaurant; folk night Sun, quiz Weds, storytelling Thurs, free wi-fi; children and dogs welcome, great views from sunny garden, lovely village and surrounding walks, bedrooms, open all day. *(J D O Carter, Christian Mole)*

TROUTBECK NY3827

Troutbeck Inn (017684) 83635

A5091/A66; CA11 0SJ Former railway hotel with small bar, lounge and log-fire restaurant, a couple of Jennings ales and good food cooked by landlord-chef, efficient friendly service; children and dogs (in bar) welcome, seven bedrooms plus four self-catering cottages in converted stables, open all day in season. *(Daniel Power)*

ULDALE NY2436

Snooty Fox (016973) 71479

Village signed off B5299 W of Caldbeck; CA7 1HA Comfortable and welcoming two-bar village inn; ample helpings of good-quality home-cooked food (not Weds) using local ingredients, up to four well kept changing ales including a summer brew named for the pub, decent selection of whiskies, friendly attentive staff, fox hunting memorabilia; winter pool, free wi-fi; children in dining areas, dogs in snug, nice location with garden at back, three bedrooms, closed lunchtimes. *(Dave Sutton)*

ULVERSTON SD2878

★ **Farmers Arms** (01229) 584469

Market Place; LA12 7BA Convivial attractively modernised town pub; front bar with comfortable sofas, contemporary wicker chairs and original fireplace, quickly changing ales and a dozen wines by the glass, good varied choice of popular food from sandwiches and deli boards up, second bar leading to big raftered dining area (children here only); unobtrusive background music, Thurs quiz; seats on attractive heated front terrace, lots of colourful tubs and hanging baskets, Thurs market day (pub busy then), bedrooms and self-catering cottages, open all day from 9am. *(Charles Todd, Simon Cleasby)*

UNDERBARROW SD4692

Punchbowl (01539) 568234

From centre of Kendal at town hall, turn left into Beast Banks signed for Underbarrow, then follow Underbarrow Road; LA8 8HQ Small friendly open-plan village local, beamed bar with mix of furniture including leather sofas on stone floor, woodburner, Hawkshead and a couple of local guests, good choice of enjoyable freshly prepared food, mezzanine restaurant; free wi-fi; children and dogs (in bar) welcome, picnic-sets and covered balcony outside, handy for walkers, open all day Fri-Sun and Weds, closed Tues. *(Sandra King)*

WASDALE HEAD   NY1807
Wasdale Head Inn (019467) 26229
NE of Wast Water; CA20 1EX Mountain hotel worth knowing for its stunning fellside setting; roomy walkers' bar with welcoming fire, several local ales and good choice of wines, ample helpings of enjoyable home-made food; residents' bar, lounge and panelled restaurant; children and dogs welcome, nine bedrooms, self-catering apartments in converted barn and camping, open all day. *(Alf Wright)*

WETHERAL   NY4654
Wheatsheaf (01228) 560686
Handy for M6 junctions 42/43; CA4 8HD Popular 19th-c village pub, three well kept changing ales and enjoyable home-made food (not Mon, Tues) including daily specials, good friendly service; Tues quiz, TV; children and dogs welcome, pretty village, picnic-sets in small garden, open all day. *(Dave Sutton)*

WREAY   NY4349
Plough (016974) 75770
Village signed from A6 N of Low Hesket; CA4 0RL Pretty village's 18th-c beamed pub, modernised split-level interior with pine tables and chairs on wood or flagstone floors, some exposed stonework, woodburner, good choice of enjoyable freshly prepared food including specials, well kept Cumberland, Hawkshead and a guest from brick-fronted canopied bar, efficient friendly service; live acoustic music Tues; children welcome, closed Mon and Tues lunchtimes, no food Mon. *(Ruth May)*

Derbyshire

KEY ★ Star Pub 🍲 Top Quality Food 🍺 Great Beer
🍷 Good Wines £ Bargain Meals 🛏 Good Bedrooms 🍴 Serves Food

ASHOVER
SK3462 Map 7
Old Poets Corner 🍺 £ 🛏
(01246) 590888 – www.oldpoets.co.uk

Butts Road (B6036, off A632 Matlock–Chesterfield); S45 0EW

**Hard-working owners keep interesting real ales (some own brew)
and ciders in characterful village; hearty food; bedrooms**

Even fleeting visitors are made to feel like the most valued of regulars
by the enthusiastic licensees in this comfortably unpretentious local.
Many are here for the fine ales that include their own Ashover Light Rale,
Coffin Lane Stout, Littlemoor Citra, Poets Tipple, Red Lion and Zoo, plus
guests from breweries such as Abbeydale, Blackjack, Blue Monkey, Gadds,
Harviestoun, Kelham Island, Oakham, Roosters, Salopian, Sarah Hughes
and Titanic; they hold beer festivals in March and October. Also, a terrific
choice of 12 farm ciders, a dozen fruit wines, 20 malt whiskies and belgian
beers. The informal bar has an easy-going atmosphere and a mix of chairs
and pews, while a small room opening off the bar has a stack of newspapers
and vintage comics; background music. French doors lead to a tiny balcony
with a couple of tables. They hold regular acoustic, folk and blues sessions
(posters advertise forthcoming events) as well as quiz nights, poetry evenings
and morris dancers. The bedrooms are attractive and there's a holiday
cottage sleeping up to eight.

🍴 Fairly priced, honest food includes sandwiches and baguettes, breaded brie wedges,
crispy stuffed potato skins, beef cobbler, burgers with toppings and chips, butternut
squash wellington, a trio of sausages and a Sunday carvery; curry night is Sunday.
Benchmark main dish: steak in ale pie £11.25. Two-course evening meal £15.50.

Own brew ~ Licensees Kim and Jackie Beresford ~ Real ale ~ Open 12-midnight ~ Bar food
12-2, 6-9; 12-5, 6-9.30 Fri, Sat; 12-4, 6-9 Sun ~ Restaurant ~ Children welcome away from
bar ~ Dogs allowed in bar and bedrooms ~ Wi-fi ~ Acoustic evenings Tues, Sun; quiz Weds ~
Bedrooms: £76/£84.50 *Recommended by Peter Pilbeam, John and Mary Warner, Andrew Vincent,
Miles Green, Malcolm Phillips*

BRADWELL
SK1782 Map 7
Samuel Fox 🍲 🍷 🛏
(01433) 621562 – www.samuelfox.co.uk

B6049; S33 9JT

**Friendly pub in the Hope Valley with real ales and fine food,
good service and neat bars; comfortable bedrooms**

After enjoying one of the wonderful walks in the surrounding Peak District National Park, head to this well kept stone inn for refreshment. The open-plan bar and interlinked dining rooms have a wide mix of customers and although there's quite an emphasis on the interesting food, regulars do pop in for a pint of local ale and a chat. Red and dogtooth upholstered tub chairs are grouped around tables on striped carpet or wooden flooring, country scenes hang on papered walls above a grey dado, curtains are neatly swagged and there are several open brick fireplaces. Bradfield Farmers Bitter and Intrepid Explorer on handpump, ten wines by the glass from a good list and a farm cider, served by helpful, courteous staff; board games. The neat restaurant is similarly furnished but with red plush dining chairs. At the front of the building, white metal seating is arranged around small ornamental trees and there are some wooden seats too. The bedrooms are restful and comfortable. No dogs inside. Wheelchair access.

Making impressive use of local produce, the food includes game terrine with pear and mustard compote, celeriac arancini with soused sardines, fennel and sumac, white radish with szechuan pepper, goats cheese and pickled aubergine, confit duck leg and pink roasted breast with port wine sauce and roasted carrots, sea bream fillet with chickpeas and roasted red pepper, pheasant with parsnip bonbons and cavolo nero, and puddings such as white chocolate cheesecake with mango, passion fruit and coconut and black forest trifle. *Benchmark main dish: braised beef cheek in red wine sauce with pickled red cabbage £16.00. Two-course evening meal £22.00.*

Free house ~ Licensee John Duckett ~ Real ale ~ Open 6-11 Wed, Thurs; 12-3, 6-11 Fri, Sat; 1-8 Sun; closed Mon, Tues, lunchtimes Weds, Thurs, all Jan ~ Bar food 6-9 Weds, Thurs; 12-2.30, 6-9 Fri, Sat; 1-8 Sun ~ Restaurant ~ Children welcome ~ Wi-fi ~ Bedrooms: £95/£130 *Recommended by W K Wood, John and Mary Warner, Miles Green, Colin and Daniel Gibbs*

BRASSINGTON
Olde Gate £

SK2354 Map 7

(01629) 540448 – www.oldgateinnbrassington.co.uk
Village signed off B5056 and B5035 NE of Ashbourne; DE4 4HJ

Lovely old interior, candlelit at night, with tasty, fairly priced food, real ales and country garden

Like a step back in time, you almost expect a Dickens character to pop into this unspoilt old pub. It's full of character with mullioned windows, a 17th-c kitchen range with gleaming copper pots, a venerable wall clock, rush-seated old chairs and antique settles (note the ancient one in black solid oak), beams hung with pewter mugs and shelves lined with embossed Doulton stoneware flagons. There's a panelled Georgian room and, to the left of a small hatch-served lobby, a cosy beamed room with stripped panelled settles, scrubbed-top tables and a blazing fire under a huge mantelbeam. Marstons Pedigree and up to three guests on handpump; cribbage, dominoes, cards. The inviting garden has tables that look out to idyllic silvery-walled pastures, and there are benches in the small front yard. The large car park has level access into the pub.

Tasty food (the Value Award is for lunchtime food) includes lunchtime sandwiches and baguettes, fried mackerel with gooseberry and elderflower dressing, pigeon breast on bubble and squeak with port syrup, trio of local sausages with onion gravy, cheese, leek and potato cakes with leek compote, steak in Guinness pie, beer-battered fish and chips, duo of lamb (cannon and mini shepherd's pie) with rosemary jus, and puddings such as apple and cinnamon crumble and black cherry and white chocolate torte. *Benchmark main dish: slow-cooked oxtail in red wine £12.50. Two-course evening meal £18.50.*

Marstons ~ Lease Melanie Cachart ~ Real ale ~ No credit cards ~ Open 12-3, 5-11;
5-11 Mon; 12-midnight Fri, Sat; 12-11 Sun; closed Mon lunchtime ~ Bar food 12-3, 6-9 ~
Restaurant ~ Well behaved children welcome ~ Dogs allowed in bar ~ Wi-fi
Recommended by Ralph Beaumont, Kathleen I'Anson

BRETTON
SK2078   Map 7

Barrel

(01433) 630856 – www.thebarrelinn.co.uk

*Signposted from Foolow, which itself is signposted from A623 just E of junction
with B6465 to Bakewell; can also be reached from either the B6049 at Great Hucklow,
or the B6001 via Abney, from Leadmill just S of Hathersage; S32 5QD*

**Remote dining pub with traditional décor, popular food and
friendly staff; bedrooms**

On a clear day you can see five counties from this popular pub as it's
on the edge of an isolated ridge in excellent walking country. Inside,
it's divided into several spic and span areas by stubs of massive knocked-
through stone walls. The cosy, dark oak-beamed bar is charmingly traditional
with gleaming copper and brass, a warming fire, patterned carpet, low
doorways and stools lined up at the counter. Marstons Pedigree and EPA
and Wychwood Hobgoblin on handpump, 28 malt whiskies, a farm cider
and wines by the glass, all served by friendly, smartly dressed staff; maybe
background radio. The outdoor seats on the front terrace by the road and
in a courtyard garden are nicely sheltered from the inevitable breeze at this
height. The bedrooms are clean and comfortable.

Pubby food includes sandwiches, chicken liver pâté with chutney, stilton
mushrooms, beer-battered fish and chips, a seasonal vegetarian risotto, lambs liver
and onions, steaks, winter pheasant and venison, and puddings such as bakewell tart
or sticky toffee pudding. *Benchmark main dish: steak in ale pie £11.95. Two-course
evening meal £19.00.*

Free house ~ Licensee Philip Cone ~ Real ale ~ Open 11-3, 6-11; 11-11 Sat, Sun ~ Bar food
12-2, 6-9; 12-9 Sat, Sun ~ Well behaved children welcome ~ Wi-fi ~ Bedrooms: /£90
Recommended by Liz and Brian Barnard, Simon Day, Anne Taylor

CHELMORTON
SK1170   Map 7

Church Inn 🍺 £ ⇌

(01298) 85319 – www.thechurchinn.co.uk

*Village signposted off A5270, between A6 and A515 SE of Buxton; keep on up through
village towards church; SK17 9SL*

**Cosy, convivial, traditional inn beautifully set in High Peak walking
country; good value food; bedrooms**

The hospitable licensees have been here for nearly 20 years now – in fact,
the landlady was born in the village. They've created a warmly friendly
old inn and our readers enjoy their visits very much, returning regularly. The
chatty, low-ceilinged bar has an open fire and is traditionally furnished with
built-in cushioned benches and simple chairs around polished cast-iron-
framed tables (a couple still with their squeaky sewing treadles). Shelves
of books, Tiffany-style lamps and house plants in the curtained windows,
atmospheric Dales photographs and prints and a coal-effect stove in the
stripped-stone end wall all add a cosy feel. Abbeydale Moonshine, Adnams
Southwold, Marstons Pedigree and guests such as Leatherbritches Ashbourne
IPA and Thornbridge Jaipur on handpump and nine wines by the glass;
darts in a tile-floored games area on the left; TV and board games. The inn is

opposite a mainly 18th-c church and is prettily tucked into woodland with fine views over the village and hills beyond from good teak tables on a two-level terrace. The cottagey bedrooms are comfortable and the breakfasts good.

Reasonably priced food includes sandwiches, black pudding fritters with spiced chutney, prawn cocktail, lasagne, steak and kidney pie, vegetable curry with naan bread, chicken wrapped in bacon with creamy mushroom sauce, beer-battered haddock and chips, lamb shank with red wine and rosemary sauce, and puddings. *Benchmark main dish: rabbit pie £12.95. Two-course evening meal £16.00.*

Free house ~ Licensees Julie and Justin Satur ~ Real ale ~ Open 12-3.30, 6-11; 12-11 Sat; 12-11 Sun ~ Bar food 12-2.30, 6-8.30; 12-8.30 Fri-Sun ~ Children welcome ~ Dogs allowed in bar ~ Wi-fi ~ Quiz night Mon 9pm ~ Bedrooms: £55/£80 *Recommended by J A Snell, Mr and Mrs R Shardlow, Ann and Tony Bennett-Hughes*

CHINLEY
Old Hall ★ 🍺 🛏

SK0382 Map 7

(01663) 750529 – www.old-hall-inn.co.uk
Village signposted off A6 (very sharp turn) E of New Mills; also off A624 N of Chapel-en-le-Frith; Whitehough Head Lane, off B6062; SK23 6EJ

Fine range of ales and ciders in splendid building with lots to look at and good country food; comfortable bedrooms

Do poke your nose into the dining room here (even if you only want a drink) as it's surprisingly grand, with a great stone chimney soaring into high eaves, refectory tables on a parquet floor, lovely old mullioned windows and a splendid minstrels' gallery. The warm bar – basically four small friendly rooms opened into a single area tucked behind a massive central chimney – contains open fires, broad flagstones, red patterned carpet, sturdy country tables and a couple of long pews and various other seats. Marstons Burton Bitter and guests from breweries such as Marble, Howard Town, Peak, Redwillow, Storm, Thornbridge and Whim on handpump, as well as some interesting lagers on tap, 20 malt whiskies, eight cask ciders, a rare range of bottled ciders and around 50 bottled (mostly belgian) beers. They hold a beer festival with music in September. Also, around a dozen new world wines by the glass and friendly, helpful service. The pretty walled garden has picnic-sets under sycamore trees. Some of the attractive bedrooms look over the garden and there's also a self-catering cottage.

As well as a weekday early-bird menu, the good food includes sandwiches, salt and pepper king prawns with sweet chilli sauce, chicken liver and bacon pâté with red onion marmalade, spring onion and asparagus risotto, chicken in lemon butter sauce with parmentier potatoes, spiced lamb rump with moroccan-style couscous and roasted mediterranean vegetables, and puddings such as rhubarb and lemon posset and sticky toffee pudding with hot fudge sauce. *Benchmark main dish: steak and kidney pudding £11.00. Two-course evening meal £15.00.*

Free house ~ Licensee Daniel Capper ~ Real ale ~ Open 12-midnight ~ Bar food 12-2, 5-9 (9.30 Fri, Sat); 12-7.30 Sun ~ Restaurant ~ Children welcome ~ Dogs allowed in bar ~ Wi-fi ~ Bedrooms: £75/£89 *Recommended by Brian and Anna Marsden, Susan Jackman, Ann and Tony Bennett-Hughes, Mary Joyce*

'Children welcome' means the pub says it lets children inside without any special restriction. If it allows them in, but to restricted areas such as an eating area or family room, we specify this. Places with separate restaurants often let children use them, and hotels usually let children into public areas such as lounges. Some pubs impose an evening time limit – let us know if you find one earlier than 9pm.

FENNY BENTLEY SK1750 Map 7

Coach & Horses

(01335) 350246 – www.coachandhorsesfennybentley.co.uk

A515 N of Ashbourne; DE6 1LB

Cosy inn with pretty country furnishings, roaring open fires and food all day

Our readers are full of praise for the way the friendly Dawson family run this comfortable former coaching inn. The traditional interior has all the trappings you'd expect of a country pub, from roaring log fires, exposed brick hearths and flagstone floors to black beams hung with pewter mugs, and hand-made pine furniture that includes wall settles with floral-print cushions. There's also a conservatory dining room and a cosy front dining room. Marstons Pedigree and a changing guest ale on handpump, a couple of farm ciders and eight wines by the glass; the landlord is knowledgeable about malt whiskies – he stocks around two dozen; quiet background music. A side garden by an elder tree (with views across fields) has seats and tables, and there are modern tables and chairs under cocktail parasols on a front roadside terrace. It's a short walk from the Tissington Trail, a popular cycling/walking path along a former railway line that is best joined at the nearby picture-book village of Tissington. No dogs inside.

 As well as sandwiches and baguettes (until 5pm), the well thought-of food includes smoked mackerel pâté, apple and black pudding stack with black pepper sauce, cumberland sausage ring with orange and cranberry sauce, butternut squash, tomato and basil bake topped with goats cheese, chicken with bacon, cheddar and barbecue sauce, hake with creamy garlic and tarragon sauce, and puddings. *Benchmark main dish: lamb rump with crushed minted potatoes and red wine and mushroom sauce £14.50. Two-course evening meal £20.00.*

Free house ~ Licensees John and Matthew Dawson ~ Real ale ~ Open 11-11 ~ Bar food 12-9 ~ Restaurant ~ Children welcome ~ Wi-fi *Recommended by Steve and Suzanne Griffiths, Joy Griffiths, Martin Day, Noel Thomas*

GREAT LONGSTONE SK1971 Map 7

Crispin

(01629) 640237 – www.thecrispingreatlongstone.co.uk

Main Street; village signed from A6020, N of Ashford in the Water; DE45 1TZ

Spotless traditional pub with emphasis on good, fairly priced pubby food; good drinks choice too

There's always quite a collection of customers here – walkers, cyclists and families – who've been enjoying the beautiful surrounding countryside; the pub is helpfully open all day. Décor throughout is traditional: brass or copper implements, decorative plates, a photo collage of regulars, horsebrasses on the beams in the red ceiling, cushioned built-in wall benches and upholstered chairs and stools around polished tables on red carpet, and a fire. A corner area is snugly partitioned off and there's a separate, more formal dining room on the right; darts, board games and maybe faint background music. Robinsons Dizzy Blonde, Double Hop, Red Jester, Unicorn and White Label Porter on handpump, Weston's Old Rosie cider and quite a choice of wines and whiskies. There are picnic-sets out in front (one under a heated canopy) set well back above the quiet lane, and more in the garden.

 Their incredible value OAP weekday menu is still on offer, plus sandwiches, chicken liver pâté, omelettes, battered haddock and chips, a pie of the day, various curries, chilli con carne, steaks with trimmings, and puddings. *Benchmark main dish: hake with chorizo and salsa £14.95. Two-course evening meal £20.00.*

Robinsons ~ Tenant Paul Rowlinson ~ Real ale ~ Open 12-3, 6-midnight; 12-midnight Sat; 12-10.30 Sun ~ Bar food 12-2.30, 6-9 ~ Restaurant ~ Children welcome ~ Dogs welcome ~ Wi-fi *Recommended by Ann and Tony Bennett-Hughes, John and Mary Warner, Malcolm and Pauline Pellatt*

HASSOP
SK2272   Map 7

Eyre Arms

(01629) 640390 – www.eyrearms.com

B6001 N of Bakewell; DE45 1NS

Comfortable, family-run 17th-c former farmhouse with decent food and beer, and pretty views from the garden

It's especially appealing here in warm weather: the hanging baskets are lovely and the delightful garden (with its gurgling fountain) looks straight out to fine Peak District countryside. Inside, the low-ceilinged beamed rooms are snug and cosy with log fires and traditional furnishings that include cushioned oak settles, comfortable plush chairs, a longcase clock, old pictures and lots of brass and copper. The small public bar has an unusual collection of teapots, as well as Bradfield Farmers Blonde, Peak Swift Nick and a guest such as Brampton Best Bitter on handpump, eight wines by the glass and 20 malt whiskies; darts, board games and background music. The dining room is dominated by a painting of the Eyre coat of arms above the stone fireplace.

Honest, pubby food includes sandwiches, deep-fried garlic mushrooms, thai-style crab cakes with sweet pepper sauce, aubergine and mushroom lasagne, rabbit pie, scampi and chips, lamp chops with red wine gravy, chicken breast stuffed with local stilton and leeks in creamy sauce, sirloin steak with a choice of sauces, and puddings such as sticky toffee pudding and bakewell pudding. *Benchmark main dish: steak and kidney pie £11.95. Two-course evening meal £18.00.*

Free house ~ Licensees Nick and Lynne Smith ~ Real ale ~ Open 11-3, 6-11; 12-10.30 Sun; closed Mon evenings in winter ~ Bar food 12-2, 6-8.30; 12-3, 6-9 Sat; 12-8 Sun ~ Children welcome ~ Dogs allowed in bar ~ Wi-fi *Recommended by Ann and Tony Bennett-Hughes, Caroline Prescott, Emma Scofield*

HATHERSAGE
SK2380   Map 7

Plough

(01433) 650319 – www.theploughinn-hathersage.co.uk

Leadmill; B6001 towards Bakewell; S32 1BA

Derbyshire Dining Pub of the Year

Comfortable dining pub with tasty food, beer and wine and seats in a waterside garden; bedrooms

The seats on the terrace by this 16th-c inn have wonderful valley views and the nine-acre grounds are on the banks of the River Derwent – the pretty garden slopes down to the water. The cosy, traditionally furnished rooms have rows of dark wooden chairs and tables (with cruets showing the emphasis on dining) and a long banquette running almost the length of one wall, and bright tartan and oriental patterned carpets; also, a big log fire, a woodburning stove and decorative plates on terracotta walls. The neat dining room is slightly more formal. They have a good wine list (with 21 by the glass), 20 malt whiskies and Black Sheep Best, Bradfield Farmers Blonde and

Greene King Old Speckled Hen on handpump; quiet background music. The well equipped beamed bedrooms in a barn conversion make this a good base for exploring the Peak District.

 A wide choice of well presented food includes sandwiches, seared foie gras with home-made sweet pickle, scallops and lasagne of jerusalem and globe artichokes, pizzas with a choice of toppings, wild mushroom risotto with white truffle and parmesan, slow-cooked pork belly with butternut squash dauphinoise, braised leeks and cider and rosemary sauce, pot-roast pheasant with a wellington of braised leg, roast shallots and garlic and parsley risotto, red mullet with aubergine caviar, roasted pepper and rosemary emulsion, and puddings such as bakewell pudding with blackberry compote and custard and chocolate mousse cake with boozy black cherry and vanilla mascarpone. *Benchmark main dish: rib-eye steak £23.00. Two-course evening meal £24.00.*

Free house ~ Licensees Bob, Cynthia and Elliott Emery ~ Real ale ~ Open 11.30-11; 12-10.30 Sun ~ Bar food 12-9.30; 12-8.30 Sun ~ Restaurant ~ Children welcome ~ Dogs welcome ~ Wi-fi ~ Bedrooms: £80/£105 *Recommended by Ann and Tony Bennett-Hughes, Richard Cole, Tim and Sarah Smythe-Brown, Ben and Diane Bowie, Peter Wilson*

HAYFIELD
SK0388 Map 7
Lantern Pike

(01663) 747590 – www.lanternpikeinn.co.uk
Glossop Road (A624 N) at Little Hayfield, just N of Hayfield; SK22 2NG

Relaxing retreat from the surrounding moors of Kinder Scout, with reasonably priced food; bedrooms

It's quite possible that the interior hasn't changed much since the late Tony Warren (the creator of *Coronation Street*) used to visit this homely place; he based his characters on some of the locals. The traditional red plush bar proudly displays photos of the original cast, many of whom were also regulars here. There's a warm fire, an array of antique clocks and a montage of local photographs. Copper Dragon Golden Pippin and Timothy Taylors Landlord on handpump; TV and background music. The tables on the stone-walled terrace look over a big-windowed weaver's house towards Lantern Pike Hill. Dogs may be allowed in at the licensees' discretion, and if clean; good walks in the Peak District National Park.

 The popular food, listed on blackboards, includes sandwiches, deep-fried calamari, chicken pâté, fidget (vegetarian) pie, salmon pasta in tomato and basil sauce, lambs liver and onions, chicken chasseur, baked cod loin with parsley sauce, local steaks with chips, and puddings such as blackcurrant cheesecake and bread and butter pudding. *Benchmark main dish: chilli con carne £10.95. Two-course evening meal £14.00.*

Enterprise ~ Lease Stella and Tom Cuncliffe ~ Real ale ~ Open 12-3, 5-11; 12-11 Sat, Sun; closed Mon lunchtime ~ Bar food 12-2.30, 5-8.30; all day weekends ~ Restaurant ~ Children welcome ~ Dogs allowed in bar ~ Wi-fi ~ Bedrooms: £61/£72 *Recommended by Malcolm and Pauline Pellatt, Gus Swan, Alf Wright*

HAYFIELD
SK0387 Map 7
Royal 🏨

(01663) 742721 – www.theroyalathayfield.com
Market Street; SK22 2EP

Big, bustling inn with fine panelled rooms, friendly service and thoughtful choice of drinks and food; bedrooms

Very much the centre of local life and with a genuinely pubby feel, this traditional stone building is enjoyed just as much by visitors. The oak-panelled bar and lounge areas have open fires, a fine collection of seats from long settles with pretty scatter cushions through elegant upholstered dining chairs to tub chairs and chesterfields, around an assortment of solid tables on rugs and flagstones; house plants and daily papers. Thwaites Original and guests such as Dark Star Hophead, Happy Valley Kinder Falldown, High Peak Pale Ale and Howard Town Longdendale Lights on handpump (they hold a beer festival in October), nine wines by the glass and three farm ciders; background music, TV and board games. The sunny front terrace is spacious, and the bedrooms are spotlessly clean and comfortable; breakfasts are good.

A thoughtful choice of food from a large menu includes sandwiches, chicken and mushroom terrine, prawn and crayfish cocktail, sharing platters, macaroni cheese with garlic bread, sausages with wholegrain mustard mash and onion gravy, lamb hotpot, chicken curry, beef bourguignon with herb dumplings, salmon fillet with white wine and dill sauce, and puddings such as chocolate fudge cake and crème brûlée. *Benchmark main dish: steak in ale pie £9.50. Two-course evening meal £13.50.*

Free house ~ Licensees Mark Miller and Lisa Davis ~ Real ale ~ Open 11-11 (11.30 Fri, Sat); 11-10.30 Sun ~ Bar food 12-2.30, 6-8.30; 12-9 Sat; 12-7 Sun ~ Children welcome ~ Dogs welcome ~ Wi-fi ~ Irish folk band most Thurs evenings ~ Bedrooms: £60/£80
Recommended by Carol and Barry Craddock, Hilary and Neil Christopher

HURDLOW
Royal Oak ◖

SK1265   Map 7

(01298) 83288 – www.peakpub.co.uk
Monyash–Longnor Road, just off A515 S of Buxton; SK17 9QJ

Bustling, carefully renovated pub in rural spot with beamed rooms, friendly staff and tasty, all-day food

Attractively presented food is served all day in this hospitable pub, which is a huge bonus for the walkers, cyclists and horse riders who crowd in. Friendly, helpful staff serve Sharps Doom Bar, Whim Hartington Bitter and a guest or two such as Thornbridge Lord Marples on handpump, seven wines by the glass and two farm ciders. The two-roomed beamed bar has an open fire in a stone fireplace, lots of copper kettles, bed warming pans, horsebrasses and country pictures, cushioned wheelback chairs and wall settles around dark tables, and stools against the counter; background music. The attractive dining room has country dining chairs, wheelbacks, a cushioned pine settle in one corner on bare floorboards, pretty curtains and another open fire. For large groups, there's also a flagstoned cellar room with benches on either side of long tables. The terraced garden has plenty of seats and picnic-sets on the grass. Both the self-catering barn with bunk bedrooms and the campsite are very popular.

A wide range of good food at fair prices includes sandwiches, sweet chilli chicken wings, beer-battered crab cakes with tartare sauce, sharing platters, butternut squash, spinach and walnut lasagne, lambs liver and bacon on leek mash with red wine gravy, pork fillet in Grand Marnier cream sauce and black pudding mash, salmon and prawns in white wine sauce, thai chicken curry, mixed grill, and puddings such as apple and mixed berry crumble and white chocolate cheesecake. *Benchmark main dish: beef and stilton pie £11.50. Two-course evening meal £17.00.*

Free house ~ Licensee Paul White ~ Real ale ~ Open 10am-11pm; 8.30am-midnight Sat; 8.30am-11pm Sun ~ Bar food 10-9 ~ Children welcome ~ Dogs welcome ~ Wi-fi
Recommended by Brian and Anna Marsden, Emma Scofield, Daphne and Robert Staples

INGLEBY   SK3427 Map 7

John Thompson 🍺 £ 🛏

(01332) 862469 – www.johnthompsoninn.com

*NW of Melbourne; turn off A514 at Swarkestone Bridge or in Stanton by Bridge; can
also be reached from Ticknall (or from Repton on B5008); DE73 7HW*

**Own-brew pub that strikes the right balance between attentive
service, roomy comfort and good value lunchtime food**

This is the longest established microbrewery in the country and it's been
in every edition of this *Guide* since it began in 1983. The John Thompson
brews launched in 1977 and friendly staff now serve JTS XXX, Rich Porter,
St Nicks and Summer Gold. The simple but comfortable and immaculately
kept modernised lounge has ceiling joists, some old oak settles, button-back
leather seats, sturdy oak tables, antique prints and paintings and a log-effect
gas fire; background music. A couple of smaller, cosier rooms open off;
piano, games machine, board games, darts, TV, and pool in the conservatory.
There are lots of tables by flower beds on the neat lawns or you can sit on
the partly covered terrace, surrounded by pretty countryside. Breakfast is
left in your fridge if you stay in one of the self-catering chalet lodges. Dogs
are allowed in the conservatory.

🍴 Honest straightforward food – available lunchtime only – includes sandwiches,
baked potatoes, cheese and broccoli pasta bake, a choice of salads, a carvery, and
puddings such as bread and butter pudding and fruit crumble. *Benchmark main dish:
roast beef carvery £8.95.*

Own brew ~ Licensee Nick Thompson ~ Real ale ~ Open 11.30-2.30, 6-10 (11 Fri); 11.30-11
Sat; 12-10.30 Sun; evening opening 6.30 in winter; closed Mon except bank holidays ~
Bar food 12-2 ~ Restaurant ~ Children until 9pm ~ Dogs allowed in bar ~ Wi-fi
Recommended by Steve and Suzanne Griffiths, Dennis Jones, Peter Pilbeam, John Beeken

KIRK IRETON   SK2650 Map 7

Barley Mow 🍺 🛏

(01335) 370306

Village signed off B5023 S of Wirksworth; DE6 3JP

**Welcoming old inn that focuses on real ale and conversation;
bedrooms**

Once you've found this quite unspoilt and unchanging mid 18th-c pub, you
won't want to leave – especially given the genuine welcome you'll get
from the long-serving, kindly landlady, who's been here 40 years. The small
main bar is relaxed and pubby with chatty locals, a roaring coal fire, antique
settles on tiles or built into panelling, four slate-topped tables and shuttered
mullioned windows. Another room has built-in cushioned pews on oak
parquet and a small woodburning stove; a third has more pews, low beams
and big landscape prints. In casks behind a modest wooden counter are
five well kept ales from breweries such as Abbeydale, Blue Monkey, Burton
Bridge, Peak, Storm and Whim; french wines and farm cider too. There are
two pub dogs. Outside you'll find a good-sized garden, a couple of benches
at the front, and a shop in what used to be the stable. This hilltop village is
very pretty and within walking distance of Carsington Water. Bedrooms are
comfortable, and readers enjoy the good breakfasts served in the stone-
flagged kitchen. Dogs may be allowed in bedrooms if clean, but not at
breakfast; the landlady tell us they have a newfoundland that is confined
but does not like other dogs on her patch.

🍴 Very inexpensive lunchtime filled rolls are the only food; the decent evening meals (no choice) are for overnight guests.

Free house ~ Licensee Mary Short ~ Real ale ~ No credit cards ~ Open 12-2, 7-11 (10.30 Sun) ~ Bar food lunchtime rolls only ~ Well behaved, supervised children lunchtime only ~ Dogs allowed in bar ~ Bedrooms: £45/£65 *Recommended by Ann and Colin Hunt, Luke Morgan, Maddie Purvis, John and Hilary Murphy*

LADYBOWER RESERVOIR   SK2084 Map 7
Yorkshire Bridge 🍺
(01433) 651361 – www.yorkshire-bridge.co.uk
A6013 N of Bamford; S33 0AZ

Just south of the dam, with several real ales, friendly staff, tasty food and fine views; bedrooms

Just a short stroll from the Ladybower Dam and with wonderful walks from the front door, this is a friendly, family-run place. The cosy bar has a woodburning stove, countless tankards hanging from beams, lots of china plates, photographs and paintings on red walls, horsebrasses and copper items, and red plush dining chairs around a mix of tables on red patterned carpeting. There's a lot of space in several other rooms – including a light and airy garden room with fine valley views – and an assortment of seating ranging from wicker and metal to bentwood-style chairs around all sorts of wooden tables, on carpeting or flagstones, plus many more decorative plates and photos. Friendly staff serve Bombs Gone (named for the pub from Bradfield), Abbeydale Moonshine, Acorn Barnsley Bitter, Bradfield Farmers Blonde and Peak Bakewell Best Bitter on handpump, and nine wines by the glass. Dogs are allowed in some bedrooms, but not in the bar at mealtimes.

🍴 Quite a choice of tasty food includes sandwiches, chicken liver pâté, crayfish and avocado cocktail, brie, sun-dried tomato and red pepper quiche, chicken caesar salad, gammon steak with egg or pineapple, burger with toppings and chips, bass fillet with prawn and lemon butter, and puddings such as chocolate millionaires meringue pie and bakewell pudding. *Benchmark main dish: steak and kidney pie £10.75. Two-course evening meal £18.00.*

Free house ~ Licensee John Illingworth ~ Real ale ~ Open 11-11 (10.30 Sun) ~ Bar food 12-2.30, 5.30-8.30 (9 Fri, Sat); 12-8.30 Sun ~ Children welcome ~ Dogs allowed in bar and bedrooms ~ Wi-fi ~ Bedrooms: £60/£96 *Recommended by Hilary Forrest, Mark Hamill, Brian and Anna Marsden*

OLD BRAMPTON   SK3171 Map 7
Fox & Goose 🍷
(01246) 566335 – www.thefoxandgooseinn.com
Off A619 Chesterfield–Baslow at Wadshelf; S42 7JJ

Fine panoramic views for bustling pub with a restful bar, inventive food in light and airy restaurant, helpful staff and seats outside

It's believed that there was a resting place here 500 years ago on the old London–Manchester road, and this carefully restored pub still welcomes travellers today – but in much more comfort and style. The character beamed bar has a woodburning stove in a big stone fireplace, mate's chairs and button-back wall seating surrounding a mix of wooden tables on large flagstones, and Bradwell Farmers Blonde and Peak Bakewell Best Bitter and Chatsworth Gold on handpump and a dozen wines by the glass served by friendly staff. A small snug leads off with heavy beams, button-back wall seats, beige carpeting and a small fireplace, and there's also a dining room with double-sided plush banquette seating. If eating, most customers head for the airy Orangery restaurant with contemporary high-backed plush chairs around polished tables and lovely panoramic views through big picture windows. Outside, there are plenty of seats and tables under parasols on a terrace and decked area, and picnic-sets on gravel.

🍴 Highly thought-of food includes sandwiches, home-cured whisky and citrus salmon with pickled cucumber and horseradish crème fraîche, duck liver parfait with shallot chutney, bulgar wheat risotto with smoked cherry tomatoes, mascarpone, goats cheese mousse and tarragon oil, sausages of the day with caramelised apple and confit onion sauce, beer-battered haddock and chips, duck breast with star anise carrot purée and orange thyme jus, and puddings such as chocolate ganache tart and crème brûlée; they also offer a two- and three-course set lunch (not Sunday). *Benchmark main dish: pie of the day £12.95. Two-course evening meal £20.00.*

Free house ~ Licensee Craig Lynch ~ Real ale ~ Open 12-9; 12-11 Sat ~ Bar food 12-3, 5-9; 12-9 Fri, Sat; 12-6 Sun; not Mon Jan, Feb ~ Restaurant ~ Children welcome ~ Dogs allowed in bar ~ Wi-fi ~ Live music Sat evening *Recommended by Harvey Brown, Maddie Purvis, James Landor*

OVER HADDON
Lathkil ◗

SK2066 Map 7

(01629) 812501 – www.lathkil.co.uk

Village and inn signposted from B5055 just SW of Bakewell; DE45 1JE

Long-serving owners of traditional pub with super views, a good range of beers and well liked food; bedrooms

Many cyclists and walkers use the comfortable, warm bedrooms here as a base for exploring the Peak District National Park; breakfasts are hearty. The views are spectacular and can be enjoyed from seats in the walled garden and windows in the bar. The airy room on the right as you enter has a nice fire in an attractively carved fireplace, old-fashioned settles with upholstered cushions, chairs, black beams, a delft shelf of blue and white plates and some original prints and photographs. On the left, the sunny spacious dining area doubles as an evening restaurant and there's a woodburning stove. Adnams Ghost Ship, Blue Monkey BG Sips, Peak Summer Sovereign, Whim Hartington Bitter and Wincle Red Diesel on handpump, a reasonable range of wines (including mulled wine) and a decent selection of malt whiskies; background music, darts, TV and board games. Dogs are welcome, but muddy boots must be left in the lobby.

🍴 Enjoyable food includes sandwiches, goats cheese, pear and candied pecan salad, duck and orange pâté, spinach and ricotta cannelloni, venison and blackberry casserole, salmon parcel with tomato and ginger jam, steak and kidney pie, duck breast with cumberland sauce, rack of lamb with marmalade and mustard crumble topping, and puddings such as lemon meringue pie and a cheesecake of the day. *Benchmark main dish: chicken stuffed with sun-dried tomatoes and parma ham with stilton sauce £12.50. Two-course evening meal £19.00.*

Free house ~ Licensee Alice Grigor-Taylor ~ Real ale ~ Open 11-11; 12-10.30 Sun ~ Bar food 12-2 (2.30 weekends), 6.30-8.30 ~ Restaurant ~ Children welcome but over-10s only in the bar ~ Dogs allowed in bar and bedrooms ~ Wi-fi ~ Bedrooms: $65/$80 *Recommended by Ann and Tony Bennett-Hughes, Ann and Colin Hunt*

Cribbage is a card game using a block of wood with holes for matchsticks or special pins to score with; regulars in cribbage pubs are usually happy to teach strangers how to play.

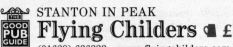

STANTON IN PEAK

SK2364 Map 7

Flying Childers 🍺 £

(01629) 636333 – www.flyingchilders.com

Village signposted from B6056 S of Bakewell; Main Road; DE4 2LW

Top notch beer and inexpensive simple bar lunches in a warm-hearted, unspoilt pub – a delight

In a beautiful steep stone village, this cottagey pub is named after an unbeatable racehorse of the early 18th c. The friendly landlord keeps Wells Bombardier and a couple of guests from breweries such as Abbeydale and Storm on handpump, and several wines by the glass. The best room in which to enjoy them is the snug little right-hand bar, virtually built for chat with its dark beam-and-plank ceiling, dark wall settles, single pew, plain tables, a hot coal and log fire, a few team photographs, dominoes and cribbage; background music. There's a bigger, equally unpretentious bar on the right. As well as seats out in front, there are picnic-sets in the well tended back garden. The surrounding walks are very fine and both walkers and their dogs are warmly welcomed; they keep doggie treats behind the bar.

 Simple lunchtime-only food cooked by the landlady includes filled rolls and toasties, home-made soups and weekend dishes such as liver and bacon, casseroles and local sausages.

Free house ~ Licensees Stuart and Mandy Redfern ~ Real ale ~ No credit cards ~ Open 12-2 (3 weekends), 7-11; closed Mon and Tues lunchtimes ~ Bar food 12-2 ~ Children in lounge bar only ~ Dogs allowed in bar ~ Live acoustic music and quiz nights (phone for details)
Recommended by Ann and Tony Bennett-Hughes, Jeremy Snow, Max Simons

WOOLLEY MOOR

SK3661 Map 7

White Horse 🌟 ♀ 🛏

(01246) 590319 – www.thewhitehorsewoolleymoor.co.uk

Badger Lane, off B6014 Matlock–Clay Cross; DE55 6FG

Attractive old dining pub with good food and drinks in pretty countryside; bedrooms

With Ogston Reservoir just a couple of minutes' drive away, this is a good choice for lunch. It's a neat and uncluttered place; the bar, snug and dining room have wooden dining chairs and tables, leather stools and sofas on flagstoned or wooden floors, a woodburning stove (in the bar), an open fire (in the dining room), boldly patterned curtains and blinds and little to distract the cream walls. Peak Bakewell Best Bitter and Chatsworth Gold on handpump and 13 wines by the glass. In the front garden you'll find picnic-sets under parasols on gravel, and boules. Contemporary bedroom suites (each with a private balcony) are well equipped and have floor-to-ceiling windows that give lovely views over the rolling countryside.

 Imaginative food includes ciabatta, crab dumplings in lime, ginger and coconut broth, haggis with crispy bacon and poached egg on toast, butternut squash, pea and rosemary risotto, lemonade-battered scampi with chunky chips, chicken breast with chive mash and mushroom and thyme sauce, calves liver with puy lentils and smoked bacon, braised carrots and shallots, local lamb rump with basil mash and red wine sauce, and puddings such as dark rum crème brûlée and orange polenta cake with clotted cream. *Benchmark main dish: crispy pork belly with spring onion mash and smoked bacon sauce £13.95. Two-course evening meal £20.50.*

Free house ~ Licensees David and Melanie Boulby ~ Real ale ~ Open 12-11; 12-6 Sun; closed Mon except bank holidays ~ Bar food 12-1.45, 6-8.45; 12-4 Sun ~ Restaurant ~ Children welcome ~ Wi-fi ~ Bedrooms: £139/£149 *Recommended by Jo Garnett, Dr Simon Innes, Derek and Sylvia Stephenson, Helena and Trevor Fraser*

Also Worth a Visit in Derbyshire

Besides the fully inspected pubs, you might like to try these pubs that have been recommended to us and described by readers. Do tell us what you think of them: feedback@goodguides.com

---

ALDERWASLEY   SK3153
Bear (01629) 822585
Left off A6 at Ambergate on to Holly Lane (turns into Jackass Lane), then right at end (staggered crossroads); DE56 2RD
Unspoilt country inn with beamed cottagey rooms, one with large glass chandelier over assorted tables and chairs, another with tartan-covered wall banquettes and double-sided woodburner, other décor includes staffordshire china ornaments, old paintings/engravings and a grandfather clock, Sharps Doom Bar, Timothy Taylors Landlord, Thornbridge Jaipur and guests, several wines by the glass (decent list) and malt whiskies, generously served food (all day Fri-Sun); children and dogs (in bar) welcome, seats in lovely garden with fine views, decent bedrooms plus two self-catering cottages, open all day. *(Stephen Shepherd)*

ASHFORD IN THE WATER SK1969
★ **Ashford Arms** (01629) 812725
Church Street; DE45 1QB Attractive 18th-c inn set in pretty village, good quality reasonably priced food including Weds steak night (32oz rump if you're really hungry), well kept Black Sheep and two local guests, nice wines, restaurant and dining conservatory; free wi-fi; children and dogs welcome, plenty of tables outside, eight comfortable bedrooms, open all day Sun (food till 5pm). *(Daphne and Robert Staples)*

ASHFORD IN THE WATER SK1969
★ **Bulls Head** (01629) 812931
Off A6 NW of Bakewell; Church Street (B6465, off A6020); DE45 1QB
Traditional 17th-c pub in attractive unspoilt village run by same family since 1953; cosy two-room beamed and carpeted bar with fires, one or two character gothic seats, spindleback and wheelback chairs around cast-iron-framed tables, local photographs and country prints on cream walls, four Robinsons ales and good choice of traditional food (not Tues evening), friendly efficient service; background music, daily papers; children welcome, dogs in bar, overshoes for walkers, hardwood tables and benches in front and in good-sized garden behind with boules and Jenga, open all day weekends in summer. *(Ann and Colin Hunt, Brian and Anna Marsden)*

ASTON-UPON-TRENT   SK4129
Malt (01332) 792256
M1 junction 24A on to A50, village signed left near Shardlow; The Green
(one-way street); DE72 2AA Comfortably modernised village pub with enjoyable good value food (not Sun evening, less choice Mon, Tues), well kept Bass, Marstons Pedigree, Sharps Doom Bar and three guests, friendly atmosphere; Tues quiz and some live music, TV; children and dogs welcome, back terrace, open all day. *(Peter Barrett)*

BAKEWELL   SK2168
Castle Inn (01629) 812103
Bridge Street; DE45 1DU Popular Georgian-fronted bay-windowed pub (actually dates from the 16th c) with well kept Greene King ales and a guest, decent competitively priced traditional food, three candlelit rooms with two open fires, flagstones, stripped stone and lots of pictures, good friendly service; background music; children and dogs welcome, level inside for wheelchairs but steps at front, tables out by road, attractive River Wye walks close by, four comfortable bedrooms, good breakfast, open (and food) all day, gets busy Mon market day. *(John Wooll)*

BAMFORD   SK2083
Anglers Rest (01433) 659317
A6013/Taggs Knoll; S33 0BQ Friendly community-owned pub with good local beers and tasty home-made food, café part and post office; Weds quiz and some live music including folk; children, walkers and dogs welcome, open all day. *(Luke Morgan)*

BASLOW   SK2572
Devonshire Arms (01246) 582551
A619; DE45 1SR Modernised village inn with opened-up bar and dining areas; a couple of Peak ales, Timothy Taylors Landlord and good wines by the glass, well liked imaginative food together with more traditional choices, friendly staff; rooms fan out from central bar with partitioning and swagged curtains creating cosy niches, range of seating including tub chairs, chesterfields and button-back leather wall banquettes, flagstones, tiles and carpeting, woodburner, coffee shop; background music, TV, free wi-fi; children and dogs (in bar) welcome, 11 comfortable bedrooms, open (and food) all day. *(Anne and Ben Smith, Neil Allen, Jo Garnett)*

BASLOW   SK2572
Wheatsheaf (01246) 582240
Nether End; DE45 1SR Cheerful Marstons inn (former coaching house) with comfortable carpeted interior, popular reasonably priced pub food including good children's menu, four well kept ales, prompt friendly service; free wi-fi; plenty of seats

outside and play area, bedrooms, handy for Chatsworth House, open all day. *(James Lander)*

BEELEY SK2667

★**Devonshire Arms** (01629) 733259

B6012, off A6 Matlock–Bakewell; DE4 2NR Lovely 18th-c stone coaching inn in attractive Peak District village near Chatsworth House; original part with black beams, flagstones, stripped stone and cheerful log fires, contrasting ultra-modern bistro/conservatory, up to five well kept changing ales, several wines by the glass and good range of malt whiskies, imaginative food (not cheap) using local ingredients; background music; children welcome, dogs in bar and some of the 14 bedrooms, open all day. *(Hilary Forrest, David Carr)*

BIRCHOVER SK2362

★**Druid** (01629) 653836

Off B5056; Main Street; DE4 2BL Welcoming 17th-c stone pub at edge of village; traditional quarry-tiled bar with open fire, dining areas either side plus more modern downstairs restaurant with wood-strip floor, good varied menu changing regularly including some unusual choices, up to five very well kept ales (tasters offered), Hogan's cider; background music and some live folk and jazz, free wi-fi; children welcome, dogs in bar, tables out in front on two levels, more seats in recently landscaped back garden, good area for walks, Nine Ladies stone circle nearby, open all day. *(Ben and Diane Bowie)*

BIRCHOVER SK2362

Red Lion (01629) 650363

Main Street; DE4 2BN Friendly early 18th-c stone-built pub with popular good value italian-influenced food (landlord is from Sardinia), also make their own cheese and have a deli next door, Sun carvery, well kept ales (up to five in summer) and four ciders, glass-covered well inside, woodburners; acoustic music session Sun evening; children and dogs welcome, nice rural views from outside seats, popular with walkers, open all day weekends, closed Mon, Tues. *(Max Simons)*

BONSALL SK2758

★**Barley Mow** (01629) 825685

Off A5012 W of Cromford; The Dale; DE4 2AY Basic one-room stone-built local with friendly colourful atmosphere, beams, pubby furnishings and woodburner, pictures and plenty of bric-a-brac, well kept local ales and real ciders, hearty helpings of good value food from short daily changing menu (be prepared to share a table); live music Fri and Sat, outside loos; children and dogs welcome, nice little front terrace, events such as hen racing and world record-breaking day, popular with UFO enthusiasts, walks from the pub, camping, open all day

weekends, closed Mon and lunchtimes Tues-Fri. *(Julie Braeburn)*

BONSALL SK2758

Kings Head (01629) 822703

Yeoman Street; DE4 2AA Welcoming 17th-c stone-built village local with two cosy beamed rooms, pubby furniture including cushioned wall benches on carpet or tiles, various knick-knacks and china, woodburners, three Batemans ales and good value home-made food, restaurant; karaoke last Sat of month, darts; children and dogs welcome, seats out at front and in back courtyard, handy for Limestone Way and other walks, open all day weekends, closed Mon lunchtime. *(Richard Stanfield)*

BRACKENFIELD SK3658

Plough (01629) 534437

A615 Matlock–Alfreton, about a mile NW of Wessington; DE55 6DD Much modernised 16th-c former farmhouse in lovely setting, welcoming three-level beamed bar with cheerful log-effect gas fire, well kept ales and plenty of wines by the glass, good popular food including weekday lunchtime set deal and blackboard specials, appealing lower-level restaurant extension; children welcome, large neatly kept gardens with terrace, closed Mon, otherwise open all day (food till 6pm Sun). *(Mr and Mrs R Shardlow)*

BUXTON SK0573

Old Sun (01298) 23452

High Street; SK17 6HA Revamped 17th-c coaching inn with several cosy linked areas, six well kept Marstons-related ales and good choice of wines by the glass, generous helpings of straightforward home-made food (not Sun evening, Mon-Thurs lunchtimes), low beams, panelling, bare boards and flagstones, soft lighting, old local photographs, open fire; background music, Sun quiz; children till 7pm, no dogs inside, roadside terrace, open all day. *(J A Snell, Ann and Tony Bennett-Hughes, Barry Collett)*

BUXTON SK0573

Tap House (01298) 214085

Old Court House, George Street; SK17 6AT Buxton brewery tap with their cask and craft range plus guests, also good selection of bottled beers, wines and spirits, tasty well priced food including some cooked in smoker, various interesting teas and coffees, friendly knowledgeable staff; daily newspapers; children welcome, some outside seating, open all day (till 1am Fri, Sat). *(Michael Mellers)*

CALVER SK2374

Derwentwater Arms (01433) 639211

In centre, bear left from Main Street into Folds Head; Low Side; S32 3XQ Elevated stone-built village pub with big windows looking down across car park to cricket pitch, good fairly priced pubby food from lunchtime baguettes to daily specials, three well kept ales including Adnams and Peak, friendly helpful service; darts; children, walkers and dogs (in bar) welcome, terraces on slopes below (disabled access from back car park), next door holiday cottage, open all day weekends. *(Brian and Anna Marsden)*

CASTLETON SK1582
Bulls Head (01433) 620256
Cross Street (A6187); S33 8WH
Imposing building spreading through several attractive linked areas, handsome panelling and pictures, appealing mix of comfortable seating including sofas and easy chairs, heavy drapes and coal fires, well kept Robinsons ales, popular food from sandwiches and hot ciabattas to pub standards and specials, helpful friendly service; background music; no dogs, some roadside picnic-sets, five bedrooms, open (and food) all day. *(James Lander)*

CASTLETON SK1482
George (01433) 620238
Castle Street; S33 8WG Busy old pub with flagstoned bar and restaurant, well kept Courage Best and other Charles Wells ales, good choice of malts, enjoyable reasonably priced pubby food including range of home-made pies, ancient beams and stripped stone, copper and brass, log fires; children and dogs welcome, tables out at front and behind, castle views, good walks, bedrooms, open all day, food all day Sat, till 6pm Sun. *(Max Simons)*

CASTLETON SK1583
Olde Cheshire Cheese
(01433) 620330 *How Lane; S33 8WJ*
Cosy 17th-c inn with two linked beamed and carpeted areas, six interesting ales such as Acorn, Bradfield and Peak, good range of reasonably priced wholesome food and decent house wines, quick friendly service, two gas woodburners, lots of photographs, toby jugs, plates and brassware, back dining room where children welcome; background and some live music, free wi-fi; dogs allowed in bar, ten bedrooms, parking across road, open (and food) all day. *(Eddie Edwards)*

CASTLETON SK1582
⭐ **Olde Nags Head** (01433) 620248
Cross Street (A6187); S33 8WH Small solidly built hotel dating from 17th c, interesting antique oak furniture and coal fire in civilised beamed and flagstoned bar, adjoining snug with leather sofas, steps down to restaurant, well kept Black Sheep, Sharps Doom Bar and guests, nice coffee and good locally sourced food, friendly helpful staff; live music Sat; children and dogs (in bar) welcome, nine comfortable bedrooms, good

breakfast, open all day. *(Steve and Suzanne Griffiths, Martin Day, Stuart Paulley)*

CHESTERFIELD SK3871
Chesterfield Arms (01246) 236634
Newbold Road (B6051); S41 7PH
Friendly 19th-c pub with 12 or more real ales including Everards Tiger, also craft beers, six ciders and good choice of wines and whiskies, basic snacks along with pie and curry nights, open fire, oak panelling and stripped wood/flagstoned floors, conservatory linking barn room; Weds quiz, live music last Thurs of month; dogs welcome, outside tables on decking, open all day (from 4pm Mon-Weds). *(Andrew Vincent)*

CHESTERFIELD SK3671
Manor (01246) 237555
Old Road, Brampton; near the school; S4 3QT Converted manor house down tree-lined drive, bar with tartan-upholstered armchairs by open fire, high stools around equally high tables, leather banquettes down one side creating booths, wood and flagstoned floors with chequered tiles by servery, ales such as Brampton and Peak, second room with tartan wall seating and a wide mix of dining chairs, good range of food from sandwiches and sharing plates up including Sun carvery and themed evenings, friendly staff; Tues quiz, Fri live music, fruit machine, TV; children welcome, tables under big parasols on front terrace, second terrace by play area, open all day. *(Andrew Vincent)*

CHESTERFIELD SK3670
Rose & Crown (01246) 563750
Old Road; S40 2QT Popular Brampton Brewery pub with their full range plus Everards and two changing guests, Weston's cider, enjoyable home-made food (not weekend evenings) from baguettes up, helpful staff and hands-on landlord, spacious traditional refurbishment with leather banquettes, panelling, wood or carpeted floors, brewery memorabilia and cast-iron Victorian fireplace, cosy snug area; Tues quiz, trad jazz first Sun of month, free wi-fi; tables outside, open all day. *(Trevor Cooper)*

CHINLEY SK0482
Paper Mill (01663) 750529
Whitehough Head Lane; SK23 6EJ
Under same management as next door Old Hall (see Main Entries); good selection of ales, craft kegs and plenty of bottled belgian beers, simple bar snacks including cheeseboards and mini ploughman's, also a raclette room (must book in advance – minimum eight people), good choice of teas and coffees, friendly helpful staff, flagstones, woodburners and open fire, local artwork for sale; TV for major sporting events; children,

walkers and dogs welcome, seats out at front and on split-level back terrace, plenty of good local walks, four bedrooms, closed weekdays till 5pm, open all day weekends. *(Ben and Diane Bowie)*

CLIFTON
SK1645
Cock (01335) 342654
Cross Side, opposite church; DE6 2GJ
Unpretentious two-bar beamed village local, comfortable and friendly, with jovial landlord, enjoyable reasonably priced home-made pub food from baguettes up, well kept Marstons Pedigree, Timothy Taylors Landlord and a couple of guests, decent choice of wines by the glass, separate dining room; quiz first Tues of month, darts; children, walkers and dogs welcome, garden with play equipment, closed Mon lunchtime. *(James Lander)*

COMBS
SK0378
Beehive (01298) 812758
Village signposted off B5470 W of Chapel-en-le-Frith; SK23 9UT Roomy, neat and comfortable, with emphasis on good freshly made food (all day Sun) from baguettes to steaks and interesting specials, also very good value weekday set menu, ales including Marstons Pedigree and a house beer from Wychwood, good choice of wines by the glass, log fire, heavy beams and copperware; background music, TV, Tues quiz; plenty of tables out in front, by lovely valley tucked away from main road, good walks, one-bed holiday cottage next door, open all day. *(G Whitehurst, Brian and Anna Marsden)*

CRICH
SK3454
Cliff (01773) 852444
Cromford Road, Town End; DE4 5DP
Unpretentious little two-room roadside pub, well kept ales such as Blue Monkey, Buxton, Dancing Duck and Sharps, generous helpings of good value straightforward food (not weekend evenings or Mon), welcoming staff and friendly regulars, two woodburners; maybe Sun folk night; children and dogs welcome, great views and walks, handy for National Tramway Museum, open all day weekends, closed weekday lunchtimes. *(Robert Turnham)*

CROWDECOTE
SK1065
Packhorse (01298) 83618
B5055 W of Bakewell; SK17 0DB Small three-room 16th-c pub in lovely setting, welcoming landlord and staff, good reasonably priced home-made food from weekday light bites and sandwiches up, four well kept changing ales, split-level interior with brick or carpeted floors, stripped-stone walls, open fire and two woodburners; Thurs quiz, pool and darts; children and dogs welcome, tables out behind, beautiful views and a popular walking route, closed Mon, Tues. *(Peter Barrett)*

DERBY
SK3538
Abbey Inn (01332) 558297
Darley Street; DE22 1DX Former abbey gatehouse opposite park (pleasant riverside walk from centre), massive 15th-c or older stonework remnants, brick floor, studded oak doors, coal fire in big inglenook, stone spiral staircase to upper bar (not always staffed) with oak rafters and tapestries, bargain Sam Smiths and reasonably priced bar food; the lavatories with their beams, stonework and tiles are worth a look too; children and dogs (downstairs) welcome, open all day. *(Luke Morgan)*

DERBY
SK3635
Alexandra (01332) 293993
Siddals Road; DE1 2QE Imposing Victorian pub, popular locally; two simple rooms with traditional furnishings on bare boards or carpet, railway prints/memorabilia, well kept Castle Rock and several quickly changing microbrewery guests, lots of continental bottled beers with more on tap, snack food such as pork pies and cobs; background music; children and dogs welcome, nicely planted backyard, 1960s locomotive cab in car park, four bedrooms, open all day. *(Luke Morgan)*

DERBY
SK3535
Babington Arms (01332) 383647
Babington Lane; DE1 1TA Large open-plan Wetherspoons with 16 real ales and four proper ciders, good friendly service, usual well priced food, comfortable seating with steps up to relaxed back area; TVs, free wi-fi; children welcome, seats out at front by pavement, open all day from 8am for breakfast. *(Andrew Vincent)*

DERBY
SK3536
Brewery Tap (01332) 366283
Derwent Street/Exeter Place; DE1 2ED
19th-c Derby Brewing Co pub (aka Royal Standard) with unusual bowed end, ten ales including five of their own from curved brick counter, lots of bottled imports, decent good value food all day (till 5pm Sun) from sandwiches and baked potatoes up, open-plan bare-boards interior with two high-ceilinged drinking areas, small upstairs room and roof terrace overlooking the Derwent; live music Tues; open all day (till 1am Fri, Sat). *(Peter Barrett)*

DERBY
SK3635
Brunswick (01332) 290677
Railway Terrace; close to Derby Midland Station; DE1 2RU One of Britain's oldest railwaymen's pubs, up to 16 ales including Everards and selection from own microbrewery, real ciders and good choice of bottled beers, cheap traditional lunchtime food including good sandwiches, high-ceilinged panelled bar, snug with coal fire, chatty front parlour, interesting

old train photographs and prints; quiz Mon, jazz upstairs Thurs, darts, TV, games machine, free wi-fi; dogs welcome, walled beer garden and side terrace, open all day. *(Dr J Barrie Jones)*

DERBY SK3435
Exeter Arms (01332) 605323
Exeter Place; DE1 2EU Victorian survivor amid 1930s apartment blocks and car parks; recently extended into next-door cottage, but keeping its traditional character including tiled-floor snug with curved wall benches and polished open range, friendly staff, well kept Dancing Duck, Marstons and two guests, good all-day food (till 6pm Sun) from snacks and pubby choices up; quiz Mon, summer live music Sat in small garden with outside bar (beer festivals), open all day (till midnight Fri, Sat). *(Luke Morgan)*

DERBY SK3534
Falstaff (01332) 342902
Silver Hill Road, off Normanton Road; DE23 6UJ Big Victorian red-brick corner pub (aka the Folly) brewing its own good value ales, two friendly bars with interesting collection of memorabilia including brewerania, games room; children (till 6pm) and dogs welcome, outside seating area, open all day. *(Richard Stanfield)*

DERBY SK3436
Five Lamps (01332) 348730
Duffield Road; DE1 3BH Corner pub with opened-up but well divided interior around central servery, wood-strip or carpeted floors, panelling, leather button-back bench seats and small balustraded raised section, a dozen well kept ales such as Everards, Oakham, Peak and Whim along with a house beer from Derby, real ciders, decent good value pubby food (not Sun evening); background music, TV; a few picnic-sets outside, open all day (till midnight Fri, Sat). *(Paul Scofield)*

DERBY SK3536
Olde Dolphin (01332) 267711
Queen Street; DE1 3DL Quaint 16th-c timber-framed pub just below cathedral, four small dark unpretentious rooms including appealing snug, big bowed black beams, shiny panelling, opaque leaded windows, lantern lights and coal fires, half a dozen predominantly mainstream ales, reasonably priced bar food and upstairs evening restaurant (Thurs-Sat), carvery Sun; quiz nights; no under-14s inside, sizeable outside area for drinkers/smokers, open all day. *(Luke Morgan)*

DERBY SK3335
Rowditch (01332) 343123
Uttoxeter New Road (A516); DE22 3LL Popular character local with own microbrewery (well kept Marstons Pedigree and guests too), friendly landlord, two bars and attractive little snug on right, coal fire;

no children, dogs welcome at weekends, pleasant back garden, closed weekday lunchtimes. *(Max Simons)*

DERBY SK3536
Silk Mill (01332) 349160
Full Street; DE1 3AF Refurbished 1920s pub keeping traditional feel, central bar with lounge and skylit dining area off, plush banquettes, cushioned stools and cast-iron-framed tables on wood floors, open fires, one or two quirky touches such as fish wallpaper, a stuffed crocodile and antler chandelier, good choice of real ales and ciders, several wines by the glass, enjoyable food (all day weekdays, till 8pm Sun) from sandwiches and sharing boards up, friendly service; daily newspapers and free wi-fi; open all day. *(Tim and Sarah Smythe-Brown)*

DUFFIELD SK3543
Pattern Makers Arms
(01332) 842844 *Crown Street, off King Street; DE56 4EY* Welcoming Edwardian backstreet local with well kept Bass (from the jug), Marstons, Timothy Taylors and guests, bargain lunchtime food (under-10s eat free Mon-Sat), pubby furniture on wood or carpeted floors, upholstered banquettes, some stained-glass and etched windows; background music, TV, darts, pool and other games, Sun quiz; beer garden behind, open all day Fri-Sun. *(Andrew Vincent)*

EARL STERNDALE SK0966
★ Quiet Woman (01298) 83211
Village signed off B5053 S of Buxton; SK17 0BU Old-fashioned unchanging country local in lovely Peak District countryside, simple beamed interior with plain furniture on quarry tiles, china ornaments and coal fire, well kept Marstons Bitter and guests, own-label bottled beers (available in gift packs), good pork pies, family room with pool, skittles and darts; no dogs inside, picnic-sets out in front along with budgies, hens, ducks and donkeys, you can buy free-range eggs, local poetry books and even hay, good hikes across nearby Dove Valley towards Longnor and Hollinsclough, small campsite next door with caravan for hire. *(Ann and Tony Bennett-Hughes, Ann and Colin Hunt, M J Winterton)*

EDALE SK1285
Old Nags Head (01433) 670291
Off A625 E of Chapel-en-le-Frith; Grindsbrook Booth; S33 7ZD Relaxed well used traditional pub at start of Pennine Way, four well kept local ales, food from sandwiches up including carvery, friendly service, log fire, flagstoned area for booted walkers, airy back family room; TV, pool and darts; dogs welcome, front terrace and garden, two self-catering cottages, open (and food) all day, can get very busy weekends. *(David Eberlin)*

EDLASTON   SK1842

Shire Horse (01335) 342714

*Off A515 S of Ashbourne, just beside
Wyaston; DE6 2DQ* Timbered pub with
good mix of drinkers and diners in large
bar with open fire and separate restaurant/
conservatory (being refurbished as we
went to press), friendly helpful staff, popular
fairly priced food (not Sun evening)
including specials board, Marstons Pedigree
and Sharps Doom Bar, good house wines;
children and dogs (in bar) welcome, tables
out in front and in back garden with terrace,
peaceful spot and nice views, open all day Sun.
(Colin Bateman)

ELMTON   SK5073

★**Elm Tree** (01909) 721261

Off B6417 S of Clowne; S80 4LS Popular
softly lit country pub run well by enthusiastic
owners, good choice of enjoyable nicely
presented food all day (till 6pm Sun) from
simple inexpensive dishes up, weekday
lunchtime set menu, well kept Black Sheep
plus one or two guests, several ciders
and wide range of wines, good friendly
service even when busy, stripped stone and
panelling, log fire, back barn restaurant
(mainly for functions); children and dogs
(in bar) welcome, garden tables, play area,
closed Tues. *(Derek and Sylvia Stephenson)*

EYAM   SK2276

Miners Arms (01433) 630853

*Off A632 Chesterfield–Chapel-en-le-Frith;
Water Lane; S32 5RG* Three-roomed
17th-c beamed inn with enjoyable food
(not Sun evening) from sandwiches up
including good lamb tagine, Greene King and
Theakstons ales, friendly efficient service; TV,
background music, free wi-fi; children and
dogs welcome, picnic-sets out at front and
in back garden, nice walks nearby especially
below Froggatt Edge, seven bedrooms, open
all day. *(Dave Braisted)*

FOOLOW   SK1976

★**Bulls Head** (01433) 630873

*Village signposted off A623 Baslow–
Tideswell; S32 5QR* Friendly pub by
green in pretty upland village; simply
furnished flagstoned bar with interesting
collection of photographs including some
saucy Edwardian ones, Black Sheep, Peak
and two guests, over 30 malts, good food
(all day Sun) with more elaborate choices
Sat evening, OAP weekday lunch deal, step
down to former stables with high ceiling
joists, stripped stone and woodburner, sedate
partly panelled dining room with plates on
delft shelves; background music; children,
walkers and dogs welcome, side picnic-sets
with nice views, paths from here out over
rolling pasture enclosed by dry stone walls,
three bedrooms, closed Mon. *(Ann and Tony
Bennett-Hughes)*

FROGGATT EDGE   SK2476

★**Chequers** (01433) 630231

A625, off A623 N of Bakewell; S32 3ZJ
Roadside dining pub surrounded by lovely
countryside; opened-up bar and eating areas,
cushioned settles, farmhouse and captain's
chairs around mix of tables, antique prints,
longcase clock and woodburner, well liked
interesting food (all day weekends) along
with more traditional choices, home-made
chutneys and preserves for sale, Bradfield,
Peak and a guest ale, several wines by the
glass, friendly helpful staff; background
music; children welcome, no dogs inside,
garden with Froggatt Edge escarpment up
through woods behind, six comfortable clean
bedrooms, good breakfast, open all day.
(Tim and Sarah Smythe-Brown)

FROGGATT EDGE   SK2577

Grouse (01433) 630423

*Longshaw, off B6054 NE of Froggatt;
S11 7TZ* Nicely old-fashioned beamed pub
in same family since 1965, carpeted front
bar with wall benches and other seating, log
fire, back bar with coal-effect gas fire, small
conservatory, enjoyable hearty home-made
food (all day Sun, not Mon evening) from nice
sandwiches to blackboard specials, four well
kept Marstons-related beers and over 40 malt
whiskies, friendly prompt service; children
(in back room) and dogs welcome, terrace
seating, lovely views and good moorland
walks, open all day weekends. *(James Lander)*

GLOSSOP   SK0394

Star (01457) 853072

Howard Street; SK13 7DD Unpretentious
corner alehouse opposite station with four
well kept changing ales and Weston's Old
Rosie cider, no food, traditional layout
including flagstoned tap room with hatch
service, old local photographs; dogs welcome
(resident alsatian called Heidi), open all
day from 4pm (2pm Fri, noon Sat, Sun).
(Andrew Vincent)

GRINDLEFORD   SK2378

Sir William (01433) 630303

B6001, opposite war memorial; S32 2HS
Popular refurbished pub-hotel under
welcoming newish management; good food
from sandwiches up, Greene King ales and
guests, friendly helpful service, restaurant;
Sun quiz, free wi-fi; children, walkers
and dogs (in a couple of areas) welcome,
splendid view especially from terrace, eight
comfortable bedrooms. *(W K Wood)*

HARDWICK HALL   SK4663

★**Hardwick Inn** (01246) 850245

*Quite handy for M1 junction 29;
S44 5QJ* Popular golden-stone pub dating
from the 15th c at south park gate of
Hardwick Hall (NT); several linked rooms
including proper bar, open fires, fine range
of some 220 malt whiskies and plenty of

wines by the glass, well kept Black Sheep, Peak, Theakstons and a Brampton ale badged for the pub, generous helpings of good reasonably priced bar food plus carvery restaurant, long-serving licensees and efficient friendly staff; unobtrusive background music; children allowed away from bar areas, dogs in one part, tables out at front and in pleasant back garden, open all day. *(Luke Morgan)*

HARTINGTON
SK1260
Charles Cotton (01298) 84229
Market Place; SK17 0AL Popular stone-built hotel in attractive village centre; large comfortable bar-bistro with open fire, enjoyable food from lunchtime sandwiches and snacks up (more restaurant evening choice), Jennings, Whim and a beer badged for the pub from Wincle, nice wines and italian coffee, friendly helpful service, restaurant and summer tearoom; background and some live music; children, walkers and dogs (in bar) welcome, seats out at front and in small back garden, 17 bedrooms, open all day. *(Barry Collett)*

HARTINGTON
SK1260
Devonshire Arms (01298) 84232
Market Place; SK17 0AL
Traditional unpretentious two-bar pub in attractive village, welcoming and cheerful, with generous helpings of enjoyable home-made food (smaller servings available), ales such as Black Sheep and Jennings, log fires; maybe background music; children and dogs welcome, tables out in front facing duck pond, more in small garden, good walks, open (and food) all day weekends. *(Steve and Suzanne Griffiths, Brian and Anna Marsden)*

HATHERSAGE
SK2381
★**Scotsmans Pack** (01433) 650253
School Lane, off A6187; S32 1BZ Bustling inn equally popular with drinkers and diners; dark panelled rooms with lots of interesting knick-knacks, upholstered gingham stools and dining chairs, cushioned wall seats and assortment of tables, woodburner, five well kept Marstons-related ales and enjoyable food including daily specials; background and some live music, quiz night Thurs, TV, darts; picnic-sets on terrace overlooking trout stream, plenty of surrounding walks, five bedrooms, open all day. *(Julie Braeburn)*

HEAGE
SK3750
Black Boy (01773) 856799
Old Road (B6013); DE56 2BN
Modernised village pub-restaurant with popular good value food including fish specials in bar and upstairs dining area,

well kept changing ales and real cider, friendly staff, open fire; children welcome, no dogs, small outside seating area, open all day. *(Max Simons)*

HOGNASTON
SK2350
★**Red Lion** (01335) 370396
Off B5035 Ashbourne–Wirksworth; DE6 1PR Traditional 17th-c village inn with open-plan beamed bar, three fires, attractive mix of old tables, curved settles and other seats on ancient flagstones, good well presented home-made food from shortish menu in bar and conservatory, nice wines by the glass, Marstons Pedigree and guests; background music; picnic-sets in field behind, boules, handy for Carsington Water, three good bedrooms, big breakfast. *(Andrew Vincent)*

HOLBROOK
SK3645
★**Dead Poets** (01332) 780301
Chapel Street; village signed off A6 S of Belper; DE56 0TQ Friendly drinkers' local with up to nine real ales (some served from jugs), traditional ciders and good range of other drinks, helpful knowledgeable landlord, filled cobs and good value weekday bar food, simple cottagey décor with beams, stripped-stone walls and broad flagstones, high-backed settles forming booths, big log fire, plenty of tucked-away corners, woodburner in snug, children allowed in back conservatory till 8pm; quiet background music, no credit cards; dogs welcome, seats out at back, open all day Fri-Sun. *(James Lander)*

HOPE
SK1783
★**Cheshire Cheese** (01433) 620381
Off A6187, towards Edale; S33 6ZF
16th-c traditional stone inn with snug oak-beamed rooms on different levels, open fires, red carpets or stone floors, straightforward furnishings and gleaming brasses, up to five ales such as Abbeydale, Bradfield and Peak, a dozen malt whiskies and enjoyable food from sandwiches and pub favourites up, friendly service; Weds quiz, folk night first and third Thurs of month; children welcome, dogs in bar, good local walks in the summits of Lose Hill and Win Hill or the cave district around Castleton, four bedrooms, limited parking, open all day weekends in summer, closed Mon. *(David Carr)*

HORSLEY WOODHOUSE
SK3944
Old Oak (01332) 881299
Main Street (A609 Belper–Ilkeston); DE7 6AW Busy roadside local linked to nearby Bottle Brook and Leadmill microbreweries, their ales and guests plus weekend back bar with another eight well priced beers tapped from the

---

Places with gardens or terraces usually let children sit there – we note in the text the very few exceptions that don't.

cask, farm ciders, basic snacks (can also bring your own food), beamed rooms with blazing coal fires; occasional live music; children and dogs welcome, hatch to covered courtyard tables, nice views, closed weekday lunchtimes till 4pm, open all day weekends. *(Ben and Diane Bowie)*

ILKESTON   SK4742
Dewdrop (0115) 932 9684
Station Street, Ilkeston junction, off A6096; DE7 5TE Large Victorian red-brick corner local in old industrial area, not strong on bar comfort but popular for its well kept beers (up to eight) such as Acorn, Blue Monkey, Bobs and Oakham, simple bar snacks, back lounge with fire and piano, connecting lobby to front public bar with pool, darts and TV, some Barnes Wallis memorabilia; sheltered outside seating at back, walks by former Nottingham Canal, open all day weekends, closed weekday lunchtimes. *(Peter Barrett)*

ILKESTON   SK4641
Spanish Bar (0115) 930 8666
South Street; DE7 5QJ Busy recently refurbished bar with half a dozen well kept/priced ales, traditional ciders and bottled belgian beers, friendly efficient staff, evening overspill room; Tues quiz; dogs welcome, small back garden and skittle alley, open all day. *(Peter Barrett)*

KING'S NEWTON   SK3826
Hardinge Arms (01332) 863808
Not far from M1 junction 23A, via A453 to Isley, then off Melbourne/Wilson Road; Main Street; DE73 8BX Bright and spacious old pub with chunky low beams and brick, wood and flagstone floors, enjoyable bar and evening restaurant food, Mon steak night, well kept Bass, Timothy Taylors and a guest, good wine range, quick friendly service; children in eating areas, bedrooms in converted stables, good breakfast, handy for Donington Park and East Midlands Airport, open all day, no food Sun evening. *(Peter Hawkins)*

LADYBOWER RESERVOIR   SK1986
Ladybower Inn (01433) 651241
A57 Sheffield–Glossop, just E of junction with A6013; S33 0AX Recently taken over by Batemans and handy for the huge nearby reservoir; their ales and a couple of guests, enjoyable pubby food from sandwiches up, friendly service, various traditionally furnished carpeted areas, cast-iron fireplaces, Lancaster Bomber pictures recalling the Dambusters' practice runs on the reservoir; background music, darts, free wi-fi; children and dogs (in bar) welcome,

picnic-sets out at front, annexe bedrooms, open (and food) all day. *(Martin Day, Lindy Andrews)*

LITTLE LONGSTONE   SK1971
Packhorse (01629) 640471
Off A6 NW of Bakewell via Monsal Dale; DE45 1NN Three comfortable linked beamed rooms, pine tables on flagstones, well kept Thornbridge ales and a guest, popular generously served home-made food from daily changing blackboard including good Sun lunch, affordably priced wine list, friendly accommodating service, coal fires; Thurs quiz; children, dogs and hikers welcome (on Monsal Trail), terrace in steep little back garden, open (and food) all day weekends. *(Ann and Tony Bennett-Hughes, Dave and Alison Baker)*

LITTON   SK1675
Red Lion (01298) 871458
Village signposted off A623, between B6465 and B6049 junctions; also signposted off B6049; SK17 8QU Welcoming traditional village pub, two linked front rooms with low beams, panelling and open fires, bigger stripped-stone back room, three well kept ales and enjoyable home-made food from sandwiches to daily specials; dogs allowed, seats and tables in front with more on village green, good walks in nearby Dales, open (and food) all day. *(Brian and Anna Marsden, Malcolm and Pauline Pellatt, Alan Johnson, Barry Collett)*

LULLINGTON   SK2513
Colvile Arms (01827) 373212
Off A444 S of Burton; Main Street; DE12 8EG Popular 18th-c village pub with high-backed settles in simple panelled bar, cosy comfortable beamed lounge, pleasant atmosphere and friendly staff, well kept Bass, Marstons Pedigree and a guest, no food except cobs; soft background music; picnic-sets on small sheltered back lawn, closed lunchtimes apart from Sun. *(Luke Morgan)*

MAKENEY   SK3544
★ **Holly Bush** (01332) 841729
From A6 heading N after Duffield, take first right after crossing River Derwent, then first left; DE56 0RX Unspoilt 17th-c two-bar village pub (former farmhouse) with three blazing fires (one in old-fashioned range by snug's curved high-backed settle), beams and black panelling, tiled and flagstone floors, well kept changing ales (some served from jugs), craft beers and real cider, enjoyable lunchtime food (not Mon, Tues) from rolls and pork pies up, lobby with hatch service; beer festivals and occasional live music; children, walkers

---

If you stay overnight in an inn or hotel, they are allowed to serve you an alcoholic drink at any hour of the day or night.

and dogs welcome, picnic-sets outside, open all day. *(Paul Scofield)*

MARSTON MONTGOMERY   SK1338
Crown   (01889) 591430
On corner of Thurvaston Road and Barway; DE6 2FF Recently refurbished red-brick beamed village pub, clean and bright, with friendly helpful staff, popular good value food (till 7.30pm Sun, not Mon), three real ales including Marstons Pedigree and several wines by the glass, restaurant; some live music; children and dogs welcome, disabled access, terrace tables, seven good bedrooms, open all day (Mon from 3pm). *(Andrew Vincent)*

MATLOCK   SK2960
Thorn Tree   (01629) 580295
Jackson Road, Matlock Bank; DE4 3JQ Superb valley views to Riber Castle from this homely 19th-c stone-built local, Bass, Greene King, Nottingham, Timothy Taylors and guests, simple well cooked food (Tues-Fri lunchtimes, Sun 5-6.30pm, Weds pie night), friendly staff and regulars; free wi-fi; children and dogs welcome, closed Mon lunchtime, open all day Fri-Sun. *(Max Simons)*

MILLERS DALE   SK1473
Anglers Rest   (01298) 871323
Just down Litton Lane; pub is PH on OS Sheet 119 map reference 142734; SK17 8SN Creeper-clad pub in lovely quiet riverside setting on Monsal Trail; two bars and dining room, log fires, Adnams, Storm and two usually local guests, enjoyable simple food, cheery helpful service, reasonable prices, darts, pool; muddy walkers and dogs in public bar; children welcome, wonderful gorge views and river walks, self-catering apartment, open all day Sat, till 5pm Sun. *(Ann and Tony Bennett-Hughes)*

MILLTOWN   SK3561
Miners Arms   (01246) 590218
Off B6036 SE of Ashover; Oakstedge Lane; S45 0HA L-shaped stone dining pub with good freshly made food from well priced blackboard menu (booking advised), nice wines and one changing real ale, friendly staff, restored spotlessly kept interior, log fires; children welcome, no dogs inside, attractive country walks from the door, closed Mon-Weds (open Weds in Dec). *(Peter Barrett)*

MONSAL HEAD   SK1871
★**Monsal Head Hotel**   (01629) 640250
B6465; DE45 1NL Outstanding hilltop location for this friendly inn; cosy stables bar with stripped timber horse-stalls, harness and brassware, cushioned oak pews, farmhouse chairs and benches on flagstones, big open fire, good selection of mainly local ales including one badged for them from Pennine, german bottled beers and plenty of wines by the glass, enjoyable locally sourced food from lunchtime sandwiches

up (they may ask to keep your credit card while you eat), elegant restaurant; children (over 3), muddy walkers and well behaved dogs welcome, big garden, stunning views of Monsal Dale with its huge viaduct, seven comfortable bedrooms, open all day till midnight. *(Ann and Colin Hunt)*

MONYASH   SK1566
★**Bulls Head**   (01629) 812372
B5055 W of Bakewell; DE45 1JH Rambling stone pub with high-ceilinged rooms, straightforward traditional furnishings including plush stools lined along bar, horse pictures and a shelf of china, log fire, four real ales such as Black Sheep and Peak Chatsworth Gold, restaurant with high-backed dining chairs on heated stone floor, popular traditional food (all day weekends) from sandwiches and baked potatoes up, friendly service, small back room with darts, board games and pool; background music; children and dogs welcome, plenty of picnic-sets under parasols in big garden, gate leading to well equipped public play area, good surrounding walks, open all day in high summer, all day Fri-Sun other times. *(Ann and Colin Hunt)*

MOORWOOD MOOR   SK3656
White Hart   (01629) 534888
Inns Lane; village signed from South Wingfield; DE55 7NU Cleanly updated country inn with good food including deals in bar and restaurant, helpful attentive staff, well kept Sharps Doom Bar, Timothy Taylors Landlord and a couple of local guests; children welcome, ten modern bedrooms, open (and food) all day. *(Derek and Sylvia Stephenson)*

NEW MILLS   SJ9886
Fox   (0161) 427 1634
Brook Bottom Road; SK22 3AY Tucked-away old-fashioned country local at end of single-track road, Robinsons ales and good value pub food (no credit cards), log fire; darts and pool; children and dogs welcome, lots of tables outside, good walking area, open all day Fri-Sun, closed Mon evening. *(Max Simons)*

NEWTON SOLNEY   SK2825
Brickmakers Arms   (01283) 702558
Main Street (B5008 NE of Burton); DE15 0SJ Friendly end-of-terrace beamed village pub owned by Burton Bridge Brewery and under new licensees; four of their well kept ales and a couple of guests including Timothy Taylors Landlord, real ciders and plenty of bottled beers, no food, two rooms off bar, one with original panelling and delft shelf displaying jugs and plates, pubby furniture, built-in wall seats and coal fires, area with books; Mon quiz, Tues bingo, Thurs poker; tables on terrace, open all day weekends, closed lunchtimes during the week. *(Julie Braeburn)*

OCKBROOK
SK4236
Royal Oak (01332) 662378
Off B6096 just outside Spondon; Green Lane; DE72 3SE 18th-c village local run by same friendly family since 1953; good value honest food (not weekend evenings) from good lunchtime cobs to steaks, well kept Bass and interesting guest beers, tile-floored tap room, carpeted snug, inner bar with Victorian prints, larger and lighter side room, nice old settle in entrance corridor, open fires; darts and dominoes, some live music; children welcome, dogs in the evening, disabled access, sheltered cottage garden and cobbled front courtyard, separate play area, open all day weekends. *(Ben and Diane Bowie)*

OSMASTON
SK1943
Shoulder of Mutton (01335) 342371
Off A52 SE of Ashbourne; DE6 1LW Down-to-earth red-brick beamed pub with post office/shop, three well kept ales including Marstons Pedigree, enjoyable generous home-made food, good friendly service; fortnightly quiz Sun, free wi-fi; picnic-sets in attractive garden, farmland views, peaceful pretty village with thatched cottages, duck pond and good walks. *(Andrew Vincent)*

PARWICH
SK1854
★Sycamore (01335) 390212
By church; DE6 1QL Chatty old country pub with cheerful welcoming landlady, Robinsons ales and good honest home-made food, log fire in neat traditional back bar, pool in small front hatch-served games room, another room serving as proper village shop; free wi-fi; children and dogs welcome, tables in front courtyard, picnic-sets on neat side grass, good walks, open all day weekends. *(Peter Barrett)*

PILSLEY
SK2371
★Devonshire Arms (01246) 583258
Village signposted off A619 W of Baslow, and pub just below B6048; High Street; DE45 1UL Civilised little country inn on the Chatsworth Estate; gentle contemporary slant with flagstoned bar and several fairly compact areas off (each with own character), log fires in three fireplaces, comfortable seating and big modern paintings, well stocked bar with four local ales and several wines by the glass, good from lunchtime open sandwiches up using Estate produce, friendly efficient staff; children and dogs welcome, a few tables outside, Chatsworth farm shop at the top of lane, bedrooms, open all day. *(Malcolm and Pauline Pellatt, Ann and Colin Hunt, Stephen Woad)*

REPTON
SK3027
Boot (01283) 346047
Boot Hill; DE65 6FT Recently restored 18th-c beamed inn (sister to the Dragon at Willington); own good microbrews

(tasting notes provided) and very well liked interesting food (booking advised, particularly at weekends) including breakfast till 11pm and set lunch deal, friendly efficient young staff, modernised L-shaped interior; live music Fri and Sat, quiz Sun; children and dogs (in bar area) welcome, split-level walled garden, nine bedrooms, open all day. *(Clive and Fran Dutson, Stephen Shepherd)*

REPTON
SK3026
Bulls Head (01283) 704422
High Street; DE65 6GF Lively village pub with interesting décor in various interconnecting bars, beams and pillars, mix of wooden dining chairs, settles and built-in wall seats with scatter cushions, squashy sofas, bare boards, flagstones and log fires, driftwood sculptures, animal hide décor and an arty bull's head, ales from Marstons, Shardlow and Purity, 15 wines by the glass and 20 malt whiskies, popular food including wood-fired pizzas, cheerful staff, upstairs restaurant; background music, free wi-fi; children and dogs (in bar) welcome, sizeable heated terrace with neatly set tables and chairs under big parasols, open (and food) all day. *(Stephen Shepherd)*

RIPLEY
SK3950
Talbot Taphouse (01773) 742626
Butterley Hill; DE5 3LT Full range of local Amber ales and changing guests kept well by knowledgeable landlord, also traditional ciders, draught belgian and bottled beers, long narrow panelled room with comfy chairs, open fire in brick fireplace, bar billiards and table skittles, friendly atmosphere; open early afternoon Fri-Sun, from 5pm other days. *(James Lander)*

ROWSLEY
SK2565
★Peacock (01629) 733518
Bakewell Road; DE4 2EB Civilised small 17th-c country hotel; comfortable seating in spacious modern lounge, inner bar with log fire, bare stone walls and some Robert 'Mouseman' Thompson furniture, good if not cheap food from lunchtime sandwiches to restaurant meals, Peak ales, nice wines and well served coffee, pleasant helpful staff; attractive riverside gardens, trout fishing, 14 good bedrooms. *(Tim and Sarah Smythe-Brown)*

SHARDLOW
SK4430
Malt Shovel (01332) 792066
3.5 miles from M1 junction 24, via A6 towards Derby; The Wharf; DE72 2HG Welcoming canalside pub in 18th-c former maltings, interesting odd-angled layout with cosy corners, Marstons Pedigree and a beer badged for the pub, good value tasty home-made food from sandwiches and baked potatoes to specials such as notable beetroot-cured salmon, evening food Thurs only (thai menu), quick friendly service, beams, panelling and central open fire; live music

Sun, free wi-fi; children and dogs welcome, lots of terrace tables by Trent & Mersey Canal, pretty hanging baskets, open all day. *(Dr D J and Mrs S C Walker, John Beeken)*

SHARDLOW   SK4429
Old Crown (01332) 792392
Off A50 just W of M1 junction 24; Cavendish Bridge, E of village; DE72 2HL Good value pub with half a dozen well kept Marstons-related ales and decent choice of malt whiskies, pubby food (not Sun evening, Mon) from sandwiches and baguettes up, beams with masses of jugs and mugs, walls covered with other bric-a-brac and breweriana, big inglenook; quiz Mon, fortnightly live music Tues; children and dogs welcome, garden with play area, open all day. *(Peter Barrett)*

SHELDON   SK1768
★ ## Cock & Pullet (01629) 814292
Village signed off A6 just W of Ashford; DE45 1QS Charming no-frills village pub with low beams, exposed stonework, flagstones and open fire, cheerful mismatch of furnishings, large collection of clocks and various representations of poultry (some stuffed), well kept Black Sheep, Sharps and Timothy Taylors, good simple food from shortish menu, reasonable prices and nice staff, pool and TV in plainer public bar; quiet background music, no credit cards; children and dogs welcome, seats and water feature on pleasant back terrace, pretty village just off Limestone Way and popular all year with walkers, clean bedrooms, open all day. *(Ann and Tony Bennett-Hughes)*

SHIRLEY   SK2141
Saracens Head (01335) 360330
Church Lane; DE6 3AS Modernised late 18th-c dining pub in attractive village; good range of interesting well presented food from pubby to more expensive restaurant dishes, four Greene King ales, speciality coffees, simple country-style dining furniture and two pretty working art nouveau fireplaces; background music; children and dogs (in bar area) welcome, picnic-sets out in front and on back terrace, open all day Sun. *(Julie Braeburn)*

SOUTH WINGFIELD   SK3755
Old Yew Tree (01773) 833626
B5035 W of Alfreton; Manor Road; DE55 7NH Friendly 16th-c village pub with enjoyable reasonably priced home-made food (not Sun evening) including lunchtime/ early evening deal, Bass, a local guest (two at weekends) and a proper cider, log fire, beams and carved panelling, separate restaurant area; Sat night entertainment, TV, free wi-fi; children, walkers and dogs welcome, some modern rattan-style furniture outside, open all day Fri-Sun, closed Mon and Tues lunchtimes. *(Robert Turnham)*

STONEDGE   SK3367
Red Lion (01246) 566142
Darley Road (B5057); S45 0LW Revamped bar-bistro (former 17th-c coaching inn) on edge of the Peak District; good attractively presented food (pricey for the area) from sandwiches up using local ingredients including own vegetables, real ales such as Peak and good choice of wines, bare stone walls, flagstones and wood floors, some substantial timbers, lounge area with comfortable seating and open fire; picnic-sets out under parasols at back, 27 bedrooms in adjacent modern hotel, open all day. *(Derek and Sylvia Stephenson)*

SUDBURY   SK1632
Vernon Arms (01283) 585329
Off A50/A515; Main Road; DE6 5HS Rambling 17th-c brick pub with enjoyable reasonably priced food including good Sun roasts, four Marstons-related ales, friendly service, three main rooms with stairs to bar, log fires; background music; children and dogs welcome, good big garden, handy for Sudbury Hall (NT), open all day. *(Dennis Jones)*

SUTTON CUM
DUCKMANTON   SK4371
Arkwright Arms (01246) 232053
A632 Bolsover–Chesterfield; S44 5JG Friendly mock-Tudor pub with bar, pool room (dogs welcome here) and dining room, all with real fires, good choice of well priced food (not Sun evening), up to 16 changing ales, ten real ciders and four perries (beer/ cider festivals Easter/Aug bank holidays); TV, games machine; children welcome, seats out at front and on side terrace, attractive hanging baskets, play equipment, open all day. *(Tim and Sarah Smythe-Brown)*

THORPE   SK1650
Old Dog (01335) 350990
Spend Lane/Wintercroft Lane; DE6 2AT Fully refurbished bistro-style village pub (18th-c coaching inn – was the Dog & Partridge), lively and friendly, with popular food (not Sun evening, Mon, Tues) from sensibly short menu including good burgers, four well kept changing ales, good attentive service, candlelit tables on flagstones, woodburners; background music; children, walkers and dogs welcome, covered eating area outside, handy for Dovedale and Tissington Trail, open all day. *(Brian and Anna Marsden)*

TICKNALL   SK3523
★ ## Wheel (01332) 864488
Main Street (A514); DE73 7JZ Stylish contemporary décor in bar and upstairs restaurant, enjoyable interesting home-made food (all day weekends) including daily specials, friendly attentive staff, well kept Marstons Pedigree and a

guest; children welcome, no dogs inside, nice outside area with café tables on raised deck, near entrance to Calke Abbey (NT). *(Tim and Sarah Smythe-Brown)*

TIDESWELL   SK1575
Horse & Jockey (01298) 872211
Queen Street; SK17 8JZ Friendly and relaxed family-run local, beams, flagstones, cushioned wall benches and coal fire in small public bar's traditional open range, bare boards, button-back banquettes and woodburner in lounge, well kept Sharps, Tetleys and a couple of local guests, decent reasonably priced food, stripped-stone dining room; children and dogs welcome, six bedrooms, good walks, open all day. *(Andrew Vincent)*

WARDLOW   SK1875
★Three Stags Heads (01298) 872268
Wardlow Mires; A623/B6465; SK17 8RW Basic unchanging pub (17th-c longhouse) of great individuality; old country furniture on flagstones, heating from cast-iron kitchen ranges, old photographs, long-serving plain-talking landlord, locals in favourite corners, well kept Abbeydale ales including house beer Black Lurcher (brewed at a hefty 8% ABV), lots of bottled beers, simple food on home-made plates (licensees are potters and have a small gallery), may be free roast chestnuts or cheese on the bar, folk music Sun afternoon; no credit cards or mobile phones; well behaved children and dogs welcome (resident lurchers), hill views from front terrace, good walking country, only open Fri evening and all day weekends. *(Ann and Tony Bennett-Hughes)*

WHITTINGTON MOOR   SK3873
Derby Tup 07506 000989
Sheffield Road; B6057 just S of A61 roundabout; S41 8LS Popular Castle Rock local with their ales along with Pigeon Fishers (landlord owns the brewery) and several guests, also craft beers, up to seven ciders and good range of other drinks, simple furniture, coal fire and lots of standing room as well as two side snugs, lunchtime sandwiches and snacks (full Sun lunch) and some themed nights; live music including jam sessions first and third Thurs of month; children, walkers and dogs welcome, seats out on small back deck, open all day and can

get very busy weekend evenings and match days. *(Max Simons)*

WILLINGTON   SK2928
Dragon (01283) 704795
The Green; DE65 6BP Renovated and extended pub backing on to Trent & Mersey Canal, enjoyable well cooked food (all day Fri-Sun) from sandwiches and sharing boards to pub favourites and grills, Bass, Marstons Pedigree, Sharps Doom Bar and a couple of microbrews from sister pub the Boot at Repton; weekend live music, sports TV, free wi-fi; children and dogs welcome, picnic-sets out overlooking canal, moorings, open all day. *(Luke Morgan)*

WINSTER   SK2460
★Bowling Green (01629) 650219
East Bank, by NT Market House; DE4 2DS Traditional old stone pub with good chatty atmosphere, character landlord and welcoming staff, enjoyable reasonably priced home-made food, at least three well kept changing local ales and good selection of whiskies, end log fire, dining area and family conservatory (dogs allowed here too); nice village with good surrounding walks, closed Mon, Tues and lunchtimes apart from Sun. *(Ann and Tony Bennett-Hughes)*

WINSTER   SK2360
Miners Standard (01629) 650279
Bank Top (B5056 above village); DE4 2DR Simply furnished 17th-c stone local, friendly and relaxed, with bar, snug and restaurant, well kept ales such as Greene King, Marstons and Wychwood, good value honest pub food (not Sun evening), big woodburner, lead-mining photographs and minerals, lots of brass, a backwards clock and ancient well; background music; children (away from bar) and dogs welcome, attractive view from garden, campsite next door, interesting stone-built village below, open all day. *(James Lander)*

WIRKSWORTH   SK2854
Royal Oak (01629) 823000
North End; DE4 4FG Friendly old-fashioned terraced local, five well kept ales including Bass, Timothy Taylors Landlord and Whim Hartington, no food apart from filled rolls, some bric-a-brac and interesting old photographs; pool room; only open evenings from 8pm and Sun lunchtime. *(Max Simons)*

Post Office address codings confusingly give the impression that a few pubs are in Derbyshire, when they're really in Cheshire (which is where we list them).

Devon

KEY ★ Star Pub   🍽 Top Quality Food   🍺 Great Beer

🍷 Good Wines   £ Bargain Meals   🛏 Good Bedrooms   🍴 Serves Food

---

BRAMPFORD SPEKE

SX9298   Map 1

Lazy Toad 🍽

(01392) 841591 – www.thelazytoadinn.co.uk

Off A377 N of Exeter; EX5 5DP

Well run dining pub in pretty village with particularly good food, real ales, friendly service and pretty garden

The friendly licensees here work hard to ensure that both drinkers and diners enjoy this 18th-c inn. The interconnected bar rooms have beams, standing timbers and slate floors, a comfortable sofa by an open log fire and cushioned wall settles and high-backed wooden dining chairs around a mix of tables; the cream-painted brick walls are hung with lots of pictures. Hanlons Yellowhammer, Otter Bitter and St Austell Tribute on handpump and several wines by the glass are served by attentive staff; the irish terrier is called Rufus. The courtyard (once used by the local farrier and wheelwright) has green-painted picnic-sets, with more in the walled garden. It's worth wandering around this charming village of thatched cottages and there are fine walks beside the River Exe and on the Exe Valley Way and Devonshire Heartland Way. Please note, they no longer offer bedrooms.

🍽 Carefully crafted food includes sandwiches, ham hock terrine with cauliflower piccalilli and butternut squash dressing, salmon gravadlax with beetroot and dill and wholegrain mustard crème fraîche, goats cheese and red onion in pastry with spinach and wild mushroom sauce, cod with lemon and chive cream and spaghetti vegetables, duck two-ways with creamed savoy cabbage and red wine jus, corn-fed chicken with swede and apple mash and mustard cream sauce, and puddings such as vanilla crème brûlée and baked cheesecake with cointreau oranges. *Benchmark main dish: fillet of beef with garlic and rocket dauphinoise and green peppercorn sauce £21.95. Two-course evening meal £18.00.*

Free house ~ Licensees Harriet and Mike Daly ~ Real ale ~ Open 12-3, 6-11; 12-4 Sun; closed Sun evening, Mon ~ Bar food 12-2, 6.30-9; 12-2.30 Sun ~ Children welcome ~ Dogs allowed in bar ~ Wi-fi *Recommended by Lindy Andrews, Hilary and Neil Christopher, Bob and Margaret Holder, Comus and Sarah Elliott*

BRANSCOMBE

SY2088   Map 1

Masons Arms 🛏

(01297) 680300 – www.masonsarms.co.uk

Main Street; signed off A3052 Sidmouth–Seaton, then bear left into village; EX12 3DJ

Rambling low-beamed rooms, woodburning stoves, a fair choice of real ales, popular food and seats on quiet terrace; spotless bedrooms

As the sea is just a stroll away and the pretty village is worth exploring, this popular place does get very busy – it's worth booking a table in advance. The rambling main bar is the heart of the place with comfortable seats and chairs on slate floors, ancient ships' beams, a log fire in a massive hearth, St Austell Proper Job and Tribute and guest beers such as Branscombe Vale Summa That and Otter Bitter on handpump and ten wines by the glass. A second bar also has a slate floor, a fireplace with a two-sided woodburning stove and stripped pine; the two dining rooms are smartly furnished. A quiet flower-filled front terrace, with thatched-roof tables, extends into a side garden. The neatly kept and comfortable bedrooms are above the inn or in converted cottages overlooking the gardens (dogs are allowed in these rooms).

Featuring much local produce, the food includes lunchtime sandwiches, chicken liver pâté with spiced tomato chutney, deep-fried crispy squid with sweet chilli sauce, smoked salmon caesar salad, mussels with white wine, garlic and cream and fries, vegetarian chickpea burger with aubergine purée, roasted red pepper salsa and fries, beer-battered fish and chips, local rump steak with a choice of sauces and chips, and puddings. *Benchmark main dish: steak and kidney pie £12.00. Two-course evening meal £19.50.*

St Austell ~ Managers Simon and Alison Ede ~ Real ale ~ Open 11-11; 12-10.30 Sun ~ Bar food 12-2.15, 6.30-9 ~ Restaurant ~ Children welcome ~ Dogs allowed in bar and bedrooms ~ Wi-fi ~ Bedrooms: /£115 *Recommended by Mr and Mrs J Watkins, Colin McLachlan, Alastair and Sheree Hepburn*

BUCKLAND MONACHORUM SX4968 Map 1
Drake Manor 🍺 £ 🛏

(01822) 853892 – www.drakemanorinn.co.uk
Off A386 via Crapstone, just S of Yelverton roundabout; PL20 7NA

Nice little village pub with snug rooms, popular food, quite a choice of drinks and pretty back garden; bedrooms

Our readers always enjoy their visits to this charming little pub and the long-serving landlady offers a genuine welcome to both visitors and regulars. The heavily beamed public bar on the left has a chatty, easy-going feel, brocade-cushioned wall seats, prints of the village from 1905 onwards, horse tack and a few ship badges and a woodburning stove in a very big stone fireplace; a small door leads to a low-beamed cubbyhole. The snug Drakes Bar has beams hung with tiny cups and big brass keys, a woodburning stove in another stone fireplace, horsebrasses and stirrups, and a mix of seats and tables (note the fine stripped-pine high-backed settle with hood). On the right is a small beamed dining room with settles and tables on flagstones. Darts, euchre and board games. Dartmoor Jail Ale, Otter Amber and Sharps Doom Bar on handpump, ten wines by the glass, 15 malt whiskies and apple juice using apples from the village. There are picnic-sets in the prettily planted and sheltered back garden and the front floral displays are much admired; morris men perform regularly in summer. The bedrooms are comfortable and they also have an attractive self-catering apartment. Buckland Abbey (National Trust) is close by.

Enjoyable food includes goats cheese mousse with beetroot, chicory and pear salad, duck and chilli jam spring rolls with sweet chilli sauce, trio of sausages (pork and leek, pork and honey, venison and pear) with creamy mash, gravy and beer-battered onion rings, mediterranean vegetable lasagne, seafood pancake in white wine and garlic cream sauce, slow-cooked ox cheek with horseradish mash, and puddings such as chocolate fondant with cream cheese ice-cream and caramelised peanuts and lemon posset with italian meringue and lemon sorbet. *Benchmark main dish: slow-cooked pork belly with boulangère potatoes, apple and black pudding purée and cider jus £13.95. Two-course evening meal £15.00.*

Punch ~ Lease Mandy Robinson ~ Real ale ~ Open 11.30-2.30, 6.30-11; 11.30-11.30 Fri, Sat; 12-11 Sun ~ Bar food 12-2 (2.30 Sun), 6.30-9.30; 11.30-2.30, 6.30-10 Fri, Sat ~ Restaurant ~ Children allowed in restaurant and area off main bar ~ Dogs allowed in bar ~ Wi-fi ~ Bedrooms: /£90 *Recommended by Mr and Mrs J Watkins, Peter Andrews, Jeremy Snaithe*

 CHAGFORD   SX7087   Map 1

Three Crowns ⇔

(01647) 433444 – www.threecrowns-chagford.co.uk
High Street; TQ13 8AJ

Stylishly refurbished bar and lounges in ancient inn, conservatory restaurant and good food and drinks; smart bedrooms

A stunning thatched 13th-c former manor house on the edge of Dartmoor, this blends ancient and modern features with great effectiveness. The bar has leather armchairs and stools in front of a big log fire, built-in panelled wall seats with bright scatter cushions, a few leather tub chairs and pretty curtains with tassled tie-backs. Dartmoor Jail Ale and St Austell Proper Job and Tribute on handpump and 11 wines by the glass, served by friendly, efficient staff. The dining lounges have all sorts of leather, plush or carved wooden chairs and settles around an assortment of tables, and big gilt-edged mirrors over fireplaces. Throughout these rooms are painted beams, standing timbers, pale flagstones, rugs, exposed stone walls hung with photographs and prints, and various copper kettles, pots and warming pans; background music, TV and board games. There's also a conservatory-style dining area with various furnishings; the courtyard has sturdy tables and chairs among box topiary. Bedrooms are stylish, well equipped and comfortable and breakfasts good and generous. Parking is limited but there's also a nearby pay-and-display car park.

Some kind of food is served from breakfast onwards: sandwiches, chicken liver parfait with tomato salsa, cod, crab and ginger fishcakes with lime butter sauce, sausages with black pudding and onion gravy, butternut squash risotto with goats cheese, salmon with tomato risotto and courgette ribbons, burger with toppings, relish and fries, lemon and thyme free-range chicken with madeira sauce, herb-crusted cod with braised fennel and red pepper butter sauce, and puddings such as vanilla crème brûlée and lemon posset. *Benchmark main dish: beer-battered fish and chips £12.95. Two-course evening meal £20.00.*

St Austell ~ Manager Lisa Hoogerverst ~ Real ale ~ Open 11am-midnight; 12-12 Sun ~ Bar food 12-2.30, 6-9 (9.30 Fri, Sat) ~ Restaurant ~ Children welcome ~ Dogs allowed in bar and bedrooms ~ Wi-fi ~ Bedrooms: £100/£135 *Recommended by Gerry Price, Isobel Mackinlay, Peter Andrews, George Sanderson*

 COCKWOOD   SX9780   Map 1

Anchor ♀ ◧

(01626) 890203 – www.anchorinncockwood.com
Off, but visible from, A379 Exeter–Torbay, after Starcross; EX6 8RA

Busy dining pub specialising in seafood (other choices available), with up to six real ales

Even in midwinter, this ex-seamen's mission remains immensely popular, and you must arrive early to be sure of a table – and even a parking space. It's in a fine spot fronting the little harbour with its bobbing boats, swans and ducks, and tables on a sheltered verandah overlook the water.

As well as an extension made up of mainly reclaimed timber and decorated with over 300 ship emblems, brass and copper lamps and nautical knick-knacks, there are several small, low-ceilinged, rambling rooms with black panelling and good-sized tables in various nooks; the snug has a cheerful winter coal fire. Otter Ale, St Austell Tribute and Tintagel Castle Gold plus a couple of guests such as Caledonian Deuchars IPA and Exeter Avocet on handpump (beer festivals at Easter and Halloween), eight wines by the glass and 40 malt whiskies; background music, darts, cards and board games.

They specialise in fish: 22 ways of serving River Exe mussels and five ways of serving local scallops, as well as sandwiches and baguettes, crab and brandy broth, blue cheese and garlic mushrooms in creamy sauce, steak in ale pie, five-bean curry with quorn and lentils bali-style, chicken on spicy tomato, leek and pepper sauce, ray wing steamed with chilli, cherry tomatoes and basil, gurnard on smoked bacon and creamed leek reduction, and puddings such as sticky toffee pudding and Baileys pannacotta. *Benchmark main dish: cold seafood medley £18.95. Two-course evening meal £25.00.*

Heavitree ~ Lease Malcolm and Katherine Protheroe, Scott Hellier ~ Real ale ~ Open 11-11; 11.30-10.30 Sun ~ Bar food 12-9 (10 Fri, Sat) ~ Restaurant ~ Children welcome if seated and away from bar ~ Dogs allowed in bar *Recommended by Patrick and Daphne Darley, Toby Jones, Patricia Hawkins*

COLEFORD
SS7701 Map 1

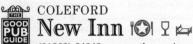

New Inn 🍽 ♈ ⇔

(01363) 84242 – www.thenewinncoleford.co.uk
Just off A377 Crediton–Barnstaple; EX17 5BZ

Ancient thatched inn with interestingly furnished areas, well liked food and real ales and welcoming licensees; bedrooms

Our readers continue to enjoy staying in the well equipped and comfortable bedrooms here, and the breakfasts are very good indeed. The U-shaped building has the servery in the 'angle' with interestingly furnished areas leading off it: ancient and modern settles, cushioned stone wall seats, some character tables (a pheasant worked into the grain of one) and carved dressers and chests. Also, paraffin lamps, antique prints on the white walls, landscape-decorated plates on one beam and pewter tankards on another. Captain, the chatty parrot, may greet you with a 'hello' or even a 'goodbye'. Otter Ale and Sharps Doom Bar on handpump, local cider, 15 wines by the glass and a dozen malt whiskies; background music, darts and board games. There are chairs and tables on decking beneath a pruned willow tree by the babbling stream, and more in a covered dining area. At 600 years old, this warmly friendly place is one of the oldest 'new' inns in the country.

The popular food includes venison and pork terrine with cranberry and orange compote, grilled goats cheese on poached pear with honey, walnut oil and orange dressing, aubergine and sweet potato moussaka with tomato and onion passata and feta, bass fillets on oriental noodles with red pepper, mangetout and spinach, slow-cooked lamb shank with red wine, pink peppercorn and mushroom sauce, chicken with crème fraîche and wholegrain mustard and tarragon sauce on potatoes, and puddings such as treacle tart and double chocolate torte. *Benchmark main dish: trio of fish in dill butter sauce £14.50. Two-course evening meal £20.00.*

Free house ~ Licensees Carole and George Cowie ~ Real ale ~ Open 12-3, 6-11 (10.30 Sun) ~ Bar food 12-2, 6.30-9.30 ~ Restaurant ~ Children welcome ~ Dogs allowed in bar ~ Wi-fi ~ Monthly quiz, summer hog roasts and bi-annual sea shanty singers ~ Bedrooms: £69/£89
Recommended by David Longhurst, Sally and David Champion, Jeremy Snaithe

DALWOOD

ST2400 Map 1

Tuckers Arms ⭐

(01404) 881342 – www.thetuckersarms.co.uk

Village signposted off A35 Axminster–Honiton; keep on past village; EX13 7EG

13th-c thatched inn with friendly, hard-working licensees, real ales and interesting bar food

A lovely sight in summer with colourful window boxes, hanging baskets and tubs, this pretty thatched longhouse is reached down narrow high-hedged lanes in hilly pasture country. The beamed and flagstoned bar has a bustling, friendly atmosphere, traditional furnishings including assorted dining chairs, window seats and wall settles, and a log fire in an inglenook fireplace with numerous horsebrasses on the wall above. The back bar has an enormous collection of miniature bottles and there's also a more formal dining room; lots of copper implements and platters. Branscombe Vale Branoc and Otter Bitter and Amber on handpump, several wines by the glass and up to 20 malt whiskies; background music and a double skittle alley. There are seats in the garden. Apart from the church, this is the oldest building in the parish.

 The reliably good and highly thought-of food includes lunchtime sandwiches, beetroot and goats cheese cake, pork belly wrapped in pancetta with apricot, cider and raisin chutney, sausage and mash with onion gravy, ham and eggs, steak in ale pie, spinach and ricotta cannelloni with tomato and white sauce, a daily changing fish dish such as crab and mixed seafood chowder, and puddings such as chocolate fudge cake and treacle tart. *Benchmark main dish: rib of beef with green beans wrapped in bacon, sautéed potatoes, peppercorn cream sauce and gravy £15.95. Two-course evening meal £20.00.*

Free house ~ Licensee Tracey Pearson ~ Real ale ~ Open 11.30-3, 6.30-11.30 ~ Bar food 12-2, 6.30-9 ~ Restaurant ~ Well behaved children in restaurant ~ Dogs allowed in bar ~ Wi-fi ~ Bedrooms: £45/£69.50 *Recommended by Tom Stone, Edward Nile, Julie Swift, Dr A McCormick*

DARTMOUTH

SX8751 Map 1

Royal Castle Hotel ♀ 🛏

(01803) 833033 – www.royalcastle.co.uk

The Quay; TQ6 9PS

350-year-old hotel by the harbour with a genuine mix of customers, real ales and good food; comfortable bedrooms

This is a most enjoyable place to stay (breakfasts are excellent) and some of the stylish bedrooms overlook the water; dogs, welcome in all rooms, get treats and a toy; they also have their own secure parking. As the place was originally two Tudor merchant houses (although the façade is Regency), there's a great deal of character and many original features – some of the beams are said to have come from the wreckage of the Spanish Armada. The two ground-floor bars are quite different. The traditional Galleon bar (on the right) has a log fire in a Tudor fireplace, some fine antiques and maritime pieces, quite a bit of copper and brass and plenty of chatty locals. The Harbour Bar (to the left of the flagstoned entrance hall) is contemporary in style and rather smart, with a big-screen TV and live acoustic music on Thursday evenings. The more formal restaurant looks over the river; background music. Dartmoor Jail Ale, Otter Amber, Sharps Doom Bar and a weekly guest such as Fullers on handpump and 28 wines by the glass; service is helpful and friendly.

Using the best local seasonal produce for the popular brasserie-style menu, dishes include sandwiches (until 5.30pm), spiced potted crab, fried chicken with asian coleslaw, sharing platters, goats cheese salad with roasted beetroot, butternut squash, chicory and pickled onion, a pie of the week, burgers with toppings, relish and fries, pad thai noodles with chicken, mussels in cider and cream, steaks with a choice of potatoes and sauces, and puddings; their Sunday carvery is very highly thought-of. *Benchmark main dish: seafood tagliatelle £13.95. Two-course evening meal £20.00.*

Free house ~ Licensees Nigel and Anne Way ~ Real ale ~ Open 8am-11pm (10.30pm Sun) ~ Bar food 8am-10pm ~ Restaurant ~ Children welcome ~ Dogs allowed in bar ~ Wi-fi ~ Live acoustic music Thurs evening, jazz Sun afternoon ~ Bedrooms: £130/£180 *Recommended by Richard Tilbrook*

DODDISCOMBSLEIGH
Nobody Inn ♀

SX8586 Map 1

(01647) 252394 – www.nobodyinn.co.uk
Off B3193; EX6 7PS

Busy old pub with plenty of character, a fine range of drinks, well liked bar food and friendly staff; bedrooms

In summer, try to bag one of the picnic-sets in the pretty garden with views of the surrounding wooded hill pastures. Inside, the beamed lounge bar of two character rooms contains handsomely carved antique settles, windsor and wheelback chairs, all sorts of wooden tables, guns and hunting prints in a snug area by one of the big inglenook fireplaces, and fresh flowers; board games. An extraordinary range of drinks includes a beer named for the pub from Branscombe Vale and two changing guests such as Bays Topsail and Piddle Martyrs Relief on handpump, 30 wines by the glass from a list of 200, 270 malt whiskies and three farm ciders. The restaurant is more formal. Do visit the local church, which has some of the best medieval stained glass in the west country.

Tasty food includes panko-crumbed squid with chilli mayonnaise, ham hock and madeira-soaked date terrine with madeira syrup, brie and red onion marmalade flan with coleslaw and sweet potato fries, rabbit with celeriac fondant, glazed onions and chestnuts and rabbit sauce, rack of ribs in honey, soy, paprika, lime and ginger with fries, fish of the day with sauce véronique, and puddings such as chocolate brownie with chocolate sauce and orange posset. *Benchmark main dish: steak in ale pie £11.95. Two-course evening meal £23.00.*

Free house ~ Licensee Susan Burdge ~ Real ale ~ Open 11-11; 12-10.30 Sun ~ Bar food 12-2.30, 6-9 (9.30 Fri, Sat); 12-3, 6-9 Sun ~ Restaurant ~ Children welcome away from main bar; no under-5s in restaurant ~ Dogs allowed in bar ~ Wi-fi ~ Bedrooms: £65/£99 *Recommended by Martin Jones, Peter Brix, S G N Bennett, Piotr Chodzko-Zajko, Stephen Shepherd*

EXETER
Fat Pig 🍺

SX9192 Map 1

(01392) 437217 – www.fatpig-exeter.co.uk
John Street; EX1 1BL

Lively pub with own-brew beers, home-distilled spirits, big-flavoured food and a buoyant atmosphere

Run with enthusiasm and with a genuine, cheerful welcome to all, this renovated Victorian pub has hit the ground running. They brew their own beers, have a newly opened distillery and only use local produce for their enjoyable, hearty food. The big-windowed bar is simply furnished:

elegant stools against a tiled counter, more stools and long cushioned pews by sturdy pale wooden tables on bare boards, an open fire in a pretty fireplace, blackboards listing food choices and lots of mirrors. There's also a red-painted and red quarry-tiled conservatory with a happy jumble of hops and house plants, books and old stone bottles on shelves, more mirrors, and long benches and settles scattered around rustic tables. Fat Pig John Street Ale, Pigmalion and Steam Hammer on handpump, good wines by the glass, around 100 malt whiskies and their Exeter Distillery gins (they have three), vodka and apple pie moonshine.

They source their rare-breed meat from nearby farms, shoot local game and make their own sausages, black pudding and dry-cured ham; their smokehouse is put to good use: crispy smoked chicken with barbecue sauce, salt cod with a soft egg and mustard dressing, ratatouille and parmesan polenta, local fish pie, pork burger with smoked cheddar and pear ketchup, whisky and cola-smoked ham hock salad, smoked beef shoulder with gherkins and coleslaw, and puddings such as dark chocolate tart and banana and honeycomb mess. *Benchmark main dish: home-smoked platter £17.50. Two-course evening meal £21.00.*

Free house ~ Licensee Paul Timewell ~ Real ale ~ Open 5-11; 4-11.30 Fri; 12-11 Sat; 12-6 Sun ~ Bar food 5-9 (10 Fri); 12-10 Sat; 12-4 Sun ~ Restaurant ~ Children allowed until 6pm ~ Dogs welcome ~ Wi-fi *Recommended by Geoffrey Sutton, Colin and Daniel Gibbs*

EXETER
Rusty Bike ◀

SX9293 Map 1

(01392) 214440 – www.rustybike-exeter.co.uk
Howell Road; EX4 4LZ

Bustling, quirky pub tucked away in a backstreet, with ales from own-brew sister pub, hearty food and lively atmosphere

Although only open from 5pm (except on Sundays when it's open midday to 7pm), this lively and interesting place draws in customers of all ages, keen to enjoy the good food, thoughtful choice of drinks and regular events. The large open-plan bar has bench seating, long wall pews and church chairs around a medley of tables on stripped boards, big modern art pieces on the walls, table football, books piled on to shelves and windowsills, and a lovely carved counter where they dispense Fat Pig John Street Ale, Nelsons Fanny and Pigmalion on handpump (brewed at their sister pub, the Fat Pig – see above), their own Exeter Distillery vodka, gin and apple pie moonshine, 18 wines by the glass, 80 malt whiskies and farm cider; board games. The Snug is similarly furnished and has a vast, ornate mirror on one wall, and there's also a separate restaurant with elegant chairs around chunky tables and doors to an outside terrace.

Using carefully sourced and very local (and sometimes foraged) produce, the enjoyable rustic-style food includes potted beef and chutney, snail popcorn and aioli, butternut squash and rosemary risotto, cheeseburger with tomato relish and chips, cod fillet with tomato, fennel and capers, ox liver and smoked bacon, very good steaks with a choice of sauce and potato, and puddings such as chocolate tart with whisky syrup and cherry sorbet and apple crumble with a shot of apple pie moonshine on the side. *Benchmark main dish: pork loin with wild garlic and wild mushroom sauce £17.50. Two-course evening meal £19.00.*

Free house ~ Licensee Paul Timewell ~ Real ale ~ Open 5-11 (midnight Sat); closed lunchtimes except Sun ~ Bar food 6-10; 12-7 Sun ~ Restaurant ~ Children welcome until 8pm ~ Dogs welcome ~ Wi-fi *Recommended by Edward May, Alison and Michael Harper, Roger and Donna Huggins, Donald Allsopp*

FROGMORE
Globe 🛏

SX7742 Map 1

(01548) 531351 – www.theglobeinn.co.uk

A379 E of Kingsbridge; TQ7 2NR

Extended and neatly refurbished inn with bar and several dining areas, real ales, popular food and seats outside; comfortable bedrooms

Once again, our readers have enjoyed staying in the well equipped, airy bedrooms while exploring the surrounding area; breakfasts are generous. The neatly kept bar has a double-sided woodburner with horsebrass-decorated stone pillars on either side, another fireplace filled with logs, cushioned settles, chunky farmhouse chairs and built-in wall seating around a mix of tables on wooden flooring, and a copper diving helmet. Attentive staff serve Otter Ale, Skinners Betty Stogs and South Hams Eddystone on handpump and several wines by the glass. The slate-floored games room has a pool table and darts. There's also a comfortable lounge with an open fire, cushioned dining chairs and tables on red carpeting, a big leather sofa, a model yacht and a large yacht painting – spot the clever mural of a log pile. Teak tables and chairs sit on the back terrace, with steps leading up to another level with picnic-sets; the summer window boxes are very pretty.

 Quite a choice of food includes baguettes, grilled goats cheese and mushroom tart, tiger prawns in garlic butter, local pasty, home-cooked ham and eggs, pizzas, vegetarian lasagne, a curry of the day, whole lemon sole with parsley and caper butter, pork fillet stuffed with fig and blue cheese on apple rösti with honey fig dressing, steak burger with relish and chips, and puddings. *Benchmark main dish: seafood pancake £11.95. Two-course evening meal £19.00.*

Free house ~ Licensees John and Lynda Horsley ~ Real ale ~ Open 12-11; 12-2.30, 6-11; 12-2.30, 6.30-10.30 Sun in winter; closed Mon lunchtime in winter ~ Bar food 12-2, 6-9 ~ Restaurant ~ Children welcome ~ Dogs allowed in bar and bedrooms ~ Wi-fi ~ Bedrooms: £70/£85 *Recommended by Hilary and Neil Christopher, S G N Bennett, Rod and Chris Pring*

GEORGEHAM
Rock ⭐ ♥ �glass

SS4639 Map 1

(01271) 890322 – www.therockinn.biz

Rock Hill, above village; EX33 1JW

Beamed pub with good food, five real ales, plenty of room inside and out and a relaxed atmosphere

The bustling bar in this 17th-c pub is the heart of the place. It's sizeable and heavy beamed and divided in two by a step. The pubby top part has half-planked walls, an open woodburning stove in a stone fireplace and captain's and farmhouse chairs around wooden tables on quarry tiles; the lower area has panelled wall seats, some built-in settles forming a cosy booth, old local photographs and ancient flatirons. Leading off here is a red-carpeted dining room with attractive black and white photographs of North Devon folk. Friendly young staff serve local Braunton #2 Bitter alongside Exmoor Gold, St Austell Tribute, Sharps Doom Bar and Timothy Taylors Landlord on handpump and more than a dozen wines by the glass; background music and board games. The light and airy back dining conservatory has high-backed wooden or modern dining chairs around tables under a vine, with a little terrace beyond. There are picnic-sets at the front beside pretty hanging baskets and tubs; wheelchair access.

 Enjoyable food includes lunchtime sandwiches, salmon and crab cakes with asian slaw and sweet chilli sauce, sharing platters, a pie of the week, lemon and rosemary chicken salad with crispy bacon, garlic croutons and boiled egg, broccoli and stilton tart with apple, french beans and toasted walnuts, spanish burger with chorizo, parma ham, manchego, garlic aioli and chips, monkfish wrapped in parma ham with seafood bouillabaisse sauce, and puddings such as apple and rhubarb crumble with vanilla custard and sticky toffee pudding with butterscotch sauce. *Benchmark main dish: spaghetti with king prawns, clams, white wine, garlic, chilli and parsley £16.95. Two-course evening meal £20.00.*

Punch ~ Lease Daniel Craddock ~ Real ale ~ Open 11am-11.30pm (midnight Sat); 12-11.30 Sun ~ Bar food 12-2.30, 6-9; 12-8.30 Sun ~ Restaurant ~ Children welcome ~ Dogs allowed in bar ~ Wi-fi *Recommended by Bob and Margaret Holder, John Jenkins, Stephen Shepherd, Margaret McDonald*

HAYTOR VALE   SX7777   Map 1
Rock ★ 🅘🅞🅣 ♀ 🛏

(01364) 661305 – www.rock-inn.co.uk

Haytor signposted off B3387 just W of Bovey Tracey, on good moorland road to Widecombe; TQ13 9XP

Civilised Dartmoor inn with lovely food, real ales and seats in pretty garden; comfortable bedrooms

At lunchtime, this civilised and particularly well run inn is at its most informal – which suits walkers from Dartmoor National Park very well. The two neatly kept, linked, partly panelled bar rooms have lots of dark wood and red plush, polished antique tables with candles and fresh flowers, old-fashioned prints and decorative plates, and warming winter log fires (the main fireplace has a fine Stuart fireback). Dartmoor IPA and Jail Ale on handpump, 15 wines (plus champagne and sparkling rosé) by the glass and 20 malt whiskies. There's also a light and spacious dining room in the lower part of the inn and a residents' lounge. The large, pretty garden opposite has some seats, with more on the little terrace next to the pub. Smart, beamed bedrooms have either garden or moor views and breakfasts are excellent. You can park at the back of the building.

🅘🅞🅣 Excellent food includes sandwiches, ham hock terrine with piccalilli, goats cheese mousse with balsamic poached fig, venison burger with beetroot and chilli relish and chips, stone bass with celeriac purée and chorizo butter, butternut squash, leek and sage risotto with crème fraîche and parmesan, lamb rump with dauphinoise potatoes and red wine sauce, confit pork belly with hispi cabbage and bacon, fondant potato and red wine sauce, and puddings such as triple-layer chocolate and passion-fruit tart with orange sorbet; they also offer a two- and three-course set evening menu. *Benchmark main dish: rib-eye steak with mushrooms, peppercorn sauce and chips £17.95. Two-course evening meal £20.00.*

Free house ~ Licensee Christopher Graves ~ Real ale ~ Open 10am-11pm; 12-10.30 Sun ~ Bar food 12-2, 7-9 (8.30 Sun) ~ Restaurant ~ Children welcome away from main bar ~ Dogs allowed in bedrooms ~ Wi-fi ~ Bedrooms: £80/£100 *Recommended by Dr and Mrs J D Abell, Kim Skuse*

HORNDON   SX5280   Map 1
Elephants Nest 🍺 £ 🛏

(01822) 810273 – www.elephantsnest.co.uk

If coming from Okehampton on A386, turn left at Mary Tavy Inn, then left after about 0.5 miles; pub signposted beside Mary Tavy Inn, then Horndon signposted; on OS Sheet it's named as the New Inn; PL19 9NQ

Isolated old inn with some interesting original features, real ales and changing food; good bedrooms

Many people use the attractively furnished and deeply comfortable bedrooms here as a base while exploring the area – the breakfasts are especially good. It's a remote old inn on the lower slopes of Dartmoor with a warmly friendly landlord; the main bar has lots of beer pump clips on the beams, high bar chairs by the bar counter, Dartmoor Jail Ale, Otter Amber, Palmers IPA and St Austell Proper Job on handpump, a couple of farm ciders, several wines by the glass and 15 malt whiskies. Two other rooms have an assortment of wooden dining chairs around a mix of tables, and throughout there are bare stone walls, flagstones, horsebrasses and three woodburning stoves. The spreading, pretty garden (with an area reserved for adults only) has picnic-sets under parasols and looks across dry-stone walls to pastures and rougher moorland above.

🍴 Highly thought-of food includes lunchtime sandwiches, pork terrine with cumberland sauce, king prawns in lemon, garlic, chilli and parsley butter, caramelised shallot and goats cheese tarte tatin, burger with red onion marmalade and fries, fillet of smoked haddock topped with welsh rarebit, chicken breast stuffed with taleggio and rosemary, wrapped in pancetta in light creamy sauce, herb-crusted lamb with crushed minted peas, and puddings such as mixed fruit crumble and sticky toffee pudding with toffee sauce. *Benchmark main dish: steak and kidney pudding £14.95. Two-course evening meal £21.00.*

Free house ~ Licensee Hugh Cook ~ Real ale ~ Open 12-3, 6.30-11 (10.30 Sun) ~ Bar food 12-2.15, 6.30-9 ~ Restaurant ~ Children welcome away from bar ~ Dogs welcome ~ Wi-fi ~ Bedrooms: £87.50/£97.50 *Recommended by Wendy Breese, Colin McLachlan, M G Hart, Stephen Shepherd*

IDDESLEIGH   SS5608   Map 1

Duke of York 🛏

(01837) 810253 – www.dukeofyorkdevon.co.uk
B3217 Exbourne–Dolton; EX19 8BG

Unfussy old place with simple furnishings, tasty food and a fair choice of drinks; charming bedrooms

Plenty of chatty regulars crowd into the unspoilt bar of this long, thatched 15th-c inn – and there's a welcome for visitors too. The homely character is helped along by rocking chairs, cushioned benches built into the wall's black-painted wooden dado, stripped tables and other simple country furnishings, banknotes pinned to beams, and a large open fireplace. Bays Topsail, Otter Bitter and Teignworthy Neap Tide tapped from the cask and a dozen wines by the glass. It can get pretty cramped at peak times. The dining room has a huge inglenook fireplace. Through a small coach arch is a little back garden with some picnic-sets. Three bedrooms are in the pub, with three more just a minute's walk away. Michael Morpurgo, author of *War Horse*, got the inspiration to write the novel after talking to World War I veteran Wilfred Ellis in front of the fire here almost 30 years ago.

🍴 Hearty food includes sandwiches, port and stilton mushrooms, duck liver and orange parfait, leek and mushroom bake, sausages with mash and caramelised onion gravy, chicken wrapped in smoked bacon with chasseur sauce, gammon with pineapple and egg, fish pie, and puddings. *Benchmark main dish: steak and kidney pudding £13.95. Two-course evening meal £15.00.*

Free house ~ Licensee John Pittam ~ Real ale ~ Open 11-midnight ~ Bar food 12-2, 7-9 ~ Restaurant ~ Children welcome ~ Dogs allowed in bar and bedrooms ~ Bedrooms: £50/£75 *Recommended by John Marsh, Alan and Alice Morgan, Simon and Alex Knight*

KINGSBRIDGE

Dodbrooke Inn 🍺 £

SX7344 Map 1

(01548) 852068

Church Street, Dodbrooke (parking some way off); TQ7 1DB

Bustling local with friendly licensees, chatty locals and well regarded food and drink

The friendly licensees have been running this bustling, quaint local for over 25 years now and customers of all ages are made most welcome. It's a small terraced pub in a quiet residential area and the traditional bar has built-in cushioned stall seats and plush cushioned stools around pubby tables, some horse harness, local photographs and china jugs, a log fire and an easy-going atmosphere. Bass, Sharps Doom Bar and a couple of guests such as Dartmoor Jail Ale and Youngs Bitter on handpump, local cider and eight wines by the glass. You can sit in the covered courtyard, which might be candlelit in warm weather.

 Fair value food includes sandwiches, deep-fried whitebait with tartare sauce, scallops and crispy bacon, ham and egg, beef stroganoff, beer-battered cod and french fries, sausage in a basket, minted lamb shank, and puddings. *Benchmark main dish: steaks with a choice of sauces £13.95. Two-course evening meal £15.00.*

Free house ~ Licensees Michael and Jill Dyson ~ Real ale ~ Open 12-2, 5-11; 12-2.30, 7-10.30 Sun; closed Mon-Weds lunchtimes ~ Bar food 12-1.30, 5.30-8.30 ~ Children welcome if over 5 ~ Wi-fi *Recommended by Brian and Sally Wakeham, Sandra and Nigel Brown*

MARLDON

Church House 🍽⭐ ♚

SX8663 Map 1

(01803) 558279 ~ www.churchhousemarldon.com

Off A380 NW of Paignton; TQ3 1SL

Pleasant inn with spreading bar rooms, particularly good food, fine choice of drinks and seats on three terraces

Our readers very much enjoy dining in this traditional 15th-c pub – but the friendly welcome from the licensees is quite a draw too. The attractively furnished, spreading bar with its woodburning stove has several different areas radiating off the big semicircular bar counter: unusual windows, some beams, dark pine and other nice old dining chairs around solid tables and yellow leather bar chairs. Leading off here is a cosy little candlelit room with four tables on bare boards, a dark wood dado and stone fireplace. There's also a restaurant with a large stone fireplace and, at the other end of the building, a similarly interesting room, split into two, with a stone floor in one part and a wooden floor (and big woodburning stove) in the other. The old barn holds yet another restaurant, with displays by local artists. Otter Ale, Dartmoor Legend and Teignworthy Neap Tide on handpump, 18 wines by the glass, ten malt whiskies and a farm cider; background music. There are picnic-sets on three carefully maintained grassy terraces behind the pub, and the village cricket field is opposite.

 Interesting food includes lunchtime sandwiches and baguettes, tiger prawns in lemon, garlic and rosemary oil, pork pâté with spiced clementine chutney, roasted courgette and red pepper tagliatelle with goats cheese pesto, lunchtime omelettes, corn-fed chicken breast filled with wild garlic and mozzarella mousse and topped with tomato sauce, pork loin with bubble and squeak and grain mustard sauce, and puddings such as strawberry-scented crème caramel and roasted fig and frangipane tart with mulled wine syrup amd vanilla mascarpone. *Benchmark main*

dish: slow-cooked lamb shoulder with dauphinoise potatoes and redcurrant sauce £16.50. Two-course evening meal £21.00.

Enterprise ~ Lease Julian Cook ~ Real ale ~ Open 11.30-3, 5.30-11 (11.30 Fri, Sat; 12-3, 5.30-10.30 Sun ~ Bar food 12-2, 7-9.30 (9 Sun) ~ Restaurant ~ Children welcome ~ Dogs allowed in bar *Recommended by John and Mary Warner, Harvey Brown, Mike and Mary Carter, Jane and Kai Horsburgh*

MORETONHAMPSTEAD SX7586 Map 1
Horse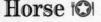

(01647) 440242 – www.thehorsedartmoor.co.uk
George Street; TQ13 8NF

Attractive mediterranean-style courtyard behind simply furnished town pub, with a good choice of drinks and excellent food

Our readers are full of warm praise for this interesting place run by a genuinely friendly landlady and her chef husband. The bar has leather chesterfields and deep armchairs in front of a woodburning stove, all manner of wooden chairs, settles and tables on carpet or wooden floorboards, rustic tools and horse tack alongside military and hunting prints on the walls and a dresser offering home-made cakes and local cider and juice for sale. There are stools by the green-planked counter where they serve Dartmoor Legend, Marstons Pedigree New World and a couple of guest beers on handpump, a dozen wines by the glass, ten malt whiskies, two farm ciders and quite a few coffees. A long light room leads off from here, and there's also a high-ceilinged barn-like back dining room; do look at forthcoming events as there's always something going on, from live bands to art shows. The sheltered inner courtyard, with metal tables and chairs, is popular with customers in warm weather.

 Delicious and interesting food includes lunchtime sandwiches and panini, confit salmon with pickled cucumber and beetroot jelly, fried lamb with red cabbage marmalade, lunchtime frittatas, sharing platters, moules frites, chicken caesar salad, jerusalem artichoke and wild mushroom lasagne, braised wild boar with gnocchi gratin and glazed root vegetables, poached and roasted guinea fowl breast and crispy leg with quince purée, brussels sprout fricassée and garlic oyster mushrooms, and puddings such as orange tart with caramelised orange and Grand Marnier crème anglaise and prune and almond clafoutis with almond ice-cream. *Benchmark main dish: pizzas with a choice of toppings £10.50. Two-course evening meal £16.50.*

Free house ~ Licensees Nigel Hoyle and Malene Graulund ~ Real ale ~ Open 12-3.30, 5-midnight; closed Mon lunchtime ~ Bar food 12.30-2.30, 6.30-9 ~ Restaurant ~ Children welcome ~ Dogs allowed in bar ~ Wi-fi ~ Live folk last Mon of month *Recommended by Isobel Mackinlay, Phoebe Peacock, Anne and Ben Smith, Millie and Peter Downing*

POSTBRIDGE SX6780 Map 1
Warren House

(01822) 880208 – www.warrenhouseinn.co.uk
B3212 0.75 miles NE of Postbridge; PL20 6TA

Straightforward old pub, relaxing for a drink or meal after a Dartmoor hike

As a refuge for walkers crossing Dartmoor, this isolated pub is invaluable. There's a lot of local character and the place was built to serve the once busy tin mining community. The cosy bar is straightforward, with simple furnishings such as easy chairs and settles beneath the beamed ochre ceiling, old pictures of the inn on partly panelled stone walls and dim lighting (powered by the pub's own generator); one of the open fires is said to have been kept alight since 1845. There's also a family room. Otter Ale plus guests such as Butcombe Bitter, Cotleigh 25 and Ringwood Old Thumper on handpump, local farm cider and malt whiskies; background music and board games. The picnic-sets on both sides of the road have moorland views.

 Bar food includes homity (vegetarian) pie, gammon and pineapple, spicy chicken with cajun dip, breaded plaice with chips, local lamb shank in red wine and rosemary sauce, smoked haddock and spring onion fishcakes with chips, and puddings. *Benchmark main dish: rabbit pie £13.25. Two-course evening meal £18.50.*

Free house ~ Licensee Peter Parsons ~ Real ale ~ Open 11-11; 12-10.30 Sun; 11-3 Mon, Tues in winter ~ Bar food 12-9 (8.30 Sun); 12-2.30 Mon, Tues in winter ~ Restaurant ~ Children in family room only ~ Dogs allowed in bar *Recommended by Edward May, Neil Allen, Charlie May*

RATTERY
SX7461   Map 1
Church House
(01364) 642220 – www.thechurchhouseinn.co.uk
Village signposted from A385 W of Totnes, and A38 S of Buckfastleigh; TQ10 9LD

Ancient place with friendly landlord plus a good range of drinks, popular bar food and peaceful views

The craftsmen who built the Norman church were probably housed in the original building here, and parts of it still survive – notably the spiral stone steps behind a little stone doorway on your left. The rooms have plenty of character: massive oak beams and standing timbers in the homely open-plan bar, large fireplaces (one with a cosy nook partitioned around it), traditional pubby chairs and tables on patterned carpet, some window seats and prints and horsebrasses on plain white walls. The dining room is separated by heavy curtains and there's a lounge too. Drinks include Dartmoor Jail Ale, Hanlons Stormstay, Otter Bitter and a changing guest on handpump, 19 malt whiskies and a dozen wines by the glass. The garden has picnic-sets on the large hedged-in lawn and peaceful views of the partly wooded surrounding hills.

 Well prepared food includes lunchtime sandwiches, ham hock terrine with fried quail egg and piccalilli, tiger prawn tempura with chilli and ginger dip, sharing boards, wild mushroom risotto, beer-battered fish of the day with chips, venison haunch with dauphinoise potatoes, pickled cabbage and red wine jus, smoked haddock and salmon fish pie, duck breast with sweet potato and cherry jus, and puddings such as lemon meringue pie and syrup sponge pudding with custard. *Benchmark main dish: slow-roasted free-range pork belly with mustard mash and cider cream sauce £13.50. Two-course evening meal £19.50.*

Free house ~ Licensees John and William Edwards ~ Real ale ~ Open 11-11 ~ Bar food 12-2.30, 6.30-9 ~ Restaurant ~ Children welcome ~ Dogs allowed in bar ~ Wi-fi
Recommended by Barry Collett, Hugh Roberts, Lynda and Trevor Smith

SALCOMBE
SX7439   Map 1
Victoria ♀
(01548) 842604 – www.victoriainn-salcombe.co.uk
Fore Street; TQ8 8BU

Friendly, bustling town-centre pub with plenty of character, west country ales, good food and back garden; bedrooms

Genuinely welcoming to all, this is a well run place with hands-on, hard-working licensees. It's an attractive 19th-c pub on two floors opposite the harbour car park, with pretty flowering summer window boxes and a large, sheltered, tiered back garden with a play area for children and maybe chickens. The beamed bar has an open fire in a big stone fireplace, huge flagstones and traditional furnishings that take in mate's chairs, built-in wall seats with scatter cushions and upholstered stools around sturdy tables. St Austell Proper Job, Tribute and a beer named for the pub and a guest such as Exmoor Fox on handpump, 19 wines by the glass, a prosecco menu and six gins; background music and board games. Several bright dining rooms lead off with all manner of painted and wooden cushioned dining chairs around polished tables on stripped floorboards, lots of prints and mirrors above a blue dado, bookcase and china plate wallpaper and quite a collection of nautical items – lanterns, oars, glass balls, ropework and so forth. Upstairs has similar tables and chairs and button-back leather chesterfields and armchairs. The quirky, comfortable bedrooms are in their Hobbit House in the garden, reached up a short flight of iron steps; no breakfasts but cafés and restaurants nearby.

Using local seasonal produce, the pleasing food includes sandwiches, twice-baked cheddar and chive soufflé, potted crab, vegetarian burger with toppings, beetroot and red onion chutney and chips, pea and ham seafood chowder with crispy pancetta and truffle oil, chicken breast with chive mash and brandy and wild mushroom sauce, lamb two-ways (seared rump and lamb confit) with mint jelly and red wine sauce, and puddings such as lemon and white chocolate tart and sticky toffee pudding with clotted cream. *Benchmark main dish: beer-battered fish and chips £12.00. Two-course evening meal £21.00.*

St Austell ~ Licensee Tim and Liz Hore ~ Real ale ~ Open 11-11 ~ Bar food 12-9 ~ Children welcome ~ Dogs allowed in bar ~ Wi-fi ~ Bedrooms: /£70 *Recommended by Elizabeth and Peter May, Edward and William Johnston*

SANDFORD
Lamb 🍺 🛏

SS8202 Map 1

(01363) 773676 – www.lambinnsandford.co.uk
The Square; EX17 4LW

16th-c inn with several real ales and decent wines by the glass, very good food and seats in garden; well equipped bedrooms

A fine choice of drinks, interesting food and a genuine welcome draw in a friendly crowd of both regulars and visitors to this charming place. The beamed bar has a log fire in a stone fireplace with red leather sofas beside it, cushioned window seats, a settle and various dining chairs around a few tables on patterned carpet; towards the back is a handsome carved chest, a table of newspapers and magazines and a noticeboard of local news and adverts. Exeter Avocet, Otter Bitter, St Austell Proper Job and Teignworthy Reel Ale on handpump, nine wines by the glass, cocktails, farm cider and 20 malt whiskies. The linked dining area has a woodburning stove, a cushioned wall pew, all manner of nice old wooden dining chairs and tables (each with a church candle) and similarly heavy beams; the large, cheerful animal paintings (which are also hung in the bedrooms) are by the landlord's wife. There's also a simpler public bar and a skittle alley. They hold free weekend film shows. The cobbled, three-level garden has fairy lights and simple seats and tables, and there are picnic-sets on grass beyond the hedge. The bedrooms are comfortable, modern and well equipped. Nearby parking is at a premium but the village car park is just a few minutes' walk up the small lane to the right.

Impressive food from a sensibly short menu includes lunchtime ciabattas, duck liver parfait with red onion marmalade, local crab won ton with mangetout and shellfish bisque, sausages and mash with onion gravy, pesto, artichoke and sunblush tomato tagliatelle, chorizo burger with onion rings and skinny fries, oxtail tortellini with seared scallop, celeriac rémoulade and red wine jus, poached and roasted poussin with confit leg, wild garlic gnocchi and watercress, and puddings such as fruit crumble and sticky toffee pudding with toffee sauce. *Benchmark main dish: venison port pie with garlic mash £11.85. Two-course evening meal £19.50.*

Free house ~ Licensee Mark Hildyard ~ Real ale ~ Open 10am-11pm (midnight); 10.30-10.30 Sat ~ Bar food 12-2.15, 6-9.15; 12-2.30, 6.30-8.30 Sun ~ Restaurant ~ Children welcome ~ Dogs welcome ~ Wi-fi ~ Open mike night first Fri of month, folk night first Tues ~ Bedrooms: £69/£89 *Recommended by Douglas Power*

 SIDBURY   SY1496 Map 1

Hare & Hounds ◀

(01404) 41760 – www.hareandhounds-devon.co.uk
3 miles N of Sidbury, at Putts Corner; A375 towards Honiton, crossroads with B3174; EX10 0QQ

Large, well run pub with log fires, beams and attractive layout, popular daily carvery and a big garden

This large roadside place is so popular that you must book a table in advance at lunchtime, when most customers are here for the exceptionally highly thought-of carvery. They also keep Otter Ale and Bitter and St Austell Tribute tapped from the cask and eight wines by the glass. There are two log fires (and rather unusual wood-framed leather sofas complete with pouffes), heavy beams, fresh flowers, and red plush cushioned dining chairs, window seats and leather sofas around plenty of tables on carpeting or bare boards. The newer dining extension, with a central open fire, leads on to a decked area; the seats here, and the picnic-sets in the big garden, have marvellous views down the Sid Valley to the sea at Sidmouth.

As well as the highly regarded carvery using the best local meat, they also offer a wide choice of dishes such as sandwiches, baguettes and panini, prawn cocktail with smoked salmon, deep-fried camembert with spiced peach chutney, chicken, beef or vegetable burger with a choice of toppings, coleslaw and chips, steak and kidney pudding, turkey curry, haddock, salmon and cod bake with a cheese topping, sweet and sour pork on rice, and puddings. *Benchmark main dish: daily carvery £10.35. Two-course evening meal £15.00.*

Heartstone Inns ~ Managers Graham Cole and Lindsey Chun ~ Real ale ~ Open 10am-11pm ~ Bar food 12-9 ~ Children welcome but no under-12s in bar ~ Dogs allowed in bar ~ Wi-fi *Recommended by Roy Hoing, William Slade, Julie Braeburn*

SOUTH ZEAL   SX6593 Map 1

Oxenham Arms ⇔

(01837) 840244 – www.theoxenhamarms.com
Off A30/A382; EX20 2JT

Wonderful 15th-c inn with lots of history, character bars, real ales, enjoyable food and big garden; bedrooms

This ancient place is just the spot to unwind after the busy A30. First licensed in 1477, it was built to combat the pagan power of the Neolithic standing stone that still forms part of the wall in the room behind the bar (there are actually 20 feet of stone below the floor). The heavily beamed and partly panelled front bar has elegant mullioned windows and Stuart fireplaces, all sorts of chairs and built-in wall seats with scatter cushions around low oak tables on bare floorboards, and bar stools against the counter where friendly staff serve Exeter 'fraidNot, Hunters Crispy Pig, a Red Rock beer named for the pub and a guest from Dartmoor on handpump; also, seven wines by the glass, 65 malt whiskies, 25 ports and three farm ciders. A small room has beams, wheelback chairs around polished tables, decorative plates and another open fire. The imposing curved stone steps lead up to the four-acre garden where there are plenty of seats and fine views; there are also seats under parasols out in front. Some of the bedrooms have four-poster beds. Charles Dickens, snowed up one winter, wrote a lot of *The Pickwick Papers* here. You can walk straight from the door on to the moor and they provide details of walking tours.

Good food includes king prawns on cucumber, orange and chilli salad, ham and bacon terrine with chutney, chickpea and potato curry, home-cooked honey and mustard ham with eggs, a pie of the day, beer-battered fish and chips, chicken with prosciutto, spinach and cheese sauce, venison steak with sweet potato and mushroom hash and blueberry and sloe gin jus, and puddings such as chocolate tart and vanilla crème brûlée. *Benchmark main dish: wild boar and apple sausages and mash £10.25. Two-course evening meal £18.00.*

Free house ~ Licensees Simon and Lyn Powell ~ Real ale ~ Open 11-11 ~ Bar food 12-2.30, 6-9; 12-5 afternoon tea and sandwiches ~ Restaurant ~ Children welcome ~ Dogs allowed in bar ~ Wi-fi ~ Bedrooms: /£115 *Recommended by Ron Corbett, Ian Herdman, David and Stella Martin, Comus and Sarah Elliott, Dr A McCormick*

SPARKWELL
Treby Arms ⭐

SX5857 Map 1

(01752) 837363 – www.thetrebyarms.co.uk
Off A38 at Smithaleigh, W of Ivybridge, Sparkwell signed from village; PL7 5DD

Devon Dining Pub of the Year

Village pub offering carefully crafted food, real ales, good wines and a friendly welcome

The food cooked by 2012 *MasterChef* winner Anton Piotrowski is so delicious that most customers come to this little village pub to eat. But there's a bar area used by locals for a pint and a chat, which keeps the atmosphere nicely informal. This small room has stools against the counter, simple wooden dining chairs and tables, a built-in cushioned window seat and a woodburning stove in a stone fireplace with shelves of cookery and guidebooks piled up on either side. Dartmoor Jail Ale and Hanlon Yellowhammer on handpump, several good wines by the glass from a list with helpful notes, 20 malt whiskies and local cider served by friendly, competent staff. Off to the right is the dining room with another woodburning stove, old glass and stone bottles on the mantelpiece and captain's and wheelback chairs around rustic tables; there's another carpeted dining room upstairs. The sunny front terrace has seats and tables.

Beautifully presented food using first class local, seasonal produce includes bar nibbles such as black pudding scotch egg, venison cigars and wild mushrooms on toast with an egg – also chilli, soy and mirin-glazed gurnard with marmite and parsnip purée and chilli-glazed cauliflower stem, slow-braised oxtail with pickled apple, quail egg yolk and truffle mash, local chicken bargain bucket with barbecue beans, honey and soy breast, coleslaw and chicken oyster salad, white wine-battered haddock with chip shop treats, and puddings such as chocolate caramel centre with banana parfait, banana chips and caramelised banana and yorkshire forced rhubarb with frangipane, custard and rhubarb sorbet. *Benchmark main dish: cocoa venison with chervil root, raisins, hazelnuts and madeira sauce £28.00. Two-course evening meal £31.00.*

Free house ~ Licensees Anton and Clare Piotrowski ~ Real ale ~ Open 12-3, 6-11; 12-11 Fri, Sat; 12-10.30 Sun; closed Mon ~ Bar food 12-2, 6-9 ~ Restaurant ~ Children welcome ~ Dogs allowed in bar ~ Wi-fi *Recommended by John Evans, Isobel Mackinlay, Kate Moran, Sally and David Champion*

SPREYTON

SX6996 Map 1

Tom Cobley

(01647) 231314 – www.tomcobleytavern.co.uk
Dragdown Hill; W out of village; EX17 5AL

Huge range of quickly changing real ales and ciders and wide choice of food in friendly and busy village pub

Up to 14 real ales are well kept on handpump or tapped from the cask here by the engaging landlord and his cheerful staff. These change all the time, but the main breweries are Dartmoor, Hanlon, Hunters, Otter, St Austell and Teignworthy; also, up to 14 farm ciders and perries and quite a range of malt whiskies. The comfortable little bar has straightforward pubby furnishings and an open fire, and local photographs and country scenes on the walls. A large back dining room has beams and background music. There are seats in the tree-shaded garden and more out in front by the quiet street. The bedrooms (some sharing bathrooms) are good value.

Honest, traditional food includes lunchtime sandwiches and open ciabattas, home-made brie pasties with cranberry sauce, deep-fried whitebait, burgers with toppings, coleslaw and chips, home-cooked ham and eggs, cottage pie, lamb and mint pudding, pork loin steaks in cream mushroom sauce, lambs liver and bacon with onion gravy, a mixed grill, and puddings. *Benchmark main dish: home-made pies £9.95. Two-course evening meal £17.00.*

Free house ~ Licensees Roger and Carol Cudlip ~ Real ale ~ Open 12-3, 6-11 (midnight Sat); 12-4, 7-11 Sun; closed Mon lunchtime ~ Bar food 12-2, 7-9 ~ Restaurant ~ Children welcome ~ Dogs allowed in bar ~ Bedrooms: £40/£80 *Recommended by Ian Herdman, Comus and Sarah Elliott, Edward and William Johnston*

STAVERTON

SX7964 Map 1

Sea Trout

(01803) 762274 – www.theseatroutinn.co.uk
Village signposted from A384 NW of Totnes; TQ9 6PA

Bustling old inn not far from the river, friendly owners, real ales, tasty food and back garden; bedrooms

There's a lot to do and see around this welcoming, partly 15th-c inn – so it makes sense to stay overnight in the clean, comfortable bedrooms that overlook the garden or the country lane; breakfasts are good. Fishing is available on the nearby River Dart (you can get daily permits). The neatly kept, beamed lounge has fishing flies and stuffed fish on the walls, and traditional tables and chairs on the part-carpeted and part-wood floor. The simpler locals' bar has wooden wall and other seats, a stag's head, guns and horsebrasses, a huge stuffed pike, a wood-burning stove and a cheerful mix of locals and visitors. Palmers 200, Copper Ale and Dorset Gold on handpump, 11 wines by the glass and several malt whiskies; background music and board games. There's also a smart, panelled restaurant and a conservatory. The attractive back garden has seats and tables.

Popular food includes sandwiches, creamy garlic mushrooms, half pint of prawns with lemon and chive mayonnaise, halloumi, red pepper and tomato linguine, beer-battered fresh fish and chips, cumberland sausages with chive mash and caramelised onion gravy, thai red chicken curry, a pie of the day, bream fillet with hazelnut and cheese crumble with scallop, leek and pea risotto, and puddings such as pear, stem ginger and cardamom sponge pudding and vanilla crème brûlée with cinnamon doughnuts. *Benchmark main dish: Sunday roast £11.95. Two-course evening meal £21.00.*

Palmers ~ Tenants Nigel and Simon Hewhouse ~ Real ale ~ Open 11-11 (midnight Sat) ~ Bar food 12-2 (3 Sun), 7-9 ~ Restaurant ~ Children welcome ~ Dogs allowed in bar and bedrooms ~ Wi-fi ~ Bedrooms: £80/£110 *Recommended by Peter Pilbeam, Mike and Margaret Banks, George Sanderson*

TIPTON ST JOHN   SY0991   Map 1
Golden Lion
(01404) 812881 – www.goldenliontipton.co.uk
Pub signed off B3176 Sidmouth–Ottery St Mary; EX10 0AA

Busy village pub with three real ales, well liked food and plenty of seats in the attractive garden

The food cooked here by the chef-landlord is very popular, so you must book a table in advance. There's a good mix of both locals and visitors and the main bar, split into two, has a comfortable, relaxed atmosphere, as does the back snug. Throughout are paintings by west country artists, art deco prints, Tiffany lamps and, hanging from the beams, hops, copper pots and kettles. A few tables are kept for those just wanting a pint and a chat. Otter Ale and Bitter and Sharps Doom Bar on handpump and 12 wines by the glass; background music. There are seats on the terracotta-walled terrace with outside heaters and grapevines and more seats on the grass edged by pretty flowering borders. Dog walkers and smokers may use a verandah.

 Good quality food includes lunchtime sandwiches, moules marinière, home-smoked duck salad with onion marmalade, vegetable lasagne, steak and kidney pudding, duck breast with oriental plum sauce, liver and bacon, venison pie, slow-roasted lamb shank, plaice with garlic butter, steak frites, and puddings such as fruit crumble and sticky toffee pudding. *Benchmark main dish: beer-battered cod and chips £10.50. Two-course evening meal £20.00.*

Heavitree ~ Tenants François and Michelle Teissier ~ Real ale ~ Open 12-2.30, 6-10 (11 Fri, Sat); closed Sun evening ~ Bar food 12-2, 6-8.30 ~ Children welcome
Recommended by Steve and Claire Harvey, Diane Abbott, Charles Todd

UGBOROUGH   SX6755   Map 1
Anchor ♀ ⇤
(01752) 690388 – www.anchorinnugborough.co.uk
Off A3121; PL21 0NG

A wide mix of customers for well run, gently civilised old inn, beamed rooms, good food and drink and seats outside; bedrooms

If you want to explore nearby Dartmoor National Park, you could stay in the comfortable, attractive and individually furnished bedrooms in this 17th-c pub – six are in the main inn and four in courtyard cabins. Throughout, the décor is light and contemporary with modern art on pale-painted walls and a relaxed and friendly atmosphere. The beamed bar has an open fire, leather sofas and dining chairs around a mix of tables on wooden flooring, and stools against the planked bar counter where they keep Sharps Doom Bar and Quercus Devon Amber on handpump and several wines by the glass; background music, TV and board games. The two-level beamed restaurant has elegant rattan dining chairs and wooden tables on flagstones in one part and more traditional dark wooden furniture on the lower area; there is a woodburning stove in a big fireplace.

Rewarding food includes sandwiches, salt and pepper local cuttlefish with tomato, chilli and red pepper salsa, duck liver parfait with truffle butter and onion relish, butternut squash risotto with crispy sage and parmesan, beer-battered hake and chips, pork and leek sausages with onion rings and red wine sauce, duck breast with fondant potato, butternut squash purée and plum jus, chicken breast with potato rösti, wild mushrooms and red wine jus, and puddings such as Baileys crème brûlée and apple tarte tatin with Rémy Martin sauce. *Benchmark main dish: local sirloin steak with onion rings, flat mushroom, chips and a choice of sauces £17.85. Two-course evening meal £20.00.*

Free house ~ Licensee Sarah Cuming ~ Real ale ~ Open 11-11 ~ Bar food 12-3, 6.30-9; 12-3, 6-9 Fri, Sat; 12-3, 6-8 Sun ~ Restaurant ~ Children welcome ~ Dogs allowed in bar ~ Wi-fi ~ Bedrooms: /£75 *Recommended by Charles Todd, Ben and Diane Bowie, Sandra King*

WIDECOMBE
Rugglestone ◀

SX7276 Map 1

(01364) 621327 – www.rugglestoneinn.co.uk
Village at end of B3387; pub just S – turn left at church and NT church house, OS Sheet 191 map reference 720765; TQ13 7TF

Charming local with a couple of bars, cheerful customers, friendly staff, four real ales and traditional pub food

A complete contrast to the busy tourist village just down the road, this remains a tucked-away gem. The unspoilt bar has just four tables, a few window and wall seats, a one-person pew built into the corner beside a nice old stone fireplace (with a woodburner) and a good mix of customers. The rudimentary bar counter dispenses Bays Gold, Dartmoor Legend, Otter Amber and a beer named for the pub (from Teignworthy) tapped from the cask; local farm cider and a decent small wine list. The room on the right is slightly bigger and lighter in feel, with beams, another stone fireplace, stripped-pine tables and a built-in wall bench; there's also a small dining room. To reach the picnic-sets in the garden you have to cross a bridge over a little moorland stream. They have a holiday cottage to rent.

Good, popular food includes sandwiches, deep-fried brie with redcurrant jelly, local potted crab, large pasty, cheese and spinach cannelloni in garlic, herb and tomato sauce, ham and eggs, steak and stilton pie, beer-battered fresh haddock and chips, and puddings. *Benchmark main dish: fish pie £10.50. Two-course evening meal £16.00.*

Free house ~ Licensees Richard and Vicki Palmer ~ Real ale ~ Open 11.30-3, 6-11.30; 11.30-3, 5-midnight Fri; 11.30am-midnight Sat; 11.30-11 Sun ~ Bar food 12-2, 6.30-9 ~ Restaurant ~ Children allowed away from bar area ~ Dogs welcome *Recommended by John Hammond, Elizabeth and Peter May, Peter Pilbeam*

WOODBURY SALTERTON
Diggers Rest

SY0189 Map 1

(01395) 232375 – www.diggersrest.co.uk
3.5 miles from M5 junction 30: A3052 towards Sidmouth, village signposted on right about 0.5 miles after Clyst St Mary; also signposted from B3179 SE of Exeter; EX5 1PQ

Bustling village pub with real ales, well liked food and country views from the terraced garden

There are walks around Woodbury Common and in the surrounding Otter Valley, so this thatched former cider house makes a good pit stop. The main bar has antique furniture, local art on the walls and a cosy seating area by the open fire. The modern extension is light and airy and opens on to the garden. Exeter Lighterman, Otter Ale and a guest from Powder Keg on handpump, 13 wines by the glass and Weston's cider; service is attentive and efficient. Background music, darts, TV and board games. The window boxes and flowering baskets are pretty in summer.

A changing choice of food includes smoked mackerel and dill fishcakes with lemon mayonnaise, sautéed chicken livers with red wine and balsamic jus and caramelised onion toast, beef and pork burger with chorizo, toppings, relish and chips, moules marinière with fries, creamy peas, asparagus and feta on pasta, duck breast with thyme-scented fondant potato, celeriac purée and red wine jus, and puddings such as vanilla pannacotta with mixed berry jelly and flapjack crumble and sticky toffee pudding with caramelised banana and butterscotch sauce; they also offer a two- and three-course set weekday menu. *Benchmark main dish: pie of the day £12.75. Two-course evening meal £19.00.*

Heartstone Inns ~ Licensee Marc Slater ~ Real ale ~ Open 11-3, 5.30-11; 11-11 Sat; 12-10.30 Sun ~ Bar food 12-2.15, 6-9 ~ Restaurant ~ Children welcome ~ Dogs welcome ~ Wi-fi ~ Live music, check website for dates *Recommended by Roger and Donna Huggins, Roy Hoing, Mike and Margaret Banks*

Also Worth a Visit in Devon

Besides the fully inspected pubs, you might like to try these pubs that have been recommended to us and described by readers. Do tell us what you think of them: feedback@goodguides.com

ABBOTSKERSWELL　　　SX8568
Court Farm (01626) 361866
Wilton Way; look for the church tower; TQ12 5NY
Attractive neatly extended 17th-c longhouse tucked away in picturesque hamlet, various rooms off long beamed and paved main bar, good mix of furnishings, woodburners, well priced popular food (worth booking) including weekday lunchtime bargains, friendly helpful service, several ales including Bass and Otter, farm cider and decent wines; background music, pool and darts; children welcome, picnic-sets in pretty lawned garden, open all day (food all day Thurs-Sun). *(Sandra and Nigel Brown)*

APPLEDORE　　　SS4630
Beaver (01237) 474822
Irsha Street; EX39 1RY Relaxed harbourside pub with lovely estuary view from popular raised dining area, well priced food especially fresh local fish, prompt friendly service, good choice of west country ales, farm cider, decent house wines and great range of whiskies; background and some live music including jazz, pool in smaller games room, TV; children and dogs (in bar) welcome, disabled access (but no nearby parking), tables on small sheltered water-view terrace. *(William Slade)*

APPLEDORE　　　SS4630
Seagate (01237) 472589
The Quay; EX39 1QS Refurbished 17th-c quayside inn, good food from lunchtime baguettes to fresh fish specials, smaller appetites catered for, four real ales, two ciders and ten wines by the glass, friendly helpful service; children and dogs welcome, terraces seating front and back, ten updated bedrooms (some with estuary view), open all day from 8am. *(Tom Stone)*

ASHILL　　　ST0811
Ashill Inn (01884) 840506
M5 junction 27, follow signs to Willand, then left to Uffculme and Craddock on B3440; Ashill signed to left; pub in centre of village; EX15 3NL Popular 19th-c village pub, cosy and friendly, with well kept local ales and good home-cooked food including daily specials (booking advised), reasonable prices, black beams, woodburner in stone fireplace, modern dining extension overlooking small garden; some live music, darts and skittles, TV; children welcome, closed Mon lunchtime, no food Sun evening. *(Guy Vowles)*

ASHPRINGTON   SX8157
Durant Arms (01803) 732240
Off A381 S of Totnes; TQ9 7UP
Comfortably refurbished 18th-c village
inn with enjoyable home-cooked food and
three well kept ales, good friendly service,
slate-floored bar with stag's head above
woodburner, china on delft shelf, other
connecting rooms; vintage juke box; children,
walkers and dogs welcome, four bedrooms
(one in courtyard annexe), closed Sun
evening, Mon. *(Anne and Ben Smith)*

ASHPRINGTON   SX8056
Watermans Arms (01803) 732214
*Bow Bridge, on Tuckenhay Road;
TQ9 7EG* Whitewashed 17th-c creekside
inn; beamed and quarry-tiled main bar area,
built-in cushioned wall seats and wheelbacks
around stripped tables, log fire, dining room
with fishing-related décor, comfortable
lounge area down steps, four Palmers ales
and several wines by the glass, good choice
of traditional seasonal food from sandwiches
and baked potatoes up; background music;
children and dogs (in bar) welcome, seats
out by the water (maybe kingfishers) and in
garden, 15 bedrooms (some in purpose-built
annexe), open all day. *(Mike and Margaret
Banks)*

AVONWICK   SX6958
★ Turtley Corn Mill (01364) 646100
*0.5 miles off A38 roundabout at SW end
of South Brent bypass; TQ10 9ES*
Carefully converted watermill with series of
linked areas, mix of wooden dining chairs
and chunky tables, bookcases, church
candles and oriental rugs or dark flagstones,
woodburners, various prints and some framed
78rpm discs, big windows looking out over
grounds, Hanlons, Otter, St Austell and
Summerskills, nine wines by the glass and 30
malt whiskies, wide choice of brasserie-style
food, free wi-fi; children and
dogs (in bar) welcome, extensive garden with
well spaced picnic-sets, giant chess set and
small lake, four bedrooms, open (and food)
all day from 8.30am for breakfast. *(John
Evans, B J Harding, Lynda and Trevor Smith)*

AXMOUTH   SY2591
★ Harbour Inn (01297) 20371
B3172 Seaton–Axminster; EX12 4AF
Ancient thatched pub by estuary; heavily
beamed bar rooms with bare boards and
stripped stone walls, huge inglenook, lots of
model boats, old pictures, photographs and
accounts of shipwrecks, other partitioned
dining/seating areas including carpeted part
with armchairs by woodburner, Badger ales
and several wines by the glass, large helpings
of enjoyable good value food from sandwiches
and deli boards up, friendly service;

background music; children and dogs (in
bar) welcome, modern furniture on terrace,
picnic-sets on grass, open (and food) all day
from 9am. *(Roger and Donna Huggins)*

AYLESBEARE   SY0490
Halfway (01395) 232273
*A3052 Exeter–Sidmouth, junction with
B3180; EX5 2JP* Modernised roadside
dining pub (same owners as the Bowd in
Sidmouth), well cooked food from fairly
priced pub favourites up including home-
made american-style burgers, good fresh fish/
seafood and other daily specials, Sun carvery,
well kept Otter Bitter and Greene King
Abbot, efficient friendly service, Dartmoor
views from restaurant and raised outside
seating area; children welcome, open (and
food) all day. *(Roger and Donna Huggins)*

BAMPTON   SS9622
Quarrymans Rest (01398) 331480
Briton Street; EX16 9LN Village pub with
beamed and carpeted main bar, leather sofas
in front of inglenook woodburner, dining
chairs and some housekeepers' chairs around
wooden tables, enjoyable home-made food
and four well kept west country ales, friendly
service, steps up to comfortable stripped-
stone dining room with high-backed leather
chairs and heavy pine tables; pool and games
machines; children and dogs welcome,
picnic-sets in pretty back garden, more seats
in front, four bedrooms, open all day.
(S G N Bennett, John and Sarah Perry)

BAMPTON   SS9522
Swan (01398) 332248
Station Road; EX16 9NG Popular beamed
village inn with spacious bare-boards bar,
woodburners in two inglenooks, three
changing local beers, decent wines and good
home-made food (not Mon) from interesting
varied menu, efficient friendly service;
children and dogs welcome, well appointed
bedrooms, big breakfast, closed Mon
lunchtime otherwise open all day.
(David Longhurst)

BANTHAM   SX6643
★ Sloop (01548) 560489
*Off A379/B3197 NW of Kingsbridge;
TQ7 3AJ* Welcoming 14th-c split-level pub
close to fine beach and walks, popular and
relaxed, with good mix of customers in black-
beamed stripped-stone bar, country tables
and chairs on flagstones, blazing woodburner,
well kept St Austell and a guest ale, enjoyable
food from nice sandwiches to good fresh
fish, friendly efficient service, restaurant;
background music; children and dogs
welcome, seats out at back, five bedrooms,
open all day in summer. *(Theocsbrian, Bob and
Margaret Holder, Lynda and Trevor Smith, Jane
and Kai Horsburgh)*

We say if we know a pub has background music.

BEER ST2289

Anchor (01297) 20386

Fore Street; EX12 3ET Sea-view inn with good choice of enjoyable food including local fish, Greene King, Otter and good value wines, refurbished open-plan interior with large eating area, friendly staff; background music, sports TV, free wi-fi; children well looked after, lots of tables in clifftop garden over road, six reasonably priced bedrooms, open (and food) all day. *(John Coatsworth, Roger and Donna Huggins)*

BEESANDS SX8140

★**Cricket** (01548) 580215

About 3 miles S of A379, from Chillington; in village turn right along foreshore road; TQ7 2EN Friendly popular pub-restaurant with pebbly Start Bay beach just over the sea wall; light airy new england-style décor with dark wood or leather chairs around big solid tables, stripped-wood flooring by the bar, patterned carpet in the restaurant, relaxed chatty atmosphere with a few tables kept for drinkers, Otter and St Austell ales, local cider and 14 wines by the glass, very good food with emphasis on fish/seafood; background music, TVs, free wi-fi; children and dogs (in bar) welcome, picnic-sets by sea wall, light attractive bedrooms (some overlooking sea), South West Coast Path runs through the village, open all day, food all day in high summer. *(Helen and Brian Edgeley, Richard Tilbrook, Bob and Margaret Holder, Dave Braisted, Jane and Kai Horsburgh)*

BELSTONE SX61293

Tors (01837) 840689

A mile off A30; EX20 1QZ Popular small Victorian granite pub-hotel in peaceful Dartmoor-edge village, family-run and welcoming, with long carpeted bar divided by settles, well kept ales such as Dartmoor and Sharps, over 60 malt whiskies and good choice of wines, enjoyable food from baguettes to specials, cheerful prompt service, restaurant; children welcome and dogs (they have their own), disabled access, seats out on nearby grassy area overlooking valley, good walks, bedrooms, open all day in summer. *(Chris and Angela Buckell)*

BERE FERRERS SX4563

Old Plough (01822) 840358

Long dead-end road off B3257 S of Tavistock; PL20 7JL 16th-c pub in secluded River Tavy village; stripped stone and panelling, low beam-and-plank ceilings, slate flagstones and woodburner, enjoyable good value home-cooked food including decent vegetarian choice, well kept Hunters, Sharps Doom Bar and a couple of guests, real cider, warm local atmosphere, steps down to cosy restaurant; live music; children and dogs welcome, garden overlooking estuary, open all day Sun. *(Tom Stone)*

BERRYNARBOR SS5546

Olde Globe (01271) 882465

Off A399 E of Ilfracombe; EX34 9SG Rambling dimly lit rooms geared to family visitors (cutlasses, swords, shields and rustic oddments), good choice of reasonably priced straightforward food including Sun carvery, Exmoor and St Austell ales, friendly service, ancient walls and flagstones, high-backed oak settles and antique tables, lots of old pictures, open fire and woodburner, more modern family room, play areas inside and out; background and summer live music; dogs welcome, tables on paved front terrace and side lawn, pretty village, open all day in season from 9.30am. *(Charles Todd)*

BICKLEIGH SS9307

Fishermans Cot (01884) 855237

A3072; EX16 8RW Greatly extended thatched riverside pub with wide choice of good local food and well kept Marstons ales, reasonable prices, friendly helpful service, lots of round tables on stone and carpet, pillars, plants and some panelled parts, fishing bric-a-brac, raised dining area, charming view over shallow rocky race below 1640 Exe bridge; background music, can get busy especially weekends and with coach parties; dogs welcome, terrace and waterside lawn, 19 good bedrooms, open all day. *(Dave Braisted)*

BISHOP'S TAWTON SS5629

★**Chichester Arms** (01271) 343945

Signed off A377 outside Barnstaple; East Street; EX32 0DQ Friendly 15th-c cob and thatch pub, good generous well priced food from sandwiches/baguettes to fresh local fish, quick obliging service even when crowded, St Austell Tribute, Charles Wells Bombardier and a guest, decent wines, heavy low beams, large stone fireplace, restaurant; free wi-fi; children and dogs welcome, awkward disabled access but staff very helpful, picnic-sets on front terrace and in back garden, open all day. *(Peter and Jean Hoare)*

BLACKAWTON SX8050

★**Normandy Arms** (01803) 712884

Signposted off A3122 W of Dartmouth; TQ9 7BN Restaurant pub and most here for the very good (if not cheap) food in two main dining areas, high-backed chairs around wooden tables on slate floors, drinkers' area with leather tub chairs and sofas by woodburner, a couple of local ales, good wines by the glass and cocktails; benches out in front and picnic-sets in small garden across lane, pretty village (May worm-charming competition), three bedrooms, closed Mon, lunchtimes Tues-Sat and Sun evening. *(William Slade)*

BOVEY TRACEY SX8178

Cromwell Arms (01626) 833473

Fore Street; TQ13 9AE Welcoming 17th-c

beamed inn with popular good value food and up to five St Austell ales, several areas including separate restaurant; quiz Tues and Sun, games machines, free wi-fi; children and dogs (in bar) welcome, disabled access/facilities, small garden with decking and pergola, 14 bedrooms, open all day. *(Elizabeth and Peter May)*

BRANSCOMBE SY1888
Fountain Head (01297) 680359
Upper village, W of Branscombe at Street; OS Sheet 192 map reference SY188889; EX12 3BG Unchanging nicely old-fashioned 14th-c tavern; room on left (former smithy) with forge tools and horseshoes on high oak beams, cushioned pews and mate's chairs, log fire in original raised hearth with tall central chimney, a couple of Branscombe Vale beers and a guest, local cider and several wines by the glass, enjoyable fair-priced food; irregularly shaped snug room on right has another log fire, white-painted plank ceiling with unusual carved ceiling rose, brown-varnished panelling and flagstone floor, local artwork for sale; live summer entertainment Sun evenings, darts and board games; children (away from bar) and dogs (in bar) welcome, seats on terrace, good coastal walks, open all day Sun. *(John Coatsworth, Roger and Donna Huggins, Revd R P Tickle)*

BRATTON CLOVELLY SX4691
Clovelly (01837) 871447
From S (A30), turn left at church, pub is on the right; EX20 4JZ Friendly 18th-c village pub with cosy bar and two dining rooms, generous helpings of popular reasonably priced traditional food, well kept Dartmoor, St Austell and a guest, cheerful staff, woodburner, games room; may be live jazz second Mon of month; children and dogs welcome, 17th-c wall paintings in Norman church, open all day weekends. *(M G Hart)*

BRAUNTON SS5135
Braunton (01271) 816547
A361 towards Barnstaple; EX31 4AX Former castellated manor house (now a Vintage Inn) with great estuary views; good choice of fairly priced food including evening set menu (Mon-Thurs), real ales and plenty of wines by the glass, friendly staff; children welcome, no dogs inside, large front garden taking in the view, open all day. *(Adrian Johnson)*

BRAYFORD SS7235
★ Poltimore Arms (01598) 710381
Yarde Down; 3 miles towards Simonsbath; EX36 3HA Ivy-clad 17th-c beamed pub – so remote it generates its own electricity and water is from a spring; good home-made food including daily specials (best to book) and two or three changing ales tapped from the cask, friendly helpful staff, traditional furnishings, woodburner in

inglenook, two attractive restaurant areas separated by another woodburner, good country views; free wi-fi; children and dogs (in bar) welcome, picnic-sets in side garden, shop and gallery, open all day. *(Julie Braeburn)*

BRENDON SS7547
★ Rockford Inn (01598) 741214
Rockford; Lynton–Simonsbath Road, off B3223; EX35 6PT Homely and welcoming little 17th-c beamed inn surrounded by fine walks and scenery (sister to the Manor House at Ditcheat, Somerset); neatly linked rooms with cushioned settles, wall seats and other straightforward furniture, country prints and horse tack, open fires, good helpings of enjoyable well priced pubby food (not Mon lunchtime), well kept ales such as Clearwater and Cotleigh tapped from the cask, Adlestone's and Thatcher's ciders, decent wines by the glass, lots of pump clips and toby jugs behind counter; background music, board games; children and dogs (in bar) welcome, seats across the road overlooking East Lyn river, well appointed bedrooms, open all day. *(Theocsbrian)*

BRENDON SS7648
Staghunters (01598) 741222
Leedford Lane; EX35 6PS Idyllically set family-run hotel with gardens by East Lyn river, good choice of enjoyable reasonably priced food, up to five well kept ales such as Cotleigh, Exmoor and Otter, friendly efficient staff, bar with woodburner, restaurant; can get very busy, though quiet out of season; children, walkers and dogs welcome, riverside tables, 12 good value bedrooms, open all day weekends (and weekdays if busy). *(Bob and Margaret Holder)*

BRIXHAM SX9256
Blue Anchor (01803) 469165
Fore Street/King Street; TQ5 8AH Friendly harbourside local, some recent refurbishment but keeping old-fashioned character, plenty of nautical hardware, interesting old photographs and log fire, well kept ales and enjoyable generously served traditional food from sandwiches up, two small dining rooms – one a former chapel down steps; weekend live music; children welcome, dogs allowed in some areas, open all day. *(David Delaney)*

BRIXHAM SX9256
★ Maritime (01803) 853535
King Street (up steps from harbour – nearby parking virtually non-existent); TQ5 9TH Single bar packed with bric-a-brac, chamber-pots hanging from beams, hundreds of key fobs, cigarette cards, pre-war ensigns, toby jugs, mannequins, astronomical charts, even a binnacle by the door, Hunters Half Bore and Pheasant Plucker, over 80 malt whiskies, no food or credit cards, long-serving landlady, lively terrier called George and Mr

Tibbs the parrot; background music, small TV, darts and board games; well behaved children and dogs allowed, fine views over harbour, six bedrooms (not ensuite), closed lunchtime. *(Millie and Peter Downing)*

BRIXHAM   SX9256
New Quay (01803) 883290
King Street; TQ5 9TW Newly refurbished early 18th-c pub tucked down side street; well kept changing west country beers and ciders from board-fronted servery, good range of wines by the glass and gins, friendly helpful staff, beam and plank ceiling, spindleback chairs and mix of old tables on slate tiles, warming woodburner, fairly traditional menu using fresh local produce, upstairs restaurant with another woodburner and old town views; no under-18s in bar after 7.30pm, dogs welcome in bar, closed Sun evening, Mon and Tues, open from 5.30pm other days. *(David Delaney)*

BROADCLYST   SX9997
New Inn (01392) 461312
Wimple Road; EX5 3BX Friendly former 17th-c farmhouse with stripped brickwork, boarded ceiling, low doorways and log fires, well cooked reasonably priced pubby food, Dartmoor, Hanlons, Otter and Sharps, good attentive service, small restaurant; skittle alley; children and dogs welcome, garden with play area, open all day. *(Philip Kingsbury)*

BROADCLYST   SX9897
Red Lion (01392) 461271
B3121, by church; EX5 3EL Refurbished 16th-c pub under same owners as the Hunters at Newton Tracey; heavy beams, flagstones and log fires, St Austell and a local guest, enjoyable well priced traditional food (special diets catered for) in bar and restaurant, good cheerful service; children and dogs welcome, picnic-sets out in front below wisteria, more in small enclosed garden across quiet lane, nice village and 15th-c church, not far from Killerton (NT), open all day weekends. *(Jeremy Snaithe)*

BROADHEMBURY   ST1004
Drewe Arms (01404) 841267
Off A373 Cullompton–Honiton; EX14 3NF Extended partly thatched family-run pub dating from the 15th c; carved beams and handsome stone-mullioned windows, woodburner and open fire, mix of furniture (some perhaps not matching age of building), modernised bar area, five well kept local ales and seven wines by the glass, enjoyable pubby food (all day weekends), friendly helpful service, skittle alley; children and dogs welcome, terrace seats, more up

steps on tree-shaded lawn, nice setting near church in pretty village, open all day. *(Tom Stone)*

BUCKFAST   SX7467
Abbey Inn (01364) 642343
Buckfast Road, off B3380; TQ11 0EA Lovely position perched on bank of River Dart; partly panelled bar with woodburner, three St Austell ales and Healey's cider, enjoyable reasonably priced pubby food from sandwiches and baguettes up, Sun carvery, big dining room with more panelling and river views; background music, free wi-fi; well behaved children and dogs (in bar) welcome, terrace and bedrooms overlooking the water, open all day. *(B J Harding)*

BUCKLAND BREWER   SS4220
★ ## Coach & Horses (01237) 451395
Village signposted off A388 S of Monkleigh; OS Sheet 190 map reference 423206; EX39 5LU Friendly old thatched pub with heavily beamed bar, comfortable seats, handsome antique settle and inglenook woodburner, smaller lounge with log fire in second inglenook, Exmoor Gold, Otter Ale and Sharps Doom Bar, local ciders, decent food including curries, small back games room (darts and pool) and skittle alley/function room; background music, games machine, occasional sports TV, free wi-fi; children and dogs (in bar) welcome, picnic-sets on front terrace and in side garden, holiday cottage. *(Bob and Margaret Holder)*

BUDLEIGH SALTERTON   SY0681
Feathers (01395) 442042
High Street; EX9 6LE Old town-centre inn with bustling local atmosphere in long beamed lounge/dining bar, well kept St Austell Tribute and three guests, enjoyable reasonably priced pubby food (not Sun evening) including specials, friendly staff, public bar with pool, darts and TV, skittle alley; Sun quiz, some live music; children and dogs welcome, nice secluded little garden, four bedrooms, open all day. *(Roger and Donna Huggins)*

BURGH ISLAND   SX6444
Pilchard (01548) 810514
300 metres across tidal sands from Bigbury-on-Sea; walk, or summer sea tractor if tide's in; TQ7 4BG Sadly, the splendid beamed and flagstoned upper bar with its lanterns and roaring log fire is reserved for guests at the associated flamboyantly art deco hotel, but the more utilitarian left-hand bar is still worth a visit for the unbeatable setting high above the sea swarming below this tidal island; Sharps, Thwaites and an ale named for the pub, lunchtime baguettes, Fri curry night;

If you know a pub is ever open all day, please tell us.

children and dogs welcome, tables outside, as well as some down by beach, open all day. *(Charles Todd)*

BUTTERLEIGH   SS9708
Butterleigh Inn (01884) 855433
Off A396 in Bickleigh; EX15 1PN
Traditional heavy-beamed country pub, friendly and relaxed with good mix of customers, enjoyable reasonably priced pubby food (not Mon) including Sun carvery, four well kept ales such as Cotleigh and Otter, good choice of wines, unspoilt lived-in interior with two big fireplaces, back dining room; free wi-fi; children and dogs welcome, picnic-sets in large garden, four comfortable bedrooms, closed Sun evening, Mon lunchtime. *(Patricia Hawkins)*

CADELEIGH   SS9107
★Cadeleigh Arms (01884) 855238
Village signed off A3072 W of junction with A396 Tiverton–Exeter at Bickleigh; EX16 8HP Attractive and friendly old pub owned by the local community; well kept Cotleigh, Dartmoor, St Austell and a guest, fresh locally sourced food (not Sun evening) from favourites up, carpeted room on left with bay-window seat and ornamental stove, flagstoned room to the right with high-backed settles and log fire in big fireplace, valley views from airy dining room down a couple of steps; background music, games room (pool and darts) and skittle alley; children and dogs welcome, picnic-sets on gravel terrace with barbecue, more on gently sloping lawn, closed Mon lunchtime. *(George Sanderson)*

CALIFORNIA CROSS   SX7053
California (01548) 821449
Brown sign to pub off A3121 S of A38 junction; PL21 0SG Neatly kept 18th-c or older beamed dining pub, red carpets, panelling and stripped stone, plates on delft shelving and other bits and pieces, log fire, good choice of enjoyable food from baguettes to steaks in bar and family area, popular Sun lunch (best to book), separate evening restaurant (Weds-Sun) and small snug, St Austell Tribute, Sharps Doom Bar and a local guest, traditional cider and decent wines by the glass, good friendly service; background music, free wi-fi; dogs welcome, attractive garden and back terrace, open all day. *(Anne and Ben Smith)*

CHAGFORD   SX7087
Ring o' Bells (01647) 432466
Off A382; TQ13 8AH Welcoming old pub with beamed and panelled bar, four well kept ales including Dartmoor, traditional fairly priced home-made food, good friendly service, woodburner in big fireplace; some live music, free wi-fi; well behaved children and dogs welcome, sunny walled garden, nearby moorland walks, four comfortable bedrooms, open all day. *(Dr A McCormick)*

CHALLACOMBE   SS6941
Black Venus (01598) 763251
B3358 Blackmoor Gate–Simonsbath; EX31 4TT Low-beamed 16th-c pub with two or three well kept changing ales, Thatcher's cider and decent wines by the glass, enjoyable fairly priced food from sandwiches to popular Sun lunch, friendly helpful staff, pews and comfortable chairs, woodburner and big fireplace, roomy attractive dining area, games room with pool and darts; free wi-fi; children and dogs welcome, garden play area, lovely countryside and good walks from the door, open all day in summer. *(Lynda and Trevor Smith)*

CHERITON BISHOP   SX7792
★Old Thatch Inn (01647) 24204
Off A30; EX6 6JH Attractive thatched village pub with welcoming relaxed atmosphere, rambling beamed bar separated by big stone fireplace (woodburner), Otter, Dartmoor and a couple of guests, ciders such as Sandford's, good freshly prepared food from owner-chef, efficient friendly service, restaurant; free wi-fi; children and dogs welcome, nice sheltered garden, two comfortable clean bedrooms. *(Charles Todd)*

CHITTLEHAMHOLT   SS6420
★Exeter Inn (01769) 540281
Off A377 Barnstaple–Crediton, and B3226 SW of South Molton; EX37 9NS 16th-c thatched coaching inn with good food from sandwiches and traditional choices up, well kept ales such as Exmoor and Otter (some tapped from the cask), local ciders and good wine choice, friendly staff, barrel seats by open stove in huge fireplace, beams dotted with hundreds of matchboxes, shelves of old bottles, traditional games, lounge with comfortable seating and woodburner, dining room and barn-style conservatory; background music; children and dogs welcome, gravel terrace, three bedrooms and four self-catering units. *(Sandra and Nigel Brown)*

CHRISTOW   SX8385
★Teign House (01647) 252286
Teign Valley Road (B3193); EX6 7PL Former farmhouse in country setting, open fire in beamed bar, very good freshly made food from pub favourites up, also an asian menu, friendly helpful staff, up to five well kept local ales, own Brimblecombe's cider and nice wines, dining room; some live music; well behaved children and dogs welcome, garden and camping field, open all day weekends. *(Charles Todd)*

CHUDLEIGH   SX8679
Bishop Lacey (01626) 854585
Fore Street, just off A38; TQ13 0HY Partly 14th-c low-beamed church house, three well kept west country beers and enjoyable reasonably priced home-made

food including some good curries, cheerful obliging staff, two bars, log fire; children and dogs welcome, open all day. *(Tom Stone)*

CHULMLEIGH   SS6814
Red Lion   (01769) 580384
East Street; EX18 7DD Nicely updated and well divided 17th-c coaching inn, beams and open fires, enjoyable fairly priced food including burgers and pizzas, St Austell, Sharps and a guest, friendly helpful service; background and some live music, darts; children welcome, five bedrooms, open all day Fri-Sun, closed Mon lunchtime.
(George Sanderson)

CHURCHSTOW   SX7145
Church House   (01548) 852237
A379 NW of Kingsbridge; TQ7 3QW Attractive building dating from the 13th c, heavy black beams and stripped stone, enjoyable home-made food including daily specials and popular carvery (Weds-Sat evenings, Sun lunchtime, booking advised), St Austell ales and decent wines, friendly staff, back conservatory with floodlit well; children welcome, dogs in certain areas, tables on big terrace. *(Tom Stone)*

CLAYHIDON   ST1615
Half Moon   (01823) 680291
On main road through village; EX15 3TJ Attractive old village pub with warm friendly atmosphere, wide choice of good home-made food from sharing boards up, well kept Otter and a couple of guests, farm cider, good wine list, comfortable bar with inglenook log fire; some live music; children and dogs welcome, picnic-sets in tiered garden over road, lovely valley views, closed Sun evening, Mon.
(Mr and Mrs R G Spiller, Mrs Zara Elliott, David Thirkettle, Guy Vowles)

CLAYHIDON   ST1817
Merry Harriers   (01823) 421270
3 miles from M5 junction 26, A38 Wellington; follow to Ford Street and Hemyock, left to Chard and pub is in 2 miles; EX15 3TR Roadside country pub with several small linked carpeted areas, comfortably cushioned pews and farmhouse chairs, woodburner, Exmoor, Otter and a guest ale, Thatcher's cider, enjoyable traditional food in two beamed dining rooms with quarry tiles and lightly timbered white walls, friendly helpful staff; skittle alley; children and dogs welcome, sizeable garden with small play area, good surrounding walks, open all day Sat, closed Sun evening, Mon. *(William Ruxton, Bob and Margaret Holder, Philip Kingsbury, Dave Braisted, Guy Vowles)*

CLOVELLY   SS3124
Red Lion   (01237) 431237
The Quay; EX39 5TF Rambling 18th-c building in lovely position on curving quay below spectacular cliffs; beams, flagstones, log fire and interesting local photographs in character back bar (dogs on leads allowed here), well kept Country Life and Sharps, bar food and upstairs restaurant, efficient service; great views, 11 attractive bedrooms (six more in Sail Loft annexe), own car park for residents and diners, open all day.
(Patricia Hawkins)

CLYST HYDON   ST0201
★**Five Bells**   (01884) 277288
W of village, just off B3176 not far from M5 junction 28; EX15 2NT Thatched and beamed dining pub under same owners as the Jack in the Green at Rockbeare; smart interior with several different areas including raised dining part, woodburner in large stone fireplace, really good attractively presented food including weekday set lunch, efficient friendly service, four well kept ales such as Butcombe and Otter, games room with pool and sports TV; live jazz last Sun of month; children welcome, dogs in bar, disabled access/loo, lovely cottagey garden, country views, open all day Sun. *(Barrie and Anne King, Paul and Sonia Broadgate)*

COCKINGTON   SX8963
Drum   (01803) 690264
Cockington Lane; TQ2 6XA Bustling Vintage Inn in thatched and beamed tavern (designed by Lutyens to match this quaintly touristy Torquay-edge medieval village); roomy well divided wood-floor bar with open fires, St Austell, Otter and Sharps, good choice of wines by the glass, their usual food including set menu choices, friendly service; children and dogs welcome, tables on terrace and in attractive back garden by 500-acre park, open all day. *(Mike and Margaret Banks)*

COCKWOOD   SX9780
★**Ship**   (01626) 890373
Off A379 N of Dawlish; EX6 8NU Comfortable traditional 17th-c pub set back from estuary and harbour – gets very busy in season; good value freshly made food including good fish specials, five ales such as Hanlons, Otter and St Austell, friendly staff and locals, partitioned beamed bar with big log fire and ancient oven, decorative plates and seafaring memorabilia, small restaurant; background music; children and dogs welcome, nice steep-sided garden, open all day, food all day Sun. *(Matt Worthington)*

COLYTON   SY2494
Kingfisher   (01297) 552476
Off A35 and A3052 E of Sidmouth; Dolphin Street; EX24 6NA Low-beamed 16th-c village pub with three well kept ales such as Sharps and Skinners, popular reasonably priced food, stripped stone, plush seats and elm settles, back restaurant; pub games and skittle alley, outside gents'; children and dogs welcome, terrace tables, garden with water feature, boules, open all day. *(Roger and Donna Huggins)*

COMBE MARTIN SS5846
Pack o' Cards (01271) 882300
High Street; EX34 0ET Unusual 'house of cards' building constructed in the late 17th c to celebrate a substantial gambling win – four floors, 13 rooms and 52 windows; snug bar area and various side rooms, St Austell Tribute, Charles Wells Bombardier and a guest, enjoyable inexpensive pub food including children's choices and good Sun roast, friendly helpful service, restaurant; dogs welcome, pretty riverside garden with play area, six comfortable bedrooms, generous breakfast, open all day. *(R T and J C Moggridge)*

COMBEINTEIGNHEAD SX9071
Wild Goose (01626) 872241
Off unclassified coast road Newton Abbot–Shaldon, uphill in village; TQ12 4RA Refurbished 17th-c pub under friendly family management; five west country ales in spacious back beamed lounge, agricultural bits and pieces on the walls, good freshly made food including daily specials, front bar with big fireplace, more beams, standing timbers and some flagstones, step down to area with another large fireplace, further cosy room with tub chairs; background and fortnightly live music, Sun quiz, TV projector for major sporting events; children and dogs welcome, back garden with nice country views, open all day weekends. *(Millie and Peter Downing)*

COUNTISBURY SS7449
Blue Ball (01598) 741263
A39, E of Lynton; EX35 6NE Beautifully set heavy-beamed rambling pub, friendly licensees, good range of generous local food in bar and restaurant, three or four ales including Exmoor and one badged for them, decent wines and proper ciders, log fires; background music, TV, free wi-fi; children, dogs and walkers welcome, views from terrace tables, good nearby cliff walks (pub provides handouts of four circular routes), comfortable bedrooms, open all day. *(Tom Stone)*

CREDITON SS8300
Crediton Inn (01363) 772882
Mill Street (follow Tiverton sign); EX17 1EZ Small friendly local (the 'Kirton') with long-serving landlady, well kept Hanlons Yellowhammer and up to nine quickly changing guests (Nov beer festival), cheap well prepared weekend food, home-made scotch eggs other times, back games room/skittle alley; free wi-fi; open all day Mon–Sat. *(Anon)*

CROYDE SS4439
Manor House Inn (01271) 890241
St Marys Road, off B3231 NW of Braunton; EX33 1PG Friendly family pub with cheerful efficient service, three well kept west country ales, good choice of enjoyable fairly priced food from lunchtime sandwiches to blackboard specials, carvery Weds and Sun, cream teas, restaurant and dining conservatory; background and live music, sports TV, games end, skittle alley; free wi-fi; dogs welcome in bar, disabled facilities, attractive terraced garden with good big play area, open all day. *(William Slade)*

CROYDE SS4439
Thatch (01271) 890349
B3231 NW of Braunton; Hobbs Hill; EX33 1LZ Lively thatched pub near great surfing beaches (can get packed in summer); rambling and roomy with beams and open fire, settles and other good seating, enjoyable pubby food from sandwiches and baked potatoes up, well kept changing local ales, morning coffee, teas, cheerful young staff, smart restaurant with dressers and lots of china; background and live music; children in eating areas, dogs in bar, flower-filled suntrap terraces and large gardens shared with neighbouring Billy Budds, good play area, simple clean bedrooms, self-catering cottage, open (and food) all day. *(Adrian Johnson)*

CULMSTOCK ST1013
Culm Valley (01884) 840354
B3391, off A38 E of M5 junction 27; EX15 3JJ Friendly 18th-c pub refurbished under present licensees; country-style décor with hotchpotch of furniture, rugs on wood floors and some interesting bits and pieces, good choice of food from varied menu, four real ales including Otter, local cider and plenty of wines by the glass, small front conservatory; free wi-fi; children and dogs (in bar) welcome, totem pole outside, tables on raised grassed area (former railway platform) overlooking old stone bridge over River Culm, covered smokers' area behind, open all day Fri–Sun. *(Charles Todd)*

DARTINGTON SX7861
★Cott (01803) 863777
Cott signed off A385 W of Totnes, opposite A384 turn-off; TQ9 6HE Long 14th-c thatched pub with heavy beams, flagstones, nice mix of old furniture and two inglenooks (one with big woodburner), good home-made locally sourced food from traditional choices up in bar and restaurant, three well kept ales including local Hunters and Greene King, Ashridge's cider, nice wines by the glass, friendly helpful service; live music Sun; children and dogs welcome, wheelchair access (with help into restaurant), picnic-sets in garden and on pretty terrace, five comfortable bedrooms, open all day. *(John Evans, Mike and Margaret Banks)*

DARTMOUTH SX8751
★Cherub (01803) 832571
Higher Street; walk along riverfront, right into Hauley Road and up steps

at end; TQ6 9RB Ancient building (Dartmouth's oldest) with two heavily timbered upper floors jettying over the street, many original interior features, oak beams, leaded lights, tapestried seats and big stone fireplace, up to six well kept ales including a house beer from St Austell in bustling bar, low-ceilinged upstairs restaurant, good food from pub favourites to fish specials, efficient friendly service; background music; children welcome (no pushchairs), dogs in bar, open all day. *(Richard Tilbrook)*

DARTMOUTH   SX8751
Floating Bridge (01803) 832354
Opposite Upper Ferry, use Dart Marina Hotel car park; Coombe Road (A379); TQ6 9PQ Bustling quayside pub in lovely spot, bar with lots of stools by windows making most of waterside view, black and white photographs of local boating scenes, St Austell Tribute, Sharps Doom Bar and guests, several wines by the glass, straightforward pub food including sandwiches, bare-boards dining room with leather-backed chairs around wooden tables; children and dogs (in bar) welcome, pretty window boxes, seats out by the river looking at busy ferry crossing, more on sizeable roof terrace, open (and food) all day. *(Steve and Liz Tilley, John Harris)*

DITTISHAM   SX8654
★ **Ferry Boat** (01803) 722368
Manor Street; best to park in village car park and walk down (quite steep); TQ6 0EX Cheerful riverside pub with lively mix of customers; beamed bar with log fires and straightforward pubby furniture, lots of boating bits and pieces, tide times chalked on wall, flags on ceiling, picture-window view of the Dart, at least three real ales such as Otter and Sharps, a dozen wines by the glass, good range of tasty home-made food including pie of the day and various curries, efficient service; background and some live music; children and dogs welcome, moorings for visiting boats on adjacent pontoon and bell to summon ferry, good walks, open (and food) all day. *(Richard Tilbrook, Steve and Liz Tilley, Dave Braisted, Lynda and Trevor Smith)*

DITTISHAM   SX8654
Red Lion (01803) 722235
The Level; TQ6 0ES Lovely location looking down over attractive village and River Dart; welcoming atmosphere, decent food including daily specials, Dartmoor, Palmers and a summer guest, carpeted bar and restaurant, open fires; also incorporates village store, tiny post office, library and craft shop; children and dogs welcome, eight bedrooms (some with river view), open from 8.30am, may shut Weds and weekend afternoons in winter. *(Tom Stone)*

DREWSTEIGNTON   SX7390
Drewe Arms (01647) 281409
Off A30 NW of Moretonhampstead;

EX6 6QN Pretty thatched village pub under welcoming management; unspoilt room on left with basic wooden wall benches, stools and tables, original serving hatch, ales such as Dartmoor and Otter from tap room casks, local cider, enjoyable sensibly priced pubby food including daily specials, two dining areas, one with Rayburn and history of Britain's longest serving landlady (Mabel Mudge), another with woodburner, darts and board games, live music and quiz nights in back Long Room; free wi-fi; children and dogs welcome, seats under umbrellas on front terrace and in garden, pretty flowering tubs and baskets, two four-poster bedrooms, four bunk rooms, on Dartmoor Trail and handy for Castle Drogo (NT), open (and food) all day in summer. *(Gerry Price, Mr and Mrs J Watkins)*

EAST ALLINGTON   SX7648
Fortescue Arms (01548) 521215
Village signed off A381 Totnes–Kingsbridge, S of A3122 junction; TQ9 7RA Pretty 19th-c village pub under newish management; two-room bar with eclectic mix of tables and chairs on black slate floor, some brewery memorabilia, St Austell and Dartmoor ales, eight wines by the glass, restaurant with own bar, high-backed dining chairs around pine tables, enjoyable well priced (particularly lunchtime) traditional food, good friendly service; background and occasional live music, free wi-fi; children and dogs (in bar) welcome, tables out at front with more on sheltered terrace, two bedrooms planned, closed Mon and lunchtime Tues. *(Elizabeth and Peter May)*

EAST BUDLEIGH   SY0684
Sir Walter Raleigh (01395) 442510
High Street; EX9 7ED Friendly little 16th-c low-beamed village local, well kept changing west country beers and good traditional food, restaurant down step; children and dogs on leads welcome, parking some way off, wonderful medieval bench carvings in nearby church, handy too for Bicton Park gardens. *(Bertie Yarwood)*

EAST DOWN   SS5941
Pyne Arms (01271) 850055
Off A39 Barnstaple–Lynton near Arlington; EX31 4LX Old pub tucked away in small hamlet, cosy carpeted bar with lots of alcoves, woodburner, sensibly priced traditional food and daily specials, Exmoor, St Austell and a guest ale, good choice of wines, flagstoned area with sofas, conservatory; background music, free wi-fi; children and dogs welcome, small enclosed garden, good walks, handy for Arlington Court (NT), three bedrooms, open all day weekends, closed Mon lunchtime. *(Sandra and Nigel Brown)*

EAST PRAWLE   SX7836
Pigs Nose (01548) 511209
Prawle Green; TQ7 2BY Relaxed and

quirky three-room 16th-c pub, lots of interesting bric-a-brac and pictures, mix of old furniture with jars of wild flowers and candles on tables, low beams, flagstones and open fire, local ales tapped from the cask, farm ciders and enjoyable simple pubby food, small family area with unusual toys, pool and darts; unobtrusive background music, hall for live bands (landlord was 1960s tour manager); friendly pub dogs (others welcome and menu for them), tables outside, pleasant spot on village green, closed Sun evening in winter. *(Tom Stone)*

EXETER SX9390
Double Locks (01392) 256947
Canal Banks, Alphington, via Marsh Barton Industrial Estate; EX2 6LT Unsmart, individual and remotely located by ship canal, Wells & Youngs and guests, farm cider in summer, bar food; background music, live at weekends; children and dogs welcome, seats out on grass or decking with distant view to city and cathedral (nice towpath walk out), big play area, camping, open all day. *(Charles Todd)*

EXETER SX9292
Georges Meeting House
(01392) 454250 *South Street; EX1 1ED* Wetherspoons in grand former 18th-c chapel; bare-boards interior with three-sided gallery, stained glass and tall pulpit at one end, eight real ales from long counter, their usual good value food; children welcome, tables in attractive side garden under parasols, open all day from 8am. *(Roger and Donna Huggins)*

EXETER SX9292
★ Hour Glass (01392) 258722
Melbourne Street; off B3015 Topsham Road; EX2 4AU Old-fashioned bow-cornered pub tucked away in surviving Georgian part above the quay; good inventive food including vegetarian from shortish regularly changing menu, up to five well kept ales (usually one from Otter) and extensive range of wines and spirits, friendly relaxed atmosphere, beams, bare boards and mix of furnishings, assorted pictures on dark red walls and various odds and ends including a stuffed badger, open fire in small brick fireplace; background and live music; children away from bar and dogs welcome (resident cats), open all day weekends, closed Mon lunchtime. *(Roger and Donna Huggins)*

EXETER SX9193
★ Imperial (01392) 434050
New North Road (above St David's Station); EX4 4AH Impressive 19th-c mansion in own six-acre hillside park with sweeping drive, various different areas including two clubby little side bars, fine old ballroom with elaborate plasterwork and gilding, light and airy former orangery with unusual mirrored end wall, interesting pictures, up to 14 real ales, standard good value Wetherspoons menu; popular with students and can get very busy; plenty of picnic-sets in grounds and elegant garden furniture in attractive cobbled courtyard, open all day. *(Roger and Donna Huggins)*

EXETER SX9192
Mill on the Exe (01392) 214464
Bonhay Road (A377); EX4 3AB Former paper mill in good spot by pedestrian bridge over weir; spacious opened-up interior on two floors (each with bar), bare boards, old bricks, beams and timbers, four well kept ales including St Austell, good house wines, popular food from snacks and sharing boards up, Sun carvery, large airy conservatory with feature raised fire; children and dogs welcome, river views from balcony tables, spiral stairs down to waterside terrace (summer barbecues), open (and food) all day. *(Julie Braeburn)*

EXETER SX9292
Old Fire House (01392) 277279
New North Road; EX4 4EP Relaxed city-centre pub in Georgian building behind high arched wrought-iron gates; up to ten real ales, several ciders and good choice of bottled beers and wines, bargain food including late-night pizzas, friendly efficient staff, arranged over two floors with dimly lit beamed rooms and simple furniture; background music, live weekends and popular with young crowd (modest admission charge Fri, Sat night), Mon quiz; picnic-sets in front courtyard, open all day till late (3am Thurs-Sat). *(David Crook, Roger and Donna Huggins)*

EXETER SX9292
Prospect (01392) 273152
The Quay; EX2 4AN Early 19th-c pub in good quayside position, well kept ales such as Exmoor, Otter and St Austell, friendly efficient young staff, usual food, plenty of comfortable tables including raised river-view dining area, rather cavernous back part; background and occasional live music; children welcome, tables out by historic ship-canal basin, open (and food) all day. *(Anon)*

EXMINSTER SX9686
★ Turf Hotel (01392) 833128
From A379 S of village, follow the signs to the Swan's Nest , then continue to end of track, by gates; park and walk right along canal towpath – nearly a mile; EX6 8EE Remote but popular waterside pub reached by 20-minute towpath walk, cycle ride or 60-seater boat from Topsham quay (15-minute trip); several little rooms – end one with slate floor, pine walls, built-in seats and woodburner, simple room along corridor serves ales such as Exeter, Otter and Hanlons, local cider/juices and ten wines by the glass, interesting locally sourced food, friendly staff; background

music, board games; children and dogs welcome, big garden with picnic-sets and summer barbecues, arrive early for a seat in fine weather, bedrooms and a yurt for hire, good breakfast, open all day in summer, best to check other times. *(Hilary and Neil Christopher, Peter Kirkman)*

EXMOUTH
SY0080

Bicton Inn (01395) 272589
Bicton Street; EX8 2RU Traditional 19th-c backstreet corner local with friendly buoyant atmosphere, up to eight well kept ales and a proper cider, no food; regular live music including folk nights, pool, darts and other pub games; children and dogs welcome, open all day. *(William Slade)*

EXMOUTH
SX9980

Grapevine (01395) 222208
Victoria Road; EX8 1DL Popular red-brick corner pub (calls itself a pub-bistro), light and spacious with mix of wooden tables and seating, rugs on bare boards, modern local artwork, own Crossed Anchors beers plus changing west country guests, plenty of bottled imports and nice choice of wines by the glass, tasty well presented food including daily special, friendly service and relaxed atmosphere; background music, live bands Fri, charity quiz Mon, free wi-fi; children and dogs welcome, open all day (from 4pm Mon-Weds). *(George Sanderson)*

EXMOUTH
SY9980

Grove (01395) 272101
Esplanade; EX8 1BJ Roomy high-gabled Victorian pub set back from beach, traditional furnishings, caricatures and local prints, enjoyable pubby food including local fish specials, friendly staff, Youngs ales and guests kept well, decent house wines, attractive fireplace at back, sea views from appealing upstairs dining room and balcony; background music, quiz Thurs; children welcome, picnic-sets in front garden, open all day (food all day weekends). *(PL)*

GEORGEHAM
SS4639

Kings Arms (01271) 890240
B3231 (Chapel Street) Croyde–Woolacombe; EX33 1JJ Welcoming comfortably modernised village pub with red walls, slate floors and leather sofas by big woodburner, good freshly cooked food using local ingredients, efficient friendly service, St Austell Tribute and a couple of local guests, good choice of wines, upstairs dining area with tables out on sunny balcony, some traditional pub games; background and live music; children and dogs welcome, small front terrace screened from road, open all day. *(Stephen Shepherd)*

HARBERTON
SX7758

★**Church House** (01803) 863707
Off A381 S of Totnes; next to church; TQ9 7SF Ancient village inn (dates to the

13th c), well kept ales including Quercus and a house beer from Hunters, local cider and ten wines by the glass, good fairly priced food (not Sun evening), friendly efficient service, unusually long bar with blackened beams, medieval latticed glass and oak panelling, attractive 17th- and 18th-c pews and settles, woodburner in big inglenook, separate dining room; quiz and live music nights; children and dogs welcome (resident golden retriever), sunny walled back garden, refurbished bedrooms, open all day Sun, closed Mon lunchtime. *(Sandra and Nigel Brown)*

HATHERLEIGH
SS5404

Tally Ho (01837) 810306
Market Street (A386); EX20 3JN Good generous food (not Sun evening) from ciabattas up, curry night Weds and Sun, good value wines, real ales such as local Clearwater and St Austell, attractive heavy-beamed and timbered linked rooms, sturdy furnishings, big log fire and woodburner, traditional games, restaurant, busy Tues market day (beer slightly cheaper then); background music, open mike night third Weds of month, darts; children and dogs welcome, tables in nice sheltered garden, three good value pretty bedrooms, open all day. *(George Sanderson)*

HEMYOCK
ST1313

Catherine Wheel (01823) 680224
Cornhill; EX15 3RQ Popular and friendly village pub with bar, lounge and restaurant, Otter and Sharps Doom Bar, Thatcher's cider and plenty of wines by the glass, good interesting food (not Sun evening, Mon), fresh flowers on tables, leather sofas by woodburner; darts, pool and skittle alley, free wi-fi; children welcome, closed Mon lunchtime. *(Patrick and Daphne Darley, Guy Vowles)*

HOLSWORTHY
SS3304

Rydon Inn (01409) 259444
Rydon (A3072 W); EX22 7HU Comfortably extended family-run dining pub, clean and tidy, with enjoyable food and well kept local ales, good friendly service, raftered bar with thatched servery, woodburner in stone fireplace; background music; children and dogs welcome, disabled facilities, views over lake from conservatory and deck, well tended garden, open all day. *(Millie and Peter Downing)*

HONITON
ST1599

Heathfield (01404) 45321
Walnut Road; EX14 2UG Ancient thatched and beamed pub in contrasting residential area, well run and spacious, with Greene King ales and good value food from varied menu including the Heathfield Whopper (20oz rump steak), Sun carvery, cheerful prompt service; skittle alley; children welcome, seven bedrooms, open all day Fri-Sun. *(Bob and Margaret Holder)*

HONITON   SY1198
★ **Holt** (01404) 47707
High Street, W end; EX14 1LA
Charming little bustling pub run by two
brothers, relaxed and informal, with just
one room downstairs, chunky tables and
chairs on slate flooring, brown leather
sofas, shelves of books, coal-effect
woodburner, full range of Otter beers
(the family founded the brewery), bigger
brighter upstairs dining room with similar
furniture on pale floorboards, very good
tapas and other inventive food; cookery
classes and quarterly music festivals; well
behaved children welcome, dogs in bar,
closed Sun, Mon. *(David and Judy Robison,
Revd R P Tickle, Dennis and Doreen Haward)*

HOPE COVE   SX6740
Hope & Anchor (01548) 561294
Tucked away by car park; TQ7 3HQ
Revamped seaside inn on two floors; open
kitchen serving decent choice of popular
food from sharing plates to local fish, St
Austell ales and a guest such as Quercus,
several wines by the glass, helpful amiable
young staff, flagstones and bare boards, two
woodburners, dining room views to Burgh
Island; background music, free wi-fi; children
and dogs welcome, sea-view tables out on
decked balcony and terrace, 11 refurbished
bedrooms, open (and food) all day from 8.30
for breakfast. *(Theocsbrian)*

HORNS CROSS   SS3823
★ **Hoops** (01237) 451222
*A39 Clovelly–Bideford, W of village;
EX39 5DL* Pretty thatched and beamed
inn dating from the 13th c, friendly and
relaxed, with traditionally furnished bar,
log fires in sizeable fireplaces and some
standing timbers and partitioning, more
formal restaurant with attractive mix of
tables and chairs, some panelling, exposed
stone and another open fire, Hoops Bitter
(from Country Life) and Hoops Best and
Light (from Forge), over a dozen wines by
the glass, enjoyable fairly straightforward
food using local suppliers; welcoming helpful
staff; may be background music; children
and dogs allowed, picnic-sets under parasols in
enclosed courtyard, more seats on terrace
and in two acres of gardens, 13 well equipped
bedrooms, open (and food) all day. *(Elizabeth
and Peter May)*

HORSEBRIDGE   SX4074
★ **Royal** (01822) 870214
*Off A384 Tavistock–Launceston;
PL19 8PJ* Dimly lit ancient local with
dark half-panelling, log fires, slate floors,
scrubbed tables and interesting bric-a-brac,
good reasonably priced food, friendly staff,
well kept Dartmoor, St Austell and Skinners
poured from the cask, real cider; no children
in the evening, dogs welcome, picnic-sets on
front and side terraces and in big garden,

quiet rustic spot by lovely old Tamar bridge,
popular with walkers and cyclists.
(Patricia Hawkins)

IDE   SX9090
Huntsman (01392) 272779
High Street; EX2 9RN Welcoming recently
refurbished thatched and beamed country
pub, tasty sensibly priced home-made food
using local suppliers from sandwiches to good
value Sun lunch, three west country beers,
friendly attentive service; some live music;
children welcome, picnic-sets in pleasant
garden. *(Dave Sadler)*

IDE   SX8990
Poachers (01392) 273847
*3 miles from M5 junction 31, via A30;
High Street; EX2 9RW* Cosy beamed pub
in quaint village, Branscombe Vale Branoc
and five changing west country guests
from ornate curved wooden bar, enjoyable
home-made food, mismatched old chairs
and sofas, various pictures and odds and
ends, big log fire, restaurant; free wi-fi;
dogs welcome (they have a boxer), tables
in pleasant garden with barbecue, three
comfortable bedrooms, open all day (till late
Fri, Sat). *(Dave Sadler)*

IDEFORD   SX8977
★ **Royal Oak** (01626) 852274
2 miles off A380; TQ13 0AY
Unpretentious little 16th-c thatched and
flagstoned village local, friendly helpful
service, a couple of changing local ales,
generous helpings of tasty well priced pub
food, navy theme including interesting
Nelson and Churchill memorabilia, beams,
panelling and big open fireplace; children
and dogs welcome, tables out at front
and by car park over road, closed Mon
lunchtime. *(Tom Stone)*

ILFRACOMBE   SS5247
George & Dragon (01271) 863851
Fore Street; EX34 9ED One of the oldest
pubs here (14th c) and handy for the
harbour, clean and comfortable with friendly
local atmosphere, ales such as Exmoor,
Sharps and Shepherd Neame, decent wines,
traditional food including local fish, beams,
stripped stone and open fireplaces, lots of
ornaments, china etc; background and some
live music (bring your own instruments),
Tues quiz, no mobile phones; children and
dogs welcome, open all day and can get very
busy weekends. *(William Slade)*

ILFRACOMBE   SS5247
Ship & Pilot (01271) 863562
Broad Street, off harbour; EX34 9EE
Bright yellow pub near harbour attracting
friendly mix of regulars and visitors, six
well kept changing ales (usually have Bass)
and good range of proper ciders/perry, no
food apart from rolls, traditional open-plan
interior with lots of old photos; weekend live

music, juke box, a couple of TVs for sport, darts; dogs welcome, tables outside, open all day. *(Dave Sadler)*

ILSINGTON   SX7876
Carpenters Arms (01364) 661629
Old Town Hill; TQ13 9RG Unspoilt little 18th-c local next to the village church, beams and flagstones, country-style pine furniture, brasses, woodburners, enjoyable generously served home-made food and well kept changing ales, friendly atmosphere; darts; children, well behaved dogs and muddy boots welcome, tables out at front, good surrounding walks, no car park, open all day weekends, closed Mon. *(Tom Stone)*

INSTOW   SS4730
Boat House (01271) 861292
Marine Parade; EX39 4JJ Modern high-ceilinged bar/restaurant with huge tidal beach just across lane and views to Appledore, wide choice of good food including plenty of fish/seafood, two well kept local ales and decent wines by the glass, friendly prompt service, lively family bustle; background music; roof terrace. *(David Field)*

KENNFORD   SX9186
Seven Stars (01392) 834887
Centre of village; EX6 7TR Recently reopened/updated little village pub, three west country beers and good value simple food including pies and pizzas, friendly atmosphere; Thurs quiz, live music, pool, darts and sports TV; children and dogs welcome, open all day. *(George Sanderson)*

KENTISBEARE   ST0606
Keepers Cottage (01884) 266247
Not far from M5 junction 28, via A373; EX15 2EB Friendly old family-run thatched cottage with stripped-stone walls and low ceilings, good choice of tasty generously served food (local suppliers listed), real ales tapped from the cask and traditional cider, attentive service, log fire; dogs welcome, picnic-sets outside. *(Roger and Donna Huggins)*

KILMINGTON   SY2698
New Inn (01297) 33376
Signed off Gammons Hill; EX13 7SF Traditional thatched local (originally three 14th-c cottages) under friendly licensees; good food (not Mon) and well kept Palmers ales; skittle alley and boules court, monthly quiz night; picnic-sets in large garden with tree-shaded areas, closed Mon lunchtime. *(David Longhurst)*

KILMINGTON   SY2798
★ Old Inn (01297) 32096
A35; EX13 7RB Bustling 16th-c thatched and beamed pub, family-run and welcoming, with generous helpings of good sensibly priced food using local suppliers, well kept Branscombe Vale, Otter and a guest, decent

choice of wines, attentive amiable service, small character front bar with traditional games (there's also a skittle alley), back lounge with leather armchairs by inglenook log fire, small restaurant; children welcome, wheelchair access, terrace and lawned area, closed Sun evening. *(Guy Vowles, Steve and Claire Harvey, Phil and Jane Villiers)*

KING'S NYMPTON   SS6819
Grove (01769) 580406
Off B3226 SW of South Molton; EX37 9ST Welcoming 17th-c thatched pub in conservation village; beamed bar with bookmarks hanging from ceiling, simple furniture on flagstones, bare stone walls and log fire, ales such as Clearwater, Exe Valley and Hunters, local cider, 25 wines (including champagne) by the glass and 65 malt whiskies, good food (not Sun evening) cooked by landlady; free wi-fi; children and dogs (in bar) welcome, self-catering cottage, closed Mon lunchtime. *(Mr and Mrs D Mackenzie, Lynda and Trevor Smith)*

KINGSKERSWELL   SX8666
★ Bickley Mill (01803) 873201
Bickley Road, follow Maddacombe Road from village, under new ring road, W of Kingskerswell; TQ12 5LN Restored 13th-c mill tucked away in lovely countryside; rambling beamed rooms with open fires and rugs on wood floors, variety of seating from rustic chairs and settles to sofas piled with cushions, modern art and black and white photos on stone walls, good well presented food including pub favourites from sensibly priced menu, a couple of Bays ales and 14 wines by the glass, friendly helpful staff; monthly jazz Sun lunchtime, free wi-fi; children and dogs (in bar) welcome, seats on big terrace, also a subtropical hillside garden, good modern bedrooms, open all day. *(Mike and Mary Carter, Kate Moran, Kim Skuse)*

KINGSTON   SX6347
Dolphin (01548) 810314
Off B3392 S of Modbury (can also be reached from A379 W of Modbury); TQ7 4QE Peaceful 16th-c inn with knocked-through beamed rooms, traditional furniture on red carpeting, open fire, woodburner in inglenook fireplace, Otter, St Austell, Sharps and Timothy Taylors, a farm cider, straightforward food; children and dogs welcome, seats in garden, pretty tubs and summer window boxes, quiet village with several tracks leading down to the sea, three bedrooms in building across road, closed some Sun evenings in winter. *(Steve Whalley, Theocsbrian)*

KINGSWEAR   SX8851
★ Ship (01803) 752348
Higher Street; TQ6 0AG Attractive old beamed local by church, plenty of atmosphere and kind cheerful service, well

kept Adnams, Otter, St Austell and guests from horseshoe bar, Addlestone's cider and nice wines, popular food including good local fish (best views from restaurant up steps), nautical bric-a-brac and local photographs, tartan carpets and two log fires; occasional live music, big-screen sports TV; children and dogs welcome, a couple of river-view tables outside, open all day in summer (all day Fri-Sun winter). *(Richard Tilbrook)*

LAKE   SX5288
★Bearslake   (01837) 861334
A386 just S of Sourton; EX20 4HQ Rambling thatch and stone pub (former longhouse dating from the 13th c), leather sofas and high bar chairs on crazy-paved slate floor at one end, three more rooms with woodburners, toby jugs, farm tools and traps, stripped stone, well kept ales such as Dartmoor and Otter, good range of spirits, decent wines and enjoyable food, beamed restaurant; wi-fi through most of the building; children allowed, large sheltered streamside garden, Dartmoor walks, six comfortable bedrooms, good breakfast, closed Sun evening, otherwise open all day.
(David Longhurst)

LANDSCOVE   SX7766
Live & Let Live   (01803) 762663
SE end of village by Methodist chapel; TQ13 7LZ Friendly open-plan village local with decent freshly made food and well kept ales such as Teignworthy, impressive collection of miniatures, log fire; children and dogs welcome, tables on small front deck and in little orchard across lane, good walks, closed Mon. *(Julie Braeburn)*

LIFTON   SX3885
★Arundell Arms   (01566) 784666
Fore Street; PL16 0AA Good imaginative food in substantial country-house fishing hotel including set lunch, warmly welcoming and individual, with nice staff and sophisticated service, good choice of wines by the glass, morning coffee and afternoon tea; also adjacent Courthouse bar, complete with original cells, doing good fairly priced pubby food (not Sun evening, Mon) including children's meals, well kept St Austell Tribute and Dartmoor Jail, darts and some live music; can arrange fishing tuition – also shooting, deer-stalking and riding; 25 bedrooms, useful A30 stop. *(Charlotte Gladstone-Millar)*

LITTLEHEMPSTON   SX8162
Pig & Whistle   (01803) 863733
Newton Road (A381); TQ9 6LT Large welcoming former coaching inn, enjoyable traditional food and ales such as Dartmoor and Teignworthy, long bar with beams and stripped stone, extensive dining area; free wi-fi, children welcome, decked front terrace, two bedrooms, open all day. *(Mike and Margaret Banks)*

LOWER ASHTON   SX8484
Manor Inn   (01647) 252304
Ashton signposted off B3193 N of Chudleigh; EX6 7QL Well run country pub under friendly hard-working licensees, good quality sensibly priced food including lunchtime set menu, well kept ales such as Dartmoor, Otter and St Austell, good choice of wines, open fires in both bars, back restaurant in converted smithy; dogs welcome, disabled access, garden picnic-sets with nice rural outlook, open all day Sun, closed Mon. *(Charles Todd)*

LUPPITT   ST1606
★Luppitt Inn   (01404) 891613
Back roads N of Honiton; EX14 4RT Unspoilt basic farmhouse pub tucked away in lovely countryside, an amazing survivor, with chatty long-serving landlady, tiny room with corner bar and a table, another not much bigger with fireplace, cheap Otter tapped from the cask, intriguing metal puzzles made by a neighbour, no food or music, lavatories across the yard; closed lunchtimes and all day Sun. *(Tom Stone)*

LUSTLEIGH   SX7881
★Cleave   (01647) 277223
Off A382 Bovey Tracey– Moretonhampstead; TQ13 9TJ Busy thatched pub in lovely Dartmoor National Park village; low-ceilinged beamed bar with granite walls and log fire, attractive antique high-backed settles, cushioned wall seats and wheelbacks on red patterned carpet, Dartmoor, Otter and a guest, enjoyable home-cooked food, good friendly service, back room (formerly the old station waiting room) converted to light and airy bistro with pale wooden furniture on wood-strip floor, doors to outside eating area; children and dogs (in bar) welcome, more seats in sheltered garden, good circular walks, open (and food) all day, till 9pm (7pm) Sun. *(Caroline Prescott, Anne and Ben Smith)*

LUTON   SX9076
★Elizabethan   (01626) 775425
Haldon Moor; TQ13 0BL Tucked-away much-altered low-beamed dining pub (once owned by Elizabeth I); wide choice of good well presented food including daily specials and popular Sun lunch, three well kept ales and several reasonably priced wines by the glass, friendly attentive service, thriving atmosphere; children welcome, pretty front garden, open all day Sun. *(Charles Todd)*

Virtually all pubs in this book sell wine by the glass. We mention wines if they are a cut above the average.

LYDFORD
SX5184

Castle Inn (01822) 820241
Off A386 Okehampton–Tavistock;
EX20 4BH Tudor inn owned by St Austell,
traditional twin bars with big slate flagstones,
bowed low beams and granite walls, high
backed settles and four inglenook log fires,
notable stained-glass door, hearty helpings
of good well priced popular food, friendly
helpful staff, restaurant; free wi-fi; children
and dogs welcome in certain areas, seats at
front and in sheltered back garden, lovely
NT river gorge nearby, eight bedrooms, open
all day. *(David Longhurst)*

LYMPSTONE
SX9884

Swan (01395) 272644
The Strand, by station entrance;
EX8 5ET Old beamed pub with enjoyable
home-made food including local fish and
bargain weekday set lunch, split-level dining
area with big log fire, half a dozen west
country ales, short but well chosen wine
list, coffee and cream teas; pool, free wi-fi;
children welcome, picnic-sets out at front,
popular with cyclists (bike racks provided),
open all day. *(Patricia Hawkins)*

LYNMOUTH
SS7249

Rising Sun (01598) 753223
Harbourside; EX35 6EG Nice old pub
in wonderful position overlooking harbour;
beamed and stripped-stone bar bustling
with locals and tourists, good fire, three
Exmoor ales and a guest, popular food
from comprehensive menu (emphasis on
fish), upmarket hotel side with attractive
restaurant; background music; dogs
welcome, well behaved children till 7.30pm,
gardens behind, bedrooms in cottagey old
thatched building, parking can be a problem
(expensive during the day, sparse at night),
open all day. *(Richard and Penny Gibbs)*

LYNTON
SS7248

Beggars Roost (01598) 753645
Manor Hotel; EX35 6LD Refurbished
stone-built country pub reopened in 2015
after two-year closure; good freshly made
food and well kept ales including Exmoor
and an own-label beer brewed by Marstons,
friendly helpful staff; children and dogs
welcome, good bedrooms in hotel side, also
camping next door, open all day. *(Ben Jones)*

LYNTON
SS6548

Hunters (01598) 763230
Pub well signed off A39 W of Lynton;
EX31 4PY Large refurbished Edwardian
country inn set in four-acre grounds (roaming
peacocks), superb Heddon Valley position by
NT information centre down very steep hill,
great walks including to the sea; two bars
one with woodburner, up to six ales including
Exmoor and Heddon Valley (brewed for
them locally), good range of other drinks and
enjoyable well priced food from fairly pubby

menu, efficient friendly service, dining room
overlooking back garden; quiz and music
nights, pool, board games, free wi-fi; children
and dogs welcome, ten bedrooms, open all day.
(Theocsbrian)

MEAVY
SX5467

★ Royal Oak (01822) 852944
Off B3212 E of Yelverton; PL20 6PJ
Partly 15th-c pub taking its name from the
800-year-old oak on green opposite; heavy
beamed L-shaped bar with church pews, red
plush banquettes, old agricultural prints
and church pictures, smaller locals' bar with
flagstones and big open-hearth fireplace,
separate dining room, good reasonably priced
food served by friendly staff, four well kept
ales including Dartmoor, farm ciders, a dozen
wines by the glass and several malt whiskies;
background music, board games; children
and dogs (in bar) welcome, picnic-sets out
in front and on the green, pretty Dartmoor-
edge village, open all day. *(Margaret and Peter
Staples, Lynda and Trevor Smith)*

MERTON
SS5212

Malt Scoop (01805) 603924
New Street; EX20 3EA Thatched former
farmhouse (a pub since the early 19th c),
renovated interior with original slate floors
and inglenook, enjoyable generously served
bar food at fair prices using local produce,
separate restaurant menu (Thurs-Sun),
St Austell ales, friendly service; free wi-fi;
children and dogs welcome, two bedrooms,
open all day Fri-Sun. *(Anon)*

MOLLAND
SS8028

London (01769) 550269
*Village signed off B3227 E of South
Molton; EX36 3NG* Proper Exmoor
inn at its busiest in the shooting season;
two small linked rooms by old-fashioned
central servery, local stag-hunting pictures,
cushioned benches and plain chairs around
rough stripped trestle tables, Exmoor Ale,
attractive beamed room on left with famous
stag story on the wall, panelled dining room
on right with big curved settle by fireplace
(good hunting and game bird prints),
enjoyable home-made food using fresh local
produce including seasonal game (not Sun
evening, no credit cards), small hall with
stuffed animals; fine Victorian lavatories;
children and dogs welcome, picnic-sets in
cottagey garden, untouched early 18th-c box
pews in church next door, two bedrooms,
closed Mon lunchtime. *(Millie and Peter
Downing)*

MONKLEIGH
SS4520

Bell (01805) 938285
A388; EX39 5JS Welcoming thatched and
beamed 17th-c village pub with carpeted bar
and small restaurant, well kept Dartmoor
and a couple of guests, enjoyable reasonably
priced food including daily specials and
Sun carvery, friendly staff; background

music, quiz nights, darts; children (till 9pm) and dogs (treats for good ones) welcome, wheelchair access, garden with raised deck, views and good walks, closed Mon. *(Charles Todd)*

MORCHARD BISHOP   SS7607
London Inn   (01363) 877222
Signed off A377 Crediton–Barnstaple; EX17 6NW Prettily placed 16th-c village coaching inn under mother and daughter licensees, thriving local atmosphere, good generous home-made food (best to book weekends), Fullers London Pride and a local guest, helpful friendly service, low-beamed open-plan carpeted bar with woodburner in large fireplace, small dining room; pool, darts and skittles; children and dogs welcome, closed Mon lunchtime. *(Julie Braeburn)*

MORELEIGH   SX7652
New Inn   (01548) 821326
B3207, off A381 Kingsbridge–Totnes in Stanborough; TQ9 7JH Cosy old-fashioned country local with friendly landlady (same family for several decades), large helpings of enjoyable home-made food at reasonable prices, Timothy Taylors Landlord tapped from the cask and a weekend guest, character old furniture, nice pictures and good inglenook log fire; only open from 6.30pm (7pm Sun). *(Paul and Karen Cornock)*

MORTEHOE   SS4545
Chichester Arms   (01271) 870411
Off A361 Ilfracombe–Braunton; EX34 7DU Blue-shuttered former 16th-c vicarage; enjoyable local food including daily specials, well kept west country ales, quick friendly service, panelled lounge, dining room and pubby locals' bar with darts and pool, interesting old local photographs; skittle alley and games machines in summer children's room, dogs welcome in bar, tables out in front and in paved side garden, lovely coast walk, open all day. *(Tom Stone)*

NEWTON ABBOT   SX8671
Olde Cider Bar   (01626) 354221
East Street; TQ12 2LD Basic old-fashioned cider house under newish management, plenty of atmosphere, around 30 interesting reasonably priced ciders (some very strong), a couple of perries, more in bottles, good country wines from the cask too, baguettes, pasties etc, friendly staff, stools made from cask staves, barrel seats and wall benches, flagstones and bare boards; regular live folk music, small back games room with bar billiards; dogs welcome, terrace tables, open all day. *(Millie and Peter Downing, Charles Todd)*

NEWTON ABBOT   SX8468
Two Mile Oak   (01803) 812411
A381 2 miles S, at Denbury/ Kingskerswell crossroads; TQ12 6DF Appealing two-bar beamed coaching inn, black panelling, traditional furnishings

and candlelit alcoves, inglenook and woodburners, well kept Bass, Dartmoor and Otter tapped from the cask, nine wines by the glass, enjoyable well priced pubby food from sandwiches and baked potatoes up (special diets catered for), decent coffee, cheerful staff; background music; children and dogs welcome, round picnic-sets on terrace and lawn, open all day. *(Roger and Donna Huggins, S Holder)*

NEWTON FERRERS   SX5447
Dolphin   (01752) 872007
Riverside Road East: Newton Hill off Church Park (B3186) then left; PL8 1AE Shuttered 18th-c pub in attractive setting; L-shaped bar with a few low black beams, pews and benches on slate floors and some white plank panelling, open fire, up to four well kept ales including St Austell, decent wines by the glass, enjoyable traditional food including good fish and chips and daily specials, friendly staff; children and dogs (in bar) welcome, terraces over lane looking down on River Yealm and yachts, open all day in summer when can get packed, parking limited. *(Jeremy Snaithe)*

NEWTON ST CYRES   SX8798
Beer Engine   (01392) 851282
Off A377 towards Thorverton; EX5 5AX Former railway hotel brewing its own beers since the 1980s and continuing well under friendly newish management; good home-made food including specials and popular Sun lunch, log fire in bar; children welcome, seats on decked verandah, steps down to garden, open all day. *(Charles Rodd)*

NEWTON TRACEY   SS5226
★ Hunters   (01271) 858339
B3232 Barnstaple–Torrington; EX31 3PL Extended 15th-c pub with massive low beams and two inglenooks, good reasonably priced food from pub standards up including smaller appetites menu, well kept St Austell Tribute and Sharps Doom Bar, decent wines, efficient friendly service, skittle alley/overflow dining area; soft background music; children and dogs welcome, disabled access using ramp, tables on small terrace behind, open all day weekends. *(Jeff Davies)*

NOMANSLAND   SS8313
Mount Pleasant   (01884) 860271
B3137 Tiverton–South Molton; EX16 8NN Informal country local with good mix of customers, huge fireplaces in long low-beamed main bar, well kept ales such as Cotleigh, Exmoor and Sharps, several wines by the glass, Weston's cider, good range of enjoyable freshly cooked food (special diets catered for), friendly attentive service, happy mismatch of simple well worn furniture including comfy old sofa, candles on tables, country pictures, daily papers, cosy dining room (former smithy with original forge),

darts in public bar; background music; well behaved children and dogs welcome, picnic-sets and play area in back garden. (Patricia Hawkins)

NOSS MAYO   SX5447
★**Ship** (01752) 872387
Off A379 via B3186, E of Plymouth; PL8 1EW Charming setting overlooking inlet and visiting boats (can get crowded in good weather); thick-walled bars with bare boards and log fires, six well kept west country beers including local Summerskills, good choice of wines and malt whiskies, popular food from wide-ranging menu, friendly efficient service, lots of local pictures and charts, books, newspapers and board games, restaurant upstairs; children welcome, dogs downstairs, plenty of seats on heated waterside terrace, parking restricted at high tide, open (and food) all day. (John Evans, Philip Crawford, Jan Gould, Lynda and Trevor Smith, Tom and Ruth Rees)

OAKFORD   SS9121
Red Lion (01398) 351592
Rookery Hill; EX16 9ES Friendly refurbished 17th-c village coaching inn (partly rebuilt in Georgian times); well kept ales such as Otter, reasonably priced pubby food including Thurs OAP lunch deal and Sun carvery till 3pm, woodburner in big inglenook; children, walkers and dogs welcome, four comfortable bedrooms, open all day Sun till 8pm, closed Mon lunchtime. (Jeff Davies)

OTTERY ST MARY   SY0995
Volunteer (01404) 814060
Broad Street; EX11 1BZ Centrally placed early 19th-c pub, traditional front bar with darts and open fire, more contemporary restaurant behind, four gravity fed beers including Otter, good reasonably priced home-made food (not Sun evening), friendly service; upstairs loos; open all day. (Roger and Donna Huggins)

PARKHAM   SS3821
★**Bell** (01237) 451201
Rectory Lane; EX39 5PL Spotlessly kept thatched village pub with three communicating rooms (one on lower level), beams and standing timbers, pubby furniture on red patterned carpet, brass, copper and old photographs, grandfather clock, woodburner and small coal fire, model ships and lanterns hanging above bar serving Exmoor, Otter and Sharps, a dozen malt whiskies, popular food; darts, free wi-fi; well behaved children welcome, dogs in bar, picnic-sets on covered back terrace with fairy lights, open (and food) all day Sun. (Peter Brix)

PARRACOMBE   SS6644
★**Fox & Goose** (01598) 763239
Off A39 Blackmoor Gate–Lynton; EX31 4PE Popular rambling Victorian pub, hunting and farming memorabilia and interesting old photographs, well kept Cotleigh and Exmoor, traditional cider and several wines by the glass, good freshly made food from interesting varied blackboard menus, also takeaway pizzas, friendly staff, log fire, separate dining room; children and dogs welcome, small front verandah, riverside terrace and garden room, three bedrooms, open all day in summer. (Charles Todd)

PETER TAVY   SX5177
★**Peter Tavy Inn** (01822) 810348
Off A386 near Mary Tavy, N of Tavistock; PL19 9NN Old stone village inn tucked away at end of little lane, bustling low-beamed bar with high-backed settles on black flagstones, mullioned windows, good log fire in big stone fireplace, snug dining area with carved wooden chairs, hops on beams and plenty of pictures, up to five well kept west country ales, Winkleigh's cider and good wine/whisky choice, well liked food from varied menu including OAP lunch (not Sun) and early evening deal, friendly attentive service, separate restaurant; children and dogs welcome, picnic-sets in pretty garden, peaceful moorland views, open all day weekends. (Helen and Brian Edgeley, Mrs Zara Elliott, Stephen Shepherd, Phil and Jane Villiers)

PLYMOUTH   SX4953
Bridge (01752) 403888
Shaw Way, Mount Batten; PL9 9XH Modern two-storey bar-restaurant with terrace and balcony overlooking busy Yacht Haven Marina, enjoyable food from sandwiches and pub favourites up, nice choice of wines by the glass, St Austell Tribute and Sharps Doom Bar, impressive fish tank upstairs; children welcome, well behaved dogs downstairs, open all day from 9am for breakfast. (William Slade)

PLYMOUTH   SX4854
Dolphin (01752) 660876
Barbican; PL1 2LS Unpretentious chatty local with good range of well kept cask-tapped ales including Bass and St Austell, open fire, Beryl Cook paintings (even one of the friendly landlord), no food but can bring your own; dogs welcome, open all day. (John Poulter)

PLYMOUTH   SX4854
Ship (01752) 667604
Quay Road, Barbican; PL1 2JZ Waterside corner pub with opened-up bare-boards interior, St Austell ales and enjoyable fairly

---

If you have to cancel a reservation for a bedroom or restaurant, please telephone or write to warn them. You may lose your deposit if you've paid one.

traditional home-made food, harbour views from upstairs restaurant, friendly attentive service; children and dogs (in bar) welcome, full wheelchair access, seats outside under umbrellas, open (and food) all day. *(Mike and Margaret Banks)*

PLYMOUTH   SX4753
Waterfront (01752) 226961
Grand Parade; PL1 3DQ Former 19th-c yacht club in good spot by Plymouth Sound, recently restored after severe storm damage and under same management as the Pandora at Mylor Bridge (Cornwall Main Entry), varied choice of enjoyable food from sandwiches and sharing boards up, St Austell ales and guests, 20 wines by the glass; children and dogs welcome, decked terrace with superb views, open (and food) all day. *(George Sanderson)*

PLYMTREE   ST0502
Blacksmiths Arms (01884) 277474
Near church; EX15 2JU Friendly 19th-c beamed and carpeted village pub with good reasonably priced food cooked by landlord, three well kept changing local ales and decent choice of wines by the glass; pool room and skittle alley; children welcome, dogs on leads (their leonberger is called Jagermeister), garden with boules and play area, open all day Sat, till 4pm Sun, closed weekday lunchtimes. *(Tom Stone)*

POUNDSGATE   SX7072
Tavistock Inn (01364) 631251
B3357 continuation; TQ13 7NY Picturesque old pub liked by walkers (plenty of nearby hikes), beams and other original features such as narrow-stepped granite spiral staircase, original flagstones and ancient log fireplaces, St Austell Tribute, Sharps Doom Bar and a summer guest, enjoyable traditional food served by friendly staff; children and dogs welcome, tables on front terrace and in quiet back garden, pretty flower boxes, open (and food) all day in summer. *(Sandra and Nigel Brown)*

PUSEHILL   SS4228
Pig on the Hill (01237) 459222
Off B3226 near Westward Ho!; EX39 5AH Extensively revamped restauranty pub (originally a cowshed); good choice of fresh well presented food (booking advised evenings and weekends), friendly helpful service, Country Life and local guests, games room with skittle alley; background music; children and dogs (in bar) welcome, disabled facilities, good views from terrace tables and picnic-sets on grass, play area, boules, open all day. *(Martyn Stringer)*

RINGMORE   SX6545
Journeys End (01548) 810205
Signed off B3392 at Pickwick Inn, St Anns Chapel, near Bigbury; best to park opposite church; TQ7 4HL Ancient

village inn (dates from the 13th c) with friendly chatty licensees, character panelled lounge and other linked rooms, Sharps Doom Bar and local guests tapped from the cask, farm cider, decent wines, well executed nicely presented food from good shortish menu (not Sun evening, best to book in summer), log fires, family dining conservatory with board games; dogs welcome throughout, recently revamped garden, attractive setting near thatched cottages and not far from the sea, open all day weekends, closed Mon. *(Sharon and John Hancock, Philip Crawford, Theocsbrian)*

ROBOROUGH   SS5717
New Inn (01805) 603247
Off B3217 N of Winkleigh; EX19 8SY Tucked-away 16th-c thatched village pub, cheerful and busy, with well kept Teignworthy and a couple of guests, ten proper ciders and several wines by the glass, good variety of enjoyable locally sourced food, beamed bar with woodburner, tiny back room leading up to dining room, friendly helpful staff; children and dogs welcome, seats on sunny front terrace, open all day Fri-Sun, closed lunchtimes Mon, Tues. *(Douglas Power)*

ROCKBEARE   SY0195
★ **Jack in the Green** (01404) 822240
Signed from A30 bypass E of Exeter; EX5 2EE Neat welcoming dining pub run well by long-serving owner; flagstoned lounge bar with comfortable sofas, ales such as Butcombe, Otter and Sharps, local cider, a dozen wines by the glass (over 100 by the bottle), first class food from interesting menu including excellent puddings, emphasis on larger dining side with old hunting/shooting photographs and leather chesterfields by big woodburner, good friendly service; background music; well behaved children welcome, no dogs inside, disabled facilities, plenty of seats in courtyard, open all day Sun, closed 25 Dec-5 Jan, quite handy for M5. *(Patrick and Daphne Darley, John Evans)*

SALCOMBE   SX7439
Fortescue (01548) 842868
Union Street, end of Fore Street; TQ8 8BZ Proper pub with five linked nautical-theme rooms, enjoyable good value food including local fish (bargain winter lunchtime deals Mon-Fri), prompt cheerful service, well kept ales such as Bass, Courage and Otter, decent wines, good woodburner, old local black and white shipping pictures, big public bar with games, small dining room; children welcome, courtyard picnic-sets. *(Brian and Janet Braby)*

SAMPFORD COURTENAY   SS6300
New Inn (01837) 82247
B3072 Crediton–Holsworthy; EX20 2TB Attractive 16th-c thatched restaurant and bar, good interesting food from landlord-chef at reasonable prices, local ales and cider,

relaxed friendly atmosphere with candlelit tables, beams and log fires; garden picnic-sets, picturesque village. *(Elizabeth and Peter May)*

SANDY PARK   SX7189
Sandy Park Inn (01647) 433267
A382 Whiddon Down–Moretonhampstead; TQ13 8JW
Hospitable little thatched and beamed inn; built-in varnished wall settles around nice tables, stools by counter serving Dartmoor, Otter and a couple of guests, good fairly traditional food cooked by landlord including fresh fish, small dining room on left, inner snug; open mike night third Sun of month; children and dogs welcome, big garden with fine views, three comfortable bedrooms, open all day (food till 7pm Sun). *(Jeff Davies)*

SHALDON   SX9371
Café Ode (01626) 873427
Ness Drive; TQ14 0HP Eco café in converted stables high above the bay with nice view; good quality food with some interesting choices such as fried sand eels, own Two Beach ales, friendly young staff; children welcome, seats outside and large car park with electric car charging points, closed Sun-Thurs evenings, open till 9pm Fri, Sat (winter hours may vary). *(S Holder)*

SHALDON   SX9372
Clifford Arms (01626) 872311
Fore Street; TQ14 0DE Attractive 18th-c open-plan pub on two levels, clean and bright, with good range of home-made blackboard food including Fri seafood, up to four mainly local ales and eight wines by the glass, low beams and stone walls, wood or carpeted floors, log fire; live jazz Mon and first Sun lunchtime of the month; children over 5 welcome, front terrace and decked area at back with palms, pleasant seaside village. *(Millie and Peter Downing)*

SHALDON   SX9472
London Inn (01626) 872453
Bank Street/The Green; TQ14 8AW
Popular bustling pub opposite bowling green in pretty waterside village, ample helpings of good reasonably priced food using local suppliers, Otter and St Austell ales, friendly efficient service; background music, pool; children and dogs (in bar) welcome, open all day. *(Charles Todd)*

SHALDON   SX9371
Ness House (01626) 873480
Ness Drive; TQ14 0HP Updated Georgian hotel on Ness headland overlooking Teign estuary, comfortable nautical-theme bar with mixed furniture on bare boards, log fire, Badger ales and decent wines by the glass, friendly young staff, quite pricey popular food in narrow beamed restaurant or small conservatory, afternoon teas; free wi-fi; children welcome, no dogs, disabled

facilities, terrace with lovely views, picnic-sets in back garden, nine bedrooms, open all day. *(Tom Stone)*

SHEBBEAR   SS4309
Devils Stone Inn (01409) 281210
Off A3072 or A388 NE of Holsworthy; EX21 5RU Neatly kept 17th-c beamed village pub reputed to be one of England's most haunted; seats in front of open woodburner, one L-shaped pew and second smaller one, flagstone floors, St Austell Tribute and a couple of local guests, decent wines, enjoyable food in dining room across corridor, plain back games room with pool and darts; picnic-sets on front terrace and in garden behind, next to actual Devil's Stone (turned by villagers on 5 Nov to keep the devil at bay), eight bedrooms (steep stairs to some), can arrange fishing and shooting, open all day weekends; up for sale as we went to press so things could change. *(Millie and Peter Downing)*

SHEEPWASH   SS4806
★ **Half Moon** (01409) 231376
Off A3072 Holsworthy–Hatherleigh at Highampton; EX21 5NE Ancient inn loved by anglers for its 12 miles of River Torridge fishing (salmon, sea and brown trout), small tackle shop and rod room with drying facilities; simply furnished main bar, lots of beams, log fire in big fireplace, well kept St Austell, Sharps and a local guest, several wines by the glass, wide choice of enjoyable food including good vegetarian options and blackboard specials, friendly service, separate extended dining room; bar billiards; children and dogs welcome, 13 bedrooms (four in converted stables), generous breakfast, tiny Dartmoor village off the beaten track. *(Charles Todd)*

SIDFORD   SY1389
★ **Blue Ball** (01395) 514062
A3052 just N of Sidmouth; EX10 9QL
Handsome thatched pub in same friendly family for over 100 years; central bar with three main areas each with log fire, pale beams, nice mix of wooden dining chairs around circular tables on patterned carpet, prints, horsebrasses and plenty of bric-a-brac, well kept Bass, Otter, St Austell and Sharps, popular bar food, pleasant attentive service, chatty public bar, board games, darts and skittle alley; background music and games machine; children and dogs welcome, flower-filled garden, terrace and smokers' gazebo, coastal walks close by, bedrooms, open all day from 8am for breakfast. *(Roger and Donna Huggins)*

SIDFORD   SY1390
Rising Sun (01395) 513722
School Street; EX10 9PF Friendly two-bar traditional local, well kept Bass, Branscombe Vale, Otter and a winter guest (guest cider in summer), well priced home-made pubby

food including good fish and chips, mix of tables and chairs on wood floors, old local photographs on white walls, open fires; some live music, pool, darts, silent TV; children (away from bar) and dogs welcome, steep garden behind, parking at nearby Spar (free after 6pm), open all day weekends. *(Roger and Donna Huggins)*

SIDMOUTH ST1287

Anchor (01395) 514129

Old Fore Street; EX10 8LP Welcoming family-run pub popular for its fresh fish and other good value food, well kept Caledonian ales including one named for them, decent choice of wines, good friendly service, large carpeted L-shaped room with nautical pictures, steps down to restaurant; darts; tables out in front, more in back beer garden with stage for live acts, open (and food) all day. *(Roger and Donna Huggins)*

SIDMOUTH SY1090

Bowd (01395) 513328

Junction B3176/A3052; EX10 0ND Large thatched and beamed dining pub with enjoyable sensibly priced food (all day Sun) including daily carvery, a couple of Otter ales and Sharps Doom Bar, friendly helpful staff, flagstoned interior with standing timbers and alcoves; children welcome, plenty of seats in big garden, play area, open all day. *(Roger and Donna Huggins)*

SIDMOUTH SY1287

Dukes (01395) 513320

Esplanade; EX10 8AR More brasserie than pub, but long bar on left has Branscombe Vale and a couple of guests, good food all day specialising in local fish (best to book in the evening), friendly efficient young staff, linked areas including conservatory and flagstoned eating area (once a chapel), smart contemporary décor; big-screen TV, daily papers; children welcome, disabled facilities, prom-view terrace tables, bedrooms in adjoining Elizabeth Hotel, open all day (may be summer queues). *(Roger and Donna Huggins)*

SIDMOUTH SY1287

★**Swan** (01395) 512849

York Street; EX10 8BY Cheerful old-fashioned town-centre local, well kept Youngs ales and enjoyable good value blackboard food from sandwiches up, friendly helpful staff, lounge bar with interesting pictures and memorabilia, darts and woodburner in bigger light and airy public bar with boarded walls and ceilings, daily newspapers, separate dining area; no under-14s, dogs welcome, flower-filled garden with smokers' area, open all day. *(Roger and Donna Huggins)*

SILVERTON SS9503

Lamb (01392) 860272

Fore Street; EX5 4HZ Flagstoned local run well by friendly landlord, Exe Valley,

Otter and a local guest tapped from stillage casks, inexpensive home-made pubby food including specials, separate eating area; skittle alley, free wi-fi; children and dogs welcome, handy for Killerton (NT), open all day weekends. *(George Sanderson)*

SLAPTON SX8245

★**Queens Arms** (01548) 580800

Sands Road corner, before church; TQ7 2PN Smartly kept one-room village local with welcoming staff and regulars, good straightforward inexpensive food cooked by landlord, four ales including Dartmoor and Otter, snug comfortable corners, roaring log fire, fascinating World War II photos and scrapbooks, dominoes and draughts; children and dogs welcome, lots of tables in lovely suntrap stepped garden. *(Sandra and Nigel Brown)*

SLAPTON SX8245

★**Tower** (01548) 580216

Off A379 Dartmouth–Kingsbridge; TQ7 2PN A short stroll from some fine beaches and backed by Slapton Ley nature reserve, this old inn has a low-beamed bar with settles, armchairs and scrubbed oak tables on flagstones or bare boards, log fires, well kept Butcombe, Dartmoor, Otter and St Austell (less choice out of season), local cider and several wines by the glass, good food including fresh fish, friendly accommodating staff; free wi-fi; children and dogs (in bar) welcome, picnic-sets in pretty back garden overlooked by ivy-covered ruins of 14th-c chantry, comfortable bedrooms reached by external stone staircase, good breakfast, lane up to the pub is very narrow and parking can be tricky particularly at peak times, closed Sun evening in winter and first two weeks of Jan. *(Peter Pilbeam, Alfie Bayliss, Nigel Smith and Karen Stafford-Smith)*

SOURTON SX5390

★**Highwayman** (01837) 861243

A386, S of junction with A30; EX20 4HN Unique place – a quirky fantasy of dimly lit stonework and flagstone-floored burrows and alcoves, all sorts of things to look at, one room a make-believe sailing galleon; a couple of local ales, proper cider and maybe organic wines, lunchtime sandwiches, home-made pasties and platters (evening food mainly for residents), friendly chatty service; nostalgic background music; children allowed in certain areas, outside fairy-tale pumpkin house and an old-lady-who-lived-in-a-shoe, period bedrooms with four-posters and half-testers, bunkrooms for walkers/cyclists. *(David Longhurst)*

SOUTH BRENT SX6960

Oak (01364) 72133

Station Road; TQ10 9BE Friendly village pub with well priced traditional and modern food, three well kept local ales and good choice of wines by the glass, welcoming helpful service, comfortable open-plan bar with some leather sofas, restaurant; Weds folk night, quiz first Thurs of month; children and dogs welcome, small courtyard, five bedrooms, little nearby parking, open all day weekends, closed Mon and Tues lunchtimes. *(David and Teresa Frost)*

SOUTH POOL   SX7740
Millbrook (01548) 531581
Off A379 E of Kingsbridge; TQ7 2RW
As we went to press, new people were taking over this well liked 17th-c village local by Salcombe estuary – reports please; small beamed bars, main one with inglenook, dining area with woodburner, pubby tables and chairs, food has been imaginative and the three ales kept well; terrace overlooking the water, may open all day. *(Nick Lawless, Richard Tilbrook)*

STICKLEPATH   SX6494
★ #### Devonshire (01837) 840626
Off A30 at Whiddon Down or Okehampton; EX20 2NW Welcoming old-fashioned 16th-c thatched village local next to Finch Foundry museum (NT); low-beamed slate-floor bar with big log fire, longcase clock and easy-going old furnishings, key collection, sofa in small snug, well kept low-priced ales tapped from the cask, farm cider, good value sandwiches, soup and home-made pasties from the Aga, games room, lively folk night first Sun of month; £1 fine for using mobile phone; dogs welcome (pub has its own), wheelchair access from car park, good walks, bedrooms, open all day Fri, Sat. *(Chris and Angela Buckell)*

STOKE FLEMING   SX8648
Green Dragon (01803) 770238
Church Street; TQ6 0PX Popular and friendly village local with yachtsman landlord, well worn-in beamed and flagstoned interior, boat pictures and charts, sleepy dogs and cats, snug with sofas, armchairs, grandfather clock and open fire, well kept ales such as Bass, Otter and Wadworths, Addlestone's and Aspall's ciders, good choice of wines by the glass and enjoyable local food including fresh fish and seasonal game, prompt service; children welcome, tables out on partly covered heated terrace, lovely garden with play area, handy for coast path. *(Maureen Wood, Richard Tilbrook)*

STOKE GABRIEL   SX8457
Church House (01803) 782384
Off A385 just W of junction with A3022; Church Walk; TQ9 6SD Popular early 14th-c pub; lounge bar with fine medieval beam-and-plank ceiling, black oak partition wall, window seats cut into thick butter-coloured walls, woodburner in huge fireplace, look out for the ancient mummified cat, well kept Bass, Sharps Doom Bar and a guest, enjoyable good value food, also little locals' bar; background music, Sun quiz; well

behaved children and dogs welcome, picnic-sets on small front terrace, old stocks (pub used to incorporate the village courthouse), limited parking, open all day. *(William Slade)*

STOKENHAM   SX8042
Church House (01548) 580253
N of A379 towards Torcross; TQ7 2SZ Extended old pub overlooking village green behind, three open-plan areas, low beams, mix of seating on flagstones, lots of knick-knacks, Otter ales and a guest, well liked food from good sandwiches up using local produce, dining conservatory; live music including jazz; children and dogs (in bar) welcome, picnic-sets on lawn with play area, interesting church next door. *(Jeff Davies)*

STOKENHAM   SX8042
Tradesmans Arms (01548) 580996
Just off A379 Dartmouth–Kingsbridge; TQ7 2SZ Picturesque partly thatched 14th-c pub; traditional low-beamed cottagey interior with log fire, well kept west country beers and decent choice of wines, locally sourced food including daily specials, restaurant; children and dogs welcome, seats over lane on raised area looking down on village green, nice bedrooms. *(Nick Lawless, Sam)*

STRETE   SX8446
Kings Arms (01803) 770380
A379 SW of Dartmouth; TQ6 0RW Welcoming former 1830s hotel under new management; bar with dining area up steps, log fire, enjoyable freshly made food from sandwiches and sharing boards up, three real ales including Otter, cocktails, good coffee and cream teas; children and dogs welcome, back terrace and garden with lovely views over Start Bay, open all day Sun till 9pm (food till 6pm), closed Mon lunchtime. *(Patricia Hawkins)*

TEIGNMOUTH   SX9372
Olde Jolly Sailor (01626) 772864
Set back from Northumberland Place; TQ14 8DE Town's oldest pub (said to date from the 12th c), comfortable low-ceilinged interior with stripped-stone walls, various nooks and crannies, well kept Dartmoor Jail, Sharps Doom Bar and guests, enjoyable pubby food (not Sun evening) including good sandwiches; live jazz Mon, sports TV, free wi-fi; children and dogs welcome, seats in front courtyard, more behind with estuary views, open all day. *(Roger and Donna Huggins, Brian Glozier)*

THORVERTON   SS9202
Thorverton Arms (01392) 860205
Village signed off A396 Exeter–Tiverton; EX5 5NS Spacious 16th-c coaching inn with five adjoining areas including log-fire bar and restaurant, good well presented home-made food at reasonable prices, three real ales including Otter, welcoming landlord and efficient friendly staff; pool;

children and dogs (in bar) welcome, wisteria-draped terrace and sunny garden, pleasant village, six comfortable bedrooms, nice breakfast. *(Elizabeth and Peter May)*

TOPSHAM SX9688

★ **Bridge Inn** (01392) 873862

2.5 miles from M5 junction 30: Topsham signposted from exit roundabout; in Topsham follow signpost (A376) Exmouth, on the Elmgrove Road, into Bridge Hill; EX3 0QQ Very special old drinkers' pub (16th-c former maltings painted a distinctive pink), in landlady's family for five generations and with up to nine well kept ales tapped from the cask; quite unchanging and completely unspoilt with friendly staff and locals, character small rooms and snugs, traditional furniture including a nice high-backed settle, woodburner, the 'bar' is landlady's front parlour (as notice on the door politely reminds customers), simple food; live folk and blues, but no background music, mobile phones or credit cards; children and dogs welcome, picnic-sets overlooking weir. *(Roger and Donna Huggins)*

TOPSHAM SX9687

★ **Globe** (01392) 873471

Fore Street; 2 miles from M5 junction 30; EX3 0HR Handsome 16th-c coaching inn mixing original features with contemporary touches; beamed bar with old prints on red-painted panelling, armchairs in a corner and suede tub and pubby chairs around dark tables on bare boards, open fire in small brick fireplace with logs piled to one side, second pale-panelled bar with traditional furniture on tartan carpet and woodburner, St Austell ales and several wines by the glass, highly regarded interesting food along with more standard choices, helpful friendly staff, another log fire and huge candlesticks in elegant dining room; free wi-fi; children and dogs (in bar) welcome, big terrace with seats under parasols, well equipped modern bedrooms, good breakfast, open (and food) all day. *(Mike Swan, Toby Jones)*

TOPSHAM SX9688

Passage House (01392) 873653

Ferry Road, off main street; EX3 0JN Relaxed 18th-c pub with traditional black-beamed bar and slate-floored lower dining area, good food from sandwiches to local fish, well kept ales and decent wines, friendly service; quiz nights, free wi-fi; children and dogs welcome, peaceful terrace looking over moorings and river (lovely at sunset) to nature reserve beyond, open all day. *(William Slade)*

TORBRYAN SX8266

★ **Old Church House** (01803) 812372

Pub signed off A381; TQ12 5UR Character 13th-c former farmhouse with attractive bar (popular with locals), benches built into fine panelling, settle and other

seats by big log fire, Hunters, Skinners, St Austell and a guest, several wines by the glass and around 35 malt whiskies, good variety of well liked tasty food, cheerful helpful staff, discreetly lit lounges, one with a splendid deep Tudor inglenook; background and occasional live music; free wi-fi; children and dogs welcome, comfortable bedrooms (woodburner in one), good breakfast. *(Jeremy Snaithe)*

TORCROSS SX8242

Start Bay (01548) 580553

A379 S of Dartmouth; TQ7 2TQ More fish and chip restaurant than pub but does sell Bass, Otter, local wine and cider; very much set out for eating and exceptionally busy at peak times with staff coping well, food is enjoyable and sensibly priced; wheelback chairs around dark tables, country pictures, some photographs of storms buffeting the building, winter coal fire, small drinking area by counter, large family room; no dogs during food times, seats outside (highly prized) looking over pebble beach and wildlife lagoon, open all day. *(Anne and Ben Smith)*

TORQUAY SX9265

★ **Cary Arms** (01803) 327110

Beach Road: off B3199 Babbacombe Road, via Babbacombe Downs Road; turn steeply down near Babbacombe Theatre; TQ1 3LX Charming higgledy-piggledy hotel reached down a tortuously steep lane; small, glass-enclosed entrance room with large ship lanterns and cleats, beamed grotto-effect bar overlooking the sea, rough pink granite walls, alcoves, hobbit-style leather chairs around carved wooden tables, slate or bare-board floors, woodburner, Bays, Hanlons and Otter, two local ciders and nine good wines by the glass, enjoyable if not particularly cheap food; free wi-fi; children and dogs (in bar) welcome, plenty of outside seating on various terraces, outside bar, barbecue and pizza oven, steps down to quay with six mooring spaces, boutique-style bedrooms, self-catering cottages (glorious views) and chic beach huts and shore suites, open all day. *(Hilary and Neil Christopher, Caroline Prescott)*

TORQUAY SX9166

Crown & Sceptre (01803) 328290

Petitor Road, St Marychurch; TQ1 4QA Friendly two-bar local with six well kept ales including Butcombe, St Austell and Otter, proper cider, interesting naval memorabilia and chamber-pot collection, basic good value lunchtime food, snacks any time; regular live music including jazz Tues, folk Fri; children and dogs welcome, two gardens, open all day Fri-Sun. *(Geoffrey Sutton)*

TORQUAY SX9163

Hole in the Wall (01803) 200755

Park Lane, opposite clock tower; TQ1 2AU Ancient two-bar local tucked away near harbour, reasonably priced usual food including good fresh fish, seven well kept ales such as Bays, Butcombe, Otter and Sharps, Blackawton cider, good friendly service, smooth cobbled floors, low beams and alcoves, lots of nautical brassware, ship models, old local photographs and chamberpots, restaurant/function room (band nights); can get very busy weekends; some seats in alley out at front, open all day. *(Tony Scott, Roger and Donna Huggins)*

TORRINGTON   SS4919
Black Horse (01805) 622121
High Street; EX38 8HN Popular twin-gabled former coaching inn; beams hung with stirrups in smallish bar with solid furniture and woodburner, lounge with striking ancient oak partition wall, back restaurant, five well kept ales including Courage and St Austell, generous helpings of tasty home-made food served by friendly staff; background music, darts and shove-ha'penny; children and dogs welcome, disabled access, three bedrooms, open all day. *(Martyn Stringer)*

TOTNES   SX8060
Albert (01803) 863214
Bridgetown; TQ9 5AD Unpretentious slate-hung pub near the river, small bar and two other rooms, low beams, flagstones, panelling, some old settles and lots of knick-knacks, friendly landlord brewing his own good Bridgetown ales, real cider and plenty of whiskies, honest reasonably priced pub food, friendly local atmosphere; quiz and music nights, darts, free wi-fi; dogs welcome, paved beer garden behind. *(Sandra and Nigel Brown)*

TOTNES   SX7960
Bay Horse (01803) 862088
Cistern Street; TQ9 5SP Welcoming traditional two-bar inn dating from the 15th c, four well kept local ales such as Dartmoor and New Lion, ciders such as Sandford Orchards, simple lunchtime food; background and regular live music including good Sun jazz; children and dogs welcome, nice garden behind, three bedrooms, good breakfast, open all day. *(Tom Stone)*

TOTNES   SX7960
★Kingsbridge Inn (01803) 863324
Leechwell Street; TQ9 5SY Attractive rambling 17th-c pub-restaurant run by two brothers; black beams, timbering and white-painted stone walls, big woodburner, enjoyable fairly traditional food from changing blackboard menu, Butcombe, Otter and nice choice of wines, good friendly service; live music every other Sat, other events such as film and tango nights in upstairs Piano Bar; children and dogs welcome, tables on back deck, closed Sun evening, Mon, but may open all day in summer. *(Roger and Donna Huggins)*

TOTNES   SX8060
★Royal Seven Stars (01803) 862125
Fore Street, The Plains; TQ9 5DD Good town-centre bar and coffee bar in well run civilised old hotel, friendly and easy-going, with well kept ales and enjoyable generously served food all day from breakfast on, separate brasserie/grill room with adjoining champagne bar; covered and heated tables out in front, river across busy main road, 21 bedrooms. *(George Sanderson)*

TOTNES   SX8059
★Steam Packet (01803) 863880
St Peters Quay, on W bank (ie not on Steam Packet Quay); TQ9 5EW Quayside inn with three distinct bar areas, light oak floor, some bare-stone and brick walls, dark half-panelling and delft shelving, squashy leather sofa in one part against wall of books, fireplace at either end, Dartmoor Jail, Sharps Doom Bar and a guest, proper cider and a dozen wines by the glass, popular fairly priced traditional food (all day Sun), friendly staff coping well at busy times, conservatory restaurant; background music, TV, free wi-fi; children and dogs welcome, seats on terrace overlooking River Dart, bedrooms, open all day. *(Mike and Margaret Banks, Julie Braeburn)*

UGBOROUGH   SX6755
Ship (01752) 892565
Off A3121 SE of Ivybridge; PL21 0NS Friendly dining pub extended from cosy 16th-c flagstoned core, well divided open-plan eating areas a step down from neat bar with woodburner, enjoyable food from bar meals to imaginative restaurant dishes and blackboard specials (plenty of fish), cheerful efficient service, well kept Palmers, St Austell and a local guest, nice house wines; background music; children welcome, dogs in bar, tables out in front, open all day Fri-Sun in summer. *(John Evans, Philip Crawford, Lynda and Trevor Smith)*

WEARE GIFFARD   SS4722
Cyder Press (01237) 425517
Tavern Gardens; EX39 4QR Welcoming village local with St Austell ales and enjoyable fairly priced home-made food, black beams and timbers, inglenook woodburner; quiz nights and Tues acoustic music; children (till 8.30pm) and dogs welcome, seats outside, beautiful countryside and handy for Tarka Trail, two bedrooms, closed Mon and Tues lunchtimes. *(Elizabeth and Peter May)*

WEMBURY   SX5349
Odd Wheel (01752) 863052
Knighton Road; PL9 0JD Modernised village pub with five well kept west country ales, good fairly traditional food from sandwiches and ciabattas up, reasonable prices including good value set lunch Mon-Fri, friendly helpful service, back

restaurant; pool, darts, sports TV, free wi-fi; children and dogs (in bar) welcome, seats out on decking, fenced play area, open (and food) all day weekends. *(Hugh Roberts, Philip Crawford)*

WEMBWORTHY   SS6609
Lymington Arms (01837) 83572
Lama Cross; EX18 7SA Large early 19th-c beamed dining pub in pleasant country setting, wide choice of food including some interesting specials, character landlady and friendly staff, well kept Sharps Doom Bar and a west country guest, Winkleigh farm cider, decent wines, comfortably plush seating and red tablecloths in partly stripped-stone bar, big back restaurant; children welcome, picnic-sets outside, closed Sun evening, Mon and Tues (and may shut early if quiet). *(Patricia Hawkins)*

WESTON   ST1400
★**Otter** (01404) 42594
Off A373, or A30 at W end of Honiton bypass; EX14 3NZ Big busy family pub with heavy low beams, enjoyable good value food (best to book) from baguettes and sharing boards up including several vegetarian options, carvery Thurs and Sun lunchtimes, smaller appetites menu and daily deals, cheerful helpful staff, well kept Otter and a guest, carpeted opened-up interior with good log fire; background music, pool; dogs allowed in one area, disabled access, picnic-sets on big lawn leading to River Otter, play area, open all day, food all day weekends. *(Robert Watt, Bob and Margaret Holder)*

WHIMPLE   SY0497
New Fountain (01404) 822350
Off A30 Exeter–Honiton; Church Road; EX5 2TA Two-bar beamed village pub sympathetically refurbished under newish licensees, friendly local atmosphere, good home-made food (not Mon) using local ingredients, well kept Teignworthy and a guest, woodburner; children and well behaved dogs welcome, some outside seating, local heritage centre in car park (open Weds, Sat), pub closes Mon lunchtime. *(Charles Todd)*

WIDECOMBE   SX7176
Old Inn (01364) 621207
B3387 W of Bovey Tracey; TQ13 7TA Busy dining pub (get there before about 12.30pm in summer to miss the coach-loads), spacious beamed interior including side conservatory with large central woodburner, enjoyable fairly standard food served by

friendly staff, well kept Badger, Dartmoor and a guest; free wi-fi; children and dogs welcome, nice garden with water features and pleasant terrace, great walks from this pretty moorland village, open (and food) all day. *(Mike and Margaret Banks)*

WONSON   SX6789
★**Northmore Arms** (01647) 231428
Between Throwleigh and Gidleigh; EX20 2JA Far from smart and a favourite with those who take to its idiosyncratic style (not all do); two simple old-fashioned rooms, log fire and woodburner, low beams and stripped stone, well kept ales such as Dartmoor tapped from the cask, farm cider and decent house wines, good honest home-made food, darts and board games; free wi-fi; children and dogs welcome, picnic-sets outside, beautiful remote walking country, closed Sun evening. *(Millie and Peter Downing)*

YEALMPTON   SX5851
Rose & Crown (01752) 880223
A379 Kingsbridge–Plymouth; PL8 2EB Central bar counter, all dark wood and heavy brass, leather-seated stools and mix of furnishings on stripped-wood floors, emphasis on popular bar and restaurant food including lunchtime/early evening set menu (not available Sun or Mon evening), friendly service, three St Austell ales, quite a few wines by the glass and decent coffee; children welcome, dogs in bar, tables in walled garden with pond, also a lawned area, open (and food) all day. *(John Evans)*

LUNDY

LUNDY   SS1344
★**Marisco** (01271) 870870
Get there by ferry (Bideford and Ilfracombe) or helicopter (Hartland Point); EX39 2LY One of England's most isolated pubs – yet surprisingly busy most nights, great setting, steep trudge up from landing stage, galleried interior with lifebelts and shipwreck salvage, open fire, two St Austell ales named for the island and its spring water on tap, Weston's cider and reasonably priced house wines, good basic food using Lundy produce and lots of fresh seafood, friendly staff, books and games; no mobile phones; children welcome, tables outside, souvenir shop doubling as general store for the island's few residents, open (and food) all day from breakfast on. *(William Slade)*

Dorset

KEY ★ Star Pub | 🌟 Top Quality Food | 🍺 Great Beer
🍷 Good Wines | £ Bargain Meals | 🛏 Good Bedrooms | 🍴 Serves Food

---

ASKERSWELL
SY5393 Map 2

Spyway £ 🛏

(01308) 485250 – www.spyway-inn.co.uk

Off A35 Bridport–Dorchester; DT2 9EP

Extremely popular family-run inn with a genuine welcome, unspoilt décor, real ales, well liked food and fine views; bedrooms

With a charming, hard-working landlord and friendly staff, this country inn is always full of cheerful customers. The unspoilt little rooms are cosily filled with old-fashioned high-backed settles, cushioned wall and window seats and some tub chairs. Old photos of the pub and rustic scenes are displayed on the walls and jugs hang from the beams; the warm Rayburn is a bonus on chilly days. Otter Ale, Bitter and Amber and Branscombe Vale Branoc on handpump, ten wines by the glass and farm cider are served by friendly staff. The dining area has old oak beams and timber uprights, red-cushioned dining chairs around dark tables on patterned carpet, horse tack and horsebrasses on the walls, and a woodburning stove. Two smaller rooms lead off from here. There are marvellous views of the downs and coast from seats on the back terrace and in the garden, and a small children's play area. The comfortable bedrooms look over the grounds and breakfasts are excellent. The steep lane outside continues up Eggardon Hill, one of the highest points in the region.

🍴 Rewarding food includes sandwiches, mozzarella fritters with sweet chilli dip, scallops with bacon and garlic, butternut squash risotto, steak in ale pie, chicken curry, slow-roasted lamb shank with red wine gravy, bass fillets with cabbage and bacon and sautéed potatoes, chicken breast stuffed with haggis with whisky cream sauce, and puddings. *Benchmark main dish: liver and bacon with red wine and onion gravy £11.50. Two-course evening meal £17.00.*

Free house ~ Licensee Tim Wilkes ~ Real ale ~ Open 12-3, 6-11 ~ Bar food 12-3, 6-9 ~ Restaurant ~ Children welcome ~ Wi-fi ~ Bedrooms: £50/£80 *Recommended by Comus and Sarah Elliott, Tom and Jill Jones, Dennis and Doreen Haward, Peter J and Avril Hanson, P and J Shapley, Tracey and Stephen Groves, Colin McLachlan*

BOURTON
ST7731 Map 2

White Lion

(01747) 840866 – www.whitelionbourton.co.uk

High Street, off old A303 E of Wincanton; SP8 5AT

Stone inn built in 1723, with beamed bar and dining room, pleasing food and ales and seats in the garden; bedrooms

An early 18th-c former coaching inn, this is a handsome place with a welcoming landlord and friendly, efficient staff. The bar is traditionally furnished and the two-level dining room has nice old wooden chairs around a medley of tables. Throughout, there are beams, bare boards, fine flagstones, stripped stone and half-panelling, bow window seats, church candles and a log fire in an inglenook fireplace. Otter Amber and a couple of guest beers such as Isle of Purbeck Fossil Fuel and Keystone Bedrock on handpump and several wines by the glass; background music. The back terrace and raised lawn have picnic-sets. Bedrooms are comfortable and breakfasts good. Stourhead (National Trust) is close by.

Well liked food includes sandwiches, smoked fish platter with sweet dill dressing, pâté with redcurrant and port jelly, macaroni cheese with garlic bread, burger with toppings, onion rings and chips, rare-breed sausages with mash and red onion gravy, coq au vin, bass fillets with herb butter, a curry of the day, and puddings. *Benchmark main dish: steak and kidney pie £13.50. Two-course evening meal £20.00.*

Free house ~ Licensee William Stuart ~ Real ale ~ Open 11.30-11 (10.30 Sun) ~ Bar food 12-2 (3 Sat), 6-9; 12-3, 7-9 Sun ~ Restaurant ~ Children welcome ~ Dogs welcome ~ Wi-fi ~ Bedrooms: /£80 *Recommended by Colin and Maggie Fancourt, Edward Mirzoeff*

CERNE ABBAS
New Inn 🍴⭐ 🍷 🛏️

ST6601 Map 2

(01300) 341274 – www.thenewinncerneabbas.co.uk
Long Street; DT2 7JF

Carefully refurbished former coaching inn with character bar and two dining rooms, friendly licensees, local ales and inventive food; fine bedrooms

It is thought this fine old place orginated in the 15th c as a guesthouse for the abbey (built by Benedictine monks). It then became a coaching inn, and there remains a great deal of character and original features throughout, including lovely mullioned windows, heavy oak beams and a pump and mounting block in the former coachyard. The bar has a solid oak counter, an appealing mix of old dining tables and chairs on slate or polished wooden floors, settles built into various nooks and crannies and a woodburner in the opened-up Yorkstone fireplace. Palmers Copper, Dorset Gold and IPA on handpump, a dozen wines by the glass, several malt whiskies and local cider. The dining room is furnished in a similar style; background music. There are seats on the terrace and picnic-sets beneath mature fruit trees or parasols in the back garden. Bedrooms, in the charming 16th-c main building and the converted stable block, are smart and well equipped. You can walk from the attractive stone-built village to the prehistoric Cerne Abbas Giant chalk carving and on to other villages.

Highly rewarding food includes sandwiches, twice-baked cheese soufflé, crispy pork belly with skate wing, braised gem and caper butter sauce, jerusalem artichoke risotto, chicken with foie gras, stuffed leg, thyme croquettes and spinach and wild mushroom sauce, cod with roast garlic mash, baby leeks and onion velouté, sirloin steak with Café de Paris butter and triple-cooked chips, and puddings such as pistachio cheesecake with maple syrup and vanilla ice-cream and caramelised banana tart with banana bavarois and passion-fruit sorbet. *Benchmark main dish: bass with fennel, liquorice, pancetta and dill £17.50. Two-course evening meal £22.00.*

Palmers ~ Tenant Julian Dove ~ Real ale ~ Open 12-11; 12-3, 6-11 in winter ~ Bar food 12-2, 7-9 (8.30 Sun) ~ Restaurant ~ Children welcome ~ Dogs allowed in bar and bedrooms ~ Wi-fi ~ Bedrooms: £85/£95 *Recommended by Andrew Reed, J R Wildon, Dr Martin Owton, Mrs P Sumner, Alan Johnson, P and J Shapley, Clive and Fran Dutson*

CHETNOLE   ST6008   Map 2

Chetnole Inn ⇔

(01935) 872337 – www.thechetnoleinn.co.uk

Village signed off A37 S of Yeovil; DT9 6NU

Attractive country pub with beams and huge flagstones, real ales, popular food and seats in the back garden; bedrooms

The bar at this nicely run beamed inn has a relaxed country kitchen feel with wheelback chairs and pine tables on huge flagstones and a woodburning stove. Friendly staff serve Butcombe Rare Breed, Wriggle Valley Gold, Yeovil Star Gazer and a weekly guest beer on handpump and there's a fair choice of wines. Popular with locals, the snug has a leather sofa near another woodburner and stools against the counter; dogs are allowed in here. The airy dining room has more wheelback chairs around pale wooden tables on stripped floorboards and a small open fire. At the back, a delightful garden has picnic-sets and a view over fields. The comfortable bedrooms overlook the old church.

Enjoyable food includes home-made duck cakes with hoisin, ginger and sweet chilli and mango relish, home-cured salmon with potato salad and horseradish cream, asparagus and goats cheese risotto, a pie of the day, burger with toppings, tomato chutney and fries, smoked haddock and pea tagliatelle, chicken breast with new potatoes and bacon, roasted cherry tomatoes and chicken broth, and puddings such as vanilla crème brûlée and sticky toffee pudding with toffee sauce and honey and ginger ice-cream. *Benchmark main dish: slow-braised pork belly with root vegetable mash, paprika potatoes and tomato jus £12.95. Two-course evening meal £20.00.*

Free house ~ Licensees Simon and Maria Hudson ~ Real ale ~ Open 11-3, 6-11; 11-11 Sat; 12-4 Sun ~ Bar food 12-2, 6.30-9 ~ Restaurant ~ Children welcome ~ Dogs allowed in bar ~ Wi-fi ~ Bedrooms: /£105 *Recommended by Geoffrey Sutton, Peter Barrett, Clive and Fran Dutson*

CHIDEOCK   SY4191   Map 1

Anchor ⇔

(01297) 489215 – www.theanchorinnseatown.co.uk

Off A35 from Chideock; DT6 6JU

Stunning beach position for carefully renovated inn, lots of character, well kept ales and popular food and seats on front terrace; light, airy bedrooms

What really distinguishes this thoughtfully refurbished old pub is its splendid position, almost straddling the Dorset Coast Path and nestling beneath the 617-foot Golden Cap pinnacle. Just a few steps from the beach, seats and tables on the spacious front terrace are ideally placed for views, but you'll have to get there early in summer to bag a spot. Inside, plenty of original character has been kept in the three smallish, light rooms: padded wall seating, nice old wooden chairs and stools around scrubbed tables on bare boards, a couple of woodburning stoves (one under a huge bressumer beam), tilley lamps, model ships and lots of historic photographs of the pub, the area and locals. From the wood-panelled bar they serve Palmers 200, Best, Copper and Dorset Gold on handpump, seven wines by the glass and cocktails; background music. The attractive, airy bedrooms are decorated with nautical touches using driftwood and ropework and overlook the sea. You can park for free in front of the pub or across the road for £4 (refundable against a spend of £20 or more in the pub).

Well liked food includes sandwiches, chicken and truffle terrine with carrot jam, szechuan and vodka squid with cured vegetables, platters, smoked tofu and roast vegetable burger with halloumi and chips, slow-braised beef and kidney casserole, confit duck leg with bubble and squeak and jus, char-roasted pork with butter beans, chorizo, apples, black pudding croquette and sherry reduction, and puddings such as rhubarb and lemon eton mess and chocolate and pistachio délice with raspberry and mint. *Benchmark main dish: malt vinegar and sea herb-battered fish and chips £13.00. Two-course evening meal £20.50.*

Palmers ~ Tenant Paul Wiscombe ~ Real ale ~ Open 10am-11pm ~ Bar food 12-9; 12-3, 6-9 Mon-Thurs Nov-Mar ~ Children welcome ~ Dogs allowed in bar ~ Wi-fi ~ Bedrooms: £115/£130 *Recommended by Lucy Ryan, Sheila Topham, Richard and Penny Gibbs, Richard Tilbrook*

CHIDEOCK   SY4292   Map 1

George

(01297) 489419 – www.georgeinnchideock.co.uk
A35 Bridport–Lyme Regis; DT6 6JD

Comfortably traditional local with a thriving feel and well liked food and drink

A cheerful mix of both holidaymakers and locals crowd into this heavily thatched old village inn creating a lively atmosphere. The cosy, low-ceilinged, carpeted bar is nicely traditional, with Palmers 200, Copper, Dorset Gold, IPA and a guest beer on handpump, six wines by the glass and farm cider, warm log fires and brassware and pewter tankards hanging from dark beams. There are wooden pews and long built-in tongue-and-groove banquettes, cream walls hung with old tools and high shelves of bottles, plates and mugs; background music, TV, bar billiards, darts and board games. The garden room opens on to a pretty walled garden with a terrace and a much used wood-fired oven.

As well as their wood-fired pizza evenings on Thursdays, the tasty food includes sandwiches, half pint of prawns with lemon mayonnaise, home-made chorizo scotch egg, home-cooked local ham with free-range eggs, burger with toppings, caramelised onion chutney and chips, vegetarian linguine, local steaks, and puddings. *Benchmark main dish: beer-battered fish of the day £11.50. Two-course evening meal £19.00.*

Palmers ~ Tenant Jamie Smith ~ Real ale ~ Open 12-3, 6-11 ~ Bar food 12-2.30, 6-9.30 ~ Restaurant ~ Children welcome except in snug bar ~ Dogs allowed in bar ~ Wi-fi *Recommended by Andrew Stone, Edward May*

CHURCH KNOWLE   SY9381   Map 2

New Inn ♀

(01929) 480357 – www.newinn-churchknowle.co.uk
Village signed off A351 N of Corfe Castle; BH20 5NQ

Partly thatched former farmhouse with plenty of seating in various rooms, open fires, a thoughtful choice of drinks, good food and a friendly landlord

Walkers regularly stop off at this usefully placed, partly thatched 16th-c inn in a quiet village beneath a fold of the Purbeck Hills and not far from the Dorset coast path. The linked character bar rooms are full of interest: brass and copper measuring jugs, bed warmers, pots and pans, horsebrasses, venerable board games and books, stone jars, china plates, a glass cabinet filled with household items from years ago, tilley lamps, the odd mangle and set of scales, a coastguard flag and an old diver's helmet. The main bar has an open fire in a stone fireplace, high-backed black leather dining chairs and cushioned wall settles around heavy rustic tables on red patterned carpet and quite a few stools against the counter. Dorset Jurassic, Sharps Doom Bar and a guest such as Ringwood Best on handpump, six wines by the glass and farm cider; there's a wine shack from which you can choose your own wines, and also a wide choice of teas, coffees and local soft drinks. The similarly furnished dining room leads off here. Outside are picnic-sets on the lawn, and there's also a campsite. Corfe Castle ruins are nearby.

Using local ingredients, the popular food includes sandwiches, twice-baked three cheese soufflé, deep-fried salt and pepper squid and whitebait with sweet chilli dip, home-cooked honey-glazed ham and free-range eggs, cottage pie, game bourguignon, chicken curry, lambs liver and bacon in red onion reduction, smoked haddock with free-range poached egg and hollandaise sauce, and puddings such as crème brûlée and gooseberry and elderflower ice-cream and plum and ginger crumble. *Benchmark main dish: roast of the day £10.95. Two-course evening meal £19.00.*

Punch ~ Tenants Maurice and Matthew Estop ~ Real ale ~ Open 11-3, 6 (5 high season)-11; closed Mon Nov-Feb ~ Bar food 12-2, 7-9 ~ Restaurant ~ Children welcome ~ Wi-fi
Recommended by R Halliday, Peter Pilbeam, Dr J J H Gilkes, Alan and Angela Scouller, Jane and Kai Horsburgh

CRANBORNE

SU0513 Map 2

Inn at Cranborne 🛏

(01725) 551249 – www.theinnatcranborne.co.uk
Wimborne Street (B3078 N of Wimborne); BH21 5PP

Neatly refurbished old inn with a friendly atmosphere, good choice of drinks, highly rated food and seats outside; comfortable bedrooms

Our readers enjoy their visits to this well run all-rounder. The rambling bars have heavy beams, open doorways, the odd standing timber and a chatty, relaxed atmosphere. The main bar area, divided into two by a partition, is a favourite place to sit: grey-planked and tartan-cushioned built-in wall seats and assorted chairs (farmhouse, wheelback, ladderback) on parquet flooring, flagstones or rugs, nightlights on each table and a woodburner in an inglenook fireplace. Badger First Call and a guest such as Tanglefoot on handpump and several wines by the glass served by friendly, helpful staff; background music, TV, darts and board games. The dining areas spread back from here, with similar furnishings and a little brick fireplace; there's also a second bar with white-painted or wooden furniture and another woodburning stove. Plenty of coaching prints on grey walls above a darker grey dado, and church candles. Outside, you'll find benches, seats and tables on neat gravel. The comfortable, well equipped bedrooms are clean and bright and the breakfasts very good. Thomas Hardy visited the pub while writing *Tess of the D'Urbervilles*.

The good interesting food uses produce from within a 30-mile radius: lunchtime sandwiches, smoked trout pâté with capers, pecan-crusted goats cheese with Pimms jelly and macerated fruit, blue cheese and parsley risotto with an egg, steak burger with toppings, onion relish and fries, free-range chicken with pea and bean cassoulet and mint and pine nut pesto, bream with lovage pasta and clams, chilli and cherry vine tomato sauce, and puddings such as quince and pear crumble with sauce anglaise and dark chocolate mousse with orange curd, honeycomb and chocolate oil. *Benchmark main dish: fish pie £10.95. Two-course evening meal £19.50.*

Badger ~ Tenant Jane Gould ~ Real ale ~ Open 11-11; 11-10 Sun ~ Bar food 12-2, 6-9; 12-2.30, 6-9.30 Fri, Sat; 12-2.30, 6-9 Sun ~ Restaurant (evening only) ~ Children welcome ~ Dogs welcome ~ Wi-fi ~ Bedrooms: £75/£99 *Recommended by Ian Malone, Peter Brix, Alison and Michael Harper*

EVERSHOT
Acorn 🌟 � 🛏

(01935) 83228 – www.acorn-inn.co.uk

Off A37 S of Yeovil; DT2 0JW

400-year-old inn in a pretty village with character rooms, log fires and knick-knacks and friendly licensees; bedrooms

This is an enjoyable place to stay: each of the attractive bedrooms is individually decorated and has a Thomas Hardy name; breakfasts are first class and guests can use the facilities at the nearby Summer Lodge hotel. The public bar has a log fire, lots of beer mats on beams, big flagstones and high chairs against the counter where they serve Dartmoor Legend and a guest beer on handpump, 39 wines by the glass and over 100 malt whiskies; dogs are looked after with a bowl of water and biscuits behind the bar. A second bar has comfortable beige leather wall banquettes and little stools around tables set with fresh flowers, and a turkish rug on nice old quarry tiles. This leads to a bistro-style dining room with ladderback chairs around oak tables; the slightly more formal restaurant is similarly furnished. There's also a comfortable lounge with armchairs, board games and shelves of books and a skittle alley. Throughout are open fires, wood panelling, pretty knick-knacks, all manner of copper and brass items, water jugs, wall prints and photographs; background music, TV and darts. The walled garden has picnic-sets under a fine beech tree, and there are numerous nearby walks. The pub is immortalised as the Sow & Acorn in Thomas Hardy's *Tess of the D'Urbervilles*.

 From a seasonally aware menu, the good food includes sandwiches, confit duck, chorizo and spring onion terrine with rhubarb purée, fresh crab, lime, coriander and chilli bruschetta, local estate venison sausages with cheesy mash and onion gravy, honey and ginger-roasted chicken on wild mushroom and parmesan risotto with red wine jus, puy lentil cottage pie with sweet potato and butternut squash mash, burgers with toppings, home-made ketchup and triple-cooked chips, and puddings such as dark chocolate brownie with salt caramel sauce and marmalade and mascarpone ice-cream and rhubarb pannacotta with rhubarb vodka. *Benchmark main dish: slow-roasted lamb shoulder £17.00. Two-course evening meal £20.00.*

Free house ~ Licensee Alex Mackenzie ~ Real ale ~ Open 11-11; 12-10.30 Sun ~ Bar food 12-2, 7-9 ~ Restaurant ~ Children welcome ~ Dogs welcome ~ Wi-fi ~ Bedrooms: £89/£110
Recommended by Nick Sharpe, Charlie May, Tracey and Stephen Groves, Clive and Fran Dutson

FARNHAM
Museum 🌟 ♱ 🛏

(01725) 516261 – www.museuminn.co.uk

Village signposted off A354 Blandford Forum–Salisbury; DT11 8DE

Partly thatched, smart inn with appealing rooms, brasserie-style food, real ales and fine wines, and seats outside; comfortable bedrooms

At the heart of this civilised place is a proper little bar with beams, flagstones, a big inglenook fireplace and quite an assortment of dining chairs around plain or painted wooden tables. Bar stools line the counter where friendly staff serve Isle of Purbeck Best, Ringwood Best and a guest from Waylands Sixpenny 6D on handpump, several wines by the glass, a dozen malt whiskies and farm cider. Leading off here is a simply but attractively furnished dining room with cushioned window seats, a long dark leather button-back wall seat, similar chairs and tables on bare floorboards and quite a few photographs on patterned wallpaper; there's also a quiet lounge with armchairs around a low table in front of an open fire, books on shelves and board games. A terrace has cushioned seats and tables under parasols. Four of the bedrooms are in the 17th-c pub itself, four others are in the converted stables; they also have a large, thatched self-catering cottage.

 Using top local, seasonal produce, the modern food includes sandwiches, twice-baked montgomery cheddar cheese soufflé, mussels in leeks and creamy white wine sauce, rabbit and leek pie, salt-baked beetroot gnocchi with creamed spinach and leeks, mascarpone and parmesan, burger with toppings, chips and garlic mayonnaise, local venison with sweet potato rösti, spring greens, glazed fig and jus, salmon and smoked haddock fishcake with buttered spinach, hollandaise and poached egg, and puddings such as bitter hot chocolate fondant with chocolate ice-cream and baked vanilla and lemon zest cheesecake with tea-soaked prunes. *Benchmark main dish: slow-cooked pork belly with champ mash and jus £13.95. Two-course evening meal £24.00.*

Free house ~ Licensee Lee Hart ~ Real ale ~ Open 11.30-11 ~ Bar food 12-2.30 (3 Sat), 6-9.30; 12-3.30, 6-9 Sun ~ Restaurant Fri and Sat evenings, Sun lunch ~ Children welcome ~ Dogs allowed in bar ~ Wi-fi ~ Bedrooms: /£110 *Recommended by Mungo Shipley, Dr Simon Innes, Peter Pilbeam*

KINGSTON
SY9579 Map 2

Scott Arms

(01929) 480270 – www.thescottarms.com
West Street (B3069); BH20 5LH

Wonderful views from a large garden, rambling character rooms, real ales and interesting food and an easy-going atmosphere; bedrooms

The views of Corfe Castle and the Purbeck Hills from the big, attractive garden are quite magnificent; there's also rustic-style seating and an outside summer kitchen with a jerk shack for caribbean-style food (the landlady is jamaican). Inside, the bar areas and more formal dining room are on several levels with stripped stone and brickwork, flagstones and bare boards, beams and high rafters, seats ranging from sofas and easy chairs through all manner of wooden chairs around tables of varying sizes and open fires; stairs lead up from the bar to a small minstrels' gallery-like area with sofas facing one another across a table. Bath Gem, Butcombe Bitter, Dorset Jurassic and Ringwood Best on handpump, 11 wines by the glass and local cider; background music, board games and darts. The two bedrooms are attractively decorated, and they have a self-catering apartment too. The surrounding area has many good walks.

Tasty food includes sandwiches, prawn cocktail, field mushroom stuffed with blue cheese and pine nuts, smoked mackerel caesar salad, local sausages with mash and gravy, free-range chicken with wild mushroom cream sauce and dauphinoise potatoes, moroccan-style vegetable stew with couscous and harissa yoghurt, beer-battered haddock and chips, and puddings such as apple and pear crumble and chocolate brownie. *Benchmark main dish: beer-battered haddock and chips £13.95. Two-course evening meal £19.95.*

Greene King ~ Lease Ian, Simon and Cynthia Coppack ~ Real ale ~ Open 11-11 ~ Bar food 12-2.30, 6-8.30 ~ Children welcome ~ Dogs allowed in bar ~ Wi-fi ~ Bedrooms: £90/£105 *Recommended by Jo Garnett, Gus Swan, Jenny and Brian Seller, Peter Meister, Peter Harrison*

Bedroom prices are for high summer. Even then you may get reductions for more than one night, or (outside tourist areas) weekends. Winter special rates are common, and many inns reduce bedroom prices if you have a full evening meal.

MIDDLEMARSH   ST6607 Map 2

Hunters Moon

(01963) 210966 – www.hunters-moon.org.uk

A352 Sherborne–Dorchester; DT9 5QN

Plenty of bric-a-brac in several linked areas, reasonably priced food and quite a choice of drinks; comfortable bedrooms

Traditional and cosy, this bustling former coaching inn is run by friendly hands-on licensees and their cheerful staff. The beamed bar rooms are filled with a great variety of tables and chairs on red patterned carpet, an array of ornamentation from horsebrasses and horse tack to pretty little tea cups hanging from beams, and lighting in the form of converted oil lamps; the atmosphere is properly pubby. Booths are formed by some attractively cushioned settles, walls are of exposed brick, stone and some panelling and there are three log fires (one in a capacious inglenook); background music, children's books and toys and board games. Butcombe Bitter and Gold and Wells Bombardier Burning Gold on handpump, farm cider and 16 wines by the glass. A neat lawn has picnic-sets, including some circular ones.

 Good food includes sandwiches, duck and pork terrine with red onion chutney, smoked salmon, prawn and crayfish with horseradish crème fraîche, burgers with toppings, coleslaw and chips, vegetable lasagne, local sausages with onion marmalade and gravy, chilli con carne, pork chops with cider and thyme gravy, scampi and chips, chicken in wine, mushroom and tarragon sauce, and puddings such as dark chocolate marquise and poached pear with cinnamon eton mess. *Benchmark main dish: pie of the day £9.95. Two-course evening meal £19.00.*

Enterprise ~ Lease Dean and Emma Mortimer ~ Real ale ~ Open 10.30-2.30, 6 (5 Fri)-11; 10.30am-11pm Sat, Sun ~ Bar food 12-2, 6-9; all day weekends ~ Children welcome ~ Dogs welcome ~ Wi-fi ~ Bedrooms: £65/£75 *Recommended by Peter Brix, Dr Simon Innes, Rob Anderson*

NETTLECOMBE   SY5195 Map 2

Marquis of Lorne

(01308) 485236 – www.themarquisoflorne.co.uk

Off A3066 Bridport–Beaminster, via West Milton; DT6 3SY

Attractive country pub with enjoyable food and drink, friendly licensees and seats in big garden; bedrooms

The big mature garden here really comes into its own in warm weather with its pretty herbaceous borders, picnic-sets under apple trees and a rustic-style play area. The comfortable, bustling main bar has a log fire, mahogany panelling, old prints and photographs and neatly matching chairs and tables. Two dining areas lead off, the smaller of which has another log fire. The wooden-floored snug (liked by locals) has board games, table skittles and background music, and they keep Palmers Copper, Dorset Gold and IPA on handpump, with ten wines by the glass from a decent list. Eggardon Hill, one of Dorset's most spectacular Iron Age hill forts with views over the coast and surrounding countryside, is within walking distance.

Highly regarded food includes sandwiches, tiger prawns in chilli and coriander tempura batter, chicken and duck liver pâté with spiced pears, butternut squash, sweet potato and spinach curry, mustard and brown sugar-baked ham with free-range eggs, pheasant sausages with onion jus and mash, salmon fillet on spinach with lobster and crab cream, local venison cutlets on bubble and squeak, and puddings. *Benchmark main dish: half shoulder of lamb with honey, mint and garlic confit £17.25. Two-course evening meal £20.00.*

Palmers ~ Tenants Stephen and Tracey Brady ~ Real ale ~ Open 11.30-2.30, 6-10.30 ~ Bar food 12-2, 6-9 ~ Restaurant ~ Children welcome ~ Dogs allowed in bar ~ Wi-fi ~ Bedrooms: £85/£95 *Recommended by Colin McLachlan, Belinda Stamp, Nick Sharpe*

PLUSH   ST7102   Map 2

Brace of Pheasants 🏮⭐ ♀ 🛏

(01300) 348357 – www.braceofpheasants.co.uk

Village signposted from B3143 N of Dorchester at Piddletrenthide; DT2 7RQ

Dorset Dining Pub of the Year

16th-c thatched pub with friendly service, generously served food and pleasant garden; comfortable bedrooms

Our readers enjoy this 16th-c inn and the friendly licensees make sure both locals and visitors receive a genuine welcome. The bustling, beamed bar has windsor chairs around good solid tables on patterned carpeting, a few standing timbers, a huge heavy-beamed inglenook at one end with cosy seating inside, and a good warming log fire at the other. Flack Manor Double Drop, Ringwood Best and Sunny Republic Dolphin Amber are tapped from the cask and they offer a fine choice of wines with 18 by the glass, and two proper farm ciders. A decent-sized garden includes a terrace and a lawn sloping up towards a rockery. Attractively fitted out and comfortable, the bedrooms are in a converted bowling alley; each has a little outdoor terrace. The pub is well placed for walks – a pleasant bridleway behind the building leads to the left of the woods and over to Church Hill.

⭐ Listing their local suppliers, the very good food includes sandwiches, lambs kidneys with creamy mustard sauce, beer-battered pigeon strips with red onion marmalade, butternut squash and chickpea tagine with herbed couscous, wild boar and apple sausages with onion gravy, smoked chicken with creamy blue cheese and marsala sauce, thyme-stuffed gilthead bream with dill pollen and herb butter, local venison with madeira reduction and bubble and squeak, and puddings such as sticky toffee pudding with caramel sauce and chocolate and black cherry torte with clotted cream. *Benchmark main dish: beer-battered fish and chips £12.50. Two-course evening meal £21.00.*

Free house ~ Licensees Phil and Carol Bennett ~ Real ale ~ Open 12-3, 7-11 (10.30 Sun) ~ Bar food 12-2, 7-9 ~ Children welcome ~ Dogs allowed in bar ~ Wi-fi ~ Bedrooms: £105/£115 *Recommended by David and Carole Newton, PLC, Barry Collett, Mr and Mrs P R Thomas, Peter Harrison*

SHERBORNE   ST6316   Map 2

Digby Tap 🍺 £

(01935) 813148 – www.digbytap.co.uk

Cooks Lane; park in Digby Road and walk round corner; DT9 3NS

Regularly changing ales in simple alehouse, open all day with very inexpensive beer and food

Handy for the glorious golden-stone abbey, this is an old-fashioned, unchanging alehouse with a lively, chatty and warmly welcoming atmosphere and is much loved by customers of all ages and from every walk of life. The straightforward flagstone bar, with its cosy corners, is full of understated character; the small games room has a pool table and a quiz machine, and there's also a TV room; mobile phones are banned. The food is extraordinarily good value and the fine range of ales includes Black Sheep

Bitter, Cottage Conquest, Otter Bitter and Wriggle Valley Ryme Rambler on handpump. Also, several wines by the glass and a choice of malt whiskies.

 Generously served and amazingly cheap, the straightforward food (lunchtime only) includes sandwiches and toasties, three-egg omelettes, sausages with free-range eggs, burgers, and specials such as fish pie, sausage casserole and a mixed grill. *Benchmark main dish: ham, egg and chips £5.50.*

Free house ~ Licensees Oliver Wilson and Nick Whigham ~ Real ale ~ No credit cards ~ Open 11-11; 12-11 Sun ~ Bar food 12-2; not Sun ~ Children welcome until 6pm ~ Dogs allowed in bar ~ Wi-fi *Recommended by Edward May, Tracey and Stephen Groves, Neil Allen*

SHROTON   ST8512   Map 2
Cricketers
(01258) 860421 – www.thecricketersshroton.co.uk
Off A350 N of Blandford (village also called Iwerne Courtney); follow signs; DT11 8QD

Country pub with real ales, well liked food and pretty garden; nice views and walks nearby

The back garden here is secluded and pretty with seats on a terrace and lawn, and there are picnic-sets at the front. Inside, the bright, divided bar has a woodburning stove in a stone fireplace, cushioned high-backed windsor and ladderback chairs in one area and black leather ones in another, all sorts of tables, a settle with scatter cushions, and red and cream walls decorated with cricket bats and photos of cricket teams; there's also a cosy little alcove and a spreading dining area towards the back. Friendly staff serve Butcombe Bitter, Otter Amber and Salisbury English Ale on handpump (they hold a beer festival on the early May Bank Holiday weekend) and several wines by the glass; background music. Walks up to the Iron Age ramparts on the summit reveal terrific views and the pub sits on the Wessex Ridgeway; walkers must leave muddy boots outside.

 Food is popular and includes baguettes, rare-breed pork pâté with pickled pears, deep-fried whitebait with tartare sauce, thai-style mushroom, spinach and coconut curry, beer-battered cod and chips, mustard and herb chicken thighs with roasted fennel and green bean salad and lemon and oil dressing, navarin of lamb with seasonal vegetables, and puddings such as chocolate nemesis and steamed ginger pudding with ginger ice-cream. *Benchmark main dish: pie of the day £10.95. Two-course evening meal £18.00.*

Heartstone Inns ~ Licensees Joe and Sally Grieves ~ Real ale ~ Open 12-3, 6-11; 12-11 Sun ~ Bar food 12-2.30, 6.30-9; no food Sun evening Sept-May ~ Children welcome ~ Wi-fi *Recommended by Paul Denny, John Pritchard, Sophie Ellison*

TARRANT MONKTON   ST9408   Map 2
Langton Arms
(01258) 830225 – www.thelangtonarms.co.uk
Village signposted from A354, then head for church; DT11 8RX

Charming pub with friendly staff, real ales, good food, plenty of dining space and seats outside; bedrooms

This is a picturesque spot next to a 15th-c church and in a pretty village, and our readers enjoy their visits to this busy thatched pub very much. The bars have a few beams, high-backed tartan dining chairs around wooden tables on carpeting, a cushioned window seat, a few high chairs against the light oak counter and Flack Manor Double Drop and guests such as Red Rock Devon County and Waylands Sixpenny Rushmore Gold on handpump, ten wines by the glass, ten malt whiskies and a farm cider. The two connected, beamed dining rooms, furnished with cushioned wooden chairs around white-clothed tables, lead into a light and airy conservatory; country prints, dried flower arrangements, background music, TV and board games. In fine weather, you can sit out in front or at teak tables in the flower-filled back garden; there's also a well equipped play area. The comfortable bedrooms occupy brick buildings around the attractive courtyard, with four in a neighbouring cottage.

 Using meat from their own farm and game from local gamekeepers, the popular food includes baguettes, duck liver parfait with plum chutney, creamy garlic mushrooms topped with brie, sharing platters, twice-baked cheese soufflé, trio of home-made game sausages with apple mash and red wine and onion gravy, king prawn and smoked salmon tart, venison bourguignon, chicken stuffed with leek and thyme with creamy white wine sauce, and puddings such as vanilla crème brûlée and chocolate torte with pistachio ice-cream. *Benchmark main dish: steak in ale pie £15.95. Two-course evening meal £23.00.*

Free house ~ Licensee Barbara Cossins ~ Real ale ~ Open 10am (11am Sat)-midnight; 12-11 Sun ~ Bar food 12-2.30, 6-9.30; all day weekends ~ Restaurant ~ Children welcome ~ Dogs allowed in bar and bedrooms ~ Wi-fi ~ Bedrooms: £80/£100 *Recommended by David and Carole Newton, Colin McLachlan, Tony and Rosemary Swainson*

TRENT ST5818 Map 2
Rose & Crown 🎯 🛏
(01935) 850776 – www.roseandcrowntrent.co.uk
Opposite the church; DT9 4SL

Character thatched pub with a friendly licensee, cosy rooms, open fires, a good choice of drinks and well thought-of food; bedrooms

The pretty bedrooms here (in a converted byre) are much enjoyed by our readers and breakfasts are first class. The cosy little bar on the right has big comfortable sofas and stools around a low table in front of an open fire, fresh flowers and candlelight. The bar opposite is furnished with nice old wooden tables and chairs on quarry tiles, and stools against the counter where they serve Wadworths Bishops Tipple, IPA, 6X and Horizon and a guest beer on handpump and 14 wines by the glass; board games. Two other connected rooms have similar wooden tables and chairs, settles and pews, a grandfather clock, pewter tankards and more fireplaces. Throughout are all sorts of pictures, including Stuart prints commemorating the fact that Charles II sought refuge in this village after the Battle of Worcester. The simply furnished back dining room leads to the garden with seats and tables and fine views (and sunsets); there are some picnic-sets at the front. The church opposite is lovely.

Much liked food includes sandwiches, salt and pepper squid with asian dressing, local pigeon with pomegranate and parma ham, mustard-glazed ham with free-range eggs, burger with toppings, coleslaw and triple-cooked chips, calves liver with sage fritters, smoked bacon and onions, duck breast with parmentier potatoes, caramelised shallots and beetroot, monkfish wrapped in parma ham with braised lentils and saffron mayonnaise, and puddings such as banana, peanut and chocolate délice with caramelised banana ice-cream and passion-fruit crème brûlée. *Benchmark main dish: venison wellington with madeira sauce £21.50. Two-course evening meal £20.50.*

Wadworths ~ Tenant Nick Lamb ~ Real ale ~ Open 11-11 ~ Bar food 12-2.30, 6-9 ~ Children welcome ~ Dogs welcome ~ Wi-fi ~ Bedrooms: £65/£85 *Recommended by J R Wildon, Martin and Anne Terry, Tracey and Stephen Groves, Liz and Martin Eldon*

WEST BAY

West Bay 🌟 🍴 🛏

SY4690 Map 1

(01308) 422157 – www.thewestbayhotel.co.uk

Station Road; DT6 4EW

Relaxed seaside inn with emphasis on seafood; bedrooms

There are two unspoilt beaches on either side of the busy little harbour (much visited since the two *Broadchurch* TV series were filmed here) and you can watch the comings and goings of the boats while enjoying a pint or a fresh fish meal. The fairly simple front part of the building, with bare boards, a coal-effect gas fire and a mix of sea and nostalgic prints, is separated by an island servery from the cosier carpeted dining area, which has more of a country kitchen feel; background music and board games. Although it's spacious enough never to feel crowded, booking is essential in season. Palmers 200, Best, Copper, Dorset Gold and a seasonal guest are served on handpump alongside good house wines (including eight by the glass) and several malt whiskies. There are tables in a small side garden and more in the large main garden. Several local teams meet to play in the pub's 100-year-old skittle alley. Bedrooms are quiet and comfortable.

Go for the fresh fish and shellfish, which includes crab pâté, fishcakes with sweet chilli aioli, mussels done three different ways, local scallops with smoked bacon and garlic butter, gilthead bream fillet with oriental stir-fry and beer-battered local white fish with chips; non-fishy dishes include home-cooked honey-roast ham and free-range eggs, spinach crêpes stuffed with ratatouille, chicken breast with roasted red pesto in a bap, beef stroganoff, pork belly in creamy honey and wholegrain mustard sauce, and puddings. *Benchmark main dish: whole grilled fish of the day £16.95. Two-course evening meal £20.50.*

Palmers ~ Tenant Samuel Good ~ Real ale ~ Open 12-11 (midnight Sat, 10 Sun); 12-3, 6-11 Nov-Mar in winter ~ Bar food 12-2 (3 weekends), 6-9; 12-3, 6-8 Sun~ Children welcome until 8pm ~ Dogs allowed in bar ~ Wi-fi ~ Bedrooms: £85/£115 *Recommended by Comus and Sarah Elliott, Steve and Liz Tilley*

WEST STOUR

Ship 🌟 🍷 🍴 🛏

ST7822 Map 2

(01747) 838640 – www.shipinn-dorset.com

A30 W of Shaftesbury; SP8 5RP

Civilised and pleasantly updated roadside dining inn offering a wide range of food and ales; bedrooms

The friendly landlord here keeps his ale well and we get warm feedback on the food too. The neatly kept rooms include a smallish but airy bar on the left with cream décor, a mix of chunky farmhouse furniture on dark boards and big sash windows that look beyond the road and car park to rolling pastures. The smaller flagstoned public bar has a good log fire and low ceilings. Butcombe Bitter, Ringwood Best and Waylands Sixpenny 6d Original on handpump, 14 wines by the glass and four farm ciders. During their summer beer festival they showcase a dozen beers and ten ciders, all from the west country. On the right, two carpeted dining rooms with stripped pine dado, stone walls and shutters are similarly furnished in a pleasantly informal style, and have some attractive contemporary cow prints; TV, numerous board games and background music. The bedlington terriers are called Douglas and Toby. Bedrooms are attractive and comfortable and you'll get pastoral views and a particularly good and hearty breakfast. Good surrounding walks.

A wide choice of interesting food includes lunchtime sandwiches and ciabatta, corned beef hash topped with poached egg, goats cheese, potato and chive croquettes with romesco sauce, butternut, leek and asparagus risotto with deep-fried leeks, pork and chorizo slider with beetroot slaw, fries and onion rings, rabbit, smoked bacon and leek hotpot, kedgeree, guinea fowl with parsley, fennel and garlic butter and bacon and cabbage bubble and squeak, and puddings such as dark chocolate and coffee mousse and pear and apple crumble with vanilla pod custard. *Benchmark main dish: scallops, tiger prawn, salmon and smoked haddock pie £14.95. Two-course evening meal £20.00.*

Free house ~ Licensee Gavin Griggs ~ Real ale ~ Open 12-3, 6-11.30; 12-midnight Sat; 12-10.30 Sun ~ Bar food 12-2.30, 6-9; not Sun evening ~ Restaurant ~ Well behaved children in restaurant and lounge ~ Dogs allowed in bar ~ Wi-fi ~ Bedrooms: £60/£90
Recommended by Peter Brix, Lindy Andrews, Anthony Wilkinson, Valerie Sayer, Tom and Ruth Rees

WEYMOUTH
SY6878   Map 2

Red Lion ◀ £
(01305) 786940 – www.theredlionweymouth.co.uk
Hope Square; DT4 8TR

Bustling place with sunny terrace, a smashing range of drinks, tasty food and lots to look at

This is known as the lifeboatmen's pub as it's closest to the RNLI station, and there are numerous pictures and artefacts relating to the lifeboat crews and their boats. The refurbished bare-boards interior, kept cosy with candles, has a cheerful, lively atmosphere, all manner of wooden chairs and tables, cushioned wall seats, some unusual, maroon-cushioned high benches beside equally high tables, the odd armchair here and there, and plenty of bric-a-brac on stripped-brick walls. Some nice contemporary touches include the woven timber wall and loads of mirrors wittily overlapped. Dorset Jurassic, Greene King Abbot, Lifeboat Bitter (named for the pub, brewed by Otter, with 10p per pint going towards the RNLI), Red Lion Bitter (also named for the pub, from Dorset) and St Austell Tribute on handpump, over 80 rums (they have a rum 'bible' to explain them) and 12 wines by the glass. Service is helpful and friendly; daily papers, board games and background music. There are plenty of seats outside that stay warmed by the sun well into the evening. The pub is owned by Tim Bird and Mary McLaughlin, who also own the Three Greyhounds in Allostock, Cholmondeley Arms in Cholmondeley and Bulls Head and Church Inn in Mobberley (all in Cheshire) and Fitzherbert Arms in Swynnerton (Staffordshire).

Much liked food includes baps, smoked mackerel pâté, pulled pork hash cake with bacon and egg, butternut squash, bean and vegetable stew with herb dumplings, burger with toppings, tomato and caramelised onion chutney and chips, mussels in white wine, shallots and cream with fries, steak in ale pie, slow-roast duck leg with spiced red cabbage and port wine gravy, and puddings such as chocolate brownie and sticky date and toffee pudding with rum and raisin ice-cream. *Benchmark main dish: seafood platter for two £21.95. Two-course evening meal £20.00.*

Free house ~ Licensee Brian McLaughlin ~ Real ale ~ Open 12-11 (10.30 Sun) ~ Bar food 12-9; may not serve food afternoon in winter ~ Children welcome until 7pm ~ Wi-fi ~ Live music outside Sun 2pm in summer *Recommended by Edward May, John Harris, Alison and Michael Harper, JPC*

The details at the end of each featured entry start by saying whether the pub is a free house, or if it belongs to a brewery or pub group (which we name).

WIMBORNE MINSTER   SZ0199 Map 2

Green Man £

(01202) 881021 – www.greenmanwimborne.com

Victoria Road, at junction with West Street (B3082/B3073); BH21 1EN

Cosy, warm-hearted town tavern with simple food at very fair prices

This is a cheery, traditional town pub with customers dropping in and out all day. The four small linked areas have maroon plush banquettes and polished dark pub tables, copper and brass ornaments, red walls, Wadworths 6X, IPA and Swordfish on handpump and a farm cider. One room has a log fire in a sizeable brick fireplace, another has a coal-effect gas fire, and there are two dart boards, a silenced games machine, background music and TV; the Barn houses a pool table. Their little border terrier is called Cooper. In summer, the award-winning flowering tubs, hanging baskets and window boxes are quite amazing – there are more on the heated back terrace.

Bargain food (lunchtime only) includes sandwiches and toasties, a full english breakfast, beef, vegetable or chicken burger with chips, sausages with egg or baked beans, scampi and chips, thai-style prawn and cod fishcake with chilli dip, and lamb shank in red wine and rosemary sauce. *Benchmark main dish: Sunday roast £8.95.*

Wadworths ~ Tenant Andrew Kiff ~ Real ale ~ Open 10am-11.30pm (midnight Sat) ~ Bar food 10-2 ~ Restaurant ~ Children welcome until 7.30pm ~ Dogs allowed in bar
Recommended by Alfie Bayliss, Steve Whalley, Patricia Hawkins

WORTH MATRAVERS   SY9777 Map 2

Square & Compass ★ ◖

(01929) 439229 – www.squareandcompasspub.co.uk

At fork of both roads signposted to village from B3069; BH19 3LF

Unchanging country tavern with masses of character, in the same family for many years; lovely sea views and fine nearby walks

At peak times you'll find a queue of customers at the serving hatches in this much loved gem, but the charming Newman family (who have run the pub for over a century) cope with warm friendliness and efficiency. Our readers love the place and the fact that it remains quite unchanging and totally unspoilt. A couple of simple rooms have straightforward furniture on flagstones and wooden benches around the walls, a woodburning stove, a stuffed albino badger and a loyal crowd of chatty locals. Bristol Beer Factory Milk Stout, Butcombe Haka, Hattie Brown New Moonlite, Otter Head and Palmers Copper tapped from the cask, and home-produced and ten other farm ciders are passed through the two serving hatches to customers in the drinking corridor; also, 20 malt whiskies. Darts and shove-ha'penny. From the local stone benches out in front there's a fantastic view over the village rooftops down to the sea. There may be free-roaming chickens and other birds clucking around and the small (free) museum exhibits local fossils and artefacts, mostly collected by the current landlord and his father. Wonderful walks lead to some exciting switchback sections of the coast path above St Aldhelm's Head and Chapman's Pool – you'll need to park in the public car park ($2 honesty box) 100 metres along the Corfe Castle road.

Bar food is limited to home-made pasties and pies.

Free house ~ Licensees Charlie Newman and Kevin Hunt ~ Real ale ~ No credit cards ~ Open 12-11 ~ Bar food all day ~ Children welcome ~ Dogs welcome ~ Live music Fri and Sat evenings, Sun lunchtime *Recommended by Peter Meister, David and Stella Martin, Robert Watt, David and Judy Robison, Adrian Johnson, Alan Johnson, Steve Whalley, Anne Evans*

Also Worth a Visit in Dorset

Besides the fully inspected pubs, you might like to try these pubs that have been recommended to us and described by readers. Do tell us what you think of them: feedback@goodguides.com

BISHOP'S CAUNDLE   ST6913
White Hart (01963) 23301
A3030 SE of Sherborne; DT9 5ND
Smallish 17th-c roadside pub with reworked carpeted interior, dark beams, panelling, stripped stone and log fire, good well presented food from varied menu including daily specials, Sharps Doom Bar and local guests, friendly service, restaurant; skittle alley; children and dogs welcome, country views from garden, closed Sun evening, Mon. *(Peter Barrett)*

BOURNEMOUTH   SZ1092
Cricketers Arms (01202) 551589
Windham Road; BH1 4RN Well preserved Victorian pub near station, separate public and lounge bars, tiled fireplaces and lots of dark wood, etched windows and stained glass, Fullers London Pride and two quickly changing guests, good weekend lunchtimes only; fortnightly Mon folk night; free wi-fi; children and dogs welcome, picnic-sets out in front, open all day. *(George Sanderson)*

BOURNEMOUTH   SZ0891
Goat & Tricycle (01202) 314220
West Hill Road; BH2 5PF Interesting split-level rambling Edwardian local (two former pubs knocked together); Wadworths ales and guests from pillared bar's impressive rank of ten handpumps, real cider, reasonably priced pubby food, friendly staff; background music, Sun quiz, free wi-fi; no under-18s, dogs welcome, good disabled access, part-covered yard, open (and food) all day. *(Geoffrey Sutton)*

BRIDPORT   SY4692
Bull (01308) 422878
East Street B3162; DT6 3LF Bustling former Georgian coaching inn, comfortable armchairs in front of open fire in reception, second fire in bar with dark turquoise wall banquettes and white-painted dining chairs around dark tables, flowers and candlelight, a couple of beers from Otter, good wines by the glass and ten malt whiskies, informal dining room with similar furnishings, popular food from good sandwiches up, cosy cocktail bar tucked away upstairs; free wi-fi; children and dogs (in bar) welcome, sheltered back courtyard and separate cider and pizza Stable bar (see below), 19 comfortable bedrooms, good breakfast, open all day from 8am.
(Comus and Sarah Elliott, Steve and Liz Tilley)

BRIDPORT   SY4692
George (01308) 423187
South Street; DT6 3NQ Relaxed old town pub under welcoming new management; good food from open kitchen, well kept Palmers and several wines by the glass, efficient friendly service; children and dogs (in bar) welcome, disabled facilities, open all day, from 10am market days (Weds, Sat) for popular brunch. *(Ian Jenkins)*

BRIDPORT   SY4692
Ropemakers (01308) 421255
West Street; DT6 3QP Long rambling town-centre pub with lots of pictures and memorabilia, well kept Palmers ales and enjoyable home-made food from nice sandwiches up, regular weekend live music, Tues quiz, free wi-fi; children and dogs welcome, tables in back courtyard, open all day except Sun evening. *(Comus and Sarah Elliott)*

BRIDPORT   SY4692
★**Stable** (01308) 426876
At the back of the Bull Hotel; DT6 3LF
Not a pub in any sense, but this lively cider/pizza bar is great fun and popular with customers of all ages; lofty barn-like room with rough planked walls and ceiling, big steel columns, two long rows of pale wooden tables flanked by wide benches, steps up to raised end area with cushioned red wall benches, over 80 ciders, St Austell Proper Job and six wines by the glass, good hand-made pizzas and other food such as pies, upstairs room (not always open); background music, free wi-fi; children and dogs welcome, open (and food) all day weekends, from 5pm weekdays (all day during school holidays). *(Edward May)*

BRIDPORT   SY4692
Tiger (01308) 427543
Barrack Street, off South Street; DT6 3LY Cheerful and attractive open-plan Victorian beamed pub with Sharps Doom Bar and five quickly changing guests, real ciders, no food except breakfast for residents; skittle alley, darts, sports TV, free wi-fi; dogs welcome, seats in heated courtyard, six bedrooms, open all day. *(Comus and Sarah Elliott)*

BUCKHORN WESTON   ST7524
★**Stapleton Arms** (01963) 370396
Church Hill; off A30 Shaftesbury–Sherborne via Kington Magna; SP8 5HS Handsome Georgian inn with large civilised bar, sofas in front of fine stone fireplace, mix of other seating on flagstones or bare boards including farmhouse and chapel chairs around scrubbed tables, modern artwork on dark red walls, ales from Butcombe, Keystone and Plain, proper cider, 32 wines by the glass and 16 malt whiskies, good interesting food

along with more traditional choices, separate elegantly furnished restaurant; some live music, free wi-fi; children and dogs (in bar) welcome, seats out at front and in charming back garden, good nearby walks, comfortable well equipped bedrooms, open all day weekends. *(Mr Yeldahm, Mr and Mrs J Watkins, Kate Moran)*

BURTON BRADSTOCK SY4889
Anchor (01308) 897228
B3157 SE of Bridport; DT6 4QF Cheerful helpful staff in pricey but good seafood restaurant, other local food including nice steaks, village pub part too with blackboard choices from baguettes up, ales such as Dorset, St Austell and Sharps, decent wines by the glass and several malt whiskies; live music second Sun of month, games including table skittles; children and dogs (in bar) welcome, two bedrooms, open all day. *(Comus and Sarah Elliott)*

CHARMOUTH SY3693
Royal Oak (01297) 560277
Off A3052/A35 E of Lyme Regis; The Street; DT6 6PE Three-room split-level village local, popular and friendly, with enjoyable reasonably priced food and well kept Palmers ales, good service; quiz and music nights, traditional pub games; children and dogs welcome, open all day weekends. *(George Sanderson)*

CHEDINGTON ST4805
Winyards Gap (01935) 891244
A356 Dorchester–Crewkerne; DT8 3HY Attractive dining pub surrounded by NT land with spectacular view over Parrett Valley into Somerset; enjoyable food from sandwiches to daily specials, also Sun carvery and good value OAP weekday lunch, four well kept changing ales, local ciders, friendly helpful service, bar with woodburner, steps down to restaurant, skittle alley/dining room; children and dogs welcome, tables on front lawn under parasols, good walks, comfortable bedrooms, open all day weekends. *(Liz and Martin Eldon)*

CHILD OKEFORD ST8213
★Saxon (01258) 860310
Signed off A350 Blandford–Shaftesbury and A357 Blandford–Sherborne; Gold Hill; DT11 8HD Welcoming 17th-c village pub; quietly clubby snug bar with log fire, two dining rooms, Butcombe, Otter and guests, nice choice of wines, well liked reasonably priced home-made food including good Sun roast, efficient service; children and dogs (in bar) welcome, attractive back garden, good walks on neolithic Hambledon Hill, four comfortable bedrooms. *(Robert Watt)*

CHRISTCHURCH SZ1593
Rising Sun (01202) 486122
Purewell; BH23 1EJ Comfortably updated old pub specialising in authentic thai food,

Flack Manor and Sharps Doom Bar from L-shaped bar, good choice of wines by the glass, pleasant helpful young staff; terrace with palms and black rattan-style furniture under large umbrellas, open all day. *(Kate Moran)*

CORFE CASTLE SY9681
Castle Inn (01929) 480208
East Street; BH20 5EE Welcoming little two-room pub mentioned in Hardy's *The Hand of Ethelberta*, fairly pubby food using local supplies including popular Fri fish night, good service, up to three ales such as Dorset, Ringwood and Sharps, heavy black beams, exposed stone walls, flagstones and log fire; children welcome, no dogs inside, back terrace and big sunny garden with mature trees, steam train views, open all day. *(Robert Watt)*

CORFE CASTLE SY9682
Greyhound (01929) 480205
A351; The Square; BH20 5EZ Bustling picturesque old pub in centre of this tourist village; three small low-ceilinged panelled rooms, steps and corridors, well kept ales such as Palmers, Ringwood and Sharps, local cider, good choice of interesting food from sandwiches and light dishes up, highish prices, traditional games including Purbeck longboard shove-ha'penny, family room; background and weekend live music; dogs welcome, garden with large decked area, great views of castle and countryside, pretty courtyard opening on to castle bridge, open all day. *(Jeff Davies)*

DEWLISH SY7798
Oak (01258) 837352
Off A354 Dorchester–Blandford Forum; DT2 7ND Welcoming red-brick village pub, two or three well kept local ales and enjoyable good value food including specials and popular Sun lunch, friendly helpful service, woodburner and open fire in bar, small dining room; winter quiz; children welcome, good-sized garden behind, two bedrooms and self-catering cottage. *(PJ, Guy Vowles)*

DORCHESTER SY6990
★Blue Raddle (01305) 267762
Church Street, near central short-stay car park; DT1 1JN Cheery pubby atmosphere in long carpeted and partly panelled bar, well kept ales such as Butcombe, Cerne Abbas, Fullers and St Austell, local ciders, good wines and coffee, enjoyable simple home-made lunchtime food (not Sun, Mon, Tues), evenings Thurs-Sat only, coal-effect gas fires; background and live folk music (Weds fortnightly), darts and crib teams; no under-14s, dogs welcome, good disabled access apart from one step, closed Mon lunchtime. *(Comus and Sarah Elliott, Steve and Liz Tilley, Barry Collett)*

EAST CHALDON
SY7983

Sailors Return (01305) 854441

Village signposted from A352 Wareham–Dorchester; from village green, follow Dorchester, Weymouth signpost; note that the village is also known as Chaldon Herring; OS sheet 194 map reference 790834; DT2 8DN Thatched village pub with five real ales such as Palmers, Otter and Ringwood, local cider and enjoyable food from short menu including fresh local fish and Weds pie night, flagstoned bar and various dining areas; winter Mon quiz; children and dogs welcome in the bar (there's a friendly pub dog), picnic-sets out at front and in side garden, useful for coast path, open all day summer (all day weekends winter). *(Andrew Stone)*

EAST MORDEN
SY9194

★**Cock & Bottle** (01929) 459238

B3075 W of Poole; BH20 7DL Popular extended dining pub with wide choice of good if not cheap food (best to book), separate bar with open fire, well kept Badger ales and nice selection of wines by the glass, efficient cheerful service; children and dogs allowed in certain areas, outside seating and pleasant pastoral outlook, closed Sun evening. *(David and Carole Newton)*

EAST STOUR
ST8123

Kings Arms (01747) 838325

A30, 2 miles E of village; The Common; SP8 5NB Extended dining pub with popular food from scottish landlord-chef including bargain lunch menu and all-day Sun carvery (best to book), St Austell Tribute, Sharps Doom Bar and a guest, decent wines and good selection of malt whiskies, friendly efficient staff, open fire in bar, airy dining area with light wood furniture, scottish pictures and Burns quotes; gentle background music; children welcome, dogs in bar, good disabled access, picnic-sets in big garden, bluebell walks nearby, three bedrooms, open all day weekends. *(Roy Hoing)*

FERNDOWN
SZ0697

Kings Arms (01202) 577490

Ringwood Road; BH22 9AA Refurbished restauranty pub with well liked food including good steaks, early-bird deal (Mon-Thurs 4.30-7pm), three real ales such as Ringwood Best and good selection of wines by the glass, friendly helpful staff; children welcome, rattan-style furniture on part-covered terrace, open (and food) all day. *(Peter Barrett)*

FERNDOWN
SU0500

Old Thatch (01202) 877192

Wimborne Road, Uddens Cross (old A31); BH21 7NW Extended low thatched pub-restaurant, enjoyable food cooked to order including decent vegetarian choices and specials board, popular Sun carvery, well kept Ringwood Best with guests such as Fullers and Sharps, good range of wines, friendly uniformed staff, well divided open-plan interior, beams, flagstones, stripped-wood and carpeted floors, large back restaurant area; background music, fruit machine; children welcome, dogs in bar part, garden picnic-sets (some under parasols), big car park. *(Ian Malone)*

FIDDLEFORD
ST8013

Fiddleford Inn (01258) 472886

A357 Sturminster Newton–Blandford Forum; DT10 2BX Beamed roadside pub refurbished under new owners; three linked areas with modern charcoal paintwork blending with traditional furnishings, old flagstones, carpets and some exposed stone, double aspect woodburner, well kept ales including one labelled for the pub, shortish choice of good well presented food, friendly young staff; monthly live music; children and dogs welcome, big fenced garden, four bedrooms, open all day. *(Colin and Maggie Fancourt, S J C Chappell)*

FONTMELL MAGNA
ST8616

★**Fontmell** (01747) 811441

A350 S of Shaftesbury; SP7 0PA Imposing dining pub with rooms, much emphasis on the enterprising modern cooking, but also some more straightforward dishes, good wine list, local ales including a house beer (Mallyshag) from Keystone, small bar area with stripy stools, comfy sofas and easy chairs, some bold colours, restaurant with shelves of books and wine bottles, windows overlooking fast-flowing stream that runs under the building; garden across road with two wood-fired pizza ovens, six comfortable well appointed bedrooms, open all day in summer, closed Mon and Tues lunchtimes in winter; for sale as we went to press – so may be changes. *(Sophie Ellison)*

GUSSAGE ALL SAINTS
SU0010

Drovers (01258) 840084

8 miles N of Wimborne; BH21 5ET Partly thatched community-owned pub, refurbished and scheduled to reopen shortly after we went to press – reports please.

HIGHCLIFFE
SZ2193

Galleon (01425) 279855

Lymington Road; BH23 5EA Smart contemporary interior with leather sofas, light wood floors and open fires, good choice of well prepared food from snacks and pub favourites up including daily specials, local ales such as Ringwood, reasonable prices and good service, conservatory opening on to terrace and sunny garden; background music – live most weekends, Tues quiz; children welcome, play area and summer barbecues, open all day (till midnight Fri, Sat). *(David and Sally Frost)*

HINTON ST MARY   ST7816
White Horse   (01258) 472723
Just off B3092 a mile N of Sturminster; DT10 1NA Welcoming traditional little village pub, good varied choice of food from changing menu cooked by south african landlord-chef (best to book), own-brew beers and decent house wines, unusual inglenook fireplace in cheerful bar, extended dining room; children, walkers and dogs welcome (pub dog is Pepper), picnic-sets in small well maintained garden, attractive setting, closed Sun evening, Mon. *(Dr Simon Innes)*

HURN   SZ1397
Avon Causeway   (01202) 482714
Village signed off A338, then follow Avon, Sopley, Mutchams sign; BH23 6AS Comfortable and roomy hotel/dining pub, enjoyable food from baguettes and pub favourites up, well kept Wadworths ales, helpful staff, interesting railway decorations and pullman-coach restaurant (used for functions) by former 1870s station platform; children and dogs welcome, disabled access, nice garden (some road noise) with play area, 12 good value bedrooms, near Bournemouth Airport (2 weeks free parking if you stay before or after you fly), open all day. *(Andrew Stone)*

LANGTON MATRAVERS   SY9978
Kings Arms   (01929) 422979
High Street; BH19 3HA Friendly old-fashioned village pub under enthusiastic landlord; ancient flagstoned corridor to bar, simple rooms off, one with a fine fireplace made from local marble, well kept ever-changing ales and enjoyable good value pubby food, cheerful helpful staff, splendid antique Purbeck longboard shove-ha'penny; children and dogs welcome, sunny picnic-sets outside, good walks including to Dancing Ledge, open (and food) all day. *(Jeff Davies)*

LYME REGIS   SY3391
★Harbour Inn   (01297) 442299
Marine Parade; DT7 3JF More eating than pubby with thriving family atmosphere, friendly busy staff and generally very well liked food from lunchtime sandwiches to local fish (not cheap, booking advised in season), good choice of wines by the glass, well kept Otter and St Austell, tea and coffee, clean-cut modern décor keeping original flagstones and stone walls (lively acoustic), paintings for sale, sea views from front windows; background music; dogs welcome, disabled access from street, verandah tables. *(Geoffrey Sutton)*

LYME REGIS   SY3492
Pilot Boat   (01297) 443157
Bridge Street; DT7 3QA Popular bow-fronted pub near waterfront with ongoing improvements from new management; good fairly priced food, Palmers ales and several wines by the glass, helpful friendly service, back restaurant; skittle alley; children and dogs welcome, terrace tables, bedrooms being refurbished for 2017, open (and food) all day. *(Mrs P Sumner)*

LYME REGIS   SY3391
Royal Standard   (01297) 442637
Marine Parade, The Cobb; DT7 3JF Right on broadest part of beach, properly pubby bar with log fire, fine built-in stripped high settles, local photographs and even old-fashioned ring-up tills, quieter eating area with stripped brick and pine, well kept Palmers ales, uncomplicated food from lunchtime sandwiches and baked potatoes up, friendly helpful service; background and some live music, prominent pool table, darts, free wi-fi; children and dogs welcome, good-sized suntrap courtyard with own servery and harbour views, open all day from 10am, gets very busy in season. *(Roger and Donna Huggins, Richard Tilbrook)*

LYME REGIS   SY3492
Volunteer   (01297) 442214
Top of Broad Street (A3052 towards Exeter); DT7 3QE Cosy old-fashioned pub with long low-ceilinged bar, nice mix of customers (can get crowded), a well kept house beer from Branscombe tapped from the cask and west country guests, enjoyable modestly priced food in dining lounge (children allowed here), friendly young staff, roaring fires; dogs welcome, open all day. *(Jeff Davies)*

LYTCHETT MINSTER   SY9693
★St Peters Finger   (01202) 622275
Dorchester Road; BH16 6JE Well run two-part beamed roadhouse with cheerful efficient staff, good value popular food from snacks and sharing boards up, small helpings available, Badger ales and several wines by the glass, homely mix of furnishings in different sections giving cosy feel despite its size, end log fire; children welcome, tables on big part-covered terrace, open (and food) all day. *(Richard)*

MANSTON   ST8116
Plough   (01258) 472484
B3091 Shaftesbury–Sturminster Newton, just N; DT10 1HB Welcoming good-sized traditional country pub, five real ales including Butcombe, Palmers and Sharps, enjoyable fairly priced standard food, beams, richly decorated plasterwork, ceilings and bar front, red patterned carpets, dining conservatory; live music Fri; garden and adjacent caravan site, open all day, till 8pm Sun. *(Dr Simon Innes)*

MARNHULL   ST7719
Blackmore Vale   (01258) 820701
Burton Street, via Church Hill off B3092; DT10 1JJ Welcoming old stone-built village pub, good traditional food cooked by

landlord-chef including two-course 'smaller appetites' lunch (Mon-Sat), three Badger ales and reasonably priced wines, pleasantly opened-up beamed and flagstoned dining bar with woodburner, more flagstones and oak flooring in cosy smaller bar with log fire; background music; children, walkers and dogs welcome, garden tables, open all day Sun. *(Belinda Stamp)*

MARNHULL ST7818

Crown (01258) 820224

About 3 miles N of Sturminster Newton; Crown Road; DT10 1LN Part-thatched inn dating from the 16th c (the Pure Drop in Hardy's *Tess of the D'Urbervilles*); linked rooms with oak beams, huge flagstones or bare boards, log fire in big stone hearth in oldest part, more modern furnishings and carpet elsewhere, Badger ales and enjoyable food, good friendly service, restaurant; children welcome, peaceful enclosed garden, bedrooms, open all day weekends. *(Sophie Ellison)*

MARTINSTOWN SY6488

Brewers Arms (01305) 889361

Burnside (B3159); DT2 9LB Friendly family-run village pub (former 19th-c school), attractively updated interior, with good reasonably priced home-made food from lunchtime baguettes to specials, popular Tues curry night, Palmers Copper and Sharps Doom Bar, restaurant; regular live music, Weds quiz; children and dogs welcome, picnic-sets out at front and in courtyard, good local walks, two bedrooms, closed Sun evening, Mon. *(Marianne and Peter Stevens)*

MELBURY OSMOND ST58707

Rest & Welcome (01935) 83248

Yeovil Road (A37); DT2 0NF Welcoming two-bar roadside pub (the Sheaf of Arrows in Hardy's story 'Interlopers at the Knap'), enjoyable home-made food and three mainly local ales, pubby furniture on carpet, some beams, woodburner, back skittle alley; background music; children and dogs welcome, nice garden with play area, open all day. *(Geoffrey Sutton)*

MELPLASH SY4897

Half Moon (01308) 488321

A3066 Bridport–Beaminster; DT6 3UD Thatched and shuttered 17th-c roadside pub under newish management; beams, log fire and pubby furnishings on patterned carpet, Palmers ales, well cooked interesting home-made food from shortish changing menu, friendly helpful staff; free wi-fi; children welcome, picnic-sets in mature back garden, good nearby walks, closed Sun evening, Mon. *(P and J Shapley)*

MILTON ABBAS ST8001

Hambro Arms (01258) 880233

Signed off A354 SW of Blandford; DT11 0BP Nicely updated pub in beautiful late 18th-c landscaped thatched village; two beamed bars and restaurant, well kept ales such as Dorset Piddle, Ringwood and Sharps, good food from ciabattas and panini up, prompt friendly service; children welcome, dogs in bar, tables on front terrace, four bedrooms, open all day weekends, closed Mon from early Oct to end Mar. *(Kate Moran)*

MOTCOMBE ST8426

Coppleridge (01747) 851980

Signed from The Street, follow to Mere/ Gillingham; SP7 9HW Welcoming country inn (former 18th-c farmhouse) with traditional bar and various dining rooms, good home-made food from sandwiches and ciabattas up, grill night Thurs, ales such as Butcombe and decent wines by the glass, friendly helpful staff; children welcome, dogs in bar and garden room, ten spacious courtyard bedrooms, 15-acre grounds with play area and two tennis courts, open all day. *(George Sanderson)*

MUDEFORD SZ1792

Ship in Distress (01202) 485123

Stanpit; off B3059 at roundabout; BH23 3NA Recently reopened/refurbished after fire, this 300-year-old former smugglers' pub is within walking distance of the harbour; good food from landlady-chef including plenty of fish/shellfish, well priced two-course lunch, four real ales (usually Ringwood Best) and decent wines, can eat in bar or restaurant; quiz Weds; children and dogs (in bar) welcome, seats and tables on suntrap back terrace, open all day. *(Alfie Bayliss, Katharine Cowherd)*

NORDEN HEATH SY94834

Halfway (01929) 480402

A351 Wareham–Corfe Castle; BH20 5DU Cosily laid-out partly thatched 16th-c pub; Badger beers, nice wines by the glass and enjoyable freshly cooked food including children's and vegetarian choices, good service, front rooms with flagstones, stripped stone and woodburners, snug little side area, pitched-ceiling back room; dogs welcome, picnic-sets on paved terrace and lawn, good nearby walks, open (and food) all day. *(Alan and Angela Scouller)*

OSMINGTON MILLS SY7381

Smugglers (01305) 833125

Off A353 NE of Weymouth; DT3 6HF Old partly thatched family-oriented inn, well extended, with cosy dimly lit timber-divided areas, woodburners, old local pictures, Badger ales, guests beers and several wines by the glass, food and service can be good; picnic sets on crazy paving by little stream, thatched summer bar, play area, lovely views from car park (parking charge refunded at bar), useful for coast path, four bedrooms, open (and food) all day. *(Michael Hill, Barry Collett)*

PAMPHILL ST9900

★**Vine** (01202) 882259
*Off B3082 on NW edge of Wimborne:
turn on to Cowgrove Hill at Cowgrove
sign, then left up Vine Hill; BH21 4EE*
Simple old-fashioned place run by same
family for three generations and part of
Kingston Lacy Estate (NT); two tiny bars
with coal-effect gas fire, handful of tables
and seats on lino, local photographs and
notices on painted panelling, narrow
wooden stairs up to room with darts, a
couple of real ales, local cider and foreign
bottled beers, lunchtime bar snacks; quiet
background music, no credit cards, outside
lavatories; children (away from bar) and
dogs welcome, verandah with grapevine,
sheltered gravel terrace and grassy area,
Sept pumpkin and conkers festival.
(Liz and Martin Eldon)

PIDDLEHINTON SY7197

Thimble (01300) 348270
High Street (B3143); DT2 7TD Spacious
thatched pub with log fires and deep glassed-
over well in low-beamed core, enjoyable
freshly made food from baguettes up, well kept
Palmers ales, friendly service; background
and some live music, free wi-fi; children
and dogs welcome, disabled facilities, valley
views from garden with stream, open all day
weekends. *(Andrew Stone)*

POOLE SZ0391

Bermuda Triangle (01202) 748087
*Parr Street, Lower Parkstone (just off
A35 at Ashley Cross); BH14 0JY*
Quirky bare-boards 19th-c local with four
particularly well kept changing ales, two or
three good continental lagers on tap and
many other beers from around the world,
friendly staff, no food, dark panelling,
snug old corners and lots of nautical and
other bric-a-brac, additional side and back
rooms; background music (can be loud); no
children and a bit too steppy for disabled
access, pavement picnic-sets, open all day
Fri-Sun. *(Sophie Ellison)*

POOLE SZ0391

Cow (01202) 723155
*Station Road, Ashley Cross, Parkstone;
beside Parkstone Station; BH14 8UD*
Interesting open-plan pub with airy bistro
bar, squashy sofas, leather seating cubes and
low tables on stripped-wood floors, open fire
in exposed brick fireplace, good food from
sandwiches and sharing boards through pub
favourites to grills, Greene King and four
mainly local guests, also craft beers such
as BrewDog and a dozen wines by the glass;
background music (live Thurs), Mon quiz, TV
for major sports, free wi-fi; children and dogs
welcome, enclosed heated terrace, open
(and food) all day, can get very busy.
(Geoffrey Sutton)

POOLE SZ0190

Poole Arms (01202) 673450
Town Quay; BH15 1HJ 17th-c waterfront
pub looking over harbour to Brownsea
Island, good fresh fish/seafood at fair prices,
well kept Ringwood, one comfortably old-
fashioned room with boarded ceiling and
nautical prints, good friendly service; outside
gents'; no children, picnic-sets in front of the
handsome green-tiled façade, almost next
door to the Portsmouth Hoy, open all day.
(Peter Barrett)

POOLE SZ0090

Portsmouth Hoy (01202) 673517
The Quay; BH15 1HJ Harbourside pub
with views to Brownsea Island, old-world
atmosphere with dark wood, beams and bare
boards, good food including fresh fish, well
kept Badger ales, friendly service; children
and dogs welcome, outside tables shared with
the Poole Arms, open all day. *(Peter Barrett)*

POOLE SZ0090

Rope & Anchor (01202) 675677
Sarum Street; BH15 1JW Refurbished
spit-level Wadworths pub next to Poole
Museum; good food including fresh fish, well
kept beers and some nice wines by the glass,
friendly accommodating staff; background
music (live Fri), daily papers, free wi-fi;
children and dogs welcome, seats on back
terrace, open (and food) all day. *(Dave
Braisted)*

PORTESHAM SY6085

Kings Arms (01305) 871342
Front Street; DT3 4ET Large modernised
and extended pub in pretty village, ales
such as Exmoor, Otter and St Austell,
good seasonal food from light meals and
sharing plates to specials and carve-your-
own Sun roasts, attentive friendly service,
coffee lounge with daily papers, open fires;
regular live music, quiz last Thurs of month;
children welcome, picnic-sets in sizeable
garden with stream and summer pizza oven,
three bedrooms, open (and food) all day
weekends. *(Marianne and Peter Stevens)*

PORTLAND SY6874

Boat that Rocks (01305) 823000
Portland Marina; DT5 1DX Modern bar/
restaurant by the marina, interesting range
of food including some thai and mexican
choices, good friendly service, four well kept
ales such as Piddle and Shepherd Neame,
upstairs cocktail bar; children welcome,
great boat views from balcony and terrace,
open all day. *(Jeff Davies)*

PORTLAND SY6873

Cove House (01305) 820895
*Follow Chiswell signposts – is at NW
corner of Portland; DT5 1AW* Low-
beamed 18th-c pub in superb position,
effectively built into sea defences just above

the end of Chesil Beach, great views from three-room bar's bay windows, Sharps Doom Bar and other well kept beers, pubby food (all day weekends) including good crab sandwiches, Tues steak night; background and regular live music, steep steps down to gents'; children welcome, dogs in bar, tables out by seawall, open all day. *(Jeff Davies)*

POWERSTOCK SY5196
★**Three Horseshoes** (01308) 485328
Off A3066 Beaminster–Bridport via West Milton; DT6 3TF Tucked-away Edwardian pub surrounded by good walks; cheerful cosy bar with flagstones and stripped panelling, windsor and mate's chairs around assorted tables, Palmers ales and several wines by the glass, nice food cooked by landlord, good timely service, slightly more formal dining room; children and dogs welcome, picnic-sets on back terrace with garden and country views, two comfortable bedrooms, closed Mon and maybe Sun evening if quiet. *(Comus and Sarah Elliott)*

PUDDLETOWN SY7594
Blue Vinney (01305) 848228
The Moor; DT2 8TE Large modernised village pub with beamed oak-floor bar and restaurant, good variety of popular well presented food (not Sun evening) from lunchtime baguettes up, well kept Sharps, Youngs and a beer named for the pub, friendly young staff; children welcome, terrace overlooking garden with play area, open all day Fri-Sun. *(P and J Shapley)*

PUNCKNOWLE SY5388
Crown (01308) 897711
Off B3157 Bridport–Abbotsbury; DT2 9BN 16th-c thatched inn with enjoyable food from sandwiches up including tapas, pizzas and children's meals, Palmers ales and good choice of wines by the glass, inglenook log fire at each end of low-beamed stripped-stone lounge, steps up to public bar with books and another log fire, small shop selling local produce including freshly baked bread; dogs welcome, disabled facilities, valley views from peaceful pretty back garden, good walks, one bedroom, open all day. *(Comus and Sarah Elliott)*

SANDFORD ORCAS ST6220
★**Mitre** (01963) 220271
Off B3148 and B3145 N of Sherborne; DT9 4RU Thriving tucked-away country local with welcoming long-serving licensees, three well kept changing ales, ciders such as Bridge Farm, wholesome home-made food (not Mon) from good soup and sandwiches up, flagstones, log fires and fresh flowers, small bar and larger pleasantly homely dining area; occasional open mike nights, games including shove-ha'penny and dominoes; children welcome and dogs (theirs are Finlay and Freya), pretty back garden with terrace, good local walks (on Macmillan Way and

Monarch's Way), closed Mon lunchtime. *(Dr Simon Innes)*

SHAFTESBURY ST8622
Grosvenor Arms (01747) 850850
High Street; SP7 8JA Georgian-fronted town-centre hotel (former coaching inn) with civilised bar, cheerful cushions on sofas and armchairs, settles, antlers on partly panelled walls, coir and wood floor, two Palmers ales and decent wines by the glass, cocktail list, conservatory area linking bar and spreading dining rooms, enjoyable modern food from good smoked salmon sandwiches (served till 6pm) and popular pizzas up, set lunch menu (Mon-Fri) and afternoon teas, pleasant staff; live jazz first Thurs of month; children and dogs welcome, central courtyard with fountain and metal furniture, 16 bedrooms, open all day. *(Caroline Prescott)*

SHAPWICK ST9301
Anchor (01258) 857269
Off A350 Blandford–Poole; West Street; DT11 9LB Welcoming red-brick Victorian pub owned by village consortium; popular freshly made food (booking advised) including good value set deal Mon-Thurs, Timothy Taylors Landlord and a couple of local ales, real cider, good service, scrubbed pine tables on wood floors, pastel walls and open fires; children and dogs welcome, tables out in front, more in attractive back garden with terrace, handy for Kingston Lacy (NT). *(Colin and Maggie Fancourt)*

SPETISBURY ST9102
Woodpecker (01258) 452658
A350 SE of Blandford; High Street; DT11 9DJ Popular village pub with welcoming chatty landlord, comfortable open-plan interior, good choice of enjoyable affordably priced home-made food (not Sun, Mon evenings), at least four well kept changing ales along with ciders/perries; bar billiards; seats out in small front garden. *(Geoffrey Sutton)*

STOBOROUGH SY9286
Kings Arms (01929) 552705
B3075 S of Wareham; Corfe Road opposite petrol station; BH20 5AB Popular part-thatched 17th-c village pub, well kept Purbeck, Ringwood and up to three guests, good fairly priced food in bar and restaurant from pub favourites up including interesting specials, cheerful efficient staff; children and dogs welcome, disabled access, views over marshes to River Frome from terrace tables, open all day during summer school holidays (all day Fri-Sun other times). *(M G Hart, Jenny and Brian Seller)*

STOKE ABBOTT ST4500
★**New Inn** (01308) 868333
Off B3162 and B3163 2 miles W of Beaminster; DT8 3JW Welcoming 17th-c

thatched pub with good home-cooked food including daily specials, well kept Palmers ales, woodburner in big inglenook, beams, brasses and copper, some handsome panelling, flagstoned dining room; children and dogs (in bar) welcome, wheelchair access, two attractive gardens, unspoilt quiet thatched village with good surrounding walks, street fair third Sat in July, closed Sun evening, Mon. *(Liz and Martin Eldon)*

STOURPAINE   ST8609
White Horse (01258) 453535
Shaston Road; A350 NW of Blandford; DT11 8TA Traditional country local extended from early 18th-c core (originally two cottages), popular food from landlord-chef including deals, good friendly service, well kept Badger ales and sensible wine list, open-plan layout with scrubbed pine tables on bare boards, woodburners, games part with pool, post office and shop; well behaved children welcome, dogs in bar, seats out at front and on back deck, open all day. *(Robert Watt)*

STOURTON CAUNDLE   ST7115
Trooper (01963) 362405
Village signed off A30 E of Milborne Port; DT10 2JW Pretty little stone-built pub in lovely village setting (Enid Blyton's house opposite); friendly staff and atmosphere, well kept changing beers (their microbrewery is currently closed), real ciders and good range of gins, food Weds and Fri (fish and chips) evenings only, tiny low-ceilinged bar, stripped-stone dining room, darts, dominoes and shove-ha'penny, skittle alley; background and some live music (folk and jazz), sports TV, outside gents'; children, walkers and dogs welcome, a few picnic-sets out in front, pleasant side garden with play area, camping, closed Mon and lunchtimes Tues-Thurs. *(Kate Moran)*

STRATTON   SY6593
Saxon Arms (01305) 260020
Off A37 NW of Dorchester; The Square; DT2 9WG Traditional (though recently built) flint-and-thatch local, open-plan, bright and spacious with light oak tables and comfortable settles on flagstones or carpet, log fire, well kept Butcombe, Timothy Taylors Landlord and two guests, good value wines, tasty generous food including good choice of specials, large comfortable dining section on right; background music, traditional games; children and dogs welcome, terrace tables overlooking village green, open (and food) all day Fri-Sun. *(George Sanderson)*

STUDLAND   SZ0382
Bankes Arms (01929) 450225
Off B3351, Isle of Purbeck; Manor Road; BH19 3AU Very popular spot above fine beach, outstanding country, sea and cliff views from huge garden over road with lots of seating; comfortably basic big bar with raised

drinking area, beams, flagstones and good log fire, well kept changing ales including own Isle of Purbeck, local cider, nice wines by the glass and enjoyable freshly made food from baguettes up, darts and pool in side area; background music, machines, sports TV; over-8s and dogs welcome, just off coast path and can get very busy on summer weekends, parking complicated (NT car park), good-sized comfortable bedrooms, open (and food) all day. *(Jenny and Brian Seller)*

STURMINSTER MARSHALL   SY9500
Red Lion (01258) 857319
Opposite church; off A350 Blandford–Poole; BH21 4BU Attractive village pub opposite handsome church; bustling local atmosphere, wide variety of enjoyable food including good value set menu (Tues-Thurs, Sun evening), special diets catered for, well kept Badger ales and nice wines, roomy U-shaped bar with log fire, good-sized dining room in former skittle alley; background music; children and dogs welcome, disabled access, back garden with wicker furniture and picnic-sets, open all day Sun, closed Mon. *(Peter Barrett)*

STURMINSTER NEWTON   ST7813
Bull (01258) 472435
A357, S of centre; DT10 2BS Refurbished thatched and beamed 16th-c riverside pub, Badger ales and enjoyable good value home-made food; children and dogs welcome, roadside picnic-sets, more in secluded back garden, closed Wed, open all day weekends. *(Dr Simon Innes)*

TOLPUDDLE   SY7994
Martyrs (01305) 848249
Former A35 W of Bere Regis; DT2 7ES Village dining pub built in the 1920s, enjoyable home-made food including Fri fish and chips and Sun carvery, two or three Badger ales, friendly accommodating staff, opened-up bare-boards interior; background music; children welcome, good disabled access, small front terrace and garden behind, open (and food) all day. *(Mrs P Sumner)*

UPLODERS   SY5093
Crown (01308) 485356
Signed off A35 E of Bridport; DT6 4NU Stone-built village corner pub, log fires, dark low beams, flagstones and mix of old furniture including stripped pine, grandfather clock, good fairly traditional home-made food using local suppliers, three changing ales; background music; children and dogs welcome, tables in attractive two-tier garden, closed Mon. *(Peter Barrett, Andrew Stone)*

WAREHAM   SY9287
Kings Arms (01929) 552503
North Street (A351, N end of town); BH20 4AD Traditional stone and thatch

town local, well kept Ringwood and guests, decent good value pubby food, friendly staff, back serving counter and two bars off flagstoned central corridor, beams and inglenook log fire; live music at weekends, darts; children and dogs welcome, garden behind with picnic-sets, open all day. *(George Sanderson)*

WAREHAM SY9287

Old Granary (01929) 552010

The Quay; BH20 4LP
Fine old brick building in good riverside position – can get very busy; emphasis on dining but two small beamed rooms by main door for drinkers, enjoyable fairly standard food at reasonable prices, well kept Badger ales and good wines by the glass, friendly efficient young staff, airy dining room with leather high-backed chairs and pews around pale wood tables, brick walls and new oak standing timbers, two further rooms with big photographs of the pub, woodburners; quiet background music; children welcome, seats out overlooking water and on covered roof terrace, boats for hire over bridge, limited nearby parking, open all day from 9am (10am Sun). *(Alan and Angela Scouller)*

WAREHAM FOREST SY9089

★**Silent Woman** (01929) 552909

Wareham–Bere Regis; Bere Road; BH20 7PA Long neatly kept dining pub divided by doorways and standing timbers, good variety of enjoyable carefully prepared food including daily specials, Badger ales kept well and plenty of wines by the glass, friendly helpful young staff, traditional furnishings, farm tools and stripped masonry; background music; no children inside, dogs welcome, wheelchair access, plenty of picnic-sets outside including a covered area, walks nearby; a popular wedding venue, so best to check it's open. *(M G Hart, Glenwys and Alan Lawrence)*

WAYTOWN SY4797

Hare & Hounds (01308) 488203

Between B3162 and A3066 N of Bridport; DT6 5LQ Attractive 18th-c country local up and down steps, friendly staff and regulars, well kept Palmers tapped from the cask, local cider, generous helpings of enjoyable good value food (not Sun evening) including popular Sun lunch, open fire, two small cottagey rooms and pretty dining room; children and dogs welcome, lovely Brit Valley views from sizeable well maintained garden, play area, occasional barbecues and live music. *(Sophie Ellison)*

WEST BEXINGTON SY5386

Manor Hotel (01308) 897660

Off B3157 SE of Bridport; Beach Road; DT2 9DF Relaxing quietly set hotel with long history and fine sea views; good choice of enjoyable food (highish prices)

in beamed cellar bar, flagstoned restaurant or Victorian-style conservatory, well kept Otter, Thatcher's cider and several wines by the glass; children welcome, dogs on leads (not in restaurant), charming well kept garden, close to Chesil Beach, 13 bedrooms. *(Liz and Martin Eldon)*

WEST LULWORTH SY8280

Castle Inn (01929) 400311

B3070 SW of Wareham; BH20 5RN Pretty 16th-c thatched inn in lovely spot near Lulworth Cove, good walks and lots of summer visitors; beamed flagstoned bar with well kept changing local ales, at least 40 ciders/perries, generous pubby food, maze of booth seating divided by ledges, cosy more modern-feeling lounge bar, pleasant restaurant; background music; children and dogs (particularly) welcome, front terrace, long attractive garden behind on several levels, 12 bedrooms, open (and food) all day. *(Jeff Davies)*

WEST LULWORTH SY8280

Lulworth Cove (01929) 400333

Main Road; BH20 5RQ Modernised inn with good range of enjoyable reasonably priced food from baguettes up, well kept Badger ales and several wines by the glass, seaside theme bar with bare boards and painted panelling; free wi-fi; children and dogs welcome, picnic-sets on sizeable terrace, short stroll down to cove, 12 bedrooms (some with sea-view balcony), open (and food) all day. *(Comus and Sarah Elliott, Jenny and Brian Seller)*

WEST STAFFORD SY7289

Wise Man (01305) 261970

Signed off A352 Dorchester–Wareham; DT2 8AG 16th-c thatched and beamed pub near Hardy's Cottage (NT); open-plan interior with flagstone and wood floors, enjoyable locally sourced food (not Sun evening) including some interesting choices, Butcombe, Timothy Taylors and guests from central bar, good choice of wines by the glass, friendly attentive staff; children and dogs welcome, disabled facilities, plenty of seats outside, lovely walks nearby, open all day weekends. *(Sophie Ellison)*

WEYMOUTH SY6778

Boot 07809 440772

High West Street; DT4 8JH Friendly unspoilt old local near the harbour; beams, bare boards, panelling, hooded stone-mullioned windows and coal fires, cosy gently sloping snug, ten well kept ales including Ringwood and other Marstons-related beers (tasting trays available), real cider and good selection of malt whiskies, no food apart from pork pies and pickled eggs, regulars bring their own food on Sun to share; live music Tues, quiz Weds; free wi-fi; disabled access, pavement tables, open all day. *(Jeff Davies)*

WEYMOUTH   SY6778

Ship (01305) 773879

Custom House Quay; DT4 8BE Neatly
modernised and extended waterfront pub
with several nautical-theme open-plan levels,
well kept Badger ales and several wines by
the glass from long bar, enjoyable good value
usual food from sandwiches and baguettes
up, upstairs evening restaurant (weekends
only out of season), friendly helpful staff;
unobtrusive background music; dogs welcome
in bar (biscuits for them), wheelchair
accessible downstairs, some quayside seating
and pleasant back terrace, open all day.
(Jeff Davies)

WIMBORNE MINSTER   SZ0199

Minster Arms (01202) 840700

West Street; BH21 1JS Revamped old
corner pub (former Pudding & Pie) with
log fires, leather sofas and an assortment of
tables and chairs on wood floors, three real
ales and well liked food from short seasonal
menu, good friendly service; open (and food)
all day. *(Adam Simmonds, Ian Malone)*

WIMBORNE MINSTER   SU0100

⋆ **Olive Branch** (01202) 884686

*East Borough, just off Hanham Road
(B3073, just E of its junction with
B3078); BH21 1PF* Handsome smartly
refurbished townhouse, spacious interior
with various dining areas serving good
value food, one with beams and view into
kitchen, another more canteen-like with
long tables and benches, relaxed atmosphere
and friendly young staff, Badger beers in

comfortable bar with woodburner; rattan and
other tables in mediterranean-style garden,
open all day from 8am (9am Sun). *(Michael
Butler, Roger and Donna Huggins)*

WINKTON   SZ1696

Fishermans Haunt (01202) 477283

B3347 N of Christchurch; BH23 7AS
Comfortable big-windowed riverside inn on
fringes of New Forest; four well kept Fullers/
Gales beers and good range of other drinks,
enjoyable food using local produce such as
venison, good helpful service, two log fires,
restaurant views of River Avon; background
music; children and dogs (in bar) welcome,
disabled facilities, tables among shrubs in
quiet back garden, heaters in covered area,
12 bedrooms, good breakfast, open all day.
*(David and Sally Frost, Paul Rampton, Julie
Harding)*

**WINTERBORNE
STICKLAND**   ST8304

Crown (01258) 881042

North Street; DT11 0NJ Welcoming
thatched village pub, two rooms separated
by servery, smaller one with inglenook
woodburner, high-backed settle and dark
tables and chairs on patterned carpet, the
other with low beams, more tables and chairs
and darts, well kept Ringwood and guests, a
local cider and good value traditional food
from sandwiches and light dishes up, prompt
cheerful service; monthly live music Fri, quiz
second Tues of month, free wi-fi; children and
dogs welcome, pretty back terrace and steps
up to lawned area with village view, open all
day Fri-Sun. *(Liz and Martin Eldon)*

Post Office address codings confusingly give the impression that some pubs are in
Dorset, when they're really in Somerset (which is where we list them).

Essex

ARKESDEN
TL4834 Map 5

Axe & Compasses 🍷

(01799) 550272 – www.axeandcompasses.co.uk

Off B1038; CB11 4EX

Comfortable, thatched pub with Greene King beers and popular food; seats outside

In a particularly lovely village, this is a rambling thatched country inn with a friendly, relaxed atmosphere. The oldest part (dating from the 17th c) has low-slung ceilings, original floor tiles, upholstered comfortable chairs, cushioned wall seats and settles around polished tables, an open fire in a brick fireplace and stools against the counter on wooden flooring. The smart, neat dining room is in the old stables with photographs of the pub and surrounding area on the walls. Greene King IPA and Old Speckled Hen and a changing guest beer on handpump, a very good wine list (with 15 by the glass) and around two dozen malt whiskies. There's a side terrace with seats and tables and pretty hanging baskets, and some benches at the front.

🍴 Pleasing food includes lunchtime sandwiches (not Sun), scallops with mushrooms, white wine and cream, feta cheese filo parcels with sweet cherry tomato dressing, vegetarian tartlet, lamb kebabs with greek salad, salmon and smoked haddock fishcakes with dill and lemon butter sauce, chicken, leek and bacon crumble, beef stew and dumplings, duck breast on pak choi with ginger and lemongrass sauce, and puddings. *Benchmark main dish: steak, kidney and mushroom pie £14.95. Two-course evening meal £24.00.*

Greene King ~ Tenants Themis and Diane Christou ~ Real ale ~ Open 11.30-2.30, 6-11; 12-3, 6-8.30 Sun ~ Bar food 12-2, 7-9; not Sun evening in winter ~ Restaurant ~ Children welcome
Recommended by Mrs P J Pearce, Charlie Parker, Ruth May

CHRISHALL
TL4439 Map 5

Red Cow 🍺

(01763) 838792 – www.theredcow.com

High Street; off B1039 Wendens Ambo–Great Chishill; SG8 8RN

Bustling, well run local with beamed rooms, four real ales, well liked food and seats in attractive garden

Popular and welcoming, this 16th-c thatched pub is run by hands-on licensees and their friendly staff. The atmospheric bar and dining room are heavily beamed and timbered, there's a woodburning stove and an open fire, all sorts of wooden dining chairs around tables of every size on bare floorboards, and a comfortable sofa and armchairs. Adnams Southwold, Morlands Old Speckled Hen, Timothy Taylors Landlord and Woodfordes Wherry on handpump, eight wines by the glass, Aspall's cider and cocktails; they hold a music and beer festival in May. Terracing has picnic-sets and the garden is pretty. The pub is handy for the Icknield Way.

 Using some home-grown and other local produce, the tasty food includes lunchtime panini, creamy garlic mushrooms, smoked salmon and lobster cocktail, sharing boards, a pie of the day, pulled roast ham and free-range eggs, sausages and mash with rich gravy, spiced lentil and feta filo tart, coq au vin, roast saddle of lamb with creamed greens, dauphinoise potatoes and mint jus, and puddings such as vanilla cheesecake with poached rhubarb and chocolate brownie with chocolate sauce; Thursday is tapas night. *Benchmark main dish: steak burger with toppings, relish and chips £12.50. Two-course evening meal £20.00.*

Free house ~ Licensees Toby and Alexis Didier Serre ~ Real ale ~ Open 12-3, 6 (5 Fri)-11; 12-11 Sat; 12-8 Sun; closed Mon ~ Bar food 12-2, 6-9; 12-9 Sat; 12-3 Sun ~ Restaurant ~ Children welcome ~ Dogs allowed in bar ~ Wi-fi ~ Live music last Fri of month
Recommended by R Anderson, Mrs Margo Finlay, Jörg Kasprowski

FEERING
TL8720   Map 5

Sun ⌷ £

(01376) 570442 – www.suninnfeering.co.uk
Just off A12 Kelvedon bypass; Feering Hill (B1024 just W of Feering proper); CO5 9NH

Striking 16th-c pub with six real ales, well liked food and pleasant garden

Always deservedly busy, the spreading slate-floored bar is relaxed, unpretentious and civilised, with two big woodburning stoves – one in the huge central inglenook fireplace, another by an antique winged settle on the left. Throughout, the timbered and jettied pub has handsomely carved black beams and timbers galore, and attractive wild-flower murals in a frieze above the central timber divider. Half a dozen ales on handpump include Shepherd Neame Bishops Finger, Goldings, Master Brew Bitter, Spitfire and Whitstable Bay Pale, plus a guest beer – and they hold summer and winter beer festivals; also, 11 wines by the glass, ten malt whiskies and 14 gins served by cheerful staff. A brick-paved back courtyard has tables, heaters and a shelter; in the garden beyond, tall trees shade green picnic-sets.

 Popular food using locally sourced produce includes lunchtime sandwiches, pork rillettes with cornichons and toasted sourdough, shell-on tiger prawns with garlic, chilli and coriander, home-cooked ham in mustard and honey with free-range eggs, beer-battered haddock with triple-cooked chips, beef or walnut burger with toppings and brioche bun, spicy chilli beef with cheese, and puddings. *Benchmark main dish: beef, mushroom and stilton pie £11.50. Two-course evening meal £16.00.*

Shepherd Neame ~ Tenant Andy Howard ~ Real ale ~ Open 12-3, 5.30-11; 12-midnight Sat; 12-10.30 Sun ~ Bar food 12-2.30, 6-9 (9.30 Fri, Sat); 12-8 Sun ~ Children welcome away from bar ~ Dogs welcome ~ Wi-fi *Recommended by Edward Mirzoeff, Mrs Margo Finlay, Jörg Kasprowski, Ray White*

FULLER STREET
TL7416   Map 5

Square & Compasses ⚙ ⌷

(01245) 361477 – www.thesquareandcompasses.co.uk
Back road Great Leighs–Hatfield Peverel; CM3 2BB

Neatly kept country pub with two woodburning stoves, four ales and enjoyable food

This gently civilised pub is in attractive countryside and handy for the Essex Way long-distance footpath. As well as a small extension for walkers and dogs, the L-shaped beamed bar has two woodburning stoves in inglenook fireplaces, and friendly staff serve Colchester No.1, Crouch Vale Essex Boys Best Bitter and Mighty Oak Captain Bob tapped from the cask, Bertie's dry cider and 18 wines by the glass; background jazz. The dining room features shelves of bottles and decanters against timbered walls, and an appealing variety of dining chairs around dark wooden tables set with linen napkins, on carpeting. Tables out in front on decking offer gentle country views.

 Using local, seasonal produce, the interesting food includes sandwiches, scallops with pea purée and truffle oil, duck liver and port pâté with chutney, fennel and carrot cheesecake with parmesan base, fish pie of smoked haddock, cod and salmon, pork sausages with spring onion mash and onion gravy, whole grilled dover sole with lemon and parsley butter, pheasant wrapped in smoked bacon with wild mushrooms, potato rösti and game sauce, and puddings such as lemon tart and vanilla pannacotta with orange and almond sauce and red wine poached pear. *Benchmark main dish: steak in ale pie £11.95. Two-course evening meal £20.50.*

Free house ~ Licensee Victor Roome ~ Real ale ~ Open 11.30-11; 12-midnight Sat; 12-11 Sun ~ Bar food 12-2 (2.30 Sat), 6.30-9.30; 12-6 Sun ~ Restaurant ~ Well behaved children welcome ~ Dogs allowed in bar *Recommended by Mrs Margo Finlay, Jörg Kasprowski, Evelyn and Derek Walter, Anne and Ben Smith, Alf Wright*

FYFIELD   TL5706 Map 5

Queens Head 🍴 ♈

(01277) 899231 – www.thequeensheadfyfield.co.uk
Corner of B184 and Queen Street; CM5 0RY

Friendly old pub with seats in riverside garden, a good choice of drinks and highly thought-of food

Many customers come to this relaxed and friendly 15th-c pub to enjoy the particularly tasty food, but it's good for drinkers too: they keep Adnams Broadside and Southwold and a guest such as Fullers London Pride on handpump and several good wines by the glass. The compact, low-beamed, L-shaped bar has exposed timbers, pretty lamps on nice sturdy elm tables and comfortable seating from wall banquettes to attractive, unusual high-backed chairs, some in a snug little side booth. In summer, two facing fireplaces have church candles instead of a fire; background music. The upstairs restaurant is more formal. On sunny days it's best to arrive early to bag a seat in the prettily planted back garden that runs down to the sleepy River Roding; the pub is usefully open all day at weekends.

Impressive food includes crispy quail with tamarind and tempura baby vegetables, chicken and tarragon ravioli with girolle mushrooms and artichoke purée, tomato and tallegio arancini with onion, tomato and garlic sauce, duo of lamb (shepherd's pie and rump) with butter bean cassoulet and mint oil, halibut with white truffle gnocchi, confit tomato and samphire and artichoke velouté, slow-cooked pork belly with salt and pepper cuttlefish, bell pepper and chilli salsa and cauliflower purée, and puddings such as baked new york cheesecake with red berry compote and salted caramel tart with marshmallow and praline. *Benchmark main dish: cod bourguignon £17.00. Two-course evening meal £23.00.*

Free house ~ Licensee Daniel Lamprecht ~ Real ale ~ Open 11-3.30, 6-11; 11-11 Sat; 12-10.30 Sun; closed Mon ~ Bar food 12-2.30 (4 Sat), 6.30-9.30; 12-6 Sun ~ Restaurant ~ Children welcome away from bar ~ Wi-fi ~ Folk music monthly (best to phone) *Recommended by Mrs Margo Finlay, Jörg Kasprowski, Mark Hamill, Beth Aldridge*

GOLDHANGER

TL9008 Map 5

Chequers

(01621) 788203 – www.thechequersgoldhanger.co.uk

Church Street; off B1026 E of Heybridge; CM9 8AS

Cheerful and neatly kept pub with six real ales, traditional furnishings, friendly staff and tasty food

You can be sure of a genuinely warm and friendly welcome here and our readers always enjoy their visits. The nice old corridor with its red and black floor tiles leads to six rambling rooms, including a spacious lounge with dark beams, black panelling and a huge sash window overlooking the graveyard, a traditional dining room with bare boards and carpeting and a games room with bar billiards; woodburning stove, open fires, TV and background music. Youngs IPA and five guests from breweries such as Adnams, Crouch Vale, St Austell and Sharps on handpump; they also hold spring and autumn beer festivals. Also, 16 wines by the glass, ten malt whiskies and several farm ciders. There are picnic-sets under umbrellas in the courtyard with its grapevine. Do look at the fine old church next door.

Good, popular food includes sandwiches, duck, orange and cognac pâté with cumberland sauce, crispy garlic and rosemary-coated brie with balsamic onion chutney, local ham and free-range eggs, macaroni cheese and spinach bake, burger with toppings, coleslaw, barbecue relish and chips, smoked haddock, king prawn and salmon pie with cheesy mash topping, chicken curry, lamb and mint pudding with red wine gravy, and puddings such as chocolate pot and lemon meringue pie. *Benchmark main dish: steak in stout pie £11.50. Two-course evening meal £18.50.*

Punch ~ Lease Philip Glover and Dominic Davies ~ Real ale ~ Open 11-11; 12-11 Sun ~ Bar food 12-3, 6.30-9; not Sun evening or Mon bank holiday evening ~ Restaurant ~ Children welcome except in tap room ~ Dogs allowed in bar ~ Wi-fi *Recommended by John and Mary Warner, Ray White, George Atkinson*

HATFIELD BROAD OAK

TL5416 Map 5

Dukes Head ♀

(01279) 718598 – www.thedukeshead.co.uk

B183 Hatfield Heath–Takeley; High Street; CM22 7HH

Relaxed, well run dining pub with enjoyable food in an attractive layout of nicely linked separate areas

In warm weather, head for the back garden with its sheltered terrace and chairs around teak tables under cocktail parasols; there are also picnic-sets at the front corner of the building which has some nice pargeting. Rambling around the central woodburner and side servery are various cosy seating areas: good solid wooden dining chairs around a variety of chunky stripped tables with a comfortable group of armchairs and a sofa at one end, and a slightly more formal area at the back on the right. Cheerful prints on the wall and some magenta panels in the mostly cream décor make for a buoyant mood. Greene King IPA, Sharps Doom Bar and Timothy Taylors Landlord on handpump and 30 wines by the glass from a good list, served by cheerful staff; background music and board games. Sam and Zac the pub dogs welcome other canines and there are always dog biscuits behind the bar.

Interesting food includes trout gravadlax with fresh crab salad and bloody mary dresssing, field mushroom and spinach stack with red onion marmalade and a crispy parmesan poached egg, local sausages with thyme and shallot gravy, free-range chicken saltimbocca with wild mushroom and pancetta linguine, fish pie topped with cheddar mash, beer-battered fish and chips, burger with toppings, coleslaw and skinny fries, and puddings such as chocolate and macadamia nut brownie and lemon syllabub with lemon jelly and candied zest; they also offer a two- and three-course set menu (weekday lunchtimes and Mon-Thurs evenings). *Benchmark main dish: king prawn spaghetti £13.75. Two-course evening meal £25.00.*

Enterprise ~ Lease Liz Flodman ~ Real ale ~ Open 11.30-11; 10.30-11 Sat; 10.30-10 Sun ~ Bar food 12-2.30, 6-9.30; 10.30-10 Sat; 10.30-9 Sun ~ Restaurant ~ Children welcome ~ Dogs allowed in bar ~ Wi-fi *Recommended by Isobel Mackinlay, Harvey Brown, Julie Braeburn, Jeremy Snaithe*

HORNDON-ON-THE-HILL   TQ6783 Map 3

Bell 🌟 ♀ 🍺 🛏

(01375) 642463 – www.bell-inn.co.uk

M25 junction 30 into A13, then left after 7 miles on to B1007, village signposted from here; SS17 8LD

Essex Dining Pub of the Year

Lovely historic pub with fine food and a very good range of drinks; attractive bedrooms

This is a first class all-rounder (and run by the same friendly family for more than 75 years) and we get consistent praise on all aspects of the place from our enthusiastic readers. The heavily beamed, panelled bar maintains a strongly pubby appearance with high-backed antique settles and benches, rugs on flagstones and highly polished oak floorboards, and an open log fire. Look out for the curious collection of ossified hot-cross buns hanging along a beam in the saloon bar. The first was put there in 1906 to mark the day (a Good Friday) that Jack Turnell became licensee; the tradition continues to this day, with the oldest available person in the village hanging the bun each year. The timbered restaurant has numerous old copper pots and pans hanging from beams. An impressive range of drinks includes Greene King IPA, Sharps Doom Bar and guests such as Crouch Vale Yakima Gold, Greene King IPA Reserve on handpump, and over 114 well chosen wines (16 by the glass). Two giant umbrellas cover the courtyard, which has very pretty summer hanging baskets. Centuries ago, many important medieval dignitaries would have stayed here as it was the last inn before travellers heading south could ford the Thames at Highams Causeway. Today, it remains a lovely place to stay with individually styled, thoughtfully equipped bedrooms of all sizes.

🌟 Excellent food includes lunchtime sandwiches, shin of beef ravioli on balsamic red onions, maple-poached pancetta and straw potatoes, crab and tea-smoked salmon pâté with fennel, red pepper jam and red pepper coulis, smoked cheese, leek and spring onion pithivier with caramelised onion purée, roast suckling pig with sage, chicken, bacon and butternut terrine with crispy pork rillette and apple purée, local venison and mustard filo pie, and puddings such as apple tart with peanut butter parfait, caramel sauce, almond brittle and chocolate stick and Baileys pastry cream-filled profiteroles with hot chocolate fudge sauce and white chocolate parfait. *Benchmark main dish: calves liver and bacon on chickpea, chorizo and button mushroom cassoulet £15.80. Two-course evening meal £25.95.*

Free house ~ Licensee John Vereker ~ Real ale ~ Open 11-11; 12-10.30 Sun ~ Bar food 12-2, 6.30-10; 12-2, 6-10 Sat; 12-2, 7-10 Sun ~ Restaurant ~ Children welcome ~ Dogs allowed in bar and bedrooms ~ Wi-fi ~ Bedrooms: /£90 *Recommended by Mrs Margo Finlay, Jörg Kasprowski, John and Enid, Mervyn and Susan English, Sarah Roberts, Valerie Sayer*

LITTLE WALDEN

TL5441 Map 5

Crown ▦ £ ⇞

(01799) 522475 – www.thecrownlittlewalden.co.uk

B1052 N of Saffron Walden; CB10 1XA

Bustling 18th-c cottage pub with a warming log fire, hearty food and bedrooms

'This never disappoints,' says one reader with much enthusiasm – and it's the sort of place that once found, you'll keep returning to; it's very much the hub of the community and particularly well run by the friendly, helpful landlord and his courteous staff. The low-ceilinged rooms have a cosy, chatty atmosphere and traditional furnishings, with book-room-red walls, floral curtains, bare boards, navy carpeting, cosy warm fires and an unusual walk-through fireplace. A higgledy-piggledy mix of chairs ranges from high-backed pews to little cushioned armchairs spaced around a good variety of closely arranged tables, mostly big, some stripped. The small red-tiled room on the right has two small tables. Three changing beers, including Adnams Broadside and Southwold and Woodfordes Wherry, are tapped straight from casks racked up behind the bar; TV, disabled access. Tables on the terrace have views over the surrounding tranquil countryside. Our readers love staying overnight here and the breakfasts are excellent.

 Fair priced popular food includes lunchtime sandwiches and baguettes, crayfish cocktail, garlic mushrooms, honey-roast ham and eggs, spinach and ricotta cannelloni, moussaka, steak and mushroom pie, crispy battered fish and chips, 10oz rib-eye steak, and puddings such as treacle pudding with custard and spicy apple crumble. *Benchmark main dish: caribbean-style prawn curry £10.95. Two-course evening meal £18.00.*

Free house ~ Licensee Colin Hayling ~ Real ale ~ Open 11.30-3, 6-11; 12-10.30 Sun ~ Bar food 12-2, 7-9; not Sun or Mon evenings ~ Restaurant ~ Children welcome ~ Dogs welcome ~ Wi-fi ~ Live jazz Weds ~ Bedrooms: /£75 *Recommended by Sara Fulton, Roger Baker, Adrian Johnson, David Twitchett*

LITTLEY GREEN

TL6917 Map 5

Compasses ▦

(01245) 362308 – www.compasseslittleygreen.co.uk

Village signposted off B1417 Felsted road in Hartoft End (opposite former Ridleys Brewery), about a mile N of junction with B1008 (former A130); CM3 1BU

Charming brick tavern – a prime example of what is now an all too rare breed; bedrooms

They keep a fantastic choice of drinks in the companionable bar here: Bishop Nick Ridleys Rite (brewed in Felsted by the landlord's brother) as well as guests from Adnams, Crouch Vale, Mighty Oak, Red Fox, Skinners, Tyne Bank and two weekend guest ales, all tapped from casks in a back cellar. In summer and at Christmas they hold beer festivals featuring dozens of beers, alongside festivities that may include vintage ploughing in the field opposite. Also, Fosseway and Tumpy Ground farm ciders, perries from Cornish Orchards and Gwynt y Ddraig and eight wines by the glass. The bar has very traditional brown-painted panelling and wall benches, plain chairs and tables on quarry tiles, with chat and laughter rather than piped music. There's a piano, darts and board games in one side room, and decorative mugs hanging from beams in another. There are picnic-sets out on the sheltered side grass and the garden behind, with a couple of long tables on the front cobbles by the quiet lane. Bedrooms are in a small newish block.

❚❚ A big blackboard shows the day's range of huffers: big rolls with a hearty range of hot or cold fillings. They also serve ploughman's, baked potatoes and a few sensibly priced dishes such as chicken liver pâté, beer-battered fish and chips, a curry, gammon and egg, and rib-eye steak. *Benchmark main dish: huffers £9.00. Two-course evening meal £14.50.*

Free house ~ Licensee Jocelyn Ridley ~ Real ale ~ Open 12-3, 5.30-11.30; 12-11.30 Thurs-Sun ~ Bar food 12-2.30 (4 Sat, 5 Sun), 7-9.30 ~ Children welcome ~ Dogs welcome ~ Wi-fi ~ Live folk music every third Mon ~ Bedrooms: /£70 *Recommended by Simon Day, Paul Scofield, David Longhurst*

MARGARETTING TYE   TL6801   Map 5
White Hart ◀ £ 🛏
(01277) 840478 – www.thewhitehart.uk.com
From B1002 (just S of A12/A414 junction) follow Maldon Road for 1.3 miles, then turn right immediately after river bridge, into Swan Lane, keeping on for 0.7 miles; The Tye; CM4 9JX

Cheery pub with a fine choice of ales, good food, plenty of customers and a family garden; bedrooms

Our readers enjoy their visits here very much – whether dropping in for a pint, a meal or to stay overnight in one of the comfortable bedrooms. The open-plan but cottagey rooms have walls and wainscoting painted in chalky traditional colours that match well with the dark timbers and mix of old wooden chairs and tables; a stuffed deer head is mounted on the chimney breast above a woodburning stove. Tapped straight from the cask, the fine range of ales includes Adnams Southwold and Broadside, Mighty Oak IPA and Oscar Wilde and a couple of guests such as Farmers Ales Pucks Folly and Woodfordes Wherry; they hold beer festivals in July and November. Also, a german wheat beer, interesting bottled beers, quite a range of spirits and winter mulled wine. The neat carpeted back conservatory is similar in style to the other rooms, and the front lobby has a bookcase of charity paperbacks. Darts, board games and background music. There are plenty of picnic-sets out on grass and terracing around the pub, with a sturdy play area, a fenced duck pond and views across the fields; lovely sunsets.

❚❚ Rewarding food includes smoked chicken terrine wrapped in pancetta with red onion marmalade, calamari in garlic butter with sweet chilli dip, spinach, ricotta and pine nut ravioli with roast cherry tomato and parmesan sauce, tandoori chicken with mint raita, salmon fillet on crab, lemon and coriander crushed potatoes with salsa verde, calves liver and bacon with gravy, steamed ginger pudding with poached rhubarb and caramelised banoffi pie with pistachio praline. *Benchmark main dish: steak in ale pie £12.95. Two-course evening meal £17.50.*

Free house ~ Licensee Elizabeth Haines ~ Real ale ~ Open 11.30-3.30, 5.30-midnight; 11.30-midnight Sat; 12-midnight Sun; 11.30-3.30, 6-11 weekdays in winter; closed Mon ~ Bar food 12-2.30, 6-9 (9.30 Fri); 12-3.30, 6-9.30 Sat; 12-7.30 Sun ~ Restaurant ~ Well behaved children welcome ~ Dogs allowed in bar ~ Wi-fi ~ Bedrooms: /£80 *Recommended by David Twitchett, Mervyn and Susan English, Mrs Margo Finlay, Jörg Kasprowski*

SAFFRON WALDEN   TL5338   Map 5
Eight Bells ♉
(01799) 522790 – www.8bells-pub.co.uk
Bridge Street; B184 towards Cambridge; CB10 1BU

Beautiful bar and dining rooms, helpful, courteous staff, enjoyable food and drink and seats in the garden

The very good food continues to draw plenty of customers to this handsomely timbered black and white Tudor inn – but they also keep Fullers London Pride, St Austell Tribute and Woodfordes Wherry on handpump, ten wines by the glass and several malt whiskies. Staff are friendly and the atmosphere is relaxed and gently civilised. The open-plan beamed bar area has leather armchairs, chesterfield sofas and old wooden settles on bare floorboards, a coal-effect gas fire in a brick fireplace and interesting old photographs. The back dining part is in a splendidly raftered and timbered barn with modern dark wood furniture and upholstered wall banquettes, a woodburning stove built into a log-effect end wall and display cabinets with old books, candlesticks and so forth; background music. There are seats and tables outside and a raised decked area. Audley End (English Heritage) is nearby, as are some decent walks. Sister pub is the Cricketers Arms at Rickling Green (in Also Worth a Visit).

The interesting menu includes crab and avocado tian with tomato fondant and dill crème fraîche, goats cheese fritters with sherry onion compote and honey, grazing boards, pie of the week, saffron, pea and courgette risotto with tomato and red pepper salsa and ricotta, gammon and fried duck egg with pease pudding, cannon of local lamb with confit potato terrine, vegetable ragoût and mint jus, fillet of turbot with potato gnocchi, capers, salsify and samphire and cockle velouté, and puddings. *Benchmark main dish: burger with toppings, dill pickle and skinny fries £13.50. Two-course evening meal £20.00.*

Cozy Pub Company ~ Lease Leanne Langman ~ Real ale ~ Open 10am-11pm (midnight Sat); 10am-10.30pm Sun ~ Bar food 12-9.30; 12-6 Sun ~ Restaurant ~ Children welcome ~ Dogs allowed in bar ~ Wi-fi *Recommended by Hilary and Neil Christopher, Andrew Stone, Max Simons*

SOUTH HANNINGFIELD

Old Windmill ⭐ ♥   TQ7497   Map 5

(01268) 712280 – www.brunningandprice.co.uk/oldwindmill
Off A130 S of Chelmsford; CM3 8HT

Extensive, invitingly converted pub with interesting food and a good range of drinks

Cosy, rambling areas are created by a forest of stripped standing timbers and open doorways here and there's always an abundance of chatty, cheerful customers. An agreeable mix of highly polished old tables and chairs are spread throughout as are frame-to-frame pictures on cream walls, woodburning stoves and homely pot plants. Deep green or dark red dado and a few old rugs dotted on the glowing wood floors provide splashes of colour; other areas are more subdued with beige carpeting. Phoenix Brunning & Price Original and five guests such as Milton Pegasus, Mighty Oak Kings, Slaters Rye IPA, Trumans Swift and XT Three on handpump, with a dozen wines by the glass, 70 malt whiskies and a good range of spirits; background music. A back terrace has tables and chairs under parasols and there are picnic-sets on the lawn, and a few more seats out in front.

Reliably good food includes sandwiches (until 5pm), smoked salmon with horseradish pannacotta and bloody mary dressing, goats cheese, basil and red pepper terrine with black olive tapenade, pork and leek sausages with onion gravy, steak burger with toppings, coleslaw and chips, pumpkin and beetroot tabbouleh with lemon and thyme yoghurt, salmon laksa in green thai curry sauce with lime and coconut rice, chicken and ham hock casserole, and puddings such as baked vanilla cheesecake with blueberry compote and sticky toffee pudding with toffee sauce. *Benchmark main dish: steak in ale pie £13.95. Two-course evening meal £21.00.*

Brunning & Price ~ Manager Nick Clark ~ Real ale ~ Open 11.30-11; 12-10.30 Sun ~
Bar food 12-10 (9.30 Sun) ~ Restaurant ~ Children welcome ~ Dogs allowed in bar ~ Wi-fi
Recommended by David Twitchett, Max Simons, Jeremy Snow

STOCK

TQ6999   Map 5

Hoop ◖

(01277) 841137 – www.thehoop.co.uk

B1007; from A12 Chelmsford bypass take Galleywood, Billericay turn-off; CM4 9BD

**Happy weatherboarded pub with interesting beers, nice food
and a large garden**

This is a refreshingly unmodern village pub with Adnams Bitter and guests
from Billericay, Harveys and Youngs on handpump or tapped from the
cask; they also hold a beer festival at the end of May featuring 100 real
ales, 80 ciders, a hog roast and a barbecue. The open-plan bar has beams
and standing timbers (hinting at the original layout when it was once three
weavers' cottages), pubby tables and chairs and a happy bustle of cheery
locals and visitors. The dining room up in the timbered eaves is a fine room
with an open fire in a big brick-walled fireplace, napery and elegant high-
backed wooden chairs on bare boards. Prettily bordered with flowers, the
large sheltered back garden has picnic-sets and a covered seating area.
Parking is limited, so it's worth arriving early.

Tasty, popular food includes sandwiches, chickpea fritters with dukkah,
pomegranate and mango yoghurt, prawn and crab cocktail, a pie of the day, treacle-
cured ham and duck eggs, burger with toppings and skinny fries, calves liver with crispy
bacon and onion rings, slow-braised beef cheek with crispy onions, brill fillet with
slow-roasted plum tomato and baby leeks, and puddings such as treacle tart and warm
chocolate fondant with salted caramel ice-cream. *Benchmark main dish: toad in the
hole with mash and gravy £10.95. Two-course evening meal £16.00.*

Free house ~ Licensee Michelle Corrigan ~ Real ale ~ Open 11-11; 12-10.30 Sun ~ Bar food
12-2.30, 6-9; 12-9.30 Sat; 12-5 Sun ~ Restaurant ~ Children welcome on left-hand side of bar
~ Dogs allowed in bar ~ Wi-fi *Recommended by Edward Mirzoeff, John and Enid, Sandra and
Nigel Brown, Brian and Sally Wakeham*

Also Worth a Visit in Essex

Besides the fully inspected pubs, you might like to try these pubs that
have been recommended to us and described by readers. Do tell us what
you think of them: feedback@goodguides.com

ARDLEIGH   TM0429

★Wooden Fender (01206) 230466
A137 towards Colchester; CO7 7PA
Pleasantly extended and furnished old pub
with friendly attentive service, beams and log
fires, good freshly made food from sharing
plates through grills to daily specials, Greene
King and guests, decent wines; children
welcome in large dining area, dogs in bar,
good-sized garden with play area, open all
day Fri, Sat, till 9pm Sun. *(Simon Day)*

AYTHORPE RODING   TL5915

★Axe & Compasses (01279) 876648
B184 S of Dunmow; CM6 1PP
Attractive weatherboarded roadside pub,

neatly kept and cosy, with beams, stripped
brickwork and rugs on pale boards,
leatherette settles, stools and dark country
chairs around a few pub tables, original
part (on the left) has a two-way fireplace
marking off a snug raftered dining area,
good quality popular food including deals,
Adnams, Sharps and a guest on handpump
or tapped from the cask, Weston's ciders
and 13 wines by the glass, well trained
happy staff; background music, board
games; small back garden with stylish
modern furniture, views across fields
to windmill, open all day from 9am for
breakfast. *(Evelyn and Derek Walter, Tina
and David Woods-Taylor, Ray White)*

BELCHAMP ST PAUL   TL7942
Half Moon (01787) 277402
Cole Green; CO10 7DP Quaint 16th-c
thatched pub overlooking green, popular
reasonably priced home-made food (not
Sun evening, Mon), well kept Greene King
IPA and guests, decent wines by the glass,
friendly helpful staff, snug beamed interior
with log fire, restaurant; Aug beer/music
festival; children welcome, no dogs inside,
tables out in front and in back garden, open
all day weekends. *(Julie Braeburn)*

BIRCHANGER   TL5122
★Three Willows (01279) 815913
*Under a mile from M11 junction 8:
A120 towards Bishop's Stortford, then
almost immediately right to Birchanger
Village; don't be waylaid earlier by the
Birchanger Services signpost; CM23 5QR*
Welcoming dining pub feeling nicely tucked
away; spacious carpeted bar with lots of
cricketing memorabilia, well furnished
smaller lounge bar, Greene King ales and
good range of popular fairly traditional
food including plenty of fresh fish, efficient
friendly service; children welcome, dogs
allowed in bar area, picnic-sets out in front
and on lawn behind (some motorway and
Stansted Airport noise), good play area,
closed Sun evening. *(John Preddy)*

BISHOPS GREEN   TL6317
Spotted Dog (01245) 231598
High Easter Road; CM6 1NF Pretty
18th-c thatched pub-restaurant in quiet rural
hamlet; good well presented food cooked
by landlord-chef including cheaper set
menu choices (not Fri, Sat evenings or Sun
lunchtime), friendly attentive staff, Greene
King IPA and a guest beer, contemporary
beamed interior with high-backed leather
chairs at well spaced tables; background
music; children welcome, rattan-style
furniture outside behind picket fence, closed
Sun evening. *(Pauline Beardsell)*

BLACKMORE END   TL7430
Bull (01371) 851740
*Off A131 via Bocking Church Street and
Beazley End; towards Wethersfield;
CM7 4DD* Tucked-away village dining pub
dating from the 15th c, cleanly restored
opened-up interior with beams, stone or
wood floors and back-to-back woodburners in
central brick fireplace, enjoyable food from
bar snacks and pub favourites up, Adnams
and a couple of guests, decent wines, friendly
helpful staff; children welcome, no dogs
inside, tables in side garden, closed Mon,
otherwise open all day (till midnight Fri, Sat).
(J B and M E Benson)

BOREHAM   TL7409
Lion (01245) 394900
Main Road; CM3 3JA Stylish bistro-bar
with rooms, popular affordably priced food

(order at bar) from snacks to daily specials,
several wines by the glass, bottled beers and
up to six well kept changing ales, efficient
friendly staff, conservatory; monthly comedy
club; children welcome, no dogs inside, open
all day. *(Sandra and Nigel Brown)*

BULMER TYE   TL8438
★Bulmer Fox (01787) 312277
A131 S of Sudbury; CO10 7EB Popular
pub-bistro with good fairly priced food from
varied menu, neatly laid tables with forms
to write your order (can also order at the
bar), Adnams and Greene King IPA, friendly
well trained staff, bare boards with one or
two 'rugs' painted on them, pastel colours
and lively acoustics, quieter side room and
intimate central snug, home-made chutneys,
preserves etc for sale; children welcome,
sheltered back terrace with arbour.
(Mrs Carolyn Dixon)

BURNHAM-ON-CROUCH   TQ9495
★White Harte (01621) 782106
The Quay; CM0 8AS Cosy old-fashioned
17th-c hotel on water's edge overlooking
yacht-filled River Crouch; partly carpeted
bars with down-to-earth charm, assorted
nautical bric-a-brac and hardware, other
traditionally furnished high-ceilinged
rooms with sea pictures on brown panelled
or stripped brick walls, cushioned seats
around oak tables, enormous winter log
fire, enjoyable food including daily specials,
Adnams and Crouch Vale, friendly efficient
service; children and dogs welcome, outside
seating jettied over the water, 19 bedrooms
(eight with river view), good breakfast, open
all day. *(Ian Phillips)*

CASTLE HEDINGHAM   TL7835
Bell (01787) 460350
St James Street B1058; CO9 3EJ Beamed
and timbered three-bar pub dating from the
15th c, unpretentious and unspoilt (well run
by same family for over 45 years), Adnams,
Mighty Oak and guests served from the cask
(July and Nov beer festivals), popular pubby
food and turkish specials; background and
Fri live music (lunchtime jazz last Sun of
month); dogs welcome, children away from
public bar, garden with hops and covered
area, handy for Hedingham Castle, open all
day Fri-Sun. *(Jeremy King)*

CHAPPEL   TL8928
Swan (01787) 222353
*Wakes Colne; off A1124 Colchester–
Halstead; CO6 2DD* Ancient oak-beamed
dining pub with enjoyable food including
stone-baked pizzas and good value set menu
(Mon-Thurs), well kept Adnams and local
ales, friendly attentive service, modernised
interior with soft lighting and inglenook log
fire; monthly live music; cobbled courtyard,
view of Victorian viaduct from spreading
garden by River Colne, open all day Fri-Sun.
(Ruth May)

CHELMSFORD   TL7006
Golden Fleece (01245) 256752
Dukes Street; CM1 1JP Popular recently
refurbished corner pub, good choice of beers
including local ales (tasting trays available),
enjoyable reasonably priced pub food from
doorstep sandwiches and sharing plates up,
friendly staff; live music, DJ and quiz nights,
sports TV; children welcome, covered outside
seating area, open all day (till 2am Fri, Sat).
(Andrew Bosi)

CHELMSFORD   TL7006
Orange Tree (01245) 262664
Lower Anchor Street; CM2 0AS
Bargain lunchtime bar food (also curry
night Thurs) in spacious no-frills local, well
kept Dark Star, Mighty Oak, Plain, Skinners
and four guests (some tapped from the
cask); Tues charity quiz; dogs welcome in
public bar, back terrace, handy for county
cricket ground, open all day, no food Sun
evening. *(Tony Hobden)*

CHELMSFORD   TL7006
Queens Head (01245) 265181
Lower Anchor Street; CM2 0AS Lively
well run Victorian corner local with very
well kept Crouch Vale beers and interesting
guests, summer farm cider and good value
wines, friendly staff, bargain home-made
food weekday lunchtimes from baguettes up,
bare boards and winter log fires; Weds quiz,
Feb meeting of the Essex Beardsman; dogs
welcome, picnic-sets in colourful courtyard,
handy for county cricket ground, open all
day. *(Andrew Bosi)*

CHIGWELL ROW   TQ4693
Two Brewers (020) 8501 1313
Lambourne Road; IG7 6ET Spacious
Home Counties pub with relaxed atmosphere,
all manner of tables and chairs and wall
banquettes on flagstones or bare boards,
heavy draped curtains, lots of pictures,
photos and gilt-edged mirrors, two-way
fireplace, good choice of real ales and wines
by the glass, enjoyable food from varied
menu, cheerful young staff; children and dogs
welcome, nice three-mile circular walk from
the pub, open (and food) all day. *(Max Simons)*

CLAVERING   TL4832
★Cricketers (01799) 550442
B1038 Newport–Buntingford; CB11 4QT
Busy dining pub with plenty of old-fashioned
charm, inventive food and signed cookbooks
by Jamie Oliver (his parents own it); main
area with very low beams and big open
fireplace, bays of deep purple button-backed

banquettes and padded leather dining chairs
on dark floorboards, split-level back part
with carpeted dining areas and some big
copper and brass pans on dark beams and
timbers, three Adnams beers and 19 wines
by the glass; background music, free wi-fi;
children welcome, attractive front terrace
with wicker-look seats around teak tables,
bedrooms, handy for Stansted Airport, open
all day from 7am, food all day Sun. *(Mrs
Margo Finlay, Jörg Kasprowski, Ray White)*

COGGESHALL   TL8224
★Compasses (01376) 561322
*Pattiswick, signed off A120 W;
CM77 8BG* More country restaurant than
pub with enjoyable well presented food
using local produce from light lunches up,
also weekday set deals and children's meals,
Adnams, Woodfordes and maybe local Bishop
Nicks, good wine choice, cheerful attentive
young staff, neatly comfortable spacious
beamed bars, barn restaurant; some live
music; plenty of lawn and orchard tables,
rolling farmland beyond, open all day.
(Charlie Parker)

COLCHESTER
Fat Cat (01206) 577990
Butt Road; CO3 3BZ Small corner pub
(sister to the Ipswich and Norwich Fat Cats)
with eight well kept ales including their own
and wide range of other beers all marked-up
on blackboard, enjoyable inexpensive food
(not Mon-Weds), friendly helpful staff; beer
festivals, Sun quiz, sports TV; dogs welcome,
open all day. *(Max Simons)*

COLNE ENGAINE   TL8530
Five Bells (01787) 224166
*Signed off A1124 (was A604) in Earls
Colne; Mill Lane; CO6 2HY* Welcoming
village pub with list of landlords back to
1579, enjoyable home-made food using
local produce, own-baked bread, six well
kept changing ales including Adnams (Nov
festival), friendly service, bare boards
or carpeted floors, woodburners, old
photographs, high-raftered dining area
(former slaughterhouse), public bar with
pool and sports TV; some live music, free
wi-fi; children, walkers and dogs welcome,
disabled facilities, attractive front terrace
with gentle Colne Valley views, open (and
food) all day. *(Mrs Margo Finlay, Jörg
Kasprowski)*

COOPERSALE STREET   TL4701
★Theydon Oak (01992) 572618
*Off B172 E of Theydon Bois; or follow
Hobbs Cross Open Farm brown sign off*

Please tell us if the décor, atmosphere, food or drink at a pub is different
from our description. We rely on readers' reports to keep us up to date:
feedback@goodguides.com, or (no stamp needed) The Good Pub Guide,
FREEPOST RTJR-ZCYZ-RJZT, Perrymans Lane, Etchingham TN19 7DN.

B1393 at N end of Epping; CM16 7QJ
Attractive old weatherboarded dining
pub, very popular for its good food (all day
Sat, Sun till 5pm) from pubby choices up
including Mon-Weds evening deal, a house
beer from Dominion and five changing
guests, friendly prompt service (they ask to
keep a credit card if you're eating), beams
and masses of brass, copper and old brewery
mirrors, two woodburners, restaurant;
background music; children welcome, no
dogs inside, tables on side terrace and in
fenced garden with small stream, lots of
hanging baskets, separate play area, open
all day. *(Brian Glozier)*

COPTHALL GREEN   TL4200
Good Intent (01992) 712066
*Upshire Road, E of Waltham Abbey;
EN9 3SZ* Welcoming traditional family-run
pub on edge of Epping Forest (just north
of M25); enjoyable food including daily
specials in bar or upstairs restaurant, well
kept McMullens, friendly accommodating
service; Weds live music, Thurs quiz;
children and dogs welcome, some picnic-sets
outside. *(Jeremy Snaithe)*

DANBURY   TL7705
Griffin (01245) 699024
A414, top of Danbury Hill; CM3 4DH
Renovated 16th-c pub with well divided
interior, beams and some carved woodwork,
mix of new and old furniture on wood, stone
or carpeted floors, log fires, enjoyable food
from pub standards, deli boards and pizzas
up, changing real ales and nice choice
of wines by the glass, friendly service;
background and occasional live music;
children welcome, terrace seating, views,
open all day (till 9pm Sun). *(Max Simons)*

DEDHAM   TM0533
★Sun (01206) 323351
High Street (B2109); CO7 6DF Stylish
Tudor coaching inn opposite church; popular
food with some italian influences (should
book at peak times), impressive wine
selection with many by the glass/carafe, well
kept Adnams, Crouch Vale and two guests,
Aspall's cider, afternoon teas, pleasant
young staff, historic panelled interior with
high carved beams, handsome furnishings
and splendid fireplaces, split-level dining
room; background music, TV; children and
dogs (in bar) welcome, picnic-sets on quiet
back lawn with mature trees and view of
church, characterful panelled bedrooms,
good Flatford Mill walk, open all day.
(Hugh Roberts)

DUNMOW   TL6222
★Angel & Harp (01371) 859259
*Church Road, Church End; B1057
signposted to Finchingfield/The
Bardfields, off B184 N of town; CM6 2AD*
Usefully open all day, this comfortable old
place has linked rooms rambling around

through standing timbers and doorways,
mix of seating including armchairs, sofas
and banquettes, stools line each side of the
free-standing zinc 'counter' serving Adnams,
Nethergate, a guest beer and eight wines
by the glass, good range of popular food
(booking advised), friendly obliging service,
substantial brick fireplace and some fine old
floor tiles in low-ceilinged main area, steps
up to interesting raftered room with one huge
table, also attractive extension with glass
wall overlooking flagstoned courtyard and
grassed area beyond; background music, free
wi-fi; children and dogs (in bar) welcome,
open from 9am (10am Sun). *(Tina and David
Woods-Taylor, Ruth May, Ian Herdman)*

DUNMOW   TL6221
Black Horse (01279) 876298
Chelmsford Road; CM6 3LT Recently
renovated and extended roadside village
pub, beamed interior with one or two
quirky touches, well liked reasonably priced
home-cooked food (not Sun evening), a
couple of ales such as Sharps Doom Bar and
Woodfordes Wherry, friendly accommodating
staff; children and small dogs welcome,
beach-theme garden, open all day Fri-Sun,
closed Mon. *(Charlie Parker)*

DUTON HILL   TL6026
Three Horseshoes (01371) 870681
*Off B184 Dunmow–Thaxted, 3 miles N
of Dunmow; CM6 2DX* Friendly
traditional village local, well kept Mighty
Oak and a couple of guests (late May Bank
Holiday beer festival), central fire, aged
armchairs by fireplace in homely left-hand
parlour, lots of interesting memorabilia,
darts and pool in small public bar, no food;
dogs welcome, old enamel signs out at front,
garden with pond and nice views, closed
lunchtimes Mon-Thurs. *(Max Simons)*

EDNEY COMMON   TL6504
Green Man (01245) 248076
Highwood Road; CM1 3QE Comfortable
country pub-restaurant, good well presented
food from interesting changing menu cooked
by chef-owners, extensive wine list (several
by the glass), a couple of real ales, friendly
attentive staff, carpeted interior with black
beams and timbers; children welcome,
tables out at front and in garden, closed Sun
evening, Mon. *(Phil and Jane Hodson)*

EPPING FOREST   TL4501
Forest Gate (01992) 572312
Bell Common; CM16 4DZ Friendly open-
plan pub dating from the 17th c and run by
the same family for over 50 years; beams,
flagstones and panelling, big woodburner,
well kept Adnams and guests from brick-
faced bar, some basic inexpensive food;
dogs welcome, tables on front lawn popular
with walkers, bedrooms and adjacent rather
upmarket restaurant. *(Max Simons)*

FINCHINGFIELD   TL6832
Fox   (01371) 810151
The Green; CM7 4JX Pargeted 16th-c
building with spacious beamed bar, exposed
brickwork and central fireplace, patterned
carpet, floor tiles by counter serving Adnams
Southwold and guests, good choice of wines
by the glass, popular freshly made food (not
Sun evening) from sandwiches and pub
favourites up, afternoon teas; background
and some live music; children and dogs
welcome, picnic-sets in front overlooking
village duck pond, open all day. *(David
Twitchett)*

FINGRINGHOE   TM0220
Whalebone   (01206) 729307
*Off A134 just S of Colchester centre,
or B1025; CO5 7BG* Old pub geared
for dining, airy country-chic rooms with
cream-painted tables on oak floors, fresh
flowers and log fire, good local food from
interestingly varied menu, nice sandwiches
too, well kept beers such as Adnams, friendly
helpful staff, barn function room; background
music; children and dogs welcome, charming
back garden with peaceful valley view, front
terrace, handy for Fingringhoe Wick nature
reserve, open all day Sat, till 6pm Sun.
(Mrs Margo Finlay, Jörg Kasprowski)

GESTINGTHORPE   TL8138
★ Pheasant   (01787) 461196
Off B1058; CO9 3AU Civilised country
pub with old-fashioned character in small
opened-up beamed rooms, settles and
mix of other furniture on bare boards,
books and china platters on shelves,
woodburners in nice brick fireplaces,
Adnams Southwold, a house beer from
Woodfordes and an occasional guest, nine
wines by the glass, good food using local
and some home-grown produce; children
and dogs (in bar) welcome, seats outside
under parasols with views over fields, five
stylish bedrooms, closed Mon lunchtime,
otherwise open all day (but they do take
days off Jan-May – best to phone or check
website). *(Walter and Susan Rinaldi-Butcher)*

GREAT CHESTERFORD   TL5142
Crown & Thistle   (01799) 530278
*1.5 miles from M11 junction 9A;
pub signposted off B184, in High
Street; CB10 1PL* Substantial building
refurbished and under new management;
decorative plasterwork inside and out,
particularly around the early 16th-c
inglenook, low-ceilinged area by bar
serving ales such as Adnams, Fullers and
Sharps, fairly priced pubby food including
burgers and stone-baked pizzas, long
handsomely proportioned dining room;
children and dogs (in bar) welcome,
suntrap back courtyard, closed, Sun
evening, Mon. *(Sandra and Nigel Brown)*

GREAT EASTON   TL6126
Green Man   (01371) 852285
*Mill End Green; pub signed 2 miles N
of Dunmow, off B184 towards Lindsell;
CM6 2DN* Popular well looked-after country
dining pub down long winding lane; linked
beamed rooms including log-fire bar, good
food (best to book weekends) from pub
favourites and tapas up, real ales, decent
wines by the glass and cocktails, friendly
helpful service; children welcome, dogs in
bar, good-sized garden with terrace, open all
day Sat, closed Sun evening, Mon. *(Mrs Margo
Finlay, Jörg Kasprowski)*

GREAT HENNY   TL8738
Henny Swan   (01787) 267953
Henny Street; CO10 7LS Welcoming
dining pub in great location on River Stour;
redecoration by present licensees with bar,
lounge and restaurant, open fires, well kept
Adnams, Woodfordes and a couple of guests,
proper cider and plenty of wines by the glass,
good food from separate bar and restaurant
menus, friendly efficient service; background
music; children welcome, terrace and
waterside garden, summer boat trips, open
(and food) all day. *(Dr Peter Crawshaw)*

HASTINGWOOD   TL4807
★ Rainbow & Dove   (01279) 415419
*0.5 miles from M11 junction 7;
CM17 9JX* Pleasantly traditional low-
beamed pub with three small rooms,
built-in cushioned wall seats and mate's
chairs around pubby tables, stripped stone
and cream or green paintwork, golfing
memorabilia, woodburner in original
fireplace, three or four changing ales, good
choice of wines by the glass and enjoyable
fairly priced food, friendly licensees and staff;
background music, darts; children and dogs
welcome, tables out under parasols, country
views, open all day Sat, closed Sun and Mon
evenings. *(Ruth May)*

HATFIELD HEATH   TL5115
Thatchers   (01279) 730270
Stortford Road (A1005); CM22 7DU
Thatched and weatherboarded 16th-c dining
pub at end of large green, good popular food
(best to book weekends) from varied menu,
well kept Greene King IPA, St Austell Tribute
and two guests from long counter, several
wines by the glass, good friendly service,
woodburners, beams, some copper and brass
and old local photographs; background
music; children in back dining area, no dogs
inside, tables out in front behind picket
fence, open all day weekends (food till
7pm Sun). *(Charlie Parker)*

HENHAM   TL5428
Cock   (01279) 850347
Church End; CM22 6AN Welcoming
old timbered place striking good balance
between community local and dining pub,

nice choice of well priced home-made food (not Sun evening), Greene King IPA, a beer from Saffron (brewed in the village) and Sharps Doom Bar, open good open fires, restaurant with leather-backed chairs on wood floor, sports TV in snug; children welcome, dogs in bar, seats out at front and in tree-shaded garden behind, open all day Fri-Sun. (Max Simons)

HERONGATE   TQ6491
★**Olde Dog** (01277) 810337
Billericay Road, off A128 Brentwood–Grays at big sign for Boars Head; CM13 3SD Welcoming weatherboarded country pub dating from the 16th c, long attractive dark-beamed bar and separate dining areas, exposed brickwork and open fires, uneven wood floors and open fires, well kept ales tapped from the cask including a house beer from Crouch Vale, popular food from sandwiches up (all day Sat, till 7pm Sun), friendly staff; dogs welcome in one area, pleasant front terrace and big garden, open all day. (Mrs Margo Finlay, Jörg Kasprowski, Paul Rampton, Julie Harding)

HOWLETT END   TL5834
White Hart (01799) 599030
Thaxted Road (B184 SE of Saffron Walden); CB10 2UZ Comfortable pub-restaurant with two smartly set modern dining rooms either side of small tiled-floor bar, good food from sandwiches and light dishes up, Nethergate Growler and nice choice of wines, friendly helpful service; children welcome, terrace and big garden, quiet spot, closed Sun evening, Mon. (Jeremy Snaithe)

LANGHAM   TM0232
Shepherd (01206) 272711
Moor Road/High Street; CO4 5NR Refurbished 1920s village pub, L-shaped bar with areas off, wood floors and painted half-panelling, large OS map covering one wall, comfortable sofas, woodburner, two Adnams beers and a guest, plenty of wines by the glass and good selection of other drinks, enjoyable food (not Sun, Mon evenings) from sharing plates up, efficient friendly service; quiz first Tues of month, occasional live music; children and dogs (in bar) welcome, side garden, open all day Fri, Sat, till 8pm Sun. (Max Simons)

LEIGH-ON-SEA   TQ8385
★**Crooked Billet** (01702) 480289
High Street; SS9 2EP Homely old pub with waterfront views from big bay windows, packed on busy summer days when service can be frantic but friendly, well kept Adnams, Nicholsons, Sharps and changing guests including seasonals, enjoyable standard Nicholsons menu, log fires, beams, panelled dado and bare boards, local fishing pictures and bric-a-brac; background music; children allowed if eating but no under-21s after 6pm,

side garden and terrace, seawall seating over road shared with Osborne's good shellfish stall (plastic glasses for outside), pay-and-display parking by flyover, open all day. (Jeff Stevens)

LITTLE BROMLEY   TM1028
Haywain (01206) 390004
Bentley Road; CO11 2PL Welcoming family-run 18th-c pub popular with locals and visitors, carpeted interior with various cosy areas leading off from main bar, beams, exposed brickwork and open fires, well kept Adnams Southwold and three regional guests, generous helpings of enjoyable home-made food (booking recommended evenings/weekends) including vegetarian choices, good friendly service; closed Sun evening, all day Mon, Tues lunchtime. (Max Simons)

LITTLE WALTHAM   TL7013
★**White Hart** (01245) 360205
The Street; CM3 3NY Handsome village pub with contemporary open-plan rooms; wood, slate and tartan-carpeted floors, seating from woven cane chairs (topped with a fur) through wall banquettes and cushioned window seats to upholstered armchairs, fireplaces (some piled high with logs), metal deer heads, antler chandeliers and candles in tall glass lanterns, Adnams, Nethergate and guests, Weston's cider and good wines by the glass, popular reasonably priced food including deals, efficient friendly service; free wi-fi; children and dogs (in bar) welcome, garden with cheerfully coloured metal chairs and parasols along with rattan-style seating and picnic-sets, open (and food) all day from 9am. (Tina and David Woods-Taylor, Lindy Andrews, Mrs Margo Finlay, Jörg Kasprowski)

LOUGHTON   TQ4296
Victoria (020) 8508 1779
Smarts Lane; IG10 4BP Welcoming flower-decked Victorian local with good helpings of enjoyable home-made food, five real ales including Sharps Doom Bar and Timothy Taylors Landlord, decent range of whiskies, chatty panelled bare-boards bar with small raised end dining area; children and dogs welcome, pleasant neatly kept front garden, Epping Forest walks, open all day weekends. (Jeff Stevens)

MATCHING GREEN   TL5310
Chequers (01279) 731276
Off Downhall Road; CM17 0PZ Red-brick Victorian pub-restaurant in picturesque village, not particularly cheap but very enjoyable traditional and mediterranean-style food from good lunchtime ciabattas up, also fixed-price weekday lunch, vegetarian menu and children's choices, friendly helpful staff dressed in black, nice wines from comprehensive list, cocktails and three well kept ales including Greene King and Woodfordes; background music and

occasional cabaret/tribute nights; disabled facilities, quiet spot overlooking large green, good local walks, open all day Fri-Sun, closed Mon. *(Roger and Pauline Pearce)*

MATCHING TYE   TL5111
Fox (01279) 731335
The Green; CM17 0QS Long 18th-c village pub opposite tiny green, decent range of popular well priced food including good Sun roast, Greene King IPA, Shepherd Neame Spitfire and a guest; welcoming service, various areas including beamed restaurant and raftered barn room, comfortable dark wood furniture, brasses, woodburners; live music and quiz nights, TV; children welcome, 12 bedrooms. *(Mrs Margo Finlay, Jörg Kasprowski)*

MESSING   TL8919
Old Crown (01621) 815575
Signed off B1022 and B1023; Lodge Road; CO5 9TU Attractive late 17th-c village pub near fine church; good interesting food (not Sun evening) from light lunches up, well kept Adnams, cheerful helpful staff; shop/deli behind, open all day. *(David Twitchett)*

MILL GREEN   TL6401
★**Viper** (01277) 352010
The Common; from Fryerning (which is signposted off N-bound A12 Ingatestone bypass) follow Writtle signposts; CM4 0PT Delightfully unpretentious country local; cosy unchanging rooms with spindleback and country kitchen chairs around neat little tables, tapestried wall seats and log fire, the fairly basic tap room is even more simple with parquet floor and coal fire, beyond is another room with sensibly placed darts; two beers named for the pub plus Animal Big Bang, Canterbury Brewers Nitro Engenius and Mighty Oak Oscar Wilde, Weston's cider/perry, straightforward lunchtime food; Easter and Aug beer festivals; children (at one end of bar) and dogs welcome, pretty cottagey garden (mass of summer colour) and lots of hanging baskets and window boxes, some seats on lawn, open all day weekends (busy with walkers and cyclists then). *(David Twitchett, Maddie Purvis)*

MISTLEY   TM1131
★**Thorn** (01206) 392821
High Street (B1352 E of Manningtree); CO11 1HE Popular for American chef-landlady's good food (especially seafood), but there's also a friendly welcome if you just want a drink or coffee; high black beams give a clue to the building's age (Matthew Hopkins, the notorious 17th-c witchfinder general, based himself here), décor, though, is crisply up to date – bentwood chairs and mixed dining tables on terracotta tiles around central bar, cream walls above blue dado, colourful modern artwork, end brick

fireplace with woodburner; newspapers and magazines, cookery classes; front pavement tables looking across to Robert Adam's swan fountain, interesting waterside village, 11 comfortable bedrooms, open all day. *(Ray White)*

MOUNT BURES   TL9031
★**Thatchers Arms** (01787) 227460
Off B1508; CO8 5AT Well run modernised pub with good local food cooked to order, set lunch deal Tues-Fri, three or four well kept ales including Adnams Southwold and Crouch Vale Brewers Gold, cheerful efficient staff; background music, film nights; children and dogs welcome, plenty of picnic-sets out behind, peaceful Stour Valley views, closed Sun evening, Mon, otherwise open all day. *(Charlie Parker)*

NEWPORT   TL5234
Coach & Horses (01799) 540292
Cambridge Road (B1383); CB11 3TR Welcoming beamed village pub with good freshly made food including specials, friendly prompt service, well kept Adnams, Timothy Taylors, Woodfordes and a guest; background music, free wi-fi; children welcome, garden with play boat, open all day Fri, Sat, till 6pm Sun. *(Ruth May)*

NORTH SHOEBURY   TQ9286
Angel (01702) 589600
Parsons Corner; SS3 8UD Conversion of timbered and partly thatched former post office/blacksmiths beside busy roundabout; Greene King, Woodfordes and a couple of guests, popular food including daily specials, small quarry-tiled entrance bar flanked by tartan-carpeted dining rooms, step up to back bar with wood floor and some old local pictures, woodburner; background music, free wi-fi; children and dogs allowed in certain areas, disabled facilities, seats out at front, open all day weekends. *(Jeff Stevens)*

PAGLESHAM   TQ9492
Plough & Sail (01702) 258242
East End; SS4 2EQ Relaxed 17th-c weatherboarded dining pub in pretty spot, popular fairly traditional food at affordable prices, friendly service, well kept changing ales, local cider and decent house wines, low black beams and big log fires, pine tables, lots of brasses and pictures, traditional games; background music; children welcome, front picnic-sets and attractive side garden, open all day Sun. *(Mrs Margo Finlay, Jörg Kasprowski)*

PAGLESHAM   TQ9293
★**Punchbowl** (01702) 258376
Church End; SS4 2DP Weatherboarded 16th-c former sailmaker's loft with low beams and stripped brickwork, pews, barrel chairs and lots of brass, local pictures, lower room laid for dining, Adnams Southwold, Sharps

Doom Bar and a couple of guests, popular fairly priced food including good OAP menu (Tues, Thurs), friendly attentive staff; background music; children usually welcome if eating but check first, no dogs inside, picnic-sets in front by lane, open (and food) all day Sun. (George Atkinson)

PELDON TL9916

Plough (01206) 735808

Lower Road; CO5 7QR Welcoming little weatherboarded village pub continuing well under son of previous licensees (some refurbishment and bar and restaurant areas swapped over), good choice of well liked generous food, Greene King London Glory, Sharps Doom Bar and decent wines by the glass, friendly efficient service, beams and woodburners, cosy restaurant; children and dogs welcome (their friendly victorian bulldog is Ponto), picnic-sets in back garden, open all day Sun, closed Mon lunchtime. (Sandra and Nigel Brown)

PELDON TM0015

Rose (01206) 735248

B1025 Colchester–Mersea (do not turn left to Peldon village); CO5 7QJ Friendly old inn with dark bowed beams, standing timbers and little leaded-light windows, some antique mahogany and padded leather wall banquettes, arched brick fireplace, Adnams, Greene King and Woodfordes, several wines by glass and generally well liked food (not Sun evening), cosy restaurant and smart airy garden room; children welcome away from bar, plenty of seats in spacious garden with pretty pond, comfortable country-style bedrooms, open all day (till 8pm Sun). (Dave Braisted)

PENTLOW TL8146

Pinkuah Arms (01787) 280857

Pinkuah Lane; CO10 7JW Contemporary refurbishment for this beamed country pub (aka Pinkers), well liked food (not Sun evening, Mon) from pub favourites to more restauranty dishes, good value lunchtime set menu and other deals, Adnams, Greene King, Timothy Taylors and Woodfordes kept well, friendly efficient service; quiz last Tues of month; children and dogs (in bar) welcome, garden and terrace with modern furniture, open all day. (Adele Summers, Alan Black)

PURLEIGH TL8401

Bell (01621) 828348

Off B1010 E of Danbury, by church at top of hill; CM3 6QJ Cosy rambling beamed and timbered pub with fine views over the marshes and Blackwater estuary; bare boards, hops and brasses, inglenook log fire, well kept ales such as Adnams and Mighty Oak, plenty of wines by the glass

(some local), good sensibly priced home-made food including specials, friendly staff; cinema and local art exhibitions in adjoining barn; children welcome, picnic-sets on side grass, good walks (on St Peter's Way), closed Sun evening, Mon. (Jeremy Snaithe)

RICKLING GREEN TL5129

Cricketers Arms (01799) 543210

Just off B1383 N of Stansted Mountfichet; CB11 3YG Brick-built beamed dining pub under same management as the Eight Bells in Saffron Walden (see Main Entries); enjoyable food from varied competitively priced menu, a couple of changing ales and good selection of wines, cheerful helpful staff, split-level modernised interior; children and dogs (in bar) welcome, pleasant outside seating area overlooking cricket green, ten bedrooms, open all day. (Charles Gysin)

RIDGEWELL TL7340

White Horse (01440) 785532

Mill Road (A1017 Haverhill–Halstead); CO9 4SG Comfortable beamed village pub with up to four well kept changing ales (some tapped from the cask), real ciders and decent wines by the glass, good generous food including lunchtime set menu (Tues-Sat), friendly service; background music, free wi-fi; well behaved children welcome, no dogs, tables out on terrace, modern bedroom block with good disabled access, closed Mon lunchtime and Tues afternoon, otherwise open all day. (Jeff Stevens)

ROMFORD TQ5088

Mawney Arms (01708) 761162

Mawney Road; RM7 7HT Popular open-plan Ember Inn with good value food and four real ales, friendly atmosphere; Sun quiz; seats out at front and in garden behind, open (and food) all day. (Robert Lester)

SAFFRON WALDEN TL5438

Cross Keys (01799) 522207

High Street; CB10 1AX Former medieval coaching inn with interesting jettied exterior, attractively updated inside with bar, restaurant and coffee shop, enjoyable well presented food including daily specials and good value set lunch (Mon-Fri), friendly service, ales such as Sharps Doom Bar, well chosen wines; children welcome, nine bedrooms, open all day. (Dr Michael Smith)

SAFFRON WALDEN TL5438

Old English Gentleman

(01799) 523595 Gold Street; CB10 1EJ Busy 19th-c red-brick town-centre pub, bare boards, panelling and log fires, plenty of inviting nooks and crannies, well kept Adnams Southwold, Woodfordes Wherry and

Pubs close to motorway junctions are listed at the back of the book.

a couple of guests, plenty of wines by the glass and good choice of enjoyable lunchtime food from sandwiches and deli boards up, friendly staff; background music, TV; children welcome, part-covered heated terrace with modern furniture, open all day (till 1am Fri, Sat). *(Sandra and Nigel Brown)*

SOUTHEND — TQ8885
Pipe of Port (01702) 614606
Tylers Avenue, off High Street; SS1 1JN
Cellar bar (not strictly a pub) with plenty of atmosphere, sawdust and candlelight, well liked food including signature pies and good value set menu, excellent range of affordably priced wines and other drinks from craft beers to cocktails, friendly knowledgeable staff; wine tasting evenings; usually closed Sun. *(Dave Braisted)*

SOUTHMINSTER TQ9699
Station Arms (01621) 772225
Station Road; CM0 7EW Popular weatherboarded local with unpretentious L-shaped bar, bare boards and panelling, friendly chatty atmosphere, well kept Adnams Southwold and several guests (beer festivals Jan, May); live blues and folk nights; back courtyard, open from midday (all day Sat from 2pm). *(Simon Day)*

STAPLEFORD TAWNEY TL5001
★ Mole Trap (01992) 522394
Tawney Common; signed off A113 N of M25 overpass – keep on; OS Sheet 167 map reference 500013; CM16 7PU Tucked-away, yet popular, little country pub with unpretentious carpeted beamed bar (mind your head as you go in), brocaded wall seats and plain pub tables, steps down to similar area, log fires, well kept Fullers London Pride and changing guests, reasonably priced down-to-earth food (not Sun and Mon evenings), cheery swift service; no credit cards, maybe quiet background radio; children welcome away from bar, small dogs allowed at quiet times, garden with rural views. *(David Twitchett)*

STEEPLE BUMPSTEAD TL6841
Fox & Hounds (01440) 731810
Chapel Street; CB9 7DQ Welcoming 15th-c beamed village pub, popular home-made food (booking advised) from varied menu including good value Mon evening two-course deal, well kept Greene King IPA and three quickly changing guests, several wines by the glass, good friendly service, small restaurant with pine furniture, log fire; some seats out in front behind picket fence, more on little terrace behind, open all day Fri-Sun (no food Sun evening). *(Adele Summers, Alan Black)*

STISTED TL7923
Dolphin (01376) 321143
A120 E of Braintree, by village turn; CM77 8EU Old mansard-roofed roadside pub with cheerful heavily beamed and timbered bar, well liked home-cooked food including set menu choices, Greene King ales tapped from the cask, brasses, antlers and lots of small prints, log fire, bright extended eating area on left; background music; children and dogs welcome, seats out at front and in pretty back garden with covered area, views over fields, open (and food) all day. *(Ray White)*

STOCK TQ6998
Bakers Arms (01277) 840423
Common Road, just off B1007 Chelmsford–Billericay; CM4 9NF Popular open-plan beamed pub with good home-made food including some mediterranean influences, friendly attentive service, ales such as Crouch Vale, Adnams and Greene King, airy dining room with french windows to enclosed terrace, more seats out at front and in side garden; children welcome, open all day (food all day Fri-Sun). *(John and Enid)*

STOW MARIES TQ8399
★ Prince of Wales (01621) 828971
B1012 between South Woodham Ferrers and Cold Norton; CM3 6SA Cheery atmosphere in traditional weatherboarded pub with several little unspoilt low-ceilinged rooms, bare boards and log fires, conservatory dining area, half a dozen widely sourced ales, bottled/draught belgian beers including fruit ones and a couple of ciders, enjoyable food (all day Sun) with some interesting specials, home-made pizzas (winter Thurs) from Victorian baker's oven; live jazz (third Fri of month); children in family room, terrace and garden tables, summer Sun barbecues, four good bedrooms in converted stable, open all day. *(David Heath)*

TAKELEY TL5421
Green Man (01279) 879181
The Street; CM22 6QU Small well renovated village pub, ales such as Sharps and Charles Wells, nice wines by the glass and good well presented food, also coffee shop serving lovely cakes; free wi-fi; children and dogs welcome, handy for Hatfield Forest (NT) and Stansted Airport, five bedrooms, open all day. *(Ray White)*

THEYDON BOIS TQ4598
Bull (01992) 812145
Station Approach; CM16 7HR Cosy beamed pub dating from the 17th c, polished wood and carpeted floors, log fire, three well kept ales including Wells Bombardier, several wines by the glass and good home-made food from sandwiches to blackboard specials (booking advised, especially weekends), friendly staff; sports TV; children and dogs (in bar) welcome, paved beer garden, open all day, no food Sun evening. *(Roger and Pauline Pearce)*

UPSHIRE   TL4100
Horseshoes (01992) 712745
Horseshoe Hill, E of Waltham Abbey;
EN9 3SN Welcoming Victorian village pub
with small bar area and dining room, good
freshly made food from chef-landlord with
some emphasis on fish, well kept McMullens
beers, friendly helpful staff; children and
dogs (in bar) welcome, garden overlooking
Lea Valley, more tables out in front, good
walks, open all day, no evening food Sun
or Mon (snacks only Mon lunchtime).
(Max Simons)

WENDENS AMBO   TL5136
★Bell (01799) 540382
B1039 W of village; CB11 4JY Cottagey
local with cheery landlord and friendly
bustle in low-ceilinged bars, brasses on
ancient timbers, wheelback chairs at neat
tables, winter log fire, Growler, Oakham and
Woodfordes, farmhouse cider and perry, and
several wines by the glass, well liked food
(not Sun evening, Mon); free wi-fi; children
and dogs welcome, three-acre garden with
seats under parasols on paved terrace, pond
leading to River Uttle, woodland walk and
timber play area, open all day Fri-Sun, closed
Mon lunchtime. *(Sandra and Nigel Brown)*

WICKHAM ST PAUL   TL8336
★Victory (01787) 269364
SW of Sudbury; The Green; CO9 2PT
Attractive and spacious old dining pub,
varied choice of good freshly made food
(not Sun evening), OAP lunch deal Tues-Fri,
friendly efficient service, Adnams and guests
from brick-fronted bar, beams and timbers,
leather sofas and armchairs, inglenook
woodburner; background music, pool and
darts; children welcome, neat garden
overlooking village cricket green, open all
day Fri-Sun, closed Mon. *(Adele Summers,
Alan Black)*

WIDDINGTON   TL5331
★Fleur de Lys (01799) 543280
Signed off B1383 N of Stansted;
CB11 3SG Welcoming unpretentious low-
beamed and timbered village pub, enjoyable
locally sourced food (not Sun evening, Mon,
Tues evening) in bar and dining room from
sandwiches to very good (if pricey) steaks,
set lunch deal Weds, Thurs (cheaper for
over-60s), well kept Adnams, Woodfordes and
a couple of guests chosen by regulars, decent
wines, dim lighting, tiled and wood floors,
inglenook log fire; pool and other games in
back bar; children and dogs welcome, picnic-
sets in pretty garden, open all day Fri-Sun,
closed Mon lunchtime. *(Mrs Margo Finlay,
Jörg Kasprowski)*

WIVENHOE   TM0321
Black Buoy (01206) 822425
Off A133; CO7 9BS Village pub owned by
local consortium; open-plan partly timbered
bare-boards bar, well kept ales such as
Colchester, Mighty Oak and Red Fox, a craft
keg, Aspall's cider and several wines by
the glass, good sensibly priced home-made
food (not Sun evening) from lunchtime
sandwiches to daily specials, cheerful service,
open fires, upper dining area glimpsing river
over roofs; well behaved children and dogs in
certain areas, seats out on brick terrace, two
bedrooms, open all day. *(Jeff Stevens)*

Gloucestershire

KEY ★ Star Pub   🍽️ Top Quality Food   🍺 Great Beer

♀ Good Wines   £ Bargain Meals   🛏️ Good Bedrooms   🍴 Serves Food

---

 BARNSLEY   SP0705   Map 4

Village Pub 🍽️ ♀ 🛏️

(01285) 740421 – www.thevillagepub.co.uk

B4425 Cirencester–Burford; GL7 5EF

Bustling pub with first class food, a good choice of drinks and seats in the back courtyard; bedrooms

As this lovely country pub is so popular with customers of all ages, it's wise to book a table in advance. The low-ceilinged bar rooms are smart and contemporary with pale paintwork, flagstones and oak floorboards, heavy swagged curtains, plush chairs, stools and window settles around polished candlelit tables, three open fireplaces and country magazines and newspapers and – as it's at the heart of the village – a cheerful crowd of regulars. Corinium Gold, North Cotswold Best and a guest from Force on handpump, an extensive wine list with a dozen by the glass and farm cider. The sheltered back courtyard has solid wooden furniture under parasols, outdoor heaters and its own servery. The individually decorated bedrooms are extremely comfortable and breakfasts are especially good.

🍽️ Particularly good food using the best local produce includes rabbit and ham hock terrine with pickled mushrooms and chutney, smoked mackerel pâté with soft-boiled egg, smoky onion tart with stilton crumble, local pheasant with celeriac gratin, sea bream with chorizo, red pepper and chickpeas, cider-braised pork belly with apple, black pudding, crackling and mustard mash, rosemary and garlic marinated angus sirloin with béarnaise sauce, and puddings such as chocolate nemesis with fruit sorbet and apple crumble with toffee custard. *Benchmark main dish: rare-breed burger with toppings, bacon jam, pickles and chips £15.00. Two-course evening meal £21.00.*

Free house ~ Licensee Michael Mella ~ Real ale ~ Open 11-11 ~ Bar food 12-2.30, 6-9.30; 12-2, 6-10 Sat; 12-9 Sun ~ Children welcome ~ Dogs allowed in bar ~ Wi-fi ~ Bedrooms: $119/$129 *Recommended by Steve and Liz Tilley, Richard Cole, Alan and Angela Scouller, Wilburoo, Richard Tilbrook, Mrs Zara Elliott, Michael Doswell*

 BLEDINGTON   SP2422   Map 4

Kings Head 🍽️ ♀ 🍺 🛏️

(01608) 658365 – www.kingsheadinn.net

B4450 The Green; OX7 6XQ

16th-c inn with atmospheric furnishings, super wines by the glass, real ales and delicious food; smart bedrooms

Our readers always enjoy their visits to this former cider house very much. It's friendly, civilised and a thoroughly good all-rounder. The main bar is the beating heart of the place and is full of ancient beams and other atmospheric furnishings (high-backed wooden settles, gate-leg or pedestal tables) and has a warming log fire in a stone inglenook; sporting memorabilia of rugby, racing, cricket and hunting. To the left, a drinking area has built-in wall benches, stools and dining chairs around wooden tables, rugs on bare boards and a woodburning stove. Hook Norton Best and guests from breweries such as Butcombe, Flying Monk, Hook Norton and Purity on handpump, a super wine list with ten by the glass, 20 malt whiskies and an extensive gin collection; background music, board games and cards. There are seats out in front and rattan-style armchairs around tables in the lovely back courtyard garden with a pagoda; maybe free-ranging bantams and ducks. This is a delightful place to stay and the setting – opposite the green in a tranquil village – is very pretty. The same first class licensees also run the Swan at Swinbrook (in Oxfordshire).

 Imaginative food uses local organic and free-range produce: lunchtime open sandwiches, pigeon breast with celeriac purée, crispy bacon and jus, loin of venison carpaccio with parmesan and orange and juniper dressing, steak and kidney pudding, battered cod with pea purée and skinny chips, wild mushroom and spinach risotto with smoked cheese, breast of chicken with confit leg, hispi cabbage and vegetable broth, ling fillet with tomato and chorizo ragoût and tagliatelle, and puddings such as rhubarb cheesecake with rhubarb ripple ice-cream and spiced carrot cake with olive oil pannacotta and orange granita. *Benchmark main dish: local sirloin steak with roasted tomato chutney and skinny chips £24.00. Two-course evening meal £22.00.*

Free house ~ Licensees Nicola and Archie Orr-Ewing ~ Real ale ~ Open 11-11 ~ Bar food 12-2, 6.30-9 ~ Restaurant ~ Children welcome ~ Dogs allowed in bar ~ Wi-fi ~ Bedrooms: £80/£100 *Recommended by Bernard Stradling, Richard Tilbrook, Richard Cole, Mike and Mary Carter, Jamie and Sue May, Alun and Jennifer Evans, P and J Shapley, Stephen Funnell*

BOURTON-ON-THE-HILL
SP1732   Map 4
Horse & Groom 🏅 ⧉
(01386) 700413 – www.horseandgroom.info
A44 W of Moreton-in-Marsh; GL56 9AQ

Gloucestershire Dining Pub of the Year

Handsome Georgian inn with a fine range of drinks, excellent food, friendly staff and lovely views from seats outside; smart bedrooms

Despite the numerous accolades and awards won over the years, the two brothers running this special place have not changed any of their core values or philosophies – everyone is made to feel welcome. The pubby bar is light, airy and simply furnished with a pleasing mix of farmhouse and other wooden chairs, settles, cushioned wall and window seats and tables on bare boards, a woodburning stove in a stone fireplace, Goffs Jouster and guests such as Purity Pure UBU and Wickwar BOB on handpump, 22 wines by the glass, local Hogan's farm cider, locally brewed lagers from the Cotswold Brewing Company, home-made elderflower cordial and local gin. There are plenty of original features throughout; board games. Dining areas spread off from here – again, with a very attractive variety of dining chairs and rustic tables, rugs here and there, snug little corners, an open fire, and horse paintings and prints on pale-painted or exposed stone walls. The large back garden has lots of seats under parasols and fine countryside views. This is a special place to stay, with individually styled, well equipped bedrooms and good breakfasts. It's best to arrive early to be sure of a space in the smallish car park. Batsford Arboretum is not far away.

 Excellent food (they list their suppliers on the menu) includes chicken liver parfait with quince jelly, wild mushroom and spinach risotto balls with roasted butternut squash purée, pine nuts and parmesan, malaysian chicken curry, slow-cooked lamb shank with roasted root vegetables, smoked lardons and rosemary gravy, whole lemon sole with chimichurri sauce, rare-breed rib-eye steak with tarragon, mustard and shallot butter, and puddings such as treacle tart with jersey cream and banana, chocolate and peanut cheesecake. *Benchmark main dish: beer-battered cod with minted pea purée and tartare sauce £13.75. Two-course evening meal £20.50.*

Free house ~ Licensee Tom Greenstock ~ Real ale ~ Open 11-2.30 (3 Sat), 6-11; 12-3.30 Sun; closed Sun evening except bank holiday weekends ~ Bar food 12-2, 7-9 (9.30 Fri, Sat); 12-2.30 Sun ~ Restaurant ~ Children welcome ~ Wi-fi ~ Bedrooms: $80/$120
Recommended by Richard Tilbrook, John Jenkins, J R Wildon, Mrs J Ekins-Daukes, K H Frostick, Richard Cox

BROCKHAMPTON
SP0322   Map 4

Craven Arms 🍺

(01242) 820410 – www.thecravenarms.co.uk
Village signposted off A436 Andoversford–Naunton – look out for inn sign at head of lane in village; can also be reached from A40 Andoversford–Cheltenham via Whittington and Syreford; GL54 5XQ

Friendly village pub with a convivial landlord, tasty bar food, real ales and seats in a big garden; bedrooms

With a warm welcome and a happy, chatty atmosphere, this is all you could wish for in an attractive old country pub. The character bars have low beams, roughly coursed thick stone walls and some tiled flooring; although it's largely been opened out to give a sizeable eating area off the smaller bar servery, there's a feeling of several communicating rooms. The furniture is mainly pine, with comfortable leather sofas, wall settles and tub chairs; also, gin traps, various stuffed animal trophies and a woodburning stove. There's Otter Bitter, Butcombe Legless Bob (named for the landlord, with 20p per pint going to Diabetes UK) and Ramsbury Bitter on handpump, eight wines by the glass and a farm cider, served by attentive staff; board games. The large garden has plenty of seats and the views are lovely. Two bedrooms have been newly reopened; good surrounding walks.

As well as their interesting barbecue-style 'hot rock' meat and fish choices with all sorts of sauces and dips, the highly thought-of food includes mussels in white wine, garlic and chilli cream, baked local blue brie with fig chutney, local ham and free-range eggs, wild mushroom, sunblush tomato and feta loaf, steak in ale pie, chicken in a basket with chipotle ketchup and fries, old spot sausages with bubble and squeak and gravy, fish of the day with celeriac fondant and rocket purée, and puddings. *Benchmark main dish: slow-cooked lamb with red wine jus and dauphinoise potatoes £18.00. Two-course evening meal £19.00.*

Free house ~ Licensee Barbara Price ~ Real ale ~ Open 12-3, 6-11; 12-11 Sat; 12-5 Sun; closed Sun evening, Mon ~ Bar food 12-2 (2.30 Sat), 6.30-9; 12.30-3 Sun ~ Restaurant ~ Children welcome ~ Dogs allowed in bar ~ Wi-fi ~ Bedrooms: /$80
Recommended by Tom McLean, Richard Tilbrook, Katherine Matthews, Ian Duncan

---

People named as recommenders after the full entries have told us that the pub should be included. But they have not written the report – we have, after anonymous on-the-spot inspection.

CHELTENHAM

SO9624 Map 4

Royal Oak ♀ ◖

(01242) 522344 – www.royal-oak-prestbury.co.uk

Off B4348 just N; The Burgage, Prestbury; GL52 3DL

Cheerful pub with popular food, several real ales and wine by the glass, and seats in the sheltered garden

Particularly well run and warmly friendly, this bustling pub is a big hit with our readers – both for the good food and well kept ales. There are plenty of amiable locals and the congenial low-beamed bar has fresh flowers and polished brasses, a comfortable mix of seating including chapel chairs on parquet flooring, some interesting pictures on the ochre walls and a woodburning stove in a stone fireplace. Dark Star Hophead, Harveys Best, Timothy Taylors Landlord and Wye Valley Bitter on handpump and seven wines by the glass; efficient, helpful service; background music. Dining room tables are nicely spaced so that you don't feel crowded, and the skittle alley doubles as a function room; they hold a lot of fun events such as beer, sausage, cider and cheese festivals. There are seats and tables under canopies on the heated terrace and in a sheltered garden. Sister pub is the Gloucester Old Spot in Coombe Hill.

As well as lunchtime doorstep sandwiches, the enjoyable food includes ciabattas, pigeon breast and black pudding salad, ham hock terrine with chutney, steak burger with toppings, barbecue sauce and chips, walnut and cashew nut roast with balsamic and dijon pan gravy, chicken stuffed with smoked bacon and mushroom mousse with red wine sauce, trio of bass, salmon and tuna on samphire and spinach with chorizo and tomato sauce, venison haunch steak with venison sausage, wholegrain mustard sauce and sautéed potatoes, and puddings. *Benchmark main dish: rolled pork belly with apricot and sausage meat stuffing, bubble and squeak and rich gravy £15.00. Two-course evening meal £22.00.*

Free house ~ Licensees Simon and Kate Daws ~ Real ale ~ Open 11-11; 12-10.30 Sun ~ Bar food 12-2, 6-9; 12-8 Sun ~ Restaurant ~ Children welcome in dining room and before 8pm in bar ~ Wi-fi *Recommended by Gordon and Jenny Quick, Ian Herdman, Andy Dolan, Victor Sumner, Roger and Donna Huggins*

CHIPPING CAMPDEN

SP1539 Map 4

Eight Bells ◖

(01386) 840371 – www.eightbellsinn.co.uk

Church Street (one-way – entrance off B4035); GL55 6JG

Lovely inn with massive timbers and beams, log fires, quite a choice of bar food, real ales and seats in a large terraced garden; bedrooms

If you stay in the attractive and comfortable bedrooms here (the breakfasts are highly regarded), you could then take the Cotswold Way, which leads to Bath. The candlelit bars have heavy oak beams, massive timber supports and stripped-stone walls with cushioned pews, sofas and solid dark wood furniture on broad flagstones, and log fires in up to three restored stone fireplaces; the atmosphere throughout is cheerful and bustling. A glass panel in the dining room floor reveals the passage from the church by which Roman Catholic priests escaped the Roundheads. Hook Norton Hooky, Goffs Jouster, Purity Pure UBU and Wye Valley HPA on handpump from the fine oak bar counter, seven wines by the glass and two farm ciders; background music and board games. There's a large terraced garden with plenty of seats, and striking views of the almshouses and church.

Food is good and uses seasonal, local produce: lunchtime ciabattas (not Sun), sardines in garlic and parsley butter, chicken liver parfait with chutney, butternut squash, spinach and tomato risotto, minted lamb and potato pie, pork faggots with creamy mash and onion gravy, creamy chicken curry, bass on tagliatelle with mediterranean-style tomato and pepper sauce, and puddings such as dark chocolate and Cointreau tart and sticky toffee pudding with butterscotch sauce. *Benchmark main dish: 8oz rib-eye steak with onion rings and chips £21.50. Two-course evening meal £20.50.*

Free house ~ Licensee Neil Hargreaves ~ Real ale ~ Open 12-11 (10.30 Sun) ~ Bar food 12-2, 6.30-9; 12-2.30, 6.30-9.30 Fri, Sat; 12-9 Sun ~ Restaurant ~ Well behaved children welcome in dining room but not in bar after 7pm; must be over 6 in bedrooms ~ Dogs allowed in bar ~ Wi-fi ~ Bedrooms: £75/£115 *Recommended by Sharon and John Hancock, Richard Tilbrook, W M Lien, Guy Vowles*

CIRENCESTER
Fleece 🛏

SP0202 Map 4

(01285) 658507 ~ www.thefleececirencester.co.uk
Market Place; GL7 2NZ

Carefully renovated inn with various bars and lounges, courteous staff, enjoyable food and drink and seats on terrace; character bedrooms

There's plenty of room in the various bars, lounges and airy dining areas here and all are different in style. Wheelback and mate's chairs and high bar stools and tables around the counter, wicker tub and high-backed yellow or orange dining chairs around an assortment of wooden tables, shelves of glassware and pottery, and french windows that open on to the terrace where there are white metal tables and chairs under parasols. Throughout, there are bare floorboards, contemporary pale paintwork, plenty of prints and fresh flowers and good lighting; background music. Efficient, courteous staff serve Thwaites Wainwright and guests from Cotswold Lion and Flying Monk on handpump, several wines by the glass and good coffees and teas. The comfortable, attractive and well equipped bedrooms (some with much character) make a good base for exploring the lovely town and surrounding countryside; breakfasts are hearty.

Good, all-day food includes sandwiches, chicken liver and foie gras parfait with fig and balsamic chutney, tempura tiger prawns with sweet chilli dip, chicken caesar salad, crab linguine with spring onions and herbs, roasted mediterranean vegetable strudel with tomato and herb sauce, pork and leek sausages with creamy thyme mash and onion gravy, bass fillets on wilted spinach with lemon hollandaise, and puddings such as chocolate pannacotta with home-made honeycomb and iced mango and pineapple parfait with lime meringue. *Benchmark main dish: steak burger with toppings, smoked tomato chutney and fries £12.95. Two-course evening meal £20.00.*

Free house ~ Licensee Paul Hodgkinson ~ Real ale ~ Open 12-11 ~ Bar food 12-9.30 ~ Restaurant ~ Children welcome ~ Dogs allowed in bar and bedrooms ~ Wi-fi ~ Bedrooms: /£109 *Recommended by Lindy Andrews, Jo Garnett, Giles and Annie Francis, R T and J C Moggridge, Guy Vowles*

'Children welcome' means the pub says it lets children inside without any special restriction. If it allows them in, but to restricted areas such as an eating area or family room, we specify this. Places with separate restaurants often let children use them, and hotels usually let children into public areas such as lounges. Some pubs impose an evening time limit – let us know if you find one earlier than 9pm.

COOMBE HILL   SO8926 Map 4

Gloucester Old Spot ★ ◖

(01242) 680321 – www.thegloucesteroldspot.co.uk

Exit M5 junction 11 and use satnav GL51 9SY; access from junction 10 is restricted;
GL51 9SY

The country local comes of age – a model for today's country pubs

As this cheerful, carefully restored country pub is close to Cheltenham
Racecourse, it gets pretty packed on race days and it's best to book
a table in advance then. The quarry-tiled beamed bar has chapel chairs
and other seats around assorted tables (including one in a bow-windowed
alcove) and opens into a lighter, partly panelled area with cushioned settles
and stripped kitchen tables. Purity Mad Goose, Timothy Taylors Landlord
and Wye Valley Butty Bach on handpump, seven decent wines by the glass
and farm cider and perry – all served by young, friendly staff. Decoration is
in unobtrusive good taste, with winter log fires. A handsome separate dining
room has similar country furniture, high stripped-brick walls, dark flagstones
and candlelight. Outside, there are chunky benches and tables under parasols
on a terrace, with some oak barrel tables on brickwork and pretty flowers
in vintage buckets and baskets; heaters for cooler weather. Sister pub is the
Royal Oak in Prestbury, near Cheltenham.

Pleasing food from their new kitchen includes cobs, crispy pressed pork shoulder
with scallops, parsnip purée and salsa verde, chicken liver parfait with fig and
orange chutney, mushroom, brie and spinach wellington with creamed leeks and
tarragon, smoked haddock fishcakes with curried leeks and poached egg, duck leg confit
with red wine reduction and dauphinoise potatoes, toulouse sausages with bubble and
squeak, red onion compote and jus, and puddings; they also offer a two- and three-
course set lunch. *Benchmark main dish: pork stuffed with black pudding, pork liver
faggot and devilled sauce £15.50. Two-course evening meal £21.75.*

Free house ~ Licensees Simon Daws and Hayley Flaxman ~ Real ale ~ Open 10am-11pm
(10.30pm Sun) ~ Bar food 12-2, 6-9; 12-8 Sun ~ Restaurant ~ Children welcome ~ Dogs
allowed in bar ~ Wi-fi *Recommended by Chris and Val Ramstedt, Dr and Mrs A K Clarke,
Mike and Mary Carter, Revd Michael Vockins*

COWLEY   SO9714 Map 4

Green Dragon ▥ ⇐

(01242) 870271 – www.green-dragon-inn.co.uk

*Off A435 S of Cheltenham at Elkstone, Cockleford sign; OS Sheet 163 map reference
970142; GL53 9NW*

**17th-c inn with character bars, separate restaurant, popular food,
real ales and seats on terraces; bedrooms**

Customers come here from far and wide to enjoy the good food and
thoughtful range of drinks. It's an attractive, stone-fronted old inn and the
two beamed bars have plenty of character and a cosy, nicely old-fashioned
feel. There are big flagstones and wooden floorboards, candlelit tables and
winter log fires in two stone fireplaces, and staff are consistently friendly
and helpful. Hook Norton Old Hooky, Sharps Doom Bar and guests such as
Butcombe Bitter and Sharps Atlantic on handpump, 12 wines by the glass
and ten malt whiskies; background music. The furniture and the bar itself in
the upper Mouse Bar were made by Robert Thompson – little mice run over
the hand-carved tables, chairs and mantelpiece; there's also a small upstairs
restaurant and a separate skittle alley. Bedrooms are comfortable and well
appointed and breakfasts are generous. There are seats outside on terraces
and this is good walking country. No wheelchair access or disabled facilities.

Highly thought-of food includes lunchtime sandwiches (not Sun), crayfish cocktail, smoked duck breast with mozzarella, figs and orange dressing, rare-breed sausages with mash and gravy, spinach and ricotta tortellini with basil pesto, steak and kidney pudding, free-range chicken with field mushroom and brandy cream sauce, venison pie, swordfish loin with sweetcorn, chilli, peppers, lime and cream sauce, and puddings such as banoffi pie and crème brûlée. *Benchmark main dish: duck breast with plum and red wine sauce £17.95. Two-course evening meal £23.00.*

Buccaneer Holdings ~ Managers Simon and Nicky Haly ~ Real ale ~ Open 11-11; 12-10.30 Sun ~ Bar food 12-2.30 (3 Sat), 6-10; 12-3.30, 6-9 Sun ~ Restaurant ~ Children welcome ~ Dogs allowed in bar ~ Wi-fi ~ Bedrooms: £70/£95 *Recommended by Tom McLean, Chris and Val Ramstedt, Brian Glozier, Mrs Zara Elliott, Chris and Angela Buckell*

DIDMARTON
Kings Arms ♀ ⌂
ST8187 Map 2

(01454) 238245 – www.kingsarmsdidmarton.co.uk
A433 Tetbury road; GL9 1DT

Bustling pub with enjoyable food, a good choice of drinks and pleasant back garden; bedrooms

This 17th-c former coaching inn has had a thoughtful refurbishment recently. Several knocked-through beamed bar rooms work their way around a big central counter (where there are high chairs and stools against the counter), with grey-painted half panelling, armchairs by a log fire in a stone fireplace, settles and window seats with scatter cushions, bare boards here and flagstones and rugs there, and a mix of farmhouse chairs and benches around wooden tables of all shapes and sizes. Church candles on shelves or in lanterns, antlers, prints and fresh flowers create interest; the jack russell is called Spoof. There's also a restaurant with another open fire. Bath Gem, Flying Monk Elmers and Wychwood Hobgoblin on handpump, and good wines by the glass; darts. Plenty of seats and picnic-sets in the pleasant back garden. Bedrooms are individually furnished and comfortable and they also have self-catering cottages in a converted barn and stable block. The pub is handy for Westonbirt Arboretum.

Using prime local ingredients, the fine choice of food (specials are handwritten on a big blackboard) includes lunchtime sandwiches, ballotine of ham hock with parsley, caper and celeriac rémoulade, home-smoked duck with plum dressing and french bean and hazelnut salad, burger with chorizo, cheese and chips, monkfish with mixed bean and chorizo casserole, lamb rump with garlic and lemon potatoes and bagna cauda (a type of warm dip), and puddings such as dark chocolate brownie and passion-fruit délice with mango sorbet; they also offer a two- and three-course set lunch. *Benchmark main dish: confit rare-breed pork belly with black pudding arancini, pancetta and apple purée £13.95. Two-course evening meal £20.00.*

Free house ~ Licensee Mark Birchall ~ Real ale ~ Open 11-11; 12-10.30 Sun ~ Bar food 12-2, 6-9; 12-3, 6-8 Sun ~ Restaurant ~ Children welcome ~ Dogs allowed in bar and bedrooms ~ Wi-fi ~ Bedrooms: /£95 *Recommended by Harvey Brown, Geoffrey Sutton, Ruth May*

DURSLEY
Old Spot ◀
ST7598 Map 4

(01453) 542870 – www.oldspotinn.co.uk
Hill Road; by bus station; GL11 4JQ

Unassuming and cheery town pub with a fine range of ales, regular beer festivals and good value lunchtime food

This is one of those pubs that has a healthy local following but also attracts serious pub-goers from far and wide. The front door opens into a deep-pink small room with stools on shiny quarry tiles beside a pine-boarded bar counter, and old enamel beer signs on the walls and ceiling; there's a profusion of porcine paraphernalia. A small room leads off on the left and the little wood-floored room to the right has a stone fireplace. A step goes down to a cosy Victorian tiled snug and (to the right) a meeting room. A fine choice of drinks includes up to eight real ales, 30 malt whiskies, three farm ciders, half a dozen wines by the glass and artisan spirits. The beers on handpump include Otter Bitter and Uley Old Ric, with guests such as Otter Bright, Palmers Copper and 200, and a couple from Flying Monk; they hold two annual beer festivals. Staff are cheerful and enthusiastic. The heated and covered garden has seats (soon to be replaced by new ones). Wheelchair access. Sister pub is the Old Badger in Eastington.

🍴 Decent lunchtime-only food includes sandwiches (the soup and sandwich deal is popular), grazing boards, slow-roast pork belly with smoked pancetta and white bean cassoulet, salmon and smoked haddock fishcakes with tartare sauce, steak in ale pie, leek, red onion and pepper tart, and puddings such as chocolate brownie with dark chocolate sauce and treacle tart with chantilly cream. *Benchmark main dish: trio of sausages with onion gravy and mash £10.95.*

Free house ~ Licensee Ellie Sainty ~ Real ale ~ Open 11-11 (midnight Sat); 12-11 Sun ~ Bar food 12-3; 12-4 Sun ~ Children welcome away from bar area before 9pm ~ Dogs allowed in bar ~ Wi-fi *Recommended by Mike Swan, Martin Jones, Chris and Angela Buckell, Steve Crick*

EASTINGTON
SO7705 Map 4
Old Badger 🍺

(01453) 822892 – www.oldbadgerinn.co.uk
Alkerton Road, a mile from M5 junction 13; GL10 3AT

Friendly, traditionally furnished pub with plenty to look at, five real ales, tasty food and seats in attractive garden

The fine choice of drinks here, served by helpful and chatty staff, might include real ales from breweries such as Castle Combe, Moles, Otter, Sarah Hughes, Strands, Uley and Wye Valley on handpump, ten wines by the glass, a dozen malt whiskies and farm cider; they hold beer and cider festivals with local musicians and brewery trips. The split-level connected rooms have an informal, easy-going feel and feature two open fires and traditional furnishings such as built-in planked and cushioned wall seats, settles and farmhouse chairs around all sorts of tables, quarry tiles and floorboards. There are stone bottles, bookshelves, breweriana on red or cream walls and even a stuffed badger. The nicely landscaped garden has benches and picnic-sets on a terrace, a lawn and under a covered gazebo; the flowering tubs and window boxes are pretty. Sister pub is the Old Spot in Dursley. Wheelchair access to top bar/dining area only; disabled loos are shared with baby-changing facilities.

🍴 Well liked pubby food includes lunchtime sandwiches, tapas (patatas bravas, lamb kofta with tzatziki, harissa spiced chicken and panko squid rings), burger with toppings, coleslaw and chips, cottage pie, thai noodle broth with fresh fish, steaks with a choice of sauces, and puddings such as dark chocolate brownie with salted caramel sauce and rhubarb pannacotta. *Benchmark main dish: beer-battered fish and chips £11.95. Two-course evening meal £17.00.*

Free house ~ Licensees Ellie Sainty and Julie Gilborson ~ Real ale ~ Open 12-11 ~ Bar food 12-2.30, 6-9; 12-3 Sun ~ Children welcome away from bar area ~ Dogs welcome ~ Wi-fi ~ Live music monthly Sat *Recommended by Alison and Michael Harper, Clive and Fran Dutson, John Harris, Chris and Angela Buckell, David Houlihan*

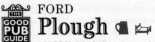

FORD

SP0829 Map 4

Plough 🍺 🛏

(01386) 584215 – www.theploughinnford.co.uk

B4077 Stow–Alderton; GL54 5RU

16th-c inn in horse-racing country with a bustling atmosphere, first class service, good food and well kept beer; bedrooms

Once our readers discover this honey-coloured stone pub they tend to come back on a regular basis. You can be sure of a genuine welcome from the helpful, friendly licensees whether you're a visitor or a regular – the inn is opposite a well known racehorse trainer's yard so many of the customers belong to the racing fraternity. The beamed and stripped-stone bar has a chatty atmosphere, racing prints and photos, old settles and benches around big tables on uneven flagstones, oak tables in a snug alcove and open fires and woodburning stoves. Darts, TV (for the races) and background music. Donnington BB and SBA on handpump, eight wines by the glass and a dozen malt whiskies. There are picnic-sets under parasols and pretty hanging baskets at the front, and a large back garden with a children's play fort. Bedrooms are comfortable and clean (the quietest ones are away from the pub) and there are views of the gallops; breakfasts are highly thought-of. It gets packed on race days. Cotswold Farm Park is nearby.

 Good, popular food using local meat and game includes baguettes, seared scallops with chorizo sausage and lemon oil, pigeon breast with garlic and lime butter, vegetarian wellington with mushroom sauce, pie of the day, gammon steak with free-range eggs or pineapple, local chicken breast with sage and onion stuffing and bread sauce, creamy fish pie, local game casserole, and puddings such as sticky toffee pudding and a seasonal crumble. *Benchmark main dish: half crispy roasted gressingham duck with orange sauce £17.95. Two-course evening meal £19.50.*

Donnington ~ Tenant Rebecca Chanin ~ Real ale ~ Open 9am-10.30pm ~ Bar food 12.15-2.15, 6-9.15; all day Fri-Sun ~ Restaurant ~ Children welcome ~ Dogs allowed in bar ~ Wi-fi ~ Bedrooms: £70/£80 *Recommended by Sara Fulton, Roger Baker, Guy Vowles, K H Frostick, Richard Tilbrook*

GLOUCESTER

SO8318 Map 4

Café René 🍺

(01452) 309340 – www.caferene.co.uk

Southgate Street; best to park in Blackfriars car park (Ladybellegate Street) and walk through passageway – pub entrance is just across road; GL1 1TP

Unusual and interestingly placed bar with fair value food all day, and good choice of drinks

Certainly not a pub – but an interesting old bar with a good range of drinks and food that's reached via a flagstoned passageway beside the partly Norman church of St Mary de Crypt. There's some stripped brick and timbering plus an internal floodlit well with water trickling down into its depths, and a very subterranean feel – black beams, dim lighting, no windows. The long bar counter is made of dozens of big casks, and they keep five changing real ales tapped from the cask, from breweries such as Arbor, Kinver, Malvern Hills, Otter, Wickwar and Wychwood, plus farm ciders and a good choice of wines by the glass (decoration consists mainly of great banks of empty wine bottles); service remains friendly and efficient even when really pushed. One antique panelled high-backed settle joins the usual pub tables and wheelback chairs on carpet, and there's a sizeable dining area on the right. Well reproduced background music, a silenced games machine and big-screen TV. There are plenty of picnic-sets under parasols out by the churchyard. They hold a popular rhythm and blues festival at the end of July.

All-day tasty food includes lunchtime sandwiches, beer-battered fish and chips, fresh pasta with a changing vegetarian sauce, a pie of the day, trio of sausages with red onion gravy and mustard mash, caribbean lamb curry, chargrilled dishes such as baby back ribs in barbecue sauce and cajun chicken, and puddings. *Benchmark main dish: steaks with a choice of potatoes and sauces £12.50. Two-course evening meal £15.00.*

Free house ~ Licensee Paul Soden ~ Real ale ~ Open 11am-midnight (later Fri, Sat) ~ Bar food 12-10 ~ Restaurant ~ Wi-fi ~ Live music Weds, Fri evenings
Recommended by Julian Richardson, Daphne and Robert Staples, Maddie Purvis

KILCOT   SO6925 Map 4
Kilcot Inn 🛏
(01989) 720707 – www.kilcotinn.com
2.3 miles from M50 junction 3; B4221 towards Newent; GL18 1NG

Attractively reworked small country inn, kind staff, enjoyable local food and drink; bedrooms

The breakfasts here get high praise from our readers and use local bacon and free-range eggs, and the bedrooms are light, airy and comfortable. The open-plan bar and dining areas have stripped beams, bare boards and dark flagstones, sunny bay-window seats, homely armchairs by one of the two warm woodburning stoves, tables with padded dining chairs and daily papers. Stools line the brick counter where the hard-working landlord and his courteous staff serve Wye Valley Butty Bach and a changing guest ale on handpump, four draught ciders and perry (with more by the bottle), 20 malt whiskies, local wine and organic fruit juice; TV and maybe background music. The front terrace has picnic-sets under cocktail parasols, with more out behind. There's a smart shed for bicycle storage.

High quality food includes lunchtime sandwiches, mussels in white wine, cream, garlic and parsley, devilled lambs kidneys with brandy cream sauce, root vegetable stew with couscous, mint and tomato, cider-battered fish of the day with chips, burger with toppings, home-made relish and skinny fries, faggots with onion gravy, red cabbage and creamed potatoes, pheasant wrapped in parma ham with smoked bacon, truffle oil and roast shallot purée, and puddings such as rhubarb crème brûlée and bread and butter pudding. *Benchmark main dish: duck breast with confit duck leg croquette and beetroot, turnip and wild garlic pesto £16.50. Two-course evening meal £20.00.*

Free house ~ Licensee Mark Lawrence ~ Real ale ~ Open 9am-11pm; reduced Sun openings Jan/Feb ~ Bar food 12-2.30, 6-9 (9.30 Thurs-Sat); 12-3 Sun ~ Restaurant ~ Children welcome ~ Dogs allowed in bar ~ Wi-fi ~ Bedrooms: £75/£85 *Recommended by Mike Swan, Emma Scofield, R T and J C Moggridge, Mike and Mary Carter, Nigel and Sue Foster, Richard Kennell*

LOWER SLAUGHTER   SP1622 Map 4
Slaughters Country Inn ♀ 🛏
(01451) 822143 – www.theslaughtersinn.co.uk
Village signposted off A429 Bourton-on-the-Water to Stow-on-the-Wold; GL54 2HS

Comfortable streamside inn with enticing food, real ales, attractive dining bar and fine grounds; bedrooms

This splendid stone inn has lovely spacious grounds with tables and chairs under parasols on terraces, and lawns that sweep down to the little River

Eye that flows slowly along the front of the building. The spreading bar
has a good mix of locals and visitors in several low-beamed linked rooms,
plus well spaced tables on polished flagstones and a variety of seats from
simple chairs to soft sofas. Log fires, medieval-motif curtains for mullioned
windows, shelves of board games, a few carefully placed landscape pictures
or stuffed fish on cream or puce walls add up to understated refinement –
and what really sets the style of the place is the thoroughly professional and
efficient service. Brakspears Bitter and Wychwood Hobgoblin on handpump,
and a dozen good wines by the glass. The smart evening restaurant looks
over a sweep of lawn and the sheep pasture beyond. The comfortable, stylish
bedrooms make a fine base for exploring the area; some are in the main
house, some across the courtyard. This is a lovely Cotswold village.

Impeccably presented food includes lunchtime club sandwiches, salt beef hash
with poached egg and cauliflower piccalilli, mustard-cured salmon with cucumber,
grapefruit and fennel, baked piperade (onions, peppers and tomatoes) with potato
gnocchi and parmesan, burger with toppings, pickle and fries, onions, pepper and
tomatoes, mussels in white wine, garlic and chilli, spiced lamb chump with baba
ganoush (smoky aubergine dip) and salsa verde, and puddings such as vanilla crème
brûlée and dark chocolate mousse with raspberry sorbet. *Benchmark main dish:
beer-battered fish and chips £14.50. Two-course evening meal £24.00.*

Free house ~ Licensee Stuart Hodges ~ Real ale ~ Open 11-11 ~ Bar food 12-3, 6.30-9;
afternoon tea 3-5.30 ~ Restaurant ~ Children welcome ~ Dogs allowed in bar and
bedrooms ~ Wi-fi ~ Bedrooms: /£190 *Recommended by R K Phillips, Nigel and Sue Foster,
George Atkinson*

NAILSWORTH
ST8699 Map 4

Weighbridge ⭐🍴 🍷

(01453) 832520 – www.weighbridgeinn.co.uk
B4014 towards Tetbury; GL6 9AL

**Bustling pub with cosy old-fashioned bar rooms, a fine choice
of drinks and food, friendly service and sheltered garden**

The famous two-in-one pies here continue to draw in customers – but the
friendly welcome and real ales play their par too. The relaxed bar has
three cosily old-fashioned rooms with open fires, stripped-stone walls and
antique settles, country chairs and window seats. The black-beamed ceiling
of the lounge bar is thickly festooned with black ironware – sheep shears,
gin traps, lamps and a large collection of keys, many from the old Longfords
Mill opposite the pub. Upstairs is a raftered hayloft with an engaging mix
of rustic tables. No noisy games machines or background music. Uley Old
Spot, Wadworths 6X and a couple of guest beers such as Bath Gem and
Great Western Maiden Voyage on handpump, 18 wines (and champagne and
prosecco) by the glass, farm cider, 12 malt whiskies and 20 gins. A sheltered
landscaped garden at the back has picnic-sets under umbrellas. Good
disabled access and facilities.

 The two-in-one pies (also available for home baking) come in a divided bowl
– one half contains the filling of your choice (perhaps steak, kidney and stout,
salmon in cream sauce, or root vegetables with beans and pulses in tomato sauce) with
a pastry topping, the other half with home-made cauliflower cheese (or broccoli mornay
or root vegetables). Also, lunchtime baguettes, prawn cocktail, creamy mushrooms
on toast, burger with toppings, coleslaw and fries, aubergine moussaka, slow-braised
lamb shank with red wine and mint sauce, and puddings such as black forest trifle and
fruit crumble. *Benchmark main dish: two-in-one pies £12.40. Two-course evening
meal £18.00.*

Free house ~ Licensee Mary Parsons ~ Real ale ~ Open 12-11 (10.30 Sun) ~ Bar food 12-9 ~
Restaurant ~ Children allowed away from the bars ~ Dogs welcome ~ Wi-fi
Recommended by Tom and Ruth Rees, Colin and Daniel Gibbs, Sandra Morgan

 ## NETHER WESTCOTE SP2220 Map 4
Feathered Nest ★
(01993) 833030 – www.thefeatherednestinn.co.uk
Off A424 Burford to Stow-on-the-Wold; OX7 6SD

**Caring service, a happy atmosphere, attractive surroundings
and exceptional food and drink; lovely bedrooms**

The food here is accomplished and beautifully presented, and for many
customers it's the main reason for their visit – but it would be a shame
to miss out on the companionable bar. This is cosy and friendly with Purity
Pure UBU and a guest beer on handpump, 22 wines by the glass from an
impressive list and some pubby dining choices too; service is exemplary.
Softly lit, this largely stripped-stone bar has real saddles as bar stools (some
of the country's best racehorse trainers live locally), a carved settle among
other carefully chosen seats, dark flagstones and low beams. This opens into
an ochre-walled high-raftered room with deeply comfortable sofas by a vast
log fire; background music and TV. Two attractively decorated dining rooms,
both on two levels, have a pleasing mix of antique tables in varying sizes, and
a lively, up-to-date atmosphere. A flagstoned terrace and heated shelter have
teak tables and wicker armchairs, and a spreading lawn bounded by floodlit
trees has groups of rustic seats, with the Evenlode Valley beyond. This is
a lovely place to stay, in individually decorated, well equipped rooms, and
breakfasts are delicious.

Championing local produce, the impressive food choices include veal with
sweetbreads, white asparagus, peas and sorrel, bass with mango, pisco, radish,
chilli and coriander, skate with cauliflower, potato terrine, capers, chicken skin and red
wine, and guinea fowl with duck liver, morel mushrooms, raviolo, wild garlic and cream
sauce; more modest bar dishes include burger with toppings and fries, beer-battered
fish and chips, a ham board with soft-boiled egg, pickles, chutneys and home-baked
bread, and puddings such as sticky toffee pudding with lemon curd, pecan nuts and
clotted cream and pear with pistachio, olive oil and rosemary ice-cream; they also offer
a two- and three-course set menu. *Benchmark main dish: ibérico pork with chorizo,
garlic mushrooms, romesco sauce and chips £30.00. Two-course evening meal £35.00.*

Free house ~ Licensee Amanda Timmer ~ Real ale ~ Open 11-11 (7.30 Sun); closed Mon
except bank holidays ~ Bar food 12-2.30, 6-9.30; 12-3.30 Sun; not Sun evening except bank
holidays ~ Restaurant ~ Children welcome ~ Dogs allowed in bar ~ Wi-fi ~ Bedrooms:
£165/£195 *Recommended by Bernard Stradling, Caroline and Oliver Sterling, Daphne and
Robert Staples*

 ## NEWLAND SO5509 Map 4
Ostrich
(01594) 833260 – www.theostrichinn.com
*Off B4228 in Coleford; or can be reached from the A466 in Redbrook, by turn-off
at the England/Wales border – keep bearing right; GL16 8NP*

**Super range of beers in welcoming country pub, with spacious bar,
open fire and good interesting food**

Parts of this friendly old inn date back to the 13th c, though much of what
you see inside is 17th-c. The low-ceilinged bar is spacious but cosily
traditional, with a chatty, relaxed atmosphere, a roaring log fire, creaky

floors, window shutters, candles in bottles on the tables, miners' lamps on uneven walls, and comfortable furnishings that include cushioned window seats, wall settles and rod-backed country kitchen chairs. The charming, warmly friendly landlady and her helpful staff keep a fine choice of real ales on handpump from breweries such as Bath, Cotswold Lion, Otter, RHC, Wye Valley and a couple of changing guests. Also, several wines by the glass and a couple of farm ciders; newspapers to read, perhaps quiet background jazz and board games. The walled garden has picnic-sets, with more out in front, and the pub is popular with walkers and their dogs. The church, known as the Cathedral of the Forest, is worth a visit.

Popular and very good, the food includes duck liver parfait and duck mousse with red onion marmalade, goose rillettes with gooseberry and elderflower jelly, smoked haddock in cream, egg and horseradish topped with dauphinoise potatoes and mozzarella, pasta with tomato and basil sauce topped with parmesan, pork ribs in tangy sauce with garlic bread, corn-fed chicken with smoked pancetta and madeira sauce and potato rösti, rack of lamb with mint and pea cream, and puddings. *Benchmark main dish: salmon and spinach fishcakes with parsley sauce £12.50. Two-course evening meal £18.00.*

Free house ~ Licensee Kathryn Horton ~ Real ale ~ Open 12-3, 6.30-11; 12-3, 6-midnight Sat; 12-4, 6.30-10.30 Sun ~ Bar food 12-2.30, 6.30 (6 Sat)-9.30 ~ Restaurant ~ Children welcome ~ Dogs allowed in bar *Recommended by Gordon and Ann Robinson, Miss B D Picton, Amaya Arias-Garcia, Roger and Donna Huggins, Millie and Peter Downing, Julian Thorpe*

NORTHLEACH
Wheatsheaf 🌟 🍷 🛏
SP1114 Map 4

(01451) 860244 – www.cotswoldswheatsheaf.com
West End; the inn is on your left as you come in following the sign off A429, just SW of the junction with A40; GL54 3EZ

Attractive stone inn with contemporary food, real ales, candles, fresh flowers and a relaxed atmosphere; stylish bedrooms

As this bustling and friendly former coaching inn is open all day, a cheerful mix of customers is always popping in and out. The airy, big-windowed linked rooms have high ceilings, antique and contemporary artwork, church candles and fresh flowers, an attractive mix of dining chairs, big leather button-back settles and stools around wooden tables, flagstones in the central bar and wooden floors laid with turkish rugs in the dining rooms; also, three open fires. Bath Gem, Hook Norton Old Hooky, Sharps Own and Wye Valley HPA on handpump, a dozen wines by the glass from a fantastic list of around 300 and local cider; background music, TV and board games. There are seats in the pretty back garden and they can arrange fishing on the River Coln. The comfortable bedrooms are individually styled and breakfasts are much enjoyed. Dogs are genuinely welcomed and they even keep a jar of pigs' ears behind the bar for them. This is a lovely little town with a fine old market square.

Highly rated food includes twice-baked cheddar soufflé, carpaccio of orange, fennel, avocado and pine nuts and mint, wild mushroom risotto with parmesan, beer-battered whiting and fries, crispy duck leg with braised red cabbage and spiced plum sauce, calves liver with tomato sauce, anchovies, capers and crispy sage, ox cheek, rib and oyster pie, and puddings such as yoghurt, honey and rose pannacotta with poached figs and blood orange and almond pudding with white custard. *Benchmark main dish: red mullet with mackerel, confit fennel and langoustines £19.00. Two-course evening meal £22.00.*

Free house ~ Licensees Sam and Georgina Pearman ~ Real ale ~ Open 12-11; 11-11 Sat; 12-10 Sun ~ Bar food 12-3, 6-10.30; 12-4, 6-10 Sun ~ Restaurant ~ Children welcome ~

Dogs welcome ~ Wi-fi ~ Bedrooms: £130/£150 *Recommended by Alan and Angela Scouller,*
Dave Braisted, Bernard Stradling, Giles and Annie Francis

OAKRIDGE LYNCH   SO9103 Map 4

Butchers Arms

(01285) 760371 – www.butchersarmsoakridge.com
Off Eastcombe–Bisley Road E of Stroud; GL6 7NZ

**Bustling country pub with nice old bars and dining room, real ales,
food cooked by the landlady and seats in a big garden**

Attractive, friendly and relaxed, the beamed bar in this well run 18th-c pub
has an open fire in a big stone fireplace with large copper pans to each
side, an attractive medley of chapel and other country chairs around tables
of various sizes on wooden floorboards, and modern art on exposed stone
walls. Stools line the central counter where they keep Wadworths 6X and IPA
and a changing guest beer on handpump and several wines by the glass. The
dining room is similarly furnished, with hunting prints and old photos on pale
walls above a grey dado, a longcase clock and stone bottles on windowsills.
The big garden with valley views has picnic-sets and other seats and tables.
They have a self-catering cottage next to the pub. This is a small village
surrounded by lovely countryside and good walks.

Pleasing country food cooked by the landlady includes smoked trout pâté, hot
spicy chicken wings with blue cheese dip, cottage pie, moules frites, chicken
caesar salad, home-cured ham and eggs, irish burger with toppings, coleslaw and fries,
scallops on chilli, coriander and garlic marinated carrot and courgette ribbons with
parsnip purée, lamb shank with minted mash, honey-glazed carrots and red wine jus,
and puddings such as warm chocolate brownie and lemon tart. *Benchmark main dish:
rib-eye steak with fries £16.95. Two-course evening meal £19.00.*

Wadworths ~ Tenants Philip and Alison McLaughlin ~ Real ale ~ Open 12-3, 6-11; 12-11 Sat,
Sun; may close earlier Sun in winter; closed Mon except bank holidays ~ Bar food 12-2, 6-9;
not Sun evening, Mon ~ Restaurant ~ Children welcome ~ Dogs allowed in bar ~ Wi-fi
Recommended by Andrew Stone, Rob Anderson, David and Stella Martin

OLDBURY-ON-SEVERN   ST6092 Map 2

Anchor ♀ ◖ £

(01454) 413331 – www.anchorinnoldbury.co.uk
Village signposted from B4061; BS35 1QA

**Friendly country pub with tasty bar food, a thoughtful range of drinks
and a pretty garden with hanging baskets**

You can walk to the River Severn and along numerous footpaths and
bridleways and then come to this bustling village pub to enjoy the fine
choice of drinks: Bass, Butcombe Bitter, Great Western Maiden Voyage and
St Austell Trelawny on handpump, a dozen wines by the glass, three farm
ciders and around 80 malt whiskies with helpful tasting notes. The neat
lounge has black beams and stonework, cushioned window seats and a range
of other wooden chairs, gate-leg tables, oil paintings of local scenes and a big
log fire. The Village Bar has old and farming photographs on the walls, and
there's a contemporary dining room towards the back of the building. The
garden is pretty in summer, with lovely hanging baskets and window boxes
and seats under parasols and trees. Wheelchair access to the dining room
and a disabled lavatory. Nearby St Arilda's church is interesting, set on an
odd little knoll.

🍴 Quite a choice of food includes sandwiches, grilled halloumi with beetroot, watercress and pomegranate salad, crayfish mayonnaise, sausages with pancetta crisp and caramelised red onion gravy, goan fish curry, chicken breast in mushroom and brandy sauce with potato rösti, duck breast with port and orange sauce and dauphinoise potatoes, local estate venison with green peppercorn sauce, and puddings such as crème brûlée and sticky toffee pudding; they also offer a two- and three-course set menu (not Sunday lunchtime). *Benchmark main dish: home-made pies £10.95. Two-course evening meal £15.95.*

Free house ~ Licensees Michael Dowdeswell and Mark Sorrell ~ Real ale ~ Open 11.30-2.30, 6-10.30; 11.30-11 Fri, Sat; 12-10 Sun ~ Bar food 12-2 (2.30 Sat), 6-9; 12-3, 6-8 Sun ~ Restaurant ~ Children in dining room only ~ Dogs allowed in bar ~ Wi-fi ~ Bedrooms: £45/£75 *Recommended by Caroline Prescott, Chris and Angela Buckell, Chris and Val Ramstedt, Amaya Arias-Garcia*

SHEEPSCOMBE   SO8910 Map 4

Butchers Arms £

(01452) 812113 – www.butchers-arms.co.uk
Village signed off B4070 NE of Stroud; or A46 N of Painswick (but narrow lanes); GL6 7RH

Country pub with open fire and woodburner, plenty to look at, several real ales and enjoyable food; fine views

Tucked away down narrow lanes, this is a busy rural pub with a welcome for all. One half of the bar has parquet flooring, the other has old quarry tiles – as well as a woodburning stove, farmhouse chairs and stools around scrubbed tables, two big bay windows with cushioned seats and low beams clad with horsebrasses; also, delft shelves lined with china, brass and copper cups, lamps and blow torches (there's even a pitchfork) and walls decorated with hunting prints and photos of the village and surrounding area. Leading off here is a high-ceilinged room with exposed-stone walls hung with maps of local walks (there are many) and wheelback and mate's chairs around tables on bare boards. The more formal restaurant is carpeted and has an open log fire. Otter Ale, Prescott Hill Climb and Wye Valley HPA on handpump, ten wines by the glass and Weston's cider; daily papers, chess, cribbage and draughts. The view over the lovely steep beechwood valley is terrific, and the seats outside make the most of it. The area was apparently once a hunting ground for Henry VIII.

🍴 As well as lunchtime sandwiches, the seasonal food includes sandwiches, free-range duck leg confit with balsamic onion-dressed leaves, breaded deep-fried whitebait with tartare sauce, sharing platters, pork, apple and sage sausages with onion gravy and grain mustard mash, a pie of the week, salmon, cod and dill fishcakes with lemon mayonnaise, specials such as mushroom, spinach, stilton and chestnut tartlet and slow-braised lamb shank with bacon and thyme jus and leek mash, and puddings such as white and dark chocolate cheesecake and banoffi pie. *Benchmark main dish: local steak burger with toppings, coleslaw and chips £10.50. Two-course evening meal £17.50.*

Free house ~ Licensees Mark and Sharon Tallents ~ Real ale ~ Open 11.30-3, 6.30-11; 11.30-11.30 Sat; 12-10.30 Sun ~ Bar food 12-2.30, 6.30-9.30; all day Sat; 12-8 (6 in winter) Sun ~ Restaurant ~ Children welcome ~ Dogs allowed in bar ~ Wi-fi
Recommended by R T and J C Moggridge, Edward May, Miles Hooper

---

The star-on-a-plate award, ⭐🍴, distinguishes pubs where the food is of exceptional quality. The knife-and-fork symbol just means the pub serves food.

STOW-ON-THE-WOLD
SP1925 Map 4
Porch House 🌟 ♀ 🛏
(01451) 870048 – www.porch-house.co.uk
Digbeth Street; GL54 1BN

Fine old character inn with carefully refurbished bars and dining areas, and imaginative food; comfortable bedrooms

It's said that part of this building was a hospice built in 947 by order of the Duke of Cornwall. A stone house was then built on the site in the 16th c, incorporating the original saxon timber structure. It's been beautifully restored, creating plenty of space for both drinking and dining, with beams (some hop-draped), big flagstones or bare floorboards, exposed stone walls and open fireplaces. The bar areas have all sorts of cushioned wooden and upholstered chairs, little stools and settles with scatter cushions around myriad tables, church candles and lanterns, books on shelves and stone bottles on windowsills and two woodburning stoves; the cosy snug is similarly furnished but has sofas and armchairs too. A beer named for the pub (from Brakspears) plus Brakspears Bitter, Oxford Gold and Special on handpump, good wines by the glass, home-brewed ginger ale and home-made lemonade all served by courteous, helpful staff. There's a dining room with upholstered, high-backed chairs (some with striking blue cushions), and also a conservatory. The atmosphere throughout is informal and gently civilised. A raised terrace has rattan chairs and cushioned wall benches around rustic tables intermingled with more contemporary seats. Bedrooms are individually designed and stylish and breakfasts particularly good. This is a lovely small town.

Rewarding food includes lunchtime sandwiches, saltimbocca pigeon with cauliflower and caper vinaigrette, beetroot-cured salmon with pickled golden beetroot, horseradish and dill, burger with toppings, special sauce and chips, braised broccoli, goats cheese, beetroot and granola, rosemary and garlic chicken with french fries, whole plaice with crab, samphire and cherry tomatoes, local lamb rump with mint, capers and goats curd, and puddings such as chocolate mousse with salted caramel ice-cream and orange and rhubarb fool. *Benchmark main dish: barbary duck breast with blackberry jus and dauphinoise potatoes £17.50. Two-course evening meal £21.00.*

Free house ~ Licensee Alex Davenport Jones ~ Real ale ~ Open 8am-11.30pm; 8am-10.30pm Sun ~ Bar food 12-3, 6.30-9.30; 12-9.30 Sat; 12-9 Sun ~ Restaurant ~ Children welcome ~ Dogs allowed in bar and bedrooms ~ Wi-fi ~ Bedrooms: /£99 *Recommended by Belinda Stamp, Nick Sharpe, Mike and Mary Carter, Maddie Purvis*

TETBURY
ST8494 Map 4
Gumstool 🌟 ♀ 🛏
(01666) 890391 – www.calcotmanor.co.uk
Part of Calcot Manor Hotel; A4135 W of town, just E of junction with A46; GL8 8YJ

Civilised bar with relaxed atmosphere, super choice of drinks and enjoyable food; bedrooms

First class food and several real ales continue to draw our readers to this well run bar-brasserie (attached to the very smart Calcot Manor Hotel). It has an easy-going atmosphere and the cleverly divided and stylish layout gives a feeling of intimacy without losing the overall sense of contented bustle: flagstones, elegant wooden dining chairs and tables, well chosen pictures and drawings on mushroom-coloured walls, and leather tub armchairs and stools. Butcombe Bitter, St Austell Tribute and Wadworths

6X on handpump, two dozen interesting wines by the glass and several malt whiskies; background music. Westonbirt Arboretum is not far away.

Prices are fair given the setting and the food is excellent – they now have a fireside grill too: twice-baked arbroath smokie and montgomery cheddar cheese soufflé, grilled scallops with brioche crumb, lemon and herb butter, local sausages with crispy shallots and red onion jam, lemon and thyme chicken breast with couscous and chilled asparagus, roasted lamb rump with sorrel mash and sun-dried tomatoes, whole lemon sole with samphire and nut brown butter sauce, and puddings such as orange posset with crispy meringue and warm treacle tart with crème fraîche. *Benchmark main dish: smoked haddock fishcakes with spinach, poached egg and lemon and herb butter £15.00. Two-course evening meal £64.00.*

Free house ~ Licensees Paul Sadler and Richard Ball ~ Real ale ~ Open 12-11 ~ Bar food 12-2 (2.30 Sat), 6-9.30; 12-4, 6-9 Sun ~ Children welcome ~ Wi-fi ~ Bedrooms: £174/£199
Recommended by Bernard Stradling, Mr and Mrs P R Thomas, Dr and Mrs A K Clarke, Andrew Vincent, Tom and Ruth Rees

TETBURY
ST8993   Map 4
Royal Oak 🏮 ♀ 🍺 🛏
(01666) 500021 – www.theroyaloaktetbury.co.uk
Cirencester Road; GL8 8EY

Golden-stone former coaching inn with a good mix of customers, character bar and upstairs dining room and seats outside; bedrooms

What stands out most to visitors here is the genuine welcome from the helpful, courteous staff and the easy-going, friendly atmosphere; they're kind to dogs too. It's a lovely 18th-c building and the careful renovations mean that original features blend easily with up-to-date touches. The open-plan rambling bar has a roaring log fire at one end, several snug areas, green leather padded built-in wall seats, stools and a variety of chairs around dark tables on wide floorboards, elbow tables dotted here and there, and a handsome carved counter where they serve Bath Gem, Moor So'Hop, Stroud Tom Long and a couple of guests such as Gloucester Spring Deity and Stroud Lightweight on handpump, ten wines by the glass, a farm cider, interesting spirits and a good choice of teas and coffee; the pretty piano does get used. Upstairs, the beamed and timbered dining room has a fine raftered ceiling, dark polished furniture on more wide floorboards, creamy yellow paintwork, fresh flowers and candlelight. Outside are seats and tables under parasols on terraces and a lawn; in summer, a trailer serves mexican street food; boules. The bedrooms – spotlessly kept and full of character – are across a cobbled courtyard, and breakfasts are extremely good. You can walk from the door into the woods.

Highly enjoyable food includes lunchtime sandwiches, tiger prawns with mango and tomato salad, cucumber and chilli maki rolls with plum sauce and oriental salad, porcini mushroom and herb burger with coleslaw and fries, beer-battered fish of the day and chips, chopped salad with grilled chicken, crispy bacon, free-range egg, avocado and shaved parmesan, roasted salmon with pickled clams and asparagus, and chocolate terrine with vanilla-poached apricots, praline and mango sorbet and rhubarb and lemon curd with ginger cheesecake. *Benchmark main dish: organic burger with toppings and chips £12.00. Two-course evening meal £20.00.*

Free house ~ Licensees Kate Lewis and Chris York ~ Real ale ~ Open 11-11 (11.30pm Fri, Sat); 12-11 Sun ~ Bar food 12-2.30, 5-9.30; 12-5 Sun ~ Restaurant ~ Children welcome until 8pm unless in restaurant ~ Dogs allowed in bar and bedrooms ~ Wi-fi ~ Live music Sun (best to phone) ~ Bedrooms: /£90 *Recommended by Caroline Prescott, Edward May, Nick Sharpe, Chris and Angela Buckell*

UPPER ODDINGTON

SP2225 Map 4

Horse & Groom ★ ♀

(01451) 830584 – www.horseandgroom.uk.com

Village signposted from A436 E of Stow-on-the-Wold; GL56 0XH

16th-c Cotswold inn with enterprising food, lots of wines by the glass, local beers and comfortable, character bars; bedrooms

Reliably well run, this pretty place is always deservedly busy and our readers are quick to praise the hard-working, hands-on landlord and the genuine welcome he offers all his customers. The bar has pale polished flagstones, a handsome antique oak box settle among other more modern seats, some nice armchairs at one end, oak beams in the ochre ceiling, stripped-stone walls and a log fire in the inglenook fireplace; the comfortable lounge is similarly furnished. Goffs Lancer, Purity Mad Goose and Wye Valley Bitter on handpump, 25 wines (including champagne and sweet wines) by the glass, 20 malt whiskies and gin, vodka, lager and cider from the local Cotswold Brewing Company. There are seats and tables under green parasols on the terrace and in the pretty garden. Some of the individually styled, different sized bedrooms are in the main house, some are in the 'cottage'; first class breakfasts.

 Food is interesting and uses local, seasonal produce: sandwiches and wraps, pigeon breast with poached pear and black pudding, lardons and red wine syrup, smoked salmon and crayfish with lemon mayonnaise, butternut squash and butter bean casserole with bulgar wheat and yoghurt, old spot sausages with grain mustard mash and red onion marmalade gravy, confit duck leg with noodles, stir-fried vegetables and sweet and sour sauce, lamb curry with onion bhaji and rice, and puddings such as lemon posset with blackcurrant sorbet and coconut milk rice pudding with caramelised pineapple. *Benchmark main dish: chicken, ham and mushroom pie £14.75. Two-course evening meal £23.50.*

Free house ~ Licensees Simon and Sally Jackson ~ Real ale ~ Open 12-3, 5.30-11; 12-3, 6.30-10.30 Sun; closed first two weeks Jan ~ Bar food 12-2, 6.30 (7 Sun)-9 ~ Children welcome ~ Dogs allowed in bar ~ Wi-fi ~ Bedrooms: £85/£110 *Recommended by Bernard Stradling, R L Borthwick, David Travis*

WESTON SUBEDGE

SP1241 Map 4

Seagrave Arms ★ ♀ 🛏

(01386) 840192 – www.seagravearms.com

B4632; GL55 6QH

Golden-stone inn with charming hands-on owner, friendly staff and impressive food; contemporary bedrooms

At 400 years old, this is a handsome country inn with a lot of character. There's a cosy little bar with a chatty atmosphere, an open fire, ancient flagstones, half-panelled walls and padded window seats, Hook Norton Hooky and Wychwood Jester Jack on handpump and 14 wines (plus prosecco and champagne) by the glass, served by helpful, friendly staff; background music, TV and board games. The two dining rooms have an appealing mix of wooden chairs and tables on floorboards. Outside, there are wicker chairs and tables on neat gravel at the front of the building and more seats in the back garden. Most of the well equipped, modern bedrooms are in the main house, with others in the converted stables; breakfasts are good and hearty. The Cotswold Way is nearby, so this place is popular with walkers and their dogs – especially at lunchtime.

🌟 The sensibly short menu plus fine daily specials cooked by the landlord includes lunchtime sandwiches and dishes such as partridge and pigeon sausage with smoked almond, plum and cumberland sauce, crab risotto with crème fraîche, salt-baked swede with wild mushrooms, truffle and pesto, burger with gherkins, toppings and fries, ox cheek with charred onion, carrot and smoked garlic, venison with bacon and onion potatoes, and cauliflower cheese, and puddings such as caramelised white chocolate ganache and rice pudding with prunes, grapes and sorrel; they also offer a two- and three-course set lunch. *Benchmark main dish: beer-battered fish and chips with tartare sauce £14.00. Two-course evening meal £22.00.*

Free house ~ Licensees Hannah Brown and Newstead Sayer ~ Real ale ~ Open 12-11; 12-9 Sun ~ Bar food 12-2.30, 6-9.30; 12-9.30 Sat; 12-8 Sun ~ Restaurant ~ Children welcome ~ Dogs allowed in bar and bedrooms ~ Wi-fi ~ Bedrooms: £70/£105 *Recommended by Nick Sharpe, Alison and Michael Harper, Susan Jackman, Dave Braisted*

WINCHCOMBE
SP0228 Map 4

Lion 🌟 ♀ 🛏

(01242) 603300 ~ www.thelionwinchcombe.co.uk
North Street; GL54 5PS

Historic inn in fine town with drinking and dining spaces in character rooms, fresh flowers and candlelight and seats on pretty terraces; warm, TV-free bedrooms

To make the most of exploring this lovely area, stay in the individually decorated country-style bedrooms here – two with their own staircases and one in a converted hayloft. Dating from the 15th c, this is a stylish former coaching inn with plenty of rustic-chic furnishings and an appealing and relaxed atmosphere. There are exposed golden-stone walls, portraits and gilt-edged mirrors on pale paintwork, flagstones, armchairs, scatter cushions on wall seats, stools and elegant wooden dining chairs around all shapes and sizes of table, jugs of fresh flowers and plenty of big stubby candles. Brakspears Oxford Gold, North Cotswold Windrush Ale, Prescott Chequered Flag and Wye Valley Butty Bach on handpump, good wines by the glass served by smiling, courteous staff; daily papers and background music. Wood and metal seats and tables sit on various terraced areas among shrubs and climbers and there are more seats on grass. Sudeley Castle is within walking distance and Cheltenham Racecourse is nearby.

🌟 Highly rewarding food includes confit pork belly with pomme purée, pancetta, apple and black pudding, baked filo pastry with brie and rosemary, confit garlic and quince marmalade, sausage and mash with red onion gravy, slow-cooked ribs with chilli and coriander potato skins, rabbit fillet stuffed with vegetables, confit leg, garlic mash and raisin and cranberry sauce, line-caught sea trout with ratatouille and lemon and caper sauce, and puddings. *Benchmark main dish: slow-cooked wagyu beef with wild mushrooms and beef jus £16.50. Two-course evening meal £21.00.*

Free house ~ Licensee Sue Chalmers ~ Real ale ~ Open 11-11 ~ Bar food 12-3, 6-9 (10 Fri); 12-4, 6-10 Sat; 12-4, 6-9 Sun ~ Restaurant ~ Children welcome ~ Dogs allowed in bar and bedrooms ~ Wi-fi ~ Bedrooms: /£99 *Recommended by Guy Vowles, Richard Tilbrook*

Real ale to us means beer that has matured naturally in its cask – not pressurised or filtered. We name all real ales stocked. We usually name ales preserved under a light blanket of carbon dioxide too, though purists – pointing out that this stops the natural yeasts developing – would disagree (most people, including us, can't tell the difference!).

Also Worth a Visit in Gloucestershire

Besides the fully inspected pubs, you might like to try these pubs that have been recommended to us and described by readers. Do tell us what you think of them: feedback@goodguides.com

---

ALDERTON SP9933

Gardeners Arms (01242) 620257

Beckford Road, off B4077 Tewkesbury–Stow; GL20 8NL Attractive recently refurnished thatched Tudor pub, enjoyable fairly standard food from lunchtime sandwiches up, good value set menu Mon-Sat, breakfast from 9.30am (10am Sun), good service by welcoming young staff, Sharps Doom Bar and two or three well local kept guests, real ciders, decent wines and good whisky/gin selection, various modernised areas, one featuring an old well, log fire, steps down to dining section; monthly quiz, live music Fri; children welcome, dogs in some parts, wheelchair access from main entrance, tables on sheltered terrace, good-sized grassy garden with boules, handy for GWR steam railway (Toddington), Stanway House and Sudeley Castle, open (and food) all day Sun. *(Chris and Angela Buckell, Martin and Alison Stainsby, Theocsbrian)*

ALDSWORTH SP1510

Sherborne Arms (01451) 844346

B4425 Burford–Cirencester; GL54 3RB Rural pub (former 17th-c stone farmhouse) set down from the road and run by same family since 1984; enjoyable good value home-made food including signature lamb and apricot casserole, often a weekday meal deal, two or three changing ales and proper cider, friendly service, beams, stripped stone and log fire, smallish bar and big dining area, conservatory, games/function room; background music, film night first Mon of month; children and dogs welcome, disabled access, pleasant front garden with smokers' shelter, closed Sun evening, Mon. *(Alan and Angela Scouller)*

AMBERLEY SO8401

Amberley Inn (01453) 872565

Steeply off A46 Stroud–Nailsworth – gentler approach from N Nailsworth; GL5 5AF Popular well located old stone inn with beautiful views and good local walks, two comfortable bars, snug and more formal restaurant, well kept Stroud ales, enjoyable locally sourced food from bar snacks up (special diets catered for), friendly helpful staff; surcharge if paying by credit card; children and dogs (in bar) welcome, side terrace and back garden, 11 bedrooms. *(Millie and Peter Downing)*

AMBERLEY SO8401

Black Horse (01453) 872556

Off A46 Stroud–Nailsworth to Amberley; left after Amberley Inn, left at war memorial; Littleworth; best to park by war memorial and walk down; GL5 5AL Two-bar pub with spectacular valley views from small conservatory and terraced garden; mix of pine furniture on wood and slate floors, exposed stone walls, modern artwork and two woodburners, up to five real ales such as Sharps, Stroud and Wickwar, Weston's cider and good range of gins, enjoyable reasonably priced fairly traditional food (not Sun evening) from sandwiches up, nice staff; outside gents'; children, walkers and dogs welcome, wheelchair access (highish step by gate), picnic-sets on front grass, more in split-level back garden, parking can be tricky, open all day. *(Chris and Angela Buckell)*

AMPNEY CRUCIS SP0701

Crown of Crucis (01285) 851806

A417 E of Cirencester; GL7 5RS Modernised roadside inn with spacious split-level bar, beams and log fires, good choice of enjoyable food including competitively priced dish of the day (weekday lunchtimes), Sharps Doom Bar and a guest, decent house wines, friendly helpful service; children and dogs welcome, disabled facilities, lots of tables out on grass by car park, quiet modern bedrooms around courtyard, good breakfast, cricket pitch over stream, open (and food) all day. *(R L Borthwick, R K Phillips)*

APPERLEY SO8627

Farmers Arms (01452) 780307

Lower Apperley (B4213); GL19 4DR Extended country pub with beams, big open fire and split-level carpeted dining area, generous helpings of good well priced home-made food from traditional favourites up, Wadworths ales, friendly atmosphere; some live music including summer tribute band festival; children welcome, picnic-sets on terrace and in garden overlooking fields, closed Sun evening, Mon. *(Beth Aldridge)*

ASHLEWORTH SO8125

Queens Arms (01452) 700395

Village signposted off A417 at Hartpury; GL19 4HT The charming south african licensees (here for 18 years) have sold this former Main Entry pub – news please.

ASHLEWORTH QUAY SO8125

Boat (01452) 700272

Ashleworth signposted off A417 N of Gloucester; quay signed from village; GL19 4HZ Tiny unpretentious alehouse under friendly licensees; front flagstoned parlour with built-in settle by scrubbed deal table, old-fashioned kitchen range, elderly fireside chairs, mats on flagstones, cribbage and dominoes, back quarry-tiled dining room with fireplace, cosy snug, up to ten mostly local ales and around eight ciders, pubby food from rolls up; children, dogs and muddy boots welcome, tricky for wheelchairs (staff will help), sunny crazy-paved front courtyard, more seats at side of building, River Severn moorings, open all day summer (all day Fri-Sun, closed Mon and lunchtime Weds in winter). *(David Travis)*

AUST   ST5788
Boars Head (01454) 632278
0.5 miles from M48 junction 1,
off Avonmouth Road; BS35 4AX 16th-c village pub handy for the 'old' Severn bridge, Marstons-related ales and decent house wines, well priced food including deals, good friendly service, linked rooms and alcoves, beams, some stripped stone and a huge log fire, old prints and bric-a-brac; background music, free wi-fi; children (in eating area) and dogs (in bar); wheelchair access, attractive sheltered garden, covered area for smokers, open all day Sun with food till 4pm. *(Beth Aldridge)*

AYLBURTON   SO6101
Cross (01594) 842823
High Street; GL15 6DE Popular family-run village pub, good choice of food from sandwiches and sharing plates through pub favourites to daily specials, changing ales such as Bath, Butcombe and Wye Valley, several wines by the glass and a dozen whiskies, welcoming helpful staff, open-plan split-level flagstoned bar, beams, modern furniture alongside high-backed settles, old local photographs, woodburners in large stone fireplaces, high-raftered dining room; free wi-fi; children and dogs welcome, wheelchair access from car park, pleasant garden with play area, open all day Fri-Sun. *(Alf Wright)*

BIBURY   SP1006
Catherine Wheel (01285) 740250
Arlington; B4425 NE of Cirencester;
GL7 5ND Bright cheerful dining pub in this famously beautiful village; enjoyable fresh food from sandwiches and pizzas up, well kept Hook Norton, Sharps and a guest, friendly attentive service, open-plan main bar and smaller back rooms, low beams, stripped stone, log fires, raftered dining room; children and dogs welcome, picnic-sets in front and in good-sized garden, handy for country and riverside walks, four bedrooms, open (and food) all day. *(Maddie Purvis)*

BISLEY   SO9006
Bear (01452) 770265
Village signed off A419 E of Stroud;
GL6 7BD Interesting 17th-c colonnaded inn (originally a courthouse); L-shaped bar

with low ceiling, old oak settles, brass and copper implements around extremely wide stone fireplace, five well kept ales including Butcombe and Charles Wells, enjoyable pubby food, friendly staff, separate stripped-stone family area; outside gents', ladies' upstairs; dogs welcome, small flagstoned courtyard, stone mounting blocks in garden across quiet road, one bedroom, open all day Sat and Sun. *(Ian Duncan)*

BLAISDON   SO7016
Red Hart (01452) 830477
Village signposted off A4136 just SW
of junction with A40 W of Gloucester;
OS Sheet 162 map reference 703169;
GL17 0AH Bustling village pub with plenty to look at in flagstoned main bar and attractive carpeted restaurant: woodworking and farming tools on magnolia walls and hanging from beams, old photographs of prize farm stock, a framed inventory of the pub in 1903 and lots of books, pot plants and some interesting prints, candles on traditional tables, cushioned wall and window seats, ales from Bespoke, Cotswold Spring, Otter and Wye Valley, local cider and ten wines by the glass, popular food from traditional choices up; background music, board games, free wi-fi; children welcome (family dining area), dogs in bar, wheelchair access, picnic-sets on terrace and in garden with play area, pretty summer window boxes, little church nearby also worth a visit. *(Chris and Angela Buckell)*

BOURTON-ON-THE-WATER SP1621
Coach & Horses (01451) 798478
A429 Stow Road; GL54 2HN Welcoming old roadside inn with ales such as Hook Norton Lion and Sharps Doom Bar in small convivial bar, enjoyable food and good friendly service, separate restaurant; TV; children and dogs (in bar) welcome, outside seating, five bedrooms in former stables, open all day. *(Peter and Jean Hoare)*

BRIMPSFIELD   SO9413
★**Golden Heart** (01242) 870261
Nettleton Bottom (not shown on road maps, so instead we list the pub under the name of the nearby village); on A417 N of the Brimpsfield turning northbound; GL4 8LA Traditional old roadside inn with low-ceilinged bar divided into five cosy areas, log fire in huge inglenook, exposed stone walls and wood panelling, well worn built-in settles and other old-fashioned furnishings, brass items, typewriters and banknotes, parlour on right with decorative fireplace leading into further room, four well kept ales such as Brakspears, Cotswold Lion, Jennings and Ringwood, several wines by the glass, popular sensibly priced food from extensive blackboard menu including unusual choices like ostrich, kangaroo and camel, friendly

---

Tipping is not normal for bar meals, and not usually expected.

staff; children and dogs welcome, seats and tables on suntrap terrace with pleasant valley views, nearby walks, two barn-conversion bedrooms, open all day weekends and school holidays. *(Gordon and Jenny Quick, Tom McLean, Ian Herdman, Richard Tilbrook, Giles and Annie Francis)*

BROAD CAMPDEN SP1537
★**Bakers Arms** (01386) 840515
Village signed from B4081 in Chipping Campden; GL55 6UR Friendly 17th-c stone pub doing well under welcoming new licensees; tiny beamed character bar with stripped-stone walls and inglenook woodburner, half a dozen well kept ales such as North Cotswold, Stanway, Wickwar and Wye Valley, simply furnished beamed dining room, popular pubby food (not Sun evening, Mon) plus blackboard specials; folk night last Weds of month, darts and board games; children (away from bar) and dogs (in bar) welcome, picnic-sets on terraces and in back garden, delightful Cotswold village and good nearby walks, open all day weekends, closed Mon lunchtime. *(Beth Aldridge)*

BROADWELL SP2027
Fox (01451) 870909
Off A429, 2 miles N of Stow-on-the-Wold; GL56 0UF Golden-stone pub above broad village green; traditional furnishings and flagstones in log-fire bar, jugs hanging from beams, interesting bits and pieces on stripped-stone walls, well kept Donnington BB and SBA, lots of rums, winter mulled wine, enjoyable generously served food (not Sun evening) cooked by ex-military chef-landlord, efficient friendly staff, two carpeted dining areas; background music, darts, board games; children and dogs (in bar) welcome, picnic-sets on gravel in sizeable back garden, aunt sally, paddock with horse called Herman, camping. *(Dennis and Doreen Haward, Alun and Jennifer Evans)*

BROCKWEIR SO5301
Brockweir Inn (01291) 689548
Signed just off A466 Chepstow–Monmouth; NP16 7NG Welcoming country local near River Wye; beams and stripped stonework, quarry tiles, sturdy settles and woodburner, nice snug with parquet floor and open fire, four well kept ales including local Kingstone and Wye Valley, three ciders, enjoyable food (not Sun evening), small back dining area and room upstairs 'Devil's Pulpit' with games and books; live music first Tues of month; children and dogs welcome, little walled garden with clay oven, good walks, open all day weekends. *(Millie and Peter Downing)*

CAMP SO9111
★**Fostons Ash** (01452) 863262
B4070 Birdlip–Stroud, junction with Calf Way; GL6 7ES Popular open-plan dining pub (part of the small Cotswold Food

Club group), light and airy, with good food from interesting light dishes and sharing plates up, real ales such as Goffs, Greene King and Stroud, nice range of wines by the glass, welcoming helpful staff, one end with easy chairs and woodburner; background music, daily papers; children welcome, rustic tables in attractive garden with heated terrace and play area, good walks, open all day (food all day Sun). *(Guy Vowles)*

CHARLTON KINGS SO9620
Royal (01242) 228937
Horsefair, opposite church; GL53 8JH Big 19th-c pub with clean modern décor, good realistically priced food (not Sun evening) in bar or dining conservatory, several well kept ales (tasting trays available) and decent wines, prompt friendly service; children and dogs welcome, picnic-sets in garden overlooking church, open all day. *(Guy Vowles)*

CHEDWORTH SP0608
Hare & Hounds (01285) 720288
Fosse Cross – A429 N of Cirencester, some way from village; GL54 4NN Rambling stone-built restaurant pub on Fosse Way, good interesting food, well kept Arkells and nice wines, efficient service, low beams and wood floors, soft lighting, cosy corners and little side rooms, two big log fires, small conservatory; children (away from bar) and dogs welcome, disabled facilities, ten courtyard bedrooms. *(Dennis and Doreen Haward)*

CHEDWORTH SP0512
Seven Tuns (01285) 720630
Village signposted off A429 NE of Cirencester; then take second signposted right turn and bear left towards church; GL54 4AE Refurbished 17th-c village pub (reopened 2015 after two-year closure) in remote valley close to famous Roman villa (NT); well kept ales such as Hook Norton and Otter, enjoyable food from pub favourites up including good value Sun lunch, friendly helpful staff, linked rooms with flagstone and wood floors, restored furniture along with newer comfortable seating, some curious artwork, embroideries and other bits and pieces, woodburners; upstairs skittle alley with darts and big-screen sports TV, open mike night last Tues of the month; children and dogs welcome, outside seating front and back, good walks, open all day Fri-Sun. *(Giles and Annie Francis, Richard Tilbrook)*

CHELTENHAM SO9622
Hewlett Arms (01242) 228600
Harp Hill, Battledown; GL52 6QG Compact split-level pebbledashed pub refurbished under present management, good home-made food (not Sun evening) from lunchtime ciabattas to specials, various deals, well kept changing ales and decent range of wines by the glass, good cheerful

service; background music; children and dogs welcome, picnic-sets under parasols in sunny front garden, open all day. *(Ian Duncan)*

CHELTENHAM SO9421

Jolly Brewmaster (01242) 772261

Painswick Road; GL50 2EZ Popular convivial local with open-plan linked areas around big semicircular counter, fine range of changing ales and ciders, friendly obliging young staff, newspapers, log fire; quiz nights Mon, Weds; dogs welcome, coachyard tables, open from 2.30pm (midday Sat, Sun). *(Ian Duncan)*

CHELTENHAM SO9522

Old Restoration (01242) 522792

High Street; GL50 1DX Much altered 17th-c beamed pub, five well kept changing ales (cheaper on Mon) and a couple of ciders, good reasonably priced food, friendly attentive staff, open fires; Mon quiz, sports TVs, darts; children (away from bar) and dogs welcome, open all day. *(Roger and Donna Huggins)*

CHELTENHAM SO9624

★ **Plough** (01242) 222180

Mill Street, Prestbury; GL52 3BG Convivial unspoilt thatched village local tucked away behind church; comfortable front lounge, service from corner corridor hatch in flagstoned back tap room, grandfather clock, old local photographs and big log fire, two or three well kept ales including Bath Gem and a house beer from Wickwar, proper ciders and good value home-made food (not Sun evening, Mon), friendly service; live folk Thurs; lovely big flower-filled back garden with boules, open all day in summer, closed lunchtimes Mon, Tues in winter. *(Beth Aldridge)*

CHELTENHAM SO9321

Royal Union (01242) 519098

Hatherley Street; GL50 2TT Backstreet local with large bar and cosy snug up steps, around eight well kept ales plus craft kegs, reasonably priced wines and good range of whiskies and gins, enjoyable food (Weds-Sat evenings, Sun lunchtime) including sharing dishes for up to ten people (must book), informal restaurant in former skittle alley; Sun evening jazz/blues, Thurs quiz; well behaved children allowed (no under-5s), courtyard behind, open all weekends, from 4pm weekdays. *(Guy Vowles, Beth Aldridge)*

CHELTENHAM SO9522

Sandford Park (01242) 571022

High Street; GL50 1DZ Former nightclub converted to a popular pub, three bar areas and upstairs function room, up to nine real ales along with craft and continental beers, several ciders and good value home-cooked food from short menu (not Sun evening, Mon lunchtime), friendly staff; Sun quiz, bar billiards; large back garden, open all day. *(Guy Vowles, Theocsbrian)*

CHIPPING CAMPDEN SP1539

Kings (01386) 840256

High Street; GL55 6AW Eclectic décor in 18th-c hotel's bar-brasserie and separate restaurant, good food from lunchtime sandwiches and pubby dishes to more upmarket choices, friendly helpful service, well kept Hook Norton Hooky and good choice of wines by the glass, afternoon teas, daily papers and nice log fire; secluded back garden with picnic-sets and terrace tables, 12 comfortable bedrooms, open all day. *(Millie and Peter Downing)*

CHIPPING CAMPDEN SP1539

Noel Arms (01386) 840317

High Street; GL55 6AT Handsome 16th-c inn with beamed and stripped-stone bar, nice food from sandwiches to steaks, some good curries too from sri lankan chef (curry night last Thurs of month), well kept Hook Norton and local guests, good choice of wines by the glass, friendly efficient staff, coffee bar (from 9am), conservatory and separate restaurant; children and dogs welcome, sunny courtyard tables, 28 well appointed bedrooms, good breakfast, open all day. *(David Travis)*

CHIPPING SODBURY ST7381

Bell (01454) 325582

Badminton Road (A432); BS37 6LL Welcoming late 18th-c family-run inn, ales such as Butcombe Gold, Sharps Doom Bar and Wadworths 6X from ornate wooden counter, three ciders and decent choice of wines, wide choice of good pub food including set lunch deal Mon-Fri and other deals, friendly efficient young staff, dining rooms either side of bar area, some stripped stone and timbering, sofas and open fires; background music, TV; children welcome, four bedrooms, open all day Thurs-Sun. *(Paul and Sonia Broadgate, Stephen Woad)*

CHIPPING SODBURY ST7282

Horseshoe 07780 505563

High Street; BS37 6AP Welcoming unpretentious little drinkers' pub in former stationers', seven well kept ales and six ciders, low priced pubby lunchtime food Fri, fortnightly curry night Weds, otherwise rolls on the bar (you can also bring your own food), comfortable sofas and settles; sports TV; dogs welcome, garden behind, open all day (till midnight weekends). *(Roger and Donna Huggins)*

A star symbol before the name of a pub shows exceptional character and appeal. It doesn't mean extra comfort. Even quite a basic pub can win a star, if it's individual enough.

CIRENCESTER   SP0103
Drillmans Arms (01285) 653892
Gloucester Road, Stratton; GL7 2JY
Unpretentious two-room roadside local,
cheerful and welcoming, with long-serving
landlady, well kept Sharps Doom Bar
and three quickly changing guests, basic
lunchtime food, low beams and woodburner;
skittle alley, darts and pool; dogs welcome,
tables out by small front car park, open all
day Sat. *(Ian Duncan)*

CIRENCESTER   SP0201
Marlborough Arms (01285) 651474
Sheep Street; GL7 1QW Busy bare-boards
pub with eight well kept ales including Box
Steam and North Cotswold, also proper
ciders and continental draught/bottled beers,
friendly landlord and good mix of customers,
reasonably priced traditional lunchtime
food (not Mon), brewery memorabilia, pump
clips and shelves of bottles, open fire; live
music and quiz nights, sports TV; enclosed
back courtyard, open all day (till 10pm Sun,
Mon). *(Giles and Annie Francis, Tom McLean)*

CLIFFORD'S MESNE   SO6922
Yew Tree (01531) 820719
*From A40 W of Huntley, turn off at 'May
Hill 1, Clifford's Mesne 2.5' signpost –
pub eventually signed up steep narrow
lane on left; Clifford's Mesne also
signposted off B4216 S of Newent – pub
then signed on right; GL18 1JS*
Tucked away on the slopes of May Hill (NT)
and under new family management; smallish
two-room beamed bar with attractive mix
of settles and character chairs around
various tables, unusual stone floor and big
woodburner, steps up to carpeted dining
room, Sharps, Wickwar and Wye Valley, pubby
food cooked by landlady, friendly service;
children and dogs welcome, views from
teak tables on side terrace, steps down to
sturdy play area, closed Sun evening, Mon,
otherwise open all day. *(Chris and Angela
Buckell, Mike and Mary Carter, R T and J C
Moggridge)*

COATES   SO9600
★Tunnel House (01285) 770280
*Follow Tarlton signs (right then left)
from village, pub up rough track on
right after railway bridge; OS Sheet 163
map reference 965005; GL7 6PW* Lively
bow-fronted stone house by entrance to
derelict canal tunnel; rambling character
rooms with beams, exposed stonework and
flagstones, good mix of furnishings and plenty
to look at including old enamel signs, railway
lamps, racing tickets, stuffed animals, even
an upside-down card table (complete with
cards and drinks) fixed to the ceiling, sofas
by log fire, Box Steam, Uley and Sharps,
a couple of Thatcher's ciders and several
wines by the glass, wide range of popular
food including daily specials, good service,

more conventional dining extension and back
conservatory; background music, free wi-fi;
children and dogs welcome, disabled access/
loos, impressive views from front terrace, big
garden down to canal, good nearby walks,
open (and food) all day. *(Sharon and John
Hancock, Chris and Angela Buckell)*

COLD ASTON   SP1219
Plough (01451) 822602
*Aka Aston Blank; off A436 (B4068) or
A429 SW of Stow-on-the-Wold; GL54 3BN*
Attractive little 17th-c village pub restored
and updated under present owners; low
beams, stone and wood floors, inglenook
woodburner, emphasis on enjoyable freshly
cooked food (not Mon) using local suppliers
from sharing boards to charcoal-grilled
steaks, well kept Cotswold Spring, Prescott,
Stroud and a guest (some tapped from
the cask), decent choice of wines, good
friendly service; children and dogs welcome,
teak tables and chairs on new terraces,
three well appointed bedrooms, open all
day Fri, Sat, closed Sun evening, Mon
lunchtime. *(Theocsbrian)*

COLEFORD   SO5710
Angel (01594) 835638
Market Place; GL16 8AE Old hotel's pubby
bar, lots of little alcoves, nooks and crannies,
leaded internal windows, leather bound
books in some places, a couple of well kept
ales such as Sharps Atlantic, bar food and
restaurant (separate evening menu), friendly
helpful staff; nine bedrooms, open all day.
(Dr J Barrie Jones, Dave Braisted)

COLESBOURNE   SO9913
Colesbourne Inn (01242) 870376
*A435 Cirencester–Cheltenham;
GL53 9NP* Civilised 19th-c grey-stone
gabled coaching inn, good choice of popular
home-made food from baguettes and
wraps up, friendly helpful staff, well kept
Wadworths ales and lots of wines by the glass,
linked partly panelled rooms, log fires, soft
lighting, comfortable mix of settles, softly
padded seats and leather sofas, candlelit
back dining room; TV above fireplace; dogs
welcome, views from attractive back garden
and terrace, nine bedrooms in converted
stable block, good breakfast. *(Dennis and
Doreen Haward)*

COMPTON ABDALE   SP0717
★Garniche at the Puesdown
(01451) 860262 *A40 outside village;
GL54 4DN* Spacious series of linked stylish
bars and eating areas, mainly stripped-stone
walls, rafter-effect or beamed ceilings,
rugs on bare boards, chesterfield sofas and
armchairs, high-backed dining chairs around
mix of tables, log fire and woodburner, a
couple of Hook Norton ales and maybe a
guest, pubby lunchtime food with more
elaborate evening choices, breakfast for
non-residents, morning coffee and afternoon

tea; gift shop; children welcome, dogs in bar, tables in pretty back garden, three comfortable ground-floor bedrooms, closed Sun evening, Mon, otherwise open (and food) all day. *(Millie and Peter Downing)*

DOYNTON ST7174

Cross House (0117) 329 5830

High Street; signed off A420 Bristol–Chippenham E of Wick; BS30 5TF Welcoming 18th-c village pub with ales such as Bath Gem and Sharps Doom Bar, summer cocktails and well priced enjoyable food cooked by landlady, carpeted beamed bar, some stripped stone, simple pub furniture and woodburner, cottagey dining room; Tues quiz, board games; children welcome, dogs in bar (two pub cats), picnic-sets out by the road, near fine walking country and Dyrham Park (NT), closed Mon, otherwise open all day. *(Taff Thomas)*

DYMOCK SO6931

Beauchamp Arms (01531) 890266

B4215; GL18 2AQ Friendly parish-owned village pub with well kept ales such as Butcombe, local ciders and popular good value traditional food (not Sun evening, Mon) including fresh fish Weds, cheerful helpful staff, three smallish rooms, log fire; children and dogs welcome, pleasant little garden with pond, local walks among daffodils and bluebells, church with corner devoted to the Dymock Poets, closed Mon lunchtime. *(Maddie Purvis)*

EASTLEACH TURVILLE SP1905

★**Victoria** (01367) 850277

Off A361 S of Burford; GL7 3NQ Open-plan low-ceilinged rooms around central servery, attractive seats built in by log fire, unusual Queen Victoria pictures, well kept Arkells, a guest beer and several good value wines by the glass, shortish choice of enjoyable sensibly priced pub food (not Sun evening) including weekday set lunch, prompt friendly service; background music; children and dogs welcome, small pleasant front garden with picnic-sets overlooking picturesque village (famous for its spring daffodils), good walks, open all day Sat. *(R K Phillips, Bernard Stradling)*

EBRINGTON SP1839

★**Ebrington Arms** (01386) 593223

Off B4035 E of Chipping Campden or A429 N of Moreton-in-Marsh; GL55 6NH 17th-c Cotswold-stone pub in attractive village by green; character beamed bar with ladderback chairs and cushioned settles on flagstones, some seats built into airy bow window, fine inglenook fireplace, own Yubberton ales plus local guests, nine wines by the glass and a proper cider, similarly furnished dining room with

another inglenook (original ironwork), good interesting food along with pub favourites; children and dogs (in bar) welcome, arched stone wall sheltering terrace picnic-sets, more on lawn, handy for Hidcote (NT) and Kiftsgate Court Gardens, well equipped country-style bedrooms, small car park (other nearby parking can be limited), open all day. *(Michael Doswell, Sharon and John Hancock, Richard Tilbrook, Clive and Fran Dutson)*

EDGE SO8409

Edgemoor (01452) 813576

Gloucester Road (A4173); GL6 6ND Spaciously modernised 19th-c dining pub with panoramic valley view across to Painswick from picture windows and pretty terrace, up to four well kept local ales and good food from reasonably priced varied menu, friendly efficient service, restaurant; children welcome, no dogs inside, good nearby walks, closed Sun evening in winter. *(Chris and Val Ramstedt)*

ELKSTONE SO9610

★**Highwayman** (01285) 821221

Beechpike; A417 6 miles N of Cirencester; GL53 9PL Interesting 16th-c building with rambling interior, low beams, stripped stone and log fires, cosy alcoves, antique settles among more modern furnishings, generous helpings of enjoyable food (gluten-free options) from lunchtime sandwiches up, Arkells beers and good house wines, friendly service; free wi-fi; children and dogs welcome, disabled access, outside play area, bedrooms, closed Sun evening, Mon. *(Alf Wright)*

FAIRFORD SP1501

★**Bull** (01285) 712535

Market Place; GL7 4AA Civilised stone hotel with comfortably old-fashioned pubby furnishings in chatty main bar, beams, timbering and open fire, Arkells ales and decent fairly straightforward food, friendly service, nice little residents' lounge with big stone fireplace; children and dogs (in bar) welcome, bedrooms, worth visiting the church which has Britain's only intact set of medieval stained-glass windows, open all day. *(Ian Duncan)*

FORTHAMPTON SO8731

Lower Lode Inn (01684) 293224

At the end of Bishop's Walk by river; GL19 4RE Brick-built 15th-c coaching inn with River Severn moorings and plenty of waterside tables (prone to winter flooding); beams, flagstones and traditional seating, woodburners, enjoyable pubby food including Sun carvery, half a dozen well kept interesting beers, friendly helpful staff, restaurant, back pool room; children

---

If we know a pub has an outdoor play area for children, we mention it.

and dogs welcome, disabled facilities, four bedrooms and campsite, open all day. *(Millie and Peter Downing)*

FOSSEBRIDGE   SP0711
Fossebridge Inn (01285) 720721

A429 Cirencester to Stow-on-the-Wold; GL54 3JS Newish management for this 17th-c former coaching inn with four acres of attractive lawned riverside gardens; two original bar rooms with log fires, beams, stripped-stone walls and flagstones, all sorts of chairs, stools and tables, copper implements, Wadworths 6X and a couple of guests (not cheap), several wines by glass, popular traditional food, two other rather grand dining rooms; background music can be obtrusive, TV; children, walkers and dogs welcome, nine bedrooms and two self-catering cottages, Chedworth Roman Villa (NT) nearby, open (and food) all day. *(Dr A Y Drummond)*

FRAMPTON COTTERELL   ST6681
Globe (01454) 778286

Church Road; BS36 2AB Popular white-painted pub next to church; large knocked-through bar-dining area with black beams and some stripped stone, usual furniture on parquet or carpet, woodburner in old fireplace, six well kept ales including Butcombe, Fullers and St Austell, Ashton Press and Thatcher's ciders, well chosen wine list, enjoyable fairly priced pubby food from well filled panini up, attentive friendly staff; background music, Tues quiz; children and dogs welcome, wheelchair access via side door, disabled/baby changing facilities, big grassy garden with play area and smokers' gazebo, on Frome Valley Walkway, open all day. *(Chris and Angela Buckell)*

FRAMPTON MANSELL   SO9202
★**Crown** (01285) 760601

Brown sign to pub off A491 Cirencester–Stroud; GL6 8JG Welcoming 17th-c country pub (former cider house) with pretty outlook; good food including daily specials, six well kept local ales such as Butcombe, Stroud and Uley, friendly helpful young staff, stripped stone and heavy beams, rugs on bare boards, two log fires and a woodburner, restaurant; children and dogs welcome, disabled access, picnic-sets in sunny front garden, 12 bedrooms in separate block, open all day from midday. *(Giles and Annie Francis, Tom and Ruth Rees)*

FRAMPTON ON SEVERN   SO7407
Three Horseshoes (01452) 742100

The Green (B4071, handy for M5 junction 13, via A38); GL2 7DY Cheerfully unpretentious 18th-c pub by splendid green; welcoming staff and locals, well kept Sharps, Timothy Taylors and Uley from small counter, proper ciders/perry, good value home-made food including speciality pies, lived-in interior with parquet flooring,

cushioned wall seats and open fire in large brick fireplace, quieter back lounge/dining room; folk nights, darts; children, walkers and dogs welcome, wheelchair access, picnic-sets out in front, garden behind with two boules pitches, views over River Severn to Forest of Dean, parking can be tricky (narrow road), open all day weekends. *(Richard Tilbrook, Chris and Angela Buckell)*

GLASSHOUSE   SO7121
★**Glasshouse Inn** (01452) 830529

Off A40 just W of A4136; GL17 0NN Much extended beamed red-brick pub with series of small linked rooms, ochre walls and boarded ceilings, appealing old-fashioned and antique furnishings, hunting pictures and taxidermy, cavernous black hearth, well kept ales including cask-tapped Butcombe and Sharps, Weston's cider, good reasonably priced wines, some interesting malt whiskies and a couple of decent gins, enjoyable home-made food from sandwiches and basket meals up (no bookings except Sun lunch), good friendly service, big flagstoned conservatory; background music; no under-14s (in bars) or dogs, good disabled access, neat garden with rustic furniture, interesting topiary, flower-decked cider presses and lovely hanging baskets, nearby paths up wooded May Hill (NT), three self-catering lodges, closed Sun evening. *(Chris and Angela Buckell)*

GLOUCESTER   SO8318
Fountain (01452) 522562

Westgate Street; GL1 2NW Tucked-away 17th-c pub off pedestrianised street, well kept ales such as Butcombe, Fullers, Hook Norton, St Austell and Severn Vale, Weston's cider, reasonably priced pubby food from baguettes up, carpeted bar with handsome stone fireplace, some black beams and panelling, pubby furniture and built-in wall benches; background music; children welcome away from bar, disabled access, flower-filled courtyard, handy for cathedral and open all day. *(Theocsbrian)*

GLOUCESTER   SO8218
Lord High Constable of England (01452) 302890

Llanthony Warehouse, Llanthony Road; GL1 2EH Relatively new Wetherspoons on east side of the docks; spacious and comfortable with high raftered ceiling, good range of real ales and craft beers, their usual good value food; TVs, free wi-fi; children welcome, outside area overlooking canal, open all day from 8am. *(Theocsbrian)*

GLOUCESTER   SO8318
New Inn (01452) 522177

Northgate Street; GL1 1SF Lovely beamed medieval building with galleried courtyard, Butcombe, Sharps and up to eight guests including smaller local breweries, decent wines, bargain daily lunchtime carvery and other good value food, friendly efficient service, coffee shop, restaurant; soft background music (live Fri, disco Sat), sports TV, free wi-fi; children welcome, no dogs, wheelchair access to restaurant only, 33 affordably priced bedrooms, handy for cathedral, open all day. *(Dave Braisted, Richard Tilbrook)*

GREAT RISSINGTON   SP1917

★**Lamb** (01451) 820388

Turn off A40 W of Burford to the Barringtons; keep straight on past Great Barrington until Great Rissington is signed on left; GL54 2LN Cotswold-stone village inn with two-roomed bar, pubby furniture on red carpet, woodburner, chairs against counter serving Brakspears, Wychwood Hobgoblin and a beer badged for the pub, decent wines by the glass and several malt whiskies, second woodburner in restaurant with agricultural tools on the walls, well liked interesting food along with a few pub standards; background music, TV; children and dogs (in bar) welcome, seats in sheltered hillside garden where Wellington bomber crashed in 1943 (see plaque and memorabilia), attractive circular walk, 14 bedrooms, open all day. *(Bernard Stradling, Michael and Jenny Back)*

GRETTON   SP0130

Royal Oak (01242) 604999

Off B4077 E of Tewkesbury; GL54 5EP Golden-stone pub under new management; bar with painted kitchen chairs, leather tub chairs and pale wooden tables on bare boards or flagstones, open fires, airy dining room and conservatory, candelabras, antlers and big central woodburner, ales such as Box Steam, Brakspears, Cotswold Spring, Jennings and Wye Valley, plenty of wines by the glass, generally well liked food from pub favourites to specials; background music; children and dogs (in bar) welcome, wheelchair access but not to raised dining room, seats on back terrace with views over village to Dumbleton Hills and Malverns, play area and bookable tennis court, GWR steam trains run along bottom of garden in summer, open all day. *(R T and J C Moggridge, Chris and Angela Buckell, B R Merritt, Theocsbrian)*

GUITING POWER   SP0924

★**Farmers Arms** (01451) 850358

Fosseway (A429); GL54 5TZ Nicely old-fashioned with stripped stone, flagstones, lots of pictures and warm log fire, well kept cheap Donnington BB and SBA, wide blackboard choice of enjoyable honest food cooked by landlord including good rabbit pie and reasonably priced Sun roasts, welcoming prompt service, carpeted back dining part; games area with darts, dominoes, cribbage and pool, skittle alley; children welcome, garden with quoits, lovely village, good walks, bedrooms. *(Michael and Jenny Back, Richard Tilbrook)*

GUITING POWER   SP0924

Hollow Bottom (01451) 850392

Village signposted off B4068 SW of Stow-on-the-Wold (still called A436 on many maps); GL54 5UX Friendly bustle in this recently refurbished old stone cottage popular with the racing fraternity; opened-up beamed bar with new wood flooring and woodburner in unusual pillared stone fireplace, horse-racing pictures, ales such as Butcombe Rare Breed, Greene King IPA and Old Speckled Hen, several wines by the glass and 15 malt whiskies, popular all-day food from flatbreads, sharing boards and pizzas up, pleasant helpful service; background music; children and dogs welcome, disabled access/facilities, seats under awning at front, decked terrace behind with own bar, nearby walks, four bedrooms, car park down steep slope, open all day. *(P and J Shapley)*

HAM   ST6898

Salutation (01453) 810284

On main road through village; GL13 9QH Welcoming unpretentious three-room country local; brasses on beams, horse and hunt pictures on Artex walls, high-backed settles, bench seats and other pubby furniture, six well kept local ales including home-brewed Tileys, nine real ciders/perries and good range of bottled beers, limited choice of simple low-priced lunchtime food such as ham, egg and chips (own pigs, hens and potatoes), folk night first Thurs of month and other live music, traditional games including shove-ha'penny, skittle alley, free wi-fi; wheelchair access, beer garden with views over deer park, handy for Berkeley Castle, open all day weekends, closed Mon lunchtime. *(Chris and Angela Buckell, Steve Crick)*

HARTPURY   SO7924

Royal Exchange (01452) 700273

A417 Gloucester–Ledbury; GL19 3BW 19th-c country pub with fresh modern interior, good food (not Sun evening) from sharing plates up, Wye Valley ales and guests, local cider/perry, friendly young staff; occasional live music, sports TV; children and dogs (in bar) welcome, fine views from garden with terrace and covered deck, open all day Fri-Sun, closed Mon lunchtime. *(David Travis)*

HAWKESBURY UPTON   ST7786

★**Beaufort Arms** (01454) 238217

High Street; GL9 1AU Unpretentious 17th-c pub in historic village; welcoming landlord and friendly chatty atmosphere, up to five well kept changing local ales and good range of ciders, popular no-nonsense food (no starters, small helpings available), extended uncluttered dining lounge on right, darts in more spartan stripped-brick bare-boards bar, interesting local and brewery memorabilia, lots of pictures (some for sale); skittle alley, free wi-fi; well behaved children allowed, dogs in bar, disabled access throughout and facilities, picnic-sets in smallish enclosed garden, on Cotswold Way and handy for Badminton Horse Trials, open all day. *(Martin and Margaret Thorpe)*

HILLESLEY   ST7689
Fleece (01453) 520003
Hawkesbury Road/Chapel Lane;
GL12 7RD Comfortably updated old stone-roofed pub owned by the local community; well kept mainly local ales, Thatcher's cider, good wines by the glass and decent gins, happy hour (3-7pm Mon-Fri), enjoyable good value pub food along with some interesting specials, friendly chatty staff and locals, bar with coir matting and some polished boards, mix of pubby furniture, cushioned benches and wall seats, woodburner, steps down to dining room and snug; quiz first Sun of month, acoustic music second Sun, darts, free wi-fi; children, walkers and dogs welcome (leave muddy boots in porch), wheelchair access to bar only, back garden with play area and smokers' shelter, small village in lovely countryside near Cotswold Way, open all day. *(Chris and Angela Buckell)*

HINTON DYRHAM   ST7376
★ Bull (0117) 937 2332
2.4 miles from M4 junction 18; A46
towards Bath, then first right (opposite
the Crown); SN14 8HG 17th-c stone pub in nice setting; main bar with two huge fireplaces, low beams, oak settles and pews on ancient flagstones, stripped-stone back area and simply furnished carpeted restaurant, food from pub standards to specials, well kept Wadworths ales; background music; children and dogs welcome, difficult wheelchair access (steps at front, but staff willing to help), seats on front balcony and in sizeable sheltered upper garden with play equipment, handy for Dyrham Park (NT), open all day weekends (food till 6pm Sun), closed Mon. *(Alf Wright)*

KEMBLE   ST9899
Thames Head (01285) 770259
A433 Cirencester–Tetbury; GL7 6NZ
Cream-painted roadside pub with opened-up modernised interior around central servery; faux black beams, stripped-stone walls and some rough-boarded dados/wall seats, fairly rustic furniture on tartan carpet, shelves of books, stoneware jugs and a bust of Old Father Thames, intriguing little front alcove, two open fires, popular reasonably priced food, well kept Arkells and good value wines, friendly chatty staff; background music, skittle alley; children and dogs (in bar area) welcome, wheelchair access using ramp, disabled loo, tables outside, four barn-conversion bedrooms, good breakfast, walk (crossing railway line) to nearby Thames source, open (and food) all day. *(Dennis and Doreen Haward)*

KILKENNY   SP0118
Kilkeney Inn (01242) 820341
A436, 1 mile W of Andoversford;
GL54 4LN Spacious recently refurbished beamed pub (originally five stone cottages), stripped-stone and some plank-clad walls, wheelback, tub and leather dining chairs around tables on slate, wood or carpeted floors, open fire and woodburner, conservatory, Charles Wells beers, real cider and decent wines by the glass, well liked food from new owner-chef including signature 'slow-cooked' dishes, buzzy atmosphere and good service; background music; children welcome, wheelchair access from car park, lovely Cotswold views from tables out at front, back garden, one well appointed bedroom, closed Sun evening, Mon.
(Richard Tilbrook, Chris and Angela Buckell)

KINETON   SP0926
Halfway House (01451) 850344
Signed from B4068 and B4077 W of
Stow-on-the-Wold; GL54 5UG Welcoming 17th-c beamed village inn under new management; enjoyable food from sandwiches and pub standards to more ambitious choices, well kept Donnington BB and SBA, Addlestone's cider and decent wines, separate dining area, log fire; pool and darts; children and dogs welcome, picnic-sets in sheltered back garden with pergola, good walks, bedrooms, open (and some food) all day. *(Richard Tilbrook)*

KINGSCOTE   ST8196
★ Hunters Hall (01453) 860393
A4135 Dursley–Tetbury; GL8 8XZ Tudor beams, stripped stone, big log fires and plenty of character in individually furnished linked rooms, oak settles along with some sofas and easy chairs, wide choice of good home-made food, well kept Greene King and Uley, friendly attentive service, flagstoned back bar with darts, pool and TV; children and dogs welcome, big garden with play area, 13 bedrooms, open all day. *(Maddie Purvis)*

KNOCKDOWN   ST8388
Holford Arms (01454) 238669
A433; GL8 8QY Welcoming 16th-c beamed pub; stripped-stone walls, flagstone or wood floors, leather sofas, armchairs and cushioned wall/window seats, candles on old dining tables, woodburner in huge stone fireplace, ales such as Greene King, Flying Monk and Stroud, own Sherston's cider and good well balanced wine list, enjoyable food from sandwiches up including good value Sun lunch (own rare-breed pork), pleasant helpful service; background and live music (bluegrass Fri), skittle alley; children and dogs welcome, disabled access (no loos), picnic sets in side garden, six bedrooms and campsite, handy for Westonbirt Arboretum, Highgrove and Badminton Horse Trials, closed Sun evening, Mon lunchtime and

Tues, otherwise open all day. *(Chris and Angela Buckell)*

LECHLADE SU2199
New Inn (01367) 252296
Market Square (A361); GL7 3AB
Refurbished 17th-c brick coaching inn close to the church, roomy front bar with large log fire, Greene King Morlands Original and a couple of guests, good value pubby food from sandwiches/panini up, back restaurant, friendly helpful staff; background music; children and dogs (in bar) welcome, big garden down to Thames, good walks, 30 bedrooms, open all day. *(Anita Kaila, Balinder Ladhar)*

LECHLADE SU2199
Swan (01367) 253571
Burford Street; GL7 3AP Welcoming 16th-c inn with linked rooms around central servery; beam-and-plank ceilings, bare boards or carpeted floors, various odds and ends including old gramophones, musical instruments, farming memorabilia and enamel signs, even a couple of vintage petrol pumps, good log fires in two big stone fireplaces, restaurant part with modern pine furniture, Halfpenny and Old Forge beers (brewed at their sister pubs) and good choice of wines by the glass, sensibly priced food (not Sun evening) including generous sandwiches and range of burgers; four bedrooms, handy for Thames Path walkers, open all day. *(Beth Aldridge)*

LEIGHTERTON ST8290
★**Royal Oak** (01666) 890250
Village signposted off A46 S of Nailsworth; GL8 8UN New owners as we went to press for this handsome mullioned-windowed village pub; rambling beamed bar with two log fires, stripped stonework and pastel paintwork, carefully chosen furniture from stylish dining chairs to comfy sofas, ales from Bath and Butcombe, traditional cider and several wines by the glass, food has been good; disabled access, sheltered side courtyard with teak and metal furniture, handy for Westonbirt Arboretum and nearby walks. *(Michael Doswell, Tom and Ruth Rees, Peter Brix, Alf Wright)*

LITTLE BARRINGTON SP2012
★**Inn For All Seasons** (01451) 844324
A40 3 miles W of Burford; OX18 4TN Handsome old coaching inn with attractive comfortable lounge bar, low beams, stripped stone and flagstones, old prints, log fire, very good food with an emphasis on fish, a couple of ales such as Otter and St Austell, lots of wines by the glass and malt whiskies, good friendly service, restaurant and conservatory, cookery school; background music, quiz nights; children and dogs (in bar) welcome, picnic-sets in garden with aunt sally, walks from door, ten bedrooms, open all day weekends. *(R K Phillips)*

LITTLETON-UPON-SEVERN ST5989
★**White Hart** (01454) 412275
3.5 miles from M48 junction 1; BS35 1NR Sympathetically refurbished 17th-c farmhouse with three main rooms; log fires and nice mix of country furnishings, loveseat in inglenook, flagstones at front, huge tiles at back, fine old White Hart Inn Simonds Ale sign, family room and snug, well kept Youngs ales and guests, good range of ciders (including their own) and of other drinks, popular food cooked by landlord from bar snacks and traditional choices to more adventurous specials, good service; children and dogs welcome (theirs is Ralph), wheelchair access, tables on front lawn, more behind by orchard, vegetable patch and roaming poultry (eggs for sale), walks from the door, open all day, food all day Sun. *(Chris and Angela Buckell)*

LONGBOROUGH SP1729
Coach & Horses (01451) 830325
Ganborough Road; GL56 0QU Traditional little 17th-c stone-built local, up to three well kept/priced Donnington ales, Weston's cider and enjoyable pubby food including good ploughman's, friendly landlord and staff, leather armchairs on flagstones, inglenook woodburner, darts, dominoes and cribbage; background music, quiz last Sun of month; children and dogs welcome, tables out at front looking down on stone cross and pretty village, two simple clean bedrooms, handy for Sezincote house and gardens, open all day Fri-Sun. *(Richard Tilbrook, Christian Mole, Mrs J Ekins-Daukes)*

LOWER ODDINGTON SP2326
★**Fox** (01451) 870862
Signed off A436; GL56 0UR Smart 16th-c creeper-clad inn with emphasis on good food (mix of modern and traditional) at sensible prices, Hook Norton and Sharps Doom Bar, nice wines, well trained personable staff, little country-style flagstoned rooms with assorted chairs around pine tables, hunting figures and pictures, inglenook fireplace, elegant restaurant; background music; children and dogs (in bar) welcome, white tables and chairs on heated terrace in cottagey garden, pretty village, three bedrooms. *(Bernard Stradling, Alun and Jennifer Evans, Richard Tilbrook)*

LOWER SWELL SP1725
Golden Ball (01451) 833886
B4068 W of Stow-on-the-Wold; GL54 1LF Welcoming 17th-c stone-built village local under newish management; Donnington ales from the pretty nearby brewery, reasonably priced generously served food from shortish menu including good baguettes, neatly kept beamed interior with some cosy nooks, woodburner; background music, sports TV, darts; children and dogs welcome, small

garden and raised deck/balcony, good walks, one bedroom, open all day weekends, no food Sun evening. *(Richard Tilbrook, Michael and Jenny Back)*

MARSHFIELD   ST7773
★**Catherine Wheel** (01225) 892220

High Street; signed off A420 Bristol–Chippenham; SN14 8LR Attractive Georgian-fronted building in unspoilt village, high-ceilinged bare-stone front part with medley of settles, chairs and stripped tables, charming dining room with impressive open fireplace, cottagey beamed back area warmed by woodburners, well kept Butcombe, Cotswold Spring and Sharps, interesting wines and other drinks, enjoyable sensibly priced food from pub favourites up including set menus; darts and dominoes, live music last Thurs of month, free wi-fi; well behaved children and dogs welcome, wheelchair access with help, flower-decked backyard, three bedrooms, open all day. *(Millie and Peter Downing)*

MAYSHILL   ST6882
New Inn (01454) 773161

Badminton Road (A432 Frampton Cotterell–Yate); BS36 2NT Popular largely 17th-c coaching inn with two comfortably carpeted bar rooms leading to restaurant, good choice of enjoyable generously served food, friendly staff, three well kept changing ales, Weston's cider and decent wines by the glass, log fire; children and dogs welcome, garden with play area, open all day Fri-Sun. *(Maddie Purvis)*

MEYSEY HAMPTON   SU1199
Masons Arms (01285) 850164

Just off A417 Cirencester–Lechlade; High Street; GL7 5JT Popular recently refurbished 17th-c village pub, good attractively presented food at reasonable prices (all day Sun), well kept Arkells, friendly helpful staff, longish open-plan beamed bar with big inglenook log fire at one end, tiled and boarded floors, scrubbed oak and pastel paintwork, restaurant; children and dogs (in bar) welcome, tables out on green, comfortable bedrooms, parking can be tricky, open all day weekends from midday (from 8.30am weekdays with a break 3-5pm). *(Revd Michael Vockins, Sara Fulton, Roger Baker)*

MINCHINHAMPTON   SO8500
Old Lodge (01453) 832047

Nailsworth–Brimscombe – on common, fork left at pub's sign; OS Sheet 162 map reference 853008; GL6 9AQ Welcoming dining pub (part of the Cotswold Food Club group) with civilised bistro feel, wood floors, stripped-stone walls, modern décor and furnishings, good food from pub favourites up, well kept beers such as Otter and Stroud, decent wines by the glass; children welcome, tables on neat lawn looking over NT common

with grazing cows and horses, six bedrooms, open all day (food all day weekends). *(David and Stella Martin)*

MISERDEN   SO9308
Carpenters Arms (01285) 821283

Off B4070 NE of Stroud; GL6 7JA Welcoming traditional country pub with opened-up low-beamed bar, stripped-stone walls, log fire and woodburner, some interesting old photographs, two Wye Valley ales (one badged for the pub) and a guest, decent wines and ample helpings of enjoyable reasonably priced food using local/home-grown produce, good vegetarian choices, friendly staff; folk night second and last Weds of month, quiz Thurs; children and dogs welcome, seats out in front and to the side, popular with walkers and handy for Miserden Park, open (and food) all day. *(Giles and Annie Francis)*

MORETON-IN-MARSH   SP2032
Black Bear (01608) 652992

High Street; GL56 0AX Unpretentious beamed and stripped-stone corner pub run by friendly welcoming family, no-frills locals' bar serving Donnington ales, generous helpings of tasty good value home-made food in airy dining room; sports TVs; children welcome. *(Richard Tilbrook)*

MORETON-IN-MARSH   SP1729
Coach & Horses (01451) 830208

Ganborough (on A424 about 2.5 miles N of Stow-on-the-Wold); GL56 0QZ This Donnington country pub (Main Entry last year) was closed for refurbishment as we went to press – news please.

MORETON-IN-MARSH   SP2032
Inn on the Marsh (01608) 650709

Stow Road next to duck pond; GL56 0DW Interesting 19th-c beamed bar with comfortable layout and dutch flavour to the bric-a-brac, models, posters etc, inglenook woodburner, dutch chef-landlady cooking good value national specialities alongside pub favourites, well kept Marstons-related beers and guests, cheerful welcoming staff, modern conservatory restaurant; may be background music; children and dogs welcome, seats at front and in back garden, closed Sun and Mon lunchtimes. *(Ian Duncan)*

MORETON-IN-MARSH   SP2032
Redesdale Arms (01608) 650308

High Street; GL56 0AW Relaxed 17th-c hotel (former coaching inn); alcoves and big stone fireplace in comfortable solidly furnished panelled bar on right; darts in flagstoned public bar, Wickwar ales, decent wines and coffee, enjoyable food from breakfast on served by courteous helpful staff, spacious child-friendly back brasserie and dining conservatory; background music, TVs, games machine; heated floodlit

courtyard, 34 comfortable bedrooms (newer ones in mews), open all day from 8am.
(Colin and Daniel Gibbs)

MORETON-IN-MARSH   SP2032
White Hart Royal (01608) 650731

High Street; GL56 0BA Substantial 17th-c coaching inn with Charles I connection; cosy beamed quarry-tiled bar with fine inglenook and nice old furniture, adjacent smarter panelled room with Georgian feel, separate lounge and restaurant, Hook Norton and a guest ale, good choice of wines, well liked food from sandwiches and pub favourites up including children's choices, good friendly service; background music; courtyard tables, 28 bedrooms, good breakfast, open all day.
(David Travis)

NAILSWORTH   ST8499
Britannia (01453) 832501

Cossack Square; GL6 0DG Large open-plan pub (part of the small Cotswold Food Club chain) in former manor house; popular bistro food (best to book evenings) including bargain weekday lunch menu, takeaway pizzas, friendly service, well kept Hook Norton, Wadworths and guests, good choice of wines by the glass, big log fire; picnic-sets in front garden, open all day (food all day weekends). *(Ian Duncan)*

NAILSWORTH   ST8499
Egypt Mill (01453) 833449

Off A46; heading N towards Stroud, first right after roundabout, then left; GL6 0AE Converted 16th-c mill with working waterwheels; split-level brick and stone floor bar, stripped beams and some hefty ironwork in comfortable carpeted lounge, seating ranging from elegant dining chairs to cushioned wall seats and sofas, well kept ales such as Wickwar and Wye Valley, a dozen wines by the glass and generally well liked reasonably priced food; background music, TV; children welcome, plenty of tables in floodlit garden overlooking millpond, nicely equipped bedrooms (some with fine beams and timbering), open (and food) all day. *(Dr and Mrs A K Clarke)*

NAUNTON   SP1123
★ **Black Horse** (01451) 850565

Off B4068 W of Stow-on-the-Wold; GL54 3AD Welcoming locals' pub with well kept/priced Donnington BB and SBA, Weston's cider and good home-made food from traditional favourites to daily specials such as seasonal game, efficient service, black beams, stripped stone, flagstones and log fire, dining room; background music, darts and dominoes; children and dogs welcome, small seating area outside, charming village and fine Cotswold walks (walking groups asked to pre-order food), open all day Fri-Sun. *(Michael and Jenny Back, Richard Tilbrook, John Jenkins, Dennis and Doreen Haward)*

NIBLEY   ST6982
Swan (01454) 312290

Badminton Road; BS37 5JF Part of small local pub group, friendly and relaxed, with good food from snacks to daily specials, Bath, Butcombe and Cotswold Spring, real cider and over a dozen wines by the glass, good service, modernised interior with fireside leather sofas one side, dining tables the other, separate restaurant; background music; children and dogs (in bar) welcome, garden picnic-sets, open all day. *(Colin and Daniel Gibbs)*

NORTH CERNEY   SP0208
★ **Bathurst Arms** (01285) 832150

A435 Cirencester–Cheltenham; GL7 7BZ This handsome pub (previous Main Entry) was being taken over as we went to press – reports please; original beamed and panelled bar with flagstones, window seats and fireplace at each end (one with woodburner is huge), oak-floored room off with country tables and high-backed settles, restaurant with another woodburner, has served Hook Norton, Ramsbury and a guest, plenty of wines by the glass and good food; garden with River Chun running through it, lovely surrounding walks and handy for Cerney House Gardens. *(W M Lien, Dennis and Doreen Haward, R T and J C Moggridge, Dave Braisted)*

NORTH NIBLEY   ST7596
New Inn (01453) 543659

E of village itself; Waterley Bottom; GL11 6EF Former cider house in secluded rural setting popular with walkers, well kept Moles, Wickwar and a weekend guest from antique pumps, fine range of ciders and perries (more in bottles), enjoyable food cooked by landlord from lunchtime sandwiches and good ploughman's up, lounge bar with cushioned windsor chairs and high-backed settles, partly stripped-stone walls, simple cosy public bar with darts (no children here after 6pm), cider festivals and other events (maybe local mummers); no credit cards; dogs welcome, hitching rail and trough for horses, picnic-sets and swings on lawn, covered decked area with pool table, two bedrooms, open all day weekends, closed Mon lunchtime (evening too in winter). *(David Travis)*

OLD DOWN   ST6187
★ **Fox** (01454) 412507

3.9 miles from M5 junction 15/16; A38 towards Gloucester, then Old Down signposted; turn left into Inner Down; BS32 4PR Tucked-away yet popular family-owned country pub; ales from Bath, Butcombe, Exmoor and Sharps, real cider and several wines by the glass, good reasonably priced traditional food (not Sun evening) from baguettes up, friendly helpful staff and warm local atmosphere, low-beams, carpeted, wood or flagstone floors, magnolia walls with beige dados, log fire, plain modern wooden furniture, dark green faux leather wall seats in bar, snug family room; live music first Sat of month; dogs welcome, good disabled access (no loos), long verandah with grapevine, front and back gardens, play area, open all day Sun. *(Chris and Angela Buckell)*

OLD SODBURY ST7581

★ **Dog** (01454) 312006

3 miles from M4 junction 18, via A46 and A432; The Hill (a busy road); BS37 6LZ Welcoming old pub with popular two-level bar, low beams, stripped stone and open fire, good food from sandwiches and baked potatoes to fresh fish and steaks, friendly young staff, well kept ales such as Wickwar, good wine and soft drinks choice; children and dogs welcome, big garden with barbecue and play area, bedrooms, open all day. *(Stephen Woad, Tom and Ruth Rees)*

PAINSWICK SO8609

Falcon (01452) 814222

New Street; GL6 6UN Handsome stone-built inn dating from the 16th c; sympathetically updated and comfortable open-plan layout with bar and two dining areas, good, popular food including daily specials, four well kept beers and good choice of wines by the glass, friendly young staff; Fri live music; children and dogs welcome, 12 comfortable bedrooms, opposite churchyard famous for its 99 yews. *(Millie and Peter Downing)*

PARKEND SO6107

Fountain (01594) 562189

Just off B4234; GL15 4JD Unpretentious 18th-c village inn by terminus of restored Lydney–Parkend steam railway; well kept Goffs, Sharps and Wye Valley, Weston's cider, wines in glass-sized bottles, enjoyable home-made traditional food including Sun carvery, welcoming helpful staff, assorted chairs and settles in two linked rooms, old tools, bric-a-brac, photographs and framed local history information, coal fire; quiz and live music nights; children, walkers and dogs welcome, wheelchair access, side garden, eight bedrooms and bunkhouse, open all day Sat. *(Alf Wright)*

PARKEND SO6308

Rising Sun (01594) 562008

Off B4431; GL15 4HN Perched on wooded hillside and approached by roughish single-track drive – popular with walkers and cyclists; open-plan carpeted bar with modern pub furniture, Wickwar BOB and several guests, real ciders and well priced straightforward food from sandwiches and baked potatoes up, friendly service, lounge/games area with pool and machines; children and dogs welcome, wheelchair access with

help, views from balcony and terrace tables under umbrellas, big woodside garden with play area and duck pond, self-catering accommodation, open (and food) all day. *(Colin and Daniel Gibbs)*

POULTON SP1001

Falcon (01285) 850878

London Road; GL7 5HN Bistro feel with good popular food from landlord-chef including lunchtime set menu, well kept local ales and nice wines by the glass, friendly attentive service and easy-going atmosphere; well behaved children welcome, closed Sun evening, Mon. *(Tom and Ruth Rees)*

QUENINGTON SP1404

Keepers Arms (01285) 750349

Church Road; GL7 5BL Community local in pretty Cotswold village, cosy and comfortable, with stripped stone, low beams and log fires, friendly helpful landlord and staff, good fairly priced food in bar and restaurant from sandwiches to popular Sun lunch, good value steak night Weds, well kept changing local beers and a traditional cider; dogs welcome, picnic-sets out in front, three bedrooms, closed Mon and Tues lunchtimes. *(Giles and Annie Francis, Dennis and Doreen Haward, R K Phillips)*

SALFORD HILL SP2629

Greedy Goose (01608) 646551

Junction A44/A436, near Chastleton; GL56 0SP Old roadside country dining pub with contemporary interior, enjoyable food from sandwiches and stone-baked pizzas up, three North Cotswold ales, friendly staff; children and dogs welcome, seats out at front and in back decked/gravelled area, camping, open all day. *(Katherine Matthews)*

SAPPERTON SO9403

Bell (01285) 760298

Village signposted from A419 Stroud–Cirencester; OS Sheet 163 map reference 948033; GL7 6LE Welcoming 250-year-old pub-restaurant, beams, flagstones and log fires, well kept ales such as Bath, Flying Monk, Hook Norton and Stroud, plenty of wines by the glass including Bollinger, generally well liked food from sharing boards and pub favourites to more ambitious choices, good service; children and dogs welcome, seats out in front and in back courtyard garden, tethering for horses, plenty of surrounding walks, open all day (till 9pm Sun). *(Beth Aldridge)*

SAPPERTON SO9303

Daneway Inn (01285) 760297

Daneway; off A419 Stroud–Cirencester; GL7 6LN The long serving licencees at this quietly tucked-away unspoilt local (a regular in the *Guide* for many years) have retired, the pub was closed for refurbishment as we went to press – news please.

SELSLEY SO8303
Bell (01453) 753801
Bell Lane; GL5 5JY Attractively updated
16th-c village inn under newish ownership;
good well presented food cooked by landlord-
chef from pub favourites up, Stroud, Uley
and a local guest, several wines by the glass
including champagne and some 30 gins,
friendly relaxed service, three connecting
rooms, open fire and woodburner, also garden
room dining extension; children, walkers
and dogs welcome, lovely valley views from
terrace tables, near Selsley Common and
Cotswold Way, two comfortably refurbished
bedrooms, closed Sun evening (and 3-5pm
Mon-Thurs in winter). *(Chris and Val
Ramstedt)*

SHIPTON MOYNE ST8989
Cat & Custard Pot (01666) 880249
*Off B4040 Malmesbury–Bristol; The
Street; GL8 8PN* Popular early 18th-c pub
(some recent renovation) in picturesque
village, several well kept ales such as Hook
Norton, Wadworths and Wickwar, decent
wines and enjoyable pubby food including
blackboard specials, friendly prompt service,
deceptively spacious inside with several
dining areas, beams and bric-a-brac, hunting
prints, cosy back snug, woodburner; children,
walkers and dogs welcome, disabled access/
facilities, shaded tables out on front lawn,
handy for Beaufort Polo Club, Highgrove
and Westonbirt Arboretum, open all day
weekends. *(Michael and Jenny Back, Chris and
Angela Buckell)*

SIDDINGTON SU0399
Greyhound (01285) 653573
*Ashton Road; village signed from A419
roundabout at Tesco; GL7 6HR*
Beamed village pub with linked rooms,
flagstones or carpet, some bare stone walls,
big log fires and woodburner, enjoyable
good value food from sandwiches/baguettes
up (smaller appetites catered for), well
kept Wadworths ales and plenty of wines
by the glass; background music; children
welcome, garden tables, open all day
weekends. *(Katherine Matthews)*

SLAD SO8707
Woolpack (01452) 813429
B4070 Stroud–Birdlip; GL6 7QA
Popular early 19th-c hillside village pub
with lovely valley views; four unspoilt little
connecting rooms, interesting photographs
including some of Laurie Lee who was a
regular (his books for sale), log fire, good
imaginative food (not Sun evening) along
with pub favourites and Mon pizza night, well
kept Uley ales and guests, local farm cider/
perry and decent wines by the glass, friendly
prompt service; some live music; children,
walkers and dogs welcome, nice garden
taking in the view, open all day. *(Chris and
Val Ramstedt)*

SLIMBRIDGE SO7204
Tudor Arms (01453) 890306
*Shepherds Patch; off A38 towards
Slimbridge Wetlands Centre; GL2 7BP*
Much extended red-brick pub just back from
canal swing bridge; welcoming and popular,
with several local ales, eight ciders/perries
and good wines by the glass, enjoyable food
(all day bar meals) from baguettes and
baked potatoes to daily specials, prompt
friendly service, linked areas with wood,
flagstone or carpeted floors, some leather
chairs and settles, comfortable dining room,
conservatory; darts, pool and skittle alley;
children and dogs (in back bar) welcome,
disabled facilities, picnic-sets outside (some
on covered terrace), boat trips, 12 annexe
bedrooms, caravan site off car park, open
all day. *(Colin and Daniel Gibbs)*

SNOWSHILL SP0933
Snowshill Arms (01386) 852653
Opposite village green; WR12 7JU
Unpretentious country pub in honeypot
village (so no shortage of customers);
well kept Donnington ales and reasonably
priced straightforward (but tasty) food from
sandwiches up, prompt friendly service,
beams, log fire, stripped stone and neat array
of tables, charming village views from bow
windows, local photographs; skittle alley;
children and dogs welcome, big back garden
with little stream and play area, handy for
Snowshill Manor (NT), lavender farm and
Cotswold Way walks. *(Eddie Edwards)*

SOMERFORD KEYNES SU0195
Bakers Arms (01285) 861298
*On main street through village;
GL7 6DN* Pretty little 17th-c stone-built
pub with catslide roof; four well kept ales
including Butcombe, Sharps and Stroud,
Addlestone's cider, good house wines,
generous helpings of enjoyable traditional
food, friendly service, lots of pine tables in
two linked areas, fire in big stone fireplace;
children and dogs welcome, nice garden with
play area, lovely village, handy for Cotswold
Water Park, open (and food) all day except
Sun when shuts at 6pm. *(Martin Day)*

SOUTHROP SP2003
★**Swan** (01367) 850205
Off A361 Lechlade–Burford; GL7 3NU
Creeper-clad 17th-c dining pub in attractive
village-green setting; bustling chatty bar with
simple tables and chairs, Bath Gem, Hook
Norton Hooky and Sharps Doom Bar, 15 wines
by the glass from well chosen list, highly
regarded creative cooking using home-grown
produce (must book), two low-ceilinged
front dining rooms with tweed-upholstered
chairs around nice mix of old tables, cushions
on settles, rugs on flagstones, open fires,
candles and fresh flowers; skittle alley, free
wi-fi; children and dogs welcome, tables in
sheltered back garden, good surrounding

walks, self-catering cottages, open all day Sat, till 4pm Sun. *(Alun and Jennifer Evans)*

ST BRIAVELS   SO5504
George (01594) 530228
High Street; GL15 6TA Old Wadworths pub with their beers and a couple of guests, enjoyable pubby food including good Sun lunch, friendly helpful service, rambling linked black-beamed rooms with attractive old-fashioned décor, woodburner in big stone fireplace, restaurant with another woodburner; children and dogs welcome, flagstoned terrace over former moat of neighbouring Norman fortress, four bedrooms, open all day weekends when can get very busy. *(Tom and Ruth Rees, Bob and Margaret Holder)*

STANTON   SP0634
★ Mount (01386) 584316
Village signposted off B4632 SW of Broadway; keep on past village on no-through road up hill, bear left; WR12 7NE 17th-c pub with fine views over village towards the welsh mountains; flagstoned bars with heavy beams in low ceilings, inglenook log fire, Donnington BB and SBA, good wines by the glass and enjoyable food from generous baguettes up, prompt friendly service, picture-window restaurant taking in the view; darts and board games, free wi-fi; well behaved children and dogs welcome, seats on terrace and in quiet garden, good walks – Cotswold Way and Wyche Way nearby, open all day weekends in summer, closed Sun evening, Mon in winter. *(Richard Tilbrook, M G Hart, S Holder, Guy Vowles, Phil and Jane Villiers)*

STAUNTON   SO7829
Swan (01452) 840323
Ledbury Road (A417), on mini roundabout; GL19 3QA Revamped village pub owned by local farming family (also have the Royal Exchange at Hartpury); enjoyable well priced food (including own lamb) from ciabattas and deli boards up, ales such as Butcombe and Wye Valley, Weston's cider, bar with sofas and woodburner, spacious restaurant and modern conservatory, attached barn for functions; live music last Sat of month, free wi-fi; children and dogs welcome, pretty garden, open all day Fri-Sun, closed Mon and Tues lunchtimes (no evening food on these days). *(Millie and Peter Downing)*

STAUNTON   SO5412
White Horse (01594) 834001
A4136; GL16 8PA Village pub on edge of Forest of Dean close to welsh border, welcoming and relaxed, with good freshly prepared food in bar or restaurant, well kept local ales and ciders, friendly helpful service; small shop; children and dogs welcome, disabled access, picnic-sets in good-sized garden with pod accommodation, open

all day Sat, till 5pm Sun, closed Mon and lunchtime Tues. *(Alf Wright)*

STOW-ON-THE-WOLD   SP1925
★ Bell (01451) 870916
Park Street; A436 E of centre; GL54 1AJ Creeper-clad dining pub with comfortable homely décor, good well presented food from bar snacks to fish specials (best to book), friendly efficient service, lots of wines by the glass including champagne, a couple of Youngs ales and a guest, proper beamed and flagstoned bar with woodburner and piano; under-16s in dining part only, dogs welcome, picnic-sets outside, five bedrooms, eight more in nearby townhouse, open (and some food) all day. *(Richard Tilbrook, Bill Webster)*

STOW-ON-THE-WOLD   SP1925
Kings Arms (01451) 830364
The Square; GL54 1AF Revamped 16th-c coaching inn; black-beamed bar with wood floor, stripped stone and painted panelling, woodburner, Greene King ales (including one badged for the pub) and a guest, enjoyable up-to-date food here or in upstairs Chophouse restaurant with saggy oak floor, leopard-skin bar stools and ink-spot tables, friendly service; children and dogs welcome, ten bedrooms including three courtyard 'cottages', open all day. *(Katherine Matthews)*

STOW-ON-THE-WOLD   SP1925
★ Talbot (01451) 870934
The Square; GL54 1BQ Cheerfully bustling one-bar pub in good position on market square; light and airy modern décor with relaxed café-bar feel, well liked interesting food including good set lunch, four Wadworths ales and several wines by the glass, cocktails, afternoon teas and proper coffee, huge mirror over big log fire, upstairs function room (and lavatories); background and occasional live music; no children inside, a few courtyard tables, open all day (till 1am Sat, 6.30pm Sun). *(Richard Tilbrook)*

STROUD   SO8505
Ale House (01453) 755447
John Street; GL5 2HA Fine range of well kept beers and ciders/perries (third-of-a-pint tasting glasses available), enjoyable food including signature curries and good value Sun lunch, main high-ceilinged part with sofa by big open fire, other rooms off; well behaved dogs welcome (biscuits for them), small side courtyard, farmers' market Sat, open all day Fri-Sun. *(Guy Vowles)*

SWINEFORD   ST6969
Swan (0117) 932 3101
A431, right on the Somerset border; BS30 6LN Popular 19th-c stone-built pub with well kept Bath Ales and a guest, decent ciders and carefully chosen range of other drinks including interesting wines and Penderyn welsh whisky, good food from pub favourites up (some imaginative choices),

helpful friendly staff, updated interior with light coloured furniture on quarry tiles or coir, pastel paintwork and dark-green panelled dado, raised back dining area, open fire, daily newspapers; children and dogs welcome, wheelchair access, picnic-sets out at front and in large sunny garden with play area, open all day, food all day Fri-Sun. *(Taff Thomas, Chris and Angela Buckell, Michael Doswell)*

TETBURY   ST8893
Close (01666) 502272
Long Street; GL8 8AQ Old stone hotel's contemporary bar, comfortable and stylish with blazing log fire, enjoyable food from sandwiches up, also brasserie and more formal dining room, coffee and afternoon teas, charming staff; children welcome, tables in lovely garden behind, open all day. *(Dr W I C Clark)*

TETBURY   ST8893
Priory (01666) 502251
London Road; GL8 8JJ Civilised restaurant-pub-hotel; central log fire in comfortable high-raftered stone-built former stables, enjoyable food (booking advised) with emphasis on interesting local produce, even a local slant to their good wood-fired pizzas, cheerful service, three well kept local ales including Uley, proper ciders and several wines by the glass, comfortable coffee lounge; children very welcome, dogs in bar, wheelchair access (staff helpful), roadside terrace picnic-sets, 14 bedrooms, open all day. *(Colin and Daniel Gibbs)*

TETBURY   ST8993
★ **Snooty Fox** (01666) 502436
Market Place; GL8 8DD High-ceilinged stripped-stone hotel lounge, four well kept local ales, a real cider and good house wines, enjoyable all-day bar food from sandwiches up, leather sofas and elegant fireplace, nice side room and anteroom, restaurant; background music; children and dogs welcome, a few sheltered tables out in front, 12 bedrooms. *(Taff Thomas)*

TEWKESBURY   SO8932
Nottingham Arms (01684) 276346
High Street; GL20 5JU Popular old black and white fronted bare-boards local, timbered bar with well kept St Austell, Sharps and Wye Valley, Weston's cider, enjoyable home-made food at reasonable prices including good Sun lunch, back dining room, friendly efficient service; music and quiz nights; children and dogs welcome, open all day. *(Dave Braisted)*

TEWKESBURY   SO8932
Royal Hop Pole (01684) 274039
Church Street; GL20 5RT Wetherspoons conversion of old inn (some parts dating from the 15th c), their usual value-minded all-day food and drink, good service; free wi-fi;

terrace seating and lovely garden leading down to river, 28 bedrooms, open from 7am. *(Theocsbrian, Dave Braisted)*

TEWKESBURY   SO8932
Theoc House (01684) 296562
Barton Street; GL20 5PY Old pub now more like a café/wine bar but with local ales, good range of food including tapas and vegetarian choices, reasonable prices, spacious split-level interior, books and board games; live jazz second and last Weds of month, free wi-fi; children and dogs welcome, open (and food) all day from 8.30am breakfast. *(Theocsbrian)*

TODDINGTON   SP0432
Pheasant (01242) 621271
A46 Broadway–Winchcombe, junction with A438 and B4077; GL54 5DT Large stone-built roadside pub with modern open-plan interior, tartan carpets, blue panelled dados and log fire, Donnington ales and enjoyable good value food, friendly attentive staff; children and dogs (in bar area) welcome, handy for preserved Gloucestershire Warwickshire Railway Station, open all day. *(Theocsbrian)*

TOLLDOWN   ST7577
Crown (01225) 891166
1 mile from M4 junction 18 – A46 towards Bath; SN14 8HZ Cosy heavy-beamed stone pub on crossroads; most here for the good food (all day Sun) from sandwiches and pub favourites to more upmarket choices, efficient welcoming staff, Wadworths ales, Thatcher's cider and plenty of wines by the glass, warm log fires, candles on pine tables, wood, coir and quarry-tiled floors, animal prints on green rough plaster walls, some bare stonework; children and dogs (in bar) welcome, disabled access/loos, sunny beer garden, nine bedrooms in building behind, handy for Dyrham Park (NT), open all day. *(Chris and Angela Buckell)*

ULEY   ST7998
Old Crown (01453) 860502
The Green; GL11 5SN Unspoilt 17th-c pub prettily set by village green just off Cotswold Way; long narrow room with settles and pews on bare boards, step up to partitioned-off lounge, six well kept local ales including Uley, decent wines by the glass and small choice of well liked pubby food from baguettes up, friendly service, open fire; children and dogs welcome, a few picnic-sets in front and attractive garden behind, four bedrooms, open all day. *(Maddie Purvis, Katherine Matthews)*

WESTONBIRT   ST8690
Hare & Hounds (01666) 881000
A433 SW of Tetbury; GL8 8QL Substantial roadside hotel with separate entrance to pub; good food from snacks and sharing boards up, well kept regional ales

and ciders, lots of wines by the glass and good selection of malts and other spirits, prompt polite service, flagstoned bar with another panelled one to the left, series of interconnecting rooms with polished wood floors, woodburner in two-way fireplace, some leather sofas and banquettes, more formal restaurant; children welcome, muddy boots and dogs in bar, disabled access/facilities, shaded tables out on front paved area, pleasant gardens, 42 bedrooms (some in outbuildings), handy for Arboretum, open all day and gets very busy (especially weekend lunchtimes). *(Chris and Angela Buckell)*

WHITMINSTER   SO7607
Fromebridge Mill (01452) 741796
Fromebridge Lane (A38 near M5 junction 13); GL2 7PD Comfortable mill-based dining pub with interconnecting rooms, beams, bare brick walls, flagstone and carpeted floors, some tables overlooking river, well kept Greene King and guests, several wines by the glass and good selection of gins, popular food including lunchtime carvery (evenings too at weekends), helpful pleasant staff; children welcome, no dogs inside, disabled access and loos, picnic-sets in big garden with play area, pretty waterside setting, footbridge from car park, open (and food) all day, can get very busy. *(Chris and Angela Buckell)*

WILLERSEY   SP1039
★Bell (01386) 858405
B4632 Cheltenham–Stratford, near Broadway; WR12 7PJ Imposing neatly modernised 17th-c stone pub, popular home-made food from sandwiches and bar meals up, ales such as Purity UBU and Mad Goose, good friendly service; children welcome, dogs in bar (theirs is Beau), overlooks village green and duck pond, lots of tables in big garden, good local walks (Cotswold Way), five bedrooms in outbuildings, open all day weekends. *(Dave Braisted)*

WINCHCOMBE   SP0228
Plaisterers Arms (01242) 602358
Abbey Terrace; GL54 5LL Traditional old split-level pub with beams and stripped stonework, well kept Timothy Taylors Landlord, Wye Valley and a guest, enjoyable pubby food served by friendly staff, two chatty front bars both with steps down to

dimly lit lower back dining area, some stall tables, Hogarth prints, bric-a-brac and flame-effect fire; TV, darts and piano; children and dogs welcome, play area in long secluded back garden, five simple bedrooms (tricky stairs). *(Steve and Liz Tilley, Richard Woods)*

WINCHCOMBE   SP0228
★White Hart (01242) 602359
High Street (B4632); GL54 5LJ Popular 16th-c inn with big windows looking out over village street, mix of chairs and small settles around pine tables, bare boards and grey-green paintwork, cricketing memorabilia, well kept Goffs and other ales such as Prescott, Wadworths and Wickwar, wine shop at back (corkage added if you buy to drink on premises), wide choice by the glass too, specialist sausage menu (including vegetarian) and other enjoyable food, good friendly service, separate restaurant, log fire; sports TV; children and dogs (in bar and bedrooms) welcome, open all day from 9am (10am Sun). *(Steve and Liz Tilley, Guy Vowles)*

WITHINGTON   SP0315
Mill Inn (01242) 890204
Off A436 or A40; GL54 4BE Idyllic streamside setting for this mossy-roofed old stone inn, plenty of character with nice nooks and corners, beams, wood/flagstone floors, two inglenook log fires and woodburner, well kept/priced Sam Smiths tapped from the cask and ample helpings of enjoyable traditional food including basket meals, four dining rooms, cheerful staff coping well at busy times; children and dogs welcome, picnic-sets in big garden, splendid walks, open all day in summer (all day Sat, closed Sun evening in winter). *(Dennis and Doreen Haward, Richard Tilbrook)*

WOOLASTON COMMON   SO5900
Rising Sun (01594) 529282
Village signed off A48 Lydney–Chepstow; GL15 6NU Traditional 17th-c stone village pub on fringe of Forest of Dean, friendly and welcoming, with enjoyable reasonably priced home-made food including signature pies, well kept Butcombe, Wye Valley and a guest, good helpful service; children and dogs welcome, seats out at front and in large back garden, open all day weekends in summer, closed Mon and Tues lunchtimes. *(Teresa Reith)*

Post Office address codings confusingly give the impression that some pubs are in Gloucestershire, when they're really in Warwickshire (which is where we list them).

Hampshire

AMPORT
Hawk Inn 🛏

SU2944   Map 2

(01264) 710371 – www.hawkinnamport.co.uk

Off A303 at Thruxton interchange; at Andover end of village just before Monxton; SP11 8AE

Relaxed rambling pub with contemporary furnishings in front bar and dining areas, helpful staff and well thought-of food; bedrooms

This very pleasing, rambling old place is handy for visitors to the famous Hawk Conservancy Trust, which is just down the road. The comfortable front bar is open-plan and modern, with brown leather armchairs and plush grey sofas by a low table, a log fire in a brick fireplace and sisal matting on bare boards. To the left, a tucked-away snug room has horse-racing photographs, shelves of books and a TV. Two dining areas have smart window blinds, black leather cushioned wall seating and elegant wooden chairs (some carved) around pale tables, big oil paintings on pale walls above a grey dado, and a woodburning stove. Black-topped stools line the counter, where courteous staff serve Upham Punter, Stakes Ale and Tipster and a guest ale on handpump and quite a few wines by the glass. The sunny sandstone front terrace has picnic-sets looking across the lane to more seating on grass that leads down to Pill Hill brook. Bedrooms are up to date and comfortable.

🍴 As well as breakfasts (7.30-10.30am weekdays, 8.30-10.30am weekends), the good food includes sandwiches, smoked duck with red wine poached pear and pecan praline, chicken liver and port pâté with chutney, sharing boards, courgette pancakes with wild mushrooms, blue cheese, spinach and pistachios, venison and mushroom pie, burger with fries and coleslaw, lemon and tarragon corn-fed chicken with fondant potato, savoy cabbage, onion purée and red wine sauce, salmon fillet with roasted red peppers, fennel, curried chickpeas and chorizo, and puddings. *Benchmark main dish: lamb rump with dauphinoise potatoes, butternut squash and red wine jus £22.00. Two-course evening meal £21.00.*

Free house ~ Licensee Becky Anderson ~ Real ale ~ Open 7.30am-11pm; 8.30am-11pm Sat; 8.30am-10.30pm Sun ~ Bar food 12-2.30, 6-9 (9.30 Fri, Sat) ~ Children welcome ~ Dogs allowed in bar ~ Wi-fi ~ Bedrooms: /£90 *Recommended by Emma Scofield, Gus Swan, Edward Mirzoeff*

BANK

SU2806 Map 2

Oak 🍺

(023) 8028 2350 – www.oakinnlyndhurst.co.uk

Signposted just off A35 SW of Lyndhurst; SO43 7FE

New Forest pub with a good mix of customers, popular food and interesting décor

Our readers always enjoy this bustling pub – especially after a walk. There's a warm welcome for all from the friendly staff and the L-shaped bar has bay windows with built-in red-cushioned seats, and two or three little pine-panelled booths with small built-in tables and bench seats. The rest of the bare-boarded bar has low beams and joists, candles in brass holders on a row of stripped old and newer blond tables set against the wall and all manner of bric-a-brac: fishing rods, spears, a boomerang, old ski poles, brass platters, heavy knives and guns. There are cushioned milk churns along the bar counter and little red lanterns among hop bines above the bar. Fullers London Pride, HSB and Gales Seafarers and a changing local guest on handpump and 14 wines by the glass; background music. The pleasant side garden has picnic-sets and long tables and benches by big yew trees.

 Rewarding food includes doorstep sandwiches, battered soft-shell crab with sweet chilli and tamarind jam, game terrine wrapped in bacon with pickled vegetables and quince jelly, burger with toppings, onion marmalade and chips, rosemary and honey butternut squash with piperade and chestnut and pumpkin-filled gnocchi, pheasant breast with sweetcorn purée, wild mushrooms and shallot sauce, a daily fresh dish, and puddings. *Benchmark main dish: pie of the day £13.95. Two-course evening meal £20.00.*

Fullers ~ Manager Carlos Dias ~ Real ale ~ Open 11.30-3, 5.30-11; 11.30-11 Sat; 12-10.30 Sun ~ Bar food 12-2.30, 6-9 (9.30 Fri); 12-5, 6-9.30 (9 Sun) Sat ~ Children welcome until 6pm; must be over 10 after 6pm ~ Dogs allowed in bar ~ Wi-fi *Recommended by B R Merritt, Katharine Cowherd, M G Hart, Mr and Mrs D Hammond, Alastair and Sheree Hepburn, Phil and Jane Villiers, Jane and Kai Horsburgh*

BAUGHURST

SU5860 Map 2

Wellington Arms 🏅 ♀ 🛏

(0118) 982 0110 – www.thewellingtonarms.com

Baughurst Road, S of village; RG26 5LP

Hampshire Dining Pub of the Year

Pretty, small country pub-with-rooms, exceptional cooking and a friendly welcome; bedrooms

As always, this delightful little country inn is run with great care by the friendly licensees and their courteous staff – and our readers love it. Of course, most people are here for the excellent food but they do keep a couple of ales such as Longdog Bunny Chaser and West Berkshire Good Old Boy on handpump, ten wines by the glass and a farm cider; background music. The dining room is attractively decorated with an assortment of cushioned oak dining chairs around a mix of polished tables on terracotta tiles, pretty blinds, brass candlesticks, flowers and windowsills stacked with cookery books. The garden has teak furniture and herbaceous borders. The four bedrooms are charming and very well equipped.

 Food is very special and makes good use of their own vegetables, bees and livestock: rabbit, pork and pheasant terrine with spiced apple chutney, baked potato gnocchi with garlic, twice-baked cheddar soufflé on braised young leeks with double cream and parmesan, caramelised butternut squash, walnuts and sage, skate wing with brown butter and capers, roast rack of lamb on sicilian caponata with pine nuts, pork chop on sticky red cabbage with parsnip crisps, and puddings such as jelly of their own elderflower cordial with rhubarb ripple ice-cream and baked caramel custard with oranges in cinnamon syrup; they may offer a two- and three-course set lunch. *Benchmark main dish: venison pot pie with celery and shallots £16.00. Two-course evening meal £23.00.*

Free house ~ Licensees Simon Page and Jason King ~ Real ale ~ Open 9-3, 6-11; 9-4 Sun ~ Bar food 12-1.30, 6.30-8.30 (9 Fri, Sat); 12-4 Sun ~ Children welcome ~ Dogs welcome ~ Wi-fi ~ Bedrooms: /£100 *Recommended by Mrs P Sumner, Ron Corbett, Kate Moran, Mark Morgan, Ben and Diane Bowie*

BEAULIEU
Montagu Arms
SU3902 Map 2

(01590) 614986 – www.montaguarmshotel.co.uk
Almost opposite Palace House; SO42 7ZL

Separate Monty's Bar, open all day for both drinks and food

The solidly built and civilised Montagu Arms hotel has a separate little bar called Monty's with its own entrance. Usefully open all day, this simply furnished bar has panelling, bare floorboards, bay windows and a mix of pale tables surrounded by tartan-cushioned dining chairs; winter log fire. There are still a couple of stools against the bar counter where they keep Ringwood Best and Fortyniner and a seasonal guest on handpump and several wines by the glass, served by cheerful, helpful bar staff. Across the entrance hall is a smarter panelled dining room. Do visit the hotel's tucked-away back garden, which is quite charming in warm weather.

Popular food includes lunchtime sandwiches (until 5pm weekends), mackerel pâté with grape chutney, crispy goats cheese with pickled beetroot, apple and beetroot purée and candied walnuts, local sausages with onion gravy, vegetarian cottage pie, a pasta and a risotto dish of the day, slow-cooked beef with horseradish dumplings, pork belly with braised red cabbage and sultanas, dauphinoise potatoes and apple sauce, a daily fresh fish dish, and puddings. *Benchmark main dish: battered haddock and chips £12.95. Two-course evening meal £20.00.*

Free house ~ Licensee Sunil Kanjanghat ~ Real ale ~ Open 11-11 (10.30 Sun); 11-3, 6-11 in winter ~ Bar food 12-2.30 (3 weekends), 6.30-9.30 ~ Restaurant ~ Children welcome ~ Dogs allowed in bar ~ Wi-fi ~ Bedrooms: £139/£159 *Recommended by Rob Anderson, Rona Mackinlay, Simon Day*

BIGHTON
English Partridge 🏆 ♀
SU6134 Map 2

(01962) 732859 – www.englishpartridge.co.uk
Bighton Dean Lane; village signed off B3046 N of Alresford; SO24 9RE

Character bars in friendly country pub with good wines and beers and highly enjoyable food

Although this charming little country pub is extremely popular locally, you can be sure that visitors are just as warmly welcomed. At the front, a small simple room to the left of the door is just right for walkers and their dogs, with a warm open fire, a few chairs and tables and stools against the counter. The main bar has a wonderful ancient parquet floor, a black dado with hunting prints, local shoot photographs and game bird pictures on the walls above, a stuffed pheasant in a glass cabinet, a woodburning stove in a brick inglenook, a fireplace filled with candles, and all sorts of dining chairs and tables. Flowerpots Perridge Pale and Triple fff Altons Pride and Moondance on handpump, ten wines by the glass, eight gins, farm cider and Somerset cider brandy; darts, board games and maybe unobtrusive background music. Through an open doorway, the back dining room has long built-in wall seats with scatter cushions, similar chairs and tables (each set with a candle in a candlestick), a huge deer's head and a boar's head, antlers, shooting and hunting photographs and fish and bird prints. The garden has a terrace with tables and chairs under parasols.

Highly regarded food includes lunchtime sandwiches, baked mini camembert with chilli jam, game pâté with tomato chutney, potato and onion tortilla with salad, lamb and rosemary sausages with onion gravy, chicken and leek pie, beer-battered haddock, and puddings such as chocolate brownie with chocolate sauce and sticky toffee pudding with butterscotch sauce; Friday is fish night, when the £10.95 deal includes a glass of wine. *Benchmark main dish: burger with toppings and triple-cooked chips £12.00. Two-course evening meal £19.00.*

Free house ~ Licensee David Young ~ Real ale ~ Open 12-3, 5-11; 12-11 Sat; 12-8 Sun; closed Mon, Tues except summer school holidays ~ Bar food 12-2.30, 6.30-9.30; 12-3 Sun ~ Children welcome ~ Dogs allowed in bar ~ Wi-fi *Recommended by Tony and Jill Radnor, M G Hart, Ann and Colin Hunt, Helene Grygar*

BRANSGORE

Three Tuns

SZ1997   Map 2

(01425) 672232 – www.threetunsinn.com

Village signposted off A35 and off B3347 N of Christchurch; Ringwood Road, opposite church; BH23 8JH

Pretty thatched pub with proper old-fashioned bar and good beers, a civilised main dining area and inventive food

Run by helpful, friendly licensees, this 17th-c thatched pub has a good choice of beers and inventive food. On the right is a separate traditional regulars' bar that seems almost taller than it is wide, with an impressive log-effect stove in a stripped-brick hearth, some shiny black panelling and individualistic pubby furnishings. The roomy low-ceilinged and carpeted main area has a fireside 'codgers' corner', as well as a good mix of comfortably cushioned low chairs around a variety of dining tables. Otter Amber, Ringwood Fortyniner and Razorback plus guests such as Skinners Betty Stogs and Cornish Knocker Ale on handpump, a dozen wines by the glass and farm cider; they hold a beer festival in September. The hanging baskets are lovely in summer and there are picnic-sets on an attractive, extensive, shrub-sheltered terrace with more tables on the grass looking over pony paddocks; pétanque. The Grade II listed barn is popular for parties and they hold a civil ceremonies licence.

Accomplished food includes sandwiches, corned beef hash fritters with home-made brown sauce and slaw, mussels in garlic, cider, chilli, ginger and cream, gnocchi with mushroom, cep purée, crispy black cabbage and truffle oil, corn-fed breadcrumbed chicken with bacon, curried popcorn, sweet potato, banana and coconut gel, venison stew with porcini dumplings, a fish dish of the day, and puddings such as orange and almond tart with brown butter ice-cream and pavlova with pineapple. *Benchmark main dish: slow-cooked pork with compressed apples and dijonnaise sauce £13.95. Two-course evening meal £19.95.*

Enterprise ~ Lease Nigel Glenister ~ Real ale ~ Open 11-11; 12-10.30 Sun ~ Bar food 12-2.15, 6.30-9.15; 12-9.15 weekends and bank holidays ~ Restaurant ~ Children welcome

~ Dogs allowed in bar ~ Wi-fi *Recommended by Glenwys and Alan Lawrence, Brian and Anna Marsden, Anne and Ben Smith*

CADNAM
SU2913 Map 2

White Hart ♀ ◖

(023) 8081 2277 – www.brunningandprice.co.uk/whitehartcadnam

Old Romsey Road, handy for M27 junction 1; SO40 2NP

Extended New Forest pub with busy bar and dining rooms, a warm welcome, good choice of drinks and tasty food

Smartly done up and extended, this bustling place is always full of both locals and visitors. The bar with its long curved counter is at the heart of things, with an open fire, stools and tables on parquet flooring, Phoenix Brunning & Price, Cottage Conquest Session IPA and Duchess, Hop Back Golden Best, Upham Punter and a guest or two on handpump and good wines by the glass served by helpful, friendly staff. There's also a cosy area with a woodburning stove in a nice old brick fireplace, rugs and comfortable leather armchairs. Various dining rooms lead off with more rugs on carpet or tiles, all manner of cushioned dining chairs and wooden tables, painted wooden dados with frame-to-frame country pictures and photographs on pale walls above, house plants on windowsills, mirrors and elegant metal chandeliers. The back terrace and garden have plenty of chairs and tables and there's a children's play area with a painted tractor.

Popular all-day food includes sandwiches, smoked ham croquettes with piccalilli dressing, mushroom and goats cheese fritter with pickled carrot salad and walnut dressing, parmesan and pine nut gnocchi with roasted mediterranean vegetables and basil pesto, crispy beef salad with sweet chilli and cashew nuts, fish pie, chicken, ham and leek pie, pork and leek sausages with onion gravy, and puddings such as glazed lemon tart with lemon sorbet and hot waffle with toffee sauce, banana and honeycomb ice-cream. *Benchmark main dish: steak burger with toppings, coleslaw and chips £12.45. Two-course evening meal £20.00.*

Brunning & Price ~ Manager Sorrel Taylor ~ Real ale ~ Open 10.30am-11pm (10.30pm Sun) ~ Bar food 12-10 (9 Sun) ~ Restaurant ~ Children welcome ~ Dogs allowed in bar ~ Wi-fi
Recommended by Gerry and Rosemary Dobson, Tom Stone, Christopher Mannings

DROXFORD
SU6018 Map 2

Bakers Arms ⊙◖ ◖

(01489) 877533 – www.thebakersarmsdroxford.com

High Street; A32 5 miles N of Wickham; SO32 3PA

Welcoming, opened-up and friendly pub with good beers, interesting cooking and cosy corners

Bowman brewery is just a mile away and their ales and maybe a couple of guests are well kept on handpump here. It's a friendly pub with an easy-going atmosphere and is attractively laid out with the central bar as the main focus: Bowman Swift One and Wallops Wood and Ringwood Old Thumper on handpump, local cider and 15 wines by the glass from a short, carefully chosen list. Well spaced tables on carpet or neat bare boards are spread around the airy L-shaped open-plan bar, with low leather chesterfields and an assortment of comfortably cushioned chairs at one end; a dark panelled dado, dark beams and joists and a modicum of country oddments emphasise the freshness of the crisp white paintwork; good log fire and board games. To one side, with a separate entrance, is the village post office. There are picnic-sets outside. There are some lovely walks along and around the nearby River Meon.

As well as a two-course set menu (the price includes a drink), the enjoyable food includes sandwiches, black pudding and chorizo salad, spiced lamb ball salad with minty yoghurt dressing, pork sausages with onion gravy, baked crab with lemon mayonnaise and skinny fries, creamy goats cheese, chestnut and spinach linguine, pheasant breast with pheasant bonbon, sauté potatoes and game gravy, local chalkstream trout with white wine butter sauce, and puddings such as pecan and almond tart and chocolate brownie with butterscotch ice-cream. *Benchmark main dish: braised local beef pie £14.00. Two-course evening meal £20.00.*

Free house ~ Licensees Adam and Anna Cordery ~ Real ale ~ Open 12-3, 6-11; 12-4 Sun ~ Bar food 12-2.30, 6.30-9.30; 12-3 Sun ~ Well behaved children welcome ~ Dogs allowed in bar ~ Wi-fi *Recommended by R Halliday, Kate Moran, Phil and Jane Villiers, Sophie Ellison, Ann and Colin Hunt*

EAST STRATTON
SU5339   Map 2
Northbrook Arms 🍺
(01962) 774150 – www.thenorthbrookarms.com
Brown sign to pub off A33 4 miles S of A303 junction; SO21 3DU

Half a dozen beers and tasty food in pretty pub on family estate; bedrooms

There's been some redecoration for this attractive brick-built village pub. The traditional tiled-floor beamed bar on the right has beams and standing timbers, quite a mix of chairs and tables and up to five real ales on handpump such as Branscombe Vale Best Bitter, Butcombe Bitter, Triple fff Altons Pride and Sharps Cornish Coaster; quite a few wines by the glass too. The left-hand carpeted part is slightly more formal, ending in a dining room beyond a little central hall; background music. The skittle alley is in the former stables. You can sit in the pretty country garden to the side or on the village green opposite. Fine nearby walks.

Seasonally changing food includes lunchtime sandwiches, goats cheese wellington with orange and beetroot purée, roast garlic and chicken liver pâté with chutney, local sausages with sweet pickled onions and mash, a pie of the day, confit pork belly with sage dauphinoise potatoes, crispy shallots and calvados and apple sauce, hake fillet wrapped in pancetta on crushed lemon and dill potatoes, and puddings such as cheesecake of the day with fruit coulis and dark chocolate brownie with white chocolate sauce. *Benchmark main dish: chilli chicken kebab with mango, lime and coriander salsa £12.95. Two-course evening meal £19.50.*

Free house ~ Licensee Ian Ashton ~ Real ale ~ Open 11-11 (10.30 Sun) ~ Bar food 12-3, 6-9; 12-9 Sat; 12-6 Sun ~ Restaurant ~ Children welcome ~ Dogs welcome ~ Wi-fi ~ Bedrooms: $80/$90 *Recommended by Sara Fulton, Roger Baker, Simon and Alex Knight*

EASTON
SU5132   Map 2
Chestnut Horse ♈
(01962) 779257 – www.thechestnuthorse.com
3.6 miles from M3 junction 9: A33 towards Kings Worthy, then B3047 towards Itchen Abbas; Easton signposted on right – bear left in village; SO21 1EG

This smart 16th-c pub is the hub of this pretty village of thatched cottages – and the hands-on landlady offers a friendly welcome to all

The interior, although open-plan, has a pleasantly rustic and cosy feel with a series of intimate separate areas; the snug décor takes in candles and fresh flowers on the tables, log fires in open fireplaces and comfortable furnishings. The black beams and joists are hung with all sorts of jugs, mugs and chamber-pots, and there are pictures of wildlife and the local area. Badger First Call and K&B Sussex Bitter and a guest beer on handpump, up to a dozen wines by the glass and 20 malt whiskies. The smallish sheltered decked area has seats and tables and colourful flowering tubs and baskets, and there are picnic-sets at the front. Walks in the nearby Itchen Valley.

 Good food includes smoked duck with soy dressing, noodles and carrot purée, confit pork belly with parma ham, caramelised apples and celeriac rémoulade, spinach and ricotta cannelloni, burger with toppings and fries, cod cheeks with creamed leeks, pomme purée, spinach and pancetta crumb, herb-crusted rack of lamb with sweetbreads, olive tapenade and boulangère potatoes, and puddings such as carrot cake with sweet carrot gel and buttermilk ice-cream and vanilla crème brûlée; they also offer a two-course set menu at lunch and early evening (not Saturday evening or Sunday). *Benchmark main dish: beer-battered fresh cod and chips £14.00. Two-course evening meal £19.00.*

Badger ~ Tenant Karen Wells ~ Real ale ~ Open 12-4, 5.30-11; 12-11 Fri-Sun ~ Bar food 12-2.30, 6-9.30; 12-8 Sun ~ Restaurant ~ Children welcome ~ Dogs allowed in bar ~ Wi-fi
Recommended by Richard Tilbrook, Helen and Brian Edgeley, Ann and Colin Hunt, John Hills, Malcolm and Jane Levitt, M G Hart, Dr and Mrs Paul Cartwright, Katharine Cowherd

FRITHAM
Royal Oak 🍺
SU2314   Map 2

(023) 8081 2606
Village signed from M27 junction 1; SO43 7HJ

Rural New Forest spot with traditional rooms, log fires, seven real ales and simple lunchtime food

The appeal of this charming brick and cob thatched pub lies in its simple rural rusticity. It's in a lovely spot right in the middle of the New Forest and part of a working farm, so there are ponies and pigs out on the green and plenty of livestock nearby. The three neatly kept black-beamed rooms are straightforward but full of proper traditional character, with prints and pictures involving local characters on the white walls, restored panelling, antique wheelback, spindleback and other old chairs and stools with colourful seats around solid tables on oak floors, and two roaring log fires. The back bar has several books; darts and board games. Up to seven real ales are tapped from the cask including one named for the pub (from Bowman), Bowman Swift One, Eight Arch Parabolic, Flack Manor Double Drop, Hop Back Summer Lightning, Stonehenge Danish Dynamite and a guest ale from Kingstone. Also, nine wines by the glass (mulled wine in winter), 14 country wines, local cider and a September beer festival; service remains friendly and efficient even when packed (which it often is). Summer barbecues may be held in the neatly kept big garden, which has a marquee for poor weather and a pétanque pitch. They have three shepherd's huts to rent for overnight stays.

🍴 Good value, limited food – lunchtime only – consists of wholesome winter soup, a particularly good pork pie, quiche and sausages. *Benchmark main dish: home-cooked pork pie ploughman's £8.50.*

Free house ~ Licensees Neil and Pauline McCulloch ~ Real ale ~ Open 11-11; 12-10.30 Sun; 11-3, 5.30-11 weekdays in winter ~ Bar food 12-2.30 (3 weekends) ~ Children welcome ~ Dogs welcome *Recommended by Sheila Topham, Adrian Johnson, Peter Meister*

Bedroom prices are for high summer. Even then you may get reductions for more than one night, or (outside tourist areas) weekends. Winter special rates are common, and many inns reduce bedroom prices if you have a full evening meal.

HIGHCLERE
Yew Tree ♀ ⇔

SU4358 Map 2

(01635) 253360 – www.theyewtree.co.uk

Hollington Cross; RG20 9SE

Friendly country inn with character rooms, a good choice of drinks, enjoyable food and seats in garden; bedrooms

The atmosphere in this 17th-c country inn is one of easy informality. The main door opens into a heavy-beamed character bar with leather tub chairs and a leather sofa facing one another across a low table in front of a two-way fireplace housing a chiminea stove, and stools and high chairs against the counter (church candles in chunky candlesticks on either side). Ringwood Best, Two Cocks 1643 Cavalier and Upham Punter on handpump and good wines by the glass, served by friendly, helpful staff. Leading off to the left is a room with antlers and stuffed squirrels on the mantelpiece above an inglenook fireplace, books piled on shelves, a pale button-back leather window seat, a mix of wooden and painted dining chairs around nice old tables on red and black tiles or carpet, and, at one end, a tartan and leather wall banquette; unobtrusive background music. Dining rooms to the left of the bar, divided by hefty timbers, have high-backed tartan seating creating booths and more wooden or painted chairs around a mix of tables on flagstones or sisal carpet. Doors lead to the garden, where there's an outside bar and a variety of elegant metal and teak seats and tables on gravel or raised decking. Well equipped and comfortable bedrooms (two on the ground floor) are named after trees; breakfasts are good. Highclere Castle is just a few minutes away.

Attractively presented food includes lunchtime sandwiches (not Sunday), mackerel fillet with new potatoes, spring onion and radish salad, venison terrine with red onion marmalade, fresh tagliatelle with purple sprouting broccoli, ricotta and wild garlic pesto, chicken caesar salad, burger with toppings, red onion marmalade, coleslaw and chips, roast cod with prawn, mussel, potato and fresh herb chowder, rack of lamb with braised red cabbage, lyonnaise potatoes and rosemary jus, and puddings such as frozen hazelnut parfait with dark chocolate cream and millionaire's shortbread. *Benchmark main dish: crispy pork belly £16.95. Two-course evening meal £21.00.*

Free house ~ Licensees Simon Davis and Tori Sambrook ~ Real ale ~ Open 9am-11pm ~ Bar food 12-2.30, 6.30-9.30 (7-8.30 Sun) ~ Children welcome ~ Dogs allowed in bar and bedrooms ~ Wi-fi ~ Bedrooms: /£99 *Recommended by Neill Allen, Emma Scofield, Barbara Brown*

HOOK
Hogget ◀

SU7153 Map 2

(01256) 763009 – www.thehogget.co.uk

1.1 miles from M3 junction 5; A287 N, at junction with A30 (car park just before traffic lights); RG27 9JJ

Well run and accommodating, a proper pub moving with the times and giving good value

There are plenty of visitors as well as lots of regular customers at this very cheerful and chatty place. The various rooms ramble around the central servery so there's plenty of space for all; the wallpaper, lighting and carpet pattern, plus high-backed stools and bar tables on the right at the back, give an easy-going and homely feel – as does the way the layout provides several smallish distinct areas. Ringwood Fortyniner and Razorback and Wychwood Dirty Tackle on handpump, 13 wines by the glass plus prosecco and plenty of neatly dressed staff; daily papers, background music and books (often cookbooks) on shelves. A sizeable terrace has sturdy tables and chairs, including some in a heated covered area.

❚❚❚ Good food includes lunchtime sandwiches (not Sunday), chilli, garlic and parsley tiger prawns, hoisin crispy duck salad, roasted pumpkin and thyme risotto, crab, chilli and fennel linguine, chilli con carne, a pie of the day, chicken with olives, cheese and mushroom sauce on spaghetti, rib-eye steak with a choice of sauces and triple-cooked chips, and puddings such as warm salted caramel fondue with pineapple, banana and marshmallows and white chocolate cheesecake with peanut praline. *Benchmark main dish: steak burger with toppings and triple-cooked chips £12.00. Two-course evening meal £20.00.*

Marstons ~ Lease Tom and Laura Faulkner ~ Real ale ~ Open 12-3, 6-11; 12-11 Sat; 12-6 Sun ~ Bar food 12-2.30, 6.30-9; all day Sat; 12-6 Sun ~ Restaurant ~ Children welcome but not after 7pm Fri and Sat ~ Dogs allowed in bar ~ Wi-fi *Recommended by Caroline Prescott, Lindy Andrews, Mrs P Sumner*

HORDLE
SZ2996 Map 2

Mill at Gordleton 🍴 ♀ ⛵

(01590) 682219 – www.themillatgordleton.co.uk
Silver Street; SO41 6DJ

Charming tucked-away country inn with friendly bar, exceptional food and pretty waterside gardens; comfortable bedrooms

The comfortable, individually furnished bedrooms here make a perfect base for exploring the area – it's on the edge of the New Forest, so there are plenty of nearby walks; breakfasts are excellent. The little panelled bar on the right is popular with locals (often with a dog) and has leather armchairs and Victorian-style mahogany dining chairs on parquet flooring, a feature stove, a pretty corner china cupboard, Ringwood Best and Upham 1st Drop on handpump, 18 good wines by the glass, 22 malt whiskies and a rack of daily papers. This overflows into a cosy lounge, and there's also a spacious second bar by the sizeable beamed restaurant extension (an attractive room with contemporary art and garden outlook). The gardens are really lovely, featuring an extensive series of interestingly planted areas looping about pools and a placid winding stream, dotted with intriguing art objects and with plenty of places to sit, from intimate pairs of seats to teak or wrought-iron tables on the main waterside terrace (which is beautifully illuminated at night).

⬟ Excellent food using local organic produce includes lunchtime rolls, twice-baked crab and cheddar soufflé with herb cream, potted ham with soft-boiled duck egg and brioche soldiers, steamed vegetable dumplings with sesame and ginger stir-fry vegetables and soy dip, local cumberland sausages with braised ham hock, mash and red wine jus, fillet of monkfish and tiger prawns with vegetable biryani, spiced cabbage, pomegranate and mint raita, and puddings such as five-spiced chocolate fondant with white chocolate and cardamom sauce and grapefruit sorbet and mango cheesecake with raspberry sauce; they also offer a two- and three-course set menu (not Sunday). *Benchmark main dish: fillet of beef with thyme-braised potato, artichoke, chicory and cep jus £28.95. Two-course evening meal £35.00.*

Upham ~ Tenant Thomas Lyon-Shaw ~ Real ale ~ Open 11-11; 12-10.30 Sun ~ Bar food 12-2.15, 7-9.15; 12-3, 6.30-8.15 Sun ~ Restaurant ~ Children welcome ~ Dogs allowed in bar ~ Wi-fi ~ Bedrooms: /£150 *Recommended by Michael Hill, Christopher and Elise Way, Gerry and Rosemary Dobson*

We say if we know a pub has background music.

HURSLEY

SU4225 Map 2

Kings Head 🍷 🍺 🛏

(01962) 775208 – www.kingsheadhursley.co.uk

A3090 Winchester–Romsey; SO21 2JW

Creeper-covered pub with an easy, friendly atmosphere, interestingly furnished rooms, well kept ales, good wines and enjoyable food; lovely bedrooms

With welcoming, helpful staff, character rooms and a thoughtful choice of both drinks and food, this former coaching inn is a winner. The bar to the left has shutters by a cushioned window seat, high-backed plush green chairs and chunky leather stools around scrubbed tables on black floor slates, one high table with equally high chairs, a raised fireplace with church candles on the mantelpiece and stools against the S-shaped, grey-painted counter. Bowman Swift One, Flack Manor Double Drop, Ringwood Best, Sharps Doom Bar and Upham Sprinter on handpump and 21 wines by the glass; background music, a piano, daily papers and board games. A character lower room has a fine end brick wall, a woodburning stove and wall banquettes with leather and tartan upholstery, and cushioned settles on floorboards. You can hire out the atmospheric downstairs skittle alley. The smartly updated courtyard garden has wooden or metal seats and tables on brickwork or gravel, parasols and heaters. The comfortable, thoughtfully equipped bedrooms (named after previous owners of the Hursley Estate) have antiques and original fireplaces. The ancient village church is opposite.

 Enterprising food includes sandwiches, twice-baked cheese soufflé, sardines on tomato toast, gammon and eggs, chicken caesar salad, asparagus ravioli with basil pesto, slow-roasted local venison loin with fennel seed and pepper crust, parsnip purée and red wine sauce, bass fillet with tiger prawns, smoked haddock and spring onion cake and lemon and dill hollandaise, pheasant, chestnut and orange pie, and puddings such as plum tarte tatin with vanilla bean ice-cream and chocolate mousse with coffee cream. *Benchmark main dish: burger with cabbage slaw, cheese and skinny chips £12.90. Two-course evening meal £22.00.*

Free house ~ Licensees Mark and Penny Thornhill ~ Real ale ~ Open 11-11; 12-10.30 Sun ~ Bar food 12-3, 6-9; 12-9.30 Sat; 12-8 Sun ~ Restaurant ~ Children welcome ~ Dogs allowed in bar ~ Wi-fi ~ Bedrooms: £85/£100 *Recommended by Jack and Hilary Burton, Valerie Sayer, Tim King*

LISS

SU7826 Map 2

Jolly Drover 🛏

(01730) 893137 – www.thejollydrover.co.uk

London Road, Hill Brow; B2070 S of town, near B3006 junction; GU33 7QL

Friendly, comfortable pub with plenty of locals and visitors, real ales, popular food and seats outside; good bedrooms

Traditional and particularly well run by long-serving, enthusiastic licensees, this cheerful place has a good mix of locals and visitors. The neatly carpeted low-beamed bar has leather tub chairs and a couple of chesterfield sofas in front of an inglenook log fire, daily papers, board games and Bowman Wallops Wood, Sharps Doom Bar and Timothy Taylors Landlord on handpump and a dozen wines by the glass. The various areas, with understated décor mainly in muted terracotta or pale ochre tones, include two back dining sections, one of which opens on to a terrace with teak furniture and a lawn with picnic-sets beyond. The neat bedrooms are in two barn conversions.

🍴 Good, honest food includes sandwiches and baps, smoked salmon and prawn platter, mushroom pâté, home-cooked ham and free-range eggs, chicken breast with bacon and stilton sauce, lasagne, lambs liver, onions and bacon, mixed nut roast with cranberry sauce, tempura-battered hake with chips, local sausages with onion gravy, and puddings such as fruit crumble with custard and banoffi pie. *Benchmark main dish: steak in ale pie £12.00. Two-course evening meal £18.00.*

Enterprise ~ Lease Barry and Anne Coe ~ Real ale ~ Open 10.30-3, 5.30-11; 12-4 Sun ~ Bar food 12-2.15, 6-9.30; 12-3 Sun ~ Restaurant ~ Children welcome ~ Wi-fi ~ Bedrooms: £70/£90 *Recommended by Mr and Mrs J Watkins, Michael and Margaret Cross, Colin and Daniel Gibbs*

LITTLETON
SU4532   Map 2

Running Horse 🛏

(01962) 880218 – www.runninghorseinn.co.uk
Main Road; village signed off B3049 NW of Winchester; SO22 6QS

Carefully renovated country pub with several dining areas, woodburning stove in the bar, enjoyable food and cabana in garden; pretty bedrooms

Staff here are courteous and friendly and the atmosphere is chatty and easy-going. Spreading dining areas are attractively furnished with an appealing variety of chairs and tables on big flagstones or bare boards, there are button-backed banquettes in a panelled alcove, a much prized cushioned seat in a bay window plus wooden armchairs around a table, and polo photographs on red walls. Also, unusual wine-bottle ceiling lights, old books on rustic bookshelves, antlers and big mirrors. A brick fireplace holds a woodburning stove, and leather-topped stools line the bar counter where they keep Upham Punter and Tipster and a changing guest on handpump, 14 wines by the glass and a farm cider. The front and back terraces have green metal tables and chairs, and there are picnic-sets on the back grass by a spreading sycamore, and a popular cabana with cushioned seats. Bedrooms are pretty, and breakfasts are open to non-residents. This is sister pub to the Thomas Lord in West Meon.

🍴 Well thought-of food includes black pudding scotch egg with mayonnaise, blow-torched scallop with mussels and samphire, butternut squash risotto with gorgonzola and gremolata, chicken kiev with girolle mushrooms and shallot and chive emulsion, burger with toppings, beer-battered shallots and coleslaw, salmon fillet with quinoa, samphire and tomato and herb passata, and puddings such as cider brandy tart with chantilly cream, and dark chocolate and salt caramel fondant with hazelnut ice-cream. *Benchmark main dish: beer-battered fish and chips £12.50. Two-course evening meal £19.00.*

Upham ~ Licensee Anita Peel ~ Real ale ~ Open 11-11 (10.30 Sun) ~ Bar food 12-2.30, 6.30-9.30; 12-3.30, 6.30-9 Sun ~ Restaurant ~ Children welcome ~ Dogs allowed in bar ~ Wi-fi ~ Bedrooms: /£105 *Recommended by Ian Herdman, M G Hart, Terry and Eileen Stott*

LONGSTOCK
SU3537   Map 2

Peat Spade ♀

(01264) 810612 – www.peatspadeinn.co.uk
Off A30 on W edge of Stockbridge; SO20 6DR

Former coaching inn with imaginative food, real ales and some sporting decor; stylish bedrooms

Fishermen from far and wide come to this attractive, well run pub to try their luck on the River Test just 100 metres away – it's world famous for its fly fishing. The bars have lots of hunting and fishing pictures and prints and the odd stuffed fish on green walls and several old wine bottles dotted here and there. Both the bar and dining room have pretty windows, an interesting mix of dining chairs around miscellaneous tables on bare boards and candlelight. Upham Punter and Tipster and a weekly guest ale on handpump, 12 wines by the glass, 19 gins and 28 malt whiskies; background music, TV and board games. Seating on the terrace or in the garden ranges from modern rattan-style through traditional wooden chairs and tables to a sunken area with wall seats around a fire pit. Bedrooms are stylish and contemporary.

Well presented, interesting food includes sandwiches, smoked duck breast with celeriac rémoulade, candied walnuts, pear and sweetcorn, hot and cold smoked local trout with horseradish and pickled cucumber, jerusalem and globe artichoke tart with butternut squash, watercress and feta, corn-fed chicken with chive butter sauce and dauphinoise potatoes, scallop, king prawn and salmon fish pie, dry-aged beefburger with wild mushrooms, truffle mayonnaise and fries, and puddings such as lemon verbena parfait with grapefruit jelly and orange ice-cream and salted caramel cheesecake with milk ice-cream. *Benchmark main dish: sharing local charcuterie board £23.00. Two-course evening meal £23.00.*

Upham ~ Licensee Nikki Swulinska ~ Real ale ~ Open 8am-11pm (10.30pm Sun) ~ Bar food 12-2.30, 6.30-9.30; 12-4, 6-9 Sun ~ Well behaved children welcome ~ Dogs allowed in bar and bedrooms ~ Wi-fi ~ Bedrooms: /£145 *Recommended by Richard Kennell, Ian Herdman, Mrs Julie Thomas, Edward Mirzoeff, Guy Vowles*

LOWER FROYLE

Anchor 🏅 ♀ 🛏

SU7643 Map 2

(01420) 23261 – www.anchorinnatlowerfroyle.co.uk
Village signposted N of A31 W of Bentley; GU34 4NA

Smart country pub with lots to look at, real ales, good wines and imaginative bar food; bedrooms

Just the place for lunch after a lovely walk, this is a stylish pub with civilised yet informal bar rooms. There are log fires, candlelight, low beams and standing timbers, flagstones in the bar itself and stripped wood floors elsewhere, sofas and armchairs dotted here and there, and a mix of attractive tables and dining chairs. Throughout are all sorts of interesting knick-knacks, books, copper items, horsebrasses and lots of pictures and prints on contemporary paintwork. High bar chairs line the counter where they keep Triple fff Altons Pride and Moondance and a guest such as Marstons EPA on handpump and nice wines by the glass. This is a stylish and comfortable place to stay overnight and breakfasts are first class. Chawton Cottage (Jane Austen's house) is ten minutes away.

Enticing food includes lunchtime sandwiches, pigeon breast with sauerkraut, bacon, almonds and jus, octopus carpaccio with crispy pig's ear, pickled grapes and spiced tomato, roasted cauliflower and truffle tortellini with cocoa bean cassoulet and confit shallot, beer-battered haddock and triple-cooked chips, prawn and chorizo cassoulet with bacon and sage crumb, corn-fed chicken breast with pearl barley and smoked ham hock croquette, almond and cumin purée, and puddings such as chocolate cake with raspberry purée and popcorn and apple délice with grenadine meringue. *Benchmark main dish: hogget (mature lamb) with imam bayildi (turkish-style aubergines) and goats cheese cigar, apricot £18.50. Two-course evening meal £21.00.*

Free house ~ Licensee Kiran Shukla ~ Real ale ~ Open 11-11 (10.30 Sun) ~ Bar food 12-2.30, 6.30-9 Mon-Thurs; 12-2.30, 6.30-9.30 Fri; 12-3, 6.30-9.30 Sat; 12-4, 6-8 Sun ~

Restaurant ~ Children welcome ~ Dogs allowed in bar and bedrooms ~ Wi-fi ~ Bedrooms: /£130 *Recommended by Mrs P Sumner, Susan and Callum Slade, Elizabeth and Peter May*

LOWER WIELD   SU6339   Map 2
Yew Tree ⊙ ✪ ♟ £

(01256) 389224 – www.the-yewtree.org.uk

Turn off A339 NW of Alton at 'Medstead, Bentworth 1' signpost, then follow village signposts; or off B3046 S of Basingstoke, signposted from Preston Candover; SO24 9RX

Bustling country pub with a delightful, hard-working landlord, relaxed atmosphere and super choice of wines and food; sizeable garden

Our readers continue to enthuse about their visits to this very well run pub – with particular praise for the charming, hands-on landlord and his staff and the very fair prices. A small flagstoned bar area on the left has pictures above a stripped-brick dado, a ticking clock and a log fire. There's carpet around to the right of the serving counter (with a couple of stylish wrought-iron bar chairs); throughout there's a mix of tables, including quite small ones for two, and miscellaneous chairs. Drinks include 13 wines by the glass from a well chosen list (with summer rosé and Louis Jadot burgundies), a beer named for the pub (from Triple fff) and Bowman South Sea Spice on handpump, local Silverback gin and a locally made lager from Andwell. Outside, there are solid tables and chunky seats on the front terrace, picnic-sets in a sizeable side garden, pleasant views and a cricket field across the quiet lane; nearby walks.

 At very fair prices, the highly regarded food includes smoked trout and horseradish pâté with lime and pepper mayonnaise, roasted red pepper and mushroom rarebit tartlet, local venison burger with toppings and chips, lasagne, cajun-crusted cod fillet on sun-dried tomato and crushed new potatoes with red pesto, half shoulder of lamb with rosemary and red wine jus and dauphinoise potatoes, specials such as feta and olive-stuffed chicken breast wrapped in parma ham with tomato and roasted aubergine sauce, and puddings such as rhubarb, apple and berry crumble and pineapple and white chocolate bread and butter pudding. *Benchmark main dish: chicken, chorizo and smoked bacon pie £10.95. Two-course evening meal £15.50.*

Free house ~ Licensee Tim Gray ~ Real ale ~ Open 12-3, 6-11; 12-10.30 Sun; closed Mon, closed first two weeks Jan ~ Bar food 12-3, 6.30-9 ~ Children welcome ~ Dogs allowed in bar ~ Wi-fi *Recommended by Ann and Colin Hunt, Geoffrey Sutton, Tony and Jill Radnor, Julian Thorpe*

LYMINGTON   SZ3295   Map 2
Angel & Blue Pig 🛏

(01590) 672050 – www.angel-lymington.com

High Street; SO41 9AP

Bustling, friendly inn with plenty of space in several connected rooms, four real ales, enjoyable food and helpful staff; bedrooms

To guarantee a table you must book in advance at this well run, busy pub as it's in the middle of a very popular tourist town. To the right of the door, a cosy front room has comfortable sofas and armchairs around a big chest, rugs on bare boards and an open fire; this leads into a pubby, flagstoned area with high tables and chairs and built-in leather wall seats. The two interconnected rooms to the left of the entrance – one carpeted, one with rugs on quarry tiles – have beams and timbers, upholstered dining chairs around a variety of tables, an old range in a brick fireplace, a large boar's head, lots of books on shelves and a bookshelf mural;

throughout are numerous hunting prints and porcine bits and pieces. At the back, overlooking the terrace where there are seats and tables under blue parasols, is yet another area with some nice old leather armchairs beside a woodburning stove and the serving counter where they keep Banks's Sunbeam, Blonde Angel (named for the pub from Ringwood) and Ringwood Razorback on handpump, 16 wines by the glass and a choice of coffees; service is cheerful and helpful. The stylish modern bedrooms are comfortable and well equipped, and breakfasts are good.

Brasserie-style food is served all day and includes lunchtime ciabattas, bloody mary prawn cocktail with tomato jelly, chicken satay skewers, vegetarian shepherd's pie, honey-glazed ham with duck egg, triple-cooked chips and pineapple relish, gloucester old spot sausages with mash, bacon and onion gravy, spatchcock piri-piri chicken with coleslaw, salmon with pak choi, peppers, spring onion and sautéed potatoes, Josper oven 35-day-aged steaks, and puddings such as raspberry ripple baked alaska and rhubarb and ginger cheesecake with white chocolate crumb. *Benchmark main dish: pulled beef burger with chorizo jam, mustard mayonnaise and skinny fries £12.95. Two-course evening meal £20.50.*

Free house ~ Licensee Matt England ~ Real ale ~ Open 9.30am-11pm (midnight Fri, Sat); 9.30am-10.30pm Sun ~ Bar food 12-10 (9 Sun) ~ Restaurant ~ Children welcome ~ Dogs allowed in bar ~ Wi-fi ~ Live music last Fri of month ~ Bedrooms: £70/£90
Recommended by Brian and Anna Marsden, Valerie Sayer

NORTH WALTHAM   SU5645   Map 2
Fox 🍷 £

(01256) 397288 – www.thefox.org
3 miles from M3 junction 7: A30 southwards, then turn right at second North Waltham turn, just after Wheatsheaf; pub also signed from village centre; RG25 2BE

Traditional flint country pub, very well run, with tasty food and drink and a nice garden

In summer, the colourful garden here is a big draw. A pergola walkway leads to the pub from a gate on the lane, the flower boxes and baskets are immaculate and there are picnic-sets under cocktail parasols in three separate areas. Inside, the low-ceilinged bar on the left has Andwell Gold Muddler, Brakspears Bitter, West Berkshire Good Old Boy and a guest beer on handpump, lots of bottled ciders plus Aspall's cider on draught; 13 wines by the glass, 22 malt whiskies and quite a collection of miniatures. The big woodburning stove, parquet floor, simple padded country kitchen chairs, and 'Beer is Best' and poultry prints above the dark dado – all give a comfortably old-fashioned feel, in which perhaps the vital ingredient is the polite and friendly efficiency of the hands-on landlord. The separate dining room, with high-backed leather chairs on a blue tartan carpet, is larger. Walks include a pleasant one to Jane Austen's church at Steventon.

Tasty food includes sandwiches, game pâté with apple and ale chutney, butterfly king prawns baked in lime and chorizo butter, home-cooked honey and mustard ham and eggs, barbecue rack of ribs with triple-cooked chips, steak in Guinness pie, pasta with chilli and tomato sauce, chicken in wild mushroom and tarragon cream sauce, slow-cooked lamb shank in rosemary and red wine, salmon en croûte with dill sauce, and puddings such as Mars Bar cheesecake and sticky toffee pudding with toffee sauce. *Benchmark main dish: local venison with creamed swede, glazed shallots and port glaze £16.50. Two-course evening meal £21.50.*

Free house ~ Licensees Rob and Izzy MacKenzie ~ Real ale ~ Open 11-11 (10.30 Sun) ~ Bar food 12-2.30, 6.30-9.30; 12-3, 6.30-8.30 Sun ~ Restaurant ~ Children welcome ~ Dogs allowed in bar ~ Wi-fi *Recommended by Glen Locke, Simon and Mandy King, Melanie and David Lawson*

NORTH WARNBOROUGH

Mill House ♀ ◖

SU7352 Map 2

(01256) 702953 – www.brunningandprice.co.uk/millhouse

A mile from M3 junction 5: A287 towards Farnham, then right (brown sign to pub)
on to B3349 Hook Road; RG29 1ET

Converted mill with an attractive layout, inventive modern food,
good choice of drinks and lovely waterside terraces

Handy for the M3, this sizeable raftered mill building is especially well
run by efficient, courteous staff. Several linked areas on the main upper
floor have heavy beams, plenty of well spaced tables in a variety of sizes
and styles, rugs on polished boards or beige carpet, coal-effect gas fires in
pretty fireplaces and a profusion of (often interesting) pictures. A section
of floor is glazed to reveal the rushing water and mill wheel below, and a
galleried section on the left looks down into a dining room, given a more
formal feel by panelling. The well stocked bar has Phoenix Brunning &
Price Original, Fuzzy Duck Cunning Stunt, Hogs Back TEA, Triple fff Altons
Pride and West Berkshire Tamesis on handpump, a fine range of 50 malt
whiskies, 18 wines by the glass and local farm cider; background music and
board games. The extensive back garden has lots of solid tables and chairs
on terraces, even more picnic-sets on grass and attractive landscaping
around the sizeable millpond; there's a couple of swings too.

 Rewarding food includes sandwiches, seared scallops with pea purée and
shredded ham hock, crispy pork cheek with parma ham and rhubarb compote,
feta and mint quiche with potato and spring onion salad, pork and leek sausages
with onion gravy, steak burger with walnut coleslaw, toppings and chips, bass with
tagliatelle, garlic spinach, baby leeks, mussels and saffron sauce, cumin and chilli
chicken with roast sweet potatoes and tzatziki, and puddings such as pecan pie
and chocolate brownie. *Benchmark main dish: braised lamb shoulder with red
wine and rosemary sauce and dauphinoise potatoes £17.95. Two-course evening
meal £22.00.*

Brunning & Price ~ Lease Ben Walton ~ Real ale ~ Open 11-11 ~ Bar food 12-10 (9.30 Sun)
~ Restaurant ~ Children welcome ~ Dogs allowed in bar ~ Wi-fi *Recommended by Richard
Dilnot, David Fowler, Edward Mirzoeff*

PETERSFIELD

Old Drum ⓘ ♀ ◖

SU7423 Map 2

(01730) 300544 – www.theolddrum.co.uk

Chapel Street; GU32 3DP

Restored 18th-c inn with friendly staff and atmosphere in bars
and dining room, interesting ales and food and seats in back
garden; bedrooms

Right in the centre of town, this bustling, friendly pub is the oldest in the
area. The airy L-shaped bar has all manner of antique dining chairs and
tables on bare boards, with a comfortable chesterfield and armchair by an
open fire (there are three fires in all) and prettily upholstered stools against
the counter. Bowman Swift One and Wallops Wood, Dark Star American
Red and Hophead and Suthwyk Liberation on handpump, 16 wines by the
glass, ten malt whiskies and farm cider and perry; background jazz and
board games. A cosy beamed dining room leads off, with more interesting
old cushioned chairs and tables on bare boards; and throughout there are
prints and mirrors and the odd stag's head on pale paintwork or exposed
bricks, modern lighting and fresh flowers. The back courtyard garden has

chairs and tables and plants in raised flower beds. Bedrooms are stylish and comfortable and breakfasts are well thought-of.

 Rewarding food includes lunchtime sandwiches, beef carpaccio with wild rocket, parmesan and comice pear, smoked salmon tartare with dill mustard sauce, gnocchi with browned butter, sage, walnuts and parmesan sauce, burger with toppings, gherkins and chips, fresh fish of the day with celeriac purée and pomegranate beurre blanc, chargilled chicken with tzatziki, leaves and pitta bread, beef fillet with dauphinoise potatoes and bordeaux butter sauce, and puddings such as chocolate fondant with chocolate swirl ice-cream tiramisu. *Benchmark main dish: beer-battered fish and chips £13.00. Two-course evening meal £21.00.*

Free house ~ Licensee Maria Solovieth ~ Real ale ~ Open 10am-11pm; 10-8 Sun ~ Bar food 12-3, 6-9; 12-4 Sun ~ Restaurant ~ Children welcome until 8pm ~ Dogs allowed in bar ~ Wi-fi ~ Bedrooms: £90/£120 *Recommended by Lindy Andrews, R T and J C Moggridge, Ann and Colin Hunt*

PETERSFIELD   SU7227   Map 2
Trooper 🏵 ◫ ⌂
(01730) 827293 – www.trooperinn.com
From A32 (look for staggered crossroads) take turning to Froxfield and Steep; pub 3 miles down on left in big dip; GU32 1BD

Courteous landlord, popular food, decent drinks, persian knick-knacks and local artists' work; attractive bedrooms

Our readers come here on a regular basis for the good food and the genuine welcome from the charming landlord and his friendly staff. The bar has a log fire in a stone fireplace, all sorts of cushioned dining chairs around dark wooden tables, old film star photos, paintings by local artists (for sale), little persian knick-knacks here and there, several ogival mirrors, lit candles and fresh flowers; there's also a sun room with lovely downland views, carefully chosen background music, board games, newspapers and magazines. Bowman Swift One, Ringwood Best and Triple fff Moondance on handpump, good wines by the glass and several gins. The attractive raftered restaurant has french windows to a paved terrace with views across the open countryside, and there are lots of picnic-sets on an upper lawn. The horse rail in the car park is reserved 'for horses, camels and local livestock'. Bedrooms are neatly kept and breakfasts are good. The inn backs on to Ashford Hangers nature reserve.

 Very good food includes lunchtime sandwiches and baguettes, smoked salmon with horseradish cream and capers, meatballs in spicy tomato sauce, sharing platters, stilton, pear and celery bread and butter pudding, lebanese pulled lamb with sweet potato fries, local sausages with onion gravy and beer-battered onion rings, free-range chicken and leek pie, moroccan-style mussels, brill fillet with spiced potatoes and parsley, coriander and lemon butter sauce, and puddings such as chocolate fruit and nut baked cheesecake and sticky toffee pudding with toffee sauce. *Benchmark main dish: slow-roasted lamb shoulder £19.50. Two-course evening meal £25.00.*

Free house ~ Licensee Hassan Matini ~ Real ale ~ Open 12-3, 6-11; 12-4 Sun; closed Sun evening, Mon lunchtime except bank holidays ~ Bar food 12-2, 6.30-9; 12-2.30 Sun ~ Restaurant ~ Children welcome ~ Dogs allowed in bar ~ Wi-fi ~ Bedrooms: £69/£99 *Recommended by Christopher and Elise Way, Bede Feltham, Melanie and David Lawson*

Real ale may be served from handpumps, electric pumps (not just the on-off switches used for keg beer) or – common in Scotland – tall taps called founts (pronounced 'fonts') where a separate pump pushes the beer up under air pressure.

PETERSFIELD   SU7129 Map 2

White Horse

(01420) 588387 – www.pubwithnoname.co.uk

Up on an old downs road about halfway between Steep and East Tisted, near Priors Dean – OS Sheet 186 or 197 map reference 715290; GU32 1DA

Much-loved old place with a great deal of simple character, friendly licensees and fantastic range of beers

Up to ten real ales are kept on handpump in this unspoilt old pub. One or two are named for the pub plus Adnams Ghost Ship, Belvoir Rare Breed, Butcombe Bitter, Fullers London Pride, Ringwood Boondoggle and Fortyniner and quickly changing guests; they also serve lots of country wines, a dozen wines by the glass, 20 malt whiskies and two farm ciders. They hold a beer festival in June and a cider festival in September. The two parlour rooms remain charming and idiosyncratic: open fires, oak settles and a mix of dark wooden dining chairs, nice old tables (including some drop-leaf ones), various pictures, farm tools, rugs, a longcase clock, a couple of fireside rocking chairs and so forth. The beamed dining room is smarter with lots of pictures on the white or pink walls. There are some rustic seats outside and also camping facilities.

Tasty food includes breakfasts (8.30am-midday), sandwiches and ciabattas, smoked salmon, haddock and prawn fishcakes with mustard cream sauce, honey-glazed ham and free-range eggs, vegetarian burger with caramelised onions and harissa dip, sausages with colcannon potatoes, onion marmalade and rich gravy, green thai chicken curry, smoked trout, crab and scallop risotto with roasted lemon dressing, and puddings such as double chocolate and raspberry brownies with raspberry sorbet and chocolate sauce and fruit crumble with custard. *Benchmark main dish: steak in ale pie £14.00. Two-course evening meal £20.00.*

Gales (Fullers) ~ Managers Georgie and Paul Stuart ~ Real ale ~ Open 12-11 ~ Bar food 12-2.30, 7-9; all day weekends ~ Restaurant ~ Children welcome ~ Dogs allowed in bar
Recommended by Lindy Andrews, Isobel Mackinlay, Ann and Colin Hunt, Tony and Jill Radnor

PORTSMOUTH   SZ6399 Map 2

Old Customs House £

(023) 9283 2333 – www.theoldcustomshouse.com

Vernon Buildings, Gunwharf Quays; follow brown signs to Gunwharf Quays car park; PO1 3TY

Well converted historic building in a prime waterfront development with real ales and well liked food

Spacious, rambling and usefully open all day, this fine Grade I listed building is very handy for shopping in the extensive modern waterside complex (of which it is part). The big-windowed high-ceilinged rooms have nautical prints and photographs on pastel walls, coal-effect gas fires, nice unobtrusive lighting and well padded chairs around sturdy tables of varying sizes on bare boards; the sunny entrance area has leather sofas. Broad stairs lead up to a carpeted restaurant with similar décor. Fullers ESB, HSB, London Pride and Gales Seafarers and a couple of changing guests on handpump, a decent range of wines by the glass and good coffees and teas. Staff are efficient, the background music well reproduced and the games machines silenced. Picnic-sets out in front are just metres from the water; the bar has disabled access and facilities. The graceful Spinnaker Tower (170 metres high with staggering views from its observation decks) is just around the corner.

🍴 As well as breakfasts (from 9am), the popular food includes smoked duck breast with chicory and orange salad and walnut dressing, scallops with chorizo and pea purée, sharing platters, a pie of the day, flat mushroom and goats cheese burger with pickle and chips, tea and hop smoked haddock with bubble and squeak, poached egg and hollandaise, chicken breast with bacon, wild mushrooms, charred gem lettuce, red pepper and tarragon aioli, and puddings such as crème brûlée and chocolate brownie with chocolate sauce. *Benchmark main dish: beer-battered fish and chips £12.95. Two-course evening meal £18.00.*

Fullers ~ Manager Marc Duvauchelle ~ Real ale ~ Open 9.30am-11pm ~ Bar food 9.30am-9pm ~ Children welcome ~ Dogs allowed in bar ~ Wi-fi *Recommended by Charlie May, John Harris, Neil Allen, Tony Scott, Tony and Wendy Hobden, Ann and Colin Hunt*

 ROCKBOURNE · SU1118   Map 2

Rose & Thistle

(01725) 518236 – www.roseandthistle.co.uk
Signed off B3078 Fordingbridge–Cranborne; SP6 3NL

Homely cottage with hands-on landlord and friendly staff, informal bars, real ales and good food, and seats in garden

This is just the place to come after visiting the nearby Roman villa. It's a 16th-c, warm and cosy thatched pub (originally two cottages) with beams, timbers and old flagstones. The bar has homely dining chairs, stools and benches around a mix of old pubby tables, Butcombe Gold, Sharps Doom Bar and a changing local ale on handpump, ten wines by the glass and three farm ciders; board games. The restaurant has a log fire in each of its two rooms (one in a big brick inglenook), old engravings and cricket prints and an informal and relaxed atmosphere. There are benches and tables under lovely hanging baskets at the front of the building, with picnic-sets under parasols on grass; good nearby walks. This is a pretty village on the edge of the New Forest.

🍴 As well as lunchtime sandwiches, the well regarded food includes duck and Armagnac terrine with onion marmalade, twice-baked cheese soufflé, burger with toppings, gherkins and chips, homity pie (vegetarian), chicken breast on crushed peas and enoki mushrooms with shallot and red wine jus, confit rare-breed pork belly with spring onion mash, black pudding and cider jus, chocolate and cointreau cheesecake with mango and passion-fruit coulis and queen of puddings. *Benchmark main dish: steak and kidney pudding £15.95. Two-course evening meal £22.00.*

Free house ~ Licensee Chris Chester-Sterne ~ Real ale ~ Open 11-3, 6-10.30; 11-10.30 Sat; 12-8 Sun ~ Bar food 12-2.15, 7-9.15; 12-2.15 Sun ~ Restaurant ~ Children welcome ~ Dogs allowed in bar ~ Wi-fi *Recommended by Christopher Mannings, Mike Swan, Ian Duncan*

 SPARSHOLT · SU4331   Map 2

Plough 🏅 ♀

(01962) 776353 – www.ploughinnsparsholt.co.uk
Village signposted off B3049 (Winchester–Stockbridge), a little W of Winchester; SO21 2NW

Neatly kept dining pub with interesting furnishings, an extensive wine list, highly rated bar food and big garden

Our readers very much enjoy their visits to this well run country pub for both a drink after a walk and for a very good meal. The landlord and his staff are warmly hospitable and the main bar has an interesting mix of wooden tables and farmhouse or upholstered chairs plus farm tools, scythes and pitchforks attached to the ceiling; Wadworths 6X, Bishops Tipple, Horizon and IPA on handpump, and 17 wines (and champagne) by the glass from an extensive list. The dining tables on the left look over fields and beyond to woodland. Outside, there are plenty of seats on the terrace and lawn and a children's play fort; disabled access and facilities.

 Top quality food includes chilli and lime tiger prawns with mango salsa, kidneys and smoked bacon in mushroom and port sauce, wild mushroom and courgette tagliatelle with parmesan, pork and chive sausages with parsley mash and red wine gravy, chicken green thai curry, slow-cooked lamb shoulder with dauphinoise potatoes and mustard and mint jus, bass fillet with sunblush tomatoes, olives, leeks and balsamic syrup, and puddings such as lemon posset with ginger crumb and chocolate brownie. *Benchmark main dish: beef and mushroom in ale pie £13.95. Two-course evening meal £22.00.*

Wadworths ~ Tenant Richard Crawford ~ Real ale ~ Open 9.30am-11pm; 10.30am-11pm Sat, Sun ~ Bar food 12-2.30, 6-9; 12-8.30 Sun ~ Children welcome *Recommended by R and S Bentley, Andrew Stone, Dr and Mrs Paul Cartwright, David Jackman, Maren Webb, Phil and Jane Villiers*

ST MARY BOURNE
Bourne Valley ♀ ⇌

SU4250 Map 2

(01264) 738361 – www.bournevalleyinn.com
Upper Link (B3048); SP11 6BT

Bustling country inn with plenty of space, an easy-going atmosphere and enjoyable food and drink; good bedrooms

This is an attractively updated old red-brick inn with plenty of space in rambling, characterful rooms. It's very popular locally but there's a warm welcome for visitors too, and dogs and children are very much part of the scene at lunchtime. The bar areas have sofas, all manner of wooden dining chairs and tables on coir or bare boards, empty wine bottles lining shelves and windowsills, and a warm log fire; at one end a deli counter serves coffee and cake, afternoon tea and picnic hampers. Ringwood Best, Sharps Doom Bar, Upham 1st Drop and a guest beer on handpump and lots of wines by the glass served by helpful, friendly staff; background music and TV. The large barn extension, complete with rafters and beams, rustic partitioning and movable shelves made from crates, has big tables surrounded by leather, cushioned and upholstered chairs, more coir carpeting, a second open fire and doors that lead out to a terrace with picnic-sets and other seating. The comfortable, contemporary bedrooms are named after local lakes, brooks and rivers. Good nearby walks.

Using the best local produce, the modern food starts with breakfast (8.30-10.30am), crab scotch egg with fennel, mooli, parmesan and salsa verde, ham hock with cheddar cream, truffle crumble and pickled onions, venison sausages with celeriac purée, wild mushrooms and blackberry jus, smoked haddock and leek risotto with poached egg, wild mushroom cannelloni, pheasant chasseur with tarragon mash and creamed savoy cabbage, pork belly with burnt apple and braised red cabbage, and puddings such as gin and tonic jelly with lime sorbet and sticky toffee pudding with toffee sauce. *Benchmark main dish: cheese burger with onion rings and fries £11.95. Two-course evening meal £21.00.*

Free house ~ Licensee Ryan Stacey ~ Real ale ~ Open 8.30am-11pm ~ Bar food 12-3, 6-9 (9.30 weekends) ~ Children welcome ~ Dogs welcome ~ Wi-fi ~ Bedrooms: £75/£85
Recommended by Mr and Mrs A H Young, Jack and Hilary Burton, Charles Welch

STEEP
SU7525 Map 2

Harrow ¶ £

(01730) 262685 – www.harrow-inn.co.uk

Take Midhurst exit from Petersfield bypass, at exit roundabout take first left towards Midhurst, then first turning on left opposite garage, and left again at Sheet church; follow over dual carriageway bridge to pub; GU32 2DA

Unchanging, simple place with long-serving landladies, beers tapped from the cask, unfussy food and cottage garden; no children inside

We've been coming here (as have many of our readers) for years and love the place as much as we did on our first visit. It's been in the same family for 87 years and remains quite unspoilt and unchanging with no pandering to modern methods – no credit cards, no waitress service, no restaurant, no music and the rose-covered loos are outside. Everything revolves around village chat and the friendly locals are likely to involve you in light-hearted conversation. Adverts for logs sit next to calendars of local views (on sale in support of local charities) and news of various quirky competitions. The small public bar has hops and dried flowers (replaced every year) hanging from the beams, built-in wall benches on the tiled floor, stripped-pine wallboards, a good log fire in the big inglenook and wild flowers on scrubbed deal tables; dominoes. Bowman Swift One, Dark Star Hophead, Flack Manor Double Drop, Hop Back GFB, Langham Hip Hop and Ringwood Best are tapped straight from casks behind the counter, and they have local wine and apple juice; staff are polite and friendly, even when under pressure. The big garden has seats on paved areas surrounded by cottage garden flowers and fruit trees. The Petersfield bypass doesn't intrude much on this idyll, though you'll need to follow the directions above to find the pub. No children inside and dogs must be on leads. They sell honesty-box flowers outside for Macmillan nurses.

Honest food includes sandwiches, hot scotch egg, hearty pea and ham soup, quiches, and puddings such as summer lemon crunch cheesecake and winter treacle tart. *Benchmark main dish: rare beef ploughman's £11.30. Two-course evening meal £16.00.*

Free house ~ Licensees Claire and Denise McCutcheon ~ Real ale ~ No credit cards ~ Open 12-2.30, 6-11; 11-3, 6-11 Sat; 12-3, 7-10.30 Sun; closed Sun evening in winter ~ Bar food 12-2, 7-9; not Sun evening ~ Dogs allowed in bar *Recommended by Tony and Jill Radnor, Edward May, Alfie Bayliss, Ann and Colin Hunt*

TOTFORD
SU5737 Map 2

Woolpack 🎬 ♀ 🛏

(01962) 734184 – www.thewoolpackinn.co.uk

B3046 Basingstoke–Alresford; SO24 9TJ

Charming pub with carefully refurbished rooms, plenty of character, first class food and drink and seats outside; lovely bedrooms

Country folk are fond of this handsome flint and brick pub with its easy-going and gently civilised atmosphere. The bar has wide floorboards, leather button-back armchairs, little stools and wooden chairs around a mix of tables, and high chairs against the counter where they offer Ramshead (a beer named for them from Marstons), Palmers Copper and a weekly changing guest beer on handpump, 15 wines by the glass and a rather special bloody mary. Leading off here is a dining room with flagstones and carpet, a raised fireplace with guns, bellows and other country knick-knacks above it and chunky tables and chairs. Throughout the other rooms are rugs on flagstones, exposed brick and stone work, a few bits of timbering and beamery, church candles, lots of photographs, some cosy booth seating and high-back upholstered dining chairs and leather wall seats around a medley of tables. The pool table converts into a dining table when they're really busy. Outside, on the terrace, on gravel and on grass are teak tables and chairs and picnic-sets under parasols, and distant views. The bedrooms, named after game birds, are extremely comfortable and well equipped.

 In addition to breakfast (9-10.30am daily) and wood-fired pizzas (summer Sundays 5.30-8.30pm), the rewarding food includes lunchtime sandwiches (not Sunday), baked camembert with onion chutney and radish salad, smoked duck breast with fennel and orange, pork faggots with mash and onion gravy, smoked trout potato cake with crispy bacon and poached egg, beef and sweet potato curry with spiced rice, peanuts and crispy shallots, rose veal escalope with fondant potato and pepper tapenade, and puddings such as apple and cinnamon crumble and hot chocolate pudding with honeycomb ice-cream. *Benchmark main dish: pie of the day £12.50. Two-course evening meal £22.00.*

Free house ~ Licensee Andrew Cooper ~ Real ale ~ Open 11-11 (midnight Sat); 12-10.30 Sun ~ Bar food 12-2.30 (3 Sat), 6.30-9; 12-4, 6.30-8.30 Sun ~ Restaurant ~ Children welcome ~ Dogs welcome ~ Wi-fi ~ Bedrooms: /£100 *Recommended by Michael Cooper, Hilary and Neil Christopher, Julian Richardson*

WEST MEON
SU6424 Map 2

Thomas Lord ♀

(01730) 829244 – www.thethomaslord.co.uk
High Street; GU32 1LN

Cricketing knick-knacks in character bar rooms, a smarter dining room, helpful staff, local beers, well thought-of food and pretty garden

Cyclists and walkers enjoy this village pub after spending time in the lovely nearby countryside of the Meon Valley. The relaxed, friendly bar has a leather chesterfield and armchairs beside a log fire, wooden chairs, animal-hide stools and corner settles on parquet flooring, and Timothy Taylors Landlord, Upham Punter, Sprinter, Stakes Ale and Tipster on handpump, a dozen wines by the glass and seasonal cocktails, served by chatty, helpful staff. There's plenty of cricketing memorabilia as the place is named after the founder of Lord's Cricket Ground: bats, gloves, balls, shoes, stumps, photographs and prints, and even stuffed squirrels playing the game in a display cabinet above the counter. A small room leads off the bar with similar furnishings, a brace of pheasant in the fireplace and antlers above; background music and board games. The dining room is slightly more formal, with long wide tartan benches beside long tables, green cushioned chairs, a big clock above another fireplace and ruched curtains; another little room has a large button-back banquette, tables and a rustic mural. Plenty of candles throughout – in nice little teacups with saucers, in candlesticks, in silver glassware, in moroccan-style lanterns and in fireplaces. The sizeable garden has picnic-sets, herbaceous borders, an outdoor pizza oven, a barbecue area, a chicken run and a kitchen garden. Sister pub is the Running Horse in Littleton.

🍴 Using their own eggs and home-grown produce, the interesting food includes sandwiches, brown and white crab with citrus textures, ham hock terrine and crispy egg, roast chicken breast with leg pasty, truffle cauliflower and braised leeks, confit pork belly with roasted apple and shallots, wild sea trout with beetroot, horseradish and red chard, venison haunch and sausage with roasted butternut squash, chocolate and pumpkin seeds, and puddings such as lemon meringue pie and blackberry cheesecake.; they also offer a two- and three-course set weekday lunch. *Benchmark main dish: dry-aged burger with barbecue sauce with truffle and parmesan fries £12.50. Two-course evening meal £19.00.*

Upham ~ Licensee Clare Winterbottom ~ Real ale ~ Open 12-11 (midnight Sat); 12-10.30 Sun ~ Bar food 12-2.30, 6-9.30 (10 Fri, Sat); 12-4, 6-9 Sun ~ Restaurant ~ Children welcome ~ Dogs allowed in bar ~ Wi-fi *Recommended by Peter Brix, Anne and Ben Smith, James Landor*

WINCHESTER
Wykeham Arms 🍽️ 🍷 🛏️

SU4829 Map 2

(01962) 853834 – www.wykehamarmswinchester.co.uk
Kingsgate Street (Kingsgate Arch and College Street are now closed to traffic; there is access via Canon Street); SO23 9PE

Tucked-away pub with lots to look at, several real ales, many wines by the glass and highly thought-of food; lovely bedrooms

This fine city pub is between the cathedral and Winchester College and remains a first class all-rounder. The series of bustling rooms have all sorts of interesting collections and three log fires – as well as 19th-c oak desks retired from the College, kitchen chairs, deal tables with candles and big windows with swagged curtains. A snug room at the back, known as the Jameson Room (after the late landlord Graeme Jameson), is decorated with a set of Ronald Searle 'Winespeak' prints. A second room is panelled. Fullers HSB, London Pride, Gales Seafarers, Olivers Island and a guest such as Flowerpots Goodens Gold on handpump, 25 wines by the glass, 29 malt whiskies, a couple of farm ciders and quite a few ports and sherries; the tea list is pretty special. There are tables on a covered back terrace and in a small courtyard. This is a fine place to stay overnight and some of the individually styled bedrooms have four-posters; the two-level suite has its own sitting room.

⭐ Highly accomplished food includes lunchtime sandwiches, roast breast of quail with crispy leg, pear and red cabbage ketchup, smoked venison carpaccio with pickled beetroot, horseradish custard and watercress purée, burger with toppings, coleslaw and fries, roast cauliflower with chestnut and swiss chard gratin, parmesan and a herb crust, shredded duck salad with bulgar wheat, pomegranate, mint and orange, roasted turbot with pancetta, girolle mushrooms, samphire and seaweed butter sauce, and puddings such as lemon and lavender cake with raspberries, white chocolate and lemon curd and banana custard tart with caramel popcorn, malt milkshake and peanut brittle; they also offer a two- and three-course set menu (Monday-Saturday lunchtimes; Monday-Thursday 6-7pm) *Benchmark main dish: confit pork belly with chorizo hash and roasted swede £16.50. Two-course evening meal £21.00.*

Fullers ~ Manager Jon Howard ~ Real ale ~ Open 11-11 (10.30 Sun) ~ Bar food 12-3, 6-9.30; 12-3.30, 6.30-9 Sun ~ Restaurant ~ Dogs allowed in bar and bedrooms ~ Wi-fi ~ Bedrooms: £99/£156 *Recommended by Conor McGaughey, Neil and Angela Huxter, Ann and Colin Hunt, Dr and Mrs J D Abell, Phil and Jane Villiers, Jane and Kai Horsburgh*

Bedroom prices are for high summer. Even then you may get reductions for more than one night, or (outside tourist areas) weekends. Winter special rates are common, and many inns reduce bedroom prices if you have a full evening meal.

Also Worth a Visit in Hampshire

Besides the fully inspected pubs, you might like to try these pubs that have been recommended to us and described by readers. Do tell us what you think of them: feedback@goodguides.com

ALRESFORD
SU5832

Bell (01962) 732429

West Street; SO24 9AT Comfortable and welcoming Georgian coaching inn, good popular food including weekday fixed-price menu and plenty of daily specials, friendly attentive service, up to five well kept changing ales and extensive choice of wines by the glass, spic and span interior with bare boards, scrubbed tables and log fire, daily papers, separate smallish dining room, occasional live music (mainly jazz); children welcome, dogs in bar (resident spaniels Freddie and Teddy), attractive sunny back courtyard, six bedrooms, closed Sun evening, otherwise open all day (till 6pm Sun). *(Tony and Jill Radnor, Ann and Colin Hunt, David and Judy Robison, Tony and Wendy Hobden)*

ALRESFORD
SU5832

Globe (01962) 733118

Bottom of Broad Street (B3046) where parking is limited; SO24 9DB Popular old tile-hung pub (sister to the Chestnut Horse at Easton – see Main Entries); enjoyable food (all day Sun) including weekday lunchtime/early evening deal and Thurs 'prosecco, beer and curry', Otter and a couple of guests, friendly staff; some live music (Mon ukulele session) and other events; children and dogs welcome, nice garden overlooking Alresford Pond, good walks, open all day. *(Neill Allen)*

ALRESFORD
SU5832

Swan (01962) 732302

West Street; SO24 9AD Long narrow bar in refurbished 18th-c hotel (former coaching inn), painted panelling and some rustic stall seating, well kept ales such as Itchen Valley, Sharps and Triple fff, decent wines, tea and coffee, popular reasonably priced food including good Sun roasts, efficient friendly service, two dining rooms (one more formal); children welcome, café-style table on terrace, 22 bedrooms, open all day. *(Val and Alan Green)*

AMPFIELD
SU4023

★ **White Horse** (01794) 368356

A3090 Winchester–Romsey; SO51 9BQ Snug low-beamed front bar with candles and soft lighting, inglenook log fire and comfortable country furnishings, spreading beamed dining area behind, well kept Greene King, guest ales and several nice wines by the glass, good food including all-day snacks, efficient service, locals' bar with another inglenook; background music; children and dogs welcome, pergola-covered terrace and high-hedged garden with plenty of

picnic-sets, cricket green beyond, good walks in Ampfield Woods and handy for Hillier Gardens, open all day. *(Tom Stone)*

ARFORD
SU8236

Crown (01428) 712150

Off B3002 W of Hindhead; GU35 8BT Low-beamed pub with log fires in several areas including local-feel bar and cosy upper dining room, well kept changing ales and decent wines by the glass, good food from pub favourites in a contemporary style to blackboard specials and a variety of local cheeses, friendly staff; children welcome in eating areas, picnic-sets in peaceful dell by little stream over the road. *(Charles Welch)*

BARTON STACEY
SU4341

Swan (01962) 760470

Village signed off A303; SO21 3RL Welcoming refurbished beamed coaching inn, good affordably priced food from pubby choices up, three changing ales, bar with brick and timber walls, light wood floor and inglenook, back restaurant; children and dogs (in bar) welcome, picnic-sets on front gravel, open all day Fri and Sat, till 10pm Sun. *(Rona Mackinlay)*

BASING
SU6653

Bartons Mill (Millstone)

(01256) 331153 *Bartons Lane, Old Basing; follow brown signs to Basing House; RG24 8AE* Busy converted watermill in tucked-away spot – lots of tables out by River Loddon looking across to viaduct through scrubland; Wadworths range kept well and a guest, Kingstone Press cider and several wines by the glass, decent food (all day Sun) from sandwiches and deli boards up, friendly staff, dimly lit beamed and flagstoned interior; may be background music, Thurs quiz, free wi-fi; children and dogs welcome, handy for Basing House ruins, open all day. *(Valerie Sayer)*

BATTRAMSLEY
SZ3098

Hobler (01590) 623944

Southampton Road (A337 S of Brockenhurst); SO41 8PT Old roadside pub with several rooms, modern décor and furnishings alongside ancient heavy beams, wood and stone floors and log fire, good food from sandwiches and sharing plates up using fresh local ingredients, weekday set menu till 6pm, well kept Ringwood, Timothy Taylors and plenty of wines by the glass, friendly efficient service; children welcome, nice garden with some tables under cover, good New Forest walks, open (and food) all day. *(Phil and Jane Villiers)*

BEAUWORTH SU5624

Milbury's (01962) 771248

*Off A272 Winchester–Petersfield;
SO24 0PB* Traditional old tile-hung country
pub, beams, panelling and stripped stone,
massive 17th-c incredibly deep well, galleried area, up
to five changing ales and straightforward
reasonably priced food, efficient service;
skittle alley; children in eating areas, garden
with fine downland views, good walks, two
bedrooms. *(Ann and Colin Hunt)*

BENTLEY SU7844

Star (01420) 23184

Centre of village on old A31; GU10 5LW
Small friendly village pub with good
reasonably priced food (not Sun evening)
from sandwiches and pizzas up, ales
such as Flowerpots, Triple fff and Sharps,
decent wines, open fire in brick fireplace,
restaurant; quiz first Mon of the month, free
wi-fi; children and dogs welcome, garden
with heated gazebos, open all day from 9am
for breakfast. *(Tom Stone)*

BISHOP'S WALTHAM SU5517

Barleycorn (01489) 892712

Lower Basingwell Street; SO32 1AJ
Relaxed 18th-c two-bar village local; popular
generously served pub food at reasonable
prices, good friendly service, well kept
Greene King ales and a guest, decent wines,
spic and span interior with beams and some
low ceiling panelling, open fires; children
and dogs welcome, large garden with back
smokers' area, open all day. *(Ann and
Colin Hunt)*

BISHOP'S WALTHAM SU5517

★ **Bunch of Grapes** (01489) 892935

*St Peter's Street – near entrance to
central car park; SO32 1AD* Neat civilised
little pub in quiet medieval street, smartly
furnished keeping individuality and unspoilt
feel (run by same family for a century), good
chatty landlord and regulars, Goddards and
guests tapped from the cask, own wines from
nearby vineyard, no food; charming walled
garden behind, opening times may vary.
(Phil and Jane Villiers)

BLACKNEST SU7941

Jolly Farmer (01420) 22244

*Binsted Road/Blacknest Road;
GU34 4QD* Bright and airy beamed dining
pub with pleasant relaxed atmosphere, good
food from lunchtime sandwiches and sharing
boards up, well kept Fullers beers, friendly
staff, wood and flagstone floors, sofas by log
fire, function room with skittle alley; children
and dogs welcome, picnic-sets in attractive

fenced garden, sheltered terrace and play
area, open all day. *(I D Barnett)*

BOLDRE SZ3198

★ **Red Lion** (01590) 673177

Off A337 N of Lymington; SO41 8NE
New Forest-edge dining pub with five black-
beamed rooms; three log fires, old cooking
range in cosy bar, pews, sturdy cushioned
dining chairs and tapestried stools, rural
landscapes on rough-cast walls, other rustic
bits and pieces including heavy-horse
harness, copper and brass pans and some
ferocious-looking traps, good home-made
food from varied menu, well kept Ringwood
and guests, friendly service; opposite village
green with seats out among flowering tubs
and hanging baskets, more tables in back
garden, self-catering apartment, open all
day Sun. *(Michael and Jenny Back, Gavin and
Helle May, M G Hart, Phil and Jane Villiers)*

BRAISHFIELD SU3724

Wheatsheaf (01794) 368652

*Village signposted off A3090 on NW edge
of Romsey; SO51 0QE* Friendly beamed
pub with four well kept beers and tasty
home-cooked food, cosy log fire; background
and some live music, sports TV, pool; children
and dogs welcome, garden with nice views,
woodland walks nearby, close to Hillier
Gardens, open all day. *(Phil and Jane Villiers)*

BRAMBRIDGE SU4721

Dog & Crook (01962) 712129

*Near M3 junction 12, via B3335; Church
Lane; SO50 6HZ* Cheerful bustling 18th-c
pub with beamed bar and cosy dining room,
enjoyable traditional food, Gales, Ringwood
and Sharps, several wines by the glass,
friendly speedy service; background music,
TV, regular events including monthly quiz,
karaoke and summer music nights; children
and dogs welcome, garden with decking and
arbour, Itchen Way walks nearby, open all day.
(Charles Welch)

BRAMDEAN SU6127

Fox (01962) 771363

A272 Winchester–Petersfield; SO24 0LP
Welcoming 17th-c part-weatherboarded
roadside pub; open-plan bar with black
beams and log fires, well kept ales such as
St Austell Tribute and Sharps Doom Bar,
farmhouse ciders and several wines by the
glass, good traditional home-made food
served promptly by friendly staff; some
live music; children and dogs welcome,
walled-in terraced area and spacious lawn
under fruit trees, three shepherd huts, good
surrounding walks, open (and food) all day
Fri-Sun. *(Helen and Brian Edgeley, Richard
Tilbrook, John Evans, Ann and Colin Hunt)*

BREAMORE SU1517
Bat & Ball (01725) 512252
Salisbury Road; SP6 2EA Dutch-gabled red-brick roadside pub, enjoyable reasonably priced food including fajitas and other mexican dishes, some south african influences too, well kept Ringwood ales, friendly service, two linked bar areas and restaurant; dogs welcome, pleasant side garden, Avon fishing and walks (lovely ones up by church and stately Breamore House), bedrooms in two apartments, open (and food) all day. *(Sam Hyde)*

BROCKENHURST SU3000
Filly (01590) 623449
Lymington Road (A337 Brockenhurst–Lymington); SO42 7UF Spotless roadside pub with enjoyable well presented food (all day weekends) from varied menu including good steaks, friendly welcoming staff, up to four changing local ales and decent selection of well priced wines, bare-boards bar with oak beams, carriage-lamp lighting and attractive fireplace, two dining rooms; occasional weekend jazz; children and dogs (in bar and garden room) welcome, sheltered tables outside and boules pitch, New Forest walks, five bedrooms, good breakfast, open all day. *(David and Sally Frost)*

BROOK SU2713
★ Green Dragon (023) 8081 3359
B3078 NW of Cadnam, just off M27 junction 1; SO43 7HE Thatched New Forest dining pub dating from the 15th c; popular food from pubby favourites to good specials, well kept Ringwood, Wadworths and guests, several wines by the glass, friendly helpful staff, linked areas with beams, log fires and traditional furnishings, lots of pictures and other bits and pieces including some old leather 'bends' showing brand marks of forest graziers; children and dogs (not in restaurant) welcome, disabled access from car park, attractive small terrace, garden with play area and paddocks beyond, picturesque village, open all day in summer, all day Sun other times. *(David and Sally Frost, B R Merritt, PL, Sir Michael and Lady Jackson, Phil and Jane Villiers)*

BROUGHTON SU3032
Tally Ho (01794) 301280
High Street, opposite church; signed off A30 Stockbridge–Salisbury; SO20 8AA Welcoming village pub with light airy bar and separate eating area, well kept ales such as Ringwood, Sharps and Timothy Taylors, good food from pub favourites up (more elaborate evening choice), friendly service;

children welcome, charming secluded back garden, good walks, open all day (no food Sun evening). *(Ann and Colin Hunt)*

BUCKLERS HARD SU4000
Master Builders House
(01590) 616253 *M27 junction 2 follow signs to Beaulieu, turn left on to B3056, then left to Bucklers Hard; SO42 7XB* Sizeable hotel in lovely spot overlooking river; character main bar with heavy beams, log fire and simple furnishings, rugs on wooden floor, mullioned windows, interesting list of shipbuilders dating from 18th c, Ringwood Best and guests, stairs down to room with a fireplace at each end, enjoyable food, afternoon teas, prompt friendly service; children and dogs welcome, small gate at bottom of garden for waterside walks, summer barbecues, 26 bedrooms. *(Gerry and Rosemary Dobson)*

BURGHCLERE SU4660
Carpenters Arms (01635) 278251
Harts Lane, off A34; RG20 9JY Friendly little village pub under new ownership, enjoyable sensibly priced home-made food (not Sun evening) from sandwiches up, Arkells and an occasional guest, good country views (Watership Down) from conservatory and terrace, log fire; background music; children, walkers and dogs welcome, tricky wheelchair access, handy for Sandham Memorial Chapel (NT) with its Stanley Spencer murals, and Highclere Castle, six comfortable annexe bedrooms, open all day. *(Mr and Mrs J Watkins)*

BURITON SU7320
Five Bells (01730) 263584
Off A3 S of Petersfield; GU31 5RX Low-beamed 17th-c pub with big log fire and some ancient stripped masonry, popular food (not Sun evening) from sandwiches to daily specials, Badger ales and good wines by the glass; background music; children and dogs welcome, nice garden and sheltered terraces, pretty village with good local walks, self-catering in converted stables, open all day. *(Tom Stone)*

BURLEY SU2202
White Buck (01425) 402264
Bisterne Close; 0.7 miles E, OS Sheet 195 map reference 223028; BH24 4AZ Extensively refurbished 19th-c mock-Tudor hotel; well kept Fullers ales in long bar with two-way log fires at either end, seats in big bow window, comfortable part-panelled shooting-theme snug with stags head, spacious well divided dining area on different levels, good choice of enjoyable attractively

presented food (not overly expensive) and nice wines, helpful personable staff; background music, free wi-fi; children and dogs welcome, terraces and spacious lawn, lovely New Forest setting with superb walks towards Burley itself and over Mill Lawn, good bedrooms, open all day. *(Conor McGaughey, Glenwys and Alan Lawrence)*

BURSLEDON   SU4909
Jolly Sailor (023) 8040 5557
Off A27 towards Bursledon Station, Lands End Road; handy for M27 junction 8; SO31 8DN Steps down to brick-built Badger dining pub worth knowing for its prime location overlooking yachting inlet, their ales (tasting trays available) and decent wine choice, food cooked to order and can be good, beams, bare boards and log fires; dogs welcome, nice outside seating area, tidal moorings, open (and some food) all day. *(Taff Thomas)*

CADNAM   SU3114
Compass (023) 8081 2237
Winsor Road, off Totton–Cadnam road at Bartley crossroads; OS Sheet 195 map reference 317143; SO40 2HE Popular 16th-c flower-decked local off the beaten track, friendly and chatty, with well kept ales and reasonably priced gluten-free only menu including free puddings with mains, brasses on beams, pubby furniture on bare boards, woodburner in brick fireplace; dogs very welcome (food for them – their characterful jack russell is Boris), side garden with decorative arbour, open all day (food all day weekends). *(Ann and Ben Smith)*

CADNAM   SU2913
Sir John Barleycorn
(023) 8081 2236 *Off Southampton Road; by M27 junction 1; SO40 2NP* Picturesque low-slung thatched dining pub extended from cosy beamed and timbered medieval core, varied menu from sandwiches and light choices up, meal deals, friendly service, well kept Fullers ales, two log fires, modern décor and stripped wood flooring; background music; children welcome, no dogs inside, suntrap benches in front and out in colourful riverside garden, open (and food) all day. *(Sam Hyde)*

CHALTON   SU7316
★**Red Lion** (023) 9259 2246
Off A3 Petersfield–Horndean; PO8 0BG Largely extended timber and thatch dining pub, interesting old core around inglenook (dates to the 12th c and has been a pub since the 1400s); wide range of popular food from sandwiches and sharing plates up, well kept Fullers/Gales beers and lots of country wines, friendly helpful service from smart young staff; children and dogs welcome, good disabled access and facilities, nice views from neat rows of picnic-sets on rectangular lawn by large car park, good walks, handy for

Queen Elizabeth Country Park, open (and food) all day. *(Val and Alan Green, Tony and Wendy Hobden, R Halliday)*

CHAWTON   SU7037
Greyfriar (01420) 83841
Off A31/A32 S of Alton; Winchester Road; GU34 1SB Popular flower-decked beamed dining pub opposite Jane Austen's House; decent food (till 7pm Sun) from lunchtime sandwiches and bar snacks up, Fullers ales, welcoming relaxed atmosphere with comfortable seating and sturdy pine tables in neat linked areas, open fire in restaurant end; background music, quiz nights; children welcome till 9pm, dogs in bar, small garden with terrace, good nearby walks, open all day. *(Neil Allen)*

CHERITON   SU5828
★**Flower Pots** (01962) 771318
Off B3046 towards Beauworth and Winchester; OS Sheet 185 map reference 581282; SO24 0QQ Unspoilt country local in same family since 1968; three or four good value own-brew beers tapped from the cask (brewery tours by arrangement), enjoyable reasonably priced home-made food (not Sun evening or bank holiday evenings, and possible restrictions during busy times) including range of casseroles and popular Weds curry night, cheerful welcoming staff, extended plain public bar with covered well, another straightforward but homely room with country pictures on striped wallpaper and ornaments over small log fire; no credit cards or children; dogs welcome, seats on pretty front and back lawns (some under apple trees), heated marquee, vintage motorcycles Weds lunchtime, two bedrooms. *(Tony and Jill Radnor)*

CHILBOLTON   SU3939
Abbots Mitre (01264) 860348
Off A3051 S of Andover; SO20 6BA Traditional 19th-c brick-built village pub refurbished under new owners; five well kept local ales and decent wines by the glass, enjoyable food from sandwiches and pubby choices up including daily specials, friendly service; picnic-sets outside, River Test and other walks (circular one from the pub), open (and food) all day. *(Terry Gilmour)*

CHILWORTH   SU4118
Chilworth Arms (023) 8076 6247
Chilworth Road (A27 Southampton–Romsey); SO16 7JZ Modernised Mitchells & Butlers dining pub, good choice of popular food from sharing plates and home-made pizzas up, weekday fixed-price menu till 6pm, Sharps Doom Bar and Timothy Taylors Landlord, lots of wines by the glass including champagne, cocktails, comfortable bar, log fires, conservatory-style restaurant; background music; children welcome, disabled access/facilities, large neat garden with terrace, open all day. *(Simon and Mandy King)*

CHURCH CROOKHAM   SU8151
Tweseldown   (01252) 613976
Beacon Hill Road; GU52 8DY Flower-decked 19th-c pub with lounge and public bars plus a sizeable split-level barn restaurant, Courage, Fullers, Triple fff and a guest, good choice of wines by the glass, enjoyable home-cooked food from standards to specials, cheerful service, horse-racing décor (Tweseldown Racecourse nearby), log fires; various events including Thurs folk night and Sun quiz, pool, darts and fruit machine; children and dogs welcome, rose garden with heated smokers' shelter, open all day. *(Ann and Ben Smith)*

COPYTHORNE   SU3115
Empress of Blandings
(023) 8081 2321   *Copythorne Crescent, just off A31; SO40 2PE* Roomy pub-restaurant with PG Wodehouse/pig theme (note spelling on Hall & Woodhouse sign), enjoyable moderately priced food and some cosy corners, Badger ales, good friendly service; free wi-fi; children welcome, dogs in one area, picnic-sets in front and back gardens, open (and food) all day. *(Glenwys and Alan Lawrence)*

CRONDALL   SU7948
Plume of Feathers   (01252) 850245
The Borough; GU10 5NT Attractive 15th-c brick and timber village pub popular for its good range of generous home-made food from standards up, friendly helpful staff, well kept Greene King and some unusual guests, nice wines by the glass, beams and dark wood, red carpet, prints on cream walls, restaurant with log fire in big brick fireplace; soft background music; free wi-fi; children welcome, picnic-sets in back terrace garden (bookable barbecues), picturesque village, three bedrooms, open all day Sun. *(Charles Welch)*

CROOKHAM   SU7952
Exchequer   (01252) 615336
Crondall Road; GU51 5SU Welcoming smartly refurbished dining pub, popular reliable home-made food from lunchtime sandwiches to blackboard specials in bar and restaurant, Mon steak and grill night, four local ales and good choice of wines by the glass, also cider and lager from local Hogs Back, daily papers, children and dogs welcome, woodburner; terrace tables, near Basingstoke Canal, open (and food) all day Fri-Sun. *(Mike and Jayne Bastin)*

CURDRIDGE   SU5314
Cricketers   (01489) 784420
Curdridge Lane, off B3035 just under a mile NE of A334 junction; SO32 2BH Open-plan split-level Victorian village dining pub, popular food (all day weekends) from lunchtime sandwiches to specials, well kept Greene King and a guest, several wines by the glass, friendly staff; background music; children and dogs welcome, picnic-sets on front lawn, pleasant walks, open all day except Mon in winter. *(Ann and Colin Hunt)*

DROXFORD   SU6118
Hurdles   (01489) 877451
Brockbridge, just outside Soberton; from A32 just N of Droxford take B2150 towards Denmead; SO32 3QT Modernised dining pub (former station hotel) with well liked food including early evening deal (Mon-Thurs); high ceilings and stripped floorboards, leather chesterfield and armchairs by log fire in one room, dining areas with eye-catching wallpaper and stripy chairs around shiny tables, well kept Bowmans and a guest, decent wines by the glass and good coffee, friendly service; background music; children and dogs (in bar) welcome, neat terraces (one covered and heated), flight of steps up to picnic-sets on sloping lawn by tall trees, open all day. *(Jane and Kai Horsburgh)*

DUMMER   SU5846
Queen   (01256) 397367
Under a mile from M3 junction 7; take Dummer slip road; RG25 2AD Comfortable beamed pub, well divided with lots of softly lit alcoves, Andwell, Otter and Sharps, decent choice of wines by the glass, popular food from lunchtime sandwiches and light dishes up, friendly service, big log fire, Queen and steeplechase prints; background music, free wi-fi; children welcome in restaurant, picnic-sets under parasols on terrace and in extended back garden, attractive village with ancient church. *(Rona Mackinlay)*

DUNBRIDGE   SU3126
Mill Arms   (01794) 340401
Barley Hill (B3084); SO51 0LF Much extended 18th-c coaching inn opposite station, welcoming informal atmosphere in spacious high-ceilinged rooms, scrubbed pine tables and farmhouse chairs on oak or flagstone floors, several sofas, two log fires, local ales such as Flack Manor and enjoyable food, dining conservatory; darts and two skittle alleys; children and dogs (in bar) welcome, big garden, plenty of walks in surrounding Test Valley, six comfortable bedrooms, open all day from 10am (till 5pm Sun). *(Ann and Ben Smith)*

DUNDRIDGE   SU5718
★ Hampshire Bowman   (01489) 892940
Off B3035 towards Droxford, Swanmore, then right at Bishop's Waltham signpost; SO32 1GD Chatty mix of customers at this homely relaxed country pub, five well kept local ales tapped from the cask, summer farm cider and good value food (all day Fri-Sun) from generous sandwiches and hearty pub dishes to specials using local produce, good cheerful service, stable bar and cosy unassuming original one; no mobile phones

(£1 fine in charity box); children and dogs (they have two) welcome, tables on heated terrace and peaceful lawn, play equipment, hitching post for horses, popular with walkers and cyclists, open all day. *(Ann and Colin Hunt, Val and Alan Green)*

DURLEY   SU5116
Farmers Home (01489) 860457
B3354 and B2177; Heathen Street/ Curdridge Road; SO32 2BT Comfortable red-brick beamed country pub, spacious but cosy, with two-bay dining area and restaurant, enjoyable food including good steaks and popular Sun lunch, friendly service, room for drinkers too with well kept Gales HSB, Ringwood and decent wines, woodburner; children and dogs (in bar) welcome, big garden with pergola and play area, nice walks, open (and food) all day. *(Phil and Jane Villiers)*

DURLEY   SU5217
★ Robin Hood (01489) 860229
Durley Street, just off B2177 Bishop's Waltham–Winchester – brown signs to pub; SO32 2AA Quirky open-plan beamed pub with well prepared food from varied blackboard menu (order at bar), Greene King and a guest ale, nice wines, good informed service from accommodating staff, log fire and leather sofas in bare-boards bar, dining area with stone floors and mix of old pine tables and chairs, bookcase door to loos; background music; children and dogs welcome, disabled facilities, decked terrace with barbecue, garden with play area and country views, open all day Sun. *(Roy and Gill Payne, Joy Griffiths, Phil and Jane Villiers)*

EAST BOLDRE   SU3700
Turf Cutters Arms (01590) 612331
Main Road; SO42 7WL Small dimly lit 18th-c New Forest local behind white picket fence, lots of beams and pictures, nicely worn-in furnishings on bare boards and flagstones, log fire, enjoyable home-made food from ciabattas up (worth booking evenings/weekends), well kept Ringwood ales and a guest, good friendly service and chatty relaxed atmosphere; children and dogs welcome, picnic-sets in large back garden, good heathland walks, bedrooms in nearby converted barn, open all day. *(Peter Meister)*

EAST END   SZ3696
★ East End Arms (01590) 626223
Back road Lymington–Beaulieu, parallel to B3054; SO41 5SY Simple friendly pub (owned by former Dire Straits bass guitarist), determinedly unfussy bar with chatty locals and log fire, Ringwood Best or Fortyniner and several wines by the glass, enjoyable freshly made food (not Sun evening) served by cheerful helpful staff, attractive dining room; occasional live music, free wi-fi; children and dogs (in bar) welcome, picnic-sets in terraced garden,

pretty cottagey bedrooms, open all day in summer (till 10pm Sun). *(Charles Welch)*

EAST MEON   SU6822
★ Olde George (01730) 823481
Church Street; signed off A272 W of Petersfield, and off A32 in West Meon; GU32 1NH Atmospheric heavy-beamed village inn with well liked food from sandwiches and light lunches to more restaurant choices, good service from smartly dressed staff, Badger ales and decent selection of wines by the glass, cosy areas around central counter, inglenook log fires; children and dogs welcome, nice back terrace, five bedrooms, good breakfast, pretty village with fine church and surrounding walks, open all day Sun. *(Ann and Colin Hunt, Mrs Julie Thomas)*

EAST WORLDHAM   SU7438
Three Horseshoes (01420) 83211
Cakers Lane (B3004 Alton–Kingsley); GU34 3AE Welcoming early 19th-c brick and stone roadside pub, comfortable and attractive, with good range of enjoyable sensibly priced food including daily specials, Fullers/Ringwood ales and one or two guests, good wines by the glass, friendly helpful staff, log fires; free wi-fi; children and dogs welcome, pleasant secluded garden with lots of picnic-sets, five well appointed bedrooms, open all day Sat, till 5pm Sun. *(Tony and Jill Radnor)*

EASTON   SU5132
Cricketers (01962) 791044
Off B3047; SO21 1EJ Light and airy traditional local in centre of village; enjoyable home-made food in bar and smallish restaurant including well priced set menu, Ringwood and other Marstons-related ales, welcoming atmosphere, mix of wooden table and chairs on carpet, various odds and ends such as cricketing and fishing memorabilia, bare-boards area with sports TV, open fire and small woodburner; background and live music, fortnightly Sun quiz; children and dogs welcome, front terrace with heated smokers' shelter, handy for Itchen Way walks, two bedrooms, open all day. *(Ann and Colin Hunt)*

ECCHINSWELL   SU4959
Royal Oak (01635) 297355
Ecchinswell Road; RG20 4UH Cosy traditional pub popular under present welcoming management; bar with open fire, window seats and plush-topped stools around tables on bare boards, country prints and books on shelves, second room with another fire, dining room with country kitchen chairs around mix of tables on pale boards, enjoyable fair value food, well kept ales and good friendly service; TV; children welcome, picnic-sets out at front and in garden. *(Dawn Saunders, Dr W I C Clark)*

ELLISFIELD
SU6345

★**Fox** (01256) 381210

Green Lane; S of village off Northgate Lane; RG25 2QW Simple tucked-away country pub with friendly atmosphere; mixed collection of stripped tables, country chairs and cushioned wall benches on bare boards and old floor tiles, some exposed masonry, open fires in plain brick fireplaces, Wadworth ales, enjoyable sensibly priced home-made food; outside gents'; children and dogs welcome, picnic-sets in nice garden, good walking country near snowdrop and bluebell woods, open all day. *(Sam Hyde)*

EMERY DOWN
SU2808

★**New Forest** (023) 8028 4690

Village signed off A35 just W of Lyndhurst; SO43 7DY Well run 18th-c weatherboarded village pub in one of the best parts of the Forest for walking; good choice of well liked honest home-made food including local venison, popular Sun roasts (should book), friendly helpful uniformed staff, Ringwood and guests, real cider and several wines by the glass, coffee and tea; attractive softly lit separate areas on varying levels, each with own character, old pine and oak furniture, hunting prints and two log fires; background music; children and dogs welcome, covered heated terrace and pleasant little garden on three levels, good value clean bedrooms, open (and food) all day, can get very busy weekends. *(Sara Fulton, Roger Baker)*

EMSWORTH
SU7405

Blue Bell (01243) 373394

South Street; PO10 7EG Friendly and relaxed little 1940s red-brick pub close to the quay, old-fashioned lived-in interior with lots of memorabilia, good choice of popular reasonably priced home-made food including fresh fish, best to book weekends, bar nibbles Sun lunchtime, Sharps Doom Bar and well kept local guests; dogs welcome, seats on small front terrace, Sun market in adjacent car park, open all day. *(Ann and Colin Hunt, Michael Butler)*

EMSWORTH
SU7405

Coal Exchange (01243) 375866

Ships Quay, South Street; PO10 7EG Friendly little L-shaped Victorian local near harbour, well kept Fullers/Gales beers along with Butcombe and other guests, good value home-made lunchtime food, themed nights including Tues curry and Weds pizza, well worn-in bar with fire each end, low ceilings; live music Weds and Sat; children and dogs welcome, tables outside and smokers' shelter, handy for Wayfarers Walk and Solent Way, open all day Fri-Sun. *(Ann and Colin Hunt)*

EMSWORTH
SU7505

Lord Raglan (01243) 372587

Queen Street; PO10 7BJ Traditional 18th-c flint pub with wide choice of enjoyable home-made food from daily changing menu, well kept Fullers/Gales beers, good friendly service, log fire, restaurant; live music Sun evening, free wi-fi; dogs welcome, pleasant waterside garden behind, open all day weekends. *(Ann and Ben Smith)*

EVERSLEY
SU7762

Tally Ho (0118) 973 2134

Fleet Hill; RG27 0RR Home Counties pub in extended old brick farmhouse, friendly chatty atmosphere, four real ales, lots of wines by the glass and enjoyable bistro-style food, beams and wood floors, built-in wall seats and cushioned dining chairs around wooden tables; children and dogs (in bar) welcome, tables on terrace and lawn, swings and play tractor, open (and food) all day. *(Tom Stone)*

EVERSLEY CROSS
SU7861

Chequers (0118) 402 7065

Chequers Lane; RG27 0NS Stylish Peach Pub dating in part from the 14th c, well kept Hogs Back and guests, carefully chosen wines and gins, good seasonal food from deli boards to daily specials, Thurs tapas night, friendly service; children welcome, tables out at front under parasols, open all day from 9.30am for breakfast. *(Tom Stone)*

EVERTON
SZ2994

Crown (01590) 642655

Old Christchurch Road; pub signed just off A337 W of Lymington; SO41 0JJ Quietly set restaurant-pub on edge of New Forest, good local food cooked by landlord-chef including daily specials, friendly service, Greene King and Ringwood ales, decent wines, two attractive dining rooms off tiled-floor bar, log fires; children welcome, wheelchair access, picnic-sets on front terrace behind picket fence and in garden behind, closed Mon. *(Jim and Caroline Storey)*

EXTON
SU6120

★**Shoe** (01489) 877526

Village signposted from A32 NE of Bishop's Waltham; SO32 3NT Popular brick-built country pub on South Downs Way; three linked rooms with log fires, good well presented food from traditional favourites to more imaginative restaurant-style dishes including fresh fish and seasonal game, well kept Wadworths ales and a guest, good friendly service; children and dogs welcome, disabled facilities, seats under parasols at front, more in garden

We say if we know a pub allows dogs.

across lane overlooking River Meon, open all day weekends. *(Ann and Colin Hunt)*

FAREHAM   SU5806
Cams Mill (01329) 287506
Cams Hall Estate, off A27; PO16 8UP Large waterside Fullers pub (oak-framed re-creation of former tidal mill); roomy interior including high-raftered and galleried eating area, popular food, well kept ales and friendly young staff, Fareham Creek views from big windows and terrace; free wi-fi; children and dogs welcome, nice circular creekside walk, open (and food) all day. *(David and Judy Robison, Ann and Colin Hunt)*

FAREHAM   SU5806
Cob & Pen (01329) 221624
Wallington Shore Road, not far from M27 junction 11; PO16 8SL Cheerful old corner local near Wallington River; four well kept ales including Fullers, St Austell and Sharps, decent choice of enjoyable well priced home-made food (all day weekends), log fire; some live music, TV, machines and darts; children and dogs welcome, large garden with play area and summer barbecues, open all day. *(Ann and Colin Hunt)*

FAREHAM   SU5806
Golden Lion (01329) 234061
High Street; PO16 7AE Traditional 19th-c town local, well kept Fullers/Gales beers from dark wood servery, dining part to the right with decent reasonably priced pubby food from sandwiches and baked potatoes up, good friendly service; charity quiz Thurs, free wi-fi; children and dogs welcome, courtyard garden, open all day (till 6pm Sun). *(Ann and Colin Hunt)*

FARNBOROUGH   SU8756
★ ## Prince of Wales (01252) 545578
Rectory Road, near station; GU14 8AL Ten well kept ales including five quickly changing guests at this welcoming Victorian local, three small linked areas with exposed brickwork, carpet or wood floors, open fire and some antiquey touches, generous lunchtime pubby food, also Mon pie night and Fri evening fish and chips, good friendly service; quiz first Sun of month, some live music; well behaved children and dogs welcome, terrace and smokers' gazebo, open all day Fri-Sun. *(Roger and Donna Huggins)*

FAWLEY   SU4603
Jolly Sailor (023) 8089 1305
Ashlett Creek, off B3053; SO45 1DT Cottagey waterside pub near small boatyard and sailing club, straightforward good value bar food, Ringwood Best and a guest, cheerful service, mixed pubby furnishings on bare boards, raised log fire, second bar with darts and pool; children and dogs welcome, tables outside looking past creek's yachts and boats to busy shipping channel, good shore walks, handy for Rothschild rhododendron

gardens at Exbury, open all day, no food Mon or evenings Tues and Sun. *(Sam Hyde)*

FINCHDEAN   SU7312
George (023) 9241 2257
Centre of village; PO8 0AU Red-brick pub dating from the 18th c, beamed front bar, separate dining area with conservatory, enjoyable fairly priced food (all day weekends – till 8pm Sun) from bar snacks up, Thurs curry night, well kept mainstream ales such as Adnams, Butcombe and Sharps, good friendly service, live music; children and dogs (in bar) welcome, picnic-sets out in front and in garden behind, good nearby walks, open all day till 10pm (midnight Fri, Sat). *(Val and Alan Green)*

FROGHAM   SU1712
Foresters Arms (01425) 652294
Abbotswell Road; SP6 2JA Refurbished New Forest pub (part of the Little Pub Group); enjoyable good value food from lunchtime baguettes and bagels up, well kept Wadworths ales and a guest, good friendly service, cosy rustic-chic interior with rugs on wood or flagstone floors, woodburners in brick fireplaces, pale green panelling, mix of old and new furniture including settles and pews, antlers and grandfather clock; children, walkers and dogs (in bar) welcome, picnic-sets out at front under pergola and on lawn, maybe donkeys, open all day Fri-Sun. *(Phil and Jane Villiers)*

GOODWORTH CLATFORD   SU3642
Royal Oak (01264) 324105
Longstock Road; SP11 7QY Comfortably modern L-shaped bar with welcoming staff, good carefully sourced food from pub staples up, Flack Manor and Ringwood ales, good choice of wines by the glass; Weds quiz night; children welcome, sheltered and very pretty dell-like garden with picnic sets, attractive Test Valley village and good River Anton walks, closed Sun evening. *(Jim and Caroline Storey)*

GOSPORT   SZ6198
Fighting Cocks (023) 9252 9885
Clayhall Road, Alverstoke; PO12 2AJ Cosy and welcoming local in residential area doing well under present management, Wadworths ales and enjoyable good value pub food, friendly helpful service; children and dogs welcome (pub spaniels are Sophie and Henry), big garden with play equipment, open all day. *(Charles Welch)*

GOSPORT   SU6101
Jolly Roger (023) 9258 2584
Priory Road, Hardway; PO12 4LQ Popular extended waterfront pub with fine harbour views, traditional beamed bar with four well kept ales and decent house wines, good choice of home-made food from bar and restaurant menus, efficient friendly young staff, lots of bric-a-brac, log fire,

attractive dining area with conservatory; children welcome, disabled access/facilities, seats outside, open all day. *(Neil and Anita Christopher, Ann and Colin Hunt)*

GOSPORT   SZ6100

Queens 07974 031671

Queens Road; PO12 1LG Classic bareboards corner local with half a dozen ales such as Oakleaf, Ringwood and Titanic kept in top condition by long-serving landlady, popular Oct beer festival, three areas off bar with good log fire in interesting carved fireplace, sensibly placed darts, TV room; closed lunchtimes Mon-Thurs, open all day Sat. *(Ann and Colin Hunt)*

GRAYSHOTT   SU8735

Fox & Pelican (01428) 604757

Headley Road; GU26 6LG Large village pub improved under present management; Fullers/Gales beers and a guest, enjoyable food (all day Fri, Sat, till 4pm Sun) from lunchtime sandwiches and light dishes up, good friendly service, linked areas with comfortable seating on wood or carpeted floors, open fire in large fireplace, dining conservatory; quiz and tapas Thurs, darts, sports TV, games machines; children and dogs welcome, wheelchair access, tables on paved terrace and lawn, fenced play area, open all day. *(Ann and Colin Hunt, John and Bernadette Elliott)*

GREYWELL   SU7151

Fox & Goose (01256) 702062

Near M3 junction 5; A287 towards Odiham, then first right to village; RG29 1BY Traditional two-bar village pub popular with locals and walkers, country kitchen furniture, open fire, enjoyable home-made pubby food from good lunchtime sandwiches up, Sun roast till 6pm, three well kept ales including Sharps Doom Bar; children and dogs welcome, good-sized back garden and camping field, River Whitewater and Basingstoke Canal walks, open all day. *(Valerie Sayer)*

HAMBLE   SU4806

Bugle (023) 8045 3000

3 miles from M27 junction 8; SO31 4HA Bustling little 16th-c village pub by River Hamble, beamed and timbered rooms with flagstones and polished boards, church chairs, woodburner in fine brick fireplace, bar stools along herringbone-brick and timbered counter, a beer named for the pub from Itchen Valley and a couple of guests (often Flack Manor), popular food (all day Sun); background music, TV; children welcome, dogs in bar, seats on terrace with view of boats, open all day. *(Alastair and Sheree Hepburn)*

HAMBLE   SU4806

King & Queen (023) 8045 4247

3 miles from M27 junction 8; High Street; SO31 4HA Popular with locals and visiting yachtsmen, this cheerful bustling pub has a simply furnished bar with log fire at one end, sofas and painted settles with scatter cushions, steps down to two small dining rooms, white-painted and plain wooden chairs, candelabra on straightforward tables, big yachting photographs, fairy lights, bunting and pennants, woodburner, three changing ales, good wines, cocktails and some 30 different rums, generous helpings of enjoyable food from sandwiches and pizzas up, friendly hard-working young staff; children and dogs welcome, sunny front garden with planked tables and picnic-sets (some under parasols), open all day. *(Taff Thomas)*

HAMBLE   SU4806

Olde Whyte Harte (023) 8045 2108

High Street; 3 miles from M27 junction 8; SO31 4JF Welcoming and popular oldfashioned village pub, big inglenook log fire, flagstones and low dark 17th-c beams, small cottagey restaurant area, generous freshly made pubby food including daily specials, Fullers/Gales beers and a guest from stonefaced counter, good wines by the glass; background music, occasional community oriented events; children and dogs welcome, small walled garden, handy for nature reserve, open (and food) all day. *(Jim and Caroline Storey)*

HAMBLE   SU4806

Victory (023) 8045 3105

High Street; SO31 4HA Split-level 18th-c red-brick pub with four well kept ales and enjoyable reasonably priced bar food, cheerful welcoming staff, nautical theme including Battle of Trafalgar mural (find the hidden faces), beams and half-panelling, wood, flagstone and carpeted floors; darts, sports TV; children and dogs welcome, terrace picnic-sets, open all day. *(Taff Thomas)*

HAMBLEDON   SU6716

★ Bat & Ball (023) 9263 2692

Broadhalfpenny Down; about 2 miles E towards Clanfield; PO8 0UB Extended dining pub opposite historic cricket pitch, log fires and comfortable modern furnishings in three linked rooms, lots of cricketing memorabilia (the game's rules are said to have been written here), enjoyable food from well priced snacks up, Fullers ales, good friendly service, panelled restaurant; children and dogs welcome, tables on front terrace, garden behind with lovely downs views, good walks, open all day. *(Ann and Colin Hunt)*

HAMBLEDON   SU6414

Vine (023) 9263 2419

West Street; PO7 4RW 400-year-old beamed village local, well kept Ringwood and enjoyable sensibly priced homemade food (not Sun-Tues evenings) from baguettes up, friendly staff, clean interior with well and two-way log fire; some live music; nice garden with small covered deck, good walks. *(Ann and Colin Hunt, Val and Alan Green)*

HAVANT SU7206

Wheelwrights Arms (023) 9247 6502

Emsworth Road; PO9 2SN Sizeable and stylishly decorated red-brick Victorian pub, well kept beers and good range of popular food including OAP lunch deal Mon-Thurs, friendly service; children welcome, open all day. *(Tom Stone)*

HAWKLEY SU7429

Hawkley Inn (01730) 827205

Off B3006 near A3 junction; Pococks Lane; GU33 6NE Traditional tile-hung village pub with seven well kept mainly local ales from central bar, good home-made food (not Sun evening) such as rabbit casserole, friendly staff, open fires (large moose head above one), rugs on flagstones, old pine tables and assorted chairs; children and dogs welcome, covered seating area at front, picnic-sets in big back garden, useful for walkers on Hangers Way, six comfortable bedrooms, open all day weekends. *(Tony and Jill Radnor)*

HAYLING ISLAND SU7201

Maypole (023) 9246 3670

Havant Road; PO11 OPS Sizeable two-bar 1930s roadside local, family-run and friendly, with good reasonably priced home-made pub food including Fri fish night, well kept Fullers/Gales beers, parquet floors and polished panelling, plenty of good seating, open fires; Thurs quiz, darts; children and dogs welcome, garden picnic-sets and play equipment, closed Sun evening. *(Neil Allen)*

HECKFIELD SU7260

New Inn (0118) 932 6374

B3349 Hook–Reading (former A32); RG27 0LE Rambling open-plan dining pub with enjoyable pubby food (all day weekends) from sandwiches and baked potatoes up, well kept Badger ales and good choice of wines by the glass, efficient friendly service, attractive layout with some traditional furniture in original core, two log fires, restaurant; jazz first Thurs of month, quiz and curry last Thurs; children welcome, good-sized heated terrace, 16 comfortable bedrooms in extension, open all day. *(Jim and Caroline Storey)*

HERRIARD SS6744

Fur & Feathers (01256) 384170

Pub signed just off A339 Basingstoke–Alton; RG25 2PN Victorian country pub, clean, light and airy, with popular fresh food from local produce, four well kept ales including Sharps Doom Bar and good choice of wines, friendly staff, smallish bar with stools along counter, dining areas either side, pine furniture on stripped-wood flooring,

painted half-panelling, old photographs and farm tools, two woodburners; background music; garden behind, open all day Fri and Sat, till 6pm Sun, closed Mon. *(Neill Allen)*

HOUGHTON SU3432

★**Boot** (01794) 388310

Village signposted off A30 in Stockbridge; SO20 6LH Updated well maintained country pub with cheery log-fire bar and more formal dining room, well kept Flack Manor, Ringwood and a guest, Weston's cider, good bar and restaurant food (not Sun evening) from baguettes to blackboard specials, friendly helpful staff; children and dogs welcome, picnic-sets out in front and in spacious tranquil garden by lovely (unfenced) stretch of River Test, outside summer grill (great tiger prawns), good walks, opposite Test Way walking/cycle path, open all day Fri-Sun. *(Helen and Brian Edgeley, John Allman)*

HURSTBOURNE TARRANT SU3853

George & Dragon (01264) 736277

The Square (A343); SP11 0AA Welcoming refurbished village pub (former 16th-c coaching inn); various areas off low-beamed core, modern pubby furniture on quarry tiles or carpet, woodburners, good freshly made seasonal food including weekday set lunch, local Betteridges and a guest such as Platform 5, good choice of wines and other drinks; small secluded terrace, eight bedrooms, pretty village in walking country, open all day from 8am (11am-10pm Sun). *(Simon Pyle)*

KEYHAVEN SZ3091

★**Gun** (01590) 642391

Keyhaven Road; SO41 0TP Busy rambling 17th-c pub looking over boatyard and sea to Isle of Wight; low-beamed bar with nautical bric-a-brac and plenty of character (less in family rooms and conservatory), good fairly standard food including local crab, well kept Ringwood, Sharps, Timothy Taylors and Charles Wells tapped from the cask, Weston's cider, lots of malt whiskies, prompt service from helpful young staff; bar billiards; tables out in front and in big back garden with swings and fish pond, you can stroll down to small harbour and walk to Hurst Castle, open all day Sat, closed Sun evening. *(M G Hart, David and Judy Robison, Bob and Margaret Holder)*

KINGSCLERE SU5258

Swan (01635) 299342

Swan Street; RG20 5PP Nicely refurbished 15th-c beamed village inn (Bel & The Dragon group), emphasis on dining with good bar and restaurant food including Josper grills, weekend brunch, three real ales, cocktails and good selection of wines by the glass including champagne, friendly helpful staff; children welcome, nine bedrooms, good surrounding walks, open all day. *(Valerie Sayer)*

LANGSTONE SU7104

★ **Royal Oak** (023) 9248 3125

Off A3023 just before Hayling Island bridge; Langstone High Street; PO9 1RY Charmingly placed waterside dining pub overlooking tidal inlet and ancient wadeway to Hayling Island, boats at high tide, wading birds when it goes out; Greene King ales and good choice of wines by the glass, reasonably priced food with all-day sandwiches and snacks, recently refurbished interior retaining spacious flagstoned bar and linked dining areas, log fire; nice garden with pond, good coast paths nearby, open all day. *(Tom Stone)*

LINDFORD SU8036

Royal Exchange (01420) 488118

Liphook Road; GU35 0NX Major revamp by Red Mist creating large bar and bright dining room, enjoyable food from sandwiches and sharing boards to good specials, set lunch deal, real ales including a house beer from Andwell, craft beers, plenty of wines by the glass and good selection of vodkas and gins, efficient friendly service; children welcome, seats outside, open all day Fri-Sun. *(John Evans)*

LINWOOD SU1910

High Corner (01425) 473973

Signed from A338 via Moyles Court, and from A31; BH24 3QY Big rambling pub in splendid New Forest position at end of track; popular and welcoming with some character in original upper log-fire bar, big back extensions for the summer crowds, nicely partitioned restaurant, verandah lounge and other rooms, good helpings of enjoyable home-made food, well kept Wadworths ales and Weston's cider, friendly staff; children and dogs welcome, horses too (stables and paddock available), extensive wooded garden with play area, seven comfortable bedrooms, open all day summer and weekends. *(Peter Meister, Phil and Jane Villiers)*

LITTLE LONDON SU6259

Plough (01256) 850628

Silchester Road, off A340 N of Basingstoke; RG26 5EP Tucked-away local, cosy and unspoilt, with log fires, low beams and mixed furnishings on brick or tiled floors (watch the step), well kept Palmers, Ringwood and interesting guests tapped from the cask, good value baguettes; bar billiards and darts; dogs welcome, attractive garden, handy for Pamber Forest and Calleva Roman remains. *(Rona Mackinlay)*

LONG SUTTON SU7447

Four Horseshoes (01256) 862488

Signed off B3349 S of Hook; RG29 1TA Welcoming unpretentious country pub with loyal band of regulars; open plan with black beams and two log fires, long-serving landlord cooking uncomplicated bargain food such as lancashire hotpot and fish and chips, friendly landlady serving three changing ales; live jazz second and fourth Tues of month; children and dogs welcome, disabled access, small glazed-in front verandah, picnic-sets and play area on grass over road, closed Mon, Tues lunchtimes. *(Tony and Jill Radnor)*

LONGPARISH SU4344

Cricketers (01264) 720335

B3048, off A303 just E of Andover; SP11 6PZ Friendly village local with connecting rooms and cosy corners, beams, bare boards and flagstones, two woodburners (one double aspect), assorted cricketing memorabilia, enjoyable freshly made food (not Sun or Mon evenings) from reassuringly short menu, well kept Wadworths ales; children and dogs welcome, nice back garden, open all day Fri-Sun. *(Mel Spear, Edward Mirzoeff)*

LYMINGTON SZ3295

Kings Head (01590) 672709

Quay Hill; SO41 3AR Friendly dimly lit old pub in steep cobbled lane of smart small shops; well kept Fullers London Pride, Ringwood, Timothy Taylors Landlord and a couple of guests, several wines by the glass, good choice of enjoyable home-made food from sandwiches up including vegetarian specials, pleasant helpful staff, nicely mixed old-fashioned furnishings in rambling beamed and bare-boarded rooms, log fire and woodburner; background music, daily papers; children and dogs welcome, nice little sunny courtyard behind, open all day and can get very busy. *(Jim and Caroline Storey)*

LYMINGTON SZ3394

Mayflower (01590) 672160

Kings Saltern Road; SO41 3QD Newly refurbished pub by Lymington Marina; high-ceilinged front rooms with patterned wallpaper or turquoise paintwork, built-in wall seats and leather-seated dining chairs around dark wooden tables, candles and fresh flowers, logs piled into fireplace, two back rooms with yachting photos on planked walls, books, model yachts and big modern lanterns, raised woodburner, three changing ales and good wines, enjoyable food served by friendly well-trained young staff; children and dogs welcome, covered terrace, garden with heavy rustic tables and benches, open (and food) all day. *(Neill Allen)*

LYNDHURST SU2908

Fox & Hounds (023) 8028 2098

High Street; SO43 7BG Big busy low-beamed pub, comfortable and much modernised/extended, good choice of popular food including weekend brunch, Fullers/Gales beers and a guest, plenty of wines by the glass, cheerful helpful service, rambling interior with exposed brick and standing timbers, wood and stone floors, attached café/deli; live music Sat, Mon quiz, free wi-fi; children and dogs welcome, disabled facilities, tables in courtyard with murals and enamel signs, covered seating in old barn, open (and food) all day. *(Anne and Ben Smith)*

LYNDHURST   SU2908
Waterloo Arms (023) 8028 2113
Pikes Hill, just off A337 N; SO43 7AS
Thatched 17th-c New Forest pub with low beams, stripped-brick walls and log fire, two Ringwood beers and Sharps Doom Bar, pubby food including blackboard specials, friendly staff, comfortable bar and roomy back dining area; Tues quiz and Sun live music; children and dogs welcome, terrace and nice big garden, open (and food) all day. *(Tom Stone)*

MAPLEDURWELL   SU6851
★ **Gamekeepers** (01256) 322038
Off A30, not far from M3 junction 6; RG25 2LU Dark-beamed dining pub with good upmarket food (not cheap and they add a service charge) from regularly changing blackboard menu, also some pubby choices and lunchtime baguettes, welcoming helpful landlord and friendly efficient staff, three well kept local ales including Andwell, good coffee, a few sofas in flagstoned and panelled core, well spaced tables in large dining room; background music, TV; children welcome, terrace and garden, lovely thatched village with duck pond, good walks, open all day weekends. *(Guy Consterdine)*

MARCHWOOD   SU3809
Pilgrim (023) 8086 7752
Hythe Road, off A326 at Twiggs Lane; SO40 4WU Popular picturesque thatched pub (originally three 18th-c cottages), enjoyable sensibly priced food from lunchtime sandwiches up, well kept Fullers ales and decent wines, friendly helpful staff, open fires; children and dogs welcome, tree-lined garden with round picnic-sets, 14 stylish bedrooms in building across car park, open all day. *(Phil and Jane Villiers)*

MATTINGLEY   SU7357
Leather Bottle (0118) 932 6371
3 miles from M3 junction 5; in Hook, turn right-and-left on to B3349 Reading Road (former A32); RG27 8JU Old red-brick chain pub with good food from varied menu, three local ales including Andwell and plenty of wines by the glass, well spaced tables in linked areas, black beams, flagstones and bare boards, inglenook log fire, extension opening on to covered terrace; background music; children and dogs (in bar) welcome, disabled access/facilities, two garden areas, open (and food) all day. *(Anne and Ben Smith)*

MEONSTOKE   SU6120
Bucks Head (01489) 877313
Village signed just off A32 N of Droxford; SO32 3NA Cleanly refurbished and opened up tile-hung pub in lovely village setting with ducks on pretty little River Meon; stone floors and log fires, popular traditional food, well kept Greene King and guests; children and dogs welcome, small walled gardens either side, one overlooking river, good walks, five bedrooms, open all day weekends (till 8pm Sun). *(Ann and Colin Hunt)*

MICHELDEVER   SU5138
Half Moon & Spread Eagle
(01962) 774339 *Brown sign to pub off A33 N of Winchester; SO21 3DG*
Simply furnished 18th-c beamed village local, bare-boards bar with woodburner, horsebrasses and old banknotes pinned overhead, five real ales, ample helpings of enjoyable well priced food in carpeted dining side from baguettes up, steps up to games area with pool and shelves of books; regular quiz nights; children and dogs welcome, sheltered back terrace and garden, pleasant walks nearby, open all day Sat, Sun till 8pm, closed Mon lunchtime. *(Charles Welch)*

MILFORD-ON-SEA   SZ2891
Beach House (01590) 643044
Park Lane; SO41 0PT Civilised well placed Victorian hotel-dining pub owned by Hall & Woodhouse; restored oak-panelled interior, entrance hall bar with Badger First Gold, Tanglefoot and a guest, nice wines by the glass and enjoyable sensibly priced food from lunchtime baguettes and sharing boards up, friendly attentive service, magnificent views from dining room and terrace; children welcome, dogs in bar, grounds down to the Solent looking out to the Needles, 15 bedrooms, open (and food) all day. *(David and Sally Frost)*

MINLEY MANOR   SU8357
Crown & Cushion (01252) 545253
A327, just N of M3 junction 4A; GU17 9UA Attractive little pub dating from 1512, two well kept Shepherd Neame ales and good fairly priced food including a few far eastern choices, prompt cheerful service, Sun carvery in big separate raftered and flagstoned rustic 'meade hall' with huge log fire; children welcome, no dogs inside, heated terrace overlooking own cricket pitch, open (and food) all day. *(KC)*

MINSTEAD   SU2810
★ **Trusty Servant** (023) 8081 2137
Just off A31, not far from M27 junction 1; SO43 7FY Attractive 19th-c red-brick pub in pretty New Forest hamlet with interesting church (Sir Arthur Conan Doyle buried here), wandering cattle and ponies, plenty of easy walks; two-room bare-boards bar and big dining room, open fires, well kept local ales and good reasonably priced food from doorstep sandwiches to local game, welcoming efficient service even when busy; children and dogs welcome, terrace and big sloping garden, open (and food) all day. *(Tom and Jill Jones)*

NEW CHERITON   SU5827

★**Hinton Arms** (01962) 771252
A272 near B3046 junction; SO24 0NH Neatly kept popular country pub with cheerful accommodating landlord and friendly staff, three or four real ales including Bowman Wallops Wood and a house beer brewed by Hampshire, decent wines by the glass, good generous pub food from sandwiches to daily specials, sporting pictures and memorabilia; TV lounge; well behaved children and dogs welcome, terrace and big garden, lots of colourful tubs and hanging baskets, very handy for Hinton Ampner House (NT). *(Tony and Jill Radnor)*

ODIHAM   SU7450

Bell (01256) 702282
The Bury, off Church Street; RG29 1LY Unspoilt two-bar local in pretty square opposite church and stocks, simple and welcoming, with three well kept changing ales and good value straightforward lunchtime food, beams and log fire; dogs allowed on the lead, picnic-sets out in front, closed Mon lunchtime, otherwise open all day. *(Ann and Colin Hunt)*

PETERSFIELD   SU7423

George (01730) 233343
The Square; GU32 3HH Old building in square with café-style tables outside, clean contemporary interior, enjoyable food including well filled sandwiches, sharing plates and home-made burgers, three well kept ales, good choice of wines by the glass and decent coffee, friendly young staff; some weekend live music; children welcome, attractive courtyard garden with own bar, open all day from 9am for breakfast. *(Jim and Caroline Storey)*

PETERSFIELD   SU7423

Good Intent (01730) 263838
College Street; GU31 4AF Homely 16th-c coaching inn, friendly and chatty, with five well kept Fullers/Gales beers and enjoyable freshly made pubby food (not Sun evening) including range of O'Hagans sausages, low black beams, pine tables and built-in upholstered benches, separate large restaurant, log fires; background and live music, quiz Mon; children and dogs welcome, seats on front terrace, narrow entrance to small back car park, three bedrooms, open all day. *(Neill Allen)*

PETERSFIELD   SU7423

Square Brewery (01730) 264291
The Square; GU32 3HJ Friendly town-centre Fullers pub recently refurbished in rustic/modern style, five of their ales kept well and short choice of enjoyable sensibly priced food including good sandwiches;

monthly quiz first Thurs of month, live music Sat, free wi-fi; children and dogs welcome, seats out in front and in courtyard garden behind, open all day from 9am for breakfast. *(Val and Alan Green)*

PHOENIX GREEN   SU7555

Phoenix (01252) 842484
London Road, A30 W of Hartley Wintney; RG27 8RT 18th-c pub with lots of beams, timber dividers, rugs on bare boards and big end inglenook, good freshly made food from varied daily changing menu with steaks a particular speciality, four well kept ales, a couple of good ciders and 16 wines by the glass, friendly prompt service, back dining room; several themed nights and club dinners; pleasant outlook from sunny garden (hats and sun cream provided). *(Chris and Claire Taylor)*

PILLEY   SZ3298

★**Fleur de Lys** (01590) 672158
Off A337 Brockenhurst–Lymington; Pilley Street; SO41 5QG Ancient thatched and beamed village pub (11th-c origins) attractively refurbished under current owners; good popular restauranty food from shortish menu (booking advised), Courage Directors, Sharps Doom Bar and a guest, efficient friendly service, inglenook log fires; well behaved children and dogs welcome, pretty garden with old well, fine forest and heathland walks, open all day Sun till 8pm, closed Mon. *(Rona Mackinlay)*

PORTSMOUTH   SZ6399

Bridge Tavern (023) 9275 2992
East Street, Camber Dock; PO1 2JJ Flagstones, bare boards and lots of dark wood, comfortable furnishings, maritime theme with good harbour views, Fullers ales, sensibly priced food including plenty of fish dishes; nice waterside terrace, open all day. *(Ann and Colin Hunt, Tony Scott)*

PORTSMOUTH   SZ6399

Dolphin (023) 9282 3595
High Street, Old Portsmouth opposite cathedral; PO1 2LU Spacious old beamed pub – known as 'the country pub in town' and furnished accordingly; half a dozen well kept ales (some expensive), enjoyable food including good vegetarian options, friendly smartly dressed staff; children and dogs welcome, small terrace behind, open all day. *(Ann and Colin Hunt)*

PORTSMOUTH   SU6501

George (023) 9275 3885
Queen Street, near dockyard entrance; PO1 3HU Spotless old inn (Grade I listed) with two rooms, one set for dining, log fire, glass-covered well and maritime pictures, well kept Greene King Abbot, Sharps Atlantic

---

There are report forms at the back of the book.

and Doom Bar, well priced food (not Sun evening, Mon lunchtime) from sandwiches up, friendly staff; eight bedrooms, handy for dockyard and HMS *Victory*, open all day. *(Ann and Colin Hunt)*

PORTSMOUTH SU6706

George (023) 9222 1079

Portsdown Hill Road, Widley; PO6 1BE Old-fashioned one-bar Georgian local with village feel, seven well kept ales such as Adnams, Flowers, Greene King and Ringwood, popular pubby food including good ploughman's, helpful pleasant staff; live music Tues, quiz Sun; dogs welcome, views of Hayling Island, Portsmouth and Isle of Wight, hill walks across the road, open all day. *(Pat and Stewart Gordon)*

PORTSMOUTH SZ6399

Pembroke (023) 9282 3961

Pembroke Road; PO1 2NR Traditional well run corner local with good buoyant atmosphere, comfortable and unspoilt under long-serving licensees, Bass, Fullers London Pride and Greene King Abbot from L-shaped bar, simple cheap food including fresh rolls, coal-effect gas fire; darts and weekend live music; open all day (break 4-7pm Sun). *(Ann and Colin Hunt)*

PORTSMOUTH SU6300

Ship Anson (023) 9282 4152

Victory Road, The Hard (opposite Esplanade Station, Portsea); PO1 3DT No-frills mock-Tudor pub close to dockyard entrance, spacious and comfortable, with well kept Greene King ales and a guest, generous pub food at bargain prices including coffee and cake, buoyant local atmosphere; fruit machines, sports TVs; children welcome, seats outside overlooking ferry port, very handy for HMS *Victory*, open all day. *(Richard Tilbrook)*

PORTSMOUTH SZ6299

Still & West (023) 9282 1567

Bath Square, Old Portsmouth; PO1 2JL Great location with superb views of narrow harbour mouth and across to Isle of Wight, especially from glazed-in panoramic upper family area and waterfront terrace; nautical bar with fireside sofas, Fullers ales and good choice of wines by the glass, enjoyable food from sandwiches and sharing plates to good fish dishes; background music, free wi-fi; handy for Historic Dockyard, nearby pay-and-display parking, open all day from 9am (11.30am Sun). *(Ann and Colin Hunt, Dr and Mrs J D Abell)*

PORTSMOUTH SU6400

White Swan (023) 9289 1340

Guildhall Walk; PO1 2DD Popular mock-Tudor pub (Brewhouse & Kitchen) visibly brewing its own good beers, also decent choice of well priced food (all day Fri-Sun) from sandwiches and sharing boards up; live

music Sun lunchtime; children welcome, open all day. *(Ann and Colin Hunt, Phil and Jane Villiers)*

PRESTON CANDOVER SU6041

Purefoy Arms (01256) 389777

B3046 Basingstoke–Alresford; RG25 2EJ By the time the *Guide* is published, the spanish licensees who offered excellent food and made this a popular Main Entry will have left – news please.

RINGWOOD SU1504

Railway (01425) 473701

Hightown Road; BH24 1NQ Traditional two-bar Victorian local spruced up under present licensees, up to four well kept changing ales (usually one from nearby Ringwood), enjoyable home-made food including range of burgers, also vegan/vegetarian menu, friendly service; Thurs quiz, darts; children and dogs welcome, nice enclosed garden with play area, vegetable patch, ducks and chickens, open all day (Sun till 9pm). *(Jim and Caroline Storey)*

ROMSEY SU3523

Dukes Head (01794) 514450

A3057 out towards Stockbridge; SO51 0HB Attractive 16th-c roadside dining pub with warren of small comfortable linked rooms, big log fire, enjoyable generously served food including affordable lunchtime specials, ales such as Flack Manor and Sharps, cheerful staff; children welcome, sheltered back terrace and pleasant garden, pretty hanging baskets, handy for Sir Harold Hillier Gardens, open all day weekends. *(Ann and Colin Hunt)*

ROMSEY SU3521

Old House at Home (01794) 513175

Love Lane; SO51 8DE Attractive 17th-c thatched pub surrounded by new development; friendly and bustling, with comfortable low-beamed interior, wide choice of freshly made sensibly priced bar food including popular Sun lunch, well kept Fullers/Gales ales and guests, Aspall's cider, cheerful efficient service; regular folk sessions; children and dogs (in bar) welcome, split-level back terrace, open all day (no food Sun evening). *(Ann and Colin Hunt, R K Phillips)*

ROMSEY SU3520

Three Tuns (01794) 512639

Middlebridge Street (but car park signed straight off A27 bypass); SO51 8HL Food is the star at this old village pub but they do keep Andwell, Flack Manor, Flowerpots and Upham, local cider and 11 wines by the glass; bar with cushioned bow-window seat, red leather seating around dark wooden tables on flagstones, beer mats pinned to the walls and church candles in fireplace, dining areas either side, one with a huge stuffed fish over another fireplace, the other with prints on yellow walls above a black dado, a few rugs scattered around, heavy beams and antler chandeliers; background music, board games, free wi-fi; children and dogs welcome, back terrace with picnic-sets under parasols, more seats in front by the tiny street, open all day, no food Sun evening. *(Andrew Stone, John Harris)*

ROTHERWICK SU7156

Coach & Horses (01256) 768976

Signed from B3349 N of Hook; also quite handy for M3 junction 5; RG27 9BG Friendly 17th-c pub with traditional beamed front rooms, good value locally sourced pubby food and well kept Badger ales, log fire and woodburners, newer back dining area; children, dogs and muddy boots welcome, tables out at front and on terrace behind overlooking fields, pretty flower tubs and baskets, good walks, open all day Sat, Sun till 6pm, closed Mon. *(Tom Stone)*

ROTHERWICK SU7156

Falcon (01256) 765422

Off B3349 N of Hook, not far from M3 junction 5; RG27 9BL Open-plan country pub with good freshly made food using local suppliers (highish prices), Wed fish night, friendly efficient service, well kept ales such as Otter and Ringwood, good selection of wines, rustic tables and comfy sofa in bare-boards bar, well laid flagstoned dining area, log fires; free wi-fi; children and dogs welcome, disabled access, tables out in front and in back garden, open all day. *(Tom Stone)*

SHALDEN SU7043

Golden Pot (01420) 80655

B3349 Odiham Road N of Alton; GU34 4DJ Airy light décor with timbered walls, bare boards and log fires, enjoyable food from baguettes up including themed nights, friendly service, a couple of ales such as Sharps Doom Bar and Triple fff Altons Pride, local artwork for sale in smallish restaurant; background music, skittle alley; children and dogs welcome, benches out in covered area at front, garden with play area, open all day. *(Valerie Sayer)*

SHEDFIELD SU5613

Samuels Rest (01329) 832213

Upper Church Road (signed off B2177); SO32 2JB Cosy unspoilt village local under welcoming licensees, good straightforward home-made food and well kept Wadworths beers, nice eating area away from bar, conservatory; aviary with chatty parrot; garden and terrace, lovely church. *(Ann and Colin Hunt)*

SHEDFIELD SU5513

Wheatsheaf (01329) 833024

A334 Wickham–Botley; SO32 2JG Friendly no-fuss local with well kept Flowerpots and guests tapped from the cask, proper cider, short sensible choice of

enjoyable bargain lunches (evening food Tues and Weds), good service, woodburner and darts in public bar, smaller lounge; live music Sat; dogs welcome, garden, handy for Wickham Vineyard, open all day. *(Ann and Ben Smith)*

SHERFIELD ENGLISH SU3022

Hatchet (01794) 322487

Romsey Road; SO51 6FP Beamed and panelled 18th-c pub with good choice of popular fairly priced food including two-for-one steak deal (Tues, Thurs evenings) and OAP lunch (Mon, Tues), four well kept ales such as Dartmoor, St Austell, Sharps and Timothy Taylors, good wine choice, friendly hard-working staff, long bar with cosy area down steps, woodburner, more steps up to second bar with darts, TV and juke box; monthly quiz; children and dogs welcome, outside seating on two levels, play area, open all day weekends. *(Jim and Caroline Storey)*

SHIPTON BELLINGER SU2345

Boot (01980) 842279

High Street; SP9 7UF Village pub with vast range of enjoyable reasonably priced food including chinese, thai, italian and mexican alongside traditional english dishes, friendly staff; background music; children welcome, back garden with decked area, open all day Sun. *(Neill Allen)*

SOPLEY SZ1596

Woolpack (01425) 672252

B3347 N of Christchurch; BH23 7AX Pretty thatched 17th-c dining pub with rambling open-plan low-beamed bar, enjoyable traditional food plus daily specials and range of sandwiches and wraps, Ringwood and Wadworths ales, Thatcher's cider and good choice of wines by the glass, modern dining conservatory overlooking weir; Mon quiz night; children in eating areas, dogs in certain parts, terrace and charming garden with weeping willows, duck stream and footbridges, open (and food) all day. *(Charles Welch)*

SOUTHAMPTON SU4111

Dancing Man (023) 8083 6666

Bugle Street/Town Quay; SO14 2AR Ancient listed building with plenty of atmosphere and character, up to 12 interesting beers including eight from on-site brewery (tours available), shortish choice of enjoyable home-made food (all day Fri-Sun) from bar snacks and pies up, good friendly service, sweeping staircase to upper dining area with own bar and fine raftered ceiling; dogs welcome (menu for them), disabled access and lift, open all day. *(Phil and Jane Villiers)*

SOUTHAMPTON SU4111

★ Duke of Wellington (023) 8033 9222

Bugle Street (or walk along city wall from Bar Gate); SO14 2AH Striking timber-framed building dating from the

14th c (cellars even older); heavy beams and fine log fire, up to nine well kept Wadworths ales (tasting trays available), plenty of wines by the glass and good fairly priced food (not Sun evening), friendly helpful service; background music (live jazz Fri), free wi-fi; children welcome, sunny streetside picnic-sets, handy for Tudor House & Garden, open all day. *(Phil and Jane Villiers)*

SOUTHAMPTON SU4213
Rockstone (023) 8063 7256
Onslow Road; SO14 0JL Popular relaxed place with well liked generous food from signature burgers to asian street food (booking advised), good variety of real ales, craft beers and ciders from well stocked bar, friendly hard-working staff; some live music; children welcome, seats out at front, open all day (till 1am Fri, Sat). *(Phil and Jane Villiers)*

SOUTHAMPTON SU4313
South Western Arms
(023) 8032 4542 *Adelaide Road, by St Denys station; SO17 2HW* Friendly backstreet corner local with ten well kept changing ales, also good choice of bottled beers and whiskies, friendly staff and easy-going atmosphere, bare boards and brickwork, lots of woodwork, toby jugs, pump clips and stag's head on beams, old range and earthenware, darts, pool and table football in upper gallery allowing children; some live music, beer festivals; dogs welcome on leads, picnic-sets in walled beer garden, open all day. *(Sam Hyde)*

SOUTHAMPTON SU4213
White Star (023) 8082 1990
Oxford Street; SO14 3DJ Smart modern bar with banquettes and open fire, comfortable sofas and armchairs in secluded alcoves by south-facing windows, bistro-style dining area, good up-to-date food including brunch, Itchen Valley ales and a guest, nice wines by the glass and lots of cocktails, efficient attentive staff (may ask to keep a credit card while you eat); sunny pavement tables on pedestrianised street, 13 boutique bedrooms, open all day. *(Rona Mackinlay)*

SOUTHSEA SZ6498
Belle Isle (023) 9282 0515
Osbourne Road; PO5 3LR Popular corner café-bar-restaurant in former shop, interesting interior with continental feel, three real ales, international bottled beers, cocktails and eclectic blackboard menu, decent coffee; children welcome, some seats out at front, open all day. *(Ann and Colin Hunt)*

SOUTHSEA SZ6698
Eastney Tavern (023) 9282 6246
Cromwell Road; PO4 9PN Bow-fronted corner pub just off the seafront, spacious and comfortable, with various eating areas (plenty of room for drinkers too), popular good value food, three real ales including

Greene King IPA and decent choice of wines by the glass, cheerful staff and good buoyant atmosphere; Tues quiz, Fri live music, sports TV; children and dogs welcome, seats in courtyard garden, nearby parking difficult, closed Mon lunchtime, otherwise open all day. *(Ann and Colin Hunt)*

SOUTHSEA SZ6499
Eldon Arms (023) 9229 7963
Eldon Street/Norfolk Street; PO5 4BS Tile-fronted Victorian backstreet pub under welcoming management, Fullers London Pride, St Austell Tribute and guests, simple food, old pictures and advertisements, attractive mirrors, shelves of books and assorted bric-a-brac; some live music, bar billiards, darts and pool; children welcome, tables in back garden, open all day. *(Ann and Colin Hunt, Phil and Jane Villiers)*

SOUTHSEA SZ6499
★Hole in the Wall (023) 9229 8085
Great Southsea Street; PO5 3BY Friendly unspoilt little local in old part of town, excellent range of well kept/priced ales including cask-tapped Oakleaf Hole Hearted, Thatcher's cider, speciality local sausages, meat puddings and other simple good value food (evenings Tues-Sat, lunchtime Fri), nicely worn boards, dark pews and panelling, old photographs and prints, hundreds of pump clips on ceiling, little snug behind the bar and sweet shop; daily papers, quiz night Thurs, Oct beer festival; small outside area at front with benches, side garden, open all day from 4pm (noon Fri, 2pm Sat and Sun). *(Ann and Colin Hunt)*

SOUTHSEA SZ6598
Leopold (023) 9282 9748
Albert Road; PO4 0JT Traditional green-tiled corner local with ten well kept ales (tasters offered), good choice of ciders and over 100 bottled beers including good selection from BrewDog, bright interior with hundreds of pump clips on the walls and pictures of old Portsmouth, no food; Mon quiz, unobtrusive TVs each end, games machines, darts; walled beer garden behind, open all day. *(Ann and Colin Hunt)*

SOUTHSEA SZ6498
Meat & Barrel (023) 9217 6291
Palmerston Road; PO5 3PT Sizeable bar-restaurant under same ownership as Southsea's Belle Isle, fine range of real ales and craft beers (tasters offered), friendly knowledgeable staff, enjoyable food including range of burgers and various sausage and mash combinations; children welcome, open all day. *(Ann and Colin Hunt)*

SOUTHSEA SZ6698
Sir Loin of Beef (023) 9282 0115
Highland Road, Eastney; PO4 9NH Spic and span one-room corner pub with friendly staff and buoyant atmosphere, at least eight

well kept frequently changing ales (tasters offered) including Gales and Titanic, no food, interesting submarine pictures and artefacts; bar billiards, juke box, some live music; open all day. *(Sam Hyde)*

SOUTHSEA SZ6499
Wine Vaults (023) 9286 4712
Albert Road, opposite King's Theatre; PO5 2SF Bustling Fullers pub with several chatty rooms on different floors, main panelled bar with long plain counter and pubby furniture, seven well kept ales and decent choice of food including pizzas and range of burgers, good service, separate restaurant; background music, sports TV, table football; children welcome, dogs in bar, smokers' roof terrace, open (and food) all day. *(Ann and Colin Hunt)*

SOUTHWICK SU6208
Golden Lion (023) 9221 0437
High Street; just off B2177 on Portsdown Hill; PO17 6EB Welcoming two-bar 16th-c beamed pub (where Eisenhower and Montgomery came before D-Day); up to seven well kept local ales including two from Suthwyk using barley from surrounding fields, four ciders and a dozen wines by the glass, enjoyable locally sourced home-made food (not Sun or Mon evenings) from snacks up in bar and dining room, cosy lounge bar with sofas and log fire, live music including Tues jazz; good outside loos; children and dogs welcome, picnic-sets on grass at side, picturesque Estate village with scenic walks, next to Southwick Brewhouse shop/museum (over 250 bottled beers), open all day Sat, till 7pm Sun. *(Ann and Colin Hunt, Val and Alan Green)*

SOUTHWICK SU6208
Red Lion (023) 9237 7223
High Street; PO17 6EF Smartly kept low-beamed village dining pub with good choice of well liked food (best to book), Fullers/Gales beers and a guest, several wines by the glass, efficient friendly staff even though busy; children welcome, good walks, open all day weekends. *(Ann and Colin Hunt)*

STOCKBRIDGE SU3535
Greyhound (01264) 810833
High Street; SO20 6EY Substantial inn reworked as civilised pub-restaurant, log fires each end of bow-windowed bar (restaurant to the right), scrubbed old tables on woodstrip floor, dark low beams, good range of well liked food especially fish, set menu and daily specials, three real ales including a house beer from Ringwood, good wine and whisky choice, friendly efficient staff (service charge added to bills); tables in charming Test-side garden behind, children and dogs allowed, bedrooms and fly fishing, open all day. *(John Evans, Mr and Mrs A Curry, Edward Mirzoeff)*

STOCKBRIDGE SU3535
★Three Cups (01264) 810527
High Street; SO20 6HB Lovely low-beamed building dating from 1500, spruced up and added to yet keeping country inn feel, some emphasis on dining with lots of smartly set pine tables, but also high-backed settles, rustic bric-a-brac and three well kept ales (two from local brewers), good interesting food along with more pubby choices, helpful amiable service, nice wines by the glass, extended 'orangery' restaurant; children and dogs welcome, vine-covered verandah and charming cottage garden with streamside terrace, eight bedrooms, open all day. *(Val and Alan Green, Tony and Jill Radnor)*

STRATFIELD TURGIS SU6960
Wellington Arms (01256) 882214
Off A33 Reading–Basingstoke; RG27 0AS Handsome old country hotel dating from the 17th c, restful and surprisingly pubby tall-windowed two-room bar, part flagstoned, part carpeted, with leather chesterfields by open fire, two well kept Badger ales, good food and service; children and dogs welcome, garden, 27 comfortable bedrooms, open all day. *(Derek Stafford)*

STROUD SU7223
Seven Stars (01730) 264122
Winchester Road; set back from A272 Petersfield–Winchester; GU32 3PG Neatly modernised and extended open-plan flint and brick pub, panelling, beams, wood and flagstone floors, good log fires, separate counter for ordering wide choice of good value popular food from well filled baguettes up, brisk but friendly service, four well kept Badger ales and good wine list, large restaurant; free wi-fi; children and dogs (in bar) welcome, outside tables, good if strenuous walking, open all day. *(Val and Alan Green)*

SWANMORE SU5716
Brickmakers (01489) 890954
Church Road; SO32 2PA Large restyled 1920s pub in centre of village, friendly and relaxed, with four well kept ales such as Bowman and Fullers, decent wines and good all-day food (till 6pm Sun) cooked by landlord-chef including popular Sun roasts and OAP weekday lunch deal, cheerful efficient service, leather sofas by log fire, dining area with local artwork; Tues quiz, some live music; children and dogs welcome (pub's dog is Rosie), garden with raised deck, nearby walks, open all day. *(Val and Alan Green, Ann and Colin Hunt)*

SWANMORE SU5816
Hunters (01489) 877214
Hillgrove; SO32 2PZ Popular rambling old dining pub on edge of village, friendly long-serving licensees and nice staff, wide choice of good honest freshly made food

including enjoyable Sun lunch, home-baked bread, well kept Bowman and a guest tapped from the cask, lots of wines by the glass, bank notes, carpentry and farm tools on the walls; background music; children and dogs welcome, big garden with play area, nice walks north of the village, open all day weekends (can be very busy then). *(Val and Alan Green)*

SWANMORE   SU5815
Rising Sun (01489) 896663
Droxford Road; signed off A32 N of Wickham and B2177 S of Bishop's Waltham, at Hillpound E of village centre; SO32 2PS Former brick coaching inn under newish friendly management; comfortable seating by log fire in low-beamed carpeted bar, pleasant roomier dining area with brick barrel vaulting in one part, local ales and good range of wines by the glass, enjoyable reasonably priced pub food including daily specials, attentive service; children and dogs (in bar) welcome, picnic-sets on side grass with a play area, Kings Way long-distance path nearby, open all day Sun with food till 6pm. *(Ann and Colin Hunt, Val and Alan Green)*

SWANWICK   SU5109
Elm Tree (01489) 579818
Swanwick Lane, off A3051 not far from M27 junction 9; SO31 7DX Welcoming two-bar pub with generous helpings of enjoyable good value food including Tues steak night, prompt friendly service, well kept Flowerpots, Sharps Doom Bar and a guest, dining extension; darts, free wi-fi; children and dogs welcome, tables in small garden, handy for Swanwick Lakes Nature Reserve, open all day. *(Ann and Colin Hunt)*

SWAY   SZ2898
Hare & Hounds (01590) 682404
Durns Town, just off B3055 SW of Brockenhurst; SO41 6AL Bright, airy and comfortable New Forest family dining pub with popular generously served food including daily specials, well kept ales such as Itchen Valley, Ringwood, St Austell and Timothy Taylors, good friendly service, low beams and central log fire; background music, Sun quiz; dogs welcome, picnic-sets and play frame in neatly kept garden, open all day. *(Ann and Ben Smith)*

THRUXTON   SU2945
White Horse (01264) 772401
Mullens Pond, just off A303 eastbound; SP11 8EE Attractive old thatched pub (tucked below A303 embankment) with emphasis on enjoyable freshly made food,

good friendly service, plenty of wines by the glass and well kept ales such as Greene King, spacious comfortably modernised interior with very low beams, woodburner and separate dining area; regular live music and other events; good-sized garden and terrace, summer barbecues, four bedrooms, closed Sun evening. *(B J Harding)*

TICHBORNE   SU5730
★ Tichborne Arms (01962) 733760
Signed off B3047; SO24 0NA Thatched pub (rebuilt in the 1930s) in rolling countryside; half-panelled bare-boards bar with interesting pictures and other odds and ends, candlelit pine tables and raised woodburner, Palmers and guests tapped from the cask, local cider, good traditional home-made food from doorstep sandwiches up, locals' bar with piano, darts and open fire; children and dogs welcome, sheltered terrace, more seats in big garden growing own vegetables, close to Wayfarers Walk and Itchen Way, open all day Sat, till 7.30pm Sun. *(Tony and Jill Radnor)*

TIMSBURY   SU3325
Bear & Ragged Staff
(01794) 368602 *A3057 towards Stockbridge; pub marked on OS Sheet 185 map reference 334254; SO51 0LB* Roadside dining pub with good choice of popular food including blackboard specials, friendly service, lots of wines by the glass, three Fullers/Gales beers and a guest, good-sized beamed interior with log fire; children welcome in eating part, tables in extended garden with play area, handy for Mottisfont (NT), good walks, open all day. *(David Hartshorne, Phil and Jane Villiers)*

TITCHFIELD   SU5305
Queens Head (01329) 842154
High Street; off A27 near Fareham; PO14 4AQ Welcoming early 17th-c family-run pub with enjoyable home-made food and four well kept ales, cosy bar with old local pictures, window seats and warm winter fire in central brick fireplace, small redecorated dining room; Sun quiz, function room for nostalgic dinner-dance and theatre nights; children welcome, picnic-sets in prettily planted backyard, pleasant conservation village near nature reserve and walks to coast, open all day. *(Jim and Caroline Storey)*

TITCHFIELD   SU5405
Wheatsheaf (01329) 842965
East Street; off A27 near Fareham; PO14 4AD Welcoming old pub with well kept ales such as Flowerpots and Palmers, good popular food (all day Sun) including

---

small-plates menu and Tues steak night, bow-windowed front bar, back restaurant extension, log fires; background music; terrace, open all day. *(Ann and Colin Hunt)*

TWYFORD SU4824

★**Bugle** (01962) 714888

B3355/Park Lane; SO21 1QT Modern pub with good enterprising food (highish prices) from daily changing menu, also lunchtime sandwiches/snacks and Mon evening set deal, attentive friendly young staff, well kept ales from Bowman, Flowerpots and Upham, nice wines by the glass, woodburner; background music; attractive verandah seating area, good walks nearby, three country-style bedrooms, good breakfast, open all day (no food Sun evening). *(Rona Mackinlay)*

TWYFORD SU4824

Phoenix (01962) 713322

High Street (B3335); SO21 1RF Cheerful open-plan local with raised dining area and big inglenook log fire, jovial long-serving landlord and friendly attentive staff, eight well kept ales including Greene King, good value wines and large helpings of enjoyable traditional food; background music, sports TV, quiz nights, skittle alley; children welcome, side terraces, open all day Weds-Sun. *(Richard Heath, Mary Smith)*

UPHAM SU5320

Brushmakers Arms (01489) 860231

Shoe Lane; village signed from Winchester–Bishops Waltham downs road, and from B2177; SO32 1JJ Welcoming low-beamed village pub under new management (some redecoration); L-shaped bar divided by central woodburner, cushioned settles and chairs around mix of tables, brushes and related paraphernalia, little back snug, enjoyable locally sourced home-made food from daily changing menu, Bowman, Fullers and two local guests, good choice of wines; quiz first Weds of month, folk session third Sun (from 5pm); children and dogs welcome, big garden with picnic-sets on sheltered terrace and tree-shaded lawn, good nearby walks, open all day weekends. *(Ann and Colin Hunt, Phil and Jane Villiers)*

UPPER CLATFORD SU3543

Crook & Shears (01264) 361543

Off A343 S of Andover, via Foundry Road; SP11 7QL Cosy and welcoming 17th-c thatched pub, well kept Otter and Ringwood ales, Thatcher's cider and reasonably priced traditional food (not Sun evening) from good baguettes to enjoyable Sun roasts, also OAP weekday lunch deal and Tues steak night, friendly attentive service, open fires and woodburner, small dining room, back skittle alley with own

bar; children and dogs welcome, pleasant secluded garden behind, closed Mon lunchtime. *(Jim and Caroline Storey)*

UPPER FARRINGDON SU7135

Rose & Crown (01420) 588231

Off A32 S of Alton; Crows Lane – follow 'Church, Selborne, Liss' signpost; GU34 3ED Airy 19th-c village pub under hospitable licensees, L-shaped bar with bare boards and log fire, a couple of Triple fff ales along with Sharps Doom Bar and a guest, good reasonably priced home-cooked food (not Sun evening) including pizzas, friendly helpful service, back dining room; children, walkers and dogs welcome, wide views from attractive garden, open all day weekends. *(Valerie Sayer)*

UPTON GREY SU6948

Hoddington Arms (01256) 862371

Signed off B3349 S of Hook; Bidden Road; RG25 2RL Nicely updated 18th-c beamed pub, good food from varied menu (sometimes themed), local ales such as Andwell along with a beer named for them (Hodd), a dozen wines by the glass, friendly staff, events including live music, french movie nights and beer/cider festivals; children and dogs welcome, big enclosed garden with terrace, quiet pretty village with interesting Gertrude Jekyll garden, good walking/cycling, open all day Fri-Sun. *(Tony and Jill Radnor)*

VERNHAM DEAN SU3456

George (01264) 737279

Centre of village; SP11 0JY Rambling open-plan 17th-c beamed and timbered pub with notable eyebrow windows, some exposed brick and flint, inglenook log fire, well kept Flack Manor, Greene King, Hop Back and a guest such as local Betteridges, popular home-made pubby food, Mon fish and steak deals, good friendly service; variety of events including Aug beer festival; children and dogs welcome, pretty garden behind, lovely thatched village and fine walks, open all day (Sun till 5pm). *(David and Judy Robison)*

WALHAMPTON SZ3396

Walhampton Arms (01590) 673113

B3054 NE of Lymington; aka Walhampton Inn; SO41 5RE Large comfortable Georgian-style family roadhouse handy for Isle of Wight ferry; popular well priced food including carvery in raftered former stables and two adjoining areas, pleasant lounge, Ringwood and Flack Manor ales and traditional cider, cheerful helpful staff; two monthly quizzes; attractive courtyard, good walks, open (and food) all day. *(Sam Hyde)*

Places with gardens or terraces usually let children sit there – we note in the text the very few exceptions that don't.

WALTHAM CHASE   SU5614
Black Dog (01329) 832316
Winchester Road; SO32 2LX
Old brick-built pub with low-ceilinged
carpeted front bar, three well kept Greene
King ales and a guest, over a dozen wines
by the glass and good well priced food
(all day Sun), cheerful service, log fires,
back restaurant; some live music, sports
TV; children and dogs welcome, colourful
hanging baskets, tables in good-sized neatly
kept garden with play area, open all day
weekends. *(Ann and Colin Hunt)*

WELL   SU7646
⋆**Chequers** (01256) 862605
*Off A287 via Crondall, or A31 via Froyle
and Lower Froyle; RG29 1TL* Appealing
low-beamed country dining pub; very good
restaurant-style food (some quite pricey)
including fresh fish/seafood, also brasserie
menu and lunchtime sandwiches, Badger
ales and good choice of wines, friendly
efficient service, wood floors, panelling and
log fires; free wi-fi; bench seating on vine-
covered front terrace, spacious back garden
overlooking fields. *(Tony and Jill Radnor, Peter
and Adriana Gill)*

WEST TYTHERLEY   SU2730
Black Horse (01794) 340308
North Lane; SP5 1NF Compact unspoilt
village local, chatty and welcoming, with
traditional beamed bar, a couple of long
tables, woodburner in big fireplace, nicely set
dining area off, four mainly local ales and a
real cider, enjoyable reasonably priced food
including good Sun roasts; quiz last Weds
of month, skittle alley; children and dogs
welcome, open all day Sun till 7.30pm,
closed Mon. *(Tom Stone)*

WHERWELL   SU3839
Mayfly (01264) 860283
*Testcombe (over by Fullerton, not in
Wherwell itself); A3057 SE of Andover,
between B3420 turn-off and Leckford
where road crosses River Test; OS
Sheet 185 map reference 382390;
SO20 6AX* Busy pub with decking and
conservatory overlooking fast-flowing River
Test; spacious beamed and carpeted bar with
fishing paraphernalia, rustic pub furnishings
and woodburner, Fullers ales and extensive
range of wines by the glass, good choice of
food too (must book for a good table), prices
generally on the high side and surcharge
added if you pay by credit card; background
music; well behaved children and dogs
welcome, open (and food) all day. *(Helen and
Brian Edgeley, Martin Day, R Halliday)*

WHERWELL   SU3840
White Lion (01264) 860317
B3420; SP11 7JF Early 17th-c multi-level
beamed village inn, popular and friendly,
with good choice of enjoyable food including

speciality pies, well kept Sharps, Timothy
Taylors and a guest, real ciders and several
wines by the glass, cheery helpful staff, open
fire, comfy leather sofas and armchairs,
dining rooms either side of bar; background
music; well behaved children welcome, dogs
on leads, sunny courtyard with good quality
furniture, Test Way walks, six bedrooms,
open all day from 7.30am (breakfast for
non-residents). *(D J and P M Taylor, Michael
and Jenny Back)*

WHITSBURY   SU1219
Cartwheel (01725) 518362
*Off A338 or A354 SW of Salisbury;
SP6 3PZ* Welcoming tucked-away red-brick
pub, ample helpings of good well presented
home-made food (not Sun evening),
Ringwood ales (tasting trays available),
pitched high rafters in one part, lower
beams elsewhere, snug little side areas;
maybe background music; children and dogs
welcome, garden with slide, open all day
Fri-Sun, closed Mon evening. *(Neill Allen)*

WICKHAM   SU5711
Greens (01329) 833197
*The Square, at junction with A334;
PO17 5JQ* Civilised restauranty place
with clean-cut modern décor, small bar
with leather sofa and armchairs on light
wood floor, extensive wine choice and a
couple of real ales, obliging young staff,
step down to split-level balustraded dining
areas with good imaginative food including
cheaper lunchtime/early evening set menus;
background music; children welcome if
eating, pleasant lawn overlooking water
meadows, closed Sun evening, Mon.
(Lachlan Milligan)

WINCHESTER   SU4829
Bishop on the Bridge
(01962) 855111 *High Street/Bridge
Street; SO23 9JX* Neat efficiently run
red-brick Fullers pub, their well kept beers
(not cheap) and decent food from ciabattas
up, leather sofas, old local prints; free wi-fi;
children and dogs welcome, nice back
terrace overlooking River Itchen, open
all day. *(Gerry and Rosemary Dobson, Val and
Alan Green)*

WINCHESTER   SU4828
⋆**Black Boy** (01962) 861754
*B3403 off M3 junction 10 towards city,
then left into Wharf Hill; no nearby
daytime parking – 220 metres from car
park on B3403; SO23 9NQ* Splendidly
eccentric décor at this chatty old-fashioned
pub, floor-to-ceiling books, lots of big
clocks, mobiles made of wine bottles or
spectacles, stuffed animals including a
baboon and dachshund, two log fires, orange-
painted room with big oriental rugs on red
floorboards, barn room with open hayloft,
five local beers kept well, straightforward
home-made food (not Sun evening, Mon,

Tues lunchtime) including sandwiches; table football and board games; supervised children and dogs welcome, slate tables out in front and seats on attractive secluded terrace, ten bedrooms in adjoining building, open all day. *(Ann and Colin Hunt, Phil and Jane Villiers)*

WINCHESTER   SU4829

Eclipse (01962) 865676

The Square, between High Street and cathedral; SO23 9EX Picturesque unspoilt 16th-c local with massive beams and timbers in two small cheerful rooms, four well kept ales such as Butcombe and Sharps, proper ciders and decent choice of wines by the glass, good value traditional lunchtime food including popular Sun roasts, oak settles and open fire; children in back area, seats outside, handy for cathedral, open all day. *(Val and Alan Green)*

WINCHESTER   SU4829

★**Old Vine** (01962) 854616

Great Minster Street; SO23 9HA Popular big-windowed town bar with well kept ales such as Bowman, Flowerpots, Ringwood and St Austell, high beams, worn oak boards, smarter and larger dining side with good choice of up-to-date food plus sandwiches and pub staples, efficient friendly service even though busy, modern conservatory; faint background music; by cathedral, with sheltered terrace, partly covered and heated, charming bedrooms, open all day. *(Helen and Brian Edgeley, Glenwys and Alan Lawrence, Val and Alan Green)*

WOLVERTON   SU5658

George & Dragon (01635) 298292

Towns End; just N of A339 Newbury–Basingstoke; RG26 5ST Extended 17th-c pub in remote rolling country (good walks), interesting layout with cosy linked areas, low beams, flagstones and log fire, good choice of enjoyable food from sandwiches to specials, beers such as Fullers, Greene King and Wadworths, decent wines, friendly attentive service; children and dogs welcome, big garden with terrace, ten bedrooms in separate block, good breakfast. *(J V Dadswell, Tony and Jill Radnor)*

Please keep sending us reports. We rely on readers for news of new discoveries, and particularly for news of changes – however slight – at the fully described pubs: feedback@goodguides.com, or (no stamp needed) The Good Pub Guide, FREEPOST RTJR-ZCYZ-RJZT, Perrymans Lane, Etchingham TN19 7DN.

Herefordshire

 CAREY   SO5631   Map 4

Cottage of Content

(01432) 840242 – www.cottageofcontent.co.uk

Village signposted from good back road betweeen Ross-on-Wye and Hereford E of A49, through Hoarwithy; HR2 6NG

Country furnishings in a friendly rustic cottage with interesting food, real ales and seats on terraces; bedrooms

Nicely tucked away in a tranquil spot near the River Wye, this medieval inn was once three labourers' cottages. The place has much character and you can be sure of a warm welcome from the helpful, friendly licensees. There's a multitude of beams and country furnishings such as stripped-pine kitchen chairs, long pews beside one big table and various old-fashioned tables on flagstones or bare boards. Hobsons Best and Wye Valley Butty Bach on handpump and local cider and perry during the summer; background music. Picnic-sets sit on the flower-filled front terrace and in the rural-feeling garden at the back. The bedrooms are quiet and the breakfasts good.

Very highly thought-of food includes sandwiches, goats cheese and red onion marmalade tartlet, smoked mackerel pâté wrapped in smoked salmon and seaweed with dill dressing, a pie of the day, honey-roast ham and egg, pork chop with apricot and pine nut stuffing with boulangère potatoes, fish dish of the day, lamb shoulder confit with celeriac, root vegetable and rosemary navarin, and puddings such as chocolate pot with Baileys cream and orange and Cointreau crème brûlée; they have tapas on Friday evenings (5.30-7pm). *Benchmark main dish: hake fillet with gremolata crust on seafood paella £15.50. Two-course evening meal £21.00.*

Free house ~ Licensees Richard and Helen Moore ~ Real ale ~ Open 12-2.30, 6.30 (6 Weds, 5.30 Fri)-11; 12-3.30 Sun; closed Sun evening, Mon, winter Tues, one week Feb, one week Oct ~ Bar food 12-2, 6.30-9; 12-2 Sun ~ Restaurant ~ Children welcome ~ Dogs allowed in bar ~ Bedrooms: £65/£85 *Recommended by Derek Stafford, Dr Michael Smith, Barry Collett, Peter J and Avril Hanson, Mike and Mary Carter*

 EARDISLEY   SO3149   Map 6

Tram £

(01544) 327251 – www.thetraminn.co.uk

Corner of A4111 and Woodseaves Road; HR3 6PG

Character pub with welcoming licensees, a cheerful mix of customers and good food and beer

As this handsome old place is always deservedly busy, you'd be best to book a table in advance. There's a cheerful mix of both drinkers and diners (all genuinely welcomed by the convivial licensees and their smiling staff) and the beamed bar on the left has warm local character, especially in the cosy back section behind sturdy standing timbers. Here, regulars congregate on the bare boards by the counter, which serves Clun Pale Ale, Hobsons Best and Wye Valley Butty Bach on handpump and three local organic ciders. Elsewhere there are antique red and ochre floor tiles, a handful of nicely worn tables and chairs, a pair of long cushioned pews enclosing one much longer table, a high-backed settle, old country pictures and a couple of pictorial Wye maps. There's a small dining room on the right, a games room (with pool and darts) in a converted brewhouse and a covered terrace; background music. The outside gents' is extremely stylish; the sizeable, neatly planted garden has picnic-sets on the lawn; pétanque. The famous black and white village is a big draw too.

Rewarding food includes baguettes, chicken and pork pâté with home-made chutney, grilled field mushrooms with cheesy rarebit filling, roasted beetroot, carrot and caramelised onion tart with red onion marmalade, local honey baked ham and eggs, free-range chicken with sweet potato stuffing, sag aloo, curry sauce and onion bhaji, steak and mushroom in ale pie, and puddings such as lemon posset and chantilly cream and Malteser cheesecake. *Benchmark main dish: 28-day-aged 6oz sirloin steak with onion rings, mushrooms and chips £12.50. Two-course evening meal £20.00.*

Free house ~ Licensees Mark and Kerry Vernon ~ Real ale ~ Open 12-3, 6-midnight; 12-4, 7-10.30 Sun; closed Mon except bank holidays ~ Bar food 12-3, 6-9; 12-3 Sun ~ Restaurant ~ Children welcome ~ Dogs allowed in bar ~ Wi-fi *Recommended by Darren and Jane Staniforth, Martin Day, David and Judy Robison, John and Jennifer Spinks, Mike and Mary Carter*

KILPECK   SO4430   Map 6

Kilpeck Inn ♀

(01981) 570464 – www.kilpeckinn.com
Village and church signposted off A465 SW of Hereford; HR2 9DN

Imaginatively extended country inn in fascinating village; bedrooms

Green values matter a lot to the licensees here: they have hi-spec insulation, underfloor heating run by a wood pellet boiler, solar heating panels and a rainwater recycling system; food and drinks are sourced as locally as possible. The beamed bar with dark slate flagstones rambles happily around to provide several tempting corners, with an antique high-backed settle in one and tall stools around a matching chest-high table in another. This opens into two cosily linked dining rooms on the left, with high panelled wainscoting. Wobbly Gold and Wye Valley Butty Bach on handpump, seven wines by the glass and farm cider; background music. The neat back grass has picnic-sets. If you stay overnight, you can make the most of the interesting nearby castle ruins and the unique romanesque church.

The popular food, cooked by the landlord, includes sandwiches, local mussels in cider and sage cream sauce, crab croquette, oak-smoked salmon and lemon mayonnaise, burger with toppings, pickle and chips, wild mushroom risotto, venison and chestnut mushroom casserole with swede mash and sage dumplings, duck breast, confit leg and orange stuffing with dauphinoise potatoes and red wine jus, beer-battered hake and chips, and puddings such as vanilla rice pudding with apricot and fig jam and double chocolate and walnut brownie. *Benchmark main dish: slow-roast pork belly with bacon and borlotti beans £13.75. Two-course evening meal £20.00.*

Free house ~ Licensee Ross Williams ~ Real ale ~ Open 12-3, 5.30-11; 12-11 Sat; 12-4 Sun; closed Sun evening, Mon ~ Bar food 12-2, 6.30-9; 12.30-3 Sun ~ Restaurant ~

Children welcome ~ Dogs allowed in bar ~ Wi-fi ~ Bedrooms: /£90 *Recommended by Miss B D Picton, Hugh Roberts, Melanie and David Lawson*

LEDBURY

SO7137   Map 4

Feathers 🏅 ♀ ⚑

(01531) 635266 ~ www.feathers-ledbury.co.uk
High Street (A417); HR8 1DS

Handsome old hotel with chatty relaxed bar, more decorous lounge, good food and friendly staff; comfortable bedrooms

At first glance, you might be surprised to find this elegantly striking timbered hotel in these pages, but travellers have been welcomed here for over 400 years and the convivial back bar-brasserie is full of a cheerful mix of drinkers and diners. Those wanting a pint and a chat congregate at one end: long beams covered in a mass of hop bines, prints and antique sale notices on stripped panelling, and stools lining the counter where they keep Fullers London Pride and a couple of guests such as Malvern Hills Black Pear and Otter Bitter on handpump, good wines by the glass from an extensive list and 40 malt whiskies; staff are first class. In the main section, full of contented diners, there are cosy leather easy chairs and sofas by the fire, flowers and oil lamps on stripped kitchen and other tables, and comfortable bays of banquettes and other seats. The sedate lounge is just right for afternoon tea, with high-sided armchairs and sofas in front of a big log fire, and daily papers. In summer, the sheltered back terrace has seats and tables under parasols and abundant plant pots and hanging baskets. The bedrooms are individually furnished and stylish.

 Seasonal produce is at the heart of the attractively presented food: ham hock with poached quail eggs and parsley oil, salt and pepper squid and whitebait with paprika mayonnaise, butternut squash and caramelised red onion tarte tatin with seared halloumi, beef and thyme burger with toppings, spicy tomato relish and chips, fishcakes with lemon and chervil mayonnaise, mustard and honey marinated rack of lamb with rosemary dauphinoise and jus, and puddings. *Benchmark main dish: beer-battered haddock and chips £13.50. Two-course evening meal £23.00.*

Free house ~ Licensee David Elliston ~ Real ale ~ Open 10am-11pm (10.30pm Sun) ~ Bar food 12-2 (2.30 Fri, Sat), 6.30-9.30 (10 Fri-Sun) ~ Restaurant ~ Children welcome ~ Dogs allowed in bar and bedrooms ~ Wi-fi ~ Bedrooms: £99.50/£155 *Recommended by David Carr, Comus and Sarah Elliott, Jeremy Snow, Jack and Hilary Burton*

LITTLE COWARNE

SO6050   Map 4

Three Horseshoes ♀

(01885) 400276 – www.threehorseshoes.co.uk
Pub signposted off A465 SW of Bromyard; towards Ullingswick; HR7 4RQ

Long-serving licensees and friendly staff in bustling country pub with good food using home-grown produce; bedrooms

Having run this carefully kept place for 27 years now, a good many of their customers are well known to the friendly licensees, but you can be sure of an equally kindly welcome as a newcomer. The L-shaped, quarry tiled middle bar has upholstered settles, wooden chairs and tables, old local photographs above the woodburning stove, hop-draped beams and local guidebooks. Opening off one side is the garden room with wicker armchairs around tables, and views over the terraced seating area and well kept garden; leading off the other side is the games room, with pool, darts, juke box, games machine and cribbage. Wye Valley Bitter and Butty Bach and a guest such as Greene King Old Speckled Hen on handpump, local Oliver's cider and perry, 11 wines by the glass and home-made elderflower cordial. A popular Sunday lunchtime carvery is offered in the stripped-stone, raftered and spacious restaurant extension. There are well sited tables and chairs on the terrace and in the neat, prettily planted garden. The bedrooms are accessed by outside stairs. Disabled access.

Cooked by the licensees' son using local and home-grown produce (you can buy their home-made preserves and chutneys at the bar), the highly regarded food includes sandwiches, prawn and haddock smokies, garlic mushrooms in creamy sauce, cheese, leek, celery, apple and walnut filo parcel, herb-crusted salmon fillet, roast rack of lamb with red wine gravy, pheasant breast with orange and port sauce, chicken breast in stilton and mushroom sauce, and puddings such as stem ginger crème brûlée and chocolate truffle torte. *Benchmark main dish: steak in ale pie £13.00. Two-course evening meal £19.50.*

Free house ~ Licensees Norman and Janet Whittall ~ Real ale ~ Open 11-3, 6.30-11.30; 11-3, 6-midnight Sat; 12-4, 7-9.30 Sun; closed Tues, winter Sun evening ~ Bar food 12-2, 6.30-9 ~ Restaurant ~ Children welcome ~ Wi-fi ~ Bedrooms: $40/$70 *Recommended by Mr Brian Wells, Julian Richardson, John Sargeant*

MICHAELCHURCH ESCLEY   SO3133 Map 6
Bridge Inn 🛏
(01981) 510646 – www.thebridgeinnmichaelchurch.co.uk
Off back road SE of Hay-on-Wye, along Escley Brook valley; HR2 0JW

Character riverside inn with warm, simply furnished bar and dining rooms, local drinks, hearty food and seats by the water; bedrooms

In warm weather, you can sit outside this remote inn – delightfully tucked away down a steep lane in an attractive valley – and watch ducks and maybe brown trout on the river. There's a relaxed homely atmosphere in the simply furnished bar, which has hops on dark beams, pine pews and dining chairs around rustic tables, a big woodburning stove and Wye Valley Butty Bach and Country Pale Ale on handpump, good wines by the glass and local cider served by the friendly landlord. Background music. Two dining areas, with contemporary paintwork, have prints on the walls. The bedrooms in the 17th-c farmhouse (one minute's walk away) are warm and comfortable and there's a cosy sitting room too; they also have a yurt and a shepherd's hut for hire. Stunning nearby walks.

Good, interesting food includes kimchi pork, chorizo and cannellini bean salad, beef and bacon in ale pie, aubergine and red pepper tagine with spinach, apricot and red onion potatoes, chicken wrapped in serrano ham with creamy garlic sauce, pork and pear meatloaf with deep-fried duck fillets, prawn salad and pickled vegetables, persian lamb, deep-fried hake with wakame and sesame tartare sauce, and puddings such as 'banoffi lova' (a mix between banoffi pie and a pavlova) and chocolate fudge brownie with chocolate sauce. *Benchmark main dish: beef in ale pie £13.75. Two-course evening meal £20.00.*

Free house ~ Licensee Glyn Bufton ~ Real ale ~ Open 12-3, 5.30-11; 6.30-11 Mon; 12-11 Sat; 12-10.30 Sun; closed Mon lunchtime ~ Bar food 12-2.30, 5.30 (6.30 Mon)-8.30; 12-3, 5.30-9.30 Sat; 12-4, 5.30-8.30 Sun ~ Restaurant ~ Children welcome ~ Dogs allowed in bar ~ Wi-fi ~ Live bands monthly (see website) ~ Bedrooms: /$95 *Recommended by Simon Daws, Paul Scofield, Geoffrey Sutton*

The 🍺 symbol shows pubs that keep their beer unusually well, have a particularly good range or brew their own.

ROSS-ON-WYE   SO5924 Map 6

Kings Head 🛏

(01989) 763174 – www.kingshead.co.uk

High Street (B4260); HR9 5HL

Welcoming bar in well run market-town hotel with real ales and tasty food; good bedrooms

On a pretty street at the centre of town stands this friendly old hotel, parts of which are said to date from the 14th c. The little beamed and panelled bar on the right has traditional pub furnishings, including comfortably padded bar seats and an antique cushioned box settle, stripped floorboards and a couple of black leather armchairs by a log-effect fire. Wye Valley Bitter and Butty Bach and a guest beer such as Sharps Doom Bar on handpump, three farm ciders, and several wines by the glass at sensible prices. The beamed lounge bar on the left, also with bare boards, has some timbering, soft leather armchairs, padded bucket seats and shelves of books, and there's also a big carpeted dining room; unobtrusive background music. The sheltered back courtyard has contemporary tables and chairs. Bedrooms are comfortable and breakfasts good.

 Pleasing food includes sandwiches, potted shrimps with lime aioli, ham hock and parsley terrine with piccalilli, sharing boards, a pie of the day, mushroom and butternut squash hotpot, local apple and pork sausages with red onion gravy, slow-roast pork belly with black pudding, chorizo cassoulet and fondant potato, free-range chicken with sweet potato purée, smoked bacon and port and stilton sauce, and puddings such as lemon and cardamom posset and bread and butter pudding. *Benchmark main dish: lamb loin with fondant potatoes, beetroot purée and lamb jus £17.25. Two-course evening meal £21.00.*

Free house ~ Licensee James Vidler ~ Real ale ~ Open 11-11; 12-10.30 Sun ~ Bar food 12-2.10, 6.30-9 ~ Restaurant ~ Children welcome ~ Dogs allowed in bar and bedrooms ~ Wi-fi ~ Bedrooms: £60/£85 *Recommended by Ann and Tony Bennett-Hughes, David Carr, Dr J Barrie Jones, Helena and Trevor Fraser*

SYMONDS YAT   SO5616 Map 4

Saracens Head 🍴 🛏

(01600) 890435 – www.saracensheadinn.co.uk

Symonds Yat E; HR9 6JL

Lovely riverside spot with seats on waterside terraces, a fine range of drinks and interesting food; comfortable bedrooms

With Wye Valley views and nearby Forest of Dean walks, this busy 17th-c inn is extremely popular with lovers of the outdoors. The hands-on, welcoming landlord and his able, friendly staff keep a close eye on things – even at peak times, it all runs along smoothly. There's a buoyant atmosphere and plenty of chatty customers in the flagstoned bar, where they serve Sharps Doom Bar, Wye Valley Butty Bach and HPA and guests such as Bespoke Over a Barrel, Kingstone Classic Bitter and Wadworths 6X on handpump, a dozen wines by the glass, 20 malt whiskies and several ciders. TV, background music and board games. There's also a cosy lounge and a modernised bare-boards dining room, as well as fine old photos of the area and fresh flowers in jugs. The terraces by the River Wye have plenty of seats, though you'll need to arrive early in fine weather to bag one. Bedrooms in the main building have views over the water, and a boathouse annexe has two more contemporary rooms. One way to reach the inn is on the little hand ferry (pulled by one of the staff). Disabled access to the bar and terrace.

🍴 Rewarding food includes sandwiches, pulled duck and noodle salad with soy and plum dressing, cod fishcakes with jalapeno mayonnaise, a pie of the day, haunch of venison with potato rösti, celeriac purée and juniper jus, grilled whole plaice with caper and lemon butter, beef ribs with barbecue sauce, free-range chicken with leeks, pancetta, borlotti beans and gruyère crust, and puddings such as baked vanilla and strawberry cheesecake with coconut sorbet and cinnamon baked pear with limoncello and cider sorbet. *Benchmark main dish: burger with toppings, relish, celeriac rémoulade and chips £14.95. Two-course evening meal £20.50.*

Free house ~ Licensees P K and C J Rollinson ~ Real ale ~ Open 11-11; 11-10.30 Sun ~ Bar food 12-2.30, 6.30-9 ~ Restaurant ~ Children welcome but not in bedrooms ~ Dogs allowed in bar ~ Wi-fi ~ Bedrooms: £59/£89 *Recommended by John Ecklin, Steve Whalley, Kate Moran, Chris and Angela Buckell, Guy Vowles, Julian Richardson*

TILLINGTON
Bell 🍺

SO4645   Map 6

(01432) 760395 – www.thebelltillington.com
Off A4110 NW of Hereford; HR4 8LE

Relaxed and friendly pub with a snug character bar opening into civilised dining areas – good value

The Williams family run this popular pub extremely well and it's always deservedly busy. The snug parquet-floored bar on the left has assorted bucket armchairs around low chunky mahogany-coloured tables, brightly cushioned wall benches, team photographs and shelves of books; the black beams are strung with dried hops. Hobson Town Crier, Wye Valley Bitter and a guest beer on handpump, cider made on site, several wines by the glass and locally produced spirits from Chase, all served by notably cheerful staff; daily papers, unobtrusive background music. The bar opens into a comfortable bare-boards dining lounge with stripy plush banquettes and a coal fire. Beyond that is a pitched-ceiling restaurant area with more banquettes and big country prints; through slatted blinds you can see a sunken terrace with contemporary tables, and a garden with teak tables, picnic-sets and a play area for children.

🍴 Good quality food includes lunchtime sandwiches, ham hock hash with fried egg, crispy soy duck with cashew nuts, home-made vegetarian quiche of the day, spicy chicken with couscous, chilli, lime and coriander, monkfish and scallop on seafood risotto, liver and bacon with mash and onion gravy, stuffed saddle of lamb with potato and parsnip rösti and proper gravy, and puddings such as Mars Bar cheesecake and rum brûlée with raisins. *Benchmark main dish: steak in ale pie £12.50. Two-course evening meal £20.00.*

Free house ~ Licensee Glenn Williams ~ Real ale ~ Open 11-11 (midnight Sat); 12-10.30 Sun ~ Bar food 12-2.30, 6-9; all day Sat; 12-3 Sun ~ Restaurant ~ Children welcome ~ Dogs allowed in bar ~ Wi-fi *Recommended by Paul and Sonia Broadgate, Lindy Andrews, Dave Braisted, John and Jennifer Spinks, Andy Dolan*

TITLEY
Stagg 🍴⭐ 🍷 🛏

SO3359   Map 6

(01544) 230221 – www.thestagg.co.uk
B4355 N of Kington; HR5 3RL

Herefordshire Dining Pub of the Year

Terrific food in three dining rooms, real ales and a fine choice of other drinks, and seats in the two-acre garden; comfortable bedrooms

Of course, most customers are here for the exceptional food but there's a pubby little bar at the heart of the place too. This convivial bar has plenty of chatty locals, a gently civilised feel and a really interesting choice of drinks served by courteous and genuinely welcoming staff. Ludlow Gold and Wye Valley Butty Bach on handpump, 11 house wines by the glass (plus a carefully chosen bin list), cocktails, local cider and perry, a huge list of gins and several whiskies. Throughout, furnishings are simple: high-backed elegant wooden or leather dining chairs around a medley of tables on bare boards, candlelight and (in the bar) 200 jugs hanging from the ceiling. The two-acre garden has seats on a terrace and a croquet lawn. There are bedrooms above the pub and in a Georgian vicarage four minutes' walk away; super breakfasts. The inn is surrounded by good walking country and is handy for the Offa's Dyke Path.

 The delicious food, using their own eggs, home-grown vegetables and fruit and local produce, includes sandwiches, cured salmon with cornish crab and avocado, local snails with mushroom, watercress and garlic butter, crispy duck leg with carrot, swede, potato fondant and kumquat, roast tomato risotto with olive tapenade and goats cheese, cod fillet with spinach, samphire, olive tapenade and parmentier potatoes, pork belly with black pudding with pistachio nuts, apple, greens and noisette potato, and puddings such as chocolate mousse with chocolate sorbet, white chocolate ice-cream and chocolate meringue and treacle tart with yoghurt sorbet. *Benchmark main dish: local rump steak with béarnaise sauce and chips £16.90. Two-course evening meal £26.00.*

Free house ~ Licensees Steve and Nicola Reynolds ~ Real ale ~ Open 12-3, 6.30-11; 12-3, 7-10.30 Sun; closed Mon, Tues, one week Jan/Feb, two weeks Nov ~ Bar food 12-2, 6.30-9 (9.30 Sat); 12-3, 7-8.30 Sun ~ Restaurant ~ Children welcome ~ Dogs allowed in bar and bedrooms ~ Wi-fi ~ Bedrooms: $80/$100 *Recommended by Lindy Andrews, Harvey Brown, Mike and Mary Carter, Simon and Alex Knight, Dave Sutton*

UPPER COLWALL
SO7643 Map 4

Chase £

(01684) 540276 ~ www.thechaseinnmalvern.co.uk
Chase Road, brown sign to pub off B4218 Malvern–Colwall, first left after hilltop on bend going W; WR13 6DJ

Gorgeous sunset views from cheerful country tavern's garden, good drinks and cost-conscious food

It's particularly worth visiting this nicely traditional pub on a clear day: the seats and tables on the steep series of small, pretty back terraces look across Herefordshire and even as far as the Black Mountains and the Brecon Beacons. Inside, the atmosphere is chatty and companionable. There's an array of gilt cast-iron-framed and treadle sewing tables, a great variety of seats (from a wooden-legged tractor seat to a carved pew), an old black kitchen range and plenty of decorations – china mugs, blue glass flasks, lots of small pictures; bar billiards. Four well kept ales are tapped from the cask, such as Bathams Best, Brains Rev James, Ringwood Fortyniner and Woods Beauty, and friendly staff also serve several wines by the glass. Plenty of good surrounding walks.

With some lunchtime dishes costing under £10, the tasty food includes sandwiches, chilli king prawns, honey-roast ham and free-range eggs, red pepper and tomato risotto, chicken caesar salad, moroccan-style lamb shank with orange and coriander couscous, steak and kidney pie, pork chop with braised fennel and gorgonzola sauce, and puddings. *Benchmark main dish: beer-battered cod and chips £11.50. Two-course evening meal £19.00.*

Free house ~ Licensee Duncan Ironmonger ~ Real ale ~ Open 12-3, 5-11; 12-11 Sat; 12-10.30 Sun ~ Bar food 12-2 (2.30 weekends), 6.30-9 ~ Children welcome ~ Dogs allowed in bar ~ Wi-fi *Recommended by Charlie Parker, Colin and Daniel Gibbs, Simon Day*

WALFORD

SO5820   Map 4

Mill Race ⭐ ♀

(01989) 562891 – www.millrace.info

B4234 Ross-on-Wye to Lydney; HR9 5QS

Contemporary furnishings in uncluttered rooms, good quality food, real ales, served by attentive staff, and terrace tables

Our readers very much enjoy their meals in this whitewashed pub – especially before or after a walk (the pub has leaflets describing pleasant ones nearby). It's all very civilised and stylish, with a row of strikingly high arched windows, comfortable leather armchairs and sofas on flagstones, and smaller chairs around broad pedestal tables. Photographs of the local countryside hang on the mainly cream or red walls and there's good unobtrusive lighting. One wall, stripped back to the stonework, contains a woodburning stove that's open to the comfortable, compact dining area on the other side; background music. From the granite-topped modern bar counter, friendly staff serve Wye Valley Bitter and a changing guest such as Hillside Legless Cow on handpump, farm cider and 22 fairly priced wines by the glass. There are seats on the terrace with views towards Goodrich Castle (English Heritage), and more seats and tables in the garden.

 Much of the produce comes from their nearby 1,000-acre farm and woodlands (cattle, rare-breed pigs, turkeys, geese, pheasant and ducks) and they list other local suppliers on their website: twice-baked cheese soufflé, crispy shredded beef with chilli and sesame dressing, aubergine parmigiana, smoked haddock fishcakes with spinach, poached egg and lemon butter sauce, burger with toppings, onion jam, celeriac slaw and chips, chicken kiev, beef bourguignon, and puddings such as almond tart with roast plums and amaretto ice-cream and banoffi caramel sundae. *Benchmark main dish: beer-battered haddock and chips £12.00. Two-course evening meal £20.00.*

Free house ~ Licensee Luke Freeman ~ Real ale ~ Open 11.30-3, 6-11; 11.30-11.30 Sat; 12-11 Sun ~ Bar food 12-2 (3 Sat), 6.30-9; 12-3, 4-8 Sun ~ Restaurant ~ Children welcome ~ Dogs allowed in bar ~ Wi-fi *Recommended by John Ecklin, Hilary De Lyon and Martin Webster, William Slade*

WALTERSTONE

SO3424   Map 6

Carpenters Arms

(01873) 890353 – www.thecarpentersarmswalterstone.com

Follow Walterstone signs off A465; HR2 0DX

Unchanging country tavern in the same family for many years

Vera Watkins has now retired but still helps out in this charming little unspoilt stone cottage (which was run by her mother for many years), and the traditional rooms remain unchanged from year to year. There are beams, broad polished flagstones, a roaring fire in a gleaming black range (complete with hot-water tap, bread oven and salt cupboard) and warming ancient settles against stripped-stone walls. Wadworths 6X and a guest such as Breconshire Brecon County tapped straight from the cask. The snug main dining room has mahogany tables and oak corner cupboards, and another little dining area has old oak tables and church pews on more flagstones. The outside lavatories are cold but in character.

Straightforward food includes sandwiches, a changing soup, pies such as salmon and leek or beef in Guinness, various curries, and puddings. *Benchmark main dish: 10oz sirloin steak with stilton or pepper sauce £17.95. Two-course evening meal £18.00.*

Free house ~ Licensee Vera Watkins ~ Real ale ~ No credit cards ~ Open 12-3, 6.30-10.30 (11 Fri); 12-11 Sat; 12-4, 6.30-10.30 Sun ~ Bar food 12-2, 7-9 ~ Restaurant ~ Children welcome *Recommended by R T and J C Moggridge, James Landor*

WOOLHOPE

SO6135 Map 4

Butchers Arms 🏅 ⚲ ◀

(01432) 860281 – www.butchersarmswoolhope.com
Off B4224 in Fownhope; HR1 4RF

Pleasant country inn in peaceful setting, with an inviting garden, interesting food and a fine choice of real ales

With enjoyable food cooked by the landlord, local ales and a friendly welcome, it's not surprising our readers like this half-timbered pub so much. The bar has very low beams, built-in cushioned wall seats, farmhouse chairs and stools around a mix of old tables (some set for dining) on carpet, hunting and horse pictures on cream walls and an open fire in a big fireplace; there's also a little beamed dining room, similarly furnished. Wye Valley Bitter and Butty Bach and Ledbury Gold on handpump, six wines by the glass from a good list, 14 malt whiskies and a couple of farm ciders. There are picnic-sets in a pretty, streamside garden. To really appreciate the surroundings, turn left as you come out of the pub and take the tiny left-hand road at the end of the car park; this turns into a track and then a path, and the view from the top of the hill is quite something.

Popular, tasty food includes pigeon and black pudding, bacon and apple, smoked salmon, crayfish and avocado salad with lemon dressing, thai green vegetable curry, lamb and beef meatballs with tomato, basil and garlic sauce on tagliatelle, roast lamb rump with redcurrant and thyme jus, bass fillet with courgette ribbons and hollandaise sauce, pork belly with smoked bacon, black pudding and apple sauce, and puddings such as dark chocolate cheesecake and cherry bakewell tart. *Benchmark main dish: rabbit, apple and cider pie £12.95. Two-course evening meal £17.00.*

Free house ~ Licensee Philip Vincent ~ Real ale ~ Open 11-3, 6-11; 12-3.30 Sun; closed Sun evening, Mon except bank holidays ~ Bar food 12-2.30, 6-9; 12-2.30 Sun ~ Restaurant ~ Children welcome ~ Dogs allowed in bar ~ Wi-fi *Recommended by Des Mannion, Harvey Brown, David and Stella Martin, Ben and Diane Bowie*

WOOLHOPE

SO6135 Map 4

Crown

(01432) 860468 – www.crowninnwoolhope.co.uk
Village signposted off B4224 in Fownhope; HR1 4QP

Cheery village local with fine range of local ciders and perries, and popular food

'This is a favourite with our walking group,' says one reader enthusiastically. And indeed, it's a cheerful, busy pub with honest food and well kept ales. It's been redecorated since the last *Guide* and there are now painted farmhouse and other wooden chairs, upholstered settles and rustic tables on wooden flooring, an open fire and a woodburning stove, some standing timbers and stools against the bar counter; background music, darts and board games. As well as Ledbury Bitter, Wye Valley HPA and a guest ale on handpump, the landlord makes four farm ciders (and keeps a couple of guest ciders) and serves around two dozen bottled ciders and perrys from within a 15-mile radius; they hold a May Day Bank Holiday festival with live music, beer, cider and perry. In summer, there's a bar in the lovely big garden, which has a fire pit and a particularly comfortable smokers' shelter with cushions and darts; marvellous views. Disabled access.

Using local suppliers, the enjoyable seasonal food includes lunchtime baguettes, haddock and prawn smokie, twice-baked cheese soufflé with garlic mushrooms, cider-braised ham and duck eggs, goats cheese and field mushroom stack, chicken with bacon and spring onion sauce and sautéed potatoes, a fresh fish dish of the day, rib of beef and basil burger with toppings, chilli ketchup and fries, and puddings such as chocolate fudge sundae and apple and blackberry crumble; they also hold a monthly Thursday evening tasting menu. *Benchmark main dish: steaks (choose the size, sauce and choice of potato) £16.00. Two-course evening meal £20.50.*

Free house ~ Licensees Matt and Annalisa Slocombe ~ Real ale ~ Open 12-3, 6-11; 12-midnight Fri, Sat; 12-11 Sun ~ Bar food 12-2, 6-9 (9.30 Fri); 12-2.30, 6-9.30 Sat; 12-3.30, 6-9 Sun ~ Restaurant ~ Children welcome ~ Wi-fi *Recommended by Katherine Matthews, Harvey Brown, Alfie Bayliss, Martin Day, Guy Vowles*

Also Worth a Visit in Herefordshire

Besides the fully inspected pubs, you might like to try these pubs that have been recommended to us and described by readers. Do tell us what you think of them: feedback@goodguides.com

ALLENSMORE SO4533
Three Horseshoes (01981) 570329
B4348; HR2 9AS Flower-decked 17th-c timbered dining pub with enjoyable fairly pubby food from sandwiches and baked potatoes to grills, bargain OAP weekday lunch and early evening deal, well kept Wye Valley and guests in cosy drinking area, friendly efficient staff; children welcome, good walking country, three bedrooms, open (and food) all day. *(R T and J C Moggridge)*

ALMELEY SO3351
Bells (01544) 327216
Off A480, A4111 or A4112 S of Kington; HR3 6LF Welcoming old country local with original jug-and-bottle entry lobby and carpeted beamed bar with woodburner, second bar has been converted to village shop/deli, a couple of well kept ales such as Three Tuns and Woods, traditional cider/perry, generous home-made food (not evenings) from sandwiches and rolls; children and dogs welcome, garden with decked area and boules, on Wyche Way long distance path, open all day. *(Guy Vowles)*

AYMESTREY SO4265
★ **Riverside Inn** (01568) 708440
A4110, at N end of village, W of Leominster; HR6 9ST Terrace and tree-sheltered garden making most of lovely waterside spot by ancient stone bridge over the Lugg; cosy rambling beamed interior with some antique furniture alongside stripped country kitchen tables, warm fires, well kept Hobsons, Wye Valley and a guest, local ciders, good lunchtime bar food and more expensive evening menu using rare-breed meat and own fruit and vegetables, warm friendly atmosphere with welcoming landlord and staff; quiet background music; children welcome, dogs in bar, bedrooms (fly fishing for residents), good breakfast, closed Sun evening, Mon lunchtime (all day Mon in winter). *(Mike and Mary Carter, Roy and Gill Payne)*

BISHOPS FROME SO6648
Green Dragon (01885) 490607
Just off B4214 Bromyard–Ledbury; WR6 5BP Welcoming village pub with four linked rooms, unspoilt rustic feel, beams, flagstones and log fires (one in fine inglenook), half a dozen ales including Otter, Timothy Taylors and Wye Valley, real ciders, enjoyable traditional food Tues-Sat evenings and Sun lunchtime; children and dogs welcome, tiered garden with smokers' shelter, on Herefordshire Trail, closed weekday lunchtimes, open all day Sat. *(Mark Morgan)*

BOSBURY SO6943
Bell (01531) 640285
B4220 N of Ledbury; HR8 1PX Traditional village pub with log fires in both bars, Otter, Wye Valley Butty Bach and a guest, three ciders and good choice of wines by the glass, dining area serving popular sensibly priced traditional food (not Sun

evening, Mon, Tues) including Sun carvery, friendly staff; pool and darts, fortnightly quiz Mon; children and dogs welcome, large garden with covered terrace and play equipment, open all day weekends, closed Mon and Tues lunchtimes. *(William Slade)*

BRINGSTY COMMON   SO6954
★**Live & Let Live** (01886) 821462
Off A44 Knightwick–Bromyard 1.5 miles W of Whitbourne turn; take track southwards at Black Cat inn sign, bearing right at fork; WR6 5UW Bustling 17th-c timber and thatch cottage; cosy flagstoned bar with scrubbed or polished tables, cushioned chairs, long stripped pew and high-backed winged settle by log fire in cavernous stone fireplace, earthenware jugs hanging from low beams, old casks built into hop-strung bar counter, three well kept ales including Wye Valley Butty Bach, local ciders/ apple juice and decent wines by the glass, good fairly traditional food served by friendly efficient staff, two dining rooms upstairs under steep rafters; children and dogs welcome, glass-topped well and big wooden hogshead as terrace tables, peaceful views from picnic-sets in former orchard, handy for Brockhampton Estate (NT), closed Mon, otherwise open all day (best to check winter hours). *(Alan and Angela Scouller, Richard Stanfield)*

BROMYARD DOWNS   SO6755
★**Royal Oak** (01885) 482585
Just NE of Bromyard; pub signed off A44; HR7 4QP Beautifully placed low-beamed 18th-c pub with wide views; open-plan carpeted and flagstoned bar, log fire and woodburner, dining room with huge bay window, well kept Malvern Hills, Purity and Woods, real cider, enjoyable food (special diets catered for), friendly service; background music, pool and darts; children, walkers and dogs welcome, picnic-sets on nice front terrace, swings, closed Sun evening, Mon (open all day bank holiday weekends). *(Margaret McDonald)*

BUSH BANK   SO4551
Bush (01432) 830206
A4110 S of Knapton; HR4 8EH Welcoming country pub set back from the road; enjoyable good value home-cooked food including sharing dishes served on miniature picnic tables and ferris wheels, well kept Wye Valley and guests, good friendly service, comfortably modernised carpeted interior, some bare stone and timbering, old local photographs, copper and brass, woodburner; children welcome, terrace with contemporary rattan-style furniture. *(Nigel and Sue Foster)*

CANON PYON   SO4648
Nags Head (01432) 830725
A4110; HR4 8NY Welcoming 17th-c timbered roadside pub; beamed bar with log fire, flagstoned restaurant and overspill/

function room, popular pubby food (not Sun evening), well kept ales such as Otter and Wye Valley, pleasant attentive service; traditional pub games; dogs and children welcome, extensive garden with play area, open all day Sun till 7pm, closed Mon lunchtime, Tues. *(Mark Morgan)*

CLIFFORD   SO2445
Castlefields (01497) 831554
B4350 N of Hay-on-Wye; HR3 5HB Rebuilt and enlarged family pub retaining some old features including a glass-covered well, popular fairly priced food and a couple of changing ales, friendly helpful staff, red-carpeted floors, woodburner in two-way stone fireplace, restaurant; pool, darts and various community-based events; lovely country views, camping, closed all day Mon, Tues afternoon, otherwise open all day. *(Dr Michael Smith)*

CLODOCK   SO3227
Cornewall Arms (01873) 860677
N of Walterstone; HR2 0PD Wonderfully old-fashioned and unchanging country local in remote hamlet by historic church and facing Black Mountains, stable-door bar with open fire each end, a few mats and comfortable armchairs on stone floor, lots of ornaments and knick-knacks, photos of past village events, books for sale, games including darts and devil among the tailors, bottled Wye Valley and cider, no food or credit cards; dogs welcome, erratic opening hours. *(Paul Scofield)*

COLWALL   SO7440
Wellington (01684) 540269
A449 Malvern–Ledbury; WR13 6HW Welcoming pub with good sensibly priced food from standards up including local beef and game (special diets catered for), well kept Goffs Tournament, a couple of guest ales and nice wines by the glass, comfortably lived-in two-level beamed bar with red patterned carpet and log fire, spacious relaxed back dining area; some live music, daily newspapers; children and dogs welcome, picnic-sets on neat grass above car park, good local walks, closed Sun evening, Mon. *(Jeremy Snow)*

DORSTONE   SO3141
★**Pandy** (01981) 550273
Pub signed off B4348 E of Hay-on-Wye; HR3 6AN Ancient inn (12th-c origins) by village green, traditional rooms with low beams, stout timbers and worn flagstones, various alcoves and vast open fireplace, ales such as Three Tuns and Wye Valley, good reasonably priced often interesting food (not Sun evening) from daily changing menu, friendly staff; children and dogs (in bar) welcome, side garden with picnic-sets and play area, four good bedrooms in purpose-built timber lodge (now run independently, but breakfast in the pub),

closed Mon lunchtime, otherwise open all day.
(Melanie and David Lawson, Mr Yeldahn)

EWYAS HAROLD   SO3828
Temple Bar (01981) 240423
Village centre signed from B4347;
HR2 0EU Welcoming family-run village
pub, good freshly made food from bar snacks
to interesting well presented restaurant
dishes (weekly changing menu), Wye Valley
Butty Bach and HPA, a guest beer plus local
cider, contemporary interior keeping original
features such as oak beams, flagstones and
log fire; disabled access, three comfortable
bedrooms, hearty breakfast, open all day
weekends. *(Miss A M Kerruish)*

FOWNHOPE   SO5734
★ Green Man (01432) 860243
B4224; HR1 4PE Striking 15th-c black and
white dining inn; beams, standing timbers
and big log fire in bare-boards bar, button-
back wall benches, bentwood and windsor
chairs at slabby-topped tables, restaurant
with inglenook woodburner, separate
function room, good well presented food from
interesting menu, three Wye Valley ales, good
wines and coffee, friendly helpful service;
background music; children welcome, no
dogs, ramped wheelchair access from car
park, attractive quiet garden, bedrooms and
self-catering cottages, open (and some food)
all day. *(David Fowler)*

FOWNHOPE   SO5734
New Inn (01432) 860350
B4224, centre of village; HR1 4PE
Neat little local set back from the road;
good pubby lunchtime food (not weekends)
cooked by landlady, occasional steak
nights, well kept Hobsons, Wye Valley and
a guest, efficient friendly service, small
dining area; children and walkers welcome,
tables outside, picturesque village with
unusual church and nice views, open all day
weekends. *(R T and J C Moggridge)*

GARWAY   SO4622
Garway Moon (01600) 750270
Centre of village, opposite the green;
HR2 8RQ Attractive 18th-c pub in pretty
location overlooking common; good locally
sourced food served by friendly staff with
themed nights, well kept ales including
Butcombe, Kingstone and Wye Valley, local
ciders, beams and exposed stonework,
woodburner, restaurant; quiz last Sun of
month; children, dogs and muddy boots
welcome, garden with play area, three
bedrooms, open all day weekends, closed
lunchtimes Mon and Tues. *(William Slade)*

GORSLEY   SO6726
★ Roadmaker (01989) 720352
0.5 miles from M50 junction 3; village
signposted from exit – B4221; HR9 7SW
Popular 19th-c village pub run well by group
of retired gurkhas; large carpeted lounge

bar with central log fire, excellent good
value nepalese food here and in evening
restaurant, also Sun roasts and other english
choices, well kept ales such as Brains and
Butcombe, efficient courteous service; quiz
first Sun of month; children welcome, no
dogs, terrace with water feature, open all day.
(Alastair Cox)

HAREWOOD END   SO5227
Harewood End Inn (01989) 730637
A49 Hereford to Ross-on-Wye; HR2 8JT
Interesting old inn with comfortable panelled
dining lounge and separate restaurant, good
choice of enjoyable home-made food from
lunchtime sandwiches up, well kept ales
such as Black Sheep and Wychwood, decent
wines, welcoming attentive staff; area with
pool, darts and TV, free wi-fi; children and
dogs welcome, nice garden and walks, five
bedrooms, closed Mon. *(Geoffrey Sutton)*

HEREFORD   SO5139
Barrels (01432) 274968
St Owen Street; HR1 2JQ Friendly 18th-c
coaching inn and former home to the Wye
Valley brewery, their well kept keenly priced
ales from barrel-front counter (beer/music
festival end Aug), Thatcher's cider, no food,
cheerful efficient staff and good mix of
customers (very busy weekends); pool room,
big-screen sports TV, background and some
live music; partly covered courtyard behind,
open all day. *(Richard Searle)*

HEREFORD   SO5039
★ Lichfield Vaults (01432) 266821
Church Street; HR1 2LR Popular place,
a pub since the 18th c (the Dog, then)
in picturesque pedestrianised area near
cathedral; dark panelling, some stripped
brick and exposed joists, impressive
plasterwork in big-windowed front room,
traditionally furnished with dark pews,
padded pub chairs and a couple of heavily
padded benches, hot coal stove, charming
greek landlord and friendly staff, five well
kept ales such as Adnams, Caledonian and
Sharps, enjoyable food from sandwiches up
including greek dishes, good Sun roasts, daily
papers; faint background music, live blues/
rock last Sun of month, TV projector for
sports (particularly rugby), games machines;
children welcome, no dogs, picnic-sets in
pleasant back courtyard, open all day.
(Robert Wivell, Andy Dolan, Richard Searle)

HOARWITHY   SO5429
New Harp (01432) 840900
Off A49 Hereford to Ross-on-Wye;
HR2 6QH Open-plan village dining pub
with cheerful bustling atmosphere, enjoyable
well presented local food from chef-landlord,
friendly helpful service, Wye Valley ales and
Weston's cider (maybe their own organic
cider in summer), pine tables on slate tiles,
two woodburners, darts; background and
some live music; children, walkers and dogs

welcome, pretty tree-sheltered garden with stream, picnic-sets and decked area, little shop and Mon morning post office, unusual italianate Victorian church, open all day Fri-Sun. *(Barry Collett)*

KENTCHURCH   SO4125
★**Bridge Inn** (01981) 240408
B4347 Pontrilas–Grosmont; HR2 0BY Ancient rustic pub bordering the River Monnow (and Wales), welcoming staff and warm local atmosphere, good reasonably priced home-made food, well kept Otter and a couple of guests, big log fire in bar, pretty little back restaurant overlooking the river (two miles of trout fishing); terrace and waterside garden with pétanque, handy for Herefordshire Trail, closed Sun evening, Mon, Tues. *(Melanie and David Lawson)*

KINGSLAND   SO4461
★**Corners** (01568) 708385
B4360 NW of Leominster, corner of Lugg Green Road; HR6 9RY Comfortably updated, partly black and white 16th-c village inn with snug nooks and corners, log fires, low beams, dark red plasterwork and some stripped brick, comfortable bow-window seat and group of dark leather armchairs in softly lit carpeted bar, well kept Hobsons, Wye Valley and decent selection of wines, big side dining room in converted hay loft with rafters and huge window, enjoyable reasonably priced food from pubby choices up, cheerful attentive service; children welcome, no garden, comfortable bedrooms in modern block behind. *(Mark Morgan)*

KINGTON   SO3056
★**Olde Tavern** (01544) 239033
Victoria Road, just off A44 opposite B4355 – follow sign to 'Town Centre, Hospital, Cattle Market'; pub on right opposite Elizabeth Road, no inn sign but 'Estd 1767' notice; HR5 3BX Gloriously old-fashioned with hatch-served side room opening off small plain parlour and public bar, plenty of dark brown woodwork, big windows, settles and other antique furniture on bare floors, gas fire, old local pictures, china, pewter and curios, well kept Hobsons, Ludlow, Wye Valley and a guest, Weston's cider, beer festivals, friendly atmosphere, no food; children and dogs welcome, little yard at back, open all day weekends, closed Mon-Thurs lunchtimes. *(William Slade)*

KINGTON   SO2956
Oxford Arms (01544) 230322
Duke Street; HR5 3DR Well worn-in (not to everyone's taste) beamed inn with woodburners in main bar on left and dining area on right, simple lounge with sofas and armchairs, Woods Shropshire Lad and a couple of guests, enjoyable reasonably priced food including Weds pie and Thurs surf-and-turf nights, good friendly service; some live music, summer beer festivals, pool; children

and dogs welcome, terrace picnic-sets, bedrooms, open all day Fri-Sun, closed Mon, Weds and lunchtimes Tues, Thurs. *(William Slade, Jeremy Snow)*

KINGTON   SO2956
Royal Oak (01544) 230484
Church Street; HR5 3BE Cheerful and welcoming 17th-c pub with new thai restaurant opening as we went to press; well kept Ringwood, Wye Valley and a guest, Somersby's cider, two little open fires, darts and sports TV in public bar; some live music; children and dogs (in bar) welcome, garden with terrace, handy for Offa's Dyke walkers, three neat simple bedrooms, open all day weekends, closed Mon and Tues lunchtimes (Mon-Thurs lunchtimes in winter). *(Richard Tilbrook)*

KINGTON   SO2956
Swan (01544) 230510
Church Street; HR5 3AZ Smartly modernised 17th-c dining pub by the square; enjoyable freshly made food (not Sun evening) from lunchtime sandwiches up, Sun brunch, three local ales and good choice of wines, enthusiastic young staff, split-level interior with three different eating areas, beams and standing timbers, woodburner in central stone fireplace; background music, free wi-fi; children welcome. *(Guy Vowles)*

LEDBURY   SO7137
★**Prince of Wales** (01531) 632250
Church Lane; narrow passage from Town Hall; HR8 1DL Friendly old black and white local prettily tucked away down narrow cobbled alley, seven well kept ales, foreign draught/bottled beers and Weston's cider, knowledgeable staff, simple low-priced home-made food from sandwiches up, low beams, nooks and crannies, shelves of books, long back room; background music, live folk Weds; a couple of tables in flower-filled backyard, open all day. *(Dave Braisted, Comus and Sarah Elliott)*

LEDBURY   SO7137
Seven Stars (01531) 635800
Homend (High Street); HR8 1BN Convivial 16th-c beamed and timbered pub with good well presented food from interesting sensibly short menu, three well kept ales including Wye Valley, friendly helpful staff, bar area with comfortable seating and cosy open fire, dining room behind; some live music, free wi-fi; children and dogs welcome, disabled access, walled terrace, three bedrooms. *(Jeremy Snow)*

LEDBURY   SO7137
Talbot (01531) 632963
New Street; HR8 2DX Comfortable 16th-c black and white fronted coaching inn; log-fire bar with Wadworths ales and guests, plenty of wines by the glass and good fairly traditional food from sharing boards and

lunchtime sandwiches up, regular deals, friendly efficient service, oak-panelled dining room; courtyard tables, 13 bedrooms (six in converted stables), open all day. *(Paul Scofield)*

LEINTWARDINE   SO4073
Lion (01547) 540203
High Street; SY7 0JZ Restored inn beautifully situated by packhorse bridge over River Teme; helpful efficient staff and friendly atmosphere, good well presented food from varied menu including some imaginative choices (can be pricey), Tues steak night, popular two-room restaurant, well kept beers such as Ludlow and Wye Valley; children welcome, safely fenced riverside garden with play area, eight attractive bedrooms, can arrange fishing trips, open all day (till 8pm Sun). *(Margaret McDonald)*

LEINTWARDINE   SO4073
★ **Sun** (01547) 540705
Rosemary Lane, just off A4113; SY7 0LP Fascinating 19th-c time warp: benches and farmhouse tables by coal fire in wallpapered brick-floored front bar (dogs welcome here), well kept Hobsons tapped from the cask and an occasional guest (Aug beer festival), another fire in snug carpeted parlour, pork pies and perhaps a lunchtime ploughman's (can bring food from adjacent fish and chip shop), friendly staff and cheery locals; open mike night last Fri of month; new pavilion-style building with bar and garden room, closed Mon lunchtime. *(Jeremy Snow)*

LEOMINSTER   SO4959
★ **Grape Vaults** (01568) 611404
Broad Street; HR6 8BS Compact two-room character pub, popular and friendly, with well kept ales including Ludlow, tasty good value traditional food (not Sun evening), good service, coal fire, beams and stripped woodwork, original dark high-backed settles and round copper-topped tables on bare boards, old local prints and posters, bottle collection, shelves of books in snug; tiny gents'; dogs welcome, open all day. *(Richard Tilbrook, Guy Vowles)*

LINTON   SO6525
Alma (01989) 720355
On main road through village; HR9 7RY New licensees and some refurbishment for this cheerful village local, up to five well kept ales and enjoyable simple pub food (not Sun, Mon), friendly service, front bar with open fire, restaurant, small back room with pool; live music (mainly acoustic) first Thurs of the month, also June festival, quiz last Sun of month; children and dogs welcome, good-sized garden behind with nice view, closed Mon lunchtime. *(Mike and Mary Carter)*

LUGWARDINE   SO5441
Crown & Anchor (01432) 850630
Just off A438 E of Hereford; Cotts Lane; HR1 4AB Cottagey timbered pub dating from the 18th c, ample helpings of enjoyable food from traditional favourites up, well kept Wye Valley and a guest beer, decent wines, good friendly service, various smallish opened-up rooms, inglenook log fire; children and dogs (in bar) welcome, seats in front and back gardens, open all day. *(Andy Dolan)*

MUCH DEWCHURCH   SO4831
Black Swan (01981) 540295
B4348 Ross-on-Wye to Hay-on-Wye; HR2 8DJ Roomy and attractive beamed local (partly 14th-c) with welcoming long-serving licensees; well kept Timothy Taylors Landlord and three local guests, Weston's cider and decent wines, enjoyable straightforward home-made food using local produce (no credit cards), log fires in cosy well worn bar and lounge with eating area, pool room with darts, TV, juke box; Thurs folk night; children and dogs welcome, seats on front terrace, open all day Sun. *(Geoffrey Sutton)*

MUCH MARCLE   SO6634
Royal Oak (01531) 660300
On A449 Ross-on-Wye to Ledbury; HR8 2ND Roadside country pub with lovely views, good reasonably priced food (till 7.30pm Sun) using meat from local farms, lunchtime deals, grill night Mon, prompt friendly service, well kept Brakspears and Marstons Pedigree, Weston's cider, pleasant lounge with open fire, library room and large back dining area; skittle alley; children and dogs welcome, garden and terrace seating, two bedrooms. *(Paul Scofield)*

ORLETON   SO4967
★ **Boot** (01568) 780228
Off B4362 W of Woofferton; SY8 4HN Popular pub with beams, timbering, even some 16th-c wattle and daub, inglenook fireplace in charming cosy traditional bar, steps up to further bar area, good-sized two-room dining part, varied choice of interesting well presented food from good sandwiches/baguettes up, friendly quick service, Hobsons, Wye Valley and a local guest (July beer/music festival), real ciders; children and dogs welcome, seats in garden under huge ash tree, fenced-in play area, open all day weekends. *(Robert W Buckle, Peter J and Avril Hanson)*

PEMBRIDGE   SO3958
New Inn (01544) 388427
Market Square (A44); HR6 9DZ Timeless ancient inn overlooking small black and white town's church, unpretentious three-room bar with antique settles, beams, worn flagstones and impressive inglenook log

fire, well kept changing ales, farm cider and generous helpings of popular good value food, friendly service, quiet little family dining room; traditional games, downstairs lavatories; no dogs, simple bedrooms and two resident ghosts. *(William Slade)*

PETERSTOW SO5524
Red Lion (01989) 730546
A49 W of Ross; HR9 6LH Roadside country pub with good sensibly priced food cooked by landlord (smaller appetites catered for), good range of well kept ales and ciders, friendly staff, open-plan pub with large dining area and modern conservatory, log fires; board games, quiz first Mon of month; children and dogs welcome, back play area, camping, open all day. *(Paul Scofield)*

PRESTON SO3841
Yew Tree (01981) 500359
Village W of Hereford; HR2 9JT Small tucked-away pub handy for River Wye, simple and welcoming, with two quickly changing ales tapped from the cask and real cider, good value home-made bar food including weekday early evening deal for two and Fri steak night; live music, free wi-fi; children and dogs welcome, bunkhouse, open (and food) all day. *(Darren and Jane Staniforth)*

ROSS-ON-WYE SO5924
Mail Rooms (01989) 760920
Gloucester Road; HR9 5BS Open-plan Wetherspoons conversion of former post office, their usual well priced food and up to five ales including Greene King, Weston's cider and good choice of wines, friendly service; silent TV, free wi-fi; children welcome till 8pm, decked back terrace, open all day from 8am. *(David Carr)*

ROSS-ON-WYE SO6024
White Lion (01989) 562785
Wilton Lane; HR9 6AQ Friendly riverside pub dating from 1650, well kept Wye Valley and a couple of guests, enjoyable traditional food at reasonable prices, good service, big fireplace in carpeted bar, stone-walled gaol restaurant (building once a police station); free wi-fi; children and dogs welcome, lots of tables in garden and on terrace overlooking the Wye and historic bridge, bedrooms and camping, open all day. *(Melanie and David Lawson)*

SELLACK SO5526
Lough Pool (01989) 730888
Off A49; HR9 6LX Welcoming black and white cottage under newish management, some refurbishment but keeping character; bars with beams and standing timbers, rustic furniture on flagstones, open fire

and woodburner, well kept Wye Valley ales and a guest, local farm ciders/perries and several wines by the glass, good food from traditional to more upmarket choices cooked by landlord-chef, back restaurant; well behaved children and dogs (in bar) allowed, good surrounding walks, closed Sun evening, Mon. *(William Slade)*

ST OWEN'S CROSS SO5424
White Mughal (01989) 730821
Junction A4137 and B4521, W of Ross-on-Wye; HR2 8LQ Half-timbered 16th-c dining pub; huge inglenook fireplaces, dark beams and timbers, various nooks and crannies, mix of furniture including old pews, ales such as Wye Valley from pewter counter, good north indian food in bar and restaurant (also authentic hungarian goulash and some pubby choices); children welcome, dogs in bar, spacious sheltered garden with play things and views to Black Mountains, two four-poster bedrooms, closed Sun evening, Mon. *(Mark Morgan)*

STAPLOW SO6941
Oak (01531) 640954
Bromyard Road (B4214); HR8 1NP Popular roadside village pub, two snug bar areas with beams, flagstones and woodburners, open-kitchen restaurant serving good (if not bargain) food from lunchtime sandwiches up, Bathams, Ledbury, Wye Valley and a guest, good choice of wines, cheerful quick service; occasional live music; children and dogs welcome, garden picnic-sets, four comfortable bedrooms, open all day. *(Jeremy Snow)*

STAUNTON ON WYE SO3844
Portway (01981) 500474
A438 Hereford to Hay-on-Wye, by Monnington turn; HR4 7NH Modernised 16th-c beamed inn with good food including Fri steak night and bargain OAP lunch Tues and Thurs, Ludlow Gold, Sharps Doom Bar and Wye Valley, log-fire bar, lounge and restaurant; background music, TV, pool; children welcome, picnic-sets in sizeable garden among fruit trees, nine bedrooms, open all day. *(Dave Braisted)*

STIFFORDS BRIDGE SO7348
Red Lion (01886) 880318
A4103 3 miles W of Great Malvern; WR13 5NN Refurbished beamed roadside pub; good choice of tasty well priced pubby food (not Sun evening) including Mon specials, Greene King, Malvern Hills and Wye Valley, real ciders, friendly helpful staff; some live music; children and dogs welcome, tables in nicely kept garden, open all day. *(Geoffrey Sutton)*

If you report on a pub that's not a featured entry, please tell us any lunchtimes or evenings when it doesn't serve bar food.

STOCKTON CROSS   SO5161

★ **Stockton Cross Inn**   (01568) 612509

Kimbolton; A4112, off A49 just N of Leominster; HR6 0HD Cosy half-timbered 16th-c drovers' inn, heavily beamed interior with huge log fire and woodburner, handsome antique settle, old leather chairs and brocaded stools, cast-iron-framed tables, well kept Wye Valley ales and guests, Robinson's cider, enjoyable food from pub favourites up, good friendly service; children and dogs welcome, pretty garden, handy for Berrington Hall (NT), open all day. *(Mark Morgan)*

SUTTON ST NICHOLAS   SO5345

Golden Cross   (01432) 880274

Corner of Ridgeway Road; HR1 3AZ Thriving modernised pub with enjoyable good value food from ciabattas up, OAP lunch deal Mon-Fri, Wye Valley Butty Bach and two regularly changing guests from stone-fronted counter, good friendly service, clean décor, some breweriana, relaxed upstairs restaurant; live music Fri, pool and darts; children and dogs welcome, disabled facilities, no-smoking garden behind, pretty village and good surrounding walks, open all day Fri-Sun. *(Paul Scofield)*

SYMONDS YAT   SO5515

Old Ferrie   (01600) 890232

Ferrie Lane, Symonds Yat West; HR9 6BL Unpretentious old inn set in picturesque spot by River Wye with own hand-pulled ferry; decent choice of enjoyable food including lunchtime sharing boards, Wye Valley ales and local cider, friendly helpful staff, log fires; games room; children welcome, waterside terrace, canoeing and good walks, bedrooms, two bunkhouses, open all day. *(Margaret McDonald)*

TRUMPET   SO6639

Trumpet Inn   (01531) 670277

Corner A413 and A438; HR8 2RA Modernised black and white timbered pub dating from the 15th c, well kept Wadworths ales and plenty of wines by the glass, good food (all day Sat, till 7pm Sun) from sandwiches to specials, Mon steak night, efficient service, carpeted interior with beams, stripped brickwork and log fires, restaurant; free wi-fi; children and dogs (in bar) welcome, tables in big garden behind, campsite with hard standings, open all day. *(Paul Scofield)*

UPTON BISHOP   SO6326

Moody Cow   (01989) 780470

B4221 E of Ross-on-Wye; HR9 7TT Tucked-away dining pub with updated rustic décor; L-shaped bar with sandstone walls, slate floor and woodburner, biggish raftered restaurant and second more intimate eating area, good freshly made food (highish prices, some dishes available in smaller helpings), well kept ales and decent wines including local ones, friendly efficient service; children, dogs and boots welcome, garden growing own fruit/vegetables, courtyard bedroom up spiral staircase, closed Sun evening, Mon. *(William Slade)*

WELLINGTON   SO4948

Wellington   (01432) 830367

Village signed off A49 N of Hereford; HR4 8AT Red-brick Victorian pub-restaurant; bar with big high-backed settles, antique farm and garden tools, historical photographs of the village and woodburner in brick fireplace, Butcombe, Goffs, Wye Valley and a guest, enjoyable fairly traditional food (not Sun evening) cooked by landlord-chef, candlelit stable restaurant and conservatory; background music; children welcome, dogs in bar, nice back garden, closed Mon, and may shut early Sun if quiet. *(Paul Scofield)*

WELLINGTON HEATH   SO7140

Farmers Arms   (01531) 634776

Off B4214 just N of Ledbury – pub signed right, from top of village; Horse Road; HR8 1LS Roomy open-plan beamed pub refurbished under present licensees, enjoyable generously served food (booking advised) including daily specials and two-course lunch menu (Wed-Fri), various themed nights, Otter, Wye Valley Butty Bach and a guest, friendly staff; free wi-fi; children and dogs welcome, picnic-sets on paved terrace, good walking country, open all day weekends, closed Mon and lunchtime Tues. *(Melanie and David Lawson)*

WEOBLEY   SO4051

Salutation   (01544) 318443

Off A4112 SW of Leominster; HR4 8SJ Old beamed and timbered inn at top of delightful village green, enjoyable food cooked by chef-landlord from bar snacks up including set lunch/early evening deal, well kept ales such as Otter, Thwaites and Wye Valley, Robinson's cider, pleasant helpful service, two bars and restaurant, inglenook fire; quiz/curry night first Weds of month; children welcome, sheltered back terrace, three bedrooms, good breakfast, open all day. *(Mark Morgan)*

WIGMORE   SO4168

Oak   (01568) 770424

Ford Street; HR6 9UJ Restored 16th-c coaching inn mixing original features with

---

Post Office address codings confusingly give the impression that a few pubs are in Herefordshire when they're really in Gloucestershire or even Wales (which is where we list them).

contemporary décor, well liked interesting food (not Tues) from sensibly short menu including lunchtime sandwiches, Hobsons and guests such as Greene King, traditional cider, cheerful helpful service; children and dogs welcome, two spacious bedrooms, closed Mon and lunchtime Tues. *(Paul Scofield)*

WINFORTON SO2946

Sun (01544) 327677

A438; HR3 6EA Friendly unpretentious village pub offering enjoyable freshly cooked food all sourced locally, Wye Valley Butty Bach and real ciders, country-style beamed areas either side of central servery, stripped stone and woodburners; background music;

children and dogs welcome, garden picnic-sets, closed Sun evening, Mon (also Tues in winter). *(John Sargeant)*

YARPOLE SO4664

Bell (01568) 780537

Just off B4361 N of Leominster; HR6 0BD Old black and white pub under new management; beamed and carpeted lounge with log fire, large high-raftered restaurant in former cider mill (the stone press remains), good variety of enjoyable well priced food including tapas, ales such as Sharps and Wye Valley, friendly staff; some live music; children welcome, garden picnic-sets, handy for Croft Castle (NT), open all day weekends. *(Ann and Tony Bennett-Hughes)*

'Children welcome' means the pub says it lets children inside without any special restriction. If it allows them in, but to restricted areas such as an eating area or family room, we specify this. Places with separate restaurants often let children use them, and hotels usually let children into public areas such as lounges. Some pubs impose an evening time limit – let us know if you find one earlier than 9pm.

Hertfordshire

ASHWELL   TL2739   Map 5
Three Tuns 🍴⭐ 🍷

(01462) 743343 – www.thethreetunsashwell.co.uk

Off A505 NE of Baldock; High Street; SG7 5NL

Bustling inn with a fair choice of drinks, tasty food served by helpful staff and substantial garden; attractive bedrooms

Built in the reign of Queen Anne, this pretty building was converted to an inn in 1806. The airy bar has an open fire, a long settle and cushioned wooden dining chairs around tables (each set with a flowering plant in a small pot), bare floorboards, a few high chairs around equally high tables and pictures on pale walls above a blue dado. The atmosphere is friendly and relaxed. Greene King IPA, Hook Norton Old Hooky, Woodfordes Wherry and Harviestoun Bitter & Twisted on handpump, a dozen wines by the glass and 15 gins; background music. The long Victorian-style dining room has a woodburning stove, built-in wall seats and more cushioned wooden dining chairs around a mix of tables, and rugs on floorboards. There are seats on the terrace and in the substantial garden with apple trees. Bedrooms are comfortable (one is dog-friendly) and attractive and the breakfasts are good. This is a charming village.

🍴⭐ First-rate, inventive food includes lunchtime sandwiches, pigeon with tarragon croquette, coffee gel, bacon popcorn and raspberries, crab salad with tomato consommé gratina, cucumber tartare, watermelon and cucumber jelly, chicken caesar salad, pearl barley and parmesan risotto with wild nettle purée, calves liver with bacon, braised red cabbage and jus, fillet of bream with fennel and beetroot escabeche, saffron potatoes, crispy tentacles and bitter orange gel, and puddings such as dark chocolate mousse with frozen chocolate air, salted caramel, smoked yoghurt and yoghurt sorbet and rhubarb, orange and ginger crumble with vanilla custard. *Benchmark main dish: beer-battered fish and chips £11.95. Two-course evening meal £20.00.*

Greene King ~ Lease Tim Lightfoot ~ Real ale ~ Open 11.45-11 (6 Sun) ~ Bar food 12-2.30, 6-9; 12-4, 6-10 Sat; 12-5 Sun ~ Restaurant ~ Children welcome ~ Dogs allowed in bar ~ Wi-fi ~ Bedrooms: /£100 *Recommended by Mrs Margo Finlay, Jörg Kasprowski, David Jackman, Diane Abbott*

BARNET
TQ2599 Map 5

Duke of York ♀

(020) 8449 0297 – www.brunningandprice.co.uk/dukeofyork

Barnet Road (A1000); EN5 4SG

Big place with reasonably priced bistro-style food and nice garden

The spreading rooms in this rather grand place have been cleverly divided up using open doorways and stairs, and big windows and mirrors keep everything light and airy. There's a friendly, easy-going atmosphere and an eclectic mix of furniture on tiled or wooden flooring, hundreds of prints and photos on cream walls, fireplaces and thoughtful touches such as table lamps, books, rugs, fresh flowers and pot plants. Stools line the impressive counter where friendly staff serve Phoenix Brunning & Price Original plus guests such as Mighty Oak Fools Gold and Oscar Wilde, Portobello American Pale Ale and Trumans Zephyr on handpump, 20 wines by the glass, 70 whiskies and farm cider; background music. The garden is particularly attractive, with seats, tables and picnic-sets on a tree-surrounded terrace and lawn, and a tractor in the good play area.

Brasserie-style food includes sandwiches, venison, rabbit and thyme faggot with juniper jus, pork belly with quinoa, pomegranate, almonds, fig and mint, sticky pork ribs with soused asian salad, honey-roast ham and free-range eggs, prawn and squid linguine, wild mushroom risotto, chicken, ham hock and leek pie, steak burger with toppings, coleslaw and chips, and puddings such as white chocolate cheesecake with passion-fruit sorbet and summer pudding. *Benchmark main dish: slow-braised lamb shoulder with dauphinoise potatoes and gravy £16.95. Two-course evening meal £20.00.*

Brunning & Price ~ Manager John Johnston ~ Real ale ~ Open 11.30-11; 11.30-10.45 Sun ~ Bar food 12-10 (9 Sun) ~ Children welcome ~ Dogs allowed in bar ~ Wi-fi
Recommended by Susan and John Douglas, Charles Gysin, Sally and David Champion

BERKHAMSTED
SP9807 Map 4

Highwayman ♀

(01442) 285480 – www.highwaymanberkhamsted.com

High Street; HP4 1AQ

Bustling town pub, newly refurbished, with plenty of room for both drinking and dining

As this attractively refurbished town pub is usefully open all day, customers are constantly popping in and out – after shopping, to meet friends for lunch or for a chat and a pint after work. Food does play a major part, but the relaxed bar is a social place with Fullers London Pride and Sharps Doom Bar plus guests such as St Austell Tribute and Tring Drop Bar Pale Ale on handpump and good wines by the glass. There are upholstered and leather chairs around all sorts of tables, lots of church candles in stubby holders and big windows overlooking the street; young staff are cheerful and helpful. The dining room has dark green leather wall seating, cushioned dining chairs around tables with barley twist legs on bare boards and a bookcase mural at one end. Up some stairs, a mezzanine with rustic wooden walls offers more seating. There are seats and tables outside on the back terraced garden.

Brasserie-style food includes crispy goats cheese parcel with pea and broad bean salad and tomato and chilli dressing, chilli and ginger squid with coriander, grilled courgette, aubergine and smoked paprika and red pepper dressing, a pie of the week, moules marinière with chips, lamb cutlets with moroccan-style vegetables, yellow split peas and almond and coriander couscous, duck breast with confit leg, dauphinoise potatoes and citrus sauce, and puddings such as deep-baked lemon tart with crème fraîche and pistachio soufflé with chocolate ice-cream. *Benchmark main dish: beef stroganoff £13.50. Two-course evening meal £21.00.*

White Brasserie Company ~ Manager Mike White ~ Real ale ~ Open 11-11; 9am-11pm Sat; 9am-10.30pm Sun ~ Bar food 12-10 (10.30 Fri); 9-11am, 12-10.30 Sat; 9-9 Sun ~ Restaurant ~ Children welcome ~ Dogs allowed in bar ~ Wi-fi ~ Live music monthly (see website) *Recommended by Lindy Andrews, Sandra Hollies, Liz and Martin Eldon*

COTTERED
Bull
TL3229   Map 5

(01763) 281243 – www.thebullcottered.co.uk
A507 W of Buntingford; SG9 9QP

Busy dining pub in nice village, recently refurbished rooms, easy-going feel, several ales, interesting food and seats in sizeable garden

There's a rather pretty view of a row of charming thatched cottages from seats at the front of this well run village dining pub, and more seats and tables under fine old trees in the big attractive back garden. The interior has been refurbished recently and the interconnected bar and dining rooms have bare boards throughout, contemporary paintwork, a woodburning stove and a log-effect gas fire, all sorts of upholstered or cushioned dining chairs around dark wooden tables, tartan armchairs and button-back banquettes; fresh flowers, candles in big white lanterns, country prints above wooden dados and stone bottles and carpentry planes dotted here and there. Greene King IPA and Abbot on handpump and nine decent wines served by helpful staff; unobtrusive background music.

 Very good food includes lunchtime sandwiches and toasties, crispy pork croquettes with beetroot, apple and pear, smoked haddock and spinach risotto, chicken in cream, wine, garlic and mushroom sauce, calves liver with bacon and sage, a pie of the day, burgers with toppings and a choice of sauce, bass fillet with crab-crushed new potatoes, butternut squash purée and chorizo crumb, and puddings such as espresso crème brûlée and bread and butter pudding. *Benchmark main dish: bass with ginger, soy, chilli and garlic £18.95. Two-course evening meal £18.50.*

Greene King ~ Tenant Darren Perkins ~ Real ale ~ Open 11.30-3, 6.30-11; 12-10.30 Sun ~ Bar food 12-2, 7-9 ~ Restaurant ~ Children welcome but no highchairs or changing facilities ~ Wi-fi ~ Dinner dance monthly *Recommended by Gordon Neighbour, Alan and Angela Scouller, Mrs Margo Finlay, Jörg Kasprowski*

EPPING GREEN
Beehive
TL2906   Map 5

(01707) 875959 – www.beehiveeppinggreen.co.uk
Off B158 SW of Hertford, via Little Berkhamsted; back road towards Newgate Street and Cheshunt; SG13 8NB

Cheerful bustling country pub, popular for its good value food

The fresh fish delivered daily from Billingsgate is a big highlight here – though the seasonally changing daily specials are just as popular. It's an attractive weatherboarded country pub with a traditional interior. The low-ceilinged, beamed bar has a friendly, informal atmosphere, ornamental brasses and a woodburning stove in a panelled corner, and serves Greene King Abbot and IPA and a changing local guest on handpump alongside a good range of ten wines by the glass; background music. Between the low building and quiet country road is a neat lawn and decked area, with plenty of tables for enjoying the summer sunshine; good woodland walks nearby.

🍴 Fresh fish is delivered daily for the smoked salmon, scallops and bacon, oak-smoked haddock topped with poached egg, fish pie and fresh crab, bass and skate. There are also sandwiches, burger with bacon, brie and chips, lamb shoulder in minted gravy, gammon and egg, steak and kidney pie, and puddings. *Benchmark main dish: beer-battered cod and chips £11.95. Two-course evening meal £18.00.*

Free house ~ Licensee Martin Squirrell ~ Real ale ~ Open 12-3, 5.30-11; 12-10.30 Sun ~ Bar food 12-2.30, 6-9.30 (9 in winter); 12-4, 6-8.30 Sun ~ Children welcome
Recommended by Revd R P Tickle, Julie Wilkinson, Alison and Michael Harper, Luke Morgan

FLAUNDEN

Bricklayers Arms ⭐ ♀

TL0101   Map 5

(01442) 833322 – www.bricklayersarms.com

4 miles from M25 junction 18; village signposted off A41 – from village centre follow Boxmoor, Bovingdon road and turn right at Belsize, Watford signpost into Hogpits Bottom; HP3 0PH

● ●
Hertfordshire Dining Pub of the Year

Cosy country restaurant with fairly elaborate food; very good wine list

In an inviting, peaceful spot, this is a civilised 18th-c dining pub. The mainly open-plan interior has stubs of knocked-through oak-timbered walls that indicate the original room layout, and the well refurbished low-beamed bar is snug and comfortable, with a roaring log fire in winter. Stools line the brick counter where they keep Sharps Doom Bar and guests like Paradigm Win-Win and Tring Side Pocket for a Toad on handpump, and an extensive wine list with 25 by the glass; background music. In summer, the terrace and beautifully kept old-fashioned garden has seats and tables. Just up the Belsize road, a path on the left leads through delightful woods to a forested area around Hollow Hedge. The pub is just 15 minutes by car from the Warner Bros Studios where the *Harry Potter* films were made; you can tour the studios but must book in advance.

🍽 The creative food, using home-smoked meat and fish, includes guinea fowl terrine with horseradish sauce gribiche and a cumin and paprika muffin, king scallops with creamed pea purée and home-pickled vegetables, a vegetarian dish of the day, chicken breast with cardamom and yoghurt seasoning, chicken thigh croquette and barbecued vegetable sauce, cod cooked in almond milk with crispy skin and steamed leeks, lamb cannon with wholegrain mustard jus and fried caper flowers, and puddings such as chocolate and honey fondant with pistachio ice-cream and lemon tart with pannacotta and raspberry ice-cream. *Benchmark main dish: slow-cooked ox cheeks in local ale with mixed bean mash and citrus zest gravy £18.95. Two-course evening meal £22.00.*

Free house ~ Licensee Alvin Michaels ~ Real ale ~ Open 12-11.30 (12.30am Sat); 12-9.30 Sun ~ Bar food 12-2.30, 6.30-9.30; 12-7 Sun ~ Restaurant ~ Children welcome ~ Dogs allowed in bar ~ Wi-fi *Recommended by Peter and Jan Humphreys, David Longhurst*

'Children welcome' means the pub says it lets children inside without any special restriction. If it allows them in, but to restricted areas such as an eating area or family room, we specify this. Some pubs may impose an evening time limit. We do not mention limits after 9pm as we assume children are home by then.

FRITHSDEN
Alford Arms ⭐🏅 ♀

TL0109   Map 5

(01442) 864480 – www.alfordarmsfrithsden.co.uk

A4146 from Hemel Hempstead to Water End, then second left (after Red Lion)
signed Frithsden, then left at T junction, then right after 0.25 miles; HP1 3DD

Thriving dining pub with a chic interior, good food from
imaginative menu and a thoughtful wine list

Lovely National Trust woodland surrounds this pretty Victorian pub, so
many of the lunchtime customers are walkers – at other times, there's a
cheerful mix of both locals and diners. The elegant, understated interior has
simple prints on pale cream walls, with blocks picked out in rich heritage
colours, and an appealing mix of antique furniture (from Georgian chairs
to old commode stands) on bare boards and patterned quarry tiles. Sharps
Doom Bar and a couple of guests such as Chiltern Beechwood and Tring Side
Pocket for a Toad on handpump; also, 24 wines by the glass from a european
list (quite a few sweet ones too) and a good choice of spirits; background
jazz and darts. There are plenty of tables outside.

 Rewarding and interesting, the food includes charred mackerel with pickled
cucumber and yoghurt dressing, rabbit and pistachio terrine with pear and local
elderberry chutney, cauliflower gratin with gruyère, butternut squash croquettes and
grain mustard dressing, free-range local sausage of the day, ale-glazed pork fillet with
braised barley, roast shallots and carrot crush, black bream with haricot beans, smoked
ham hock and crispy serrano ham, and puddings such as dark chocolate délice with
honeycomb and polenta shortbread and banana and praline spring roll with cinnamon
ice-cream and toffee sauce. *Benchmark main dish: coq au vin with parsnip purée*
£16.50. Two-course evening meal £22.50.

Salisbury Pubs ~ Lease Darren Johnston ~ Real ale ~ Open 11-11; 12-10.30 Sun ~
Bar food 12-2.30, 6.30-9.30; 12-3, 6-10 Fri, Sat; 12-9 Sun ~ Restaurant ~ Children welcome ~
Dogs allowed in bar ~ Wi-fi *Recommended by Alf Wright, Daniel King, Sandra Hollies*

HARPENDEN
White Horse

TL1312   Map 5

(01582) 469290 – www.thewhitehorseharpenden.co.uk
Redbourn Lane, Hatching Green (B487 just W of A1081 roundabout); AL5 2JP

Smart up-to-date dining pub with civilised bar side

Behind this extended, white-weatherboarded pub is a huge sunny terrace
with plenty of contemporary seats and tables under parasols. Inside,
the chatty bar is split-level (one part was once the stables) with prints on
burnt orange-painted plank panelling, stools around tables with taller ones
against the counter, and an open fire. Haresfoot Wild Boy, Sharps Doom Bar
and Tring Bring Me Sunshine on handpump and several wines by the glass,
served by friendly, helpful staff; background music and board games. The
airy, stylish dining room has tartan-upholstered dining chairs, cushioned wall
seats and settles around pale wooden tables on floorboards, and black and
white photographs on the walls.

🍴 Some sort of food is available all day: crab, avocado and lobster mayonnaise,
twice-baked blue cheese soufflé with candied walnut and chicory salad, free-range
sausages with mash and onion gravy, wild mushroom and gruyère tart with creamed
leeks, sticky braised beef cheek with celeriac and horseradish purée, chargrilled tuna
loin with spinach and radish and broad bean salsa, 28-day dry-aged steaks with a choice
of sauces, and puddings such as Valrhona milk chocolate mousse with coffee cream and

banoffi cheesecake with butterscotch sauce; they also offer a two- and three-course set weekday menu (12-6). *Benchmark main dish: chicken with sweet potato hash, cabbage and chorizo jus £14.75. Two-course evening meal £20.50.*

Peach Pub Company ~ Manager Alex Callinan ~ Real ale ~ Open 9.30am-11pm (11.30pm Sat, 10.30pm Sun) ~ Bar food 12-9.30 (8.30 Sun) ~ Restaurant ~ Children welcome ~ Dogs allowed in bar ~ Wi-fi *Recommended by Edward May, Isobel Mackinlay, Sandra and Nigel Brown*

HERTFORD HEATH TL3510 Map 5
College Arms 🍴⭐ ♀

(01992) 558856 – www.thecollegearmshertfordheath.com
London Road; B1197; SG13 7PW

Light and airy rooms with contemporary furnishings, friendly service, good, interesting food and real ales; seats outside

On the edge of a village and backed by woodland, this is a popular and civilised place for a drink or a meal. The bar has long cushioned wall seats and pale leather dining chairs around tables on rugs or wooden floorboards, and a modern bar counter where they serve Adnams Ghost Ship and Titanic Plum Porter on handpump and 20 wines by the glass; background jazz. Another area has more long wall seats and an open fireplace piled with logs, and there's a charming little room with brown leather armchairs, a couple of cushioned pews, a woodburning stove in an old brick fireplace, hunting-themed wallpaper and another rug on floorboards. The elegant, partly carpeted dining room contains a real mix of antique dining chairs and tables. The back terrace has tables, seats and a long wooden bench among flowering pots and a children's play house.

 Good, interesting food includes sandwiches, mackerel pâté with cucumber carpaccio, sweet crispy chilli lamb, wild mushroom risotto, pie of the day, seared stone bass fillet with mustard crust, pancetta and potato terrine, crispy leeks and creamy red wine jus, roasted lamb rump with crispy wild mushroom and lettuce sauce, pork belly with braised beetroot, crackling and red wine jus, 32-day aged 10oz rib-eye with garlic portobello mushroom and a choice of sauces, and puddings such as apple and toffee crumble with cinnamon ice-cream and white and milk chocolate tart with orange syrup. *Benchmark main dish: beer-battered fish and chips £12.50. Two-course evening meal £22.00.*

Punch ~ Lease Andy Lilley ~ Real ale ~ Open 11-11 (midnight Sat); 12-8 Sun ~ Bar food 12-3, 6-9 (9.30 Fri); 12-4, 6-9.30 Sat; 12-7 Sun ~ Restaurant ~ Children welcome ~ Dogs allowed in bar ~ Wi-fi ~ Live music last Fri of month *Recommended by Sandra Morgan, Colin and Daniel Gibbs, Douglas Power, WAH*

POTTERS CROUCH TL1105 Map 5
Holly Bush 🍺 £

(01727) 851792 – www.thehollybushpub.co.uk
2.25 miles from M25 junction 21A: A405 towards St Albans, then first left, then after a mile turn left (ie away from Chiswell Green), then at T junction turn right into Blunts Lane; can also be reached fairly quickly, with a good map, from M1 junctions 6 and 8; AL2 3NN

Well tended cottage with gleaming furniture, well kept Fullers beers, good value food and an attractive garden

Though this neatly kept pub seems to stand alone on a quiet little road, it's only a few minutes' drive from the centre of St Albans. There are quite a few antique dressers (several filled with plates), a number of comfortably cushioned settles, a fox's mask, some antlers, a fine old clock with a lovely chime, daily papers and (on the right as you enter) a big fireplace. In the evening, neatly placed candles cast glimmering light over darkly varnished tables, all sporting fresh flowers. The long, stepped bar has particularly well kept Fullers ESB, London Pride, Seafarers and a Fullers seasonal beer on handpump, served by helpful staff who remain friendly even when pushed. The fenced-off back garden has plenty of sturdy picnic-sets on a lawn surrounded by handsome trees.

Popular food includes lunchtime sandwiches, toasties and deli platters, brussels pâté with apple and ale chutney, lamb koftas with tzatziki, wild mushroom and asparagus pie, chilli con carne, beef, chicken or spicy bean burgers with toppings, coleslaw and chips, moroccan lamb tagine with couscous, smoked haddock fishcakes with spinach and roasted vine tomatoes, and puddings such as rhubarb and custard cake and date and ginger sticky toffee pudding. *Benchmark main dish: steak in ale pie £12.50. Two-course evening meal £15.00.*

Fullers ~ Tenants Steven and Vanessa Williams ~ Real ale ~ Open 12-2.30, 6-11; 12-3, 7-10.30 Sun ~ Bar food 12-2 (2.30 Sun), 6-9; not Sun-Tues evenings ~ Children welcome
Recommended by Mrs Zara Elliott, Tina and David Woods-Taylor

PRESTON
Red Lion 🍺 £

TL1824   Map 5

(01462) 459585 – www.theredlionpreston.co.uk
Village signposted off B656 S of Hitchin; The Green; SG4 7UD

Homely village local with changing beers, fair-priced food and neat colourful garden

A few picnic-sets on the grass in front of this community-owned village pub face lime trees on the peaceful village green opposite – while the pergola-covered back terrace and good-sized sheltered garden, with its colourful herbaceous border, have seats and picnic-sets (some shade is provided by a tall ash tree). The main room on the left, with grey wainscot, has sturdy, well varnished furniture including padded country kitchen chairs and cast-iron-framed tables on patterned carpet, a generous window seat, a log fire in a brick fireplace and fox-hunting prints. The somewhat smaller room on the right has steeplechase prints, varnished plank panelling and brocaded bar stools on flagstones around the servery; darts and dominoes. Fullers London Pride and Youngs Bitter on handpump with guests such as Oakham Akhenaten, Oldershaw Grantham Dark and Tring Drop Bar Pale Ale; also, four farm ciders, 11 wines by the glass (including an english house wine), a perry and winter mulled wine.

 Fair priced food includes stilton-stuffed mushrooms, garlic and chilli prawns, spinach and mushroom lasagne, rabbit and cider casserole, moussaka, plaice in caper butter, liver and bacon with onion gravy, fish pie, chicken curry, and puddings such as chocolate fudge cake and bakewell tart. *Benchmark main dish: chilli crab with spaghetti £9.00. Two-course evening meal £14.00.*

Free house ~ Licensee Raymond Lambe ~ Real ale ~ Open 12-2.30, 5.30-11; 12-midnight Sat; 12-10.30 Sun ~ Bar food 12-2, 6.30-8.30; not Sun evening, Mon ~ Children welcome ~ Dogs welcome ~ Wi-fi *Recommended by Lindy Andrews, Alfie Bayliss, Anne Taylor, Alan and Angela Scouller*

The 🍺 symbol shows pubs that keep their beer unusually well, have a particularly good range or brew their own.

REDBOURN

TL1011   Map 5

Cricketers

(01582) 620612 – www.thecricketersofredbourn.co.uk

3.2 miles from M1 junction 9; A5183 signed Redbourn/St Albans, at second roundabout follow B487 for H Hempstead, first right into Chequer Lane, then third right into East Common; AL3 7ND

Good food and beer in attractively updated pub with a bar and two restaurants

This nicely placed village pub has a relaxed front bar with a country-style décor: comfortable tub chairs, cushioned bench seating and high-backed bar stools on pale brown carpet, and a woodburning stove. They serve five quickly changing ales on handpump such as St Austell Tribute and Tring Side Pocket for a Toad with guests such as Sharps Doom Bar and Tring Brock Bitter, 16 wines by the glass, farm cider, several malt whiskies and good coffee; well reproduced background music. This bar leads back into an attractive, comfortably refurbished and unusually shaped modern restaurant; there's also an upstairs contemporary restaurant for private parties or functions. The side garden has plenty of seating and summer barbecues; there are lots of nearby walks and cycle routes. They can help with information on the museum next door.

Well thought-of food includes sandwiches, devilled chicken livers on toasted ciabatta, grilled sardines stuffed with ricotta and baby spinach, artichoke, leek and potato gratin with gruyère, cheeseburger with toppings and chips, kleftiko lamb shank with peppers and pecorino, chicken stuffed with parma ham, asparagus and gorgonzola with wild mushroom sauce, beer-battered cod and chips, daube of beef with dauphinoise potatoes, and puddings such as chocolate fondant and rhubarb crumble. *Benchmark main dish: crayfish and chilli £13.90. Two-course evening meal £20.00.*

Free house ~ Licensees Colin and Debbie Baxter ~ Real ale ~ Open 12-11 (midnight Sat); 12-10.30 Sun ~ Bar food 12-3, 6-9; 12-5 Sun ~ Restaurant ~ Children welcome ~ Dogs allowed in bar ~ Wi-fi *Recommended by Richard Kennell, Sarah Roberts, Carol and Barry Craddock*

SARRATT

TQ0499   Map 5

Cricketers ♀ 🍺

(01923) 270877 – www.brunningandprice.co.uk/cricketers

The Green; WD3 6AS

Plenty to look at in rambling rooms, up to six real ales, nice wines, enjoyable food and friendly staff; seats outside

Once three charming old cottages, this cleverly refurbished pub has interlinked rooms with numerous little snugs and alcoves – perfect for a quiet drink. There's all manner of antique dining chairs and tables on rugs or stripped floorboards, comfortable armchairs or tub seats, cushioned pews, wall seats and two open fires in raised fireplaces. Also, cricketing memorabilia, fresh flowers, large plants and church candles, Phoenix Brunning & Price Original, Paradigm Win-Win, Tring Side Pocket for a Toad and a couple of guests on handpump, good wines by the glass, 27 gins and 50 malt whiskies; background music and board games. Several sets of french windows open on to the back terrace where there are tables and chairs, with picnic-sets on grass next to a colourfully painted tractor; seats at the front overlook the village green and duck pond.

🍴 Interesting food includes sandwiches, smoked salmon tartare with a poached egg, keta salmon and hollandaise, pigeon with wild mushroom risotto and parmesan crisp, chicken caesar salad, cheese and potato pie with wholegrain mustard sauce, cumberland pork sausages with onion gravy and mash, smoked haddock and salmon fishcakes with tomato and spring onion salad, pork fillet with truffle mash, caramelised apples, black pudding and calvados jus, and puddings such as orange and Cointreau jelly with pink grapefruit sorbet and white chocolate cheesecake with blackcurrant sorbet. *Benchmark main dish: beer-battered fish and chips £12.75. Two-course evening meal £20.00.*

Brunning & Price ~ Licensee David Stowell ~ Real ale ~ Open 10am-11pm; 9am-11pm (10.30pm Sun) Sat ~ Bar food 12-9.30 ~ Restaurant ~ Children welcome ~ Dogs allowed in bar ~ Wi-fi *Recommended by Brian Glozier, John Harris, Martin Jones, Mrs Margo Finlay, Jörg Kasprowski*

ST ALBANS
Verulam Arms 🍺

TL1407   Map 5

(01727) 836004 – www.the-foragers.com
Lower Dagnall St; AL3 4QE

Unusual pub with foraged ingredients for both food and drink

The foragers who run this unusual town pub are a team of hunters and gatherers using wild game, fruit and fungi for their interesting food. They also brew their own ale with wild ingredients and make home-made liqueurs and cocktails such as woodruff and apple vodka or a martini that uses sloe gin, vermouth and douglas fir syrup (a sort of christmas tree-with-grapefruit taste); you can also buy tickets to join them on their foraging walks. Furnishings and décor are simple: scrubbed tables surrounded by all manner of old dining chairs on floorboards, fireplaces with big gilt-edged mirrors above, a few prints on sage green paintwork, large blackboards with daily specials listed, frosted windows and candles. High chairs line the counter where they serve their own Foragers Sling Shot and two guests plus ales from local breweries such as Oakham and Tring on handpump; also, beers from all over the world, tapped from the cask and in bottles, and cider. The gravelled garden has brightly painted picnic-sets and a heated awning where they grow hops and grapes.

🍴 Inventive and certainly different, the seasonal food includes sloe gin-cured salmon with british wasabi of horseradish and lady's smock with pickled sea vegetables and wholemeal crisps, shredded slow-cooked muntjac and blue cheese risotto rice balls with leek mayonnaise and hedgerow syrup, sharing boards, venison and beef burger cooked to a roman recipe and topped with onion jam, pickles and tomatoes, root vegetables, baby vegetables and nut roast on spring shoots pesto, browned leeks and goats cheese, mussels, queen scallops and root vegetable broth with sea purslane and seaweed and finished with smoky highland whisky, and puddings such as cheesecake using seasonal plants and sticky toffee pudding; they also offer a two- and three-course set menu (Mon-Thurs and lunchtimes Fri, Sat). *Benchmark main dish: pressed pork belly with crab apple and scrumpy cider purée topped with alexander seeds £14.50. Two-course evening meal £21.00.*

Free house ~ Licensee George Fredenham ~ Real ale ~ Open 12-11 (midnight Fri, Sat.) ~ Bar food 12-3, 6.30-9 (10 Fri, Sat); 12-4 Sun ~ Restaurant ~ Well behaved children welcome ~ Dogs welcome ~ Wi-fi *Recommended by Kate Moran, Patricia Hawkins, Edward Nile*

Real ale may be served from handpumps, electric pumps (not just the on-off switches used for keg beer) or – common in Scotland – tall taps called founts (pronounced 'fonts') where a separate pump pushes the beer up under air pressure.

WATTON-AT-STONE
TL3019 Map 5

Bull

(01920) 831032 – www.thebullwatton.co.uk

High Street; SG14 3SB

Bustling old pub with beamed rooms, candlelight and fresh flowers, real ales served by friendly staff and enjoyable food

As it's open all day and in a pretty village, this well run old pub has a good mix of customers dropping in and out. The huge inglenook fireplace is in the middle with a leather button-back chesterfield and armchairs on either side, a leather banquette beside a landscape-patterned wall, and solid dark wooden dining chairs and plush-topped stools around all sorts of tables on bare boards. The atmosphere is relaxed and friendly, there are fresh flowers, and friendly staff serve Adnams Ghost Ship, St Austell Proper Job and Sharps Doom Bar on handpump and good wines by the glass; background music. Near the entrance are some high bar chairs along counters by the windows; from here, it's a step up to a charming little room with just four tables, wooden dining chairs, a wall banquette, decorative logs in a fireplace, books on shelves, board games and an old typewriter. At the other end of the building is an elegantly furnished dining room with carpet and a slate floor. Paintwork throughout is contemporary. Outside there are church chairs and tables on a covered terrace, picnic-sets on grass and a small, well equipped play area for children.

Enjoyable food includes sandwiches, ham hock and apple rillettes with apple purée, cured salmon with beetroot, dill oil and radish, vegetarian burger with toppings, straw fries and home-made tomato ketchup, beer-battered fish and chips, piri-piri chicken with spinach and sweet potato, sweet potato purée and confit tomato, duck breast with chicory tarte tatin, carrot and cumin purée and hazelnut jus, and puddings such as orange pannacotta with chocolate mousse, basil and chocolate soil and sticky toffee pudding with butterscotch sauce. *Benchmark main dish: slow-roast pork belly £15.00. Two-course evening meal £18.00.*

Punch ~ Lease Alastair and Anna Bramley ~ Real ale ~ Open 9.30am-11pm; 12-6 Sun; closed Sun evening ~ Bar food 12-3 (4 Sat), 6-10; 12-4 Sun ~ Restaurant ~ Children welcome ~ Dogs allowed in bar ~ Wi-fi *Recommended by Sally Wright, James Landor, Daphne and Robert Staples*

Also Worth a Visit in Hertfordshire

Besides the fully inspected pubs, you might like to try these pubs that have been recommended to us and described by readers. Do tell us what you think of them: feedback@goodguides.com

ALDBURY SP9612
Greyhound (01442) 851228
Stocks Road; village signed from A4251 Tring–Berkhamsted, and from B4506; HP23 5RT
Picturesque village pub with some signs of real age inside; inglenook in cosy traditional beamed bar, more contemporary area with leather chairs, airy oak-floored back restaurant with wicker chairs at big tables, Badger ales and a dozen wines by the glass, generally well liked food from lunchtime sandwiches, sharing plates and pubby choices up, set menu Mon-Thurs; children welcome, dogs in bar, front benches facing green with whipping post, stocks and duck pond, suntrap gravel courtyard, eight bedrooms (some in newer building behind), open all day, food all day weekends (till 7.30pm Sun). *(Conor McGaughey, Tracey and Stephen Groves)*

ALDBURY SP9612
★**Valiant Trooper** (01442) 851203
Trooper Road (towards Aldbury Common); off B4506 N of Berkhamsted; HP23 5RW Cheery traditional pub with

appealing beamed bar, red and black floor tiles, built-in wall benches, a pew and small dining chairs around country tables, two further rooms (one with inglenook) and back barn restaurant, enjoyable generously served food (all day Sat, not Sun or Mon evenings), Chiltern, Fullers, Tring and a couple of guests, five ciders and several wines by the glass, friendly helpful staff; background music, free wi-fi; children and dogs (in bar) welcome, enclosed garden with wooden adventure playground, well placed for Ashridge Estate beechwoods, open all day. *(Conor McGaughey, Richard Kennell)*

ALDENHAM   TQ1498
Round Bush (01923) 855532
Roundbush Lane; WD25 8BG Cheery and bustling traditional village pub with plenty of atmosphere, two front rooms and back restaurant, popular generously served food at fair prices, well kept Charles Wells ales and a guest such as St Austell, friendly efficient staff; quiz first Weds of month, live music last Fri, darts; children and dogs welcome, big enclosed garden with play area, good walks, open (and food) all day. *(Sarah Roberts)*

ARDELEY   TL3027
★ **Jolly Waggoner** (01438) 861350
Off B1037 NE of Stevenage; SG2 7AH Traditional beamed pub with lots of nooks and corners, inglenook log fire, up to four well kept changing ales (usually one from Buntingford), plenty of wines by the glass including some organic ones, good reasonably priced home-made food with much sourced from farm opposite (rare-breed meat), friendly service, restaurant with linen tablecloths; children and dogs welcome, large garden, open all day, food all day Sat, till 7pm Sun. *(Mrs Margo Finlay, Jörg Kasprowski)*

ASHWELL   TL2639
Bushel & Strike (01462) 742394
Off A507 just E of A1(M) junction 10, N of Baldock, via Newnham; Mill Street opposite church, via Gardiners Lane (car park down Swan Lane); SG7 5LY Smartly modernised 19th-c village dining pub (originally a brewery), good interesting food (Sun till 6pm) from chef-landlord including set lunch and occasional themed nights, Charles Wells ales and nice selection of wines by the glass, friendly service; picnic-sets on lawn and small terrace with view of church, closed Mon, otherwise open all day (till 10pm Sun). *(Dave Sutton)*

AYOT GREEN   TL2213
Waggoners (01707) 324241
Off B197 S of Welwyn; AL6 9AA Former 17th-c coaching inn under french owners; good food from snacks and pubby choices in cosy low-beamed bar to more upmarket french cooking in comfortable restaurant extension, frequent meal deals, friendly attentive staff, good wine list, real ales;

attractive and spacious suntrap back garden with sheltered terrace – some A1(M) noise, wooded walks nearby. *(Alf Wright)*

AYOT ST LAWRENCE   TL1916
Brocket Arms (01438) 820250
Off B651 N of St Albans; AL6 9BT Attractive 14th-c low-beamed inn with good traditional food (special diets catered for) in bar and restaurant, friendly helpful staff, six real ales including Greene King, Sharps and one badged for them from Nethergate, wide choice of wines by the glass, inglenook log fires; live music including jazz and open mike nights, quiz second Sun of the month; children welcome, dogs in bar, nice suntrap walled garden with play area, handy for George Bernard Shaw's house (Shaw's Corner – NT), six comfortable bedrooms, open all day, no food Sun evening. *(Liz and Martin Eldon, WAH)*

BALDOCK   TL2433
Orange Tree (01462) 892341
Norton Road; SG7 5AW Unpretentious old two-bar pub with up to 13 well kept ales including Buntingford and Greene King, real ciders such as Apple Cottage and large selection of whiskies, good value locally sourced home-made food (all day Sat, till 6pm Sun) including range of pies and blackboard specials, friendly young staff, games room with bar billiards; quiz Tues, folk club Weds; children welcome and dogs (theirs is Arthur), garden with play area and chickens, open all day Thurs-Sun. *(John Pritchard)*

BARKWAY   TL3834
Tally Ho (01763) 848071
London Road (B1368); SG8 8EX Little village-edge pub with clean modern décor, light wood flooring, log fire in central brick fireplace, three changing ales and good range of other drinks, all-day food (not Sun evening), friendly efficient staff; children welcome, decked seating area at front, picnic-sets and weeping willow in garden beyond car park, open all day from 9am (till 7pm Sun). *(Ross Balaam)*

BENINGTON   TL3023
Bell (01438) 869827
Town Lane; just past post office, towards Stevenage; SG2 7LA Traditional 16th-c pub in very pretty village, local beers such as Buntingford and enjoyable caribbean food (licensees are from Trinidad), low beams, sloping walls and big inglenook; occasional folk nights and other events; big garden with country views, handy for Benington Lordship Gardens, open all day Sun (food till 6pm), closed Mon. *(Daniel King)*

BERKHAMSTED   SP9907
Rising Sun (01442) 864913
George Street; HP4 2EG Victorian canalside pub known locally as the Riser,

five well kept ales including one badged for them by Tring, 30 ciders/perries (three beer/cider festivals a year) and interesting range of spirits, two very small traditional rooms with a few basic chairs and tables, coal fire, snuff and cigars for sale, no food apart from ploughman's and monthly pop-up restaurant, friendly service; background music, Thurs quiz; children and dogs welcome, chairs out by canal and well worn seating in covered side beer garden, colourful hanging baskets, open all day in summer, closed winter lunchtimes Mon-Thurs. *(Taff Thomas)*

BISHOP'S STORTFORD   TL5021
Nags Head (01279) 654553
Dunmow Road; CM23 5HP Well restored 1930s art deco pub (Grade II listed), McMullens ales from island servery and plenty of wines by the glass, wide choice of enjoyable reasonably priced food, lots of smallish well spaced tables, good service; quiz last Weds of month, free wi-fi; children welcome, no dogs inside, garden with play area, open all day. *(Sarah Roberts)*

BRAUGHING   TL3925
Axe & Compass (01920) 821610
Just off B1368; The Street; SG11 2QR Nice country pub in pretty village with ford; enjoyable freshly prepared food (till 6pm Sun) from varied menu, Weds steak night, own-baked bread, well kept ales including Harveys and several wines by the glass, friendly uniformed staff, mix of furnishings on wood floors in two roomy bars, lots of old local photographs, log fires, restaurant with little shop selling home-made produce; well behaved children and dogs welcome, garden overlooking playing field, outside bar. *(Dave Sutton)*

BRAUGHING   TL3925
Golden Fleece (01920) 823555
Green End (B1368); SG11 2PE 17th-c dining pub with good freshly made food (special diets catered for) from chef-landlord including some imaginative choices, popular tapas night last Weds of the month, Adnams Southwold and guests, plenty of wines by the glass, cheerful service, bare-boards bar and two dining rooms, beams and timbers, good log fire; quiz first Sun of month, summer beer festival; children welcome, circular picnic-sets out in front, back garden with metal furniture on split-level paved terrace, play area, open all day weekends (food till 6pm Sun). *(Sarah Roberts)*

BRICKET WOOD   TL1302
Gate (01923) 678944
Station Road/Smug Oak Lane; AL2 3PW Popular family pub refurbished under new management; good sensibly priced home-cooked food including british tapas, Charles Wells and guests, friendly service, log fire bar and side dining area; free wi-fi; dogs welcome, garden, open all day. *(Dave Sutton)*

BUSHEY   TQ1394
Horse & Chains (020) 8421 9907
High Street; WD23 1BL Comfortably modernised dining pub with woodburner in big inglenook, good choice of wines by the glass, real ales and enjoyable bar food from sandwiches and sharing plates up, also separate restaurant menu, themed nights and Sun brunch, kitchen view from compact dining room, good friendly service; children welcome, open (and food) all day. *(Jane Woodward)*

CHORLEYWOOD   TQ0395
★ Black Horse (01923) 282252
Dog Kennel Lane, The Common; WD3 5EG Welcoming old country pub popular for its good value generous food (smaller helpings available) from good sandwiches to daily specials, bargain OAP meals, five well kept ales including Adnams, Wadworths and Charles Wells, decent wines, tea and coffee, good cheery service even when busy, low dark beams and two log fires in thoroughly traditional rambling bar, daily papers; open mike night second Sun of month, TV, free wi-fi; children, walkers and dogs welcome, picnic-sets overlooking common, parking can be difficult, open all day, no food Sun evening. *(Roy Hoing)*

CHORLEYWOOD   TQ0294
Land of Liberty Peace & Plenty
(01923) 282226 *Long Lane, Heronsgate, just off M25 junction 17; WD3 5BS* Traditional 19th-c drinkers' pub in leafy outskirts, half a dozen well kept interesting ales and good choice of cider/perry, snacky food such as pasties, simple layout, darts, skittles and board games; background jazz, TV (on request), no mobile phones or children inside; dogs on leads welcome, garden with pavilion, open all day. *(Sandra Hollies)*

CHORLEYWOOD   TQ0295
Stag (01923) 282090
Long Lane/Heronsgate Road; WD3 5BT Open-plan Edwardian dining pub with good varied choice of food from sandwiches and tapas up, well kept McMullens ales and several wines by the glass, friendly attentive service, bar and eating areas extending into conservatory, woodburner in raised hearth; daily papers, free wi-fi; children and dogs welcome, tables on back lawn, open all day, food all day Weds-Sun, handy for M25 (junction 17). *(Jake, Brian Glozier, Richard Kennell)*

CHORLEYWOOD   TQ0396
White Horse (01923) 282227
A404 just off M25 junction 18; WD3 5SD Recently refurbished black-beamed roadside pub, enjoyable fairly pubby food (all day Sun) from lunchtime sandwiches up, Weds steak night, a house beer from Greene King along

with local guests, friendly helpful staff, big log fire; children and dogs (in bar) welcome, small back terrace, open all day. *(Mr and Mrs J Watkins)*

COLNEY HEATH   TL2007
Plough (01727) 823720
Sleapshyde; handy for A1(M) junction 3; A414 towards St Albans, double back at first roundabout then turn left; AL4 0SE
Cosy 18th-c low-beamed thatched local with friendly chatty atmosphere, good value generous home-made food (not Sun-Tues evenings) from lunchtime baked potatoes up, well kept Greene King, St Austell and a guest, friendly efficient staff, big log fire, small brighter back dining area; charity quiz first Tues of month, darts and dominoes, sports TV, free wi-fi; children welcome, no dogs during food times, front and back terraces, picnic-sets on lawn overlooking fields, open all day weekends. *(Robert Turnham)*

ESSENDON   TL2608
Candlestick (01707) 261322
West End Lane; AL9 6BA Peacefully located country pub under same ownership as the nearby Woodman at Wildhill; emphasis on dining but also three well kept beers and several wines by the glass, relaxed friendly atmosphere, good value freshly prepared bar and restaurant food, comfortable clean interior with faux black timbers, log fires; children and dogs welcome, plenty of seats outside, good walks, closed Mon and Tues otherwise open all day (till 8pm Sun).
(Paul Humphreys, Peter and Jean Hoare, Jestyn Phillips)

FLAUNDEN   TL0100
Green Dragon (01442) 832269
Flaunden Hill; HP3 0PP Comfortable and chatty 17th-c beamed pub in same family for three generations; partly panelled extended lounge, back restaurant and traditional little tap bar, log fire, popular good value food (not Mon) with emphasis on thai dishes, Fullers, St Austell and Youngs, friendly helpful service; background music, darts and other pub games; children and dogs welcome, hitching rail for horses, well kept garden with smokers' shelter, pretty village, only a short diversion from Chess Valley Walk, closed Sun evening, Mon lunchtime. *(Sarah Roberts)*

GILSTON   TL4313
Plume of Feathers (01279) 424154
Pye Corner; CM20 2RD Old beamed corner pub with decent choice of well priced food (all day Fri-Sun) including cook-your-own meat on a volcanic rock, Courage Best, Adnams Broadside and local guests, Weston's cider and maybe a mulled winter one, good choice of wines by the glass, pleasant staff, carpeted interior with brass-hooded log

fire; background music, free wi-fi; children welcome, seats on terrace and fenced grassy area with play equipment. *(Quentin and Carol Williamson)*

GOSMORE   TL1827
Bull (01462) 440035
High Street; SG4 7QG Popular 17th-c village pub, beams and open fires, good often imaginative food (not Mon) cooked by landlord-chef, Fullers, Sharps and a guest, friendly welcoming service, small back dining area; no under-14s in bar after 6pm or on Sun lunchtime, terrace tables, closed Sun evening, Mon lunchtime. *(Hugo Jeune)*

GREAT HORMEAD   TL4030
Three Tuns (01763) 289405
B1038/Horseshoe Hill; SG9 0NT
Old thatched and timbered country pub-restaurant in lovely surroundings; enjoyable home-made food including blackboard specials, Buntingford Twitchell and a couple of guests, good choice of wines by the glass and local gin, small linked areas, huge inglenook with another great hearth behind, back conservatory extension; free wi-fi; children and dogs welcome, nice secure garden, open all day Sun till 7pm. *(Mrs Zara Elliott)*

HALLS GREEN   TL2728
Rising Sun (01462) 790487
NW of Stevenage; from A1(M) junction 9 follow Weston signs off B197, then left in village, right by duck pond; SG4 7DR
Welcoming 18th-c beamed and carpeted country pub with good value traditional home-made food (not Sun evening) in bar or conservatory restaurant, well kept McMullens ales, friendly helpful service, woodburner and open fire; children and dogs (in bar) welcome, disabled access, big garden with terrace, boules and plenty for kids including swings and playhouse, closed Mon, otherwise open all day. *(Jestyn Phillips)*

HATFIELD   TL2308
Eight Bells (01707) 272477
Park Street, Old Hatfield; AL9 5AX
Attractive old beamed pub (two buildings knocked together) with Charles Dickens association; small rooms on different levels, wood floors and open fire, three well kept ales including Sharps and Wells, good value food; background music (live Tues, Sat), games machine, free wi-fi; children and dogs welcome, tables in backyard, closed Mon. *(Dr W I C Clark)*

HATFIELD   TL2308
Horse & Groom (01707) 264765
Park Street, Old Hatfield; AL9 5AT
Friendly old town local with up to half a dozen well kept ales (beer festivals), good

---

value pubby lunchtime food (free Tues and Sat nights if you buy a pint), dark beams and good winter fire, old local photographs, darts and dominoes; sports TV; dogs welcome, a few tables out behind, handy for Hatfield House, open all day. *(Daniel King)*

HEMEL HEMPSTEAD   TL0411
Crown & Sceptre   (01442) 234660
Bridens Camp; leaving on A4146, right at Flamstead/Markyate sign opposite Red Lion; HP2 6EY Traditional rambling pub, welcoming and relaxed, with well kept Greene King ales, up to six guests and local cider, generous helpings of good reasonably priced pubby food (not Sun evening), cheerful efficient staff, dining room with woodburner; children allowed, dogs in outside bar/games room, picnic-sets out at front and in pleasant garden, good walks, open all day weekends. *(Peter and Jan Humphreys)*

HEMEL HEMPSTEAD   TL0604
Paper Mill   (01442) 288800
Stationers Place, Apsley; HP3 9RH Recently built canalside pub on site of former paper mill; spacious open-plan interior with upstairs restaurant, Fullers ales and a couple of guests (usually local), food from sandwiches and sharing plates up, friendly staff, log fire; comedy, quiz and live music nights, free wi-fi; children welcome, tables out on balcony and by the water, open all day. *(Alf Wright)*

HERTFORD   TL3212
Old Barge   (01992) 581871
The Folly; SG14 1QD Red-brick bay-windowed pub by River Lee Navigation canal, clean quaint interior arranged around central bar, wood and flagstone floors, some black beams and log fire, Sharps Doom Bar and four guests, real ciders/perry, enjoyable reasonably priced food (not Sun evening) from sandwiches up, friendly staff; background and live music, Sun quiz, newspapers, games machines; children welcome, a few tables out in front, more to the side, open all day. *(Quentin and Carol Williamson)*

HIGH WYCH   TL4614
Rising Sun   (01279) 724099
Signed off A1184 Harlow–Sawbridgeworth; CM21 0HZ Opened-up 19th-c red-brick village local, up to five well kept ales including Courage, Mighty Oak and Oakham tapped from the cask, friendly staff and regulars, woodburner, no food; live music and monthly quiz nights, darts; walkers and dogs welcome, small side garden, closed Tues lunchtime. *(Liz and Martin Eldon)*

HITCHIN   TL1828
Half Moon   (01462) 452448
Queen Street; SG4 9TZ Welcoming tucked-away local with well kept Adnams, Youngs

and half a dozen guests, real cider/perry and plenty of wines by the glass, good value food including tapas and burgers, some themed nights, beer festivals Apr and Oct; open all day (till 1am Fri, Sat). *(M and J White)*

HITCHIN   TL1929
Radcliffe Arms   (01462) 456111
Walsworth Road; SG4 9ST Busy modernised Victorian pub-restaurant with good freshly made food from bar snacks up (some quite pricey), Mon meal deals, local Buntingford ales and extensive wine list (many by the glass), friendly staff, bar area with central counter, conservatory; some live music; children welcome, dining terrace with further seating for drinkers, open all day from 9am for breakfast, no food Sun evening. *(Daniel King)*

HITCHIN   TL5122
Victoria   (01462) 432682
Ickleford Road, at roundabout; SG5 1TJ Popular wedge-shaped Victorian corner local, Greene King ales and a couple of guests, Aspall's cider, enjoyable reasonably priced home-cooked food; events including live music and quiz nights, barn function room; children welcome, seats in sunny beer garden, open all day. *(Daniel King)*

HUNSDON   TL4114
Fox & Hounds   (01279) 843999
High Street; SG12 8NJ Village dining pub with good enterprising food from chef-landlord, not cheap but they do offer a weekday set menu, friendly efficient service, Adnams Southwold, a local guest beer and wide choice of wines by the glass, organic fruit juices too, beams, panelling and fireside leather sofas, more formal restaurant with chandelier and period furniture, bookcase door to lavatories; children welcome, dogs in bar, heated covered terrace, closed Sun evening, Mon. *(Sarah Roberts)*

LEY GREEN   TL1624
Plough   (01438) 871394
Plough Lane, Kings Walden; SG4 8LA Small brick-built rural local, plain and old-fashioned, with chatty regulars, two well kept Greene King ales and a guest, simple low-priced food (not Weds); folk session Tues (band second of month), more live music Sat; big informal garden with verandah, peaceful views, good walks nearby, closed lunchtimes Mon and Tues, otherwise open all day. *(Conor McGaughey)*

LITTLE HADHAM   TL4322
Nags Head   (01279) 771555
Hadham Ford, towards Much Hadham; SG11 2AX Popular and welcoming 16th-c country dining pub with small linked heavily black-beamed rooms, enjoyable sensibly priced food from snacks up including good Sun roasts, close-set tables in small bar with Greene King ales and decent wines,

restaurant down a couple of steps; occasional quiz nights; children in eating areas, tables in pleasant garden. *(Mrs Margo Finlay, Jörg Kasprowski)*

LONG MARSTON   SP8915
Queens Head (01296) 668368
Tring Road; HP23 4QL Welcoming beamed village local with well kept Fullers beers and enjoyable good value food from pub favourites up (not Sun evening), helpful friendly service, open fire; children welcome, seats on terrace, good walks nearby, two bedrooms in annexe, open all day. *(Alf Wright)*

MUCH HADHAM   TL4219
★ **Bull** (01279) 842668
High Street; SG10 6BU Neatly kept old dining pub with good home-made food from sandwiches to daily specials, nice choice of wines by the glass including champagne, well kept Brakspears and guests, cheerful efficient service even at busy times, inglenook log fire in unspoilt bar with locals and their dogs, roomy civilised dining lounge and back dining room; children welcome, good-sized garden, Henry Moore Foundation nearby, open all day weekends (food till 6.30 Sun). *(Dave Sutton)*

NORTHAW   TL2702
Sun (01707) 655507
B156; on green opposite the church; EN6 4NL Appealing décor in 16th-c pub by village green; opened-up bar with curved counter and stained-glass gantry, some green-painted panelling and open fire, ales such as Buntingford, Red Squirrel and Saffron, craft beers, Aspall's cider and 13 wines by the glass, enjoyable food from interestingly varied menu (highish prices), snug with another fireplace and two dining rooms with exposed brick walls and mix of old furniture; background music, free wi-fi; children and dogs (in bar) welcome, picnic-sets on back terrace, more on grass, open all day (till 6pm Sun), closed Mon. *(Caroline Prescott, Alf Wright)*

NUTHAMPSTEAD   TL4134
★ **Woodman** (01763) 848328
Off B1368 S of Barkway; SG8 8NB Tucked-away thatched and weatherboarded village pub with comfortable unspoilt core, 17th-c low beams/timbers and nice inglenook log fire, dining extension, enjoyable home-made food (not Sun evening, Mon) from traditional choices up, Buntingford, Greene King and Woodfordes tapped from the cask, friendly service, interesting USAF memorabilia and outside memorial (near World War II airfield); children in family room with soft play area, dogs in bar,

benches out overlooking tranquil lane, two comfortable bedrooms, open all day Tue-Sat, Sun til 7pm, closed Mon. *(Sandra Hollies)*

RICKMANSWORTH   TQ0594
Feathers (01923) 770081
Church Street; WD3 1DJ Quietly set off the high street, beams, panelling and soft lighting, well kept Fullers London Pride, Tring and two guests, good wine list, varied choice of freshly prepared seasonal food (all day) from sandwiches up including lunchtime deal, good friendly young staff coping well when busy; children till 5pm, picnic-sets out behind. *(Brian Glozier)*

RICKMANSWORTH   TQ0592
Rose & Crown (01923) 773826
Woodcock Hill/Harefield Road, off A404 E of Rickmansworth at Batchworth; WD3 1PP Wisteria-clad low-beamed country pub attractively refurbished under newish owners, Fullers London Pride and a guest, enjoyable traditional home-cooked food, afternoon teas, friendly attentive staff, airy dining room and conservatory, open fires; children, dogs and muddy boots welcome, peaceful garden and terrace with views, open all day. *(Daniel King)*

RIDGE   TL2100
Old Guinea (01707) 660894
Crossoaks Lane; EN6 3LH Welcoming modernised country pub with good pizzeria alongside traditional bar, St Austell Tribute, proper italian coffee, open fire; children welcome, dogs in bar, large garden with far-reaching views, open all day (food till 10pm). *(Liz and Martin Eldon)*

ROYSTON   TL3540
Old Bull (01763) 242003
High Street; SG8 9AW Coaching inn dating from the 16th c with bow-fronted Georgian façade; roomy high-beamed bar, exposed timbers and handsome fireplaces, wood flooring, plenty of tables and some easy chairs, papers and magazines, dining area with wall-sized photographs of old Royston, enjoyable pubby food including good value Sun carvery, Greene King ales and a guest, several wines by the glass, helpful pleasant service; background music and live folk (second and last Fri of month); children welcome, dogs in bar, suntrap courtyard, 11 bedrooms, open all day from 8am (till 1am Fri, Sat). *(John Pritchard)*

RUSHDEN   TL3031
Moon & Stars (01763) 288330
Mill End; off A507 about a mile W of Cottered; SG9 0TA Cottagey low-beamed pub in peaceful country setting, good well

---

If you report on a pub that's not a featured entry, please tell us any lunchtimes or evenings when it doesn't serve bar food.

priced home-made food (not Mon) in bar or small dining room, Adnams Southwold and a guest, friendly service; children and dogs (in bar) welcome, large back garden, closed Sun evening, Mon (and Tues lunchtime in winter). *(Alf Wright)*

SARRATT   TQ0499
★**Boot** (01923) 262247
The Green; WD3 6BL Early 18th-c dining pub with good food (all day Sat, not Sun evening) from lunchtime sandwiches and sharing plates up, weekend breakfast from 9.30am, also tapas and pizzas Fri and Sat evening, three well kept ales and good choice of wines by the glass, friendly young staff, rambling bar with unusual inglenook, restaurant extension; children and (in some parts) dogs welcome, good-sized garden with polytunnel growing own produce, pleasant spot facing green, handy for Chess Valley walks, open all day. *(Tom and Ruth Rees, Ross Balaam, Chris and Pauline Sexton)*

SARRATT   TQ0498
Cock (01923) 282908
Church End: a very pretty approach is via North Hill, a lane N off A404, just under a mile W of A405; WD3 6HH Comfortably traditional 17th-c pub; latched back door opening directly into homely tiled snug with cluster of bar stools, vaulted ceiling and original bread oven, archway through to partly oak-panelled lounge with lovely inglenook log fire, red plush chairs at oak tables, lots of interesting artefacts and several namesake pictures of cockerels, Badger ales and decent choice of enjoyable food (not Sun evening) including OAP deal, restaurant in converted barn; background music (live Sun afternoon), free wi-fi; children and dogs (in bar) welcome, picnic-sets in front looking over quiet lane towards churchyard, more on sheltered lawn and terrace with open country views, play area, open all day. *(Tom and Ruth Rees, Roy Hoing)*

SAWBRIDGEWORTH   TL4814
Orange Tree (01279) 722485
West Road; CM21 0BP Dining pub on leafy outskirts, good freshly cooked food from interestingly varied menu including pub favourites and daily specials, set lunch deal and some themed nights, McMullens ales, friendly staff; children welcome, side garden, closed Mon. *(Mrs Margo Finlay, Jörg Kasprowski)*

ST ALBANS   TL1406
Fighting Cocks (01727) 869152
Abbey Mill Lane; through abbey gateway – you can drive down; AL3 4HE Ancient octagonal building (former dovecote) by River Ver; enjoyable food (not Sun evening) from landlord-chef including good Sun lunch, up to eight well kept changing ales such as Harviestoun, Leeds, Purity and Woodfordes, friendly helpful service, sunken Stuart

cockfighting pit (now a dining area), low heavy beams and panelling, copper-canopied inglenook log fire; weekend live music, darts; children and dogs welcome, attractive public park beyond garden, open all day. *(Sandra Hollies)*

ST ALBANS   TL1406
Garibaldi (01727) 894745
Albert Street; left turn down Holywell Hill past White Hart – car park left at end; AL1 1RT Busy little Victorian backstreet local with well kept Fullers/Gales beers and a guest, good wines by the glass and reasonably priced tasty food with daily specials (till 4.30pm Sun), friendly staff; live music, sports TV, free wi-fi; children and dogs welcome, picnic-sets on enclosed terrace, lots of window boxes and flowering tubs, closed Mon lunchtime, otherwise open all day. *(Dave Sutton)*

ST ALBANS   TL1507
Mermaid (01727) 568912
Hatfield Road; AL1 3RL Bay-windowed pub with several seating areas (including window seats) arranged around central servery, half a dozen well kept ales, a dozen ciders/perries and good selection of bottled beers, friendly knowledgeable staff, small menu serving Pieminister pies and selection of curries; background and live music, sports TV, darts; beer garden behind, open all day. *(Dave Sutton)*

ST ALBANS   TL1307
Six Bells (01727) 856945
St Michaels Street; AL3 4SH Rambling old pub with five well kept beers including Oakham, Timothy Taylors and Tring, reasonably priced home-made pubby food (not Sun evening) from lunchtime sandwiches up, cheerful helpful staff, low beams and timbers, log fire, quieter panelled dining room; weekly live music, some quiz nights; children and dogs welcome, small back garden, handy for Verulamium Museum, open all day. *(Dave Sutton)*

ST ALBANS   TL1406
White Hart Tap (01727) 860974
Keyfield, round corner from Garibaldi; AL1 1QJ Friendly 19th-c corner local with half a dozen well kept ales (beer festivals), decent choice of wines by the glass and reasonably priced fresh food (all day Sat, not Sun evening), good fish and chips Fri; some live music, Weds quiz; tables outside, open all day. *(Dave Sutton)*

THERFIELD   TL3337
Fox & Duck (01763) 287246
Signed off A10 S of Royston; The Green; SG8 9PN Open-plan 19th-c bay-windowed pub in peaceful village setting with picnic-sets on small front green, good food (not Sun evening) from pub favourites up, Greene King and a couple of guests, friendly helpful staff,

country chairs and sturdy stripped-top tables on stone flooring, smaller boarded area on left with darts, carpeted back restaurant; children welcome, garden behind with gate to park (play equipment), pleasant walks nearby, open all day weekends, closed Mon. *(Mrs Margo Finlay, Jörg Kasprowski)*

TITMORE GREEN   TL2126
Hermit of Redcoats (01438) 747333
Redcoates Green; SG4 7JR Large attractively updated red-brick Victorian pub, good locally sourced food (not Sun evening) from light lunchtime choices up, Greene King ales, plenty of wines by the glass and extensive range of gins, efficient friendly service; children, dogs and muddy boots welcome, seats out in front behind picket fence, spacious garden, open all day. *(Sarah Roberts)*

TRING   SP9313
Grand Junction Arms
(01442) 891400 *Bulbourne; B488 towards Dunstable, next to BWB works; HP23 5QE* Busy canalside pub on two levels; four well kept ales and good range of wines by the glass, enjoyable reasonably priced food cooked to order from pub favourites to more adventurous choices, friendly staff, local artwork for sale; Sun quiz, some live music; children welcome, big garden with play equipment, fruit trees and beehives, open all day, no food Sun evening. *(Taff Thomas)*

TRING   SP9211
Kings Arms (01442) 823318
King Street; by junction with Queen Street (which is off B4635 Western Road – continuation of High Street); HP23 6BE Cheerful family-run backstreet pub built in the 1830s; five well kept ales including Tring, real cider and decent choice of malt whiskies, good value food (not Sun evening) from pub favourites up including daily specials, stools around cast-iron tables, cushioned pews, some pine panelling and two warm coal fires (unusually below windows), separate courtyard restaurant; darts, free wi-fi; children till 8.30pm, no dogs inside, open all day weekends. *(Alf Wright)*

TRING   SP9211
Robin Hood (01442) 824912
Brook Street (B486); HP23 5ED Welcoming traditional local with four Fullers/Gales beers and a couple of guests kept well, good value pubby food (all day Sat), pop-up thai restaurant Sun evening, cosy atmosphere and genial service, several well cared for smallish linked areas, main bar

with banquettes and standard pub chairs on bare boards or carpet, conservatory with woodburner; background music, free wi-fi; children welcome, dogs in bar (resident yorkshire terrier and westie), small back terrace, public car park nearby, open all day Fri-Sun. *(Tony and Wendy Hobden)*

WARESIDE   TL3915
Chequers (01920) 467010
B1004; SG12 7QY Proper old-fashioned country local with down-to-earth landlady, three well kept ales such as Adnams and Buntingford, good straightforward home-made food at reasonable prices including vegetarian options, meat from local farmers, friendly staff, log fire; children, walkers and dogs welcome. *(Caroline Prescott)*

WELL END   SU8987
Black Lion (01628) 520421
Marlow Road; SL8 5PL Simple comfortably furnished pub with nice atmosphere, well kept ales such as Aylesbury, Brakspears and Rebellion, good wines (landlord has separate wine business) and enjoyable reasonably priced pub food, friendly helpful staff, log fire; quiz Thurs, pool; children welcome, picnic-sets outside, open all day, no food Sun evening, Mon. *(Paul Baxter)*

WESTMILL   TL3626
Sword Inn Hand (01763) 271356
Village signed off A10 S of Buntingford; SG9 9LQ Beamed 14th-c colour-washed pub in pretty village next to church; good food in bar and pitched-ceiling dining room from snacks to evening specials, welcoming attentive service, Greene King IPA and two guests from brick-faced counter, pine tables on bare boards or tiles, log fires; children and dogs (in one part of bar) welcome, attractive outside seating area, four comfortable bedrooms in outbuilding, open all day Fri, Sat, closed Sun evening. *(Mrs Margo Finlay, Jörg Kasprowski)*

WHEATHAMPSTEAD   TL1716
Cross Keys (01582) 832165
Off B651 at Gustard Wood 1.5 miles N; AL4 8LA Friendly 17th-c brick pub attractively placed in rolling wooded countryside, enjoyable reasonably priced pubby food (not Sun-Tues evenings) in bar and beamed restaurant including good Sun roasts, four well kept ales such as Adnams and Greene King, inglenook log fire; quiz second Mon of month; children, walkers and dogs welcome, picnic-sets in large garden with play area, three bedrooms, open all day weekends. *(Ron and June Buckler)*

Post Office address codings confusingly give the impression that some pubs are in Hertfordshire, when they're really in Bedfordshire, Buckinghamshire or Cambridgeshire (which is where we list them).

WHEATHAMPSTEAD TL1712
Wicked Lady (01582) 832128
Nomansland Common; B651 0.5 miles S; AL4 8EL Chain dining pub with clean contemporary décor, wide range of food including weekday fixed-price menu till 6pm, well kept Adnams, Fullers and Timothy Taylors, plenty of wines by the glass, cocktails, friendly attentive young staff, various rooms and alcoves, low beams and log fires, conservatory; garden with pleasant terrace, open (and food) all day. *(Dave Sutton)*

WIGGINTON SP9310
Greyhound (01442) 824631
Just S of Tring; HP23 6EH Friendly family-run village pub, four well kept ales including Tring, ample choice of good food from snacks and pubby choices to daily specials, cheerful efficient service, restaurant; monthly quiz and live music nights, TV, free wi-fi; children and dogs welcome, back garden with fenced play area, handy for Ridgeway walks, three clean modern bedrooms, open all day, food all day too apart from Sun evening. *(Ross Balaam, Roy Hoing)*

WILDHILL TL2606
Woodman (01707) 642618
Off B158 Brookmans Park–Essendon; AL9 6EA Simple tucked-away country local with friendly staff and regulars, well kept Greene King and four guests, open-plan bar with log fire, two smaller back rooms (one with TV), straightforward weekday bar lunches; darts; children and dogs welcome, plenty of seating in big garden. *(Liz and Martin Eldon)*

WILLIAN TL2230
★ **Fox** (01462) 480233
A1(M) junction 9; A6141 W towards Letchworth then first left; SG6 2AE Civilised contemporary dining pub; pale wood tables and chairs on stripped boards or big ceramic tiles, paintings by local artists, good inventive food along with more traditional choices, Adnams, Sharps, Woodfordes and a couple of guests, good wine list (14 by the glass), attentive friendly young staff; background music, summer beer festival, TV; children and dogs (in bar) welcome, side terrace with smart tables under parasols, picnic-sets in good-sized back garden below handsome 14th-c church tower, open all day (no food Sun evening). *(Sarah Roberts, Simon Jenkinson)*

WILLIAN TL2230
Three Horseshoes (01462) 685713
Baldock Lane, off Willian Road, handy for A1(M), junction 9; SG6 2AE Welcoming traditional village local with enjoyable generously served pubby food at reasonable prices, well kept Greene King and guests, log fires; occasional quiz nights; children and dogs welcome, terrace and small sunny garden, lots of colourful hanging baskets, open (and food) all day. *(Simon Jenkinson)*

WILSTONE SP9014
Half Moon (01442) 826410
Tring Road, off B489; HP23 4PD Traditional old village pub, clean and comfortable, with good value pubby food (all day Tue-Sat) from sandwiches/panini up, well kept ales including Malt, Tring and XT, friendly efficient staff, big log fire, low beams, old local pictures and lots of brasses; may be background radio, games including scrabble, dominoes and darts, free wi-fi; children and dogs welcome, some seats out in front and in good-sized back garden, handy for Grand Union Canal walks. *(Conor McGaughey)*

WINKWELL TL0206
Three Horseshoes (01442) 862585
Just off A4251 Hemel–Berkhamsted; Pouchers End Lane, just over canal swing-bridge; HP1 2RZ 16th-c pub worth knowing for its charming setting by unusual swing-bridge over Grand Union Canal; low-beamed three-room core with inglenooks, traditional furniture including settles, a few sofas, three Charles Wells ales and good selection of wines by the glass, food from british tapas to burgers (they may ask to keep a credit card while you eat), bay-windowed extension overlooking canal; background music, comedy and quiz nights; children welcome, picnic-sets out by the water, open (and food) all day. *(Taff Thomas)*

Isle of Wight

 BEMBRIDGE   SZ6587 Map 2

Crab & Lobster 🍴⭐

(01983) 872244 – www.crabandlobsterinn.co.uk

Foreland Fields Road, off Howgate Road (which is off B3395 via Hillway Road);
PO35 5TR

Clifftop views from terrace and delicious seafood; bedrooms

The fine view over the Solent from this busy pub perched on a coastal
bluff are best enjoyed from picnic-sets on the terrace – but you'll need
to arrive early on a sunny day to bag one. The interior is roomier than you
might expect and decorated in a parlour-like style, with lots of yachting
memorabilia, old local photographs and a blazing winter fire; darts, dominoes
and cribbage. Helpful, cheerful staff serve Goddards Fuggle-Dee-Dum,
Sharps Doom Bar and Upham Punter on handpump, a dozen wines by the
glass, 16 malt whiskies and good coffee. Two of the light and airy bedrooms
look over the sea. The shore is just a stroll away.

🍴⭐ As well as excellent seafood – crab and prawn cocktail, moules marinière,
hot seafood platters, lobster salad and seafood pie – the popular food includes
lunchtime sandwiches, a pâté of the day, burgers with toppings, coleslaw and fries, a pie
of the day, steaks with onion rings and chips, and puddings such as mixed berry eton
mess and chocolate brownie with vanilla ice-cream. *Benchmark main dish: seafood
mixed grill £17.95. Two-course evening meal £22.00.*

Enterprise ~ Lease Caroline and Ian Quekett ~ Real ale ~ Open 11-11; 12-10.30 Sun ~
Bar food 12-2.30, 6-9; 12-9 weekends ~ Children welcome ~ Dogs allowed in bar ~ Wi-fi ~
Bedrooms: £90/£115 *Recommended by D J and P M Taylor, Jack and Hilary Burton, Daniel King*

 HULVERSTONE   SZ3984 Map 2

Sun 🍺

(01983) 741124 – www.sun-hulverstone.com

B3399; PO30 4EH

**Fine setting and views over the sea for picture-postcard pub,
a good mix of walkers and cyclists in bustling bar, real ales and tasty
food and plenty of outside seats**

With lovely views over the Channel, this pretty, thatched pub has lots
of picnic-sets in a secluded, split-level cottagey garden looking across
to the sea. The low-ceilinged bar has a nice mix of character furniture
(including a fine old settle) on flagstones and floorboards, brick and stone

walls, and horsebrasses and ironwork around a woodburning stove.
Brakspears Bitter, Greene King Abbot, Sharps Doom Bar and Youngs
Special on handpump and several wines by the glass. Large windows in
the traditionally furnished and carpeted dining room take in the fine view.

 Tasty traditional food includes chicken liver pâté with tomato chutney, moules
marinière, a pie and a curry of the day, vegetarian lasagne, chicken with
bacon, mozzarella and barbecue sauce, beer-battered cod and chips, gammon with
egg and pineapple, loin of pork with wholegrain mustard sauce, local steaks, and
puddings. *Benchmark main dish: lambs liver and bacon with red wine jus £11.45.
Two-course evening meal £18.00.*

Enterprise ~ Lease Rob Benwell ~ Real ale ~ Open 11.30-11 (10 Sun) ~ Bar food 12-9 (8.30
Sun) ~ Restaurant ~ Children welcome ~ Dogs allowed in bar ~ Live music Fri/Sat evenings
Recommended by Mungo Shipley, Mrs Jillian Chave, Alfie Bayliss, Tracey and Stephen Groves

SHALFLEET
New Inn 🍴 ☆ ♀

SZ4089   Map 2

(01983) 531314 – www.thenew-inn.co.uk
A3054 Newport–Yarmouth; PO30 4NS

Isle of Wight Dining Pub of the Year

Bustling pub with seafood specialities and good beers and wines

Only a stroll from the quay, this is an 18th-c former fishermen's haunt
with quite an emphasis on fish dishes. The rambling rooms have plenty
of character, with warm fires, yachting photographs and pictures, boarded
ceilings and scrubbed pine tables on flagstone, carpet or slate floors.
Goddards Scrumdiggity, Ringwood Best and Sharps Doom Bar on handpump,
11 wines by the glass and farm cider; background music. There may be
double sittings in summer; dogs are only allowed in areas with stone floors.
This is sister pub to the Fishbourne Inn at Fishbourne and Boathouse in
Seaview (both in Also Worth a Visit).

 Using produce from the island and the sea surrounding it, the popular food
includes sandwiches and baguettes, half pint of prawns, spicy breadcrumbed brie
with berry coulis, a pie of the day, local sausages with wholegrain mustard mash, crispy
onions and jus, tagliatelle with slow-roast tomato and saffron sauce with chilli, beer-
battered fish of the day with chips, whole plaice with nut brown butter, slow-roast pork
belly with rosemary jus, local lobster (half or whole), and puddings. *Benchmark main
dish: fish pie £11.95. Two-course evening meal £17.00.*

Enterprise ~ Lease Martin Bullock ~ Real ale ~ Open 10am-11pm; 10am-10.30pm Sun ~
Bar food 12-2.30, 6-9.30 ~ Children welcome ~ Dogs allowed in bar ~ Wi-fi
Recommended by Penny and Peter Keevil, David Longhurst, Ruth May

SHORWELL
Crown 🍺

SZ4582   Map 2

(01983) 740293 – www.crowninnshorwell.co.uk
B3323 SW of Newport; PO30 3JZ

**Popular pub with an appealing streamside garden and play area,
pubby food and several real ales**

In warm weather, the peaceful tree-sheltered garden here is just the place
to head for. There's a little stream that broadens into a small trout-filled
pool, plenty of closely spaced picnic-sets and white garden chairs and
tables on grass, and a decent children's play area. Four opened-up rooms

spread around a central bar with carpet, tiles or flagstones, and there's a warm welcome for all. Adnams Broadside, Goddards Fuggle-Dee-Dum, Sharps Doom Bar, St Austell Proper Job and Timothy Taylors Landlord on handpump, 11 wines by the glass and a farm cider. The beamed, knocked-through lounge has blue and white china on an attractive carved dresser, country prints on stripped-stone walls and a winter log fire with a fancy tilework surround. Black pews form bays around tables in a stripped-stone room off to the left, with another log fire; background music and board games. This is an attractive rural setting.

As well as opening for weekend breakfasts (from 9am), the tasty food includes sandwiches and baguettes, prawn cocktail, garlic mushrooms, sharing platters, macaroni cheese, pizzas with a choice of toppings, chilli con carne, a curry of the day, a pie of the day, a choice of steaks, and puddings. *Benchmark main dish: beer-battered fish and chips £11.95. Two-course evening meal £18.50.*

Enterprise ~ Lease Nigel and Pam Wynn ~ Real ale ~ Open 11.30-11 ~ Bar food 12-9.30 ~ Children welcome ~ Dogs welcome ~ Wi-fi *Recommended by Toby Jones, Martin Jones, Tracey and Stephen Groves*

Also Worth a Visit in Isle of Wight

Besides the fully inspected pubs, you might like to try these pubs that have been recommended to us and described by readers. Do tell us what you think of them: feedback@goodguides.com

ARRETON   SZ5386
★**White Lion** (01983) 528479
A3056 Newport–Sandown; PO30 3AA
Old white-painted former coaching inn with lightened-up beamed interior, bar with stripped-wood floor and comfortable seats by log fire, Sharps Doom Bar, Timothy Taylors Landlord and a guest, several wines by the glass and good choice of well liked fairly priced food, friendly helpful staff, restaurant; children and dogs welcome, pleasant garden with view of ancient church, good walks, open (and food) all day. *(David Longhurst)*

BEMBRIDGE   SZ6488
Pilot Boat (01983) 872077
Station Road/Kings Road; PO35 5NN
Welcoming little harbourside pub shaped like a boat – even has portholes; bare-boards interior with deep red walls and log fire, good food from sandwiches to local seafood, well kept Goddards and guests, friendly efficient service; sports TV; children and dogs welcome, disabled access, tables out overlooking water or in pleasant courtyard behind, well placed for coast walks, five bedrooms, open all day. *(Max Simons)*

BONCHURCH   SZ5778
★**Bonchurch Inn** (01983) 852611
Bonchurch Shute; from A3055 E of Ventnor turn down to Old Bonchurch; opposite Leconfield Hotel; PO38 1NU
Quirky former stables with restaurant run by welcoming italian family (here since 1984); congenial bar with narrow-planked ship's decking and old-fashioned steamer-style seats, Courage ales tapped from the cask, decent wine list, bar food and good italian dishes, charming helpful service, fairly basic family room, darts, shove-ha'penny and other games; background music; dogs welcome, delightful continental-feel central courtyard (parking here can be tricky), holiday flat. *(Steve Grey)*

BRADING   SZ6086
Bugle (01983) 407359
High Street (A3055 Sandown–Ryde); PO36 0DQ Refurbished pub with three roomy beamed areas; painted or wooden chairs around tables of all sizes, tartan wall seating, button-back banquettes and a bright flowery sofa, wood or tiled floors, chunky candles and open fires, decent choice of good pubby food from baguettes to popular Sun carvery, three local ales; weekly live music; dogs welcome (menu for them), attractive garden. *(Peter Barrett)*

CARISBROOKE   SZ4687
★**Blacksmiths Arms** (01983) 529263
B3401 1.5 miles W; PO30 5SS Friendly family-run hillside pub, scrubbed tables in neat beamed and flagstoned front bars, superb Solent views from airy bare-boards family dining extension, ales such as Adnams, Island and Timothy Taylors, decent wines and cider, good food including fresh fish; children, dogs and walkers welcome (Tennyson Trail nearby), terrace tables and smallish back garden with same view, play area, open all day. *(Steve Grey)*

COWES   SZ4995
Duke of York (01983) 295171
Mill Hill Road; PO31 7BT Welcoming
inn with popular generously served pub food
including good fish and chips, well kept ales
such as Goddards, Ringwood and Sharps,
lots of nautical bits and pieces; free wi-fi;
children and dogs welcome, bedrooms.
(Jack and Hilary Burton)

COWES   SZ5092
★**Folly** (01983) 297171
*Folly Lane signed off A3021 just S of
Whippingham; PO32 6NB* Glorious
Medina estuary views from bar and waterside
terrace of this cheery laid-back place;
timbered ship-like interior with simple
wood furnishings, wide range of enjoyable
sensibly priced food from breakfast on (may
be queues at peak times but staff cope well),
Greene King ales and a guest; background
and live music, TV, fruit machine; children
and dogs welcome, long-term parking,
showers and weather forecasts for sailors,
water taxi, open (and food) all day. *(D J and
P M Taylor, Richard Kennell)*

COWES   SZ4996
Union (01983) 293163
*Watch House Lane, in pedestrian centre;
PO31 7QH* Old-town inn tucked back from
the seafront; well kept Fullers/Gales beers
and good value freshly made food, friendly
helpful young staff, cosy areas around central
bar, log fire, dining room and conservatory;
Weds quiz; children and dogs welcome,
tables outside, six comfortable clean
bedrooms. *(David Longhurst)*

CULVER DOWN   SZ6385
Culver Haven (01983) 406107
*Seaward end, near Yarborough
Monument; PO36 8QT* Superb Channel
views from this isolated clifftop pub, clean
and modern, with popular fairly priced home-
made food, well kept changing ales such as
Goddards, Timothy Taylors and Wadworths,
several wines by the glass and good coffee,
friendly service, big restaurant; children
and dogs welcome, small terrace, good
walks. *(Steve Grey)*

FISHBOURNE   SZ5592
Fishbourne Inn (01983) 882823
*From Portsmouth car ferry turn left into
Fishbourne Lane (no through road);
PO33 4EU* Half-timbered mock-Tudor pub
(sister to the Boathouse at Seaview and New
Inn at Shalfleet – a Main Entry); open-plan
rooms with wooden and high-backed dining
chairs around tables on slate floor, leather
sofas, country pictures on part-panelled

walls, big model yacht and woodburner,
smart dining room with wood flooring,
Goddards Fuggle-Dee-Dum, Ringwood Best
and Sharps Doom Bar, eight wines by the
glass from extensive list, enjoyable all-day
food from lunchtime sandwiches/baguettes
up, friendly service; background music (live
July, Aug), free wi-fi; children and dogs (in
bar) welcome, bedrooms, handy for Wightlink
ferry terminal, open from 9am. *(Mungo
Shipley, Max Simons, David Longhurst)*

FRESHWATER   SZ3487
Red Lion (01983) 754925
*Church Place; from A3055 at E end
of village by Freshwater Garage mini
roundabout follow Yarmouth signpost,
then take first real right turn signed to
Parish Church; PO40 9BP* Bay-windowed
red-brick pub on quiet village street, popular
with locals and visitors; well kept ales such as
Goddards Fuggle-Dee-Dum, Sharps Doom Bar
and West Berkshire Good Old Boy, 11 wines
by the glass and enjoyable good value food
from varied blackboard menu, open-plan bar
with country-style furnishings on flagstones
or bare boards, woodburner; children under
10 at landlord's discretion, dogs welcome, a
couple of picnic-sets out at front with view of
church, more tables in carefully tended back
garden growing own herbs and vegetables,
good walking on the nearby Freshwater Way.
(John Jenkins, M G Hart)

GODSHILL   SZ5281
★**Taverners** (01983) 840707
High Street (A3020); PO38 3HZ
Welcoming 17th-c pub with good food cooked
by landlord-chef, emphasis on fresh local
produce (some home-grown), booking
advised weekends, well kept ales including
Sharps and a house beer from Yates, plenty
of wines by the glass and some interesting
home-made liqueurs, good friendly service,
spacious bar and two front dining areas,
beams, bare boards and slate floors,
woodburner; children and dogs welcome in
certain parts, garden with terrace and play
area, own shop, limited parking, handy for
the Model Village, open all day, closed Sun
evening (except bank and school summer
holidays). *(D J and P M Taylor)*

GURNARD   SZ4796
Woodvale (01983) 292037
Princes Esplanade; PO31 8LE Large
1930s inn with splendid picture-window
views of the Solent (great sunsets), good
choice of food from sandwiches and
baguettes to daily specials, Fullers London
Pride, Ringwood Fortyniner and a couple of
guests, plenty of wines by the glass, friendly
staff; weekend live music, Mon quiz; children

We include some hotels with a good bar that offers facilities comparable
to those of a pub.

and dogs welcome, garden with terrace and summer barbecues, five bedrooms, open all day. *(Jack and Hilary Burton)*

HAVENSTREET SZ5590
White Hart (01983) 883485
Off A3054 Newport–Ryde; Main Road; PO33 4DP Welcoming old red-brick village pub with good choice of popular food (all day Sun, special diets catered for) from sandwiches to Ringwood and Goddards ales, cosy log-fire bar and carpeted dining area; children and dogs welcome, tables in secluded garden behind, open all day. *(Peter Barrett)*

NEWCHURCH SZ5685
★ Pointer (01983) 865202
High Street; PO36 0NN Well run old two-room pub by Norman church, generous helpings of good fairly priced local food including blackboard specials (booking advised in season), Mon meal deal, well kept Fullers ales and a guest, friendly service; children and dogs welcome, views from pleasant back garden, boules, open (and food) all day. *(Max Simons)*

NEWPORT SZ5089
Bargemans Rest (01983) 525828
Little London; PO30 5BS Quayside pub with spreading bare-boards interior packed with nautical memorabilia, good choice of generous reasonably priced pubby food including vegetarian and gluten-free options, Goddards, Ringwood and four guests; frequent live music, free wi-fi; children (away from bar) and dogs welcome, part-covered terrace overlooking Medina river, handy for Quay Arts Centre, open (and food) all day. *(D J and P M Taylor)*

NEWPORT SZ4989
Newport Ale House 07791 514668
Holyrood Street; PO30 5AZ Steps up to intimate one-room pub with friendly chatty atmosphere, stools and leatherette bucket chairs on bare boards, half-panelling and some striking wallpaper, well kept changing ales tapped from the cask by knowledgeable landlord, pies, rolls and sandwiches; some live music, darts; dogs welcome, open all day. *(Lisa Robertson)*

NINGWOOD SZ3989
★ Horse & Groom (01983) 760672
A3054 Newport–Yarmouth, a mile W of Shalfleet; PO30 4NW Carefully extended roomy pub liked by families; comfortable leather sofas grouped around low tables on flagstones, sturdy tables and chairs well spaced for relaxed dining, winter log fire, Ringwood Best and a couple of guests, a dozen wines by the glass, popular fair value food served by friendly staff; background music, games machine, board games, free wi-fi; dogs allowed in bar, garden with well equipped play area including bouncy castle and crazy golf, nearby walks, open all day. *(Mrs J Ekins-Daukes, Penny and Peter Keevil)*

NITON SZ5075
★ Buddle (01983) 730243
St Catherine's Road, Undercliff; off A3055 just S of village, towards St Catherine's Point; PO38 2NE Stone pub surrounded by NT land with sea views from clifftop garden; traditional bar rooms with heavy black beams, captain's chairs and wheelbacks around solid wooden tables on big flagstones or carpet, some cushioned wall seating, open fire in broad stone fireplace with massive mantelbeam, ales such as Goddards, Island, Sharps, Yates and Youngs, traditional cider and several wines by the glass, food from sandwiches to daily specials; background and regular live music, free wi-fi; children and dogs welcome, picnic-sets on stone terraces and in neatly kept sloping garden, handy for coast path, open (and food) all day. *(Jack and Hilary Burton)*

NORTHWOOD SZ4983
Travellers Joy (01983) 298024
Off B3325 S of Cowes; PO31 8LS Friendly pub with simple contemporary interior; up to eight well kept ales including Brains Rev James and Island Wight Gold (tasters offered), enjoyable reasonably priced food from sandwiches and pubby choices to daily specials, long bar with log fire, dining conservatory, pool room; Sun quiz and some live music; children, walkers and dogs welcome, garden with pétanque and play area, open (and food) all day. *(Peter Barrett)*

SANDOWN SZ5984
Caulkheads (01983) 403878
Avenue Road; PO36 8AY Emphasis on family dining but liked by locals for a drink too; wide choice of pubby food including pizzas and several real ales, simply furnished airy room with dark farmhouse-style chairs and benches around tables on stripped boards, books and stone bottles on shelves, regulars' bar with pool, darts and fruit machine; picnic-sets under umbrellas in back garden. *(David Longhurst)*

SEAVIEW SZ5992
★ Boathouse (01983) 810616
On B3330 Ryde–Seaview; PO34 5BW Extended blue-painted Victorian pub just across from the beach (sister to the Fishbourne Inn at Fishbourne and New Inn at Shalfleet – a Main Entry); bar with sturdy leather stools and tub-like chairs around circular wooden tables, large model yacht on mantelpiece above open fire, fresh flowers and candles, Goddards, Sharps Doom Bar and 13 wines by the glass, well liked good value food from interesting snacks and sandwiches to specials, elegantly furnished dining room; background music, free wi-fi; children and

dogs (in bar) welcome, seats on terrace overlooking Solent, airy sea-view bedrooms, open all day from 9am. *(John Jenkins, Peter Barrett, Jack and Hilary Burton)*

SEAVIEW   SZ6291
Seaview Hotel (01983) 612711
High Street; off B3330 Ryde–Bembridge; PO34 5EX Small gently civilised but relaxed hotel, traditional wood furnishings, seafaring paraphernalia and log fire in pubby bare-boards bar, comfortable more refined front bar, well kept Fullers and a guest, good wine list including some local choices, enjoyable pub food (smaller helpings available) and more elaborate restaurant menu using produce from their farm, pleasant staff (may ask for a credit card if you run a tab); background music, TV; children welcome, dogs in bar, sea glimpses from tables on tiny front terrace, 13 bedrooms (some with sea views, seven in modern back annexe), open all day. *(Ian Malone)*

SHANKLIN   SZ5881
★ Fishermans Cottage (01983) 863882
Bottom of Shanklin Chine; PO37 6BN Thatched cottage in terrific setting tucked into the cliffs on Appley beach, steep zigzag walk down beautiful chine; spotless little rooms with low beams, flagstones and stripped-stone walls, old local pictures, Island beers and good value pub food including plenty of fish; background and some live music; children and dogs welcome, sun-soaked terrace overlooking sea, lovely walk to Luccombe, open all day, closed Oct-Mar. *(Colin and Maggie Fancourt)*

SHANKLIN   SZ5881
Steamer (01983) 862641
Esplanade; PO37 6BS Busy nautical-theme bar, fun for holiday families, with good range of real ales and enjoyable well priced food including local seafood and imaginative specials, cheery on-the-ball staff, live music most weekends; fine sea views from covered floodlit terrace, eight bedrooms, open all day. *(Colin and Maggie Fancourt)*

ST HELENS   SZ6289
Vine (01983) 872337
Upper Green Road; PO33 1UJ Victorian pub overlooking cricket green; enjoyable home-cooked food (all day Sat, Sun) including stone-baked pizzas, ales such as Island and Ringwood, cheerful helpful staff; weekend live music, Weds quiz, pool, free wi-fi; children and dogs welcome, play area across road, open all day. *(Max Simons)*

VENTNOR   SZ5677
Perks (01983) 857446
High Street; PO38 1LT Little bar packed with interesting memorabilia behind shop-window front, well kept ales including Bass and good range of wines, popular well priced home-made food from sandwiches and baked potatoes up, bargain OAP two-course lunch, fast friendly service; open all day. *(David Longhurst)*

VENTNOR   SZ5677
★ Spyglass (01983) 855338
Esplanade, SW end; road down is very steep and twisty, and parking nearby can be difficult – best to use pay-and-display (free in winter) about 100 metres up the road; PO38 1JX Perched above the beach with a fascinating jumble of seafaring memorabilia in snug quarry-tiled interior, Ringwood ales and guests, popular food including fish dishes (well filled crab sandwiches), friendly helpful service; background music, live daily in summer; children welcome, dogs in bar, sea-wall terrace with lovely views, coast walk towards the Botanic Garden, heftier hikes on to St Boniface Down and towards the eerie shell of Appuldurcombe House, four sea-view bedrooms, open all day. *(D J and P M Taylor, Colin and Maggie Fancourt)*

WHITWELL   SZ5277
White Horse (01983) 730375
High Street; PO38 2PY Popular extended old pub (dates from 1454) with enjoyable good value food from pub staples to daily specials, well kept ales such as Goddards and Yates, good friendly service, carpeted beamed bar with exposed stonework, restaurant; Mon quiz, darts and pool; children and dogs welcome, picnic-sets among fruit trees in big garden with play area, open all day (food all day weekends). *(Jack and Hilary Burton)*

YARMOUTH   SZ3589
Bugle (01983) 760272
The Square; PO41 0NS Old coaching inn with long frontage and several linked rooms; chesterfields by open fire in low-ceilinged panelled lounge, farmhouse-style furniture in dining areas, books on shelves (and book wallpaper), restaurant with high-backed leather chairs around mix of tables on bare boards or carpet, generous helpings of enjoyable pub food (all day summer, all day weekends winter) including daily fresh fish dishes, ales from Goddards, Island and Yates, quick cheerful service, traditionally furnished bar, conservatory; background music; children and dogs welcome, picnic-sets and lots of hanging baskets in courtyard garden, seven bedrooms, handy for the ferry, open all day. *(Richard Kennell)*

YARMOUTH   SZ3589
Wheatsheaf (01983) 760456
Bridge Road, near ferry; PO41 0PH Opened-up and modernised Victorian pub with enjoyable well priced food including good burgers, cheerful service, Goddards, Ringwood and a guest; pool; children and dogs welcome, handy for the harbour, open (and food) all day. *(Steve Grey)*

Kent

THE GOOD PUB GUIDE   BIDBOROUGH   TQ5643   Map 3

Kentish Hare ♀

(01892) 525709 – www.thekentishhare.com

Bidborough Ridge; TN3 0XB

Plenty of drinking and dining space in well run pub with local ales, good wines, enjoyable food and attentive staff

The easy-going and friendly atmosphere here is appealing to both drinkers and diners. The main bar has leather armchairs grouped around an open fire with antlers above, some unusual stools made of corks, bookcase wallpaper and carved stools against the counter where they keep a beer named for them from Tonbridge plus Coppernob (also from Tonbridge) and Harveys Best on handpump, 30 wines by the glass, a locally brewed lager, cocktails and a farm cider. A cosy middle room has a modern two-way woodburner at one end with leather sofas and armchairs beside it, old photographs of the pub, local people and the area, lamps made from fire extinguishers, and wallpaper depicting old leather suitcases. On the other side of the woodburner is a second bar, with attractive chunky wooden chairs and cushioned settles around various tables on wide dark floorboards; some in small booths. The airy back restaurant is similarly furnished with industrial-style lights hanging from painted joists, pots of fresh flowers and candles, exposed brick walls and an open kitchen; background music. A decked terrace with contemporary tables and chairs overlooks a lower terrace with picnic-sets.

🍴 Food is very good: confit salmon with teriyaki, pickled mouli, daikon cress, salmon roe and pak choi, pork fritter with veal jus, anchovy and grilled baby gem, baked mushroom with pearl barley, spinach and duck egg, haddock risotto with poached egg, leeks and grain mustard sauce, saddle of lamb, braised lamb shoulder, sweetbread and salt-baked celeriac, lemon sole with brown shrimp butter, and puddings such as peanut butter parfait with banana sorbet and aerated chocolate and rum baba with mango salsa and coconut; they also offer a two- and three-course set menu. *Benchmark main dish: duck breast with butternut squash and sage in red wine sauce £18.95. Two-course evening meal £18.00.*

Free house ~ Licensees Chris and James Tanner ~ Real ale ~ Open 11-3, 5-11; 11-11 Sat; 11-6 Sun; closed Sun evening, Mon ~ Bar food 12-2.30, 6-9.30; 12-4 Sun ~ Restaurant ~ Children welcome (under-5s eat free) ~ Dogs allowed in bar ~ Wi-fi *Recommended by Nigel and Jean Eames, Edward May, Julian Richardson, Charlie Parker*

We accept no free drinks or meals and inspections are anonymous.

BIDDENDEN

TQ8238 Map 3

Three Chimneys 🌟 ☆ 🍷 🛏

(01580) 291472 – www.thethreechimneys.co.uk

Off A262 at pub sign, a mile W of village; TN27 8LW

Kent Dining Pub of the Year

Pubby beamed rooms of considerable individuality, log fires, imaginative food and big, pretty garden; comfortable bedrooms

Two lovely new bedrooms, each with their own terrace, have been opened up in this fine old pub; breakfasts are very good. The small, low-beamed bar and dining rooms are civilised but informal with plenty of character. They're simply done out with plain wooden furniture and old settles on flagstones and coir matting, some harness and sporting prints on the stripped-brick walls and good log fires. The public bar on the left is quite down to earth, with darts, dominoes and cribbage. Well trained, attentive staff serve Adnams Southwold, Harveys Best and a guest such as Westerham British Bulldog tapped from the cask, 15 wines plus sparkling wine and champagne by the glass, local Biddenden cider and 13 malt whiskies. A candlelit bare-boards restaurant has rustic décor and french windows that open into a conservatory; seats in the pretty garden. Sissinghurst gardens (National Trust) are nearby.

 Excellent food uses the best local, seasonal produce: deep-fried breadcrumbed brie with apple and celery salad and cumberland sauce, cheddar rarebit on toast with parma ham and sunblush tomato salad, three-cheese and onion croquettes on creamed leeks with mushroom fricassée, rack of lamb with butternut squash, dauphinoise potatoes and jus, salmon fillet with crab, dill and lemon croquette, aubergine purée and spiced saffron, tomato and red pepper sauce, duck breast with roasted carrot and swede, parmentier potatoes and rich jus, and puddings. *Benchmark main dish: smoked haddock on creamed leeks with tarragon and mushroom velouté £18.95. Two-course evening meal £25.00.*

Free house ~ Licensee Craig Smith ~ Real ale ~ Open 11.30-11 ~ Bar food 12-9; lighter afternoon menu ~ Restaurant ~ Children welcome ~ Dogs allowed in bar ~ Wi-fi ~ Bedrooms: £80/£120 *Recommended by Alan Cowell, John Evans, Martin Day, Miss A E Dare, Andrew Bosi*

CHIDDINGSTONE CAUSEWAY

TQ5146 Map 3

Little Brown Jug

(01892) 870318 – www.thelittlebrownjug.co.uk

B2027; TN11 8JJ

Bustling pub with interconnected bar and dining rooms, open fires, five real ales and enjoyable food; seats outside

Set in rolling countryside, this is a friendly pub with seats and tables on a terrace, picnic-sets on grass, several 'dining huts' (bookable in advance for £25) and a children's play area. Inside, the beamed front bar has rugs on bare boards or tiled floors, a roaring log fire, leather chesterfield sofas and chunky stools in one corner and high chairs against the carved counter where they keep Greene King IPA and Abbot, Harviestoun Bitter & Twisted and Larkins Traditional on handpump and good wines by the glass; background music and board games. Throughout, various dining areas merge together with open doorways and timbering, more open fires, hundreds of prints, framed old cigarette cards, maps and photos on painted walls, books on shelves, houseplants, old stone bottles and candles on windowsills, big mirrors and all manner of cushioned wooden dining chairs, wall seats and settles with scatter cushions and polished dark wood or rustic tables.

🍴 A wide choice of good food includes sandwiches, moules marinière, baked camembert studded with garlic and rosemary, corned beef hash with home-made baked beans and fried egg, asparagus, broad bean and minted pea risotto, beer-battered fish and chips, steak burger with toppings, skinny fries and aioli, lambs liver, crispy bacon and onion gravy, grilled whole plaice with lemon and caper butter, and puddings such as mixed berry eton mess and chocolate brownie with dark chocolate sauce. *Benchmark main dish: half shoulder of lamb with honey-mustard glaze and herb crumb and gravy £18.95. Two-course evening meal £20.00.*

Whiting & Hammond ~ Lease Duke Chidgey ~ Real ale ~ Open 10am-11.30pm; 9am-midnight Fri, Sat; 9am-10.30pm Sun ~ Bar food 12-9.30; 9am-9.30pm Fri-Sun ~ Restaurant ~ Children welcome ~ Dogs allowed in bar ~ Wi-fi *Recommended by Mike Swan, Emma Scofield, Peter Meister, Christian Mole, Tony Scott*

CHIPSTEAD
George & Dragon 🏵️ ❦ ♉

TQ5056 Map 3

(01732) 779019 – www.georgeanddragonchipstead.com
Near M25 junction 5; 39 High Street; TN13 2RW

Excellent food in popular village dining pub with three real ales, friendly, efficient service and seats in garden

Most customers are here for the particularly good food, but drinkers who want a pint and a chat are made just as welcome. The opened-up bar has heavy black beams and standing timbers, grey-green panelling, framed articles on the walls about their suppliers, and an easy-going, friendly atmosphere; background music. In the centre, a comfortable sofa and table sit in front of a log fire, with a tiny alcove to one side housing a built-in wall seat and just one table and chair. Westerham Grasshopper and Georges Marvellous Medicine and a weekly changing guest such as Westerham Puddledock Porter on handpump and 21 wines by the glass served by courteous, helpful staff. Up a step to each side are two small dining areas with more panelling, an attractive assortment of nice old chairs around various tables on bare floorboards and two more (unused) fireplaces. Upstairs is a sizeable timbered dining room with similar furnishings and a cosy room that's just right for a private party. The back garden has benches, modern chrome and wicker chairs and tables under parasols, and raised beds for flowers, herbs and vegetables. Wheelchair access to garden only.

🏵️ Interesting food using carefully sourced local produce includes sandwiches, smoked mackerel mousse with cucumber 'cannelloni' and squid ink dough balls with pea shoot and lemon balm salad, pork and chicken liver terrine with indian-spiced cauliflower, shaved fennel, golden raisins and spiced tomato chutney, mushroom, sage and smoked cheddar risotto, burger with toppings, harissa mayonnaise and chips, lamb rump with rainbow carrots, courgette, sweet potato and salsa verde, hake with pistachio and pine nut crust, chive crushed new potatoes and watercress vichyssoise, and puddings such as chocolate cheesecake with raspberry coulis and rhubarb and stem ginger crumble with custard. *Benchmark main dish: slow-cooked pork belly with caramelised onion gravy and savoy cabbage £15.00. Two-course evening meal £21.00.*

Free house ~ Licensee Ben James ~ Real ale ~ Open 11-11 (10.30 Sun) ~ Bar food 12-3 (4 weekends), 6-9.30 (8.30 Sun) ~ Restaurant ~ Children welcome ~ Dogs allowed in bar ~ Wi-fi *Recommended by Gordon and Margaret Ormondroyd, Mrs Margo Finlay, Jörg Kasprowski, Dave Braisted, Simon and Mandy King*

GOUDHURST
TQ7037 Map 3

Green Cross

(01580) 211200 – www.greencrossinn.co.uk

East off A21 on to A262 (Station Road); TN17 1HA

Down-to-earth bar with real ales and more formal back restaurant

The little two-roomed front bar in this popular place is properly pubby and easy-going, though most people are here for the marvellous fish and shellfish. There are stripped-wood floors, dark wood furnishings, wine bottles on windowsills, hop-draped beams, brass jugs on the mantelshelf above the fire, and a few plush bar stools by the counter; background music. Harveys Best and half a dozen wines by the glass. Attractive in an old-fashioned sort of way, the back dining room is a little more formal with flowers on tables, dark beams in cream walls and country paintings for sale. You can sit out on a small terrace at the side of the pub.

Smashing food majoring on fish and shellfish includes linguine with queen scallops in vermouth, tarragon and cream sauce, moules marinière, huge dressed cock crab, seafood paella, skate wing with black butter, capers and butter, and whole bass with spring onion, soy and white wine; non-fishy dishes include chicken liver parfait with red onion marmalade and slow-cooked pork belly with crackling, apple sauce and gravy; also, puddings such as mulberry crème brûlée and sticky toffee pudding with toffee sauce. *Benchmark main dish: avocado and crab bake £9.05. Two-course evening meal £20.00.*

Free house ~ Licensees Lou and Caroline Lizzi ~ Real ale ~ Open 12-3, 6-11; closed Sun evening ~ Bar food 12-2, 7-9 ~ Restaurant ~ Children welcome ~ Wi-fi *Recommended by Harvey Brown, Emma Scofield, Allan Lloyd and family, Alan and Alice Morgan*

ICKHAM
TR2258 Map 3

Duke William

(01227) 721308 – www.thedukewilliamickham.com

Off A257 E of Canterbury; The Street; CT3 1QP

Friendly and gently civilised country pub with character rooms, good food and ales and seats in pretty garden; bedrooms

This is a well run country pub that our readers enjoy greatly. The spreading bar has huge oak beams and stripped joists, seats that range from country kitchen to cushioned settles with animal-skin throws, all manner of tables on stripped wooden floors and a log fire with a low barrel table in front of it. Seats line the bar where friendly staff serve Shepherd Neame Whitstable Bay Pale Ale, Tonbridge Rustic and a local guest from breweries such as Old Dairy, Pig & Porter and Romney Marsh on handpump, eight wines by the glass and several gins. The low-ceilinged dining room is similarly furnished, there's a snug with a TV and table football, and a conservatory overlooking the garden and fields beyond. Throughout, paintwork is contemporary, tables are set with fresh flowers and candles in stone bottles and there are interesting paintings, prints and china plates on the walls; background music and board games. Modern seats and tables are set under parasols on the partly covered terrace, with picnic-sets and a children's play area on grass. Bedrooms (named after the owner's culinary heroes) are attractively and simply furnished and breakfasts are generous. Canterbury is just ten minutes by car.

Rewarding food using local, seasonal produce includes sandwiches, potted shrimps with toasted sourdough, pork pâté with tomato chutney, leek and potato sausage roll with parsley sauce, beer-battered cod and chips, fillet of plaice with mussel and celeriac broth, honey mustard ham with home-made baked beans and a fried egg, lamb neck curry, and puddings such as chocolate pot with honeycomb and sour cream and rhubarb crumble; they usually offer a weekend brunch (11am-3pm). *Benchmark main dish: braised pig cheeks and black pudding suet pudding with apple sauce and crackling £15.75. Two-course evening meal £21.00.*

Free house ~ Licensee Mark Sargeant ~ Real ale ~ Open 11-11 (midnight Sat); 11-10.30 Sun ~ Bar food 12-3, 5.30 (6.30 Sat)-9.30; 11-5 Sun ~ Restaurant ~ Live music every second Weds ~ Dogs allowed in bar ~ Wi-fi ~ Bedrooms: /£100 *Recommended by Claire Adams, Glenwys and Alan Lawrence, Nigel Havers, Colin Humphreys*

IVY HATCH
Plough ♀
TQ5854 Map 3

(01732) 810100 – www.theploughivyhatch.co.uk
High Cross Road; village signed off A227 N of Tonbridge; TN15 0NL

Country pub with highly thought-of food, real ales and seats in landscaped garden

There are rewarding walks all around this village pub – through woodland and along the greensand escarpment near One Tree Hill; come here for refreshment afterwards. The various rooms have pale wooden floors, leather chesterfields grouped around an open fire, quite a mix of cushioned dining chairs around assorted tables, and high bar chairs by the wooden bar counter where they keep Tonbridge Blonde Ambition, Ringwood Best and Westerham Spirit of Kent on handpump, 12 wines by the glass and farm cider. There's also a conservatory; background music and board games. Seats in the landscaped garden are surrounded by cob trees; pétanque. Ightham Mote (National Trust) is very close.

As well as breakfasts (9am-midday, from 10am weekends), the interesting choice of food includes sandwiches, crispy chorizo, quinoa, pomegranate, rocket and orange salad, mussels in cream, garlic, shallots and herbs, wild boar and apple sausages with mash, red onion marmalade, and red wine gravy, gurnard with ratte potatoes, spinach and caper beurre noisette, guinea fowl with tarragon and garlic brioche pudding, crispy bacon and red wine jus, and puddings such as chocolate and orange brownie with mascarpone and rhubarb fool. *Benchmark main dish: burger in home-made brioche bun with red pepper ketchup, coleslaw and chips £13.50. Two-course evening meal £21.00.*

Free house ~ Licensee Miles Medes ~ Real ale ~ Open 9am-11pm; 10am-11pm Sat; 10-6 Sun ~ Bar food 12-2.45, 6-9.30; 12-5.30 Sun ~ Restaurant ~ Children welcome ~ Wi-fi *Recommended by Bob and Margaret Holder, Peter Brix, Lindy Andrews*

LANGTON GREEN
Hare ♀ ◖
TQ5439 Map 3

(01892) 862419 – www.brunningandprice.co.uk/hare
A264 W of Tunbridge Wells; TN3 0JA

Interestingly decorated Edwardian pub with a fine choice of drinks and imaginative food

This is a particularly well run and highly popular pub that's always deservedly busy. The high-ceilinged rooms are light and airy, with rugs on bare boards, built-in wall seats, stools and old-style wooden tables and chairs, dark dados below pale-painted walls covered in old photographs and prints, old romantic pastels and a huge collection of chamber-pots hanging from beams. Greene King IPA and London Glory, Hardys & Hansons Olde Trip and two changing guest ales on handpump, 30 wines by the glass, 75 malt whiskies, 25 gins and a farm cider; background music and board games. French windows open on to a big terrace with pleasant views of the tree-ringed village green. Parking in front of the pub is limited but you can park in the lane to one side.

Enjoyable brasserie-style food includes sandwiches, smoked salmon and crab roulade, duck samosa with sweet chilli sauce and sesame noodle salad, wild mushroom risotto with herb oil, local sausages with mash and gravy, red mullet, sea trout, mussel and cod cheek bouillabaisse with aioli, chicken, ham and leek pie, steak burger with toppings, coleslaw and chips, rump steak with horseradish butter and chips, and puddings such as crème brûlée and sticky toffee pudding with toffee sauce. *Benchmark main dish: lamb shoulder with dauphinoise potatoes and mint jus £16.95. Two-course evening meal £21.50.*

Brunning & Price ~ Manager Tina Foster ~ Real ale ~ Open 11-11; 11am-midnight Fri, Sat; 12-10.30 Sun ~ Bar food 12-9.30 (10 Fri, Sat, 9 Sun) ~ Restaurant ~ Children welcome ~ Dogs allowed in bar ~ Wi-fi *Recommended by Mrs J Ekins-Daukes, Gerry and Rosemary Dobson, R and S Bentley*

MATFIELD
Wheelwrights Arms 🏮 ♀ 🍺

TQ6541 Map 3

(01892) 722129 – www.thewheelwrightsarmsfreehouse.co.uk
The Green; TN12 7JX

Cosy, character village pub with friendly staff, good food, up to seven real ales and decent wines; seats on a front terrace

Run by enthusiastic and hard-working licensees, this attractive weatherboarded pub is extremely popular locally but with a genuine welcome for visitors too. There are hop-strung beams, traditional dark pubby tables and chairs on bare floorboards (one bench has a half wheel as its back), church candles and leather armchairs in front of a woodburning stove; background music. Canterbury Ales The Pardoners Ale, Dark Star Antares, Greene King Abbot, Larkins Traditional, Westerham Finchcocks Original and Whitstable Native on handpump, 13 good wines by the glass, local lager, cider brewed in the village and several whiskies and gins; helpful, courteous service. The dining room leads off the bar with a decorative woodburner in an inglenook fireplace, horse tack, old soda siphons and other knick-knacks dotted about, and some old photos of the pub and village along with cricketing prints and cartoons on the walls. At the front are hanging baskets and modern seats and tables.

Cooked by the landlord, the particularly good food includes sandwiches, seared scallops with haggis croquette, neeps, tatties, apple and sage, duck liver pâté with duck leg and pistachio terrine, duck ham and orange gel, baba ganoush with curried cauliflower burger and harissa yoghurt, wild boar sausages with shallot crisps and golden raisin chutney, cod loin with clams, pancetta, chicken broth and crispy potato shells, and puddings such as rhubarb and white chocolate cheesecake with ginger cake crumb and rhubarb and stem ginger ice-cream and apple and cinnamon parfait with hazelnut praline, syrup sponge and chantilly cream. *Benchmark main dish: vitelotte potato gnocchi with wild garlic cream and home-made Boursin-style cheese £12.95. Two-course evening meal £25.00.*

Free house ~ Licensees Rob and Gem Marshall ~ Real ale ~ Open 12-11; 12-9 Sun; closed Mon except bank holidays ~ Bar food 12-2.15, 6.30-8.45; 12-3.45 Sun~ Restaurant ~ Well behaved children welcome ~ Dogs allowed in bar ~ Wi-fi *Recommended by Mrs Ruth Lewis, Claire Adams, Peter Pilbeam, James Allsopp*

MEOPHAM
Cricketers
TQ6364 Map 3

(01474) 812163 – www.thecricketersinn.co.uk
Wrotham Road (A227); DA13 0QA

Busy village pub with friendly staff, plenty to look at, several real ales, good wines and well thought-of food

Opposite the village green, this is a busy, well run village pub with plenty of space for both drinking and dining. The bar has cushioned wall settles, a medley of old-style wooden dining chairs and tables, a raised fireplace, newspapers to read and Bexley Bob, Sharps Doom Bar, Tring Robin Redbreast and a guest ale on handpump and around a dozen wines by the glass. Glass partitioning separates an end room that has bookshelves either side of another fireplace, rugs on bare floorboards and big house plants. Down steps to one side of the bar is a sizeable dining room with another raised fireplace and similar chairs and tables on more rugs and boards. Throughout, there are frame-to-frame photos, prints and paintings, and church candles on each table; background music. A family room at the end has doors that open to sizeable outdoor seating areas with contemporary black rattan-style seats under parasols overlooking a windmill; there are a few seats out in front too.

Popular food includes sandwiches (until 6pm), duck liver parfait with red onion jam, southern fried chicken with red pepper relish, steak burger with toppings, onion rings, coleslaw and fries, pie of the day, smoked haddock in mustard sauce with poached egg, chicken wrapped in parma ham with mushroom arancini and thyme sauce, confit pork belly with ham hock and black pudding bonbons and apple purée, and puddings such as orange and honey-scented cheesecake with vanilla syrup and apple and rhubarb crumble. *Benchmark main dish: beer-battered cod and chips £13.95. Two-course evening meal £19.00.*

Whiting & Hammond ~ Manager Scott Hawkes ~ Real ale ~ Open 9am-11pm (midnight Fri, Sat) ~ Bar food 9-11, 12-9.30; 9am-9.30pm Fri, Sat; 9am-9pm Sun ~ Restaurant ~ Children welcome ~ Dogs allowed in bar ~ Wi-fi *Recommended by Gordon and Margaret Ormondroyd, Dave Braisted, B and M Kendall*

PENSHURST
Bottle House
TQ5142 Map 3

(01892) 870306 – www.thebottlehouseinnpenshurst.co.uk
Coldharbour Lane; leaving Penshurst SW on B2188 turn right at Smarts Hill signpost, then bear right towards Chiddingstone and Cowden; keep straight on; TN11 8ET

Country pub with friendly service, a good choice of drinks, tasty food and sunny terrace; nearby walks

After enjoying a walk in the surrounding rolling countryside, come to this cottagey place for lunch. The bars have all sorts of joists and beams (a couple of particularly low ones are leather padded) and the open-plan rooms are split into cosy areas by numerous standing timbers. Pine wall boards and bar stools are ranged along the timber-clad copper-topped counter where they keep Dark Star American Pale Ale, Larkins Traditional and Tonbridge Coppernob on handpump and 19 wines by the glass from a good list. There's also a hotchpotch of wooden tables (with fresh flowers and candles), fairly closely spaced chairs on dark boards or coir, a woodburning stove and photographs of the pub and local scenes; background music. Some of the walls are of stripped stone. The sunny, brick-paved terrace has teak chairs and tables under parasols, and olive trees in white pots; parking is limited.

⬣ Pleasing food includes sandwiches, pulled pork scotch egg, hot flaked smoked salmon, asparagus and chive hollandaise, baked goats cheese salad with beetroot salsa and pesto dressing, beef in red wine pie, confit duck leg with champ mash, sautéed mushrooms and bacon and garlic jus, monkfish, salmon and king prawn thai red curry, slow-roasted barbecue ribs with skinny fries, chicken with chorizo, spinach and pine nut creamy linguine, and puddings such as chocolate brownie with toffee sauce and mango and passion-fruit brûlée. *Benchmark main dish: slow-cooked pork belly with creamed cabbage and bacon, dauphinoise potatoes and cider jus £15.50. Two-course evening meal £20.00.*

Free house ~ Licensee Paul Hammond ~ Real ale ~ Open 11-11; 11-10.30 Sun ~ Bar food 12-10 (9 Sun) ~ Restaurant ~ Children welcome ~ Dogs allowed in bar *Recommended by Richard Kennell, Tina and David Woods-Taylor, Martin Day, B and M Kendall, Christian Mole, Bob and Margaret Holder*

PENSHURST
Leicester Arms 🛏

TQ5243 Map 3

(01892) 871617 ~ www.theleicesterarmshotel.com
High Street; TN11 8BT

Refurbished old place in lovely village with plenty of space, local ales, good food and friendly staff; bedrooms

The beamed and timbered bar rooms are to the right of the entrance hall, and our favourite is the middle room. Here, there's a roaring fire in an open woodburner (two armchairs in front), an attractive mix of cushioned wooden dining chairs around dark tables, a lovely, wonky brick floor and, on the walls, a vast ornate gilt mirror and arty twisted vine stems (it sounds unusual but looks most attractive). From here, steps lead up to an airy dining room with half panelling and contemporary paintwork, bookshelves wallpaper, similar tables and chairs on rugs and wooden flooring and big windows. The front bar has another open woodburning stove, button-back wall seating and traditional seats and tables on wide floorboards, church candles and fresh flowers, lots of suspended saddles and horsey wallpaper; background music and board games. Harveys Best, Larkins Traditional and a guest from Tonbridge on handpump and several wines by the glass. To the left of the entrance hall is a more formal purple-painted and panelled restaurant. The bedrooms are comfortable; some have four-posters and some look over to the rather fine village church. Penshurst Place is nearby.

🍴 Reliably good food includes sandwiches, potted shrimps with cayenne butter, local game terrine with indian-style chutney, local sausages with mash, red onion marmalade and gravy, wild mushroom risotto, beer-battered cod with chips, duck breast with parsnip purée, red onion tart and roasted plums, flatiron steak with garlic butter and frites, and puddings such as chocolate fondant with salted caramel, cherry coulis and black cherry sorbet and fig and honey pannacotta with banoffi ice-cream. *Benchmark main dish: steak burger with tomato chutney, aioli and skinny chips £12.50. Two-course evening meal £18.50.*

Free house ~ Licensee Richard Barrett ~ Real ale ~ Open 10am-11pm (midnight Sat); 11-10 Sun ~ Bar food 12-3, 6.30-10; not Sun evening ~ Restaurant ~ Children welcome ~ Dogs allowed in bar and bedrooms ~ Wi-fi ~ Bedrooms: £75/£85 *Recommended by Isobel Mackinlay, Edward May, Nigel Havers, Lionel Smith*

Please let us know what you think of a pub's bedrooms: feedback@goodguides.com or (no stamp needed) The Good Pub Guide, FREEPOST RTJR-ZCYZ-RJZT, Perrymans Lane, Etchingham TN19 7DN.

PLUCKLEY
TQ9243 Map 3

Dering Arms 🌟⌑ ♀ ⇥

(01233) 840371 – www.deringarms.com

Pluckley station, which is signposted from B2077; or follow Station Road (left turn off Smarden Road in centre of Pluckley) for about 1.3 miles S, through Pluckley Thorne; TN27 0RR

Handsome building with stylish main bar, carefully chosen wines, three ales, good fish dishes and roaring log fire; comfortable bedrooms

This is a comfortable place to stay overnight and the breakfasts are highly regarded. A fine building with an imposing frontage, mullioned arched windows and dutch gables, it was originally built as a hunting lodge on the Dering Estate. The high-ceilinged, stylishly plain main bar has a solid country feel with a variety of wooden furniture on flagstones, a roaring log fire in a great fireplace, country prints and some fishing rods. The smaller half-panelled back bar has similar dark wood furnishings, plus an extension with a woodburning stove, comfortable armchairs, sofas and a grand piano; board games. Goachers Gold Star and a beer named for the pub from Goachers on handpump, 11 good wines by the glass from a fine list, local cider, 30 malt whiskies and 20 cognacs. Classic car meetings (the landlord James has a couple of classic motors) are held here on the second Sunday of the month.

 There's an emphasis on fish and shellfish (though non-fishy dishes are offered as well): oysters, moules marinière, duck rillettes, local sausages with mustard mash and onion gravy, fillet of black bream with samphire and beurre blanc, guinea fowl and mushroom pie, whole crab salad, coq au vin, monkfish with bacon, orange and cream sauce, and puddings such as apple, sultana and calvados tart with vanilla ice-cream and sticky toffee pudding with walnut sauce. *Benchmark main dish: bass with minted leeks and bacon on red wine sauce £14.95. Two-course evening meal £25.00.*

Free house ~ Licensee James Buss ~ Real ale ~ Open 11.30-3.30, 6-11; 12-4 Sun; closed Sun evening, Mon ~ Bar food 12-2.30 (3 Sat), 6.30-9; 12-3 Sun ~ Restaurant ~ Children welcome ~ Dogs allowed in bar ~ Bedrooms: £85/£95 *Recommended by Isobel Mackinlay, Jeremy Snow, Sandra Morgan*

SEVENOAKS
TQ5055 Map 3

Kings Head ♀

(01732) 452081 – www.kingsheadbesselsgreen.co.uk

Bessels Green; A25 W, just off A21; TN13 2QA

Bustling pub with open-plan, character rooms, quite a choice of ales, good food and seats in garden

The little bar here is liked by chatty locals and has black and white floor tiles, stools against the counter and friendly staff who serve Caledonian Deuchars IPA and Fullers London Pride, as well as guests such as Blackjack Jabberwocky, Dark Star Hophead, Old Dairy Blue Top and St Austell Tribute on handpump and a dozen wines by the glass. An attractive small room with a two-way open fire leading off here is dog-friendly. Spreading dining areas fan out from the bar with a wide mix of cushioned dining chairs, button-back wall seats and settles with scatter cushions around rustic or dark wooden tables on bare board or tile floors. Also, open fires, frame-to-frame prints, old photos and maps on painted walls, house plants, church candles and old bottles on windowsills, and bookshelves; background music. Outside there are teak tables and chairs on a terrace, picnic-sets on grass and one or two circular 'dining huts' (bookable in advance for £25).

Popular food includes sandwiches, rabbit, ham hock and serrano ham terrine with piccalilli, prawn, crab and avocado tian with bloody mary dressing, beer-battered cod and chips, chicken caesar salad, roasted cauliflower, hazelnut and sunblush tomato on spaghetti, steak burger with toppings, relish and skinny fries, chicken, ham and leek pie, and puddings such as profiteroles with dark chocolate sauce and lemon tart with raspberry chantilly cream. *Benchmark main dish: shoulder of lamb with dauphinoise potatoes and redcurrant and port sauce £18.95. Two-course evening meal £21.00.*

Whiting & Hammond ~ Manager Jamie Owen ~ Real ale ~ Open 11-11 (midnight Sat); 11-10.30 Sun ~ Bar food 12-9.30 (9 Sun); breakfast 9-11.30am weekends ~ Children welcome ~ Dogs allowed in bar ~ Wi-fi *Recommended by Gordon and Margaret Ormondroyd, B and M Kendall, Carol and Barry Craddock*

SEVENOAKS
White Hart ⭐ ♀

TQ5352   Map 3

(01732) 452022 – www.brunningandprice.co.uk/whitehart
Tonbridge Road (A225 S, past Knole); TN13 1SG

Well run coaching inn with lots to look at in character rooms, rewarding food, and friendly, helpful staff

Service with a smile, well liked food and a thoughtful choice of drinks keep customers coming back on a regular basis to this carefully renovated old place. The many rooms (with open fires and woodburning stoves) are connected by open doorways and steps. All manner of nice wooden dining chairs around tables of every size sit on rugs or bare floorboards, cream walls are hung with lots of prints and old photographs (many of local scenes or schools) and there are fresh flowers and plants, daily papers, board games and plenty of chatty, cheerful customers. Phoenix Brunning & Price Original and Old Dairy Blue Top plus guests from breweries such as Empire, Harveys, Timothy Taylors, Tonbridge and Westerham on handpump, 20 good wines by the glass, 50 malt whiskies and a farm cider. At the front of the building are picnic-sets under parasols, and there are also wooden benches and chairs around tables under more parasols on the back terrace.

 Good, modern food includes sandwiches, smoked salmon with fennel pannacotta, chicken liver pâté with apple and ginger chutney, cauliflower and aubergine dhal with chilli flatbread and red onion and coriander bhaji, harissa-spiced pork belly with pomegranate, almonds, fig and mint salad, steak and ale in mushroom pie, chicken breast with fondant potato, smoked bacon, baby onion and sherry sauce, and puddings such as roasted plums with marmalade ice-cream and meringue and chocolate and salted caramel tart with raspberry sorbet. *Benchmark main dish: fish pie £13.95. Two-course evening meal £22.00.*

Brunning & Price ~ Manager Chris Little ~ Real ale ~ Open 11-11; 12-10.30 Sun ~ Bar food 12-10 (9 Sun) ~ Children welcome away from bar until 7pm ~ Dogs allowed in bar ~ Wi-fi *Recommended by B J Harding, Martin Day, B and M Kendall, Alan Cowell, Gordon and Margaret Ormondroyd*

SHIPBOURNE
Chaser ♀

TQ5952   Map 3

(01732) 810360 – www.thechaser.co.uk
Stumble Hill (A227 N of Tonbridge); TN11 9PE

Busy country pub with lots to look at in rambling rooms, log fires, good choice of drinks, enjoyable food and seats outside

The comfortably opened-up bar and dining areas here have a gently civilised and friendly feel – helped along by the courteous, obliging staff. There are stripped wooden floors, frame-to-frame pictures, maps and old photos on the walls above pine wainscoting, house plants and antique glass bottles on windowsills, several roaring log fires, shelves of books and an eclectic mix of solid wood tables (each set with a church candle) surrounded by prettily cushioned dining chairs. Greene King IPA, Larkins Traditional, Sharps Cornish Coaster and York Guzzler on handpump, good wines by the glass, 20 malt whiskies and two farm ciders; background music. A striking, school chapel-like room at the back has wooden panelling and a high timber-vaulted ceiling. French windows open on to an enclosed central courtyard with wicker-style tables and chairs on large flagstones and plants in wall pots; this has a retractable awning and a woodburning stove and creates extra family dining space. A side garden with hedges and shrubs has picnic-sets and is overlooked by the church. You can use the small back car park or park in the lane opposite by the green-cum-common; local walks.

Extremely popular food includes sandwiches, smoked salmon mousse with pickled fennel, capers and chervil and lemon dressing, pigeon breast with bubble and squeak, cauliflower purée and red wine sauce, aubergine, courgette and tomato parmigiana, steak burger with toppings, red onion and garlic mayonnaise and chips, chicken, leek and pancetta pie, herb-crusted cod loin with clam and pea velouté and crispy parma ham, and puddings such as banoffi pie with chocolate sauce and key lime pie with lemon sorbet. *Benchmark main dish: braised lamb shank and chorizo in red wine, broad bean and butter bean stew and cheesy mash £18.95. Two-course evening meal £20.00.*

Whiting & Hammond ~ Manager Craig White ~ Real ale ~ Open 11-11; 9am-midnight (10.30 Sun) Sat ~ Bar food 12-9.30; 9am-9.30pm Thurs, Sat; 9-9 Sun ~ Children welcome ~ Dogs allowed in bar ~ Wi-fi *Recommended by Tina and David Woods-Taylor, Gordon and Margaret Ormondroyd, Penny and David Shepherd*

SISSINGHURST

Milk House 🔯 🛏️

TQ7937 Map 3

(01580) 720200 – www.themilkhouse.co.uk
The Street; TN17 2JG

Bustling village inn of character with well kept ales, enjoyable food and seats in big garden; restful bedrooms

Handy for Sissinghurst Castle (National Trust) and its beautiful gardens, this is just the place to head for afterwards. Through the notable entrance hall, turn right for the companiable bar. This has grey-painted beams, a grey plush sofa by a handsome Tudor fireplace and candles in hurricane jars; unusual touches include the book mural wallpaper, milk churns on windowsills, wickerwork used on the bar counter and for lampshades, and a wire cow. Daily papers, board games and background music. Dark Star American Pale Ale, Harveys Best and a guest from local breweries such as Old Dairy, Tonbridge and Westerham on handpump, 14 wines by the glass, local cider and gin and several malt whiskies, all served by friendly, helpful staff. The restaurant to the left is similarly furnished and there's also a small room leading off, just right for a private party. A large terrace outside the bar has sturdy tables and chairs under green parasols, there's an outdoor pizza/flatbread oven, picnic-sets and a children's play hut beside a fenced-in pond. The bedrooms are comfortable and well equipped and the breakfasts very good.

As well as tea, coffee and cake from 9am and home-baked pizzas and flatbreads, the interesting food includes sandwiches, home-smoked trout with chive and tarragon tart with chicory and crispy spring onion salad, chicken, pistachio and apricot ballotine with parsnip and honey purée and kale crisps, wild mushroom and marjoram risotto cakes with crispy egg and parmesan, burger with toppings, tomato chutney and skinny fries, nut milk-marinated halibut with chilli, lemon and crab risotto, leeks and a saffron reduction, and puddings such as sloe gin frangipane tart with clotted cream ice-cream and baklava cheesecake with berry kissel. *Benchmark main dish: local pork and herb sausages with spinach mash, red onion marmalade and red wine jus £10.00. Two-course evening meal £22.00.*

Mint Pub Company ~ Managers Dane and Sarah Allchorne ~ Real ale ~ Open 9am-11pm; 9am-midnight Fri, Sat ~ Bar food 12-3, 6-9; light snacks in afternoon ~ Restaurant ~ Children welcome ~ Dogs allowed in bar ~ Wi-fi ~ Live music winter Weds from 6pm ~ Bedrooms: /£120 *Recommended by Peter and Carole Jordan, Amy Dillman, Christian Mole, Ian Meeson, Mary Joyce, Sandra Hollies*

SPELDHURST
George & Dragon 🏮 ☆ ♀

TQ5541 Map 3

(01892) 863125 – www.speldhurst.com
Village signed from A264 W of Tunbridge Wells; TN3 0NN

Handsome old pub with beams, flagstones and huge fireplaces, local beers, good food and attractive outside seating areas

Based around a 13th-c manorial hall, this is a lovely half-timbered building with some fine original features: heavy beams (installed during 'modernisation' in 1589 – until then, the room went up to the roof), some of the biggest flagstones you'll ever see and a massive stone fireplace. To the right of the rather splendid entrance hall, a half-panelled room is set for dining with a mix of old wheelback and other dining chairs and a cushioned wall pew around several tables, small pictures on the walls and horsebrasses on one huge beam. A doorway leads to another dining room with similar furnishings and a second big inglenook. Those wanting a drink and a chat tend to head to the room on the left of the entrance (you can eat in here too), where there's a woodburning stove in a small fireplace, high-winged cushioned settles and various wooden tables and dining chairs on a stripped wood floor; background music. The restaurant is upstairs. Harveys Best, Larkins Traditional and a guest beer on handpump, 16 wines by the glass and a farm cider, served by friendly, efficient staff. Teak tables, chairs and benches sit on a nicely planted gravel terrace in front of the pub, while at the back is a covered area with big church candles on wooden tables and a lower terrace with seats around a 200-year-old olive tree; more attractive planting here and some modern garden design.

 Food is rewarding and includes sandwiches, gin-cured salmon with beetroot, avocado, grapefruit and radish, braised pork knuckle with mustard, celeriac rémoulade and crispy egg, local sausages with mash, onion jam and cider gravy, loin of local roe deer with braised red cabbage, pear and dauphinoise potatoes, stone bass with pak choi, linguine, lemongrass, coconut and kaffir lime cream, and puddings such as dark chocolate mousse with honeycomb, space dust and clementine and battenberg with toasted marzipan and honey ice-cream. *Benchmark main dish: salt marsh rump and breast of lamb with smoked aubergine and almonds £22.00. Two-course evening meal £24.00.*

Free house ~ Licensee Julian Leefe-Griffiths ~ Real ale ~ Open 12-11 ~ Bar food 12-2.30 (3 Sat), 6.30-9.30; 12-4 Sun ~ Restaurant ~ Children welcome ~ Dogs allowed in bar ~ Wi-fi *Recommended by Martin Day, Hunter and Christine Wright, Mary Joyce, Peter and Emma Kelly*

STALISFIELD GREEN

TQ9552 Map 3

Plough 🌟◎ 🍺

(01795) 890256 – www.theploughinnstalisfield.co.uk

Off A252 in Charing; ME13 0HY

Ancient country pub with rambling rooms, open fires, interesting local ales and smashing food

The imaginative food here is very highly regarded, but drinkers are made just as welcome and the atmosphere is easy-going and friendly. The hop-draped rooms ramble around, up and down, with open fires in brick fireplaces, interesting pictures, books on shelves, farmhouse and other nice old dining chairs around a mix of pine or dark wood tables on bare boards, and the odd milk churn dotted about; background music. Hopdaemon Incubus, Old Dairy Blue Top, Westerham Finchcocks Original and a guest beer on handpump, 14 wines by the glass, a dozen malt whiskies, four local ciders and a fair choice of gins, vodkas and bourbons. The pub appears to perch on its own amid downland farmland, and picnic-sets on a simple terrace overlook the village green below.

 Cooked by the landlord, the inventive food includes lunchtime rolls, sautéed chicken livers with polenta croutons and madeira jus, smoked salmon pâté with brown crab mayonnaise and guacamole, beer-battered fish and chips, vegetarian moussaka with lentils and chickpeas, confit pork belly and cured tenderloin with chorizo puy lentils, pave of scottish salmon with fennel pollen and cockle velouté, and puddings such as burnt cream, lemon curd and meringue and sticky toffee pudding with toffee sauce; they also offer a two- and three-course set lunch. *Benchmark main dish: pie of the day £13.50. Two-course evening meal £20.00.*

Free house ~ Licensees Richard and Marianne Baker ~ Real ale ~ Open 12-3, 6-11; 12-3, 5-11 Weds, Fri; 12-11 Sat; 12-6 Sun; closed Sun evening, Mon; first week Jan ~ Bar food 12-2 (2.30 Sat), 6-9; 12-3.30 Sun ~ Restaurant ~ Children welcome in designated areas ~ Dogs allowed in bar ~ Live music every two months *Recommended by Toby Jones, Martin Jones, Luke Morgan, Susan and Callum Slade, Pauline and Mark Evans*

STODMARSH

TR2160 Map 3

Red Lion 🛏

(01227) 721339 – www.theredlionstodmarsh.com

High Street; off A257 just E of Canterbury; CT3 4BA

Interesting country pub with lots to look at, good choice of drinks and well liked food; bedrooms

With comfortable bedrooms and hearty breakfasts, this friendly country pub is handy for Stodmarsh National Nature Reserve. The bar rooms have country kitchen chairs and tables, books on shelves and windowsills, tankards hanging from beams, a big log fire and plenty of candles and fresh flowers. Greene King IPA and a guest such as Wychwood Goddess tapped from the cask, eight wines by the glass and a farm cider; background music. There are seats and tables in the back garden.

🍴 Interesting food includes ham hock terrine with pickles, king prawns in garlic and chilli oil, roast vegetable tart with onion marmalade, free-range chicken with chorizo mash, wilted spinach and chicken jus, beer-battered cod and chips, duck breast with boulangère potatoes, truffled celeriac purée and parsnip crisps, whisky-cured pork ribs with barbecue sauce and onion rings, and puddings such as white chocolate fondant with raspberry sorbet and crème brûlée. *Benchmark main dish: local lamb with carrot and carroway purée, dauphinoise potatoes and lamb jus £17.95. Two-course evening meal £20.50.*

Free house ~ Licensee Jeremy Godden ~ Real ale ~ Open 11.30-11; 11.30-midnight Fri, Sat; 12-10.30 Sun ~ Bar food 12-3, 6-9.30; 12-9.30 Sat, Sun ~ Children welcome ~ Dogs allowed in bar ~ Wi-fi ~ Bedrooms: £90/£95 *Recommended by Anneke and Bert Bannink, Philip Meek and Jessica Sproxton Miller*

STONE IN OXNEY
Ferry ◀

TQ9428 Map 3

(01233) 758246 – www.oxneyferry.com
Appledore Road; N of Stone-cum-Ebony; TN30 7JY

Bustling small cottage with character rooms, candlelight, open fires, real ales and popular food

In a lovely marshland setting, this pretty 17th-c cottage has plenty of room inside for both diners and drinkers. The main bar has hop-draped painted beams, a green dado and stools against the counter where they serve a beer named for the pub (from Westerham), Harveys Best, Sharps Doom Bar and a guest from the local Three Legs Brewing Company on handpump, eight wines by the glass and farm ciders. To the right is a cosy eating area with wheelback chairs and a banquette around a few long tables, a log fire in an inglenook and candles in wall sconces on either side. To the left of the main door is a dining area with big blackboards on red walls, a woodburning stove beneath a large bressumer beam and high-backed light wooden dining chairs around assorted tables; up a couple of steps, a smarter dining area has modern chandeliers. Throughout, there are wooden floors, all sorts of pictures and framed maps, a stuffed fish, beer flagons, an old musket and various brasses. Background music, TV, games machine, darts and pool in the games room. In warm weather the tables and benches on the front terrace and seats in the back garden are much prized; a river runs along the bottom and sunsets can be lovely. Disabled access in the bar and on the terrace.

Good food includes sandwiches, pigeon breast with blueberry jus and beetroot purée, rosemary-infused baked baby camembert with onion marmalade, potato gnocchi in stilton and pear sauce, chargrilled chicken salad in peanut butter and sweet chilli sauce, beer-battered cod and chips, parmesan-coated guinea fowl on herb-roasted parmentier potatoes, wild boar steak with wild mushroom and madeira sauce, and puddings such as whisky bread and butter pudding and orange and dark chocolate crème brûlée. *Benchmark main dish: steak and chorizo burger with toppings, spicy tomato chutney, coleslaw and dripping chips £12.95. Two-course evening meal £19.00.*

Free house ~ Licensee Paul Withers Green ~ Real ale ~ Open 11-11; 12-10 Sun ~ Bar food 12-3, 6-9; 12-9 Sat; 12-8 Sun ~ Restaurant ~ Children welcome in restaurant and games room ~ Dogs allowed in bar ~ Wi-fi *Recommended by Bill Adie, Lindy Andrews, Julie Swift*

TUNBRIDGE WELLS
Black Pig ⭐

TQ5839 Map 3

(01892) 523030 – www.theblackpig.net
Grove Hill Road; TN1 1RZ

Busy town pub with real ales, rewarding food, friendly service and seats outside

Very popular locally but with a genuine welcome for visitors too, this is a bustling town pub with cheerful staff. The long narrow bar has a woodburning stove in a brick fireplace with leather sofas to each side, bookshelves, a large antelope head and some unusual friesian cow wallpaper, and a few tables and chairs on bare boards; an overflow room up some steps to the right has wooden chairs around heavy, dark tables and more books on shelves. Harveys Best on handpump and good wines by the glass. If dining, most customers head for the character room to the left of the bar: a mix of contemporary wallpaper and panelling, oriental paintings, large flower arrangements and candles, button-back wall banquettes and an assortment of wooden tables and chairs on more floorboards and an open kitchen. A back terrace has seats and tables on gravel.

Good, interesting food includes sandwiches, rabbit rillettes, scotch egg, bass and sardine fritters with pickled daikon and saffron and sweetcorn mayonnaise, sharing boards, mediterranean vegetable and goats cheese strudel with garlic butter, local wild game platter with beetroot fondant, carrot purée and juniper berry jus, roast bream with gnocchi in white wine and thyme velouté, and puddings such as apple and pear crumble and sticky toffee pudding with caramelised banana and toffee sauce. *Benchmark main dish: pork belly with dauphinoise potatoes, apple sauce and jus £14.00. Two-course evening meal £21.00.*

Free house ~ Licensee Ajay Sandhu ~ Real ale ~ Open 12-11 (10 Sun, Mon) ~ Bar food 12-2.30, 7-9.30 (10 Fri); 12-3, 6-10 Sat; 12-9 Sun ~ Restaurant ~ Children welcome ~ Dogs allowed in bar ~ Wi-fi *Recommended by Edward May, Lindy Andrews, Yann, Katherine Matthews*

TUNBRIDGE WELLS
Sankeys

TQ5839   Map 3

(01892) 511422 ~ www.sankeys.co.uk
Mount Ephraim (A26 just N of junction with A267); TN4 8AA

Pubby street-level bar, real ales, decent food, cheerful feel; downstairs brasserie (wonderful fish and shellfish) and seats on sunny back terrace

Light and airy with a cheerful atmosphere, the pubby bar here has comfortably worn leather sofas and pews around all sorts of tables on bare boards, a fine collection of rare enamel signs and antique brewery mirrors, and old prints, framed cigarette cards and lots of old wine bottles and soda siphons; a big flat-screen TV (for rugby only) and background music. There's a constantly changing range of real ales, craft beers, fruit beers, lagers and ciders, and they always feature local Larkins Traditional and Tonbridge Coppernob on handpump; also, 16 wines by the glass and a wide choice of spirits. Downstairs is the informal fish restaurant with its bistro-style décor; from here, french windows lead on to an inviting suntrap deck with wicker and chrome chairs around wooden tables.

Food in the upstairs bar includes sandwiches, baguettes and tortilla wraps, grazing boards, honey-roasted ham and free-range eggs, caesar or quinoa salad, chilli con carne, local sausages and mash with onion gravy, smoked haddock, prawns and free-range eggs, beer-battered haddock and chips, and several ways of doing mussels. The excellent à la carte fish and shellfish menu is only served downstairs – our Food Award is for this. *Benchmark main dish: burgers with toppings and home-baked buns £7.00. Two-course evening meal £20.00.*

Free house ~ Licensee Matthew Sankey ~ Real ale ~ Open 12-1am; 12-11 Sun ~ Bar food 12-3, 6-10; 12-10 Sat; 12-8 Sun ~ Restaurant ~ Children welcome ~ Dogs allowed in bar ~ Wi-fi *Recommended by Edward May, Harvey Brown, Alfie Bayliss*

'Children welcome' means the pub says it lets children inside without any special restriction. If it allows them in, but to restricted areas such as an eating area or family room, we specify this. Some pubs may impose an evening time limit. We do not mention limits after 9pm as we assume children are home by then.

ULCOMBE
TQ8550 Map 3

Pepper Box

(01622) 842558 – www.thepepperboxinn.co.uk

Fairbourne Heath; signposted from A20 in Harrietsham, or follow Ulcombe signpost from A20, then turn left at crossroads with sign to pub, then right at next minor crossroads; ME17 1LP

Friendly country pub with lovely log fire, well liked food, fair choice of drinks and seats in a pretty garden

With attentive and convivial licensees welcoming both locals and visitors, this well run country pub is always deservedly busy. The homely bar has standing timbers and a few low beams (some hung with hops), copper kettles and pans on windowsills, and nice horsebrasses on the fireplace's bressumer beam; two leather sofas are set beside the splendid inglenook fireplace with its lovely log fire. A side area, furnished more functionally for eating, extends into the opened-up beamed dining room with a range in another inglenook and more horsebrasses. Shepherd Neame Master Brew and guests such as Early Bird and Whitstable Bay Pale Ale on handpump and 15 wines by the glass; background music. In summer, the hop-covered terrace and shrub-filled garden (looking out over a great plateau of rolling arable farmland) is just the place to relax after a walk along the nearby Greensand Way footpath. The village church is worth a look.

Well liked, interesting food includes lunchtime sandwiches, lamb and kaffir lime kebabs with chilli and mint yoghurt, chicken liver and pistachio parfait with pear and raisin chutney, courgettes baked and stuffed with pine nuts, tomato, mozzarella and basil, local sausages with mash and onion gravy, a pie of the day, crab cakes with red pepper and paprika and lime mayonnaise, chicken ballotine with tarragon butter, smoked bacon, mushrooms and marsala sauce, and puddings such as crème brûlée of the day and white chocolate and Baileys cheesecake. *Benchmark main dish: five-spice duck in honey with stir-fried noodles and vegetables in soy sauce £15.00. Two-course evening meal £19.00.*

Shepherd Neame ~ Tenant Sarah Pemble ~ Real ale ~ Open 11-3, 6-11; 12-5 Sun ~ Bar food 12-2.15, 6.30-9.30; 12-3 Sun ~ Restaurant ~ Children over 7 only ~ Dogs allowed in bar
Recommended by Martin Day, Peter Meister, Tina and David Woods-Taylor, Christian Mole, Quentin and Carol Williamson

WHITSTABLE
TR1066 Map 3

Pearsons Arms ♀

(01227) 773133 – www.pearsonsarmsbyrichardphillips.co.uk

Sea Wall off Oxford Street after road splits into one-way system; public parking on left as road divides; CT5 1BT

Seaside pub with an emphasis on imaginative food, several local ales and good mix of customers

This is a rewarding place for either a drink or an enjoyable meal. It's a weatherboarded, beachside pub with two front bars, divided by a central chimney: cushioned settles, captain's chairs and leather armchairs on a stripped-wood floor, driftwood walls and big flower arrangements on the bar counter. Nethergate Growler, Sharps Doom Bar, Timothy Taylors Landlord and Whitstable East India Pale Ale on handpump, 14 wines by the glass and an extensive choice of cocktails; background music. A cosy lower room has a bookcase mural and a couple of big chesterfields and dining chairs around plain tables on a stone floor. Up a couple of flights of stairs, the restaurant has sea views, mushroom-coloured paintwork, contemporary wallpaper, more driftwood and church chairs and pine tables on nice wide floorboards.

🍴 Good, interesting food includes lunchtime sandwiches, salmon ballotine with wasabi crème fraîche and pickled cucumber, pork terrine with apple purée and piccalilli, burger with toppings, sauce, coleslaw and chips, cod fillet with crispy cod cheek, confit potato and mussel and saffron broth, sea bream with lemon and sorrel gnocchi, caper dressing and crab and chive brown butter, and puddings such as chocolate and banana mousse with caramel-glazed bananas and hazelnut and caramel ice-cream and rhubarb and custard tart with rhubarb ripple ice-cream; they also offer a two- and three-course set lunch. *Benchmark main dish: fish pie £14.75. Two-course evening meal £20.50.*

Enterprise ~ Lease Jake Alder ~ Real ale ~ Open 12-midnight (11 Sun) ~ Bar food 12-2.30, 6.30-9.30 ~ Restaurant ~ Children welcome ~ Dogs allowed in bar ~ Wi-fi ~ Live music Tues, Sun evenings *Recommended by Adrian Johnson, Ian Herdman, Roy Hoing*

 WYE   TR0546   Map 3

Kings Head

(01233) 812418 – www.kingsheadwye.co.uk

Church Street; TN25 5BN

Simply furnished, bustling pub – good food, ales and wines by the glass – and bright bedrooms

---

At the top of the handsome high street close to the church, this is a bustling, friendly inn with a good mix of locals and visitors. The bare-boards bar is divided by a two-way log fire, with a long brown button-back wall banquette in one part and armchairs beside the fire on the other side by a glass-topped trunk table. There are low-backed button-back pale grey chairs around all sorts of tables and pale-painted high chairs beside the counter where they keep Shepherd Neame Spitfire and Whitstable Bay Pale Ale on handpump and six good wines by the glass, plus an array of olives, cheese straws, cupcakes and so forth; service is efficient and helpful. In one corner, there's a dresser where they sell flavoured olive oils and jams. The dining room has one long wall banquette and painted kitchen chairs around pine tables and an open fire at one end with a pile of logs to one side. Throughout, there are rustic, bare-board walls, church candles, photographs of the local area, daily papers and background jazz. There are seats in a small back courtyard and the bedrooms are airy and simply furnished.

🍴 Well liked food includes sandwiches, duck liver parfait with quail egg salad, crab croquettes with crab mayonnaise, lunchtime arnold bennett omelette, falafel with spiced yoghurt, tabbouleh and flatbread, ox cheek and smoked bacon pie, beer-battered fish and chips, slow-cooked barbecue ribs with coleslaw, chorizo baked beans and blue cheese and buttermilk dressing, and puddings such as rhubarb and custard trifle and lemon posset with blueberry compote. *Benchmark main dish: beer-battered fresh fish of the day and chips £12.00. Two-course evening meal £18.00.*

Shepherd Neame ~ Tenant Scott Richardson ~ Real ale ~ Open 7.30am-10pm; 7.30am-11pm Fri, Sat ~ Bar food 12-3, 6-9; 12-10 Sat; 12-7 Sun ~ Restaurant ~ Children welcome ~ Dogs welcome ~ Wi-fi ~ Live music Weds evening ~ Bedrooms: /£90 *Recommended by James Allsopp, Julie Braeburn, Tony Smaithe*

A few pubs try to make you leave a credit card at the bar, as a sort of deposit if you order food. This is a bad practice, and the banks and credit card firms warn you not to let your card go like this.

Also Worth a Visit in Kent

Besides the fully inspected pubs, you might like to try these pubs that have been recommended to us and described by readers. Do tell us what you think of them: feedback@goodguides.com

APPLEDORE   TQ9529

Black Lion (01233) 758206

The Street; TN26 2BU Bustling 1930s village pub with good generously served food (all day Fri-Sun), lamb from Romney Marsh and local fish, four or five well kept ales including Goachers, Biddenden cider, welcoming helpful staff, partitioned back eating area, log fire; background music, events such as bank holiday hog roasts; children welcome, tables out on green, attractive village and good Military Canal walks, open all day. *(Julie Swift)*

BADLESMERE   TR0154

Red Lion (01233) 740320

A251, S of M2 junction 6; ME13 0NX Spacious partly 16th-c roadside country pub run by mother and daughter, friendly local atmosphere, Gadds and two or three guests from hop-strung bar, enjoyable well priced home-made food (not Sun evening) using local produce, beams, bare boards and stripped brickwork, books and board games; background music, free wi-fi; children and dogs welcome, large garden with paddock for camping, closed Mon, otherwise open all day (till 7pm Sun). *(Thomas Green)*

BARHAM   TR2050

Duke of Cumberland (01227) 831396

The Street; CT4 6NY Open-plan pub close to village green, enjoyable home cooking including good Sun roasts, well kept Harveys, Greene King, Timothy Taylors and a guest, friendly staff, plain tables and chairs on bare boards or flagstones, hops and log fire; live music, quiz nights, board games and darts; children welcome, dogs in bar, garden with boules and play area, three bedrooms, handy for A2, open all day, food all day weekends. *(Jim Jacks)*

BEARSTED   TQ8055

Oak on the Green (01622) 737976

The Street; ME14 4EJ Well run pub with bustling friendly atmosphere, two hop-festooned bar areas, bare boards and half-panelling, wide choice of home-made food including some mexican dishes, a house beer from 1648, Fullers London Pride and two local guests, restaurant (they also own the smaller fish restaurant next door); children and dogs (in bar) welcome, disabled access, seats out at front under big umbrellas, open (and food) all day. *(Conor McGaughey)*

BENENDEN   TQ8032

★**Bull** (01580) 240054

The Street; by village green; TN17 4DE Relaxed informal atmosphere in bare-boards or dark terracotta-tiled rooms, pleasing mix of furniture, church candles on tables, log fire in brick inglenook, friendly hands-on licensees, ales such as Dark Star, Harveys, Larkins and Old Dairy from carved wooden counter, Biddenden cider, more formal dining room, tasty generously served food (not Sun evening) including speciality pies and popular Sun carvery, various offers; background music (live Thurs and Sun), quiz nights; children and dogs (in bar) welcome, picnic-sets out in front behind white picket fence, back garden, open all day. *(Peter and Emma Kelly)*

BETHERSDEN   TQ9240

George (01233) 820235

The Street; TN26 3AG Tile-hung village local with good buoyant atmosphere, well kept Brakspears, Harveys, Greene King Old Speckled Hen and a guest, generous sensibly priced food including good value carvery (Sun, Weds), large public bar with open fire, smaller lounge next to dining area; pool, free wi-fi; children and dogs welcome, open all day, no food Sun evening, Mon lunchtime. *(Tony and Wendy Hobden)*

BOUGH BEECH   TQ4846

★**Wheatsheaf** (01732) 700100

B2027, S of reservoir; TN8 7NU Attractive 14th-c pub with emphasis on good freshly cooked food including children's meals, three Westerham ales along with Harveys and good choice of wines, friendly attentive service, beams and timbering, bare boards and log fires (one in a huge fireplace), high ceilinged dining room, more tables upstairs; dogs welcome, nice outside seating area and good walks including circular one around Bough Beech Reservoir, open all day (food till 6pm Sun). *(Mrs J Ekins-Daukes, Martin Day, B J Harding, Christian Mole)*

BOXLEY   TQ7758

Kings Arms (01622) 755177

1 mile from M20 junction 7; opposite church; ME14 3DR Cosy dining pub in pretty village at foot of downs, largely 16th/17th-c, with good choice of traditional food from lunchtime baguettes to weekly specials, four well kept ales including

---

We say if we know a pub has background music.

Harveys and Thwaites, low black beams, red chesterfields by big brick fireplace; background music, monthly quiz; children and dogs welcome, picnic-sets and play area in appealing garden, good local walks, open (and food) all day. *(Martin Day)*

BOYDEN GATE   TR2265
★ **Gate Inn** (01227) 860498
Off A299 Herne Bay–Ramsgate – follow 'Chislet, Upstreet' sign opposite Roman Gallery; Chislet also signed off A28 Canterbury–Margate at Upstreet – after right turn into Chislet main street, keep right on to Boyden; CT3 4EB Rustic pub with unpretentious quarry-tiled bar rooms, cushioned pews around character tables, hop-strung beams, attractively etched windows and double aspect log fire, Shepherd Neame and occasional guests from tap room casks, popular sensibly priced pubby food including signature Gatewich sandwich, bare-boards restaurant in former bakery, woodburner; Weds quiz and some live folk nights; children and dogs (in bar) welcome, sheltered garden bounded by two streams, ducks and chickens, open (and food) all day weekends. *(Penny and David Shepherd)*

BRABOURNE   TR1041
★ **Five Bells** (01303) 813334
East Brabourne; TN25 5LP Popular 16th-c inn at foot of North Downs; opened-up interior with hop-strung beams, standing timbers and ancient brick walls, all manner of dining chairs and tables on stripped boards, wall seats here and there, two log fires, quirky decorations including candles in upturned bottles on the walls and a garland-draped mermaid figurehead, four well kept changing local ales, Biddenden cider and selection of kentish wines, well liked food from varied menu, friendly service, shop selling local produce, monthly arts and crafts market; some live music, unisex loos; children and dogs welcome, comfortable if eccentric bedrooms, open all day from 9am for breakfast. *(Richard and Penny Gibbs, Bob Hinchley)*

BRASTED   TQ4654
Stanhope Arms (01959) 561970
Church Road; TN16 1HZ Welcoming old village pub next to the church, Greene King ales and enjoyable pubby food (not Mon), cosy traditional bar with darts, bright cheerful restaurant; children and dogs welcome (resident labradors), back garden with summer barbecues and bat and trap, open all day. *(Alan Cowell)*

BRENCHLEY   TQ6841
★ **Halfway House** (01892) 722526
Horsmonden Road; TN12 7AX Beamed 18th-c inn with attractive mix of rustic and traditional furnishings on bare boards, old farm tools and other bric-a-brac, two log fires, cheerful staff and particularly friendly landlord, up to a dozen well kept changing

ales tapped from the cask, enjoyable traditional home-made food including popular Sun roasts, two eating areas; children and dogs welcome, picnic-sets and play area in big garden, summer barbecues and beer festivals, two bedrooms, open all day (no food Sun evening). *(Peter Meister)*

BROADSTAIRS   TR3868
Four Candles 07947 062063
Sowell Street; CT10 2AT Quirky one-room micropub in former shop, good selection of local beers chalked on blackboard including own brews, kentish wines, high tables and stools on sawdust floor, bucket lightshades and various odds and ends including pitchfork handles (the Two Ronnies' famous sketch was inspired by a Broadstairs ironmonger), local cheese and pork pies, friendly chatty service; closed weekday lunchtimes. *(Sandra Morgan)*

BROOKLAND   TQ9724
Woolpack (01797) 344321
On A259 from Rye, about a mile before Brookland, take the first right turn signposted Midley where the main road bends sharp left, just after the expanse of Walland Marsh; OS Sheet 189 map reference 977244; TN29 9TJ Welcoming 15th-c cottage refurbished under newish family management; lovely uneven brick floor in ancient entrance lobby, quarry-tiled main bar with low beams (thought to have come from local wrecks) and massive inglenook, dining room, good value generously served traditional food from sandwiches and baked potatoes up (no bookings), Shepherd Neame ales and several wines by the glass, pub cat; children welcome, picnic-sets in good-sized garden, open (and food) all day weekends. *(M and J White, DF and NF, Conrad Freezer, B and M Kendall)*

BURMARSH   TR1032
Shepherd & Crook (01303) 872336
Shear Way, next to church; TN29 0JJ Traditional 16th-c marshside village local with smuggling history; well kept Hop Fuzz, Old Dairy and maybe a guest, Weston's cider, good straightforward home-made food at low prices, prompt friendly service, interesting photographs and blow lamp collection, open fire; bar games, some live music; children and dogs welcome, seats on side terrace, closed Mon, Tues, otherwise open all day (Sun till 6pm). *(B and M Kendall)*

CANTERBURY   TR1458
Dolphin (01227) 455963
St Radigunds Street; CT1 2AA Busy modernised dining pub with plenty of tables in light spacious bar, enjoyable fairly traditional home-made food from baguettes up, Sharps Doom Bar, Timothy Taylors Landlord and guests such as Gadds, nice wines including country ones, friendly staff, bric-a-brac on delft shelf, board games,

flagstoned conservatory; free wi-fi; children welcome, dogs at management's discretion, disabled access, picnic-sets in good-sized back garden, open all day (food all day Sat). *(Julie Swift)*

CANTERBURY
TR1457
Foundry (01227) 455899
White Horse Lane; CT1 2RU Pub in former 19th-c iron foundry, light and airy interior on two floors, six Canterbury Brewers beers from visible microbrewery plus local guests, craft lagers and kentish cider, enjoyable well presented pubby food till 6pm including platters and good sandwiches, helpful cheerful staff; disabled access, small courtyard area, open all day (till late Fri, Sat). *(Martin Gowing)*

CANTERBURY
TR1457
Parrot (01227) 454170
Church Lane – the one off St Radigunds Street, 100 metres E of St Radigunds car park; CT1 2AG Ancient heavy-beamed pub with wood and flagstone floors, stripped masonry, dark panelling and big open fire, Shepherd Neame ales and well liked food including pre-theatre menu, extensive wine list, friendly service, upstairs vaulted restaurant; nicely laid out courtyard with central barbecue, open all day. *(Jim Jacks)*

CAPEL
TQ6444
Dovecote (01892) 835966
Alders Road; SE of Tonbridge; TN12 6SU Cosy pub in nice country surroundings with open fire, beams and some stripped brickwork, up to six cask-tapped ales including Harveys, Weston's cider, enjoyable well priced food (not Sun evening, Mon) from pitched-ceiling dining end, friendly helpful staff; live acoustic music Mon, quiz every other Weds; well behaved children allowed, no dogs inside, lots of picnic-sets in back garden with terrace and play area, bat and trap, open all day Tues-Sun, closed Mon. *(Martin Day)*

CHARTHAM
TR1054
Artichoke (01227) 738316
Rottington Street; CT4 7JQ Attractive timbered pub dating from the 15th c, enjoyable reasonably priced home-made food (till 5pm Sun) from sandwiches and baked potatoes up, OAP lunch deal, well kept Shepherd Neame ales, good service, carpeted log-fire bar, dining area with light wood tables (one built around a glass-topped well); quiz last Thurs of the month, darts and bat and trap; children welcome, picnic-sets in back garden, open all day. *(Christopher Mannings)*

CHIDDINGSTONE CAUSEWAY
TQ5247
Greyhound (01892) 870275
Charcott, off back road to Weald; TN11 8LG Updated red-brick village local with good food cooked by landlord-chef from pub favourites up, well kept Harveys and a couple of guests, friendly staff, log fire; children and dogs welcome, picnic-sets out in front and in garden, useful for walkers, open all day weekends. *(Martin Day)*

CHILHAM
TR0653
★**White Horse** (01227) 730355
The Square; CT4 8BY 15th-c pub in picturesque village square; handsome ceiling beams and massive fireplace with lancastrian rose carved on mantel beam, chunky light oak furniture on pale wood flooring and more traditional pubby furniture on quarry tiles, four well kept ales including a house beer from Canterbury Brewers, enjoyable food (all day Sat, not Sun evening) with more adventurous evening choices, amiable helpful service; live music and quiz nights; children welcome, dogs in bar (friendly pub alsatian is Sean), handy for the castle, open all day. *(Sandra Morgan)*

CHILLENDEN
TR2653
★**Griffins Head** (01304) 840325
SE end of village; 2 miles E of Aylesham; CT3 1PS Attractive 14th-c beamed and timbered pub surrounded by nice countryside, gently upscale local atmosphere in two bars and flagstoned back dining room, big log fire, full range of Shepherd Neame ales, good wine list and decent choice of popular home-made food, attentive friendly service; no under-8s, dogs welcome, summer weekend barbecues in pretty garden, vintage car meetings first Sun of the month, open all day. *(Thomas Green)*

CHIPSTEAD
TQ4956
★**Bricklayers Arms** (01732) 743424
Chevening Road; TN13 2RZ Attractive popular place overlooking lake and green, wide choice of good fairly priced pub food (not Sun evening), well kept Harveys from casks behind long counter, efficient cheerful service and relaxed chatty atmosphere, heavily beamed flagstoned bar with open fire and fine racehorse painting, larger back restaurant; Tues quiz and monthly live music; children and dogs welcome, seats out in front, open all day. *(Martin Day, Tina and David Woods-Taylor, Mr and Mrs A Dempster, Tony Scott)*

CONYER QUAY
TQ9664
Ship (01795) 520881
Conyer Road; ME9 9HR Renovated and extended 18th-c creekside pub owned by adjacent Swale Marina; bare boards and open fires, enjoyable home-cooked food including weekend breakfast from 10am, Adnams, Shepherd Neame and guests; live folk first and third Tues of month, jazz/blues dinner third Thurs; children and dogs welcome, useful for boaters, walkers (on Saxon Shore Way) and birders, seats out at front, open all day weekends (Sun till 9.30pm). *(Claire Adams)*

COWDEN TQ4640

Fountain (01342) 850528

Off A264 and B2026; High Street; TN8 7JG Good sensibly priced food from sandwiches up (not Sun evening) in attractive tile-hung beamed village pub, steps steps up to unpretentious dark-panelled bar, well kept Harveys and decent wines by the glass, friendly helpful staff, old photographs on cream walls, good log fire, mix of tables in adjoining room, woodburner in small back dining area with one big table; background music, Thurs quiz; children, walkers and dogs welcome, picnic-sets on small terrace and lawn, pretty village, open all day Sun. *(Jim Jacks)*

COWDEN TQ4642

★**Queens Arms** (01342) 850598

Cowden Pound; junction B2026 with Markbeech Road; TN8 5NP Friendly little Victorian time warp known as Elsie's after former long-serving landlady – present local owner has thankfully kept things much the same; two simple unpretentious rooms with open fires, a well kept/priced ale from Larkins, no food, darts, shove-ha'penny and other traditional games, piano, folk music (second and third Tues of month and some Sats), morris dancers and Christmas mummers; dogs welcome, open Mon, Tue 5-10.30pm, Weds, Thurs 5-7.30pm, Fri 5-9pm, Sat 5-7.30pm (longer if music), Sun 12-3pm. *(Tony Scott)*

CROCKHAM HILL TQ4450

Royal Oak (01732) 866335

Main Road; TN8 6RD Chatty old village pub owned by Westerham brewery, their ales kept well and good value fairly standard food (till 7pm Sun) from sandwiches and sharing plates up, friendly hard-working staff, mix of furniture including comfy leather sofas on stripped-wood floor, painted panelling, original Tottering-by-Gently cartoons and old local photographs, log fire in right-hand bar; occasional live music, darts; children, walkers and dogs welcome, small garden behind car park, handy for Chartwell (NT), open all day weekends. *(Malcolm and Jane Levitt)*

CRUNDALE TR0949

★**Compasses** (01227) 700300

Sole Street; CT4 7ES Welcoming country pub with really good imaginative food cooked by landlord-chef using local ingredients including good value set lunch, well kept Shepherd Neame ales and maybe a guest, traditional interior with hop-strung beams and woodburner in brick inglenook, back restaurant; children, walkers and dogs (in bar) welcome, big garden with play equipment, closed Mon (including bank holidays), otherwise open all day (till 6pm Sun). *(Julie Swift)*

DARGATE TR0761

Dove (01227) 751360

Village signposted from A299; ME13 9HB Tucked-away 18th-c restauranty pub with rambling rooms, good food (some quite expensive), Shepherd Neame ales and guests, nice wines by the glass, efficient pleasant service, plenty of stripped-wood tables, woodburner in brick and stone fireplace; live music last Fri of month; children, walkers and dogs welcome, sheltered garden with bat and trap, summer classic car meetings, open all day Fri, Sat. *(Peter and Emma Kelly)*

DARTFORD TQ5473

Malt Shovel (01322) 224381

Darenth Road; DA1 1LP Cheerful 17th-c waney-boarded pub with two traditional bars and conservatory, well kept St Austell, Youngs, and a guest, good generously served home-made food lunchtimes (not Mon, Tues) and Fri, Sat evenings, friendly helpful staff; free wi-fi; children and dogs welcome, tables on paved part-covered terrace, closed Mon lunchtime, otherwise open all day. *(Quentin and Carol Williamson, A N Bance)*

DEAL TR3751

Berry (01304) 362411

Canada Road; CT14 7EQ Small no-frills local opposite old Royal Marine barracks, welcoming enthusiastic landlord serving fine selection of well kept changing ales (tasting notes on slates, regular festivals), kentish farm cider and perry, no food, L-shaped carpeted bar with coal fire; Fri quiz, darts teams, pool and some live music; dogs welcome, small vine-covered back terrace, open all day (from 2pm Tues). *(Alan and Alice Morgan)*

DEAL TR3752

Bohemian (01304) 361939

Beach Street opposite pier; CT14 6HY Refurbished seafront bar with five real ales, around 70 bottled beers and huge selection of spirits, popular traditional home-made food including Sun roasts, friendly helpful staff, L-shaped room with mismatched furniture (some découpage tables), polished wood floor, lots of pictures, mirrors, signs and other odds and ends (customers encouraged to donate items), sofas and weekend papers, similar décor in upstairs cocktail bar with good sea views; background music; children and dogs welcome, sunny split-level deck behind and heated smokers' gazebo, open all day (from 9am Sun) and can get very busy, particularly at weekends. *(Alan and Alice Morgan)*

DEAL TR3752

Just Reproach 07432 413226 .

King Street; CT14 6HX Popular and genuinely welcoming micropub in former corner shop; simple drinking room with sturdy tables on bare boards, stools and cushioned benches, friendly knowledgeable service from father and daughter team, three or four changing small brewery ales tapped from the cask, also real ciders and some organic wines, locally made cheese, friendly chatty atmosphere; no mobile phones; dogs welcome, closed Sun evening. *(Alan and Alice Morgan, Jim Jacks)*

DEAL   TR3753
Prince Albert *(01304) 375425*
Middle Street; CT14 6LW Compact 19th-c corner pub in conservation area, bowed entrance doors, etched-glass windows and fairly ornate interior with assorted bric-a-brac, three changing local ales, popular food especially Sun carvery in back dining area, friendly staff; small garden behind, bedrooms, closed lunchtimes except Sun, no food Mon, Tues. *(Jim Jacks)*

DEAL   TR3753
Ship *(01304) 372222*
Middle Street; CT14 6JZ Traditional dimly lit two-room local in historic maritime quarter; five well kept ales including Dark Star and Ramsgate served by friendly landlord, no food, bare boards and lots of dark woodwork, stripped brick and local ship and wreck pictures, evening candles, cosy panelled back bar, open fire and woodburner; live music Thurs; dogs welcome, small pretty walled garden, open all day. *(Alan and Alice Morgan)*

DOVER   TR3241
Blakes *(01304) 202194*
Castle Street; CT16 1PJ Small flagstoned cellar bar down steep steps, brick and flint walls, dim lighting, woodburner, Adnams and six changing guests, farm ciders and perries, over 50 malt whiskies and several wines by the glass, decent lunchtime bar food from sandwiches up, panelled carpeted upstairs restaurant (food all day), friendly staff; well behaved children welcome, dogs in bar, side garden and suntrap back terrace, four bedrooms, open all day. *(Christopher Mannings)*

DUNGENESS   TR0916
Pilot *(01797) 320314*
Battery Road; TN29 9NJ Single-storey, mid 20th-c seaside café-bar by shingle beach; well kept Adnams, Courage, Harveys and a guest, decent choice of good value food from nice sandwiches to fish and chips, friendly efficient service (even when packed), open-plan interior divided into three areas, dark plank panelling (including the slightly curved ceiling), lighter front part overlooking beach,

prints and local memorabilia, books for sale (proceeds to RNLI); background music, free wi-fi; children welcome, picnic-sets in side garden, open all day till 10pm (9pm Sun). *(M and J White, B and M Kendall)*

DUNKS GREEN   TQ6152
★Kentish Rifleman *(01732) 810727*
Dunks Green Road; TN11 9RU Relaxing Tudor country pub with bare-boards bar and two carpeted dining areas, rifles on low beams, cosy log fire, well kept ales such as Harveys, Tonbridge, Westerham and Whitstable, Biddenden cider, enjoyable reasonably priced food (service charge added) from light meals to popular Sun roasts, friendly efficient staff; children and dogs welcome, tables in pretty garden with well, good walks from the door, one bedroom, open all day Fri-Sun, no food Sun or Mon evenings. *(Malcolm and Jane Levitt, Bob and Margaret Holder, B and M Kendall)*

EAST PECKHAM   TQ6548
Man of Kent *(01622) 871345*
Tonbridge Road; TN12 5LA Traditional tile-hung pub dating from the 16th c, low black beams, mix of pubby furniture on carpet or slate tiles, fresh flowers, big two-way woodburner in central fireplace, ales such as Harveys, Timothy Taylors, Tonbridge and Sharps, enjoyable well priced home-made food (all day Sat, not Sun evening) from sandwiches and pizzas up; children welcome, terrace seating by River Bourne, nearby walks, open all day. *(Phil and Jane Hodson)*

FAVERSHAM   TR0161
Bear *(01795) 532668*
Market Place; ME13 7AG Traditional late Victorian Shepherd Neame pub (back part dates from the 16th c), their ales kept well and occasional guests, pubby lunchtime food (evenings Tues-Thurs), friendly relaxed atmosphere, locals' front bar, snug and back dining lounge (all off side corridor); quiz last Mon of month, free wi-fi; a couple of pavement tables, open all day. *(Conor McGaughey)*

FAVERSHAM   TR0160
Elephant *(01795) 590157*
The Mall; ME13 8JN Well run traditional town pub, friendly and chatty, with four or five good changing ales mainly from smaller Kent brewers, a local cider too, no food (can bring your own), single bare-boards bar with central log fire and cosy seating areas, dim lighting; juke box and some live music, games machine; children and dogs welcome, peaceful suntrap back garden with pond,

---

Real ale may be served from handpumps, electric pumps (not just the on-off switches used for keg beer) or – common in Scotland – tall taps called founts (pronounced 'fonts') where a separate pump pushes the beer up under air pressure.

open all day Sat, till 7pm Sun, from 3pm weekdays, closed Mon. *(Claire Adams)*

FAVERSHAM TR0161
Sun (01795) 535098
West Street; ME13 7JE Rambling 15th-c pub in pedestrianised street, unpretentious feel in small low-ceilinged partly panelled rooms, scrubbed tables and big inglenook, well kept Shepherd Neame ales and enjoyable bar food, smart restaurant attached; unobtrusive background music; wheelchair access possible (small step), pleasant back courtyard, eight bedrooms, open all day. *(Sam Phillips)*

FAVERSHAM TR0161
Vaults (01795) 591817
Preston Street; ME13 8PA Centrally placed old pub (more spacious than it looks) with half a dozen well kept ales (at least one local) and a couple of real ciders, cheerful helpful staff, enjoyable good value food (all day Fri, Sat and till 4pm Sun) including nice steaks and carve-your-own Sun roasts; quiz and curry first Mon of the month, traditional games; children and dogs welcome, big back garden, open all day. *(Ben Martin)*

FINGLESHAM TR3353
★ Crown (01304) 612555
Just off A258 Sandwich–Deal; The Street; CT14 0NA Popular neatly kept low-beamed country local dating from the 16th c, good value generous home-made food from usual pub dishes to interesting specials, afternoon tea, friendly helpful service, well kept local ales such as Ramsgate, Biddenden cider, softly lit split-level carpeted bar with stripped stone and inglenook log fire, two other attractive dining rooms; children and dogs welcome, lovely big garden with play area and bat and trap, campsite, open all day Fri-Sun. *(Peter and Emma Kelly)*

FOLKESTONE TR2336
British Lion (01303) 251478
The Bayle, near churchyard; CT20 1SQ Popular 18th-c flower-decked pub nestling behind parish church, comfortable and cosy, with four well kept ales and a couple of real ciders, big helpings of good value traditional food, friendly helpful service; children welcome, tables out in small yard, open all day Sun. *(Sandra Morgan)*

FORDCOMBE TQ5240
Chafford Arms (01892) 731731
B2188, off A264 W of Langton Green; TN3 0SA Picturesque 19th-c tile-hung pub, well kept Harveys and Larkins, enjoyable pubby food from sandwiches and baguettes up, lounge bar, locals' bar (dogs allowed – their black lab is Charlie) and dining room; free wi-fi; children welcome, picnic-sets on front terrace and in attractive sheltered back garden with Weald views, 1930s telephone

box in car park, closed Sun evening, Mon lunchtime, otherwise open all day. *(Tony Scott)*

FORDWICH TR1759
George & Dragon (01227) 710661
Off A28 at Sturry; CT2 0BX Handsome old Home Counties pub on the banks of the River Stour in Britain's smallest town; spreading character rooms with beams and timbers, rugs on polished boards or flagstones, assortment of nice old chairs and tables (one a giant bellows), armchairs either side of open fire, Phoenix Brunning & Price, Shepherd Neame and guests, good wines by the glass and well liked brasserie-style food, pleasant helpful staff; children and dogs welcome, disabled access/facilities, picnic-sets and a play tractor in garden, open (and food) all day. *(Penny and David Shepherd)*

FRITTENDEN TQ8141
Bell & Jorrocks (01580) 852415
Corner of Biddenden Road/The Street; TN17 2EJ Simple 18th-c tile-hung and beamed village local, well kept Harveys, Woodfordes Wherry and a couple of guests (Apr beer festival), Weston's and Thatcher's ciders, good home-made food (not Sun evening, Mon, Tues), friendly welcoming atmosphere, log fire with propeller from german bomber above; live music and other events, sports TV, kentish darts; children and dogs welcome, open all day. *(Sam Phillips)*

GOODNESTONE TR2554
★ Fitzwalter Arms (01304) 840303
The Street; NB this is in E Kent not the other Goodnestone; CT3 1PJ Old lattice-windowed beamed village pub, rustic bar with wood floor and open fire, Shepherd Neame ales and local wines, carpeted dining room with another fire, enjoyable reasonably priced home-made food (not Sun evening), friendly service; shove-ha'penny and bar billiards; well behaved children and dogs welcome, terrace with steps up to peaceful garden, lovely church next door and close to Goodnestone Park Gardens, three bedrooms, open all day. *(Julie Swift)*

GOUDHURST TQ7337
Goudhurst Inn (01580) 212605
Junction of A262 and B2084; TN17 1DX Refurbished Victorian roadside pub under newish owners, light modern interior, enjoyable food from pub favourites up, three well kept ales, good choice of wines including some from own nearby Hush Heath vineyard (also make their own cider), friendly young aproned staff, bare-boards bar, restaurant and dining conservatory; live music last Fri of month, big-screen TV for major sports; children and dogs welcome, Weald view from paved terrace with pizza/barbecue shack, four comfortable bedrooms, good breakfast, open all day from 7am. *(Alf Wright)*

GOUDHURST TQ7237
Star & Eagle (01580) 211512
High Street; TN17 1AL Steps up to
striking medieval building, now a small hotel,
next to the church; settles and Jacobean-
style seats in heavily beamed open-plan
carpeted areas, log fires, intriguing smuggling
history, good choice of enjoyable food
(some prices on the high side), well kept
Brakspears, Harveys and Wychwood, friendly
if not always speedy service, restaurant;
children welcome, no dogs inside, tables out
at back with lovely views, attractive village,
11 character bedrooms, good breakfast, open
all day. *(Allan Lloyd and family)*

GROOMBRIDGE TQ5337
★ Crown (01892) 864742
B2110; TN3 9QH Charming tile-hung
wealden inn with snug low-beamed bar,
old tables on worn flagstones, panelling,
bric-a-brac, fire in sizeable brick inglenook,
well kept Harveys, Larkins and a guest,
enjoyable food (all day Sat, till 7pm Sun)
from traditional choices up including plenty
of gluten-free options, good friendly service,
refurbished two-room restaurant with
smaller inglenook; background music, free
wi-fi; children and dogs (in bar) welcome,
tables on narrow brick terrace overlooking
steep green, more seats in garden behind,
four bedrooms, handy for Groombridge Place
gardens, open all day. *(Martin Day, D Marsh,
Hunter and Christine Wright)*

HAWKHURST TQ7531
★ Great House (01580) 753119
*Gills Green; pub signed off A229 N;
TN18 5EJ* Stylish white-weatherboarded
restauranty pub (part of the Elite group);
good variety of well liked if not always cheap
food, ales such as Harveys, Old Dairy and
Sharps from marble counter, polite efficient
service, sofas, armchairs and bright scatter
cushions in chatty bar, stools against counter
used by locals, dark wood dining tables and
smartly upholstered chairs on slate floor
beside log fire, steps down to airy dining
room with Aga (they cook on it) and doors
out to terrace; background music, jazz
afternoons and other events; children and
dogs (in bar) welcome, open all day (food all
day weekends). *(Nicci Carruthers)*

HAWKHURST TQ7630
Queens (01580) 754233
Rye Road (A268 E); TN18 4EY Fine
Georgian fronted inn (building actually
dates to the 16th c) set back from the road;
revamped main bar with heavy beams and
bare boards, some barrel tables with high
modern chairs, armchairs either side of

inglenook woodburner, dining area and
cosy snug, well liked food from bar meals
up, ales such as Old Dairy, Rockin Robin
and Sharps, decent wines by the glass,
good friendly service, separate restaurant
to left of entrance with another inglenook;
background music; children welcome, tables
out in front, seven refurbished bedrooms,
open all day. *(Edwina Watts)*

HERNE TR1865
Butchers Arms (01227) 371000
Herne Street (A291); CT6 7HL
The UK's first micropub (converted from a
butchers in 2005), up to half a dozen well
kept changing ales (mainly local) tapped
from backroom casks, tasters offered by
friendly former motorbike-racing landlord,
good local cheeses, just a couple of benches
and butcher's-block tables (seats about
ten), lots of bric-a-brac; dogs welcome,
disabled access, tables out under awning,
open 12-1.30pm, 6-9pm, closed Sun evening,
Mon. *(Thomas Green)*

HERNHILL TR0660
Red Lion (01227) 751207
*Off A299 via Dargate, or A2 via
Boughton Street and Staplestreet;
ME13 9JR* Pretty Tudor pub by church
and attractive village green, some recent
refurbishment under new management but
keeping character; densely beamed with
antique-style tables and chairs on flagstones
or parquet, log fires, fairly traditional food
from sharing boards up using local produce,
well kept ales such as Sharps and Shepherd
Neame, decent wines, friendly helpful staff,
upstairs restaurant; soft background music;
children and dogs welcome, seats in front
and in big garden, open all day. *(Christopher
Mannings)*

HEVER TQ4743
Greyhound (01732) 862221
Uckfield Lane; TN8 7LJ This welcoming
19th-c country pub was being renovated
after a fire as we went to press – it should
have reopened by the time you read this; has
served good value food and three well kept
ales such as Harveys; handy for Hever Castle,
reports please.

HEVER TQ4744
Henry VIII (01732) 862457
By gates of Hever Castle; TN8 7NH
Predominantly 17th-c with some fine oak
panelling, wide floorboards and heavy beams,
inglenook fireplace, Henry VIII touches
to décor, emphasis on enjoyable mainly
traditional food from baguettes up, well kept
Shepherd Neame ales, friendly efficient staff,
restaurant; no dogs even in garden; outside

Half pints: by law, a pub should not charge more for half a pint than half the price
of a full pint, unless it shows that half-pint price on its price list.

covered area with a couple of leather sofas, steps down to deck and pondside lawn, bedrooms, open all day. *(Tony Scott)*

HIGH HALDEN TQ8937
Chequers (01233) 850503
A28, Ashford Road; TN26 3LP
Atmospheric 17th-c pub under same ownership as the Oak on the Green at Bearsted; hop-draped beams, rustic dining tables on bare boards, log fire, generous helpings of enjoyable food from extensive menu including lunchtime deal, changing ales, friendly service; children and dogs welcome, open (and food) all day. *(Thomas Green)*

HODSOLL STREET TQ6263
Green Man (01732) 823575
Signed off A227 S of Meopham; turn right in village; TN15 7LE Friendly family-run village pub with traditional furnishings in neat mainly carpeted rooms around central bar, painted half-panelling, old framed photographs and woodburner in standalone fireplace, Harveys, Sharps, Timothy Taylors and a guest, wide choice of enjoyable blackboard food from sandwiches/baguettes up including popular two-course weekday lunch deal; background and live music, quiz Mon, free wi-fi; children and dogs welcome, picnic-sets in front overlooking small green, more tables and climbing frame on back lawn, open (and food) all day Fri-Sun. *(Mrs J Ekins-Daukes)*

HOLLINGBOURNE TQ8455
Dirty Habit (01622) 880880
B2163, off A20; ME17 1UW
Ancient dimly lit beamed pub in Elite Pubs group (as are the Great House in Hawkhurst, Gun at Gun Hill etc); ales including Harveys and Shepherd Neame, several wines by the glass and popular food (all day weekends) served by friendly staff, main bar area with armchairs and stools on slate floor, panelled end room with mix of tables and chairs, low beamed dining room and a further raftered eating area with brick floor and woodburner; children welcome, good outside shelter with armchairs and sofas, on North Downs Way (leaflets for walkers) and handy for Leeds Castle, open all day. *(Penny and David Shepherd)*

HOLLINGBOURNE TQ8354
★Windmill (01622) 889000
M20 junction 8, A20 towards Lenham then left on to B2163 – Eyhorne Street; ME17 1TR Most people here for the impressive food but there is a small back bar serving Sharps Doom Bar, a guest beer and up to 15 wines by the glass; light and airy main room with white-painted beams, animal skins on bare boards and log fire in low inglenook, mix of furniture including armchairs, heavy settles with scatter cushions, red leather banquette and dark wood dining tables and

chairs, two further dining rooms (steps up to one), candles and fresh flowers; background music (live Weds), free wi-fi; children and dogs (in bar) welcome, back terrace, summer barbecues, open all day. *(Alan Cowell, Martin Day, Miss A E Dare)*

IDE HILL TQ4851
Cock (01732) 750310
Off B2042 SW of Sevenoaks; TN14 6JN Pretty village-green local dating from the 15th c, chatty and friendly, with two recently refurbished bars (steps between), Greene King ales and a beer badged for the pub, enjoyable well priced traditional food, cosy in winter with good inglenook log fire; children and dogs welcome, picnic-sets out at front, handy for Chartwell (NT) and nearby walks, open all day. *(Paul Scott)*

IDEN GREEN TQ8031
★Woodcock (01580) 240009
Not the Iden Green near Goudhurst; village signed off A268 E of Hawkhurst and B2086 at W edge of Benenden; in village follow Standen Street sign, then fork left into Woodcock Lane; TN17 4HT Part-weatherboarded 17th-c country pub in quiet spot with good surrounding walks; low-ceilinged bar with a couple of big standing timbers, stripped-brick walls hung with horse tack, inglenook woodburner, Greene King ales and a guest, seven wines by the glass, enjoyable food including blackboard specials, small panelled dining room; free wi-fi; children and dogs (in bar) welcome, pretty cottage garden, open all day, till 7pm Sun, closed Mon lunchtime. *(Conrad Freezer)*

IGHTHAM TQ5956
★George & Dragon (01732) 882440
The Street, A227; TN15 9HH Ancient half-timbered pub with bright spacious interior, enjoyable if not particularly cheap food from snacks to daily specials, well kept Shepherd Neame ales and decent wines, friendly attentive staff, sofas among other furnishings in long main bar, heavy-beamed end room, woodburner and open fires, restaurant; children and dogs welcome, back terrace, handy for Ightham Mote (NT), good walks, open all day from 10am for breakfast, no food Sun evening. *(Bob and Margaret Holder, Alan Cowell, Gordon and Margaret Ormondroyd, Quentin and Carol Williamson)*

IGHTHAM COMMON TQ5855
★Harrow (01732) 885912
Signposted off A25 just W of Ightham; pub sign may be hard to spot; TN15 9EB Smart and comfortable with emphasis on good imaginative food from daily changing menu, also some traditional choices and Sunday roasts, relaxed cheerful bar area to the right with candles and fresh flowers, dining chairs on herringbone wood floor, winter fire, charming little antiquated conservatory and more formal dining room,

well kept Loddon and nice wines by the glass; background music; children welcome (not in dining room Sat evening), pretty little pergola-enclosed back terrace, handy for Ightham Mote (NT), closed Sun evening to Weds. *(Jim Jacks)*

IGHTHAM COMMON   TQ5955
Old House (01732) 886077
Redwell, S of village; OS Sheet 188 map reference 591559; TN15 9EE Basic two-room country local tucked down narrow lane, no inn sign, beams, bare bricks and huge inglenook, half a dozen interesting changing ales from tap room casks, no food; darts; dogs welcome, closed weekday lunchtimes, opens 7pm and may shut early if quiet. *(Sandra Morgan)*

KENNINGTON   TR0245
Old Mill (01223) 661000
Mill Lane; TN25 4DZ Updated and much extended dining pub dating from the early 19th c (same owners as the Oak on the Green at Bearsted); good choice of generously served food (some quite expensive), also lighter appetites menu Mon-Thurs till 5pm, a house beer from 1648, Fullers London Pride and local guests, good friendly service; children welcome, plenty of terrace and garden seating, open (and food) all day. *(Thomas Green)*

KILNDOWN   TQ7035
Globe & Rainbow (01892) 890803
Signed off A21 S of Lamberhurst; TN17 2SG Welcoming pub with small cheerful bar serving Harveys, guest ales and well chosen wines, bare-boards dining room with woodburner, enjoyable freshly made food from snacks up; children and dogs welcome, country views from decking out by cricket pitch, open all day Tues-Sat, till 7pm Sun, closed Mon. *(Claire Adams)*

KINGSDOWN   TR3748
Kings Head (01304) 373915
Upper Street; CT14 8BJ Tucked-away split-level local with two cosy bars and L-shaped extension (children welcome here), black timbers, lots of old photographs on faded cream walls, a few vintage amusement machines, woodburner, Greene King IPA and two mainly local guests, popular reasonably priced food including blackboard specials, friendly landlord and staff; background and occasional live music, darts; dogs welcome, small side garden, skittle alley, open all day Sun, closed weekdays till 5pm. *(Thomas Green)*

KINGSTON   TR2051
Black Robin (01227) 830230
Elham Valley Road, off A2 S of Canterbury at Barham signpost; CT4 6HS Refurbished 18th-c pub named after a notorious highwayman who was hanged nearby; kentish ales and good helpings of enjoyable home-made food

from shortish menu (can eat in bar or back restaurant extension), friendly helpful staff; background and live music including some established folk artists, quiz second Tues of month, sports TV; children and dogs welcome, disabled access, seats out on decking, open all day (till midnight Fri, Sat). *(Alan and Alice Morgan)*

LADDINGFORD   TQ6848
Chequers (01622) 871266
The Street; ME18 6BP Friendly old beamed and weatherboarded village pub with good sensibly priced food from sandwiches and sharing boards up, some themed nights, well kept Adnams Southwold and three guests (Apr beer festival); children and dogs welcome, big garden with play area, shetland ponies in paddock, Medway walks nearby, one bedroom, open all day weekends. *(Jim Jacks)*

LAMBERHURST   TQ6735
Vineyard (01892) 890222
Lamberhurst Down; S of village signed off A21; TN3 8EU Pretty 17th-c dining pub by green and vineyards, same ownership as the Great House in Hawkhurst (Elite Pubs); main bar has most character with a few stools by counter serving Harveys, Sharps and a guest, log fire in brick fireplace with boar's head above, wall banquette draped with animal hide, cushioned leather armchairs and mix of dining furniture on flagstones or bare boards, enjoyable bistro-style food (all day Fri-Sun), friendly staff, long narrow room off with similar tables and chairs, equestrian pictures and antlers over fireplace, large ham for carving, sketched wallpaper of local landmarks, more formal panelled restaurant; seats and tables on terrace by car park, bedroom extension, open all day. *(Mrs Margo Finlay, Jörg Kasprowski, Martin Day)*

LEIGH   TQ5646
Plough (01732) 832149
Powder Mill Lane/Leigh Road, off B2027 NW of Tonbridge; TN11 9AJ Attractive opened-up Tudor country pub, lattice windows, hop-strung beams and parquet flooring, some cushioned pews and farmhouse chairs, massive grate in two-way inglenook, well kept Tonbridge Coppernob and up to three local guests, popular home-cooked food, friendly helpful staff, small flagstoned room behind servery with old mangle and darts; quiz third Thurs of month; children and dogs welcome, picnic-sets in garden with play area, old barn for weddings and other functions, open all day Sun till 9pm, closed Mon-Weds. *(Peter and Emma Kelly)*

LINTON   TQ7550
Bull (01622) 743612
Linton Hill (A229 S of Maidstone); ME17 4AW Comfortably modernised 17th-c dining pub; good choice of food from sandwiches and light dishes to pub favourites

and grills, popular Sun carvery, fine fireplace in nice old beamed bar, carpeted restaurant, well kept Shepherd Neame ales, friendly efficient service; children and dogs (in bar) welcome, side garden overlooking church, splendid far-reaching views from back decking, two gazebos, open all day. *(Claire Adams)*

LITTLE CHART   TQ9446
Swan (01233) 840011

The Street; TN27 0QB Attractive 15th-c village pub under new management; notable arched Dering windows, open fires and clean fresh décor in unspoilt front bar and good-sized dining area, flowers on tables, enjoyable home-made food, three well kept beers such as Old Dairy and decent wines by the glass, friendly staff; children and dogs (in bar) welcome, nice riverside garden, closed Mon, otherwise open all day (till 10pm Sun). *(Miss A E Dare)*

LOWER HARDRES   TR1453
⋆**Granville** (01227) 700402

Faussett Hill, Street End; B2068 S of Canterbury; CT4 7AL Spacious pub freshened up under new management; contemporary furnishings in several linked areas, one with unusual central fire under large conical hood, also a proper public bar with farmhouse chairs, settles and woodburner, enjoyable food (not Sun evening) from baguettes and pub favourites to more restauranty dishes (booking advised), good value set lunch, up to three Shepherd Neame ales including Master Brew, 13 wines by the glass, friendly helpful staff; background music, maybe live jazz Tues, artwork for sale; children and dogs welcome, seats on small sunny terrace and in garden under large spreading tree, open all day. *(Alan Cowell)*

LUDDESDOWNE   TQ6667
⋆**Cock** (01474) 814208

Henley Street, N of village – OS Sheet 177 map reference 664672; off A227 in Meopham, or A228 in Cuxton; DA13 0XB Early 18th-c country pub under friendly long-serving no-nonsense landlord, at least six ales such as Adnams, Goachers, St Austell and one brewed for the pub by local Musket brewery, german beers too, a small selection of straightforward food including large filled rolls and basket meals, rugs on polished boards in pleasant bay-windowed lounge, beams and panelling, quarry-tiled locals' bar, woodburners, pews and other miscellaneous furnishings, aircraft pictures, masses of beer mats and bric-a-brac ranging from stuffed animals to model cars, back dining conservatory; Tues quiz, bar billiards and darts; no children inside or on part-covered heated back terrace, dogs

welcome, big secure garden, good walks, open all day. *(Thomas Green)*

LYDDEN   TR2645
Bell (01304) 830296

Canterbury Road (B2060 NW of Dover); CT15 7EX Welcoming busy dining pub with good choice of well cooked interesting food along with pub favourites, meal deals including popular Weds grill night (must book), well kept ales such as Sharps, friendly attentive staff, carpeted beamed bar with scrubbed pine tables, woodburner in large brick fireplace, restaurant; ale and cheese festival June, skittle alley; children welcome, picnic-sets in big sloping garden with play equipment, handy for A2, open (and food) all day Sun. *(Peter Meister)*

MARDEN   TQ7547
Stile Bridge (01622) 831236

Staplehurst Road (A229); TN12 9BH Friendly roadside pub with five well kept ales and lots of bottled beers, proper ciders too and extensive range of gins, good traditional food; events including beer festivals, live music and comedy nights; dogs welcome in bar, back garden, open all day (till 7pm Sun). *(Sam Phillips)*

MARGATE   TR3570
Lifeboat 07837 024259

Market Street; CT9 1EU Corner ale and cider house with cosy dimly lit front bar, barrel tables on sawdust floor, larger back room with open fire, stillage-served local beers and excellent choice of kentish ciders/perries, good value food including locally sourced cheeses, sausages, pies and seafood, friendly helpful service; regular live music, quiz Weds; seats out at front, handy for Turner Contemporary, open all day. *(Kevin, Peter Meister)*

MATFIELD   TQ6642
Poet at Matfield (01892) 722416

Maidstone Road; TN12 7JH Attractively refurbished 17th-c beamed pub-restaurant named for Siegfried Sassoon who was born nearby; south african chef cooking good food from interesting varied menu (can be pricey and they add a service charge), ales such as Old Dairy and Tonbridge, nice wines and kentish gins, friendly efficient staff; open all day from 9.30am, closed Sun evening. *(Martin Day)*

MERSHAM   TR0438
Farriers Arms (01233) 720444

The Forstal/Flood Street; TN25 6NU Large opened-up community-owned pub, beers from own microbrewery including seasonal ales, enjoyable home-made food from sandwiches to daily specials, children's

---

There are report forms at the back of the book.

menu and some themed nights, restaurant; live music and other events including May beer festival; pleasant streamside garden behind, pleasant country views, open all day (till 1am Fri, Sat). *(Julie Swift)*

NEWENDEN   TQ8327
White Hart (01797) 252166
Rye Road (A268); TN18 5PN Popular 16th-c weatherboarded local; long low-beamed bar with big stone fireplace, dining areas off serving enjoyable reasonably priced pub food including good Sun roasts and themed evenings, well kept Harveys, Old Dairy, Rother Valley and guests, friendly helpful young staff, back games area with pool; background music, quiz nights, sports TV; children and dogs welcome, boules in large garden, near river (boat trips to NT's Bodiam Castle), six bedrooms, open all day. *(Sandra Morgan)*

NEWNHAM   TQ9557
★ George (01795) 890237
The Street; village signed from A2 W of Ospringe, outside Faversham; ME9 0LL Old pub with spreading open-plan rooms, beams, stripped brickwork and polished floorboards, candles and lamps on handsome tables, two inglenooks (one with woodburner), Shepherd Neame ales, real cider and ten wines by glass, well liked food; monthly live music; children welcome, seats in spacious tree-sheltered garden, James Pimm (creator of Pimms) was born in the village, closed Sun evening. *(Gerald and Brenda Culliford, Roger and Anne Newbury)*

NONINGTON   TR2551
Royal Oak (01304) 841012
Holt Street; CT15 4HT Cleanly refurbished village pub-restaurant set up from the road, friendly welcoming staff, good pub food including range of burgers and daily specials, four well kept beers such as Fullers, Sharps, Wantsum and Whitstable; some live music; children and dogs welcome, picnic-sets on front deck looking over to village pond, more seats and play area in nice back garden, summer barbecues and outside bar, open all day, food all day Sat, till 5pm Sun. *(Peter and Emma Kelly)*

NORTHBOURNE   TR3352
Hare & Hounds (01304) 369188
Off A256 or A258 near Dover; The Street; CT14 0LG Welcoming 17th-c village pub under newish management; good italian food including range of smaller plates, some pubby choices as well, two or three real ales such as Dark Star and Harveys from brick-faced servery, good choice of wines, bare-boards and flagstoned bar separated by a couple of archways, nice log fire; children and dogs welcome, paved terrace and garden with play area, closed Mon, otherwise open all day. *(Jim Jacks)*

OARE   TR0163
★ Shipwrights Arms (01795) 590088
S shore of Oare Creek, E of village; signed from Oare Road/Ham Road junction in Faversham; ME13 7TU Remote marshland tavern with plenty of character; three dark simple little bars separated by standing timbers, wood partitions and narrow door arches, medley of seats from tapestry-cushioned stools to black panelled built-in settles forming booths, flags and boating pennants on ceiling, wind gauge above main door (takes reading from chimney), up to six kentish beers tapped from the cask (pewter tankards over counter), simple home-cooked food (not Sun or Mon evening); background local radio; children (away from bar area) and dogs welcome, large garden with bat and trap, path along Oare Creek to Swale estuary, lots of surrounding bird life, closed Sun and Mon evenings. *(Penny and David Shepherd)*

OARE   TR0063
Three Mariners (01795) 533633
Church Road; ME13 0QA Comfortable simply restored 18th-c pub with good reputation for food including fresh fish, evening set menu option, Shepherd Neame ales and plenty of wines by the glass, beams, bare boards and log fire; children and dogs (in bar) welcome, attractive garden overlooking Faversham Creek, good walks, open all day. *(Colin McLachlan)*

OLD ROMNEY   TR0325
Rose & Crown (01797) 367500
Swamp Road off A259; TN29 9SQ Friendly bay-windowed pub with good value tasty food, well kept Greene King ales and Biddenden cider, helpful staff, dining conservatory; TV, pool and darts; children welcome, pretty garden with play area and boules, chalet bedrooms, Romney Marsh view, closed Sun evening, Mon and Tues, otherwise open all day. *(Sandra Morgan)*

PENSHURST   TQ4943
★ Rock (01892) 870296
Hoath Corner, Chiddingstone Hoath, on back road Chiddingstone–Cowden; OS Sheet 188 map reference 497431; TN8 7BS Tiny welcoming cottage with undulating brick floor, simple furnishings and woodburner in fine brick inglenook, well kept Larkins and good home-made food from varied menu, large stuffed bull's head for ring the bull, up a step to smaller room with long wooden settle by nice table; walkers and dogs welcome, picnic-sets out in front and on back lawn. *(Martin Day)*

PENSHURST   TQ5241
★ Spotted Dog (01892) 870253
Smarts Hill, off B2188 S; TN11 8EP Quaint weatherboarded pub first licensed in 1520 so plenty of signs of age; heavy low

beams and timbers, attractive moulded panelling, big inglenook fireplace, hops, horsebrasses and lots of country pictures, traditional furniture on bare boards or carpet, Harveys, Larkins, Tonbridge and Youngs, several wines by the glass, popular pubby food (not Sun evening); free wi-fi; children and dogs (in bar) welcome, terrace seating on several levels with good views over miles of countryside, open all day (till 10pm Sun). *(Mrs J Ekins-Daukes)*

PETT BOTTOM   TR1652
Duck (01227) 830354
Off B2068 S of Canterbury, via Lower Hardres; CT4 5PB Popular tile-hung pub in attractive downland spot; long bare-boards bar with scrubbed tables, pine panelling and two log fires, very good freshly cooked food (not Sun evening, Mon) including weekday set lunch, friendly helpful service, two or three well kept beers such as Old Dairy and Timothy Taylors Landlord, Biddenden cider and good wine choice; quiz last Sun of the month; children and dogs welcome, seats and old well out in front, garden behind where Ian Fleming used to sit making notes for his James Bond novels (see blue plaque), camping close by, shut Mon, otherwise open all day. *(Sam Phillips, Jim Jacks)*

PETTERIDGE   TQ6640
Hopbine (01892) 722561
Petteridge Lane; NE of village; TN12 7NE Unspoilt tiled and weatherboarded cottage in quiet hamlet, two small rooms with open fire between, traditional pubby furniture, hops and horsebrasses, three well kept local ales, enjoyable good value home-made food including wood-fired pizzas, friendly staff, steps up to simple back part with brick fireplace; outside gents'; terrace seating, open all day Fri-Sun. *(Christopher Mannings)*

PLAXTOL   TQ6054
★ Golding Hop (01732) 882150
Sheet Hill (0.5 miles S of Ightham, between A25 and A227); TN15 0PT Secluded old-fashioned country local with hands-on plain-talking landlord; simple dimly lit two-level bar, cask-tapped Adnams and guests kept well, local farm ciders (sometimes their own), short choice of basic good value bar food (not Mon or Tues evenings), old photographs of the pub, woodburners; bar billiards, portable TV for major sporting events; no children inside, suntrap streamside lawn and well fenced play area over lane, good walks; still for sale as we went to press. *(Thomas Green)*

PLUCKLEY   TQ9245
Black Horse (01233) 841948
The Street; TN27 0QS Attractive medieval pub behind Georgian façade (the Hare & Hounds in *The Darling Buds of May*); five log fires including vast inglenook, beams, bare boards and flagstones, dark half-panelling

and distinctive mullioned windows, ales such as Greene King, Harveys and Shepherd Neame, enjoyable traditional food from baguettes to good Sun roasts, Thurs steak night, friendly attentive service, roomy carpeted dining areas, Gatling machine gun by the loos; background music; children and dogs welcome, spacious informal garden by tall sycamores, play area, good local walks, open all day. *(Peter Meister)*

PLUCKLEY   TQ9144
Rose & Crown (01233) 840048
Mundy Bois – spelled Monday Boys on some maps – off Smarden Road SW of village centre; TN27 0ST Popular 17th-c tile-hung pub with good food (all day Sun) from french chef, three well kept beers such as Adnams and Harveys, friendly attentive service, main bar with massive inglenook, small snug and restaurant; background music, beer festival Aug; children and dogs welcome, pretty garden and terrace with views, play area, open all day. *(Caroline Prescott)*

RAMSGATE   TR3764
Artillery Arms (01843) 853202
West Cliff Road; CT11 9JS Old-fashioned little corner local on two levels, chatty and welcoming, with half a dozen well kept interesting beers, artillery prints/ memorabilia and fine listed windows depicting Napoleonic scenes; dogs welcome, wheelchair access, open all day. *(Jim Jacks)*

RAMSGATE   TR3764
Conqueror 07890 203282
Grange Road/St Mildred's Road; CT11 9LR Cosy single-room micropub in former corner shop, welcoming enthusiastic landlord serving three changing ales straight from the cask, also local cider and apple juice, friendly chatty atmosphere, large windows (may steam up when busy) and old photos of the cross-channel paddle steamer the pub is named after; dogs welcome, closed Sun evening, Mon. *(Claire Adams)*

RAMSGATE   TR3765
Great Tree (01843) 590708
Margate Road; CT11 7SP Quirky relaxed place with unusual café-bar décor, four real ales and 20 or so proper ciders, also interesting teas and good coffee, local artwork on show along with regular events including jazz, opera (puerto rican landlady is a trained singer), film and poetry evenings; children (away from the bar) and dogs welcome, closed Weds and weekday lunchtimes, open all day Sun. *(Simone Stream)*

RAMSGATE   TR3664
Sir Stanley Gray (01843) 599590
Pegwell Road; CT11 0NJ Over the road from the Pegwell Bay Hotel and connected by a tunnel; fine sea and coastline views from carpeted bar with plush seating and mock

beams, open fire, wide choice of popular food, friendly service, ales including local Gadds; regular live music, free wi-fi; children welcome, disabled access, terrace tables, open (and food) all day. *(Sam Phillips)*

RINGLESTONE TQ8755

Ringlestone Inn (01622) 859900
Ringlestone Road, signed Doddington off B2163 NE of Hollingbourne; ME17 1NX
Tucked-away former monks' hospice, an inn by 1615, furnished to match the antiquity of its worn brick floor, stripped masonry, sturdy beams and inglenook log fire, enjoyable if not particularly cheap food including range of pies, Shepherd Neame ales, farm cider, country wines and liqueurs; can get very busy in summer; children and well behaved dogs welcome, big attractive garden with play area, open all day Sat, till 5pm Sun, closed Tues. *(A N Bance)*

ROCHESTER TQ7468

Coopers Arms (01634) 404298
St Margaret's Street; ME1 1TL Ancient jettied building behind cathedral, cosily unpretentious with two comfortable beamed bars, low-priced pub food and good range of well kept beers, list of landlords back to 1543 and ghostly tales of a monk reputedly walled-up here (mannequin marks the spot); live music (Sun) and quiz nights; tables in attractive courtyard, open all day. *(Tony Scott)*

ROLVENDEN TQ8431

Bull (01580) 241212
Regent Street; TN17 4PB Welcoming tile-hung cottage with woodburner in fine brick inglenook, high-backed leather dining chairs around rustic tables on stripped boards, built-in panelled wall seats, ales from Harveys and Old Dairy, kentish wines and enjoyable food (not Sun evening in winter) from pub favourites and pizzas up, pale oak tables in dining room, friendly helpful service; background music; children and dogs (in bar) welcome, a few picnic-sets at front, more seats in sizeable back garden, open all day. *(Alan and Alice Morgan)*

ROLVENDEN LAYNE TQ8530

Ewe & Lamb (01580) 241837
Maytham Road; TN17 4NP Beamed, bare-boards pub with well kept Adnams, Harveys and a guest, enjoyable home-made food from baguettes up including lots of gluten-free choices, themed nights, friendly efficient service, back restaurant, log fires; children and dogs welcome, seats out at front behind white picket fence, open all day. *(V Brogden)*

SANDWICH TR3358

★**George & Dragon** (01304) 613106
Fisher Street; CT13 9EJ Popular 15th-c backstreet dining pub run by two brothers (one cooks), very good often imaginative food from open kitchen (booking advised), well kept Wantsum, Otter and a couple of guests,

nice choice of wines by the glass, good friendly service, open-plan beamed interior with blazing fire; children and dogs (in bar) welcome, pretty back terrace, open all day Sat, closed Sun evening. *(Di and Mike Gillam, Alan Casey)*

SARRE TR2564

Crown (01843) 847808
Ramsgate Road (A253) off A28; CT7 0LF Historic 15th-c inn (Grade I listed) sandwiched between two main roads; front bar and other rambling rooms including restaurant, beams and log fires, well kept Shepherd Neame ales and decent fairly priced wines, own cherry brandy (the pub is known locally as the Cherry Brandy House), generous helpings of enjoyable locally sourced food from sandwiches up, good friendly service; children welcome, side garden (traffic noise), comfortable surprisingly quiet bedrooms, open all day. *(Allan Lloyd and family)*

SEASALTER TR0864

★**Sportsman** (01227) 273370
Faversham Road, off B2040; CT5 4BP Restaurany dining pub just inside seawall – rather unprepossessing from outside but surprisingly light and airy; imaginative contemporary cooking using plenty of seafood (not Sun evening, Mon, must book and not cheap), home-baked breads, good wine choice including english, a couple of well kept Shepherd Neame ales, knowledgeable landlord and friendly staff; two plain linked rooms and long conservatory, scrubbed pine tables, wheelback and basket-weave dining chairs on wood floor, local artwork; children welcome, plastic glasses for outside, wide views over marshland with grazing sheep and (from seawall) across to Sheppey, small caravan park one side, wood chalets the other, open all day Sun. *(Martin Day)*

SELLING TR0455

Rose & Crown (01227) 752214
Follow Perry Wood signs; ME13 9RY Tucked-away traditional 16th-c country pub with beams and two inglenooks, well kept Adnams, Harveys and a guest, pub food from sandwiches up, friendly service, games such as cribbage and shut the box; background music, quiz first Weds of month; children welcome, dogs on leads in bar, back garden with play area and bat and trap, nice walks (Pulpit viewing platform nearby), open all day Sun, closed Mon evening. *(Christopher Mannings)*

SEVENOAKS TQ5555

★**Bucks Head** (01732) 761330
Godden Green, just E; TN15 0JJ Welcoming and relaxed flower-decked pub with neatly kept bar and restaurant area, good freshly cooked blackboard food from baguettes to Sun roasts, well kept Shepherd Neame and a guest, beams, panelling and

splendid inglenooks; children and dogs welcome, front terrace overlooking informal green and duck pond, pretty back garden with mature trees, pergola and views over quiet country behind Knole (NT), popular with walkers. *(Sam Phillips)*

SEVENOAKS   TQ5355
Halfway House (01732) 463667
2.5 miles from M25 junction 5; TN13 2JD Nicely updated old roadside pub with friendly staff and regulars, good competitively priced food from sensibly short menu, three changing ales, local wines and interesting flavoured vodkas, upper bar with record player and LPs (can bring your own), some live music too; handy for the station, parking can be tricky, open all day (no food Mon). *(Sam Phillips, Alf Wright)*

SHOREHAM   TQ5161
Two Brewers (01959) 522800
High Street; TN14 7TD Busy family-run village pub with two modernised beamed rooms, back part more restauranty, popular freshly made food from sharing plates to Sun roasts, three well kept changing kentish ales, friendly helpful staff, snug areas with comfortable seating, two woodburners; regular live music; handy for walkers, seats out in front behind picket fence, open all day Sat, till 6pm Sun, closed Mon, Tues. *(Martin Day)*

SNARGATE   TQ9928
★ Red Lion (01797) 344648
B2080 Appledore–Brenzett; TN29 9UQ Unchanging 16th-c pub in same family for over 100 years, simple old-fashioned charm in three timeless little rooms with original cream wall panelling, heavy beams in sagging ceilings, dark pine Victorian farmhouse chairs on bare boards, an old piano and coal fire, local cider and four or five ales including Goachers tapped from casks behind unusual free-standing marble-topped counter, no food, traditional games like toad in the hole, nine men's morris and table skittles; children in family room, dogs in bar, outdoor lavatories, cottage garden, closed Mon evening. *(Peter and Emma Kelly, Anon)*

ST MARGARET'S BAY   TR3744
★ Coastguard (01304) 853051
Off A256 NE of Dover; keep on down through the village to the bottom of the bay, pub off on right by the beach; CT15 6DY At bottom of a steep winding road with lovely sea views (France visible on a clear day) from prettily planted balcony and beachside seating, newly refurbished bar with four changing ales, bottled continental beers, over 40 whiskies and a carefully chosen wine list (some from Kent), straightforward pubby food including seafood specials, more fine views from restaurant with close-set tables on wood-strip floor; background music, free wi-fi (mobile phones

pick up french signal); children and dogs allowed in certain areas, good walks, open all day. *(Tony Scott)*

ST MARY IN THE MARSH   TR0627
Star (01797) 362139
Opposite church; TN29 0BX Remote down-to-earth pub with Tudor origins; straightforward reasonably priced lunchtime food, well kept ales including Youngs from brick-faced bar, friendly service, inglenook woodburner; bar billiards and darts, free wi-fi; children and dogs welcome, tables in nice garden, good value beamed bedrooms with Romney Marsh views, lovely setting opposite ancient church (Edith Nesbit, author of *The Railway Children*, buried here), popular with walkers and cyclists. *(Claire Adams)*

STAPLEHURST   TQ7846
Lord Raglan (01622) 843747
About 1.5 miles from town centre towards Maidstone, turn right off A229 into Chart Hill Road opposite Chart Cars; OS Sheet 188 map reference 785472; TN12 0DE Country pub with cosy chatty area around narrow bar counter, hop-strung low beams, big log fire and woodburner, mix of comfortably worn dark wood furniture, good reasonably priced home-cooked food, Goachers, Harveys and a guest, farm cider and perry, good wine list; children and dogs welcome, reasonable wheelchair access, tables on terrace and in side orchard, Aug onion festival, closed Sun. *(Sandra Morgan)*

STOWTING   TR1241
★ Tiger (01303) 862130
3.7 miles from M20 junction 11; B2068 N, then left at Stowting signpost, straight across crossroads, then fork left after 0.25 miles and pub is on right; coming from N, follow 'Brabourne, Wye, Ashford' signpost to right at fork, then turn left towards Posting and Lyminge at T junction; TN25 6BA Peaceful 17th-c country pub near the Wye Downs and North Downs Way; traditionally furnished bare-boards rooms with woodburners, some faded rugs on stone floor towards the back, candles in bottles, books, paintings and brewery memorabilia, local ales such as Shepherd Neame Master Brew, Biddenden cider and several wines by the glass, well liked food (not Sun evening) including daily specials; children and dogs (in bar) welcome, wheelchair access with help, seats on front terrace, closed Mon, Tues, otherwise open all day. *(Ian Herdman, Chris and Jo Nicholls, Glenwys and Alan Lawrence, Malcolm Greening)*

TENTERDEN   TQ8833
White Lion (01580) 765077
High Street; TN30 6BD Comfortably updated beamed and timbered 16th-c inn behind Georgian façade, enjoyable food

including Josper grills and pizzas from open kitchen, mainly local ales such as Old Dairy and a beer badged for them, good choice of other drinks including cocktails, big log fire, friendly helpful staff; background music; heated terrace overlooking street, nicely refurbished bedrooms, good breakfast, open (and food) all day. *(Dave Braisted)*

THURNHAM   TQ8057
★ **Black Horse** (01622) 737185

Not far from M20 junction 7; off A249 at Detling; ME14 3LD Large busy dining pub with enjoyable food from good sandwiches up, three well kept ales including Westerham, farm ciders such as Biddenden, friendly efficient uniformed staff, alcove seating, timbers and hop-strung beams, bare boards and log fires, back restaurant; children, walkers (by Pilgrims Way) and dogs welcome, pleasant garden with partly covered terrace, nice views, comfortable modern bedroom block, open (and food) all day. *(Penny and David Shepherd)*

TOYS HILL   TQ4752
★ **Fox & Hounds** (01732) 750328

Off A25 in Brasted, via Brasted Chart and The Chart; TN16 1QG Traditional country pub continuing well under present welcoming licensees; bar area separated by two-way woodburner, plain tables and chairs on dark boards or stone floor, hunting prints, old photographs, plates and copper jugs, modern carpeted dining extension with big windows overlooking tree-sheltered garden, enjoyable home-made pubby food (not Sun evening) from lunchtime sandwiches up, well kept Greene King ales and several wines by the glass, friendly efficient staff; background music, darts, free wi-fi; children and dogs (in bar) welcome, roadside verandah used by smokers, good local walks and views, handy for Chartwell and Emmetts Garden (both NT), open all day Fri-Sun. *(Brian Glozier)*

TUDELEY   TQ6145
Poacher & Partridge (01732) 358934

Hartlake Road; TN11 0PH Refurbished in smart country style by Elite Pubs (Great House in Hawkhurst, Dirty Habit at Hollingbourne etc); light interior with pizza oven, wide range of good food (all day weekends) including daily specials, Tues steak night, ales such as Sharps Doom Bar and Timothy Taylors Landlord, good choice of wines by the glass, friendly attentive staff; live music including afternoon jazz; children welcome, outside bar and grill, play area, near interesting church with Chagall stained glass (note roof paintings at pub's entrance), local walks (leaflets provided), open all day. *(Nigel and Jean Eames)*

TUNBRIDGE WELLS   TQ5837
Bull (01892) 263489

Frant Road; TN2 5LH Friendly 19th-c pub towards the outskirts of town; two

modernised linked areas with one or two quirky touches, chunky pine tables and kitchen chairs on stripped-wood floor, a couple of leather sofas by open fire, well kept Shepherd Neame ales, generous helpings of enjoyable home-cooked food from changing menu (not Sun evening, Mon); children (till 8.30pm) and dogs welcome, seats out on fenced roadside terrace, closed Mon lunchtime, otherwise open all day. *(Jim Jacks)*

TUNBRIDGE WELLS   TQ5838
Compasses (01892) 530744

Little Mount Sion; TN1 1YP Old pub tucked up from High Street and backing on to park; split-level beamed rooms around central bar, bare boards or carpet, log fires (one in large brick fireplace), some stained and frosted glass, six well kept ales including Greene King and a beer badged for the pub, well priced food from snacks up, proper coffee; background music, free wi-fi, bar billiards; children and dogs welcome, teak and rattan-style furniture on good-sized front terrace, open (and food) all day. *(Jim Jacks, Sam Phillips)*

TUNBRIDGE WELLS   TQ5839
Sussex Arms (01892) 549579

Nevill Street, off Frant Road; TN2 5TE Informal tucked-away place behind the Pantiles (if using side door make sure you choose the right handle); opened-up areas around bar serving good selection of ales, craft beers and ciders, enjoyable lunchtime food (12-4pm Thurs-Sun in winter) from shortish menu, friendly staff and good mix of customers, cellar bar for functions; live and background music (some from old vinyl), Thurs quiz, bar billiards; children and dogs welcome, seats on glass-covered terrace, open all day (till 1am Fri, Sat). *(Sam Phillips)*

UNDERRIVER   TQ5552
★ **White Rock** (01732) 833112

SE of Sevenoaks, off B245; TN15 0SB Attractive village pub with good food from pubby choices up (all day weekends, best to book), well kept Harveys, Westerham and a guest, decent wines, beams, bare boards and stripped brickwork in cosy original part with adjacent dining area, another bar in modern extension with woodburner; background and some live music, pool; children welcome, dogs may be allowed but ask first, small front garden, back terrace and large lawn with boules and bat and trap, pretty churchyard and walks nearby, open all day in summer, all day weekends winter. *(Martin Day, Tina and David Woods-Taylor)*

UPNOR   TQ7671
Ship (01634) 290553

Upnor Road, Lower Upnor; ME2 4UY Smallish mock-Tudor pub overlooking Medway and boats; good home-cooking including fish specials, ales such as Sharps, Shepherd Neame and Charles Wells, friendly staff, carpeted interior with marine knick-knacks; children welcome, picnic-sets out at front and in garden behind, open all day. *(Dave Braisted)*

UPPER UPNOR TQ7570

Tudor Rose (01634) 714175

Off A228 N of Strood; High Street; ME2 4XG 16th-c pub down narrow cobbled street just back from the river next to Upnor Castle (best to use village car park at top); cosy beamed rooms with mix of old furniture and some nautical bits and pieces, Shepherd Neame ales and an occasional guest, popular pubby food (not Sun evening) from baguettes up, good friendly service; children welcome, seats out at front made from an old boat, large enclosed garden behind with arbour, open all day. *(Christopher Mannings)*

WAREHORNE TQ9832

Woolpack (01233) 732900

Off B2067 near Hamstreet; TN26 2LL Part-weatherboarded 16th-c dining pub now under same ownership as the Five Bells at Brabourne and the Globe in Rye (in Sussex); interesting revamped interior with beams, inglenook fire and lots of quirky touches, local ales and well liked food including daily specials, friendly hard-working staff; children and dogs welcome, bench seating out at front overlooking quiet lane and 15th-c church, five stylish bedrooms, open all day. *(Peter Meister, Alf Wright)*

WEALD TQ5250

Windmill (01732) 463330

Windmill Road; TN14 6PN Popular and friendly village pub with six well kept ales including Larkins, local ciders and tasty home-cooked food, good service, traditional hop-strung interior with etched windows and two fires, mix of seating including old pews and carved settles by candlelit tables, jugs and bottles on delft shelves, snug dining area; live music and quiz nights; children welcome, nice back garden, closed Mon lunchtime, otherwise open all day. *(Martin Day)*

WEST MALLING TQ6857

Bull (01732) 842753

High Street; ME19 6QH Friendly old pub with good selection of mainly local ales and reasonably priced traditional home-made food (not Sun-Weds evenings), hop-strung beams, bare boards and big log fire, refurbished restaurant; live music first Sat of month, quiz Mon, beer festivals; children and dogs welcome, open all day Fri-Sun. *(Thomas Green)*

WESTBERE TR1862

Old Yew Tree (01227) 710501

Just off A18 Canterbury–Margate; CT2 0HH Heavily beamed 14th-c pub in pretty village, simply furnished bare-boards

bar, inglenook log fire, good reasonably priced food from varied menu, Shepherd Neame Master Brew and a guest, friendly helpful staff; quiz first Weds of the month, open mike last Weds; picnic-sets in garden behind, open all day weekends, closed Mon. *(Julie Swift)*

WESTERHAM TQ4453

General Wolfe (01959) 562104

High Street, W side of village; TN16 1RQ Attractive 16th-c weatherboarded pub with long cottagey room, beams, woodburner and separate snug, Greene King ales and a local guest, popular sensibly priced food (not Sun-Tues evenings) including one or two unusual choices; open mike night Sun and other live music, quiz Weds; dogs welcome, seats out on raised back deck, open all day. *(Tony Scott)*

WESTERHAM TQ4454

Grasshopper on the Green

(01959) 562926 *The Green; TN16 1AS* Old black-beamed pub (small former coaching house) facing village green, three linked bar areas with log fire at back, well kept ales including Westerham, popular pubby food from sandwiches up, helpful pleasant service, restaurant upstairs; sports TV, free wi-fi; children and dogs welcome, seating out at front and in back garden with play area, open all day. *(Tony and Wendy Hobden, Martin Day)*

WESTGATE-ON-SEA TR3270

Bake & Alehouse 07913 368787

Off St Mildred's Road down alley by cinema; CT8 8RE Micropub in former bakery; simple little bare-boards room with a few tables (expect to share when busy), four well kept interesting ales tapped from the cask, real ciders – maybe a warm winter one (Monks Delight), kentish wines, local cheese, sausage rolls and pork pies, friendly chatty atmosphere; closed Sun evening, Mon. *(Claire Adams)*

WESTWELL TQ9847

Wheel (01233) 712430

The Street; TN25 4LQ Traditional brick-built village pub under friendly new management (some refurbishment); popular home-made food from bar snacks up, well kept Shepherd Neame ales and decent choice of wines, beams and log fire, small shop; children and dogs (in bar) welcome, good-sized garden, close to Pilgrims Way, closed, Sun evening, Mon. *(Jim Jacks)*

WHITSTABLE TR1066

Black Dog

High Street; CT5 1BB Quirky micropub (former deli) with five changing ales and several artisan ciders tapped from back room, friendly staff may offer tasters, snacky food, narrow dimly lit Victorian-feel bar with high tables and benches along two sides, intriguing mix of pictures and other bits and pieces on green walls, prominent chandelier suspended from red ceiling; eclectic background music and occasional folk sessions; open all day. *(Dr Martin Owton)*

WHITSTABLE   TR1066
Old Neptune (01227) 272262
Marine Terrace; CT5 1EJ Great view over Swale estuary from this popular unpretentious weatherboarded pub set right on the beach (rebuilt after being washed away in 1897 storm); Harveys, Whitstable and a guest, lunchtime food from shortish menu including seafood specials, friendly young staff; weekend live music; children and dogs welcome, picnic-sets on the shingle (plastic glasses out here and occasional barbecues), fine sunsets, can get very busy in summer, open all day. *(B and M Kendall)*

WICKHAMBREAUX   TR2258
Rose (01227) 721763
The Green; CT3 1RQ Attractive 16th-c and partly older pub with enjoyable home-made food (more elaborate evening menu including Thurs steak night), Greene King IPA and three guests (May/Aug beer festivals), real ciders, friendly helpful staff, small bare-boards bar with log fire in big fireplace, dining area beyond standing timbers with woodburner, hop-strung beams, panelling and stripped brick; quiz second Weds of the month; children and dogs welcome, enclosed side garden and small courtyard, nice spot across green from church and watermill, open all day, no food Sun evening. *(Christopher Mannings)*

WILLESBOROUGH STREET   TR0341
Blacksmiths Arms (01233) 623975
The Street; TN24 0NA Beamed village pub dating in part to the 17th c, Fullers London Pride and a couple of guests, good traditional home-cooked food (not Sun evening) from sandwiches and snacks up, daily blackboard specials, friendly service, open fires including inglenook; children and dogs welcome, picnic-sets in good-sized garden with play area, handy for M20 (junction 10), open all day. *(Tony and Vivien Smith)*

WORTH   TR3356
St Crispin (01304) 612081
Signed off A258 S of Sandwich; CT14 0DF Dating from 15th c with low beams, stripped brickwork and bare boards, enjoyable traditional home-made food including bargain OAP weekday lunch in bar, carpeted restaurant or back conservatory (dogs allowed here), four real ales such as Black Sheep, Fullers, Sharps and Timothy Taylors, central log fire; children welcome away from bar, nice big garden behind with terrace and play area, seven bedrooms (three

in motel-style extension), lovely village position, open all day, food all day too except Sun evening. *(Peter and Emma Kelly)*

WROTHAM   TQ6159
Bull (01732) 789800
1.7 miles from M20 junction 2 – Wrotham signed; TN15 7RF Restored 14th-c coaching inn with enjoyable if not always cheap food including smokehouse/barbecue menu, large beamed bar with well spaced tables, real ales such as Dark Star, craft beers and good wine list, welcoming helpful service, separate restaurant; Fri live music; children welcome, 11 comfortable bedrooms, open all day, food all day weekends. *(Gordon and Margaret Ormondroyd)*

WYE   TR0546
New Flying Horse (01233) 812297
Upper Bridge Street; TN25 5AN 17th-c Shepherd Neame inn with beams and inglenook, enjoyable food including fixed-price menu in bar and restaurant, friendly accommodating staff; Sun quiz, occasional live music; children welcome, good-sized pretty garden with play area and miniature thatched pub (a former Chelsea Flower Show exhibit), nine bedrooms (some in converted stables), open all day. *(Thomas Green)*

WYE   TR0446
Tickled Trout (01233) 812227
Signed off A28 NE of Ashford; TN25 5EB Popular summer family pub by River Stour; rustic-style carpeted bar with beams, stripped brickwork, stained-glass partitions and open fire, spacious conservatory/restaurant, good choice of enjoyable food including OAP lunch (Mon-Thurs), ales such as Canterbury, Old Dairy and Sharps, kentish ciders and several wines by the glass, friendly helpful staff; live music Sun evening, quiz first Weds of month, free wi-fi; children and dogs welcome, tables on terrace and riverside lawn, open (and food) all day including breakfast from 9am. *(Thomas Green, Alf Wright)*

YALDING   TQ6950
★ Walnut Tree (01622) 814266
B2010 SW of Maidstone; ME18 6JB Timbered village pub with split-level main bar, fine old settles, a long cushioned mahogany bench and mix of dining chairs on brick or carpeted floors, chunky wooden tables with church candles, interesting old photographs, big inglenook log fire, well kept Black Sheep, Harveys and Skinners, good bar food and more inventive restaurant menu, OAP lunchtime discount Mon-Fri, attractive raftered dining room with high-backed leather dining chairs on parquet flooring; background and occasional live music, TV; a few picnic-sets out by road, open all day. *(Peter and Emma Kelly)*

Lancashire

with Greater Manchester, Merseyside and Wirral

KEY ★ Star Pub | 🍽 Top Quality Food | 🍺 Great Beer

🍷 Good Wines | £ Bargain Meals | 🛏 Good Bedrooms | 🍴 Serves Food

---

BASHALL EAVES   SD6943   Map 7

THE GOOD PUB GUIDE

Red Pump 🍽 🛏

(01254) 826227 – www.theredpumpinn.co.uk

NW of Clitheroe, off B6478 or B6243; BB7 3DA

Beautifully placed country inn with a cosy bar, highly thought-of food in more contemporary dining rooms and changing beers; bedrooms

You can stay in the individually decorated and comfortable bedrooms here or in their new glamping yurts surrounded by lovely Forest of Bowland countryside; breakfasts are good and generous and residents can fish in the nearby river. The chatty, helpful licensees create a cheerful atmosphere and there are two pleasantly up-to-date dining rooms and a traditional, cosy central bar: bookshelves, cushioned settles and wheelbacks on flagstones, and log fires. The three regional beers on handpump change weekly and might include Black Sheep Best, Bowland Hen Harrier and Moorhouses White Witch, plus eight wines by the glass and several malt whiskies; background music and board games. The views from seats in the terraced gardens (where they grow their own herbs) are splendid.

🍽 Pleasing food includes sandwiches, home-cured salmon with caper and lemon dressing, lambs kidneys with spinach and bacon on soda bread, roasted vegetable and goats cheese vol-au-vent, shin of beef in red wine with horseradish mash, grilled chicken marinated in thyme and garlic with a white wine, mushroom and cream sauce, bass with spinach and lobster sauce and crushed potatoes, slow-roast pork belly with chorizo and cannellini bean cassoulet, and puddings such as rhubarb and raspberry pannacotta and sticky toffee and date pudding with butterscotch sauce. *Benchmark main dish: 40-day-aged-steak £21.00. Two-course evening meal £19.00.*

Free house ~ Licensees Frances and Jonathan Gledhill ~ Real ale ~ Open 12-2, 5.30-11; 12-11 Sat; 12-10 Sun; closed Mon, winter Tues ~ Bar food 12-2, 6-9; 12-7 Sun ~ Restaurant ~ Children welcome ~ Dogs allowed in bar and bedrooms ~ Wi-fi ~ Bedrooms: £102/£120
Recommended by Jo Garnett, Nick Sharpe, Daniel King, Tim and Sarah Smythe-Brown

BAY HORSE   SD4952   Map 7

THE GOOD PUB GUIDE

Bay Horse 🛏

(01524) 791204 – www.bayhorseinn.com

1.2 miles from M6 junction 33: A6 southwards, then off on left; LA2 0HR

18th-c former coaching inn with log fires, comfortable bar and restaurant, rewarding food, local ales and friendly staff; bedrooms

The bedrooms in the converted barn over the road from this civilised family-run dining pub are comfortable and just right if you want to explore the area or need to break a journey while on the nearby motorway. The cosily pubby beamed bar has cushioned wall banquettes in bays, lamps on windowsills, and a good log fire. Moorhouses Pendle Witches Brew, Thwaites Wainwright and Timothy Taylors Golden Best on handpump and ten wines by the glass served by friendly, efficient staff. The smarter restaurant has cosy corners, fresh flowers, a woodburning stove and lovely views over the garden – where there are plenty of seats and tables.

Enjoyable food includes sandwiches, gin- and seaweed-cured salmon with horseradish and cucumber, terrine of truffled chicken and wild mushrooms with herb mayonnaise, aubergine with lentils, quinoa, goats cheese, spinach and herb oil, pork and leek sausages with mash and onion gravy, chicken with dry-cured bacon, asparagus and truffle butter, hake fillet with creamy leeks and mussels, slow-cooked duck legs with roast figs and port sauce, and puddings such as chocolate torte with salted caramel and caramel ice-cream and vanilla pannacotta with rhubarb. *Benchmark main dish: lamb rump with puy lentils, carrot purée, madeira jus and truffles £18.75. Two-course evening meal £22.00.*

Mitchells ~ Tenant Craig Wilkinson ~ Real ale ~ Open 12-3, 6-11; closed Mon, Tues; second week Jan, second week Nov ~ Bar food 12-2, 6-9; 12-3, 6-8 Sun ~ Restaurant ~ Children welcome ~ Dogs allowed in bar *Recommended by Claire Adams, Nigel Havers, Alf Wright*

BISPHAM GREEN

Eagle & Child 🌟 ♀ 🍺

SD4813 Map 7

(01257) 462297 – www.ainscoughs.co.uk
Maltkiln Lane (Parbold–Croston road, off B5246); L40 3SG

Gently civilised pub with antiques, enterprising food, an interesting range of beers and appealing rustic garden

Facing the village green, this is a bustling all-rounder that our readers enjoy very much. The largely open-plan bar is carefully furnished with several handsomely carved antique oak settles (the finest made in part, it seems, from a 16th-c wedding bed-head), a mix of small old oak chairs, an attractive oak coffer, old hunting prints and engravings and hop-draped low beams. Also, red walls, coir matting, oriental rugs on ancient flagstones in front of a fine old stone fireplace and counter; the pub dogs are called Betty and Doris. Friendly young staff serve Bowland Hen Harrier, Coniston Bluebird Bitter, Hawkshead Windermere Pale, Southport Carousel, Thwaites Original and Wainwright and Wychwood Hobgoblin on handpump, farm cider, ten wines by the glass and around 30 malt whiskies. A popular beer festival is usually held on the early May Bank Holiday weekend. The spacious garden has a well tended but unconventional bowling green; beyond is a wild area that's home to crested newts and moorhens. They also run a shop in a handsome side barn selling interesting wines and pottery, plus a proper butcher and a deli. This is part of the Ainscoughs group.

Rewarding food includes sandwiches, smoked haddock with buttered spinach and poached egg, seared scallops with celeriac purée, black pudding and chorizo, burger with toppings, bacon jam, onion rings and pickles, wild mushroom and spinach risotto with white truffle oil, salmon with pasta and rocket pesto, chicken breast with morel mushrooms, truffle and olive mash, duck breast with black cherry jus and dauphinoise potatoes, and puddings such as chocolate brownie with chocolate sauce and treacle tart. *Benchmark main dish: steak and mushroom in ale pie £12.75. Two-course evening meal £19.50.*

Free house ~ Licensee Peter Robinson ~ Real ale ~ Open 12-11 (10.30 Sun) ~ Bar food 12-2, 5.30-9; 12-9 Sat; 12-8 Sun ~ Children welcome ~ Dogs welcome ~ Live music monthly Fri evening *Recommended by R T and J C Moggridge, Martin Sargeant, W K Wood, Beth Aldridge, Julian Richardson*

DOWNHAM
Assheton Arms 🌟🍽 🍷

SD7844 Map 7

(01200) 441227 – www.seafoodpubcompany.com/the-assheton-arms
Off A59 NE of Clitheroe, via Chatburn; BB7 4BJ

Lancashire Dining Pub of the Year

Fine old inn with plenty of dining and drinking space, a friendly welcome, several real ales and creative food; bedrooms

This is a genuinely friendly old place with helpful staff and an easy-going atmosphere. A small front bar, with a hatch to the kitchen, has tweed-upholstered armchairs and stools on big flagstones around a single table, a woodburning stove surrounded by logs, and drawings of dogs and hunting prints on grey-green walls. Off to the right, a wood-panelled partition creates a cosy area where there are similarly cushioned pews and nice old chairs around various tables on a rug-covered wooden floor, and a couple of window chairs. The main bar, up a couple of steps, has old photographs of the pub and the village on pale walls and a marble bar counter where they serve Moorhouses White Witch, Thwaites Wainwright and Timothy Taylors Landlord on handpump, a dozen wines by the glass and farm cider; background music and board games. A two-level restaurant has carpet or wooden flooring, two fireplaces (one with a woodburning stove and the other with a lovely old kitchen range) and hunting prints. The setting at the top of a steep hill is very pretty, and picnic-sets and tables and chairs make the most of this. The comfortable bedrooms are in the former post office and in two cottages. Do note the lovely church opposite. This is part of the Seafood Pub Company.

Excellent food includes smoked salmon with scampi fritters, charred cucumber and brown shrimp mayonnaise, spicy quinoa cakes with sweet potato, chargrilled spring onions, dried tomatoes and tzatziki, satay chicken salad with peanut and mint dressing and shredded vegetables, brisket and blue cheese pudding with sticky roast beetroot and roast ale gravy, goan king prawn curry, piggy grill (gammon rib-eye with fried duck egg, pork fillet wrapped in streaky bacon, pineapple and grain mustard ketchup glazed pork belly with mash, black pudding fritter), cod tagine with crab koftas, toasted couscous, pickled lemon, pomegranate and rose petal harissa, and puddings such as After Eight choc ice with chocolate mousse and chocolate crumble and passion-fruit and blackberry mess with mini meringues. *Benchmark main dish: whole bass with smoked salmon, prawn and shellfish butter sauce £19.50. Two-course evening meal £21.50.*

Free house ~ Licensee Jocelyn Neve ~ Real ale ~ Open 12-11 (midnight Sat, 10.30 Sun) ~ Bar food 12-9 (10 Fri, Sat, 8 Sun) ~ Restaurant ~ Children welcome ~ Dogs allowed in bar ~ Wi-fi *Recommended by Richard Cox, Steve Whalley, W K Wood, Julie Swift, Caroline Sullivan, Millie and Peter Downing*

Real ale to us means beer that has matured naturally in its cask – not pressurised or filtered. We name all real ales stocked. We usually name ales preserved under a light blanket of carbon dioxide too, though purists – pointing out that this stops the natural yeasts developing – would disagree (most people, including us, can't tell the difference!).

FORMBY SD3109 Map 7

Sparrowhawk ♀ ◖

(01704) 882350 – www.brunningandprice.co.uk/sparrowhawk

Southport Old Road; brown sign to pub just off A565 Formby bypass, S edge of Ainsdale; L37 0AB

Light and airy pub with interesting décor, good food and drinks choices and wooded grounds

You'll find plenty of space for drinking and dining in the open-plan linked areas that spread out from the central bar here, and there's a bustling atmosphere at any time of day. The various rooms have plenty of interest, from attractive prints on pastel walls, church candles, flowers and snug leather fireside armchairs in library corners through tables with rugs on dark boards by big bow windows and a comfortably carpeted conservatory dining room; background music. A wide choice of drinks includes 21 wines by the glass, 89 malt whiskies, 49 gins and Phoenix Brunning & Price Original, Salopian Oracle, Titanic Plum Porter and a couple of guest beers on handpump. A flagstoned side terrace has sturdy tables, and several picnic-table sets are nicely spread on the woodside lawns by a set of swings and an old Fergie tractor (painted green instead of the usual grey). A walk from the pub to coastal nature reserves might just yield red squirrels, still hanging on in this area.

 As well as weekend brunches (9.30-11am), the good, brasserie-style food includes sandwiches, grilled sardines with confit tomatoes and black olive tapenade, red pepper and goats cheese pannacotta with dried tomato and artichoke salad, honey-roast ham and free-range eggs, local sausages with mash and onion gravy, tandoori grilled halloumi with toasted coconut, pineapple, lime and mint salad, teriyaki bass with crispy wasabi rice balls and soy and sesame dressing, fish pie, and puddings such as rhubarb and custard trifle with apricot sauce and baked cherry and amaretti cheesecake with cherry compote. *Benchmark main dish: lamb shoulder with roast potatoes and gravy £16.95. Two-course evening meal £20.00.*

Brunning & Price ~ Manager Iain Hendry ~ Real ale ~ Open 10.30am-11pm; 10.30-10.30 Sun ~ Bar food 12-10 (9.30 Sun) ~ Children welcome ~ Dogs allowed in bar ~ Wi-fi *Recommended by Peter Pilbeam, Sandra Morgan, Colin Humphreys*

GREAT MITTON SD7138 Map 7

Aspinall Arms ⊕ ♀ ◖

(01254) 826555 – www.brunningandprice.co.uk/aspinallarms

B6246 NW of Whalley; BB7 9PQ

Cleverly refurbished and extended riverside pub with cheerful friendly service and a fine choice of drinks and food

The setting by the River Ribble for this well run pub is lovely, and in warm weather the picnic-sets on grass overlooking the water and seats and tables on the terrace make the most of the view. Various rambling rooms and snugger corners inside have a chatty, easy-going atmosphere, with customers dropping in and out all day. Seating ranges from attractively cushioned old-style dining chairs through brass-studded leather ones to big armchairs and sofas around an assortment of dark tables. Floors are flagstoned, carpeted or wooden and topped with rugs, while the pale-painted or bare stone walls are hung with an extensive collection of prints and local photographs. Dotted about are large mirrors, house plants, stone bottles and bookshelves and there are both open fires and a woodburning stove. From the central servery, friendly and helpful staff serve Phoenix Brunning & Price Original,

Hawkshead Lakeland Gold, Lancaster Blonde, Moorhouses Aspinall Witch (named for the pub) and Phoenix Monkeytown Mild on handpump, 15 wines by the glass, 50 gins, an amazing 150 malt whiskies and a farm cider; background music and board games.

 Rewarding food includes sandwiches, crispy duck salad with hoisin, watermelon and chilli cashews, orange- and dill-cured salmon with pickled fennel, orange, lemon dressing and tarragon cream, spinach, asparagus and blue cheese quiche, steak and kidney suet pudding, sea bream fillet with crab and salmon croquette, samphire and hollandaise, grilled lamb cutlets with red wine reduction and minted jersey royals, and puddings such as dark chocolate torte with espresso martini cream and salted caramel and bread and butter pudding with apricot sauce. *Benchmark main dish: beer-battered fish and chips £12.75. Two-course evening meal £20.00.*

Brunning & Price ~ Manager Chris Humphries ~ Real ale ~ Open 10.30am-11pm; 10.30-10.30 Sun ~ Bar food 12-10 (9.30 Sun) ~ Restaurant ~ Children welcome ~ Dogs allowed in bar ~ Wi-fi *Recommended by Steve Whalley, W K Wood, John and Sylvia Harrop, Peter Meister*

LITTLE ECCLESTON
SD4240 Map 7

Cartford 🌟 🍴 🛏

(01995) 670166 – www.thecartfordinn.co.uk
Cartford Lane, off A586 Garstang–Blackpool, by toll bridge; PR3 0YP

Attractively refurbished riverside coaching inn with a thoughtful choice of drinks and food; waterside bedrooms

This is a prettily placed 17th-c coaching inn on the bank of the River Wyre – tables in the garden overlook the water (crossed by a toll bridge), the Trough of Bowland and the peaks of the Lake District. Inside, the unusual four-level layout blends both traditional and contemporary elements with an appealing mix of striking colours, natural wood and polished floors, while the log fire and eclectic choice of furniture create a comfortable and relaxed feel in the bar lounge; background music. Hawkshead Lakeland Gold, Lancaster Black, Moorhouses Pride of Pendle and a beer named for the pub (from Moorhouses) on handpump, alongside speciality bottled beers, ten wines by the glass, a dozen gins and a dozen malt whiskies. There's also another cosy lounge and a riverside restaurant. The individually decorated bedrooms have a tranquil river view too.

 Very good food includes lunchtime sandwiches, barbecue ribs, fresh crab caesar salad, sharing platters, cumberland-style sausages with mash and onion gravy, moules frites, wild garlic and pea orzo pasta with roast vine tomatoes, basil and pine nuts, corn-fed chicken breast with saffron fondant potatoes, butternut squash purée and white wine and chive cream sauce, porchetta with smoky bean casserole, pork belly, gremolata and coriander, a fish dish of the day, and puddings such as crème brûlée of the day and salted maple and pecan pie with ginger ice-cream. *Benchmark main dish: oxtail and beef skirt in ale pudding £14.95. Two-course evening meal £21.00.*

Free house ~ Licensees Patrick and Julie Beaume ~ Real ale ~ Open 12-11 (midnight Sat, 10 Sun); closed Mon lunchtime ~ Bar food 12-2, 5.30-9 (10 Fri, Sat); 12-8.30 Sun ~ Restaurant ~ Children welcome until 9pm ~ Wi-fi ~ Bedrooms: £70/£120
Recommended by Caroline Prescott, Isobel Mackinlay, Dave, Steve Whalley, W K Wood

MANCHESTER
SJ8297 Map 7

Wharf ♀ 🍴

(0161) 220 2960 – www.brunningandprice.co.uk/thewharf
Blantyre Street/Slate Wharf; M15 4SW

Big wharf-like pub with large terrace overlooking the water and a fine range of drinks and food

Although this huge place is open-plan and on several levels, there are enough cosy nooks and alcoves to keep some sense of cosiness. Downstairs is more pubby and informal with groups of high tables and chairs, while the restaurant upstairs has table service. Throughout there's an appealing variety of pre-war-style dining chairs around quite a choice of dark wooden tables on rugs and shiny floorboards, hundreds of interesting prints and posters on bare-brick or painted walls, old stone bottles, church candles, house plants and fresh flowers on windowsills and tables, bookshelves and armchairs here and there, and large mirrors over open fires. Despite the crowds, the hard-working staff remain unfailingly helpful and friendly. They serve Phoenix Brunning & Price Original and Weetwood Cheshire Cat plus up to eight quickly changing guest ales on handpump, such as Beartown Polar Eclipse, Cotleigh Redfire, Milestone Raspberry Wheat Beer, Mobberley HedgeHopper, Pennine Real Blonde, Tatton White Queen and Three Castles Try Me, as well as farm cider, 19 wines by the glass and over 50 malt whiskies. The large front terrace has plenty of wood and chrome tables and chairs around a fountain, and picnic-sets overlooking the canal basin.

Pleasing food includes sandwiches, a trio of salmon (smoked salmon roulade, smoked salmon potato salad, smoked salmon mousse), chicken liver pâté with plum and ginger chutney, pea and mint arancini with thai asparagus, rocket and sun-dried tomatoes, chicken, ham hock and leek pie, hake with herb crumble and mussel provençale sauce, spiced lamb rump with butternut squash, couscous, chargrilled peppers and coriander yoghurt, and puddings such as crème brûlée and treacle tart. *Benchmark main dish: cod with prawns, baby vegetables and shellfish bisque £16.25. Two-course evening meal £20.00.*

Brunning & Price ~ Manager Siobhan Youngs ~ Real ale ~ Open 10.30am-11pm (midnight Sat); 10.30-10.30 Sun ~ Bar food 12-10; 9am-10pm Sat; 9am-9.30pm Sun ~ Restaurant ~ Children welcome ~ Dogs allowed in bar ~ Wi-fi ~ Live music Fri evening
Recommended by Ruth May, Edward May, Rosie and John Moore, Susan and Callum Slade, Tony Hobden

MELLOR
Millstone 🍺 🛏

(01254) 813333 – www.millstonehotel.co.uk
The Mellor near Blackburn; Mellor Lane; BB2 7JR

SD6530   Map 7

Enthusiastic chef-patron in smart, popular dining pub with rewarding food, real ales and seats outside; bedrooms

Our readers enjoy all aspects of their visits to this extended stone coaching inn. It's a comfortable place to stay overnight; the bedrooms (some are in a separate block across the car park) are well equipped and the breakfasts good. There's extensive panelling on both sides of the central bar, and the dining rooms have comfortable seats around polished tables. At busy meal times, the whole space is opened into one big happy eating area around the bar itself, which has a handful of tables, settles, a housekeeper's chair and rugs on bare boards; log fires and background music. Lancaster Bomber, Thwaites Original and a guest beer on handpump and a dozen wines by the glass; service is informally friendly and helpful. A side terrace has seats and tables under parasols.

Cooked by the enthusiastic landlord, the highly thought-of food includes sandwiches, duck spring rolls with cucumber and sesame salad and sticky plum sauce, goats cheese and cranberry mousse, steak burger with toppings, coleslaw and chips, filo parcel of wild mushrooms, spinach and pine nuts with shallot and roast tomato sauce, steak and kidney in ale pudding, roast cod with cockles in white wine cream broth, and puddings such as sticky toffee pudding with toffee sauce and crème brûlée.

Benchmark main dish: beer-battered fish and chips £9.95. Two-course evening meal £20.00.

Thwaites ~ Manager Alan Holliday ~ Real ale ~ Open 9am-midnight; 9am-10.30 Sun ~ Bar food 12-9.30 (9 Sun) ~ Restaurant ~ Children welcome ~ Wi-fi ~ Bedrooms: £70/£80
Recommended by William and Ann Reid, Brian and Anna Marsden, W K Wood, Edward Mirzoeff

SAWLEY   SD7746 Map 7
Spread Eagle 🛏
(01200) 441202 – www.spreadeaglesawley.co.uk
Village signed just off A59 NE of Clitheroe; BB7 4NH

Nicely refurbished pub with quite a choice of food, riverside restaurant and four real ales; bedrooms

Just across a country lane from the River Ribble and close to the substantial ruins of a 12th-c cistercian abbey stands this attractive old coaching inn. There's a pleasing mix of nice old and quirky modern furniture – anything from an old settle and pine tables to new low chairs upholstered in animal print fabric – all set off well by the grey rustic stone floor. Low ceilings, cosy sectioning, a warming fire and cottagey windows keep it all feeling intimate. The dining areas are more formal, with modern stripes and a bookshelf mural; background music. A beer named for the pub (from Bowland), Dark Horse Hetton Pale Ale, Moorhouses Pride of Pendle and Thwaites Wainwright on handpump and several wines by the glass. If you want to explore the exhilarating walks in the Forest of Bowland, stay in the individually furnished and comfortable bedrooms.

🍴 Food is good and includes sandwiches, chinese-spiced duck terrine with plum sauce, salmon and herb rillette with new potato salad, sausages with mash and onion gravy, chicken on potato purée with chive cream sauce and asparagus ravioli, ragoût of vegetarian mince with potato gnocchi and basil oil, mussels in cider cream with skinny fries and garlic mayonnaise, chargrilled gammon with egg and pineapple, and puddings such as bread and butter ice-cream terrine with apricot sorbet and vanilla pannacotta with gingerbread, apple purée and spiced syrup. *Benchmark main dish: steak pie £11.95. Two-course evening meal £20.00.*

Individual Inns ~ Managers Greg and Natalie Barns ~ Real ale ~ Open 11-11 (midnight Sat); 12-10.30 Sun ~ Bar food 12-2, 5.30-9; 12-7 Sun ~ Restaurant ~ Children welcome ~ Dogs allowed in bar and bedrooms ~ Wi-fi ~ Bedrooms: £92/£110 *Recommended by Ruth May, Brian and Janet Ainscough, Ann and Tony Bennett-Hughes, Anne Taylor*

THORNTON HOUGH   SJ2979 Map 7
Red Fox 🍷 🍺
(0151) 353 2920 – www.brunningandprice.co.uk/redfox
Liverpool Road; CH64 7TL

Big spreading pub with character rooms, a fine choice of beers, wines, gins and whiskies, courteous staff serving enjoyable food and large back garden

With its own drive and grounds, this is a substantial brick and sandstone pub on the edge of a village of striking mock-Elizabethan estate workers' houses. The big, spacious main bar is reached up stairs from the entrance: large central pillars divide the room into smaller areas with high stools and tables in the middle, dark wooden tables and chairs to each side and deep leather armchairs and fender seats by the large fireplace. This leads into a long, airy carpeted dining room with two rows of painted iron supports, hefty leather and wood chairs around highly polished tables and a raised fire pit; doors from here lead out to a terrace. Two additional dining rooms are similarly furnished, one with an elegant chandelier hanging from a fine moulded ceiling, the other with a huge metal elephant peeping through large house plants. Throughout there are photographs, prints and pictures covering the walls, big plants, stone bottles and shelves of books. Friendly, cheerful staff serve Phoenix Brunning & Price Original and Facers Sunlight Sunny Bitter with guests such as Brightside The Optimist, Castle Rock Red Riding Hood, Cheshire Brew Brothers Earls Eye Amber and Merlin Castle Black Stout on handpump, 21 wines by the glass, 165 malt whiskies, 100 gins and seven farm ciders; background music and board games. At the back, terraces have good quality wooden chairs and tables under parasols with steps down to picnic-sets around a fountain on a spreading lawn, and country views.

🍴 Good modern food includes sandwiches, scallops with ham fritters, pea purée and lemon dressing, basil pannacotta with tomato salad and black olive tapenade, daube of venison with parsnip and potato gratin and port and cranberry jus, smoked haddock and salmon fishcakes with tomato and spring onion salad, crispy jerk beef with pineapple salsa, jamaican rice and ginger beer dressing, cumin and chilli chicken with tzatziki and roast sweet potato, and puddings such as lemon tart with raspberry coulis and apple and blackberry crumble. *Benchmark main dish: lamb shoulder with carrot mash, mint gravy and dauphinoise potatoes £16.95. Two-course evening meal £23.00.*

Brunning & Price ~ Manager David Green ~ Real ale ~ Open 10.30am-11pm (10.30pm Sun) ~ Bar food 12-10 (9.30 Sun) ~ Restaurant ~ Children welcome ~ Dogs allowed in bar ~ Wi-fi *Recommended by Edward May, Isobel Mackinlay, Lionel Smith, Jack and Hilary Burton*

UPPERMILL
Church Inn 🍺 £

SD0006   Map 7

(01457) 820902 – www.churchinnsaddleworth.co.uk
From the main street (A607), look out for the sign for Saddleworth Church, and turn off up this steep narrow lane – keep on up; OL3 6LW

Community pub with big range of own-brew beers at unbeatable bargain prices and tasty food; children very welcome

Cheerful, friendly and well run – and with fantastic own brews to boot – this is a first-class pub and always deservedly busy. The big, unspoilt, L-shaped main bar has high beams and some stripped stone, settles, pews, a good individual mix of chairs, lots of attractive prints, staffordshire and other china on a high delft shelf, jugs, brasses and so forth. They keep up to 11 of their own Saddleworth beers – though, if the water levels from the spring aren't high enough for brewing, they bring in guests such as Black Sheep and Copper Dragon. Some of their own seasonal ales are named after the licensee's children, only appearing around their birthdays; two home-brewed lagers on tap too. TV (for sporting events) and unobtrusive background music. A conservatory opens on to the terrace. The local bellringers arrive on Wednesdays to practise with a set of handbells kept here; anyone can join the morris dancing on Thursdays. Children enjoy all the animals, including rabbits, chickens, dogs, ducks, geese, alpacas, horses, 14 peacocks in the next-door field and some cats that live in an adjacent barn; dogs are made to feel very welcome. It's next to an isolated church, with fine views down the valley.

🍴 Honest, fair-priced food includes sandwiches, creamy garlic mushrooms, pâté and toast, chicken, steak or vegetarian fajitas with wraps, sour cream, salsa and guacamole, a roast of the day, lasagne, lamb shank in minted gravy, steak and mushroom in ale pie, mixed grill, and puddings such as jam roly-poly and apple crumble. *Benchmark main dish: beer-battered fish and chips £9.50. Two-course evening meal £12.00.*

Own brew ~ Licensee Christine Taylor ~ Real ale ~ Open 12-midnight (1am Sat) ~ Bar food 12-3, 5-9; 12-9 Fri-Sun and bank holidays ~ Restaurant ~ Children welcome ~ Dogs allowed in bar ~ Wi-fi *Recommended by Gordon and Margaret Ormondroyd, Colin and Daniel Gibbs, Kate Moran, Peter Barrett*

 WADDINGTON   SD7243 Map 7

Lower Buck

(01200) 423342 – www.lowerbuck.co.uk

Edisford Road; BB7 3HU

Hospitable village pub with reasonably priced food and five real ales

Close to Ribble Valley walks and tucked away behind the church, this little stone building is a proper chatty local. The several small, neatly kept cream-painted bars and dining rooms, each with a warming coal fire, have plenty of cheerful customers, good solid chairs and settles on carpet or stripped wooden floors and lots of paintings. Welcoming staff serve up to five real ales on handpump, such as Bowland Hen Harrier, IPA and Pheasant Plucker, Moorhouses Premier Bitter and Timothy Taylors Landlord, and ten wines by the glass; darts and pool. There are picnic-sets out on cobbles at the front and in the sunny back garden.

Tasty food includes sandwiches, duck liver pâté with onion marmalade, smoked salmon with capers and lemon, steak in ale pie, sausages and mash with onion gravy, cheese and tomato quiche with chips, hotpot with pickled cabbage, and puddings such as steamed syrup sponge with custard and sticky toffee pudding with butterscotch sauce. *Benchmark main dish: beer-battered fish and chips £10.50. Two-course evening meal £19.00.*

Free house ~ Licensee Andrew Warburton ~ Real ale ~ Open 11-11; 11-midnight Fri, Sat ~ Bar food 12-2.30, 5-9; 12-9 Sat, Sun and bank holidays ~ Children welcome ~ Dogs allowed in bar ~ Wi-fi *Recommended by Caroline Prescott, Isobel Mackinlay, Ruth May, Geoffrey Sutton*

 WHITEWELL   SD6546 Map 7

Inn at Whitewell ★ 🎖 🍷 🍺 🛏

(01200) 448222 – www.innatwhitewell.com

Most easily reached by B6246 from Whalley; road through Dunsop Bridge from B6478 is also good; BB7 3AT

Fine manor house with smartly pubby atmosphere, top quality food, exceptional wine list, real ales and professional, friendly service; luxury bedrooms

As our readers constantly tell us, this is a special place and a first-class all-rounder. Many of them stay overnight in the lovely bedrooms (several have open fires) – and they also have a self-catering holiday house. It's an elegant and civilised old manor house; the bar rooms have handsome old wood furnishings, including antique settles, oak gate-leg tables and sonorous clocks, set off beautifully against powder blue walls neatly hung with big appealing prints. The pubby main bar has roaring log fires in attractive stone fireplaces and heavy curtains on sturdy wooden rails; one area has a selection of newspapers and magazines, local maps and guidebooks. There's a piano for anyone who wants to play, and board games. The view from the riverside bar and adjacent terrace is idyllic. Early evening sees a cheerful bustle that later settles to a more tranquil and relaxing atmosphere. Drinks include a marvellous wine list of around 230 wines with 17 by the glass (reception has a good wine shop), 24 whiskies, eight gins, organic ginger beer, lemonade and fruit juices and Bowland Hen Harrier, Moorhouses Blond Witch, Timothy Taylors Landlord and a guest beer on handpump. They own several miles of trout, salmon and sea trout fishing on the River Hodder; picnic hamper on request.

Excellent food using the best local, seasonal produce includes lunchtime sandwiches, potted crab with cucumber pickle and avocado purée, chicken satay salad with carrot and mangetout, roasted sesame seeds and crispy onions, gnocchi with spinach, vine tomatoes and red onions and parmesan topping, cumberland sausages and champ with fried egg, goosnargh corn-fed chicken with celeriac purée, baby onions and smoked bacon jus, bass fillet with goats cheese and spinach couscous, crushed tomatoes and harissa, and puddings such as lemon cheesecake with blackcurrant compote and plum and almond tart with crème anglaise. *Benchmark main dish: fish pie £11.50. Two-course evening meal £18.00.*

Free house ~ Licensee Charles Bowman ~ Real ale ~ Open 11am-midnight ~ Bar food 12-2, 7.30-9.30 ~ Restaurant ~ Children welcome ~ Dogs allowed in bar and bedrooms ~ Wi-fi ~ Bedrooms: £95/£132 *Recommended by Ian Herdman, John and Sylvia Harrop, Richard Cox, Steve Whalley, John Poulter, W K Wood*

WORSLEY   SD7401   Map 7
Worsley Old Hall ♀ ◖
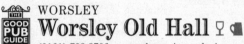

(0161) 703 8706 – www.brunningandprice.co.uk/worsleyoldhall
A mile from M60 junction 13: A575 Walkden Road, then after roundabout take first left into Worsley Park; M28 2QT

Very handsomely converted landmark building, now a welcoming pub scoring high on all counts

If you want a break from the nearby M60, come to this civilised and grand timbered mansion. It's been carefully restored and has some lovely original architectural features: a gracefully arched inglenook and matching window alcove, handsome staircase, heavy beams and glowing mahogany panelling. The relaxed and chatty main area spreads generously around the feature central bar, where exceptionally well trained staff serve 17 good wines by the glass, over 100 malt whiskies, 38 gins and Phoenix Brunning & Price Original and Brightside Brindley Blonde on handpump with guests such as Battlefield 1066, Merlin Dark Magic, Weetwood Eastgate Ale, George Wright Blonde Moment. There's also the usual abundance of well chosen prints, fireside armchairs and a wide collection of cushioned dining chairs and wooden tables, and rugs on oak parquet; board games and background music. A big flagstoned terrace has heavy teak tables and a barbecue area, while the neat lawn beyond has a fountain among the picnic-table sets. The Worsley Bridgewater Canal heritage area is a ten-minute walk away.

Interesting food is served all day and includes sandwiches, char siu pork belly with pak choi, radish and pickled ginger salad, spicy deep-fried squid with patatas bravas and chorizo, butternut squash and brie wellington with dauphinoise potatoes, steak burger with toppings, coleslaw and chips, steak in ale pudding, rosemary and garlic chicken with pasta, wild mushrooms, bacon and spinach, salmon with mussels, samphire and seaweed butter, and puddings such as dark chocolate brownie with chocolate sauce and eccles cake with honeycomb ice-cream. *Benchmark main dish: beer-battered haddock and chips £12.95. Two-course evening meal £20.00.*

Brunning & Price ~ Manager David Green ~ Real ale ~ Open 9am-11pm (10.30pm Sun) ~ Bar food 12-10 (9.30 Sun) ~ Restaurant ~ Children welcome ~ Dogs allowed in bar ~ Wi-fi *Recommended by Gerry and Rosemary Dobson, Michael Butler, Dr and Mrs A K Clarke, W K Wood, Brian and Anna Marsden, Alun and Jennifer Evans*

Also Worth a Visit in Lancashire

Besides the fully inspected pubs, you might like to try these pubs that have been recommended to us and described by readers. Do tell us what you think of them: feedback@goodguides.com

ARKHOLME   SD5872
★ **Redwell** (015242) 21008
B6254 Over Kellet–Arkholme; LA6 1BQ
Nicely renovated 17th-c country pub-restaurant; spacious bar with wooden tables and chairs on flagstones, sofas by woodburner, very good individual cooking from landlord-chef including ingredients from next-door smokehouse, home-baked bread, well kept ales such as Tirril and good choice of other drinks, friendly attentive service, separate restaurant; background music; children welcome, muddy boots and dogs in bar, tables outside, seven bedrooms, open (and food) all day. *(Michael Doswell)*

BARLEY   SD8240
★ **Barley Mow** (01282) 690868
Barley Lane; BB12 9JX Bars and dining rooms resembling a hunting lodge; animal hide chairs and cushions, antlers and stuffed animals including a big boar's head, exposed-stone, cream-coloured or planked walls, woodburners (one in a raised two-sided fireplace), mix of furniture including long rustic wall seats on carpet, bare boards or flagstones, Moorhouses, Thwaites and Timothy Taylors, eight wines by the glass and well liked hearty food; background music, TV, board games, free wi-fi; children and dogs (in bar) welcome, comfortable bedrooms, open (and food) all day. *(Isobel Mackinlay, Charlie Parker)*

BARLEY   SD8240
Pendle (01282) 614808
Barley Lane; BB12 9JX Friendly 1930s stone pub in shadow of Pendle Hill, three cosy rooms, two log fires, and six well kept regional ales including Moorhouses, simple substantial food (all day weekends) using local produce including lamb from family farm, conservatory; garden, lovely village and good walking country, bedrooms, open all day Fri-Sun. *(David Heath)*

BARNSTON   SJ2783
★ **Fox & Hounds** (0151) 648 7685
3 miles from M53 junction 3: A552 towards Woodchurch, then left on A551; CH61 1BW Well run and welcoming early 20th-c pub; local Brimstage, Theakstons and guests, 60 malt whiskies and hearty home-made food (all day weekends, not Mon evening), roomy carpeted bay-windowed lounge with built-in banquettes and plush-cushioned captain's chairs around solid tables, old local prints and collection of police and other headgear, charming quarry-tiled corner with antique range, copper kettles, built-in pine kitchen cupboards, enamel food bins and earthenware, small traditional locals' bar with collection of horsebrasses and metal ashtrays, snug where children allowed; dogs welcome in bar, picnic-sets at back among tubs and hanging baskets, open all day. *(Ann and Tony Bennett-Hughes, Roger and Anne Newbury)*

BARTON   SD5137
Sparling (01772) 860830
A6 N of Broughton; PR3 5AA
Contemporary dining pub with well liked imaginative food including set deals, roomy bar with comfortable sofas and other seats, plenty of tables in linked areas off, wood and flagstone floors, modern fireplaces, real ales such as Thwaites Wainwright and good choice of wines by the glass, friendly efficient young staff; free wi-fi; children welcome, handy for M6. *(Charlie Parker)*

BELMONT   SD6715
Black Dog (01204) 811218
Church Street (A675); BL7 8AB Nicely set Holts pub with enjoyable food, well kept beers and friendly staff, recently refurbished retaining traditional character, coal and gas fires, picture-window dining extension; children and dogs welcome, seats outside with moorland views above village, attractive part-covered smokers' area, good walks, three decent well priced bedrooms, open (and food) all day. *(Hilary Forrest)*

BLACKBURN   SD6525
★ **Oyster & Otter** (01254) 203200
1.8 miles from M65 junction 3: A674 towards Blackburn, turn right at Feniscowles mini roundabout, signposted to Darwen and Tockholes, into Livesey Branch Road; BB2 5DQ Distinctive clapboard and stone building in modern new england style; cushioned dining booths by big windows on one side, other cosy seating areas divided by shoulder-high walls and large central hearth, end part with comfy sofas, very good food including signature fish/seafood from open kitchen, Thwaites Wainwright, a guest ale and ten wines by the glass, helpful young staff in

aprons; background music (live third Fri of month), free wi-fi; children welcome, seats on decking above road, open (and food) all day. *(Jo Garnett, Pat and Tony Martin, W K Wood, Douglas Power)*

BLACKSTONE EDGE   SD9617
★ **White House** (01706) 378456
A58 Ripponden–Littleborough, just W of B6138; OL15 0LG Beautifully placed moorland pub with fine panoramic views, emphasis on good value hearty food from sandwiches up, prompt friendly service and a warm welcoming atmosphere, four real ales including Theakstons, belgian bottled beers and decent choice of wines, carpeted main bar with fire, other areas off, most tables used for dining; children welcome till 9pm, no dogs, open (and food) all day Sun. *(George Sanderson)*

BOLTON   SD7112
Brewery Tap (01204) 302837
Belmont Road; BL1 7AN Two-room corner tap for Bank Top, their full range kept well and a guest, knowledgeable friendly staff, no food; free wi-fi; children (until 7pm) and dogs welcome, seats outside, open all day. *(Charles Welch)*

BRINDLE   SD5924
★ **Cavendish Arms** (01254) 852912
3 miles from M6 junction 29, via A6 and B5256 (Sandy Lane); PR6 8NG Traditional village pub dating from the 15th c on corner adjacent to church; beams, cosy snugs with open fires, stained-glass windows, carpets throughout, good inexpensive home-made food (all day weekends) from sandwiches up, Banks's, Marstons and two guest ales, friendly helpful service; children welcome, dogs in tap room, heated canopied terrace with water feature, more tables in side garden, good walks, open all day. *(Gordon and Margaret Ormondroyd)*

BROUGHTON   SD4838
Plough at Eaves (01772) 690233
A6 N through Broughton, first left into Station Lane under a mile after traffic lights, then left after 1.5 miles, Eaves Lane; PR4 0BJ Pleasantly unpretentious old country tavern with two beamed homely bars, well kept Thwaites ales and good choice of enjoyable reasonably priced food, friendly accommodating service, lattice windows and traditional furnishings, old guns over woodburner in one room, log fire in dining bar with conservatory; background music; children welcome, front terrace and spacious side/back garden, well equipped play area, open (and food) all day weekends. *(Julie Swift)*

BURY   SD8008
Swan & Cemetery (0161) 764 1508
Manchester Road; BL9 9NS Recently renovated Thwaites pub with two bars and restaurant, their ales kept well and reasonably priced, enjoyable food from extensive menu including good choice of fish dishes, prompt friendly service; Weds quiz; seats out on south-facing back deck, open all day. *(Gerry and Rosemary Dobson)*

BURY   SD8313
Trackside (0161) 764 6461
East Lancashire Railway station, Bolton Street; BL9 0EY Welcoming busy station bar by East Lancs steam railway; bright, airy and clean with ten real ales including a house beer from local Outstanding, also bottled imports, real ciders and great range of whiskies, enjoyable home-made food (not Mon, Tues); folk night last Thurs of month; children (till 7pm) and dogs welcome, platform tables under canopy, open all day. *(P A Lord)*

CARNFORTH   SD5173
Longlands (01524) 781256
Tewitfield, about 2 miles N; A6070, off A6; LA6 1JH Family-run village inn with good food in bar and airy restaurant from pizzas and pub favourites up, four local beers, friendly staff; children and dogs welcome (their black lab is Ronnie); bedrooms and self-catering cottages, Lancaster Canal and M6 nearby, open all day. *(John Evans)*

CHEADLE HULME   SJ8785
Church Inn (0161) 485 1897
Ravenoak Road (A5149 SE); SK8 7EG Popular old family-run pub with decent food from varied menu including deals, well kept Robinsons beers and nice selection of wines by the glass, gleaming brass on panelled walls, warming coal fire, pleasant staff and locals, back restaurant; live music most Sun evenings; children welcome, seats outside (some under cover), car park across road, open all day. *(Lionel Smith)*

CHIPPING   SD6141
★ **Dog & Partridge** (01995) 61201
Hesketh Lane; crossroads Chipping–Longridge with Inglewhite–Clitheroe; PR3 2TH Comfortable old-fashioned and much altered 16th-c dining pub in grand countryside, long-serving owners, enjoyable food (all day Sun), ales such as Thwaites and Tetleys, friendly service, beams, exposed stone walls and good log fire, small armchairs around close-set tables in main lounge, restaurant; free wi-fi; children welcome, no dogs inside, open all day Sun, closed Mon, Tues evening. *(George Sanderson)*

CHORLTON CUM HARDY   SJ8193
Horse & Jockey (0161) 860 7794
Chorlton Green; M21 9HS Comfortably refurbished pub with mock-Tudor façade, light and modern with several different seating areas around central bar, own-brewed Bootleg ales, Holts and guests, plenty of wines by the glass, knowledgeable chatty staff, good choice of food from sandwiches

and deli boards through burgers and hotdogs up, further dining areas upstairs (evening/weekends); live music and quiz nights, TV; children allowed till 9pm, dogs very welcome, plenty of tables on front terrace looking across to green, open (and food) all day. *(Rosie and John Moore)*

CLAUGHTON   SD5666
★ **Fenwick Arms** (01524) 221157
A683 Kirkby Lonsdale–Lancaster; LA2 9LA Civilised 250-year-old black and white pub in Lune Valley, mainly popular for its particularly good fish and seafood; smartly refurbished with white-painted beams in wonky ceilings, open fires (one in a black range) and painted panelling, upholstered and antique-style dining chairs around all shapes of tables on carpet or bare boards, window seats with scatter cushions, Thwaites Wainwright, Timothy Taylors Landlord and a guest, 14 wines by the glass and a good choice of spirits, efficient friendly staff; background music, free wi-fi; children and dogs (in bar) welcome, picnic-sets on front terrace, nine comfortable modern bedrooms, open (and food) all day. *(Lindy Andrews, Dr Simon Innes, Ray and Winifred Halliday, Maddie Purvis, John Sargeant, Steve Whalley)*

CLITHEROE   SD7441
New Inn (01200) 423312
Parson Lane; BB7 2JN Traditional old-fashioned local with ten or more well kept ales from central bar, friendly knowledgeable staff, cosy rooms with log fires; live music including fortnightly irish sessions Sun afternoon; dogs welcome, seats out front and back, open all day. *(John Poulter)*

COLNE   SD8940
Black Lane Ends (01282) 863070
Skipton Old Road, Foulridge; BB8 7EP Country pub tucked away in quiet lane, good sensibly priced food from large menu, well kept real ales including Timothy Taylors Landlord, cheerful attentive staff, two massive fires, small restaurant; children welcome, garden with play area and good Pennine views, handy for canal and reservoir walks. *(Maddie Purvis)*

DELPH   SD9809
Royal Oak (01457) 874460
Off A6052 about 100 metres W of White Lion, turn up steep Lodge Lane and keep on up into Broad Lane; OL3 5TX Welcoming traditional 18th-c pub opposite old moorland church in steep narrow winding lane, great views of surrounding valleys, real fires in three small rooms, comfortable solid furniture, four well kept ales including

Millstone and Moorhouses, no food; closed Mon and lunchtimes apart from Sun when open 12-6pm. *(Charlie Parker)*

DENSHAW   SD9710
Printers Arms (01457) 874248
Oldham Road; OL3 5SN Above Oldham in shadow of Saddleworth Moor, modernised interior with small log-fire bar and three other rooms, popular good value food including bargain set menu (till 6.30pm, 4pm Sat, not Sun), Black Sheep and Timothy Taylors Golden Best, several wines by the glass, friendly efficient young staff; children welcome, lovely views from two-tier beer garden, open (and food) all day. *(Stuart Paulley)*

DENSHAW   SD9711
★ **Rams Head** (01457) 874802
2 miles from M62 junction 22; A672 towards Oldham, pub N of village; OL3 5UN Sweeping moorland views from this welcoming roadside dining pub (don't be put off by its rather austere exterior); really good food (all day weekends) including seasonal game and seafood, well kept ales such as Marstons and Timothy Taylors, efficient friendly service, four thick-walled little rooms, beam-and-plank ceilings, panelling, oak settles and built-in benches, log fires, coffee shop and adjacent delicatessen selling local produce; soft background music; children welcome (not Sat evening), closed Mon. *(Gordon and Margaret Ormondroyd)*

DENTON   SJ9395
Lowes Arms (0161) 336 3064
Hyde Road (A57); M34 3FF Thriving 19th-c pub with up to four well kept ales such as local Hornbeam and Phoenix (the on-site brewery remains closed), jovial community-spirited landlord and helpful friendly staff, wide choice of good reasonably priced food including daily specials, bar with pool and darts, restaurant; children and dogs welcome, tables outside, smokers' shelter, open all day. *(Jack and Hilary Burton)*

DIGGLE   SE0007
Diggle (01457) 872741
Village signed off A670 just N of Dobcross; OL3 5JZ Sturdy four-square hillside inn overlooking west end of Standedge Canal tunnel; good value all-day food (till 7.30pm Sun) from snacks up, well kept ales such as Black Sheep, Copper Dragon, Millstone and Timothy Taylors, helpful staff; picnic-sets among trees, quiet spot just below the moors, four bedrooms, open (and food) all day. *(John Sargeant)*

We include some hotels with a good bar that offers facilities comparable to those of a pub.

DOBCROSS SD9906
Swan (01457) 873451
The Square; OL3 5AA Renovated low-beamed 18th-c pub, three areas off small central bar, all with open fires, flagstones and upholstered bench seating, five Marstons-related beers and enjoyable home-made food including specials, friendly atmosphere; folk, theatre and comedy evenings in upstairs function room; children and dogs welcome, tables out at front, attractive village below moors, open all day weekends, closed Mon lunchtime. *(Patricia Hawkins)*

DOLPHINHOLME SD5153
Fleece (01524) 791233
A couple of miles from M6 junction 33; W of village; Chipping Lane/Anyon Road; LA2 9AQ Extensively renovated old stone inn (parts date from the 16th c), various rooms including black-beamed bar with rugs on flagstones and log fire with unusual copper canopy, four well kept regularly changing ales and decent wines by the glass, popular sensibly priced food (good value set lunch), friendly efficient service, dining lounge with some modern booth seating and sofas in front of woodburner, little shop selling local produce; children and dogs welcome, modern rattan-style furniture on terrace, Trough of Bowland views, nine comfortable well appointed bedrooms, excellent breakfast, closed Mon, otherwise open all day. *(Richard Heath)*

DUNHAM TOWN SJ7488
Axe & Cleaver (0161) 928 3391
School Lane; WA14 4SE Big 19th-c country house converted into spacious open-plan Chef & Brewer, good value popular food from light lunchtime choices and sharing plates up (best to book Sun lunch), three well kept ales, friendly service; children welcome, garden picnic-sets, handy for nearby Dunham Massey (NT), open (and food) all day. *(Jeremy King)*

DUNHAM TOWN SJ7288
Vine (0161) 928 3275
Barns Lane, Dunham Massey; WA14 5RU Tucked-away old-fashioned little village local with friendly staff and regulars, well kept Sam Smiths and several ciders, enjoyable generously served lunchtime food; dogs welcome, tables outside, handy for Dunham Massey (NT), open all day. *(Hilary Forrest)*

EDENFIELD SD7919
Coach (01706) 825000
Market Street; BL0 OHJ Refurbished and extended 19th-c dining pub, enjoyable food from sandwiches and sharing plates up, good value weekday set lunch and afternoon teas, local ales, over a dozen wines by the glass and good range of gins, friendly relaxed atmosphere; free wi-fi; children welcome, disabled access/facilities, closed Mon, otherwise open (and food) all day. *(Charles Welch)*

FENCE SD8237
Fence Gate (01282) 618101
2.6 miles from M65 junction 13; Wheatley Lane Road, just off A6068 W; BB12 9EE Imposing 18th-c dining pub with good choice of enjoyable food, five real ales and several wines by the glass, service not always speedy, refurbished panelled bar with pewter counter and woodburner in large stone fireplace, contemporary brasserie plus various function rooms, look out for their display of over 600 gins; background and regular live music; children welcome, rattan-style furniture out at front, open all day. *(Charlie Parker)*

FENCE SD8237
★ White Swan (01282) 611773
Wheatley Lane; BB12 9QA Whitewashed village dining pub with comfortably renovated Victorian-style interior, highly regarded imaginative food (not cheap) from short daily changing menu, good service, four well kept Timothy Taylors ales from curved polished wood servery, nice wines, own infused spirits and good coffee, old pictures of the pub, some antlers and stuffed animal heads, wall lights and chandeliers, fireplace at each end; children welcome, outside seating on two levels with wooden tables, open all day, no food Mon. *(Steve Whalley)*

GARSTANG SD4945
Th'Owd Tithebarn (01995) 604486
Off Church Street; PR3 1PA Creeper-clad tithe barn with big terrace overlooking Lancaster Canal marina and narrow boats; linked high-raftered rooms with red patterned carpet or flagstones, upholstered stools, armchairs and leather tub seats around assorted shiny tables, lots of cartwheels, rustic lamps, horse tack and a fine old kitchen range, four changing ales, fair value wines by the glass and enjoyable well priced pubby food from hot and cold sandwiches to grills and specials, friendly staff; Tues quiz, TV, free wi-fi; children and dogs (in bar) welcome, open all day (food all day weekends). *(Rosie and John Moore)*

GISBURN SD8248
White Bull (01200) 415805
Main Street (A59); BB7 4HE Spacious refurbished roadside pub; opened-up dining rooms on either side of entrance, more room further back to right of bar, taupe-painted walls and stone-effect wallpaper, nice mix of dark furniture on polished wood or flagstone floors, some beams and whitewashed standing timbers, good attractively presented food cooked by chef-owner from pub standards up, four well kept ales (including a Holts beer named for the pub) from semi-circular

counter with cherry wood top, friendly service; children and dogs (in one section) welcome, narrow access to large back car park, open all day. *(Steve Whalley)*

GOOSNARGH   SD5738
★ **Horns**   (01772) 865230

On junction of Horns Lane and Inglewhite Road; pub signed off B5269, towards Chipping; PR3 2FJ Early 18th-c inn (same family ownership since 1952) with neatly kept carpeted rooms including a rare 'parlour' behind the servery, popular home cooking from pub standards to local duck and game, own Goosnargh ales and an occasional microbrewery guest, plenty of wines by the glass and good choice of malts, courteous helpful service, log fires; background music; children welcome, dogs in garden only, six bedrooms in converted stone barn (some with road noise), caravan park, not far from M6, open (and food) all day Sun, closed Mon lunchtime. *(Steve Whalley)*

GOOSNARGH   SD5636
Stags Head   (01772) 446185

Whittingham Lane (B5269); PR3 2AU Old roadside pub under welcoming new management; lots of separate areas rambling around central servery, open fires, good well presented interesting food (all day weekends, not Mon) at reasonable prices including daily specials and meal deals, attentive courteous service, Theakstons Best and guests such as Robinsons, restaurant; children and dogs welcome, tables out in pleasant garden, closed Mon lunchtime, otherwise open all day. *(Frances Wilson)*

GREAT ECCLESTON   SD4240
★ **Farmers Arms**   (01995) 672018

Halsall Square (just off A586); PR3 0YE Popular attractively refurbished country pub not far from Fylde Coast and Blackpool; smart dining areas, on two floors, with painted panelled walls and eclectic collection of seating including cushioned settles on carpet or polished boards, woodburners in stone fireplaces, Thwaites Wainwright, Timothy Taylors Landlord and a guest, around 14 wines by the glass and highly regarded interesting food with emphasis on fish/seafood and grills, good friendly service; free wi-fi; children and dogs (in bar) welcome, teak furniture on sheltered terrace, open (and food) all day. *(Lindy Andrews, Dr Simon Innes, Gordon and Margaret Ormondroyd)*

GREAT MITTON   SD7139
★ **Three Fishes**   (01254) 826888

Mitton Road (B6246, off A59 NW of Whalley); BB7 9PQ Stylish and contemporary with plenty of cosy corners; areas by bar are elegantly traditional with two big stone fireplaces and rugs on polished floors, other individually furnished rooms with some exposed stonework, very

good attractively presented food, Marstons, Moorhouses, Reedley Hallows and Thwaites, a dozen wines by the glass and 15 malt whiskies, friendly smartly dressed young staff and good chatty atmosphere; background music, free wi-fi; children and dogs (in bar) welcome, terrace and garden with fine Ribble Valley views, open (and food) all day. *(Graham and Elizabeth Hargreaves, Steve Whalley, W K Wood)*

GREENFIELD   SD9904
King William IV   (01457) 873933

Chew Valley Road (A669); OL3 7DD Welcoming 19th-c village local with half a dozen well kept ales including local Greenfield and Millstone, enjoyable home-made food (not Mon, Tues or lunchtimes Weds, Thurs); sports TV; children and dogs welcome, tables on walled front terrace, open all day. *(John Sargeant)*

GREENFIELD   SD9904
Railway Hotel   (01457) 872307

Shaw Hall Bank Road, opposite station; OL3 7JZ Friendly four-room stone pub with half a dozen well kept mainly local ales, no food, old local photographs and open fire; live music Thurs, Fri and Sun, games bar with darts and pool; on the Transpennine Rail Ale Trail, open all day. *(Julie Swift)*

HESKIN GREEN   SD5315
Farmers Arms   (01257) 451276

Wood Lane, N of M6 junction 27); PR7 5NP Popular country pub under long-serving family, good choice of well priced, generously served home-made food in two-level dining area including weekend breakfasts from 9am, ales such as Black Sheep, Jennings, Prospect and Timothy Taylors, heavy black beams, sparkling brasses, china and stuffed animals, darts in public bar; background music, open mike nights and other regular events, Sky TV; children welcome, dogs in bar/lounge, big colourful garden with play area, more tables front and side, five good value bedrooms, open all day. *(Maddie Purvis)*

HEST BANK   SD4766
★ **Hest Bank Inn**   (01524) 824339

Hest Bank Lane; off A6 just N of Lancaster; LA2 6DN Good choice of enjoyable reasonably priced food from pub favourites up in picturesque three-bar coaching inn, nice setting close to Morecambe Bay, well kept ales such as Black Sheep and Thwaites, decent wines, friendly helpful young staff, separate restaurant area with pleasant conservatory; children welcome, plenty of tables out by Lancaster Canal, open all day. *(Roy and Gill Payne)*

HORNBY   SD5868
Castle   (01524) 221204

Main Street; LA2 8JT Bustling, sizeable Georgian inn with interesting modernised interior, bar with leather sofas and open fires, bistro and restaurant, tasty reasonably priced food from sandwiches, pub favourites and pizzas up, Black Sheep, Bowland and guests, good selection of other drinks, friendly helpful staff; courtyard tables, six boutique bedrooms, open all day. *(Michael Butler)*

HURST GREEN   SD6837

★ **Shireburn Arms** (01254) 826678
Whalley Road (B6243 Clitheroe–Goosnargh); BB7 9QJ Welcoming 17th-c hotel with peaceful Ribble Valley views from big airy restaurant and neatly kept garden, enjoyable food (all day weekends) from sandwiches and traditional dishes to daily specials, leather armchairs, sofas and log fire in beamed and flagstoned lounge bar with linked dining area, two well kept ales such as Lancaster and Thwaites, several wines by the glass, friendly helpful service, daily papers; children and dogs welcome, pretty Tolkien walk from here, 22 comfortable bedrooms, open all day from 9am for coffee.
(Steve Whalley)

HYDE   SJ9493

Joshua Bradley (0161) 406 6776
Stockport Road, Gee Cross; SK14 5EZ Victorian mansion house handsomely converted to pub-restaurant keeping panelling, moulded ceilings and imposing fireplaces, good range of well priced popular food, Hydes and a couple of guest beers in fine condition, friendly efficient staff, conservatory; children welcome, heated terrace, play area, open (and food) all day.
(Hilary Forrest)

HYDE   SJ9595

Sportsman (0161) 368 5000
Mottram Road; SK14 2NN Welcoming Victorian local with Rossendale ales and lots of changing guests (frequent beer festivals), bargain bar food, popular upstairs cuban restaurant, bare boards and open fires, pub games; children and dogs welcome, back terrace with heated smokers' shelter, open all day. *(Charlie Parker)*

IRBY   SJ2586

★ **Irby Mill** (0151) 604 0194
Mill Lane, off Greasby Road; CH49 3NT Converted miller's sandstone cottage (original windmill demolished 1898), friendly and welcoming, with eight well kept ales including Caledonian Deuchars IPA, Greene King Abbot and Charles Wells Bombardier, good choice of wines by the glass, ample helpings of popular reasonably priced food from sandwiches up, efficient service, two low-beamed traditional flagstoned rooms and extended carpeted dining area, log fire, interesting old photographs and history; tables on terraces and revamped side area, good local walks, open (and food) all day, gets crowded evenings/weekends when parking limited. *(Clive Watkin)*

LANCASTER   SD4761

★ **Borough** (01524) 64170
Dalton Square; LA1 1PP Popular city-centre pub, stylish and civilised, with chandeliers, dark leather sofas and armchairs, lamps on antique tables, high stools and elbow tables, eight ales including some from on-site microbrewery, lots of bottled beers, big dining room with central tables and booths along one side, enjoyable food with much emphasis on local suppliers, daily specials and meal deals, jams and local produce for sale; upstairs comedy night Sun; children and dogs welcome, lovely tree-sheltered garden, bedrooms, open (and food) all day from 8am for breakfast. *(Paul Humphreys)*

LANCASTER   SD4761

Sun (01524) 66006
Church Street; LA1 1ET Hotel's refurbished bar, ten well kept ales including five from Lancaster, plenty of continental beers and good choice of wines by the glass, popular food from doorstep sandwiches, deli boards and pub staples up, exposed stonework, panelling and several fireplaces, conservatory; background music, TV; children welcome away from servery, tables on walled and paved terrace, 16 comfortable bedrooms, open all day. *(Rosie and John Moore)*

LANCASTER   SD4761

Water Witch (01524) 63828
Parking in Aldcliffe Road behind Royal Lancaster Infirmary, off A6; LA1 1SU Attractive conversion of 18th-c canalside stables, flagstones, stripped stone, rafters and pitch-pine panelling, half a dozen well kept changing ales, fairly traditional food from sandwiches and deli boards up including weekday lunch deal, upstairs restaurant; Thurs quiz, free wi-fi; children in eating areas, picnic-sets out by water, moorings, open (and food) all day.
(Rosie and John Moore, Lionel Smith)

LANESHAW BRIDGE   SD9141

Alma (01282) 857830
Emmott Lane, off A6068 E of Colne; BB8 7EG Attractively renovated 18th-c inn with popular food, several wines by the glass and four real ales including Moorhouses Pride of Pendle, flagstoned bar, friendly staff, part-panelled lounge with rugs on bare boards, open fires, large garden room extension; background music; well behaved children and dogs welcome, ten comfortable well appointed bedrooms, open (and food) all day, breakfast for non-residents.
(David Heath, John and Eleanor Holdsworth)

LATHOM   SD4510

Ring o' Bells (01704) 893157
In Lathom, turn right into Ring o' Bells Lane; L40 5TE Up for sale as we went to press, this has been a good family-friendly

canalside pub; linked rooms filled with fine antique furniture, rugs on flagstones, paintings, prints and large mirrors on walls, staffordshire dogs and decorative plates above open fires, ales such as Cumberland, Lancaster, Moorhouses and Thwaites, good wines by the glass and over 25 whiskies, fair priced interesting food (all day weekends), downstairs room and indoor/outdoor children's play areas; background music (live last Fri of month), TV, darts, board games, free wi-fi; dogs allowed in bar, seats outside, vegetable garden and orchard, open all day. *(Jo Garnett)*

LITTLEBOROUGH   SD9517

Moorcock (01706) 378156

Halifax Road (A58); OL15 0LD Long roadside inn high on the moors with far-reaching views, friendly and popular, with wide range of good value food (all day Thurs-Sun) from sandwiches and pub favourites up in flagstoned bar or restaurant, four well kept beers; sports TV; terrace tables taking in the view, seven comfortable reasonably priced bedrooms, open all day. *(George Sanderson)*

LIVERPOOL   SJ3489

Baltic Fleet (0151) 709 3116

Wapping, near Albert Dock; L1 8DQ Unusual bow-fronted pub with six interesting beers including Wapping (brewed in the cellar), real ciders and several wines by the glass, simple well cooked/priced lunchtime food such as traditional scouse, bare boards, big arched windows, simple mix of furnishings and some nautical paraphernalia, fires in parlour and snug; background music, TV; children welcome in eating areas, dogs in bar, back terrace, open all day. *(David Thorpe)*

LIVERPOOL   SJ3589

Belvedere (0151) 709 0303

Sugnall Street; L7 7EB Unspoilt 19th-c two-room pub with friendly chatty atmosphere, original features including etched glass and coal fires, four well kept changing ales such as Brimstage and Liverpool Organic, good selection of bottled beers, real cider and fine choice of gins (excellent gin and tonic); dogs welcome, open all day. *(Helen McLagan)*

LIVERPOOL   SJ3589

Cracke (0151) 709 4171

Rice Street; L1 9BB Friendly unchanging local with five well kept ales including Phoenix and Thwaites, traditional cider, no food, small unspoilt bar with bare boards and bench seats, snug and bigger back room with unusual Beatles diorama, local artwork and some photos of John Lennon who used to drink here; juke box, sports TV; picnic-sets in sizeable tree-shaded back garden, open all day. *(Lionel Smith)*

LIVERPOOL   SJ3590

Crown (0151) 707 6027

Lime Street; L1 1JQ Well preserved art nouveau showpiece; fine tiled fireplace and copper bar front, dark leather banquettes, panelling and splendid ornate ceiling, smaller back room with another good fireplace, impressive staircase sweeping up under cupola to handsome area with ornate windows, five real ales and good range of low-priced food; sports TV; open all day from 8am for breakfast, very handy for the train station. *(Lionel Smith)*

LIVERPOOL   SJ3589

Dispensary (0151) 709 2160

Renshaw Street; L1 2SP Small busy central pub worth knowing for its very well kept beers (up to ten), good choice of bottled imports too, no food, bare boards and polished panelling, wonderful etched windows, comfortable raised back bar with coal fire, some Victorian medical artefacts; background music, silent TVs, notices on house rules; open all day. *(Lionel Smith, Charlie Parker)*

LIVERPOOL   SJ3589

Fly in the Loaf (0151) 708 0817

Hardman Street; L1 9AS Former bakery with smart gleaming bar serving Okells, guest ales and several foreign beers, enjoyable simple home-made food at low prices, efficient, friendly service, long refurbished room with panelling and some raised sections; background music, sports TV, upstairs lavatories; open all day, till midnight Fri, Sat. *(Charlie Parker)*

LIVERPOOL   SJ3490

Hole In Ye Wall (0151) 227 3809

Off Dale Street; L2 2AW Character 18th-c pub (the city's oldest) with thriving local atmosphere in high-beamed panelled bar, half a dozen changing ales fed by gravity from upstairs (no cellar as pub is on Quaker burial site), baguettes, pies, burgers and so forth, friendly staff, plenty of woodwork, stained glass and old Liverpool photographs, coal-effect gas fire in unusual brass-canopied fireplace; live music evenings Mon, Fri and Sat, traditional singalong Sun, sports TV; children allowed till 5pm, no dogs, open all day. *(Lionel Smith, George Sanderson)*

LIVERPOOL   SJ3490

Hub (0151) 709 2401

Hanover Street; L1 4AA Bar-bistro in bow-fronted corner building; light modern interior with wood flooring and big windows, good fairly priced food from extensive menu, decent wines and five real ales including Liverpool Organic, friendly staff; children welcome, open all day and can get very busy. *(David H Bennett)*

LIVERPOOL SJ3490
Lion (0151) 236 1734
Moorfields, off Tithebarn Street; L2 2BP
Beautifully preserved ornate Victorian
tavern, great changing beer choice and
over 80 malt whiskies, good value simple
lunchtime food including home-made pork
pies, open sandwiches and baguettes,
friendly staff, sparkling etched glass and
serving hatches in central bar, unusual
wallpaper and matching curtains, big
mirrors, panelling and tilework, two small
back lounges one with fine glass dome,
coal fire; quiz night Tues; open all day.
(George Sanderson)

LIVERPOOL SJ3590
Ma Egerton's Stage Door
(0151) 345 3525 *Pudsey Street,
opposite side entrance to Lime Street
station; L1 1JA* Victorian pub behind the
Empire Theatre and named after a former
long-serving landlady/theatrical agent;
refurbished but keeping old-fashioned
character with green leather button-back
banquettes (note the bell pushes), swagged
curtains, wood floors, panelling and small
period fireplace, lots of celebrity pictures and
other memorabilia, a couple of changing ales
and enjoyable food including sharing plates
and pizzas, friendly staff; Mon quiz night;
open all day. *(David H Bennett)*

LIVERPOOL SJ3589
Peter Kavanaghs (0151) 709 3443
*Egerton Street, off Catherine Street;
L8 7LY* Character Victorian pub popular
with locals and students; interesting décor
in several small rooms, old-world murals,
stained glass and all kinds of bric-a-brac (lots
hanging from ceiling), piano, wooden settles
and real fires, well kept Greene King Abbot
and guests, friendly licensees; open all day
(till 1am Fri, Sat). *(George Sanderson)*

LIVERPOOL SJ3589
Philharmonic Dining Rooms
(0151) 707 2837 *36 Hope Street;
corner of Hardman Street; L1 9BX*
Beautifully preserved Victorian pub with
wonderful period detail; centrepiece
mosaic-faced counter, heavily carved and
polished mahogany partitions radiating out
under intricate plasterwork ceiling, main
hall with stained glass of Boer War heroes
Baden-Powell and Lord Roberts, rich
panelling, mosaic floor and copper panels
of musicians above fireplace, other areas
including two side rooms called Brahms
and Liszt, the original Adamant gents' is
also worth a look, ten real ales, several
wines by the glass and decent choice of
malt whiskies, fair-priced food, service may
suffer at busy times; background music and
machines; children welcome till 7pm, open
(and food) all day. *(David Field, Susan and
John Douglas)*

LIVERPOOL SJ3589
Roscoe Head (0151) 709 4365
Roscoe Street; L1 2SX Unassuming old
local with cosy bar, snug and two other
spotless unspoilt little rooms, friendly
long-serving landlady, well kept Jennings,
Tetleys and five guests, inexpensive home-
made lunches (not weekends), interesting
memorabilia and traditional games such as
crib; quiz nights Tues and Thurs; open all day
till midnight. *(Jack and Hilary Burton)*

LIVERPOOL SJ3490
Ship & Mitre (0151) 236 0859
Dale Street; L2 2JH Friendly local with
fine art deco exterior and ship-like interior,
up to a dozen unusual changing ales (many
beer festivals), real ciders and more than
70 bottled beers, decent choice of good value
food (all day Fri-Sun) such as wraps, burgers
and all-day breakfast, upstairs function room
with original 1930s décor; well behaved
children (till 7pm) and dogs welcome, open
all day. *(Charlie Parker)*

LIVERPOOL SJ3490
★Thomas Rigbys (0151) 236 3269
Dale Street; L2 2EZ Spacious beamed and
panelled Victorian pub, mosaic flooring, old
tiles and etched glass, Okells ales and three
changing guests from impressively long bar,
also good range of imported draught and
bottled beers, steps up to main area, table
service from attentive staff, reasonably
priced hearty home-made food till 7pm;
sports TV; disabled access, seats in big
courtyard, open all day. *(Jack and Hilary
Burton)*

LIVERPOOL SJ3490
White Star (0151) 231 6861
*Rainford Gardens, off Matthew Street;
L2 6PT* Popular traditional local dating
from the 18th c; cosy bar with lots of
woodwork, boxing photographs, White Star
shipping line and Beatles memorabilia (they
used to rehearse in back room), well kept
ales including Bowland and Draught Bass,
basic snacky food, friendly staff; sports TV;
wheelchair access (ladies' is upstairs),
open all day. *(Lionel Smith)*

LONGRIDGE SD6038
★Derby Arms (01772) 782370
*Chipping Road, Thornley; 1.5 miles
N of Longridge on back road to
Chipping; PR3 2NB* Creeper-clad village
pub with attractively refurbished bar and
connecting dining rooms, wide floorboards
or grey carpet, woodburner and open fire,
all manner of seating including high-backed
chairs, settles with scatter cushions, wall
banquettes and leather-topped stools,
Copper Dragon, Thwaites and Timothy
Taylors Boltmaker from stylish oak-planked
servery, good food including chargrills
and daily fish specials, cheerful helpful

service; free wi-fi; children and dogs (in bar) welcome, good quality furniture on front terrace behind picket fence, comfortable airy bedrooms, open (and food) all day, breakfast for non-residents. *(Gilly and Frank Newman, Steve Whalley)*

LONGRIDGE SD6037

New Drop (01254) 878338

Higher Road, Longridge Fell, parallel to B6243 Longridge–Clitheroe; PR3 2YX Pleasant modernised dining pub in lovely moors-edge country overlooking Ribble Valley, good choice of popular reasonably priced food, decent wines and three well kept ales (usually Bowland Hen Harrier), friendly service; children welcome, open all day Sun, closed Mon. *(Julie Swift)*

LYDGATE SD9704

★**White Hart** (01457) 872566

Stockport Road; Lydgate not marked on some maps and not the one near Todmorden; take A669 Oldham–Saddleworth, right at brow of hill to A6050 after almost 2.5 miles; OL4 4JJ Smart up-to-date dining pub overlooking Pennine moors, mix of locals in bar or simpler end rooms and diners in elegant brasserie with smartly dressed staff, high quality food (not cheap), Lees, Timothy Taylors and a guest beer, 16 wines by the glass, old beams and exposed stonework contrasting with deep red or purple walls and modern artwork, open fires, newspapers; various events and a popular wedding/conference venue; children welcome, dogs in bar, picnic-sets on back lawn making most of position, 12 bedrooms, open all day. *(Charles Welch)*

LYTHAM SD3627

Queens (01253) 737316

A584/Bath Street; FY8 5LB Refurbished Victorian pub-restaurant-hotel with outdoor seating looking across green to sea and windmill, well kept ales including Theakstons Best, enjoyable food (all day weekends) from sandwiches to daily specials, friendly relaxed atmosphere; children welcome and dogs (treats for them), ten bedrooms, open all day. *(Alf Wright)*

LYTHAM SD3627

★**Taps** (01253) 736226

A584 S of Blackpool; Henry Street – in centre, one street in from West Beach; FY8 5LE Cheerful town pub a couple of minutes from the beach; around ten well kept ales including Greene King, proper cider, friendly knowledgeable staff, simple lunchtime food (not Sun); redecorated open-plan bar with bare-boards or tiled floor, stripped-brick walls, open giant clocks and crystal chandeliers, open fires, new dining

area leading through to sunny terrace; quiz Mon, TV for major sports; children allowed till 7.30pm, parking nearby difficult – best to use West Beach car park on seafront (free Sun), open all day. *(Steve Whalley)*

MANCHESTER SJ8498

Angel (0161) 833 4786

Angel Street, off Rochdale Road; M4 4BR Friendly place on edge of the Northern Quarter, good value home-made food (not Sun evening), ten well kept ales including Bobs, bottled beers and a couple of ciders/perries, piano in bare-boards bar, smaller upstairs restaurant with two log fires and local artwork; live acoustic music Tues, free wi-fi; children and dogs welcome, back beer garden, open all day (till 2am Fri, Sat). *(P A Lord)*

MANCHESTER SJ8398

Ape & Apple (0161) 839 9624

John Dalton Street; M2 6HQ Large open-plan pub with five well kept good value Holts beers plus guests, hearty traditional bar food including deals, comfortable seating, bare boards, carpet and tiles, lots of old prints and posters, upstairs restaurant/function room, friendly atmosphere; Weds comedy night, juke box, games machines; children and dogs welcome, heated central courtyard, open all day (till 9pm Sun). *(Rosie and John Moore)*

MANCHESTER SJ8498

Bar Fringe (0161) 835 3815

Swan Street; M4 5JN Popular long bare-boards bar specialising in continental beers, also six changing ales from smaller breweries and real cider, friendly staff, basic snacks till 4pm (no food weekends), daily papers, shelves of empty beer bottles, posters and cartoons on the walls, motorcycle hanging above the door; rock juke box; no children or dogs, tables out behind, open all day. *(Maddie Purvis)*

MANCHESTER SJ8397

★**Britons Protection** (0161) 236 5895

Great Bridgewater Street, corner of Lower Mosley Street; M1 5LE Lively unpretentious pub with rambling rooms and notable tiled murals of 1819 Peterloo Massacre (took place nearby); plush little front bar with tiled floor, glossy brown and russet wall tiles, solid woodwork and ornate red and gold ceiling, two cosy inner lounges, both served by hatch, with attractive brass wall lamps and solidly comfortable furnishings, coal-effect gas fire in simple art nouveau fireplace, five ales including Jennings, Robinsons and a Thwaites beer named for the pub from massive counter with heated footrail, also some 330 malt whiskies, straightforward lunchtime food Mon-Fri; occasional storytelling and live

---

If we know a pub has an outdoor play area for children, we mention it.

music; children till 5pm, tables in enclosed back garden, handy for Bridgewater Hall concerts, open all day (very busy lunchtime and weekends). *(Dr and Mrs A K Clarke)*

MANCHESTER SJ8498
Castle (0161) 237 9485
Oldham Street, about 200 metres from Piccadilly, on right; M4 1LE Restored 18th-c pub well run by former *Coronation Street* actor; simple traditional front bar, small snug, Robinsons ales and guests from fine bank of handpumps, Weston's Old Rosie cider, back room for regular live music and other events, overspill space upstairs; nice tilework outside, open all day till late. *(Charles Welch)*

MANCHESTER SJ8497
Circus (0161) 236 5818
Portland Street; M1 4GX Traditional little two-room local with friendly staff serving well kept Tetleys and Robinsons from tiny corridor bar (or may be table service), leatherette wall benches and panelling, back room has football memorabilia and period fireplace; sports TV; open all day and can get crowded. *(Charles Welch, George Sanderson)*

MANCHESTER SJ8398
City Arms (0161) 236 4610
Kennedy Street, off St Peters Square; M2 4BQ Proper old-fashioned local with handsome tiled façade and corridor, eight quickly changing ales, belgian bottled beers and bargain lunches, friendly service, coal fires, bare boards and banquettes, panelling and masses of pump clips; background music, TV, games machine; wheelchair access but steps down to back lounge, open all day. *(P A Lord)*

MANCHESTER SJ8397
Dukes 92 (0161) 839 8642
Castle Street, below the bottom end of Deansgate; M3 4LZ Recently refurbished former stables overlooking canal basin, friendly informal atmosphere, modern furnishing on light tiled floor, exposed brickwork, stairs up to stylish gallery bar leading to roof terrace, two Seven Bro7hers ales, decent wines and wide range of spirits, good food choice from bar snacks and pizzas up; background music, DJs Fri and Sat, live music Sun; children welcome, no dogs inside, waterside tables on big terrace with outside bar/kitchen, open all day (till 1am Fri, Sat). *(George Sanderson)*

MANCHESTER SJ8194
Font (0161) 871 2022
Manchester Road, Chorlton; M21 9PG Relaxed split-level bar with regularly changing beers including eight real ales and 16 craft kegs, also extensive bottled range and traditional ciders, fair-priced cocktails too, eclectic choice of enjoyable food (till 9pm) from deli boards to interesting salads

and spicy african stews; weekend DJs, free wi-fi; children and dogs welcome, seats out at front behind railings, open all day (till 1am Fri, Sat). *(Mark and Sarah Bannister)*

MANCHESTER SJ8397
Knott (0161) 839 9229
Deansgate; M3 4LY Friendly modern glass-fronted café-bar under railway arch by Castlefield heritage site; seven well kept ales including Castle Rock and Marble, also lots of craft beers and continental imports, enjoyable good value food; background music; upstairs balcony overlooking Rochdale Canal, open (and food) all day. *(Patricia Hawkins)*

MANCHESTER SJ8499
★ Marble Arch (0161) 832 5914
Rochdale Road (A664), Ancoats; centre of Gould Street, just E of Victoria station; M4 4HY Cheery own-brew pub with fine listed Victorian interior; long narrow bar with wonderful lightly barrel-vaulted ceiling, extensive glazed brickwork, marble and tiling, sloping mosaic floor and frieze advertising various drinks, old stone bottles on shelves, their good Marble beers plus a couple of guests (brewery visible from windows in back dining room – tours by arrangement), well liked home-made food from varied menu (including separate cheese menu); background music; children welcome, small garden, open all day (till midnight Fri, Sat). *(Nick Lawless)*

MANCHESTER SJ8398
★ Mr Thomas's Chop House
(0161) 832 2245 *Cross Street; M2 7AR* Interesting late 19th-c pub with well preserved features; good generously served food including signature corned beef hash, friendly staff, ales such as Holts and Lees and decent wines by the glass, front bar with panelling, original gas lamp fittings and framed cartoons, stools at wall and window shelves, back green-tiled eating areas with rows of tables on black and white Victorian tiles, archways and high ceilings; seats out at back, open all day. *(Charlie Parker)*

MANCHESTER SJ8298
New Oxford (0161) 832 7082
Bexley Square, Salford; M3 6DB Red-brick Victorian corner pub with up to 16 well kept changing ales (chalked on blackboard), plus extensive range of draught and bottled continental beers, real ciders too, light airy feel in small front bar and back room, coal fire, low-priced basic food till 6pm; open mike and quiz nights, juke box, free wi-fi; café-style seating out in square, open all day. *(Julie Swift)*

MANCHESTER SJ8398
Oast House (0161) 829 3830
Crown Square, Springfields; M3 3AY Quirky mock-up of a kentish oast surrounded by modern high-rise; rustic lofty interior with

bare boards, timbers and plenty of tables, real ales and good selection of bottled beers and wines, enjoyable fairly priced food from deli boards to barbecue and rotisserie grills, friendly helpful young staff, busy cheerful atmosphere; nightly live music; children welcome, spacious outside seating area, open all day (till 2am Fri, Sat). *(Charlie Parker)*

MANCHESTER SJ8397
Paramount (0161) 233 1820
Oxford Street; M1 4BH Spacious Wetherspoons worth knowing for its interesting range of well priced beers, friendly service, usual food; TVs, free wi-fi; children welcome, open all day from 7am. *(D W Stokes)*

MANCHESTER SJ8284
Parkfield (0161) 766 3923
Park Lane; M45 7GT Welcoming dining pub with good variety of food from sandwiches and pub staples to restauranty choices, all-day Sun roasts, three regional ales and good wine list, cocktails, freshly ground coffee; some live music; children and dogs welcome, garden behind, open all day. *(George Sanderson)*

MANCHESTER SJ8397
★ **Peveril of the Peak** (0161) 236 6364
Great Bridgewater Street; M1 5JQ Vivid art nouveau external tilework and three sturdily furnished old-fashioned bare-boards rooms, interesting pictures, lots of mahogany, mirrors and stained or frosted glass, log fire, four ales such as Copper Dragon, Seven Bro7hers, Skinners and Timothy Taylors from central servery, cheap basic lunchtime food; table football, pool, background music, TV; children welcome, pavement tables, usually open all day. *(Lionel Smith)*

MANCHESTER SJ8498
Port Street Beer House
(0161) 237 9949 *Port Street; M1 2EQ* Fantastic range of international beers on draught and in bottles along with well kept real ales, good service from knowledgeable staff, no food, can get very busy but more room upstairs; events such as 'meet the brewer'; open all day weekends, from 2pm Fri, 4pm other days. *(Dave Ellis)*

MANCHESTER SJ8397
Rain Bar (0161) 235 6500
Great Bridgewater Street; M1 5JG Bare boards and lots of woodwork in former umbrella works, well kept Lees ales and plenty of wines by the glass, wide choice of enjoyable good value food, friendly relaxed atmosphere, nooks and corners, coal fire in small snug, large upstairs bar/function room; background music, Weds quiz; good back

terrace overlooking spruced-up Rochdale Canal, handy for Bridgewater Hall, open (and food) all day. *(Dr and Mrs A K Clarke)*

MANCHESTER SJ8398
★ **Sams Chop House** (0161) 834 3210
Back Pool Fold, Chapel Walks; M2 1HN Thriving downstairs dining pub (offshoot from Mr Thomas's Chop House) with original Victorian décor, generous helpings of good plain english food including weekend brunch, formal waiters, well kept beers and good wine choice, a former haunt of LS Lowry (his statue sits contemplatively at the bar), back restaurant with black and white tiled floor; background music, sports TV; some pavement tables, open all day. *(Dave Ellis)*

MANCHESTER SJ8498
Smithfield (0161) 819 2767
Swan Street; M4 5JZ Simply presented pub on edge of the Northern Quarter recently taken over by the Blackjack brewery, their ales and guests from six handpumps, also a dozen craft kegs, real cider and good selection of spirits, straightforward food such as sausages and pies, three main areas with vintage mismatched furniture on wood floors, traditional games including darts, shove-ha'penny and table skittles; dogs welcome, open all day weekends, from 1pm Fri, 4.30pm other days. *(Phil Hilton)*

MARPLE SJ9389
Hare & Hounds (0161) 427 0293
Dooley Lane (A627 W); SK6 7EJ Dining pub above River Goyt with modern layout and décor, tasty traditional food at reasonable prices from sandwiches up, Hydes ales and a guest, friendly service; background music; well behaved children welcome, outside seating, open (and food) all day. *(Ed Green)*

MARPLE SJ9588
Ring o' Bells (0161) 427 2300
Church Lane; by Macclesfield Canal, bridge 2; SK6 7AY Popular old-fashioned local with assorted memorabilia in four linked rooms, well kept Robinsons ales and well thought-of food at reasonable prices; quiz nights and some live music including brass bands in the waterside garden, own narrowboat, one bedroom, open all day. *(Ed Green)*

MARPLE BRIDGE SJ9889
Hare & Hounds (0161) 427 4042
Mill Brow; from end of Town Street in centre, turn left up Hollins Lane and keep on uphill; SK6 5LW Comfortable civilised and well run stone-built country pub in lovely spot, good ambitious modern food including grazing menu, well kept Robinsons ales and nice wines, log fires; quite small

---

We say if we know a pub allows dogs.

inside and can get crowded; garden behind, open all day weekends, closed Mon-Thurs lunchtimes. *(Charlie Parker)*

MELLOR SJ9888
Devonshire Arms (0161) 427 2563

This is the Mellor near Marple, S of Manchester; heading out of Marple on the A626 towards Glossop, Mellor is the next road after the B6102, signposted off on the right at Marple Bridge; Longhurst Lane; SK6 5PP Newish management for this Robinsons pub; front bar with old leather-seated settles and open fire, two small back rooms with Victorian fireplaces, well kept ales and fair-priced pubby food including Tues steak night and Fri fish evening, friendly helpful staff; children and dogs welcome, garden with pond crossed by japanese bridge, large pergola, play area on small tree-sheltered lawn, open all day weekends. *(Hilary Forrest)*

MORECAMBE SD4264
Midland Grand Plaza

(01524) 424000 *Marine Road W; LA4 4BZ* Classic art deco hotel in splendid seafront position; comfortable if unorthodox contemporary furnishings in spacious sea-view Rotunda Bar, rather pricey but enjoyable food from interesting lancashire tapas to restaurant meals (popular and very good afternoon tea), good service; children welcome, 44 bedrooms, open all day. *(George Sanderson)*

MORECAMBE SD4364
Palatine (01524) 410503

The Crescent; LA4 5BZ Comfortable Edwardian seafront pub with enjoyable reasonably priced food including deli boards, pizzas and pub standards (good lancashire hotpot), four Lancaster ales and guests, good friendly staff, leather armchairs and some high tables with stools on wood floor, upstairs panelled sea-view dining lounge; seats out in front, open all day (till 1am Fri, Sat). *(George Sanderson)*

NETHER BURROW SD6175
★Highwayman (01524) 273338

A683 S of Kirkby Lonsdale; LA6 2RJ Substantial 17th-c stone pub in pretty Lune Valley countryside, modern well divided flagstoned interior with some intimate corners, a couple of big log fires, very good food from sandwiches and bar snacks up, Thwaites ales, 14 wines by the glass and good range of other drinks, friendly efficient service; children and dogs (in bar) welcome, big terrace and lovely gardens, open (and food) all day. *(Barbara and Peter Kelly, John Poulter)*

NEWTON SD6950
★Parkers Arms (01200) 446236

B6478 7 miles N of Clitheroe; BB7 3DY Arch-windowed cream pub on edge of village, friendly welcome and good locally sourced food from lunchtime sandwiches (home-baked bread) to imaginative specials, can eat in bar or restaurant, four real ales including Bowland, good range of wines and decent coffee, wood and flagstone floors, log fires; children and well behaved dogs welcome, lovely views from picnic-sets on front lawn, one bedroom, open all day weekends, closed Mon, Tues. *(Graham and Carol Parker, Ray and Winifred Halliday, Dr Peter Crawshaw)*

PLEASINGTON SD6528
★Clog & Billycock (01254) 201163

Village signposted off A677 Preston New Road on W edge of Blackburn; Billinge End Road; BB2 6QB Attractive carefully modernised and extended old village pub, light and airy with flagstoned floors and high ceilings, cosier room with high-backed settles and fireplace at one end, good variety of well liked food including Fri fish and chips, small bar area serving Thwaites ales and several wines by the glass; background music, free wi-fi; children and dogs welcome, small garden with awning-covered terrace, open (and food) all day. *(Gordon and Margaret Ormondroyd, W K Wood)*

RABY SJ3179
★Wheatsheaf (0151) 336 3416

Raby Mere Road, The Green; from A540 heading S from Heswall, turn left into Upper Raby Road, village about a mile further; CH63 4JH Up to nine well kept ales in pretty 17th-c black and white thatched pub, simply furnished rambling rooms with homely feel, cosy central bar and nice snug formed by antique settles around fine old fireplace, small coal fire in more spacious room, well liked reasonably priced bar food including good range of sandwiches/toasties, à la carte menu in large former cowshed restaurant, good friendly service, conservatory; children welcome, dogs in bar, picnic-sets on terrace and in pleasant back garden, open all day and gets very busy at weekends, no food Sun or Mon evenings. *(Roger and Anne Newbury)*

RAMSBOTTOM SD8016
Eagle & Child (01706) 557181

Whalley Road (A56); BL0 0DL Friendly well run pub with good freshly made food (booking advised) using locally sourced produce including own vegetables, well kept Thwaites ales, real cider and decent choice of wines by the glass, good service; children welcome, interesting garden with valley views over roof tops to Holcombe Moor and Peel Tower, open all day Fri and Sat, till 7pm Sun. *(W K Wood)*

RAMSBOTTOM SD8017
★Fishermans Retreat (01706) 825314

Twine Valley Park/Fishery signed off A56 N of Bury at Shuttleworth; Bye Road; BL0 0HH Remote yet busy pub-restaurant with highly thought-of food (some quite pricey) using produce from surrounding Estate and trout lakes (they can arrange fishing), also have own land where they raise cattle; mountain lodge-feel bar with beams and bare stone walls, five well kept ales including Copper Dragon, Moorhouses, Timothy Taylors and Thwaites, over 300 malt whiskies and good wine list, small family dining room and restaurant/function room extension, helpful friendly staff; a few picnic-sets with lovely valley views, closed Mon, otherwise open (and food) all day. *(Rosie and John Moore)*

RAMSBOTTOM SD7816
Major (01706) 826777

Bolton Street; BL0 9JA Welcoming end-of-terrace local with four well kept ales and enjoyable inexpensive pub food including bargain meal deal (Weds, Thurs), friendly obliging staff, old local pictures, two-way woodburner; Tues quiz, pool, darts, sports TV; children and dogs welcome, beer garden, closed lunchtimes Mon and Tues, otherwise open all day (no food Mon, Tues, lunchtime Weds and after 5.45pm Sun). *(R T and J C Moggridge)*

RAWTENSTALL SD8213
Buffer Stops (0161) 764 7790

Bury Road; in East Lancashire Railway station; BB4 6EH Platform bar at Rawtenstall heritage station, five well kept changing ales, real cider/perry and selection of bottled beers, snacky food, popular with locals and railway enthusiasts, good friendly service; children welcome in former waiting room, platform tables, open all day (till 9pm Mon, Tues). *(P A Lord, Steve Whalley)*

RILEY GREEN SD6225
★ **Royal Oak** (01254) 201445

A675/A6061; PR5 0SL Cosy low-beamed four-room pub (former coaching inn) extended by present owners; good freshly made food served by friendly efficient staff, four Thwaites ales and maybe a guest from long back bar, ancient stripped stone, open fires, seats from high-backed settles to plush armchairs on carpet, lots of nooks and crannies, impressive woodwork and some bric-a-brac, comfortable dining rooms; children and dogs welcome, picnic-sets at front and in side beer garden, short walk from Leeds & Liverpool Canal, footpath to Hoghton Tower, open all day, food all day weekends. *(Maddie Purvis)*

ROCHDALE SD8913
Baum (01706) 352186

Toad Lane (off Hunters Lane), next to the Rochdale Pioneers (Co-op) Museum; OL12 0NU In surviving cobbled street and plenty of old-fashioned charm, seven well kept changing ales and lots of bottled beers, good value food all day (Sun till 6pm) from sandwiches and tapas up including daily

roast, cheerful young staff, bare boards, old advertising signs, conservatory; free wi-fi; children and dogs welcome, garden with pétanque, open all day (till midnight Fri, Sat). *(P A Lord)*

ROMILEY SJ9390
Duke of York (0161) 406 9988

Stockport Road; SK6 3AN Popular former coaching inn with four well kept beers including Thwaites and Charles Wells Bombardier, good reasonably priced food (not Sun evening, Mon) in beamed bar or upstairs restaurant, friendly efficient staff; seats out at front behind white picket fence, open all day. *(Stuart Paulley)*

ROMILEY SJ9390
Platform 1 (0161) 406 8686

Stockport Road next to station; SK6 4BN Popular pub revamped in modern/traditional style, open and airy with tiled floor, some high tables and chairs, six mostly local ales including a well priced house beer, enjoyable good value pubby food from sandwiches up, bargain OAP deal 12-5pm weekdays, friendly service, carpeted upstairs restaurant called Platform 2; small decked seating area outside, open (and food) all day (last orders for food 6.45pm Sun). *(Ed Green)*

ROUGHLEE SD8440
Bay Horse (01282) 696558

Blacko Bar Road; handy for M65 junction 13; BB9 6NP Modern renovation for this old village pub; slate floor bar/dining area to the right, leather sofas and light open feel, carpeted dining room to the left with view into back kitchen, good food (all day weekends) including interesting daily specials, short well priced wine list, four local ales, friendly competent staff; children welcome, pretty village in beautiful valley near Pendle Hill, good walking country. *(George Sanderson)*

SCARISBRICK SD4011
Heatons Bridge Inn (01704) 840549

Heatons Bridge Road; L40 8JG Pretty 19th-c pub by bridge over Leeds & Liverpool Canal (popular with boaters), good value generous home-made food (till 6pm Sun, not Mon, Tues), well kept Black Cat, Tetleys and a guest, friendly welcoming staff, four traditional cosy areas and dining room; free wi-fi; children and dogs welcome, pretty hanging baskets, garden with play area and World War II pillbox (pub hosts two vintage military vehicle events during the year), open all day. *(Dave Braisted)*

SCOUTHEAD SD9605
Three Crowns (0161) 624 1766

Huddersfield Road; OL4 4AT Refurbished stone dining pub with well liked food from snacks and pub favourites up, good value OAP set menu till 6.30pm Mon-Sat, cheerful efficient service, well kept ales and decent choice of wines, local artwork and photographs; children welcome, open (and food) all day. *(Charles Welch)*

STALYBRIDGE SJ9598
★ **Station Buffet** (0161) 303 0007
The Station, Rassbottom Street; SK15 1RF Charming Victorian buffet bar; period advertisements, old photographs of the station and other railway memorabilia on wood-panelled and red walls, fire below etched-glass mirror, Millstone, Timothy Taylors Landlord and six quickly rotating guests, two proper ciders, seven wines by glass and ten malt whiskies, very good value straightforward food (no credit cards), newish conservatory, plus extension into what was the ladies' waiting room and part of the station-master's quarters with original ornate ceilings and Victorian-style wallpaper; live folk Sat evening, free wi-fi; children and dogs welcome, open (and food) all day. *(P A Lord)*

STOCKPORT SJ8990
★ **Arden Arms** (0161) 480 2185
Millgate Street/Corporation Street, opposite pay car park; SK1 2LX Cheerful Victorian pub in handsome dark-brick building, several well preserved high-ceilinged rooms off island bar (one tiny old-fashioned snug accessed through servery), tiling, panelling and two coal fires, good sensibly priced food (not Mon-Wed evenings) from lunchtime sandwiches to interesting specials, half a dozen well kept Robinsons ales, friendly efficient service; background music (live Sat in summer), quiz nights, free wi-fi; children and dogs welcome, tables in sheltered courtyard with smokers' shelter, open all day. *(John Wooll)*

STOCKPORT SJ8989
Armoury (0161) 477 3711
Shaw Heath, by roundabout; SK3 8BD Friendly traditionally refurbished 19th-c local with well kept Robinsons ales; darts, sports TV, free wi-fi; open all day and busy on Edgeley Park match days. *(Ed Green)*

STOCKPORT SJ8990
Crown (0161) 480 5850
Heaton Lane, Heaton Norris; SK4 1AR Busy but welcoming partly open-plan Victorian pub popular for its well kept changing ales (up to 16), also bottled beers and real cider, three cosy lounge areas off bar, spotless stylish décor, wholesome bargain lunches; frequent live music, darts; tables in cobbled courtyard, huge viaduct soaring above, open all day. *(Ed Green, Lionel Smith)*

STOCKPORT SJ8890
Magnet (0161) 429 6287
Wellington Road North; SK4 1HJ Busy pub with 14 cask ales including own Watts beers, farm cider, pizza van Fri evenings, pool and juke box in one of the five rooms; live acoustic music first Fri of month; open all day Fri-Sun, from 4pm other days. *(Lionel Smith)*

STOCKPORT SJ8990
Swan With Two Necks
(0161) 480 2341 *Princes Street; SK1 1RY* Traditional narrow pub with welcoming local atmosphere; front panelled bar, back room with button-back wall benches, stone fireplace and skylight, drinking corridor, well kept Robinsons ales and decent lunchtime food (not Sun, Mon) from sandwiches up; small outside area, open all day Fri, Sat, other days till 7pm (6pm Sun). *(Ed Green)*

STRINES SJ9686
Sportsmans Arms (0161) 427 2888
B6101 Marple–New Mills; SK6 7GE Comfortable roadside local with panoramic Goyt Valley view from picture-window lounge bar, good changing ale range and enjoyable well priced honest food including specials, small separate bar, log fire; folk night first Weds of month; children and dogs welcome, tables out on side decking, heated smokers' shelter, open all day weekends. *(Tony Hobden)*

TATHAM SD6169
Tatham Bridge Inn (01524) 221326
B6480, off A683 Lancaster–Kirkby Lonsdale; LA2 8NL Popular old pub with cosy low-beamed bar, well kept ales such as Black Sheep, Tetleys and York, good range of enjoyable fairly priced home-cooked food, friendly helpful staff, dining rooms along corridor and upstairs; well behaved dogs welcome, bedrooms. *(Charlie Parker)*

THORNTON HOUGH SJ3080
Seven Stars (0151) 336 4574
Church Road; CH63 1JW Comfortable 19th-c roadside village pub, three well kept changing ales and generous helpings of enjoyable fairly priced pubby food, friendly helpful service, restaurant; Weds quiz, free wi-fi; children welcome, no dogs, disabled access/facilities, picnic-sets out at front and on side lawn, well placed for walkers and cyclists on Millennium cycle route, open (and food) all day. *(Theocsbrian)*

TOCKHOLES SD6623
Black Bull (01254) 581381
Between Tockholes and Blackburn; BB3 0LL Welcoming 19th-c country pub on crossroads high above Blackburn; home to the Three B's Brewery with their good beers including Black Bull Bitter from brick-fronted counter (tasting trays available), no food, opened-up neat interior with dark blue patterned carpet and leaf wallpaper, cushioned wall seats and high-backed chairs, woodburner, snug to left of entrance with another fire; background music; seats outside (some under cover – including new summerhouse), good view, open all day weekends, otherwise from 4pm, closed Mon, Tues. *(Steve Whalley)*

TOCKHOLES   SD6621
Royal   (01254) 705373
Signed off A6062 S of Blackburn, and off A675; Tockholes Road; BB3 0PA Friendly old pub with unpretentious little rooms and big open fires, four well kept ales such as local Three B's from tiny back servery, well priced pubby food including some blackboard specials (good steak night Weds); children, walkers and dogs welcome, big garden with views from sheltered terrace, good walks including to Darwen Tower, closed Mon, otherwise open all day. *(Dr Kevan Tucker)*

TUNSTALL   SD6073
Lunesdale Arms   (01524) 274203
A683 S of Kirkby Lonsdale; LA6 2QN Welcoming relaxed atmosphere at this attractive 18th-c dining pub; opened-up bare-boards interior with good mix of stripped tables and chairs, woodburner in solid stone fireplace, snugger little flagstoned back part and games area with pool, Black Sheep and a couple of guests, enjoyable sensibly priced food from weekly changing menu; children and dogs (in bar) welcome, pretty Lune Valley village, church has Brontë family associations, closed Mon. *(Jack and Hilary Burton)*

UPPERMILL   SE0006
Cross Keys   (01457) 874626
Church Road, off Runninghill Gate; OL3 6LW Welcoming low-beamed 18th-c moorland local up long steep lane, clean and tidy, with flagstoned bar, log fire in old cooking range, carpeted dining room and separate barn for functions, generous well cooked pub food at reasonable prices, well kept Lees ales; folk club Sun; children and dogs welcome, terrace tables (some under cover), adventure playground, lovely Saddleworth Hills setting with Tame Valley views, good walks, open all day, food all day Fri-Sun. *(Gordon and Margaret Ormondroyd)*

WADDINGTON   SD7243
Higher Buck   (01200) 423226
The Square; BB7 3HZ Welcoming pub in picturesque village; smartly modernised open-plan interior with airy new england feel and good mix of seating, nice food including pub favourites (all day Sun till 8pm), well kept Thwaites from pine servery, good friendly service; background music; children welcome, tables out on front cobbles and in small back courtyard, seven attractively refurbished bedrooms, open all day. *(Steve Whalley)*

WADDINGTON   SD7243
★ Waddington Arms   (01200) 423262
Clitheroe Road (B6478 N of Clitheroe); BB7 3HP Character inn with four linked bars, left one snugget with blazing woodburner in huge fireplace, other low-beamed rooms have fine oak settles, chunky stripped-pine tables and lots to look at including antique and modern prints and vintage motor-racing posters, generous helpings of popular tasty food, well kept Moorhouses and four guests, good choice of wines by the glass and a dozen malt whiskies, friendly helpful staff; children and dogs welcome, wicker chairs on sunny front terrace looking over to village church, more seats on two-level back terrace and neat tree-sheltered lawn, comfortable bedrooms, good walks in nearby Forest of Bowland, open all day. *(Graham and Carol Parker)*

WALLASEY   SJ3094
Queens Royal   (0151) 691 1010
Marine Promenade opposite the lake; CH45 2JT Welcoming double-fronted Victorian seafront hotel with airy modernised bar, six regional ales from island servery, enjoyable food including well priced early evening menu and popular Sun carvery, afternoon teas, good friendly service; children welcome, front terrace with striking sea views, comfortable bedrooms, open (and food) all day. *(Susan and John Douglas)*

WEST BRADFORD   SD7444
Three Millstones   (01200) 443339
Waddington Road; BB7 4SX Attractive old building, but more restaurant than pub with all tables laid for dining; popular food from owner-chef including set deals and daily specials in four comfortable linked areas, beams, timbers and warming fires in two grand fireplaces, ales such as Bowland and Moorhouses, good choice of wines, friendly efficient service; five newly opened bedrooms, closed Sun evening, Mon, Tues. *(John and Eleanor Holdsworth, John and Sylvia Harrop)*

WEST KIRBY   SJ2186
White Lion   (0151) 625 9037
Grange Road (A540); CH48 4EE Friendly proper pub in interesting 18th-c sandstone building, several small beamed areas on different levels, Black Sheep, Courage and a couple of quickly changing guests, good value simple bar lunches (not Sun), coal stove; no children, attractive secluded back garden up steep stone steps, fish pond, parking in residential side streets, open all day. *(George Sanderson)*

WHALLEY   SD7336
★ Swan   (01254) 822195
King Street; BB7 9SN Modernised 17th-c former coaching inn with friendly staff, good mix of customers in big bar, a couple of Bowland ales and Timothy Taylors Landlord, enjoyable food from fairly standard menu (Sun till 7pm), further room with leather sofas and armchairs on bare boards; background music; children and dogs (in bar) welcome, picnic-sets on back terrace and on grass strips by car park, six bedrooms named after nearby

rivers and attractions, open all day.
(Gordon and Margaret Ormondroyd)

WHEATLEY LANE   SD8338
★**Sparrowhawk**   (01282) 603034
*Wheatley Lane Road; towards E end
of village road, which runs N of and
parallel to A6068; one way to reach it is
to follow Fence signpost, then turn off at
Barrowford signpost; BB12 9QG*
Comfortably civilised 1930s feel in imposing
black and white pub; oak panelling, parquet
flooring and leather tub chairs, domed
stained-glass skylight, six well kept ales
including Reedley Hallows from cushioned
leatherette counter, nice wines by the glass
and good food from sandwiches and light
lunches up, friendly young staff; background
and live music, comedy nights; children
welcome, dogs in bar, heavy wooden tables
on spacious front terrace with good views to
the moors beyond Nelson and Colne, open
(and food) all day. *(Bev, Maddie Purvis)*

WHEELTON   SD6021
★**Dressers Arms**   (01254) 830041
*Briers Brow; off A674, 2.1 miles from
M61 junction 8; PR6 8HD* Popular old
stone-built pub restored a couple of years
ago after devastating fire; five well kept ales
such as Black Sheep, Tetleys and Thwaites,
good choice of enjoyable reasonably priced
food including Sun carvery, friendly attentive
service; children and dogs welcome, open
(and food) all day. *(Patricia Hawkins)*

WISWELL   SD7437
★**Freemasons Arms**   (01254) 822218
*Village signposted off A671 and A59 NE
of Whalley; pub on Vicarage Fold,
a gravelled pedestrian passage between
Pendleton Road and Old Back Lane in
village centre (don't expect to park very
close); BB7 9DF* Civilised dining pub with
three linked rooms; antique sporting prints
on cream or pastel walls, rugs on polished
flagstones, carved oak settles and variety
of chairs around handsome stripped or
salvaged tables, candles and log fires, Bank
Top, Lancaster, Reedley Hallows and a guest,
well chosen wines and good imaginative

food (all day Sun till 7pm), efficient friendly
service from uniformed staff, more rooms
upstairs; children and dogs (in bar) welcome,
flagstoned front terrace with heaters and
awning, open all day weekends, closed Mon
and first two weeks of Jan. *(Caroline Prescott,
Emma Scofield, John and Mary Warner, Alison
and Michael Harper)*

WOODFORD   SJ8882
Davenport Arms   (0161) 439 2435
A5102 Wilmslow–Poynton; SK7 1PS
Popular red-brick country local (aka
the Thief's Neck) run by same family
since 1932; well kept Robinsons ales and
enjoyable lunchtime food from snacks up
(evening menu Thurs-Sat), friendly service,
refurbished snug rooms, log fires; children
and dogs welcome, tables on front terrace
and in nice back garden with play area,
open all day. *(Lee McLean)*

WRIGHTINGTON   SD5011
Rigbye Arms   (01257) 462354
*3 miles from M6 junction 27; off A5209
via Robin Hood Lane and left into High
Moor Lane; WN6 9QB* 17th-c dining pub
in attractive moorland setting, welcoming
and relaxed, with wide choice of reliably
good sensibly priced food including game
menu and Thurs steak night, hot and cold
sandwiches too, friendly prompt service
even at busy times, well kept Black Sheep,
Tetleys and Timothy Taylors, decent wines,
several carpeted rooms including cosy tap
room, open fires, separate evening restaurant
(Weds-Sat); free wi-fi; children welcome,
garden, bowling green, regular car club
meetings, open (and food) all day Sun.
(George Sanderson)

WRIGHTINGTON BAR   SD5313
Corner House   (01257) 451400
B5250, N of M6 junction 27; WN6 9SE
Opened-up 19th-c corner pub-restaurant;
good food (all day weekends) from traditional
to more upscale choices, meal deals and daily
specials, real ales and good quality wines,
plenty of tables in different modernised
areas; children welcome, seats outside,
open all day. *(Ed Green, Julie Swift)*

> Post Office address codings confusingly give the impression that some pubs
> are in Lancashire when they're really in Cumbria or Yorkshire
> (which is where we list them).

Leicestershire

and Rutland

KEY	★ Star Pub	🍴★ Top Quality Food	🍺 Great Beer
🍷 Good Wines	£ Bargain Meals	🛏 Good Bedrooms	🍴 Serves Food

BREEDON ON THE HILL
SK4022 Map 7

Three Horseshoes 🍴★

(01332) 695129 – www.thehorseshoes.com

Main Street (A453); DE73 8AN

Comfortable pub with friendly licensees and emphasis on popular food

This thoughtfully run 18th-c dining pub has been nicely restored and decorated to make the most of its attractive structure. The clean-cut central bar has a stylishly simple feel with heavy worn flagstones, green walls and ceilings, a log fire, pubby tables and a dark wood counter. Marstons Pedigree and a guest beer on handpump and decent house wines served by chatty, helpful staff. Beyond the bar is a dining room with maroon walls, dark pews and tables, while a two-room dining area on the right has a comfortably civilised and chatty feel with big antique tables set quite closely together on coir matting, and colourful modern country prints and antique engravings on canary yellow walls. Even at lunchtime there are lit candles in elegant modern holders. The farm shop sells their own and other local produce: eggs, jams, meat, smoked foods and chocolates. Look out for the quaint conical village lock-up opposite.

🍴★ Good, enjoyable food includes sandwiches, smoked salmon with dill mayonnaise, grilled goats cheese with piccalilli, roast vegetable casserole, local sausages with onion gravy, chicken in stilton sauce with garlic mash, duck breast with sweet potato, beef and mushroom casserole, blackened salmon with crème fraîche, steaks with a choice of sauces, and puddings such as lemon cheesecake and chocolate whisky trifle. *Benchmark main dish: beer-battered fish and chips £10.75. Two-course evening meal £19.00.*

Free house ~ Licensees Ian Davison, Jennie Ison, Stuart Marson ~ Real ale ~ Open 11.30-2.30, 5.30-10.30 (11 Sat); 12-3 Sun; closed Sun evening, Mon ~ Bar food 12-2, 5.30-9; 12-3 Sun ~ Restaurant ~ Children welcome ~ Dogs allowed in bar ~ Wi-fi
Recommended by Belinda Stamp, John Harris, Jeremy Snow, Brian and Anna Marsden

BUCKMINSTER
SK8822 Map 7

Tollemache Arms 🍴★

(01476) 860477 – www.tollemache-arms.co.uk

B676 Colsterworth–Melton Mowbray; Main Street; NG33 5SA

Emphasis on good food in stylishly updated pub; bedrooms

As there's plenty to do nearby, it makes sense to stay in the comfortable, well equipped bedrooms in this impressive 19th-c stone-built country pub; breakfasts are good. Table and standard lamps, big bunches of flowers and the smell of baking bread from the kitchen create a homely feel, and there's plenty of wood throughout – floors, hand-made pews, chairs and tables, with leather armchairs beside an open fire in the bar. Next to the main restaurant is a library with shelves of books and leather sofas and armchairs; background music. Grainstore Rutland Bitter, Marstons Pedigree and Oakham JHB on handpump, a good choice of wines by the glass and several malt whiskies. There are plenty of teak tables and chairs in the sizeable garden. This is a lovely village.

 Tempting food includes sandwiches, smoked salmon roulade, ham hock terrine with spiced apple chutney, beer-battered cod and chips, tandoori-spiced tofu with cajun potatoes, beef and mushroom stroganoff, burger with sweet onion marmalade and chips, seafood in white wine, garlic and cream, steaks with a choice of sauces, and puddings such as elderflower cheesecake with fruit compote and sticky toffee pudding with butterscotch sauce; they also have a takeaway menu. *Benchmark main dish: chicken breast stuffed with halloumi and wrapped in bacon on chorizo, red pepper and bacon stew £14.50. Two-course evening meal £19.00.*

Free house ~ Licensee Sarah Turner ~ Real ale ~ Open 11-3, 6 (5 Fri)-11; 11-11 Sat; 12-5 Sun; closed Sun evening, Mon ~ Bar food 12-3, 6-9; 12-9 Sat; 12-4 Sun ~ Restaurant ~ Children welcome ~ Dogs allowed in bar ~ Wi-fi ~ Bedrooms: /£75 *Recommended by Barry Collett, Nick Judkins, Valerie Sayer, Toby Jones*

CLIPSHAM
SK9716 Map 8

Olive Branch ★ ♀ ◀ 🛏

(01780) 410355 – www.theolivebranchpub.com

Take B668/Stretton exit off A1 N of Stamford; Clipsham signposted E from exit roundabout; LE15 7SH

Leicestershire Dining Pub of the Year

An exceptional place for a drink, a meal or an overnight stay; bedrooms

Once again, this first class, civilised inn gets top marks from our readers, who enjoy every aspect of the place. Made up of former labourers' cottages, the various small and charmingly attractive rooms have a relaxed country atmosphere, dark joists and beams, rustic furniture, an interesting mix of pictures (some by local artists), candles on tables, and a cosy log fire in a stone inglenook fireplace; background music. A carefully chosen range of drinks includes a beer named for the pub and a couple of guests from Grainstore and Timothy Taylors on handpump, an enticing wine list (with 17 by the glass), a thoughtful choice of spirits and cocktails (they make their own using seasonal ingredients) and several british and continental bottled beers. Service is efficient and genuinely friendly. Outside, there are tables, chairs and big plant pots on a pretty little terrace, with seating on the neat lawn, sheltered in the crook of the two low buildings. The restful bedrooms (in a renovated Georgian house across the road) are extremely comfortable and the breakfasts are delicious. It can get pretty busy at peak times. The wine shop also sells their own jams and chutneys, you can order individual dishes to take away and they can even organise food for a dinner party to be enjoyed at home.

 The delicious food is cooked by Mr Hope, one of the owners: sandwiches, pigeon breast with pickled mushrooms, parsley purée and confit egg yolk, smoked haddock with dill gnocchi, wilted spinach and clams, butternut squash risotto, duck breast with swede gratin and braised fennel, pave of cod with lemon, couscous and kale (purée, pickled, tempura), sirloin of rose veal with black truffle potato purée, bone marrow fritter and red wine sauce, and puddings such as honeycomb mousse with chocolate textures and beurre noisette ice-cream and jamaican ginger cake with spiced pineapple and pink grapefruit sorbet; they also offer a two- and three-course set lunch. *Benchmark main dish: roast cutlet and braised shoulder of lamb with sweet potato rösti and french-style peas £22.50. Two-course evening meal £26.50.*

Free house ~ Licensees Sean Hope and Ben Jones ~ Real ale ~ Open 12-3, 6-11; 12-11 Sat; 12-10.30 Sun ~ Bar food 12-2, 6.30-9.30; 12-3, 7-9 Sun ~ Children welcome ~ Dogs allowed in bar and bedrooms ~ Wi-fi ~ Bedrooms: £97.50/£115 *Recommended by Malcolm and Jane Levitt, Carol Borthwick, Paul Scofield, Simon Day, Barry Collett*

COLEORTON
SK4117 Map 7

George

(01530) 834639 ~ www.georgeinncoleorton.co.uk
Loughborough Road (A512 E); LE67 8HF

Attractively traditional homely pub with dining area, honest food and drink and large garden

There's a good welcoming atmosphere in this attractive pub, and the bar on the right is nicely laid out to give the feel of varied and fairly small separate areas. As well as a dark panelled dado with lots of local photographs on the walls above, there are shelves of books, pews and wall seats with scatter cushions, a leather sofa and tartan-upholstered tub chairs by the woodburning stove and church candles on tables. Leatherbritches Goldings, Marstons Pedigree and Tollgate Billy's Best Bitter on handpump and ten wines by the glass served by friendly staff. A bigger room on the left has another woodburning stove and plenty to look at; background music. The spreading back garden has sturdy tables and chairs.

Fair value food includes toasted ciabattas and baguettes, crayfish and prawn cocktail, lamb kofta with tzatziki, omelettes, sharing boards, thai green chicken curry, broccoli and montgomery cheddar tart, steak in ale pie, smoked haddock with creamy wild mushroom sauce, lambs liver and bacon, gammon with pineapple fritter, fried egg and chips, and puddings such as black forest cheesecake with cherry jus and Baileys bread and butter pudding. *Benchmark main dish: beer-battered fish and chips £12.00. Two-course evening meal £18.00.*

Free house ~ Licensees Mark and Janice Wilkinson ~ Real ale ~ Open 12-3, 5.30-11; 12-11 Fri, Sat; 12-9 Sun ~ Bar food 12-2, 6-9; 12-7 Sun ~ Restaurant ~ Well behaved children welcome ~ Dogs allowed in bar ~ Wi-fi *Recommended by Comus and Sarah Elliott, Lesley and Peter Barrett*

GREETHAM
SK9314 Map 7

Wheatsheaf ⭐ ♀

(01572) 812325 ~ www.wheatsheaf-greetham.co.uk
B668 Stretton–Cottesmore; LE15 7NP

Warmly friendly stone pub with interesting food, real ales, a dozen wines, and seats in front and back gardens

The welcoming and helpful licensees of this particularly well run pub create a cheerful atmosphere that their many customers enjoy very much. The linked L-shaped rooms have both a log fire and a blazing open stove, traditional settles and cushioned captain's chairs around tables of varying sizes, and Brewsters Decadence, Greene King IPA and Nene Valley DXB on handpump, a dozen wines by the glass and home-made cordials; background music. A games room has TV, darts, pool and board games. The pub dogs are a dachshund and a labradoodle, and visiting dogs are welcome in the bar. There are chunky picnic-sets on the front lawn and more seats on a back terrace by a pretty stream with a duck house; pétanque. They sell their own pickles, chutneys and chocolates; ramp for wheelchairs.

Extremely good and very popular food includes lunchtime sandwiches (not Sunday), rabbit and wild mushroom lasagne, mussels with white wine, shallot and cream sauce, pasta with butternut squash, pine nuts and crispy sage, cod fillet with crab sauce and potato rösti, duck breast with lentils, spinach and horseradish cream, mackerel fillets with bacon, spinach and sweet mustard, lamb rump with parsnip purée and minted red wine sauce, and puddings such as white chocolate, orange and cardamom crème brûlée and sticky ginger pudding with toffee sauce. *Benchmark main dish: crispy pork belly with chorizo, apple sauce and sautéed potatoes £15.50. Two-course evening meal £21.50.*

Punch ~ Lease Scott and Carol Craddock ~ Real ale ~ Open 12-3, 6-11; 12-11 Fri, Sat; 12-10.30 Sun; closed Mon except bank holidays; two weeks Jan ~ Bar food 12-2 (2.15 Sat), 6.30-9; 12-3 Sun ~ Restaurant ~ Children welcome ~ Dogs allowed in bar ~ Wi-fi
Recommended by Michael and Jenny Back, Maddie Purvis, John and Mary Warner

LYDDINGTON SP8797 Map 4

Marquess of Exeter

(01572) 822477 – www.marquessexeter.co.uk
Main Street; LE15 9LT

Stone inn with contemporary décor, real ales and excellent food; bedrooms

The spacious open-plan areas in this handsome, friendly inn have understated but stylish furnishings; the fine flagstone floors, thick walls, beams and exposed stonework are left to speak for themselves. There's a mix of old tables and chairs, smart fabrics, leather sofas, pine chests and old barrels that might always have been here. In winter, it's all warmed by several open fires – one a quite striking piece in dark iron. A beer named for the pub (from Ringwood) and Brakspears Oxford Gold on handpump and around a dozen wines by the glass. Outside, a terrace has seats and picnic-sets, with more in the tree-sheltered gardens that seem to merge with the countryside beyond. The pub is named after the Burghley family, which has long owned this charming village (Burghley House is about 15 miles away).

Food is imaginative and cooked by the landlord: salmon gravadlax with beetroot vinaigrette, apple, horseradish and caper cream, terrine of local pork and chorizo with tarragon and tomato salsa, mushroom, spinach and gorgonzola risotto, beer-battered cod and chips, lemon-marinated chicken with grilled vegetables and lemon butter, lamb rump with crispy seaweed and dauphinoise potatoes, linguine with clams, mussels, tomatoes, chilli and garlic, and puddings such as chocolate tart with pear jelly and honeycomb and stem ginger ice-cream and coconut and rum pannacotta with pineapple and lime salsa; they also offer a two- and three-course set lunch. *Benchmark main dish: rib of beef with pommes frites and béarnaise sauce (for two people) £48.50. Two-course evening meal £21.00.*

Marstons ~ Lease Brian Baker ~ Real ale ~ Open 11-11 (midnight Sat); 12-10.30 Sun ~ Bar food 12-2.30, 6.30-9.30; 12-3.30, 6.30-9 Sun ~ Restaurant ~ Children welcome ~ Dogs allowed in bar and bedrooms ~ Wi-fi ~ Bedrooms: £79.50/£99 *Recommended by Alan Sutton, Peter Andrews, Philippa & Felix, Julie Braeburn*

OAKHAM   SK8509 Map 4

Grainstore ◀ £

(01572) 770065 – www.grainstorebrewery.com

Station Road, off A606; LE15 6RE

Super own-brewed beers in a converted railway grain warehouse, cheerful customers and pubby food

The ten own-brews in this former Victorian grain store are the reason so many customers are here, and staff will usually offer a sample or two to help you decide which to drink. They're served traditionally on handpump at the left end of the bar counter and through swan necks with sparklers on the right. Following the traditional tower system of production, the beer is brewed on the upper floors of the building directly above the down-to-earth bar; during working hours, you'll hear the busy noises of the brewery rumbling overhead. They offer beer takeaways and hold a beer festival (with over 80 real ales and live music) on the August Bank Holiday weekend; there's also a farm cider, several wines by the glass and 15 malt whiskies. Décor is plain and functional, with well worn wide floorboards, bare ceiling boards above massive joists supported by red metal pillars, a long brick-built bar counter with cast-iron stools, tall cask tables and simple elm chairs; games machine, darts, board games, giant Jenga and bottle-walking. In summer, the huge glass doors are pulled back, opening on to a terrace with picnic-sets. You can book a brewery tour (though not on Friday or Saturday evenings) – tickets are available online. Disabled access.

The popular food includes sandwiches, sharing platters, rack of baby back ribs with barbecue sauce, coleslaw and pickles, sausages with onion and ale gravy, beer-battered haddock goujons and chips, home-baked ham and eggs, wild mushroom tagliatelle, cajun chicken with onion rings and skinny fries, and puddings such as banoffi split and sticky toffee pudding; they also have offers such as weekend breakfasts (9.30-11am), Tuesday burger night, Wednesday pie and pint evening and Thursday 'two mains and a jug of beer' night. *Benchmark main dish: steak and ale burger with toppings and fries £9.00. Two-course evening meal £12.00.*

Own brew ~ Licensee Peter Atkinson ~ Real ale ~ Open 12-11 (midnight Fri); 9am-midnight Sat; 9am-11pm Sun ~ Bar food 12-3, 6-9; 9-9 Sat; 9-5 Sun ~ Children welcome ~ Dogs welcome ~ Wi-fi ~ Live music twice a month, comedy monthly *Recommended by Barry Collett, Anne and Ben Smith*

OAKHAM   SK8608 Map 4

Lord Nelson ★ ♀ ◀

(01572) 868340 – www.kneadpubs.co.uk

Market Place; LE15 6DT

Splendidly restored and full of interest, usefully open all day, real ales and ciders and enjoyable food

There are half a dozen rooms in this handsome place spread over two floors. You can choose from cushioned church pews, leather elbow chairs, long oak settles, sofas, armchairs – or, to watch the passing scene, a big bow-window seat; carpet, bare boards and ancient red and black tiles, plus paintwork in soft shades of ochre, canary yellow, sage or pink and William Morris wallpaper. There's plenty to look at too, from intriguing antique *Police News* and other prints – plenty of Nelson, of course – to the collections of mullers, copper kettles and other homely bric-a-brac in the heavy-beamed former kitchen with its Aga. But the main thing is simply the easy-going, good-natured atmosphere. Castle Rock Harvest Pale and Fullers London Pride with guests such as Navigation Last Knight, North Yorkshire

Archbishop Lee's Ruby Ale and Warwickshire Duck Soup on handpump; also three farm ciders and 17 wines by the glass. Background music and TV.

 Well liked food includes sandwiches, pigs in blankets and duck-fat potatoes with mustard mayonnaise, home-made scotch egg with piccalilli, sharing boards, cauliflower and lentil curry, lamb kofta meatballs in harissa tomato sauce and lemon and roasted pepper couscous, chorizo and barbecue chicken lasagne, asian-style salmon with wasabi mash, five-spice pak choi and red thai coconut sauce, lambs liver, crispy bacon and pearl onion sauce, and puddings such as treacle tart and apple crumble. *Benchmark main dish: pizzas with a choice of toppings £8.95. Two-course evening meal £15.00.*

Knead Pubs ~ Managers Danielle Usher and Lee Jones ~ Real ale ~ Open 10am-11pm; 12-11 Sun ~ Bar food 12-2.30,6-9; 12-5, 6-9 Sat; 12-8 Sun ~ Children welcome ~ Dogs allowed in bar ~ Wi-fi *Recommended by Barry Collett, Nigel Havers, James Landor*

PEGGS GREEN
SK4117 Map 7
New Inn £
(01530) 222293 – www.thenewinnpeggsgreen.co.uk
Signposted off A512 Ashby–Shepshed at roundabout, then turn immediately left down Zion Hill towards Newbold; pub is 100 metres on the right, with car park on opposite side of road; LE67 8JE

Intriguing bric-a-brac in unspoilt pub, friendly welcome, well liked food at fair prices and real ales; cottagey garden

Since 1978 this cheerful pub has been run by the same friendly family who have been collecting old bric-a-brac since then; it covers almost every inch of the walls and ceilings in the two cosy tiled front rooms, and is worth close inspection. The little room on the left, a bit like an old kitchen parlour (called the Cabin), has china on the mantelpiece, lots of prints and photographs, three old cast-iron tables, wooden stools and a small stripped kitchen table. The room to the right has attractive stripped panelling and more appealing bric-a-brac. The small back 'Best' room (good for private meetings) has a stripped-wood floor and a touching display of old local photographs including some colliery ones. Bass, Marstons Pedigree and a quickly changing guest beer on handpump; background music and board games. There are plenty of seats in front of the pub, with more in the peaceful back garden. Do check the unusual opening and food service times carefully.

 Incredibly cheap food includes hot and cold cobs, chunky soup, sausages in onion gravy, corned beef hash, ham and eggs, and smoked haddock; Tuesday is pie night, Wednesday brings a pizza van to the car park and Friday is Dine Inn, when there are more elaborate food choices on offer. *Benchmark main dish: faggots and peas £5.90.*

Enterprise ~ Lease Maria Christina Kell ~ Real ale ~ Open 12-2.30, 5.30-11; 12-3, 6.30-11 Sat; 12-3, 7-10.30 Sun; closed Tues-Thurs lunchtimes ~ Bar food 12-2, 6-8 Mon; 12-2 Fri, Sat; filled rolls might be available at other times ~ Well behaved children welcome ~ Dogs welcome ~ Wi-fi ~ Live folk club second Mon of month, quiz Thurs *Recommended by Anne and Ben Smith, Edward Nile, William Pace*

SILEBY
SK6015 Map 7
White Swan
(01509) 814832 – www.whiteswansileby.co.uk
Off A6 or A607 N of Leicester; in centre turn into King Street (opposite church), then after mini roundabout turn right at Post Office signpost into Swan Street; LE12 7NW

Exemplary town local, a boon to its chatty regulars, with tasty home cooking and a friendly welcome

The very good value food and the genuine can-do attitude of the helpful staff make this honest local a special place. It's been run for over 30 years by Mrs Miller and our readers are consistent in their praise. It has all the touches that mark the best of between-the-wars estate pub design, such as an art deco-tiled lobby, polychrome-tiled fireplaces, shiny red Anaglypta ceiling and a comfortable layout of linked but separate areas including a small restaurant (now lined with books). Packed with bric-a-brac from bizarre hats to decorative plates and lots of prints, it quickly draws you in thanks to the genuinely bright and cheerful welcome. Sharps Doom Bar and maybe a guest beer on handpump and six wines by the glass. The pub is especially popular with walkers from Cossington Meadows and those moored at Sileby Marine.

Popular food includes prawn cocktail, mushrooms in creamy stilton sauce, tomato and mushroom pasta, gammon and egg, chicken breast in barbecue sauce with cheese and bacon, beef and mushroom in ale pie, salmon and prawn pancake with stilton cheese sauce, steaks with a choice of sauces and chips, and puddings. *Benchmark main dish: beef cobbler £13.95. Two-course evening meal £17.00.*

Free house ~ Licensee Theresa Miller ~ Real ale ~ Open 6-10 Tues-Thurs; 12-2, 6-11 Fri; 6-11 Sat; 12-3 Sun; closed Sun evening, all day Mon, lunchtimes Tues-Thurs, Sat ~ Bar food 6-8.30 Tues-Thurs, Sat; 12-1.30, 6-8.30 Fri; 12-1.30 Sun ~ Children welcome ~ Dogs allowed in bar ~ Wi-fi *Recommended by Harvey Brown, Emma Scofield*

STATHERN
SK7731 Map 7

Red Lion ⭑ ♀

(01949) 860868 – www.theredlioninn.co.uk

Off A52 W of Grantham via the brown-signed Belvoir road (keep on towards Harby; Stathern is signposted on left); or off A606 Nottingham–Melton Mowbray via Long Clawson and Harby; LE14 4HS

Country-style dining pub with fine range of drinks and imaginative food; good garden with a play area

New owners have taken over this bustling place and some refurbishments have taken place. The lounge bar on the right has a woodburning stove and leads to a more traditional flagstoned bar with an open fire, beams, oak doors, comfortable seating and photos of the village. The small snug, with tables set for eating, connects to a long, narrow restaurant and then out to a suntrap terrace and a lawn where there are good quality seats and tables. Fullers London Pride and a changing guest from Brewsters on handpump, 25 wines and champagnes by the glass, and a fine choice of spirits. Behind the car park is an unusually big play area with swings and climbing frames.

Interesting food includes sandwiches, pork and rabbit terrine with dill pickles, king scallops topped with gruyère, parmesan and panko crust, vegetable tart with peppers and crispy mozzarella, roast chicken (crispy rillettes, ballotine and breast) in chasseur sauce, venison haunch in port sauce with roasted beetroot, halibut fillet on bouillabaisse risotto topped with shellfish and sea herbs, lamb shoulder and cutlet with provençale vegetables, and puddings such as iced nougatine parfait and whole orange and pistachio cake with milk ice-cream. *Benchmark main dish: 55-hour pork belly £19.00. Two-course evening meal £27.00.*

Free house ~ Licensees Mark Barbour and Karen Hammond ~ Real ale ~ Open 12-11 ~ Bar food 12-9; 12-6 Sun ~ Restaurant ~ Children welcome ~ Dogs allowed in bar ~ Wi-fi *Recommended by Comus and Sarah Elliott, Sarah Roberts, Geoffrey Sutton, Christopher Mannings*

The 🍺 symbol shows pubs that keep their beer unusually well, have a particularly good range or brew their own.

SUTTON CHENEY
Hercules Revived ⭐ ♀

SK4100 Map 4

(01455) 699336 – www.herculesrevived.co.uk

Off A447 3 miles S of Market Bosworth; CV13 0AG

Attractively furnished bar and upstairs dining rooms, highly thought-of food, real ales and helpful staff

You'll feel equally warmly welcomed in this 18th-c former coaching inn whether you're popping in for a pint and a chat or for a very good meal. The long bar is easy-going and has brown leather wall seating with attractive scatter cushions, upholstered brown and white checked or plain wooden church chairs around various tables, rugs on wooden flooring, fresh flowers, prints and ornamental plates on creamy yellow walls and a big open fire; background music. There are high leather chairs against the rough hewn counter, where they serve Church End What the Foxs Hat and Sharps Doom Bar on handpump and ten wines by the glass. Upstairs, each of the interlinked, grey-carpeted dining rooms (one wall is a giant map of the area) have their own colour scheme and tartan dining chairs around dark wooden tables. There are picnic-sets with parasols on the little back terrace, with views across a meadow to the church.

Interesting food includes wild mushrooms, spinach and mustard on toast with poached egg, cajun-spiced chicken with maple, pineapple and sweetcorn, soda-battered fish and chips, smoked applewood polenta with chickpeas, squash, courgette and peppers, salmon with samphire, broccoli, gnocchi and cockle chive sauce, duck breast and confit leg with carrot and potato rösti and cherry anise sauce, and puddings such as banana pannacotta with roasted pecans and dark chocolate and praline brioche pudding with orange and crème fraîche. *Benchmark main dish: beef stew with cheddar mash and red cabbage £12.95. Two-course evening meal £10.00.*

Free house ~ Licensee Oliver Warner ~ Real ale ~ Open 12-3.30, 6-11; 12-11 Sat; 12-9.30 Sun ~ Bar food 12-2.30, 6-9 (8 Sun) ~ Restaurant ~ Children welcome ~ Dogs allowed in bar
Recommended by Lindy Andrews, Alison and Michael Harper, Pauline and Mark Evans

SWITHLAND
Griffin 🍺

SK5512 Map 7

(01509) 890535 – www.griffininnswithland.co.uk

Main Street; between A6 and B5330, between Loughborough and Leicester; LE12 8TJ

A good mix of cheerful customers and well liked food in a well run, busy pub

After a walk in Bradgate Park or Swithland Wood, come to this bustling country pub for lunch. It's a friendly place with a warm welcome for all. The three beamed communicating rooms are cosy and traditional with some panelling, leather armchairs and sofas, cushioned wall seating, a woodburner, a nice mix of wooden tables and chairs and lots of bird prints. Stools line the counter where Adnams Southwold, Everards Original and Tiger and a guest such as Wadworths Bishops Tipple are well kept on handpump; also, a couple of farm ciders, several malt whiskies and wines by the glass from a good list; background music. The terrace, screened by plants, has wicker seats, and there are more seats in the streamside garden overlooking open fields, as well as painted picnic-sets outside the Old Stables. They also have a café/deli selling local produce and artisan products. Good wheelchair access and disabled facilities.

 Good food includes mussels in cider and cream, fried black pudding topped with cheddar and wholegrain mustard rarebit, spiced butternut squash and baby spinach risotto, a trio of local sausages with mash and gravy, venison, wild mushroom and ale pie, calves liver and onion with marsala wine sauce, beer-battered haddock and chips, and puddings such as white chocolate brownie with raspberry ripple ice-cream and raspberry sherbert and pear and honey tarte tatin with vanilla ice-cream. *Benchmark main dish: beer-battered haddock and chips £12.75. Two-course evening meal £20.00.*

Everards ~ Tenant John Cooledge ~ Real ale ~ Open 12-11 (10.30 Sun) ~ Bar food 12-2, 5.30-9; 12-9 Sat; 12-8 Sun ~ Restaurant ~ Children welcome ~ Dogs allowed in bar ~ Wi-fi
Recommended by Ian Herdman, Edward Nile, William Pace, David Longhurst

WING

Kings Arms 🍴⭐ ♀ 🛏

SK8902 Map 4

(01572) 737634 – www.thekingsarms-wing.co.uk
Village signposted off A6003 S of Oakham; Top Street; LE15 8SE

Nicely kept old pub with big log fires, super choice of wines by the glass and good modern cooking; bedrooms

If you stay here you can choose between the Old Bake House (the village's former bakery) or Orchard House (just up their private drive) – both have well equipped, comfortable rooms, and breakfasts are particularly good. This is a civilised former farmhouse with a neatly kept and invitingly attractive long bar, two large log fires (one in a copper-canopied central hearth), various nooks and crannies, nice old low beams and stripped stone, and flagstone or wood-strip floors. Friendly, helpful staff serve almost three dozen wines by the glass, as well as Black Sheep, Courage Directors, Grainstore Cooking and Shepherd Neame Spitfire on handpump, local cider, home-made liqueurs and a dozen malt whiskies; dominoes and cards. There are seats out in front, and more in the sunny yew-sheltered garden; the car park has plenty of space. You'll find a medieval turf maze just up the road and it's only a couple of miles to one of England's two osprey hotspots.

 First class food uses produce from their own smokehouse, home-baked bread and home-made pickles, chutneys, preserves and so forth: lunchtime sandwiches, home-smoked trout trio with sweet pickled beetroot and potato salad, smoked pigeon breast and black pudding with apricot, redcurrant and onion relish, chicken caesar salad, burgers with toppings and fries, paneer, mushroom and spinach curry, fish pie, smoked ham in honey and cider with eggs, and puddings such as chocolate mousse and creme brûlée with berry compote. *Benchmark main dish: beer-battered fish and chips £13.50. Two-course evening meal £20.00.*

Free house ~ Licensee David Goss ~ Real ale ~ Open 12-3, 6.30-11; 12-11 Sat; 12-3 Sun; closed Sun evening, Mon lunchtime ~ Bar food 12-2, 6.30-8.30 (9 Fri, Sat) ~ Restaurant ~ Children welcome ~ Dogs allowed in bar and bedrooms ~ Wi-fi ~ Bedrooms: £75/£100
Recommended by John Davis, Colin Chambers, Pat and Stewart Gordon, Susan Jackman, Mary Joyce, Peter Andrews

WYMONDHAM

Berkeley Arms 🍴⭐

SK8518 Map 7

(01572) 787587 – www.theberkeleyarms.co.uk
Main Street; LE14 2AG

Well run village pub with interesting food, interlinked beamed rooms, a relaxed atmosphere and sunny terrace

The hands-on, hard-working licensees keep their friendly golden-stone inn in tip top form and our readers enjoy their visits here. There's a welcoming, relaxed atmosphere, knick-knacks, magazines, table lamps and cushions – and at one end (in front of a log fire), two wing chairs on patterned carpet beside a low coffee table. The red-tiled or wood-floored dining areas, dense with stripped beams and standing timbers, are furnished in a kitchen style with light wood tables and red-cushioned chunky chairs. Marstons Pedigree and guests such as Batemans XB, Castle Rock Harvest Pale, Marstons Pedigree and Timothy Taylors Golden Best on handpump, 11 wines by the glass and local cider. Outside, on small terraces to either side of the front entrance, picnic-sets get the sun nearly all day long. There are good surrounding walks.

Cooked by the landlord, the imaginative food includes sandwiches, mussels with coconut milk, chilli, coriander and lemongrass, pigeon breast with poached apple and pancetta salad and hazelnut dressing, potato gnocchi with courgettes, tomato and olive sauce, local sausages with mash and red onion gravy, chicken breast with wild garlic and wild mushroom risotto, cod fillet with shrimp and dill sauce, and puddings such as dark chocolate mousse with coffee cream and honeycomb and rice pudding with caramel poached pear; they also offer a two- and three-course set evening menu. *Benchmark main dish: braised lamb shoulder with ratatouille, potato gratin and rosemary sauce £17.00. Two-course evening meal £23.00.*

Free house ~ Licensee Louise Hitchen ~ Real ale ~ Open 12-3, 6-11; 12-5 Sun; closed Sun evening, Mon; first two weeks Jan, two weeks summer ~ Bar food 12-1.45, 6.30-9; 12-3 Sun ~ Restaurant ~ Children welcome ~ Dogs allowed in bar *Recommended by Barry Collett, Neil Allen, John and Mary Warner, Max Simons, David Travis*

Also Worth a Visit in Leicestershire

Besides the fully inspected pubs, you might like to try these pubs that have been recommended to us and described by readers. Do tell us what you think of them: feedback@goodguides.com

AB KETTLEBY   SK7519
Sugar Loaf (01664) 822473
Nottingham Road (A606 NW of Melton); LE14 3JB Beamed roadside pub with modern open-plan carpeted bar, bare-boards end with coal-effect gas fire, airy dining conservatory, enjoyable reasonably priced food including Sun carvery, four real ales, friendly attentive service; darts; children welcome, no dogs inside, seats on small side terrace, open (and food) all day. *(Lindy Andrews)*

BELMESTHORPE   TF0410
Blue Bell (01780) 763859
Village signposted off A16 just E of Stamford; PE9 4JG Cottagey 17th-c stone pub in attractive remote hamlet; good keenly priced home-made food and decent range of well kept ales such as Grainstore, friendly welcoming staff, comfortable dining areas either side of central bar, beams and huge inglenook; seats in garden. *(Barry Collett)*

BLABY   SP5697
Bakers Arms (0116) 278 7253
Quite handy for M1 junction 21; The Green; LE8 4FQ Tucked-away thatched pub dating from 1485, lots of low beams, nooks and crannies in linked rooms, exposed

brickwork and stone fireplaces, wide choice of good interesting food (not Sun evening) from sandwiches and bar snacks up, Everards ales, restored 19th-c bakery, bread-making courses and other events such as psychic nights; children welcome, garden picnic-sets, open all day. *(Edward Nile)*

BRANSTON   SK8129
★**Wheel** (01476) 870376
Main Street near the church; NG32 1RU Beamed 18th-c stone-built village pub with good food cooked by chef-landlord including set lunch and early evening deal, three well kept changing ales such as Batemans from central servery (May beer festival), proper cider and good choice of wines, friendly smartly dressed staff, woodburner and open fires; background music and occasional live music; children welcome, dogs in bar, attractive garden, splendid countryside near Belvoir Castle, open all day (till 8pm Sun). *(Comus and Sarah Elliott)*

BRAUNSTON   SK8306
Blue Ball (01572) 722135
Off A606 in Oakham; Cedar Street opposite church; LE15 8QS Pretty 17th-c thatched and beamed dining pub, good food (not Sun evening) including deals, well kept Marstons-related ales and decent

wines (happy hour 5.30-6.30pm Fri), friendly welcoming staff, log fires, leather furniture and country pine in linked rooms, small conservatory, artwork for sale; monthly jazz Sun lunchtime; free wi-fi; children welcome, painted furniture outside on decking, attractive village, open all day Sat, till 8pm Sun. *(Patrick and Barbara Knights, Barry Collett)*

BRAUNSTON SK8306
Old Plough (01572) 722714
Off A606 in Oakham; Church Street; LE15 8QT Comfortably opened-up black-beamed village local, well kept Fullers London Pride, Grainstore and a couple of guests, enjoyable good value pub food (not Sun evening), friendly efficient service, log fire, back dining conservatory; darts, free wi-fi; children, dogs and muddy boots welcome, tables in sheltered back garden with pétanque, five bedrooms, open all day weekends. *(R L Borthwick, Barry Collett)*

BRUNTINGTHORPE SP6089
★ **Joiners Arms** (0116) 247 8258
Off A5199 S of Leicester; Church Walk/ Cross Street; LE17 5QH More restaurant than pub with most of the two beamed rooms set for eating, drinkers have area by small light oak bar with open fire; civilised relaxed atmosphere, candles on tables, elegant dining chairs and big flower arrangements, first class imaginative food efficiently served by friendly staff, cheaper set lunch menu, plenty of wines by the glass including champagne, one mainstream ale such as Greene King or Sharps; picnic-sets in front, closed Sun evening, Mon. *(Sarah Roberts)*

BURROUGH ON THE HILL SK7510
Grants (01664) 452141
Off B6047 S of Melton Mowbray; Main Street; LE14 2JQ Cosy old pub with own Parish ales (brewed next door) including the fearsomely strong Baz's Bonce Blower, well liked food served by smiley helpful staff, open fires, restaurant and games room; Tues quiz and occasional live music, sports TV, free wi-fi; children and dogs welcome, tables in garden, good walk to nearby Iron Age fort, open all day weekends, closed Mon lunchtime. *(Phil and Jane Hodson)*

BURTON OVERY SP6797
Bell (0116) 259 2365
Main Street; LE8 9DL Good interesting choice of well priced food (not Mon) from lunchtime sandwiches up in L-shaped open-plan bar and dining room (used mainly for larger parties), log fire, comfortable sofas, ales such as Langton and Timothy Taylors Landlord, pleasant unobtrusive service; children welcome, nice garden and lovely

village, open all day weekends, closed Mon and Tues lunchtimes. *(R L Borthwick)*

CALDECOTT SP8693
Plough (01536) 770284
Main Street; LE16 8RS Welcoming pub in attractive ironstone village; carpeted bar with banquettes and small tables leading to spacious eating area, log fires, four well kept changing beers such as Grainstore and Langton, wide range of popular inexpensive food including blackboard specials, prompt service; children and dogs welcome, good-sized garden at back, closed weekday lunchtimes. *(Max Simons)*

COLEORTON SK4016
Angel (01530) 834742
The Moor; LE67 8GB Friendly homely pub with good range of enjoyable reasonably priced food including carvery (weekday lunchtimes, Weds evening), well kept beers such as Marstons Pedigree, hospitable attentive staff, beams and open fire; tables outside, open (and food) all day Thurs-Sun. *(Lindy Andrews)*

CROXTON KERRIAL SK8329
Geese & Fountain (01476) 870350
A607 SW of Grantham; NG32 1QR Modernised 17th-c coaching inn with enjoyable food from sandwiches and pizzas up, five local ales, several craft beers, organic wines and some interesting spirits, friendly welcoming service, log fire in big open-plan beamed bar, dining room and garden room; children, walkers and dogs welcome, secure bike racks for cyclists, picnic-sets in inner courtyard and sloping garden with views, seven good bedrooms (separate block), closed in winter Tues and Weds lunchtime. *(JP)*

DADLINGTON SP4097
Dog & Hedgehog (01455) 213151
The Green, opposite church; CV13 6JB Popular red-brick village dining pub with good choice of well regarded food, friendly staff and hands-on character landlord, rebadged ales from brewers such as Quartz and Tunnel, nice wines, restaurant; children and dogs welcome, garden looking down to Ashby de la Zouch Canal, closed Sun evening, otherwise open all day. *(Gareth Woods, Mike and Margaret Banks)*

DISEWORTH SK4524
Plough (01332) 810333
Near East Midlands Airport and M1 junction 23A; DE74 2QJ Extended 16th-c beamed pub, well kept Bass, Greene King, Marstons and guests, low-priced traditional food (not Sun evening), friendly staff, bar and spacious well divided restaurant, log

---

Half pints: by law, a pub should not charge more for half a pint than half the price of a full pint, unless it shows that half-pint price on its price list.

fires; dogs welcome, paved terrace with steps up to lawn, handy for Donington Park race track, open all day. *(James Landor)*

EAST LANGTON   SP7292
★ **Bell** (01858) 545278
Off B6047; Main Street; LE16 7TW
Appealing creeper-clad beamed country inn buzzing with locals and families (particularly at weekends), well kept Fullers, Greene King, Langton and a guest, nice wines, good well presented food including daily specials and popular Sun carvery, friendly efficient staff, long low-ceilinged stripped-stone bar, spacious restaurant, modern pine furniture, log fires; picnic-sets on sloping front lawn, bedrooms. *(Gerry and Rosemary Dobson, Mike and Margaret Banks, Barry Collett)*

EXTON   SK9211
★ **Fox & Hounds** (01572) 812403
The Green; signed off A606 Stamford–Oakham; LE15 8AP Handsome 17th-c village inn refurbished by present owners; high-ceilinged candlelit lounge with big stone fireplace and comfortable seating, good food here or in more formal restaurant, Grainstore, Greene King and a guest, nice wines by the glass; soft background music and daily papers; children welcome, no dogs, sheltered walled garden overlooking pretty paddocks, three bedrooms, handy for Rutland Water and the gardens at Barnsdale, open all day in summer. *(David Heath)*

FOXTON   SP6989
★ **Foxton Locks** (0116) 279 1515
Foxton Locks, off A6 3 miles NW of Market Harborough (park by bridge 60/62 and walk); LE16 7RA Busy place in great canalside setting at foot of spectacular flight of locks; large comfortably reworked L-shaped bar, popular pubby food including Sun carvery, converted boathouse (not always open) for snacks, friendly efficient service, well kept ales such as Greene King, Sharps and Theakstons; some live music, free wi-fi; children and dogs welcome, glassed-in dining 'terrace' overlooking the water, steps down to fenced waterside lawn, good walks, open (and food) all day. *(Gerry and Rosemary Dobson)*

GADDESBY   SK6813
Cheney Arms (01664) 840260
Rearsby Lane; LE7 4XE Friendly red-brick country pub set back from the road; bar with bare-boards and terracotta-tiled floor, well kept Everards and a guest from brick-faced servery, open fires including inglenook in more formal dining room, big helpings of popular reasonably priced food (not Sun evening, Mon) from good lunchtime baguettes up, Thurs steak night; sports TV, free wi-fi; children welcome, walled back garden with smokers' shelter, lovely medieval church nearby, four bedrooms, closed Mon lunchtime. *(Sarah Roberts)*

GILMORTON   SP5787
Grey Goose (01455) 552555
Lutterworth Road; LE17 5PN Popular bar-restaurant with good range of enjoyable freshly made food from lunchtime sandwiches up, early-bird weekday deals and Sun carvery, ales such as Grainstore and several wines by the glass including champagne, good friendly staff coping well at busy times, light contemporary décor, stylish wood and metal bar stools mixing with comfortable sofas and armchairs, woodburner in stripped-brick fireplace; modern furniture on terrace, closed Sun evening, otherwise open all day. *(Simon Day)*

GLASTON   SK8900
Old Pheasant (01572) 822326
A47 Leicester–Peterborough, E of Uppingham; LE15 9BP Attractive much-extended stone inn; beamed bar with inglenook and some comfortable leather armchairs, well kept Grainstore from central brick servery, good range of generously served food including Weds grill night, steps up to restaurant; bar billiards; children welcome, picnic-sets on sheltered terrace, good value bedrooms, open (and food) all day. *(Paul A Moore)*

GREAT BOWDEN   SP7488
Red Lion (01858) 463571
Off A6 N of Market Harborough; Main Street; LE16 7HB Attractively modernised dining pub with good well presented food using local produce (some from own garden), carefully chosen wines and three real ales including a house beer from Langton, friendly attentive service; background music; children welcome, no dogs during food times, tables out on deck and lawn, open all day, no food Sun evening, Mon. *(James Landor)*

GREETHAM   SK9214
Plough (01572) 813613
B668 Stretton–Cottesmore; LE15 7NJ Traditional village pub, comfortable and welcoming, with good home-made food including popular nightly themed specials, breakfast Sat, can eat in cosy lounge or fire-divided restaurant, Grainstore, Timothy Taylors and three guests, helpful friendly service; children and dogs welcome, garden behind, good local walks and not far from Rutland Water, open all day Thurs-Sun. *(Lindy Andrews)*

GRIMSTON   SK6821
Black Horse (01664) 812358
Off A6006 W of Melton Mowbray; Main Street; LE14 3BZ Steps up to popular old village-green pub on two levels, welcoming licensees and friendly locals, well kept Adnams, Marstons and a couple of guests, decent wines, enjoyable fairly priced traditional food from baguettes to blackboard specials, open fire; darts; children welcome,

pétanque in back garden, attractive village with stocks and 13th-c church, closed Sun evening. *(James Landor)*

GUMLEY SP6890
Bell (0116) 279 0126
NW of Market Harborough; Main Street; LE16 7RU Friendly beamed village local, L-shaped bar with hunting prints and two open fires, Timothy Taylors Landlord, Woodfordes Wherry and guests, fair-priced home-cooked food including blackboard specials, weekday lunch deal and Weds steak night; live music, sports TV; children and dogs welcome, pond in terrace garden, local walks and cycle routes, open (and food) all day weekends. *(Max Simons)*

HALLATON SP7896
Bewicke Arms (01858) 555734
On Eastgate, opposite village sign; LE16 8UB Attractive recently refurbished 17th-c thatched dining pub; highly regarded food from interesting sensibly short menu making use of local ingredients, professional friendly service, ales such as Grainstore and Timothy Taylors, proper cider and good selection of wines, bar dining areas and restaurant, log fires and woodburners, memorabilia from ancient inter-village bottle-kicking match (still held on Easter Mon); children welcome, disabled facilities, big terrace overlooking paddock, play area, three bedrooms in converted stables, café, shop, open all day, no food Sun evening, Mon. *(Edward Nile)*

HARBY SK7531
Nags Head (01949) 869629
Main Street; LE14 4BN Popular old beamed pub with four comfortably refurbished linked rooms, popular good value pubby food (not Sun evening) including burger menu and Tues evening deals, two Marstons-related ales and a guest, friendly service, real fires; live music first Fri of month, sports TV, free wi-fi; picnic-sets in large garden, interesting Vale of Belvoir village, open all day Fri-Sun, closed Mon lunchtime. *(Phil and Jane Hodson)*

HINCKLEY SP4293
Railway (01455) 612399
Station Road; LE10 1AP Friendly chatty pub owned by the Steamin' Billy Brewing Company, their ales (contract-brewed nearby by Belvoir) and guests from seven pumps, also draught continentals and real cider, sensibly priced food including Thurs steak night, friendly young staff, open fires, darts; dogs welcome, beer garden behind, handy for train station. *(Lindy Andrews)*

HOBY SK6717
Blue Bell (01664) 434247
Main Street; LE14 3DT Attractive well run thatched pub with good range of popular realistically priced food (smaller appetites catered for), friendly attentive uniformed staff, four well kept Everards ales and two guests, good choice of wines by the glass, teas/coffees, open-plan and airy with beams, comfortable traditional furniture, old local photographs; background music, skittle alley and darts; children, walkers and dogs welcome, picnic-sets in valley-view garden with boules, open all day, food all day weekends. *(Edward Nile)*

HOUGHTON ON THE HILL SK6703
Old Black Horse (0116) 241 3486
Main Street (just off A47 Leicester– Uppingham); LE7 9GD Welcoming village pub with enjoyable home-made food (not Sun evening, Mon) including Thurs pie night, well kept Everards, a guest beer and decent wines by the glass, opened up inside into distinct modernised areas, mix of bare boards, tiles and carpet, some panelling; background and live music, regular quiz nights, sports TV, darts; children and dogs welcome, attractive big garden with boules, open all day Fri and Sun. *(Max Simons)*

HUNGARTON SK6907
Black Boy (0116) 259 5410
Main Street; LE7 9JR Large partly divided restauranty bar with open fire, good well priced food cooked to order by landlord-chef (weekend booking advised), various themed nights, changing ales such as Greene King, Fullers and Charles Wells, cheerful welcoming staff; background music; picnic-sets on decking, closed Sun evening, Mon lunchtime. *(Max Simons)*

ILLSTON ON THE HILL SP7099
★**Fox & Goose** (0116) 259 6340
Main Street, off B6047 Market Harborough–Melton Mowbray; LE7 9EG Individual little two-bar village local, simple, comfortable and friendly, with hunting pictures and assorted oddments including some stuffed animals, woodburner and coal fire, well kept Everards, a couple of guest beers and good choice of other drinks, enjoyable generously served home-made food (Thurs-Sat evenings only); darts and table tennis; children, walkers and dogs welcome, disabled access, Sept onion growing competition, open all day weekends, closed weekday lunchtimes. *(James Landor)*

KIRBY MUXLOE SK5104
Royal Oak (0116) 239 3166
Main Street; LE9 2AN Modernish village pub with good food from sandwiches and pub favourites to more inventive dishes, lunchtime/early evening set deal and Tues steak night, Everards ales including one badged for them and a guest, good wine choice, sizeable restaurant; Mon quiz and monthly live jazz; children and dogs (in bar) welcome, disabled facilities, picnic-sets outside, 15th-c castle ruins nearby. *(Sarah Roberts)*

KNIPTON SK8231
Manners Arms (01476) 879222
Signed off A607 Grantham–Melton Mowbray; Croxton Road; NG32 1RH Handsome Georgian hunting lodge reworked as comfortable country inn, bare-boards bar with log fire, four well kept ales and nice choice of wines by the glass, good food here or in sizeable restaurant with attractive conservatory, friendly helpful staff; background music; terrace with ornamental pool, lovely views over pretty village, ten comfortable individually furnished bedrooms, open all day. *(Simon Day)*

KNOSSINGTON SK8008
Fox & Hounds (01664) 452129
Off A606 W of Oakham; Somerby Road; LE15 8LY Attractive 18th-c ivy-clad village dining pub, beamed bar with log fire and cosy eating areas, well liked food (best to book) from traditional choices to blackboard specials, Fullers London Pride, attentive friendly service; no under-8s, dogs welcome, big back garden, closed Sun evening, Mon and lunchtimes Tues-Thurs. *(Max Simons)*

LEICESTER SK5804
Ale Wagon (0116) 262 3330
Rutland Street/Charles Street; LE1 1RE Basic 1930s two-room corner local with nine well kept real ales including own Hoskins Brothers beers, a traditional cider, no food apart from baps, coal fire, upstairs function room; background music; handy for Curve Theatre and station, open all day, closed Sun lunchtime. *(John Poulter)*

LEICESTER SK5804
Criterion (0116) 262 5418
Millstone Lane; LE1 5JN 1960s building with dark wood and carpeted main room, up to a dozen ales, 100 bottled beers and a couple of real ciders, good value stone-baked pizzas (not Sun) plus some other snacky food, room on left with games and old-fashioned juke box; regular live music and quiz nights, annual comedy festival; picnic-sets outside, open all day. *(Edward Nile)*

LEICESTER SK5804
Globe (0116) 253 9492
Silver Street; LE1 5EU Some refurbishment but keeping original character, lots of woodwork in partitioned areas off central bar, bare boards and some Victorian mosaic floor tiles, mirrors and working gas lamps, four Everards ales along with three guests, two real ciders and over a dozen wines by the glass, friendly staff, enjoyable well priced food from bar snacks up, function room upstairs; background music (not in snug); children and dogs welcome, metal café-style tables out in front, open all day (Sun till 6pm). *(Edward Nile)*

LEICESTER SK5804
★ Rutland & Derby Arms
(0116) 262 3299 *Millstone Lane; nearby metered parking; LE1 5JN* Neatly kept modern town bar with open-plan interior; comfortable bar chairs by long counter, padded high seats including a banquette by chunky tall tables, some stripped brickwork and a few small prints of classic film posters, popular all-day food, Everards and guests, 20 wines by the glass and good range of malt whiskies and other drinks, helpful staff; background music, live acoustic session last Fri of month, free wi-fi; children welcome, sunny courtyard with tables under parasols, more seats on upper terrace, closed Sun, otherwise open all day (1am Fri, Sat). *(Jeff Davies)*

LEICESTER SK5803
Swan & Rushes (0116) 233 9167
Oxford Street/Infirmary Square; LE1 5WR Triangular-shaped pub with up to ten well kept ales including Batemans and Oakham, extensive range of bottled beers and real cider served by friendly knowledgeable staff, thriving local atmosphere in two rooms with big oak tables, low-priced home-made food (not Sun) including stone-baked pizzas; themed beer and cider festivals, Thurs quiz, maybe Sat live music, bar billiards, pool and darts; dogs welcome, sunny back terrace, open all day and very busy on match days. *(Simon Day)*

LEICESTER FOREST WEST SK5001
Bulls Head (01455) 822252
Hinckley Road (A47); LE9 9JE Opened-up and fully refurbished roadside pub, Everards ales and guests kept well, several wines by the glass, popular good value home-made food including lunchtime set menu (Mon-Fri); children welcome, disabled access/facilities, seats out at front and in nice enclosed back garden with play area, open all day, food till 5.30pm Sun. *(Andy Dolan)*

LONG WHATTON SK4823
Royal Oak (01509) 843694
The Green; LE12 5DB Smartly updated dining pub with good well presented modern food along with pub favourites, early-bird menu 5.30-6.30pm, Sun pie night, three well kept ales and decent choice of wines by the glass, friendly efficient staff; bedrooms in separate building, open all day. *(Ken and Lynda Taylor)*

LOUGHBOROUGH SK5319
Swan in the Rushes (01509) 217014
The Rushes (A6); LE11 5BE Bare-boards town local with three smallish high-ceilinged rooms, good value Castle Rock and plenty of interesting changing guests, real cider and over 30 malt whiskies, well priced food (not

Sun evenings) including Pieminister pies and vegetarian options, open fire and daily papers, refurbished upstairs craft/world beer bar with roof terrace; good juke box, and some live music, free wi-fi; children welcome in eating areas, tables outside, open all day. *(Lindy Andrews)*

LOUGHBOROUGH SK5319
Tap & Mallet (01509) 210028
Nottingham Road; LE11 1EU Basic friendly pub with well kept Abbeydale, Batemans, Salopian and interesting microbrew guests, also foreign beers and Weston's cider, coal fire; juke box, darts and pool; walled back garden with pets corner, open all day Sat, closed lunchtime other days. *(Edward Nile)*

LYDDINGTON SP8796
★ **Old White Hart** (01572) 821703
Village signed off A6003 N of Corby; LE15 9LR Popular and welcoming 17th-c inn across from small green; softly lit front bar with heavy beams in low ceiling, just a few tables, glass-shielded log fire, Greene King IPA and a guest, good food (not Sun evening in winter) including own sausages and cured meats (landlord is a butcher), half-price offer Mon-Thurs, efficient obliging service, attractive restaurant, further tiled-floor room with rugs, lots of fine hunting prints and woodburner; children welcome, seats by heaters in pretty walled garden, eight floodlit boules pitches, handy for Bede House and good nearby walks, ten bedrooms, open all day (may be a break Sun afternoon). *(Michael Sargent, Mike and Margaret Banks, Peter Andrews)*

MANTON SK8704
Horse & Jockey (01572) 737335
St Mary's Road; LE15 8SU Welcoming early 19th-c stone pub with updated low-beamed interior, modern furniture on wood or stone floors, woodburner, well kept ales such as Grainstore and Greene King plus a house beer (Fall at the First), decent fairly priced food from baguettes to blackboard specials, cheery if not always speedy service; background music; children and dogs welcome, colourful tubs and hanging baskets, terrace picnic-sets (they ask for a card if you eat out here), nice location, on Rutland Water cycle route (racks provided), open all day in summer (all day Fri, Sat, till 7pm Sun in winter). *(Barry Collett, P and D Carpenter, Mike and Margaret Banks)*

MARKET OVERTON SK8816
Black Bull (01572) 767677
Opposite the church; LE15 7PW Attractive low-beamed thatch and stone pub (dates from the 17th c) in pretty village well placed for Rutland Water, welcoming

licensees and staff, good home-made food (booking advised) from pub staples up in long carpeted bar and two separate dining areas, well kept Black Sheep and a couple of guests, woodburner, banquettes and sofas; some background and live music; children and dogs welcome, tables out in front by small carp pool, two recently redecorated bedrooms, open all day Sun till 6pm, closed Mon. *(Barry Collett, M and GR)*

MEDBOURNE SP7992
★ **Nevill Arms** (01858) 565288
B664 Market Harborough–Uppingham; LE16 8EE Handsome stone-built Victorian inn nicely located by stream and footbridge; good bar and restaurant food served by friendly helpful staff, well kept ales such as Adnams, St Austell and Charles Wells, craft beers and good choice of wines by the glass including champagne, beams and mullion windows, woodburners (one in stone inglenook), modernised restaurant with light wood furniture on white tiles; children and dogs (in bar) welcome, streamside picnic-sets, back terrace and stable-conversion café (9am-4pm), ten bedrooms, open all day. *(Barry Collett)*

MELTON MOWBRAY SK7519
Anne of Cleves (01664) 481336
Burton Street, by St Mary's Church; LE13 1AE Monks' chantry dating from the 14th c and gifted to Anne of Cleves by Henry VIII; heavy beams and mullioned windows, chunky tables, character chairs and settles on flagstones, tapestries on burnt orange walls, log fire, well kept Everards and guests, decent wines and ample helpings of enjoyable food, small end dining room; background music; tables in pretty little walled garden with flagstone terrace, open all day. *(Sarah Roberts)*

MELTON MOWBRAY SK7518
Boat (01664) 500969
Burton Street; LE13 1AF Chatty and welcoming one-room local with four well kept ales and lots of malt whiskies, no food, panelling and open fire; darts; dogs welcome, open all day Thurs-Sun, closed Mon lunchtime. *(Sarah Roberts, Jeff Davies)*

MOUNTSORREL SK5715
Swan (0116) 230 2340
Loughborough Road, off A6; LE12 7AT Log fires, old flagstones and stripped stone, friendly staff and locals, enjoyable well priced often interesting food from baguettes up (best to book evenings), monthly themed nights such as cambodian and portuguese, Theakstons and other well kept ales, Weston's cider and good choice of wines, pine tables and gingham cloths in neat dining area and restaurant; dogs welcome in bar, pretty

---

walled back garden down to canalised River Soar, open all day weekends. *(Max Simons)*

MOWSLEY SP6488
Staff of Life (0116) 240 2359
Village signposted off A5199 S of Leicester; Main Street; LE17 6NT Gabled village pub with roomy fairly traditional bar, high-backed settles on flagstones, wicker chairs on shiny wood floor and stools around unusual circular counter, woodburner, Bass and Thwaites Wainwright, a dozen wines by the glass and decent whisky choice, well liked interesting mid-priced food (not Sun evening), set deal (Tues, Weds), good service; background music; well behaved children welcome (no under-12s Fri and Sat nights), no dogs, seats out in front and on nice leaf-shaded deck, open all day Sun, closed Mon and weekday lunchtimes. *(Lindy Andrews)*

NORTH LUFFENHAM SK9303
Fox (01780) 720991
Pinfold Lane; LE15 8LE Recently refurbished sister pub to the Horse & Jockey at Manton; flagstoned bar with woodburner, four well kept ales and several wines by the glass from light wood servery, lounge with comfortable seating on wood floor, exposed stone walls and another woodburner, good quality food in spacious dining room with modern furnishings, friendly prompt service; darts and TV upstairs; children and dogs welcome, paved terrace with large planters and picnic-sets under parasols, pretty village, open all day weekends, closed Mon and Tues lunchtimes. *(Barry Collett)*

OADBY SK6202
★Cow & Plough (0116) 272 0852
Gartree Road (B667 N of centre); LE2 2FB Converted farm buildings with extraordinary collection of brewery memorabilia in two dark back rooms – enamel signs and mirrors advertising long-forgotten beers, an aged brass cash register, furnishings and fittings salvaged from pubs and another churches (there's some splendid stained glass behind the counter), own Steamin' Billy beers and several guests, two real ciders and a dozen malt whiskies, good pubby food plus some interesting specials, long front extension and conservatory; background music, live jazz Weds lunchtime, TV, darts and board games, free wi-fi; children and dogs welcome, picnic-sets in the old yard, open all day, no food Sun evening. *(Barry Collett)*

OAKHAM SK8508
Three Crowns (01572) 757441
Northgate, next to Methodist church; LE15 6QS Cheery town pub serving full range of Steamin' Billy ales, spacious L-shaped bar with mix of tables and chairs, comfortable sofas, no food apart from lunchtime cobs. *(Barry Collett)*

OAKHAM SK8508
Wheatsheaf (01572) 723458
Northgate; Church Street end; LE15 6QS Popular attractive 17th-c local near church, well kept Everards and guests, good selection of wines by the glass and generous pubby food including specials, cheerful comfortable bar with open fires, quieter lounge, back conservatory; some live music; pretty suntrap courtyard, open all day Fri-Sun. *(Barry Collett)*

OLD DALBY SK6723
Crown (01664) 820320
Debdale Hill; LE14 3LF Stylishly revamped 16th-c dining pub with intimate rustic rooms up and down steps (same owners as the Curzon Arms in Woodhouse Eaves and Windmill at Wymeswold); popular interesting food along with traditional choices, also own-smoked dishes and good value weekday set menu, up to four real ales and plenty of wines by the glass, friendly staff; children, muddy boots and dogs welcome, attractive garden with covered area, open all day Fri-Sun, food all day Sat, till 6pm Sun. *(James Landor)*

REDMILE SK7935
★Windmill (01949) 842281
Off A52 Grantham–Nottingham; Main Street; NG13 0GA Snug low-beamed bar with sofas, easy chairs and log fire in large raised hearth, comfortable roomier dining areas with woodburners, wide choice of good home-made food from sandwiches, burgers and stone-baked pizzas up (maybe game from local Belvoir Estate), well kept ales such as Adnams, Newby Wyke and Oldershaws, good wines by the glass; children welcome, sizeable well furnished front courtyard, open (and food) all day. *(Edward Nile)*

ROTHLEY SK5812
Woodmans Stroke (0116) 230 2785
Church Street; LE7 7PD Family-run 18th-c thatched pub with good value weekday lunchtime bar food from sandwiches up, well kept changing ales and good wines by the glass including champagne, friendly service, beams and settles in front rooms, open fire, old local photographs plus rugby and cricket memorabilia; sports TV; pretty front hanging baskets, cast-iron tables in attractive garden with heaters, pétanque, open all day Sat. *(Mike and Margaret Banks)*

RYHALL TF0310
Wicked Witch (01780) 763649
Bridge Street; PE9 4HH Refurbished dining pub with good upmarket weekly changing set menus from chef-proprietor including occasional themed evenings, Banks's Mansfield and maybe a guest, nice wines; children welcome till 7pm, tables in back garden, closed Sun evening, Mon. *(Lindy Andrews)*

SADDINGTON
SP6591

Queens Head (0116) 240 2536

*S of Leicester between A5199 (ex A50)
and A6; Main Street; LE8 0QH*
Welcoming village pub with well kept
Everards, nice wines and good attractively
presented food (all day Sat, till 6pm Sun),
cleanly updated interior on different levels,
country and reservoir views from dining
conservatory and sloping terrace; Sun quiz,
free wi-fi; children welcome, farm shop
(9am-2pm), open all day Weds-Sun.
(Mike and Margaret Banks)

SEATON
SP9098

George & Dragon (01572) 747773

Main Street; LE15 9HU Stone-built pub
dating from the 17th c; two cosy split-level
bars (one a former bakery) and separate
restaurant, three real ales including Bass and
Grainstore, good traditional home-made food
(half-price mains Tues-Fri), attentive service
and friendly local atmosphere; children
welcome, outside tables, unspoilt hilltop
village with good views of Harringworth
Viaduct, bedrooms, open all day Sat, Sun
till 7pm, closed Mon. *(Philip Meek)*

SHAWELL
SP5480

White Swan (01788) 860357

*Main Street; village signed down
declassified road (ex A427) off A5/A426
roundabout – turn right in village; not
far from M6 junction 1; LE17 6AG*
Attractive little 17th-c beamed dining pub
with clean contemporary interior, good
interesting food from landlord-chef along
with some pub staples, local Dow Bridge ales
and guests, lots of wines by the glass, themed
food and wine tasting evenings, champagne
breakfast Sat, restaurant; children welcome,
open (and food) all day, kitchen closes 6pm
Sun. *(James Landor)*

SHEARSBY
SP6290

Chandlers Arms (0116) 247 8384

*Fenny Lane, off A50 Leicester–
Northampton; LE17 6PL* Comfortable old
creeper-clad pub in attractive village, seven
well kept ales including Dow Bridge (tasting
trays, July beer festival), a summer cider and
good value pubby food (not Sun evening);
background music, monthly quiz, table
skittles; secluded raised garden overlooking
green, open Sun till 7pm, closed Mon and
lunchtime Tues. *(Lindy Andrews)*

SILEBY
SK6015

Horse & Trumpet (01509) 812549

*Barrow Road, opposite church;
LE12 7LP* Friendly beamed village pub
renovated by the Steamin' Billy group, their
beers and guests kept well, real cider, fresh
cobs; some live music including jazz second
Mon of month, skittle alley, darts; well
behaved dogs welcome, terrace picnic-sets,
open all day. *(Sarah Roberts)*

SOMERBY
SK7710

★**Stilton Cheese** (01664) 454394

*High Street; off A606 Oakham–Melton
Mowbray, via Cold Overton, or
Leesthorpe and Pickwell; LE14 2QB*
Good friendly staff in enjoyable ironstone
pub with beamed bar/lounge, comfortable
furnishings on red patterned carpets, country
prints, plates and copper pots, stuffed badger
and pike, Grainstore, Marstons, Tetleys and
two guests, 30 malt whiskies, good reasonably
priced pubby food along with daily specials,
restaurant; children welcome, seats on
terrace, peaceful setting on edge of pretty
village. *(Mike and Margaret Banks, Phil and
Jane Hodson)*

SOUTH LUFFENHAM
SK9401

★**Coach House** (01780) 720166

Stamford Road (A6121); LE15 8NT
Refurbished old inn with stripped-stone and
flagstoned bar, scatter cushions on small
pews, log fire, three real ales including
Adnams and Greene King, decent wines
by the glass, good well priced food served
by friendly staff, separate snug with neat
built-in seating, smarter more modern
dining room; children and dogs (in bar)
welcome, small back deck, seven bedrooms,
open all day Sat, till 5pm Sun, closed Mon
lunchtime. *(Jeff Davies)*

SPROXTON
SK8524

Crown (01476) 861608

Coston Road; LE14 4QB Friendly fairly
compact 19th-c stone-built inn with spotless
well laid-out interior, good reasonably
priced food from bar snacks to restaurant
dishes cooked by landlord-chef, three well
kept changing ales, good wines and coffee,
light airy bar with woodburner, lounge area
and restaurant with glassed-off wine store;
children and dogs (in bar) welcome, lovely
sunny courtyard, attractive village and good
local walks, three bedrooms, open all day
weekends, closed lunchtimes Mon-Thurs.
(Simon Day)

STRETTON
SK9415

★**Jackson Stops** (01780) 410237

*Rookery Lane; a mile or less off A1, at
B668 (Oakham) exit; follow village sign,
turning off Clipsham Road into Manor
Road, pub on left; LE15 7RA* Attractive
thatched former farmhouse with plenty of
character; meandering rooms filled with
period features, black-beamed country bar
with wall timbering, coal fires and elderly
settle on worn tile and brick floor, a couple
of Grainstore ales, eight wines by the glass
and ten malt whiskies, smarter airy room
on right with mix of ancient and modern
tables on dark blue carpet, corner fire, two
dining rooms, one with stripped-stone walls
and old open cooking range, well liked food
including deals, warm friendly service;
rare nurdling bench (a game involving old

pennies), background music; children and dogs (in bar) welcome, closed Sun evening, Mon. *(John and Sylvia Harrop, Barry Collett, Gordon and Margaret Ormondroyd, Mike and Margaret Banks)*

THORNTON   SK4607
Reservoir (01530) 382433
Main Street; LE67 1AJ Busy pub with pleasant modern décor, popular home-made food from varied menu (not Sun evening) including good value set lunch, steak night Weds, Steamin' Billy ales, friendly efficient service, restaurant; children welcome, dogs and muddy boots in bar, good circular walk around Thornton Reservoir. *(Hilary Edwards)*

THORPE LANGTON   SP7492
★ **Bakers Arms** (01858) 545201
Off B6047 N of Market Harborough; LE16 7TS Civilised thatched restauranty pub with small bar; consistently good imaginative food (must book) from regularly changing menu including several seafood dishes, cottagey beamed linked areas and stylishly simple country décor, a well kept ale and good choice of wines by the glass, friendly efficient staff, maybe a pianist; no under-12s or dogs, picnic-sets in back garden with country views, closed Sun evening, Mon and weekday lunchtimes. *(Gerry and Rosemary Dobson)*

THRUSSINGTON   SK6415
Star (01664) 424220
Village signposted off A46 N of Syston; The Green; LE7 4UH Neatly modernised 18th-c village inn, L-shaped bar with low stripped beams, broad floorboards and inglenook woodburner, unusual double-sided high-backed settle, Belvoir Star Bitter, Timothy Taylors Landlord and a guest, ten wines by the glass, steps up to skylit dining room, popular all-day food; background music, quiz Sun, TV, free wi-fi; children and dogs (in bar) welcome, side garden and flagstoned terrace, bedrooms, open all day from 9am. *(Simon Day)*

TUGBY   SK7600
Fox & Hounds (0116) 259 8188
A47 6 miles W of Uppingham; LE7 9WB Attractively modernised village-green dining pub, good well priced food (all day Sat, till 6pm Sun) from bar snacks up, efficient welcoming staff, ales such as Courage, Grainstore and Sharps, compact open-plan interior with stripped beams and quarry tiles, dining part with light-wood furniture and woodburner; background music, TV; fenced terrace by car park, open all day Fri-Sun. *(R L Borthwick, Barry Collett)*

UPPINGHAM   SP8699
Falcon (01572) 823535
High Street East; LE15 9PY Quietly refined old coaching inn, welcoming and relaxed, with oak-panelled bar, spacious nicely furnished lounge and restaurant, roaring fire and big windows overlooking market square, good food (not Sun evening) from bar snacks up, three Grainstore ales, efficient friendly service; children welcome, dogs in bar, back garden with terrace, bedrooms (some in converted stable block), open all day. *(John and Sylvia Harrop, Barry Collett)*

UPPINGHAM   SP8699
Vaults (01572) 823259
Market Place next to church; LE15 9QH Attractive old pub with compact modernised interior; enjoyable reasonably priced traditional food served by friendly staff, four real ales including Adnams Broadside, Marstons Pedigree and a house beer from Grainstore, several wines by the glass, two pleasant little upstairs dining rooms; background music, sports TVs; children and dogs welcome, some tables out overlooking picturesque square, four bedrooms (booking from nearby Falcon Hotel), open all day. *(Barry Collett)*

WALTHAM ON THE WOLDS   SK8024
Royal Horseshoes (01664) 464346
Melton Road (A607); LE14 4AJ Attractive sympathetically restored stone and thatch pub in centre of village; good varied choice of generous affordably priced blackboard food, well kept Castle Rock, Sharps and three guests, interesting wine list and some 30 gins, two main rooms with beams and open fires; children welcome, no dogs inside, courtyard tables, good value comfortable bedrooms in annexe, hearty breakfast, open all day weekends. *(Michael Doswell)*

WELHAM   SP7692
Old Red Lion (01858) 565253
Off B664 Market Harborough–Uppingham; Main Street; LE16 7UJ Popular comfortably updated corner dining pub (part of the King Henry's Tavern group); beamed rooms, some on different levels, including unusual barrel-vaulted back area, leather sofas by log fire, Fullers London Pride and Greene King IPA, nice selection of wines, decent coffee and extensive choice of enjoyable fairly pubby food including good steaks and Sun carvery, efficient friendly staff; children and walkers welcome (ramblers' menu), no dogs, open (and food) all day. *(Guy and Caroline Howard)*

WHITWICK   SK4316
Three Horseshoes (01530) 837311
Leicester Road; LE67 5GN Unpretentious and unchanging local with long quarry-tiled bar, old wooden benches and open fires, tiny snug to the right, well kept Bass and Marstons Pedigree, no food, piano, darts, dominoes and cards; outside loos; no proper pub sign so easy to miss. *(Max Simons)*

WOODHOUSE EAVES SK5214
Curzon Arms (01509) 890377
Maplewell Road; LE12 8QZ Cheerful old beamed pub in pretty Charnwood Forest village; popular food (not Sun evening) from lunchtime sandwiches and pub favourites up, also good value weekday set menu, Sharps Doom Bar, Timothy Taylors Landlord and a couple of guests, several wines by the glass, good friendly service, attractive up-to-date décor with interesting collection of wall clocks, carpeted dining room; background music, free wi-fi; children, walkers and dogs welcome, ramp for disabled access, good-sized front lawn and terrace, open all day weekends. *(Ian Herdman)*

WOODHOUSE EAVES SK5214
Old Bulls Head (01509) 890255
Main Street; LE12 8RZ Big contemporary open-plan M&B dining pub, clean and tidy, with good choice of food including pizzas, pasta and grills, weekday set menu till 6pm, good wine list and well kept ales such as Brains Rev James, Marstons Pedigree and Sharps Doom Bar, friendly helpful staff; well behaved children welcome, outside seating, nice village setting and handy for Charnwood Forest and Bardon Hill, open (and food) all day. *(Graham H Ashworth)*

WOODHOUSE EAVES SK5313
Wheatsheaf (01509) 890320
Brand Hill; turn right into Main Street, off B591 S of Loughborough; LE12 8SS New owners for this brick and stone creeper-clad country pub with its pretty window boxes and tubs; traditionally furnished beamed bar areas with open fires, black and white motor-racing photographs on the walls, dining rooms with high-backed chairs around mix of tables, ales such as Adnams, Charnwood, Fullers and Timothy Taylors, several wines by the glass and good food; children welcome, dogs in bar if not too busy, seats outside under parasols, bedrooms in cottage annexe, open all day Sat, closed Sun evening. *(Ian Herdman, P and D Carpenter)*

WYMESWOLD SK6023
Windmill (01509) 881313
Brook Street; LE12 6TT Bustling side-street village pub with enjoyable good value home-made food (not Sun evening) from lunchtime snacks up, three well kept rotating ales, good cheerful service even though busy; children welcome, dogs in bar, back garden with decked area, open all day Fri, Sat, till 9pm Sun. *(Martin Day, Mike and Mary Carter)*

Post Office address codings confusingly give the impression that some pubs are in Leicestershire, when they're really in Cambridgeshire (which is where we list them).

Lincolnshire

KEY	⭐ Star Pub	🍽 Top Quality Food	🍺 Great Beer
🍷 Good Wines	£ Bargain Meals	🛏 Good Bedrooms	🍴 Serves Food

BARNOLDBY LE BECK TA2303 Map 8
Ship 🍽 🍷

(01472) 822308 – www.the-shipinn.com

Village signposted off A18 Louth–Grimsby; DN37 0BG

Tranquil refined dining pub with plenty to look at

Although many customers are here for the good, interesting food, there's a thoughtful choice of drinks and quite a collection of Edwardian and Victorian bric-a-brac too: stand-up telephones, violins, a horn gramophone, a bowler and top hats, old racquets, riding crops and hockey sticks. Heavy dark-ringed drapes swathe the windows and the furnishings fit in well, with pretty cushions on comfortable dark green wall benches, heavily stuffed green plush Victorian-looking chairs on a green fleur de lys carpet and a warming winter coal fire. Batemans XB, Black Sheep and Tom Woods Best Bitter on handpump, up to a dozen malt whiskies and good wines by the glass; background music. A fenced-off sunny area behind has hanging baskets and a few picnic-sets under parasols. This is a charming village.

🍽 Rewarding food includes sandwiches, scallops with chorizo and aioli, grilled honey-glazed goats cheese with pear ketchup, open vegetarian lasagne with basil oil and parmesan, slow-roasted blade of beef with horseradish mash, caramelised onion purée and red wine jus, duck breast with slow-cooked root vegetables and berry and cinnamon sauce, fish pie, lamb shank with sautéed cabbage and redcurrant reduction, and puddings such as white chocolate parfait with honeycomb and caramel salted bonbon. *Benchmark main dish: beer-battered fish and chips £10.95. Two-course evening meal £17.00.*

Free house ~ Licensee Michele Hancock ~ Real ale ~ Open 12-3, 6-11; 12-6 Sun ~ Bar food 12-2, 7-9; 12-5 Sun ~ Restaurant ~ Children welcome ~ Wi-fi
Recommended by Tim Rosamond, Tom Stone, Margaret McDonald

BASTON TF1113 Map 8
White Horse 🍽 🍷 🍺

(01778) 560923 – www.thewhitehorsebaston.co.uk

Church Street; PE6 9PE

Blue-painted and refurbished village pub with four real ales, friendly staff and good, popular food

Carefully restored, this 18th-c village pub is run by a friendly family. Using reclaimed farm materials (the bricks in the bay window, the boards in the ceiling, some of the beams and the huge piece of sycamore that acts as the counter in the snug bar), it's an interesting place with a good mix of customers. The main bar has built-in wall seats with scatter cushions, windsor and farmhouse chairs and stools around all sorts of tables on wooden flooring, a woodburning stove in a brick fireplace (with big logs piled into another) and horse-related items on pale paintwork; background music, TV, darts and board games. The dining area is similarly furnished. Stools line the blue-painted counter where they keep Adnams Southwold, Castle Rock Harvest Pale, Grainstore Calcutta and Hopshackle American Pale Ale on handpump, a dozen wines by the glass, several gins and ten malt whiskies; the resident springer spaniel is called Audrey. There are seats and tables on a side terrace.

Highly regarded food includes sandwiches, crab beignet with fennel purée and lemon and dill pastille, house-cured duck breast with broad beans and port and walnut dressing, beer-battered fish and chips, mushroom and ricotta ravioli with pesto and pine nuts, burger with sweet and sour relish and chips, a fresh fish dish of the day, and puddings such as honey brûlée with pistachio cake and walnut tart with fig and vanilla ice-cream. *Benchmark main dish: slow-roast pork belly with seared scallops, braised lentils and samphire £14.95. Two-course evening meal £20.00.*

Free house ~ Licensees Ben and Germaine Larter ~ Real ale ~ Open 4-11 Mon, Tues; 12-11 Wed, Thurs; 12-midnight Fri, Sat; 12-10.30 Sun ~ Bar food 5.30-9 Tues; 12-2.30, 5.30-9 Wed-Fri; 12-9 Sat; 12-6 Sun ~ Restaurant ~ Children welcome until 9pm only ~ Dogs allowed in bar ~ Wi-fi *Recommended by Michael and Jenny Back, Chris and Val Ramstedt, Patrick and Barbara Knights*

GEDNEY DYKE
Chequers 🖤❗ ♀
TF4125 Map 8

(01406) 366700 – www.the-chequers.co.uk
Off A17 Holbeach–Kings Lynn; PE12 0AJ

Smart dining pub with small bar, stylish restaurant rooms and imaginative food

Much emphasis is placed on the first class food in this stylish and friendly fenland village pub – but there's a warm welcome for those just wanting a chat and a pint too. The beamed bar has seats against the counter where they serve Greene King Abbot and Woodfordes Wherry on handpump, 12 wines and champagne by the glass and a wide range of spirits. There are several high chairs around equally high tables and an open fire. The smart, linked, carpeted dining rooms and conservatory have high-backed cream or black dining chairs around white-clothed tables, and throughout there's bare brick here and there and good lighting; service is helpful and courteous. The back terrace and fenced-off garden have plenty of seats and tables.

Top quality food includes crispy whitebait with garlic mayonnaise, ham hock terrine with caramelised apple, cauliflower cheese arancini with leek mash and truffled leeks, steak burger with toppings, red onion chutney and triple-cooked chips, lamb shank with roast celeriac, puy lentils and lamb jus, salmon fillet with charred baby gem and pea and carrot purée, and puddings such as glazed white chocolate and passion-fruit crème brûlée and lemon cheesecake. *Benchmark main dish: beer-battered cod and triple-cooked chips £11.00. Two-course evening meal £18.50.*

Free house ~ Licensee Gareth Franklin ~ Real ale ~ Open 11.30-3, 5-11 (midnight Sat); 12-5 Sun; closed Sun evening, Mon, Tues; first week Jan ~ Bar food 12-2, 6-9; 12-3 Sun ~ Restaurant ~ Children welcome ~ Dogs allowed in bar ~ Wi-fi *Recommended by Hilary and Neil Christopher, Carol and Barry Craddock, Charles Welch*

GREAT LIMBER

New Inn 🌟 ♀ 🛏

TA1308 Map 8

(01469) 569998 – www.thenewinngreatlimber.co.uk

High Street; DN37 8JL

Rather grand but with a civilised and easy-going atmosphere in bar and dining rooms, marvellous food, fine wines and large back garden; bedrooms

Part of the Brocklesby Estate, this handsome place is thriving following its reopening and refurbishment. The focus is on the excellent food and fine bedrooms, but there's a proper working bar liked by locals for a pint and a chat, quiz evenings or a game of darts. Here, there are windsor chairs, red button-back wall seating, some upholstered tub seats and oak tables on pale floorboards, neatly stacked logs to either side of one fireplace and shelves of books by another, and chairs against the counter where efficient, friendly staff serve Batemans XXXB, Tom Woods Old Codger and Wadworth IPA on handpump and a dozen wines by the glass. A snug little corner has a curved high-backed wall seat just right for a small group. The dining room is split into two, with cushioned wooden chairs in one part and comfortable red chairs and long wall seats with pretty scatter cushions in another. Throughout, the walls are hung with modern art, black and white photos and big mirrors; background music and TV. The landscaped back garden has both picnic-sets and tables and chairs. Bedrooms are comfortable and tranquil and breakfasts highly thought-of.

 Using organic produce from the Estate's kitchen garden, the impressive food starts with breakfasts (for non-residents too – 7.30-9.30am weekdays, 8-10am weekends) plus lunchtime sandwiches, black pudding and cheese hash browns with caramelised pear, duck breast with crispy duck leg croquettes, cherries and almonds, venison sausages with truffle mash and onion rings, parsnip, celeriac and fennel risotto, red mullet with squid, oven-dried tomatoes, wild fennel and pickled mushrooms, and puddings such as white chocolate mousse with white chocolate sorbet and dill cucumber and lemon tart with marmalade ice-cream. *Benchmark main dish: guinea fowl with boudin blanc and celeriac purée £18.00. Two-course evening meal £28.00.*

Free house ~ Licensee Alex Carter ~ Real ale ~ Open 12-11.30; 12-10.30 Sun ~ Bar food 12-2.30, 6.30-9; 12-6 Sun; not Mon lunchtime ~ Restaurant ~ Dogs allowed in bar ~ Wi-fi ~ Bedrooms: £80/£96 *Recommended by Miles Green, Andrew Vincent, Mark Morgan*

HEIGHINGTON

Butcher & Beast 🍺 £

TF0369 Map 8

(01522) 790386 – www.butcherandbeast.co.uk

High Street; LN4 1JS

Traditional village pub with terrific range of drinks, pubby food and a pretty garden by stream

The award-winning hanging baskets and tubs outside this cheerful village pub make quite a show in summer, and for warmer weather there are picnic-sets on a lawn that runs down to a stream. The simply decorated bar has button-back wall banquettes, pubby furnishings and stools along the counter where the hard-working, hands-on licensees keep half a dozen ales such as Batemans XB, XXXB and a seasonal guest plus Bass and changing beers from Everards and Hop Back; also two farm ciders, eight wines by the glass, 30 gins and 20 malt whiskies; occasional TV. The Snug has red-cushioned wall settles and high-backed wooden dining chairs, and the beamed dining room (extended this year) is neatly set with an attractive medley of wooden or painted chairs around chunky tables on floorboards, and a woodburning stove; throughout, the cream or yellow walls are hung with old village photos and country pictures.

 Reasonably priced, honest food includes prawn cocktail, garlic mushrooms, pasta filled with mushrooms and ricotta with sun-dried tomatoes and truffle oil, chicken strips in creamy apricot and stilton sauce, moules frites, burgers with toppings and chips, thai cod and prawn fishcakes with sweet chilli sauce, steaks with a choice of sauce, and puddings such as white and dark chocolate cheesecake and lemon sponge. *Benchmark main dish: steak in ale pie £11.25. Two-course evening meal £17.00.*

Batemans ~ Tenants Mal and Diane Gray ~ Real ale ~ Open 12-11 (10.30 Sun) ~ Bar food 12-2, 5-8.30; 12-2.30, 6-8 Sun ~ Restaurant ~ Children welcome away from bar ~ Dogs allowed in bar ~ Wi-fi *Recommended by Chris Johnson, William Pace, Sandra Morgan*

HOUGH-ON-THE-HILL SK9246 Map 8
Brownlow Arms ⭐ ♀ 🛏
(01400) 250234 – www.thebrownlowarms.com
High Road; NG32 2AZ

Lincolnshire Dining Pub of the Year

Refined country house with beamed bar, real ales, imaginative food and graceful terrace; bedrooms

After the busy A1, this smart old stone inn is such a relief with its warm welcome and proper values. Our readers also love staying in the well equipped and comfortable bedrooms, and breakfasts are highly rated. The comfortable beamed bar has plenty of panelling, some exposed brickwork, local prints and scenes, a large mirror, and a pile of logs beside a big fireplace. Seating is on elegant, stylishly mismatched upholstered armchairs, and the carefully arranged furnishings give the impression of several separate and cosy areas. Served by impeccably polite staff, the ales on handpump are Black Sheep and Timothy Taylors Landlord, there are ten wines by the glass and up to 20 malt whiskies; background music.

Good and enterprising food includes lunchtime sandwiches (not Sunday), home-cured maple and whisky gravadlax with beetroot concasse, cream cheese and fennel and dill crisps, pigeon breast with sautéed celeriac, chorizo, kale and red wine jus, roasted red pepper filo tart with grilled goats cheese and courgettes, beer-battered haddock and chips, duck breast with spiced ginger beer sauce and stir-fried vegetables, trio of lamb (cannon, seared liver, shepherd's pie) with rosemary jus, and puddings such as passion-fruit and raspberry bavarois with raspberry pastilles and passion-fruit sorbet and triple chocolate brownie with chocolate sauce and rocky road ice-cream. *Benchmark main dish: saddle of venison with butternut squash purée, blackberries and dark chocolate jus £27.50. Two-course evening meal £25.00.*

Free house ~ Licensee Paul L Willoughby ~ Real ale ~ Open 12-2.30, 6-11; 6-11 Tues; 12-3.30 Sun; closed Sun evening, Mon ~ Bar food 12-2, 6.30-9.30; 12-2.30 Sun ~ Restaurant ~ Children welcome but must be over 8 in evening ~ Wi-fi ~ Bedrooms: £70/£110
Recommended by Brian and Janet Ainscough, John Davis, Alan Clark, Michael Doswell, John Preddy, Charles Fraser, George Sanderson

---

Please keep sending us reports. We rely on readers for news of new discoveries, and particularly for news of changes – however slight – at the fully described pubs: feedback@goodguides.com, or (no stamp needed) The Good Pub Guide, FREEPOST RTJR-ZCYZ-RJZT, Perrymans Lane, Etchingham TN19 7DN.

INGHAM
SK9483 Map 8

Inn on the Green ⭐

(01522) 730354 – www.innonthegreeningham.co.uk

The Green; LN1 2XT

Nicely modernised place serving thoughtfully prepared food; chatty atmosphere

If it's just a drink and a chat that you want, head for the locals' bar with its informal, pubby feel and log fire; several tables there may also be occupied by those enjoying the tasty food. Caring staff serve Sharps Doom Bar and two guests, such as Pheasantry Best Bitter and Tom Woods Old Codger, on handpump, ten wines by the glass, 15 malt whiskies, 32 gins and home-made cordials. The beamed and timbered dining room is spread over two floors, with lots of exposed brickwork, local prints and a warm winter fire. The lounge between these rooms has leather sofas and background music, and a bar counter where you can buy home-made jams, marmalade and chutney. There are attractive views across the village green.

 Pleasing food includes sandwiches, goats cheese bonbon with roasted beetroot and olive tapenade, pork belly with wild mushrooms and blue cheese sauce, vegetable stack with girolle mushrooms and truffle dressing, pie of the day, chicken kiev with fries and coleslaw, cod loin with coconut rice and laksa curry sauce, duck breast with smoked bacon and apple, and puddings such as chocolate tart with confit oranges and burnt orange caramel and layered goan coconut pancake cake with coconut jelly and passion-fruit sorbet; they also offer a two- and three-course set menu (lunchtime and 6-6.55pm). *Benchmark main dish: braised blade of beef with horseradish croquette £15.50. Two-course evening meal £18.00.*

Free house ~ Licensees Andrew Cafferkey and Sarah Sharpe ~ Real ale ~ Open 11.30-3, 6-11; 12-10.30 Sun; closed Mon ~ Bar food 12-1.45 (3.30 Sun), 6-8.45 ~ Restaurant ~ Children welcome ~ Wi-fi *Recommended by Richard Cole, Miss Barr, Caroline Sullivan, Christopher Mannings*

KIRKBY LA THORPE
TF0945 Map 8

Queens Head ⭐ £

(01529) 305743 – www.thequeensheadinn.com

Village and pub signposted off A17, just E of Sleaford, then turn right into Boston Road cul-de-sac; NG34 9NU

Reliable dining pub very popular for its good food and helpful, efficient service

Gently traditional and neatly comfortable, this is highly regarded locally but draws in plenty of visitors too. There are open fires, elaborate flower arrangements and plenty of courteous dark-waistcoated staff, and the carpeted bar has stools along the counter, button-back banquettes, sofas and captain's chairs around shiny dark tables. The smart, beamed restaurant has high-backed orange-upholstered dining chairs around linen-set tables on carpet, heavy curtains and a woodburning stove; there's also a popular dining conservatory. Nice decorative touches take in thoughtful lighting, big prints, china plates on delft shelves and handsome longcase clocks (it's quite something when they all chime at midday). Batemans XB and a guest such as Black Sheep on handpump; background music. Easy disabled access.

At lunchtime, the particularly good food includes several dishes at £9.95 (hence our Value Award): braised saddle of local rabbit with root vegetables and juniper and merlot jus, whole flounder with brown shrimp and lemon butter, venison pie in red wine gravy, and slow-cooked lamb with creamed greens and minted redcurrant jus;

also, pork and juniper berry terrine with red onion chutney, crêpe of wild mushrooms, spinach and brie cream sauce, twice-cooked cider pork belly with black pudding fritter, sausage and apple mash, and puddings such as Baileys crème brûlée and sticky ginger and date pudding with butterscotch sauce. *Benchmark main dish: steak and kidney pudding £14.95. Two-course evening meal £20.00.*

Free house ~ Licensee John Clark ~ Real ale ~ Open 12-3, 6-11; 12-10.30 Sun ~ Bar food 12-2.30, 6-9.30; 12-8.30 Sun ~ Restaurant ~ Children welcome until 7pm ~ Dogs allowed in bar ~ Wi-fi *Recommended by Phoebe Peacock, Andrew Stone, David Travis, Patricia Hawkins*

STAMFORD
George of Stamford

TF0306 Map 8

(01780) 750750 – www.georgehotelofstamford.com
High Street, St Martins (B1081 S of centre, not the quite different central pedestrianised High Street); PE9 2LB

Handsome coaching inn with traditional bar, several dining areas and lounges, excellent staff and top class food and drink; bedrooms

This lovely place was built in 1597 for Lord Burghley (whose splendid nearby Elizabethan house is well worth visiting) and it has plenty of genuine character. It remains exceptionally well run with professional but friendly staff and a civilised yet informal atmosphere. The various areas are furnished with all manner of seats from leather, cane and antique wicker to soft sofas and easy chairs, and there's a room to suit every occasion. The central lounge is particularly striking with sturdy timbers, broad flagstones, heavy beams and massive stonework. The properly pubby little York Bar at the front has Adnams Broadside, Black Sheep and Grainstore Triple B on handpump alongside 20 wines from an exceptional list and 30 malt whiskies. There's an amazing oak-panelled restaurant (jacket or tie required) and a less formal Garden Room restaurant, which has well spaced furniture on herringbone glazed bricks around a central tropical planting. The seats in the charming cobbled courtyard are highly prized and the immaculately kept walled garden is beautifully planted; there are also sunken lawns – and croquet. Individually and thoughtfully decorated bedrooms and splendid breakfasts.

The simplest food option is the York Bar snack menu with sandwiches (their toastie is especially good), a proper ploughman's and a plate of smoked salmon with capers. First class food in the restaurants includes chicken liver pâté with cumberland sauce, prawn and crab cocktail, moroccan-style lamb tagine, butternut squash risotto with parmesan crisp, beer-battered haddock and chips, confit duck leg cassoulet with sauerkraut, shellfish platter, and puddings. *Benchmark main dish: roast sirloin of beef with trimmings £24.95. Two-course evening meal £24.00.*

Free house ~ Licensee Chris Pitman ~ Real ale ~ Open 11-11; 12-10.30 Sun ~ Bar food 12-2, 7-9 ~ Restaurant ~ Children must be over 8 in panelled dining room ~ Dogs allowed in bar and bedrooms ~ Wi-fi ~ Bedrooms: £120/£195 *Recommended by Richard Tilbrook, Lizzie Lander, Miss B D Picton, Caroline Sullivan, Hilary and Neil Christopher*

STAMFORD
Tobie Norris

TF0307 Map 8

(01780) 753800 – www.kneadpubs.co.uk
St Pauls Street; PE9 2BE

A warren of ancient rooms, a good period atmosphere, a fine choice of drinks, enjoyable food and seats outside

The best has been made of this building's great age: worn flagstones, meticulously stripped stonework, a huge hearth for one room's woodburning stove and steeply pitched rafters in one of the two upstairs rooms – it's been beautifully restored. The charming series of little rooms are full of character and have a wide variety of furnishings from pews and wall settles to comfortable armchairs and a handsomely panelled shrine to Nelson and the Battle of Trafalgar. Attentive, friendly staff serve Adnams Mosaic, Castle Rock Harvest Pale Ale and guests such as St Austell Tribute and Thornbridge Jaipur on handpump, farm cider and several wines by the glass. A snug end conservatory opens to a narrow but sunny two-level courtyard with seats and tables.

Enjoyable food includes lunchtime sandwiches and wraps, nibbles such as pigs in blankets with salt and garlic potatoes and mustard mayonnaise and honey and smoked bacon dough balls, sharing boards, home-made stone-baked pizzas with lots of toppings, cauliflower and lentil curry, pressed ham hock and treacle-glazed fried ham with duck eggs, bass, gnocchi and pea fricassée with caper, dill and white wine sauce, and puddings such as spiced apple crumble and chocolate and caramel sundae. *Benchmark main dish: indian-style burger with sag aloo and sweet onion bhaji £14.95. Two-course evening meal £19.00.*

Free house ~ Licensees Tim Chantrell and Gemma Rogerson ~ Real ale ~ Open 11-11 (midnight Fri, Sat) ~ Bar food 12-2.30, 6-9; 12-5, 6-9 Sat ~ Children welcome until 8pm; no pushchairs ~ Dogs welcome ~ Wi-fi *Recommended by Anne and Ben Smith, Andrew Stone, Dr J Barrie Jones, Barry Collett*

WOOLSTHORPE
Chequers ⭐ ♀

SK8334 Map 8

(01476) 870701 – www.chequersinn.net

Woolsthorpe near Belvoir, signposted off A52 or A607 W of Grantham; NG32 1LU

Interesting food at comfortably relaxed inn with good drinks and appealing castle views from outside tables; bedrooms

The oldest parts of this inn date from 1640 when it was a farm and the village bakery – the original oven is still here. The heavily beamed main bar has two big tables (one a massive oak construction), a comfortable mix of seating including some handsome leather chairs and banquettes, and a huge boar's head above a good log fire in the big brick fireplace. Among cartoons on the wall are some of the illustrated claret bottle labels from the series commissioned from famous artists. There are more leather seats in a dining area on the left and a corridor leads off to the light and airy main restaurant, decorated with contemporary pictures, and then to another bar; background music. Grainstore Rutland Bitter, St Austell Tribute and a couple of guest beers on handpump, around 30 wines by the glass, 50 malt whiskies, 20 gins, a seasonal cocktail list and a farm cider. There are good quality teak tables, chairs and benches outside and, beyond these, some picnic-sets on the edge of the pub's cricket field, with views of Belvoir Castle. If you want to explore the lovely Vale of Belvoir, it makes sense to stay in the comfortable bedrooms in the converted stables next door.

Creative food includes sandwiches, foie gras with mandarin purée and gingerbread crouton, scallops with wild mushrooms, parsnip purée and parsnip crisps, goats cheese, beetroot and spinach tart, a pie of the day, local sausages with mash and onion gravy, sea bream fillet and tiger prawn katsu curry, steak frites with garlic butter, duck with beetroot champ mash, confit oranges and glazed cherries, and puddings such as dark chocolate and coffee mousse with kirsch cherry ice-cream and marshmallow with pineapple carpaccio and lime sorbet. *Benchmark main dish: rib of beef with béarnaise sauce and chips (for two) £39.00. Two-course evening meal £20.00.*

Free house ~ Licensee Justin Chad ~ Real ale ~ Open 12-11 (midnight Sat); 12-10.30 Sun ~ Bar food 12-2.30, 6-9.30; 12-4, 6-8.30 Sun ~ Restaurant ~ Children welcome ~ Dogs allowed in bar and bedrooms ~ Wi-fi ~ Bedrooms: £50/£70 *Recommended by David Heath, Jo Garnett, Edward Nile, William Pace*

Also Worth a Visit in Lincolnshire

Besides the fully inspected pubs, you might like to try these pubs that have been recommended to us and described by readers. Do tell us what you think of them: feedback@goodguides.com

---

ALLINGTON   SK8540
★**Welby Arms** (01400) 281361
The Green; off A1 at N end of Grantham bypass; NG32 2EA Welcoming, well run and well liked inn with helpful friendly staff, large simply furnished bar divided by stone archway, beams and joists, log fires (one in attractive arched brick fireplace), comfortable plush wall banquettes and stools, up to six changing ales, over 20 wines by the glass and plenty of malt whiskies, good popular food including blackboard specials, civilised back dining lounge; background music; children welcome, tables in walled courtyard with pretty flower baskets, picnic-sets on front lawn, comfortable bedrooms, open all day Sun. *(Roger and Pauline Pearce, Gordon and Margaret Ormondroyd)*

ASLACKBY   TF0830
Robin Hood & Little John
(01778) 440681 *A15 Bourne–Sleaford; NG34 0HL* Old mansard-roofed roadside country pub under new management; split-level bar with beams, flagstones and woodburners, popular fairly pubby food including vegetarian choices and daily specials, Greene King Abbot and guests, friendly staff, separate more modern oak-floored restaurant; children and dogs (in bar) welcome, tricky wheelchair access, three-level terrace, open (and food) all day weekends. *(Miles Green)*

BARHOLM   TF0810
Five Horseshoes (01778) 560238
W of Market Deeping; village signed from A15 Langtoft; PE9 4RA Welcoming old-fashioned village local, cosy and comfortable, with beams, rustic bric-a-brac and log fire, well kept Adnams, Oakham and four guests, good range of wines, Fri pizza van; pool room with TV, some live music; children and dogs welcome, garden and shady arbour, play area, open all day weekends (from 1pm Sat), closed weekday lunchtimes. *(Ian and Tina Humphrey)*

BASSINGHAM   SK9160
Five Bells (01522) 788269
High Street; LN5 9JZ Cheerful old country pub with well liked food including good value set menu (booking advised), Greene King

IPA and a couple of guests, several brandies, efficient friendly service, bare-boards interior with hop-draped beams, cosy log fires and lots of brass and bric-a-brac, some quotations on the walls and a well in one part; children and dogs (particularly) welcome, open all day (food till 7pm Sun). *(Tony and Maggie Harwood)*

BELCHFORD   TF2975
★**Blue Bell** (01507) 533602
Village signed off A153 Horncastle–Louth; LN9 6LQ 18th-c dining pub with cosy comfortable bar, Batemans, Worthington and guests, Thatcher's cider, good traditional and modern food, efficient friendly service, restaurant; children and dogs welcome, picnic-sets in terraced back garden, good base for Wolds walks and Viking Way (remove muddy boots), open all day Sun, may close second and third weeks in Jan. *(David Travis)*

BICKER   TF2237
Red Lion (01775) 821200
A52 NE of Donnington; PE20 3EF Nicely decorated 17th-c village pub, enjoyable home-made food including set lunch and popular Sun carvery, also a 'Lincolnshire tapas' menu, friendly helpful service, Adnams Southwold, Courage Directors and a guest, bowed beams (some painted), exposed brickwork and half panelling, wood and flagstone floors, woodburners, part-raftered restaurant; quiz first Weds of month; children welcome, no dogs inside, rattan-style furniture on brick terrace with pergola, lawned garden, closed Mon, Tues, otherwise open all day (Sun till 7pm). *(Mrs Julie Thomas)*

BILLINGBOROUGH   TF1134
★**Fortescue Arms** (01529) 240228
B1177, off A52 Grantham–Boston; NG34 0QB Popular beamed village pub with old stonework, exposed brick, panelling and big see-through fireplace in carpeted rooms, tables in bay windows overlooking high street, well kept Greene King and a guest, enjoyable pubby food including weekday meal deal, good friendly service even at busy times, Victorian prints, brass and copper, a stuffed badger and pheasant, dining rooms at each end; children and dogs welcome, picnic-sets and rattan-style furniture in sheltered courtyard with

flowering tubs, useful big car park, open (and food) all day weekends. *(Mrs Julie Thomas)*

BOSTON   TF3244
Mill (01205) 352874
Spilsby Road (A16); PE21 9QN Popular roadside pub with enjoyable reasonably priced food (not Tues) including some italian choices, Batemans XB and a guest, friendly italian landlord and staff; children welcome, tables out in front. *(James Allsopp)*

BURTON COGGLES   SK9725
Cholmeley Arms (01476) 550225
Village Street; NG33 4JS Well kept ales such as Fullers London Pride, Grainstore and Greene King Abbot in small beamed pubby bar with warm fire, generous helpings of good reasonably priced home-made food (not Sun evening), friendly efficient service, restaurant; farm shop, four bedrooms in separate building overlooking garden, handy for A1, open all day weekends, closed lunchtimes Mon, Tues. *(Caroline Sullivan)*

CAYTHORPE   SK9348
Red Lion (01400) 272632
Signed just off A607 N of Grantham; High Street; NG32 3DN Popular village pub with good fairly traditional home-made food (booking advised) including early-bird deal (Weds-Fri 6-7pm), Tues fish and chips night, friendly helpful staff, well kept Adnams and Everards, good sensibly priced wine, bare-boards bar with light wood counter, black beams and roaring fire, modern restaurant; back terrace by car park. *(Margaret McDonald)*

CHAPEL ST LEONARDS   TF5672
Admiral Benbow (01754) 871847
The Promenade; PE24 5BQ Small bare-boards beach bar serving three real ales and good choice of foreign bottled beers, ciders too, sandwiches and snacks, cushioned bench seats, stools and barrel tables, lots of bric-a-brac and nautical memorabilia on planked walls and ceiling; children and dogs welcome, picnic-sets out on mock-up galleon, great sea views, open all day summer, all Fri-Sun winter. *(Miles Green)*

CLAYPOLE   SK8449
Five Bells (01636) 626561
Main Street; NG23 5BJ Friendly brick-built village pub, good-sized beamed bar with smaller dining area beyond servery, well kept Greene King IPA and mainly local guests, a couple of ciders, good value home-made food including range of burgers and daily specials; pool and darts; children welcome, dogs in bar, grassy back garden with play area, four bedrooms, closed Mon lunchtime, otherwise open all day. *(David Travis)*

CLEETHORPES   TA3009
No 2 Refreshment Room
07905 375587 *Station Approach beneath the clock tower; DN35 8AX* Small comfortable station bar with well kept Hancocks HB, Rudgates Mild, Sharps Doom Bar and guests, real cider too, friendly staff, interesting old pictures of the station, historical books on trains and the local area, no food but they do a free Sun evening buffet; tables out under heaters, open all day from 7.30am. *(James Allsopp)*

CLEETHORPES   TA3008
Nottingham House (01472) 505150
Sea View Street; DN35 8EU Seafront pub with lively main bar, lounge and snug, seven well kept ales including Tetley Mild, Timothy Taylors Landlord and Wychwood Hobgoblin, Weston's ciders, good reasonably priced food from sandwiches and pub favourites up in bar or upstairs restaurant, helpful friendly staff; live acoustic music first Mon and third Tues of month; children and dogs welcome, refurbished bedrooms, good breakfast, open all day. *(Chris Johnson)*

CLEETHORPES   TA3108
★ **Willys** (01472) 602145
Highcliff Road; south promenade; DN35 8RQ Popular mock-Tudor seafront pub with panoramic Humber views, open-plan interior with tiled floor and painted brick walls, own good ales from visible microbrewery, also changing guests and belgian beers, enjoyable home-made bargain bar lunches (evening food Mon-Thurs), friendly service and good mix of customers; children welcome, no dogs at food times, a few tables out on the prom, open all day (till late Fri, Sat). *(Chris Johnson)*

COLEBY   SK9760
Bell (01522) 813778
Village signed off A607 S of Lincoln, turn right and right into Far Lane at church; LN5 0AH Restauranty pub with wide variety of top notch food from owner-chef including early-bird menu (Weds-Fri), welcoming cheerful staff, well kept Timothy Taylors and several wines by the glass (not cheap), bar and three dining areas; children over 8 welcome, terrace tables, village on Viking Way with lovely fenland views, three bedrooms, open evenings Weds-Sat and lunchtime Sun. *(Miles Green)*

CONINGSBY   TF2458
Leagate Inn (01526) 342370
Leagate Road (B1192 southwards, off A153 E); LN4 4RS Heavy-beamed 16th-c fenland pub run by same family for over 25 years; three cosy linked rooms, medley of

---

It's very helpful if you let us know up-to-date food prices when you report on pubs.

furnishings including high-backed settles around the biggest of three log fires, ancient oak panelling, dim lighting, attractive dining room, even a priest hole; enjoyable well priced food from extensive menu, Adnams, Batemans and Charles Wells ales, friendly service; free wi-fi; children welcome (they eat free 6-7pm Mon-Fri); dogs in bar, pleasant garden with play area, site of old gallows at front, eight motel bedrooms, open (and food) all day Sun. *(David Travis)*

DONINGTON ON BAIN TF2382
Black Horse (01507) 343640
Main Road; between A153 and A157, SW of Louth; LN11 9TJ Roadside village inn doing well under welcoming new management; two carpeted bars (back one with low beams) and restaurant with open fires and woodburner, good locally sourced food cooked by landlord-chef including daily specials, well kept John Smiths and guests, proper cider; games room with pool, darts and dominoes, free wi-fi; children and dogs (in bars) welcome, picnic-sets in back garden, eight motel-style bedrooms, on Viking Way and handy for Cadwell Park race circuit, closed Mon and Tues lunchtimes. *(Miles Green)*

DRY DODDINGTON SK8546
★ **Wheatsheaf** (01400) 281458
Main Street; 1.5 miles off A1 N of Grantham; NG23 5HU Spotless 16th-c village pub under newish owners; front bar (basically two rooms) with woodburner, variety of built-in wall seats, settles and little wooden stools, windows looking out to green and lovely 14th-c church with its crooked tower, Greene King Abbot and IPA, several wines by the glass and enjoyable food from varied menu including themed nights, slight slope down to comfortable extended dining room (once a cow byre perhaps dating to the 13th c); background music, free wi-fi; children and dogs (in bar) welcome, side disabled access, neat tables under parasols on front terrace, closed Mon. *(Dr D J and Mrs S C Walker, John Saul)*

FOSDYKE TF3132
Ship (01205) 260764
Moulton Washway; A17; PE12 6LH Useful roadside pub with popular reasonably priced food from varied menu, Sun carvery, two Adnams beers and Batemans XB, friendly staff, simple pine and quarry tile décor, woodburner, quiz every other Mon; children welcome, garden tables, open all day. *(Margaret McDonald)*

FULBECK SK9450
Hare & Hounds (01400) 272322
The Green (A607 Leadenham-Grantham); NG32 3JJ Converted 17th-c maltings overlooking attractive village green, modernised linked areas, log fire, highly regarded food from ciabattas and pub favourites up, friendly attentive service, well

kept ales such as Brakspears and Marstons Pedigree, affordable wine list, raftered upstairs function room; terrace seating, eight good bedrooms in adjacent barn conversion, closed Sun evening. *(William and Ann Reid)*

GAINSBOROUGH SK8189
Eight Jolly Brewers (01427) 611022
Ship Court, Silver Street; DN21 2DW Small drinkers' pub in former warehouse, eight interesting real ales, traditional cider and plenty of bottled beers, friendly staff and locals, beams and bare brick, more room upstairs and live music Thurs; seats outside, open all day. *(Miles Green)*

IRNHAM TF0226
Griffin (01476) 550201
Bulby Road; NG33 4JG Welcoming old stone-built pub in nice village setting, enjoyable generously served home-made food (not Sun evening), Oakham and a couple of guests such as Navigation, good helpful service, three rooms (two for dining), log fires; background music; children welcome, no dogs inside (resident bassett is Bertie), classic car meet first Weds of month (spring/summer), four comfortable bedrooms, closed Mon, Tues. *(James Allsopp)*

KIRKBY ON BAIN TF2462
★ **Ebrington Arms** (01526) 354560
Main Street; LN10 6YT Popular village pub with good value traditional food (not Mon, booking advised), half a dozen well kept ales such as Adnams, Batemans and Sharps, friendly service, beer mats on low 16th-c beams, carpets and banquettes, open fire, restaurant behind; background music, darts; children and dogs welcome, wheelchair access, tables out in front by road, lawn to the side with play equipment, campsite next door, closed Mon lunchtime. *(Miles Green)*

LINCOLN SK9871
Dog & Bone (01522) 522403
John Street; LN2 5BH Comfortable and welcoming backstreet local with six well kept ales including Batemans, real cider and good value Sunday lunch (third Sun of the month), log fires, various things to look at including collection of valve radios, local artwork and exchange library of recent fiction; background and live music, quiz nights, beer festivals; dogs welcome (theirs is Blade), picnic-sets on back terrace, open all day Fri-Sun, from 4.30pm other days. *(Caroline Sullivan)*

LINCOLN SK9771
Jolly Brewer (01522) 528583
Broadgate; LN2 5AQ Popular no-frills pub with unusual art deco interior, good choice of well kept ales such as Idle Valley, Tom Woods and Welbeck Abbey, real cider, no food; regular live music including Weds open mike night; back courtyard with covered area, open all day (till 8pm Sun). *(Miles Green)*

LINCOLN
SK9771

Strugglers (01522) 535023
Westgate; LN1 3BG Cosily worn-in beer lovers' haunt tucked beneath the castle walls, built in 1841 and once run by the local hangman (note the pub sign); half a dozen or more well kept ales including Bass and Timothy Taylors, bare boards throughout with lots of knick-knacks and pump clips, two open fires (one in back snug); some live acoustic music; no children inside, dogs welcome, steps down to sunny back courtyard with heated canopy, open all day (till 1am Fri, Sat). *(Richard Tilbrook)*

LINCOLN
SK9771

Victoria (01522) 541000
Union Road; LN1 3BJ Old-fashioned local just outside the castle gates, eight real ales including Bass and Castle Rock, foreign draught and bottled beers and real cider, simply furnished tiled front lounge with pictures of Queen Victoria, coal fire, basic lunchtime food, friendly staff and good mix of customers (gets especially busy lunchtime and later in the evening); live music Sat; children and dogs welcome, seats on heated terrace, play area, good castle views, open all day till midnight (1am Fri, Sat). *(James Allsopp)*

LINCOLN
SK9771

Widow Cullens Well (01522) 523020
Steep Hill; just below cathedral; LN2 1LU Ancient reworked building on two floors (upstairs open to the rafters), cheap Sam Smiths beers and enjoyable food including children's choices, chatty mix of customers (busy evening and weekends), friendly service but can slow at peak times and they add a surcharge if you pay by card, beams, stone walls and log fire, back extension with namesake well; dogs welcome, terrace seating, open all day. *(David Travis)*

LINCOLN
SK9771

★ Wig & Mitre (01522) 535190
Steep Hill; just below cathedral; LN2 1LU Civilised café-style dining pub with plenty of character and attractive period features over two floors; big-windowed downstairs bar, beams and exposed stone walls, pews and Gothic furniture on oak boards, comfortable sofas in carpeted back area, quieter upstairs dining room with views of castle walls and cathedral, antique prints and caricatures of lawyers/clerics, well liked food from breakfast on including good value set menus and some interesting seasonal dishes, extensive choice of wines by the glass from good list, Everards Tiger and a couple of guests, friendly service; children and dogs welcome, open 8am-midnight. *(Philip Kingsbury, Richard Tilbrook, Brian and Anna Marsden)*

LONG BENNINGTON
SK8344

★ Reindeer (01400) 281382
Just off A1 N of Grantham – S end of village, opposite school; NG23 5DJ Intimate atmosphere in attractively traditional 17th-c low-beamed pub run by popular long-serving landlady; consistently good food (fair value considering the quality) from sandwiches up in bar and more formal restaurant, can get very busy so best to book, well kept ales such as Timothy Taylors Landlord, nice wines, good friendly service, coal-effect stove in stone fireplace; background music; picnic-sets under parasols on small front terrace, closed Sun evening, Mon. *(Brian and Janet Ainscough, Mike and Margaret Banks)*

LONG BENNINGTON
SK8344

Royal Oak (01400) 281332
Main Road; just off A1 N of Grantham; NG23 5DJ Popular local with good-sized bar serving well kept Marstons and Mansfield ales, several wines by the glass and good sensibly priced home-made food including specials, friendly helpful staff; children welcome, seats out in front and in big back garden with play area, path for customers to river, open all day. *(Margaret McDonald)*

LOUTH
TF4083

Waggon & Horses (01507) 450364
A157; South Reston; LN11 8JQ Welcoming roadside pub with good range of reasonably priced home-cooked food including daily specials and Sun carvery, bargain OAP lunch Weds, Sat breakfast, well kept Batemans and guests, decent wine list, friendly helpful service, comfortable panelled lounge bar with porcelain horse-and-cart models, brassware and collection of old photographs, open fire, well laid-out restaurant (children welcome here), conservatory; pool and darts; garden with play area, camping, open all day from 8.30am (afternoon break Sun). *(Roy and Lindsey Fentiman)*

LOUTH
TF3287

Wheatsheaf (01507) 606262
Westgate, near St James Church; LN11 9YD Welcoming traditional 17th-c low-beamed pub, half a dozen well kept ales including Bass, Greene King and Tom Woods, real cider, enjoyable pubby food served by friendly helpful young staff, coal fires in all three bars, old photographs; children welcome, no dogs, tables outside, open all day and can get busy. *(David Travis)*

MARKET DEEPING
TF1310

Bull (01778) 343320
Market Place; PE6 8EA Bustling local run by welcoming ex-footballer landlord; cosy

---

If you know a pub is ever open all day, please tell us.

low-ceilinged alcoves, little corridors and interesting heavy-beamed medieval Dugout Bar, well kept Everards Tiger and Original and a couple of guests including Adnams, enjoyable lunchtime food, restaurant, upstairs games room; sports TV, free wi-fi; children in eating areas, seats in coachyard, open all day. *(Miles Green)*

MARKET RASEN   TF1089
Aston Arms (01673) 842313
Market Place; LN8 3HL Popular market-square pub serving generous helpings of inexpensive food, Theakstons, Wells Bombardier and a guest, friendly staff, beamed bar, lounge and games area; children and well behaved dogs welcome, side terrace, open all day. *(Phil and Jane Hodson)*

MINTING   TF1873
Sebastopol (01507) 578577
Off A158 Lincoln–Horncastle; LN9 5RT Updated red-brick village pub; good attractively presented food from imaginative menu using Lincolnshire suppliers, well kept Batemans, a local guest and nice wines by the glass, friendly staff, small bar with open fire and comfortable seats on patterned slate floor, beamed restaurant with strip-wood flooring and cheerfully upholstered chairs by light wood tables; charity quiz first Weds of month; children welcome, resident westie called Snoopy, picnic-sets on front terrace, self-catering barn conversion, closed Sun evening, Mon (and Tues, Weds in winter). *(James Allsopp)*

NORTON DISNEY   SK8859
Green Man (01522) 789804
Main Street, off A46 Newark–Lincoln; LN6 9JU Old beamed village pub-restaurant under new management; enjoyable food from chef-landlord including pub standards and daily specials, good Sun roasts, Black Sheep, Brains Rev James and a guest, friendly staff, opened-up modernised interior; tables out in front and in spacious back garden, closed Sun evening, Mon lunchtime. *(Susie Hennings)*

SCAMPTON   SK9579
Dambusters (01522) 731333
High Street; LN1 2SD Welcoming pub with several beamed rooms around central bar, masses of interesting Dambusters and other RAF memorabilia, generous helpings of reasonably priced straightforward food (not Sun evening), also home-made chutneys, pâté and biscuits for sale, six interesting ales including own microbrews (ceiling covered in beer mats), short list of well chosen wines, pews and chairs around tables on wood floor, log fire in big two-way brick fireplace, more formal seating at back; children and dogs welcome (their black labrador is Bomber), very near Red Arrows runway viewpoint, closed Mon, otherwise open all day (till 7pm Sun). *(John and Sylvia Harrop)*

SKENDLEBY   TF4369
Blacksmiths Arms (01754) 890662
Off A158 about 10 miles NW of Skegness; PE23 4QE Cottagey-fronted 17th-c pub with cosy old-fashioned two-room bar, low beams and log fire, view into cellar from servery, well kept Batemans XB, a house beer from Horncastle and guest, good home-made food served by friendly helpful staff, back dining extension with deep well; Mon quiz; children and dogs welcome, unsuitable for wheelchairs, wolds views from back garden, closed Sun evening (not last of month when live band) and Mon lunchtime. *(Miles Green)*

SKILLINGTON   SK8925
Cross Swords (01476) 861132
The Square; NG33 5HB Traditional 19th-c stone pub on crossroads in delightful village, welcoming and homely, with good food cooked by landlord-chef from bar snacks to restaurant dishes, lunchtime carvery Tues-Fri, a couple of changing ales; background music, no under-10s or dogs; three annexe bedrooms, closed Sun evening, Mon lunchtime. *(Susie Hennings)*

SOUTH FERRIBY   SE9921
Hope & Anchor (01652) 635334
Sluice Road (A1077); DN18 6JQ Refurbished nautical theme pub under newish ownership; bar, snug and back dining area with wide views over confluence of Rivers Ancholme and Humber (plenty for bird-watchers), good locally sourced food (all day Fri, Sat, not Sun evening, Mon) from pub standards to more restauranty choices including 40-day-aged steaks (not cheap), Theakstons, Tom Woods and a guest, several wines by the glass including champagne, good friendly service; children and dogs welcome, disabled access/facilities, outside tables, closed Mon lunchtime, otherwise open all day. *(Caroline Sullivan)*

SOUTH RAUCEBY   TF0245
Bustard (01529) 488250
Main Street; NG34 8QG Modernised 19th-c stone-built pub with good food from varied menu, three well kept ales including one badged for them from Batemans, plenty of wines by the glass, friendly efficient staff, flagstoned bar with log fire, steps up to bare-stone restaurant (former stables); quiz nights, live jazz third and last Weds of month; children welcome, attractive sheltered garden, open all day Sat, closed Sun evening, Mon. *(David Travis, Susie Hennings)*

SPALDING   TF2422
Priors Oven 07972 192750
Sheep Market; PE11 1BH Friendly micropub in ancient building (former bakery), small octagonal room with vaulted ceiling, island bar serving up to six changing ales, local ciders and maybe english wines,

no food, spiral stairs up to comfortable lounge with period fireplace; open all day. *(James Allsopp)*

STAMFORD TF0207
All Saints Brewery – Melbourn Brothers (01780) 7521865
All Saints Street; PE9 2PA Well reworked old building (core is a medieval hall) with warren of rooms on three floors; upstairs bar serving bottled fruit beers from adjacent early 19th-c brewery and low-priced Sam Smiths on handpump, enjoyable food from pub favourites up including set deals and good vegetarian options, friendly staff, ground-floor dining area with log fire and woodburner, top floor with leather sofas and wing chairs; children and dogs welcome, picnic-sets in cobbled courtyard, brewery tours, open all day. *(Susie Hennings)*

STAMFORD TF0306
★ Bull & Swan (01780) 766412
High Street, St Martins; PE9 2LJ Handsome former staging post with three traditional linked rooms; low beams, rugs on bare boards, portraits in gilt frames on painted or stone walls, several open fires and good mix of seating including high-backed settles, leather banquettes and bow-window seats, Adnams Southwold, Sharps Doom Bar and guests such as Grainstore and Nene Valley, 20 wines by the glass and 30 malt whiskies, well liked food from panini and sharing boards up, helpful staff; background music, free wi-fi; children and dogs welcome, tables in back coachyard, character bedrooms named after animals, open all day. *(John Harris, Andrew Stone)*

STAMFORD TF0207
Jolly Brewer (01780) 755141
Foundry Road; PE9 2PP Welcoming unpretentious 19th-c stone-built pub with six well kept ales including own Bakers Dozen, traditional cider too and wide range of interesting whiskies (some from india and japan), low-priced simple food, nice open fire; regular beer festivals and quiz nights, sports TV, pool, darts and other games; open all day. *(Susie Hennings)*

SURFLEET TF2528
Mermaid (01775) 680275
B1356 (Gosberton Road), just off A16 N of Spalding; PE11 4AB Welcoming and traditional with two high-ceilinged carpeted rooms, huge sash windows, banquettes, captain's chairs and spindlebacks, Adnams and a couple of guests, good choice of fairly standard popular food including a monthly themed night, friendly attentive service, restaurant; background music; pretty terraced garden with summer bar and seats under thatched parasols, children's play area walled from River Glen, moorings, four bedrooms, open all day Sat in summer, closed Sun evening. *(Michael and Jenny Back)*

SWINESHEAD TF2340
Wheatsheaf (01205) 820349
Market Place; P320 3LJ Welcoming 18th-c family-run inn; enjoyable food (not Sun evening, Mon, Tues lunchtime) including weekday early-bird deal 5-6.30pm, well kept Batemans XB and guests, friendly helpful staff, beamed bar areas either side of central servery (interesting carved frontage one side), panelled back dining room with high-backed leather chairs, open fires; background music, TVs, games machines, darts; children welcome, garden behind with play area, four comfortable affordable bedrooms, good breakfast, open all day Fri-Sun, closed Mon lunchtime. *(Tim and Katie Oliver)*

TATTERSHALL THORPE TF2159
Blue Bell (01526) 342206
Thorpe Road; B1192 Coningsby–Woodhall Spa; LN4 4PE Ancient low-beamed pub (said to date from the 13th c) with friendly cosy atmosphere, RAF memorabilia including airmen's signatures on the ceiling (pub was used by the Dambusters), big open fire, three well kept ales such as local Horncastle, Thwaites Lancaster Bomber and Tom Woods Bomber County, some nice wines and enjoyable well priced pubby food, small dining room; some live music; garden tables, bedrooms, closed Mon (and Sun evening in winter). *(David Travis)*

TETFORD TF3374
White Hart (01507) 533255
East Road, off A158 E of Horncastle; LN9 6QQ Friendly bay-windowed village pub dating from the 16th c, Brains Rev James and a couple of guests, good value generous pubby food, pleasant inglenook bar with curved-back settles and slabby elm tables on red tiles, other areas including pool room; regular live music; children and dogs welcome, sheltered back lawn with guinea pigs and rabbits, pretty countryside, bedrooms, closed Mon. *(Susie Hennings)*

THEDDLETHORPE ALL SAINTS TF4787
★ Kings Head (01507) 339798
Pub signposted off A1031 N of Maplethorpe; Mill Road; LN12 1PB Long 16th-c thatched pub with cheerful helpful landlord; carpeted two-room front lounge with very low ceiling, brass platters on timbered walls, antique dining chairs and tables, easy chairs by log fire, central bar (more low beams) with well kept ales such as Batemans and a local cider, coal fire with side oven, shelves of books, stuffed owls and country pictures, long dining room, good local food from sandwiches and sharing plates to steaks and fresh Grimsby fish, Sun carvery; one or two picnic-sets in front area, more on lawn, open all day Sat, closed Sun evening, Mon. *(Roy and Lindsey Fentiman)*

THREEKINGHAM TF0836
Three Kings (01529) 240249
Just off A52 12 miles E of Grantham; Saltersway; NG34 0AU Former coaching inn with big entrance hall, fire and pubby furniture in comfortable beamed lounge, panelled restaurant plus bigger dining/function room, good choice of enjoyable home-made food including Thurs steak night, Bass, Timothy Taylors Landlord and guests, friendly efficient staff; Weds quiz; children and dogs (in bar) welcome, sunny paved terrace and small lawned area, various car club meetings, closed Mon.
(Tim and Katie Oliver)

WAINFLEET TF5058
★ Batemans Brewery (01754) 882009
Mill Lane, off A52 via B1195; PE24 4JE Circular bar in brewery's ivy-covered windmill tower, Batemans ales in top condition, czech and belgian beers on tap too, ground-floor dining area with cheap food including baguettes and a few pubby dishes, popular Sun carvery, plenty of old pub games (more outside), lots of brewery memorabilia and plenty for families to enjoy; no dogs inside, entertaining brewery tours and shop, tables on terrace and grass, open 11.30am-4pm (2.30pm in winter), closed Mon, Tues. *(Miles Green)*

WEST DEEPING TF1009
Red Lion (01778) 347190
King Street; PE6 9HP Stone-built pub under friendly family management; long low-beamed bar with four well kept ales including Fullers London Pride and local Hopshackle, popular freshly made food (not Sun evening) from baguettes up including weekday evening meal deal, back dining extension, stripped stone and open fire; occasional live music, free wi-fi; children welcome, no dogs inside, tables in back garden with terrace and fenced play area, vintage car/motorcycle meetings, open all day Sat, till 4pm Sun, closed Mon.
(Howard and Margaret Buchanan)

WILSFORD TF0043
Plough (01400) 230304
Main Street; NG32 3NS Traditional old two-bar village pub next to church, beams and open fires, a couple of real ales, nice range of wines and good choice of well presented bar food (till 7.30 Sun), pleasant friendly service, dining conservatory; pool and other games in adjoining room; children welcome, small walled back garden, good local walks, open all day Fri and Sun.
(Pat and Stewart Gordon)

WITHAM ON THE HILL TF0516
Six Bells (01778) 590360
Village signed from A6121, SW of Bourne; PE10 0JH Well restored Edwardian stone inn, smart comfortable bar with woodburner, enjoyable food (not Sun evening) including wood-fired pizzas, well kept Bass and guests, good friendly service; children and dogs (in bar) welcome, picnic-sets on front terrace, nice village, three well appointed bedrooms, good breakfast, closed Sun evening, Mon. *(Tim and Katie Oliver)*

WOODHALL SPA TF1963
Village Limits (01526) 353312
Stixwould Road; LN10 6UJ Modernised country pub-restaurant on village outskirts; good locally sourced food cooked by landlord-chef from pub standards up, well kept ales including own badged beers from local Horncastle microbrewery, friendly service, smallish beamed bar with banquettes, dining room with light wood furniture on wood-strip floor; children welcome, eight courtyard bedrooms, closed Mon lunchtime (and possibly Sun and Mon evenings in winter). *(David Travis)*

Post Office address codings confusingly give the impression that a few pubs are in Lincolnshire, when they're really in Cambridgeshire (which is where we list them).

Norfolk

KEY ★ Star Pub 🌟 Top Quality Food 🍺 Great Beer

🍷 Good Wines £ Bargain Meals 🛏 Good Bedrooms 🍴 Serves Food

BAWBURGH
Kings Head 🌟 🍷 🍺 🛏

(01603) 744977 – www.kingshead-bawburgh.co.uk

Harts Lane; A47 just W of Norwich then B1108; NR9 3LS

Busy, small-roomed pub with five real ales, good wines by the glass, interesting food and friendly service; bedrooms

Friendly, helpful staff and a cheerful atmosphere continue to draw praise from our readers for this 17th-c pub in a pretty village. The small rooms have plenty of low beams and standing timbers, leather sofas and an attractive assortment of old dining chairs and tables on wood-strip floors; also, a knocked-through open fire and a couple of woodburning stoves in the restaurant areas. Adnams Southwold and Broadside, Tring Moongazer and Woodfordes Reedlighter and Wherry on handpump, ten wines by the glass and 12 malt whiskies; service is friendly and helpful. Background music, TV and board games. There are seats in the garden and the pub is opposite a little green. The six bedrooms are comfortable and pretty.

🌟 Good, extremely popular food includes confit chicken potato cake with fried egg, home-made brown sauce and gremolata, dressed crab rolled in cucumber with avocado mousse and basil mayonnaise, crispy spiced polenta with grilled halloumi and vegetables, duo of local pork (fillet and braised belly) with home-made black pudding, sautéed cabbage and apple sauce, cod fillet with confit potatoes, squid noodles and samphire with lemongrass velouté, charred fillet of beef cottage pie with puréed carrots, confit shallots and pan jus, and puddings such as strawberry bavarois with poached strawberries and yoghurt jelly and custard pannacotta with poached rhubarb and stem ginger ice-cream. *Benchmark main dish: steak burgers with toppings, red cabbage coleslaw and chips £11.00. Two-course evening meal £20.00.*

Free house ~ Licensee Anton Wimmer ~ Real ale ~ Open 11-11; 12-10.30 (8 in winter) Sun ~ Bar food 12-2, 5.30-9; 12-3, 6-9 Sun; no food Sun evenings Nov-Mar ~ Restaurant ~ Children welcome ~ Dogs allowed in bar ~ Wi-fi ~ Bedrooms: £90/£110 *Recommended by Tina and David Woods-Taylor, David Fowler, David Travis, Edward Nile*

BURSTON
Crown 🍺

(01379) 741257 – www.burstoncrown.com

Village signposted off A140 N of Scole; Mill Road; IP22 5TW

Friendly, relaxed village pub usefully open all day, with a warm welcome, real ales and well liked bar food

On a chilly day, the best place to sit here is the heavily beamed, quarry-tiled bar room with its comfortably cushioned sofas in front of a woodburning stove in a huge brick fireplace; there are also stools by a low chunky wooden table, and newspapers and magazines. Locals tend to gather in an area by the bar counter where they serve Adnams Broadside and Southwold and guests such as Castle Rock Starling and Cottage Pacific on handpump or tapped from the cask, six wines by the glass and nine malt whiskies. The public bar on the left has a nice long table and panelled settle on an old brick floor in one alcove, a pool table, and more tables and chairs towards the back near a dartboard. Both rooms are hung with paintings by local artists; background music and board games. The simply furnished, beamed dining room has another big brick fireplace. Outside, there's a smokers' shelter, seats and tables on a terrace and in the secluded garden where there's also a play area for children.

Using their smokehouse for some dishes, the good food cooked by the landlord includes sandwiches, tiger prawns in chilli and garlic butter, chicken liver parfait with red onion marmalade, pie of the week, spinach, tomato and feta cheese filo parcels with tomato sauce, chicken schnitzel with spicy coleslaw and chips, beer-battered cod and chips, pork marinated in lime, soy and onions with fried rice and oriental salad, and puddings. *Benchmark main dish: rib-eye steak with café de paris butter £18.30. Two-course evening meal £19.50.*

Free house ~ Licensees Bev and Steve Kembery ~ Real ale ~ Open 12-11; 10.30am-11pm Sat; 12-10.30 Sun ~ Bar food 12 (10.30 Sat)-2, 6.30-9; 12-4 Sun; not Mon ~ Restaurant ~ Children welcome ~ Dogs allowed in bar ~ Wi-fi ~ Live music Thurs 8.30pm, every second Sun from 5pm *Recommended by Ruth May, Caroline Sullivan, Patricia Hawkins*

CASTLE ACRE
Ostrich
TF8115   Map 8

(01760) 755398 – www.ostrichcastleacre.com
Stocks Green; PE32 2AE

Friendly old village pub with original features, fine old fireplaces, real ales and tasty food; bedrooms

Although largely rebuilt during the 18th c, there are still features to search out that date back a couple of hundred years earlier – such as the original masonry, beams and trusses. The L-shaped, low-ceilinged front bar (on two levels) has a woodburning stove in a huge old fireplace, lots of wheelback chairs and cushioned pews around pubby tables on a wood-strip floor and gold patterned wallpaper; it's a step up to an area in front of the bar counter where there are similar seats and tables and a log fire in a brick fireplace. Greene King Abbot, IPA, Speckled Hen and a beer named for the pub on handpump, around a dozen wines by the glass and several malt whiskies. There's a separate dining room with another brick fireplace. The sheltered garden has picnic-sets under parasols and the inn faces the tree-lined village green; nearby are the remains of a Norman castle and a Cluniac monastery (English Heritage).

Popular food includes lunchtime sandwiches, twice-baked blue cheese soufflé with pear and watercress salad, duck and sweet potato hash cake, poached egg and home-made brown sauce, sharing platters, butternut squash risotto with parmesan, braised ham hock with grain mustard mash, pineapple purée, charred corn, crispy egg and cider sauce, cod with chorizo, butter beans, mussels and gremolata crumb, local venison loin with coffee, salsify, bacon and chocolate jus, and puddings. *Benchmark main dish: steak burger with toppings and chips £13.95. Two-course evening meal £19.00.*

Greene King ~ Tenant Tiffany Turner ~ Real ale ~ Open 10am-11pm; 10am-midnight Sat ~
Bar food 12-3, 6-9 ~ Restaurant ~ Children welcome ~ Dogs allowed in bar ~ Wi-fi ~ Live
music last Sun of month ~ Bedrooms: £75/£85 *Recommended by David Jackman,
Graham and Elizabeth Hargreaves, Hilary De Lyon and Martin Webster*

EAST RUDHAM   TF8228 Map 8
Crown 🌟 🍷 🛏

(01485) 528530 – www.crowninnnorfolk.co.uk
A148 W of Fakenham; The Green; PE31 8RD

**Smart and attractive open-plan seating areas, cosy back sitting room,
very good food, real ales and friendly atmosphere; bedrooms**

Standing at the head of the village green, this is a stylish, gently civilised
place with open-plan seating areas. At the end of the main room a log
fire is flanked by a grandfather clock on one side and bookshelves on the
other, with wood and brown leather dining chairs around a mix of tables
and rugs on stripped floorboards. The other end is slightly more informal,
with another bookshelf beside a second fireplace, a pubby part with white-
painted, cushioned built-in seats, and high chairs against the handsome
slate-topped counter where they keep Adnams Broadside, Black Sheep,
Woodfordes Wherry and a changing guest on handpump and 20 wines by
the glass; staff are friendly and helpful. There's also a cosy lower area to
the back of the building with comfortable leather sofas and armchairs and
a flat-screen TV; an upstairs dining room has a high-pitched ceiling and
a woodburning stove. The gravelled terrace at the front has seats under
parasols. Bedrooms are airy and comfortable and breakfasts are hearty.

🌟 Rewarding food includes whisky-cured salmon with pickled beetroot, crisp ham
hock and egg with charred pineapple and merlot vinegar, wild mushroom risotto,
burger with toppings and chips, beer-battered fish and chips, chicken with leeks,
tarragon and herb gnocchi, cocoa-marinated venison with potato terrine and pickled
grapes, spiced duck with carrot purée, and puddings such as Baileys crème brûlée and
tiramisu. *Benchmark main dish: lamb rump with rosemary potatoes and red wine
sauce £17.00. Two-course evening meal £21.00.*

Free house ~ Licensee Tristram McEwen ~ Real ale ~ Open 11-11; 11am-midnight Sat ~
Bar food 12-2.30, 6-9 (9.30 Sat); 12-8 Sun ~ Children welcome ~ Dogs welcome ~ Wi-fi ~
Bedrooms: /£110 *Recommended by Ruth May, Derek and Sylvia Stephenson, Tom Stone,
Margaret McDonald*

GREAT MASSINGHAM   TF7922 Map 8
Dabbling Duck 🌟 🍺

(01485) 520827 – www.thedabblingduck.co.uk
Off A148 King's Lynn–Fakenham; Abbey Road; PE32 2HN

**Unassuming from the outside but with character bars and warm fires,
real ales and interesting food; comfortable bedrooms**

The setting here is rather nice with big duck ponds on the adjacent and
sizeable village green – tables and chairs on the pub's front terrace take
in this view, and there are more seats and a play area in the enclosed back
garden. The relaxed bars have leather sofas and armchairs by woodburning
stoves (three in all), a mix of antique wooden dining tables and chairs on
flagstones or stripped-wooden floors, a very high-backed settle, 18th- and
19th-c quirky prints and cartoons, and plenty of beams and standing timbers.
At the back of the pub is the Blenheim room, just right for a private group,
and there's also a candlelit dining room. Adnams Broadside and Ghost Ship,

Beeston Worth the Wait and Woodfordes Wherry on handpump and a dozen wines by the glass, served from a bar counter made of great slabs of polished tree trunk; background music, TV, darts and board games. The bedrooms are named after famous local sportsmen and airmen from the World War II air base in Massingham. Wheelchair access.

 Food is attractively presented and includes sandwiches, duck liver pâté with orange and pink peppercorn marmalade, marinated squid with chorizo mayonnaise and chickpea relish, rib burger with toppings, bacon jam and dripping fries, truffle and gruyère gratin with celeriac purée and beer-pickled mushrooms, malt-glazed chicken with maple-bacon parsnips and pancetta sauce, fillet of bream with crayfish, dashi velouté and saffron potatoes, and puddings such as clotted cream rice pudding with raspberry sorbet and chocolate and ale cake with beer sauce and malt ice-cream. *Benchmark main dish: duck pie with maple syrup and tarragon £12.00. Two-course evening meal £20.00.*

Free house ~ Licensee Dominic Symington ~ Real ale ~ Open 11-11 (10.30 Sun) ~ Bar food 12-2.30, 6.30-9 (9.30 Fri, Sat); all day Sun ~ Restaurant ~ Children welcome ~ Dogs allowed in bar and bedrooms ~ Wi-fi ~ Bedrooms: £75/£90 *Recommended by Simon and Mandy King, Millie and Peter Downing, Patricia Hawkins, Tracey and Stephen Groves*

HOLKHAM
Victoria ♀ 🛏

TF8943 Map 8

(01328) 711008 – www.victoriaatholkham.co.uk
A149 near Holkham Hall; NR23 1RG

Smart, handsome inn with pubby bar, plenty of character dining space, thoughtful choice of drinks, friendly staff and enjoyable food; bedrooms

With the vast stretch of Holkham Sands beach just minutes away, this upmarket yet informal and friendly place has an outside bar and a seafood shack and plenty of outdoor seating for busy, sunny lunchtimes; you'll need to get here early (or late) to bag a table. Inside, there's a proper bare-boards bar to the left that's popular with locals, while a spreading dining and sitting area has an appealing variety of antique-style dining chairs and tables on rugs and stripped floorboards, antlers and antique guns, and sofas by a big log fire. There's also a small drawing room to the right of the main entrance (for hotel guests only) with homely furniture, an open fire and an honesty bar. Adnams Broadside and Ghost Ship and Woodfordes Wherry on handpump, 20 wines by the glass, good coffee and efficient, polite service. An airy conservatory dining room, decorated in pale beige, leads out to a back courtyard with green-painted furniture. Some of the stylish bedrooms have views of the sea and breakfasts are good and generous.

Using Estate and other local produce, the very good food is served all day from 8am for breakfast: smoked haddock fishcake with salsa verde, chicken and bacon terrine with tomato chutney, venison sausages with champ mash and caramelised onion, wild mushroom risotto, burger with toppings and chips, pork tenderloin with potato galette and caramelised apple, sea trout with sauce provençale and chateau potatoes, and puddings such as chocolate torte and apple bavarois with honeycomb. *Benchmark main dish: salmon en croûte with spinach and brown shrimp beurre blanc £17.25. Two-course evening meal £25.00.*

Free house ~ Licensee Lord Coke ~ Real ale ~ Open 11-11; 12-10.30 Sun ~ Bar food 8am-9pm ~ Restaurant ~ Children welcome ~ Dogs welcome ~ Wi-fi ~ Bedrooms: £135/£195 *Recommended by Tracey and Stephen Groves, W K Wood, Jestyn Phillips, Julian Richardson*

 KING'S LYNN

Bank House 🌟 ♀ ⇌

TF6119 Map 8

(01553) 660492 – www.thebankhouse.co.uk

*Kings Staithe Square via Boat Street and along the quay in one-way system;
PE30 1RD*

Georgian bar-brasserie with plenty of history and character, airy rooms, real ales and imaginative food from breakfast onwards; bedrooms

This is a splendid quayside spot and the Corn Exchange theatre and arts centre is just five minutes away. Usefully open all day, the various stylish rooms are busy with customers popping in and out for drinks and meals. The elegant bar (once the bank manager's office – the building was Barclays Bank's first opening in 1780) has sofas and armchairs, a log fire with fender seating and Adnams Broadside and Southwold and Wychwood Hobgoblin on handpump, 26 wines by the glass, ten whiskies and cocktails; background music. The restaurant has fine antique chairs and tables on bare boards, an airy brasserie has sofas and armchairs around low tables and a big brick fireplace, and two other areas (one with fine panelling, the other with a half-size billiards table) have more open fires. The atmosphere throughout is bustling and welcoming and service is helpful and courteous. An outside area is flanked by magnificent wrought-iron gates, with fire pits for warmth on chillier evenings, and the riverside terrace (lovely sunsets) has an open-air bar. Sister pub is the Rose & Crown in Snettisham.

 Modern brasserie food using tip top local produce includes sandwiches, gin-cured salmon gravadlax with cucumber salsa, five-spice pork terrine with sweet and sour oranges, sharing platters, spelt risotto with roast pepper, rocket, harissa and grilled halloumi, steak burger with toppings, barbecue sauce and fries, pork T-bone in ginger and molasses marinade with cabbage salad and sweet potato fries, red mullet fillet with chive gnocchi and romesco sauce, and puddings such as lemon tart with berry compote and raspberry sorbet and orange and apricot bread and butter pudding with crème anglaise; they also offer breakfasts (7-10am; 7.30-midday Sun). *Benchmark main dish: smoked haddock with pasta, parmesan, kale and crushed wasabi peas £14.25. Two-course evening meal £20.00.*

Free house ~ Licensee Anthony Goodrich ~ Real ale ~ Open 11-11 (10.30 Sun); 12-9.30 Sat; 12-8.30 Sun ~ Bar food 12-9.30 (8.30 Sun) ~ Restaurant ~ Children welcome ~ Dogs allowed in bar ~ Wi-fi ~ Bedrooms: £85/£115 *Recommended by Colin Humphreys, John Wooll, R C Vincent, David Longhurst, Anne and Ben Smith, Ian Duncan*

LARLING

Angel 🍺 ⇌

TL9889 Map 5

(01953) 717963 – www.angel-larling.co.uk

*From A11 Thetford–Attleborough, take B1111 turn-off and follow pub signs;
NR16 2QU*

Good-natured chatty atmosphere in busy pub with several real ales and tasty bar food; bedrooms

The same friendly family have run this 17th-c inn since 1913 and they still have the original visitors' books from 1897 to 1909. The comfortable 1930s-style lounge on the right has squared panelling, cushioned wheelback chairs, a nice long cushioned, panelled corner settle and some good solid tables for eating; also, a collection of whisky-water jugs on a delft shelf over the big brick fireplace, a woodburning stove, a couple of copper kettles and some hunting prints. Adnams Southwold and four guests from breweries such as Lacons, Oakham, Swannay and Woodfordes on handpump, 100 malt whiskies and ten wines by the glass; they hold an August beer festival with more than 100 real ales and ciders, live music and a barbecue. The quarry-tiled black-beamed public bar has a good local feel, with darts, juke box, games machine, board games and background music. There's a neat grass area behind the car park with picnic-sets around a big fairy-lit apple tree and a fenced play area. The four-acre meadow is a caravan and camping site from March to October. Plenty of surrounding walks and good bird-watching.

🍴 Well liked food includes sandwiches, prawn cocktail, creamy mushroom pot, chicken and bacon caesar salad, sausage, egg and chips, tiger prawn balti, broccoli and cream cheese bake, barbecue rack of pork ribs, smoked haddock provençale, mixed grill, and puddings such as chocolate fudge cake and treacle sponge. *Benchmark main dish: steak and kidney pie £11.95. Two-course evening meal £17.00.*

Free house ~ Licensee Andrew Stammers ~ Real ale ~ Open 10am-11pm ~ Bar food 12-9.30 (10 Fri, Sat) ~ Restaurant ~ Children welcome ~ Wi-fi ~ Bedrooms: £60/£90
Recommended by Hilary and Neil Christopher, Andrew Stone, Patricia Hawkins

MORSTON
Anchor 🏅 ♀

TG0043   Map 8

(01263) 741392 – www.morstonanchor.co.uk
A149 Salthouse–Stiffkey; The Street; NR25 7AA

Quite a choice of rooms filled with bric-a-brac and prints, real ales and enjoyable food

---

The friendly hands-on licensees run this bustling place with great enthusiasm – they really care about their pub and their customers, and it shows. Three traditional rooms on the right have straightforward seats and tables on original wooden floors, coal fires, local 1950s beach photographs and lots of prints and bric-a-brac. Adnams Old Ale, local Winters Golden and Woodfordes Wherry on handpump, 22 wines by the glass and 13 gins; background music, darts and board games. The contemporary airy extension on the left, with comfortable benches and tables, leads into the more formal restaurant where local art is displayed on the walls. You can sit outside at the front of the building. If parking is tricky at the pub, there's an overflow around the corner off-road and a National Trust car park five minutes' walk away. The surrounding area is wonderful for bird-watching and walking, and you can book seal-spotting trips here.

⭐ The food, using the best local produce, is highly regarded and includes sandwiches, scallops with braised pig's cheek, cauliflower and vanilla purée, twice-baked blue cheese soufflé with poached pears, toasted walnuts and blue cheese cream, burger with toppings, red onion jam, home-made kimchi slaw and skinny fries, cheese gnocchi with butternut squash, wild mushrooms and rocket and pine nut pesto, lamb suet pudding with red cabbage and jus, and puddings such as crème brûlée with honeycomb ice-cream and apple and rhubarb crumble with custard. *Benchmark main dish: beer-battered fish of the day with triple-cooked chips £12.95. Two-course evening meal £18.00.*

Free house ~ Licensees Harry Farrow and Rowan Glennie ~ Real ale ~ Open 9am-11pm; 9am-10pm Sun; closed Sun evening Jan-Apr ~ Bar food 12-3, 6-9 ~ Restaurant ~ Children welcome ~ Dogs allowed in bar ~ Wi-fi *Recommended by Peter Meister, Roy Hoing, David Carr, Derek and Sylvia Stephenson, Brian Glozier*

We checked prices with the pubs as we went to press in summer 2016.
They should hold until around spring 2017.

NORTH CREAKE
Jolly Farmers

TF8538 Map 8

(01328) 738185 – www.jollyfarmersnorfolk.co.uk

Burnham Road; NR21 9JW

Friendly village local with three cosy rooms, open fires and woodburners, well liked food and several real ales

Nothing is too much trouble for the thoughtful licensees in this well run former coaching inn. There are three cosy and relaxed rooms, including the main bar with a large open fire in a brick fireplace, a mix of pine farmhouse and high-backed leather dining chairs around scrubbed pine tables on quarry tiles and pale yellow walls. Beside the wooden bar counter are some high bar chairs, and they keep Woodfordes Nelsons Revenge and Wherry tapped from the cask, 11 wines by the glass and a dozen malt whiskies; service is helpful and friendly. There's also a cabinet of model cars. A smaller bar has pews and a woodburning stove, while the red-walled dining room has similar furniture to the bar and another woodburner. There are seats outside on the terrace.

 Rewarding food includes baked brie with apple chutney, savoury crab pot with cheese topping, mushrooms en croûte with brie, hazelnuts and wild mushroom sauce, honey ham and eggs, chicken caesar salad, lambs liver and bacon in red wine gravy, mussels with cider and wholegrain mustard, sirloin steak with a choice of sauces and chips, and puddings such as lemon posset in brandy snap baskets and dark chocolate, cherry and cherry wine tart. *Benchmark main dish: slow-cooked lamb with mint and redcurrant glaze and dauphinoise potatoes £13.50. Two-course evening meal £18.50.*

Free house ~ Licensees Adrian and Heather Sanders ~ Real ale ~ Open 12-2.30, 7-11; 12-7 Sun; closed Mon, Tues ~ Bar food 12-2, 7-9; 12-5.30 Sun ~ Children welcome ~ Dogs allowed in bar *Recommended by Christopher and Elise Way, Philip and Susan Philcox, Barbara Brown, Derek and Sylvia Stephenson*

NORWICH
Fat Cat

TG2109 Map 5

(01603) 624364 – www.fatcatpub.co.uk

West End Street; NR2 4NA

A place of pilgrimage for beer lovers and open all day; lunchtime rolls and pies

A visit to this lively pub is akin to coming to a private beer festival. There's usually an extraordinary range of up to 32 quickly changing ales and the knowledgeable landlord and his helpful staff can guide you through the choices. On handpump or tapped from the cask in a stillroom behind the bar – big windows reveal all – are their own beers (Fat Cat Bitter, Hell Cat, Honey Ale, Marmalade Cat, Stout Cat and Wild Cat), as well as guests from breweries such as Crouch Vale, Fullers, Oakham and Timothy Taylors – and many more choices from across the country. You'll also find imported draught beers and lagers, over 50 bottled beers from around the world and 20 ciders and perries. The no-nonsense furnishings include plain scrubbed pine tables and simple solid seats, lots of brewery memorabilia, bric-a-brac and stained glass. There are tables outside.

Bar food consists of rolls and good pies at lunchtime (not Sunday).

Own brew ~ Licensee Colin Keatley ~ Real ale ~ No credit cards ~ Open 12-11 (midnight Fri); 11-midnight Sat ~ Bar food Filled rolls available until sold out; not Sun ~

Children allowed until 6pm ~ Dogs allowed in bar ~ Wi-fi *Recommended by Edward May, Mike Swan, Miles Green, Sophie Ellison*

OXBOROUGH   TF7401   Map 5

Bedingfeld Arms

(01366) 328300 – www.bedingfeldarms.co.uk
Near church; PE33 9PS

Attractively furnished Georgian inn with restful rooms, thoughtful choice of drinks, enjoyable food and good service; bedrooms

To make best use of the surrounding walks and cycling routes, why not stay in the lovely bedrooms here – four bedrooms are in the inn and five in the coach house annexe; breakfasts are extremely good. The relaxed, wood-floored bar has green leather chesterfields, leather tub chairs and window seats around tables of varying heights, an open fire in a marble fireplace with a large gilt mirror above, fresh flowers and candles, and high chairs against the long bar counter. The airy dining room, with more fresh flowers and candles, is furnished with high-backed wooden and cushioned chairs around antique tables, wall seating with scatter cushions and bird prints on pale grey walls. Adnams Broadside, Wells Bombardier Burning Gold and Woodfordes Wherry on handpump and ten wines by the glass served by courteous, helpful staff; TV for major sporting events, background music. A new covered verandah extension (using local oak trees) has been added since the last edition of the *Guide*, with leather arm and dining chairs, and the garden has seats and tables and a view of the church. Oxburgh Hall (National Trust) is opposite.

The tempting food uses lamb and game from their farm, some home-grown vegetables and other local, seasonal produce: ham hock terrine with onion chutney, seared scallops, pea purée, black pudding and crispy bacon, pea, mint, spinach, goats cheese and pearl barley risotto, burger with toppings, relish and chips, chilli salmon fillet with vegetable tian, dauphinoise potatoes and hollandaise, venison wellington with grilled apricot, spinach and butternut squash, and puddings such as dark chocolate brownie with chocolate sauce and hazelnut nougat glacé with lemon sorbet and mango coulis. *Benchmark main dish: fresh fish dish of the day £14.95. Two-course evening meal £25.00.*

Free house ~ Licensees Stephen and Catherine Parker ~ Real ale ~ Open 11-11; 11-midnight Sat ~ Bar food 12-3, 6-9; 8-8 Sun ~ Restaurant ~ Well behaved children welcome ~ Dogs allowed in bar and bedrooms ~ Wi-fi ~ Bedrooms: £78.50/£88
Recommended by Mike Swan, John Harris, Maddie Purvis, Julie Braeburn

RINGSTEAD   TF7040   Map 8

Gin Trap

(01485) 525264 – www.thegintrapinn.co.uk
Village signed off A149 near Hunstanton; OS Sheet 132 map reference 707403; PE36 5JU

Bustling country pub with plenty of room in character bars for both eating and drinking and seats outside; bedrooms

Close to the Peddars Way, this is an attractive 17th-c coaching inn with friendly licensees. The original beamed bar has farmhouse and mate's chairs around solid pine tables on bare boards, yellow tartan window seats, pub photos on the walls, horse tack, coach lamps and a woodburning stove. A step leads up to a quarry-tiled room with similar furnishings and then on to a conservatory. There's also a character back snug with red-painted walls and nice old floor tiles. Adnams Ghost Ship and Southwold, Woodfordes Wherry and a guest such as Tipples Redhead on handpump, good wines by the glass and around 30 gins. The back garden has picnic-sets and a children's play area and there are more seats out in front. Bedrooms are comfortable and well equipped.

Popular food includes twice-baked goats cheese and chive soufflé with beetroot jam, chicken satay skewers, butternut squash tagine, beer-battered fish and chips, buttermilk chicken breast with coleslaw and sweet potato fries, lemon sole with caper and cream sauce and rosemary potatoes, slow-roast lamb shank with wholegrain mustard mash and balsamic onions, and puddings such as apple and calvados tart and a cheesecake of the day. *Benchmark main dish: rump burger with toppings, onion rings, coleslaw and chips £13.50. Two-course evening meal £21.00.*

Free house ~ Licensees Dave Wann and Annelli Taylor ~ Real ale ~ Open 11.30-11; 11.30-2.30, 6-11 in winter ~ Bar food 12-2, 6-8.30; 12-2.30, 6-9 Fri, Sat; 12-4, 6-8 Sun ~ Restaurant ~ Children welcome ~ Dogs allowed in bar and bedrooms ~ Wi-fi ~ Bedrooms: /£99
Recommended by Tracey and Stephen Groves, Philip and Susan Philcox, O Thompson

---

SALTHOUSE
Dun Cow 🏅 ◖

TG0743   Map 8

(01263) 740467 – www.salthouseduncow.com
A149 Blakeney–Sheringham (Purdy Street, junction with Bard Hill); NR25 7XA

Relaxed village pub, a good all-rounder and with enterprising food

Once they've found this place, our readers tend to return on a regular basis. And on a sunny day, the picnic-sets on the front grass looking across the bird-filled salt marshes towards the sea are the perfect place to be; there are more seats in a sheltered back courtyard and an orchard garden beyond. Inside, the flint-walled bar consists of a pair of high-raftered rooms opened up into one area, with stone tiles around the counter where regulars congregate, and a carpeted seating area with a fireplace at each end. Also, scrubbed tables, one very high-backed settle, country kitchen chairs and elegant red-padded dining chairs, with big sailing ship and other prints. Adnams Broadside, Norfolk Brewhouse Moon Gazer Golden Ale and Woodfordes Reedlighter and Wherry on handpump, 19 wines by the glass, 14 malt whiskies and a good relaxed atmosphere. The bedrooms are self-catering.

Food is particularly good: sandwiches (until 5pm), goats cheese croquettes with pickled beetroot chutney, local crab and coriander scotch egg with curried mayonnaise, chickpea, spinach, lentil and coconut dhal with paneer fritter, steak in ale casserole with dumplings, chargrilled swordfish caesar salad, milk and sage-braised pork belly with chorizo, butter bean, spinach and tomato stew, cheese burger with bacon and fries, steak of the day, and puddings such as crème brûlée and treacle tart with custard. *Benchmark main dish: half local garlic lobster with fries £17.00. Two-course evening meal £20.00.*

Punch ~ Lease Daniel Goff ~ Real ale ~ Open 11-11 ~ Bar food 12-9 ~ Children welcome ~
Dogs welcome ~ Wi-fi *Recommended by Brian Glozier, Neil and Angela Huxter, DF and NF*

SNETTISHAM
Rose & Crown 🏅 ♀ 🛏

TF6834   Map 8

(01485) 541382 – www.roseandcrownsnettisham.co.uk
Village signposted from A149 King's Lynn–Hunstanton just N of Sandringham; coming in on the B1440 from the roundabout just N of village, take first left into Old Church Road; PE31 7LX

Particularly well run inn with log fires and interesting furnishings, imaginative food, a fine range of drinks and stylish seating on heated terrace; well equipped bedrooms

As ever, our readers love all aspects of this excellent pub. The two main bars have distinct character and simple charm, with an open fire and woodburning stove, old quarry tiles or coir flooring, cushioned wall seating and wooden tables and chairs, candles on mantelpieces and daily papers. There are stools against the bar where locals enjoy Adnams Southwold and Broadside, Lancaster Bomber, Marstons Pedigree, Ringwood Boondoggle and Woodfordes Wherry on handpump; also, 14 wines by the glass, ten malt whiskies and local cider and fruit juices served by neatly dressed, courteous staff. A small wooden-floored back room has old sports equipment, the landlord's sporting trophies and photos of the pub's cricket team. The civilised little restaurant (decorated in soft greys) has cushions and picture mounts with splashes of bright green and flowers in old galvanised watering cans sitting on windowsills. At the back of the building, two rooms make up the bustling Garden Room, with sofas, wooden farmhouse and white-painted dining chairs around a mix of tables, church candles in large lanterns, attractive striped blinds and doors that lead to the pretty walled garden. Here there are plenty of contemporary seats and tables under cream parasols, outdoor heaters, colourful herbaceous borders and a wooden galleon-shaped climbing fort for children. Bedrooms are spacious and well appointed and breakfasts very good. Disabled lavatories and wheelchair ramp. This is sister pub to the Bank House in King's Lynn.

 Using the best local produce, the top class food includes sandwiches, scallops with cauliflower and tonka bean purée, venison and black pudding scotch egg with parsnip and apple rémoulade, barbecue chicken and pulled pork burger with onion rings and fries, chargrilled halloumi with roast vine tomato and basil risotto, cod fillet with puy lentils and turnip and pancetta stew, pork fillet with jerusalem artichoke purée, burnt leeks, pommes dauphine and jus, and puddings such as chocolate torte with turkish delight and pistachio brittle and honey pannacotta with poached rhubarb, pear and granola. *Benchmark main dish: steak burger with red onion relish, onion rings and fries £13.50. Two-course evening meal £21.00.*

Free house ~ Licensee Anthony Goodrich ~ Real ale ~ Open 11-11; 11-10.30 Sun ~ Bar food 12-9 (9.30 Fri, Sat); 12-8.30 Sun ~ Restaurant ~ Children welcome ~ Dogs welcome ~ Wi-fi ~ Bedrooms: $100/$120 *Recommended by John Wooll, R C Vincent, DF and NF, Roy Hoing, Tracey and Stephen Groves, Tom Carver, Roger and Donna Huggins, Tony Scott*

STANHOE   TF8037 Map 8
Duck 🏴 ♀ 🛏
(01485) 518330 – www.duckinn.co.uk
B1155 Docking–Burnham Market; PE31 8QD

Smart candlelit country dining pub with popular food, real ales and appealing layout; bedrooms

With such good food on offer in this neatly kept pub, most customers are here to dine. But drinkers are made just as welcome and there's an entrance bar where those wanting just a chat and a pint can feel at home. This bar has pale grey paintwork, cushioned edwardian-style chairs around wooden tables on dark floor slates, and stools against the panelled counter where they serve Adnams Ghost Ship and Elgoods Cambridge on handpump from a fine slab-topped counter and a dozen wines by the glass. A small wooden-floored area leads off, with a woodburning stove in an old brick fireplace and modern artwork, and this in turn opens into two dining rooms: cushioned chairs and farmhouse tables on more slates or coir carpeting, scatter cushions on wall seating and local seascapes on the walls. The small garden has picnic-sets under a fruit tree, and seats and tables in a garden room with fairy lights and candles; more seats and tables set out on the front gravel. The bedrooms are well appointed and comfortable. Good disabled access and lavatory.

 First class food includes sandwiches, scallops with squid ink fettuccine, dashi and dill, pigeon breast with black pudding, celeriac purée and wild mushrooms, leek and cheese gratin with new potato beignet and pecan caramel, beer-battered cod and chips, free-range chicken with pumpkin risotto, hazelnut, pancetta and parmesan, fillet of hake with mussels, brown shrimps and saffron nage, and puddings such as dark chocolate and orange tart with orange mascarpone and sticky toffee apple pudding with toffee sauce. *Benchmark main dish: beer-battered fish and chips £13.00. Two-course evening meal £21.00.*

Elgoods ~ Tenants Sarah and Ben Handley ~ Real ale ~ Open 11-11; 12-10.30 Sun ~ Bar food 12-2.30, 6-9; 12-8 Sun ~ Restaurant ~ Children welcome ~ Dogs allowed in bar ~ Wi-fi ~ Bedrooms: £90/£135 *Recommended by Christopher and Elise Way, Tracey and Stephen Groves, Mrs J H Godding, R Halliday, Ian Duncan, Sarah Flynn*

THORNHAM
Orange Tree 🌟 ♟ 🛏

TF7343 Map 8

(01485) 512213 – www.theorangetreethornham.co.uk
Church Street/A149; PE36 6LY

Norfolk Dining Pub of the Year

Nice combination of friendly bar and good contemporary dining, plus suntrap garden; bedrooms

The most pubby part of this highly popular and well run place is at the front in the sizeable bar. This is bustling and friendly with white-painted beams, red leather chesterfields in front of a log fire, flowery upholstered or leather and wooden dining chairs and red or stripy plush wall seats around a mix of tables on wood or quarry-tiled floors; background music, board games and flat-screen TV. Helpful, attentive staff serve Adnams Southwold, Woodfordes Wherry and a guest beer on handpump, 35 wines by the glass and 19 gins. A little dining room leads off here with silver décor, buddha heads and candles, and the two-part restaurant is simple and contemporary in style. In warm weather, the front garden is much in demand: lavender beds and climbing roses, lots of picnic-sets under parasols, outdoor heaters and a small smart corner pavilion. At the back of the building is a second outdoor area with children's play equipment. The bedrooms (our readers particularly recommend those in the Old Bakery) make a good base for this lovely stretch of the north Norfolk coast; breakfasts are good. They're kind to dogs and have a doggie menu plus snacks.

Imaginative food includes sandwiches, tempura soft-shell mangrove crab, pork belly carpaccio and seared king scallop with salt caramel and apple purée, pea, feta and lemon fritters with spiced fennel and red pepper slaw, lemon and mint gel and wild garlic pesto, seafood spaghetti, chickpea, preserved lemon and feta burger with creamy thyme and mustard coleslaw and mint and yoghurt dressing, salt marsh lamb (best end, shoulder and rump) with buckwheat, buttermilk curd, sumac, pomegranate and pistachio crust, and puddings such as chocolate devil and banana sticky toffee pudding with toffee sauce and banoffi ice-cream. *Benchmark main dish: free-range chicken and wild mushroom pie £14.95. Two-course evening meal £23.50.*

Punch ~ Lease Mark Goode ~ Real ale ~ Open 11-11; 12-10.30 Sun ~ Bar food 12-9.30 ~ Restaurant ~ Children welcome ~ Dogs allowed in bar and bedrooms ~ Wi-fi ~

Bedrooms: £80/£89 *Recommended by Gordon and Margaret Ormondroyd, Chris Johnson, John Harris, Neil Allen, Tracey and Stephen Groves*

THORPE MARKET
TG2434   Map 8

Gunton Arms ♀

(01263) 832010 – www.theguntonarms.co.uk

Cromer Road; NR11 8TZ

Impressive place with an easy-going atmosphere, open fires and antiques, real ales, interesting food and friendly staff; bedrooms

Run with individuality ,this is an interesting and rather grand country house surrounded by a 1,000-acre deer park; but they do have a bar and a fine range of drinks – and it's fun. The large entrance hall sets the scene; throughout, the atmosphere is easy-going and friendly, but definitely gently upmarket. Simply furnished, the bar has dark pubby chairs and tables on a wooden floor, a log fire, a long settle beside a pool table, and high stools against the mahogany counter where they serve Adnams Southwold and Broadside, Woodfordes Wherry and a guest beer on handpump, ten wines by the glass, 22 malt whiskies and two ciders; staff are chatty and helpful. Heavy curtains line an open doorway into a dining room, where vast antlers hang above a big log fire (they often cook over this) and there are straightforward chairs around scrubbed tables on stone tiles. There's also a lounge with comfortable old leather armchairs and a sofa on a fine rug in front of yet another log fire, some genuine antiques, big house plants and standard lamps, as well as a more formal restaurant with candles and napery and two homely sitting rooms for hotel residents. Many of the walls are painted dark red and hung with assorted artwork and big mirrors; background music, darts, TV and board games. The bedrooms have many original fittings, but no TV or tea-making facilities.

Rustic, hearty food using Estate produce includes sandwiches, deep-fried cod cheeks with caper mayonnaise, stuffed saddle of rabbit with quince jelly and pickles, sea trout with seashore vegetables and brown shrimps, pork tenderloin skewer marinated in sherry and bay leaf, red deer curry, crab pasta with chilli and coriander, rib of beef cooked over the fire, and puddings such as chocolate truffle torte with raspberry and rhubarb and vanilla cheesecake. *Benchmark main dish: venison sausages with mash and onion gravy £14.50. Two-course evening meal £24.00.*

Free house ~ Licensee Simone Baker ~ Real ale ~ Open 12-11; 12-10.30 Sun ~ Bar food 12-3, 6-10 (9 Sun) ~ Restaurant ~ Children welcome ~ Dogs allowed in bar and bedrooms ~ Wi-fi ~ Bedrooms: /£130 *Recommended by David Carr, William and Megan, David Twitchett, Tracey and Stephen Groves, David Jackman*

WARHAM
TF9441   Map 8

Three Horseshoes ★ ◀

(01328) 710547 – www.warhamhorseshoes.co.uk

Warham All Saints; village signed from A149 Wells-next-the-Sea to Blakeney, and from B1105 S of Wells; NR23 1NL

Interesting, simple furnishings in unspoilt pub, pubby food, real ales and seats outside; bedrooms

This is a step back into the past. It's an old-fashioned pub dating from 1720 and the gas-lit simple rooms look unchanged since the 1920s. There are stripped deal or mahogany tables (one marked for shove-ha'penny) on stone floors, red leatherette settles built around partly panelled walls in the public bar, royalist photographs, a longcase clock with a clear piping strike and open fires in Victorian fireplaces. The traditional local game of twister is nailed to the ceiling showing whose round it is. Norfolk Brewhouse Moon Gazer Dark Mild, Woodfordes Wherry and a guest ale on handpump or tapped from the cask and local cider served by friendly staff. There's a courtyard garden with flower tubs and a well. There are five basic bedrooms next door in what was the post office.

 Home-cooked food includes sandwiches, hearty soups, beans on toast, pies such as rabbit or mushroom and nut, pheasant or pigeon casserole, home-cooked gammon, and puddings such as crumbles and tarts with custard. *Benchmark main dish: pie of the day £10.80. Two-course evening meal £16.00.*

Free house ~ Licensee Iain Salmon ~ Real ale ~ Open 12-2.30 (3 weekends), 6-11 ~ Bar food 12-2, 6-8 ~ Children welcome away from bar area but not allowed in bedrooms ~ Dogs welcome ~ Wi-fi ~ Bedrooms: £40/£60 *Recommended by Peter Meister, David Field, Roy Hoing, Gus Swan, Derek and Sylvia Stephenson*

WIVETON
Wiveton Bell ⭐ 🛏

TG0442 Map 8

(01263) 740101 – www.wivetonbell.co.uk
Blakeney Road; NR25 7TL

Busy dining pub where drinkers are welcomed too, local beers, consistently enjoyable food and seats outside; bedrooms

The mainly open-plan rooms here have some fine old beams, an attractive mix of dining chairs around wooden tables on a stripped-wood floor, a log fire and prints on yellow walls. The sizeable conservatory has smart beige dining chairs around wooden tables on coir flooring. Friendly, attentive staff serve Norfolk Brewhouse Moon Gazer Amber Ale and Dark Mild, Woodfordes Wherry and Yetmans Amber on handpump, and a dozen wines by the glass. Picnic-sets on the front grass look across to the church; at the back, stylish wicker tables and chairs on several decked areas are set among decorative box hedging. Character bedrooms are comfortable and well equipped and a continental breakfast hamper is delivered to your room each morning; three of the rooms have their own small terrace. There's also a self-catering cottage to rent.

 Attractively presented, rewarding food includes ham hock and black pudding terrine with sweet pickled baby onions and apple purée, local blue cheese with red wine poached pear aned candied walnut salad, local shiitake mushroom risotto with truffle oil, chicken caesar salad, herb-crusted hake fillet with lemon and dill crushed potatoes, salsify cooked in red wine and caper beurre noisette, chicken with wild mushroom and tarragon fricassée and crispy pancetta, steak burger with toppings, onion rings, home-made relish and chips, and puddings such as crumble of the day with vanilla anglaise and chocolate brownie with chocolate ice-cream. *Benchmark main dish: slow-braised local pork belly £15.95. Two-course evening meal £25.00.*

Free house ~ Licensee Berni Morritt ~ Real ale ~ Open 12-11 (10.30 Sun) ~ Bar food 12-2.15, 6-9.15 ~ Children welcome ~ Dogs allowed in bar ~ Wi-fi ~ Bedrooms: /£130
Recommended by John Wooll, Roy Hoing, David Jackman, Barbara Brown, Peter and Emma Kelly

WOLTERTON
Saracens Head ⭐ 🛏

TG1732 Map 8

(01263) 768909 – www.saracenshead-norfolk.co.uk
Wolterton; Erpingham signed off A140 N of Aylsham, on through Calthorpe; NR11 7LZ

Remote inn with stylish bars and dining room and seats in courtyard; good bedrooms

Hidden away down country lanes, this is a civilised Georgian inn that our readers enjoy very much. The two-room bar is simple but stylish with high ceilings, light terracotta walls and tall windows with cream and gold curtains – all lending a feeling of space, though it's not large. There's a mix of seats from built-in wall settles to wicker fireside chairs, as well as log fires and flowers. Woodfordes Wherry and a changing guest such as Panther Black Panther on handpump and several wines by the glass. The windows look on to a charming old-fashioned gravel stableyard with plenty of chairs, benches and tables. A pretty six-table parlour on the right has another big log fire. The bedrooms are comfortable and up to date.

 Extremely good, interesting food using the best local produce includes crispy duck salad with watermelon, lime, chilli and mint, pigeon and pork terrine with rhubarb and apple chutney, wild sea trout with pea risotto and lemon and white wine sauce, savoury cheesecake with roast vegetables, basil and balsamic, local loin of lamb with redcurrant sauce, wilted spinach and fondant potato, and puddings such as chocolate nemesis with pistachio ice-cream and treacle tart; they offer an autumn and winter two- and three-course set lunch. *Benchmark main dish: loin of local lamb with red onion tarte tatin and red wine and rosemary jus £17.50. Two-course evening meal £21.00.*

Free house ~ Licensees Tim and Janie Elwes ~ Real ale ~ Open 11-3, 6-10.30; closed Mon and Tues lunchtimes in winter ~ Bar food 12-2, 6-8.30; 12-2, 6-8 Sun, Mon ~ Restaurant ~ Children welcome ~ Dogs allowed in bar and bedrooms ~ Wi-fi ~ Bedrooms: £70/£100
Recommended by Philip and Susan Philcox, John Evans, David Jackman

WOODBASTWICK   TG3214   Map 8
Fur & Feather 🍺
(01603) 720003 ~ www.thefurandfeatherinn.co.uk
Off B1140 E of Norwich; NR13 6HQ

Full range of first class Woodfordes brewery ales, friendly service and popular bar food

As it's next door to Woodfordes brewery, the ales in this thatched, cottagey place are kept in tip top condition. Tapped from the cask there's Bure Gold, Mardlers, Nelsons Revenge, Once Bittern, Sundew and Wherry. You can also visit the brewery shop. Efficient, helpful staff also serve a dozen wines by the glass and ten malt whiskies. The style and atmosphere are not what you'd expect of a brewery tap – it's set out more like a comfortable and roomy dining pub with wooden chairs and tables on tiles or carpeting, plus sofas and armchairs; background music. There are seats and tables in the pleasant garden. This is a delightful pub in a lovely Estate village.

Rewarding food includes sandwiches and baps, pressed parsley and ham hock terrine with horseradish relish, potted hot smoked salmon with piccalilli, vegetarian shepherd's pie, steak and mushrooms in ale in a giant yorkshire pudding, seafood medley, burgers with toppings, coleslaw and chips, venison pie, whole pheasant with bacon-wrapped sausages and gravy, slow-cooked pork belly with smoky bacon beans and crackling, and puddings such as jam sponge with custard and lemon posset. *Benchmark main dish: steak and kidney pudding £13.75. Two-course evening meal £20.00.*

Woodfordes ~ Tenant Tim Ridley ~ Real ale ~ Open 10-10 ~ Bar food 12-9 (8 Sun) ~ Restaurant ~ Children welcome ~ Wi-fi *Recommended by David Carr, Christopher Maxse, Roy Hoing, Geoffrey Sutton*

Also Worth a Visit in Norfolk

Besides the fully inspected pubs, you might like to try these pubs that have been recommended to us and described by readers. Do tell us what you think of them: feedback@goodguides.com

AYLMERTON TG1840
Roman Camp (01263) 838291
Holt Road (A148); NR11 8QD Large late 19th-c mock-Tudor roadside inn; comfortable panelled bar, cosy sitting room off with warm fire, and light airy dining room, decent choice of enjoyable sensibly priced food from sandwiches up, well kept Adnams, Greene King and a guest, friendly helpful service from uniformed staff; children welcome, attractive sheltered garden behind with sunny terraces and pond, 15 bedrooms.
(Dr Simon Innes)

AYLSHAM TG1926
★ **Black Boys** (01263) 732122
Market Place; off B1145; NR11 6EH Small friendly hotel with imposing Georgian façade and informal open-plan beamed bar, popular generously served food from snacks up including good Sun roasts, various meal deals, Adnams, guest ales and decent wines, comfortable seating and plenty of tables on carpet or bare boards, helpful young uniformed staff coping well at busy times; children and dogs welcome, seats in front by marketplace, more behind, bedrooms, big cooked breakfast, open (and food) all day.
(John Wooll, John Evans)

BANNINGHAM TG2129
★ **Crown** (01263) 733534
Colby Road; opposite church by village green; NR11 7DY Welcoming 17th-c beamed pub in same family for 25 years; good choice of popular affordably priced food (they're helpful with gluten-free diets), well kept Greene King and local guests, decent wines, friendly well trained staff, log fires and woodburners; TV, free wi-fi; children and dogs welcome, disabled access, garden jazz festival Aug, open (and food) all day weekends. *(David Twitchett)*

BARTON BENDISH TF7105
Berney Arms (01366) 347995
Off A1122 W of Swaffham; Church Road; PE33 9GF Attractive dining pub in quiet village, good freshly made food from sandwiches and pub favourites to more inventive dishes, good value set menu too, service prompt and welcoming, Adnams beers and several wines by the glass, afternoon teas, restaurant; regular quiz nights; children and dogs (in bar) welcome,

pleasant garden, good bedrooms in converted stables and forge, open all day, food all day Sun.
(Sarah Flynn)

BINHAM TF9839
Chequers (01328) 830297
B1388 SW of Blakeney; NR21 0AL Long low-beamed 17th-c local away from the bustle of the coastal pubs; comfortable bar with coal fires at each end, Adnams Southwold, Norfolk Brewhouse Moon Gazer Golden and guests, enjoyable pub food at reasonable prices, friendly staff; various games; children and dogs welcome, picnic-sets in front and on back grass, interesting village with huge priory church, open all day weekends. *(Roy Hoing)*

BLAKENEY TG0243
Kings Arms (01263) 740341
West Gate Street; NR25 7NQ A stroll from the harbour to this chatty 18th-c pub, three simple low-ceilinged connecting rooms and airy garden room, Adnams, Greene King, Marstons and guests, generous wholesome food from breakfast on; children and dogs welcome, big garden, bedrooms, open all day from 9.30am (midday Sun). *(David Carr)*

BLAKENEY TG0243
White Horse (01263) 740574
Off A149 W of Sheringham; High Street; NR25 7AL Friendly inn popular with locals and holidaymakers; long split-level carpeted bar with fine-art equestrian prints and paintings, high-backed brown leather dining and other chairs around light oak tables, Adnams ales and a dozen wines by the glass, well liked food including local fish/shellfish; wine tasting events; children and dogs welcome, wheelchair access to upper bar and dining conservatory only, seats in suntrap courtyard and pleasant paved garden, short stroll to harbour, bedrooms, open all day.
(Simon and Mandy King)

BLICKLING TG1728
Bucks Arms (01263) 732133
B1354 NW of Aylsham; NR11 6NF Handsome Jacobean inn well placed by gates to Blickling Hall (NT); small proper bar, lounge set for eating with woodburner, smarter more formal dining room with another fire, decent range of beers including Woodfordes, several wines by the glass and enjoyable food from varied menu, friendly

---

If you stay overnight in an inn or hotel, they are allowed to serve you an alcoholic drink at any hour of the day or night.

attentive young staff; background music; children and dogs welcome, tables out on lawn, lovely walks nearby, three bedrooms, open all day (food all day Sun). *(R C Vincent, David Twitchett, John Wooll, Tom and Ruth Rees)*

BODHAM STREET
TG1240
Red Hart (01263) 588270
The Street; NR25 6AD Old family-run village pub with well liked fairly traditional home-cooked food, ales including Woodfordes Wherry, efficient relaxed service; pool, sports TV; children and dogs welcome (menus for both), open all day. *(Patricia Hawkins)*

BRAMERTON
TG2905
Waters Edge (01508) 538005
Mill Hill, N of village, by river; NR14 7ED Clean modern refurbishment for this pub-restaurant in great spot overlooking bend of River Yare; good (not especially cheap) food including daily specials, ales such as Greene King and Woodfordes, plenty of wines by the glass including champagne, efficient friendly service; children welcome, wheelchair access, picnic-sets on waterside deck, moorings, open all day weekends, closed Mon in winter. *(Lionel Smith)*

BRANCASTER
TF7743
★Ship (01485) 210333
London Street (A149); PE31 8AP Bustling roadside inn, part of the small Flying Kiwi chain; compact bar with built-in cushioned and planked wall seats, Jo C's ales and guests from oak counter, nice wines by the glass, several dining areas with woodburner in one and neatly log-piled fireplace in another, good modern food served by friendly helpful staff, contemporary paintwork throughout, pale settles and nice mix of other furniture on rugs and bare boards, bookcases, shipping memorabilia and lots of prints; background music, TV, daily papers; children and dogs welcome, gravelled seating area with circular picnic-sets out by car park, attractive well equipped bedrooms, open all day. *(Tracey and Stephen Groves, Paulgermany)*

BRANCASTER STAITHE
TF7944
★Jolly Sailors (01485) 210314
Main Road (A149); PE31 8BJ Unpretentious pub set in prime bird-watching territory on edge of NT dunes and salt flats, chatty mix of locals and visitors in simply furnished bars, wheelbacks, settles and cushioned benches around mix of tables on quarry tiles, photographs and local maps on the walls, woodburner, their own Brancaster ales (brewery not on site) and guests, several wines by the glass, sizeable back dining room with popular food including pizzas (price reasonable for the area); children and dogs welcome, plenty of picnic-sets and play equipment in peaceful back garden, ice-cream hut in summer, vine-covered terrace, open all day (food all

day in season). *(Neil and Angela Huxter, John Wooll, Derek and Sylvia Stephenson, Tracey and Stephen Groves)*

BRANCASTER STAITHE
TF8044
★White Horse (01485) 210262
A149 E of Hunstanton; PE31 8BY Popular restauranty place, but does have proper informal front locals' bar; own good Brancaster ales and guests, lots of wines by the glass and good range of gins, log fire, pine furniture, historical photographs and bar billiards, middle part with comfortable sofas and newspapers, splendid views over tidal marshes from airy dining conservatory and new raised lounge, enjoyable bar and restaurant food including 'tapas' and plenty of fish (they ask for a credit card if you run a tab); children welcome, dogs in bar, seats on sundeck taking in the view, more under cover on heated front terrace, nice beaches, coast path at bottom of garden, open (and food) all day. *(John Wooll, Tracey and Stephen Groves, DF and NF, Roy Hoing)*

BROCKDISH
TM2179
Old Kings Head (01379) 668843
The Street; IP21 4JY Light and airy old pub at centre of village; several well kept changing ales including Adnams and Norfolk Brewhouse, decent wines by the glass and over 40 gins, enjoyable food with Italian slant including good pizzas, friendly helpful staff, L-shaped beamed bar with comfortable leather sofa, tub chairs, some scrubbed wooden tables and pews on bare boards, log fire, steps up to smaller seating area, café serving good coffee and cakes, local art for sale; live music nights; popular with Angles Way walkers, dogs welcome in bar, a few tables out at the side, closed Mon, otherwise open (and food) all day, shuts 9pm Sun. *(Sheila Topham)*

BROOKE
TM2899
Kings Head (01508) 550335
Norwich Road (B1332); NR15 1AB Welcoming 17th-c village pub with popular freshly cooked food from traditional choices up, good friendly service, four real ales and excellent choice of wines by the glass, maybe a norfolk whisky, light and airy bare-boards bar with log fire, eating area up a step; quiz last Sun of month, occasional theatre nights, free wi-fi; children welcome, tables in sheltered garden, open all day (from 9.30am weekends for breakfast). *(Ian Duncan)*

BROOME
TM3591
Artichoke (01986) 893325
Yarmouth Road; NR35 2NZ Unpretentious split-level roadside pub with up to ten well kept ales (some from tap room casks) including Adnams, belgian fruit beers and excellent selection of whiskies, good traditional home-made food in bar or dining room, friendly helpful staff, wood and flagstone floors, log fire in big

fireplace; dogs welcome, garden picnic-sets, smokers' shelter, closed Mon otherwise open all day (shuts weekday afternoons in winter). *(Edward Nile)*

BURNHAM MARKET   TF8342
Hoste (01328) 738777
The Green (B1155); PE31 8HD
Character front bar in smart hotel with informal chatty feel, leather dining chairs, settles and armchairs (note the glass-topped suitcase table), wood-effect flooring, farming implements and cartoons on the walls, woodburner, Greene King and Woodfordes, 19 wines by the glass from extensive carefully chosen list and several malt whiskies, good if not cheap food including lunchtime sandwiches, courteous service, elegant dining rooms, bustling conservatory and smart airy back restaurant, art gallery upstairs; children and dogs (in bar) welcome, attractive garden, luxurious bedrooms, open all day from 9am. *(Walter and Susan Rinaldi-Butcher)*

BURNHAM MARKET   TF8342
Nelson (01328) 738321
Creake Road; PE31 8EN Dining pub with nice food from pizzas to more ambitious dishes in bar and restaurant, interesting vegetarian options and OAP lunch deal (Tues, Thurs), pleasant efficient uniformed staff, well kept Woodfordes Wherry and guests from pale wood servery, extensive wine list, L-shaped bar with leather sofas and armchairs, local artwork for sale; children and dogs welcome, terrace picnic-sets under parasols, four bedrooms (two in converted outbuilding), open all day. *(Tracey and Stephen Groves)*

BURNHAM THORPE   TF8541
★ Lord Nelson (01328) 738241
Off B1155 or B1355, near Burnham Market; PE31 8HL Neatly kept 17th-c pub with lots of Nelson memorabilia (he was born in this sleepy village); antique high-backed settles on worn red tiles in small bar, smoke ovens in original fireplace, little snug leading off, two dining rooms one with flagstones and open fire, well liked sensibly priced bar food, Greene King, Woodfordes and a guest tapped from the cask, several wines by the glass, secret rum-based recipes (Nelson's Blood and Lady Hamilton's Nip); children and dogs welcome, good-sized play area and pétanque in long back garden, open all day in summer, closed Mon evening (except school/bank holidays). *(Derek and Sylvia Stephenson, R Halliday)*

CHEDGRAVE   TM3699
White Horse (01508) 520250
Norwich Road; NR14 6ND Welcoming pub with Timothy Taylors Landlord and four other well kept ales, decent wines by the glass and good choice of enjoyable sensibly priced food including healthy options menu (pre-order) and themed nights, friendly attentive young staff, log fire and sofas in bar, restaurant; events such as live music, monthly quiz and beer festivals, pool and darts; children and dogs welcome, garden picnic-sets, open all day. *(Barbara Brown)*

CLEY-NEXT-THE-SEA   TG0443
★ George (01263) 740652
Off A149 W of Sheringham; High Street; NR25 7RN Large red-brick village inn overlooking the salt marshes; small carpeted front bar with long settle and sturdy dark wooden chairs, photographs of Norfolk wherries and other local scenes, Greene King, Woodfordes, Yetmans and a guest, 13 wines by the glass and well liked locally sourced food, candle-lit dining rooms, good friendly service; newspapers and free wi-fi; children and dogs (in bar) welcome, tables in little garden across lane, comfortable bedrooms, open all day, food all day summer. *(Dr Simon Innes, Carol and Barry Craddock, Lionel Smith)*

CLEY-NEXT-THE-SEA   TG0443
Three Swallows (01263) 740526
Holt Road off A149; NR25 7TT Popular refurbished local, log fires in bar and dining room, stripped-pine tables, enjoyable reasonably priced pubby food (all day Sun) from sandwiches up, various themed nights during the week, well kept Adnams, Greene King and Woodfordes from unusual richly carved bar, cheerfully busy staff; children and dogs welcome, disabled access, metal tables and chairs out at front facing green, big garden with surprisingly grandiose fountain, aviary and heated smokers' shelter, four annexe bedrooms, good breakfast, handy for the salt marshes, open all day. *(Simon Watkins)*

COCKLEY CLEY   TF7904
Twenty Churchwardens
(01760) 721439 *Off A1065 S of Swaffham; PE37 8AN* Friendly informal pub in converted school next to church, three linked beamed rooms, good open fire, popular well-priced food including nice home-made pies, well kept Adnams Southwold; newspapers, second-hand books for sale, no credit cards; children and dogs welcome, tiny unspoilt village. *(Lionel Smith)*

COLTISHALL   TG2719
Kings Head (01603) 737426
Wroxham Road (B1354); NR12 7EA Popular dining pub close to River Bure and moorings, imaginative food from owner-chef (especially fish/seafood), also bar snacks, lunchtime set menu and children's choices, well kept Adnams and good wines by the glass, friendly efficient service, open fire, fishing nets and stuffed fish including a monster pike and bill from marlin caught by landlord, cookery school; background music; seats outside (noisy road), four bedrooms. *(Gilly and Frank Newman)*

CONGHAM   TF7123
Anvil   (01485) 600625
St Andrews Lane; PE32 1DU Tucked-away modern country pub with welcoming licensees, wide choice of tasty generously served home-made food (smaller helpings available), good value Sun carvery, quick friendly service, three or more well kept ales (at least one local), reasonable prices; live music and quiz nights; children welcome, picnic-sets in small walled front garden, campsite, open all day weekends, closed Mon Oct-April. *(R C Vincent)*

CROMER   TG2242
Red Lion   (01263) 514964
Off A149; Tucker Street/Brook Street; NR27 9HD Substantial refurbished Victorian hotel with elevated sea views, original features including panelling and open fires, five well kept ales in bare-boards flint-walled bar, good food from sandwiches and platters up including daily specials, efficient friendly service, restaurant and conservatory; background music; children and dogs welcome, disabled facilities, tables in back courtyard, 14 bedrooms, open all day. *(Revd R P Tickle, Tony and Maggie Harwood, Anne Evans)*

DOWNHAM MARKET   TF6003
Railway Arms   (01366) 386636
At railway station, Railway Road; PE38 9EN Cosy station bar with tiny adjoining rooms, one with glowing coal fire, another with second-hand bookshop, ales tapped from the cask and several good ciders, tea, coffee and some snacky food, friendly staff; board games; best to check opening times. *(Patricia Hawkins)*

EAST WINCH   TF6916
Carpenters Arms   (01553) 841228
A47 Lynn Road; PE32 1NP Useful roadside pub with good value home-made food including daily specials in bar or separate restaurant, several beers and ciders, friendly helpful service; children welcome, no dogs inside, open (and food) all day. *(R C Vincent)*

EDGEFIELD   TG0934
★ Pigs   (01263) 587634
Norwich Road; B1149 S of Holt; NR24 2RL Friendly bustling pub with carpeted bar, Adnams, Greene King, Woodfordes and a house beer from Wolf tapped from casks, arches through to simply furnished area with mixed chairs and pews on broad pine boards, airy dining extension in similar style split into stalls by standing timbers and low brick walls, nice variety of well priced food (all day Sun) including Norfolk tapas, games room with bar billiards, also children's playroom; background music; dogs allowed in bar, good wheelchair access, rustic furniture on big covered front terrace,

adventure playground, boules, ten bedrooms (seven with spa facilities including sauna and outside bath), open all day from 8am (breakfast for non-residents). *(Peter Meister, Tracey and Stephen Groves)*

ELSING   TG0516
Mermaid   (01362) 637640
Church Road; NR20 3EA Welcoming 17th-c pub in quiet little village, L-shaped carpeted bar with woodburner, well kept Adnams, Woodfordes and guests tapped from the cask, enjoyable home-made food including range of pies and suet puddings (signature steak and kidney roly-poly), indian and thai curries also available, friendly helpful service; pool and other games such as dominoes and shut the box, free wi-fi; children and dogs welcome, handy for walkers on Wensum Way, nice garden, 14th-c church opposite with interesting brasses, closed Mon lunchtime. *(Shaun Mahoney)*

GAYTON   TF7219
Crown   (01553) 636252
Lynn Road (B1145/B1153); opposite church; PE32 1PA Low-beamed village pub with plenty of character, three main areas and a charming snug, good value food including buffet lunch (Mon-Sat) and carvery (all day Sun, Tues-Fri evenings), well kept Greene King ales, friendly service, sofas and good log fire, games room; children welcome in restaurant, dogs in bar, disabled access, attractive sheltered garden, four bedrooms, open (and food) all day. *(David Travis)*

GELDESTON   TM3990
★ Locks   (01508) 518414
Off A143/A146 NW of Beccles; off Station Road S of village, obscurely signed down long rough track; NR34 0HW Remote candlelit pub at navigable head of River Waveney; ancient tiled-floor core with beams and big log fire, changing ales tapped from casks and decent food including burgers, vegetarian dishes and Fri curry night, large extension for summer crowds; regular live music, no credit cards; children welcome, riverside garden, moorings, open all day in summer (winter: all day Fri, Sat and till 7pm Sun, closed Mon-Weds and Thurs lunchtime). *(Barbara Brown)*

GREAT BIRCHAM   TF7632
★ Kings Head   (01485) 578265
B1155, S end of village (called and signed Bircham locally); PE31 6RJ Handsome Edwardian hotel (up for sale as we went to press) with cheerful contemporary little bar, comfortable sofas, tub chairs and log fire, Adnams Broadside, Woodfordes Wherry and a couple of quickly changing guests, 15 wines by the glass, 18 malt whiskies and over 50 gins, lounge areas and airy modern restaurant with enjoyable varied choice of food, friendly helpful staff; free wi-fi; children and dogs welcome,

tables out in front and behind, nice country views, comfortable bedrooms and excellent breakfast, open all day from 7am. *(Ruth May, Donald Allsopp, Julie Swift)*

GREAT CRESSINGHAM   TF8401
★**Windmill** (01760) 756232
Village signed off A1065 S of Swaffham; Water End; IP25 6NN Shuttered red-brick pub with interesting pictures and bric-a-brac in warren of rambling linked rooms, plenty of cosy corners, good value tasty bar food from baguettes to chargrills, half a dozen ales including Adnams, Greene King and a house beer (Windy Miller) brewed by Purity, good choice of wines by the glass, 60 malt whiskies and decent coffee, friendly efficient staff, pool room and other pub games; background music (live country & western Tues), big sports TV in side snug; children and dogs welcome, large garden with picnic-sets and good play area, caravan parking, bedroom extension, open all day. *(Paul Rampton, Julie Harding)*

GREAT HOCKHAM   TL9592
Eagle (01953) 498893
Harling Road; IP24 1NP Friendly 19th-c red-brick corner local, half a dozen well kept ales including Adnams, Greene King and Woodfordes, pubby food all day Fri, Sat and till 6pm Sun, just lunchtime snacks other days; fortnightly quiz Weds, pool, darts, free wi-fi; children and dogs welcome, open all day Fri-Sun. *(Dr Simon Innes)*

GREAT YARMOUTH   TG5207
Mariners (01493) 332299
Howard Street S; NR30 1LN Dutch-gabled two-room pub popular for its excellent range of real ales and ciders, bar food such as pies and pasties, extended menu Fri, good service; frequent events including live music and beer/cider festivals; open all day. *(Edward Nile)*

HARPLEY   TF7825
Rose & Crown (01485) 521807
Off A148 Fakenham–Kings Lynn; Nethergate Street; PE31 6TW Friendly old village pub competently run by welcoming licensees, nice range of good sensibly priced home-made food, well kept Woodfordes Wherry and guests, Aspall's cider, modernised interior with open fires; children and dogs welcome, garden picnic-sets, closed Sun evening, all day Mon, Tues lunchtime. *(Derek and Sylvia Stephenson, John Wooll)*

HEYDON   TG1127
★**Earle Arms** (01263) 587376
Off B1149; NR11 6AD Popular old dutch-gabled pub overlooking green and church in delightfully unspoilt Estate village; well kept Adnams, Woodfordes and a guest, enjoyable food from varied if not extensive menu using local fish and meat (gluten-free choices marked), decent wine list, friendly efficient service, racing prints, some stuffed animals

and good log fire in old-fashioned candlelit bar, more formal dining room; children and dogs welcome, picnic-sets in small cottagey back garden, open all day Sun (no evening food then), closed Mon. *(Philip and Susan Philcox, David Twitchett)*

HICKLING   TG4123
Greyhound (01692) 598306
The Green; NR12 0YA Small popular village pub with welcoming open fire, good choice of enjoyable food in bar and neat restaurant, well kept local ales and ciders, friendly long-serving landlord; well behaved children and dogs welcome, seats out at front and in pretty back garden with terrace, handy for nature reserve. *(Roy Hoing)*

HINGHAM   TG0202
White Hart (01953) 850214
Market Place, just off B1108 W of Norwich; NR9 4AF Georgian-fronted coaching inn under new management; character rooms arranged over two floors, beams and standing timbers, stripped floorboards with oriental rugs, mix of furniture including comfortable sofas in quiet corners, lots of prints and photographs, woodburners, galleried long room up steps from main bar with egyptian frieze, upstairs dining/function room, good choice of well liked food including british tapas, four real ales, lots of wines by the glass and cocktails, friendly service; background music, bar billiards; children welcome, dogs downstairs, modern benches and seats in gravelled courtyard, pretty village with huge 14th-c church, five newly refurbished bedrooms, open all day, food all day weekends. *(Carol and Barry Craddock)*

HOLME-NEXT-THE-SEA   TF7043
White Horse (01485) 525512
Kirkgate Street; PE36 6LH Attractive old-fashioned place, cosy and rambling, with warm log fires, ample choice of fair priced food including local fish, friendly efficient service, Adnams, Greene King and decent wines, refurbished side extension; children and dogs welcome, small back garden, more seats out in front and on lawn opposite, play area, open all day (afternoon break in winter). *(David Travis)*

HOLT   TG0738
Feathers (01263) 712318
Market Place; NR25 6BW Relaxed hotel with popular locals' bar comfortably extended around original panelled area, open fire, antiques in attractive entrance/reception area, good choice of enjoyable fairly priced food including blackboard specials, friendly helpful service, Greene King ales and decent wines, good coffee, restaurant and dining conservatory; background music; children welcome, no dogs, 13 comfortable bedrooms, open all day. *(John Evans)*

HORSEY   TG4622
★**Nelson Head** (01493) 393378
Off B1159; The Street; NR29 4AD
Unspoilt nicely tucked-away red-brick
country pub, impressive range of beers (some
direct from the cask, Sept festival) as well
as ciders, good sensibly priced bar food (not
Sun evening in winter) from sandwiches and
snacks to daily specials, friendly chatty staff,
good log fire and lots of interesting bric-a-
brac including various guns, small side dining
room; quiet background music; children
welcome, well behaved dogs in bar, outside
seating including in field opposite, good coast
walks (seals), open all day. *(Dr Simon Innes)*

HORSTEAD   TG2619
Recruiting Sergeant (01603) 737077
B1150 just S of Coltishall; NR12 7EE
Light, airy and spacious roadside pub,
enjoyably generously served food from fresh
wraps and jacket potatoes up including good
fish choice, efficient friendly service even
though busy, up to half a dozen changing
ales such as Adnams, Greene King, Timothy
Taylors and Woodfordes, plenty of wines by
the glass, big open fire; children welcome,
terrace and garden tables, bedrooms, open
all day. *(Dr Simon Innes)*

HUNWORTH   TG0735
Hunny Bell (01263) 712300
Signed off B roads S of Holt; NR24 2AA
Welcoming 18th-c beamed pub; neat bar with
cushioned country chairs around wooden
tables including a couple of long slabby
ones, stone floor and woodburner, cosy snug
with homely furniture on old worn tiles
and original stripped-brick walls, another
woodburner in high-raftered bare-boards
dining room, enjoyable food from fairly pubby
menu, ales such as Adnams, Greene King and
Woodfordes, friendly helpful service; children
welcome, wheelchair access, picnic-sets on
terrace overlooking village green, more
seats in garden among fruit trees.
(Simon and Mandy King)

INGHAM   TG3926
★**Swan** (01692) 581099
*Off A149 SE of North Walsham; signed
from Stalham; NR12 9AB* Smart 14th-c
thatched dining pub nicely placed for
Broads and coast; rustic main area divided
by massive chimneybreast with woodburner
on each side, low beams and hefty standing
timbers, bare boards or parquet, some old
farm tools, quieter small brick-floored part
with leather sofas, good well presented
restaurant-style food including set menu
choices, seasonal ingredients from own farm,
well kept Woodfordes, local cider and good
selection of wines, friendly service; children
welcome, picnic-sets on sunny back terrace,
more at side, five comfortable bedrooms
in converted stables, good breakfast.
(Roy Hoing)

ITTERINGHAM   TG1430
★**Walpole Arms** (01263) 587258
*Village signposted off B1354 NW of
Aylsham; NR11 7AR* Beamed 18th-c pub
close to Blickling Hall (NT); good modern
cooking using fresh local ingredients (some
from own farm) along with more traditional
choices, efficient friendly service, well
kept Adnams, Woodfordes and nice wines
by the glass, sizeable open-plan bar with
woodburner, stripped-brick walls and dark
wood dining tables on red carpet, light
airy restaurant opening on to vine-covered
terrace; jazz nights and Weds quiz; children
welcome, dogs in bar, two-acre landscaped
garden, open all day Sat, closed Sun evening.
(Agnes Broda)

KENNINGHALL   TM0485
Red Lion (01953) 887849
*B1113 S of Norwich; East Church Street;
NR16 2EP* 16th-c pub with stripped beams,
bare boards and old floor tiles, enjoyable
good value home-made food from baguettes
and baked potatoes up, Sun brunch, well
kept Greene King IPA, Woodfordes Wherry
and guests, friendly helpful young staff, bar
with woodburner, cosy panelled snug and
back restaurant; regular live music and quiz
nights, free wi-fi; children (not in bar) and
dogs welcome, tables out by back bowling
green, bedrooms in former stable block, open
all day Fri-Sun. *(Lionel Smith)*

KING'S LYNN   TF6120
Crown & Mitre (01553) 774669
Ferry Street; PE30 1LJ Old-fashioned
unchanging pub in great riverside spot,
lots of interesting naval and nautical
memorabilia, up to six well kept ales (the
long-serving landlord still hopes to brew his
own), good value straightforward home-made
food, river-view back conservatory; no credit
cards; well behaved children and dogs
welcome, quayside tables. *(John Wooll)*

KING'S LYNN   TF6119
Marriotts Warehouse
(01553) 818500 *South Quay; PE30 5DT*
Bar-restaurant-café in converted 16th-c brick
and stone warehouse; well liked/priced food
from lunchtime sandwiches and light dishes
up (greater evening choice), good range of
wines, beers such as Sharps Doom Bar and
Woodfordes Wherry, cocktails, small upstairs
bar with river views; children welcome,
quayside tables, open all day from 10am.
(Dr Simon Innes)

LETHERINGSETT   TG0638
★**Kings Head** (01263) 712691
A148 (Holt Road) W of Holt; NR25 7AR
Popular country house-style inn with
character rooms; bars with rugs on tiles,
hunting/coaching prints and open fires,
well kept Adnams, Norfolk Brewhouse
and Woodfordes, decent wines by the glass

and good interesting food from generous sandwiches up, friendly efficient staff, partly skylit bare-boards dining room with built-in wall seating, farm tools on cream-painted flint and cob walls, back area under partly pitched ceiling with painted rafters; background music, free wi-fi; children and dogs welcome, picnic-sets out at front and on side lawn, up-to-date bedrooms, open all day, food all day Sun till 7.30pm. *(Tracey and Stephen Groves, Dr Simon Innes, Anne and Ben Smith, Gordon and Margaret Ormondroyd, David Jackman, Charles Gysin)*

LITTLE PLUMSTEAD   TG3112
Brick Kilns (01603) 720043
Norwich Road (B1140); NR13 5JH Pink-painted beamed country dining pub, wide choice of enjoyable fairly priced food including fish menu and plenty of options for special diets, well kept Adnams and a guest, good friendly service, bare-boards bar, carpeted restaurant and flagstoned conservatory overlooking paddock with horses, goats and donkeys; children welcome, well behaved dogs in bar, three bedrooms, open all day. *(Patricia Hawkins)*

LYNG   TG0617
Fox (01603) 872316
The Street; NR9 5AL Old beamed village pub with several refurbished linked areas and separate restaurant, ample helping of good inexpensive home-made food, Tues steak night, Thurs OAP lunch offer, ales such as Adnams and Woodfordes, friendly staff; pool and giant chessboard in one part; children and dogs (in front bar) welcome, enclosed garden with view of church, open (and food) all day in summer, closed Mon lunchtime winter. *(Richard Kennell)*

MARSHAM   TG1924
Plough (01263) 735000
Old Norwich Road; NR10 5PS Welcoming 18th-c inn with split-level open-plan bar, enjoyable food using local produce (special diets catered for) including good value set lunch, Adnams Southwold and a couple of local guests, friendly helpful staff; free wi-fi; children welcome, dogs in garden only, comfortable bedrooms, open all day. *(Ian Duncan)*

MUNDFORD   TL8093
Crown (01842) 878233
Off A1065 Thetford–Swaffham; Crown Road; IP26 5HQ Unassuming 17th-c pub, warmly welcoming, with heavy beams and huge fireplace, interesting local memorabilia, Courage Directors and one or two guests, over 50 malt whiskies, enjoyable generously served food at sensible prices, spiral iron stairs to two restaurant areas (larger one has separate entrance accessible to wheelchairs), locals' bar with sports TV; children and dogs welcome, back terrace and garden with wishing well, Harley-Davidson

meeting first Sun of month, bedrooms (some in adjoining building), also self-catering accommodation, open all day. *(Lionel Smith)*

NEW BUCKENHAM   TM0890
Inn on the Green (01953) 860172
Chapel Street; NR16 2BB Modern renovation of late Victorian red-brick pub by little green close to the Kings Head; good freshly prepared food from pub favourites to more restaurant dishes including blackboard specials, Adnams and Woodfordes, good selection of wines, pleasant efficient staff; children (away from bar) and dogs (in bar) welcome, terrace tables, handy for Banham Zoo. *(Quentin and Carol Williamson)*

NEW BUCKENHAM   TM0890
Kings Head (01953) 861247
Market Place; NR16 2AN Refurbished 17th-c pub by small green opposite medieval market cross, ales such as Adnams Southwold and Greene King Abbot, generous helpings of enjoyable reasonably priced pubby food, friendly helpful service, modern open-plan bar with beams and inglenook, big back dining area; quiz nights; pool; five bedrooms. *(Edward Nile)*

NORTH TUDDENHAM   TG0413
Lodge (01362) 638466
Off A47; NR20 3DJ Modernised dining pub with local ales and enjoyable home-made food from traditional favourites up, meal deal Tues, friendly attentive service; quiz nights; children welcome, tables outside (some on decking), open all day, closed Sun evening, Mon. *(Carol and Barry Craddock)*

NORTHREPPS   TG2439
Foundry Arms (01263) 579256
Church Street; NR27 0AA Welcoming village pub with good reasonably priced traditional food (not Sun evening, Mon) from generous sandwiches up, well kept Adnams, Woodfordes and decent choice of wines, good friendly service, woodburner, smallish restaurant; pool and darts in separate area; children and dogs welcome, picnic-sets in back garden, open all day. *(Lana Wood)*

NORWICH   TG2309
Adam & Eve (01603) 667423
Bishopgate; follow Palace Street from Tombland, N of cathedral; NR3 1RZ Ancient pub dating from at least 1240 when used by workmen building the cathedral, has a Saxon well beneath the lower bar floor and striking dutch gables (added in 14th and 15th c); old-fashioned small bars with tiled or parquet floors, cushioned benches built into partly panelled walls and some antique high-backed settles, three ales including Adnams and Theakstons, Aspall's cider and around 40 malt whiskies, traditional pubby food (not Sun evening), friendly service; background music; children allowed in snug till 7pm, no dogs inside, picnic-sets out among pretty

tubs and hanging baskets, open all day, closed 25 and 26 Dec, 1 Jan. *(Ian Phillips)*

NORWICH TG2408
Coach & Horses (01603) 477077
Thorpe Road; NR1 1BA Light and airy tap for Chalk Hill brewery (tours available), friendly staff, good value generous home-made food from rolls and paninis up, lunch deals and Sat brunch, L-shaped bare-boards bar with open fire, pleasant back dining area; sports TVs, gets very busy on home match days; disabled access possible (not to lavatories), front terrace, open all day. *(David Carr)*

NORWICH TG2210
Duke of Wellington (01603) 441182
Waterloo Road; NR3 1EG Friendly rambling local with up to 22 well kept quickly changing ales including Oakham and Wolf, many served from tap room casks, foreign bottled beers too, no food apart from sausage rolls and pies (can bring your own), real fire; traditional games, folk music Tues evening; well behaved dogs welcome, nice back terrace (Aug beer festival), open all day. *(Ian Duncan)*

NORWICH TG2308
Edith Cavell (01603) 765813
Tombland/Princes Street; NR3 1HF Corner pub-restaurant named after the gallant Norfolk nurse; enjoyable fairly priced food from sandwiches to good steaks cooked on hot rocks, three real ales including a house beer from Wolf, friendly helpful service, smallish bar, upstairs restaurant (and loos); diagonally across from Erpingham Gate into cathedral green, open all day (till 1am Fri, Sat). *(John Wooll)*

NORWICH TG2310
Fat Cat Tap (01603) 413153
Lawson Road; NR3 4LF 1970s shed-like building home to the Fat Cat brewery and sister pub to the Fat Cat (see Main Entries) and Fat Cat & Canary; their beers and up to 12 guests along with draught continentals, lots of bottled beers and eight or more local ciders/perries, no food apart from rolls and pork pies; live music Fri night and Sun afternoon, fortnightly quiz Thurs; children (till 6pm) and dogs welcome, seats out front and back, open all day. *(David Carr)*

NORWICH TG2309
★ Kings Head (01603) 620468
Magdalen Street; NR3 1JE Traditional Victorian local with friendly licensees and good atmosphere in two simply furnished bare-boards bars (front one is tiny), a dozen very well kept changing regional ales including a house beer from Winters, good choice of imported beers and a local cider, no food except pork pies, bar billiards in back bar; open all day. *(Tracey and Stephen Groves, David Carr)*

NORWICH TG2208
Plough (01603) 661384
St Benedicts Street; NR2 4AR Friendly little city-centre pub owned by Grain, their ales and guests kept well, good wines and cocktails, knowledgeable staff, food limited to sausage pie and summer barbecues, simply updated split-level interior with bare boards and open fire; background music; good spacious beer garden behind, open all day. *(Dr Simon Innes)*

NORWICH TG2308
Ribs of Beef (01603) 619517
Wensum Street, S side of Fye Bridge; NR3 1HY Welcoming and comfortable with nine real ales including Adnams and Oakham, four traditional ciders and good wine choice, deep leather sofas and small tables upstairs, attractive smaller downstairs room with river view, generous well priced lunchtime food (till 5pm weekends), quick cheerful service; Sun live music, monthly quiz; children welcome, tables out on narrow waterside walkway, open all day. *(David Carr)*

NORWICH TG2308
St Andrews Brew House
(01603) 305995 *St Andrews Street; NR2 4TP* Interesting newly opened place visibly brewing its own beers, also plenty of guest ales, craft kegs and bottled beers, utilitarian bare-boards interior with exposed ducting, rough masonry walls and eclectic mix of seating including some button-back booths, popular sensibly priced food from british tapas and sharing boards up, busy efficient staff, upstairs function room; background music, sports TV, Tues quiz and occasional comedy nights; children welcome, pavement tables, open all day, breakfast from 8am Mon-Fri. *(Tracey and Stephen Groves)*

NORWICH TG2308
Take Five (01603) 763099
Opposite cathedral gate; NR3 1HF Old black and white timber-fronted building, a mix of wine bar, pub and restaurant; four or five mainly local ales and decent wines, enjoyable well priced home-made food with good vegetarian choice, friendly efficient service, nice open fire; children welcome, closed Sun, otherwise open (and food) all day. *(Barbara Brown)*

NORWICH TG2309
Wig & Pen (01603) 625891
St Martins Palace Plain; NR3 1RN Popular 17th-c beamed pub opposite cathedral close; good value generous food from doorstep sandwiches up, prompt friendly service, six ales including Adnams, Fullers, Humpty Dumpty and Woodfordes, well priced wines; background music, sports TVs, May beer festival; metal café-style furniture out at front, open all day (till 6pm Sun). *(Revd R P Tickle)*

OLD HUNSTANTON
TF6842
Lodge (01485) 532896
Old Hunstanton Road (A149); PE36 6HX
Old red-brick roadside pub with clean
contemporary décor, popular food in bar or
restaurant from pizzas and pub favourites
up, well kept local beers such as Woodfordes
Wherry and good choice of wines by the
glass, friendly helpful staff, plenty of seating
on wood floors including booths and sofas
by woodburner; children and dogs (in bar)
welcome, tables on covered terrace and small
lawn, 16 good bedrooms, open all day.
(Tracey and Stephen Groves)

OVERSTRAND
TG2440
Sea Marge (01263) 579579
High Street; NR27 0AB Substantial half-
timbered sea-view hotel (former Edwardian
country house) with separate entrance to
spacious bar area, good food from ciabattas
to local seafood including weekday deal till
6pm, real ales and decent wines by the
glass, panelled restaurant with more upmarket
menu; children welcome, no dogs during food
times, five-acre grounds with terraced lawns
down to clifftop and steep steps to coast path
and beach, 25 comfortable bedrooms.
(David Carr, David Jackman)

OVERSTRAND
TG2440
White Horse (01263) 579237
High Street; NR27 0AB Comfortably
modernised red-brick pub with good choice
of well liked food in bar, dining room or barn
restaurant (also used for functions), up to
five well kept regional ales, friendly attentive
staff, pool room; background music, silent
sports TV; children and dogs welcome, picnic-
sets in front, more in garden behind with
play equipment (may be bouncy castle), eight
bedrooms, short walk to beach, open all day
from 8am. *(David Jackman)*

ROYDON
TF7022
Three Horseshoes (01485) 600666
*The one near King's Lynn; Lynn Road;
PE32 1AQ* Refurbished brick and stone
village pub under same ownership as nearby
Congham Hall Hotel; pleasant pastel décor
with simple wood furniture, stone-floor bar
and split-level part-carpeted restaurant,
woodburner in each, good uncomplicated
food (all day Sun) from reasonably priced
blackboard menu, weekday OAP lunch
deal, three ales including Greene King and
Woodfordes, friendly helpful staff; children
and dogs (in bar) welcome, tables outside,
closed Mon, Tues, otherwise open all day.
(John Wooll, R C Vincent)

SCULTHORPE
TF8930
Hourglass (01328) 856744
The Street; NR21 9QD Restauranty place
with long open room combining light modern
style with some dark beams, good choice of

enjoyable fairly priced food including OAP
lunch deal (Mon, Tues), Adnams Broadside
and Woodfordes Wherry, quick friendly
service. *(Edward Nile)*

SCULTHORPE
TF8930
★ **Sculthorpe Mill** (01328) 856161
*Inn signed off A148 W of Fakenham,
opposite village; NR21 9QG* Welcoming
dining pub in rebuilt 18th-c mill, appealing
riverside setting with seats out under
weeping willows and in attractive garden
behind; light, airy and relaxed with leather
sofas and sturdy tables in bar/dining area,
good reasonably priced food from sandwiches
to daily specials, attentive service, Greene
King ales and good house wines, upstairs
restaurant; background music, six comfortable
bedrooms, open all day in summer (all day
weekends winter). *(John Wooll)*

SEDGEFORD
TF7036
King William IV (01485) 571765
*B1454, off A149 Kings Lynn–
Hunstanton; PE36 5LU* Homely inn
handy for beaches and bird-watching; bar
and dining areas decorated with paintings
of north Norfolk coast and migrating birds,
high-backed dark leather dining chairs
around pine tables on slate tiles, log fires,
Adnams, Greene King and Woodfordes, ten
wines by the glass, straightforward food;
children welcome (no under-4s in main
restaurant after 6.30pm), dogs allowed in
bar and a couple of the bedrooms, seats on
terrace and under parasols on grass, also an
attractive covered dining area surrounded
by flowering tubs, closed Mon lunchtime,
otherwise open all day. *(Roy Hoing)*

SHERINGHAM
TG1543
Lobster (01263) 822716
High Street; NR26 8JP Almost on seafront
and popular with locals and tourists,
friendly panelled bar with log fires and
seafaring décor, wide range of ales including
Adnams, Greene King and Woodfordes, two
or three ciders and decent wines by the
glass, generous reasonably priced bar food,
restaurant with seasonal seafood including
lobster and crab; some live music; children
and dogs welcome, two courtyards, open all
day. *(Brian Glozier)*

SHOULDHAM
TF6708
Kings Arms (01366) 347410
The Green; PE33 0BY Prettily placed
community-owned pub, sympathetically
renovated (if a little sparse at present), with
well kept changing ales tapped from the cask
and generously served pubby food (not Sun
evening, Mon), pleasant staff, café; some live
music, quiz last Sun of the month; children
and dogs welcome, classic car/motorcycle
meetings first Sun of month, Sept beer
festival, open all day weekends, closed Mon
lunchtime. *(Henry Fryer)*

SMALLBURGH   TG3324
Crown (01692) 536314
A149 Yarmouth Road; NR12 9AD
Character thatched and beamed village inn
dating from the 15th c, well kept Adnams,
Fullers, Timothy Taylors, Woodfordes and a
guest, enjoyable home-made food in log-fire
bar and small dining room, regular african
themed nights (friendly landlady is from the
Ivory Coast); darts, monthly quiz; children
and dogs welcome, picnic-sets in pretty
back garden, Aug anglo-african festival,
two bedrooms, open all day (food all day
summer). *(Ian Duncan)*

SOUTH LOPHAM   TM0481
White Horse (01379) 688579
A1066 Diss–Thetford; The Street;
IP22 2LH Friendly beamed village pub
with well kept Adnams, Woodfordes and an
occasional guest, enjoyable home-made food
including vegetarian options and blackboard
specials, log fires; live music, karaoke and
quiz nights, TV; children welcome, big garden
with play area, handy for Bressingham
Gardens, open all day. *(Carol and Barry
Craddock)*

SOUTH WALSHAM   TG3613
Ship (01603) 270049
The Street (B1140); NR13 6DQ
Welcoming modernised village pub in same
small group as the Bucks Arms in Blickling
and Recruiting Sergeant at Horstead;
good fresh food (all day Sun till 7.30pm)
from sandwiches and traditional choices
up including several fish dishes, efficient
friendly service, well kept Adnams and
Woodfordes, stripped bricks and beams,
restaurant; children welcome, tables on
front elevated terrace and on tiered back
one, open all day Fri-Sun, closed Mon in
winter. *(Carol Avery)*

SOUTHREPPS   TG2536
★ ## Vernon Arms (01263) 833355
Church Street; NR11 8NP Popular
old-fashioned brick and cobble village
pub, welcoming and relaxed, with good
home-made food including steaks and
well priced crab (booking recommended),
also good Sun roasts and takeaway fish
and chips (Tues-Sat evenings), friendly
helpful staff, well kept Adnams, Greene
King, Woodfordes and a guest, good choice
of wines and malt whiskies, big log fire;
darts and pool, occasional live music; tables
outside, children, dogs and muddy walkers
welcome, open all day, no evening food Sun
or Mon. *(Dr D J and Mrs S C Walker)*

SPORLE   TF8411
Peddars Inn (01760) 788101
The Street; PE32 2DR Welcoming beamed
pub with inglenook bar, dining room and
little conservatory, good sensibly priced food
from pub favourites to specials, well kept

Adnams and a couple of local guests, Aspall's
cider, friendly service; occasional live music
and charity quiz nights; children and dogs
welcome, a few seats outside on grass, well
placed for Peddars Way walkers, open all day
Sat, closed Sun evening, Mon and lunchtime
Tues. *(Philip and Susan Philcox)*

STIFFKEY   TF9643
Red Lion (01328) 830552
A149 Wells–Blakeney; NR23 1AJ
Popular cheerful old pub; front bar with
tiled floor and inglenook, cushioned pews
and other pubby seats, local landscape
photos, room off with scatter cushions on
settles, another room with dark panelling
and splendid winged settle, Greene
King and Woodfordes ales, generally
well liked food (all day Sun) from pubby
choices to local fish/shellfish (local
mussels a speciality), friendly service,
two back dining rooms, one a flint-walled
conservatory; children and dogs welcome,
big partly covered gravelled courtyard,
more tables on covered deck, ten bedrooms
in modern block with own balconies or
terraces, nearby coastal walks, open all day.
(Dr D J and Mrs S C Walker, Roy Hoing)

STOW BARDOLPH   TF6205
Hare Arms (01366) 382229
Just off A10 N of Downham Market;
PE34 3HT Cheerful bustling village pub
under long-serving licensees; bar with
traditional pub furnishings and interesting
bric-a-brac, log fire, Greene King ales and
a couple of well kept guests, nine wines by
glass and several malt whiskies, well liked
food (all day Sun), two refurbished dining
rooms and family conservatory, pub cats;
children welcome in some parts, no dogs
inside, plenty of seats in front and back
gardens, maybe wandering peacocks, Church
Farm Rare Breeds Centre nearby, open (and
food) all day weekends. *(Denis and Margaret
Kilner, Tracey and Stephen Groves)*

SURLINGHAM   TG3107
Ferry House (01508) 538659
Ferry Road: far end by river; NR14 7AR
Welcoming unpretentious pub by River Yare;
well kept regional ales and generous helpings
of good inexpensive home-made food from
baguettes up, helpful accommodating service,
central woodburner in brick fireplace; some
live music; children and dogs welcome, very
busy with boats and visitors in summer – free
mooring, picnic-sets on waterside lawn,
handy for RSPB reserve, open (and food)
all day. *(Denis and Margaret Kilner)*

SWAFFHAM   TF8109
Kings Arms (01760) 723244
Market Place; PE37 7LA Refurbished
17th-c coaching inn, enjoyable food from
snacks and sharing boards up, good selection
of drinks including well kept Adnams,
restaurant and champagne/cocktail bar;

friendly staff, children welcome, courtyard tables, closed Sun evening, Mon, Tues, otherwise open all day. *(Matt, John Wooll)*

SWANTON MORLEY   TG0217
Darbys (01362) 637647
B1147 NE of Dereham; NR20 4NY
Cosy unspoilt red-brick local (formerly two farm cottages), half a dozen ales tapped from the cask including Adnams, Beeston and Woodfordes, fair value pubby food, long bare-boards country-style bar with gin traps and farming memorabilia, log fire and bread oven, step up to attractive dining room with stripped-wood furniture, another small room with glassed-over well; background radio, TV, free wi-fi; children and dogs welcome, wheelchair access (easiest through french doors), back garden with picnic-sets and play area, campsite, open all day Fri-Sun. *(Shaun Mahoney, Simon and Mandy King)*

TACOLNESTON   TM1495
★ Pelican (01508) 489521
Norwich Road (B1113 SW of city); NR16 1AL Former 17th-c coaching inn, chatty timbered bar with relaxed comfortable atmosphere, good log fire, sofas, armchairs and old stripped settle on quarry tiles, candles and flowers on tables, some booth seating, up to four well kept changing ales, Aspall's cider and 36 malt whiskies, winter mulled wine, restaurant area with high-backed leather chairs around oak tables, good choice of enjoyable food from pub favourites up, friendly service, shop selling local produce and bottled norfolk/suffolk ales; background music; children and dogs welcome, plenty of tables on decking behind, sheltered lawn beyond, bedrooms, open all day summer, closed weekday lunchtimes winter. *(Patricia Hawkins)*

THOMPSON   TL9296
Chequers (01953) 483360
Griston Road, off A1075 S of Watton; IP24 1PX Picturesque 16th-c thatched dining pub tucked away in attractive setting, enjoyable food including bargain weekday lunch offer and regular themed nights, ales such as Greene King and Woodfordes, helpful staff and friendly atmosphere, series of quaint rooms with low beams, inglenooks and some stripped brickwork; children welcome, dogs in bar, seats out in front and in back garden with swing, bedroom block, open (and food) all day Sun. *(David Travis)*

THORNHAM   TF7343
★ Lifeboat (01485) 512236
A149 by Kings Head, then first left; PE36 6LT New owners and refurbishment for this popular 16th-c inn; plenty of atmosphere in two pubby main bars, beams, lots of horse tack and farming implements, big lamps, brass measuring jugs, and chairs and settles around dark sturdy tables on quarry tiles, one bench has an antique penny-

in-the-hole game, woodburners, cosy tap bar and spreading more formal restaurant, four real ales including Greene King and Woodfordes, enjoyable food from sandwiches and pub favourites up, two-level conservatory with steps up to terrace garden; children and dogs welcome, play area, more seats out at the front, 13 bedrooms (front ones with marshland views), good walks to the sea, open all day, food all day weekends. *(Derek and Sylvia Stephenson, Ian Phillips, Brian and Janet Ainscough, Tracey and Stephen Groves, Paulgermany)*

WALSINGHAM   TF9336
Bull (01328) 820333
Common Place/Shire Hall Plain; NR22 6BP Rather quirky pub in pilgrimage village; bar with various odds and ends including half-size statue of Charlie Chaplin, pictures of archbishops and clerical visiting cards, welcoming landlord and friendly efficient staff, tasty food (not Sat and Sun evenings) from inexpensive menu, three well kept changing ales, log fire, typewriter in snug, old-fashioned cash register in gents'; free wi-fi; children welcome, courtyard and attractive flowery terrace by village square, dovecote stuffed with plastic lobsters and crabs, outside games room, nice snowdrop walk in nearby abbey garden, bedrooms, open all day. *(John Wooll)*

WEASENHAM ST PETER   TF8522
Fox & Hounds (01328) 838868
A1065 Fakenham–Swaffham; The Green; PE32 2TD Traditional 18th-c beamed local with bar and two dining areas (one with inglenook woodburner), spotless and well run by friendly family, three changing ales, good reasonably priced home-made food (not Sun evening), pubby furniture and carpets throughout, brasses and lots of military prints; children welcome, big well maintained garden and terrace, closed Mon. *(Edward Nile)*

WELLS-NEXT-THE-SEA   TF9143
Albatros 07979 087228
The Quay; NR23 1AT Bar on 1899 quayside clipper, charts and other nautical memorabilia, Woodfordes ales served from the cask, dutch food including speciality pancakes, seats on deck with good views of harbour and tidal marshes; live weekend music; children and dogs welcome, not good for disabled, cabin accommodation with shared showers, open (and food) all day. *(John Wooll, John Poulter)*

WELLS-NEXT-THE-SEA   TF9143
Bowling Green (01328) 710100
Church Street; NR23 1JB Welcoming 17th-c pub in quiet spot on outskirts, Greene King, Woodfordes and a guest, generous helpings of reasonably priced traditional food, bargain OAP lunch Tues, L-shaped bar with corner settles, flagstone and brick floor,

two woodburners, raised dining end; children and dogs welcome, sunny back terrace, two bedrooms in converted barn, also self-catering accommodation. *(Lionel Smith)*

WELLS-NEXT-THE-SEA   TF9143
Crown   *(01328) 710209*
The Buttlands; NR23 1EX Smart old coaching inn (part of Flying Kiwi group) overlooking tree-lined green; rambling bar on several levels with beams and standing timbers, grey-painted planked wall seats and brown leather dining chairs on stripped floorboards, Jo C's Norfolk Ale along with Adnams and Woodfordes, several wines by the glass, enjoyable modern food including daily specials, friendly accommodating staff, airy dining room and elegant more formal restaurant; background music; children and dogs (in bar) welcome, 12 bedrooms, open all day from 8am for breakfast. *(David Carr, Derek and Sylvia Stephenson)*

WELLS-NEXT-THE-SEA   TF9143
Edinburgh   *(01328) 710120*
Station Road/Church Street; NR23 1AE Traditional 19th-c pub near main shopping area, enjoyable home-made food and three well kept ales including Woodfordes, open fire, sizeable restaurant, also 'lifeboat' dining room decorated in RNLI colours; background music, free wi-fi; children and dogs welcome, disabled access, courtyard with heated smokers' shelter, three bedrooms, open all day. *(David Carr)*

WELLS-NEXT-THE-SEA   TF9143
★ Globe   *(01328) 710206*
The Buttlands; NR23 1EU Handsome Georgian inn a short walk from the quay; plenty of space and nice atmosphere in opened-up contemporary rooms, tables on oak boards, big bow windows, well kept Adnams beers, thoughtful wine choice and enjoyable food including Weds steak night, good service; background music, jazz evenings; children and dogs welcome, attractive courtyard with pale flagstones,

more seats at front overlooking green, seven bedrooms (more planned), open all day. *(Derek and Sylvia Stephenson, David Carr)*

WEST ACRE   TF7815
Stag   *(01760) 755395*
Low Road; PE32 1TR Small family-run local with three or more well kept changing ales in appealing unpretentious bar, good value home-made food, efficient friendly service, neat dining room; quiz third Sun of month; attractive spot in quiet village, closed Mon. *(John Wooll)*

WEYBOURNE   TG1143
Ship   *(01263) 588721*
A149 W of Sheringham; The Street; NR25 7SZ Popular refurbished village pub; well kept Woodfordes Wherry and two local guests, good wine choice, big bar with pubby furniture and woodburner, two dining rooms, good reasonably priced home-made food (not Mon, should book weekends) from lunchtime sandwiches through pub favourites to local seafood, efficient friendly young staff; background music, free wi-fi; well behaved children welcome, dogs in bar, seats out at front and in nice side garden handy for Muckleburgh military vehicle museum, open all day in season. *(M and GR)*

WYMONDHAM   TG1001
★ Green Dragon   *(01953) 607907*
Church Street; NR18 0PH Picturesque heavily timbered medieval pub with plenty of character; small beamed bar and snug, bigger dining area, interesting pictures, log fire under Tudor mantelpiece, four well kept changing ales and over 50 whiskies, winter mulled wine, big helpings of popular good value food including daily specials (best to book), friendly helpful staff, upstairs function room (open mike night third Sun of month, ukulele group third Tues, quiz Thurs); children and dogs welcome, garden behind with raised deck, near glorious 12th-c abbey church, open all day (food all day Fri-Sun). *(Barbara Brown)*

Post Office address codings confusingly give the impression that a few pubs are in Norfolk, when they're really in Cambridgeshire or Suffolk (which is where we list them).

Northamptonshire

ASHBY ST LEDGERS   SP5768   Map 4

Olde Coach House 🛏

(01788) 890349 – www.oldecoachhouse.co.uk

Main Street; 4 miles from M1 junction 18; A5 S to Kilsby, then A361 S towards Daventry; village also signed off A5 N of Weedon; CV23 8UN

Much character in ex-farmhouse with real ales, good wines, well liked food and plenty of outside seating; bedrooms

In an attractive village ancient enough to be mentioned in the Domesday Book, this carefully updated inn has an opened-up bar on the right that's full of original charm, with stools against the counter where they keep Wells Bombardier, Youngs Bitter and a guest beer on handpump and 16 wines by the glass, served by friendly staff. Several dining areas, all very relaxed, take in paintwork ranging from white and light beige to purple, and flooring that includes stripped wooden boards, original red and white tiles and beige carpeting. All manner of pale wooden tables are surrounded by assorted church chairs, high-backed leather dining chairs and armchairs, with comfortable squashy leather sofas and pouffes in front of a log fire. There are hunting pictures, large mirrors, an original old stove and fresh flowers; background music and TV. The back garden has picnic-sets among shrubs and trees, modern tables and chairs out in front under pretty hanging baskets, and a dining courtyard. This is a lovely place to stay with 11 of the well equipped, contemporary bedrooms located in the converted stables; breakfasts are good. The nearby church is of interest.

🍴 Quite a choice of reliably good food includes sandwiches, scallops with black pudding and pea purée, a choice of tapas-style dishes, pumpkin gratin with rosemary and goats cheese in tomato sauce, burgers with toppings, aioli and chips, venison with celeriac purée and braised red cabbage, bass with chorizo and butter beans, braised lamb shoulder and cutlet with redcurrant and rosemary jus, and puddings such as baked lemon ricotta cheesecake with raspberry sorbet and chocolate and orange bread and butter pudding. *Benchmark main dish: steak in ale pie £12.95. Two-course evening meal £18.00.*

Quicksilver Management ~ Lease Mark Butler ~ Real ale ~ Open 12-11 ~ Bar food 12-2.30, 6-9.30 ~ Restaurant ~ Children welcome ~ Dogs allowed in bar ~ Wi-fi ~ Bedrooms: /£75
Recommended by Mungo Shipley, Anne and Ben Smith, George Atkinson, Mike and Mary Carter

---

People named as recommenders after the full entries have told us that the pub should be included. But they have not written the report – we have, after anonymous on-the-spot inspection.

FARTHINGHOE
SP5339   Map 4

Fox 🛏

(01295) 713965 – www.foxatfarthinghoe.co.uk

Just off A422 Brackley–Banbury; Baker Street; NN13 5PH

Bustling stone inn with a neat bar and dining rooms, tasty food, helpful service and seats in the garden; bedrooms

Carefully restored and spruced-up, this golden-stone pub has plenty of space for both drinking and eating. The dark beamed bar has stools and a log fire in a stripped-stone fireplace, and the dining areas have seats ranging from leather tub chairs to banquettes, cushioned wall seats with scatter cushions and quite a range of wooden dining chairs – all around rustic wooden tables; mirrors and country prints on pastel walls. Courage Directors and Youngs Bitter on handpump, nine wines by the glass and a good choice of gins; background music. The terrace and lawn have picnic-sets under a giant parasol. Bedrooms in an adjoining barn conversion are quiet and comfortable, and one is suitable for disabled customers.

Popular food includes duck liver parfait with redcurrant and cranberry jelly, smoked salmon and prawn parcel with pickled cucumber, mixed bean burger with onion rings, coleslaw, mango salsa and chips, pork and leek sausages with mash and onion gravy, chicken breast with mushroom and tarragon mousse and fondant potato, chilli con carne, and puddings such as chocolate and cherry roulade with raspberry sorbet and sticky toffee pudding with toffee sauce. *Benchmark main dish: local sirloin steak with a choice of sauce and chips £23.00. Two-course evening meal £19.00.*

Charles Wells ~ Lease Neil Bellingham ~ Real ale ~ Open 12-11; 12-10.30 Sun ~ Bar food 12-2.30, 6-9.30; 12-4, 6-8 Sun ~ Restaurant ~ Children welcome ~ Dogs allowed in bar ~ Wi-fi ~ Bedrooms: £65/£75 *Recommended by Jo Garnett, Daniel King, Edward Nile*

FARTHINGSTONE
SP6155   Map 4

Kings Arms 🍺 £

(01327) 361604

Off A5 SE of Daventry; village signed from Litchborough; NN12 8EZ

Individual place with cosy traditional interior, carefully prepared food and lovely garden

The hard-working landlord in this little gem of a pub keeps his ever-changing beers in top condition and sources interesting choices from far and wide. It's a traditional pub with a wide mix of chatty customers and the cosy flagstoned bar has a huge log fire, comfortable homely sofas and armchairs near the entrance, whisky-water jugs hanging from oak beams, and lots of pictures and decorative plates on the walls. A games room at the far end has darts, dominoes, cribbage, table skittles and board games. Dent Aviator Ale, Wickwar BOB and Woodfordes Wherry on handpump and a short but decent wine list. Look out for the interesting newspaper-influenced décor in the outside gents'. The handsome gargoyled stone exterior is nicely weathered and very pretty in summer when the hanging baskets are at their best; there are seats on a tranquil terrace among plant-filled, painted tractor tyres and recycled art, and they've recorded over 200 species of moth and 20 different types of butterfly. This is a picturesque village and good walks nearby include the Knightley butterfly Way. It's worth ringing ahead to check the opening and food times.

Tasty food – served weekend lunchtimes only – includes sandwiches, popular cheese, meat and fish platters, cassoulets and casseroles, and puddings such as gingerbread pudding and meringues. *Benchmark main dish: salmon fishcakes £8.95.*

Free house ~ Licensees Paul and Denise Egerton ~ Real ale ~ Open 7-11 Mon-Thurs;
6.30-midnight Fri; 12-11.30 Sat; 12-6, 9-11 Sun; closed Mon, weekday lunchtimes ~ Bar food
12-2.30 weekends; maybe evening snacks ~ Children welcome ~ Dogs allowed in bar ~ Wi-fi
Recommended by Sharon and John Hancock, George Atkinson, Ian Duncan, Katherine Matthews

FOTHERINGHAY

Falcon ⭐ ♀

TL0593   Map 5

(01832) 226254 – www.thefalcon-inn.co.uk
Village signposted off A605 on Peterborough side of Oundle; PE8 5HZ

● ●
Northamptonshire Dining Pub of the Year

**Upmarket dining pub with a good range of drinks and modern
british food, and attractive garden**

Both drinkers and diners are warmly welcomed in this stylish pub and
the gently civilised atmosphere appeals to all. There are winter log fires
in stone fireplaces, fresh flowers, cushioned slatback armchairs, bucket
chairs and comfortably cushioned window seats and bare floorboards. The
Orangery restaurant opens on to a charming lavender-surrounded terrace
with lovely views of the huge church behind and of the attractively planted
garden; plenty of seats under parasols. The thriving little locals' tap bar has
a fine choice of drinks including Fullers London Pride, Greene King IPA
and a guest such as Nobbys Swift Nick on handpump, 16 good wines by the
glass and several malt whiskies; darts team and board games. This is a lovely
village (Richard III was born here) with plenty of moorings on the River
Nene; the ruins of Fotheringhay Castle, where Mary, Queen of Scots was
executed, is nearby.

 Enterprising food includes open sandwiches, smoked ham hock and rabbit
terrine with piccalilli, tempura tiger prawns with sweet chilli dip, a pie and a
burger of the day, vegetable risotto, corn-fed chicken with butternut squash purée,
dauphinoise potatoes and salsa verde, red mullet fillets on mediterranean vegetable
couscous with saffron aioli, and puddings such as lemon curd tartlet and seasonal fruit
crumble; they also offer a two- and three-course set menu (not Saturday evening or
Sunday lunchtime). *Benchmark main dish: salmon, crab and dill fishcakes £11.50.
Two-course evening meal £22.00.*

Free house ~ Licensee Sally Facer ~ Real ale ~ Open 12-11; 12-5 Sun (12-10 Sun June-
Sept) ~ Bar food 12-2, 6-9; 12-3 Sun (12-3, 5-8.30 Sun June-Sept) ~ Restaurant ~ Children
welcome ~ Dogs allowed in bar ~ Wi-fi *Recommended by Miss B D Picton, Ian Herdman,
Michael Sargent, Mike and Margaret Banks, Charles Fraser*

GREAT BRINGTON
Althorp Coaching Inn 🍺

SP6664   Map 4

(01604) 770651 – www.althorp-coaching-inn.co.uk
*Off A428 NW of Northampton, near Althorp Hall; until recently known as the
Fox & Hounds; NN7 4JA*

**Friendly golden-stone thatched pub with some fine architectural
features, tasty popular food, well kept real ales and sheltered garden**

The fine range of well kept real ales on handpump in this 16th-c former
coaching inn might include Greene King IPA, Phipps NBC India Pale
Ale, St Austell Tribute, Sharps Doom Bar and a couple of guest beers; the
extended dining area gives views of the 30 or so casks racked in the cellar.
Also, eight wines by the glass and a dozen malt whiskies. The ancient bar
has all the traditional features you'd wish for, from a dog or two sprawled

by the huge log fire, to old beams, sagging joists and an appealing mix of country chairs and tables (maybe with fresh flowers) on broad flagstones and bare boards. There are snug alcoves, nooks and crannies with some stripped-pine shutters and panelling, two fine log fires and an eclectic medley of bric-a-brac from farming implements to an old clocking-in machine and country pictures. A function room in a converted stable block is next to the lovely cobbled and paved courtyard (also accessible by the old coaching entrance) with sheltered tables and tubs of flowers; there's more seating in the charming garden.

Quite a variety of food includes sandwiches and baguettes (not Sunday lunchtime), game terrine with port jelly, baked camembert with red onion chutney, sharing platters, pea and asparagus risotto, burger with toppings and chips, corn-fed chicken stuffed with sun-dried tomato and goats cheese with tomato sauce, a pie of the day, beer-battered fish and chips, steaks with a choice of sauces and chips, and puddings such as lemon tart with raspberry sorbet and raspberry coulis and Baileys cream profiteroles with chocolate sauce. *Benchmark main dish: pork belly with mulled red cabbage, parsnip purée and jus £14.95. Two-course evening meal £21.00.*

Free house ~ Licensee Michael Krempels ~ Real ale ~ Open 11am–midnight; 12–11 Sun ~ Bar food 12–3, 6–9.30; 12–8.30 Sat; 12–8 Sun ~ Restaurant ~ Children welcome ~ Dogs allowed in bar ~ Wi-fi *Recommended by George Atkinson, Gerry and Rosemary Dobson, Luke Morgan, John and Sarah Webb*

LOWICK
Snooty Fox ♀
SP9780 Map 4

(01832) 733434 – www.thesnootyfoxlowick.com
Off A6116 Corby–Raunds; NN14 3BH

Bustling village pub with plenty of seating space, real ales, quite a choice of food and friendly staff

At the heart of a peaceful village, this solidly built 17th-c pub is popular for its highly thought-of food. The spacious lounge bar has a woodburning stove in a sizeable fireplace, handsomely moulded dark oak beams, leather sofas, stools and bucket armchairs on big terracotta tiles, and stripped stonework. A formidable carved counter has a beer named for the pub (from Marstons), Digfield Fools Nook, Marstons Pedigree and Wychwood Hobgoblin on handpump, lots of wines by the glass and a farm cider. The more formal dining rooms have high-backed leather and other dining chairs around quite a choice of chunky tables on pale wooden floorboards; background music. There are picnic-sets under parasols on the front grass and a children's play area.

Pleasing food includes lunchtime sandwiches, open ravioli with pheasant ragoût, devilled whitebait and lemon mayonnaise, wild mushroom, spinach and goats cheese vol-au-vent with a poached egg and pimento cream, free-range pork sausages with mash and onion gravy, beer-battered cod and chips, bass fillets with creamy tomato sauce, king prawns, tarragon and deep-fried courgettes, trio of lamb cutlets with port and redcurrant jus, and puddings such as turkish delight cheesecake and chocolate mousse tart with raspberry sorbet; they also offer a two-course set lunch. *Benchmark main dish: duck breast on blackberry and marsala sauce with smoked garlic mash and honeyed carrots £18.95. Two-course evening meal £22.00.*

Free house ~ Licensee Carmen Sharpe ~ Real ale ~ Open 12–3, 5–11; 12–11 Sat, Sun; closed Mon ~ Bar food 12–2 (3 Sun), 6–9 (9.30 Sat) ~ Restaurant ~ Children welcome ~ Dogs allowed in bar ~ Wi-fi *Recommended by Michael Sargent, George Atkinson, Clive and Fran Dutson, Mike and Margaret Banks, Peter Andrews*

NORTHAMPTON

SP7559 Map 4

Malt Shovel  £

(01604) 234212 – www.maltshoveltavern.com

Bridge Street (approach road from M1 junction 15); no parking in nearby street, best to park in Morrisons central car park; far end – passage past Europcar straight to back entrance; NN1 1QF

Friendly, well run real ale pub with bargain lunches and over a dozen varied beers

Of course, everyone comes to this lively tavern for the fantastic ales but it's a genuine place with a cheerful feel, fairly priced food and knowledgeable, enthusiastic staff. Up to 13 real ales are served from a battery of handpumps lined up on the long counter: Frog Island Best Bitter, Fullers London Pride, Greene King New Horizons IPA and XX Mild, Hook Norton Old Hooky, JW Lees Moonraker, Nobbys Best, Oakham Bishops Farewell and JHB, and Phipps NBC India Pale Ale. They also stock belgian draught and bottled beers, 50 malt whiskies, 17 rums, 17 vodkas and 17 gins and Cheddar Valley farm cider; regular beer festivals. It's also home to quite an extensive collection of carefully chosen brewing memorabilia – look out for the rare Northampton Brewery Company star, displayed outside the pub, and some high-mounted ancient beer engines; darts, daily papers and background music. The secluded backyard has tables and chairs and a smokers' shelter; disabled facilities.

Lunchtime-only food includes wraps and baguettes, filled baked potatoes, three-cheese and broccoli bake, shepherd's pie, burger and chips, gammon and egg, lambs liver and bacon casserole, and pork belly with spring onion mash and red cabbage. *Benchmark main dish: goat curry £6.50.*

Free house ~ Licensee Mike Evans ~ Real ale ~ Open 11.30-3, 5-11; 11.30-11 Fri, Sat; 12-10.30 Sun ~ Bar food 12-2; not Sun ~ Well behaved children welcome in bar ~ Dogs allowed in bar ~ Wi-fi ~ Blues Weds evening *Recommended by Richard Kennell, George Atkinson, Dr J Barrie Jones, Caroline Sullivan*

OUNDLE

TL0388 Map 5

Ship  £

(01832) 273918 – www.theshipinn-oundle.co.uk

West Street; PE8 4EF

Bustling down-to-earth pub with interesting beers and good value pubby food; bedrooms

Two brothers run this traditional town local, which has always been popular for its genuinely welcoming and lively atmosphere. Off to the left of the central corridor, the heavily beamed lounge consists of cosy areas with a mix of leather and other seats, sturdy tables and a warming log fire in a stone inglenook. A charming little panelled snug at one end has button-back leather seats. The wood-floored public bar has poker evenings on Wednesdays, while the terrace bar has pool, darts, TV, board games and background music. Friendly staff serve Brewsters Hophead, Caledonian Deuchars IPA, Nene Valley NVB Bitter and Sharps Doom Bar on handpump, eight wines by the glass and several malt whiskies. The wooden tables and chairs out on the series of small sunny, covered terraces are lit at night.

Reasonably priced pubby food includes baguettes and rolls, pâté of the day, chilli nachos with guacamole and salsa, beer-battered haddock and chips, sausages with mash and onion gravy, chilli con carne with sour cream and cheese, burger with toppings, coleslaw and fries, ham, eggs and chips, and puddings; steak night is

Wednesday and burger evening is Thursday. *Benchmark main dish: steak in ale pie £9.95. Two-course evening meal £14.00.*

Free house ~ Licensees Andrew and Robert Langridge ~ Real ale ~ Open 11am-11.30pm; 12-11 Sun ~ Bar food 12-3, 6-9; 12-6 Sun ~ Children welcome ~ Dogs welcome ~ Wi-fi ~ Live folk music second Mon of month ~ Bedrooms: £39/£69 *Recommended by Phoebe Peacock, Andrew Stone, Julie Swift*

SPRATTON
SP7170 Map 4

Kings Head
(01604) 847351 – www.kingsheadspratton.co.uk
Brixworth Road, off A5199 N of Northampton; NN6 8HH

Part brasserie, part bar with contemporary furnishings, an easy-going atmosphere, real ales and rewarding food; seats outside

'Three in one' is how this enterprising place describes itself – bar, restaurant and coffee shop. It works well. There are pale flagstones and ancient stripped stonework mixing well with handsome new wood flooring and up-to-date décor, plus leather chesterfields, an antique settle, café chairs around stripped brasserie-style tables and a woodburning stove in a brick fireplace. Friendly staff serve St Austell Tribute, Sharps Doom Bar and a guest such as Phipps NBC India Pale Ale on handpump, eight wines by the glass and artisan spirits; background music and darts. The back coffee shop has a glass wall overlooking a courtyard laid out with modern metal and wood tables and chairs.

Interesting food includes lunchtime sandwiches, ham hock terrine with black pudding crumble, pea soup and mint oil, chilli crab with candied chicory, brown crab mayonnaise and orange gel, roasted beetroot and goats cheese risotto, mackerel with charred spring onions, radishes and courgette, crispy scallop roe and dill mayonnaise, lamb rump and crispy shoulder with peas, broad beans and baby spinach, and puddings; the coffee shop offers home-made cakes and scones, milkshakes and speciality teas and coffee. *Benchmark main dish: beer-battered fish and chips £15.50. Two-course evening meal £22.00.*

Free house ~ Licensee Natalie Tompkins ~ Real ale ~ Open 12-3, 6-11; 12-11.30 Fri, Sat; 12-10.30 Sun ~ Bar food 12-2.30, 6-9 (9.30 Fri, Sat); 12-5 Sun; coffee shop 8.30-5; 12-5 Sun ~ Restaurant ~ Children welcome ~ Dogs allowed in bar ~ Wi-fi *Recommended by George Atkinson, Gerry and Rosemary Dobson, Mike and Margaret Banks, Edward May*

Also Worth a Visit in Northamptonshire

Besides the fully inspected pubs, you might like to try these pubs that have been recommended to us and described by readers. Do tell us what you think of them: feedback@goodguides.com

ABTHORPE SP6446
★**New Inn** (01327) 857306
Signed from A43 at first roundabout S of A5; Silver Street; NN12 8QR
Traditional partly thatched country local run by cheery farming family, fairly basic rambling bar with dining area down a couple of steps, four well kept Hook Norton beers and Weston's cider, good pubby food (not Sun evening) using own meat and home-grown herbs, set menu choices, beams, stripped stone and inglenook woodburner, darts and table skittles; quiz last Sun of month, occasional live music, free wi-fi; children, dogs and muddy boots welcome, garden tables, bedrooms in converted barn (short walk across fields), open all day Fri-Sun, closed Mon and Tues lunchtimes.
(Ian Duncan)

APETHORPE TL0295
Kings Head (01780) 470627
Kings Cliffe Road; PE8 5DG Roomy stone-built pub in conservation village; log fire in comfortable bar, Fullers London Pride

and three local guests, sensibly short choice of enjoyable home-cooked food including bar snacks and daily specials, friendly efficient service, big dining area, little café serving breakfast from 9am; seasonal events, TV; children, walkers and dogs welcome, some seats out at front and in nice sheltered courtyard behind, open all day Sat, till 7pm Sun, closed Mon lunchtime. *(Luke Morgan)*

ARTHINGWORTH   SP7581
Bulls Head (01858) 525637
Kelmarsh Road, just above A14 by A508 junction; pub signed from A14; LE16 8JZ Steps up to much extended black-beamed pub with various seating areas in L-shaped bar, pubby furniture and upholstered banquettes on patterned carpet, woodburner, fairly standard good value food including midweek lunch deal, well kept Thwaites and a couple of guests (May beer festival), efficient cheery service, restaurant; background music, TV, darts and skittles, free wi-fi; disabled access (from back) and facilities, terrace picnic-sets, eight bedrooms in separate block, handy for Kelmarsh Hall, open all day weekends (food till 7.30pm Sun). *(Gerry and Rosemary Dobson)*

ASHTON   TL0588
Chequered Skipper (01832) 273494
The one NE of Oundle, signed from A427/A605 roundabout; PE8 5LD Handsomely rebuilt thatched pub on chestnut-tree green of elegant Estate village; well kept changing local ales and good home-made food from snacks and stone-baked pizzas up, helpful friendly young staff, spacious open-plan layout with dining areas either side; children welcome, well behaved dogs in bar, good 4-mile circular walk, open all day weekends. *(Michael and Jenny Back, Peter Andrews)*

AYNHO   SP5133
Cartwright (01869) 811885
Croughton Road (B4100); handy for M40 junction 10; OX17 3BE Spotless 16th-c coaching inn with linked areas, contemporary furniture on wood or tiled floors, some exposed stone walls, leather sofas by big log fire in small bar, ales such as Adnams and Butcombe, nice wines and coffee, good well presented food including set deals, friendly efficient uniformed staff; background music, daily newspapers, TV and free wi-fi; children welcome, a few seats in pretty corner of part-cobbled coachyard, 21 bedrooms, good breakfast, pleasant village with apricot trees growing against old cottage walls, open all day. *(George Atkinson)*

AYNHO   SP4932
★ **Great Western Arms**
(01869) 338288 *On B4031 1.5 miles E of Deddington, 0.75 miles W of Aynho, adjacent to Oxford Canal and Old Aynho station; OX17 3BP* Attractive old pub

with series of linked cosy rooms; fine solid country tables on broad flagstones, golden stripped-stone walls, warm cream and deep red plasterwork, fresh flowers and candles, log fires, well kept Hook Norton and guests, good wines by the glass and enjoyable fairly pubby food served by friendly attentive young staff, elegant dining area on right, extensive GWR collection including lots of steam locomotive photographs, daily papers and magazines; background music, skittle alley, pool; children and dogs welcome, white cast-iron furniture in back former stable courtyard, moorings on Oxford Canal and nearby marina, bedrooms, open all day, food all day Sun. *(Michael Sargent)*

BADBY   SP5558
Windmill (01327) 311070
Village signposted off A361 Daventry–Banbury; NN11 3AN Attractive 17th-c thatched and beamed village pub, flagstoned bar area with woodburner in huge inglenook, up to five well kept changing ales, decent wines and good choice of popular reasonably priced home-made food from lunchtime sandwiches up, welcoming helpful staff, restaurant extension; background and occasional live music; children and dogs welcome, terrace out by pretty green, nice walks (Badby bluebell woods close by), eight good bedrooms, open all day. *(Graham and Elizabeth Hargreaves, Sara Fulton, Roger Baker)*

BARNWELL   TL0584
Montagu Arms (01832) 273726
Off A605 S of Oundle, then fork right at Thurning/Hemington sign; PE8 5PH Attractive old stone-built pub with well kept Adnams, Digfield (brewed in village) and guests, real ciders, good helpings of enjoyable home-cooked food (not Sun evening, Mon), cheerful staff, log fire, low beams, flagstones or tile and brick floors, back dining room and conservatory; children and dogs welcome, big garden with play area, pleasant streamside village, nice walks, open all day weekends, closed Mon lunchtime. *(Miles Green)*

BRAUNSTON   SP5465
Admiral Nelson (01788) 891900
Dark Lane, Little Braunston, overlooking Lock 3 just N of Grand Union Canal tunnel; NN11 7HJ 18th-c ex-farmhouse in peaceful setting by canal and hump bridge; good freshly made food (not Sun evening) from sandwiches/baguettes and traditional favourites up, well kept ales including one brewed for them by local Merrimen, efficient service, L-shaped bar with log fire and two seating areas to the right (sofas at low tables), a couple of steps down to cosy dining alcove, brick-partitioned restaurant extension to the left with sturdy tables and high-backed leather chairs; some live music including Aug festival, hood skittles and darts, free wi-fi; well behaved children and dogs welcome, wheelchair access, lots of

waterside picnic-sets, closed Mon lunchtime in winter, otherwise open all day. *(Richard Kennell, Clive and Fran Dutson, Simon and Mandy King)*

BRAYBROOKE
SP7684

Swan (01858) 462754 *Griffin Road; LE16 8LH* Nicely kept thatched pub with good drinks choice including Everards ales, popular sensibly priced food (not Sun evening) from sandwiches and pub favourites up, friendly attentive staff, fireside sofas, soft lighting, beams and some exposed brickwork, restaurant; quiet background music; children and dogs welcome, disabled facilities, pretty hedged garden with covered terrace, open all day Fri-Sun, closed Mon. *(Mike and Margaret Banks)*

BRIXWORTH
SP7470

Coach & Horses (01604) 880329 *Harborough Road, just off A508 N of Northampton; NN6 9BX* Welcoming early 18th-c stone-built beamed pub, popular good value food from fairly straightforward menu plus more adventurous specials including seasonal game, lunchtime and early evening set deals, well kept Marstons-related ales, prompt friendly service, log-fire bar with small dining area off, back lounge; tables on gravelled terrace behind, bedrooms in converted outbuildings, charming village with famous Saxon church, open (and food) all day Sun; for sale so could be changes. *(Gerry and Rosemary Dobson, Mike and Margaret Banks)*

BUGBROOKE
SP6756

Wharf Inn (01604) 832585 *The Wharf; off A5 S of Weedon; NN7 3QB* Well situated McManus pub by Grand Union Canal; large beamed water-view restaurant, tiled and carpeted bar with small informal raised eating area, lots of stripped brickwork, enjoyable food from varied menu (till 7pm Sun), good friendly service, five changing ales and 24 wines by the glass; background music; children and dogs (in bar) welcome, disabled facilities, plenty of tables on big waterside lawn, moorings, open (and food) all day. *(Gerry and Rosemary Dobson)*

CHACOMBE
SP4943

★**George & Dragon** (01295) 711500 *Handy for M40 junction 11, via A361; Silver Street; OX17 2JR* Welcoming pub dating from the 17th c with beams, flagstones, panelling and bare stone walls, two inglenook woodburners and deep glass-covered well, good popular food (not Sun evening) in three dining areas from lunchtime baguettes and traditional choices up, vegetarian options, two-for-one burger deal Mon evening, good service, Everards ales and a guest from brass-topped counter, several wines by the glass and decent coffee; background music (live last Fri of month), charity quiz last Sun; children and dogs (in bar) welcome, picnic-sets on suntrap terrace, pretty village with interesting church, open all day. *(George Atkinson)*

CHAPEL BRAMPTON
SP7366

★**Brampton Halt** (01604) 842676 *Pitsford Road, off A5199 N of Northampton; NN6 8BA* Popular well laid out McManus pub on Northampton & Lamport Railway (which is open some weekends) in much extended former stationmaster's house; large restaurant, railway memorabilia and train theme throughout, wide choice of enjoyable generous food (smaller helpings available) from sandwiches to blackboard specials, meal deal Mon-Thurs, well kept Fullers London Pride, Sharps Doom Bar and four guests (beer festivals), several wines by the glass, cheerful attentive service even when very busy; background music, TV in bar; children welcome, no dogs inside, lots of tables in big garden with awnings and heaters, summer barbecues and maybe marquee, pretty views over small lake, Nene Way walks, open (and food) all day. *(Gerry and Rosemary Dobson, George Atkinson)*

CLIPSTON
SP7181

Bulls Head (01858) 525268 *B4036 S of Market Harborough; LE16 9RT* Welcoming village pub with popular good value food, Everards ales and up to five guests, log fire and heavy beams (coins inserted by World War II airmen); background music, TV, Tues quiz/curry night; children and dogs welcome, terrace tables, three comfortable bedrooms, open all day weekends. *(William Pace)*

COLLINGTREE
SP7555

Wooden Walls of Old England (01604) 760641 *1.2 miles from M1 junction 15; High Street; NN4 0NE* Cosy thatch and stone village pub dating from the 15th c and named as a tribute to the navy; four well kept Marstons-related ales and good choice of wines by the glass, generous helpings of enjoyable home-made food (not Sun evening), friendly staff, beams and open fire; sports TV, table skittles, free wi-fi; big back garden with terrace, open all day Fri-Sun, closed Mon. *(Ian Duncan)*

COLLYWESTON
SK9902

★**Collyweston Slater** (01780) 444288 *The Drove (A43); PE9 3PQ* Roomy 17th-c main road inn with enjoyable generously served pub food (all day Sun when can get very busy), well kept Everards ales and decent wines, friendly service, contemporary interior with brown leather sofas and easy chairs, smart modern two-part dining room and two or three more informal areas, one with a raised stove in dividing wall, beams, stripped stone and mix of dark flagstones, bare boards and carpeting; background music, TV, darts; children welcome, teak furniture on flagstoned terrace, boules, three bedrooms, open all day. *(Terry Davis)*

CRICK   SP5872

★ **Red Lion** (01788) 822342

1 mile from M1 junction 18; in centre of village off A428; NN6 7TX Nicely worn-in stone and thatch coaching inn run by same family since 1979; traditional low-ceilinged bar with lots of old horsebrasses (some rare) and tiny log stove in big inglenook, straightforward low-priced lunchtime food, more elaborate evening menu (not Sun) including popular steaks, plenty for vegetarians too, Adnams Southwold, Greene King Old Speckled Hen, Wells Bombardier and a guest, good friendly service; Sun quiz, free wi-fi; children (under-12s lunchtime only) and dogs welcome, picnic-sets on terrace and in Perspex-covered coachyard with pretty hanging baskets. *(Miles Green)*

DUDDINGTON   SK9800

Royal Oak (01780) 444267

High Street, just off A43; PE9 3QE Stone-built inn on edge of pretty village; modern bar area with leather sofas and chairs on flagstones, panelling and log fire, three Grainstore ales from brick servery, restaurant with stone walls, oak floor and light oak furniture, enjoyable food from pub favourites up including weekday set lunch; background music; children welcome, disabled facilities, tables on small grassy area at front, six bedrooms, open (and food) all day Fri-Sun. *(Patricia Hawkins)*

EAST HADDON   SP6668

★ **Red Lion** (01604) 770223

High Street; village signposted off A428 (turn right in village) and off A50 N of Northampton; NN6 8BU Substantial and elegant golden-stone thatched hotel with sizeable dining room, log-fire lounge and bar, emphasis on well presented imaginative food and most tables set for dining, but they do keep Charles Wells ales in good condition and offer over a dozen wines by the glass, generally efficient friendly service; background music; children welcome, attractive grounds including walled side garden, cookery school, seven comfortable bedrooms and two-bed cottage, good breakfast, closed Sun evening. *(Gerry and Rosemary Dobson)*

EASTON ON THE HILL   TF0104

Blue Bell (01780) 763003

High Street; PE9 3LR Welcoming stone-built village pub with strong italian leaning to menu and staff, good food (not Sun evening, Mon), three changing ales and plenty of wines by the glass, pleasant atmosphere, restaurant; pool and TV in games area, May beer festival; children welcome, picnic-sets in good-sized sheltered garden behind, closed Mon lunchtime. *(Colin McLachlan)*

EASTON ON THE HILL   TF0104

★ **Exeter Arms** (01780) 756321

Stamford Road (A43); PE9 3NS Carefully renovated 18th-c pub with friendly easy-going atmosphere; country-feel bar with cushioned captain's chairs, wall/window seats and copper pans above woodburner, tractor seats by counter serving Grainstore, Oakham and several wines by the glass, good food (not Sun evening) from varied menu, restaurant and airy orangery opening on to sunken terrace; free wi-fi; children and dogs (in bar) welcome, picnic-sets on lawn, light, comfortable bedrooms, open all day from 9am (till 9pm Sun). *(Phoebe Peacock, Caroline Prescott, William Pace)*

ECTON   SP8263

Worlds End (01604) 414521

A4500 Northampton–Wellingborough; NN6 0QN Extended 17th-c roadside inn (sister to the Olde Coach House at Ashby St Ledgers – see Main Entries); contemporary décor in L-shaped bar and dining room down steps, well liked food from ciabattas, sharing boards, pizzas and pubby choices up, good value set menu, Hook Norton, Sharps and often a guest (weekday happy hour 5-7pm), good selection of wines by the glass, friendly service; background music (live Fri); children welcome, no dogs, garden with decked terrace, 20 bedrooms in separate block, open all day (till 9pm Sun). *(Mike and Margaret Banks, George Atkinson, Gerry and Rosemary Dobson)*

EYDON   SP5450

★ **Royal Oak** (01327) 263167

Lime Avenue; village signed off A361 Daventry–Banbury, and from B4525; NN11 3PG Interestingly laid-out 17th-c ironstone dining pub under newish management, some lovely period features including fine flagstone floors and leaded windows, cosy snug in right with cushioned benches built into alcoves, seats in bow window, inglenook log fire, long corridor-like central bar linking three other small characterful rooms, very good well presented food (not Sun evening) from owner-chef, friendly attentive staff; children and dogs welcome, terrace seating (some under cover), open all day. *(David Travis)*

GRAFTON REGIS   SP7546

★ **White Hart** (01908) 542123

A508 S of Northampton; NN12 7SR Thatched roadside dining pub with several linked rooms, good pubby food (not Sun evening) including range of home-made soups and popular well priced Sun roasts (best to book), Greene King ales and Aspall's cider, good wines by the glass, friendly helpful staff coping well when busy, restaurant with open fire and separate menu; background music;

children and dogs welcome (they have a couple of boxers and a parrot), terrace tables and gazebo in good-sized garden, closed Mon. *(Miles Green)*

GREAT BILLING   SP8162
Elwes Arms (01604) 407521
High Street; NN3 9DT Thatched stone-built 16th-c village pub, two bars (steps between), wide choice of good value tasty food (all day weekends) including weekday lunchtime deal, Black Sheep, Wadworths 6X and Shepherd Neame Spitfire, friendly service, pleasant dining room (children allowed); background music, quiz Thurs and Sun, sports TV, darts, free wi-fi; no dogs, garden tables and nice covered decked terrace, play area, open all day Weds-Sun. *(Ian Duncan)*

GREAT CRANSLEY   SP8276
Three Cranes (01536) 790287
Loddington Road; NN14 1PY Small stone-built village pub run by same family for 27 years; small carpeted bar with dining area to right leading to little conservatory, well kept Banks's Bitter and Marstons Pedigree, enjoyable reasonably priced home-made food including monthly themed nights, prompt friendly service; free wi-fi; children welcome, dogs in garden only, closed Mon (except for quiz night first Mon of the month) and weekday lunchtimes. *(Luke Morgan)*

GREAT EVERDON   SP5957
Plough (01327) 361606
Next to church; NN11 3BL Small fairly simple bare-boards pub in tucked-away village; bar with a couple of steps down to lounge/dining area, open fire and woodburner, Greene King IPA, Gun Dog Jack's Spaniels, Sharps Doom Bar and a guest, decent wines, short choice of good reasonably priced lunchtime food cooked by landlady (more substantial meals Fri evening and Sun lunchtime – must book), friendly obliging staff; fortnightly quiz Tues; dogs welcome, some seats out in front, more in spacious garden behind, stables shop (the Furrow) selling old furniture, collectables and plants, good walks nearby, open all day. *(George Atkinson)*

GREENS NORTON   SP6649
Butchers Arms (01327) 350488
High Street; NN12 8BA Comfortable family-run village pub with enjoyable reasonably priced food from sandwiches and pizzas up, lunchtime carvery Weds and Sun, ales including St Austell and Sharps, pleasant chatty staff, games room with pool, darts and skittles; background and some live music, fortnightly quiz Sun; children (till 9pm) and dogs allowed, disabled access, picnic-sets and play area outside, pretty village near Grafton Way walks, closed lunchtimes Mon, Tues. *(George Atkinson)*

HACKLETON   SP8054
White Hart (01604) 870271
B526 SE of Northampton; NN7 2AD Comfortably traditional 18th-c country pub; wide choice of enjoyable food from sandwiches and baked potatoes up, curry night Tues, friendly helpful staff, Fullers London Pride, Greene King IPA and a guest, decent choice of wines and other drinks, flagstoned bar with log fire, dining area up steps, beams, stripped stone and brickwork, illuminated well; background music, TV, pool and hood skittles; supervised children and dogs welcome, disabled access, picnic-sets in sunny garden, open all day, no food Sun evening. *(Miles Green)*

HARRINGTON   SP7780
Tollemache Arms (01536) 711770
High Street; off A508 S of Market Harborough; NN6 9NU Pretty thatched and beamed Tudor pub revamped under new licensees (also have the Red Lion at East Haddon); enjoyable food including sharing boards, pizzas and selection of burgers, Charles Wells ales and a guest, good choice of wines by the glass, cocktails and a local artisan gin, friendly attentive staff; children and dogs (in bar) welcome, back garden with country views, lovely quiet ironstone village, handy for Carpetbagger Aviation Museum, open all day weekends (till 8pm Sun). *(Gerry and Rosemary Dobson, Mike and Margaret Banks)*

HELLIDON   SP5158
Red Lion (01327) 261200
Stockwell Lane, off A425 W of Daventry; NN11 6LG Welcoming wisteria-clad inn on edge of village opposite small green; bar with woodburner, cosy lounge and softly lit low-ceilinged stripped-stone dining area, ample helpings of enjoyable home-made food served by helpful friendly staff including themed nights, four changing ales, hood skittles and pool in back games room; children and dogs welcome, a few picnic-sets on front grass, windmill vineyard and pleasant walks nearby, six bedrooms, open all day weekends. *(David Travis)*

HIGHAM FERRERS   SP9668
Griffin (01933) 312612
High Street; NN10 8BW Welcoming 17th-c pub-restaurant (bigger than it looks) with good food including fresh fish and popular Sun carvery (till 5pm), five well kept rotating ales and good selection of wines and malt whiskies, comfortable front bar with log fire, large back restaurant and dining conservatory, friendly service; free wi-fi; tables on heated terrace, open all day Fri-Sun. *(Dr W I C Clark)*

HINTON-IN-THE-HEDGES   SP5536
Crewe Arms (01280) 705801
Off A43 W of Brackley; NN13 5NF Updated 17th-c stone-built village pub, well

kept ales including Hook Norton, enjoyable
home-made food (not Sun evening) from
bar snacks to specials, good friendly service,
log fire; background music; dogs welcome,
picnic-sets in garden, two comfortable bothy
bedrooms, open all day. *(Tony Rice)*

KETTERING SP8778
Alexandra Arms (01536) 522730
Victoria Street; NN16 0BU Backstreet
real ale pub with up to 14 changing quickly,
hundreds each year, knowledgeable landlord,
basic opened-up bar with pump clips
covering walls and ceiling, back games room
with darts, hood skittles and TV, some snacky
food; quiz night Weds; a couple of picnic-sets
out in front, small beer garden behind, open
all day (from 2pm Mon-Thurs). *(William Pace)*

KILSBY SP5671
★ George (01788) 822229
*2.5 miles from M1 junction 18: A428
towards Daventry, left on to A5 – pub
off on right at roundabout; CV23 8YE*
Popular pub (handy for motorway) with
welcoming relaxed atmosphere; proper
old-fashioned public bar, wood-panelled
lounge with plush banquettes and coal-effect
gas stove opening into smarter comfortably
furnished area, well kept Adnams, Fullers,
Timothy Taylors and a guest, fine range of
malt whiskies, enjoyable good value home-
made food including daily specials, cheerful
staff coping well at busy times; trad jazz
lunch first Sun of month, quiz nights, free-
play pool tables, darts, TV; children welcome
if eating, dogs in bar, garden picnic-sets, six
bedrooms. *(Luke Morgan)*

KISLINGBURY SP6959
Cromwell Cottage (01604) 830288
High Street; NN7 4AG Sizeable recently
redecorated dining pub tucked away near
River Nene; modernised comfortable bar/
lounge with open fire and some beams, civil
war themed pictures, maps and a large mural
on one wall, smart dining room, popular food
(booking advised) from snacks to specials
including weekend brunch from 9am, well
kept changing ales and nice wines, neat
cheerful staff; no dogs, plenty of seats on
paved terrace, open (and food) all day.
(Mike and Margaret Banks, George Atkinson)

KISLINGBURY SP6959
Sun (01604) 833571
*Off A45 W of Northampton; Mill Road;
NN7 4BB* Welcoming thatch and ironstone
village pub popular with locals and visitors
alike; ales such as Greene King, Hoggleys,
St Austell and Sharps, enjoyable fairly
traditional food (not Sun evening) including
Tues pizza night, L-shaped bar/lounge and
small separate dining area; quiz last Sun of
month, sports TV, free wi-fi; children and
dogs welcome, disabled access, a few picnic-
sets out in front, open all day Fri-Sun.
(Miles Green)

LITCHBOROUGH SP6353
Old Red Lion (01327) 830064
*Banbury Road, just off former B4525
Banbury–Northampton; opposite church;
NN12 8JF* Attractive beamed pub owned by
local farming family and doubling as village
shop; four rooms including cosy flagstoned
bar with woodburner in big inglenook, ales
such as Grainstore and Oakham, shortish
choice of generously served food (not Sun
evening, Mon) from sandwiches up, friendly
relaxed atmosphere, barn-conversion
restaurant at back; skittles and pool; children
welcome, popular with walkers, terrace
seating, open all day. *(George Atkinson)*

LITTLE BRINGTON SP6663
★ Saracens Head (01604) 770640
*4.5 miles from M1 junction 16, first
right off A45 to Daventry; also signed
off A428; Main Street; NN7 4HS* Friendly
old village pub with enjoyable fairly priced
food (not Sun evening, Mon) from lunchtime
sandwiches up, well kept Greene King IPA,
Timothy Taylors Landlord and a guest,
several wines by the glass, roomy U-shaped
beamed lounge with woodburner, flagstones,
bare boards and tiled floors, chesterfields
and lots of old prints, book-lined dining room
(proper napkins); gentle background music;
plenty of tables out on gravel/paved area with
country views, walks nearby and handy for
Althorp House and Holdenby House.
*(George Atkinson, Gerry and Rosemary Dobson,
Mike and Margaret Banks)*

LITTLE HARROWDEN SP8671
Lamb (01933) 673300
*Orlingbury Road/Kings Lane – off A509
or A43 S of Kettering; NN9 5BH*
Popular pub in delightful village; split-level
carpeted lounge bar with log fire and brasses
on 17th-c beams, dining area, good promptly
served food, Wells Eagle and a couple of
guests, short sensibly priced wine list, games
bar with darts, hood skittles and machines;
background music, Fri quiz, free wi-fi;
children welcome, small raised terrace and
garden, open all day weekends. *(Tony Rice)*

MOULTON SP7866
Telegraph (01604) 648228
West Street; NN3 7SB Spacious old stone-
built village pub, welcoming and popular,
with good promptly served food (not Sun
evening) from sandwiches and pizzas up, well
kept Fullers, Sharps and a couple of guests,
maybe an interesting craft keg, log fire in bar,
back restaurant extension; children welcome,
open all day Fri-Sun. *(Michael Nicholas)*

NASSINGTON TL0696
Queens Head (01780) 784006
Station Road; PE8 6QB Early 19th-c stone
dining pub in delightful village; softly lit
beamed bar with mix of old tables and chairs
on bare boards, large oriental rug in front of

roaring fire, reasonably priced food from bar snacks to imaginative restaurant dishes using local ingredients, pleasant helpful uniformed staff, nice choice of wines by the glass, ales such as Greene King, Nene Valley and Oakham, afternoon teas, separate restaurant; children welcome, pretty garden by River Nene, narrow entrance to car park can be tricky, ten chalet bedrooms, open all day. *(David Travis)*

NETHER HEYFORD   SP6658
Olde Sun (01327) 340164

1.75 miles from M1 junction 16; village signposted left off A45 westbound; Middle Street; NN7 3LL Popular quirky place with small atmospheric linked rooms, bric-a-brac packed into nooks and crannies and hanging from the ceilings including brassware, 1930s cigarette cards, railway memorabilia, advertising signs and World War II posters, nice old cash till on one of the two counters serving Banks's, Greene King, Marstons and a guest, well priced honest food (not Sun evening), courteous helpful service, beams and low ceilings (one painted with fine sunburst), partly glazed dividing panels, steps between some areas, rugs on parquet, red tiles or flagstones, big inglenook log fire, games room with hood skittles and darts; background music; children and dogs welcome, lots of old farm equipment outside, open all day Fri-Sun. *(Martin Day, John Evans, George Atkinson)*

NORTHAMPTON   SP7560
Albion Brewery Bar (01604) 946606

Kingswell Street; NN1 1PR Tap for the revived 19th-c Albion Brewery (visible through glass partition, tours available); half a dozen Phipps/Hoggleys ales in top condition plus a guest and local cider, also their own Kingswell gin, enjoyable good value food from snacks up, friendly staff, pitched-ceiling bar with big windows and reclaimed fittings (many from closed Phipps pubs), traditional games including Northamptonshire skittles and bar billiards; live music (upstairs concert venue planned); disabled access/loo, open all day Fri, Sat, closed Sun and Mon evenings. *(Richard Kennell)*

NORTHAMPTON   SP7261
Hopping Hare (01604) 580090

Harlestone Road (A428), New Duston; NN5 6PF Spacious Edwardian pub-restaurant-hotel on edge of housing estate; contemporary, stylish and comfortable, with good nicely presented food from lunchtime sandwiches and pub favourites to sharing boards and up-to-date restauranty dishes, well kept Adnams, Black Sheep and a guest, good choice of wines by the glass including champagne, neatly dressed friendly staff; background music, daily newspapers, free wi-fi; tables out on deck, 18 modern bedrooms, open all day, food all day weekends (and weekdays during school summer holidays). *(Gerry and Rosemary Dobson, George Atkinson)*

NORTHAMPTON   SP7560
Lamplighter (01604) 631125

Overstone Road; NN1 3JS Popular Victorian corner pub in the Mounts area, friendly and welcoming, with wide choice of draught and bottled beers, good value generously served food including range of burgers; regular live music, quiz Weds; children welcome if eating, picnic-sets in heated courtyard, open all day (till 1am Fri, Sat). *(Miles Green, Tony Rice)*

NORTHAMPTON   SP7661
Olde England 07742 069768

Kettering Road, near the racecourse; NN1 4BP Quirky conversion of Victorian corner shop over three floors (steepish stairs to upper level and down to cellar bar), ground-floor room with assorted tables and chairs on bare boards, 20 well kept changing ales and similar number of ciders from hatch on stairs, lots of pictures with medieval or Arthurian themes, plus the odd banner, flag and suit of armour, bargain food with more extensive choice at weekends when pub is at its busiest, friendly staff and broad mix of customers; cards and board games, folk music, quiz nights and poetry readings; children and dogs welcome, closed Mon-Fri lunchtimes, otherwise open all day. *(George Atkinson)*

NORTHAMPTON   SP7560
Wig & Pen (01604) 622178

St Giles Street; NN1 1JA Long L-shaped beamed room with bar running most of its length, up to a dozen well kept ales (tasters offered) including Adnams, Fullers and Greene King, traditional ciders and good choice of bottled beers, whiskies and gins, generous servings of enjoyable nicely presented food (not weekend evenings) from sandwiches, tapas and deli boards up, brunch from 10am, friendly young staff; Tues jazz and other live music, sports TVs; split-level walled garden, handy for Guildhall and Derngate Theatre, open all day (till 1.30am Fri, Sat) and busy on Saints rugby days. *(George Atkinson, Dr J Barrie Jones)*

OLD   SP7873
White Horse (01604) 781297

Walgrave Road, N of Northampton between A43 and A508; NN6 9QX Popular and welcoming village pub refurbished under present management, good reasonably priced food from short menu supplemented by some interesting daily specials, three well kept generally local ales, proper ciders and decent wines by the glass, friendly efficient staff; quiz night first Thurs of month, live music last Fri, free wi-fi; well behaved children and dogs welcome, garden and deck overlooking 13th-c church, open all day Sat, till 7pm Sun, closed Mon. *(Gerry and Rosemary Dobson)*

OUNDLE   TL0388
Talbot (01832) 273621
New Street; PE8 4EA Handsome former
merchant's house, now a hotel; various rooms
including comfortably modernised bar, a couple
of real ales such as Black Sheep and Digfield,
enjoyable food from sandwiches and sharing
plates up, good service, restaurant; children
welcome, seats in courtyard and garden,
40 bedrooms, open all day. *(Ross Balaam)*

RAVENSTHORPE   SP6670
Chequers (01604) 770379
Chequers Lane; NN6 8ER Cosy old
creeper-clad brick pub with L-shaped bar
and restaurant, well kept ales including
Oakham, Sharps and Thwaites, good choice
of generous sensibly priced food from light
snacks to steaks and daily specials, friendly
attentive staff, banquettes, cushioned pews
and sturdy tables, coal-effect fire; children
welcome, partly covered side terrace, play
area and separate building for Northants
skittles, handy for Ravensthorpe Reservoir
and Coton Manor Gardens, open all day
weekends. *(George Atkinson)*

RUSHDEN   SP9566
Station Bar (01933) 318988
Station Approach; NN10 0AW Not a pub,
part of station HQ of Rushden Historical
Transport Society (non-members can sign in
for £1); bar in former ladies' waiting room
with gas lighting, enamel signs and railway
memorabilia, seven well kept ales including
Oakham and Phipps, tea and coffee, filled
rolls and perhaps some hot food, friendly
staff; also museum and summer train rides,
table skittles in a Royal Mail carriage;
open all day weekends, closed weekday
lunchtimes. *(Ian Duncan)*

RUSHTON   SP8483
Thornhill Arms (01536) 710251
Station Road; NN14 1RL Rambling
family-run dining pub opposite lovely village's
cricket green, popular food including keenly
priced set menu (weekday evenings, Sat
lunchtime) and carvery (Sun, Mon evening),
gluten-free menu, prompt friendly service, up
to four well kept ales, several neatly laid-out
dining areas including smart high-beamed
back restaurant, open fire; children welcome,
garden with decked area, open all day Sun.
(David Travis)

SLIPTON   SP9579
★ Samuel Pepys (01832) 731739
*Off A6116 at first roundabout N of
A14 junction, towards Twywell and
Slipton; NN14 3AR* Old reworked stone
pub with long modernised bar, heavy low
beams, wood flooring, log fire and great
central pillar, up to four well kept ales
including local Digfield, decent choice of
ciders and wines by the glass, good variety
of popular food including daily specials and

weekday OAP lunch deal, friendly helpful
service, dining room extending into roomy
conservatory with country views; background
music; children and dogs (in bar) welcome,
wheelchair access from car park using ramp,
well laid-out sheltered garden with heated
terrace, open all day weekends (till 7pm Sun
in winter). *(Mike and Margaret Banks, Clive and
Fran Dutson)*

STAVERTON   SP5461
Countryman (01327) 311815
Daventry Road (A425); NN11 6JH
Beamed and carpeted dining pub with
popular food from smallish menu including
some interesting vegetarian options, Great
Oakley, Wells Bombardier and a guest, good
friendly service even when busy, bar divided
by brick pillars, restaurant; background
music; children and dogs (in bar) welcome,
disabled access, some tables out at front and
in small garden behind, open (and food) all
day Sun. *(George Atkinson)*

STOKE BRUERNE   SP7449
Boat (01604) 862428
*3.5 miles from M1 junction 15 – A508
towards Stony Stratford, then signed on
right; Bridge Road; NN12 7SB* Old-world
flagstoned bar in picturesque canalside spot
by lock, half a dozen Marstons-related ales
and maybe a local guest, Thatcher's cider,
enjoyable fairly standard food (not Sun
evening) from baguettes up including deals,
friendly service, more modern central-
pillared back bar and bistro, comfortable
upstairs bookable restaurant with separate
menu, shop for boaters; background music;
children and dogs welcome, disabled
facilities, tables out by towpath opposite
canal museum, trips on own narrowboat,
open all day and can get very busy in summer,
especially weekends when parking nearby
difficult. *(Gerry and Rosemary Dobson)*

STOKE DOYLE   TL0286
★ Shuckburgh Arms (01832) 272339
*Village signed (down Stoke Hill) from
SW edge of Oundle; PE8 5TG* Relaxed
17th-c pub in quiet hamlet; four traditional
rooms with some modern touches, low black
beams in bowed ceilings, pictures on pastel
walls, lots of pale tables on wood or carpeted
floors, stylish art deco seats and elegant
dining chairs, inglenook woodburner, ales
such as Nene Valley and Nobbys from
granite-top bar, well selected wines and good
popular food including two-course deal,
helpful attentive staff; soft background
music; children welcome, garden with decked
area and play frame, bedrooms in separate
modern block, closed Sun evening, Mon.
(Peter Andrews)

SUDBOROUGH   SP9682
Vane Arms (01832) 730033
Off A6116; Main Street; NN14 3BX
Old thatched pub in pretty village, low

beams, stripped stonework and inglenook fires, well kept Everards Tiger and guests, enjoyable freshly cooked food, friendly staff, restaurant; well behaved dogs welcome in bar, disabled access, terrace tables, three bedrooms in nearby building, closed Sun evening. *(Tony Rice)*

SULGRAVE SP5545
★**Star** (01295) 760389
Manor Road; E of Banbury, signed off B4525; OX17 2SA Handsome creeper-clad inn of character; log fire in fine inglenook, working shutters, old doors and flagstones, moss- or plum-coloured walls, mix of antique, vintage and retro furniture, candles and polished copper creating nice old-fashioned feel, Hook Norton, two guest beers and seven wines by the glass, good well presented/priced food with some emphasis on fish, friendly staff, dining room has working range where breakfasts are cooked, snug was the old farmhouse kitchen; children and dogs (in bar) welcome, neat back garden with vine-covered trellis, short walk to Sulgrave Manor (George Washington's ancestral home), four bedrooms, open all day Sat, till 9pm Sun (5pm winter), closed Mon. *(Andrew Stone, George Atkinson)*

THORNBY SP6675
★**Red Lion** (01604) 740238
Welford Road; A5199 Northampton–Leicester; NN6 8SJ Popular old country pub with interesting choice of up to five well kept/priced changing ales, good home-cooked food (not Sun evening, Mon) from standards up including popular steak and stilton pie, smaller helpings available for some dishes, prompt friendly service, beams and log fire, lots of old local photos, back dining area; children and dogs welcome, garden picnic-sets, open all day weekends when can get very busy (booking advised Sat night), closed Mon lunchtime. *(George Atkinson, Gerry and Rosemary Dobson, Mike and Margaret Banks)*

THORPE MANDEVILLE SP5344
★**Three Conies** (01295) 711025
Off B4525 E of Banbury; OX17 2EX Attractive and welcoming 17th-c ironstone pub, well kept Hook Norton ales and good choice of enjoyable locally sourced food (not Sun evening, Mon), beamed bare-boards bar with some stripped stone, mix of old tables and comfortable seating, log fires, large dining room; background music (live Fri), TV, hood skittles; children and dogs welcome, disabled facilities, tables out in front, more behind on decking and lawn, closed Mon lunchtime, otherwise open all day.
(Miles Green)

TOWCESTER SP7047
Folly (01327) 354031
A5 S, opposite racecourse; NN12 6LB Early 18th-c thatched and beamed restauranty pub opposite racecourse; good

food (booking advised) from pub favourites to more expensive restaurant-style dishes, gluten-free menu too, good selection of wines and beer, friendly helpful staff, small bar with steps up to dining area; children welcome till 8pm, picnic-sets outside, open all day Sun till 9pm, closed Mon. *(Mike Kavaney)*

TOWCESTER SP6948
Towcester Mill (01327) 437060
Chantry Lane; NN12 6YY Old mill tucked away behind market square and surrounded by redevelopment; nice little beamed bare-boards bar acting as tap for on-site brewery (tours Mon and Tues evenings – book ahead), seven ales including a couple of guests, also good range of ciders and country wines, friendly knowledgeable staff, fish and chips Thurs evening (pies at other times); shop selling their beers, June and Sept beer/music festivals; walkers and dogs welcome, garden behind with seats by millrace and pond, open all day summer (winter from 5pm Mon-Fri, all day Sat, till 5pm Sun).
(Ian Herdman)

TURWESTON SP6037
Stratton Arms (01280) 704956
E of crossroads in village; pub itself just inside Buckinghamshire; NN13 5JX Friendly chatty local in picturesque village, five well kept ales including Otter and good choice of other drinks, enjoyable reasonably priced traditional food Fri-Sun (not Sun evening), low ceilings and two log fires, small restaurant; background music, sports TV; children and dogs welcome, large pleasant garden by Great Ouse with barbecue and play area, camping, open all day Weds, Fri and Sat, till 8pm other days, closed Tues.
(Ian Duncan)

TWYWELL SP9578
Old Friar (01832) 732625
Lower Street, off A14 W of Thrapston; NN14 3AH Well run popular pub with enjoyable good value food including deals, carvery all day Sun and Tues-Sat evenings, Greene King and a couple of guests, cheerful attentive service, modernised split-level interior with beams and some exposed stonework; children and dogs welcome, garden with good play area, open all day Fri-Sun, food all day weekends including Sat breakfast. *(Mike and Margaret Banks)*

UPPER BODDINGTON SP4853
Plough (01327) 260364
Warwick Road; NN11 6DH Renovated 18th-thatched village inn keeping much of its original character, small beamed and flagstoned bar, lobby with old local photos, Greene King IPA, Shepherd Neame Spitfire and a guest, good value fairly traditional food (curry night Tues) in restaurant, snug or intimate 'Doll's Parlour' named after former veteran landlady, friendly efficient service,

woodburners; quiz first Sun of month,
occasional live music and beer festivals,
free wi-fi; children and dogs welcome, five
bedrooms (some sharing bathroom), usually
closed weekday lunchtimes, open all day
weekends, no food Sun evening, Mon.
(Clive and Fran Dutson)

WADENHOE   TL0183
★ **Kings Head** (01832) 720024
*Church Street; village signposted
(in small print) off A605 S of Oundle;
PE8 5ST* Beautifully placed 17th-c country
pub with picnic-sets on sun terrace and
among trees on grassy stretch by River Nene
(moorings); uncluttered partly stripped-stone
bar with woodburner in fine inglenook, pale
pine furniture and a couple of cushioned
wall seats, simple bare-boards public bar
and attractive little beamed dining room
with more pine furniture, three changing
ales, several wines by the glass and good well
presented food, friendly efficient service,
games room with darts, dominoes and table
skittles; children and dogs welcome, open
all day in summer (otherwise all day Fri,
Sat, till 6pm Sun, closed Mon).
(Edward and William Johnston)

WALGRAVE   SP8072
Royal Oak (01604) 781248
*Zion Hill, off A43 Northampton–
Kettering; NN6 9PN* Welcoming old stone-
built village local, good well presented food
(best to book) including some interesting
specials, very popular two-for-one Tues
evening deal on main courses, well kept
Adnams, Greene King and three guests,
decent wines, friendly prompt service,
long three-part carpeted beamed bar,
small lounge, restaurant extension behind;
children welcome, small garden with play
area, open all day Sun. *(Gerry and Rosemary
Dobson)*

WEEDON   SP6458
★ **Narrow Boat** (01327) 340333
*3.9 miles from M1 junction 16: A45
towards Daventry, left on to A5, pub
then on left after canal, at Stowe Hill –
junction Watling Street/Heyford Lane;
NN7 4RZ* Big draw here is the Grand Union
Canal position – plenty of seats on covered
deck and in garden sloping down to the
water, outside summer bar and children's
play trail; rambling interior with comfortable
dark banquettes and padded chairs around
neat tables, woodburner, a couple of Charles
Wells ales and several wines by the glass,
wide choice of generously served food (all
day weekends), carpeted conservatory with
heavy curtains for cooler nights; background
music; children and dogs (in bar) welcome,
disabled facilities, well equipped comfortable
bedrooms in separate block, open all day.
*(Michael Butler, Mike and Margaret Banks,
Ian Herdman)*

WELFORD   SP6480
Wharf Inn (01858) 575075
*Pub just over Leicestershire border;
NN6 6JQ* Spacious castellated Georgian
folly in delightful setting by two Grand
Union Canal marinas; six well kept ales such
as Grainstore, Marstons, and Oakham in
unpretentious bar, popular reasonably priced
food (all day Sun) including good steak
and kidney pudding and some interesting
specials, efficient enthusiastic service,
pleasant dining section; children and dogs
welcome, wheelchair access using portable
ramps, disabled loo, big waterside garden
and good local walks (leaflet available), open
all day. *(Dennis and Doreen Haward, Simon and
Mandy King, Gerry and Rosemary Dobson)*

WELTON   SP5866
White Horse (01327) 702820
*Off A361/B4036 N of Daventry; behind
church, High Street; NN11 2JP* Beamed
17th-c village pub on different levels, well
kept Adnams, Purity, Oakham and a guest,
local cider and nice house wines, reasonably
priced food (not Sun evening, Mon, Tues)
including good value steak deal, friendly
staff, woodburners, separate games bar
with darts and skittles, small dining room;
fortnightly Sun quiz; children and dogs
welcome in one part, attractive garden and
terrace, open all day Fri-Sun, closed Mon
and Tues lunchtimes. *(Hilary Colpus)*

WHITTLEBURY   SP6943
Fox & Hounds (01327) 858048
High Street; NN12 8XJ Double-fronted
19th-c village bar-restaurant, smartly
refurbished modern interior with wood
flooring and comfy stylish seating, four real
ales including local Gun Dog and one badged
for the pub, good well presented food from
thick-cut sandwiches and sharing boards up,
friendly helpful service; children and dogs
welcome, picnic-sets on suntrap gravelled
terrace, handy for Silverstone, open all day
weekends. *(George Atkinson)*

YARDLEY HASTINGS   SP8656
★ **Rose & Crown** (01604) 696276
*Just off A428 Bedford–Northampton;
NN7 1EX* Spacious and popular 18th-c
dining pub in pretty village; flagstones,
beams, stripped stonework and quiet
corners, step up to big comfortable dining
room, flowers on tables, good well presented
food from interesting daily changing menu
along with bar snacks and pubby choices,
good value set menu too, efficient friendly
young staff, six real ales including a house
beer from local Hart Family, four ciders
and decent range of wines; background and
occasional live music, daily newspapers;
children welcome till 9pm, dogs in bar,
tables under parasols in split-level garden,
boules, open all day (from 5pm Mon).
(Mike and Margaret Banks, S Holder)

Northumbria

BLANCHLAND   NY9650 Map 10

Lord Crewe Arms ★ ♀ 🍺 🛏

(01434) 675469 – www.lordcrewearmsblanchland.co.uk

B6306 S of Hexham; DH8 9SP

Wonderful historic building, with unique Crypt bar, cosy dining rooms and spacious character restaurant; comfortable, well equipped bedrooms

---

The history and tremendous age of this fine old hotel are reason enough to come here. But add to this particularly good food, real ales and a genuine welcome and you have somewhere pretty special. It was built as a guest house in 1235 for the neighbouring Premonstratensian monastery and the architecture is remarkable. The unique Crypt bar is a medieval vaulted room sculpted by thick stone walls, lit by candlelight and with family crests on the ceiling. There are high wooden stools by wall shelves and against the armour-plated counter, cushioned settles and plush stools around a few little tables, with Hadrian Border Tyneside Blonde, Wylam Red Kite and Lord Crewe Brew (named for the pub from Wylam) on handpump, 14 wines by the glass, 30 malt whiskies and a farm cider; darts and board games. One character sitting area has a leather sofa and two big tartan armchairs on flagstones in front of a large open fire, while the grand yet informal restaurant features a fine old wooden floor, cushioned wall seating and leather-cushioned dining chairs around oak-topped tables, fresh flowers, antlers on the walls and a big central candelabra. The bedrooms are lovely. Derwent Reservoir is nearby.

 Inventive and particularly good food includes home-cured smoked salmon, devilled lambs kidneys with roasted cauliflower, creamed local spelt with dippy yolk and chives, roast lamb chump with anchovies and crushed anya potatoes, local fish with brown shrimps, spinach and whipped potatoes, pork rib chop with chorizo, grelot onions and fried potato cake, grilled flatiron steak with peppercorn sauce and fries, and puddings such as raspberry bakewell pudding and treacle tart with stewed gooseberries and clotted cream. *Benchmark main dish: spit-roast whole roast chicken for two with garlic butter and fries £34.00. Two-course evening meal £20.00.*

Free house ~ Licensee Tommy Mark ~ Real ale ~ Open 7.30am-11pm ~ Bar food 12-2.30, 6-9; 12-3, 6-9.30 Sat; 12-3.30, 6.30-8.30 Sun ~ Restaurant ~ Children welcome ~ Dogs allowed in bar and bedrooms ~ Wi-fi ~ Bedrooms: £90/£99 *Recommended by Dr Terry Murphy, Barry Collett, David and Betty Gittins, Comus and Sarah Elliott*

CARTERWAY HEADS

NZ0452 Map 10

Manor House Inn

(01207) 255268 – www.themanorhouseinn.com

A68 just N of B6278, near Derwent Reservoir; DH8 9LX

Handy after a walk, with a traditional bar, comfortable lounge, bar food and five real ales; bedrooms

Our readers enjoy their visits to this friendly country inn where there's always a good mix of customers. Homely and old-fashioned, the locals' bar has an original boarded ceiling, pine tables, chairs and stools, old oak pews and a mahogany counter. The carpeted lounge bar (warmed by a woodburning stove) and restaurant are comfortably pubby with wheelback chairs, stripped-stone walls and picture windows that make the most of the lovely setting. Allendale Pennine Pale, Mordue Five Bridges and a guest beer on handpump, alongside ten wines by the glass, 20 malt whiskies and Weston's Old Rosie cider; darts, board games and background music. Derwent Valley and Reservoir are close by and there are stunning views over the water and beyond from picnic sets on the terrace. The comfortable bedrooms also have fine views.

Rewarding food includes pigeon with black pudding and apple salad and plum reduction, citrus-cured bass with aioli, cheddar and wild garlic soufflé, burger with toppings, onion rings and fries, tuna niçoise salad, lamb rump with creamed mash and madeira jus, venison with wild mushroom, whisky and cream sauce, and puddings such as rosemary pannacotta with citrus sugar and chocolate fondant with salted caramel. *Benchmark main dish: bavette steak with shallot purée, confit shallot and asparagus £18.00. Two-course evening meal £20.00.*

Enterprise ~ Licensee Chris Baxter ~ Real ale ~ Open 12-11 (10.30 Sun) ~ Bar food 12-3, 6-9; 12-4 Sun ~ Restaurant ~ Children welcome ~ Dogs allowed in bar and bedrooms ~ Wi-fi ~ Bedrooms: £60/£85 *Recommended by Adrian Johnson, Lesley and Peter Barrett, Robert Wivell*

COTHERSTONE

NZ0119 Map 10

Fox & Hounds

(01833) 650241 – www.cotherstonefox.co.uk

B6277; DL12 9PF

Bustling inn with cheerful beamed bar, good food and quite a few wines by the glass; bedrooms

This Georgian country inn occupies an attractive spot by the village green and is surrounded by fine walks. The cheerful, simply furnished beamed bar has a partly wooden floor (elsewhere it's carpeted), a good winter log fire, thickly cushioned wall seats and local photographs and country pictures in its various alcoves and recesses. Bitter End Lakeland Best Gold, Black Sheep and a changing guest from Tirril on handpump alongside eight wines by the glass and around 15 malt whiskies from smaller distilleries. Don't be surprised by the unusual loo attendant – an african grey parrot called Reva. There are seats outside on a terrace and quoits.

Tasty food includes smoked salmon, prawn and melon platter, cheese and hazelnut pâté with caramelised onion relish, vegetable bake, steak and black pudding in ale pie, smoked mackerel prawn and salmon fishcake, lambs liver, crispy bacon, mustard mash and gravy, beer-battered fresh haddock and chips, and puddings; you can have takeaway fish and chips on Tues and Fri evenings (6-8.30pm). *Benchmark main dish: chicken filled with local cheese in creamy leek sauce £10.50. Two-course evening meal £16.00.*

Free house ~ Licensee Nichola Swinburn ~ Real ale ~ Open 12-3, 6-11 (10.30 Sun); closed
Mon-Weds lunchtimes Nov-Easter ~ Bar food 12-2, 6-9 ~ Restaurant ~ Children welcome ~
Dogs allowed in bar and bedrooms ~ Wi-fi ~ Bedrooms: £47.50/£80 *Recommended by WAH,
Adrian Johnson, Miles Green, Julian Richardson*

CRASTER
NU2519 Map 10

Jolly Fisherman

(01665) 576461 – www.thejollyfishermancraster.co.uk

Off B1339, NE of Alnwick; NE66 3TR

Stunning views, very good food and plenty of seasonal visitors

The surrounding coastal walks are very much worth exploring – including
one from this well run inn along the cliff to Dunstanburgh Castle (English
Heritage). The bustling bar, full of locals and ramblers, has a winter fire,
leather button-back wall banquettes and upholstered and wooden dining
chairs around hefty tables on bare boards, a few stools scattered here and
there, and photographs and paintings in gilt-edged frames on the walls. Black
Sheep, Mordue Workie Ticket, Timothy Taylors Landlord and a changing
guest on handpump served by friendly staff. From big windows in the
upstairs dining room you look down on the pretty harbour and out to sea.
Seats and tables in the garden have the same outlook – and get snapped up
pretty quickly. They have a couple of fishermen's cottages and an apartment
for rent and have opened a café and gift shop opposite the pub.

 As well as their famous crab sandwiches and crab soup, the enjoyable food
includes potted pheasant with whisky jelly and celeriac rémoulade, creamy moules
marinière, venison, pigeon and pheasant pie, bouillabaisse, organic pork belly with
dauphinoise potatoes, crackling and apple relish, skate wing with brown shrimp, caper
and sage butter, sirloin steak with pink peppercorns, watercress purée and beef dripping
chips, and puddings such as sticky ginger sponge and lemon posset. *Benchmark main
dish: fresh fish board £9.95. Two-course evening meal £20.50.*

Punch ~ Lease David Whitehead ~ Real ale ~ Open 11-11 (midnight Fri); 11am-1am Sat;
12-10.30 Sun ~ Bar food 11-3, 5.30-9; 12-3, 5-9 Sun; not Sun evening in winter ~ Restaurant
~ Children welcome ~ Dogs allowed in bar ~ Wi-fi *Recommended by John and Sylvia Harrop,
Comus and Sarah Elliott, Barry Collett, Pat and Stewart Gordon*

DIPTONMILL
NY9261 Map 10

Dipton Mill Inn ♟ 🍺 £

(01434) 606577 – www.diptonmill.co.uk

S of Hexham; off B6306 at Slaley; NE46 1YA

Own-brew beers, good value bar food and waterside terrace

Tucked away in a little hamlet, this bustling country local is much
loved for its home-brewed ales and tasty, fair-priced food. The neatly
kept snug bar has genuine character, dark ply panelling, low ceilings, red
furnishings, a dark red carpet and two welcoming open fires. All six of the
nicely named beers from the family-owned Hexhamshire Brewery are well
kept on handpump: Blackhall English Stout, Devils Elbow, Devils Water, Old
Humbug, Shire Bitter and Whapweasel. Also, 14 wines by the glass, 21 malt
whiskies, Weston's Old Rosie and a guest cider. The garden is peaceful and
pretty with its sunken crazy-paved terrace by a restored mill stream and
attractive planting; Hexham Racecourse is not far away and there are nice
woodland walks nearby.

Amazing value food includes sandwiches, chicken liver pâté, smoked salmon and prawns, mince and dumplings, cheese and onion flan, lambs liver and sausages, chicken with sherry sauce, haddock with tomato and basil, lamb steak in wine with mustard, and puddings such as syrup sponge and apple crumble. *Benchmark main dish: steak pie £7.50. Two-course evening meal £11.00.*

Own brew ~ Licensee Mark Brooker ~ Real ale ~ No credit cards ~ Open 12-2.30, 6-11; 12-3 Sun ~ Bar food 12-2, 6.30-8.30; 12-2 Sun ~ Children welcome ~ Wi-fi
Recommended by Comus and Sarah Elliott, Martinthehills, Stephen Woad

DURHAM
NZ2742   Map 10

Victoria 🍺

(0191) 386 5269 – www.victoriainn-durhamcity.co.uk
Hallgarth Street (A177, near Dunelm House); DH1 3AS

Unchanging and neatly kept Victorian pub with royal memorabilia, cheerful locals and well kept regional ales; bedrooms

This little gem with its long-serving owners remains as charmingly unspoilt and immaculately kept as ever. The layout is original and the décor Victorian and three small rooms lead off a central bar: mahogany, etched and cut glass and mirrors, colourful William Morris wallpaper over a high panelled dado, some maroon plush seats in little booths, leatherette wall seats and long narrow drinkers' tables. Also, coal fires in handsome iron and tile fireplaces, photographs and articles showing a real pride in the pub, lots of period prints and engravings of Queen Victoria, and staffordshire figurines of her and the Prince Consort. Big Lamp Bitter, Durham White Gold, Saltaire Chocolate Stout, Wylam Gold Tankard and York Otherside IPA on handpump, over 35 irish whiskeys, 50 scottish malts and cheap house wines; dominoes. Credit cards are accepted only for accommodation. No food.

Free house ~ Licensee Michael Webster ~ Real ale ~ No credit cards ~ Open 11.45-11; 12-2, 7-10.30 Sun ~ Children welcome ~ Dogs welcome ~ Bedrooms: £60/£83
Recommended by Denis and Margaret Kilner, Colin and Daniel Gibbs, Andrew Stone

ELLINGHAM
NU1625   Map 10

Pack Horse 🛏

(01665) 589292 – www.packhorseinn-ellingham.co.uk
Signed off A1 N of Alnwick; NE67 5HA

Stone-built inn with attractive rooms, good food, friendly staff and pretty garden; bedrooms

This is a delightful little pub in a peaceful village and the pretty bedrooms make a good base for exploring the lovely coastline and nearby castles. The flagstoned bar has masses of jugs hanging from beams, a long settle and upholstered stools around pubby tables, a log fire and tall stools against the counter where friendly staff serve Black Sheep and Timothy Taylors Landlord on handpump; background music. The snug has a woodburning stove in a big stone fireplace with a stag's head above and captain's chairs and other seats on bare floorboards. The restaurant is divided into two with high-backed black leather chairs around pale tables on tartan carpet. As well as picnic-sets in the enclosed garden, there's an area where they grow their own vegetables for use in the pub kitchen.

 Very good food includes sandwiches, thai beef salad, ham hock terrine with parma ham, egg and apple sauce, prawn, chorizo and tomato tagliatelle, beer-battered haddock and chips, duck pie, bass with vegetable stir-fry, tempura prawn and sweet chilli sauce, pork belly with black pudding fritter, roast lamb with thyme and garlic, scallops and port sauce, and puddings such as chocolate brownie sundae and vanilla crème brûlée. *Benchmark main dish: slow-cooked beef in bourguignon sauce £12.95. Two-course evening meal £20.00.*

Free house ~ Licensee Oliver Simpson ~ Real ale ~ Open 12-2, 6-11; 12-3, 7-10 Sun; closed first two weeks Feb ~ Bar food 12-2, 6-9 (8.30 in winter); 12-3 Sun ~ Restaurant ~ Children welcome ~ Dogs allowed in bar and bedrooms ~ Wi-fi ~ Bedrooms: £60/£80 *Recommended by Claire Adams, Nigel Havers, David Travis*

GILSLAND   NY6366 Map 10
Samson

(016977) 47880 – www.thesamson.co.uk
B6318, E end of village; CA8 7DR

Friendly village pub in wonderful countryside, cheerful atmosphere in cosy bar, local ales and enjoyable food; bedrooms

Our readers have been quick to voice their enthusiasm for this charming little pub – on all aspects. The cosy bar has a chatty, easy-going atmosphere, red-patterned carpeting, swagged curtains, woodburning stoves, cushioned settles, traditional chairs and stools around sewing machine-treadle and other pubby tables and plush stools at the carved wooden counter. Allendale Pennine Pale and a guest from Hesket Newmarket on handpump and several wines by the glass served by friendly staff; throughout the year they hold quiz nights, themed evenings and live music events. In the dining room are beige tartan-upholstered chairs around white-clothed tables on wide floorboards and prints on red or yellow walls. There are picnic-sets on the back lawn. Bedrooms are warm and attractive and make a good base for exploring nearby Hadrian's Wall – and Hadrian's Wall National Trail and Cycleway is close by as well. They also run Willowford Farm B&B just outside the village.

They use their own lamb and other organic local produce for the pleasing food: smoked salmon mousse, pork belly bite with black pudding, crackling and apple sauce, tomato risotto with crispy halloumi and basil dressing, local sausages on mash with caramelised onion gravy, mackerel fillet in tomato, red pepper and black olive sauce, shepherd's pie, hoisin chicken with stir-fried vegetables and noodles, and puddings such as elderflower pannacotta and chocolate orange sponge with chocolate orange sauce and madagascan vanilla ice-cream. *Benchmark main dish: rare-breed beef burger with toppings, smoky relish and chips £11.95. Two-course evening meal £19.50.*

Free house ~ Licensees Liam McNulty and Lauren Harrison ~ Real ale ~ Open 12-10.30 ~ Bar food 12-2.30, 6-8.30 ~ Children welcome ~ Dogs allowed in bar ~ Wi-fi ~ Acoustic night second Sun of month ~ Bedrooms: £60/£80 *Recommended by Carol and Barry Craddock, Caroline Prescott, Michael Doswell, Comus and Sarah Elliott*

HEDLEY ON THE HILL   NZ0759 Map 10
Feathers 🏮 ⚲ 🍺

(01661) 843607 – www.thefeathers.net
Village signposted from New Ridley, which is signposted from B6309 N of Consett; OS Sheet 88 map reference 078592; NE43 7SW

Northumbria Dining Pub of the Year

Imaginative food, interesting beers from small breweries and friendly welcome in quaint tavern

There's always something going on in this bustling hilltop pub – anything from piano lessons to a knitting club to star gazing – and the hands-on, friendly licensees offer a genuine welcome to all. The two neat, homely bars are properly pubby, with open fires, tankard-hung beams, stripped stonework, solid furniture including settles, and old black and white photographs of local places and farm and country workers. Quickly changing beers include Mordue Workie Ticket and guests such as Consett Ale Works Red Dust, Fullers London Pride, Hadrian Border Gladiator Bitter, Northumberland Pit Pony, Orkney Red MacGregor and Wylam Northern Kite on handpump, as well as six farm ciders, 28 wines by the glass and 33 malt whiskies. They hold an Easter beer/food festival with a barrel race, a farmers' market and a barbecue; darts and dominoes. The picnic-sets in front are a nice place to sit and watch the world drift by.

Using local, seasonal and carefully sourced produce and baking bread daily, the delicious food includes home-made black pudding with poached duck egg and devilled gravy, kipper and whisky pâté with toast, local sausages with real ale gravy, roast butternut squash risotto with cheese and hazelnuts, cod with braised fennel and saffron velouté, dry-cured bacon chop with broad beans and peas and gooseberry ketchup, ox cheek in stout with malted onions and salsify, and puddings such as dark chocolate torte with chocolate sauce and steamed marmalade pudding with custard. *Benchmark main dish: roast haunch of roe deer £16.00. Two-course evening meal £21.00.*

Free house ~ Licensees Rhian Cradock and Helen Greer ~ Real ale ~ Open 6-11 Mon-Weds; 12-11 Thurs-Sat; 12-10.30 Sun; closed Mon-Weds lunchtimes; closed first two weeks Jan ~ Bar food 6-8.30 Weds; 12-2.30, 6-8.30 Thurs-Sat; 12-4.30 Sun; no food Mon, Tues ~ Children welcome ~ Wi-fi ~ Live local folk music monthly Sun evening *Recommended by Peter and Eleanor Kenyon, Comus and Sarah Elliott, Dr Simon Innes, Claire Adams*

MICKLETON
Crown 🍺

NY9724 Map 10

(01833) 640381 – www.thecrownatmickleton.co.uk
B6277; DL12 0JZ

Bustling, friendly pub with hands-on owners, an easy-going atmosphere in connected rooms and seats in garden

Set in lovely countryside, this well run pub has a good mix of both locals and visitors and a warm welcome is offered to all by the friendly family in charge. The simply furnished bars and dining areas have a mix of cushioned settles, upholstered, leather and wooden dining chairs around all sorts of tables on polished floorboards, country prints and photographs on the walls and a woodburning stove flanked by two leather armchairs. Stools line the bar counter where they keep Jennings Bitter, Banks's Bitter and local guests such as Pennine Hair of the Dog and Sonnet 43 Steam Beer Amber Ale on handpump, and good wines by the glass. There are rustic picnic-sets in the front garden with fine views. They have two self-catering properties for rent and a campsite.

Reliably good food includes sandwiches, Morecambe Bay brown shrimps with spiced butter, creamy garlic mushrooms, steak burger with toppings, onion rings, sauce and chips, pulled pork with red slaw and skinny fries, moules frites, chicken ballotine with black pudding, carrot purée and merlot and bacon jus, portuguese fish stew, and puddings such as chocolate pot with honeycomb and caramel latte ice-cream and rhubarb pavlova with poached rhubarb and rhubarb gel. *Benchmark main dish: twice-cooked rare-breed steak with creamy peppercorn sauce and chips £16.95. Two-course evening meal £18.00.*

Free house ~ Licensee Joyce Rowbotham ~ Real ale ~ Open 12-midnight; 12-9 Sun ~
Bar food 12-9; 12-6 Sun ~ Children welcome ~ Dogs welcome ~ Wi-fi ~ Bedrooms: /£75
Recommended by Gerry Price, Lesley and Peter Barrett, Michael Doswell

NEWTON NZ0364 Map 10
Duke of Wellington 🏅 ♀ 🍺 🛏

(01661) 844446 – www.thedukeofwellingtoninn.co.uk
Off A69 E of Corbridge; NE43 7UL

**Big stone pub with modern and traditional furnishings, five real ales,
good wines by the glass and highly thought-of food; bedrooms**

Our readers stay in the comfortable, well equipped bedrooms of this
welcoming inn regularly – and very much enjoy the food and ales too.
The bustling bar has leather chesterfields, built-in cushioned wall seats,
farmhouse chairs and tables on honey-coloured flagstones, a woodburning
stove with a shelf of books to one side, and rustic stools against the counter
where they keep Greene King Old Speckled Hen and Hadrian Border
Tyneside Blonde with guests from local breweries such as Anarchy, Mordue
and Wylam on handpump, a dozen wines by the glass and 12 malt whiskies;
TV, darts, dominoes and daily papers. The L-shaped restaurant has elegant
tartan and wood dining chairs around pale tables on bare boards, modern
art on exposed stone walls, and french windows that lead out to the terrace.
Paintwork throughout is contemporary. Seats on the back terrace have lovely
views across the Tyne Valley. They hold regular wine-tasting evenings and
quiz and music nights.

As well as breakfasts for non-residents (8-10am), the impressive all-day food
includes tempura king prawns with mussel popcorn, scampi tail with fennel and
compressed apple, twice-baked chilli cheese soufflé with parmesan cream, vegetable
gallette with wild mushroom forestière, sweet potato purée, tomato fondue and herb oil,
confit chicken and chestnut mushroom pie, burger with toppings, onion rings, coleslaw
and fries, sea bream with soused mackerel, samphire, saffron potatoes and black
grape sauce, and puddings such as grenadine roast rhubarb with ginger mousse, crème
pâtissière and double ginger ice-cream and peanut butter cheesecake with raspberry
jelly and peanut butter-filled macaroons; they also offer a two- and three-course set
menu (12-6pm). *Benchmark main dish: best end of lamb with confit shoulder,
haggis-stuffed shoulder, dauphinoise potatoes and red wine jus £21.95. Two-course
evening meal £23.00.*

Free house ~ Licensee Rob Harris ~ Real ale ~ Open 11-11 ~ Bar food 12-9; 12-6
(5 in winter) Sun ~ Restaurant ~ Children welcome ~ Dogs allowed in bar ~ Wi-fi ~
Bedrooms: £95/£120 *Recommended by Pat and Stewart Gordon, Comus and Sarah Elliott,
Katherine Matthews, Lionel Smith*

NEWTON-BY-THE-SEA NU2424 Map 10
Ship 🍺

(01665) 576262 – www.shipinnnewton.co.uk
Low Newton-by-the-Sea, signed off B1339 N of Alnwick; NE66 3EL

**In a charming square of fishermen's cottages with good simple food
and own-brew beers; best to check winter opening times**

You can walk along the massive stretch of empty, beautiful beach with
views all the way to Dunstanburgh Castle from this row of converted
fishermen's cottages; tables outside the pub look across the sloping village
green and down to the sea. Their own-brew ales on handpump remain a big
draw as well; these usually include five at any one time from a choice of

26 – maybe Ship Inn Dolly Daydream, Hop Monster, Red Herring, Sandcastles at Dawn and Squid Ink. The plainly furnished but cosy bare-boards bar on the right has nautical charts on dark pink walls, while another simple room on the left has beams, hop bines, some bright modern pictures on stripped-stone walls and a woodburning stove in a stone fireplace; darts, dominoes. It can get extremely busy at peak times, so it's best to book in advance – and there might be a queue for the bar. No nearby parking from May to September, but there's a car park up the hill.

Using local, seasonal produce the well regarded food includes lunchtime sandwiches, stotties and ciabattas, kipper pâté, grilled halloumi with basil, roasted peppers and tomatoes, roasted vegetable, olive and brie tart, slow-roasted pork belly with salt and pepper kale, haddock fillet with salsa verde and herb butter, rib-eye steak with onion marmalade and horseradish, and puddings such as apple crumble and lemon tart. *Benchmark main dish: crab salad £17.95. Two-course evening meal £22.00.*

Own brew ~ Licensee Christine Forsyth ~ Real ale ~ Open 11-11; 12-10 Sun; check website or phone for winter variations ~ Bar food 12-2.30, 7-8; not Sun-Tues evenings ~ Children welcome ~ Dogs welcome ~ Wi-fi ~ Live folk last Mon of month, other live music last Sun of month *Recommended by Comus and Sarah Elliott, Noel and Judy Garner*

NORTH SHIELDS
NZ3668 Map 10

Staith House 🎯 ♀

(0191) 270 8441 – www.thestaithhouse.co.uk
Fish Quay/Union Road; NE30 1JA

**Smashing food and real ales in refurbished dining pub
with friendly staff and seats outside**

Although most customers are here for the particularly good food, you will find Caledonian Deuchars IPA, Robinsons Dizzy Blonde and Theakstons Lightfoot Bitter on handpump and ten wines by the glass, served by enthusiastic staff. The attractive interior blends stripped wood, brickwork and stone with upholstered armchairs and dining chairs, captain's chairs and tartan wall seating, a medley of wooden tables and slate flooring and bare boards; to one end are some high bar chairs around equally high tables. Above the white woodburning stove are candles on a big mantlebeam and a large, rustic mirror, while the walls have ships' lamps and old photographs of the Tyne. Picnic-sets and solid benches and tables sit on side terraces and the hanging baskets look pretty against the blue-painted pub walls.

Cooked by the landlord (a former *MasterChef* finalist), the sensibly short choice of first class food includes chorizo scotch egg with aioli, tongue and cheek terrine with horseradish and pickled onions, steak and kidney casserole with root vegetable mash and crispy onions, stone bass fillet with oyster mayonnaise, roasted cucumber and wasabi beurre blanc, lamb rump with ewe's milk curd, samphire and spinach, and puddings such as dark chocolate and peanut butter terrine with caramelised walnut ice-cream and sticky toffee pudding with caramel sauce. *Benchmark main dish: seared bass with black pudding, chorizo and seaweed butter £19.00. Two-course evening meal £22.00.*

Free house ~ Licensee John Calton ~ Real ale ~ Open 12-10; 12-11.30 Sat; 12-9 Sun ~ Bar food 12-3, 6-9 (9.30 Sat); 12-4.30 Sun ~ Children welcome ~ Dogs allowed in bar ~ Wi-fi ~ Live music Sun 3pm *Recommended by Comus and Sarah Elliott, Peter Pilbeam, Patricia Hawkins*

Anyone claiming to arrange, or prevent, inclusion of a pub in the *Guide* is a fraud. Pubs are included only if recommended by readers and if our own anonymous inspection confirms that they are suitable.

ROMALDKIRK
NY9922 Map 10

Rose & Crown ★ 🍴 ⚲ 🛏

(01833) 650213 – www.rose-and-crown.co.uk

Just off B6277; DL12 9EB

Handsome old inn with accomplished cooking, attentive service and a fine choice of drinks; bedrooms

The comfortable bedrooms (in the main building of this 18th-c inn, the courtyard or Monk's Cottage) make a civilised base for the area, and breakfasts are highly thought-of. The beamed bar area has lots of brass and copper, old-fashioned seats facing a warming log fire, a Jacobean oak settle, a grandfather clock, and old farm tools and black and white pictures of Romaldkirk on the walls. Black Sheep and Thwaites Wainwright on handpump, 11 wines by the glass and 20 malt whiskies. The hall has wine maps and other interesting prints, a cosy little snug has sofas and armchairs by a woodburning stove and there's an oak-panelled restaurant. Picnic-sets line the front terrace. The village church is interesting and the exceptional Bowes Museum and High Force waterfall are nearby; the owners provide an in-house guide for days out in the area, and a *Walking in Teesdale* book.

 Imaginative food includes honey-glazed goats cheese with beetroot, apple, hazelnuts and gingerbread, king scallops with carrot purée, curry emulsion, cured pork fat and coriander, steak in ale pie, wild mushroom and cheese wellington with roasted vegetables and red wine sauce, salmon with seared langoustine, smoked champ potato, roasted cauliflower and white wine sauce, pork shoulder wrapped in parma ham with pork sausages, baked apple, sautéed potatoes and port jus, and puddings such as white chocolate pannacotta with passion fruit and sticky toffee pudding with toffee sauce. *Benchmark main dish: lamb loin with crispy belly, artichoke, beetroot, mint and redcurrant jus £19.00. Two-course evening meal £24.00.*

Free house ~ Licensee Cheryl Robinson ~ Real ale ~ Open 11-11 ~ Bar food 12-2.30, 6.30-9 ~ Restaurant ~ Children welcome but under-8s must leave by 8pm ~ Dogs allowed in bar and bedrooms ~ Wi-fi ~ Bedrooms: £110/£135 *Recommended by WAH, Gerry Price, Mark Hamill, Julie Swift*

SEAHOUSES
NU2232 Map 10

Olde Ship ★ 🍺 £ 🛏

(01665) 720200 – www.seahouses.co.uk

Just off B1340, towards harbour; NE68 7RD

Lots of atmosphere and maritime memorabilia in busy little inn; views across harbour to Farne Islands; bedrooms

There's always a cheerful, bustling atmosphere in this harbourside inn, which was first licensed in 1812 to serve the herring fishermen – the same friendly family have owned it since then. The old-fashioned bar has a rich assemblage of nautical bits and pieces, and even the floor is made of scrubbed ship's decking: lots of shiny brass fittings, ship's instruments and equipment, a knotted anchor made by local fishermen and sea pictures and model ships (including fine ones of the North Sunderland lifeboat and the Seahouses' Grace Darling lifeboat). There's also a model of the Forfarshire, the paddle steamer that local heroine Grace Darling went to rescue in 1838 (you can read more of the story in the pub), and even the ship's nameboard. An anemometer takes wind-speed readings from the top of the chimney. It's all gently lit by stained-glass sea-picture windows, lantern lights and a winter open fire. Simple furnishings include built-in leatherette pews around one end, stools and cast-iron tables. Black Sheep, Greene King Old

Speckled Hen, Hadrian Border Farne Island and Theakstons Best Bitter on handpump (summer guests too), a good wine list and several malt whiskies; background music and TV. The battlemented side terrace (you'll also find fishing memorabilia out here) and one window in the sun lounge look across the harbour to the Farne Islands; if you find yourself here as dusk falls, the light of the Longstones lighthouse shining across the fading evening sky is a charming sight. The pub is not really suitable for children – though there is a little family room, and children are welcome (as are walkers) on the terrace. You can book boat trips to the Farne Islands at the harbour, and there are bracing coastal walks, notably to Bamburgh, Grace Darling's birthplace.

The sensibly short menu includes sandwiches and panini, duck and orange pâté, salt and pepper squid with garlic mayonnaise, vegetable lasagne, rack of barbecue baby pork ribs with chips, bass fillet with mediterranean tomato sauce, chicken breast stuffed with apple, apricot and raisins wrapped in bacon with creamy brandy sauce, fresh crab salad, and puddings such as golden sponge and apple and blackberry pie. *Benchmark main dish: smoked fish chowder £10.50. Two-course evening meal £16.00.*

Free house ~ Licensees Judith Glen and David Swan ~ Real ale ~ Open 11-11; 12-11 Sun ~ Bar food 12-2.30, 7-8.30 ~ Restaurant ~ Children allowed in lounge and dining room if eating, but must be over 10 if staying ~ Wi-fi ~ Bedrooms: £47/£94 *Recommended by Peter Smith and Judith Brown, Comus and Sarah Elliott, Noel and Judy Garner, John and Sylvia Harrop*

STANNERSBURN
NY7286 Map 10

Pheasant £ ⇔

(01434) 240382 – www.thepheasantinn.com
Kielder Water road signposted off B6320 in Bellingham; NE48 1DD

Friendly village inn with quite a mix of customers, homely bar food and streamside garden; bedrooms

'Delightful' and 'charming' are words used by our readers to describe this family-run inn. It's been gently redecorated and updated since the last edition of the *Guide*, but the low-beamed lounge still has ranks of old local photographs on stripped stone and panelling, brightly polished surfaces, shiny brasses, dark wooden pubby tables and chairs and upholstered stools ranged along the counter; there are several open fires. The separate public bar is simpler and opens into another snug seating area with beams and panelling. The friendly licensees and courteous staff serve Timothy Taylors Landlord and a changing guest from Wylam on handpump, wines by the glass, 38 malt whiskies and a couple of farm ciders. There are picnic-sets in the streamside garden, and a pony paddock too. Staying overnight in the comfortable and well equipped courtyard bedrooms gives you time to explore the beautiful surrounding countryside, and they've now got a self-catering cottage; Kielder Water is nearby.

Tasty food includes sandwiches, ham hock terrine with chutney, twice-baked cheese soufflé, spinach and ricotta cannelloni, home-cooked ham salad with new potatoes, crisp haddock fillets with chips, salmon with hot pepper marmalade and crème fraîche, chicken with tomato, garlic and basil sauce on tagliatelle with parmesan, steak and kidney or game pie, and puddings such as lemon cheesecake and brioche bread and butter pudding with cream. *Benchmark main dish: slow-roast local lamb with rosemary and redcurrant jus £14.25. Two-course evening meal £20.50.*

Free house ~ Licensees Walter and Robin Kershaw ~ Real ale ~ Open 12-3, 6-11; closed Mon, Tues Nov-Mar ~ Bar food 12-2.30, 6-8.30 ~ Restaurant ~ Children welcome ~ Dogs allowed in bedrooms ~ Wi-fi ~ Bedrooms: £70/£99 *Recommended by Michael Doswell, John Poulter, Comus and Sarah Elliott, Peter Smith and Judith Brown*

STANNINGTON
GOOD PUB GUIDE
St Marys Inn ⏛ 🛏

NZ1881   Map 10

(01670) 293293 – www.stmarysinn.co.uk

*Turn left in Stannington village and past the church, follow Green Lane
to St Marys Lane; NE61 6BL*

**Interesting old building with woodburning stoves in bar and dining
rooms, original and modern features blending well, thoughtful drinks
and enjoyable food; bedrooms**

Once part of a former Victorian asylum, this red-brick, gabled building
with a clock tower has been carefully refurbished recently. Although it's
a big place with a series of connected rooms (each with individual character
and plenty of cosy corners), the bar remains at the heart of all activity. It's
here that regulars (and a dog or two) feel at home with daily papers, board
games, seats by a woodburning stove and stools against the long oak-topped
bar where friendly staff serve St Mary's Ale (from Wylam) and guests such as
Anarchy Blonde Star and Timothy Taylors Landlord on handpump, 15 wines
by the glass and 50 malt whiskies. Several dining rooms have contemporary
paintwork or flowery wallpaper, all sorts of wooden or leather dining chairs
and long cushioned settles around tables of varying size on parquet flooring,
more woodburning stoves, brightly coloured blinds, and copper kettles and
pans and interesting artwork. The courtyard garden has modern seats and
tables. Bedrooms are light, modern and comfortable and breakfasts are
generous. The inn is handy for the A1.

 A wide choice of food includes sandwiches, moules marinière, lamb koftas with
harissa and flatbread, chicken caesar salad, rare-breed sausages with roast baby
shallots and gravy, vegetable and lentil curry with smoked yoghurt and lime pickle,
venison haunch with beetroot, redcurrants and kale, corn-fed chicken with black
truffle emulsion, and puddings such as caramel tart with glazed banana and cream
cheese ice-cream and sticky toffee pudding; they also offer breakfast and afternoon
tea. *Benchmark main dish: beer-battered cod and chips £13.50. Two-course evening
meal £21.00.*

Free house ~ Licensee Scott Davidson ~ Real ale ~ Open 7am-11pm ~ Bar food 10-9.30;
12-8 Sun ~ Restaurant ~ Children welcome ~ Dogs allowed in bar and bedrooms ~ Wi-fi ~
Bedrooms: $80/$100 *Recommended by Comus and Sarah Elliott, Tim and Sarah Smythe-Brown,
Michael Doswell*

WARK
GOOD PUB GUIDE
Battlesteads 🍺 🛏

NY8676   Map 10

(01434) 230209 – www.battlesteads.com

B6320 N of Hexham; NE48 3LS

**Eco pub with good local ales, fair value interesting food and
a relaxed atmosphere; comfortable bedrooms**

The nicely restored carpeted bar of this pretty pub has a woodburning
stove with a traditional oak surround, low beams, comfortable seats
including some deep leather sofas and easy chairs, and old *Punch* country
life cartoons on the terracotta walls above a dark dado. As well as 13
wines by the glass, 20 malt whiskies and a farm cider, they keep four good
changing local ales such as Durham Magus, Hadrian Border Secret Kingdom,
High House Farm Nels Best and Sonnet 43 India Pale Ale on handpump at
the heavily carved dark oak bar counter; service is excellent. Background
music and TV. There's also a restaurant, a spacious conservatory and tables
on the terrace. Some of the ground-floor bedrooms have disabled access,

and they're licensed to hold civil marriages. The owners are extremely conscientious about the environment and gently weave their beliefs into every aspect of the business. They grow their own produce, have a charging point in the car park for electric cars and use a biomass boiler.

Using their own and other carefully sourced produce, the food includes sandwiches, rabbit rillettes with jerusalem artichoke, pork belly and prune terrine with beetroot chutney, baby leek and smoked brie pie, venison chilli with home-made nachos, dry-cured gammon with free-range egg and pease pudding, halibut with wild mushrooms, charred cucumber and brown shrimps, lamb cutlet with mini shepherd's pie and pressed rump, and puddings such as chocolate brownie with warm chocolate sauce and treacle tart with rhubarb compote. *Benchmark main dish: cajun chicken with prawns, bacon, cream and sautéed potatoes £11.75. Two-course evening meal £22.00.*

Free house ~ Licensees Richard and Dee Slade ~ Real ale ~ Open 11-11 ~ Bar food 12-3, 6.30-9 ~ Restaurant ~ Children welcome ~ Dogs allowed in bar and bedrooms ~ Wi-fi ~ Bedrooms: £70/£115 *Recommended by John and Sylvia Harrop, Comus and Sarah Elliott, Mark Hamill, R L Borthwick, Peter Smith and Judith Brown*

THE GOOD PUB GUIDE

WINSTON

NZ1416 Map 10

Bridgewater Arms

(01325) 730302 – www.thebridgewaterarms.com

B6274, just off A67 Darlington–Barnard Castle; DL2 3RN

Carefully renovated former schoolhouse with quite a choice of appealing food, three real ales and seats outside

A good mix of both drinkers and diners gather in this carefully converted Victorian schoolhouse and the atmosphere is informal and friendly. The high-ceilinged bar has an open log fire, cushioned settles and chairs, a wall lined with bookcases, and high chairs against the counter where they keep Jennings Cumberland, Marstons Pedigree and Rudgate Jorvik Blonde on handpump, a dozen wines by the glass and 12 malt whiskies. The two rooms of the restaurant have high-backed black leather dining chairs around clothed tables on stripped wooden flooring or tartan carpet, wine bottles lining a delft shelf and various prints and pictures on pale yellow walls. There are some picnic-sets at the front and the fine old bridge across the River Tees is just a stroll away.

Fish and shellfish plays a big part in the food here: crab, langoustine and spring onion thermidor, creamy moules marinière, bass and king scallops on stir-fried greens with lime crème fraîche and sweet chilli sauce, and grilled seafood platter; they also have partridge breast, confit leg, bacon and foie gras, venison loin with wild mushrooms, pancetta and heritage carrots, sirloin steak with peppercorn sauce and chips, and puddings such as chocolate pudding with chocolate sauce and Armagnac-soaked prune frangipane tart with salted caramel ice-cream. *Benchmark main dish: john dory fillets on seafood and saffron risotto with samphire £24.00. Two-course evening meal £23.00.*

Free house ~ Licensee Paul Grundy ~ Real ale ~ Open 12-3.30, 6-11; closed Sun, Mon ~ Bar food 12-2, 6-9 ~ Restaurant ~ Well behaved children welcome ~ Wi-fi *Recommended by Isobel Mackinlay, Edward May, Edward and William Johnston, Dave Sutton*

Please tell us if the décor, atmosphere, food or drink at a pub is different from our description. We rely on readers' reports to keep us up to date: feedback@goodguides.com, or (no stamp needed) The Good Pub Guide, FREEPOST RTJR-ZCYZ-RJZT, Perrymans Lane, Etchingham TN19 7DN.

Also Worth a Visit in Northumbria

Besides the fully inspected pubs, you might like to try these pubs that have been recommended to us and described by readers. Do tell us what you think of them: feedback@goodguides.com

---

ACOMB   NY9366

Miners Arms (01434) 603909

Main Street; NE46 4PW Friendly little 18th-c village pub with good value traditional food (not Sun evening, Mon) including popular Sun roasts, Wylam, Yates and guests, comfortable settles in carpeted bar, huge fire in stone fireplace, back dining area; folk night first Mon of month, quiz last Thurs; children and dogs welcome, a couple of tables out in front, more in back courtyard, open all day weekends, closed weekday lunchtimes. *(Andrew Stone)*

ALLENDALE   NY8355

Golden Lion (01434) 683225

Market Place; NE47 9BD Friendly 18th-c two-room pub with enjoyable good value traditional food, well kept Wylam, Timothy Taylors and three guests, games area with pool and darts, upstairs weekend restaurant; occasional live music; children and dogs welcome, Allendale Fair first weekend June, New Year's Eve flaming barrel procession, open all day (till late Fri, Sat). *(Comus and Sarah Elliott)*

ALNMOUTH   NU2410

★ **Red Lion** (01665) 830584

Northumberland Street; NE66 2RJ Friendly former coaching inn with peaceful sheltered garden and raised deck giving wide views over Aln estuary; pleasant relaxed bar with heavy black beams, classic leather wall banquettes and window seats, old local photographs on dark mahogany brown panelling, cheerful fires, well kept ales such as Black Sheep, Roosters, Tempest and Tyne Bank, half a dozen wines by the glass, popular often interesting food from good panini up, stripped-brick restaurant with flagstones and woodburner; background and monthly live music, free wi-fi; children and dogs (in bar) welcome, comfortable well equipped bedrooms, open all day from 9.30am. *(Barry Collett, Comus and Sarah Elliott, Noel and Judy Garner)*

ALNMOUTH   NU2410

Sun (01665) 830983

Northumberland Street; NE66 2RA Comfortable banquettes in long low-beamed bar with open fire one end, woodburner the other, carpet or bare boards, sturdy candlelit pine tables and plenty to look at including driftwood decorations, small contemporary dining area, generous helpings of well priced traditional food from sandwiches and hot baguettes up, ales such as Adnams and Black Sheep, good coffee, friendly staff and chatty locals; background music; children welcome, attractive seaside village, four bedrooms. *(Barry Collett, Michael Doswell)*

ALNWICK   NU1813

John Bull (01665) 602055

Howick Street; NE66 1UY Popular chatty drinkers' pub, essentially front room of early 19th-c terraced house, good selection of well kept changing ales, real cider, extensive choice of bottled belgian beers and well over 100 malt whiskies; fortnightly live music Mon, darts and dominoes; closed weekday lunchtimes. *(Donald Allsopp)*

ALNWICK   NU1813

Plough (01665) 602395

Bondgate Without; NE66 1PN Smart contemporary pub-boutique hotel in Victorian stone building (under same management as the Jolly Fisherman at Craster – see Main Entries); well kept Timothy Taylors Landlord and a guest in lively front bar, several wines by the glass, good food (not Sun evening) in bar, bistro or upstairs restaurant, friendly helpful staff; children and dogs welcome, pleasant streetside raised terrace, seven bedrooms, open all day. *(Barry Collett)*

ALNWICK   NU1813

Tanners Arms (01665) 602553

Hotspur Place; NE66 1QF Welcoming little drinkers' pub with three well kept local ales and a decent glass of wine, flagstones and stripped stone, warm woodburner, plush stools and wall benches, small tree in the centre of the room; juke box and some live acoustic music, TV; dogs welcome, open all day weekends, closed weekday lunchtimes. *(Donald Allsopp)*

AMBLE   NU2604

Wellwood Arms (01665) 714646

High Street, off A1068; NE65 0LD Open-plan dining pub with good value food including pub favourites, evening carvery (all day Sun) and Weds steak night, ales such as Timothy Taylors Landlord, friendly staff; background music, sports TV; children and dogs welcome, four bedrooms, open all day. *(Tom Stevenson)*

ANICK   NY9565

★ **Rat** (01434) 602814

Village signposted NE of A69/A695 Hexham junction; NE46 4LN Popular country pub with cosy traditional bar; coal fire in kitchen range, cottagey knick-knacks such as floral chamber-pots hanging from beams, china and glassware on a delft shelf, well kept Allendale, Blythe, Hexhamshire, Tyne Bank, Timothy Taylors and Wylam, farm cider, a dozen wines by the glass (including champagne) and a local gin, good well presented interesting food (not Sun evening), efficient service, conservatory; background music and some live folk, free wi-fi; children welcome, charming garden with dovecote, statues and lovely North Tyne Valley views, limited parking (you can park around the village green), open all day. *(GSB, Comus and Sarah Elliott, Noel and Judy Garner, Michael Doswell)*

AYCLIFFE   NZ2822
★ **County** (01325) 312273
The Green, Aycliffe; just off A1(M) junction 59, off A167 at West Terrace and then right to village green; DL5 6LX
Smart inn with open-plan rooms in red, green and cream, seating from cushioned dining chairs to tartan banquettes, stripy carpets, painted ceiling joists and log fires, highly regarded imaginative food in minimalist wood-floored restaurant, ales such as Durham, Hawkshead, Oakham and Ossett, 11 wines by the glass, friendly service; free wi-fi; children welcome, metal tables and chairs out at front, attractive bedrooms, open all day, food all day Sun, useful A1 stop. *(Alison Langton, Edward Nile, Tom Stone, Donald Allsopp)*

BAMBURGH   NU1834
★ **Castle** (01668) 214616
Front Street; NE69 7BW Clean and comfortably old-fashioned pub with friendly welcoming staff, generous helpings of popular reasonably priced food including good crab sandwiches, a couple of well kept ales and decent house wines, expanded dining area to cope with summer visitors, local artwork for sale, open fires (one in old range); children welcome, no dogs inside, circular picnic-sets in nice beer garden, open (and food) all day. *(Derek and Sylvia Stephenson, Comus and Sarah Elliott)*

BAMBURGH   NU1834
Lord Crewe Arms (01668) 214243
Front Street; NE69 7BL Small early 17th-c hotel prettily set in charming coastal village dominated by Norman castle; updated bar and restaurant (Wynding Inn) with painted joists and panelling, bare stone walls and light wood floor, warm woodburner, beers from Northumberland and Charles Wells, good varied menu; sheltered garden with castle view, short walk from splendid sandy beach, 17 comfortable bedrooms. *(Comus and Sarah Elliott)*

BARDON MILL   NY7566
Twice Brewed (01434) 344534
Military Road (B6318 NE of Hexham); NE47 7AN Large busy inn well placed for fell walkers and major Hadrian's Wall sites; half a dozen ales including local microbrews and two badged for them by

Yates, over 50 rums, 20 malt whiskies and seven reasonably priced wines by the glass, good value hearty pub food from baguettes to blackboard specials, quick cheerful service, local photographs and art for sale; quiet background music; children welcome, no dogs, picnic-sets in back garden, 14 bedrooms, open all day. *(John Poulter, John and Sylvia Harrop)*

BARRASFORD   NY9173
★ **Barrasford Arms** (01434) 681237
Village signposted off A6079 N of Hexham; NE48 4AA Bustling sandstone inn with owner-chef's highly praised interesting food including good value set lunch, welcoming local atmosphere and friendly helpful staff, traditional log-fire bar with old photographs and bric-a-brac, up to three real ales such as Sharps and Wylam, two dining rooms, one with wheelback chairs around neat tables and stone chimneybreast hung with guns and copper pans, the other with comfortably upholstered dining chairs; background music, TV, darts; children welcome, plenty of nearby walks, handy for Hadrian's Wall, 11 bedrooms and well equipped bunkhouse, open all day weekends (no food Sun evening), closed Mon. *(John and Sylvia Harrop)*

BEADNELL   NU2229
Beadnell Towers (01665) 721211
The Wynding, off B1340; NE67 5AY Large slightly old-fashioned pub-hotel with unusual mix of furnishings, good food in log-fire bar or restaurant including local fish/seafood (can get busy with summer tourists and booking advised), well kept ales such as Black Sheep, Hadrian Border and Jarrow, decent wines from shortish list, pleasant staff; some live music; children welcome, seats outside, ten bedrooms (a bit of a climb to some), open all day weekends. *(Derek and Sylvia Stephenson, Comus and Sarah Elliott)*

BEAMISH   NZ2154
Beamish Hall (01207) 233733
NE of Stanley, off A6076; DH9 0YB Converted stone-built stables in courtyard at back of hotel, popular and family friendly (can get crowded), five or six beers from own microbrewery (tours available), decent wines and enjoyable food including some interesting choices, uniformed staff; regular events such as live music, barbecues and a summer festival; plenty of seats outside, big play area, open (and food) all day. *(Peter Smith and Judith Brown)*

BEAMISH   NZ2055
Black Horse (01207) 232569
Red Row (off Beamishburn Road NW, near A6076); OS Sheet 88 map reference 205541; DH9 0RW Late 17th-c country dining pub with contemporary/rustic interior, heritage colours blending with beams,

flagstones and some exposed stonework, enjoyable fairly traditional food (not Sun evening) from hot or cold sandwiches up, half a dozen well kept changing beers and decent wines by the glass, friendly attentive staff, cosy fire-warmed front room extending to light spacious dining area with central bar, another dining room upstairs, airy conservatory; children welcome, dogs in bar, restful views from big paved terrace, more tables on grass, open all day. *(Peter Smith and Judith Brown)*

BERWICK-UPON-TWEED   NT9952

Barrels   (01289) 308013

Bridge Street; TD15 1ES Small friendly pub with interesting collection of pop memorabilia and other bric-a-brac, some eccentric furniture including barber's chair in bare-boards bar, red banquettes in back room, a house ale from Tyne Bank and five well kept changing guests, also foreign bottled beers; regular live music and DJs in basement bar, good quality background music; open all day, may open from 2pm Jan, Feb. *(Tony Scott)*

CATTON   NY8257

★**Crown**   (01434) 618351

B6295, off A686 S of Haydon Bridge; NE47 9QS Welcoming 18th-c village pub in good walking country; inner bar with stripped-stone and bare boards, dark tables, mate's chairs and a traditional settle, good log fire, well kept Allendale beers and enjoyable home-cooked blackboard food, efficient staff, extension with folding glass doors opening on to small garden, lovely Allen Valley views; bar billiards, quiz Tues, folk night Thurs; children and dogs welcome, open all day summer (all day weekends, from 5pm weekdays in winter). *(Comus and Sarah Elliott)*

CHATTON   NU0528

Percy Arms   (01668) 215244

B6348 E of Wooller; NE66 5PS Sympathetically refurbished stone-built country inn (same owners as the Northumberland Arms at Felton); good well presented food (not Sun evening) in flagstoned log-fire bar or light panelled dining room, well kept ales such as Allendale, Coquetdale and Hadrian Border, good whisky choice, efficient friendly staff, open fire and woodburner; Weds quiz, May beer festival, darts; children and dogs (in bar) welcome, picnic-sets on small front lawn, five well appointed bedrooms, good breakfast, quiet village with sweeping views of the Cheviot Hills, open all day. *(Comus and Sarah Elliott, Michael Doswell)*

CHESTER-LE-STREET   NZ2753

Lambton Worm   (0191) 387 1162

North Road; DH3 4AJ Interesting 1930s building on outskirts of town with striking union jack front door, spacious bare-boards bar with dark walls and heavily draped windows, comfortable button-back banquettes and some intimate candlelit booths, plenty to look at including pictures fixed to the ceiling and tale of the giant Lambton Worm, own Sonnet 43 beers, enjoyable food from separate bar and restaurant menus, friendly service, large more formal back dining room with dark half-panelling, ornate gilt ceiling and pictures of film stars and former prime ministers on red walls; Tues quiz, live acoustic music Fri; children welcome, 14 bedrooms, open all day. *(Tom Stevenson)*

CORBRIDGE   NY9964

★**Angel**   (01434) 632119

Main Street; NE45 5LA Imposing coaching inn at end of broad street facing handsome Tyne Bridge; sizeable modernised main bar with light wood tables and chairs, leather wall benches, blue-grey walls, up to six local ales including Wylam, Weston's cider, a dozen wines by the glass and 30 malts, popular all-day food (not Sun evening) including interesting specials and good value weekday set lunch, friendly efficient uniformed staff, separate oak-panelled lounge with button-back armchairs, sofa and big stone fireplace, daily papers, stripped masonry in raftered back restaurant; children welcome, seats on front cobbles below wall sundial, bedrooms, open all day from 7.30am (8.30am Sun) for breakfast. *(Comus and Sarah Elliott, Ian Herdman)*

CORBRIDGE   NY9864

★**Black Bull**   (01434) 632261

Middle Street; NE45 5AT Rambling 18th-c beamed pub with four linked rooms, mix of traditional pub furniture including leather banquettes, wood, flagstone or carpeted floors, log fires (one in open hearth with gleaming copper canopy), ceramic collection in front room and information about Hadrian's Wall, enjoyable pubby food, three Greene King ales, a guest beer and good choice of wines by the glass, efficient cheery service; children welcome, seats out on two-level terrace, open all day. *(Ian Herdman, Comus and Sarah Elliott)*

CORBRIDGE   NY9868

★**Errington Arms**   (01434) 672250

About 3 miles N of town; B6318, on A68 roundabout; NE45 5QB Busy 18th-c stone-built pub by Hadrian's Wall attracting good mix of diners and walkers; beamed bars with pine panelling, stone and burgundy walls, farmhouse and other chairs around pine tables on strip-wood flooring, log fire and woodburner, good choice of popular fresh food from interesting sandwiches up, well kept Jennings and Wylam ales, several wines by the glass, plenty of friendly helpful staff; background music; children welcome, a few picnic-sets out in front, closed Sun evening, Mon. *(Pat and Stewart Gordon, Comus and Sarah Elliott, Martin Day)*

CORNHILL-ON-TWEED   NT8539
Collingwood Arms   (01890) 882424
Main Street; TD12 4UH Restored and
comfortably updated Georgian stone hotel;
nice little bar with decent wines, around
25 malt whiskies and a well kept local ale
such as Alnwick, good choice of reasonably
priced food in adjoining dining room or more
pricey restaurant, friendly helpful staff, open
fires; children and dogs (in bar) welcome,
tables out in lovely grounds, local fishing
and shooting, 15 well appointed bedrooms
(named after ships from the Battle of
Trafalgar), good breakfast, open all day.
(Pat and Stewart Gordon)

CRAMLINGTON   NZ2373
Snowy Owl   (01670) 736111
*Just off A1/A19 junction via A1068;
Blagdon Lane; NE23 8AU* Large Vintage
Inn, relaxed and comfortable, with their
usual all-day food, friendly efficient young
staff, Black Sheep and a couple of guests,
plenty of wines by the glass, softly lit
rooms with beams, flagstones and stripped
stone, interesting mix of furnishings and
decorations, three log fires; background
music; disabled access, bedrooms in
adjoining Innkeepers Lodge. *(Comus and
Sarah Elliott)*

CROOKHAM   NT9138
Blue Bell   (01890) 820252
*Pallinsburn; A697 Wooler–Cornhill;
TD12 4SH* Welcoming 18th-c roadside
country pub with enjoyable freshly prepared
food and well kept ales such as Fyne and
Greene King, friendly attentive service; dogs
welcome, comfortable clean bedrooms, good
breakfast. *(Katherine Matthews)*

DARLINGTON   NZ2814
Number Twenty 2   (01325) 354590
Coniscliffe Road; DL3 7RG Long
Victorian pub with high ceiling, wood
and carpeted floors, exposed brickwork
and striking red and gold wallpaper,
up to 13 quickly changing ales (tasters
offered) including own Village Brewer
range supplied by Hambleton, draught
continentals and decent wine selection,
snacky food till 7pm in back part, good
friendly service; closed Sun, otherwise
open all day. *(Colin Chambers)*

DINNINGTON   NZ2073
White Swan   (01661) 872869
Prestwick Road; NE13 7AG Large open-
plan pub-restaurant very popular for its wide
range of good value food including gluten-free
menu, reasonably priced wines and a well
kept changing ale, efficient friendly service
even at busy times; background music;

family area (children's menu till 5.30pm),
no dogs inside, disabled facilities, orangery
and attractive garden with pond, handy for
Newcastle Airport, open all day weekends
(till 9pm Sun). *(Colin and Daniel Gibbs)*

DUNSTAN   NU2419
Cottage   (01665) 576658
*Off B1339 Alnmouth–Embleton;
NE66 3SZ* Comfortable single-storey
beamed inn, enjoyable reasonably priced
food (smaller helpings available) from
fairly standard menu, three well kept ales,
restaurant and conservatory; live music, quiz
nights, free wi-fi; children and dogs welcome,
attractive garden with terrace and play area,
ten bedrooms, open all day. *(John and
Sylvia Harrop)*

DURHAM   NZ2742
Bishop Langley   (0191) 386 4779
*North Road/Framwellgate Bridge;
DH1 4PW* Recently refurbished pub in
great riverside position with fine castle and
cathedral views; up to five real ales including
Sharps Doom Bar and several bottled beers,
enjoyable well priced food from short menu
(all day Fri and Sat, till 6pm other days),
friendly helpful staff; background and some
live music; children welcome, large roof
terrace making most of the view, open all day.
(Richard Tilbrook)

DURHAM   NZ2742
Dun Cow   (0191) 386 9219
Old Elvet; DH1 3HN Unchanging
backstreet pub in pretty 16th-c black and
white timbered cottage, tiny chatty front bar
with wall benches, corridor to long narrow
back lounge with banquettes, well kept ales
such as Black Sheep, Camerons and Copper
Dragon, good value simple food, friendly staff;
background music, Mon quiz; children and
dogs welcome, open all day except Sun in
winter. *(Julie Swift)*

DURHAM
Head of Steam   (0191) 386 6060
Reform Place, North Road; DH1 4RZ
Hidden-away pub close to the river, modern
open-plan interior on two floors, good range
of well kept changing ales, real ciders
and plenty of bottled continental beers,
competitively priced food till early evening
(4pm Sun) including burgers and pizzas;
background music (live upstairs); outside
tables, open all day. *(Dr J Barrie Jones,
Peter Smith and Judith Brown)*

DURHAM   NZ2742
Market Tavern   (0191) 386 2069
Market Place; DH1 3NJ Narrow Taylor
Walker in the heart of old Durham;
traditionally refurbished interior including

Pubs close to motorway junctions are listed at the back of the book.

some cosy leather seating booths, six changing ales and a proper cider, enjoyable pubby food, friendly efficient service; popular with students (university-run folk night Weds); looks out on marketplace at front and to indoor market at back, open (and food) all day. *(Dr J Barrie Jones, Richard Tilbrook)*

DURHAM   NZ2642
Old Elm Tree (0191) 386 4621
Crossgate; DH1 4PS Comfortable friendly old pub on steep hill across from castle, two-room main bar and small lounge, four well kept ales including Caledonian Deuchars IPA and Wychwood Hobgoblin (occasional beer festivals), reasonably priced home-made food, open fires, folk and quiz nights; dogs welcome, small back terrace, open all day. *(Peter Smith and Judith Brown)*

DURHAM   NZ2742
Swan & Three Cygnets
(0191) 384 0242 *Elvet Bridge; DH1 3AG*
Victorian pub in good bridge-end spot high above river, city views from big windows and terrace, bargain lunchtime food and Sam Smiths ales, helpful friendly young staff, popular with locals and students; open all day. *(Dr J Barrie Jones)*

EARSDON   NZ3273
Beehive (0191) 252 9352
Hartley Lane; NE25 0SZ Popular nicely renovated 18th-c country pub with cosy linked rooms, low beams, soft lighting and one or two quirky touches, three well kept local ales (tasting trays available), good fairly priced home-made food (best to book weekends) from sandwiches, light dishes and sharing boards up, friendly service (can slow at busy times); background and some live music; children welcome, dogs in certain areas, garden with summer bar, play area and pygmy goats, open (and food) all day, kitchen shuts 6pm Sun. *(Martinthehills, Michael Doswell)*

EDMUNDBYERS   NZ0150
Punch Bowl (01207) 255545
B6278; DH8 9NL Small village's community local under newish management; well kept ales and good choice of enjoyable reasonably priced food including daily specials and good Sun roasts, friendly attentive service, café area; Thurs quiz, free wi-fi; children and dogs (in bar) welcome, fishing on nearby Derwent Reservoir (permits available from the pub), six modernised bedrooms, good breakfast, open all day. *(John Poulter, Robert Wivell)*

EGGLESCLIFFE   NZ4213
Pot & Glass (01642) 651009
Church Road; TS16 9DQ Friendly little 17th-c village pub with up to seven well kept ales including Black Sheep and Caledonian Deuchars IPA, good value straightforward food (some themed nights); monthly folk

club; children welcome, picnic-sets on back terrace with play area, lovely setting behind church, open all day Sun, closed Mon lunchtime. *(Tim Mayers)*

EGLINGHAM   NU1019
★ **Tankerville Arms** (01665) 578444
B6346 Alnwick–Wooler; NE66 2TX
Traditional 19th-c stone pub with contemporary touches and cosy friendly atmosphere; beams, bare boards and some stripped stone, banquettes and warm fires, well kept Hadrian Border and a guest, good wines, nicely presented often imaginative food from shortish menu, raftered split-level restaurant; free wi-fi; children, dogs and walkers welcome, lovely country views from back garden, attractive village, three bedrooms, closed lunchtimes Mon, Tues. *(Comus and Sarah Elliott, Michael Doswell)*

EMBLETON   NU2322
Dunstanburgh Castle Hotel
(01665) 576111 *B1339; NE66 3UN*
Comfortable hotel in attractive spot near magnificent coastline, good choice of enjoyable bar and restaurant food using local meat and fish, good for vegetarians too, efficient friendly service, local ales and decent wines (five by the glass), two lounges for coffee with open fires; children welcome, seats in nice garden, bedrooms and self-catering cottages, open all day. *(John and Sylvia Harrop)*

EMBLETON   NU2322
Greys (01665) 576983
Stanley Terrace off W T Stead Road, turn at the Blue Bell; NE66 3UY Welcoming pub with carpeted bar and cottagey back dining room, open fires; well priced home-made food (wider evening choice) including good crab sandwiches and local fish, interesting range of well kept regional beers; juke box; children and dogs welcome, small walled back garden, raised decking with village views, open all day. *(Derek and Sylvia Stephenson)*

ESH   NZ1944
Cross Keys (0191) 373 1279
Front Street; DH7 9QR Friendly 18th-c village local with hearty helpings of well liked good value food (not Sun evening), half a dozen ales such as Big Lamp, Black Sheep and Brains, afternoon teas; children welcome, colourful hanging baskets at front, good country views from behind, closed Mon, otherwise open all day. *(Jim and Sue James)*

FELTON   NU1800
Northumberland Arms
(01670) 787370 *West Thirston; B6345, off A1 N of Morpeth; NE65 9EE* Stylish 19th-c inn across road from River Coquet (same owners as the Percy Arms at Chatton); beams, stripped stone/brickwork and woodburner in roomy open-plan lounge

bar, flagstones and nice mix of furnishings including big sofas, restaurant with mix of light wood tables on bare boards, good sensibly priced food from bar snacks and standard dishes up (best to book), bread from their own bakery, three or four well kept mainly local beers and nice wines by the glass from short well chosen list; Thurs quiz, monthly folk night (fourth Tues); children welcome, dogs in bar, six good bedrooms, open (and food) all day. *(GSB)*

FROSTERLEY NZ0236
★**Black Bull** (01388) 527784
Just off A689 W of centre; DL13 2SL
Unique in having its own peal of bells (licensee is a campanologist); great atmosphere in three interesting traditional beamed and flagstoned rooms with coal fires, landlord's own fine photographs and three grandfather clocks, four well kept local ales, farm cider and perry, carefully chosen wines and malt whiskies, good food using local and organic ingredients (best to book evenings), popular Sun lunch; occasional acoustic live music; well behaved children and dogs welcome, attractive no-smoking terrace with wood-fired bread oven and old railway furnishings (opposite steam line station), closed Sun evening to Weds, otherwise open all day. *(Tom Stone)*

GATESHEAD NZ2563
Central (0191) 478 2543
Half Moon Lane; NE8 2AN Unusual 19th-c wedge-shaped pub (Grade II listed) restored by the Head of Steam group; well preserved features including notable buffet bar, great choice of changing local ales, real ciders and lots of bottled beers, low-priced food such as burgers from short menu, upstairs function rooms and roof terrace, live music; open all day (till 1am Fri, Sat). *(Peter Smith and Judith Brown)*

GREAT WHITTINGTON NZ0070
Queens Head (01434) 672516
Village signed off A68 and B6018 N of Corbridge; NE19 2HP Handsome golden-stone village pub; dark leather chairs around sturdy tables, some stripped-stone walls and soft lighting, nice hunting mural above old fireplace in long narrow bar, Wylam ales, popular chinese restaurant at back (early evening deals); background music; children and dogs (in bar) welcome, picnic-sets under parasols on little front lawn, closed lunchtimes (all day Mon in winter). *(Julie Swift)*

GRETA BRIDGE NZ0813
★**Morritt** (01833) 627232
Hotel signposted off A66 W of Scotch Corner; DL12 9SE Striking 17th-c country house hotel popular for weddings

and the like; properly pubby bar with big windsor armchairs and sturdy oak settles around traditional cast-iron-framed tables, open fires and remarkable 1946 mural of Dickensian characters by JTY Gilroy (known for Guinness advertisements), big windows looking on to extensive lawn, Thwaites Major Morritt (named for them) and Timothy Taylors Landlord, 19 wines by the glass from extensive list, bar and restauarant food, afternoon teas, friendly staff; background music; children and dogs (in bar and bedrooms) welcome, attractively laid-out split-level garden with teak tables and play area, open all day. *(Barry Collett, WAH)*

HALTWHISTLE NY7166
Milecastle Inn (01434) 321372
Military Road; B6318 NE – OS Sheet 86 map reference 715660; NE49 9NN
New owners for this sturdy stone-built pub on remote moorland road running alongside Hadrian's Wall; small rooms off beamed bar, brasses, horsey and local landscape prints, two log fires, ales such as Big Lamp, a few wines by the glass, traditional food, small comfortable restaurant; children have been welcome, tables and benches in big sheltered garden with dovecote and stunning views, two self-catering cottages. *(Comus and Sarah Elliott, Hilary and Neil Christopher, Max Simons)*

HART NZ4634
White Hart (01429) 265468
Just off A179 W of Hartlepool; Front Street; TS27 3AW Welcoming end of terrace nautical-theme pub with old ship's figurehead outside, fires in both bars, wide choice of popular fairly traditional food cooked by friendly landlady, takeaways available, ales such as Copper Dragon; live music; children welcome, no dogs inside, open all day. *(Katherine Matthews)*

HAYDON BRIDGE NY8364
★**General Havelock** (01434) 684376
Off A69 Corbridge–Haltwhistle; B6319 (Ratcliffe Road); NE47 6ER Old darkly painted pub, a short stroll upstream from Haydon Bridge itself; L-shaped bar with a couple of changing ales and decent choice of wines by the glass, well thought-of freshly made food (not Sun evening, Mon) from shortish menu including daily specials, stripped-stone barn dining room and terrace with fine South Tyne river views; children and dogs (in bar) welcome, open most of the day (short afternoon break). *(Geof Cox, Comus and Sarah Elliott, Louella Miles)*

HEXHAM NY9464
Heart of Northumberland
(01434) 608013 *Market Street; NE46 3NS* Reopened and refurbished after long closure; five real ales and lots of ciders,

---

We say if we know a pub has background music.

short menu of well cooked pub favourites, good cheerful service; children welcome; more reports please. *(Comus and Sarah Elliott)*

HIGH HESLEDEN   NZ4538
Ship   (01429) 836453
Off A19 via B1281; TS27 4QD Popular Victorian inn with half a dozen well kept changing ales and good food cooked by landlady including some interesting specials, friendly service and atmosphere, sailing ship models including big one hanging with lanterns from boarded ceiling, log fire; sea views over farmland from garden, six bedrooms in new block, closed Mon and lunchtimes apart from Sat. *(Des Mannion)*

HOLWICK   NY9126
Strathmore Arms   (01833) 640362
Back road up Teesdale from Middleton; DL12 0NJ Attractive and welcoming old stone-built country pub in beautiful scenery just off Pennine Way; four well kept ales including a house beer (Strathmore Gold) brewed by Mithril, low-priced traditional food all day, home-baked bread, beams, flagstones and open fire; live music Fri, quiz first Weds of month, pool, free wi-fi; well behaved dogs welcome, popular with walkers, four bedrooms, closed Tues. *(Michael Doswell)*

HOLY ISLAND   NU1241
Crown & Anchor   (01289) 389215
Causeway passable only at low tide, check times (01289) 330733; TD15 2RX Comfortably unpretentious pub-restaurant by the priory; a couple of well kept Hadrian Border ales and enjoyable traditional home-made food including specials (maybe local oysters), friendly helpful staff, cosy little bar with open fire, more roomy modern back dining room; children and dogs (in bar) welcome, garden with lovely views (they may ask for a credit card if you eat out here), four bedrooms, open all day. *(Trevor, Tim Mayers)*

HOLY ISLAND   NU1241
Ship   (01289) 389311
Marygate; TD15 2SJ Nicely set pub (busy in season) with beamed bar, wood floors, stone walls and maritime memorabilia, big stove, steps down to carpeted lounge/dining area, fairly pubby menu including fish/seafood, Hadrian Border Holy Island Blessed Bitter badged for them plus one or two guests, 30 malt whiskies; background music; children welcome and usually dogs (but do ask first), sheltered sunny garden, four bedrooms, may close at quiet times. *(Andrew Stone)*

HORSLEY   NZ0965
Lion & Lamb   (01661) 852952
B6528, just off A69 Newcastle–Hexham; NE15 0NS 18th-c former coaching inn; main bar with scrubbed tables, stripped stone, flagstones and panelling, up to four changing ales and a real cider, good food from sandwiches and hearty traditional choices up including summer seafood and winter game, also tapas, efficient service, bare-boards restaurant; children and dogs (not evenings) welcome, Tyne views from attractive sunny garden with roomy terrace, play area, open all day. *(Michael Doswell, Comus and Sarah Elliott)*

HURWORTH-ON-TEES   NZ2814
★ Bay Horse   (01325) 720663
Church Row; DL2 2AQ Popular dining pub (best to book, particularly weekends) with very good imaginative food, quite pricey but they do offer a fixed-price alternative (lunchtimes Mon-Sat, evenings Mon-Thurs), also vegetarian menu and children's meals, three well kept changing ales, extensive wine list, smiling efficient young staff, sizeable bar with good open fire, restaurant; seats on back terrace and in well tended walled garden beyond, charming village by River Tees, open all day. *(Peter Hacker)*

HURWORTH-ON-TEES   NZ3110
Otter & Fish   (01325) 720019
Off A167 S of Darlington; Strait Lane; DL2 2AH Pleasant village setting across road from the River Tees; up-to-date open-plan layout with flagstones and stripped wood, open fires and church candles, nice mix of dining furniture, comfortable armchairs and sofas by bar, good well presented local food including set deals and decent vegetarian and children's choices (wise to book especially weekends), friendly helpful staff, ales such as Black Sheep and several wines by the glass; closed Sun evening. *(Colin and Daniel Gibbs)*

KENTON BANKFOOT   NZ2068
Twin Farms   (0191) 286 1263
Main Road; NE13 8AB Roomy Fitzgerald pub in elegant period-rustic style, recycled stone, timbers etc, real fires, several pleasant softly lit areas off central bar, enjoyable reasonably priced food from sandwiches and sharing boards to imaginative specials, well kept changing ales and good selection of wines by the glass, friendly efficient service; background music, Mon quiz; children welcome, disabled facilities, garden and terrace, handy for A1 and airport, open all day. *(R T and J C Moggridge, Peter and Eleanor Kenyon)*

KNARSDALE   NY6754
Kirkstyle   (01434) 381559
Signed off A689; CA8 7PB Welcoming 18th-c country pub in lovely spot looking over South Tyne Valley to hills beyond; enjoyable reasonably priced food (not Mon) including some interesting specials, well kept Yates and a summer guest, dining room, games area with darts and pool; dogs very welcome, quoits team, handy for Pennine Way, South Tyne Trail and South Tynedale Railway

(Lintley terminus), closed Sun evening, Mon lunchtime (and Tues except school summer holidays), may shut from 9pm if quiet. *(Comus and Sarah Elliott)*

LANGDON BECK   NY8531
Langdon Beck Hotel
(01833) 622267 *B6277 Middleton–Alston; DL12 0XP* Isolated unpretentious inn with two cosy bars and spacious lounge, well placed for walks including Pennine Way; good choice of enjoyable generous food using local Teesdale beef and lamb, Jarrow Rivet Catcher and Ringwood Best, friendly helpful staff, interesting rock collection in 'geology room'; events including Easter 'egg jarping', late May beer festival and Langdonbury music festival (July); wonderful fell views from garden, seven bedrooms (some sharing bathrooms), open all day, closed Mon in winter. *(Jim and Sue James)*

LANGLEY ON TYNE   NY8160
Carts Bog Inn (01434) 684338
A686 S, junction B6305; NE47 5NW Isolated 18th-c moorside pub with heavy beams and stripped-stone walls, old photographs, spindleback chairs around mix of tables on red carpet, nice open fire, good range of enjoyable generous food from sandwiches up including signature Bog Pie (steak and mushroom suet pudding) and popular Sun lunch (best to book), two or three well kept local ales, friendly efficient young staff, games room with pool and darts; children and dogs welcome, picnic-sets in big garden with views, quoits, open all day weekends, closed Mon (and Tues in winter). *(John Poulter)*

LESBURY   NU2311
Coach (01665) 830865
B1339; NE66 3PP Picturesque stone pub at heart of pretty village; low-beamed rooms with pubby furniture on tartan carpet, dark leather stools by counter serving Black Sheep and Timothy Taylors Landlord, part off to left with sofas and armchairs, small dining room and a further seating area with woodburner and tub-like chairs, popular home-made food including daily specials, friendly staff; background music; children welcome, dogs in some parts, seats out in front and on terrace, pretty flowering tubs and baskets, handy for Alnwick Castle, open all day. *(Donald Allsopp)*

LONGFRAMLINGTON   NU1301
Village Inn (01665) 570268
Just off A697; Front Street; NE65 8AD Friendly 18th-c stone inn arranged into three distinct areas; tasty freshly prepared pub food including good Sun carvery, own-brewed VIP beers along with local guests; some live music, Mon quiz, pool room; comfortable bedrooms and self-catering cabins (just outside the village), open all day. *(Tim Mayers)*

LONGHORSLEY   NZ1494
Shoulder of Mutton (01670) 788236
East Road; A697 N of Morpeth; NE65 8SY Comfortable bar and restaurant with welcoming staff, good choice of enjoyable reasonably priced food from lunchtime baguettes up, popular Sun carvery till 6pm (must book), Courage Directors, Caledonian Deuchars IPA and a guest, good selection of other drinks; background music, TV, fruit machine; children and dogs (in bar) welcome, picnic-sets in back garden, three bedrooms, open all day (food all day Tues-Sat). *(Guy and Caroline Howard)*

MIDDLETON   NZ0685
Ox (01670) 772634
Village signed off B6343, W of Hartburn; NE61 4QZ Warmly welcoming Georgian country pub in small tucked-away village, a couple of local ales such as Acton and Wylam, tasty straightforward home-made food (not Sun evening); children and dogs welcome, seats outside, handy for Wallington (NT), open all day weekends, closed weekday lunchtimes. *(Julie Swift)*

MILFIELD   NT9333
Red Lion (01668) 216224
Main Road (A697 Wooler–Cornhill); NE71 6JD Comfortable 18th-c coaching inn with good fairly priced food from chef-owner including popular Sun carvery, well kept ales such as Black Sheep and Thwaites, a dozen wines by the glass and decent coffee, friendly efficient service; children welcome, pretty garden by car park at back, two bedrooms, good breakfast, open all day weekends. *(Michael Doswell)*

MORPETH   NZ1986
Tap & Spile (01670) 513894
Manchester Street; NE61 1BH Cosy and easy-going two-room pub with up to eight well kept ales such as Caledonian, Everards, Hadrian Border and Mordue, Weston's Old Rosie cider and country wines, short choice of good value lunchtime food Fri and Sat, friendly staff, traditional pub furniture and interesting old photographs, quieter back lounge (children allowed here) with coal-effect gas fire, board and other games; good local folk music Sun afternoon, quiz Mon, ukulele band Tues, unobtrusive background music, sports TV; dogs welcome in front bar, open all day Fri-Sun. *(Colin and Daniel Gibbs)*

By law, pubs must show a price list of their drinks. Let us know if you're inconvenienced by any breach of this law.

NETHERTON NT9807
Star (01669) 630238
Off B6341 at Thropton, or A697 via Whittingham; NE65 7HD Simple unchanging village local run by charming long-serving landlady (licence has been in her family since 1917), large high-ceilinged room with wall benches and many original features, friendly regulars, range of bottled beers, no food, music, children or dogs; quiz first Weds of the month; open evenings only from 7.30pm, closed Mon and Thurs. *(Steve Kingsdon)*

NEWBROUGH NY8768
Red Lion (01283) 575785
Stanegate Road; NE47 5AR Former coaching inn with light airy feel and buoyant atmosphere; log fire, flagstones and half-panelling, old local photographs plus some large paintings, good sensibly priced food (not Sun evening) in bar and two dining areas from well filled baguettes up (more elaborate evening menu), a couple of well kept local ales, friendly efficient service, games room with pool and darts, little shop selling local crafts and artwork; children and dogs (not at food times) welcome, garden behind with decking, good local walks and on NCN cycle route 72, five bedrooms, open all day. *(Michael Doswell)*

NEWCASTLE UPON TYNE NZ2464
★Bacchus (0191) 261 1008
High Bridge E, between Pilgrim Street and Grey Street; NE1 6BX Smart, spacious and comfortable Fitzgerald pub with ocean liner look; two-level interior with lots of varnished wood, pillars, ship and shipbuilding photographs, good value lunchtime food (not Sun) from sandwiches and panini to pubby mains and some unusual specials, nine very well kept changing ales (beer festivals), plenty of bottled imports, farm cider and splendid range of whiskies, decent coffee too, friendly helpful staff; background music; disabled facilities, handy for Theatre Royal, open all day and can get very busy. *(Peter Smith and Judith Brown, Jeremy King)*

NEWCASTLE UPON TYNE NZ2464
Bodega (0191) 221 1552
Westgate Road; NE1 4AG Majestic Edwardian drinking hall next to Tyne Theatre; Big Lamp, Durham and six guest ales, real cider and bottled beers, friendly service, snug front cubicles, spacious back area with two magnificent stained-glass cupolas; background music, Thurs quiz, big-screen TVs (very busy on match days), darts, free wi-fi; open all day. *(Roger and Donna Huggins)*

NEWCASTLE UPON TYNE NZ2563
★Bridge Hotel (0191) 232 6400
Castle Square, next to high-level bridge; NE1 1RQ Big, well divided, high-ceilinged bar around servery with replica slatted snob screens, Black Sheep, Caledonian Deuchars IPA and seven guests kept well, real cider, friendly staff, bargain generous lunchtime food (not weekends), magnificent fireplace, great river and bridge views from raised back area, live music upstairs including long-standing Mon folk club; background music, sports TV, games machines; flagstoned back terrace overlooking part of old town wall, open all day. *(Peter Smith and Judith Brown)*

NEWCASTLE UPON TYNE NZ2563
Bridge Tavern (0191) 261 9966
Under the Tyne Bridge; NE1 3UF Bustling former Newcastle Arms under same ownership as the Town Wall; airy interior with brick walls and lots of wood, industrial-style ceiling, view into back microbrewery (joint venture with Wylam), ten beers including guests (tasting trays available), well liked often imaginative food (all day, till 7pm Fri-Sun) from snacks and sharing boards up, friendly helpful staff; background music; well behaved children and dogs allowed before 7pm, upstairs bar and good roof terrace, open all day (till 1am Fri, Sat). *(GSB, Peter Smith and Judith Brown, Comus and Sarah Elliott)*

NEWCASTLE UPON TYNE NZ2563
Broad Chare (0191) 211 2144
Broad Chare, just off quayside opposite law courts; NE1 3DQ Traditional feel although only recently converted to a pub, british-leaning food from bar snacks such as crispy pigs' ears and Lindisfarne oysters to hearty main courses like steak and kidney pudding, four real ales including a house beer from Wylam (Writer's Block), good choice of bottled beers, wines and whiskies, bare-boards bar and snug, old local photographs, upstairs dining room; background music; children welcome till 7pm (later upstairs), no dogs, next door to the Live Theatre, open all day (no food Sun evening). *(Steve Kingsdon)*

NEWCASTLE UPON TYNE NZ2464
Centurion (0191) 261 6611
Central Station, Neville Street; NE1 5HL Glorious high-ceilinged Victorian décor with tilework and columns in former first class waiting room, well restored with comfortable leather seats giving club-like feel, Black Sheep, Caledonian Deuchars IPA, Jarrow Rivet Catcher and a couple of guests, friendly staff; background music, big-screen sports TV; useful café-deli next door, open all day. *(Roger and Donna Huggins, Alan and Jane Shaw, Comus and Sarah Elliott)*

NEWCASTLE UPON TYNE NZ2464
City Tavern (0191) 232 1308
Northumberland Road; NE1 8JF Revamped half-timbered city-centre pub on different levels, ten real ales including two house beers brewed by Newcastle and Theakstons, decent wine list and some 60

gins, enjoyable food from reasonably priced varied menu including plenty for vegetarians, friendly staff; children and dogs welcome, open (and food) all day, kitchen closes 7pm Sun. *(Comus and Sarah Elliott, Steve Kingsdon)*

NEWCASTLE UPON TYNE NZ2664
Cluny (0191) 230 4474
Lime Street; NE1 2PQ Bar-café-music venue in interesting 19th-c mill/warehouse (part of the Head of Steam group); low-priced home-made food including various burgers and hot dogs, Sun brunch, up to eight well kept ales, good selection of other beers, ciders and some exotic rums, sofas in comfortable raised area with daily papers and art magazines, back gallery featuring local artists; background music and regular live bands (also in Cluny 2 next door); children (till 7pm) and dogs allowed, picnic-sets out on green, striking setting below Metro Bridge, parking nearby can be difficult, open (and food) all day. *(Steve Kingsdon)*

NEWCASTLE UPON TYNE NZ2563
★ Crown Posada (0191) 232 1269
The Side; off Dean Street, between and below the two high central bridges (A6125 and A6127); NE1 3JE City's oldest pub, just a few minutes' stroll from the castle; long narrow room with elaborate coffered ceiling, stained-glass counter screens and fine mirrors with tulip lamps on curly brass mounts (matching the great ceiling candelabra), long green built-in leather wall seat flanked by narrow tables, old photos of Newcastle and plenty of caricatures, Allendale, Hadrian Border, Highland, Titanic and Wylam, may do sandwiches, heating from fat low-level pipes, music from vintage record player; no credit cards; well behaved children in front snug till 6pm, open all day (midnight Fri, Sat) and can get packed at peak times. *(Peter Smith and Judith Brown)*

NEWCASTLE UPON TYNE NZ2664
Cumberland Arms (0191) 265 1725
James Place Street; NE6 1LD Friendly, unspoilt and traditional; half a dozen well kept mainly local ales along with a good range of craft beers and ciders/perries, two annual beer festivals, limited choice of good value snacky food, obliging staff, bare boards and open fires; events most nights including regular folk sessions, ukulele band Thurs; dogs welcome, tables out overlooking Ouseburn Valley, four bedrooms, open all day weekends, from 5pm Mon-Weds (3pm Thurs, Fri). *(Denis and Margaret Kilner)*

NEWCASTLE UPON TYNE NZ2664
Free Trade (0191) 265 5764
St Lawrence Road, off Walker Road (A186); NE6 1AP Splendidly basic and unpretentious with outstanding views up river from big windows, terrace tables and seats on grass; up to nine real ales,

traditional ciders and plenty of bottled beers and whiskies, good sandwiches/pasties, regular pizza nights, original Formica tables and coal fire, free juke box, warm friendly atmosphere; steps down to back room and loos; open all day. *(Andrew Stone)*

NEWCASTLE UPON TYNE NZ2266
Old George (0191) 260 3035
Cloth Market, down alley past Pumphreys; NE1 1EZ Attractive refurbished 16th-c pub (former coaching inn) in cobbled yard, beams and panelling, comfortable armchairs by open fire, well kept/priced ales including Bass, plenty of wines by the glass and cocktails, good value food served by friendly staff; background music at one end, DJ Fri and Sat, open mike Thurs and Sun, sports TV, free wi-fi; children welcome, open all day (till 2am Fri, Sat). *(Richard Tilbrook)*

NEWCASTLE UPON TYNE NZ2463
Town Wall (0191) 232 3000
Pink Lane; across from Central Station; NE1 5HX Newish pub in handsome listed building; spacious bare-boards interior with dark walls, button-back banquettes and mix of well spaced tables and chairs, pictures in heavy gilt frames, up to 12 ales (one badged for them), good choice of bottled beers and several wines by the glass, well priced food including sharing boards, burgers and pub favourites, basement overspill/function room; background music, free wi-fi; well behaved children and dogs welcome, open all day (till 1am Fri, Sat), food till 7pm Fri-Sun. *(Comus and Sarah Elliott)*

NEWTON-BY-THE-SEA NU2325
★ Joiners Arms (01665) 576112
High Newton-by-the-Sea, by turning to Linkhouse; NE66 3EA Updated open-plan village pub-restaurant; flagstoned bar with big front windows and open fire, wood-clad dining area behind, good well presented food from interesting sandwiches and sharing plates up, four local ales including Anarchy, carefully chosen wines and cocktails, cheerful helpful uniformed staff; background music; children and dogs welcome, picnic-sets out at front and back, good coastal walks, five stylish bedrooms, open all day, food all day during school summer holidays. *(Comus and Sarah Elliott)*

NEWTON-ON-THE-MOOR NU1705
Cook & Barker Arms
(01665) 575234 *Village signed from A1 Alnwick–Felton; NE65 9JY* Traditional stone-built country inn; beamed bar with stripped-stone and partly panelled walls, broad-seated settles around oak-topped tables, horsebrasses, coal fires, Black Sheep, Timothy Taylors and a guest, extensive wine list, popular food using meat from own farm (good weekday set lunch deal), friendly staff, separate

restaurant with french windows opening on to terrace; background music, TV; children welcome, no dogs, 18 reasonably priced bedrooms and nearby self-catering cottage, good breakfast, Boxing Day hunt starts here, open all day. *(J R Wildon, John and Sylvia Harrop, Peter Smith and Judith Brown)*

NORTH SHIELDS   NZ3568
Quay Taphouse (0191) 259 2023
Bell Street; NE30 1HF Clean and airy quayside pub with good value food including sharing platters and tapas, a couple of changing ales, several wines by the glass and decent coffee, quick friendly service; weekend live music; children welcome, open all day. *(Donald Allsopp)*

PONTELAND   NZ1771
Badger (01661) 867931
Street Houses; A696 SE, by garden centre; NE20 9BT Early 18th-c Vintage Inn with warren of rooms and alcoves, good log fire, well kept beers such as Bass, Black Sheep and Timothy Taylors, decent range of wines by the glass, their usual all-day food, helpful friendly service; background music; children welcome, handy for Newcastle Airport, open all day. *(Comus and Sarah Elliott)*

PONTELAND   NZ1773
Blackbird (01661) 822684
North Road opposite church; NE20 9UH Imposing ancient stone pub doing well under present management; open-plan interior with mix of furniture including several high tables, button-back banquettes, wood, slate and tartan-carpeted floors, striking old map of Northumberland and etching of Battle of Otterburn either side of fireplace, larger Tudor stone fireplace in unusual Tunnel Room, enjoyable food from bar snacks to restaurany dishes, six real ales including one badged for them and over 50 gins, friendly service; background music, sports TV, free wi-fi; children and dogs welcome, picnic-sets out at front, more tables on back lawn, open all day, food till 5pm Sun. *(Michael Doswell)*

RENNINGTON   NU2118
★ Horseshoes (01665) 577665
B1340; NE66 3RS Comfortable and welcoming family-run pub with nice local feel (may be horses in car park), a couple of well kept ales including Hadrian Border Farne Island, decent wines by the glass and ample helpings of enjoyable locally sourced food, friendly efficient service, simple neat bar with flagstones and woodburner, carpeted restaurant; darts, free wi-fi; children welcome, picnic-sets out on small front lawn, attractive quiet village near

coast, Aug scarecrow competition, closed Mon. *(Guy and Caroline Howard)*

RIDING MILL   NZ0161
Wellington (01434) 682531
A695 just W of A68 roundabout; NE44 6DQ Popular 17th-c pub (Chef & Brewer) in pretty village; wide choice of enjoyable fairly priced food, three real ales and decent wines by the glass, friendly helpful staff, beams and two big log fires; background music; children welcome, disabled access/facilities, plenty of outside seating, nearby walks and river, open (and food) all day. *(Comus and Sarah Elliott)*

ROCHESTER   NY8497
Redesdale Arms (01830) 520668
A68 3 miles W of Otterburn; NE19 1TA Isolated old roadside inn (aka the First & Last) surrounded by unspoilt countryside, warm and cosy, with enjoyable food such as venison hotpot cooked by landlord, Allendale ales, friendly attentive staff; ten bedrooms, open (and food) all day. *(Comus and Sarah Elliott, Peter and Eleanor Kenyon)*

SEATON SLUICE   NZ3477
Kings Arms (0191) 237 0275
West Terrace; NE26 4RD Friendly busy old pub in pleasant seaside location perched above tidal Seaton Sluice Harbour; good range of beers and enjoyable pubby food (not Sun evening) including gluten-free menu, beamed and carpeted bar with old photographs and woodburner at each end, restaurant; children welcome, a few picnic-sets on sunny front grass, more seats in enclosed beer garden behind, open all day. *(Eddie Edwards, Arthur Shackleton)*

SHINCLIFFE   NZ2940
Seven Stars (0191) 384 8454
High Street N (A177 S of Durham); DH1 2NU Comfortable and welcoming 18th-c village inn, varied choice of good generous food from pub favourites up, weekday set menu and other deals, three well kept ales, coal-effect gas fire in lounge bar, panelled dining room; children in eating areas, dogs in bar, some picnic-sets outside, eight bedrooms, open all day Tues-Sun, closed Mon lunchtime. *(Jim and Sue James)*

SLALEY   NY9757
Rose & Crown (01434) 673996
Church Close; NE47 0AA Welcoming 17th-c pub owned by the village, enjoyable good value food from sandwiches up including some chinese, indian and italian dishes, local ales such as Allendale, beams and log fires; Sun quiz; children and dogs welcome, garden with long country views, two

---

All *Guide* inspections are anonymous. Anyone claiming to be a *Good Pub Guide* inspector is a fraud. Please let us know.

bedrooms, open all day in summer, no food Sun evening, may be reduced choice Mon. *(Tim Mayers)*

SLALEY NY9658

★**Travellers Rest** (01434) 673231

B6306 S of Hexham (and N of village); NE46 1TT Attractive stone-built country pub, spaciously opened up, with farmhouse-style décor, beams, flagstones and polished wood floors, huge fireplace, comfortable high-backed settles forming discrete areas, friendly uniformed staff, popular good value food (not Sun evening) in bar or quieter dining room, good children's menu, real ales such as Allendale, Black Sheep and Caledonian; dogs welcome, tables outside with well equipped adventure play area on grass behind, three good value bedrooms, open all day. *(Andrew Stone)*

SOUTH SHIELDS NZ3567

Alum Ale House (0191) 427 7245

Ferry Street (B1344); NE33 1JR Welcoming 18th-c bow-windowed pub adjacent to North Shields ferry, open-plan bare-boards bar with a dozen well kept Marstons-related ales, fire in old range; music and quiz nights; seats on front deck overlooking the river, handy for marketplace, open all day. *(Julie Swift)*

SOUTH SHIELDS NZ3566

Steamboat (0191) 454 0134

Mill Dam/Coronation Street; NE33 1EQ Friendly 19th-c corner pub with eight well kept changing ales, lots of nautical bric-a-brac, bar ceiling covered in flags, raised seating area and separate lounge; near river and marketplace, open all day. *(John Poulter)*

STANNINGTON NZ2179

★**Ridley Arms** (01670) 789216

Village signed off A1 S of Morpeth; NE61 6EL Extended village pub handy for A1; several separate areas, each with different mood and style, proper front bar with open fire and cushioned settles, stools along counter serving up to nine local ales including Alnwick and Hadrian Border, a dozen wines by the glass and good coffee, decent choice of enjoyable reasonably priced food, pleasant helpful staff, several dining areas with comfortable upholstered bucket chairs around dark tables on bare boards or carpet, cartoons and portraits on cream, panelled or stripped-stone walls; background music, Tues quiz, free wi-fi; children welcome, good disabled access, picnic-sets in front and on back terrace, open (and food) all day. *(Michael Doswell, Comus and Sarah Elliott)*

SUNDERLAND NZ4057

Ivy House (0191) 567 3399

Worcester Terrace; SR2 7AW Friendly Victorian corner pub off the beaten track, five well kept changing ales, interesting bottled beers and good range of spirits,

popular reasonably priced food from open kitchen including burgers and pizzas; background and live music, Weds quiz, sports TV; open all day. *(Andrew Stone)*

TYNEMOUTH NZ3669

Hugos at the Coast (0191) 257 8956

Front Street; NE30 4DZ Popular Sir John Fitzgerald pub with open-plan split-level interior, four changing ales and good choice of wines, freshly prepared bar food from sandwiches up, reasonable prices and cheerful service; Weds quiz, TV, darts; some pavement seating, open all day, food till 6pm (4pm Sun). *(Peter and Eleanor Kenyon)*

WARDEN NY9166

Boatside (01434) 602233

Village signed N of A69; NE46 4SQ Old stone-built pub refurbished after recent flooding, modern décor but still cosy, enjoyable fairly priced food from varied menu, a couple of local ales and decent selection of new world wines, good friendly service; sports TV; children welcome, small neat enclosed garden, attractive spot by Tyne Bridge, bedrooms in adjoining cottages (some self-catering), open (and food) all day. *(Comus and Sarah Elliott)*

WARENFORD NU1429

White Swan (01668) 213453

Off A1 S of Belford; NE70 7HY Simply decorated friendly bar with a couple of changing ales such as Alnwick and Greene King, steps down to cosy restaurant with William Morris wallpaper, good carefully presented imaginative food (reduced lunchtime choice), cheerful efficient service, warm fires; children and dogs (in bar) welcome, open all day Sun. *(Michael Doswell)*

WARKWORTH NU2406

Hermitage (01665) 711258

Castle Street; NE65 0UL Rambling former coaching inn with good choice of popular home-made food including carvery (Fri and Sat evenings, Sun lunchtime), Jennings Cumberland and three guests, decent range of wines, friendly staff, quaint décor with fire in old range, small upstairs restaurant; background and some live music; children and dogs welcome, attractive setting with benches and hanging baskets out in front, five bedrooms, open (and food) all day. *(Pat and Stewart Gordon)*

WELDON BRIDGE NZ1398

★**Anglers Arms** (01665) 570271

B6344, just off A697; village signposted with Rothbury off A1 N of Morpeth; NE65 8AX Traditional coaching inn nicely located by bridge over River Coquet; two-part bar with cream walls or oak panelling, shiny black beams hung with copper pans, profusion of fishing memorabilia, taxidermy and a grandfather clock, some unexpectedly low tables with matching chairs, sofa by coal fire, Shepherd Neame Spitfire, Timothy Taylors Landlord and Youngs Bitter, around 36 malt whiskies and decent wines, well liked, generous food, friendly staff; background music; children and dogs (in bar) welcome, attractive garden and good play area with assault course, fishing rights, comfortable bedrooms, open (and food) all day. *(Ian Herdman, Comus and Sarah Elliott)*

WEST WOODBURN   NY8986
Bay Horse (01434) 270218
A68; NE48 2RX Modernised 18th-c roadside inn with horse-theme décor, Belhaven and other Greene King ales, decent wines and good range of reasonably priced food including Sun carvery, friendly service, can eat in carpeted log-fire bar or separate restaurant; background music; children and dogs welcome, riverside garden, seven bedrooms. *(J V Dadswell)*

WHALTON   NZ1281
Beresford Arms (01670) 775273
B6524; NE61 3UZ Pub-restaurant in attractive village; popular reasonably priced home-made food (some dishes available in smaller sizes), Jarrow and a couple of local guests, friendly helpful staff, high-backed chairs at sturdy candlelit pine tables, tartan carpet, old photographs, separate stables restaurant; darts and dominoes; children and dogs (in bar) welcome, disabled access, four comfortable bedrooms, open all day, food till 4pm Sun. *(Peter and Eleanor Kenyon)*

WHITFIELD   NY7857
Elks Head (01434) 345282
Off A686 SW of Haydon Bridge; NE47 8HD Extended old stone pub attractively set in steep wooded valley, light and spacious, with bar and two dining areas,

good value tasty food, Fullers London Pride and a couple of local guests, several wines by the glass, friendly helpful service; children and dogs (in bar) welcome, picnic-sets in small pretty front garden by little river, scenic area with good walks, ten bedrooms (some in adjacent cottage), open all day summer. *(Comus and Sarah Elliott)*

WHORLTON   NZ1014
Fernavilles Rest (01833) 627341
High Stakes, N of village green; DL12 8XD Recently refurbished old stone pub on green of pretty village; log-fire bar and well divided half-panelled restaurant, popular reasonably priced food including bargain set menu (lunchtime/early evening), a house beer from local Mithril and two guests kept well, friendly smartly dressed young staff; children, walkers and dogs welcome (their black lab is Ralph), three good value comfortable bedrooms, near historic narrow suspension bridge over the Tees and handy for Bowes Museum, open all day (till 5pm Sun). *(GSB, Michael Doswell)*

WYLAM   NZ1164
★Boathouse (01661) 853431
Station Road, handy for Newcastle–Carlisle railway; across Tyne from village (and George Stephenson's Birthplace – NT); NE41 8HR Convivial two-room pub with a dozen real ales, 14 ciders (some tapped from the cellar) and good choice of malt whiskies, snacky food, friendly helpful young staff, light interior with one or two low beams and woodburner; fortnightly open mike night (Tues), juke box, sports TV; children and dogs welcome, seats outside, close to station and river, open all day (evenings can be very busy). *(Comus and Sarah Elliott)*

Nottinghamshire

CAYTHORPE   SK6845 Map 7
Black Horse 🍺 £

(0115) 966 3520 – www.caythorpebrewery.co.uk

Turn off A6097 0.25 miles SE of roundabout junction with A612, NE of Nottingham; into Gunthorpe Road, then right into Caythorpe Road and keep on; NG14 7ED

Quaintly old-fashioned little pub brewing its own beer, simple interior and enjoyable homely food; no children, no credit cards

The same friendly family have run this old country local for three generations. It's a homely place and the uncluttered carpeted bar has just five tables, along with brocaded wall banquettes and settles, decorative plates on a delft shelf, a few horsebrasses attached to the ceiling joists and a coal fire. Cheerful regulars might occupy the few bar stools to enjoy Caythorpe Bitter and a seasonal ale brewed in outbuildings here and served alongside a couple of guests such as Caythorpe Dover Beck and Greene King Abbot Ale on handpump; nine wines by the glass too. Off the front corridor is a partly panelled inner room, with a wall bench running all the way round three unusual, long, copper-topped tables; there are several old local photographs, darts and board games. Down on the left, an end room has just one huge round table. There are seats outside. The pub is close to the River Trent where there are waterside walks.

▯▯ Good value home-cooked food (you'll need to book a table in advance) includes sandwiches, prawn cocktail, mushrooms on toast with creamy rosemary sauce, three-egg omelettes, lamb chops with creamed potato, gammon and eggs, baked salmon with asparagus and parsley sauce, and puddings such as walnut sticky toffee pudding and treacle sponge with custard. *Benchmark main dish: fresh fish in parsley sauce with chips £11.00. Two-course evening meal £17.00.*

Own brew ~ Licensee Sharron Andrews ~ Real ale ~ No credit cards ~ Open 12-3, 6-11; 12-5, 8-11 Sun; closed Mon except bank holidays ~ Bar food 12-2, 6-8.30; not Sat evening, Sun ~ Dogs allowed in bar *Recommended by Peter and Jean Hoare, Sally and David Champion, Dave Braisted*

CLAYWORTH   SK7288 Map 7
Blacksmiths ▯▯

(01777) 818171 – www.blacksmithsclayworth.com

Town Street; DN22 9AD

Interestingly refurbished dining pub with enthusiastic licensees, stylish décor and good, inventive food; bedrooms

Young licensees Will and Leah undertook the task of totally revamping this village pub after it had been shut for two years and reopening it as an interesting local pub and dining place. The bar has leather chesterfields and armchairs and upholstered cube seats by a woodburning stove, slate floor tiles and décor that includes cowbells here and there and a pair of skis (a nod to the publicans' seven years in Switzerland). Theakstons Best and Timothy Taylors Landlord on handpump served by well trained staff. The dining areas have a stylish, contemporary feel with some bold paintwork, cushioned walls seats and high-backed chairs around a mix of tables, dramatic flower arrangements and candles in large glass jars; stairs lead up to a private dining area with a balcony overlooking the countryside. In the sunny walled garden there are plenty of tables and chairs. The Chesterfield Canal, which circles the village, is popular with bird-watchers, walkers and cyclists.

Creative, well presented food includes lunchtime sandwiches (not Sunday), king scallops with trotter bonbon, crispy ear and burnt apple purée, pigeon breast with carrot caramel, hazelnuts and creamed cabbage, beetroot gnocchi with girolle mushrooms, courgettes and goats cheese, glazed beef short-rib with potato terrine, bone marrow croquette and baby onions, venison loin with crispy kale, mushroom purée, burnt onion and parsley root, and puddings such as black forest fondant with kirsch cherries, cherry ice-cream, pistachio curd and white chocolate chantilly and buttermilk pannacotta with rhubarb and honeycomb. *Benchmark main dish: burger with toppings and chips £12.95. Two-course evening meal £22.00.*

Free house ~ Licensees Will and Leah Frankland ~ Real ale ~ Open 12-3, 5.30-11; 12-8 Sun; closed Mon; 10 days Jan ~ Bar food 12-2.30, 6-9 (9.30 Fri, Sat); 12-4.30 Sun ~ Children welcome ~ Wi-fi ~ Bedrooms: /£100 *Recommended by Dan Thawley, Peter and Emma Kelly, Brian and Sally Wakeham, Stephen Woad*

COLSTON BASSETT
SK6933 Map 7
Martins Arms ★ ♀ ◀
(01949) 81361 – www.themartinsarms.co.uk
Village signposted off A46 E of Nottingham; School Lane, near market cross in village centre; NG12 3FD

Nottinghamshire Dining Pub of the Year

Smart dining pub with impressive food, good range of drinks including seven real ales and attractive grounds

Although most customers in this former farmhouse are here for the excellent food, they do keep a fine choice of drinks too: Bass, Black Sheep, Belhaven Grand Slam, Black Sheep, Greene King IPA, Marstons Pedigree and Timothy Taylors Landlord on handpump, 22 wines by the glass or carafe (including prosecco, champagne and sweet wines), Belvoir organic ginger beer and 17 malt whiskies; staff are neatly uniformed. There's a civilised and comfortably relaxed atmosphere, warm log fires in Jacobean fireplaces, fresh flowers and candlelight, and it's smartly decorated with period fabrics and colours, antique furniture and hunting prints; dominoes and cards. The main dining room is now painted in a warm red with new gold silk curtains. The lawned garden (with summer croquet and barbecues) backs on to National Trust parkland. Do visit the church opposite and Colston Bassett Dairy (just outside the village), which produces and sells its own stilton cheese.

Highly enjoyable food includes lunchtime sandwiches, belly pork with smoked eel, rarebit, apples and piccalilli, home-smoked salmon with yuzu, fennel, chargrilled cucumber, keta and seaweed cracker, burger with stilton, short rib, relish, truffle and parmesan chips, black pudding sausages with mixed grains and red wine jus, stone bass with crab mousse, ratte potato, passion fruit, samphire and butter sauce, venison loin with beetroot, parsnip, black pudding and chocolate, and puddings such as rhubarb crumble soufflé and pineapple pannacotta with roast pineapple and coconut sorbet. *Benchmark main dish: pork cutlet with braised cheek, cauliflower cheese, smoked ham croquettes and confit egg yolk £19.00. Two-course evening meal £24.00.*

Free house ~ Licensees Lynne Strafford Bryan and Salvatore Inguanta ~ Real ale ~ Open 12-3 (3.30 Sat), 6-11; 12-4, 7-10.30 Sun ~ Bar food 12-2, 6-9; 12-2.30 Sun ~ Restaurant ~ Children welcome ~ Wi-fi *Recommended by Caroline Prescott, Ian Duncan, Barbara Brown, Elizabeth and Peter May, Sandra King*

GRINGLEY ON THE HILL
Blue Bell
SK7390 Map 7

(01777) 816303 – www.bluebellinngringley.co.uk
High Street, just off A361 Bawtry–Gainsborough; DN10 4RF

Village pub with friendly owners, refurbished bars, real ales and wines by the glass, highly thought-of food and seats in garden

Very much the social hub of the village, this busy pub has a good mix of both regulars and visitors who are all genuinely welcomed by the hands-on licensees and their helpful staff. The various interconnected rooms are on different levels with pale painted beams, bare boards and striped carpeting, carved wood and smart leather dining chairs around sturdy tables, mirrors and prints on wallpapered or painted walls, and open fires. Theakstons Black Bull and a couple of guests such as Adnams Lighthouse and Butcombe Bitter on handpump, 30 whiskies and bourbons, a good choice of gins and wines by the glass; background music and TV. The back garden has picnic-sets under cocktail parasols, a children's play fort and a summer marquee. The acoustic and jazz sessions are very popular.

Well regarded food includes panko-breaded king prawns with sweet chilli dip, pulled pork with caramelised red onion chutney, sharing platters, mushroom and stilton tart with sweet potato, spinach and coconut curry, burgers with toppings, onion rings, a choice of sauces and chips, tomato and basil chicken, a fish dish of the day, mixed grill, and puddings such as sticky toffee pudding and cheesecake of the week. *Benchmark main dish: steak and stilton in ale pie £9.95. Two-course evening meal £16.00.*

Enterprise ~ Tenants Adam and Louise Kay ~ Real ale ~ Open 12-11; 3-11 Mon, Tues ~ Bar food 12-2, 6-9; 12-9 Sat; 12-4 Sun; not Sun evening, all Mon, Tues lunchtime ~ Restaurant ~ Children welcome ~ Wi-fi ~ Live music some Fri, Sat evenings (best to phone) *Recommended by Edward May, Jo Garnett, Richard Cole, Charles Fraser*

Also Worth a Visit in Nottinghamshire

Besides the fully inspected pubs, you might like to try these pubs that have been recommended to us and described by readers. Do tell us what you think of them: feedback@goodguides.com

AWSWORTH　　　　　　SK4844
Gate (0115) 932 9821
*Main Street, via A6096 off A610
Nuthall–Eastwood bypass; NG16 2RN*
Friendly Victorian free house with good range of well kept ales including Burton Bridge, bar with woodburner, coal fire in lounge, some snacky food; skittle alley; dogs welcome, disabled facilities, back courtyard and roof terrace, near site of once-famous railway viaduct, open all day. *(Chris Stevenson)*

You can send reports directly to us at feedback@goodguides.com

BAGTHORPE   SK4751
Dixies Arms (01773) 810505
A608 towards Eastwood off M1 junction 27, right on B600 via Sandhill Road, left into School Road; Lower Bagthorpe; NG16 5HF Friendly unspoilt 18th-c brick local with D H Lawrence connections; beams and tiled floors, well kept Greene King Abbot, Theakstons Best and a guest, no food, entrance bar with tiny snug, good fire in small part-panelled parlour's fine fireplace, longer narrow room with toby jugs, darts and dominoes; live music Sat, quiz Sun, free wi-fi; children and dogs (on leads) welcome, picnic-sets out at front, big garden and play area behind, open all day. *(Mike Benton)*

BEESTON   SK5236
Crown (0115) 925 4738
Church Street; NG9 1FY Everards pub with 14 real ales, real ciders/perry and good choice of other drinks, no hot food but fresh cobs and snacks; front snug and bar with quarry-tiled floor, carpeted parlour with padded wall seats, Victorian décor and new polished bar in lounge, beams, panelling and bric-a-brac including an old red telephone box; weekend live music, regular quiz nights and beer festivals; dogs welcome, terrace tables (some under cover), open all day. *(Mike Benton)*

BEESTON   SK5336
★ Victoria (0115) 925 4049
Dovecote Lane, backing on to railway station; NG9 1JG Genuine down-to-earth all-rounder (former red-brick station hotel) attracting good mix of customers; up to 16 real ales (regular beer festivals), two farm ciders, 120 malt whiskies and 30 wines by the glass, good sensibly priced food (order at bar) from varied blackboard menu including plenty for vegetarians, efficient service, three fairly simple unfussy rooms with original long narrow layout (last one for diners only), solid furnishings, bare boards and stripped woodwork, stained-glass windows, some breweriana, open fires; live music and other events including July VicFest, newspapers and board games; children welcome till 8pm, dogs in bar, seats out on covered heated area overlooking platform (trains pass just a few feet away), limited parking, open (and food) all day. *(Clive and Fran Dutson, Dr Martin Owton)*

BINGHAM   SK7039
Horse & Plough (01949) 839313
Off A52; Long Acre; NG13 8AF Former 1818 Methodist chapel with low beams, flagstones and stripped brick, comfortable open-plan seating including pews, prints and old brewery memorabilia, half a dozen well kept ales (tasters offered), real cider and good wine choice, enjoyable reasonably priced bar food and popular upstairs grill room (Weds-Sat evenings, Sun lunchtime) with open kitchen, good friendly service; background music; children and dogs welcome, disabled facilities, open all day. *(Jeff Davies)*

BUNNY   SK5829
Rancliffe Arms (0115) 984 4727
Loughborough Road (A60 S of Nottingham); NG11 6QT Substantial early 18th-c former coaching inn with linked dining areas, emphasis on good food including popular carvery (Mon, Weds, Sat and Sun) with excellent range of fresh vegetables, friendly prompt service, chunky country chairs around mixed tables on flagstones or carpet, well kept changing range of Marstons-related beers in comfortable log-fire bar with sofas and armchairs; background music; children welcome, decking outside, open all day Fri-Sun. *(Gerry and Rosemary Dobson)*

CAR COLSTON   SK7242
Royal Oak (01949) 20247
The Green, off Tenman Lane (off A46 not far from A6097 junction); NG13 8JE Good well priced traditional pubby food (not Sun evening) in biggish 19th-c pub opposite one of England's largest village greens, four well kept Marstons-related ales and decent choice of wines by the glass, woodburner in lounge bar with tables set for eating, public bar with unusual barrel-vaulted brick ceiling, spotless housekeeping; skittle alley; children and dogs welcome, picnic-sets on spacious back lawn, heated smokers' den, camping, open all day Fri-Sun. *(Comus and Sarah Elliott)*

CAUNTON   SK7459
★ Caunton Beck (01636) 636793
Newark Road; NG23 6AE Reconstructed low-beamed dining pub made to look old using original timbers and reclaimed oak; scrubbed pine tables and country kitchen chairs, open fire, three real ales including Oakham JHB and over two dozen wines by the glass, well presented popular food from breakfast on, cheerful obliging staff and nice relaxed atmosphere; daily newspapers, free wi-fi; children and dogs (in bar) welcome, seats on flowery terrace, open all day from 8.30am, handy for A1. *(Jim and Sue James)*

CLIPSTONE   SK6064
Dog & Duck (01623) 822138
B6030 Mansfield–Ollerton; NG21 9BT Extended roadside country dining pub with

---

Places with gardens or terraces usually let children sit there – we note in the text the very few exceptions that don't.

quirky opulent décor; good choice of home-made food from ciabattas and pub favourites up, early-bird menu 4-6pm Mon-Fri, well kept Caledonian Deuchars IPA , Theakstons Old Peculier and occasional guest, decent wines, friendly young staff, conservatory; background and some live music; children and dogs very welcome, play area (may be bouncy castle), disabled facilities though some steps, tables outside, open (and food) all day. *(Martin and Alison Stainsby)*

CUCKNEY   SK5671
Greendale Oak (01623) 844441
A616, E of A60; NG20 9NQ Doing well since recent refurbishment, good sensibly priced food all day (till 7pm Sun) from sandwiches, sharing boards and pizzas up, weekday deal (4-6.30pm) on some main courses, eight real ales including Everards, good friendly service, restaurant; children welcome, no dogs inside, sturdy bench seating on front terrace, garden behind, open all day (till 1am Fri-Sun).
(Derek and Sylvia Stephenson)

EDWINSTOWE   SK6266
Forest Lodge (01623) 824443
Church Street; NG21 9QA Friendly 18th-c inn with enjoyable home-made food in pubby bar or restaurant, good service, five well kept ales including Wells Bombardier and a house beer from Welbeck Abbey, log fire; children welcome, 13 bedrooms, handy for Sherwood Forest. *(Mike Benton)*

FARNDON   SK7652
Boathouse (01636) 676578
Off A46 SW of Newark; keep on towards river – pub off Wyke Lane, just past the Riverside pub; NG24 3SX Big-windowed contemporary bar-restaurant overlooking the Trent, emphasis on food but they do serve a couple of changing ales, good choice of wines and some interesting cocktails, main area indeed reminiscent of a boathouse with high ceiling trusses supporting bare ducting, simple modern tables and upholstered chairs, shallow step up to second similarly furnished dining area, good variety of well liked food including early-bird deal, neat young staff; background and Sun live music, July garden party with live bands, free wi-fi; children welcome, wicker chairs around teak tables on heated terrace, own moorings, open all day, food all day Sun. *(Ian Duncan)*

FISKERTON   SK7351
Bromley Arms (01636) 830789
Main Street; NG25 0UL Popular Trentside pub with modernised opened-up interior, fairly compact bar area with upholstered stools and leather armchairs/sofas, two-way fireplace, three well kept Greene King ales plus a beer badged for the pub, decent range of wines by the glass, river-view dining part with upholstered chairs on patterned carpet

(some matching wallpaper), substantial helpings of enjoyable fairly priced food (discount 4-6pm Mon-Fri), friendly helpful service; background music, live acoustic session Thurs; children welcome, rattan-style furniture on narrow walled terrace, picnic-sets by edge of wharf giving best views, open (and food) all day and can get very busy in summer. *(Clive and Fran Dutson, Gerry and Rosemary Dobson)*

GRANBY   SK7436
★Marquis of Granby (01949) 859517
Off A52 E of Nottingham; Dragon Street; NG13 9PN Popular and friendly 18th-c pub in attractive Vale of Belvoir village, tap for Brewsters with their ales and interesting guests from chunky yew counter, no food apart from Fri evening fish and chips, two small comfortable rooms with broad flagstones, some low beams and striking wallpaper, open fire; children and dogs welcome, open all day weekends, from 4pm Mon-Fri. *(Laura Reid)*

HALAM   SK6754
Waggon (01636) 813109
Off A612 in Southwell centre, via Halam Road; NG22 8AE Modernised and opened-up 17th-c beamed pub with several cosy areas, Thwaites beers and a couple of changing guests, Kingstone Press cider, enjoyable all-day food (till 5pm Sun) from lunchtime light bites to grills, friendly welcoming staff; children and dogs (in one area) allowed, terrace picnic-sets, open all day. *(Brian and Anna Marsden)*

HARBY   SK8870
Bottle & Glass (01522) 703438
High Street; village signed off A57 W of Lincoln; NG23 7EB Refurbished dining pub with pair of bay-windowed front bars, well kept ales including own microbrews and good choice of wines, small area with squashy sofas and armchairs and more formal restaurant; children welcome, dogs in bar, modern wrought-iron furniture on back terrace, picnic-sets on grass beyond, open all day. *(Chris Stevenson)*

KIMBERLEY   SK4944
★Nelson & Railway (0115) 938 2177
Station Road; handy for M1 junction 26 via A610; NG16 2NR Welcoming Victorian beamed pub in same family for over 40 years, popular and comfortable, with very well liked attractively priced home-made food from snacks to blackboard specials, well kept Greene King ales and guests, mix of Edwardian-looking furniture, brewery prints (was tap for defunct Hardys & Hansons Brewery) and railway signs, dining extension; juke box, games machine, darts, free wi-fi; children and dogs allowed, nice front and back gardens, 11 good value bedrooms, proper breakfast, open all day, food all day Sat, till 6pm Sun. *(Stephen Woad)*

KIMBERLEY   SK5044
Stag (0115) 938 3151
Nottingham Road; NG16 2NB Friendly
18th-c traditional local spotlessly kept by
good landlady; two cosy rooms, small central
counter and corridor, low beams, dark
panelling and settles, old Shipstones Brewery
photographs, table skittles and working
vintage slot machines, well kept Adnams,
Timothy Taylors Landlord and three guests
(May beer festival), no food; children and
dogs welcome, attractive back garden with
play area, opens 5pm (1.30pm Sat, midday
Sun). *(Jeff Davies)*

LAMBLEY   SK6345
Woodlark (0115) 931 2535
Church Street; NG4 4QB Welcoming
interestingly laid-out village local; neatly
furnished bare-brick beamed bar, extension
into next house giving comfortable lounge/
dining area, popular good value freshly made
food (not Sun evenings), downstairs steak
bar (Fri, Sat evenings), well kept Castle
Rock, Sam Smiths, Timothy Taylors and
a guest, open fire; traditional pub games;
children and dogs welcome, tables on side
terrace, open all day. *(Mike Benton)*

LAXTON   SK7266
★Dovecote (01777) 871586
Off A6075 E of Ollerton; NG22 0NU
Red-brick pub handy for A1; cosy country
atmosphere in three traditionally furnished
dining areas, well liked food including
notable steak and ale pie and good value
Sun lunch, well kept Castle Rock and guests,
proper cider and several wines by the glass,
friendly efficient staff; background music,
free wi-fi; children welcome, no dogs inside,
small front terrace and sloping garden with
views towards church, interesting village still
using the medieval 'strip farming' method,
two bedrooms, open all day Sun (food till
7.30pm). *(Malcolm Phillips, Derek and Sylvia
Stephenson)*

LOWDHAM   SK6646
Worlds End (0115) 966 3857
Plough Lane; NG14 7AT Small 18th-c
village pub with long carpeted beamed bar/
dining room, enjoyable traditional home-
made food (all day Fri, Sat, not Sun evening),
friendly service, three changing ales from
brick-faced counter, open fire; background
music, free wi-fi; children and dogs welcome,
some covered seats out at front among
colourful tubs and baskets, picnic-sets on
lawned area, open all day. *(Laura Reid)*

MANSFIELD   SK5561
Il Rosso (01623) 623031
Nottingham Road (A60); NG18 4AF
Restauranty pub with good italian-influenced
food including early-bird deal, three well
kept ales, good service; regular live music,
sports TV, free wi-fi; children welcome,

no dogs inside, two terraces (one with
retractable awning), open all day from 8am
for breakfast. *(Derek and Sylvia Stephenson)*

MANSFIELD   SK5363
Railway Inn (01623) 623086
*Station Street; best approached by
viaduct from near Market Place;
NG18 1EF* Friendly traditional local with
four changing ales, real cider and good
bargain home-made food (till 5pm Sun),
two little front rooms leading to main bar,
another cosy room at back, laminate flooring
throughout; some live music; children and
dogs welcome, small courtyard and beer
garden, handy for Robin Hood Line station,
open all day. *(Chris Stevenson)*

MAPLEBECK   SK7160
Beehive
*Signed down pretty country lanes from
A616 Newark–Ollerton and from A617
Newark–Mansfield; NG22 0BS*
Unpretentious little beamed country tavern
in nice spot, welcoming chatty landlady,
tiny front bar with slightly bigger side room,
traditional furnishings and antiques, open
fire, a couple of well kept ales, no food;
children and dogs welcome, tables on small
terrace with flower tubs and grassy bank
running down to stream, play area, may be
closed weekday lunchtimes, busy weekends
and bank holidays. *(Ian Duncan)*

MORTON   SK7251
Full Moon (01636) 830251
*Pub and village signed off Bleasby–
Fiskerton back road, SE of Southwell;
NG25 0UT* Attractive old brick pub
tucked away in remote hamlet close to
River Trent; modernised pale-beamed
bar with two roaring fires, comfortable
armchairs, eclectic mix of tables and
other simple furnishings, Timothy Taylors
Landlord and guests, nine wines by the
glass, enjoyable food (not Sun evening)
including good value lunchtime/early
evening weekday set menu, separate
carpeted restaurant; background music,
board games, free wi-fi; children and dogs
(in bar) welcome, picnic-sets out at front,
more on a peaceful back terrace and
sizeable lawn with sturdy play equipment,
open all day weekends. *(Jim and Sue James)*

NEWARK   SK7953
Just Beer 07983 993747
*Swan & Salmon Yard, off Castle Gate
(B6166); NG24 1BG* Welcoming one-room
micropub tucked down alley, four or five
interesting quickly changing beers from
brick bar, real cider/perry, limited range of
other drinks, bright airy minimalist décor
with some brewery memorabilia, half a
dozen tables on stone floor, eclectic mix of
customers; darts, dominoes and board games;
dogs welcome, open all day (from 1pm
weekdays). *(Ian Duncan)*

NEWARK SK7953
Prince Rupert (01636) 918121
Stodman Street, off Castle Gate; NG24 1AW Ancient renovated timber-framed pub near market, several small rooms on two floors, beams, exposed brickwork and many original features, old furniture including high-backed settles, assorted bric-a-brac, mirrors and signs, conservatory, well kept Brains, Oakham and three guests, Weston's cider, blackboard choice of wines by the glass, pubby food plus speciality pizzas with some unusual toppings, friendly staff, live music most weekends, open mike third Thurs of the month; children and dogs welcome, seats in small courtyard, open all day (till 1am Fri, Sat). *(Tony and Maggie Harwood)*

NORMANTON ON THE WOLDS SK6232
Plough (0115) 937 2401
Off A606 5 miles S of Nottingham; NG12 5NN Ivy-clad pub on edge of village, warm and welcoming, with good freshly made food from extensive menu including nice steaks and popular Sun lunch (booking advised), Black Sheep, Fullers London Pride, Wells Bombardier and a couple of guests, friendly uniformed staff, fires in bar and extended restaurant; soft background music; children welcome, big garden with play area and summer barbecues, open all day, no food Sun evening. *(Chris Stevenson)*

NOTTINGHAM SK5739
★Bell (0115) 947 5241
Angel Row; off Market Square; NG1 6HL Deceptively large pub with late Georgian frontage concealing two much older timber-framed buildings; front Tudor Bar with glass panels protecting patches of 300-year-old wallpaper, larger low-beamed Elizabethan Bar with half-panelled walls and maple parquet flooring, and upstairs Belfry with more heavy panelling and 15th-c crown post; up to a dozen real ales including Greene King and Nottingham from remarkable deep sandstone cellar (can arrange tours), ten wines by the glass, reasonably priced straightforward bar food; background and regular live music including trad jazz, TV, silent fruit machine; children welcome in some parts, pavement tables, open all day (till 1am Sat). *(Laura Reid)*

NOTTINGHAM SK5843
Bread & Bitter (0115) 960 7541
Woodthorpe Drive; NG3 5JL In former suburban bakery still showing ovens, three bright and airy bare-boarded rooms, defunct brewery memorabilia, around a dozen well kept ales including Castle Rock, good range of bottled beers, traditional cider and decent wine choice, reasonably priced pub food from cobs to specials, friendly staff; quiz/curry night Mon, live music every other Tues; well

behaved children and dogs welcome, open (and food) all day, kitchen closes 7pm Sun. *(Laura Reid, Ian Duncan)*

NOTTINGHAM SK5739
Canalhouse (0115) 955 5060
Canal Street; NG1 7EH Converted wharf building with bridge over indoors canal spur (complete with narrowboat), lots of bare brick and varnished wood, huge joists on steel beams, long bar serving Castle Rock and three guests, well over 100 bottled beers and good choice of wines, sensibly priced food from snacks up including range of burgers; background music (can be loud); masses of tables out on attractive waterside terrace, open all day (till 1am Fri, Sat), food till 7pm Sun. *(Ian Duncan)*

NOTTINGHAM SK5739
Cock & Hoop (0115) 948 4414
High Pavement opposite Galleries of Justice; NG1 1HF Cosy panelled front bar with fireside armchairs and flagstoned cellar bar attached to recently reopened Lace Market Hotel; characterful décor, enjoyable fairly priced food from sandwiches to good Sun roasts, Sharps Doom Bar and several local guests; children and dogs welcome, covered outside seating area, 42 bedrooms (ones by the street can be noisy at weekends), open (and food) all day. *(Mike Benton)*

NOTTINGHAM SK5739
★Cross Keys (0115) 941 7898
Byard Lane; NG1 2GJ Restored Victorian city-centre pub on two levels, lower carpeted part with leather banquettes, panelling and chandeliers, upper area with old wooden tables and chairs and some bucket seats on bare boards, interesting pictures/prints and more pendant lighting, well kept Navigation ales and a couple of guests, good reasonably priced food from breakfast on, friendly service, upstairs function/dining room; sports TV; seats outside, open all day from 9am. *(Mike Benton, Ian Duncan)*

NOTTINGHAM SK5739
Fellows Morton & Clayton
(0115) 950 6795 *Canal Street (part of inner ring road); NG1 7EH* Flower-decked former canal warehouse, up to nine well kept ales such as Black Sheep, Fullers, Nottingham, Sharps and Timothy Taylors, good value pubby food (not evenings Sun-Weds), softly lit downstairs bar with alcove seating, wood floors and lots of exposed brickwork, two raised areas, upstairs restaurant/function room; monthly quiz first Thurs, several sports TVs, free wi-fi; open all day, till midnight Fri, Sat. *(Tony Hobden)*

NOTTINGHAM SK5642
Gladstone (0115) 912 9994
Loscoe Road, Carrington; NG5 2AW Welcoming mid-terrace backstreet local with

half a dozen well kept ales such as Castle Rock, Fullers, Oakham and Timothy Taylors, good range of malt whiskies, comfortable lounge with reading matter, basic bar with old sports memorabilia and darts, upstairs folk club Weds, quiz Thurs; background music, sports TV, free wi-fi; tables in back garden among colourful tubs and hanging baskets, open all day weekends, closed weekday lunchtimes. *(Ian Duncan)*

NOTTINGHAM SK5640

Hand & Heart (0115) 958 2456

Derby Road; NG1 5BA Unexceptional exterior but unusual inside with bar and dining areas cut deep into back sandstone; a house beer from Dancing Duck, Maypole and guests, two real ciders and good wine and whisky range, enjoyable fairly priced traditional food from sandwiches and snacks up, set lunch deal Mon-Sat, tasting menu first Mon of month, friendly helpful service, glassed-in upstairs room overlooking street; background and interesting live music Thurs; children welcome till 7pm if eating, dogs in bar, open all day (late licence Fri, Sat). *(Laura Reid)*

NOTTINGHAM SK5542

Horse & Groom (0115) 970 3777

Radford Road, New Basford; NG7 7EA Eight good changing ales and a real cider in popular open-plan local by former Shipstones Brewery, still with their name and other memorabilia, good value straightforward food from sandwiches up, snug with open fire; live music and quiz nights; open all day weekends, from 4pm weekdays. *(Ian Duncan)*

NOTTINGHAM SK5739

★ **Keans Head** (0115) 947 4052

St Marys Gate; NG1 1QA Cheery pub in attractive Lace Market area; fairly functional single room with simple wooden café furnishings on wooden boards, some exposed brickwork and red tiling, low sofa by big windows overlooking street, stools by wood counter and small fireplace, Castle Rock and three guests, draught belgian and interesting bottled beers, 20 wines by the glass, around 60 malt whiskies and lots of teas/coffees, tasty fairly traditional food (not Sun evening), friendly service; background music, daily papers and free wi-fi; children welcome till 7pm, church next door worth a look, open all day. *(Peter Smith and Judith Brown)*

NOTTINGHAM SK5539

King William IV (0115) 958 9864

Manvers Street/Eyre Street, Sneinton; NG2 4PB Victorian corner local (the King Billy) with plenty of character, well kept Oakham and six guests from circular bar, also craft beers and real cider, good fresh

cobs and sausage rolls, friendly staff; irish folk session Thurs, silenced sports TV, pool upstairs; dogs welcome, new roof terrace, handy for cricket, football and rugby grounds, open all day (from 2pm Mon). *(Ian Duncan)*

NOTTINGHAM SK5740

★ **Lincolnshire Poacher**

(0115) 941 1584 *Mansfield Road; up hill from Victoria Centre; NG1 3FR* Impressive range of drinks at this popular down-to-earth pub (attracts younger evening crowd), 13 well kept ales including Castle Rock, lots of continental draught/bottled beers, half a dozen ciders and over 70 malt whiskies, shortish choice of reasonably priced uncomplicated food; big simple traditional front bar with wall settles, wooden tables and breweriana, plain but lively room on left and corridor to chatty panelled back snug with newspapers and board games, conservatory overlooking tables on large heated back area; live music Weds, Sun, free wi-fi; children (till 8pm) and dogs welcome, open all day (till midnight Thurs-Sat). *(Laura Reid, Mike Stevenson)*

NOTTINGHAM SK5541

★ **Lion** (0115) 970 3506

Lower Mosley Street, New Basford; NG7 7FQ Around ten real ales (tasters available) including Bass and Castle Rock from one of the city's deepest cellars (glass viewing panel – can be visited at quiet times), also plenty of craft beers and proper ciders, good well priced burger/hot dog menu; big open-plan room with feel of separate areas, bare bricks and polished dark oak boards, old brewery pictures and posters, open fires; regular live music including popular Sun lunchtime jazz, Weds quiz; children welcome till 6pm, no dogs, disabled facilities, garden with terrace and smokers' shelter, open all day. *(Ian Duncan)*

NOTTINGHAM SK5739

Malt Cross (0115) 941 1048

St James's Street; NG1 6FG Former Victorian music hall with vaulted glass roof and gallery looking down on bar area, bare boards and ornate iron pillars, comfortable sofas, good selection of drinks including some interesting real ales, decent well priced food from shortish menu, teas, coffees and daily newspapers; quiz and music nights; cellars converted into art gallery/workshop areas, ancient caves (tours available); open all day (till 9pm Sun). *(Laura Reid)*

NOTTINGHAM SK5739

Newshouse (0115) 952 3061

Canal Street; NG1 7HB Friendly two-room 1950s Castle Rock pub with blue tiled exterior, their ales and half a dozen changing

---

If you know a pub is ever open all day, please tell us.

guests, belgian and czech imports, decent fresh lunchtime food (Mon-Sat), mix of bare boards and carpet, local newspaper/radio memorabilia, beer bottles on shelves, darts, table skittles and bar billiards; background music, big-screen sports TV; a few tables out in front, open all day and popular on match days. *(Chris Stevenson)*

NOTTINGHAM SK5739

★ **Olde Trip to Jerusalem**

(0115) 947 3171 *Brewhouse Yard; from inner ring road follow 'The North, A6005 Long Eaton' signpost until in Castle Boulevard, then right into Castle Road; pub is on the left; NG1 6AD* Unusual rambling pub seemingly clinging to sandstone rock face, largely 17th-c and a former brewhouse supplying the hilltop castle; downstairs bar carved into the stone with dark panelling and simple built-in seats, tables on flagstones, some rocky alcoves, Greene King IPA and H&H Olde Trip plus guests, good value food all day, efficient staff dealing well with busy mix of customers; popular little tourist shop with panelled walls soaring into dark cavernous heights; children welcome, seats and ring the bull in snug courtyard, open all day (till midnight Fri, Sat). *(Peter Smith and Judith Brown)*

NOTTINGHAM SK5640

Organ Grinder (0115) 970 0630

Alfreton Road; NG7 3JE Tap for Blue Monkey with up to nine well kept ales including guests, a couple of ciders and a perry, good local pork pies, open-plan interior with bare boards and woodburner; sports TV; well behaved dogs welcome, seats out behind, open all day. *(Ian Duncan)*

NOTTINGHAM SK5540

Plough (0115) 970 2615

St Peters Street, Radford; NG7 3EN Friendly 1930s local with its own good value Nottingham ales brewed behind, also guest beers and traditional cider, weekday sandwiches, two bars (one carpeted, the other with terrazzo flooring), banquettes, old tables and chairs, bottles on delft shelving, coal fires; Thurs quiz, TV, traditional games including outside skittle alley; dogs welcome (may get a treat), beer garden with covered smokers' area, open all day. *(Jeff Davies)*

NOTTINGHAM SK5739

Salutation (0115) 947 6580

Hounds Gate/Maid Marian Way; NG1 7AA Low beams, flagstones, ochre walls and cosy corners including two small quiet rooms in ancient lower back part, plusher modern front lounge, up to eight real ales and good choice of draught/bottled ciders, quickly served food till 8pm (6pm Sun), helpful friendly staff (ask them to show you the haunted caves below the pub); background rock music and live bands

upstairs; open all day (till 2am Fri, Sat). *(Jeff Davies, Ian Duncan)*

NOTTINGHAM SK5640

Trent Bridge (0115) 977 8940

Radcliffe Road; NG2 6AA Good Wetherspoons in sizeable Victorian pub next to the cricket ground (very busy on match days), comfortably refurbished linked rooms with panelling and cricketing memorabilia, several well kept ales and decent good value food, efficient friendly staff; sports TVs, free wi-fi; children welcome, open all day from 8am. *(Ian Duncan)*

NOTTINGHAM SK5838

Trent Navigation (0115) 986 5658

Meadow Lane; NG2 3HS Welcoming tile-fronted Victorian pub close to canal and home to the Navigation Brewery, their beers and guests from half a dozen pumps along with ciders/perries, popular food including deals, regular live music (Fri blues) and well attended Sun quiz; sports TVs (pub is next to Notts County FC); children welcome, brewery shop at back, open all day. *(Phil and Jane Hodson)*

NOTTINGHAM SK5739

★ **Vat & Fiddle** (0115) 985 0611

Queens Bridge Road; alongside Sheriffs Way (near multi-storey car park); NG2 1NB Open-plan 1930s brick pub – tap for next door Castle Rock Brewery; varnished pine tables, bentwood chairs and stools on parquet or terrazzo flooring, some brewery memorabilia and interesting photographs of demolished local pubs, up to a dozen real ales including guests, bottled continentals, traditional ciders and over 30 malt whiskies, decent food (not Sun evening) including range of burgers and Thurs curry night, modern dining extension, visitors' centre with own bar; some live music, free wi-fi; children and dogs welcome, picnic-sets out at front by road, open all day (till midnight Fri-Sat). *(Laura Reid)*

RADCLIFFE ON TRENT SK6439

Horse Chestnut (0115) 933 1994

Main Road; NG12 2BE Smart pub with plenty of Victorian/Edwardian features, well kept Brewsters, Fullers, St Austell and four guests, decent wines by the glass and sensibly priced home-made food (not Sun evening) including some italian choices (good pizzas), friendly service, two-level main bar, parquet and mosaic floor, panelling, big mirrors and impressive lamps, handsome leather wall benches and period fireplaces; some live music; children and dogs welcome, disabled access, terrace seating, open all day, food all day Fri, Sat. *(Jim and Sue James)*

RAMPTON SK7978

Eyre Arms (01777) 248771

Main Street; DN22 0HR Shuttered red-brick village pub with enjoyable good value food from chef-owner including extensive specials menu and weekday lunchtime bargains, well kept local ales, friendly helpful service, refurbished dining area overlooking pleasant garden, locals bar with pool; open all day. *(David and Ruth Hollands)*

RUDDINGTON SK5733
Three Crowns (0115) 846 9613
Easthorpe Street; NG11 6LB Open-plan pub known locally as the Top House, well kept Fullers, Nottingham and three guests (beer festivals), good indian food in back Three Spices evening restaurant; open all day weekends, closed lunchtimes Mon and Tues. *(Ian Duncan)*

SCAFTWORTH SK6692
King William (01302) 710292
A631 Bawtry–Everton; DN10 6BL Popular red-brick country pub with friendly relaxed atmosphere, good well presented home-made food (best to book Sun lunch), Theakstons Best and a couple of regional guests, good choice of wines by the glass, bar, snug and two dining rooms with old high-backed settles, plain tables and chairs and log fires; background music; children and dogs welcome, big back garden with swings, open all day Fri-Sun, from 4.30pm other days. *(Chris Stevenson)*

SELSTON SK4553
★Horse & Jockey (01773) 781012
Handy for M1 junctions 27/28; Church Lane; NG16 6FB Interesting pub on different levels dating from the 17th c, low heavy beams, dark flagstones, individual furnishings and good log fire in cast-iron range, friendly staff, Greene King Abbot and Timothy Taylors Landlord poured from the jug and up to four guests, real cider, no food, games area with darts and pool; folk night Weds, quiz Sun; dogs welcome, terrace and smokers' shelter, pleasant rolling country. *(Laura Reid)*

SOUTHWELL SK7054
★Final Whistle (01636) 814953
Station Road; NG25 0ET Popular railway-themed pub commemorating the long defunct Southwell line; ten well kept ales including Bass, Everards, Oakham and two house beers from Ashover (beer festivals), real ciders/perries, foreign bottled beers and good range of wines, cheeseboard and other snacky food, traditional opened-up bar with tiled or wood floor, settles and armchairs in quieter carpeted room, corridor drinking area, two open fires, panelling, lots of railway memorabilia and other odds and ends; quiz Tues and Sun, folk night second Thurs of

month; children and dogs welcome, back garden with wonderful mock-up of 1920s platform complete with track and buffers, on Robin Hood Way and Southwell Trail, open all day. *(Brian and Anna Marsden)*

THURGARTON SK6949
Red Lion (01636) 830351
Southwell Road (A612); NG14 7GP Cheery pub dating from the 16th c with split-level beamed bars and restaurant, a couple of changing ales from dark-panelled bar, good choice of enjoyable reasonably priced food including specials, comfortable banquettes and other seating on patterned carpets, lots of nooks and crannies, grandfather clock, open fires; children welcome, no dogs inside, attractive back garden on two levels, open (and food) all day weekends. *(Jim and Sue James)*

TUXFORD SK7471
Fountain (01777) 872854
Lincoln Road on edge of village near railway line; NG22 0JQ Comfortably updated family dining pub with welcoming atmosphere, enjoyable affordably priced food (not Sun evening) from pub favourites and grills to daily specials, local ales and ciders such as Welbeck Abbey and Scrumpy Wasp, friendly service; free wi-fi; picnic-sets out in fenced area, open all day Fri-Sun, closed lunchtimes Mon, Tues. *(Derek and Sylvia Stephenson)*

UPTON SK7354
★Cross Keys (01636) 813269
Main Street (A612); NG23 5SY 17th-c pub in fine spot with rambling heavy-beamed bar, log fire in brick fireplace, own Mallard ales (brewed in Maythorne) and good home-made food (not Sun evening) from lunchtime sandwiches to specials, friendly staff, back extension; seats on decked terrace, British Horological Institute opposite, open all day Fri-Sun, closed Mon and Tues lunchtimes. *(Ian Duncan)*

WEST BRIDGFORD SK5838
Larwood & Voce (0115) 981 9960
Fox Road; NG2 6AJ Well run open-plan dining pub (part of the small Moleface group); good locally sourced home-made food in bar and restaurant area including some imaginative choices, plenty of wines by the glass, cocktail menu and three well kept ales, cheerful staff; sports TV; children welcome away from bar, seats out on raised deck with heaters, on the edge of the cricket ground and handy for Nottingham Forest FC, open all day, from 10am weekends for breakfast. *(Peter Smith and Judith Brown, Vanessa and Jerry Hockin)*

Post Office address codings confusingly give the impression that a few pubs are in Nottinghamshire, when they're really in Derbyshire (which is where we list them).

WEST BRIDGFORD   SK5938

Poppy & Pint (0115) 981 9995

Pierrepont Road; NG2 5DX Converted
former British Legion Club backing on to
bowling green and tennis courts; large bar
with raised section and family area, around a
dozen real ales including Castle Rock and a
couple of ciders, decent food from breakfast
on; monthly folk night and other events; dogs
welcome in bar, open all day from 9.30am
(10am Sun). *(Mike Benton)*

WEST BRIDGFORD   SK5837

★ ## Stratford Haven (0115) 982 5981

Stratford Road, Trent Bridge; NG2 6BA
Good Castle Rock pub; bare-boards front bar
leading to linked areas including airy skylit
back part with relaxed local atmosphere,
their well kept ales and many guests
(monthly brewery nights), interesting
bottled beers, farm ciders and good wine
and whisky choice, wide range of well priced
home-made food including themed nights,
fast friendly service; some live music
(nothing loud), Sun quiz, daily papers;
children (during the day) and dogs welcome,
tables outside, handy for cricket ground and

Nottingham Forest FC (busy on match days),
open (and food) all day. *(Laura Reid)*

WEST STOCKWITH   SK7994

White Hart (01427) 892672

Main Street; DN10 4EY Small refurbished
country pub at junction of Chesterfield Canal
with River Trent, own good Idle beers from
next-door brewery plus guests, enjoyable well
priced traditional food (not Sun evening),
friendly atmosphere; live music Fri, pool
and sports TV; children and dogs welcome,
garden overlooking the water, open all day.
(Sam Greetham)

WYSALL   SK6027

Plough (01509) 880339

*Keyworth Road; off A60 at Costock, or
A6006 at Wymeswold; NG12 5QQ*
Attractive 17th-c beamed village local;
popular good value lunchtime food from
shortish menu, cheerful staff, Bass, Greene
King Abbot, Timothy Taylors Landlord and
three guests, rooms either side of bar with
nice mix of furnishings, soft lighting, big log
fire; Tues quiz, pool; french doors to pretty
terrace with flower tubs and baskets, open
all day. *(George Sanderson)*

Oxfordshire

KEY ★ Star Pub 🎯 Top Quality Food 🍺 Great Beer
🍷 Good Wines £ Bargain Meals 🛏 Good Bedrooms 🍽 Serves Food

ASTHALL   SP2811 Map 4

Maytime 🎯 🛏

(01993) 822068 – www.themaytime.com
Off A40 at W end of Witney bypass, then first left; OX18 4HW

Carefully renovated Cotswold-stone inn with individually furnished bar and dining rooms, good food and seats outside; smart bedrooms

A 17th-c former coaching inn with its own smithy, this is now a carefully refurbished inn of much character. The lofty bar has exposed roof trusses, flagstones, leather sofas, cushioned wall seats and stools against the counter where friendly staff serve Dark Star Hophead and Mantle Cwrw Teifi on handpump, good wines by the glass and a fine collection of 69 gins; background music and board games. Several white-painted beamed rooms lead off on several levels with cushioned window seats, a mix of tartan upholstered and traditional wooden chairs around tables of varying size on black slates or bare boards, and pictures on painted or stone walls; one room has a glass ceiling. The pub springer is called Alfie. Seats and tables sit under parasols on the back terrace with more seats in the extended garden overlooking the River Windrush. This is a lovely place to stay, with stylish, smart and well equipped bedrooms and highly thought-of breakfasts; there are good walks from the door.

🎯 Interesting, very popular food includes sandwiches, pigeon breast with blackberry, puy lentils and pancetta crisp, potted chicken liver parfait with celeriac rémoulade, pea and broad bean risotto, home-baked honey and mustard ham with free-range eggs, bass fillet with sautéed baby squid, smoked aubergine, parmentier potatoes and saffron velouté, local venison with lyonnaise potatoes and red wine jus, and puddings such as cardamom pannacotta with tropical fruit coulis and chocolate brownie with lemon curd chocolate sphere, raspberry gel and chantilly cream. *Benchmark main dish: sage and wild boar burger with toppings, onion rings and skinny chips £12.50. Two-course evening meal £21.00.*

Free house ~ Licensee Dominic Wood ~ Real ale ~ Open 11-11 ~ Bar food 12-2.30 (3 weekends), 6-9.30 ~ Restaurant ~ Children welcome but not in bedrooms ~ Dogs allowed in bar ~ Wi-fi ~ Live music 3-5pm every second Sun ~ Bedrooms: £85/£95
Recommended by Liz Bell, William and Megan, Sophia and Hamish Greenfield

---

Real ale may be served from handpumps, electric pumps (not just the on-off switches used for keg beer) or – common in Scotland – tall taps called founts (pronounced 'fonts') where a separate pump pushes the beer up under air pressure.

BANBURY
SP4540 Map 4

Olde Reindeer 🍺 £

(01295) 270972 – www.yeoldereindeer.co.uk

Parsons Street, off Market Place; OX16 5NA

Interesting town pub with a friendly welcome, real ales and simple food

This is a splendid old inn, full of history and with a chatty mix of shoppers and regulars. The front bar has a good, bustling atmosphere, heavy 16th-c beams, very broad polished oak floorboards, a magnificent carved overmantel for one of the two roaring log fires and traditional solid furnishings; some interesting breweriana too. It's worth looking at the handsomely proportioned Globe Room used by Oliver Cromwell as his base during the Civil War. Quite a sight, it still has some very fine 17th-c carved dark oak panelling. Hook Norton Hooky, Cotswold Lion, Old Hooky, Hooky Mild and a couple of guest beers on handpump, 12 wines by the glass, fruit wines and several malt whiskies. The little back courtyard has tables and benches under parasols, aunt sally and pretty flowering baskets.

🍴 Traditional food at fine value includes pâté with red onion chutney, breaded whitebait with lemon mayonnaise, pork sausages with mash and caramelised onion gravy, a vegetarian dish of the day, a pie of the day, grilled bacon chop with bubble and squeak and poached egg, chicken kiev, beer-battered fish and chips, and puddings such as hot chocolate fudge cake and fruit crumble. *Benchmark main dish: venison burger with relish and chips £10.00. Two-course evening meal £15.00.*

Hook Norton ~ Tenant Jeremy Money ~ Real ale ~ Open 11-11 (midnight Fri, Sat); 12-10.30 Sun ~ Bar food 12-3, 6-9; 12-3 Sun ~ Children welcome until 8pm ~ Dogs allowed in bar ~ Live music Sat from 9pm; jam night Sun *Recommended by Rosie and John Moore, George Atkinson, Edward Edmonton,*

BESSELS LEIGH
SP4501 Map 4

Greyhound 🍷 🍺

(01865) 862110 – www.brunningandprice.co.uk/greyhound

A420 Faringdon–Botley; OX13 5PX

Cotswold-stone inn with rambling rooms, up to half a dozen real ales, lots of wines by the glass and enjoyable food

Our readers love their visits to this handsome old pub and the knocked-through rooms have plenty of character and interest: the half-panelled walls are covered in all manner of old photographs and pictures, individually chosen cushioned dining chairs, leather-topped stools and dark wooden tables are grouped on carpeting or rug-covered floorboards, and there are books on shelves, glass and stone bottles on windowsills, big gilt mirrors, three fireplaces (one housing a woodburning stove) and sizeable pot plants. Wooden bar stools line the counter where they serve Phoenix Brunning & Price Original, Cottage Black Diamond, Loddon Ferrymans Gold, Prescott Summer Seasons Best and White Horse Village Idiot on handpump, 14 wines by the glass, 102 malt whiskies and a farm cider. By the back dining extension is a white picket fence-enclosed garden with picnic-sets under green parasols; the summer window boxes and hanging baskets are very pretty.

🍴 Highly regarded food includes sandwiches, sardine fillets wrapped in parma ham with spicy tomato salsa, asparagus with crispy egg and hollandaise, sharing boards, wild boar and chorizo meatballs with tomato and basil sauce on pasta, bass fillet with lobster and crayfish bisque and vegetable ribbons, steak burger with toppings, coleslaw and chips, shredded lamb with olive, artichoke and feta salad and mint yoghurt dressing, and puddings such as white chocolate, strawberry and amaretto cheesecake and sticky toffee pudding with toffee sauce. *Benchmark main dish: crispy beef salad with chilli and cashew nuts £12.75. Two-course evening meal £20.00.*

Brunning & Price ~ Manager Darren Snell ~ Real ale ~ Open 11-11; 11.30-10.30 Sun ~ Bar food 12-10 (9.30 Sun) ~ Well behaved children welcome ~ Dogs allowed in bar ~ Wi-fi *Recommended by Neil and Angela Huxter, Tracey and Stephen Groves, Richard Tilbrook, Taff Thomas, Nigel and Sue Foster*

BRIGHTWELL BALDWIN
Lord Nelson 🌟 ♀

SU6594   Map 4

(01491) 612497 – http://thenelsonbrightwell.co.uk
Off B480 Chalgrove–Watlington, or B4009 Benson–Watlington; OX49 5NP

Attractive inn with several character bars, real ales, good wines by the glass and enjoyable well thought-of food; bedrooms

The atmosphere in this bustling 300-year-old inn is relaxed and friendly, and helped along by the cheerful mix of both drinkers and diners. The bar has candles and fresh flowers, wine bottles on windowsills, horsebrasses on standing timbers, lots of paintings on white or red walls, wheelback and other dining chairs around assorted dark tables and a big brick inglenook fireplace. One cosy room has cushions on comfortable sofas, little lamps on dark furniture, ornate mirrors and portraits in gilt frames; background music. Rebellion IPA and Roundhead on handpump, 20 wines (including champagne) by the glass, a dozen malt whiskies and winter mulled wine. There are seats and tables on the back terrace and in the willow-draped garden.

From a thoughtful menu and using local produce, food includes sandwiches, twice-baked cheese soufflé, pigeon breast with smoked bacon, black pudding and red wine jus, baked aubergine with tomatoes, garlic and fresh herbs topped with cheese with sweet potato fries, burger with toppings, coleslaw and skinny fries, sausages on champ mash with onion gravy, half duck with orange sauce, red cabbage and dauphinoise potatoes, half lobster thermidor with skinny fries, and puddings. *Benchmark main dish: fillet of beef wellington £20.00. Two-course evening meal £24.00.*

Free house ~ Licensees Roger and Carole Shippey ~ Real ale ~ Open 12-3, 6-11; 12-5 Sun; 12-5 in winter ~ Bar food 12-2, 6-10; 12-4 Sun ~ Restaurant ~ Children welcome ~ Dogs allowed in bar ~ Wi-fi ~ Bedrooms: £75/£100 *Recommended by Colin McLachlan, Roy Hoing, Valerie Sayer*

BURFORD
Highway ♀ 🛏

SP2512   Map 4

(01993) 823661 – www.thehighwayinn.co.uk
High Street (A361); OX18 4RG

Comfortable old inn with a good choice of wines and well liked bar food; comfortable bedrooms

There are all sorts of interesting touches in the bars here, but the main feature is the pair of big windows overlooking the bustle of the pretty High Street; each consists of several dozen panes of old float glass and has a long cushioned window seat. Do notice the stag candlesticks for the rather close-set tables on well worn floorboards, the neat modern dark leather chairs, the nice old station clock above the big log fire in a pleasingly simple stone fireplace and the careful balance of ancient stripped stone with filigree black and pale blue wallpaper. A small corner counter has Hook Norton Hooky and a guest such as Box Steam Piston Broke on handpump, 20 wines (including champagne) by the glass and 13 malt whiskies; they hold a beer festival and barbecue in the second week of June. Background music, TV and board games. On the right, a second bar room, with another big window seat, is carpeted but otherwise similar in style; there's also a downstairs cellar bar that's open for tapas at the weekend. A few picnic-sets stand above the pavement at the front. The bedrooms are individually decorated in a country house style and breakfasts are good.

Interesting food includes lunchtime sandwiches and panini, loin of rabbit on fennel salad with marsala prunes, black pudding and pancetta, breadcrumbed calamari with garlic and paprika mayonnaise, moroccan-spiced nut roast with apricot and date couscous and mint yoghurt, southern fried chicken burger with sweet chilli and fries, a pie of the day, beer-battered haddock and chips, confit duck leg with dark cherry and chocolate jus and dauphinoise potatoes, and puddings. *Benchmark main dish: mini lamb rack, shoulder bonbon and redcurrant and red wine jus £17.00. Two-course evening meal £20.50.*

Free house ~ Licensees Dan, Jane and Michelle Arnell ~ Real ale ~ Open 12-11.30 (midnight weekends); closed first two weeks Jan ~ Bar food 12-2, 7-9 ~ Restaurant ~ Children welcome ~ Dogs allowed in bar and bedrooms ~ Wi-fi ~ Bedrooms: £90/£130
Recommended by Ross Balaam, Ray and Janet Anstis, Roy Hoing

BURFORD
SP2412   Map 4

Lamb 🏅 ♈ 🍷 🛏

(01993) 823155 – www.cotswold-inns-hotels.co.uk/lamb
Village signposted off A40 W of Oxford; Sheep Street (B4425, off A361); OX18 4LR

Lovely old inn with a bustling bar, real ales and an extensive wine list, interesting bar and restaurant food, and pretty gardens; bedrooms

At the heart of this civilised, 500-year-old inn is a cosy bar with an unchanging, restful atmosphere. There are armchairs on rugs and flagstones in front of log fires, china plates on shelves, Hook Norton Hooky and Wickwar Cotswold Way on handpump, an extensive wine list with 18 by the glass and 26 malt whiskies. The roomy beamed main lounge is charmingly traditional with distinguished old chairs, oak tables, seats built into stone-mullioned windows, polished floorboards, fresh flowers and antiques and other fine decorations. A pretty terrace with teak furniture leads down to neatly kept lawns surrounded by flowers, shrubs and small trees. The garden, enclosed by the warm stone of the surrounding buildings, is a real suntrap. They're kind to dogs and even have a special menu for them.

Tempting, reliably good food includes sandwiches, ham hock terrine with piccalilli, eggs benedict, sausage and mash with red onion gravy, wild mushroom linguine, burger with toppings and skinny chips, moules marinière, chicken with truffled mash and jus, bass fillet with white wine sauce, and puddings such as white chocolate, banana and pistachio bread and butter pudding with pistachio ice-cream and lemon posset with berry coulis. *Benchmark main dish: lamb shank with mash and minted vegetables £16.95. Two-course evening meal £22.00.*

Cotswold Inns & Hotels ~ Manager Bill Ramsay ~ Real ale ~ Open 12-11 ~ Bar food 12-9.30 ~ Restaurant ~ Children welcome ~ Dogs allowed in bar and bedrooms ~ Wi-fi ~ Bedrooms: £175/£185 *Recommended by Richard Tilbrook, George Atkinson*

We say if we know a pub has background music.

CHURCHILL   SP2824   Map 4

Chequers

(01608) 659393 – www.thechequerschurchill.com

Church Road; B4450 Chipping Norton to Stow-on-the-Wold (and village signed off A361 Chipping Norton–Burford); OX7 6NJ

Simple furnishings in spacious bars and dining rooms, a friendly relaxed atmosphere, up to six ales and popular food

This busy village inn is Cotswold stone at its most golden. There's a relaxed and friendly bar with plenty of chatty customers, an armchair and other comfortable chairs around an old trunk in front of an inglenook fireplace, some exposed stone walls, cushioned wall seats, and a mix of wooden and antique leather chairs around nice old tables on bare floorboards. Rugs are dotted about and stools line the counter presided over by a big stag's head: a beer named for the pub (from Chadlington) plus Butcombe Bitter, Crate Rye, Hook Norton Hooky, JW Lees Manchester Pale Ale and Sharps Cornish Coaster on handpump, 12 wines by the glass, 11 malt whiskies, mocktails and a farm cider; darts and background music. At the back is a large extension with soaring rafters, big lantern lights, long button-back leather banquettes and other seating, while upstairs is another similarly and simply furnished dining area and a room just right for a private party. The terraced back garden has been enlarged this year and has lots of good quality wooden chairs and tables. The church opposite is impressive.

Extremely good food includes devilled kidneys on toast, twice-baked cheddar soufflé, asian-style duck salad, caramelised onion and braised chicory tart with cheese and hazelnuts, beer-battered whiting and chips, braised ibérico pig cheeks with parsnip purée and morcilla (spanish sausage), beef short rib, bone marrow and shallot pie, gurnard fillet with shaved fennel, orange, chicory and mint, steaks with quite a choice of sauces, and puddings. *Benchmark main dish: calves liver with bacon, mash and red wine sauce £16.00. Two-course evening meal £23.00.*

Free house ~ Licensee Peter Creed ~ Real ale ~ Open 11am-midnight ~ Bar food 12-3, 6-9.30 ~ Restaurant ~ Children welcome ~ Dogs welcome ~ Wi-fi *Recommended by Bernard Stradling, Roger White, Helena and Trevor Fraser*

EAST HENDRED   SU4588   Map 2

Eyston Arms

(01235) 833320 – www.eystonarms.co.uk

Village signposted off A417 E of Wantage; High Street; OX12 8JY

Attractive bar areas with low beams, flagstones, log fires and candles, imaginative food and helpful service

Always busy and welcoming, this is a well run place and although many customers are here to enjoy the very good food, locals do pop in for just a drink and a chat. There are seats at the bar and they keep a few tables free for drinkers keen to try the Hook Norton Hooky, Wadworths 6X and a guest ale on handpump, ten wines by the glass and 15 malt whiskies. Several separate-seeming candlelit areas have contemporary paintwork and modern country-style furnishings, low ceilings and beams, stripped timbers and the odd standing upright, nice tables and chairs on flagstones and carpet, some cushioned wall seats and an inglenook fireplace; background music. Picnic-sets outside overlook the pretty lane and there are seats set out in the back courtyard garden.

Imaginative food includes potted ham and rabbit with plum chutney, smoked salmon with cucumber and horseradish pannacotta, steak and chorizo burger with toppings, pickled courgettes, chipotle mayonnaise and string chips, spinach and asparagus gnocchi with wild mushroom, white wine and cream sauce, pigeon breast with bacon lardons, walnuts, asparagus and grain mustard dressing, seared scallop and king prawn salad with roasted red peppers, and puddings such as almond and rhubarb tart and chocolate and polenta cake with pistachio custard. *Benchmark main dish: rare roast local beef with string chips £15.95. Two-course evening meal £22.00.*

Free house ~ Licensees George Dailey and Daisy Barton ~ Real ale ~ Open 9am-11pm (10pm Sun) ~ Bar food 12-9 (light menu 2-5); 12-8 Sun (light menu 4-8) ~ Restaurant ~ Children welcome ~ Dogs allowed in bar ~ Wi-fi *Recommended by Nigel and Sue Foster, Sally Wright, John Sargeant*

FILKINS
SP2304 Map 4

Five Alls 🌟 🍺

(01367) 860875 – www.thefiveallsfilkins.co.uk
Signed off A361 Lechlade–Burford; GL7 3JQ

Thoughtfully refurbished inn with creative food, quite a range of drinks, a friendly welcome and seats outside; bedrooms

Impressive food can be enjoyed in the elegant and individually furnished dining rooms here – but there's also a beamed bar liked by locals. This has a cosy area with three leather chesterfields grouped around a table by an open fire, an informal dining space with farmhouse chairs and cushioned pews around tables on bare boards and a nice little window seat for two. Stools line the bar where friendly staff serve a beer named for the pub (from Wychwood), Brakspears Bitter and Oxford Gold and Butcombe Bitter on handpump, 16 wines by the glass and six malt whiskies. Décor in the dining room includes some unusual postage-stamp wallpaper, an attractive mix of chairs and tables on rugs, floorboards and flagstones, plus chandeliers, church candles, fresh flowers and modern artwork on pale-painted walls; background music and TV. The back terrace has chunky tables and chairs under parasols and there are a few picnic-sets at the front. Bedrooms are comfortable and attractively refurbished.

 Cooked by the landlord, the delicious food includes sandwiches, potted shrimps and smoked trout with melba toast, chicken liver and foie gras parfait with plum and apple chutney, caramelised onion, sage and gruyère tart, calves liver with bubble and squeak, pancetta, beetroot and brown mint butter, moroccan lamb tagine with couscous, chickpeas and harissa, cod with chorizo, mussels, broad beans and wild garlic, and puddings such as banoffi tart and baked alaska; they also offer a two- and three-course set menu (Mon-Thurs). *Benchmark main dish: local pork with crackling, artichokes, field mushrooms and confit potatoes £17.00. Two-course evening meal £25.00.*

Free house ~ Licensee Sebastian Snow ~ Real ale ~ Open 12-11; 12-9 Sun ~ Bar food 12-3, 6-10; not Sun evening ~ Restaurant ~ Children welcome ~ Dogs allowed in bar ~ Wi-fi ~ Bedrooms: £95/£120 *Recommended by Liz Bell, Charles Fraser, Carol and Barry Craddock*

GORING
SU5980 Map 2

Miller of Mansfield 🌟 🍷 🍺

(01491) 872829 – www.millerofmansfield.com
High Street; RG8 9AW

First class food and drink in handsome inn with easy-going bars and dining rooms; bedrooms

In a lovely village surrounded by pretty countryside, this is a handsome 18th-c coaching inn run by hands-on, professional licensees. They've worked hard to create exactly the atmosphere they want, which is one of easy, friendly informality backed up by excellent food and a carefully chosen choice of drinks. Décor in the beamed bars is simple and unfussy: armchairs around open fires or in bay windows, plain wooden tables, bare floorboards, exposed stone and brick walls and a few prints and gilt-edged mirrors; one end bar just has a few chairs and big barrels for tables. Hook Norton Hooky, Sharps Cornish Coaster and West Berkshire Good Old Boy on handpump and 16 wines by the glass from a thoughtful list; service is courteous and helpful. The dining rooms are painted in yellow or cream and have antique-style or contemporary dining chairs on more boards; background music. The multi-level terraced garden has solid furniture among flowering tubs with parasols for hot days. The bedrooms are individually decorated and well equipped. Woodland walks are a few minutes' away.

 Accomplished food using the best seasonal produce and cooked by the chef-owner includes sandwiches, cured salmon with pickled cucumber, lime granita and honey and soy dressing, chicken parfait, cocks comb, black pudding and egg yolk on brioche, cauliflower and cumin lasagne with hazelnuts and golden raisins, local muntjac pie, oak-smoked cod with parsley purée, salsify and caper fish sauce, and puddings such as caramelised chocolate mousse with malt ice-cream and pear tarte tatin with salted caramel; they also offer a two- and three-course set lunch. *Benchmark main dish: rare-breed sirloin steak with bone marrow sauce, confit shallots and puffed creamy spelt £23.00. Two-course evening meal £30.00.*

Enterprise ~ Lease Mary and Nick Galer ~ Real ale ~ Open 10am-11pm; 11am-10pm Sun ~ Bar food 12-2.30, 6-9; 12-2.30, 6-8 Sun ~ Restaurant ~ Children welcome ~ Dogs allowed in bar and bedrooms ~ Wi-fi ~ Bedrooms: $80/$120 *Recommended by Sally Wright, Nigel Havers, Sarah Roberts*

HEADINGTON
SP5407 Map 4
Black Boy
(01865) 741137 – www.theblackboy.uk.com
Old High Street/St Andrews Road; off A420 at traffic lights opposite B4495; OX3 9HT

Enterprising dining pub with good, enjoyable food and useful summer garden

Up-to-date food and furnishings draw many customers into this stylish place. There are black leather seats on dark parquet, big mirrors, silvery patterned wallpaper, nightlights in fat opaque cylinders and glittering bottles behind the long bar counter. It's light and airy in feel, particularly at the two tables in the big bay window; just to the side are lower, softer seats beside an open fire. Crisp white tablecloths and bold black and white wallpaper lend the area on the left a touch of formality. Everards Crown and York Guzzler on handpump, 20 wines by the glass, ten malt whiskies and several coffees and teas. Behind the building is an appealing terrace, with picnic-sets under alternating black and white parasols on smart pale stone chippings, and a central seat encircling an ash tree.

Rewarding food includes lunchtime sandwiches, beetroot-infused gravadlax with cucumber and dill crème fraîche, smoked haddock fishcakes with chive beurre blanc and wilted spinach, spiced potato and chickpea burger with cheese and fries, chicken with garlic and thyme mash, french-style peas and jus, swordfish with mango and chilli salsa beer-battered fish and chips, and puddings such as orange and cardamom brûlée and iced white chocolate mousse with raspberry sorbet. *Benchmark main dish: crayfish and broad bean risotto £11.95. Two-course evening meal £21.00.*

Greene King ~ Lease Abi Rose and Chris Bentham ~ Real ale ~ Open 12-3, 5-11 ~ Bar food 12-2.45, 6-9.15 ~ Restaurant ~ Children welcome ~ Wi-fi *Recommended by John Poulter, Susan Eccleston, Neil Allen*

HIGHMOOR

SU6984 Map 2

Rising Sun

(01491) 640856 – www.risingsunwitheridgehill.co.uk

Witheridge Hill, signposted off B481; OS Sheet 175 map reference 697841; RG9 5PF

Friendly village pub with a welcoming landlord, character bars and eating areas, and good food and drink; seats in garden

To be sure of a table, it's best to book in advance as this charming 17th-c pub is always full of chatty customers – all made welcome by the friendly landlord. The cosy bar has beams, old red and white floor tiles, a comfortable sofa, lots of walking sticks in a pot by the woodburning stove, books on the windowsill and leather stools against the counter where they serve Brakspears Bitter and a couple of guests such as Marstons Pedigree and Ringwood Best on handpump and a dozen wines by the glass; background music. The three interlinked eating areas have rugs on bare boards, pictures on dark red walls and seating that includes captain's and farmhouse chairs, chunky benches and cushioned wall seats around an assortment of tables; one section has a log fire in a small brick fireplace. There are picnic-sets and white metal chairs and tables in the pleasant back garden. Good surrounding walks.

Food is enjoyable and includes lunchtime sandwiches and little snacks such as scrambled egg on toast, calamari rings and bacon nachos, deep-fried breaded brie with mango chutney, black pudding, crispy bacon and fried bantam egg, sweet potato and baby spinach pot roast with goats cheese, bangers and mash with onion gravy, burger with toppings, red onion chutney and chips, bass with prawn, caper and lemon butter, slow-cooked belly with apple mash, crackling and cider jus, and puddings. *Benchmark main dish: steak and mushroom in Guinness pie £12.75. Two-course evening meal £19.00.*

Brakspears ~ Tenant Simon Duffy ~ Real ale ~ Open 12-3, 5-11; 12-11 Sat; 12-9 Sun ~ Bar food 12-2, 6-9; 12-2.30, 6-9.30 Sat; 12-3 Sun ~ Restaurant ~ Children welcome ~ Dogs allowed in bar ~ Wi-fi *Recommended by John Pritchard, Jeremy Snaithe, Sandra King*

KELMSCOTT

SU2499 Map 4

Plough 🛏

(01367) 253543 – www.theploughinnkelmscott.com

NW of Faringdon, off B4449 between A417 and A4095; GL7 3HG

Lovely spot for tranquil pub with character bar and dining rooms, attractive furnishings and friendly owners; bedrooms

This pretty 17th-c country pub is in a peaceful hamlet by the upper Thames; moorings are just a few minutes' away. The small traditional beamed front bar has ancient flagstones and stripped stone walls, along with a good log fire and the relaxed chatty feel of a real village pub. Butcombe Bitter, Hook Norton Hooky and Sharps Doom Bar on handpump, good wines by the glass and maybe farm cider. The dining room has elegant wooden or painted dining chairs around all sorts of tables, striped and cushioned wall seats, cartoons on exposed stone walls, rugs on the floor and plants on windowsills. The garden has seats and tables (some under cover). Bedrooms are comfortable and breakfasts are good. The Oxfordshire Cycleway runs close by and the inn is handy for Kelmscott Manor (open Wednesdays and Saturdays April-October).

Cooked by the landlord, the highly thought-of food includes sandwiches, twice-baked cheese soufflé, sautéed wild mushrooms on toast with poached egg and truffle oil, goats cheese, spinach and red onion tart, moules frites in cider, mallard two-ways with chestnuts and bacon, chargrilled rib-eye steak with triple-cooked potato wedges and béarnaise sauce, and puddings such as dark rum and chocolate mousse tart and sticky date and ginger pudding with toffee sauce. *Benchmark main dish: lamb pie £16.50. Two-course evening meal £24.00.*

Free house ~ Licensee Sebastian Snow ~ Real ale ~ Open 12-11 ~ Bar food 12-2.30, 6-9.30 (not Mon evening); 12-3, 6-10 Sat; 12-7 Sun ~ Restaurant ~ Children welcome ~ Dogs allowed in bar ~ Wi-fi ~ Bedrooms: £70/£90 *Recommended by R K Phillips, Liz Bell*

KINGHAM
SP2624 Map 4

Plough 🏅 ♀ 🛏

(01608) 658327 – www.thekinghamplough.co.uk

Village signposted off B4450 E of Bledington; or turn S off A436 at staggered crossroads a mile SW of A44 junction – or take signed Daylesford turn off A436 and keep on; The Green; OX7 6YD

Friendly dining pub combining an informal pub atmosphere with creative food; bedrooms

Of course, the exceptional food cooked by the landlady is the main draw to this Cotswold-stone inn but the little bar is properly pubby and keeps an interesting choice of drinks. It has some nice old high-backed settles and brightly cushioned chapel chairs on broad dark boards, candles on stripped tables and cheerful farmyard animal and country prints; at one end is a big log fire, at the other a woodburning stove. A snug one-table area is opposite the servery where they keep Hook Norton Hooky and a guest such as Wye Valley HPA on handpump, eight wines by the glass, home-made cordials, 14 malt whiskies and local cider. The fairly spacious and raftered two-part dining room is up a few steps. The bedrooms are comfortable and pretty and the breakfasts very good.

Championing local produce, the fantastic modern dishes include rabbit terrine with potato bread and tarragon butter, crab and watercress cocktail, potato croquette with local asparagus, confit duck yolk egg, herbs and lemon butter, bass with mussels, sea lettuce and cider stew, lamb loin and braised shoulder with crispy sweetbreads, carrots and pea shoots, hanger steak with bone marrow butter, onion rings and triple-cooked chips, and puddings such as chocolate mousse and cornflake cream and rhubarb and stem ginger baked alaska. *Benchmark main dish: pork, lamb or beef wellington £26.00. Two-course evening meal £30.00.*

Free house ~ Licensees Emily Watkins and Miles Lampson ~ Real ale ~ Open 12-11 (midnight Sat); 12-10 Sun ~ Bar food 12-2 (2.30 Sat), 6.30-9; 12-3 Sun (light meals 6-8) ~ Restaurant ~ Children welcome ~ Dogs allowed in bar and bedrooms ~ Wi-fi ~ Bedrooms: £110/£145 *Recommended by Belinda May, David Jackman, Neil and Angela Huxter, Richard Tilbrook*

KIRTLINGTON
SP4919 Map 4

Oxford Arms 🏅 ♀

(01869) 350208 – www.oxford-arms.co.uk

Troy Lane, junction with A4095 W of Bicester; OX5 3HA

Civilised and friendly stripped-stone pub with enjoyable food using local produce and good wine choice

This sturdy 19th-c stone pub, in a lovely village, is popular with our readers. The long line of recently refurbished linked rooms is divided by a central stone hearth with a great round stove, and by the servery itself – where you'll find Black Sheep and Hook Norton Hooky on handpump, an interesting range of 13 wines by the glass, nine malt whiskies, farm cider and organic soft drinks. Past the bar area with its cushioned wall pews, creaky beamed ceiling and age-darkened floor tiles, dining tables on parquet have neat red chairs; beyond that, leather sofas cluster round a log fire at the end. Also, church candles, fresh flowers and plenty of stripped stone. A sheltered back terrace has teak tables under giant parasols with heaters – as well as white metal furniture and picnic-sets on neat gravel. The geranium-filled window boxes are pretty.

Good, enjoyable food includes sandwiches, potted shrimps with toast, salmon and prawn fishcakes with sweet chilli sauce, a risotto of the day, daube of rare-breed beef with buttered pasta, pigeon salad with black pudding and bacon, fillet of wild bass with green beans and lemon oil, lamb steak with garlic butter and dauphinoise potatoes, and puddings such as dark rum and chocolate mousse and almond and plum tart with vanilla ice-cream. *Benchmark main dish: venison burger with chutney and triple-cooked chips £15.00. Two-course evening meal £24.00.*

Punch ~ Lease Bryn Jones ~ Real ale ~ Open 12-3, 6-11; 12-3 Sun; closed Sun evening, bank holiday Mon evening ~ Bar food 12-2.30, 6.30-9; 12-3 Sun ~ Restaurant ~ Well behaved children welcome ~ Dogs welcome *Recommended by Dr Peter Crawshaw, Mr and Mrs J Watkins, Brian and Sally Wakeham*

LONGWORTH
Blue Boar ♀
SU3899 Map 4

(01865) 820494 – www.blueboarlongworth.co.uk
Tucks Lane; OX13 5ET

Smashing old pub with good wines and beer, and enjoyable food

This handsome country pub is close to the Thames, and there's also a circular two-mile walk from the front door. Inside, it's warmly traditional and the three low-beamed, characterful small rooms have a bustling but easy-going atmosphere and a good mix of locals and visitors. There are brasses, hops and assorted knick-knacks (skis, an old clocking-in machine) on the walls and ceilings, scrubbed wooden tables and benches, faded rugs and floor tiles, fresh flowers on the bar and two blazing log fires (the one by the bar is noteworthy). The main eating area is the red-painted room at the end and there's a quieter restaurant extension too. Brakspears Bitter and Otter Ale on handpump, 20 malt whiskies and a dozen wines by the glass. There are tables outside in front and on the back terrace.

Well thought-of food includes sandwiches, skewered king prawns with aioli, antipasti sharing board, crispy stone-baked pizzas, lamb and chickpea curry, beer-battered fish and chips, tarragon-stuffed chicken breast with gnocchi, wild mushrooms and spinach, lemon and herb-crusted cod loin with ratatouille, and puddings such as white chocolate and cranberry panettone bread and butter pudding with vanilla custard and apple and blackberry crumble. *Benchmark main dish: burger with toppings, aioli and chips £11.95. Two-course evening meal £20.00.*

Free house ~ Licensee Paul Dailey ~ Real ale ~ Open 12-11; 12-10 Sun ~ Bar food 12-2.30, 6.30-9.30 (10 Fri, Sat); 12-3, 6.30-9 Sun ~ Restaurant ~ Children allowed lunchtime only ~ Dogs allowed in bar ~ Wi-fi *Recommended by Carol and Barry Craddock, John Pritchard, Neil and Angela Huxter*

Please keep sending us reports. We rely on readers for news of new discoveries, and particularly for news of changes – however slight – at the fully described pubs: feedback@goodguides.com, or (no stamp needed) The Good Pub Guide, FREEPOST RTJR-ZCYZ-RJZT, Perrymans Lane, Etchingham TN19 7DN.

MILTON-UNDER-WYCHWOOD SP2618 Map 4

Hare ♀

(01993) 835763 – www.themiltonhare.co.uk
High Street; OX7 6LA

Renovated stone inn with linked bar and dining rooms, attractive contemporary furnishings, real ales, pleasing food and seats in the garden

Locals are thrilled that this village pub (closed for several years) has now been reopened and completely refurbished. There's a bar and a couple of little drinking areas warmed by a woodburning stove and various dining areas leading off: wooden floors, dark grey painted or exposed stone walls, painted beams, big gilt-edged mirrors and seating that includes stools, wooden or leather dining chairs, long button-back wall seats and cushioned settles around tables of every size – each set with a little glass oil lamp. Splashes of bright colour here and there brighten things considerably. Throughout, there's all manner of hare paraphernalia – photos, paintings, statues, a large glass case with stuffed boxing hares, motifs on scatter cushions and so forth. Stools line the counter where friendly, well trained staff serve Hook Norton Hooky and guests such as Bath Summers Hare and North Cotswold Shagweaver on handpump and good wines by the glass; on Fridays at 5pm it's champagne happy hour. The garden has tables, benches and chairs on a terrace and on a lawn.

As well as daily fresh fish dishes such as whole dressed cornish crab, moules frites and tuna, prawn and smoked salmon sushi with soy, shallot and chilli dip, the rewarding food includes lunchtime sandwiches, shallot and thyme scotch egg with wild garlic mayonnaise, chicken liver parfait with red onion marmalade, superfood salad with pomegranate dressing, confit duck leg with bacon and shallots, red wine sauce and dauphinoise potatoes, free-range chicken wrapped in parma ham with creamed peas and pancetta, and puddings such as espresso crème brûlée with vanilla-sugared doughnuts and rhubarb and apple crumble. *Benchmark main dish: skate wing with local asparagus and lemon and parsley butter £17.50. Two-course evening meal £24.00.*

Free house ~ Licensees Sue and Rachel Hawkins ~ Real ale ~ Open 12-3, 5.30-11; 11-11 Sat, Sun ~ Bar food 12-2.30, 6-9 (9.30 Sat); 12-9 Sun ~ Restaurant ~ Children welcome but not in the bar at weekends ~ Dogs allowed in bar ~ Wi-fi ~ Live acoustic music Sun evening
Recommended by Liz Bell, Tim and Sarah Smythe-Brown, Liz and Martin Eldon

OXFORD SP5106 Map 4

Bear ◀

(01865) 728164 – www.bearoxford.co.uk
Alfred Street/Wheatsheaf Alley; OX1 4EH

Delightful pub with friendly staff, two cosy rooms, six real ales and well liked bar food

The oldest drinking house in the city, this is a charming little tavern tucked away from the tourist trail. The two small rooms are beamed, partly panelled and have a chatty, bustling atmosphere (in term time it's often packed with students), winter coal fires, thousands of vintage ties on the walls and up to six real ales from handpumps on the fine pewter bar counter: Fullers ESB, HSB, London Pride and Olivers Island and a guest from Shotover. Staff are friendly and helpful; board games. There are seats under parasols in the large terraced back garden where summer barbecues are held.

🍴 Bar food includes sandwiches, breaded whitebait with aioli, scotch egg with piccalilli and ale chutney, sharing platters, ham and egg, sausages and mash with red wine gravy, a quiche of the day, burgers with toppings and chips, steaks, and puddings such as chocolate brownie and treacle sponge with custard. *Benchmark main dish: beer-battered cod and chips £11.95. Two-course evening meal £16.00.*

Fullers ~ Manager James Vernede ~ Real ale ~ Open 11-11 (midnight Fri, Sat); 11.30-10.30 Sun ~ Bar food 12-4, 5-8 (8.30 Thurs); 12-9 Fri-Sun ~ Children welcome but no pushchairs inside ~ Dogs welcome ~ Wi-fi *Recommended by Gus Swan, MarkandDi, Carol and Barry Craddock, Daniel England, Richard Tilbrook*

OXFORD
Perch ♀

SP4907 Map 4

(01865) 728891 – www.the-perch.co.uk
Binsey Lane, on right after river bridge leaving city on A420; OX2 0NG

A fine mix of customers for beautifully set inn with riverside gardens, local ales, popular food and friendly service

In summer, this thatched 17th-c limestone pub is a special place with a lovely garden running down to the Thames Path where there are moorings. A partly covered terrace has seats and tables, there are picnic-sets on the lawn, a summer bar and an attractively furnished marquee. The heavily beamed bar has red leather chesterfields in front of a woodburning stove, a very high-backed settle, little stools around tables and fine old flagstones. Hook Norton Hooky and guests such as Loose Cannon Gunners Gold and White Horse Bitter on handpump and plenty of wines by the glass. Leading off here are the dining areas with bare floorboards, scatter cushions on built-in wall seats, wheelbacks and other chairs around light tables, a second woodburner with logs piled to the ceiling next to it, and a fine brass chandelier. Service is helpful and friendly; they hold an annual beer and cider festival, outdoor film evenings in summer and a folk festival. It's said that this might be one of the first places that Lewis Carroll gave public readings of *Alice's Adventures in Wonderland*.

🍴 Reliably good food includes lunchtime sandwiches, potted kiln-smoked salmon with watercress mousse, rabbit, chicken and smoked bacon terrine with grape and apple chutney, pea, baby spinach and wild garlic croquettes with tomato chutney, moules frites, burger with toppings and triple-cooked chips, sea trout with spring onion, parsley and cockle butter, and puddings such as rhubarb and custard eton mess and dark chocolate mousse with honeycomb shortbread crumble and caramelised orange. *Benchmark main dish: suet crust pie of the day £13.95. Two-course evening meal £22.00.*

Free house ~ Licensee Jon Ellse ~ Real ale ~ Open 10.30am-11pm ~ Bar food 12-10 (9 Sun) ~ Restaurant ~ Children welcome ~ Dogs welcome ~ Wi-fi *Recommended by Colin McKerrow*

OXFORD
Punter

SP5005 Map 4

(01865) 248832 – www.thepunteroxford.com
South Street, Osney (off A420 Botley Road via Bridge Street); OX2 0BE

Easy-going atmosphere in bustling pub overlooking the water with plenty of character and enjoyable food

There's a boathouse feel to this cheerful place – which is apt given its position on Osney Island with views over the Thames. Run by an enthusiastic landlord and his friendly staff, the lower area has attractive rugs on flagstones and an open fire, while the upper room has more rugs on bare boards and a single big table surrounded by oil paintings – just right for a private group. Throughout are all manner of nice old dining chairs around an interesting mix of tables, art for sale on whitewashed walls and a rather fine stained-glass window. Greene King Fireside, Morlands Original and Old Golden Hen on handpump from the tiled counter and several wines by the glass; board games.

 Rewarding food includes scotch egg with piccalilli, venison rillettes with orange and cranberry marmalade, spelt, jerusalem artichoke, sun-dried tomato and blue cheese risotto, merguez sausage and kale pasta bake with ricotta cheese, venison goulash with polenta dumplings and sour cream, panko-breadcrumbed fish and chips, and puddings; they also offer a couple of £5 lunch dishes. *Benchmark main dish: burger with toppings, tomato relish and frites £12.00. Two-course evening meal £20.00.*

Greene King ~ Lease Tom Rainey ~ Real ale ~ Open 12-midnight; 12-11.30 Sun ~ Bar food 12-3, 6-10; 12-10 Sat; 12-9 Sun ~ Children welcome ~ Dogs welcome ~ Wi-fi
Recommended by Harvey Brown, Phoebe Peacock, Richard Tilbrook

OXFORD   SP5107   Map 4
Rose & Crown ◄

(01865) 510551 – www.rose-n-crown.com
North Parade Avenue; very narrow, so best to park in a nearby street; OX2 6LX

Lively friendly local with a fine choice of drinks and proper home cooking

A good mix of customers of all ages enjoy this bustling local with its charming old-fashioned atmosphere, and the long-serving licensees give the place a great deal of individuality. The front door opens into a passage with a small counter and shelves of reference books for crossword buffs. This leads to two rooms: a cosy one at the front overlooking the street, and a panelled back room housing the main bar and traditional pub furnishings. Adnams Southwold, Hook Norton Old Hooky, Shotover Scholar and Vale Two Cities on handpump, around 30 malt whiskies and 20 wines by the glass (including champagne and sparkling wine). The pleasant walled and heated back courtyard can be covered with a huge awning; at the far end is a 12-seater dining/meeting room. The loos are basic.

 Honest food at fair prices includes sandwiches, potted shrimps and crab, hot rissoles of chickpeas with tzatziki, omelettes, ham, sausage, bacon and egg, steak and kidney pie, honey-glazed chicken or venison burger, both with chips, and puddings such as apple pie and chocolate cake with ice-cream. *Benchmark main dish: pint of sausages with chips and english mustard £11.00. Two-course evening meal £20.00.*

Free house ~ Licensees Andrew and Debbie Hall ~ Real ale ~ No credit cards ~ Open 11am-midnight (1am Sat) ~ Bar food 12-2.15, 6-9 ~ Well behaved and accompanied children may sit in courtyard until 5pm ~ Wi-fi ~ Live jazz twice monthly Sun
Recommended by Andy Dolan, John Harris, Barbara Brown

RAMSDEN   SP3515   Map 4
Royal Oak ♀ ◄

(01993) 868213 – www.royaloakramsden.com
Village signposted off B4022 Witney–Charlbury; OX7 3AU

Busy pub with long-serving licensees, large helpings of varied food, carefully chosen wines and seats outside; bedrooms

For nearly 30 years now, the same licensees have run their village pub with enthusiasm and care. The unpretentious rooms are relaxed and friendly with all manner of wooden tables, chairs and settles, cushioned window seats, exposed stone walls, bookcases with old and new copies of *Country Life* and, when the weather gets cold, a cheerful log fire. Butts Barbus Barbus, Hook Norton Hooky and Loose Cannon Recoil on handpump, 40 wines by the glass from a carefully chosen list and three farm ciders. Folding doors from the restaurant give easy access to the back terrace and there are some tables and chairs out in front. The bedrooms are in a converted coach house and stable block. The village church is opposite.

Tasty food includes smoked haddock with whisky cream sauce topped with cheddar, baked field mushrooms with goats cheese, burger with toppings and fries, pie of the week, calves liver and bacon on sweet potato mash with caramelised onions, jamaican curry of the week, salmon fillet with confit fennel, truffle potatoes and champagne velouté, rack of lamb with roast garlic mash and redcurrant and rosemary jus, and puddings. *Benchmark main dish: steak and kidney pudding £16.00. Two-course evening meal £20.00.*

Free house ~ Licensee Jon Oldham ~ Real ale ~ Open 11.30-3, 6.30-11; 11.30-11 Sat; 12-10.30 Sun ~ Bar food 12-2.30, 7-10; 12-10 Sat; 12-9 Sun ~ Restaurant ~ Children welcome ~ Dogs allowed in bar ~ Wi-fi ~ Bedrooms: £55/£85 *Recommended by Lindy Andrews, Tim King, Charles Welch*

SHILTON
Rose & Crown ⭐

SP2608   Map 4

(01993) 842280 – www.shiltonroseandcrown.com
Just off B4020 SE of Burford; OX18 4AB

Simple and appealing little pub with particularly good food, real ales and fine wines

Consistently high standards keep this pretty, 17th-c stone pub as popular as ever. It's a friendly place and the small front bar has an unassuming but civilised feel, low beams and timbers, exposed stone walls, a log fire in a big fireplace and half a dozen or so farmhouse chairs and tables on the red tiled floor. There are usually a few locals at the planked counter where they serve Butcombe Rare Breed, Hook Norton Old Hooky and Youngs Bitter on handpump, along with ten wines by the glass, seven malt whiskies and farm cider. A second room, similar but bigger, is used mainly for eating, and has another fireplace. An attractive side garden has picnic-sets. This is a lovely Cotswolds village.

The landlord-chef cooks the popular food which includes lunchtime ciabattas, game terrine with gherkins, gravadlax with dill and mustard sauce, lentil and red pepper moussaka, lambs liver and bacon with mash, ham and egg, smoked haddock, salmon and prawn fish pie, minute steak with garlic butter and chips, and puddings such as prune, Armagnac and almond tart and chocolate and walnut brownie with chocolate sauce. *Benchmark main dish: steak and mushroom in ale pie £13.50. Two-course evening meal £19.00.*

Free house ~ Licensee Martin Coldicott ~ Real ale ~ Open 11.30-3, 6-10.30; 11.30-11 Sat; 12-10 Sun ~ Bar food 12-2 (2.45 weekends and bank holidays), 7-9 ~ Children welcome lunchtime only ~ Dogs allowed in bar *Recommended by R K Phillips, John Evans*

People named as recommenders after the full entries have told us that the pub should be included. But they have not written the report – we have, after anonymous on-the-spot inspection.

SHIPLAKE
SU7779 Map 2

Baskerville 🏆 ♿ 🛏

(0118) 940 3332 – www.thebaskerville.com

Station Road, Lower Shiplake (off A4155 just S of Henley); RG9 3NY

Emphasis on imaginative food but a proper public bar too, interesting sporting memorabilia and a pretty garden; bedrooms

Particularly well run and homely in a smart way, you can be sure of a genuine welcome here. There are a few beams, red leather tub chairs, pale wood dining chairs and tables on oak floors or patterned carpet, plush red banquettes by the windows and a couple of log fires in brick fireplaces. Flowers and large house plants are dotted about, and the red walls are hung with a fair amount of sporting memorabilia and pictures (especially old rowing photos – Henley is very near) as well as signed rugby shirts and photos (the pub has its own rugby club) and maps of the Thames. Also, bar chairs line the light, modern counter where they keep Loddon Ferrymans Gold and Hoppit, Rebellion IPA and Sharps Doom Bar on handpump, 15 wines by the glass from a thoughtfully chosen list, 40 malt whiskies and farm cider, all served by neat staff; they support WaterAid by charging £1 for a jug of iced water and at the time of writing have raised £6,000. Background music and TV. There's a separate dining room and a small room for private parties. The pretty garden has a covered barbecue area, teak furniture under huge parasols, some rather fun statues cut from box hedging and a timber play frame. The bedrooms are well equipped and comfortable and the breakfasts extremely good.

 As well as lunchtime open sandwiches, the rewarding food includes smoked haddock soufflé with cheddar sauce, devilled lambs kidneys with crispy shallots, feta and spinach puff pastry roll with salsa verde, 28-day dry-aged burger with toppings, worcestershire mayonnaise and fries, chicken, ham and leek pie, king scallops with black pudding, pea purée, pancetta crisp and truffle oil, lamb shank with champ mash and red wine jus, bouillabaisse with rouille, and puddings such as profiteroles with chocolate sauce and baked alaska. *Benchmark main dish: beer-battered cod and triple-cooked chips £14.50. Two-course evening meal £24.00.*

Free house ~ Licensee Allan Hannah ~ Real ale ~ Open 11-11; 12-10.30 Sun ~ Bar food 12-9.30 (10 Fri, Sat); 12-3.30 Sun ~ Restaurant ~ Children welcome but not after 7pm Fri and Sat ~ Dogs allowed in bar and bedrooms ~ Wi-fi ~ Bedrooms: £100/£110
Recommended by Simon Collett-Jones, Richard Kennell, Allan Lloyd and family

SPARSHOLT
SU3487 Map 2

Star 🏆 🛏

(01235) 751873 – www.thestarsparsholt.co.uk

Watery Lane; OX12 9PL

Oxfordshire Dining Pub of the Year

Delicious food, real ales and good wines by the glass, helpful friendly staff and seats in the garden; bedrooms

Of course, most customers come to this inviting and compact 16th-c pub for the excellent food – but they do have a simply furnished bar where they keep Purity Gold and Sharps Doom Bar on handpump and several wines by the glass; staff are efficient and friendly. The dining rooms have pale farmhouse chairs around chunky tables on floorboards or big flagstones, hops on beams, an open fire and old stone bottles and plants dotted about. The atmosphere is easy-going and informal; background music and board games. The two pub dogs are called Minnie and Ella. There are seats in the back garden (and a new kitchen garden) and eight attractive, contemporary bedrooms in a smartly converted barn. You can enjoy walks along the Ridgeway and a carpet of spring snowdrops in the churchyard.

 From a seasonal menu using local produce, the delicious food includes lunchtime sandwiches, foie gras and confit duck leg ballotine with prune and Armagnac chutney and macadamia nut, beef blade terrine with watercress, pickled shallot and horseradish ice-cream, parmesan and truffle gnocchi with morel mushrooms and truffle cream, burger with carrot and cabbage slaw, toppings and fries, home oak-smoked sea trout with pea, chorizo and charred gem fricassée, and puddings such as sticky toffee soufflé with salted caramel parfait and butterscotch and dark and caramel chocolate délice with coffee ice-cream. *Benchmark main dish: roast brill with parsley root and lemon and white wine cream £23.50. Two-course evening meal £25.00.*

Free house ~ Licensee Caron Williams ~ Real ale ~ Open 12-11 (midnight Sat); 12-11 Sun ~ Bar food 12-2.30, 6.30-9 (9.30 Fri, Sat); 12-8 Sun ~ Restaurant ~ Children welcome ~ Dogs welcome ~ Wi-fi ~ Bedrooms: £85/£95 *Recommended by John Harris, Diane Abbott, Ben and Diane Bowie, Liz Bell*

STANFORD IN THE VALE
SU3393 Map 4
Horse & Jockey ♀ £
(01367) 710302 – www.horseandjockey.org
A417 Faringdon–Wantage; Faringdon Road; SN7 8NN

Bustling, traditional village local with real character, highly thought-of and good value food and well chosen wines; bedrooms

The friendly, hard-working licensees in this charming pub offer a warm welcome to all. It's an interesting place and since this is racehorse-training country (and given the pub's name) there are big Alfred Munnings racecourse prints, card collections of Grand National winners and other horse and jockey pictures on the walls. The place is split into two sections: a contemporary dining area and an older part with flagstones, wood flooring, low beams and raftered ceilings. There are old high-backed settles and leather armchairs, a woodburning stove in a big fireplace and an easy-going atmosphere. A beer named for the pub (from Greene King), Greene King Molecule of Life and St Austell Tribute on handpump, carefully chosen wines by the glass and a dozen malt whiskies; background music. As well as tables under a heated courtyard canopy, there's a separate enclosed and informal garden. The bedrooms, which are housed in another building behind the pub, are quiet and comfortable.

Home cooking at fair prices includes sandwiches with home-made crisps, chicken liver pâté with fruit chutney, salt, pepper and chilli tempura king prawns with sweet chilli sauce, sharing boards, chicken caesar salad, stone-baked pizzas, wild mushroom stroganoff, pork and leek sausages on thyme mash with caramelised onion gravy, burger with toppings, smoked chilli relish and skinny fries, and puddings such as chocolate brownie with ice-cream and lemon posset with pistachio ice-cream. *Benchmark main dish: spiced breadcrumbed medallions of chicken with smoked paprika, spiced beans, onion rings and fries £11.50. Two-course evening meal £18.00.*

Greene King ~ Lease Charles and Anna Gaunt ~ Real ale ~ Open 11-3, 5-midnight; 11am-12.30am Sat; 11-11 Sun ~ Bar food 12-2.30, 6.30-9 (9.30 Fri, Sat) ~ Restaurant ~ Children welcome ~ Dogs allowed in bar ~ Wi-fi ~ Open mike first Weds of month ~ Bedrooms: £65/£80 *Recommended by Peter Barrett, Luke Morgan, James Landor*

There are report forms at the back of the book.

STONESFIELD

SP3917 Map 4

White Horse

(01993) 891063 – www.whitehorsestonesfield.co.uk

Village signposted off B4437 Charlbury–Woodstock; Stonesfield Riding; OX29 8EA

Neatly kept little pub with a relaxed atmosphere and enjoyable food and beer

As this attractively upgraded small country pub is on the Oxfordshire Way long-distance path, it's just the place for a weekend lunch. There's a friendly, uncluttered feel – just a few pieces of contemporary artwork on green and cream paintwork, and the cosy bar has a woodburning stove, country-style chairs and plush or leather stools around solid tables on bare boards, Ringwood Best Bitter on handpump and six wines by the glass; background music. The pink-walled dining room has similar but more elegant furnishings and an open fire; a nice touch is the inner room with just a pair of Sheraton-style chairs around a single mahogany table. Doors open on to a neat walled garden with picnic-sets and interesting plants in pots, and they've redesigned the courtyard this year. It's handy for the Roman villa at nearby North Leigh (English Heritage) but do note that the pub has restricted opening hours.

The popular food uses their own free-range eggs and some home-grown produce: sandwiches, smoked salmon pâté, goats cheese, walnut and pear salad, mediterranean vegetable lasagne, burger with relish and chips, lime-glazed chicken with shallot and mushroom stuffing and sautéed potatoes, salmon fillet with parmesan and parsley crust and creamy mushroom sauce, and puddings such as double chocolate brownie and brioche bread and butter pudding with blackberry coulis. *Benchmark main dish: pie of the day £12.95. Two-course evening meal £19.00.*

Free house ~ Licensees John and Angela Lloyd ~ Real ale ~ Open 5-11; 12-3, 6-11 Sat; 12-3 Sun; closed Sun evening, Mon, lunchtimes Tues-Fri; first week Jan ~ Bar food 6.30-9 Fri; 12-2, 6.30-9 Sat; 12-2 Sun ~ Restaurant ~ Children welcome ~ Dogs allowed in bar ~ Wi-fi
Recommended by Isobel Mackinlay, Gus Swan, Edward May

SWERFORD

SP3830 Map 4

Masons Arms

(01608) 683212 – www.masons-arms.com

A361 Banbury–Chipping Norton; OX7 4AP

Well liked food and fair choice of drinks in bustling dining pub with relaxed atmosphere and country views

The friendly bar here is welcoming at any time of year with a big brown leather sofa facing a couple of armchairs in front of a log fire in a stone fireplace, rugs on pale wooden floors, Brakspears Bitter and Jennings Cumberland on handpump and 12 wines by the glass. The light and airy dining extension has pastel-painted dining chairs around nice old tables on beige carpet, and steps lead down to a cream-painted room with chunky tables and contemporary pictures. Around the other side of the bar is another spacious dining room with great views by day, candles at night and a civilised feel; background music. In warm weather, head for the picnic-sets on grass in the neat back garden and enjoy the pretty views over the Oxfordshire countryside.

The fish specials here might include thai prawn salad, moules marinière, seafood tagliatelle and tempura red mullet with sweet potato chips, wasabi pea purée and mango salsa; non-fishy choices include baked brie filo parcels with cranberry and red onion chutney, beef casserole with horseradish dumpling, chicken in sweet and sour sauce on a sizzling skillet, burger with toppings, roasted chipotle pepper relish and chips, and puddings; they also offer a two- and three-course set lunch. *Benchmark main dish: roasted pollock wrapped in pancetta on bubble and squeak £15.95. Two-course evening meal £20.00.*

Free house ~ Licensee Louise Davies ~ Real ale ~ Open 11-3, 6-11; 11-6 Sun ~ Bar food 12-2.15, 6-9 (9.30 Sat); 11-6 Sun ~ Restaurant ~ Children welcome ~ Dogs allowed in bar ~ Wi-fi *Recommended by M J Winterton, Maddie Purvis, Daphne and Robert Staples*

 SWINBROOK   SP2812   Map 4

Swan ⭐ ♟ 🛏

(01993) 823339 – www.theswanswinbrook.co.uk
Back road a mile N of A40, 2 miles E of Burford; OX18 4DY

Smart old pub with handsome oak garden rooms, antiques-filled bars, local beers and contemporary food; bedrooms

In warm weather, the outdoor seats and circular picnic-sets make the best of this 400-year-old stone pub's position by a bridge over the River Windrush. It's a civilised place and owned by the Devonshire Estate – there are plenty of interesting Mitford family photographs blown up on the walls. The little bar has simple antique furnishings, settles and benches, an open fire and (in an alcove) a stuffed swan; locals drop in here for a pint and a chat. A small dining room leads off from the bar to the right of the entrance, and there are also two garden rooms with high-backed beige and green dining chairs around pale wood tables and views across the garden and orchard. Hook Norton Hooky and a couple of changing guests from breweries such as Cotswold Lion and Flying Monk on handpump, nine wines by the glass, farm ciders and local draught lager; background music, board games and TV. The elegant bedrooms are in a smartly converted stone barn beside the pub, with five by the water. The Kings Head in Bledington (Gloucestershire) is run by the same first class licensees.

🎯 Using the best seasonal local produce, the inviting food includes lunchtime sandwiches, beetroot-cured salmon with celeriac rémoulade, pork and game terrine with pear chutney, gnocchi with butternut squash, goats cheese, mushrooms and spinach and hazelnut pesto, steak and mushroom in ale pie, crispy fishcake with poached egg and hollandaise sauce, pork belly with black pudding bacon and sage jus, whole plaice with crab and chilli, lemon and coriander butter, and puddings such as rhubarb and apple crumble and chocolate fondant with caramel ice-cream. *Benchmark main dish: beer-battered fresh fish and chips £14.00. Two-course evening meal £22.00.*

Free house ~ Licensees Archie and Nicola Orr-Ewing ~ Real ale ~ Open 11-11 ~ Bar food 12-2, 7-9; 12-3, 7-8.30 Sun ~ Restaurant ~ Children welcome ~ Dogs allowed in bar ~ Wi-fi ~ Bedrooms: £100/£125 *Recommended by Bernard Stradling, Tom McLean, Colin McLachlan, Edward Mirzoeff, Richard Tilbrook*

TADPOLE BRIDGE   SP3200   Map 4

Trout 🎯 ♟ 🛏

(01367) 870382 – www.trout-inn.co.uk
Back road Bampton–Buckland, 4 miles NE of Faringdon; SN7 8RF

Busy country inn with waterside garden and moorings, civilised bar and dining rooms and a fine choice of drinks and food; bedrooms

As this good-looking 17th-c inn is on the banks of the Thames (there are moorings for six boats), you'll need to book a table in advance. It's been smartly refurbished and the bar has a large stuffed trout, exposed stone walls, beams and standing timbers, a woodburning stove with logs neatly piled to one side, leather armchairs and stools, scatter cushions on window seats, and wooden floors and flagstones. Upholstered stools line the blue painted counter where courteous, friendly staff serve a beer named for the pub (from Ramsbury), Banks's Bitter and Thwaites Lancaster Bomber on handpump, ten wines by the glass from a wide-ranging, carefully chosen list, 21 malt whiskies and two farm ciders. The dining rooms have green- and brown-checked chairs around a mix of nice wooden tables, fresh flowers and candlelight; the pale wood or blue painted tongue-and-groove walls are hung with trout and stag prints, oars and mirrors. The pretty garden has good quality chairs and tables under parasols, and the six bedrooms (three open on to a small courtyard) are attractive and comfortable.

 Appetising food includes lunchtime sandwiches, warm ham hock with broccoli and capers, pickled herring with horseradish, cucumber and dill, local sausages of the day with red wine sauce, parmesan gnocchi with wild mushrooms and artichoke velouté, beer-battered haddock and chips, lamb chump and braised shoulder with salsa verde, rainbow trout with crayfish butter and fries, and puddings such as banana soufflé with rum and raisin ice-cream and rhubarb crème brûlée. *Benchmark main dish: guinea fowl with sweet potato and buttered leeks £17.50. Two-course evening meal £24.00.*

Free house ~ Licensee Ricardo Canestra ~ Real ale ~ Open 12-11.30 ~ Bar food 12-2.30, 6-9; 12-2.30, 6.30-9.30 Fri, Sat; 12-3, 6-8 Sun ~ Restaurant ~ Children welcome ~ Dogs welcome ~ Wi-fi ~ Bedrooms: /£130 *Recommended by Mr and Mrs P R Thomas, John Poulter, Roy Davies, Neil and Angela Huxter, Richard Tilbrook*

WOLVERCOTE
Jacobs Inn

SP4809 Map 4

(01865) 514333 – www.jacobs-inn.com
Godstow Road; OX2 8PG

Cheerful pub with enthusiastic staff, simple furnishings, inventive cooking and seats in the garden

The robust, interesting food, lively and informal atmosphere and slightly quirky décor are all enjoyed by our readers. The simply furnished bar has leather armchairs and chesterfields, some plain tables and benches, wide floorboards, a small open fire and high chairs at the counter where they keep Brakspears Bitter, Wychwood Dirty Tackle and Hobgoblin and a guest beer on handpump, 13 wines by the glass, a good choice of spirits and lots of teas and coffees; background music. You can eat at plain wooden tables in a grey panelled area with an open fire or in the smarter knocked-through dining room. This has standing timbers in the centre, a fire at each end and shiny, dark wooden chairs and tables on floorboards; there are standard lamps, stags' heads, a reel-to-reel tape recorder, quite a few mirrors, and deli items for sale. Several seating areas outside have good quality tables and chairs arranged under parasols, picnic-sets on decking, and deckchairs and more picnic-sets on grass.

Using home-reared pigs, free-range eggs and other local, seasonal produce, the food features big rustic flavours; dishes include sandwiches, crab with crème fraîche on toasted sourdough, duck rillettes with celeriac slaw, sausages with champ mash and rosemary gravy, wild boar burger with a choice of sauces and chips, pork T-bone steak with mustard sauce, grilled whole bass with carrot mash, samphire and sorrel sauce, and puddings such as chocolate and stout cake with vanilla ice-cream and caramel pannacotta; they also offer a two- and three-course set lunch. *Benchmark main dish: home-made pies £14.00. Two-course evening meal £20.00.*

Marstons ~ Lease Damion Farah and Johnny Pugsley ~ Real ale ~ Open 9am-11pm ~
Bar food 9am-10pm ~ Restaurant ~ Children welcome ~ Dogs allowed in bar ~ Wi-fi
Recommended by John Evans, William Slade, Thomas Green, Michael and Margaret Cross

WOODSTOCK
Kings Arms 🎯 £ 🛏

SP4416   Map 4

(01993) 813636 – www.kings-hotel-woodstock.co.uk
Market Street/Park Lane (A44); OX20 1SU

**Bustling town-centre hotel with well liked food, a wide choice
of drinks and an enjoyable atmosphere; comfortable bedrooms**

'A really good place' and 'delighted to recommend this again' are just two
of the enthusiastic comments from our readers on this stylish town-
centre pub. The unfussy bar has a cheerful mix of locals and visitors, an
appealing variety of old and new furnishings including brown leather seats
on the stripped-wood floor, smart blinds and black and white photographs;
at the front is an old wooden settle and a modern woodburning stove. The
neat restaurant has high-backed black leather dining chairs around a mix
of tables on black and white floor tiles, and piles of neatly stacked logs on
either side of another woodburning stove; background music. Brakspears
Bitter, Jennings Cumberland and Thwaites Lancaster Bomber on handpump,
11 wines (plus champagne) by the glass and 35 malt whiskies. There are
seats and tables on the street outside.

Good, enjoyable food includes sandwiches, pork-seasoned scallops with pea
and ham fritter, duck scotch egg with spring onions and duck egg mayonnaise,
caramelised shallot and tomato tart with blue cheese, ham and free-range egg with
potato and celeriac hash and brown caper butter, free-range chicken breast with
mushrooms, pearl barley and buttered broad beans, baked cod with seafood broth,
saffron and samphire, and puddings such as lemon curd cheesecake with candied lemon
and coffee buttermilk pudding with hazelnut and coffee macaroon; they also offer a two-
and three-course set menu (Monday-Thursday 12-2.30, 6-6.45). *Benchmark main dish:
pork belly stuffed with black pudding and apple, onion purée and sautéed potatoes
£15.75. Two-course evening meal £24.00.*

Free house ~ Licensees David and Sara Sykes ~ Real ale ~ Open 7am-11pm ~ Bar food
12-2.30, 6-9; 12-5, 6-9 Sun ~ Restaurant ~ Children welcome in bar and restaurant but no
under-12s in bedrooms ~ Dogs allowed in bar ~ Wi-fi ~ Bedrooms: £85/£150
Recommended by Neil and Angela Huxter, Phil and Helen Holt, Richard Tilbrook

Also Worth a Visit in Oxfordshire

Besides the fully inspected pubs, you might like to try these pubs that
have been recommended to us and described by readers. Do tell us what
you think of them: feedback@goodguides.com

ABINGDON   SU4997
Brewery Tap (01235) 521655
Ock Street; OX14 5BZ
Former tap for defunct Morland Brewery but
still serving Original along with changing
guests (autumn beer festival), proper ciders
and good choice of wines, enjoyable well
priced food from bar snacks to popular Sun
roasts, stone floors and panelled walls, two
log fires; background and weekend live
music, Tues quiz, darts, free wi-fi; children

and dogs welcome, enclosed courtyard (aunt
sally), three bedrooms, open all day (till 1am
Fri, Sat). *(Jack Trussler)*

ADDERBURY   SP4735
★ **Red Lion** (01295) 810269
*The Green; off A4260 S of Banbury;
OX17 3NG* Attractive 17th-c stone
coaching inn with good choice of enjoyable
well priced food (all day weekends)
including deals, helpful friendly staff, Greene
King ales, good wine range and coffee,

linked bar rooms with high stripped beams, panelling and stonework, big inglenook log fire, old books and Victorian/Edwardian pictures, more modern restaurant extension; background music, games area; children (in eating areas) and dogs welcome, picnic-sets out on roadside terrace, 13 character bedrooms, good breakfast, open all day in summer. *(Sandra King)*

ALVESCOT SP2704
Plough (01993) 842281
B4020 Carterton–Clanfield, SW of Witney; OX18 2PU Stone-built village pub freshened up and improved under newish management, Wadworths ales and enjoyable food from sandwiches and pub standards up, good friendly service; children welcome, dogs in bar, back terrace and garden with play area, open (and food) all day. *(Carol and Barry Craddock)*

ARDINGTON SU4388
Boars Head (01235) 835466
Signed off A417 Didcot–Wantage; OX12 8QA Modernised 17th-c timber-framed pub with good value popular food from daily changing menu (more evening choice), friendly attentive staff, well kept ales including Loose Cannon, Fullers London Pride and one badged for them, low beams and log fires; background music (maybe live piano); children and dogs (in one area) welcome, terrace seating, peaceful attractive village. *(Helene Grygar)*

ARDLEY SP5427
Fox & Hounds (01869) 346883
B430 (old A43), just SW of M40 junction 10; OX27 7PE Roadside pub dating from the early 19th c with later additions, long opened-up low-beamed dining lounge, big fireplaces each end, enjoyable home-made food from lunchtime snacks to daily specials, two changing ales and good wine choice, helpful friendly staff, another open fire in cosy carpeted bar; children welcome, no dogs inside, attractive beer garden, bedrooms, open (and food) all day weekends. *(Phil and Jane Hodson, Dave Braisted)*

ASCOTT UNDER WYCHWOOD SP2918
Swan (01993) 832332
Shipton Road; OX7 6AY Comfortable and welcoming 17th-c coaching inn, two Hook Norton ales and a guest, good home-cooked food (not Sun or Mon evenings) in bar or raftered restaurant; soft background jazz, folk club first and third Sat of month, Mon quiz; children and dogs welcome, six bedrooms, closed Mon lunchtime. *(Colin McKerrow)*

ASHBURY SU2685
Rose & Crown (01793) 710222
B4507/B4000; High Street; SN6 8NA Friendly 16th-c coaching inn with roomy open-plan beamed bar, three well kept Arkells beers and decent range of wines by the glass, good food from 'grazing platters' and pub favourites up, polished woodwork, traditional pictures, chesterfields and pews, raised section with further oak tables and chairs, games room with table tennis, pool and darts, separate restaurant; background and occasional live music, quiz nights, sports TV; children and dogs welcome, disabled facilities, tables out at front and in garden behind, lovely view down pretty village street of thatched cottages, handy for Ridgeway walks, eight bedrooms, open all day summer. *(Carol and Barry Craddock)*

ASTON TIRROLD SU5586
Sweet Olive (01235) 851272
Aka Chequers; Fullers Road; village signed off A417 Streatley–Wantage; OX11 9EN New owners for this rustic dining pub; main room with wall settles, mate's chairs and sturdy tables on quarry tiles or slate floor, small brick fireplace, well liked if not cheap food from varied menu, good wines by the glass, ales such as Sharps, Wells and West Berkshire, friendly service; background music; picnic-sets in small cottagey garden. *(Edward Edmonton)*

BANBURY SP4540
Three Pigeons (01295) 275220
Southam Road; OX16 2ED Well renovated 17th-c coaching inn handy for town centre; several small rooms surrounding central bar, beams, flagstones, bare boards and woodburners, good friendly atmosphere, shortish choice of well prepared food (all day weekends) from doorstep sandwiches to restaurant dishes, also set menu, three changing ales, decent selection of wines by the glass and around 30 malt whiskies, proper coffee too; children welcome, tables under parasols on paved terrace, three bedrooms, useful but limited parking, open all day. *(JHBS)*

BECKLEY SP5611
★Abingdon Arms (01865) 351311
Signed off B4027; High Street; OX3 9UU Welcoming old dining pub in lovely unspoilt village; comfortably modernised simple lounge, smaller public bar with antique carved settles, open fires, well kept Brakspears and guests, fair range of good reasonably priced wines, enjoyable home-made food from smallish menu including good Sun roasts, friendly efficient service;

We include some hotels with a good bar that offers facilities comparable to those of a pub.

background and some live music; children and dogs welcome, big garden dropping away from floodlit terrace to trees, summer house, superb views over RSPB Otmoor reserve and good walks, open all day weekends. *(Dennis and Doreen Haward, Peter J and Avril Hanson)*

BEGBROKE   SP4713
Royal Sun (01865) 374718
A44 Oxford–Woodstock; OX5 1RZ
Welcoming old stone-built pub with modernised bare-boards interior, wide choice of enjoyable good value food from snacks to Sun carvery, well kept Hook Norton and a guest, good friendly service; may be background music, big-screen sports TV, free wi-fi; children welcome, no dogs inside, tables on terrace and in small garden, open all day. *(Simon Sharpe)*

BLEWBURY   SU5385
Red Lion (01235) 850403
Nottingham Fee – narrow turning N from A417; OX11 9PQ Attractive red-brick downland village pub; enjoyable generously served home-made food including speciality fresh fish, well kept Brakspears, good choice of wines and decent coffee, efficient friendly service, beams, tiled floor and big log fire, separate dining area; children and dogs (in bar) welcome, peaceful enclosed back garden, pretty surroundings, two bedrooms. *(Thomas Green)*

BLOXHAM   SP4235
★ **Joiners Arms** (01295) 720223
Old Bridge Road, off A361; OX15 4LY
Golden-stone 16th-c inn with rambling rooms, white dining chairs around pale tables on wood floor, plenty of exposed stone, open fires, Marstons, Ringwood and guests, enjoyable traditional food including deals (popular Tues steak night), old well in raftered room off bar; Weds quiz; children and dogs welcome, pretty window boxes, seats out under parasols on various levels – most popular down steps by stream (playhouse there too), open all day from 10am for breakfast. *(Tim King)*

BRIGHTWELL   SU5890
Red Lion (01491) 837373
Signed off A4130 2 miles W of Wallingford; OX10 0RT Busy village local playing active part in the community; four or five well kept ales (regulars Loddon and West Berkshire), wines from nearby vineyard, enjoyable good value home-made food including proper pies, friendly efficient staff, two-part bar with snug seating by log fire, dining extension to the right; dogs welcome, seats out at front and in back garden, open all day Sun till 9pm. *(John Pritchard)*

BRITWELL SALOME   SU6793
Red Lion (01491) 613140
B4009 Watlington–Benson; OX49 5LG
Brick and flint pub under new management

– same owners as the Red Lion at Upper Basildon (see Main Entries in Berkshire); freshly modernised bar and dining room in pastel greys, assorted tables and chairs on wood or carpeted floors, open fires, ales such as West Berkshire and XT, real cider and good choice of wines by the glass, well liked food from varied menu including good seafood and charcuterie plates, friendly efficient service; children welcome, seats in courtyard garden, closed Sun evening. *(Dennis and Doreen Haward)*

BROUGHTON   SP4238
★ **Saye & Sele Arms** (01295) 263348
B4035 SW of Banbury; OX15 5ED
Attractive old stone house part of the Broughton Estate with castle just five minutes away; sizeable bar with polished flagstones, cushioned window seats and dark wooden furnishings, a few brasses, three real ales including Sharps Doom Bar and nine wines by the glass, good food cooked by landlord, friendly service, two carpeted dining rooms with exposed stone walls, open fires, over 240 ornate water jugs hanging from beams; children welcome, no dogs inside, picnic-sets and hanging baskets on terrace, neat lawn with tables under parasols, pergola and smokers' shelter, aunt sally, closed Sun evening. *(P and J Shapley)*

BUCKLAND   SU3497
★ **Lamb** (01367) 870484
Off A420 NE of Faringdon; SN7 8QN
Carefully run 18th-c stone-built dining pub in lovely Estate village, highly regarded interesting food cooked by chef-owner, can eat in low-beamed bar with log fire or restaurant, a couple of changing local ales and good choice of wines by the glass, friendly helpful staff; well behaved children and dogs welcome (resident cocker is Oats), seats in courtyard and pleasant tree-shaded garden, good walks (close to Thames Path), three comfortable well equipped bedrooms, closed Sun evening, Mon. *(Isobel Mackinlay, Nick Sharpe)*

BURFORD   SP2512
Angel (01993) 822714
Witney Street; OX18 4SN Long heavy-beamed dining pub in interesting 16th-c building, warmly welcoming with roaring log fire, good popular food from sandwiches and pub favourites up, Hook Norton ales and well chosen wines; Aug beer festival, TV; children and dogs welcome, big secluded garden, three comfortable bedrooms, good english breakfast, open (and food) all day. *(Bernard Stradling)*

BURFORD   SP2512
Mermaid (01993) 822193
High Street; OX18 4QF Handsome beamed dining pub with flagstones, panelling, stripped stone and nice log fire, decent food (all day weekends) at sensible

prices including local free-range meat and fresh fish, friendly service, well kept Greene King ales and a guest, bay window seating at front, further airy back dining room and upstairs restaurant; background music (live Fri), quiz first Mon of month, darts; children welcome, tables out at front and in courtyard behind, open all day. *(Paul and Sue Merrick)*

CAULCOTT
SP5024
★ **Horse & Groom** (01869) 343257
Lower Heyford Road (B4030); OX25 4ND Pretty 16th-c roadside thatched cottage, L-shaped red-carpeted room with log fire in big inglenook (brassware under its long bressumer) and plush-cushioned settles, chairs and stools around a few dark tables at low-ceilinged bar end, White Horse Bitter and a couple of guests, decent house wines, good food (not Sun evening) cooked by french owner-chef, also O'Hagans sausage menu, dining room at far end with jugs hanging on black joists, decorative plates, watercolours and original drawings, small side sun lounge, shove-ha'penny and board games; well behaved over-5s welcome, awkward for disabled customers (some steps and no car park), picnic-sets in nice little front garden, closed Mon. *(George Atkinson)*

CHADLINGTON
SP3222
Tite (01608) 676910
Off A361 S of Chipping Norton; Mill End; OX7 3NY Friendly renovated 17th-c country pub; bar with eating areas either side, beams and stripped stone, pubby furniture including spindleback chairs and settles, flagstones and bare boards, woodburner in large fireplace, well kept Sharps Doom Bar and a couple of guests, Weston's cider and a dozen wines by the glass, enjoyable fairly traditional home-cooked food (not Sun evening), good service; occasional live music, winter quiz nights; well behaved children and dogs welcome, lovely shrub-filled garden with split-level terrace, good walks nearby, open all day. *(Richard Stanfield, Colin McKerrow, Bernard Stradling)*

CHALGROVE
SU6397
Red Lion (01865) 890625
High Street (B480 Watlington–Stadhampton); OX44 7SS Attractive beamed village pub owned by local church trust since 1637; good home-made seasonal food (not Sun evening) from interesting menu, popular pudding evening second Tues of the month, well kept Butcombe, Fullers London Pride, Rebellion Mild and two guests, friendly helpful staff, quarry-tiled bar with big open fire, separate carpeted restaurant; children and dogs welcome, attractive front

and back gardens, open all day Sun (and Sat if busy). *(Thomas Green)*

CHARLTON-ON-OTMOOR
SP5615
Crown (01865) 331850
Signed off B4027 in Islip; High Street, opposite church; OX5 2UQ Refurbished 17th-c village local with welcoming relaxed atmosphere, bar and separate restaurant, good interesting food from landlord-chef, well kept Rebellion and a guest ale, decent wines; children welcome. *(Tim Roberts)*

CHARNEY BASSETT
SU3794
Chequers (01235) 868642
Chapel Lane off Main Street; OX12 0EX Welcoming 18th-c village-green pub with spacious modernised interior, Brakspears and Wychwood ales, enjoyable fairly priced food from lunchtime sandwiches and baguettes to steaks (booking advised), log fire; children and dogs (in bar) welcome, picnic-sets in small garden, three bedrooms, open all day. *(Sandra King)*

CHAZEY HEATH
SU6979
Packhorse (0118) 972 2140
Off A4074 Reading–Wallingford by B4526; RG4 7UG Attractive 17th-c beamed village dining pub (part of Home Counties group); good choice of well liked food from sandwiches and light dishes up, local ales, plenty of wines by the glass and some interesting gins, polished tables on wood and rug floors, built-in leatherette banquettes, shelves of books and lots of framed pictures, big log fire in raised hearth; background music; children and dogs (in main bar) welcome, disabled facilities, parasol-shaded tables in back garden, handy for Mapledurham house and watermill, open (and food) all day. *(John Cadge)*

CHECKENDON
SU6684
★ **Black Horse** (01491) 680418
Village signed off A4074 Reading–Wallingford; RG8 0TE Charmingly old-fashioned country tavern (tucked into woodland away from main village) kept by same family for 110 years; relaxing and unchanging series of rooms, back one with West Berkshire and White Horse tapped from the cask, one with bar counter has some tent pegs above the fireplace (they used to be made here), homely side lounge with some splendidly unfashionable 1950s-style armchairs and another room beyond that, only baguettes and pickled eggs; no credit cards; children allowed but must be well behaved, dogs welcome, seats on verandah and in garden, popular with walkers and cyclists. *(Edward Edmonton)*

A star symbol before the name of a pub shows exceptional character and appeal.
It doesn't mean extra comfort. Even quite a basic pub can win a star,
if it's individual enough.

CHIPPING NORTON
Blue Boar (01608) 643525   SP3127
High Street/Goddards Lane; OX7 5NP
Spacious former coaching inn (first licensed
in 1683); good helpings of enjoyable well
priced food (all day weekends), up to six well
kept Marstons-related ales, friendly helpful
staff, woodburner in big stone fireplace,
raftered back restaurant and airy flagstoned
garden room; background music (live
weekends), Thurs quiz, darts, sports TV, fruit
machine; children welcome, open all day.
(Liz and Martin Eldon)

CHIPPING NORTON
Chequers (01608) 644717   SP3127
Goddards Lane; OX7 5NP Bustling
traditional town pub with three softly lit
beamed rooms, no frills but comfortable
and full of character, flagstones, low ochre
ceilings and log fire (not always lit), up to
eight mainly Fullers ales, 15 wines by the
glass and enjoyable food (not Sun evening)
from shortish menu, friendly staff, airy
conservatory restaurant behind; TV, free
wi-fi; children and dogs (in bar) welcome,
theatre next door, open all day. *(Richard
Stanfield, Richard Tilbrook)*

CHIPPING NORTON
Crown & Cushion (01608) 642533   SP3127
High Street; OX7 5AD Welcoming little
bar at back of handsome old-fashioned
16th-c hotel, log fire, beams, some flagstones
and stripped stone, well kept/priced Hook
Norton Hooky, enjoyable good value bar
food including bargain OAP deal Tues, nice
coffee, cheerful helpful staff, separate bistro
restaurant; children welcome, tables in
sheltered suntrap courtyard, 40 bedrooms,
open all day. *(R C Vincent, Pat and Graham
Williamson)*

CHISLEHAMPTON
Coach & Horses (01865) 890255   SU5998
*B480 Oxford–Watlington, opposite
B4015 to Abingdon; OX44 7UX* Extended
16th-c coaching inn with two homely and
civilised beamed bars, big log fire, sizeable
restaurant with polished oak tables and
wall banquettes, good choice of popular
reasonably priced food (not Sun evening),
friendly obliging service, three well kept ales
usually including Hook Norton; background
music; neat terraced gardens overlooking
fields by River Thame, some tables out in
front, bedrooms in courtyard block, open all
day (closed 3-7pm Sun). *(Roy Hoing,
Mr and Mrs P R Thomas, Mike and Mary Carter,
Andy Dolan)*

CHRISTMAS COMMON
Fox & Hounds (01491) 612599   SU7193
Off B480/B481; OX49 5HL Welcoming
old Chilterns pub in lovely countryside,
spacious front barn restaurant serving good
value home-made food from open kitchen

including Tues evening set deal, Brakspears
and a guest, decent wines and some gins
flavoured with herbs from the garden,
two compact beamed rooms simply but
comfortably furnished, bow windows, red
and black floor tiles and big inglenook, snug
little back room too; board games; children,
walkers and dogs welcome, rustic benches
and tables outside, open all day. *(Bill Gulliver
and Harry Thomson)*

CHURCH ENSTONE
★ **Crown** (01608) 677262   SP3725
*Mill Lane; from A44 take B4030
turn-off at Enstone; OX7 4NN* Pleasant
bar in popular 17th-c beamed country
pub, straightforward furniture, old
local photographs on stone walls, some
horsebrasses, log fire in large fireplace, well
kept Hook Norton and guests, good fairly
priced food cooked by landlord from pub
favourites up, friendly service, carpeted
dining room with red walls, slate-floored
conservatory; children welcome, dogs in
bar, white metal furniture on front terrace
overlooking lane, picnic-sets in sheltered back
garden, closed Sun evening. *(Andy Dolan)*

CLANFIELD
Clanfield Tavern (01367) 810117   SP2802
*Bampton Road (A4095 S of Witney);
OX18 2RG* Pleasantly extended 17th-c
stone pub (former coaching inn) adjacent
to the Plough; opened-up beamed interior
keeping feel of separate areas, mostly
carpeted with mix of pubby furniture
including some old settles (built-in one
by log fire), smallish bar with comfortable
seating in snug flagstoned area with
woodburner, Marstons-related ales and
enjoyable reasonably priced food (all day Sat,
not Sun evening) including gluten-free menu,
more contemporary dining conservatory;
background music, free wi-fi; children
welcome, dogs in bar, picnic-sets on small
flower-bordered lawn looking across to
village green, open all day (till 9pm Sun).
(R K Phillips)

CLANFIELD
Plough (01367) 810222   SP2802
Bourton Road; OX18 2RB Substantial
old stone inn with lovely Elizabethan façade,
civilised atmosphere and plenty of character,
log fires in comfortable beamed lounge bar,
various dining areas, good food, particularly
fish and seasonal game, well kept Hook
Norton Hooky and a guest, good wine list and
over 180 gins (can organise tasting sessions),
attentive service; children and dogs welcome,
attractive gardens with teak tables on sunny
front terrace, 12 bedrooms, open all day.
(Wilburoo, R K Phillips)

CRAWLEY
★ **Lamb** (01993) 708792   SP3412
Steep Hill; just NW of Witney; OX29 9TW
Relaxed 18th-c stone-built dining pub with

very good if not particularly cheap food from owner-chef, friendly attentive staff, beamed bar with polished boards and lovely inglenook log fire, Brakspears and Wychwood ales, various dining areas with cushioned settles, high-backed chairs and built-in wall seats, exposed stone walls throughout, prints, paintings, antlers and church candles; dogs welcome in bar, views from tables on back terrace and lawn, summer barbecues and wood-fired pizzas, pretty village, good walks (on Palladian Way), open all day Sat, closed Sun evening, Mon. *(Carol and Barry Craddock, Guy Vowles)*

CROWELL   SU7499
Shepherds Crook (01844) 355266
B4009, 2 miles from M40 junction 6; OX39 4RR Welcoming and popular old village pub, good varied choice of freshly prepared food (not Sun evening) including daily specials, up to half a dozen ales such as Adnams, Rebellion, St Austell and Timothy Taylors, extensive wine list (ten by the glass), 30 or so whiskies, beamed bar with stripped brick and flagstones, woodburner, high-raftered dining area; 'jazz & dinner' evenings, quiz nights; children and dogs welcome, tables out on front terrace and small green, nice walks, open all day. *(Taff Thomas)*

CUMNOR   SP4503
Bear & Ragged Staff
(01865) 862329 *Signed from A420; Appleton Road; OX2 9QH* Extensive restaurant-pub dating from 16th c, contemporary décor in linked rooms with wood floors and painted beams, good food from sandwiches and sharing plates (create your own) through pub favourites up, Thurs steak night, friendly efficient service, flagstoned bar with log fire, well kept Greene King ales and good wine choice, airy garden room; background music, TV, free wi-fi; children welcome, decked terrace and fenced play area, nine bedrooms, open (and food) all day. *(Tim King)*

CURBRIDGE   SP3208
Lord Kitchener (01993) 772613
Lew Road (A4095 towards Bampton); OX29 7PD Extensively renovated and modernised roadside pub, wide range of enjoyable food including gluten-free choices, Greene King ales and several wines by the glass, good friendly service; children welcome, closed Sun evening, Mon. *(Helene Grygar)*

CUXHAM   SU6695
Half Moon (01491) 612165
4 miles from M40 J6; S on B4009, then right on B480 at Watlington; OX49 5NF 16th-c thatched and beamed pub in sleepy village surrounded by fine countryside; sensibly priced italian-leaning food including good pizzas, Hook Norton Hooky and several wines by the glass, proper italian coffee,

friendly accommodating staff; free wi-fi; children and dogs welcome, nice garden behind, open (and food) all day. *(Bill Gulliver and Harry Thomson)*

DEDDINGTON   SP4631
★**Deddington Arms** (01869) 338364
Off A4260 (B4031) Banbury–Oxford; Horse Fair; OX15 0SH Beamed and timbered 16th-c hotel in charming village with lots of antiques shops and good farmers' market (last Sat of month); very well liked food including set lunch/evening menus in sizeable contemporary back dining room, comfortable more traditional bar with mullioned windows, flagstones and log fire, good food here too including sandwiches, Adnams, Hook Norton and a couple of guests, plenty of wines by the glass, attentive friendly service; unobtrusive background music, free wi-fi; children welcome, comfortable chalet bedrooms around courtyard, good breakfast, nice local walks, open all day. *(Gerry and Rosemary Dobson, Chris and Rachel Marshall, George Atkinson)*

DEDDINGTON   SP4631
Unicorn (01869) 338838
Market Place; OX15 0SE Refurbished 17th-c inn with beamed L-shaped bar, cosy snug, inglenook log fire, candlelit restaurant, interesting modern food (not Sun evening) cooked by the landlord, three Charles Wells ales and good choice of wines by the glass, friendly service; background music (not in snug); well behaved children and dogs welcome, cobbled courtyard leading to long walled back garden, six bedrooms, open all day (all day weekends in winter) and from 9am for good farmers' market (last Sat of month). *(Thomas Green)*

DENCHWORTH   SU3891
Fox (01235) 868258
Off A338 or A417 N of Wantage; Hyde Road; OX12 0DX Comfortable 17th-c thatched and beamed pub in pretty village, good sensibly priced food from extensive menu including Sun carvery (best to book), friendly efficient staff, well kept Greene King ales and good choice of reasonably priced wines, plush seats in low-ceilinged connecting areas, two log fires, old prints and paintings, airy dining extension; children and dogs welcome, tables under umbrellas in pleasant sheltered garden with heated terrace, play area and aunt sally. *(R K Phillips)*

DORCHESTER-ON-THAMES   SU5794
Fleur de Lys (01865) 340502
Just off A4074 Maidenhead–Oxford; High Street; OX10 7HH Traditional 16th-c coaching inn opposite abbey; knocked through split-level bar/dining area with open fire and woodburner, plain wooden tables and interesting old photographs of the pub, good imaginative evening set menu

(not Sun), more straightforward lunchtime food, friendly efficient service, two changing ales; children (away from bar) and dogs welcome, picnic-sets on front terrace, more in back garden with play area and aunt sally, five bedrooms, closed Sun evening to Tues lunchtime. *(John Pritchard)*

DUCKLINGTON SP3507
Bell (01993) 700341
Off A415, a mile SE of Witney; Standlake Road; OX29 7UP Pretty thatched and beamed village local, good value home-made food including stone-baked pizzas, decent vegetarian options and Sun carvery, bargain OAP lunch deal Mon-Sat, Greene King ales, friendly service, big stripped-stone and flagstoned bar with scrubbed tables, log fires and glass-covered well, old local photographs and farm tools, hatch-served public bar, roomy back restaurant with bells hanging from beams; background music, quiz first Sun of month, sports TV, pool, free wi-fi; children welcome, seats outside and aunt sally, five bedrooms, open all day (till 9.30pm Sun), no food Sun evening. *(Dennis and Doreen Haward)*

EAST HENDRED SU4588
Plough (01235) 833213
Off A417 E of Wantage; Orchard Lane; OX12 8JW Timbered 16th-c village pub with good value traditional food (not Sun evening), Greene King-related ales and decent choice of wines by the glass, efficient friendly service, lofty raftered main room with interesting farming memorabilia, side dining area; background and regular live music, sports TV, pool, machines; well behaved children and dogs allowed, lovely enclosed back garden, attractive village, open all day weekends, closed Mon. *(S and L McPhee)*

EATON SP4403
Eight Bells (01865) 862261
Signed off B4017 SW of Oxford; OX13 5PR Cosy unpretentious old pub with relaxed local atmosphere, two small low-beamed bars with open fires and a dining area, five well kept ales including Loose Cannon, traditional low-priced food (not Sun evening) served by friendly helpful staff; pleasant garden with aunt sally, nice walks, open all day Fri-Sun, closed Mon. *(Tim King, Jack Trussler)*

EPWELL SP3540
★ **Chandlers Arms** (01295) 780153
Sibford Road, off B4035; OX15 6LH Welcoming little 16th-c stone pub renovated and doing well under present licensees; good freshly made food (booking advised) from sandwiches and bar meals up, well kept Fullers London Pride and Hook Norton, proper coffee, bar with country-style furniture, two dining areas, good

attentive service; children welcome, no dogs, pleasant garden with aunt sally and summer entertainment, attractive out-of-the-way village near Macmillan Way long-distance path, open all day. *(Bernard Stradling, Dennis and Doreen Haward, Clive and Fran Dutson, Guy Vowles)*

EWELME SU6491
Shepherds Hut (01491) 836636
Off B4009 about 6 miles SW of M40 junction 6; High Street; OX10 6HQ Extended bay-windowed village pub with beams, bare boards and woodburner, enjoyable home-made food (not Sun evening) from ciabattas up, Greene King ales and a guest, friendly helpful staff, back dining area; children, walkers and dogs welcome, terrace picnic-sets with steps up to lawn and play area, open all day. *(Anthony Waters, David Lamb)*

EXLADE STREET SU6582
★ **Highwayman** (01491) 682020
Just off A4074 Reading-Wallingford; RG8 0UA Whitewashed brick building with two beamed bar rooms, mainly 17th-c (parts older), with interesting rambling layout and mix of furniture, inglenook woodburner, good freshly cooked food from landlord-chef including lunchtime set menu, three well kept beers and plenty of wines by the glass, friendly efficient service, airy conservatory dining room; soft background music; children and dogs welcome, terrace and garden with fine views, closed Sun evening, Mon. *(Bill Gulliver and Harry Thomson, John Pritchard)*

FERNHAM SU2991
★ **Woodman** (01367) 820643
A420 SW of Oxford, then left into B4508 after about 11 miles; village another 6 miles on; SN7 7NX Friendly 17th-c country pub with heavily beamed character main rooms, various odds and ends such as milkmaids' yokes, leather tack, coach horns and an old screw press, candlelit tables made from casks and a big open fire, also some comfortable newer areas, up to eight changing ales tapped from the cask, several malt whiskies and decent choice of wines by the glass, very well liked food from sandwiches up including good value set lunch and Tues steak night, pleasant helpful service; background music, 'film and dinner' evenings; children and dogs (in bar) welcome, disabled facilities, terrace seats, good walks below the downs, open all day Fri-Sun. *(R K Phillips)*

FIFIELD SP2318
Merrymouth (01993) 831652
A424 Burford-Stow; OX7 6HR Simple but comfortable roadside inn dating from 13th c, L-shaped bar with bay-window seats, flagstones and low beams, some walls stripped back to old masonry, warm stove, generous food cooked by landlord

including fish specials, well kept ales such as Brakspears and Hook Norton, decent choice of wines, friendly staff; background music, free wi-fi; children and dogs welcome, tables on terrace and in back garden, nice views, nine stable-block bedrooms, good breakfast. *(Richard Stanfield, Stanley and Annie Matthews)*

FINSTOCK SP3616

★ **Plough** (01993) 868333

Just off B4022 N of Witney; High Street; OX7 3BY Thatched and low-beamed village pub with long rambling bar, leather sofas by massive stone inglenook, pictures of local scenes and some historical documents connected with the pub, roomy dining room with candles on stripped-pine tables, popular home-made pubby food (best to book), two or three well kept ales including Adnams Broadside, traditional cider, several wines by the glass and decent choice of whiskies, friendly helpful staff; soft background music, bar billiards; children and dogs (in bar) welcome, seats in neatly kept garden with aunt sally, woodland walks and along River Evenlode, open all day Sat, closed Sun evening, Mon lunchtime. *(S and L McPhee)*

FRINGFORD SP6028

Butchers Arms (01869) 277363

Off A421 N of Bicester; Main Street; OX27 8EB Welcoming partly thatched creeper-clad local in Flora Thompson's 'Candleford' village; enjoyable traditional food including good Sun roasts (three sittings, best to book), well kept Brakspears, Hook Norton and Sharps, charming efficient service, unpretentious interior with L-shaped bar and back dining room, good log fire; picnic-sets out at front beside village cricket green. *(Dave Snowden)*

FYFIELD SU4298

★ **White Hart** (01865) 390585

Main Road; off A420 8 miles SW of Oxford; OX13 5LW Grand medieval hall with soaring eaves, huge stone-flanked window embrasures and minstrels' gallery, contrasting cosy low-beamed side bar with woodburner in large inglenook, fresh flowers and evening candles, civilised friendly atmosphere and full of history; good imaginative modern food (not Sun evening, best to book) cooked by licensee-chef using home-grown produce, Loose Cannon and a couple of guests, around 12 wines by the glass and several malt whiskies; background music; well behaved children welcome, elegant furniture under umbrellas on spacious heated terrace, lovely gardens, good Thames-side walks, open all day weekends, closed Mon. *(Thomas Green)*

GALLOWSTREE COMMON SU6980

Reformation (0118) 972 3126

Horsepond Road; RG4 9BP Friendly and welcoming black-beamed village local,

enjoyable varied choice of home-made food, Brakspears and a couple of Marstons-related guests, plenty of wines by the glass, open fires, conservatory; some live music, other events such as tractor runs and log-splitting competitions; children and dogs welcome, garden with 'shipwreck' play area, closed Sun evening, Mon. *(Liz and Martin Eldon)*

GODSTOW SP4809

★ **Trout** (01865) 510930

Off A40/A44 roundabout via Wolvercote; OX2 8PN Pretty 17th-c Mitchells & Butlers dining pub in lovely riverside location (gets packed in fine weather); good choice of food from varied menu including set weekday deal till 6pm (booking essential at busy times), four beamed linked rooms with contemporary furnishings, flagstones and bare boards, log fires in three huge hearths, Brakspears, Sharps and a guest, several wines by the glass; background music; children and dogs (in bar) welcome, plenty of terrace seats under big parasols, footbridge to island (may be closed), abbey ruins opposite, car park fee refunded at bar, open (and food) all day. *(Edward Edmonton)*

GORING SU5980

★ **Catherine Wheel** (01491) 872379

Station Road; RG8 9HB Friendly 18th-c village pub with two cosily traditional bar areas, especially the more individual lower room with its dark beams and inglenook log fire, popular home-made food (not Sun evening) from seasonal menu, well kept Brakspears and other Marstons-related ales, Thatcher's cider, back restaurant, notable doors to lavatories; monthly quiz and some live music, TV, free wi-fi; children and dogs welcome, sunny garden and gravel terrace, handy for Thames Path, open all day. *(M A Borthwick)*

GORING SU5980

John Barleycorn (01491) 872509

Manor Road; RG8 9DP Friendly low-beamed cottagey local with cosy unpretentious lounge bar and adjoining dining room, popular good value pubby food (not Sun evening) from lunchtime sandwiches up, Brakspears, Ringwood Fortyniner and a guest, seven wines by the glass, cheerful swift service, public bar with log fire and bar billiards; children welcome, enclosed beer garden, short walk to the Thames, three bedrooms, open all day. *(Paul Humphreys, Taff Thomas)*

GOZZARD'S FORD SU4698

Black Horse (01865) 390530

Off B4017 NW of Abingdon; N of A415 by Marcham–Cothill road; OX13 6JH Ancient pub in tiny hamlet, some refurbishment under present management, decent choice of popular home-made food including several fish dishes, well kept ales such as Greene King IPA, Loose Cannon and

Morlands, good friendly service, comfortable beamed main bar partly divided by stout timbers and low steps, end woodburner, separate bare-boards public bar with pool, darts and TV; weekend live music; children and dogs welcome, large garden, open all day. (John Pritchard)

GREAT TEW   SP3929
★ **Falkland Arms** (01608) 683653
The Green; off B4022 about 5 miles E of Chipping Norton; OX7 4DB Part-thatched 16th-c golden-stone pub in lovely village, unspoilt partly panelled bar with high-backed settles, stools and plain tables on flagstones or bare boards, lots of mugs and jugs hanging from beam-and-plank ceiling, interesting brewerania, dim converted oil lamps and shutters for stone-mullioned latticed windows, open fire in fine inglenook, Wadworths and guests, Weston's cider, country wines and 30 malt whiskies, snuff for sale, locally sourced freshly made food, friendly service, separate dining room; folk night Sun; children and dogs welcome, tables out at front and under parasols in back garden, six bedrooms and cottage, open all day from 8am (breakfast for non-residents). (Dr W I C Clark)

HAILEY   SP3414
★ **Bird in Hand** (01993) 868321
Whiteoak Green; B4022 Witney–Charlbury; OX29 9XP Attractive 17th-c extended stone inn, good food including some welsh influences from owner-chef (best to book summer weekends), set lunch deal Tues and Weds, helpful friendly service, well kept ales such as Brains and Hook Norton, several wines by the glass, beams, timbers and stripped stone, comfortable armchairs on polished boards, large log fire, cosy corners in carpeted restaurant, witty references to Wales and rugby dotted about, lovely Cotswold views; parasol-shaded terrace tables, 16 bedrooms in modern block around grass quadrangle, good breakfast, open all day from 8am. (Paul and Sue Merrick)

HAILEY   SU6485
★ **King William IV** (01491) 681845
The Hailey near Ipsden, off A4074 or A4130 SE of Wallingford; OX10 6AD Popular fine old pub in lovely countryside, beamed bar with good sturdy furniture on tiles in front of big log fire, three other cosy seating areas opening off, enjoyable freshly made food (not Sun evening) from baguettes to specials, Brakspears and guests tapped from the cask, helpful friendly staff; children and dogs welcome, terrace and large garden enjoying wide-ranging peaceful views, good

walking (Chiltern Way and Ridgeway), leave muddy boots in porch, open all day weekends. (Bob and Margaret Holder)

HAILEY   SP3512
★ **Lamb & Flag** (01993) 702849
B4022 a mile N of Witney; Middletown; OX29 9UB Rambling 17th-c stone-built village pub with plenty of character, beams, some ancient flagstones and inglenook woodburner, enjoyable freshly made food at affordable prices including good Sun lunch, friendly attentive staff, well kept Thwaites Lancaster Bomber and guests, good choice of wines by the glass; children and dogs welcome, lovely garden, open all day weekends, closed Mon and lunchtimes Tues, Weds. (Keith and Caroline Bowerman)

HAMPTON POYLE   SP5015
Bell (01865) 376242
From A34 S, take Kidlington turn and village signed from roundabout; from A34 N, take Kidlington turn, then A4260 to roundabout, third turning signed for Superstore (Bicester Road); village signed from roundabout; OX5 2QD Front bar with three snug rooms, lots of big black and white photo-prints, sturdy simple furnishings, scatter cushions and window seats, a stove flanked by bookshelves one end, large fireplace the other, open kitchen with feature pizza oven in biggish inner room, spreading restaurant with plenty of tables on pale limestone floor, inventive food including cheaper weekday set menu, good choice of wines by the glass, ales such as Hook Norton and Wye Valley, efficient uniformed staff and cheerful buzzy atmosphere; background music; children and dogs (in bar) welcome, modern seats on sunny front terrace by quiet village lane, nine good bedrooms, open all day. (Gerry Price, S and L McPhee)

HANWELL   SP4343
Moon & Sixpence (01295) 730544
Main Street; OX17 1HN Refurbished stone-built pub in attractive village setting, good food cooked by owner-chef from pub favourites up including set menu choices, comfortable bar and dining areas with view into kitchen, friendly staff, well kept Charles Wells ales and several wines by the glass from good list; children welcome, disabled access, seats on back terrace, open till 6pm Sun. (Gerry and Rosemary Dobson)

HEADINGTON   SP5406
Butchers Arms (01865) 742470
Wilberforce Street; OX3 7AN Welcoming backstreet local with good mix of customers, refurbished bare-boards interior, well kept Fullers beers and good value tasty food

---

Half pints: by law, a pub should not charge more for half a pint than half the price of a full pint, unless it shows that half-pint price on its price list.

(not Sun evening), roaring fire; children and dogs welcome, disabled access, heated terrace with smokers' shelter, open all day Fri-Sun. *(Tim King)*

HENLEY   SU7682
Anchor (01491) 574753
Friday Street; RG9 1AH Beamed pub just back from the river; uncluttered gently upmarket feel, wood and stone floors, tall tables, leather sofas and numbered dining tables with flowers, popular food from panini and sharing plates up, Brakspears Bitter and a guest, several wines by the glass; children welcome, smart sunny terrace at back, open all day. *(Mungo Shipley)*

HENLEY   SU7682
Angel on the Bridge (01491) 410678
Thames-side, by the bridge; RG9 1BH
17th-c and worth knowing for its prime Thames-side position (packed during the regatta); small front bar with log fire, downstairs back bar and adjacent restaurant, beams, uneven floors and dim lighting, Brakspears ales and maybe a guest such as Ringwood, good choice of wines by the glass, enjoyable food from sandwiches and pubby choices up, cheerful staff; tables under parasols on popular waterside deck (plastic glasses here), moorings for two boats, open all day, at least in summer. *(Thomas Green)*

HENLEY   SU7582
★**Three Tuns** (01491) 410138
Market Place; RG9 2AA Small heavy-beamed front bar with fire, all tables set for eating (stools by counter for drinkers), well kept Brakspears and guests such as Ringwood, good well presented home-made food (not Sun evening), also good value weekday set lunch, nice wines, friendly attentive service, lighter panelled back dining area with painted timbers and wood floor; live music Sun; children and dogs (in bar) welcome, tables in attractive little back courtyard, closed Mon, otherwise open all day. *(Paul Humphreys, Tracey and Stephen Groves)*

HOOK NORTON   SP3534
★**Gate Hangs High** (01608) 737387
N towards Sibford, at Banbury–Rollright crossroads; OX15 5DF Tucked-away old stone pub with cosy low-ceilinged bar, traditional furniture on bare boards, attractive inglenook, good reasonably priced home-made food from bar snacks to daily specials, well kept Hook Norton ales and a guest, decent wines, friendly helpful service, side dining extension; background music; children and dogs (in bar) welcome, pretty

courtyard and country garden, four bedrooms, camping, quite near Rollright Stones (EH), open all day. *(S and L McPhee)*

HOOK NORTON   SP3533
Sun (01608) 737570
High Street; OX15 5NH Recently refurbished pub in centre of village; beamed and flagstoned bar with big fireplace, two dining areas, good range of enjoyable food from sandwiches and platters up, well kept Hook Norton and several wines by the glass, friendly helpful staff; children and dogs welcome, tables out in front and on back terrace, six comfortable bedrooms (ones above bar can be noisy), hearty breakfast, open all day (till 6pm Sun).
(Helene Grygar)

HORNTON   SP3945
Dun Cow (01295) 670524
West End; OX15 6DA Traditional 17th-c thatch and ironstone village pub, friendly and relaxed, with sensibly short choice of good fresh food (not Sun evening, Mon or Tues) from lunchtime sandwiches up using local suppliers, Hook Norton, St Austell and Wells Bombardier, a dozen wines by the glass; quiz first Weds of the month; children and dogs welcome, appealing small garden behind, open all day weekends, closed lunchtimes Mon, Tues (in winter lunchtimes Mon-Thurs). *(Lionel Smith)*

KIDMORE END   SU6979
New Inn (0118) 972 3115
Chalkhouse Green Road; signed from B481 in Sonning Common; RG4 9AU
Extended black and white pub by village church; beams and big log fire, enjoyable freshly made food, well kept Brakspears ales and decent wines by the glass, pleasant restaurant; children welcome, tables in large sheltered garden with pond, six bedrooms, open all day Mon-Sat, till 5pm Sun.
(Tim King)

KINGHAM   SP2523
★**Wild Rabbit** (01608) 658389
Church Street; OX7 6YA Former 18th-c farmhouse with plenty of rustic chic, antique country furniture, limestone floors, exposed stone walls, beams and huge fireplaces, contemporary artwork and fresh flowers, Hook Norton Hooky and a couple of guests, several wines by the glass including champagne, good food in bar or more upmarket choices (not cheap) in spacious brasserie-style restaurant with kitchen view, pleasant helpful young staff; children welcome, dogs in bar, paved front terrace with topiary rabbits, 12 sumptuously

---

If you report on a pub that's not a featured entry, please tell us any lunchtimes or evenings when it doesn't serve bar food.

appointed individual bedrooms, open all day. *(Bernard Stradling, Liz Bell)*

LAUNTON
SP6022
Bull (01869) 248158
Just E of Bicester; Bicester Road; OX26 5DQ Cleanly modernised, part-thatched 17th-c village pub, enjoyable good value food including OAP lunchtime deal (Mon-Fri) and Tues steak night, Greene King IPA and a couple of guests, friendly staff; background music, Sun quiz; children and dogs welcome, wheelchair access from car park, garden with terrace, open all day. *(Dennis and Doreen Haward)*

LEWKNOR
SU7197
★**Olde Leathern Bottel**
(01844) 351482 *Under a mile from M40 junction 6; off B4009 towards Watlington; OX49 5TH* Popular and friendly family-run pub, two heavy-beamed bars with understated décor and rustic furnishings, open fires, well kept Brakspears and Marstons, several wines by the glass, tasty pub food and specials served quickly, family room separated by standing timbers; dogs welcome, splendid garden with plenty of picnic-sets under parasols, play area and boules, handy for walks on Chiltern escarpment. *(David Lamb, R K Phillips)*

LONG HANBOROUGH
SP4214
★**George & Dragon** (01993) 881362
A4095 Bladon–Witney; Main Road; OX29 8JX Substantial pub with original two-room bar (17th-c or older), low beams, stripped stone and two woodburners, Charles Wells ales and decent range of wines, roomy thatched restaurant extension with comfortably padded dining chairs around sturdy tables, wide choice of well liked food from lunchtime sandwiches and baked potatoes up, prompt friendly service; background music, Weds 'quiz and fizz' night; children and dogs (in bar) welcome, large back garden with picnic-sets among shrubs, tables beneath canopy on separate sheltered terrace, summer barbecues, shuts 8pm Sun. *(Carol and Barry Craddock)*

LONGCOT
SU2790
King & Queen (01793) 784348
Shrivenham Road, off B4508; SN7 7TL Friendly beamed pub with good food cooked by landlord-chef, three well kept ales including Loose Cannon and two proper ciders; occasional live music, pool and darts, free wi-fi; children and dogs (they have a couple) welcome, terrace tables, six bedrooms, closed Mon lunchtime. *(R K Phillips, George Paton)*

MAIDENSGROVE
SU7288
Five Horseshoes (01491) 641282
Off B480 and B481, W of village; RG9 6EX Character 16th-c dining pub set high in the Chilterns; rambling bar with

low ceiling and log fire, good food (not Sun evening) from changing menu including home-smoked salmon and seasonal game, set lunch Tues-Fri, friendly service, well kept Brakspears and good choice of wines by the glass, airy conservatory restaurant; regular jazz evenings; children and dogs (in bar) welcome, plenty of tables in suntrap garden with rolling countryside views, good walks, open all day Sat, Sun, closed Mon. *(Susan and John Douglas)*

MARSH BALDON
SU5699
Seven Stars (01865) 343337
The Baldons signed off A4074 N of Dorchester; OX44 9LP Competently run, community-owned beamed pub on edge of village green; good food all day including plenty of gluten-free and vegetarian choices (notable fish and chips), well kept Fullers, Loose Cannon and a couple of local guests, helpful staff coping well at busy times, refurbished bar areas, seats by corner fire, raftered barn restaurant; children, dogs and walkers' muddy boots welcome, seats outside overlooking fields and horses, open all day (till midnight Fri, Sat). *(Neil and Angela Huxter)*

MINSTER LOVELL
SP3211
★**Old Swan & Minster Mill**
(01993) 774441 *Just N of B4047 Witney–Burford; OX29 0RN* Lovely 15th-c building with much emphasis on hotel/restaurant side but with unchanging tranquil little bar; stools at wooden counter, Brakspears Oxford Gold, North Cotswold Windrush and Wychwood Hobgoblin, good wines by the glass from fine list, 23 malt whiskies, various teas and coffees, inventive food from sandwiches up, prompt friendly service; attractive low-beamed rooms lead off with log fires in huge fireplaces, rugs on bare boards or ancient flagstones, leather tub chairs, comfortable armchairs and sofas, antiques, prints, lots of horsebrasses, swords, even a suit of armour; background music, live jazz first Sun of month; children and dogs (in bar) welcome, 65-acre grounds with tennis, croquet and fishing on River Windrush, luxurious bedrooms. *(Edward May, Isobel Mackinlay, Richard Kennell)*

MURCOTT
SP5815
★**Nut Tree** (01865) 331253
Off B4027 NE of Oxford, via Islip and Charlton-on-Otmoor; OX5 2RE Beamed and thatched 15th-c dining pub, good imaginative cooking (not cheap) using own produce including home-reared pigs, neat friendly young staff, Vale, two guests beers and carefully chosen wines; background music; children and dogs (in bar) welcome, terrace and pretty garden, unusual gargoyles on front wall (modelled loosely on local characters), closed Sun evening, Mon and Tues. *(R A and E J Harkness)*

NEWBRIDGE
SP4001
Maybush (01865) 300101
A415 7 miles S of Witney; OX29 7QD
Recently revamped 18th-c eco dining pub in lovely Thames-side setting by ancient bridge; clean modern interior with light stone floors, some stripped beams and woodburners in two-way fireplaces, good well presented food, a couple of real ales such as Sharps Doom Bar, craft beers from Cotswold and decent wines by the glass, friendly attentive staff; children and dogs (in bar) welcome, waterside terrace and garden, on the Thames Path, moorings and shepherd's hut accommodation, closed Sun evening, Mon, otherwise open all day.
(Lindy Wildsmith)

NEWBRIDGE
SP4001
Rose Revived (01865) 300221
A415 7 miles S of Witney; OX29 7QD
Recently refurbished 16th-c ivy-clad pub on the banks of the Thames (Greene King Old English Inn); fresh modern décor mixing with beams and stone fireplaces, enjoyable well priced food including deals, good friendly service; free wi-fi; children and dogs (in one part) welcome, disabled access/facilities, lovely big riverside garden with play area, moorings, seven bedrooms, open (and food) all day. *(Natalie)*

NORTH HINKSEY
SP4905
Fishes (01865) 249796
Off A420 just E of A34 ring road; N Hinksey Lane, then pass church into cul-de-sac signed to rugby club; OX2 0NA
Popular brick and tile Victorian pub (part of the Peach group) set in three acres of wooded grounds; extended open-plan interior with conservatory, good choice of enjoyable food from sandwiches and deli boards up, well kept Greene King ales and a guest, plenty of wines by the glass and nice selection of gins, friendly helpful staff; children welcome, dogs in bar and snug, tables out at front, on back deck and in streamside garden with summer barbecues and tipi, open (and food) all day from 9.30am for breakfast. *(S and L McPhee)*

NORTH MORETON
SU5689
Bear at Home (01235) 811311
Off A4130 Didcot–Wallingford; High Street; OX11 9AT Dating from the 16th c with traditional bar, cosy fireside areas and dining part with stripped-pine furniture, lots of beams, carpeted floors, pictures on rough walls; friendly service from father and daughter team, enjoyable sensibly priced home-made food including daily specials, Timothy Taylors, a beer for the pub from West Berkshire and a couple of local guests (July beer festival), Weston's cider and a dozen wines by the glass; Mon quiz; children and dogs welcome, appealing back garden overlooking cricket pitch, aunt sally,

pretty village, open all day Sat, closed Sun evening. *(Bill Gulliver and Harry Thomson)*

NORTHMOOR
SP4202
Red Lion (01865) 300301
B4449 SE of Stanton Harcourt; OX29 5SX Renovated 15th-c village pub owned by the local community, good range of well presented freshly made food, up to four ales such as Brakspears, Cotswold Lion, Hook Norton and Wychwood, plenty of wines by the glass, friendly young staff, cosy atmosphere with heavy beams and bare stone walls, scrubbed tables, open fire one end, woodburner the other; summer movie nights and car boot sales, free wi-fi; children, walkers and dogs welcome, garden tables, open all day Sat, closed Sun evening, Mon. *(Helene Grygar)*

OXFORD
SP5106
Chequers (01865) 727463
Off High Street; OX1 4DH Narrow 16th-c courtyard pub tucked away down small alleyway, several areas on three floors with interesting architectural features, beams, panelling and stained glass, eight or so well kept ales and enjoyable good value Nicholsons menu, afternoon tea, friendly service; walled garden, open (and food) all day. *(Thomas Green)*

OXFORD
SP5106
★ Eagle & Child (01865) 302925
St Giles; OX1 3LU Long narrow Nicholsons pub dating from the 16th c with two charmingly old-fashioned panelled front rooms, well kept Brakspears, Hook Norton and interesting guests, good choice of food from sandwiches to Sun roasts, friendly service and bustling atmosphere, stripped-brick back dining extension and conservatory, Tolkien and C S Lewis connections (the Inklings writers' group used to meet here); games machine; children allowed in back till 8pm, open (and food all day). *(Ian Herdman, Roger and Donna Huggins, David Thornton, Tony Scott)*

OXFORD
SP5105
Head of the River (01865) 721600
Folly Bridge; between St Aldates and Christ Church Meadow; OX1 4LB
Civilised well renovated pub by river, boats for hire and nearby walks; spacious split-level downstairs bar with dividing brick arches, flagstones and bare boards, well kept Fullers/Gales beers and good choice of wines by the glass, popular pubby food from sandwiches up, good service; background music, daily papers; tables on stepped heated waterside terrace, 12 bedrooms, open all day. *(Martin Day, Andy Dolan)*

OXFORD
SP5203
Isis Farmhouse (01865) 243854
Off Donnington Bridge Road; no car access; OX4 4EL Early 19th-c former

farmhouse in charming waterside spot (accessible only to walkers/cyclists), relaxed lived-in interior with two woodburners, short choice of enjoyable home-made food (sensible prices, no credit cards), Appleford and a guest ale, nice wines and interesting soft drinks, afternoon teas with wonderful home-baked cakes; some live music; children and dogs welcome, terrace and garden picnic-sets, canoe hire, short walk to Iffley Lock and nearby lavishly decorated early Norman church, open all day Thurs-Sat in summer (Fri-Sun in winter) and all bank holidays including Christmas, may close in bad weather. *(Thomas Green, Sandra King)*

OXFORD SP5106
Kings Arms (01865) 242369
Holywell Street/Parks Road; OX1 3SP Relaxed corner pub dating from the early 17th c opposite the New Bodleian Library; popular with locals and students (Wadham College owns it), various cosy rooms up and down stairs, lots of panelling and pictures, open fires, well kept Youngs ales and guests, several wines by the glass, pubby food from baked potatoes and sandwiches up; free wi-fi; children and dogs welcome, a few pavement tables, open (and food) all day. *(Andy Dolan)*

OXFORD SP5006
Kite (01865) 248546
Mill Street; OX2 0AL Refurbished Victorian backstreet pub under new management; half a dozen or so real ales including Greene King and XT, a couple of ciders and decent range of wines, enjoyable generously served food from lunchtime ciabattas and sharing boards up, friendly staff, cosy candlelit décor, dining room with woodburner; weekly live music, board games; children and dogs on leads welcome, sheltered terrace (maybe summer barbecues), five bedrooms, open all day and handy for station. *(Richard Tilbrook)*

OXFORD SP5106
Lamb & Flag (01865) 515787
St Giles/Banbury Road; OX1 3JS Old pub owned by nearby college, modern airy front room with light wood panelling and big windows over street, more atmosphere in back rooms with stripped stonework and low-boarded ceilings, a beer by Palmers for the pub (L&F Gold), Skinners Betty Stogs and guests, real cider/perry, some lunchtime food including sandwiches and home-made pies, Thomas Hardy's *Jude the Obscure* connection; open all day. *(Andy Dolan)*

OXFORD SP5006
Old Bookbinders (01865) 553549
Victor Street; OX2 6BT Dark and mellow family-run local tucked away in the Jericho area; friendly and unpretentious, with old fittings and lots of interesting bric-a-brac, Greene King ales and three guests, decent choice of whiskies and

other spirits, enjoyable french-leaning food including speciality crêpes and lunchtime/early evening set menu; board games and shove-ha'penny, Tues quiz, open mike night Sun; children, dogs and students welcome, entertaining features such as multiple door handles to the gents', closed Mon and lunchtimes Tues, Weds, otherwise open all day. *(Andy Dolan)*

OXFORD SP5105
Royal Blenheim (01865) 242355
Ebbes Street; OX1 1PT Popular airy 19th-c corner pub, opened by Queen Victoria during her Golden Jubilee, and now the tap for the White Horse Brewery; their range and many interesting guests, good value straightforward food (all day weekends) including some decent vegetarian options, Sun breakfast, friendly chatty staff, single room with original tiled floor and raised perimeter booth seating; big-screen sports TV, Weds quiz, Mon knitting club; open all day (till midnight Fri, Sat). *(S and L McPhee)*

OXFORD SP5106
Turf Tavern (01865) 243235
Bath Place; via St Helens Passage, between Holywell Street and New College Lane; OX1 3SU Interesting character pub hidden away behind high walls, small dark-beamed bars with lots of snug areas, up to a dozen constantly changing ales including Greene King, Weston's cider and winter mulled wine, popular reasonably priced food from sandwiches up, pleasant helpful service; newspapers and free wi-fi; children and dogs welcome, three walled-in courtyards (one with own bar), open (and food) all day. *(Andy Dolan, Tony Scott)*

OXFORD SP5106
White Horse (01865) 204801
Broad Street; OX1 3BB Bustling place squeezed between parts of Blackwell's bookshop; small narrow bar with snug raised back alcove, low beams and timbers, beautiful view of the Clarendon Building and Sheldonian Theatre, half a dozen ales including Brakspears, Sharps, Shotover and a house beer from Marstons, enjoyable home-made food, friendly staff; open all day and popular with students. *(Barry Collett, Roger and Donna Huggins)*

PISHILL SU7190
★Crown (01491) 638364
B480 Nettlebed–Watlington; RG9 6HH 15th-c inn at heart of the Chilterns; beamed bars with old local photographs, prints and maps, some panelling and nice mix of wooden tables and chairs, Brakspears and Rebellion ales, seven wines by the glass and a dozen malt whiskies, tasty generously served food, good service, knocked-through back area with standing timbers and three log fires (not always lit); priest hole is said to be one of the largest in the country; well

behaved children welcome, dogs in bar, seats in pretty garden with thatched barn for functions, lots of nearby walks, self-catering cottage, closed Sun evening. *(Edward Edmonton)*

PLAY HATCH   SU7477

Shoulder of Mutton

(0118) 947 3908   *W of Henley Road (A4155) roundabout; RG4 9QU* Dining pub with low-ceilinged log-fire bar and large back conservatory restaurant, good food including signature mutton dishes and set menus, well kept Greene King and guests such as nearby Loddon, reasonably priced house wines, friendly attentive service; children welcome, picnic-sets in carefully tended walled garden with well, closed Sun evening, Mon. *(John Pritchard)*

ROKE   SU6293

Home Sweet Home   (01491) 838249

Off B4009 Benson–Watlington; OX10 6JD Wadworths country pub with two smallish bars, heavy stripped beams, big log fire and traditional furniture, carpeted room on right leading to restaurant area, good food including set menu Tues-Sat, friendly staff; background music, Rokefest music/beer festival late May Bank Holiday; children and dogs welcome, low-walled front garden, open all day Sun till 8pm (food till 3pm), closed Mon. *(Colin McLachlan)*

ROTHERFIELD GREYS   SU7282

★ **Maltsters Arms**   (01491) 628400

Can be reached off A4155 in Henley, via Greys Road passing Southfields long-stay car park; or follow Greys Church signpost off B481 N of Sonning Common; RG9 4QD New owners for this Chilterns country pub; comfortable wall banquettes front bar with beamed comfortable wall banquettes and woodburner, linked lounge and restaurant, Brakspears and other Marstons-related beers, Aspall's cider and eight wines by the glass, good sensibly priced food from fairly pubby menu, friendly staff; background music; children and dogs (in bar) welcome, terrace tables under big heated canopy, picnic-sets on grass looking over paddocks and rolling countryside, good walks nearby and handy for Greys Court (NT), open all day Sun. *(Penny and Peter Keevil, Ross Balaam, R K Phillips, David Lamb)*

ROTHERFIELD PEPPARD   SU7081

Unicorn   (01491) 628674

Colmore Lane; RG9 5LX Attractive country pub under same owners as the Little Angel, Henley (see Also Worth a Visit in Berkshire) and Cherry Tree, Stoke Row; bustling bar with open fire, Brakspears ales and good wines by the glass, dining room with high-backed chairs around mix of tables on stripped boards, well liked interesting food including lunchtime sandwiches and daily specials, Thurs tapas evening, friendly

service; dogs welcome (pub dogs are Alfie and Betsy), seats out in front and in pretty back garden, open all day weekends. *(Jack Trussler)*

SHENINGTON   SP3742

Bell   (01295) 670274

Off A422 NW of Banbury; OX15 6NQ Unpretentious 17th-c two-room pub with popular home-made food, well kept Hook Norton Hooky and good range of wines by the glass, friendly service, heavy beams, some flagstones, stripped stone and pine panelling, two woodburners; children in eating areas and dogs in bar, picnic-sets out at front, charming quiet village with good surrounding walks, closed Sun evening, Mon. *(Thomas Green)*

SHIPTON-UNDER-WYCHWOOD   SP2717

★ **Lamb**   (01993) 830465

High Street; off A361 to Burford; OX7 6DQ Mother and son team at this handsome stone inn, beamed bar with oak-panelled settle, farmhouse chairs and polished tables on wood-block flooring, stripped-stone walls, church candles and log fire, Greene King IPA and a couple of guests, good wines (plenty by the glass) and well liked food including children's menu and Weds pie night, pleasant friendly service, restaurant area; free wi-fi; dogs allowed in bar (they have their own), wheelchair access, garden with modern furniture on terrace, five themed bedrooms, open all day. *(R K Phillips)*

SHIPTON-UNDER-WYCHWOOD   SP2717

Wychwood Inn   (01993) 831185

High Street; OX7 6BA Under same ownership as the Lamb (see previous entry); contemporary décor in open-plan bar/dining area, more period character in flagstoned public bar with black beams and inglenook, up to eight real ales including one badged for them and plenty of wines by the glass, enjoyable food from wraps to grills, friendly young staff; sports TV, darts; children and dogs welcome, picnic-sets on small terrace, shop in glassed-in coach entrance, five bedrooms, open all day. *(Bernard Stradling)*

SHUTFORD   SP3840

George & Dragon   (01295) 780320

Church Lane; OX15 6PG Ancient stone pub set down from church; cosy L-shaped bar with flagstones and impressive fireplace, five well kept ales including Hook Norton, decent choice of wines by the glass and good locally sourced bar and restaurant food (not Sun evening-Tues), friendly service; live music and quiz nights, separate room for sports TV, darts and dominoes; children and dogs (in bar) welcome, small garden overlooking village, open all day weekends, closed Mon and lunchtimes Tues-Thurs. *(Sandra King)*

SIBFORD GOWER   SP3537
Wykham Arms   (01295) 788808
Signed off B4035 Banbury to Shipston-on-Stour; Temple Mill Road; OX15 5RX
Cottagey 17th-c thatched and flagstoned dining pub, good food (not Sun evening) from light lunchtime menu up, friendly attentive staff, two well kept changing ales and over 20 wines by the glass, comfortable open-plan interior with low beams and stripped stone, glass-covered well, inglenook; children and dogs welcome, country views from big garden, lovely manor house opposite and good walks nearby, open all day Sun, closed Mon.
(S and L McPhee)

SOULDERN   SP5231
Fox   (01869) 345284
Off B4100; Fox Lane; OX27 7JW Early 19th-c pub set in delightful village, open-plan beamed interior with woodburner in two-way fireplace, enjoyable fairly priced food including themed nights, well kept Hook Norton, guest ales and several wines by the glass, friendly attentive service; regular live music; terrace and walled garden, aunt sally, four bedrooms, open all day Sat, till 4pm Sun.
(Jack Trussler)

SOUTH NEWINGTON   SP4033
Duck on the Pond   (01295) 721166
A361; OX15 4JE Spotless roadside dining pub with small flagstoned bar and linked carpeted eating areas up a step, well liked food (not Sun evening) from lunchtime ciabattas up including some good vegetarian choices and popular Sun lunch, Hook Norton Hooky and a couple of guests, cheerful pleasant staff, lots of duck-related items, woodburner; children welcome, no dogs inside, spacious grounds with tables on deck and lawn, pond with waterfowl and little River Swere winding down beyond, open all day weekends, closed Mon. *(George Atkinson)*

SOUTH STOKE   SU5983
Perch & Pike   (01491) 872415
Off B4009 2 miles N of Goring; RG8 0JS Renovated 17th-c brick and flint pub just a field away from the Thames; low-beamed flagstoned bar with open fire, well kept Brakspears and decent wines by the glass, enjoyable home-made food from varied changing menu, friendly helpful staff, sizeable restaurant in converted barn; children welcome, dogs in bar and snug (theirs is Alfie), tables on terrace and flower-bordered lawn, four bedrooms, open all day Sat, till 6pm Sun. *(Tim King)*

STANTON ST JOHN   SP5709
Talk House   (01865) 351654
Middle Road/Wheatley Road (B4027 just outside village); OX33 1EX Attractive part-thatched dining pub; older part on left with steeply pitched rafters soaring above stripped-stone walls, mix of old dining chairs and big stripped tables, large rugs on flagstones; rest of building converted more recently but in similar style with massive beams, flagstones or stoneware tiles, and log fires below low mantelbeams, good if not cheap food from sandwiches up (not Sun), three Fullers ales and several wines by the glass; children welcome, inner courtyard with teak tables and chairs, a few picnic-sets on side grass, bedrooms, open all day except Sun evening. *(Liz and Martin Eldon)*

STEEPLE ASTON   SP4725
★ Red Lion   (01869) 340225
Off A4260 12 miles N of Oxford; OX25 4RY Cheerful village pub with neatly kept beamed and partly panelled bar, antique settle and other good furnishings, well kept Hook Norton ales and decent wines by the glass, enjoyable food from shortish menu including pizzas, obliging young staff, back conservatory-style dining extension; Mon quiz; well behaved children welcome till 7pm, dogs in bar, suntrap front garden with lovely flowers and shrubs, parking may be awkward, open all day Sat, till 5pm Sun. *(Robert Watt)*

STEVENTON   SU4691
North Star
Stocks Lane, The Causeway, central westward turn off B4017; OX13 6SG Very traditional little village pub through yew tree gateway; tiled entrance corridor, main area with ancient high-backed settles forming booth in front of brick fireplace, three well kept ales from side tap room, hatch service to another room with plain seating, a couple of tables and coal fire, simple lunchtime food, friendly staff; dogs welcome, tables on front grass, aunt sally, open all day weekends, closed weekday lunchtimes. *(Lionel Smith)*

STOKE LYNE   SP5628
Peyton Arms   07546 066160
From minor road off B4110 N of Bicester fork left into village; OX27 8SD Beautifully situated and largely unspoilt one-room stone alehouse, character landlord (Mick the Hat) and loyal regulars, very well kept Hook Norton from casks behind small corner bar, no food apart from filled rolls, inglenook fire, tiled floor and lots of

---

Post Office address codings confusingly give the impression that some pubs are in Oxfordshire, when they're really in Berkshire, Buckinghamshire, Gloucestershire or Warwickshire (which is where we list them).

memorabilia, games area with darts and pool; no children or dogs; pleasant garden with aunt sally, open all day weekends till 7pm, closed weekday lunchtimes apart from Tues, and may shut early if quiet. *(Maddie Purvis)*

STOKE ROW   SU6884
Cherry Tree (01491) 680430
Off B481 at Highmoor; RG9 5QA
Sympathetically modernised 18th-c pub-restaurant (originally three cottages), enjoyable often interesting food from sharing platters to daily specials, Fri fish and chips, Brakspears ales and decent wines by the glass, helpful friendly staff, small linked rooms mainly set for dining, heavy low beams, stripped boards and flagstones; background music, TV in bar; well behaved children and dogs welcome, lots of tables in attractive garden, nearby walks, four good bedrooms in converted barn, nice breakfast, open all day (food all day Sun). *(Bob and Margaret Holder, Katharine Cowherd)*

STOKE ROW   SU6884
★Crooked Billet (01491) 681048
Nottwood Lane, off B491 N of Reading – OS Sheet 175 map reference 684844; RG9 5PU Nice place, but more restaurant than pub; charming rustic layout with heavy beams, flagstones, antique pubby furnishings and great inglenook log fire, crimson Victorian-style dining room, very good interesting food (all day weekends) cooked by owner-chef using local ingredients, cheaper set lunches Mon-Fri, helpful friendly staff, Brakspears Oxford Gold tapped from the cask (no counter), good wines, relaxed homely atmosphere; weekly live music often including established artists; children very welcome, big garden by Chilterns beechwoods, open all day. *(Colin McLachlan)*

SUNNINGWELL   SP4900
Flowing Well (01865) 735846
Just N of Abingdon; OX13 6RB
Refurbished timbered pub in former 19th-c rectory; popular food including british tapas, range of burgers and other pub favourites, a couple of Greene King ales and a guest, good choice of wines; children welcome, dogs in bar, large heated raised terrace, more seats in garden with small well, open (and food) all day. *(Jack Trussler)*

SWINFORD   SP4308
Talbot (01865) 881348
B4044 just S of Eynsham; OX29 4BT
Roomy and comfortable 17th-c beamed pub, well kept Arkells tapped from cooled casks and good choice of wines, enjoyable reasonably priced pubby food including deals, Sun carvery, friendly staff, long attractive flagstoned bar with some stripped stone, cheerful log-effect gas fire, charity quiz second Mon of month; children and dogs welcome, garden with decked area overlooking Wharf Stream, nice walk along

lovely stretch of the Thames towpath, moorings quite nearby, 11 bedrooms, open all day. *(Rosie and John Moore)*

THAME   SP7105
Cross Keys (01844) 218202
Park Street/East Street; OX9 3HP
Friendly one-bar 19th-c corner local, eight well kept ales including own Thame beers (not always available) and half a dozen ciders, no food apart from scotch eggs but can bring your own; regular comedy and quiz nights; courtyard garden, open all day weekends. *(Thomas Green)*

THAME   SP7006
★Thatch (01844) 214340
Lower High Street; OX9 2AA
Characterful timbered and thatched 16th-c dining pub (part of the Peach group); good interesting food from deli boards to daily specials, well kept ales, nice wines and some interesting gins, friendly personable service, cosy bar and appealing collection of little higgledy-piggledy rooms, heavy beams, old quarry tiles, flagstones and double-sided inglenook, smart contemporary furnishings and bold paintwork; children welcome, prettily planted terraced garden with tables under parasols, open (and food) all day. *(Alf Wright)*

TOOT BALDON   SP5600
★Mole (01865) 340001
Between A4074 and B480 SE of Oxford; OX44 9NG Light open-plan restaurranty pub with very good if not cheap food (booking advisable), friendly attentive service, nice wines by the glass, Hook Norton and a guest, leather sofas by bar, neat country furniture or more formal leather dining chairs in linked eating areas including conservatory, stripped 18th-c beams and big open fire; background music; children welcome, no dogs inside, lovely gardens, open all day. *(S and L McPhee)*

UFFINGTON   SU3089
Fox & Hounds (01367) 820680)
High Street; SN7 7RP Traditional beamed village local with three changing ales and enjoyable fairly priced home-made food including daily specials, friendly attentive staff, new garden room extension with view of White Horse Hill; live music and quiz nights, free wi-fi; children and dogs welcome, picnic-sets outside, handy for Tom Brown's School Museum, four ground-floor bedrooms, open all day, no food Sun evening. *(Tina and David Woods-Taylor)*

WALLINGFORD   SU6089
Partridge (01491) 839305
St Marys Street; OX10 0ET More restaurant than pub, contemporary and airy, with comfortably modern furnishings including bar stools, leather sofas and armchairs on bare boards, open fires, good

well presented food (not especially cheap) from sharing plates to popular Sun roasts, well chosen wines, neat helpful staff; children welcome, pleasant back terrace, four bedrooms (three sharing bathroom), may be possible to park in St Leonard's Lane off Thames Street, closed Mon, lunchtimes Tues-Sat and Sun evening. *(Colin McLachlan)*

WANTAGE SU3987
King Alfreds Head (01235) 771595
Market Place; OX12 8AH Updated pub set back from market square, reasonable choice of good well priced food including one or two specials, Sun carvery, ales such as St Austell and plenty of wines by the glass, helpful friendly staff, linked areas, leather sofas by log fire; background music, sports TV, free wi-fi; children and dogs welcome, sizeable beer garden with summer barbecues and some live music, open all day. *(R K Phillips)*

WANTAGE SU3987
★ Royal Oak (01235) 763129
Newbury Street; OX12 8DF Popular two-bar corner local with well kept West Berkshire ales (some named for the friendly knowledgeable landlord) along with Wadworths 6X and plenty of guests, excellent range of ciders and perries too, lots of decorative pump clips, old ship photographs, darts; several group meetings such as choral society and cribbage; closed weekday lunchtimes. *(Jack Trussler)*

WARBOROUGH SU6093
Six Bells (01865) 858265
The Green S; just E of A329, 4 miles N of Wallingford; OX10 7DN Thatched 16th-c pub opposite village cricket green, well kept Brakspears and enjoyable fairly pubby food (not Sun or Mon evenings) from sandwiches and sharing boards up, friendly attentive staff, low beams and attractive country furnishings in small linked areas off bar, bare boards, stripped stone and big log fire; tables out in front and in pleasant orchard garden behind, open all day weekends. *(John Pritchard, Roy Hoing, Paul Humphreys)*

WARDINGTON SP4946
Hare & Hounds (01295) 750645
A361 Banbury–Daventry; OX17 1SH Comfortable and welcoming traditional village local, well kept Hook Norton ales and enjoyable home-made food including bargain OAP lunch offer, low-ceilinged bar leading to dining area, woodburner; quiz nights, darts and dominoes; children and dogs welcome, garden with play area and aunt sally, open all day Fri, Sat, till 8pm Sun. *(Simon Sharpe)*

WATLINGTON SU6994
Fat Fox (01491) 613040
Shireburn Street; OX49 5BU Centrally placed 17th-c inn with beamed inglenook bar and separate restaurant, nice food from

changing menu using local produce, four real ales including Brakspears and good choice of wines by the glass, friendly helpful staff; free wi-fi; children and dogs (in bar) welcome, Ridgeway walks, nine bedrooms (seven in converted back barn), good breakfast, handy for M40 (junction 3), open all day. *(Taff Thomas)*

WEST HANNEY SU4092
Plough (01235) 868909
Just off A338 N of Wantage; Church Street; OX12 0LN Refurbished 16th-c thatched and beamed village pub now owned by the local community; light modern décor, four well kept ales including Greene King IPA, generous helpings of popular home-made food (not Sun evening, Mon), friendly service; children and dogs welcome, nice walled garden behind, good walks from the door, open all day weekends. *(John Harris, Jo Garnett)*

WHITCHURCH SU6377
Ferry Boat (0118) 984 2161
High Street, near toll bridge; RG8 7DB Welcoming comfortably updated 18th-c pub with airy log-fire bar and restaurant, good variety of enjoyable home-made food including stone-baked pizzas, friendly prompt service, real ales such as Black Sheep and Timothy Taylors, several wines by the glass; background music, free wi-fi; children welcome away from bar, well behaved dogs in bar only, café-style seating in courtyard garden, closed Sun evening, Mon. *(Paul Humphreys)*

WITNEY SP3509
Angel (01993) 703238
Market Square; OX28 6AL Unpretentious 17th-c town local with wide choice of enjoyable well priced food from good sandwiches up, Marstons-related ales including a house beer from Wychwood and occasional guest, efficient friendly service even when packed, beams and open fire; background music (live Fri), sports TVs; lovely hanging baskets, back terrace with smokers' shelter, parking nearby can be difficult, open all day. *(S and L McPhee)*

WITNEY SP3509
★ Fleece (01993) 892270
Church Green; OX28 4AZ Smart civilised town pub (part of the Peach group), popular for its wide choice of good often imaginative food from sandwiches and deli boards up, fixed-price menu too (Mon-Fri 12-6pm), friendly helpful service, Greene King and a couple of guests, decent coffee, leather armchairs on wood floors, restaurant; background and occasional live music, daily papers; children welcome, café-style tables out at front overlooking green, ten affordable comfortable bedrooms, good breakfast, open (and food) all day from 9am. *(Mrs B H Adams, R K Phillips)*

WITNEY SP3509
Hollybush (01993) 708073
Corn Street; OX28 6BT Popular modernised 18th-c pub under same ownership as the Horseshoes across the road; front bar with woodburner in big fireplace, settles and window seats, various dining areas off, good food from sandwiches and deli boards up, evening meal deal Sun and other offers, three well kept ales including a house beer from Greene King, good wine selection, efficient friendly staff; background music, free wi-fi; children and dogs welcome, open (and food) all day. *(Edward Edmonton)*

WITNEY SP3510
Horseshoes (01993) 703086
Corn Street, junction with Holloway Road; OX28 6BS Attractive 16th-c stone-built pub with enjoyable freshly made food (all day weekends) from pubby choices up, also a gluten-free menu, deli counter and weekday set lunch deal, three changing ales and decent wines by the glass, heavy beams, stripped-stone walls and log fires, separate back dining room; children and dogs welcome, tables on sunny terrace, open all day. *(Thomas Green)*

WOLVERCOTE SP4909
Plough (01865) 556969
First Turn/Wolvercote Green; OX2 8AH Comfortably worn-in pubby linked areas, armchairs and Victorian-style carpeted bays in main lounge, well kept Greene King ales, farm cider and decent wines by the glass, friendly helpful staff and bustling atmosphere, enjoyable good value usual food in flagstoned stables dining room and library (children allowed here), OAP meal deal, traditional snug, woodburner; dogs welcome in bar, picnic-sets on part-decked terrace looking over rough meadow to canal and woods, open all day Fri-Sun. *(Simon Sharpe)*

WOODSTOCK SP4417
Black Prince (01993) 811530
Manor Road (A44 N); OX20 1XJ Old pub with one modernised low-ceilinged bar, timbers, stripped stone and log fire, suit of armour, good value home-made food from sandwiches to specials, well kept St Austell,

Sharps and guests, friendly service; some live music, outside lavatories; children, walkers and dogs welcome, tables in pretty garden by small River Glyme, aunt sally, nearby right of way into Blenheim Palace parkland, open all day. *(Malcolm Phillips)*

WOODSTOCK SP4416
Woodstock Arms (01993) 811251
Market Street; OX20 1SX Warmly welcoming 16th-c pub with long narrow bar and end dining area, enjoyable home-made food (not Sun evening), three well kept Greene King ales and good wine choice, prompt helpful service, heavy beams, stripped stone and log fire in splendid fireplace; background music; children and dogs welcome, sunny courtyard, open all day. *(Tim King)*

WOOLSTONE SU2987
White Horse (01367) 820726
Off B4507; SN7 7QL Appealing partly thatched pub with Victorian gables and latticed windows, plush furnishings, spacious beamed and part-panelled bar, two big open fires, Arkells ales and enjoyable food from lunchtime open sandwiches up, wood-fired pizzas Thurs and Sun, restaurant; free wi-fi; well behaved children and dogs allowed, plenty of seats in front and back gardens, secluded interesting village handy for White Horse and Ridgeway, six bedrooms, open all day. *(S and L McPhee)*

WOOTTON SP4320
Killingworth Castle (01993) 811401
Glympton Road; B4027 N of Woodstock; OX20 1EJ Under same ownership as the Ebrington Arms (Ebrington, Gloucestershire – Also Worth a Visit); striking three-storey 17th-c coaching inn with simply furnished candlelit rooms, built-in wall seats and mix of chairs around farmhouse tables on bare boards, woodburner in stone fireplace and another fire, own Yubberton ales plus local guests, cider and lager from Cotswold, good range of spirits featuring smaller british producers, popular interesting food (themed evenings), friendly staff; garden with circular picnic-sets under green parasols, bedrooms, open all day from 9am. *(Gerry Price, Bernard Stradling)*

Please tell us if the décor, atmosphere, food or drink at a pub is different from our description. We rely on readers' reports to keep us up to date: feedback@goodguides.com, or (no stamp needed) The Good Pub Guide, FREEPOST RTJR-ZCYZ-RJZT, Perrymans Lane, Etchingham TN19 7DN.

Shropshire

KEY   ★ Star Pub   🍴 Top Quality Food   🍺 Great Beer

🍷 Good Wines   £ Bargain Meals   🛏 Good Bedrooms   🍴 Serves Food

 BRIDGNORTH   SO7192 Map 4

Old Castle 🍺 £

(01746) 711420 – www.oldcastlebridgnorth.co.uk
West Castle Street; WV16 4AB

Cheerful town pub, relaxed and friendly, with generous helpings of good value pubby food, well kept ales and good-sized suntrap terrace

A big plus for this traditional pub (once two cottages) is the sunny back terrace with picnic-sets, lovely hanging baskets, big pots of flowers, shrub borders and decking at the far end that gives an elevated view over the west side of town; children's playthings. The low-beamed open-plan bar is properly pubby with some genuine character: you'll find tiles and bare boards, cushioned wall banquettes and settles around cast-iron-framed tables, and bar stools arranged along the counter where the friendly landlord and his staff serve Hobsons Town Crier, Sharps Doom Bar, Thwaites Lancaster Bomber and Wye Valley HPA on handpump. A back conservatory extension has darts, pool and a games machine; background music and big-screen TV for sports events. Do walk up the street to see the ruined castle – its 20-metre Norman tower tilts at such an extraordinary angle that it makes the leaning tower of Pisa look like a model of rectitude.

🍴 Good pubby food choices at fair prices include sandwiches and baguettes, devilled whitebait, chicken dippers with barbecue sauce, butternut squash risotto, burgers with onion rings and chips, beef bourguignon, chilli con carne, fish pie with prawns, minted lamb shank with peas and gravy, a mixed grill and puddings. *Benchmark main dish: steak in ale pie £9.25. Two-course evening meal £14.00.*

Punch ~ Tenant Bryn Charles Masterman ~ Real ale ~ Open 11.30-11; 11.30-10.30 Sun ~ Bar food 12-3, 6.30-8.30 ~ Children welcome ~ Dogs welcome ~ Wi-fi
Recommended by Geoff and Ann Marston, Andrew and Michele Revell

CARDINGTON   SO5095 Map 4

Royal Oak

(01694) 771266 – www.at-the-oak.com
Village signposted off B4371 Church Stretton–Much Wenlock, pub behind church; also reached via narrow lanes from A49; SY6 7JZ

Heaps of character in well run and friendly rural pub with seasonal bar food and real ales

Tucked away in a lovely spot, this is said to be Shropshire's oldest continuously licensed pub. It's been enjoyed by our readers for many years and the rambling low-beamed traditional bar has a roaring winter log fire, a cauldron, black kettle and pewter jugs in a vast inglenook fireplace, aged standing timbers from a knocked-through wall, and red and green tapestry seats solidly capped in elm; board games and dominoes. Ludlow Best and Sharps Doom Bar with guests such as Hobsons Town Crier and Wye Valley Butty Bach on handpump, eight wines by the glass, ten gins, several malt whiskies and farm cider. A comfortable dining area has exposed old beams and studwork. This is glorious country for walks, such as the one to the summit of Caer Caradoc, a couple of miles to the west (ask for directions at the pub), and the front courtyard makes the most of its beautiful position.

Tasty food includes baguettes, smoked mackerel pâté, devilled kidneys with chilli sauce dressing, beer-battered cod and chips, mushroom and spinach lasagne, gammon with egg or pineapple, beef bourguignon with horseradish mash, chicken or prawn curry, duck breast with a plum, shallot and red wine sauce, and puddings. *Benchmark main dish: fidget pie (gammon in spiced cider with apples) £12.25. Two-course evening meal £16.50.*

Free house ~ Licensees Steve and Eira Oldham ~ Real ale ~ Open 12-2.30, 6-11; 12-11 Sat, Sun; 12-4 Sun in winter; closed Mon except bank holidays ~ Bar food 12-2.30, 6-9 ~ Restaurant ~ Children welcome ~ Dogs allowed in bar ~ Wi-fi *Recommended by Peter Meister, Dave Braisted, Charles Todd*

CHETWYND ASTON

SJ7517   Map 7

Fox 🏠 ♟ ♀ ◧

(01952) 815940 – www.brunningandprice.co.uk/fox
Village signposted off A41 and A518 just S of Newport; TF10 9LQ

Civilised dining pub with generous helpings of well liked food and a fine array of drinks served by ever attentive staff

Although this handsome Edwardian pub is large and spreading, there are cosy corners too – all filled with a cheerful crowd of customers. The linked rooms (one with a broad arched ceiling) has plenty of tables in varying shapes and sizes, some quite elegant, and a loosely matching diversity of comfortable chairs on parquet, polished boards or attractive floor tiles. Masses of prints and photographs line the walls, there are three open fires, and big windows and careful lighting contribute to the relaxed atmosphere; board games. Bar stools line the long bar counter where courteous, efficient staff keep around 18 wines by the glass, 40 malt whiskies, 20 gins and Phoenix Brunning & Price Original, Three Tuns XXX, Woods Shropshire Lad and three quickly changing guests from breweries such as Purple Moose, Rowton and Woods on handpump. The large back garden is quite lovely, with a sunny terrace, picnic-sets tucked into the shade of mature trees and extensive views across quiet country fields. Good disabled access.

The attractively presented and very good food includes sandwiches, red wine-cured salmon with fennel pannacotta, slow-braised lamb croquette with minted pea purée, confit tomato, cucumber and yoghurt, crab linguine with lime, chilli and coriander, thai sweet potato, aubergine and spinach curry, steak in ale pie, duck breast and faggot with treacle-glazed carrots and port and plum jus, smoked haddock and salmon fishcakes, and puddings such as chocolate brownie with chocolate fudge sauce and hazelnut ice-cream. *Benchmark main dish: steak burger with toppings, coleslaw and chips £12.95. Two-course evening meal £20.50.*

Brunning & Price ~ Manager Samantha Forrest ~ Real ale ~ Open 11am-11.30pm; 11-11 Sun ~ Bar food 12-10; 12-9.30 Sun ~ Children welcome ~ Dogs allowed in bar ~ Wi-fi *Recommended by Phoebe Peacock, John Evans, Tony Smaithe*

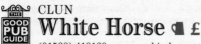

CLUN
SO3080 Map 6

White Horse ◗ £

(01588) 418139 – www.whi-clun.co.uk

The Square; SY7 8JA

Bustling local with own-brewed and guest ales and good value traditional food; bedrooms

The own-brewed Clun beers here are as popular as ever and include Citadel Strong Ale, Loophole, Pale Ale and Solar, with guests such as Hobsons Best and Wye Valley Butty Bach on handpump, served by attentive staff. They also keep five wines by the glass, a few malt whiskies and farm cider. There's always a friendly mix of both regulars and visitors. The low-beamed front bar is cosy and friendly and warmed in winter by a cosy inglenook woodburning stove; from here, a door leads into a separate little dining room with a rare plank and munton screen. In the games room at the back you'll find a TV, games machine, darts, pool, juke box and board games; small garden. The bedrooms are quiet and comfortable.

Reasonably priced food includes sandwiches, potted wild boar with port and cranberries, creamy garlic mushrooms, pork sausages with mash and gravy, red bean and coconut pottage, lasagne, beer-battered haddock and chips, liver and bacon casserole, 28-day-aged steaks with onion rings and chips, and puddings such as chocolate brownie and marmalade bread and butter pudding. *Benchmark main dish: steak and kidney pudding £11.95. Two-course evening meal £15.00.*

Own brew ~ Licensee Jack Limond ~ Real ale ~ No credit cards ~ Open 10am-midnight ~ Bar food 12-2 (3 Sat), 6.30-8.30; 12.30-2.30, 6.30-8.30 Sun ~ Restaurant ~ Children welcome ~ Dogs allowed in bar and bedrooms ~ Wi-fi ~ Live music every second Fri ~ Bedrooms: £42.50/£70 *Recommended by Mike and Jean Turner, Andy Dolan, Lance and Sarah Milligan*

COALPORT
SJ7002 Map 4

Woodbridge ♀ ◗

(01952) 882054 – www.brunningandprice.co.uk/woodbridge

Village signposted off A442 1.5 miles S of A4169 Telford roundabout; down in valley, turn left across narrow bridge into Coalport Road, pub immediately left; TF8 7JF

Superb Ironbridge Gorge site for extensive handsomely reworked pub, an all-round success

Big windows here look out on a lovely section of a wooded gorge and the many tables and chairs on the big raised deck look over the River Severn. The spreading series of linked rooms are comfortable and civilised with log fires and Coalport-style stoves, rugs on broad boards as well as tiles or carpet, black beams in the central part and plenty of polished tables and cosy armchair corners. A mass of mainly 18th- and 19th-c prints line the walls and the historic pictures, often of local scenes, are well worth a look; background music. Phoenix Brunning & Price Original and guests such as Hobsons Twisted Spire, Three Tuns XXX, Timothy Taylors Landlord and Woods Parish Bitter on handpump, 16 wines by the glass, 45 malt whiskies and 15 gins; service is quick and friendly.

Pleasing food includes sandwiches, baked camembert with spiced carrot and apricot compote, chicken liver pâté with ginger and plum chutney, crab and leek quiche with crème fraîche potato salad, honey-roast ham with free-range eggs, chicken with pancetta and butternut squash risotto, whole bream with chilli, anchovy and herb butter and greens, sesame pork belly with pak choi, pickled ginger and watermelon salad, and puddings such as passion-fruit and white chocolate cheesecake with lemon sorbet and sticky toffee pudding with toffee sauce. *Benchmark main dish: lamb shoulder with dauphinoise potatoes, carrot mash and gravy £17.95. Two-course evening meal £22.00.*

Brunning & Price ~ Manager Vrata Krist ~ Real ale ~ Open 11.30-11; 11.30-midnight Fri, Sat; 11.30-10.30 Sun ~ Bar food 12-10 (9.30 Sun) ~ Restaurant ~ Children welcome ~ Dogs allowed in bar ~ Wi-fi *Recommended by R Anderson, Lynda and Trevor Smith, Dave Braisted, Max Simons, David Seward*

HODNET
Bear 🍺 ⌂

SJ6128   Map 6

(01630) 685214 – www.bearathodnet.co.uk
Drayton Road (A53); TF9 3NH

Black and white timbered former coaching inn with beamed rooms, four real ales, enjoyable food and seats outside; bedrooms

We know this nice old village inn will do well as it's run by a professional, hands-on landlord who has worked wonders on other pubs in these pages. The rambling, open-plan main room has heavy 16th-c beams and timbers creating separate areas, wooden tables and chairs on rugs or flagstones, and a woodburning stove in a large stone fireplace (there are three other open fires as well); there's a former bear pit under the floor. The smaller, beamed and quarry-tiled bar has Black Sheep, Rowton Portly Stout and Salopian Shropshire Gold on handpump, 14 wines by the glass, 30 malt whiskies and around 20 gins served by friendly staff; the pub jack russell is called Jack. The garden has picnic-sets and a play area, and the refurbished bedrooms are well equipped and comfortable. Hodnet Hall Gardens are opposite and the inn is handy for Hawkstone Park; good walks in lovely surrounding countryside.

🍴 Enjoyable food includes lunchtime sandwiches, wild mushrooms in cream and white wine sauce on garlic toasted sourdough, prawn cocktail, honey-glazed ham and egg, roasted mediterranean vegetable frittata, steak burger with toppings, coleslaw and chips, chicken with dauphinoise potatoes and red wine gravy, bass fillet with roasted red pepper and tomato sauce, and puddings such as triple chocolate brownie with white chocolate sauce and coconut ice-cream and sticky toffee pudding with butterscotch sauce; they also offer a two- and three-course set lunch (Mon-Thurs). *Benchmark main dish: pie of the day £12.95. Two-course evening meal £18.00.*

Free house ~ Licensees Gregory and Pia Williams ~ Real ale ~ Open 12-11; 12-9 Sun ~ Bar food 12-3, 6-9; 12-4 Sun ~ Restaurant ~ Children welcome ~ Dogs allowed in bar ~ Wi-fi ~ Bedrooms: £60/£120 *Recommended by Roger and Anne Newbury, Maddie Purvis, Paul Scofield*

IRONBRIDGE
Golden Ball ⌂

SJ6703   Map 4

(01952) 432179 – www.goldenballironbridge.co.uk
Brown sign to pub off Madeley Road (B4373) above village centre – pub behind Horse & Jockey, car park beyond on left; TF8 7BA

Low-beamed, partly Elizabethan pub with popular food and drink; bedrooms

Tucked away in a steep little hamlet of other ancient buildings, this is a friendly inn. There are worn boards, red-cushioned pews, one or two black beams, a dresser of decorative china and a woodburning stove. Otter Bitter, Wye Valley HPA and a guest or two on handpump, quite a few belgian bottled ales, wines by the glass and a farm cider; background music and TV.

A pretty fairy-lit pergola path leads to the door and a sheltered side courtyard has tables under parasols. This is a comfortable place to stay overnight and the breakfasts are good. You can walk down to the River Severn, and beyond – but it's pretty steep getting back up.

A choice of tasty food includes smoked salmon and caper salad, chicken liver pâté with home-made chutney, wild mushroom, spinach and ricotta filo parcel, chicken wrapped in bacon on spiced bean cassoulet, beer-battered cod with chips, rump steak with cracked pepper sauce, sautéed mushrooms and chips, and puddings such as rhubarb and ginger tart and chocolate fudge cake. *Benchmark main dish: pie of the day £9.95. Two-course evening meal £18.00.*

Enterprise ~ Lease Jessica Janke ~ Real ale ~ Open 12-11; 12-10.30 Sun ~ Bar food 12-9; 12-7 Sun ~ Restaurant ~ Children welcome ~ Dogs allowed in bar and bedrooms ~ Wi-fi ~ Live band Fri monthly, open mike second Sun of month ~ Bedrooms: £60/£65
Recommended by Mark Morgan, George Sanderson, Dr Simon Innes

MAESBURY MARSH
Navigation

SJ3125   Map 6

(01691) 672958 – www.thenavigation.co.uk
Follow Maesbury Road off A483 S of Oswestry; by canal bridge; SY10 8JB

Versatile and friendly canalside pub with cosy bar and local seasonal produce in a choice of dining areas

Picnic-sets outside this 18th-c wharf building are arranged beside the Montgomery Canal, and windows in the dining room also overlook the water. As well as running a traditional pub, the friendly hands-on licensees have a book exchange, a shop where you can buy fresh local produce (including fish and shellfish) and a two-pint takeaway service. The quarry-tiled bar on the left has squishy brown leather sofas by a traditional black range blazing in a big red-brick fireplace, little upholstered cask seats around three small tables, and dozens of wrist- and pocket-watches hanging from the beams. A couple of steps lead up to a carpeted area beyond a balustrade, with armchairs and sofas around low tables, and a piano; off to the left is a dining area with paintings by local artists. The main beamed dining room, with some stripped stone, is beyond another small bar (they serve cocktails here) with a coal-effect gas fire – and an amazing row of cushioned carved choir stalls complete with misericord seats. Salopian Darwin's Origin and Stonehouse Cambrian Gold on handpump, 11 wines by the glass, nine malt whiskies (one from Wales) and a farm cider (in summer); quiet background music and board games.

Using free-range meat and local produce, the tasty food includes lunchtime sandwiches, chicken liver pâté with damson jelly, lamb kofta with mint yoghurt, home-made fettucine arrabiata with olive and mushrooms, toulouse sausage casserole with beans and tomatoes, chicken breast wrapped in bacon with leeks and mushrooms in white wine sauce, a roast of the day, and puddings such as vanilla rice pudding with home-made jam and chocolate and pistachio torte; they also offer a two- and three-course set menu. *Benchmark main dish: beer-battered fish and chips £11.95. Two-course evening meal £22.00.*

Free house ~ Licensees Brent Ellis and Mark Baggett ~ Real ale ~ Open 12-2, 6-11; 12-6 Sun; closed Sun evening, all day Mon, lunchtime Tue, first two weeks Jan ~ Bar food 12-2, 6-8.30; 12-2 Sun ~ Restaurant ~ Children welcome ~ Dogs allowed in bar ~ Wi-fi ~ Folk music last Weds of month *Recommended by Clive and Fran Dutson, Isobel Mackinlay, Jeremy Snow*

SHIPLEY

SO8095 Map 4

Inn at Shipley ♀ ◀

(01902) 701639 – www.brunningandprice.co.uk/innatshipley

Bridgnorth Road; A454 W of Wolverhampton; WV6 7EQ

Light and airy country pub – a good all-rounder

Carefully extended, this is a handsome 18th-c building with rambling rooms and a civilised atmosphere. Several woodburning stoves and log fires surround the central bar – one in a big inglenook in a cosy, traditionally tiled black-beamed end room and another by a welcoming set of wing and other leather armchairs. All sorts of dining chairs are grouped around a variety of well buffed tables, rugs are set on polished boards, attractive pictures are hung frame to frame and big windows let in plenty of daylight; church candles, careful spotlighting and chandeliers add atmosphere. The various areas are interconnected but manage to also feel distinct and individual; upstairs is a separate private dining room. Phoenix Brunning & Price Original, Holdens Golden Glow, Salopian Oracle, Three Tuns XXX, Titanic Plum Porter and Woods Shropshire Lad on handpump, 17 wines by the glass, 80 malt whiskies, 70 gins and two farm ciders; good neatly dressed staff, background music and board games. There are plenty of sturdy tables outside, some on a sizeable terrace with a side awning, others by weeping willows on the main lawn behind the car park, and more set out on smaller lawns around the building.

 Good, modern food includes sandwiches, confit salmon with cucumber ketchup and wasabi rice cake, baked camembert with chutney, king prawn and chorizo linguine, red pepper and feta lasagne, thai-spiced hake fillet with crispy crab won ton and coriander citrus dressing, chicken, ham and leek pie, braised lamb shoulder with dauphinoise potatoes, carrot and swede purée and rosemary gravy, and puddings such as salted caramel and chocolate tart with raspberry sorbet and profiteroles with dark chocolate sauce. *Benchmark main dish: beer-battered haddock and chips £12.75. Two-course evening meal £20.00.*

Brunning & Price ~ Manager Marc Eeley ~ Real ale ~ Open 10.30am-11pm; 10.30-10.30 Sun ~ Bar food 12-10 (9.30 Sun) ~ Restaurant ~ Children welcome ~ Dogs allowed in bar ~ Wi-fi
Recommended by Isobel Mackinlay, Lynda and Trevor Smith, Edward Nile

SHREWSBURY

SJ4812 Map 6

Armoury ⊛ ♀ ◀

(01743) 340525 – www.brunningandprice.co.uk/armoury

Victoria Quay, Victoria Avenue; SY1 1HH

Vibrant atmosphere in interestingly converted riverside warehouse with tempting all-day food

They certainly keep a fine range of drinks in this 18th-c former warehouse – Phoenix Brunning & Price Original, Longden The Golden Arrow, Salopian Oracle, Woods Shropshire Lad and a couple of guest beers on handpump, 17 wines by the glass, 100 malt whiskies, a dozen gins, lots of rums and vodkas, a variety of brandies and a farm cider. The spacious open-plan interior has long runs of big arched windows with views across the broad River Severn – but, despite its size, it also has a personal feel, helped by the eclectic décor, furniture layout and cheerful bustle. A mix of wood tables and chairs are grouped on stripped-wood floors, the huge brick walls display floor-to-ceiling books or masses of old prints mounted edge to edge, and there's a grand stone fireplace at one end. Colonial-style fans whirr away on the ceilings, which are supported by green-painted columns, and small wall-mounted glass cabinets display smokers' pipes. The hanging baskets are quite a sight in summer. The pub doesn't have its own car park, but there are plenty of parking places nearby.

 Highly regarded food includes sandwiches, crayfish and prawn salad with lemon mayonnaise, ox tongue with wilted spinach, beetroot and sweet pickles, lentil cottage pie topped with sweet potato, chicken and bacon caesar salad, harissa hake with tunisian couscous and lime and coriander yoghurt, duck breast with leek and potato rösti and passion-fruit sauce, steak, mushroom and ale pudding, lamb shoulder with carrot purée and red wine gravy, and puddings such as chocolate mousse cake with caramelised banana and banana ice-cream and crème brûlée. *Benchmark main dish: braised lamb shoulder with carrot purée and red wine gravy £16.95. Two-course evening meal £22.00.*

Brunning & Price ~ Manager Emily Waring ~ Real ale ~ Open 12-11 (10.30 Sun) ~ Bar food 12-10 (9.30 Sun) ~ Children welcome ~ Dogs allowed in bar ~ Wi-fi
Recommended by Steve Whalley, Claire Adams, Sandra Hollies

SHREWSBURY
SJ4912   Map 6

Lion & Pheasant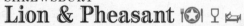

(01743) 770345 – www.lionandpheasant.co.uk
Follow City Centre signposts across the English Bridge; SY1 1XJ

Shropshire Dining Pub of the Year

Civilised bar and upstairs restaurant in comfortable, neatly updated and well placed inn; bedrooms

This is lovely place to stay in comfortable rooms – some of which provide glimpses of the River Severn below the nearby English Bridge – and breakfasts are good. It's an appealing, thoughtfully run 16th-c inn with a mix of original features blending seamlessly with more contemporary touches. The big-windowed bar consists of three linked levels, the lowest of which has armchairs on dark flagstones by a big inglenook; elsewhere, there's a cushioned settee, but most of the seats are at sturdy stripped tables on dark floorboards. A few modern paintings, plentiful flowers and church candles brighten up the restrained cream and grey décor, as do the friendly staff and background music. Salopian Oracle and Shropshire Gold and Three Tuns XXX on handpump and 14 wines by the glass. Off quite a warren of corridors, the restaurant (you can eat from its menu in the bar too) is in the older back part of the building with beams and timbering. Outside, there are seats and tables under parasols with olive trees and flowering pots dotted about.

 Imaginative food includes sandwiches, smoked honey-glazed quail breast with black pudding, quail egg and beetroot, cured salmon with gribiche sauce, potato gnocchi with lovage, fried duck egg, crispy purple kale and sauce choron (béarnaise sauce with tomato purée), burger with toppings, chilli relish and triple-cooked chips, brill with glazed king oyster mushrooms, baby leeks, dauphinoise potatoes and butter sauce, and puddings such as iced peanut butter parfait with caramelised banana, peanut brittle and banana ice-cream and chocolate, hazelnut and coffee mousse with amaretto ice-cream and silver leaf; they also offer an early-bird menu (6-7pm Sun-Thurs, 6-6.45pm Fri). *Benchmark main dish: pork fillet with glazed cheek, potato terrine, rhubarb and crackling crumble £18.00. Two-course evening meal £26.00.*

Free house ~ Licensee Jim Littler ~ Real ale ~ Open 10am-11pm ~ Bar food 12-2.30, 6-9.30 ~ Restaurant ~ Children welcome ~ Wi-fi ~ Bedrooms: £99/£119
Recommended by Isobel Mackinlay, Edward May, Peter Harrison

Also Worth a Visit in Shropshire

Besides the fully inspected pubs, you might like to try these pubs that have been recommended to us and described by readers. Do tell us what you think of them: feedback@goodguides.com

---

ADMASTON   SJ6313
Pheasant (01952) 251989
Shawbirch Road; TF5 0AD Red-brick Victorian pub with good locally sourced food (all day Sat, till 7pm Sun), three or four well kept ales including Salopian and Woods, pleasant staff; Thurs quiz; children welcome, garden with picnic-sets and play area, open all day. *(Mark Morgan)*

ALBRIGHTON   SJ8104
Shrewsbury Arms (01902) 373003
High Street; WV7 3LA Brick and timber dining pub with good home-cooked food from light dishes and sharing plates up, deals including weekday set lunch, Sharps Doom Bar and up to three local guests, friendly helpful staff; live music Fri, Sat; children and dogs welcome, garden tables, open (and food) all day. *(Mrs B H Adams, Mark Writtle)*

ASTON MUNSLOW   SO5187
Swan (01584) 841415
Off B4368, in lane NW of village; SY7 9ER Former 14th-c coaching inn under newish welcoming family, bar and two dining areas, black beams and open fires, enjoyable good value traditional food including bargain OAP lunch (Tues), well kept ales such as Hobsons, Ludlow and Wye Valley, chatty helpful service; pool room; children welcome, garden with shady areas, open all day weekends, closed Mon lunchtime. *(Steve and Jane Payne)*

BISHOP'S CASTLE   SO3288
★**Castle Hotel** (01588) 638403
Market Square, just off B4385; SY9 5BN Substantial coaching inn at top of lovely market town, clubby little beamed and panelled bar with log fire, larger rooms off with big Victorian engravings and another fire, well kept Clun, Hobsons, Six Bells and Three Tuns, local cider, ten wines by the glass (maybe one from nearby vineyard) and 30 malt whiskies, popular food served by friendly staff, handsome panelled dining room; background music, darts and board games; children and dogs welcome, pretty hanging baskets at front, garden behind with terrace seating, pergolas and climbing plants, surrounding walks, nice spacious bedrooms, good breakfast, useful big car park, open all day. *(Paul and Kate O'Donnell, Richard Tilbrook, David Field, Mr and Mrs D J Nash)*

BISHOP'S CASTLE   SO3288
★**Six Bells** (01588) 630144
Church Street; SY9 5AA Friendly 17th-c pub with character landlord and own-brew beers (microbrewery tours available); smallish no-frills bar with mix of well worn furniture, old local photographs and prints, bigger room with stripped-stone walls, benches around plain tables on bare boards and inglenook woodburner, country wines and summer cider, July beer festival, sandwiches only lunchtimes Mon-Sat, good value home-made food Thurs-Sat evenings, Sun roast; no credit cards; well behaved children and dogs welcome, café in brewery, open all day. *(Sandra Hollie)*

BISHOP'S CASTLE   SO3288
★**Three Tuns** (01588) 638797
Salop Street; SY9 5BW Extended old pub adjacent to unique four-storey Victorian brewhouse (a brewery said to have existed here since 1642); busy chatty atmosphere in public, lounge and snug bars, Three Tuns beers (including 1642) from old-fashioned handpumps (cheaper 5-7pm Fri), several wines by the glass, tasty good value food (not Sun evening) from sandwiches up, friendly young staff, modernised dining room done out in smart oak and glass; lots going on including film club, music nights, July beer festival and maybe morris men or a brass band in the garden; children and dogs welcome, open all day. *(Mike and Eleanor Anderson)*

BRIDGES   SO3996
Bridges (01588) 650260
Bridges, W of Ratlinghope; SY5 0ST Old renovated beamed country pub owned by Three Tuns with their full range in excellent condition, bare-boards bar to right, large dining room to left, woodburner, fairly traditional home-made food (not Sun evening, winter Mon), helpful friendly staff; regular live music; children welcome, dogs in room off bar, tables out by the little River Onny (some on raised deck), bedrooms, also camping and youth hostel nearby, great walking country, open (and food) all day. *(Mark Morgan)*

BRIDGNORTH   SO6890
★**Down** (01746) 789539
The Down; B4364 Ludlow Road 3 miles S; WV16 6UA Good value roadside dining pub

---

We checked prices with the pubs as we went to press in summer 2016.
They should hold until around spring 2017.

overlooking rolling countryside, enjoyable food including popular daily carvery, efficient friendly service, a house beer (Down & Out) from Three Tuns and a couple of local guests; background music; children welcome, nine comfortable bedrooms, open all day. (Claire Adams)

BRIDGNORTH   SO7193
Kings Head (01746) 762141
Whitburn Street; WV16 4QN 17th-c timbered coaching inn with high-raftered back stable bar, good food here from 5pm (all day weekends) or in all-day restaurant with separate menu, friendly staff, Hobsons and Wye Valley plus a couple of guests, winter mulled wine, log fires, beams and flagstones, pretty leaded windows; children and dogs welcome, courtyard tables, open all day (food all day weekends). (Claire Adams)

BRIDGNORTH   SO7192
★**Railwaymans Arms** (01746) 764361
Severn Valley Station, Hollybush Road (off A458 towards Stourbridge); WV16 5DT Bathams, Hobsons and plenty of other well kept ales in chatty old-fashioned converted waiting room at Severn Valley steam railway terminus, bustling on summer days; old station signs and train nameplates, superb mirror over fireplace, may be simple summer snacks, Sept beer festival; children and dogs welcome, wheelchair access with help, tables out on platform – the train to Kidderminster (station bar there too) has an all-day bar and bookable Sun lunches, open all day. (Claire Adams)

BRIDGNORTH   SO7192
White Lion (01746) 763962
West Castle Street; WV16 4AB Fairly compact 18th-c two-bar pub with seven well kept ales including own Hop & Stagger brews, Thatcher's cider, reasonably priced simple food such as home-made scotch eggs and butcher-made pies, friendly helpful staff, comfortable carpeted lounge with open fire; regular events including folk club (first Tues of month), storytelling (second Tues) and charity quiz (last Tues); children and dogs welcome, lawned garden with terrace, four good value clean bedrooms (no breakfast), open all day. (Dave Braisted)

BRIDGNORTH   SO7093
Woodberry (01746) 762950
Victoria Road/Sydney Cottage Drive; WV16 4LF Fully refurbished dining inn with good choice of enjoyable locally sourced food, ales such as Hobsons, friendly efficient service; background music, free wi-fi; children welcome, comfortable bedrooms and good breakfast, open (and food) all day. (Paul Scofield)

BROMFIELD   SO4877
★**Clive** (01584) 856565
A49, 2 miles NW of Ludlow; SY8 2JR Sophisticated minimalist bar-restaurant

taking its name from Clive of India who once lived here; emphasis mainly on the imaginative well presented food but also Hobsons and Ludlow ales, several wines by the glass and a bar menu, welcoming well trained staff, dining room with light wood tables, door to sparsely furnished bar with metal chairs, glass-topped tables and sleek counter, step down to room with soaring beams and rafters, exposed stonework and woodburner in huge fireplace; background music, free wi-fi; children welcome, tables under parasols on secluded terrace, fish pond, 15 stylish bedrooms, good breakfast, open all day. (Mike and Mary Carter)

BUCKNELL   SO3574
★**Baron** (01547) 530549
Chapel Lawn Road; just off B4367 Knighton Road; SY7 0AH Modernised family-owned country inn, friendly and efficiently run, with enjoyable good value home-made food from panini and pizzas up, well kept Ludlow and Wye Valley, log fire in carpeted front bar, back dining room with old cider press and grindstone, conservatory; free wi-fi; children welcome, peaceful setting with lovely views from big garden, five bedrooms, camping field, open all day Sat, closed Sun evening and lunchtimes Mon-Thurs. (Brian and Jacky Wilson)

BURWARTON   SO6185
★**Boyne Arms** (01746) 787214
B4364 Bridgnorth–Ludlow; WV16 6QH Handsome Georgian coaching inn with welcoming cheerful staff, enjoyable generous food (not Sun evening, Mon) including good value deals and Fri steak night, up to three real ales such as Battlefield, Otter and Timothy Taylors, Robinson's and Thatcher's cider, decent coffee, separate restaurant and public bar (dogs allowed here), function room with pool and other games; children welcome, good timber adventure playground in pretty garden, hitching rail for horses, open all day weekends, closed Mon lunchtime. (Sandra Hollie)

CHURCH STRETTON   SO4593
Bucks Head (01694) 722898
High Street; SY6 6BX Old town pub with several good-sized modernised areas including restaurant, up to four well kept Marstons ales, decent good value pubby food plus vegetarian options, friendly attentive staff, black beams and timbers, mixed dark wood tables and chairs; newspapers, free wi-fi; garden with picnic-sets, four bedrooms, open all day (1am Fri, Sat). (Claire Adams)

CHURCH STRETTON   SO4593
Housmans (01694) 724441
High Street; SY6 6BX Buzzing and welcoming restaurant-bar with good wine and cocktail lists plus a couple of well kept ales from Three Tuns, food mainly tapas-style sharing plates but also good value weekday

set lunch, local art on walls; occasional live jazz and other acoustic music; children welcome, open all day weekends. *(Mark Morgan)*

CLAVERLEY   SO8095
Woodman (01746) 710553
B4176/Danford Lane; WV5 7DG Rural 19th-c red-brick dining pub; contemporary beamed interior arranged around central bar, good popular food (must book) using local produce – some from farm opposite, well kept Black Sheep and Enville, lots of wines by the glass and interesting range of gins, good well organised service; terrace and garden tables, closed Sun evening. *(Paul Humphreys, Paul and Sue Merrick)*

CLUN   SO3080
Sun (01588) 640559
High Street; SY7 8JB Beamed and timbered 15th-c pub with traditional flagstoned public bar, woodburner in inglenook, larger carpeted lounge bar, enjoyable home-made food (not Sun evening) from lunchtime sandwiches up, four well kept Three Tuns ales, friendly helpful staff; children and dogs (in bar) welcome, paved back terrace, peaceful village and lovely rolling countryside, six bedrooms (some in converted outbuildings), open all day Fri-Sun, closed lunchtimes Mon-Thurs. *(Paul Scofield)*

CLUNTON   SO3381
Crown (01588) 660265
B4368; SY7 0HU Welcoming old country local with three well kept ales including Hobsons and Stonehouse, enjoyable generously served food cooked by landlord (Thurs-Sat evenings), also Weds fish and chips and good value Sun lunch, log fire in cosy flagstoned bar, dining room, games room with TV; folk night last Mon of month; small garden, open all day Fri-Sun, closed lunchtimes other days. *(Tony Smaithe)*

COALPORT   SJ6902
Shakespeare (01952) 580675
High Street; TF8 7HT Welcoming early 19th-c inn by pretty Severn gorge park, timbering, bare stone walls and tiled floors, well kept Everards, Hobsons, Ludlow and a guest, good value generously served food from sandwiches through pub standards to international dishes; children welcome, picnic-sets in tiered garden with play area, handy for Coalport China Museum, four bedrooms, open all day weekends, closed weekdays till 5pm. *(Geoff and Ann Marston)*

CORFTON   SO4985
Sun (01584) 861239
B4368 Much Wenlock–Craven Arms; SY7 9DF Lived-in unchanging three-room country local with own good Corvedale ales (including an unfined beer), friendly long-serving landlord often busy in back brewery,

decent pubby food from baguettes to steaks, lots of breweriana, basic quarry-tiled public bar with darts, pool and juke box, quieter carpeted lounge, dining room with covered well, tourist information; children and dogs (in bar) welcome, good wheelchair access throughout and disabled loos, tables on terrace and in large garden with good play area. *(Robert W Buckle)*

CRAVEN ARMS   SO5485
Tally Ho (01584) 841811
Bouldon; SY7 9DP Welcoming tucked-away pub owned by group of villagers; good local beers such as Hobsons and big helpings of enjoyable freshly made pub food at very reasonable prices, service with a smile; dogs welcome, country views from nice garden. *(Paul Sayers)*

ELLESMERE   SJ3034
Red Lion (01691) 622632
Church Street; SY12 0HD Popular and welcoming 16th-c coaching inn next to church; ample helpings of good value tasty food from sandwiches up, Thwaites ales, friendly helpful service; Sun quiz; children welcome, comfortable bedrooms (courtyard ones suitable for disabled), good breakfast, open (and food) all day. *(John Wooll)*

GRINDLEY BROOK   SJ5242
Horse & Jockey (01948) 662723
A41; SY13 4QJ Extended 19th-c roadside pub with enjoyable good value food from varied menu, friendly helpful service, eight well kept ales including a house beer from Woods named after resident chocolate labrador Blaze, teas and coffees, well divided open-plan interior with mix of furniture on wood or carpeted floors, some interesting bits and pieces, woodburners; sports TV, pool; children, dogs and muddy boots welcome, play area on side lawn, handy for Sandstone Trail and Llangollen Canal, open (and food) all day. *(Andrew and Michele Revell)*

GRINSHILL   SJ5223
★**Inn at Grinshill** (01939) 220410
Off A49 N of Shrewsbury; SY4 3BL Civilised early Georgian country inn; comfortable 19th-c panelled bar with log fire in raised two-way hearth, Greene King and a couple of local guests, spacious modern restaurant with view into kitchen producing some very good food, friendly caring staff; background music; children and dogs welcome, pleasant back garden with plenty of tables and chairs, nice walks from the door, six comfortable clean bedrooms, closed Sun evening, Mon, Tues. *(Mark Morgan)*

HIGHLEY   SO7483
Ship (01746) 861219
Severnside; WV16 6NU Refurbished 18th-c inn in lovely riverside location, enjoyable pubby food including bargain OAP weekday lunch and early-bird deal, Sun carvery, five

real ales; children welcome, tables on raised front deck, handy for Severn Way walks (and Severn Valley Railway), fishing rights, bedrooms, open all day. *(Stephen Shepherd)*

HOPE   SJ3401
Stables (01743) 891344
Just off A488 3 miles S of Minsterley; SY5 0EP Hidden-away little 17th-c beamed country pub (former drovers' inn), friendly and welcoming, with nice home-made food and a couple of well kept ales such as Wye Valley Butty Bach, newspapers, log fires; dogs welcome (their irish wolfhound is Murphy) fine views from garden, two bedrooms and a 'shepherd's hut' for glamping enthusiasts, closed weekday lunchtimes. *(Paul Scofield)*

HOPTON WAFERS   SO6376
Crown (01299) 270372
A4117; DY14 0NB Attractive 16th-c creeper-clad inn, comfortably lived-in with beams and inglenook, good food (all day Sun) in three separate dining rooms, weekday set deal lunchtime/early evening, ales such as Ludlow and Wye Valley, good choice of wines and decent coffee, cheerful helpful staff, relaxed atmosphere; free wi-fi; children and dogs welcome, inviting garden with terraces, duck pond and stream, 18 bedrooms (11 in new adjoining building), open all day. *(Ross Balaam)*

IRONBRIDGE   SJ6603
★Malthouse (01952) 433712
The Wharfage (bottom road alongside Severn); TF8 7NH Converted 18th-c malthouse wonderfully located in historic gorge, spacious bar with iron pillars supporting heavy pine beams, lounge/dining area, up to three well kept changing ales and good reasonably priced food from baguettes up, friendly staff; live music Fri, Sat; children and dogs welcome, terrace tables, 14 individually styled bedrooms and self-catering cottage, open (and food) all day. *(Geoff and Ann Marston)*

KNOCKIN   SJ3322
Bradford Arms (01691) 682358
B4396 NW of Shrewsbury; SY10 8HJ Sizeable neatly kept village local with notable three-faced roof clock, popular good value pubby food (best to book) and well kept Marstons-related beers, friendly welcoming staff, games rooms; TV, free wi-fi; children and dogs welcome, garden behind by car park, open (and food) all day. *(Mark Morgan)*

KNOWBURY   SO5874
Bennetts End (01584) 890220
Hope Bagot Lane; SY8 3LL Extended 17th-c country pub with very well liked freshly made food from reasonably priced menu, well kept local ales, real cider and decent wines, friendly enthusiastic staff, cosy rooms with log fires, restaurant; children and dogs welcome, garden overlooking farmland

and 18th-c aqueduct, good local walks, open all day Sat, closed Sun evening and weekday lunchtimes (although may open in summer). *(Paul Sayers, Kevin Booker, Julia Atkins)*

LEEBOTWOOD   SO4798
★Pound (01694) 751477
A49 Church Stretton–Shrewsbury; SY6 6ND Thatched cruck-framed building dating from 1458 – thought to be oldest in the village; stylishly modern bar rooms with minimalist fixtures and wooden furnishings, good interesting food cooked by chef-owner from light meals up, also pub favourites, a couple of real ales from Ludlow and nice wines by the glass, friendly efficient service; background music; seats on flagstoned terrace; disabled parking (level access to bar), closed Sun evening, Mon. *(Paul Scofield)*

LEIGHTON   SJ6105
Kynnersley Arms (01952) 510233
B4380; SY5 6RN Victorian building built on remains of ancient corn mill; coal fire and woodburner in main opened-up area, armchairs and sofas in back part with stairs to lower level containing mill machinery (there's also a 17th-c blast furnace), five well kept mainly local ales including Salopian Shropshire Gold and a house beer (Next of Kyn) from Woods, traditional food along with pizzas and pasta dishes, Sun carvery, friendly helpful staff; background and occasional live music, sports TV, pool, free wi-fi; children and dogs welcome, good walks nearby, open all day. *(Lance and Sarah Milligan)*

LEINTWARDINE   SO4175
★Jolly Frog (01547) 540298
A4113 Ludlow–Knighton, E edge of village; The Toddings; SY7 0LX Cheerful well run bar-bistro in glorious countryside; front bar with just a few tables on light oak boards, check tablecloths and red leatherette dining chairs, woodburner at each end and frenchified décor (kepis and other hats hanging from stripped beams, Paris street signs and a Metro map), similarly furnished dining room up a few steps, ales such as Otter and Three Tuns, good wines by the glass and well liked food from wood-fired pizzas to fresh fish/seafood, friendly professional staff; background music, free wi-fi; children welcome, inner courtyard with tables under sail canopy, more seating on upper deck with wide pastoral views, closed Mon. *(Dave Braisted, Steve Whalley, Clive Watkin)*

LITTLE STRETTON   SO4491
Green Dragon (01694) 722925
Village well signed off A49 S of Church Stretton; Ludlow Road; SY6 6RE Popular village pub at foot of Long Mynd; enjoyable good value food in bar or adjacent dining area (well behaved children allowed here), well kept Wye Valley beers and guests, proper cider, friendly efficient young staff, warm

woodburner; stone-floored area for booted walkers, tables outside and play area, handy for Cardingmill Valley (NT), open (and food) all day. *(Peter Meister)*

LITTLE STRETTON   SO4492
⋆**Ragleth** (01694) 722711
Village well signed off A49 S of Church Stretton; Ludlow Road; SY6 6RB
Characterful opened-up 17th-c dining pub; light and airy bay-windowed front bar with eclectic mix of old tables and chairs, some exposed brick and timber work, huge inglenook in heavily beamed brick and tile-floored public bar, four mainly local beers such as Hobsons, good food including plenty of fish dishes, cheerful attentive owners and staff; background music, TV, darts and board games; children welcome, dogs in bar, lovely garden with tulip tree-shaded lawn and good play area, thatched and timbered church and fine hill walks nearby, open all day Sat (summer) and Sun. *(Ray and Winifred Halliday, Mr and Mrs D J Nash)*

LITTLE WENLOCK   SJ6507
Huntsman (01952) 503300
Wellington Road; TF6 5BH Welcoming modernised village pub, good food (till 7pm Sun) from lunchtime ciabattas and pub standards up, Fri fish night, four well kept/priced changing ales and good selection of wines, black beamed bar with stone floor and central log fire, carpeted restaurant with high-backed upholstered chairs at light wood tables and woodburner in big fireplace; children and dogs (in bar) welcome, terrace seating, bedrooms, handy for Wrekin walks, open (and food) all day. *(Mr and Mrs D J Nash)*

LUDLOW   SO5174
Blue Boar (01584) 878989
Mill Street; SY8 1BB Recently renovated former coaching inn with lots of linked areas, well kept ales such as Black Sheep, Hobsons and Three Tuns, good choice of wines by the glass and enjoyable well priced home-made food (not Sun evening), friendly helpful young staff; upstairs live music, film and quiz nights; children and dogs welcome, back suntrap courtyard, bedrooms, open all day. *(Roy and Gill Payne)*

LUDLOW   SO5174
⋆**Charlton Arms** (01584) 872813
Ludford Bridge, B4361 Overton Road; SY8 1PJ Bustling place by massive medieval bridge with fine views over River Teme from two balconies; character bar with pubby furniture on brick floors, double-sided woodburner, hop-hung counter serving Ludlow, Wye Valley and 11 wines by the glass, comfortable two-roomed lounge, dining room, enjoyable well presented food from traditional choices up, friendly service; background and monthly live music, board games, free wi-fi; children and dogs (in bar) welcome, well equipped cosy bedrooms

with river views, good breakfast, open all day. *(Richard Tilbrook, Roy and Gill Payne, GSB, Paul Sayers, John Jenkins, Ian Herdman)*

LUDLOW   SO5174
Church Inn (01584) 872174
Church Street, behind Butter Cross; SY8 1AW This popular town centre pub (Main Entry last year) was being refurbished under new owners as we went to press – reports please.

LUDLOW   SO5174
Queens (01584) 879177
Lower Galdeford; SY8 1RU Welcoming and popular 19th-c family-run pub, good reasonably priced food with emphasis on fresh local produce (booking advised, particularly Sun lunchtime), four well kept ales including Hobsons, Ludlow and Wye Valley, helpful friendly service, long narrow oak-floor bar, steps down to vaulted-ceiling dining area; some live music; children welcome (not in bar after 6pm), dogs allowed in one area, modern seating on enclosed deck, courtyard accommodation, open all day. *(Roy and Gill Payne)*

LUDLOW   SO5175
Unicorn (01584) 873555
Corve Street, bottom end; SY8 1DU Small half-timbered 17th-c coaching inn, character bar with hop-festooned beams and part panelled walls, tasty fairly traditional food from good sharing boards up, well kept ales such as Ludlow, friendly service from hands-on landlady, back dining room; live folk first Fri of the month, charity quiz first Sun; children and dogs welcome, terrace among willows by river, open (and food) all day. *(Richard Tilbrook, Paul Sayers)*

MAESBURY   SJ3026
Original Ball (01691) 654880
Maesbury Road; SY10 8HB Refurbished old brick-built pub, hefty beams, woodburner in central fireplace, Marstons Pedigree and Stonehouse Station Bitter, decent wines and enjoyable reasonably priced pub food including Sun carvery, friendly helpful staff; some live music, TV, pool; children and dogs welcome, open all day weekends, from 4pm other days. *(Claire Adams, Geoff and Ann Marston)*

MARKET DRAYTON   SJ6734
Red Lion (01630) 652602
Great Hales Street; TF9 1JP Extended 17th-c coaching inn now tap for Joules Brewery; back entrance into attractive modern bar with light wood floor and substantial oak timbers, traditional dark-beamed part to the right, updated but keeping original features, with pubby furniture on flagstones, brewery mirrors and signs, woodburner, more breweriana in dining/function room to left featuring 'Mousey' Thompson carved oak panelling

and fireplace; Joules Blonde, Pale Ale, Slumbering Monk and a seasonal beer (tasting trays available), good selection of wines, fairly straightforward home-made food and Sun carvery till 4pm; some live music; picnic-sets outside, brewery tours 7pm Mon-Thurs, open all day. *(Andrew and Michele Revell)*

MARTON SJ2802

★ **Sun** (01938) 561211

B4386 NE of Chirbury; SY21 8JP
Welcoming family-run dining pub, clean and neatly kept, with high standard of cooking including seasonal game and good fresh fish, light and airy black-beamed bar with comfortable sofa and traditional furnishings, woodburner in big stone fireplace, Hobsons Best and several wines by the glass, chunky pale tables and ladder-back chairs in restaurant; children welcome, dogs in bar (but do ask first), front terrace, closed Sun evening, Mon and lunchtime Tues.
(Roger and Anne Newbury)

MUCH WENLOCK SO6299

Gaskell Arms (01952) 727212

High Street (A458); TF13 6AQ 17th-c coaching inn with comfortable old-fashioned lounge divided by brass-canopied log fire, enjoyable straightforward bar food at fair prices, friendly attentive service, three well kept ales such as Ludlow, Salopian and Wye Valley, brasses and prints, civilised beamed restaurant, locals' bar; background music; well behaved children allowed, no dogs, disabled facilities, spacious walled garden behind with terrace, 14 bedrooms (some recently refurbished), open all day.
(Paul Scofield)

MUCH WENLOCK SO6299

★ **George & Dragon** (01952) 727312

High Street (A458); TF13 6AA Busy town pub filled with fascinating collection of pub paraphernalia – old brewery and cigarette advertisements, bottle labels, beer trays and George and the Dragon pictures, also 200 jugs hanging from beams; main quarry-tiled room with antique settles and open fires in two attractive Victorian fireplaces, timbered back dining room, Greene King, Hobsons, St Austell, Shepherd Neame and Thwaites, big helpings of well priced food (not Weds or Sun evenings), good friendly service; background and some live music; children and dogs (in bar) welcome, pay-and-display car park behind, open all day. *(Mark Morgan)*

MUNSLOW SO5287

★ **Crown** (01584) 841205

B4368 Much Wenlock–Craven Arms; SY7 9ET Former courthouse with imposing exterior and pretty back façade showing Tudor origins; lots of nooks and crannies, split-level lounge bar with old-fashioned mix of furnishings on broad flagstones, old bottles and country pictures, bread oven by log fire, traditional snug with another fire, eating area with tables around central oven chimney, more beams, flagstones and stripped stone, good food from sandwiches and sharing plates through pubby choices to restauranty dishes, popular Sun lunch, steak nights Tues and Weds, ales such as Otter, Three Tuns and Wye Valley, local bottled cider and nice wines, helpful efficient staff, friendly bustling atmosphere; background music; children welcome, level wheelchair access to bar only, bedrooms, closed Sun evening, Mon.
(Dr Peter Crawshaw, Robert W Buckle)

NEENTON SO6387

Pheasant (01746) 787955

B4364 Bridgnorth–Ludlow; WV16 6RJ Refurbished village pub owned by the local community; three or four well kept ales including Hobsons and over a dozen wines by the glass, good fairly priced home-made food from shortish menu, friendly young staff, comfortable seating by inglenook woodburner, oak-framed dining extension; free wi-fi; children and dogs (in bar) welcome, tables in orchard garden, three bedrooms, open all day weekends, closed Mon. *(Lynda and Trevor Smith, John and Jennifer Spinks)*

NESSCLIFFE SJ3819

Old Three Pigeons (01743) 741279

Off A5 Shrewsbury–Oswestry (now bypassed); SY4 1DB Friendly 16th-c pub with two bar areas and restaurant, good fairly priced food including fresh fish and plenty of daily specials, Thurs spanish night, three well kept local ales (maybe one from on-site microbrewery), nice wines by the glass, black beams, wood floors and warm log fires; children and dogs (in bar) welcome, picnic-sets in garden with fountain and covered area, opposite Kynaston's Cave, good cliff walks, open all day. *(Sandra Hollie)*

NORTON SJ7200

★ **Hundred House** (01952) 730353

A442 Telford–Bridgnorth; TF11 9EE Family-run inn with rambling rooms, hops and dried flowers hanging from beams, log fires in handsome fireplaces (one with great Jacobean arch and fine old black cooking pots), variety of chairs and settles with patchwork leather cushions, steps up to partly panelled eating area, well kept ales including Three Tuns, proper cider and good choice of wines and whiskies, highly regarded if not cheap food (all day Sun) using local Estate beef and game, good service; background music, free wi-fi; children and

---

dogs (in bar) welcome, pretty back garden, bedrooms with antique four-posters and trademark velvet-cushioned swings, open all day. *(Alfie Bayliss, R T and J C Moggridge, Charlie May)*

PICKLESCOTT   SO4399
Bottle & Glass (01694) 751252
Off A49 N of Church Stretton; SY6 6NR
Remote 17th-c country pub with plenty of character in quarry-tiled bar and lounge/ dining areas, low black beams, oak panelling and log fires, assortment of old tables and chairs, good traditional home-made food (not Sun evening) from baps up, will cater for special diets, well kept ales such as Hobsons and Woods, friendly helpful service; TV; children welcome, dogs in bar, seats out on raised front area, good walks, three bedrooms, open till 7pm Sun, closed Mon lunchtime (and evening winter). *(Carol Avery)*

SHAWBURY   SJ5621
Fox & Hounds (01939) 250600
Wytheford Road; SY4 4JG Light and spacious 1960s pub, various opened-up areas including black-lined dining room with woodburner, rugs and assorted dark furniture on wood floors, cream-painted dados and lots of pictures, good fairly priced food from light lunches and sharing boards to daily specials, meal deals, four or five well kept ales and good choice of wines, efficient helpful service; children welcome, picnic-sets on terrace and lawn, open (and food) all day. *(Tony Smaithe)*

SHIFNAL   SJ74508
White Hart (01952) 461161
High Street; TF11 8BH Nine well kept interesting ales in chatty 17th-c timbered pub, quaint and old-fashioned with separate bar and lounge, good home-made lunchtime food (not Sun), several wines by the glass, friendly welcoming staff; no credit cards; couple of steep steps at front door, back terrace and beer garden, open all day. *(Mark Morgan)*

SHREWSBURY   SJ4912
Admiral Benbow (01743) 244423
Swan Hill; SY1 1NF Great choice of regional ales, also ciders and bottled belgian beers, friendly staff; darts, free wi-fi; no children, beer garden behind, closed lunchtimes except Sat. *(Jeff Davies)*

SHREWSBURY   SJ4812
Boat House Inn (01743) 231658
New Street/Quarry Park; leaving centre via Welsh Bridge/A488 turn into Port Hill Road; SY3 8JQ Refurbished pub in lovely position by footbridge to Severn park, river views from long bar and terrace tables; pastel blue panelling, painted tables and chairs on bare boards, some beams and timbering, log fire, well kept regional ales

and enjoyable food from sandwiches to grills, friendly staff; background music, TV; children welcome, no dogs inside, summer bar on decked riverside terrace, open all day. *(Lance and Sarah Milligan)*

SHREWSBURY   SJ4812
Bricklayers Arms (01743) 366032
Copthorne Road/Hafren Road; SY3 8NL Spotless 1930s suburban pub (walkable from the town centre) owned by Joules, their beers in top condition and generous helping of popular traditional food including good Sun lunch, cheerful efficient service, bare boards, panelling and open fire, screens and gleaming stained glass, one wall with examples of different bricklaying patterns; children and dogs welcome, picnic-sets out in front, open all day Thurs-Sun, from 4pm other days. *(Robert W Buckle)*

SHREWSBURY   SJ4913
Dolphin (01743) 247005
A49 0.5 mile N of station; SY1 2EZ Traditionally refurbished little 19th-c pub with friendly welcoming staff and good mix of regulars and visitors, well kept Joules and a couple of guests, short choice of good bar snacks/simple meals, reasonable prices, original features including gas lighting, log fires; music and charity quiz nights, darts, free wi-fi; dogs welcome; seats on sunny back deck, open all day. *(Lance and Sarah Milligan)*

SHREWSBURY   SJ4912
Loggerheads (01743) 360275
Church Street; SY1 1UG Chatty old-fashioned local with panelled back room, flagstones, scrubbed-top tables, high-backed settles and coal fire, three other rooms with lots of prints, bare boards and more flagstones, quaint linking corridor and hatch service for the Marstons-related ales, no food, friendly service; weekly live folk music; dogs welcome (in some areas), open all day. *(Sandra Hollie)*

SHREWSBURY   SJ4912
Nags Head (01743) 362455
Wyle Cop; SY1 1XB Attractive old two-room pub, small, unpretentious and welcoming, with good range of well kept beers, no food; TV, juke box; dogs welcome, remains of ancient timbered building (used as a smokers' shelter) and garden behind, open all day (till 1am Fri, Sat). *(Jeff Davies)*

SHREWSBURY   SJ4812
Shrewsbury Hotel (01743) 236203
Mardol/Mardol Quay; SY1 1PU Refurbished partly open-plan Wetherspoons (former coaching inn) opposite the river, eight well kept/priced ales and their usual good value food, helpful friendly service; TVs for subtitled news, free wi-fi; children welcome, tables out in front, 22 bedrooms (residents' car park), open all day from 8am. *(Ian Phillips)*

SHREWSBURY   SJ4912

★ **Three Fishes** (01743) 455229
Fish Street; SY1 1UR Timbered and
heavily beamed 16th-c pub in quiet cobbled
street, small tables around three sides of
central bar, flagstones, old pictures, half
a dozen well kept beers from mainstream
and smaller brewers, good value wines and
enjoyable fairly priced food (not Sun) from
baguettes to blackboard specials ordered
from separate servery, good friendly service
even when busy; no mobile phones; open all
day Fri-Sun. *(Lance and Sarah Milligan)*

STIPERSTONES   SJ3600

★ **Stiperstones Inn** (01743) 791327
*Village signed off A488 S of Minsterley;
SY5 0LZ* Cosy traditional pub useful for a
post-walk drink or up dramatic quartzite ridge
of the Stiperstones; small carpeted lounge
with comfortable leatherette wall banquettes
and lots of brassware on ply-panelled walls,
plainer public bar with darts, TV and fruit
machine, a couple of real ales such as
Hobsons and Stonehouse, good value bar food
usefully served all day, also afternoon teas
with freshly baked cakes and home-made
jams, friendly helpful service; background
music; children and dogs (in bar and garden)
welcome, two comfortable bedrooms, open
all day. *(Paul Scofield)*

STOTTESDON   SO6782

Fighting Cocks (01746) 718270
High Street; DY14 8TZ New owners for
this welcoming old half-timbered community
pub in unspoilt countryside, some gentle
refurbishment in progress; carpeted split-
level interior with low ceilings and log fire,
good home-made food using local produce,
well kept Hobsons and a couple of guests,
real ciders; live music and occasional charity
quiz nights; children and dogs welcome
(their collie is Buddy), nice views from
garden and good walks, small shop behind,
open all day weekends, closed Mon.
(Mark Morgan)

UPTON MAGNA   SJ5512

Haughmond (01743) 709918
Pelham Road; SY4 4TZ Welcoming
refurbished village pub; log-fire bar with
painted beams, oak-strip flooring and carpet,
a house beer (Antler) brewed by Marstons
and two local guests from brick servery, good
food in brasserie and more upmarket and
expensive Basil's restaurant (open evenings
Thurs-Sat), village shop; children welcome
(until 9pm), dogs in bar, great view to the
Wrekin from attractive back garden, handy

for Haughmond Hill walks and Attingham
Park (NT), five bedrooms, open all day
weekends. *(Geoff and Ann Marston)*

WALL UNDER HEYWOOD   SO5092

Plough (01694) 771833
B4371; SY6 7DS Welcoming country pub
with good generously served food including
Sun carvery, five well kept ales such as Big
Shed, Greene King and Hobsons, log fire and
various odds and ends in small front bar, snug
with darts, comfortable 'piano' lounge and
dining conservatory; live music including Sun
lunchtime jazz; children and dogs welcome,
tables in back garden, good local walks, open
all day. *(Paul Bright)*

WELLINGTON   SJ6511

Cock (01952) 244954
*Holyhead Road (B5061 – former A5);
TF1 2DL* Welcoming 18th-c coaching
inn with well kept Hobsons and five
quickly changing guests usually from
small breweries, handpulled cider and
extensive range of bottled beers, friendly
knowledgeable staff, some food such as pies,
big fireplace; free wi-fi; dogs welcome, beer
garden with covered area, bedrooms, closed
lunchtime Mon-Weds, otherwise open all day.
(Claire Adams)

WELLINGTON   SJ6410

Old Orleton (01952) 255011
*Holyhead Road, off M54
junction 7); TF1 2HA* Modernised 17th-c
red-brick coaching inn with restaurant
and bar, well presented food from good
varied menu including vegetarian options,
a couple of Hobsons beers and Weston's
cider, welcoming helpful staff; nice view of
the Wrekin, ten well appointed comfortable
bedrooms, good breakfast. *(Mark Morgan)*

WELLINGTON   SJ6411

Pheasant (01952) 260683
Market Street; TF1 1DT Renovated
town-centre pub with own Wrekin beers
(can arrange tours of the microbrewery)
alongside guests including Everards, real
cider and home-produced gin, enjoyable good
value lunchtime food, friendly staff; children
welcome, disabled access and facilities, beer
garden, open all day. *(Bill Jones, Brian Banks)*

WELSHAMPTON   SJ4335

Sun (01948) 710847
A495 Ellesmere–Whitchurch; SY12 0PH
Friendly village pub with good choice of
enjoyable reasonably priced food (order
at bar), real ales such as Stonehouse; live
music and quiz nights; children and dogs
welcome, big back garden, 15-minute walk

Please tell us if any pub deserves to be upgraded to a featured entry – and why:
feedback@goodguides.com, or (no stamp needed) The Good Pub Guide,
FREEPOST RTJR-ZCYZ-RJZT, Perrymans Lane, Etchingham TN19 7DN.

to Llangollen/Shropshire Union Canal, three bedrooms, open (and food) all day. *(Tony Smaithe)*

WHITCHURCH   SJ5441
Anchor (01948) 663806
Pepper Street; SY13 1BG Renovated 17th-c pub tucked down small side street, spic and span bare-boards bar and flagstoned restaurant, well kept Sharps Doom Bar and three guests, enjoyable reasonably priced food including imaginative vegetarian choices, courteous attentive staff; free wi-fi; children welcome, tables in small courtyard, six comfortable bedrooms, open all day. *(Robert W Buckle)*

WHITCHURCH   SJ5441
Black Bear (01948) 663800
High Street/Bargates; SY13 1AZ Black and white building opposite church (a pub since 1667), half a dozen well kept interesting beers including Phoenix, enjoyable home-made food from open sandwiches up, characterful interior and good atmosphere; live acoustic music second Tues of the month; children and dogs (in bar) welcome, beer garden behind, open all day weekends. *(John and Hazel Sarkanen)*

WHITCHURCH   SJ5441
Old Town Hall Vaults
(01948) 662251 *St Marys Street; SY13 1QU* Red-brick 19th-c Joules local (birthplace of composer Sir Edward German), four of their ales and a guest, good value straightforward food from snacks up, main room divided into distinct areas with bar in one corner, oak panelling, stained glass, mirrors and signs, sturdy furniture including bench seating and cast-iron-framed tables, log fires, further room with glazed ceiling; outside listed gents'; dogs welcome, partly covered yard with barrel tables, open all day. *(Clive and Fran Dutson, Giles and Annie Francis)*

WHITCHURCH   SJ5345
Willey Moor Lock (01948) 663274
Tarporley Road; signed off A49 just under 2 miles N; SY13 4HF Large opened-up pub in picturesque spot by Llangollen Canal; two log fires, low beams and countless teapots and toby jugs, cheerful chatty atmosphere, half a dozen changing local ales and around 30 malt whiskies, good value quickly served pub food from sandwiches up; background music, games machine, no credit cards (debit cards accepted); well behaved dogs in some areas, terrace tables, secure garden with big play area. *(Tony Smaithe)*

WISTANSTOW   SO4385
Plough (01588) 673251
Off A49 and A489 N of Craven Arms; SY7 8DG Welcoming village pub adjoining the Woods brewery, their beers in peak condition and enjoyable home-made food including daily specials (all day Sat, till 7.30 Sun), friendly efficient service, smallish bar, airy high-ceilinged modern restaurant, games part with darts, dominoes and pool; background music, sports TV, free wi-fi; children and dogs (in bar) welcome, some tables outside, open all day Fri-Sun, closed Tues. *(Andrew and Michele Revell)*

Post Office address codings confusingly give the impression that some pubs are in Shropshire, when they're really in Cheshire (which is where we list them).

Somerset

ASHCOTT ST4337 Map 1

Ring o' Bells 🍺

(01458) 210232 – www.ringobells.com

High Street; pub well signed off A39 W of Street; TA7 9PZ

Friendly village pub with homely décor in several bars, separate restaurant, tasty bar food and changing local ales

As the RSPB reserve Ham Wall is nearby, this traditional 18th-c pub is a popular lunch spot for bird-watchers. It's been run for many years by the same family and the three main bars, on different levels, are all comfortable, with maroon plush-topped stools, cushioned mate's chairs and dark wooden pubby tables on patterned carpet, horsebrasses along the bressumer beam above a big stone fireplace and a growing collection of hand bells; background music. Black Rock Pale and Flowerpots Bitter on handpump, eight wines by the glass and local farm cider. There's also a separate restaurant, a skittle alley/function room, and plenty of picnic-sets outside on the terrace and in the garden.

🍴 Honest food includes sandwiches, brie fritters with cranberry sauce, fresh grilled sardines, celery, almond and cashew nut roast with cheese sauce, home-cooked ham and free-range egg, lambs liver and mushrooms in cider, scampi with chips, chicken breast stuffed with sun-dried tomatoes and basil, gurnard fillet with courgette tagliatelle and pesto, and puddings such as sherry trifle and chocolate meringue pie. *Benchmark main dish: pie of the day £10.95. Two-course evening meal £16.50.*

Free house ~ Licensees John and Elaine Foreman and John Sharman ~ Real ale ~ Open 12-2.30, 7-11; 12-3, 7-10.30 Sun ~ Bar food 12-2, 7-10 ~ Restaurant ~ Children welcome ~ Dogs allowed in bar ~ Wi-fi *Recommended by Belinda Stamp, Martin Jones, Edward May, Patrick and Daphne Darley*

BABCARY ST5628 Map 2

Red Lion 🏆 🍷 🛏

(01458) 223230 – www.redlionbabcary.co.uk

Off A37 S of Shepton Mallett; 2 miles or so N of roundabout where A37 meets A303 and A372; TA11 7ED

Thatched pub with comfortable rambling rooms, interesting food and local beers and seats outside; bedrooms

Several distinct areas in this busy thatched inn work their way around the bar counter. To the left is a longish room with dark red walls, a squashy leather sofa and two winged armchairs around a low table by an open fire –

plus a few well spaced tables and captain's chairs. There are elegant rustic wall lights, clay pipes in a display cabinet, local papers or magazines to read and board games. A more dimly lit public bar with lovely dark flagstones has a high-backed old settle and other more straightforward chairs; table skittles and background music. In the good-sized dining room a large stone lion's head sits on a plinth above a big open fire, and tables and chairs are set on polished boards. There's Lyme Regis Cobb Bitter, Otter Ale and Teignworthy Reel Ale on handpump, 18 wines by the glass and cocktails. The Den, set in a pretty courtyard, has light modern furnishings, a summer wood-fired pizza oven and a brasserie-style menu, and doubles as a party, wedding and conference venue. The long informal garden has a play area and plenty of seats. The bedrooms are comfortable and well equipped and the pub is handy for the Fleet Air Arm Museum at Yeovilton, the Haynes Motor Museum in Sparkford and for shopping at Clarks Village in Street. Wheelchair access.

 Well thought-of food includes lunchtime sandwiches, crayfish cocktail, duck liver parfait, roasted swede risotto with spinach and truffle oil, sausages and mash with red wine jus, salmon fishcake with wilted spinach and lemon mayonnaise, confit pork belly with butter beans, crackling and honey and cider jus, duck with potato and pancetta terrine and jus, line-caught bass with celeriac purée, bacon and red wine sauce, and puddings such as crème brûlée and banoffi pie with coconut ice-cream. *Benchmark main dish: steak burger with toppings, pickles and fries £12.75. Two-course evening meal £20.00.*

Free house ~ Licensee Charles Garrard ~ Real ale ~ Open 12-3, 6-midnight ~ Bar food 12-2.30, 6.30-9.30 (9 Sun) ~ Restaurant ~ Children welcome ~ Dogs allowed in bar ~ Wi-fi ~ Bedrooms: £90/£110 *Recommended by Helen and Brian Edgeley, Bob and Margaret Holder, Daphne and Robert Staples*

BATH
Chequers
ST7465 Map 2

(01225) 360017 – www.thechequersbath.com

Rivers Street; BA1 2QA

City-centre pub with friendly staff, pretty upstairs restaurant and enjoyable food and beers

Located in the centre of Bath, this bustling 19th-c pub is a popular spot. The bar has velvet-cushioned wall pews, chapel, farmhouse and kitchen chairs around all sorts of tables (each set with flowers) on parquet flooring, wedgwood blue paintwork and some fine plasterwork and a coal-effect gas fire in a white-painted fireplace. Bath Gem and Butcombe Bitter on handpump and several wines by the glass. The recently refurbished and attractive little restaurant upstairs has leather-seated chapel chairs and wall pews around candlelit tables, a wooden floor and a huge window into the kitchen. In warm weather there are picnic-sets under awning on the pavement.

Good, interesting food includes rabbit and hare terrine with pickles and pistachio, cured salmon mousse with smoked eel, lotus root and teriyaki sauce, potato gnocchi with crispy egg, wild mushrooms and butternut squash, game pie with chips, pork belly, cheek, faggot and tenderloin with black pudding, bulgar wheat and pickled apple, hake with cockles, cauliflower textures and mint, duck breast and confit leg with burnt and hay-baked celeriac, turnip and borlotti beans, and puddings such as dark chocolate fondant with raspberries and white chocolate and burnt passion-fruit custard with mango and coconut. *Benchmark main dish: venison haunch with blackberries £24.95. Two-course evening meal £26.50.*

Bath Pub Company ~ Lease Joe Cussens ~ Real ale ~ No credit cards ~ Open 12-11 ~ Bar food 6-9.30 Mon-Fri; 12-2, 6-10 Sat; 12-4, 6-9 Sun ~ Restaurant ~ Children welcome ~

Dogs allowed in bar ~ Wi-fi *Recommended by Dr Simon Innes, Comus and Sarah Elliott, Luke Morgan, Richard Mason*

BATH
Hare & Hounds

ST7467 Map 2

(01225) 482682 – www.hareandhoundsbath.com

Lansdown Road, Lansdown Hill; BA1 5TJ

Lovely views from back terrace with plenty of seating, relaxed bar areas, real ales, nice food and helpful staff

'A great find,' says one of our readers with enthusiasm. One of the big pluses here is the wonderful extended view down over villages and fields from windows in the bar and from seats and tables on the decked back terrace; if you head down some steps from the terrace there's a garden with more seats and tables. The atmosphere in the single long bar is relaxed and friendly, helped along by cheerful staff. There are chapel chairs and long cushioned wall settles around pale wood-topped tables on bare boards, minimal decoration on pale walls above a blue-grey dado and an attractively carved counter where they serve a beer named for the pub (from Caledonian), Butcombe Bitter and Theakstons Vanilla Stout on handpump and several wines by the glass; background music. There's a bronze hare and hound at one end of the mantelpiece over a log fire, and a big mirror above. A little side conservatory is similarly furnished, with dark slate flagstones.

Food is good and starts with breakfast (8.30-11.30am), followed by sandwiches, scallops with black pudding, cauliflower purée and hazelnut butter, game terrine with spiced pear and fig chutney, aubergine and red pepper tagine with tzatziki, beer-battered haddock and chips, burger with toppings, coleslaw and skinny chips, duck breast and confit leg with parsnip purée, braised red cabbage and port jus, and puddings such as chocolate brownie and vanilla crème brûlée. *Benchmark main dish: pork belly with mustard mash and savoy cabbage £14.00. Two-course evening meal £21.00.*

Bath Pub Company ~ Lease Joe Cussens ~ Real ale ~ Open 8.30am-11pm (10.30pm Sun) ~ Bar food 8.30-11, 12-3, 5.30-9; 8.30-11, 12-8 Sun ~ Children welcome ~ Dogs welcome ~ Wi-fi *Recommended by Dr and Mrs A K Clarke, Michael Doswell, Sally and David Champion, Richard Mason*

BATH
Marlborough

ST7465 Map 2

(01225) 423731 – www.marlborough-tavern.com

35 Marlborough Buildings/Weston Road; BA1 2LY

Open all day and with plenty of customers; candles, fresh flowers, cheerful staff and good food

This easy-going place is very central, it's useful that it's open every day for coffee from 8am (9am weekends). The U-shaped bar is always busy and the cheerful staff keep things buzzing along nicely. There are bare boards throughout, church candles in sizeable jars on windowsills and on the mantelpiece above a fireplace strung with fairy lights and plenty of tea-lights; each table has a single flower in a vase. Seating ranges from thick button-back wall seats to chapel, kitchen and high-backed cushioned dining chairs; background music. Chunky bar stools line the counter, where they serve Butcombe Bitter and guests such as Box Steam Piston Broke and Butcombe Moxee IPA on handpump and several wines by the glass. The little courtyard side garden is a suntrap in summer and there are benches and chairs around tables among the various plantings.

Reliably good food includes pork rillettes with apricot chutney, honey-truffled goats cheese, shallot purée, figs and apple crisps, duo of pork with panko black pudding, broccoli purée, wholegrain mash and red wine jus, butternut squash and wild mushroom risotto with truffle oil, burger with toppings, relish, coleslaw and fries, beer-battered ling with triple-cooked chips, lamb rump with curried lentils, cumin and cauliflower purée, onion bhaji and raita, and puddings such as lemon posset with almond crumble and trio of chocolate with blackberry purée. *Benchmark main dish: chicken with wild garlic mash, mushroom purée, and red wine jus £17.50. Two-course evening meal £22.00.*

Free house ~ Licensees Joe Cussens and Justin Sleath ~ Real ale ~ Open 9am-11pm ~ Bar food 12-2.30 (3 Sat), 6-9.30; 12-7 Sun ~ Children welcome ~ Dogs welcome ~ Wi-fi
Recommended by Peter Barrett, Dr and Mrs A K Clarke, James Allsopp

BATH
Old Green Tree
ST7564   Map 2

(01225) 448259
Green Street; BA1 2JZ

Tiny, unspoilt local with six real ales and lots of cheerful customers

Our readers continue to praise this charming little 18th-c tavern, which remains as unspoilt as ever. The three small rooms – with oak panelling and low ceilings of wood and plaster – include a comfortable lounge on the left as you go in, its walls decorated with wartime aircraft pictures (in winter) and local artists' work (in spring and summer). There's a back bar as well; the big skylight lightens things attractively. Half a dozen beers on handpump might include Green Tree Bitter (named for the pub by Blindmans Brewery), Butcombe Bitter and RCH Pitchfork, with guests such as Plain Inncognito and Stonehenge Spire Ale; also, seven wines by the glass from a nice little list with helpful notes, 36 malt whiskies and a farm cider. The gents' is basic and down steep steps. No children and no dogs.

Lunchtime-only food includes sandwiches, soup, pâté, sausages with ale and onion gravy, vegetable curry, burger with toppings and chips and lambs liver with bacon and roast garlic mash. *Benchmark main dish: sausage and mash with onion gravy £8.50.*

Free house ~ Licensee Tim Bethune ~ Real ale ~ No credit cards ~ Open 11-11; 12-6.30 Sun ~ Bar food 12-2.30 (3 Sat); not evenings or Sun *Recommended by Ben and Diane Bowie, Taff Thomas, Dr J Barrie Jones, Melanie and David Lawson, Richard Mason*

BATH
Star
ST7565   Map 2

(01225) 425072 – www.abbeyales.co.uk/www.star-inn-bath.co.uk
Vineyards; The Paragon (A4), junction with Guinea Lane; BA1 5NA

Quietly chatty and unchanging old town local, the brewery tap for Abbey Ales

In quiet steep streets of undeniably handsome if well worn stone terraces, yet handy for the main shopping area, this old pub gives a strong sense of the past. The four small linked rooms have many original features such as traditional wall benches (one is known as Death Row), panelling, dim lighting and open fires. Abbey Bellringer plus guests such as Abbey Black Friar, Banfield Tunnel Vision, Bass and St Austell Proper Job tapped from the cask, several wines by the glass, 30 malt whiskies and Cheddar Valley cider; darts, shove-ha'penny, cribbage and board games – and complimentary snuff.

The place gets particularly busy at weekends and is around five minutes' walk from the city centre.

🍴 Food consists of filled rolls.

Punch ~ Lease Paul Waters and Alan Morgan ~ Real ale ~ Open 12-2.30, 5.30-midnight; noon-1am Fri, Sat; 12-midnight Sun ~ Bar food ~ Children welcome ~ Dogs welcome ~ Wi-fi ~ Singing session Sun evening, irish folk Fri evening, quiz first Sun of month
Recommended by Taff Thomas, Andrew and Michele Revell, Jack and Hilary Burton, Dr J Barrie Jones

BISHOPSWOOD
ST2512　Map 1

Candlelight 🌟 🍺

(01460) 234476 – www.candlelight-inn.co.uk
Off A303/B3170 S of Taunton; TA20 3RS

Friendly, hard-working licensees in neat dining pub with real ales and farm cider, enjoyable imaginative food and seats in the garden

Always friendly thanks to the personable landlord at the helm, this is a gently civilised pub that's handy for the A303. The neatly kept, more or less open-plan rooms are separated into different areas by standing stone pillars and open doorways. The beamed bar has high chairs by the counter where they serve a fine range of drinks: Bass and Otter Bitter with guests such as Teignworthy Gun Dog and Yeovil Star Gazer tapped from the cask, eight wines by the glass, a couple of farm ciders and winter drinks such as hot Pimms, whisky toddies and hot chocolate. Also, captain's chairs, pews and cushioned window seats around a mix of wooden tables on sanded floorboards, and a small ornate fireplace. To the left is a comfortable area with a button-back sofa beside a big woodburner, wheelback chairs and cushioned settles around wooden tables set for dining, with country pictures, photos, a hunting horn and bugles on the granite walls; background music and shove-ha'penny. On the other side of the bar is a similarly furnished dining room. Outside, a decked area has picnic-sets and a neatly landscaped garden has a paved path winding through low walls set with plants.

🌟 Enjoyable food includes sandwiches, ham hock terrine with fig chutney, home-cured venison with radicchio, pear, walnut and parmesan, wild mushroom and chestnut fricassée in puff pastry with wild garlic pesto, pork tenderloin with bubble and squeak, apple fondant and cider jus, cod fillet with parmesan and walnut crust and haricot bean and chorizo cassoulet, rack of lamb with fennel, olive, anchovy and red pepper ragoût with rosemary jus, and puddings such as passion-fruit parfait with tropical fruit salad and chocolate and praline terrine with berry jelly. *Benchmark main dish: duck breast with duck bonbons, pak choi, celeriac purée and juniper jus £18.00. Two-course evening meal £20.00.*

Free house ~ Licensees Tom Warren and Debbie Lush ~ Real ale ~ Open 12-2.30 (3 Sat), 6-11; 12-11 Sun; closed Mon, first week Nov ~ Bar food 12-2, 7-9; 12-2.30, 7-9.30 Fri, Sat ~ Well behaved children welcome away from bar area ~ Dogs allowed in bar ~ Wi-fi
Recommended by Patrick and Daphne Darley, Hugh Roberts, Roy Hoing

BRISTOL
ST5873　Map 2

Highbury Vaults 🍺 £

(0117) 973 3203 – www.highburyvaults.co.uk
St Michaels Hill, Cotham; BS2 8DE

Cheerful town pub with up to eight real ales, good value tasty bar food and friendly atmosphere

Good value food, a fine range of quickly changing real ales and a warm welcome are the mainstays of this unpretentious pub. On handpump, the beers might be Youngs Bitter and London Gold plus guests such as Ashley Down Landlord's Best, Bath Gem, Cotswold Spring Stunner, St Austell Tribute and Teignworthy Mad Hatters; also, six wines by the glass and eight malt whiskies. They offer hot sausage rolls from the oven on Thursday and Friday evenings at 10pm. The little front bar, with a corridor beside it, leads through to a series of small rooms: wooden floors, green and cream paintwork and old-fashioned furniture and prints (including plenty of royal family period engravings and lithographs in the front room). A model railway runs on a shelf the full length of the pub, with tunnels through the walls; bar billiards, TV and board games. The attractive back terrace has tables built into a partly covered flowery arbour; disabled access to main bar (but not the loos).

🍴 Reasonably priced food includes filled rolls, baked potatoes, burgers with coleslaw, tortilla chips and salsa, beef in ale pie, lasagne, fish pie and daily specials. *Benchmark main dish: chilli con carne £6.95. Two-course evening meal £14.00.*

Youngs ~ Manager Bradd Francis ~ Real ale ~ Open 12-midnight (11 Sun) ~ Bar food 12-2, 5.30-8.30; 12-3 Sun ~ Children welcome ~ Wi-fi *Recommended by Carol and Barry Craddock, Lindy Andrews, John and Mary Warner*

CHARLTON HORETHORNE
Kings Arms 🎯 🛏️

ST6623   Map 2

(01963) 220281 – www.thekingsarms.co.uk

B3145 Wincanton–Sherborne; DT9 4NL

Bustling inn with relaxed bars and more formal restaurant, good ales and wines and enjoyable food; bedrooms

The hands-on landlord here remains as enthusiastic as ever and his staff are friendly and efficient. It's a smart place and the main bar has an appealing assortment of local art (all for sale) on dark mulberry or cream walls, nice old carved wooden dining chairs and pine pews around a mix of tables, a slate floor and a woodburning stove. Leading off is a cosy room with sofas and newspapers on low tables. Butcombe Bitter, Wadworths 6X and a guest beer on handpump are served from the rather fine granite bar counter; they also keep 14 wines by the glass, nine malt whiskies and local farm cider. To the left of the main door is an informal dining room with Jacobean-style chairs and tables on a pale wooden floor and more local artwork. The back restaurant (past the open kitchen which is fun to peek into) has decorative wood and glass mirrors, wicker or black leather high-backed dining chairs around chunky, polished, pale wooden tables on coir carpeting, and handsome striped curtains. The attractive courtyard at the back of the inn has chrome and wicker chairs around teak tables under green parasols; a smokers' shelter overlooks a croquet lawn. The comfortable bedrooms are well equipped and contemporary.

⭐ Imaginative food includes sandwiches, smoked chicken and ham hock terrine with piccalilli, tempura king prawns with chilli dipping sauce, steak burger with crumbled stilton and red onion marmalade, cod with puy lentils, chorizo, baby spinach and madeira jus, saffron, courgette and pea risotto, Josper-cooked loin of pork with stir-fried broccoli, sugar snap peas, samphire and sesame ginger and egg noodles, venison steak with pomme purée, marinated beetroot and port jus, and puddings such as key lime pie with blueberry sorbet and carrot cake with beetroot ice-cream and carrot curd. *Benchmark main dish: free-range duck leg with charred peaches, white onion purée, dauphinoise potatoes and sherry jus £19.00. Two-course evening meal £24.00.*

Free house ~ Licensee Tony Lethbridge ~ Real ale ~ Open 7am-11pm ~ Bar food 12-2.30, 7-9.30; 12-2.30, 7-10 Fri, Sat; 12-2.30, 7-9 Sun ~ Restaurant ~ Children welcome ~ Dogs allowed in bar ~ Wi-fi ~ Bedrooms: /£135 *Recommended by Michael Hill, Edward Mirzoeff, Maddie Purvis, Claire Adams, Bob West*

CHURCHILL

ST4459   Map 1

Crown 🍺 £

(01934) 852995 –

The Batch; in village, turn off A368 into Skinners Lane at Nelson Arms; BS25 5PP

Unchanging small cottage with friendly customers and staff, super range of real ales and homely lunchtime food

For those keen on more modern comforts, this rural cottage might not appeal. It's an untouched, simple old pub and for lovers of the unspoilt – it's perfect. There are seven real ales tapped from the cask, including Bath Gem, Butcombe Bitter, Otter Bitter, Palmers IPA, RCH IPA, St Austell Tribute and a quickly changing guest; several wines by the glass and five local ciders too. The small and rather local-feeling stone-floored and cross-beamed room on the right has a big log fire in a large stone fireplace, chatty and friendly customers and steps that lead up to another seating area. The left-hand room – with a slate floor, window seats and a log burner – leads through to the Snug. There's no noise from music or games (except perhaps dominoes). The outside lavatories are basic. There are garden tables at the front, more seats on the back lawn and hill views; the Mendip morris men visit in summer and some of the best walking on the Mendips is nearby. There isn't a pub sign outside, but no one seems to have a problem finding the place.

 Traditional, lunchtime-only food includes sandwiches (the rare roast beef is popular), beef casserole, cauliflower cheese, lasagne and puddings. *Benchmark main dish: chilli beef £6.40.*

Free house ~ Licensee Brian Clements ~ Real ale ~ No credit cards ~ Open 11-11; 12-10.30 Sun ~ Bar food 12-2.30 ~ Children welcome away from bar ~ Dogs allowed in bar ~ Wi-fi *Recommended by Hugh Roberts, Taff Thomas, Millie and Peter Downing*

CLAPTON-IN-GORDANO

ST4773   Map 1

Black Horse 🍺 £

(01275) 842105 – www.thekicker.co.uk

4 miles from M5 junction 19; A369 towards Portishead, then B3124 towards Clevedon; in North Weston opposite school, turn left signposted Clapton, then in village take second right, may be signed 'Clevedon, Clapton Wick'; BS20 7RH

Unpretentious old pub with lots of cheerful customers, friendly service, real ales, cider and simple lunchtime food; pretty garden

Customers of all ages enjoy this old-fashioned 14th-c tavern where, thankfully, nothing changes. The partly flagstoned, partly red-tiled main room has winged settles and built-in wall benches around narrow, dark wooden tables, window seats, a big log fire with stirrups and bits on the mantelbeam, and amusing cartoons and photographs of the pub. A window in an inner snug retains metal bars from the days when this room was the petty sessions gaol; also, high-backed settles – one with a marvellous carved and canopied creature, another with an art nouveau copper insert reading 'East, West, Hame's Best' – lots of mugs hanging from black beams and numerous small prints and photographs. A simply furnished room is the only place that families are allowed; background music. Bath Gem, Butcombe Bitter, Courage Best, Exmoor Gold and Otter Bitter on handpump or tapped from the cask, six wines by the glass and three farm ciders. There are rustic tables and benches in the garden, with more to one side of the car park – the summer flowers are quite a sight. Paths from the pub lead up Naish Hill or to Cadbury Camp (National Trust) and there's access to local cycle routes.

¶¶ Honest lunchtime-only food includes baguettes and baps with lots of hot and cold fillings and daily specials such as soup, local faggot and peas, beef in red wine, pork and cider, and paprika chicken. *Benchmark main dish: corned beef hash £8.25.*

Enterprise ~ Lease Nicholas Evans ~ Real ale ~ Open 11-11; 12-9.30 Sun ~ Bar food 12-2.30; not evenings or Sun ~ Children in family room only ~ Dogs welcome ~ Wi-fi
Recommended by John Pritchard, Roy Hoing, Chris and Angela Buckell, R T and J C Moggridge, Taff Thomas

COMBE HAY   ST7359   Map 2

Wheatsheaf 🏅 ⧗ 🛏

(01225) 833504 – www.wheatsheafcombehay.co.uk
Village signposted off A367 or B3110 S of Bath; BA2 7EG

Somerset Dining Pub of the Year

Smart and cheerful country dining pub with first class food and drink; attractive bedrooms

Many customers are here to enjoy the impressive food or to stay in the stylishly simple and spacious bedrooms. But they also welcome walkers with their dogs, and drinkers can sit in a central area by a big fireplace, where there are sofas on dark flagstones and daily papers and current issues of *The Field* and *Country Life* on a low table. Friendly staff serve Butcombe Bitter and Gold and Otter Bright on handpump, 16 wines by the glass from a very good list, 18 malt whiskies and a farm cider. Other areas have stylish high-backed grey wicker dining chairs around chunky modern dining tables, on parquet or coir matting. It's fresh and bright, with block-mounted photo-prints, contemporary artwork and mirrors with colourful ceramic mosaic frames (many for sale) on white-painted stonework or robin's-egg blue plaster walls. The sills of the many shuttered windows house anything from old soda siphons to a stuffed kingfisher and a Great Lakes model tugboat. Glinting glass wall chandeliers and nightlights in entertaining holders supplement the ceiling spotlights; background music and a cheerful cocker spaniel. The two-level front garden has picnic-sets and a fine view over the church and valley; good surrounding walks.

🏅 Stylish food includes sandwiches, ham hock and black pudding terrine with piccalilli, rabbit and red wine risotto with rabbit liver parfait, pigeon crown with leg croquette, golden raisins and capers, burger with toppings and skinny chips, chicken breast with wild mushroom sauce, a fish dish of the day, lamb rump with aubergine and tomato moussaka, steak rossini with foie gras, fondant potato and truffle jus, and puddings such as dark chocolate mousse and treacle tart with apple and elderflower sorbet; they also offer a two- and three-course set weekday evening menu. *Benchmark main dish: fish stew £18.00. Two-course evening meal £20.00.*

Free house ~ Licensee Ian Barton ~ Real ale ~ Open 10.30-3, 6-11; 12-3 Sun; closed Sun evening, Mon except bank holidays, first week Jan ~ Bar food 12-2.30, 6.30-9 ~ Restaurant ~ Children welcome ~ Dogs welcome ~ Wi-fi ~ Bedrooms: /$120 *Recommended by Mrs Julie Thomas, Nick Lawless, Richard Mason, George Sanderson, Julian Thorpe*

The 🍺 symbol shows pubs that keep their beer unusually well, have a particularly good range or brew their own.

CORTON DENHAM

ST6322 Map 2

Queens Arms 🌟 ♟ 🍺 🛏

(01963) 220317 – www.thequeensarms.com

Village signposted off B3145 N of Sherborne; DT9 4LR

Handsome 18th-c inn with super choice of drinks, interesting food and a sunny garden; comfortable, stylish bedrooms

This is an elegant looking, honey-coloured stone inn with a gently civilised atmosphere. The bustling, high-beamed bar has rugs on flagstones and two big armchairs in front of an open fire, some old pews, barrel seats and a sofa, church candles and large bowls of flowers. There's also a couple of separate restaurants – one with cushioned wall seating and chunky leather chairs around dark wooden tables, mirrors down one side and a drop-down cinema screen (screenings are held twice a month). A beer named for the pub (from Gyle 59) plus Gyle 59 Toujours, and guests from breweries such as Otter, Teignworthy and Yeovil on handpump, 22 wines (including champagne) by the glass from a carefully chosen list, 57 malt whiskies, 26 gins, unusual bottled beers from Belgium, Germany and the US and four local apple juices. A south-facing back terrace has teak tables and chairs under parasols (or heaters, if it's cool) and colourful flower tubs. The bedrooms are comfortable and have lovely country views and breakfasts are particularly good. There are fine surrounding walks and the pub offers a list of walking and running routes.

 Using their own pigs, cows and hens, the rewarding food includes sandwiches, beetroot and gin-cured salmon with crab apple jelly, cider-braised pork belly with black pudding and apple and shallot purée, honey-roast ham and eggs, rib burger with home-cured bacon, pickles and chips, wild mushroom and butternut squash risotto, braised lamb shoulder and Guinness pie, roasted cod with brown shrimps, mussels, leeks and sea greens, and puddings such as rhubarb and custard sundae and chocolate fondant with salted caramel ice-cream; afternoon tea is offered 3-5.30pm daily. *Benchmark main dish: wine-battered fish and chips £13.95. Two-course evening meal £25.00.*

Free house ~ Licensees Jeanette and Gordon Reid ~ Real ale ~ Open 10am-midnight (11pm Sun) ~ Bar food 12-3, 6-9 ~ Restaurant ~ Children welcome ~ Dogs allowed in bar and bedrooms ~ Bedrooms: £90/£120 *Recommended by Carol and Barry Craddock, Stuart Reeves, Miles Green*

CROSCOMBE

ST5844 Map 2

George 🍺 🛏

(01749) 342306 – www.thegeorgeinn.co.uk

Long Street (A371 Wells–Shepton Mallet); BA5 3QH

Warmly welcoming, family-run coaching inn with charming canadian landlord, enjoyable food, good local beers and attractive garden; bedrooms

'What a wonderful pub for a thirsty traveller,' says one reader, very happy with the fine range of drinks. As well as four farm ciders, they keep King George the Thirst (from Blindmans), Butcombe Rare Breed, Cotleigh Osprey and Yeovil Summerset on handpump or tapped from the cask, ten wines by the glass and home-made elderflower cordial. It's a very well run and genuinely friendly inn and the main bar has a good mix of locals and visitors, stripped stone, dark wooden tables and chairs and more comfortable seats, a settle by one of the log fires in the inglenook fireplaces, and the family's grandfather clock; a snug area has a woodburning stove.

The attractive dining room has more stripped stone, local artwork and family photographs on burgundy walls and high-backed cushioned dining chairs around a mix of tables. The back bar has canadian timber and a pew reclaimed from the local church, and there's a family room with games and books for children. Darts, a skittle alley, board games, shove-ha'penny and a canadian wooden table game called crokinole. The pub dog Tessa has been joined by Pixy the labrador/spaniel cross. Outside is an attractive, sizeable garden with seats on a heated and covered terrace, flower borders, a grassed area, a wood-fired pizza oven (used on Fridays) and chickens; children's swings. We've received very positive comments on the accommodation this year – and breakfasts are good.

Food is good and includes ham hock and caper terrine with a scotch quail egg, tempura king prawns with soy and chilli dressing, vegetable curry with accompaniments, a pie of the day, pressed ox tongue with pickled vegetables, dauphinoise potatoes and horseradish jus, duck leg with sautéed carrots and ginger and madeira reduction, local steaks with toppings and sauces (steak night is Wednesday), and puddings such as apple and berry crumble and rum and raisin bread and butter pudding. *Benchmark main dish: scallops in garlic butter with balsamic reduction £15.95. Two-course evening meal £20.50.*

Free house ~ Licensees Peter and Veryan Graham ~ Real ale ~ Open 10-3, 6-11; 11-11 Sat, Sun ~ Bar food 12-2.30, 6-9; 12-8 Sun ~ Restaurant ~ Children welcome ~ Dogs allowed in bar ~ Wi-fi ~ Bedrooms: £60/£80 *Recommended by Ann and Colin Hunt, Taff Thomas, Ray White, Dr J Barrie Jones*

DULVERTON
SS9127 Map 1

Woods ★ ⦿ ♥

(01398) 324007 – www.woodsdulverton.co.uk
Bank Square; TA22 9BU

Smartly informal place with exceptional wines, real ales, first rate food and a good mix of customers

The good ship Woods sails merrily on with high praise for all aspects of the place from our enthusiastic readers. There are satisfied diners to the right and happy lunchtime drinkers nursing their pints to the left; as the pub is on the edge of Exmoor, there are plenty of good sporting prints on salmon pink walls, antlers and other hunting trophies, stuffed birds and a couple of salmon rods. By the bar counter are bare boards, daily papers, tables partly separated by stable-style timbering and masonry dividers, and (on the right) a carpeted area with a woodburning stove in a big fireplace; maybe unobjectionable background music. The marvellous drinks choice includes Otter Ale and St Austell Cornish Best and Proper Job tapped from the cask, farm cider, many sherries and some unusual spirits – but it's the stunning wine list that draws the most attention. Mr Groves, the landlord, reckons he could put 1,000 different wines up on the bar and will open any of them (with a value of up to £100) for just a glass. He is there every night and will happily chat to tables of restaurant customers about any wines they might be interested in. Big windows look on to the quiet town centre (there's also a couple of metal tables on the pavement) and a small suntrap back courtyard has a few picnic-sets.

Excellent food using their own farm produce includes sandwiches, seared mackerel fillet with cucumber linguine, spring onion, chilli and lime, confit duck and foie gras terrine with red onion marmalade and pickled wild mushrooms, goats cheese, asparagus and wild garlic risotto with caramelised walnut salad, cod fillet with shrimps, herb salad and caper nut brown butter, lamb loin and slow-roast shoulder with artichoke purée, fondant potato and thyme sauce, rib-eye steak with slow-roast tomato, fries and bordelaise butter, and puddings such as glazed lemon tart with coconut sorbet and citrus confit and stem ginger pannacotta with poached rhubarb and apricot sorbet. *Benchmark main dish: changing home-reared pork dish £16.50. Two-course evening meal £22.00.*

Free house ~ Licensee Patrick Groves ~ Real ale ~ Open 12-3, 6-11.30; 12-4, 7-11.30 Sun ~ Bar food 12-2, 6 (7 Sun)-9.30 ~ Restaurant ~ Children welcome ~ Dogs welcome ~ Wi-fi
Recommended by M G Hart, Richard and Penny Gibbs, Ian and Rose Lock, Lynda and Trevor Smith

DUNSTER
SS9943 Map 1

 # Luttrell Arms ⭐🍷🛏

(01643) 821555 – www.luttrellarms.co.uk
High Street; A396; TA24 6SG

Character bars and dining areas in lovely antiques-filled hotel, a thoughtful choice of drinks, enjoyable food and seats in courtyard and garden; luxurious bedrooms

In an interesting and pretty town on the edge of Exmoor National Park, this is a rather special place with some fine medieval features. The Old Kitchen Bar has the workings of the former kitchen with meat hooks on the beamed ceiling and a massive log fire and bread oven. The main bar – popular locally – has swords and guns on the wall above a huge fireplace, cushions on antique chairs, horsebrasses, copper kettles, plates and warming pans, animal furs dotted here and there, a stag's head and an antler chandelier, and various country knick-knacks. Exmoor Ale, Otter Amber and Sharps Doom Bar on handpump, 28 good wines by the glass, a dozen malt whiskies and three farm ciders; staff are courteous and helpful. There's also the Boot Bar with a lovely panelled wall seat and rugs on quarry tiles, a small snug and a deeply comfortable sitting room with one beautiful panelled wall, a woodburning stove and plenty of armchairs, sofas and window seats; board games. The lovely garden is on several levels with seats on lawns or terraces and haunting castle views; a little galleried courtyard has metalwork chairs and tables. Some of the bedrooms are opulent with four-posters, antiques and carved fireplaces; breakfasts are first class.

🔲 Highly regarded food includes sandwiches, citrus-cured salmon with pickled cucumber, yoghurt and horseradish, whipped goats cheese mousse with beetroot, apple and celery, a pie of the week, honey-roast ham and duck eggs, garlic chicken kiev with macaroni cheese, beans and chicken velouté, pork three-ways (confit belly, braised cheek, faggot) with charred cauliflower purée and caper jus, bass fillet with bombay potatoes, samphire and saffron sauce, and puddings such as treacle tart with lemon curd and dark chocolate fondant with cherry purée and cherry ice-cream. *Benchmark main dish: beer-battered fish and chips £12.00. Two-course evening meal £18.00.*

Free house ~ Licensee Tim Waldren ~ Real ale ~ Open 11-11; 12-11 Sun ~ Bar food 7.30am-9.30pm ~ Restaurant ~ Children welcome ~ Dogs allowed in bar and bedrooms ~ Wi-fi ~ Bedrooms: £100/£140 *Recommended by Martin Jones, Isobel Mackinlay, Rosie and John Moore, Elizabeth and Peter May*

EXFORD
SS8538 Map 1

 # Crown 🛏

(01643) 831554 – www.crownhotelexmoor.co.uk
The Green (B3224); TA24 7PP

17th-c coaching inn in pretty moorland village, character bar with real ales and enjoyable food and big back garden; comfortable bedrooms

Set in the middle of Exmoor, this family-run inn is just the place to head for after a walk. The two-room bar is easy-going and has a log fire in a big stone fireplace, plenty of stuffed animal heads and hunting prints on grey walls, some hunting-themed plates and old photographs of the area, cushioned benches and other traditional pubby tables and chairs on bare boards. There are stools against the counter where they serve Exmoor Ale and Gold and St Austell Tribute on handpump, 16 wines by the glass, 15 malt whiskies, ten gins and farm cider; TV and board games. The dining room is rather smart. At the front of the building are some tables and chairs with more on a back terrace – there's also a stream threading its way past gently sloping lawns in the three-acre garden. The bedrooms are warm and comfortable, they're very dog-friendly, have stabling for horses and can arrange riding, fishing, shooting, hunting, wildlife-watching, cycling and trekking.

Tasty food using west country produce includes lunchtime baguettes and sandwiches, twice-baked cheese soufflé with red onion jam, tiger prawns with saffron and tomato sauce, wild boar and apple sausages with wholegrain mustard mash and caramelised onion sauce, braised lamb shoulder with loin, spinach, cauliflower purée and lamb jus, bass on spaghetti in tomato fondue with sauce vierge, and puddings such as blueberry soufflé with champagne sorbet and creamy rice pudding with salted caramel. *Benchmark main dish: beef in ale pie £13.95. Two-course evening meal £19.00.*

Free house ~ Licensees Sara and Dan Whittaker ~ Real ale ~ Open 12-11 ~ Bar food 12-2.30, 6-9 ~ Restaurant ~ Children welcome ~ Dogs allowed in bar and bedrooms ~ Wi-fi ~ Bedrooms: £75/£135 *Recommended by Geoff and Ann Marston, William Slade*

FROME
ST7747   Map 2
Archangel
(01373) 456111 – www.archangelfrome.com
King Street; BA11 1BH

Ancient place with contemporary design, several eating and drinking areas, a bustling atmosphere, rewarding food, and drink and courtyard seats; bedrooms

In a historic market town, this old place, which dates back to the Domesday Book, opened its doors as an inn in 1311. It's quite a surprise inside. They've kept the ancient beams and walls and added contemporary artwork and touches of glass, steel, slate and leather throughout. The bar is bustling and convivial with a good mix and age range of customers sitting on wall banquettes or at high tables and chairs dotted around the room; the brick walls are painted white and there's a strip of blue neon lighting at ground level. They keep Ramsbury Same Again, Ringwood Boondoggle and a guest ale on handpump, good wines by the glass and a large cocktail list. Stairs lead up to the restaurant with its rather dramatic glass-enclosed mezzanine cube, there are mustard yellow and pale green leather chairs around a mix of tables on big floorboards, high rafters lined with electric candles and a large carved angel on a plinth; background music. A long slate-floored passageway links this main part to a two-roomed snug area that has big leather sofas and armchairs and an open fire, and a small, rather cosy dining room. The central courtyard has colourful tables and chairs and a mediterranean feel.

Food includes lunchtime sandwiches, rope-grown mussels in cider and thyme, chicken livers with pancetta and toasted brioche, gnocchi with roast chicory, hazelnuts and parmesan, chicken caesar salad, beer-battered fish and chips, a pie of the day, roast cod with celeriac boulangère, lamb rump with braised neck croquette, rosemary mash and broccoli purée, salmon fillet with roast cauliflower, butter beans, chorizo and parsley oil, and puddings such as rhubarb and ginger cheesecake and dark chocolate brownie. *Benchmark main dish: duck breast with griddled sweet potato, spring onion and spinach and a duck egg £16.95. Two-course evening meal £23.00.*

Free house ~ Licensee Ross Nicol ~ Real ale ~ Open 7am-11pm (midnight Sat) ~ Bar food 12-2.30, 6-9.30; 12-5, 6-9.30 weekends ~ Restaurant ~ Children welcome ~ Dogs allowed in bar and bedrooms ~ Wi-fi ~ Bedrooms: £70/£90 *Recommended by Geoff and Ann Marston, Lance and Sarah Milligan*

HINTON ST GEORGE
ST4212 Map 1
Lord Poulett Arms 🏅 ♀ 🛏
(01460) 73149 – www.lordpoulettarms.com
Off A30 W of Crewkerne and off Merriott road (declassified – former A356, off B3165) N of Crewkerne; TA17 8SE

Thatched 17th-c stone inn with top class food, good choice of drinks and pretty garden; attractive bedrooms

The several attractive and cosy linked bar areas in this civilised inn have hop-draped beams, walls made of honey-coloured stone or painted in bold Farrow & Ball colours, and rugs on bare boards or flagstones; also, open fires (one in an inglenook, another in a raised fireplace that separates two rooms), antique brass candelabra, fresh flowers and candles, and some lovely old farmhouse, windsor and ladderback chairs around fine oak or elm tables. Branscombe Vale Bitter, Otter Ale and St Austell Trelawny on handpump, 13 wines by the glass, home-made cordial, some interesting spirits and local bottled cider and perry; background music, chess and backgammon. The pub cat is called Honey. Outside, beneath a wisteria-clad pergola, are white metalwork tables and chairs in a mediterranean-style, lavender-edged gravelled area, and picnic-sets in a wild flower meadow; boules. Bedrooms are pretty and the breakfasts splendid. This is a peaceful and attractive village with nice surrounding walks.

 As well as a two- and three-course menu of the day, the imaginative food includes sandwiches, mussels in curry and coconut sauce, local duck leg with pink grapefruit, endive, toasted almonds and mustard dressing, cumin-dusted cauliflower with spiced dhal and garlic butter, cider-battered fish and chips, pie of the day, burger with rarebit, pickles and chips, a fish dish of the day, slow-cooked pork belly with spelt spaetzle, mustard cream and pickled vegetable salad, and puddings such as dark chocolate délice with burnt orange sorbet and praline and peanut butter mousse with peanut streusel, raspberry gel and 'jumbleberry' sorbet. *Benchmark main dish: lamb rump with shoulder shepherd's pie and rosemary jus £19.50. Two-course evening meal £23.00.*

Free house ~ Licensees Steve Hill and Michelle Paynton ~ Real ale ~ Open 12-11 ~ Bar food 12-2.30, 6.30-9.15; 12-3, 7-9.15 Sun ~ Children welcome ~ Dogs allowed in bar ~ Wi-fi ~ Live music summer Sun afternoons ~ Bedrooms: £65/£95 *Recommended by Ian Malone, Tim and Sarah Smythe-Brown, Charles Todd*

HOLCOMBE
ST6649 Map 2
Holcombe Inn 🏅 🛏
(01761) 232478 – www.holcombeinn.co.uk
Off A367; Stratton Road; BA3 5EB

Charming inn with far-reaching views, cosy bars, a wide choice of drinks and good food; lovely bedrooms

A thoroughly enjoyable all-rounder, this well run place remains a big hit with our readers. The cosy room to the right of the main entrance has sofas around a central table and an open woodburning stove. To the left is the bar: fine old flagstones, window seats and chunky captain's chairs around pine-topped tables, and a carved wooden counter where they serve Bath Gem, Butcombe Bitter and Otter Bitter on handpump, 21 wines and champagne by the glass, 25 malt whiskies, cocktails and a thoughtful choice of local drinks (cider, vodka, sloe gin, various juices); board games and background music. A two-way woodburning stove also warms the dining room, which is partly carpeted and partly flagstoned, and has partitioning creating snug seating areas, a mix of high-backed patterned or leather and brass-studded dining chairs around all sorts of tables; daily newspapers. A little sitting area leads off here and serves specialist teas and coffees. The bedrooms are well equipped and some have views over peaceful farmland to Downside Abbey's school; there are picnic-sets on a terrace and side lawn, and the sunsets can be stunning.

 Rewarding and very popular, the food includes sandwiches, crispy duck samosa with hoisin, soy and honey reduction, seared tiger prawns on chilli, ginger and noodle salad, sharing boards, mushroom stroganoff, honey-roast ham and eggs, smoked salmon in creamy sauce with pasta, olives, spinach and tomatoes, guinea fowl with bacon and roast garlic stuffing, creamed leeks and jus, brill fillet on prawn and herb risotto and samphire, neck and noisette of lamb with vegetable tagine, quinoa and braising juices, and puddings such as lime and lemon cheesecake and eton mess chocolate melt. *Benchmark main dish: pie of the day £13.95. Two-course evening meal £21.95.*

Free house ~ Licensee Julie Berry ~ Real ale ~ Open 8am-11pm ~ Bar food 12-2.30, 6-9; 12-9 Fri-Sun ~ Restaurant ~ Children welcome ~ Dogs allowed in bar and bedrooms ~ Wi-fi ~ Bedrooms: £75/£120 *Recommended by Cynthia Awad, Isobel Mackinlay, Lyn and Geoff Hallchurch*

HUISH EPISCOPI   ST4326   Map 1
Rose & Crown ⬤ £
(01458) 250494
Off A372 E of Langport; TA10 9QT

17th-c pub with local cider and real ales, simple food and a friendly welcome from long-serving licensees

The same friendly family have run this unspoilt thatched inn for more than 146 years; it's known locally as 'Eli's' after the licensees' grandfather. There's no bar as such, just a central flagstoned still room where drinks are served: Teignworthy Reel Ale and a couple of guests such as Glastonbury Mystery Tor and Hop Back Summer Lightning, local farm cider and Somerset cider brandy. The casual little front parlours, with their unusual pointed-arch windows, have family photographs, books, cribbage, dominoes, shove-ha'penny and bagatelle and attract a good mix of both locals and visitors. A much more orthodox big back extension has pool, a games machine and a juke box. There are plenty of seats and tables in the extensive outdoor area and two lawns – one is enclosed and has a children's play area; you can camp (by arrangement to pub customers) on the adjoining paddock. There's also a separate skittle alley, a large car park, morris men (in summer) and fine nearby river walks; the site of the Battle of Langport (1645) is not far.

Fairly priced traditional food includes sandwiches, good soups, cottage pie, a vegetarian tart, pork, apple and cider cobbler, chicken in tarragon sauce, and puddings such as sticky toffee pudding and apple crumble. *Benchmark main dish: steak in ale pie £8.75. Two-course evening meal £13.00.*

Free house ~ Licensees Maureen Pittard, Stephen Pittard and Patricia O'Malley ~ Real ale ~ No credit cards ~ Open 11.30-2.30, 5.30-11; 11.30-11.30 Fri, Sat; 12-10.30 Sun ~ Bar food

12-2, 5.30-7.30; not Sun evening ~ Children welcome ~ Dogs welcome ~ Wi-fi ~ Live music last Thurs of month, folk singaround third Sat of month (except June-Aug)
Recommended by Robert Colledge, David Longhurst, Lindy Andrews

KINGSDON
ST5126   Map 2

Kingsdon Inn

(01935) 840543 – www.kingsdoninn.co.uk
At Podimore roundabout on A303, follow signs to Langport (A372) then right on B3151; TA11 7LG

Charming old thatched pub with low-ceilinged rooms, west country beers, friendly staff and well thought-of food; bedrooms

If you want to escape the A303, head for this warmly friendly former cider house where you can be sure of a good meal. The main bar has a woodburning stove, built-in wooden and cushioned wall seats with pretty scatter cushions, farmhouse and wheelback chairs around scrubbed kitchen tables set with candles and fresh flowers, and red quarry tiles on the floor; background classical music and TV. Some steps lead up to a carpeted dining area with a few low sagging beams, half-panelled walls and similar furnishings; one table is snugly set into a former inglenook fireplace. The stools on pale tiles against the counter are popular, and courteous, helpful staff serve Butcombe Bitter and St Austell Tribute on handpump, 14 wines by the glass and local farm cider. There's a second dining area plus an attractive separate restaurant with another woodburning stove. The garden has picnic-sets on grass, a herb garden and a small cottagey path leading to the front door. The pub is handy for the Fleet Air Arm Museum.

 The rewarding food uses local produce, and the bread, ice-creams and crackers for cheese are made in-house: smoked duck caesar salad with parmesan, wild boar with pasta and black truffle oil, massaman vegetable curry, burger with spicy tomato relish and chips, cider-braised crispy pork belly with caramelised red onions and five spice-infused cooking juices, parma ham-wrapped rose veal with mozzarella-stuffed rump, carrot purée and cep velouté, and puddings such as roasted fig, caramelised fig financier and fig compote with amaretto ice-cream and toasted almond, caramel and white chocolate parfait with raspberry sorbet and raspberry mousse. *Benchmark main dish: crab and ale rarebit with fries £11.00. Two-course evening meal £20.00.*

Game Bird Inns ~ Managers Adam Cain and Cinzia Lezzi ~ Real ale ~ Open 12-3, 6-11; 12-3, 7-10.30 Sun ~ Bar food 12-2, 6.30-9; 12-3, 7-10.30 Sun ~ Children welcome ~ Dogs allowed in bar and bedrooms ~ Wi-fi ~ Bedrooms: £65/£95 *Recommended by P and J Shapley, Ian Herdman, Mrs Zara Elliott, Andrew Vincent*

MELLS
ST7249   Map 2

Talbot

(01373) 812254 – www.talbotinn.com
W of Frome, off A362 or A361; BA11 3PN

Carefully refurbished and interesting old coaching inn, real ales and good wines, inventive food and seats in courtyard; lovely bedrooms

Showing noticeable attention to detail, the bedrooms in this handsome former coaching inn are smart and stylish and breakfasts are excellent. The bustling candlelit bar is nicely informal with various wooden tables and chairs on big quarry tiles, a woodburning stove in a stone fireplace, and stools (much used by locals) against the counter where friendly, helpful staff serve a beer named for the pub (from Keystone), Butcombe Bitter and a couple of guests such as Butcombe Big IPA and Hop Back Citra on handpump, several good wines by the glass and a farm cider. The two interconnected dining rooms have brass-studded leather chairs around wooden tables, a log fire with candles in fine clay cups on the mantelpiece above and lots of coaching prints on the walls; quiet background music and board games. There's a mediterranean air to the courtyard with its pale green metalwork chairs and tables. Off here, in separate buildings, are the enjoyable, rustic-feeling sitting room with sofas, chairs and tables, smart magazines, a huge mural and vast glass bottles (free films or popular TV programmes are shown here on Sunday evenings), and the grill room, where food is cooked simply on a big open fire overlooked by 18th-c portraits. Until the dissolution of the monasteries in the early 16th c, this village was owned by Glastonbury Abbey – do visit the lovely church where Siegfried Sassoon is buried; the walled gardens opposite the inn are very pretty. This is sister pub to the Beckford Arms at Fonthill Gifford (Wiltshire).

Accomplished food includes sandwiches, lamb and veal fritter with harissa yoghurt and charred onions, cured sea trout with radishes, carrots, sour cream and crispy nettles, beer-battered fish and chips, pearl barley risotto with sweetbreads, wild garlic and parmesan, cod, lemon and dill fregola with romanesco purée and roasted crab bisque, pork chop with creamed potato, kale and anchovy and parsley butter, and puddings such as white chocolate cheesecake with quince sorbet and hazelnut granola and blood orange jelly with meringue, lemon curd, basil and vanilla ice-cream. *Benchmark main dish: burger with toppings and chips £12.50. Two-course evening meal £20.00.*

Free house ~ Licensee Matt Greenlees ~ Real ale ~ Open 8am-11pm ~ Bar food 12-3, 6-9.30 ~ Restaurant ~ Children welcome ~ Dogs welcome ~ Wi-fi ~ Bedrooms: /£100
Recommended by Miss B D Picton, Ann and Colin Hunt, David and Judy Robison, S G N Bennett, Edward Mirzoeff, Chris and Angela Buckell, Richard Mason

 MIDFORD   ST7660   Map 2
Hope & Anchor
(01225) 832296 – www.hopeandanchormidford.co.uk
Bath Road (B3110); BA2 7DD

Welcoming old pub with popular food and several real ales

Parts of this friendly place date from the 17th c and as it's at the heart of the Cam Valley it makes a fine spot for a lunch break. Open-plan and neatly kept by the long-serving licensees, it has a civilised bar plus a heavy-beamed restaurant with a long cushioned settle against red-patterned wallpaper, a mix of dark wooden dining chairs and tables on flagstones and a woodburning stove. The back conservatory is modern, stylish and popular with families. Otter Amber, Sharps Doom Bar and a guest on handpump, 11 wines by the glass and a farm cider are served by courteous staff. Outside, there are seats on the sheltered back terrace which has an upper tier. The pub is on the Colliers Way cycling/walking path and near walks on the disused Somerset & Dorset Railway.

Generous helpings of carefully chosen food include lunchtime panini, deep-fried camembert with onion marmalade, smoked salmon and prawn salad with lemon and dill dressing, home-cooked ham and eggs, pork and leek sausages with onion and mushroom cream sauce, duck with stir-fried vegetables and plum sauce on noodles, paprika pork fillet with creamed leeks and stilton, cajun chicken salad with peppers, tomatoes, courgettes and avocado, and puddings such as eton mess with strawberry coulis and chocolate brownie with white chocolate sauce. *Benchmark main dish: steak and mushroom in ale pie £12.50. Two-course evening meal £21.00.*

Free house ~ Licensee Richard Smolarek ~ Real ale ~ Open 11.30-3, 6-11; 11.30-11 Sat,
Sun ~ Bar food 12-2 (3 weekends), 6-9.30 ~ Restaurant ~ Children welcome ~ Dogs allowed
in bar ~ Wi-fi *Recommended by Harvey Brown, Julian Richardson, Tim King*

MILVERTON
ST1225 Map 1

Globe

(01823) 400534 – www.theglobemilverton.co.uk
Fore Street; TA4 1JX

**Bustling and friendly inn with a welcome for all, good ales,
quite a choice of tasty food and seats outside; bedrooms**

Although locals do pop in for a pint of Otter Bitter, Quantock Ale or
a guest beer on handpump served by cheerful, helpful staff, most
customers are here for the very good food. This is a handsome former
coaching inn and the opened-up rooms have solid rustic tables surrounded
by an attractive mix of wooden or high-backed black leather chairs, artwork
on pale-painted walls above a red dado, and a big gilt-edged mirror above
a woodburning stove in an ornate fireplace; background music and board
games. Bar chairs line the counter where they keep ten wines by the glass
and local farm cider. The sheltered outside terrace has raffia-style chairs and
tables and cushioned wall seating under parasols. The two bedrooms are
comfortable and breakfasts are continental.

Local produce is at the heart of everything; the smashing seasonal food includes
sandwiches, spiced lamb and feta filo parcels with harissa yoghurt, tempura
tiger prawns with sweet chilli sauce, smoked haddock and pea risotto with poached
egg, potato and parsnip gnocchi with cheddar, sage and apple, fish and leek pie, burger
with toppings and chips, duck breast with ratatouille, cornish cod with bacon and bean
cassoulet, and puddings. *Benchmark main dish: honey-glazed slow-roasted pork belly
with shallots and garlic £14.95. Two-course evening meal £20.00.*

Free house ~ Licensees Mark and Adele Tarry ~ Real ale ~ Open 12-3, 6-11 (11.30 Sat);
12-3 Sun; closed Sunday evening, Mon lunchtime ~ Bar food 12-2, 6.30-9 ~ Restaurant ~
Children welcome ~ Dogs allowed in bar ~ Wi-fi ~ Bedrooms: £60/£65 *Recommended by
Lyn and Geoff Hallchurch, Valerie Sayer, Colin and Daniel Gibbs*

MONKSILVER
ST0737 Map 1

Notley Arms

(01984) 656095 – www.notleyarmsinn.co.uk
B3188; TA4 4JB

**Bustling friendly pub with a good mix of regulars and visitors,
enjoyable food and drink and seats in streamside garden; bedrooms**

Very well run by friendly licensees, this pub is in a lovely village on the
edge of Exmoor National Park. Each of the open-plan bar rooms has
its own atmosphere: two open fires plus two woodburning stoves (the one
in the lounge is fronted by chesterfield sofas), cushioned window seats
and settles, an appealing collection of old dining chairs around mixed
wooden tables on slate tiles or flagstones, original paintings on cream walls
and panelling, and fresh flowers, church candles and big stone bottles;
background music. Tractor seats line the bar where they keep Exmoor Ale,
St Austell Tribute and Sleaford Pleasant Pheasant on handpump, 30 wines
by the glass, 20 malt whiskies and farm cider; staff are courteous and helpful.
At the bottom of the neat garden is a clear-running stream and plenty of
picnic-sets on grass; a heated, circular wooden pavilion is just right for
a party of 12; boules. The attractive and comfortable bedrooms are in the
former coach house; one is suitable for disabled customers.

Very good food includes sandwiches, free-range scotch egg with sweet chilli sauce, whipped goats cheese mousse with beetroot and celery salad, rare-breed sausages with onion gravy, artichoke, palm heart and pine nut pithivier with spinach and basil oil, venison steak burger with coleslaw and triple-cooked chips, bream fillet on crab and prawn cannelloni with butternut squash, 10oz steak with wild mushroom and pepper sauce, and puddings such as chocolate fondant with blackberry ice-cream and banana and almond parfait with raspberry coulis and mango sorbet. *Benchmark main dish: fillet of hake with pea and sorrel risotto and beurre blanc £17.00. Two-course evening meal £20.00.*

Free house ~ Licensees Simon and Caroline Murphy ~ Real ale ~ Open 8am-11pm ~ Bar food 12-2, 6-9 ~ Restaurant ~ Children welcome ~ Dogs welcome ~ Wi-fi ~ Bedrooms: £59/£64 *Recommended by Richard and Penny Gibbs, Mike and Lynne Steane, Bob and Margaret Holder, Mike and Mary Carter, Lynda and Trevor Smith*

MONKTON COMBE   ST7761   Map 2
Wheelwrights Arms 🛏️
(01225) 722287 – www.wheelwrightsarms.co.uk
Just off A36 S of Bath; Church Cottages; BA2 7HB

18th-c stone pub with cheerful customers, helpful landlord and staff, good food and seats outside; comfortable bedrooms

Bath is nearby and the peaceful village here is surrounded by picturesque hills and valleys, so it's not surprising that this friendly place gets booked up pretty quickly. At one end of the bar-dining room is an open fire in a raised fireplace with logs piled on either side, cushioned and wood-planked built-in wall seats, rush-seated or cushioned high-backed dining chairs around tables (each set with a small lamp), parquet flooring or carpet, and old photographs and oil paintings (the one above the fireplace of a dog is particularly nice). The middle room has some pretty frieze work, a high shelf of wooden wader birds and stools against the green-painted counter where they keep Butcombe Bitter and Otter Bitter on handpump, 15 wines by the glass and farm cider; background jazz and board games. A small end room is just right for a group. The gravelled terraces have wood and metal tables and chairs and picnic-sets. This is an enjoyable place to stay and the bedrooms, in a restored annexe, are quiet, well equipped and comfortable.

🍴 Extremely tasty food includes sandwiches, ham hock, potato and parsley terrine, gin and tonic-cured salmon with pickled cucumber and lemon crème fraîche, wild mushroom, spinach and parmesan risotto, sausages of the day with mash and gravy, cornish fish stew with saffron potato and aioli, local game ragoût with pasta and gremolata, and puddings such as orange and ginger treacle tart and sticky toffee pudding with butterscotch sauce. *Benchmark main dish: beer-battered fish and chips £13.50. Two-course evening meal £23.00.*

Free house ~ Licensee David Munn ~ Real ale ~ Open 8am-11pm ~ Bar food 12-2, 6-9.30 ~ Children welcome ~ Dogs allowed in bar ~ Wi-fi ~ Bedrooms: £85/£160 *Recommended by Dr Simon Innes, Carol and Barry Craddock, Richard Mason*

ODCOMBE   ST5015   Map 2
Masons Arms 🍺 🛏️
(01935) 862591 – www.masonsarmsodcombe.co.uk
Off A3088 or A30 just W of Yeovil; Lower Odcombe; BA22 8TX

Own-brew beers and tasty food in pretty thatched cottage; bedrooms

Bedrooms here are well equipped and comfortable and the breakfasts are good and hearty – our readers recommend them. It's a popular place with own-brew beers served by friendly staff. The simple little bar has joists and a couple of standing timbers, a mix of cushioned dining chairs around all sorts of tables on cream and blue patterned carpet, and a couple of tub chairs and a table in the former inglenook fireplace. Up a step is a similar area, while more steps lead down to a dining room with a squashy brown sofa and a couple of cushioned dining chairs in front of a woodburning stove; the sandstone walls are hung with black and white local photographs and country prints. Their own ales are Odcombe No.1, Roly Poly and seasonal beers on handpump, they make their own sloe and elderflower cordials, have 11 wines by the glass and serve farm cider. There's a thatched smokers' shelter and picnic-sets in the garden, plus a vegetable patch and chicken coop and a campsite.

Using home-grown and other local produce, the good food includes sandwiches, smoked haddock scotch egg with curried mayonnaise, mushroom risotto, dry-cured gammon steak with duck egg, corn-fed chicken breast stuffed with sunblush tomatoes on pesto tagliatelle, burger with toppings and triple-cooked chips, duck leg with chorizo and pancetta cassoulet and butter bean purée, and puddings such as chocolate and amaretto mousse and sloe gin crème brûlée; brunch is served 8am-2pm daily. *Benchmark main dish: liver and bacon with bubble and squeak £14.75. Two-course evening meal £20.00.*

Own brew ~ Licensees Drew Read and Paula Tennyson ~ Real ale ~ Open 8am-3pm, 6-midnight ~ Bar food 12-2, 6.30-9.30 ~ Children welcome ~ Dogs welcome ~ Wi-fi ~ Bedrooms: £60/£90 *Recommended by Mr and Mrs P R Thomas, Edward Lubbock, JPC, S G N Bennett*

PITNEY
Halfway House 🍺 £

ST4527 Map 1

(01458) 252513 – www.thehalfwayhouse.co.uk
Just off B3153 W of Somerton; TA10 9AB

Bustling, friendly local with nine real ales, local ciders and good simple food

As ever, our readers love their visits here. It's an unpretentious village local with a fine range of up to ten regularly changing beers. The atmosphere is chatty and easy-going and there's a good cross-section of cheerful customers in the three old-fashioned rooms which have communal tables, roaring log fires and a homely feel underlined by a profusion of books, maps and newspapers. Tapped from the cask, the ales might include Bays Gold, Branscombe Vale Summa This, Butcombe Rare Breed, Dark Star American Pale Ale, Exmoor Gold, Hop Back Summer Lightning, Otter Bright, Teignworthy Reel Ale and Whitstable East India Pale Ale; also, four farm ciders, a dozen malt whiskies and several wines by the glass; board games. There are tables outside.

Fairly priced simple food includes lunchtime sandwiches, ham and eggs, faggots with mash and onion gravy, a pie of the day, venison burger with red onion jam and chips, a casserole of the day and chilli beef. *Benchmark main dish: beer-battered fish and chips £9.50. Two-course evening meal £16.00.*

Free house ~ Licensee Mark Phillips ~ Real ale ~ Open 11.30-3, 4.30-11; 11.30-3, 4.30-midnight Fri, Sat; 12-11 Sun ~ Bar food 12-2.30, 7-9.30; 1-5 Sun ~ Children welcome ~ Dogs welcome ~ Wi-fi *Recommended by Bob and Margaret Holder, Richard and Penny Gibbs, Mr Yeldahn, S G N Bennett*

Tipping is not normal for bar meals, and not usually expected.

PRIDDY ST5250 Map 2

Queen Victoria £

(01749) 676385 – www.thequeenvicpriddy.co.uk

Village signed off B3135; Pelting Drove; BA5 3BA

Stone-built country pub with open fires and woodburners, friendly atmosphere, real ales and honest food; seats outside

There's plenty of room for all here, both inside and out – it's very popular locally and also with walkers (plus their dogs) and cyclists. The various dimly lit rooms and alcoves have a lot of character and plenty of original features, and customers are chatty and cheerful. One room leading off the main bar has a log fire in a big old stone fireplace with a huge cauldron to one side. There are flagstoned or slate floors, bare stone walls (the smarter dining room is half panelled and half painted), horse tack, farm tools and photos of Queen Victoria. Furniture is traditional: cushioned wall settles, farmhouse and other solid chairs around all manner of wooden tables, a nice old pew beside a screen settle making a cosy alcove, and high chairs next to the bar counter where they serve Butcombe Bitter and Rare Breed and Fullers London Pride on handpump, two farm ciders, eight malt whiskies and nine wines by the glass. There are seats in the front courtyard and more across the lane where there's also a children's playground. There is access for wheelchairs.

Good value traditional food includes baguettes, smoked salmon and prawn cocktail, deep-fried brie wedges with plum sauce, ham and eggs, brie and beetroot tart, beefburger and scampi with chips, a curry of the day, lasagne, chilli beef, and puddings. *Benchmark main dish: beef in ale pie £9.95. Two-course evening meal £13.00.*

Butcombe ~ Tenant Mark Walton ~ Real ale ~ Open 12-11; 12-10.30 Sun ~ Bar food 12-2, 6-9 (all day end May-Sept); 12-9 Sat; 12-8 Sun ~ Children welcome ~ Dogs welcome ~ Wi-fi ~ Live folk second Mon of month; folk festival July *Recommended by Chris and Angela Buckell, Dave Sutton, Sophie Ellison*

SOMERTON ST4828 Map 2

White Hart

(01458) 272273 – www.whitehartsomerton.com

Market Place; TA11 7LX

Attractive old place with several bars, open fires, spacious dining room and enjoyable food; bedrooms

As this partly 16th-c pub is in a lovely village, it makes sense that it opens at 9am and serve breakfasts until 11am. The main bar has long wall seats with attractive scatter cushions, stools around small tables and big mirrors on the wall. Bath Gem, Cheddar Potholer and guests such as Blindmans Golden Spring and Yeovil Star Gazer on handpump, farm ciders and 14 wines by the glass, served by friendly staff. A doorway leads to a cosy room with a leather sofa, armchairs, a chest table and an open fire, and another snug bar is similarly furnished, while a simpler room has straightforward wooden dining chairs and tables, a little brick fireplace and some stained glass. Throughout, there are rugs on parquet flooring (some plain bare boards too), church candles, contemporary paintwork and interesting lighting – look out for the antler chandelier with its pretty hanging lampshades; background music and board games. Outside, the flower-filled terrace has tables and chairs under parasols with more on grass. Some of the airy, well equipped and comfortable bedrooms overlook the square and church.

🍴 Interesting brasserie-style food (much of it cooked in a wood-fired oven) includes chorizo sausage rolls with apple and fennel slaw, devilled crab on toast with pickled red onion salad, mushroom, leek and cider pie, rare-breed burger with toppings, truffle mayonnaise and chips, chicken stuffed with wild garlic and cheese with crispy coppa ham, polenta and grilled spring onions, lemon sole with gherkin, caper and dill butter, and puddings such as marmalade bread and butter pudding and chocolate and salted caramel tart with home-made ice-cream and honeycomb. *Benchmark main dish: pork belly with orange gremolata £16.50. Two-course evening meal £22.00.*

Free house ~ Licensee Kirsty Schmidt ~ Real ale ~ Open 9am-11pm (10.30pm Sun) ~
Bar food 12-3, 6 (5 Sat)-9.45; 12-9 Sun ~ Restaurant ~ Children welcome ~ Dogs
allowed in bar and bedrooms ~ Wi-fi ~ Live music monthly ~ Bedrooms: /£85
Recommended by Martin Jones, Isobel Mackinlay, Hugh Roberts, Peter and Emma Kelly

STANTON WICK

ST6162   Map 2

Carpenters Arms 🍽⭐ 🍷 🛏

(01761) 490202 – www.the-carpenters-arms.co.uk
Village signposted off A368, just W of junction with A37 S of Bristol; BS39 4BX

Bustling, friendly dining pub on country lane with enjoyable food, helpful staff and fine choice of drinks; nice bedrooms

This attractive little stone pub is in peaceful countryside with good nearby walks. You can be sure of a warm welcome from the landlord and his attentive staff. Coopers Parlour on the right has a couple of beams, seats around heavy tables on a tartan carpet and attractive curtains; in the angle between here and the bar area is a wide woodburning stove in an opened-through fireplace. The bar has wall settles with cushions, stripped-stone walls and a big log fire in an inglenook. There's also a snug inner room (brightened by mirrors in arched recesses) and a restaurant with leather sofas, easy chairs and a lounge area at one end. Bath Gem, Butcombe Bitter and Sharps Doom Bar on handpump, ten wines by the glass (and some interesting bin ends) and several malt whiskies; TV in the snug. There are picnic-sets on the front terrace along with pretty flower beds, hanging baskets and tubs. Bedrooms are quiet and comfortable.

🍽 Assured cooking includes dishes such as sandwiches, salmon fishcake with saffron and garlic mayonnaise, chicken liver and wild mushroom pâté with plum and apple chutney, mussel, prawn and crayfish linguine with white wine and chive cream sauce, thai chicken curry, lamb rump with dauphinoise potatoes and red wine and rosemary sauce, braised beef on horseradish mash with wild mushroom and red wine sauce, and puddings such as maple and pecan tart with salted caramel ice-cream and chocolate brownie. *Benchmark main dish: 8oz rib-eye steak with a choice of sauces and straw fries £18.95. Two-course evening meal £21.00.*

Buccaneer Holdings ~ Manager Simon Pledge ~ Real ale ~ Open 11-11; 12-10.30 Sun ~
Bar food 12-2.30, 6-9.30 (10 Fri, Sat); 12-9 Sun ~ Restaurant ~ Children welcome ~
Dogs allowed in bar ~ Wi-fi ~ Bedrooms: £75/£110 *Recommended by Taff Thomas,
Mr and Mrs J Watkins, William and Ann Reid, Dr and Mrs A K Clarke, Mr and Mrs P R Thomas*

WATERROW

ST0525   Map 1

Rock 🍽 🛏

(01984) 623293 – www.rockinnwaterrow.co.uk
B3227 Wiveliscombe–Bampton; TA4 2AX

Handsome inn with local ales, interesting food and a nice mix of customers; comfortable bedrooms

Our readers enjoy staying in the pretty, cottagey bedrooms here – and breakfasts are good. It's a striking timbered inn built into the rock face on the edge of Exmoor National Park and the relaxed and informal bar area has dining chairs and cushioned window seats around scrubbed kitchen tables on tartan carpet, sympathetic lighting and a log fire in a stone fireplace. High black leather bar chairs line the copper-topped bar counter where they serve Quantock Wills Neck, St Austell Tribute and a guest from Otter on handpump, several wines by the glass, a dozen malt whiskies and farm cider; background music, darts and board games. The elegant restaurant is up some steps from the bar with pale grey-painted panelled walls, and there's also a snug with a big leather sofa and leather armchairs. There are seats under umbrellas out in front. Parking outside is limited but there is more on the far side of the main road over the bridge.

Cooked by the landlord, the high quality food using seasonal produce includes sandwiches, white crab layered with avocado and smoked salmon, baked local brie fondant with a melting centre and pickled beetroot, sweet potato gnocchi with spinach, chestnuts and grilled artichoke, loin of rabbit with braised lettuce and pomme purée, free-range chicken breast with creamed wild garlic, asparagus and truffle macaroni cheese, slow-cooked blade of rare-breed beef marinated in black garlic with cheddar mash and black treacle sauce, and puddings. *Benchmark main dish: shepherd's pie £12.95. Two-course evening meal £23.00.*

Free house ~ Licensees Daren and Ruth Barclay ~ Real ale ~ Open 12-3, 6-11; closed Sun evening, all day Mon, Tues lunchtime ~ Bar food 12-2, 6.30-9 ~ Restaurant ~ Children welcome ~ Dogs welcome ~ Wi-fi ~ Bedrooms: £65/£85 *Recommended by Paul Fitzpatrick, Mike and Mary Carter, Mrs K M King, Pat Mitchell*

WEDMORE

ST4348 Map 1

Swan 🍽️ ⚑ 🍺

(01934) 710337 – www.theswanwedmore.com
Cheddar Road, opposite Church Street; BS28 4EQ

Bustling place with a friendly, informal atmosphere, lots of customers, efficient service and tasty food; bedrooms

There's a lively, buoyant atmosphere here as customers drop in and out all day – for breakfasts, morning coffee and afternoon tea and lunchtime and evening bar food. Mirrors dotted about give the open-plan layout a feeling of even more space and the main bar has all sorts of wooden tables and chairs on floorboards, a wall seat with attractive scatter cushions, a woodburning stove, suede stools against the panelled counter and a rustic central table with daily papers; background music. Bath Gem, Cheddar Potholer, Otter Bitter and a guest beer on handpump, 20 wines by the glass and two farm ciders are served by quick, friendly staff. At one end of the room, a step leads down to an area with rugs on huge flagstones, a leather chesterfield, armchairs and brass-studded leather chairs, then down another step to more sofas and armchairs. The airy dining room has attractive high-backed chairs, tables set with candles in glass jars and another woodburner. There are plenty of seats and tables on the terrace and lawn, and the metal furniture among flowering tubs at the front of the building gives a continental feel.

Some sort of good food is served all day: sandwiches on home-made bread, ham hock and pheasant terrine with chutney, crispy cuttlefish with caper mayonnaise, chilli bean burger with pickles and marinated ricotta, slow-roasted duck leg with polenta, butternut caponata, crispy salami and wild mushrooms, hake fillet with saffron potatoes, mussels and leek and cider sauce, local venison ragoût with squash purée, and puddings such as rocky road sundae with toffee sauce and chocolate and salted caramel tart with ice-cream and honeycomb. *Benchmark main dish: whole plaice with tartare sauce and chips £16.50. Two-course evening meal £21.00.*

Free house ~ Licensee Natalie Zvonek-Little ~ Real ale ~ Open 9am-11pm (10.30 Sun) ~ Bar food 9am-10pm; snacks in afternoon ~ Restaurant ~ Children welcome ~ Dogs allowed in bar ~ Wi-fi ~ Bedrooms: /£100 *Recommended by Taff Thomas, John and Mary Warner, R T and J C Moggridge*

 ### WRAXALL
Battleaxes

ST4971   Map 2

(01275) 857473 – www.flatcappers.co.uk
Bristol Road B3130, E of Nailsea; BS48 1LQ

Bustling pub with relaxed dining and drinking areas, helpful staff and good food; big bedrooms with contemporary bathrooms

The spacious interior in this interesting stone-built Victorian pub is split into separate areas: polished floorboards or flagstones, portraits and pictures on walls above painted and panelled dados, mirrors on boldly patterned wallpaper, fresh flowers and house plants, books on windowsills and church candles. The bar has leather-topped stools against the counter where they keep a beer named for the pub (from Three Castles), Butcombe Bitter and a guest ale on handpump and several wines by the glass; background music. Throughout there are long pews with scatter cushions, church chairs and a medley of other wooden dining chairs around chunky tables and groups of leather armchairs; it's all very easy-going. There are picnic-sets outside and some of the spacious bedrooms have country views. Tyntesfield (National Trust) is nearby. Wheelchair access using ramps.

Tasty food includes sandwiches (until 5pm, not Sun), smoked haddock scotch egg with cauliflower purée, chicken and duck liver pâté with pickled wild mushrooms, butternut and sage ravioli with almond sauce, rump burger with relish and triple-cooked chips, corn-fed chicken with rösti potato and wild mushroom and shallot sauce, stone bass in tomato bisque with clams and haricot beans, and puddings such as sticky toffee pudding with butterscotch and pecan sauce and dark chocolate and fudge fondant with salted caramel ice-cream; steak night is Wednesday and breakfasts are served from 8am. *Benchmark main dish: local venison wellington with parsnip purée and juniper jus £18.50. Two-course evening meal £21.00.*

Flatcappers ~ Manager Ben Paxton ~ Real ale ~ Open 8am-11pm ~ Bar food 8am-10pm (9pm Sun) ~ Children welcome ~ Dogs allowed in bar ~ Wi-fi ~ Bedrooms: /£80
Recommended by Dr Simon Innes, Gus Swan, R T and J C Moggridge

WRINGTON
Plough

ST4762   Map 2

(01934) 862871 – www.theploughatwrington.co.uk
2.5 miles off A370 Bristol–Weston, from bottom of Rhodiate Hill; BS40 5QA

Welcoming pub with bustling bar and two dining rooms, good food, well kept beer and seats outside

As this neatly kept and well run village pub is so popular, it's best to book a table in advance. The bar is chatty and convivial, with locals perched on stools against the counter where they keep Butcombe Bitter (the brewery is in the village), Black Sheep and Youngs Special on handpump and 18 wines by the glass served by friendly and efficient staff. The two dining rooms (the one at the back has plenty of big windows overlooking the gazebo and garden) have open doorways and throughout you'll find (three) winter fires, slate or wooden floors, beams and standing timbers, plenty of pictures on the planked, red or yellow walls and all manner of high-backed leather or wooden dining or farmhouse chairs around tables of many sizes. Also, fresh flowers, table skittles and a chest of games. There are picnic-sets at the front and on the back grass; boules. They hold a farmers' market on the second Friday of the month. This is sister pub to the Rattlebone at Sherston (Wiltshire). Disabled access.

🍴 Appealing food includes sandwiches, creamy smoked haddock with spinach, cheese and poached egg, game terrine with wild mushrooms and pickled shallots, pork, apple and cider sausages with cheddar and spring onion mash and onion gravy, roasted beetroot with quinoa, hazelnuts, pomegranate and spinach with beetroot dressing, duck breast with carrot and cumin purée and orange jus, and puddings such as dark chocolate délice with bourbon crumbs and salted caramel sauce and orange crème brûlée with apricots. *Benchmark main dish: lamb rump with apricot herb crust and shoulder with pea purée and jus £13.95. Two-course evening meal £17.00.*

Youngs ~ Tenant Jason Read ~ Real ale ~ Open 12-3, 5-11; 12-midnight Fri, Sat; 12-11 Sun ~ Bar food 12-2.30, 6-9.30; 12-5 Sun ~ Restaurant ~ Children welcome ~ Dogs welcome ~ Wi-fi *Recommended by Chris and Angela Buckell, Bob and Margaret Holder, Dr and Mrs A K Clarke, Michael Doswell, Tracey and Stephen Groves*

Also Worth a Visit in Somerset

Besides the fully inspected pubs, you might like to try these pubs that have been recommended to us and described by readers. Do tell us what you think of them: feedback@goodguides.com

ACTON TURVILLE   ST8080
Fox & Hounds (01454) 218224
Tormarton Road (B4039); GL9 1HW
Busy traditional village pub, good home-made food from varied menu including popular Sun roasts with up to ten different vegetables, well kept changing ales, local cider and keenly priced wines, good coffee too, efficient friendly service, panelled main bar with a few contemporary touches, rooms off including plainer snug; children welcome. *(Michael Doswell)*

APPLEY   ST0721
Globe (01823) 672327
Hamlet signposted from the network of back roads between A361 and A38, W of B3187 and W of Milverton and Wellington; OS Sheet 181 map reference 072215; TA21 0HJ Traditional 15th-c village pub; entrance corridor with serving hatch, simple pubby furnishings in beamed front room, another with 1930s railway posters and GWR bench, further room with easy chairs, three local ales and traditional cider, good range of sensibly priced home-made food including specials, friendly service; skittle alley; children, walkers and dogs welcome, picnic-sets in garden with play area, path opposite leading to River Tone, closed Sun evening, Mon, otherwise open all day. *(Bob and Margaret Holder)*

AXBRIDGE   ST4354
Lamb (01934) 732253
The Square; off A371 Cheddar–Winscombe; BS26 2AP Big rambling carpeted pub with heavy 15th-c beams and timbers, stone and roughcast walls, large stone fireplaces, old settles, unusual bar front with bottles set in plaster, Butcombe and a guest, well chosen wine and good coffee, generous food (all day Sat, till 6pm Sun) from sandwiches and baked potatoes up, lunch deal (Tues, Thurs), they may ask for a credit card if you run a tab, board games, table skittles and alley; sports TV; children and dogs allowed, seats out at front and in small sheltered back garden, medieval King John's Hunting Lodge (NT) opposite, open all day. *(Ann and Colin Hunt, Roger and Donna Huggins)*

BACKWELL   ST4969
George (01275) 462770
Farleigh Road; A370 W of Bristol; BS48 3PG Modernised and extended main road dining pub (former coaching inn), popular food in bar and restaurant from sandwiches and sharing boards up, two-for-one pizzas before 6pm Mon-Sat, well kept Bath, Butcombe, St Austell and a guest, good choice of wines; background music in some areas; children and dogs welcome, gravel terrace and lawn behind, seven bedrooms, open all day. *(Simon Sharpe)*

BARROW GURNEY ST5367

Princes Motto (01275) 472282

B3130, just off A370/A38; BS48 3RY
Cosy and welcoming, with unpretentious
local feel in traditional tap room, long lounge/
dining area up behind, four Wadworths ales
with Butcombe as guest, modestly priced
simple lunchtime food (all day Fri, breakfast
available Sat), log fire, some panelling, cricket
team photographs, jugs and china; dogs
welcome, pleasant garden with terrace, open
all day. *(Taff Thomas)*

BATCOMBE ST6839

★ Three Horseshoes (01749) 850359

*Village signposted off A359 Bruton–
Frome; BA4 6HE* Handsome honey-
coloured stone inn with long narrow main
room, beams, local pictures, built-in
cushioned window seats and nice mix of
tables, woodburner one end, open fire the
other, Butcombe, Wild Beer and a couple of
guests, local ciders, around a dozen wines
by the glass and several malt whiskies,
very good food (best to book, especially
weekends), efficient service, attractive
stripped-stone dining room; open mike
night last Thurs of month; children and dogs
welcome, three simple but pretty bedrooms,
lovely church next door, open all day
weekends. *(Ann and Colin Hunt)*

BATH ST7464

Bath Brew House (01225) 805609

James Street West; BA1 2BX Interesting
spaciously converted pub visibly brewing its
own James Street beers, also guest ales and
craft kegs, food from open kitchen including
spit-roasts, various events such as comedy
nights in upstairs room with own bar and
sports TV; well behaved children and dogs
allowed in some areas, sizeable split-level
beer garden with covered eating area,
summer barbecues, open (and food) all day.
(Dr and Mrs A K Clarke)

BATH ST7565

Bell (01225) 460426

Walcot Street; BA1 5BW Long narrow split-
level pub owned by the local community;
nine real ales and traditional cider, some
basic good value food, lots of pump clips
and gig notices, a couple of fires (one gas),
bar billiards and table football; packed and
lively in the evenings with regular live music
and DJ sets, board game nights, free wi-fi;
canopied garden, even has its own laundrette,
open all day. *(James Allsopp)*

BATH ST7564

Boater (01225) 464211

*Argyle Street, by Pulteney Bridge;
BA2 4BQ* Refurbished Fullers pub in good
spot near river, fairly traditional bare-boards
bar with at least five well kept ales, fine
range of draught/bottled craft beers and
good choice of wines by the glass, popular
fairly priced food from lunchtime sandwiches
and pub favourites up, quick friendly service,
upstairs restaurant with nice view of weir,
cosy cellar bar; children and dogs welcome,
sizeable back terrace on two levels, open all
day (till 1am Fri, Sat). *(Dr and Mrs A K Clarke)*

BATH ST7564

★ Coeur de Lion (01225) 463568

*Northumberland Place, off High Street
by W H Smith; BA1 5AR* Tiny stained-
glass-fronted single-room pub, simple, cosy
and friendly, with candles and log-effect gas
fire, well kept Abbey ales and guests, good
well priced traditional food from snacks
and baguettes up (vegetarian options),
Christmas mulled wine, more room and loos
upstairs; may be background music; tables
out in charming flower-filled flagstoned
pedestrian alley, open all day, food till 6pm.
(Dr and Mrs A K Clarke)

BATH ST7564

★ Crystal Palace (01225) 482666

Abbey Green; BA1 1NW Spacious
two-room Fullers pub, rugs on wood floors
and comfortable mix of seating, panelled
walls and groups of pictures, popular sensibly
priced food from lunchtime sandwiches up,
Somerset cheese and port menu, speedy
friendly service, four well kept ales from
plank-faced bar, log fire, garden room
opening on to nice sheltered courtyard;
background music, sports TV, free wi-fi;
children and dogs welcome, handy for Roman
Baths and main shopping areas, open (and
food) all day. *(Roger and Anne Newbury,
Dr and Mrs A K Clarke)*

BATH ST7464

Garricks Head (01225) 318368

*St Johns Place/Westgate, beside Theatre
Royal; BA1 1ET* Civilised and relaxed
dining pub; bar with tall windows, wheelback
and other chairs around wooden tables on
bare boards, candles and a couple of sizeable
brass chandeliers, gas-effect coal fire with
fine silver meat domes on wall above, four
interesting regional ales, real ciders and
decent wines by the glass, proper cocktails,
good food including pre-theatre menu,
separate smartly set dining room; may be soft
background jazz; children and dogs (in bar)
welcome, pavement tables, open all day.
(Charles Todd)

BATH ST7564

Graze (01225) 429392

Behind Bath Spa station; BA1 1SX
Spacious Bath Ales bar-restaurant (part
of the city's Vaults development) arranged
over upper floor and served by lift; modern
steel and glass construction with leather
chairs and benches on wood-strip flooring,
slatted ceiling with exposed ducting and
pendant lighting, good selection of beers
(some from on-site microbrewery, can be
pricey), extensive range of wines and spirits,

enjoyable food cooked in open kitchen from light dishes to Josper grills, good value weekday set lunch; children welcome, disabled facilities, two sizeable terraces overlooking Bath one side, the station the other, life-size models of cows, pigs and chickens, open all day from 8am (9am weekends) for breakfast. *(Chris and Angela Buckell, Dr and Mrs A K Clarke)*

BATH ST7465

Hall & Woodhouse (01225) 469259

Old King Street; BA1 2JW Conversion of stone-fronted warehouse/auction rooms; big open-plan interior on two floors, steel girders and glass, palms and chandeliers, mix of modern and traditional furniture including old-fashioned iron-framed tables with large candles and some simple bench seating, parquet and slate floors, Badger ales from full-length servery on the right, sweeping stairs up to another bar and eating area (disabled access via lift), roof terrace, decent choice of food from pub favourites to specials, helpful chatty staff; gets very busy with after-work drinkers when standing room only, open (and food) all day from 8am (9am weekends). *(Dr and Mrs A K Clarke)*

BATH ST7465

★ **Hop Pole** (01225) 446327

Albion Buildings, Upper Bristol Road; BA1 3AR Bustling family-friendly Bath Ales pub, their beers and guests kept well, decent wines by the glass and good choice of whiskies and other spirits, nice food (all day Fri-Sun) from sandwiches and traditional favourites up in bar and former skittle alley restaurant, friendly helpful staff, settles and other pub furniture on bare boards in four linked areas, lots of dark woodwork, ochre walls, some bric-a-brac; background music, Mon quiz; discreet sports TV; wheelchair access to main bar area only, pleasant two-level back courtyard with boules, fairy-lit vine arbour and heated summerhouses, opposite Victoria Park (great kids' play area), open all day. *(Chris and Angela Buckell, Taff Thomas)*

BATH ST7565

King William (01225) 428096

Thomas Street/A4 London Road; BA1 5NN Small corner dining pub with well cooked food from short daily changing menu, four local ales and good choice of wines by the glass, chunky old tables on bare boards, steep stairs up to simple attractive dining room; background music; children and dogs welcome, open all day weekends. *(Dr and Mrs A K Clarke)*

BATH ST7565

Pig & Fiddle (01225) 460868

Saracen Street; BA1 5BR Lively place (particularly weekends) with half a dozen well kept ales and fairly simple food including range of burgers, reasonable

prices and friendly staff, two big open fires, bare boards and collection of sporting memorabilia, steps up to bustling servery and little dining area, games part; live music and DJ nights, several TVs for sport; picnic-sets on big heated terrace, open all day, food till early evening. *(Dr and Mrs A K Clarke)*

BATH ST7565

Pulteney Arms (01225) 463923

Daniel Street/Sutton Street; BA2 6ND Cosy, cheerful and largely unspoilt 18th-c pub, Fullers London Pride, Otter, Timothy Taylors Landlord and guests, Thatcher's cider, enjoyable well priced fresh food including Fri fish night, lots of Bath RFC memorabilia, traditional furniture on wooden floors, old gas lamps, woodburner; background music, sports TV; pavement tables and small back terrace, handy for Sydney Gardens and Holburne Museum, open all day Fri-Sun. *(Giles and Annie Francis, Taff Thomas, Dr and Mrs A K Clarke)*

BATH ST7464

Raven (01225) 425045

Queen Street; BA1 1HE Small buoyant 18th-c city-centre free house, two well kept ales for the pub from Blindmans and four guests, craft beers and a changing cider, decent wines by the glass too, limited choice of food (good Pieminister pies), quick friendly service, bare boards, some stripped stone and an open fire, newspapers, quieter upstairs bar; storytelling evenings and monthly talks on science and the arts; no under-14s or dogs; open all day. *(Comus and Sarah Elliott, Dr and Mrs A K Clarke)*

BATH ST7466

Richmond Arms (01225) 316725

Richmond Place, off Lansdown Road; BA1 5PZ Cosy 18th-c bow-windowed pub in quiet setting off the tourist track; well liked sensibly priced home-made food (not Sun evening, Mon) including daily specials, Butcombe, Sharps Doom Bar and a guest, ciders from Symonds and Thatcher's, lots of wines by the glass, friendly service, mix of tables and chairs on bare boards, local artwork for sale; monthly quiz; children and dogs welcome, enclosed pretty front garden, may be summer barbecues, open all day. *(Dr and Mrs A K Clarke)*

BATH ST7364

Royal Oak (01225) 481409

Lower Bristol Road; near Oldfield Park station; BA2 3BW Friendly roadside pub with well kept Butts, Downton and up to five guests, good range of ciders/perries and bottled beers, no food, two bare-boards bar areas with open fires; regular live music, Tues quiz; dogs welcome (they have two huskies), side beer garden, open all day (from 2pm Mon-Thurs). *(Taff Thomas)*

BATH ST7564
Royal Oak (01225) 466909
A36 Pulteney Road; BA2 4HN
Refurbished community pub popular with
Bath RFC supporters and busy on match days,
Bath, Butcombe and a guest, Orchard Pig
cider, burgers and other reasonably priced
pub food (weekend lunchtimes, and evenings
Tues-Sat); sports TVs, quiz first Tues of
month, free wi-fi; outside seating (summer
barbecues), open all day weekends, from
4pm Tues-Fri, closed Mon. *(Taff Thomas)*

BATH ST7464
Salamander (01225) 428889
John Street; BA1 2JL Busy city local tied
to Bath Ales, their full range and a guest
kept well, good choice of wines by the glass,
bare boards, black woodwork and ochre walls,
popular pub food from sandwiches up (more
choice evenings/weekends), friendly helpful
young staff, upstairs restaurant with open
kitchen; background music, daily papers;
children till 8pm, no dogs, open all day (till
1am Fri, Sat). *(Comus and Sarah Elliott, Taff
Thomas, Dr and Mrs A K Clarke, Richard Mason)*

BATH ST7564
Volunteer Riflemans Arms
(01225) 425210 *New Bond Street Place;
BA1 1BH* Friendly little city-centre pub
with leather sofas and a few close-set tables,
wartime/military posters, open fire, well
kept ales including a house beer from Moles,
a couple of draught ciders and good value
tasty lunchtime food, small upstairs dining
room and roof terrace; background music;
pavement tables, open all day. *(Lance and
Sarah Milligan)*

BATH ST7564
White Hart (01225) 338053
Widcombe Hill; BA2 6AA Bistro-style
pub (sister to Fox & Badger at Wellow)
with scrubbed pine tables on bare boards,
candles and fresh flowers, good imaginative
if not cheap food, well kept Butcombe from
traditional panelled counter, proper cider
and plenty of wines by the glass, quick
friendly service; background music; children
and dogs welcome, pretty bare garden,
bedrooms (some sharing bathroom), open all
day (Sun till 5pm). *(Julian Richardson)*

BATHFORD ST7866
Crown (01225) 852426 *Bathford
Hill, towards Bradford-on-Avon, by
Batheaston roundabout and bridge;
BA1 7SL* Welcoming bistro pub with
good blackboard food including weekday
set deals, ales such as Bath and Timothy
Taylors Landlord, nice wines, charming
french landlady; children and dogs welcome,

tables out in front and in back garden with
pétanque, open all day. *(Taff Thomas,
Dr and Mrs A K Clarke)*

BICKNOLLER ST1139
Bicknoller Inn (01984) 656234
Church Lane; TA4 4EW Welcoming
old thatched pub nestling below the
Quantocks, traditional flagstoned front bar
with woodburner, side room and large back
restaurant with open kitchen, good food from
pub favourites up, Sun carvery, four well
kept Palmers ales and a couple of real ciders,
skittle alley; children and dogs (in bar)
welcome, courtyard and nice back garden,
boules, attractive village, open till 6pm Sun,
closed Mon lunchtime. *(Peter Rogan)*

BLAGDON ST5058
New Inn (01761) 462475
*Signed off A368; Park Lane/Church
Street; BS40 7SB* Lovely view over
Blagdon Lake from seats in front; well kept
Wadworths and guests, decent wines and
enjoyable reasonably priced food, bustling
bars with two inglenook log fires, heavy
beams hung with horsebrasses and tankards,
comfortable antique settles and mate's
chairs among more modern furnishings, old
prints and photographs, plainer side bar; no
under-10s, dogs welcome, wheelchair access
best from front. *(M G Hart)*

BLAGDON HILL ST2118
Blagdon Inn (01823) 421296
4 miles S of Taunton; TA3 7SG
Refurbished village pub with several linked
bar and dining areas (one room upstairs);
mix of elegant and traditional furnishings,
flagstone or carpeted floors, local art for
sale, inglenook log fire, imaginative well
presented food from co-owner/chef using
local and own produce, good wine list, ales
such as Butcombe, Thatcher's cider, friendly
prompt service; children and dogs welcome,
picnic-sets in front, more seats on terrace
from upper dining room, adjoining fields with
pigs, sheep and chickens, open all day Sat,
closed Sun evening, Mon. *(Guy Vowles)*

BLEADON ST3457
★ Queens Arms (01934) 812080
*Just off A370 S of Weston; Celtic
Way; BS24 0NF* Popular 16th-c beamed
village pub; informal chatty atmosphere
in carefully divided areas, generous
reasonably priced food (not Sun evening)
from lunchtime baguettes to steaks, friendly
service, Butcombe and other well kept
ales tapped from the cask, local cider
and decent wines by the glass, flagstoned
restaurant and stripped-stone back bar
with woodburner, sturdy tables and winged
settles, old hunting prints; children (away

---

*If you stay overnight in an inn or hotel, they are allowed to serve you an
alcoholic drink at any hour of the day or night.*

from bar) and dogs (not in restaurant) welcome, partial wheelchair access, picnic-sets on pretty heated terrace, open all day. *(Rosie and John Moore)*

BRISTOL ST5773

Alma (0117) 973 5171

Alma Vale Road, Clifton; BS8 2HY
Two-bar pub with west country beers, Aspall's and Thatcher's ciders and several wines by the glass, good range of whiskies too, very well liked imaginative food along with more standard choices including Sun roasts, friendly hard-working staff, dark panelled traditionally furnished front bar with wood flooring, more contemporary back room with bright modern wallpaper and local artwork on display, thriving upstairs theatre (10% food discount for ticket holders); background music, jazz pianist Sun; easy wheelchair access, small paved terrace behind (not late evening), open all day. *(Chris and Angela Buckell, Clive Watkin)*

BRISTOL ST5873

Bank (0117) 930 4691

John Street; BS1 2HR Small proper single-bar pub, centrally placed (but off the beaten track) and popular with office workers; four changing local ales (may include a porter), real ciders and enjoyable well priced food till 4pm including sandwiches, burgers and one or two unusual choices, comfortable bench seats, newspapers, books on shelf above fireplace; background and regular live music, quiz nights, free wi-fi; dogs welcome, wheelchair access, tables under umbrellas in paved courtyard, open all day (till 1am Thurs-Sat). *(Taff Thomas)*

BRISTOL ST5972

Barley Mow (0117) 930 4709

Barton Road; The Dings; BS2 0LF
Late 19th-c Bristol Beer Factory pub in old industrial area close to floating harbour; well kept changing ales, excellent selection of craft kegs and bottled beers, proper cider and decent choice of wines by the glass, enjoyable good value food (not Sun evening) from short menu catering for vegetarians, cheerful chatty staff, simply refurbished interior with wood floors, off-white walls and painted panelled dados, cushioned wall seats and pubby furniture, various odds and ends dotted about, open fire in brick fireplace; Mon quiz, free wi-fi; disabled access, open all day (till 10pm Sun). *(William Slade)*

BRISTOL ST5872

Beer Emporium (0117) 379 0333

King Street opposite the Old Vic; BS1 4EF Cellar bar-restaurant with two vaulted rooms; long stone-faced counter under stained-glass skylight, 12 regularly changing ales/craft beers (tasters offered) plus over 150 in bottles from around the world, good selection of malt whiskies and

other spirits, interesting wine list, coffees and teas, italian food (not Sun) including range of pizzas, cheerful chatty staff; some live music; disabled loos, open all day till 2am (2pm-1am Sun), can get crowded. *(Taff Thomas)*

BRISTOL ST5774

Blackboy (0117) 973 5233

Whiteladies Road; BS8 2RY Modernised dining pub with good well presented food from chef-owner, several offers including set lunch and themed evenings, relaxed friendly atmosphere, back eating area with light wood furniture, small front bar with sewing-machine tables, armchairs and open fire, ales such as Butcombe, St Austell and Timothy Taylors, friendly attentive service; open all day. *(William Slade)*

BRISTOL ST5872

BrewDog (0117) 927 9258

Baldwin Street, opposite church; BS1 1QW Corner bar serving own BrewDog beers and guests from other craft breweries (draught and bottled), knowledgeable young staff offer tasters, limited but interesting selection of substantial bar snacks, starkly modern feel with exposed brick, stainless-steel furniture and granite surfaces; can get noisily busy; wheelchair access, open all day till midnight. *(James Allsopp)*

BRISTOL ST5872

Bristol Brewhouse & Kitchen

(0117) 973 3793 *Cotham Hill, Clifton; BS6 6JY* Lively chain pub visibly brewing its own beers, good range of other drinks too, decent reasonably priced food from large sharing plates up (some cooked in fire pit in middle of bar), lunchtime meal deal, good friendly service, upstairs room with lots of draught ciders and collection of vinyl records to play; events such as brewing masterclasses and Mon quiz; children and dogs welcome, no wheelchair access, picnic-sets in garden across road, open (and food) all day. *(Richard and Penny Gibbs)*

BRISTOL ST5874

Chums 07757 681261

Chandos Road; BS6 6PF Newly opened micropub in former corner shop, mismatched furniture on boarded floor, painted half-panelling and lots of modern artwork for sale, six real ales (listed on blackboard) from pine-planked servery, real ciders including Gwatkin's and range of bottled belgian beers, snacky food; mobile phones discouraged; wheelchair access with difficulty (staff will help), open all day weekends, from 4pm other days. *(Chris and Angela Buckell)*

BRISTOL ST5873

Colston Yard (0117) 376 3232

Upper Maudlin Street/Colston Street; BS1 5BD Refurbished pub on site of the old Smiles Brewery, five real ales and interesting range of bottled beers, open plan bare-boards interior around central bar, leather stools and banquettes, some high tables and drinking shelves, exposed brickwork and wood/stone-clad walls, enjoyable food such as burgers and pizzas, friendly staff; background music; children welcome, disabled access/loos, a few pavement tables, closed Sun and Mon, otherwise open all day. *(Taff Thomas, Bob and Margaret Holder)*

BRISTOL ST5872
Commercial Rooms (0117) 927 9681
Corn Street; BS1 1HT Spacious colonnaded Wetherspoons (former early 19th-c merchants' club) in good location; main part with lofty stained-glass domed ceiling, large oval portraits of Bristol notables and gas lighting, comfortable quieter back room with ornate balcony, note the unusual wind gauge above horseshoe servery; good changing choice of real ales, local ciders and nice chatty bustle (busiest weekend evenings), their usual food and low prices; ladies' with chesterfields and open fire; children welcome, no dogs, side wheelchair access and disabled facilities, open all day from 8am and till late Fri-Sun. *(D J and P M Taylor, Chris and Angela Buckell)*

BRISTOL ST5872
Cornubia (0117) 925 4415
Temple Street opposite fire station; BS1 6EN Tucked-away 18th-c real ale pub with fine selection including a good locally brewed house beer, also interesting bottled beers, farm ciders and perry, snacky food such as pasties and pork pies, friendly helpful service, walls and ceilings covered in pump clips, union jacks and other patriotic memorabilia, open fire and an aquarium for turtles; Thurs blues night, quiz first Tues of month; dogs welcome, not suitable for wheelchairs, picnic-sets in secluded front beer garden (summer barbecues), boules pitch, closed Sun evening, otherwise open all day. *(Taff Thomas)*

BRISTOL ST5772
Cottage (0117) 921 5256
Baltic Wharf, Cumberland Road; BS1 6XG Converted harbour master's office on wharf near Maritime Heritage Centre, comfortable and roomy with fine views of Georgian landmarks and Clifton suspension bridge, popular generous pub food from sandwiches up at reasonable prices, well kept Butcombe ales and a guest, real cider and nice wines, good service even when busy; background music; children welcome, portable ramps for wheelchairs, waterside terrace tables, access through sailing club,

on foot along waterfront or by round-harbour ferry, open all day. *(Taff Thomas, M G Hart)*

BRISTOL ST5773
Eldon House (0117) 922 1271
Lower Clifton Hill, Clifton; BS8 1BT Extended terrace-end Clifton pub; bare boards and mix of wooden tables and chairs, circular stone-walled dining area with glazed roof, snug with original stained glass and half-door servery, well kept Bath Ales and a couple of guests, several wines by the glass, decent good value food (not Sun evening) including blackboard specials, friendly staff; background music (live Sun), Mon quiz, free wi-fi; children allowed till 8pm, open all day Fri-Sun, closed lunchtimes Mon-Weds. *(Taff Thomas)*

BRISTOL ST5876
Gloucester Old Spot
(0117) 924 7693 *Kellaway Avenue; BS6 7YQ* Popular refurbished community pub with opened-up interior, main bar with ales such as Butcombe, Exmoor and Timothy Taylors from dark wood horseshoe servery, decent wines and enjoyable good value food (not Sun evening) from sandwiches and sharing boards up, friendly staff, back bar with dark green tiles, large parquet-floored dining lounge opening on to verandah and AstroTurf beer garden; Tues quiz, free wi-fi; children and dogs welcome, wheelchair access using portable ramp (staff will help), play area with wendy house, open all day from 9am for breakfast. *(Chris and Angela Buckell)*

BRISTOL ST5872
Golden Guinea (0117) 987 2034
Guinea Street; BS1 6SX Steps up to cosy backstreet pub, well kept changing ales and real ciders, simple bargain home-made food, roasts last Sun of the month, friendly staff, pews, wing armchairs and farmhouse tables on bare boards, some flock wallpaper and contemporary street art; live music, comedy and quiz nights; seats out in front and behind, closed lunchtimes Mon and Tues, otherwise open all day. *(Taff Thomas, James Allsopp)*

BRISTOL ST5975
Grace (0117) 924 4334
Gloucester Road, Bishopston; BS7 8BG Friendly relaxed place with well liked food including tapas-style dishes and good Sun roasts, real ales/craft beers, cocktails and good wines by the glass, nice coffee too, one room with simple furniture on wood or stone floors, original Victorian fireplace and arched stained-glass windows; children welcome, enclosed decked garden behind, open (and food) all day. *(Claire Bush)*

It's very helpful if you let us know up-to-date food prices when you report on pubs.

BRISTOL ST5772
Grain Barge (0117) 929 9347
Hotwell Road; BS8 4RU Converted 100-ft
barge owned by Bristol Beer Factory, their
ales kept well and fair priced food including
good sandwiches, burgers and Sun roasts,
steak night Thurs, great harbour views from
seats out on top deck, tables and sofas in
wood floor bar below, also a 'hold bar' for
functions and Fri live music, art exhibitions;
popular with younger crowd; open all day.
(Taff Thomas, Steve and Liz Tilley)

BRISTOL ST5873
Green Man (0117) 925 8062
Alfred Place, Kingsdown; BS2 8HD
Cosy local with country pub feel, bare boards
and dark woodwork, well kept Dawkins and
guests, real cider, several wines by the glass
and around 60 gins, extensive burger menu
and good Sun roasts, friendly knowledgeable
staff; background and live music, Weds quiz,
free wi-fi; dogs welcome, wheelchair access
possible with help, open all day Fri and Sat,
till 9pm Sun, from 4pm other days.
(Dan Beswick)

BRISTOL ST5772
★ Hope & Anchor (0117) 929 2987
Jacobs Wells Road, Clifton; BS8 1DR
Welcoming 18th-c pub opposite 11th-century
Jacobs Well, half a dozen changing ales from
central bar, nice wines and good choice of
malt whiskies, tables of various sizes (some
shaped to fit corners) on bare boards, darker
back area, enjoyable food including home-
made pizzas, friendly staff; background and
occasional live music, Sun quiz; children
welcome, disabled access, attractive tiered
back garden, parking nearby can be tricky,
open (and food) all day. *(Taff Thomas)*

BRISTOL ST5873
Horts City Tavern (0117) 925 2520
Broad Street; BS1 2EJ Open-plan 18th-c
Youngs pub, their well kept ales and Bath
Gem, good fairly priced food including
burgers and pizzas, big windows overlooking
street, 26-seat cinema at back (free entry
if you have a meal); background music,
sports TV; tables in cobbled courtyard,
open (and food) all day. *(Julian Richardon,
James Allsopp)*

BRISTOL ST5874
Kensington Arms (0117) 944 6444
Stanley Road; BS6 6NP Dining pub in
centre of Redland serving good interesting
food from light lunches up, well kept Greene
King and guests, plenty of wines by the glass,
cheerful accommodating staff and nice
buoyant atmosphere; may be background
music; children and dogs welcome, disabled
facilities (no wheelchair access to dining
room, but can eat in bar), heated terrace,
open all day. *(Simon Sharpe)*

BRISTOL ST5872
King Street Brewhouse
(0117) 405 8948 *Welsh Back; BS1 4RR*
Popular newly opened bar in the city's
'Beermuda Triangle' close to the river; glass
and boarded frontage with steps or lift up to
mezzanine bar, bare boards and reclaimed
wood walls, long tables and bench seating,
floor in front of tiled servery embedded with
pennies, their own beers from glassed-off
back microbrewery, also changing local
ales, decent range of ciders, gins and malt
whiskies, good if not particularly cheap wine
list, extensive food choice from sandwiches
and small plates up, helpful young staff;
sports TV one end; children welcome,
disabled loos/baby changing (key at bar),
some pavement seating, open (and food)
all day. *(Chris and Angela Buckell)*

BRISTOL ST5972
Kings Head (0117) 929 2338
Victoria Street; BS1 6DE Welcoming and
relaxed little 17th-c pub, big front window
and splendid mirrored bar-back, corridor to
cosy panelled snug with serving hatch, five
well kept ales including Castle Rock, Harveys
and Sharps, range of pies, toby jugs on joists,
old-fashioned local prints and photographs;
pavement tables, open all day.
(D J and P M Taylor)

BRISTOL ST5276
Lamplighters (0117) 279 3754
*End of Station Road, Shirehampton;
BS11 9XA* Popular 18th-c riverside pub;
well kept Bath Ales and a guest, Thatcher's
ciders, teas and coffees, competitively priced
traditional food including children's choices,
OAP meal deals and themed nights, modern
bar furniture on carpet or bare boards,
some faux leather sofas and armchairs,
pastel walls with darker greeny-blue dados,
bold patterned wallpaper here and there,
mezzanine dining area and cellar bar (not
always open); disabled access/facilities,
picnic-sets on paved front terrace, limited
parking nearby (beware the high spring
tides), riverside walks, open all day.
(Chris and Angela Buckell)

BRISTOL ST5673
Mall (0117) 974 5318
The Mall, Clifton; BS8 4JG Relaxed
corner pub with well kept changing ales,
interesting continental beers and lots of
wines by the glass, enjoyable modern pub
food, tall windows ornate ceiling, some
panelling and mix of old furniture on wood
floors, downstairs bar; Thurs quiz, free wi-fi;
small garden behind (summer barbecues),
open all day till midnight. *(Taff Thomas)*

BRISTOL ST5772
Nova Scotia (0117) 929 7994
*Baltic Wharf, Cumberland Basin;
BS1 6XJ* Old local on S side of floating

harbour with views to Clifton and Avon Gorge; Courage Best and guests, local scrumpy and generous helpings of enjoyable pub food, four linked areas, snob screen, mahogany and mirrors, nautical charts as wallpaper, welcoming relaxed atmosphere and friendly regulars; wheelchair access with help through snug's door, plenty of tables out by water, bedrooms sharing bathroom. *(Taff Thomas, Chris and Angela Buckell)*

BRISTOL ST5872
Old Duke (0117) 927 7137
King Street; BS1 4ER Corner pub in interesting cobbled area between docks and Bristol Old Vic; named after Duke Ellington and festooned with jazz posters, plus one or two instruments, good bands nightly and Sun lunchtime, four real ales including Otter and Sharps, simple food, usual pub furnishings; open all day (till 1am Fri, Sat), gets packed evenings. *(Taff Thomas)*

BRISTOL ST5872
Old Fish Market (0117) 921 1515
Baldwin Street; BS1 1QZ Imposing brick-built former fish market, relaxed friendly atmosphere, well kept Fullers/Gales beers from handsome wooden counter, fine range of whiskies and gins, food from pizzas up including various chowders; background music, Sun live jazz, sports TVs, free wi-fi; open all day (food all day weekends). *(Taff Thomas)*

BRISTOL ST5772
Orchard
Hanover Place, Spike Island; BS1 6XT Friendly unpretentious corner local with up to eight well kept stillaged ales and great range of ciders, food from snacks up in bar or upstairs dining room, woodburner; live music including Mon blues jam and Tues jazz, quiz Thurs, sports TV (pub gets very busy on match days); tables out in front, handy for SS *Great Britain*, open all day (from 9am weekends for breakfast). *(Simon Sharpe)*

BRISTOL ST5672
Portcullis (0117) 908 5536
Wellington Terrace; BS8 4LE Compact two-storey pub in Georgian building close to Clifton Bridge, well kept Dawkins and several changing guests, farm ciders, fine range of wines by the glass and spirits, tapas-style food, good friendly staff, flame-effect gas fire, dark wood and usual pubby furniture; free wi-fi; dogs welcome, tricky wheelchair access, garden behind on upper level, closed weekday lunchtimes, open all day weekends. *(Rosie and John Moore)*

BRISTOL ST5772
Pump House (0117) 927 2229
Merchants Road; BS8 4PZ Spacious well converted dockside building (former 19th-c pumping station); charcoal-grey brickwork, tiled floors and high ceilings, good food

in bar and smart candlelit mezzanine restaurant, ales such as Bath, Butcombe and St Austell, decent wines from comprehensive list and huge choice of gins, friendly staff, cheerful atmosphere; waterside tables, open all day. *(Taff Thomas, James Allsopp)*

BRISTOL ST5872
Royal Naval Volunteer
(0117) 316 9237 King Street; BS1 4EF Modernised 17th-c pub in cobbled street, wide range of draught and bottled british beers, ciders/perries and a dozen wines by the glass, friendly knowledgeable staff, good interesting food in back restaurant; weekend live music, sports TV; dogs welcome, terrace seating. *(Taff Thomas)*

BRISTOL ST5972
Seven Stars (0117) 927 2845
Thomas Lane; BS1 6JG Unpretentious one-room real ale pub near harbour (and associated with Thomas Clarkson and slave trade abolition), popular with students and local office workers, up to eight well kept changing ales (20 from a featured county on first Mon-Thurs of the month), some interesting malts and bourbons, dark wood and bare boards, old local prints and photographs, no food – can bring in takeaways; weekend folk music, juke box, pool, games machine; dogs welcome, disabled access (but narrow alley with uneven cobbles and cast-iron kerbs), open all day. *(Chris and Angela Buckell, Taff Thomas)*

BRISTOL ST5872
Small Bar
King Street; BS1 4DZ Real ale/craft beer pub with over 30 choices including own Left Handed Giant, all served in smaller glasses (up to two-thirds of a pint), good range of bottled beers too, friendly knowledgeable staff, enjoyable food such as burgers and hotdogs along with vegetarian/vegan choices, simple décor with bare boards and flagstones, roughly exposed brickwork here and there and wood plank walls, some barrel tables and a couple of old fireplaces, upstairs area with armchairs, sofas and shelves of books; background music; open all day (till 1am Fri, Sat). *(Julian Richardson)*

BRISTOL ST5871
Steam Crane (0117) 923 1656
North Street; BS3 1HT Fine selection of ales/craft beers and well liked food including good burgers and Sun roasts, friendly staff, large bare-boards room with patterned wallpaper above cerise dado, mismatching furniture including leather sofas, chandeliers and maybe local artwork for sale; background music, live bands, swing nights and DJs, sports TV; children welcome, seats on back terrace, open all day (till 1am Fri, Sat), food all day Sun. *(Taff Thomas)*

BRISTOL ST5872

Three Tuns (0117) 907 0689

St Georges Road; BS1 5UR Popular city-centre pub; seven real ales including local Arbor, craft kegs and interesting selection of bottled beers, several ciders too, cajun/creole-influenced menu, pine tables on bare boards, a couple of small leather sofas in alcoves, open fire; regular events including art exhibitions, music, Weds quiz and Sun magic night; covered and heated back terrace down steps, near cathedral, open all day. *(Simon Sharpe)*

BRISTOL ST5773

Victoria (0117) 974 5675

Southleigh Road, Clifton; BS8 2BH Refurbished little two-room pub under new management, popular and can get crowded, with half a dozen or more changing small brewery ales including a couple from Dawkins, interesting bottled belgian beers, local cider and good selection of gins, basic snacks such as pies and sausage rolls, big mirrors and open fire; free wi-fi; dogs welcome, disabled access (a few low kerbs/steps), open all day weekends, from 4pm Mon-Fri. *(Chris and Angela Buckell)*

BRISTOL ST5973

Volunteer (0117) 955 8498

New Street, near Cabot Circus; BS2 9DX Tucked-away local with friendly laid-back atmosphere, good choice of changing ales/craft beers, a couple of ciders and decent wines by the glass, well liked reasonably priced home-made food including range of burgers and popular Sun roasts; live music and beer festivals; children and dogs welcome, walled garden behind, open all day. *(Taff Thomas)*

BRISTOL ST5976

Wellington (0117) 951 3022

Gloucester Road, Horfield (A38); BS7 8UR Roomy 1920s red-brick pub recently refurbished and opened up; well kept Bath Ales and guests, craft beers, local cider and good choice of other drinks including half a dozen gins, enjoyable food till 10pm, pleasant efficient service; children welcome, disabled access/loos, sunny terrace, popular boutique bedrooms (best to book early), open all day (from 9am weekends for breakfast) and very busy on Bristol RFC/Rovers match days. *(Chris and Angela Buckell)*

BRISTOL ST5873

White Lion (0117) 927 7744

Quay Head, Colston Avenue; BS1 1EB Small friendly city-centre pub with simple bare-boards bar, four Wickwar ales and a guest, range of Pieminister pies, good coffee, daily newspapers and free wi-fi; spiral stairs down to lavatories; café-style pavement tables under awning. *(Taff Thomas)*

BROADWAY ST3215

Bell (01460) 52343

Broadway Lane; TA19 9RG Welcoming village pub attracting good mix of locals and visitors, flagstones and open fires, comfortable leather sofas and armchairs, well priced traditional menu, ales such as Courage, Youngs and St Austell, skittle alley; children and dogs welcome, seats out in front and on back terrace, good value bedrooms, open all day Fri-Sun. *(Martin and Alison Stainsby)*

BURROW BRIDGE ST3530

King Alfred (01823) 698379

Main Road, by the bridge; TA7 0RB Old-fashioned local under new ownership, relaxed friendly atmosphere in flagstoned bar, well kept ales such as Butcombe and Otter, local ciders and decent wines by the glass, landlord-chef's good food (not Sun evening) from pub standards up, comfortable dining room upstairs with view over River Parrett and Somerset Levels, roof terrace; live music and quiz/curry nights; dogs welcome, open all day Fri, Sun till 9pm, closed Mon. *(Mr Yeldahn, Susan Crabbe, Bob and Margaret Holder)*

BUTLEIGH ST5133

Rose & Portcullis (01458) 850287

Sub Road/Barton Road; BA6 8TQ Welcoming stone-built country pub with enjoyable good value home-made food (not Sun evening), five well kept ales and several local ciders, helpful friendly staff, bar and airy dining extension; children and dogs welcome, tables outside. *(Stuart Reeves)*

CASTLE CARY ST6432

George (01963) 350761

Just off A371 Shepton Mallet–Wincanton; Market Place; BA7 7AH Old-fashioned thatched country-town hotel (former 15th-c coaching inn), popular front bar with big inglenook, bistro bar and restaurant, well liked food from sandwiches to good steaks and up, real ales including Greene King, decent wines, friendly staff; children welcome, 17 bedrooms (some in courtyard), open all day. *(Richard Tilbrook)*

CHEDDAR ST4553

Gardeners Arms (01934) 742235

Silver Street; BS27 3LE Tucked away in the old part of the village (originally three farmworkers' cottages), generous helpings of popular home-made food from baguettes

---

Places with gardens or terraces usually let children sit there – we note in the text
the very few exceptions that don't.

to good Sun roasts, well kept Butcombe Bitter and Sharps Doom Bar, friendly service, two-room beamed dining area, interesting old local photographs, woodburner; children and dogs welcome, a couple of picnic-sets out at front, more in garden behind, closed Mon, otherwise open all day. *(Taff Thomas)*

CHEDDAR ST4653
White Hart (01934) 741261
The Bays; BS27 3QN Welcoming village local with well kept beers, traditional ciders and enjoyable fairly priced home-made food from good ploughman's to Sun carvery, log fire; live music and quiz nights, free wi-fi; children welcome, picnic-sets out in front and in back garden with play area, open (and food) all day. *(Taff Thomas)*

CHEW MAGNA ST5763
Pelican (01275) 331777
South Parade; BS40 8SL Friendly buoyant atmosphere at this welcoming village pub; opened-up modern interior with polished wood flooring, candles on chunky tables, some old pew chairs and high-backed settles, leather armchairs by woodburners in stone fireplaces, well kept changing ales such as Butcombe, Otter and St Austell, local cider, plenty of wines by the glass and some unusual malt whiskies, good fairly priced food including daily specials, efficient service; children and dogs welcome, wheelchair access from back courtyard, grassy beer garden, open all day (Sun till 6pm). *(Taff Thomas, Chris and Angela Buckell, M G Hart)*

CHEW MAGNA ST5861
★ Pony & Trap (01275) 332627
Knowle Hill, New Town; from B3130 in village, follow 'Bishop Sutton, Bath' signpost; BS40 8TQ Michelin-starred dining pub in nice rural spot near Chew Valley Lake; really good imaginative food from snacks and some lunchtime pubby choices through to beautifully presented restaurant dishes (must book), professional friendly service, Butcombe ales and a guest, front bar with cushioned wall seats and built-in benches on parquet, old range in snug area on left, dark plank panelling and housekeeper's chair in corner, lovely pasture views from two-level back dining area with white tables on slate flagstones; children welcome, dogs in bar, modern furniture on back terrace, picnic-sets on grass with chickens in runs below, front smokers' shelter, good walks. *(Steve and Liz Tilley, Taff Thomas, Mr and Mrs A H Young, Ian and Rose Lock)*

CHEWTON MENDIP ST5953
Waldegrave Arms (01761) 241384
High Street (A39); BA3 4LL Friendly village pub run by the same family for over 30 years, enjoyable generously served traditional food from sandwiches up, well kept local ales

such as Butcombe, Cottage and Cheddar; quiz nights and darts leagues; dogs welcome in bar, colourful window boxes and hanging baskets, flower-filled garden behind, open (and food) all day Sun. *(R T and J C Moggridge)*

CHILCOMPTON ST6451
Somerset Wagon (01761) 232732
B3139; Broadway; BA3 4JW Cosy and welcoming 19th-c pub (former railway inn), Wadworths ales, Addlestone's and Thatcher's ciders, decent wines and well liked good value food, efficient friendly service even when packed, pleasant olde-worlde areas off central bar, lots of settles, log fire; some live music; children and dogs welcome, small front garden, open all day Sun. *(Ian Phillips)*

CHISELBOROUGH ST4614
★ Cat Head (01935) 881231
Cat Street; leave A303 on A356 towards Crewkerne; take the third left (at 1.4 miles) signed Chiselborough, then left after 0.2 miles; TA14 6TT Character 15th-c hamstone pub refurbished under good new licensees; bar and two dining areas, flagstones, mullioned windows and two permanently lit woodburners (one in fine inglenook), well liked/priced fairly traditional food cooked by landlady, a couple of local ales such as Sharps and Butcombe; classical background music; children and dogs (in bar) welcome, picnic-sets in lovely back garden, closed Sun evening, Mon. *(Rosie and John Moore, Simon Sharpe)*

COMBE FLOREY ST1531
★ Farmers Arms (01823) 432267
Off A358 Taunton–Williton, just N of main village turn-off; TA4 3HZ Pretty thatched and beamed 15th-c village pub sympathetically refurbished by new owners; five ales including Exmoor and Patriot (landlord owns the brewery), farm ciders and plenty of wines by the glass, good if not always cheap food including tapas and Josper grills, friendly staff; live acoustic music, free wi-fi; children and dogs welcome, charming cottagey garden with picnic-sets and flowering tubs, Taunton–Minehead steam railway runs close by, open all day, no food Sun evening. *(Ian Jenkins, Richard and Penny Gibbs)*

COMPTON DANDO ST6464
Compton Inn (01761) 490321
Court Hill; BS39 4JZ Welcoming stone-built village pub in lovely setting; enjoyable home-made food (not Sun evening), well kept Butcombe, Sharps and a guest, wood-floored bar with dining area at each end (one down a couple of steps), two-way woodburner in stone fireplace; charity quiz first Mon of month, TV; children, walkers and dogs welcome, picnic-sets out in front, garden behind with boules, open all day. *(David Longhurst)*

COMPTON MARTIN ST5457

Ring o' Bells (01761) 221284

A368 Bath–Weston; BS40 6JE
Old village pub with traditional beamed front bar, log fire in big inglenook, pubby seats on flagstones, steps leading up to spacious back area with oak boards, stripped-stone walls and various odds and ends including gold discs and signed celebrity photos, Butcombe and a guest ale, good wine and whisky choice, enjoyable food (not Sun evening) from sandwiches up; background and live music (artists such as Coldplay, Duran Duran and Kylie Minogue have played here), monthly quiz, board games, free wi-fi; children allowed till 8.30pm, dogs in bar, big garden backing on to Mendip Hills, play area, good surrounding walks, two spacious bedrooms, open all day Thurs-Sun.
(Gus Swan, Neil Allen)

CONGRESBURY ST4363

★ **Plough** (01934) 877402

High Street (B3133); BS49 5JA Popular old-fashioned character local – a pub since the 1800s; half a dozen well kept changing west country ales such as Butcombe, St Austell and Twisted Oak, ciders from Moles and Thatcher's, quick smiling service, generous helpings of well cooked food (not Sun evening) including daily specials, several small interconnecting rooms off flagstoned main bar, mix of old and new furniture, built-in pine wall benches, old prints, photos, farm tools and some morris dancing memorabilia, log fires; Sun quiz; no children inside, dogs welcome, wheelchair access from car park, garden with rustic furniture and boules. *(Hugh Roberts, Bob and Margaret Holder, Taff Thomas)*

CORFE ST2319

White Hart (01823) 421388

B3170 S of Taunton; TA3 7BU Friendly traditional 17th-c village pub with enjoyable sensibly priced pubby food (not Tues) including some vegetarian options, curry night last Thurs of the month, well kept ales such as Butcombe and Exmoor, beams, hot woodburner and open fire; bar billiards, skittle alley; dogs welcome, open all day Sat, closed Tues lunchtime. *(Charles Todd)*

CROSS ST4254

New Inn (01934) 732455

A38 Bristol–Bridgwater, junction A371; BS26 2EE Steps up to friendly roadside pub with five well kept ales (discount Thurs evening), good choice of enjoyable fairly traditional food from baguettes and baked potatoes up; Mar beer festival; children and dogs welcome, nice hillside garden with play area, open (and food) all day. *(Hugh Roberts)*

CROWCOMBE ST1336

Carew Arms (01984) 618631

Just off A358 Taunton–Minehead; TA4 4AD Interesting 17th-c beamed country inn attracting good mix of customers; hunting trophies, huge flagstones and good inglenook log fire in small lived-in front bar, five well kept ales such as Exmoor, Otter and St Austell, real cider, enjoyable reasonably priced home-made food including specials, friendly service, dining room allowing children, skittle alley; dogs, walkers and cyclists welcome, garden tables, six bedrooms, open all day in summer (all day Fri-Sun in winter). *(Ian and Rose Lock, S G N Bennett)*

CULBONE HILL SS8247

Culbone (01643) 862259

Culbone Hill; A39 W of Porlock, opposite Porlock Weir Toll Road; TA24 8JW Set high on Exmoor and perhaps more restaurant-with-rooms than pub; good food including themed nights, up to three well kept local ales and decent choice of malt whiskies, good friendly service; children welcome, terrace with wonderful views over Lorna Doone valley, five well appointed bedrooms, open all day, food all day weekends and in high season. *(Melanie and David Lawson)*

DINNINGTON ST4013

Dinnington Docks (01460) 52397

NE of village; Fosse Way; TA17 8SX Good cheery atmosphere in large old-fashioned rural local, unspoilt and unfussy, with good choice of inexpensive genuine home cooking including fresh fish Fri, well kept Butcombe and guests, farm ciders, friendly attentive staff, memorabilia to bolster myth that there was once a railway line and dock here, log fire, family room; some live music, skittle alley in adjoining building; large garden behind, good walks, open all day. *(S Holder)*

DITCHEAT ST6236

★ **Manor House** (01749) 860276

Signed off A37 and A371 S of Shepton Mallet; BA4 6RB Pretty 17th-c red-brick village inn (sister to the Rockford Inn at Brendon, Devon); buoyant atmosphere and popular with jockeys from nearby stables, enjoyable home-made food from sandwiches and pubby bar meals to more sophisticated choices, well kept Butcombe and guests, friendly helpful staff, unusual arched doorways linking big flagstoned bar to comfortable lounge and restaurant, open fires; skittle alley; children welcome, tables on back grass, handy for Royal Bath & West showground, five bedrooms, good breakfast, open all day. *(William Slade)*

Pubs close to motorway junctions are listed at the back of the book.

DOWLISH WAKE   ST3712
New Inn (01460) 52413
Off A3037 S of Ilminster, via Kingstone;
TA19 0NZ Comfortable and welcoming
dark-beamed village pub, enjoyable home-
made food including blackboard specials,
well kept Butcombe and Otter, local cider,
friendly helpful staff, woodburners in stone
inglenooks, pleasant dining room; quiz first
Sun of the month; dogs welcome, attractive
garden and village, Perry's cider mill and
shop nearby, four bedrooms in separate
annexe. *(James Allsopp)*

DULVERTON   SS9127
Bridge Inn (01398) 324130
Bridge Street; TA22 9HJ Welcoming
unpretentious little pub next to River Barle;
reasonably priced food using local suppliers,
up to four well kept ales including Exmoor,
some unusual imported beers, Addlestone's
cider and 30 malt whiskies, comfortable
sofas, woodburner; folk night third Sat of
month, fortnightly quiz Sun; children and
dogs welcome, two terraces, open all day
summer (all day Fri-Sun, closed Mon evening
winter). *(Vera Smith)*

DUNDRY   ST5666
Carpenters (0117) 964 6423
Wells Road; BS41 8NE Cleanly renovated
village pub with well kept ales such as
Bath and Butcombe, Thatcher's cider and
enjoyable fairly priced traditional food
including specials, helpful friendly staff;
children and dogs welcome, picnic-sets on
lawn, open all day Fri, Sat, till 6pm Sun,
closed Mon lunchtime. *(Taff Thomas)*

DUNDRY   ST5566
Dundry Inn (0177) 964 1722
Church Road, off A38 SW of Bristol;
BS41 8LH Renovated roomy village pub,
half-panelled bar with cushioned window
seats and comfy armchairs on oak floor,
steps up to stone-tiled dining area with
open fire, Bath, Butcombe and Sharps,
enjoyable imaginative food along with pubby
choices; well behaved children welcome, no
wheelchair access, picnic-sets in enclosed
church-side garden with outstanding views
over Bristol and beyond, two bedrooms,
handy for airport, closed Sun evening, Mon.
(Rosie and John Moore)

DUNSTER   SS9843
★ Stags Head (01643) 821229
West Street (A396); TA24 6SN Friendly
helpful staff in unassuming 16th-c roadside
inn, enjoyable good value food including daily
specials, Exmoor and a guest ale, beams,
timbers and inglenook log fire, steps up to
small back dining room; dogs welcome in bar
area, comfortable simple bedrooms, good
breakfast, closed Weds lunchtime.
(James Allsopp)

EAST HARPTREE   ST5453
Castle of Comfort (01761) 221321
B3134, SW on Old Bristol Road; BS40 6DD
Welcoming family-managed former coaching
inn set high in the Mendips (last stop before
the gallows for some past visitors); hefty
timbers and exposed stonework, cushioned
settles and other pubby furniture on
carpet, log fires, Butcombe, Sharps and a
guest, ample helpings of reasonably priced
traditional food including good steaks,
friendly staff; children (away from bar) and
dogs welcome, wheelchair access, big garden
with raised deck and play area, fine walks
nearby. *(Charles Todd)*

EAST LAMBROOK   ST4218
Rose & Crown (01460) 240433
Silver Street; TA13 5HF Stone-built dining
pub spreading extensively from compact
17th-c core with inglenook log fire, friendly
staff and relaxed atmosphere, decent choice
of freshly made food using local suppliers,
takeaway fish and chips, Palmers ales and
nine wines by the glass, restaurant extension
with old glass-covered well, skittle alley;
quiz and curry night third Thurs of month;
children and dogs (in bar) welcome, picnic-
sets on neat lawn, opposite East Lambrook
Manor Garden, closed Sun evening, Mon.
(Simon Sharpe)

EAST WOODLANDS   ST7944
★ Horse & Groom (01373) 462802
Off A361/B3092 junction; BA11 5LY
Small pretty pub (aka the Jockey) tucked
away down country lanes, friendly and
relaxed, with good choice of enjoyable well
priced food including some real bargains,
quickly changing ales and real ciders, pews
and settles in flagstoned bar, woodburner in
comfortable lounge, big dining conservatory;
traditional games; children welcome in
eating areas, dogs in bar, disabled access,
nice front garden with more seats behind,
handy for Longleat. *(James Allsopp)*

EVERCREECH   ST6336
Natterjack (01749) 860253
A371 Shepton Mallet–Castle Cary;
BA4 6NA Former Victorian station
hotel (line closed 1966), good choice of
popular generous food at reasonable prices,
Butcombe and a couple of guests, real cider
and good range of wines, welcoming landlord
and cheerful efficient staff, long bar with
eating areas off; dogs welcome, lots of tables
under parasols in big neatly kept garden,
five bedrooms in restored cider house, open
all day. *(Julian Richardson)*

EXFORD   SS8538
★ Exmoor White Horse
(01643) 831229 *B3224; TA24 7PY*
Popular and welcoming old three-storey
creeper-clad inn, more or less open-plan bar

with good log fire, high-backed antique settle among more conventional seats, scrubbed deal tables, hunting prints and local photographs, Exmoor ales, Thatcher's cider and over 150 malt whiskies, good locally sourced bar and restaurant food including Sun carvery; children and dogs welcome, tables outside by river, pretty village, Land Rover Exmoor safaris, 28 comfortable bedrooms, open all day from 8am. *(Richard and Penny Gibbs, Lynda and Trevor Smith)*

FAULKLAND   ST7555
★ **Tuckers Grave** (01373) 834230
A366 E of village; BA3 5XF Tiny cider house, unspoilt and unchanging, with chatty locals and warm friendly atmosphere; flagstoned entrance opening into simple room with casks of Butcombe and Thatcher's Cheddar Valley cider in alcove on left, perhaps lunchtime sandwiches, two high-backed settles facing each other across a single table on right, side room with shove-ha'penny, open fires, skittle alley; children welcome in one area, lots of tables and chairs on attractive back lawn, good views, closed Mon lunchtime (except bank holidays). *(Taff Thomas)*

FRESHFORD   ST7960
Inn at Freshford (01225) 722250
Off A36 or B3108; BA2 7WG Roomy old stone-built village pub in lovely spot near River Frome; well kept Box Steam and guests, interesting ciders and good wines, generous helpings of well prepared food served by pleasant young staff; live music including Thurs jazz; children and dogs welcome, wheelchair access, pretty hillside garden overlooking valley, good waterside walks. *(Nick Lawless, Chris and Angela Buckell)*

FROME   ST7748
Griffin (01373) 467766
Milk Street; BA11 3DB Unpretentious bare-boards bar with etched glass and open fires, long counter serving good Milk Street beers brewed here by friendly landlord, hot food Weds (usually a themed night) and Sun, easy-going mixed crowd; regular live music, Mon quiz; small garden, open till 1am Fri, Sat, closed lunchtimes except Sun. *(Peter Barrett)*

GLASTONBURY   ST4938
George & Pilgrim (01458) 831146
High Street; BA6 9DP Comfortable 15th-c inn with magnificent carved stone façade and some interesting features, carpeted bar with handsome stone fireplace, moulded beams, oak panelling and traceried stained-glass bay window, St Austell and guests, restaurant, OAP meal deal Mon-Thurs and other offers; 14 bedrooms, open all day. *(Ann and Colin Hunt)*

GLASTONBURY   ST5039
Who'd A Thought It (01458) 834460
Northload Street; BA6 9JJ Interesting pub filled with oddments and memorabilia – red phone box (complete with mannequin), bicycle chained to the ceiling, lots of enamel signs and old photographs, coal fire in old range, beams, flagstones, stripped brick and pine panelling, well kept Palmers ales and decent wines by the glass, enjoyable freshly cooked food; free wi-fi; children and dogs welcome, terrace picnic-sets, five comfortable bedrooms, open all day. *(Simon Sharpe)*

HALLATROW   ST6357
★ **Old Station** (01761) 452228
A39 S of Bristol; BS39 6EN Former 1920s station hotel with extraordinary collection of bric-a-brac including railway memorabilia, musical instruments, china cows, post boxes, even half an old Citroën, wide mix of furnishings, Brains Rev James, Butcombe Bitter and a guest, several wines by the glass, popular varied choice of good value food cooked by landlord, Pullman carriage restaurant, cheerful helpful service; children and dogs (in bar) welcome, café-style furniture on decking, picnic-sets on grass, also crazy golf, football pitch and polytunnel growing own vegetables, five bedrooms in converted outbuilding (no breakfast), open all day Fri-Sun. *(Ian and Rose Lock)*

HARDWAY   ST7234
★ **Bull** (01749) 812200
Off B3081 Bruton–Wincanton at brown sign for Stourhead and King Alfred's Tower; Hardway; BA10 0LN Charming beamed 17th-c country dining pub, good popular food (not Sun evening, Mon) in comfortable bar and character dining rooms, well kept Butcombe and Otter, farm cider and reasonably priced wines by the glass, friendly long-serving landlord and good informal service, log fire; unobtrusive background music; children and dogs welcome, tables and barbecues in lovely garden behind, more seats in pretty rose garden over road, closed Sun evening and Mon in winter. *(Michael Hill, Stuart Reeves)*

HASELBURY PLUCKNETT   ST4711
White Horse (01460) 78873
North Street; TA18 7RJ Popular open-plan village dining pub, good enterprising food cooked by chef-landlord from bar snacks up

---

We mention bottled beers and spirits only if there is something unusual about them – imported belgian real ales, say, or dozens of malt whiskies; so do please let us know about them in your reports.

including set menu choices, west country ales tapped from the cask, local ciders and ten wines by the glass, friendly helpful service, candlelit tables on flagstones or bare boards, leather sofa by inglenook log fire; children and dogs welcome, pretty back terrace with roses and old well, closed Sun evening, Mon. *(Gareth and Dorothy Thomas)*

HILLFARANCE ST1624
Anchor (01823) 461334
Oake; pub signed off Bradford-on-Tone to Oake road; TA4 1AW Comfortable village pub with dining area off attractive two-part bar, good choice of enjoyable food including Sun carvery, nice friendly atmosphere, three local ales; children welcome, garden with play area, bedrooms and holiday apartments, closes 10pm Mon-Thurs, 11pm Fri, Sat, open all day Sun till 9.30pm. *(Bob and Margaret Holder)*

★ HINTON BLEWETT ST5956
Ring o' Bells (01761) 452239
Signed off A37 in Clutton; BS39 5AN Charming low-beamed stone-built country local opposite village green, old-fashioned bar with solid furniture including pews, log fire, good value food (not Sun evening) cooked by landlady, obliging service, Butcombe, Fullers and guests, good wines by the glass, dining room; children, walkers and dogs welcome, good view from tables in sheltered front yard, open all day in summer. *(Taff Thomas)*

HINTON CHARTERHOUSE ST7758
Rose & Crown (01225) 722153
B3110 about 4 miles S of Bath; BA2 7SN 18th-c village pub under new management; partly divided bar, fine panelling, cushioned wall seats and bar stools, farmhouse chairs around chunky tables on red carpeting, woodburner in ornate carved stone fireplace (smaller brick one on other side), Butcombe, Fullers and maybe a guest, several wines by glass, enjoyable food from sandwiches to grills, Sun carvery, long dining room and steps to lower area with unusual beamed ceiling; background music; children and dogs welcome, picnic-sets under parasols in terraced garden, bedrooms, open all day. *(David and Stella Martin, Mark Sykes)*

HOLCOMBE ST6648
Duke of Cumberland
(01761) 233731 *Edford Hill; BA3 5HQ* Modernised riverside pub with enjoyable fairly priced food including home-made pizzas, Blindmans, Butcombe, Wadsworth and a guest, ciders such as Long Ashton and Thatcher's, friendly helpful staff, flagstoned bar with easy chairs by log fire, table skittles and other traditional games, also a skittle alley in the dining area; background and some live music, sports TV; children and dogs welcome, small waterside garden, open all day. *(Ian Phillips)*

HORSINGTON ST7023
Half Moon (01963) 370140
Signed off A357 S of Wincanton; BA8 0EF Beamed pub dating from the 17th c, light and airy knocked-through bars, stripped stone and oak floors, inglenook log fires, enjoyable sensibly priced pubby food, up to six well kept ales, decent wines and a dozen gins, friendly helpful service, evening restaurant; traditional music first Weds of month, skittle alley, free wi-fi; children and dogs welcome, disabled access, attractive sloping front garden and big back one, good walks nearby, ten bedrooms in separate buildings behind, closed Sun evening, best to check winter hours. *(Stuart Reeves)*

HORTON ST3214
★ Five Dials (01460) 55359
Hanning Road; off A303; TA19 9QH Cleanly updated village pub run by friendly helpful couple, popular reasonably priced home-made food including good steaks and fish, Otter, Sharps Doom Bar and a guest, local ciders and good choice of wines by the glass, restaurant; children and dogs welcome, six comfortable bedrooms, open all day Fri-Sun, closed Mon. *(Evelyn and Derek Walter)*

KELSTON ST7067
Old Crown (01225) 423032
Bitton Road; A431 W of Bath; BA1 9AQ 17th-c creeper-clad inn with four small traditional rooms, beams and polished flagstones, carved settles and cask tables, logs burning in ancient open range, two more coal-effect fires, well kept Butcombe ales and real cider, enjoyable fairly priced food in bar and small restaurant, good value lunchtime set menu and other deals; children and dogs welcome, wheelchair access with help, picnic-sets under apple trees in sheltered sunny back garden, play area, four bedrooms in converted outbuildings, open all day. *(Taff Thomas)*

KENN ST4169
Drum & Monkey (01275) 873433
B3133 Yatton–Clevedon; BS21 6TJ Welcoming village pub with good choice of food including well priced set deals and themed nights, three well kept ales such as Sharps, real cider, friendly helpful service, bar with wood-strip floor, inglenook log fire one end, woodburner the other, lofty restaurant and dining conservatory, snug with TV and darts; live music including tribute bands and Sun evening jazz, quiz Weds; children and dogs (in bar) welcome, a couple of stocks outside, open all day. *(Taff Thomas)*

KEYNSHAM ST6669
★ Lock-Keeper (0117) 986 2383
Keynsham Road (A4175 NE of town); BS31 2DD Welcoming riverside pub with

plenty of character, bare boards and relaxed worn-in feel, simple left-hand bar with big painted settle, cushioned wall benches, trophy cabinet and old local photographs, two more little rooms with assorted cushioned dining chairs, more photographs and rustic prints, Wells and Youngs ales plus guests, good quality wines, whiskies and gins, nice coffee too, popular well priced bar food served by cheerful helpful young staff, light modern conservatory (quite different in style); live music Fri, Sat; children welcome, dogs in bar, disabled access/facilities, teak furniture and giant parasols on big heated deck overlooking water, steps down to picnic-sets on grass, outside bar and barbecue, pétanque, open all day. *(Taff Thomas, Chris and Angela Buckell, Dr and Mrs A K Clarke, Tony Hobden)*

KINGSTON ST MARY ST2229
Swan (01823) 451383

Lodes Lane, in centre of village; TA2 8HW Cosy 17th-c roadside village pub, neat and tidy, with long knocked-through panelled bar, modern furniture on carpets, black-painted beams and rough plastered walls with signed cricket bats (landlord is keen cricketer), big stone fireplaces, popular home-made pubby food (not Sun evening), well kept Dartmoor, Exmoor and Sharps, Thatcher's Cheddar Valley cider, cheerful helpful staff; background music; children welcome, no dogs inside, front wheelchair access, garden with play area, skittle alley, handy for Hestercombe Gardens. *(Bob and Margaret Holder, Chris and Angela Buckell)*

KNAPP ST3025
Rising Sun (01823) 491027

Village W of North Curry (pub signed from here); TA3 6BG Tucked-away 15th-c longhouse surrounded by lovely countryside; handsome beams, flagstones and two inglenooks with woodburners, Exmoor and Sharps Doom Bar, proper cider, good food with emphasis on fish/seafood, seasonal game too, friendly helpful staff; children and dogs welcome, sunny little front terrace, open all day Sat, closed Sun evening (except first Sun of month when there's a quiz), Mon, Tues lunchtime. *(Mr Yeldahn)*

KNOLE ST4825
Lime Kiln (01458) 241242

A372 E of Langport; TA10 9JH Creeper-clad beamed 17th-c country pub set back from the road, good range of well priced locally sourced food, some main courses available in smaller helpings, ales such as Butcombe, Otter and Ringwood, Thatcher's Cheddar Valley cider, friendly attentive staff, flagstoned bar and large carpeted dining room, inglenook log fire; children welcome, pleasant garden with southerly views, open (and food) all day weekends. *(Helen and Brian Edgeley)*

LANGFORD BUDVILLE ST1122
★ **Martlet** (01823) 400262

Off B3187 NW of Wellington; TA21 0QZ Cosy, comfortable and cottagey with friendly landlady and staff, good generously served food (becomes more restaurant in evenings with fewer drinkers), popular OAP lunch deal Weds-Fri, well kept/priced local ales including Exmoor, inglenook, beams and flagstones, central woodburner, steps up to dining room, conservatory; children welcome, terrace picnic-sets, closed Sun evening, Mon and lunchtime Tues. *(S G N Bennett)*

LANGPORT ST4625
★ **Devonshire Arms** (01458) 241271

B3165 Somerton–Martock, off A372 E of Langport; TA10 9LP Handsome gabled inn (former hunting lodge) on village green; simple flagstoned back bar with high-backed chairs around dark tables, up to three west country ales tapped from the cask, several wines by the glass and local cider brandy, stylish main room with comfortable leather sofas and glass-topped log table by fire, scatter cushions on long wall bench, church candles, elegant dining room with wicker chairs and pale wood tables on broad boards, good interesting food from lunchtime sandwiches up (local suppliers listed), charming efficient service, maybe evening pianist; wheelchair access from car park, teak furniture out at front, pretty box-enclosed courtyard behind with water-ball feature, more seats on raised terraces, nice bedrooms, good breakfast. *(Richard and Penny Gibbs)*

LONG ASHTON ST5370
Bird in Hand (01275) 395222

Weston Road; BS41 9LA Stone-built dining pub with good locally sourced food from bar meals to imaginative restaurant dishes, well kept Bath Gem, St Austell Tribute and two guests, Ashton Press cider, nice wines, friendly welcoming young staff, spindleback chairs and blue-painted pine tables on wood floors, open fire and woodburner; children and dogs welcome, side terrace, parking can be tricky, open all day. *(Rosie and John Moore)*

LONG ASHTON ST5370
Miners Rest (01275) 393449

Providence Lane; BS41 9DJ Welcoming three-room country pub, comfortable and unpretentious, with well kept Butcombe and an occasional guest such as Sharps Doom Bar tapped from the cask, five good traditional ciders, generous helpings of simple inexpensive lunchtime food, cheerful prompt service, local mining memorabilia, log fire, darts; no credit cards; well behaved children and dogs welcome, wheelchair access with some heroics, vine-covered verandah and suntrap terrace, open all day. *(David Longhurst)*

LOWER GODNEY   ST4742
Sheppey Inn   (01458) 831594
Tilleys Drove; BA5 1RZ Revamped
character pub attracting good mix of
customers; at least six local ciders tapped
from the barrel along with local ales and
craft beers, imaginative choice of well liked
food, some cooked in charcoal oven, plain
furniture on bare boards, black beams,
stripped-stone walls and open fire, stuffed
animals, old local photographs and modern
artwork, long simply furnished dining area
with pitched ceiling; regular live music;
children welcome, seats on deck overlooking
small river. *(Julian Richardson)*

LUXBOROUGH   SS9837
Royal Oak   (01984) 641498
*Kingsbridge; S of Dunster on minor
roads into Brendon Hills; TA23 0SH*
Friendly landlord and refurbishment for
this atmospheric old inn set deep in Exmoor
National Park; compact beamed bar with
ancient flagstones, several rather fine
settles, scrubbed kitchen tables and huge
brick inglenook, back bar with cobbled floor,
some quarry tiles and stone fireplace, cosy
side room set for eating plus two further
dining rooms, Exmoor and a couple of guests,
generous food from pub favourites to more
upmarket choices including seasonal game;
pool, shove-ha'penny and board games in
back room, also a radiogram with stack
of old LPs; children and dogs welcome,
seats in lovely sunny back courtyard, eight
bedrooms, good walks nearby including
Coleridge Way, open all day weekends (no
food Sun evening), closed Mon and weekday
lunchtimes. *(Richard and Penny Gibbs, Lynda
and Trevor Smith)*

LYDFORD ON FOSSE   ST5630
Cross Keys   (01963) 240473
Just off A37; TA11 7HA Renovated
beamed and flagstoned pub with good
traditional home-made food (not Sun
evening) including generous ploughman's
and award-winning pies, cheerful service,
half a dozen well kept ales tapped from the
cask, proper ciders and nice wines by the
glass, connecting rooms (main dining area at
front), chunky rustic furniture and log fires
in substantial old fireplaces; live music and
other events in function room; children and
dogs welcome, disabled access/loos, seats
on covered terrace and in sunny garden,
six comfortable well equipped bedrooms,
camping field, popular with Fosse Way
walkers. *(Richard Tilbrook, Dave Grindley,
Chris and Angela Buckell)*

MINEHEAD   SS9746
Old Ship Aground   (01643) 703516
Quay West; TA24 5UL Friendly Edwardian
harbourside pub owned by local farming
family; Marstons-related ales and a guest
such as Cotleigh, Thatcher's cider, enjoyable
food using own meat and other local produce,
Sun carvery, helpful pleasant service
even when busy, faux black beams, pubby
furniture and window-seat views; background
music (live Fri), free wi-fi; children and
dogs welcome, wheelchair access via side
door, disabled loo, outside tables overlooking
harbour, 12 bedrooms, open all day.
(Revd R P Tickle)

MONTACUTE   ST4917
Kings Arms   (01935) 822255
Bishopston; TA15 6UU Extended
17th-c inn next to church; stripped-stone
bar with comfortable seating and log fire,
contemporary restaurant, three real ales
including Greene King, enjoyable food from
bar snacks to restaurant dishes, friendly
staff; background music, quiz second Sun of
the month; pleasant garden behind,
15 bedrooms (most with own bathrooms),
handy for Montacute House (NT).
(A H Baker)

NAILSEA   ST4469
Blue Flame   (01275) 856910
*Netherton Wood Lane, West End;
BS48 4DE* Small friendly 19th-c farmers'
local with two unchanging lived-in rooms,
coal fire, well kept ales from casks behind
bar, traditional ciders, fresh rolls and pork
pies, pub games; outside lavatories including
roofless gents', limited parking (may be filled
with Land Rovers and tractors); children's
room, sizeable informal garden, open all day
weekends, closed lunchtimes Mon, Tues.
(Taff Thomas)

NORTH CURRY   ST3125
Bird in Hand   (01823) 490248
*Queens Square; off A378 (or A358)
E of Taunton; TA3 6LT* Friendly village
pub with cosy main bar, old pews, settles,
benches and yew tables on flagstones,
some original beams and timbers, good
inglenook log fire, well kept ales and
decent wines by the glass, enjoyable
good value food in separate dining part;
background music; children, dogs and
muddy boots welcome, open all day Sun.
(Bob and Margaret Holder)

NORTON ST PHILIP   ST7755
★ George   (01373) 834224
A366; BA2 7LH Wonderful building full
of history and interest – an inn for over 700
years; heavy beams, timbering, stonework
and panelling, vast open fires, distinctive
furnishings, plenty of 18th-c pictures, fine
pewter and heraldic shields, Wadworths
ales and enjoyable food from varied
menu, good friendly service; children and
particularly dogs welcome, appealing
galleried courtyard, atmospheric bedrooms
(some reached by Norman turret), worth
strolling over meadow to attractive
churchyard, open all day. *(R K Phillips,
Mark Sykes, Dr and Mrs A K Clarke)*

NUNNEY ST7345
George (01373) 836458
Church Street; signed off A361 Shepton Mallet–Frome; BA11 4LW Smart 17th-c coaching inn set in quaint village with ruined castle; comfortably modern open-plan lounge with beams, stripped stone and woodburner in big fireplace, good well presented food from sharing plates, pizzas and burgers up, Wadworths ales and a guest, nice wines by the glass and good coffee, friendly helpful staff, separate restaurant; children and dogs (in bar) welcome, attractive split-level walled garden, rare 'gallows' inn sign spanning road, nine bedrooms, open all day. *(Ann and Colin Hunt, Revd Michael Vockins)*

OVER STRATTON ST4315
★ Royal Oak (01460) 240906
Off A303 via Ilminster turn at South Petherton roundabout; TA13 5LQ Friendly thatched family dining pub, enjoyable reasonably priced food including bargain two-course lunch (Tues-Sat), well kept Badger ales, linked rooms with attractive rustic décor, flagstones, thick stone walls and prettily stencilled beams, scrubbed kitchen tables, pews and settles, log fires; tables outside, secure play area, closed Mon. *(Bob and Margaret Holder)*

PITMINSTER ST2219
Queens Arms (01823) 421529
Off B3170 S of Taunton (or reached direct); near church; TA3 7AZ Popular village pub-restaurant with good competitively priced food from varied menu (best to book), also set deal Tues-Sat, well kept west country ales and decent wines; downstairs skittle alley; closed Sun evening, Mon. *(Patrick and Daphne Darley, Bob and Margaret Holder)*

PORLOCK SS8846
★ Ship (01643) 862507
High Street; TA24 8QD Picturesque old thatched pub with beams, flagstones and big inglenook log fires, popular reasonably priced food from sandwiches up, well kept ales such as Cotleigh, Exmoor, Otter and St Austell, friendly service, back dining room, small locals' front bar with games; children welcome, attractive split-level sunny garden with decking and play area, nearby nature trail to Dunkery Beacon, five bedrooms, open all day; known as the Top Ship to distinguish it from the Ship at Porlock Weir. *(Tom McLean)*

PORLOCK WEIR SS8846
★ Ship (01643) 863288
Porlock Hill (A39); TA24 8PB Unpretentious thatched pub in wonderful spot by peaceful harbour – can get packed; long and narrow with dark low beams, flagstones and stripped stone, simple pub furniture, woodburner, west country ales

including Exmoor, real ciders and a perry, good whisky and soft drinks choice, enjoyable pubby food served promptly by friendly staff, games rooms across small backyard, tea room; background music and big-screen TV; children and dogs welcome, sturdy picnic-sets in front and at side, good coast walks, three decent bedrooms, limited free parking but pay and display opposite; calls itself the Bottom Ship to avoid confusion with the Ship at Porlock. *(Peter Barrett)*

PORTISHEAD ST4576
★ Windmill (01275) 818483
M5 junction 19; A369 into town, then follow Sea Front sign and into Nore Road; BS20 6JZ Busy dining pub perched on steep hillside with panoramic Severn estuary views; curving glass frontage rising two storeys (adjacent windmill remains untouched), contemporary furnishings, four Fullers ales and a couple of guests, plenty of wines by the glass, decent range of enjoyable food from sandwiches and baked potatoes to daily specials, early-bird deal 3-7pm Mon-Fri (6pm Sat), efficient friendly staff; children welcome, dogs allowed in bar, disabled access including chair lift, metal furniture on tiered lantern-lit terraces and decking, open (and food) all day. *(Chris and Angela Buckell)*

PRIDDY ST5450
★ Hunters Lodge (01749) 672275
From Wells on A39 pass hill with TV mast on left, then next left; BA5 3AR Welcoming and unchanging farmers', walkers' and potholers' pub above Ice Age cavern, in same family for generations, well kept local beers tapped from casks behind bar, Thatcher's and Wilkin's ciders, simple cheap food, log fires in huge fireplaces, low beams, flagstones and panelling, old lead mining photographs; live folk music; no mobiles or credit cards; children and dogs in family room, wheelchair access, garden picnic-sets. *(Taff Thomas, M G Hart)*

PRISTON ST6960
Ring o' Bells (01761) 471467
Village SW of Bath; BA2 9EE Unpretentious old stone pub with large knocked-through bar, good reasonably priced traditional food cooked by licensees using nearby farm produce, real ales from small local brewers including a house beer from Blindmans, quick friendly service, flagstones, beams and good open fire; skittle alley; children, dogs and muddy boots welcome, benches out at front overlooking little village green (maypole here on May Day), good walks, two bedrooms, closed Mon and lunchtimes Tues-Thurs. *(Taff Thomas)*

RICKFORD ST4859
Plume of Feathers (01761) 462682
Very sharp turn off A368; BS40 7AH Cottagey 17th-c local with enjoyable reasonably priced home-made food in bar

and dining room, friendly service, well kept Butcombe and guests, local cider and good choice of wines, black beams and half-panelling, mix of furniture including cast-iron tables and settles, log fires; table skittles, darts and pool; well behaved children and dogs welcome, rustic tables on narrow front terrace, pretty streamside hamlet, bedrooms, open all day. *(Dr and Mrs A K Clarke)*

RIMPTON ST6021
White Post Inn (01935) 851525
Rimpton Hill, B3148; BA22 8AR
Small pub straddling Dorset border (boundary actually runs through the bar) and modernised by chef-owner; good well presented imaginative food from reworked pub favourites up, local ales and ciders, interesting list of spirits including a milk vodka, friendly helpful staff, cosy bar with sofas and woodburner, fine country views from restaurant and back terrace; children welcome, three bedrooms, open all day Sat, closed Sun evening, Mon. *(Melanie and David Lawson)*

RODNEY STOKE ST4850
Rodney Stoke Inn (01749) 870209
A371 Wells–Weston; BS27 3XB
Comfortable dining pub with modern décor, extensive choice of good generously served food, local real ale, friendly accommodating service, airy high-beamed restaurant extension; children welcome, roadside terrace and back garden with play area, camping, open (and food) all day Sun. *(Julian Richardson)*

SALTFORD ST6968
Jolly Sailor (01225) 873002
Off A4 Bath–Keynsham; Mead Lane; BS31 3ER Worth knowing for its great River Avon setting by lock and weir; good range of food from bar snacks and pub favourites to more imaginative choices, Weds and Thurs curry nights, Wadworths ales and guests, flagstones, low beams and two log fires, conservatory dining room overlooking the water; background music, daily newspapers; children and dogs (in bar) allowed, disabled access/facilities, paved lockside terrace, open (and food) all day. *(Chris and Angela Buckell, Dr and Mrs A K Clarke)*

SANDFORD ST4159
Railway (01934) 611518
Station Road; BS25 5RA Revamped by Thatcher's with their full range of ciders, real ales such as Butcombe and plenty of wines by the glass, lofty flagstoned bar with long oak counter, comfortable bare-boards area off with exposed stone walls and open fire, attractive timber-framed dining

extension; free wi-fi; children and dogs welcome, outside seating on two levels, open all day. *(Taff Thomas)*

SHEPTON MONTAGUE ST6731
★ Montague Inn (01749) 813213
Village signed off A359 Bruton–Castle Cary; BA9 8JW Simply but tastefully furnished dining pub with welcoming licensees, popular for civilised meal or just a drink, stripped-wood tables and kitchen chairs, inglenook log fire, nicely presented often interesting food including daily specials, well kept ales such as Bath, Cottage and Wadworths tapped from the cask, farm ciders, good wine and whisky choice, friendly well informed young staff, bright spacious restaurant extension behind; children and dogs (in bar) welcome, disabled access, garden and big terrace with teak furniture, maybe summer Sun jazz, peaceful farmland views, closed Sun evening. *(Edward Mirzoeff)*

SIMONSBATH SS7739
★ Exmoor Forest Inn (01643) 831341
B3223/B3358; TA24 7SH Friendly family-run inn beautifully placed in remote countryside; split-level bar with circular tables by counter, larger area with cushioned settles, upholstered stools and mate's chairs around mix of tables, hunting trophies, antlers and horse tack, woodburner, good reasonably priced traditional food alongside more imaginative choices including local game, well kept ales such as Clearwater, Exmoor and Otter, real cider, good range of wines and malt whiskies, airy dining room, residents' lounge; children and dogs welcome, seats in front garden, fine walks along River Barle, own trout and salmon fishing, ten comfortable bedrooms, open all day in high season. *(Bob and Margaret Holder, Paul Baxter)*

SOUTH CHERITON ST6924
White Horse (01963) 370394
A357 Wincanton–Blandford; BA8 0BL Renovated 17th-c roadside pub under friendly family management, well kept ales, craft beers and decent range of wines by the glass, good home-made food (not Sun evening) in bar or restaurant (separate menus), cheerful service, local artwork for sale; some live music, skittle alley; children and dogs welcome, picnic-sets in small back garden, open all day weekends. *(Stuart Reeves)*

SPAXTON ST2336
Lamb (01278) 671350
Barford Road, Four Forks; TA5 1AD Welcoming simply furnished little pub at foot of the Quantocks, open-plan beamed

---

All *Guide* inspections are anonymous. Anyone claiming to be a *Good Pub Guide* inspector is a fraud. Please let us know.

bar with woodburner, well kept beers and enjoyable good value food (not Sun evening) cooked by landlady including notable local steaks, booking advised; quiz last Sun of month; tables on lawn behind, closed all day Mon and lunchtimes apart from Sun. *(PLC)*

STANTON DREW ST5963
Druids Arms (01275) 332230
Off B3130; BS39 4EJ Refurbished pub in stone-circle village (there are some standing stones in the garden); linked flagstoned rooms with low black beams, bare stone walls and green dados, cushioned window seats and pubby furniture, candles here and there, open fires, tractor-seat stools by pale wood bar serving Butcombe and Sharps Doom Bar, Thatcher's cider and modest wine list, enjoyable often creative food (not Sun evening) from bar snacks up, OAP lunch deal; quiz second Mon of month; children welcome, front wheelchair access using portable ramp, picnic-sets out by lane and in garden backing on to 14th-c church, open all day. *(Chris and Angela Buckell, Taff Thomas)*

STAPLE FITZPAINE ST2618
Greyhound (01823) 480227
Off A358 or B3170 S of Taunton; TA3 5SP Rambling country pub with popular food from varied menu (best to book evenings), well kept Badger ales and good wines by the glass, welcoming helpful staff, flagstones and inglenooks, nice mix of settles and chairs, olde-worlde pictures, farm tools and so forth; children and dogs welcome, comfortable well equipped bedrooms, good breakfast, open all day. *(Sara Fulton, Roger Baker)*

STOGUMBER ST0937
White Horse (01984) 656277
Off A358 at Crowcombe; TA4 3TA Friendly old village local with well kept ever-changing west country ales, real ciders and decent home-made food, carpeted beamed bar with raised end section, old local photographs, log fire, separate restaurant, games room with pool; quiet back terrace, two bedrooms accessed by external staircase, open all day. *(Bob and Margaret Holder)*

STOKE ST GREGORY ST3527
Rose & Crown (01823) 490296
Woodhill; follow North Curry signpost off A378 by junction with A358 – keep on to Stoke, bearing right in centre, passing church and follow lane for 0.5 miles; TA3 6EW Popular dining pub with good food (best to book) and two or three local ales, friendly helpful staff, more or less open-plan, with stools by curved brick and wood counter, long high-raftered flagstoned dining room and two further beamed eating areas, one with glass-covered well; background music; children welcome, seats on sheltered front terrace, one bedroom. *(Alistair Forsyth)*

TARR SS8632
★ Tarr Farm (01643) 851507
Tarr Steps – narrow road off B3223 N of Dulverton; deep ford if you approach from the W (inn is on E bank); TA22 9PY Fine Exmoor position for this 16th-c inn above River Barle's medieval clapper bridge; compact unpretentious bar rooms with good views, leather chairs around slabby rustic tables, some stall and wall seating, game bird pictures on wood-clad walls, three woodburners, well kept Exmoor ales and several wines by the glass, good food using local produce, residents' end with smart evening restaurant, friendly helpful service, pleasant log-fire lounge with dark leather armchairs and sofas; children and dogs welcome, slate-topped stone tables outside making most of setting, extensive grounds, good bedrooms (no under-10s), open all day but may be closed early Feb. *(M G Hart, Bob and Margaret Holder)*

TAUNTON ST2525
Hankridge Arms (01823) 444405
Hankridge Way, Deane Gate (near Sainsbury's); just off M5 junction 25 – A358 towards city, then right at roundabout, right at next roundabout; TA1 2LR Interesting nicely restored Badger dining pub based on 16th-c former farmhouse – quite a contrast to the modern shopping complex surrounding it; different-sized linked areas, beams, timbers and big log fire, popular food from lunchtime sandwiches through pubby choices up, well kept ales and decent wines by the glass, friendly young staff; background music; dogs welcome, plenty of tables in pleasant outside area. *(Simon Sharpe)*

TAUNTON ST2225
Plough (01823) 324404
Station Road; TA1 1PB Popular little pub with three or four local ales including Otter tapped from cooled casks, up to ten racked ciders with more on draught and seven wines by the glass, simple food all day till 10pm including range of pies, bare boards, panelling, candles on tables, cosy nooks and open fire, hidden door to lavatories; background music (live weekends), popular quiz Tues; dogs welcome, handy for station, open all day (till 3am Fri, Sat). *(William Slade)*

TAUNTON ST2223
Vivary Arms (01823) 272563
Wilton Street; across Vivary Park from centre; TA1 3JR Popular low-beamed 18th-c local (Taunton's oldest), good value fresh food from light lunches up in snug plush lounge and small dining room, takeaway fish and chips, friendly helpful young staff, well kept ales including Butcombe, decent wines, interesting collection of drink-related items; pool

and darts; lovely display of hanging baskets and flowers. *(Bob and Margaret Holder, Alistair Forsyth)*

TINTINHULL ST5019
★ **Crown & Victoria** (01935) 823341
Farm Street, village signed off A303; BA22 8PZ Handsome golden-stone inn, carpeted throughout, with high bar chairs by light oak counter serving four well kept ales including Butcombe and Sharps, farmhouse furniture and big woodburner, good popular food using free range/organic ingredients, efficient friendly service, dining room with more pine tables and chairs, former skittle alley also used for dining, end conservatory; well behaved children welcome, disabled facilities, big garden with play area, five bedrooms, handy for Tintinhull Garden (NT), closed Sun evening. *(Charles Todd)*

TRULL ST2122
Winchester Arms (01823) 284723
Church Road; TA3 7LG Cosy streamside village pub with good value generous food including blackboard specials and popular Sun lunch, curry night first Weds of the month, west country ales and ciders, friendly helpful service, small dining room; Sun quiz, skittle alley; garden with decked area and summer barbecues, six bedrooms. *(James Allsopp)*

UPTON ST0129
Lowtrow Cross Inn (01398) 371220
A3190 E of Upton; TA4 2DB Welcoming old pub run by mother and son; character low-beamed bar with log fire and woodburner, bare boards and flagstones, two country-kitchen dining areas, one with enormous inglenook, generous helpings of tasty home-made food (not Mon, lunchtime Tues), ales such as Cotleigh and Otter, ciders from Sandford Orchards and Thatcher's, good mix of locals and diners; children and dogs welcome, lovely surroundings, three bedrooms, camping next door, closed Mon lunchtime (Sun evening, Mon, Tues in winter). *(Simon Sharpe)*

VOBSTER ST7049
★ **Vobster Inn** (01373) 812920
Lower Vobster; BA3 5RJ Spacious old stone-built dining pub with popular reasonably priced food (special diets catered for) including fresh fish and regular meal deals, good friendly service, Butcombe, Ashton Press cider and nice wines by the glass, three comfortable open-plan areas with antique furniture, plenty of room for just a drink; children and dogs (in bar) welcome, seats on lawn, boules, four bedrooms, closed Sun evening, Mon. *(David Longhurst)*

WAMBROOK ST2907
Cotley Inn (01460) 62348
Off A30 W of Chard; don't follow the small signs to Cotley itself; TA20 3EN Refurbished old stone pub under welcoming licensees; light and airy beamed bar with flagstones and double-sided woodburner, carpeted dining areas off, two further fires, well kept Otter ales and a guest tapped from the cask, enjoyable reasonably priced traditional food, friendly attentive service; background music, skittle alley; children and dogs welcome, lovely view from terrace tables, nice garden below, quiet spot with plenty of surrounding walks, tethering for horses, closed Sun evening, Mon lunchtime. *(Bob and Margaret Holder)*

WASHFORD ST0440
White Horse (01984) 640415
Abbey Road/Torre Rocks; TA23 0JZ Welcoming and popular old local, good selection of well kept ales and enjoyable reasonably priced pubby food including specials and deals, can eat in bar or separate restaurant, log fires; pool; large smokers' pavilion over road next to trout stream, field with interesting collection of fowl and goats, bedrooms, good traditional breakfast. *(Richard and Penny Gibbs)*

WATCHET ST0743
Pebbles (01984) 634737
Market Street; TA23 0AN Popular, welcoming and relaxed little bar in former shop near Market House Museum and harbour; extensive range of regional ciders (tasters offered), also cask-tapped ales such as Exmoor, Moles and Otter and good choice of whiskies, cider brandies and other drinks, friendly helpful staff, no food but can bring your own (plates and cutlery supplied; fish and chip shop next door); regular live music (some impromptu) including folk and jazz, sea shanty and poetry evenings, free wi-fi; dogs on leads welcome, open all day (from 3pm Weds). *(Richard and Penny Gibbs)*

WATCHET ST0643
Star (01984) 631367
Mill Lane (B3191); TA23 0BZ Late 18th-c beamed pub at end of lane just off Watchet harbour; main flagstoned bar with other low-ceilinged side rooms, some exposed stonework and rough wood partitioning, mix of traditional furniture including oak settles, window seats, local artwork for sale, woodburner in ornate fireplace, good selection of pubby food mostly sourced locally including fresh fish, four well kept west country ales, Sheppy's cider and a few malt whiskies, cheerful efficient staff; background music; children and dogs

---

Virtually all pubs in this book sell wine by the glass. We mention wines if they are a cut above the average.

welcome, wheelchair access, picnic-sets out in front and in sloping beer garden behind, handy for marina and West Somerset Railway. *(Chris and Angela Buckell)*

WELLOW   ST7358
Fox & Badger (01225) 832293
Signed off A367 SW of Bath; BA2 8QG
Opened-up village pub under same owners as the White Hart at Widcombe Hill, Bath; good mix of customers, flagstones one end, bare boards the other, some snug corners, woodburner in massive hearth, Butcombe, Fullers, Greene King and Sharps, four ciders, wide range of good food (booking advised weekends), friendly accommodating service; children and dogs welcome, picnic-sets in covered courtyard, open all day Fri, Sat, closed Sun evening. *(Alistair Holdoway, Taff Thomas)*

WELLS   ST5445
★ City Arms (01749) 673916
High Street; BA5 2AG Bustling town-centre pub with up to seven well kept ales, three ciders and enjoyable reasonably priced food from varied menu including themed nights, friendly service, modernised main bar and restaurant areas; background music; children and dogs welcome, cobbled courtyard and some reminders that the building was once a jail, first-floor terrace, four bedrooms, open (and food) all day. *(R K Phillips, Dr J Barrie Jones)*

WELLS   ST5445
Crown (01749) 673457
Market Place; BA5 2RF Former 15th-c coaching inn overlooked by cathedral, various bustling areas with light wooden flooring, plenty of matching chairs and cushioned wall benches, Butcombe, Palmers, St Austell and Sharps, popular food from sandwiches up in bar and bistro, friendly efficient service; background music, TV; children until 8pm, dogs in bar, small heated courtyard, 15 bedrooms, open all day. *(Ann and Colin Hunt, Richard Tilbrook, Steve and Liz Tilley)*

WELLS   ST5546
★ Fountain (01749) 672317
St Thomas Street; BA5 2UU Relaxed restaurant place with big comfortable bar, interesting décor and large open fire, quite a choice of popular food here or in upstairs dining room (booking advised weekends), Mon steak night, Tues OAP lunch, ales such as Bath, Butcombe and Sharps, several wines by the glass, courteous helpful staff; unobtrusive background music; children welcome, pretty in summer with window

boxes and blue shutters, handy for cathedral and moated Bishop's Palace, closed Sun evening, Mon lunchtime. *(Hugh Roberts, Ann and Mike Bolton, Ian Phillips, R K Phillips, Stephen Funnell)*

WEST BAGBOROUGH   ST1733
★ Rising Sun (01823) 432575
Village signed off A358 NW of Taunton; TA4 3EF Charming beamed village pub under new management; small flagstoned bar to right of massive main door serving west country ales, smart cosy dining room with attractive mix of chairs around a few dark wood tables, good if not especially cheap food including daily specials, friendly service, pleasant back snug, upstairs room with trusses in high pitched ceiling, refectory tables and oriental rug on wood floor; children and dogs welcome, teak seats outside by lane, two bedrooms, no car park, closed Sun evening. *(Bob and Margaret Holder)*

WEST HATCH   ST2719
Farmers Arms (01823) 480980
Slough Green, W of village; TA3 5RS Welcoming tucked-away pub (former farmhouse) with four neatly kept linked rooms mostly set for dining, beams, stripped boards and exposed stonework, country pine furniture, leather sofas by woodburner, good popular home-made food from bar and restaurant menus, four west country ales and plenty of wines by the glass, afternoon teas, cheerful helpful service; monthly live music; children welcome, seats on terrace and small lawn, good local walks, five bedrooms, open all day. *(Richard and Patricia Jefferson, Hugh Roberts, Bob and Margaret Holder)*

WEST HUNTSPILL   ST3145
Crossways (01278) 783756
A38, between M5 junctions 22 and 23; TA9 3RA Rambling 17th-c tile-hung pub with six well kept mostly local ales (tasting trays available), good choice of enjoyable generously served food at reasonable prices, cheerful efficient staff (they may ask for a credit card if you run a tab), split-level carpeted areas with beams and log fires, skittle alley; pool, TV; children and dogs welcome, disabled facilities, garden with play area and heated smokers' shelter, seven bedrooms, open all day. *(R K Phillips)*

WEST MONKTON   ST2628
★ Monkton (01823) 412414
Blundells Lane; signed from A3259; TA2 8NP Popular and welcoming village dining pub with good choice of freshly made food including some south african influences (best to book weekends), bare-boards bar

---

Cribbage is a card game using a block of wood with holes for matchsticks or special pins to score with; regulars in cribbage pubs are usually happy to teach strangers how to play.

with central woodburner and snug off, separate restaurant with strip-wood floor, Exmoor, Otter and Sharps Doom Bar, Orchard Pig and Thatcher's ciders, nine wines by the glass, good friendly service; children and dogs welcome, wheelchair access from the front, lots of tables in big garden bounded by stream, play area. *(Bob and Margaret Holder)*

WEST PENNARD ST5438
Lion (01458) 832941
A361 E of Glastonbury; Newtown; BA6 8NH Traditional stone-built 16th-c village inn; bar and dining areas off small flagstoned black-beamed core, enjoyable pubby food plus daily specials, Sun carvery, Butcombe, Otter and Sharps, inglenook woodburner and open fires; background and live folk music; children and dogs welcome, tables on big forecourt, skittle alley, good nearby walks, seven refurbished bedrooms in converted side barn. *(Rosie and John Moore)*

WIDCOMBE ST2216
Holman Clavel (01823) 421070
Culmhead, on ridge road W of B3170, follow sign for Blagdon; 2 miles S of Corfe; TA3 7EA Country local dating from the 14th c and under new management; friendly and relaxed with good food from varied menu, Butcombe Bitter and Gold plus a guest, local ciders such as Tricky's, flagstoned bar with woodburner in big fireplace, room off has a long dining table (seats 24); some live music; children, dogs and muddy boots welcome, handy for Blackdown Hills, open all day Fri-Sun, closed Tues. *(William Slade)*

WINCANTON ST7028
Nog Inn (01963) 32998
South Street; BA9 9DL Welcoming old split-level pub with Otter, Sharps and a couple of guests, real cider and continental beers, good reasonably priced traditional food including Sun carvery (not summer) and blackboard specials, bare boards, carpet and flagstones, pump clips on ceiling, log fires; background and some live music, comedy nights, charity quiz (second Thurs of month), darts; well behaved children and dogs welcome, pleasant back garden with heated smokers' shelter, open (and food) all day. *(Lance and Sarah Milligan)*

WINFORD ST5262
Crown (01275) 472388
Crown Hill, off Regil Road; BS40 8AY Popular old pub in deep country with linked beamed rooms, mix of pubby furniture including settles on flagstones or quarry tiles, old pictures and photographs on rough walls, copper and brass, leather sofas in front of big open fire, enjoyable generous home-made food (all day Sun) at very reasonable prices, Butcombe and Wadworths and a guest, good choice of wines by the

glass, friendly attentive landlord and staff; table skittles and skittle alley; children and dogs welcome, wheelchair access with help, tables out in front and in back garden, closed Mon lunchtime, otherwise open all day. *(Taff Thomas)*

WINSFORD SS9034
★ Royal Oak (01643) 851455
Off A396 about 10 miles S of Dunster; TA24 7JE Prettily placed thatched and beamed Exmoor inn, enjoyable well priced home-made food (greater evening choice), Exmoor ales and west country ciders, friendly helpful staff, carpeted bar with woodburner in big stone fireplace, large bay window seat looking across to village green and foot and packhorse bridges over River Winn, restaurant and other lounge areas; children and dogs (in bar) welcome, disabled facilities, eight good bedrooms some with four-posters. *(Bob and Margaret Holder, Phil Bartley)*

WITHAM FRIARY ST7440
★ Seymour Arms (01749) 850742
Signed from B3092 S of Frome; BA11 5HF Well worn-in unchanging flagstoned country tavern, in same friendly family since 1952; two simple rooms off 19th-c hatch-service lobby, panelled benches and open fires, well kept Cheddar Potholer and an occasional guest, Rich's local cider tapped from back room, low prices, no food but can bring your own; bar billiards, darts and table skittles; children and dogs welcome, garden by main rail line, village cricket pitch over the road, open all day. *(Taff Thomas)*

WITHYPOOL SS8435
★ Royal Oak (01643) 831506
Village signed off B3233; TA24 7QP Prettily placed country inn – where R D Blackmore stayed while writing *Lorna Doone*; lounge with raised working fireplace, comfortably cushioned wall seats and slat-backed chairs, sporting trophies, paintings and copper/brass ornaments, enjoyable food here and in restaurant, well kept Exmoor ales, friendly helpful service, character locals' bar; walkers and dogs welcome (leave muddy boots in porch), children in eating areas, wooden benches on terrace, attractive riverside village with lovely walks, grand views from Winsford Hill just up the road, eight bedrooms (twisting staircase to top floor), open all day, but may close for a week in Feb. *(Lynda and Trevor Smith)*

WOOKEY ST5245
★ Burcott (01749) 673874
B3139 W of Wells; BA5 1NJ Beamed roadside pub with two simply furnished old-fashioned front bar rooms, flagstones, some exposed stonework and half-panelling, lantern wall lights, old prints, woodburner, a couple of real ales such as Hop Back Summer

Lightning and a proper cider, enjoyable food (not Mon evening, or Tues evening in winter) from snacks up in bar and restaurant (children allowed here), good service, small games room with built-in wall seats; soft background music, no dogs; wheelchair access, front window boxes and tubs, picnic-sets in sizeable garden with Mendip Hills views, four self-catering units in converted stables, closed Sun evening, Mon. *(Taff Thomas)*

WOOKEY HOLE   ST5347
Wookey Hole Inn (01749) 676677
High Street; BA5 1BP Open-plan family dining pub usefully placed opposite the caves, welcoming and relaxed, with unusual contemporary décor, wood or tiled floors, tables with paper cloths for drawing on (crayons provided), two woodburners, good food from pub favourites to daily specials, three changing local ales, several belgian beers, ciders and perry, efficient friendly staff; background music; dogs allowed, pleasant garden with various sculptures, five individually styled bedrooms, open all day apart from Sun evening. *(Ann and Colin Hunt)*

WOOLVERTON   ST7954
Red Lion (01373) 830350
Set back from A36 N of village; BA2 7QS Spacious modernised pub with beams, panelling and lots of stripped wood, candles and log-effect fire, well kept Wadworths, decent wines by the glass and good choice of enjoyable food from baguettes up including stone-baked pizzas and children's meals, friendly quick service, locals' bar with fire (dogs allowed here); background music, free

wi-fi; plenty of tables outside, play area, open all day Fri, Sat, till 9pm Sun. *(William Slade)*

WRAXALL   ST4971
★ Old Barn (01275) 819011
Just off Bristol Road (B3130) in grounds of Wraxall House; BS48 1LQ Idiosyncratic gabled barn conversion, scrubbed tables, school benches and soft sofas under oak rafters, stripped boards and flagstones, various pictures and odds and ends, welcoming atmosphere and friendly service, five well kept ales including Butcombe, Fullers and Palmers tapped from the cask, farm ciders, good wines by the glass, simple sandwiches, unusual board games; occasional background music and sports TV; dogs welcome, nice garden with terrace barbecue (bring your own meat) and smokers' shelter, open all day. *(Taff Thomas, Steve and Liz Tilley)*

YARLINGTON   ST6529
Stags Head (01963) 440393
Pound Lane; BA9 8DG Old low-ceilinged and flagstoned country pub tucked away in rustic hamlet; well kept Bass, Greene King and Otter from small central bar, woodburner, chapel chairs and mixed pine tables on left, carpeted dining area on right with big log fire, modern landscape prints and feature cider-press table, second dining room with doors on to terrace, enjoyable food from traditional choices up including monthly themed nights, good friendly service; background music; well behaved children welcome, dogs in bar, picnic-sets in sheltered back garden with small stream, maybe summer morris men, three bedrooms, closed Sun evening. *(Robert Watt)*

Real ale to us means beer that has matured naturally in its cask – not pressurised or filtered. We name all real ales stocked. We usually name ales preserved under a light blanket of carbon dioxide too, though purists – pointing out that this stops the natural yeasts developing – would disagree (most people, including us, can't tell the difference!).

Staffordshire

ALSTONEFIELD SK1355 Map 7

George  ♀

(01335) 310205 – www.thegeorgeatalstonefield.com

Village signed from A515 Ashbourne–Buxton; DE6 2FX

**Simply furnished and friendly pub in a pretty Peakland village,
real ales and enjoyable food and seats outside**

In the middle of a quiet farming hamlet and opposite the village green, this
is a welcoming stone-built pub run by a long-serving family. There's an
easy-going atmosphere in the chatty bar which has low beams and quarry
tiles, old Peak District photographs and pictures, a log fire, Marstons Burton
Bitter and Pedigree New World Pale Ale and guests such as Brakspears
Oxford Gold and Ringwood Best Bitter on handpump and a dozen wines
by the glass; service is friendly and helpful. As well as a little snug, there's
a neat dining room with a woodburning stove, simple farmhouse furniture,
candlelight and fresh flowers. There are picnic-sets at the front with more
seats in a big, sheltered back stable yard.

 Particularly good food uses local produce and some grown in their own organic
garden: lunchtime sandwiches, corn-fed chicken and pistachio terrine, sautéed
wild mushrooms and duck egg on toasted sourdough, truffled macaroni cheese with
mushrooms and spinach, venison burger with toppings, gherkins and chips, rare-breed
sausages with chive mash, onion marmalade and gravy, confit duck leg with sticky red
cabbage, truffle and black pepper mash, a fresh fish dish of the day with crispy capers
and crab beignet, and puddings such as dark chocolate fondant cake with peanut
butter ice-cream and brittle and rhubarb and stem ginger cheesecake with rhubarb
compote. *Benchmark main dish: steak pie £16.00. Two-course evening meal £25.00.*

Marstons ~ Tenant Emily Brighton ~ Real ale ~ Open 11.30-3, 6-11; 11.30-11 Fri, Sat;
12-9.30 Sun ~ Bar food 12-2.30, 6.30-9 ~ Restaurant ~ Children welcome ~ Dogs allowed
in bar ~ Wi-fi *Recommended by Joy Griffiths, Belinda May, Edward Nile*

BREWOOD SJ8708 Map 4

Oakley ♀

(01902) 859800 – www.brunningandprice.co.uk/oakley

Kiddemore Green Road; ST19 9BQ

**Cleverly extended and refurbished bar and dining areas in
substantial pub, with lots to look at, interesting food and drink
and seats on long terrace**

The spreading terrace behind this newly opened pub has flowering tubs, raised beds and overlooks a lake, so its many seats and benches are quickly snapped up in warm weather. Inside, the open-plan rooms have been furnished with thought and care and the many windows and pastel paintwork keep it all very light and airy. Partitioning and metal standing posts split larger areas into cosier drinking and dining spaces. Throughout there are big house plants in pots with smaller ones on windowsills, mirrors above open fires (some in pretty Victorian fireplaces), books on shelves, elegant metal chandeliers, standard lamps, stubby candles and fresh flowers. Seating ranges from groups of leather armchairs to all manner of cushioned wooden dining chairs around character tables, the walls (some half-panelled) are hung with hundreds of prints, and flooring consists of rugs on big boards and, in the restaurant, carpet. From the long counter, friendly, helpful staff serve Phoenix Brunning & Price Original, Salopian Oracle and Wye Valley Butty Bach with guests such as Stonehouse Station Bitter and Titanic Plum Porter on handpump, a dozen wines by the glass, 86 whiskies, 71 gins and 68 rums; background music. There's a rack outside for cyclists. Disabled parking and lavatories.

Pleasing modern food includes sandwiches, rabbit, leek and bacon pasty with piccalilli, scallops with crab and lemon fritters and pea purée, chicken satay salad with pineapple, chinese leaves and peanuts, honey-roast ham with free-range eggs, wild mushroom tortellini with king oyster mushrooms and madeira broth, thai red fish curry, ox cheek bourguignon with horseradish mash, lamb rump with mint potato cakes and salsa verde, and puddings such as rhubarb and ginger trifle and baked white chocolate cheesecake with peach purée. *Benchmark main dish: braised lamb shoulder with dauphinoise potatoes and rosemary gravy £16.95. Two-course evening meal £21.00.*

Brunning & Price ~ Manager John Duncan ~ Real ale ~ Open 11-11 (10.30 Sun) ~ Bar food 12-10 (9.30 Sun) ~ Restaurant ~ Children welcome ~ Dogs allowed in bar ~ Wi-fi
Recommended by Hilary and Neil Christopher, James Landor, Kate Moran

CAULDON
SK0749 Map 7

Yew Tree ★★ £

(01538) 309876 – www.yewtreeinncauldon.co.uk
Village signposted from A523 and A52 about 8 miles W of Ashbourne; ST10 3EJ

A unique collection of curios in friendly pub with good value snacks and bargain beer; very eccentric

This extraordinary roadside local is a treasure trove of fascinating curiosities and antiques, the most impressive pieces being the working polyphons and symphonions – 19th-c developments of the musical box, some taller than a person, each with quite a repertoire of tunes and elaborate sound-effects. There are also two pairs of Queen Victoria's stockings, an amazing collection of ceramics and pottery including a Grecian urn dating back almost 3,000 years, penny-farthing and boneshaker bicycles and the infamous Acme Dog Carrier. Seats include 18th-c settles, plenty of little wooden tables and a four-person oak church choir seat with carved heads that came from St Mary's church in Stafford. Look out for the array of musical instruments ranging from a one-string violin (phonofiddle) through pianos and sousaphones to the aptly named serpent. Drinks are very reasonably priced, so it's no wonder the place is popular with locals. Burton Bridge Bitter, Rudgate Ruby Mild and a guest or two on handpump, ten interesting malt whiskies, eight wines by the glass and farm cider; they hold a music and beer festival in July and a vintage vehicle rally in September. Darts, table skittles and board games. There are seats outside the front door and in the cobbled stable yard, and they have a basic campsite for pub customers and a small caravan for hire. The pub is almost hidden from view by a towering yew tree.

The modest menu includes sandwiches, locally made pies, vegetable or beef chilli, beef stew with mash, and puddings. *Benchmark main dish: pie and mash £7.00. Two-course evening meal £10.00.*

Free house ~ Licensee Alan East ~ Real ale ~ Open 12-3, 6-11; 12-midnight Sat; 12-11 Sun; closed weekday lunchtimes in winter ~ Bar food 12-3, 6-9; 12-9 weekends ~ Children allowed in polyphon room ~ Dogs allowed in bar ~ Wi-fi ~ Live folk music first Tues of month
Recommended by Dr Simon Innes, Mungo Shipley, Helen McLagan, Alf Wright

CHEADLE
SK0342   Map 7

Queens at Freehay

(01538) 722383 – www.queensatfreehay.co.uk

A mile SE of Cheadle; take Rakeway Road off A522 (via Park Avenue or Mills Road), then after 1 mile turn into Counslow Road; ST10 1RF

Gently civilised dining pub with three real ales and attractive garden

Our readers continue to enjoy their visits to this 18th-c pub with its welcoming landlord and friendly atmosphere. The neat rooms have some cottagey touches that blend in well with the modern refurbishments. The comfortable lounge bar has pale wood tables on stripped wood floors, small country pictures and curtains with matching cushions, and opens via an arch into a simple light, airy dining area with elegant chairs and tables on tartan carpeting. Helpful staff serve Peakstones Rock Alton Abbey and a couple of guest beers such as Ringwood Boondoggle and Thwaites Lancaster Bomber on handpump and nine wines by the glass; some seating is set aside for those who want just a drink and a chat. In warm weather, the attractive and immaculately kept little back garden is a fine place to sit, with picnic-sets among mature shrubs and flowering tubs.

Good enjoyable food includes chicken liver, bacon and rosemary pâté with cider, apple and onion chutney, herb-breaded brie with balsamic tomato ketchup, spicy bean and sweet potato burger with toppings and chips, harissa chicken in an onion, tomato, red pepper, chickpea and apricot sauce with couscous, battered cod and chips, barnsley lamb chops with minted gravy and potatoes of the day, and puddings such as chocolate orange cheesecake and strawberry and champagne eton mess; they also offer several dishes in smaller helpings. *Benchmark main dish: beef in red wine pie £12.95. Two-course evening meal £16.00.*

Free house ~ Licensee Adrian Rock ~ Real ale ~ Open 12-3, 6-11; 12-4, 6.30-10.30 Sun ~ Bar food 12-2, 6-9.30; 12-2.30, 6.30-9.30 Sun ~ Restaurant ~ Children welcome ~ Wi-fi
Recommended by Dr Simon Innes, Victor Sumner

ELLASTONE
SK1143   Map 7

Duncombe Arms ⭐ ♥ ♀

(01335) 324275 – www.duncombearms.co.uk

Main Road; DE6 2GZ

Staffordshire Dining Pub of the Year

Nooks and crannies here and there, a thoughtful choice of drinks, friendly staff and lovely food; seats outside

Notably friendly, this stylishly refurbished village pub offers a genuine welcome to all its customers ranging from damp walkers to those out for a special meal – and there's somewhere interesting to sit whatever the occasion. There are beams here and there, bare brick, exposed stone and painted walls, open fires and woodburners, horse prints and photos, big bold paintings of pigs, sheep, cows and chickens, large clocks and fresh flowers, church candles on mantelpieces, in big glass jars and on tables – and flooring that ranges from carpet to flagstones to bare floorboards and brick. Furnishings are just as eclectic: long leather button-back and cushioned wall seats, armchairs, all manner of wooden or upholstered dining chairs and tables made from mahogany, pine and even driftwood. Black Sheep, Marstons Pedigree and a beer named for the pub on handpump, 20 wines by the glass from a fine list, a dozen gins and 18 malt whiskies; background music and board games. An attractive terrace has wooden or rush seats around tables under parasols, braziers for cooler evenings and a view down over the garden to Worthy Island Wood.

Creative food includes lunchtime sandwiches, home-made beans on toast with crispy egg, confit salmon with potato salad, pickled shallots and salad cream, jerusalem artichoke risotto with roasted salsify and mushrooms, burger with toppings and skinny fries, roasted pork rump with creamed pearl barley and onion and mustard sauce, cod fillet with rope-grown mussels, crispy potatoes and warm tartare sauce, local steaks with peppercorn sauce and triple-cooked chips, and puddings such as dark chocolate tart with blackberries, honeycomb and blackberry sorbet and spiced parkin cake with treacle ice-cream, rhubarb and custard. *Benchmark main dish: beer-battered fish and chips £13.00. Two-course evening meal £22.00.*

Free house ~ Licensees Johnny and Laura Greenall ~ Real ale ~ Open 12-11; 12-midnight Sat; 12-10.30 Sun ~ Bar food 12-2.30, 6-9; 12-2.30, 5.30-10 Fri, Sat; 12-8 Sun ~ Restaurant ~ Children welcome ~ Dogs allowed in bar ~ Wi-fi *Recommended by Brian and Anna Marsden, Mrs J Hollaway, Millie and Peter Downing*

LONGDON GREEN
Red Lion ♀ 📖

SK0813   Map 7

(01543) 490410 – www.brunningandprice.co.uk/redlion
Hay Lane; WS15 4QF

Large, well run pub with interesting furnishings, a fine range of drinks, enjoyable food and spreading garden

In summer, this handsome pub is especially popular as it has a large garden with seats and tables on a suntrap terrace, picnic-sets on grass, a gazebo and swings and a play tractor for children; you can also watch cricket matches on the village green opposite. The interior has been extended and thoughtfully opened up, but the bar remains the heart of the place, with spreading rooms and nooks and crannies leading off. One dining room has skylights, rugs on nice old bricks, house plants lining the windowsill, an elegant metal chandelier and a miscellany of cushioned dining chairs around dark wooden tables. Similar furnishings fill the other rooms, and the walls are covered with old photos, pictures and prints relating to the local area and big gilt-edged mirrors; background music and board games. Open fires include a raised central fire pit. You'll find Phoenix Brunning & Price Original, Backyard Blonde, Blythe Bagots Bitter, Castle Rock Elsie Mo and Salopian Lemon Dream on handpump, 20 wines by the glass, 50 malt whiskies, 30 gins and two farm ciders. Staff are friendly, courteous and helpful.

From a well judged menu, food includes sandwiches, warm smoked mackerel with apple jelly and lemon chantilly cream, a charcuterie board for sharing, blue cheese, fig and jerusalem artichoke quiche, steak in ale pie, chicken with pancetta and wild mushroom tagliatelle and truffle oil, smoked haddock and salmon fishcakes with tomato salad, steak burger with toppings, coleslaw and chips, venison rump with watercress purée and game jus, and puddings such as berry crumble with custard and crème brûlée. *Benchmark main dish: beer-battered fish and chips £12.75. Two-course evening meal £20.00.*

Brunning & Price ~ Manager Chloe Turner ~ Real ale ~ Open 10.30am-11pm (10.30pm Sun) ~ Bar food 12-10 (9.30 Sun) ~ Restaurant ~ Children welcome ~ Dogs allowed in bar ~ Wi-fi
Recommended by Belinda May, Peter Brix, Susan Jackman, Luke Morgan

SALT
Holly Bush £

SJ9527   Map 7

(01889) 508234 – www.hollybushinn.co.uk
Village signposted off A51 S of Stone (and A518 NE of Stafford); ST18 0BX

Delightful medieval pub with all-day food

Decked with brightly coloured flowers in summer, this charming thatched pub is in a pretty village. It's a friendly place with a good mix of customers, with a standing-only serving section from where several cosy areas spread out with high-backed cushioned pews, old tables and more conventional seats. The oldest part has a heavy-beamed and planked ceiling (some of the beams are attractively carved), a woodburning stove and a salt cupboard built into a big inglenook, with other nice old-fashioned touches including copper utensils, horsebrasses and an ancient pair of riding boots on the mantelpiece. A modern back extension, with beams, stripped brickwork and a small coal fire, blends in well. Adnams Southwold, Marstons Pedigree and a guest ale on handpump, alongside ten wines by the glass. They operate a secure locker system for credit cards, which they'll ask to keep if you run a tab. Outside, the back is beautifully tended and filled with flowers, with rustic picnic-sets on a big lawn.

Food is fairly priced and hearty and uses local produce; options include baked camembert with apricot reserve, prawn cocktail, a vegetarian dish of the day, cajun-style burger with toppings, coleslaw and beer-battered onion rings, free-range pork chops with cheese, beer and mustard topping, venison in red wine casserole, greek-style lamb, a mixed grill, and puddings. *Benchmark main dish: steak in ale pie £10.45. Two-course evening meal £15.00.*

Admiral Taverns ~ Licensees Geoffrey and Joseph Holland ~ Real ale ~ Open 12-11 (10.30 Sun) ~ Bar food 12-9.30 (9 Sun) ~ Children welcome ~ Wi-fi *Recommended by Dave Braisted, Steve and Liz Tilley, Stephen Shepherd, Ian and Rose Lock*

SWYNNERTON
Fitzherbert Arms ♀ ◀

SJ8535   Map 7

(01782) 796782 – www.fitzherbertarms.co.uk
Off A51 Stone–Nantwich; ST15 0RA

Thoughtfully renovated pub with character rooms, interesting décor, local ales and rewarding food; seats outside with country views

After a major restoration, this charming village pub has reopened – the frontage is fun with a stack of old beer barrels between two large glass windows and box topiary. It's on Lord Stafford's estate at the centre of Swynnerton and a circular walk (details on their website) guides you from the pub car park and back again – just in time for lunch; dogs will be greeted with a biscuit and a water bowl. On entering through an impressive glass door, the bar sits at the centre to the right, with a raised fireplace styled like a furnace and blacksmiths' tools and relics. Down a step to the left is the older part of the pub with button-back leather armchairs beside a two-way fireplace, rugs on flagstones, hops and some fine old brickwork. Fitzherbert Best (from Weetwood) and Swynnerton Stout (from Titanic) on handpump with a couple of guests from breweries within a 35-mile radius; also, 15 good wines by the glass, a fantastic and carefully chosen array of 30 ports with helpful notes (they hold port tasting evenings – phone for details) and a farm cider from the Apple County Cider Company. Staff are helpful and friendly. The beamed dining room has similar furnishings to the bar (a nice mix of old dining chairs and tables) plus window seats with scatter cushions, gilt-edged mirrors, black and white photographs and chandeliers; background music and board games. Do look out for the glass-topped giant bellows and anvil tables, door handles made of old smithy's irons, and candles in old port bottles. Outside, a covered oak-timbered terrace has contemporary seats around rustic tables, heaters, fairy-lit shrubs in pots and country views; there are more seats in a small hedged garden too. The pub is owned by Tim Bird and Mary McLaughlin, who also own the Three Greyhounds Inn in Allostock, Bulls Head and Church Inn in Mobberley (all Cheshire) and Red Lion in Weymouth (Dorset).

Interesting food includes mussels with cider and bacon, confit duck with fried egg and grain mustard sauce, sharing plates, burger with toppings, coleslaw and chips, caramelised onion tart with walnut and cheese crust and sautéed potatoes, venison with prunes, port, crispy onions and creamy mash, bass en papillote with cherry tomatoes and courgettes, and puddings such as chocolate and hazelnut brownie, chocolate sauce and pistachio ice-cream and apple and rhubarb crumble with vanilla custard. *Benchmark main dish: calves liver with sautéed new potatoes, sticky onion gravy and braised red cabbage £13.95. Two-course evening meal £19.00.*

Free house ~ Licensee Leanne Wallis ~ Real ale ~ Open 12-11 (10.30 Sun) ~ Bar food 12-9 (9.30 Fri, Sat); 12-8.45 Sun ~ Children welcome but no under 10s after 7pm ~ Dogs allowed in bar ~ Wi-fi *Recommended by Margaret McDonald, Patricia Hawkins, Diane Abbott*

WRINEHILL   SJ7547 Map 7
Hand & Trumpet ♀ ◉
(01270) 820048 ~ www.brunningandprice.co.uk/hand
A531 Newcastle – Nantwich; CW3 9BJ

All-day food in big attractive dining pub with a good choice of ales and wines by the glass, served by courteous staff

---

Whether it's a drink and a chat you're after or an enjoyable meal, this substantial pub is just the place. The linked, open-plan areas work their way around the long, solidly built counter, with a mix of dining chairs and sturdy tables on polished tiles or stripped-oak boards with rugs. There are nicely lit prints and mirrors on cream walls between a mainly dark dado, plenty of house plants, open fires and deep red ceilings. Original bow windows and a large skylight keep the place light and airy, and french windows open on to a spacious balustraded deck with teak tables and chairs. From here, there is a pleasant view down to ducks swimming on a big pond in the sizeable garden. Friendly attentive staff serve Phoenix Brunning & Price Original, Big Shed Engineers Best, Lancaster Northern Hemisphere Hopped Ale, Slaters Haka and a couple of guest beers on handpump, as well as 16 wines by the glass, 20 gins and about 70 whiskies; board games. Good disabled access and facilities.

Interesting food includes sandwiches, five-spice pork ribs with tomato and chilli sauce, king prawn, smoked salmon and crab with dill, cucumber and seafood dressing, chicken, ham and leek pie, field mushroom and goats cheese burger with coleslaw and sweet potato fries, teriyaki salmon with stir-fried noodles and vegetables, duck breast and confit leg with fondant potato and pickled rhubarb sauce, and puddings such as hot waffle with caramelised banana and banana ice-cream and dark chocolate torte with raspberry cream. *Benchmark main dish: braised lamb shoulder with dauphinoise potatoes and redcurrant and red wine gravy £17.95. Two-course evening meal £19.00.*

Brunning & Price ~ Manager John Unsworth ~ Real ale ~ Open 12-11 (10.30 Sun) ~ Bar food 12-9 ~ Children welcome ~ Dogs allowed in bar ~ Wi-fi *Recommended by Laura Reid, Dr and Mrs A K Clarke, Chris Stevenson*

Also Worth a Visit in Staffordshire

Besides the fully inspected pubs, you might like to try these pubs that have been recommended to us and described by readers. Do tell us what you think of them: feedback@goodguides.com

ABBOTS BROMLEY   SK0824
Coach & Horses (01283) 840256
High Street; WS15 3BN Modernised 18th-c village pub with good choice of well liked home-made food from baguettes and pizzas up, beamed bar with stone floor and button-back banquettes, dark wood pubby furniture in carpeted restaurant, log fire, three well kept ales such as St Austell and Marstons and several wines by the glass, friendly helpful staff; children and dogs (in bar) welcome, pleasant garden with circular picnic-sets, open all day Sun (food till 5pm), closed Mon. *(Mike Benton)*

ABBOTS BROMLEY   SK0824
Goats Head (01283) 840254
Market Place; WS15 3BP Black and white 16th-c village pub under new management; four well kept ales including St Austell Tribute, several wines by the glass and enjoyable home-made food (not Sun evening) including lots of fish options, opened-up beamed interior with oak floors, traditional furnishings and fire in big inglenook; children and dogs (in one bar area) welcome, teak furniture on deck and sheltered lawn looking up to church tower, closed Mon lunchtime, otherwise open all day. *(Mike Benton)*

ALSAGERS BANK   SJ8048
Gresley Arms (01782) 722469
High Street; ST7 8BQ At the top of Alsagers Bank with wonderful far-reaching views from the back, welcoming and popular, with eight or more interesting ales from smaller breweries and several real ciders, good value pubby food including bargain Thurs night (must book) and eat-for-£1 Mon if you buy a drink, traditional slate-floor bar with beams and open fire, comfortable lounge, picture-window dining room taking in the view, and a lower family room; Mon quiz; walkers and dogs welcome, garden picnic-sets, Apedale Heritage Centre nearby, open all day Thurs-Sun, from 3pm other days, no food lunchtimes (apart from Sun), Tues, Weds or evening Sun. *(Brian and Anna Marsden)*

BLACKBROOK   SJ7638
Swan with Two Necks
(01782) 680343 *Nantwich Road (A51); ST5 5EH* Country pub-restaurant with smart modern décor in open-plan split-level dining areas, good well presented food (booking advised) from sharing boards up, Timothy Taylors Landlord, three guest ales and plenty of wines by the glass including champagne, efficient friendly service (they may ask for a credit card if running a tab); background music; children welcome, comfortable tables out on decking, open (and food) all day. *(Laura Reid)*

BLITHBURY   SK0819
Bull & Spectacles (01889) 504201
Uttoxeter Road (B5014 S of Abbots Bromley); WS15 3HY Friendly 17th-c pub with good choice of enjoyable generously served food including bargain lunchtime Hot Table (half a dozen or so generous main dishes with help-yourself vegetables, and some puddings), also good value steak night (Mon, Thurs), a couple of changing ales such as Hook Norton Lion and Wells Bombardier, good service; children and dogs welcome, next door to reindeer farm, open all day Sun. *(Chris Stevenson)*

BRAMSHALL   SK0534
Robin Hood (01889) 566032
Leigh Road; ST14 5BH Modernised dining pub with generous helpings of enjoyable good value food from pub favourites up, well kept ales including one badged for them, afternoon teas; children welcome, open (and food) all day Fri-Sun. *(Margaret and Peter Staples)*

BURSLEM   SJ8649
Leopard (01782) 819644
Market Place; ST6 3AA Traditional Victorian city-centre pub with three rooms including a snug, good choice of enjoyable home-made food (Tues-Sun lunchtimes, Fri and Sat evenings), Bass and up to five changing guests, well priced wines, friendly

helpful service; live music, ghost tours in derelict hotel part; open all day. *(Luke Morgan)*

BURTON UPON TRENT SK2523

★**Burton Bridge Inn** (01283) 536596
Bridge Street (A50); DE14 1SY
Friendly down-to-earth local with good Burton Bridge ales from brewery across old-fashioned brick yard; simple little front area leading into adjacent bar with pews, plain walls hung with notices, awards and brewery memorabilia, 16 malt whiskies and lots of country wines, small beamed and oak-panelled lounge with simple furniture and flame-effect fire, upstairs dining room and skittle alley, short choice of low-priced lunchtime food Thurs-Sat; no credit cards; children welcome, dogs in bar, open all day Fri, Sat, closed Mon lunchtime. *(Hilary and Neil Christopher)*

BURTON UPON TRENT SK2423

★**Coopers Tavern** (01283) 532551
Cross Street; DE14 1EG Friendly old-fashioned 19th-c backstreet local tied to Joules – was tap for the Bass brewery and still has some glorious ephemera including mirrors and glazed adverts; homely and warm with coal fire, straightforward front parlour, back bar doubling as tap room with up to half a dozen guest beers (including Bass) and good selection of ciders/perries, pork pies only but can bring your own food (or take beer to next-door curry house); live music including Tues folk night; children and dogs welcome, small back garden, open all day Thurs-Sun, from 5pm Mon, 3pm Tues and Weds. *(Hilary and Neil Christopher)*

BURTON UPON TRENT SK2423

Old Cottage Tavern (01283) 511615
Rangemoor Street/Byrkley Street; DE14 2EG Friendly unpretentious corner local acting as tap for Burton Old Cottage, their ales in top condition and three guests, bars front and back and a snug, upstairs games room with skittle alley; folk nights; bedrooms, open all day. *(Hilary and Neil Christopher)*

CANNOCK WOOD SK0412

Park Gate (01543) 682223
Park Gate Road, S side of Cannock Chase; WS15 4RN Large red-brick dining pub with popular food including various deals and children's menu, ales such as St Austell, Sharps and Thwaites, rustic feel bar with woodburner, other comfortably modernised areas and conservatory; background and occasional live Irish music; dogs allowed in bar, nice secluded back garden with plenty of picnic-sets and play area, by Castle

---

Ring Iron Age hill fort, good Cannock Chase walks, open all day. *(Kate Moran)*

CHEDDLETON SJ9752

Black Lion (01538) 360620
Leek Road, by the church; ST13 7HP Refurbished 19th-c village local, well kept Bass, Welbeck Abbey and two guests, freshly made traditional lunchtime food (snacks such as local pork pies in the evening), woodburner; some live music, pool and darts; dogs welcome, seats out in front and in fenced back garden. *(James Landor)*

CHEDDLETON SJ9751

Boat (01538) 360521
Basford Bridge Lane, off A520; ST13 7EQ Cheerful unpretentious canalside local handy for Churnet Valley steam railway, flint mill and country park; long bar with low plank ceiling, well kept Marstons-related ales and enjoyable honest food from sandwiches to good steaks, dining room behind; children welcome, dogs in bar, seats out overlooking Caldon Canal, open all day. *(Chris and Dorothy Stock)*

CODSALL SJ8603

Codsall Station (01902) 847061
Chapel Lane/Station Road; WV8 1BY Converted vintage waiting room and ticket office of working station, comfortable and welcoming, with well kept Holdens ales and a couple of guests, good value pubby food (sandwiches only Sun) including blackboard specials, lots of railway memorabilia, open fire, conservatory; terrace seating, open all day Fri-Sun. *(Stephen Shepherd, Mark Writtle)*

CONSALL SK0049

Black Lion (01782) 550294
Consall Forge, OS Sheet 118 map reference 000491; best approach from Nature Park, off A522, using car park 0.5 miles past Nature Centre; ST9 0AJ Traditional take-us-as-you-find-us place tucked away in rustic canalside spot by restored steam railway station; generous helpings of enjoyable pub food, five well kept ales including Peakstones Rock and several ciders, flagstones and good coal fire; background music; children and dogs welcome, seats out overlooking canal, area for campers and shop for boaters, good walks, open (and food) all day, can get very busy weekend lunchtimes. *(Chris Stevenson)*

COPMERE END SJ8029

Star (01785) 850279
W of Eccleshall; ST21 6EW Friendly two-room 19th-c country local with well kept Bass, Titanic Anchor, Wells Bombardier and

---

Anyone claiming to arrange, or prevent, inclusion of a pub in the *Guide* is a fraud. Pubs are included only if recommended by readers and if our own anonymous inspection confirms that they are suitable.

a couple of guests, good choice of reasonably priced food from sandwiches up, open fire and woodburner, piano; children and dogs welcome, tables and play area in back garden overlooking mere, good walks, open all day weekends, closed Mon. *(Luke Morgan)*

DENSTONE SK0940
Tavern (01889) 590847
College Road; ST14 5HR Welcoming 17th-c stone-built pub, comfortable lounge with antiques, good food including freshly made pizzas (Fri, Sat evenings) and Sun carvery, well kept Marstons ales and good range of wines by the glass, pleasant service, dining conservatory; some live music; children welcome, picnic-sets out at front among tubs and hanging baskets, village farm shop and lovely church, open all day Fri-Sun, closed Mon. *(Laura Reid)*

DUSTON SP7262
Hopping Hare (01604) 580090
Hopping Hill Gardens; NN5 6PF Imposing red-brick former manor surrounded by housing; largish bar adjacent to entrance, log fires and lots of different dining areas, well kept Adnams, Black Sheep and a guest, good range of wines by the glass and nicely presented food from good varied menu including plenty of gluten-free choices, attentive friendly service; children welcome, seats out on decking, 19 bedrooms, open all day, food all day weekends. *(Gerry and Rosemary Dobson)*

ECCLESHALL SJ8329
Old Smithy (01785) 850564
Castle Street; ST21 6DF Pub-restaurant with comfortable clean modern décor, popular freshly made food (all day Sun) at fair prices including decent vegetarian options, four mainstream ales and good choice of other drinks, friendly efficient staff, maybe Mon evening pianist; children welcome, open all day. *(James Landor)*

ECCLESHALL SJ8329
Royal Oak (01785) 859065
High Street; ST21 6BW Old beamed and colonnaded coaching inn restored by Joules brewery and run by father and son team; their well kept ales and enjoyable locally sourced food including Mon and Tues bargains, welcoming chatty staff; dogs welcome, beer garden, open all day. *(Mike Benton)*

FLASH SK0267
Travellers Rest/Knights Table
(01298) 236695 *A53 Buxton–Leek; SK17 0SN* Isolated main-road pub and one of the highest in Britain, clean and friendly, with good reasonably priced traditional food (not Sun evening) including home-made pies, four well kept ales and good selection of wines, beams, bare stone walls and open fires, medieval knights theme; free wi-fi;

children very welcome, great Peak District views from back terrace, classic car meeting last Thurs of month, bedrooms, closed Mon, otherwise open all day. *(John Wooll)*

FRADLEY SK1414
White Swan (01283) 790330
Fradley Junction; DE13 7DN Refurbished pub (aka the Mucky Duck) in good canalside location at Trent & Mersey and Coventry junction; Everards ales and three guests, enjoyable reasonably priced food including pizzas, cheery traditional public bar with woodburner and open fire, quieter lounge and lower vaulted dining room (former stable); Thurs folk night, open mike Sun; children and dogs welcome, waterside tables, classic car/motorbike meetings, open all day. *(Hilary and Neil Christopher)*

GNOSALL SJ8220
Boat (01785) 822208
Gnosall Heath, by Shropshire Union Canal Bridge 34; ST20 0DA Popular little canalside pub run by friendly family, comfortable first-floor bar with curved window seat overlooking narrowboats, decent choice of reasonably priced pub food (not Sun evening, reduced choice Mon evening), Marstons-related ales, open fire; children and dogs welcome, tables out by canal, moorings and nice walks, open all day weekends, closed Mon lunchtime. *(Diane Abbott)*

HANLEY SJ8847
Coachmakers Arms (01782) 262158
Lichfield Street; ST1 3EA Chatty traditional 19th-c town local with four small rooms and drinking corridor, five well kept ales including Bass, darts, cards and dominoes, original seating and local tilework, open fires; children and dogs welcome, open all day (remains under threat of demolition). *(Laura Reid)*

HARTSHILL SJ8645
Jolly Potters 07875 586902
Hartshill Road (A52); ST4 7NH Friendly drinkers' pub under newish management (some refurbishment), traditional layout with four rooms off corridor, three or four well kept ales including Bass and Black Sheep, good selection of gins, no food (may be summer barbecues/hog roasts); acoustic open mike night Tues; dogs very welcome, small garden and terrace, open from 3pm Fri-Sun (4pm other days). *(James Landor)*

HAUGHTON SJ8620
Bell (01785) 780301
A518 Stafford–Newport; ST18 9EX Refurbished 19th-c village pub with good value popular food (not Sun or Mon evenings, best to book), lunchtime deal Mon-Sat, five well kept ales including Marstons, Timothy Taylors and a house beer from Jennings, friendly attentive service even when busy, restaurant behind; children welcome, no

dogs inside, picnic-sets in back garden, open all day Fri-Sun. *(Kate Moran)*

HIGH OFFLEY   SJ7725
Anchor (01785) 284569
Off A519 Eccleshall–Newport; towards High Lea, by Shropshire Union Canal Bridge 42; Peggs Lane; ST20 0NG
Built around 1830 to serve the Shropshire Union Canal and little changed in the century or more this family has run it; two small simple front rooms, one with a couple of fine high-backed settles on quarry tiles, Wadworths 6X and Weston's cider, sandwiches on request, owners' sitting room behind bar, occasional weekend sing-alongs; outbuilding with semi-open lavatories (swallows may fly through); no children inside, lovely garden with hanging baskets and notable topiary anchor, small shop, moorings (near Bridge 42), caravans/camping, closed Mon-Thurs in winter. *(Helen McLagan)*

HIMLEY   SO8990
★Crooked House (01384) 238583
Signed down long lane from B4176 Gornalwood–Himley, OS Sheet 139 map reference 896908; DY3 4DA Extraordinary sight, building thrown wildly out of kilter by mining subsidence, one side 4-ft lower than the other and slopes so weird that things appear to roll up them; public bar (dogs allowed here) with grandfather clock and hatch serving Banks's and other Marstons-related ales, lounge bar, good food from snacks and pub standards to more unusual choices, cheery service, some local antiques in level extension, conservatory; children welcome in eating areas, big outside terrace, closed Mon, otherwise open all day (till 6pm Sun). *(Dave Braisted)*

HULME END   SK1059
Manifold Inn (01298) 84537
B5054 Warslow–Hartington; SK17 0EX
Fairly isolated stone coaching inn near River Manifold, enjoyable traditional home-made food at reasonable prices, four well kept ales such as Leatherbritches, Marstons, Thwaites and Whim, pleasant friendly staff, log fire in traditional carpeted bar, adjacent restaurant and conservatory; background music, TV; children and dogs (in some parts) welcome, disabled facilities, tables outside, ten bedrooms (eight in converted barns), self-catering cottage, good walks including Manifold Trail, open all day. *(Derek and Sylvia Stephenson)*

KIDSGROVE   SJ8354
★Blue Bell (01782) 774052
Hardingswood; off A50 NW edge of town; ST7 1EG Simple friendly pub (looks more like a house) with half a dozen thoughtfully chosen and constantly changing ales from smaller breweries, around 30 bottled continentals, up to three draught farm ciders and a perry, filled rolls weekends only; four small, carpeted rooms, unfussy and straightforward, with blue upholstered benches and basic pub furniture, gas-effect coal fire; may be background music and the occasional folk session, no credit cards; dogs and well behaved children welcome, tables in front and on little back lawn, close to Trent & Mersey and Macclesfield Canal junction, open all day Sun, closed Mon and weekday lunchtimes. *(Hilary and Neil Christopher)*

KNIGHTON   SJ7240
White Lion (01630) 647300
B5415 Woore–Market Drayton; TF9 4HJ
Modernised roadside pub with enjoyable food (not Mon) including tapas, three Theakstons ales, friendly attentive service, open fires, dining conservatory; background music; children welcome but no dogs inside, small outside seating area, open all day. *(Mike Benton)*

LEEK   SJ9856
★Wilkes Head 07976 592787
St Edward Street; ST13 5DS Friendly three-room local dating from the early 18th c (still has back coaching stables), owned by Whim with their ales and interesting guests, real ciders and good choice of whiskies, filled rolls, gas fire and lots of pump clips, pub games, juke box in back room, regular live music organised by musician landlord; children allowed in one room (not really a family pub), dogs welcome but do ask first, fair disabled access, garden with stage, open all day except Mon lunchtime. *(James Landor)*

LICHFIELD   SK0705
Boat (01543) 361692
From A5 at Muckley Corner, take A461 signed Walsall; pub is on right just before M6 Toll; WS14 0BU Most emphasis on food with huge floor-to-ceiling menu boards, views into kitchen and dishes ranging from lunchtime sandwiches through light snacks to interesting main choices; entrance part with leather club chairs and sofas around coffee tables and potted palms, split-level bar/dining areas with sturdy modern pine furniture on carpet, views of canal, three well kept changing ales and a dozen wines by the glass; background music; children and dogs (in bar) welcome, wheelchair access, garden with seats on raised deck, open (and food) all day Sun. *(Luke Morgan)*

LICHFIELD   SK1109
Duke of York (01543) 300386
Greenhill/Church Street; WS13 6DY
Old beamed pub with split-level front bar, cosy carpeted lounge and converted back stables, inglenook woodburners, well kept Joules ales and guests, simple lunchtime food (not Sun) served by pleasant staff; some live music, May beer festival; no children but dogs allowed, terrace picnic-sets behind and own bowling green, open all day. *(Luke Morgan)*

LICHFIELD   SK1308
Horse & Jockey (01543) 262924
*Tamworth Road (A51 Lichfield–
Tamworth); WS14 9JE* Cosy old-fashioned
pub with wide range of popular freshly
prepared food including good home-made
pies and fish specials (booking advisable),
ales such as Castle Rock, Marstons and
Sharps, good friendly service, open fire; darts;
children welcome if eating, no dogs, open all
day Sun. *(Luke Morgan, Mike Benton)*

LITTLE BRIDGEFORD   SJ8727
Mill (01785) 282710
*Worston Lane; near M6 junction 14;
turn right off A5013 at Little Bridgeford;
ST18 9QA* Useful dining pub in attractive
1814 watermill, enjoyable sensibly priced
food in bar and restaurant including
children's menu and Sun carvery, ales such
as Greene King and Marstons, good friendly
service; Thurs quiz; nice grounds with
adventure playground and nature trail (lakes,
islands etc); open all day. *(Luke Morgan)*

LONGNOR   SK0965
Old Cheshire Cheese (01298) 83218
High Street; SK17 0NS Welcoming and
relaxed 17th-c village pub, three well kept
Robinsons ales and enjoyable good value food
including blackboard specials and Weds steak
night, open fire, bric-a-brac and pictures
in traditional main bar, two dining rooms,
pool and TV in separate rooms; free wi-fi;
children, walkers and dogs welcome, tables
out in front and on back grass, four bedrooms
in converted stables over road, closed Mon,
otherwise open all day. *(Brian and Anna
Marsden)*

MARCHINGTON   SK1330
Dog & Partridge (01283) 820394
Church Lane; ST14 8LJ Flower-decked
18th-c village pub with various beamed and
tile-floored rooms, Bass and three changing
guests (beer festivals), good food (not Sun
evening) including themed nights and
bargain two-course lunch deal, good value
wines, attentive friendly staff, real fires and
some interesting bits and pieces; background
music, free wi-fi; children and dogs (in bar)
welcome, tables under parasols in paved back
terrace by car park, open all day Sun with
live music from 5pm. *(Paul Humphreys)*

MEERBROOK   SJ9960
Lazy Trout (01538) 300385
Centre of village; ST13 8SN Popular
country dining pub with enjoyable sensibly
priced food including daily specials, friendly
helpful staff, small bar area with five well
kept ales such as Greene King, Marstons
and Wincle from curved stone counter,
comfortable dining lounge to the right with
log fire, second quarry-tiled dining room to
the left with pine furniture and old cooking
range; juke box; children welcome, dogs and

muddy boots in some parts, seats out at front
by quiet lane and in appealing garden behind
with splendid views to the Roaches and Hen
Cloud, good walks, open (and food) all day.
*(Brian and Anna Marsden, Dr D J and
Mrs S C Walker, Malcolm and Pauline Pellatt)*

PENKRIDGE   SJ9214
Littleton Arms (01785) 716300
*St Michaels Square/A449 – M6 detour
between junctions 12 and 13; ST19 5AL*
Cheerfully busy dining pub-hotel (former
coaching inn) with contemporary open-
plan layout, good variety of enjoyable well
presented food from sandwiches and sharing
boards to popular Sun lunch, nice wines by
the glass and five well kept changing ales
from island servery, friendly accommodating
staff; background music; children and dogs
(in bar area) welcome, ten bedrooms, open
all day. *(Laura Reid)*

SEIGHFORD   SJ8725
Hollybush (01785) 281644
*3 miles from M6 junction 14 via A5013/
B5405; ST18 9PQ* Modernised and
extended beamed pub owned by the village
and leased to Titanic, their ales and guests,
good value locally sourced pubby food (all
day Fri and Sat, till 7pm Sun) from lunchtime
sandwiches and light choices up; monthly
charity quiz, portable skittle alley; children
and dogs welcome, beer garden, open all day
Fri-Sun. *(James Landor)*

SHEEN   SK1160
Staffordshire Knot (01298) 84329
Off B5054 at Hulme End; SK17 0ET
Welcoming traditional 17th-c stone-built
village pub, nice mix of old furniture on
flagstones or red and black tiles, stag's head
and hunting prints, two log fires in hefty
stone fireplaces, good interesting food cooked
by landlady, well kept local Whim Hartington
and reasonably priced wines, friendly helpful
staff; closed Mon. *(Mike Benton)*

STAFFORD   SJ9323
Swan (01785) 258142
Greengate Street; ST16 2JA Modernised
18th-c two-bar coaching inn, well kept
Marstons-related ales and guests, good
sensibly priced bar and brasserie food
including themed evenings (Tues vegetarian/
vegan, Weds steak, Thurs fish), coffee shop,
friendly helpful staff; courtyard with rattan-
style furniture, 31 bedrooms, open (and food)
all day. *(Jeff Davies)*

STOKE-ON-TRENT   SJ8649
Bulls Head (01782) 834153
St Johns Square, Burslem; ST6 3AJ
Old-fashioned two-room tap for Titanic
with up to ten ales (including guests) from
horseshoe bar, also good selection of belgian
beers, ciders and wines, well cared-for
interior with varnished tables on wood or
carpeted floors, coal fire; bar billiards, table

skittles and good juke box; drinking area outside (may be barbecue if Port Vale are at home), open all day Fri-Sun, closed till 3pm Mon, Tues. *(Chris Stevenson)*

STOKE-ON-TRENT SJ8745
Glebe (01782) 860670
35 Glebe Street, by the Civic Centre; ST4 1HG Well restored 19th-c Joules corner pub, their ales, real cider and good reasonably priced wines from central mahogany counter, William Morris leaded windows, bare boards and panelling, some civic portraits and big fireplace with coat of arms above, wholesome bar food (not Sun, Mon evening) from good doorstep sandwiches up, friendly staff; quite handy for station, open all day. *(Dr J Barrie Jones)*

STONE SJ8933
Wayfarer (01785) 811023
The Fillybrooks (A34 just N); ST15 0NB Sizeable 1930s pub beside dual-carriageway, contemporary décor and same owners as the Swan with Two Necks at Blackbrook; good food from varied menu including sharing plates and stone-baked pizzas, beers such as Joules, Salopian, Sharps and Timothy Taylors, lots of wines by the glass including champagne, friendly attentive staff; children welcome, no dogs inside, terrace seating, open (and food) all day. *(Mike Benton)*

STOWE SK0027
★**Cock** (01889) 270237
Off A518 Stafford–Uttoxeter; ST18 0LF Popular bistro-style conversion of old beamed village pub (calls itself Bistro le Coq), well executed french food (not Mon) from sensibly short set menus, good affordably priced wines, small bar area serving real ale, friendly efficient service; well behaved children welcome, closed Sun evening, Mon lunchtime. *(Chris Stevenson)*

TAMWORTH SK2004
Market Vaults (01827) 66552
Market Street next to Town Hall; B79 7LU Friendly traditional little pub with front bar and raised back lounge, dark oak, brass and original fireplaces, well kept Joules Pale Ale and seven guests, up to 16 real ciders and bargain lunchtime food; regular live music, Weds quiz, TV; nice garden behind, open all day (from 2pm Mon). *(Mike Benton)*

TRYSULL SO8594
Bell (01902) 892871
Bell Road; WV5 7JB Extended 18th-c red-brick village pub next to church, cosy bar, inglenook lounge and large high-ceilinged

back dining area, well kept Holdens, Bathams and a guest, reasonably priced wines and generally well liked food, friendly service; children and dogs (in bar) welcome, paved front terrace, open all day Fri-Sun. *(Paul Humphreys)*

WETTON SK1055
Olde Royal Oak (01335) 310287
Village signed off Hulme End–Alstonefield road, between B5054 and A515; DE6 2AF Welcoming old stone pub in lovely NT countryside – a popular stop for walkers; traditional bar with white ceiling boards above black beams, small dining chairs around rustic tables, log fire in stone fireplace, carpeted sun lounge, four well kept changing ales and good selection of malt whiskies, fairly priced home-made food from sandwiches up; background and live music, darts, dominoes and shove-ha'penny; children and dogs welcome, picnic-sets in shaded garden, closed Mon, otherwise open (and food) all day. *(James Landor)*

WHEATON ASTON SJ8512
Hartley Arms (01785) 840232
Long Street (canalside, Tavern Bridge); ST19 9NF Popular roomy pub in pleasant spot just above Shropshire Union Canal (Bridge 19), good affordably priced food from landlord-chef including specials, set lunch and Sun carvery, well kept Bank's and guests, efficient friendly service; acoustic music night Mon; children welcome, picnic-sets outside, open all day. *(Luke Morgan)*

WHITTINGTON SK1608
Dog (01543) 432601
The one near Lichfield; Main Street; WS14 9JU Beamed 18th-c village inn with good freshly made food (not Sun evening, Mon) from sensibly short menu including lunchtime deal, well kept Bass, Black Sheep and Greene King, decent choice of wines by the glass, open fire; sports TV; children welcome, no dogs inside, seats on small terrace, three bedrooms, open all day. *(Chris Stevenson)*

YARNFIELD SJ8632
Labour in Vain (01785) 760072
Yarnfield Road; ST15 0NJ Refurbished village pub under new family management, good varied choice of well liked food including set lunch menu, ales such as Bass, welcoming helpful staff, modern décor with wood-strip floors, some exposed stonework and double-aspect woodburner; background music; children welcome, open all day, no food Mon, Tues or after 7pm Sun. *(Hilary and Neil Christopher)*

Post Office address codings confusingly give the impression that some pubs
are in Staffordshire, when they're really in Cheshire or Derbyshire
(which is where we list them).

Suffolk

ALDEBURGH
Cross Keys

TM4656 Map 5

(01728) 452637

Crabbe Street; IP15 5BN

16th-c pub with seats outside near the beach, chatty atmosphere, friendly licensee and local beers; bedrooms

If you want to bag one of the seats on the sheltered back terrace with views across the promenade to the water, it's best to arrive promptly at peak times. This is a traditional pub and the low-ceilinged interconnecting bars have a cheerful, bustling atmosphere, a welcome from the obliging landlord, antique and other pubby furniture, miscellaneous paintings on the walls and log fires in two inglenook fireplaces. Adnams Southwold, Broadside and Ghost Ship on handpump, decent wines by the glass and several malt whiskies; background music and games machine. The bedrooms are attractively furnished.

🍴 Tasty food includes sandwiches, smoked mackerel pâté, goats cheese tart, ham and eggs, steak and kidney pie, fresh fish dishes such as mussels, whole plaice, hake and skate wing with brown butter, and puddings such as fruit crumble and sticky toffee pudding. *Benchmark main dish: fresh local fish and chips £11.00. Two-course evening meal £18.00.*

Adnams ~ Tenants Mike and Janet Clement ~ Real ale ~ Open 11am-midnight; 12-midnight Sun ~ Bar food 12-3, 6.30-9; not Sun evening ~ Children welcome ~ Dogs welcome ~ Wi-fi ~ Bedrooms: £75/£95 *Recommended by Nick Sharpe, Peter Pilbeam, Alan Cowell, Ian Herdman*

BURY ST EDMUNDS
Old Cannon 🍺 🛏

TL8564 Map 5

(01284) 768769 – www.oldcannonbrewery.co.uk

Cannon Street, just off A134/A1101 roundabout at N end of town; IP33 1JR

Busy own-brew town pub with local drinks and interesting bar food; bedrooms

Looking more like a stylish private townhouse than a pub, this cheerful place brews its own beers with the brewery actually in the bar. There are two huge gleaming stainless-steel brewing vessels and views up to a steel-balustraded open-plan malt floor above the counter; Old Cannon Best and Gunner's Daughter and seasonal ales such as Black Pig, Blonde Bombshell, Bow Chaser, Brass Monkey, Hornblower and Rusty Gun on handpump. Also ten wines by the glass and carefully chosen spirits. A row of chunky old bar stools line the ochre-painted counter, and there's an appealing assortment of old and new chairs and tables and upholstered banquettes on well worn bare boards; background music. The comfortable bedrooms are in the old brewhouse across the courtyard. Behind, through the old coach arch, is a good-sized cobbled courtyard with hanging baskets and stylish metal tables and chairs.

 Well thought-of food includes rolls, confit chicken and leek parfait with spiced pear chutney, potato and ham hock hash with a crispy egg and tomato velouté, minted pea pesto, peas and mangetout with tomatoes and spaghetti, burger with toppings, sweet and sour marmalade and chips, hot salmon and dill fishcakes with feta, chilli and sorrel hollandaise, moroccan-style chicken tagine, and puddings such as rhubarb and stem ginger crumble and cheesecake of the day. *Benchmark main dish: local sausages with colcannon mash and onion gravy £14.00. Two-course evening meal £20.00.*

Own brew ~ Licensee Garry Clark ~ Real ale ~ Open 12-11 (10 Sun) ~ Bar food 12-9; 12-3 Sun ~ Restaurant ~ Children must be over 10 ~ Wi-fi ~ Bedrooms: £95/£130
Recommended by Barry Collett, Martin Day, Katherine Matthews, Jack Trussler

CHELMONDISTON
TM2037   Map 5

Butt & Oyster

(01473) 780764 – www.debeninns.co.uk/buttandoyster
Pin Mill – signposted from B1456 SE of Ipswich; continue to bottom of road; IP9 1JW

Chatty old riverside pub with pleasant views, good food and drink and seats on the terrace

From windows in the bar or from seats on the terrace, this simple old bargeman's pub has fine views over the River Orwell; it's named for the flounders and oysters that used to be caught here. The half-panelled little smoke room is pleasantly worn and unfussy with high-backed and other old-fashioned settles on a tiled floor. There's also a two-level dining room with country kitchen furniture on bare boards, and pictures and boat-related artefacts on the walls above the dado. Adnams Southwold and Mosaic and a couple of guests tapped from the cask by friendly, efficient staff, several wines by the glass and local cider; board games. The annual Thames Barge Race (end June/early July) is fun. The car park can fill up pretty quickly.

 Fish dishes play a big role here but they have non-fishy choices too: sandwiches, shrimps in garlic butter, scallops and chorizo salad, chicken caesar salad, beef or pork and apple burger with tomato chutney and chips, fritto misto with coleslaw and sweet chilli dip, local sausages with mash and gravy, malaysian seafood curry, lamb chops with dauphinoise potates and minted gravy, and puddings. *Benchmark main dish: beer-battered cod and chips £11.95. Two-course evening meal £18.00.*

Adnams ~ Lease Steve Lomas ~ Real ale ~ Open 9am-11pm ~ Bar food 9am-9.30pm ~ Restaurant ~ Children welcome ~ Dogs allowed in bar ~ Wi-fi *Recommended by Pat and Tony Martin, Mike and Mary Carter, Richard and Penny Gibbs*

DUNWICH
TM4770   Map 5

Ship 🍺 🛏

(01728) 648219 – www.shipatdunwich.co.uk
St James Street; IP17 3DT

Friendly, well run and pleasantly traditional pub in a coastal village, tasty bar food and local ales; bedrooms

This old brick pub (much of the charming village is under the sea due to coastal erosion) was once the haunt of smugglers and seafarers. Today, there's a cheerful mix of both regulars and visitors and the landlord and his friendly staff offer a welcome to all. The traditionally furnished main bar has benches, pews, captain's chairs and wooden tables on a tiled floor, a woodburning stove (left open in cold weather) and lots of sea prints. Adnams Southwold and guests from breweries such as Grainstore, Green Jack, Humpty Dumpty and Woodfordes are served from antique handpumps at the handsomely panelled bar counter, as well as several wines by the glass; board games. A simple conservatory looks on to a back terrace, and the large garden is very pleasant, with well spaced picnic-sets, two large anchors and an enormous fig tree. The comfortable bedrooms make an excellent base for exploring the area and breakfasts are hearty. The RSPB reserve at Minsmere and nearby Dunwich Museum are worth visiting and there are good walks in Dunwich Forest.

Enjoyable food includes a choice of home-made scotch eggs, local smoked sprats with beetroot relish and horseradish cream, blue cheese, walnut and chive pâté with home-pickled vegetables, free-range baked ham with free-range eggs, cod, haddock and salmon pie, beer-battered haddock or cod and chips, pork sausages with mash, onion rings and red wine gravy, and puddings such as chocolate and beetroot cake with mascarpone and berries and bakewell tart with custard. *Benchmark main dish: slow-cooked pork belly with leek gratin, apple and date purée and red wine gravy £14.95. Two-course evening meal £21.50.*

Free house ~ Licensee Matt Goodwin ~ Real ale ~ No credit cards ~ Open 11-11 ~ Bar food 12-3, 6-9; 12-9 Sun ~ Restaurant evening only ~ Children welcome ~ Dogs allowed in bar and bedrooms ~ Bedrooms: £85/£115 *Recommended by Tracey and Stephen Groves, Barry Collett, Denis and Margaret Kilner, Millie and Peter Downing, Donald Allsopp, Ian Herdman*

EASTBRIDGE
Eels Foot 🛏

TM4566 Map 5

(01728) 830154 – www.theeelsfootinn.co.uk
Off B1122 N of Leiston; IP16 4SN

Country local with hospitable atmosphere, fair value food and Thursday evening folk sessions; bedrooms

As this simple, friendly place borders the freshwater marshes and RSPB Minsmere is nearby, it attracts plenty of bird-watchers and walkers – particularly at lunchtime; a footpath leads directly to the sea. There are light modern furnishings on stripped-wood floors in the upper and lower parts of the bar, a warming fire, Adnams Southwold, Broadside, Ghost Ship, Mosaic and a guest ale on handpump, 11 wines by the glass, several malt whiskies and a farm cider; darts in a side area, board games, cribbage and a neat back dining room. The terrace has seats and tables and there are benches set out in the delightful big back garden. Bedrooms are comfortable, attractive and peaceful and are in a separate building (one room has wheelchair access); breakfasts are tasty. They're now a certified Caravan Club site and can provide electric hook-ups.

Good quality, home-cooked food includes several gluten-free options: king prawns in garlic butter, moules marinière, stuffed butternut squash, lasagne, welsh rarebit, a pie of the day, beer-battered fish and chips, winter casseroles, and puddings such as sticky toffee pudding and tiramisu. *Benchmark main dish: slow-cooked pork belly with spring onion mash and cider jus £13.25. Two-course evening meal £18.00.*

Adnams ~ Tenant Julian Wallis ~ Real ale ~ Open 12-3, 6-11; 12-11 Fri; 11.30-11 Sat; 11.30-11.30 Sun ~ Bar food 12-2.30, 6-9; 12-9 Fri-Sun ~ Children welcome ~ Dogs welcome ~ Wi-fi ~ Live folk music Thurs and last Sun of month ~ Bedrooms: £80/£105
Recommended by Roy Hoing, Mary Joyce, Max Simons

IPSWICH
TM1844 Map 5

Fat Cat ⬤

(01473) 726524 – www.fatcatipswich.co.uk

Spring Road, opposite junction with Nelson Road (best bet for parking is up there); IP4 5NL

Fantastic range of changing real ales in a well run town pub, with a garden

With an extraordinary range of up to 18 real ales from around the country on handpump or tapped from the cask, this cheery and busy town pub remains a beer lover's dream. There might be Adnams Southwold, Crouch Vale Brewers Gold and Yakima Gold, Dark Star Hophead, Earl Soham Albert, Exmoor Gold, Fat Cat Honey Cat, Hop Back Summer Lightning, Mighty Oak Holly Daze, Navigation Eclipse, Pheasantry Mikado Mild, St Austell Tribute, Skinners Betty Stogs, Titanic Plum Porter and Woodfordes Wherry. They also stock quite a few belgian bottled beers, farm cider and seven wines by the glass. The bars have a mix of café chairs and stools, unpadded wall benches and cushioned seats around cast-iron and wooden pub tables, bare floorboards, lots of enamel brewery signs and posters on canary-yellow walls; board games and shove-ha'penny. There's also a spacious back conservatory and several picnic-sets on the terrace and lawn. There is very little nearby parking. Well behaved dogs are welcome but they must be kept on a lead.

🍴 They keep a supply of rolls, spicy scotch eggs and sausage rolls made in their small kitchen and are happy for you to bring in takeaway food (not Friday or Saturday).

Free house ~ Licensees John and Ann Keatley ~ Real ale ~ No credit cards ~ Open 12-11; 11am-midnight Sat; 12-midnight Sun ~ Bar food all day while it lasts ~ Dogs welcome ~ Wi-fi *Recommended by Edward May, Mike Swan, Peter Brix, Daphne and Robert Staples, James Landor*

LONG MELFORD
TL8646 Map 5

Black Lion 🏨 ♀ 🛏

(01787) 312356 – www.blacklionhotel.net

Church Walk; CO10 9DN

Well appointed hotel with relaxed and comfortable bar, good modern food, attentive staff and seats in pretty garden; bedrooms

In a strikingly handsome village street and opposite the green, this Georgian hotel is a civilised spot for a drink or meal. The back bar, liked by locals for a pint and a chat, has comfortable sofas, leather wing armchairs, an open fire and Adnams Southwold on handpump and 18 carefully chosen wines by the glass; background music. The dining rooms have attractive antique or high-backed leather chairs around candlelit tables, oil paintings, another open fire and heavy curtains. In warm weather you can take morning coffee and afternoon tea in the appealing Victorian walled garden. The individually decorated bedrooms are well equipped and comfortable and make a fine base for exploring the area.

 Good, appetising food includes breakfasts for non-residents (7.30-9.30am weekdays, 8.30-10am weekends); also lobster mousse with a fennel scone and pickled samphire, chicken liver pâté with onion marmalade, roasted red pepper and basil arancini with parmesan velouté, lambs liver and crispy bacon with red onion gravy, beer-battered cod and fries, corn-fed chicken with butter fondant, anchovy fritters, duck egg and gribiche sauce, duck breast with potato gnocchi, yellow carrot, orange and star anise jus, and puddings such as crème brûlée and date pudding with salted caramel, banana cream and saffron popcorn. *Benchmark main dish: beer-battered fish and chips £13.95. Two-course evening meal £24.00.*

Ravenwood Group ~ Licensee Craig Jarvis ~ Real ale ~ Open 7.30am (8.30am weekends)-11pm ~ Bar food 12-2, 7-9.30 ~ Restaurant ~ Children welcome ~ Dogs allowed in bar and bedrooms ~ Wi-fi ~ Bedrooms: £102/£125 *Recommended by Alison and Michael Harper, Bill Adie, John Harris*

MIDDLETON
TM4267 Map 5

Bell ⬤ £

(01728) 648286

Off A12 in Yoxford via B1122 towards Leiston; also signposted off B1125 Leiston–Westleton; The Street; IP17 3NN

Thatch and low beams, friendly landlord, good beer and popular good value food – a peaceful spot

The grand flint tower of the village church overlooks this pretty cream-washed pub and there are picnic-sets out in front under parasols. On the left, the traditional bar has a warm welcome from the character landlord, a log fire in a big hearth, old local photographs, a low plank-panelled ceiling, and bar stools and pew seating; Adnams Southwold, Broadside and Ghost Ship tapped from the cask and nine wines by the glass. On the right, an informal two-room carpeted lounge/dining area has padded mate's and library chairs around dark tables under low black beams, with pews by a big woodburning stove and modern seaside brewery prints. Dogs are welcomed with treats and a bowl of water. Camping is available in the broad meadow behind. RSPB Minsmere is nearby, as are walks along the coast.

 Good value food served in generous helpings includes lunchtime sandwiches, cajun-spiced crumbed chicken goujons with honey-mustard dip, sweet potato and butternut squash risotto, sausage and mash, liver and bacon, pork cheek ragoût on bubble and squeak, chicken with red wine, bacon, mushroom and black pudding sauce, and puddings such as banana split and rice pudding flavoured with bay, cinnamon and fruit compote. *Benchmark main dish: beer-battered cod and chips £9.95. Two-course evening meal £18.00.*

Adnams ~ Tenants Nicholas and Trish Musgrove ~ Real ale ~ Open 12-3, 6-11 (midnight Fri); 12-midnight Sat; 12-9 Sun; closed Mon ~ Bar food 12-2, 6-9; 12-5 Sun ~ Restaurant ~ Well behaved children allowed away from bar ~ Dogs allowed in bar ~ Wi-fi *Recommended by Peter Smith and Judith Brown, Anne Taylor, Andrew Vincent*

PETTISTREE
TM2954 Map 5

Greyhound 🎯

(01728) 746451 – www.greyhoundinnpettistree.co.uk

The Street; brown sign to pub off B1438 S of Wickham Market, 0.5 miles N of A12; IP13 0HP

Neatly kept village pub with enjoyable food and drink; seats outside

Hard-working, friendly licensees run this bustling pub and there's a welcome for all. It's basically just two smallish rooms with open fires, some rather low beams, chunky farmhouse chairs and cushioned settles around dark wooden tables on bare floorboards and candlelight. Earl Soham Victoria Bitter and guests such as Adnams Ghost Ship and Crouch Vale Brewers Gold on handpump, several wines by the glass and quite a few malt whiskies; it's best to book in advance to be sure of a table. The well kept side garden has picnic-sets under parasols, with more beside the gravelled front car park. The village church is next door.

Cooked by the landlady using local produce, the interesting food includes treacle and malt whisky-cured salmon with dill cream, crispy baked goats cheese with chilli pepper jam, lamb, cumin and mint burger with mustard mayonnaise and chips, basil gnocchi with spinach pesto and roasted peppers, slow-roasted pork belly in cider with black pudding, dauphinoise potatoes and cider gravy, whole roasted plaice with confit and roasted fennel and tomato and red pepper salsa, hanger steak in rosemary and garlic with chips, and puddings such as whisky marmalade ice-cream with shortbread and meringue with nectarines, chantilly cream and berry coulis. *Benchmark main dish: sea trout with parsley mash, confit roasted fennel and seaweed butter £13.00. Two-course evening meal £20.00.*

Free house ~ Licensees Stewart and Louise McKenzie ~ Real ale ~ Open 12-3, 6-11; 12-4 Sun; closed Sun evening, Mon, two weeks Jan ~ Bar food 12-2.30, 6-9; 12-3 Sun ~ Restaurant ~ Children welcome ~ Dogs allowed in bar ~ Wi-fi *Recommended by Michael Williamson, Peter Brix, George Sanderson*

REDE

Plough

(01284) 789208

Village signposted off A143 Bury St Edmunds–Haverhill; IP29 4BE

TL8055 Map 5

Well liked and promptly served food in a 16th-c pub, with several wines by the glass and friendly service

This is a fine spot at the end of the village green with little sound except birdsong. The quaint, partly thatched and cream-washed pub has a cheerful landlord and the pretty bar is traditional with low beams, comfortable seating and a solid-fuel stove in a brick fireplace. Changing ales include Butcombe Bitter, Fullers London Pride, Harveys Best and Ringwood Best Bitter on handpump and they keep several wines by the glass; background music. There are picnic-sets set out in the sheltered cottagey garden and also at the front.

Good food includes game terrine, salt and pepper squid with chilli sauce, ham and eggs, calves liver and bacon, oxtail casserole, chicken with pears and roquefort cheese, rabbit stew, a fresh fish dish of the day, and puddings such as apple lattice tart and bread and butter puddings. *Benchmark main dish: slow-cooked rioja lamb £13.95. Two-course evening meal £19.00.*

Admiral Taverns ~ Tenant Brian Desborough ~ Real ale ~ Open 11-3, 6.30-11.30; 12-3, 7-11 Sun ~ Bar food 12-2, 7-9; 12-2 Sun ~ Restaurant ~ Children welcome until 8pm ~ Wi-fi *Recommended by R A P Cross, Lindy Andrews, Christopher Mannings*

SIBTON

White Horse 🍴 ♗ ⛃

(01728) 660337 – www.sibtonwhitehorseinn.co.uk

Halesworth Road/Hubbard's Hill, N of Peasenhall; IP17 2JJ

TM3570 Map 5

Particularly well run inn with nicely old-fashioned bar, good mix of customers, real ales and imaginative food; bedrooms

The licensees running this busy village inn are hands-on and hard-working and offer a genuine welcome to all. The appealing bar has a roaring log fire in a large inglenook fireplace, horsebrasses and tack on the walls, old settles and pews, and they serve Adnams Southwold, Wolf Golden Jackal and Woodfordes Wherry on handpump, nine wines by the glass and 15 malt whiskies from an old oak-panelled counter. Beer festivals are held in June and August and a viewing panel reveals the working cellar and its ancient floor. Steps lead up past an old partly knocked-through timbered wall into a carpeted gallery, and there's also a smart dining room and a secluded (and popular) dining terrace. There are plenty of seats in the sizeable garden. The bedrooms, housed in a separate building next door, are warm, contemporary and well equipped.

 Using local, seasonal produce and making everything in-house, the particularly good food includes lunchtime sandwiches, local kiln-roasted salmon with soused leek, grapefruit, feta, avocado and tarragon, ballotine of quail with apricot and sage couscous and cumin-spiced tomato chutney, beetroot and wild garlic risotto with roast jerusalem artichoke and port reduction, home-cooked ham with free-range egg and sweet and sour pineapple, beer-battered cod and twice-cooked chips, local pork with fennel and potato cake, pea and broad bean fricassée and buttered samphire, and puddings such as iced milk chocolate parfait with caramelised banana, filo biscuit and coffee reduction and ginger parkin with poached pear, caramel sauce and maple syrup ice-cream. *Benchmark main dish: local pork loin with smoked belly, black pudding, dauphinoise potatoes and mustard jus £14.50. Two-course evening meal £20.00.*

Free house ~ Licensees Neil and Gill Mason ~ Real ale ~ Open 12-3, 6-11; 12-3.30, 6.30-11 Sun; closed Mon lunchtime, one week Jan ~ Bar food 12-2, 6.30-9; 12-2.30, 7-8.30 Sun ~ Restaurant ~ Well behaved children welcome but must be over 7 in evening; not in bedrooms ~ Dogs allowed in bar ~ Wi-fi ~ Music and beer festival in summer, barbecue Fri evening in summer ~ Bedrooms: $80/$95 *Recommended by Lindy Andrews, Isobel Mackinlay, Thomas Green, Simon Rodway, R L Borthwick*

SOUTHWOLD
Crown 🏵 ⏣ 🍷 🍺 🛏

TM5076   Map 5

(01502) 722275 – www.adnams.co.uk/hotels/the-crown
High Street; IP18 6DP

Comfortable hotel with relaxed bars, a fine choice of drinks, interesting food and seats outside; bedrooms

Of course, this isn't a pub in the true sense, it's a civilised hotel – but those in the know head for the back bar. Here, there's an informal, chatty atmosphere with locals and dogs, oak panelling, some fine antique tables and chairs on bare boards, very well kept Adnams Southwold, Broadside, Ghost Ship and Old Ale on handpump, plenty of wines by the glass from a splendid list, ten malt whiskies and interesting spirits; staff are courteous and friendly. The beamed front bar has a stripped curved high-backed settle and smaller dark varnished settles, kitchen and other chairs and a restored, carved wooden fireplace. Seats in a sunny sheltered corner are very pleasant. This is a special place to stay in comfortable, character bedrooms and breakfasts are especially recommended.

 Enjoyable, rewarding food includes lunchtime ciabatta sandwiches, crab with watercress, mango and chilli salsa, pork and apple terrine with date chutney, butternut squash, goats cheese and lentil parcel with tomato relish, omelette arnold bennett, venison sausages with herb mash and red wine jus, partridge with garlic mash, savoy cabbage, parsnip and blackberry jus, bass with confit potato, fig, parma ham, goats curd and a port and tarragon dressing, and puddings such as dark chocolate délice with orange compote and orange sorbet and apple, blackberry and prosecco jelly with thyme crème fraîche. *Benchmark main dish: calves liver with bacon, onion purée and dauphinoise potatoes £20.00. Two-course evening meal £24.00.*

Adnams ~ Manager Jenny Knights ~ Real ale ~ Open 11-11 ~ Bar food 12-2.30, 6.30 (6 in summer)-9 ~ Children welcome ~ Dogs allowed in bar ~ Bedrooms: $135/$205
Recommended by Colin McLachlan, Phil and Jane Villiers, Brian and Sally Wakeham, John and Enid

SOUTHWOLD
TM4975 Map 5

Harbour Inn ♀ ◀

(01502) 722381 – www.harbourinnsouthwold.co.uk

Blackshore, by the boats; from A1095, turn right at the Kings Head, and keep on past the golf course and water tower; IP18 6TA

Great spot down by the boats with lots of outside tables and interesting interior; popular food with emphasis on local seafood

You can walk from here along the Blyth estuary to Walberswick (where the Bell is under the same good management as this pub) via a footbridge and return by the one-man ferry. The back bar is nicely nautical with dark panelling and built-in wall seats around scrubbed tables, and cheerful staff serve 16 wines by the glass, along with Adnams Southwold, Broadside, Ghost Ship and a guest such as Oyster Stout on handpump. The low ceiling is draped with ensigns, signal flags, pennants and a line strung with ancient dried fish, and there's a quaint old stove, rope fancywork, local fishing photographs and even portholes with water bubbling behind them; they have their own weather station for walkers and sailors. The lower front bar, with a tiled floor and panelling, is broadly similar, while the large, elevated dining room has panoramic views of the harbour, lighthouse, brewery and churches beyond the marshes. Picnic-sets on the terrace look over the boats on the estuary; there are also seats and tables behind the pub, which look out over the marshy commons to the town.

Food is popular and includes sandwiches, potted kipper pâté, terrine of ham hock with piccalilli, grilled spiced mackerel on chickpea, tomato, red onion, mint and coriander salad, trio of sausages with redcurrant gravy, vegetarian cottage pie topped with cheesy mash, coconut and panko-breadcrumbed salmon fishcake with creamy thai-spiced sauce, chicken, leek and mushroom pudding, monkfish and prawn goan-style curry, and puddings such as sticky toffee pudding with butterscotch sauce and rapsberry and passion-fruit eton mess. *Benchmark main dish: beer-battered cod and chips £12.00. Two-course evening meal £19.00.*

Adnams ~ Tenant Nick Attfield ~ Real ale ~ Open 11-11 ~ Bar food 12-9 ~ Children welcome away from top bar ~ Dogs allowed in bar ~ Folk singers Thurs and Sun evenings
Recommended by Phoebe Peacock, Barry Collett, Sheila Topham, Bob and Margaret Holder, Simon Rodway

STOKE-BY-NAYLAND
TL9836 Map 5

Crown ★ ♀ ⇐

(01206) 262001 – www.crowninn.net

Park Street (B1068); CO6 4SE

Suffolk Dining Pub of the Year

Smart dining pub with attractive modern furnishings, imaginative food, real ales and a great wine choice; good bedrooms

'A thoroughly good all-rounder,' say our readers with enthusiasm about this civilised and easy-going inn. The extensive open-plan dining bar is well laid out to give several distinct-feeling areas: a sofa and easy chairs on flagstones near the serving counter, a couple of armchairs under heavy beams by the big woodburning stove, one sizeable table tucked nicely into a three-sided built-in seat and a lower side room with more beams and cheerful floral wallpaper. Tables are mostly stripped veterans, with high-backed dining chairs, but there are more modern chunky pine tables at the back; also, contemporary artwork (mostly for sale) and daily papers.

Served by friendly staff, there's Adnams Southwold, Crouch Vale Brewers Gold, Woodfordes Wherry and a changing guest such as Lacons Falcon Ale on handpump and Aspall's cider. Wine is a key feature, with 30 by the glass and hundreds more from the glass-walled 'cellar shop' in one corner – you can buy there to take away too. The sheltered flagstoned back terrace has comfortable teak furniture, heaters, big terracotta-coloured parasols and a peaceful view over rolling, lightly wooded countryside. Bedrooms are well equipped and comfortable. Good disabled access. This pretty village is worth exploring and there are plenty of well-marked surrounding footpaths.

 As well as breakfasts for non-residents (7.30-10.30am), the tempting food includes house-cured salmon with sweet mustard and dill dressing, crispy duck and watercress salad with radish, spring onions and asian dressing, caramelised onion tart with walnut and parmesan crust and creamy leek sauce, smoked haddock fillet in red wine with wilted spinach, poached egg and mash, braised goat shoulder with roasted garlic mash, free-range chicken breast with peanuts, chilli, lime and yoghurt and shallot, herb and lemon tabbouleh and puddings such as banana tatin with banana gel and banoffi parfait and a trio of chocolate; they also offer a two- and three-course set lunch. *Benchmark main dish: beer-battered haddock and chips £13.95. Two-course evening meal £20.00.*

Free house ~ Licensee Richard Sunderland ~ Real ale ~ Open 11-11; 12-10.30 Sun ~ Bar food 12-2.30, 6-9.30 (10 Fri, Sat); all day Sun ~ Children welcome ~ Dogs allowed in bar ~ Wi-fi ~ Bedrooms: £95/£135 *Recommended by Christopher and Elise Way, Mrs Carolyn Dixon, Mrs Margo Finlay, Jörg Kasprowski, MDN, Alan Cowell*

STRATFORD ST MARY
Swan 🏆 ♥ ⬛

TM0434 Map 5

(01206) 321244 – www.stratfordswan.com
Lower Street; CO7 6JR

Excellent food and drink in 16th-c coaching inn; riverside seats

With creative food and a great interest in beers, wines and spirits, this lovely timbered inn is much enjoyed by a wide mix of customers. They keep Adnams Ghost Ship, Swannay Orkney IPA and Oakham JHB on handpump, nine craft ales, 130 bottled beers from around the world, 14 wines by the glass, 53 malt whiskies, 11 vodkas, 19 gins, a farm cider and several interesting bottled ones. There's a log fire in a Tudor brick fireplace in one of the two beamed bars and a coal fire in the other, and an eclectic range of old furniture on parquet or brick floors; board games. The compact and timbered back restaurant is rather elegant. Outside, there are teak tables and chairs under parasols on a terrace, more seats arranged on a big lawn and, across the road, some tables under willow trees by the River Stour (where there's a landing stage).

 Inventive food is paired with wine and ales on the menu and includes fish soup with rouille, pigs head croquette with gribiche sauce, aubergine parmigiana, salmon fillet with spinach and beurre blanc, spiced braised lamb shoulder with lentil and turnip purée, whole boned stuffed pigeon with mash and kale, and puddings such as tonka bean pannacotta with sour cherries and saffron pear frangipane tart. *Benchmark main dish: rib-eye steak with sliced potato cake and garlic butter £21.25. Two-course evening meal £22.00.*

Free house ~ Licensee Jane Dorber ~ Real ale ~ Open 11-11; closed Mon, Tues ~ Bar food 12-3, 6-9 ~ Restaurant ~ Children welcome ~ Dogs allowed in bar ~ Wi-fi
Recommended by Gus Swan, Charlie May, Phoebe Peacock, Maddie Purvis, Jack and Hilary Burton

You can send reports directly to us at feedback@goodguides.com

UFFORD

Crown ♀

TM2952 Map 5

(01394) 461030 – www.theuffordcrown.com

High Street; IP13 6EL

Bustling pub with a good mix of customers, real ales, enjoyable food and friendly atmosphere; seats outside

Very much a family business, this is a friendly pub with plenty of room for both drinking and dining. The bar and dining areas have cushioned wooden dining chairs and leather wall banquettes around a medley of dark tables on bare boards or carpeting, books on shelves, modern ceiling lights and open fires in brick fireplaces. Stools line the counter where they serve Adnams Southwold and Earl Soham Victoria Bitter on handpump and a dozen good wines by the glass; maybe daily papers. At the front of the building are some tables and chairs and the back terrace and garden have plenty of picnic-sets under parasols. This is sister pub to the Ramsholt Arms at Ramsholt.

Cooked by the landlady's brother, the tempting seasonal food includes lunchtime sandwiches, spiced lobster in coconut noodle soup, chicken liver and foie gras parfait with fig chutney, linguine with pistachio pesto, spinach and sunblush tomatoes, sausage and mash with caramelised onion gravy, maple syrup and Jack Daniels-glazed baby back ribs with frites, and puddings such as dark chocolate fondant with salted caramel ice-cream and ginger and pineapple upside-down cake with vanilla ice-cream. *Benchmark main dish: crispy pork belly with greens, apple sauce and jus £14.00. Two-course evening meal £20.50.*

Free house ~ Licensees Max and Polly Durrant ~ Real ale ~ Open 12-3, 5 (4 Fri)-11; 12-11 Sat; 12-10.30 Sun; closed Tues ~ Bar food 12-2, 6-9; 12-3, 6-8 Sun ~ Restaurant ~ Children welcome ~ Dogs allowed in bar ~ Wi-fi *Recommended by Liz and Martin Eldon, Jack Trussler, Sandra King*

WALBERSWICK

Anchor 🏮⭐ ♀ 🛏

TM4974 Map 5

(01502) 722112 – www.anchoratwalberswick.com

The Street (B1387); village signed off A12; IP18 6UA

Friendly, bustling pub with good food and thoughtful choice of drinks; bedrooms

Drinkers and diners are equally well served here – though many customers are here to enjoy the interesting food. The simply furnished front bar, divided into snug halves by a two-way open fire, has big windows, heavy stripped tables on original oak flooring, sturdy built-in green leather wall seats and nicely framed black and white photographs of fishermen that are displayed on colour-washed panelling; daily papers and board games. Helpful, friendly staff serve Adnams Ghost Ship and a guest or two on handpump, 50 bottled beers and around 20 wines by the glass; they hold a beer festival in August. The extensive dining area stretches back from a small, more modern-feeling lounge. There are plenty of seats in the attractive garden, and an outdoor bar and wood-fired pizza oven serving the flagstoned terraces. The six spacious chalet-style rooms in the garden have views of either the water or beach huts and sand dunes, while from the bedrooms in the main house you can hear the sea just a few hundred metres away; dogs are allowed in some rooms. As well as the coast path, there's a pleasant walk to Southwold.

Using the best local, seasonal produce, the inventive food includes fish soup with rouille, pork, rabbit and pistachio terrine with chutney, polenta, goats cheese, mushroom and wood-roasted vegetables, lamb stew with olives and capers, a changing roasted fresh fish dish, veal schnitzel with pickled cabbage and sautéed potatoes, pork belly with mustard mash and bacon lentils, and puddings such as lime cheesecake with passion-fruit curd and tonka bean and buttermilk pannacotta with poached rhubarb. *Benchmark main dish: whole crab linguine with chilli and garlic £14.75. Two-course evening meal £20.00.*

Boudica Inns ~ Lease Mark and Sophie Dorber ~ Real ale ~ Open 11-11 ~ Bar food 12-3, 6-9 ~ Restaurant ~ Children welcome ~ Dogs allowed in bar and bedrooms ~ Wi-fi ~ Bedrooms: £120/£145 *Recommended by Denis and Margaret Kilner, Sheila Topham, Thomas Green, Simon Rodway*

WALBERSWICK
TM4974 Map 5

Bell 🌟 ♟ 🍺 🛏

(01502) 723109 – www.bellinnwalberswick.co.uk
Just off B1387; IP18 6TN

Interesting and thriving 16th-c inn with good food and drinks choice, friendly atmosphere and nice garden; cosy bedrooms

There's a lot of original character in the rooms of this 600-year-old inn. The charming, rambling bar has antique curved settles, cushioned pews and window seats, scrubbed tables, two huge fireplaces (one with an elderly woodburning stove watched over by a pair of staffordshire china dogs) and a chatty atmosphere. The fine old flooring encompasses sagging ancient bricks, broad boards, flagstones and black and red tiles. Friendly staff serve 16 good wines by the glass, several malt whiskies and Adnams Southwold, Broadside, Ghost Ship, Mosaic and Oyster Stout on handpump; background music and darts. Don't miss the classic *New Yorker* wine cartoons in the lavatories. The Barn Café is open during the school holidays for light snacks, cakes, teas and so forth. A big, neatly planted sheltered garden behind has smart oak tables and chairs under blue parasols and a view over the dunes to the sea; pétanque. The rowing-boat ferry to Southwold is nearby (there's a footbridge a bit further away). Bedrooms, some with sea or harbour views, are attractively decorated, and breakfasts are good. This is sister pub to the Harbour Inn in Southwold.

🌟 From a well judged menu, the accomplished cooking includes sandwiches, bloody mary crayfish and prawn cocktail, baked camembert with rosemary, garlic and sea salt, mixed mushroom and spinach tagliatelle in caramelised onion and cream sauce, steak and mushroom in ale pie, mussels in cider, leek and saffron chowder, chicken schnitzel in bacon and parmesan crumb with white wine, mushroom and tarragon cream sauce, confit duck leg with braised puy lentils and bacon and sautéed potatoes, and puddings such as apple and cinnamon pannacotta crumble and chocolate and walnut brownie. *Benchmark main dish: fish pie £12.00. Two-course evening meal £20.00.*

Adnams ~ Tenant Nick Attfield ~ Real ale ~ Open 11-11 ~ Bar food 12-2.30, 6-9 ~ Children welcome away from bar ~ Dogs allowed in bar and bedrooms ~ Wi-fi ~ Bedrooms: £85/£95 *Recommended by Peter Pilbeam, Giles and Annie Francis, George Sanderson, Julian Richardson, R L Borthwick*

WALDRINGFIELD
TM2844 Map 5

Maybush

(01473) 736215 – www.debeninns.co.uk/maybush
Off A12 S of Martlesham; The Quay, Cliff Road; IP12 4QL

Busy pub with tables outside by the riverbank; nautical décor and a fair choice of drinks and fair value food

This spot is a haven for bird-watchers and ramblers, and river cruises are available nearby (though you have to pre-book). The picnic-sets overlooking the River Deben get snapped up pretty quickly, though some of the tables inside by the windows have the same view. The spacious knocked-through bar is divided into separate areas by fireplaces or steps. There's a nautical theme, with an elaborate ship's model in a glass case and a few more in a light, high-ceilinged extension – as well as lots of old lanterns, pistols and aerial photographs; background music and board games. Adnams Southwold and Ghost Ship on handpump and a fair choice of wines available by the glass; board games.

 Popular food includes sandwiches, deep-fried breaded brie with red onion chutney, garlic-marinated king prawn skewer with sweet chilli dip, vegetable lasagne, sausages on mash with cider gravy, gammon with pineapple and free-range egg, barbecue chicken with bacon and smoked cheese, pork and apple burger with toppings and chips, bass fillets with ratatouille and fondant potato, and puddings such as chocolate brownie and cherry bakewell tart. *Benchmark main dish: beer-battered cod and chips £11.95. Two-course evening meal £17.50.*

Adnams ~ Lease Steve and Louise Lomas ~ Real ale ~ Open 9am-11pm ~ Bar food 9am-9.30pm ~ Restaurant ~ Children welcome ~ Dogs allowed in bar ~ Wi-fi
Recommended by Bob and Margaret Holder, Mark Morgan, Tim King

WESTLETON
Crown 🏅 ♀ 🛏
TM4469   Map 5

(01728) 648777 – www.westletoncrown.co.uk
B1125 Blythburgh–Leiston; IP17 3AD

Bustling old inn with a cosy chatty bar, carefully chosen drinks and interesting food; bedrooms

The heart of this stylish old coaching inn remains the attractive little bar with its lovely log fire and plenty of original features. Locals drop in here for a pint and a chat, which keeps the atmosphere informal and relaxed, and they serve Adnams Southwold and three guest beers from breweries such as Green Jack, Norfolk and Woodfordes on handpump, 20 wines by the glass from a thoughtful list and 11 malt whiskies; background music and board games. There's also a parlour, a dining room and a conservatory, with all manner of wooden dining chairs and tables and historic photographs on some fine old bare-brick walls. The charming terraced garden has plenty of seats and tables. Bedrooms are comfortable and spotlessly maintained (some are in the main inn, others are in converted stables and cottages); the breakfasts are excellent.

🌟 Food is inventive and includes sandwiches, pressed ham hock terrine with spiced plum chutney, salmon and cod fishcakes with horseradish cream, sweet potato, spinach, parmesan and rocket risotto, beer-battered fish and chips, chicken with bacon, peppers and madeira cream sauce, moroccan-braised lamb shank with vegetable tagine and coriander couscous, 28-day-aged sirloin steak with peppercorn sauce, and puddings such as lemon posset with wild berry sorbet and crushed meringue and ginger pudding with toffee sauce. *Benchmark main dish: slow-cooked pork belly £17.00. Two-course evening meal £23.00.*

Free house ~ Licensee Gareth Clarke ~ Real ale ~ Open 7am (7.30am Sun)-11pm ~ Bar food 12-2.30, 6.30-9.30 ~ Restaurant ~ Children welcome ~ Dogs allowed in bar and bedrooms ~ Wi-fi ~ Bedrooms: £90/£95 *Recommended by Peter Smith and Judith Brown, Tracey and Stephen Groves, Roy Hoing, Andrew Vincent, Ian Herdman*

WHEPSTEAD
White Horse

TL8258 Map 5

(01284) 735760 – www.whitehorsewhepstead.co.uk

Off B1066 S of Bury; Rede Road; IP29 4SS

Charming country pub with attractively furnished rooms and well liked food and drink

New licensees had just taken over as we went to press and were planning future refurbishments. This is a 17th-c building with several Victorian additions and the dark-beamed bar still has a woodburning stove in a low fireplace, stools around pubby tables on a tiled floor, and Adnams Southwold and a guest from St Peters on handpump. Linked rooms have country kitchen tables and chairs on antique floor tiles and some traditional wall seats and rather fine old farmhouse chairs. The neat sheltered back terrace has seats and tables and there are also picnic-sets on grass.

The changing menu includes ham with bubble and squeak, a poached egg and chive hollandaise, smoked mackerel pâté, local sausages with mash and onion gravy, sweet potato and cauliflower curry, ale-braised beef with red onion jam, moroccan-style lamb with red pepper couscous, beer-battered fish and chips, and puddings such as double chocolate cheesecake and butterscotch and raisin tart. *Benchmark main dish: bass fillets with crayfish and garlic butter £14.95. Two-course evening meal £19.00.*

Free house ~ Licensees Hana and Lee Saunders ~ Real ale ~ Open 11.30-3, 7-11; 11.30-3 Sun; closed Sun evening ~ Bar food 12-2, 7-9 ~ Restaurant ~ Children welcome ~ Dogs welcome ~ Wi-fi *Recommended by Peter Pilbeam, Lindy Andrews, Tim King*

Also Worth a Visit in Suffolk

Besides the fully inspected pubs, you might like to try these pubs that have been recommended to us and described by readers. Do tell us what you think of them: feedback@goodguides.com

ALDEBURGH TM4656
White Hart (01728) 453205
High Street; IP15 5AJ Friendly one-room local in former high-ceilinged reading room, panelling, stained-glass windows and open fire, Adnams ales and guests, decent wines by the glass, summer pizzas in back courtyard; no children inside, dogs welcome, open all day. *(Jack Trussler)*

ALDRINGHAM TM4461
Parrot & Punchbowl
(01728) 830221 *B1122/B1353 S of Leiston; IP16 4PY* Welcoming 17th-c beamed country pub, good fairly priced traditional food catering for special diets, well kept Adnams Southwold, Woodfordes Wherry and a guest, two-level restaurant; live music; children and dogs (in bar) welcome, nice sheltered garden, also family garden with adventure play area. *(James Landor)*

BADINGHAM TM3068
White Horse (01728) 638280
A1120 S of village; IP13 8JR Welcoming 15th-c low-beamed pub (former coaching inn), generous helpings of good reasonably priced food including themed nights and OAP lunch Mon-Thurs, Earl Soham and three guests, Aspall's and Weston's ciders, inglenook log fire and a couple of woodburners; charity quiz first Tues of month, local band last Tues; children, dogs and muddy boots welcome, neat bowling green and nice rambling garden, two bedrooms accessed by spiral staircase, open all day Sun. *(Dr Peter Crawshaw)*

BARHAM TM1251
Sorrel Horse (01473) 830327
Old Norwich Road; IP6 0PG Friendly open-plan beamed and timbered country inn with good log fire in central chimneybreast,

---

The star-on-a-plate award, |✪|, distinguishes pubs where the food is of exceptional quality. The knife-and-fork symbol just means the pub serves food.

well kept ales including Greene King, popular home-made pubby food (all day weekends); free wi-fi; children and dogs welcome, disabled facilities, picnic-sets on side grass with big play area, bedrooms in converted barn, open all day Weds-Sun. *(Floras23)*

BILDESTON   TL9949
Crown (01449) 740510
B1115 SW of Stowmarket; IP7 7EB
Picturesque 15th-c timbered country inn; smart beamed main bar with leather armchairs and inglenook log fire, back area with contemporary artwork, more formal dining room, ales such as Adnams and Greene King, good choice of wines, gins and cocktails, interesting well liked food from sandwiches and reworked pub favourites up including a tasting menu, afternoon tea with glass of champagne; children welcome, disabled access and parking, tables laid for eating in appealing central courtyard, more in large beautifully kept garden with decking, 13 bedrooms. *(Mrs Carolyn Dixon)*

BILDESTON   TL9949
Kings Head (01449) 741434
High Street; IP7 7ED Small 16th-c beamed village pub with own good beers (brewery behind – can view by appointment) plus local guests, enjoyable well priced home-made food (Fri evening, Sat, Sun lunchtime), pleasant chatty staff, wood floor bar with inglenook woodburner; games evenings and live music, quiz last Thurs of month; children welcome, back garden with terrace and play equipment, open all day weekends, closed Mon, Tues and lunchtimes Weds-Fri. *(Mary Joyce)*

BLAXHALL   TM3656
Ship (01728) 688316
Off B1069 S of Snape; can be reached from A12 via Little Glemham; IP12 2DY
Charming country setting for this popular and friendly low-beamed 18th-c pub; good reasonably priced traditional food in bar and restaurant, well kept Adnams Southwold, Woodfordes Wherry and guests; some live music including Mon sing-along folk session in side room with piano, also June folk festival; children in eating areas, dogs in bar, eight chalet bedrooms, good breakfast, open all day weekends. *(Donald Allsopp)*

BOXFORD   TL9640
Fleece (01787) 211183
Broad Street (A1071 Sudbury–Ipswich); CO10 5DX Old coaching inn (partly 15th-c) with plenty of character; beautiful Corder Room with attractive period furniture, dark panelled wainscoting, William Morris wallpaper and sweeping red curtains,

beamed bar on left with woodburner in terracotta-tiled front part, bare-boards back area has pews and other seats around old stripped tables and big fireplace, Adnams and Sharps, local cider and 11 wines by the glass, enjoyable food (not Sun evening, Mon); free wi-fi; children and dogs (in bar) welcome, open all day Fri-Sun; changing hands as we went to press, so may be changes. *(Peter Pilbeam, Ian Duncan, Charles Fraser)*

BRAMFIELD   TM3973
Queens Head (01986) 784214
The Street; A144 S of Halesworth; IP19 9HT New owners and refurbishment for this popular village pub which was about to reopen as we went to press – reports please; various rooms with heavy beams, timbering and exposed brickwork, impressive fireplace in high-raftered lounge, separate bar also with log fires; tiered garden, next to interesting church.

BRENT ELEIGH   TL9348
★ Cock (01787) 247371
A1141 SE of Lavenham; CO10 9PB
Timeless and friendly thatched country pub, Adnams, Greene King Abbot and a guest, organic farm cider, enjoyable traditional food cooked by landlady, cosy ochre-walled snug and second small room, antique floor tiles, lovely coal fire, old photographs of village (church well worth a look); darts, shove-ha'penny and toad in the hole; well behaved children and dogs welcome, picnic-sets up on side grass with summer hatch service, one bedroom, open all day Fri-Sun. *(Mrs Carolyn Dixon)*

BROCKLEY GREEN   TL7247
★ Plough (01440) 786789
Hundon Road; CO10 8DT Friendly neatly kept knocked-through bar, beams, timbers and stripped brick, scrubbed tables and open fire, good food from lunchtime sandwiches and deli boards up, Tues steak night, cheerful efficient staff, three changing ales, good choice of wines by the glass and several malt whiskies, restaurant; Thurs quiz, beer festivals Apr and Sept; children and dogs welcome, attractive grounds with peaceful country views, comfortable bedrooms, open all day weekends. *(Adele Summers, Alan Black)*

BUNGAY   TM3389
Castle (01986) 892283
Earsham Street; NR35 1AF Pleasantly informal 16th-c dining inn with good interesting food from chef-owner including regular themed nights; opened-up beamed interior with restaurant part at front, two open fires, friendly efficient staff, Earl

---

A star symbol before the name of a pub shows exceptional character and appeal. It doesn't mean extra comfort. Even quite a basic pub can win a star, if it's individual enough.

Soham Victoria and a guest, Aspall's cider, nice choice of wines by the glass, afternoon teas, french windows to pretty courtyard garden; children welcome, dogs in bar area, four comfortable bedrooms, open all day in summer (till 4pm Sun). *(Liz and Martin Eldon)*

BURY ST EDMUNDS TL8463
Dove (01284) 702787
Hospital Road; IP33 3JU Friendly 19th-c alehouse with rustic bare-boards bar and separate parlour, half a dozen well kept mainly local beers and some real ciders; quiz third Sun of the month; folk night third Mon; some seats out at front, closed weekday lunchtimes. *(Julian Richardson)*

BURY ST EDMUNDS TL8564
★**Nutshell** (01284) 764867
The Traverse, central pedestrian link off Abbeygate Street; IP33 1BJ Tiny simple local with timeless interior (can be a crush at busy times), lots of interest such as a mummified cat (found walled up here) hanging from dark brown ceiling along with companion rat, bits of a skeleton, vintage bank notes, cigarette packets, military and other badges, spears and a great metal halberd, one short wooden bench along shopfront corner windows, a cut-down sewing-machine table and an elbow rest running along a rather battered counter, Greene King ales, no food; background music, steep narrow stairs up to lavatories; children (till 7pm) and dogs welcome, open all day. *(Barry Collett, Jack Trussler)*

BURY ST EDMUNDS TL8564
One Bull (01284) 848220
Angel Hill; IP33 1UZ Smartly refurbished pub with own Brewshed beers and local guests, extensive choice of wines by the glass and good food from sandwiches and sharing boards up, friendly helpful staff; free wi-fi; children till 6pm in bar (8pm restaurant), closed Sun evening, otherwise open all day. *(Jeremy King)*

BURY ST EDMUNDS TL8563
★**Rose & Crown** (01284) 755934
Whiting Street; IP33 1NP Cheerful black-beamed corner local with long-serving affable licensees, bargain simple lunchtime home cooking (not Sun), particularly well kept Greene King ales (including XX Mild) and guests, pleasant lounge with lots of piggy pictures and bric-a-brac, good games-oriented public bar, rare separate off-sales counter; background radio, no credit cards or under-14s; pretty back courtyard, open all day weekdays. *(Jack Trussler)*

BUXHALL TM9957
★**Crown** (01449) 736521
Off B1115 W of Stowmarket; Mill Road; IP14 3DW A pub of two halves; steps down to cosy low-beamed bar on left with

woodburner in brick inglenook, timbered dining area beyond, well kept Adnams Broadside, Earl Soham Victoria and nice choice of wines by the glass, light airy dining room to the right with its own bar and another woodburner, good interesting attractively presented food (not particularly cheap), friendly service; children and dogs welcome, plenty of tables on terrace with views over open country (ignore the pylons), herb garden, closed Sun evening, Mon. *(R A P Cross, Jeremy King)*

CAVENDISH TL8046
Bull (01787) 280245
A1092 Long Melford–Clare; CO10 8AX Traditional old pub with heavy beams, timbers and open fires, Nethergate Suffolk County and up to four guests, a real cider on handpump too, enjoyable reasonably priced pub food (not Sun evening), good friendly service; charity quiz first Sun of month; children in eating areas, no dogs inside, paved back terrace with steps up to car park (useful in this picturesque honeypot village), open all day weekends, closed Tues. *(Mary Joyce)*

CAVENDISH TL8046
★**George** (01787) 280248
A1092; The Green; CO10 8BA Restaurant 16th-c inn with contemporary feel in two bow-windowed front areas, beams and timbers, big woodburner in stripped-brick fireplace, very well liked food from interesting varied menu including set deals, two Nethergate ales and plenty of wines by the glass, Aspall's cider, back servery and further eating area, charming young staff, daily newspapers; children and well behaved dogs welcome, stylish furniture on sheltered back terrace, tree-shaded garden with lovely village church behind, five bedrooms up rather steep staircase, good breakfast, open all day except Sun evening. *(Marianne and Peter Stevens, Ray White)*

CHELSWORTH TL9848
Peacock (01449) 743952
B1115 Sudbury–Needham Market; IP7 7HU Prettily set village dining pub with lots of Tudor brickwork and exposed beams, separate pubby bar with grandfather clock and inglenook woodburner, local ales and tasty home-cooked food from lunchtime sandwiches/baguettes up, friendly service; children and dogs welcome, four bedrooms, attractive small garden, closed Sun evening. *(Charles Fraser)*

CHILLESFORD TM3852
★**Froize** (01394) 450282
B1084 E of Woodbridge; IP12 3PU Restaurant rather than pub and open only when they serve food (not Mon or evenings Sun-Thurs), reliably good if not cheap buffet-style food from owner-chef using carefully sourced local produce including seasonal

game, nice wines by the glass and well kept Adnams, warmly welcoming service, little deli next to bar; occasional live folk music; seats on terrace, no dogs inside. *(Ian Duncan)*

CREETING ST MARY   TM1155
Highwayman (01449) 760369
A140, just N of junction with A14;
IP6 8PD Attractively modernised 17th-c pub with two bars and pleasant galleried barn extension, welcoming landlord and friendly relaxed atmosphere, good freshly cooked food from landlady-chef, well kept H&H Olde Trip and Woodfordes Wherry, decent wines; unobtrusive background music; children welcome, no dogs inside, tables on gravel terrace and back lawn with pretty pond, closed Sun evening, Mon. *(David Twitchett)*

CRETINGHAM   TM2260
Bell (01728) 685419
The Street; IP13 7BJ Attractive and welcoming old pub with good traditional home-made food from sandwiches up, well kept ales such as Adnams and Earl Soham, nice wines by the glass, bare-boards bar, dining tables in tiled second room, beams and timbers, leather sofa and armchairs by woodburner; regular live music; dogs welcome in snug, garden picnic-sets. *(Donald Allsopp)*

EARL SOHAM   TM2263
Victoria (01728) 685758
A1120 Yoxford–Stowmarket; IP13 7RL Simple two-bar pub popular with locals, well kept Earl Soham beers (used to be brewed here) and reasonably priced home-cooked food, friendly service, kitchen chairs and pews, scrubbed country tables, tiled or bare board floors, panelling and open fire; outside gents'; children and dogs welcome, seats out in front and on raised back lawn, handy for working windmill at Saxted, open all day Fri-Sun (May-Sept). *(Neil, Jack Trussler)*

EAST BERGHOLT   TM0734
Kings Head (01206) 298190
Burnt Oak, towards Flatford Mill;
CO7 6TL Refurbished 17th-c village dining pub, good freshly made food including lunchtime set deal and regular themed nights, Adnams, Crouch Vale and guests, good choice of wines, pleasant staff; children and dogs welcome, side garden and terrace, handy for Flatford Mill (NT), closed Mon and Tues, open all day weekends from 9.30am for breakfast. *(Carolyn Dixon)*

EASTON   TM2858
White Horse (01728) 746456
N of Wickham Market on back road to Earl Soham and Framlingham;
IP13 0ED This attractive early 18th-c pub was closed for refurbishment under new owners as we went to press – reports please.

EDWARDSTONE   TL9542
★ **White Horse** (01787) 211211
Mill Green, just E; village signed off A1071 in Boxford; CO10 5PX
Unpretentious pub with own good Mill Green beers and guests, various sized bars with lots of beer mats, rustic prints and photos on walls, second-hand tables and chairs including an old steamer bench and panelled settle on bare boards, woodburner and open fire, well liked food (booking advised); bar billiards, darts, ring the bull and other games, regular beer/music festivals; children and dogs welcome, end terrace with sturdy teak furniture, attractive smokers' shelter, makeshift picnic-sets on grass, two scandinavian-style self-catering 'cottages' plus campsite with shower block, open (and food) all day in summer. *(Mrs Margo Finlay, Jörg Kasprowski, Jeremy King)*

EYE   TM1473
Queens Head (01379) 870153
Cross Street; IP23 7AB Popular three-room beamed pub; Adnams and local guests tapped from the cask (July beer festival), 11 wines by the glass and good fairly priced food (not Sun evening) cooked by landlord including fish specials, friendly accommodating staff, interesting local artwork, woodburner, background music; children and dogs (theirs is Franco) welcome, garden with play area, open all day (Sun till 9pm), breakfast from 8.30am. *(Bev Page)*

FELIXSTOWE   TM2734
Fludyers Arms (01394) 691929
Undercliff Road E; IP11 4SH Restored and extended Edwardian pub-hotel on seafront, opened-up bare boards bar, several dining areas including panelled restaurant, Adnams, Woodfordes and guests, popular food from bar snacks up including set menu, good friendly service; events such as live jazz; children welcome, sea views from heated front terrace, 12 bedrooms and mews apartment, open (and food) all day. *(Mrs M S Forbes)*

FELIXSTOWE FERRY   TM3237
Ferry Boat (01394) 284203
Off Ferry Road, on the green; IP11 9RZ Much-modernised 17th-c pub tucked between golf links and dunes near harbour, martello tower and summer rowing-boat ferry; enjoyable fair value pub food including good fish dishes, friendly efficient staff, well kept Adnams Southwold, Woodfordes Wherry and a guest, decent coffee, warm log fire; background music; children and dogs welcome, tables out in front, on green opposite and in fenced garden, good coast walks, open all day weekends and busy in summer. *(Julian Richardson)*

FRAMLINGHAM   TM2863
Crown (01728) 723521
Market Hill; IP13 9AP Stylishly updated
16th-c beamed coaching inn, good food from
lunchtime sandwiches and pizzas up, Greene
King and guests, several wines by the glass,
friendly helpful staff, open fires; background
and some live acoustic music, free wi-fi;
children and dogs welcome, tables in back
courtyard, 14 bedrooms, open all day.
(Brian and Sally Wakeham)

FRAMLINGHAM   TM2862
Station Hotel (01728) 723455
Station Road (B1116 S); IP13 9EE
Simple high-ceilinged big-windowed bar
with scrubbed tables on bare boards, half-
panelling and woodburner, well kept Earl
Soham ales and good choice of house wines,
popular freshly cooked food from interesting
menu, also wood-fired pizzas Thurs-Sat
evenings, friendly relaxed atmosphere,
back snug with tiled floor; children and
dogs welcome, picnic-sets in pleasant
garden. *(Sandra King)*

FRESSINGFIELD   TM2677
★ Fox & Goose (01379) 586247
*Church Street; B1116 N of Framlingham;
IP21 5PB* Relaxed dining pub in beautifully
timbered 16th-c building next to church,
very good food served in cosy informal
heavy-beamed rooms and upstairs restaurant,
friendly efficient service, good wines by the
glass, Adnams and a guest tapped from the
cask in side bar; faint background music;
children welcome, downstairs disabled
facilities, tables out by duck pond,
closed Mon. *(Jeff Davies)*

FRISTON   TM4160
Old Chequers (01728) 688039
*Just off A1094 Aldeburgh–Snape;
IP17 1NP* Refurbished under friendly new
licensees; brightened-up L-shaped bar with
wood flooring and woodburner, enjoyable
home-made food and well kept ales such
as Adnams, Greene and Woodfordes from
brick-faced servery; well behaved children
and dogs welcome, sunny back terrace,
nice circular walks to Aldeburgh and
Snape, closed Mon, otherwise open all day
(not Tues lunchtime, and till 8pm Sun in
winter). *(Tracey and Stephen Groves)*

GREAT BRICETT   TM0450
Red Lion (01473) 657799
B1078, E of Bildeston; IP7 7DD
Extended old beamed pub serving very
good vegetarian and vegan food at
competitive prices (nothing for meat
eaters), children's menu and takeaways
too, real ales such as Greene King; dogs

welcome in bar, garden with deck and play
equipment, closed Mon. *(Jack Trussler)*

GREAT GLEMHAM   TM3461
Crown (01728) 663693
*Between A12 Wickham Market–
Saxmundham and B1119
Saxmundham–Framlingham; IP17 2DA*
Traditionally restored early 19th-c red-brick
village pub; two big fireplaces and some nice
old suffolk furniture on wood and quarry-tiled
floors, mostly local beers from old brass
handpumps, good interesting food (not Sun
evening, Tues) along with pub favourites,
back coffee lounge with freshly baked cakes,
friendly helpful staff; some acoustic music,
monthly quiz, darts, table skittles, free wi-fi;
well behaved children and dogs welcome,
disabled facilities, cast-iron furniture on
back lawn, self-catering cottage, open all
day weekends, closed Tues lunchtime.
(Brian and Sally Wakeham)

GREAT WRATTING   TL6848
Red Lion (01440) 783237
School Road; CB9 7HA Popular village pub
with a couple of ancient whale bones flanking
the entrance; bar with log fire and lots of
copper and brass, well kept Adnams and
generous helpings of enjoyable pubby food,
friendly welcoming staff, restaurant; children
and dogs welcome, big back garden, open all
day Sat. *(Adele Summers, Alan Black)*

GRUNDISBURGH   TM2250
★ Dog (01473) 735267
*The Green; off A12 via B1079 from
Woodbridge bypass; IP13 6TA* Friendly
pink-washed pub with villagey public bar,
log fire, settles and dark wooden carvers
around pubby tables on tiles, Adnams, Earl
Soham, Woodfordes and a guest, half a dozen
wines by the glass, popular good value food
including daily specials, themed nights and
set lunch (Tues-Sat), carpeted lounge linking
to bare-boards dining room; children and
dogs welcome, picnic-sets out in front by
flowering tubs, more seats in wicker-fenced
mediterranean-feel back garden, play
area, open all day Fri-Sun, closed Mon.
(Ian Duncan)

HADLEIGH   TM0242
Kings Head (01473) 828855
High Street; IP7 5EF Modernised
Georgian-fronted pub (building is actually
much older) with popular food from daily
changing menu including good wood-fired
pizzas, Adnams, Greene King, Crouch Vale
and guests, Aspall's cider, friendly helpful
staff; Apr beer festival and themed food
weeks; dogs welcome in some areas, open
all day from 9.30am (midday Sun).
(Mrs Carolyn Dixon)

If you report on a pub that's not a featured entry, please tell us any lunchtimes
or evenings when it doesn't serve bar food.

HADLEIGH   TM0242
Ram (01473) 822880
Market Place; IP7 5DL Smartly updated
bar-restaurant (sister to the Swan at Long
Melford and Greyhound at Lavenham) facing
Georgian corn exchange; good well presented
food (not particularly cheap) including set
menu, brunch from 10am, plenty of wines by
the glass from extensive list, cocktails and
a beer from Greene King, efficient service;
children welcome, small courtyard garden
behind, open all day (Sun till 7pm).
(Mrs Carolyn Dixon)

HARTEST   TL8352
Crown (01284) 830250
B1066 S of Bury St Edmunds; IP29 4DH
Old pub by church behind pretty village
green; good food (all day Sun) from
sandwiches and sharing boards up, popular
Weds pie and pint night, own Brewshed
beers plus a couple from Greene King, plenty
of wines by the glass, friendly attentive
uniformed staff, well modernised split-level
beamed interior (note the coins left by
departing WW1 soldiers), good log fire in
big fireplace; free wi-fi; children (not in bar
after 8pm) and well behaved dogs welcome,
tables on big back lawn and in sheltered side
courtyard, good play area, open all day.
(Marianne and Peter Stevens)

HASKETON   TM2450
Turks Head (01394) 610343
*Top Road; follow village signs taking
B1079 from second Woodbridge
roundabout; IP13 6JG* Fresh modern
décor in this recently refurbished country
dining pub; flagstoned bar with white-painted
beams and woodburner in large fireplace,
changing local ales, Aspall's cider and good
range of wines, dining room with wood
floors, blue walls and pitched ceiling, good
food from sensibly short but varied menu
including interesting bar snacks, efficient
friendly service; children and dogs (in bar
and snug) welcome, landscaped garden, open
all day (till 8pm Sun). *(David Stewart)*

HAWKEDON   TL7953
★ Queens Head (01284) 789218
*Off A143 at Wickham Street, NE of
Haverhill; and off B1066; IP29 4NN*
Flint Tudor pub in pretty setting looking
down broad peaceful green to interesting
largely Norman village church; quarry-
tiled bar with dark beams and ochre walls,
plenty of pews and chapel chairs around
scrubbed tables, elderly armchairs by
antique woodburner in huge fireplace,
cheerful helpful staff, Adnams, Woodfordes
and guests, proper cider/perry and nice
choice of wines, good popular food (not Mon,
Tues) using home-reared meat, dining area
stretching back with country prints and a
couple of tusky boars' heads; some live music;
picnic-sets out in front, more on back terrace

overlooking rolling country, little shop (Fri
and Sat mornings) selling their own bacon,
pies, casseroles etc, open all day Fri-Sun,
closed lunchtimes Mon-Thurs. *(R A P Cross)*

HOLBROOK   TM1636
Compasses (01473) 328332
Ipswich Road; IP9 2QR Simple spacious
village pub with enjoyable straightforward
food including children's choices, prompt
friendly service, well kept Adnams and
Sharps Doom Bar, Aspall's cider, big log fire,
restaurant; quiz first Fri of the month; seats
out at front under cover, garden with play
area, good walks nearby. *(David and Judy
Robison)*

IPSWICH   TM1644
Dove Street (01473) 211270
St Helens Street; IP4 2LA Over 20 well
kept quickly changing ales including their
own brews (regular beer festivals), farm
ciders, bottled beers and good selection
of whiskies, low priced simple pub food
including substantial pork pies, hot drinks,
bare-boards bar, carpeted snug and back
conservatory; dogs welcome, children till
7pm, seats on heated covered terrace, two
bedrooms and brewery shop across the road,
open (and food) all day. *(Tony Hobden)*

IPSWICH   TM1645
Greyhound (01473) 252862
Henley Road/Anglesea Road; IP1 3SE
Popular 19th-c pub close to Christchurch
Park; cosy front bar, corridor to larger
lounge/dining area, five well kept Adnams
ales and a couple of guests, good home
cooking including bargain weekday lunch
and daily specials, quick friendly service; Sun
quiz, sports TV, free wi-fi; children welcome,
picnic-sets under parasols on back terrace,
open all day Fri-Sun (breakfast Sun from
10am). *(Liz and Martin Eldon)*

IPSWICH   TM1747
Railway Inn (01473) 252337
*Westerfield Road close to the station;
IP6 9AA* Refurbished roadside pub popular
locally for its good reasonably priced food (all
day weekends) including set menus and daily
specials, three well kept ales from Adnams
and several wines by the glass, pleasant
attentive service; quiz last Weds of month;
children and dogs (in bar area) welcome,
four bedrooms, outside tables and colourful
hanging baskets, open all day Fri-Sun.
(Jack Trussler)

IPSWICH   TM1744
Woolpack (01473) 215862
Tuddenham Road; IP4 2SH Welcoming
traditional red-brick pub dating from the
1600s, Adnams and four other well kept
beers, several wines by the glass and good
coffee, popular fairly priced home-cooked
food including blackboard specials, two bars,
snug and back dining area, corner with piano

and board games; live music and quiz nights; dogs welcome, seats on heated front terrace, opposite Christchurch Park, open all day from 9.30am for breakfast. *(Jack Trussler)*

KERSEY   TM0044
Bell (01473) 823229
Signed off A1141 N of Hadleigh; The Street; IP7 6DY Welcoming black and white Tudor pub in notably picturesque village with ford; good value traditional home-made food (not Mon evening), Adnams Broadside, Greene King IPA and a guest, friendly helpful service, low-beamed log-fire bar with dining area, restaurant; children and dogs (in bar) welcome, attractive sheltered back terrace, open all day. *(Paul and Marion Watts, Mrs Margo Finlay, Jörg Kasprowski)*

KESGRAVE   TM2346
Kesgrave Hall (01473) 333741
Hall Road; IP5 2PU Country hotel with comfortably contemporary bare-boards bar, Adnams and a couple of guests from granite-topped servery, several wines by the glass and cocktails, popular often imaginative food in open-kitchen brasserie (no booking so best to arrive early), friendly efficient young staff; children and dogs welcome, attractive heated terrace with huge retractable awning, 23 stylish bedrooms, open (and food) all day. *(Mike and Mary Carter)*

LAVENHAM   TL9149
Greyhound (01787) 249553
High Street; CO10 9PZ Well modernised 14th-c pub under same management as the Swan at Long Melford and Ram at Hadleigh; Greene King IPA and four guests, over a dozen wines by the glass and some interesting gins, good food from varied menu including vegetarian choices and brunch from 10am, friendly attentive service, opened-up (but cosy) beamed interior with inglenook woodburner and plenty of contemporary touches; children and dogs (in bar) welcome, back terrace, open (and food) all day. *(Mrs Carolyn Dixon)*

LAVENHAM   TL9149
Swan (01787) 247477
High Street; CO10 9QA Smart hotel incorporating handsome medieval buildings; appealing network of beamed and timbered alcoves and more open areas, tiled-floor inner bar with log fire and memorabilia from its days as the local for US 48th Bomber Group, well kept Adnams and a guest, lots of wines by the glass from extensive list and good interesting food, can eat in bar, informal brasserie or lavishly timbered restaurant, efficient friendly young staff; children and dogs welcome, sheltered courtyard garden,

45 bedrooms, open all day. *(Bill Adie, Mrs Carolyn Dixon, Marianne and Peter Stevens)*

LAXFIELD   TM2972
★ **Kings Head** (01986) 798395
Gorams Mill Lane, behind church; IP13 8DW Unspoilt thatched pub with no bar counter – Adnams ales and a guest poured in tap room; interesting little chequer-tiled front room dominated by three-sided booth of high-backed settles in front of old range fire, two other rooms with pews, old seats and scrubbed deal tables, well liked tasty food including good home-made pies (kitchen may close early if quiet), friendly helpful staff; children and dogs welcome, neatly kept garden with arbour and small pavilion for cooler evenings, boules, two bedrooms, open all day (till 7pm Sun). *(Sandra King)*

LAXFIELD   TM2972
Royal Oak (01986) 798666
High Street; IP13 8DH Extended Tudor pub next to 14th-c church; beams, old quarry tiles and inglenook, half a dozen well kept ales including Adnams and Woodfordes, good value food (not Sun evening) served by friendly staff; quiz and music nights; children and dogs welcome, tables out in front, open all day. *(Donald Allsopp)*

LINDSEY TYE   TL9846
★ **Red Rose** (01449) 741424
Village signposted off A1141 NW of Hadleigh; IP7 6PP Old hall house with neatly kept main bar, low beams and standing timbers, assortment of wooden tables and chairs, red leather sofas by log fire in brick fireplace, second similarly furnished room with another big fireplace, good reliable food (not Sun evening) , Adnams and Mauldons ales, 11 wines by the glass, friendly service; free wi-fi; children and dogs welcome, flowering tubs and a few picnic-sets out in front, more seating behind, open all day Sun. *(Mrs Margo Finlay, Jörg Kasprowski, Mrs Carolyn Dixon, Rona Mackinlay, Valerie Sayer)*

LONG MELFORD   TL8645
Crown (01787) 377666
Hall Street; CO10 9JL Partly 17th-c inn with four well kept ales including Adnams and Greene King, central servery with unusual bar chairs, log fire, some stripped brickwork and tartan carpet, oak-floored restaurant with high-backed chairs and vibrant red walls, good locally sourced food (all day Sun) from bar snacks up, friendly helpful service; tables under parasols on attractive split-level terrace, 12 well equipped bedrooms, open all day. *(Martin Day)*

Places with gardens or terraces usually let children sit there – we note in the text the very few exceptions that don't.

LONG MELFORD
TL8645
Swan (01787) 464545
Hall Street; CO10 9JQ Well run beamed
dining pub (same group as Greyhound at
Lavenham and Ram at Hadleigh); good
imaginative food (best to book) including
vegetarian choices, brunch from 10am, well
selected wines, interesting gins, cocktails
and a couple of real ales, obliging service,
split-level interior with pastel décor and
some unusual wallpaper, high-backed dining
chairs and mix of tables on wood or carpeted
floors, log fire; unobtrusive background
music; children welcome, tables out on
terrace and lawn, four good bedrooms
in next-door building, open all day.
(Hayley Ransome)

LOWESTOFT
TM5593
Triangle (01502) 582711
St Peters Street; NR32 1QA Popular
two-bar tap for Green Jack ales, guest beers
too and real cider, regular beer festivals,
breweriana and open fire; live music Fri, pool
and TV in back bar; open all day (till 1am
Fri, Sat). *(Charles Fraser)*

MELTON
TM2850
Olde Coach & Horses
(01394) 384851 *Melton Road; IP12 1PD*
Attractively modernised beamed former
staging inn, good choice of enjoyable fairly
priced food from sandwiches, snacks and
sharing plates up (special diets catered
for), lunchtime meal deal Mon-Sat, Adnams
and decent wines by the glass, good friendly
service; July beer festival, free wi-fi; children
welcome, dogs in wood-floored area, tables
out under parasols among colourful hanging
baskets and planters, open all day from 9am
for breakfast. *(Julian Richardson)*

MONKS ELEIGH
TL9647
Swan (01449) 763163
A1141 NW of Hadleigh; IP7 7AU
Refurbished thatched and beamed pub
overlooking small village green (same owners
as Anchor at Nayland and Angel at Stoke-
by-Nayland), good interesting food (not Sun
evening) using locally sourced ingredients,
some cooked/smoked over charcoal, Adnams
Southwold and a guest, plenty of wines by
the glass including champagne, friendly
accommodating staff; children welcome, dogs
in bar, open all day Fri and Sat, till 9pm Sun,
closed Mon. *(Mrs Carolyn Dixon, MDN, Lesley
Bernard Rose)*

MOULTON
TL6964
Packhorse (01638) 751818
Bridge Street; CB8 8SP Stylishly revamped
and more restaurant-with-rooms than pub;

good popular (if pricey) food from owner-chef
including some inventive choices (must
book), carve your own Sun roast at the table,
well kept Adnams, Woodfordes and a guest,
good wines by the glass, pleasant attentive
service; dogs welcome, adjacent to delightful
15th-c bridge across the Kennett and handy
for Newmarket races, four bedrooms, open
all day. *(John and Enid, Caroline Prescott,
M and GR)*

NAYLAND
TL9734
★ Anchor (01206) 262313
*Court Street; just off A134 – turn-off
S of signposted B1087 main village
turn; CO6 4JL* Friendly pub by River
Stour under same ownership as the Angel
at Stoke-by-Nayland and Swan at Monks
Eleigh; bare-boards bar with assorted wooden
dining chairs and tables, big gilt mirror on
silvery wallpaper one end, another mirror
above pretty fireplace at the other, five
changing ales and several wines by the glass,
interesting food (some home-smoked) along
with more standard dishes, Fri evening tapas,
two other rooms behind and steep stairs up
to cosy restaurant; quiz last Sun of month;
children welcome, dogs in bar, terrace
tables overlooking river, open all day.
(Lesley Bernard Rose)

NEWBOURNE
TM2743
★ Fox (01473) 736307
*Off A12 at roundabout 1.7 miles N of
A14 junction; The Street; IP12 4NY*
Pink-washed 16th-c pub decked in summer
flowers; low-beamed bar with slabby elm
and other dark tables on tiled floor, stuffed
fox in inglenook, comfortable carpeted
dining room with various mirrors, Adnams
Southwold, guest ales and decent wines
by the glass, good choice of popular food
including lunchtime set menu, friendly
efficient service; background music, free
wi-fi; children and dogs (in bar) welcome,
wheelchair access, attractive grounds with
rose garden and pond, open (and food)
all day. *(Brian and Sally Wakeham)*

ORFORD
TM4249
★ Jolly Sailor (01394) 450243
Quay Street; IP12 2NU Welcoming old pub
under mother and daughter team; several
snug rooms with exposed brickwork, boating
pictures and other nautical memorabilia, four
well kept Adnams beers and popular sensibly
priced food from lunchtime sandwiches up,
friendly efficient service, unusual spiral
staircase in corner of flagstoned main bar
by brick inglenook, horsebrasses and local
photographs, two cushioned pews and long
antique stripped-deal table; maybe local
sea shanty group, free wi-fi; children and

We checked prices with the pubs as we went to press in summer 2016.
They should hold until around spring 2017.

dogs welcome, tables on back terrace and lawn with views over marshes, popular with walkers and bird-watchers, bedrooms, open all day weekends. *(Brian Glozier, Roger and Pauline Pearce, Penny Lang, Phil and Jane Villiers, Bob and Margaret Holder)*

ORFORD   TM4249
★ **Kings Head** (01394) 450271
Front Street; IP12 2LW Friendly village inn surrounded by fine walks and lovely coastline; partly 700 years old and plenty of authentic atmosphere, snug main bar with heavy low beams straightforward furniture on red carpeting, Adnams ales and several wines by the glass, enjoyable home-made food from generously filled sandwiches to daily specials, dining room with nice old stripped-brick walls and rugs on ancient boards, woodburners; children and dogs welcome, three bedrooms open all day Fri-Sun. *(Derek and Sylvia Stephenson)*

POLSTEAD   TL9938
Cock (01206) 263150
Signed off B1068 and A1071 E of Sudbury, then pub signed; Polstead Green; CO6 5AL Welcoming 16th-c beamed and timbered village local; bar with woodburner, Greene King IPA and two guests, good choice of wines and enjoyable reasonably priced home-made food from lunchtime sandwiches up, helpful friendly staff, light and airy barn restaurant; background music; children and dogs welcome, disabled facilities, picnic-sets overlooking small green, open all day Sat, closed Sun evening. *(Mary Joyce)*

RAMSHOLT   TM3041
Ramsholt Arms (01394) 411209
Signed off B1083; Dock Road; IP12 3AB Lovely isolated spot overlooking River Deben and under same management as the Crown at Ufford (see Main Entries); modernised open-plan bar with log fire, enjoyable food from lunchtime sandwiches up, Adnams, a couple of guest beers and decent choice of wines by the glass; children and dogs welcome, plenty of tables outside taking in the view, handy for bird walks and Sutton Hoo (NT), open all day in high summer and busy at weekends, best to check other times (may close Jan). *(Jack Trussler)*

REYDON   TM4977
★ **Randolph** (01502) 723603
Wangford Road (B1126 just NW of Southwold); IP18 6PZ Stylish inn with quite an emphasis on dining and bedroom side; bar with high-backed leather dining chairs around chunky wooden tables on parquet floor, a couple of comfortable armchairs and sofa, prints of the pub from 1910 and photographs of Southwold beach, Adnams beers, more high-backed chairs in carpeted dining room with pretty Victorian fireplace, enjoyable food from

short but varied menu including lunchtime sandwiches and snack baskets, pleasant staff; background music, TV; children welcome, dogs in small back bar, wheelchair access, picnic-sets on decked area and grass, ten bedrooms and self-catering bungalow, good breakfast, open all day. *(Liz and Martin Eldon)*

ROUGHAM   TL9063
★ **Ravenwood Hall** (01359) 270345
Off A14 E of Bury St Edmunds; IP30 9JA Country-house hotel with two compact bar rooms, tall ceilings, patterned wallpaper and big heavily draped windows overlooking sweeping lawn with stately cedar, back area set for eating with upholstered settles and dining chairs, sporting prints and log fire, very good well presented food (own smoked meats and fish), well kept Adnams, good choice of wines and malt whiskies, pleasant attentive staff, comfortable lounge area with horse pictures, a few moulded beams and early Tudor wall decoration above big inglenook, separate more formal restaurant; background music; children and dogs welcome, teak furniture in garden, swimming pool and croquet, big enclosures for geese, pygmy goats and shetland ponies, 14 bedrooms, open 9am-midnight. *(Julian Richardson)*

SAXTEAD GREEN   TM2564
Old Mill House (01728) 685064
B1119; The Green; IP13 9QE Roomy dining pub across green from windmill; beamed carpeted bar and neat country-look flagstoned restaurant extension, good choice of generous well priced fresh food (all day Sun) including daily carvery, good friendly service, well kept Greene King ales and decent wines; discreet background music; children very welcome, attractive garden with terrace and good play area, open all day Sun. *(Sandra King)*

SHOTTISHAM   TM3244
Sorrel Horse (01394) 411617
Hollesley Road; IP12 3HD Charming 15th-c thatched community-owned local; well kept Adnams, Earl Soham, Woodfordes and guests tapped from casks, decent choice of home-made traditional food including deals, attentive helpful young staff, good log fire in tiled-floor bar with games area (bar billiards), woodburner in attractive dining room; fortnightly Weds quiz, free wi-fi; children and dogs welcome, tables out on sloping front lawn and in small garden behind, open all day weekends. *(Donald Allsopp)*

SNAPE   TM3958
★ **Crown** (01728) 688324
Bridge Road (B1069); IP17 1SL Small well laid-out 15th-c beamed pub with brick floors, inglenook log fire and fine double suffolk settle, well kept Adnams ales, good fresh food using local ingredients

including own meat (reared behind the pub), reasonable prices, efficient friendly young staff; folk night last Thurs of month, darts, free wi-fi; children and dogs welcome, garden, two bedrooms. *(Simon Rodway)*

SNAPE   TM4058
★ **Golden Key** (01728) 688510
Priory Lane; IP17 1SA Welcoming traditionally furnished village pub; low-beamed lounge with old-fashioned settle and straightforward tables and chairs on chequerboard tiled floor, log fire, small snug and two cosy dining rooms, well kept Adnams ales, local cider and a dozen wines by the glass, good food from monthly changing menu (reasonably priced for the area), cheerful attentive service; children and dogs welcome, two terraces with pretty hanging baskets and seats under large parasols, handy for the Maltings, three comfortable bedrooms, good breakfast, open all day weekends.
(Peter Smith and Judith Brown, Sara Fulton, Roger Baker, Derek and Sylvia Stephenson, Phil and Jane Villiers, Simon Rodway)

SNAPE   TM3957
★ **Plough & Sail** (01728) 688413
The Maltings, Snape Bridge (B1069 S); IP17 1SR Nicely placed dining pub (part of the Maltings complex) airily extended around original 16th-c core, mostly open-plan with good blend of traditional and modern furnishings, well kept Adnams Bitter, Woodfordes Wherry and guests, a dozen wines by the glass including champagne and good bistro-style food (pre- and post-concert menus), spacious dining room, upstairs restaurant, efficient well organised service; background music; children and dogs (in bar) welcome, teak furniture on flower-filled terrace, picnic-sets at front, open all day.
(Edward Mirzoeff, Tracey and Stephen Groves, Phil and Jane Villiers, Simon Rodway)

SOUTH ELMHAM   TM3385
★ **St Peters Brewery** (01986) 782288
St Peter South Elmham; off B1062 SW of Bungay; NR35 1NQ Beautifully but simply furnished manor dating from the 13th c (much extended in 1539) with own St Peters ales and bottled beers, enjoyable food from sensibly short menu, afternoon teas, good friendly service, bar and dining hall with dramatic high ceiling, elaborate woodwork and flagstoned floor, antique tapestries, woodburner in fine fireplace, two further rooms reached up steepish stairs; children and dogs (in bar) welcome, outside tables overlooking original moat, open all day Fri and Sat, till 6pm Sun, Weds and Thurs, closed Mon, Tues (although may open in

high summer), they do host weddings and other events, so best to check. *(Liz and Martin Eldon)*

SOUTHWOLD   TM5076
★ **Lord Nelson** (01502) 722079
East Street, off High Street (A1095); IP18 6EJ Busy local near seafront with partly panelled traditional bar and two small side rooms, coal fire, light wood furniture on tiles, lamps in nice nooks and corners, interesting Nelson memorabilia including attractive nautical prints and fine model of HMS *Victory*, five well kept Adnams ales, several wines by the glass and decent pubby food, good service even when packed; board games, free wi-fi; children (away from the bar) and dogs welcome, disabled access not perfect but possible, seats out in front with sidelong view of the sea, sheltered and heated back garden with Adnams brewery in sight, open all day. *(Barry Collett, Giles and Annie Francis, Sheila Topham, Simon Rodway)*

SOUTHWOLD   TM5076
★ **Red Lion** (01502) 722385
South Green; IP18 6ET Cheerful pubby front bar with big windows looking over green towards the sea, sturdy wall benches and bar stools on flagstones, well kept Adnams including seasonals, quieter back room with mate's chairs, cushioned pews and polished dark tables on pale woodstrip flooring, seaside cartoons by Giles, Mac and the like, good range of popular reasonably priced food served by friendly neatly dressed staff, three linked dining rooms; background music (live Sun afternoon); tables out in front and in small sheltered back courtyard, next to the Adnams retail shop. *(James Landor)*

SOUTHWOLD   TM5076
Sole Bay (01502) 723736
East Green; IP18 6JN Busy pub near Adnams brewery, their full range kept well and good wine choice, cheerful efficient staff, enjoyable reasonably priced simple food including good fish and chips, airy interior with well spaced tables, conservatory; sports TV; children and dogs welcome, disabled facilities, picnic-sets outside, moments from sea and lighthouse, open (and food) all day. *(James Landor, Mary Joyce)*

SOUTHWOLD   TM5076
Swan (01502) 722186
Market Place; IP18 6EG Relaxed comfortable back bar in smart Adnams-owned hotel, their full range kept well plus bottled beers and good choice of wines and whiskies, enjoyable bar food including lunchtime set menu (Mon-Sat), cheerful

---

Please tell us if any pub deserves to be upgraded to a featured entry – and why: feedback@goodguides.com, or (no stamp needed) The Good Pub Guide, FREEPOST RTJR-ZCYZ-RJZT, Perrymans Lane, Etchingham TN19 7DN.

competent staff, coffee and teas in luxurious chintzy front lounge, restaurant; nice garden, 42 bedrooms (some in separate block), good breakfast. *(Mary Joyce)*

STANSFIELD TL7851
Compasses (01284) 789263
High Street; CO10 8LN Simple little country pub with good often interesting food cooked by character landlord (some ingredients from next door farm), own-brewed beers and local guests, beams, bare boards and large woodburner; walkers and dogs welcome, outside tables with lovely rural views, open all day weekends, closed Mon, Tues. *(Julian Richardson)*

STOKE ASH TM1170
White Horse (01379) 678222
A140/Workhouse Road; IP23 7ET Sizeable 17th-c roadside coaching inn, beams and inglenook fireplaces, generous helpings of good reasonably priced pub food all day from 8am, well kept Adnams, Greene King and Woodfordes, local Calvors lager and Aspall's cider, efficient service from friendly young staff; children welcome, bedrooms in modern annexe, open (and food) all day. *(Jeff Davies)*

STOKE-BY-NAYLAND TL9836
★ ## Angel (01206) 263245
B1068 Sudbury–East Bergholt; CO6 4SA Elegant and comfortable 17th-c inn (same owners as Swan at Monks Eleigh and Anchor at Nayland); lounge with handsome beams, timbers and stripped brickwork, leather chesterfields and wing armchairs around low tables, pictures of local scenes, more formal room with deep glass-covered well, chatty bar with straightforward furniture on red tiles, well kept Banks's Mansfield and a guest, ten wines by the glass, wide range of enterprising food (all day weekends) served promptly by friendly uniformed staff; children and dogs (in bar) welcome, seats on sheltered terrace, six individually styled bedrooms, good breakfast, open all day. *(Mrs Carolyn Dixon, MDN, Dr Michael Smith, Lesley Bernard Rose)*

STUTTON TM1434
Gardeners Arms (01473) 328868
Manningtree Road, Upper Street (B1080); IP9 2TG Cottagey roadside pub on edge of small village, well kept Adnams Southwold and guests, enjoyable home-made food including daily specials and OAP meals, friendly helpful service, cosy L-shaped bar with log fire, side dining room and larger area stretching to the back, lots of bric-a-brac, film posters and musical instruments; children and dogs (on leads) welcome, two-tier back garden with pond, open all day Sun, closed Mon. *(Ian Duncan)*

SUDBURY TL8741
Brewery Tap (01787) 370876
East Street; CO10 2TP Corner tap for Mauldons brewery, their range and guests kept well, good choice of malt whiskies, bare boards and scrubbed tables, some food (can bring your own); darts, cribbage and bar billiards, live music, quiz third Weds of month; dogs welcome, open all day. *(Donald Allsopp)*

SWEFFLING TM3464
White Horse (01728) 664178
B1119 Framlingham–Saxmundham; IP17 2BB Traditional little two-room country pub, friendly and laid-back, with woodburner in one room, range in the other, up to three well kept changing east anglian beers served from tap room door, real cider and some interesting local wines and spirits, simple food such as ploughman's and locally made winter pies; some live acoustic music, bar billiards, darts and other traditional games; children and dogs welcome, self-catering cottage and campsite with yurts, closed lunchtimes apart from Sun. *(Charles Fraser)*

SWILLAND TM1852
Moon & Mushroom (01473) 785320
Off B1078; IP6 9LR Popular 16th-c country local serving East Anglian beers from racked casks behind long counter, old tables and chairs on quarry tiles, log fire, enjoyable good value home-made food such as rabbit pie and local venison; quiz first Weds of month; children and dogs welcome, heated terrace with grapevines and roses, closed Sun evening, Mon. *(Brian and Sally Wakeham)*

THELNETHAM TM0178
White Horse (01379) 898779
Village signed off B1111 in Hopton; IP22 1JN Friendly family-run country pub off the beaten track but popular, good well presented freshly made food (not Sun evening-Tues), up to four local ales, real cider and nice wines; live music Tues; children, walkers and dogs welcome, open all day weekends, closed Mon, Tues lunchtime. *(Julian Richardson)*

THORNDON TM1469
Black Horse (01379) 678523
Off A140 or B1077, S of Eye; The Street; IP23 7JR Friendly 17th-c village pub with enjoyable food including good value lunchtime carvery, also indian and fish and chip takeaways, three well kept local ales, beams, lots of timbering, stripped brick and big fireplaces; well behaved children welcome, tables on lawn, country views behind, open all day Sun till 9pm. *(Mary Joyce)*

THORNHAM MAGNA TM1070
Four Horseshoes (01379) 678777
Off A140 S of Diss; Wickham Road; IP23 8HD Extensive thatched dining pub dating from the 12th c, well divided dimly lit carpeted bar, Greene King ales

and good choice of wines and whiskies, enjoyable reasonably priced food with main courses available in two sizes, popular Sun carvery, friendly helpful staff, very low heavy black beams, country pictures and brass, big log fireplaces, illuminated interior well; background music; children and dogs welcome, disabled access, handy for Thornham Walks and interesting thatched church, picnic-sets on big sheltered lawn, seven comfortable bedrooms, open all day. *(Ian Duncan)*

THORPENESS   TM4759
★ **Dolphin** (01728) 454994
Just off B1353; Old Homes Road; village signposted from Aldeburgh; IP16 4FE
Neatly kept extended dining pub in interesting seaside village (all built in the early 1900s); main bar with scandinavian feel, pale wooden tables and assortment of old chairs on broad modern quarry tiles, log fire, Adnams, Woodfordes and a guest, several wines by the glass, more traditional public bar with pubby furniture on stripped-wood floor, built-in cushioned wall seats and old local photographs, airy dining room with country kitchen-style furniture, good food and friendly service; background music, TV, free wi-fi; children and dogs welcome, good-sized garden with terrace, bedrooms, open all day weekends in summer. *(Peter Meister, Tracey and Stephen Groves, Simon Rodway)*

THURSTON   TL9165
Fox & Hounds (01359) 232228
Barton Road; IP31 3QT Rather imposing former 19th-c station inn, well kept Adnams Broadside, Greene King IPA and four guests, pubby furnishings in carpeted lounge (back part set for dining), ceiling fans and lots of pump clips, big helpings of reasonably priced pubby food (not Sun evening or Mon lunchtime), friendly service, bare-boards public bar with pool, darts and machines; background and some live music, quiz nights; dogs welcome, picnic-sets on grassed area by car park and on small covered side terrace, pretty village, self-catering apartment, open all day Fri-Sun. *(Julian Richardson)*

TUDDENHAM   TM1948
★ **Fountain** (01473) 785377
The Street; village signed off B1077 N of Ipswich; IP6 9BT Popular well run dining pub in nice village; several linked café-style rooms with heavy beams and timbering, stripped floors, wooden dining chairs around light tables, open fire, lots of prints (some by cartoonist Giles who spent time here after World War II), wide choice of well cooked food (all day Sun till 7pm) including set menus, Adnams Bitter and good selection of

wines by the glass, decent coffee, pleasant helpful service; background music; no under-10s in bar after 6.30pm, wicker and metal chairs on covered heated terrace, rows of picnic-style tables under parasols on sizeable lawn, may close first week of Jan. *(Brian and Sally Wakeham)*

UFFORD   TM2952
White Lion (01394) 460770
Lower Street (off B1438, towards Eyke); IP13 6DW 16th-c village pub near quiet stretch of River Deben; home to the Uffa Brewery with their beers and guests tapped from the cask, enjoyable generous home-made food (own pigs, free-range hens and bees), raised woodburner in large central fireplace, captain's chairs and spindlebacks around simple tables, shop/deli; regular events including quiz nights, beer festivals and vintage car rallies; nice views from outside tables, summer barbecues, closed Sun evening, Mon lunchtime. *(Charles Fraser)*

WANGFORD   TM4679
Angel (01502) 578636
Signed just off A12 by B1126 junction; High Street; NR34 8RL Handsome old coaching inn with airy beamed and carpeted bar, enjoyable good value food from sandwiches up, pleasant efficient service, Adnams, Brakspears, Greene King and up to two guests, decent wines, family dining room; dogs welcome (resident standard poodle), seven comfortable bedrooms (the church clock sounds on the quarter), good breakfast, open all day Sun (and other days if busy). *(Jeff Davies)*

WENHASTON   TM4274
Star (01502) 478240
Hall Road; IP19 9HF Friendly well run 19th-c country pub, Adnams Southwold and guests, good wine choice and wide range of enjoyable inexpensive home-made food; children, dogs and muddy boots welcome, sizeable lawn with boules, nice views, open all day Sun. *(David Field)*

WESTLETON   TM4469
White Horse (01728) 648222
Darsham Road, off B1125 Blythburgh–Leiston; IP17 3AH Friendly and relaxed traditional pub with good home-cooked food from blackboard menu including specials, four well kept Adnams ales, unassuming high-ceilinged bar with central fire, steps down to stone-floored back dining room; quiz nights, darts; children and dogs welcome, picnic-sets in cottagey garden with climbing frame, more out by village duck pond, four bedrooms, good breakfast, open all day Fri-Sun. *(Peter Meister, Ian Herdman)*

Post Office address codings confusingly give the impression that some pubs
are in Suffolk, when they're really in Cambridgeshire, Essex or Norfolk
(which is where we list them).

WOODBRIDGE   TM2648
Cherry Tree (01394) 384627
Opposite Notcutts Nursery, off A12;
Cumberland Street; IP12 4AG Opened-up
17th-c pub (bigger than it looks) with well
kept Adnams and guests, good wines by
the glass and ample helpings of reasonably
priced tasty food including specials, friendly
service, beams and two log fires, mix of pine
furniture, old local photographs; Thurs quiz
and regular beer festivals; children and dogs
(in bar) welcome, garden with play area,
three bedrooms in converted barn, good
breakfast (for non-residents too), open all day.
(Peter Smith and Judith Brown)

WOODBRIDGE   TM2748
Crown (01394) 384242
Thoroughfare/Quay Street; IP12 1AD
Stylish 17th-c dining inn, well kept ales
such as Adnams from glass-roofed bar (boat
suspended above counter), lots of wines by
the glass and cocktails, good imaginative
food from light meals up including set menu,
afternoon teas, pleasant young staff, various
eating areas with contemporary furnishings;
live jazz second Thurs of month; children and
dogs (in bar) welcome, courtyard tables, ten
well appointed bedrooms, open all day.
(Liz and Martin Eldon)

WOODBRIDGE   TM2749
Kings Head (01394) 387750
Market Hill; IP12 4LP Opened-up town
pub with handsome Elizabethan beams and
log fire in massive central chimneybreast,
Adnams ales and good home-made food
from baguettes up, dining room down a
couple of steps; background music; well
behaved children and dogs (menu for them)
welcome, disabled facilities, tables on heated
terrace, open all day weekends, no food Sun
evening. *(Pat and Tony Martin)*

WOODBRIDGE   TM2749
Olde Bell & Steelyard
(01394) 382933 *New Street, off*
Market Square; IP12 1DZ Ancient and
unpretentious timber-framed pub with two
smallish beamed bars and compact dining
room, brassware and old china, log fire,
Greene King ales and guests from canopied
servery, traditional ciders, enjoyable home-
made food from huffers up, friendly staff;
traditional games including bar billiards,
sports TV, free wi-fi; children and dogs
welcome, disabled access, back terrace,
steelyard still overhanging street, open till late
Fri and Sat. *(Peter Smith and Judith Brown)*

WOOLPIT   TL9762
Swan (01359) 240482
The Street; IP30 9QN Welcoming old
coaching house pleasantly situated in village
square, heavy beams and painted panelling,
mixed tables and chairs on carpet, roaring
log fire one end, good inventive food from
daily changing blackboard menu, prompt
friendly service, well kept Adnams from slate-
top counter and lots of wines by the glass;
may be soft background music; walled garden
behind, four bedrooms in converted stables,
closed Sun, Mon. *(Jeremy King)*

Surrey

BUCKLAND
Pheasant ♀ 🍺

TQ2250 Map 3

(01737) 221355 – www.brunningandprice.co.uk/pheasant
Reigate Road (A25 W of Reigate); RH3 7BG

Busy roadside pub with a thoughtful range of drinks and food served by friendly young staff, character rooms and seats on terrace and lawn

Carefully extended from its 18th-c heart, this is now an attractive weatherboarded pub with a bustling atmosphere and friendly, helpful staff. The various interconnected areas are split up by timbering and painted standing pillars and throughout there are wall-to-wall prints and pictures, gilt-edged mirrors, house plants, old stone bottles and elegant metal chandeliers. A couple of dining rooms at one end, separated by a two-sided open fire, have captain's chairs and cushioned dining chairs around a mix of tables on bare boards and rugs. The busy bar has a long high table with equally high chairs, another two-way fireplace with button-back leather armchairs and sofas in front of it and stools against the counter where they keep Brunning & Price Phoenix Original plus guests such as Harveys Best, Hogs Back TEA, Pilgrim Surrey Bitter, Surrey Hills Shere Drop and Titanic Plum Porter on handpump, 23 wines by the glass, 60 whiskies and 41 gins; background music and board games. Of the two further dining rooms, one has a big open fire pit in the middle. On the terrace is another open fire pit surrounded by built-in seats plus solid tables and chairs, while the lawn has plenty of picnic-sets and a play tractor for children.

🍴 Enterprising food includes sandwiches, pigeon breast with pearl barley risotto and baby beetroot, potted smoked salmon, mackerel and trout with pickled vegetables, vegetable cassoulet with grilled halloumi, smoked haddock fishcake with poached egg and hollandaise, steak in ale pie, lemon and thyme-marinated chicken salad with feta, cucumber and skordalia (a greek potato dish), moules frites, and puddings such as lemon posset with strawberry salad and chocolate brownie with chocolate sauce. *Benchmark main dish: braised lamb shoulder with sticky red cabbage and rosemary gravy £16.95. Two-course evening meal £20.00.*

Brunning & Price ~ Manager Beth Wells ~ Real ale ~ Open 9am-11pm (10.30pm Sun) ~ Bar food 9am-10pm ~ Restaurant ~ Children welcome ~ Dogs allowed in bar ~ Wi-fi
Recommended by Mrs Margo Finlay, Jörg Kasprowski, John Branston, Donald Allsopp, Ann and Chris Heaps

If we know a pub has an outdoor play area for children, we mention it.

CHIDDINGFOLD

SU9635   Map 3

Swan 🛏

(01428) 684688 – www.theswaninnchiddingfold.com

Petworth Road (A283 S); GU8 4TY

Open-plan light and airy rooms in well run inn, with local ales, modern food and seats in terraced garden; bedrooms

Especially busy on Goodwood race days, this stylishly updated tile-hung inn is popular with both locals and visitors. The bar has an open fire in an inglenook fireplace with leather armchairs in front and antlers above, wooden tables and chairs and cushioned wall seats on pale floorboards and leather-topped stools against the counter where they keep Upham Tipster and Stakes on handpump, 19 wines by the glass and a good choice of spirits. Staff are helpful and friendly. The dining room leads off here with modern chairs and chunky tables set with fresh flowers on more bare boards. Outside, a three-tiered terraced garden has plenty of seats and tables. Bedrooms are well equipped and comfortable and breakfasts are highly thought-of. There's plenty to do and see nearby.

🍴 Tempting food includes chicken and foie gras terrine with apple purée, potted shrimps, ballotine of rabbit with wild garlic, herbed gnocchi, jerusalem artichokes and broad beans, burger with toppings and shoestring fries, chermoula chicken with red onion, spinach roasted chickpea salad and lemon yoghurt dressing, cod fillet with vegetable spaghetti, fennel fritter and salsa verde, crayfish linguine with chilli and garlic, and puddings such as dark chocolate, marzipan and caramel délice with toffee popcorn and lemon sorbet and banana bread and butter pudding with poppy seed ice-cream. *Benchmark main dish: whole roast plaice with parmentier potatoes and herb brown butter £16.95. Two-course evening meal £22.00.*

Upham ~ Managers Zach and Sinead Leach ~ Real ale ~ Open 9am-11pm ~ Bar food 10-3, 6.30-9.30 (9 Sun) ~ Children welcome ~ Dogs allowed in bar ~ Wi-fi ~ Bedrooms: /£165
Recommended by Helena and Trevor Fraser, Tim and Sarah Smythe-Brown, Sally and David Champion

CHILWORTH

TQ0347   Map 2

Percy Arms ⭐🍴 🍷

(01483) 561765 – www.thepercyarms.net

Dorking Road; GU4 8NP

Popular, well run pub, liked by families on Sunday lunchtime, with stylish décor, modern paintwork, attentive staff and highly regarded food; lots of outside seating

On our Sunday lunchtime visit, even the two tables with cubed tartan stools, rustic planked chairs and a button-back leather armchair in the entrance hall were taken – it's pretty essential to book a table in advance. It's an extended and attractively decorated pub and to the right of the bar is a small room with logs piled neatly above a woodburning stove, a long slate-topped table lined with an equally long pew and cushioned bench and an L-shaped settle with scatter cushions by one other table; TV. The flagstoned bar has similar furnishings plus a high table and chairs in a corner and tartan-cushioned chairs against the counter where very efficient staff served a beer named for the pub (from Greene King), Greene King IPA, Abbot and a guest beer on handpump and 16 wines by the glass. To the left of the entrance are two dining rooms down steps with upholstered tub and high-backed chairs on bare boards or rugs, and a self-service carvery. Down more steps and leading off the bar, other dining rooms have alcoves with built-in cushioned wall seats, high-backed spindle and other chairs on wooden floors, antler chandeliers and doors out to a decked terrace; another terrace has plenty of picnic-sets. Paintwork is contemporary, pictures have large rustic frames and here and there are antlers and animal skins. The two-part garden is connected by a bridge over a small stream and has children's play equipment and lots more picnic-sets.

As well as offering breakfasts to non-residents (7.30-11am weekdays, from 8.30 weekends), the interesting food includes south african specialities such as boerewors (a sausage) with polenta wedges and chakalaka (a spicy vegetable dish), a sharing board, durban-style prawn curry, and bobotie (a spicy ground beef dish with a fluffy egg topping); also, lunchtime sandwiches (not Sunday), salt and pepper squid with aioli, thai sticky beef salad, beer-battered cod and chips, a full or half rack of pork ribs, burgers such as chicken and chorizo or portobello mushroom with chips, and puddings such as chocolate fondant with berry pannacotta and limoncello glacé; they also offer a two-course set lunch. *Benchmark main dish: 35-day dry-aged steaks with a choice of sauces, red onion salsa and chips £23.95. Two-course evening meal £22.00.*

Greene King ~ Lease Janine Hunter ~ Real ale ~ Open 7am-10pm; 8am-11pm Sat; 8am 10pm Sun ~ Bar food 12-3, 6-10; 12-10 Sat; 12-9 Sun ~ Children welcome ~ Dogs allowed in bar ~ Wi-fi *Recommended by Julie Braeburn, Charles Todd, Sandra and Nigel Brown, Ian Phillips*

CHIPSTEAD
White Hart ♀

TQ2757   Map 3

(01737) 554455 – www.brunningandprice.co.uk/whitehartchipstead
Hazelwood Lane; CR5 3QW

Plenty to look at in open-plan rooms, thoughtful choice of drinks, interesting food and friendly staff

Opposite rugby playing fields with far distant views, this is a well run, busy pub in a pretty village. There's a raftered dining room to the right with elegant metal chandeliers, rough-plastered walls, an open fire in a brick fireplace and a couple of carved metal standing uprights. Helpful staff serve Phoenix Brunning & Price Original, Pilgrim Surrey Bitter and Sharps Doom Bar with guests such as Dark Star Partridge and Twickenham Wolf of the Woods on handpump, 16 wines by the glass, over 25 gins and up to 60 malt whiskies; background music and board games. The long room to the left is light and airy, with wall panelling at one end, a woodburning stove and numerous windows overlooking the seats on the terrace. Throughout, there's a fine mix of antique dining chairs and settles around all sorts of tables, rugs on bare boards or flagstones, hundreds of interesting cartoons, country pictures, cricketing prints and rugby team photographs, large, ornate mirrors and, arranged on the windowsills and mantelpieces, old glass and stone bottles, clocks, books and plants.

Reliably good food includes sandwiches, king prawn and kiln-smoked salmon cocktail, chicken liver pâté with fig and plum chutney, cheddar, potato and onion pie with home-made baked beans, steak burger with toppings, coleslaw and chips, pork sausages with mash and onion gravy, chicken curry with coconut rice, cod with butternut squash purée and crispy bacon, lamb shoulder with dauphinoise potatoes and gravy, rump steak with horseradish butter, and puddings such as crème brûlée and bread and butter pudding with apricot sauce. *Benchmark main dish: fish pie with french-style peas £13.50. Two-course evening meal £20.00.*

Brunning & Price ~ Manager Damien Mann ~ Real ale ~ Open 11.30-11; 12-10.30 Sun ~ Bar food 12-10 (9.30 Sun) ~ Restaurant ~ Children welcome ~ Dogs allowed in bar ~ Wi-fi *Recommended by Fr Robert Marsh, Paul A Moore, John Branston*

CHOBHAM

SU9761   Map 2

White Hart ♀ ◧

(01276) 857580 – www.brunningandprice.co.uk/whitehartchobham

High Street; GU24 8AA

Brick-built village inn with cheerful customers and a thoughtful choice of food and drink

Dating from the early 16th c, this handsome place is one of the oldest buildings in the village. The opened-up bar has white-painted beams, standing pillars, rugs on parquet or wide boards, an assortment of dark wooden dining chairs and tables, and armchairs beside two fireplaces. High chairs line the counter where cheerful, well trained staff serve Phoenix Brunning & Price Original, Dark Star Original, Thurstons Horsell Gold, Tillingbourne Falls Gold and Twickenham Spring Ale on handpump, and a fine choice of wines and around 50 gins and 50 whiskies. An L-shaped dining room has a leather wall banquette and leather and brass-studded dining chairs around a mix of tables and lots of old photos and prints on exposed brick or painted walls. There's also a carpeted, comfortable dining room with similar furniture and a big elegant metal chandelier. The little garden at the side has seats under parasols.

 Good quality modern food includes sandwiches, smoked salmon and crab arancini with dill crème fraîche, crispy goats cheese with beetroot salad and toasted hazelnuts, open vegetable ravioli with sage butter, steak in ale pie, thai seafood laksa with noodles, chicken and chorizo schnitzel with polenta chips and rémoulade sauce, sea bream with green vegetable vignole (an italian stew) and pancetta, duo of duck breast and leg with celeriac dauphinoise, kale and red cherry sauce, and puddings such as glazed lemon tart with raspberry sorbet and sticky toffee pudding with toffee sauce. *Benchmark main dish: cheese and potato pie with wholegrain mustard and chive sauce £11.95. Two-course evening meal £20.00.*

Brunning & Price ~ Manager Nikki Szabo ~ Real ale ~ Open 11-11; 12-10.30pm Sun ~ Bar food 12-10; 9am-10pm Sat; 9am-9.30pm Sun ~ Restaurant ~ Children welcome ~ Dogs allowed in bar ~ Wi-fi *Recommended by Ian Phillips, Dr Simon Innes, Simon Collett-Jones*

ELSTEAD

SU9044   Map 2

Mill at Elstead

(01252) 703333 – www.millelstead.co.uk

Farnham Road (B3001 just W of village, which is itself between Farnham and Milford); GU8 6LE

Fascinating building with big attractive waterside garden, Fullers beers and well liked food

Rising four storeys, this sensitively converted, largely 18th-c watermill is in a rather special setting above the prettily banked River Wey. Picnic-sets are dotted about by the water (floodlit at night) which includes a lovely millpond, swans and weeping willows. A series of rambling linked bar areas on the spacious ground floor have big windows that make the most of the view, and there's a restaurant upstairs. You'll find brown leather armchairs and antique engravings by a longcase clock, neat modern tables and dining chairs on bare boards, big country tables on broad ceramic tiles, iron pillars, stripped masonry and a log fire in a huge inglenook. Fullers London Pride, ESB and Olivers Island with a guest such as Hogs Back Surrey Nirvana on handpump, 15 wines by the glass and several malt whiskies and gins; background music, board games and TV.

🍴 Pleasing food includes sandwiches, corned beef hash with black pudding and a fried egg, smoked duck salad with walnuts, dates, pumpkins seeds and soy sauce, wild and chestnut mushroom cottage pie, corn-fed chicken with truffle and wild mushroom pasta in a creamy sauce, hop and tea-smoked haddock and cod fishcake with fennel salad, venison haunch with braised red cabbage and rich chocolate jus, and puddings such as apple and blackberry crumble with cinnamon ice-cream and brandy-soaked bread and butter pudding with custard. *Benchmark main dish: beer-battered fish and chips £11.95. Two-course evening meal £19.00.*

Fullers ~ Manager Paul Stephens ~ Real ale ~ Open 11-11; 12-10.30 Sun ~ Bar food 12-3, 5-9; 12-9 Sat; 12-7 Sun ~ Restaurant ~ Children welcome ~ Dogs welcome ~ Wi-fi ~ Quiz night Weds *Recommended by Christopher and Elise Way, Geoff and Ann Marston, Edward and William Johnston*

ENGLEFIELD GREEN
Bailiwick ♀ 🍺
SU9869 Map 2

(01784) 477877 – www.brunningandprice.co.uk/bailiwick
Wick Road; TW20 0HN

Fine position by parkland for busy pub, with lots of interest in various bars and dining rooms, well liked food and drink and super staff

The seats and tables on the small front terrace here overlook ancient woodland, and a circular walk from this busy pub follows the south-east corner of Windsor Great Park – you can also see the polo lawns, Virginia Water lake and the vast expanses of landscaped parkland. Smaller than many of the other Brunning & Price pubs, it has an open-plan bar area at the front where dogs are allowed: cushioned dining tables around wooden tables on rugs and bare boards, a pretty Victorian fireplace with a large mirror above and stools against the counter where knowledgeable, warmly friendly staff serve Phoenix Brunning & Price Original, Dorking Gold, Trumans Swift and Twickenham Champions Ale on handpump, 21 good wines by the glass and farm cider. Steps lead down to a dining area and on again to a bigger room with caramel-coloured leather dining chairs, banquettes and every size of table. Throughout there are elegant metal chandeliers, prints and black and white photographs, lots of house plants and windowsills full of old stone and glass bottles. There's no car park attached to the pub, but there are 20 free spaces in the long lay-by on Wick Road; if these are full there's a large pay-on-entry car park alongside.

🍴 As well as weekend breakfasts (9-11.30am), quite a choice of popular food includes sandwiches (until 5pm), blue cheese and hazelnut cheesecake with fig chutney and grape and celery salad, a charcuterie board, caramelised onion, spinach and brie quiche, steak burger with toppings, coleslaw and chips, chicken and ham hock pie, king prawn and chorizo linguine, harissa-spiced pork belly with pomegranate, fig and mint salad, and puddings such as hot waffle with caramelised banana, toffee sauce and banana ice-cream. *Benchmark main dish: braised lamb shoulder with carrot purée, mash and rosemary gravy £17.95. Two-course evening meal £21.00.*

Brunning & Price ~ Manager Paolo Corgiolu ~ Real ale ~ Open 10am-11pm; 9am-11pm Sat, Sun ~ Bar food 12-9.30 (9 Sun) ~ Children welcome but only in downstairs dining room after 6pm; no prams ~ Dogs allowed in bar ~ Wi-fi *Recommended by Sophie Ellison, Donald Allsopp, Miles Green*

The star-on-a-plate award, 🌟, distinguishes pubs where the food is of exceptional quality. The knife-and-fork symbol just means the pub serves food.

ESHER
TQ1566 Map 3

Marneys

(020) 8398 4444 – www.marneys.com

Alma Road (one-way), Weston Green; heading N on A309 from A307 roundabout, after Lamb & Star pub turn left into Lime Tree Avenue (signposted to All Saints Parish Church), then left at T junction into Chestnut Avenue; KT10 8JN

Country-feeling pub with good value food and attractive garden

A good local following enjoys the chatty low-beamed bar in this charming small pub – and it's handy for Hampton Court Palace. Fullers London Pride, Sharps Doom Bar and Youngs Original on handpump, 16 wines by the glass, ten malt whiskies and perhaps horse-racing on the unobtrusive corner TV. To the left, past a little cast-iron woodburning stove, the dining area has big pine tables, pews, pale country kitchen chairs and cottagey blue-curtained windows; background music. There are seats and wooden tables on the front terrace, which has views over the wooded common, village church and duck pond, and more seats on the decked area in the pleasantly planted sheltered garden.

 At fair prices for the area, the well liked food includes sandwiches, box-baked camembert with chutney, pint of prawns with aioli, steak in ale pie, thai-style salmon fishcakes with sweet chilli sauce, salmon gravadlax with horseradish cream, cumberland sausages with mustard mash and onion gravy, lamb burger with goats cheese and caramelised onions with fries, and puddings such as sticky toffee pudding and chocolate brownie with ice-cream. *Benchmark main dish: beef burger with toppings and fries £10.95. Two-course evening meal £20.00.*

Free house ~ Licensee Thomas Duxberry ~ Real ale ~ Open 11-11; 12-10.30 Sun ~ Bar food 12-2.30, 6-9; 12-3.30 Sun; not Fri-Sun evenings ~ Restaurant ~ Children welcome away from bar ~ Dogs allowed in bar ~ Wi-fi *Recommended by Belinda May, Julie Braeburn*

MICKLEHAM
TQ1753 Map 3

Running Horses 🏵 ♀ 🛏

(01372) 372279 – www.therunninghorses.co.uk

Old London Road (B2209); RH5 6DU

Country pub with plenty of customers in bar and dining rooms, enjoyable food and drink and seats on big front terrace; bedrooms

On a warm day, the front terrace here is a fine place to sit among the pretty flowering tubs and hanging baskets, and there's a peaceful view of the old church with its strange stubby steeple. Inside, the stylish and spacious bar has cushioned wall settles and other dining chairs around straightforward tables on parquet flooring, racing cartoons and Hogarth prints on the walls, lots of race tickets hanging from a beam and a log fire in an inglenook fireplace; some wood-panelled booths have red leather banquettes. Stools line the counter where friendly, helpful staff serve a beer named for the pub (from Banks's), Brakspears Bitter and Oxford Gold, Fullers London Pride and Ringwood Boondoggle on handpump and around 20 wines by the glass; background music. The panelled restaurant has an attractive mix of upholstered and wooden dining chairs around a medley of tables on tartan carpet. Parking is in a narrow lane although you can also park on the main road.

🏵 Rewarding food includes lunchtime sandwiches, ham hock terrine with crispy quail egg, devilled crab on toast with lemon, soft cheese, cep mushroom, white onion, spinach and root vegetable tart, confit duck leg with champ mash, button onions and port, salmon fillet with samphire and brown shrimp and herb butter, guinea fowl breast with peas, broad beans, asparagus and minted new potatoes, and puddings such as hot chocolate mousse with salted caramel ice-cream and tiramisu roulade with cherry ice-cream. *Benchmark main dish: calves liver with creamed mash, bacon, sherry shallots and red wine £15.00. Two-course evening meal £24.00.*

Brakspears ~ Manager Iain Huddy ~ Real ale ~ Open 12-11 ~ Bar food 12-3, 6-9 (10 Fri, Sat); 12-6 Sun ~ Restaurant ~ Children welcome but must be over 10 in bar area ~ Dogs allowed in bar ~ Wi-fi ~ Bedrooms: /£135 *Recommended by Conor McGaughey, Sheila Topham, Tony Scott, Ian Phillips, Ron Corbett, David and Sally Frost*

MILFORD
SU9542 Map 2

Refectory ♀ ◧

(01483) 413820 – www.brunningandprice.co.uk/refectory
Portsmouth Road; GU8 5HJ

Beamed and timbered rooms of much character, six real ales and other thoughtful drinks and well liked food

Originally a cattle barn, this handsome place then became an antiques shop and tea room before Brunning & Price carefully restored and extended it into this lovely pub. The L-shaped, mainly open-plan rooms are spacious and interesting with exposed stone walls, stalling and standing timbers creating separate seating areas, strikingly heavy beams and a couple of big log fires in fine stone fireplaces. A two-tiered and balconied part at one end has a wall covered with huge brass platters; elsewhere there are nice old photographs and a variety of paintings. Dining chairs and dark wooden tables are grouped on wooden, quarry-tiled or carpeted floors, and there are bookshelves, big pot plants, stone bottles on windowsills and fresh flowers. High wooden bar stools line the long counter where they serve Phoenix Brunning & Price Original, Hogs Back TEA, Dark Star Hophead and three guests from breweries such as Cottage, Langham and Tillingbourne on handpump, a dozen wines by the glass, around 80 malt whiskies and two farm ciders. The back courtyard – adjacent to the characterful pigeonry – has teak tables and chairs. Wheelchair facilities and disabled parking.

The well judged menu includes sandwiches, chicken liver parfait with date and pear chutney, smoked haddock kedgeree, arancini balls with soft quail egg, mussels with leeks, cider and cream, cauliflower, chickpea and spinach tagine with moroccan-style rice, steak burger with toppings, coleslaw and chips, chicken and asparagus pie with creamy tarragon sauce, beer-battered haddock and chips, and puddings such as banoffi eton mess and chocolate brownie with chocolate sauce. *Benchmark main dish: malaysian fish stew with sticky coconut rice £15.95. Two-course evening meal £21.00.*

Brunning & Price ~ Manager Lee Parry ~ Real ale ~ Open 10.30am-11pm; 12-11 Sun ~ Bar food 12-10 (9.30 Sun) ~ Restaurant ~ Children welcome ~ Dogs allowed in bar ~ Wi-fi *Recommended by Martin and Alison Stainsby, Ron Corbett, Tony Scott*

SHAMLEY GREEN
TQ0343 Map 3

Red Lion

(01483) 892202 – www.redlionshamleygreen.com
The Green; GU5 0UB

Pleasant dining pub with popular tasty food and nice gardens

The highly rated food is the main draw to this friendly pub, but they do keep Youngs IPA and a couple of guests such as Greene King Morlands Old Golden Hen and Sharps Doom Bar on handpump, and 11 wines by the glass; staff are helpful and attentive. The two interconnected bars are fairly traditional with a mix of new and old wooden tables, chairs and cushioned settles on bare boards and red carpet, stripped standing timbers, fresh white walls, deep red ceilings and open fires; background music. There are plenty of hand-made rustic tables and benches outside, both at the front and at the back – which is more secluded and has seats on a heated, covered terrace and grassed dining areas.

 Good, tasty food includes warm scallop and bacon salad, crispy duck salad with oranges and hoisin dressing, greek spinach and feta pie with fries, sausages and mash with onion gravy, chilli con carne, beer-battered haddock and chips, lamb shank in red wine sauce with redcurrant jelly and mash, skate in lemon and caper butter, chicken breast stuffed with feta cheese, sun-dried tomatoes, garlic and rosemary with fries, and puddings. *Benchmark main dish: veal schnitzel in lemon garlic butter topped with a fried egg £15.95. Two-course evening meal £20.50.*

Punch ~ Lease Debbie Ersser ~ Real ale ~ Open 11.30-11; 12-10 Sun (12-8 in winter) ~ Bar food 12-2.30 (3 weekends), 6.30-9.30; 12-3, 6.30-8.30 Sun; no food Sun evening in winter ~ Restaurant ~ Children welcome ~ Dogs allowed in bar ~ Wi-fi
Recommended by Graeme Bennet

SUNBURY
Flower Pot 🛏

TQ1068   Map 3

(01932) 780741 – www.theflowerpothotel.co.uk
1.6 miles from M3 junction 1; follow Lower Sunbury sign from exit roundabout, then at Thames Street turn right; pub on next corner, with Green Street; TW16 6AA

Former coaching inn with appealing, contemporary bar and dining room, real ales and all-day food; bedrooms

Although not actually on the river, this handsome place with its elegant wrought-iron balconies and pretty summer hanging baskets is in a villagey area with waterside walks. The airy bar has leather tub chairs around copper-topped tables, high chairs upholstered in brown and beige tartan around equally high tables in pale wood, attractive flagstones, contemporary paintwork and stools against the counter; there's also a couple of comfortably plush burgundy armchairs. The bar leads into a dining area with pale blue-painted and dark wooden cushioned dining chairs around an assortment of partly painted tables on bare boards, artwork on papered walls and a large gilt-edged mirror over an open fireplace; candles in glass jars, fresh flowers, background music and newspapers. Brakspears Bitter and Oxford Gold and a guest beer such as Wychwood Dirty Tackle on handpump and 15 wines by the glass. A side terrace has wood and metal tables and chairs. The bedrooms are smart and comfortable.

 As well as breakfast for non-residents, the popular food includes sandwiches, hake and prawn fishcakes with sweet chilli sauce, wild boar, rum and ginger pâté with chutney, sharing boards, stone-baked pizzas, burger with toppings, coleslaw and chips, bass fillet with chargrilled mediterranean vegetables and tomato dressing, 28-day-aged rump steak with a choice of sauces and crispy onion rings, and puddings such as lemon drizzle cake with mango sorbet and strawberry and raspberry eton mess. *Benchmark main dish: spicy half baby chicken with rosemary and sea salt fries and coleslaw £13.95. Two-course evening meal £20.00.*

Authentic Inns ~ Tenant Simon Bailey ~ Real ale ~ Open 7am-11pm; 8am-11pm Sat, Sun ~ Bar food 7-3, 6-9 (10 Fri, Sat); 8am-9pm Sun ~ Restaurant ~ Children welcome ~ Dogs allowed in bar ~ Wi-fi ~ Live music last Sat of month ~ Bedrooms: /£99
Recommended by Edward Edmonton, Pauline and Mark Evans

WALTON ON THE HILL

TQ2255 Map 3

Blue Ball

(01737) 819003 – www.theblueball.co.uk

Not far from M25 junction 8; Deans Lane, off B2220 by pond; KT20 7UE

Popular pub with spreading drinking and dining areas, helpful staff, well liked food and drink and lots of outside seating

Opposite Banstead Heath, this sizeable pub has been thoughtfully renovated. The entrance bar has a chatty atmosphere, a good welcome from cheerful staff and colourful leather-topped stools at the counter. there are rugs on bare boards, house plants on windowsills, all manner of old pictures and photographs on the walls, antique-style cushioned, farmhouse and high-backed kitchen chairs around tables of every size, and a sizeable wine cage. A beer named for the pub (from Caledonian), Caledonian Deuchars IPA, Courage Directors and Jennings Cumberland on handpump and good wines by the glass. Leading back from here, several dining rooms have multi-coloured button-back leather banquettes, similar chairs and tables on more rugs and wooden floors, bookshelves, gilt-edged mirrors and a big central conical open fire. On our Sunday visit, there were plenty of cheerful family groups enjoying roast lunches; background music. The outside terrace has lots of seats and tables plus a fire pit under a gazebo, and you can hire cabanas for a private group (you must book in advance, especially in warm weather when they're extremely popular).

Pleasing food includes sandwiches (until 5pm), salt and pepper squid with aioli, baked figs wrapped in parma ham with stilton, walnut and rocket salad, ham and egg, butternut squash, sage and pine nut risotto with goats cheese, beer-battered cod and chips, lemon and thyme chargrilled chicken with roasted mediterranean vegetables on ciabatta croûte, lamb shoulder with honey and mustard glaze, dauphinoise potatoes and redcurrant and rosemary sauce, and puddings such as chocolate and hazelnut tart and sticky toffee pavlova with toffee sauce. *Benchmark main dish: beer-battered fish and chips £13.95. Two-course evening meal £19.50.*

Whiting & Hammond ~ Manager Martin Slocombe ~ Real ale ~ Open 10am-11pm; 9am-midnight Sat; 9am-10.30pm Sun ~ Bar food 12-9.30; 9am-9.30pm Sat; 9-9 Sun ~ Restaurant ~ Children welcome ~ Dogs allowed in bar ~ Wi-fi *Recommended by Caroline Sullivan, Valerie Sayer, Charlie Parker*

WEST END

SU9461 Map 2

The Inn West End

(01276) 858652 – www.the-inn.co.uk

Just under 2.5 miles from M3 junction 3; A322 S, on right; GU24 9PW

Surrey Dining Pub of the Year

Plenty of dining and drinking space in carefully refurbished rooms, excellent wines and inventive food; bedrooms

Wine plays a big part here, with 20 by the glass from a fantastic list of around 500 – Iberia is the speciality – and a shop where you browse and perhaps decide to take a bottle or two home with you; there are also several sherries, sweet wines and port. It's an airy place with a relaxed, friendly atmosphere throughout, all helped along by the enthusiastic and hard-working licensees. The bar has white-painted beams, slatted and cushioned wooden benches and elegant chairs around a mix of tables on bare floorboards, pretty curtains, a big central barrel and chairs against the counter where they keep Fullers London Pride, Otter Bitter and Thurstons

Horsell Gold on handpump. Do ask about the unusual clock. There's an extended restaurant and a lounge area with books on shelves, daily papers and an open fire; Sunny and Teddy are the pub dogs. The pretty garden and terrace have plenty of seats for when the weather is warm. Bedrooms are extremely well equipped and comfortable – two allow dogs and one has disabled facilities. No children.

As well as breakfasts (7.30-10.30am; 8.30-11am weekends), morning coffee and afternoon tea, the first class food using local producers and ingredients includes ham hock terrine with piccalilli and treacle soda bread, fritto misto with rouille, wild mushroom risotto with chives and parmesan, venison burger with toppings, house sauce and chips, smoked haddock kedgeree, crispy buttermilk pheasant with sweet potato and house slaw, glazed shin of beef with truffle mash, pollock with scottish langoustine and pickled chilli, and puddings such as chamapgne and berry jelly with blackberry granita and chocolate fondant with pistachio ice-cream; they also offer two- and three-course set menus. *Benchmark main dish: game (using snipe, woodcock, mountain or brown hare, all types of deer) casserole £13.50. Two-course evening meal £20.00.*

Free house ~ Licensees Gerry and Ann Price ~ Real ale ~ Open 7.30am-11pm (midnight Fri); 12-10.30 Sun ~ Bar food 12-2.30, 6-9.30 ~ Restaurant ~ Dogs allowed in bedrooms ~ Wi-fi ~ Bedrooms: /£90 *Recommended by Guy Vowles, Guy Consterdine, Edward Mirzoeff*

Also Worth a Visit in Surrey

Besides the fully inspected pubs, you might like to try these pubs that have been recommended to us and described by readers. Do tell us what you think of them: feedback@goodguides.com

---

ALBURY   TQ0447

★**Drummond Arms** (01483) 202039
Off A248 SE of Guildford; The Street; GU5 9AG Modernised 19th-c pub in pretty village; ales such as Adnams, Courage, Sharps and Hogs Back, good choice of wines and enjoyable food from sandwiches and sharing plates up, cheerful courteous service, opened-up bar with leather chesterfields, log fire and newspapers, parquet-floored dining room, conservatory; children welcome, good-sized pretty back garden by little River Tillingbourne, duck island, summer barbecues and hog roasts, pleasant walks nearby, nine bedrooms, open all day (food all day weekends). *(Nigel and Sue Foster)*

ALFOLD   TQ0435
Alfold Barn (01403) 752288
Horsham Road, A281; GU6 8JE Beautifully preserved 16th-c building with bar and restaurant, good locally sourced home-made food from daily changing menu with some emphasis on fish (maybe lobster and crab), friendly attentive service, up to three well kept ales from nearby breweries, beams and rafters, mixed furniture on flagstones or carpet, warming log fires; children welcome, garden with play area and animals including Rosie the goat, closed Sun evening, Mon. *(Mike Benton)*

ALFOLD   TQ0334
Three Compasses (01483) 275729
Dunsfold Road; GU6 8HY Reworked 400-year-old pub with interesting 1940s theme (plenty to look at); well kept Otter, Sharps Doom Bar and a guest, enjoyable freshly made food (not Sun evening, Mon) in bar and restaurant area, games room with darts, table skittles and bar billiards; Mon swing/jive classes; children and dogs welcome, good-sized garden with play area, on back lane to former Dunsfold Aerodrome (now Dunsfold Park with little museum), Wey & Arun Canal nearby, open all day in summer, closed Sun evening. *(Sandra King)*

BATTS CORNER   SU8140
Blue Bell (01252) 792801
Batts Corner; GU10 4EX Busy tucked-way country pub with linked stone-floor rooms, light fresh décor and mix of furniture including sofas by big log fire, well kept Hogs Back TEA, Triple fff Moondance and guests such as Frensham, good home-made food from sandwiches to popular Sun lunch (must book), helpful friendly staff; children and dogs on leads welcome, attractive spacious garden with rolling views, summer barbecues and good play area, handy for Alice Holt Forest, open all day Fri and Sat, till 8pm Sun. *(Tony and Jill Radnor, Patric Curwen)*

If you know a pub is ever open all day, please tell us.

BETCHWORTH   TQ2149
Dolphin (01737) 842288
Off A25 W of Reigate; The Street;
RH3 7DW Cosy 16th-c beamed local in
picturesque village on Greensand Way;
neat front bar with inglenook log fire
and plain tables on ancient flagstones,
snug and a further panelled bar with
chiming grandfather clock, nice old
local photographs, well kept Surrey Hills
and Youngs, decent choice of wines and
enjoyable fair-priced traditional food (all day
weekends) including daily specials, friendly
efficient young staff, restaurant; children,
walkers and dogs welcome, front and side
terraces, back garden, fine Pre-Raphaelite
pulpit in church opposite, open all day.
(John Evans, Ian Phillips)

BLETCHINGLEY   TQ3250
Red Lion (01883) 743342
Castle Street (A25), Redhill side;
RH1 4NU Modernised well looked-after
beamed village dining pub, good reasonably
priced home-made food such as steak and
kidney pudding, friendly staff, well kept
Greene King ales and good choice of wines
by the glass; children welcome (under-10s
till 7pm), heated part-covered terrace, secret
garden, summer barbecues, open all day.
(Geoffrey Kemp)

BLETCHINGLEY   TQ3250
Whyte Harte (01883) 743231
2.5 miles from M25 junction 6, via A22
then A25 towards Redhill; RH1 4PB
Low-beamed Tudor inn with good well
presented food served by friendly staff,
three changing ales and plenty of wines
by the glass, big inglenook log fire in
extensive open-plan bar, separate dining
area; background music; children and
dogs welcome, lovely beer garden, eight
bedrooms, good breakfast, attractive
village street (shame about the traffic),
open all day. *(Simon Sharpe)*

BLINDLEY HEATH   TQ3645
Red Barn (01342) 830820
Tandridge Lane, just off B2029, which
is off A22; RH7 6LL Splendid farmhouse/
barn conversion; contemporary furnishings
mixing with 17th-c beams and timbers,
central glass-sided woodburner with
soaring flue, large model plane suspended
from rafters, one wall with shelves of
books, another hung with antlers, clever
partitioning creating cosier areas too; red
cooking range and big wooden tables in
farmhouse-style room, adjacent bar with
sofas by large fireplace, one or two real ales
and good wine list, food and service can
be good; background and some live music;
children and dogs (in bar) welcome, solid
granite tables on lawn, open all day.
(Tony Scott)

BRAMLEY   TQ0044
★**Jolly Farmer** (01483) 893355
High Street; GU5 0HB Family-run village
pub with traditional beamed interior packed
with collections of plates, old bottles, enamel
signs, sewing machines, prints, antique tools
and so on, timbered semi-partitions and open
fire, Bowman, Youngs and up to six guests,
a couple of real ciders and 14 wines by the
glass, fairly pubby food including good Sun
carvery; background music, board games, free
wi-fi; children and dogs (in bar) welcome,
tables by car park, walks up St Martha's Hill
and handy for Winkworth Arboretum (NT),
bedrooms, open all day. *(Tom and Ruth Rees,*
TomH, Mrs Zara Elliott, Peter Hailey)

BROCKHAM   TQ1949
Inn on the Green (01737) 845101
Brockham Green; RH3 7JS Restaurant
pub facing village green (part of the small
Grumpy Mole group), good food from
traditional choices up including cook-your-
own steaks on a hot stone, helpful friendly
service, well kept Fullers London Pride
and Surrey Hills Shere Drop, several wines
by the glass, afternoon teas, conservatory;
children welcome, picnic-sets out at front,
garden behind, open all day, food all day
weekends. *(Milena Duncan, Malcolm Phillips)*

BROCKHAM   TQ1949
Royal Oak (01737) 843241
Brockham Green; RH3 7JS Nice spot on
charming village green below North Downs;
bare-boards bar and light airy dining area,
well kept Adnams, Sharps, Wells and Wye
Valley, enjoyable freshly cooked pub food at
reasonable prices, good service from warmly
welcoming staff, newspapers and log fires;
children and dogs allowed, tables out in
front looking across to fine church, more
seats in back garden, handy for Greensand
Way. *(Conor McGaughey, Ian Phillips)*

BROOK   SU9238
Dog & Pheasant (01428) 682763
Haslemere Road (A286); GU8 5UJ
Popular friendly pub looking across busy
road to cricket green, long beamed bar
divided up by standing timbers, cushioned
wall settles, open fire in brick fireplace, four
well kept ales such as Ringwood and Sharps
from linenfold counter, dining area on right,
further room to left with big inglenook, well
liked food including Weds grill night; children
welcome, picnic-sets on back decking and
grass, play equipment, open all day (till 6pm
Sun). *(Pauline and Mark Evans)*

BURROWHILL   SU9763
Four Horseshoes (01276) 857581
B383 N of Chobham; GU24 8QP Busy
refurbished pub attractively set by village
green, beams and log fires, three well kept
ales including one badged for them, popular

food served by cheerful staff, modern dining extension; children, dogs and muddy boots welcome, tables out at front (some under ancient yew), open all day (Sun till 7pm). *(Mr and Mrs Johnson-Poensgen)*

CARSHALTON   TQ2764
Hope (020) 8240 1255
West Street; SM5 2PR Chatty community-owned local; Downton, Windsor & Eton and five guests, also craft beers, real cider/perry and over 50 bottled beers, generous low-priced pubby food (limited evening choice), 1950s feel U-shaped bar with open fire, lots of pump clips, larger back room with bar billiards; live acoustic music first Weds of month, regular beer and cider festivals; garden, open all day. *(Conor McGaughey)*

CATERHAM   TQ3254
Harrow (01883) 343260
Stanstead Road, Whitehill; CR3 6AJ Simple 16th-c beamed pub high up in open country by North Downs Way; L-shaped bare-boards bar and carpeted back dining area, several real ales (sometimes tapped from the cask), enjoyable food including daily specials, friendly service and good local atmosphere; beer festivals; children and dogs welcome, garden picnic-sets, popular with walkers and cyclists, open all day, no food Sun evening. *(Edward Edmonton)*

CHARLESHILL   SU8844
Donkey (01252) 702124
B3001 Milford–Farnham near Tilford; coming from Elstead, turn left as soon as you see pub sign; GU10 2AU Old-fashioned beamed dining pub with enjoyable home-made food including set menus and other deals, up to three well kept changing ales and good choice of wines by the glass, prompt friendly service, conservatory restaurant; children and dogs welcome, attractive garden, much-loved donkeys Pip and Dusty in paddock, good walks, open all day weekends. *(Jim and Sue James)*

CHIDDINGFOLD   SU9635
★ **Crown** (01428) 682255
The Green (A283); GU8 4TX This is a particularly lovely 700-year-old timbered building with strong sense of history; bar and interconnected dining rooms with massive beams (some over 2-ft thick), oak panelling, moulded plasterwork and fine stained-glass windows, magnificently carved fireplace, mate's and other pubby chairs, cushioned wall seats and some nice antique tables, lots of portraits, simple split-level back public bar with open fire, up to five changing ales and several wines by the glass, enjoyable often interesting food (all day Fri-Sun); children (there's a playroom) and dogs welcome in certain areas, seats outside looking across village green to interesting church, more tables in sheltered central courtyard, character creaky bedrooms, open all day

from 7am (8am Sun) for breakfast. *(Chris and Pauline Sexton, Alastair and Sheree Hepburn)*

CHIDDINGFOLD   SU94323
Mulberry (01428) 644460
Petworth Road (A283 S); GU8 4SS Relaxed country pub owned by DJ Chris Evans, attractive rambling bar with a couple of steps down to dining area, log fires (one in huge inglenook), enjoyable if not always cheap food, two well kept ales and good choice of wines by the glass, friendly staff; live music, free wi-fi; children and dogs (in some areas) welcome, tables on covered verandah, picnic-sets among fruit trees on lawn with play area, three well equipped bedrooms in separate block, open (and food) all day. *(Mike Benton)*

CHIPSTEAD   TQ2757
Ramblers Rest (01737) 552661
Outwood Lane (B2032); CR5 3NP Mitchells & Butlers country dining pub with contemporary furnishings in partly 14th-c rambling building, low beams (old and new), flagstones, panelling and log fires, enjoyable up-to-date and more traditional food including popular Sun lunch, Adnams, Sharps and a guest, interesting continental beers, Aspall's cider and good value wines by the glass, young friendly staff, dining extension; children and dogs welcome, disabled access (from front) and loos, big garden with pretty terrace and attractive views, nice local walks, open (and food) all day. *(Sheila Topham, Mrs Julie Thomas, Tony Scott)*

CHIPSTEAD   TQ2555
Well House (01737) 830640
Chipstead signed with Mugswell off A217, N of M25 junction 8; CR5 3SQ Originally three 16th-c cottages (converted from tea rooms to pub in 1955); log fires in all three rooms, low beams and rustic décor, bric-a-brac and pewter tankards hanging from ceiling, well kept Adnams, Fullers, Surrey Hills and local guests, Millwhite's cider, food from ciabattas up (not Sun evening), friendly staff, small conservatory, resident ghost called Harry the Monk; dogs allowed (they have cats), large pleasing hillside garden with ancient well (reputed to be mentioned in the Domesday Book), delightful country setting, open all day. *(Conor McGaughey)*

CHURT   SU8538
Crossways (01428) 714323
Corner of A287 and Hale House Lane; GU10 2JE Friendly down-to-earth local attracting good mix of customers; quarry-tiled public bar and carpeted saloon with panelling and plush banquettes, good beer range (some served direct from the cellar) and four real ciders, enjoyable well priced pub lunches (not Sun) including home-made pies, evening food Weds only, cheerful young staff; darts, TV, beer/cider festivals;

no under-10s inside, dogs welcome, picnic-sets in lawned garden, open all day Fri, Sat. *(Tony and Jill Radnor)*

CLAYGATE TQ1563

★ **Foley** (01372) 462021

Hare Lane; KT10 0LZ Beautifully restored 19th-c Youngs pub; pubby part at front with wooden tables and chairs on bare boards, leather armchairs and sofas by Victorian fireplace, lots of interconnected sitting and dining areas leading off, their well kept ales and a guest, 30 wines by the glass, interesting spirits and good range of coffees and teas, highly thought-of food from open kitchen; background music, daily papers and free wi-fi; children and dogs (in bar) welcome, seats on two-level terrace, well equipped modern bedrooms, open (and food) all day including breakfast from 7.30am (8.30am Sun). *(Sandra King)*

CLAYGATE TQ1563

Hare & Hounds (01372) 465149

The Green; KT10 0JL Renovated flower-decked Victorian/Edwardian village pub, good sensibly priced french food along with some pub favourites in bar or smaller restaurant, nice wines and well kept changing ales including local Brightwater, friendly caring service; Sun quiz, some live music, free wi-fi; children and dogs welcome, disabled access/loo, tables on attractive front terrace and in small back garden with play area, open (and food) all day. *(Sean)*

COBHAM TQ1159

Running Mare (01932) 862007

Tilt Road; KT11 3EZ Attractive old flower-decked pub overlooking green (can get very busy); well kept Fullers, Hogs Back and Youngs, good food including popular Sun lunch, efficient friendly service, two timbered bars and restaurant; regular live music; children very welcome, a few tables out at front and on rose-covered back terrace, open all day. *(Pauline and Mark Evans)*

COLDHARBOUR TQ1544

Plough (01306) 711793

Village signposted in the network of small roads around Leith Hill; RH5 6HD Former 17th-c beamed coaching house refurbished and opened up under welcoming new management; own-brewed Leith Hill ales and guests, proper cider and a dozen wines by the glass, food in bar or restaurant (new kitchen opening as we went to press); background music, Thurs quiz, TV, free wi-fi; children and dogs welcome, seats out at front and on new back terrace overlooking fields, revamped bedrooms, open all day. *(Mike Benton)*

COMPTON SU9646

★ **Withies** (01483) 421158

Withies Lane; pub signed from B3000; GU3 1JA Civilised gently old-fashioned 16th-c pub with atmospheric low-beamed bar, some 17th-c carved panels between windows, splendid art nouveau settle among old sewing-machine tables, log fire in massive inglenook, well kept Adnams, Greene King, Hogs Back and Sharps, very well liked food (can be pricey and they add a service charge), efficient bow-tied staff; children welcome, seats on terrace, under apple trees and creeper-hung arbour, flower-edged neat front lawn, on edge of Loseley Park and close to Watts Gallery, closed Sun evening. *(Helen and Brian Edgeley, Ron Corbett, Susan and John Douglas, Dr W I C Clark)*

CRANLEIGH TQ0539

★ **Richard Onslow** (01483) 274922

High Street; GU6 8AU Busy Peach group pub with cheerful small bar, leather tub chairs and built-in sofa, slate-floored drinking area, Firebird, Hook Norton, Sharps and Surrey Hills, a proper cider and ten wines by the glass, good interesting food in two dining rooms with open fires and sizeable restaurant with pale tables on wood floor, modern flowery wallpaper and big windows overlooking the street; background music, board games, free wi-fi; children and dogs (in bar) welcome, seats out at front and in terraced back garden, ten smart well equipped bedrooms, open (and food) all day from 7am (7.30am weekends) for breakfast. *(Christopher and Elise Way, Mike Benton, Jim and Sue James)*

DORKING TQ1649

Cricketers (01306) 889938

South Street; RH4 2JU Chatty and relaxed little Fullers local, well kept Chiswick, London Pride, ESB and a guest, simple food (Tues-Sat lunchtimes, Thurs-Sat evenings) including good sandwiches, friendly service, cricketing memorabilia on stripped-brick walls; events including beer festivals, Scalextric championship and onion-growing competition, darts, sports TV, free wi-fi; nice split-level suntrap back terrace, open all day. *(Conor McGaughey)*

DORKING TQ1649

Old House At Home (01306) 889664

West Street; RH4 1BY Bustling old Youngs pub with opened-up beamed interior, enjoyable food from bar snacks up, friendly staff; Fri live music; dogs welcome, back terrace with heated beach huts, closed Mon lunchtime, otherwise open all day (till 10pm Sun). *(Edward and William Johnston)*

DORMANSLAND TQ4042

Old House At Home (01342) 836828

West Street; RH7 6QP Friendly 19th-c village pub with beamed log-fire bar, traditional furniture on parquet floor, horsebrasses above unusual barrel-fronted counter serving Shepherd Neame ales, enjoyable well priced food (not Sun evening) including fresh pizzas, carpeted restaurant and plainer room with darts and TV; some live music; children and dogs (in bar) welcome, a few picnic-sets out in front, beer garden behind, closed Mon lunchtime, otherwise open all day. *(Tony Scott)*

DORMANSLAND   TQ4042
Plough (01342) 832933
Plough Road, off B2028 NE; RH7 6PS Friendly traditional old pub in quiet village, well kept Fullers, Harveys and Sharps, Weston's cider and decent wines, good choice of enjoyable lunchtime bar food including specials, thai restaurant (Mon-Sat), log fires and original features; children welcome, disabled facilities, good-sized garden, open all day. *(Tony Scott)*

DUNSFOLD   TQ0036
Sun (01483) 200242
Off B2130 S of Godalming; GU8 4LE Old double-fronted pub with four rooms (brighter at the front), beams and some exposed brickwork, scrubbed pine furniture and two massive log fires, ales such as Adnams, Harveys and Sharps, decent wines, enjoyable home-made pub food at reasonable prices including popular Sun lunch (best to book), good friendly service; Sun quiz, darts; children and dogs welcome, seats on terrace and common opposite, good walks. *(Sandra King)*

EASHING   SU9543
★ Stag on the River (01483) 421568
Lower Eashing, just off A3 southbound; GU7 2QG Civilised, gently upmarket riverside inn with Georgian façade masking much older interior; attractively opened-up rooms including charming old-fashioned locals' bar with armchairs on red and black quarry tiles, cosy log-fire snug beyond, Hogs Back TEA, one or two Marstons-related ales and a beer badged for the pub, Hazy Hog cider, plenty of emphasis on food with several linked dining areas including river room up a couple of steps, attentive courteous staff; children welcome, dogs in bar, extensive terrace with wicker or wooden furniture under parasols (some by weir), picnic-sets on grass, seven bedrooms, open all day. *(Jim and Sue James)*

EAST CLANDON   TQ0551
★ Queens Head (01483) 222332
Just off A246 Guildford–Leatherhead; The Street; GU4 7RY Busy dining pub in same small group as Duke of Cambridge at Tilford, Stag at Eashing and Wheatsheaf in Farnham, well liked food (best to book) from light dishes to good daily specials, set lunch deal (Mon-Thurs), a beer badged for them and changing guests such as Ringwood and Surrey Hills from fine elm-topped counter, also Hazy Hog cider and nice wines by the glass, good friendly service, comfortable linked rooms, log fire in big inglenook; daily newspapers and free wi-fi, silent TV in bar;

children welcome, tables out in front and on side terrace, handy for Hatchlands (NT), open all day Fri and Sat, till 9pm Sun. *(John Evans, Tom and Ruth Rees, Ron Corbett, John Allman)*

EFFINGHAM   TQ1153
Plough (01372) 458121
Orestan Lane; KT24 5SW Popular refurbished Youngs pub with well kept ales and enjoyable home-made food including Sun roasts and children's menu, plenty of wines by the glass, friendly efficient staff, open interior around central bar, grey-painted beams, delft shelving and half-panelling, wood floors, two coal-effect gas fires; plenty of tables on forecourt and in pretty garden with fruit trees, disabled access and parking, handy for Polesden Lacey (NT), closed Sun evening. *(Nick Higgins)*

ELSTEAD   SU9043
Woolpack (01252) 703106
B3001 Milford–Farnham; GU8 6HD Comfortably modernised tile-hung dining pub run by italian family, enjoyable home-cooked food including stone-baked pizzas, Thurs italian night, Sat fish night and Sun carvery, cask-tapped ales and decent wines by the glass, friendly efficient service, long main bar, restaurant, open fires; children welcome, garden with picnic-sets, open all day Sun. *(D J and P M Taylor)*

EPSOM   TQ2160
Rising Sun (01372) 740809
Heathcote Road; KT18 5DX Refurbished Victorian backstreet pub, open-plan but with cosy bare-boards front bar area, St Austell, Youngs and a couple of guests, several wines by the glass, enjoyable home-made food including some imaginative additions to traditional menu, efficient courteous service, open fire; disabled access/loos, nice garden with covered section, barbecues, open all day. *(Jeff Davies)*

EPSOM   TQ2158
Rubbing House (01372) 745050
Langley Vale Road (on Epsom Downs Racecourse); KT18 5LJ Restauranty pub popular for its fantastic racecourse views – can get very busy but staff cope well; attractive modern décor, good value promptly served food including children's menu, tables perhaps a little close together, Greene King and Sharps ales, serious wine list, upper balcony for Derby days; background music; seats out by the course, open all day. *(Mike Benton)*

FARNHAM   SU8346
Wheatsheaf (01252) 717135
West Street; GU9 7DR Stylishly updated old pub in same group as the Queens Head at East Clandon, Stag at Eashing and Duke of Cambridge at Tilford; good food (all day Fri-Sun) from open kitchen including

weekday set menu, gluten-free diets catered for, well kept local ales such as Hogs Back, craft beers and good choice of wines and whiskies, friendly helpful staff; free wi-fi; children welcome, seats in back courtyard, open all day (from 9am weekends for breakfast), no nearby parking. *(Nick Higgins)*

FICKLESHOLE   TQ3960
White Bear (01959) 573166
Featherbed Lane/Fairchildes Lane; off A2022 just S of A212 roundabout; CR6 9PH Long 16th-c country dining pub with lots of small rooms, beams, flagstones and open fires, fair value traditional food (orders taken at the bar), Brakspears, Pilgrim and a couple of guests; children and well behaved dogs welcome, picnic-sets and stone bear on front terrace, sizeable back garden with pond and summer weekend 'burger shack', open all day, food till 7pm Sun. *(Edward Edmonton)*

FRIDAY STREET   TQ1245
Stephan Langton (01306) 730775
Off B2126; RH5 6JR Refurbished 1930s pub prettily placed in tucked-away hamlet; good home-made food from sandwiches up including two-course evening deal Tues and Weds, well kept local Tillingbourne beers and guests, nice wines and fine gin selection, friendly staff; children and dogs welcome, wooded setting with pond, good nearby walks, closed Mon, otherwise open all day (till 7pm Sun). *(Martin Day)*

GODALMING   SU9643
Star (01483) 417717
Church Street; GU7 1EL Friendly 17th-c local in cobbled pedestrian street, cosy low-beamed and panelled L-shaped bar, up to eight well kept changing ales (four tapped from the cask) including Greene King, five proper ciders/perries, simple bar food (not weekend evenings), more modern back room; Mon folk night, Sun quiz; no dogs, heated back terrace, open all day. *(Sandra King)*

GOMSHALL   TQ0847
Compasses (01483) 202506
Station Road (A25); GU5 9LA Popular village pub with simple bar and much bigger comfortable dining room, good value home-made food, well kept Fullers London Pride, Otter Bitter and Surrey Hills Shere Drop, decent wines by the glass, friendly helpful service; background and weekend live music, Aug 'Gomstock' festival; children and dogs welcome, pretty garden sloping down to roadside mill stream, open (and food) all day, closes around 8pm Sun. *(Tony Scott)*

GOMSHALL   TQ0847
Gomshall Mill (01483) 203060
Station Road; GU5 9LB Attractive timber-framed and weatherboarded medieval mill with interesting multi-level interior, part of the Home Counties group and quite

restauranty; good sensibly priced food from extensive menu including sandwiches and children's meals, four well kept ales and several wines by the glass, nice cafetière coffee, friendly helpful staff; terrace with view of River Tillingbourne running under the building, open all day. *(Richard Kennell)*

GRAYSWOOD   SU9134
Wheatsheaf (01428) 644440
Grayswood Road (A286 NE of Haslemere); GU27 2DE Welcoming family-run dining pub with light airy décor, enjoyable freshly made food in bar and restaurant, good range of well kept beers, friendly helpful staff; quiz first Tues of the month; front verandah, side terrace, seven bedrooms in extension, good breakfast. *(Jeff Davies)*

GUILDFORD   SU9949
Weyside (01483) 568024
Shalford Road, Millbrook; across car park from Yvonne Arnaud Theatre, beyond boatyard; GU1 3XJ Big riverside pub (former Boatman) refurbished by Youngs, their ales and enjoyable food from sharing dishes and pub favourites up, friendly service, large split-level bar dropping down to back dining conservatory, also barn-room restaurant; children and dogs welcome, terrace overlooking River Wey, open all day. *(Mike Benton)*

GUILDFORD   SU9949
White House (01483) 302006
High Street; GU2 4AJ Refurbished Fullers pub in pretty waterside setting, their ales and good range of wines, enjoyable food from small plates up, sizeable bar with conservatory, upstairs rooms and roof terrace; children welcome, a few picnic-sets by River Wey, open (and food) all day. *(Tony Scott)*

HEADLEY   TQ2054
★Cock (01372) 377258
Church Lane; KT18 6LE Relaxed opened-up pub in same group as the Stag at Eashing and Queens Head at East Clandon; light airy modern refurbishment (parts date to the 18th c) with open fires and comfortable seating, good food (all day Fri-Sun) from lunchtime sandwiches and sharing plates up, steak and grill night Mon, a house beer (Red Mist) and a couple of guests, interesting wines including champagne by the glass, friendly attentive service; children welcome, dogs in one area, disabled access using lift from upper car park, terrace tables under parasols, attractive setting and good woodland walks, open all day. *(John Evans)*

HOLMBURY ST MARY   TQ1144
Kings Head (01306) 730282
Pitland Street; RH5 6NP Welcoming old pub tucked away in hillside village, good food

(not Sun evening) cooked by landlord-chef, well kept Dark Star Hophead, Otter and a guest, bare boards, exposed brickwork and two log fires; background music, darts, outside gents'; children and dogs welcome, pretty spot with a few seats out at front, more in big sloping back garden, good walks, open all day weekends (till 9pm Sun), closed Mon. *(Ian Phillips)*

HORLEY   TQ2742
Olde Six Bells (01293) 825028

Quite handy for M23 junction 9, off Horley turn from A23; Church Road – head for the church spire; RH6 8AD Ancient stone-roofed Vintage Inn – part of the heavy-beamed open-plan bar was probably a medieval chapel and some masonry may date from the 9th c; their usual good value food, Fullers London Pride, Sharps Doom Bar and a guest, log fires, upstairs overflow raftered dining room, conservatory; children welcome, tables out by bend in River Mole, open all day. *(Tony Scott)*

HORSELL   SU9859
Cricketers (01483) 762363

Horsell Birch; GU21 4XB Country pub popular for its good sensibly priced food including Sun carvery, cheerful efficient service, Shepherd Neame ales, plenty of wines by the glass and good range of gins, various areas including back dining extension with booth seating, log fires; live jazz Mon, quiz every other Tues; children welcome, no dogs inside, wheelchair access, picnic-sets out at front overlooking Horsell Common, big back garden with barbecue and good play area, open all day. *(Tim and Sarah Smythe-Brown)*

HORSELL   SU9959
Plough (01483) 714105

Off South Road; Cheapside; GU21 4JL Small local overlooking wooded heath, friendly and relaxed, with well kept Dartmoor, Sharps and a guest, reasonably priced home-made food (not Sun evening or Mon) including daily specials and weekday set menu, Thurs steak night, L-shaped bar with woodburner; Weds quiz; families and dogs (theirs is Buddy) welcome, tables in pretty garden with play area, open all day, breakfast from 8.30am Thurs-Sun. *(Sandra King)*

HORSELL   SU9959
★ Red Lion (01483) 768497

High Street; GU21 4SS Large and very popular with light airy feel, split-level bar with comfortable sofas and easy chairs, clusters of pictures on cream-painted walls, Fullers London Pride, St Austell Tribute and a guest from long wooden servery, a dozen wines by the glass, back dining room with exposed brick walls, old pews and blackboards listing the good bistro-style food, efficient service; children allowed till

early evening, ivy-clad passage to garden and comfortable tree-sheltered terrace, good walks, open all day. *(Colette Grace)*

HORSELL COMMON   TQ0160
Sands at Bleak House

(01483) 756988 *Chertsey Road, The Anthonys; A320 Woking–Ottershaw; GU21 5NL* Smart contemporary pub-restaurant on edge of Horsell Common; grey sandstone for floor and face of bar counter, brown leather sofas and cushioned stools, two dining rooms with dark wood furniture, woodburners, good well presented food (can be pricey) including set menu, Andwell, Hogs Back and Sharps, friendly attentive uniformed staff; background music, TV, free wi-fi; children welcome, courtyard with picnic-sets and smokers' shelter, good shortish walk to sandpits that inspired H G Wells's *The War of the Worlds*, seven bedrooms, open all day, till 6pm Sun. *(Mike Benton)*

LALEHAM   TQ0568
★ Three Horseshoes (01784) 455014

Shepperton Road (B376); TW18 1SE Bustling dining pub near pleasant stretch of the Thames; bar with white walls and contrasting deep blue woodwork, easy-going mix of tables and chairs on bare boards, log fire fronted by armchairs and squashy sofa, well kept Fullers/Gales beers and plenty of wines by the glass, popular sensibly priced food including blackboard specials (booking advised), efficient friendly staff, dining areas with assorted tables and chairs, pictures and mirrors on grey walls; soft background music, free wi-fi; children welcome till 8pm, attractive flagstoned terrace, picnic-sets on grass, open (and food) all day. *(Geoffrey Kemp, Simon Collett-Jones, Hunter and Christine Wright, Gerry and Rosemary Dobson)*

LEIGH   TQ2147
★ Seven Stars (01306) 611254

Dawes Green, south of A25 Dorking–Reigate; RH2 8NP Attractive tile-hung country dining pub serving popular sensibly priced food, comfortable beamed and flagstoned bar with traditional furnishings and inglenook, Fullers, Harveys, Sharps and Youngs from glowing copper counter, several wines by the glass, plainer public bar and sympathetic restaurant extension where children allowed; dogs welcome in bar areas, plenty of outside seating, open all day, food all day Fri, Sat and till 7pm Sun. *(Pauline and Mark Evans)*

LIMPSFIELD CHART   TQ4251
Carpenters Arms 722209

Tally Road; RH8 0TG Friendly open-plan pub owned by Westerham, their full range kept well (tasting trays available), popular home-made food (not Sun evening) from light lunches up, friendly helpful staff, garden room; free wi-fi; tables on terrace and lawn, delightful setting by village common, lovely walks and handy for Chartwell (NT), open all day weekends. *(Mike Benton)*

MICKLEHAM   TQ1753
King William IV (01372) 372590
Just off A24 Leatherhead–Dorking; Byttom Hill; RH5 6EL Steps up to small nicely placed country pub, well kept Hogs Back TEA, Surrey Hills Shere Drop and a guest, enjoyable food from lunchtime sandwiches to blackboard specials, friendly attentive service, pleasant outlook from cosy plank-panelled front bar, carpeted dining area with grandfather clock and log fire; background music, live jazz Sun evening; children and dogs welcome, plenty of tables in pretty terraced garden (some in open-sided timber shelters), lovely panoramic views of the Mole Valley, open (and food) all day. *(Jeff Davies)*

MOGADOR   TQ2453
Sportsman (01737) 246655
From M25 up A217 past second roundabout, then Mogador signed; KT20 7ES Modernised and extended low-ceilinged pub on edge of Walton Heath (originally 16th-c royal hunting lodge), well kept ales including Sharps and Wells, good food from varied interesting menu, friendly attentive service, restaurant with raised section; children welcome (no pushchairs), dogs in bar, seating out on common, front verandah and back lawn, popular with walkers and riders, open all day. *(Tony Scott)*

NUTFIELD   TQ3050
Queens Head (01737) 823619
A25 E of Redhill; RH1 4HH Welcoming three-room beamed pub with good locally sourced food (not Sun evening) including deals, well kept Harveys, Sharps and guests such as Pilgrim and Surrey Hills, plenty of wines by the glass, log fires; regular live music, Sun quiz, darts, daily newspapers; tables out on terrace and side lawn, maybe summer barbecues, open all day. *(Ian Phillips)*

OCKLEY   TQ1337
★Punchbowl (01306) 627249
Oakwood Hill, signed off A29 S; RH5 5PU Attractive 16th-c tile-hung country pub with slabby Horsham stone roof; friendly landlord and welcoming relaxed atmosphere, wide choice of good value generously served food (all day Sat, not Sun evening), Badger ales, central bar with huge inglenook, polished flagstones and low beams, collections of brass spiles, horsebrasses and cigarette lighters, restaurant area to left and another bar to right with sofas, armchairs and TV; children and dogs welcome, picnic-sets in pretty garden, quiet spot with good walks including Sussex Border Path, open all day. *(Jim and Sue James)*

OUTWOOD   TQ3246
★Bell (01342) 842989
Outwood Common, just E of village; off A23 S of Redhill; RH1 5PN Attractive 17th-c extended dining pub; smartly rustic beamed bar with oak and elm furniture (some Jacobean in style), soft lighting, low beams and vast stone inglenook, Fullers London Pride, ESB and a guest, 20 wines by the glass and wide range of spirits, popular food from pub standards up (best to book, especially evenings when drinking-only space limited); background music, free wi-fi; children and dogs (in bar) welcome, well maintained garden looking out past pine trees to rolling fields, open all day, food all day weekends. *(Tony Scott)*

OUTWOOD   TQ3146
Dog & Duck (01342) 842964
Prince of Wales Road; turn off A23 at station sign in Salfords, S of Redhill – OS Sheet 187 map reference 312460; RH1 5QU Relaxed beamed country pub with fairly priced home-made food in bar or restaurant, friendly welcoming service, well kept Badger ales from brick-faced servery, decent wines, warm winter fires; monthly quiz and live music nights; children welcome, garden with duck pond and play area. *(Tony Scott)*

OXTED   TQ4048
Royal Oak (01883) 722207
Caterfield Lane, Staffhurst Wood, S of town; RH8 0RR Popular country pub, cheerful and comfortable, with ales such as Adnams, Larkins and Sharps, also good range of ciders including Biddenden and Weston's, enjoyable locally sourced home-made food (not Sun or Mon evenings), back dining room, open fire; children and dogs welcome, nice garden with lovely views across fields, open all day Fri-Sun. *(Simon Rodway)*

PUTTENHAM   SU9347
Good Intent (01483) 810387
Signed off B3000 just S of A31 junction; The Street/Seale Lane; GU3 1AR Convivial beamed village local, Otter, Sharps, Timothy Taylors and three guests, popular reasonably priced traditional food (not Sun, Mon evenings) including good sandwiches, big log fire in cosy front bar with alcove seating, some old farming tools and photographs of the pub, parquet-floored dining area; darts, free wi-fi; well behaved children and dogs welcome (they have a dog), small sunny garden, good walks, open all day weekends. *(Alan and Shirley Sawden, Mrs J Ekins-Daukes)*

PYRFORD LOCK   TQ0559
Anchor (01932) 342507
3 miles from M25 junction 10 – S on A3, then take Wisley slip road and go on past RHS Wisley garden; GU23 6QW

Light and airy waterside dining pub (can get very busy and may be queues), good value food from sandwiches up, Badger ales and several wines by the glass, simple tables on bare boards, quieter more comfortable panelled back area, narrowboat memorabilia, pleasant oak-framed conservatory with raised woodburner, daily papers; children welcome, dogs in some areas, splendid terrace by bridge and locks on River Wey Navigation, moorings, large car park across road, handy for RHS Wisley, open (and food) all day. *(Ian Phillips, Tony Hobden)*

REDHILL   TQ2750
Garland (01737) 764612
Brighton Road; RH1 6PP Friendly 19th-c Harveys corner local, their full range kept well including seasonals, enjoyable well priced traditional food cooked by landlord (lunchtimes, Fri evening, Sun till 4pm); live music Sat, bar billiards, darts, free wi-fi; children (till 7.30pm) and well behaved dogs welcome, picnic-sets in back garden, open all day. *(Tony Scott, Tony Hobden)*

REDHILL   TQ2850
Home Cottage (01737) 762771
Redstone Hill; RH1 4AW Stylishly updated 19th-c Youngs pub, their ales and guests, several wines by the glass (can be pricey) and good variety of enjoyable food in bar or restaurant; children welcome, nice garden with covered terrace, open (and food) all day. *(PL)*

REDHILL   TQ2749
Plough (01737) 766686
Church Road, St Johns; RH1 6QE Friendly early 17th-c beamed pub with lots of bits and pieces to look at including copper and brass hanging from the ceiling, Fullers, Youngs and a couple of guests, enjoyable sensibly priced blackboard food (not Sun evening), open fire; Weds quiz; no under-10s inside, dogs welcome, back garden and terrace (barbecues and spit roasts), open all day. *(Tony Scott)*

REIGATE HEATH   TQ2349
Skimmington Castle (01737) 243100
Off A25 Reigate–Dorking via Flanchford Road and Bonny's Road; RH2 8RL Nicely located small country pub with emphasis on enjoyable home-made food from good baguettes up (can get very busy and best to book), well kept Harveys, St Austell and a couple of guests, friendly efficient service, snug beamed and panelled rooms, log fires; children, dogs and muddy boots welcome, seats out on three sides (some heaters), open all day, food till 7pm Sun. *(Tony Scott, Ian Phillips)*

RIPLEY   TQ0556
★Anchor (01483) 211866
High Street; GU23 6AE Former 16th-c almshouse with clean modern décor in low-ceilinged linked areas, reminders here and there of Ripley's cycling heritage, good interesting food from bar snacks up, quite pricey but they do offer a lunchtime set menu (not Sun), Timothy Taylors Landlord and local guests, several wines by the glass including champagne; children welcome, rattan-style furniture in sunny decked courtyard, closed Mon, otherwise open all day (till 9pm Sun). *(Gerry Price, Christopher and Elise Way, Geoffrey Kemp)*

RIPLEY   TQ0456
Seven Stars (01483) 225128
Newark Lane (B367); GU23 6DL Neat and comfortable 1930s pub with snug areas, enjoyable food from extensive menu, Brakspears, Fullers, Sharps and Shepherd Neame, good wines and coffee, red patterned carpet, gleaming brasses and open fire; quiet background music; picnic-sets and heated wooden booths in well tended garden, river and canalside walks, closed Sun evening. *(Mike Benton)*

ROWLEDGE   SU8243
Cherry Tree (01252) 792105
Cherry Tree Road; off A325 just S of Farnham; GU10 4AB Welcoming 17th-c village pub with good traditional food from sandwiches up including set menu choices, well kept Greene King ales, friendly helpful service, beams and log fires; children and dogs welcome, tables on front terrace, more in lawned garden with old well, handy for Birdworld and Alice Holt Forest, open (and food) all day weekends, closed Mon. *(Jim and Sue James)*

SEND   TQ0156
New Inn (01483) 762736
Send Road, Cartbridge; GU23 7EN Well placed old pub by River Wey Navigation, long bar and dining room, Adnams, Fullers, Greene King, Sharps and a guest, good choice of enjoyable generously served food (something available all day) from sandwiches, through grills to blackboard specials, friendly helpful service, beams and log-effect gas fires; children and dogs welcome, large waterside garden with moorings, can get very busy in the summer. *(John Pritchard, Roger and Pauline Pearce)*

SHALFORD   SU9946
Parrot (01483) 561400
Broadford Road; GU4 8DW Big welcoming inn with wide range of popular freshly made food, Fullers London Pride, Sharps Doom Bar and Surrey Hills Shere Drop, good friendly service, rows of neat pine dining tables, some easy chairs around low tables, pleasant conservatory; free wi-fi; children welcome till 8pm, attractive garden with hanging baskets, picnic-sets under parasols, five ensuite bedrooms in separate building, handy for Loseley Park. *(Sandra King)*

SHALFORD   TQ0047
Queen Victoria   01483 561733
Station Row; GU4 8BY Tile-hung bay-
windowed local with compact modernised
interior around central bar, enjoyable
reasonably priced food (all day Sat, not Sun
evening, Mon) from lunchtime sandwiches
up, a beer badged for the pub along with
Otter and a weekend guest, woodburner;
some live music, TV; children welcome, seats
out at front and on back terrace, open all day.
(Tony and Wendy Hobden)

SHALFORD   TQ0047
Seahorse   (01483) 514351
*A281 S of Guildford; The Street;
GU4 8BU* Gently upmarket Mitchells &
Butlers dining pub with wide range of food
including popular set menu (weekdays till
6pm), friendly young staff, Adnams and
Sharps Doom Bar, good choice of wines and
other drinks, contemporary furniture and
artwork, two-way log fire, smart dining room,
comfortable part near entrance with sofas
and huge window; picnic-sets in big lawned
garden, covered terrace, handy for Shalford
Mill (NT), open all day. *(Richard Tilbrook)*

SHAMLEY GREEN   TQ0343
Bricklayers Arms   (01483) 898377
Guildford Road, S of the green; GU5 0UA
Red-brick village pub with five well kept
ales such as Exmoor, Hogs Back and Surrey
Hills, enjoyable pubby food (not Sun evening)
including fish and steak specials (Fri, Sat),
U-shaped layout with bare boards, carpets
and flagstones, exposed brick and stripped
wood, old local photographs, sofas by
woodburner, games area with pool, darts and
machines; quiz and poker nights, TV; children
and dogs welcome, a couple of picnic-sets out
in front, more seats behind, open all day.
(Ian Phillips)

SHEPPERTON   TQ0866
Red Lion   (01932) 244526
Russell Road; TW17 9HX In good
position across from the Thames, bistro-style
renovation (oldest part a pub since the
18th c), well cooked/presented food (all day
weekends) from varied regularly changing
menu, Sat brunch and popular Sun lunch,
Fullers, Theakstons and a guest, good
range of other drinks, friendly helpful staff;
children and dogs welcome, modern furniture
on picket-fenced front terrace, more seats
over road on riverside deck, open (and food)
all day. *(Gerry and Rosemary Dobson)*

SHERE   TQ0747
White Horse   (01483) 202518
*Shere Lane; signed off A25 3 miles E
of Guildford; GU5 9HS* Splendid Chef &
Brewer with uneven floors, massive beams
and timbers, Tudor stonework, oak wall seats
and two log fires (one in huge inglenook),
several rooms off small bar, good range of

enjoyable food including deals, Greene King
IPA and a couple of guests, Weston's cider
and plenty of wines by the glass, good service;
children welcome, dogs seats out at front
and in big garden behind, beautiful film-set
village, open (and food) all day. *(Ian Phillips,
Tony Scott)*

SHERE   TQ0747
William Bray   (01483) 202044
Shere Lane; GU5 9HS Dining pub with
good well presented locally sourced food,
four real ales such as Brakspears, Ringwood
and Surrey Hills and decent range of wines,
friendly helpful staff, roomy contemporary
bar with stone floor and woodburner, more
formal airy restaurant with comfortable
leather chairs; background and fortnightly
live music (Tues); children and dogs
welcome, split-level front terrace and pretty
landscaped side garden, useful car park, open
(and some food) all day. *(Nick Higgins)*

SHOTTERMILL   SU8832
Mill   (01428) 643183
*Liphook Road (B2131, off A287 W
of Haslemere); GU27 3QE* Recently
refurbished and extended 17th-c pub, low
beamed bar and more spacious modern
restaurant, popular food (all day Sun) from
sandwiches, sharing plates and pizzas up,
Wadworths ales and large choice of wines by
the glass, friendly service; free wi-fi; children
and dogs welcome, terrace and garden behind,
open all day. *(Martin and Alison Stainsby)*

STAINES   TQ0371
Bells   (01784) 454240
Church Street; TW18 4ZB Comfortable
and sociable Youngs pub in old part of town,
their well kept ales and a guest, decent
choice of wines and good promptly served
fresh food (special diets catered for), central
fireplace; dogs allowed in bar, tables in nice
back garden with heated terrace, limited
roadside parking, open all day weekends
(no food Sun evening). *(Edward Edmonton)*

STOKE D'ABERNON   TQ1259
★ **Old Plough**   (01932) 862244
Station Road, off A245; KT11 3BN
Popular nicely updated 300-year-old pub
in same group as the Onslow Arms at West
Clandon, Red Lion at Horsell and Three
Horseshoes in Laleham; good freshly made food
including daily specials, Fullers/Gales beers
and a couple of guests including Surrey Hills,
plenty of wines by the glass, competent friendly
staff, restaurant with various knick-knacks;
newspapers and free wi-fi; children (not in
bar after 7.30pm) and dogs welcome, seats out
under pergola in attractive garden, open
(and food) all day. *(Charles North)*

SUTTON ABINGER   TQ1045
Volunteer   (01306) 730985
*Water Lane; just off B2126 via Raikes
Lane, 1.5 miles S of Abinger Hammer;*

RH5 6PR Picturesque family-run pub in delightful setting above clear stream, low-ceilinged linked rooms, log fires, enjoyable traditional food from sandwiches up, Badger ales and several wines by the glass, good friendly service, restaurant; children and dogs welcome, terrace and suntrap lawns stepped up behind, nice local walks, open all day Sat, Sun till 5pm. *(Pauline and Mark Evans)*

SUTTON GREEN   TQ0054
Olive Tree (01483) 729999
Sutton Green Road; GU4 7QD New owners for this big rambling country dining pub; bar area with leather sofas by open fire, Fullers, Hogs Back and Timothy Taylors, good range of wines by the glass and well liked food from open sandwiches to daily specials, friendly helpful service, spreading dining room with clean-cut décor; children and dogs (in bar) welcome, tables out behind, open all day. *(Peter Sutton, Peter Brix, David Jackman, Nigel and Sue Foster)*

TADWORTH   TQ2355
★Dukes Head (01737) 812173
Dorking Road (B2032 opposite common and woods); KT20 5SL Roomy and comfortably modernised 19th-c pub, popular for its good varied choice of food (booking advised), five well kept ales including Fullers, Youngs and a house beer (KT20) from Morlands, Aspall's cider, good choice of wines by the glass, helpful friendly staff, three dining areas and two big inglenook log fires; background music, Weds quiz; children welcome, dogs in some areas, lots of hanging baskets and plenty of tables in well tended terrace garden, open (and food) all day, till 8pm (6.30pm Sun). *(John Branston)*

THAMES DITTON   TQ1567
Albany (020) 8972 9163
Queens Road, signed off Summer Road; KT7 0QY Mitchells & Butlers bar-with-restaurant in lovely Thames-side position, light airy modern feel, with good variety of food from sharing plates and pizzas to more upscale dishes, weekday lunchtime and early evening fixed-price menu, good choice of wines by the glass, cocktails and ales such as Hop Back, St Austell and Sharps, cheerful efficient young staff, log fire, river pictures, daily papers; disabled access/loo, nice balconies and two-level heated deck overlooking river to Hampton Court Palace grounds, moorings, open all day. *(Tony Scott, Simon and Mandy King, Tom and Ruth Rees)*

THAMES DITTON   TQ1667
Red Lion (020) 8398 8662
High Street; KT7 0SF Revamped and extended pub with enjoyable home-made food from regularly changing menu, decent wines and coffee, ales such as Surrey Hills and Twickenham from servery clad in reclaimed doors, cheerful young staff, mismatched furniture in bare-boards bar,

back conservatory; children welcome, seats on split-level enclosed terrace with Lego wall, open (and food) all day. *(Tom and Ruth Rees)*

THURSLEY   SU9039
★Three Horseshoes (01252) 703268
Dye House Road, just off A3 SW of Godalming; GU8 6QD Pretty tile-hung pub owned by village consortium; convivial beamed front bar with log fire, well kept Hogs Back TEA and guests, 12 wines by the glass, good popular food (not Sun evening) served by friendly competent staff, dining room with paintings for sale; background music; well behaved children welcome, dogs in bar, attractive two-acre garden with pleasant views over common and Saxon church, play fort, open all day Sat, till 8pm Sun. *(Christopher and Elise Way, Hunter and Christine Wright, Ian Phillips)*

TILFORD   SU8742
Duke of Cambridge (01252) 792236
Tilford Road; GU10 2DD Recently refurbished dining pub in same small local group as the Queens Head at East Clandon, Stag at Eashing and Wheatsheaf at Farnham; nice food from varied menu including gluten-free and children's choices, good selection of wines and gins (some local), ales such as Hogs Back and Surrey Hills, helpful service; May charity music festival; children and dogs welcome, terrace and garden with outside bar/grill, good play area, open all day. *(Mike Benton)*

VIRGINIA WATER   SU9968
Rose & Olive Branch
(01344) 843713 *Callow Hill; GU25 4LH* Small unpretentious red-brick pub with good choice of popular food including speciality pies and several vegetarian options, two Greene King ales and a guest, decent wines, friendly busy staff; background music; children welcome, tables on front terrace and in garden behind, good walks, open (and food) all day weekends. *(Edward and William Johnston)*

WALLISWOOD   TQ1138
Scarlett Arms (01306) 627243
Signed from Ewhurst–Rowhook back road, or off A29 S of Ockley; RH5 5RD Cottagey 16th-c village pub with low beams and flagstones, simple furniture and two log fires (one in big inglenook), Badger ales, well priced traditional food (not Sun evening) including malaysian menu, friendly helpful staff, dining room behind; background music; children and dogs welcome, tables out at front and in garden under parasols, good walks, open all day Fri, Sat, till 9.30pm Sun, closed Mon lunchtime. *(Sandra King)*

WALTON-ON-THAMES   TQ1068
Weir (01932) 784530
Towpath, Waterside Drive, off Sunbury Lane; KT12 2JB Edwardian pub in

nice Thames-side spot with big terrace overlooking river, weir and steel walkway, decent choice of food all day (till 7.30pm Sun) from snacks up, Greene King, Sharps and a couple of guests, traditional décor, river pictures, newspapers; children and dogs welcome, lovely towpath walks, six bedrooms. *(Jim and Sue James)*

WARLINGHAM   TQ3955
Botley Hill Farmhouse
(01959) 577154 *S on Limpsfield Road (B269); CR6 9QH* Refurbished 16th-c country pub set high on the North Downs; low-ceilinged linked rooms up and down steps, fresh flowers and candles, enjoyable food (till 6.30pm Sun) from standards up, well kept local ales such as Pilgrim and Westerham tapped from the cask (tasters offered), nice wines by the glass, good friendly service, big log fireplace in one room, tea shop selling local produce; children and dogs welcome, disabled access, terrace and garden with fine views, good local walks, open all day, breakfast from 9am. *(Jeff Davies)*

WEST CLANDON   TQ0451
★ Bulls Head (01483) 222444
A247 SE of Woking; GU4 7ST
Comfortably old-fashioned village pub based around 1540s timbered hall-house, popular good value pubby food (not Sun evening) including proper home-made pies, friendly helpful staff, ales from Sharps, Surrey Hills and Youngs, good coffee, small lantern-lit beamed front bar with open fire and some stripped brick, old local prints and bric-a-brac, simple raised back inglenook dining area, games room with darts and pool; children and dogs welcome, disabled access from car park, play area in neat little garden, nice walks. *(Nick Higgins)*

WEST CLANDON   TQ0452
★ Onslow Arms (01483) 222447
A247 SE of Woking; GU4 7TE Busy modernised pub with heavily beamed rambling rooms leading away from central bar; wooden dining chairs and tables on wide floorboards, painted panelling, all sorts of copper implements, hunting horns and pictures, leather chesterfields in front of open fire, ales including Sharps, Surrey Hills and a house beer brewed by Caledonian, good popular food from lunchtime sandwiches and traditional choices up; live music Weds, TV, daily papers and free wi-fi; children (till early evening) and dogs welcome, pretty courtyard garden with tables under parasols, open (and food) all day. *(Christopher and Elise Way, Gordon and Margaret Ormondroyd, Mrs J Ekins-Daukes)*

WEST HORSLEY   TQ0853
Barley Mow (01483) 282693
Off A246 Leatherhead–Guildford at Bell & Colvill garage roundabout; The Street; KT24 6HR Welcoming tree-shaded

traditional pub, low beams, mix of flagstones, bare boards and carpet, two log fires, well kept ales such as Fullers, Greene King and Surrey Hills, decent wines, good thai food along with more conventional lunchtime menu, barn function room; background music; children and dogs welcome, picnic-sets in good-sized garden, open all day, no food Sun. *(Mike Benton)*

WEST HORSLEY   TQ0752
King William IV (01483) 282318
The Street; KT24 6BG Comfortable and welcoming early 19th-c village pub; low entrance door to front and side bars, beams, flagstones and log fire, back conservatory restaurant, good variety of enjoyable food (not Sun evening) including gluten-free menu, four real ales such as Courage and Surrey Hills, decent choice of wines by the glass and good coffee; background and live music, quiz nights, free wi-fi; children and dogs welcome, disabled access, small sunny garden with deck and play area, open all day. *(Simon Sharpe)*

WEYBRIDGE   TQ0765
Minnow (01932) 831672
Thames Street/Walton Lane; KT13 8NG Busy bay-windowed Mitchells & Butlers dining pub; contemporary pastel décor with some unusual decorative panels, chunky tables and chairs on gleaming flagstones, sofas and armchairs, two-way log fire in raised hearth, popular food including fixed-price weekday menu till 6pm, ales such as Fullers, Timothy Taylors and Youngs, good wines by the glass, friendly staff; children welcome, big front terrace with heaters, open all day. *(Mike Benton)*

WEYBRIDGE   TQ0965
Oatlands Chaser (01932) 253277
Oatlands Chase; KT13 9RW Large newly refurbished Mitchells & Butlers pub in quiet residential street, light contemporary décor with several eating areas, log fires, good reasonably priced food including weekday set menu (till 6pm), friendly efficient service, Fullers, St Austell and Sharps, good wine choice, interesting gins and cocktails; children welcome, disabled access, lots of tables out at front, 19 smart bedrooms, open (and food) all day. *(Ian Phillips)*

WEYBRIDGE   TQ0765
★ Old Crown (01932) 842844
Thames Street; KT13 8LP Comfortably old-fashioned three-bar pub dating from the 16th c, good value traditional food (not Sun-Tues evenings) from sandwiches to fresh fish, Courage, Youngs and a guest kept well (not cheap), good choice of wines by the glass, friendly efficient service, family lounge and conservatory, coal-effect gas fire; may be sports TV in back bar with Lions RFC photographs, silent fruit machine; secluded terrace and smokers' shelter, steps down

to suntrap garden overlooking Wey/Thames confluence, mooring for small boats, open all day. (Jim and Sue James)

WEYBRIDGE   TQ0664
Queens Head (01932) 839820
Bridge Road; KT13 8XS 18th-c pub owned by Raymond Blanc's White Brasserie Company, emphasis on dining with good food including well priced lunchtime/ early evening set menu (not Sun), but also a proper bar serving real ales and plenty of wines by the glass, friendly staff; soft background music, newspapers; children welcome, a couple of picnic-sets outside, open (and food) all day. (Mike Benton)

WINDLESHAM   SU9464
Brickmakers (01276) 472267
Chertsey Road (B386, W of B383 roundabout); GU20 6HT Airy red-brick country dining pub, updated linked areas in pastel shades or vibrant reds, light wood furniture on flagstone and wood floors, two-way woodburner, good freshly prepared food (all day Fri-Sun when best to book) using local suppliers, Courage Best, Fullers London Pride and Sharps Doom Bar, good choice of wines by the glass and decent coffee, efficient friendly service, conservatory; well behaved children allowed, appealing garden with pergola, open all day from 9am for breakfast. (Gerry Price, Colette Grace)

WITLEY   SU9439
White Hart (01428) 683695
Petworth Road; GU8 5PH Picture-book beamed Tudor pub, well kept St Austell Tribute, Youngs Bitter and a guest, craft beers, plenty of wines by the glass and extensive range of whiskies, good food including signature home-smoked/chargrilled meats, friendly helpful staff, bar, restaurant and cosy panelled snug with inglenook (where George Eliot used to drink); children and dogs welcome, tables on cobbled terrace and in garden, nice walks nearby, open all day Tues-Sat, till 6pm Sun, closed Mon lunchtime. (Tim and Sarah Smythe-Brown)

WOKING   TQ0058
Herbert Wells (01483) 722818
Chertsey Road; GU21 5AJ Corner Wetherspoons named after H G Wells, busy with shoppers yet with lots of cosy areas and side snugs, fine selection of beers and ciders and their usual competitively priced all-day food, friendly helpful staff, old local pictures; free wi-fi and daily papers; children welcome, a few pavement tables, open from 8am. (Tony Hobden)

WONERSH   TQ0145
Grantley Arms (01483) 893351
The Street; GU5 0PE Attractively refurbished and extended 16th-c village dining pub under new ownership; opened-up contemporary beamed bar with areas off, up to half a dozen ales and interesting wine list including english choices, nicely presented food (separate bar and restaurant menus – can be expensive), friendly helpful staff, more formal evening restaurant (Tues-Sat, plus Sun lunchtime), private dining in former bakery; Mon quiz; children and dogs (in bar) welcome, ramp for wheelchairs, disabled loo, terrace tables, open all day. (Sandra King)

WOOD STREET   SU9550
Royal Oak (01483) 235137
Oak Hill; GU3 3DA Popular 1920s village local with half a dozen well kept ales including Ringwood, good value traditional home-cooked food (not Mon), bargain OAP lunch Thurs, friendly staff; music and quiz nights, free wi-fi; dogs welcome, good-sized garden. (Alan and Shirley Sawden)

WORPLESDON   SU9854
Jolly Farmer (01483) 234658
Burdenshott Road, off A320 Guildford– Woking, not in village; GU3 3RN Old Fullers pub in pleasant country setting, their well kept ales in beamed and flagstoned bar with small log fire, fairly traditional food from lunchtime sandwiches up (they may ask to swipe your credit card if running a tab), bare-boards dining extension under pitched roof; background music, free wi-fi; children and dogs welcome, garden tables under parasols and pergola, open all day, food all day weekends. (Nick Higgins)

WRECCLESHAM   SU8344
Bat & Ball (01252) 792108
Bat & Ball Lane, South Farnham; approach from Sandrock Hill and Upper Bourne Lane, then narrow steep lane to pub; GU10 4SA Fairly traditional pub tucked away in hidden valley; decent range of enjoyable food (all day weekends) from pubby choices up including good puddings display, six well kept local ales (June beer and music festival), plenty of wines by the glass, friendly helpful staff; Tues charity quiz, open mike night last Thurs of month; children and dogs welcome, disabled facilities, tables out on attractive terrace with vine arbour and in garden with substantial play fort, open all day. (Jeff Davies)

WRECCLESHAM   SU8244
Royal Oak (01252) 728319
The Street; GU10 4QS 17th-c black-beamed village local with enjoyable good value home-made food, Greene King IPA and a couple of guests, friendly helpful staff, log fire; Sun quiz, sports TV, darts; children and dogs welcome, big garden with play area, open all day. (Tony and Jill Radnor)

Sussex

KEY ★ Star Pub 🍽️ Top Quality Food 🍺 Great Beer

 🍷 Good Wines £ Bargain Meals 🛏️ Good Bedrooms 🍴 Serves Food

ALFRISTON   TQ5203 Map 3
George 🍷
(01323) 870319 – www.thegeorge-alfriston.com
High Street; BN26 5SY

Venerable 14th-c timbered inn with comfortable, heavily beamed bars, good wines and several real ales; bedrooms

This fine old place with plenty of character is just a few steps away from the bucolic village green. The long bar, dominated by a huge stone inglenook fireplace with a winter log fire (or summer flower arrangement), has massive hop-hung low beams, soft lighting, lots of copper and brass, and settles and chairs around sturdy stripped tables. Greene King Abbot, Dark Star Hophead and Theakstons XB on handpump, 14 wines by the glass (including champagne and a pudding wine), ten gins, board games and background music; good service. The lounge has comfortable sofas, standing timbers and rugs on the wooden floor, and the restaurant is cosy and candlelit. There are seats in the spacious flint-walled garden, and the beamed bedrooms are comfortable; there's no car park but you can park a couple of minutes away. This is a lovely village to wander around and two long-distance paths (the South Downs Way and Vanguard Way) cross here; the quietly beautiful Cuckmere Haven is nearby.

🍴 Food is popular and available all day: smoked salmon and prawn parcel, serrano ham, fig and buffalo mozzarella salad, sharing boards, chickpea, sweetcorn and bean burger with pickles, chargrilled chicken with tomato and basil pasta, calves liver with crispy pancetta and shallot gravy, sea bream fillets with butter bean and chorizo stew, moroccan-style lamb chop with mint couscous, and puddings such as pear and raspberry crumble and chocolate and salted caramel ganache tart. *Benchmark main dish: braised short rib of beef with roasted root vegetables and horseradish mash £16.50. Two-course evening meal £20.00.*

Greene King ~ Lease Roland and Cate Couch ~ Real ale ~ Open 11-11; 12-11 weekends ~ Bar food 12-9 ~ Restaurant ~ Children welcome ~ Dogs welcome ~ Wi-fi ~ Bedrooms: /£100
Recommended by Tony and Wendy Hobden, Mr and Mrs P R Thomas, Tony and Jill Radnor, John Beeken

---

Please let us know what you think of a pub's bedrooms: feedback@goodguides.com
or (no stamp needed) The Good Pub Guide, FREEPOST RTJR-ZCYZ-RJZT,
Perrymans Lane, Etchingham TN19 7DN.

ALFRISTON

TQ5203 Map 3

Star 🛏

(01323) 870495 – www.thestaralfriston.co.uk

High Street; BN26 5TA

Ancient inn with original features, plenty of space for drinking and dining, helpful staff and enjoyable food; bedrooms

The handsome timbered frontage of this 13th-c inn is decorated with fine medieval carvings, and the striking red lion on the corner – known as Old Bill – was probably the figurehead from a wrecked Dutch ship. The character front bar has heavy dark beams, cushioned settles, stools and captain's chairs around pubby tables on bare floorboards, a log fire in the Tudor fireplace and tankards hanging over the counter where they serve beers from Harveys and Long Man on handpump and ten wines by the glass. Steps down to the left lead into a big two-level bar (one level has a lovely herringbone brick floor) with rustic tables, chapel chairs and both an open fire and woodburning stove; there's a door through to yet another room with book-mural wallpaper, plush burgundy armchairs and sofas, another woodburner and a TV. Some medieval artefacts are hung on the walls. The comfortable and contemporary bedrooms – newly furnished – are at the back of the building; this is a good base for walking, and the village is well worth a stroll around.

 Well thought-of food includes sandwiches, crispy pig cheeks with pickled cabbage and capers, moules marinière, tiger prawn and chorizo spaghetti with white wine and tarragon, hop and ale sausages with red wine gravy, free-range chicken and smoked ham pie, burgers with toppings and triple-cooked chips, lambs liver with bacon, mash and roast onion gravy, and puddings such as parkin pudding with salted caramel sauce and apple and blackberry crumble. *Benchmark main dish: beer-battered local cod and chips £11.95. Two-course evening meal £19.00.*

Free house ~ Licensee Julie Garvin ~ Real ale ~ Bar food ~ Restaurant ~ Children welcome ~ Dogs allowed in bar ~ Wi-fi ~ Live music Fri evenings ~ Bedrooms: /£92
Recommended by John Beeken, David and Judy Robison, John and Mary Warner

CHARLTON

SU8812 Map 2

Fox Goes Free ♀

(01243) 811461 – www.thefoxgoesfree.com

Village signposted off A286 Chichester–Midhurst in Singleton, also from Chichester–Petworth via East Dean; PO18 0HU

Comfortable old pub with beamed bars, popular food and drink and big garden; bedrooms

This is a lovely place to while away a lunchtime – especially in good weather when you can sit at one of the picnic-sets under the apple trees in the attractive back garden with the South Downs as a backdrop; there are rustic benches and tables on the gravelled front terrace too. The bar, the first of several cosy separate rooms, has old irish settles, tables and chapel chairs and an open fire. Standing timbers divide up a larger beamed bar, which has a huge brick fireplace and old local photographs on the walls. A dining area overlooks the garden. The family extension is a clever conversion from horse boxes and the stables where the 1926 Goodwood winner was once housed; darts, board games, TV and background music. A beer named for the pub (from Arundel), Langham Hip Hop and Saison and Listers Best Bitter on handpump, 15 wines by the glass and Addlestone's cider. You can walk up to Levin Down nature reserve, or stroll around the Iron Age hill fort on the

Trundle with huge views to the Isle of Wight; the Weald & Downland Open Air Museum and West Dean Gardens are nearby too.

 From a seasonal menu (they make their own bread, ice-creams and chips), the enjoyable food includes lunchtime ciabattas (not Sunday lunchtime), potted ham hock with home-pickled vegetables, smoked salmon, crab and avocado roulade with apple and fennel salad, home-cooked honey-roasted ham and eggs, a vegetarian risotto of the day, burger with toppings, harissa mayonnaise and chips, chicken breast stuffed with chorizo and topped with tomato sauce, bass fillets with spinach, sunblush tomatoes and béarnaise sauce, and puddings such as white chocolate pannacotta and orange chocolate mousse. *Benchmark main dish: pie of the day £12.50. Two-course evening meal £18.00.*

Free house ~ Licensee David Coxon ~ Real ale ~ Open 11am-11pm (midnight Sat); 12-11 Sun ~ Bar food 12-2.30, 6.15-9.45; 12-10 weekends ~ Restaurant ~ Children welcome ~ Dogs allowed in bar ~ Wi-fi ~ Live music first Weds of month ~ Bedrooms: £70/£95
Recommended by Richard and Judy Winn, J A Snell, Roy Hoing, Katharine Cowherd, Caroline Sullivan

CHILGROVE
White Horse 🏵 ⭐ ♟ 🛏
(01243) 519444 – www.thewhitehorse.co.uk

SU8214   Map 2

B2141 Petersfield–Chichester; PO18 9HX

18th-c whitewashed inn with original features, a thoughtful choice of drinks, first class food and plenty of outside seating; bedrooms

A gently civilised place for a drink or a meal, this is a handsome coaching inn with plenty of room for both – and a cheerful mix of customers. The bar area has leather armchairs in front of a woodburning stove and daily papers on the light oak counter where friendly staff serve a beer named for the pub (from Marstons), Help for Heroes (also from Marstons), Langham Hip Hop and and a guest from Ballards on handpump and 18 good wines by the glass. Just off here, a room with leather button-back wall seats and mate's and other dark wooden dining chairs has all sorts of country knick-knacks: stuffed animals, china plates, riding boots, flower paintings, dog drawings, stone bottles and books on shelves. The dining room to the other side of the bar has a huge painting of a galloping white horse, a long suede wall banquette, high-backed settles creating stalls, elegant chairs, lots of mirrors and big metal chandeliers. Throughout, there are fat candles in lanterns, flagstones and coir carpet, beams and timbering, and animal-skin throws; background music and board games. A two-level terrace has dark grey rattan-style seats around glass-topped tables under parasols among pretty flowering tubs; an area up steps has rustic benches and tables and there are picnic-sets on grass at the front. Each of the comfortable, contemporary and light bedrooms has a little private courtyard (two also have a hot tub). There are good surrounding walks.

🏵 The pleasing and attractively presented food uses the best local produce: sandwiches, goats cheese and honey mousse with raspberry jelly, chilli salt squid with aioli, herb polenta and mushroom stuffed aubergine with spinach and parmesan purée, smoked haddock rarebit with caper cream, burger with toppings, red cabbage slaw and fries, a pie of the day, roast guinea fowl with beetroot pearl couscous, pancetta and basil oil, and puddings. *Benchmark main dish: slow-roast suckling pig with herb stuffing, apple sauce and wild mushroom jus £19.50. Two-course evening meal £20.00.*

Free house ~ Licensee Niki Burr ~ Real ale ~ Open 8am-11pm; 8.30am-midnight Sat, Sun ~ Bar food 12-3, 6-9 (9.30 Fri); 12-9.30 Sat; 12-9 Sun ~ Restaurant ~ Children welcome ~ Dogs allowed in bar and bedrooms ~ Wi-fi ~ Live jazz Sun 2.30 ~ Bedrooms: £60/£90
Recommended by Mungo Shipley, Nick Sharpe, Mark Hamill

COPTHORNE TQ3240 Map 3

Old House 🍷 ⛺

(01342) 718529 – www.theoldhouseinn.co.uk

B2037 NE of village; RH10 3JB

**Charming old place with plenty of character, real ales,
enjoyable food and attentive staff; attractive bedrooms**

This is a lovely old inn housed in a timbered higgledy-piggledy building
with nooks and crannies in several interconnected rooms. The
immediately warming little bar has an easy-going feel, a brown leather
chesterfield, armchairs and carved wooden chairs around all sorts of tables,
a big sisal mat on flagstones, a decorative fireplace and nightlights. Ringwood
Razorback, Sharps Doom Bar and a guest from Copthorne on handpump,
several good wines by the glass and a couple of huge glass flagons holding
Sipsmith vodka and gin. Off to the left is a charming small room with a
woodburning stove in an inglenook fireplace and two leather armchairs in
front, white-painted beams in a low ceiling (this is the oldest part, dating
from the 16th c), cushioned settles and pre-war-style cushioned dining chairs
around varying tables. A teeny back room, like something you'd find on an
old galleon, has button-back wall seating up to the roof, a few chairs and
heavy ropework. The dining rooms are beamed (some painted) and timbered
with parquet, quarry tiles or sisal flooring, high-backed leather and other
dining chairs, more wall seating and fresh flowers and candles; background
music and board games. Heavy rustic tables and benches in a terraced
garden and smartly comfortable bedrooms in a converted barn. Gatwick
Airport is nearby.

🍽 Highly regarded food includes home-cured salmon with scrambled duck egg and
watercress purée, pork and black pudding scotch egg with curried mayonnaise,
tofu and courgette burger with sweet potato fries, corn-fed chicken with chorizo and
parmesan polenta, lamb rump with roasted vegetables and rosemary jus, and puddings
such as molten chocolate fondant with mint choc chip ice-cream and raspberry
pannacotta with raspberry sorbet; they also offer a two- and three-course set weekday
lunch. *Benchmark main dish: shin of beef and marrowbone pie £14.50. Two-course
evening meal £22.00.*

Free house ~ Licensee Stephen Godsave ~ Real ale ~ Open 11-11; 12-10 Sun ~ Bar food
12-3, 6-9 (8 Sun) ~ Restaurant ~ Children welcome ~ Dogs allowed in bar ~ Wi-fi ~
Bedrooms: /£90 *Recommended by Isobel Mackinlay, Michael Rugman, Sophie Ellison*

DANEHILL TQ4128 Map 3

Coach & Horses 🏅 🍷

(01825) 740369 – www.coachandhorses.co

Off A275, via School Lane towards Chelwood Common; RH17 7JF

**Well run dining pub with bustling bars, welcoming staff,
very good food and ales and a big garden**

In warm weather, the adults-only terrace beneath a huge maple tree is quite
a draw, and the big garden has picnic-sets, a children's play area and fine
views of the South Downs. Inside, the little bar to the right has half-panelled
walls, simple furniture on polished floorboards, a woodburner in a brick
fireplace and a big hatch to the bar counter: Harveys Best and a guest from
a local brewery such as Long Man on handpump, local Black Pig farmhouse
cider and a dozen wines by the glass including prosecco and Bluebell
sparkling wine from Sussex. A couple of steps lead down to a half-panelled
area with a mix of dining chairs around characterful wooden tables (set with

flowers and candles) on a fine brick floor, and changing artwork on the walls; cribbage, dominoes and cards. Down another step is a dining area with stone walls, beams, flagstones and a woodburning stove.

Food is imaginative and includes sandwiches, ham hock and puy lentil terrine with tarragon mustard aioli, grilled chilli prawns, smoked salmon and spring onion risotto, calves liver and bacon with mash and caramelised onions, moules frites, burger with toppings, smoked bacon relish and chips, grilled toulouse sausages with roasted provençale vegetables and salsa verde, stone bass with roast salsify, new potatoes, chicory and red onion and caper vinaigrette, guinea fowl breast with pearl barley and smoked bacon cream, and puddings such as apple and rhubarb crumble. *Benchmark main dish: crisp pork belly with pancetta hash and charred onion £14.50. Two-course evening meal £20.00.*

Free house ~ Licensee Ian Philpots ~ Real ale ~ Open 12-3, 5.30-11; 12-11 Sat; 12-10.30 Sun ~ Bar food 12-2 , 6.30-9 (9.30 Fri, Sat); 12-3 Sun ~ Restaurant ~ Well behaved children welcome but not on adult terrace ~ Dogs allowed in bar ~ Wi-fi *Recommended by Nick Lawless, R and S Bentley, Mr and Mrs R A Bradbrook*

DIAL POST
Crown 🏵

TQ1519   Map 3

(01403) 710902 – www.crowninndialpost.co.uk
Worthing Road (off A24 S of Horsham); RH13 8NH

Tile-hung village pub with interesting food and a good mix of drinkers and diners; bedrooms

The friendly licensees here are equally welcoming to locals and visitors alike and this creates a cheerful, bustling atmosphere. The beamed bar has a couple of standing timbers, brown squashy sofas, pine tables and chairs on the stone floor, a small woodburning stove in a brick fireplace, and Greyhound Beer, Long Man Best Bitter and a changing ale from Hammerpot on handpump served from the attractive herringbone brick counter; eight wines by the glass plus prosecco, champagne and a pudding wine. To the right of the bar, the restaurant (with more beams) has an ornamental woodburner in a brick fireplace, a few photographs, chunky pine tables, chairs, a couple of cushioned pews and a shelf of books; steps lead down to an additional dining room; board games. The pub dog is called Chops. The straightforwardly furnished dining conservatory, facing the village green, is light and airy. There are picnic-sets in the garden behind the pub.

Reliably good food includes sandwiches, seared scallops with cauliflower purée, black pudding and parmesan crisp, home-cured bresaola with celeriac rémoulade, caramelised onion, goats cheese and spinach tart with beetroot fritters, smoked haddock with spinach and a fish velouté, confit chicken leg with chorizo, bean and saffron ragoût, beer-battered cod and chips, and puddings such as rice pudding with sherry-macerated golden raisin and dark chocolate meringue with blueberry compote and chantilly cream. *Benchmark main dish: burgers with toppings and chips £11.50. Two-course evening meal £18.00.*

Free house ~ Licensees James and Penny Middleton-Burn ~ Real ale ~ Open 12-3, 6-11; 12-4 Sun ~ Bar food 12-2.15, 6-9 (9.30 Fri, Sat); 12-3 Sun ~ Restaurant ~ Children welcome but must be dining after 7pm ~ Dogs welcome ~ Wi-fi ~ Bedrooms: £51/£69
Recommended by Tony and Wendy Hobden, Richard Tilbrook, R and M Thomas

We mention bottled beers and spirits only if there is something unusual about them – imported belgian real ales, say, or dozens of malt whiskies; so do please let us know about them in your reports.

DITCHLING
Bull 🍴 ♀ 🍺 🛏

TQ3215 Map 3

(01273) 843147 – www.thebullditchling.com

High Street (B2112); BN6 8TA

500-year-old local in centre of village with three bars and dining rooms, a good choice of ales and popular food; bedrooms

This ancient and atmospheric pub is said to get its name from the papal bull designating it as a safe house for pilgrims and travellers to the great monastery at Lewes. The beamed main room on the right is a cosy haven in winter with a log fire in a sizeable inglenook fireplace, and efficient staff greet you at the bar counter where they serve Bedlam Benchmark, Timothy Taylors Landlord and guests such as Dark Star Revelation, Gun Project Babylon and 360° Pale #39 on handpump, 22 wines by the glass and a large choice of spirits. There are benches, scrubbed wooden tables and leather chesterfields on bare boards, and modern artwork and historic photos of the village on the walls; daily papers and background music. Two other rooms lead off to the left from the main entrance. You can sit in the garden under apple trees or on a terrace; the kitchen garden provides fruit, vegetables and herbs for the pub's menu. The bedrooms are well equipped and comfortable.

 Food is good and includes sandwiches, roasted camembert with tomato chutney, cured salmon with dill potato cake and fennel and beetroot salad, butternut squash, brie and pine nut pithivier, celeriac and sage beurre noisette, chicken ham hock and mushroom pie, smoked haddock chowder with poached duck egg, braised lamb shoulder with rosemary and dauphinoise potatoes, and puddings such as banana parfait with peanut butter ice-cream and poached pear with hazelnut pannacotta. *Benchmark main dish: beer-battered cod and chips £13.50. Two-course evening meal £21.00.*

Free house ~ Licensee Dominic Worrall ~ Real ale ~ Open 11-11 (10.30 Sun) ~
Bar food 12-2.30, 6-9.30; 12-9.30 Sat; 12-9 Sun ~ Restaurant ~ Children welcome ~
Dogs allowed in bar ~ Wi-fi ~ Quiz night second Sun of month ~ Bedrooms: /£140
Recommended by Nick Sharpe, Tony Scott, B and M Kendall

DONNINGTON
Blacksmiths 🛏

SU8501 Map 2

(01243) 785578 – www.the-blacksmiths.co.uk

B2201 S of Chichester; PO20 7PR

Neatly refurbished country pub with light rooms, attractive furnishings, enjoyable food and drink and seats outside; bedrooms

This spic and span white-painted pub, close to the Chichester Canal towpath, has been carefully refurbished from top to toe, and it looks lovely. The bar has pale wooden wall seats with scatter cushions, plush-topped stools and metal-legged tables on wide floorboards, an open fire, a rail hung with old hammers and other tools, and high wicker chairs against the counter where friendly staff serve a couple of changing ales from Arundel or Langham on handpump, alongside ten wines by the glass. Off to one side is a dining room with button-back grey leather wall seats beside an open fire, grey leather or wooden chairs around simple wooden tables, and watercolour pictures on the walls. To the other side of the bar is another dining room with similar furnishings and an alcove that's just right for a little group. A terrace, edged by neatly stacked logs and surrounded by glass panels to keep out the wind, has teak tables and chairs under parasols, a fire pit and far-reaching country views; they grow their own produce and keep chickens. Bedrooms are airy, attractive and comfortable, and breakfasts are good.

Using produce from their farm and kitchen garden and their own eggs, the rewarding food includes lunchtime sandwiches, tempura squid with chilli jam, twice-baked blue cheese soufflé, red pepper and halloumi or beef burgers with toppings, coleslaw and chips, sausages of the day with red wine jus, lamb curry, slow-cooked pork belly with crispy doughnut cheek and apple and raisin purée, buttermilk chicken with creamy mushrooms, gratin potatoes and cashew nut crumble, and puddings such as orange and almond polenta tart with mango sorbet and chocolate brownie with espresso ice-cream. *Benchmark main dish: fish of the day £16.00. Two-course evening meal £20.00.*

Free house ~ Licensees Will and Mariella Fleming ~ Real ale ~ Open 11-11; 11-5 Sun ~ Bar food 12-2.30, 6-9.30; 12-4, 6-10 Sat; 12-4 Sun ~ Restaurant ~ Children welcome ~ Dogs allowed in bar and bedrooms ~ Wi-fi ~ Live music Sun evenings in summer; see website ~ Bedrooms: £90/£110 *Recommended by Alan and Alice Morgan, Tony Smaithe, Simon and Alex Knight*

DUNCTON
Cricketers

SU9517 Map 3

(01798) 342473 – www.thecricketersduncton.co.uk
Set back from A285; GU28 0LB

Charming old coaching inn with friendly licensees, real ales, popular food and suntrap back garden

Handy for Goodwood, this old inn dates from at least the 1600s and got its present name from the 19th-c owner John Wisden, the cricketer who published the famous *Wisden Cricketers' Almanack*. The traditional bar has a display of cricketing memorabilia, a few standing timbers, simple seating and an open woodburning stove in an inglenook fireplace. Steps lead down to a dining room with farmhouse chairs around wooden tables. Dark Star Partridge, Langham Hip Hop, Triple fff Moondance and a guest from Firebird on handpump, nine wines by the glass and two farm ciders. There are picnic-sets out in front beneath the flowering window boxes and more on decked areas and under parasols on the grass in the picturesque back garden.

 Pleasing food includes lunchtime sandwiches (not Sunday), sticky duck salad, duo of mackerel, ham and eggs, trio of sausages with mash and onion gravy, tapenade-stuffed chicken breast stuffed with sautéed potatoes, wild mushroom, spinach and goats cheese risotto, beer-battered fresh haddock and chips, sizzling pork, pear and parsnip skillet, and puddings. *Benchmark main dish: steak and mushroom in ale pie £10.95. Two-course evening meal £19.00.*

Inn Company ~ Manager Martin Boult ~ Real ale ~ Open 11-11; 12-10.30 Sun ~ Bar food 12-2.30, 6-9; 12-9 Sat, Sun; brunch 11-midday (not Sun), hot snacks 3-6 ~ Children welcome ~ Dogs allowed in bar ~ Wi-fi *Recommended by Peter Barrett, Ruth May, Simon Sharpe*

EARTHAM
George ♀ ◖

SU9309 Map 2

(01243) 814340 – www.thegeorgeeartham.com
Signed off A285 Chichester–Petworth, from Fontwell off A27, from Slindon off A29; PO18 0LT

170-year-old pub in tucked-away village with country furnishings and contemporary touches, local ales and enjoyable food

There are some lovely walks and cycle routes in the rolling South Downs around this well run, friendly pub. The light and airy bar has a cheerful mix of customers and is prettily decorated with scatter cushions on a long wall pew, painted dining chairs around wood-topped tables (each set with fresh flowers and candles) on parquet flooring. There are sofas, armchairs, a dresser with country knick-knacks, beams, timbering, paintings on cream-painted walls above a grey-planked dado, stone bottles and books and three open fires; background music and board games. A beer named for the pub (from Otter) and guests such as Goldmark Liquid Gold, Hogs Back Surrey Nirvana and Langham Decennium 10 on handpump, 13 wines by the glass, 20 gins, 20 malt whiskies and farm cider. The large garden has picnic-sets on grass and seats and tables under a gazebo. Easy disabled access.

Creative food includes smoked salmon with quail eggs, wild mushrooms and poached egg on artisan toast, a pie of the day, lambs liver and bacon, thai green vegetable curry, pork tenderloin with turnip and potato dauphinoise and wholegrain mustard and madeira sauce, local venison wrapped in parma ham with vegetable medley and red wine jus, and puddings such as passion-fruit cheesecake and local stout sticky toffee pudding. *Benchmark main dish: steak burger with toppings, coleslaw and skinny fries £12.50. Two-course evening meal £18.00.*

Free house ~ Licensees James and Anita Thompson ~ Real ale ~ Open 11.30-11; 12-6 Sun; closed Mon ~ Bar food 12-3, 6-9; 12-4 Sun ~ Restaurant ~ Children welcome ~ Dogs allowed in bar *Recommended by Nick Sharpe, Alf Wright, Lionel Smith*

EAST DEAN   TV5597 Map 3

Tiger ♀ ⇐

(01323) 423209 – www.beachyhead.org.uk
Off A259 Eastbourne–Seaford; BN20 0DA

Pretty old pub with two little bars and a dining room, an informal and friendly atmosphere and own-brewed beers; bedrooms

The walks to the coast and along the clifftops of the Seven Sisters and up to Belle Tout Lighthouse and Beachy Head are splendid, so this charming old pub is always packed. The delightful cottage-lined green position is also a big draw and in warm weather customers sit on the grass here or at picnic-sets on the flower-filled terrace. You need to arrive early to be sure of a seat and they only take table reservations from October to March. The focal point of the little beamed main bar is the open woodburning stove in a brick inglenook, surrounded by polished horsebrasses; there are just a few rustic tables with benches, simple wooden chairs, a window seat and a long cushioned wall bench. The walls are hung with fish prints and a stuffed tiger's head, and a couple of hunting horns hang above the long bar counter. Friendly, attentive staff serve their own-brewed Beachy Head Legless Rambler and South Downs Ale (brewery tours available on request), Harveys Best, Long Man Golden Tipple and Long Blonde and St Austell Tribute on handpump, and nine wines by the glass. Down a step on the right is a small room with an exceptionally fine high-backed curved settle, a couple of other old settles and nice old chairs and wooden tables on coir carpeting; on the walls there's an ancient map of Eastbourne and Beachy Head and photographs of the pub. The dining room to the left of the main bar has a cream woodburner and hunting prints. Bedrooms are comfortable and breakfasts good.

As well as breakfasts from 8am, the food includes sandwiches, deep-fried whitebait, pâté of the day, beer-battered haddock and chips, stuffed pepper on moroccan-style couscous, chicken in provençale sauce with green beans, a fresh fish dish of the day, rump steak with garlic butter and chips, and puddings such as lemon posset and chocolate brownie. *Benchmark main dish: burger with relish, onion rings and chips £11.50. Two-course evening meal £20.50.*

Free house ~ Licensee Rebecca Vasey ~ Real ale ~ Open 8am-11pm ~ Bar food 12-3, 6-9 ~
Restaurant ~ Children welcome ~ Dogs allowed in bar ~ Wi-fi ~ Bedrooms: /£130
Recommended by Martin Day, David and Judy Robison

ERIDGE GREEN   TQ5535   Map 3
Nevill Crest & Gun ♀ ◖

(01892) 864209 – www.brunningandprice.co.uk/nevillcrestandgun
A26 Tunbridge Wells–Crowborough; TN3 9JR

**Handsome old building with lots of character, plenty to look at,
six real ales and enjoyable modern food**

This 500-year-old former farmhouse has been cleverly opened up and
extended with standing timbers and doorways keeping some sense
of separate rooms. Throughout, there are heavy beams (some carved),
panelling, rugs on wooden floors and woodburning stoves and open fires in
three fireplaces (the linenfold carved bressumer above one is worth seeking
out). Also, all manner of individual dining chairs around dark wood or
copper-topped tables, lots of pictures, maps and photographs relating to the
local area, and windowsills crammed with toby jugs, stone and glass bottles
and plants. Phoenix Brunning & Price Original, Hurst Founders Best Bitter,
Larkins Traditional, Long Man Best Bitter, Old Dairy Red Top, Tonbridge
Coppernob and Westerham Grasshopper on handpump, 15 wines by the glass
and 70 malt whiskies; daily papers, board games and background music.
There are a few picnic-sets in front of the building and teak furniture on the
back terrace, next to the newer dining extension with its large windows, light
oak rafters, beams and coir flooring.

Interesting food includes sandwiches, ham hock and tarragon croquettes with
piccalilli, crispy beef salad with chilli, watermelon and cashews, crab quiche with
horseradish and crème fraîche potato salad, pork and leek sausages with red wine and
onion gravy, braised lamb shoulder with dauphinoise potatoes and rosemary gravy, sea
trout with gnocchi, clams and seaweed butter, and puddings such as dark chocolate
brownie with salted caramel ice-cream and bread and butter pudding with apricot
sauce. *Benchmark main dish: rosemary and garlic chicken on pasta with wild
mushrooms and bacon £13.95. Two-course evening meal £19.00.*

Brunning & Price ~ Manager Ian Huxley ~ Real ale ~ Open 11-11 ~ Bar food 12-9 ~
Children welcome ~ Dogs allowed in bar ~ Wi-fi *Recommended by Hilary and Neil Christopher,
Edward May, Isobel May*

EWHURST GREEN   TQ7924   Map 3
White Dog

(01580) 830264 – www.thewhitedogewhurst.co.uk
*Turn off A21 to Bodiam at S end of Hurst Green, cross B2244, pass Bodiam Castle,
cross river then bear left uphill at Ewhurst Green sign; TN32 5TD*

**Welcoming family-run village pub with a nice little bar,
several real ales and popular food; bedrooms**

The view over Bodiam Castle (National Trust) from the seats and tables in
the back garden is stunning; do arrive early on a warm day. The bar has a
roaring log fire in an inglenook fireplace, hop-draped beams, wood panelling,
farm implements, horsebrasses and a mix of chairs and tables on old brick or
flagstoned floors. There's also a high-backed cushioned settle by the counter
where they keep four real ales from breweries such as Harveys, Old Dairy,
Pig & Porter and Tonbridge on handpump and 20 wines by the glass. A dining
room has sturdy wooden tables and chairs on more flagstones and the games

room has darts and pool; background music. The bedrooms are light and airy and one has a view over the castle.

Quite a choice of food includes sandwiches, thai-style fishcakes with spicy cucumber relish, pigeon breast with rhubarb compote, pot-roasted rabbit in creamy mustard and cider sauce, gnocchi with tomato and basil sauce topped with cheese, pork cheek with crispy ham hock bonbon and mustard apple sauce, whole bass with rosemary and sweet potato fries, local lamb with redcurrant and port sauce and mustard mash, and puddings such as plum crumble with crème anglaise and white chocolate brownie with chocolate sauce. *Benchmark main dish: grilled mackerel fillets with chilli jam on wild garlic mash £12.95. Two-course evening meal £20.00.*

Free house ~ Licensees Harriet and Dale Skinner ~ Real ale ~ Open 12-11 (11.30 Sat); 12-3, 6-11 in winter ~ Bar food 12-2 (2.30 weekends), 6.30-9 (9.30 Sat) ~ Restaurant ~ Children welcome ~ Dogs allowed in bar and bedrooms ~ Wi-fi ~ Bedrooms: /£95
Recommended by David Jackman, Rob Newland

FIRLE
Ram ◀

TQ4607   Map 3

(01273) 858222 – www.raminn.co.uk
Village signed off A27 Lewes–Polegate; BN8 6NS

Bustling country pub with three open fires, character rooms, good food and drink and seats in garden; bedrooms

There's usually a cheerful crowd of locals and walkers in this 500-year-old country inn, part of the Firle Estate. The main bar has a log fire, captain's and mate's chairs and a couple of gingham armchairs around dark pubby tables on bare boards or quarry tiles, gilt-edged paintings on dark brown walls, Harveys Best and guest beers such as Dark Star Hophead, Long Man Golden Tipple and Sharps Doom Bar on handpump, 21 wines by the glass and eight malt whiskies; service is welcoming and helpful. A cosy bar leads off here with another log fire, olive green built-in planked and cushioned wall seats and more dark chairs and tables on parquet flooring. Throughout, there are various ceramic ram's heads or skulls, black and white photos of the local area, candles in hurricane jars and daily papers; darts and toad in the hole. The back dining room is up some steps and overlooks the flint-walled garden where there are tables and chairs on a terrace and picnic-sets on grass; more picnic-sets under parasols at the front. The bedrooms are comfortable and the breakfasts good.

As well as lunchtime ciabattas, the menu includes venison medallions with celeriac purée, roast figs and crispy bocconcini (tiny mozzarella balls), sharing boards, roast butternut squash, goats cheese and marjoram cannelloni with blackened tomato sauce, beer-battered haddock and fries, confit wild rabbit arancini with wild mushrooms, sage butter and red wine jus, 21-day-aged sirloin steak with confit shallots and green peppercorn jus, and puddings such as salted caramel crème brûlée and white chocolate and ginger torte with rhubarb jam. *Benchmark main dish: burger with coleslaw and fries £12.00. Two-course evening meal £20.00.*

Free house ~ Licensee Hayley Bayes ~ Real ale ~ Open 9am-11pm ~ Bar food 9am-9.30pm ~ Children welcome away from bar ~ Dogs welcome ~ Wi-fi *Recommended by Michael Rugman, Douglas Power*

'Children welcome' means the pub says it lets children inside without any special restriction. If it allows them in, but to restricted areas such as an eating area or family room, we specify this. Some pubs may impose an evening time limit. We do not mention limits after 9pm as we assume children are home by then.

FLETCHING

Griffin 🍴⭐ 🍷 🛏 TQ4223 Map 3

(01825) 722890 – www.thegriffininn.co.uk

Village signposted off A272 W of Uckfield; TN22 3SS

Busy, gently upmarket inn with a fine wine list, real ales, bistro-style bar food and a big garden; pretty bedrooms

This is a handsome village and this civilised inn is very much its focal point. The beamed and quaintly panelled bar rooms have blazing log fires, old photographs and hunting prints, straightforward close-set furniture including some captain's chairs, and china on a delft shelf. A small bare-boarded serving area is off to one side and there's a cosy separate bar with sofas and a TV. The place gets pretty packed at weekends. Harveys Best and guests such as Beachy Head Legless Rambler and Gun Scaramanga on handpump, plus 20 wines by the glass from a good list (including champagne, prosecco and sweet wine); they hold a monthly wine club with supper (on a Thursday evening). At the bottom of the two-acre garden behind the pub is an outside bar and wood oven, tables and chairs under parasols and a stunning view over Sheffield Park; there more seats on a sandstone terrace. The bright and pretty bedrooms are comfortable and the breakfasts good. There are ramps for wheelchairs.

 Food is first class and includes lamb kofta with minted broad bean, green bean and lentil salad, tempura monkfish with spicy red pepper jam, butternut squash linguine with spinach, tomatoes, chilli and parmesan, wild boar and apple sausages with mustard mash and claret jus, fresh crab pasta with fennel, capers, chilli and garlic, duck breast with parmentier potatoes, chorizo and jus, and puddings such as vanilla pannacotta with limoncello syrup and chocolate brownie with chocolate sauce. *Benchmark main dish: beer-battered local cod and chips £13.50. Two-course evening meal £20.00.*

Free house ~ Licensees James Pullan and Samantha Barlow ~ Real ale ~ Open 12-11; 12-midnight Sat; 12-10.30 Sun ~ Bar food 12-2.30 (2.45 weekends), 7-9.30 (9 Sun) ~ Restaurant ~ Children welcome ~ Dogs allowed in bar ~ Wi-fi ~ Piano player Fri and Sat evenings, Sun lunch ~ Bedrooms: £70/£100 *Recommended by Alan Cowell, Carol and Barry Craddock, Daniel King*

FRIDAY STREET

Farm at Friday Street 🍷 🍺 TV6203 Map 3

(01323) 766049 – www.farmfridaystreet.com

B2104, Langney; BN23 8AP

Handsome 17th-c house with lots to look at, efficient staff serving popular food and drink and seats outside

There's plenty of both dining and drinking areas in what was once a farmhouse (although houses have replaced the fields that used to surround it) and the atmosphere is friendly and easy-going. The old core has many newer extensions, but it's been done well – the open-plan rooms are split by brick pillars into cosier areas with sofas, stools and all manner of wooden dining chairs and tables on bare boards, creamy coloured flagstones, oak or carpet. Throughout, there are open fires, big house plants, stubby church candles, frame-to-frame prints and pictures and farming implements. Caledonian Deuchars IPA, Langham Best Bitter, Long Man Long Blonde, St Austell Tribute and Sharps Doom Bar on handpump and 14 wines by the glass. The dining room is on two levels with timbered walls, glass partitions, a raised conical roof and an open kitchen. The front lawn has plenty of picnic-sets for warm weather.

Good quality, interesting food includes crab spring roll with crispy noodles and mango and chilli salsa, baked camembert with garlic and rosemary with cranberry compote, vegetable tagine, pork and leek sausages with mash and onion gravy, burger with toppings, barbecue sauce and skinny fries, smoked haddock mornay tart with soft-boiled egg and caper potato salad, braised half shoulder of lamb with dauphinoise potatoes and red wine and rosemary jus, and puddings such as banana parfait with butterscotch sauce and white chocolate pannacotta with honey jelly and popping candy. *Benchmark main dish: bass fillet, crayfish and pea risotto £15.50. Two-course evening meal £20.00.*

Whiting & Hammond ~ Manager Paul Worman ~ Real ale ~ Open 9am-11pm (10.30pm Sun) ~ Bar food 12-9.30 (9 Sun) ~ Restaurant ~ Children welcome ~ Dogs allowed in bar ~ Wi-fi
Recommended by John Harris, Anne and Ben Smith, Peter and Elizabeth May

HASTINGS
Crown ♀ ◀
TQ8109   Map 3

(01424) 465100 – www.thecrownhastings.co.uk
All Saints Street, Old Town; TN34 3BN

Informal and friendly corner pub with interesting food, local ales and simple furnishings – a good find

With an easy-going and gently quirky feel, this is a bustling little corner pub in the Old Town and just up from the sea. The simply furnished bar has bare boards, plain chairs around tables inlaid with games and set with posies of flowers, a log fire and plenty of windows to keep everything light (despite the dark paintwork); a snug has leather armchairs in front of another open fire, a couple of tables, and books and house plants on a windowsill and mantelpiece; board games. Stools line the counter where they keep four changing ales from breweries such as Bedlam, Franklins, Old Dairy and Three Legs on handpump, 15 good wines by the glass, 17 gins, 17 whiskies and local cider; service is friendly and helpful. There's a dining area at one end of the bar with scatter cushions on wall seats, mismatched chairs and some sizeable tables. Local art hangs on the walls (some for sale) and on our visit one window was hung with bright neckties and lined with shelves of local pottery, greetings cards and hand-made purses; daily papers and background jazz or blues music. Dogs and children receive a genuinely warm welcome. There are a few picnic-sets at the front.

As well as good weekend brunches (11am-2pm), the enterprising food includes lunchtime sandwiches on home-made ciabatta, spicy nduja (spreadable italian pork sausage) and salami hash brown with fried egg and home-made ketchup, sea spinach and wild garlic fritter with tomato and cayenne dip, roast squash and goats cheese wellington with roast root vegetable ratatouille, fish pie with parsley mash, wild mallard (breast, confit leg, crispy wing) with mushrooms, fondant parsnip and gravy, cod fillet with braised carrot and bay purée, and puddings such as cardamom and cinnamon chocolate slice and Sussex honey sponge pudding with vodka toffee sauce and salted caramel ice-cream. *Benchmark main dish: local pork chop with swede purée, braised chicory and pan juices £14.00. Two-course evening meal £20.00.*

Free house ~ Licensees Tess Eaton and Andrew Swan ~ Real ale ~ Open 11-11 (10.30 Sun) ~ Bar food 12-10 (9.30 Sun) ~ Children welcome ~ Dogs welcome ~ Wi-fi
Recommended by Alice Wright, Jenny Shepherd

It's very helpful if you let us know up-to-date food prices when you report on pubs.

 **HEATHFIELD**   TQ5920   Map 3

Star 🍺

(01435) 863570 – www.starinnoldheathfield.co.uk

Church Street, Old Heathfield, off A265/B2096 E; TN21 9AH

Pleasant old pub with bustling, friendly atmosphere, well liked food, a decent choice of drinks and seats in lovely garden

The irregular stonework at the bottom of this pub shows its great age – it was built in 1328 as a resting place for pilgrims on their way along this high ridge across the Weald to Canterbury. There are ancient heavy beams, built-in wall settles and window seats, panelling, inglenook fireplaces and a roaring winter log fire; a doorway leads to a similarly decorated room set up more for eating with wooden tables and chairs (one table has high-backed white leather dining chairs) and a woodburning stove. An upstairs dining room has a striking barrel-vaulted ceiling (it was originally a dormitory for masons working on the reconstruction of the church after a fire in 1348). Harveys Best and guests such as Jennings Sneck Lifter and Whitstable East India Pale Ale on handpump and 11 wines by the glass; background music. The very prettily planted garden has rustic furniture under smart umbrellas and lovely views of rolling pasture dotted with sheep and lined with oak trees.

Well liked food includes devilled whitebait with tartare sauce, chicken liver parfait, home-cured gammon and free-range eggs, free-range pork and ale sausages with balsamic onion gravy, steak and mushroom pie, goat curry with caramelised plantain and hot pepper sauce, tiger prawn and crayfish linguine with champagne sauce, game bourguignon with parsnip mash, and puddings such as plum and almond tart and chocolate mousse. *Benchmark main dish: fresh local fish and chips £12.50. Two-course evening meal £20.00.*

Free house ~ Licensees Mike and Sue Chappell ~ Real ale ~ Open 11.30-11; 12-10.30 Sun ~ Bar food 12-2.30, 6.30-9; 12-3, 6-8.30 Sun ~ Restaurant ~ Children welcome ~ Dogs welcome ~ Wi-fi *Recommended by Martin Day, Claire Adams, James Landor*

 HENLEY   SU8925   Map 2

Duke of Cumberland Arms 🏅 🍺

(01428) 652280 – www.dukeofcumberland.com

Off A286 S of Fernhurst; GU27 3HQ

Charming country pub with two character dining rooms, local beers and enjoyable food

It's hard to imagine that the lane on which this pretty little stone-built 16th-c cottage stands was once the main road from London to Chichester – coaches would stop here and change horses. Two small rooms have big scrubbed oak tables on brick or flagstoned floors, low ceilings, rustic decorations and an open fire. Harveys Best, Langham Best Bitter and Hip Hop and London Beer Factory Chelsea Blonde tapped from the cask and several wines by the glass; background music and board games. A dining extension has a light and more modern feel plus cosy sofas in front of a woodburning stove and fine views. From seats and picnic-sets on decking and in the charming big, tiered garden there are more beautiful Surrey Hills views; the many ponds contain trout.

Interesting food includes sandwiches, salt and pepper squid with garlic mayonnaise, baked goats cheese with honey and thyme roasted root vegetables, prawn, pea and crayfish risotto, chargrilled chicken with chorizo, avocado, mozzarella and sunblush tomato salad, venison ragoût with home-made pasta, herb-crusted lamb rack with dauphinoise potatoes and mint jus, whole lemon sole with lemon, caper and parsley butter, and puddings such as flambé pineapple with rum toffee sauce and coconut ice-cream and Valrhona chocolate sphere with marshmallow and salted caramel ice-cream. *Benchmark main dish: confit free-range pork belly with apple and calvados glaze and thyme and port jus £18.95. Two-course evening meal £25.00.*

Free house ~ Licensee Simon Goodman ~ Real ale ~ Open 11.45-11.30; 12-10.30 Sun ~ Bar food 12-2, 7-9; not Sun or Mon evenings ~ Restaurant ~ Well behaved children welcome ~ Dogs allowed in bar ~ Wi-fi *Recommended by John Evans, Miss A E Dare, S G N Bennett, John Davis*

HIGH HURSTWOOD
TQ4925 Map 3

Hurstwood 🏵 ♀

(01825) 732257 – www.thehurstwood.com

Hurstwood Road off A272; TN22 4AH

Friendly dining pub with chatty bar area, first class food and seats in the garden

The main emphasis here is on the excellent food – but regulars do drop in for a pint and a chat and they keep Harveys Best and IPA and Sharps Doom Bar on handpump, ten good wines by the glass and a fair choice of spirits and cocktails; staff are attentive. The U-shaped and beamed open-plan interior has high spindleback chairs against the counter, and an area beside the log fire in the tiled Victorian fireplace with a couple of leather sofas, armchairs and two tables. The dining areas have tables set with red gingham napkins, little plants and church candles in rustic ironwork candlesticks, chairs that range from farmhouse to captain's to cushioned dining ones on bare boards, hunting prints and other artwork on pale painted walls above a grey dado, various lamps and lanterns, and a piano (which does get played). French windows at one end open out to decking with seats and tables, which leads down to a grassed area with more seats.

 Delicious food includes sandwiches (not Sunday), pickled mackerel with cucumber and gin, chicken livers with cherries, whipped goats cheese with strawberries and candied beetroot, chicken caesar salad with anchovies, gnocchi with ricotta, spinach, broad beans and pine nuts, pig cheeks with swede mash, pak choi and port jus, bass fillets with lemon-roasted fennel, capers and beurre blanc, and puddings such as chocolate cheesecake with chocolate mousse and triple chocolate ice-cream and orange polenta cake with orange syrup. *Benchmark main dish: crab linguine £14.95. Two-course evening meal £22.00.*

Free house ~ Licensees Martin and Lenka Spanek ~ Real ale ~ Open 11.30-11; 12-5.30 Sun; closed Sun evening except bank holidays ~ Bar food 12-2.30, 6.30-9.30; 12-3 Sun ~ Children welcome ~ Dogs allowed in bar ~ Wi-fi *Recommended by Nick Sharpe, Charles Welch, Marianne and Peter Stevens, Miles Green*

HORSHAM
TQ1730 Map 3

Black Jug ♀

(01403) 253526 – www.brunningandprice.co.uk/blackjug

North Street; RH12 1RJ

Busy town pub with wide choice of drinks, efficient staff and rewarding food

There's a good mixed crowd of office workers, theatre-goers and couples here and the atmosphere is always lively. The single, large, early 20th-c room has a long central bar, a nice collection of sizeable dark wood tables and comfortable chairs on a stripped-wood floor, bookcases and interesting old prints and photographs above a dark wood-panelled dado on cream walls; board games. A spacious, bright conservatory has similar furniture and lots of hanging baskets. Harveys Best and Marstons Pedigree New World with guests such as Courage Directors and Butcombe Haka on handpump, 16 wines by the glass, 150 malt whiskies, 30 rums and farm cider. The pretty, flower-filled back terrace has plenty of garden furniture; parking is in the council car park next door, as the small one by the pub is reserved for staff and deliveries only.

Attractively presented food includes sandwiches, potted smoked mackerel with fennel and pickled cucumber salad, pigeon with black pudding bonbons and celeriac purée, moules marinière, cauliflower, aubergine and paneer dhal with chilli flatbread and coriander bhaji, steak in ale pie, salmon fillet with egg noodles and sesame and spring onion broth, lamb shoulder with dauphinoise potatoes and roasted carrots, confit duck leg with chorizo, butter bean and vegetable cassoulet, and puddings such as coconut and lime arancini with mango jelly and dark chocolate cheesecake with raspberry sorbet. *Benchmark main dish: beer-battered fish and chips £12.95. Two-course evening meal £20.50.*

Brunning & Price ~ Tenant Alastair Craig ~ Real ale ~ Open 11.30-11; 12-10.30 Sun ~ Bar food 12-10 (9.30 Sun) ~ Children welcome till 5pm ~ Dogs allowed in bar ~ Wi-fi
Recommended by Tony Scott, Simon Day, Millie and Peter Downing

HORSTED KEYNES
Crown 🏵 ♀

TQ3828 Map 3

(01825) 791609 – www.thecrown-horstedkeynes.co.uk
The Green; RH17 7AW

Super food in beamed 16th-c inn, character bar with real ales, fine wines and seats outside; bedrooms

Of course, much emphasis is placed on the highly thought-of food here (cooked by the chef-patron), but there's also a proper bar with heavy beams, big flagstones, a huge inglenook fireplace, simple furniture and chairs against the counter where they keep Harveys Best, Long Man Copper Hop and St Austells Tribute on handpump and 20 wines by the glass; staff are helpful and convivial. There's also a two-way fireplace with a leather sofa on one side and spreading dining areas on the other, with all manner of high-backed wooden and leather dining chairs around rustic-style tables on red-patterned carpet, more beams and timbering and bare brick walls. Seats in the terraced back garden overlook the village green and cricket pitch and there are picnic-sets at the front. The four comfortable bedrooms are decorated in a pretty country style.

Accomplished cooking includes sandwiches, chicken liver and foie gras parfait with red onion and chilli jam, potted crab with rosette of smoked salmon and dill crème fraîche, butternut squash, leek and parmesan risotto with truffle oil, beer-battered fish and chips, chicken, mushroom and leek pie, rump burger with toppings and chips, bass fillets with spring onion potoatoes, cockles, prawns and lemon butter, and puddings such as passion-fruit and white chocolate cheesecake with mango chilli salsa and mango sorbet and dark chocolate brownie with chocolate sauce and caramel ice-cream. *Benchmark main dish: calves liver and bacon with red wine jus £16.00. Two-course evening meal £22.00.*

Free house ~ Licensee Mark Raffan ~ Real ale ~ Open 12-3, 6-11; 12-5 Sun; closed Mon ~ Bar food 12-2.30, 6-9; 12-4.30 Sun ~ Restaurant ~ Children welcome ~ Dogs allowed in bar ~ Wi-fi ~ Bedrooms: £70/£90 *Recommended by Sally and David Champion, Penny and David Shepherd, Sophia and Hamish Greenfield, Geoff and Ann Marston*

LICKFOLD
SU9226 Map 2

Lickfold Inn ⭑○⭑ ♉

(01789) 532535 – www.thelickfoldinn.co.uk

NE of Midhurst, between A286 and A283; GU28 9EY

Sussex Dining Pub of the Year

Tudor country pub with impressive food in bars and upstairs restaurant, friendly staff, a thoughtful choice of drinks and attractive garden

It's a surprise to find this little gem tucked away in the countryside with such inventive and delicious food on offer. But this is no straightforward restaurant – it's a proper pub with a working bar and a great deal of easy-going character. The two bar rooms have heavy Tudor beams, a fine herringbone brick floor, comfortable sofas to each side of a woodburning stove, chapel chairs, armchairs, Georgian settles and more sofas with scatter cushions and nice old tables (some with fine in-laid panels); it's fun to be able to watch the kitchen hard at work behind a big glass window. Bowman Lapwing and Swift One and Langham Best Bitter on handpump, a dozen wines by the glass and several gins. Upstairs, the restaurant has more heavy beams, pale grey upholstered dining chairs around dark polished wood tables on bare boards, a few standing timbers and another woodburning stove. Outside, a terrace has plenty of seats and tables and there's also a garden across the drive on several levels with more seats, and a big enclosure of chickens.

 Using the best local, seasonal produce, the imaginative food includes enterprising bar nibbles that change daily plus foie gras parfait with rhubarb, salmon with cucumber, gin and seaweed, rapeseed tortellini with pumpkin and whey, hake with treacle bacon, salsify and wild mushrooms, pork loin with pigs head and onions, beef with oyster and salt-baked celeriac, and puddings such as bitter chocolate and blood orange and rosewater set cream with lychees and rapsberries; they also offer a two- and three-course set lunch. *Benchmark main dish: lamb with rape greens, yoghurt and gorse £26.00. Two-course evening meal £32.00.*

Free house ~ Licensee Tom Sellers ~ Real ale ~ Open 11.30-10; 11.30-11.30 Sat; 11.30-8.30 Sun; closed Mon, winter Tues, first two weeks Jan ~ Bar food 12-2, 7-9 ~ Restaurant ~ Children welcome ~ Dogs allowed in bar ~ Wi-fi *Recommended by Jack Trussler, Andrew and Michele Revell, Brian and Sally Wakeham*

LURGASHALL
SU9327 Map 2

Noahs Ark

(01428) 707346 – www.noahsarkinn.co.uk

Off A283 N of Petworth; GU28 9ET

Busy old pub in nice spot with neatly kept rooms, real ales and pleasing food using local produce

An inn since 1537, this old place is in a lovely spot overlooking the village green and cricket pitch. Inside, the simple, traditional bar, popular with locals, has a bustling atmosphere and bar stools by the counter where they serve Greene King IPA and Abbot and a guest such as Hogs Back TEA on handpump, 20 wines by the glass and a fine bloody mary. There are also beams, a mix of wooden chairs and tables, parquet flooring and an inglenook fireplace. Open to the top of the rafters, the dining room is spacious and airy with church candles and fresh flowers on light wood tables; a couple of comfortable sofas face each other in front of an open woodburning stove; background music and board games. The pub's border terrier is called Gillie and visiting dogs may get a dog biscuit. There are tables set out in a large side garden.

|¶| Well regarded food includes sandwiches, deep-fried crab puffs with shaved fennel salad and wilted garlic mayonnaise, chorizo scotch egg with home-made brown sauce, creamy chestnut mushroom pie with a crispy poached egg and chive sauce, free-range chicken leg with cream mash and garlic bread sauce, creamy moules marinière with frites, lamb rump with boulangère potatoes and cumberland jelly, and puddings such as passion-fruit crème brûlée and chocolate financier with popcorn and salted caramel ice-cream. *Benchmark main dish: burger with toppings, coleslaw and chips £12.75. Two-course evening meal £20.00.*

Greene King ~ Lease Henry Coghlan and Amy Whitmore ~ Real ale ~ Open 11-11; 11-midnight Sat; 12-10 (8 in winter) Sun ~ Bar food 12-2.30, 7-9.30; 12-3 Sun ~ Restaurant ~ Children welcome ~ Dogs allowed in bar ~ Wi-fi *Recommended by Colin McKerrow, Alastair and Sheree Hepburn, Edward May*

 MARK CROSS   TQ5831   Map 3
Mark Cross Inn ♀
(01892) 852423 – www.themarkcross.co.uk
A267 N of Mayfield; TN6 3NP

Sizeable pub with interconnected rooms, real ales and popular food, and good views from seats in the garden

In warm weather, the benches and tables on the terrace and the picnic-sets on grass get snapped up quickly by customers keen to enjoy the far-reaching views; there's also a children's play fort. Inside, it's a big place on several linked levels but kept cosy with church candles and open fires, shelves lined with books and stone bottles, gilt-edged mirrors, big clocks, large house plants and fresh flowers. There's all manner of seating from farmhouse, mate's and cushioned dining chairs to settles and stools grouped around dark shiny tables on rugs and bare boards, and the walls are lined almost frame to frame with photographs, prints, paintings and old newspaper cuttings. Helpful staff serve Caledonian Deuchars IPA, Fullers London Pride, Long Man Best and Shepherd Neame Spitfire on handpump and good wines by the glass; daily papers and background music.

|¶| As well as brunch (9-11am Thurs-Sun), the generously served all-day food includes sandwiches (until 6pm), ham hock and leek terrine with pickles, box-baked camembert with red onion marmalade, thai vegetable curry, burger with toppings, sweet mustard mayonnaise and fries, beer-battered cod and chips, free-range chicken with fondant potato, pea purée and madeira and mushroom jus, flat-iron steak with stuffed tomatoes, onion confit and skinny fries, and puddings such as chocolate brownie with chocolate sauce and strawberry pannacotta. *Benchmark main dish: braised shoulder of local lamb with herb and honey crust, gratin potatoes and red wine sauce £18.95. Two-course evening meal £21.00.*

Whiting & Hammond ~ Manager Amy Glenie ~ Real ale ~ Open 9am-11pm (midnight Fri, Sat); 9am-10.30pm Sun ~ Bar food 12-9.30 (9 Sun) ~ Restaurant ~ Children welcome ~ Dogs allowed in bar ~ Wi-fi *Recommended by Charles Welch, Caroline Sullivan, Edward Nile*

 **OVING**   SU9005   Map 2
Gribble Inn 🍺
(01243) 786893 – www.gribbleinn.co.uk
Between A27 and A259 E of Chichester; PO20 2BP

Own-brewed beers in bustling village pub with well liked bar food and pretty garden

For over 30 years, this 16th-c thatched pub has brewed its own ales. On handpump, these might include Fuzzy Duck, Gribble Ale, Pig's Ear, Plucking Pheasant, Quad Hopper, Reg's Tipple and three seasonal ales, such as Sussex Quad Hopper or strong Wobbler Ale; they also stock 30 gins, 30 vodkas and unusual rums. The chatty bar features a lot of heavy beams and timbering while the other various linked rooms have a cottagey feel and sofas around two roaring log fires; board games. The barn houses a venue for parties. There are seats outside in a covered area and more chairs and tables in the pretty garden with its apple and pear trees.

Using local, seasonal ingredients, the varied food includes gruyère cheese soufflé, home-smoked pigeon with poached pear and chestnuts, burger with toppings and chips, home-cooked ham and free-range eggs, beer-battered haddock and chips, slow-braised beef short ribs with root vegetable mash, rabbit leg with seared loin, mushroom duxelles and braised red cabbage, confit duck leg with braised gem lettuce and home-brewed cherry brandy jus, and puddings. *Benchmark main dish: slow-roast pork belly with mash and bacon £14.95. Two-course evening meal £18.00.*

Badger ~ Licensees Simon Wood and Nicola Tester ~ Real ale ~ Open 11-11; 12-9 Sun ~ Bar food 12-9; 12-4 Sun ~ Restaurant ~ Children welcome away from bar ~ Dogs allowed in bar ~ Wi-fi *Recommended by Dave Snowden, John Beeken, Ian and Barbara Rankin*

PETWORTH

SU9721 Map 2

Angel ⭐ 🍴 🍺 🛏

(01798) 342153 – www.angelinnpetworth.co.uk
Angel Street; GU28 0BG

Medieval building with 18th-c façade, chatty atmosphere in beamed bars, friendly service and good, interesting food; bedrooms

This is a smart town pub with the feel of a country inn, and we continue to get keen reports from our readers. The interconnected rooms have kept many of their original features. The front bar has beams, a log fire in an inglenook fireplace and an appealing variety of old wooden and cushioned dining chairs and tables on wide floorboards. It leads through to the main room with high chairs by the counter where they keep a beer named for the pub (from Langham) plus a guest such as Dorking Smokestack Lightnin' and Firebird Pacific Gem on handpump, 22 wines by the glass from an extensive list and a good range of malt whiskies and gins; board games. Staff are courteous and helpful. There's also high-backed brown leather and antique chairs and tables on pale wooden flooring, the odd milk churn and french windows to a three-level terrace garden. The cosy and popular back bar is similarly furnished, with a second log fire. If you'd like to stay overnight, bedrooms are comfortable and the breakfasts good.

Well thought-of food includes lunchtime sandwiches, sloe gin and beetroot-cured salmon with dill blini, confit lamb belly croquettes with wild garlic mayonnaise, red chard and jerusalem artichoke risotto, crispy skin free-range chicken with ginger broth and kale, guinea fowl salad with croutons, lardons and garlic dressing, calves liver with bacon, mash and gravy, confit duck leg with cherry jus and dauphinoise potatoes, venison and chestnut mushroom pie, skate wing with nut brown caper butter, and puddings. *Benchmark main dish: fish pie £14.00. Two-course evening meal £21.50.*

Free house ~ Licensee Murray Inglis ~ Real ale ~ Open 10.30am-11pm; 11.30-10.30 Sun ~ Bar food 12-2.30, 6.30-9.30; 12-2.30, 6-9 Sun ~ Children welcome ~ Dogs welcome ~ Wi-fi ~ Live jazz summer Sun 4pm ~ Bedrooms: £100/£140 *Recommended by David Jackman, Mr and Mrs P R Thomas, Tracey and Stephen Groves, John Evans*

RINGMER

TQ4313 Map 3

Cock 🍺 £

(01273) 812040 – www.cockpub.co.uk

Uckfield Road – blocked-off section of road off A26 N of village turn-off; BN8 5RX

Country pub with a wide choice of popular bar food, real ales in character bar and plenty of seats in the garden

You can be sure of a warm welcome in this 16th-c former coaching inn from the friendly licensees and their helpful staff. The unspoilt bar has traditional pubby furniture on flagstones, heavy beams, a log fire in an inglenook fireplace, Harveys Best and a couple of guests such as Beachy Head Legless Rambler and Dark Star Hophead on handpump, 12 wines by the glass and a dozen malt whiskies. There are also three dining areas; background music. Outside, on the terrace and in the garden, are lots of picnic-sets with views across open fields to the South Downs. The owners' dogs are called Bailey and Tally, and visiting dogs are offered a bowl of water and a chew. This is sister pub to the Highlands at Uckfield.

 An extensive choice of popular food includes sandwiches, deep-fried camembert with cranberry sauce, tiger prawns in garlic butter, honey-roast ham with free-range eggs, chickpea, courgette and coconut curry, local venison sausages with onion gravy, chicken florentine with spinach and cheese sauce, grilled whole plaice and chips, pork fillet in cream and dijon mustard sauce, and puddings such as spotted dick and treacle tart. *Benchmark main dish: steak in ale pie £11.75. Two-course evening meal £18.00.*

Free house ~ Licensees Ian, Val, Nick and Matt Ridley ~ Real ale ~ Open 11-3, 6-11.30; 11-10.30 Sun ~ Bar food 12-2 (2.30 Sat), 6-9.30; 12-8.30 Sun ~ Restaurant ~ Well behaved children welcome but no toddlers ~ Dogs allowed in bar ~ Wi-fi *Recommended by Ann and Colin Hunt, John Beeken, William Pace*

ROBERTSBRIDGE

TQ7323 Map 3

George 🛏

(01580) 880315 – www.thegeorgerobertsbridge.co.uk

High Street; TN32 5AW

Former coaching inn with good food and ales and seats in courtyard garden; comfortable bedrooms

Quietly civilised and well run, this handsome old village inn is popular with both locals and visitors. There's a log fire in a brick inglenook fireplace with a leather sofa and a couple of armchairs in front – just the place for a quiet pint and a chat – plus high bar stools by the counter where they serve Harveys Best and Franklins English Garden on handpump, good wines by the glass and a farm cider. A dining area leads off here with elegant high-backed beige tartan or leather chairs around a mix of tables (each with fresh flowers and a tea-light) on stripped floorboards and more tea-lights in a small fireplace; background music. The back terrace has plenty of seats and tables. Bedrooms are comfortable and the breakfasts tasty.

 Good, enjoyable food includes chorizo and thyme terrine with chutney, baby camembert stuffed with rosemary and garlic, sharing platters, ham and free-range eggs, cheese burger with toppings, relish and chips, pumpkin, butternut squash and brie tart, chicken wrapped in smoked bacon with creamy herb sauce, lamb steak with roasted root vegetable purée and minted jus, tempura cod and chips, and puddings such as lemon posset and a chocolate dish of the day. *Benchmark main dish: slow-roasted local pork with wholegrain mustard and cider sauce £14.50. Two-course evening meal £20.00.*

Free house ~ Licensees John and Jane Turner ~ Real ale ~ Open 12-11; 12-9 Sun;
closed Mon ~ Bar food 12-2.30, 6.30-9; 12-7 Sun ~ Children welcome but must be
accompanied by an adult at all times ~ Dogs allowed in bar ~ Wi-fi
Recommended by David Jackman, Peter Meister, Valerie Sayer

RYE
Ship
TQ9120   Map 3

(01797) 222233 – www.theshipinnrye.co.uk
The Strand, at the foot of Mermaid Street; TN31 7DB

**Informal and prettily set old inn with unusual furnishings,
local ales and tasty food; bedrooms**

This 16th-c inn was once used as a warehouse for storing goods seized
from smugglers – it's now an easy-going place with an unusual blend
of quirkiness and comfort. The ground floor is opened up, from the sunny
big-windowed front part to a snugger section at the back, with a log fire in
the stripped-brick fireplace below a stuffed boar's head. Flooring varies from
one area to the next: composition, stripped boards, flagstones, a bit of carpet
in the armchair corner. There are beams and timbers, and a mixed bag of
rather second-hand-feeling furnishings – a cosy group of overstuffed leather
armchairs and sofa, random stripped or Formica-topped tables and various
café chairs – that suit it nicely, as do the utilitarian bulkhead wall lamps.
Long Man Best Bitter, Old Dairy Gold Top and Rother Valley Boadicea on
handpump and several wines by the glass; board games. In addition to the
simply furnished but comfortable bedrooms, the pub rents a 300-year-old
single-storey cottage and 500-year-old house. There are picnic-sets and
a couple of cheerful oilcloth-covered tables out by the quiet lane.

As well as weekend breakfasts (8-11.30am), the good food includes lunchtime
sandwiches, duck egg scotch egg with fennel salad, hot wings with chilli sauce
and buttermilk dip, breaded haddock and fries, bacon chop with fried potatoes and
egg, curried sweet potato and aubergine with herb yoghurt, venison with pancetta,
confit garlic and cabbage, hake fillet with chestnut mushrooms and lemon butter,
and puddings. *Benchmark main dish: burger with toppings, chipotle mayonnaise
and fries £13.75. Two-course evening meal £19.00.*

Enterprise ~ Lease Karen Northcote ~ Real ale ~ Open 8am-11pm (10.30pm Sun) ~
Bar food 12-3 (3.30 weekends), 6-10; light snacks 3.30-5 weekends ~ Children welcome ~
Dogs allowed in bar and bedrooms ~ Wi-fi ~ Bedrooms: £90/£110 *Recommended by David
Jackman, Stephen Shepherd, Peter Meister, Paul Rampton, Mike and Eleanor Anderson,
Julie Harding*

RYE
Ypres Castle ◀
TQ9220   Map 3

(01797) 223248 – www.yprescastleinn.co.uk
Gun Garden; steps up from A259, or down past Ypres Tower; TN31 7HH

**Traditional pub with several real ales, quite a choice of bar food
and seats in garden**

Perched beside a stepped path just beneath the medieval Ypres Tower,
this bustling pub has views down over the River Rother from its
sheltered garden. Inside, it's unpretentious and traditional: the main bar has
wall banquettes with pale blue cushions, an open fire in a stone fireplace
with a mirror above and easy chairs in front, assorted chairs and tables
(each set with a modern oil lamp) and local artwork. Stools line the blue-
panelled counter where they keep Harveys Best and guests such as Adnams

Broadside, Long Man Long Blonde, Old Dairy Copper Top and Timothy Taylors Landlord on handpump, eight wines by the glass and farm cider; background music and board games. The back dining room has paintings and pictures of Rye and similar furnishings to the bar; there's another dining room at the front.

 Quite a choice of pleasing food includes baguettes, crayfish and avocado salad, quiche of the day, roasted vegetable and red onion marmalade tower topped with goats cheese, honey-roast ham with duck egg and chips, smoked haddock, salmon and pea fishcakes with wilted spinach, local lamb hotpot with mash, and puddings such as chocolate fudge cake and apple crumble. *Benchmark main dish: burger with toppings, an egg and chips £10.50. Two-course evening meal £18.00.*

Free house ~ Licensee Garry Dowling ~ Real ale ~ Open 12-11 (10.30 Sun) ~ Bar food 12-3, 6-9 (8 Fri); 12-3 Sun ~ Children welcome ~ Dogs welcome ~ Wi-fi ~ Live music Fri and Sun evenings *Recommended by M and J White, Stephen Shepherd, Jo Garnett, Tony Scott*

 SALEHURST　　　　　　　　　　　　　　　　　　TQ7424　Map 3

Salehurst Halt ◖ £

(01580) 880620 – www.salehursthalt.co.uk

Village signposted from Robertsbridge bypass on A21 Tunbridge Wells–Battle; Church Lane; TN32 5PH

Bustling country local in quiet hamlet with easy-going atmosphere, real ales, well liked bar food and seats in pretty back garden

There's always a cheerful crowd of chatty locals here – especially on Wednesday evenings when the bellringers from the church next door pile in. To the right of the door is a small stone-floored area with a couple of tables, a settle, a TV and an open fire. Furniture includes a nice long scrubbed pine table, a couple of sofas and a mix of more ordinary pubby tables and wheelback and mate's chairs on the wood-strip floor; occasional background music, board games and books on shelves. Dark Star American Pale Ale, Harveys Best and Isfield Flapjack on handpump, farm cider, several malt whiskies and eight wines by the glass. The cottagey and charming back garden has views over the Rother Valley and the summer barbecues and pizzas from the wood-fired oven are extremely popular; a terrace has metal chairs and tiled tables.

Food is highly thought-of and includes home-cured gravadlax, chicken liver parfait with chutney, lager-battered fish and chips, spinach, squash and goats cheese pie, burgers with toppings and chips, fresh fish of the day, pork schnitzel with fennel, green bean and olive salad, lemon and thyme chicken with couscous, and puddings such as salted caramel torte and rhubarb bakewell sponge. *Benchmark main dish: goat curry £12.00. Two-course evening meal £19.00.*

Free house ~ Licensee Andrew Augarde ~ Real ale ~ Open 12-11.30 (10.30 Sun); closed Mon ~ Bar food 12-2.30, 7-9.30; 12.30-3 Sun ~ Children welcome ~ Dogs allowed in bar ~ Wi-fi *Recommended by Peter Meister, B and M Kendall, Nick Sharpe*

SOUTH HARTING　　　　　　　　　　　　　　　　　SU7819　Map 2

White Hart ⇛ ♀

(01730) 825124 – www.the-whitehart.co.uk

B2146 SE of Petersfield; GU31 5QB

Charming old village pub, carefully renovated, with a good mix of locals and visitors, enjoyable food and ales, and seats in garden; bedrooms

If you stay in the comfortable, character bedrooms here you can make the most of the lovely surrounding countryside – and Uppark (National Trust) is close by. It's a 16th-c, sympathetically renovated village inn with plenty of charm. The bars and dining area have beams and standing timbers, a couple of woodburning stoves and an open fire, bare boards and flagstones, and an attractive mix of cushioned wooden dining chairs, cushioned window seats and settles, leather armchairs and all sorts of rustic tables; there's a mural of a white hart, country prints, antlers, candles and fresh flowers. Friendly staff serve Upham Punter and Tipster and a guest beer such as Wadworths 6X on handpump, 17 wines by the glass (from Berry Brothers of London), a dozen malt whiskies and farm cider. The terrace and garden have seats and picnic-sets under parasols, and there's a fine magnolia.

As well as serving breakfasts to non-residents (7.30-10am weekdays, 8-10am weekends), the good, interesting food uses the best local, seasonal produce: baguettes, moules marinière, duck liver parfait with smoked duck bacon and pineapple, sharing boards, thai corn cakes with butternut foam and baby corn, burger with celeriac and horseradish slaw and fries, sea bream with marinated grapes, baby fennel, Pernod butter and potato galette, guinea fowl breast with confit wing, potato pressing and chicken emulsion, and puddings such as rhubarb soufflé with rhubarb custard ice-cream and popcorn parfait with caramelised banana, banana bread and peanut praline. *Benchmark main dish: ham hock, duck egg and chips £12.50. Two-course evening meal £21.00.*

Upham ~ Manager Dana Tase ~ Real ale ~ Open 7.30am-11pm; 8am-11pm Sat, Sun ~ Bar food 12-3, 6-9 (9.30 Fri, Sat); 12-3, 6-8.30 Sun ~ Restaurant ~ Children welcome ~ Dogs allowed in bar and bedrooms ~ Wi-fi ~ Live music (see website); quiz first Sun of month 5.30pm ~ Bedrooms: £104/£124 *Recommended by Douglas Power, Anne and Ben Smith, Daphne and Robert Staples*

TICEHURST
Bell 🏠
TQ6830 Map 3

(01580) 200234 – www.thebellinticehurst.com
High Street; TN5 7AS

Carefully restored inn with heavily beamed rooms, real ales and good wines by the glass, popular food and friendly service; bedrooms

There's plenty of history and character here and the renovations were done with great care. The heavily beamed bar has an inglenook fireplace, tables surrounded by a mix of cushioned wooden dining chairs on bare boards, some quirky decorations such as a squirrel in a rocking chair, and stools by the counter where cheerful staff serve Firebird Heritage XX, Harveys Best and Long Man Long Blonde on handpump, seven wines by the glass and a dozen malt whiskies. The dining room continues from the bar and is similarly furnished, with the addition of cushioned wall settles and an eclectic choice of paintings on the red walls; background music. A snug has comfortable sofas grouped around a low table in front of another open fire, interesting wallpaper, a large globe, an ancient typewriter and various books and pieces of china. What was the carriage room holds a long sunken table with benches on either side (perfect for an informal party) and there's an upstairs function room too. At the back is a courtyard garden with seats and tables and built-in cushioned seating up steps on an upper part. The bedrooms in the coaching inn are comfortable and very individually decorated and there are also separate lodges, each with their own little garden built around a fire pit.

Pleasing food includes lunchtime sandwiches, pheasant terrine with spiced apple chutney, moules marinière, pea and mint risotto, rabbit loin, liver and kidney with beetroot gratin and game jus, beer-battered fish and triple-cooked chips, baby chicken with romesco sauce, butterflied black bream with roasted cherry tomatoes, beef short rib with barbecue sauce and mash, ox liver with bacon and sweet red onion, and puddings such as dark chocolate fondant with pistachio ice-cream and coconut crème brûlée. *Benchmark main dish: burger with cheese and triple-cooked chips £13.50. Two-course evening meal £20.00.*

Free house ~ Licensee Howard Canning ~ Real ale ~ Open 7am-midnight ~ Bar food 12-3, 6-9.30; 12-4, 6-9 Sun ~ Restaurant ~ Children welcome ~ Dogs allowed in bar and bedrooms ~ Wi-fi ~ Bedrooms: /$150 *Recommended by David Jackman, Roger and Anne Newbury, Martin Day, Carol and Barry Craddock*

TILLINGTON
SU9621 Map 2
Horse Guards 🎯 ♟ 🛏

(01798) 342332 – www.thehorseguardsinn.co.uk

Off A272 Midhurst–Petworth; GU28 9AF

300-year-old inn with beams, panelling and open fires in rambling rooms, inventive food and charming garden; cottagey bedrooms

With a gently civilised atmosphere, excellent food and a thoughtful range of drinks, it's not surprising that we get consistently high praise from our readers for this 18th-c inn. The neatly kept, beamed front bar has good country furniture on bare boards, a chesterfield in one corner and a lovely view beyond the village to the Rother Valley from a seat in the big panelled bow window. High bar chairs line the counter where they keep Harveys Best and Langham Halfway to Heaven on handpump, 17 wines by the glass, home-made sloe gin and local farm juices. Other rambling beamed rooms have similar furniture on brick floors, rugs and original panelling and there are fresh flowers throughout; background music and board games. In warm weather the leafy, lush and sheltered garden has picnic-sets, day beds, deck chairs and even a hammock, and there's also a charming terrace. The cosy country bedrooms are comfortable and breakfasts are good. Constable and Turner both painted the medieval church with its unusual spire; Petworth House (National Trust) is nearby.

Delicious food includes lunchtime sandwiches, half pint of home beech- and oak-smoked shell-on prawns with bloody mary mayonnaise, deep-fried parsnips with honey and mustard dip, spiced pork and pigeon burger with cucumber and mint yoghurt, cauliflower and cheddar cake with celeriac, rocket and red onion salad and walnut dressing, paella with chorizo, salmon, mullet, cod, mussels, clams, prawns and rosemary, tamarind and soy pork shoulder with sticky rice, pak choi and asian peanut salad, and puddings such as sticky ginger parkin with muscovado sauce and cinnamon ice-cream and rhubarb mess with rose water and almond meringue. *Benchmark main dish: venison haunch with spelt, pearl barley, root vegetable and linseed and lentil risotto £17.50. Two-course evening meal £22.00.*

Enterprise ~ Lease Sam Beard ~ Real ale ~ Open 12-midnight ~ Bar food 12-2.30, 6.30-9 (9.30 Fri); 12-3, 6-9.30 Sat; 12-3.30, 6.30-9 Sun ~ Children welcome ~ Dogs welcome ~ Wi-fi ~ Bedrooms: £90/$100 *Recommended by Ron and June Buckler, John Evans, Richard Dilnot, Ann and Colin Hunt, Richard Tilbrook, Miss A E Dare*

UCKFIELD
TQ4720 Map 3
Highlands

(01825) 762989 – www.highlandsinn.co.uk

Eastbourne Road/Lewes Road; TN22 5SP

Busy, well run pub with plenty of space, real ales and well thought-of food; seats outside

Our favourite spot in this big, bustling place is the area around the bar counter where customers chat over a pint or a glass of wine or read the newspapers: high tartan benches, high leather chairs around equally high tables and armchairs here and there. Harveys Best and a couple of guests such as Black Cat Original and Dark Star Hophead on handpump, 15 wines by the glass and a dozen malt whiskies. Service from friendly, helpful young staff is good. The large, spreading restaurant on the right is split into two by a dividing wall with bookcase wallpaper, and has painted rafters in high ceilings, big glass lamps and walls decorated with local photographs and animal pictures. Also, all manner of cushioned dining and painted farmhouse chairs, long chesterfield sofas, upholstered banquettes and scatter cushions on settles around wooden tables on the part carpeted, part wooden and part ceramic flooring; background music. There's also an end bar with more long chesterfields, a pool area, TV, fruit machine and an open fire. Outside is a decked smoking shelter, a children's play area and picnic-sets on a terrace and on grass. This is sister pub to the Cock at Ringmer.

Food is very popular and includes sandwiches, ham hock terrine with piccalilli, baked camembert with chutney, roasted vegetable lasagne, a pie of the day, lamb, beef or chicken burger with toppings, coleslaw and fries, smoked haddock in creamy cheese, leek and mustard sauce, gammon steak with a fried egg and pineapple, calves liver and bacon with red onion gravy, and puddings such as milk chocolate and orange bavarois with nut and coconut bonbon and banoffi pie. *Benchmark main dish: chicken breast topped with cheese and bacon in barbecue cream sauce £10.95. Two-course evening meal £19.00.*

Ridley Inns ~ Managers Ian, Val, Nick and Matt Ridley ~ Real ale ~ Open 11-11 (midnight Sat); 11-10.30 Sun ~ Bar food 12-2.30, 6-9.30; 12-9.30 Sat; 12-6 Sun ~ Restaurant ~ Children welcome ~ Dogs allowed in bar ~ Wi-fi *Recommended by Mike and Eleanor Anderson, Tony and Wendy Hobden*

WARNINGLID
Half Moon ♀

TQ2425 Map 3

(01444) 461227 ~ www.thehalfmoonwarninglid.co.uk
B2115 off A23 S of Handcross or off B2110 Handcross–Lower Beeding; RH17 5TR

Simply furnished pub with real ales, rewarding food, lots of wines by the glass and seats in sizeable garden; bedrooms

Although there's obviously a strong emphasis on the imaginative food here, the lively locals' bar has a proper pubby atmosphere, straightforward wooden furniture on bare boards and a small Victorian fireplace; a room just off here has oak beams and flagstones. A couple of steps lead down to the dining areas, which have a mix of wooden chairs, cushioned wall settles and nice old tables on floorboards, plank panelling and bare brick, and old village photographs; there's also another open fire and a glass-covered well. Adnams Broadside, Harveys Best and Hurst Founders Best Bitter on handpump, around 18 wines by the glass, several malt whiskies and a farm cider. The sheltered, sizeable garden has picnic-sets on a lawn and a spectacular avenue of trees with uplighters that glow at night-time. Bedrooms are contemporary and comfortable and the breakfasts highly rated.

Well liked food includes smoked salmon with horseradish and potato salad, chicken liver parfait with chutney, chicken curry, local sausages with mash and onion gravy, burgers with toppings and chips, chargrilled halloumi with ratatouille, beer-battered cod and chips, and puddings such as double chocolate brownie with white chocolate ice-cream and sticky toffee pudding. *Benchmark main dish: calves liver and bacon with red onion marmalade gravy £14.50. Two-course evening meal £21.00.*

Free house ~ Licensee James Amico ~ Real ale ~ Open 11.30-3, 5.30-11; 11.30-11 Sat;
12-9 Sun ~ Bar food 12-2, 6-9.30; 12-3 Sun ~ Restaurant ~ Children welcome ~ Dogs allowed
in bar ~ Wi-fi ~ Bedrooms: /£120 *Recommended by John Harris, Belinda May, Sophie Ellison,
Andrew Stone*

WEST HOATHLY

TQ3632   Map 3

Cat 🏅 ⚐ 🛏

(01342) 810369 – www.catinn.co.uk

Village signposted from A22 and B2028 S of East Grinstead; North Lane; RH19 4PP

**16th-c inn with old-fashioned bar, airy dining rooms, local real ales,
tempting food and seats outside; lovely bedrooms**

You must certainly book a table in advance at this busy old place as
it's extremely popular. The friendly hands-on landlord welcomes both
drinkers and diners and the lovely old bar has beams, proper pubby tables
and chairs on an old wooden floor, and a fine log fire in an inglenook
fireplace. Harveys Best and Old Ale and guests such as Black Cat Original
and Larkins Traditional on handpump, as well as local cider and apple juice
and 20 wines by the glass (plus five locally made sparkling ones); look out
for the glass cover over the 75-ft well. The light, airy dining rooms have a
nice mix of wooden dining chairs and tables on pale wood-strip flooring, and
throughout there are hops, china platters, brass and copper ornaments and
a gently upmarket atmosphere. The contemporary-style garden room has
glass doors that open on to a terrace with teak furniture. The cocker spaniel
is called Harvey. Bedrooms are comfortable, pretty and well equipped, and
breakfasts are good. Steam train enthusiasts can visit the Bluebell Railway,
and the Priest House in the village is a fascinating museum in a cottage
endowed with an extraordinary array of ancient anti-witch symbols.
Parking is limited.

 Particularly good food using local suppliers includes sandwiches, scotch egg with
smoked bacon mayonnaise, bacon and leek fishcake with a poached egg and
béarnaise sauce, burger with toppings, confit onion and chips, corn-fed chicken with
potato terrine, turnip and mustard velouté, lamb rump with boulangère potatoes and
red onion and port purée, sea trout with samphire, spring onion, baby gem and beurre
blanc, and puddings such as bread and butter pudding with crème anglaise and treacle
tart with vanilla ice-cream. *Benchmark main dish: steak and mushroom in ale pie
£14.75. Two-course evening meal £25.00.*

Free house ~ Licensee Andrew Russell ~ Real ale ~ Open 12-11; 12-4 Sun ~ Bar food 12-2,
6-9; 12-2.30, 6-9.30 Fri, Sat; 12-2.30 Sun ~ Children over 7 welcome ~ Dogs allowed in bar
and bedrooms ~ Wi-fi ~ Bedrooms: £85/£120 *Recommended by Nick Lawless, S G N Bennett,
Martin Day, Tina Wright, Tony Scott*

WITHYHAM

TQ4935   Map 3

Dorset Arms ⚐ 🛏

(01892) 770278 – www.dorset-arms.co.uk

B2110; TN7 4BD

**Friendly, bustling inn with beamed rooms, real ales and good wines,
interesting food and seats in garden; bedrooms**

Part of the Buckhurst Estate, this 18th-c inn is owned by the current Lord
De La Warr, and although there is a strong emphasis on the particularly
good food, it's a proper pub with a working bar. To the left, the friendly and
informal beamed bar has fender seats around an open fire, scatter cushions
on a built-in wall seat, a couple of armchairs, a few simple seats and tables,

and darts. Harveys Best and a couple of guests such as Adnams Southwold and Long Man Long Blonde on handpump and good wines by the glass, served by friendly, courteous staff. The dining room has a cottagey feel with pretty curtains, bookshelves to each side of a small fireplace, horse pictures and paintings, rosettes and pieces of china, a long red leather wall seat and wheelback and farmhouse chairs around dark wooden tables. A small room leads off with high-backed red leather chairs around more dark tables, a big ornate gilt-edged mirror, antlers and a chandelier; a lower room with contemporary seats and tables has a retractable roof. As well as seats on the front terrace and picnic-sets on grass, there are steep steps that lead up to a lawned garden with more picnic-sets. The six bedrooms are attractively decorated and comfortable.

🍴 Rewarding food includes crab on toast, scotch egg with mustard mayonnaise, smoked aubergine and purple sweet potato with feta cheese and olives, burger with toppings and chips, Estate sausages and mash, chicken, bacon and avocado salad, whole lemon sole with brown shrimps, samphire and frites, duck breast with roasted root vegetables and honey and five-spice dressing, bavette steak and frites, and puddings such as chocolate and hazelnut brownie with hot fudge sauce and lemon posset. *Benchmark main dish: griddled flat-iron chicken with frites and salad £13.00. Two-course evening meal £20.00.*

Free house ~ Licensee Charlie Blundell ~ Real ale ~ Open 12-11 (10.30 Sun) ~ Bar food 12-2.30, 6-9; 12-9 Sat; 12-8 Sun ~ Restaurant ~ Children welcome ~ Dogs allowed in bar and bedrooms ~ Wi-fi ~ Bedrooms: /£105 *Recommended by Nigel and Jean Eames, Gerry and Rosemary Dobson*

Also Worth a Visit in Sussex

Besides the fully inspected pubs, you might like to try these pubs that have been recommended to us and described by readers. Do tell us what you think of them: feedback@goodguides.com

ALBOURNE — TQ2514
Ginger Fox (01273) 857888
Take B2117 W from A23; pub at junction with A281; BN6 9EA
Thatched country dining pub with simple rustic interior, emphasis on restaurant side (there is a small bar area serving local ales such as Harveys), highly regarded modern cooking, not cheap but they also do a good value two-course lunch menu (Mon-Fri), lots of wines by the glass from good list, friendly professional service; children welcome, attractive garden with South Downs views, play area, open all day. *(John Evans)*

ALCISTON — TQ5005
Rose Cottage (01323) 870377
Village signposted off A27 Polegate–Lewes; BN26 6UW Part tile-hung pub (two cottages) under new licensees; simple furnishings in bar and dining rooms, beams, log fires and some country bric-a-brac, good popular food from pub favourites up, Burning Sky, Harveys and a guest, several wines by the glass, friendly helpful service; children and dogs welcome, tables in front garden, you can walk straight to the South Downs from here, three self-catering apartments, closed Sun evening. *(Stuart and Diana Hughes, Michael Rugman)*

ALFOLD BARS — TQ0333
Sir Roger Tichborne
(01403) 751873 *B2133 N of Loxwood; RH14 0QS* Renovated and extended beamed country pub keeping original nooks and crannies, five well kept ales including local Firebird and Youngs, popular well presented food (not Sun evening) from varied reasonably priced menu, friendly prompt service, flagstones and log fires, restaurant; children welcome, dogs in bar, back terrace and sloping lawn with lovely rural views, good walks, open all day. *(Tony and Wendy Hobden)*

ALFRISTON — TQ5203
Olde Smugglers (01323) 870241
Waterloo Square; BN26 5UE Black-beamed 14th-c village inn under new management; wood and brick floors, panelling and various nooks and crannies, sofas by big inglenook, Harveys and a couple of guests, Weston's Old Rosie cider and half a dozen wines by the glass, reasonably priced traditional food (all day summer, all day Fri-Sun winter) from sandwiches to daily specials, conservatory; background music,

live last Weds of month; children and dogs welcome, tables on back suntrap terrace and lawn, four bedrooms (two sharing bathroom), open all day. *(Tony Scott, John Beeken)*

AMBERLEY   TQ0211
Bridge (01798) 831619
Houghton Bridge, off B2139; BN18 9LR Welcoming open-plan dining pub, comfortable and relaxed, with pleasant bar and two-room dining area, candles on tables, log fire, wide range of popular reasonably priced food (not Sun evening) from good sandwiches up, well kept ales including Harveys, cheerful efficient young service; children and dogs welcome, seats out in front, more tables in enclosed side garden, handy for station, open all day. *(Tony Scott)*

AMBERLEY   TQ0313
Sportsmans (01798) 831787
Crossgates; Rackham Road, off B2139; BN18 9NR Popular 17th-c pub with enjoyable fairly priced food and three well kept ales including Harveys, friendly efficient young staff, three bars including brick-floored one with darts, great views over Amberley Wildbrooks nature reserve from pretty back conservatory restaurant and tables outside; dogs welcome, good walks, five neat bedrooms, open all day. *(Tony Scott, Alastair and Sheree Hepburn)*

ANGMERING   TQ0604
Lamb (01903) 774300
The Square; BN16 4EQ Airy updated village coaching inn, enjoyable food (not Sun evening) from varied menu including good value two-course lunch, ales such as Fullers and Harveys from light wood servery, good choice of wines by the glass, friendly service, painted half-panelling and wood-strip floors, inglenook log fire in bar, woodburner on raised plinth in restaurant; children welcome, modernised bedrooms, open all day. *(Andrew Stone)*

ANGMERING   TQ0704
Spotted Cow (01903) 783919
High Street; BN16 4AW Up to six well kept ales including Harveys, Sharps and Timothy Taylors, decent wines by the glass and good choice of popular food from traditional choices up, efficient friendly service, smallish bar to the left, long dining extension with large conservatory on right, two fires; occasional live music, regular quiz nights, free wi-fi; children and dogs (in bar) welcome, disabled access (outside gents'), hedged garden with pretty flower borders, also lower garden with country views, boules and play area, nice walk to Highdown Hill fort, open all day Fri-Sun. *(John Beeken, Tony and Wendy Hobden)*

ARDINGLY   TQ3430
★ **Gardeners Arms** (01444) 892328
B2028 2 miles N; RH17 6TJ Well liked

food from sandwiches and pub favourites up in old linked rooms, Badger beers, pleasant efficient service, standing timbers and inglenooks, scrubbed pine on flagstones and broad boards, old local photographs, mural in back part, lighted candles and nice relaxed atmosphere; children and dogs welcome, disabled facilities, café-style furniture on pretty terrace and in side garden, opposite South of England showground and handy for Borde Hill Garden and Wakehurst Place (NT), open all day. *(Martin Day)*

ARLINGTON   TQ5407
Yew Tree (01323) 870590
Off A22 near Hailsham, or A27 W of Polegate; BN26 6RX Neatly modernised Victorian village pub under long-serving family; generous helpings of popular good value home-made food (booking advised), well kept Harveys and Long Man, decent wines, prompt friendly service, log fires, hop-covered beams and old local photographs, darts in thriving bare-boards bar, plush lounge, comfortable conservatory; children welcome, nice big garden with play area, paddock with farm animals, good local walks. *(John Beeken, Tony Scott)*

ARUNDEL   TQ0208
★ **Black Rabbit** (01903) 882828
Mill Road, Offham; keep on and don't give up; BN18 9PB Refurbished riverside pub in lovely spot near wildfowl reserve with timeless views of water meadows and castle – well organised for families and can get very busy; long bar with eating areas at either end, good choice of enjoyable reasonably priced food from baguettes and sharing boards up, well kept Badger ales and decent wines by the glass, good friendly service, log fires, newspapers; background music, Tues quiz; dogs welcome, covered tables and pretty hanging baskets out at front, extensive terrace across road overlooking river, play area, boat trips and good walks, open (and food) all day. *(John Beeken)*

ARUNDEL   TQ0107
Red Lion (01903) 882214
High Street; BN18 9AG Centrally placed red-brick pub with good value food including moules frites menu and Sat breakfast (from 10am), four well kept ales such as Arundel, Dark Star, Fullers and Sharps, Thatcher's cider, bare-boards front bar with leather sofas either side of welcoming fire (huge red lion above), back restaurant; regular live music, sports TV, free wi-fi; children and dogs welcome (pub dog is Roxy), garden behind with sandpit, open (and food) all day. *(Tony and Wendy Hobden, Jestyn Phillips)*

ARUNDEL   TQ0107
Swan (01903) 882314
High Street; BN18 9AG Georgian inn's comfortably relaxed L-shaped bar, well kept Fullers/Gales beers and occasional guests,

popular fairly priced food including deals, friendly efficient young staff, wood flooring, sporting memorabilia and old photographs, open fire, connecting restaurant; 14 bedrooms, no car park (pay-and-display opposite), open all day. *(Dr and Mrs J D Abell, Jestyn Phillips)*

ASHURST   TQ1816
★**Fountain** (01403) 710219
B2135 S of Partridge Green; BN44 3AP
Attractive 16th-c pub with plenty of character; rustic tap room on right with log fire in brick inglenook, country dining chairs around polished tables on flagstones, opened-up snug with heavy beams and another inglenook, Harveys Best and guests, several wines by the glass, generally well liked home-cooked food (all day weekends) from varied menu, skittle alley/function room; children (not in front bar) and dogs welcome, seats on front brick terrace, pretty garden with raised herb beds, orchard and duck pond, summer barbecues, open (and food) all day. *(Alastair and Sheree Hepburn, Tony Scott)*

BALLS CROSS   SU9826
★**Stag** (01403) 820241
Village signed off A283 at N edge of Petworth; GU28 9JP Cheery unspoilt 17th-c country pub; cosy flagstoned bar with log fire in huge inglenook, a few seats and bar stools, Badger beers and several wines by the glass, second tiny room and appealing old-fashioned bare-boards restaurant, fishing rods, country knick-knacks and old photographs, enjoyable pubby food (not Mon and Sun evenings), good service; bar skittles, darts and board games in separate room, outside loos; well behaved children allowed away from main bar, dogs welcome, seats out in front and in pretty back garden, open all day weekends. *(Colin McKerrow)*

BARCOMBE   TQ4416
Anchor (01273) 400414
Barcombe Mills; BN8 5BS Late 18th-c pub with lots of tables out by winding River Ouse (boat hire), well kept ales including Harveys and enjoyable reasonably priced pubby food, friendly smartly dressed staff, two beamed bars, restaurant and small front conservatory; children and dogs welcome, self-catering chalet, open all day and can get crowded summer weekends. *(Sally Taylor)*

BARCOMBE CROSS   TQ4212
Royal Oak (01273) 400418
Off A275 N of Lewes; BN8 5BA
Welcoming family-run village pub with good mix of locals and visitors, up to five well kept Harveys ales and reasonably priced wines, enjoyable generously served food from bar snacks up (not Sun evening-Weds, pizza van Mon evening), friendly helpful service, long bar with restaurant attached, beams, bare boards and open fire, local art for sale; skittle

alley; children and dogs welcome, a few tables out in front and in small tree-shaded garden, open all day. *(John Beeken)*

BARNS GREEN   TQ1227
Queens Head (01403) 730436
Chapel Road; RH13 0PS Welcoming traditional tile-hung village pub, good generous home-made food from short menu (all day Sat, till 7pm Sun), five well kept ales including Fullers, Harveys, Long Man and St Austell, good range of wines by the glass; live music and quiz nights, Aug classic car event; children and dogs welcome, tables out at front and in back garden with play area, open all day. *(Peter Barrett)*

BERWICK   TQ5105
★**Cricketers Arms** (01323) 870469
Lower Road, S of A27; BN26 6SP
Charming brick and flint local with three small unpretentious bars, huge supporting beam in each low ceiling, simple country furnishings on quarry tiles, cricketing pictures and bats, two log fires, friendly staff, four Harveys ales tapped from the cask, country wines and good coffee, well cooked uncomplicated food at reasonable prices, old Sussex coin game toad in the hole; children in family room only, dogs welcome, delightful cottagey front garden with picnic-sets among small brick paths, more seats behind, Bloomsbury Group wall paintings in nearby church and handy for Charleston, good South Downs walks, open all day summer, closed weekday afternoons winter. *(Alan Cowell, Tony Scott, John Beeken)*

BILLINGSHURST   TQ0830
Blue Ship (01403) 822709
The Haven; hamlet signposted off A29 just N of junction with A264, then follow signpost left towards Garlands and Okehurst; RH14 9BS Unspoilt pub in quiet country spot, beamed and brick-floored front bar, scrubbed tables and wall benches, inglenook woodburner, cask-tapped Badger ales served from hatch, good home-made food from pub favourites up, two small carpeted back rooms; darts, bar billiards, shove-ha'penny, cribbage and dominoes; children and dogs welcome, tables out at front and in side garden with play area, camping, closed Sun evening, Mon. *(Tony Scott)*

BILLINGSHURST   TQ0725
Limeburners (01403) 782311
Lordings Road, Newbridge (B2133/ A272 W); RH14 9JA Friendly characterful local in converted row of cottages, three Fullers ales and enjoyable fairly priced pubby food (not Sun evening) from snacks up, part-carpeted bar with horsebrasses on dark beams and inglenook at each end; background music, quiz nights, TV, bar billiards; children and dogs welcome, picnic-sets in pleasant front garden with play area, campsite behind. *(Tony Smaithe)*

BILLINGSHURST   TQ0825
Olde Six Bells (01403) 782124
High Street (A29); RH14 9QS
Picturesque partly 14th-c timbered pub,
updated interior with large bar and split-
level restaurant, flagstone and wood floors,
inglenook log fire, four well kept Badger ales
and enjoyable reasonably priced pubby food
from baguettes and baked potatoes up, games
room; children and dogs welcome, disabled
access/loo, roadside garden and terrace, open
all day, food all day Sat and till 5pm Sun.
(Tony and Wendy Hobden)

BINSTED   SU9806
Black Horse (01243) 553325
*Binsted Lane; about 2 miles W of
Arundel, turn S off A27 towards Binsted;
BN18 0LP* Modernised 17th-c dining
pub with good varied choice of food from
sandwiches up, ales such as Harveys and
local Listers, wood-floored bar and separate
dining room; monthly live music; children
and dogs welcome, plenty of outside seating
on terrace with covered well, lawn and in
open-fronted oak-framed building, valley
views over golf course, closed Sun evening,
Mon. *(Tony and Wendy Hobden)*

BLACKBOYS   TQ5220
★ Blackboys Inn (01825) 890283
B2192, S edge of village; TN22 5LG
Old weatherboarded inn set back from road;
main bar to the right with beams, timbers,
dark wooden furniture and log fire, locals'
bar to left with lots of bric-a-brac, Harveys
ales including seasonals, several wines by the
glass and wide choice of enjoyable food (all
day Sat, till 7pm Sun), panelled dining areas;
background and some live music; children
and dogs (in bar) welcome, sizeable garden
with seats under trees, on terrace and under
cover by duck pond, good walks (Vanguard
Way passes the pub, Wealdway close by),
open all day. *(Simon Sharpe)*

BODIAM   TQ7825
Castle Inn (01580) 830330
*Village signed from B2244; opposite
Bodiam Castle; TN32 5UB* Bustling
country pub very handy for Bodiam Castle
(NT), Shepherd Neame ales and a couple
of guests, good choice of wines, popular
reasonably priced food from sandwiches up,
friendly helpful service, plain tables and
chairs in snug bar, log fire, back restaurant;
picnic-sets on big sheltered terrace, open
all day. *(Stephen Shepherd, Conrad Freezer)*

BOGNOR REGIS   SZ9201
Royal Oak (01243) 821002
*A259 Chichester Road, North Bersted;
PO21 5JF* Old-fashioned two-bar beamed
local (aka the Pink Pub), well kept ales such
as Long Man and Shepherd Neame, shortish
choice of popular reasonably priced food till
6.30pm (2.30pm Sun), friendly service; Thurs

quiz, bar billiards, darts, sports TV; children
and dogs welcome (pub boxer is Alfie).
(Ruth May)

BOLNEY   TQ2623
Bolney Stage (01444) 881200
*London Road, off old A23 just N of
A272; RH17 5RL* Sizeable 16th-c black
and white dining pub (part of the Home
Counties group) with good varied choice of
popular food, four changing ales (blackboard
descriptions) and good selection of wines
by the glass, friendly prompt service, low
beams and polished flagstones, nice mix of
old furniture, woodburner and big two-way
log fire; children and dogs (in main bar)
welcome, disabled facilities, tables on
terrace and lawn, play area, handy for
Sheffield Park (NT), Bluebell Railway and
a useful M23/A23 stop, open (and food) all
day. *(David Jackman, Tony and Wendy Hobden,
Tony Scott, Alastair and Sheree Hepburn)*

BOLNEY   TQ2622
Eight Bells (01444) 881396
The Street; RH17 5QW Popular village
pub with wide choice of good sensibly priced
food from baguettes up, bargain OAP lunch
Tues, Weds, efficient friendly young staff, well
kept Harveys and a couple of guests, decent
choice of wines, brick-floored bar with eight
handbells suspended above servery, second
flagstoned bar set for eating, open fires,
timbered dining extension; bar billiards,
pool and darts; children welcome, disabled
facilities, tables out on deck under huge
canopy, outside bar and play area, various
events including annual pram race (Easter
Mon), three bedrooms in separate beamed
cottage. *(John Beeken, Ross Balaam, Tony Scott)*

BOSHAM   SU8003
★ Anchor Bleu (01243) 573956
High Street; PO18 8LS Waterside inn
overlooking Chichester Harbour; two simple
bars with low ochre ceilings, worn flagstones
and exposed timbered brickwork, lots of
nautical bric-a-brac, robust furniture (some
tables close together), up to six real ales and
popular sensibly priced bar food, efficient
friendly staff (they may ask for a credit
card if you run a tab), upstairs dining room;
children and dogs welcome, seats on front
terrace and raised back one (access through
massive wheel-operated bulkhead door),
lovely views over sheltered inlet, can park
by water but note tide times, church up lane
figures in Bayeux Tapestry, village and shore
worth exploring, open all day in summer and
can get very crowded. *(Dr and Mrs J D Abell,
Roy Hoing)*

BOSHAM   SU8105
White Swan (01243) 696465
*A259 roundabout; Station Road;
PO18 8NG* Refurbished 18th-c dining pub
with enjoyable sensibly priced food (not
Sun evening), four well kept ales including

Hop Back Summer Lightning, good-sized flagstoned bar, restaurant beyond with old bread oven, darts in snug; fortnightly quiz Weds, sports TV; children and dogs welcome in certain areas, open all day. *(Anne and Ben Smith)*

BREDE   TQ8218
Red Lion (01424) 882188
A28 opposite church; TN31 6EJ Popular family-run beamed village pub; plain tables and chairs on bare boards, candles and inglenook log fire, good competitively priced home-made food (should book) including local fish and Sun carvery, own-baked bread, well kept Harveys, Sharps, Youngs and guests, short good value wine list, friendly efficient service even when busy, back dining area decorated with sheet music and instruments (occasional live music); children and dogs welcome, garden behind with roaming chickens (eggs for sale), narrow entrance to car park, open all day Fri-Sun. *(Conrad Freezer, V Brogden)*

BRIGHTON   TQ3104
★ **Basketmakers Arms** (01273) 689006
Gloucester Road – the E end, near Cheltenham Place; off Marlborough Place (A23) via Gloucester Street; BN1 4AD Cheerful bustling backstreet local with eight pumps serving Fullers/Gales beers and guests, decent wines by the glass, over 100 malt whiskies and good choice of other spirits, well liked/priced bar food, two small low-ceilinged rooms, lots of interesting old tins, enamel signs, photographs and posters; background music; children welcome till 8pm, dogs on leads, a few pavement tables, open all day (till midnight Fri, Sat). *(Phil and Jane Villiers)*

BRIGHTON   TQ3004
Brighton Beer Dispensary
(01273) 205797 *Dean Street; BN1 3EG*
Popular little terraced pub jointly owned by Brighton Bier and Late Knights Brewery, their ales along with many guests, craft beers and an extensive bottled range, four hand-pulled ciders too, well informed friendly staff, bar snacks and burgers plus Sun roasts, small back conservatory; quiz nights; open all day and can get packed. *(Andrew Stone)*

BRIGHTON   TQ3005
Chimney House (01273) 556708
Upper Hamilton Road; BN1 5DF
Red-brick corner pub in residential area, bare-boards interior arranged around central bar, one or two quirky touches such as antler chandeliers, good innovative food from open kitchen using local ingredients (some foraged), three real ales including Harveys, home-made jams, chutney and bread for sale; folk night Sun; children and dogs welcome,

closed Mon, otherwise open all day, no food Sun evening. *(Robert MacGregor)*

BRIGHTON   TQ3104
Colonnade (01273) 328728
New Road, off North Street; by Theatre Royal; BN1 1UF Small richly restored theatre bar with ornate frontage – note Willie the 19th-c automaton in small bay window; shining brass and mahogany, plush banquettes, velvet swags and gleaming mirrors, interesting pre-war playbills and signed theatrical photographs, three well kept ales including Fullers London Pride, good range of wines and interesting gins; downstairs lavatories; pavement seats overlooking Pavilion gardens, open all day. *(A N Bance)*

BRIGHTON   TQ3004
Craft Beer Company
(01273) 723736 *Upper North Street; BN1 3FG* Busy corner pub with fine selection of interesting draught and bottled beers, friendly knowledgeable staff, pubby food from snacks up, simple L-shaped bar with raised back section; closed weekday lunchtimes, open all day weekends. *(Andrew Stone)*

BRIGHTON   TQ3004
★ **Evening Star** (01273) 328931
Surrey Street; BN1 3PB Chatty drinkers' pub with good mix of customers, simple pale wood furniture on bare boards, up to four well kept Dark Star ales (originally brewed here) and lots of changing guests including continentals (in bottles too), traditional ciders/perries and country wines, lunchtime baguettes, friendly staff coping well at busy times; background and some live music; pavement tables, open all day. *(Peter Meister)*

BRIGHTON   TQ2804
Foragers (01273) 733134
3 Stirling Place, Hove; BN3 3YU Relaxed Victorian corner pub, good food (not Sun evening) from varied menu including some unusual choices (emphasis on organic sustainable produce – some foraged), well kept Harveys and interesting range of wines and spirits, friendly service; children welcome, picnic-sets out at front, garden behind, open all day. *(Mr and Mrs A Dempster)*

BRIGHTON   TQ3203
Ginger Dog (01273) 620990
College Place, Kemptown; BN2 1HN
Restauranty Kemptown pub, part of the small Gingerman group – Ginger Pig (Brighton), Ginger Fox (Albourne); highly regarded modern food from changing menu (not especially cheap), good wines, cocktails and three local beers, well informed friendly service, fairly traditional bare-boards

---

Tipping is not normal for bar meals, and not usually expected.

interior; children and dogs welcome, open all day. *(Charles North)*

★ **Ginger Pig** (01273) 736123
Hove Street; BN3 2TR Bustling place just minutes from the beach; informal bare-boards bar area with plush stools and simple wooden dining chairs around mixed tables, armchairs and sofas here and there, Harveys Best and a guest, nice wines by the glass and interesting local spirits and soft drinks, raised restaurant part with long button-back wall seating and more wooden tables and chairs, contemporary cow paintings, enterprising modern food served by friendly attentive staff; background jazz; children welcome, open all day. *(Martin Day, Val and Alan Green)*

Hand in Hand (01273) 699595
Upper St James's Street, Kemptown; BN2 1JN It may be Brighton's smallest pub, but the canary yellow exterior makes it hard to miss; own-brewed ales along with five well kept changing guests, plenty of bottled beers and a real cider, dimly lit bar with a few tables and benches, tie collection and lots of newspaper cuttings on the walls, photographs including Victorian nudes on the ceiling, food limited to local sausage rolls, cheerful service and colourful mix of customers; interesting background music (live jazz Sun), veteran fruit machine; dogs welcome, open all day and can get crowded. *(Peter Meister)*

★ **Jolly Poacher** (01273) 683967
Ditchling Road; BN1 4SG Emphasis on owner-chef's imaginative food prepared in open kitchen; plenty of rustic character in U-shaped bar-cum-dining room with high-backed cushioned wooden chairs around mix of tables on wide boards, modern artwork on pale walls above grey-green dado, contemporary lights hanging from high ceiling, a couple of fireplaces, Harveys Best, 11 good wines by the glass and cocktails (two-for-one 4-7pm); background music, free wi-fi; children and dogs welcome, metal furniture on narrow side terrace, closed Mon, otherwise open all day. *(Lindy Andrews, Harvey Brown)*

Lion & Lobster (01273) 327299
Sillwood Street; BN1 2PS Backstreet pub spread across three floors, softly lit interior with quirky portraits on red walls, well kept ales such as Dark Star and Harveys, extensive choice of food (booking recommended) including daily specials and late-night menu; regular jazz evenings, Mon quiz, sports TV; large terrace on two levels (can get very busy in summer), open (and food) all day, till 2am Fri and Sat. *(Tony Scott)*

Stanmer House (01273) 680400
Stanmer Park; BN1 9QA Whiting & Hammond pub-restaurant in 18th-c parkland mansion; three impressive front rooms with button-back leather chesterfields on bare boards or marble, ornate fireplaces, gilt-edged mirrors and chandeliers, stone lions/metal sculptures in wall recesses, old local photographs and shelves of books, well kept Park Life (brewed for them by Turners) and guests, 16 wines by the glass, enjoyable interesting food and popular afternoon teas, dining rooms (to left) with Victorian and Edwardian-style chairs around heavy dark tables, big portraits, church candles and opulent flower arrangements; children and dogs (in some parts) welcome, rustic furniture on terrace and around garden's pond, contemporary seats on front flagstones, open (and some food) all day from 9am, shuts 6pm Mon-Weds in winter. *(Mungo Shipley, John Harris)*

Ash Tree (01424) 892104
Off A271 (was B2204) W of Battle; 1st northward road W of Ashburnham Place, then 1st fork left, then bear right into Brownbread Street; TN33 9NX Tranquil 17th-c country local tucked away in isolated hamlet, enjoyable affordably priced home-made food including specials, good choice of wines and well kept ales such as Harveys Best, cheerful service, cosy beamed bars with nice old settles and chairs, stripped brickwork, interesting dining areas with timbered dividers, good inglenook log fires; quiz first Tues of month; children (in eating area) and dogs welcome, pretty garden, open all day. *(Julian Richardson)*

★ **George** (01903) 883131
Off A27 near Warningcamp; BN18 9RR Busy 17th-c community-owned pub with attractively updated beamed interior; ales such as Arundel, Hammerpot and Harveys, wide range of wines including local fizz, some interesting gins, cocktails and decent coffee, good freshly made food from shortish daily changing menu including range of sussex cheeses, efficient courteous service; free wi-fi; children and dogs welcome, picnic-sets out in front, hilltop village with splendid views down to Arundel Castle and river, open all day weekends, may close Sun evening in winter. *(John Davis, Mike and Marion Higgins, Celia Caulkin)*

Rose & Crown (01435) 882600
Inn sign on A265; TN19 7ER Old tile-hung local tucked down lane (parking can be tricky) in pretty village, well kept Harveys, decent wines and enjoyable food served by friendly staff, very low

ceilings with banknotes stuck to beams near servery, pubby furniture on patterned carpet, inglenook log fire, separate restaurant with another inglenook, glass-covered well just inside front door; children and dogs welcome, small side garden and pleasant back terrace, bedrooms, handy for Batemans (NT), open all day weekends. *(Martin Day, Tony Scott, Richard Kennell)*

BURY TQ0013

Squire & Horse (01798) 831343

Bury Common; A29 Fontwell–Pulborough; RH20 1NS 16th-c roadside dining pub with very good attractively presented food from australian chef, well kept Harveys and a guest, good choice of wines, several partly divided beamed areas, plush wall seats, hunting prints and ornaments, log fire; children welcome, no dogs inside, pleasant garden and pretty terrace (some road noise), open all day Sun. *(Peter Barrett)*

BYWORTH SU9821

★ **Black Horse** (01798) 342424

Off A283; GU28 0HL Popular chatty country pub with smart simply furnished bar, pews and scrubbed tables on bare boards, pictures and old photographs, open fires, four ales including Flowerpots and Fullers, Weston's Old Rosie cider, decent food (not Sun evening) from light lunchtime dishes up, children's menu, back restaurant with nooks and crannies and old range, spiral staircase to heavily beamed function/dining room, games room with pool and darts; dogs allowed in bar, attractive garden with tables on steep grassy terraces, lovely Downs views, stable-block bedrooms, open all day. *(John Davis, Ann and Colin Hunt)*

CHALVINGTON TQ5209

Yew Tree Inn (01323) 811326

Chalvington Road, between Chalvington and Golden Cross; BN27 3TB Isolated low-beamed 17th-c country pub; flagstones, stripped brickwork, and inglenook, enjoyable well priced home-made food (not Sun evening) from lunchtime baguettes up, well kept Harveys and guests, conservatory; children and dogs welcome, good-sized terrace, extensive grounds with play area, own cricket pitch and camping, good walks, open all day (till 6pm Sun). *(Andrew and Michele Revell)*

CHICHESTER SU8605

Chichester Inn (01243) 783185

West Street; PO19 1RP Georgian pub (quieter than the city-centre ones) with half a dozen local ales such as Dark Star and Harveys, good value pubby food from snacks up, friendly service, smallish front lounge with plain wooden tables and chairs, sofas by open fire, larger back public bar; regular live music plus comedy nights and jive/lindy hop classes, sports TV, pool; courtyard garden with smokers' shelter, four bedrooms, open all day. *(Tony and Wendy Hobden)*

CHICHESTER SU8504

Crate & Apple (01243) 539336

Westgate; PO19 3EU Newish pub in former restaurant, good freshly made food from varied menu, local ales, good range of wines by the glass and several gins, friendly attentive service, modern/rustic décor with simple tables and chairs on wood or stone floors, painted dados, leather sofas by woodburner; children welcome, sunny front terrace with umbrellas, more seats behind, closed Sun evening, otherwise open all day. *(Miss A E Dare, Charlotte Bull, Craig Adfield)*

CHICHESTER SU8604

Eastgate (01243) 774877

The Hornet (A286); PO19 7JG Welcoming town pub with light airy interior extending back, three Fullers ales and a guest, well cooked affordably priced traditional food, cheerful prompt service, woodburner; background and weekend live music, darts, pool and cribbage; children and dogs welcome, small heated back terrace, open all day. *(Phil and Jane Villiers)*

CHICHESTER SU8605

Park Tavern (01243) 785057

Priory Road; PO19 1NS Friendly buoyant pub in pleasant spot opposite Priory Park, good choice of Fullers/Gales beers and enjoyable reasonably priced home-made food, smallish front bar, extensive back eating area; quiz Tues, live music Sun; dogs welcome (they have two), open all day. *(Phil and Jane Villiers)*

CHIDDINGLY TQ5414

★ **Six Bells** (01825) 872227 *Village signed off A22 Uckfield–Hailsham; BN8 6HE* Lively unpretentious village local run well by hardworking hands-on landlord; small linked bars with interesting bric-a-brac, local pictures and posters, old furniture, cushioned window seats and log fires, family extension giving much-needed extra space, well kept Courage Directors, Harveys Best and a guest, decent wines by the glass and a farm cider, bargain food; good weekend live music, free wi-fi; dogs welcome in bar, seats at the back by big raised goldfish pond, boules, monthly vintage and kit-car meetings, church opposite with interesting Jefferay Monument, open (and food) all day Fri-Sun. *(Simon Sharpe)*

CHIDHAM SU7804

Old House at Home (01243) 572477

Off A259 at Barleycorn pub in Nutbourne; Cot Lane; PO18 8SU Neat 18th-c red-brick pub in remote unspoilt farm hamlet; good choice of popular food from open sandwiches to fish specials, lunchtime set menu, several wines by the glass and at least four real ales including a house beer from Langham, friendly service, low beams and timbering, log fire; children allowed in eating areas, tables on front terrace and in attractive back garden, Chichester Harbour walks nearby, open all day. *(Tony and Jill Radnor, David and Judy Robison, J A Snell)*

CHILGROVE   SU8116
★ **Royal Oak** (01243) 535257
Off B2141 Petersfield–Chichester, signed Hooksway; PO18 9JZ Unchanging country pub close to South Downs Way; two simple cosy bars with huge log fires, country kitchen furniture and cottagey knick-knacks, Bowman, Exmoor and Fullers, good honest food, homely dining room with woodburner, plainer family room; background music (live last Fri of month), cribbage, dominoes and shut the box, free wi-fi; dogs welcome in bar (pub staffies are Twiglet and Amber – the parrot is Gilbert), pretty garden with picnic-sets under parasols, closed Sun evening, Mon and throughout Nov. *(Peter Brix, Martin Jones, Tony and Jill Radnor)*

CLAPHAM   TQ1105
Coach & Horses (01903) 694721
Arundel Road (A27 Worthing–Arundel); BN13 3UA Friendly 18th-c former coaching inn beside dual carriageway; well liked food including blackboard specials and set-menu choices, four changing ales (always one from Arundel), local gins and vodka, refurbished interior with comfortable seating by open fire, flagstoned dining area to left of bar; background music, quiz last Weds of month; children and dogs welcome, tables under parasols on back terrace, play area, open all day, food all day Sun. *(Tony and Wendy Hobden)*

COCKING CAUSEWAY   SU8819
Greyhound (01730) 814425
A286 Cocking–Midhurst; GU29 9QH Pretty 18th-c tile-hung pub set back from the road, enjoyable good value home-made food (all day weekends – should book), four changing ales such as Irving, Listers, Long Man and Shepherd Neame, open-plan but cosy beamed and panelled bar with alcoves, log fire, pine furniture in big back dining conservatory; monthly quiz; children and dogs welcome, grassed area at front with picnic-sets and huge eucalyptus, sizeable garden and play area behind, open all day. *(Tony and Wendy Hobden)*

COLEMANS HATCH   TQ4533
★ **Hatch** (01342) 822363
Signed off B2026, or off B2110 opposite church; TN7 4EJ Quaint and appealing little weatherboarded Ashdown Forest pub dating from 1430, big log fire in quickly filling beamed bar, small back dining room with another fire, good freshly made food (not Sun evening) from varied menu, well kept Harveys, Larkins and one or two guests, friendly staff and good mix of customers

including families and dogs; picnic-sets on front terrace and in beautifully kept big garden, not much parking so get there early. *(Tony Scott)*

COMPTON   SU7714
Coach & Horses (023) 9263 1228
B2146 S of Petersfield; PO18 9HA Welcoming 17th-c two-bar local in charming downland village, not far from Uppark (NT), beams, panelling, shuttered windows and log fires, up to five changing ales including a house beer from Ballards, good food cooked by landlord-chef; bar billiards; dogs welcome, tables out by village square, nice surrounding walks, closed Mon. *(Julian Richardson)*

COOLHAM   TQ1423
★ **George & Dragon** (01403) 741320
Dragons Green, Dragons Lane; pub signed off A272; RH13 8GE Tile-hung cottage surrounded by fine countryside; cosy bar with massive unusually low beams (see if you can decide whether date cut into one is 1677 or 1577), heavily timbered walls, traditional furniture and log fire in big inglenook, Dark Star Hophead, Harveys Best, Skinners Betty Stogs and a guest, decent wines by the glass and enjoyable food (not Sun, Mon or Tues evenings), dining room with pale farmhouse chairs around rustic tables on wood floor; children and dogs (in bar) welcome, pretty garden, two attractive double bedrooms in converted outbuilding, open all day Fri-Sun. *(Mungo Shipley, Nick Sharpe)*

COOTHAM   TQ0714
Crown (01903) 742625
Pulborough Road (A283); RH20 4JN Extended roadside village pub with L-shaped bar on two levels, Harveys and a couple of guests, wide choice of popular food from bar snacks up (smaller helpings available), also set menus, friendly service, two open fires, large back dining area, games room (darts and pool); children and dogs welcome, big garden with play area and goats, handy for Parham House, open all day Sun till 10pm. *(Tony and Wendy Hobden)*

COUSLEY WOOD   TQ6533
★ **Old Vine** (01892) 782271
B2100 Wadhurst–Lamberhurst; TN5 6ER Popular 16th-c weatherboarded pub freshened-up under new management; linked rooms with heavy beams and open timbering, attractive old pine tables surrounded by farmhouse chairs, several settles, wood or brick flooring (restaurant area is carpeted), well kept ales and several wines by the glass from green painted servery, enjoyable good value home-made food from sandwiches up; background and occasional live music; children and dogs welcome, picnic-sets on front terrace, three refurbished bedrooms, open all day Fri, Sat, closed Sun evening, Mon lunchtime. *(Helena and Trevor Fraser)*

COWFOLD　　　　　　　　　TQ2122
Hare & Hounds　(01403) 865354
Henfield Road (A281 S); RH13 8DR
Small friendly village pub with well kept
Dark Star, Harveys and a guest, good value
traditional home-made food including
Thurs OAP lunch, flagstoned bar with log
fire, little room off to the right, carpeted
dining room to the left; children and
dogs welcome, a couple of picnic-sets
out in front, back terrace, open all day
weekends. *(Tony and Wendy Hobden)*

CUCKFIELD　　　　　　　　TQ3025
Rose & Crown　(01444) 414217
London Road; RH17 5BS Popular
17th-c former coaching inn run by father
and son team, good if not cheap food from
interesting regularly changing menus, well
kept Harveys and a guest, local Hepworth
lagers and good choice of wines, friendly
staff; children and dogs welcome, tables
out in front and in nice garden behind,
closed Mon, otherwise open all day (Sun
till 9pm). *(Phil and Jane Hodson)*

DALLINGTON　　　　　　　　TQ6619
★ Swan　(01424) 838242
Woods Corner, B2096 E; TN21 9LB
Popular old local with cheerful chatty
atmosphere, well kept Harveys and a
guest, decent wines by the glass and good
blackboard food, efficient friendly service,
bare-boards bar divided by standing timbers,
mixed furniture including cushioned settle
and high-backed pew, old enamel signs (on
walls and floor), candles in bottles, swan
ornaments, big woodburner, simple back
restaurant with far-reaching views to the
coast; occasional background music, board
games; children and dogs welcome, steps
down to loos and garden. *(Peter Meister)*

DELL QUAY　　　　　　　　SU8302
Crown & Anchor　(01243) 781712
*Off A286 S of Chichester – look out for
small sign; PO20 7EE* 19th/20th-c beamed
pub in splendid spot overlooking Chichester
Harbour – best at high tide and quiet times
(can be packed on sunny days and parking
difficult); comfortable bow-windowed lounge
and panelled public bar (dogs welcome), two
log fires, well kept Youngs and a couple of
guests, lots of wines by the glass including
champagne, enjoyable freshly made food
from pub favourites to specials, friendly staff;
children and dogs welcome, views from large
terrace, nice walks, open (and food) all day.
(Ian Phillips, J A Snell)

DENTON　　　　　　　　　　TQ4502
Flying Fish　(01273) 515440
Denton Road; BN9 0QB Welcoming
17th-c flint village pub, enjoyable food from
baguettes up, well kept Shepherd Neame ales
and guests including Harveys, friendly helpful
staff; poker night Thurs; picnic-sets out by

road and on back deck looking up to sloping
garden, handy for South Downs Way, open
all day. *(Ruth May)*

EAST ASHLING　　　　　　SU8207
Horse & Groom　(01243) 575339
B2178; PO18 9AX Busy country pub with
five well kept ales including Dark Star, Hop
Back and Youngs, decent choice of wines by
the glass, good food from sandwiches and
baguettes up, reasonable prices, unchanging
front drinkers' bar with old pale flagstones
and inglenook range, carpeted area with
scrubbed trestle tables, airy extension with
solid country kitchen furniture; children and
dogs allowed in some parts, garden picnic-
sets under umbrellas, 11 bedrooms (some
in barn conversion), open all day Sat, closed
Sun evening. *(Ross Balaam)*

EAST CHILTINGTON　　　　TQ3715
★ Jolly Sportsman　(01273) 890400
*2 miles N of B2116; Chapel Lane – follow
sign to 13th-c church; BN7 3BA* Inventive
modern food cooked by landlord in this
civilised place; small character log-fire bar
for drinkers, Dark Star and Harveys tapped
from the cask, excellent range of malt
whiskies, cognacs and armagnacs and very
good wine list, smart but cosy restaurant
with contemporary light wood furniture and
modern landscapes, garden room; free wi-fi;
children and dogs (in bar) welcome, front
garden with rustic tables under trees, more
seats on big back lawn with views towards
the Downs, open all day Sat, till 4pm Sun,
closed Mon. *(Nick Sharpe, Isobel Mackinlay,
Mrs Julie Thomas, Ollie, Sally Taylor)*

EAST DEAN　　　　　　　　SU9012
Star & Garter　(01243) 811318
*Village signed with Charlton off A286
in Singleton; also signed off A285;
PO18 0JG* Airy dining pub in peaceful
village-green setting; pleasant bar and
restaurant with exposed brickwork, panelling
and oak floors, furnishings from sturdy
stripped tables and country kitchen chairs
through chunky modern to antique carved
settles, Arundel ales tapped from the cask
and several wines by the glass, good food
including local fish/seafood, friendly service;
background music; children and dogs (in
bar) welcome, teak furniture on heated
terrace, smokers' shelter, steps down to
walled lawn with picnic-sets, near South
Downs Way, bedrooms, open (and food) all
day weekends. *(Tony Smaithe, Brian and Sally
Wakeham)*

EAST HOATHLY　　　　　　TQ5116
Foresters Arms　(01825) 840208
*Off A22 Hailsham–Uckfield; South
Street; BN8 6DS* Friendly village pub
with enjoyable freshly made food from pub
favourites up (not Sun evening or Mon), four
well kept Harveys ales and several wines by
the glass; darts; children and dogs welcome,

disabled facilities, garden with picnic-sets and play area, open all day weekends, closed Mon lunchtime. (*Conrad Freezer*)

EAST HOATHLY   TQ5216
Kings Head (01825) 840238
High Street/Mill Lane; BN8 6DR Creeper-clad 17th-c pub on crossroads (was the village school), own 1648 ales (brewed next door) plus Harveys Best, long open-plan room with wood floor, brick walls and log fire, pubby furniture including upholstered settles, enjoyable reasonably priced traditional food, friendly staff and good mix of locals and visitors, function room; TV, free wi-fi; children and dogs welcome, steps up to walled back garden, open all day.
(*John Beeken*)

EAST LAVANT   SU8608
★**Royal Oak** (01243) 527434
Pook Lane, off A286; PO18 0AX Pretty dining pub with low beams, crooked timbers and exposed brickwork in open-plan rooms, log fires and church candles, drinking part at front with wall seats and sofas, one or two changing ales tapped from the cask, many wines by the glass and some 20 malt whiskies, dining area with leather chairs and scrubbed pine tables, imaginative food including specials, good friendly service; background music, free wi-fi; children and dogs (in bar) welcome, flagstoned front terrace with far-reaching views to the Downs, more seats to the side and back, stylish bedrooms and self-catering cottages, car park across the road, handy for Goodwood, open 7.30am-10.30pm. (*Mrs J Ekins-Daukes, John Evans, I Short, Tracey and Stephen Groves, Miss A E Dare, Graham Forbes*)

EASTBOURNE   TV6098
Bibendum (01323) 735363
Grange Road/South Street opposite Town Hall; BN21 4EU Roomy 19th-c corner pub with wine bar feel, good choice of beers and decent food, friendly helpful staff, restaurant; seats out in front, open (and food) all day.
(*Ruth May*)

EASTBOURNE   TV6199
Marine (01323) 720464
Seaside Road (A259); BN22 7NE Comfortable spacious pub under welcoming long-serving licensees, near the seafront and well known for its extravagant Christmas decorations; panelled bar, lounge with sofas and tub chairs, log fire, three well kept ales and good choice of wines, whiskies and brandies, generous helpings of good freshly made food, back conservatory; children welcome, terrace and covered smokers' area, open (and food) all day Sun. (*Alan Johnson*)

EASTBOURNE   TV6097
Pilot (01323) 723440
Holywell Road, Meads; just off front below approach from Beachy Head;

BN20 7RW Busy renovated corner inn with good fairly priced home-cooked food from lunchtime sandwiches up, well kept Harveys Best, Sharps Doom Bar and a guest, good selection of wines by the glass, friendly staff; free wi-fi; children welcome, dogs in bar, seats out in front and in nice split-level beer garden behind, walks up to Beachy Head, three bedrooms, open all day.
(*Mr and Mrs A Dempster*)

EASTERGATE   SU9405
Wilkes Head (01243) 543380
Just off A29 Fontwell–Bognor; Church Lane; PO20 3UT Small friendly red-brick local with two traditional bars and back dining extension, beams, flagstones and inglenook log fire, enjoyable reasonably priced blackboard food from sandwiches up, Adnams Southwold, several guest ales and proper cider; acoustic music night second Sun of the month, beer festivals, darts; children welcome, tables in big garden with play area, open all day weekends. (*Tony and Wendy Hobden*)

ELSTED   SU8320
Elsted Inn (01730) 813662
Elsted Marsh; GU29 0JT Attractive and welcoming Victorian country pub, enjoyable reasonably priced food (not Sun evening, Mon) from shortish menu, three or four changing ales and decent wines by the glass, friendly accommodating service, two log fires, nice country furniture on bare boards, old Goodwood racing photos (horses and cars), dining area at back; children and dogs (in bar) welcome, plenty of seating in lovely enclosed Downs-view garden with big terrace, four bedrooms, open all day Fri and Sat, till 9pm Sun, closed Mon lunchtime. (*James Stock*)

ELSTED   SU8119
★**Three Horseshoes** (01730) 825746
Village signed from B2141 Chichester–Petersfield; from A272 about 2 miles W of Midhurst, turn left heading W; GU29 0JY A congenial bustle at this pretty white-painted old pub, beamed rooms, log fires and candlelight, ancient flooring, antique furnishings and interesting prints and photographs, up to five ales tapped from the cask such as Bowman, Flowerpots, Langham and Youngs, summer cider, very well liked food from blackboard menu, good friendly service; children allowed, dogs in bar, two delightful connecting gardens with plenty of seats, lovely roses and fine Downs views, good surrounding walks. (*Tony and Jill Radnor, John Evans, Miss A E Dare, S G N Bennett*)

ERIDGE STATION   TQ5434
★**Huntsman** (01892) 864258
Signed off A26 S of Eridge Green; TN3 9LE Country local with two opened-up rooms, pubby furniture on bare boards, some tables with carved/painted board

games including own 'Eridgeopoly', hunting pictures, three Badger ales and over a dozen wines by the glass, popular bar food (not Sun evening, Mon) including fresh fish, seasonal game and home-grown produce, friendly staff; children and dogs welcome, picnic-sets and heaters on decking, outside bar, more seats on lawn among weeping willows, open all day weekends, closed Mon lunchtime. *(Jamie Green)*

FALMER   TQ3508
Swan (01273) 681842
Middle Street (just off A27 bypass);
BN1 9PD Long thin building with seating areas either side of small central bar (model train runs above it), unpretentious and in same family for last century, Palmers and local guests, straightforward sensibly priced lunchtime food (evenings Thurs and Fri), friendly staff and homely atmosphere; music and quiz nights, sports TV; dogs welcome, seats on little terrace, near Sussex University (student discounts), closed Mon evening, otherwise open all day. *(Tony and Wendy Hobden, Robert Kennedy)*

FERNHURST   SU9028
Red Lion (01428) 643112
The Green, off A286 via Church Lane;
GU27 3HY Friendly wisteria-clad 16th-c pub tucked quietly away by green and cricket pitch near church; heavy beams and timbers, attractive furnishings, inglenook woodburner, good food (not Sun evening) from sandwiches and snacks up, well kept Fullers/Gales beers and a guest, decent wines, cheerful helpful service, restaurant; children and dogs welcome, seats out in front and in back garden with well, walks from the door, open all day. *(Andy and Sallie James)*

FERRING   TQ0903
Henty Arms (01903) 241254
Ferring Lane; BN12 6QY Popular 19th-c local with six well kept changing ales and generous helpings of well priced food (can get busy so best to book), breakfast from 9am Tues-Sat, friendly staff, opened-up lounge/dining area, log fire, separate bar with TV and games including bar billiards; children and dogs welcome, garden tables, Oct conker tournament with morris dancers, open (and food) all day. *(Tony and Wendy Hobden)*

FINDON   TQ1208
Gun (01903) 873206
High Street; BN14 0TA Low-beamed pub with opened-up bar area and restaurant, enjoyable food including good value burger night (Mon), french night (Tues) and popular Sun lunch, four well kept Marstons-related beers, friendly staff, log fire; free wi-fi; children and dogs (in bar) welcome, sheltered garden, pretty village below Cissbury Ring (NT), Sept sheep fair, open all day, no food Sun evening. *(Andrew and Michele Revell)*

FISHBOURNE   SU8304
Bulls Head (01243) 839895
Fishbourne Road (A259 Chichester–Emsworth); PO19 3JP Former 17th-c farmhouse with traditional interior, copper pans on black beams, some stripped brick and panelling, paintings of local scenes, good log fire, well kept Fullers/Gales beers and popular reasonably priced home-made food, friendly efficient service, intimate dining room; background music and daily newspapers; children welcome, dogs in bar, tables on small covered deck, four bedrooms in former skittle alley, handy for Fishbourne Roman villa, open all day weekends. *(John Beeken)*

FITTLEWORTH   TQ0118
Swan (01798) 865429
Lower Street (B2138, off A283 W of Pulborough); RH20 1EL Pretty tile-hung dining inn with beamed main bar, mix of furniture including windsor chairs, high-backed stools and button-backed banquettes on wood flooring, wall of pictures and old pub sign one end, big inglenook log fire the other, Harveys, Sharps Doom Bar and a guest, several wines by the glass and traditional cider, good food from pubby choices up in bar and separate panelled restaurant, set lunch deal Mon-Fri, efficient friendly staff; background music, free wi-fi, children and dogs welcome, big back lawn with plenty of tables, good walks nearby, 14 comfortable well priced bedrooms, open all day weekends. *(John Davis, Colin McKerrow, Alastair and Sheree Hepburn)*

FLETCHING   TQ4223
Rose & Crown (01825) 722884
High Street; TN22 3ST Welcoming individually decorated 16th-c village pub; heavy chandeliers hanging from beamed ceiling, oil paintings on boldly coloured walls, eclectic mix of furniture on parquet or brick flooring, candles and fresh flowers, a couple of leather armchairs by big open fire, good imaginative food including vegetarian choices in bar or restaurant, well kept Harveys and nice wines by the glass, friendly helpful service; children and dogs welcome, tables in pretty garden, closed Mon, otherwise open all day. *(Jamie and Sue May)*

FRANT   TQ5835
Abergavenny Arms (01892) 750233
A267 S of Tunbridge Wells; TN3 9DB Attractively refurbished beamed dining pub under welcoming new management, good freshly cooked food from varied menu including themed evenings, six well kept local ales such as Harveys, Larkins, Long Man and Tonbridge, good choice of wines by the glass and several interesting gins, friendly efficient staff, leather sofas by big woodburner in brick inglenook, three separate dining areas; background music, daily papers; children

welcome, terrace seating on different levels, front part looking over road to Eridge Park (good walks), open (and food) all day. *(Martin Day, Gavin Markwick)*

FULKING TQ2411
Shepherd & Dog (01273) 857382
Off A281 N of Brighton, via Poynings; BN5 9LU 17th-c bay-windowed pub in beautiful spot below the Downs; low beams, panelling and inglenook, fine range of real ales and craft beers including Downland (brewed a couple of miles away), also bottled beers, ciders and plenty of wines by the glass, enjoyable food from tapas-style plates up, friendly efficient young staff; beer, cider and 'gin and jazz' festivals; children and dogs welcome, terrace and pretty streamside garden with own bar, straightforward climb to Devils Dyke, open all day, food till 6pm Sun. *(Tony and Wendy Hobden)*

FUNTINGTON SU7908
★Fox & Hounds (01243) 575246
Common Road (B2146); PO18 9LL Bustling old bay-windowed pub with updated beamed rooms in grey/green shades, welcoming log fires, good food from open sandwiches and snacks to daily specials and popular Sun carvery (booking advised weekends), well kept Dark Star, Timothy Taylors and guests, lots of wines by the glass and good coffee, friendly service, comfortable spacious dining extension; free wi-fi; children and dogs welcome, tables out in front and in walled back garden, village shop, open (and food) all day, from 9am weekends for breakfast. *(David Jackman, I Short)*

GUN HILL TQ5614
★Gun (01825) 872361
Off A22 NW of Hailsham, or off A267; TN21 0JU Big 15th-c country dining pub with good bistro-style food and efficient friendly service; large central bar with nice old brick floor, stools against counter, Aga in corner, small grey-panelled room off with rugs on bare boards, animal skins on cushioned wall benches and mix of scrubbed and dark tables, logs piled into tall fireplace, well kept Harveys and Timothy Taylors, decent wines by the glass, close-set tables in two-room cottagey restaurant, beams and open fires, old bottles and glasses along gantry, gun prints and country pictures; background music; children welcome, picnic-sets in garden and on lantern-lit front terrace, Wealdway walks, open all day Sun. *(M and GR)*

HALNAKER SU9008
★Anglesey Arms (01243) 773474
A285 Chichester–Petworth; PO18 0NQ Georgian pub belonging to the Goodwood Estate; bare boards, settles and log fire, well kept Otter, Youngs and a couple of guests, decent wines, good varied if not particularly cheap food including local organic produce

---

and Selsey fish, friendly accommodating service, simple but smart L-shaped dining room (children allowed) with woodburners, stripped pine and some flagstones; traditional games; dogs welcome in bar, tables in big tree-lined garden, good nearby walks, open all day Fri-Sun. *(Peter Barrett)*

HAMMERPOT TQ0605
★Woodman Arms (01903) 871240
On N (eastbound) side of A27; BN16 4EU Pretty thatched pub with beams, timbers and inglenook woodburner, good choice of well liked food (smaller helpings available) including popular Sun lunch, three or four Fullers/Gales beers and decent wines by the glass, attentive friendly staff, comfortable bar with snug to the left, restaurant to the right; occasional live music, free wi-fi; children welcome if eating, no dogs inside, tables in nice garden, open till 5pm Sun. *(PL, Tony and Wendy Hobden)*

HANDCROSS TQ2529
Royal Oak (01444) 401406
Horsham Road (A279, off A23); RH17 6DJ Traditional comfortably refurbished tile-hung village pub, well kept Fullers, Harveys and a guest, good choice of enjoyable food (not Mon evening), friendly helpful staff; fortnightly quiz Tues, free wi-fi; children and dogs welcome, seats out at front and on small terrace overlooking fields and woods, handy for Nymans (NT), open all day Fri-Sun. *(Mrs P R Sykes)*

HANDCROSS TQ2328
Wheatsheaf (01444) 400472
B2110 W; RH13 6NZ Welcoming country pub with Badger ales and good range of generous home-made food using local produce, efficient staff (they may ask to swipe a card if running a tab), two simply furnished bars with lots of horse tack and farm tools, log fires, caged parrot called Smirnoff; children welcome, garden with covered terrace and play area, near Nymans (NT), open all day (till 7pm Sun). *(Tony Scott)*

HARTFIELD TQ4634
Gallipot (01892) 770008
B2110 towards Forest Row; TN7 4AJ Traditional stone and weatherboarded country pub, long narrow beamed interior with central bar and fire at one end, good home-made food from baguettes to daily specials (not many tables so best to book), three well kept local beers including Harveys, friendly helpful staff; some live music; children and dogs welcome, pleasant sloping garden behind with good views, handy for Pooh Bear country, open all day. *(Colin Bateman, Mrs J Ekins-Daukes)*

HASTINGS TQ8109
Dolphin (01424) 431197
Rock-a-Nore, off A259 at seafront; TN34 3DW Friendly tile-hung pub facing

the fishermen's huts, smallish carpeted interior with masses of fishing/maritime paraphernalia, enjoyable food including fresh fish, well kept Dark Star, Harveys, Youngs and three guests; background and regular live music, quiz Thurs; raised front terrace, open all day, food till 6pm (9pm Mon). *(Tony and Wendy Hobden)*

HASTINGS TQ8209
First In Last Out (01424) 425079
High Street, Old Town; TN34 3EY
Congenial and chatty pub serving its own FILO beers (brewed close by) and a guest ale, good fairly priced food (not Sun, lunchtime Mon) from varied menu including evening tapas (Mon) and indian thali (Thurs), friendly helpful staff, open-plan carpeted bar with 1970s Artex walls, dark wood booths and feature central raised log fire, lighter back dining room; regular live music, quiz first Sun of month; open all day. *(Mike and Eleanor Anderson, Dave and Jan Pilgrim, Tony and Wendy Hobden)*

HERMITAGE SU7505
★ Sussex Brewery (01243) 371533
A259 just W of Emsworth; PO10 8AU
Bustling little 18th-c pub on the West Sussex/Hampshire border; small bare-boards bar with good fire in brick inglenook, simple furniture, flagstoned snug, well kept Youngs ales and guests, ten wines by the glass and hearty food including speciality sausages (even vegetarian ones), small upstairs restaurant; children and dogs welcome, picnic-sets in back courtyard, open all day. *(Andrew Stone)*

HOOE TQ6910
Red Lion (01424) 892371
Denbigh Road; off B2095; TN33 9EW
Attractive old local behind screen of pollarded lime trees – originally a farmhouse but a pub since the 17th c, plenty of original features including hop-strung beams, flagstones and two big inglenooks (some refurbishment by present owners), generous helpings of popular home-cooked food (worth booking), well kept Harveys, a guest and plenty of continental beers, good friendly service, main bar and back snug, overflow function room and further eating space upstairs; children and dogs welcome, seats out at front and in garden behind, open all day. *(Nigel and Jean Eames)*

HOUGHTON TQ0111
★ George & Dragon (01798) 831559
B2139 W of Storrington; BN18 9LW
13th-c beams and timbers in attractive spic and span bar rambling up and down steps, note the elephant photograph above the fireplace, good Arun Valley views from back extension, well liked reasonably priced food, Marstons-related ales and decent wines by the glass, good friendly service; background music; children and dogs welcome, seats on

decked terrace taking in the views and in charming sloping garden, good walks, open all day Fri and Sat, till 9pm Sun. *(Tony Scott, Alastair and Sheree Hepburn)*

HUNSTON SU8601
Spotted Cow (01243) 786718
B2145 S of Chichester; PO20 1PD
Friendly modernised village pub with beams, flagstones and big log fires, good choice of enjoyable food (not Sun, Mon evenings) including specials, Fullers/Gales beers, small front bar, roomier side lounge with armchairs, sofas and low tables, airy high-ceilinged restaurant; may be background music; children (if eating) and dogs welcome, good disabled access, pretty garden, handy for towpath walkers, open all day. *(Brian and Sally Wakeham)*

HURSTPIERPOINT TQ2816
New Inn (01273) 834608
High Street; BN6 9RQ Popular 16th-c beamed village pub under new ownership, Harveys and a couple of guests, good wines by the glass and enjoyable food from pub favourites up, friendly staff, linked areas including oak-panelled back bar with log fire and more formal restaurant with large skylight; quiz first Tues of the month, sports TV; children and dogs welcome, good sized enclosed garden with terrace and play area, open all day, food all day Sat, till 4pm Sun. *(Simon Sharpe)*

ICKLESHAM TQ8716
★ Queens Head (01424) 814552
Off A259 Rye–Hastings; TN36 4BL
Friendly well run country pub, extremely popular locally (and at weekends with cyclists and walkers), open-plan areas around big counter, high timbered walls, vaulted roof, shelves of bottles, plenty of farming implements and animal traps, pubby furniture on brown pattered carpet, other areas with inglenooks and a back room with old bicycle memorabilia, up to eight well kept ales including Greene King and Harveys, local cider, several wines by the glass and good choice of reasonably priced home-made food (all day weekends); background jazz and blues (live 4-6pm Sun); well behaved children till 8.30pm, dogs welcome, picnic-sets, boules and play area in peaceful garden with fine Brede Valley views, you can walk to Winchelsea, open all day. *(Tony and Wendy Hobden, Tony Scott, V Brogden, Peter Meister)*

ICKLESHAM TQ8716
★ Robin Hood (01424) 814277
Main Road; TN36 4BD Friendly family-run beamed pub with buoyant local atmosphere, good value unpretentious home-made food (all day Sun) including blackboard specials, up to seven well kept changing ales (always have Greene King IPA) and three proper ciders, hops overhead, lots of copper bric-a-brac, log fire, games area with pool, back

dining conservatory; free wi-fi; children and dogs (in bar) welcome, big garden with play area and boules, fine Brede Valley views, open all day Fri-Sun. *(Julian Richardson)*

ISFIELD TQ4417

Laughing Fish (01825) 750349

Station Road; TN22 5XB Opened-up Victorian local with affable landlord and cheerful efficient staff, enjoyable good value home-cooked food (not Sun evening) including specials board and some good vegetarian options, well kept Greene King ales with three local guests (always one from Isfield), open fire, bar billiards and other traditional games, various events including entertaining beer race Easter Mon; children and dogs welcome, disabled access, small pleasantly shaded walled garden with enclosed play area, field for camping, right by Lavender Line railway (pub was station hotel), open all day. *(Ann and Colin Hunt, John Beeken)*

JEVINGTON TQ5601

Eight Bells (01323) 484442

Jevington Road, N of East Dean; BN26 5QB Village pub in good walking country, simple furnishings, heavy beams, panelling, parquet floor and inglenook, popular home-made food from sandwiches up, well kept ales including Harveys; background music (live Mon), Tues quiz; children and dogs welcome, front terrace and secluded Downs-view garden, adjacent cricket field, open all day. *(Martin Day)*

KINGSTON TQ3908

★ **Juggs** (01273) 472523

Village signed off A27 by roundabout W of Lewes; BN7 3NT Popular tile-hung village pub with heavy 15th-c beams and very low front door, lots of neatly stripped masonry, sturdy wooden furniture on bare boards and stone slabs, log fires, smaller eating areas including a family room, reliable fairly priced food from sandwiches and pub standards up, well kept Harveys and Shepherd Neame, good wines and coffee, friendly helpful young staff; background music, fortnightly quiz; dogs welcome, disabled access/facilities, lots of outside tables including covered area with heaters (they ask to swipe a credit card if you eat here), tubs and hanging baskets, play area, nice Downs walks, open all day. *(John Beeken, Ian Phillips, PL)*

LEWES TQ4110

Black Horse (01273) 473653

Western Road; BN7 1RS Bow-windowed pub with knocked-through bar keeping traditional feel, two log fires, wood floor, panelling and lots of old pictures, half a dozen ales mainly from smaller local brewers and some interesting gins, enjoyable home-made food including tapas, friendly service; quiz nights, sports TV, bar billiards and toad

in the hole; children welcome, beer garden, open (and food) all day. *(Tony Scott)*

LEWES TQ4210

Gardeners Arms (01273) 474808

Cliffe High Street; BN7 2AN Unpretentious little bare-boards local opposite brewery shop, lots of beer mats on gantry, homely stools, built-in wall seats and plain scrubbed tables around three narrow sides of bar, dog water bowl by blocked-up fireplace, Harveys and five interesting changing guests, farm ciders, some lunchtime food including sandwiches, pasties and pies, bar nibbles on Sun, photos of Lewes bonfire night; background music, TV, darts; no children; open all day. *(Sophia and Hamish Greenfield)*

LEWES TQ4210

★ **John Harvey** (01273) 479880

Bear Yard, just off Cliffe High Street; BN7 2AN Bustling tap for nearby Harveys brewery, four of their beers including seasonals kept in top condition, some poured from the cask, good well priced food (not Sun evening) from lunchtime sandwiches, baked potatoes and ciabattas up, regular themed nights, friendly efficient young staff, flagstoned beamed bar with woodburner and huge vat halved to make two snug seating areas, lighter room on left, upstairs restaurant/function room; live music first Sun of the month; a few tables outside, open all day. *(Peter Meister, Tony Scott)*

LEWES TQ4110

★ **Lewes Arms** (01273) 473152

Castle Ditch Lane/Mount Place – tucked behind castle ruins; BN7 1YH Cheerful unpretentious little local with five well kept Fullers ales and two guests, 30 malt whiskies and plenty of wines by the glass, generous helpings of enjoyable reasonably priced bar food including good Sun roasts, tiny front bar on right with stools along curved counter and bench window seats, two other simple rooms hung with photographs and information about the famous Lewes bonfire night, beer mats pinned over doorways, poetry and folk evenings and more obscure events like pea throwing and dwyle flunking; background music; children (away from front bar) and dogs welcome, picnic-sets on attractive split-level back terrace, open all day (till midnight Fri, Sat). *(Conor McGaughey, J A Snell, Ann and Colin Hunt, Tony Scott)*

LEWES TQ4110

★ **Pelham Arms** (01273) 476149

At top of High Street; BN7 1XL Popular 17th-c beamed pub, good well presented food (booking advised) including some interesting vegetarian choices, friendly efficient service, three Badger ales, character rambling interior with inglenook; vintage swing night first Thurs of month; children till 8pm, dogs in bar areas, small courtyard garden, open all day. *(Ann and Colin Hunt)*

LEWES TQ4110
Rights of Man (01273) 486894
High Street; BN7 1YE Central Harveys
pub close to the law courts, five of their ales
kept well and enjoyable food including tapas,
spruced-up Victorian-style décor with a series
of booths, another bar at the back and roof
terrace; background music, free wi-fi; open
all day. *(Peter Barrett)*

LEWES TQ4210
★**Snowdrop** (01273) 471018
South Street; BN7 2BU Welcoming pub
tucked below the chalk cliffs; narrowboat
theme with brightly painted servery and
colourful jugs, kettles, lanterns etc hanging
from curved planked ceiling, wide mix of
simple furniture on parquet flooring, old
sewing machines and huge stone jars, slightly
bohemian atmosphere; well kept range
of ales including Dark Star and Harveys,
a couple of ciders and hearty helpings of
enjoyable reasonably priced food (good
vegetarian options), nice coffee, cheerful
efficient staff (may ask for a credit card if
running a tab), more tables in upstairs room
(spiral stairs) with bar billiards and darts;
background music – live jazz Mon; dogs very
welcome (menu for them), outside seating on
both sides with pretty hanging baskets, open
all day. *(Ann and Colin Hunt, Peter Meister,
Robert W Buckle)*

LINDFIELD TQ3425
Bent Arms (01444) 483146
High Street; RH16 2HP Surprisingly
spacious 16th-c village coaching inn with low
black beams, timbers and some stained glass,
most tables set for their popular affordably
priced food including lunchtime sandwiches
and ploughman's using own bread, good value
evening set menu, three well kept Badger
ales, friendly service; children welcome,
sizeable back garden with covered area, nine
bedrooms and cottage. *(Mrs P R Sykes,
Tony and Wendy Hobden, Tony Scott)*

LITLINGTON TQ5201
Plough & Harrow (01323) 870632
*Between A27 Lewes–Polegate and A259
E of Seaford; BN26 5RE* Neatly extended
17th-c flint village pub, large beamed bar
with smaller rooms off, half a dozen well kept
ales including at least three from Long Man,
decent wines by the glass and good selection
of food from lunchtime pub staples to more
enterprising dishes using local ingredients,
friendly attentive service; monthly live music
and Aug beer festival; children and dogs
welcome, attractive back garden, good walks
(on South Downs Way), open all day, food all
day weekends. *(John Beeken)*

LITTLEHAMPTON TQ0202
★**Arun View** (01903) 722335
*Wharf Road; W towards Chichester;
BN17 5DD* Refurbished pub in lovely
harbour spot with busy waterway directly
below windows, popular good value food (all
day Sun) from sandwiches/ciabattas to good
fresh fish, brunch Mon-Sat from 10.30am,
well kept Arundel, Fullers and Ringwood,
several wines by the glass, cheerful helpful
staff, flagstoned and panelled back bar with
banquettes and dark wood tables, large
dining conservatory; background and monthly
live music, TVs, pool; children welcome,
disabled facilities, flower-filled terrace,
interesting waterside walkway to coast,
four bedrooms, open all day. *(Peter Meister,
Tony and Wendy Hobden)*

LITTLEHAMPTON TQ0202
Steam Packet (01903) 715994
River Road; BN17 5BZ Renovated 19th-c
corner pub just across from the Arun View;
open-plan interior providing several separate
seating areas, well kept ales such as Courage,
Langham and Timothy Taylors, enjoyable food
from snacks to daily specials; quiz Thurs,
jazz Fri; seats out in small area facing river,
raised back garden, open all day, no food Sun
evening. *(Tony Scott, Tony and Wendy Hobden)*

LITTLEWORTH TQ1921
Windmill (01403) 710308
*Sign for pub off the B2135 N of
Partridge Green; village signed off A272
southbound, W of Cowfold; RH13 8EJ*
Refurbished brick and tile inn dating from
the 17th c, two flagstoned bars, one with
inglenook log fire, the other with woodburner,
beams and lots of old farming tools etc on
walls and ceiling, enjoyable home-made food
(all day weekends) from sandwiches and pub
standards up, well kept Harveys and a couple
of guests, restaurant; bar billiards, darts, TV;
children welcome, picnic-sets in peaceful
garden overlooking fields, bedrooms, open
all day. *(Anne and Ben Smith)*

LODSWORTH SU9321
Halfway Bridge Inn (01798) 861281
*Just before village, on A272 Midhurst–
Petworth; GU28 9BP* Restauranty 17th-c
coaching inn with character rooms, good
oak chairs and individual mix of tables,
log fires (one in polished kitchen range),
interconnecting restaurant areas with beams
and wooden floors, generally well liked food
(all day weekends), Langham, Long Man
and Sharps Doom Bar, wide range of wines
by the glass; background music, newspapers
and free wi-fi; children and dogs (in bar)
welcome, small back terrace, seven bedrooms
in former stable yard, open all day. *(Brian
and Sally Wakeham)*

LODSWORTH SU9223
Hollist Arms (01798) 861310
Off A272 Midhurst–Petworth; GU28 9BZ
In lovely spot by village green and under
friendly newish management; small snug
room on right with open fire, public bar on
left serving local Langham, two guest beers

and a dozen wines by the glass, enjoyable fairly traditional food (not Sun evening) including some european influences, L-shaped dining room with wood-strip floor, inglenook and comfortable seating area, interesting prints and paintings (some by the chef); children and dogs welcome, steps up to cottagey back garden, picnic-sets on terrace or you can sit under a huge horse chestnut on the green, good walks nearby, open all day. *(Peter Barrett)*

LOWER BEEDING   TQ2225
Crabtree (01403) 892666
Brighton Road; RH13 6PT Family-run pub with Victorian façade but much older inside with Tudor beams and huge inglenook (dated 1537), simple light modern décor, dining room in converted barn, good interesting food (not Sun evening) using local seasonal produce, friendly service, well kept Badger beers and good selection of wines by the glass including english fizz; children welcome, dogs in bar, landscaped garden, with fine country views, handy for Nymans (NT), open all day. *(Jamie Green)*

LYMINSTER   TQ0204
Six Bells (01903) 713639
Lyminster Road (A284), Wick; BN17 7PS Unassuming 18th-c flint pub with open bar and separate dining room, well kept Fullers London Pride, Sharps Doom Bar and good house wines, generous helpings of enjoyable food cooked by landlord (best to book weekends), friendly efficient staff, low black beams, wood floor and big inglenook with horsebrasses, pubby furnishings; background music, free wi-fi; children and dogs (in one area) welcome, terrace and garden seating. *(John Beeken)*

MAYFIELD   TQ5826
Middle House (01435) 872146
High Street; TN20 6AB Handsome 16th-c timbered inn, L-shaped beamed bar with massive fireplace, several well kept ales including Harveys, local cider and decent wines, quiet lounge area with leather chesterfields around log fire in ornate carved fireplace, good choice of enjoyable food, friendly staff coping well at busy times, attractive panelled restaurant; background music; children welcome, terraced back garden with lovely views, five bedrooms, open all day. *(Tony Scott)*

MAYFIELD   TQ5927
★ **Rose & Crown** (01435) 872200
Fletching Street; TN20 6TE Pretty 16th-c weatherboarded pub set down lane from village centre; two cosy front character rooms with coins stuck to low ceiling boards, bench seats built into partly panelled walls and

simple furniture on floorboards, inglenook log fire, tankards above bar serving Harveys and a guest, several wines by the glass, decent all-day food (till 7pm Sun) including tapas night last Thurs of the month, further small room behind servery and larger carpeted one down steps; live music Sat, Tues quiz, free wi-fi; children (till 8.30pm) and dogs welcome, raised front terrace, decked back garden, open all day (till midnight Fri, Sat). *(Ruth May)*

MID LAVANT   SU8508
★ **Earl of March** (01243) 533993
A286 Lavant Road; PO18 0BQ Updated and extended with emphasis on eating, but seats for drinkers in flagstoned log-fire bar, well kept Harveys, Timothy Taylors and a guest such as Long Man, nice wines by the glass including champagne and english fizz, good if pricey food with much sourced locally, plush dining area and conservatory with seafood bar, pleasant staff; free wi-fi; children and dogs welcome, delightful location with view up to Goodwood from neatly kept garden, local walks, open all day. *(Miss A E Dare, Mrs J Ekins-Daukes)*

MILLAND   SU8328
Rising Sun (01428) 741347
Iping Road junction with main road through village; GU30 7NA Busy 20th-c red-brick Fullers pub, three of their ales and varied choice of fresh well presented food including specials and weekday lunchtime/ early evening offers, friendly helpful staff, three linked rooms including cheery log-fire bar and bare-boards restaurant; live music first Fri of month, free wi-fi; children and dogs welcome, extensive lawns attractively divided by tall yew hedge, canopied heated terrace and smokers' gazebo, good walking area, open all day weekends. *(Tony Smaithe)*

MILTON STREET   TQ5304
★ **Sussex Ox** (01323) 870840
Off A27 just under a mile E of Alfriston roundabout; BN26 5RL Extended country pub (originally a 1900s slaughterhouse) with magnificent Downs views; bar area with a couple of high tables and chairs on bare boards, old local photographs, three real ales including Harveys and good choice of wines by the glass, lower brick-floored room with farmhouse furniture and woodburner, similarly furnished dining room (children allowed here), further front eating area with high-backed rush-seated chairs, popular food from traditional choices up, friendly service; dogs welcome in bar, teak seating on raised back deck taking in the view, picnic-sets in garden below and more under parasols at front, open all day weekends. *(Dr Nigel Bowles, Tony Scott)*

We say if we know a pub allows dogs.

NETHERFIELD TQ7118
Netherfield Arms (01424) 838282
Just off B2096 Heathfield–Battle;
TN33 9QD Low-ceilinged 18th-c country
dining pub with wide choice of enjoyable food
including good specials, friendly attentive
service, decent wines and a well kept ale
such as Long Man, inglenook log fire, cosy
restaurant; lovely back garden with picnic
sets, far-reaching views from front, closed
Sun evening, Mon. *(Julian Richardson)*

NEWHAVEN TQ4500
Hope (01273) 515389
Follow West Beach signs from A259
westbound; BN9 9DN Big-windowed
pub overlooking busy harbour entrance;
long bar with raised area, open fires and
comfy sofas, upstairs dining conservatory
and breezy balcony tables with even better
view towards Seaford Head, well kept ales
such as Dark Star and Harveys, good choice
of generous realistically priced food (till
7pm Sun), friendly staff; regular live music;
tables on grassed waterside area.
(Andrew Stone)

NEWICK TQ4121
Royal Oak (01825) 722506
Church Road; BN8 4JU White
weatherboarded two-bar pub on edge of
lovely village green, neat and comfortable,
with enjoyable good value food, well kept
Harveys and Long Man, friendly staff, big
open fire; children and dogs welcome
(affable pub dog), tables out in front, open
all day. *(Tony Scott)*

NUTBOURNE TQ0718
Rising Sun (01798) 812191
Off A283 E of Pulborough; The Street;
RH20 2HE Unspoilt creeper-clad village
pub dating partly from the 16th c (same
owner for 35 years); front bar with beams,
exposed brickwork and woodburner,
scrubbed tables on bare boards, some 1920s
fashion and dance posters, Fullers London
Pride, local Greyhound and a couple of
guests, good well presented food from pub
favourites up, friendly service, second bar
leading through to quarry-tiled restaurant,
cosy back family room; background and
monthly live music; dogs welcome (Chalky
is the resident lucas terrier), small pond
and smokers' shelter out behind, archway
through to lawned area. *(Richard Tilbrook,*
Tony Scott)

NUTHURST TQ1926
Black Horse (01403) 891272
Off A281 SE of Horsham; RH13 6LH
Welcoming 17th-c country pub under
newish management; low black beams,
flagstones/bare boards, inglenook log fire
and plenty of character in its several small
rooms, enjoyable good value food served
by friendly attentive staff, four real ales

including Fullers London Pride; charity quiz
Weds; children and dogs welcome, pretty
streamside back garden, more seats on front
terrace, open all day Sat, till 8pm Sun.
(Julian Richardson)

OFFHAM TQ3912
Blacksmiths Arms (01273) 472971
A275 N of Lewes; BN7 3QD Open-
plan dining pub with good food from pub
favourites up, well kept Goldstone, Harveys
and Hurst, efficient friendly service,
clean updated interior with a couple of
woodburners, one in huge end inglenook;
children and dogs (in bar) welcome, french
windows to terrace, four bedrooms (steep
stairs), open all day. *(PL)*

PARTRIDGE GREEN TQ1819
★ Green Man (01403) 710250
Off A24 just under a mile S of A272
junction – take B2135 at West Grinstead
signpost; pub at Jolesfield, N of Partridge
Green; RH13 8JT Relaxed gently upmarket
dining pub with popular enterprising food,
well chosen wines by the glass including
champagne, Dark Star and Harveys, excellent
service; unassuming front area by counter
with bentwood bar seats, stools and library
chairs around one or two low tables, old
curved high-back settle, main eating
area widening into back part with pretty
enamelled stove and pitched ceiling on left,
more self-contained room on right with
stag's head, minimal decoration but plenty of
atmosphere; cast-iron seats and picnic-sets
under parasols in neat back garden, closed
Sun evening. *(Jamie Green)*

PARTRIDGE GREEN TQ1819
Partridge (01403) 710391
Church Road/High Street; RH13 8JS
Spacious 19th-c village pub (former station
hotel) now tap for Dark Star, their full range
and maybe a guest, real cider, enjoyable
sensibly priced home-made food (not Sun,
Mon evenings) including blackboard specials
and deals, friendly relaxed atmosphere; darts
and pool; children and dogs welcome, garden
with play equipment and large terrace, open
all day. *(Tony and Wendy Hobden)*

PATCHING TQ0705
Fox (01903) 871299
Arundel Road; signed off A27 eastbound
just W of Worthing; BN13 3UJ Generous
good value home-made food including
popular Sun roasts (best to book), quick
friendly service even at busy times, two or
three well kept local ales, large dining area
off roomy panelled bar, dark pubby furniture
on patterned carpet, hunting pictures;
quiet background music; children and dogs
welcome, disabled access, colourful hanging
baskets and good-sized tree-shaded garden
with well laid-out seating, heaters and
play area, open all day Sun till 9pm.
(David Jackman, Tony and Wendy Hobden)

PATCHING TQ0805

Worlds End (01903) 871346

Former A27 Worthing–Arundel, off A280 roundabout; BN13 3UQ Long roomy pub next to Patching Pond, good range of food from baguettes up (smaller helpings available for some choices), well kept Badger beers including seasonal, friendly efficient staff, large raftered barn-style family room; good-sized garden with play area, open (and food) all day, kitchen closes 7pm Sun. *(Tony and Wendy Hobden)*

PETT TQ8713

Royal Oak (01424) 812515

Pett Road; TN35 4HG Brick and weatherboarded village pub, roomy main bar with big open fire, well kept Harveys and a couple of changing guests, popular home-made food (not Sun evening) including several fish dishes, two dining areas, efficient friendly service; monthly live music (often Irish) and quiz nights, traditional games; dogs welcome, small garden behind, open all day. *(Peter Meister)*

PETT TQ8613

Two Sawyers (01424) 812255

Pett Road, off A259; TN35 4HB Meandering low-beamed rooms including bare-boards bar with stripped tables, tiny snug, passage sloping down to restaurant, popular good value freshly made food, friendly helpful service, well kept Harveys and guests, local cider/perry and wide range of wines; background music; children welcome in restaurant, dogs in bar, suntrap front courtyard, back garden with shady trees and well spaced tables, three bedrooms, open all day. *(Peter Barrett)*

PETWORTH SU9719

Badgers (01798) 342651

Station Road (A285 1.5 miles S); GU28 0JF Restauranty dining pub with good up-to-date food including tapas, seasonal game and seafood, frequent Sun hog/lamb roasts, can eat in bar areas or restaurant, friendly accommodating staff, a couple of changing ales such as Sharps and Youngs, good choice of wines, cosy fireside area with sofas; free wi-fi; over-5s allowed in bar's eating area, stylish tables and seats on terrace by water lily pool, summer barbecues, three well appointed bedrooms, good breakfast, closed winter Sun evening. *(Helena and Trevor Fraser)*

PETWORTH SU9721

Star (01798) 342569

Market Square; GU28 0AH Airy opened-up old pub with well kept Fullers/Gales ales and decent wines, good choice of enjoyable food (not Sun evening), friendly service, log fire; free wi-fi; a few seats on terrace looking on to market square, open all day. *(Helena and Trevor Fraser)*

PETWORTH SU9722

Stonemasons (01798) 342510

North Street; GU28 9NL Attractive low-beamed 17th-c inn; enjoyable freshly made food at fair prices, two or three ales including Skinners Betty Stogs, helpful efficient staff, opened-up modernised areas in former adjoining cottages, inglenook log fires; children and dogs welcome, picnic-sets in pleasant sheltered back garden, five bedrooms, opposite Petworth House (NT) so can get busy, open all day. *(Tony and Wendy Hobden)*

PETWORTH SU9921

Welldiggers Arms (01798) 344288

Low Heath; A283 E; GU28 0HG Recently refurbished and extended after having been in same family for nearly 70 years; bar keeping oak furniture made by previous landlord's father, painted low beams, brick fireplace and old pictures, four real ales from fork handle handpumps including a house beer (Ted's Tickle) brewed by Arundel, enjoyable food from pub favourites up, modern flagstoned picture-window restaurant with open kitchen and deli counter, glassed-over illuminated well; children and dogs (in bar) welcome, tables outside with Downs views, pizza oven, 14 new bedrooms, closed Sun evening. *(Sophia and Hamish Greenfield)*

PLUMPTON TQ3613

★**Half Moon** (01273) 890253

Ditchling Road (B2116); BN7 3AF Enlarged beamed and timbered roadside dining pub with good locally sourced food from pub favourites up, local ales and plenty of wines by the glass, good friendly service, log fire with unusual flint chimneybreast; background music; children and dogs (in bar) welcome, tables in wisteria-clad front courtyard and on back terrace, big Downs-view garden with picnic area, good walks nearby, open all day (till 6pm Sun). *(Julian Richardson)*

RINGMER TQ4512

Green Man (01273) 812422

Lewes Road; BN8 5NA Welcoming 1930s roadside pub with busy mix of locals and visitors, at least six real ales from brick-faced counter including Greene King, wide range of generous good value food, efficient friendly service, long bar with log fire, large restaurant, conservatory; children and dogs welcome, terrace tables, more on lawn under trees, play area, open (and food) all day. *(John Beeken)*

RODMELL TQ4105

Abergavenny Arms (01273) 472416

Back road Lewes–Newhaven; BN7 3EZ Welcoming beamed and raftered ex-barn, large open-plan bar with wood and tiled floors, several recesses and log fire in big fireplace, good selection of enjoyable bar food (not Sun evening), well kept Harveys and one or more local guests, upstairs eating area, games room; occasional live music, free wi-fi; children welcome, large two-level back terrace, handy for Virginia Woolf's Monk's House (NT) and South Downs Way, open all day. *(John Beeken)*

ROTTINGDEAN   TQ3602
Queen Victoria (01273) 302121
High Street; BN2 7HF Welcoming 1930s mock-Tudor pub with six well kept local ales such as Harveys and Long Man, proper ciders, good range of wines by the glass and over 30 gins, enjoyable locally sourced home-made food (not Weds) from daily changing menu, vegetarians/vegans well catered for, long partitioned room with large chandeliers, painted panelling, mix of old furniture and log fire; background music, live jazz Sat lunchtime; dogs welcome, small back garden, handy for seaside walks, open all day. *(Tony and Wendy Hobden)*

ROWHOOK   TQ1234
★**Chequers** (01403) 790480
Off A29 NW of Horsham; RH12 3PY Attractive 15th-c country pub, beamed and flagstoned front bar with portraits and inglenook log fire, step up to low-ceilinged lounge, well kept Harveys and guests, decent wines by the glass and good food from chef-landlord using local ingredients including home-grown vegetables, young enthusiastic staff, separate restaurant; background music; children and dogs welcome, tables out on front terraces and in pretty garden behind, good play area, closed Sun evening. *(John Preddy, Ian and Rose Lock)*

RUSHLAKE GREEN   TQ6218
Horse & Groom (01435) 830320
Off B2096 Heathfield–Battle; TN21 9QE Pretty little village green pub under welcoming dutch licensees; L-shaped low-beamed bar with brick fireplace, small room down a step and dining room to the right with inglenook, good interesting food (more pubby at lunchtime) including some dutch dishes, Harveys, Shepherd Neame and decent wines by the glass; children and dogs welcome, cottagey garden with country views, nice walks, closed Sun evening, Mon, otherwise open all day. *(Peter Barrett)*

RUSPER   TQ1836
★**Royal Oak** (01293) 871393
Friday Street, towards Warnham – back road N of Horsham, E of A24 (OS Sheet 187 map reference 185369); RH12 4QA Old-fashioned and well worn-in tile-hung pub in very rural spot on Sussex Border Path, small carpeted top bar with leather sofas and armchairs, log fire, steps down to long beamed main bar with plush wall seats, pine tables and chairs and homely knick-knacks, well kept Surrey Hills Ranmore

and six changing guests, farm ciders and perries, short choice of enjoyable low-priced lunchtime food (evenings and Sun lunch by pre-arrangement), plain games room with darts; no children inside, a few picnic-sets on grass by road and in streamside garden beyond car park, roaming chickens (eggs for sale), bedrooms, closes at 9pm (4pm Sun). *(Tony Scott, Alastair and Sheree Hepburn)*

RUSPER   TQ2037
Star (01293) 871264
Off A264 S of Crawley; RH12 4RA Several linked rooms in rambling 15th-c beamed coaching inn, friendly and cosy, with well kept Fullers London Pride, Greene King Abbot and Sharps Doom Bar, good choice of popular food from sandwiches and light meals up including some greek dishes, wood floors, old tools on walls, fine brick inglenook; dogs welcome, small back terrace. *(Ian Phillips)*

RYE   TQ9220
★**George** (01797) 222114
High Street; TN31 7JT Sizeable hotel with popular beamed bar, mix of furniture including settles on bare boards, log fire, ales such as Dark Star, Franklins, Harveys and Old Dairy, continental beers on tap too, friendly service from neat young staff, interesting bistro-style food, big spreading restaurant to right of main door; may be background jazz; children and dogs welcome, attractive bedrooms, open all day. *(Alf Wright, Caroline Prescott)*

RYE   TQ9220
★**Globe** (01797) 225220
Military Road; TN31 7NX Small weatherboarded pub under same owners as the Five Bells at Brabourne and Woolpack at Warehorne (both in Kent); revamped interior full of quirky touches such as corrugated iron-clad walls, hanging lobster pot lights and eclectic range of furniture from school chairs to a table made from part of an old fishing boat, even hay bale seats in one area, scatter cushions, fresh flowers, candles and paraffin lamps, two log fires, good locally sourced food from open kitchen with wood-fired oven, interesting local ales and ciders (no bar counter), also some wines from nearby Chapel Down, shelves of home-made preserves for sale, quick cheerful service; unisex loos; children and dogs welcome, seats on side decking, Sat market, open all day. *(Peter Meister, Mike and Eleanor Anderson, Tracy Collins)*

RYE   TQ9220
★**Mermaid** (01797) 223065
Mermaid Street; TN31 7EY Fine old timbered inn on famous cobbled street (cellars date from 12th c, although pub was rebuilt in 1420); civilised antiques-filled bar, Victorian gothick carved chairs, older but plainer oak seats, huge working inglenook

with massive bressumer, Fullers, Greene King and Harveys, good selection of wines and malt whiskies, well liked food in bar (not Sat evening) or restaurant with more elaborate and expensive evening choices, efficient friendly service, reputedly haunted by five ghosts; background music; children welcome, seats on small back terrace, bedrooms (most with four-posters), open all day. *(DF and NF, Stephen Shepherd)*

RYE
TQ9120

★**Standard** (01797) 225231
The Mint, High Street; TN31 7EN
Ancient pub sympathetically opened up and renovated, moulded beams, exposed brickwork and panelling, brown leather and farmhouse chairs at rustic tables on quarry tiles, candles and log fires (stag's head above one), four well kept ales including nearby Three Legs, good fairly priced food using local ingredients (fish from the harbour), nice wines and decent coffee, friendly accommodating staff; outside gents'; well behaved children and dogs welcome, picnic-sets on small back terrace, five well appointed character bedrooms, open all day. *(Peter Meister, Mike and Eleanor Anderson)*

RYE HARBOUR
TQ9419

Inkerman Arms (01797) 222464
Rye Harbour Road; TN31 7TQ Friendly 19th-c end of terrace pub near nature reserve, enjoyable food including good fish and chips, Old Dairy Red Top, Gold Top and an occasional guest; children and dogs welcome, picnic-sets in sheltered back terrace with pond, open all day Fri-Sun. *(Jamie Green)*

SEDLESCOMBE
TQ7817

Queens Head (01424) 870228
The Green; TN33 0QA Attractive tile-hung village-green pub; beamed main bar on right with mixed tables and wheelback chairs on wood floor, church candles and fresh flowers, a huge cartwheel and some farming odds and ends, Harveys and Sharps Doom Bar from plank-fronted servery, side room laid for dining with brick fireplace, sofas in back lounge, another dining room to left of entrance with sisal flooring and huge working inglenook, good popular food (best to book) from shortish menu; quiet background music; children and dogs welcome, picnic-sets in garden. *(Simon Sharpe)*

SHORTBRIDGE
TQ4521

★**Peacock** (01825) 762463
Piltdown; OS Sheet 198 map reference 450215; TN22 3XA Civilised and welcoming old country dining pub with two fine yew trees flanking entrance, dark beams, timbers and big inglenook, some nice old furniture on parquet floors, good freshly made food from light dishes up (not Sun night), two or three well kept ales and decent wines by the glass, friendly attentive

staff, restaurant; children welcome, back garden and terrace. *(Tony Scott)*

SIDLESHAM
SZ8697

★**Crab & Lobster** (01243) 641233
Mill Lane; off B2145 S of Chichester; PO20 7NB Restaurant-with-rooms rather than pub but walkers and bird-watchers welcome in small flagstoned bar for light meals, Harveys, Sharps and 17 wines by the glass including champagne, stylish upmarket restaurant with good imaginative (and pricey) food including excellent local fish, competent friendly young staff; background music; children welcome, tables on back terrace overlooking marshes, smart bedrooms, self-catering cottage, open all day (food all day weekends). *(Tracey and Stephen Groves, Richard Tilbrook)*

SINGLETON
SU8713

Partridge (01243) 811251
Just off A286 Midhurst–Chichester; PO18 0EY Pretty 16th-c pub in attractive village setting; all sorts of light and dark wood tables and dining chairs on polished wooden floors, flagstones or carpet, some country knick-knacks, open fires and woodburner, well kept Fullers London Pride, Harveys Best and a summer guest, several wines by the glass, mostly well liked food, friendly if not always speedy service; background music; daily papers and board games; children and dogs welcome, plenty of seats under parasols on terrace and in walled garden, handy for Weald & Downland Open Air Museum. *(Robert Wivell)*

SLINDON
SU9708

Spur (01243) 814216
Slindon Common; A29 towards Bognor; BN18 0NE Roomy 17th-c pub with good choice of popular food from bar snacks and pub favourites up, Courage Directors and Sharps Doom Bar, friendly staff, pine tables and two big log fires, large panelled restaurant, games room with darts and pool, skittle alley; quiz fourth Weds of the month, some live music; children welcome, dogs in bar, pretty garden (traffic noise), good local walks, open all day Sun. *(Andrew and Michele Revell)*

SMALL DOLE
TQ2112

Fox (01273) 491196
Henfield Road; BN5 9XE Busy roadside village pub with good choice of well liked/priced home-made food including popular weekday set menu, quick friendly service even at busy times, Harveys and one or two guests, large dining area off roomy panelled bar, dark pubby furniture on patterned carpet, hunting pictures; quiet background music; children and dogs welcome, disabled access, colourful hanging baskets and good-sized tree-shaded garden with play area, open all day weekends (food all day Sun till 8pm). *(Tony and Wendy Hobden)*

SOUTHWATER TQ1528
Bax Castle (01403) 730369
*Two Mile Ash, a mile or so NW;
RH13 0LA* Early 19th-c country pub (some
recent refurbishment) with well liked/priced
traditional home-made food, also wood-fired
pizzas and Sun carvery, three Marstons-
related ales, friendly staff, sofas next to big
log fire, barn restaurant; background music;
children and dogs welcome, pleasant garden
with play area, near Downs Link path on
former railway track, open all day (till 9pm
Sun). *(Tony Scott, Tony and Wendy Hobden)*

STAPLEFIELD TQ2728
Jolly Tanners (01444) 400335
Handcross Road, just off A23; RH17 6EF
Split-level local by cricket green, welcoming
landlord and pub dogs, two good log fires,
padded settles, lots of china, brasses and old
photographs, Fullers, Harveys and four guests
(beer festivals), real cider, enjoyable pubby
food including range of 'sizzling' dishes,
friendly chatty atmosphere; background and
some live music; children and dogs welcome,
attractive suntrap garden, quite convenient
for Nymans (NT), open all day Fri-Sun.
(Tony Scott)

STAPLEFIELD TQ2728
Victory (01444) 400463
Warninglid Road; RH17 6EU Pretty little
shuttered dining pub overlooking cricket
green (and London to Brighton veteran car
run, first Sun in Nov), friendly welcoming
staff, good choice of popular home-made food
with smaller helpings for children, well kept
Harveys, local cider and decent wines from
zinc-topped counter, beams and woodburner;
dogs welcome, nice tree-shaded garden with
play area. *(Tony Scott)*

STEDHAM SU8522
Hamilton Arms (01730) 812555
School Lane (off A272); GU29 0NZ
Village local run by friendly thai family,
standard pub food as well as good thai bar
snacks and restaurant dishes (you can buy
ingredients in their little shop), good value
Sun buffet, reasonably priced wines and
four or more well kept ales, games room;
background music; pretty hanging baskets
on front terrace overlooking small green,
nearby walks, closed Mon, otherwise open
all day. *(Ruth May)*

STOPHAM TQ0318
★ **White Hart** (01798) 874903
*Off A283 E of village, W of Pulborough;
RH20 1DS* Fine old beamed pub by
medieval River Arun bridge, well kept
Harveys, Langham and Sharps, good food
from ciabattas, sharing plates and stone-
baked pizzas up, friendly efficient service;

summer Sun afternoon jazz; children and
dogs (in bar) welcome, waterside tables,
open all day, food all day Sat, till 6pm Sun.
(Alastair and Sheree Hepburn)

STOUGHTON SU8011
Hare & Hounds (023) 9263 1433
*Signed off B2146 Petersfield–Emsworth;
PO18 9JQ* Airy pine-clad country dining
pub with good reasonably priced fresh food
from sandwiches to Sun roasts, up to six
well kept ales and Weston's cider, cheerful
service, flagstones and big open fires, locals'
bar with darts; quiz nights; children (in
eating areas) and dogs welcome, tables on
pretty front terrace and grass behind, lovely
setting near Saxon church, good walks, open
all day Fri-Sun. *(Ann and Colin Hunt)*

SUTTON SU9715
★ **White Horse** (01798) 869221
The Street; RH20 1PS Cleanly modernised
country inn close to Bignor Roman Villa; bar
with open brick fireplace at each end, tea-
lights on mantelpieces, cushioned high bar
chairs, three well kept ales and good wines
by the glass, two-room barrel-vaulted dining
area with minimalist décor and another little
fire, good value well thought-of food from
sandwiches up, friendly helpful young staff;
children and dogs (in bar) welcome, steps up
to lawn with plenty of picnic-sets, more seats
at front, good surrounding walks, bedrooms,
closed Mon and Sun evenings. *(Julian
Richardson)*

THAKEHAM TQ1017
White Lion (01798) 813141
*Off B2139 N of Storrington; The Street;
RH20 3EP* Steps up to 16th-c pub in pretty
village (level access from back car park);
heavy beams, panelling, bare boards and
traditional furnishings, four changing ales
and decent wines by the glass, well liked
food (not Sun evening) including good
selection of blackboard specials, efficient
service, pleasant dining room with inglenook;
children and dogs welcome, nice sunny
terrace and small enclosed lawn, open all day.
(Alastair and Sheree Hepburn,Celia Caulkin)

TICEHURST TQ6831
★ **Bull** (01580) 200586
*Three Leg Cross; off B2099 towards
Wadhurst; TN5 7HH* Attractive 14th-c
country pub popular with good mix of
customers, big log fires in two heavy-beamed
old-fashioned bars, well kept Harveys and a
couple of guests, contemporary furnishings
and flooring in light airy dining extension
serving good food (not Sun evening),
friendly service; children and dogs welcome,
charming front garden (busy in summer),
bigger back one with play area, four
bedrooms, open all day. *(Peter Meister)*

There are report forms at the back of the book.

TURNERS HILL TQ3435
Crown (01342) 715218
East Street; RH10 4PT Modernised village
pub dating from the 16th c, low-beamed
bar with sofas by big log fire, steps down
to high-raftered dining area with parquet
floor and another fire, decent food from
sandwiches and pubby choices up, well kept
ales including Harveys and St Austell, good
service; children welcome, picnic-sets out
in front and in sheltered back garden, valley
views, open all day. *(Ruth May)*

TURNERS HILL TQ3435
★ **Red Lion** (01342) 715416
Lion Lane, just off B2028; RH10 4NU
Old-fashioned, unpretentious and welcoming
country local; snug parquet-floored bar
with plush wall benches and small open
fire, steps up to carpeted dining area with
inglenook log fire, cushioned pews and
settles, old photos and brewery memorabilia,
well kept Harveys ales and good home-made
food (lunchtime only – must book Sun);
live music and quiz nights; children (away
from bar) and dogs welcome, picnic-sets on
side grass overlooking village, open all day
weekends. *(Nick Lawless, Tony and Wendy
Hobden, Tony Scott, Mrs P R Sykes)*

UDIMORE TQ8818
Plough (01797) 223381
*Cock Marling (B2089 W of Rye);
TN31 6AL* Popular refurbished and
extended 17th-c roadside pub; good freshly
made food including tapas, bargain main
course deal Weds evening, well kept Harveys,
a house beer brewed by Old Dairy and a
guest, good choice of wines by the glass,
weekday happy hour (5.30-7pm), friendly
service, L-shaped main bar with wood floor,
separate back dining room, two woodburners;
children and dogs welcome, tables on good-
sized sunny back terrace, Brede Valley views,
closed Sun evening. *(Peter Meister)*

UPPER DICKER TQ5409
Plough (01323) 844859
Coldharbour Road; BN27 3QJ Extended
17th-c pub with small central beamed bar,
seats by inglenook, two dining areas off to
the left and step up to larger dining bar on
right with raised section, well kept Shepherd
Neame and Harveys, enjoyable food from
pubby choices up; background and live music
(Fri); children and dogs welcome, good-sized
garden with play area, open (and food) all
day. *(Mike and Shelley Woodroffe, Nigel and Jean
Eames, Paul A Moore)*

WADHURST TQ6431
White Hart (01892) 782850
High Street; TN5 6AP Late 19th-c village-
centre pub with L-shaped bar, squashy sofa
at one end, old local photos on grey-green
paintwork above a darker dado, wooden
and cushioned dining chairs around tables

of varying sizes on stripped wood flooring,
large map of the area covering one wall,
gilt-edged mirror above open fireplace, up to
six well kept predominantly local ales such
as Larkins, Long Man and Old Dairy, decent
wines by the glass, fairly priced food (not
Sun evening) including pizzas, friendly staff;
background music; chunky picnic-sets out in
front, more in neat crazy-paved little back
garden, open all day. *(Anne and Ben Smith)*

WALBERTON SU9705
Holly Tree (01243) 553110
The Street; BN18 0PH Grey-painted 19th-c
village pub with fun quirky décor (a mix of
gothic, bling and glitz said one reader), good
choice of enjoyable food from sandwiches
and sharing plates up, also vegetarian menu
and OAP weekday lunch deal, friendly well
trained young staff; quiz nights; children
and dogs welcome, café-style furniture and
planters on front terrace, open (and food)
all day. *(Paul Humphreys)*

WALDERTON SU7910
Barley Mow (023) 9263 1321
*Stoughton Road, just off B2146
Chichester–Petersfield; PO18 9ED*
Popular country pub with good food including
Sun carvery, ales such as Adnams, Ringwood
and Sharps, friendly service, two log fires in
U-shaped bar with roomy dining areas; skittle
alley; children welcome, big streamside back
garden, good walks (Kingley Vale nearby) and
handy for Stansted Park, open all day, food
till 6pm Sun. *(Brian and Sally Wakeham)*

WALDRON TQ5419
★ **Star** (01435) 812495
Blackboys–Horam side road; TN21 0RA
Pretty pub in quiet village across from the
church; beamed main bar with settle next to
good log fire in brick inglenook, wheelbacks
around pubby tables on old quarry tiles,
several built-in cushioned wall and window
seats, old local pictures and photographs,
high stools by central counter serving a
couple of well kept Harveys ales and a guest,
maybe own apple juice, good food including
bar snacks, pubby dishes and specials (not
Mon and Sun evenings), dining areas with
painted chairs around pine-topped tables on
parquet or bare boards, bookshelf wallpaper,
chatty local atmosphere and friendly
staff; some live music, quiz last Mon of the
month; picnic-sets in pleasant back garden,
wassailing on Twelfth Night, small café and
shop next door. *(Mike and Eleanor Anderson)*

WARBLETON TQ6018
★ **Black Duck** (01435) 830636
S of B2096 SE of Heathfield; TN21 9BD
Friendly licensees at this small renovated
pub tucked down from church; L-shaped
main room with pale oak flooring, cushioned
leather sofas in front of roaring inglenook,
beams and walls hung with horsebrasses,
tankards, musical instruments, farm tools,

even an old typewriter, high-backed dining chairs around mix of tables, popular pubby food including daily specials, bar area up a step with stools along counter, Harveys, Sharps Doom Bar and nice wines by the glass, cabinet of books and board games; background music; picnic-sets in back garden with sweeping valley views, more on front grass. *(Helena and Trevor Fraser)*

WARNHAM   TQ1533
Sussex Oak (01403) 265028
Just off A24 Horsham–Dorking; Church Street; RH12 3QW Cheerfully busy country pub with heavy beams and timbers, mix of flagstones, tiles, wood and carpeting, big inglenook log fire, well kept Fullers, Harveys, Timothy Taylors and guests from carved servery, real cider and plenty of wines by the glass, enjoyable fairly traditional food (all day weekends), high-raftered restaurant; background and some live music, Thurs quiz, darts, free wi-fi; children and dogs welcome, disabled facilities/parking, picnic-sets in large garden, good local walks, open all day. *(Christopher Maxse)*

WARTLING   TQ6509
★Lamb (01323) 832116
Village signed with Herstmonceux Castle off A271 Herstmonceux–Battle; BN27 1RY Popular family-owned country pub; small entrance bar with open fireplace, ales such as Harveys, Old Dairy and Pig & Porter, several wines by the glass from good list (nice house red), two-level beamed and timbered dining room to the left with inglenook woodburner, bigger back bar and restaurant, well liked food including blackboard specials, friendly service; children and dogs welcome, steps up to garden with chunky seats, bedrooms, closed Sun evening, otherwise open all day. *(V Brogden)*

WEST ASHLING   SU8007
Richmond Arms (01243) 572046
Just off B2146; Mill Road; PO18 8EA Village dining pub in quiet pretty setting near big millpond with ducks and geese, good interesting food (quite pricey, best to book) from bar snacks up, also wood-fired pizzas cooked in a vintage van (Fri, Sat evenings), well kept Harveys ales and plenty of wines by the glass, competent friendly staff; children welcome, two nice bedrooms, closed Sun evening, Mon and Tues. *(Tracey and Stephen Groves, John Evans)*

WEST WITTERING   SZ8099
Lamb (01243) 511105
Chichester Road; B2179/A286 towards Birdham; PO20 8QA Modernised 18th-c tile-hung country pub, three Badger ales and enjoyable home-cooked food including good Sun roasts, friendly staff coping well during busy summer months, bar with painted beams and timbers, assorted furniture on wood floor including kitchen chairs and

scrubbed pine tables, woodburner in brick fireplace, two bare-boards dining rooms off with some interesting artwork; background music; children and dogs welcome, tables out in front and in small sheltered back garden, open all day Sat, closed Sun evening. *(Andrew and Michele Revell)*

WILMINGTON   TQ5404
★Giants Rest (01323) 870207
Just off A27; BN26 5SQ Busy country pub with long wood-floored bar, adjacent open areas with simple furniture, rural pictures and pot plants, log fire, well kept/priced Long Man range and South Downs cider (made in the village), good well presented food cooked by french chef-landlord including specials and gluten-free options, friendly helpful staff; children and dogs welcome, lots of seats in front garden, more behind, surrounded by Downs walks and village famous for chalk-carved Long Man, two comfortable bedrooms up narrow stairs sharing bathroom, open all day weekends (food all day Sun). *(Tom and Jill Jones, John Beeken, Paul A Moore, Peter Meister)*

WINCHELSEA   TQ9017
New Inn (01797) 226252
German Street; just off A259; TN36 4EN Attractive 18th-c pub with L-shaped front bar mainly laid for dining, good fair-value food from sandwiches to local fish, well kept Greene King and guests, friendly helpful staff, some slate flagstones, blackened beams and log fire, separate back bar with darts and TV; background music; children welcome, pleasant tree-shaded walled garden, delightful setting opposite church (where Spike Milligan is buried), comfortable bedrooms, good breakfast. *(Peter Barrett)*

WINEHAM   TQ2320
★Royal Oak (01444) 881252
Village signposted from A272 and B2116; BN5 9AY Splendidly old-fashioned local with log fire in big inglenook, Harveys Best and guests tapped from stillroom casks, enjoyable home-cooked food (not Sun evening), jugs and ancient corkscrews on very low beams, collection of cigarette boxes and old bottles, various stuffed animals including a stoat and crocodile, more bric-a-brac and old local photographs in back parlour with views of quiet countryside; occasional folk music and morris men; children away from bar and dogs welcome, picnic-sets out at front, closed evenings 25 and 26 Dec, 1 Jan. *(Tony Scott)*

WISBOROUGH GREEN   TQ0526
Cricketers Arms (01403) 700369
Loxwood Road, just off A272 Billingshurst–Petworth; RH14 0DG Attractive old pub on edge of village green, four or five well kept ales such as Dark Star, Fullers, Harveys and St Austell, good choice of food including specials, cheerful staff, open-plan with two big woodburners and

pleasing mix of country furniture on parquet flooring, stripped-brick dining area on left; some weekend live music; children welcome, tables out in front, open all day. *(Tony Scott, Alastair and Sheree Hepburn)*

WISBOROUGH GREEN   TQ0525
Three Crowns   0333 700 7333
Billingshurst Road (A272); RH14 0DX
Well looked-after beamed pub with quirky interior, enjoyable freshly made food (all day Sun) from sharing boards and pub favourites up, prompt friendly service, well kept Harveys and a couple of guests, extensive choice of wines by the glass including champagne and good range of gins; live music and quiz nights; children welcome, sizeable tree-shaded back garden, open all day. *(Andrew Stone)*

WIVELSFIELD GREEN   TQ3519
Cock   (01444) 471668
North Common Road; RH17 7RH
Pleasant red-brick village pub, good choice of well cooked reasonably priced food (all day Sun), Harveys and guests, helpful friendly staff, two bars and restaurant, log fire; quiz nights, darts, bar billiards, pool and sports TV; children, walkers and dogs welcome, seats out in front and in garden behind, open all day. *(Patric Curwen, Alf Wright)*

WOODMANCOTE   SU7707
Woodmancote   (01243) 371019
The one near Emsworth; Woodmancote Lane; PO10 8RD Village pub with unusual contemporary décor – plenty of quirky touches; good popular food from sandwiches and sharing boards up (best to book), Weds steak night, real ales including one badged for them and several wines by the glass, restaurant; regular quiz nights; dogs welcome in bar, seats out under cover, open all day. *(Julian Richardson)*

WORTHING   TQ1502
Selden Arms   (01903) 234854
Lyndhurst Road, between Waitrose and hospital; BN11 2DB Friendly unchanging 19th-c backstreet local opposite the gasworks, welcoming long-serving licensees, six well kept ales (Jan beer festival), craft kegs and continental draught/bottled beers, bargain lunchtime food (not Sun) including doorstep sandwiches, Fri curry night, comfortably worn interior with photographs of old Worthing pubs, pump clips on ceiling, log fire; occasional live music, quiz last Weds of month, darts; dogs welcome, open all day. *(Tony and Wendy Hobden, Alastair and Sheree Hepburn)*

Warwickshire

with Birmingham and West Midlands

KEY ★ Star Pub   🍽️ Top Quality Food   🍺 Great Beer

🍷 Good Wines   £ Bargain Meals   🛏️ Good Bedrooms   🍴 Serves Food

---

ALDERMINSTER   SP2348   Map 4

Bell 🍽️ 🍷 🛏️

(01789) 450414 – www.thebellald.co.uk

A3400 Oxford–Stratford; CV37 8NY

Gently civilised 18th-c inn with sympathetically modernised character bars, a new two-storey restaurant, excellent modern cooking and thoughtful choice of drinks; bedrooms

Part of the Alscot Estate, this is a civilised Georgian coaching inn with a friendly, easy-going atmosphere. The open-plan rooms cleverly manage to create a contemporary feel that goes well with the many original features: beams, standing timbers, flagstoned or wooden floors and open fires. The bustling bar serves Alscot Ale and Monkey (named for the pub from North Cotswold), North Cotswold Shagweaver, Purity Pure UBU and a guest such as Stratford Upon Avon Stratford Gold on handpump, a dozen wines by the glass and proper cocktails (including a special bloody mary). The bar is comfortably furnished with a mix of traditional wooden chairs and tables, upholstered sofas, armchairs in front of open fires, high bar chairs by the blue-painted counter and daily papers; background music. The new two-storey restaurant is stylish and contemporary. The bottom floor, which features some stunning chandeliers, is decorated in soft pastels and silvers and has folding doors leading directly to the terrace, while the top floor has attractive chairs around polished copper tables on dark floorboards, seats on a balcony and panoramic views across the Stour Valley. Ideal for parties is a private dining room with its own decked area and lawn. An appealing courtyard and gardens have seats and tables looking over water meadows and the lovely valley. The boutique-style bedrooms are individually decorated, well equipped and comfortable.

🍽️ Using produce from the Estate, the imaginative food includes lunchtime sandwiches, sesame-seared tuna loin with king prawn and chilli fritters, pickled carrots and wasabi sauce, trio of duck salad with watercress and orange, chicken caesar salad, ricotta, spinach and almond pastilla with pea and mint risotto, navarin of lamb with herb-coated cutlet and minted lamb croquette, lemon sole and prawn paupiette with braised octopus, red cabbage purée and spelt, quinoa and baby leaf salad with red wine vinaigrette, and puddings such as white chocolate and raspberry cheesecake with raspberry coulis and flourless banana sponge with marinated banana, pistachio cream and toffee sauce. *Benchmark main dish: chicken breast burger with cheese and barbecue sauce £12.95. Two-course evening meal £20.00.*

Free house ~ Licensee Emma Holman-West ~ Real ale ~ Open 9am-11pm ~ Bar food 12-2.30, 6.30-9 (9.30 Fri, Sat); 12-3, 6.30-8.30 Sun ~ Restaurant ~ Children welcome ~

Dogs allowed in bar ~ Wi-fi ~ Bedrooms: £70/£95 *Recommended by P and J Shapley, John Harris, Susan and John Douglas*

ARMSCOTE

SP2444 Map 4

Fuzzy Duck

(01608) 682635 – www.fuzzyduckarmscote.com

Off A3400 Stratford–Shipston; CV37 8DD

Interestingly refurbished former coaching inn with real ales, a good wine list, inventive food and seats outside; bedrooms

Set in a picturesque hamlet, this Georgian coaching inn was stylishly reworked a couple of years ago and is part-pub and part-boutique inn. The bar has an open fire, high, chunky leather chairs around equally high metal tables on flagstones, with more leather chairs against the counter where friendly staff serve Purity Mad Goose and Stratford Upon Avon Stratford Gold on handpump, a dozen wines by the glass, 12 malt whiskies and a farm cider; a wall of glass-faced boxes holds bottles of spirits belonging to regular customers. Three interconnected dining rooms have a mix of dark wooden tables surrounded by leather and other elegant chairs on pale floorboards, a sofa here and there and a two-way woodburning stove in an open fireplace. Throughout, cartoons and arty photographs hang on pale or dark grey walls and flowers are arranged in big vases; background music and board games. At the back, another dining room (also used for private parties) leads to a decked terrace with basket-weave armchairs, cushioned sofas and small modern metal chairs and tables under big parasols; there's also a small lawn with fruit trees. The deeply comfortable, thoughtfully equipped and pretty bedrooms – each named after a species of duck – are supplied with their own Baylis & Harding beauty products. There are plenty of walks in the surrounding rolling countryside and Stratford-upon-Avon is close by.

 Using home-baked bread and their own ice-creams, the tempting food from seasonal menus includes rabbit leg ravioli with creamed peas, bacon and truffle oil, home-cured salmon with yoghurt, cucumber and bitter orange purée, beer-battered fish and chips, creamed mushroom, leek, parmesan and asparagus puff pastry pie, slow-roast duck leg with duck fat carrots, confit garlic and pomegranate molasses jus, sea bream fillet with chorizo and white beans and creamed shellfish sauce, and puddings such as dark chocolate fondant with pistachio ice-cream and white chocolate sauce and treacle and malt bran tart with orange butterscotch. *Benchmark main dish: local lamb rump with potato terrine, roast cauliflower and caramelised purée, olive and red wine jus £19.00. Two-course evening meal £24.00.*

Free house ~ Licensee Annabelle Lyall ~ Real ale ~ Open 10am-11pm; 11-5 Sun; closed Sun evening, Mon ~ Bar food 12-2.30, 6-9 (9.30 Fri, Sat); 12-3 Sun ~ Restaurant ~ Children welcome ~ Dogs welcome ~ Wi-fi ~ Bedrooms: £110/£160 *Recommended by Miles Green, Charles Welch, Patricia Hawkins*

BARSTON

SP1978 Map 4

Malt Shovel

(01675) 443223 – www.themaltshovelatbarston.com

3 miles from M42 junction 5; A4141 towards Knowle, then first left into Jacobean Lane/Barston Lane; B92 0JP

Well run country dining pub full of happy customers, with an attractive layout, good service and seats in sheltered garden

A favourite pub with many of our readers, this bustling place feels just right whether you're popping in for a drink and a chat or enjoying a first class meal. The light and airy bar rambles extensively around the zinc-topped central counter with big terracotta floor tiles neatly offset by dark grouting, and cream, tan and blue paintwork. Sharps Doom Bar and Wells Bombardier Burning Gold on handpump and 18 wines by the glass served by efficient, neatly dressed staff. Furnishings are comfortable throughout, with informal dining chairs and scatter-cushioned pews arranged around stripped-top tables of varying types and sizes. There are cheerful fruit and vegetable paintings on the walls, and french café-style shutters. The sheltered back garden has a weeping willow and picnic-sets, and the terrace and verandah have cushioned teak seats and tables.

Enticing food includes pigeon breast with pear and vanilla purée and balsamic shallots, tempura soft-shell crab with shiitake mushrooms, pak choi and satay sauce, mushroom and ricotta tortellini with walnut pesto and mushroom duxelles, steak in ale pudding, jamaica-spiced slow roast lamb with sweet potato, mango and ginger beer shot, corn-fed chicken with celeriac purée, pancetta, wild mushrooms and truffle oil, sole fillets with prawn and hot smoked salmon mousse and lemon beurre blanc, and puddings such as peanut butter, caramel and chocolate slice with charred banana and gooseberry bread and butter pudding with vanilla bean custard. *Benchmark main dish: baked cod with textures of broccoli, crispy ham and truffle oil £16.50. Two-course evening meal £28.00.*

Free house ~ Licensee Helen Somerfield ~ Real ale ~ Open 12-12; 12-11 Sun ~ Bar food 12-2.30, 6-9.30; 12-4 Sun ~ Restaurant ~ Children welcome away from restaurant ~ Dogs allowed in bar *Recommended by Susan and John Douglas, Peter J and Avril Hanson, Ian Herdman, Dave Braisted*

BIRMINGHAM
Old Joint Stock ◧ £
SP0686 Map 4

(0121) 200 1892 – www.oldjointstocktheatre.co.uk
Temple Row West; B2 5NY

Big bustling Fullers pie-and-ale pub with impressive Victorian façade and interior, and a small back terrace

Even when packed to the gunnels (which it always is at peak times), the efficient staff here manage to remain friendly and helpful. The interior is impressively flamboyant: chandeliers hang from the soaring pink and gilt ceiling, gently illuminated busts line the top of the ornately plastered walls and there's a splendid cupola above the centre of the room. Photographs of the historic building's past line the walls; there's also a big dining balcony reached up a grand sweeping staircase. Fullers ESB, London Pride, Olivers Island and Seafarers on handpump, and several wines by the glass; background music. Most nights something is presented in the smart purpose-built little theatre on the first floor. The small back terrace has cast-iron tables and chairs and wall-mounted heaters.

As well as breakfasts (8-11am weekdays, from 9am Saturday, from 10am Sunday), the popular food includes sandwiches (until 5pm), sharing boards, tomato, artichoke, black olive and goats cheese pasta, glazed ham and free-range eggs with piccalilli, lamb rump with basil pesto and new potatoes, chicken, pistachio and pomegranate salad, beer-battered cod and chips, and puddings such as chocolate brownie and gooseberry pie. *Benchmark main dish: pie of the day £12.95. Two-course evening meal £17.00.*

Fullers ~ Manager Paul Bancroft ~ Real ale ~ Open 8am-11pm; 9am-11pm Sat; 10am-11pm Sun ~ Bar food 12-10 ~ Restaurant ~ Children allowed until 6pm ~ Wi-fi ~ Regular live entertainment in theatre *Recommended by Sharon and John Hancock, Mrs Julie Thomas, Barry Collett, John Evans, Alan Johnson*

GAYDON
Malt Shovel

SP3654 Map 4

(01926) 641221 – www.maltshovelgaydon.co.uk

Under a mile from M40 junction 12; B4451 into village, then over roundabout and across B4100; Church Road; CV35 0ET

Bustling pub in a quiet village with a nice mix of pubby bar and smarter restaurant

There's always a good mix of customers in this cheerful village pub, all keen to enjoy the tasty food cooked by the landlord. Mahogany-varnished boards through to bright carpeting link the entrance with the bar counter to the right and a woodburning stove on the left. The central area has a high-pitched ceiling, milk churns and earthenware containers in a loft above the bar and three steps that lead up to a space with comfortable sofas overlooked by a big stained-glass window; reproductions of classic posters line the walls. Sharps Doom Bar, Shepherd Neame Spitfire, St Austell Tribute and Timothy Taylors Golden Best on handpump, with 11 wines by the glass and two farm ciders. A busy eating area has fresh flowers on a mix of kitchen, pub and dining tables; background music, darts. The pub's jack russell is called Mollie.

 Fair value food includes lunchtime sandwiches and baguettes, chicken liver pâté with chutney, smoked haddock welsh rarebit, three-egg omelettes with a choice of filling, wild boar and apple sausages in calvados and cider with baby onions, steak and kidney pudding, battered haddock and chips, slow-braised beef with bacon, mushrooms and red wine sauce, and puddings such as lemon cheesecake and sticky toffee pudding. *Benchmark main dish: pie of the day £10.95. Two-course evening meal £16.00.*

Enterprise ~ Lease Richard and Debi Morisot ~ Real ale ~ Open 11-3, 5-11; 11-11 Fri, Sat; 12-10.30 Sun ~ Bar food 12-2, 6.30-9 ~ Restaurant ~ Children welcome ~ Dogs allowed in bar ~ Wi-fi *Recommended by Joy Griffiths, Steve Whalley, M and A H, Tony Smaithe*

HAMPTON-IN-ARDEN
White Lion

SP2080 Map 4

(01675) 442833 – www.thewhitelioninn.com

High Street; handy for M42 junction 6; B92 0AA

Popular village local with a good choice of ales; bedrooms

They keep a fine range of real ales on handpump in this bustling former farmhouse: Castle Rock Harvest Pale, Hobsons Best and Town Crier, M&B Brew XI, St Austell Proper Job and Sharps Doom Bar. The carpeted bar is nice and relaxed, with a mix of furniture tidily laid out, neatly curtained small windows, low-beamed ceilings and some local memorabilia on the cream-painted walls; background music, TV and board games. The modern dining areas are fresh and airy with light wood and cane chairs on stripped floorboards. The bedrooms are quiet and comfortable. The church opposite is mentioned in the Domesday Book.

Tasty food includes sandwiches and 'les croques', spicy king prawn skewer with sweet chilli sauce, moules of the day, sharing boards, various omelettes, mushroom and pesto linguine, steak burger with toppings, coleslaw and chips, beer-battered fish and chips, hunters chicken (bacon, cheese and barbecue sauce), beef bourguignon, slow-cooked lamb shank with red wine gravy, and puddings. *Benchmark main dish: pork fillet and belly with black pudding, apple and bacon £13.00. Two-course evening meal £20.00.*

Free house ~ Licensee Chris Roach ~ Real ale ~ Open 12-11; 12-midnight Fri, Sat; 12-10.30 Sun ~ Bar food 12-2.30, 6-9.30; 12-4 Sun ~ Restaurant ~ Children welcome ~ Dogs welcome ~ Wi-fi ~ Bedrooms: £80/£90 *Recommended by Malcolm Phillips, R T and J C Moggridge, Ian and Rose Lock*

HUNNINGHAM
SP3768 Map 4

Red Lion

(01926) 632715 – www.redlionhunningham.co.uk

Village signposted off B4453 Leamington–Rugby just E of Weston, and off B4455 Fosse Way 2.5 miles SW of A423 junction; CV33 9DY

Civilised and friendly place, a good range of drinks and well liked food

Friendly and easy-going, this riverside pub has a light open-plan interior that's been cleverly sectioned and appealingly furnished. There are pews with scatter cushions, an assortment of antique dining chairs and stools around nice polished tables on bare boards (a few big rugs here and there), contemporary paintwork and walls hung with film and rock star photographs; one long wall is a papered mural of bookshelves. A cosy room has tub armchairs around an open coal fire, and they keep a beer named for the pub (from Greene King), Greene King Abbot and a changing guest on handpump, ten wines by the glass and 40 malt whiskies; background music. The garden has picnic-sets that look across to the arched 14th-c bridge over the River Leam and there's a basket of rugs for customers to take outside; more picnic-sets are set out at the front.

Good food includes sandwiches, confit duck hash with poached egg and truffled hollandaise, slow-braised pig cheeks with burnt onion purée and nduja (spicy, spreadable italian pork sausage), sharing platters, cauliflower macaroni cheese with garlic and shallots, wild mushroom-stuffed chicken with parsnip purée and blackened shallots, herb-crusted cod loin with butternut squash, samphire, fish nage and crispy seaweed, and puddings such as chocolate brownie sundae with marshmallow and fudge sauce and passion-fruit cheesecake with orange drizzle. *Benchmark main dish: dry-aged steak burger with toppings, relish and chips £12.50. Two-course evening meal £21.00.*

Greene King ~ Manager Richard Merand ~ Real ale ~ Open 11-11 (10.30 Sun) ~ Bar food 12-9 ~ Restaurant ~ Children welcome ~ Dogs allowed in bar ~ Wi-fi *Recommended by George Atkinson, Jeremy Snaithe, Sandra King*

ILMINGTON
SP2143 Map 4

Howard Arms ♀

(01608) 682226 – www.howardarms.com

Village signed with Wimpstone off A3400 S of Stratford; CV36 4LT

Lovely mellow-toned interior, lots to look at and enjoyable food and drink; bedrooms

With good nearby hill walks and a pretty setting beside the village green, this golden-stone inn is doing well under its newish licensees. Several beamed and flagstoned rooms (recently refurbished) have a nice mix of furniture ranging from pews and rustic stools to leather dining chairs around all sorts of tables, rugs on bare boards, shelves of books, candles and a log fire in a big inglenook. The range of drinks is good: Hook Norton Hooky, St Austell Proper Job, Timothy Taylors Landlord and Wye Valley HPA on handpump, 20 wines by the glass and a thoughtful choice of whiskies and brandies; background music, TV. The big back garden has seats under parasols and a colourful herbaceous border. Bedrooms are well equipped and comfortable and the breakfasts well thought-of.

🍴 Pleasing food includes sandwiches, potted crab and crayfish, ham hock terrine with roast pear salad and apricot jam, beetroot and asparagus risotto with apple crisps, burger with toppings and chips, black pudding and apple sausages with onion gravy, lamb chump with pea purée and rainbow carrots, salmon fillet with orange and chilli couscous, tiger prawns and red pepper coulis, duck breast with wild garlic vegetable broth and toasted barley, and puddings such as mississippi mud pie with chantilly cream and apple tarte tatin and vanilla ice-cream. *Benchmark main dish: calves liver with crispy bacon and red wine gravy £13.50. Two-course evening meal £20.00.*

Free house ~ Licensee Robert Jeal ~ Real ale ~ Open 9am-11pm; 11-10.30 Sun ~ Bar food 12-3, 6-9.30; 12-8 Sun ~ Restaurant ~ Children welcome ~ Dogs allowed in bar ~ Wi-fi ~ Bedrooms: £75/£90 *Recommended by Mr and Mrs A H Young, Geoff and Ann Marston, Alan and Alice Morgan*

LEAMINGTON SPA
Star & Garter 🍷 ◖

SP3166   Map 4

(01926) 359960 – www.starandgarterleamington.co.uk
Warwick Street; CV32 5LL

Bustling town-centre pub with open-plan rooms, good food and drink and friendly welcome

This fine old place is just a few minutes from the shopping heart of this bustling town and usefully open all day, so there are always customers popping in and out. It's been carefully renovated, with plenty of space for both drinking and dining, and although open-plan it has distinct cosy and quieter spots created by cleverly positioned furniture. At the front by big windows, the bar has cushioned wall seats upholstered in quirky eastern european fabric, as well as blue leather banquettes, red leather armchairs and small wooden stools around mixed tables on bare boards. High stools line the counter where they keep a beer named for the pub (from Greene King), Greene King Abbot, IPA and Morlands Old Golden Hen and St Austell Tribute on handpump, 14 wines by the glass plus champagne and prosecco, 13 gins and ten malt whiskies; background music. Leading back from here, a dining area has black, brown or red leather back-to-back banquettes down one side, elegant contemporary wooden dining chairs on more bare boards and an open kitchen. Up some steps is a second bar area with blue tub seats, bright scatter cushions and some bold paintwork. The atmosphere is lively and friendly and staff are helpful and attentive.

🍴 As well as weekend brunches (9am-midday), quite a choice of food using top quality produce includes pulled chicken croquettes with barbecue sauce, potted crab and prawns, free-range cumberland sausage and mash with onion gravy, vegetable and puy lentil pie with cheddar mash, bass with kerala curry sauce and basmati rice, lamb cutlets with vegetable and pearl barley broth and salsa verde, 28-day dry-aged steaks with a choice of sauce, and puddings such as pineapple upside-down cake with coconut ice-cream and Valrhona cheesecake with a peanut butter cookie; they also offer a two- and three-course set menu (midday-6.30pm). *Benchmark main dish: seared king scallops with crispy pork belly and black pudding £16.50. Two-course evening meal £20.50.*

Peach Pub Company ~ Lease Colin Barber ~ Real ale ~ Open 11-11; 9am-midnight Sat; 9am-10.30pm Sun ~ Bar food 12-10; 9am-10pm Sat; 9am-9pm Sun ~ Children welcome ~ Dogs allowed in bar ~ Wi-fi *Recommended by Miles Green, Donald Allsopp*

LONG COMPTON

SP2832 Map 4

Red Lion ⭐ 🛏

(01608) 684221 – www.redlion-longcompton.co.uk

A3400 S of Shipston-on-Stour; CV36 5JS

Traditional character and contemporary touches in comfortably furnished coaching inn; bedrooms

With homely log fires and a sizeable garden, this lovely old coaching inn is enjoyed by our readers throughout the year. The roomy, charmingly furnished lounge bar has some exposed stone and beams and nice rambling corners with cushioned settles among pleasantly assorted and comfortable seats and leather armchairs; there are tables on flagstones and carpets, animal prints on warm paintwork and both an open fire and a woodburning stove. Hook Norton Hooky and Wickwar Cotswold Way with a guest such as Brains The Rev James Original on handpump and a dozen wines by the glass; the chocolate labrador is called Cocoa. The simple public bar has darts, pool, a juke box and a TV; background music. There are tables out in the big back garden, with a play area. This is a charming place to stay in pretty bedrooms.

As well as a two- and three-course weekday menu, the rewarding food includes sandwiches, a charcuterie plate, smoked trout salad with pink grapefruit, avocado and horseradish crème fraîche, twice-baked cheese soufflé with apple, celery and walnut salad, beer-battered cod and chips, chargrilled chicken breast marinated in lemon, chilli, garlic and mint with spiced couscous and cucumber yoghurt, pork medallions with wild mushrooms, black pudding, crisp pancetta and creamy stilton sauce, and puddings such as banana and pecan brioche bread and butter pudding and rhubarb and vanilla crème brûlée. *Benchmark main dish: steak in ale pie £14.00. Two-course evening meal £21.00.*

Cropthorne Inns ~ Manager Lisa Phipps ~ Real ale ~ Open 10-3, 6-11; 10am-11pm Fri-Sun ~ Bar food 12-2.30, 6-9; 12-9.30 Fri, Sat; 12-9 Sun ~ Restaurant ~ Children welcome ~ Dogs welcome ~ Wi-fi ~ Bedrooms: £60/£95 *Recommended by Sarah Williamson, David Jackman, Alun and Jennifer Evans, J A Snell*

LOWER BRAILES

SP3139 Map 4

George 🍺 £

(01608) 685788 – www.georgeinnbrailes.com

B4035 Shipston–Banbury; OX15 5HN

Handsome stone inn dating from the 14th c, with cheerful landlord and customers and well liked food; bedrooms

This bustling inn was built in the 14th c to house the stonemasons constructing the interesting village church. It's a welcoming place and the back bar is beamed and panelled and has a cheerful atmosphere helped along by chatty locals. There's also a roomy front bar with dark oak chairs and tables on flagstones and an inglenook fireplace, and a separate restaurant. Hook Norton Hooky, Old Hooky and Red Rye on handpump, nine wines by the glass and farm cider; background music, TV, games machine, darts, pool, juke box and board games. There's aunt sally and picnic-sets (some blue-painted) in the sizeable and sheltered back garden and on the terrace; a few tables and chairs are out in front. The comfortable bedrooms are fair value. There are good walks to enjoy nearby.

As well as some dishes that qualify for our Value Award, the tasty food includes prawn cocktail, pork and chicken terrine with fig relish, greek salad with feta and olives, beer-battered haddock and chips, chilli con carne, pie of the day, slow-roast pork shoulder with red wine, mushroom and baby onion sauce, salmon supreme with a piquant tomato and spinach sauce, steaks with a choice of sauce, and puddings. *Benchmark main dish: steak and kidney pie £9.00. Two-course evening meal £15.00.*

Free house ~ Licensee Baggy Saunders ~ Real ale ~ Open 12-11.30; 5-11 Mon; 12-midnight Sat; 12-10.30 Sun ~ Bar food 12-2.30, 6-9; 12-3.30 Sun ~ Restaurant ~ Children welcome but not in bar after 8pm Fri, Sat ~ Dogs allowed in bar and bedrooms ~ Wi-fi ~ Bedrooms: £40/£60 *Recommended by Phoebe Peacock, Peter Brix, JHBS, R T and J C Moggridge, Richard Tilbrook*

PRESTON BAGOT SP1765 Map 4

Crabmill

(01926) 843342 – www.thecrabmill.co.uk

A4189 Henley-in-Arden to Warwick; B95 5EE

Comfortable décor, open fires and particularly good food and drink in converted mill

Our readers enjoy their visits to this rambling former cider mill very much, praising the impressive food served by helpful staff and the range of drinks. There's a gently civilised atmosphere and it's attractively decorated throughout with contemporary furnishings and warm colour combinations. A smart two-level lounge has comfortable sofas and chairs, low tables, big table lamps and a couple of rugs on bare boards. The elegant, low-beamed dining area is roomy with caramel leather banquettes and chairs at pine tables, while the beamed and flagstoned bar area has stripped-pine country tables and chairs and snug corners; open fires. From the gleaming metal bar counter they serve Purity Pure Gold and UBU and Sharps Doom Bar on handpump and nine wines by the glass; background music. There are plenty of tables (some under cover) in the large, attractive, decked garden.

Extremely good food includes sandwiches (until 3pm Mon-Thurs, until 5pm Fri, Sat; not Sun), ham hock with bubble and squeak, hispi cabbage, a poached egg, local smoked bacon and hollandaise sauce, crispy duck with spring onion, carrot, mouli and crispy vermicelli noodle salad with sweet chilli sauce, beef and baby onion in Guinness pie, masala-marinated chicken with sweet potato and spinach curry, onion bhaji and mint yoghurt, hake fillet with scallops, wild garlic and blue cheese macaroni and truffle oil, duck breast with wild mushrooms and celeriac purée, and puddings such as chocolate brownie with mint choc chip ice-cream and boozy cherries and sticky toffee pudding with salted caramel sauce. *Benchmark main dish: slow-cooked lamb shoulder with dauphinoise potatoes, onion purée and mint sauce £16.95. Two-course evening meal £21.00.*

Free house ~ Licensee Sally Coll ~ Real ale ~ Open 11-11; 12-6 Sun ~ Bar food 12-2.30, 6-9.30; 12-4 Sun ~ Restaurant ~ Children welcome ~ Dogs allowed in bar ~ Wi-fi
Recommended by Clive and Fran Dutson, Jenni Owen, Laura Reid, Lance and Sarah Milligan

SHIPSTON-ON-STOUR SP2540 Map 4

Black Horse

(01608) 238489 – www.blackhorseshipston.com

Station Road (off A3400); CV36 4BT

16th-c pub with simple country furnishings, well kept ales, an extensive choice of thai food and seats outside

The oldest and only thatched building in the village, this ancient stone tavern is chocolate-box pretty with its flowering baskets and tubs. Low-beamed, character bars lead off a central entrance passage with some fine old flagstones and floor tiles and two open fires (one an inglenook). There are also wheelbacks, stools, rustic seats and tables and built-in wall benches, half-panelled or exposed stone walls, and plenty of copper kettles, pans and bed warmers, horse tack and toby jugs. Friendly staff serve Prescott Hill Climb, Ringwood Old Thumper and Wye Valley The Hopfather on handpump, several wines by the glass, a dozen gins and ten malt whiskies; background music, TV, darts and board games. The little dining room has pale wooden tables and chairs on bare boards. There are a couple of benches on the front cobbles, contemporary seats and tables on a partly covered raised decked area at the back and picnic-sets on grass.

 The popular food is thai: tom yum soups, steamed dumplings, chicken satay, spicy salads such as seafood, lots of curries, chicken, duck and pork in tamarind, sweet soy and plum sauces, stir-fries and a big choice of dishes with noodles and rice. *Benchmark main dish: chicken, pork or prawn thai curries £7.99. Two-course evening meal £16.50.*

Free house ~ Licensee Gabe Saunders ~ Real ale ~ Open 12-3, 6-11; 6-11 Mon; 12-midnight Fri-Sun ~ Bar food 12-2.30, 6-10; not Mon ~ Restaurant ~ Children welcome ~ Dogs allowed in bar ~ Wi-fi *Recommended by Charlie May, Peter Brix, Jo Garnett*

SHIPSTON-ON-STOUR
SP2540   Map 4

Horseshoe ♠ £

(01608) 662190 – www.horseshoeshipston.com
Church Street; CV36 4AP

Cheerful local with welcoming regulars, traditional furnishings, real ales and honest food and seats outside

It's the friendly and chatty, easy-going atmosphere that our readers particularly like in this pretty 17th-c timbered coaching inn. The two rooms that form the open, carpeted bar have straightforward red-upholstered cushioned wall seats and wheelback chairs around scrubbed wooden tables, country prints on lemon-yellow walls, copper pans hanging on the bressummer beam over the open fire (with books and stone jars on shelves to one side) and stools against the counter; juke box. There's Adnams Southwold, Sharps Doom Bar and Wadworths 6X on handpump and several wines by the glass, and service is cheerful and courteous. The end dining room is similarly furnished. The back terrace has contemporary seats and tables on decking; aunt sally.

 Tasty food includes hot and cold sandwiches and baguettes, a pâté of the day, scrambled eggs on toast, all-day breakfast, spinach and ricotta cannelloni, chicken breast in stilton sauce, a pie and a curry of the day, steak and kidney pudding, beer-battered haddock and chips, and puddings. *Benchmark main dish: steaks cut to order with a choice of sauces and chips £16.95. Two-course evening meal £16.00.*

Enterprise ~ Manager Baggy Saunders ~ Real ale ~ Open 10am-11pm ~ Bar food 12-2.30, 6-9; not Sun evening ~ Children welcome ~ Dogs welcome ~ Wi-fi
Recommended by Julian Thorpe, Douglas Power

WARMINGTON
SP4147   Map 4

Falcon ♀ ♠

(01295) 692120 – www.brunningandprice.co.uk/falcon
B4100 towards Shotteswell; OX17 1JJ

Carefully extended and restored roadside pub with spreading bar and dining rooms, a fine choice of drinks and food and seats outside

Reopened as we went to press after a beautiful restoration by Brunning & Price, this 18th-c pub was originally built to take advantage of what was a busy turnpike road. It's a handsome golden-stone inn and the interconnected bar and dining areas have much character and plenty to look at. There are beams, mirrors over several open fires, rugs on pale floorboards, elegant metal chandeliers, prints and photos covering pale-painted walls, bookshelves, house plants and stone bottles. Cushioned Edwardian-style chairs and leather armchairs are grouped around a wide mix of tables and the main dining room has a central fire pit. Friendly young staff serve Phoenix Brunning & Price Original and White Monk and guests such as Cottage Goldrush, Gun Dog Ales Hotdog, Kendricks Webb Ellis and White Horse Black Horse Porter on handpump, 15 wines by the glass, 68 gins and numerous malt whiskies; background music. The garden has good quality seats and tables under a gazebo.

Attractively presented, interesting food includes sandwiches, pulled pork croquette with asian slaw and barbecue sauce, smoked salmon with bloody mary jelly, steak in ale pie, sweet potato and aubergine malaysian curry with coconut rice and tempura okra, devilled bass fillets with cucumber, watermelon and pink grapefruit salad and saffron mayonnaise, chicken breast with lemon thyme risotto, crispy parmesan and herb pesto, and puddings such as hot waffle with toffee sauce, caramelised banana and honeycomb ice-cream and berry and elderflower jelly with gin and tonic sorbet. *Benchmark main dish: braised lamb shoulder with dauphinoise potatoes and rosemary gravy £16.95. Two-course evening meal £20.50.*

Brunning & Price ~ Manager Peter Palfi ~ Real ale ~ Open 11-11 (10.30 Sun) ~ Bar food 12-10 (9.30 Sun) ~ Restaurant ~ Children welcome ~ Dogs allowed in bar ~ Wi-fi
Recommended by Peter and Emma Kelly, Melanie and David Lawson

WELFORD-ON-AVON

Bell 🌟 ♀ 🍺

SP1452 Map 4

(01789) 750353 ~ www.thebellwelford.co.uk
Off B439 W of Stratford; High Street; CV37 8EB

Warwickshire Dining Pub of the Year

Enjoyably civilised pub with appealing ancient interior, good carefully sourced food, a great range of drinks and a pretty garden with table service

As always, this particularly well run pub is a winner with our readers and every aspect of the place is first class. The attractive interior – with plenty of signs of the building's venerable age – is divided into five comfortable areas, each with its own character, from the cosy terracotta-painted bar to a light and airy gallery room with antique wood panelling, solid oak floor and contemporary Lloyd Loom chairs. Flagstone floors, stripped or well polished antique or period-style furniture and three good fires (one in an inglenook) add warmth and cosiness. Hobsons Best, Purity Pure Gold and UBU and a guest beer on handpump and 18 wines (including prosecco and champagne) by the glass. In summer, the virginia creeper-covered exterior is festooned with colourful hanging baskets. The lovely garden has solid teak furniture, a vine-covered terrace, water features and gentle lighting. This riverside village has a handsome church and pretty thatched black and white cottages and is certainly worth exploring.

Using the best seasonal produce from local producers, the highly popular food includes sandwiches, crayfish, prawn and melon cocktail, deep-fried brie with ginger and apricot compote, lunchtime omelettes with free-range eggs, chicken caesar salad with fresh anchovies, beer-battered fresh haddock and chips, faggots with mash and sage and onion gravy, gammon with fresh pineapple, mixed grill, sirloin steak with a choice of sauces, and puddings such as sticky toffee pudding and chocolate, brandy and orange truffle tart; they also offer a spicy menu on Friday evenings. *Benchmark main dish: breaded garlic chicken stuffed with smoked cheddar on sweet potato mash with wilted spinach £14.95. Two-course evening meal £21.00.*

Laurel (Enterprise) ~ Lease Colin and Teresa Ombler ~ Real ale ~ Open 11.30-3, 6-11; 11.30-11.30 Fri, Sat; 11.45-10.30 Sun ~ Bar food 11.45-2.30, 6.15-9.30 (10 Fri); 11.45-10 Sat; 12-9.30 Sun ~ Children welcome ~ Wi-fi *Recommended by Sharon and John Hancock, Hugh Roberts, Joan Cole, M G Hart, Ron Corbett, Jeff Humphries, Phil and Jane Villiers, Doreen Allen, Dave Braisted, Mr and Mrs C Skellon*

Also Worth a Visit in Warwickshire

Besides the fully inspected pubs, you might like to try these pubs that have been recommended to us and described by readers. Do tell us what you think of them: feedback@goodguides.com

ALCESTER   SP0957
Holly Bush (01789) 507370
Henley Street (continuation of High Street towards B4089; limited nearby parking); B49 5QX Welcoming 17th-c Everards pub under new management, their beers and one or two guests, three real ciders and decent choice of wines by the glass, enjoyable good value traditional food from sandwiches up, six smallish rooms with simple furniture including pews and wall benches, bare boards, flagstones and carpet, some dark panelling, two woodburners and an open fire; quiz Thurs, monthly folk night, TV, free wi-fi; children and dogs welcome, seats in pretty back garden, barbecues, open all day. *(Andrew Jones)*

ALCESTER   SP0857
Turks Head (01789) 765948
High Street, across from church; B49 5AD Nicely updated old town pub with small front room and another off corridor, well kept Wye Valley and three guests, several bottled beers and good choice of wines, enjoyable food (not Sun evening) from sharing plates and pizzas up including good fish and chips, Sat brunch; free wi-fi; children welcome, tables in walled garden behind, open all day. *(Theocsbrian, Mr and Mrs D M Fishleigh)*

ALDRIDGE   SK0900
Old Irish Harp (01922) 455968
Chester Road, Little Aston (A452 over Staffordshire border); WS9 0LP Popular modernised pub with good choice of enjoyable food including speciality rotisserie chicken, meal deal Mon-Fri, Banks's Bitter, Jennings Cumberland and Marstons Pedigree, extensive dining area; free wi-fi; children welcome, plenty of seats outside, open all day. *(Miles Green)*

ALVESTON   SP2356
Ferry (01789) 269883
Ferry Lane; end of village, off B4086 Stratford–Wellesbourne; CV37 7QX

Comfortable beamed dining pub with enjoyable food and well kept ales such as Courage and Wye Valley, friendly staff; quiz first Tues of month, occasional live music; children and dogs welcome, nice spot with seats out at front (some on raised deck), open all day Sat, closed Sun evening, Mon. *(Mr and Mrs J Watkins)*

ARDENS GRAFTON   SP1153
★**Golden Cross** (01789) 772420
Off A46 or B439 W of Stratford, corner of Wixford Road/Grafton Lane; B50 4LG Bustling 18th-c stone pub with friendly relaxed beamed bar, rugs on dark flagstones, mix of furniture including chapel chairs around pine kitchen tables, modern local photos, woodburner in big old fireplace, Purity Gold and Wells Bombardier, Thatcher's cider and ten wines by the glass, enjoyable food (some served on boards and slates), friendly efficient service, attractive dining room with unusual coffered ceiling and big mullioned bay window; background and live acoustic music (Thurs), free wi-fi; children and dogs (in bar) welcome, wheelchir access, picnic-sets in good-sized, back garden, more sturdy rustic furniture on heated terrace, nice views, open all day Fri-Sun (food all day Sat, Sun). *(Sharon and John Hancock, Stanley and Annie Matthews)*

BARSTON   SP2078
★**Bulls Head** (01675) 442830
From M42 junction 5, A4141 towards Warwick, first left, then signed down Barston Lane; B92 0JU Unassuming and unspoilt partly Tudor village pub, four well kept ales including Adnams Southwold and Purity Mad Goose, popular traditional home-made food from sandwiches to specials, cheerful helpful staff, log fires, comfortable lounge with pictures and plates, oak-beamed bar and separate dining room; children and dogs allowed, good-sized secluded garden alongside pub and barn, open all day Fri-Sun,

no food Sun evening. *(Clive and Fran Dutson, Malcolm Phillips)*

BILSTON   SO9496
Trumpet (01902) 493723
High Street; WV14 0EP Holdens pub with their ales and guests kept well, main draw is the good nightly (and Sun lunchtime) jazz, lots of musical memorabilia and photographs, friendly atmosphere. *(Jeremy Snaithe)*

BINLEY WOODS   SP3977
Roseycombe (024) 7654 1022
Rugby Road; CV3 2AY Warm and friendly 1930s pub with good choice of bargain home-made food, Bass and Theakstons; Weds quiz night, some live music; children welcome, big garden. *(Alan Johnson)*

BIRMINGHAM   SP0788
★ **Bartons Arms** (0121) 333 5988
High Street, Aston (A34); B6 4UP Magnificent listed Edwardian landmark standing alone in a rather daunting area; impressive linked richly decorated rooms from the palatial to the snug, original tilework murals, stained glass and mahogany, decorative fireplaces, sweeping stairs to handsome upstairs rooms, well kept Oakham ales from ornate island bar with snob screens, interesting imported bottled beers and frequent mini beer festivals, well priced thai food, good young staff; open all day. *(Charles Welch)*

BIRMINGHAM   SP0688
Lord Clifden (0121) 523 7515
Great Hampton Street (Jewellery Quarter); B18 6AA Fairly traditional pub with contemporary touches, leather banquettes and padded stools around dimpled copper-top tables, bustling atmosphere, wide choice of good value generous food from sandwiches to daily specials, Wye Valley and guests plus draught continentals, prompt friendly service, interesting collection of street art including Banksy's; darts in front bare-boards section, sports TVs (outside too), Thurs quiz night and weekend DJs; plenty of seats in enclosed part-covered beer garden with table tennis and table football, open all day (till late Fri, Sat). *(Charles Welch)*

BIRMINGHAM   SP0786
Old Contemptibles (0121) 200 3310
Edmund Street; B3 2HB Spacious well restored Edwardian corner pub (Nicholsons) with lofty ceiling and lots of woodwork, good choice of real ales and enjoyable well priced food including range of sausages and pies, friendly efficient young staff; upstairs lavatories; no children, handy central

location and popular at lunchtime with office workers, open all day (till 6pm Sun). *(Alan Johnson)*

BIRMINGHAM   SP0784
Old Moseley Arms (0121) 440 1954
Tindal Street; B12 9QU Tucked-away Victorian pub with five well kept ales including Enville, Salopian and Wye Valley (regular festivals), good value indian food (evenings and all day Sun); sports TVs, darts; outside seating area, handy for Edgbaston cricket ground, open all day. *(Charles Welch)*

BIRMINGHAM   SP0384
Plough (0121) 427 3678
High Street; B17 9NT Popular place with spacious modern interior (one or two steps), enjoyable range of food including stone-baked pizzas and chargrilled burgers, regular offers, well kept Purity, Wye Valley and guests, plenty of wines by the glass and some 50 whiskies, good coffee too; background music, TVs; well behaved children welcome, paved garden with covered area, open all day from 8am (9am weekends) for breakfast. *(Miles Green)*

BIRMINGHAM   SP0686
Post Office Vaults (0121) 643 7354
New Street/Pinfold Street; B2 4BA Two entrances to this simple downstairs bar with 13 interesting ciders/perries, eight real ales including Hobsons and Salopian and over 300 international bottled beers, friendly knowledgeable staff, no food but can bring your own (plates and cutlery supplied); handy for New Street station, open all day. *(Tony and Wendy Hobden)*

BIRMINGHAM   SP0686
Purecraft Bar & Kitchen
(0121) 237 5666 *Waterloo Street; B2 5TJ* Newish industrial-chic style bar, excellent range of real ales and craft kegs including several from Purity, interesting bottled beers, Dunkerton's cider and a dozen wines by the glass, open kitchen serving good food (not Sun evening) from sandwiches and deli boards up (dishes matched with beer), friendly helpful service; children welcome, open all day. *(David Thorpe)*

BIRMINGHAM   SP0687
Rose Villa (0121) 236 7910
By clocktower in Jewellery Quarter (Warstone Lane/Vyse Street); B18 6JW Listed 1920s brick building standing in splendid isolation; front saloon with impressive stained glass leading through to small but magnificent bar, floor-to-ceiling green tiles and massive tiled arch over fireplace, original parquet flooring, quirky

---

We include some hotels with a good bar that offers facilities comparable to those of a pub.

touches here and there such as antler chandeliers and a red phone box, four or five well kept ales including Sharps Doom Bar, cocktails, reasonably priced food from american diner menu; live music and DJs Fri, Sat till late – can get very busy; open all day, from 11am weekends for brunch.
(Dave Braisted, Charles Welch)

BIRMINGHAM   SP0686
★ **Wellington** (0121) 200 3115
Bennetts Hill; B2 5SN Traditionally refurbished high-ceilinged pub with 16 well kept interesting ales (listed on TV screens) including three from Black Country, also real ciders and bottled beers, experienced landlord and friendly staff, no food but plates and cutlery if you bring your own, more room and roof terrace upstairs; regular beer festivals and quiz nights, darts; open all day and can get very busy. *(Tony and Wendy Hobden, Helen McLagan, Alan Johnson)*

BRIERLEY HILL   SO9286
★ **Vine** (01384) 78293
B4172 between A461 and (nearer) A4100; immediately after the turn into Delph Road; DY5 2TN Popular Black Country pub (aka the Bull & Bladder) offering a true taste of the West Midlands; down-to-earth welcome and friendly chatty locals in meandering series of rooms, each different in character, traditional front bar with wall benches, comfortable extended snug with solidly built red plush seats, tartan-decorated back bar, well kept/priced Bathams from brewery next door, a couple of simple very cheap lunchtime dishes (no credit cards) plus cobs and snacks all day; TV, games machine, darts and dominoes; children and dogs welcome, tables in backyard, open all day. *(Miles Green)*

BROOM   SP0853
★ **Broom Tavern** (01789) 778199
High Street; off B439 in Bidford; B50 4HL Spacious 16th-c brick and timber village pub, relaxed and welcoming, with good interesting food from chef-owners including excellent Sun roasts, four well kept ales such as North Cotswold, Purity, Sharps and Wye Valley, well balanced wine list with several by the glass, good attentive (but not intrusive) service, main room divided into two parts, one with cottage-style tables and chairs, the other with oak furniture, black beams and log fire, also a snug perfect for a group of diners; Mon quiz; children welcome, tables out on grass either side, handy for Ragley Hall, open all day weekends. *(Clive and Fran Dutson, Stanley and Annie Matthews, Theocsbrian, David and Catharine Boston)*

CLAVERDON   SP2064
★ **Red Lion** (01926) 842291
Station Road; B4095 towards Warwick; CV35 8PE Upmarket beamed Tudor dining pub with highly regarded if not particularly cheap food (some middle eastern influences), well kept Hook Norton Lion and several wines by the glass, friendly staff, linked rooms including back area with country views over sheltered heated deck and gardens, log fires; children welcome, no dogs inside, open all day Sat, closed Sun evening; licence under threat as we went to press so could be changes. *(Roger Braithwaite, Clive and Fran Dutson, David and Catharine Boston)*

COVENTRY   SP3379
Establishment (024) 7622 2727
Bayley Lane; CV1 5RN Former courtroom in the cathedral quarter preserving judge's bench, witness box, dock and public gallery, also steps down to cells (now a dining area); three changing ales, decent choice of wines and cocktails, fairly extensive menu including sandwiches, sharing boards, pizzas and grills, set menu till 5pm, welcoming hard-working young staff; DJs Fri and Sat night, jazz Sun afternoon, free wi-fi; children welcome, open (and food) all day from 10am for breakfast, shuts 3am Fri, Sat. *(Alan Johnson)*

COVENTRY   SP3279
Old Windmill (024) 7625 1717
Spon Street; CV1 3BA Friendly 15th-c pub with lots of tiny rooms (known locally as Ma Brown's), exposed beams in uneven ceilings, inglenook woodburner, half a dozen well kept ales including RCH, Theakstons and Timothy Taylors, good local pork pies; live music, juke box, sports TV and games machines, darts; closed Mon lunchtime, otherwise open all day (till 1am Fri, Sat), busy at weekends. *(Julian Thorpeham)*

COVENTRY   SP3379
Town Wall (024) 7622 0963
Bond Street, among car parks behind Belgrade Theatre; CV1 4AH Busy Victorian city-centre local with half a dozen well kept ales including Adnams and Bass, Weston's cider, enjoyable food (not Sun evening, Mon) from lunchtime sandwiches to hearty dishes such as rabbit pie, unspoilt basic front bar and tiny snug, engraved windows, bigger back lounge with actor/playwright photographs and pictures of old Coventry, open fires; big-screen sports TV; no children, open all day. *(Alan Johnson)*

COVENTRY   SP3378
Whitefriars (024) 7625 1655
Gosford Street; CV1 5DL Pair of well preserved medieval townhouses, three old-fashioned rooms on both floors, lots of ancient beams, timbers and furniture, flagstones, cobbles and coal fire, five well kept changing ales, bar lunches (not weekends); Tues quiz, some live music; no children inside unless eating, smokers' shelter on good-sized back terrace, open all day (1am Fri, Sat). *(Alan Johnson)*

EASENHALL   SP4679
Golden Lion (01788) 833577
Main Street; CV23 0JA Bar in 16th-c part
of busy comfortable hotel, white-painted
beams, half-panelling and log fire, some
original wattle and daub and fine 17th-c
carved bench depicting the 12 apostles, a
couple of real ales (usually one from Charles
Wells) and good food including lunchtime/
early evening deal (Mon-Fri), prompt
friendly service, more formal restaurant;
background music; children and small dogs
welcome, disabled access/loos, tables on
side terrace and spacious lawn, 20 well
equipped bedrooms (some with four posters),
attractive village, open (and food) all day.
*(Simon Le Fort, Helen McLagan, Gerry and
Rosemary Dobson)*

EDGE HILL   SP3747
★Castle (01295) 670255
Off A422; OX15 6DJ Crenellated
octagonal tower built in 1742 as gothic
folly (marks where Charles I raised his
standard at the Battle of Edgehill); major
renovation creating bar and four dining
areas, plenty of original features including
arched windows and doorways, beams and
stone fireplaces, fantastic views (some
floor-to-ceiling windows), good food (not Sun
evening), deli bar for sandwiches, coffee and
afternoon teas, well kept Hook Norton ales,
friendly enthusiastic young staff; downstairs
lavatories; children welcome, seats in lovely
big garden with more outstanding views,
beautiful Compton Wynyates nearby, four
refurbished bedrooms, parking can be a
problem at busy times, open all day Sat,
till 7pm Sun. *(Susan and John Douglas,
Andy Dolan)*

ETTINGTON   SP2748
★Chequers (01789) 740387
Banbury Road (A422); CV37 7SR Good
enterprising food is the main draw here,
but they do keep three real ales including a
house beer from Martsons and decent range
of wines by the glass; bar and restaurant
areas with variety of comfortable and
rather elegant dining chairs, big mirrors,
a piano and richly figured velvet curtains
and wall hangings, good service and relaxed
friendly atmosphere; background music, free
wi-fi; children and dogs (in bar) welcome,
sheltered back garden with picnic-sets on
lawn and stylish furniture on terrace, open
all day Sat, till 6pm Sun, closed Mon.
*(Dr and Mrs A K Clarke, R T and J C Moggridge,
K H Frostick, Mike and Mary Carter)*

FARNBOROUGH   SP4349
Kitchen (01295) 690615
Off A423 N of Banbury; OX17 1DZ
Fully refurbished golden-stone dining pub
in NT village; bar with painted beams, wood
floor and cushioned window seats, red
woodburner in big fireplace, saddle and
tractor seat stools at blue panelled counter
serving Purity Gold and UBU, good wines by
the glass and generally well liked food from
interesting if pricey menu, two-room dining
area; jazzy background music, free wi-fi;
children and dogs welcome, neat sloping
garden with blue picnic-sets and pizza oven,
local walks, open all day weekends, closed
Tues, Weds. *(Miles Green)*

FENNY COMPTON   SP4152
Merrie Lion (01295) 771134
Brook Street; CV47 2YH Spotless early
18th-c beamed village pub; three well
kept beers including one badged for them,
decent range of wines and good freshly
made food from pubby choices up, friendly
welcoming atmosphere; quiz nights and other
events; tables outside, handy for Burton
Dassett Hills Country Park, open all day
weekends. *(Sharon and John Hancock)*

FILLONGLEY   SP2787
Cottage (01676) 540599
Black Hall Lane; CV7 8EG Popular
country dining pub on village outskirts,
good value fairly traditional food including
lunchtime and early-bird deals, beers such
as Marstons, St Austell and Timothy Taylors,
friendly caring service; back terrace and lawn
overlooking fields, closes Sun evening at 6pm.
(Geoff and Ann Marston)

FIVE WAYS   SP2270
★Case Is Altered (01926) 484206
*Follow Rowington signs at junction
roundabout off A4177/A4141 N of
Warwick, then right into Case Lane;
CV35 7JD* Convivial unspoilt old cottage
licensed for over three centuries; Old Pie
Factory, Wye Valley and three guests served
by friendly long-serving landlady, no food,
simple small main bar with fine old poster of
Lucas, Blackwell & Arkwright Brewery (now
flats), clock with hours spelling out Thornleys
Ale (another defunct brewery), and just a
few sturdy old-fashioned tables and a couple
of stout leather-covered settles facing each
other over spotless tiles, modest little back
room with old bar billiards table (takes
sixpences); no children, dogs or mobile
phones; full disabled access, stone table on
little brick courtyard, open all day Sun till
7.30pm. *(Charles Welch)*

FLECKNOE   SP5163
Old Olive Bush (01788) 891134
Off A425 W of Daventry; CV23 8AT
Unspoilt little Edwardian pub in quiet
photogenic village, friendly chatty
atmosphere, enjoyable traditional food
cooked by landlady (Weds-Sat evenings,
Sun lunchtime), well kept changing ales
and decent wines, open fire in bar with
stripped-wood floor, steps up to games
room with table skittles, small dining
room with etched-glass windows and
another fire; Thurs quiz; children welcome,

pretty garden, closed Mon, weekday lunchtimes. *(Lance and Sarah Milligan)*

FRANKTON SP4270
Friendly (01926) 632430
Just over a mile S of B4453 Leamington Spa–Rugby; Main Street; CV23 9NY Popular 16th-c village pub living up to its name, four well kept ales and good reasonably priced traditional home-made food, two low-ceilinged rooms, open fire; quiz last Thurs of month; open all day weekends, closed Mon lunchtime. *(Darren and Jane Staniforth)*

HALESOWEN SO9683
Waggon & Horses (0121) 550 4989
Stourbridge Road; B63 3TU Popular 19th-c red-brick corner pub refurbished and extended by new owners (Black Country Ales); 14 well kept interesting ales (tasting trays available) and four real ciders, friendly knowledgeable staff, limited food such as cobs and pork pies, open fire; dogs welcome, open all day. *(Nigel Espley, Tea Belly)*

HAMPTON LUCY SP2557
Boars Head (01789) 840533
Church Street, E of Stratford; CV35 8BE Welcoming unpretentious village pub with nicely decorated interior, beams and log fires, good range of changing ales and enjoyable modestly priced pubby food from sandwiches up, deli shop; children welcome, seats in enclosed back courtyard, near lovely church, and handy for Charlecote Park (NT) and M40, open all day, food all day Fri, Sat, not Sun evening. *(Susan and John Douglas)*

HARBOROUGH MAGNA SP4779
Old Lion (01788) 833238
3 miles from M6 junction 1; B4112 Pailton Road; CV23 0HQ Welcoming stylishly updated village pub, emphasis on good well presented home-cooked food from pub favourites and stone-baked pizzas to steaks and daily specials, friendly attentive staff, Greene King ales including one badged for the pub and maybe a guest, nice choice of wines; children and dogs (in bar) welcome, terrace seating, open (and food) all day Sat, till 6pm Sun. *(Jeremy Snaithe)*

HARBURY SP3759
Gamecock (01926) 258859
Chapel Street; CV33 9HT Village pub serving three well kept ales including Byatts Gold, Aspall's and Thatcher's ciders and excellent choice of wines by the glass, good traditional food along with deli boards and tapas, friendly helpful staff; children and dogs welcome, garden, open all day weekends, closed Mon, lunchtimes Tues-Fri. *(Sharon and John Hancock)*

HARTSHILL SP3394
Anchor (024) 7639 3444
Mancetter Road (B4111); CV10 0RT

Welcoming cleanly presented canalside pub run by father and son, three Everards ales and good choice of enjoyable home-made food, Sun carvery; sports TV, free wi-fi; children and dogs welcome, garden with bouncy castle, goats and chickens, open all day (till 6pm Sun). *(Ben Caunter)*

HATTON SP2367
★**Falcon** (01926) 484281
Birmingham Road, Haseley (A4177, not far from M40 junction 15); CV35 7HA Smartly updated dining pub with relaxing rooms around island bar, lots of stripped brickwork and low beams, tiled and oak-planked floors, good moderately priced food from sandwiches, sharing boards and pub favourites up, lunchtime/early evening deal Mon-Fri, friendly service, nice choice of wines by the glass and well kept Marstons-related ales, barn-style back restaurant; children welcome, disabled facilities, garden (dogs allowed here) with heated covered terrace, four bedrooms in converted barn, open (and food) all day. *(John Preddy)*

HENLEY-IN-ARDEN SP1566
★**Bluebell** (01564) 793049
High Street (A3400, off M40 junction 16); B95 5AT Impressive timber-framed dining pub with former coach entrance, well liked imaginative food (not Sun evening) served by cheerful helpful staff, rambling old beamed and flagstoned interior with contemporary furnishings creating stylish but relaxed atmosphere, big fireplace, well kept ales such as Church End and Purity, 20 wines by the glass, good coffee and afternoon teas, daily papers; may be background music, occasional art exhibitions and live music; children welcome if eating, dogs allowed, tables on back decking, open till 7.30pm Sun, closed Mon, otherwise open all day. *(Geoff and Ann Marston)*

HENLEY-IN-ARDEN SP1565
Nags Head (01564) 793120
High Street; B95 5BA Refurbished black and white-fronted pub dating in part from the 17th c, four real ales (one badged for them) and good range of wines, enjoyable food (all day Sat, till 6pm Sun) including gluten-free options, reasonable prices, pleasant attentive service; some live music, sports TV; children and dogs (in bar) welcome, seats out at back, open all day. *(Phil and Helen Holt)*

KENILWORTH SP2872
Clarendon Arms (01926) 852017
Castle Hill; CV8 1NB Busy pub opposite castle and under same ownership as next-door Harringtons restaurant; Hook Norton, Wye Valley and a couple of guests, tasty reasonably priced pub food, several rooms off long bare-boards bustling bar, largish peaceful upstairs dining room, cheerful young staff; children welcome, dogs in bar, metal tables on small raised terrace, daytime

car park fee deducted from food bill, open all day Fri-Sun. *(Tony and Wendy Hobden, Ian Herdman)*

KENILWORTH   SP2872

Cross (01926) 853840

New Street; CV8 2EZ Smart 19th-c Michelin-starred restaurant-pub with first class skilfully cooked food (not cheap), set lunch Mon-Sat, 18 wines by the glass and a couple of ales including Charles Wells Bombardier, open-plan split-level interior with view into kitchen, front bar for drinkers; terrace and small garden, open all day, no food Sun evening. *(Charles Welch)*

KENILWORTH   SP2871

Queen & Castle (01926) 852661

Castle Green; CV8 1ND Modernised beamed Mitchells & Butlers dining pub opposite castle, good range of enjoyable food including weekday set menu (till 6pm), three real ales and plenty of wines by the glass; children welcome, open all day. *(Christopher and Elise Way, Ian Herdman)*

KENILWORTH   SP2872

★Virgins & Castle (01926) 853737

High Street; CV8 1LY Maze of intimate rooms off inner servery, small snugs by entrance corridor, flagstones, heavy beams, lots of woodwork including booth seating, coal fire, four well kept Everards ales and a couple of guests, good food at reasonable prices, friendly service, restaurant, games bar upstairs; children in eating areas, disabled facilities, tables in sheltered garden, parking can be a problem, open all day. *(Dr and Mrs A K Clarke)*

LADBROKE   SP4158

★Bell (01926) 811224

Signed off A423 S of Southam; CV47 2BY Refurbished beamed country pub set back from the road, smallish bar with tub chairs by log fire, snug off with library wallpaper and another fire in little brick fireplace, three ales including Ringwood and plenty of wines by the glass, very good well presented food from pub favourites and grills up, weekday set menu, airy restaurant with light oak flooring, friendly efficient service; background music, free wi-fi; children and dogs (in bar) welcome, a few picnic-sets out in front and on side grass, pleasant surroundings, closed Sun evening, Mon. *(Clive and Fran Dutson, Mike Fountain)*

LAPWORTH   SP1871

★Boot (01564) 782464

Old Warwick Road; B4439 Hockley Heath–Warwick – 2.8 miles from M40 junction 1, but from southbound carriageway only, and return only to northbound; B94 6JU Popular upmarket dining pub near Stratford Canal, good range of food from interesting menu including weekday fixed-price offer, efficient cheerful young staff, upscale wines, Purity UBU and St Austell Tribute, stripped beams and dark panelling, big antique hunting prints, cushioned pews and bucket chairs on ancient quarry tiles and bare boards, warm fire, charming low-raftered upstairs dining room; background music; children and dogs welcome, teak tables, some under extendable canopy on side terrace, and picnic-sets on grass beyond, nice walks, open all day. *(R L Borthwick)*

LAPWORTH   SP1970

Navigation (01564) 783337

Old Warwick Road (B4439 SE); B94 6NA Modernised beamed pub by the Grand Union Canal; slate-floor bar with woodburner, bare-boards snug and restaurant, well kept ales such as Byatts, Purity, Timothy Taylors, Thwaites and Wadworths, unusually Guinness also on handpump, decent wines and reasonably priced food (all day Fri-Sun) from sandwiches and other bar choices up, breakfast from 10am weekends, friendly hard-working staff; children welcome, dogs in bar, covered terrace and waterside garden, handy for Packwood House and Baddesley Clinton (both NT), open all day. *(W M Lien, Clive and Fran Dutson)*

LEAMINGTON SPA   SP3165

Cricketers Arms (01926) 881293

Archery Road; CV31 3PT Friendly town local opposite bowling greens; enjoyable fairly priced food using meat from good local butcher, popular Sun roasts (till 6pm), also nice home-made sausage rolls and scotch eggs, well kept Slaughterhouse and a couple of guests such as Timothy Taylors from central bar, Weston's cider, some panelling and cricketing memorabilia, comfortable banquettes, open fires; darts, sports TV, fortnightly quiz Mon; children and dogs welcome, heated back terrace, open all day. *(Julian Thorpeham)*

LEEK WOOTTON   SP2868

Anchor (01926) 853355

Warwick Road; CV35 7QX Neat and well run dining lounge popular for its good fresh food including fish specials, well kept Hook Norton, Purity and two guests, good selection of affordably priced wines and soft drinks, attentive friendly service, lots of close-set tables, smaller overflow dining area; background music, sports TV; children welcome, no dogs inside, long garden behind with play area, open all day Sun. *(Ian Herdman)*

LIGHTHORNE   SP3455

Antelope (01926) 651188

Old School Lane, Bishops Hill; a mile SW of B4100 N of Banbury; CV35 0AU Attractive early 18th-c stone-built pub in pretty village setting, two neatly kept comfortable bars and separate dining area, beams, flagstones and big open fire, well kept Greene King IPA, Sharps Doom Bar and a couple of guests, enjoyable food from good sandwiches up, friendly effective service; children welcome, picnic-sets out by well and on small grassy area, open all day Fri-Sun. *(Jeff Davies)*

LITTLE COMPTON   SP2530
★ **Red Lion** (01608) 674397
Off A44 Moreton-in-Marsh to Chipping Norton; GL56 0RT Popular low-beamed 16th-c Cotswold-stone inn, good reasonably priced food cooked by landlady from pubby choices up, Donnington ales and good choice of wines by the glass, snug alcoves, inglenook woodburner; darts and pool in public bar; well behaved children and dogs welcome, pretty side garden with aunt sally, two nice bedrooms. *(K H Frostick, R K Phillips, D L Frostick)*

LONGFORD   SP3684
Greyhound (024) 7636 3046
Sutton Stop, off Black Horse Road/ Grange Road; junction of Coventry and North Oxford canals; CV6 6DF Cosy 19th-c canalside pub with plenty of character, half a dozen well kept ales including Bass and Marstons Pedigree, good range of enjoyable food including lunchtime sandwiches and home-made pies, friendly helpful staff, coal-fired stove, unusual tiny snug; children and dogs welcome, tables on attractive waterside terrace, nice spot (if you ignore the pylons), open all day. *(Lance and Sarah Milligan)*

LOWER GORNAL   SO9191
Fountain (01384) 242777
Temple Street; DY3 2PE Lively local with nine well kept ales including Greene King, Hobsons and RCH, draught continentals, real cider and country wines, enjoyable inexpensive food (not Sun evening), can eat in bar, lounge or separate restaurant; background music; children and dogs welcome, picnic-sets in gravel garden, open all day. *(Dave Braisted)*

LOWSONFORD   SP1868
Fleur de Lys (01564) 782431
Off B4439 Hockley Heath–Warwick; Lapworth Street; B95 5HJ Prettily placed by Stratford Canal, linked beamed rooms of varying sizes, log fires, good fairly priced food including range of pies, Greene King Abbot, IPA and a guest beer, plenty of wines by the glass, cocktails, friendly helpful staff; children welcome, large waterside garden, open (and food) all day. *(Chris Sallnow)*

LYE   SO9284
★ **Windsor Castle** (01384) 897809
Stourbridge Road (corner A458/A4036; car park in Pedmore Road just above traffic lights – don't be tempted to use the next-door restaurant's parking!); DY9 7DG Interesting well kept beers from

impressive row of handpumps including own Sadlers ales (brewery tours available); central flagstoned part with bar stools by counter and window shelf overlooking road, several snugger rooms off, some brewing memorabilia, enjoyable home-cooked food (not Sun evening) from deli boards up, friendly service; children and dogs welcome, disabled facilities, terrace and verandah seating, four bedrooms, handy for Lye station, open all day (from 9am Sat for breakfast). *(Douglas Power)*

NAPTON   SP4560
Folly (01926) 815185
Off A425 towards Priors Hardwick; Folly Lane, by locks; CV47 8NZ Popular beamed red-brick pub in lovely spot on Oxford Canal by Napton Locks and Folly Bridge (113): three bars on different levels, mix of furnishings and two big fireplaces (one with woodburner), lots of interesting bric-a-brac, pictures and old framed photographs, good straightforward home-made food (not Sun evening), well kept ales including Hook Norton, friendly efficient staff; children and dogs welcome. *(Clive and Fran Dutson, Adrian Johnson)*

NETHER WHITACRE   SP2292
Gate (01675) 481292
Gate Lane; B46 2DS Welcoming traditional community pub, seven well kept Marstons-related ales and good honest local food, log-fire bar, lounge and dining conservatory, games room with pool; children and dogs (in bar) welcome, garden picnic-sets, open all day, no food Mon. *(Dave Bell)*

NETHERTON   SO9488
★ **Old Swan** (01384) 253075
Halesowen Road (A459 just S of centre); DY2 9PY Victorian tavern full of traditional character and known locally as Ma Pardoe's after a former long-serving landlady; wonderfully unspoilt front bar with big swan centrepiece in patterned enamel ceiling, engraved mirrors, traditional furnishings and old-fashioned cylinder stove, other rooms including cosy back snug and more modern lounge, own well priced ales and enjoyable good value bar food (best to book/check times), upstairs restaurant; no under-16s, dogs allowed in bar, open all day. *(Nigel Espley)*

NEWBOLD ON STOUR   SP2446
White Hart (01789) 450205
A3400 S of Stratford; CV37 8TS Welcoming dining pub in same family for many years, proper pubby atmosphere, with enjoyable varied home-made food (not always Sun evening) including early-bird offer, Adnams Southwold and Purity Mad Goose, nice wines, long airy beamed bar with good log fire in large stone fireplace, flagstones and big bay windows, back bar and separate dining room; pool, darts and ring the bull;

children and dogs welcome, picnic-sets out at front and on back lawned area, open all day weekends. *(Douglas Power)*

OFFCHURCH SP3665
★**Stag** (01926) 425801

N of Welsh Road, off A425 at Radford Semele; CV33 9AQ Popular 16th-c thatched and beamed village pub; oak-floored bar with log fires, ales such as Purity and Warwickshire, a dozen wines by the glass and good interesting food served by friendly efficient young staff, more formal cosy restaurant areas with bold wallpaper, striking fabrics, animal heads and big mirrors; children and dogs (in bar) welcome, nice garden with rattan-style furniture on terrace, open all day. *(Charles Welch)*

OLD HILL SO9686
Waterfall (0121) 561 3499

Waterfall Lane; B64 6RG Friendly unpretentious two-room local, well kept Bathams, Holdens and several guests, straightforward low-priced home-made food, tankards and jugs hanging from boarded ceiling; dogs welcome, seats on small raised front area and in back garden, open all day. *(Dave Braisted)*

OXHILL SP3149
★**Peacock** (01295) 688060

Off A422 Stratford–Banbury; CV35 0QU Popular stone-built country pub with good varied menu including blackboard specials and gluten-free choices, friendly attentive young staff, a house beer from Wychwood and two guests, good selection of wines by the glass; cosy beamed bar with big solid tables and woodburner, half-panelled bare-boards dining room; unobtrusive background music; children and dogs (in bar) welcome, nice back garden, pretty village, open all day. *(Clive and Fran Dutson)*

PRINCETHORPE SP4070
Three Horseshoes (01926) 632345

High Town; junction A423/B4453; CV23 9PR Friendly old beamed village pub with Marstons EPA and Pedigree and Charles Wells Bombardier, enjoyable traditional food including blackboard specials and children's choices, good service, decorative plates, pictures, comfortable settles and chairs, two restaurant areas; free wi-fi; big garden with terrace and play area, five bedrooms, open all day Fri-Sun. *(Shaun Mahoney)*

PRIORS MARSTON SP4857
Holly Bush (01327) 260934

Off A361 S of Daventry; Holly Bush Lane; CV47 7RW 16th-c pub under new management; beams, flagstones and lots of stripped stone in rambling linked rooms, log fire and woodburners, enjoyable home-made food (not Sun or Tues evenings), Black Sheep, Hook Norton, Sharps and a guest, friendly service; Tues quiz, darts, free wi-fi;

children welcome, dogs in bar, terrace and sheltered garden (barbecues), summer beer and music festival, closed Mon-Weds lunchtimes, otherwise open all day (till 8pm Sun). *(Julian Thorpeham)*

RATLEY SP3847
Rose & Crown (01295) 678148

Off A422 NW of Banbury; OX15 6DS Ancient golden-stone village pub, charming and cosy, with five well kept changing ales (St Austell Tribute and Wells Bombardier feature regularly), blackboard list of wines, enjoyable good value food (not Sun evening, Mon) including daily specials, friendly efficient staff, carpeted black-beamed bar with woodburner each end, traditional furniture and window seats, cosy snug; background music, darts; children, walkers and dogs welcome, tables on sunny split-level terrace, aunt sally, near lovely church in sleepy village, handy for Upton House (NT), open all day Fri-Sun, closed Mon lunchtime. *(JHBS, John Allman, Clive and Fran Dutson)*

ROWINGTON SP1969
Tom o' the Wood (01564) 782252

Off B4439 N of Rowington, following Lowsonford sign; Finwood Road; CV35 7DH Spaciously modernised and extended canalside pub, good home-cooked food (not Sun evening) from sharing baskets and stone-baked pizzas up, well kept Greene King IPA and a guest, Weston's Rosie's Pig cider, friendly staff and pub labrador (Boris), conservatory; live music Fri; children and dogs welcome, tables on terrace and side lawn, open all day (may close early Sun). *(Nigel and Sue Foster)*

RUGBY SP5075
Merchants (01788) 571119

Little Church Street; CV21 3AN Open-plan pub tucked away near main shopping area, cheerfully busy, with nine quickly changing ales (some unusual for the area), real ciders and huge selection of belgian and other bottled imports, regular beer/cider/gin festivals, shortish choice of low-priced lunchtime food including speciality fish and chips, quite dark inside with beams, bare boards and mat-covered flagstones, lots of interesting breweriana; background music (live Tues), quiz last Mon of month, sports TVs; open all day, till 1am Fri, Sat. *(George Atkinson)*

RUGBY SP5075
Seven Stars (01788) 546611

Albert Square; CV21 2SH Traditionally refurbished 19th-c red-brick local with great choice of ales including B&T and Everards, personable landlord and friendly staff, main bar, lounge, snug and conservatory; occasional charity events with live music; some outside seating, open all day. *(Douglas Power)*

RUSHALL
SK03001

Manor Arms (01922) 642333
Park Road, off A461; WS4 1LG
Interesting low-beamed 18th-c pub (on much
older foundations) by Rushall Canal, three
rooms in contrasting styles, one with big
inglenook, well kept Banks's ales from pumps
fixed to the wall (there's no counter), simple
snacky food (nothing hot), friendly staff;
waterside garden with moorings, by Park
Lime Pits nature reserve. *(Miles Green)*

SEDGLEY
SO9293

★Beacon (01902) 883380
*Bilston Street; A463, off A4123
Wolverhampton–Dudley; DY3 1JE* Plain
old brick pub with own good Sarah Hughes
ales from traditional Victorian tower brewery
behind; cheery locals in simple quarry-tiled
drinking corridor, little snug on left with wall
settles, imposing green-tiled marble fireplace
and glazed serving hatch, old-fashioned
furnishings such as velvet and net curtains,
mahogany tables on patterned carpet, small
landscape prints, sparse tap room on right
with blackened range, dark-panelled lounge
with sturdy red leather wall settles and big
dramatic sea prints, plant-filled conservatory
(no seats), little food apart from cobs; no
credit cards; children allowed in some parts
including garden with play area. *(Miles Green)*

SHUSTOKE
SP2290

★Griffin (01675) 481205
*Church End, a mile E of village; 5 miles
from M6 junction 4; A446 towards
Tamworth, then right on to B4114
straight through Coleshill; B46 2LB*
Unpretentious country local with a dozen
well kept changing ales including own
Griffin (brewed in next-door barn), farm
cider and country wines, may be winter
mulled wine, standard lunchtime bar food
(not Sun); cheery low-beamed L-shaped
bar with log fires in two stone fireplaces
(one a big inglenook), fairly simple décor
including cushioned café seats, elm-topped
sewing trestles and a nice old-fashioned
settle, beer mats on ceiling, conservatory
(children allowed here); games machine;
dogs welcome, old-fashioned seats on back
grass with distant views of Birmingham, large
terrace, play area and summer marquee (live
music), camping field, open all day Sun.
(Geoff and Ann Marston)

SHUSTOKE
SP2290

Plough (01675) 481557
B4114 Nuneaton–Coleshill; B46 2AN
Old-fashioned feel with rooms arranged
around the bar, well kept Bass and three
guests, good choice of fairly straightforward
food served by friendly helpful staff, separate
dining room, black beams, open fire and

gleaming brass; pool and darts, regular quiz
nights (usually Mon); seats out at back along
with caged rabbits and exotic birds, open all
day Fri-Sun. *(Jeremy Snaithe)*

STOCKTON
SP4365

Boat (01926) 812657
A426 Southam–Rugby; CV23 8HQ
Fairly traditionally updated canalside pub
under new management, open-plan split-level
interior (raised part mainly for dining) with
dark wood furniture on wood or pale stone
floor, woodburner in brick fireplace, brewery
mirrors and advertising signs, bottles on
delft shelf, a house beer from Nethergate
and three guests, popular reasonably priced
pubby food (not Sun evening), friendly
staff, little deli; children and dogs (in bar)
welcome, picnic-sets out by the water
(moorings), garden behind with play area,
open all day. *(George Atkinson)*

STOURBRIDGE
SO9084

Duke William (01384) 440202
Coventry Street; DY8 1EP Friendly
Edwardian corner pub in semi-pedestrianised
area, own Craddocks beers from on-site
microbrewery (tour available) plus guests
and draught/bottled imports, good pie,
mash and peas menu, traditional old Black
Country feel with long corridor, open fire in
bar and cosy snug; plenty of events including
music, quiz and film nights (some in upstairs
function room); no children, beer garden,
open all day. *(Dave Braisted)*

STOURBRIDGE
SO8983

Plough & Harrow (01384) 397218
Worcester Street; DY8 1AX Friendly
little bay-windowed end of terrace local
(sister to the nearby Duke William), well
kept Craddocks ales and guests, snacky
food (nothing hot), cosy horseshoe bar
with log fires and piano; dogs welcome,
children allowed in garden, partly covered
beer garden with woodburner, close to Mary
Stevens Park, open all day. *(Dave Braisted)*

STRATFORD-UPON-AVON
SP2055

★Bear (01789) 265540
*Swans Nest Hotel, just off A3400
Banbury Road, by bridge; CV37 7LT*
Part of the Swans Nest Hotel complex; bar
with eight real ales from pewter-topped
counter including a house beer brewed by
North Cotswold, 26 wines by the glass and
several malt whiskies, good value popular
food (all day weekends), professional service,
two traditional linked rooms with china
and other bric-a-brac on delft shelf above
panelling, a couple of wing armchairs by fire
and variety of other seating including sofas,
scatter-cushioned banquettes, a character
settle and splendid long bench with baluster
legs, river views from big windows; sports

Pubs close to motorway junctions are listed at the back of the book.

TV, free wi-fi; children and dogs welcome, tables on waterside lawn (beyond service road), open all day. *(Clive and Fran Dutson, Nigel Bray)*

STRATFORD-UPON-AVON SP2054
★ **Encore** (01789) 269462
Bridge Street; CV37 6AB More modern bar than traditional pub; main beamed area with big windows, well spaced cast-iron tables, bucket armchairs and square stools on broad oak boards or pale flagstones, large charcoal sketches of local scenes, softly lit dark-walled back area with barrel and other rustic tables, stairs up to long comfortable dining room with river views, log fire, well kept Purity, Robinsons and Sharps, plenty of wines by the glass and good coffee, popular food including fixed-price weekday menu, friendly chatty staff; background music; children welcome, dogs in bar, open (and food) all day from 9.30am, can get very busy weekends. *(Hugh Roberts, Mitchell Cregor, Phil and Jane Villiers)*

STRATFORD-UPON-AVON SP2054
Garrick (01789) 292186
High Street; CV37 6AU Ancient pub with fine timbered frontage, heavy beams in irregularly shaped rooms, simple furnishings on bare boards or flagstones, enjoyable fairly priced food from sandwiches and light dishes up, well kept Greene King ales and decent wines by the glass, friendly helpful staff, small air-conditioned back dining area; background music, TV, games machine; children welcome, open (and food) all day. *(Alan Johnson)*

STRATFORD-UPON-AVON SP1955
Old Thatch (01789) 295216
Rother Street/Greenhill Street; CV37 6LE Cosy and welcoming thatched pub dating from the 15th c on corner of market square, well kept Fullers ales, nice wines and popular fairly priced food including Sun carvery, rustic décor, beams, slate or wood floors, sofas and log fire, back dining area; children welcome, covered tables outside, open all day (Sun till 6pm). *(Alan Johnson)*

STRATFORD-UPON-AVON SP2055
Old Tramway (01789) 297593
Shipston Road; CV37 7LW Mid 19th-c red-brick pub backing on to the old Moreton-in-Marsh horse-drawn tramway (now an embankment footpath); cosy fairly traditional interior with log fire, three real ales and good choice of popular reasonably priced pub food, friendly staff; sports TV, free wi-fi; children and dogs welcome, small front garden, partly covered heated terrace behind with summer bar, open (and food) all day. *(B and F A Hannam)*

STRATFORD-UPON-AVON SP2055
One Elm (01789) 404919
Guild Street; CV37 6QZ Peach pub with fresh modern décor on two floors, well liked food from sandwiches and sharing boards up, good value weekday set menu till 6pm, Purity, Sharps and one or two guests, plenty of wines by the glass and interesting range of gins, cocktails, friendly efficient service; children and dogs welcome, seats out at front and in attractive courtyard behind, open all day. *(Dr and Mrs J D Abell)*

STRATFORD-UPON-AVON SP1955
White Swan (01789) 297022
Rother Street; CV37 6NH Extensively renovated historic hotel (dates from 1450) with warren of connecting heavily beamed areas around central bar (one or two steps), good mix of seating including leather armchairs/sofas and antique settles, Shakespearean themed pictures and prints, oak panelled dining room with two fine carved fireplaces and 16th-c wall painting of Tobias and the Angel, five Fullers/Gales beers, several wines by the glass and good choice of food to suit all tastes and occasions, quick friendly service; background music, daily newspapers, free wi-fi; children welcome, seats out at front overlooking market square and to the side, character bedrooms, open (and food) all day. *(Susan and John Douglas)*

STRATFORD-UPON-AVON SP1954
Windmill (01789) 297687
Church Street; CV37 6HB Ancient pub (with town's oldest licence) beyond the striking Guild Chapel, very low beams, panelling, mainly stone floors, big fireplace (gas fire), Greene King, Purity UBU and guests, good value enjoyable food including range of burgers, friendly efficient staff; background music, sports TV, games machines; courtyard tables, open all day. *(Charles Welch)*

STRETTON-ON-FOSSE SP2238
★ **Plough** (01608) 661053
Just off A429; GL56 9QX Popular little 17th-c village local continuing well under present licensees; central servery separating small bar and snug dining area, four changing mainly local ales, good home-cooked food (not Sun evening) including blackboard specials, stripped brick/stone walls and some flagstones, low oak beams, inglenook log fire; dominoes and cribbage, free wi-fi; children welcome, no dogs, a few tables outside, open all day. *(K H Frostick)*

TANWORTH-IN-ARDEN SP1071
Warwickshire Lad (01564) 742346
Broad Lane/Wood End Lane, Wood End; B94 5DP Beamed country pub with broad choice of enjoyable food cooked by landlord-chef including good value weekday set menu (till 6pm), well kept St Austell, Wye Valley and a couple of guests, friendly efficient staff; open mike night last Sun of month; children and dogs welcome, popular with walkers (bridleway opposite), seats outside, open

(and food) all day and fairly convenient for M42 (junction 3). *(Clive and Fran Dutson, Nick Hales, Elaine Powis)*

TEMPLE GRAFTON   SP1355
Blue Boar (01789) 750010
1 mile E, towards Binton; off A422 W of Stratford; B49 6NR Welcoming stone-built dining inn with good food from sandwiches and tapas-style snacks up, set lunch Mon-Fri, well kept Banks's, Ringwood, Wychwood and a guest, afternoon teas, beams, stripped stonework and log fires, glass-covered well with goldfish, smarter dining room up a couple of steps; sports TV; children and dogs welcome, picnic-sets outside, 14 bedrooms, open all day. *(Sharon and John Hancock)*

TIDDINGTON   SP2255
Crown (01789) 297010
Main Street; CV37 7AZ Refurbished family-friendly pub with good well priced home-made food (smaller helpings available), four well kept ales including Sharps Doom Bar, darts, pool and TV in side bar; children and dogs welcome, garden with play area, open all day Fri-Sun, no food Sun evening. *(Alan Johnson)*

TIPTON   SO9492
Pie Factory (0121) 557 1402
Hurst Lane, Dudley Road towards Wednesbury; A457/A4037; DY4 9AB Eccentric décor and quirky food – the mixed grill comes on a shovel, and you're awarded a certificate if you finish their massive Desperate Dan Cow Pie (comes with pastry horns) – other pies and good value food including Sun carvery, well kept Lump Hammer house ales brewed by Enville plus a guest; background music (live weekends), TV; children welcome, bedrooms. *(Miles Green)*

UFTON   SP3762
White Hart (01926) 612428
Just off A425 Southam–Leamington; CV33 9PJ Friendly old pub in elevated roadside position next to church; modernised beamed bar with log fire, high-backed leather chairs and some booth seating, stripped-stone walls, a few steps here and there, well kept ales such as Greene King, St Austell and Slaughterhouse, several wines by the glass and enjoyable good value food, efficient service; children welcome, picnic-sets in hilltop garden with panoramic views, closed Sun evening. *(Clive and Fran Dutson)*

UPPER BRAILES   SP3039
Gate (01608) 685212
B4035 Shipston-on-Stour to Banbury; OX15 5AX Traditional low-beamed village

local, well kept Hook Norton and a guest, Weston's cider and enjoyable reasonably priced food including good fish and chips, efficient friendly service, coal fire; TV, darts; children welcome, tables in extensive back garden with play area and aunt sally, pretty hillside spot with lovely walks, two comfortable bedrooms, good breakfast, closed weekday lunchtimes, no food Sun evening, Mon. *(JHBS)*

UPPER GORNAL   SO9292
★**Britannia** (01902) 883253
Kent Street (A459); DY3 1UX Popular old-fashioned 19th-c local with friendly chatty atmosphere (known locally as Sally's after former landlady), particularly well kept/priced Bathams, coal fires in front bar and time-trapped little back room with its wonderful wall-mounted handpumps, some bar snacks including good local pork pies; sports TV; dogs welcome, nice flower-filled backyard, open all day. *(Dave Braisted)*

WALSALL   SP0198
Black Country Arms
(01922) 640588 *High Street; WS1 1QW* Imposing old town pub on three levels, great choice of well kept ales including Black Country, craft beers and real ciders, enjoyable home-made pubby food at bargain prices (till 4pm Sun, Mon), good friendly service; background and live music, quiz nights, sports TV; no dogs, small side terrace, open all day (till midnight Fri; Sat).
(Dave Braisted, Liz and Brian Barnard)

WARMINGTON   SP4147
Plough (01295) 690666
Just off B4100 N of Banbury; OX17 1BX Attractive and welcoming old stone pub under brother and sister team, some updating but keeping character and good local atmosphere, low heavy beams and exposed stone walls, comfortable chairs by inglenook woodburner, well kept Greene King ales and Sharps Doom Bar, enjoyable traditional home-made food (not Mon), extended dining room; children welcome, tables on back terrace, delightful village with pond and interesting church, closed Sun evening. *(Clive and Fran Dutson)*

WARWICK   SP2864
★**Rose & Crown** (01926) 411117
Market Place; CV34 4SH Friendly bustling Peach group inn with uncluttered modern décor, good choice of interesting sensibly priced food, well kept Purity, Sharps and a guest, good wines and coffee, cheerful efficient service; background music, newspapers; children and dogs (in front

---

Anyone claiming to arrange, or prevent, inclusion of a pub in the *Guide* is a fraud. Pubs are included only if recommended by readers and if our own anonymous inspection confirms that they are suitable.

bar) welcome, tables out under parasols, 13 comfortable bedrooms, open (and food) all day from 8am for breakfast. *(Christopher and Elise Way, Alan Johnson)*

WARWICK SP2967
★ **Saxon Mill** (01926) 492255
Guys Cliffe, A429 just N; CV34 5YN Rambling Mitchells & Butlers dining pub in charmingly set converted mill; beams and blazing log fire, smart contemporary chairs and tables on polished boards and flagstones, cosy corners with leather armchairs and big rugs, mill race and turning wheel behind glass, enjoyable food in bar and (best to book) upstairs family restaurant including good value weekday set menu (till 6pm) and weekend brunch from 9am, local beers and several wines by the glass, friendly enthusiastic service; background music; ground-floor wheelchair access and loo, tables out on terraces by broad willow-flanked river, more over bridge, delightful views across to Guys Cliffe House ruins, open (and food) all day. *(Adrian Johnson, Simon and Mandy King)*

WEST BROMWICH SO9992
Sow & Pigs (0121) 553 3127
Hill Top, towards Wednesbury; B70 0PS Saved from demolition and fully refurbished by Two Crafty Brewers, their well kept beers and up to three guests, good value food such as burgers and hot dogs (not Sun evening, Mon-Thurs lunchtime), contemporary feel but keeping original features; live music; open all day. *(Dave Cooper)*

WHICHFORD SP3134
Norman Knight (01608) 684621
Ascott Road, opposite village green; CV36 5PE Sympathetically extended beamed and flagstoned pub, with own Stratford Upon Avon beers and enjoyable home-made food, friendly service; live music including monthly folk club; children and dogs welcome, tables out by lovely village green, aunt sally, site at back for five caravans, good walks, open all day Fri, Sat, till 6pm Sun, closed Mon lunchtime. *(Douglas Power)*

WILLEY SP4885
Wood Farm (01788) 833469
Coalpit Lane; CV23 0SL Modern visitor centre attached to (and with view into) Wood Farm Brewery, up to eight of their ales and occasional guests, ample helpings of enjoyable reasonably priced food from sandwiches and baked potatoes up, cheerful helpful service, upstairs galleried function/overflow room; children welcome, no dogs, substantial terrace with country views,

camping, brewery tours (must pre-book, not Sun), open all day (till 6pm Sun). *(George Atkinson, Alan Johnson)*

WILLOUGHBY SP5267
Rose (01788) 891180
Just off A45 E of Dunchurch; Main Street; CV23 8BH Neatly decorated old thatched dining pub; low beamed and planked ceiling, wood or tiled floors, some panelling and inglenook woodburner, good range of food cooked well by italian chef-landlord including pizzas, weekday set italian menu, tapas night last Thurs of month, well kept Hook Norton and Sharps Doom Bar, reasonably priced house wines, friendly attentive young staff; children and dogs welcome, disabled facilities, seating in side garden with gate leading to park and play area, closed Sun evening, Mon. *(Clive and Fran Dutson)*

WIXFORD SP0854
Fish (01789) 778593
B4085 Alcester–Bidford; B49 6DA Old pub by pretty brick bridge over River Arrow; enjoyable reasonably priced food including bargain weekday set menu, three real ales, friendly attentive staff, contemporary bare-boards interior with plenty of quirky touches, log fire; children and dogs welcome, big riverside garden, open (and food) all day. *(B and F A Hannam)*

WOLVERHAMPTON SO9298
★ **Great Western** (01902) 351090
Corn Hill/Sun Street, behind railway station; WV10 0DG Cheerful pub hidden away in cobbled lane down from mainline station; Holdens and guest beers kept well, real cider, bargain home-made food (not Sun), helpful friendly staff, traditional front bar, other rooms including neat dining conservatory, interesting railway memorabilia, open fires; background radio, TV; children and dogs welcome, maybe summer barbecues in yard, open all day and busy with Wolves fans on match days. *(Dave Braisted)*

WOOTTON WAWEN SP1563
Bulls Head (01564) 795803
Stratford Road, just off A3400; B95 6BD Attractive black and white dining pub under new management; good choice of enjoyable traditional food from baguettes up, Marstons Pedigree, Ringwood and a guest, friendly helpful staff, Elizabethan beams and timbers, stone and quarry-tiled floors, log fires; children welcome, dogs in bar, outside tables front and back, handy for one of England's finest churches and Stratford Canal walks, open all day (till 8pm Sun). *(Charles Welch)*

Wiltshire

ALDBOURNE
SU2675 Map 2

Blue Boar 🍺 £

(01672) 540237 – www.theblueboarpub.co.uk

The Green (off B4192 in centre); SN8 2EN

Busy local with simple pubby furnishings in bar, cottagey restaurant and seats outside

Picnic-sets at the front make the most of the charming location by the pretty village green here and the window boxes are lovely in summer. The heavily beamed bar has built-in wooden window seats, tall farmhouse chairs and other red-cushioned pubby chairs on flagstones or bare boards, a woodburning stove in an inglenook fireplace with a stuffed boar's head and large clock above it, horsebrasses on the bressumer beam and a notice board with news of beer festivals and live music events. Wadworths IPA, 6X, Swordfish and a guest ale on handpump, eight wines by the glass, 17 malt whiskies and a farm cider. The back restaurant is beamed and cottagey with standing timbers, dark wooden chairs and tables on floorboards and rugs, and plates displayed on a dresser.

🍴 Traditional food at fair prices includes lunchtime sandwiches and baguettes, deep-fried breaded whitebait with tartare sauce, smoked mackerel pâté, home-cooked ham with free-range eggs, root vegetable nut roast topped with goats cheese, sausages and mash with onion gravy, lambs liver and bacon, chicken with white wine and tarragon sauce, salmon fillet with lemon and parsley butter, and puddings such as banoffi pie and lemon tart. *Benchmark main dish: steak and kidney pie £9.50. Two-course evening meal £16.50.*

Wadworths ~ Tenants Michael and Joanne Hehir ~ Real ale ~ Open 11.30-3, 5.30-11.30; 11.30am-midnight Fri, Sat; 12-11 Sun ~ Bar food 12-2 (2.30 Fri, Sat), 6.30-9; 12-4 Sun ~ Restaurant ~ Children welcome ~ Dogs allowed in bar ~ Wi-fi ~ Live music regularly (phone to check) *Recommended by Roy and Gill Payne, Julian Thorpe*

BRADFORD-ON-AVON
ST8261 Map 2

Castle 🍺

(01225) 865657 – www.flatcappers.co.uk

Mount Pleasant, by junction with A363, N edge of town; extremely limited pub parking but spaces in nearby streets; BA15 1SJ

Substantial stone inn with local ales, popular food, plenty of character and fine views; bedrooms

The unspoilt bar here has a lot of individual character, a wide range of seats (church chairs, leather armchairs, cushioned wall seating and brass-studded leather dining chairs) around chunky pine tables on dark flagstones, church candles, fringed lamps and a good log fire; daily papers, background music and board games. A bare-boards snug on the right is similar in style. Cheerful staff serve a beer named for the pub (from Three Castles Brewery), Dark Star Original, Plain Inntrigue and Sheep Dip, Quantock White Hind and Three Castles Barbury Castle on handpump and several wines by the glass; they hold a beer and music festival twice a year. The seats at the front of this handsome stone building offer sweeping town views, while in the back garden you look across lovely countryside. The boldly decorated bedrooms are comfortable and have spacious bathrooms. Back wheelchair access.

As well as breakfasts (8.30am-midday), the good food includes quite a few nibbles, sharing boards, spinach and feta strudel with onion jam, sausages of the week, cottage pie, beer-battered cod and chips, whole spring chicken with bread sauce and sautéed potatoes, fillet of sea bream with shaved fennel and aioli, slow-cooked pork belly with thyme boulangère potatoes, pea purée, apple sauce and red wine jus, and puddings such as chocolate and hazelnut brownie with chocolate sauce and knickerbocker glory. *Benchmark main dish: burgers with toppings, sauce, coleslaw and chips £9.95. Two-course evening meal £16.50.*

Free house ~ Licensee Ben Paxton ~ Real ale ~ Open 9am-11pm ~ Bar food 8.30am-10pm (9.30pm Sun) ~ Children welcome but must be seated from 7.30pm ~ Dogs allowed in bar ~ Wi-fi ~ Bedrooms: £90/£100 *Recommended by Chris and Angela Buckell, Dr and Mrs A K Clarke*

CHICKSGROVE

ST9729 Map 2

Compasses ★ ⊙ ♍ ⇔

(01722) 714318 – www.thecompassesinn.com

From A30 5.5 miles W of B3089 junction, take lane on N side signposted 'Sutton Mandeville, Sutton Row', then first left fork (small signs point the way to the pub in Lower Chicksgrove; look out for the car park); can also be reached off B3089 W of Dinton, passing the glorious spire of Teffont Evias church; SP3 6NB

Excellent all-rounder with enjoyable food, a genuine welcome, four real ales and seats in the quiet garden; attractive bedrooms

It may not be the easiest pub to find but our readers love the hidden, peaceful setting, the genuine welcome and the interesting food and drink; it's a lovely place to stay too, with comfortable rooms. The unchanging bar has plenty of real character: old bottles and jugs hanging from beams above the roughly timbered counter, farm tools and traps on the part-stripped stone walls, high-backed wooden settles forming snug booths around tables on the mostly flagstoned floor, and a log fire. Butcombe Bitter, Hop Back Taiphoon and Waylands Sixpenny 6d Gold on handpump, nine wines by the glass, eight malt whiskies and farm cider. The quiet garden behind has seating on terraces and in a flagstoned courtyard. Fine surrounding walks.

Imaginative food includes daily specials listed on boards: ciabattas, thai-style mussels, goats cheese, apricot and chive terrine with red onion marmalade, wild boar and apple sausages with red wine gravy and mash, chickpea and carrot fritters with mixed bean cassoulet, tandoori-style chicken with bombay potatoes, lentil samosa and mint yoghurt, slow-roasted pork belly with bacon dauphinoise, apple and fennel slaw and cider sauce, brill with confit chicken wings and fish bisque sauce, and puddings such as treacle tart with orange curd ice-cream and carrot cake with honey and stem ginger ice-cream. *Benchmark main dish: lamb rump with breaded mutton shoulder, minted pea purée, creamed sheeps cheese and redcurrant/port jus £16.95. Two-course evening meal £23.00.*

Free house ~ Licensee Alan Stoneham ~ Real ale ~ Open 12-3, 6-11; 12-3, 7-10.30 Sun;
closed Mon lunch Jan-Easter ~ Bar food 12-2, 7-9 ~ Children welcome ~ Dogs welcome ~
Wi-fi ~ Bedrooms: £75/£95 *Recommended by Michael Doswell, S Holder, Edward Mirzoeff*

CORSHAM ST8670 Map 2

 **Methuen Arms** 🍷⭐ 🛏

(01249) 717060 – www.themethuenarms.com
High Street; SN13 0HB

**Charming hotel with character bars, friendly staff, imaginative food,
good wines and ales, and seats outside; comfortable bedrooms**

In a bustling market town, this handsome Georgian inn is run by
professional licensees and their warmly friendly staff. It's civilised yet
informal and there's always a good mix of both drinkers and diners. The
proper little front bar has a log fire, a big old clock under a sizeable mirror,
an assortment of antique dining chairs and tables, rugs on elm floorboards
and evening candlelight. Drinks include Butcombe Bitter, Prescott Hill Climb
and St Austell Tribute on handpump, 12 wines by the glass, ten malt whiskies
and quite a few gins; background music. Across the green-painted bar
counter is a second small bar, with similar furnishings, bare boards and rugs
and a couple of armchairs. The dining room has settles (carved and plain),
high-backed dining chairs with wooden arms around old sewing-machine
tables, an open fire with tea-lights, black and white photographs of large
local houses on sage green paintwork and swagged curtains. Another room
leads off here, and there's also a restaurant at the back. The garden to the
side of the building has seats and tables.

 As well as breakfasts for non-residents (7.30-10.30am), the excellent food from
a thoughtful menu includes lunchtime sandwiches, pork and pigeon terrine with
fig and port purée, chargrilled mackerel with smoked mackerel rillettes and pickled
cucumber, leek and gruyère tart with duck egg and truffle, chicken saltimbocca with
confit leg, salsify and mushroom purée, cod with braised gem lettuce, samphire, potato
and tarragon gnocchi and shellfish cream sauce, and puddings such as spiced rum and
date sticky toffee pudding with toffee sauce and Valrhona chocolate mousse cake with
milk chocolate fudge ice-cream. *Benchmark main dish: chargrilled local lamb loin
and braised shoulder with artichoke purée, lamb and rosemary jus £21.50. Two-course
evening meal £28.00.*

Free house ~ Licensees Martin and Debbie Still ~ Real ale ~ Open 12-11 (10.30 Sun) ~
Bar food 12-3, 6-10 ~ Restaurant ~ Children welcome ~ Dogs allowed in bar ~ Wi-fi ~
Bedrooms: £90/£120 *Recommended by Mr and Mrs P R Thomas, Roger and Donna Huggins,
Dr and Mrs A K Clarke*

CRICKLADE SU1093 Map 4

Red Lion 🍺 🛏

(01793) 750776 – www.theredlioncricklade.co.uk
Off A419 Swindon–Cirencester; High Street; SN6 6DD

**16th-c inn with well liked food in two dining rooms, ten real ales,
friendly, relaxed atmosphere and big garden; bedrooms**

As well as ales from their on-site Hop Kettle microbrewery, there are
plenty of guest beers here, served by friendly staff. Their own brews
might include Hop Kettle Dawn til Dusk, Kia Ora and North Wall, while the
other changing choices might be Oakham Chemical Syndicate, Tapstone
Kush Kingdom and XT 15. They also keep 60 bottled beers, five farm ciders,
ten wines by the glass, 18 malt whiskies and 15 gins (gin hour is 5.30-6.30).

The bar has a good community atmosphere, stools by the nice old counter, wheelbacks and other chairs around dark wooden tables on red patterned carpet, an open fire and all sorts of bric-a-brac on the stone walls including stuffed fish, animal heads and old street signs. You can eat here or in the slightly more formal dining room, furnished with pale wooden farmhouse chairs and tables, beige carpeting and a woodburning stove in a brick fireplace. There are plenty of picnic-sets in the big back garden. Bedrooms are comfortable and breakfasts good. You can walk along the nearby Thames Path or around the historic and pretty town.

As well as lunchtime sandwiches (not Sunday), the enjoyable food includes sandwiches, potted brown shrimps, chicken and ham terrine with piccalilli, salt beef hash with local poached egg and crispy capers, stilton cauliflower and broccoli cheese, cod loin with curried sweet potato, braised gem lettuce and seared leeks and broad beans, flat-iron steak and skinny chips, and puddings such as chocolate fondant with dehydrated mousse and white chocolate sorbet and treacle tart with milk ice-cream. *Benchmark main dish: burger with toppings, triple-cooked chips and chilli jam £12.50. Two-course evening meal £21.00.*

Free house ~ Licensee Tom Gee ~ Real ale ~ Open 12-11 (midnight Sat); 12-10.30 Sun ~ Bar food 12-2.30, 6-9 (9.30 Fri); 12-3, 6-9.30 Sat); 12-3.30, 6-9 Sun ~ Restaurant ~ Children welcome ~ Dogs welcome ~ Wi-fi ~ Bedrooms: /£85
Recommended by Rob Henderson, Tracey and Stephen Groves, DF and NF, Phil and Jane Villiers

CRUDWELL   ST9592   Map 4
Potting Shed 🎯 ♀ 🍺
(01666) 577833 – www.thepottingshedpub.com
A429 N of Malmesbury; The Street; SN16 9EW

Civilised but relaxed dining pub with low-beamed rooms, an interesting range of drinks and creative cooking; seats in the big garden

There's a good welcome under the newish owners for all customers here, and that includes dogs who might get a treat from the bar and a greeting from the pub dog, Milton. Low-beamed rooms rambling around the bar have bare stone walls, open fires and woodburning stoves (one in a big worn stone fireplace), mixed plain tables and chairs on pale flagstones, armchairs in one corner and daily papers. Four steps lead up into a high-raftered area with wood flooring, and there's another separate, smaller room that's ideal for a lunch or dinner party. Also, lots of country prints and more modern pictures, fresh flowers, candles and some quirky, rustic decorations such as a garden-fork door handle, garden-tool beer pumps and so forth. A fine range of drinks includes Bath Gem, Butcombe Bitter, Flying Monk Elmers and Timothy Taylors Landlord on handpump, as well as 21 wines and champagne by the glass, three farm ciders, home-made seasonal cocktails and local fruit liqueurs; background music and board games. There are sturdy teak seats around cask tables as well as picnic-sets out on the side grass among weeping willows. Good access for those in need of extra assistance. They also own the hotel across the road.

Accomplished food includes sandwiches, home-cured sea trout with asparagus, almonds, tomatoes and olives, smoked duck with confit leg, orange, spring onion and pickled walnuts, beer-battered haddock with triple-cooked chips, breaded globe artichokes with crushed cauliflower and black pudding croquettes, chimichurri (argentinian herb and chilli mix) lamb cutlets with aubergine, peppers, courgettes and mint yoghurt, hake with chorizo, baby squid and spinach and parmesan potatoes, and puddings such as vanilla pannacotta with strawberry sorbet and chocolate fondant with blueberry compote. *Benchmark main dish: burger with toppings, triple-cooked chips and home-made ketchup £14.00. Two-course evening meal £20.00.*

Enterprise ~ Lease Alex Payne ~ Real ale ~ Open 11-11 ~ Bar food 12-2.30, 6-9; 12-3, 6.30-8.30 Sun ~ Restaurant ~ Children welcome ~ Dogs welcome ~ Wi-fi
Recommended by Dr W I C Clark, Taff Thomas, Geoffrey Sutton, Alistair Forsyth

EAST CHISENBURY
SU1352 Map 2

Red Lion 🍴 ♉ 🛏

(01980) 671124 – www.redlionfreehouse.com
At S end of village; SN9 6AQ

Wiltshire Dining Pub of the Year

Country inn in peaceful village run by hard-working chef-owners, contemporary décor, an informal atmosphere and excellent food; fine bedrooms

This is a special place to stay and the very well equipped, boutique-style bedrooms are in a separate building with private decks just a few metres from the River Avon; breakfasts are delicious and the bloody marys and bucks fizz are complimentary. Of course, the wonderful food in this thatched inn is the reason most customers are here (Mr and Mrs Manning are both top chefs), but they also keep a fine range of drinks. Locals congregate at high chairs by the counter for a pint and a chat: Andwell Ruddy Darter, Otter Amber and Stonehenge Pigswill on handpump, 30 wines by the glass, home-made cordial and quite a range of gins and malt whiskies. One long room is split into different areas by brick and green-planked uprights. A big woodburner sits in a brick inglenook fireplace at one end; at the other is a comfortable black leather sofa and armchairs, and in between are high-backed and farmhouse wooden dining chairs around various tables on bare boards or stone tiles, with pretty flowers and church candles dotted about. There's an additional dining room too, and a new private upstairs dining room has been added since the last *Guide*; background music. Outside, the terrace and grassed area above it have picnic-sets and tables and chairs. They make their own dog treats and can organise a packed lunch for walkers.

Using home-reared pigs, their own eggs and home-grown produce (plus other local, seasonal specialities), the exceptional food includes sandwiches, warm crab tart, chicken, ham hock and leek terrine with pear chutney, pumpkin and black truffle tortelloni with hispi cabbage, cheese and toasted hazelnuts, duck breast with leg and pistachio pastille, salt-baked swede and anise roasting juices, monkfish with curried cauliflower, raisins, almonds, quinoa and pan juices, and puddings such as coconut sticky rice with lime curd, peanut crumb, fresh coconut and lime sherbert and Valrhona chocolate brownie with caramel popcorn and banana ice-cream; they also offer a two- and three-course set weekday lunch. *Benchmark main dish: local rib-eye steak with béarnaise sauce for two people £60.00. Two-course evening meal £33.00.*

Free house ~ Licensees Britt and Guy Manning ~ Real ale ~ Open 9am-11pm ~ Bar food 12-2.30, 6-9 (9.30 Sat); 12-3, 6-8 Sun ~ Children welcome ~ Dogs allowed in bar and bedrooms ~ Wi-fi ~ Bedrooms: /£150 *Recommended by Wilburoo, R T and J C Moggridge, Ian Herdman, Penny and David Shepherd, Simon and Alex Knight*

A star after the name of a pub shows exceptional quality. It means most people (after reading the report to see just why the star has been won) would think a special trip worthwhile.

EAST KNOYLE
ST8731 Map 2
Fox & Hounds ♀
(01747) 830573 – www.foxandhounds-eastknoyle.co.uk

Village signposted off A350 S of A303; The Green (named on some road atlases),
a mile NW at OS Sheet 183 map reference 872313; or follow signpost off B3089,
about 0.5 miles E of A303 junction near Little Chef; SP3 6BN

**Pretty thatched village pub with splendid views, welcoming service,
good beers and popular, enjoyable food**

This 15th-c pub is in a charming spot by the village green and also
overlooks Blackmore Vale. Three linked areas – on different levels
around the central horseshoe-shaped servery – have big log fires, plentiful
oak woodwork and flagstones, comfortably padded dining chairs around big
scrubbed tables, and a couple of leather sofas; the furnishings are all very
individual and uncluttered. There's also a small light-painted conservatory
restaurant. Hop Back Summer Lightning, Otter Amber and Palmers Copper
Ale on handpump, a dozen wines by the glass and Thatcher's farm cider;
background music and skittle alley. There are marvellous views over into
Somerset and Dorset from plenty of picnic-sets, the nearby woods are good
for a stroll and the Wiltshire Cycleway passes through the village.

 Popular food includes rabbit and olive terrine, lamb samosas with mango chutney,
chickpea, sweet potato and spinach curry, risotto with scallops and crab, steak
and ale pie, bacon-wrapped chicken breast with gratin potato and pesto cream sauce,
flat-iron steak with peppercorn sauce and chips, and puddings such as chocolate 'lumpy
bumpy' with cream and pear and almond tart with vanilla ice-cream. *Benchmark main
dish: beer-battered cod and chips £12.00. Two-course evening meal £19.00.*

Free house ~ Licensee Murray Seator ~ Real ale ~ Open 11.30-3, 5.30-11 (10 Sun) ~
Bar food 12-2.30, 6.30-9 ~ Children welcome ~ Dogs welcome ~ Wi-fi
Recommended by Roy Hoing, Douglas Power, Valerie Sayer

EDINGTON
ST9353 Map 2
Three Daggers 🍺
(01380) 830940 – www.threedaggers.co.uk
Westbury Road (B3098); BA13 4PG

**Rejuvenated village pub with open fires, beams and candlelight,
helpful staff, enjoyable food and own-brew beers; bedrooms**

The thoughtful choice of drinks in this appealing brick pub includes their
own hand-pumped Three Daggers beers – Daggers Ale, Black, Blonde
and Edge (brewed in the farm shop building) – 14 wines by the glass, ten
malt whiskies and a couple of farm ciders. The interior is heavily beamed
and open-plan with a friendly, easy-going atmosphere: leather sofas and
armchairs at one end in front of a woodburning stove, kitchen and chapel
chairs and built-in planked wall seats with scatter cushions, leather-topped
stools against the counter, and a cosy nook with just one table. A two-way
fireplace opens into the candlelit restaurant, which has similar tables and
chairs on a dark slate floor, and lots of photos of local people and views.
Stairs lead up to another dining room with beams in a high roof and some
unusual large wooden chandeliers; background music, darts and board
games. The airy conservatory has tea-lights or church candles on scrubbed
kitchen tables and wooden dining chairs. Just beyond this are picnic-sets
on grass plus a fenced-off, well equipped children's play area. The three
bedrooms are pretty. Do visit their farm shop opposite.

Food is good and includes breakfasts (from 10am), lunchtime sandwiches, treacle-cured salmon with roast beetroot, ewes curd, pickled egg and dill cucumber, pressed ham hock, potato and celeriac rémoulade with piccalilli, wild mushroom risotto with garlic butter, burger with toppings, coleslaw and triple-cooked chips, hake fillet with chorizo and haricot beans in tomato sauce, partridge breast and legs, creamed brussel sprouts and bacon, parsnip purée and game chips, and puddings such as banoffi pie with peanut ice-cream and dark chocolate brownie with chocolate sauce. *Benchmark main dish: pulled pork with pickles £15.00. Two-course evening meal £22.00.*

Free house ~ Licensee Robin Brown ~ Real ale ~ Open 10am-11pm (10.30pm Sun) ~ Bar food 12-2.30, 6-9; 12-3, 6-9.30 Sat; 12-4, 6-8 Sun ~ Restaurant ~ Children welcome ~ Dogs allowed in bar ~ Wi-fi ~ Live music Fri/Sat evenings ~ Bedrooms: £85/£95

Recommended by Hilary and Neil Christopher, Rob Anderson, Beth Aldridge

FONTHILL GIFFORD ST9231 Map 2

Beckford Arms

(01747) 870385 – www.beckfordarms.com

Hindon Lane; from Fonthill Bishop, bear left after tea rooms through Estate gate; from Hindon follow High Street signed for Tisbury; SP3 6PX

18th-c coaching inn with character bar and restaurant, unfailingly good food, thoughtful choice of drinks and an easy-going atmosphere; comfortable bedrooms

There's an almost country-house hotel feel to this golden-stone coaching inn with its civilised yet informal atmosphere – and you can expect a friendly welcome from courteous staff. The main bar has various old wooden dining chairs and tables on parquet flooring, a huge fireplace and bar stools beside the counter where they keep an interesting range of drinks: Keystone Phoenix (named for them), Yeovil Stout Hearted and a changing guest on handpump, 15 wines by the glass, 20 malt whiskies, farm cider and winter mulled wine and cider, and cocktails such as a bellini using locally produced peach liqueur and a bloody mary using home-grown horseradish. The cosy sitting room is stylish with comfortable sofas facing one another across a low table with newspapers, a nice built-in window seat among other chairs and tables, and an open fire in a stone fireplace with candles in brass candlesticks and fresh flowers on the mantelpiece. There's also a separate restaurant and private dining room. Much of the artwork on the walls is by local artists. They host film nights on occasional Sundays and will provide water and bones for dogs (the pub dog is called Elsa). The mature rambling garden has seats on a brick terrace, hammocks under trees, games for children, a dog bath and boules. Bedrooms are well equipped and individually decorated and breakfasts are good and generous.

Using local suppliers and some home-grown produce, the imaginative food includes home-smoked trout with tarragon mayonnaise, peas and pickled radish, pigeon breast with black pudding, smoked bacon and artichoke purée, beefburger with toppings, chilli coleslaw, pickles and chips, garlic-roasted fregola with cauliflower purée, wild mushrooms and a crispy egg, slow-braised lamb shoulder with roasted shallots and celeriac purée, cod with ricotta dumplings, hollandaise sauce and artichoke crisps, and puddings such as white chocolate mousse with baked white chocolate and raspberry and mint sorbet and orange posset with ginger treacle bread and pickled blackberries. *Benchmark main dish: crispy chicken burger with bacon, avocado and chips £12.00. Two-course evening meal £12.50.*

Free house ~ Licensees Dan Brod and Charlie Luxton ~ Real ale ~ Open 8am-11pm (10.30 Sun) ~ Bar food 12-3, 6-9.30 (9 Sun) ~ Children welcome ~ Dogs welcome ~ Wi-fi

~ Bedrooms: /£95 *Recommended by Michael Sargent, Michael Doswell, S G N Bennett, Bob and Margaret Holder, Richard and Penny Gibbs, Edward Mirzoeff*

 GREAT BEDWYN   SU2764   Map 2

Three Tuns 🏵 ♀

(01672) 870280 – www.threetunsbedwyn.co.uk

Village signposted off A338 S of Hungerford, or off A4 W of Hungerford via Little Bedwyn; High Street; SN8 3NU

Carefully refurbished village pub with a friendly welcome, real ales and highly rated food

The chef-owner and his wife run this neatly kept 18th-c village inn with a great deal of care and enthusiasm. The beamed front bar is traditional and simply furnished with pubby stools and chairs on bare floorboards, and has an open fire, artwork by local artists on the walls and plenty of original features. They keep quickly changing ales from small local breweries including Three Tuns (brewed by Betteridge), a seasonal beer from Butcombe and West Berkshire Swift Pale Ale on handpump, 14 wines by the glass, several malt whiskies, gins and vodkas and Sheppy's farm cider. French doors in the back dining room lead into the garden where there are tables and chairs and an outdoor grill. The Kennet & Avon Canal runs through the village and the pub is on the edge of Savernake Forest, which has lovely walks and cycle routes.

 Cooked by the landlord using seasonal ingredients from local producers and making everything in-house, the particularly good food includes goose rillettes with gherkins, pear, pomegranate, walnut and gorgonzola salad, chanterelle mushroom and black truffle ragoût, crispy chicken thighs with jerusalem artichokes, kale and mash, cod with ibérico chorizo, roasted red peppers and aioli, venison faggots with sticky red cabbage and mash, and puddings such as vanilla burnt cream and rhubarb and passion-fruit mess with white chocolate ice-cream. *Benchmark main dish: bavette steak with roasted bone marrow, bordelaise sauce and chips £19.50. Two-course evening meal £22.00.*

Free house ~ Licensees James and Ashley Wilsey ~ Real ale ~ Open 10am-midnight; 12-6 Sun; closed Sun evening, Mon, first week Jan ~ Bar food 12.30-2.30, 6-9.30; 12.30-9.30 Fri, Sat; 12-3 Sun ~ Restaurant ~ Children welcome ~ Dogs welcome ~ Wi-fi
Recommended by Caroline Prescott, Alan and Alice Morgan, Edward and William Johnston Alfie Bayliss

HOLT   ST8561   Map 2

Toll Gate 🛏

(01225) 782326 – www.tollgateinn.co.uk

Ham Green; B3107 W of Melksham; BA14 6PX

16th-c stone pub with cheerful staff, woodburning stoves in bars, real ales and popular food; pretty bedrooms

This former weavers' shed is a friendly place with a good mix of both locals and visitors. The relaxed bar has real character with seats by a woodburner, a mix of tables and chairs on pale floorboards and plenty of paintings by local artists for sale. Box Steam Half Sovereign and Tunnel Vision (the brewery is in the village), Butcombe Bitter and Fullers London Pride with a guest such as Sharps Doom Bar on handpump, 16 wines by the glass, interesting gins and three farm ciders; background music, TV and board games. The dining room leads off the bar with high-backed leather and other cushioned chairs, a second woodburner, fresh flowers and cream window blinds. Up a few steps, the high-raftered restaurant is similarly furnished with white deer heads on a dark blue wall and church windows (this used to be a workers' chapel). The sun-shaded and paved back terrace has seats and tables, and there's a boules pitch. Bedrooms, some of which are in their old farm shop, have open fires; there's also a holiday cottage for rent. Wheelchair access to bar (but not to loos).

 Tasty food includes lunchtime ciabattas (not Sunday), chilli crab cakes with pea purée and lime vinaigrette, breaded lamb breast with caper and dijon mayonnaise, pork, onion and cider pie, burger with toppings, coleslaw and chips, chicken caesar salad, wild mushroom and spinach risotto, beer-battered fish and chips, guinea fowl kiev with mushroom, asparagus, pepper and seed crumble with chive cream, bass fillet with ratatouille, 28-day dry-aged steaks with chips and a choice of sauces, and puddings such as chocolate brownie with dark chocolate truffles, white chocolate fudge, caramel ice-cream and caramel sauce and rhubarb and apple crumble. *Benchmark main dish: stuffed pork belly with apple and mustard purée, sweet potato, leek and cheddar gratin £14.50. Two-course evening meal £19.50.*

Free house ~ Licensees Laura Boulton and Mark Hodges ~ Real ale ~ Open 10am-11pm (midnight Sat); 10-4 Sun ~ Bar food 12-2, 6.30-9; 12-9 Sat; 12-4 Sun ~ Restaurant ~ Children welcome ~ Wi-fi ~ Live music outside in summer ~ Bedrooms: £60/£70
Recommended by Comus and Sarah Elliott, Chris and Angela Buckell

LOWER CHUTE
Hatchet 🍴 🛏
SU3153 Map 2

(01264) 730229 – www.thehatchetinn.com
The Chutes well signposted via Appleshaw off A342, 2.5 miles W of Andover; SP11 9DX

Neatly kept 13th-c thatched inn with a friendly welcome for all, four beers and enjoyable food; comfortable bedrooms

Although it's tucked away down country lanes, you'll always find plenty of chatty customers in this charming rural gem, and the convivial landlord offers a warm welcome to all. The very low-beamed bar has a peaceful local feel, a splendid 16th-c fireback in a huge fireplace (and a roaring winter log fire) and various comfortable seats around oak tables; there's also an extensive restaurant. Timothy Taylors Landlord and a couple of guests such as Greene King Old Golden Hen and Triple fff Moondance on handpump, eight wines by the glass, 20 malt whiskies and several farm ciders; board games. There are seats out on a terrace and the side grass and a safe play area for children. The snug bedrooms make this a fine place to stay (dogs are welcome in one room) and breakfasts are hearty.

 Honest pubby food includes baguettes, deep-fried whitebait with tartare sauce, creamy garlic mushrooms, spinach and red pepper lasagne, chicken curry, lambs liver and bacon, fish pie, beef bourguignon, lamb rump in red wine, rosemary and redcurrant sauce with mash, and puddings. *Benchmark main dish: steak in ale pie £10.95. Two-course evening meal £19.50.*

Free house ~ Licensee Jeremy McKay ~ Real ale ~ Open 11.30-3, 6-11 (all day Fri); 12-4, 7-10.30 Sun ~ Bar food 12-2.15, 6.30-9.45; 12-3, 7-9 Sun ~ Restaurant ~ Children welcome ~ Dogs welcome ~ Wi-fi ~ Open mike night first Fri of month, quiz Tues evening ~ Bedrooms: £70/£80 *Recommended by Pip White, Hilary and Neil Christopher, S Holder*

Please keep sending us reports. We rely on readers for news of new discoveries, and particularly for news of changes – however slight – at the fully described pubs: feedback@goodguides.com, or (no stamp needed) The Good Pub Guide, FREEPOST RTJR-ZCYZ-RJZT, Perrymans Lane, Etchingham TN19 7DN.

MANTON
Outside Chance ♀

SU1768 Map 2

(01672) 512352 – www.theoutsidechance.co.uk

Village (and pub) signposted off A4 just W of Marlborough; High Street; SN8 4HW

Popular dining pub, civilised and traditional, nicely reworked with sporting theme; interesting modern food

The 20-times champion jump jockey A P McCoy co-owns this charming country pub that's usefully open all day. The three small linked rooms have hops on beams, flagstones or bare boards, and mainly plain pub furnishings such as chapel chairs and a long-cushioned pew; one room has a more cosseted feel, with panelling and a comfortable banquette. The décor celebrates unlikely horse-racing winners Caughoo, Foinavon, Mr Spooner's Only Dreams (a 100-1 winner at Leicester in 2007) and the odd-gaited little Seabiscuit who cheered many thousands of Americans with his dogged pursuit of victory during the Depression. There's a splendid log fire in the big main fireplace and maybe fresh flowers and candlelight; background music and board games. Wadworths IPA, 6X and a guest from Wadworths on handpump and eight good wines by the glass served by neatly dressed young staff; background music, board games and TV. A suntrap side terrace has contemporary tables with metal frames and granite tops, while the good-sized garden has sturdy rustic tables and benches under ash trees; they have private access to the local playing fields and children's play area. There are plenty of walks and things to see and do nearby.

 Rewarding food includes herbed scotch egg with curried mayonnaise, panko scampi with pea purée, chicken caesar salad, beer-battered haddock and triple-cooked chips, a tart of the day, potato gnocchi with mushrooms, parmesan and parsley cream with truffle, 10oz rib-eye steak with green peppercorn sauce, and puddings such as pannacotta with toffee sauce and chocolate brownie with chocolate sauce and salted caramel ice-cream. *Benchmark main dish: burger with toppings, coleslaw, red onion jam and frites £13.95. Two-course evening meal £21.00.*

Wadworths ~ Tenant Howard Spooner ~ Real ale ~ Open 12-11 ~ Bar food 12-2, 6-9; 12-3, 6-8 Sun ~ Children welcome ~ Dogs welcome ~ Wi-fi *Recommended by Wilburoo, Tina and David Woods-Taylor, Simon Rodway*

MARLBOROUGH
Lamb ◀

SU1869 Map 2

(01672) 512668 – www.thelambinnmarlborough.com

The Parade; SN8 1NE

Friendly inn with big helpings of popular food, real ales, plenty of customers and traditional pubby furnishings; comfortable bedrooms

Just off the high street and full of chatty locals, this cheerful town tavern has a good bustling atmosphere and pretty summer window boxes. The L-shaped bar has lots of hop bines, wall banquettes, wheelback chairs around wooden tables on parquet flooring, Cecil Aldin prints on red walls, candles in bottles and a two-way woodburning stove; the easy-going bulldog may be poddling about. Wadworths IPA, 6X and Horizon tapped from the cask, ten wines by the glass and 15 malt whiskies; games machine, juke box, darts and TV. There are picnic-sets and modern alloy and wicker seats and tables in the attractive back courtyard. The bedrooms are light and cottagey (some are in a former stable block) and breakfasts hearty.

Generous helpings of fair priced food includes lunchtime sandwiches and toasties, prawn cocktail, eggs benedict, butternut squash and chickpea tagine with pistachio rice, rare-breed sausages with mash and caramelised onion gravy, lamb koftas with tzatziki, hummus and stuffed vine leaves, gammon and eggs, steak and kidney in ale pie, beer-battered fresh cod and chips, and puddings such as seasonal fruit crumble and treacle tart with clotted cream ice-cream. *Benchmark main dish: 28-day dry-aged rib-eye steak with chips and a choice of sauces £16.00. Two-course evening meal £18.00.*

Wadworths ~ Tenant Vyv Scott ~ Real ale ~ Open 11-11 (11.30 Fri, Sat); 12-10.30 Sun ~ Bar food 12-2.30, 6.30-9; not Fri-Sun evenings ~ Children welcome until 8pm ~ Dogs allowed in bar and bedrooms ~ Wi-fi ~ Bedrooms: £55/£75 *Recommended by Mark Morgan, Sheila and Robert Robinson, Peter Brix*

MARSTON MEYSEY
Old Spotted Cow 🏮❗ ♀
SU1297 Map 4

(01285) 810264 – www.theoldspottedcow.co.uk
Off A419 Swindon–Cirencester; SN6 6LQ

An easy-going atmosphere in cottagey bar rooms, friendly young staff, lots to look at, well kept ales and enjoyable food; bedrooms

The main comment from readers on this smashing little pub is just how friendly the landlady and her staff are. You'll see many cows of all sorts around the bars, and some of them are actually spotted: paintings, drawings, postcards, all manner and colour of china objects and embroidery and toy ones too. The main bar has high-backed cushioned dining chairs around chunky pine tables on wooden floorboards or parquet, a few rugs here and there, an open fire at each end of the room (with comfortable sofas in front of one), fresh flowers and brass candlesticks with candles, and beer mats and bank notes pinned to beams. Butcombe Gold, Otter Bitter and Timothy Taylors Landlord on handpump, ten wines by the glass, summer farm cider and quite a few gins and malt whiskies. Two cottagey dining rooms lead off here with similar tables and chairs, a couple of long pews and a big bookshelf. There are seats and picnic-sets on the front grass and a children's play area is provided beyond a big willow tree. A classic car show is held here on the late May bank holiday.

Interesting and reliably good, the food includes sandwiches, lots of tapas dishes such as chilli king prawns, quail eggs, breaded fish balls with aioli and so forth, butternut squash curry with beetroot raita, cinnamon rice and chutney, mixed seafood linguine in fennel and white wine sauce, calves liver and bacon with root vegetable mash and red wine gravy, spicy chicken thighs with green mango salsa and kachumba (indian cucumber and tomato salad), pork escalope in madeira sauce with crushed potatoes, and puddings such as chocolate and rum trifle and steamed syrup sponge with custard. *Benchmark main dish: bubble and squeak with bacon, a poached egg and creamy mustard sauce £8.00. Two-course evening meal £18.00.*

Free house ~ Licensee Anna Langley-Poole ~ Real ale ~ Open 11-11; 11-6.30 Sun ~ Bar food 12-2, 7-9; 12-3 Sun ~ Restaurant ~ Children welcome but must be over 8 in bar ~ Dogs allowed in bar ~ Wi-fi ~ Bedrooms: /£95 *Recommended by Ben and Diane Bowie, Mr and Mrs John and Anne Selby, Edward Mirzoeff*

MONKTON FARLEIGH
Muddy Duck 🏮 🛏
ST8065 Map 2

(01225) 858705 – www.themuddyduckbath.co.uk
Signed off A363 Bradford–Bath; BA15 2QH

Grand stone building with character bar and dining room, open fire, real ales, good food and seats at the front and back; bedrooms

In a pretty village that's not far from Bath, this convivial and imposing 17th-c stone inn is much enjoyed by our readers. The bar and dining room are furnished in a similar manner, with wooden and upholstered chairs around tables of all shapes on bare boards or parquet flooring, armchairs in front of an open fire, cushioned pews, the odd duck ornament, beams, half-panelled walls and low-hanging lamps. High red leather chairs line the counter where friendly staff serve Butcombe Bitter, St Austell Proper Job and Timothy Taylors Landlord on handpump and good wines by the glass; background music and board games. In front of the building there's an impressive wisteria and picnic-sets under parasols; at the back, colourful tables and chairs sit in a fairy-lit, gravelled courtyard with views over open country. Three of the five individually decorated bedrooms have woodburning stoves and two are separate from the main building and have their own little courtyards.

 Often enterprising food includes confit duck with orange, fig and port, salmon with smoked paprika cure, peas and carrots, butternut squash lasagne with wild and chestnut mushrooms and cambozola, burger with toppings, slaw, pickles and triple-cooked chips, pollack with parmentier potatoes, bacon, peas and onion, local rare-breed beef fillet with garlic and herb butter, portobello mushrooms and french fries, and puddings. *Benchmark main dish: venison, chervil root and blueberries £18.00. Two-course evening meal £25.00.*

Punch ~ Lease Tom Lakin ~ Real ale ~ Open 12-11; 12-9 Sun ~ Bar food 12-2.30, 6-9; 12-3, 6-9.30 Sat; 12-4 Sun ~ Restaurant ~ Children welcome ~ Dogs allowed in bar ~ Wi-fi
Recommended by Taff Thomas, Sarah Roberts, Graham Waters, Dr and Mrs A K Clarke, Richard Mason

NEWTON TONY   SU2140   Map 2
Malet Arms

(01980) 629279 – www.maletarms.com
Village signposted off A338 Swindon–Salisbury; SP4 0HF

Smashing village pub with no pretensions, a good choice of local beers and highly thought-of food

We love this pub and, for many of our readers it's also a favourite. For those who like their pubs neat and tidy, it might be a little worn about the edges, but for most of us this just adds to the genuine, unspoilt character. The landlord and his staff are friendly and enthusiastic and sure to make you welcome. The low-beamed interconnecting rooms have a mix of tables of different sizes with high-winged wall settles, carved pews, chapel and carver chairs, and lots of pictures of local scenes and from imperial days. The main front windows are said to be made from the stern of a ship, and there's a log and coal fire in a huge fireplace. The snug is noteworthy for its fantastic collection of photographs and prints celebrating the local aviation history of Boscombe Down, alongside archive photographs of Stonehenge festivals of the 1970s and '80s. At the back is a homely, red-painted dining room. Four real ales on handpump come from breweries such as Butcombe, Flack Manor, Hop Back, Itchen Valley, Ramsbury, Stonehenge and Triple fff and they also keep 40 malt whiskies, eight wines by the glass and Weston's Old Rosie cider; board games. There are seats on the small front terrace with more on grass and in the back garden. The road to the pub goes through a ford, and it may be best to use an alternative route in winter when the water can be quite deep. There's an all-weather cricket pitch on the village green.

 Using seasonal game from local shoots (some bagged by the landlord), lamb raised in the surrounding fields and free-range local pork, the country cooking includes venison liver pâté with spicy home-made plum chutney, smoky devil rarebit (fjordling with smoked cheddar, horseradish, rosemary and tabasco on toast), roasted red pepper stuffed with baba ganoush (smoky aubergine dip), millionaire's fish pie (scallops, prawns, pollack and smoked salmon), venison, mushroom and Guinness pie, lamb shoulder with mash and minted pea purée, and puddings such as Toblerone cheesecake and steamed cherry sponge with custard. *Benchmark main dish: burger with toppings and chips £10.50. Two-course evening meal £18.00.*

Free house ~ Licensees Noel and Annie Cardew ~ Real ale ~ Open 11-3, 6-11; 12-4 Sun; closed Sun evening ~ Bar food 12-2.30, 6.30-9.30; 12-2.30 Sun ~ Restaurant ~ Children allowed only in restaurant or snug ~ Dogs allowed in bar *Recommended by John Allman, Roger and Donna Huggins, Steve Whalley, Edward Mirzoeff, Randy Alden*

PITTON
Silver Plough ♀ 🛏

SU2131 Map 2

(01722) 712266 – www.silverplough-pitton.co.uk
Village signed from A30 E of Salisbury (follow brown signs); SP5 1DU

Bustling country dining pub with popular, reasonably priced bar food, good drinks and nearby walks; bedrooms

With notably helpful and friendly staff, a warm atmosphere and a cheerful mix of both locals and visitors, this pub is a winner. The comfortable, nicely kept front bar has plenty to look at: black beams strung with hundreds of antique boot warmers and stretchers, pewter and china tankards, copper kettles, toby jugs, earthenware and glass rolling pins and so forth. Seats include half a dozen cushioned antique oak settles (one elaborately carved, next to a very fine reproduction of an Elizabethan oak table) around rustic pine tables. Badger First Call, K&B Sussex Bitter and Tanglefoot on handpump and 13 wines by the glass served from a bar made from a hand-carved Elizabethan overmantel. The back bar is simpler, but still has a big winged high-backed settle, cases of antique swords and some substantial pictures, and there are two woodburning stoves for winter warmth; background music. The skittle alley is for private use only. The quiet south-facing lawn has picnic-sets and other tables beneath parasols and there are more seats on the heated terrace; occasional barbecues. If you stay overnight and don't have breakfast, prices are cheaper than those given below. There are plenty of walks in the surrounding woodland and on downland paths.

Cooked by the landlord, the high quality food includes sandwiches and wraps, smoked trout pâté with watercress and lemon purée, whole baked camembert with rhubarb crust, roasted field mushroom with rarebit and herb and vegetable couscous, lemongrass and chilli chargrilled chicken with soft herb quinoa and sweet tomato ragoût, crayfish and king prawn fishcakes with smoked paprika and lime marie rose, duck leg braised in merlot and redcurrant with roasted red pepper, onion and broad bean medley, and puddings such as chocolate torte with raspberry mousse and lemon meringue crème brûlée. *Benchmark main dish: ginger ale slow-cooked pork belly with beetroot dauphinoise and gooseberry sauce £13.50. Two-course evening meal £20.50.*

Badger ~ Tenants Katie Hunter and Mike Reeves ~ Real ale ~ Open 12-3, 6-11; 12-8.30 Sun ~ Bar food 12-2, 6-9; 12-7.30 Sun ~ Restaurant ~ Children welcome ~ Dogs allowed in bar ~ Wi-fi ~ Bedrooms: £50/£60 *Recommended by Peter Meister, Tom and Ruth Rees, I D Barnett, David and Judy Robison, Edward Mirzoeff, Helen and Brian Edgeley*

The 🍺 symbol shows pubs that keep their beer unusually well, have a particularly good range or brew their own.

POULSHOT

ST9760   Map 2

Raven ◀

(01380) 828271 – www.ravenpoulshot.co.uk

Off A361; SN10 1RW

Pretty village pub with friendly licensees, enjoyable beer and food and seats in a walled back garden

The welcoming, professional licensees take great care of their pretty half-timbered pub – and of their customers too. The two cosy, black-beamed rooms are spotlessly kept with comfortable banquettes, pubby chairs and tables and an open fire. Wadworths IPA and 6X plus a changing guest tapped from the cask and 13 wines by the glass; background music in the dining room only. The jack russell is called Faith and the doberman Harvey. There are picnic-sets under parasols in the walled back garden and the pub is just across from the village green. Good nearby walks.

Food is well liked and cooked by the landlord and includes baguettes, chicken liver pâté with redcurrant jelly, asian chicken salad, ham and free-range eggs, butternut squash, chestnut mushroom and spinach lasagne, spicy lamb burger with toppings, pickled chilli and harissa mayonnaise, fish crumble, a hot meaty curry, beer-battered haddock and chips, liver and bacon with red wine gravy, and puddings such as spotted dick and custard and rhubarb eton mess. *Benchmark main dish: steak and kidney pie £11.95. Two-course evening meal £18.00.*

Wadworths ~ Tenants Jeremy and Nathalie Edwards ~ Real ale ~ Open 11.30-3, 6.30-11; 12-3.30, 7-10.30 Sun; closed Sun evening Oct-Easter, Mon end Oct-early May ~ Bar food 12-2 (2.30 Sun), 6.30-9 ~ Restaurant ~ Children welcome ~ Dogs allowed in bar ~ Wi-fi
Recommended by Charlie May, Peter and Penny Bull, Susan Eccleston

RAMSBURY

SU2771   Map 2

Bell ◎ ✿ ⇐

(01672) 520230 – www.thebellramsbury.com

Off B4192 NW of Hungerford, or A4 W; SN8 2PE

Lovely old inn with a civilised feel, character bar and dining rooms, and a thoughtful choice of both drinks and food; spotless bedrooms

Not surprisingly, this handsome and civilised 300-year-old former coaching inn does get extremely busy at peak times, so it's best to arrive early or pre-book a table in the restaurant. Throughout, the original features and contemporary paintwork and furnishings blend well together; the two rooms of the bar have tartan-cushioned wall seats and pale wooden dining chairs around assorted tables, country and wildlife paintings, interesting stained-glass windows and a woodburning stove. Neat, efficient staff serve Ramsbury Bitter, Gold and a seasonal ale plus a guest such as Muirhouse Chocolate Mild on handpump, a dozen wines by the glass and 20 malt whiskies. A cosy room between the bar and restaurant has much-prized armchairs and sofas before an open fire, a table of magazines and papers, a couple of portraits, stuffed birds and a squirrel, books on shelves and patterned wallpaper. The restaurant, smart but relaxed, is similarly furnished to the bar with white-clothed tables on bare boards or rugs, oil paintings and winter-scene photographs on beige walls; fresh flowers decorate each table. A nice surprise is the charming back café with white-painted farmhouse, tub and wicker chairs on floorboards, where they offer toasties, buns, cakes and so forth – it's very popular for morning coffee and afternoon tea. The garden has picnic-sets on a lower terrace and raised lawn, with more on a little terrace towards the front. The restful, well equipped bedrooms are named after game birds or fish.

First class food, using some home-grown produce plus seasonal ingredients from local suppliers, includes scallops with pickled cucumber and sweet potato puree, waldorf salad with nettles, lovage, walnuts and local blue cheese, burger with toppings, caramelised onion mayonnaise and triple-cooked chips, mussels in cider and cream, poached cod with champ mash, hispi cabbage and parsley sauce, roast rack of lamb with pressed potatoes, morel mushrooms and pea and mint purée, and puddings such as apple and pear crumble with bay leaf ice-cream and bakewell tart. *Benchmark main dish: beer-battered haddock and triple-cooked chips £14.00. Two-course evening meal £21.00.*

Free house ~ Licensee Alistair Ewing ~ Real ale ~ Open 12-11 (10 Sun) ~ Bar food 12-2.30, 6-9; 12-3, 6-8 Sun ~ Restaurant ~ Children welcome ~ Dogs allowed in bar ~ Wi-fi ~ Bedrooms: /£110 *Recommended by Richard Tilbrook, Hilary and Neil Christopher, James Allsopp*

ROWDE ST9762 Map 2
George & Dragon 🛏
(01380) 723053 – www.thegeorgeanddragonrowde.co.uk
A342 Devizes–Chippenham; SN10 2PN

Gently upmarket inn with good food, west country ales and a relaxed atmosphere; bedrooms

Handy for walks along the nearby Kennet & Avon Canal, this is a 16th-c former coaching inn with plenty of character. The two low-ceilinged rooms have beams, large open fireplaces, wooden dining chairs (some straightforward and others rather elegant) and wall seats with scatter cushions around candlelit tables, antique rugs and walls hung with old pictures and portraits; the atmosphere is pleasantly chatty. From the rustic bar counter, friendly staff serve Butcombe Bitter and Prescott Track Record on handpump and several wines by the glass. The pretty back garden has tables and chairs. Bedrooms are individually furnished and well equipped.

 Using plenty of cornish fish (most of which is listed on blackboards), the enjoyable food includes sandwiches, creamy tuna and caper tonnato, a changing terrine with chutney, spicy fishcakes with tartare sauce, twice-baked cheese soufflé with parmesan cream, chicken parmigiana with sautéed potatoes, thai green fish curry, pork tenderloin with herb stuffing, braised red cabbage and red wine jus, and puddings such as chocolate and raspberry roulade and fruit crumble; they also offer a two- and three-course set menu (not Fri or Sat evenings or Sun lunch). *Benchmark main dish: beer-battered fish and chips £14.00. Two-course evening meal £22.00.*

Free house ~ Licensee Christopher Day ~ Real ale ~ Open 12-3 (4 Sat), 6.30-11; 12-4 Sun; closed Sun evening ~ Bar food 12-3 (4 weekends), 6.30-10 ~ Restaurant ~ Children welcome ~ Dogs allowed in bar ~ Bedrooms: £75/£95 *Recommended by Pauline and Mark Evans, Rosie and John Moore, Sophia and Hamish Greenfield*

SHERSTON ST8585 Map 2
Rattlebone ♀
(01666) 840871 – www.therattlebone.co.uk
Church Street; B4040 Malmesbury–Chipping Sodbury; SN16 0LR

17th-c village pub with rambling rooms, real ales and good bar food using local and free-range produce; friendly staff

There's a great deal of character here as well as a bustling atmosphere helped along by chatty customers. The rambling rooms are softly lit and in the public bar and long back dining room you'll find beams, standing timbers and flagstones, pews, settles and country kitchen chairs around an assortment of tables, and armchairs and sofas by roaring fires. Butcombe

Bitter, Flying Monk Elmers and St Austell Tribute on handpump, 20 wines by the glass from a thoughtful list, local cider and home-made lemonade; background music, darts, board games, TV and games machine. Outside is a skittle alley and three boules pitches, often in use by one of the many pub teams; a boules festival is held in July, as well as mangold hurling (similar to boules, but using cattle-feed turnips) and other events. The two pretty gardens include an extended terrace where they hold barbecues and spit roasts. Wheelchair access.

Good food includes thyme-infused goats cheese brûlée, baby monkfish scampi with lemon mayonnaise, sharing boards, free-range chicken with lemon, thyme and garlic and skinny fries, asparagus and pea risotto with parmesan, a pie of the day, calves liver with crispy bacon and sage and black pudding mash, thai salmon curry, and puddings such as dark chocolate torte with orange mascarpone and honeycomb and sticky toffee pudding with toffee sauce; they also offer a two-course weekday lunch menu, a burger evening on Monday and pizza specials on Sunday evening. *Benchmark main dish: wild boar ragoût £10.50. Two-course evening meal £20.00.*

Youngs ~ Tenant Jason Read ~ Real ale ~ Open 12-3, 5-11 (midnight Fri); 12-midnight Sat; 12-11 Sun ~ Bar food 12-2.30, 6-9.30; 12-5 Sun ~ Restaurant ~ Children welcome ~ Dogs allowed in bar ~ Wi-fi ~ Live music last weekend of month *Recommended by R T and J C Moggridge, Hilary and Neil Christopher*

SOUTH WRAXALL   ST8364   Map 2
Longs Arms 🌟

(01225) 864450 ~ www.thelongsarms.com
Upper S Wraxall, off B3109 N of Bradford-on-Avon; BA15 2SB

Friendly licensees for well run and handsome old stone inn with plenty of character, real ales and first class food

The enthusiastic, convivial landlord here comes in for special praise from our readers for the thoughtfulness and care he shows all his customers. The bar has windsor and other pubby chairs around wooden tables on flagstones, a fireplace with a woodburning stove and high chairs by the counter where they keep Wadworths Horizon and 6X and a changing guest on handpump and ten wines and prosecco by the glass. Another room has cushioned and other dining chairs, a nice old settle and a wall banquette around a mix of tables on carpeting, fresh flowers and lots of prints and paintings; board games. There are tables and chairs in the pretty walled back garden, which also has raised beds and a greenhouse where they grow salad leaves and herbs.

Top notch food cooked by the landlord includes sweet cured herrings with cucumber, radish and pine nuts, crispy pork belly with chilli and peanut pickle, veal pie with mash and spring greens, twice-baked cheese soufflé, smoked salmon fishcakes, organic lamb rump with swede, broad beans, hazelnuts and mint, turbot with potato terrine and asparagus, and puddings such as salted caramel fondant with biscuit ice-cream and caramelised lemon curd with raspberry and mint. *Benchmark main dish: free-range pork belly with truffle mash, black pudding and crackling £16.50. Two-course evening meal £22.00.*

Wadworths ~ Tenants Rob and Liz Allcock ~ Real ale ~ Open 12-3.30, 5.30-11.30; 12-5 Sun; closed Sun evening, Mon, three weeks Jan ~ Bar food 12-2.30, 5.30-9.30; 12-3 Sun ~ Children welcome ~ Dogs welcome ~ Wi-fi *Recommended by Michael Doswell, Mr and Mrs A H Young, Taff Thomas, Mr and Mrs P R Thomas, Alistair Holdoway*

If we know a pub has an outdoor play area for children, we mention it.

SWINDON   SU1384 Map 2

Weighbridge Brewhouse ◀

(01793) 881500 – www.weighbridgebrewhouse.co.uk

Penzance Drive; SN5 7JL

Stunning building with stylish modern décor, own microbrewery ales, a huge wine list, a big range of popular food and helpful staff

At any one time you'll find six of their own-brew ales here, such as Weighbridge Brinkworth Village, Pooleys Gold, Poppy Red, Renegade, Swindon Pale Ale and Weighbridge Best; also, 20 wines by the glass, 30 malt whiskies and a cocktail menu. The bar area has comfortable brown leather chesterfields and wood and leather armchairs around a few tables on dark flagstones, much-used blue bar chairs against the long dimpled and polished steel counter and a sizeable carved wooden eagle on a stand. The fantastic-looking, stylishly modern open-plan dining room has a steel-tensioned high-raftered roof (the big central skylight adds even more light), attractive high-backed striped chairs and long wall banquettes, bare brick walls, candles in red glass jars on windowsills and a glass cabinet at the end displaying about 1,000 bottled beers from around the world. Metal stairs lead up to an area overlooking the dining room below with big sofas and chairs beside a glass piano; another room on the same level is used for cosier dining occasions. There are seats on an outside terrace.

🍴 Extremely popular, good food includes chicken caesar salad, spinach and mushroom pie, faggots with chive mash and onion gravy, lambs liver and bacon, beer-battered bass with lyonnaise potatoes and tartare sauce, thai-style crocodile, crispy half duck with redcurrant jelly and cherry wine, salmon and lobster tagliatelle in seafood liquor with star anise and lobster tempura, steaks with a choice of five sauces, and puddings such as mixed berry pavlova and honeycomb cheesecake with toffee sauce. *Benchmark main dish: pork tenderloin in bacon, onion, mushroom and red wine sauce with cheese dumplings £23.00. Two-course evening meal £26.00.*

Free house ~ Licensees Anthony and Allyson Windle ~ Real ale ~ Open 11.30am–midnight; 12-10.30 Sun ~ Bar food 12-2, 6-9.30; 12-8 Sun ~ Restaurant ~ Children welcome before 8pm ~ Dogs allowed in bar ~ Live music Thurs-Sat evenings *Recommended by Gus Swan, Charlie May, Sarah Roberts, Edward Edmonton*

 TOLLARD ROYAL   ST9317 Map 2

King John 🍽️ ⬅

(01725) 516207 – www.kingjohninn.co.uk

B3081 Shaftesbury–Sixpenny Handley; SP5 5PS

Pleasing contemporary furnishings in carefully opened-up pub, courteous, helpful service, good drinks and excellent food; pretty bedrooms

Opened in 1859, this was named after one of King John's hunting lodges and although regulars do drop in for a pint, most customers are here for the creative food. It's gently civilised and friendly and the open-plan L-shaped bar has a relaxed atmosphere, a log fire, nice little touches such as a rosemary plant and tiny metal buckets of salt and pepper on scrubbed kitchen tables, dog-motif cushions, a screen made up of the sides of wine boxes, and candles in big glass jars. An attractive mix of seats takes in spindlebacks, captain's and chapel chairs (some built into the bay windows) plus the odd cushioned settle, and there are big terracotta floor tiles, lantern-style wall lights, hound, hunting and other photographs, and prints of early 19th-c scientists. Ringwood Best, Sharps Doom Bar and Waylands Sixpenny

6d Gold on handpump and wines from a good list. A second log fire has fender seats on each side and leather chesterfields in front, and there's also a stuffed heron and grouse and daily papers. Outside at the front are seats and tables beneath parasols, with more up steps in the raised garden where there's also an outdoor kitchen pavilion. The bedrooms are comfortable and pretty and there's a self-catering cottage opposite.

 Often inventive food includes sandwiches, crab on toast, crispy hare risotto, fish and chips with pea fritter, twice-baked local cheddar cheese soufflé, brill fillet and ravioli with saffron velouté, smoked pork tenderloin with mash and black pudding, fillet steak with béarnaise sauce, and puddings such as apple doughnuts with mulled cider and toffee sauce and chocolate and orange fondant. *Benchmark main dish: venison haunch with potato rösti, bacon and gravy £18.95. Two-course evening meal £22.00.*

Free house ~ Licensee Lee Hart ~ Real ale ~ Open 11-11 ~ Bar food 12-2.30, 7-9.30; 12-3, 7-9 Sun ~ Restaurant ~ Children welcome ~ Dogs welcome ~ Wi-fi ~ Bedrooms: £95/£140
Recommended by Michael Hill, Emma Scofield, Colin Humphreys, Mike Kavaney

UPTON SCUDAMORE   ST8647   Map 2
Angel

(01985) 213225 – www.theangelinn.co.uk
Off A350 N of Warminster; BA12 0AG

Bustling bar and dining rooms where old and new features blend together, real ales, good wines, well thought-of food and seats in garden; attractive bedrooms

The bedrooms in this 16th-c coaching inn are well equipped and comfortable and make a good base for exploring the area – Longleat House & Safari Park are nearby. The bar has built-in tartan-cushioned wall seats, some farmhouse chairs and tables on stripped floorboards and stools against the counter where they serve Butcombe Bitter and Sharps Doom Bar on handpump and good wines by the glass; service is friendly and helpful. Steps lead up to an informal dining room with more farmhouse chairs around rustic tables on more bare boards, plus big hanging ceiling lights, sizeable paintings and fresh flowers; the upper restaurant is stylish with cushioned elegant chairs around polished tables on tartan carpet. The terraced back garden has modern chairs and tables under parasols, with sofas and more seats and tables among flower tubs and pots.

Good food includes lunchtime sandwiches, scotch egg with chilli jam, tiger prawns in garlic, shallot and sweet chilli cream with chorizo, honey and mustard ham with fried eggs, blue cheese, spinach and walnut linguine, steak burger with toppings, chilli jam and skinny fries, chicken with bubble and squeak, roasted gem lettuce and carrot purée, lamb rump with minted haricot beans, bacon crisp and jus, salmon with roasted beetroot, celeriac purée and creamed cabbage with cumin, and puddings such as brownie with chocolate and rum sauce and vanilla cream and mocha crème brûlée with chocolate ice-cream. *Benchmark main dish: cider-battered fish and triple-cooked chips £11.50. Two-course evening meal £21.00.*

Free house ~ Licensee Sharon Cornelius ~ Real ale ~ Open 11.30-3, 5.30-11 (10 Sun); see website for opening times in winter ~ Bar food 12-2, 6.30-9 ~ Restaurant ~ Children welcome ~ Dogs allowed in bar ~ Wi-fi ~ Bedrooms: £90/£100 *Recommended by Neil Allen, John Harris, Roger and Donna Huggins, Dave Sutton*

Also Worth a Visit in Wiltshire

Besides the fully inspected pubs, you might like to try these pubs that have been recommended to us and described by readers. Do tell us what you think of them: feedback@goodguides.com

BADBURY SU1980

★**Plough** (01793) 740342

A346 (Marlborough Road) just S of M4 junction 15; SN4 0EP Busy country pub well placed for M4 with wide choice of good fairly priced food, friendly efficient service, well kept Arkells and decent wines, large rambling bar with log fire, light airy dining room; background music; children and dogs welcome, tree-shaded garden with far-reaching views, open all day from 9am for breakfast, food all day Sun till 8pm.
(R K Phillips, Richard and Judy Winn)

BARFORD ST MARTIN SU0531

★**Barford Inn** (01722) 742242

B3089 W of Salisbury (Grovely Road), just off A30; SP3 4AB Welcoming 16th-c coaching inn; dark panelled front bar with big log fire, other interlinking rooms, old utensils and farming tools, beamed bare-brick restaurant, wide choice of popular reasonably priced food (not Sun evening) including deals, prompt friendly service, well kept Badger ales and decent wines by the glass; children welcome, dogs in bar, disabled access (not to bar) and loos, terrace tables, more in back garden, four comfortable annexe bedrooms, good walks, open all day.
(Michael Hill, Edward Mirzoeff)

BECKHAMPTON SU0868

Waggon & Horses (01672) 539418

A4 Marlborough–Calne; SN8 1QJ Handsome stone and thatch former coaching inn; generous fairly priced food cooked to order from varied menu in open-plan beamed bar or separate dining area, well kept Wadworths ales, good cheerful service; background music; children and dogs welcome, pleasant raised garden with play area, handy for Avebury (NT), open all day Fri-Sun. *(Sheila and Robert Robinson)*

BERWICK ST JAMES SU0739

★**Boot** (01722) 790243

High Street (B3083); SP3 4TN Welcoming flint and stone pub not far from Stonehenge; good locally sourced food from daily changing blackboard menu including some unusual bar snacks, friendly efficient staff, well kept Wadworths ales and a guest, huge log fire in inglenook at one end, sporting prints over brick fireplace the other, lit candles, small back dining room with collection of celebrity boots; children and dogs welcome, sheltered side lawn. *(Dennis and Doreen Haward)*

BERWICK ST JOHN ST9422

★**Talbot** (01747) 828222

Village signed from A30 E of Shaftesbury; SP7 0HA Unspoilt 17th-c pub in attractive village, simple furnishings and big inglenook in heavily beamed bar, Ringwood Best, Wadworths 6X and a guest, several wines by the glass, good choice of popular home-made food including decent vegetarian options, friendly service, restaurant, darts; free wi-fi; children welcome and dogs (pub has its own), seats outside, good local walks, closed Sun evening, Mon. *(Helen and Brian Edgeley)*

BIDDESTONE ST8673

★**Biddestone Arms** (01249) 714377

Off A420 W of Chippenham; The Green; SN14 7DG Spacious white-painted stone pub mostly set out for dining; very popular food from standards to specials, good vegetarian options, gluten-free choices and Sun carvery too, friendly efficient service despite being busy, well kept Sharps, Wadworths and guests, nice open fire; children and dogs (in front bar) welcome, pretty back garden, attractive village with lovely pond. *(Mr and Mrs A H Young, R K Phillips, Roger and Donna Huggins, Dr and Mrs A K Clarke)*

BIDDESTONE ST8673

White Horse (01249) 713305

The Green; SN14 7DG New hard-working owners for this 16th-c three-room local overlooking duck pond; enjoyable fairly pubby food (not Sun evening) including a few specials and menu for smaller appetites, a couple of changing local ales, friendly staff; children and dogs welcome, tables out at front and in back garden with clematis-covered pergola and play area, picturesque village, open all day Sun, closed Mon. *(Michael Doswell)*

BOX ST8168

Northey Arms (01225) 742333

A4, Bath side; SN13 8AE 19th-c stone-built dining pub with good interesting food from snacks up including children's menu, well kept Wadworths ales and plenty of wines by the glass, friendly young staff, fresh contemporary décor with chunky modern tables and high-backed rattan chairs, afternoon teas (not Sun); background music; seats in garden behind, nine smart well appointed bedrooms including five new ones, open (and food) all day from 8am for breakfast. *(Dr and Mrs A K Clarke, Gavin Markwick)*

BOX
ST8369
★**Quarrymans Arms** (01225) 743569
From Bath, A4 London Road right into Beech Road, keep left then right into Bargates Hill; from Corsham, left after Rudloe Park Hotel into Beech Road, third left on to Barnetts Hill; SN13 8HN Enjoyable unpretentious pub with friendly staff and informal relaxed atmosphere, plenty of mining-related photographs and memorabilia (once a local for Bath-stone miners – you can hire a key to visit the extensive mines or take a guided tour), well kept Butcombe, Moles, Wadworths and guests, 60 malt whiskies and several wines by the glass, decent choice of enjoyable fairly priced food (all day Sun) including daily specials; children and dogs welcome, picnic-sets on terrace with sweeping views, popular with walkers and potholers, four bedrooms, open all day. *(Taff Thomas, Dr and Mrs A K Clarke)*

BRADFORD-ON-AVON
ST8260
Barge (01225) 863403
Frome Road; BA15 2EA Large modernised stone inn set down from canal, well kept ales such as Brakspears, Fullers, Marstons and Ringwood, nice wines by the glass and enjoyable pub food including children's choices, good friendly staff and atmosphere, open-plan interior with stripped stone, flagstones and solid furniture, woodburners; wheelchair access, garden with smokers' pavilion, steps up to canalside picnic-sets, moorings, five bedrooms. *(Giles and Annie Francis, Taff Thomas, Dr and Mrs A K Clarke)*

BRADFORD-ON-AVON
ST8261
Bunch of Grapes (01225) 938088
Silver Street; BA15 1JY Attractively renovated bar-restaurant with good french-influenced cooking including set menu choices, local ales such as Butcombe along with craft beers (sampling trays), plenty of well chosen french wines, nice coffee and cakes too, friendly efficient service, upstairs dining room; children welcome, open all day. *(Mo Moncreiff-Jury)*

BRADFORD-ON-AVON
ST8161
Dog & Fox (01225) 862137
Ashley Road; BA15 1RT Welcoming unpretentious two-room pub on country outskirts, beams and painted half-panelling, well kept Bath Gem, Courage Best and Sharps Doom Bar, four draught ciders, enjoyable affordably priced traditional food, right-hand part with little serving hatch and comfy seating by woodburner, carpeted dining area behind, small bare-boards bar to the left with darts; children and dogs welcome, picnic-sets and play area in lawned garden, open all day Fri-Sun. *(Taff Thomas)*

BRADFORD-ON-AVON
ST8261
★**George** (01225) 865650
Woolley Street; BA15 1AQ Recently refurbished three-room dining pub under new ownership with good popular food from open kitchen, weekend breakfast (from 9.30am), also afternoon teas (Fri-Sun), efficient friendly service, three well kept ales and good choice of wines and whiskies, log fires, more room upstairs; children and dogs welcome, back garden on two levels, open all day Fri, Sat, till 6pm Sun. *(Taff Thomas, Alistair Holdoway)*

BRADFORD-ON-AVON
ST8260
Timbrells Yard (01225) 869492
St Margarets Street; BA15 1DE Extensive modern refurbishment for this old stone-built riverside inn; long bar with stools and chairs around mix of tables on wood floor, scatter cushions on upholstered wall/window seats, woodburner in big stone fireplace, archway through to small seating area with armchairs and sofas, steps up to airy river-view restaurant with open kitchen, beers such as Bath, Box Steam, Cheddar and Meantime, good choice of other drinks including some interesting gins, well liked food from all-day bar snacks up; tables out on paved terrace, 17 stylish bedrooms, open from 7.30am for breakfast. *(Taff Thomas)*

BROAD HINTON
SU1176
Barbury (01793) 731510
On A4361 Swindon–Devizes, E of village; SN4 9PF Roadside sister pub to the Vine Tree in Norton; long bar with woodburner at each end, a few wicker armchairs and tables on bare boards, hunting and shooting prints, Regency-striped modern armchairs around counter serving well kept/priced St Austell and a couple of guests, 30 wines by the glass, steps up to carpeted dining room, food from shortish interesting menu can be good, service not always speedy; background music, daily newspapers, free wi-fi; children and dogs welcome, seats and tables on partly covered back terrace, closed Mon lunchtime, otherwise open all day, no food Sun evening, Mon. *(Hilary and Neil Christopher, Paul A Moore)*

BROKENBOROUGH
ST9189
Horse Guards (01666) 822302
Signed from Malmesbury on Tetbury road; SN16 0HZ Well run 18th-c village dining pub with fresh modern décor, beams and some bare stone walls in cosy bar, large two-way woodburner, lower plainer back part mainly for eating, good home-made food using local ingredients including seasonal game, well kept Uley and a guest, interesting wines from shortish list, welcoming owners and friendly staff; children and dogs allowed, two comfortable bedrooms, closed Mon lunchtime. *(Michael Doswell)*

BROUGHTON GIFFORD ST8763

★**Fox** (01225) 782949

*Village signposted off A365 to B3107
W of Melksham; The Street; SN12 8PN*
Stylish chatty pub with linked areas; white-
painted beams and broad dark flagstones,
sofas and armchairs, old-fashioned dining
chairs around stripped tables, candles in
brass candlesticks, big bird and plant prints,
log fire in stone fireplace, Bath Gem and
Butcombe Bitter from pink-painted servery,
a dozen wines by the glass and several malt
whiskies and gins, good if not especially
cheap food (not Sun evening) from doorstep
sandwiches up; background music, daily
papers, board games; children and dogs
welcome, picnic-sets on back terrace,
more seats on good-sized sheltered lawn,
bedrooms, closed Mon, otherwise open all
day (till 10pm Sun). *(Michael Doswell, Taff
Thomas, Mr and Mrs A H Young, Peter Meister)*

BULKINGTON ST9458

Well (01380) 828287

High Street; SN10 1SJ Popular dining
pub with modernised open-plan interior,
good food from sandwiches and traditional
favourites up, efficient friendly service,
four real ales including Sharps and Timothy
Taylors, well priced wines; background
music, free wi-fi; children and dogs (in bar)
welcome, wheelchair access, closed Mon
except first of month when there's a themed
food night. *(Susan Eccleston)*

BURCOMBE SU0631

★**Ship** (01722) 744879

*Burcombe Lane; brown sign to pub off
A30 W of Salisbury, then turn right;
SP2 0EJ* Busy welcoming pub with most
here for the good fairly traditional food
including popular dry-aged steaks; section
by entrance with log fire, beams and leather-
cushioned wall and window seats on slate
tiles, steps up to spreading area of pale wood
dining chairs around bleached tables, more
beams (one supporting splendid chandelier),
three changing local ales, Thatcher's cider,
nice wines by the glass and good range
of gins/whiskies, friendly helpful staff;
background music, free wi-fi; children, dogs
and muddy boots welcome, picnic-sets in
informal back garden sloping down to willows
by fenced-off River Nadder, open (and food)
all day weekends. *(Paul Scofield)*

CASTLE COMBE ST8477

Castle Inn (01249) 783030

Off A420; SN14 7HN Handsome inn
centrally placed in this remarkably preserved
Cotswold village; beamed bar with big
inglenook, padded bar stools and fine old
settle, hunting and vintage motor-racing
pictures, Butcombe and Castle Combe,
decent wines by the glass, well liked bar food
and more restaurant evening menu, friendly
attentive service, two snug lounges, formal
dining rooms and big upstairs eating area
opening on to charming little roof terrace;
children welcome, no dogs inside, tables
out at front looking down idyllic main
street, fascinating medieval church clock,
11 bedrooms, limited parking, open all day
from 9.30am. *(Mr and Mrs A H Young)*

CASTLE COMBE ST8477

White Hart (01249) 782295

*Signed off B4039 Chippenham–Chipping
Sodbury; SN14 7HS* Attractive 14th-c
Wadworths pub in centre of this popular
honeypot village; beams, panelling, flagstones
and log fires, seats in stone-mullioned
window, lots of old local photographs, good
choice of enjoyable generously served food
from doorstep sandwiches up, friendly
service, modern restaurant on left; children,
walkers and dogs welcome, tables on
pavement and in sheltered courtyard, handy
for Macmillan Way and new Palladian Way,
open all day. *(Roger and Donna Huggins,
Kevin Upton)*

CHILMARK ST9732

Black Dog (01722) 716344

B3089 Salisbury–Hindon; SP3 5AH
Cosy 15th-c beamed village pub with several
linked areas, cushioned window seats,
inglenook woodburner, a suit of armour in
one part, black and white film star pictures
in another, enjoyable home-made food
from lunchtime sandwiches and pizzas up,
Wadworths ales, friendly service; free wi-fi;
children and dogs welcome, disabled access,
good-sized garden fenced from road, closed
Sun evening, also Tues Oct-Mar. *(Helen and
Brian Edgeley)*

CHOLDERTON SU2242

Crown (01980) 629247

*A338 Tidworth–Salisbury roundabout,
just off A303; SP4 0DW* Thatched low-
beamed cottage with nicely informal eating
areas in L-shaped bar, a couple of well kept
ales and good home-made food cooked by
landlord-chef including set menu Mon-Thurs,
good friendly staff, woodburner, restaurant;
quiz first Weds of month; children and dogs
welcome, picnic-sets out at front and in
garden with play area, open (and food) all
day Sun. *(Dennis and Doreen Haward)*

COMPTON BASSETT SU0372

★**White Horse** (01249) 813118

At N end of village; SN11 8RG New
management as we went to press for this
popular 18th-c village pub (previous Main
Entry); simply furnished bar with cushioned
settles and upholstered dining chairs around
assorted tables on parquet floor, woodburner,
Bath, Wadworths and up to two guests,
Orchard Pig cider, 14 wines by the glass and
decent choice of spirits including nine gins,
good freshly made local food, restaurant with
beams, joists and miscellaneous antique
tables and chairs; background music, board

games, free wi-fi; children and dogs (in bar) welcome, big garden and paddock with pigs, sheep and geese, eight attractive bedrooms in separate building, nearby walks, open all day. *(Michael Doswell, S G N Bennett)*

CORSHAM ST8670
Hare & Hounds (01249) 701106
Pickwick (A4 E); SN13 0HY Friendly old pub by mini roundabout, popular well priced food (smaller helpings available), well kept ales such as Bath Gem and Caledonian Deuchars IPA, plenty of wines by the glass, log fire; Tues quiz; children (if eating) and dogs welcome, picnic-sets on strip of lawn between car park and road, open (and food) all day. *(Dr and Mrs A K Clarke)*

CORSHAM ST8670
★ **Two Pigs** (01249) 712515
Pickwick (A4); SN13 0HY Friendly cheerfully eccentric little beer lovers' pub run by character landlord – most lively on Mon evenings when there's live blues/rock; collection of bric-a-brac in narrow dimly lit flagstoned bar, enamel signs on wood-clad walls, pig-theme ornaments and old radios, Stonehenge ales including Pigswill and a couple of guests; background blues, no food or under-21s; covered yard outside called the Sty, closed lunchtimes except Sun. *(Geoffrey Sutton)*

CORTON ST9340
★ **Dove** (01985) 850109
Off A36 at Upton Lovell, SE of Warminster; BA12 0SZ Brick pub on edge of small Wylye Valley village not far from the A303; popular well prepared food from interesting sandwiches and pub favourites to more enterprising dishes, good service, at least three well kept ales including Otter and Wadworths, Weston's cider, decent wines by the glass and good choice of malt whiskies, pleasant helpful staff, opened-up rooms with flagstones, oak boards, magnolia walls and pale green dados, lots of animal pictures/figurines, photographs of horse racing and other sporting events, flowers on good quality dining tables, newspapers and woodburner in bar, sunny conservatory; children and dogs welcome, wheelchair access/loos, picnic-sets outside, five comfortable bedrooms in courtyard annexe, open all day and can get very busy. *(Chris and Angela Buckell)*

CROCKERTON ST8642
★ **Bath Arms** (01985) 212262
Off A350 Warminster–Blandford; BA12 8AJ Welcoming old dining pub (some refurbishment), bar with plush banquettes and matching chairs, well spaced tables on parquet, beams in whitewashed ceiling, woodburner, two Wessex ales and a weekend guest, real cider and several wines by the glass, good food from interesting changing menu (booking advised), cheerful staff, two restaurant areas and a garden room;

background music, free wi-fi; children and dogs (in bar) welcome, plenty of picnic-sets in well divided garden, gets crowded during school holidays (Longleat close by), good local walks, two bedrooms, open all day (till 6pm Sun in winter). *(Mr and Mrs A H Young, John Hazel)*

DEVIZES SU0061
Bear (01380) 722444
Market Place; SN10 1HS Ancient coaching inn with big carpeted main bar, log fires, winged wall settles and upholstered bucket armchairs, steps up to room named after portrait painter Thomas Lawrence with oak-panelling and large open fireplace, well kept Wadworths, a couple of decent ciders and extensive choice of wines by the glass, good food from sandwiches and light dishes up (they may ask for a credit card if you run a tab), Bear Grills bistro, cellar bar with live music (Fri) and comedy night first Thurs of month; children welcome, dogs in front bar, wheelchair access throughout, mediterranean-style courtyard, 25 bedrooms, open all day. *(Tom and Jill Jones, JPC)*

DEVIZES SU0061
British Lion (01380) 720665
A361 Swindon roundabout; SN10 1LQ Chatty little drinkers' pub with four well kept quickly changing ales and a proper cider, bare-boards bar with brewery mirrors, gas fire, back part with pool and darts, no food; garden behind, open all day. *(Valerie Sayer)*

DONHEAD ST ANDREW ST9124
★ **Forester** (01747) 828038
Village signposted off A30 E of Shaftesbury, just E of Ludwell; Lower Street; SP7 9EE Attractive 14th-c thatched restaurant-pub in charming village; relaxed atmosphere in nice bar, stripped tables on wood floors, log fire in inglenook, alcove with sofa and magazines, Butcombe Bitter and a guest, 15 wines by the glass including champagne, very good well presented food from bar tapas up with much emphasis on fresh fish/seafood, good service, comfortable main dining room with well spaced country kitchen tables, second cosier dining room; children and dogs welcome, seats outside on good-sized terrace with country views, can walk up White Sheet Hill and past the old and 'new' Wardour castles, closed Sun evening, Mon. *(Simon and Alex Knight)*

EBBESBOURNE WAKE ST9924
★ **Horseshoe** (01722) 780474
On A354 S of Salisbury, right at signpost at Coombe Bissett; village about 8 miles further; SP5 5JF Unspoilt country pub in pretty village with plenty of regular customers, welcoming long-serving landlord and friendly staff, well kept Bowman, Otter, Palmers and guests tapped from the cask, farm cider, generous helpings of good traditional food (not Mon), neatly kept

and comfortable character bar, collection
of farm tools and bric-a-brac on beams,
conservatory extension and small restaurant;
children (away from bar) and dogs welcome,
seats in pretty little garden with views over
Ebble Valley, play area, chickens and goat in
paddock, good nearby walks, one bedroom,
closed Sun evening, Mon lunchtime.
(Michael Hill)

ENFORD   SU14351
Swan (01980) 670338
Long Street, off A345; SN9 6DD
Attractive and welcoming thatched village
pub much improved under current licensees,
comfortable beamed interior with log fire
in large fireplace, Marstons-related beers
with local guests such as Stonehenge and
Three Daggers, good locally sourced home-
made food from lunchtime sandwiches and
snacks up; darts; children, walkers and dogs
welcome (pub dogs are Digger and Pickle),
seats out on small front terrace and garden
behind, gallows-style pub sign spanning
the road, closed Mon. *(Mrs Zara Elliott,
Peter Meister)*

FARLEIGH WICK   ST8063
Fox & Hounds (01225) 863122
*A363 NW of Bradford-on-Avon;
BA15 2PU* Rambling low-beamed 16th-c
roadside pub, welcoming and clean, with
wide range of enjoyable food including good
value lunchtime set deal (Tues-Sat), can
eat in three distinct areas (largest is the
L-shaped bar), well kept Bath Gem and six
wines by the glass, polite efficient service,
oak and flagstone floors, log fire; children
and dogs (in one part) welcome, attractive
well maintained garden, closed Mon.
(Michael Doswell)

FORD   ST8474
White Hart (01249) 782213
*Off A420 Chippenham–Bristol;
SN14 8RP* Handsome 16th-c Marstons-
managed country inn; beamed bars with bare
boards or quarry tiles, lots of prints on bold
paintwork, dining and tub chairs, cushioned
wall seats, leather-padded benches and
button-back sofas, log fire and woodburner,
Bath Gem and one or two guests such as
Box Steam and Flying Monk, 20 wines by the
glass and good range of other drinks, popular
food including signature steaks cooked in
charcoal oven, friendly efficient staff; free
wi-fi; children and dogs (in bar) welcome,
front courtyard and terrace, trout stream
by small stone bridge, comfortable modern
bedrooms, open (and food) all day. *(Sara
Fulton, Roger Baker, David Jackman, Dennis and
Doreen Haward, Steve Blatchford)*

FOXHAM   ST9777
Foxham Inn (01249) 740665
NE of Chippenham; SN15 4NQ Small
tucked-away country dining pub with
simple traditional décor, enterprising food

strong on local produce along with more
straightforward bar meals, some themed
evenings, well kept ales such as Butcombe
and Sharps, good choice of wines by the
glass and nice coffee, woodburner, more
contemporary conservatory-style restaurant
with kitchen view, own bread, chutneys, jams
etc for sale; children and dogs welcome,
disabled access and facilities, terrace with
pergola, extensive views from front, two
comfortable bedrooms, closed Mon.
(Michael Doswell)

GREAT DURNFORD   SU1337
Black Horse (01722) 782270
*Follow Woodfords sign from A345 High
Post traffic lights; SP4 6AY* Traditional
red-brick country pub thriving under present
welcoming licensees; four unpretentious
rooms with lots of quirky bits and pieces,
large inglenook woodburner in one, well
kept ales including a house beer from Hop
Back, real cider, generous helpings of good
straightforward home-made food; children
and dogs welcome, big informal garden
with play area, closed Sun evening, Mon.
(Tony and Rachel Schendel)

GRITTLETON   ST8680
★**Neeld Arms** (01249) 782470
*From M4 junction 17, follow A429 to
Cirencester and immediately left, signed
Stanton St Quintin and Grittleton;
SN14 6AP* Popular and welcoming 17th-c
pub in attractive old stone-built village,
pleasantly updated open-plan rooms with
stone walls and painted panelling, nice
mix of furniture, woodburner in little brick
fireplace, inglenook on the right, ales from
Castle Combe, Flying Monk and Wadworths
from pale oak-topped counter, good varied
blackboard menu from pub favourites up,
friendly helpful service, back dining area
with another inglenook; free wi-fi; children
and dogs welcome, wheelchair access (not to
lavatories), terrace with pergola, comfortable
character bedrooms. *(David and Sue Medcalf,
Sara Fulton, Roger Baker, Simon and Mandy King,
Ruth Ridge, Mike Kavaney)*

HAMPTWORTH   SU2419
Cuckoo (01794) 390302
Hamptworth Road; SP5 2DU Welcoming
17th-c thatched New Forest pub owned
by the Hamptworth Estate; peaceful and
unspoilt, with friendly mix of customers
from farmers to families in four compact
rooms around tiny servery, up to nine ales
such as Bowman, Hop Back, Palmers and
Ringwood tapped from the cask, real ciders/
perry, simple food including sandwiches,
ploughman's, pasties and pies, basic
wooden furniture (some new tables are
being made using Estate trees), open fire
and woodburner; shove-ha'penny, shut the
box and other traditional games, live music
last Sat of month; children (till 9pm) and
dogs welcome, big garden with view of golf

course, two pétanque pitches, open all day Fri-Sun. *(Penny and David Shepherd)*

HANNINGTON   SU1793
Jolly Tar (01793) 762245
Off B4019 W of Highworth; Queens Road; SN6 7RP Old painted stone pub in pretty village, relaxing beamed bar with big log fire, steps up to flagstoned and stripped-stone dining area, good reasonably priced home-made food including popular Sun lunch (should book), well kept Arkells ales, friendly helpful service; children welcome, dogs in bar, picnic-sets on front terrace and in big garden with play area, four comfortable bedrooms, good breakfast, closed Mon lunchtime, no food Sun evening. *(Geoffrey Sutton)*

HEDDINGTON   ST9966
Ivy (01380) 859652
Off A3102 S of Calne; SN11 0PL Picturesque thatched 15th-c village local; good inglenook log fire in L-shaped bar, heavy low beams, timbered walls, assorted furnishings on parquet floor, cask-tapped Wadworths ales, good wine choice and well cooked/priced pubby food including Sun carvery, back dining room; children and dogs welcome, disabled access, picnic-sets in small side garden, open all day Sat, till 8pm Sun, closed Mon. *(Paul Scofield)*

HEYTESBURY   ST9242
Angel (01985) 840330
Just off A36 E of Warminster; High Street; BA12 0ED Beamed 16th-c coaching inn in quiet village just below Salisbury Plain, spacious and comfortably modernised, with popular food (not Sun evening, should book weekends), Greene King ales, log fire; children and dogs welcome, bedrooms, open all day (till 8pm Sun). *(Ann and Colin Hunt, Chris and Angela Buckell)*

HINDON   ST9132
Lamb (01747) 820573
B3089 Wilton–Mere; SP3 6DP Attractive refurbished old hotel; long roomy log-fire bar, two flagstoned lower sections with very long polished table, high-backed pews and settles, up steps to a third, bigger area, well kept Youngs, Wells Bombardier and a guest such as local Keystone, several wines by the glass and around 25 malt whiskies, cocktails and cuban cigars, generally well liked bar and restaurant food (service charge added), friendly helpful staff; can get very busy; children and dogs welcome, tables on roadside terrace and in garden across road with boules, 19 bedrooms, good breakfast, open all day from 7.30am for breakfast. *(Ben and Diane Bowie)*

HORNINGSHAM   ST8041
Bath Arms (01985) 844308
By tradesmen's entrance to Longleat House; BA12 7LY Handsome old creeper-clad stone inn on pretty village's sloping green, refurbished and opened up with polished wood floors and open fires, well kept ales such as Wessex, local cider and wide choice of wines, food can be good, restaurant and conservatory; wheelchair access to bar via side door, attractive garden with neat terraces, 16 bedrooms, handy for Longleat, open all day, no food Mon lunchtime. *(Belinda Stamp, John Harris)*

HORTON   SU0363
Bridge Inn (01380) 860273
Horton Road; village signed off A361 London Road, NE of Devizes; SN10 2JS Former flour mill and bakery by Kennet & Avon Canal, carpeted log-fire area on left with tables set for dining, more pubby part to right of bar with some stripped brickwork and country kitchen furniture on reconstituted flagstones, old bargee photographs and rural pictures, Wadworths ales tapped from the cask, good value food including Weds curry buffet and Sun carvery, friendly service; background music, TV; well behaved children welcome, dogs in bar, disabled facilities, safely fenced garden with picnic-sets and big play area, original grinding wheel, canal walks and moorings, bedrooms, closed Mon. *(Giles and Annie Francis)*

KILMINGTON   ST7835
Red Lion (01985) 844263
B3092 Mere–Frome, 2.5 miles S of Maiden Bradley; 3 miles from A303 Mere turn-off; BA12 6RP NT-owned country pub continuing well under present welcoming management; low-beamed flagstoned bar with cushioned wall and window seats, curved high-backed settle, woodburners in big fireplaces at either end, well kept ales such as Butcombe and Wessex, traditional ciders, enjoyable straightforward home-made food including good choice of inexpensive light lunches, newer big-windowed back dining area; children and dogs (in bar) welcome, picnic-sets in large attractive garden with fine views, White Sheet Hill (hang-gliding) and Stourhead gardens (NT) nearby, no evening food Mon or Tues (pub shuts at 9pm then). *(Edward Mirzoeff)*

KINGTON ST MICHAEL   ST9077
Jolly Huntsman (01249) 750305
Handy for M4 junction 17; SN14 6JB Roomy stone-built pub dating from the 18th c, Moles Gold, Wadworths 6X and a

---

We include some hotels with a good bar that offers facilities comparable to those of a pub.

couple of guests, proper cider and good home-made food from pub standards to unusual things like kangaroo, friendly service, carpeted interior with some scrubbed tables, comfortable sofas and good log fire; children and dogs (in bar) welcome, nine bedrooms in separate block. *(Roger and Donna Huggins)*

LACOCK ST9268

Bell (01249) 730308

E of village; SN15 2PJ Extended cottagey pub with warm welcome; local beers including a house brew from Bath Ales (beer festivals), traditional ciders, interesting wines by the glass and good selection of malt whiskies and gins, enjoyable generously served food from lunchtime platters through pub favourites and grills up, well briefed efficient young staff, linked rooms off bar including more formal restaurant and bright conservatory; children welcome away from bar, disabled access from car park, sheltered well tended garden with smokers' shelter (the Coughing Shed) and play area, open (and food) all day weekends. *(Chris and Angela Buckell, Tony and Wendy Hobden)*

LACOCK ST9168

George (01249) 730263

West Street; village signed off A350 S of Chippenham; SN15 2LH Rambling inn at centre of busy NT tourist village; low-beamed bar with upright timbers creating cosy corners, armchairs and windsor chairs around close-set tables, seats in stone-mullioned windows, some flagstones, dog treadwheel in outer breast of central fireplace, lots of old pictures and bric-a-brac, souvenirs from filming *Cranford* and *Harry Potter* in the village, Wadworths beers and Weston's cider, bar food from snacks up; background music; children and dogs welcome, tricky wheelchair access, picnic-sets on grass and in attractive courtyard with pillory and well, open all day in summer. *(Valerie Sayer)*

LACOCK ST9168

★ **Red Lion** (01249) 730456

High Street; SN15 2LQ Popular NT-owned Georgian inn, sizeable opened-up interior with log fire in big stone fireplace, bare boards and flagstones, roughly carved screens here and there and some cosy alcoves, well kept Wadworths ales, Thatcher's and Weston's ciders, enjoyable food from sandwiches and sharing plates up, good friendly service even when busy; background music; children and dogs welcome, wheelchair access to main bar area only, picnic-sets out on gravel, four modern bedrooms, open (and food) all day. *(Dave Braisted)*

LACOCK ST9367

Rising Sun (01249) 730363

Bewley Common, Bowden Hill – out towards Sandy Lane, up hill past abbey; OS Sheet 173 map reference 935679;

SN15 2PP Old stone pub with three knocked-together simply furnished rooms, beams and log fires, Moles ales, real cider and enjoyable fairly traditional food (not Sun evening) from snacks and sharing boards up, friendly attentive service; background music (live every other Weds), free wi-fi; well behaved children welcome, dogs in bar, no wheelchair access, wonderful views across Avon Valley from conservatory and two-level terrace, closed Mon evening, otherwise open all day (till 9pm Sun), winter hours may vary. *(Ben and Diane Bowie)*

LIDDINGTON SU2081

Village Inn (01793) 790314

Handy for M4 junction 15, via A419 and B4192; Bell Lane; SN4 0HE Comfortable pub with enjoyable good value food from varied menu including early-bird bargains and daily specials, well kept Arkells beers, pleasant helpful staff, linked bar areas, stripped-stone and raftered back dining extension, conservatory, log fire in splendid fireplace; well behaved children over 8 allowed in restaurant area, no under-14s in bar, disabled facilities, terrace tables, village shop in car park selling basics, two bedrooms. *(KC, R K Phillips)*

LITTLE SOMERFORD ST9784

Somerford Arms (01666) 826535

Signed off B4042 Malmesbury–Brinkworth; SN15 5JP Popular (can be noisy) modernised village pub, easy chairs in front of bar's woodburner, green-painted half-panelling and stone flooring, linked restaurant with enjoyable home-made food from varied menu, well kept changing ales and lots of wines by the glass, friendly service; children, dogs (pub boxer is Nutmeg) and muddy boots welcome, open all day. *(Paul Scofield)*

LONGBRIDGE DEVERILL ST8640

George (01985) 840396

A350/B3095; BA12 7DG Popular refurbished and extended roadside inn owned by Upham, their beers kept well and generous helpings of enjoyable freshly made food, Sun carvery, friendly enthusiastic staff, conservatory; children welcome, big riverside garden with play area, 12 bedrooms, handy for Longleat, open all day (breakfast for non residents from 8am Mon-Sat). *(Simon and Alex Knight)*

LOWER WOODFORD SU1235

★ **Wheatsheaf** (01722) 782203

Signed off A360 just N of Salisbury; SP4 6NQ Updated and extended 18th-c Badger dining pub, open airy feel, with good choice of fairly priced traditional food from sharing boards up (booking advised weekends), well kept beers, good wines and coffee, well trained genial staff, beams, panelling and exposed brickwork, mix of old furniture, log fire and woodburner;

background music, free wi-fi; children welcome in restaurant, dogs in bar, disabled loo and parking, tree-lined fenced garden with play area, pretty setting, open (and food) all day. *(Mrs Zara Elliott, Michael and Jenny Back, I D Barnett)*

LUCKINGTON   ST8384
Old Royal Ship (01666) 840222
Off B4040 SW of Malmesbury; SN14 6PA
Friendly pub by village green, opened up inside with one long bar divided into three areas, Flying Monk, Sharps and Wadworths from central servery, also farm cider and several wines by the glass, good range of food including vegetarian choices, decent coffee, neat tables, spindleback chairs and small cushioned settles on dark boards, some stripped masonry and small open fire, skittle alley; background music, quiz first Weds of month, live jazz second Weds; children welcome, garden (beyond car park) with boules, play area and plenty of seats, Badminton House close by, open all day weekends. *(Guy Vowles)*

MARDEN   SU0857
Millstream (01380) 848490
Village signposted off A342 SE of Devizes; SN10 3RH Rather smart red-brick dining pub in leafy setting at top end of this attractive village; much-liked food cooked by landlady-chef including fish/seafood specials and good value Sun lunch (best to book), well kept Wadworths ales, friendly young staff, appealing layout of linked cosy areas, beams and log fires, red-cushioned dark pews and small padded dining chairs around sturdy oak and other good tables, comfy sofas in one part; free wi-fi; children and dogs welcome (resident pointers are Sophie and Francesca), disabled access/loos, big garden down to tree-lined stream, 12th-c church worth a visit, closed Sun and Mon evenings. *(Alan and Audrey Moulds, Michael Doswell)*

NETHERHAMPTON   SU1129
★**Victoria & Albert** (01722) 743174
Just off A3094 W of Salisbury; SP2 8PU
Cosy black-beamed bar in simple thatched cottage, popular home-made food from sandwiches up, sensible prices and local supplies, three well kept changing ales, farm cider and decent wines, welcoming helpful staff, old-fashioned cushioned wall settles on ancient floor tiles, log fire, restaurant; children and dogs welcome, hatch service for sizeable terrace and garden behind, handy

for Wilton House and walks in the Nadder Valley. *(David and Laura Young)*

NORTON   ST8884
★**Vine Tree** (01666) 837654
4 miles from M4 junction 17; A429 towards Malmesbury, then left at Hullavington, Sherston signpost, then follow Norton signposts; in village turn right at Foxley signpost, which takes you into Honey Lane; SN16 0JP Civilised dining pub (sister to the Barbury in Broad Hinton), three neat small rooms, beams, old settles and unvarnished wooden tables on flagstones, sporting prints and church candles, large fireplace in central bar, woodburner in restaurant, Butcombe Bitter and Flying Monk Elmers, 40 wines by the glass, 35 gins and several malt whiskies, well liked imaginative food; children and dogs welcome, hitching rail for horses, picnic-sets and play area in two-acre garden, suntrap terrace, closed Sun evening. *(Penny and David Shepherd)*

OGBOURNE ST ANDREW   SU1871
Silks on the Downs (01672) 841229
A345 N of Marlborough; SN8 1RZ
Popular civilised restauranty pub with horse-racing theme, good variety of enjoyable food (best to book), Ramsbury Gold and a guest, proper cider and decent wines by the glass, good friendly service, stylish décor with mix of dining tables on polished wood floors, some good prints and photographs as well as framed racing silks; well behaved children allowed, no dogs inside, small decked area and garden, closed Sun evening. *(Valerie Sayer)*

PEWSEY   SU1561
Waterfront (01672) 564020
Pewsey Wharf (A345 just N); SN9 5NU
Bar-bistro in converted wharf building next to Kennet & Avon Canal, good reasonably priced food including daily specials, three well kept changing ales tapped from the cask in upstairs bar (can eat here too), good quality wines, efficient friendly staff; children and dogs (in bar) welcome, waterside picnic-sets, nice walks, open all day Fri-Sun. *(Giles and Annie Francis, Dave Snowden)*

REDLYNCH   SU2021
Kings Head (01725) 510420
Off A338 via B3080; The Row; SP5 2JT
Early 18th-c pub on edge of New Forest; three or four well kept ales including Hop Back Summer Lightning and Ringwood Best, decent house wines and coffee, good value

home-made food including OAP weekday lunch deal for two, beamed and flagstoned main bar with woodburner in large brick fireplace, small conservatory; free wi-fi; children, dogs and muddy boots welcome, picnic-sets out in front and in side garden, nice Pepperbox Hill (NT) walks nearby, closed Mon lunchtime. *(Ben and Diane Bowie)*

SALISBURY SU1430
Avon Brewery (01722) 416184
Castle Street; SP1 3SP Long narrow city bar with frosted and engraved bow window, dark mahogany and two open fires, friendly staff and regulars, well kept Ringwood Best and a Marstons-related guest, good portuguese food in back restaurant, also pub favourites; sheltered courtyard garden overlooking river, open all day. *(Valerie Sayer)*

SALISBURY SU1429
Haunch of Venison (01722) 411313
Minster Street, opposite Market Cross; SP1 1TB Ancient pub under newish management; tiny downstairs rooms dating from 1320, massive beams, stout oak benches built into timbered walls, open fire, tiny snug with unique pewter counter and rare set of antique taps for gravity-fed spirits, four real ales, generous pubby lunchtime food, more restauranty evening choice, friendly staff; halfway upstairs is panelled room with splendid fireplace and (behind glass) the mummified hand of an 18th-c card sharp still clutching cards; open all day. *(Ann and Colin Hunt)*

SALISBURY SU1429
Kings Head (01722) 342050
Bridge Street; SP1 2ND Corner Wetherspoons in nice spot by river (site of former hotel), variety of seating in large relaxed bar with separate TV area, upstairs gallery, two Greene King ales and four quickly changing guests, low-priced menu including breakfast, log fire; good value bedrooms, open all day from 7am (till 1am Thurs-Sat). *(Ann and Colin Hunt)*

SALISBURY SU1429
New Inn (01722) 326662
New Street; SP1 2PH Much-extended old building with massive beams and timbers, good choice of enjoyable home-made food from pub staples up, well kept Badger ales and decent house wines, cheerful service, flagstones, floorboards and carpet, quiet cosy alcoves, inglenook log fire; children welcome, pretty walled garden with striking view of nearby cathedral spire, three bedrooms, open all day. *(Mike Kavaney)*

SALISBURY SU1430
Wyndham Arms (01722) 331026
Estcourt Road; SP1 3AS Corner red-brick local with unpretentious modern décor, popular and friendly, with full Hop Back range (brewery was originally based here)

and a guest such as Downton, bottled beers and country wines, no food, small front and side rooms, longer main bar; darts and board games; children and dogs welcome, open all day Thurs-Sun, from 4.30pm other days. *(Tony and Rachel Schendel)*

SANDY LANE ST9668
George (01380) 850403
A342 Devizes–Chippenham; SN15 2PX Handsome 18th-c stone pub refurbished under new management, long simply furnished bar with wood floor, light blue dado and log fire, a couple of Wadworths ales and a guest, enjoyable food from sandwiches and bar meals to more expensive restauranty choices, airy back dining room with large woodburner, timber-framed conservatory; background music, TV; children and well behaved dogs welcome (their labrador is Ollie), terrace and lawn, charming thatched village, Bowood Estate walks, closed Sun evening, Mon. *(Susan Eccleston)*

SEEND ST9361
Barge (01380) 828230
Seend Cleeve; signed off A361 Devizes–Trowbridge; SN12 6QB Busy waterside pub with plenty of seats in garden making most of boating activity on Kennet & Avon Canal (moorings), rambling interior with log fires, some unusual seating in bar including painted milk churns, Wadworths ales and extensive range of wines by the glass, decent choice of well cooked/priced food, efficient service; background music, free wi-fi; children and dogs welcome, summer barbecues, open all day. *(Giles and Annie Francis, Tracey and Stephen Groves, Dr and Mrs A K Clarke)*

SEEND ST9562
Three Magpies (01380) 828389
Sells Green – A365 towards Melksham; SN12 6RN Traditional partly 18th-c roadside pub with well kept Wadworths and decent choice of wines by the glass, enjoyable home-made pubby food at reasonable prices, good friendly service, two warm fires; free wi-fi; children welcome, dogs allowed in the bar, big garden with play area, campsite next door, Kennet & Avon Canal close by, open all day. *(Giles and Annie Francis)*

SEMINGTON ST9259
Lamb (01380) 870263
The Strand; A361 Devizes–Trowbridge; BA14 6LL Modernised dining pub with various eating areas including bar with wood-strip floor and log fire, enjoyable food from pub favourites to specials including good value set menu Mon and Tues, a couple of Box Steam ales, friendly staff; background music, live acoustic night Sun; children and dogs welcome, pleasant garden with views to the Bowood Estate, play area, two self-catering cottages, open all day weekends. *(Paul Scofield)*

SHALBOURNE   SU3162

Plough (01672) 870295

Off A338; SN8 3QF Low-beamed
traditional pub by small village green, good
variety of enjoyable fairly priced food cooked
by landlord including vegetarian choices,
Butcombe and Wadworths, friendly helpful
landlady and staff, open fire in neat bar,
separate carpeted restaurant with central
woodburner; free wi-fi; children and dogs
welcome, disabled access, small garden with
play area, closed Mon. *(Geoffrey Sutton)*

SOUTH MARSTON   SU1987

Carpenters Arms (01793) 822997

Just off A420 E of Swindon; SN3 4ST
Roomy old Arkells local with warm friendly
atmosphere, good choice of enjoyable
well priced food (not Sun evening, Mon
lunchtime) including bargain two-course
lunch Tues-Fri, beamed bar with open fire,
separate carpeted restaurant, pool room;
background music; children and dogs
welcome, big back garden with terrace and
play area, nine motel bedrooms (some train
noise), caravan parking, open all day.
(Penny and David Shepherd)

STEEPLE ASHTON   ST9056

Longs Arms (01380) 870245

High Street; BA14 6EU Spotless 17th-c
coaching inn with friendly local atmosphere,
well kept Sharps and Wadworths, plenty of
wines by the glass and good choice of fresh
locally sourced food including lunchtime
sandwiches and homemade pizzas, bar with
lots of pictures and old photos, adjacent
dining area, woodburner, quiz and open mike
nights, free wi-fi; children and dogs welcome,
big garden with play area, boules, adjoining
self-catering cottage, delightful village, open
all day weekends if busy. *(Susan Eccleston)*

STIBB GREEN   SU2262

Three Horseshoes (01672) 810324

Just N of Burbage; SN8 3AE Welcoming
thatched village pub with enjoyable
affordably priced food including blackboard
specials, well kept Wadworths ales, inglenook
log fire in comfortable beamed front bar,
railway memorabilia, small dining room; dogs
welcome, seats in nice garden, closed Mon
lunchtime. *(Valerie Sayer)*

STOURTON   ST7733

Spread Eagle (01747) 840587

*Church Lawn; follow Stourhead brown
signs off B3092, N of junction with A303
W of Mere; BA12 6QE* Busy NT-owned
Georgian inn at entrance to Stourhead
Estate; spacious interior with antique settles,
solid tables and chairs, sporting prints and
handsome fireplaces, well kept Butcombe,
Wessex and interesting wines by the glass
in flagstoned bar, popular home-made food
served by efficient helpful staff, cream teas,
restaurant; background music; children
welcome, wheelchair access (step down to
dining areas), smart back courtyard with
circular picnic-sets, five bedrooms (guests
can wander freely around famous gardens
outside normal hours, picnic hampers
available), open all day. *(Alan Cowell)*

SUTTON BENGER   ST9478

Wellesley Arms (01249) 721721

*Handy for M4 junction 17, via B4122
and B4069; High Street; SN15 4RD*
Beamed 15th-c Cotswold-stone pub with
pleasant bar areas and restaurant, good
pubby food including lunchtime set menu
(Tues-Fri) and popular Sun lunch, well kept
Wadworths ales, efficient friendly service;
background music, TV; children and dogs
welcome, garden with play area and paddock,
open all day weekends (no food Sun evening),
closed Mon lunchtime. *(David Crook)*

SUTTON VENY   ST8941

Woolpack (01985) 840834

High Street; BA12 7AW Small well run
1920s village local, good blackboard food
including some inventive dishes cooked by
landlord-chef (best to book), home-made
chutneys, pickles etc for sale, Marstons
and Ringwood ales, sensibly priced wines
by the glass, charming service, modernised
interior with compact side dining area
screened from bare-boards bar, woodburner;
background music; closed Sun evening, Mon
lunchtime. *(Simon and Alex Knight)*

SWALLOWCLIFFE   ST9627

Royal Oak (01747) 870211

*Signed just off A30 Wilton–Shaftesbury;
Common Lane; SP3 5PA* Pretty part-
thatched beamed inn transformed by group
of villagers after long closure; attractive
clean décor in inglenook bar and dining
room, stylish locally made furniture on
flagstones, new oak-framed conservatory, well
liked food from snacks and pub favourites
up, Butcombe ales including one badged for
them and good range of wines by the glass,
friendly staff; children, walkers and dogs
welcome, sheltered back garden with tables
made from reclaimed timber, six comfortable
bedrooms, good walks, open all day. *(Ben and
Diane Bowie)*

Please tell us if the décor, atmosphere, food or drink at a pub is different
from our description. We rely on readers' reports to keep us up to date:
feedback@goodguides.com, or (no stamp needed) The Good Pub Guide,
FREEPOST RTJR-ZCYZ-RJZT, Perrymans Lane, Etchingham TN19 7DN.

TISBURY ST9429
Boot (01747) 870363
High Street; SP3 6PS Ancient unpretentious village local with long-serving and welcoming licensees, three well kept changing ales tapped from the cask, cider/perry, range of pizzas and reasonably priced pubby food, notable fireplace; dogs welcome, tables in good-sized back garden, closed Sun evening and lunchtimes Mon, Tues. *(Paul Scofield)*

UPAVON SU1355
Ship (01980) 630313
High Street; SN9 6EA Large thatched pub with welcoming local atmosphere, good choice of enjoyable home-made food including wood-fired pizzas (Thurs-Sat evenings), Weds steak night, friendly helpful service, well kept changing ales, a couple of traditional ciders and decent range of wines and whiskies, some interesting nautical memorabilia; occasional live acoustic music; dogs welcome, picnic-sets in front and on small side terrace, parking can be tricky. *(Geoffrey Sutton)*

WARMINSTER ST8745
Organ (01985) 211777
49 High Street; BA12 9AQ Former 18th-c inn (reopened 2006 after 93 years as a shop), front bar, snug and traditional games room, welcoming owners and chatty regulars, three regional beers including one named for them, real ciders/perries, good cheap lunchtime cheeseboard, skittle alley, local art in upstairs gallery; no under-21s, dogs welcome, open all day Sat, from 4pm other days. *(Jeff Davies)*

WARMINSTER ST8744
Snooty Fox (01985) 846505
Fore Street/Brook Street; SN7 8PW Modernised restaurant pub on the outskirts, neat clean and comfortable, with good varied choice of food cooked by owner-chef from lunchtime ciabattas and pub favourites up, ales such as Bath and Wadworths from brick-faced counter, good friendly service; seats out on terrace and small lawn, open all day Sun (till 4pm in winter), closed Mon. *(Marianne and Peter Stevens)*

WARMINSTER ST8745
★Weymouth Arms (01985) 216995
Emwell Street; BA12 8JA Charming backstreet pub with snug panelled entrance bar, log fire in fine stone fireplace, ancient books on mantelpiece, leather tub chairs around walnut and satinwood table, more seats against the walls, daily papers, Butcombe, Wadworths 6X and nice wines by the glass, second heavily panelled room with wide floorboards and smaller fireplace, candles in brass sticks, split-level dining room stretching back to open kitchen serving good interesting food from snacks up, friendly attentive service; children and dogs (in bar) welcome, seats in flower-filled back courtyard, six well equipped comfortable bedrooms, closed Mon lunchtime. *(Edward Mirzoeff, Andrew McDonald)*

WEST LAVINGTON SU0052
Bridge Inn (01380) 813213
Church Street (A360); SN10 4LD This previous Main Entry will be under new ownership by the time you read this – reports please; spacious comfortable bar mixing contemporary elements with firmly traditional fixtures including enormous brick inglenook, smaller modern fireplace at other end, cream-painted or exposed brick walls hung with pictures of the Lavingtons, timbers and an occasional step dividing up the various areas, has served good food, Sharps Doom Bar and Wadworths IPA; seats on raised back lawn.

WEST OVERTON SU1368
Bell (01672) 861099
A4 Marlborough–Calne; SN8 1QD Early 19th-c coaching inn with good imaginative cooking from owner-chef using fresh local ingredients, bar with woodburner, spacious restaurant beyond, well kept Wadworths and other local beers such as Moles, attentive friendly uniformed staff; background music; disabled access, nice secluded back garden with terrace and own bar, country views, good walks nearby, closed Sun evening, Mon. *(Mr and Mrs A H Young, Michael Doswell, Tina and David Woods-Taylor)*

WESTWOOD ST8159
★New Inn (01225) 863123
Off B3109 S of Bradford-on-Avon; BA15 2AE Traditional 18th-c country pub with several linked rooms, beams and stripped stone, scrubbed tables on slate floor, lots of pictures, imaginative good value food (not Sun evening) cooked by chef-owner together with pub staples, generous Sun lunch and some themed nights, well kept Wadworths, cheerful buzzy atmosphere; children and dogs welcome, tables in paved garden behind, pretty village with good surrounding walks, Westwood Manor (NT) opposite. *(Alistair Holdoway, Taff Thomas)*

WHITLEY ST8866
Pear Tree (01225) 704966
Off B3353 S of Corsham; SN12 8QX Attractive stone dining pub (former 17th-c farmhouse) under new management; revamped beamed interior with plenty of contemporary/rustic charm in front bar, restaurant and airy garden room, good food from varied if not cheap menu, three real ales including Bath Gem, friendly attentive service; children welcome, terrace and pretty garden, eight well equipped bedrooms (four in converted barn), open all day from 7.30am (8.30am Sun). *(Taff Thomas, Alistair Holdoway)*

WILTON   SU2661

★**Swan** (01672) 870274

The village S of Great Bedwyn; SN8 3SS
Popular light and airy 1930s pub, good well
presented seasonal food (not Sun evening)
including daily specials, two Ramsbury ales
and a local guest, farm ciders and good value
wines from extensive list, friendly efficient
staff, stripped pine tables, high-backed
settles and pews on bare boards, woodburner;
children and dogs welcome, disabled access,
front garden with picnic-sets, picturesque
village with windmill, open all day weekends.
(Tony Hobden, Mrs Zara Elliott)

WINGFIELD   ST8256

★**Poplars** (01225) 752426

*B3109 S of Bradford-on-Avon (Shop
Lane); BA14 9LN* Appealing country
pub with warm friendly atmosphere, beams
and log fires, popular sensibly priced food
from pub staples to interesting specials,
Wadworths ales (including seasonal) and
Weston's cider, cheerful quick service even
when busy, airy family dining extension; quiz
first Sun of month; nice garden and own
cricket pitch. *(Jamie Green)*

WINSLEY   ST7960

★**Seven Stars** (01225) 722204

*Off B3108 bypass W of Bradford-
on-Avon; BA15 2LQ* Handsome bustling
inn with low-beamed linked areas, light
pastel paintwork and stripped-stone walls,
farmhouse chairs around candlelit tables
on flagstones or coir, woodburner, very good
freshly made food using local suppliers,
prompt friendly service, changing west
country ales, Thatcher's and Weston's
ciders, nice wines by the glass; background
music; children and dogs (in bar) welcome,
disabled access with ramp, tables under
parasols on terrace and neat grassy
surrounds, bowling green opposite, closed
Sun evening. *(B and F A Hannam,
Michael Doswell, Alistair Holdoway)*

WINTERBOURNE
BASSETT   SU1075

White Horse (01793) 731257

Off A4361 S of Swindon; SN4 9QB
Welcoming roadside dining pub with gently
old-fashioned feel, part-carpeted bar with
plenty of wood, plush-topped stools and
cushioned dining chairs, Wadworths ales
and quite a few wines by the glass, enjoyable
home-made food including daily specials
(seasonal game) and bargain lunchtime
deal (Mon-Fri), dining rooms with country
kitchen furniture on wood floors, old
prints and paintings, woodburner in little
brick fireplace, flagstoned conservatory;
background music, bar billiards, TV, free
wi-fi; children and dogs (in bar) welcome,
tables on good-sized lawn, closed Sun
evening, Mon lunchtime (shuts at 8pm),
Tues lunchtime. *(Alf Wright)*

WOOTTON RIVERS   SU1963

Royal Oak (01672) 810322

Off A346, A345 or B3087; SN8 4NQ
Cosy 16th-c beamed and thatched pub, ales
such as Ramsbury and Wadworths 6X, plenty
of wines by the glass and enjoyable food
from lunchtime sandwiches to fish dishes,
comfortable L-shaped dining lounge with
woodburner, timbered bar and small games
area; free wi-fi; children and dogs welcome,
tables out in yard, pleasant village near
Kennet & Avon Canal, good local walks,
bedrooms in adjoining building, open (and
food) all day Sun. *(David and Judy Robison)*

ZEALS   ST7831

Bell & Crown (01747) 840404

A303; BA12 6NJ Nicely laid out beamed
dining pub, warm and friendly, with good
food cooked by chef-landlord, efficient
service, ales such as Butcombe, Palmers
and Wadworths, a dozen wines by the
glass including champagne, big log fire
in flagstoned bar, restaurant; closed Sun
evening, Mon. *(Geoffrey Sutton)*

A star symbol before the name of a pub shows exceptional character and appeal.
It doesn't mean extra comfort. Even quite a basic pub can win a star,
if it's individual enough.

Worcestershire

 BAUGHTON   SO8742   Map 4

Jockey ♀

(01684) 592153 – www.thejockeyinn.co.uk

*4 miles from M50 junction 1; A38 northwards, then right on to A4104
Upton–Pershore; WR8 9DQ*

**Smart, open-plan bar and dining rooms in elegantly updated pub
with a thoughtful choice of drinks, rewarding food, courteous staff
and seats outside**

As soon as this extended and stylishly refurbished pub opened after a
long closure, we started getting enthusiastic reports from our readers.
The interior is open-plan and contemporary with distinct drinking and
dining areas that work well. The smart dining rooms have high-backed
upholstered chairs, long button-back wall seats, a mix of pale-topped tables
and bare floorboards with décor that takes in an unusual woven wicker wall,
oil portraits, a large black and white painting of a jockey on a racehorse,
horse-racing photographs, bookshelves, stubby candles in glass lanterns,
small flowering plants in pots and up-to-date paintwork. Stools on flagstones
line the counter in the beamed bar and friendly, attentive staff serve Sharps
Doom Bar and Wye Valley Butty Bach and HPA on handpump, wines by the
glass from a good list (they have a large, glass, walk-in wine store) and lots
of cocktails; background music. Big leather armchairs, sofas and pouffes are
grouped together and there's an open fire and a neat ceiling-high stack of
logs beside a two-way woodburning stove. Outside, there are seats and tables
under heated parasols and picnic-sets on neat gravelling.

🍴 Good, enjoyable food includes lunchtime sandwiches, ham hock and black pudding
terrine with sweet pickled vegetables, smoked haddock scotch egg with aioli,
sharing boards, oriental mango, cashew and coriander salad in citrus, honey and peanut
dressing, stone-baked pizzas, wild mushroom, spinach and truffle cannelloni with
parmesan froth, beer-battered cod with triple-cooked chips, lamb loin with celeriac
mash and spiced tomato jam, steaks with skinny fries and a choice of sauces, and
puddings such as apple and pear crumble with custard and chocolate cheesecake with
dark chocolate sauce and white chocolate ice-cream; they also offer a two- and three-
course set lunch. *Benchmark main dish: burger with toppings, coleslaw and fries
£13.95. Two-course evening meal £20.00.*

Free house ~ Licensee Rebekah Seddon-Wickens ~ Real ale ~ Open 11.30-11 (11.30 Fri,
Sat); 12-6 Sun; closed Mon except bank holidays ~ Bar food 12-9 (9.30 Fri, Sat); 12-4 Sun ~
Children welcome ~ Wi-fi *Recommended by Mrs Zara Elliott, Charles Welch, Colin Humphreys*

BRANSFORD
SO8052 Map 4
Bear & Ragged Staff ♀
(01886) 833399 – www.bearatbransford.co.uk
Off A4103 SW of Worcester; Station Road; WR6 5JH

Well run dining pub with pleasant places to sit both inside and out and well liked food and drink

In a hamlet tucked away in the Teme Valley, this is a friendly, gently civilised dining pub – but there's a relaxing bar as well: Hobsons Twisted Spire and Sharps Doom Bar on handpump, ten wines by the glass, several malt whiskies and quite a few brandies and liqueurs. The restaurant is more formal with upholstered dining chairs, proper tablecloths and linen napkins. These interconnecting rooms give fine views of attractive rolling country (as do the pretty garden and terrace). In winter, there's a warming open fire; background music and darts. Good disabled access and facilities.

 Using some home-grown produce, the changing food includes sandwiches, seared scallops with black pudding, won ton crisps and watercress purée, chicken, avocado and blue cheese salad, halloumi cheese with red onion, peppers and cabbage in sticky black bean sauce, curry of the day, grilled hake with cheddar and parsley crust, creamy garlic potatoes and braised fennel, duck breast with leg bonbon, dauphinoise potatoes and passion-fruit jus, rib-eye steak with a choice of sauces and triple-cooked chips, and puddings such as vanilla crème brûlée with fruit compote and chocolate fondant with espresso cream. *Benchmark main dish: beer-battered fish and chips £12.95. Two-course evening meal £19.00.*

Free house ~ Licensee Lynda Williams ~ Real ale ~ Open 12-2.30, 6-11; 12-4 Sun ~ Bar food 12-2, 6-9; 12-2.30 Sun ~ Restaurant ~ Children welcome ~ Dogs allowed in bar ~ Wi-fi
Recommended by Brian Parry, Charles Welch

BRETFORTON
SP0943 Map 4
Fleece ★ ◖ £
(01386) 831173 – www.thefleeceinn.co.uk
B4035 E of Evesham: turn S off this road into village; pub is in central square by church; there's a sizeable car park at one side of the church; WR11 7JE

Marvellously unspoilt medieval pub owned by the National Trust; bedrooms

Many of the furnishings here are original and heirlooms of the family that owned this lovely former farm for around 500 years; it was bequeathed to the National Trust in 1977. The fine country rooms include a great oak dresser holding a priceless 48-piece set of Stuart pewter, two grandfather clocks, ancient kitchen chairs, curved high-backed settles, a rocking chair and a rack of heavy pointed iron shafts, probably for spit roasting in one of the huge inglenook fireplaces; two other log fires. As well as massive beams and exposed timbers, there are worn and crazed flagstones (scored with marks to keep out demons) and plenty of oddities such as a great cheese-press and set of cheese moulds and a rare dough-proving table; a leaflet details the more bizarre items. Malvern Hills Black Pear, Purity Mad Goose, Uley Pigs Ear, Wye Valley Bitter and a guest or two on handpump, six wines by the glass, a similar number of malt whiskies and four farm ciders; board games. They hold an asparagus auction at the end of May, as part of the Vale of Evesham Asparagus Festival, and also host the village fête on August Bank Holiday Monday. The calendar of events also includes morris dancing and the village silver band plays here regularly. The lawn, with fruit trees around a beautifully restored thatched and timbered barn, is a lovely place to sit, and there are more picnic-sets and a stone pump-trough in the front courtyard. If you're visiting to enjoy the famous historic interior, best to go midweek as it can get very busy at weekends.

 Bar food includes plenty of asparagus in season, chicken caesar salad, pork sausages with sweet and sour onions and mustard mash, lamb burger with salad and fries, cider and mustard glazed ham with free-range eggs, beer-battered cod and chips, a pie of the day, 28-day-aged steaks with a choice of sauce and twice-cooked chips, and puddings such as apple and date crumble and a changing crème brûlée. *Benchmark main dish: pork faggots with mustard mash £9.95. Two-course evening meal £15.50.*

Free house ~ Licensee Nigel Smith ~ Real ale ~ Open 10am-11pm; 10.30am-11pm Sun ~ Bar food 12-2.30, 6.30-9; 12-8 Sun ~ Children welcome ~ Dogs welcome ~ Wi-fi ~ Bedrooms: /£97.50 *Recommended by Stanley and Annie Matthews, David Carr, Steve Whalley, Revd Michael Vockins*

BROADWAY
SP0937 Map 4
Crown & Trumpet 🍺 £
(01386) 853202 – www.crownandtrumpet.co.uk
Church Street; WR12 7AE

Honest local with good real ale and decent food; bedrooms

Warmly welcoming and run by a charming landlord and his helpful staff, this is an old-fashioned, unpretentious place with a good mix of both regulars and visitors. The bustling beamed and timbered bar has a cheerful, easy-going feel, antique dark high-backed settles, large solid tables and a blazing log fire. You'll find a beer named for the pub (from Stanway) plus Prescott Chequered Flag, Stroud Tom Long and Timothy Taylors Landlord on handpump, alongside nine wines by the glass, ten malt whiskies, Black Rat perry and cider, Orchard Pig chilli and ginger or marmalade ciders, mulled wine and a good range of soft drinks. There's an assortment of pub games, including darts, cribbage, shut the box, dominoes, bar skittles and ring the bull, as well as a games machine, TV and background music. The hardwood tables and chairs outside, set among flowers on a slightly raised front terrace, are popular with walkers.

 Incredibly good value, popular food includes lunchtime baguettes and panini, mushrooms in stilton sauce on a baby bloomer, prawn cocktail with peppers, duck and apricot sausages with plum gravy, a choice of omelettes, meaty or vegetarian lasagne, gluten-free fish pie, local faggots with mushy peas, chilli con carne, chicken breast with mushroom sauce and sautéed potatoes, and puddings such as apple and cinnamon crumble and sticky toffee pudding. *Benchmark main dish: beef in plum pie £8.95. Two-course evening meal £12.00.*

Laurel (Enterprise) ~ Lease Andrew Scott ~ Real ale ~ Open 11-11 (midnight Sat); 11-11 Sun ~ Bar food 12-2.30, 5.45-9.30; 12-9.30 Fri-Sun ~ Children welcome ~ Dogs allowed in bar ~ Wi-fi ~ Live jazz/blues Thurs evening, 1960s-80s music Sat evening ~ Bedrooms: /£68 *Recommended by M G Hart, David Carr, Phil and Jane Villiers, Theocsbrian*

CHILDSWICKHAM
SP0738 Map 4
Childswickham Inn 🍽️
(01386) 852461 – www.childswickhaminn.co.uk
Off A44 NW of Broadway; WR12 7HP

Bustling dining pub with highly regarded food, good drinks choice, attentive staff and seats in neat garden

The chatty bar in this bustling pub is full of friendly regulars (often with their dogs too) and there are leather sofas and armchairs and Lancaster Northern Hemisphere Hopped Ale and Sharps Atlantic on handpump, ten wines by the glass (Friday evening special deals on champagne and prosecco), malt whiskies, and farm cider; background music. There are two dining areas, one with high-backed dark leather chairs on terracotta tiles, the other with country kitchen chairs on bare floorboards. Both have contemporary artwork on part-timbered walls painted cream or pale violet; an open fire and woodburning stove. Outside, the neat garden has rush-seated chairs and tables on decking and also separate areas under parasols. The surrounding countryside offers many lovely walks. Disabled facilities.

Rewarding food using local produce includes sandwiches, confit cajun chicken terrine with chorizo and pickled pepper relish, beef, chilli and smoked mozzarella parcel with tomato and paprika coulis, porcini mushroom, toasted smoked almonds and basil pasta in cheese sauce, beer-battered fish and chips, blue swimming crab and haddock fishcake with mustard and dill sauce, barbecue and Guinness-glazed beef short rib with maple bacon and bean cassoulet, lamb with harissa-spiced crushed sweet potato with merguez sausage and sweet onion jus, and puddings such as peanut butter and dark chocolate brownie cheesecake with strawberry jelly and rum and raisin crème brûlée; Thursday is steak night. *Benchmark main dish: sesame duck breast with saffron fondant potato, parsnip purée and spiced jus £16.95. Two-course evening meal £20.50.*

Punch ~ Tenant Carol Marshall ~ Real ale ~ Open 11.30-11; 12-11 Sun ~ Bar food 12-2, 6-9; 12-8 (6 in winter) Sun ~ Restaurant not Sun evening or Mon lunch ~ Children welcome ~ Dogs allowed in bar ~ Wi-fi *Recommended by Roy and Gill Payne, P and J Shapley, Ian Duncan*

CLENT

Fountain 🌟 ♀

SO9279 Map 4

(01562) 883286 – www.thefountainatclent.co.uk

Adams Hill/Odnall Lane; off A491 at Holy Cross/Clent exit roundabout, via Violet Lane, then right at T junction; DY9 9PU

Restauranty pub often packed to overflowing, with imaginative dishes and good choice of drinks

With a wide choice of reliably good food and well kept real ales on handpump, our readers enjoy this spotlessly kept, friendly pub. The long carpeted dining bar (consisting of three knocked-together areas) is fairly traditional, with teak chairs and pedestal tables and some comfortably cushioned brocaded wall seats. There are nicely framed local photographs on the rag-rolled pinkish walls above a dark panelled dado, pretty wall lights and candles on the tables (flowers in summer). The changing real ales include Brakspears Oxford Gold, Jennings Cocker Hoop and Marstons Burton Bitter on handpump, farm cider and most of their wines are available by the glass; also speciality teas and good coffees. Background music and skittle alley. There are tables outside on a decked area.

A wide choice of highly popular food includes wild duck with beetroot purée and hazelnuts, tiger prawns with garlic butter, linguine with truffle, mushrooms and spinach in creamy sauce, smoked haddock florentine, corn-fed chicken stuffed with chorizo on roast red pepper, rosemary and cherry tomato piperade, beef wellington, calves liver with red wine sauce and sage, steaks with a choice of six sauces, king prawn and crab risotto, and puddings such as strawberry and chocolate cheesecake and pear frangipane; they also offer a two-course lunch menu (not Sun). *Benchmark main dish: lamb pot roast £18.95. Two-course evening meal £20.00.*

Marstons ~ Lease Richard and Jacque Macey ~ Real ale ~ Open 11-11; 12-9 Sun ~
Bar food 12-2, 6-9 (9.30 Fri, Sat); 12-6 Sun ~ Children welcome ~ Wi-fi
Recommended by S Holder, Anne Taylor, Lionel Smith, Carol and Barry Craddock

CUTNALL GREEN
SO8868 Map 4
Chequers 🏅🍴 ♀
(01299) 851292 – www.chequerscutnallgreen.co.uk
Kidderminster Road; WR9 0PJ

**Bustling roadside pub with plenty of drinking and dining space
in interesting rooms and rewarding food**

Our readers have been enjoying the pretty garden here with its three 'beach huts' to hire, chairs with barrel tables and sofas, heaters and parasols. It's an interesting pub, built some 90 years ago on the site of an old coaching inn, and is a clever mix of ancient and modern: red-painted walls between beams and timbering, broad floorboards and weathered quarry tiles, and warm winter fires. There are leather sofas and tub chairs, high-backed purple and red or ladderback dining chairs around all sorts of tables, plenty of mirrors giving the impression of even more space, brass plates and mugs, candles and fresh flowers. Sharps Doom Bar, Wye Valley HPA and a guest from Marstons on handpump and 14 wines by the glass. One elegant but cosy room, known as the Players Lounge, has photographs of the landlord Mr Narbett who is a former chef for the England football team. This is sister pub to the Bell & Cross at Holy Cross.

 Food is good and interesting and includes weekend breakfasts (9-11am), sandwiches, duck rillettes with pear and apple chutney, smoked salmon with pickled crab, shaved fennel, apple sticks, avocado and lemon oil, stone-baked pizzas, burger with toppings, relish and skinny fries, a pie of the day, butternut squash, taleggio, spinach and roasted tomato pasta, chicken curry, plaice fillets with prawns, lemon-crushed potatoes and shellfish bisque, and puddings such as molten chocolate tart with popcorn, salted caramel and white chocolate ice-cream and limoncello pannacotta with blueberry and mint compote. *Benchmark main dish: slow-cooked lamb with chorizo dauphinoise potatoes, and pea and mint purée, £16.95. Two-course evening meal £20.00.*

Free house ~ Licensees Roger and Jo Narbett ~ Real ale ~ Open 12-11 (10.30 Sun) ~
Bar food 12-9 (9.15 Fri, 9.30 Sat, 8.30 Sun) ~ Restaurant ~ Children welcome ~ Dogs
allowed in bar ~ Wi-fi *Recommended by Fiona Thomas, Dave Braisted, Dr and Mrs A K Clarke,
Lynda and Trevor Smith*

HOLY CROSS
SO9278 Map 4
Bell & Cross ★ 🏅🍴 ♀
(01562) 730319 – www.bellandcrossclent.co.uk
*2 miles from M5 junction 3: A491 towards Stourbridge, then follow Clent signpost
off on left; DY9 9QL*

**A delightful old interior, good food, staff with a can-do attitude
and a pretty garden**

The perfect place for a break from the M5, this well run pub has a cosy bar where chatty locals are served by neatly dressed courteous staff. Enville Ale, Otter Bitter, Timothy Taylors Landlord, and Wye Valley HPA on handpump and 12 wines by the glass. The four attractively decorated dining rooms (with a choice of carpet, bare boards, lino or nice old quarry tiles) have a variety of moods, from snug and chatty to bright and airy; background music. Décor includes theatrical engravings on red walls, nice sporting prints on pale green walls, and racing and gun dog pictures above a black panelled dado; most rooms have coal fires. The lovely garden has a spacious lawn, and the terrace offers pleasant views – both have seating. This is sister pub to the Chequers at Cutnall Green.

Quite a choice of well liked food includes sandwiches, chilli-crusted duck with pineapple carpaccio, spring onion and lime dressing, pulled spicy chicken with soft tacos, guacamole, shredded lime and sour cream, ham, free-range eggs and skinny fries, slow-cooked lamb shoulder with chorizo dauphinoise and pea and mint purée, beer-battered cod and chips, chicken breast with candied carrots and pancetta and sage sauce, and puddings such as sticky toffee pudding with butterscotch sauce and raspberry trifle with raspberry sorbet; they also offer a two- and three-course menu (not Fri evenings or weekends). *Benchmark main dish: calves liver with bubble and squeak £15.25. Two-course evening meal £20.00.*

Enterprise ~ Lease Roger and Jo Narbett ~ Real ale ~ Open 12-3, 6-11; 12-9 Sun ~ Bar food 12-2, 6-9 (9.15 Fri, 9.30 Sat); 12-7 Sun ~ Restaurant ~ Children welcome ~ Dogs allowed in bar ~ Wi-fi *Recommended by Dr and Mrs A K Clarke, Steve Whalley, Dr D J and Mrs S C Walker, Susan and John Douglas*

KNIGHTWICK

Talbot 🎯 ♀ 🍺 🛏

SO7355 Map 4

(01886) 821235 – www.the-talbot.co.uk
Knightsford Bridge; B4197 just off A44 Worcester–Bromyard; WR6 5PH

Interesting old coaching inn with good own-brewed beer and riverside garden; bedrooms

In warm weather, it's lovely to use the tables on the lawn beside the River Teme (it's across the lane from this former coaching inn, but they serve out here too) or you can sit in front of the building on old-fashioned seats. The heavily beamed and extended lounge bar is traditionally furnished with a variety of seats from small carved or leatherette armchairs to winged settles by the windows, and there's both a warm log fire and a vast stove in a big central stone hearth. The bar opens into a light and airy garden room. Their Teme Valley microbrewery uses locally grown hops to produce Talbot Blonde, That, This, T'Other and a seasonal ale that are served on handpump and they hold regular beer festivals; also, a dozen wines by the glass and 16 malt whiskies. The back public bar has pool on a raised side area, a TV, darts, a juke box and cribbage; in contrast, the dining room is a sedate place for a quiet meal. A farmers' market takes place here on the second Sunday of the month.

They grow their own produce, forage for wild food and make the preserves, bread, raised pies and black pudding in-house for the enjoyable food, which includes sandwiches, goats cheese millefeuille with confit tomatoes, smoked pigeon and sautéed breasts with crispy bacon and tarragon vinaigrette, creamy beetroot risotto with parmesan, chicken and mushroom pie, locally shot game cassoulet with white beans, onion and paprika, salmon fillet baked in the Aga with prawn, white wine and caper butter, slow-roast pork belly with griddled black pudding and apple fritters, and puddings such as chocolate truffle cake and lemon meringue roulade; they also offer a two- and three-course set lunch. *Benchmark main dish: beer-battered fish and chips £14.00. Two-course evening meal £19.00.*

Own brew ~ Licensee Annie Clift ~ Real ale ~ Open 8am-11pm ~ Bar food 8am-9pm ~ Restaurant ~ Children welcome ~ Dogs welcome ~ Wi-fi ~ Bedrooms: £65/£110
Recommended by Alan and Angela Scouller, Dr and Mrs Paul Cartwright, Ben and Diane Bowie

---

It's very helpful if you let us know up-to-date food prices when you report on pubs.

MALVERN
Nags Head 🍺

SO7845   Map 4

(01684) 574373 – www.nagsheadmalvern.co.uk

Bottom end of Bank Street, steep turn down off A449; WR14 2JG

A delightfully eclectic layout and décor, remarkable choice of ales, tasty lunchtime bar food and warmly welcoming atmosphere

A favourite with many readers, this cheerful pub is always packed with customers keen to enjoy the marvellous range of ales and easy-going atmosphere. A series of snug, individually decorated rooms, separated by a couple of steps and with two open fires, have leather armchairs, pews sometimes arranged as booths and a mix of tables (including sturdy ones stained different colours). There are bare boards here, flagstones there, carpet elsewhere, plenty of interesting pictures and homely touches such as house plants, shelves of well thumbed books and daily papers; board games. If you struggle to choose from the 15 or so beers on handpump, you'll be offered a taster by the professional, friendly staff: Banks's Bitter, Bathams Best Bitter, Brains Rev James, Burning Sky Plateau, Burton Bridge Sovereign Gold, Connoisseur Lucem, Jennings Cumberland, Marstons Pedigree New World, Otter Bitter, Purity Pure Ubu, Ringwood Fortyniner, St Georges Charger, Dragons Blood and Friar Tuck, and Woods Shropshire Lad. Also, two farm ciders, 30 malt whiskies, a dozen gins, ten bottled craft ales/lagers and ten wines by the glass including pudding ones. The front terrace and garden have picnic-sets, benches and rustic tables as well as parasols and heaters, to cope with all weather conditions.

🍴 Tasty lunchtime food includes sandwiches, various ploughman's, home-cooked ham and eggs, beef bourguignon, mediterranean vegetable lasagne and beer-battered cod and chips, with evening meals (served in the barn extension dining room only) such as chicken liver pâté, wild mushroom and asparagus risotto, slow-braised pork belly with chorizo hash and cider glaze, oak-smoked duck breast ballotine with caramelised cabbage and shallots, fondant potato and juniper jus, seared lambs liver with smoked bacon jus, and puddings. *Benchmark main dish: beer-battered fresh cod and chips £13.80. Two-course evening meal £19.50.*

Free house ~ Licensee Alex Whistance ~ Real ale ~ Open 11am-11.15pm (11.30pm Fri, Sat); 12-11 Sun ~ Bar food 12-2.30, 6.30-8.30; 12-2.30, 7-8.30 Sun ~ Restaurant ~ Children welcome ~ Dogs welcome ~ Wi-fi *Recommended by Barry Collett, Guy Vowles, Mark Hamill, Katherine Matthews*

NEWLAND
Swan 🍺

SO7948   Map 4

(01886) 832224 – www.theswaninnmalvern.co.uk

Worcester Road (set well back from A449 just NW of Malvern); WR13 5AY

Popular, interesting pub with six real ales and seats in the big garden

Our readers enjoy their visits to this bustling, creeper-clad pub – both for the six real ales and for the tasty food. The dimly lit dark-beamed bar is quite traditional, with a forest canopy of hops, whisky-water jugs, beakers and tankards. Several of the comfortable and clearly individually chosen seats are worth a close look for their carving, and the wall tapestries are interesting. The carved counter has their own St Georges Dragons Blood and Friar Tuck plus Purity Mad Goose, Ringwood Fortyniner, a guest from Marstons and another changing guest on handpump, as well as several wines, malt whiskies and four farm ciders. On the right is a broadly similar red-carpeted dining room and beyond it, in complete contrast, an ultra-modern glass garden room; background music and board games. The garden itself is as individual as the pub, with a picnic-sets on grass, a cluster of huge wooden casks topped with flowers, even a piano doing flower-tub duty – and a set of stocks on the pretty front terrace.

Enjoyable food includes lunchtime sandwiches, baguettes and omelettes, ham hock terrine with home-made piccalilli, coconut-crusted king prawns with sweet chilli sauce, spicy chicken curry, vegetable and lentil stew with coriander dumplings, smoked haddock fishcakes with lemon mayonnaise, chilli con carne, slow-roast pork belly with leek and potato dauphinoise and gravy, and puddings. *Benchmark main dish: beef in ale pie £13.70. Two-course evening meal £20.00.*

Free house ~ Licensee James Crane ~ Real ale ~ Open 12-11.30 ~ Bar food 12-2.30, 6.30-9; 12-3, 7-9 Sun ~ Restaurant ~ Children welcome but not in bar after 8pm ~ Dogs welcome ~ Wi-fi *Recommended by Mike and Mary Carter, Jack Trussler, Chris Stevenson*

TENBURY WELLS   SO6468   Map 4
Talbot 🏅 ♀ 🛏

(01584) 781941 – www.talbotinnnewnhambridge.co.uk
Newnham Bridge; A456; WR15 8JF

Worcestershire Dining Pub of the Year

Carefully refurbished coaching inn with character bar and dining rooms and highly rated food; bedrooms

This 19th-c coaching inn is in lovely Teme Valley countryside and has a friendly, gently civilised atmosphere. There are nice old red and black and original quarry tiles, bare floorboards, open fires, hops and candlelight, with the bar and dining rooms being quite different in style. There's an assortment of dark pubby, high-backed painted wooden and comfortably upholstered dining chairs around a variety of tables, leather tub chairs and sofas here and there, bookshelves, old photographs of the local area, table lights and standard lamps, and some elegant antiques dotted about. It gets pretty busy at the weekend when you'll need to book a table in advance. Hobsons Best Bitter and Wye Valley HPA on handpump, local cider and good wines available by the glass. The bedrooms are thoughtfully decorated and well equipped and breakfasts are good.

Imaginative food includes sandwiches, pigs head with fennel, apple and coriander, scallops with cauliflower and black pepper, blue cheese, pear and walnut risotto, chicken breast with leek, mushroom and rosemary gnocchi, monkfish with spiced pearl barley, sultanas and kale, duck with turnip, pear, cider and fondant potato, pork belly with celeriac, shallots and rhubarb, and puddings such as chocolate, peanut butter and salted caramel fudge and burnt white chocolate ice-cream and clotted cream pannacotta with rhubarb and balsamic meringue. *Benchmark main dish: bass with baby gem lettuce, dauphinoise potatoes and tapenade £16.00. Two-course evening meal £24.00.*

Free house ~ Licensee Barnaby Williams ~ Real ale ~ Open 12-11; 12-9 Sun; closed first two weeks Jan ~ Bar food 12-2.30, 7-9.30; 12-7.30 Sun ~ Children welcome ~ Dogs allowed in bar ~ Wi-fi ~ Live music last Fri of month Sept-Feb ~ Bedrooms: £80/£90
Recommended by Ian Malone, Jacob Vaughan, Lance and Sarah Milligan

---

Please keep sending us reports. We rely on readers for news of new discoveries, and particularly for news of changes – however slight – at the fully described pubs: feedback@goodguides.com, or (no stamp needed) The Good Pub Guide, FREEPOST RTJR-ZCYZ-RJZT, Perrymans Lane, Etchingham TN19 7DN.

WELLAND
SO8039 Map 4

Inn at Welland ⭐ ♀

(01684) 592317 – www.theinnatwelland.co.uk

Drake Street; A4104 W of Upton upon Severn; WR13 6LN

Stylish contemporary country dining bar with good food and wines and nice tables outside

There's a lively buzz of conversation and a gently civilised atmosphere here and our readers enjoy their visits very much: cool grey paintwork, a few carefully chosen modern prints and attractive seat fabrics, with beige flagstones in the central area, wood flooring to the sides and a woodburning stove at one end. Malvern Hills Black Pear, Otter Bitter and Wye Valley Butty Bach on handpump, 21 wines by the glass including an unusually wide range of pudding wines, and two farm ciders served by neatly dressed, efficient staff; background music. The good-sized neat garden, offering tranquil views of the Malvern Hills, has tables with comfortable teak or wicker chairs, some on a biggish sheltered deck, others on individual separate terraces set into lawn. The pub is handy for the Three Counties Showground.

⭐ Making everything in-house and championing local produce, the tempting food includes crab and prawn cocktail with avocado purée, chicken liver and cognac parfait with sage and red onion chutney, sharing plates, chicken caesar salad, omelette arnold bennett, twice-baked blue cheese soufflé with parmesan cream and polenta chips, plaice fillets with asparagus and salsa verde, crisp confit pork belly with cider fondant potato, creamed leeks and smoked bacon, apples and sultanas with red wine jus, 28-day dry-aged steaks with fries, and puddings such as lime mousse with dark chocolate ganache and chantilly cream and iced nougat parfait with toasted marshmallow and pink grapefruit. *Benchmark main dish: aberdeen angus burger with toppings, triple-cooked chips and coleslaw £13.90. Two-course evening meal £22.00.*

Free house ~ Licensees David and Gillian Pinchbeck ~ Real ale ~ Open 12-4, 5.30-11; 12-4.30 Sun; closed Sun evening, Mon ~ Bar food 12-2.30, 6-9.30; 12-2.30 Sun ~ Children welcome ~ Wi-fi *Recommended by Alfie Bayliss, Caroline Prescott, R T and J C Moggridge, Richard Kennell, Dave Braisted, Chris and Val Ramstedt, Bernard Stradling*

Also Worth a Visit in Worcestershire

Besides the fully inspected pubs, you might like to try these pubs that have been recommended to us and described by readers. Do tell us what you think of them: feedback@goodguides.com

ABBERLEY SO7567

Manor Arms (01299) 890300
Netherton Lane; WR6 6BN Modernised country inn tucked away in quiet village backwater opposite fine Norman church; changing ales and good selection of wines, enjoyable food from pub favourites up, set menu and other offers, friendly service; sports TV; two-level deck with lovely valley views, good walks (on Worcestershire Way), six bedrooms, closed Mon, Tues, otherwise open all day. *(Charles Welch)*

ALVECHURCH SP0172

Weighbridge (0121) 445 5111
Scarfield Wharf; B48 7SQ Little red-brick pub (former weighbridge office) by Worcester & Birmingham Canal marina, bar and a couple of small rooms, five well kept ales including Kinver Bargee Bitter and Weatheroak Tillerman's Tipple (beer festivals), simple low-priced food (not Tues, Weds); tables outside. *(S and L McPhee)*

ASHTON UNDER HILL SO9938

Star (01386) 881325
Elmley Road; WR11 7SN Smallish pub perched above road in quiet village at foot of Bredon Hill; linked beamed rooms around bar, one with flagstones and log fire, steps up to pitch-roofed dining room with woodburner, good choice of well liked food (not Sun or Mon evenings) from generous baguettes to specials, real ales such as Black Sheep and Greene King IPA, friendly welcoming staff;

background music, TV and games machine; children and dogs welcome, picnic-sets in pleasant garden, good walks (Wyche Way passes nearby), open all day. *(Guy Vowles)*

BELBROUGHTON   SO9177
Queens (01562) 730276
Queens Hill (B4188 E of Kidderminster); DY9 0DU Old refurbished red-brick pub by Belne Brook, several linked areas including beamed slate-floor bar, very good modern food alongside pub standards, also set menu choices, three well kept beers and nice selection of wines, friendly staff coping well at busy times; disabled facilities, small roadside terrace, pleasant village and handy for M5 (junction 4), open all day weekends. *(Graham and Elizabeth Hargreaves)*

BELBROUGHTON   SO9277
Talbot (01562) 730249
Off A491; DY9 9TG Popular village pub with enjoyable good value food in bar and restaurant, set deal Mon-Weds, well kept Jennings Cocker Hoop and guests, friendly staff; gin and wine tasting evenings; garden with covered terrace, open (and food) all day. *(Dave Braisted)*

BERROW   SO7835
Duke of York (01684) 833449
Junction A438/B4208; WR13 6JQ Bustling old country pub with two spic and span linked rooms, beams, nooks and crannies and log fire, welcoming friendly staff, good food from baguettes up including fresh fish specials, well kept Banks's, Wye Valley and a guest, restaurant; big garden behind, handy for Malvern Hills. *(Theocsbrian)*

BERROW GREEN   SO7458
★**Admiral Rodney** (01886) 821375
B4197, off A44 W of Worcester; WR6 6PL Light and roomy high-beamed 17th-c dining pub, big stripped kitchen tables and two woodburners, popular reasonably priced food from varied menu (should book Fri, Sat evenings), Weds curry night, friendly fast service, well kept Birds, Wye Valley and guests, real cider/perry, charming split-level restaurant in rebuilt barn; folk music third Weds of month, skittle alley; well behaved children and dogs welcome, disabled facilities, tables outside with pretty view and heated covered terrace, good walks, three bedrooms, closed Mon lunchtime, open all day weekends. *(John and Jennifer Spinks)*

BEWDLEY   SO7775
Hop Pole (01299) 401295
Hop Pole Lane; DY12 2QH Friendly modernised family-run pub, good choice of enjoyable food (booking advised) from pub classics up including set evening menu, regular themed nights, three or four well kept Marstons-related ales and several wines

by the glass, walls decorated with old tools etc, cast-iron range in dining area; regular live music and other events such as cookery demonstrations, free wi-fi; children and dogs (not during food times) welcome, front garden with scarecrow and vegetable patch, open all day (afternoon break Mon). *(Jack Trussler)*

BEWDLEY   SO7875
★**Little Pack Horse** (01299) 403762
High Street; no nearby parking – best to use main car park, then cross B4190 (Cleobury Road), and keep walking on down narrowing High Street; DY12 2DH Friendly town pub tucked away in side street; cosy old timbered rooms with bare boards and quarry tiles, some reclaimed oak panelling, woodburner, tasty food including good pies and suet puddings, a couple of Hobsons ales and a guest, selection of bottled ciders and perries and good wine choice, cheerful helpful service, restaurant; background music, TV; children and dogs (in bar) welcome, heated outside area, open all day weekends, closed Mon-Thurs lunchtimes. *(Jamie Green)*

BEWDLEY   SO7875
Mug House (01299) 402543
Severn Side North; DY12 2EE 18th-c bay-windowed pub in charming spot by River Severn, good food from traditional choices up including set menus, can eat in bar of more upmarket evening restaurant (not Sun) with lobster tank, six well kept ales such as Bewdley, Purity, Timothy Taylors and Wye Valley (May beer festival), log fire; children (till 8pm) and dogs welcome, disabled access, glass-covered terrace behind, seven river-view bedrooms, open all day. *(Dan Hanson)*

BIRLINGHAM   SO9343
Swan (01386) 750485
Church Street; off A4104 S of Pershore, via B4080 Eckington Road, turn off at sign to Birlingham with integral 'The Swan Inn' brown sign (not the 'Birlingham (village only)' road), then left; WR10 3AQ Pretty family-run thatched and timbered cottage, updated beamed quarry-tiled bar with woodburner in big stone fireplace, well kept ales such as Hook Norton and Purity, real cider, good food from reasonably priced varied menu including fresh fish specials, friendly efficient service, dining conservatory; nice back garden, open all day Sun till 7pm, closed Mon. *(Theocsbrian, Dr and Mrs H J Field)*

BISHAMPTON   SO9445
Dolphin (01386) 462343
Main Street; WR10 2LX Comfortably updated village pub with good reasonably priced food (not Sun evening, Mon) cooked by landlord-chef including daily specials and some weekday lunchtime bargains, Tues

curry and Weds steak night, Fullers London Pride or Sharps Doom Bar with a guest such as local Pershore, well chosen wines by the glass, efficient friendly young staff; children and dogs welcome, seats on paved terrace and small raised deck, open all day Sun till 9pm, closed Mon lunchtime. *(Dave Braisted)*

BOURNHEATH SO9474

Gate (01527) 878169

Handy for M5 junction 4 via A491 and B4091; Dodford Road; B61 9JR Comfortable tiled-floor country dining pub with good american/mexican-influenced menu, real ales and craft beers such as Brakspears, Purity, Revisionist and Shipyard, plenty of wines by the glass, friendly prompt service, conservatory; children welcome, sheltered garden, open all day Fri-Sun. *(Dave Braisted)*

BREDON SO9236

★ **Fox & Hounds** (01684) 772377

4.5 miles from M5 junction 9; A438 to Northway, left at B4079, in Bredon follow sign to church; GL20 7LA Cottagey 16th-c thatched pub with open-plan carpeted bar, low beams, stone pillars and stripped timbers, central woodburner, traditional furnishings including upholstered settles, a variety of wheelback, tub and kitchen chairs around handsome mahogany and cast-iron-framed tables, elegant wall lamps, smaller side bar, Butcombe, Charles Wells Bombardier, Wadworths 6X and Wye Valley HPA, nice wines by the glass and wide choice of food including specials, fast friendly service; background music, quiz Sun evening (no food then); children welcome, dogs in bar, outside picnic-sets (some under cover), closed Mon. *(Lance and Sarah Milligan)*

BROADWAS-ON-TEME SO7555

Royal Oak (01886) 821353

A44; WR6 5NE Red-brick roadside pub with various areas including unusual lofty-raftered medieval-style dining hall, good value daily carvery and other popular food, well kept ales and decent wines by the glass, friendly helpful service; free wi-fi; children welcome, disabled access, garden with play area, open (and food) all day weekends. *(Dan Hanson)*

CALLOW END SO8349

Blue Bell (01905) 830261

Upton Road; WR2 4TY Popular Marstons local with two bars and dining area, their well kept ales and wide variety of enjoyable food including lots of specials (some good vegetarian choices), friendly welcoming staff, open fire; quiz first Sun of the month; children allowed, dogs in garden only, open all day weekends. *(Dave Braisted)*

CALLOW HILL SP0164

Brook Inn (01527) 543209

Elcocks Brook, off B4504; B97 5UD Modernised country dining pub under new management, good fairly priced food from lunchtime sandwiches and baps up, Marstons-related ales, friendly helpful staff; tables out at front and in pleasant back beer garden, open all day. *(Dave Braisted)*

CALLOW HILL SO7473

Royal Forester (01299) 266286

Near Wyre Forest visitor centre; DY14 9XW Dining pub dating in part from the 15th c, good food including set menu Mon-Thurs, friendly helpful service, well kept ales such as Hobsons and Otter, Robinson's cider, relaxed lounge bar and restaurant; live music last Fri of the month; children and dogs welcome, seats outside, seven contemporary bedrooms, open all day. *(Chris Stevenson)*

CAUNSALL SO8480

Anchor (01562) 850254

Caunsall Road, off A449; DY11 5YL Traditional unchanging two-room pub (in same family since 1927), welcoming atmosphere and can get very busy, five well kept ales such as Hobsons, Three Tuns and Wye Valley, traditional ciders and good value generously filled cobs, friendly efficient service; dogs welcome, large outside seating area behind, near Staffordshire & Worcestershire Canal. *(Brian and Anna Marsden)*

CHADDESLEY CORBETT SO8973

Swan (01562) 777302

Off A448 Bromsgrove–Kidderminster; DY10 4SD Popular old local, lively and friendly, with well kept Bathams and enjoyable good value pubby food (all day Sat, till 6pm Sun, nothing hot Mon, Tues), various rooms including large lofty lounge; Thurs jazz, TV, games machine; children and dogs welcome, picnic-sets in big lawned garden with play area and country views, handy for Harvington Hall, open all day. *(Pat and Tony Martin, Dave Braisted)*

CLAINES SO8558

Mug House (01905) 456649

Claines Lane, off A449 3 miles W of M5 junction 3; WR3 7RN Fine views from this ancient country tavern in unique churchyard setting by fields below the Malvern Hills; several small rooms around central bar, low doorways and heavy oak beams, well kept Banks's and other Marstons-related ales, simple lunchtime pub food (not Sun); no credit cards, outside lavatories; children allowed if away from servery; open all day weekends. *(Jamie Green)*

Tipping is not normal for bar meals, and not usually expected.

CROPTHORNE
SO9944
Bell (01386) 861860
Main Road (B4084); WR10 3NE Isolated rather stark looking roadside pub with contrasting brightly modernised interior, L-shaped bar with painted beams, bare boards and colourful carpet, well divided seating areas (one down a couple of steps), log fire, small back conservatory, emphasis on dining with popular freshly made food from good ploughman's up, children's choices, Sharps Doom Bar and a guest, welcoming efficient service; background music; open all day Sun till 7pm, closed Mon (and Tues in winter). *(Richard Kennell)*

CROWLE
SO9256
Chequers (01905) 381772
Crowle Green, not far from M5 junction 6; WR7 4AA Busy newly refurbished beamed dining pub (sister to the Forest at Feckenham); good food (some quite pricey) from sandwiches and one or two pubby choices up, Hook Norton, Purity St Austell and Wye Valley, craft beers such as Howling Hops, lots of wines by the glass and good range of other drinks, friendly attentive staff; children welcome, open all day. *(Dave Braisted)*

DEFFORD
SO9042
★Monkey House (01386) 750234
A4104, after passing Oak pub on right, it's the last of a small group of cottages; WR8 9BW Tiny black and white thatched cider house, a wonderful time warp and in the same family for over 150 years; ciders and a perry tapped from barrels into pottery mugs and served by landlady from a hatch, no other drinks or food (can bring your own); children welcome, no dogs (resident rottweilers), garden with caravans, sheds and Mandy the horse, small spartan outbuilding with a couple of plain tables, settle and fireplace, open Fri and Sun lunchtimes, Weds and Sat evenings. *(S and L McPhee)*

DEFFORD
SO9042
Oak (01386) 750327
Woodmancote (A4104); WR8 9BW Modernised 17th-c beamed country pub with two front bars and back restaurant, well kept Sharps Doom Bar and Wye Valley, Thatcher's cider, good fairly priced food (till 7pm Sun) including deals, themed night first Thurs of the month, friendly staff; occasional live music; children and dogs welcome, vine-covered front pergola, garden with orchard and chickens, open all day, from 9am weekends for breakfast. *(Dan Hanson)*

DODFORD
SO9372
Dodford Inn (01527) 835825
Whinfield Road; B61 9BG Recently reopened mid 19th-c red-brick country pub tucked away in six-acre grounds, fresh modern refurbishment, up to four well kept ales including Purity and Wye Valley (beer festivals), good home-made food (all day Sat, not Sun evening) from sandwiches and pizzas up, friendly staff; children welcome, no dogs inside, nice views over wooded valley from terrace tables, good walks, open all day. *(Dave Braisted)*

DROITWICH
SO8963
Gardeners Arms (01905) 772936
Vines Lane; WR9 8LU Individual place on the edge of town; cosy traditional bar to the right, bistro-style restaurant to the left with red gingham tablecloths and lots of pictures (mostly for sale), four Marstons-related ales, well priced food from varied menu including range of good local sausages, friendly attentive service; live music and quiz nights, June beer festival, also themed food evenings, whisky tastings and a cigar club; children and dogs welcome, outside seating areas on different levels below railway embankment with quirky mix of furniture, play area, camping, close to Droitwich Canal, open all day. *(Dave Braisted)*

DROITWICH
SO9063
Hop Pole (01905) 770155
Friar Street; WR9 8ED Heavy-beamed local with panelled rooms on different levels, friendly staff, well kept Enville, Malvern Hills, Wye Valley and a guest, bargain home-made lunchtime food including doorstep sandwiches; dominoes, darts and pool, live music first Sun of month; children welcome, partly canopied back garden, open all day. *(Dave Braisted, Tony and Wendy Hobden)*

DUNLEY
SO7969
Dog (01299) 822833
A451 S of Stourport; DY13 0UE Attractive creeper-clad roadside pub, good choice of enjoyable food from bar meals up, well kept Banks's, Hobsons and Wye Valley, friendly staff; children and dogs welcome, garden with play area and bowling green, three bedrooms, open all day. *(Lynda and Trevor Smith)*

ELDERSFIELD
SO8131
★Butchers Arms (01452) 840381
Village signposted from B4211; Lime Street (coming from A417, go past the Eldersfield turn and take the next one), OS Sheet 150 map reference 815314; also signposted from B4208 N of Staunton; GL19 4NX Pretty 16th-c cottage with deliberately simple unspoilt little locals' bar, ales such as St Austell, Wickwar and Wye Valley tapped from the cask, a farm cider and short but well chosen wine list, just a dozen seats in candlelit dining room and booking essential for owner-chef's highly regarded imaginative food (not cheap); no under-10s, garden picnic-sets and nice surroundings, open and food lunchtime Fri-Sun, evening Tues-Sat, closes for two weeks Dec-Jan and the latter part of Aug. *(Dan Hanson)*

EVESHAM SP0344

Old Red Horse (01386) 442784

Vine Street; WR11 4RE Attractive black and white former coaching inn, two bars with beams, bare boards and open fires, three real ales, enjoyable straightforward food at reasonable prices including weekday set deal, good cheerful service; TV and machines; nice covered inner courtyard with small pond, five bedrooms, open all day (no evening food weekends). *(George Atkinson)*

FECKENHAM SP0061

Forest (01527) 894422

B4090 Droitwich–Alcester; B96 6JE Contemporary décor and good interesting food at this village dining pub from lunchtime sandwiches and sharing boards up, well kept Hook Norton and Timothy Taylors, efficient friendly service, oak-floored bar with light-wood stools at high tables and some other more comfortable seating, panels of bookshelf wallpaper dotted about, woodburner, adjoining restaurant with upholstered booth seats, conservatory; children welcome, disabled access/facilities, rattan furniture on block-paved terrace with big outdoor fireplace, more tables on raised lawn, open all day. *(Mike and Mary Carter)*

FLADBURY SO9946

Chequers (01386) 861854

Chequers Lane; WR10 2PZ Modernised old pub in peaceful village; long beamed bar with log fire in old-fashioned range, ales such as Sharps Doom Bar and Wye Valley, Aspall's and Weston's ciders, enjoyable sensibly priced home-made food including Thurs burger night, timbered back restaurant with conservatory; background music, free wi-fi; children welcome, steps up to walled terrace, play area on lawn with country views, eight bedrooms in extension, open all day Fri-Sun, closed Mon lunchtime. *(Lance and Sarah Milligan)*

GRIMLEY SO8359

Camp House (01905) 640288

A443 5 miles N from Worcester, right to Grimley, right at village T junction; WR2 6LX Simple unspoilt old pub in same family since 1939, appealing Severn-side setting (prone to flooding) with own landing stage, generous home-made food at bargain prices, well kept Bathams and guests, Thatcher's and Robinson's ciders, friendly laid-back atmosphere; no credit cards; children and well behaved dogs welcome, attractive lawns (maybe wandering peacocks), small campsite, open all day. *(Jamie Green)*

HADLEY SO8662

Bowling Green (01905) 620294

Hadley Heath; off A4133 Droitwich–Ombersley; WR9 0AR Friendly 16th-c inn with beams and big log fire, well kept Wadworths ales and decent wines by the glass, good food (all day Sun) from sandwiches, deli boards and pizzas up, comfortable back lounge and restaurant; children welcome, tables out overlooking own bowling green (UK's oldest), eight comfortable bedrooms, nice walks (footpath starts from car park), open all day. *(Andy Dolan)*

HALLOW SO8258

Crown (01905) 640408

Main Road; WR2 6LB Large low-beamed 17th-c pub with modern/rustic décor, good food from sandwiches up including set menu choices, pizza deal Mon-Thurs, St Austell Tribute, Wye Valley Butty Bach and guest, friendly helpful staff; children welcome, no dogs inside, tables under parasols on terrace and lawn, big tipi with fire pit, open all day, food till 6pm Sun. *(Dave Braisted)*

HANBURY SO9662

Vernon (01527) 821236

Droitwich Road (B4090); B60 4DB 18th-c former coaching inn, contemporary interior and much emphasis on food, but serves real ales such as Wye Valley and Sharps in beamed bar with woodburner, nice food from light choices to more enterprising restaurant-style dishes, set lunch menu too, good friendly service; children welcome, modern terrace seating, five boutique-style bedrooms, open all day from 9.30am. *(Dan Hanson)*

HANLEY CASTLE SO8342

★ Three Kings (01684) 592686

Church End, off B4211 N of Upton upon Severn; WR8 0BL Timeless, hospitable and by no means smart – in same family for over 100 years and a favourite with those who put unspoilt character and individuality first; cheerful, homely tiled-floor tap room separated from entrance corridor by monumental built-in settle, equally vast inglenook fireplace, room on left with darts and board games, separate entrance to timbered lounge with second inglenook and neatly blacked kitchen range, leatherette armchairs, spindleback chairs and antique winged settle, well kept Butcombe, Hobsons and three guests from smaller brewers, Weston's cider and around 75 malt whiskies, simple snacks; live music; old-fashioned wood and iron seats on front terrace looking across to great cedar shading tiny green, on Wyche Way long-distance path. *(Barry Collett, Guy Vowles)*

HANLEY SWAN SO8142

Swan (01684) 311870

B4209 Malvern–Upton; WR8 0EA Contemporary rustic décor and furnishings blending well with old low beams (some painted), bare boards and log fire, extended back part set for their good well presented food (all day Sat, not Sun evening) from sandwiches/baguettes and pub favourites to more restaurant dishes, friendly helpful service, St Austell Tribute, Sharps Doom Bar and Wye Valley HPA, seven wines by the glass, new oak-framed conservatory; children and dogs welcome, disabled access/loos, seats out on paved terrace and grass, nice spot facing green and big duck pond, five comfortable good value bedrooms, open all day. *(Ian Phillips, Martin and Alison Stainsby, Dave Braisted)*

HIMBLETON   SO9458
Galton Arms   (01905) 391672
Harrow Lane; WR9 7LQ Friendly old black and white bay-windowed country pub, enjoyable food including daily specials in split-level beamed bar or restaurant, well kept Banks's, Bathams, Wye Valley and a guest, woodburner; sports TV; children and dogs welcome, picnic-sets in small part-paved garden, local walks, open all day Sun, closed Mon lunchtime. *(Dave Braisted)*

KIDDERMINSTER   SO8376
King & Castle   (01562) 747505
Railway Station, Comberton Hill; DY10 1QX Neatly recreated Edwardian refreshment room in Severn Valley Railway terminus, steam trains outside and railway memorabilia and photographs inside, simple furnishings, half a dozen ales including Bathams, cobs at the bar or reasonably priced straightforward food in adjacent dining room 9am-4pm (6pm weekends); Oct beer festival; little museum close by, open all day and busy bank holidays/railway gala days. *(Dave Braisted)*

LONGDON   SO8434
Hunters Inn   (01684) 833388
B4211 S, towards Tewkesbury; GL20 6AR Beamed and timbered country pub with flagstone floors, stripped-brickwork and log fires, good locally sourced food including aberdeen angus steaks from own farm, lunchtime set deal (Tues-Sat), Sun carvery, real ales such as Donnington and Otter, local ciders and decent wines by the glass, friendly service, raftered dining area with linen tablecloths, good views; some live music; children welcome, extensive well tended garden, closed Mon. *(Jack Trussler)*

MALVERN   SO7746
Foley Arms   (01684) 573397
Worcester Road; WR14 4QS Substantial Georgian hotel owned by Wetherspoons (former coaching inn), friendly staff and usual good value; children welcome, splendid views from sunny terrace and back bedrooms, open all day from 7am. *(David Carr)*

MALVERN   SO7746
Red Lion   (01684) 564787
St Anns Road; WR14 4RG Enjoyable food (all day weekends) from substantial sandwiches and baguettes up, also good

adjacent thai restaurant, well kept Marstons-related ales such as Ringwood, cheerful prompt service, airy modern décor with stripped pine, bare boards, flagstones and pastel colours; background and live music including frequent jazz nights; attractive partly covered front terrace, well placed for walks, open all day weekends, closed Mon-Thurs lunchtimes. *(S and L McPhee)*

MALVERN   SO7643
Wyche   (01684) 575396
Wyche Road; WR14 4EQ Comfortable busy pub near top of Malvern Hills, splendid views and popular with walkers, five local ales and decent range of affordable pubby food, good service; children and dogs welcome, four bedrooms, open all day. *(Guy Vowles)*

OMBERSLEY   SO8463
★Cross Keys   (01905) 620588
Just off A449; Main Road (A4133, Kidderminster end); WR9 0DS Carpeted bar with easy-going atmosphere, archways opening into several separate areas – nicest on left with attractive Bob Lofthouse animal etchings, beams (maybe hop-strung) and some horse tack on dark varnished country panelling, Timothy Taylors Landlord, Wye Valley HPA and occasional guest, several wines by the glass and decent coffee, comfortable back room with sofas and armchairs leading to dining conservatory, plenty of emphasis on their well liked food from baguettes to enterprising daily specials (good fish choice), friendly helpful service; unobtrusive background music; children welcome if eating, no dogs, terrace with alloy furniture under big heated canopy, open all day Sun. *(Robert W Buckle)*

OMBERSLEY   SO8463
★Kings Arms   (01905) 620142
Main Road (A4133); WR9 0EW Imposing beamed and timbered Tudor pub; spotless rambling rooms with nooks and crannies, three splendid fireplaces, low-ceilinged quarry-tiled bar with dark wood pew and stools around cast-iron tables, three dining areas, one room with Charles II coat of arms decorating the ceiling, good food and service (popular with older diners), well kept Marstons-related ales; background music; children and dogs welcome, seats on tree-sheltered courtyard, colourful hanging baskets and tubs, open all day, food all day weekends. *(Lynda and Trevor Smith)*

PENSAX   SO7368
★Bell   (01299) 896677
B4202 Abberley–Clows Top, Snead Common part of village; WR6 6AE Mock-Tudor roadside pub with good local atmosphere and friendly staff, half a dozen ever changing ales such as Hobsons (festival last weekend of June), also cider and perry, well liked good value pubby food (not Sun evening) from sandwiches up, L-shaped main

bar with traditional décor, cushioned pews and pubby tables on bare boards, vintage beer ads and wartime front pages, two open fires and woodburner, dining room with french windows opening on to deck; children and dogs (in bar) welcome, country-view garden, open all day summer weekends, closed Mon. (Lynda and Trevor Smith, Dave Braisted)

PEOPLETON   SO9350
Crown (01905) 840222
Village and pub signed off A44 at Allens Hill; WR10 2EE Cosy village pub with welcoming owners and friendly mix of drinkers and diners, beamed bar with big inglenook, well laid-out eating area, good food (must book) from sandwiches and pub favourites up including lunchtime set deal, well kept Fullers, Sharps and Wye Valley, nice wines by the glass, efficient pleasant service; surcharge added if paying by credit card; children and dogs (in bar) welcome, flower-filled back garden, open all day, no food Sun evening. (A Phelps, Revd Michael Vockins)

PERSHORE   SO9545
Angel (01386) 552046
High Street; WR10 1AF Comfortably modernised old bow-windowed coaching inn, various well cared-for areas including flagstoned bar, beams, panelling and original fireplaces, ales such as Hook Norton and Sharps, decent wines and popular good value food including lunchtime deals, good friendly service; background music, quiz first Sun of the month, TV, free wi-fi; grounds at back lead down to River Avon, 15 bedrooms, open all day. (Stanley and Annie Matthews)

PERSHORE   SO9545
★ **Brandy Cask** (01386) 552602
Bridge Street; WR10 1AJ Plain high-ceilinged bow-windowed bar with coal fire, own good beers from courtyard brewery and guests, reasonably priced generous food (not Tues) from sandwiches to steaks, friendly helpful service, dining room; well behaved children allowed, no dogs inside, terrace and koi pond in long attractive garden down to river. (Dan Hanson)

SEVERN STOKE   SO8544
Rose & Crown (01905) 371249
A38 S of Worcester; WR8 9JQ Attractive 16th-c black and white pub, low beams, good fire and various knick-knacks in character bar, some cushioned wall seats and high-backed settles among more modern pub furniture, well kept Marstons-related ales and decent choice of enjoyable sensibly priced food, good friendly service, carpeted back restaurant; fortnightly quiz Weds, monthly folk night; dogs welcome, wheelchair access with help, picnic-sets in big garden with play area, Malvern Hills views and good walks, open (and food) all day. (Chris Stevenson)

SHATTERFORD   SO7981
Bellmans Cross (01299) 861322
Bridgnorth Road (A442); DY12 1RN Welcoming 19th-c mock-Tudor dining pub with good well presented food cooked by french chef-landlord including lunchtime set menu and themed nights, restaurant with kitchen view, Enville and a couple of guests from neat timber-effect bar, good choice of wines, teas and coffees; children welcome, picnic-sets outside, handy for Severn Woods walks, open (and food) all day weekends. (Dennis and Doreen Haward)

STOKE POUND   SO9667
Queens Head (01527) 557007
Sugarbrook Lane, by Bridge 48, Worcester & Birmingham Canal; B60 3AU Smartly refurbished by the small Lovely Pubs group; fairly large bar with comfortable seating area, dedicated dining part beyond, good choice of popular food including sharing plates, wood-fired pizzas and charcoal spit-roasts, early evening discount Mon-Fri, well kept ales such as Purity, Sharps and Wye Valley, large selection of wines from glass-fronted store, helpful pleasant young staff; Thurs live music; children welcome, waterside garden with tipi, moorings, good walk up the 36 locks of Tardebigge Steps, quite handy for Avoncroft Museum, open (and some food) all day. (Charles Welch)

STOKE WORKS   SO9365
Bowling Green (01527) 861291
A mile from M5 junction 5, via Stoke Lane; handy for Worcester & Birmingham Canal; B60 4BH Friendly comfortable pub with enjoyable straightforward food at bargain prices (particularly good faggots), Banks's and a Marstons guest, wall chart showing cost of a pint over the years; children welcome, big garden with play area and well tended bowling green, open all day, no food Sun. (Dave Braisted)

TENBURY WELLS   SO5968
Pembroke House (01584) 810301
Cross Street; WR15 8EQ Striking timbered building, oldest in town, with pubby beamed bar and two dining rooms, good popular food (not Sun evening, Mon, best to book), friendly efficient staff, Hobsons Best and a guest such as Ludlow Boiling Well, woodburner, games area with pool, darts and TV; background music and some live music; children welcome, no dogs inside, smokers' shelter and pleasant garden, open all day Fri-Sun, closed Mon lunchtime. (Jamie Green)

UPHAMPTON   SO8464
Fruiterers Arms (01905) 620305
Off A449 N of Ombersley; WR9 0JW Homely country local (looks like a private house, and has been in the same family for

nearly 170 years), good value Cannon Royall ales brewed at the back of the pub and a couple of guests, farm cider and perry, simple rustic Jacobean panelled bar and lounge with comfortable armchairs, beams and log fire, lots of photographs and memorabilia, no food except filled rolls Fri-Sun; children till 9pm, dogs welcome in one area, back terrace and some seats out in front, open all day. *(S and L McPhee)*

WEATHEROAK HILL   SP0574
Coach & Horses (01564) 823386
Icknield Street – coming S on A435 from Wythall roundabout, filter right off dual carriageway a mile S, then in village turn left towards Alvechurch; not far from M42 junction 3; B48 7EA Roomy country pub (in same family since 1968) brewing its own good Weatheroak Hill beers, well kept guests too and farm ciders, good range of enjoyable food (not Sun evening) including stone-baked pizzas; proper old-fashioned tiled-floor bar with log fire (dogs allowed here), steps up to refurbished high-raftered restaurant area; children welcome, plenty of seats out on lawns and terrace, open all day. *(Dan Hanson)*

WEST MALVERN   SO7645
Brewers Arms (01684) 575408
The Dingle, signed off B4232; WR14 4BQ New owners for this attractive little two-bar beamed country local down steep path, well kept Malvern Hills, Marstons, Wye Valley and up to five guests at busy times, good value pubby food (not Sun evening, Mon), airy dining room; free wi-fi; children, walkers and dogs welcome, glorious view from small garden, open all day Fri-Sun. *(Jack Trussler)*

WILDMOOR   SO9675
Wildmoor Oak (0121) 453 2696
A mile from M5 junction 4 – first left off A491 towards Stourbridge; Top Road; B61 0RB Busy country local with good choice of enjoyable food (all day Fri-Sun) including caribbean dishes cooked by landlord, changing real ales, ciders and perries, friendly atmosphere; music nights second Fri and last Thurs of the month, free wi-fi; small sloping terrace and garden, closed Mon lunchtime, otherwise open all day (winter hours may differ). *(Dave Braisted)*

WILLERSEY   SP1039
New Inn (01386) 853226
Main Street; WR12 7PJ Friendly old stone-built local in lovely village, generous good value pub food (not Sun evening) from sandwiches up, prompt service, well kept Donnington ales, flagstoned bar with raised quarry-tiled end section, some black beams, games room with pool and darts, separate

skittle alley; background music, TV; rattan-style tables and chairs outside, good local walks, open all day. *(Guy Vowles)*

WITHYBED GREEN   SP0172
Crown (0121) 445 2300
Near Bridge 61, Worcester & Birmingham Canal; B48 7PN Tucked-away pub in row of former canal workers' cottages overlooking fields, Greene King Abbot and a couple of guests, simple low-priced food (not Sun), series of lived-in small rooms with two open fires; background music; children and dogs welcome, picnic-sets out in front and on terrace, open all day. *(Dave Braisted)*

WOLVERLEY   SO8379
Lock (01562) 850581
Wolverley Road (B4189 N of Kidderminster, by Staffordshire & Worcester Canal); DY10 3RN Roadside pub next to narrow lock; pleasant and comfortable, with enjoyable good value food (all day weekends) including range of burgers and grills, Banks's and a couple of other Marstons-related beers, cheerful staff, separate tea room; children and dogs welcome, waterside picnic-sets, handy for Kingsford Country Park, open all day. *(Dave Braisted)*

WORCESTER   SO8554
Cardinals Hat (01905) 724006
Friar Street; just off A44 near cathedral; WR1 2NA Dating from the 14th c with three small character rooms (one with fine oak panelling), half a dozen changing ales, real ciders and plenty of bottled beers, friendly well informed staff, good bar snacks and cheese/meat platters; free wi-fi; children welcome, pleasant little brick-paved terrace behind, closed Mon lunchtime, otherwise open all day. *(Jamie Green)*

WORCESTER   SO8455
Dragon (01905) 25845
The Tything (A38); WR1 1JT Recently refurbished alehouse under friendly new landlady, carpeted L-shaped bar with woodburner, six well kept Church End ales and a couple of guests, traditional cider and seven wines by the glass, just snacky food at the moment, more room (and loos) upstairs; no children welcome, dogs welcome, partly covered back terrace, open all day Fri-Sun, from 4pm other days. *(Charles Welch)*

WORCESTER   SO8454
Farriers Arms (01905) 27569
Fish Street; WR1 2HN Welcoming and relaxed old timbered pub rambling through pleasant lounge/dining area and public bar, enjoyable inexpensive food, well kept ales

---

We say if we know a pub has background music.

such as Wells Bombardier and decent house wines, good cheerful service; TV, pool, darts; beer garden, handy for cathedral, open all day. *(Charles Welch, Dan Hanson)*

WORCESTER   SO8554
King Charles II (01905) 726100
New Street; WR1 2DP Small jettied Tudor building, heavy beams, fine panelling and woodburners in carved fireplaces, settles and pews on bare boards, eight well kept ales from Craddocks and associated Bridgnorth and Two Thirsty Brewers, traditional ciders, enjoyable range of Pieminister pies served with peas and different types of mash (limited range of other food), friendly young staff, upstairs area with bench seating, old tapestry and some leather easy chairs; ask about the skeleton under the floor; open all day (food all day weekends). *(Dave Braisted, Tony and Wendy Hobden, Stephen Funnell)*

WORCESTER   SO8455
★ **Marwood** (01905) 330460
The Tything (A38); some nearby parking; WR1 1JL Easy to miss this old building, quirky and civilised with a long narrow series of small linked areas, dark flagstones and broad floorboards, stripped or cast-iron-framed tables, the odd chandelier and art deco poster, open fires, upstairs room looking across to law courts, four well kept changing ales, enjoyable food (not Sun evening) from open sandwiches and tapas up, friendly service; background music; children (not in bar after 7.30pm) and dogs welcome, sunny flagstoned courtyard, open all day (till late Sat). *(David Carr)*

WORCESTER   SO8555
Plough (01905) 21381
Fish Street; WR1 2HN Traditional corner pub with two simple rooms off entrance lobby, six well kept interesting ales including Hobsons and Malvern Hills, farm cider/perry and good whisky choice, straightforward food available Fri and Sat lunchtimes plus rolls all day weekends; outside lavatories; small back terrace with cathedral view, open all day. *(Chris Stevenson)*

WORCESTER   SO8554
Swan With Two Nicks (01905) 28190
New Street/Friar Street; WR1 2DP Rambling early 16th-c backstreet pub, plenty of character in bare-boards low-ceilinged front rooms, four changing local ales and some interesting bottled ciders, decent whisky and rum choice too, well priced food including good pies, friendly atmosphere, upstairs cocktail bar (Fri, Sat evenings), another part for live music and comedy nights; open all day. *(Dave Braisted)*

WYRE PIDDLE   SO9647
Anchor (01386) 641510
Off A4538 NW of Evesham; WR10 2JB Great position by River Avon with moorings, decking on three levels, floodlit lawn and view from airy back dining room; enjoyable well priced home-made food (not Tues, Weds) from baguettes up, beers such as Wye Valley in beamed and flagstoned bar with inglenook stove, good friendly service; children welcome, open all Fri, Sat, till 6pm Sun, closed Mon. *(Jeff Davies)*

Post Office address codings confusingly give the impression that some pubs are in Worcestershire, when they're really in Gloucestershire, Herefordshire, Shropshire or Warwickshire (which is where we list them).

Yorkshire

ASENBY
SE3975 Map 7

Crab & Lobster 🌟 🍷 🛏

(01845) 577286 – www.crabandlobster.co.uk

Dishforth Road; village signed off A168 – handy for A1; YO7 3QL

**Interesting furnishings and décor in rambling bar, inventive
restaurant food, good drinks choice and seats on attractive terrace;
smart bedrooms**

As this interesting place is so handy for the A1, our readers enjoy dropping in for a drink or a meal. Of course, it's not a straightforward pub (the main emphasis is on the hotel and restaurant side), but there's a rambling L-shaped bar where they keep Copper Dragon Golden Pippin on handpump and good wines by the glass. This bustling bar has an interesting jumble of seats, from antique high-backed and other settles through sofas and wing armchairs heaped with cushions to tall and rather theatrical corner seats; the tables are almost as much of a mix. The walls and available surfaces are a jungle of bric-a-brac including lots of race tickets, while standard and table lamps and candles keep the lighting pleasantly informal. There's also a cosy main restaurant and a dining pavilion with big tropical plants, nautical bits and pieces and Edwardian sofas; background music. The gardens have bamboo and palm trees lining the path, which leads to a gazebo; there are seats on a mediterranean-style terrace. The opulent bedrooms (based on famous hotels around the world) are in nearby Crab Manor, which has seven acres of mature gardens and a 180-metre golf hole with full practice facilities.

🌟 As well as a two- and three-course set lunch menu, the rewarding – if not cheap – food includes club sandwich, moules marinière, spare ribs in sweet and sticky orange, five-spice, bourbon, treacle and chilli sauce, wild mushroom, fennel and courgette risotto, natural cured haddock with cheesy bacon and onion mash, a poached egg and wholegrain mustard sauce, herb-crusted lamb loin with gruyère and cheddar gratin potatoes, rosemary and redcurrants, venison loin with steamed venison and cherry pudding and juniper gravy, and puddings such as white chocolate and raspberry cheesecake with orange and cranberry sauce and sticky date and toffee apple pudding with toffee sauce. *Benchmark main dish: half lobster thermidor £24.00. Two-course evening meal £28.00.*

Kymel Trading ~ Licensee Robbie King ~ Real ale ~ Open 11am-11.30pm ~ Bar food 12-2.30, 7-9; 12-2.30, 6.30-9.30 Sat ~ Restaurant ~ Children welcome ~ Wi-fi ~ Live jazz Weds evening, Sun lunchtime ~ Bedrooms: /£165 *Recommended by Pat and Graham Williamson, J R Wildon, Helena and Trevor Fraser*

BECK HOLE

NZ8202 Map 10

Birch Hall

(01947) 896245 – www.beckhole.info/bhi.htm

Off A169 SW of Whitby, from top of Sleights Moor; YO22 5LE

Extraordinary place in lovely valley with friendly landlady, real ales and simple snacks

Quite unique, this tiny pub-cum-village shop remains resolutely unchanged. It's in stunning surroundings in a beautiful steep valley village by a bridge over a river and close to Thomason Foss waterfall, so walkers with their dogs make up many of the customers. The two simple rooms have built-in cushioned wall seats, wooden tables (one embedded with 136 pennies), flagstones or composition flooring, unusual items such as a tube of toothpaste priced 1/-3d, and a model train running around a head-height shelf. Black Sheep, North Yorkshire Beckwatter and a guest such as Hambleton Goldfield on handpump and several malt whiskies and wines by the glass. The shop sells postcards, sweets and ice-creams. There are benches outside in a streamside garden and one of the wonderful nearby walks is along a disused railway. They have a self-catering cottage for hire.

Bar snacks only, such as local pork pie, butties, scones and their famous beer cake.

Free house ~ Licensee Glenys Crampton ~ Real ale ~ No credit cards ~ Open 11-11; 11-3, 7.30-11 Weds-Sun in winter; closed Mon evening in winter, all day Tues Nov-Apr ~ Bar food available during opening hours ~ Children in small family room ~ Dogs welcome
Recommended by Toby Jones, Elizabeth and Peter May, Nigel Havers, Thomas Green

BLAKEY RIDGE

SE6799 Map 10

Lion 🍺 🛏

(01751) 417320 – www.lionblakey.co.uk

From A171 Guisborough–Whitby follow Castleton, Hutton-le-Hole signposts; from A170 Kirkby Moorside–Pickering follow Keldholm, Hutton-le-Hole, Castleton signposts; OS Sheet 100 map reference 679996; YO62 7LQ

Extended pub in fine scenery and open all day; popular food; bedrooms

On cold, misty days, walkers find this isolated 16th-c inn quite a haven – but if you wish to stay here, you'll need to book well in advance. The low-beamed rambling bars have open fires, a few big high-backed rustic settles around cast-iron-framed tables, lots of small dining chairs, a nice leather sofa and stone walls hung with old engravings and photographs of the pub under snow (it can easily get cut off in winter – 40 days is the record so far). The fine choice of beers on handpump might include Black Sheep Best, Copper Dragon Golden Pippin, Theakstons Best, Old Peculier and Paradise Ale, Thwaites Wainwright and a changing guest; they have 13 wines by the glass and several malt whiskies; background music and games machine. The inn is situated at the highest point of the North York Moors National Park (1,325 feet above sea level) and the valley views are breaktaking.

Tasty, well liked food includes lunchtime sandwiches, smoked salmon and scrambled egg, creamy moules marinière, mushroom stroganoff, gammon with egg and pineapple, beer-battered haddock and chips, beef stew and dumplings, duck breast in orange sauce, chicken breast with creamy leek and bacon sauce, poached salmon fillet in creamy white wine and prawn sauce, and puddings such as jam roly-poly with custard and chocolate nut sundae. *Benchmark main dish: steak and mushroom pie £11.50. Two-course evening meal £16.00.*

Free house ~ Licensees Barry, Diana, Paul and David Crossland ~ Real ale ~ Open 10am-11pm (midnight Sat) ~ Bar food 12-10 ~ Restaurant ~ Children welcome ~ Dogs allowed in bar ~ Wi-fi ~ Bedrooms: £42.50/£86 *Recommended by WAH, Dr J Barrie Jones, , Ian Herdman, Walter and Susan Rinaldi-Butcher*

BOROUGHBRIDGE

SE3966   Map 7

Black Bull £

(01423) 322413 – www.blackbullboroughbridge.co.uk
St James Square; B6265, just off A1(M); YO51 9AR

Bustling town pub with real ales, several wines by the glass and traditional bar food; bedrooms

For many centuries, this attractive old town pub has been looking after people travelling between Scotland and England, and today it's still welcoming customers on the same route. There are lots of separate drinking and eating areas where cheerful regulars drop in for a pint and a chat. The main bar area has a big stone fireplace and comfortable seats and is served through an old-fashioned hatch; there's also a cosy snug with traditional wall settles, and a tap room, lounge bar and restaurant. John Smiths Cask, Rudgate Battle Axe and Timothy Taylors Boltmaker on handpump, six wines by the glass and 21 malt whiskies; dominoes. The borzoi dog is called Spot and the two cats Kia and Mershka. The hanging baskets are lovely.

Our Value Award is for the fair priced bar food: sausages with mash and onion gravy, battered haddock and chips, thai beef strips with stir-fried vegetables and noodles and spicy chiken goujons. They also offer tuna steak on mushrooms and red onions in arrabiata sauce topped with mozzarella, lamb shank with rosemary and redcurrant gravy, venison steak with berry glaze on bacon and blue cheese, and puddings such as banoffi meringue roulade and jam sponge with custard. *Benchmark main dish: pie of the day £9.75. Two-course evening meal £16.00.*

Free house ~ Licensee Anthony Burgess ~ Real ale ~ Open 11-11 (midnight Fri, Sat); 11.30-11 Sun ~ Bar food 12-2, 6-9 (9.30 Fri, Sat); 12-2.30, 6-9 Sun ~ Restaurant ~ Children welcome ~ Dogs welcome ~ Wi-fi ~ Bedrooms: £50/£75 *Recommended by Denis and Margaret Kilner, Andrew and Michele Revell, Melanie and David Lawson*

BRADFIELD

SK2290   Map 7

Strines Inn £ 🛏

(0114) 285 1247 – www.thestrinesinn.webs.com
From A57 heading E of junction with A6013 (Ladybower Reservoir) take first left turn (signposted with Bradfield) then bear left; with a map can also be reached more circuitously from Strines signpost on A616 at head of Underbank Reservoir, W of Stocksbridge; S6 6JE

Surrounded by fine scenery, with quite a mix of customers and traditional beer and bar food; bedrooms

With the Peak District National Park on the doorstep, the scenery surrounding this former manor house is superb. The main bar has a coal fire in a rather grand stone fireplace, black beams liberally decked with copper kettles and so forth, quite a menagerie of stuffed animals, and homely red plush-cushioned traditional wooden wall benches and small chairs; background music. Two other rooms, to the right and left, are similarly furnished. Acorn Yorkshire Pride, Jennings Cocker Hoop, Marstons Pedigree and Peak Chatsworth Gold on handpump and nine wines by the glass. There are plenty of picnic-sets outside, as well as swings, a play area, and peacocks and geese. The bedrooms have four-poster beds and a dining table (they serve breakfast in your room) and our readers appreciate staying here; the front room overlooks the Strines Reservoir.

🍴 Pubby food choices include sandwiches, giant yorkshire pudding with onion gravy, game and port pâté, macaroni cheese, burgers with salad and chips, liver and onions, lasagne, mixed grill, and puddings such as chocolate fudge cake and caramel apple pie with custard. *Benchmark main dish: steak in ale pie £9.50. Two-course evening meal £14.50.*

Free house ~ Licensee Bruce Howarth ~ Real ale ~ Open 10.30am-11pm ~ Bar food 12-9; 12-2.30, 5-8.30 weekdays in winter ~ Children welcome ~ Dogs welcome ~ Bedrooms: £65/£85 *Recommended by Dave Sutton, Edward and William Johnston, Julie Braeburn*

CONSTABLE BURTON   SE1690   Map 10
Wyvill Arms 🏅 ♀ 🍺 🛏
(01677) 450581 – www.thewyvillarms.co.uk
A684 E of Leyburn; DL8 5LH

Well run, friendly dining pub with interesting food, a dozen wines by the glass, real ales and efficient helpful service; bedrooms

Our readers enjoy staying in this former farmhouse as the bedrooms are comfortable and breakfasts generous. Downstairs, the small bar area has a finely worked plaster ceiling with the Wyvill family's coat of arms, a mix of seating and an elaborate stone fireplace with a warm winter fire. The second bar has a lower ceiling with fans, leather seating, old oak tables, various alcoves and a model train on a railway track running around the room; the reception area includes a huge leather sofa that can seat up to eight people, another carved stone fireplace and an old leaded stained-glass church window partition. Both rooms are hung with pictures of local scenes. Theakstons Best, Wensleydale Coverdale Gamekeeper and a guest beer on handpump, plus nine wines by the glass and nine malt whiskies; chess, backgammon and dominoes. There are several large wooden benches under sizeable white parasols for outdoor dining and picnic-sets by a well. Constable Burton Hall is opposite.

🍽 The high standard of cooking includes lunchtime sandwiches, ham hock, chicken and cheese terrine with pear and apple chutney, pigeon breast with wild mushrooms and madeira sauce, battered fresh fish and chips, spicy aubergine, courgette and red pepper stew, breaded chicken supreme stuffed with mozzarella cheese and smoked bacon on creamed leeks with stilton sauce, slow-cooked moroccan-style lamb shank, half a crispy duck confit with black cherry sauce, aberdeen angus steaks with a choice of sauces, and puddings such as three-way brûlée (vanilla, blueberry, strawberry) and pecan pie with vanilla ice-cream. *Benchmark main dish: steak and onion pie £13.50. Two-course evening meal £19.50.*

Free house ~ Licensee Nigel Stevens ~ Real ale ~ Open 11-3, 5.30 (6 Sun)-11; closed Mon ~ Bar food 12-2.15, 5.30-9 ~ Restaurant ~ Children welcome until 8.30 ~ Dogs allowed in bar ~ Wi-fi ~ Bedrooms: £65/£90 *Recommended by Hilary and Neil Christopher, Michael Doswell, Millie and Peter Downing, Barbara Brown*

CRAY   SD9479   Map 7
White Lion 🛏
(01756) 760262 – www.whitelioninncray.com
B6160 N of Kettlewell; BD23 5JB

Refurbished and reopened inn under newish owners, open fires in bar and dining room, a fair choice of food and seats outside; bedrooms

Some 1,100 feet up by Buckden Pike, this former drovers' hostelry is set in lovely countryside and is popular with walkers. Throughout, there are lovely big flagstones and beams and the bar has button-back leather chesterfield sofas and armchairs in front of a woodburning stove, a cushioned window seat, books on shelves and a brass chandelier; a simple little back room (good for wet dogs) has some tables and chairs. Black Sheep Best, Hop Studio Pale and Wharfedale Blonde on handpump and eight wines by the glass. The attractive dining room has antique-style dining chairs around chunky tables, an open fire, some exposed stone walling and bits and pieces of old farming equipment; background music. In warm weather you can sit at picnic-sets above the quiet steep lane or on flat limestone slabs in the middle of the shallow stream that tumbles down opposite. The airy, comfortable bedrooms are in the pub itself or in a converted barn.

 As well as lunchtime sandwiches, the tasty food includes chicken liver parfait with onion marmalade, smoked haddock and leek fishcake with lemon and dill mayonnaise, local sausages with mash and caramelised red onion gravy, beer-battered haddock and chips, wild mushroom risotto with truffle oil, game pie in red wine gravy, rack of lamb with fondant potato and rosemary and redcurrant jus, and puddings such as crème brûlée with blueberries and sticky sponge with butterscotch sauce and chantilly cream. *Benchmark main dish: pork fillet with serrano ham and black pudding £17.00. Two-course evening meal £21.00.*

Free house ~ Licensee Dennis Peacock ~ Real ale ~ Open 12-10.30 ~ Bar food 12-2.30, 6-8.30 ~ Restaurant ~ Children welcome ~ Dogs allowed in bar ~ Wi-fi ~ Bedrooms: £90/£130 *Recommended by Kate Moran, Peter and Emma Kelly, Susan and Callum Slade, Luke Morgan*

 CRAYKE   SE5670   Map 7
Durham Ox 🎖️ ⚜️ 💡 🛏️
(01347) 821506 – www.thedurhamox.com
Off B1363 at Brandsby, towards Easingwold; West Way; YO61 4TE

Friendly, well run inn, with interesting décor in old-fashioned rooms, fine drinks and smashing food; comfortable bedrooms

As well as a proper pubby bar liked by locals, this civilised inn also appeals to visitors who stay overnight and enjoy the very good food. The old-fashioned lounge bar has venerable tables, antique seats and settles on flagstones, pictures and photographs on dark red walls, interesting satirical carvings in the panelling (Victorian copies of medieval pew ends), polished copper and brass and an enormous inglenook fireplace. In the bottom bar is a framed illustrated account of local history (some of it gruesome) dating back to the 12th c, and a large framed print of the famous Durham Ox, which weighed 171 stone. The Burns Bar has a woodburning stove, exposed brickwork and large french windows that open on to a balcony. Black Sheep Best, Rudgate Grain Store, Timothy Taylors Boltmaker and a changing guest on handpump, 20 wines by the glass, a dozen malt whiskies and interesting spirits; background music and board games. There are seats in the courtyard garden, the bottom of which offers views on three sides over the Vale of York; on the fourth is a charming view to the medieval church on the hill – supposedly the very hill up which the Grand Old Duke of York marched his men. The bedrooms, in the main building or in renovated farm cottages (dogs allowed here), are well equipped, spacious and comfortable; breakfasts are very good. The nearby A19 leads straight to a park & ride for York. The pub belongs to Provenance Inns.

Using local seasonal produce and baking their own bread, the assured cooking includes sandwiches, ham hock terrine with pickled quail eggs and pea purée, confit duck leg and asparagus salad with poached duck egg, butternut squash and sage ravioli with nut brown butter, spatchcock poussin with aioli and piri piri, barbecue sticky pork rib platter with skinny fries, fresh fish dish of the day with hollandaise sauce, and puddings such as vanilla pannacotta with fruit coulis and apricot and almond frangipane with chantilly cream; they also offer an early-bird menu (5.30-6.45pm Sun-Fri). *Benchmark main dish: rib-eye steak plus all the trimmings £24.95. Two-course evening meal £25.00.*

Free house ~ Licensee Michael Ibbotson ~ Real ale ~ Open 11am-midnight; 12-11 Sun ~ Bar food 12-2.30, 5.30-9.30; 12-3, 5.30-8.30 Sun ~ Restaurant ~ Children welcome ~ Dogs allowed in bar and bedrooms ~ Wi-fi ~ Bedrooms: £100/£120 *Recommended by Gordon and Margaret Ormondroyd, Christopher and Elise Way, Walter and Susan Rinaldi-Butcher*

DOWNHOLME
Bolton Arms
SE1197   Map 10

(01748) 823716 – www.boltonarmsdownholme.com
Village signposted just off A6108 Leyburn–Richmond; DL11 6AE

Tasty food and ales in stone-built country pub; bedrooms

In warm weather particularly, this country pub really comes into its own with seats in the neat garden and picnic-sets and benches on a lower level terrace – all with magnificent views; the summer hanging baskets are very pretty too. The simply furnished, carpeted bar is down a few steps and has two smallish linked areas off the servery where they keep Timothy Taylors Landlord and Wensleydale Semer Water on handpump, ten wines by the glass and eight malt whiskies. There are comfortable plush wall banquettes, a log fire in a neat fireplace, quite a collection of gleaming brass, a few small country pictures and drink advertisements on freshly decorated walls; background music and dominoes. The dining conservatory also has wonderful views across Swaledale.

Popular food includes sandwiches, baked goats cheese on pear and fig salad, prawn cocktail, spinach and ricotta pancakes, beef stroganoff, chicken breast strips in creamy mushroom sauce, steak and mushroom pie, salmon fillet in a creamy prawn sauce, lambs liver and bacon, fresh seafood tagliatelle, and puddings such as berry eton mess and ginger sponge pudding. *Benchmark main dish: slow-cooked lamb shoulder with mint and redcurrant gravy £15.95. Two-course evening meal £17.00.*

Free house ~ Licensees Steve and Nicola Ross ~ Real ale ~ Open 11-3, 6-11 (midnight weekends); closed Tues lunchtime ~ Bar food 12-2, 7-9 ~ Restaurant ~ Children welcome ~ Dogs allowed in bedrooms ~ Wi-fi ~ Bedrooms: £45/£70 *Recommended by David Bird, Mungo Shipley, Patricia Hawkins, Caroline Sullivan*

EAST WITTON
Blue Lion 🏅 ⏐ 🛏
SE1486   Map 10

(01969) 624273 – www.thebluelion.co.uk
A6108 Leyburn–Ripon; DL8 4SN

Civilised dining pub with a proper bar, real ales, delicious food and courteous service; comfortable bedrooms

Once again, our readers have nothing but the warmest of praise for all aspects of this 18th-c coaching inn – and the welcome is just as genuine to damp dog walkers dropping in for a pint beside the fire as to those in for a special meal or overnight stay. The big squarish bar is civilised but informal with soft lighting, high-backed antique settles and old windsor chairs on turkish rugs and flagstones, ham hooks in the high ceiling decorated with dried wheat, teazles and so forth, a delft shelf filled with appropriate bric-a-brac, plus several prints, sporting caricatures and other pictures; daily papers. Black Sheep Best and Golden Sheep and Theakstons Best on handpump, an impressive wine list including a dozen (plus champagne) by the glass and 17 malt whiskies. The candlelit, high-ceilinged and elegant dining room has another open fire. Picnic-sets on the gravel outside look beyond the stone houses on the far side of the village green to Witton Fell, and there's a big attractive back garden. The comfortable bedrooms with pretty country furnishings are located in the main house and in converted stables across the courtyard (where dogs are welcome).

Wonderful food using the best seasonal local produce includes lunchtime sandwiches, rabbit arancini with tomato stew and red wine, queenie scallops with garlic butter and gruyère gratin, butternut squash and pine nut risotto with parmesan, beef in ale pudding with red wine gravy, slow-roasted honey-glazed duckling with apple gravy, salmon fillet with tarragon and brown shrimp tagliatelle, slow-cooked pork belly, pigs cheek and black pudding scotch egg, and puddings such as triple chocolate brownie with Baileys ice-cream and iced liquorice terrine with roast fig; they also offer a two- and three-course set lunch. *Benchmark main dish: grouse with bread sauce and game chips £26.50. Two-course evening meal £24.00.*

Free house ~ Licensee Paul Klein ~ Real ale ~ Open 12-11 ~ Bar food 12-2, 7-9; 12-9 Sun ~ Restaurant ~ Children welcome ~ Dogs allowed in bar and bedrooms ~ Wi-fi ~ Bedrooms: £84/£109 *Recommended by Neil and Angela Huxter, Tracey and Stephen Groves, Gordon and Margaret Ormondroyd, Simon Cleasby, Comus and Sarah Elliott, Clive and Fran Dutson*

ELSLACK
SD9249   Map 7

Tempest Arms
(01282) 842450 – www.tempestarms.co.uk
Just off A56 Earby–Skipton; BD23 3AY

Friendly inn with three log fires in stylish rooms, six real ales, good wines and well regarded food; bedrooms

The comfortable, well equipped bedrooms in this very well run 18th-c stone inn make a perfect base for exploring the beautiful scenery and walks of the Yorkshire Dales. It's a stylish but understated and cosy place with a happy mix of customers and plenty of character in the bar and surrounding dining areas: cushioned armchairs, built-in wall seats with comfortable cushions, stools, plenty of tables and three log fires – one greets you at the entrance and divides the bar and restaurant. There's quite a bit of exposed stonework, amusing prints on cream walls, half a dozen real ales such as Dark Horse Hetton Pale Ale, Naylors Brew 1641, Saltaire Blonde, Theakstons Best Bitter and Thwaites Wainwright on handpump, 12 wines by the glass, 30 malt whiskies and 20 gins; background music and board games. The tables outside are largely screened from the road by a raised bank.

Tempting, highly popular food includes sandwiches, smoked mackerel niçoise salad, chicken and ham terrine with apple chutney, sharing boards, vegetable and lentil cottage pie, chicken skewers with raita dip, bombay potatoes and coleslaw, beef bourguignon, slow-braised lamb with roasted root vegetables and mint and redcurrant gravy, goan fish and seafood curry with pineapple chutney, and puddings such as crème brûlée and sherry trifle. *Benchmark main dish: slow-cooked pork belly with apple sauce, yorkshire pudding and roast gravy £15.50. Two-course evening meal £22.00.*

Individual Inns ~ Managers Martin and Veronica Clarkson ~ Real ale ~ Open 11-11 (10.30 Sun) ~ Bar food 12-2.30, 6-9; 12-7.30 Sun ~ Restaurant ~ Children welcome ~ Dogs allowed in bar and bedrooms ~ Wi-fi ~ Bedrooms: £75/£100 *Recommended by Hilary Forrest, Claes Mauroy, John and Sylvia Harrop, S Holder, John and Eleanor Holdsworth, David Fowler*

FELIXKIRK
SE4684   Map 10

Carpenters Arms 🌟 ♀

(01845) 537369 – www.thecarpentersarmsfelixkirk.com

Village signed off A170 E of Thirsk; YO7 2DP

Stylishly refurbished village pub with spacious rooms, real ales and highly regarded food; lodge-style bedrooms

In a picturesque small village on the edge of the moors, this friendly pub was once a carpenter's workshop. The opened-up bars are spacious and relaxed with dark beams and joists, candlelight and fresh flowers, stools against the panelled counter where they keep Black Sheep Best, Timothy Taylors Boltmaker and a seasonal guest beer on handpump, around 20 wines by the glass and 18 malt whiskies, and a mix of chairs and tables on big flagstones or carpet. There's also a snug seating area with tartan armchairs in front of a double-sided woodburning stove. The red-walled dining room has a mix of antique and country kitchen chairs around scrubbed tables, and the walls throughout are hung with traditional prints, local pictures and maps; background music. There are seats and tables on a raised decked terrace overlooking the landscaped garden and picnic-sets at the front. The ultramodern, well equipped bedrooms come with a drying wardrobe for wet days and a log-effect gas fire – they make a good base for both short walks and long-distance hikes (the Cleveland Way is in the locality); dogs are welcome. This is part of the Provenance Inns group.

 Good inventive food using local produce includes sandwiches, chicken liver and mushroom parfait, marinated goats cheese with tomato, fine bean and lemon dressing, smoked duck breast with celeriac rémoulade, apple and black pudding, burger with toppings, onion rings and chips, herb-crusted free-range chicken with pea risotto and baby leeks, bass with fennel and caper salad and sauce vierge, first-class steaks with a choice of sauce, and puddings such as sticky toffee pudding with cinder toffee ice-cream and caramel sauce and glazed lemon tart with raspberry sorbet; they also offer an early-bird menu (5.30-6.45pm Sun-Fri). *Benchmark main dish: lamb rump with broad beans, pancetta and baby gem £17.95. Two-course evening meal £20.00.*

Free house ~ Licensee Michael Ibbotson ~ Real ale ~ Open 12-11 ~ Bar food 12-2.30, 5.30-9.30; 12-3, 5.30-8 Sun ~ Children welcome ~ Dogs allowed in bar and bedrooms ~ Wi-fi ~ Live music and supper second Sun of month ~ Bedrooms: /£165
Recommended by Harvey Brown, Dr Simon Innes, Jim and Sue James, Mike Benton

GRANTLEY
SE2369   Map 7

Grantley Arms 🌟 ♀

(01765) 620227 – www.grantleyarms.com

Village signposted off B6265 W of Ripon; HG4 3PJ

Relaxed and interesting dining pub with good food

There's plenty of local atmosphere and a warm welcome in this creeper-clad 17th-c country inn and the hospitable licensees are very hands-on. The front bar has a huge fireplace built of massive stone blocks and housing a woodburning stove, beams, traditional furnishings such as comfortable dining chairs and polished tables set with evening tea-lights and some of the landlady's own paintings of ponies and dogs. The back dining room has crisp linen tablecloths, decorative plates and more paintings, mainly landscapes. Theakstons Best and guests from Bradfield, Hambleton and Great Newsome on handpump, nine wines by the glass, eight malt whiskies, a local farm cider and attentive friendly service. Teak tables and chairs on the flagstoned front terrace have a pleasant outlook, and Fountains Abbey and Studley Royal Water Garden (National Trust) is nearby.

Making everything in-house, the enjoyable food includes lunchtime sandwiches and omelettes, cheddar cheese and rocket soufflé, prawn cocktail with avocado purée and lime and cucumber sorbet, butternut squash and feta cheese tart, lager-battered haddock and chips, rare-breed pork belly with apple purée, crackling and red wine sauce, a fresh fish dish of the day, and puddings such as white, dark and milk chocolate terrine with chocolate sauce and kirsch cherries and pear and ginger sponge pudding with custard; they also have a coffee morning menu (from 9am) and a two- and three-course set lunch menu (Tuesday-Saturday). *Benchmark main dish: fish pie £13.95. Two-course evening meal £19.00.*

Free house ~ Licensees Valerie Sails and Eric Broadwith ~ Real ale ~ Open 12-3, 5.30-10.30; 12-3, 5.30-11 Fri, Sat; 12-10.30 Sun; closed Mon except bank holidays ~ Bar food 12-2, 5.30-9 (9.30 Sat); 12-3.30, 5.30-8 Sun ~ Restaurant ~ Well behaved children welcome ~ Wi-fi
Recommended by Kate Moran, Rosie and John Moore, Sophia and Hamish Greenfield, Rona Mackinlay

GRINTON   SE0498   Map 10

Bridge Inn

(01748) 884224 – www.bridgeinn-grinton.co.uk
B6270 W of Richmond; DL11 6HH

Bustling pub with traditional, comfortable bars, log fires, real ales, malt whiskies and tasty bar food; neat bedrooms

On the banks of the River Swale, this former coaching inn is a popular place for a drink or a meal after enjoying one of the good local walks. There's a relaxing, comfortable atmosphere, bow-window seats and a pair of stripped traditional settles among more usual pub seats (all well cushioned), a good log fire and Ascot Single Hop, Jennings Cumberland, Thwaites Wainwright and York Yorkshire Terrier on handpump; also, eight wines by the glass, 20 malt whiskies and ten gins. On the right, a few steps lead down into a room with darts and ring the bull. On the left, past leather armchairs and a sofa next to a second log fire (and a glass chess set), is an extensive two-part dining room with décor in cream and shades of brown, and a modicum of fishing memorabilia. The bedrooms are neat, simple and comfortable, and breakfasts good. There are picnic-sets outside and the lovely church opposite is known as the Cathedral of the Dales.

Popular food includes lunchtime baguettes, smoked mackerel pâté with pickled cucumber, deep-fried brie with cranberry sauce, a risotto of the day, cajun chicken burger with smoked bacon, cheese and barbecue sauce, beer-battered cod and chips, gammon with egg or pineapple, duck breast with garlic mash and star anise jus, and puddings such as toffee apple cheesecake and three-chocolate brownie with dark chocolate rocky road and chocolate sauce. *Benchmark main dish: steak in ale pie £10.95. Two-course evening meal £17.00.*

Jennings (Marstons) ~ Lease Andrew Atkin ~ Real ale ~ Open 12-11 (midnight Sat) ~ Bar food 12-2.30, 6-9; all day weekends ~ Restaurant ~ Children welcome ~ Dogs allowed in bar and bedrooms ~ Wi-fi ~ Bedrooms: £51/£82 *Recommended by Tracey and Stephen Groves*

HALIFAX   SE1027   Map 7

Shibden Mill

(01422) 365840 – www.shibdenmillinn.com
Off A58 into Kell Lane at Stump Cross Inn, near A6036 junction; keep on, pub signposted from Kell Lane on left; HX3 7UL

300-year-old interesting pub with a cosy rambling bar, four real ales and inventive, top class bar food; luxury bedrooms

Tucked away at the bottom of a peaceful wooded valley, this 17th-c restored mill is particularly well run and much enjoyed by our readers. The rambling bar is full of nooks and crannies and the bustling atmosphere is helped along by a good mix of locals and visitors. Some cosy side areas have banquettes heaped with cushions and rugs, well spaced attractive old tables and chairs, and candles in elegant iron holders giving a feeling of real intimacy; also, antique hunting prints, country landscapes and a couple of big log fires. A beer named for them (from Moorhouses) plus Black Sheep, Little Valley Withens IPA and Stod Fold Gold on handpump and 21 wines by the glass from a wide list. There's also an upstairs restaurant; background music. Outside on the pleasant heated terrace are plenty of seats and tables, and the building is prettily floodlit at night. The bedrooms are stylish and well equipped, and there are lovely walks nearby.

Consistently top class food includes venison and chicken liver pâté with quail scotch egg and berries, cod with cauliflower couscous, sorrel and pomegranate, buckwheat and quinoa risotto with spinach and halloumi pancakes, rabbit and tarragon pie, red deer with confit potatoes, young turnips, pickled berries and cumberland sauce, battered monkfish with sweet potato chips, chilli jam and mango yoghurt, charcoal oven-cooked steaks, and puddings such as chocolate and orange soufflé with Grand Marnier custard and rum and banana baba with caramelised banana, toffee mousse and banoffi ice-cream. *Benchmark main dish: local beef fillet £25.00. Two-course evening meal £24.00.*

Free house ~ Licensee Glen Pearson ~ Real ale ~ Open 12-11 (10.30 Sun) ~ Bar food 12-2, 5.30-9; 12-2.30, 5.30-9.30 Fri, Sat; 12-7.30 Sun ~ Restaurant ~ Children welcome ~ Dogs allowed in bar ~ Wi-fi ~ Bedrooms: £100/£125 *Recommended by John and Eleanor Holdsworth, Laura Reid, Gordon and Margaret Ormondroyd*

HARTSHEAD
Gray Ox ⭐🍴 ♀

SE1822 Map 7

(01274) 872845 – www.grayoxinn.co.uk

3.5 miles from M62 junction 25; A644 towards Dewsbury, left on to A62, next left on to B6119, first left into Fall Lane, left into Hartshead Lane – pub on right; WF15 8AL

Handsome dining pub with cosy beamed bars, inventive cooking, real ales, several wines by the glass and fine views

This thoroughly enjoyable and rather smart dining pub is extremely popular for its enticing food and is always packed with cheerful customers. The main bar has a roaring log fire, beams and flagstones, bentwood chairs and leather stools around stripped-pine tables; leading off from here the comfortable carpeted dining areas have bold paintwork, some interesting wallpaper and leather dining chairs around polished tables. There's also a private dining room. Jennings Cocker Hoop, Thwaites Wainwright and a guest beer on handpump, 15 wines by the glass and a cocktail menu; background music. In warm weather the picnic-sets outside are much prized, and fine views through the latticed pub windows look across the Calder Valley to the distant outskirts of Huddersfield – the city lights are pretty at night-time.

Using the best local produce, the imaginative food includes thai-spiced tuna carpaccio with mango, lemongrass and coriander salsa and bean sprout and toasted peanut salad, roasted red pepper and goats cheese terrine with pesto dressing and garlic croûtes, corn-fed chicken breast with confit leg and wild mushroom ballotine, asparagus and broad bean risotto and chive cream, whole lemon sole with brown shrimp and brioche crumb, caesar salad and caper butter, pork belly with black pudding, roast fillet wrapped in parma ham, parsnip purée, stockpot carrots and red wine jus, and puddings such as chocolate and coffee mousse with caramel and coffee jelly and Baileys ice-cream and tonka bean crème brûlée; they also offer a two- and three-course set menu. *Benchmark main dish: beer-battered line-caught haddock and chips £13.00. Two-course evening meal £20.00.*

Banks's (Marstons) ~ Lease Bernadette McCarron ~ Real ale ~ Open 12-3, 6 (5 Fri)-midnight; 12-midnight Sat; 12-11 Sun ~ Bar food 12-2, 6-9 (9.30 Sat); 12-7 Sun ~ Restaurant ~ Children welcome ~ Wi-fi *Recommended by Brian and Anna Marsden, Gordon and Margaret Ormondroyd, Michael Butler*

HELPERBY
Oak Tree ★ ♀ 🛏
SE4370 Map 7

(01423) 789189 – www.theoaktreehelperby.com
Raskelf Road; YO61 2PH

Attractive pub with real ales in friendly bar, fine food in cosy dining rooms and seats on terrace; comfortable bedrooms

Both locals and visitors crowd into this pretty village pub keen to enjoy the good food and well kept ales. The informal bar has church chairs and elegant wooden dining chairs around a mix of wooden tables on old quarry tiles, flagstones and oak floorboards, prints and paintings on bold red walls and open fires; background music. Stools line the counter where they keep Black Sheep Best, John Smiths, Timothy Taylors Landlord and a guest or two on handpump and a dozen wines by the glass. The main dining room has a large woodburner in a huge brick fireplace, a big central flower arrangement, high-backed burgundy and graceful wooden chairs around nice old tables on oak flooring, ornate mirrors and some striking artwork on exposed brick walls. French windows lead out to the terrace where there are plenty of seats and tables for summer dining. Upstairs, a private dining room has a two-way woodburner, a sitting room and doors to a terrace. The bedrooms are comfortable and well equipped. The pub is part of Provenance Inns.

As well as first class steaks and grills, the good, modern food includes sandwiches, garlic and parsley queenie scallops with cheddar and gruyère crust, black pudding and chorizo croquettes with apple jam, pea and mint ravioli with spinach and ricotta salad, cumberland pork sausages with sweet onion and red wine gravy, beer-battered fish and chips, beef bourguignon, barnsley lamb chop with redcurrant and mint glaze and green beans, and puddings such as raspberry mousse with white chocolate truffles and sunken chocolate cake with vanilla ice-cream; they also offer an early-bird menu (before 7pm) and breakfast for non-residents (8-11.30am weekends). *Benchmark main dish: burger with toppings, red slaw, fries and garlic mayonnaise £13.00. Two-course evening meal £20.00.*

Free house ~ Licensee Michael Ibbotson ~ Real ale ~ Open 12-3, 5.30-11; 8am-11pm Sat, Sun ~ Bar food 12-2.30, 5.30-9.30 (8.30 Sun) ~ Restaurant ~ Children welcome ~ Dogs allowed in bar and bedrooms ~ Wi-fi ~ Bedrooms: /£140 *Recommended by Comus and Sarah Elliott, Dr and Mrs R G J Telfer*

HETTON
Angel ★ ♀ 🛏
SD9658 Map 7

(01756) 730263 – www.angelhetton.co.uk
Off B6265 Skipton–Grassington; BD23 6LT

Creeper-covered inn with delicious food, real ales and an excellent wine list; lovely bedrooms

Glorious countryside surrounds this mainly 18th-c former drovers' inn, and to make the most of it many customers stay in the individually styled bedrooms and suites – in a converted barn or the more modern Sycamore Bank opposite; breakfasts are excellent. The most informal area here is the bar-brasserie. This is a fine, panelled and beamed room with standing timbers, a working Victorian farmhouse range set in a big stone fireplace, copper kettles, bed warmers, horsebrasses and the odd gun or two on red-painted walls, and farmhouse and wheelback chairs around wooden tables on carpeting. Black Sheep Best and Dark Horse Craven Bitter and Hetton Pale Ale on handpump, an award-winning wine list with 20 by the glass and a large choice of malt whiskies. The two upmarket restaurant rooms, also beamed and with some timbering, have smart high-backed and plush tub dining chairs arranged around white-clothed tables, with paintings and photographs on gold-leaf wallpapered walls. Tables and chairs on the front terrace are under retractable awnings.

Excellent food using the best local, seasonal produce includes provençale fish soup, poached pear, parma ham and blue cheese salad with truffle honey and candied walnuts, jerusalem artichoke, leek and wild mushroom pie, venison sausages with thyme mash and onion gravy, salmon fillet with prawn sauce and chive mash, duck breast with chorizo and duck croquette, pak choi and orange dressing, 28-day matured sirloin steak with a choice of sauces, and puddings such as blackberry mousse with white chocolate and tarragon ice-cream, blackberry gel and blackberry and sea salt sauce and sticky toffee pudding with butterscotch sauce and crème chantilly. *Benchmark main dish: little moneybags (crisp pastry filled with seafood and lobster sauce) £8.25. Two-course evening meal £23.00.*

Free house ~ Licensee Juliet Watkins ~ Real ale ~ Open 12-11 (11.30 Sat); 12-10.30 Sun ~ Bar food 12-2.15, 6-9.30 (10 Sat); 12-2.30, 6-8.30 Sun ~ Restaurant ~ Children welcome ~ Wi-fi ~ Bedrooms: £135/£150   *Recommended by Peter Smith and Judith Brown, Clive Watkin, W K Wood, Nick Higgins*

LEDSHAM
Chequers 🏅 ♀

SE4529   Map 7

(01977) 683135 – www.thechequersinn.com
1.5 miles from A1(M) junction 42: follow Leeds signs, then Ledsham signposted; Claypit Lane; LS25 5LP

Friendly village pub with hands-on landlord, log fires in several beamed rooms, real ales and interesting food; pretty back terrace

'This is everything that a good pub should be,' says one reader with enthusiasm – and many others agree. It's neatly kept and very well run and the several small, individually decorated rooms have plenty of character, with low beams, log fires, lots of cosy alcoves, toby jugs and all sorts of knick-knacks on the walls and ceilings (cricket fans will be interested to see a large photo in one room of four yorkshire heroes). From the little old-fashioned, panelled-in central servery they offer Brown Cow Sessions Pale Ale, Leeds Best, Theakstons Best, Timothy Taylors Landlord and a guest beer on handpump and eight wines by the glass. The lovely sheltered two-level terrace at the back has lots of tables among roses, and the hanging baskets and flowers are very pretty. RSPB Fairburn Ings reserve is not far and the ancient village church is worth a visit.

Carefully crafted food includes seared scallops with black pudding and minted pea purée, chicken, chorizo and bacon on salad, corned beef hash layered with caramelised onions and potatoes, wild garlic and sweet potato risotto with parmesan, gammon steak with a duck egg, venison fillet medallions with sticky red onion sauce and fondant potato, garlic and rosemary poussin with dauphinoise potatoes and honeyed parsnips, grilled swordfish on ratatouille, duck breast with stir-fried vegetables and soy sauce, rainbow trout with lemon, capers and parsley, and puddings such as crème brûlée and chocolate chip brownie with ice-cream. *Benchmark main dish: steak and mushroom pie £13.45. Two-course evening meal £20.00.*

Free house ~ Licensee Chris Wraith ~ Real ale ~ Open 11-11; 12-6 Sun ~ Bar food 12-9; 12-5 Sun ~ Restaurant ~ Children until 8pm ~ Dogs allowed in bar ~ Wi-fi
Recommended by Alistair Forsyth, Gordon and Margaret Ormondroyd, Noel and Judy Garner, Richard Cole, Denis and Margaret Kilner, Stephen Woad

LEVISHAM
SE8390 Map 10

Horseshoe 🏅 🛏

(01751) 460240 – www.horseshoelevisham.co.uk
Off A169 N of Pickering; YO18 7NL

Friendly village pub with super food, neat rooms, real ales and seats on the village green; bedrooms

Our readers really enjoy their visits to this warmly friendly pub that's run by two brothers. The bustling bars have beams, blue banquettes, wheelback and captain's chairs around a variety of tables on polished wooden floors, vibrant landscapes by a local artist on the walls and a log fire in the stone fireplace; an adjoining snug has a woodburning stove, comfortable leather sofas and old photographs of the pub and the lovely village. Served by the courteous staff are Black Sheep and guests such as Cropton Yorkshire Moors and Timothy Taylors Golden Best on handpump, half a dozen wines by the glass and 15 malt whiskies; background music. There are seats on the attractive green, with more in the back garden. The clean, comfortable bedrooms make a good base for exploring the North York Moors National Park; breakfasts are hearty. The historic church is worth a visit. This is sister pub to the Fox & Rabbit in Lockton.

 Cooked by one of the landlords, the smashing food includes sandwiches, crab and smoked salmon terrine, deep-fried brie and parma ham parcels, nut roast with creamy white wine sauce, sausage and mash with onion gravy, deep-fried haddock and chips, chicken breast wrapped in bacon on creamed leeks, slow-roast pork belly with thyme mash, apple sauce and cider gravy, lamb shank with rosemary mash and minted gravy, and puddings such as coffee and hazelnut roulade and chocolate truffle torte. *Benchmark main dish: steak in ale pie £11.50. Two-course evening meal £19.00.*

Free house ~ Licensees Toby and Charles Wood ~ Real ale ~ Open 11-11 (10.30 Sun) ~ Bar food 12-2, 6-8.30 ~ Children welcome ~ Dogs allowed in bar ~ Wi-fi ~ Bedrooms: £45/£80
Recommended by Sara Fulton, Roger Baker, Stanley and Annie Matthews, Ian Herdman, Ian and Rose Lock, John Robinson

LINTON IN CRAVEN
SD9962 Map 7

Fountaine 🍺

(01756) 752210 – www.fountaineinnatlinton.co.uk
Off B6265 Skipton–Grassington; BD23 5HJ

Neatly kept pub with attractive furnishings, open fires, five real ales and popular food; bedrooms

The Dales countryside surrounding this friendly, civilised inn contains many fine walks and the pretty hamlet merits wandering around too. The bars have beams and white-painted joists in low ceilings, log fires (one in a beautifully carved heavy wooden fireplace), attractive built-in cushioned wall benches and stools around a mix of copper-topped tables, little wall lamps and quite a few prints on the pale walls. John Smiths, Tetleys Cask, Thwaites Original and guests such as Dark Horse Hetton Pale Ale and

Wharfedale Blonde on handpump, 17 wines by the glass and a dozen malt whiskies served by efficient staff; background music, darts and board games. The terrace, looking across the road to the duck pond, has teak benches and tables under green parasols, and the hanging baskets are most attractive. The well equipped bedrooms are in a converted barn behind the pub.

Hearty pub classics include sandwiches, pig cheek croquettes, black pudding and cheese fritter and apple purée, potted smoked mackerel with pickled cucumber and kohlrabi coleslaw, salad platters, mushroom, cranberry and brie wellington with creamy herb sauce, cumberland sausage ring with bacon, cabbage and gravy, steak pie, gammon and eggs, fresh haddock fillet with chips, half a roast duck in ginger, spring onion and honey sauce, slow-braised lamb shank in redcurrant and mint sauce, and puddings such as chocolate fudge brownie and white chocolate cheesecake. *Benchmark main dish: slow-roasted beef in ale with yorkshire pudding £13.50. Two-course evening meal £20.00.*

Individual Inns ~ Manager Christopher Gregson ~ Real ale ~ Open 11-11; 12-10.30 Sun ~ Bar food 12-9 ~ Restaurant ~ Children welcome ~ Dogs allowed in bar ~ Wi-fi ~ Bedrooms: £75/£99 *Recommended by Peter Smith and Judith Brown, Hilary Forrest, Lynda and Trevor Smith, Gordon and Margaret Ormondroyd, B and M Kendall*

LOCKTON
Fox & Rabbit

SE8488   Map 10

(01751) 460213 – www.foxandrabbit.co.uk
A169 N of Pickering; YO18 7NQ

Neatly kept pub with fine views, a friendly atmosphere, real ales and highly regarded food

Set in a lovely spot, this is an attractive pub with a warm welcome for all. The interconnected rooms have beams, panelling and some exposed stonework, wall settles and banquettes, dark pubby chairs and tables on tartan carpet, a log fire and an inviting atmosphere; log flowers, brasses, china plates, prints and old local photographs too. The locals' bar is busy and cheerful and there are panoramic views from the comfortable restaurant – it pays to arrive early to bag a window seat. Black Sheep, Cropton Yorkshire Moors and Timothy Taylors Golden Best on handpump, seven wines by the glass, 12 malt whiskies and home-made elderflower cordial; background music, games machine, pool, juke box and board games. Outside are seats under parasols and some picnic sets. The inn is in the North York Moors National Park, so there are plenty of surrounding walks. They have a caravan site. This is sister pub to the Horseshoe in Levisham.

Good food from a seasonal menu includes sandwiches, smoked salmon with beetroot and crème fraîche, chicken liver and brandy pâté with red onion marmalade, spinach and ricotta cannelloni in tomato sauce, steak in ale pie, sausages with red onion gravy, slow-braised lamb shank with parsley mash and roast cherry tomatoes, pork belly with champ mash, black pudding, apple purée and cider jus, cajun chicken pasta with mixed peppers, and puddings such as lemon and lime cheesecake and crème brûlée. *Benchmark main dish: Whitby fish and chips £12.95. Two-course evening meal £16.00.*

Free house ~ Licensees Toby and Charles Wood ~ Real ale ~ Open 11am-11.30pm ~ Bar food 12-2, 5-8.30 ~ Restaurant ~ Children welcome ~ Dogs allowed in bar ~ Wi-fi *Recommended by Stanley and Annie Matthews, Sara Fulton, Roger Baker, Michael Butler, Ian Herdman, Ian and Rose Lock*

You can send reports directly to us at feedback@goodguides.com

LOW CATTON
SE7053 Map 7

Gold Cup

(01759) 371354 – www.goldcuplowcatton.com

Village signposted with High Catton off A166 in Stamford Bridge or A1079 at Kexby Bridge; YO41 1EA

Friendly, pleasant pub with attractive bars, real ales, decent dependable food, seats in garden and ponies in paddock

For 27 years the hospitable licensees in this comfortable white-rendered house have been offering sustenance to their wide mix of customers. The neatly kept bar has a bustling atmosphere, plenty of smart tables and chairs on stripped wooden floors, quite a few pictures, an open fire at one end opposite a gas-effect stove and coach lights on the rustic-looking walls. The spacious restaurant, with solid wooden pews and tables (said to be made from a single oak tree), has pleasant views of the surrounding fields. Theakstons Best Bitter on handpump; background music and pool. There's a grassed area in the garden for children and the back paddock houses three ponies, Cinderella, Dobbin and Polly. The pub has fishing rights on the adjacent River Derwent.

Popular food includes lunchtime sandwiches, smoked salmon, prawn and crayfish cocktail, beer-battered mushrooms with garlic mayonnaise, steak burger with toppings and chips, home-baked ham in creamy stilton sauce, steak in ale pie, crispy half duck with plum and ginger sauce, bass fillets with roasted vegetables and pesto, and puddings such as bakewell tart and custard and chocolate and brandy torte; they also offer a two- and three-course set candlelit supper menu. *Benchmark main dish: cajun chicken with minted yoghurt dip £11.50. Two-course evening meal £17.00.*

Free house ~ Licensees Pat and Ray Hales ~ Real ale ~ Open 12-2.30, 6-11; 12-11 Sat; 12-10.30 Sun; closed Mon lunchtime ~ Bar food 12-2, 6-9; 12-9 Sat; 12-8 Sun ~ Restaurant ~ Children welcome ~ Dogs allowed in bar ~ Wi-fi *Recommended by Dave Braisted, Gordon and Margaret Ormondroyd*

MALHAM
SD9062 Map 7

Lister Arms

(01729) 830330 – www.listerarms.co.uk

Off A65 NW of Skipton; BD23 4DB

Friendly inn in fine countryside with cosy bars and dining room, Thwaites ales, enjoyable food and seats outside; comfortable bedrooms

The bedrooms in this handsome, creeper-covered inn are attractive, warm and comfortable with views over either the village green or the Yorkshire Dales National Park; breakfasts are good and hearty. One bar has a medley of cushioned dining chairs and leather or upholstered armchairs around antique wooden tables on slate flooring, with a big deer's head above the inglenook fireplace. A second bar has a small brick fireplace with logs piled to each side, rustic slab tables, cushioned wheelback chairs and comfortable wall seats. Thwaites Original Bitter, Lancaster Bomber, Nutty Black, Wainwright and guests such as Dark Horse Hetton Pale Ale and Settle Signal Main Line on handpump, 20 wines by the glass and Weston's farm cider. A woodburning stove stands in the fireplace of the dining room where there are swagged curtains and smartly upholstered high-backed and pale wooden farmhouse chairs around rustic tables on bare floorboards. The flagstoned and gravelled courtyard has seats and benches around tables under parasols; some overlook the small green at the front. Fine walks all around.

🍴 Generous helpings of reliably good food includes sandwiches, sharing boards, salmon and smoked mackerel terrine with lumpfish caviar, mushroom gnocchi with soft herb and butter sauce, burgers with toppings and skinny fries, local pork sausages with crispy onions and onion gravy, duck breast with egg noodles and sweet caramel and soy reduction, smoked cheddar and spinach-stuffed cod tail with pea risotto and chive cream sauce, fine steaks with a choice of sauces, and puddings such as iced pistachio and dark chocolate parfait with mint macaroon and raspberry stew and caramelised lemon tart with citrus creme fraîche and berry crisp. *Benchmark main dish: home-made pies £13.00. Two-course evening meal £21.00.*

Thwaites ~ Manager Darren Dunn ~ Real ale ~ Open 8am-11pm ~ Bar food 12-9.30 (10 Fri, Sat) ~ Restaurant ~ Children welcome ~ Dogs allowed in bar and bedrooms ~ Wi-fi ~ Bedrooms: £84/£90 *Recommended by Dr Simon Innes, Lindy Andrews, John and Sylvia Harrop*

MARTON-CUM-GRAFTON SE4263 Map 7
Punch Bowl 🏅 ⚲

(01423) 322519 – www.thepunchbowlmartoncumgrafton.com
Signed off A1 3 miles N of A59; YO51 9QY

Refurbished old inn in lovely village, with character bar and dining rooms, real ales, interesting food and seats on terrace

'As nice a pub as you could wish for,' says one of our more discerning readers. It's a handsome and particularly well run old inn with many original features: the main bar is beamed and timbered with a built-in window seat at one end, lots of red leather-topped stools, and cushioned settles and church chairs around pubby tables on flagstones or bare floorboards. Black Sheep Best, Rudgate Jorvik Blonde and Timothy Taylors Boltmaker on handpump, 20 wines by the glass and a dozen malt whiskies. Open doorways lead to five separate dining areas, each with an open fire, heavy beams and an attractive mix of cushioned wall seats and wooden or high-backed red dining chairs around antique tables on oak floors; the red walls are covered with photographs of vintage car races and racing drivers, sporting-themed cartoons and old photographs of the pub and village. Up a swirling staircase is a coffee loft and a private dining room. There are seats and tables in the back courtyard where they hold summer barbecues. The pub belongs to the Provenance Inns group.

🏅 Championing local produce, the accomplished food includes sandwiches, smoked duck with watercress and orange salad and soy, ginger and sesame dressing, chicken liver and mushroom parfait with red onion marmalade, sharing platters, wild mushroom ravioli, sea bream fillets with parmentier potatoes, braised fennel and tomato salsa, beer-battered fish and chips, roasted lamb rump with ratatouille and redcurrant jus, pork chop with sage mash, creamy cider and apple sauce and crackling crisp, and puddings such as black forest chocolate cake and vanilla cheesecake with berry compote; they also offer an early-bird menu (5.30-6.45pm; not Sun). *Benchmark main dish: chicken kiev with sweet potato fries and green beans £14.95. Two-course evening meal £23.00.*

Free house ~ Licensee Michael Ibbotson ~ Real ale ~ Open 12-3, 5-11; 12-11.30 Sat; 12-10.30 Sun ~ Bar food 12-2.30, 5.30-9.30; 12-8 Sun ~ Children welcome ~ Dogs allowed in bar ~ Wi-fi *Recommended by Gordon and Margaret Ormondroyd, Ian Duncan, Paul Scofield, Daphne and Robert Staples*

Bedroom prices are for high summer. Even then you may get reductions for more than one night, or (outside tourist areas) weekends. Winter special rates are common, and many inns reduce bedroom prices if you have a full evening meal.

MASHAM

SE2281 Map 10

Black Sheep Brewery

(01765) 680100 – www.blacksheepbrewery.co.uk

Brewery signed off Leyburn Road (A6108); HG4 4EN

Lively place with friendly staff, unusual décor in big warehouse room, well kept beers and popular food

In general, this interesting place is more of a bistro than a pub, though a huge upper warehouse room has a bar serving their own-brewed Black Sheep Best, Ale, Golden Sheep and Riggwelter plus a couple of changing guests on handpump, several wines by the glass and a fair choice of soft drinks. Most of the good-sized tables have cheery gingham tablecloths and brightly cushioned green café chairs, and there are some modern pubbier tables near the bar. The space is partly divided by free-standing partitions and there's a good deal of bare woodwork, with cream-painted rough stonework and green-painted steel girders and pillars; background music and friendly service. The tours of the sizeable brewery are popular and a glass wall lets you see into the brewing exhibition centre; there's also a shop selling beers and beer-related items from pub games and T-shirts to pottery and fudge. Picnic-sets out on the grass.

 Much liked food includes sandwiches, garlic and rosemary baked camembert with celery, apple and walnut salad, game terrine with onion marmalade, pork in ale sausages with onion gravy, macaroni, tomato and cauliflower cheese, cajun chicken with skinny fries, beer-battered fresh haddock and chips, braised lamb shank with creamy sage mash, burger with toppings, onion ring, coleslaw and fries, sticky toffee pudding with stout and toffee sauce and cinnamon doughnuts with hot chocolate sauce. *Benchmark main dish: steak in ale pie £12.50. Two-course evening meal £18.00.*

Free house ~ Licensee Paul Casterton ~ Real ale ~ Open 10-5 Sun-Weds; 10am-11pm Thurs-Sat ~ Bar food 12-2.30 Sun-Weds; 12-2.30, 6-8.30 Thurs-Sat ~ Children welcome ~ Wi-fi
Recommended by Janet and Peter Race, Jeremy Snow, Nigel Havers

MOULTON

NZ2303 Map 10

Black Bull 🏮 ⚲

(01325) 377556 – www.theblackbullmoulton.com

Just E of A1, a mile E of Scotch Corner; DL10 6QJ

Character pub with a traditional bar, a large open restaurant, good choice of drinks, high quality food and courteous efficient service; bedrooms

The friendly bar in this carefully refurbished pub has a convivial feel with high chairs against the counter where they serve Black Sheep Best, Theakstons Boltmaker and a guest beer on handpump, 18 wines by the glass and over 20 malt whiskies. There's some original panelling and leather wall seating topped with scatter cushions, and the dining area has cushioned wooden chairs around a mix of tables on pale flagstones, a couple of leather armchairs in front of a woodburner in a brick fireplace, some horse tack, and stone bottles, wooden pails and copper items on windowsills. The new dining extension with tall windows and a wooden floor has attractive brown-orange high-backed dining chairs or cushioned settles and a rather nice wire bull; background music. Doors from here lead out to a neat terrace with modern seats and tables among pots of rosemary or tall bay trees. They hope to open bedrooms in the near future. This is part of Provenance Inns.

 Highly enjoyable food from a well judged menu includes sandwiches, queenie scallops with thermidor sauce, ham hock terrine, seafood sharing platters, burger with toppings, onion rings and chips, pea and ricotta risotto, home-smoked chicken breast with baby leeks, celeriac and tarragon cream and dauphinoise potatoes, fish pie with lemon and dill velouté and cheddar topping, charcoal-grilled steaks with a choice of sauce, and puddings such as chocolate and peanut indulgence and rhubarb and ginger cheesecake; they also offer an early-bird menu (before 7pm Sun-Fri). *Benchmark main dish: bass fillet with chorizo and shellfish sauce £14.95. Two-course evening meal £20.00.*

Free house ~ Licensee Michael Ibbotson ~ Real ale ~ Open 12-3, 5-11; 12-midnight Sat; 12-11 Sun ~ Bar food 12-2.30, 5.30-9.30; 12-3, 6-9.30 Sun ~ Restaurant evening ~ Children welcome ~ Dogs allowed in bar ~ Wi-fi *Recommended by Michael Doswell, Christopher Mannings*

RIPPONDEN
Old Bridge 🍷 ◗

SE0419 Map 7

(01422) 822595 – www.theoldbridgeinn.co.uk

From A58, best approach is Elland Road (opposite the Golden Lion), park opposite the church in pub's car park and walk back over ancient hump-back bridge; HX6 4DF

Pleasant old pub by medieval bridge with relaxed communicating rooms and well liked food

The third generation of the family run this 14th-c pub which is next to a beautiful medieval packhorse bridge over the little River Ryburn; seats in the garden overlook the water. Inside, the three communicating rooms, each on a slightly different level, have oak settles built into window recesses in the thick stone walls, antique oak tables, rush-seated chairs and comfortably cushioned free-standing settles, a few well chosen pictures and prints on the panelled or painted walls and a big woodburning stove. Timothy Taylors Best, Golden Best, Landlord and Ram Tam, a couple of guests such as Phoenix Arizona and Salopian Oracle on handpump, quite a few foreign bottled beers, 15 wines by the glass, 30 malt whiskies and farm cider; quick, efficient service. If you have trouble finding the pub (there's no traditional pub sign outside), just head for the church.

The ever popular weekday lunchtime cold meat and salad buffet has been running since 1963 (they also offer soup and sandwiches at lunch). Evening and weekend choices include thyme-crusted pigeon, confit ox cheek, roast fig, spinach and wild mushroom butter, venison with roast sweet potato, pistachio crumb, porcini tuille and port wine reduction, beer-battered haddock and dripping chips, a pie of the day, sweet potato, asparagus and spinach malaysian curry, chicken supreme with confit thigh, goats cheese bonbon and thyme and honey jus, and puddings. *Benchmark main dish: seared hake with ballotine of smoked salmon and prawn and lemon beurre blanc £13.75. Two-course evening meal £20.00.*

Free house ~ Licensees Tim and Lindsay Eaton Walker ~ Real ale ~ Open 12-3, 5-11; 12-11.30 Sat; 12-10.30 Sun ~ Bar food 12-2, 5-9 (9.30 Fri, Sat); 12-4 Sun ~ Children allowed until 8pm but must be seated away from bar ~ Wi-fi *Recommended by Brian and Anna Marsden, Dr Kevan Tucker, Steve Whalley*

ROBIN HOOD'S BAY
Laurel

NZ9505 Map 10

(01947) 880400

Bay Bank; village signed off A171 S of Whitby; YO22 4SE

Delightful little pub in unspoilt fishing village with neat friendly bar and real ales; no food

Things here remain quite unchanged and the charming landlord welcomes all to his little local at the bottom of a row of fishermen's cottages. The neatly kept beamed main bar has an open fire and is decorated with old local photographs, Victorian prints and brasses and lager bottles from across the world. There's Adnams Southwold and Theakstons Best and Old Peculier on handpump; darts, board games and background music. In summer, the hanging baskets and window boxes are lovely. They rent out a self-contained apartment for two people. This is one of the prettiest and most unspoilt fishing villages on the north-east coast.

There's no food but you can bring in sandwiches from the tea shop next door and eat them in the pub.

Free house ~ Licensee Brian Catling ~ Real ale ~ No credit cards ~ Open 12-11 (10.30 Sun); 4-11 Mon-Thurs in winter ~ Children in snug bar only ~ Dogs welcome
Recommended by Diane Abbott, Elizabeth and Peter May, Simon and Alex Knight

ROECLIFFE
SE3765   Map 7

Crown 🏅 ♀ 🍺 🛏

(01423) 322300 – www.crowninnroecliffe.com
Off A168 just W of Boroughbridge; handy for A1(M) junction 48; YO51 9LY

Attractively placed pub with a civilised bar, first class enterprising food and a fine choice of drinks; charming bedrooms

Top marks once again from our readers for all aspects of this excellent pub; the hard-working Mainey family continue to welcome the cheerful crowds of both locals and visitors who fill their lovely inn. The bar has a contemporary colour scheme of dark reds and off-whites with pleasant prints carefully grouped and lit; one area has chunky pine tables on flagstones, while another, with a log fire, has dark tables on plaid carpet. Partners Working Class Hero, Timothy Taylors Landlord, Treboom Yorkshire Sparkle Really Pale Ale and a guest ale on handpump, 30 wines by the glass and 15 malt whiskies. For meals, you can choose between a small candlelit olive-green bistro with nice tables, a long-case clock and a couple of paintings, and a more formal restaurant; background music. The garden has rattan sofas and tables on decking. This is a most enjoyable place to stay in cosy, country-style bedrooms. The village green is opposite.

Enticing food using their own smokehouse and home-baked bread includes king prawn tempura with asian salad and sweet chilli dipping sauce, orange smoked duck breast, liver parfait and rillettes with kirsch cherries, calves liver with bacon and madeira jus, bass fillet with crab risotto, crispy fried crab claw, chilli tempura courgette and ginger oil, chicken breast with italian parsley gnocchi, wild mushrooms, dandelion leaves and pancetta, venison loin with potato rösti, sloe gin red cabbage and horseradish, and puddings such as belgian chocolate tart with lime zest and vanilla cream and vanilla crème brûlée with caramelised banana and chocolate and hazelnut biscotti. *Benchmark main dish: fish pie £13.95. Two-course evening meal £22.00.*

Free house ~ Licensee Karl Mainey ~ Real ale ~ Open 12-11; 12-8 Sun ~ Bar food 12-2.30, 6-9.30 12-7 Sun ~ Restaurant ~ Children welcome ~ Dogs allowed in bar and bedrooms ~ Wi-fi ~ Bedrooms: £80/£100 *Recommended by Derek and Sylvia Stephenson, Lesley and Peter Barrett, Tracey and Stephen Groves, Alistair Forsyth, Janet and Peter Race, S Holder, Simon Cleasby, Les and Sandra Brown, Comus and Sarah Elliott, Peter and Anne Hollindale, Richard Cole*

The star-on-a-plate award, 🏅, distinguishes pubs where the food is of exceptional quality. The knife-and-fork symbol just means the pub serves food.

SANCTON

SE9039 Map 7

Star 🌟 ♈ 🍺

(01430) 827269 – www.thestaratsancton.co.uk

King Street (A1034 S of Market Weighton); YO43 4QP

Cheerful bar with four real ales, more formal dining rooms with accomplished food, and a friendly, easy-going atmosphere

Don't be put off by the slightly austere exterior as, once inside, all the attributes of this much loved old pub become clear. There's a bar with a woodburning stove, traditional red plush stools around a mix of tables, and a cheerful atmosphere helped along by the enthusiastic, hard-working licensees. Ales from breweries such as Copper Dragon, Great Newsome and Wold Top are served on handpump from the brick counter and they keep 19 wines by the glass including prosecco and champagne and over 20 malt whiskies. The more formal (though still relaxed) dining rooms have comfortable high-backed dark leather dining chairs around wooden tables on carpeting, and prints on red- or cream-painted walls; background music. There are picnic-sets outside at the back. As this is at the foot of the Yorkshire Wolds Railway, many walkers and cyclists use it as a base for both a pint and a chat and a good meal.

 Highly thought-of and extremely good, the rewarding food (using home-grown ingredients and produce from village allotments) includes sandwiches, duck liver parfait with sweet onion jam, potted beef with sauerkraut, mustard hollandaise and black treacle bread, local sausages with roasted root vegetable mash and ale gravy, oak-roasted salmon caesar salad, calves liver with potato purée, bacon jam and red wine jus, spiced duck breast with leg croquette, foie gras, parsnip purée and duck jus, smoky herb-rolled pork tenderloin with black pudding crumb, leek and sage stuffed onion, creamy onion sauce and cider jus, and puddings such as rhubarb bakewell tart with parkin ice-cream and banana cake with peanut butter parfait, chocolate soil and toffee sauce; they also offer a two- and three-course set lunch (not Sun). *Benchmark main dish: steak in ale pie £14.95. Two-course evening meal £22.00.*

Free house ~ Licensees Ben and Lindsey Cox ~ Real ale ~ Open 12-3, 6-11.30; 12-11 Sun; closed Mon ~ Bar food 12-2, 6-9.30; 12-3, 6-8 Sun ~ Restaurant ~ Children welcome
Recommended by Michael Butler, Gordon and Margaret Ormondroyd, Pat and Graham Williamson

SANDHUTTON

SE3882 Map 10

Kings Arms 🍺

(01845) 587887 – www.thekingsarmssandhutton.co.uk

A167, 1 mile N of A61 Thirsk–Ripon; YO7 4RW

Cheerful pub with friendly service, interesting food and beer, and comfortable furnishings; bedrooms

On race days at nearby Thirsk racecourse, it's best to book way ahead if you want a table in this charming village inn. It's still run by the friendly father and son team and while there's quite a focus on food, there remains a traditional pubby atmosphere. The bar has an unusual circular woodburner in one corner, a high central table with four equally high stools, modern ladder-back wooden dining chairs around light pine tables, a couple of cushioned wicker armchairs, some attractive modern bar stools and photographs of the pub in years gone by. Black Sheep, Rudgate Viking, Theakstons Best, Village Brewer White Boar Bitter and Walls Gun Dog Bitter on handpump, 11 wines by the glass and efficient, friendly service. The two connecting dining rooms have similar furnishings to the bar (plus some high-backed brown leather dining chairs), arty flower photographs on cream walls and a small woodburning stove; background music, darts, board games and TV. There's a small beer garden and they have secure bike storage with air and puncture repair kits and a heated towel rail for drying wet kit.

 Generous helpings of tasty food (in the evening you can talk to the chef and choose the size of meat or fish you'd like and what sauce to go with it) includes sandwiches, prawn and smoked salmon cocktail, spicy lamb kofta with minted sour cream, mixed lentil, spinach and mushroom pie with ricotta mash topping, chilli con carne, burger with toppings and chips, fish pie, bass fillets with rosemary, lemon, sea salt and mash, lamb rack with haggis mash and whisky gravy, and puddings such as lemon curd bread and butter pudding and fruits of the forest eton mess. *Benchmark main dish: salmon, cod and prawn fishcake with sweet chilli sauce £10.50. Two-course evening meal £17.50.*

Free house ~ Licensees Raymond and Alexander Boynton ~ Real ale ~ Open 12-11 (midnight Sat); 12-10 Sun ~ Bar food 12-2.30, 5.30-9; 12-9 Sat; 12-5 Sun ~ Restaurant ~ Children welcome ~ Dogs allowed in bar ~ Wi-fi ~ Bedrooms: $45/$70
Recommended by Michael Butler, Jeremy Snaithe, Helena and Trevor Fraser

SHEFFIELD
SK4086 Map 7

Kelham Island Tavern ◀ £
(0114) 272 2482 – www.kelhamtavern.co.uk
Kelham Island; S3 8RY

Busy little local with fantastic real ales, basic but decent lunchtime food, a friendly welcome and pretty back garden

The knowledgeable, well organised and friendly staff in this busy tavern keep the 13 interesting ales on handpump in tip top condition. There's always a mild and a stout or porter on offer and their regulars include Abbeydale Deception, Acorn Barnsley Bitter, Bradfield Farmers Blonde and Pictish Brewers Gold, with guests from breweries such as Arbor, Blue Bee, Brass Castle, Dark Star, Hop Studio, North Riding, Siren Craft, Tiny Rebel and Yorkshire Dales; also, a changing craft beer, a german wheat beer, a belgian fruit beer, an interesting range of bottled ales, two farm ciders and around 30 malt whiskies. It's a busy backstreet local with a wide array of cheerful customers and pubby furnishings; dominoes and board games. The unusual flower-filled back courtyard garden has plenty of seats and tables, and the front window boxes regularly win awards.

 Tasty and very good value pubby food – served weekday lunchtimes only – includes sandwiches, locally made pork pies and lunchtime hot dishes such as casseroles, mushroom and red pepper stroganoff, burgers with chips and various curries. *Benchmark main dish: steak in ale pie £5.50.*

Free house ~ Licensee Trevor Wraith ~ Real ale ~ Open 12-midnight ~ Bar food 12-3 (not weekends) ~ Children allowed in back room ~ Dogs welcome ~ Live folk Sun evenings
Recommended by Sharon and John Hancock, Pat and Tony Martin

SOUTH DALTON
SE9645 Map 8

Pipe & Glass ⭐ ♀ 🛏
(01430) 810246 – www.pipeandglass.co.uk
West End; brown sign to pub off B1248 NW of Beverley; HU17 7PN

Yorkshire Dining Pub of the Year

Attractive dining pub with exceptional food, real ales in bar, good service, garden and front terrace; stylish bedrooms

'The perfect pub,' says one reader with huge enthusiasm – and indeed, it's a pretty inn with wonderful food, a proper bar, first class service and stylish bedrooms. What more could you want? The beamed and bow-windowed bar has copper pans hanging above a woodburning stove in the sizeable fireplace, cushioned window seats and high-backed wooden dining chairs around a mix of tables (each set with a church candle) and some old prints. There's Black Sheep, Two Chefs (named for them from Great Yorkshire) and a couple of guest beers on handpump, 15 wines by the glass, 40 malt whiskies and a farm cider. Service is prompt and friendly. Beyond, all is airy and comfortably contemporary, angling around some chunky button-back leather chesterfields and armchairs (where there's another woodburner) into a light restaurant area overlooking the park, with similar tables and chairs on bare boards; background music. There are tables on the garden's peaceful lawn and picnic-sets on the front terrace; the yew tree is said to be 500 years old. As well as two stylish rooms with their own little terrace and views over Dalton Park, there are now three luxury suites. The village is charming and its elegant Victorian church spire, 62 metres tall, is visible for miles around.

Stunning food, beautifully presented and cooked by the chef-landlord, includes lunchtime sandwiches, guinea fowl and ham hock ballotine with scampi fritter, pease pudding and air-dried ham, cider-cured wild sea trout with radishes, caviar, dill, squid ink cracker and crispy quail egg, local pork sausages with bubble and squeak and onion, ale and sage gravy, grilled and deep-fried goats cheese with baby leeks, salt-baked beetroot, smoked beetroot purée and hazelnut milk, free-range chicken breast with tarragon forcemeat, peas, gem lettuce, girolle mushrooms, crisp pancetta and champ potato, beef fillet with salt beef niçoise salad, salt beef pasty and horseradish hollandaise, and puddings such as strawberry and white chocolate cheesecake with strawberry lime and basil sorbet, black pepper and a sesame tuile and hot dark chocolate 'millionaire' pudding with salted burnt butter ice-cream. *Benchmark main dish: roast partridge with black pudding, parsnips and burnt apple purée £24.00. Two-course evening meal £30.00.*

Free house ~ Licensees Kate and James Mackenzie ~ Real ale ~ Open 12-11 (10.30 Sun); closed Mon except bank holidays ~ Bar food 12-9.30; 12-4 Sun ~ Restaurant ~ Children welcome ~ Wi-fi ~ Bedrooms: /£180 *Recommended by Mary Kirkwood, Michael Doswell, Chris Stevenson, Penny and David Shepherd, Tim and Sarah Smythe-Brown*

THORNTON WATLASS   SE2385   Map 10
Buck

(01677) 422461 – www.buckwatlass.co.uk
Village signposted off B6268 Bedale–Masham; HG4 4AH

Honest village pub with five real ales, a traditional bar and dining room, well liked food and popular Sunday jazz; bedrooms

This is very much a community pub, where you can be sure of a warm welcome from the licensees. The pleasantly traditional bar on the right has upholstered wall settles on carpet, a fine mahogany bar counter, local artwork on the walls and a brick fireplace; background music, TV and board games. The Long Room (overlooking the cricket green) has photos, prints and other memorabilia from Thornton Watlass cricket teams past and present, and is the venue for the Sunday afternoon jazz sessions. Black Sheep, Theakstons Best, Walls Gun Dog Bitter and a guest such as Small World Long Moor Pale on handpump, eight wines by the glass and a dozen interesting malt whiskies. The sheltered garden has a well equipped children's play area. The bedrooms have been recently refurbished.

🍴 Popular food includes sandwiches and wraps, deep-fried whitebait with tartare sauce, battered chicken strips with sweet chilli dip, spinach and ricotta cannelloni, lasagne, lambs liver with bacon and onion gravy, haddock on new potatoes with chorizo and red pepper sauce, gammon with egg and pineapple, chicken casserole, lamb rump with red wine and rosemary jus, steaks with a choice of sauce, and puddings. *Benchmark main dish: steak in ale pie £10.95. Two-course evening meal £15.00.*

Free house ~ Licensees Victoria and Tony Jowett ~ Real ale ~ Open 12-11 (10.30 Sun) ~ Bar food 12-2, 6-9; 12-3, 6-8.30 Sun ~ Restaurant ~ Children welcome ~ Dogs allowed in bar and bedrooms ~ Wi-fi ~ Live trad jazz some Sun lunchtimes (best to phone) ~ Bedrooms: £55/£85 *Recommended by Belinda Stamp, Dave Braisted, Richard Kennell*

WELBURN　　　　　　　　　　　　　　　　　　SE7168　Map 7

Crown & Cushion ♀ ◀

(01653) 618777 – www.thecrownandcushionwelburn.com

Off A64; YO60 7DZ

Plenty of dining and drinking space in well run inn with real ales and particularly good food – and seats outside

---

Our readers really enjoy their visits to this carefully refurbished and extended 18th-c inn. The little tap room has rustic tables and chairs on wide floorboards, high stools around an equally high central table, beams and timbering, with Black Sheep, Brass Castle Malton Amber, Rudgate Jorvik and York Guzzler on handpump and 19 wines by the glass served by friendly, helpful staff. The other attractively refurbished, interconnecting rooms are for dining and on different levels: smart high-backed chairs mix with wooden ones and an assortment of cushioned settles and wall seats around various tables on flagstones or red and black floor tiles. There are open fires and a woodburning stove, old prints of the pub and local scenes on painted or exposed stone walls and lots of horsebrasses, copper pans and kettles and old stone bottles; background music. Contemporary tables and chairs are arranged on a terrace with picnic-sets below and a long-reaching view across to the Howardian Hills. The pub is handy for Castle Howard. This is part of the Provenance Inns group.

🍴 Rewarding food includes sandwiches, queenie scallops with gruyère, cheddar and garlic butter, confit rabbit and tea-braised prune terrine, moules frites, wild mushroom and cheese pancakes with mushroom cream and truffle oil, cumberland sausage and mash with onion gravy, fish pie, barnsley lamb chop with parmentier potatoes and mint and redcurrant glaze, venison loin with port reduction and fondant potato, and puddings such as dark chocolate and coffee marquise with candied hazelnuts and salted caramel and lemon meringue parfait with blackberry compote; they also offer an early-bird menu (5.30-6.45pm). *Benchmark main dish: pork fillet, slow-roasted belly, potato and apple rösti, creamy mushroom sauce £15.95. Two-course evening meal £21.00.*

Free house ~ Licensee Michael Ibbotson ~ Real ale ~ Open 12-3, 5.30-11; 12-11 Fri-Sun ~ Bar food 12-3, 5.30-9 (9.30 Fri, Sat); 12-8 Sun ~ Restaurant ~ Children welcome ~ Dogs allowed in bar ~ Wi-fi *Recommended by Caroline Prescott, Belinda Stamp, Simon Sharpe, Pat and Graham Williamson, Mike Benton*

'Children welcome' means the pub says it lets children inside without any special restriction. If it allows them in, but to restricted areas such as an eating area or family room, we specify this. Some pubs may impose an evening time limit. We do not mention limits after 9pm as we assume children are home by then.

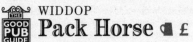

WIDDOP
SD9531 Map 7

Pack Horse ◀ £

(01422) 842803 – www.thepackhorse.org

The Ridge; from A646 on W side of Hebden Bridge, turn off at Heptonstall signpost (as it's a sharp turn, coming out of Hebden Bridge the road signs direct you around a turning circle), then follow Slack and Widdop signposts; can also be reached from Nelson and Colne, on high, pretty road; OS Sheet 103 map reference 952317; HX7 7AT

Friendly pub up on the moors and liked by walkers for generous, tasty honest food, four real ales and lots of malt whiskies

Considering its isolation high up on the moors, this friendly, traditional walkers' pub is remarkably popular as a cosy haven. The bar has welcoming winter fires, window seats cut into the partly panelled stripped-stone walls (from where you can take in the beautiful views), sturdy furnishings and horsey mementoes. Black Sheep and Thwaites Wainwright plus guests such as Cottage Conquest and Greyhawk Blonde Obsession on handpump, over 100 single malt whiskies and some irish ones, and 11 wines by the glass. The friendly golden retrievers are called Padge and Purdey. There are seats outside in the cobblestoned beer garden and pretty summer hanging baskets. They have a smart self-catering apartment for rent.

 Warming, hearty food includes sandwiches, devilled mackerel, potted duck with cranberries, macaroni cheese with garlic bread, sausage and mash with sizzled onions, beef, Guinness and mushroom pie, salmon en croûte with lobster sauce, beef bourguignon, confit duck leg with bubble and squeak, caramelised pear and rosemary and garlic jus, corn-fed chicken kiev with sautéed potatoes, and puddings. *Benchmark main dish: rack of lamb with a changing jus £13.95. Two-course evening meal £19.00.*

Free house ~ Licensee Andrew Hollinrake ~ Real ale ~ Open 12-3, 5.30-11; 12-11 Sat, Sun; closed Mon except bank holidays; no weekday lunchtime opening in winter ~ Bar food 12-2, 5.30-9; 12-7 Sun ~ Children welcome ~ Dogs welcome *Recommended by Diane Abbott, Alan and Alice Morgan, Simon and Alex Knight*

YORK
SE5951 Map 7

Maltings ◀ £

(01904) 655387 – www.maltings.co.uk

Tanners Moat/Wellington Row, below Lendal Bridge; YO1 6HU

Bustling, friendly city pub with cheerful landlord, interesting real ales and other drinks plus good value standard food

With amazing value food and around eight real ales, this busy, friendly pub is run by a jovial, hard-working landlord. The atmosphere is bustling and cheerful and the tricksy décor is strong on salvaged, somewhat quirky junk: old doors for the bar front and much of the ceiling, a marvellous collection of railway signs and amusing notices, an old chocolate dispensing machine, cigarette and tobacco advertisements alongside cough and chest remedies, what looks like a suburban front door for the entrance to the ladies', partly stripped orange brick walls and even a lavatory pan in one corner; games machine. The day's papers are framed in the gents'. The beers on handpump include Black Sheep and Golden Sheep, Elland Red River IPA, Errant Tusk, Ghost Reaper, Pheasantry Stout, Roosters Yankee and York Guzzler. They also keep six continental beers on tap, four craft beers, lots of bottled beers, six farm ciders, 15 country wines and 25 whiskies from all over the world. Nearby parking is difficult; the pub is very handy for the National Railway Museum and the station. Please note that dogs are allowed only after food service has finished.

Incredibly cheap, decent food includes sandwiches and toasties, baked potatoes with lots of fillings, mushroom and spinach lasagne, ham and egg, sausage and beans, chilli tacos, and beef in ale pie. *Benchmark main dish: cheesy chips £4.40.*

Free house ~ Licensee Shaun Collinge ~ Real ale ~ No credit cards ~ Open 11am-11.30pm; 12-10.30 Sun ~ Bar food 12-2 weekdays; 12-4 weekends ~ Children allowed only during meal times ~ Wi-fi ~ Live music Mon and Tues evenings
Recommended by Eddie Edwards, Dr J Barrie Jones, Roger and Donna Huggins

Also Worth a Visit in Yorkshire

Besides the fully inspected pubs, you might like to try these pubs that have been recommended to us and described by readers. Do tell us what you think of them: feedback@goodguides.com

ADDINGHAM   SE0749
Craven Heifer (01943) 830106
Main Street; LS29 0PL Very good food (not Sun evening, Mon) from bar snacks to upmarket restaurant choices including a seven-course tasting menu, friendly efficient service, four well kept ales such as Black Sheep and Saltaire, pebble-floored bar with restaurant areas off, open fires; cookery classes and wine tasting events; a few tables in front, seven individually styled bedrooms, open all day (Mon till 6pm). *(Simon Sharpe)*

AINDERBY STEEPLE   SE3392
Wellington Heifer (01609) 775718
A684, 3 miles from A1; opposite church; DL7 9PU Nicely refurbished late 18th-c pub with four connecting rooms, flagstone floors and log fires, comfortable scatter-cushion bench seating and sturdy tables, good range of beers and wines from carved counter, enjoyable food including good value lunchtime/early evening set menu, restaurant at end of corridor; children welcome, two well appointed bedrooms, open and food all day Sun. *(Peter Hacker, Michael Doswell)*

AINTHORPE   NZ7007
Fox & Hounds (01287) 660218
Brook Lane; YO21 2LD Traditional beamed moorland inn dating from the 16th c, tranquil setting with sheep grazing freely and wonderful views; nice open fire in unusual stone fireplace, comfortable seating, well kept Theakstons ales and good choice of wines by the glass, generous fairly priced food including daily specials, friendly staff, restaurant, games room; free wi-fi; dogs welcome (great walks from the door), seven bedrooms and attached self-catering cottage in 18th-c buildings, open all day. *(Douglas Power)*

AISLABY   SE8508
Forge (01947) 811522
Main Road, off A171 W of Whitby; YO21 1SW Refurbished mellow stone village pub with opened-up interior, light wood floor, upholstered wall benches and woodburner in brick fireplace, well kept ales such as Black Sheep from small central servery, good home-made food at sensible prices including popular Sun roasts served till 7pm, friendly accommodating staff; Tues quiz; children and dogs welcome, six bedrooms. *(John Robinson)*

ALDBOROUGH   SE4166
Ship (01423) 322749
Off B6265 just S of Boroughbridge, close to A1; YO51 9ER Attractive 14th-c beamed village dining pub adjacent to medieval church, good home-made food from sandwiches and pub standards up including early-bird deal, cheerful helpful service, well kept Black Sheep and Theakstons, extensive affordably priced wine list, some old-fashioned seats around cast-iron-framed tables, lots of copper and brass, inglenook fire, candlelit back restaurant; children and dogs welcome, a few picnic-sets outside, handy for Roman remains and museum, open all day weekends, closed Mon lunchtime, food till 6pm Sun. *(Peter Hacker)*

AMPLEFORTH   SE5878
★ **White Swan** (01439) 788239
Off A170 W of Helmsley; East End; YO62 4DA Popular stone-built village pub, beamed lounge with carpeted or slate floors, sporting prints and two-way woodburner, locals' bar with further beams and standing timbers, patterned wall seating and log fire, more formal dining area has plush furnishings and linen-clothed tables, good food from traditional choices up, Black Sheep and Theakstons, decent wines by the glass and ten malt whiskies, friendly service; background music, pool, darts and dominoes; children welcome, back terrace overlooking valley, open all day weekends. *(Simon and Alex Knight)*

APPLETON-LE-MOORS   SE7388
★ **Moors** (01751) 417435
N of A170, just under 1.5 miles E of Kirkby Moorside; YO62 6TF Traditional stone-built village pub, beamed bar with

built-in high-backed settle next to old kitchen fireplace, plenty of other seating, some sparse decorations (a few copper pans, earthenware mugs, country ironwork), three changing regional ales and over 50 malt whiskies, tasty fair value food, friendly helpful staff; background music, darts; children and dogs welcome, tables in lovely walled garden with quiet country views, walks to Rosedale Abbey or Hartoft End, eight double bedrooms, open all day. *(Ann and Tony Bennett-Hughes)*

APPLETON-LE-STREET   SE7373

Cresswell Arms (01653) 693647

B1257/Appleton Lane; YO17 6PG Modernised stone-built country inn dating from the 1800s, pleasant carpeted bar with log fire, good-sized bare-boards restaurant with pine furniture and fittings, well kept Wold Top and enjoyable pubby food (all day Sun) from sandwiches up; children welcome, ten bedrooms, closed Mon and Tues lunchtimes in winter. *(Michael Butler)*

APPLETREEWICK   SE0560

Craven Arms (01756) 720270

Off B6160 Burnsall–Bolton Abbey; BD23 6DA Character creeper-clad 16th-c beamed pub, cushioned settles and rugs on flagstones, fire in old range, gas lighting and some interesting pictures and bric-a-brac, up to eight well kept ales including a house beer from Dark Horse, several wines by the glass, home-made food from baguettes up, friendly helpful service, small dining room and splendid thatched and raftered cruck barn with gallery; free wi-fi; children, dogs and muddy boots welcome (plenty of surrounding walks), wheelchair access, nice country views from front picnic-sets, more seats in back garden, open all day. *(Hilary Forrest, Gordon and Margaret Ormondroyd)*

ARNCLIFFE   SD9371

★**Falcon** (01756) 770205

Off B6160 N of Grassington; BD23 5QE Basic no-frills country tavern in lovely setting on village green, coal fire in small bar with elderly furnishings, well kept Timothy Taylors Landlord and a guest either from handpump or tapped direct from cask to stoneware jugs in central hatch-style servery, inexpensive simple lunchtime food, friendly service, attractive watercolours, sepia photographs and humorous sporting prints, back sun room overlooking pleasant garden; quiz first Fri of month; children till 9pm and dogs welcome, four miles of trout fishing, nice walks, five bedrooms (two with own bathroom), breakfast and evening meal for residents. *(Claes Mauroy, Neil and Angela Huxter, Peter Smith and Judith Brown)*

ASKRIGG   SD9491

Crown (01969) 650387

Main Street; DL8 3HQ Open-plan local in James Herriot village, three areas off main bar, open fires (one in old-fashioned range), enjoyable simple pub food at reasonable prices including deals, Black Sheep, Theakstons and a guest, friendly buzzy atmosphere; children, walkers and dogs welcome, tables outside, open all day. *(Nick Higgins)*

ASKRIGG   SD9491

Kings Arms (01969) 650113

Signed from A684 Leyburn–Sedbergh in Bainbridge; DL8 3HQ Popular 18th-c coaching inn (the Drovers in TV's *All Creatures Great and Small*) under same ownership as the Charles Bathurst at Langthwaite and the Punch Bowl at Low Row; high-ceilinged flagstoned main bar with good log fire, traditional furnishings and décor, a couple of well kept house beers from nearby Yorkshire Dales plus Black Sheep, Theakstons and a guest, 13 wines by the glass, enjoyable reasonably priced food including some evening offers, friendly efficient service, more modern restaurant with inglenook, games room in former barrel-vaulted beer cellar; background music, TV; children and dogs (in bar) welcome, side courtyard, bedrooms run separately as part of Holiday Property Bond complex behind, open all day. *(Tracey and Stephen Groves, John and Enid)*

AUSTWICK   SD7668

★**Game Cock** (01524) 251226

Just off A65 Settle–Kirkby Lonsdale; LA2 8BB Quaint civilised place in pretty spot below Three Peaks; friendly old-fashioned beamed back bar with bare-boards and good log fire, well kept Thwaites and a guest, winter mulled wine and nice coffee, cheerful efficient staff, plenty of emphasis on french chef-owner's good fairly priced food, two refurbished restaurant areas and small conservatory-style extension; children, walkers and dogs welcome, garden with play equipment, four bedrooms, closed Mon, otherwise open all day (till 1am if busy). *(Colin Hammond)*

AYSGARTH   SE0188

Aysgarth Falls (01969) 663775

A684; DL8 3SR Creeper-clad moorland hotel refurbished under present licensees, good food and welcoming accommodating service, ales such as Black Sheep, Theakstons and Wensleydale in log-fire bar where dogs welcome, comfortable eating areas, some interesting ancient masonry at the back recalling its days as a pilgrims' inn; great scenery near broad waterfalls, 11 bedrooms, camping (adults only). *(Mary Hunstings)*

AYSGARTH   SE0088

★**George & Dragon** (01969) 663358

Just off A684; DL8 3AD Welcoming 17th-c posting inn with emphasis on good locally sourced food from sandwiches up, two big dining areas and small beamed and panelled bar with log fire, well kept ales including Black Sheep, Theakstons and a house beer from Yorkshire Dales, good choice of wines by the glass, friendly helpful staff; may be background music, free wi-fi; children and dogs (in bar) welcome, nice paved garden, lovely scenery and walks, handy for Aysgarth Falls, seven bedrooms, open all day. *(Malcolm and Jane Levitt)*

BAILDON   SE1538
Junction (01274) 582009
Baildon Road; BD17 6AB Friendly wedge-shaped local with three traditional linked rooms, seven well kept ales including own Junction brews (July festival), generous helpings of good value home-made food (weekday lunchtimes), games part with pool; live music Sun evening, Thurs quiz, sports TV; children welcome, open all day. *(Andy Barker)*

BARKISLAND   SE0419
★**Fleece** (01422) 820687
B6113 towards Ripponden; HX4 0DJ Large well renovated and extended 18th-c beamed moorland dining pub, very good popular food including weekday set menu, efficient friendly uniformed staff, Timothy Taylors Landlord and a couple of other well kept ales such as Ilkley and Stod Fold; background music; children welcome, front disabled access, lovely Pennine views from first-floor terrace and garden, summer barbecues, five bedrooms, handy for M62, open all day from 8am for breakfast, food till 7pm Sun. *(Gordon and Margaret Ormondroyd)*

BARMBY-ON-THE-MARSH   SE6828
Kings Head (01757) 630705
High Street; DN14 7HT Renovated and extended early 19th-c beamed village pub, good locally sourced food including some imaginative choices, Yorkshire tapas, Sun lunchtime carvery, four well kept local ales, bar, lounge and restaurant, deli (home-baked bread to order); children welcome, disabled access/facilities, open all day weekends, closed Mon and Tues lunchtimes. *(Laura Reid)*

BARNSLEY   SE3203
Strafford Arms (01226) 287488
Near Northern College, about 2.5 miles NW of M1 junction 36; S75 3EW Pretty stone-built village pub owned by Fine & Country Inns; opened-up contemporary interior, decent choice of food (some cooked in Josper grill) from lunchtime sandwiches and platters up, local ales such as Timothy Taylors and Bradfield, good range of wines and cocktails, friendly service, log fires including one in big Yorkshire range; Tues

quiz, free wi-fi; children, dogs and muddy boots welcome, garden with play area, on Trans Pennine Trail and by entrance to Wentworth Castle, open (and food) all day. *(Gordon and Margaret Ormondroyd)*

BEDALE   SE2688
Old Black Swan (01677) 422973
Market Place; DL8 1ED Popular old pub with attractive bay-window façade, well kept ales including Theakstons and generous helpings of good value food, friendly efficient staff, log fire; darts, pool, sports TV; children and dogs welcome, disabled facilities, small covered back terrace, Tues market, open all day. *(Jeremy Snaithe)*

BEVERLEY   TA0339
★**White Horse** (01482) 861973
Hengate, off North Bar; HU17 8BN Timeless place known locally as Nellie's; carefully preserved Victorian interior with basic little rooms huddled around central bar, brown leatherette seats (high-backed settles in one little snug) and plain chairs and benches on bare boards, antique cartoons and sentimental engravings, gas-lighting including chandelier, coal fires, more space upstairs, bargain Sam Smiths and guests, straightforward food, friendly staff; charity quiz Tues, games room; children till 7pm, no dogs inside, courtyard picnic-sets, open all day. *(Simon Sharpe)*

BEVERLEY   TA0239
Woolpack (01482) 867095
Westwood Road, W of centre; HU17 8EN Small proper pub in pair of 19th-c cottages kept spotless by welcoming landlady, highly thought-of traditional food at reasonable prices including Tues pie-and-pint night, seven well kept Marstons-related beers, open fires and simple furnishings, brasses, knick-knacks and prints, cosy snug; Thurs quiz; contemporary seats and tables in beer garden, open all day weekends. *(C A Hall)*

BILTON   SE4750
Chequers (01423) 359637
Pub signed just off B1224; YO26 7NN Quietly placed cream-washed village inn; well kept Black Sheep, Timothy Taylors and a summer guest, nice selection of wines by the glass and hearty helpings of good freshly made often interesting food from hot and cold sandwiches up, linked areas with comfortable seating including leather armchairs and banquettes, woodburner, some open shelving separating part-panelled dining room; picnic-sets in small garden with extensive country views, three bedrooms, open all day (food all day weekends). *(John and Eleanor Holdsworth, Michael Doswell)*

There are report forms at the back of the book.

BINGLEY   SE1039
Brown Cow (01274) 564345
*B6429 just W of junction with A650;
BD16 2QX* Open-plan pub in nice riverside
spot (recent renovations after flood damage),
Timothy Taylors range and good choice of
enjoyable food including various burgers,
friendly staff; quiz Tues, live music Sat;
children and dogs welcome, tables out on
sheltered terrace, open all day. *(John and
Eleanor Holdsworth)*

BINGLEY   SE1242
Dick Hudsons (01274) 552121
Otley Road, High Eldwick; BD16 3BA
Well run Vintage Inn family dining pub
named after a former landlord, their usual
reasonably priced food including set menu
choices, Black Sheep, Marstons and Timothy
Taylors, lots of wines by the glass, efficient
friendly young staff; tables outside with great
views over Baildon Moor, open all day.
*(Gordon and Margaret Ormondroyd,
John and Eleanor Holdsworth)*

BIRSTWITH   SE2459
★**Station Hotel** (01423) 770254
Off B6165 W of Ripley; HG3 3AG
Welcoming immaculately kept stone-built
Dales pub; bar, log-fire restaurant and garden
room, good sensibly priced home-made food
from extensive menu including lunchtime/
early evening set deal, four local ales and
14 wines by the glass, friendly efficient
staff; open mike and quiz nights; tables in
landscaped garden with heated smokers'
shelter, picturesque valley, five bedrooms,
open (and food) all day. *(John and Eleanor
Holdsworth)*

BISHOPTHORPE   SE5947
Woodman (01904) 706507
*Village signed just off A64 York S bypass;
Main Street; YO23 2RB* Welcoming
open-plan pub with good range of enjoyable
food cooked by landlord-chef including
OAP weekday menu and other deals, four
regional ales and decent choice of wines
by the glass, friendly efficient service,
woodburner; background music; children and
dogs welcome, seats out in front and in large
back garden with play equipment, handy for
York racecourse, open all day. *(Gordon and
Margaret Ormondroyd, Rob Jones)*

BOLTON ABBEY   SE0754
Devonshire Arms (01756) 710441
B6160; BD23 6AJ Comfortable and elegant
18th-c hotel in wonderful position on edge of
Bolton Abbey Estate; good if pricey food from
light meals up in bright modern brasserie-
bar, good service, contemporary paintings
(some for sale) on roughcast walls, colourful
armchairs around cast-iron-framed tables on
pale wood floor, well kept Copper Dragon
ales and good wines by the glass, afternoon
teas, more formal restaurant; tables in

spacious courtyard with extensive views,
Estate and Strid river valley walks, bedrooms
in old and new wings. *(WAH)*

BRADFIELD   SK2692
Old Horns (0114) 285 1207
High Bradfield; S6 6LG Welcoming
old stone pub in hill village with stunning
views; good hearty food including themed
evenings, bargain weekday lunchtime deal
and Sun carvery, can eat in part-flagstoned
bar or carpeted pitch-roofed dining room,
half a dozen predominantly Thwaites beers,
friendly helpful staff; background music, Tues
quiz, TV; children welcome, raised terrace
taking in the view, picnic-sets and play area
in garden, next to interesting 14th-c church,
good walks, open all day. *(Roger and Pauline
Pearce)*

BRADFORD   SE1533
Fighting Cock (01274) 726907
Preston Street (off B6145); BD7 1JE
Busy bare-boards traditional alehouse by
industrial estate, a dozen well kept changing
ales, foreign draught/bottled beers and real
ciders, friendly staff and lively atmosphere,
all-day sandwiches plus good simple
lunchtime hot dishes (not Sun), may be free
bread and dripping on the bar, coal fires;
dogs welcome, open all day. *(Andrew and
Michele Revell)*

BRADFORD   SE1633
Sparrow Bier Café (01677) 470411
North Parade; BD1 3HZ Bare-boards bar
with great selection of bottled beers, draught
continentals and local real ales, friendly
knowledgeable staff, good deli platters and
pies, local artwork, more tables in cellar
bar; background music; open all day.
(Douglas Power)

BRADFORD   SE1938
Stansfield Arms (0113) 250 2659
*Apperley Lane, Apperley Bridge; off
A658 NE; BD10 0NP* Popular ivy-clad
pub dating from the 16th c, enjoyable food
including daily specials and early-bird deal,
well kept Black Sheep, Timothy Taylors
Landlord and a guest, friendly helpful
service, beams, stripped stone and dark
panelling, open fires, restaurant; children
welcome, tables out on front decking,
pleasant setting, open all day till midnight
(1am Fri, Sat) and can get very busy.
(John and Eleanor Holdsworth)

BRAMHAM   SE4242
Swan (01937) 843570
Just off A1 2 miles N of A64; LS23 6QA
Unspoilt and unchanging little local up steep
hill from village square – also known as the
'Top Pub'; friendly atmosphere and good
mix of customers, well kept Black Sheep,
Hambleton and Leeds Pale, no food, two coal
fires; open all day. *(Les and Sandra Brown,
Michael Butler)*

BRANTINGHAM   SE9329
Triton (01482) 667261
Ellerker Road; HU15 1QE Spacious
comfortably refurbished and extended old
stone pub, good choice of enjoyable home-
made food in bar and restaurant, three
local ales, good friendly service; children,
walkers and dogs welcome, tables out at front
and in sheltered back garden, open all day
weekends (food all day Sat, till 6.30pm Sun).
(John Robinson)

BREARTON   SE3260
★**Malt Shovel** (01423) 862929
*Village signposted off A61 N of
Harrogate; HG3 3BX* Welcoming 15th-c
dining pub; heavily beamed rooms with two
open fires and woodburner, attractive mix
of tables and chairs on wood or slate floors,
some partitioning separating several eating
areas, good food from light lunches up,
helpful friendly staff, well kept Black Sheep,
Timothy Taylors Landlord and a guest from
linenfold oak counter, plenty of wines by the
glass, airy conservatory; children welcome,
tables under parasols in garden and pretty
summer hanging baskets, circular walks
from the pub, closed Sun evening, Mon.
(Mr and Mrs D Hammond)

BRIDGE HEWICK   SE3370
Black-a-moor (01765) 603511
*Boroughbridge Road (B6265 E of
Ripon); HG4 5AA* Roomy family-run dining
pub with wide choice of popular home-
cooked food including good value early-bird
deal (lunchtime and evening), well kept
local beers and good selection of wines,
friendly young staff, sofas and woodburner
in bar area; free wi-fi; children welcome,
comfortable bedrooms. *(Edward and William
Johnston)*

BROUGHTON   SD9450
★**Bull** (01756) 792065
A59; BD23 3AE Handsome carefully
refurbished old inn, flagstones, exposed stone
walls and lots of pale oak, built-in wall seats
and mix of dining chairs around polished
tables, open fires, good brasserie-style food
including set menu Mon-Thurs, a house beer
from Thwaites (1709 – the date the pub was
built) and three guests, a couple of proper
ciders, ten wines by the glass from extensive
list and several malt whiskies, good friendly
service; children and dogs (in bar) welcome,
rattan furniture on attractive front terrace,
garden behind, can walk through Broughton
Estate's 3,000 acres of lovely parkland, open
(and food) all day. *(Steve Whalley, John and
Sylvia Harrop, David Norris)*

BUCKDEN   SD9477
Buck (01756) 761401
B6160; BD23 5JA Steps up to large
creeper-clad stone-built pub-hotel;
modernised and extended open-plan bar, log

fire (stag's head above) and flagstones in
original core, restaurant with high-backed
chairs at linen-clothed tables, ample
helpings of enjoyable food including daily
specials, well kept Theakstons and guests,
friendly helpful staff; children and dogs
welcome, terrace with good surrounding
moorland views, popular walking spot,
12 bedrooms, good breakfast, open (and
food) all day. *(Peter Smith and Judith Brown)*

BURN   SE5928
★**Wheatsheaf** (01757) 270614
*Main Road (A19 Selby–Doncaster);
YO8 8LJ* Welcoming busy 19th-c roadside
pub; comfortable seats in partly divided
open-plan bar with masses to look at – air
force wartime memorabilia, gleaming copper
kettles, polished buffalo horns, cases of
model vans and lorries, decorative mugs
above one bow-window seat, a drying rack
over the log fire, well kept Copper Dragon,
Timothy Taylors and four guests, 20 malt
whiskies, straightforward good value food
(not Sun-Tues evenings), roast only on Sun;
games machine, TV and may be unobtrusive
background music; children and dogs
welcome, picnic-sets on terrace in small back
garden, open all day. *(Hilary Forrest)*

BURNSALL   SE0361
★**Red Lion** (01756) 720204
B6160 S of Grassington; BD23 6BU
Family-run 16th-c inn in lovely spot by River
Wharfe, refurbished panelled restaurant
with oak flooring and woodburner, more
traditional back bar, good imaginative food
together with pub favourites, well kept ales
such as Copper Dragon and Timothy Taylors,
nice wines, efficient friendly service; children
welcome, tables out on front cobbles and on
big back terrace, views across to Burnsall
Fell, comfortable bedrooms (dogs allowed in
some and the bar), fishing permits available,
open all day, food all day weekends. *(Martin
and Anne Muers)*

BURTON LEONARD   SE3263
★**Hare & Hounds** (01765) 677355
*Off A61 Ripon–Harrogate, handy for
A1(M) junction 48; HG3 3SG* Civilised
and welcoming 19th-c village dining pub;
good popular food (not Tues) from lunchtime
sandwiches up using fresh local ingredients,
set menu choices, well kept ales such as
Black Sheep and Theakstons, nice wines by
the glass and decent coffee, efficient friendly
service, cosy carpeted bar with woodburner,
large dining area beyond; children in eating
areas, pretty little back garden, closed Mon.
(Peter Hacker)

CARLTON   SE0684
Foresters Arms (01969) 640272
Off A684 W of Leyburn; DL8 4BB
Old stone pub owned by local co-operative;
log fire bar with dark low beams and
flagstones, four well kept Yorkshire-

brewed ales and good range of popular affordably priced food (not Sun evening, Mon), carpeted restaurant; events such as book club, children's cookery classes and fortnightly Tues quiz; dogs welcome, disabled access, a few picnic-sets out at front, pretty village in heart of Yorkshire Dales National Park, lovely views, three bedrooms, open all day weekends, closed Mon lunchtime (and Tues lunchtime in winter). *(Alan and Alice Morgan)*

CARLTON HUSTHWAITE   SE4976
Carlton Inn   (01845) 501265
Butt Lane; YO7 2BW Cosy modernised beamed dining pub; good fairly priced food cooked by landlady including daily specials and lunchtime/early evening set menu, cheerful helpful service, John Smiths and Theakstons, local cider, mix of country furniture including some old settles, open fire; children welcome, dogs in back bar area, garden picnic-sets, open all day Sun, closed Mon. *(Walter and Susan Rinaldi-Butcher, Dr and Mrs R G J Telfer)*

CARPERBY   SE0089
Wheatsheaf   (01969) 663216
1 mile NW of Aysgarth; DL8 4DF Friendly early 19th-c inn set in quiet Dales village and popular with walkers; cosy traditional bar with nice warm fire, three or four well kept ales including Black Sheep and Jennings, enjoyable good value home-cooked food, lounge and dining room; children and dogs welcome, 13 comfortable bedrooms (James Herriot spent his honeymoon here in 1941), good breakfast, lovely walks to Aysgarth Falls, open all day. *(Randy Alden)*

CARTHORPE   SE3083
★ Fox & Hounds   (01845) 567433
Village signed from A1 N of Ripon, via B6285; DL8 2LG Neatly kept pub under long-serving owners and emphasis on good well presented food, attractive high-raftered restaurant with lots of farm and smithy tools, Black Sheep and Worthington in L-shaped bar with two log fires, plush seating, plates on stripped beams and evocative Victorian photographs of Whitby, some theatrical memorabilia in corridors, good friendly service; background classical music; children welcome, handy for A1, closed Mon and first week Jan. *(Simon and Alex Knight)*

CATTAL   SE4455
Victoria   (01423) 330249
Station Road; YO26 8EB Bustling Victorian-themed dining pub with extensive choice of good attractively presented food (should book), charming attentive service, well kept ales including one from local Rudgate named for the landlord, good value wines; children welcome, picnic-sets in gravelled back garden, closed lunchtime (except Sun) and all day Mon, handy for the station. *(Les and Sandra Brown)*

CAWOOD   SE5737
Ferry   (01757) 268515
King Street (B1222 NW of Selby), by Ouse swing bridge; YO8 3TL Interesting 16th-c inn with several comfortable areas, low beams and stripped brickwork, woodburner in massive inglenook, enjoyable food including Fri steak night and other deals, five well kept ales; Tues bingo, Aug charity music festival, sports TV; children and dogs welcome, nice flagstone terrace and lawn down to river, bedrooms, open all day Thurs-Sun, otherwise from 4pm (until 1am Fri and Sat). *(Nick Higgins)*

CHAPEL-LE-DALE   SD7477
★ Old Hill Inn   (01524) 241256
B5655 Ingleton–Hawes, 3 miles N of Ingleton; LA6 3AR Welcoming former farmhouse with fantastic views to Ingleborough and Whernside; clean rustic interior with beams, log fires and bare-stone recesses, straightforward furniture on stripped-wood floors, nice pictures and some interesting local artefacts, Black Sheep, Dent and a guest, good wholesome food including lovely puddings (look out for the landlord's sugar sculptures), separate dining room and sun lounge, relaxed chatty atmosphere; children welcome, dogs in bar, wonderful remote surrounding walks, two bedrooms and space for five caravans, open all day Sat, closed Mon. *(Lynda and Trevor Smith)*

CLAPHAM   SD7469
New Inn   (01524) 251203
Off A65 N of Settle; LA2 8HH Stylishly renovated 18th-c riverside inn in famously pretty village, good well presented food in bar or restaurant including some interesting vegetarian options, local ales such as Copper Dragon, friendly staff, three open fires; children and dogs welcome, tables outside, walk to Ingleborough Cave or more adventurous hikes, 20 neat, attractive bedrooms. *(Michael Butler)*

CLIFTON   SE1622
★ Black Horse   (01484) 713862
Westgate/Coalpit Lane; signed off Brighouse Road from M62 junction 25; HD6 4HJ Friendly 17th-c inn-restaurant, pleasant décor, front dining rooms with good interesting food including a few pubby dishes, can be pricey, efficient uniformed service, open fire in back bar with beam-and-plank ceiling, well kept Timothy Taylors Landlord and a house beer brewed by Brass Monkey, decent wines; nice courtyard, 21 comfortable bedrooms, pleasant village, open all day. *(Michael Butler)*

CLOUGHTON   SE9798
Falcon   (01723) 870717
Pub signed just off A171 out towards Whitby; YO13 0DY Big 19th-c country inn set in five-acre grounds, well divided

opened-up interior including log-fire lounge and dining conservatory, enjoyable freshly made pubby food from sandwiches to daily specials, Theakstons and a guest, good choice of wines, distant sea view from end windows; background music; children welcome, picnic-sets in neat walled garden, good walks (leave muddy boots by the door), eight bedrooms and 11 glamping pods, closed Mon, Tues in winter. *(Ian and Jane Irving)*

CLOUGHTON NEWLANDS TA0195

Bryherstones (01723) 870744

Newlands Road, off A171 in Cloughton; YO13 0AR Traditional stone pub with several interconnecting rooms including dining room up on right and flagstoned stable-theme bar on left, very well liked food using locally sourced meat, Timothy Taylors and a house beer from Wold Top, good friendly service, games room (pool and darts); children and dogs welcome, picnic-sets and play area in sheltered back garden, closed lunchtimes Mon–Weds. *(Sandra and Nigel Brown)*

COLEY SE1226

Brown Horse (01422) 202112

Lane Ends, Denholme Gate Road (A644 Brighouse–Keighley, a mile N of Hipperholme); HX3 7SD Popular roadside pub with enjoyable reasonably priced home-made food (not Sun evening), Brakspears, Saltaire, Timothy Taylors Landlord and a guest, cheerful helpful staff, open fires, small back conservatory overlooking beer garden; children welcome, no dogs inside, open all day. *(John and Eleanor Holdsworth, Gordon and Margaret Ormondroyd)*

COLTON SE5444

★Old Sun (01904) 744261

Off A64 York–Tadcaster; LS24 8EP Top notch cooking at this extended 18th-c beamed dining pub, good wine list with plenty available by the glass, well kept Black Sheep and local guests (proper bar area), friendly competent staff; cookery demonstrations and little shop selling home-made and local produce; children welcome, seats out on sunny front terrace, bedrooms in separate building, open all day Fri–Sun, closed Mon, Tues lunchtime. *(Christian Mole, John and Eleanor Holdsworth)*

CONEYTHORPE SE3958

★Tiger (01423) 863632

2.3 miles from A1(M) junction 47; A59 towards York, then village signposted (and brown sign to Tiger Inn); bear left at brown sign in Flaxby); HG5 0RY Spreading red-carpeted bar with hundreds of pewter tankards hanging from ochre-painted joists, olde-worlde prints, china

figurines in one arched alcove, padded grey wall seats, pews and settles around sturdy scrubbed tables, open fire, more formal back dining area, tasty sensibly priced food from lunchtime sandwiches through pub favourites, also set deals, well kept Black Sheep, Copper Dragon and Timothy Taylors Landlord, good range of wines, friendly helpful staff; background music; picnic-sets on front gravel terrace and on small green opposite, open all day. *(Margaret and Peter Staples)*

COXWOLD SE5377

Fauconberg Arms (01347) 868214

Off A170 Thirsk–Helmsley, via Kilburn or Wass; easily found off A19 too; YO61 4AD 17th-c village pub with heavily beamed flagstoned bar, log fires in both linked areas (one in unusual arched fireplace in a broad low inglenook), some attractive oak chairs made by local craftsmen alongside more usual pub furnishings, old local photographs and copper implements, Theakstons and a couple of guests, proper cider and good range of malt whiskies, friendly service, traditional home-cooked food, friendly staff, elegant, gently upmarket dining room; live music some weekends, pool, free wi-fi; children welcome, dogs in bar, views from terrace over fields to Byland Abbey (EH), picnic-sets on front cobbles, eight comfortable bedrooms, open all day; for sale last we heard, so things may change. *(John Harris, Gus Swan, Richard Kennell)*

CROPTON SE7588

New Inn (01751) 417330

Village signposted off A170 W of Pickering; YO18 8HH Modernised village pub with own Great Yorkshire beers and guests (can tour brewery for £7.50 – includes a pint); public bar with plush seating, panelling and small fire, downstairs conservatory (doubles as visitor centre at busy times) and elegant restaurant with local artwork, fairly straightforward food from sandwiches up; background music, TV, games machine, darts and pool; well behaved children and dogs (in bar) welcome, garden and brewery shop, bedrooms, open all day. *(Laura Reid)*

DACRE BANKS SE1961

★Royal Oak (01423) 780200

B6451 S of Pateley Bridge; HG3 4EN Popular solidly comfortable 18th-c pub with Nidderdale views, good traditional food (not Sun or Mon evenings) along with daily specials and events such as summer seafood festivals, attentive friendly staff, well kept Greene King ales and good choice of wines by the glass, interesting selection of gins too,

---

Pubs close to motorway junctions are listed at the back of the book.

beams and panelling, log-fire dining room, games room with darts, dominoes and pool; background music, TV, free wi-fi; children welcome in eating areas, terrace and informal back garden, three bedrooms, big breakfast, open all day. *(Michael Butler)*

DANBY   NZ7008
Duke of Wellington (01287) 660351
West Lane; YO21 2LY 18th-c creeper-clad inn overlooking village green, usually four Yorkshire ales such as Copper Dragon and Daleside, enjoyable home-made food from shortish menu; clean tidy bedrooms. *(Millie and Peter Downing)*

DARLEY   SE1961
Wellington Inn (01423) 780362
B6451; Darley Head; HG3 2QQ Extended roadside stone inn with fine Nidderdale views, beams and big open fire in bar, modern restaurant with light wood floor and small conservatory, enjoyable freshly made food including weekday set lunch, well kept Black Sheep, Copper Dragon, Timothy Taylors and Tetleys, helpful friendly staff; children and dogs (in bar) welcome, seats on large grassed area, 12 bedrooms, good breakfast, open all day. *(Julie Braeburn)*

DEWSBURY   SE2622
Huntsman (01924) 275700
Walker Cottages, Chidswell Lane, Shaw Cross – pub signed; WF12 7SW Cosy low-beamed converted cottages alongside urban-fringe farm, lots of agricultural bric-a-brac and blazing log fire, small front bar, Timothy Taylors Landlord and three guests, well priced home-made food (lunchtimes Tues-Sat, evenings Thurs, Fri till 7.30pm), quiet relaxed atmosphere; open all day weekends, closed Mon. *(Michael Butler)*

DEWSBURY   SE2421
★West Riding Licensed Refreshment Rooms (01924) 459193
Station (Platform 2), Wellington Road; WF13 1HF Convivial three-room early Victorian station bar, eight well kept changing ales, foreign bottled beers and farm ciders, good value food such as burgers and pizzas, friendly staff, lots of railway memorabilia and pictures, coal fire; juke box and live music; children till 6pm in two end rooms, disabled access, on Transpennine Rail Ale Trail, open all day. *(Simon Sharpe)*

DONCASTER   SE5702
Corner Pin (01302) 340670
St Sepulchre Gate West, Cleveland Street; DN1 3AH Traditional corner pub with plush beamed lounge and cheery public bar, five well kept ales, good value traditional home-made food including popular Sun lunch; juke box, TV, Sun quiz; seats on back decking, open all day. *(Nick Higgins)*

DONCASTER   SE5703
Marketplace Alehouse
07505 829106 *Market Place; DN1 1ND* Popular little wood and tiled bar in the market square, real ales, craft beers and extensive bottled range, wines by the glass too and well liked/priced food including deli boards and tapas, friendly knowledgeable staff; unobtrusive background music; closed Sun, Mon and evening Tues, otherwise open all day. *(Nick Higgins)*

DUNNINGTON   SE6751
Windmill (01904) 481898
Hull Road (A1079); YO19 5LP Large fairly modern dining pub serving generous helpings of popular home-made food, welcoming friendly staff, good range of beers and other drinks, back conservatory; children welcome, picnic-sets in garden behind, ten bedrooms, open (and food) all day. *(Simon and Alex Knight)*

EASINGWOLD   SE5270
★George (01347) 821698
Market Place; YO61 3AD Neat, bright and airy market town hotel (former 18th-c coaching inn), quiet corners even when busy, helpful cheerful service, well kept Black Sheep, Timothy Taylors and a guest, good sensibly priced food in bar and restaurant, beams, horsebrasses and warm log fires, slightly old-fashioned feel and popular with older customers; pleasant bedrooms, good breakfast. *(Chris Stevenson)*

EAST MARTON   SD9050
Cross Keys (01282) 844326
A59 Gisburn–Skipton; BD23 3LP Spacious refurbished 17th-c pub behind small green looking down on Leeds & Liverpool Canal; black beams, bare boards and patterned carpet, woodburner in big stone fireplace, good food from hot and cold sandwiches, sharing plates and pub favourites up, well kept Copper Dragon and Greyhawk ales, friendly service, further dining area down steps; background music; children, walkers and dogs welcome, picnic-sets on front deck, near Pennine Way, open (and food) all day weekends in winter, may open all day in summer. *(Chilliski, John and Sylvia Harrop)*

EAST MORTON   SE0941
Busfeild Arms (01274) 563169
Main Road; BD20 5SP Attractive 19th-c stone-built village pub (originally a school); traditionally furnished beamed and flagstoned bar with woodburner, Saltaire, Timothy Taylors, Tetleys and a guest, good range of enjoyable well priced food including gluten-free menu, weekday early-bird deal (5.30-6.30pm), efficient cheerful service, restaurant; Thurs quiz, live music Sat, sports TV; children welcome, picnic-sets on front terrace,

three bedrooms, open all day, food till 6pm Sun. *(Gordon and Margaret Ormondroyd)*

EAST WITTON   SE1487
★ **Cover Bridge Inn**   (01969) 623250
A6108 out towards Middleham; DL8 4SQ
Cosy and welcoming 16th-c flagstoned country local, good choice of well kept Yorkshire-brewed ales and decent, generously served pub food at sensible prices, small restaurant, roaring fires; children and dogs welcome, riverside garden with play area, three bedrooms, open all day. *(Sandra and Nigel Brown)*

EBBERSTON   SE8983
Grapes   (01723) 859273
High Street (A170); YO13 9PA
Modernised roadside pub under new management, plenty of emphasis on their good well presented food from short if not particularly cheap menu, nice wines and a couple of real ales such as Greene King; children and dogs welcome. *(Sara Fulton, Roger Baker)*

EGTON   NZ8006
★ **Wheatsheaf**   (01947) 895271
Village centre; YO21 1TZ 19th-c village pub of real character, interesting pictures and collectables in small bare-boards bar with fire in old range, very good generously served food including daily specials, friendly service, Black Sheep, Timothy Taylors Landlord and a summer guest, several wines by the glass, restaurant; four bedrooms in adjacent cottage, closed Mon, no food Sun evening. *(John Robinson)*

EGTON BRIDGE   NZ8005
Horseshoe   (01947) 895245
Village signed off A171 W of Whitby; YO21 1XE Attractively placed 18th-c stone inn; open fire, high-backed built-in winged settles, wall seats and spindleback chairs, various odds and ends including a big stuffed trout (caught nearby in 1913), Theakstons Best and a couple of guests, popular food using their own eggs and vegetables and locally sourced meat; background music, free wi-fi; children welcome, dogs in side bar during mealtimes, seats on quiet terrace in nice mature garden by small River Esk, good walks (on Coast to Coast path), six bedrooms, open all day weekends. *(Melanie and David Lawson)*

EGTON BRIDGE   NZ8005
★ **Postgate**   (01947) 895241
Village signed off A171 W of Whitby; YO21 1UX Moorland village pub next to station; good imaginative food at fair prices including fresh local fish, friendly staff, well kept Black Sheep and a guest, traditional

quarry-tiled bar with beams, panelled dado and coal fire in antique range, elegant restaurant; children and dogs welcome, walled front garden with picnic-sets either side of brick path, three nice, clean bedrooms. *(Melanie and David Lawson)*

ELLAND   SE1021
Barge & Barrel   (01422) 371770
Quite handy for M62 junction 24; Park Road (A6025, via A629 and B6114); HX5 9HP Large roadside pub by Calder & Hebble Navigation, own-brew beers along with plenty of guests such as Abbeydale, Black Sheep, Milltown and Timothy Taylors, pubby food including Fri steak night, lounge bar, snug with open fire and games room; Thurs quiz and occasional live music; children welcome, waterside seats and moorings, limited parking, open all day. *(Jane Sutton)*

ELLAND   SE1019
Golden Fleece   (01422) 372704
Lindley Road, handy for M62 junction 24; HX5 0TE Comfortable country pub next to cricket field; good plentiful home-made food including daily specials, well kept local ales, cheerful service, bar with woodburner at one end, restaurant; also own nearby farm shop, closed Mon lunchtime, otherwise open all day (food all day weekends). *(Gordon and Margaret Ormondroyd)*

EMBSAY   SE0053
Elm Tree   (01756) 790717
Elm Tree Square; BD23 6RB Popular open-plan beamed village pub, hearty helpings of good value food (different lunchtime and evening menus) including blackboard specials, four well kept ales such as Tetleys and Thwaites, cheerful young staff; comfortable bedrooms, handy for Embsay Steam Railway. *(Martin Denbigh)*

FERRENSBY   SE3660
★ **General Tarleton**   (01423) 340284
A655 N of Knaresborough; HG5 0PZ Carefully renovated 18th-c coaching inn, more restaurant-with-rooms than pub, but there's an informal bar with sofas and woodburner serving well kept Black Sheep, Timothy Taylors Landlord and a dozen wines by the glass; other open-plan rooms with low beams, brick pillars creating alcoves, exposed stonework and dark leather high-backed dining chairs around wooden tables, first class modern cooking from owner-chef along with more traditional food and children's menu, pleasant well trained staff; seats in covered courtyard and tree-lined garden, pretty country views, 13 stylish bedrooms, good breakfast. *(Janet and Peter Race, Peter and Anne Hollindale)*

If you know a pub is ever open all day, please tell us.

FILEY TA1180

Bonhommes (01723) 514054

The Crescent; YO14 9JH Friendly bustling bar with several well kept ales including one badged for them, popular food such as home-made pizzas; live music and quiz nights; children and dogs welcome, open all day till late. *(Simon Sharpe)*

FINGHALL SE1889

★Queens Head (01677) 450259

Off A684 E of Leyburn; DL8 5ND Welcoming comfortable dining pub, log fires either end of low-beamed carpeted bar with stone archway, settles making stalls around big tables, four real ales such as Theakstons and Wensleydale, good food from deli boards and traditional favourites up including lunchtime and early evening set menus, efficient service, extended back dining room with Wensleydale view; children welcome, no dogs inside, disabled facilities, back garden with decking sharing same view, three bedrooms, may stay open all day on busy weekends. *(Clive and Fran Dutson)*

FIXBY SE1119

Nags Head (01727) 871100

New Hey Road, by M62 junction 24 south side, past Hilton; HD2 2EA Spacious ivy-covered chain dining pub, appealing outside and comfortable in, pubby bar with four well kept ales, wide choice of enjoyable food, friendly helpful service, linked areas with wood and slate floors, restaurant on two levels; garden tables, bedrooms in adjoining Premier Inn, open all day from 7am. *(Gordon and Margaret Ormondroyd)*

GARGRAVE SD9253

Masons Arms (01756) 749510

Church Street/Marton Road (off A65 NW of Skipton); BD23 3NL Traditional beamed pub with welcoming local atmosphere; open interior divided into bar, lounge and restaurant, log fire, ample helpings of enjoyable home-made food at very fair prices, well kept ales such as Black Sheep, Copper Dragon, Tetleys and Timothy Taylors from ornate counter, friendly efficient staff; live acoustic music first Fri of month in winter, darts; children and dogs welcome, tables out behind overlooking own bowling green, charming village on Pennine Way and not far from Leeds & Liverpool Canal, six barn conversion bedrooms, open (and food) all day. *(Beth Aldridge)*

GIGGLESWICK SD8164

★Black Horse (01729) 822506

Church Street – take care with the car park; BD24 0BE Hospitable licensees at this 17th-c village pub prettily set by church; cosy bar with gleaming copper and brass, bric-a-brac and coal-effect fire, good value generously served food, well

kept Timothy Taylors, Tetleys and guests, quick friendly service, intimate dining room; piano (often played), monthly quiz; children welcome till 9pm, no dogs, heated back terrace, smokers' shelter, three reasonably priced comfortable bedrooms, good breakfast, open all day weekends; still for sale as we went to press, but business as usual. *(Simon and Alex Knight)*

GIGGLESWICK SD8164

Harts Head (01729) 822086

Belle Hill; BD24 0BA Cheerful bustling 18th-c village inn, comfortable carpeted bar/lounge with five well kept changing real ales such as Black Sheep and Copper Dragon, good choice of enjoyable reasonably priced food, restaurant, residents' snooker room; sports TV, quiz night; children and dogs welcome, picnic-sets on sloping lawn, ten bedrooms, open all day Fri-Sun, closed lunchtimes Tues, Thurs. *(Simon and Alex Knight, Diane Abbott)*

GILLAMOOR SE6890

★Royal Oak (01751) 431414

Off A170 in Kirkbymoorside; YO62 7HX Stone-built 18th-c dining pub with interesting locally sourced food at sensible prices including daily specials, friendly staff, ales such as Black Sheep and Copper Dragon, reasonably priced wines, roomy bar with heavy dark beams, log fires in two tall stone fireplaces (one with old kitchen range), overspill dining room where dogs allowed; children welcome, eight comfortable modern bedrooms, good breakfast, attractive village handy for Barnsdale Moor walks. *(Ian and Rose Lock)*

GILLING EAST SE6176

★Fairfax Arms (01439) 788212

Main Street (B1363, off A170 via Oswaldkirk); YO62 4JH Smartly presented country inn, beamed bar with bare boards by handsome oak counter, carpeted area with woodburner, Black Sheep, Tetleys and a couple of local guests, interesting wines by the glass, two-part carpeted dining room with big hunting prints on red walls, nicely old-fashioned floral curtains and some padded oak settles, modern food plus pubby choices, neat aproned staff; picnic-sets out in front by floodlit roadside stream, pleasant village well placed for Howardian Hills and North York Moors, comfortable up-to-date bedrooms, good breakfast, open all day, food till 7pm Sun; new orangery planned. *(Rosie and John Moore)*

GILLING WEST NZ1805

White Swan (01748) 825122

High Street (B6274 just N of Richmond); DL10 5JG Welcoming 17th-c village inn with open-plan bar and dining room, log fires, well kept ales including a house beer from Mithril, good home-made food from Yorkshire tapas, through burgers and fresh fish to steaks, Sat brunch, friendly helpful staff; children and dogs welcome, courtyard tables, four bedrooms, open all day (from 4pm Tues). *(Comus and Sarah Elliott)*

GLUSBURN   SD9944
Dog & Gun   (01535) 633855
Colne Road (A6068 W); BD20 8DS
Sizeable stone-built pub, attractive inside and out, and popular for its wide choice of good generously served food, cheerful helpful staff, well kept Timothy Taylors ales, two roaring log fires; children welcome, tables out in front and on small roof terrace, open (and food) all day. *(Douglas Power)*

GOATHLAND   NZ8200
Mallyan Spout Hotel
(01947) 896486 *Opposite church; YO22 5AN* Old creeper-clad stone hotel with three spacious lounges and traditional bar, roaring fires and fine views, popular fairly priced bar food including Sun lunchtime carvery, three real ales, good malt whiskies and wines, friendly helpful staff, smart restaurant (separate evening menu); well behaved children welcome in eating areas, dogs in bar, handy for namesake waterfall, comfortable bedrooms and good buffet breakfast, open all day.
(Jane Sutton)

GOODMANHAM   SE8943
Goodmanham Arms   (01430) 873849
Main Street; YO43 3JA Unpretentious little red-brick country pub (not to everyone's taste) with three traditional linked areas, beam-and-plank ceilings, some red and black floor tiles, mix of furniture and plenty of interesting odds and ends, even a Harley-Davidson, seven real ales – three from on-site All Hallows microbrewery, unfussy food from italian owner (no starters) including a winter casserole cooked over the open fire, evening meals served 5-7pm Mon (steak and pie night then) and Fri only, occasional acoustic music; outside gents'; children and dogs welcome, good walks (on Wolds Way), open all day. *(Simon Sharpe)*

GRANGE MOOR   SE2215
Kaye Arms   (01924) 840228
Wakefield Road (A642); WF4 4BG
Smartly updated dining pub divided into three distinct areas, very popular good value food including deals, well kept ales such as Black Sheep and plenty of wines by the glass, efficient friendly service; children welcome, handy for National Coal Mining Museum, open all day weekends. *(Michael Butler, Gordon and Margaret Ormondroyd)*

GRASSINGTON   SE0064
★ Devonshire   (01756) 752525
The Square; BD23 5AD Handsome old stone hotel recently acquired by Timothy Taylors and refurbished; cheerful bustling atmosphere, good window seats and tables outside overlooking sloping village square, five of their well kept ales plus Saltaire Blonde and several wines by the glass, enjoyable well priced food from sandwiches, sharing plates and pub favourites up, helpful friendly service, woodburners in bar and spacious restaurant; background music; children and dogs (in part of bar) welcome, eight comfortably updated bedrooms, open (and food) all day. *(Peter Smith and Judith Brown, B and M Kendall)*

GRASSINGTON   SE0064
Foresters Arms   (01756) 752349
Main Street; BD23 5AA Comfortable opened-up coaching inn with friendly bustling atmosphere, six well kept regional ales such as Black Sheep and Tetley, good reasonably priced hearty food including pizzas, cheerful helpful service, log fires; popular quiz Mon, sports TV, darts and pool; children and dogs welcome, a few tables out at front, seven affordable bedrooms, good breakfast, open all day. *(Jeff Davies)*

GREAT AYTON   NZ5610
Royal Oak   (01642) 200283
Off A173 – follow village signs; High Green; TS9 6BW Popular 18th-c village inn with good promptly served food including set menu (till 6.30pm), well kept Caledonian Deuchars IPA and Theakstons, convivial bar with log fire, beam-and-plank ceiling and bulgy old partly panelled stone walls, traditional furnishings including antique settles, pleasant views of elegant green from bay windows, two linked dining rooms, back one appealingly old-fashioned and catering for tour groups; children welcome, dogs in bar, four comfortable bedrooms, handy for Cleveland Way, open (and food) all day.
(WAH)

GREAT BROUGHTON   NZ5405
Bay Horse   (01642) 712319
High Street; TS9 7HA Big creeper-clad dining pub in attractive village, wide choice of food including blackboard specials and good value set lunch, friendly attentive service, real ales such as Camerons and Jennings, restaurant; children welcome (under-5s till 8pm), seats outside, open (and food) all day weekends. *(Beth Aldridge)*

GREAT HABTON   SE7576
★ Grapes   (01653) 669166
Corner of Habton Lane and Kirby Misperton Lane; YO17 6TU Popular and genuinely welcoming beamed dining pub in small village, homely and cosy, with good cooking including fresh local fish and game, Marstons-related ales, open fire, small public bar with darts and TV; background music; a few roadside picnic-sets, nice walks, open all day Sun, closed Mon, lunchtime Tues.
(Laura Reid)

GUISELEY   SE1941
Coopers (01943) 878835
Otley Road; LS20 8AH Market Town
Tavern conversion of former Co-operative
store, open-plan bare-boards bar with good
range of well priced food from ciabattas and
snacks up, eight real ales including Okells,
Roosters and Timothy Taylors, also craft kegs,
bottled beers and decent range of wines,
good friendly service, upstairs function/
dining room; Weds open mike night; open
all day. *(Sandra and Nigel Brown)*

HALIFAX   SE0924
Three Pigeons (01422) 347001
*Sun Fold, South Parade; off Church
Street; HX1 2LX* Carefully restored,
four-room 1930s pub (Grade II listed), art
deco fittings, ceiling painting in octagonal
main area, original flooring, panelling and
tiled fireplaces with log fires, at least five
Ossett ales along with Fernandes, Rat and
sometimes Fullers, good Robinson's pies,
friendly chatty staff; tables outside, handy for
Eureka! museum and Shay Stadium (pub very
busy on match days), open all day Fri-Sun,
from 4pm other days. *(Pat and Tony Martin)*

HARDRAW   SD8691
★Green Dragon (01969) 667392
Village signed off A684; DL8 3LZ
Friendly traditional Dales pub dating from
13th c and full of character; stripped stone,
antique settles on flagstones, lots of bric-a-
brac, low-beamed snug with fire in old iron
range, another in big main bar, five well
kept ales including one badged for them
from Yorkshire Dales, generously served
food, small restaurant; annual brass band
competition and other live music; children
and dogs welcome, tables in attractive
courtyard, ten bedrooms, bunkhouse and
camping, next to Hardraw Force (England's
highest single-drop waterfall). *(Eddie
Edwards, Tracey and Stephen Groves, John and
Sylvia Harrop)*

HAROME   SE6482
★Star (01439) 770397
*High Street; village signed S of A170,
E of Helmsley; YO62 5JE* Restaurant-
with-rooms in pretty 14th-c thatched
building, but bar does have informal feel;
bowed beam-and-plank ceiling, plenty of
bric-a-brac, interesting furniture including
'Mousey' Thompson pieces, log fire and well
polished tiled kitchen range, three changing
ales and plenty of wines by the glass,
home-made fruit liqueurs, highly regarded
inventive cooking from chef-owner (not
cheap), snacks served in cocktail bar, coffee

loft in the eaves, well trained helpful staff;
background music; children welcome, seats
on sheltered front terrace, more in garden,
nine bedrooms, open all day Sun, closed Mon
lunchtime. *(Mr and Mrs Richard Osborne,
B R Merritt, J R Wildon)*

HARPHAM   TA0961
St Quintin Arms (01262) 490329
Main Street; YO25 4QY Comfortable old
village pub with enjoyable reasonably priced
home-made food (not Sun evening) including
plenty of specials, well kept Tetleys and Wold
Top, good friendly service, bar and small
dining room; sports TV, daily papers; children
welcome, sheltered garden with pond, on
National Cycle Route 1, three bedrooms,
open all day Sun, closed lunchtimes Mon
and Tues. *(Jane Sutton)*

HARROGATE   SE3155
Coach & Horses (01423) 561802
West Park; HG1 1BJ Friendly bustling pub
with half a dozen good Yorkshire-brewed ales,
over 30 gins and 80 malt whiskies, enjoyable
good value lunchtime food plus some themed
evenings, comfortable interior arranged
around central bar with booths and other
cosy areas; Fri charity raffle, Sun quiz; no
children or dogs, open all day. *(Nick Higgins)*

HARROGATE   SE2955
★Hales (01423) 725570
Crescent Road; HG1 2RS Classic Victorian
décor in 18th-c gas-lit local close to the Pump
Rooms; leather seats in alcoves, stuffed birds,
comfortable saloon and tiny snug, half a
dozen ales including Daleside, simple good
value lunchtime food, friendly helpful staff;
can get lively weekend evenings, open all day.
(Nick Higgins)

HARROGATE   SE2955
★Old Bell (01423) 507930
Royal Parade; HG1 2SZ Thriving Market
Town Tavern with up to five mainly local
beers from handsome counter, lots of bottled
continentals and impressive choice of wines
by the glass, friendly helpful staff, traditional
lunchtime snacks including sandwiches,
more elaborate evening meals upstairs, bare
boards and panelling, old sweet shop ads and
breweriana; no children, dogs welcome, open
all day. *(Nick Higgins, Simon Sharpe)*

HARROGATE   SE3155
Winter Gardens (01423) 877010
Royal Baths, Crescent Road; HG1 2RR
Interesting Wetherspoons conversion of
former ballroom in landmark building,
plenty of well kept ales and their usual good
value food, service not always speedy, many

We include some hotels with a good bar that offers facilities comparable
to those of a pub.

original features, comfortable sofas in lofty hall, upper gallery; TVs, free wi-fi; children welcome, seats on nice terrace, open all day, can be very busy late evening. *(Nick Higgins)*

HAWES
SD8789
Crown
(01969) 667212

Market Place; DL8 3RD Welcoming traditional market town local divided into four areas, open fires/woodburners and some interesting old photographs, well kept ales including four from Theakstons, hearty helpings of good value pub food served by friendly helpful staff; free wi-fi; children, walkers and dogs welcome, seats out on cobbled front forecourt and in back split-level beer garden with lovely Wensleydale views, three bedrooms, open all day. *(Eddie Edwards)*

HAWES
SD8789
White Hart
(01969) 667214

Main Street; DL8 3QL Friendly renovated 16th-c coaching inn on cobbled street, emphasis on good fairly priced food, but also four well kept regional ales, bar with fire in antique range, restaurant; children and dogs welcome, five bedrooms, open (and food) all day. *(Eddie Edwards)*

HAWNBY
SE5489
Inn at Hawnby
(01439) 798202

Aka Hawnby Hotel; off B1257 NW of Helmsley; YO62 5QS Welcoming stone-built inn set in pretty moorland village, good food from traditional choices up, ales such as Black Sheep and Great Newsome, ten wines by the glass, helpful friendly service; children welcome, dogs in bar (but must ask first), lovely views from restaurant and garden tables, good walking country (packed lunches available), nine quiet bedrooms (three in converted stables over road), open all day Fri-Sun, closed Mon, Tues in Feb, Mar. *(Melanie and David Lawson)*

HEADINGLEY
SE2736
Arcadia
(0113) 274 5599

Arndale Centre; LS6 2UE Glass-fronted Market Town Tavern in former bank, eight changing regional ales, a couple of craft kegs and over 100 bottled beers, good range of wines too, friendly knowledgeable staff, snacky food, stairs to mezzanine (pub quiz here Mon); no children; open all day. *(Peter Smith and Judith Brown)*

HEATH
SE3520
Kings Arms
(01924) 377527

Village signposted from A655 Wakefield–Normanton – or, more directly, turn off to the left opposite Horse & Groom; WF1 5SL Popular old-fashioned gas-lit pub of genuine character; fire in black range (long row of smoothing irons on the mantelpiece), plain elm stools, built-in oak settles and dark panelling, well kept Ossett

and several guests, standard food (all day Fri and Sat, till 7pm Sun), more comfortable extension preserving original style, two other small flagstoned rooms and a conservatory; summer folk events, Tues quiz, free wi-fi; children and dogs (in bar) welcome, benches out at front facing village green (surrounded by fine 18th-c stone merchants' houses), picnic-sets on side lawn and in nice walled garden, open all day (may shut early if quiet). *(C A Hall)*

HEBDEN
SE0263
Clarendon
(01756) 752446

B6265; BD23 5DE Well cared-for modernised inn surrounded by wonderful moorland walking country; bar, snug and restaurant, open fire, ales such as Black Sheep, Thwaites and Timothy Taylors, good range of enjoyable food (till 7pm Sun) from pubby choices up including blackboard specials, cheerful relaxed atmosphere; Sun quiz, Oct beer/food festival; children welcome, farm shop, five bedrooms, open all day weekends. *(Alan and Alice Morgan)*

HEBDEN BRIDGE
SD9922
Hinchcliffe Arms
(01422) 883256

Off B6138; HX7 5TA Tucked-away stone-built pub in great walking country on the Calderdale Way and near Stoodley Pike; freshly refurbished under new owners with open-plan bar to the left, restaurant on the right, three Lees ales and a guest, enjoyable fairly traditional home-made food from sandwiches up, friendly service; children and dogs (in bar) welcome, a few seats out at front, picturesque setting close to stream and Victorian church, open all day weekends (Sun till 9pm), closed Mon. *(Dr Kevan Tucker, Gordon and Margaret Ormondroyd)*

HEBDEN BRIDGE
SD9927
Old Gate
(01422) 843993

Oldgate; HX7 8JP Busy bar-restaurant with wide choice of enjoyable food served from 10am breakfast on, nine well kept ales, plenty of bottled beers and lots of wines by the glass including champagne, good friendly service, bar popular with young people, artwork by local artists, upstairs room for comedy club (second Sun of month) and other events; children welcome, tables outside, open (and food) all day. *(Jamie Green)*

HEBDEN BRIDGE
SD9827
Stubbings Wharf
(01422) 844107

About a mile W; HX7 6LU Friendly pub in good spot by Rochdale Canal with adjacent moorings, popular good value food (all day weekends, booking advised) from sandwiches and light meals up, half a dozen well kept regional ales, proper ciders, comfortable carpeted interior with local pictures on the walls; children and dogs welcome, boat trips, open all day. *(Gordon and Margaret Ormondroyd)*

HELMSLEY SE6183
Feathers (01439) 770275
Market Place; YO62 5BH Substantial old stone inn overlooking the market square, enjoyable food (all day Sat) from sandwiches to popular Sun carvery, well kept Black Sheep, Tetleys and a guest, good friendly service, several rooms with comfortable seats, oak and walnut tables (some by Robert 'Mouseman' Thompson – as is the bar counter), flagstones or tartan carpet, heavy medieval beams and huge inglenook log fire, panelled corridors; children and dogs (in bar) welcome, outside tables with heaters, 22 bedrooms, open all day. *(Chris Willers)*

HELWITH BRIDGE SD8169
Helwith Bridge Inn (01729) 860220
Off B6479 N of Stainforth; BD24 OEH Friendly unpretentious village local popular with walkers, up to eight well kept ales in flagstoned bar, enjoyable reasonably priced pub food (all day weekends), dining room with light wood furniture on bare boards; free wi-fi; children and dogs welcome, camping and basic bunkhouse, by River Ribble and Settle–Carlisle railway, open all day. *(Beth Aldridge)*

HEPWORTH SE1606
Butchers Arms (01484) 687147
Village signposted off A616 SE of Holmfirth; Towngate; HD9 1TE Old country dining pub with enjoyable french-influenced cooking including good value set menu, three well kept Yorkshire ales, decent wines by the glass and cocktails, friendly staff, flagstones by counter, bare boards elsewhere, log fire, low beams (handsomely carved in room on right); children, walkers and dogs welcome, terrace seating, open all day (till 7pm Mon). *(Douglas Power)*

HIGH HOYLAND SE2710
Cherry Tree (01226) 382541
Bank End Lane; 3 miles W of M1 junction 38; S75 4BE Split-level whitewashed village pub, well kept Acorn Barnsley Bitter, Black Sheep and a couple of guests, good range of enjoyable competitively priced food (not Sun evening), friendly young staff, beams and open fire, dining areas each end of bar and separate small restaurant; background music; children and dogs welcome, front roadside picnic-sets with lovely views over Cannon Hall Country Park, open all day. *(Michael Butler)*

HOLMFIRTH SD1408
Nook (01484) 681568
Victoria Square/South Lane; HD9 2DN Friendly tucked-away 18th-c stone local run by same family for two generations, own-brew beers and guests, low-priced home-made pubby food including good burgers, no-frills bar areas with flagstones and quarry tiles, big open fire; juke box, pool; heated streamside terrace, bedrooms, open (and food) all day. *(Nick Higgins)*

HOPPERTON SE4256
Masons (01423) 330442
Hopperton Street; HG5 8NX Revamped village dining pub with good food from pub classics to more creative dishes, a couple of real ales, friendly helpful staff, modernised interior with two fires, restaurant; background music; children and dogs (in bar) welcome, closed Mon, Tues. *(John and Eleanor Holdsworth, Graham Gill)*

HORBURY SE2918
Boons (01924) 277267
Queen Street; WF4 6LP Comfortably unpretentious flagstoned local, lively and chatty without being noisy, Clarkes, John Smiths, Timothy Taylors Landlord and up to four quickly changing guests, pleasant young staff, no food or children, rugby league memorabilia, warm fire; back tap room with pool and TV; courtyard tables, open all day Fri-Sun. *(Michael Butler)*

HORBURY SE2918
Cricketers (01924) 267032
Cluntergate; WF4 5AG Welcoming refurbished Edwardian pub, Bosuns, Timothy Taylors and six local guests including Sportsman (brewed at their sister pub in Huddersfield), also craft beers such as BrewDog, real cider and good selection of spirits, reasonably priced cheeseboards and meze platters; Weds quiz, monthly acoustic night and regular beer festivals; open all day Fri-Sun, from 4pm other days. *(Michael Butler)*

HORSFORTH SE2438
Town Street Tavern (0113) 281 9996
Town Street; LS18 4RJ Revamped Market Town Tavern with eight well kept ales and lots of draught/bottled continental beers, good food in small bar or upstairs restaurant, friendly helpful service; children and dogs (in bar) welcome, small terrace, open all day, food all day Sat, till 6pm Sun. *(Chris Stevenson)*

HUBBERHOLME SD9278
★ George (01756) 760223
Dubbs Lane; BD23 5JE Ancient little Dales inn, beautifully placed and run by friendly licensees; heavy beams, flagstones and stripped stone, enjoyable fairly priced home-made food (booking advised evenings), Black Sheep and three guests, open fire, perpetual candle on bar; outside lavatories; children allowed in dining area, well behaved dogs in bar (pub jack russell is George), terrace seating, River Wharfe fishing rights, six comfortable clean bedrooms (three in annexe), good breakfast, closed Mon lunchtime, Tues, otherwise open all day. *(Claes Mauroy)*

HUDDERSFIELD SE1416
Grove (01484) 430113
Spring Grove Street; HD1 4BP Friendly two-bar pub with huge selection of bottled beers (some gluten-free), 19 well kept/priced ales including Oakham, Timothy Taylors and Thornbridge, 120 malt whiskies and 60 vodkas, also real cider, knowledgeable staff, no food but choice of snacks from dried crickets to biltong; live music Tues and Thurs evenings, art gallery; children and dogs welcome, back terrace, open all day.
(Jeremy Snaithe)

HUDDERSFIELD SE1416
Kings Head (01484) 511058
Station, St Georges Square; HD1 1JF Victorian station building housing friendly well run pub; large open-plan room with original tiled floor, two smaller rooms off and plans for new dining room, ten well kept beers, good sandwiches and cobs; some live afternoon/evening music, Jimi Hendrix pub sign; dogs welcome, disabled access via platform 1, open all day. *(Jeremy Snaithe)*

HUDDERSFIELD SE1416
Rat & Ratchet (01484) 542400
Chapel Hill; HD1 3EB Refurbished split-level pub with own-brew beers and several guests including Ossett, good range ciders/perries too, pork pies and sausage rolls, friendly staff; open all day Fri-Sun, from 3pm other days. *(Laura Reid, Jeremy Snaithe)*

HUDDERSFIELD SE1417
Slubbers Arms (01484) 429032
Halifax Old Road; HD1 6HW Friendly V-shaped traditional three-room pub, good range of beers including Timothy Taylors from horseshoe bar, pie-and-peas menu, black and white photographs and old wartime posters, warm fire, games room; well behaved dogs welcome, terrace for smokers, open all day and busy on match days. *(Jeremy Snaithe)*

HUDDERSFIELD SE1417
Sportsman 07766 131123
St Johns Road; HD1 5AY Same owners as the West Riding Licensed Refreshment Rooms at Dewsbury; restored 1930s interior with lounge and two cosy side rooms, eight real ales and four craft beers, friendly knowledgeable staff, food such as burgers and pizzas served Fri-Sun; live music Sat; dogs welcome, handy for station, open all day.
(Laura Reid)

HUDDERSFIELD SE1415
Star (01484) 545443
Albert Street, Lockwood; HD1 3PJ Unpretentious friendly local with excellent range of competitively priced ales kept well by enthusiastic landlady, continental beers and real cider too, beer festivals in back marquee, open fire; open all day weekends, closed Mon and lunchtimes Tues-Fri.
(Jeff Davies)

HUDSWELL NZ1400
George & Dragon (01748) 518373
Hudswell Lane; DL11 6BL Popular community-owned village pub run by welcoming landlord, enjoyable good value home-made food from short menu plus a few daily specials, well kept ales including Copper Dragon, Roosters and Rudgate, various craft beers such as Revisionist and Shipyard, friendly atmosphere; small shop and library, free wi-fi; children and dogs welcome, panoramic Swaledale views from back terrace, open all day weekends (food Sun till 4pm). *(Peter and Emma Kelly)*

HULL TA1028
★ **Olde White Harte** (01482) 326363
Passage off Silver Street; HU1 1JG Ancient pub with Civil War history, carved heavy beams, attractive stained glass and two big inglenooks with frieze of delft tiles, well kept Caledonian, Theakstons and guests from copper-topped counter, 80 or so malt whiskies; old skull displayed in Perspex case (found here in the 19th c); children welcome, dogs in bar, heated courtyard, open all day.
(Simon Sharpe)

HUTTON-LE-HOLE SE7089
Crown (01751) 417343
The Green; YO62 6UA Overlooking pretty village green with wandering sheep in classic coach-trip country; enjoyable home-made pubby food (not Sun evening), Black Sheep, Tetleys and a guest, decent wines by the glass, cheerful efficient service, opened-up bar with varnished woodwork, dining area; quiz first Sun of month; children and clean dogs welcome, small site available for caravans behind, Ryedale Folk Museum next door and handy for Farndale walks, open all day Sun till 6pm, closed winter Mon, Tues. *(Alf Wright)*

ILKLEY SE1147
Bar t'at (01943) 608888
Cunliffe Road; LS29 9DZ Extended Market Town Tavern pub, eight mainly Yorkshire ales kept well, good wine and bottled beer choice, enjoyable well priced pubby food from sandwiches and snacks up, steak night first Fri of the month, candlelit cellar dining area, friendly service; upstairs loos; dogs welcome, back terrace with heated canopy, open all day, food all day Fri and Sat, till 6pm Sun. *(Pat and Tony Martin)*

By law, pubs must show a price list of their drinks. Let us know if you're inconvenienced by any breach of this law.

ILKLEY
SE1347

Wheatley Arms (01943) 816496

*Wheatley Lane, Ben Rhydding;
LS29 8PP* Smart spacious stone inn;
linked dining rooms with attractively
upholstered chairs around assorted tables,
rugs on bare boards, bold wallpaper and
two log fires, garden room and locals'
bar with tub chairs and tartan-cushioned
wall seats, Ilkley, Saltaire, Thwaites and
Wharfedale, 23 wines by the glass and
a dozen malt whiskies, popular modern
food served by efficient personable staff;
background music, live jazz first Sun
lunchtime of the month, TV, free wi-fi;
children and dogs (in bar) welcome,
terrace tables, comfortable individually
decorated bedrooms (some with private
roof terrace), good walks, open all day.
*(Gordon and Margaret Ormondroyd, Michael
Butler, Colin Humphreys, Caroline Sullivan)*

KEIGHLEY
SE0641

Boltmakers Arms (01535) 661936

East Parade; BD21 5HX Small open-plan
split-level character local, friendly and
bustling, with full Timothy Taylors range and
a guest kept well, malt whiskies and farm
cider, keen prices, limited food, lots to look
at including brewing pictures and celebrity
photos, coal fire; Tues quiz, Weds live music,
sports TV; small beer garden, short walk from
Keighley & Worth Valley Railway, open all day.
(Nick Higgins)

KELD
NY8900

Keld Lodge (01748) 886259

Butthouse Rigg (B6270); DL11 6LL
Remote former youth hostel now serving as
village inn, three well kept Black Sheep ales
and tasty sensibly priced food, good service,
various rooms including conservatory-style
restaurant with superb Swaledale views;
children and dogs welcome, popular with
Coast to Coast walkers, 11 bedrooms, open
all day. *(Douglas Power)*

KETTLESING
SE2257

★ Queens Head (01423) 770263

*Village signposted off A59 W of
Harrogate; HG3 2LB* Popular stone pub
with very good well priced traditional food,
L-shaped carpeted main bar with lots of
close-set cushioned dining chairs and tables,
open fires, little heraldic shields on the walls
along with 19th-c song sheet covers and
lithographs of Queen Victoria, delft shelf of
blue and white china, smaller bar on left with
built-in red banquettes and cricketing prints,
life-size portrait of Elizabeth I in lobby, well
kept Black Sheep, Roosters and Theakstons,
efficient friendly service; background radio;
children welcome, seats in neatly kept
suntrap back garden, benches in front by
lane, eight bedrooms, open all day Sun.
(Robert Wivell)

KETTLEWELL
SD9672

Blue Bell (01756) 760230

Middle Lane; BD23 5QX Roomy knocked-
through former coaching inn with friendly,
cheerful landlord, Copper Dragon and other
Yorkshire ales kept well, enjoyable home-
made food using local ingredients, low beams
and snug simple furnishings, old country
photographs, daily newspapers, woodburner,
restaurant; Sun quiz, TV and free wi-fi;
children, walkers and dogs welcome, shaded
picnic-sets on cobbles facing bridge over the
Wharfe, six annexe bedrooms, open (and
food) all day. *(Simon and Alex Knight)*

KETTLEWELL
SD9772

★ Kings Head (01756) 761600

The Green; BD23 5RD Refurbished old
pub tucked away near church, flagstoned
main bar with log fire in big arched
inglenook, three local ales and well chosen
wines, good affordably priced food (all day
Sun till 7pm) cooked by chef-landlord from
pub favourites to imaginative restaurant
dishes, efficient friendly service; children
welcome, no dogs inside, six renovated
bedrooms named after kings, attractive
village and good surrounding walks,
closed Mon (Sept-Apr), otherwise open
all day. *(Simon and Alex Knight)*

KETTLEWELL
SD9672

Racehorses (01756) 760233

B6160 N of Skipton; BD23 5QZ
Comfortable, civilised and friendly two-bar
inn next to River Wharf (across from the Blue
Bell); enjoyable fair value home-made food
and three well kept Timothy Taylors ales, log
fires, separate dining areas; children and
dogs (in some parts) welcome, front and
back terrace seating, pretty village handy for
Wharfedale walks, parking can be tricky, 13
good bedrooms, open all day. *(Jeremy King)*

KILBURN
SE5179

Forresters Arms (01347) 868386

*Between A170 and A19 SW of Thirsk;
YO61 4AH* Welcoming beamed inn next
to the Robert 'Mousey' Thompson furniture
workshops (early examples of his work in
both bars); roaring fires, well kept local
ales and good choice of home-made food,
restaurant; background music; children
welcome, dogs in some areas, suntrap seats
out in front, smokers' shelter behind, ten
bedrooms, open all day. *(Andrew and
Michele Revell)*

KIRBY HILL
NZ1406

Shoulder of Mutton (01748) 822772

*Off A66 NW of Scotch Corner, via
Ravensworth; DL11 7JH* Traditional
18th-c ivy-clad village inn recently taken
over by the chef; well liked food from pub
favourites up, four local beers, front bar areas
linking to long back restaurant, log fires;
children and dogs welcome, fine Holmedale

views from picnic-sets behind and bedrooms (you do hear the tuneful church bell), may open all day Sun. *(Gerry Price, Michael Doswell)*

KIRKBY FLEETHAM   SE2894
★**Black Horse** (01609) 749010
Village signposted off A1 S of Catterick; Lumley Lane; DL7 0SH New manager for this popular village pub and plenty of changes planned – news please; modernised beamed bar with flagstones, cushioned wall seats and log fire, little snug at far end, ales such as Black Sheep, Timothy Taylors and York, back dining room up a couple of steps with big bow windows on either side, enjoyable food including Tues steak night, friendly service; children and dogs (in bar) welcome, seats out at front, on side gravel terrace and in sheltered back garden, seven comfortable bedrooms, open all day.

KIRKBY OVERBLOW   SE3249
Shoulder of Mutton (01423) 871205
Main Street; HG3 1HD Creeper-clad 19th-c village pub with three linked areas, bare boards or flagstones, comfortable banquettes, open fire and woodburner, well kept ales such as Black Sheep and Timothy Taylors Landlord and plenty of wines by the glass, good freshly prepared food (all day Sun till 7pm) including early-bird menu, friendly service; quiz second Sun of month; dogs welcome, picnic-sets in back garden, closed Mon. *(John and Eleanor Holdsworth)*

KIRKBYMOORSIDE   SE6986
George & Dragon (01751) 433334
Market Place; YO62 6AA Family-run 17th-c coaching inn, front bar with beams and panelling, tub seats around wooden tables on carpet or stripped wood, log fire, good choice of well kept ales and several malt whiskies, enjoyable generously served bar food including good value lunchtime set deal, afternoon teas, good service, also a snug, bistro and more formal restaurant; background music; children welcome, seats and heaters on front and back terraces, 20 bedrooms, Weds market day, open all day. *(Chris Willers)*

KIRKHAM   SE7365
Stone Trough (01653) 618713
Kirkham Abbey; YO60 7JS Beamed country pub in beautiful setting with several cosy log-fire rooms, enjoyable food and three well kept ales such as Tetleys, Tom Woods and York, afternoon teas, restaurant; children welcome, seats on front terrace with lovely views over to Kirkham Priory (EH), good walks, convenient for Castle Howard, open all day. *(Stanley and Annie Matthews, Richard Stanfield)*

KNARESBOROUGH   SE3556
Blind Jacks (01423) 869148
Market Place; HG5 8AL Simply done multi-floor tavern in 18th-c building (pub since 1990s), old-fashioned traditional character with low beams, bare brick and floorboards, cast-iron-framed tables, pews and stools, brewery mirrors etc, good range of real ales and craft kegs including own Bad beers (no longer brewed on-site), friendly helpful staff, limited food (cheese and pâté), two small downstairs rooms, quieter upstairs; well behaved children allowed away from bar, dogs welcome, open all day weekends, from 5pm Mon, 4pm other days. *(Simon Sharpe)*

KNARESBOROUGH   SE3457
Mitre (01423) 868948
Station Road; HG5 9AA Red-brick 1920s Market Town Tavern by the station, clean fresh décor and friendly staff, up to eight real ales including Black Sheep, Roosters and Okells, interesting continental beers, enjoyable sensibly priced food in bar, side dining room and evening brasserie (Fri, Sat); live music Sun evening; children and dogs welcome, terrace tables under parasols, four bedrooms, open all day. *(B and M Kendall)*

KNAYTON   SE4388
Dog & Gun (01845) 537368
Moor Road, off A19; YO7 4AZ Attractive well cared-for family-run pub, cosy and comfortable with roaring fire at one end, tables laid for their popular traditional home-made food (best to book) including blackboard specials, Black Sheep and Copper Dragon, good friendly service; music festival Sept; children and dogs welcome, heated outside seating area, open all day weekends (food till 7pm Sun), closed Mon and lunchtimes Tues-Fri. *(Michael Doswell)*

LANGTHWAITE   NY0002
★**Charles Bathurst** (01748) 884567
Arkengarthdale, a mile N towards Tan Hill; DL11 6EN Welcoming busy 18th-c country inn with strong emphasis on dining and bedrooms, but pubby feel in long bar (sister to Punch Bowl at Low Row and Kings Arms at Askrigg); scrubbed pine tables and country chairs on stripped floors, snug alcoves, open fire, Black Sheep, Caledonian Deuchars IPA and a local guest, several wines by the glass and good choice of popular interesting food, cheerful helpful staff, dining room with views of Scar House, Robert 'Mousey' Thompson furniture, several other eating areas; background music, TV, pool and darts; children welcome, dogs in bar, lovely walks from the door and views over village and Arkengarthdale, 19 smart bedrooms (best not above dining room), open all day; worth checking there are no corporate events/weddings before you visit. *(Walter and Susan Rinaldi-Butcher)*

LANGTHWAITE   NZ0002
★**Red Lion** (01748) 884218
Just off Arkengarthdale Road, Reeth–Brough; DL11 6RE Proper pub dating from 17th c, homely and relaxing, in charming

Dales village with ancient bridge; friendly and welcoming with character landlady, lunchtime sandwiches, pasties and sausage rolls, a couple of well kept Black Sheep ales, Thatcher's cider, country wines, tea and coffee, well behaved children allowed lunchtime in low-ceilinged side snug, newspapers and postcards; the ladies' is a genuine bathroom; no dogs inside, good walks including circular ones from the pub – maps and guides for sale. *(Alan and Alice Morgan)*

LASTINGHAM SE7290

★ **Blacksmiths Arms** (01751) 417247
Off A170 W of Pickering; YO62 6TL
Popular 17th-c pub opposite beautiful Saxon church in charming village; log fire in open range, tankards hanging from beams, traditional furnishings, well kept Theakstons and other regional ales, several wines by the glass and good sensibly priced home-made food (not Sun evening), friendly prompt service, two dining rooms; background music, darts, board games; children, walkers and dogs welcome, seats out at front and in back beer garden, three bedrooms, open all day. *(Dr Peter Crawshaw, Peter and Anne Hollindale, Richard Stanfield)*

LEALHOLM NZ7607

★ **Board** (01947) 897279
Off A171 W of Whitby; YO21 2AJ
In wonderful moorland village spot by wide pool of River Esk; homely bare-boards bar on right with squishy old sofa and armchairs by big black stove, local landscape photographs on stripped-stone or maroon walls, china cabinet and piano, left-hand bar with another fire, traditional pub furniture, darts and a stuffed otter, carpeted dining room, four well kept changing ales, five ciders and dozens of whiskies, good seasonal food using meat from own farm and other local produce, friendly helpful landlady; children, dogs and muddy boots welcome, secluded waterside garden with decking, bedrooms (good breakfast) and self-catering cottage, open all day. *(Nick Higgins)*

LEAVENING SE7863

Jolly Farmers (01653) 658276
Main Street; YO17 9SA Bustling village local, friendly and welcoming, with four regional ales and popular good value traditional food (not Mon, Tues), front bar with eating area behind, separate dining room; some live music; children and dogs welcome, open all day weekends, closed weekday lunchtimes. *(Jeremy Snaithe)*

LEEDS SE2932

Cross Keys (0113) 243 3711
Water Lane, Holbeck; LS11 5WD
Welcoming early 19th-c pub; flagstones and bare boards, stripped brick, original tiling and timbers, old prints and photographs, a collection of clocks in one part, three or four interesting Yorkshire ales plus imported bottled beers, shortish choice of good well prepared food (not Sun evening), winding stairs up to function/dining room; newspapers and board games; children welcome, tables under big parasols in sheltered back courtyard, open all day. *(Nigel and Sue Foster)*

LEEDS SE3131

Garden Gate (0113) 345 1234
Whitfield Place, Hunslet; LS10 2QB
Impressive Edwardian pub (Grade II* listed) owned by Leeds Brewery with their well kept ales from rare curved ceramic counter, a wealth of other fine period features in rooms off central drinking corridor including intricate glass and woodwork, art nouveau tiling, moulded ceilings and mosaic floors; dogs welcome, tables out in front. *(Andrew and Michele Revell)*

LEEDS SE2932

★ **Grove** (0113) 243 9254
Back Row, Holbeck; LS11 5PL Unspoilt and lived-in 1930s-feel local overshadowed by towering office blocks, tables and stools in main bar with marble floor, panelling and original fireplace, large back room and snug off drinking corridor, eight well kept regional ales including Daleside and Theakstons, Weston's cider, lunchtime food (not Sat), friendly staff; regular live music including folk club; open all day. *(Jane Sutton)*

LEEDS SE2932

Midnight Bell (0113) 244 5044
Water Lane, Holbeck; LS11 5QN Leeds Brewery pub on two floors in Holbeck Urban Village, three of their ales and guests kept well, enjoyable home-made food (all day weekends including good Sun lunch), friendly staff, light contemporary décor mixing with original beams and stripped brickwork; children welcome, dogs in courtyard beer garden only, open all day. *(Diane Abbott)*

LEEDS SE3037

Mustard Pot (0113) 269 5699
Strainbeck Lane, Chapel Allerton; LS7 3QY Friendly management in relaxed easy-going dining pub, enjoyable food (all day Sun) from lunchtime sandwiches to daily specials, Marstons-related ales plus monthly guests, decent wines by the glass, mix of furniture from farmhouse tables and chairs to comfortable banquettes and leather chesterfields, half-panelling and open fire; background music; children welcome, pleasant front garden with heaters, open all day. *(Jan Sutton)*

LEEDS SE2933

Pour House 07816 481492
Canal Wharf, Holbeck; LS11 5PS
Canalside pub in old granary building, enjoyable good value food from sandwiches and sharing plates up, friendly service, ales such as Leeds, Kirkstall and Wharfe Bank,

good choice of bottled beers and other drinks, seating on two levels; open (and food) all day. *(Chris Stevenson)*

LEEDS SE3033

Scarbrough (0113) 243 4590

Bishopgate Street, opposite station; LS1 5DY Nicholsons pub with ornate tiled façade, eight well kept changing ales served by friendly knowledgeable staff, enjoyable food including good specials; sports TV; open all day and busy lunchtime, early evening. *(Andrew Bosi)*

LEEDS SE3033

Victoria (0113) 245 1386

Great George Street; LS1 3DL Opulent early Victorian pub with grand cut and etched mirrors, impressive globe lamps extending from majestic bar, carved beams, leather-seat booths with working snob screens, smaller rooms off, eight real ales and standard Nicholsons food in separate room with serving hatch, friendly efficient service; live jazz first Thurs of month; open all day. *(Peter Smith and Judith Brown)*

LEEDS SE3033

★**Whitelocks** (0113) 245 3950

Turks Head Yard, off Briggate; LS1 6HB Classic Victorian pub, a little worn around the edges but full of character; long narrow bar with tiled counter, grand mirrors, mahogany and glass screens, heavy copper-topped tables and red leather, well kept Theakstons ales and enjoyable generous food, friendly hard-working young staff; crowded at lunchtime; children welcome, tables in narrow courtyard, open (and food) all day. *(Douglas Power, Laura Reid)*

LEYBURN SE1190

Sandpiper (01969) 622206

Just off Market Place; DL8 5AT Restaurranty pub in pretty little stone cottage, beamed bar with built-in wall seats and log fire, steps up to snug with Dales photographs and woodburner by linenfold servery, ales such as Black Sheep, Rudgate and Wensleydale, ten wines by the glass and up to 75 malt whiskies, attractive restaurant with dark wooden tables and chairs on bare boards, good interesting food cooked by patron-chef from sandwiches and small plates up, pleasant efficient service; background music; children and dogs (in bar) welcome, seats on front terrace among pretty hanging baskets, comfortable well equipped bedrooms, closed Mon, some Tues in winter and for two weeks early Jan. *(Lynda and Trevor Smith, John and Enid, Michael Butler, Mary Hunstings, Clive and Fran Dutson)*

LINTHWAITE SE1014

★**Sair** (01484) 842370

Lane Top, Hoyle Ing, off A62; HD7 5SG Old-fashioned four-room pub brewing its own good value Linfit beers, pews and chairs on rough flagstones or wood floors, log-burning ranges, dominoes, cribbage and shove-ha'penny, piano and vintage rock juke box; no food or credit cards; dogs welcome, children till 8pm, plenty of tables out in front with fine Colne Valley views, restored Huddersfield Narrow Canal nearby, open all day weekends, from 5pm weekdays. *(Edward and William Johnston)*

LINTON SE3846

★**Windmill** (01937) 582209

Off A661 W of Wetherby; LS22 4HT Welcoming upmarket 16th-c inn on different levels, beams and stripped stone, antique settles around copper-topped tables, three log fires; good up-to-date food plus more traditional dishes, ales such as Theakstons Best and several wines by the glass, prompt cheerful service, restaurant and airy conservatory; background music; children and dogs (in bar) welcome, sunny back terrace and sheltered garden with pear tree raised from seed brought back from the Napoleonic Wars, two bedrooms in annexe, open all day Fri-Sun (food all day Sat, till 6pm Sun). *(Michael Butler)*

LITTON SD9074

Queens Arms (01756) 770096

Off B6160 N of Grassington; BD23 5QJ Beautifully placed 17th-c Dales pub; main bar with stone floor and beam-and-plank ceiling, old photographs on rough stone walls, coal fire, plainer carpeted dining room with woodburner, ales such as Greene King, Thwaites and Wharfedale, enjoyable freshly made food, friendly staff; children and dogs welcome, plenty of seats in two-tier garden, country views and good surrounding walks, six bedrooms, open all day weekends, closed Mon except bank holidays. *(Claes Mauroy)*

LOFTHOUSE SE1073

Crown (01423) 755206

Pub signed from main road; Nidderdale; HG3 5RZ Prettily placed Dales pub, friendly and relaxed, with hearty simple food from sandwiches up, well kept Black Sheep and Theakstons, small public bar, comfortable dining extension where children allowed, open fire; no credit cards, outside gents'; dogs welcome, good walks from the door, bedrooms. *(Claes Mauroy, B and M Kendall)*

LOW BRADFIELD SK2691

Plough (0114) 285 1280

Village signposted off B6077 and B6076 NW of Sheffield; New Road; S6 6HW Modernised old pub ideally placed for some of South Yorkshire's finest scenery; L-shaped bar with stone walls, comfortable wall banquettes and captain's chairs, log fire in big arched fireplace, well kept Bradfield, Thwaites and a guest, good value food from sandwiches and baked potatoes to grills, bargain two-for-one deals weekday lunchtimes, Sun carvery; background music,

Weds quiz, sports TV, free wi-fi; children and dogs welcome, seats on back verandah, terrace and lawn, Damflask and Agden Reservoirs close by, open (and food) all day. *(Sandra and Nigel Brown)*

LOW ROW   SD9898
★ **Punch Bowl** (01748) 886233
B6270 Reeth–Muker; DL11 6PF 17th-c country inn under same ownership as the Charles Bathurst at Langthwaite and Kings Arms at Askrigg; long bare-boards bar with peaceful view over Swaledale, stripped kitchen tables and a variety of seats including armchairs and sofa by woodburner, good food (menu on huge mirror with some interesting choices), nice wines by the glass, well kept Black Sheep ales and a guest, cheerful efficient staff, separate dining room similar in style; wide views from terrace set above road, comfortable bedrooms, good breakfast, open all day. *(Roy and Gill Payne)*

LUND   SE9748
★ **Wellington** (01377) 217294
Off B1248 SW of Driffield; YO25 9TE Smart busy pub with cosy Farmers Bar, beams, well polished wooden banquettes and square tables, quirky fireplace, plainer side room with flagstones and wine-theme décor, Yorkstone walkway to further room with village's Britain in Bloom awards; highly rated well presented food (not Sun evening and not cheap) in restaurant and bistro dining area, well kept ales including Timothy Taylors and Theakstons, good wine list, 25 malt whiskies, friendly efficient staff; background music, TV; children welcome, benches in pretty back courtyard, open all day Sun, closed Mon lunchtime. *(Pat and Stewart Gordon, Huw Jones)*

MALTON   SE7972
Spotted Cow (01653) 697568
Cattle Market; YO17 7JN Unspoilt early 18th-c pub overlooking cattle and sheep market (popular with local farmers on market days), small traditional rooms including tap room on left with tiled floor, wooden furniture and vintage brewery mirror, well kept Marstons, Tetleys and a guest; pool in back bar; dogs welcome, open from 4pm Mon, Weds and Thurs, otherwise open all day. *(Mike and Eleanor Anderson)*

MANFIELD   NZ2213
Crown (01325) 374243
Vicars Lane; DL2 2RF Traditional unpretentious village local under new management, friendly and welcoming, with eight interesting ales such as Brass Castle, Greyhawk and Village Brewer, enjoyable

home-made food, two bars and a pool room; dogs welcome, garden, good walks nearby, open all day weekends, closed lunchtimes Mon, Tues. *(Alan and Alice Morgan)*

MARSDEN   SE0411
Riverhead Brewery Tap
(01484) 841270 *Peel Street, next to Co-op; just off A62 Huddersfield–Oldham; HD7 6BR* Owned by Ossett with up to ten well kept ales including Riverhead range (microbrewery visible from bare-boards bar), bustling friendly atmosphere, airy upstairs beamed restaurant with stripped tables (moors view from some) and open kitchen, good choice of enjoyable food (not Mon) including OAP weekday lunch deal; background and some live music, Tues quiz; dogs welcome, wheelchair access, some riverside tables, open all day. *(Jeremy Snaithe)*

MASHAM   SE2280
Kings Head (01765) 689295
Market Place; HG4 4EF Handsome 18th-c stone inn (Chef & Brewer), two large modernised linked bars with stone fireplaces, well kept Black Sheep and Theakstons, nice choice of wines, good food served by friendly helpful staff, part-panelled restaurant; background music, TV; children welcome, tables out at front and in sunny back courtyard, 27 good value bedrooms, open all day. *(Michael Butler)*

MASHAM   SE2281
White Bear (01765) 689319
Wellgarth, Crosshills; signed off A6108 opposite turn into town; HG4 4EN Comfortably updated stone-built beamed inn, small public bar with full range of Theakstons ales kept well and several wines by the glass, larger lounge with welcoming coal fire, decent choice of food, from sandwiches/baguettes up, afternoon teas, friendly efficient staff, restaurant extension; background music; children and dogs (in bar) welcome, terrace tables, 14 bedrooms, open all day. *(Rosie and John Moore)*

MAUNBY   SE3586
Buck (01845) 587777
Off A167 S of Northallerton; YO7 4HD New owners for this brick-built dining pub in quiet out-of-the-way village by River Swale; good food (not Sun evening) from lunchtime sandwiches and traditional choices up (shortish menu), friendly helpful service, ales such as Theakstons and York, eight wines by the glass, carpeted beamed bar with comfy leather sofa and captain's chest in front of inviting fire, more contemporary

---

Please tell us if any pub deserves to be upgraded to a featured entry – and why: feedback@goodguides.com, or (no stamp needed) The Good Pub Guide, FREEPOST RTJR-ZCYZ-RJZT, Perrymans Lane, Etchingham TN19 7DN.

restaurant and conservatory with one huge table; children welcome, dogs in bar, open all day weekends, closed Mon, Tues. *(Michael Doswell, John and Eleanor Holdsworth)*

MENSTON SE1744
Fox (01943) 873024
Bradford Road (A65/A6038); LS29 6EB Contemporary Mitchells & Butlers dining pub in former coaching inn on busy junction, decent fairly priced food, efficient friendly staff, Black Sheep, Timothy Taylors Landlord and a guest, Aspall's cider, big fireplace, flagstones and polished boards in one part; background music, free wi-fi; two terraces looking beyond car park to cricket field, open (and food) all day. *(Beth Aldridge)*

MIDDLEHAM SE1288
Richard III (01969) 623240
Market Place; DL8 4NP Traditional 17th-c beamed inn with friendly landlady and locals, cosy front bar, Black Sheep, John Smiths and Theakstons, good range of generous food cooked by landlord, back bar and restaurant, lots of racehorse pictures; sports TV; tables out by square, six bedrooms, open all day, food all day Fri-Sun. *(Michael Butler)*

MIDDLEHAM SE1287
★ White Swan (01969) 622093
Market Place; DL8 4PE Extended coaching inn opposite cobbled market square, beamed and flagstoned entrance bar with log fire, well kept Theakstons ales, nice wines by the glass and several malt whiskies, good choice of enjoyable food (all day Sun) in modern brasserie with large fireplace or back dining room, friendly efficient staff; background music; children welcome, 17 comfortable bedrooms, hearty breakfast. *(Michael Butler)*

MIDDLESMOOR SE0974
Crown (01423) 755204
Top of Nidderdale Road from Pateley Bridge; HG3 5ST Remote unpretentious family-run inn with beautiful view over stone-built hamlet high in upper Nidderdale, warmly welcoming character landlord and good local atmosphere, well kept Black Sheep and guests, several whiskies and simple wholesome food, blazing fires in cosy spotless rooms, old photographs and bric-a-brac, homely dining room; children and dogs welcome, small garden, seven good value bedrooms, camping and self-catering cottage, open all day weekends. *(Claes Mauroy)*

MIDDLETON TYAS NZ2205
Shoulder of Mutton (01325) 377271
Just E of A1 Scotch Corner roundabout; DL10 6QX Welcoming old pub with three softly lit low-ceilinged rooms on different levels, enjoyable freshly made food from snacks to good steaks, three well kept changing ales, prompt friendly service; quiz last Weds of the month; children welcome, a useful A1/A66 stop, open all day Sun, closed Mon lunchtime. *(Millie and Peter Downing)*

MILLINGTON SE8351
Gait (01759) 302045
Main Street; YO42 1TX Honest, friendly 16th-c beamed local, five well kept regional ales and enjoyable straightforward home-made food, nice mix of old and newer furnishings, large map of Yorkshire on the ceiling, big inglenook log fire; live music or quiz Weds; children and dogs welcome, garden picnic-sets, appealing village in good Wolds walking country, closed Mon and lunchtimes Tues-Thurs. *(Simon Sharpe)*

MOORSHOLM NZ6912
Jolly Sailor (01287) 660270
A171 nearly a mile E; TS12 3LN Remotely placed dining pub with good variety of enjoyable food, well kept Black Sheep and a guest, friendly staff, long beamed and stripped-stone bar, restaurant; children and dogs welcome, tables looking out to the surrounding moors, open all day. *(WAH)*

MUKER SD9097
★ Farmers Arms (01748) 886297
B6270 W of Reeth; DL11 6QG Small down-to-earth pub in beautiful valley village popular with walkers and other visitors (can get very busy); warmly welcoming, with four well kept local ales such as Yorkshire Dales and good choice of wines by the glass, teas and coffees, enjoyable good value home-made food (delivered by dumb waiter from upstairs kitchen), good service, clean interior with warm fire, simple modern pine furniture, flagstones and panelling; soft background music, darts and dominoes; children, dogs and muddy boots welcome, hill views from terrace tables, self-catering apartment, open all day; for sale last we heard, but business as usual – news please. *(John and Enid, Roy and Gill Payne, Clive and Fran Dutson)*

NEWTON-ON-OUSE SE5160
★ Dawnay Arms (01347) 848345
Off A19 N of York; YO30 2BR 18th-c pub with two bars and airy river-view dining room, low beams, stripped masonry, open fire and inglenook woodburner, chunky pine tables and old pews on bare boards and flagstones, fishing memorabilia, highly regarded original food (till 6pm Sun), also good lunchtime sandwiches (home-baked bread), interesting vegetarian menu and children's choices, ales such as Tetleys and Timothy Taylors, good range of wines by the glass, friendly efficient service; terrace tables, lawn running down to Ouse moorings, handy for Beningbrough Hall (NT), open all day Sun till 6pm, closed Mon. *(Simon and Alex Knight)*

NORTH DALTON SE9352
Star (01377) 217688
B1246 Pocklington–Driffield; YO25 9UX Picturesque 18th-c red-brick inn next to

village pond, good range of changing ales and well cooked pubby food from new chef, open fire in pubby bar, restaurant; some live music including open mike nights; children and dogs welcome, open all day weekends, from 2pm Fri, 5pm other days. *(Jane Sutton)*

NORTH RIGTON   SE2749

Square & Compass   (01423) 733031
Hall Green Lane/Rigton Hill; LS17 0DJ Substantial stone building with smart modern interior, beamed bar serving Leeds, Theakstons and Washburn, good range of bottled beers and plenty of wines by the glass, well liked food from sandwiches, sharing boards and pizzas up, friendly efficient service by aproned staff, restaurant; children and dogs (in bar) welcome, tables on tiered terrace, peaceful village, open all day from 9am. *(Gordon and Margaret Ormondroyd)*

NORTHALLERTON   SE3794

Tithe Bar   (01609) 778482
Friarage Street; DL6 1DP Market Town Tavern with seven good mainly local ales along with plenty of continental beers, tasty well priced food including specials, friendly young staff, modernised bar split into three areas, upstairs evening brasserie; children and dogs welcome, open all day. *(Richard Tilbrook)*

NORWOOD GREEN   SE1326

Old White Beare   (01274) 676645
Signed off A641 in Wyke, or off A58 Halifax–Leeds just W of Wyke; Village Street; HX3 8QG Nicely renovated and extended 16th-c pub named after ship whose timbers it incorporates; well kept Copper Dragon, Timothy Taylors and a guest, decent choice of food (not Sun evening) including weekday fixed-price menu, good friendly service, bar with steps up to dining area, small character snug, imposing galleried flagstoned barn restaurant; children and dogs welcome, a few tables out in front and in back garden, Calderdale Way and Brontë Way pass the door, open all day. *(Michael Butler)*

NUN MONKTON   SE5057

Alice Hawthorn   (01423) 330303
Off A59 York–Harrogate; The Green; YO26 8EW Refurbished beamed dining pub in picturesque location on broad village green with pond and lovely avenue to church and Rivers Nidd and Ouse – maybe cows grazing peacefully; good imaginative food (can be pricey) using local ingredients including some from own kitchen garden, also pub favourites and set lunch/early-evening menus, local ales such as Yorkshire Heart and some nice wines, good attentive service; children welcome, open

all day Sat, Sun till 8pm, closed Mon, Tues lunchtime. *(John and Eleanor Holdsworth)*

NUNNINGTON   SE6679

Royal Oak   (01439) 748271
Church Street; at back of village, which is signposted from A170 and B1257; YO62 5US Welcoming neatly refurbished old pub, bar with high beams and some farming memorabilia on bare-stone wall, nice mix of furniture, dining area linked by double-sided woodburner, good food with some tuscan influences, Theakstons York and a guest such as Timothy Taylors, nice wines and italian coffee; bar billiards; children and dogs welcome, terrace seating, handy for Nunnington Hall (NT), open all day Sun (no evening food), closed Mon, Tues. *(Melanie and David Lawson)*

OAKWORTH   SE0138

Grouse   (01535) 643073
Harehills, Oldfield; 2 miles towards Colne; BD22 0RX Comfortable old pub in undisturbed moorland hamlet, enjoyable food from light lunches to good steaks and daily specials, well kept Timothy Taylors ales, friendly service; children and dogs (in snug) welcome, picnic-sets on terrace with lovely Pennine views, open (and food) all day. *(Andrew and Michele Revell)*

OLDSTEAD   SE5380

★ **Black Swan**   (01347) 868387
Village signed off Thirsk Bank, W of Coxwold; YO61 4BL Tucked-away 16th-c restaurant with rooms in beautiful surroundings; bar with beams, flagstones and 'Mousey' Thompson furniture, log fire, lots of wines by the glass and well kept Black Sheep, attractive back dining rooms serving first class food (Michelin starred and not cheap), good friendly service; children welcome, picnic-sets out in front, four comfortable well equipped bedrooms with own terrace, good breakfast, fine surrounding walks, closed weekday lunchtimes and two weeks in Jan. *(Nick Higgins)*

OSMOTHERLEY   SE4597

★ **Golden Lion**   (01609) 883526
The Green, West End; off A19 N of Thirsk; DL6 3AA Attractive busy old stone pub with friendly welcome, Timothy Taylors and guests, around 50 malt whiskies, roomy beamed bar on left with old pews and a few decorations, similarly unpretentious well worn-in eating area on right, weekend dining room, well liked pubby food and good service; background music; children welcome, dogs in bar, seats in covered courtyard, benches out at front overlooking village green, 44-mile Lyke Wake Walk starts here and Coast to Coast one nearby, seven comfortable

---

We say if we know a pub allows dogs.

bedrooms, open all day weekends, closed Mon and Tues lunchtimes. *(WAH, Walter and Susan Rinaldi-Butcher)*

OSMOTHERLEY SE4597

Three Tuns (01609) 883301

South End, off A19 N of Thirsk; DL6 3BN Small stylish pub-restaurant with décor inspired by Charles Rennie Mackintosh; very good freshly made food in bistro setting with pale oak furniture and panelling, friendly efficient service, flagstoned bar with built-in cushioned wall benches, stripped-pine tables and light-stone fireplace, well kept ales such as Timothy Taylors, good friendly service; children welcome, dogs in bar, seats out at front and in charming terrace garden, good nearby walks, comfortable bedrooms. *(M and GR)*

OSSETT SE2719

★ **Brewers Pride** (01924) 273865

Low Mill Road/Healey Lane (long cul-de-sac by railway sidings, off B6128); WF5 8ND Friendly local with Bobs White Lion (brewed at back of pub), Rudgate Ruby Mild and seven guests, cosy front rooms and flagstoned bar, open fires, brewery memorabilia, good well priced food (not Sun evening) including Tues night tapas, modern back dining extension (Millers Restaurant); Mon quiz, live music first Sun of month; well behaved children and dogs welcome, big back garden, near Calder & Hebble Navigation, open all day. *(Michael Butler)*

OSSETT SE2820

Old Vic (01924) 273516

Manor Road, just off Horbury Road; WF5 0AU Friendly four-room roadside pub with well kept Ossett ales and a guest such as Fullers London Pride, competitively priced home-cooked food (not Sun evening, Mon), traditional décor with old local photographs, shelves of bottles and antique range, pool room; children and dogs welcome, open all day Fri-Sun, closed lunchtime other days. *(Michael Butler)*

OSSETT SE2719

Tap (01924) 272215

The Green; WF5 8JS Tap for the Ossett Brewery; simple traditional décor with flagstones, bare boards and woodburner, mix of seating including upholstered banquettes and padded stools, photos of other Ossett pubs, their ales and guests plus competitively priced wines by the glass, friendly relaxed atmosphere; small car park (other nearby parking can be difficult), open all day Thurs-Sun, from 3pm other days. *(Michael Butler)*

OSWALDKIRK SE6278

Malt Shovel (01439) 788461

Signed off B1363/B1257 S of Helmsley; YO62 5XT Attractive former small 17th-c manor house under welcoming and helpful licensees, two cosy bars and dining room, well kept/priced Sam Smiths OBB and

enjoyable good value food (not Weds), huge log fires, heavy beams and flagstones; views from garden, open all day (and food) weekends. *(Alan and Alice Morgan)*

OTLEY SE2045

Old Cock (01943) 464424

Crossgate; LS21 1AA Traditional two-room drinkers' pub with nine mainly local ales and a couple of ciders, also foreign imports and range of gluten-free bottled beers, beer festivals, no cooked food but good pies and sausage sandwiches, more room upstairs; no under-18s, dogs welcome, open all day. *(Sandra and Nigel Brown)*

OTLEY SE2047

★ **Roebuck** (01943) 463063

Roebuck Terrace; LS21 2EY Friendly low-beamed pub modernised to a high standard, good food from sandwiches and sharing plates up including range of hearty pies, Black Sheep and five changing local beers, plenty of wines by the glass, good helpful service, log fire and woodburner, raftered restaurant with mix of old furniture including pews on wood floor; children and dogs (in bar) welcome, wheelchair access, tables out on terrace and small lawn, open all day (closed Mon in winter), food all day Sat, till 7pm Sun. *(John and Eleanor Holdsworth)*

OXENHOPE SE0335

Bay Horse (01535) 642921

Upper Town; BD22 9LN Rescued from closure a couple of years ago and returned to a bustling community pub; friendly enthusiastic licensees, good value food cooked to order and half a dozen well kept local ales; free wi-fi; children, walkers and dogs welcome, seats outside. *(Brian and Anna Marsden)*

OXENHOPE SE0434

★ **Dog & Gun** (01535) 643159

Off B6141 towards Denholme; BD22 9SN Spacious beautifully placed 17th-c moorland pub, smartly extended and comfortable, with wide choice of good generously served food from sandwiches to daily specials, welcoming attentive staff, full Timothy Taylors range kept well and good selection of malts, beamery, copper, brasses, plates and jugs, big log fire each end, padded settles and stools, glass-covered well in one dining area, wonderful views; five bedrooms in adjoining hotel, open all day weekends. *(Gordon and Margaret Ormondroyd)*

PICKERING SE7984

White Swan (01751) 472288

Market Place, just off A170; YO18 7AA Civilised and welcoming 16th-c coaching inn run by the same family for over 30 years; cosy properly pubby bar, sofas and a few tables, panelling and log fire, Black Sheep, Timothy Taylors Landlord and a dozen wines by the glass, second bare-boards room with big bow window and handsome art nouveau iron fireplace, good food (everything made in-house, even ketchup) in flagstoned restaurant and next-door deli, efficient friendly staff, residents' lounge in converted beamed barn; children and dogs (in bar) welcome, bedrooms, open all day from 7.30am. *(Pat and Graham Williamson)*

PICKHILL SE3483

★**Nags Head** (01845) 567391

A1 junction 50 (northbound) or junction 51 (southbound), village signed off A6055, Street Lane; YO7 4JG Welcoming dining inn with many tables set for eating, but bustling tap room on left (lots of ties, jugs, coach horns and ale-yards) serves Black Sheep, Rudgate, Theakstons and a guest along with 30 malt whiskies, vintage Armagnacs and ten wines by the glass, smarter lounge bar with deep green plush banquettes, pictures for sale and open fire, library-themed restaurant, good food from wide ranging menu; background music, TV, free wi-fi; well behaved children welcome till 7.30pm (after that in dining room only), dogs in bar, front verandah, boules/quoits pitch and nine-hole putting green, seven comfortable bedrooms, buffet-style breakfast, open all day. *(Michael Butler)*

POOL SE2445

★**White Hart** (0113) 203 7862

Just off A658 S of Harrogate, A659 E of Otley; LS21 1LH Popular light and airy Mitchells & Butlers dining pub (bigger inside than it looks), good food from sharing plates and pizzas to more restaurant dishes, fixed-price menu too, efficient friendly young staff, 25 wines by the glass including champagne, three well kept (if not cheap) ales such as Leeds and Timothy Taylors, stylishly simple bistro eating areas, armchairs and sofas on bar's flagstones and bare boards, welcoming log fires; plenty of tables outside, open (and food) all day. *(Michael Butler, John and Sylvia Harrop, Gordon and Margaret Ormondroyd)*

PUDSEY SE2037

Thornhill Arms (0113) 256 5492

Town Gate; LS28 5NF Fully updated 17th-c pub with wide range of enjoyable food from meze sharing plates, mexican choices, burgers and hot dogs up, real ales such as Theakstons and plenty of wines by the glass, friendly efficient staff; free wi-fi; children welcome, seats outside, open (and food) all day. *(John and Eleanor Holdsworth)*

REDMIRE SE0491

Bolton Arms (01969) 624336

Hargill Lane; DL8 4EA Welcoming village dining pub (former 17th-c farmhouse) with enjoyable fairly traditional food at reasonable prices, well kept Black Sheep, Theakstons, Wensleydale and a guest, efficient friendly service even at busy times, woodburner in comfortable carpeted bar, attractive dining

room; free wi-fi; children and dogs (in bar) welcome, disabled facilities, picnic-sets in small part-paved garden, handy for Wensleydale Railway and Bolton Castle, good walks, five bedrooms (two with views from shared balcony, others in converted outbuilding), open all day. *(Tracey and Stephen Groves, Clive and Fran Dutson)*

REETH SE0499

Buck (01748) 884210

Arkengarthdale Road/Silver Street; DL11 6SW Friendly 18th-c coaching inn adjacent to village green, ales such as Black Sheep, Copper Dragon, Ossett and Timothy Taylors, enjoyable fairly pubby food, part carpeted beamed bar with open fire, steps up to dining area; Sat live music, free wi-fi; children welcome, dogs in bar (theirs is Marley), a few tables out in front, hidden walled garden with play equipment, good walking country, ten comfortable bedrooms, open all day. *(Beth Aldridge)*

RIPLEY SE2860

Boars Head (01423) 771888

Off A61 Harrogate–Ripon; HG3 3AY Informal and relaxed old hotel, long bar-bistro with nice mix of dining chairs and tables, walls hung with golf clubs, cricket bats, some jolly cricketing/hunting drawings, a boar's head and interesting religious carving, Black Sheep, Daleside and Theakstons, 20 wines by the glass and several malt whiskies, good food including produce from the Estate (the Ingilby family have lived in next-door Ripley Castle for over 650 years), separate restaurant; children welcome, dogs in bar and bedrooms, pleasant little garden, open (and food) all day. *(Simon Sharpe)*

RIPON SE3171

★**One-Eyed Rat** (01765) 607704

Allhallowgate; HG4 1LQ Small bare-boards pub with numerous well kept ales, farm cider, draught continentals and lots of bottled beers, long narrow bar with roaring fire, cigarette cards, framed beer mats, bank notes and old plates, no food but may be free black pudding; live music and beer festivals, pool; children welcome, nice outside seating area, open all day Sat, closed Mon-Thurs lunchtimes. *(Nick Higgins)*

RIPON SE3171

Royal Oak (01765) 602284

Kirkgate; HG4 1PB Centrally placed, well run 18th-c coaching inn on pedestrianised street; smart modern décor, Timothy Taylors ales and guests kept well, good choice of wines, split-level dining area serving good food from pub staples to more enterprising restaurant dishes, lunchtime/early evening deal Mon-Fri, brisk friendly service; background music; children and dogs (in bar) welcome, seats in courtyard with retractable awning, eight bedrooms, open (and food) all day. *(Richard Tingle, Janet and Peter Race)*

RIPON SE3170

Water Rat (01765) 602251

Bondgate Green, off B6265; HG4 1QW
Small pub on two levels, prettily set by
footbridge over River Skell and near canal
basin; well kept Theakstons and three
guests, Weston's cider and interesting range
of gins, enjoyable pubby food including Sun
carvery (till 4pm), good friendly service,
conservatory; children and dogs welcome,
charming view of cathedral, ducks and weir
from riverside terrace, closed Mon, otherwise
open all day. *(Pat and Graham Williamson,
Richard Tingle)*

RIPPONDEN SE0319

Fox (01422) 825880

*Oldham Road; just off M62 junction 22;
HX6 4DP* Modern timber-fronted pub-
restaurant with wide choice of food cooked
by landlord-chef including fresh fish/seafood,
efficient service, well kept Copper Dragon
and Thwaites; live acoustic music last Thurs
of month; children welcome, seats outside,
open (and food) all day Weds to Sun, closed
Mon and Tues lunchtimes. *(Douglas Power)*

RISHWORTH SE0316

Booth Wood (01422) 825600

Oldham Road (A672); HX6 4QU
Welcoming beamed and flagstoned country
dining pub, smartened-up but keeping cosy
atmosphere; good range of enjoyable well
priced food from sandwiches to blackboard
specials, lunchtime/early evening bargains,
local Oates beers and guests, friendly staff,
some leather sofas and wing-back chairs, two
blazing woodburners; live music including
folk nights; children welcome, open all day
(from 9.30am Sun for breakfast). *(Gordon
and Margaret Ormondroyd, Stuart Paulley)*

ROBIN HOOD'S BAY NZ9504

Bay Hotel (01947) 880278

The Dock, Bay Town; YO22 4SJ
Old village inn perched on edge of the bay
with fine sea views from cosy picture-window
upstairs bar (Wainwright bar downstairs
open too if busy), ales including Caledonian
Deuchars IPA and Theakstons, reasonably
priced home-made food in bar and separate
dining area from sandwiches to blackboard
specials, log fires; background music, TV;
children and dogs welcome, popular with
walkers (at end of the 191-mile Coast to
Coast path), lots of tables outside, bedrooms,
steep road down and no parking at bottom,
open all day. *(Rosie and John Moore)*

ROBIN HOOD'S BAY NZ9505

Victoria (01947) 880205

Station Road; YO22 4RL Clifftop Victorian
hotel with great bay views, good choice of
local beers from curved counter in traditional
carpeted bar, enjoyable fresh food here, in
restaurant or large family room, also a coffee
shop/tea room; dogs welcome, useful car
park, play area and picnic-sets in big garden
overlooking sea and village, comfortable
bedrooms, good breakfast. *(Nick Higgins)*

SANDSEND NZ8612

Hart (01947) 893304

East Row; YO21 3SU Shoreside pub
with good choice of generously served
traditional food including fish/seafood
(best to book a table), well kept ales such
as Black Sheep, prompt friendly service, log
fire in beamed and flagstoned bar, upstairs
dining room; free wi-fi; children and dogs
welcome, picnic-sets on small side terrace,
open all day (till 6pm Sun). *(Jeff Davies)*

SAWDON TA9484

★**Anvil** (01723) 859896

Main Street; YO13 9DY Attractive high-
raftered former smithy with emphasis on
chef-landlord's good locally sourced food
(best to book), well kept ales from Yorkshire
brewers and nice range of wines, friendly
attentive service, feature smith's hearth with
anvil and old tools, scrubbed pine tables and
good woodburner, lower-ceilinged second bar
leading to small neat dining room; children
welcome, dogs in some parts, terrace seating,
two self-catering cottages, closed Mon,
Tues and lunchtime Weds. *(Sara Fulton,
Roger Baker)*

SAWLEY SE2467

★**Sawley Arms** (01765) 620642

*Village signposted off B6265 W of Ripon;
HG4 3EQ* Village dining pub with friendly
busy atmosphere, well liked food from
sandwiches and light meals up including
daily specials, curry night Tues, steak night
Thurs, Theakstons Best and Timothy Taylors
Landlord, a dozen wines by the glass,
welcoming helpful staff, comfortable interior
with log fire and conservatory; children
welcome, seats on terrace and in attractive
garden, close to Fountains Abbey (NT),
open (and food) all day. *(John and Eleanor
Holdsworth, Janet and Peter Race)*

SCARBOROUGH TA0588

Golden Ball (01723) 353899

Sandside, opposite harbour; YO11 1PG
Mock-Tudor seafront pub with good harbour
and bay views from highly prized window
seats (busy in summer), panelled bar with
some nautical memorabilia, well kept low-
priced Sam Smiths; family lounge upstairs,
tables out in yard, open all day. *(Simon and
Alex Knight)*

SCARBOROUGH TA0387

Valley (01723) 372593

Valley Road; YO11 2LX Family-run
Victorian pub with basement bar, up to six
well kept changing ales and eight ciders/
perries, excellent choice of bottled belgian
beers too, friendly staff, no food, more seats
upstairs and pool room; bedrooms, open
all day. *(Douglas Power)*

SCORTON   NZ2500

Farmers Arms (01748) 812533

Northside; DL10 6DW Comfortably
modernised little pub (popular locally) in
terrace of old cottages overlooking green,
well kept Black Sheep, Copper Dragon
and Courage Directors, decent wines and
enjoyable food including good rabbit pie,
fresh Whitby fish and popular Sun lunch (till
3pm), friendly accommodating staff, bar with
open fire, darts and dominoes, restaurant;
background music, fortnightly quiz and bingo
nights; children and dogs welcome, open all
day weekends, closed Mon lunchtime.
(Pat and Stewart Gordon, Ian and Rose Lock)

SCOTTON   SE3259

Guy Fawkes Arms (01423) 862598

Main Street; HG5 9HU Hospitable neatly
refurbished village pub run by two local
families, very popular food (must book)
including plenty of fish and good value set
lunch, well kept Black Sheep, Copper Dragon
and three local guests, charming staff; Mon
quiz; children and dogs (not at food times)
welcome, open all day (food all day Sat, till
7pm Sun). *(Margaret and Peter Staples,
Michael Doswell)*

SETTLE   SD8163

Lion (01729) 823459

*B6480 (main road through town), off
A65 bypass; BD24 0HB* Market town inn
with grand staircase sweeping down into
baronial-style high-beamed bar, lovely log
fire, second bar with bare boards and dark
half-panelling, lots of old local photographs
and another fire, enjoyable good value food
including deli boards and specials, well kept
Thwaites and occasional guests, decent
wines by the glass, helpful welcoming staff,
restaurant; Tues jazz, monthly quiz, silent
TV and games machine; children and dogs
welcome, courtyard tables, 14 bedrooms,
open (and food) all day. *(Michael Butler)*

SHAROW   SE3371

Half Moon (01765) 278524

Sharow Lane; HG4 5BP Nice little village
pub with well kept Black Sheep ales and
tasty home-made food from sandwiches
up, early-bird deal Tues-Thurs (5.30-7pm),
Victorian pictures and ornate gilded mirror
on grey/green walls, lots of pine furniture,
sofa and easy chairs one end, cosy dining
room the other with open fire, small gift
shop; quiz nights; children welcome, dogs in
bar area, open all day Sun till 7.45pm, closed
Mon and lunchtime Tues. *(Michael Doswell)*

SHEFFIELD   SK3487

Bath (0114) 249 5151

Victoria Street, off Glossop Road; S3 7QL
Victorian corner pub with well restored
1930s interior, two rooms and a drinking
corridor, friendly staff, well kept Thornbridge
and guests, simple snacky food including

weekend hot pork sandwiches, live music Sun
and Weds with some emphasis on jazz/blues,
Thurs quiz; open all day (from 4pm Sun).
(Martin Day, David Carr)

SHEFFIELD   SK3687

Fat Cat (0114) 249 4801

23 Alma Street; S3 8SA Cheerfully
busy little Victorian pub with a dozen
interesting beers on handpump including
next-door Kelham Island, also draught/
bottled continentals and traditional cider,
friendly knowledgeable staff, straightforward
bargain food (not Sun evening) catering for
vegetarians/vegans; Mon quiz; seats in back
courtyard, open all day. *(David Carr)*

SHEFFIELD   SK3687

Gardeners Rest (0114) 272 4978

Neepsend Lane; S3 8AT Welcoming beer-
enthusiast landlord serving his own good
Sheffield ales from light wood counter, also
several changing guests tapped from the
cask, farm cider and continental beers, no
food, old brewery memorabilia and changing
local artwork, daily papers, games including
bar billiards; live music and popular Sun
quiz; well behaved children (till 9pm) and
dogs welcome, disabled facilities, back
conservatory and tables out in quirky garden
overlooking River Don, open all day Fri-Sun,
from 3pm other days. *(Diane Abbott)*

SHEFFIELD   SK3588

Harlequin (0114) 275 8195

Nursery Street; S3 8GG Welcoming
open-plan corner pub owned by nearby Exit
33, their well kept ales and great selection
of changing guests, also bottled imports
and real ciders/perries, straightforward
cheap lunchtime food including Sun roasts;
weekend live music, Weds quiz, beer festivals;
children till 7pm and dogs welcome, outside
seating, open all day. *(Simon Sharpe)*

SHEFFIELD   SK3687

Hillsborough (0114) 232 2100

*Langsett Road/Wood Street; by Primrose
View tram stop; S6 2UB* Friendly
pub in small red-brick hotel back under
management from ten years ago; eight
mainly local ales (they plan to rebuild the
dismantled cellar brewery), several wines
by the glass and good value traditional food
(not Sun evening, Mon), bare-boards bar and
lounge, views to ski slope from attractive
back conservatory and terrace; Tues quiz,
weekend live music including folk every other
Sun, free wi-fi; children and dogs welcome,
six good value bedrooms, open all day (from
2pm Mon). *(Simon Sharpe)*

SHEFFIELD   SK3290

★ New Barrack (0114) 232 4225

*601 Penistone Road, Hillsborough;
S6 2GA* Friendly and lively with nine real
ales including Castle Rock and lots of bottled
belgian beers, traditional good value bar

food, comfortable front lounge with log fire and upholstered seats on old pine floors, tap room with another fire, new function room (own bar); live music and comedy nights, pool, darts, sports TV; children (till 9pm) and dogs welcome, attractive little walled garden, difficult parking nearby, closed lunchtimes Mon-Weds, otherwise open all day. *(Jane Sutton)*

SHEFFIELD   SK3186
Ranmoor (0114) 230 1325
Fulwood Road (across from church); S10 3GD Comfortable and welcoming open-plan 19th-c local, four well kept ales including Abbeydale and Bradfield, enjoyable food, etched bay windows, big mirrors and period fireplaces; two outside seating areas, open all day. *(Mike Benton)*

SHEFFIELD   SK3185
Rising Sun (0114) 230 3855
Fulwood Road; S10 3QA Recently extended and refurbished community pub, a dozen ales including several from Abbeydale, good selection of craft kegs too, tasty fairly priced food, friendly service; background music, quiz Weds and Sun; children welcome, a few tables out in front, more on terrace at back, open all day. *(Jane Sutton)*

SHEFFIELD   SK3586
Sheffield Tap (0114) 273 7558
Station, platform 1B; S1 2BP Busy station bar in restored Edwardian refreshment room, popular for its huge choice of world beers on draught and in bottles, also own Tapped ales from visible microbrewery and plenty of guests including Thornbridge, knowledgeable helpful staff, snacky food, spacious tiled interior with vaulted roof; open all day. *(David Carr)*

SHEFFIELD   SK3687
★ Wellington (0114) 249 2295
Henry Street; by Shalesmoor tram stop; S3 7EQ Unpretentious relaxed corner pub with up to ten changing beers including own bargain Little Ale Cart brews, bottled imports, real cider, coal fire in lounge, photographs of old Sheffield, daily papers and pub games, friendly staff; tables out behind, open all day with afternoon break on Sun. *(Simon Sharpe)*

SHELLEY   SE2112
★ Three Acres (01484) 602606
Roydhouse (not signed); from B6116 towards Skelmanthorpe, turn left in Shelley (signposted 'Flockton, Elmley, Elmley Moor'), go up lane for 2 miles towards radio mast; HD8 8LR Civilised former coaching inn with emphasis on hotel and dining side; roomy lounge with leather chesterfields, old prints and so forth, tankards hanging from main beam, well kept Copper Dragon, 40 malt whiskies and up to 17 wines by the glass from serious

(not cheap) list, several formal dining rooms, wide choice of good if expensive food from lunchtime sandwiches up, competent friendly service; conferences, weddings and events; children welcome, fine moorland setting and lovely views, smart well equipped bedrooms. *(W K Wood)*

SHEPLEY   SE1809
Farmers Boy (01484) 605355
Marsh Lane, W of village – off A629 at Black Bull (leads on past pub to A635); HD8 8AP Smart stone-built dining pub; small traditional beamed bar on right serving Black Sheep, Bradfield and Copper Dragon, bare-boards area on left with coal fire and sturdy country tables, carpeted part rambling back through plenty of neat linen-set dining tables, barn restaurant with own terrace, popular often imaginative food, not cheap but they do offer a lunchtime/early evening set menu, friendly service; children welcome, disabled access (via restaurant entrance) and loos, unobtrusive background music; picnic-sets out in front, open all day. *(Nick Higgins)*

SHIPLEY   SE1437
Fannys Ale House (01274) 591419
Saltaire Road; BD18 3JN Bare-boards alehouse on two floors, cosy and friendly, with eight well kept ales including Timothy Taylors, also bottled beers and farm ciders, gas lighting, brewery memorabilia, log fire and woodburner, back extension; dogs welcome, closed Mon lunchtime, otherwise open all day and can get crowded weekend evenings. *(Laura Reid, Edward and William Johnston)*

SHIPLEY   SE1337
Hop (01274) 582111
Bingley Road; BD18 4DH Roomy open-plan tramshed conversion, full Ossett range and guests from curved counter, good choice of enjoyable food including sandwiches, sharing boards and wood-fired pizzas, friendly helpful service; regular live music, quiz night Thurs; no under-18s after 8pm, on edge of Saltaire World Heritage Site, open all day (food all day Fri, Sat and till 7pm Sun). *(Pat and Tony Martin)*

SICKLINGHALL   SE3648
Scotts Arms (01937) 582100
Main Street; LS22 4BD Hospitable and popular 17th-c pub with enjoyable generously served food (all day weekends) including blackboard specials, rambling interior with interesting nooks and crannies, low beams, old timbers and log fires, four well kept ales including Timothy Taylors Landlord and Theakstons Old Peculier, good wine range, friendly efficient staff; free wi-fi; children welcome, disabled access/loos, big garden with teak furniture on paved terrace, open all day. *(Gordon and Margaret Ormondroyd)*

SINNINGTON   SE7485
★**Fox & Hounds** (01751) 431577
Off A170 W of Pickering; YO62 6SQ
Pretty village's popular 18th-c coaching
inn, carpeted beamed bar with two-way
woodburner, comfortable seating, various
pictures and old artefacts, imaginative
attractively presented food along with pub
favourites, friendly helpful service, well kept
Black Sheep and a guest, several wines by
the glass and some interesting whiskies,
lounge and smart restaurant; background
music, free wi-fi; children and dogs welcome,
picnic-sets out at front and in garden, ten
good comfortable bedrooms. *(Pat and Stewart
Gordon, Ralph Beaumont)*

SKIPTON   SD9851
★**Narrow Boat** (01756) 797922
*Victoria Street; pub signed down alley
off Coach Street; BD23 1JE* Lively pub
down cobbled alley, eight well kept ales, fruit
and wheat beers, farm cider/perry, dining
chairs, pews and stools around wooden tables
on bare boards, various breweriana, upstairs
galleried area with interesting canal mural,
fair-priced pubby food (all day Sat, not Sun
evening); live music Mon; children allowed if
eating, dogs welcome, picnic-sets under front
colonnade, Leeds & Liverpool Canal nearby,
open all day. *(Rosie and John Moore)*

SKIPTON   SD9851
Woolly Sheep (01756) 700966
Sheep Street; BD23 1HY Bustling narrow
pub with full Timothy Taylors range kept
well and a guest, friendly service, two
beamed bars off flagstoned passage, exposed
brickwork, stone fireplace, lots of sheep
prints and bric-a-brac, comfortable raised
lunchtime dining area at back, good choice
of enjoyable reasonably priced food (plenty
for children); wheelchair access with
help, covered decked terrace behind, six
bedrooms, good breakfast, open all day.
(Comus and Sarah Elliott)

SLEDMERE   SE9364
★**Triton** (01377) 236078
*B1252/B1253 junction, NW of Great
Driffield; YO25 3XQ* Handsome old inn
by Sledmere House, open-plan bar with old-
fashioned atmosphere, dark wooden furniture
on red patterned carpet, 15 clocks ranging
from grandfather to cuckoo, lots of willow
pattern plates, paintings and pictures, open
fire, Greene King, Timothy Taylors, Tetleys
and Wold Top, 50 different gins, generous
helpings of well liked freshly cooked food
(only take bookings in separate restaurant),
friendly helpful staff; children welcome till

8pm, five good bedrooms, massive breakfast,
open all day Sun till 9pm, closed winter Mon
lunchtime. *(Chris Stevenson)*

SLINGSBY   SE6975
Grapes (01653) 628076
*Off B1257 Malton–Hovingham; Railway
Street; YO62 4AL* Stone-built 18th-c village
pub, good sensibly priced food (not Sun
evening) from traditional menu, well kept
Black Sheep, Copper Dragon, Timothy Taylors
and Theakstons, cheerful staff, bare boards,
flagstones and painted beams, nice mix of
old furniture and some interesting bits and
pieces including a tusky boar's head above
one of the woodburners, games area with
bar billiards; tables out behind, open all day
Fri-Sun, closed Mon. *(Beth Aldridge)*

SNAITH   SE6422
Brewers Arms (01405) 862404
Pontefract Road; DN14 9JS Georgian
inn tied to local Old Mill Brewery, their
distinctive range from brick and timber-
fronted servery, decent home-made food
including fresh fish/seafood (June crab
festival), friendly helpful staff, open-plan
carpeted interior, old well complete with
skeleton; children welcome in eating areas,
attractive, good quality bedrooms, open
all day but may close early if quiet.
(Simon Sharpe)

SNAPE   SE2684
★**Castle Arms** (01677) 470270
Off B6268 Masham–Bedale; DL8 2TB
Welcoming homely pub in pretty village,
flagstoned bar with straightforward pubby
furniture, horsebrasses on beams and open
fire, Marstons-related ales, enjoyable food
including monthly themed nights, dining
room (also flagstoned) with dark tables
and chairs and another fire; children and
dogs welcome, picnic-sets out at front
and in courtyard, fine walks in Yorkshire
Dales and on North York Moors, nine good
bedrooms. *(Millie and Peter Downing)*

SOUTH KILVINGTON   SE4284
Old Oak Tree (01845) 523276
Stockton Road (A61); YO7 2NL
Spacious low-ceilinged pub with three linked
rooms and long back conservatory, large
choice of good honest food and well kept
beers served by friendly staff; tables on
sloping lawn. *(Diane Abbott)*

SOWERBY BRIDGE   SE0623
Hogs Head (01422) 836585
Stanley Street; HX6 2AH Newly opened
brewpub in former 18th-c maltings, one
large bare-boards room with heavy beams

We mention bottled beers and spirits only if there is something unusual about them
– imported belgian real ales, say, or dozens of malt whiskies; so do please let us know
about them in your reports.

and big woodburner, brewery visible behind glass, their good beers and several mainly local guests, food planned; open from 3pm weekdays, midday weekends. *(Pat and Tony Martin)*

SOWERBY BRIDGE SE0523
Works (01422) 834821
Hollins Mill Lane, off A58; HX6 2QG
Large airy bare-boards pub in converted joinery workshop by Rochdale Canal, seating from pews to comfortable sofas, at least eight well kept ales including Timothy Taylors plus a couple of ciders, good bargain home-made food from sandwiches and pub favourites to vegetarian choices and specials, Weds curry night, Sun brunch; comedy and music nights in big upstairs room; children and dogs welcome, disabled facilities, backyard (covered in poor weather), open (and food) all day. *(Pat and Tony Martin)*

STAMFORD BRIDGE SE7055
Three Cups (01759) 377381
A166 W of town; YO41 1AX Vintage Inn family dining pub with popular food including meal deals, plenty of wines by the glass and three well kept beers, friendly helpful staff, pleasant rustic décor with two blazing fires, glass-topped well in bar; disabled access, play area behind, river walks nearby, open (and food) all day. *(Pat and Graham Williamson)*

STANBURY SE0037
Old Silent (01535) 647437
Hob Lane; BD22 0HW Welcoming moorland dining inn, enjoyable fairly priced home-made food including Thurs steak night, Timothy Taylors Landlord, Theakstons Old Peculier and guests, attentive helpful service, character linked rooms with beams, flagstones, mullioned windows and open fires, restaurant and conservatory; free wi-fi; children and dogs welcome, eight bedrooms, open all day. *(John and Eleanor Holdsworth)*

STAVELEY SE3662
Royal Oak (01423) 340267
Signed off A6055 Knaresborough–Boroughbridge; HG5 9LD Popular welcoming pub in village conservation area; beams and panelling, open fires, broad bow window overlooking front lawn, well kept Black Sheep, Timothy Taylors and two local guests, several wines by the glass, good choice of enjoyable food in bar and restaurant; children welcome. *(Douglas Power)*

STILLINGTON SE5867
Bay Tree (01347) 811394
Main Street; leave York on outer ring road (A1237) to Scarborough, first exit on left signposted B1363 to Helmsley; YO61 1JU Cottagey pub-restaurant in pretty village's main street, contemporary bar areas with comfortable cushioned wall seats and leather/bamboo tub chairs around mix of tables, church candles and lanterns,

central gas-effect coal fire, real ales such as Black Sheep, several wines by the glass and interesting restaurant food from chef-owner plus good value bar snacks, steps up to cosy dining area, larger conservatory-style back restaurant; background music; seats in garden and a couple of picnic-sets at front, closed Tues and Weds. *(Jeremy Snaithe)*

STOKESLEY NZ5208
White Swan (01642) 710263
West End; TS9 5BL Good Captain Cook ales brewed at this attractive 18th-c flower-decked local, L-shaped bar with three relaxing seating areas, log fire, assorted memorabilia and nice bar counter with carved panels, speciality pies; regular live music and beer festivals; no children, dogs welcome, open all day. *(Nick Higgins)*

SUTTON UPON DERWENT SE7047
★**St Vincent Arms** (01904) 608349
Main Street (B1228 SE of York); YO41 4BN Welcoming and cheerful with seven well kept ales including Fullers, lots of wines by the glass and popular food from interesting sandwiches to good fish/seafood specials (more elaborate evening meals – need to book weekends), bustling parlour-style front bar with panelling, traditional high-backed settles, windsor chairs, cushioned bow-window seat and gas-effect coal fire, another lounge and separate dining; children and dogs (in bar) welcome, garden tables, handy for Yorkshire Air Museum. *(Michael Doswell, Margaret and Peter Staples)*

SUTTON-UNDER-WHITESTONECLIFFE SE4983
Whitestonecliffe Inn (01845) 597271
A170 E of Thirsk; YO7 2PR Well located 18th-c beamed roadside pub, enjoyable fairly priced food from traditional menu along with blackboard specials, three well kept ales including Black Sheep, friendly staff, log fire and some exposed stonework in bar, separate restaurant, games room with pool and darts; quiz last Fri of month; children and dogs welcome, six self-catering cottages, open all day weekends, closed Mon lunchtime. *(Chris Willers)*

TAN HILL NY8906
★**Tan Hill Inn** (01833) 628246
Arkengarthdale Road, Reeth–Brough, at junction Keld/West Stonesdale Road; DL11 6ED Basic old pub (Britain's highest) in wonderful bleak setting on Pennine Way, often snowbound; full of bric-a-brac and interesting photographs, simple sturdy furniture on flagstones, ever-burning big log fire with prized stone side seats, chatty atmosphere, five well kept ales including one badged for them from Dent, good cheap pubby food, family room; live weekend music; dogs welcome, seven bedrooms, bunk rooms and camping, wandering ducks and chickens,

Swaledale sheep show here last Thurs in May, open all day and can get overcrowded. *(Ian and Rose Lock)*

THIRSK   SE4282

Golden Fleece (01845) 523108
Market Place; YO7 1LL Comfortable bustling old coaching inn with decent food and afternoon tea, Black Sheep ales and good friendly service, restaurant, view across marketplace from bay windows; dogs welcome, 23 bedrooms, good breakfast. *(Laura Reid)*

THIXENDALE   SE8461

Cross Keys (01377) 288272
Off A166 3 miles N of Fridaythorpe; YO17 9TG Unspoilt country pub in deep valley below the rolling Wolds and popular with walkers; cosy and relaxed L-shaped bar with fitted wall seats, well kept Tetleys and a couple of guests, generous uncomplicated blackboard food; no children or dogs inside, views from big back garden, handy for Wharram Percy earthworks (EH), comfortable bedrooms in converted stables, good breakfast, closed Mon-Thurs lunchtimes. *(Melanie and David Lawson)*

THOLTHORPE   SE4766

New Inn (01347) 838329
Flawith Road; YO61 1SL Cleanly updated beamed village-green pub with log-fire bar and candlelit restaurant, good food (allergies catered for) from sandwiches and wood-fired pizzas up including popular Sun lunch, Fri evening fish and chip deal, John Smiths and a local guest, friendly helpful staff; small shop; children welcome, closed Mon.
(Rosie and John Moore)

THORNTON   SE0832

White Horse (01274) 834268
Well Heads; BD13 3SJ Deceptively large country pub popular for its wide choice of good food including early-bird menu, five well kept Timothy Taylors ales, pleasant helpful staff, four separate areas, two with log fires; children welcome, upstairs lavatories (disabled ones on ground level), also disabled parking, open all day, food all day weekends (till 7.45pm Sun). *(John and Eleanor Holdsworth, Gordon and Margaret Ormondroyd)*

THORNTON DALE   SE8383

New Inn (01751) 474226
The Square; YO18 7LF Friendly early 18th-c beamed coaching inn – packed weekend evenings; well kept ales and good traditional food cooked by landlord including

deals; children and dogs (in bar) welcome, courtyard tables, six bedrooms and self-catering cottage, pretty village in walking area, open all day in summer. *(Sara Fulton, Roger Baker)*

THORNTON-LE-CLAY   SE6865

White Swan (01653) 618286
Off A64 SW of Malton, via Foston; Low Street; YO60 7TG Refurbished 19th-c family-run village pub; a house beer from Helmsley with guests such as Black Sheep and York, nice wines by the glass and enjoyable well priced home-made food including daily specials, early-bird discount 5-6.30pm (not Sun), friendly helpful young staff, some local chutneys, preserves etc for sale; children welcome, large garden, attractive countryside nearby and Castle Howard, closed Mon, open all day Sun. *(Sophie and Hamish Greenfield)*

THORP ARCH   SE4346

Pax (01937) 843183
The Village; LS23 7AR Welcoming 19th-c village pub, enjoyable home-made food (notable steak and ale pie) at sensible prices, ales such as Abbeydale, Moorhouses and Roosters, friendly helpful service, two bar areas, open fire, back dining area; children and dogs welcome, useful stop for A1, open all day weekends, no food Sun evening. *(Les and Sandra Brown)*

THRESHFIELD   SD9863

Old Hall Inn (01756) 752441
B6160/B6265 just outside Grassington; BD23 5HB Old creeper-clad village inn set back from the road, enjoyable food served by attentive friendly staff, good choice of beers and wines, flagstoned bar with dining rooms either side, open fires (one in fine blacked kitchen range), high beam-and-plank ceiling, cushioned wall pews; neat garden and pretty hanging baskets, seven comfortable bedrooms, self-catering cottage, open (and food) all day. *(T Peter Wall, Gordon and Margaret Ormondroyd)*

THRINTOFT   SE3293

New Inn (01609) 771961
Thrintoft Moor Lane, off Bramper Lane; DL7 0PN Friendly 18th-c village local with good variety of generously served home-made food including popular Sun lunch, well kept Black Sheep and a guest such as Walls County Town, restaurant, open fire and woodburner; quiz first Thurs of month, free wi-fi; children welcome, no dogs inside, disabled access, front garden with two quoits pitches, closed Mon, no food Tues lunchtime. *(Steve Thornley)*

A star before the name of a pub shows exceptional quality. It means most people (after reading the report to see just why the star has been won) would think a special trip worthwhile.

TIMBLE   SE1852

★**Timble Inn** (01943) 880530

Off Otley–Blubberhouses moors road;
LS21 2NN Smartly restored 18th-c inn
tucked away in quiet farmland hamlet, good
food from pub favourites up including well
aged Nidderdale beef (booking advised),
ales such as Copper Dragon, Ilkley and
Theakstons; children welcome, no dogs at
food times, good walks from the door, seven
well appointed bedrooms, closed Sun evening
to Weds lunchtime. *(Millie and Peter Downing)*

TONG   SE2230

Greyhound (0113) 285 2427

Tong Lane; BD4 0RR Traditional low-
beamed and flagstoned local by village
cricket field, distinctive areas including cosy
dining room, generous helpings of enjoyable
good value food, ales such as Black Sheep,
Leeds, Timothy Taylors and Tetleys, several
wines by the glass, good friendly service;
tables outside, open all day (food till 5.45pm
Sun). *(Michael Butler)*

TOPCLIFFE   SE4076

Angel (01845) 578000

Off A1, take A168 to Thirsk, after 3 miles
follow signs for Topcliffe; Long Street;
YO7 3RW Part of the West Park Inns group;
softly lit bare-boards bar with log fire, real
ales and good choice of wines by the glass,
enjoyable food in carpeted grill restaurant,
weekday early-bird deal (till 6.30pm),
cheerful helpful service; background music,
comedy night (usually first Tues of month);
children welcome, nice garden, 16 bedrooms,
open all day (food all day Sun till 8pm).
(Michael Doswell)

TOTLEY   SK3080

Cricket (0114) 236 5256

Signed from A621; Penny Lane; S17 3AZ
Tucked-away 19th-c stone-built pub (part of
the BrewKitchen group) beside rustic cricket
field, much focus on dining but still a friendly
local atmosphere, pews, mixed chairs and
pine tables on bare boards and flagstones, log
fires, enjoyable blackboard food from snacks
and sharing boards up including rotisserie
chicken and own-cured meats, cheaper
lunchtime/early evening set menu (Mon-
Fri), Thornbridge ales and good choice of
wines from extensive list, happy hour Thurs,
Fri 5-7pm, friendly service; children and
dogs welcome, outside tables and summer
barbecues, Peak District views, open (and
food) all day. *(David Carr)*

TOWTON   SE4839

Rockingham Arms (01937) 530948

A162 Tadcaster–Ferrybridge; LS24 9PB
Comfortable roadside village pub, enjoyable
home-made food including early-bird menu
(5-7pm Tues-Thurs), friendly service, ales
such as Black Sheep and Theakstons, back
conservatory; children and dogs welcome,

garden tables, handy for Towton Battlefield,
closed Sun evening, Mon, otherwise open
all day. *(Jane Sutton)*

WAINSTALLS   SE0428

Cat i' th' Well (01422) 244841

From Halifax, turn left at the Crossroads
pub in Wainstalls, follow narrow road
downhill, pub is on left after steep bend
over little bridge; HX2 7TR Picturesque
country pub in fine hidden-away spot towards
the windy top of Luddenden Dean; dining
area on the left, larger flagstoned bar with
attractive fireplace on right, some 19th-c
reclaimed panelling, well kept Timothy
Taylors ales and a guest, decent home-
made food (not Tues or Weds, till 6pm Sun)
including Thurs steak night, friendly service;
Mon quiz; children and walkers welcome,
no dogs inside, handy for Calderdale Way,
open all day Fri-Sun. *(Gordon and Margaret*
Ormondroyd)

WAKEFIELD   SE3320

Bull & Fairhouse (01924) 362930

George Street; WF1 1DL Chatty and
welcoming 19th-c pub, bare-boards bar with
comfortable rooms off, open fire, well kept
Bobs White Lion, Great Heck Golden Bull
and four other changing ales (beer festivals),
no food; live weekend music, quiz Thurs,
sports TV; children welcome till 8pm, dogs on
leads, open all day Fri-Sun, from 4pm other
days. *(Jeremy Snaithe)*

WAKEFIELD   SE3320

Fernandes Brewery Tap

(01924) 386348 *Avison Yard, Kirkgate;*
WF1 1UA Owned by Ossett but still brewing
Fernandes ales in the cellar, interesting guest
beers, bottled imports and traditional ciders,
ground-floor bar with flagstones, bare brick
and panelling, original raftered top-floor bar
with unusual breweriana; monthly folk and
open mike nights, quiz Weds; dogs welcome,
open all day Fri-Sun (when some lunchtime
food available), from 4pm other days.
(Douglas Power)

WAKEFIELD   SE3220

Harrys Bar (01924) 373773

Westgate; WF1 1EL Cheery little one-room
local with good selection of real ales and
bottled beers, stripped-brick walls, open
fire; live music Mon and Weds, free wi-fi;
small back garden, open all day Sun, closed
lunchtime other days. *(Alan and Alice Morgan)*

WALKINGTON   SE9937

Dog & Duck (01482) 423026

B1230, East End; HU17 8RX Comfortably
modernised pub with popular generously
served food including blackboard specials,
four well kept Marstons-related beers,
friendly helpful service; sports TV; children
welcome, garden and terrace with pizza oven
and barbecue, charming village, open (and
food) all day. *(Nick Higgins)*

WALTON   SE4447
Fox & Hounds   (01937) 842192
Hall Park Road, off back road Wetherby–Tadcaster; LS23 7DQ Busy dining pub with good reasonably priced food from sandwiches to specials (should book Sun lunch), well kept Black Sheep, John Smiths and a guest, friendly thriving atmosphere; children welcome, handy A1 stop, closed Mon.
(Douglas Power)

WALTON   SE3517
New Inn   (01924) 255447
Shay Lane; WF2 6LA Open-plan village pub with friendly staff and buoyant atmosphere, well kept Ossett and guests, several wines by the glass and good helpings of tasty well priced food cooked by landlord, split-level back dining extension; quiz nights Sun and Mon; children welcome, dogs in bar, garden play area, open (and food) all day.
(Michael Butler)

WARLEY TOWN   SE0524
Maypole   (01422) 835861
Signed off A646 just W of Halifax; HX2 7RZ Friendly open-plan village dining pub, enjoyable good value food from fairly traditional menu including lunchtime/early evening set deal, well kept ales such as Black Sheep, pleasant young staff, two-way woodburner; children welcome, open all day Fri-Sun, closed Mon lunchtime. *(John and Eleanor Holdsworth, Pat and Tony Martin)*

WASS   SE5579
Stapylton Arms   (01347) 868280
Back road W of Ampleforth; or follow brown sign for Byland Abbey off A170 Thirsk–Helmsley; YO61 4BE New owners and refurbishment for former Wombwell Arms; two bustling bars with log fires, a beer or two from Helmsley or Theakstons, restaurant in 18th-c granary with emphasis on contemporary food; children welcome, no dogs, pretty village and surrounding countryside, near ruins of Byland Abbey (EH), bedrooms planned, has opened all day weekends.

WATH   SE3277
George   (01765) 641324
Main Street; village N of Ripon; HG4 5EN Friendly refurbished village pub with good range of enjoyable traditional food (not Sun evening) using local ingredients, ales such as Black Sheep, Rudgate and Theakstons, decent choice of wines; five comfortable bedrooms, open all day weekends, closed lunchtimes Mon and Tues.
(Jane Sutton)

WATH-IN-NIDDERDALE   SE1467
★ Sportsmans Arms   (01423) 711306
Nidderdale road off B6265 in Pateley Bridge; village and pub signposted over hump-back bridge, on right after a couple of miles; HG3 5PP Civilised, beautifully located restaurant with rooms run by long-serving owner; although most emphasis on the excellent food and bedrooms, it does have a proper welcoming bar with open fire (a highly rated ploughman's and other food here), Black Sheep and Timothy Taylors Landlord, Thatcher's cider, lots of wines by the glass from extensive list and 40 malt whiskies, helpful hospitable staff; background music; children welcome, dogs in bar, benches and tables outside, pretty garden with croquet, own fishing on River Nidd. *(Lynda and Trevor Smith, Stephen Woad)*

WEAVERTHORPE   SE9670
Blue Bell   (01944) 738204
Main Road; YO17 8EX Upscale country dining pub, quite ornate in parts, with good attractively presented food and fine choice of wines (many by the glass including champagne), well kept Tetleys and Timothy Taylors Landlord, cosy cheerful bar with unusual collection of bottles and packaging, open fire, intimate back restaurant, friendly attentive staff; 12 bedrooms (six in annexe), interesting village, closed Sun evening, Mon.
(Millie and Peter Downing)

WENSLEY   SE0989
Three Horseshoes   (01969) 622327
A684; DL8 4HJ Simple little beamed and flagstoned country pub under new management (some redecoration), well kept Black Sheep, Rudgate, Theakstons and Wensleydale, enjoyable straightforward food including sandwiches and pizzas, friendly helpful service; children and dogs welcome, lovely views from garden, popular with walkers, open all day. *(Clive and Fran Dutson)*

WENTWORTH   SK3898
Rockingham Arms   (01226) 742075
3 miles from M1 junction 36; B6090, signed off A6135; Main Street; S62 7TL Welcoming 19th-c ivy-clad inn (John Barras group), comfortable traditional furnishings, stripped stone and open fires, bar with two snug rooms off, more formal dining room, several ales including Theakstons and good choice of wines by the glass, well priced traditional food; background music, TV; dogs allowed in part, attractive garden with bowling green, 11 bedrooms, open (and food) all day. *(Michael Butler)*

If you stay overnight in an inn or hotel, they are allowed to serve you an alcoholic drink at any hour of the day or night.

WEST TANFIELD SE2678
Bruce Arms (01677) 470325
Main Street (A6108 N of Ripon);
HG4 5JJ Smart dining pub (18th-c
coaching inn) under same ownership as
the nearby Bull; good restaurant-style food
served by friendly attentive staff, well kept
Theakstons and good range of wines, gins
and malt whiskies; terrace tables, three
comfortable bedrooms, good breakfast,
closed Sun evening, Mon, Tues and lunchtime
Weds. *(Peter and Eleanor Kenyon, Michael
Butler)*

WEST TANFIELD SE2678
Bull (01677) 470678
Church Street (A6108 N of Ripon);
HG4 5JQ Busy pub in picturesque riverside
setting; flagstoned bar and slightly raised
dining area, popular fairly standard food
(all day Sat, till 7pm Sun), well kept Black
Sheep and Theakstons, pleasant service;
background and occasional Sun live music,
free wi-fi; children (away from bar) and dogs
welcome, tables on terraces in attractive
garden sloping steeply to River Ure and
its old bridge, five bedrooms, open all day
weekends. *(Michael Butler)*

WEST WITTON SE0588
Wensleydale Heifer (01969) 622322
A684 W of Leyburn; DL8 4LS Stylish
restaurant-with-rooms rather than pub, but
can pop in just for a drink; excellent food
with emphasis on fish/seafood and grills (not
cheap), also early-bird menu, good wines,
cosy informal upmarket food bar with Black
Sheep and a house beer brewed by Yorkshire,
extensive main formal restaurant, attentive
helpful service; 13 good bedrooms (back ones
quietest), big breakfast, open all day.
(Andrew and Michelle Revell)

WESTOW SE7565
Blacksmiths Arms (01653) 619606
Off A64 York–Malton; Main Street;
YO60 7NE Updated 18th-c pub with
attractive beamed bar, woodburner in
brick inglenook and original bread oven,
beers such as Copper Dragon, Tetleys
and Thwaites, enjoyable home-made food
from sandwiches and pub favourites up,
restaurant; picnic-sets on side terrace,
open all day. *(Rosie and John Moore)*

WETHERBY SE4048
Swan & Talbot (01937) 582040
Handy for A1; North Street; LS22 6NN
Comfortable traditional town pub (former
posting inn) with large bar area and
restaurant, good food from sandwiches and
sharing plates up, four well kept ales and
several wines by the glass, busy friendly staff;
background music, TV; children welcome,
courtyard tables, open all day from 9am for
breakfast. *(Nick Higgins, Jane Sutton)*

WHITBY NZ9011
Black Horse (01947) 602906
Church Street; YO22 4BH Small
traditional two-room pub, much older than
its Victorian frontage, and previously a
funeral parlour and brothel; friendly and
down to earth with five changing ales,
continental beers and a proper cider, range
of Yorkshire tapas, tins of snuff for sale; dogs
welcome, four cosy bedrooms, open all day.
(Diane Abbott)

WHITBY NZ9011
Board (01947) 602884
Church Street; YO22 4DE Busy pub in
good spot opposite fish quay, faux-beamed
bar with nice old range in one part,
banquettes and other pubby furniture on
patterned carpet, modern dining room
downstairs with fine harbour view from big
windows, well kept Caledonian Deuchars IPA
and Theakstons, good value traditional food,
friendly staff; background music, live bands
Thurs and Fri, Weds quiz, TV and games
machine; bedrooms. *(Jeff Davies)*

WHITBY NZ9011
★ Duke of York (01947) 600324
Church Street, Harbour East Side;
YO22 4DE Busy pub in fine harbourside
position, good views and handy for the
famous 199 steps leading up to abbey;
comfortable beamed lounge bar with fishing
memorabilia, Black Sheep, Caledonian and
three guests, decent wines and several malt
whiskies, enjoyable straightforward bar
food at reasonable prices, attentive service;
background music, TV, games machine;
children welcome, bedrooms overlooking
water, no nearby parking, open (and food)
all day. *(Ian and Jane Irving)*

WHITBY NZ8911
Station Inn (01947) 603937
New Quay Road; YO21 1DH Friendly
three-room bare-boards drinkers' pub across
from the station and harbour, clean and
comfortable, with good mix of customers,
eight well kept ales including a house
beer brewed by Whitby, Weston's cider and
good wines by the glass, traditional games;
background and regular live music; dogs
welcome, open all day. *(Jeff Davies)*

WHITBY NZ9011
White Horse & Griffin
(01947) 604857 *Church Street;*
YO22 4BH Historic 17th-c coaching inn;
tall narrow front bar with bare boards and
a couple of large chandeliers, ales such as
Marstons and Timothy Taylors, steps down
to low beamed bistro-style dining area with
flagstones and log fire, good food including
brunch menu, friendly staff; ten bedrooms,
close to the 199 steps to abbey, open all day.
(Randy Alden)

WIGHILL SE4746

White Swan (01937) 832217

Main Street; LS24 8BQ Fairly modern family-run village pub with two cosy front rooms and larger side extension, well kept Black Sheep, a house beer from Moorhouses and a guest, enjoyable interesting food, friendly staff; children welcome, no dogs inside, wheelchair access with help (steps down to lavatories), picnic-sets on side lawn, closed Mon, Tues lunchtime. *(Ken Wright)*

WOMBLETON SE6683

Plough (01751) 431356

Main Street; YO62 7RW Welcoming village local with good home-made food including blackboard specials, ales such as Black Sheep, John Smiths, Tetleys and Theakstons, bar eating area and restaurant; tables outside. *(Sandra and Nigel Brown)*

WORTLEY SK3099

Wortley Arms (0114) 288 8749

A629 N of Sheffield; S35 7DB 18th-c stone-built coaching inn with several comfortably furnished rooms, beams, panelling and large inglenook, good food (all day Sat) and five well kept ales including Timothy Taylors and Wentworth; occasional live music; children and dogs (in bar) welcome, nice village about ten minutes from M1, open all day (till 8pm Sun). *(Michael Butler, Stuart Paulley)*

YORK SE6051

Black Swan (01904) 686910

Peaseholme Green (inner ring road); YO1 7PR Striking black and white Tudor building; compact panelled front bar, crooked-floored central hall with fine period staircase and black-beamed back bar with vast inglenook, good choice of real ales, decent wines and generous helpings of reasonably priced pubby food from sandwiches up; background music; children welcome, useful car park behind, bedrooms, open all day. *(Jeremy Snaithe)*

YORK SE6051

★ Blue Bell (01904) 654904

Fossgate; YO1 9TF Delightfully old-fashioned little Edwardian pub, very friendly and chatty, with well kept Bradfield, Rudgate, Timothy Taylors Landlord and three guests (a dark mild always available), good value lunchtime sandwiches (not Sun), daily papers, tiny tiled-floor front bar with roaring fire, panelled ceiling and stained glass, corridor to small back room with hatch service, lamps and candles, pub games; no children, dogs welcome, open all day (but maybe just for locals on busy nights). *(Roger and Donna Huggins)*

YORK SE5951

★ Brigantes (01904) 675355

Micklegate; YO1 6JX Bar-bistro (Market Town Tavern) with shop-style frontage, wooden tables and chairs on bare boards, blue-painted half-panelling and screens forming booths, ten well kept mainly Yorkshire ales (York Brewery is in street behind), good range of bottled beers, decent wines and coffee, good food from fairly priced varied menu, quick cheerful service, upstairs function room; children and dogs welcome, open all day, food all day weekends. *(Pat and Tony Martin)*

YORK SE6051

Golden Ball (01904) 652211

Cromwell Road/Victor Street; YO1 6DU Friendly well preserved four-room Edwardian corner pub owned by local co-operative, five well kept changing ales, no food apart from bar snacks, bar billiards, cards and dominoes; live music first and third Thurs, TV; lovely small walled garden, open all day weekends, closed weekday lunchtimes. *(Jeremy Snaithe)*

YORK SE6051

Golden Fleece (01904) 625171

Pavement; YO1 9UP Popular little city-centre pub with four well kept ales including Copper Dragon and Timothy Taylors, long corridor from bar to comfortable back dining room (sloping floors – it dates from 1503), interesting décor with quite a library, lots of pictures and ghost stories; background music and occasional folk evenings; children allowed if eating, no dogs, four bedrooms, open all day. *(Jeremy Snaithe)*

YORK SE6052

Guy Fawkes (01904) 466674

High Petergate; YO1 7HP Splendid spot next to the Minster, dark panelled interior with small bar to the left, half a dozen real ales including Timothy Taylors and York, enjoyable sensibly priced food (not Sun evening) from shortish menu plus blackboard specials, good helpful service, dining rooms lit by gas wall-lights and candles, open fires; courtyard tables, 13 bedrooms, open all day. *(Laura Reid, Jeremy Snaithe)*

YORK SE6051

Harkers (01904) 672795

St Helens Square; YO1 8QN Nicholsons pub in handsome late Georgian building (basement has part of Roman gateway), spacious split-level bar with high ceilings and

---

A few pubs try to make you leave a credit card at the bar, as a sort of deposit if you order food. This is a bad practice, and the banks and credit card firms warn you not to let your card go like this.

columns, a couple of smaller rooms off, half a dozen ales including Rudgate, John Smiths and York from long counter, their usual good value food; open all day. *(Jeff Davies)*

YORK SE6052
House of Trembling Madness
(01904) 640009 *Stonegate; YO1 8AS*
Unusual place above own off-licence; impressive high-raftered medieval room with collection of stuffed animal heads from moles to lions, eclectic mix of furniture including cask seats and pews on bare boards, lovely old brick fireplace, real ales and craft beers from pulpit servery, also huge selection of bottled beers (all available to buy downstairs), good knowledgeable staff, hearty reasonably priced food including various platters; two self-catering apartments in ancient courtyard behind, open (and food) all day. *(Roger and Donna Huggins)*

YORK SE5951
★ Judges Lodging (01904) 639312
Lendal; YO1 8AQ Lovely Georgian townhouse in city centre; cellar bar with fine vaulted ceilings, upholstered dining chairs and sofas on big flagstones, through to contemporary dining room and bright airy garden room, real ales, good wines by the glass and interesting food; ground-floor 'Medicine Cabinet' with quirky men's trouser leg stools by bar counter, leather armchairs on either side of fireplace and plaster judges' heads, two more restaurants upstairs with tall window shutters, chandeliers and gilt-edged mirrors, efficient friendly staff; modern furniture out in front between lavender pots, more seating behind, well equipped comfortable bedrooms (top one with York Minster view), open and food all day.
(Lionel Smith, Beth Aldridge, Rona Mackinlay)

YORK SE6052
Lamb & Lion (01904) 612078
High Petergate; YO1 7EH Appealing Georgian inn next to Bootham Bar; five well kept local ales and nice choice of wines by the glass, good food from sandwiches to more restauaranty choices, friendly helpful staff, bare-boards bar and series of compact rooms off narrow corridors; steep steps up to attractive paved garden below city wall and looking up to the Minster, 12 bedrooms, open all day, food all day Sun. *(Marianne and Peter Stevens)*

YORK SE6052
Old White Swan (01904) 540911
Goodramgate; YO1 7LF Spacious bustling Nicholsons pub with Victorian, Georgian and Tudor-themed bars, wide choice of fair value food, eight well kept ales and good whisky choice, central glass-covered courtyard (dogs allowed here); background and monthly live music, big-screen sports TV, games machines; children welcome (till 9pm if eating), open all day. *(Jeremy Snaithe)*

YORK SE6051
Phoenix (01904) 656401
George Street; YO1 9PT Friendly little pub next to city walls, proper front public bar and comfortable back horseshoe-shaped lounge, five well kept ales for Yorkshire brewers, decent wines and simple food; live jazz two or three times a week, bar billiards; beer garden, handy for Barbican, open all day Sat, closed lunchtimes other days. *(Ken Wright)*

YORK SE6051
Pivni (01904) 635464
Patrick Pool; YO1 8BB Old black and white pub close to the Shambles, extensive range of foreign draught and bottled beers (some unusual choices), also good selection of local ales, friendly knowledgeable staff, small narrow bar, more seats upstairs, snacky food and good coffee; dogs welcome, open all day. *(Ken Wright, Nick Higgins)*

YORK SE6051
Punch Bowl (01904) 655147
Stonegate; YO1 8AN Bustling 17th-c black and white-fronted pub with small panelled rooms off corridor, good choice of well kept ales, decent wines and sensibly priced Nicholsons menu, efficient friendly service, dining room at back with fireplace; background music; a couple of tables out by pavement, open (and food) all day. *(Eddie Edwards)*

YORK SE6052
Royal Oak (01904) 628869
Goodramgate; YO1 7LG Comfortable old pub with good choice of enjoyable food including evening set menu (Mon-Thurs), well kept Greene King, Theakstons and guests, decent wines, good friendly service; background music (live Weds, Fri), quiz Sun; handy for Minster, open all day. *(Pat and Graham Williamson)*

YORK SE6052
Snickleway (01904) 656138
Goodramgate; YO1 7LS Interesting little open-plan pub behind big shop-front window, lots of antiques, copper and brass, cosy fires, five well kept ales, some lunchtime food (not Sun) including good sandwiches, cheery landlord and prompt friendly service, stories of various ghosts including Mrs Tulliver and her cat; Tues quiz; open all day. *(Ken Wright)*

YORK SE6052
Star Inn the City (01904) 619208
Museum Street; YO1 7DR Restauaranty place (sister to the Star at Harome) in wonderful central riverside setting – a former 19th-c pumping station with modern glass extension; very good but not cheap food (they also do a weekday set menu till early evening), beers including a house brew (Two Chefs) from Great Yorkshire, good range of wines by the glass and cocktails,

friendly service; open all day from 9am for breakfast. *(Richard Tilbrook)*

YORK   SE6051
Swan (01904) 634968
Bishopgate Street, Clementhorpe; YO23 1JH Unspoilt 1930s pub (Grade II listed), hatch service to lobby for two small rooms off main bar, several changing ales and ciders, friendly knowledgeable staff may offer tasters; small pleasant walled garden, near city walls, open all day weekends, closed weekday lunchtimes. *(Nick Higgins)*

YORK   SE6052
★ **Three Legged Mare** (01904) 638246
High Petergate; YO1 7EN Bustling light and airy modern café-bar with York Brewery's full range and guests kept well (12 handpumps), plenty of belgian beers too, quick friendly young staff, interesting sandwiches and some basic lunchtime hot food, back conservatory; no children, disabled facilities (other lavatories down spiral stairs), back garden with replica gallows after which pub is named, open all day till midnight (11pm Sun). *(Jane Sutton, Douglas Power)*

YORK   SE5951
Whippet (01904) 500660
Opposite Park Inn Hotel, North Street; YO1 6JD Steak and alehouse in street set back from the river, good popular food including signature dry-aged steaks, small bar area with four well kept ales from Yorkshire brewers, lots of wines by the glass, interesting cocktails and excellent range of gins, friendly well informed staff; no children, open all day. *(Pat and Graham Williamson)*

YORK   SE5951
York Tap (01904) 659009
Station Road; YO24 1AB Restored Edwardian bar at York station; high ceiling with feature stained-glass cupolas, columns and iron fretwork, bentwood chairs and stools on terrazzo floor, button-back banquettes, period fireplaces, great selection of real ales from circular counter with brass footrail, also bottled beers listed on blackboard, good pork pies (three types); seats out by platform, open all day from 10am. *(Roger and Donna Huggins)*

London

CENTRAL LONDON   Map 13

Admiral Codrington 🍷

(020) 7581 0005 – www.theadmiralcodrington.co.uk

Mossop Street; ⊖ *South Kensington; SW3 2LY*

Long-standing Chelsea landmark with easy-going bar and pretty restaurant, popular food and seats outside

Bustling and with a gently civilised atmosphere, this tucked-away pub has a good mix of customers dropping in and out all day. A central dark-panelled bar has high red chairs beside the counter with more around equally high tables on either side of the log-effect gas fire, button-back wall banquettes with cream and red patterned seats, little stools and plain wooden chairs around a medley of tables on black-painted boards, patterned wallpaper above a dado and a shelf with daily papers. There are ornate flower arrangements, a big portrait above the fire, several naval prints and quiet background music. The friendly, helpful staff serve London Beer Factory Chelsea Blonde, Upham Tipster and a guest beer on handpump, good wines by the glass and, of course, their famous bloody mary. The light and airy restaurant area is a total contrast: high-backed pretty wall seats and plush dining chairs around light tables, an open kitchen, fish prints on pale blue paintwork, a second fireplace and an impressive retractable skylight. The back garden has chunky benches and tables under a summer awning.

🍴 Enjoyable food includes smoked sea trout with warm potato and spring onion salad, smoked chicken and ham hock ballotine with piccalilli, leek and mushroom pie, beer-battered haddock and triple-cooked chips, beef fillet and shin wellington with mushroom purée, pickled girolles and stout reduction, sea bream with fennel purée, confit fennel and beurre blanc, lamb rump with olive-crushed potato, confit tomato and lamb jus, fish pot pie with thai curry sauce, 28-day-aged steaks with a choice of sauces, and puddings such as sticky toffee pudding with orange butterscotch and stem ginger ice-cream and chocolate fondant with chocolate soil, mascarpone and coconut sorbet. *Benchmark main dish: burger with toppings, coleslaw and chips £14.50. Two-course evening meal £25.00.*

Free house ~ Licensee Ben Newton ~ Real ale ~ Open 11.30-11 (midnight Weds, Thurs, 1am Fri, Sat); 12-10.30 Sun; closed 24-26 Dec ~ Bar food 12-3, 6-10 (11 Thurs, Fri); 12-4, 7-11 Sat; 12-9 Sun ~ Restaurant ~ Children welcome but not in bar after 7pm ~ Dogs allowed in bar ~ Wi-fi *Recommended by Edward May, Isobel Mackinlay, Margaret McDonald, Tom Stone*

Map 13

Alfred Tennyson 🌟 ♀

(020) 7730 6074 – www.thealfredtennyson.co.uk

Motcomb Street; ⊖ *Knightsbridge; SW1X 8LA; SW1X 8LA*

Bustling and civilised with good drinks choice, rewarding food and friendly, helpful service

The interesting food and drinks and relaxed, civilised atmosphere draw plenty of customers to this pub in a quiet residential area. Apart from one table surrounded by stools beside the bar counter, there are high-backed upholstered dining chairs around wooden tables on parquet flooring, comfortable leather wall seats and eclectic décor that encompasses 19th-c postcards to nobility, envelopes displayed address-side out, Edward Lear illustrations and World War II prints – plus antique books on windowsills. Friendly, helpful staff serve Canopy Journeyman and Cubitt 1788 (named for the pub from Canopy) on handpump, cocktails and 23 wines by the glass. The upstairs restaurant has leather chairs and wooden tables on more parquet and a huge mirror above an open fire. Above that is a room for private hire, while up again is a cosy loft used for monthly events such as cheese tastings. The front pavement has tables and chairs beneath a striped awning.

 Rewarding food includes country-style terrine with pumpkin chutney, chilli salt squid with grilled lime dressing, stuffed globe artichoke with smoked aubergine, minted yoghurt, spring onions and pine nut dressing, shepherd's pie with cheddar mash, slow-cooked rabbit leg with chorizo, tomato and green olive ragoût with grain mustard dumplings, spicy chicken burger with avocado, blue cheese and smoked tomato sauce, salmon fillet with caramelised onion, samphire and romesco sauce, and puddings such as rum and coconut cake with salted banana mousse and apple tart with caramel, brown butter and pecan ice-cream. *Benchmark main dish: lightly battered fish and chips £14.00. Two-course evening meal £24.00.*

Cubitt House ~ Lease Adam Quigley ~ Real ale ~ Open & bar food 8am-11pm; 9am-11pm Sat; 9am-10pm Sun ~ Children welcome ~ Dogs allowed in bar ~ Wi-fi
Recommended by Toby Jones, Caroline Prescott, Neil Tipler, Michael Butler

TQ2781 Map 13

Grazing Goat 🌟 ♀ 🛏

(020) 7724 7243 – www.thegrazinggoat.co.uk

New Quebec Street; ⊖ *Marble Arch; W1H 7RQ*

A good mixed crowd of customers, restful décor, a thoughtful choice of drinks and good interesting food; bedrooms

It's hard to believe that goats used to graze on this land, tucked away as it is behind busy Oxford Street. A stylish pub with a rustic feel, it has a big gilt-edged mirror above an open fire and plenty of spreading dining space with white cushioned and beige dining chairs around pale tables on bare boards, sage green or light oak-panelled walls, hanging lamps and lanterns and some goat memorabilia dotted about. Efficient, friendly staff serve Canopy Journeyman and Cubitt 1788 (named for the pub from Canopy), 23 wines by the glass and Weston's cider. The upstairs restaurant is more formal. Glass doors open on to the street where there are a few wooden-slatted chairs and tables. The bedrooms are modern and well equipped, with good bathrooms.

 Imaginative food includes smoked gurnard with pickled vegetables, samphire, sea beets and mushroom broth, globe artichoke with avocado, crispy broccoli and broad bean and mint dressing, salad of spiced crab with red kaniwa (similar to quinoa), avocado, cashew nut and lime aioli, rare-breed burger with coppa ham, smoked cheddar and red onion jam, chicken, bacon and three-cheese pie with fennel, orange and rocket salad, saddle of rabbit with leg croquette, liver pâté with caramelised onion and sage dressing, haddock with spring onion spelt, a poached egg and cockle dressing, and puddings such as rum-poached pineapple with brown sugar marshmallow and coconut sorbet and lemon and almond pudding with milk ice-cream. *Benchmark main dish: beer-battered fish and chips £14.00. Two-course evening meal £24.00.*

Cubitt House ~ Licensee Adam Quigley ~ Real ale ~ Open & bar food 7.30am-11pm (10.30pm Sun) ~ Restaurant ~ Children welcome ~ Dogs allowed in bar ~ Wi-fi ~ Bedrooms: £210/£250 *Recommended by Tim and Sarah Smythe-Brown, Charles Todd, Laura Reid*

CENTRAL LONDON   Map 13

Harp 🍺

(020) 7836 0291 – www.harpcoventgarden.com
47 Chandos Place; ⊖ ⇄ *Charing Cross* ⊖ *Leicester Square; WC2N 4HS*

Ten real ales and lots of ciders and perries in bustling narrow pub; pretty summer hanging baskets

Whatever the time of day, this little gem is always busy; at peak times, customers are happy to spill out on to the pavement or the back alley. It pretty much consists of one long narrow, very traditional bar, with lots of high bar stools along the wall counter and around elbow tables, big mirrors on the red walls, some lovely stained glass and loads of interesting, quirkily executed celebrity portraits. If you're lucky, you may be able to snare one of the prized seats by the front windows. A little room upstairs is much quieter, with comfortable furniture and a window overlooking the road below. The ten real ales on handpump are particularly well kept and quickly changing, though they always have Harveys Best, Dark Star American Pale Ale and Hophead and Fullers London Pride with guests sourced from all over the country – as well as up to nine farm ciders, three perries and quite a few malt whiskies.

Food – served lunchtime only – consists of sandwiches, sausage rolls and pork pies.

Free house ~ Licensee Sarah Bird ~ Real ale ~ Open 10.30am-11.30pm; 10.30am-midnight Fri, Sat; 12-10.30 Sun ~ Bar food 12-2 ~ Wi-fi *Recommended by Taff Thomas, Tony Scott, Edward and William Johnston, William Slade*

CENTRAL LONDON   Map 13

Lamb & Flag 🍺 £

(020) 7497 9504 – www.lambandflagcoventgarden.co.uk
Rose Street, off Garrick Street; ⊖ *Covent Garden, Leicester Square; WC2E 9EB*

Historic yet unpretentious, full of character and atmosphere, with six real ales and pubby food

This is the most characterful pub in Covent Garden, so you'll never have it to yourself – but customers spill out on to the pavement, even in winter. It's an unspoilt and, in places, rather basic old tavern: the more spartan front room leads into a cosy, atmospheric, low-ceilinged back bar with high-backed black settles and an open fire. Fullers ESB, London Pride, Olivers Island, Seafarers, Summer Ale and a seasonal beer plus a couple of guests from breweries such as Adnams and Butcombe on handpump, as well as 12 wines by the glass and 25 malt whiskies. The upstairs Dryden Room is often less crowded and has more seats (though fewer beers). There's a lively and well documented history: Dryden was nearly beaten to death by hired thugs outside, and Dickens made fun of the Middle Temple lawyers who frequented it when he was working in nearby Catherine Street.

🍴 Tasty food, served upstairs, includes sandwiches, nibbles such as lamb kofta, barbecue chicken wings and baked brie with garlic bread, sharing boards, gammon and eggs, steak in ale pie, sausage and mash with caramelised onions and gravy, burgers with toppings and chips, and puddings such as chocolate brownie and sticky toffee pudding. *Benchmark main dish: beer-battered fish and chips £12.00. Two-course evening meal £19.50.*

Fullers ~ Manager Tim Adams ~ Real ale ~ Open 11-11; 12-10.30 Sun ~ Bar food 12-9 ~ Restaurant ~ Children in upstairs dining room only ~ Dogs allowed in bar ~ Wi-fi ~ Live jazz first Sun evening of month *Recommended by Sharon and John Hancock, Tony Scott, Brian and Anna Marsden*

CENTRAL LONDON   Map 13

Old Bank of England 🍷 🍺

(020) 7430 2255 – www.oldbankofengland.co.uk
Fleet Street; ⊖ *Chancery Lane (not Sundays), Temple (not Sundays)*
⊖ ⇄ *Blackfriars; EC4A 2LT*

Dramatically converted former bank building, with gleaming chandeliers in impressive, soaring bar, well kept Fullers beers and tasty food

The interior here is quite astounding. It was once a subsidiary branch of the Bank of England and is a Grade I listed Italianate building –the soaring spacious bar has three gleaming chandeliers hanging from an exquisitely plastered ceiling that's high above an unusually tall island bar counter crowned with a clock. The end wall has huge paintings and murals that look like 18th-c depictions of Justice, but in fact, feature members of the Fuller, Smith and Turner families, who set up the brewery that owns the pub. There are well polished dark wooden furnishings, luxurious curtains swagging massive windows, plenty of framed prints and, despite the grandeur, some surprisingly cosy corners, with screens between tables creating an unexpectedly intimate feel. The quieter galleried section upstairs offers a bird's-eye view of the action; some smaller rooms (used mainly for functions) open off. Fullers ESB, IPA, London Pride, Olivers Island, Seafarers and a guest beer on handpump alongside a good choice of malt whiskies and a dozen wines by the glass. At lunchtime, the background music is generally classical or easy listening; it's louder and livelier in the evenings. There's also a garden with seats (one of the few pubs in the area to have one).

🍴 Pies have a long if rather dubious pedigree in this area: it was in the vaults and tunnels below the Old Bank and the surrounding buildings that Sweeney Todd butchered the clients destined to provide the fillings at his mistress Mrs Lovett's nearby pie shop. Somehow or other, good home-made pies have become a speciality on the menu here too: sweet potato, spinach and goats cheese, lamb with red wine, rosemary and mint, and traditional fish. They also offer breakfasts (8-11am), chicken, pistachio and pomegranate salad, beer-battered fish and chips, burger with toppings and chips, and puddings such as gooseberry pie and chocolate brownie. *Benchmark main dish: steak in ale pie £12.95. Two-course evening meal £19.50.*

Fullers ~ Manager Harry Christie ~ Real ale ~ Open 8am-11pm; closed Sun~ Bar food 12-9 Mon-Fri ~ Children welcome ~ Wi-fi *Recommended by Dr and Mrs A K Clarke, Tony Scott, Simon Collett-Jones, Richard Kennell, Barry Collett, Mrs Maureen Pye*

We mention bottled beers and spirits only if there is something unusual about them – imported belgian real ales, say, or dozens of malt whiskies; so do please let us know about them in your reports.

CENTRAL LONDON   Map 13

Olde Mitre ◀ £

(020) 7405 4751 – www.yeoldemitreholburn.co.uk

Ely Place; the easiest way to find it is from the narrow passageway beside 8 Hatton Garden; ❸ *Chancery Lane (not Sundays); EC1N 6SJ*

Hard to find but well worth it – an unspoilt old pub with lovely atmosphere, unusual guest beers and bargain toasted sandwiches

This is a real refuge from the modern city nearby – and there's been a tavern here since 1546. The cosy small rooms have lots of dark panelling as well as antique settles and (particularly in the popular back room where there are more seats) old local pictures and so forth. It gets good-naturedly packed with the City suited-and-booted between 12.30pm and 2.15pm, filling up again in the early evening, but in the early afternoons and by around 8pm is a good deal more tranquil. An upstairs room, mainly used for functions, may double as an overflow area at peak periods. They serve Adnams Broadside, Fullers London Pride, Olivers Island, Seafarers and three guest beers on handpump, and they hold three beer festivals a year; eight farm ciders and several wines by the glass. No music, TV or machines – the only games here are cribbage and dominoes. There's some space for outside drinking by the pot plants and jasmine in the narrow yard between the pub and St Etheldreda's Church (which is worth a look). Note the pub doesn't open on weekends or bank holidays. The best approach is from Hatton Garden, walking up the right-hand side away from Chancery Lane; an easily missed sign on a lamp-post points the way down a narrow alley. No children.

 Served all day, bar snacks are limited to scotch eggs, pork pies, sausage rolls and really good value toasties.

Fullers ~ Manager Judith Norman ~ Real ale ~ Open 11-11; closed weekends and bank holidays ~ Wi-fi *Recommended by Conor McGaughey, Tony Scott, N R White, Daniel England*

CENTRAL LONDON   Map 13

Orange ⊙| ♀ ⇔

(020) 7881 9844 – www.theorange.co.uk

Pimlico Road; ❸ *Sloane Square; SW1W 8NE*

London Dining Pub of the Year

Carefully restored pub with simply decorated rooms, thoughtful choice of drinks and good modern cooking; bedrooms

At the heart of Pimlico, this restored Georgian inn has an easy-going, gently civilised feel and courteous, friendly staff. The two floors of the pub itself have huge sash windows on all sides making the interconnected rooms light and airy; throughout, the décor is shabby-chic and simple and the atmosphere easy-going and chatty. The high-ceilinged downstairs bar has wooden dining chairs around pale tables on bare boards, an open fire at one end and a big carved counter where they keep Canopy Journeyman and Cubitt 1788 (named for the pub from Canopy), 23 wines by the glass, Weston's cider and a lengthy cocktail list. The dining room to the right, usually packed with cheerful customers, is decorated with prints, glass bottles and soda siphons, big house plants and a few rustic knick-knacks. Upstairs, the linked restaurant rooms are similarly furnished with old french travel posters and circus prints on cream walls, more open fireplaces, big glass ceiling lights and chandeliers and jazz playing quietly in the background. This is a comfortable place to stay in well equipped bedrooms; breakfasts are first class.

 Good modern food includes smoked quail with broad beans, fried quail egg and peanut granola, wild boar terrine with pistachio, shallot confit and toasted spelt bread, trout with fennel freekeh (a kind of grain) and razor clam and caper dressing, potato gnocchi with smoked garlic cream, calçot onions and blue cheese, salad of crab, pickled cockles, sea lettuce and oyster mayonnaise, slow-cooked rabbit pie with baked mash and chervil buttered asparagus, corn-fed chicken breast with round lettuce and pea and ham broth, and puddings such as lemon and passion-fruit tart with coconut sorbet and chocolate praline délice with popcorn and salted malt parfait. *Benchmark main dish: wood-fired pizzas £14.50. Two-course evening meal £24.00.*

Cubitt House ~ Licensee Adam Quigley ~ Real ale ~ Open & bar food 8am-11.30pm (midnight Fri, Sat); 8am-10.30pm Sun ~ Restaurant ~ Children welcome ~ Dogs allowed in bar ~ Wi-fi ~ Bedrooms: £205/£240 *Recommended by Nick Sharpe, Rosie and John Moore, Penny and David Shepherd, Elizabeth and Peter May*

CENTRAL LONDON
Punchbowl ♀

Map 13

(020) 7493 6841 ~ www.punchbowllondon.com
Farm Street; ⊖ *Green Park; W1J 5RP*

Bustling, rather civilised pub with good wines and ales, enjoyable food and helpful service

This tucked-away Mayfair pub has real character – the nicest part is at the back where several panelled booths have suede bench seating, animal scatter cushions, some etched glasswork and church candles on tables. Elegant spoked chairs are grouped around dark tables on worn floorboards, a couple of long elbow shelves are lined with high chairs and one fireplace has a coal fire while the other is piled with logs. At the front it's simpler, with cushioned bench seating and pubby tables and chairs on floor tiles. All sorts of artwork from cartoons to oil paintings line the walls and the ceiling has interesting old hand-drawn street maps; background music. Adnams Broadside, Caledonian Deuchars IPA and a beer named for the pub on handpump, good wines by the glass and professional, friendly service. The smart dining room upstairs has plush furnishings, large artworks and a huge gilt mirror above an open fire; there are private dining facilities too.

Good food includes lightly battered monkfish cheeks with crispy kale, smoked paprika and gribiche sauce, rabbit, baby leek and ham hock terrine with celeriac and apple slaw, wild boar and apple sausages with caramelised onion and wild thyme gravy, ricotta, squash and mushroom wellington with chive butter sauce, chicken with mushrooms, celeriac, roasted garlic and truffled tarragon sauce, king prawn and chorizo linguine with white wine, chilli and garlic, 28-day dry-aged rib-eye steak with béarnaise sauce and truffle chips, and puddings such as sticky toffee pudding and banana and spiced rum bread and butter pudding. *Benchmark main dish: beer-battered fish and chips £14.50. Two-course evening meal £30.00.*

Free house ~ Licensee Ben Newton ~ Real ale ~ Open 12-11 (9 Sun) ~ Bar food 12-3.30, 5.30-10; 12-10 Sat; 12-8 Sun ~ Restaurant ~ Children welcome if seated and dining ~ Dogs allowed in bar ~ Wi-fi *Recommended by Edward May, Belinda Stamp, Laura Reid, Jeff Davies*

'Children welcome' means the pub says it lets children inside without any special restriction. If it allows them in, but to restricted areas such as an eating area or family room, we specify this. Some pubs may impose an evening time limit. We do not mention limits after 9pm as we assume children are home by then.

CENTRAL LONDON   Map 13

Seven Stars ◀

(020) 7242 8521 – www.thesevenstars1602.co.uk

Carey Street; ⊖ Temple (not Sundays), Chancery Lane (not Sundays), Holborn;
WC2A 2JB

**Quirky pub with cheerful staff, an interesting mix of customers
and a good choice of drinks and food**

A favourite haunt of lawyers, Church of England music directors and
choir singers, this character pub faces the back of the law courts.
Numerous caricatures of barristers and judges line the red-painted walls of
the two main rooms and there are posters of legal-themed british films, big
ceiling fans and checked tablecloths that add a quirky, almost continental
touch. A third area, in what was formerly a legal wig shop next door, still
retains its original frontage, with a neat display of wigs in the window. It's
worth arriving early as they don't take bookings and tables get snapped up
quickly. Adnams Broadside, Harveys IPA, Sharps Cornish Coaster and a
couple of changing guests on handpump and six wines by the glass (they
import wine from France); they do a particularly good dry martini. On busy
evenings, customers overflow on to the quiet road in front; things generally
quieten down after 8pm and there can be a nice, sleepy atmosphere some
afternoons. The Elizabethan stairs up to the loos are rather steep, but there's
a good strong handrail. The pub cat, who wears a ruff, is called Peabody.
No children are allowed.

🍴 Cooked according to the landlady's fancy, the good, interesting food includes prawn
and crayfish cocktail, clam and chorizo chowder, dill-cured herrings, a vegetarian
cheesy pasta dish, pork and parmesan meatballs in broth, rabbit stew, chicken with
new potatoes and asparagus, and slow-braised lamb shank. *Benchmark main dish:
pie of the day £11.00. Two-course evening meal £15.00.*

Free house ~ Licensee Roxy Beaujolais ~ Real ale ~ Open 11-11; 12-11 Sat; 12-10 Sun;
closed some bank holidays ~ Bar food 1-9.30 ~ Wi-fi *Recommended by Brian and Anna
Marsden, Dr and Mrs A K Clarke, Dr J Barrie Jones*

CENTRAL LONDON   Map 13

Star ◀

(020) 7235 3019 – www.star-tavern-belgravia.co.uk

Belgrave Mews West, behind the German Embassy, off Belgrave Square;
⊖ Knightsbridge, Hyde Park Corner; SW1X 8HT

**Bustling local with restful bar, upstairs dining room, Fullers ales,
well liked bar food and colourful hanging baskets**

Outside peak times, there's a restful, local feel to this tucked-away pub
in its cobbled mews. The small bar is pleasant, with sash windows, a
wooden floor, stools by the counter, an open winter fire and Fullers ESB,
London Pride and Olivers Island plus a guest beer on handpump, nine wines
by the glass and a few malt whiskies. An arch leads to the main seating
area with well polished tables and chairs and good lighting; there's also an
upstairs dining room. In summer, the front of the building is covered with an
astonishing array of hanging baskets and flowering tubs. It's said that this is
where the Great Train Robbery was planned.

🍴 Popular food includes lunchtime sandwiches, port and stilton rarebit, smoked duck
with poached pears, blue cheese and walnuts, pork belly with celeriac mash, sage
and apple, mozzarella with spelt, broccoli, cranberries, chilli and hazelnuts, corn-fed
chicken with sautéed potatoes and smoked bacon, fish pie, rib-eye steak with roquefort

butter and chips, and puddings such as vanilla and ginger cheesecake and chocolate and peanut butter tart. *Benchmark main dish: beer-battered fish and chips £12.00. Two-course evening meal £19.00.*

Fullers ~ Manager Marta Lemieszewska ~ Real ale ~ Open 11-11; 12-11 Sat; 12-10.30 Sun ~ Bar food 12-3, 5-9; 12-4, 5-9 Sun ~ Restaurant ~ Children welcome ~ Dogs welcome ~ Wi-fi
Recommended by Mike and Jayne Bastin, Michael Butler, Helen McLagan

CENTRAL LONDON Map 13
Thomas Cubitt 🍴 🍷
(020) 7730 6060 – www.thethomascubitt.co.uk
Elizabeth Street; ⊖ Sloane Square ⊖ ⇌ Victoria; SW1W 9PA

Belgravia pub with a civilised but friendly atmosphere and enjoyable food and drink

Named after the legendary builder and located in well heeled Elizabeth Street, this bustling place has a bar with miscellaneous Edwardian-style dining chairs around wooden tables on stripped parquet flooring, and architectural prints and antlers on panelled or painted walls; open fires and lovely flower arrangements. Attentive staff serve Canopy Journeyman and Cubitt 1788 (named for the pub from Canopy), 23 wines by the glass, Weston's cider and cocktails. The more formal dining room upstairs has smart upholstered wooden chairs around white-clothed tables, candles in wall holders, a few prints, house plants and window blinds; background music. In warm weather, the floor-to-ceiling glass doors are pulled back to the street where there are cordoned-off tables and chairs on the pavement.

 Enterprising food inludes rare-breed pork terrine with crispy ear, pickled mustard seeds and ale chutney, home-cured bresaola with pickled onions, brisket croquettes and potato and rosemary bread, poached trout with cucumber, dill, red onion and lemon crème fraîche, orange braised chicory with potato confit, celery and cardamom purée, granola and mint yoghurt, corn-fed chicken breast with spiced broad beans and braised baby gem, bacon and pine nut dressing, rare-breed lamb shank pie with tarragon jus, dry-aged rib-eye steak with celeriac rémoulade, truffle and parmesan fries, and puddings such as pineapple with rum, brown sugar marshmallow and coconut sorbet and chocolate tart with chocolate sorbet and honeycomb. *Benchmark main dish: lamb burger with rocket pesto, smoked garlic mayonnaise and paprika fries £15.00. Two-course evening meal £24.00.*

Cubitt House ~ Licensee Adam Quigley ~ Real ale ~ Open 12-11 (10 Sun) ~ Bar food 12-10 (9 Sun) ~ Restaurant ~ Children welcome ~ Dogs allowed in bar ~ Wi-fi *Recommended by Tracey and Stephen Groves, Tim and Sarah Smythe-Brown, Peter and Emma Kelly*

NORTH LONDON TQ1493 Map 5
Hare
(020) 8954 4949 – www.hareoldredding.com
Brookshill/Old Redding; ⇌ Hatch End; HA3 6SD

Carefully modernised old pub with plenty of drinking and dining space, friendly staff and enjoyable food

This extended early 19th-c pub is attractively contemporary inside with interconnected bar and dining rooms. The bar has tartan cushions on a long leather wall seat, upholstered and leather dining chairs around a medley of tables and a long counter lined with bar stools. Fullers London Pride and a changing guest beer on handpump and several wines by the glass. The stylish brasserie has a woodburning stove, a long beige button-back leather wall seat, leather-seated chairs around simple tables, rugs on bare boards and candles in lanterns, and there's also a similarly furnished dining area with more rugs on black slates. A little room with burgundy-painted wall planking is just right for a small group. Throughout, there are church candles on substantial holders, dried lavender in rustic jugs and modern artwork. The back garden has seats and tables under a gazebo, deck chairs on the lawn and piles of blankets for cooler weather; some picnic-sets out in front.

Quite a choice of food includes potted crab with avocado, shallot and coriander guacamole, crispy goats cheese parcel with pea and broad bean salad and tomato and chilli dressing, a pie of the week, chickpea and coriander cakes with smoked aubergine and roast tomato sauce, beef bourguignon, duck breast and confit leg with dauphinoise potatoes and citrus sauce, salmon fillet with pickled vegetables and dill crème fraîche, 30-day dry-aged steaks with a choice of sauces, and puddings such as deep-baked lemon tart with crème fraîche and pistachio soufflé with chocolate ice-cream; they also offer a two-course evening set menu (not Sunday). *Benchmark main dish: steak frites £19.50. Two-course evening meal £22.00.*

White Brasserie Company ~ Manager Amanda Radcliffe ~ Real ale ~ Open 11-11 (10 Sun) ~ Bar food 12-10 (10.30 Fri, Sat); 12-9 Sun ~ Restaurant ~ Children welcome ~ Dogs allowed in bar ~ Wi-fi *Recommended by Geoff and Ann Marston, Andrew and Michele Revell, Charles Todd*

NORTH LONDON

Map 12

Holly Bush ♀ 🍺

(020) 7435 2892 – www.hollybushhampstead.co.uk
Holly Mount; ⊖ Hampstead; NW3 6SG

Unique village local, with good food and drinks, and lovely unspoilt feel

Always a favourite with our readers, this bustling old place was originally a stable block and is tucked away among some of Hampstead's most villagey streets. The old-fashioned front bar has a dark sagging ceiling, brown and cream panelled walls (decorated with vintage advertisements and a few hanging plates), open fires, bare boards and secretive bays formed by partly glazed partitions. The slightly more intimate back room, named after the painter George Romney, has an embossed red ceiling, panelled and etched glass alcoves, and ochre-painted brick walls covered with small prints; lots of board and card games. Fullers ESB, IPA, London Pride and Olivers Island plus a guest such as Adnams Ghost Ship on handpump, as well as 15 malt whiskies and 14 wines by the glass from a good wine list. The upstairs dining room has table service at the weekend, as does the rest of the pub on Sundays. There are benches on the pavement outside.

Well liked food includes lunchtime sandwiches, chicken liver pâté with onion marmalade, lamb faggot with pea and olive purée and lamb sauce, feta, avocado and quinoa salad with butternut squash, mint, coriander and pomegranate molasses dressing, salmon fillet with red sorrel, pickled beetroot, apple and celery, quail egg and crab mayonnaise, beer-battered cod and chips, confit duck leg with dauphinoise potatoes, and puddings such as apple, pear and blackberry crumble with amaretto ice-cream and chocolate fondant tart with rosewater marshmallow and vanilla ice-cream. *Benchmark main dish: beef cheek pie £16.50. Two-course evening meal £22.00.*

Fullers ~ Manager Ben Ralph ~ Real ale ~ Open 12-11 (10.30 Sun) ~ Bar food 12-10; 12-8 Sun ~ Restaurant ~ Children welcome ~ Dogs welcome ~ Wi-fi
Recommended by Dave Braisted, Tony Scott, Isobel Mackinlay, John and Mary Warner

---

We checked prices with the pubs as we went to press in summer 2016.
They should hold until around spring 2017.

NORTH LONDON   Map 12
Princess of Wales
(020) 7722 0354 ~ www.lovetheprincess.com

*Fitzroy Road/Chalcot Road; ❧ Chalk Farm via Regents Park Road and footbridge;
NW1 8LL*

**Friendly place with three different seating areas, enjoyable food,
wide choice of drinks and funky garden**

Spread over three floors, this bustling pub usefully offers some kind of food
all day at weekends. The main bar, at ground level, is open-plan and light
with big windows looking out to the street, wooden tables and chairs on bare
boards and plenty of high chairs against the counter: Sambrooks Wandle and
a beer named for the pub (also from Sambrooks) plus a changing guest ale
on handpump, 16 wines by the glass, 11 malt whiskies and good cocktails.
Upstairs, the smarter dining room has beige- and white-painted chairs,
leather sofas and stools around wooden tables on more bare boards, big gilt-
edged mirrors and chandeliers; two TVs. Orange and green plush banquettes
create a diner-like feel in the colourful Garden Room downstairs, and doors
lead out to the suntrap garden with its Bansky-style mural, framed wall
mirrors and picnic-sets (some painted pink and purple) under parasols.

Interesting food includes parma ham with roasted figs and baby mozzarella, crispy
chilli squid with aioli, pizzas, rare-breed sausages with mash and onion gravy,
salmon fillet with samphire, green beans, baby broccoli, red pepper and teriyaki sauce,
seafood linguine with white wine and chive sauce, half a roast free-range chicken with
coleslaw and chips, a pie of the day, spicy thai beef salad, and puddings such as double
chocolate and peanut butter brownie, and banoffi pie. *Benchmark main dish: smoked
burger with toppings, onion rings and chips £13.50. Two-course evening meal £20.50.*

Free house ~ Licensee Lawrence Santi ~ Real ale ~ Open 11am-midnight; 10am-midnight
Sat; 10am-11.30pm Sun ~ Bar food 12-2.30, 6-10.30; 12-10.30 weekends ~ Restaurant ~
Children welcome ~ Dogs allowed in bar ~ Wi-fi *Recommended by Edward May,
Harvey Brown, Laura Reid, Jamie Green*

SOUTH LONDON   Map 12
Earl Spencer ♀ ◁
(020) 8870 9244 ~ www.theearlspencer.co.uk

Merton Road; ❧ Southfields; SW18 5JL

Good, interesting food and six real ales in busy but friendly pub

Our readers enjoy their visits to this sizeable Edwardian pub very much –
there's a cheerful, chatty atmosphere and it's particularly well run. There
are cushioned wooden, farmhouse and leather dining tables around all sorts
of tables on bare boards, standard lamps, modern art on the walls and an
open fire. The back bar has long tables, pews and benches, and stools line the
U-shaped counter where efficient, friendly staff serve six ales on handpump.
These include Belleville Calif-Oregon Amber, By the Horns The Mayor of
Garratt, East London Foundation Bitter, Sambrooks Wandle, Wimbledon
Tower SPA and a weekly changing guest beer. Also, 20 wines by the glass,
50 british gins, 12 british vodkas and 20 malt whiskies; they also sell 23 kinds
of cigar. There are picnic-sets out on the front terrace.

Rewarding food includes pork rillettes with celeriac rémoulade, mussels
in cider, bacon, thyme and crème fraîche, chestnut, spinach and wild
mushroom wellington with goats cheese sauce, sea trout with smoked garlic and
pea purée, oriental duck leg with pak choi, soy, ginger and garlic, lamb, apricot,

almond and chickpea tagine with couscous and harissa dressing, and puddings such as dark chocolate and hazelnut terrine and sticky ginger pudding with toffee sauce. *Benchmark main dish: chargrilled bavette steak with chips and horseradish butter £15.50. Two-course evening meal £21.50.*

Enterprise ~ Lease Michael Mann ~ Real ale ~ Open 4-11 Mon-Thurs; 11am-midnight Fri, Sat; 12-10.30 Sun ~ Bar food 7-10 Mon-Thurs; 12.30-3.30, 7-10 Fri, Sat; 12.30-4, 7-9.30 Sun ~ Children welcome ~ Dogs allowed in bar ~ Wi-fi *Recommended by Mrs G Marlow, Belinda May, James Landor, Rona Mackinlay*

SOUTH LONDON
Map 12

Jolly Gardeners 🔘

(020) 8870 8417 – www.thejollygardeners.co.uk
Garrett Lane; ⇌ *Earlsfield; SW18 4EA*

High quality food in bustling corner street pub, local ales, a relaxed atmosphere and courtyard garden

With the 2010 *MasterChef* winner at the helm, this Victorian corner pub gets packed in the evenings with customers keen to enjoy the notably good food. The L-shaped front bar has high stools around equally high tables, high-backed black leather dining chairs around straightforward tables, pale floorboards and more stools at the counter where friendly, chatty staff serve Belleville Northcote Blonde and Sambrooks Wandle on handpump and a dozen wines by the glass. Similar furnishings lead back to more of a dining area where there's an open fire. Paintwork is dark grey (as is the dado), décor is minimal and the atmosphere is easy-going; background music and TV. The airy conservatory is simply furnished with cushioned wooden chairs around wood-topped tables on floorboards and doors lead out to the decked courtyard garden. Here there are heaters, big parasols and a much-used barbecue as well as wall seating with scatter cushions, picnic-sets and contemporary tables and chairs.

🔘 Using top quality produce, the interesting food includes dressed crab with pickled cucumber, avocado and tamarind yoghurt, guinea fowl roulade with foie gras, pickled vegetables, parsnip purée and crispy chicken, smoked aubergine and goats cheese ravioli, cured cod with artichokes, potato velouté and bacon dust, pressed shoulder of lamb, rainbow chard parcel of braised lamb, preserved lemon, black quinoa and vanilla mash, and puddings such as lime, mascarpone and blueberry cheesecake with blueberry coulis, lime chantilly and chocolate shavings and caramelised pineapple with tequila, lime and celery sorbet. *Benchmark main dish: three-way pork belly with carrot and lime purée, baby turnips and chimichurri £17.00. Two-course evening meal £25.00.*

The Lads Pub Co ~ Tenant Stephen Robb ~ Real ale ~ Open 12-11 (midnight Fri, Sat); 12-8 (7 in winter) Sun ~ Bar food 12-3, 6-10; 12-5 Sun ~ Restaurant ~ Children welcome ~ Dogs allowed in bar ~ Wi-fi *Recommended by Millie and Peter Downing, L Wright and V Matos, Edward Nile*

SOUTH LONDON
Map 12

Latchmere ♀

(020) 7223 3549 – www.thelatchmere.co.uk
Battersea Park Road; ⇌ *Clapham Junction; SW11 3BW*

Busy, well run pub with open-plan drinking and dining areas, enjoyable food and drink, and seats in garden; upstairs theatre

Recently refurbished, this Battersea landmark remains a cheerful, bustling place with a good mix of customers. The open-plan areas include a log fire with leather sofas to either side, a group of tub chairs in one corner, and cushioned Edwardian-style dining chairs, two-sided banquettes and red leather wall seating around wooden tables on bare floorboards. There are some model yachts, big mirrors, animal prints, photographs and posters, and evening candles. Stools line the counter where efficient, friendly staff serve Sharps Doom Bar, St Austell Liquid Sunshine and Timothy Taylors Landlord on handpump, 19 wines by the glass, and cocktails. Outside, there is a heated terraced garden that has several small booths down one side, a larger one available for a private party and plenty of tables and chairs. The award-winning theatre is located on the first floor.

🍴 Good, popular food includes lunchtime sandwiches, cheddar crème brûlée, chorizo scotch egg with smoked garlic aioli, caesar salad (you can add chicken, bass or goats cheese), a pie of the day, pork and leek sausages with onion jus, ricotta and lemon ravioli with tomato pesto and parmesan, salmon with pak choi, celeriac purée, samphire and sauce vierge, treacle-roasted beef brisket with bean salad and sweet potato fries, gremolata and pickles, and puddings; they also offer a two- and three-course pre-theatre menu (6-7pm; not Sunday). *Benchmark main dish: beer-battered hake with chips £13.50. Two-course evening meal £21.00.*

Three Cheers Pub Co ~ Manager Tom Peake ~ Real ale ~ Open 11-11; 11am-midnight Fri, Sat; 11-10.30 Sun ~ Bar food 12-2.30, 6-10.30; 12-4, 5-10.30 Sat; 12-9 Sun ~ Restaurant ~ Children welcome until 7pm ~ Dogs welcome ~ Wi-fi *Recommended by Donald Allsopp, Caroline Sullivan, Sophie Ellison, Julian Thorpe*

SOUTH LONDON
Rose & Crown �♥ TQ4563 Map 12

(01689) 869029 ~ www.the-roseandcrown.co.uk
Farnborough Way (A21); ⇌ *Chelsfield; BR6 6BT*

Sizeable pub on the edge of London with surprisingly large back garden, character bars, a wide choice of food and drink and cheerful service

You might be forgiven for thinking that a pub on a large roundabout on the outskirts of London might not be your first port of call for a drink or meal – but you'd be mistaken in this case. It's been completely renovated and refurbished to create open-plan interconnected rooms with alcoves and smaller, cosier areas too. Every shape and size of Edwardian-style dining chairs, leather tub seats, upholstered stools and coloured button-back banquettes are grouped around all manner of polished tables on rugs, bare boards or black and white tiles. Walls are hung with frame-to-frame prints and pictures, there are house plants, church candles, lots of mirrors and hundreds of books on shelves, and three log fires (one's a woodburner). On our Sunday lunchtime visit the place was humming with cheerful customers, all ably looked after by chatty, efficient and friendly staff. A beer named for the pub (from Youngs), Youngs Bitter, Blonde, Bombardier and Special and a guest from Larkins on handpump, and 16 wines by the glass. The biggest surprise is the extensive and well equipped back garden which has colourful beach huts and cabanas, chairs and tables on a terrace, picnic-sets on grass and a sizeable children's play area.

🍴 A wide choice of interesting food includes sandwiches (until 6pm), smoked corned beef and spring onion croquettes with blue cheese and confit garlic and pine kernel mayonnaise, prawn cocktail, beer-battered fish and chips, pork and leek sausages with onion and thyme gravy, steak, celery and onion pie, spelt risotto and grilled goats cheese, calves liver and black pudding bonbons with caramelised onion and red wine sauce, lemon and thyme poussin with braised baby gem and spring vegetable fricassée,

28-day-aged steaks with a choice of sauces, and puddings such as tonka bean crème brûlée and chocolate brownie with milk chocolate sauce. *Benchmark main dish: burger with toppings, american sauce and skinny fries £11.95. Two-course evening meal £20.00.*

Whiting & Hammond ~ Manager Lee Scott ~ Real ale ~ Open 11-11; 12-10.30 Sun ~ Bar food 12-9.30 (9 Sun) ~ Restaurant ~ Children welcome ~ Dogs allowed in bar ~ Wi-fi
Recommended by Christian Mole, Lionel Smith, Daphne and Robert Staples

SOUTH LONDON

Map 13

Royal Oak 🍺

(020) 7357 7173 – www.harveys.org.uk
Tabard Street/Nebraska Street; ☉ Borough ☉ ⇌ London Bridge; SE1 4JU

Old-fashioned corner house with particularly well kept beers and honest food

This bustling pub has the look and feel of a traditional London alehouse – you'd never imagine it had been painstakingly transformed by Sussex brewery Harveys just a few years ago. The place has an unpretentious air and is always packed with customers of varying ages, all keen to enjoy the full range of Harveys ales plus a guest from Fullers on handpump and Thatcher's cider. The two little L-shaped rooms (the front bar is larger and brighter, the back room cosier with dimmer lighting) meander around the central wooden servery, which has a fine old clock in the middle. The rooms are done out with patterned rugs on wooden floors, plates running along a delft shelf, black and white scenes or period sheet music on red-painted walls, and an assortment of wooden tables and chairs. There's disabled access at the Nebraska Street entrance.

Tasty food includes sandwiches, deep-fried whitebait, duck liver pâté, seasonal fresh crab salad, ham, egg and chips, rabbit in mustard sauce, game pie, goats cheese and beetroot salad, and puddings such as lemon tart and sherry trifle. *Benchmark main dish: bubble and squeak with black pudding, bacon and duck egg £9.25. Two-course evening meal £16.50.*

Harveys ~ Tenants John Porteous, Frank Taylor ~ Real ale ~ Open 11-11; 12-9 Sun ~ Bar food 12-2.45, 5-9.15; 12-8 Sun ~ Children welcome until 9pm ~ Dogs welcome
Recommended by N R White, Tony Scott, Tom Stone, Patricia Hawkins

SOUTH LONDON

Map 12

Victoria 🏨 🍴 🍷 🛏

(020) 8876 4238 – www.thevictoria.net
West Temple Sheen; ⇌ Mortlake; SW14 7RT

Excellent food in attractive inn, airy conservatory and cosy bar and seats in pretty garden; bedrooms

After a walk in nearby Richmond Park, this well run, friendly inn is just the place for lunch. The bar has leather sofas facing each other beside a fireplace, and wooden seats and tables in a bow window with more on bare boards around the counter. Sambrooks Wandle, Timothy Taylors Landlord and a guest such as Twickenham Naked Ladies on handpump, 25 wines by the glass from a good list and home-made elderflower cordial; background music. A light and airy back conservatory restaurant has dark chunky furniture and doors that open out into a pretty garden. Here, there are plenty of seats and tables under a huge parasol and an outside bar. The stylish modern bedrooms are comfortable and breakfasts good.

As well as Saturday brunch (11-3pm), the imaginative food includes tapas-like small plates such as labneh, pomegranate and nut croquante and crispy squid with sweet chilli mayonnaise, a charcuterie board, crispy pig head and hock salad with apple and pickled walnuts, rare-breed hot dog with home-made kimchi, ketjap manis (indonesian soy sauce) and crispy shallots, corn-fed chicken thigh with bhel puri salad and paratha bread, whole plaice with serrano ham and peas, asparagus and pecorino ravioli with broad beans and peas, chargrilled lamb chop with imam bayildi and tzatziki, and puddings such as milk chocolate mousse with chocolate soil, honeycomb and peanut crunch and key lime pie in a jar. *Benchmark main dish: burger with toppings and chips £12.50. Two-course evening meal £25.00.*

Enterprise ~ Lease Greg Bellamy ~ Real ale ~ Open 11-11 (10.30 Sun) ~ Bar food 12-10 ~ Restaurant ~ Children welcome ~ Dogs allowed in bar ~ Wi-fi ~ Bedrooms: £125/£135
Recommended by Simon Rodway, Jamie Green, Chris Stevenson

WEST LONDON
TQ1370 Map 3
Bell
(020) 8941 9799 ~ www.thebellinnhampton.co.uk
Thames Street, Hampton; ⇌ *Hampton; TW12 2EA*

Bustling pub by the Thames with seats outside, real ales, a good choice of food and friendly service

There's a good bustling atmosphere and a wide mix of customers in this friendly riverside pub. The interconnected rooms have wooden dining and tub chairs around copper-topped or chunky wooden tables, comfortably upholstered wall seats with scatter cushions, mirrors, old photographs and lots of church candles. From the long panelled bar counter here, helpful staff serve Caledonian Deuchars IPA and guests such as Adnams Jack Brand Mosaic Pale Ale, Sambrooks Wandle and Sharps Doom Bar on handpump, 20 wines by the glass and speciality teas and coffees. There are plenty of contemporary seats and tables in the garden, which has heaters, lighting and booth seating; summer barbecues.

Popular food includes a mexican or aromatic duck platter, arancini with peppers, peas and cheddar, beef or halloumi burgers with toppings, coleslaw and chips, barbecue pork ribs, tuna steak with mango, red onion, carrot and coconut salad, slow-braised lamb shoulder with mint and rosemary, and puddings such as eton mess and sticky toffee pudding with toffee sauce. *Benchmark main dish: piri-piri chicken with shoestring fries £13.95. Two-course evening meal £20.00.*

Authentic Inns ~ Lease Simon Bailey ~ Real ale ~ Open 11-11 (midnight Fri, Sat) ~ Bar food 12-3, 6-10; 12-10 Sat; 12-9 Sun ~ Restaurant ~ Children welcome ~ Dogs allowed in bar ~ Wi-fi ~ Live music Sat evening *Recommended by Hilary and Neil Christopher, Carol and Barry Craddock, Maddie Purvis*

WEST LONDON
Map 12
Dove ♀ ◖
(020) 8748 9474 ~ www.dovehammersmith.co.uk
Upper Mall; ⊖ *Ravenscourt Park; W6 9TA*

Character pub with a lovely riverside terrace, cosily traditional front bar and an interesting history

One of London's best known pubs, this old-fashioned riverside place is in the Guinness World Records for having the smallest bar room – the front snug, a mere 4'2" by 7'10". The bar is cosy, traditional and unchanging, with black panelling and red leatherette cushioned built-in wall settles and stools around assorted tables. It leads to a bigger, similarly furnished back room that's more geared to eating, which in turn leads to a conservatory. Fullers ESB, London Pride, Olivers Island, a changing seasonal ale plus a guest or two on handpump and 19 wines by the glass including champagne and sparkling wine. Head down steps at the back to reach the verandah with its highly prized tables looking over a low river wall to the Thames Reach just above Hammersmith Bridge; a tiny exclusive area, reached up a spiral staircase, is a prime spot for watching rowers on the water. The pub has played host to many writers, actors and artists over the years (there's a fascinating framed list on a wall); it's said to be where 'Rule Britannia' was composed and was a favourite with Turner, who painted the view of the Thames from the delightful back terrace, and with Graham Greene. The street itself is associated with the foundation of the arts and crafts movement – William Morris's old residence Kelmscott House (open to the public on certain afternoons), is nearby.

Good food includes crab tart with crispy capers, pea shoots, white crab meat and pickled shallot rings, pressed ham hock terrine with broad bean and tahini purée, confit rabbit and venison bacon caesar salad, quinoa and fennel salad with lime and coriander, burger with toppings, pickles, beetroot slaw and chips, rack and breast of lamb with pomegranate, sweetcorn and smoked almond couscous, and puddings such as mango and passion-fruit mess and rosewater jelly with chocolate soil and chantilly cream. *Benchmark main dish: beer-battered fish and chips £13.00. Two-course evening meal £21.00.*

Fullers ~ Manager Sonia Labatut ~ Real ale ~ Open 11-11; 12-10.30 Sun ~ Bar food 12-10; 12-8 ~ Children welcome ~ Dogs welcome ~ Wi-fi *Recommended by Taff Thomas, Tony Scott, Hunter and Christine Wright*

WEST LONDON

Duke of Sussex 🌟 ♀ 🍺

Map 12

(020) 8742 8801 – www.thedukeofsussex.co.uk
South Parade; ⊖ *Chiswick Park* ⇄ *South Acton; W4 5LF*

Attractively restored Victorian local with interesting bar food, a good choice of drinks and a lovely big garden

On a warm day, the unexpectedly extensive garden behind this well run pub is a real treat – there are seats and tables under parasols, nicely laid out plants, carefully positioned lighting and (if it gets cooler in the evening) heaters. The classy, simply furnished bar has some original etched glass, chapel and farmhouse chairs around scrubbed pine and dark wood tables, and huge windows overlooking Acton Green. The big horseshoe-shaped counter, lined with high bar stools, is where they serve a beer named for the pub (from Greene King), Portobello VPA, Sharps Own and Triple fff Citra Sonic on handpump, 30 wines by the glass and 15 malt whiskies. Off here is a dining room, again with simple wooden furnishings on parquet, but also six-seater booths, chandeliers, antique lamps, a splendid skylight framed by colourfully painted cherubs and a couple of large mirrors, one above a small tiled fireplace.

Imaginative food includes prawns in chilli and garlic with tomato bread, ham croquettes, goats cheese, beetroot and hazelnut salad, chicken pie for two people, hake with roast potatoes and sofrito (a spanish fragrant tomato sauce), lamb rump with chickpea salad, and puddings such as lemon meringue pie and sticky toffee pudding. *Benchmark main dish: seafood paella £14.50. Two-course evening meal £21.00.*

Greene King ~ Manager Matt Mullett ~ Real ale ~ Open 12-11 (11.30 Fri, Sat); 12-10.30 Sun ~ Bar food 12-10 (10.30 Fri, Sat); 12-9 Sun ~ Restaurant ~ Children welcome ~ Dogs allowed in bar ~ Wi-fi *Recommended by Ben and Diane Bowie, Sophia and Hamish Greenfield, Keith Mantle*

WEST LONDON
Malt House

TQ2577   Map 12

(020) 7084 6888 – www.malthousefulham.co.uk
Vanston Place; ⊖ *Fulham Broadway; SW6 1AY*

Creative food and good drinks choice in refurbished Georgian pub, stylish bar and dining areas and hidden-away garden; bedrooms

Dating from 1729, this large refurbished corner pub has a good, bustling atmosphere in its U-shaped bar. There are big windows, high ceilings, wooden or tiled floors, green leather button-back wall seating and dark wooden dining chairs around pale-topped tables and groups of sofas and armchairs dotted here and there. Planked walls are hung with water colours, there's a lot of cream paintwork and some bookshelf wallpaper. Contemporary high chairs line the counter where helpful staff serve Brakspears Bitter, Marstons Pedigree New World Pale Ale and a guest beer on handpump, eight good wines by the glass, 11 malt whiskies and a farm cider. The small paved back garden has pretty hanging baskets, fairy lights, candles in lanterns and candy-striped benches around wooden tables. Bedrooms are comfortable and light and airy.

As well as breakfasts for non-residents (from 8am), the highly thought-of food includes asian prawn salad with chilli, pickled ginger and peanuts, pork rillettes with burnt apple purée, asparagus and pecorino ravioli with cime di rapa (turnip tops) and truffle oil, burger with toppings and triple-cooked chips, yoghurt-spiced chicken breast and salad with pomegranate, mint, chilli and flatbread, whole plaice with nut butter, samphire and capers, slow-cooked charred lamb shoulder with imam bayildi and coriander yoghurt, and puddings such as rhubarb and white chocolate cheesecake with mango and passion-fruit yoghurt ice-cream and warm parkin cake with caramel sauce. *Benchmark main dish: beer-battered fish and triple-cooked chips £14.50. Two-course evening meal £22.00.*

Brakspears ~ Lease Jessica Chanter ~ Real ale ~ Open 10am-11pm; 11-11 Sun ~ Bar food 8am-2.30, 6-10; 12-9 Sun ~ Restaurant ~ Children welcome ~ Dogs welcome ~ Wi-fi ~ Bedrooms: £135/£145 *Recommended by Mike Swan, Susan Eccleston, Sally and David Champion, Geoff and Ann Marston*

WEST LONDON
Mute Swan ♀ ◧

TQ1568   Map 12

(020) 8941 5959 – www.brunningandprice.co.uk/muteswan
Palace Gate, Hampton Court Road; ⇌ *Hampton Court; KT8 9BN*

Handsome pub close to the Thames with sunny seats outside, relaxed bar, upstairs dining room and imaginative food and drinks choice

Just yards from the River Thames (though there's no view), this remains a friendly, busy and well run pub. The light and airy bar has four big leather armchairs grouped around a low table in the centre, while the rest of the room has brown leather wall seats, high-backed Edwardian-style cushioned dining chairs around dark tables and rugs on bare boards. The walls are covered in interesting photographs, maps, prints and posters and there are sizeable house plants, glass and stone bottles on the windowsills and a woodburning stove; the atmosphere is informal and relaxed. Brunning &

Price Phoenix Original, Hogs Back TEA, Sharps Coaster and Tillingbourne Falls Gold on handpump, a carefully chosen wine list with 19 by the glass, farm cider and 75 malt whiskies; staff are efficient and helpful. A metal spiral staircase – presided over by an elegant metal chandelier – leads up to the dining area where there are brass-studded caramel leather chairs around well spaced tables on bare boards or carpeting, and numerous photographs and prints. The tables and chairs on the front terrace get snapped up quickly and the pub is opposite the gates to Hampton Court Palace. There are a few parking spaces in front, but you'll probably have to park elsewhere.

Pleasing modern food includes sandwiches, rabbit spring roll with pickled carrot salad, smoked salmon with golden beetroot rösti and horseradish crème fraîche, mussels in leek, cider and cream sauce, honey and mustard glazed ham with free-range eggs, tandoori salmon with spinach dhal, spiced hasselback potatoes and crab bhajis, lemon and thyme poussin with wild garlic risotto, braised lamb shoulder with dauphinoise potatoes and red wine and rosemary sauce, and puddings such as crème brûlée and dark chocolate and hazelnut praline tart with strawberry ice-cream. *Benchmark main dish: chicken and ham hock pie £14.95. Two-course evening meal £21.00.*

Brunning & Price ~ Manager Alisha Craigwell ~ Real ale ~ Open 11-11 (midnight Fri, Sat); 11-10.30 Sun ~ Bar food 12-10 (9.30 Sun) ~ Restaurant ~ Children welcome in upstairs restaurant only ~ Dogs allowed in bar ~ Wi-fi *Recommended by Atle Helgedagsrud, Belinda May, Alf Wright*

WEST LONDON
Old Orchard ♀ ◖
Map 3

(01895) 822631 – www.brunningandprice.co.uk/oldorchard
Off Park Lane; Harefield; ⇌ *Denham (some distance away); UB9 6HJ*

Wonderful views from the front garden, a good choice of drinks and interesting brasserie-style food

The position here is pretty special: from tables on the front terrace and in the garden you look down to the narrowboats on the canal and across to the lakes that are part of the conservation area known as the Colne Valley Regional Park – it's a haven for wildlife. Inside, the open-plan rooms have an attractive mix of cushioned dining chairs around all sizes and shapes of dark wooden tables, lots of prints, maps and pictures covering the walls, books on shelves, old glass bottles on windowsills and rugs on wood or parquet flooring. One room is hung with a sizeable rug and some tapestry. There are daily papers to read, three cosy coal fires, big pot plants and fresh flowers. Half a dozen real ales on handpump served by friendly, efficient staff include Phoenix Brunning & Price Original, Mighty Oak Oscar Wilde and Tring Side Pocket for a Toad alongside guests such as Leighton Buzzard Black Buzzard, Mole Rucking Mole, Thornbridge Jaipur and Tiny Rebel One Inch Punch; also, 24 wines by the glass, 140 malt whiskies and six farm ciders. The atmosphere is civilised and easy-going.

Interesting food includes sandwiches, chicken liver parfait with spiced onion chutney, smoked salmon with brown crab purée, wasabi guacamole, apple and fennel, carrot and toasted pumpkin seed pasta with coriander oil, steak burger with toppings, coleslaw and chips, bass fillets with king prawns, roasted red peppers, blood orange and ciabatta croutons, duck breast with roasted sweet potatoes, broccoli purée, confit duck leg and pecan nut croquette, braised lamb shoulder with dauphinoise potatoes and red wine gravy, and puddings such as crème brûlée and chocolate brownie and chocolate sauce. *Benchmark main dish: pork tenderloin green curry with lemongrass cauliflower cake and spicy crackling £15.25. Two-course evening meal £22.50.*

Brunning & Price ~ Manager Dan Redfern ~ Real ale ~ Open 11.30-11; 12-10.30 Sun ~
Bar food 12-10 (9.30 Sun) ~ Children welcome ~ Dogs welcome ~ Wi-fi
Recommended by Patrick and Daphne Darley, Richard Elliott, Simon Rodway

WEST LONDON
White Horse ⭐ ♀ 🍺
Map 12

(020) 7736 2115 – www.whitehorsesw6.com
Parsons Green; ⊖ *Parsons Green; SW6 4UL*

**Cheerfully relaxed local with big terrace, excellent range
of carefully sourced drinks and imaginative food**

On summer evenings and weekends, the front terrace – overlooking
Parsons Green itself – has something of a continental feel with its
many seats and tables; there are barbecues most sunny evenings. Inside,
the stylishly modernised U-shaped bar has a gently upmarket and chatty
atmosphere, plenty of leather chesterfield sofas and wooden tables, huge
windows with slatted wooden blinds, flagstone and wood floors, and
winter coal and log fires (one in an elegant marble fireplace). There's also
an upstairs dining room with its own bar. The impressive range of drinks
takes in real ales such as Harveys Best, Oakham JHB and guest beers
such as Flack Manor Double Drop, Mallinsons Summit, Moor Confidence,
Siren Undercurrent, Thornbridge Windle and Twickenham Sundancer on
handpump, eight craft ales, six of the seven Trappist beers, around 135 other
foreign bottled beers, several malt whiskies and 20 good wines by the glass.
They hold three beer festivals a year (one celebrating the best American beer
and two spotlighting regional breweries).

 As well as breakfast, the highly enjoyable food includes sandwiches, sweet
chilli and lime-glazed squid, chicken skewers marinated in ras el hanout with
quinoa salad and coconut dressing, pork, leek and welsh rarebit sausages with spring
onion mash and red wine jus, crab cakes with coconut yoghurt dressing and baby kale,
beer-battered fresh cod and chips, chicken and avocado or quinoa and mushroom
burger with toppings and fries, mint-glazed lamb rump with grilled baby leeks and
red wine jus, 21-day-aged rib-eye steak with béarnaise sauce and fries, and puddings
such as dark chocolate brownie with vanilla pod ice-cream and carrot cake and orange
cheesecake. *Benchmark main dish: beer-battered fish and chips £14.00. Two-course
evening meal £30.00.*

Mitchells & Butlers ~ Manager Danny Daws ~ Real ale ~ Open 9.30am-11.30pm (midnight
Thurs-Sat) ~ Bar food 9.30am-10.30pm ~ Restaurant ~ Children welcome ~ Dogs welcome
~ Wi-fi *Recommended by Tony Scott, Edward May, Jim and Sue James, Jeff Davies*

WEST LONDON
Windsor Castle 🍺
Map 12

(020) 7243 8797 – www.thewindsorcastlekensington.co.uk
Campden Hill Road; ⊖ *Notting Hill Gate; W8 7AR*

**Genuinely unspoilt, with lots of atmosphere in tiny, dark rooms
and lovely summer garden**

Unchanging and full of character, there's a lot of old-fashioned charm
here, with a wealth of dark oak furnishings, sturdy high-backed built-in
elm benches, time-smoked ceilings, soft lighting and a coal-effect fire. Three
of the tiny unspoilt rooms have their own entrance from the street, but it's
much more fun trying to navigate through the minuscule doors between
them inside. Usually fairly quiet at lunchtime, it tends to be packed most
evenings. The panelled and wood-floored dining room at the back overlooks

the garden. Black Sheep, Fullers London Pride, Hop Back Summer Lightning, Harviestoun Summer Legend, Portobello Bronze Star, Sharps Doom Bar, Salopian Hop Twister and Wells Bombardier on handpump, decent house wines, farm ciders, malt whiskies and jugs of Pimms. The garden, on several levels, has tables and chairs on flagstones and feels secluded thanks to the high ivy-covered walls; heaters for cooler evenings.

🍴 Good, popular food includes sandwiches, sweet chilli and lime-glazed squid, ras el hanout chicken skewers with quinoa salad and coconut dressing, honey and mustard sweet cured bacon loin with eggs, slow-cooked short rib of beef with bone marrow sauce and mash, roasted half chicken with confit shallots and garlic, parmesan and rosemary fries and red wine jus, bass with dauphinoise potatoes, asparagus and lemon butter sauce, and puddings such as lemon and blueberry cheesecake with strawberry compote and chocolate brownie with vanilla bean ice-cream. *Benchmark main dish: beer-battered fish and chips £14.00. Two-course evening meal £23.00.*

Mitchells & Butlers ~ Manager Andrew Davidson ~ Real ale ~ Open 12-11 (10.30 Sun) ~ Bar food 12-10 (9 Sun) ~ Restaurant ~ Children in eating area of bar ~ Dogs welcome ~ Wi-fi *Recommended by Hilary and Neil Christopher, Harvey Brown, Tony Scott, Neil Allen*

Also Worth a Visit in London

Besides the fully inspected pubs, you might like to try these pubs that have been recommended to us and described by readers. Do tell us what you think of them: feedback@goodguides.com

CENTRAL LONDON

E2

Sun (020) 7739 4097
Bethnal Green Road; E2 0AN
Revamped 19th-c bar with good choice of local beers and other drinks including cocktails, friendly helpful service, padded stools around copper-topped counter with lanterns above, bare boards, exposed brickwork and some leather banquettes, bar snacks; open all day. *(Charles Todd)*

EC1

Bishops Finger (020) 7248 2341
West Smithfield; EC1A 9JR Welcoming little pub close to Smithfield Market, Shepherd Neame ales including seasonals, good range of sausages and other food in bar or upstairs room; children welcome, seats out in front, closed weekends and bank holidays, otherwise open all day and can get crowded. *(N R White, Tony Scott)*

Butchers Hook & Cleaver (020) 7600 9181 *West Smithfield; EC1A 9DY* Fullers conversion of bank and adjoining butcher's shop, their full range kept well and enjoyable pubby food including various pies, efficient service, spiral stairs to mezzanine; background music, free wi-fi; closed weekends, otherwise open (and food) all day from 8am, gets busy with after-work drinkers. *(N R White)*

Craft Beer Company (020) 7404 7049 *Leather Lane; EC1N 7TR* Corner drinkers' pub with excellent selection of real ales and craft beers plus an extensive bottled range, good choice of wines and spirits too, high stools and tables on bare boards, big chandelier hanging from mirrored ceiling, can get very busy but service remains efficient and friendly, food limited to snacks, upstairs room; open all day. *(Conor McGaughey, N R White)*

Dovetail (020) 7490 7321
Jerusalem Passage; EC1V 4JP Fairly small and can get very busy with drinkers spilling into alleyway, specialises in draught/ bottled belgian beers and serves popular food including some belgian dishes, efficient staff cope well at peak times; open all day (from 2pm Sun). *(N R White)*

Fox & Anchor (020) 7250 1300
Charterhouse Street; EC1M 6AA Beautifully restored late Victorian pub/ boutique hotel by Smithfield Market (note the art nouveau façade); long slender bar with unusual pewter-topped counter, lots of mahogany, green leather and etched glass, small back snugs, Youngs ales and guests, oyster bar and decent choice of other freshly cooked food, friendly efficient staff; six individual well appointed bedrooms, good breakfast, open all day from 7am (8am weekends). *(N R White, Tony Scott)*

★ **Hand & Shears** (020) 7600 0257
Middle Street; EC1A 7JA Traditional
unspoilt Smithfield corner pub, three rooms
and small snug arranged around central
servery, bare boards, panelling and a couple
of gas fires, interesting prints and old
photographs, up to six changing ales, friendly
service; open all day (bustling lunchtime and
early evening), closed weekends. *(N R White,
John Poulter)*

★ **Jerusalem Tavern** (020) 7490 4281
Britton Street; EC1M 5UQ Atmospheric
re-creation of a dark 18th-c tavern (1720
merchant's house with shopfront added
1810), tiny dimly lit bar, simple wood
furnishings on bare boards, some remarkable
old wall tiles, coal fires and candlelight,
stairs to a precarious-feeling (though
perfectly secure) balcony, plainer back room,
St Peters beers tapped from the cask and
in bottles, short choice of lunchtime food
including good sandwiches, friendly attentive
young staff; no children but dogs welcome,
seats out on pavement (plastic glasses if
you drink out here), open all day weekdays,
closed weekends, bank holidays and 24
Dec-2 Jan; can get very crowded at peak
times. *(Conor McGaughey, N R White, Roger and
Donna Huggins)*

Ninth Ward (020) 7833 2949
Farringdon Road; EC1R 3BN American-
themed bar-grill (has sister restaurant
in New York) with unusual New Orleans-
inspired interior (quite dark), tasty food
such as burgers and chicken wings, good
range of craft and bottled beers, cocktails,
friendly staff; background music; closed Sat
lunchtime and all day Sun, otherwise open all
day till late. *(Julie Swift)*

Old Fountain (020) 7253 2970
Baldwin Street; EC1V 9NU Popular
traditional old pub in same family since
1964; long bar serving two rooms, excellent
range of real ales and craft beers chalked
up on board, enjoyable good value food (not
Sat lunchtime) from open kitchen, main
carpeted part with wooden tables and chairs,
padded stools and fish tank; function room
for live music, darts; nice roof terrace; open
all day. *(Tony Scott)*

Old Red Cow (020) 7726 2595
Long Lane; EC1A 9EJ Cheerful little
pub close to the Barbican and within
sight of Smithfield Market, fine changing
selection of cask, craft and bottled beers,
tasters offered by friendly knowledgeable
staff, nine wines by the glass, well liked if
not particularly cheap food from sharing
boards and home-made pies to good Sun
roasts, modernised interior with larger
room upstairs; open all day and popular
with after-work drinkers, no food Sun
evening. *(Tony Scott, N R White)*

EC2

★ **Dirty Dicks** (020) 7283 5888
Bishopsgate; EC2M 4NR Refurbished
but keeping olde-worlde tavern feel in main
bar with bare boards, low beams, exposed
brickwork and some interesting old prints,
Youngs ales and guests such as Meantime and
Sambrooks, lots of wines by the glass
and good variety of enjoyable fairly priced
food, upstairs dining room, cellar cocktail
bar with barrel-vaulted ceiling; background
music; open all day (till 3am Thurs-Sat),
handy for Liverpool Street station.
(N R White, Tony Scott)

Hamilton Hall (020) 7247 3579
*Bishopsgate; also entrance from
Liverpool Street station; EC2M 7PY*
Showpiece Wetherspoons with flamboyant
Victorian baroque décor mixing with
contemporary bar counter and modern
tables and chairs, good-sized comfortable
mezzanine, lots of real ales including
interesting guests, decent wines and coffee,
their usual food and competitive pricing,
friendly staff doing their best at busy times;
silenced machines, free wi-fi, screens
showing train times; good disabled access,
café-style furniture out in front, open all
day from 7am, can get very crowded after
work. *(Tony and Wendy Hobden)*

Lord Aberconway (020) 7929 1743
Old Broad Street; EC2M 1QT Victorian
feel with high moulded ceiling, dark
panelling, some red leather bench seating
and drinking booths, six well kept ales and
reasonably priced Nicholsons menu from
sandwiches up, dining gallery; silent fruit
machine; handy for Liverpool Street station,
gets busy with after-work drinkers, open till
9.30pm Sat, closed Sun, otherwise open
all day. *(N R White)*

EC3
East India Arms (020) 7265 5121
Fenchurch Street; EC3M 4BR Standing-
room 19th-c corner pub popular with City
workers, well kept Shepherd Neame ales
served by efficient staff, small single room
with wood floor, half-panelling, old local
photographs and brewery mirrors; tables
outside, closed weekends and may shut by
9pm weekdays. *(Julie Swift, N R White)*

Hoop & Grapes (020) 7481 4583
Aldgate High Street; EC3N 1AL Originally
17th-c (dismantled and rebuilt 1983) and
much bigger inside than it looks; long
partitioned bare-boards bar with beams,
timbers, exposed brickwork and panelling,
mix of seating including some button-back
wall benches, seven real ales and standard
Nicholsons menu (popular lunchtime),
friendly efficient service; a few seats in front,
closed Sun, otherwise open (and food) all day.
(Tony Scott)

Jamaica Wine House

(020) 7929 6972 *St Michaels Alley, Cornhill; EC3V 9DS* Red-stone 19th-c pub (site of London's first coffee house) in warren of small alleys; traditional Victorian décor with ornate coffered ceiling, oak-panelling, booths and bare boards, Shepherd Neame ales and wide choice of wines, food from sharing dishes up in bar or downstairs dining room, friendly helpful service, bustling atmosphere (quietens after 8pm); closed weekends. *(Tony Scott)*

Lamb (020) 7626 2454

Leadenhall Market; EC3V 1LR Well run stand-up bar with friendly staff coping admirably with hordes of after-work drinkers, Youngs ales and good choice of wines, dark panelling, engraved glass and plenty of ledges and shelves, spiral stairs up to small carpeted gallery overlooking market's central crossing, corner servery for lunchtime carvery and other food, separate stairs to nice bright dining room (not cheap), also basement bar with shiny wall tiles and own entrance; tables out under splendid Victorian market roof – crowds here in warmer months, open (and food) all day, closed weekends. *(Tony Scott)*

Ship (020) 7702 4422

Hart Street; EC3R 7NB Tiny one-room 19th-c City pub with ornate flower-decked façade; Caledonian ales and two well kept guests, some food including sandwiches and burgers, friendly staff, limited seating and can get packed, upstairs dining room; spiral stairs down to lavatories; closed weekends. *(Charles Todd)*

Ship (020) 7929 3903

Talbot Court, off Eastcheap; EC3V 0BP Interesting Nicholsons pub tucked down alleyway; busy bare-boards bar with soft lighting and ornate décor, candles in galleried dining area, friendly efficient staff, several well kept ales including their house beer from St Austell, good value food; open all day weekdays, closed weekends. *(Tony Scott)*

Simpsons Tavern (020) 7626 9985

Just off Cornhill; EC3V 9DR Pleasingly old-fashioned place founded in 1757; small narrow panelled bar serving five real ales including Adnams, Bass and Fullers, traditional chophouse with upright stall seating (expect to share a table) and similar upstairs restaurant, good value straightforward food from sandwiches and snacks up, further bar downstairs; open weekday lunchtimes and from 8am Tues-Fri for breakfast. *(Edward Nile)*

Swan (020) 7929 6550

Ship Tavern Passage, off Gracechurch Street; EC3V 1LY Traditional Fullers pub with bustling narrow flagstoned bar, their well kept ales and lunchtime sandwiches and snacks, friendly efficient service, neatly kept Victorian panelled décor, low lighting, larger more ordinary carpeted bar upstairs; silent TV; covered alley used by smokers, open all day Mon-Fri (may be closed by 8.30pm), shuts at weekends. *(Margaret McDonald)*

EC4

★**Black Friar** (020) 7236 5474
Queen Victoria Street; EC4V 4EG An architectural gem (some of the best Edwardian bronze and marble art nouveau work to be found anywhere) and built on site of 13th-c Dominican priory; inner back room (the Grotto) with low vaulted mosaic ceiling, big bas-relief friezes of jolly monks set into richly coloured florentine marble walls, gleaming mirrors, seats built into golden marble recesses and an opulent pillared inglenook, ironic verbal embellishments such as Silence is Golden and Finery is Foolish, and opium-smoking hints modelled into the front room's fireplace; six ales including Fullers, Sharps and Nicholsons (St Austell), plenty of wines by the glass, traditional food (speciality pies); children welcome if quiet, plenty of room on wide forecourt, handy for Blackfriars station, open (and food) all day. *(Barry Collett, Paul Humphreys, Tony Scott)*

Cockpit (020) 7248 7315

St Andrews Hill/Ireland Place, off Queen Victoria Street; EC4V 5BY Plenty of atmosphere in this little corner pub near St Paul's Cathedral; as name suggests, a former cockfighting venue with surviving spectators' gallery; good selection of ales such as Adnams, St Austell and Shepherd Neame, lunchtime food; open all day. *(Jeff Davies)*

Old Bell (020) 7583 0216

Fleet Street, near Ludgate Circus; EC4Y 1DH Dimly lit 17th-c tavern backing on to St Bride's Church; stained-glass bow window, heavy black beams, bare boards and flagstones, half a dozen or more well kept changing ales from island servery (can try before you buy, tasting trays available), usual Nicholsons food, friendly helpful young staff and cheery atmosphere, various seating nooks, brass-topped tables, coal fire; background music; covered and heated outside area, open all day (may close early weekend evenings). *(Tony Scott)*

★**Olde Cheshire Cheese**
(020) 7353 6170 *Wine Office Court, off 145 Fleet Street; EC4A 2BU* Best to visit this 17th-c former chophouse outside peak times when it can be packed (early evening especially); soaked in history with warren of old-fashioned unpretentious rooms, high beams, bare boards, old built-in black benches, Victorian paintings on dark brown walls, big open fires, tiny snug and steep stone steps down to unexpected series of cosy areas and secluded alcoves, Sam Smiths

beers, all-day pubby food; Coco the profane parrot – also look out for Polly (now stuffed) who entertained distinguished guests for over 40 years; children allowed in eating area lunchtime only, closed Sun evening. *(Tony Scott, Giles and Annie Francis)*

Olde Watling (020) 7248 8935

Watling Street; EC4M 9BR Heavy-beamed and timbered post-blitz replica of pub built by Wren in 1668; interesting choice of well kept beers, standard Nicholsons menu, good service, quieter back bar and upstairs dining room; open all day. *(Charles Todd)*

SW1

Albert (020) 7222 5577

Victoria Street; SW1H 0NP Airy open-plan bar with gleaming mahogany, cut and etched glass, ornate ceiling and solid comfortable furnishings, enjoyable pubby food from sandwiches up, well kept Fullers London Pride, Charles Wells Bombardier and guests, 24 wines by the glass, efficient cheerful service, handsome staircase lined with portraits of prime ministers leading up to carvery/dining room; background music, games machine, lavatories down steep stairs; children welcome if eating, open (and food) all day. *(Tony Scott)*

Antelope (020) 7824 8512

Eaton Terrace; SW1W 8EZ Pretty little flower-decked local in Belgravia, traditional interior with snug seating areas, bare boards and panelling, mix of old and new furniture including leather bucket chairs, interesting prints, gas-effect coal fire in tiled Victorian fireplace, Fullers ales from central servery and decent house wines, upstairs dining room (children allowed) serving decent pubby food including popular Sun roasts; TVs, free wi-fi, daily papers; dogs welcome, open all day and can get crowded in the evening. *(Rosie and John Moore)*

Buckingham Arms (020) 7222 3386

Petty France; SW1H 9EU Welcoming and relaxed bow-windowed early 19th-c local, Youngs ales and a guest from long curved bar, good range of wines by the glass, well thought-of pubby food from back open kitchen, elegant mirrors and dark woodwork, stained-glass screens, stools at modern high tables, some armchairs and upholstered banquettes, unusual side corridor with elbow ledge for drinkers; background music, TV; dogs welcome, handy for Buckingham Palace, Westminster Abbey and St James's Park, open all day, till 6pm weekends. *(Tom Stone)*

Cask & Glass (020) 7834 7630

Palace Street; SW1E 5HN Snug one-room traditional pub with good range of Shepherd Neame ales, friendly staff and atmosphere, good value lunchtime toasties, old prints and shiny black panelling; quiet corner TV; hanging baskets and a few tables outside, handy for Queen's Gallery, open all day, till 8pm Sat, closed Sun. *(Charles Todd)*

Cask Pub & Kitchen (020) 7630 7225

Charlwood Street/Tachbrook Street; SW1V 2EE Modern and spacious with simple furnishings, excellent choice of real ales and craft kegs, over 500 bottled beers and decent range of wines too, friendly knowledgeable staff, good burgers and other enjoyable food (roasts on Sun), chatty atmosphere – can get packed and noisy in the evening, regular beer-related events such as Meet the Brewer; downstairs gents'; some outside seating, open all day. *(Richard Tilbrook, Tony Scott)*

Clarence (020) 7930 4808

Whitehall; SW1A 2HP Beamed corner pub (Geronimo Inn), Youngs and guests, decent wines by the glass and popular food from snacks up, friendly chatty staff, quirky cheerful décor with well spaced tables and varied seating including tub chairs and banquettes, upstairs dining area; pavement tables, open (and food) all day. *(Susan Eccleston)*

★ Fox & Hounds (020) 7730 6367

Passmore Street/Graham Terrace; SW1W 8HR Small flower-decked Youngs pub in backstreets below Sloane Square, their well kept ales and interesting guests, warm red décor with lots of old pictures, prints and photographs, wall benches and leather chesterfields, back room with skylight, coal-effect gas fire; open all day and can get crowded early evening. *(Richard and Penny Gibbs)*

★ Grenadier (020) 7235 3074

Wilton Row; the turning off Wilton Crescent looks prohibitive, but the barrier and watchman are there to keep out cars; SW1X 7NR Steps up to cosy old mews pub with lots of character and military history, but not much space (avoid 5-7pm); simple unfussy panelled bar, stools and wooden benches on bare boards, changing ales such as Fullers, Timothy Taylors, Woodfordes and Youngs from rare pewter-topped counter, famous bloody marys, well liked food on blackboard, intimate back restaurant; no mobiles or photography; children over 8 and dogs allowed, hanging baskets, sentry box and single table outside, open (and food) all day. *(Richard Tilbrook)*

Grosvenor (020) 7821 8786

Grosvenor Road; SW1V 3LA Traditional pub across from river (no views), chatty and relaxed, with three well kept ales including Sharps and nice selection of wines, enjoyable good value pub food including popular Sun roasts, friendly staff; some tables out by road, secluded beer garden behind, open (and food) all day. *(Jamie Green)*

Jugged Hare (020) 7828 1543
*Vauxhall Bridge Road/Rochester Row;
SW1V 1DX* Popular Fullers pub in former
colonnaded bank; iron pillars and dark
woodwork, large chandelier, old photographs
of London, smaller back panelled dining
room, stairs up to gallery, four well kept ales
and reasonably priced food including range
of pies, good friendly service; background
music, TVs, silent fruit machine; open all day.
(Laura Reid)

★**Lord Moon of the Mall**
(020) 7839 7701 *Whitehall; SW1A 2DY*
Popular Wetherspoons bank conversion with
elegant main room, big arched windows
looking over Whitehall, old prints and a
large painting of Tim Martin (founder of the
chain), through an arch the style is more
recognisably Wetherspoons with neatly tiled
areas, bookshelves opposite long bar, ten
real ales and their good value food (from
breakfasts up); children (if eating) and
dogs welcome, open all day from 8am (till
midnight Fri, Sat). *(Tina and David Woods-
Taylor, Stephen Shepherd, B and M Kendall)*

Morpeth Arms (020) 7834 6442
Millbank; SW1P 4RW Victorian pub
facing the Thames, roomy and comfortable,
with view across river to MI6 headquarters
from upstairs Spy Room, etched and cut
glass, lots of mirrors, paintings, prints and
old photographs (some of british spies),
well kept Youngs ales and guests, decent
choice of wines and fair value standard
food, welcoming efficient staff, built on
site of Millbank Prison and cells remain
below; background music; seats outside
(a lot of traffic), handy for Tate Britain
and Thames Path walkers, open (and food)
all day. *(Robert Lester, Nigel and Sue Foster)*

Nags Head (020) 7235 1135
Kinnerton Street; SW1X 8ED Unspoilt
and unchanging little mews pub with
no-nonsense plain-talking landlord,
low-ceilinged panelled front room with
unusual sunken counter, log-effect gas fire
in old range, narrow passage down to even
smaller bar, well kept Adnams from 19th-c
handpumps, uncomplicated food, theatrical
mementoes, what-the-butler-saw machine
and one-armed bandit; no mobiles, individual
background music; well behaved children
and dogs allowed, a few seats outside, open
(and food) all day. *(Helen McLagan, Richard
and Penny Gibbs)*

★**Red Lion** (020) 7321 0782
Duke of York Street; SW1Y 6JP Pretty
little Victorian pub, remarkably preserved
and packed with customers often spilling
out on to pavement by mass of foliage and
flowers; series of small rooms with profusion
of polished mahogany, gleaming mirrors, cut/
etched windows and chandeliers, striking
ornamental plaster ceiling, Fullers/Gales

beers, traditional food (all day weekdays,
snacks evening, diners have priority over a
few of the front tables); no children; dogs
welcome, closed Sun and bank holidays,
otherwise open all day. *(Jeff Davies)*

Red Lion (020) 7930 5826
Parliament Street; SW1A 2NH
Victorian pub by Houses of Parliament, used
by Foreign Office staff and MPs, divided
bare-boards bar with showy chandeliers
suspended from fine moulded ceiling,
parliamentary cartoons and prints, Fullers/
Gales beers and decent wines from long
counter, good range of food, efficient staff,
also clubby cellar bar and upstairs panelled
dining room; free wi-fi; children welcome,
outside bench seating, open all day (till 9pm
Sun). *(Martin Day)*

Red Lion (020) 7930 4141
*Crown Passage, behind St James's
Street; SW1Y 6PP* Cheerful traditional
little pub tucked down narrow passage near
St James's Palace; dark panelling and leaded
lights, upholstered settles and stools on
patterned carpet, lots of prints, decorative
plates and horse brasses, well kept Adnams,
St Austell and decent range of malt whiskies,
friendly service, lunchtime sandwiches (no
hot food), narrow overflow room (and ladies')
upstairs, downstairs gents'; sports TV in one
corner; colourful hanging baskets, closed
Sun, otherwise open all day. *(Michael Butler,
Tony Scott)*

Speaker (020) 7222 1749
Great Peter Street; SW1P 2HA Bustling
chatty atmosphere in unpretentious smallish
corner pub (can get packed at peak times),
well kept Timothy Taylors, Youngs and guests,
bottled beers and lots of whiskies, limited
choice of enjoyable simple food, friendly
staff, panelling, political cartoons and prints;
no mobiles, background music or children;
open (and food) all day weekdays, closed
Sat, Sun. *(Charles Todd)*

★**St Stephens Tavern** (020) 7925 2286
Parliament Street; SW1A 2JR Victorian
pub opposite Houses of Parliament and
Big Ben (so quite touristy); lofty ceilings
with brass chandeliers, tall windows with
etched glass and swagged curtains, gleaming
mahogany, charming upper gallery bar (may
be reserved for functions), four well kept
Badger ales from handsome counter with
pedestal lamps, fairly priced traditional food
including burgers and pies, friendly efficient
staff, division bell for MPs and lots of
parliamentary memorabilia; open (and food)
all day. *(Julie Swift)*

Tom Cribb (020) 7839 3801
Panton Street; SW1Y 4EA Small Shepherd
Neame corner pub named after 19th-c boxer,
tiled exterior and traditional bare-boards bar,
four real ales, limited choice of pubby food

till 6pm, welcoming service; sports TV; no children, open all day (till 9.30 Sun). *(Eddie Edwards)*

White Swan (020) 7821 8568
Vauxhall Bridge Road; SW1V 2SA Roomy corner pub handy for Tate Britain, lots of dark dining tables on three levels in long room, well cooked reasonably priced pubby food, six or more ales including Adnams, Fullers, St Austell and Youngs, decent wines by the glass, quick helpful uniformed staff; background music, can get very busy at peak times; open all day. *(John Wooll)*

SW3

★ Coopers Arms (020) 7376 3120
Flood Street; SW3 5TB Useful bolthole for King's Road shoppers (so can get busy); comfortable dark-walled open-plan bar with mix of good-sized tables on floorboards, pre-war sideboard and dresser, railway clock and moose head, Youngs and guests, good all-day bar food; well behaved children till 7pm, dogs allowed in bar, courtyard garden. *(Richard and Penny Gibbs)*

Cross Keys (020) 7351 0686
Lawrence Street; SW3 5NB Under same ownership as the Brown Cow and Sands End (both SW6); open-plan bare-boards interior with skylit back dining area, exposed brick walls and some recycled wood panelling, Greene King IPA and three guests from central servery, good modern food (not cheap) including all-day bar snacks (not weekend evenings), attentive friendly service. *(Richard and Penny Gibbs)*

Hour Glass (020) 7581 2497
Brompton Road; SW3 2DY Under same ownership as nearby Brompton Food Market deli and recently refurbished; compact wood-floored bar with open brick fireplace, red leather banquette at each end, stools along drinking shelf overlooking street, Fullers London Pride and a couple of guests, proper cider, very well liked interesting food from bar snacks up, panelled upstairs dining room with open kitchen, friendly helpful service; children and dogs (in bar) welcome, handy for V&A and other nearby museums, open (and food) all day, meals till 5pm Sun. *(Tom Stone)*

Pigs Ear (020) 7352 2908
Old Church Street; SW3 5BS Civilised L-shaped corner pub, friendly and relaxed, with short interesting choice of bar food and more elaborate evening menu, lots of wines by the glass including champagne and three changing ales, good service, tables and benches on wood floors, butterflies and 1960s posters on grey-green panelling, large mirrors and huge windows, open fire, upstairs restaurant; background music; children and dogs (in bar) welcome, open all day (food all day weekends). *(P Nick)*

Surprise (020) 7351 6954
Christchurch Terrace; SW3 4AJ Late Victorian Chelsea pub (Geronimo Inn) popular with well heeled locals; Sharps, Youngs and a house beer (HMS Surprise) from light wood servery, champagne and plenty of other wines by the glass, interesting food including british tapas-style canapé boards and set menu, friendly service, soft grey décor and comfortable furnishings with floral sofas and armchairs on sturdy floorboards, stained-glass partitioning, upstairs dining room, daily papers; open all day. *(Edward Nile)*

W1

★ Argyll Arms (020) 7734 6117
Argyll Street; W1F 7TP Popular and unexpectedly individual pub with three interesting little front cubicle rooms (essentially unchanged since 1860s), wooden partitions and impressive frosted and engraved glass, mirrored corridor to spacious back room, around eight real ales including Nicholsons, Fullers and Sharps, well liked reasonably priced food in bar or upstairs dining room overlooking pedestrianised street; background music, fruit machine; children welcome till 8pm, open (and food) all day. *(Dr Kevan Tucker, Barry Collett, Tony Scott, John Beeken)*

★ Audley (020) 7499 1843
Mount Street; W1K 2RX Classic late Victorian Mayfair pub, opulent red plush, mahogany panelling and engraved glass, chandeliers and clock in extravagantly carved bracket hanging from ornately corniced ceiling, Fullers London Pride, Sharps Doom Bar, Taylor Walker 1730 and guests from long polished bar, good choice of pub food (reasonably priced for the area), friendly efficient service, upstairs panelled dining room, cellar wine bar; quiet background music, TV, pool; children till 6pm, pavement tables, open (and food) all day. *(Tony Scott)*

Clachan (020) 7494 0834
Kingly Street; W1B 5QH Nicholsons corner pub behind Liberty (and once owned by them), ornate plaster ceiling supported by large fluted and decorated pillars, comfortable screened leather banquettes, smaller drinking alcove up three or four steps, fine selection of real ales from handsome mahogany counter, affordably priced food served all day, dining room upstairs; can get very busy. *(Giles and Annie Francis)*

Crown & Two Chairmen
(020) 7437 8192 *Bateman Street/Dean Street; W1D 3SB* Large main room with smaller area off to the right, different height tables on bare boards, Sharps, Windsor & Eton and three guests, also craft beers such as Camden Town, interesting up-to-date food from bar snacks up including weekday

breakfasts (from 10am) and Sun roasts, upstairs dining room, good mix of customers (gets busy with after-work drinkers); free wi-fi; open (and food) all day. *(Jeff Davies)*

★ **Dog & Duck** (020) 7494 0697
Bateman Street/Frith Street; W1D 3AJ
Bags of character in this tiny Soho pub – best enjoyed in the afternoon when not so packed; unusual old tiles and mosaics (the dog with tongue hanging out in hot pursuit of a duck is notable), heavy old advertising mirrors and open fire, Fullers London Pride and guests from unusual little counter and quite a few wines by the glass, enjoyable well priced food in cosy upstairs dining room where children welcome; background music; dogs allowed in bar, open (and food) all day with drinkers often spilling on to the pavement. *(Richard and Penny Gibbs)*

Flying Horse (020) 7636 8324
Oxford Street, near junction with Tottenham Court Road; W1D 1AN
Ornate late Victorian pub (formerly the Tottenham) with long narrow bar, old tiling, mirrors, mahogany fittings and so forth, also three notable murals behind glass of voluptuous nymphs, dark floorboards and leather banquettes, half a dozen real ales and enjoyable all-day food from Nicholsons menu, friendly service, bar and dining room downstairs; background music, free wi-fi; children welcome until 9pm, can get very busy at lunchtime. *(Millie and Peter Downing)*

French House (020) 7437 2477
Dean Street; W1D 5BG Small character Soho pub with impressive range of wines, bottled beers and other unusual drinks, some draught beers but no real ales or pint glasses, lively chatty atmosphere (mainly standing room), theatre memorabilia, shortish choice of modern food (Mon-Fri till 4pm) in bar or upstairs restaurant, efficient staff; no music or mobile phones; can get very busy evenings with customers spilling on to the street, open all day. *(Tom Stone)*

★ **Grapes** (020) 7493 4216
Shepherd Market; W1J 7QQ Genuinely old-fashioned pub with dimly lit bar, plenty of well worn plush red furnishings, stuffed birds and fish in display cases, some old guns, wood floors, panelling, coal fire and snug back alcove, six ales including Fullers, Sharps and a house beer from Brains, good choice of authentic thai food (not Sun evening), english food too, lots of customers (especially lunchtime and early evening) spilling out on to square; children till 6pm weekdays (anytime weekends), open all day. *(Tony Scott)*

★ **Guinea** (020) 7409 1728
Bruton Place; W1J 6NL Lovely hanging baskets and chatty customers outside this tiny 17th-c mews pub, standing room only at peak times, a few cushioned wooden seats and tables on tartan carpet, side elbow shelf and snug back area, old-fashioned prints, planked ceiling, Youngs and a guest from striking counter, famous steak and kidney pie, grills and some sandwiches (not Sat lunchtime or Sun evening), smart Guinea Grill restaurant; no children; open all day (till 8pm Sun). *(Charles Todd)*

Prince Regent (020) 7486 7395
Marylebone High Street; W1U 5JN
Victorian corner pub in Marleybone village, flamboyant (if slightly worn) bare-boards interior with richly coloured furnishings, large gilt mirrors and opulent chandeliers, four changing ales, good range of wines and decent sensibly priced home-made food, friendly staff, upstairs 'Opium Room'; quiz Mon, free wi-fi; open all day from 8am (11am weekends) for breakfast. *(Susan Eccleston)*

Running Horse (020) 7493 1275
Davies Street/Davies Mews; W1K 5JE
Stylish 18th-c pub with open-plan bare-boards bar, appealing collection of dining chairs and cushioned settles around mix of tables, tartan armchairs in front of green-tiled fireplace, ales such as Rebellion, lots of wines by the glass and good imaginative food from bar snacks up, friendly service, horse-racing prints on plain or navy-painted panelling, projector showing live televised racing, upstairs cocktail bar with button-back club chairs, brass chandeliers and more horsey prints on racing genius wallpaper; background music (can be loud), free wi-fi; children and dogs welcome, contemporary wicker seats and tables out on the pavement, closed Sun evening, otherwise open all day. *(Richard and Penny Gibbs)*

Shakespeares Head
(020) 7734 2911 *Great Marlborough Street; W1F 7HZ* Taylor Walker corner pub dating from the early 18th c (though largely rebuilt in the 1920s), dark beams, panelling and soft lighting, well kept ales including Fullers and Sharps, enjoyable pubby food from sandwiches and baked potatoes up, friendly staff, upstairs dining room overlooking Carnaby Street; open (and food) all day. *(M J Winterton)*

Three Tuns (020) 7408 0330
Portman Mews S; W1H 6HP Large bare-boards front bar and sizeable lounge/dining area with beams and nooks and crannies, Fullers, Timothy Taylors and guests, enjoyable reasonably priced pubby food, good friendly staff and vibrant atmosphere; street benches. *(Tom Stone)*

W2

Mad Bishop & Bear
(020) 7402 2441 *Paddington station; W2 1HB* Up escalators from concourse, full Fullers range kept well and good wine choice,

reasonably priced standard food quickly served including breakfast from 8am (10am Sun), airy interior with ornate plasterwork and mirrored columns, high tables and chairs on light wood or tiled floors, raised carpeted dining area with some booth seating, train departures screen; background music, TVs, games machines; tables out at front, open all day till 11pm (10.30pm Sun). *(Dr and Mrs A K Clarke, Roger and Donna Huggins, Ian Herdman)*

★**Victoria** (020) 7724 1191

Strathearn Place; W2 2NH Well run bare-boards pub with lots of Victorian pictures and memorabilia, cast-iron fireplaces, gilded mirrors and mahogany panelling, brass mock-gas lamps above attractive horseshoe bar serving Fullers ales and guests from smaller breweries, several wines by the glass and reasonably priced popular food, friendly service and chatty relaxed atmosphere; upstairs has small library/snug and replica of Gaiety Theatre bar (mostly reserved for private functions now); quiet background music, TV; pavement tables, open all day. *(Jeff Davies)*

WC1

Bountiful Cow (020) 7404 0200

Eagle Street ; WC1R 4AP This previous Main Entry pub, popular for its excellent burgers and steaks, was up for sale as we went to press – news please; informal bar with booth seating and raised area by the windows, chrome stools against counter serving Adnams ales and ten wines by the glass, smallish upper room with wicker dining chairs around oak tables, larger downstairs dining room; background music, free wi-fi; children welcome, has closed on Sun. *(Hilary and Neil Christopher, Belinda May)*

★**Cittie of Yorke** (020) 7242 7670

High Holborn; WC1V 6BN Splendid back bar rather like a baronial hall with extraordinarily extended counter, 1,000-gallon wine vats resting above gantry, bulbous lights hanging from soaring raftered roof, intimate ornately carved booths and triangular fireplace with grates on all three sides, smaller comfortable panelled room with lots of little prints of York, cheap Sam Smiths beers and reasonably priced bar food, lots of students, lawyers and City types but plenty of space to absorb the crowds; children welcome, closed Sun, otherwise open all day. *(Barry Collett, Tony Scott)*

Lady Ottoline (020) 7831 0008

Northington Street; WC1N 2JF Well restored 19th-c Bloomsbury pub; original fitted benches and some utilitarian 1940s furniture on bare boards, woodburning stove, modern artwork including portrait of Lady Ottoline Morrell who had associations with the Bloomsbury Set, enjoyable up-to-date food from short menu (not cheap), four real ales, fine range of gins and good wines,

friendly service, staircase with risqué Victorian photographs up to dining rooms; children (till 6pm) and dogs allowed, peaceful atmosphere despite TV, open all day (closed from 5pm Sun). *(Susan and John Douglas)*

★**Lamb** (020) 7405 0713

Lamb's Conduit Street; WC1N 3LZ Famously unspoilt Victorian pub with bank of cut-glass swivelling snob screens around U-shaped counter, sepia photographs of 1890s actresses on ochre panelled walls, traditional cast-iron-framed tables, snug little back room, Youngs ales and guests kept well, good choice of malt whiskies, straightforward pubby food from baguettes up; children welcome till 5pm, slatted wooden seats out in front, more in small courtyard, Foundling Museum nearby, open all day (till midnight Thurs-Sat) and can get very busy. *(Brian and Anna Marsden, Helen McLagan, Tracey and Stephen Groves)*

Museum Tavern (020) 7242 8987

Museum Street/Great Russell Street; WC1B 3BA Traditional high-ceilinged ornate Victorian pub facing British Museum, busy lunchtime and early evening, half a dozen well kept ales and several wines by the glass, standard Taylor Walker menu, friendly helpful staff; one or two tables out under gas lamps, open all day. *(Jeff Davies)*

Norfolk Arms (020) 7388 3937

Leigh Street; WC1H 9EP Atmospheric tile-fronted pub with ornate ceiling and other high Victorian features, very good tapas, a couple of well kept changing ales and nice wines, close-set tables in bustling U-shaped bar, friendly efficient service; open all day. *(Charles Todd)*

★**Princess Louise** (020) 7405 8816

High Holborn; WC1V 7EP Splendid Victorian gin palace with extravagant décor – even the gents – has its own preservation order; gloriously opulent main bar with wood and glass partitions, fine etched and gilt mirrors, brightly coloured and fruit-shaped tiles, slender Portland stone columns soaring towards the lofty and deeply moulded plaster ceiling, open fire, cheap Sam Smiths from long counter, competitively priced pubby food (not Fri-Sun) in quieter upstairs room; gets crowded early weekday evenings, no children; open all day. *(Barry Collett)*

Queens Larder (020) 7837 5627

Queen Square; WC1N 3AR Small character pub on corner of traffic-free square and cobbled Cosmo Place, also known as Queen Charlotte (it's where she stored food for her mad husband George III, who was being cared for nearby); circular cast-iron tables, wall benches and stools around attractive U-shaped bar, theatre posters on dark panelled walls, Greene King ales, decent pubby food, upstairs function room; background jazz; dogs welcome, picnic-sets and heater outside. *(Jamie Green)*

Skinners Arms (020) 7837 5621

Judd Street; WC1H 9NT Richly decorated, with glorious woodwork, marble pillars, high ceilings and ornate windows, lots of London prints on busy wallpaper, interesting layout including comfortable back seating area, coal fire, Greene King and guests from attractive long bar, enjoyable home-made food from baguettes and wraps up; unobtrusive background music, muted TV; pavement picnic-sets, handy for British Library, open all day, closed Sun. *(Roger and Donna Huggins)*

WC2 TQ2980

Admiralty (020) 7930 0066

Trafalgar Square; WC2N 5DS Handsome naval-theme pub by Trafalgar Square; button-back leather seating in booths by big windows, high stools and elbow tables, grand chandeliers and lots of interesting prints, flagstaff with white ensigns and union jacks, eight Fullers/Gales beers from traditional counter, grand steps up to mezzanine with leather-seated dining chairs at wooden tables, also atmospheric vaulted cellar bar with painted brick or planked walls, arched seating alcoves, nautical prints and knick-knacks, standard pub food including speciality pies, efficient staff; children welcome, a few pavement tables, open all day from 8am (10am weekends) for breakfast. *(David Jackman)*

Bear & Staff (020) 7930 5261

Bear Street; WC2H 7AX Traditional Nicholsons corner pub with six well kept changing ales and standard pubby food from sandwiches and sharing plates up, friendly staff, upstairs dining room named after Charlie Chaplin who was a customer; open all day. *(Caroline Sullivan)*

Cheshire Cheese (020) 7836 2347

Little Essex Street/Milford Lane; WC2R 3LD Small cosy 1920s corner pub, leaded bow windows, beams and panelling, cushioned oak settles and assorted seats on patterned carpet, bric-a-brac hanging from beams, well kept St Austell Tribute, Sharps Doom Bar and guests, good value wines and pubby food, friendly staff, games room with bar billiards, darts and table skittles, upstairs dining/function room; background music, sports TV; closed Sun, otherwise open all day. *(Tony and Wendy Hobden, David and Sally Frost)*

Coal Hole (020) 7379 9883

Strand; WC2R 0DW Well preserved Edwardian pub adjacent to the Savoy; original leaded windows, classical wall reliefs, mock-baronial high ceiling and raised back gallery, nine changing ales from central

servery, standard Nicholsons menu, wine bar downstairs; sports TV; open all day and can get very busy. *(Tony Scott, Simon Collett-Jones)*

★ Cross Keys (020) 7836 5185

Endell Street/Betterton Street; WC2H 9EB Foliage-covered Covent Garden pub with fascinating interior, masses of photographs, pictures and posters including Beatles memorabilia, all kinds of brassware and bric-a-brac from stuffed fish to musical instruments, three well kept Brodies ales and couple of guests (usually smaller London brewers), decent wines by the glass, good lunchtime sandwiches and a few bargain hot dishes; fruit machine, gents' downstairs; sheltered outside cobbled area with flower tubs, open all day. *(Millie and Peter Downing)*

Edgar Wallace (020) 7353 3120

Essex Street; WC2R 3JE Simple spacious open-plan pub dating from 18th c, eight well kept ales including one badged for them from Nethergate, enjoyable good value traditional food from sandwiches up, friendly efficient service, half-panelled walls and red ceilings, interesting Edgar Wallace memorabilia and a collection of old beer and cigarette adverts, upstairs dining room; a few high tables in side alleyway, closed weekends. *(Edward Nile)*

George (020) 7353 9638

Strand; WC2R 1AP Timbered pub near the law courts, long narrow bare-boards bar, nine real ales and a dozen wines by the glass, lunchtime food from sandwiches up, also upstairs bar/restaurant, pre-theatre meal discount till 7pm; open all day. *(Tony Scott)*

Knights Templar (020) 7831 2660

Chancery Lane; WC2A 1DT Good well managed Wetherspoons in big-windowed former bank, marble pillars, handsome fittings and plasterwork, bustling atmosphere on two levels, ever-changing range of well kept/priced ales, good wine choice and enjoyable bargain food, friendly efficient staff; free wi-fi; open all day Mon-Fri, till 5pm Sat, closed Sun. *(Ian Herdman)*

Mr Foggs (020) 7581 3992

St Martins Lane; WC2N 4EA Themed around Jules Verne's Phileas Fogg, small Victorian-style bar with appropriate pictures and stuffed animals on panelled walls, masses of bric-a-brac hanging from ceiling including model boats, bird cages, brass instruments, even an old pram, craft beers and over a dozen wines by the glass from metal-topped servery, friendly staff in period dress, enjoyable food including bar snacks, sharing plates and range of pies, atmospheric upstairs re-creation of 19th-c salon/gin parlour, swagged curtains, chinese wallpaper and chaise longues, fine selection of gins and cocktails; open all day, upstairs from 5pm (3pm Sat). *(Tim and Sarah Smythe-Brown)*

Nell Gwynne (020) 7240 5579

Bull Inn Court, off Strand; WC2R 0NP
Narrow dimly lit old pub tucked down
alleyway, character bare-boards interior with
lots of pictures (some of Nell Gwynne) on
papered walls, a few tables but it's mainly
standing room and drinkers spill outside at
busy times, ales such as Adnams, Fullers and
St Austell, some interesting bottled beers
including Camden Town and extensive range
of spirits; good juke box, TV, darts; closed
Sun, otherwise open all day. *(Brian Glozier)*

Porterhouse (020) 7379 7917

Maiden Lane; WC2E 7NA London outpost
of Dublin's Porterhouse brewery, their
interesting beers along with guests and lots
of bottled imports, good choice of wines by
the glass, pubby food; three-level labyrinth of
stairs (lifts for disabled), galleries, gleaming
copper ducting and piping, a large sonorous
open-work clock suspended from the
ceiling, neatly cased bottled beer displays;
background and live music, sports TV
(also in gents'); tables on front terrace,
open all day and can get packed evenings.
(Margaret McDonald)

Salisbury (020) 7836 5863

St Martins Lane; WC2N 4AP Gleaming
Victorian pub in the heart of the West
End, a wealth of cut-glass and mahogany,
wonderfully ornate bronze light fittings
and etched mirrors, some interesting
photographs including Dylan Thomas
enjoying a drink here in 1941, up to six well
kept ales, usual Taylor Walker menu from
sharing platters up, cheerful staff; steep
stairs down to lavatories; children allowed till
5pm, fine details on building exterior, seats in
pedestrianised side alley, open (and food)
all day. *(Susan Eccleston)*

Ship (020) 7405 1992

Gate Street; WC2A 3HP Tucked-away bare-
boards pub with roomy minimally furnished
bar, some booth seating, chesterfields by
open fire, quite dark with leaded lights,
panelling and plaster-relief ceiling, six well
kept changing ales, enjoyable bar food,
upstairs restaurant with good separate menu,
friendly service; background music; open
(and food) all day. *(Michael Zeitlyn)*

★ Ship & Shovell (020) 7839 1311

*Craven Passage, off Craven Street;
WC2N 5PH* Unusually split between two
facing buildings; well kept Badger ales
and a guest, decent reasonably priced food
including wide range of baguettes, bar
snacks and pubby choices, good friendly
service; one side brightly lit with dark wood,
etched mirrors and interesting mainly naval
pictures, plenty of tables, some stall seating
and open fire; other side (across 'Underneath
the Arches' alley) has a cosily partitioned
bar; open all day, closed Sun. *(Tony Scott,
Ian Phillips)*

Temple Brew House

(020) 7936 2536 *Essex Street; WC2R 3JF*
Popular refurbished basement bar; fine
range of beers including some from on-site
microbrewery, lots of wines by the glass and
well liked food from sandwiches, small plates
and burgers up (own smokehouse), friendly
service from enthusiastic knowledgeable
young staff; open (and food) all day.
(Edward Nile)

Wellington (020) 7836 2789

Strand/Wellington Street; WC2R 0HS
Long narrow traditional corner pub next
to the Lyceum; eight real ales including
Trumans and Sharps, a couple of craft
beers and several wines by the glass, usual
Nicholsons menu, friendly staff, quieter
upstairs bar/restaurant; sports TV; tables
outside, open all day. *(Dr Kevan Tucker,
Tony Scott)*

EAST LONDON

E1

★ Prospect of Whitby (020) 3603 4041

Wapping Wall; E1W 3SH Claims to be
oldest pub on the Thames dating from 1520
(although largely rebuilt after much later
fire), was known as the Devil's Tavern and
has a colourful history (Pepys and Dickens
used it regularly and Turner came for weeks
at a time to study the river views) – tourists
love it; L-shaped bare-boards bar with
plenty of beams, flagstones and panelling,
five changing ales served from fine pewter
counter, good choice of wines by the glass,
bar food and more formal restaurant upstairs,
cheerful helpful staff; children welcome (only
if eating after 5.30pm), unbeatable views
towards Docklands from tables on waterfront
courtyard, open all day. *(Alastair and Sheree
Hepburn, B and M Kendall)*

Town of Ramsgate (020) 7481 8000

Wapping High Street; E1W 2PN
Interesting olde-London Thames-side
setting, restricted but evocative river view
from small back floodlit terrace with mock
gallows (hanging dock was nearby), long
narrow dimly lit chatty bar with squared
oak panelling, Fullers and Youngs ales, good
choice of traditional food (all day Sun)
including daily specials and deals, friendly
helpful service; background music, Mon quiz;
children and dogs welcome, open all day.
(Tom Stone)

Water Poet (020) 7426 0495

Folgate Street; E1 6BX Big rambling
Spitalfields pub with ornate touches and
bohemian feel, enjoyable food in bar and
dining room including popular Sun roasts,
good selection of real ales and craft beers,
decent wines, friendly staff and nice mix of
customers, comfortable leather sofas and
armchairs on wood floor, basement bar/

function room (comedy club), separate games room with two pool tables; sports TV; children allowed till 7pm, large enclosed outside area (dogs welcome here) with 'barn' room and barbecue, open all day. *(Jeff Davies)*

Williams (020) 7247 5163

Artillery Lane; E1 7LS Busy pub with wide range of real ales including Greene King and several from smaller London brewers, proper ciders too, comfortable interior with several seating areas including some leather sofas, pictures of old London breweries on the walls; weekend live music; closed Sun otherwise open (and food) all day. *(Tony and Wendy Hobden)*

E2

Carpenters Arms (020) 7739 6342

Cheshire Street; E2 6EG Welcoming neatly looked-after little corner pub just off Brick Lane and once owned by the Kray twins, well kept ales including Timothy Taylors Landlord, enjoyable blackboard food; beer garden at back, closed Mon-Weds till 4pm, otherwise open all day. *(Neil Hosland-Round)*

E3

★ Crown (020) 8880 7261

Grove Road/Old Ford Road; E3 5SN Dining pub (Geronimo Inn) with relaxed welcoming bar, faux animal hide stools and chunky pine tables on polished boards, big bay window with comfortable scatter cushion seating area, books etc on open shelves, well kept Youngs and guests, good choice of wines by the glass, three individually decorated upstairs dining areas overlooking Victoria Park, imaginative food (all day Sun); background music; children and dogs welcome, open all day. *(Rona Mackinlay)*

Palm Tree (020) 8980 2918

Haverfield Road; E3 5BH Lone survivor of blitzed East End terrace tucked away in Mile End Park by Regent's Canal; two Edwardian bars around oval servery, old-fashioned and unchanging under long-serving licensees, a couple of well kept ales, lunchtime sandwiches, good local atmosphere with popular weekend jazz; no credit cards; open all day (till late Sat). *(Charles Todd)*

E14

★ Grapes (020) 7987 4396

Narrow Street; E14 8BP Relatively unchanged since Charles Dickens used it as a model for his Six Jolly Fellowship Porters in *Our Mutual Friend*; a proper traditional tavern with friendly atmosphere and good mix of customers, partly panelled bar with prints of actors, old local maps and the pub itself, elaborately etched windows, plates along a shelf, larger back area leading

to small deck looking over river towards Canary Wharf, Adnams, Marstons, Timothy Taylors and a guest, good value tasty bar food, upstairs restaurant with fine views; no children, dogs on the lead welcome, can catch Canary Wharf riverboat and enter pub via steps from foreshore, open all day. *(B and M Kendall)*

★ Gun (020) 7515 5222

Coldharbour; E14 9NS Dining pub with great views from riverside terrace of the O2 centre; smart front restaurant and two character bars – busy flagstoned drinkers' one with antique guns and log fire, cosy red-painted next-door room with leather sofas and armchairs, stuffed boar's head and modern prints, Adnams Bitter and guests, several wines by the glass and very well liked contemporary food (not cheap), efficient service from friendly staff; background music; children welcome till 8pm, open all day (may close for weddings and other events – best to check website). *(Laura Reid)*

Narrow (020) 7592 7950

Narrow Street; E14 8DJ Stylish dining pub (part of Gordon Ramsay's chain) with great Thames views from window seats and covered terrace, simple but smart bar with white walls and blue woodwork, mosaic-tiled fireplaces and colourful striped armchairs, beers such as Fullers London Pride, good wines, food from bar snacks to pricier restaurant meals, dining room also white with matching furnishings, local maps, prints and a suspended boat; background music (live Weds); children welcome, open all day. *(Andrew and Michele Revell)*

E17

Bell (020) 8523 2277

Forest Road/Chingford Road; E17 4NE Imposing Victorian corner pub with spacious open-plan interior, nice mismatch of furniture including comfy sofas, bare boards, panelling and some sturdy pillars, eight real ales, craft beers and a couple of proper ciders, generous helpings of enjoyable reasonably priced food, good friendly service; live music, DJ and quiz nights; children and dogs welcome, beer garden to the side and back, convenient for Walthamstow's William Morris Gallery, open all day. *(Rosie and John Moore)*

Queens Arms (020) 8520 9184

Orford Road; E17 9NJ Refurbished 19th-c corner pub in Walthamstow village, spacious and comfortable, with well kept ales such as Timothy Taylors Landlord and numerous wines by the glass, well liked food from interesting changing menu, friendly service and good buoyant atmosphere; background music; children very welcome, seats outside, open all day. *(Michael Butler)*

NORTH LONDON

N1

Albion (020) 7607 7450

Thornhill Road; N1 1HW Charming wisteria-clad Georgian building in Islington conservation area; attractive bare-boards interior with minimalist front bar and spacious back lounge/dining room, log fires, decent pubby dishes plus weekend brunch (9-11.30am), four beers such as Adnams, Meantime and Sharps, helpful service; tables out at front and in impressive walled back garden with pergola, open all day. *(Tom Stone)*

Camden Head (020) 7359 0851

Camden Walk; N1 8DY Comfortably preserved Victorian pub in pedestrianised street, lots of fine etched glass and mahogany panelling, unusual clock suspended from ceiling, button-back leather wall seats and a few small booths, half a dozen well kept changing ales from oval island servery, fairly priced pubby food (order at the bar), friendly staff, free nightly comedy club upstairs; trivia machine, downstairs ladies'; children welcome till 7pm, no dogs, chunky picnic-sets on front terrace, open (and food) all day. *(Charles Todd)*

Charles Lamb (020) 7837 5040

Elia Street; N1 8DE Small friendly backstreet corner pub with four well kept ales such as Dark Star and Windsor & Eton, interesting bottled beers and decent choice of wines by the glass including own-label, good blackboard food (brunch Sat from 11am), no bookings, big windows, polished boards and simple traditional furniture; background jazz; pavement tables, closed Mon and Tues lunchtimes, otherwise open all day. *(Jeff Davies)*

Craft Beer Company

(020) 7278 4560 *White Lion Street; N1 9PP* Flower-decked Islington pub with extensive choice of interesting draught and bottled beers, good range of wines and spirits too, cosy and softly lit with dark green walls, wood-strip or red carpeted floors, a couple of ornate Victorian pillars, leather armchairs under a portrait of Churchill, high tables in main bar, low ones in adjacent areas, good mix of customers; occasional live acoustic music; small side garden, open all day Fri-Sun, from 4pm other days. *(Jeff Davies)*

★ **Drapers Arms** (020) 7619 0348

Barnsbury Street; N1 1ER Welcoming simply furnished Georgian townhouse, U-shaped bar with dark wooden tables and wheelback chairs on bare boards, gilt mirrors over fireplaces, sofa and some

comfortable chairs in one part, Harveys, Otley and Sambrooks, british draught lagers and 17 carefully chosen wines by the glass from bright green counter, good imaginative modern food, stylish upstairs dining room with striking chequerboard-painted floor; background music, free wi-fi; children welcome (must be seated and dining after 6pm), dogs allowed in bar, nice paved back terrace with zinc-topped tables under large parasols, open all day. *(Paul A Moore, Belinda May)*

Duke of Cambridge (020) 7359 3066

St Peters Street; N1 8JT Well established as London's first organic pub; simply decorated busy main room with chunky wooden tables, pews and benches on bare boards, corridor past open kitchen to more formal dining room and conservatory, ales from small breweries, also organic draught lagers, ciders, spirits and wines, interesting bar food using seasonal produce (not cheap and they add a service charge), teas and coffees; children welcome, dogs in bar, open all day. *(Jeff Davies, Tom Stone)*

Earl of Essex (020) 7424 5828

Danbury Street; N1 8LE One-room pub brewing its own Earl ales, great choice of other beers too on draught and in bottles, straightforward but decent home-made food with beer recommendations listed on boards; back walled garden, open (and food) all day. *(Laura Reid)*

Hemingford Arms (020) 7607 3303

Hemingford Road; N1 1DF 19th-c ivy-clad pub filled with bric-a-brac, good choice of real ales from central servery, thai evening food plus Sunday roasts, open fire, upstairs bar/function room; live music including Mon bluegrass, sports TV, machines; picnic-sets outside, open all day. *(Jamie Green)*

Lighterman (020) 3846 3400

Granary Square, Regent's Canal; N1C 4BH Newly opened modern canalside bar/restaurant on three floors, popular food from breakfast on including wood-fired grills, good range of drinks from real ales to cocktails, efficient friendly service; seats out on wraparound balcony and waterside terrace, open (and food) all day. *(Charles Todd)*

Marquess Tavern (020) 7359 4615

Canonbury Street/Marquess Road; N1 2TB Imposing revamped Victorian pub; bare boards and a mix of furniture including sofas around big horseshoe servery, a couple of fireplaces and lots of prints (some recalling George Orwell who used to drink here), Youngs beers, good selection of wines, gins and cocktails, traditional and more adventurous food in bar or back skylit dining room with classical wall columns, large mirrors and modern lights dangling from high ceiling; background music, TV; children and dogs welcome, a few seats out behind front railings, open (and food) all day. *(Sally, Jamie Green)*

★**Parcel Yard** (020) 7713 7258
King's Cross station, N end of new concourse, up stairs (or lift); N1C 4AH Impressive restoration of listed Victorian parcel sorting office; lots of interesting bare-boards rooms off corridors around airy central atrium, pleasing old-fashioned feel with exposed pipework and ducting adding to the effect, back bar serving full range of well kept Fullers beers plus guests from long modern counter, plenty of wines by the glass, similar upstairs area with old and new furniture including comfortable sofas, railway memorabilia and some nice touches like Victorian envelope wallpaper, good bistro-pub food from bar snacks up, breakfast till 11.45am, attentive friendly service, power points to recharge phones/laptops, screens for train times, platform views; seats out at front, open all day from 8am (9am Sun). *(Peter Smith and Judith Brown, John Oates, Dr Kevan Tucker, Martin Day, Susan and John Douglas, Roger and Donna Huggins)*

Wenlock Arms (020) 7608 3406
Wenlock Road; N1 7TA Friendly corner local with excellent choice of real ales, craft beers and ciders from central servery, plenty of foreign bottled beers too, simple food, alcove seating, coal fires; darts, free wi-fi; children (until 8pm) and dogs welcome, open all day. *(Jeff Davies)*

N6

★**Flask** (020) 8348 7346
Highgate West Hill; N6 6BU Comfortable traditional Georgian pub owned by Fullers; intriguing up-and-down layout, sash-windowed bar hatch, panelling and high-backed carved settle in snug lower area with log fire, wide choice of food; picnic-sets out in front courtyard, handy for strolls around Highgate village or Hampstead Heath, open all day. *(Caroline Sullivan)*

N8
Kings Head (020) 8340 1028
Crouch End Hill/Broadway; N8 8AA Victorian corner pub with open-plan bar, cushioned window seats, leather banquettes, high stools and elbow tables on bare boards, well kept ales such as Sambrooks and Sharps, good choice of other drinks, enjoyable food including set menu, friendly helpful staff, downstairs comedy club (Thurs, Sat, Sun); background music, TV; open all day (till 2am Fri, Sat). *(Jim and Sue James)*

NW1
Bree Louise (020) 7681 4930
Cobourg Street/Euston Street; NW1 2HH No-frills corner pub with wide selection of well kept ales on handpump and gravity, good choice of ciders too and some decent reasonably priced wines, food emphasising pies (Mon-Thurs bargains), basic décor and well worn furnishings; can get very busy early evening; pavement tables, handy for Euston station, open all day. *(Tony Scott, Dr J Barrie Jones, Liz and Brian Barnard, Phil and Jane Villiers)*

★**Chapel** (020) 7402 9220
Chapel Street; NW1 5DP Corner dining pub attracting equal share of drinkers (busy and noisy in the evening); spacious rooms dominated by open kitchen, smart but simple furnishings, sofas at lounge end by big fireplace, a couple of real ales such as Adnams and Black Sheep, good choice of wines by the glass, several coffees and teas, good food from weekly changing menu, brisk friendly service; children and dogs welcome, picnic-sets in sizeable back garden, more seats on decking under heated parasols, covered smokers' area, open all day. *(Susan Eccleston)*

Constitution (020) 7380 0767
St Pancras Way; NW1 0QT Traditional standalone 19th-c pub close to Camden Lock and a quieter alternative to the busy market area; three local beers and good selection of wines by the glass, pubby lunchtime food Mon-Fri, friendly staff and enjoyable atmosphere; pool, darts and juke box, cellar bar for live music; barbecues in lovely sunny garden overlooking canal, open all day. *(Charles Todd)*

★**Doric Arch** (020) 7388 2221
Eversholt Street; NW1 2DN Virtually part of Euston station (up stairs from the bus terminus) and a welcome retreat from the busy concourse; well kept Fullers ales, guest beers and enjoyable well priced pubby food from snacks and sharing plates to specials, friendly efficient service, compact bare-boards bar with railway memorabilia and pretty Victorian fireplace, some button-back bench seating and a cosy boothed alcove, steps up to carpeted back dining area; background music, TVs (including train times); open (and food) all day. *(Dave Braisted, Dr and Mrs A K Clarke)*

Euston Tap (020) 3137 8837
Euston Road; NW1 2EF Small 19th-c neoclassical lodge in front of Euston station, good selection of ever-changing real ales and imported beers including huge bottled range, friendly knowledgeable staff, limited seating but more space and lavatory up spiral staircase; outside tables, open all day from noon; identical building opposite dedicated to ciders/perries (open from 3pm weekdays, noon Sat, 2-9pm Sun). *(Tracey and Stephen Groves, Dr and Mrs A K Clarke)*

Metropolitan (020) 7486 3489
Baker Street station, Marylebone Road; NW1 5LA Flight of steps up to

Wetherspoons in impressively ornate pillared hall (designed by Metropolitan Railway architect Charles W Clarke), lots of tables on one side, very long bar the other, leather sofas and some elbow tables, ten or more real ales, good coffee and their usual inexpensive food; games machines, free wi-fi; family area, open all day from 8am (10am Sun). *(Tony Hobden)*

Queens Head & Artichoke

(020) 7916 6206 *Albany Street; NW1 4EA* Corner pub-restaurant near Regent's Park with good fairly priced modern food including lots of smaller tapas-style plates, five well kept ales and good choice of wines from Edwardian counter, bare boards and panelling, large leaded windows, upstairs dining room; may be background music; pavement picnic-sets under awnings, open all day. *(Tom Stone)*

Tapping the Admiral

(020) 7267 6118 *Castle Road; NW1 8SU* Friendly local with fine range of well kept ales mainly from London brewers, fairly priced home-made food including range of pies; quiz Weds, live music Thurs, free wi-fi; children welcome until 7pm, pub cat called Nelson, beer garden with heaters, open all day. *(Jamie Green)*

NW3

★**Flask** (020) 7435 4580
Flask Walk; NW3 1HE Bustling local with two traditional front bars divided by unique Victorian screen, smart banquettes, panelling and lots of little prints, attractive fireplace, Youngs and a guest, plenty of wines by the glass and maybe winter mulled wine, popular all-day food, good friendly service, dining conservatory; background music, TV; children (till 8pm) and dogs welcome, seats and tables in alley, open (and food) all day. *(Roger and Donna Huggins)*

★**Spaniards Inn** (020) 8731 8406
Spaniards Lane; NW3 7JJ Busy 16th-c pub next to Hampstead Heath with charming garden – flagstoned walk among roses, side arbour with climbing plants and plenty of seats on crazy-paved terrace (arrive early weekends as popular with dog walkers and families); attractive and characterful low-ceilinged rooms with oak panelling, antique winged settles, snug alcoves and open fires, up to five real ales, continental draught beers and several wines by glass, popular fairly pubby food including range of burgers, upstairs dining room; car park fills fast and nearby parking difficult, open (and food) all day. *(Tim and Sarah Smythe-Brown)*

NW5   TQ2886

★**Bull & Last** (020) 7267 3641
Highgate Road; NW5 1QS Traditional décor with a stylish twist in this Victorian corner dining pub; single room with big

windows, colonial-style fans in planked ceiling, bulls' heads and other stuffed animals, stone fireplace one end along with collection of tankards and big faded map of London, much emphasis on their good imaginative food (not cheap), takeaway food including picnic hampers for Hampstead Heath, well kept changing ales and a house craft beer, good selection of wines, whiskies and gins, friendly staff, upstairs restaurant; children (away from bar) and dogs welcome, hanging baskets and picnic-sets by street, open all day. *(Lois Dyer)*

Junction Tavern (020) 7485 9400

Fortess Road; NW5 1AG Victorian corner pub with good interesting food in light dining room and conservatory, modern décor, St Austell, Sambrooks, Shepherd Neame and Thwaites (beer festivals), good choice of wines by the glass, friendly, helpful staff; background music; no children after 7pm, picnic-sets under big parasols in back garden, closed Mon-Thurs till 5pm. *(Jeff Davies)*

Southampton Arms 07958 780073

Highgate Road; NW5 1LE Simply furnished drinkers' pub with one long room, wall seats and stools around tables on bare boards, 11 changing beers and eight ciders, bar snacks (no credit cards); live piano some evenings, Mon quiz; garden at back and handy for the Heath, open all day. *(Tony Scott)*

SOUTH LONDON

SE1

Anchor (020) 7407 1577

Bankside; SE1 9EF In great Thames-side spot with river views from upper floors and roof terrace, beams, stripped brickwork and old-world corners, well kept Adnams, St Austell, Sharps and guests, good choice of wines by the glass, popular fish and chip bar (takeaways available) and other good value food, breakfast/tea room, can get very busy but staff cope well; background music; provision for children, disabled access, more tables under big parasols on raised riverside terrace, bedrooms in Premier Inn behind, open (and food) all day. *(B and M Kendall)*

Dean Swift (020) 7357 0748

Gainsford Street; SE1 2NE Well run single-room pub tucked away behind Tower Bridge, five cask ales, lots of craft beers and several wines by the glass, friendly well informed staff, rewarding choice of food from bar snacks to Sun roasts; sports TV; open (and food) all day. *(Rona Mackinlay)*

Fire Station (020) 7620 2226

Waterloo Road; SE1 8SB Unusual fire station conversion, busy and noisy, with two big recently refurbished knocked-through rooms, burger and pizza menu, craft beers such as Beavertown, Meantime and Revisionist, 11 wines by the glass and cocktails, friendly staff; background music; children welcome, a few tables out in front, handy for Old Vic theatre and Waterloo station, open (and food) all day from 7am (9am weekends) for breakfast. *(Susan Eccleston)*

★ **Founders Arms** (020) 7928 1899
Hopton Street; SE1 9JH Modern glass-walled building in superb location – outstanding terrace views along Thames and handy for South Bank attractions; plenty of customers (City types, tourists, theatre- and gallery-goers) spilling on to pavement and river walls, Youngs Bitter and a guest, lots of wines by the glass, extensive choice of well priced bar food all day (weekend breakfasts from 9am), tea and coffee from separate servery, cheerful service; background music; children welcome away from bar, open till midnight Fri, Sat. *(B and M Kendall, Ian Phillips)*

Garrison (020) 7089 9355
Bermondsey Street; SE1 3XB Interesting tile-fronted dining pub with idiosyncratic mix of styling, popular modern food including breakfast from 8am (9am weekends), a real ale or two but perhaps more emphasis on wine than beer, buzzy atmosphere, cinema/function room downstairs; open all day. *(Charles Todd)*

★ **George** (020) 7407 2056
Off 77 Borough High Street; SE1 1NH Tucked-away 16th-c coaching inn (mentioned in *Little Dorrit*), owned by the National Trust and beautifully preserved; lots of tables in bustling cobbled courtyard with views of the tiered exterior galleries, series of no-frills ground-floor rooms with black beams, square-latticed windows and some panelling, plain oak or elm tables on bare boards, old-fashioned built-in settles, dimpled glass lanterns and a 1797 Act of Parliament clock, impressive central staircase up to a series of dining rooms and balcony, well kept Greene King ales and a beer badged for the pub, good value traditional food from sandwiches up; children welcome away from bar, open (and food) all day. *(Tony Scott, Simon Collett-Jones, Brian Glozier, B and M Kendall)*

Horniman (020) 7407 1991
Hays Galleria, off Battlebridge Lane; SE1 2HD Spacious bright and airy Thames-side drinking hall with lots of polished wood, comfortable seating including a few sofas, upstairs seating, several real ales with unusual guests (may offer tasters), lunchtime food from soup and sandwiches up, snacks other times, service not always speedy; background music; children welcome, fine river views from outside picnic-sets, open all day. *(Tony and Wendy Hobden)*

★ **Kings Arms** (020) 7207 0784
Roupell Street; SE1 8TB Proper corner local tucked away amid terrace houses, bustling and friendly, with curved servery dividing traditional bar and lounge, bare boards, open fire and various bits and pieces including local road signs on the walls, nine well kept changing beers, good wine and malt whisky choice, welcoming helpful staff, enjoyable reasonably priced food from thai dishes to Sun roasts, big back extension with conservatory/courtyard dining area; background music; open all day. *(B and M Kendall, Simon Collett-Jones)*

★ **Market Porter** (020) 7407 2495
Stoney Street; SE1 9AA Properly pubby no-frills place opening at 6am weekdays for workers at neighbouring Borough Market, up to ten unusual real ales (over 60 guests a week) often from far-flung brewers and in top condition, particularly helpful friendly service, bare boards and open fire, beams with barrels balanced on them, simple furnishings, food in bar and upstairs lunchtime restaurant with view over market; background music; children allowed weekends till 7pm, dogs welcome, gets very busy with drinkers spilling on to the street, open all day. *(B and M Kendall, Tony Scott)*

Rake (020) 7407 0557
Winchester Walk; SE1 9AG Tiny discreetly modern Borough Market bar with amazing bottled beer range in wall-wide cooler, also half a dozen continental lagers on tap and three real ales, good friendly service; fair-sized covered and heated outside area. *(Tom Stone)*

Ring (020) 7620 0811
Blackfriars Road/The Cut, opposite Southwark tube station; SE1 8HA Popular chatty local named after the historic boxing ring that used to be opposite, single bare-boards bar with lots of boxing photographs and memorabilia, simple seating including some upholstered wall benches, Sharps Doom Bar and interesting guests, straightforward food such as burgers and hot dogs, friendly helpful service; background music, TV for major sports; picnic-sets out at front, open all day. *(Simon Collett-Jones)*

Roebuck (020) 7357 7324
Great Dover Street; SE1 4YG Cheerful unpretentious Victorian pub with open-plan bar, big windows and high ceilings, a mix of wooden chairs and tables and leather

chesterfields on bare boards, good range of beers including Meantime and Trumans, proper cider and several wines by the glass, well liked pubby food (all day Sun); upstairs lounge with own bar (Charlie Chaplin is said to have performed here as a boy), Thurs poetry readings; picnic-sets outside, open all day (till 1am Sat). *(B and M Kendall)*

Sheaf (020) 7407 9934
Southwark Street; SE1 1TY In cellars beneath the Hop Exchange, brick vaulted ceilings and iron pillars, button back benches, sofas and some high tables, lots of framed black and white photographs of former regulars, ten real ales and decent pubby food; sports TVs; open all day. *(Jeff Davies)*

Wheatsheaf (020) 7940 3880
Stoney Street; opposite Borough Market main entrance under new railway bridge; SE1 9AA Youngs pub with comfortably refurbished interior, three of their well kept beers and a guest, food from side campervan kitchen; live music; heated back garden, open (and food) all day from 9am (10 Sun). *(Jamie Green)*

White Hart (020) 7928 9190
Cornwall Road/Whittlesey Street; SE1 8TJ Backstreet corner local near Waterloo station; friendly community bustle, comfortable sofas, stripped boards and so forth, real ales, craft beers and artisan spirits, lots of bottled beers, good range of ciders and wines, sensibly priced up-to-date blackboard food as well as pub standards, Sunday bloody marys and newspapers, fresh flowers on tables; background music, free wi-fi; disabled facilities, open all day, food till early evening. *(Simon Collett-Jones, Ian Phillips)*

SE5
★Crooked Well (020) 7252 7798
Grove Lane; SE5 8SY Popular early 19th-c restaurant pub with button-back sofas, wall seats and all manner of dining chairs, really good imaginative food including two-course lunch deal (Thurs and Fri), nice wines and cocktails, Sharps Doom Bar, welcoming helpful staff; seats outside, closed Mon-Weds lunchtimes, otherwise open all day. *(Susan Eccleston)*

SE8
Dog & Bell (020) 8692 5664
Prince Street; SE8 3JD Friendly old-fashioned local tucked away on Thames Path; wood benches around bright cheerfully decorated L-shaped bar, open fire, up to half a dozen well kept ales including Fullers, bottled belgian beers, prompt friendly service, reasonably priced pub food from good sandwiches up, dining room; TV, bar billiards; tables in yard, open all day. *(Jeff Davies)*

SE9
Park Tavern (020) 8850 3216
Passey Place; SE9 5DA Traditional Victorian corner pub off Eltham High Street, eight well kept changing ales and 14 wines by the glass, log fire, friendly easy-going atmosphere; background music; pleasant little garden behind, open all day. *(Jeff Davies)*

SE10
Cutty Sark (020) 8858 3146
Ballast Quay, off Lassell Street; SE10 9PD Great Thames views from this early 19th-c Greenwich tavern, genuinely unspoilt old-fashioned bar, dark flagstones, simple furnishings including barrel seats, open fires, narrow openings to tiny side snugs, upstairs room (reached by winding staircase) with ship deck-feel and prized seat in big bow window, Youngs ales and a couple of guests, organic wines, malt whiskies and wide choice of enjoyable bar food; background music, children and dogs welcome, busy riverside terrace across narrow cobbled lane, limited but free parking if you get a space, open (and food) all day. *(Millie and Peter Downing)*

★Greenwich Union (020) 8692 6258
Royal Hill; SE10 8RT Feels more like a bar than a pub with full Meantime craft range, 150 bottled beers, unusual spirits and interesting choice of teas and coffees, good food too from varied menu, friendly brisk service; long narrow stone-flagged room with simple front area, wooden furniture, stove and daily papers, comfortable part with sofas and cushioned pews, booth seating in end conservatory; free wi-fi; well behaved children and dogs welcome, paved terrace with teak furniture, old-fashioned lamp posts and end fence painted as a poppy field, open (and food) all day. *(Taff Thomas, Tracey and Stephen Groves)*

Guildford Arms (020) 8691 6293
Guildford Grove/Devonshire Drive; SE10 8JY Bow-fronted Georgian dining pub in residential area; highly regarded creative cooking from chef-owner in bar or upstairs restaurant (tasting menus), beers such as Brockley, Meantime and Phipps, well chosen wines and cocktails, efficient well informed staff; picnic-sets under parasols in lovely back garden, open all day, food all day weekends. *(Rosie and John Moore)*

Pilot (020) 8858 5910
River Way, Blackwall Lane; SE10 0BE Refurbished early 19th-c pub surviving amid O2 development; opened-up interior on three levels with roof terrace overlooking park, well kept Fullers/Gales beers, good choice of food (all day Fri, Sat, till 6pm Sun) from pubby choices and charcoal grills to daily specials; background music, newspapers and free wi-fi;

dogs welcome, picnic-sets in front, more seating in enclosed back garden with paving, lawn and covered area, ten well equipped boutique bedrooms, open all day. *(Taff Thomas)*

Prince of Greenwich
(020) 8692 6089 *Royal Hill; SE10 8RT* Victorian pub transformed by new Sicilian owners; warm welcoming atmosphere and good italian cooking from freshly made pizzas up, quirky décor with unusual furnishings, eclectic collection of bits and pieces and lots of black and white jazz photos/posters, Fullers London Pride and Sharps Doom Bar, nice wines by the glass; live jazz and italian film nights; children and well behaved dogs welcome, closed Mon, open from 4pm Tues and Weds, 1pm Thurs, midday rest of week. *(Margaret McDonald)*

Sail Loft (020) 8222 9310
Victoria Parade, Greenwich; SE10 9FR New Thames-side pub on two floors with excellent views over to Canary Wharf, airy modern interior with floor-to-ceiling windows, Fullers/Gales beers and plenty of wines by the glass, open kitchen serving varied choice of food from bar snacks up (12.5% service charge added); background music, free wi-fi; children and dogs welcome, terrace with covered seating booths taking in the view, open all day. *(Charles Todd)*

SE12   TQ3974
Lord Northbrook (020) 8318 1127
Burnt Ash Road; SE12 8PU Opened-up, bare-boards Victorian corner pub, contemporary paintwork and lots of pictures, good mix of seating including a couple of chesterfields by Victorian fireplace, well kept Fullers/Gales beers, decent food from shortish menu, friendly staff, conservatory; dogs welcome, paved split-level back garden; open all day, food all day weekends. *(Jamie Green)*

SE15   TQ3575
Ivy House (020) 7277 8233
Stuart Road; SE15 3BE Co-operative owned pub with eight real ales and good range of craft beers and ciders, well priced food (not lunchtimes Mon, Tues) including burgers and hot dogs, old-fashioned panelled interior, stage in back room for live music, comedy and theatre nights; children (till 8pm) and dogs welcome, rack for cyclists, open all day. *(Susan Eccleston)*

Old Nuns Head (020) 7639 4007
Nunhead Green; SE15 3QQ Popular open-plan 1930s brick and timber pub on edge of small green, four well kept changing ales and enjoyable food from good burgers up, roasts only on Sun, cheerful efficient staff, Thurs quiz; children welcome, back garden and a few seats out in front, handy for fascinating gothic Nunhead Cemetery. *(Jeff Davies, Tom Stone)*

SE16
★ Mayflower (020) 7237 4088
Rotherhithe Street; SE16 4NF Unchanging cosy old riverside pub in unusual street with lovely early 18th-c church; good generous bar food including more upmarket daily specials, well kept Greene King and guests, good value wines and decent coffee, friendly young staff, black beams, panelling, nautical bric-a-brac, high-backed settles and coal fires, great Thames views from upstairs candlelit evening restaurant; background music; children welcome, fun jetty/terrace over water (barbecues), handy for Brunel Museum, open all day. *(Jeremy King, Tony Scott)*

SE22
Clockhouse (020) 8693 2901
Peckham Rye/Barry Road; SE22 9QA Light and airy restyled Victorian pub, well kept Youngs and guests, decent wines and cocktail list, enjoyable fairly priced home-cooked food, busy hard-working staff, cheerfully decorated front bar with dining area behind, upstairs function room; background music; children (till 7pm) and dogs welcome, tables on front terrace looking across to Peckham Rye, open (and food) all day. *(John Wooll)*

SE24
Florence (020) 7326 4987
Dulwich Road; SE24 0NG Refurbished tile-fronted Victorian pub in Herne Hill, own-brew beers plus guests, real cider and several wines by the glass, enjoyable food from interesting varied menu, brunch from 11am, open contemporary décor; children (till 7pm) and dogs welcome, a few tables out in front under awning, more on back terrace, open all day (till 1am Fri, Sat). *(Tom Stone)*

SW4
Bobbin (020) 7738 8953
Lillieshall Road; SW4 0LN Tucked-away 19th-c pub in Clapham Old Town, unpretentious opened-up front bar with blue-grey walls and blue-painted chairs on bare boards, button-back wall benches, ales such as Harveys and Sambrooks, enjoyable reasonably priced food including Sun lunch, flagstoned back conservatory; background music, darts and board games; sunny walled beer garden, open all day Fri-Sun, from 5pm other days. *(Jamie Greeb)*

Windmill (020) 8673 4578
Clapham Common South Side; SW4 9DE Big bustling pub by the common, contemporary front bar, quite a few original Victorian features, pillared dining room leading through to conservatory-style eating area, popular varied choice of food all day (good breakfasts, too), Wells Bombardier, Youngs Bitter and decent wines by the glass; background music, Sun quiz; children welcome, tables under umbrellas along front,

more seats in side garden, good bedrooms, open all day. *(Millie and Peter Downing)*

SW11

Eagle Ale House (020) 7228 2328

Chatham Road; SW11 6HG Attractive unpretentious backstreet local, seven changing ales including southern brewers like Harveys, Surrey Hills and Westerham, welcoming efficient service, worn leather chesterfield in fireside corner of L-shaped bar; big-screen sports TV; dogs welcome, back terrace with heated marquee, small front terrace too, open all day weekends, from 4pm other days. *(Julie Swift)*

Falcon (020) 7228 2076

St Johns Hill; SW11 1RU Lively Victorian pub with ten well kept beers from remarkably long light oak counter, period partitions, cut-glass and mirrors, subdued lighting, quieter back dining area serving good value pub food, friendly service; quiz Sun, TV; handy for Clapham Junction station, open all day. *(Tim and Sarah Smythe-Brown)*

Fox & Hounds (020) 7924 5483

Latchmere Road; SW11 2JU Victorian pub with good italian-influenced food (all day Sun, not Mon-Thurs lunchtimes), St Austell and two local ales, several wines by glass, spacious straightforward bar with big windows overlooking street, bare boards, mismatched tables and chairs, photographs on walls, fresh flowers, view of kitchen behind; background music, TV, daily newspapers; children (till 7pm) and dogs welcome, terrace picnic-sets, open all day Fri-Sun, closed Mon lunchtime. *(Jim and Sue James)*

Westbridge (020) 7228 6482

Battersea Bridge Road; SW11 3AG Draft House pub with interesting ever-changing choice of real ales, craft beers and ciders served by friendly knowledgeable staff, tasting trays available, good reasonably priced food from open kitchen, can eat in bar or back restaurant; background music (often blues/jazz), sports TV; small garden, open (and food) all day. *(Richard and Penny Gibbs)*

Woodman (020) 7228 2968

Battersea High Street; SW11 3HX Under welcoming new management and no major changes; enjoyable food from sandwiches up, Badger ales and several wines by the glass, good friendly service, has village-local feel and can get very busy (particularly in summer); children and dogs welcome, back garden with heaters and wood-fired pizza oven, open (and food) all day. *(Richard and Penny Gibbs)*

SW12

Avalon (020) 8675 8613

Balham Hill; SW12 9EB Part of the Renaissance group with popular food including weekend brunch, well kept changing ales and good choice of wines by the glass, plenty of room in split-level bar and back dining area, big murals, stuffed animals and coal fires; sports TV; children welcome, front terrace and good large garden behind, open all day (till 1am Fri, Sat). *(Susan Eccleston)*

★Nightingale (020) 8673 1637

Nightingale Lane; SW12 8NX Refurbished early Victorian local, cosy and civilised, with small front bar opening into larger back area and attractive family conservatory, well kept Youngs ales with guests such as Sambrooks and Wimbledon, enjoyable sensibly priced bar food, friendly service, open fire; dogs welcome, nice secluded back beer garden with summer barbecues, open all day. *(Jeff Davies)*

SW13

Bulls Head (020) 8876 5241

Lonsdale Road; SW13 9PY Imposing Victorian pub by the river in Barnes, popular and welcoming, with good live jazz (nightly and Sun afternoon) in back music room; comfortable open-plan areas refurbished by Geronimo Inns in their usual colourful, quirky modern style, good food and service, three real ales including Sharps and Youngs from central servery, upstairs balconied restaurant; children welcome, open (and food) all day. *(Edward Mirzoeff)*

Idle Hour (020) 8878 5555

Railway Side (off White Hart Lane between Mortlake High Street and Upper Richmond Road); SW13 0PQ Tucked-away organic dining pub, chatty and relaxed, with good interesting modern food, organic soft drinks, wines and beers, also cocktails (good bloody mary) and 30 gins, nice chunky old tables on bare boards, a profusion of wall clocks on different times, comfortable sofa by small fireplace; background music, daily papers and magazines; no children, tables with candles in small pretty yard behind, if driving, park at end of Railway Side and walk (road gets too narrow for cars), closed weekday lunchtimes. *(Edward Mirzoeff)*

Red Lion (020) 8748 2984

Castelnau; SW13 9RU Roomy 19th-c Fullers pub with enjoyable fairly priced food from varied menu (order at bar), their well kept ales and good choice of wines by the glass from stainless-steel counter, friendly staff, back dining part has most character with impressive Victorian woodwork, big arched windows and high ceiling with stained-glass skylight, comfortable fireside sofas, relaxed atmosphere; TV; children and dogs welcome, wheelchair access/loo, big garden with heated terrace and lawn (occasional outdoor theatre), open all day, food all day weekends. *(Edward Mirzoeff, Simon and Mandy King, Susan and John Douglas)*

White Hart (020) 8876 5177

The Terrace; SW13 0NR Revamped open-plan Barnes dining pub with fine river views, well kept Wells and Youngs ales along with craft beers such as Camden Town and Meantime from island servery, good selection of wines by the glass, popular food in bar or upstairs restaurant with open kitchen and balcony; seats outside, open (and food) all day. *(Edward Mirzoeff)*

SW15

Bricklayers Arms

Down cul-de-sac off Lower Richmond Road near Putney Bridge; SW15 1DD Welcoming tucked-away little 19th-c local, up to ten well kept changing ales, proper cider/ perry and good selection of english wines, enjoyable food, efficient friendly staff, long L-shaped room with pitched-roof section, pine tables on bare boards, lots of pictures on painted panelling, log fire; background music, sports TV; paved side terrace, open all day Fri-Sun, from 4pm other days; refurbishment and bedrooms planned. *(Dr Kevan Tucker, M J Winterton)*

Half Moon (020) 8780 9383

Lower Richmond Road; SW15 1EU Good long-standing music venue restyled by Geronimo Inns, Youngs and a couple of guests from elegant curved counter, food from burgers and hot dogs to more elaborate choices and a brunch menu; free lunchtime jazz, nightly gigs in back music room; open all day (till 1am Fri, Sat). *(David M Smith)*

Jolly Gardeners (020) 8789 2539

Lacy Road; SW15 1NT Slightly quirky bare-boards pub in residential Putney; gardening theme with trowels and watering cans on walls, potted flowers and botanical prints, bucket lampshades, a reclining gnome and row of colourful heated sheds in the back garden; four changing ales and several other draught beers, good selection of wines, enjoyable pubby food including Sat brunch and Sun roasts; Tues quiz, sports TV, newspapers and free wi-fi; front fairy-lit terrace, open (and food) all day. *(Tom Stone)*

★Telegraph (020) 8788 2011

Telegraph Road; SW15 3TU Big pub on Putney Heath named after 19th-c admiralty telegraph station that was sited nearby; three attractively modernised rooms with leather armchairs and sofas, rugs on wood floors, eight real ales including a beer badged for them, enjoyable bistro-style food, upstairs function/overspill rooms; background and live music, sports TV, newspapers and board games; children and dogs welcome, great rural feel garden, open all day. *(Susan and John Douglas)*

SW16

Earl Ferrers (020) 8835 8333

Ellora Road; SW16 6JF Opened-up Streatham corner pub with Sambrooks and several other well kept ales (tasters offered), interesting food along with pub standards including popular Sat brunch and Sun roasts, good friendly service, mixed tables and chairs, sofas, old photographs; pool and darts, music Mon and Thurs, quiz Weds; children welcome, some tables outside with tractor-seat stools, open all day weekends, from 5pm weekdays. *(Simon Stone)*

Railway (020) 8769 9448

Greyhound Lane; SW16 5SD Busy Streatham corner local with two big rooms (back one for families), rotating ales from London brewers such as Meantime, Redemption, Sambrooks and Trumans, enjoyable freshly made food, friendly staff, events including Tues quiz and monthly farmers' market; walled back garden, open all day (till 1am Fri, Sat). *(Jeff Davies)*

SW18

Alma (020) 8870 2537

York Road, opposite Wandsworth Town station; SW18 1TF Corner Victorian pub-hotel with well kept Wells and Youngs ales and good choice of wines from island bar, sofas and informal mix of tables and chairs on wood floor, mosaic plaques and painted mirrors, wide range of good food from bar snacks up, back restaurant, friendly helpful staff; 23 bedrooms, open all day from 7am (8am weekends). *(Mrs G Marlow)*

Cats Back (020) 8617 3448

Point Pleasant; SW18 1NN Traditionally refurbished 19th-c corner pub, Harveys first in SW London, four of their ales along with bottled beers, enjoyable food including Sun roasts, friendly staff, occasional live music; partially covered back garden with heaters, open all day weekends. *(Tom Stone)*

Ship (020) 8870 9667

Jews Row; SW18 1TB Popular riverside pub by Wandsworth Bridge; light and airy conservatory-style décor, mix of furnishings on bare boards, church candles on tables, more basic public bar, well kept Youngs ales, Sambrooks and a guest, freshly cooked interesting bistro food (not particularly cheap) in extended restaurant with own garden; children and dogs welcome, good-sized terrace with barbecue and outside bar, open all day. *(Jamie Green)*

SW19

Alexandra (020) 8947 7691

Wimbledon Hill Road; SW19 7NE Busy Youngs pub with their well kept beers and

---

There are report forms at the back of the book.

guests from central bar, good wine choice, enjoyable food from sandwiches to good Sun roasts, friendly attentive service, comfortably up-to-date décor in linked rooms; sports TVs; tables out in mews and on attractive popular roof terrace. *(Edward Nile)*

Crooked Billet (020) 8946 4942
Wimbledon Common; SW19 4RQ Busy 18th-c pub popular for its position by Wimbledon Common (almost next door to the Hand in Hand); Youngs ales and guests, good choice of wines and enjoyable up-to-date food in open-plan bar or dining room, friendly helpful staff, mix of wooden dining chairs, high-backed settles and scrubbed pine tables on oak boards, some interesting old prints, winter fire; Mon quiz, board games; children (away from bar) and dogs welcome, plastic glasses for outside, open (and food) all day. *(Laura Reid)*

Fox & Grapes (020) 8619 1300
Camp Road; SW19 4UN Popular 18th-c dining pub by Wimbledon Common; modern bistro feel but keeping some original features in the two linked areas (step between), enjoyable up-to-date food (not cheap and they add a service charge), view into kitchen from high-ceilinged upper room with its unusual chandeliers, well chosen wines by the glass, Sharps Doom Bar and guest from central servery, pleasant relaxed atmosphere; children and dogs welcome, three bedrooms, open all day, food all day Sun. *(Susan and John Douglas, Peter Sutton)*

Hand in Hand (020) 8946 5720
Crooked Billet; SW19 4RQ Friendly Youngs local on edge of Wimbledon Common, their ales and guests kept well, enjoyable home-made pubby food, several areas off central bar with leather armchairs, sofas and built in wall seats, bookshelves, photos and prints on papered walls, stubby candles and a log fire; front courtyard, benches out by common, open all day. *(Margaret McDonald)*

Sultan (020) 8544 9323
Norman Road; SW19 1BN Red-brick 1950s drinkers' pub owned by Hop Back and hidden in a tangle of suburban roads; their well kept ales and a guest such as Downton (also plans for own microbrewery), some snacky food, friendly staff and locals, big scrubbed tables, darts in public bar; nice walled beer garden with summer barbecues, open all day. *(Charles Todd)*

WEST LONDON

SW6

★**Atlas** (020) 7385 9129
Seagrave Road; SW6 1RX Busy tucked-away pub with long simple bar, plenty of panelling and dark wall benches, mix of old tables and chairs, brick fireplaces, good food

(all day Sun), four well kept ales, lots of wines by the glass and decent coffee, friendly service; background music; children (till 7pm) and dogs welcome, seats under awning on heated and attractively planted side terrace, open all day. *(Susan Eccleston)*

Brown Cow (020) 7384 9559
Fulham Road; SW6 5SA Popular rustic-style dining pub (same owner as nearby Sands End), assortment of old furniture on bare boards including butcher's block table, pendant lighting, Victorian prints of prize cows, one wall clad in distressed mirrored glass, enjoyable if not particularly cheap modern pub food from bar snacks up (including brunch), ales such as Greene King and Trumans, 'larder shop' selling home-made jams etc; dogs welcome, benches and milk churns outside, open all day. *(Susan and John Douglas)*

Eight Bells (020) 7736 6307
Fulham High Street/Ranelagh Gardens; SW6 3JS Friendly traditional pub tucked away near Putney Bridge, Fullers London Pride, Sharps Doom Bar and a guest, good value standard pub menu; sports TV; dogs welcome, seats outside under awning, close to Bishop's Park, open all day and busy with away supporters on Fulham match days. *(Dr Kevan Tucker, Susan and John Douglas)*

Harwood Arms (020) 7386 1847
Walham Grove; SW6 1QP Lively bare-boards Fulham gastropub with good food from bar snacks to enterprising full meals (not cheap), also set menu choices, a couple of well kept changing ales and extensive wine list, bar area with leather sofas; closed Mon lunchtime, otherwise open all day. *(Rosie and John Moore)*

Sands End (020) 7731 7823
Stephendale Road; SW6 2PR Fulham dining pub with mix of wooden dining chairs around medley of tables on bare boards, open fire, good modern british food from snacks up including weekend brunch, plenty of wines by the glass, Greene King IPA, Otter Amber and a couple of guests, home-made jams, chutneys etc for sale; attracts upmarket crowd and can be very busy, open (and food) all day. *(Richard Kennell)*

SW7

★**Anglesea Arms** (020) 7373 7960
Selwood Terrace; SW7 3QG Very busy 19th-c pub, well run and friendly, with mix of cast-iron tables on wood-strip floor, central elbow tables, panelling and heavy portraits, large brass chandeliers hanging from dark ceilings, big windows and swagged curtains, several booths at one end with partly glazed screens, Greene King Abbott, IPA and four guests, around 20 malt whiskies and 15 wines by the glass, interesting bar food, steps down to dining room; children welcome, dogs in

bar, heated front terrace, open all day.
(Peter Sutton)

Queens Arms (020) 7823 9293
Queens Gate Mews; SW7 5QL Popular
Victorian corner pub with open-plan bare-
boards bar, generous helpings of enjoyable
good value home-made food, decent wines
by the glass and good selection of beers
including Fullers and Sharps, friendly helpful
service; TV; children welcome, disabled
facilities, handy for Royal Albert Hall, open
all day. *(Jeff Davies)*

SW10

Chelsea Ram (020) 7351 4008
Burnaby Street; SW10 0PL Corner
Geronimo Inn, mix of furniture on bare
boards or stripy carpet including farmhouse
tables, padded stools around an old
workbench, cushioned wall seats, shelves
of books and some striking artwork, tiled
Victorian fireplace, Youngs and guests, good
all-day food including daily specials, weekend
brunch (from 11am) and popular Sun roasts,
friendly service, board games; pavement
picnic-sets, open all day. *(Jim and Sue James)*

W4

★ Bell & Crown (020) 8994 4164
Strand on the Green; W4 3PF Fullers
local with great Thames views from back bar
and conservatory, interesting food and
friendly staff, panelling and log fire, lots of
atmosphere and can get very busy weekends;
dogs welcome, terrace and towpath area,
good walks, open all day. *(Rona Mackinlay)*

★ Bulls Head (020) 8994 1204
Strand on the Green; W4 3PQ
Refurbished old Thames-side pub (served
as Cromwell's HQ during Civil War), seats by
windows overlooking the water in beamed
rooms, steps up and down, ales such as St
Austell and Sharps, several wines including
champagne by the glass, decent all-day
pubby food served by friendly helpful staff;
background music; seats out by river, pretty
hanging baskets, part of Chef & Brewer
chain. *(Jeff Davies)*

City Barge (020) 8994 2148
Strand on the Green; W4 3PH Attractively
furnished old riverside pub; light modern
split-level interior keeping a few original
features such as Victorian panelling and
open fires, good choice of ales/craft beers
and wines by the glass (prosecco on tap),
interesting food from open kitchen including
good fish choice, weekend brunch, friendly
young staff; background music; children and
dogs welcome, waterside picnic-sets facing
Oliver's Island, deckchairs on grass and more
formal terrace, open all day. *(Charles Todd)*

Roebuck (020) 8995 4392
Chiswick High Road; W4 1PU
Popular relaxed Victorian dining pub with

high ceilings and bare boards, front bar
and roomy back dining area opening on
to delightful paved garden, enjoyable well
presented food (all day Sun) from open
kitchen, daily changing menu, four real ales
and good choice of wines by the glass; dogs
welcome, open all day. *(Simon Rodway)*

Swan (020) 8994 8262
Evershed Walk, Acton Lane; W4 5HH
Cosy 19th-c local with good mix of customers
and convivial atmosphere, well liked
interesting food along with more pubby
choices, friendly staff, a dozen or so wines
by the glass, St Austell, Sambrooks and
Twickenham, two bars with wood floors and
panelling, leather chesterfields by open fire;
dogs very welcome, children till 7.30pm,
picnic-sets on good spacious terrace, open
(and food) all day weekends, from 5pm
other days. *(Laura Reid)*

Tabard (020) 8994 3492
Bath Road; W4 1LW Roomy Chiswick pub
built in 1880, pleasant chatty atmosphere, up
to ten changing ales, decent choice of wines
and all-day pubby food, friendly efficient
staff, arts and crafts interior with lots of
nooks and corners, period mirrors and high
frieze of William de Morgan tiles; fringe
theatre upstairs, free wi-fi; well behaved
children and dogs welcome, disabled access,
terrace tables by busy road, open all day.
(Rosie and John Moore)

W6

★ Anglesea Arms (020) 8749 1291
Wingate Road; W6 0UR Bustling Victorian
corner pub with good food from interesting
modern menu, four changing ales and plenty
of wines by the glass, friendly staff, roaring
fire in bare-boards panelled bar, close-set
tables in sky-lit bare-brick dining room;
children and dogs welcome, tables out by
quiet street, open all day Fri-Sun, from 5pm
other days. *(Millie and Peter Downing)*

Black Lion (020) 8748 2639
South Black Lion Lane; W6 9TJ
Welcoming old pub set back from the river;
helpful friendly staff, up to half a dozen well
kept ales such as Adnams, Fullers and St
Austell, lots of wines by the glass and good
coffee, enjoyable food from sandwiches
and tapas up, popular Sun lunch, L-shaped
interior with bare boards and half-panelling,
back skittle alley; live music Fri, children and
dogs welcome, summer barbecues in large
terrace garden, open all day. *(Neil, Edward
Mirzoeff, Simon Rodway)*

Blue Anchor (020) 8748 5774
Lower Mall; W6 9DJ Right on the Thames
a short walk from Hammersmith Bridge; two
traditional linked areas with oak floors and
panelling, mirrors one end with oars above, a
house beer from Nelsons and three well kept
guests, enjoyable food from light meals up,

pleasant river-view dining room upstairs with balcony; TV; disabled facilities, waterside pavement tables, open all day (food all day weekends). *(Edward Stone)*

Blue Boat (020) 3092 2090
Thames Path, off Chancellors Road; W6 9GD Newly built Fullers riverside pub with views over to Hammersmith Bridge and the Harrods Depository building; wide (not very deep) interior with long bar serving their full range and good choice of other drinks, lively chatty atmosphere, well divided areas including cosy part to the left with library of local interest books, assortment of old and new furniture, some booth seating, rough wood cladding, reclaimed metal pillars and exposed ceiling ducting, popular food from open kitchen served by friendly staff; french windows on to terrace with cushioned chairs, parasols and an old rowing boat; open (and food) all day from 10am for brunch. *(Susan and John Douglas, Edward Mirzoeff)*

Carpenters Arms (020) 8741 8386
Black Lion Lane; W6 9BG Good imaginative cooking at this relaxed well run corner dining pub, fine for just a drink too with plenty of wines by the glass and Adnams Bitter, friendly helpful staff and good mix of customers, simple bare-boards interior with open fire; dogs welcome, attractive garden, open all day. *(Caroline Sullivan)*

Hampshire Hog (020) 8748 3391
King Street; W6 9JT Spacious Hammersmith pub with light airy interior, plenty of emphasis on food from varied if not extensive menu, good choice of wines including 50cl carafes, cocktails, prices can be high; background music; nice big garden with some seats under cover, open (and food) all day from 10am. *(Edward Mirzoeff, Simon Rodway)*

Latymers (020) 8748 3446
Hammersmith Road; W6 7JP Big popular bar with mirrored ceiling in 1980s corner building, well kept Fullers ales and good reasonably priced thai food, friendly staff, spacious back restaurant; free wi-fi; children and dogs welcome, pavement seating, open all day. *(Susan and John Douglas)*

Pear Tree (020) 7381 1787
Margravine Road; W6 8HJ Arts and crafts building (plenty of original features) tucked away behind Charing Cross Hospital; cleanly kept cosily lived-in interior with heavy curtains, drapes on doors and cushions on well worn seating, soft lighting and candlelight, fresh flowers and crisp

white evening tablecloths, open fires, good modern pub food from bar snacks up, well kept Greene King, Sharps and Timothy Taylors, good range of wines by the glass, efficient service; background music; dogs welcome, seats in small garden, open (and food) all day Fri-Sun, closed Mon-Thurs lunchtimes. *(Susan and John Douglas)*

Queens Head (020) 7603 3174
Brook Green; W6 7BL Spacious refurbished Fullers pub dating from the early 19th c, cosy linked areas with beams and open fire, good menu from lunchtime sandwiches and bar snacks up, four well kept ales, craft beers and nice wines by the glass; Mon quiz; children and dogs welcome, big garden behind, open (and food) all day. *(Edward Nile)*

W7

Fox (020) 8567 4021
Green Lane; W7 2PJ Friendly open-plan 19th-c local in quiet cul-de-sac near Grand Union Canal, several real ales including Fullers London Pride, Sharps Cornish Coaster and Timothy Taylors Landlord, decent wines by the glass and well priced food including popular Sun lunch, panelling and stained glass, farm tools hanging from ceiling; children and dogs welcome, small side garden, horse and donkey in pub's field across the road, food/crafts market last Sat of month, towpath walks, open all day. *(Laura Reid)*

W8

★**Britannia** (020) 7937 6905
Allen Street, off Kensington High Street; W8 6UX Smartly refurbished Youngs pub with spacious front bar, pastel green walls contrasting dark panelling, patterned rugs on bare boards, banquettes, leather tub chairs and sofas, steps down to back area with wall-sized photograph of the Britannia Brewery (now demolished), dining conservatory beyond, good freshly prepared food including pub staples, spiral staircase up to overflow/function room; background music, Tues quiz, sports TV; children welcome, wheelchair access (side passage to back part), open (and food) all day. *(Simon and Mandy King)*

★**Churchill Arms** (020) 7727 4242
Kensington Church Street; W8 7LN Character long-serving irish landlord at this bustling old pub, eclectic interior dense with bric-a-brac – prints and books of butterflies, countless lamps, miners' lights, horse tack, bedpans and brasses hanging from ceiling, prints of american presidents and lots of Churchill memorabilia, a couple of interesting carved figures and statuettes

---

Places with gardens or terraces usually let children sit there – we note in the text the very few exceptions that don't.

behind central counter, well kept Fullers ales, 18 wines by the glass and good value thai food, spacious rather smart plant-filled dining conservatory; free wi-fi; children and dogs welcome, some chrome tables and chairs outside, stunning display of window boxes and hanging baskets, open (and food) all day. *(Tony Scott)*

Scarsdale (020) 7937 1811
Edwardes Square; W8 6HE Popular easy-going Georgian pub in leafy square, scrubbed pine tables, simple cushioned dining chairs, pews and built-in wall seats on bare boards, oil paintings in fancy gilt frames and old local photographs, heavily swagged curtains, coal-effect gas fires, Adnams, Fullers and a guest, 16 wines by the glass and a dozen malt whiskies, well liked food; free wi-fi; children (in dining area) and dogs welcome, seats and tables under parasols on attractive front terrace, open (and food) all day.
(Emma Scofield, Mike Swan, Tony Scott)

W9
Prince Alfred (020) 7286 3287
Formosa Street; W9 1EE Well preserved ornate Victorian pub with five separate bar areas (lots of mahogany) arranged around central servery, snob screens and duck-through doors, beautiful etched-glass bow window, Youngs ales and guests, good choice of wines by the glass, enjoyable food including some imaginative choices in airy modern dining room with large centre skylight, cellar function rooms; background music; open (and food) all day. *(Charles Todd)*

Truscott Arms (020) 7266 9198
Shirland Road; W9 2JD Sizeable carefully renovated Victorian pub with original tiles, cornices, ceiling roses and wooden flooring in various bars and dining rooms, beers such as Camden, Moncada, Redemption and Sambrooks, 40 wines by the glass, cocktails and wide choice of spirits, imaginative food from bar snacks up including short weekday set menu till 6pm, friendly service; background music, Mon quiz, free wi-fi; children and dogs (in bar) welcome, colourful tables and chairs in garden, open (and food) all day. *(Nick Sharpe, Belinda May)*

Warwick Castle (020) 7266 0921
Warwick Place; W9 2PX Popular character pub in narrow street near Little Venice; open-fronted with a few pavement tables, unspoilt rooms with comfortable lived-in feel, etched windows, panelling, open fires and some striking light fittings, friendly landlady and staff, real ales such as Greene King and guests, blackboard food from sandwiches up (all day Fri-Sun); quiz night Thurs; dogs welcome, open all day. *(Andrew and Michele Revell)*

W11
Portobello Gold (020) 7460 4910
Portobello Road, opposite Denbigh Terrace; W11 2QB The long-serving landlord at this rather quirky bohemian place is retiring, so things will change greatly – news please.

W12
Oak (020) 8741 7700
Goldhawk Road; W12 8EU Large refurbished Victorian pub serving interesting mediterranean-influenced food including speciality wood-fired pizzas, good range of beers and wine, friendly staff; open all day weekends, from 6pm other days.
(Simon Rodway)

★ Princess Victoria (020) 8749 5886
Uxbridge Road; W12 9DH Imposing former gin palace with carefully restored rather grand bar, oil paintings on slate-coloured walls, comfortable leather wall seats, parquet flooring and small fireplace, Hackney, Sambrooks and two daily changing guests from handsome marble-topped horseshoe counter, also 20 gins and excellent wine list, big dining room with plenty of original features and more paintings, good imaginative modern food, friendly staff; children and dogs (in bar) welcome, white wrought-iron tables and chairs on pretty terrace, popular artisan market in front (Sat), open all day. *(Hilary and Neil Christopher, Nick Sharpe, Simon Rodway)*

W13
Duke of Kent (020) 8991 7820
Scotch Common; W13 8DL Large refurbished open-plan pub with lots of interesting discrete areas, coal fires, several Fullers ales and guests, good food from pub standards up, friendly staff; free wi-fi; children welcome, big garden with partly covered terrace, picnic-sets and play area, open all day. *(Susan and John Douglas)*

W14   TQ2477
★ Colton Arms (020) 7385 6956
Greyhound Road; W14 9SD Unspoilt little gem, like an old-fashioned country tavern and in same family for over 40 years; main U-shaped front bar with log fire, polished brasses, fox mask, hunting crops and hunting-scene plates, fine collection of handsomely carved antique oak furniture, two tiny back rooms with own serving counters (ring bell for service), Fullers London Pride, Sharps Doom Bar and a guest, old-fashioned brass till; no food or credit cards; children (over 4) till 7pm, dogs allowed in bar, charming back terrace with neat rose arbour, next to the Queen's Club tennis courts and gardens. *(Tim and Sarah Smythe-Brown)*

We say if we know a pub allows dogs.

Crown & Sceptre (020) 7603 2007
Holland Road; W14 8BA; W14 8BA
Civilised Victorian corner pub with light airy
interior; sofas, antique-style dining chairs
and leather cube stools around wooden
tables, rugs on bare boards, gas fire, Courage
Directors, Youngs London Gold and a guest,
20 wines by the glass and extensive range
of whiskies and gins, thoughtful choice of
interesting food, friendly service, cosy cellar
bar with banquettes, candles in bottles and
big prints on rough wood walls; background
music, TV, board games; children and
dogs (in bar) welcome, pavement tables,
comfortable bedrooms, handy for Olympia,
open all day from 7.30am. *(Edward May, Neil)*

★**Havelock Tavern** (020) 7603 5374
Masbro Road; W14 0LS Busy pub in
former shop, light airy L-shaped bar with
plain unfussy décor, second smaller room,
Sambrooks Wandle, Sharps Doom Bar and
guests, wide choice of interesting wines by
the glass, well liked food cooked to order
from short changing menu, swift friendly
service; free wi-fi; children and dogs
welcome, picnic-sets on small paved terrace,
open all day. *(Tom Stone)*

OUTER LONDON

BARNET EN5 TQ2496
Black Horse (020) 8449 2230
Wood Street/Union Street; EN5 4HY
Attractively modernised 19th-c pub with
button-back leather wall seating, nice mix
of old tables and chairs, eight real ales
including own Barnet beers from back
microbrewery, good range of enjoyable food,
friendly staff; children and dogs (in bar)
welcome, terrace seating, open all day (food
all day weekends). *(Nigel and Sue Foster)*

Gate (020) 8449 7292
*Barnet Road (A411, near Hendon Wood
Lane); EN5 3LA* Modernised country
pub feel with comfortably opened-up areas,
beams and log fires, good choice of enjoyable
home-made food from lunchtime sandwiches/
ciabattas up, well kept Greene King, Sharps
and a guest, friendly staff and atmosphere;
children welcome, open (and food) all day.
(Nigel and Sue Foster)

BECKENHAM BR3 TQ3769
George (020) 8663 3468
High Street; BR3 1AG Busy weatherboarded pub with friendly efficient staff,
half a dozen real ales and enjoyable food
including breakfast (until midday); children
welcome, side garden with terrace, open
all day. *(Dan Hanson)*

Jolly Woodman (020) 8663 1031
Chancery Lane; BR3 6NR Welcoming
old-fashioned and neatly kept local in

conservation area, cosy L-shaped bar with
woodburner, five or so well kept ales such as
Harveys Best and Timothy Taylors Landlord,
good choice of whiskies, reasonably priced
home-made food (weekday lunchtimes
only) including sandwiches; dogs welcome,
pavement tables and sunny flower-filled back
courtyard, open all day (from 4pm Mon).
(B J Harding)

BEXLEY DA5 TQ4973
Kings Head (01322) 553137
Bexley High Street; DA5 1AA Dating from
14th c, linked rooms with low beams and
brasses, traditional furniture, open fires, well
kept Greene King ales and tasty pub food
including all-day breakfast, friendly staff; jazz
Mon evening; open all day. *(Ross Balaam)*

BEXLEYHEATH DA6 TQ4875
Robin Hood & Little John
(020) 8303 1128 *Lion Road; DA6 8PF*
Small 19th-c family-run local in residential
area, welcoming and spotless, with eight
well kept ales such as Adnams, Bexley,
Fullers and Harveys, popular bargain pubby
lunchtime food (not Sun); well behaved
children allowed away from the bar till
8.30pm, seats out at front and in back
garden. *(Dan Hanson)*

BIGGIN HILL TN16 TQ4359
★**Old Jail** (01959) 572979
*Jail Lane; (E off A233 S of airport and
industrial estate, towards Berry's Hill
and Cudham); TN16 3AX* Big family
garden with picnic-sets, substantial trees
and good play area for this popular country
pub (on fringe of London); traditional
beamed and low-ceilinged rooms with RAF
memorabilia, two cosy small areas to right
divided by timbers, one with big inglenook,
other with cabinet of Battle of Britain plates,
ales such as Harveys, Long Man and Sharps,
good choice of enjoyable reasonably priced
food (not Sun evening) from sandwiches up,
friendly attentive service, step up to dining
room with small open fire; background music;
dogs welcome, open all day (food all day
Thurs-Sat). *(David Jackman, David Greene,
B and M Kendall)*

BROMLEY BR1 TQ4069
Red Lion (020) 8460 2691
North Road; BR1 3LG Chatty well
managed backstreet local in conservation
area, traditional dimly lit interior with wood
floor, tiling, green velvet drapes and shelves
of books, well kept Greene King, Harveys and
guests, lunchtime food, good friendly service;
tables out in front, open all day.
(S and L McPhee)

BR2 TQ4265
Two Doves (020) 8462 1627
Oakley Road (A233); BR2 8HD Popular
Victorian local, comfortable and
unpretentious, with cheerful staff and

regulars, well kept Wells, Youngs and a guest, snacky lunchtime food such as rolls and baked potatoes, modern back conservatory and lovely garden; open all day Fri-Sun. *(B and M Kendall)*

CHELSFIELD BR6 TQ4864
Five Bells (01689) 821044
Church Road; just off A224 Orpington bypass; BR6 7RE Chatty 17th-c white weatherboarded village local, two separate bars and dining area, inglenook fireplace, well kept Courage, Harveys and a couple of guests, reasonably priced food from lunchtime sandwiches up, evening meals Thurs-Sat only, Sun breakfast 9-11am; live music including jazz and open mike nights, Tues quiz; sports TV; children welcome, picnic-sets among flowers out in front, open all day. *(Dan Hanson)*

CHISLEHURST BR7 TQ4469
Crown (020) 8467 7326
School Road; BR7 5PQ Imposing Victorian pub overlooking common, simple attractive interior with flagstoned bar and several dining areas, well kept Shepherd Neame ales and good quality food from sandwiches and traditional choices up, friendly helpful service; open mike night first Tues of month; children welcome, terrace tables, pétanque, seven bedrooms, open all day. *(David Jackman)*

Sydney Arms (020) 8467 3025
Old Perry Street; BR7 6PL Friendly pub in residential road almost opposite entrance to Scadbury Park; four mainstream beers along with a smaller brewery guest, enjoyable inexpensive pub food, two bars, dining room and big conservatory; free wi-fi; children and dogs (in bars) welcome, pleasant garden, open all day (food all day weekends). *(B J Harding)*

EASTCOTE HA5 TQ1089
Case Is Altered (020) 8866 0476
High Road/Southill Lane; HA5 2EW Attractive 17th-c pub in quiet setting adjacent to cricket ground; main bar, flagstoned snug and barn dining area, Rebellion, Sharps and guests, enjoyable all-day food (till 6pm Sun) from sandwiches and bar snacks up, friendly efficient staff; children and dogs welcome, nice front garden (very popular in fine weather – barbecues), handy for Eastcote House Gardens, open all day. *(Brian Glozier)*

HAMPTON TW12 TQ1469
Jolly Coopers (020) 8979 3384
High Street; TW12 2SJ Friendly end of terrace Georgian local with four or five well kept ales and good choice of wines, well liked freshly cooked food in back restaurant extension including good evening tapas and Sun lunch till 5pm; quiz last Tues of month; attractive terrace with climbing plants

and summer barbecues, open all day. *(Simon and Mandy King)*

HAMPTON COURT KT8 TQ1668
★ Kings Arms (020) 8977 1729
Hampton Court Road, by Lion Gate; KT8 9DD Civilised well run pub by Hampton Court itself (so can get busy with tourists), comfortable furnishings including sofas in back area, good open fires, lots of oak panelling, beams and some stained glass, well kept Badger beers and good choice of wines by the glass, friendly service, enjoyable food from sandwiches up, restaurant too (food all day weekends); background music; children and dogs welcome, picnic-sets on roadside front terrace, limited parking, 13 bedrooms, open all day. *(Emma Scofield)*

HARROW HA1 TQ1587
Castle (020) 8422 3155
West Street; HA1 3EF Edwardian Fullers pub in picturesque part, their ales and guests kept well, decent food from lunchtime sandwiches through pies to full meals, several rooms around central servery, open fires, rugs on bare boards and lots of panelling, collection of clocks in cheery front bar, more sedate back lounge; children welcome, steps up from street, nice garden behind with rattan-style seats and tables, open (and food) all day. *(Sam Phillips)*

ISLEWORTH TW7 TQ1675
London Apprentice (020) 8560 1915
Church Street; TW7 6BG Large Thames-side Taylor Walker pub, reasonably priced food from sandwiches up, well kept ales and good wine choice, log fire, pleasant friendly service, upstairs river-view restaurant; may be background music; children welcome, attractive riverside terrace with tables under parasols, open all day. *(Jim Jacks)*

KEW TW9 TQ1977
Coach & Horses (020) 8940 1208
Kew Green; TW9 3BH Attractive coaching inn overlooking green, Youngs ales and enjoyable modern food, friendly young staff, relaxed open-plan interior with armchairs, sofas and log fire, shelves of books, restaurant with kitchen view; background music, sports TV; children and dogs welcome, teak tables on front terrace, secret garden behind with chickens, nice setting and handy for Kew Gardens and National Archive (beware of parking restrictions), 31 good bedrooms, buffet breakfast, open all day. *(Tim Mayers)*

KINGSTON KT2 TQ1869
Boaters (020) 8541 4672
Canbury Gardens (park in Lower Ham Road if you can); KT2 5AU Family-friendly pub by the Thames in small park, good selection of beers such as Bedlam, BrewDog, Hogs Back, Sambrooks and Trumans, decent wines, varied choice of

enjoyable food from changing menu (service charge added), comfortable banquettes in split-level wood-floored bar; Sun evening jazz, quiz nights; riverside terrace and balcony, parking nearby can be difficult, open (and food) all day. *(David and Sally Frost)*

Canbury Arms (020) 8255 9129
Canbury Park Road; KT2 6LQ Popular open-plan pub with simple contemporary décor, bare boards and big windows, relaxed friendly atmosphere, good up-to-date food including breakfast from 9am (not Sun), helpful young staff, up to five well kept ales and good wine choice, side conservatory; regular events such as quiz and music nights, wine tasting and camera club; children and dogs welcome, white-painted picnic-sets out at front under parasols, open all day. *(David and Sally Frost)*

ORPINGTON BR6   TQ4963
★ **Bo-Peep** (01959) 534457
Hewitts Road, Chelsfield; 1.7 miles from M25 junction 4; BR6 7QL Useful M25 country-feel dining pub, old low beams and enormous inglenook in carpeted bar, two cosy candlelit dining rooms, airy side room overlooking lane and fields, well kept Sharps Doom Bar, a changing beer from Westerham and a guest, cheerful efficient staff, good helpings of enjoyable food (all day Sat, not Sun evening) from traditional choices up and weekend afternoon tea; background music; children welcome, dogs in bar, picnic-sets on big brick terrace, open all day. *(B and M Kendall)*

OSTERLEY TW7   TQ1578
Hare & Hounds (020) 8560 5438
Windmill Lane (B454, off A4 signed for Greenford); TW7 5PR Edwardian pub in nice setting opposite Osterley Park (NT), spacious recently refurbished interior with connecting rooms including pitched-ceiling back dining extension, Fullers/Gales beers, decent wines and popular food from sandwiches and small dishes up, friendly helpful staff; children and dogs welcome, disabled facilities, picnic-sets out at front on AstroTurf, big garden with glass-covered eating area and barbecue, play area with big tipi, open (and food) all day. *(Susan and John Douglas)*

RICHMOND TW9   TQ1774
Princes Head (020) 8940 1572
The Green; TW9 1LX Spacious open-plan pub overlooking cricket green, clean and well run, with low-ceilinged panelled areas off island servery, well kept Fullers ales, popular sensibly priced pub food from sandwiches up, friendly young staff and chatty locals, coal-effect fire; background music, TV, fruit machine and daily papers; children and dogs allowed in certain areas, circular picnic-sets outside, handy for Richmond Theatre, open (and food) all day. *(Tim Mayers)*

Watermans Arms (020) 8940 2893
Water Lane; TW9 1TJ Friendly old-fashioned Youngs local with their well kept ales and a couple of guests from Twickenham, enjoyable thai food plus some standard english dishes, traditional layout with open fire, red banquettes and model of a Thames barge, upstairs restaurant; no credit cards but they have an ATM machine; handy for the river; landlord may be retiring so things could change. *(Brian and Anna Marsden, Tony and Wendy Hobden)*

★ **White Cross** (020) 8940 6844
Water Lane; TW9 1TH Lovely garden with terrific Thames views, seats on paved area, outside bar and boats to Kingston and Hampton Court; two chatty main rooms with local prints and photographs, three log fires (one unusually below a window), well kept Youngs and guests from old-fashioned island servery, a dozen wines by the glass, decent bar food all day, bright and airy upstairs room (children welcome here till 6pm) with pretty cast-iron balcony for splendid river view, good mix of customers; background music, TV; dogs welcome, tides can reach the pub entrance (wellies provided). *(Miles Green)*

White Swan (020) 8940 0959
Old Palace Lane; TW9 1PG Small 18th-c cottage pub, civilised and relaxed, with rustic dark-beamed open-plan bar, well kept Otter, St Austell, Sharps and Timothy Taylors, popular freshly made food, coal-effect fires, back dining conservatory and upstairs restaurant; soft background music; children (till 6.30pm) and dogs welcome, some seats on narrow paved area at front, more in pretty walled back terrace below railway, open all day. *(Luke Morgan)*

TW10   TQ1874
White Horse (020) 8940 2418
Worple Way, off Sheen Road; TW10 6DF Large open-plan Fullers pub, their ales and good choice of wines from long aluminium counter, airy interior with pastel shades, exposed brickwork and mix of old and new furniture on bare boards including some easy chairs, enjoyable food from traditional favourites up, friendly helpful service; free wi-fi; children welcome (playground next door), two-level back terrace, open all day. *(Tim Morgan)*

ROMFORD RM1   TQ5188
Golden Lion (01708) 740081
High Street; RM1 1HR Popular former coaching inn (one of the town's oldest buildings) with spacious beamed interior, four or five well kept ales, good value pubby food from lighter meals to giant plates, friendly staff and good mix of customers; weekend live music, sports TV, free wi-fi; open (and food) all day. *(Richard Tilbrook)*

RM2   TQ5188
Ship   (01708) 741571
Main Road; RM2 5EL 17th-c black
and white pub, panelling, low beams and
woodburner in fine brick fireplace, Adnams,
Courage, Fullers, Sharps and guests, good
value food (not weekend evenings) from
sandwiches and sharing boards up; live
weekend music; children and dogs welcome,
picnic-sets in back garden under parasols,
open all day. *(Robert Lester)*

TEDDINGTON TW11   TQ1671
Kings Head   (020) 3166 2900
High Street; TW11 8HG Comfortably
updated bare-boards front bar with easy
chairs and button-back wall benches, modern
artwork and photographs on vibrant coloured
walls, woodburners, Fullers London Pride,
Meantime London Pale Ale and Sharps Doom
Bar, lots of wines by the glass including
champagne, well separated back dining
part with similar décor and open kitchen,
enjoyable interesting food including good
value set menu till 6pm (not Sun), courteous
helpful service; background music; children
welcome, seats out at front an on enclosed
back terrace, open (and food) all day.
(Robert W Buckle)

TWICKENHAM TW1   TQ1673
Crown   (020) 8892 5896
Richmond Road, St Margarets; TW1 2NH
Refurbished Georgian pub with emphasis
on good food from sandwiches and sharing
plates to restauranty choices, several large
dining areas including splendid Victorian
back hall, also well kept ales, nice wines by
the glass and decent coffee, friendly efficient
staff, open fire; newspapers and free wi-fi;
children welcome, picnic-sets in sunny
courtyard garden, open (and food)
all day. *(Taff Thomas)*

White Swan   (020) 8892 2166
Riverside; TW1 3DN Refurbished 17th-c
Thames-side pub up steep anti-flood steps;
bare-boards L-shaped bar with cosy log fire,
river views from prized bay window, Fullers,
Sharps and guests such as Twickenham,
enjoyable fairly priced food (all day Sat,
Sun till 6pm), friendly local atmosphere,
board games; live acoustic music and quiz
nights; children and dogs welcome, tranquil
setting opposite Eel Pie Island with well
used balcony and waterside terrace (liable to
flooding) across quiet lane, open all day.
(Ian Phillips, Taff Thomas)

TW2   TQ1572
Sussex Arms   (020) 8894 7468
Staines Road; TW2 5BG Traditional bare-
boards pub with 18 handpumps plus ciders
and perries from long counter, plenty in
bottles too, simple food including good home-
made pies, friendly staff, walls and ceilings
covered in beer mats and pump clips, open
fire, some live acoustic music; large back
garden with boules, open all day. *(Jeff Davies)*

UXBRIDGE UB8   TQ0582
Malt Shovel   (01895) 812797
Iver Lane, Cowley (B470); UB8 2JE
Vintage Inn by Grand Union Canal, their
usual fair-priced food including set deal, ales
such as Caledonian, Fullers and Greene King
served by pleasant staff; children welcome,
seats outside, open (and food) all day.
(Taff Thomas)

SCOTLAND

SHETLAND

ORKNEY

WESTERN ISLES
LEWIS
HARRIS
NORTH UIST
SOUTH UIST
BARRA
SKYE
RUM
COLL
TIREE
MULL
COLONSAY
JURA
ISLAY
ARRAN

SUTHERLAND
CAITHNESS
NAIRN
ROSS-SHIRE
MORAYSHIRE
BANFFSHIRE
ABERDEENSHIRE
INVERNESS-SHIRE
KINCARDINESHIRE
ANGUS
PERTHSHIRE
FIFE
KINROSS-SHIRE
CLACKMANNANSHIRE
STIRLINGSHIRE
DUNBARTON
RENFREW
ARGYLL
LOTHIAN W MID E
LANARK-SHIRE
PEEBLES
SELKIRK
BERWICKSHIRE
ROXBURGHSHIRE
AYRSHIRE
DUMFRIESSHIRE
KIRKCUDBRIGHT-SHIRE
WIGTOWNSHIRE

North Sea

NORTHUMBERLAND
TYNE & WEAR
COUNTY DURHAM
CLEVELAND
CUMBRIA
ISLE OF MAN
NORTH YORKSHIRE
LANCS
WEST YORKS
EAST YORKS
MERSEYSIDE
GTR MANCH
S YORKS
ANGLESEY
CHESHIRE
DERBYSHIRE
NOTTS
LINCOLNSHIRE
GWYNEDD
CLWYD
STAFFS
LEICS & RUTLAND
NORFOLK
SHROPS
W MIDS
WARKS
NORTHANTS
CAMBS
POWYS
HEREFORD & WORCS
BEDS
HERTS
SUFFOLK
DYFED
GLOS
OXON
BUCKS
ESSEX
GLAMORGAN
GWENT
WILTSHIRE
BERKS
LONDON
HAMPSHIRE
SURREY
KENT
SOMERSET
WEST SUSSEX
EAST SUSSEX
DEVON
DORSET
ISLE OF WIGHT
CORNWALL

Irish Sea

SCILLY ISLES

English Channel

KEY ⭐ Star Pub 🍽️ Top Quality Food 🍺 Great Beer

🍷 Good Wines £ Bargain Meals 🛏️ Good Bedrooms 🍴 Serves Food

ANCRUM NT6224 Map 10
Cross Keys 🍽️ 🍷
(01835) 830242 – www.ancrumcrosskeys.com
Off A68 Jedburgh–Edinburgh; TD8 6XH

Simply decorated village pub with a high reputation for local ales and particularly good food

Perched above Ale Water for 200 years and overlooking the village green, this cheerful pub is the hub of local life. But there are usually just as many visitors too, as the reputation of the innovative food has spread far and wide. The easy-going, simply furnished bar has dogs and regulars vying for the fire, wall seats, minimal décor and stools against the counter where they serve Born in the Borders Foxy Blonde and a guest ale from a local brewery such as Born in the Borders on handpump, a good choice of wines and a healthy number of malt whiskies; a newish side bar is for both drinking and eating. The blue-walled dining room has chunky tables and chairs on bare boards, an open kitchen and, again, minimal décor. Service is helpful and friendly. There's a back garden with picnic-sets and a gate that leads down to the water. A few tables and chairs are set out in front of the stone building.

🍽️ Creatively presented and with some unusual touches, the food uses local and foraged ingredients: crispy butterflied king prawns with sweet chilli, lime and soy dipping sauce, yakitori chicken skewers, rabbit, mushroom and smoked bacon pie, cold seafood platter, burger with toppings, coleslaw and chips, salmon fillet with lobster and crab fritter and salsa verde, chargrilled rib-eye steak with a choice of sauces, and puddings such as layered Baileys and milk chocolate pot and rhubarb and vanilla crème brûlée. *Benchmark main dish: tempura-battered haddock and chips £12.00. Two-course evening meal £19.00.*

Free house ~ Licensee John Henderson ~ Real ale ~ Open 5pm-midnight (1am Fri, Sat); 12-midnight Sun; closed weekday lunchtimes ~ Bar food 5.30-9 Weds-Sun; 12-2, 5.30-9 Sat; 12-2, 5.30-8 Sun ~ Restaurant ~ Children welcome ~ Dogs allowed in bar ~ Wi-fi
Recommended by Isobel Mackinlay, Alan and Alice Morgan, Elizabeth and Peter May

APPLECROSS NG7144 Map 11
Applecross Inn ⭐ 🛏️
(01520) 744262 – www.applecross.uk.com
Off A896 S of Shieldaig; IV54 8LR

Wonderfully remote pub on famously scenic route on west coast; particularly friendly welcome, real ales and good seafood; bedrooms

If you wish to stay here, you'll have to book months ahead as customers from all over the world will also be wanting a place. But it will be worth it for the extraordinary drive through miles of spectacularly wild, unpopulated scenery to get there and for the inn's breathtaking backdrop towards Raasay and Skye. The alternative route, along the single-track lane winding around the coast from just south of Shieldaig, has equally glorious sea loch (and then sea) views nearly all the way. The no-nonsense, welcoming bar has a woodburning stove, exposed stone walls, upholstered pine furnishings and a stone floor; An Teallach Crofters Pale Ale and Isle of

Skye Red on handpump, over 50 malt whiskies and a good, varied wine list; board games. The tables in the shoreside garden enjoy magnificent views. There's a new outdoor eating area for summer use. Some disabled facilities.

The first class fresh local fish and seafood includes squat lobsters, oysters, fresh haddock, langoustines, a seafood platter, king scallops and dressed crab with smoked salmon – but they also offer chicken liver parfait, pigeon breast, crispy bacon and pine nut salad, thai green chicken curry, venison burger with chips, duck breast in soy and honey marinade with wasabi topping, and puddings such as seasonal fruit crumble and sticky toffee pudding. *Benchmark main dish: local king scallops in garlic butter with crispy bacon £17.50. Two-course evening meal £25.00.*

Free house ~ Licensee Judith Fish ~ Real ale ~ Open 11am-11.30pm (midnight Sat); 12.30-11.30 Sun ~ Bar food 12-9 ~ Children welcome till 8.30pm ~ Dogs welcome ~ Wi-fi ~ Live music first Sun of month 3-6pm ~ Bedrooms: £85/£130. *Recommended by Barry Collett, Roy and Gill Payne, the Dutchman, M J Winterton, John and Enid*

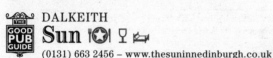

DALKEITH   NR3264   Map 11
Sun 🌟 🍷 🛏

(0131) 663 2456 – www.thesuninnedinburgh.co.uk
A7 S; EH22 4TR

Family-run inn with charming bar and restaurant, open fires, leafy garden, local ale and delicious food; comfortable, airy bedrooms

Surrounded by five acres of wooded grounds and close to the River Esk, you'd never believe you were so close to Edinburgh. The bars have been carefully renovated with walls stripped back to the original stone (or with hunting-theme wallpaper), bare floorboards and refurbished fireplaces. There are cushioned built-in settles, all sorts of wooden dining chairs around an appealing collection of tables, gilt-edged mirrors and high stools against the counter where friendly staff serve Born in the Borders Foxy Blonde and Stewart Pentland IPA on handpump and good wines by the glass; background music. Seats on the covered courtyard overlook the garden where they hold popular summer barbecues. Bedrooms are thoughtfully equipped and comfortable and breakfasts highly rated.

Enticing food cooked by the landlord and his son includes breakfasts (8.30-10.30am), sandwiches, moules marinière, confit duck leg salad with hot sauce, cottage pie, roast shallot tarte tatin with tempura sprouting broccoli and lemon thyme cream, lamb rump with shepherds pie, lamb cutlet, twice-baked pea soufflé, cauliflower purée and red wine jus, turbot fillets with crab and spring onion risotto, chilli and ginger king prawn and red pepper dressing, and puddings such as ginger cheesecake with chocolate soil and ginger ice-cream and tropical fruit salad with apple sorbet. *Benchmark main dish: beer-battered haddock and chips £10.95. Two-course evening meal £19.00.*

Free house ~ Licensee Bernadette McCarron ~ Real ale ~ Open 8.30am-11pm (midnight Sat) ~ Bar food 12-9 ~ Children welcome ~ Wi-fi ~ Bedrooms: £75/£95 *Recommended by Isobel Mackinlay, Laura Reid, Jeff Davies, Lance and Sarah Milligan*

EDINBURGH   NT2574   Map 11
Bow Bar 🍺

(0131) 226 7667
West Bow; EH1 2HH

Cosy, enjoyably unpretentious pub with an excellent choice of well kept beers

'A fine place to spend a dark, damp Edinburgh evening,' says one of our readers – and we know just what he means. It's a cheerfully traditional alehouse and a haven of old-fashioned drinking with a splendid range of real ales. The rectangular bar has an impressive carved mahogany gantry, and from the tall 1920s founts on the bar counter, knowledgeable staff dispense eight well kept real ales: regulars such as Alechemy Bowhemia Pale, Cromarty Happy Chappy and Stewart 80/- and five quickly changing guests; regular beer festivals. Also on offer are some 320 malts, including five 'malts of the moment', a good choice of rums, 60 international bottled beers and 20 gins. The walls are covered with a fine collection of enamel advertising signs and handsome antique brewery mirrors, and there are sturdy leatherette wall seats and café-style bar seats around heavy narrow tables on the wooden floor. No children allowed.

Lunchtime-only food is limited to pies.

Free house ~ Licensee Mike Smith ~ Real ale ~ Open 12-midnight; 12.30-11.30 Sun ~ Bar food 12-3 ~ Dogs welcome ~ Wi-fi *Recommended by Dr Matt Burleigh, Roger and Donna Huggins*

EDINBURGH
Kays Bar £

NT2574 Map 11

(0131) 225 1858 – www.kaysbar.co.uk
Jamaica Street West; off India Street; EH3 6HF

Cosy, enjoyably chatty backstreet pub with good value lunchtime food and an excellent choice of well kept beers

This convivial little pub is tucked away from the tourists in a backstreet and has an eclectic mix of customers and an enjoyable local feel. There are long, curving, well worn, red-plush wall banquettes and stools around cast-iron tables on red carpet, and red pillars supporting a red ceiling. Décor is simple with big casks and vats arranged along the walls, old wine and spirits merchants' notices and gas-type lamps. A quiet panelled back room (a bit like a library) leads off, with a narrow, plank-panelled pitched ceiling and a collection of books ranging from dictionaries to ancient steam-train books for boys; there's a lovely warming coal fire in winter. Seven real ales on handpump might include Caledonian Deuchars IPA and Theakstons Best, plus guests such as Caledonian Edinburgh Castle 80/-, Courage Best, Stewart Telos, Thwaites Wainwright and Timothy Taylors Landlord; they also stock more than 50 malt whiskies aged from eight to 50 years old, and ten blended whiskies; board games. In days past, the pub was owned by John Kay, a whisky and wine merchant; wine barrels were hoisted up to the first floor and dispensed through pipes attached to nipples that are still visible around the ceiling light rose. Dogs may be allowed outside food service times.

Lunchtime food is very good value and includes stovies, pâté with toast, chicken or beef curries, steak pie, chilli con carne, prawn salad, and puddings such as chocolate fudge cake. *Benchmark main dish: mince and tatties £4.95.*

Free house ~ Licensee Fraser Gillespie ~ Real ale ~ Open 11am-midnight (1am Fri, Sat); 12.30-11 Sun ~ Bar food 12-2.30; not Sun ~ Wi-fi *Recommended by Mary Kirkwood, Roger and Donna Huggins, Rona Mackinlay*

Real ale may be served from handpumps, electric pumps (not just the on-off switches used for keg beer) or – common in Scotland – tall taps called founts (pronounced 'fonts') where a separate pump pushes the beer up under air pressure.

GLASGOW
Babbity Bowster ♀

NS5965   Map 11

(0141) 552 5055 – www.babbitybowster.com

Blackfriars Street; G1 1PE

A lively mix of traditional and modern with a continental feel too; bedrooms

Built on the site of an old monastery, this is a friendly place where locals and visitors mix happily and there's no background music or TV to interrupt the chatty feel. The simply decorated, light-filled interior has fine tall windows, plush stools and cushioned ladder-back chairs around a mix of dark tables on bare boards, some wall bench seating, open fires and attractive plant prints on light paintwork. The bar opens on to a pleasant terrace with picnic-sets under parasols and there's another back terrace too. High chairs line the counter where they keep Caledonian Deuchars IPA and a couple of guests such as Fyne Ales Jarl and Williams Brothers May Bee on air-pressure tall fount, and a remarkably sound collection of wines and malt whiskies; good tea and coffee too. On Saturday evenings, the pub has live traditional scottish music, while at other times you may find games of boules in progress outside. Note the bedroom price is for the room only.

🍴 A short choice of enjoyable food includes sandwiches, croque monsieur, mussels, onions and leeks in creamy saffron sauce, haggis, neeps and tatties, a pie of the day, vegetarian moussaka, a fresh fish dish of the day, saddle of deer crusted in pepper and oatmeal with a whisky sauce, rack of lamb with dijon mustard and white wine jus, duck breast with orange and star anise, and puddings such as clootie dumpling with toffee sauce and caramelised lemon tart. *Benchmark main dish: cullen skink £6.25. Two-course evening meal £19.00.*

Free house ~ Licensee Fraser Laurie ~ Real ale ~ Open 11am-midnight; 12.30-midnight Sun ~ Bar food 12-10 ~ Restaurant ~ Children welcome if eating ~ Wi-fi ~ Live traditional music Weds afternoon, Sat early evening ~ Bedrooms: £55/£70 *Recommended by Isobel Mackinlay, Mungo Shipley, Dave Braisted, Rona Mackinlay*

GLASGOW
Bon Accord 🍺 £

NS5765   Map 11

(0141) 248 4427 – www.bonaccordweb.co.uk

North Street; G3 7DA

Remarkable choice of drinks including an impressive range of whiskies and real ales, a good welcome and bargain food

They keep an amazing 380 malt whiskies in this cheerful tavern alongside Caledonian Deuchars and nine daily changing guests sourced from breweries around Britain and served from swan-necked handpumps. Also, continental bottled beers, a farm cider and, in a remarkable display behind the counter, lots of gins, vodkas and rums. Staff are knowledgeable, so do ask for help if you need it. The several linked traditional bars are warmly understated with cream or terracotta walls, a mix of chairs and tables, a leather sofa and plenty of bar stools on polished bare boards or carpeting; TV, background music and board games. There are circular picnic-sets on a small terrace, and modern tables and chairs out in front.

🍴 Incredibly good value food includes baguettes, french fries topped with cheese and bacon, scottish breakfast, battered fresh haddock and chips, burgers with various toppings, gammon and egg, and puddings such as apple pie and clootie dumpling. *Benchmark main dish: steak pie £6.00. Two-course evening meal £9.50.*

Free house ~ Licensee Paul McDonagh ~ Real ale ~ Open 11am-midnight; 12.30-midnight
Sun ~ Bar food 11-8; 12.30-8 Sun ~ Children welcome until 8pm ~ Wi-fi ~ Live band Sat
evening *Recommended by Mary Kirkwood, Neil Allen, Helena and Trevor Fraser, Dave Sutton*

ISLE OF WHITHORN   NX4736 Map 9

Steam Packet ♀ ⇔

(01988) 500334 – www.thesteampacketinn.biz

Harbour Row; DG8 8LL

**Waterside views from friendly, family-run inn with up to eight
real ales and tasty pubby food; bedrooms**

In a pretty fishing village on the tip of the south-west peninsula, this is a
friendly, family-run inn right on the quayside. Big picture windows overlook
the bustle of yachts and inshore fishing boats – a view that's shared by some
of the bedrooms. The comfortable low-ceilinged bar is split into two: on the
right, plush button-back banquettes and boat pictures, and on the left, stools
around cast-iron-framed tables on big stone tiles, and a woodburning stove
in the bare stone wall. There's a lower beamed dining room with high-backed
leather dining chairs around square tables on wooden flooring plus another
woodburner, a small eating area off the lounge bar, and an airy conservatory
leading into the garden. As well as their own-brewed ales from the new Five
Kingdoms Brewery, they keep Belhaven IPA, Fyne Ales Jarl, Greene King
Old Speckled Hen and guests from brewers such as Kelburn and Orkney
on handpump, quite a few malt whiskies and 11 wines by the glass; TV,
dominoes and pool. You can walk from here up to the remains of St Ninian's
kirk, on a headland behind the village.

 As well as plenty of fish and seafood choices, the popular food includes cullen
skink, duck liver and cointreau pâté with chutney, vegetable curry, chicken with
chilli and garlic, a curry of the day, burger with toppings, onion rings and chips, lamb
cutlets with garlic roasted potatoes and red wine jus, sirloin steak with a choice of
sauces, and puddings such as orange and almond cake with orange syrup and mixed
berry roulade. *Benchmark main dish: beer-battered fish and chips £10.95.
Two-course evening meal £15.00.*

Free house ~ Licensee Alastair Scoular ~ Real ale ~ Open 11-11 (midnight Sat); 12-11 Sun;
11-3, 6-11 weekdays in winter ~ Bar food 12-2, 6.30-9; snacks 2-6pm Fri-Sun ~ Restaurant ~
Children welcome except in public bar ~ Dogs allowed in bar and bedrooms ~ Wi-fi ~
Folk music third Sun of month ~ Bedrooms: £30/£60 *Recommended by the Dutchman,
David and Betty Gittins, Jack Trussler, Mike Benton*

MEIKLEOUR   NO1539 Map 11

Meikleour Arms ⇔

(01250) 883206 – www.meikleourarms.co.uk

A984 W of Coupar Angus; PH2 6EB

**Traditional 19th-c inn and part of the Meikleour Estate;
a welcoming and well run base for the area; bedrooms**

Before visiting this enjoyable country inn, do visit the spectacular beech
hedge just 300 metres away which was planted over 250 years ago – it's
the tallest in the world. Once in the pub, the main lounge bar is basically two
rooms (one carpeted, the other with a stone floor) with comfortable seating,
some angling equipment and fishing/shooting pictures and open wood fires.
There's a beer named for the pub (from Inveralmond), Orkney Dark Island
and Strathbraan Look West on handpump, 50 malt whiskies and nine wines
by the glass, served by attentive, friendly staff; background music. The

panelled and tartan-carpeted dining room is elegant and more formal. Seats in the garden and on a small colonnaded verandah, with more on a sloping lawn, have distant highland views. The pretty bedrooms are comfortable, warm and well appointed and breakfasts are good. There's a lot to see and do nearby – including one of the best salmon beats in Scotland.

Food is interesting and uses Estate produce as well as some from their own walled garden: duck croquettes with plum chutney, prawn, crayfish and avocado cocktail, black pudding, bacon, mushrooms and poached egg salad, leek and asparagus quiche, lemon, rosemary and sage crumbed chicken with green bean and potato salad, pork fillet stuffed with spinach, ricotta and apricot with grain mustard sauce, cod on chorizo, spinach and potatoes, and puddings such as dark chocolate délice and pear tarte tatin with chantilly cream. *Benchmark main dish: beer-battered haddock and chips £11.95. Two-course evening meal £18.00.*

Free house ~ Licensee Greg Burgess ~ Real ale ~ Open 11-11 (midnight Sat) ~ Bar food 12-9 ~ Restaurant ~ Children welcome ~ Dogs allowed in bar and bedrooms ~ Wi-fi ~ Bedrooms: £90/£110 *Recommended by Mr and Mrs J Watkins, Les and Sandra Brown, Pat and Stewart Gordon*

MELROSE
Burts Hotel 🌟 🛏

NT5433 Map 9

(01896) 822285 – www.burtshotel.co.uk
B6374, Market Square; TD6 9PL

Scotland Dining Pub of the Year

Comfortable town-centre hotel with imaginative food and a fine array of malt whiskies; bedrooms

In the middle of a beautifully unspoilt small town with the abbey ruins just a few steps away, this is a smart place run by the same family for many years. Neat public areas are maintained with attention to detail. The welcoming red carpeted bar has a warming fire, tidy pub tables between cushioned wall seats and windsor armchairs, scottish prints on pale green walls and a long dark wood counter serving Greene King Old Speckled Hen, Born in the Borders Foxy Blonde and Timothy Taylors Landlord on handpump, 12 wines by the glass from a good wine list, a farm cider and around 80 malt whiskies. The elegant restaurant with its swagged curtains, dark blue wallpaper and tables laid with white linen offers a smarter dining experience; background music. The licensees are very hands-on. In summer you can sit out in the well tended garden. The bedrooms, though quite small, are immaculate and comfortably decorated and the breakfasts highly thought-of.

Particularly good, confident cooking that showcases the best local produce includes sandwiches (not Sun), lobster, scallop and prawn terrine with pickled cucumber and sweet pepper dressing, camembert croquettes with apple and cranberry compote, salmon fishcakes with caper and herb cream, burger with toppings, pickles, relish and chips, butternut squash, pine nut and goats cheese risotto cakes with red pepper purée, duck breast with creamed savoy cabbage, garlic mash, red wine shallots and thyme jus, bass fillets with tarragon gnocchi, cauliflower purée and brown shrimp sauce, and puddings such as dark chocolate tart with pistachio cake, poached cherries and cherry ice-cream and rum crème brûlée with banoffi bonbon, glazed bananas and rum and raisin ice-cream. *Benchmark main dish: harissa-spiced lamb rump with garlic potatoes and cumin jus £17.50. Two-course evening meal £21.00.*

Free house ~ Licensees Graham and Nick Henderson ~ Real ale ~ Open 11-2.30, 5-11; 12-2.30, 6-11 Sun; closed 1 week Jan ~ Bar food 12-2, 6-9.30 (10 Fri, Sat) ~ Restaurant ~ Children welcome ~ Dogs allowed in bar and bedrooms ~ Wi-fi ~ Bedrooms: £75/£140 *Recommended by Roy and Gill Payne, Ian Herdman, Martin Day, John Poulter, Nick Higgins*

PLOCKTON

NG8033 Map 11

Plockton Hotel ★ 🌟 🛏

(01599) 544274 – www.plocktonhotel.co.uk

Village signposted from A87 near Kyle of Lochalsh; IV52 8TN

Neat little hotel with wonderful views, very good food with emphasis on local seafood and real ales; bedrooms

After a long drive across the hills, this National Trust village is a delightful surprise. Family-run and right by Loch Carron, the hotel has tables in the front garden that look out past the village's trademark palm trees to a shore lined with colourful flowering shrubs and across the sheltered anchorage to rugged mountains. Inside, the welcoming, comfortably furnished lounge bar has window seats with views of the harbour boats, as well as antique dark red leather seating around neat Regency-style tables on a tartan carpet, and three model ships set into the woodwork and partly panelled stone walls. The separate public bar has pool, board games, TV, a games machine, juke box and background music. Cromarty Kowabunga, Highland Island Hopping and a couple of guest ales on handpump, 30 malt whiskies and several wines by the glass. Half the comfortable bedrooms have extraordinary water views, while the others, some with balconies, look over the hillside garden; breakfasts are good. There's a hotel nearby called the Plockton, so don't get the two confused.

 As well as very good fish and shellfish dishes such as salmon topped with spring onion, chilli and lime, monkfish wrapped in streaky bacon, chargrilled prawns with lemon and garlic butter, and seafood platter, the popular food includes country pâté with chutney, stilton, pear and walnut salad, haggis-stuffed burger with toppings and fries, venison casserole with redcurrant jelly and juniper berries, chicken stuffed with smoked ham and cheese in sun-dried tomato, garlic and basil sauce, and puddings. *Benchmark main dish: bass with a changing risotto £14.95. Two-course evening meal £20.50.*

Free house ~ Licensee Alan Pearson ~ Real ale ~ Open 11–midnight (11.30 Sat); 12–11 Sun ~ Bar food 12-2.15, 6-9 ~ Restaurant ~ Children welcome ~ Live music Weds evening ~ Bedrooms: £70/£140 *Recommended by M J Winterton, Barry Collett, Les and Sandra Brown, Laura Reid*

RATHO

NT1470 Map 11

Bridge 🌟 � 🍴

(0131) 333 1320 – www.bridgeinn.com

Baird Road; EH28 8RA

Canalside inn with cosy bar and airy restaurant, a thoughtful choice of drinks and enjoyable food; attractive bedrooms

The individually decorated and well equipped bedrooms in this charming inn have Union Canal views, and breakfasts are lovely. The cosy bar has an open fire with leather armchairs to either side and a larger area with a two-way fireplace and upholstered tub and cushioned wooden chairs on pale boards around a mix of tables; a contemporary and elegant dining room leads off. Belhaven St Andrews Ale, Bridge Friendly Fire ISA and a changing guest from Inveralmond on handpump, 36 wines by the glass and 50 malt whiskies. The main restaurant is light and airy with up-to-date pale oak settles, antique-style chairs and big windows overlooking the water. Seats on the terrace share the same view. A unique part of the friendly licensees' business here is their summer restaurant barge, which travels from the inn down the canal to the Almondell Aqueduct over the River Almond; there's a full kitchen team on board and you can have lunch, afternoon tea or supper.

 Using their own pork and lamb and produce grown in their walled garden, the well presented, particularly good food includes sandwiches (served with soup or fries), cullen skink, pork terrine with prosciutto, chorizo and fennel, a pie of the day, roast vegetable and puy wellington with herby mash, bass fillets with lightly spiced sweet potato purée, chorizo, scallops and sauce vierge, venison loin with braised and rolled haunch, port gel and bitter chocolate, and puddings such as citrus posset with shortbread and trio of chocolate, dark brownie, milk chocolate crémeux and white chocolate crumble. *Benchmark main dish: burger with toppings, pickles and fries £13.00. Two-course evening meal £20.00.*

Free house ~ Licensees Graham and Rachel Bucknall ~ Real ale ~ Open 9am-11pm; 11am-midnight Fri, Sat; 11-11 Sun ~ Bar food 12-3, 5-9; 12-9 Sat; 12-8 Sun ~ Restaurant ~ Children welcome but not in bar after 8pm ~ Dogs allowed in bar ~ Wi-fi ~ Live music monthly (phone for details) ~ Bedrooms: £75/£90 *Recommended by Pat and Stewart Gordon*

SHIELDAIG
NG8153   Map 11

Tigh an Eilean Hotel 🛏

(01520) 755251 – www.tighaneilean.co.uk
Village signposted just off A896 Lochcarron–Gairloch; IV54 8XN

Stunningly set hotel with separate contemporary bar, real ales and enjoyable food; tranquil bedrooms

Many of our recommended Scottish inns are in lovely settings – but the position here is particularly stunning, looking over the forested Shieldaig Island to Loch Torridon and then out to the sea beyond; if you're lucky you might see otters, sea eagles, seals or even the rare pine marten. Separate from the hotel, the bright, attractive bar is on two storeys with an open staircase; dining is on the first floor and a decked balcony has a magnificent loch and village view. The place is gently contemporary and nicely relaxed with timbered floors, timber-boarded walls, shiny bolts through exposed timber roof beams and an open kitchen. A couple of changing ales from An Teallach on handpump and up to a dozen wines by the glass; background music, TV, darts, pool and board games. Tables outside in a sheltered little courtyard are well placed to enjoy the gorgeous position. To preserve the peace and quiet, the comfortable bedrooms have no TVs and no telephones, though each has its own sitting area.

Rewarding food using top quality local produce includes shellfish delivered fresh from the jetty, as well as sandwiches, wild mushroom tortellini with pea and herb velouté, hand-dived scallops with serrano ham and toasted hazelnut and coriander beurre blanc, duck breast with mango and honey and soy sauce, rack of lamb with herb crust and lamb jus, saddle of local venison with honey-roasted pears and celeriac purée, bream in fennel, leek and saffron broth with steamed mussels and grilled scallop, and puddings such as chocolate marquise with white chocolate sauce and crème brûlée with raspberries. *Benchmark main dish: seafood stew £15.75. Two-course evening meal £18.50.*

Free house ~ Licensee Cathryn Field ~ Real ale ~ Open 11-11 (midnight Sat); closed Mon and Tues Jan ~ Bar food 12-9; 12-2.30, 6.30-9 in winter ~ Restaurant ~ Children welcome ~ Dogs allowed in bar and bedrooms ~ Wi-fi ~ Traditional live folk music Fri, Sat ~ Bedrooms: £80/£160 *Recommended by John and Enid, Rona Mackinlay, Brian and Sally Wakeham, William Slade*

If you know a pub is ever open all day, please tell us.

SLIGACHAN

NG4930   Map 11

Sligachan Hotel 🍺 🛏

(01478) 650204 – www.sligachan.co.uk

A87 Broadford–Portree, junction with A863; IV47 8SW

Spectacularly set mountain hotel with walkers' bar and plusher side, all-day food and impressive range of whiskies

The huge, modern pine-clad main bar in this stunningly set hotel falls somewhere between a basic climbers' bar and the plusher, more sedate hotel side. It's spaciously open to the ceiling rafters and has geometrically laid-out dark tables and chairs on neat carpets; pool, TV, darts, games machine and board games. As well as their own Cuillin Black Face, Eagle and Pinnacle, they keep a guest on handpump plus an incredible display of over 400 malt whiskies at one end of the counter. It can get quite lively in here some nights, but there's a more sedate lounge bar with leather bucket armchairs on plush carpets and a coal fire; background highland and islands music. The separate restaurant is in the hotel itself. The interesting little museum, well worth a visit, charts the history of the hotel and its famous climbers, with photographs and climbing and angling records. There are tables out in the garden and a big play area for children, which can be seen from the bar. The bedrooms are comfortable, bright and modern, and they also offer self-catering and have a campsite with caravan hook-ups. Dogs are allowed only in the main bar and not in the hotel's cocktail bar – but are allowed to stay in some bedrooms. Some of the most testing walks in Britain are right on the hotel's doorstep.

 Some sort of food is usually on offer all day: cullen skink, grilled local scallops with garlic butter and parsley breadcrumbs, filo pastry and feta cheese tart with ratatouille, beer-battered fish and chips, venison burger with pickles, sauce and fries, whisky-braised short rib of beef with haggis, neeps, tatties and braising juices, hake with tomato, chorizo, spinach and white beans, and puddings such as sticky toffee pudding with toffee sauce and yoghurt pannacotta with whisky jelly. *Benchmark main dish: venison casserole with mustard mash and sticky red cabbage £13.95. Two-course evening meal £16.00.*

Own brew ~ Licensee Sandy Coghill ~ Real ale ~ Open 9am-midnight; 11am-midnight Sun; closed Nov-Feb (hotel); phone for bar times ~ Bar food 7.30am-9.30pm ~ Restaurant ~ Children welcome ~ Dogs allowed in bar and bedrooms ~ Wi-fi ~ Live music every second Sat of month ~ Bedrooms: £50/£100   *Recommended by Caroline Prescott, Anne and Ben Smith, Charles Welch*

STEIN

NG2656   Map 11

Stein Inn 🛏

(01470) 592362 – www.steininn.co.uk

End of B886 N of Dunvegan in Waternish, off A850 Dunvegan–Portree; OS Sheet 23 map reference 263564; IV55 8GA

Lovely setting on Skye's northern corner for this welcoming 18th-c inn with good, simple food and lots of whiskies; a rewarding place to stay

On the west side of the island's Waternish peninsula and in a tiny waterside hamlet, this is an inn of character with marvellous views across Loch Bay. The unpretentious original public bar makes a particularly inviting retreat from the elements, with sturdy country furnishings, flagstones, beam-and-plank ceiling, partly panelled stripped-stone walls and a warming double-sided stove between the two rooms. Caledonian Deuchars IPA and a couple of local guests such as Cairngorm Trade Winds and Orkney Dark Island on handpump, eight wines by the glass and over 135 malt whiskies. Good service from smartly uniformed staff. Pool, darts, board games, dominoes and cribbage in the games area, and maybe background music. There's a lively indoor play area for children and showers for yachtsmen. Benches outside look over the water – as do all the bedrooms; it's worth pre-ordering the smoked kippers as part of the tasty breakfasts. Dogs are welcome but not during evening food service.

Food is well regarded and uses highland meat and local fish: lunchtime sandwiches (the crab is popular) and toasties, moules marinière, baked camembert with cranberry sauce, bean and nut patties with plum chutney, steak braised in ale, venison pie, salmon in vermouth and tarragon sauce, pork chop with walnut and blue cheese butter, duck breast in garlic and cider cream sauce, and puddings such as white chocolate cheesecake and apple and blueberry crumble. *Benchmark main dish: beer-battered haddock and chips £9.50. Two-course evening meal £15.00.*

Free house ~ Licensees Angus and Teresa McGhie ~ Real ale ~ Open 11am-midnight; 11-11 Sun; 12-11 in winter ~ Bar food 12-4, 6-9.30 ~ Children welcome ~ Dogs allowed in bar and bedrooms ~ Wi-fi ~ Bedrooms: £45/£77 *Recommended by Alison and Michael Harper, Rob Anderson, Daniel King*

SWINTON
Wheatsheaf 🏵️ ♟️ ⚲

NT8347   Map 10

(01890) 860257 – www.wheatsheaf-swinton.co.uk
A6112 N of Coldstream; TD11 3JJ

Civilised place with small bar for drinkers, comfortable lounges, top quality food and drinks and professional service; appealing bedrooms

Although this is more of a restaurant-with-rooms, the attentive, friendly staff also welcome customers into the little bar and informal lounges. Here they keep Belhaven IPA on handpump alongside 50 malt whiskies and 18 wines by the glass. There are comfortable plush armchairs, several nice old oak settles with cushions, a little open fire, sporting prints and china plates on the bottle-green walls in the bar and small agricultural prints and fishing-theme décor on the painted or bare-stone walls in the lounges. The dining room and front conservatory with its vaulted pine ceiling have carpet on the floor and high-backed slate-grey chairs around pale wood tables set with fresh flowers while the more formal restaurant has black leather high-backed dining chairs around clothed tables; background music. The well equipped, comfortable bedrooms have been refurbished in Farrow & Ball colours and the scottish breakfasts are good. This is an attractive village surrounded by rolling countryside and located only a few miles from the River Tweed.

As well as bar choices such as pork and chorizo burger, king prawn linguine with chilli and tomatoes, and steak in Guinness pie, the creative food might include king scallops with apple and capers and apple and port purée, ham hock terrine with piccalilli, corn-fed chicken breast with haggis bonbon and a panache of vegetables, sea bream with potato and chive salad and anchovy salsa, slow-braised pork belly and cheek with pak choi, ginger and chilli, and puddings such as white chocolate crème brûlée and orange pannacotta with spiced orange compote. *Benchmark main dish: pork loin with asian dressing £19.50. Two-course evening meal £20.00.*

Free house ~ Licensee Michael Laurence ~ Real ale ~ Open 11-11 (midnight Sat); 11-10 Sun ~ Bar food 12-2, 6-9 ~ Restaurant ~ Children welcome but under-10s only in restaurant 6-7pm ~ Dogs allowed in bar and bedrooms ~ Wi-fi ~ Bedrooms: £89/£119 *Recommended by Belinda May, Nick Sharpe, Michael Doswell*

THORNHILL   NS6699 Map 11

Lion & Unicorn

(01786) 850204 – www.lion-unicorn.co.uk

Main Street (A873); FK8 3PJ

Busy, interesting pub with emphasis on its home-made food; friendly staff and bedrooms

Parts of this neatly kept inn date from 1635 and there's an original fireplace with a log fire in a high brazier almost big enough to drive a car into. The back bar has pubby character, some exposed stone walls, wooden flooring and stools lined along the counter where they keep An Teallach Ale and Caledonian Deuchars IPA on handpump and several wines by the glass; log fires. This opens to a games room with a pool table, juke box, fruit machine, darts, TV and board games. The more restaurant-feeling beamed and carpeted front room is traditionally furnished and set for dining; background music. Outside there are benches in a gravelled garden and a lawn with a play area for children.

Popular food includes breaded mushrooms with garlic mayonnaise, haggis fritters with whisky, honey and grain mustard dip, three-cheese macaroni with parmesan crust, chicken, leek and mushroom pie, steak burger with toppings and chips, roast rib-eye of beef with yorkshire pudding and red wine gravy, beer-battered haddock and chips, chicken topped with haggis and wrapped in bacon with creamy whisky sauce, and puddings such as sticky toffee pudding and assorted ice-creams. *Benchmark main dish: pork loin with honey and mustard glaze £9.75. Two-course evening meal £19.00.*

Free house ~ Licensee Fiona Stevenson ~ Real ale ~ Open 12-midnight (1am Fri, Sat) ~ Bar food 12-9 ~ Restaurant ~ Children welcome ~ Dogs allowed in bar ~ Wi-fi ~ Bedrooms: £55/£75 *Recommended by Lindy Andrews, Anne and Ben Smith, John Evans*

WEEM   NN8449 Map 11

Ailean Chraggan ♀

(01887) 820346 – www.aileanchraggan.co.uk

B846; PH15 2LD

Changing range of seasonal food in family-run hotel; bedrooms

There are fine views from the flower-filled covered terrace and garden behind this friendly little hotel to the mountains beyond the Tay up to Ben Lawers (the highest peak in this part of Scotland). The busy bar has a chatty feel and a wide mix of customers, changing guest ales from Inveralmond and Strathbraan on handpump and over 100 malt whiskies; winter darts. There's also an adjoining neatly old-fashioned dining room and a comfortable carpeted modern lounge. The bedrooms are warm and spacious and the breakfasts very tasty; the owners can arrange fishing nearby.

Rewarding food includes local seafood and game and dishes might include sandwiches, prawn and monkfish ravioli with saffron butter, pigeon breast with black pudding and apple and celery rémoulade, venison burger with toppings and chips, beer-battered haddock and chips, scallops with white wine sauce and potato gratin, bacon-wrapped pork fillet with potato rösti and meat juices, and puddings such as crème brûlée and a changing pannacotta. *Benchmark main dish: venison haunch £17.95. Two-course evening meal £20.00.*

Free house ~ Licensee Alastair Gillespie ~ Real ale ~ Open 12-11; 4.30-11 Mon, Tues; closed Mon and Tues lunchtimes ~ Bar food 12-2, 6-8.30 (9 Sat) ~ Restaurant ~ Children welcome ~ Dogs allowed in bar and bedrooms ~ Wi-fi ~ Bedrooms: £70/£110 *Recommended by Isobel Mackinlay, Neil and Angela Huxter, John Evans*

Also Worth a Visit in Scotland

Besides the fully inspected pubs, you might like to try these pubs that have been recommended to us and described by readers. Do tell us what you think of them: feedback@goodguides.com

ABERDEENSHIRE

ABERDEEN   NJ9305
Grill (01224) 573530
Union Street; AB11 6BA Don't be put off by the exterior of this 19th-c granite building – the remodelled 1920s interior is well worth a look; long wood-floored bar with fine moulded ceiling, mahogany panelling and original button-back leather wall benches, ornate servery with glazed cabinets housing some of the 500 or so whiskies (a few dating from the 1930s, and 60 from around the world), five well kept ales including Caledonian 80/- and Harviestoun Bitter & Twisted, basic snacks; no children or dogs; open all day. *(Dave Sutton)*

ABERDEEN   NJ9406
★ **Prince of Wales** (01224) 640597
St Nicholas Lane; AB10 1HF Individual and convivial old tavern with eight changing ales from very long counter, bargain hearty food, painted floorboards, flagstones or carpet, pews and screened booths, original tiled spitoon running length of bar; live acoustic music Sun evening, quiz Mon, games machines; children over 5 welcome if eating, open all day from 10am (11am Sun). *(Laura Reid)*

ABOYNE   NO5298
★ **Boat** (01339) 886137
Charlestown Road (B968, just off A93); AB34 5EL Friendly country inn with fine views across River Dee; refurbished bare-boards bar with contemporary paintwork, scatter cushions on built-in wall seats, antlers, animal hides and scottish pictures, model train chugging its way around just below ceiling height, woodburner in stone fireplace, three well kept ales, decent wines and some 30 malt whiskies, tasty bar food from 7am breakfast on, more elaborate seasonal evening menu, spiral stairs up to roomy additional dining area; background music, games in public bar end; children welcome, dogs in bar, six comfortable well equipped bedrooms, open all day. *(Laura Reid)*

ALFORD   NJ5617
Forbes Arms (01975) 562108
A944; by the bridge; AB33 8QJ Small riverside hotel with two bars, restaurant and conservatory, good value pubby food including high teas, a changing scottish ale; projector for sports; seats in garden sloping down to River Don (fishing permits available), nine comfortable bedrooms, open all day. *(David and Betty Gittins)*

BALMEDIE   NJ9619
Cock & Bull (01358) 743249
A90 N of Balmedie; AB23 8XY Pleasant atmosphere and interesting décor in this food-led country pub, a well kept ale such as Burnside and good locally sourced food, obliging attentive service, beamed log-fire lounge, restaurant and conservatory; children and dogs (in bar) welcome, four bedrooms in converted cottage, open (and food) all day. *(Mandy Davidson)*

OLDMELDRUM   NJ8127
Redgarth (01651) 872353
Kirk Brae, off A957; AB51 0DJ Good-sized comfortable lounge with traditional décor and subdued lighting, two or three well kept ales and good range of malt whiskies (village distillery), popular reasonably priced food, friendly attentive service, restaurant; children welcome, lovely views to Bennachie, bedrooms (get booked quickly). *(William Slade)*

PENNAN   NJ8465
Pennan Inn (01346) 561201
Just off B9031 Banff–Fraserburgh; AB43 6JB Whitewashed building in long row of old fishermen's cottages, wonderful spot right by the sea – scenes from the film *Local Hero* (1983) shot here; small bar with simple furniture and exposed stone walls, modern décor in separate restaurant, enjoyable sensibly priced food from shortish menu including some thai dishes, at least one real ale, friendly service; five bedrooms, at foot of steep winding road and parking along front limited, closed Mon, shut out of season. *(Lance and Sarah Milligan)*

ANGUS

BROUGHTY FERRY   NO4630
★ **Fishermans Tavern**
(01382) 775941 *Fort Street; turning off shore road; DD5 2AD* Once a row of fishermen's cottages, this friendly pub is just steps away from the beach; up to eight well kept changing ales (May beer festival) and good range of malt whiskies, secluded lounge area with coal fire, small carpeted snug with basket-weave wall panels, another fire in back bar popular with diners for the wide choice of reasonably priced pubby food (offers available – check website), TV, fruit machine; children and dogs welcome, disabled facilities, tables on front pavement, more in secluded little walled garden, 12 bedrooms, open all day (till 1am Thurs-Sat). *(Jimmy Lothian)*

CLOVA   NO3273

Glen Clova Hotel   (01575) 550350

B955 NW of Wheen; DD8 4QS Tucked-away 19th-c hotel's unpretentious climbers' bar; flagstones, bench seats and woodburner in stone fireplace, assorted bric-a-brac and old photographs, a couple of well kept changing beers, 18 malts and plenty of wines by the glass, good food (same menu as their restaurant), friendly staff; children and dogs welcome, ten bedrooms, eight garden lodges and a bunkhouse, glorious walks nearby, open all day. *(Pat and Stewart Gordon)*

ARGYLL

ARDFERN   NM8004

Galley of Lorne   (01852) 500284

B8002; village and inn signposted off A816 Lochgilphead–Oban; PA31 8QN 17th-c drovers' inn on edge of Loch Craignish, cosy beamed and flagstoned bar with warming log fire, some black panelling and unfussy assortment of furniture including settles, up to four real ales and 50 whiskies, good choice of food from lunchtime sandwiches up, lounge bar with woodburner and spacious picture-window restaurant; background music, small pool room, darts, games machine, sports TV; good sea and loch views from sheltered terrace and deck, seven bedrooms in extension, open all day summer. *(Laura Reid)*

BRIDGE OF ORCHY   NN2939

★ Bridge of Orchy Hotel

(01838) 400208   *A82 Tyndrum–Glencoe; PA36 4AB* Spectacular spot on West Highland Way, very welcoming with good fairly priced all-day food in bar, lounge and smarter restaurant, open fires, decent choice of well kept ales, house wines and malt whiskies, interesting mountain photos; dogs welcome; ten good bedrooms, more in airy riverside annexe. *(Alison and Michael Harper)*

CAIRNDOW   NN1811

★ Cairndow Stagecoach Inn

(01499) 600286   *Village and pub signed off A83; PA26 8BN* 17th-c coaching inn in wonderful position on edge of Loch Fyne, good sensibly priced food including local venison and fresh fish, ales from nearby Fyne and over 40 malt whiskies, friendly accommodating staff; children and dogs welcome, lovely peaceful lochside garden, 13 comfortable bedrooms, six more in modern annexe with balconies overlooking the water, good breakfast, open (and food) all day. *(Roy and Lindsey Fentiman, Pat and Stewart Gordon, David J Austin)*

CONNEL   NM9034

Oyster   (01631) 710666

A85, W of Connel Bridge; PA37 1PJ 18th-c pub opposite former ferry slipway, lovely view across the water (especially at sunset), decent-sized bar with friendly highland atmosphere, log fire in stone fireplace, café with cakes, ice-cream and coffees, enjoyable food including excellent local seafood, Caledonian Deuchars IPA, good range of wines and malts, attentive service; sports TV, pool and darts; modern hotel part with 16 attractive bedrooms with separate evening restaurant. *(Alison and Michael Harper)*

GLENCOE   NN1058

★ Clachaig   (01855) 811252

Old Glencoe Road, behind NTS Visitor Centre; PH49 4HX 18th-c climbers' and walkers' inn surrounded by the scenic grandeur of Glencoe; Boots Bar with 14 scottish ales, some 300 malts and increasing range of artisan gins, vodkas and rums from across Scotland, slate-floored snug with whisky barrel-panelled walls and open fire, lounge (children allowed here) with mix of tables and booths, photos signed by famous climbers and local artwork, hearty food; background music, live bands Sat, pool, free wi-fi; dogs welcome, comfortable bedrooms in adjoining hotel plus self-catering, open (and food) all day. *(Isobel Mackinlay)*

INVERARAY   NN0908

★ George   (01499) 302111

Main Street East; PA32 8TT Very popular Georgian hotel (packed in high season) at hub of this appealing small town; pubby bar with exposed joists, bare stone walls, old tiles and big flagstones, antique settles, carved wooden benches and cushioned stone slabs along the walls, four log and peat fires, a couple of real ales and 100 malt whiskies, good food in bar and smarter restaurant, newish conservatory; live entertainment Fri, Sat; children and dogs welcome, well laid-out terraces with plenty of seats, bedrooms, Inveraray Castle and walks close by, open all day till 1am. *(William Slade)*

OBAN   NM8530

Cuan Mor   (01631) 565078

George Street; PA34 5SD Contemporary quayside bar-restaurant with lots of kitchen-style chairs and tables on bare boards, snug bar with open fire, over 100 malts and their own-brewed ales, wide choice of competitively priced food all day from sizeable menu, friendly service; children welcome, some seats outside. *(Laura Reid)*

OBAN   NM8529

Lorne   (01631) 570020

Stevenson Street; PA34 5NA Victorian décor including tiles and island bar with ornate brasswork, well kept Oban Bay ales, reasonably priced food such as pies and burgers, good service; live music and DJs at weekends, Weds quiz; children welcome, sheltered beer garden with contemporary chairs and tables, open all day till late. *(Dr Simon Innes)*

OTTER FERRY   NR9384

Oystercatcher (01700) 821229

B8000, by the water; PA21 2DH Some
renovation under new management; pub-
restaurant in old building in outstanding spot
overlooking Loch Fyne, good food using local
fish and shellfish, well kept ales including
Fyne from pine-clad bar, decent wine list,
friendly staff; dogs welcome in bar; lots of
tables out on spit, free moorings, open all day
(closed Weds). *(Darren and Jane Staniforth)*

PORT APPIN   NM9045

Pierhouse (01631) 730302

*In Appin, turn right at the Port Appin/
Lismore Ferry sign; PA38 4DE* Beautiful
location overlooking Loch Linnhe to Lismore
and beyond, smallish bar with attractive
terrace, good range of wines and beers, 90
malt whiskies and 25 gins (many scottish),
excellent seafood (plus other bar food),
picture-window restaurant taking in the fine
view, helpful friendly staff; children welcome,
12 comfortable bedrooms, moorings for
visiting yachts, open all day. *(Pat and
Stewart Gordon)*

TARBERT   NR8365

West Loch Hotel (01880) 820283

A83, a mile S; PA29 6YF Friendly
18th-c family-run inn overlooking sea loch,
comfortably updated with exposed stone
walls, pale-topped tables and high-backed
dark dining chairs, relaxing lounges with
fine views or open fire, enjoyable food using
local produce, Belhaven and good selection
of whiskies and gins, helpful cheerful service;
children and dogs welcome, eight bedrooms
(some with loch view), handy for ferry
terminal. *(M J Winterton)*

TAYVALLICH   NR7487

Tayvallich Inn (01546) 870282

B8025; PA31 8PL Small single-storey
conversion by Loch Sween specialising in
good local seafood; pale pine furnishings
on quarry tiles, local nautical charts, good
range of whiskies and usually a couple of
beers from Loch Ness, friendly atmosphere;
background music (live first Fri of month);
children and dogs welcome, a few picnic-sets
on front deck with lovely views over yacht
anchorage, open all day. *(Laura Reid)*

AYRSHIRE

DUNURE   NS2515

Dunure (01292) 500549

Just off A719 SW of Ayr; KA7 4LN
Welcoming place attractively set by ruined
harbourside castle; updated bar, lounge and
restaurant, varied food including fresh fish/
seafood, good service, nice wines but no real
ales; courtyard tables, bedrooms and two
cottages, not far from Culzean Castle (NTS).
(Alan and Alice Morgan)

SORN   NS5526

Sorn Inn (01290) 551305

*Village signed from Mauchline (A76);
Main Street; KA5 6HU* Restaurant pub
in tiny conservation village, highly regarded
imaginative food from brasserie menu served up
in two restaurant areas, also smallish bar
serving Orkney ale, friendly staff; children
and dogs (not in restaurant) welcome,
comfortable well appointed bedrooms, good
breakfast, open (and food) all day weekends,
closed Mon. *(David and Betty Gittins)*

SYMINGTON   NS3831

Wheatsheaf (01563) 830307

*Just off A77 Ayr–Kilmarnock; Main
Street; KA1 5QB* Single-storey former
17th-c posting inn, charming and cosy,
with first class food (must book weekends)
including lunchtime/early evening set
menu, efficient friendly service, log fire;
children welcome, tables outside, quiet
pretty village, open (and food) all day.
(Alan and Alice Morgan)

BERWICKSHIRE

ALLANTON   NT8654

★Allanton Inn (01890) 818260

B6347 S of Chirnside; TD11 3JZ Well run
18th-c stone-built village inn with attractive
open-plan interior, very good fairly priced
food with emphasis on fresh fish/seafood
from daily changing menu, a couple of well
kept ales such as Born in the Borders, good
wine list and speciality gins, friendly efficient
service, cosy bare boards bar with scatter
cushions on bench seats, immaculate dining
areas, log fire; background music; children
welcome, no dogs inside, picnic-sets in
sheltered garden behind, nice views, seven
bedrooms, open all day. *(Dr Peter Crawshaw,
Michael Doswell)*

AUCHENCROW   NT8560

Craw (01890) 761253

*B6438 NE of Duns; pub signed off A1;
TD14 5LS* Delightful little 18th-c village
pub in row of cream-washed slate-roofed
cottages, friendly and welcoming, with
enjoyable well presented food including fresh
fish and speciality pies, changing ales from
smaller brewers (Nov beer festival), good
wine list, beams decorated with hundreds
of pump clips, pictures on panelled walls,
woodburner, more formal back restaurant;
children welcome, tables on decking behind
and out on village green, three bedrooms
and self-catering, open all day weekends.
(Alistair Forsyth)

LAUDER   NT5347

Black Bull (01578) 722208

Market Place; TD2 6SR Comfortable
white-painted 18th-c inn festooned with
cheerful window boxes and hanging baskets,

cosy rustic-feel bar with country scenes on panelled walls, quieter room off and restaurant, well kept Stewart Edinburgh Gold and a local guest, enjoyable food using local seasonal produce, friendly service; background music, sports TV, free wi-fi; children and dogs (in bar) welcome, eight bedrooms, open (and food) all day. *(Phil and Jane Hodson)*

CAITHNESS

MEY   ND2872
Castle Arms (01847) 851244
A836; KW14 8XH 19th-c former coaching inn, enjoyable home-made food (evening restaurant but may be shut winter – check website), friendly helpful service, lounge bar with plenty of malt whiskies (no real ales), views of Dunnet Head and across Pentland Firth to the Orkneys; seven comfortable bedrooms and two suites in back extension (one with disabled facilities), well placed for N coast of Caithness, Gills Bay ferry and Castle of Mey. *(Helena and Trevor Fraser)*

DUMFRIESSHIRE

BARGRENNAN   NX3576
House O' Hill (01671) 840243
Off A714, road opposite church; DG8 6RN Small pub on edge of Galloway Forest (good mountain biking) with enthusiastic owners, interesting well cooked/priced food using local seasonal produce (best to book), a couple of real ales and good wine list, friendly helpful staff; two comfortable bedrooms (good breakfast) and self-catering cottage, open all day. *(Mike Benton)*

BEATTOCK   NT0702
Old Stables (01683) 300134
Smith Way; 0.25 mile from M74 junction 15; DG10 9QX Turreted 19th-c village-edge pub, bargain home-cooked food served by friendly staff, Belhaven beers, restaurant with gingham-clothed tables and railway memorabilia (the old Beattock line was famous for its steep gradients); pool, darts, big-screen TVs and fruit machine; covered outside seating area, three bedrooms and parking for campervans, open all day. *(Phil and Jane Hodson)*

DUMFRIES   NX9776
★**Cavens Arms** (01387) 252896
Buccleuch Street; DG1 2AH Good generously served home-made food (not Mon) from pubby standards up, seven well kept interesting ales, traditional ciders and fine choice of malts, friendly landlord and good attentive service, civilised front part with lots of wood, drinkers' area at back with bar stools, banquettes and traditional cast-iron tables, more recently added lounge/restaurant areas; discreet TV; no children

or dogs allowed, disabled facilities, small terrace at back, open all day and can get very busy. *(Dr J Barrie Jones)*

DUMFRIES   NX9775
Globe (01387) 252335
High Street; DG1 2JA Proper town pub with strong Burns connections, especially in the dark-panelled 17th-century snug and little museum-like room beyond; main part is more modern in feel; ales such as Caledonian and Sulwath, plenty of whiskies and good value pubby food (evening by arrangement), friendly service; live music Mon, children welcome in eating areas, terrace seating, open all day. *(Jimmy Lothian)*

DUNBARTONSHIRE

ARROCHAR   NN2903
Village Inn (01301) 702279
A814, just off A83 W of Loch Lomond; G83 7AX Friendly, cosy and interesting with well kept ales such as Caledonian and Fyne and several dozen malts, good hearty home-made food in simple dining area (gets booked up) with heavy beams, bare boards, panelling and roaring fire, steps down to unpretentious bar, fine sea and hill views; background music; children welcome in eating areas till 8pm, no dogs, tables out on deck and lawn, neat, comfortable bedrooms including more spacious ones in former back barn, good breakfast, open (and food) all day. *(Tim Sayers)*

EAST LOTHIAN

ABERLADY   NT4679
Old Aberlady (01875) 870503
Main Street; EH32 0NF In pretty coastal village with lots to do nearby; varied choice of enjoyable food including breakfast from 8am, Caledonian Deuchars IPA and a guest, good wine and whisky selection, friendly staff; children and dogs welcome, six bedrooms, open (and food) all day. *(Alistair Forsyth)*

GULLANE   NT4882
Golf (01620) 843259
Main Street; A198; EH31 2AB Ivy-clad inn dating from 1836 with two bars and restaurant, Belhaven IPA and maybe a guest, good food cooked by manager-chef (former *MasterChef* winner), modern décor with golfing theme, open fires; live music, sports on big projector screen in one bar along with pool and darts; children and dogs welcome, sheltered paved terrace, bedrooms (some in separate cottage), open all day from 7am. *(Elisa Cordial)*

GULLANE   NT4882
★**Old Clubhouse** (01620) 842008
East Links Road; EH31 2AF Single-storey building in nice position overlooking Gullane

Links, cosy bar and more formal dining room, seating from wooden dining chairs and banquettes to big squashy leather armchairs and sofas, Victorian pictures and cartoons, stuffed birds, sheet music covers, golfing and other memorabilia, open fires, good choice of food including specials, Caledonian Deuchars IPA, Timothy Taylors Landlord and a couple of guests, nice house wines, friendly helpful service; children and dogs (in bar) welcome, plenty of seats out at front, open (and food) all day. *(Alistair Forsyth, Paul Baxter)*

HADDINGTON
NT5173
Victoria (01620) 823332
Court Street; EH41 3JD Popular bar-restaurant with good imaginative local food cooked by chef-landlord, Belhaven ales and short but decent wine list, prompt friendly service, mix of cushioned dining chairs and wall banquettes on wooden flooring or carpets, woodburning stove; five bedrooms, open all day. *(Comus and Sarah Elliott)*

HADDINGTON
NT5173
Waterside (01620) 825674
Waterside; just off A6093, over pedestrian bridge at E end of town; EH41 4AT Attractively set riverside dining pub next to historic bridge, spacious but cosy modernised interior, enjoyable bistro-style food (steak night Thurs), three changing ales from smaller brewers and good wine choice, pleasant friendly staff; open mike Sun afternoon; children welcome (family room with toys), dogs allowed, picnic-sets out overlooking the River Tyne. *(Comus and Sarah Elliott)*

FIFE

CULROSS
NS9885
Red Lion (01383) 880225
Low Causeway; KY12 8HN Convivial old pub in pretty NTS village, good value food, a beer from Inveralmond and several wines by the glass, beams and amazing painted ceilings; seats outside, open (and food) all day. *(Brian and Anna Marsden)*

CUPAR
NO3714
Boudingait (01334) 654681
Bonnygate; KY15 4BU Bustling bar with captain's and cushion-seated chairs around dark tables on wood flooring, open fire, high chairs against counter serving a couple of changing ales, good variety of well liked reasonably priced traditional food (something available all day), friendly attentive staff; live folk and quiz nights; children welcome. *(Laura Reid)*

ELIE
NO4999
Ship (01333) 330246
The Toft, off A917 (High Street) towards harbour; KY9 1DT Refurbished inn in great position for enjoying a drink

overlooking the sandy bay; bar and two restaurants (one upstairs), generally well liked food, friendly service; children and dogs welcome, seats on terrace (own bar) looking out to stone granary and pier, maybe beach cricket, six boutique-style bedrooms, open all day. *(Brian and Anna Marsden, Pat and Stewart Gordon)*

ST ANDREWS
NO5116
Central (01334) 478296
Market Street; KY16 9NU Traditional Victorian town-centre pub (Taylor Walker) with good choice of english and scottish beers from island servery, knowledgeable friendly staff, fair-priced pubby food from sandwiches up, busy mix of customers; pavement tables, open all day. *(Laura Reid)*

INVERNESS-SHIRE

ARDGOUR
NN0163
Inn at Ardgour (01855) 841225
From A82 follow signs for Strontian A861 and take Corran Ferry across loch to the inn; note that ferry does not sail over Christmas period; PH33 7AA Traditional fairly remote roadside inn by Corran Ferry slipway; enjoyable food and decent beer and whisky choice, friendly accommodating staff, restaurant; children and well behaved dogs welcome, a few tables outside, fine Loch Linnhe views, clean bedrooms (dogs allowed in some), open all day. *(Lance and Sarah Milligan)*

AVIEMORE
NH8612
Cairngorm (01479) 810233
Grampian Road (A9); PH22 1PE Large flagstoned bar in traditional turreted hotel, lively and friendly, with good value food from wide-ranging menu using local produce, Cairngorm ales and good choice of other drinks, prompt helpful service, tartan-walled and carpeted restaurant; regular live music, sports TV; children welcome, comfortable smart bedrooms (some with stunning views), open (and food) all day. *(William Slade)*

CARRBRIDGE
NH9022
Cairn (01479) 841212
Main Road; PH23 3AS Welcoming traditionally furnished hotel bar, enjoyable pubby food using local produce, three well kept ales including Cairngorm, old local pictures, warm coal fire, separate more formal dining room; pool and sports TV; children and dogs welcome, seats and tables out in front, seven comfortable bedrooms, open all day. *(William Slade)*

DORES
NH5934
★Dores (01463) 751203
B852 SW of Inverness; IV2 6TR Traditional country pub with exposed stone walls and low ceilings in delightful spot on the shore of Loch Ness; small attractive bar

on right with two or three well kept changing scottish ales and several whiskies, two-part dining area to the left serving good food from breakfasts and pub favourites up, friendly staff; children and dogs welcome, sheltered front garden, more tables out behind taking in the spectacular view, open (and food) all day. *(The Dutchman)*

FORT WILLIAM NN1274
Ben Nevis Inn (01397) 701227
N off A82: Achintee; PH33 6TE Roomy, well converted, raftered stone barn in stunning spot by path up to Ben Nevis, good mainly straightforward food (lots of walkers so best to book), ales such as Cairngorm and Isle of Skye, prompt cheery service, bare-boards dining area with steps up to bar; live music (Tues in summer, first and third Thurs in winter); children welcome, no dogs, seats out at front and back, bunkhouse below, open all day Apr-Oct, otherwise closed Mon-Weds. *(William Slade)*

GLEN SHIEL NH0711
Cluanie Inn (01320) 340238
A87 Invergarry–Kyle of Lochalsh, on Loch Cluanie; IV63 7YW Welcoming inn in lovely isolated setting by Loch Cluanie with stunning views; friendly table service for drinks including well kept Isle of Skye and excellent malt whisky range, enjoyable food (good local game and salmon) in three knocked-together rooms and restaurant, warm log fire, two chatty parrots in lobby; children allowed, dogs too (owners have several of their own), big comfortable pine-furnished modern bedrooms, self-catering club house, good breakfast (non-residents welcome), open all day. *(Dave Sutton)*

GLENFINNAN NM9080
Glenfinnan House (01397) 722235
Take A830 off A32 to Glenfinnan, turn left after Glenfinnan Monument Visitors Centre; PH37 4LT Beautifully placed 18th-c hotel by Loch Shiel, traditional bar with well kept ales and over 50 whiskies, good well presented food including fish/seafood dishes and local venison, restaurant; lawns down to the water, comfortable bedrooms, may close during the winter. *(M J Winterton)*

GLENUIG NM6576
Glenuig Inn (01687) 470219
A861 SW of Lochailort, off A830 Fort William–Mallaig; PH38 4NG Friendly bar on picturesque bay, enjoyable locally sourced food including some from next-door smokery, well kept Cairngorm ales and a scottish cider on tap, lots of bottled beers and good range of whiskies, woodburner in dining room; dogs welcome, bedrooms in adjoining block, also bunkhouse popular with walkers and divers, moorings for visiting yachts, open (and food) all day. *(William Slade)*

INVERIE NG7500
★ Old Forge (01687) 462267
Park in Mallaig for ferry; PH41 4PL Utterly remote waterside stone pub with stunning views across Loch Nevis; comfortable mix of old furnishings, lots of charts and sailing prints, open fire, good reasonably priced bar food including fresh local seafood (excellent langoustines) and venison burgers, a well kept house beer (Remoteness IPA) and other draught beers, lots of whiskies and good wine choice, restaurant extension, live music and ceilidhs (instruments provided); the snag is getting there – boat (jetty moorings and new pier), Mallaig foot-ferry six times a day (four in winter) or 15-mile walk through Knoydart from nearest road; children and dogs welcome, six bedrooms (get booked early), closed Weds, otherwise open all day from 2.30pm, evening food only in winter. *(David Todd)*

INVERMORISTON NH4216
Glenmoriston Arms (01320) 351206
A82/A887; IV63 7YA Small civilised hotel dating in part from 1740 when it was a drovers' inn, bare-boards bar with open fire and big old stag's head, neatly laid out restaurant with antique rifles, a well kept beer such as Orkney and over 100 malt whiskies, enjoyable food from lunchtime sandwiches to local fish and shellfish (not lunchtime Oct-Mar), friendly staff; handy for Loch Ness, ten bedrooms (three in converted outbuilding). *(Dave Sutton)*

INVERNESS NH6645
Number 27 (01463) 241999
Castle Street; IV2 3DU Busy pub opposite the castle, friendly and welcoming, with plenty of draught and bottled beer and good choice of well liked/priced food including Mon steak night, restaurant at back; open (and food) all day. *(The Dutchman)*

INVERNESS NH6645
Phoenix Ale House (01463) 240300
Academy Street; IV1 1LX Bare-boards 1890s bar with fine oval servery, up to ten real ales and enjoyable well priced food, neatly furnished adjoining dining room; sports TV; open (and food) all day. *(Pat and Stewart Gordon)*

MALLAIG NM6796
Steam (01687) 462002
Davies Brae; PH41 4PU Victorian inn run by mother and daughter, good choice of food including freshly landed fish (takeaway menu too), speedy service, bar with open fire and pool, split-level restaurant with high-backed dark leather chairs around pale tables on floorboards; live music; children and dogs welcome, tables in back garden, five neat bedrooms (no breakfast). *(Tim Sayer)*

ONICH NN0263
Four Seasons (01855) 821393
Off A82, signed for Inchree, N of village;
PH33 6SE Wooden building – part of
Inchree holiday complex; bare-boards bar
with cushioned wall benches, dining area
with unusual central log fire, up to three
scottish ales and decent choice of whiskies,
generous varied evening food at reasonable
prices, local maps and guidebooks for sale,
daily weather forecast and free wi-fi; children
(till 8.30pm) and dogs welcome, hostel, lodge
and chalet accommodation, handy for Corran
Ferry, open all day in season (when can be
very busy), check winter opening.
(Mike Benton)

WHITEBRIDGE NH4815
Whitebridge (01456) 486226
B862 SW of village; IV2 6UN Old-style
hunting, shooting and fishing hotel set in
the foothills of the Monadhliath Mountains,
popular and cheerful, with good home-made
food, well kept ales such as Cairngorm,
Cromarty and Loch Ness and around 50
malts, two bars with woodburners, summer
restaurant; dogs welcome, 12 bedrooms,
open all day in summer, all day weekends
winter. *(John Poulter)*

KINCARDINESHIRE

FETTERCAIRN NO6573
Ramsay Arms (01561) 340334
Burnside Road; AB30 1XX Hotel with
decent food in tartan-carpeted bar and smart
oak-panelled restaurant, friendly service,
well kept ales and several malts including the
local Fettercairn; children welcome, picnic-
sets in garden, attractive village (liked by
Queen Victoria who stayed at the hotel),
12 comfortable bedrooms, good breakfast.
(Jack Trussler)

STONEHAVEN NO8595
★ Lairhillock (01569) 730001
Netherley; 6 miles N of Stonehaven,
6 miles S of Aberdeen, take the Durris
turn-off from the A90; AB39 3QS
Extended 200-year-old family-run inn;
cheerful beamed bar with dark woodwork,
panelled wall benches and attractive
mix of old seats, lots of brass and copper
items and nice open fire, Timothy Taylors
Landlord and guests, several wines by
the glass, good malt whiskies, interesting
food including own-smoked salmon,
spacious lounge with unusual central fire,
panoramic views from back conservatory;
children and dogs (in bar) welcome, open
all day. *(Gus Swan, Neil Allen)*

STONEHAVEN NO8785
Marine Hotel (01569) 762155
Shore Head; AB39 2JY Popular
harbourside pub with six well kept ales
including own Dunnottar brews, 170 bottled
belgian beers and plenty of whiskies, good
food especially local fish/seafood, efficient
service, large stripped-stone bar with log
fire in cosy side room, upstairs sea-view
restaurant; live acoustic music last Thurs of
month; children welcome, pavement tables,
bedrooms, open all day (till 1am Fri, Sat).
(Gus Swan)

KINROSS-SHIRE

KINNESSWOOD NO1801
Well Country Inn (01592) 840444
A911; Scotlandwell; KY13 9JA Welcoming
old pub in centre of village, comfortable
lounge with open fire, good selection of
scottish ales, malt whiskies and wines,
enjoyable food served by pleasant helpful
staff, small restaurant; children welcome,
nine bedrooms (six in separate annexe).
(J V Dadswell)

KIRKCUDBRIGHTSHIRE

CASTLE DOUGLAS NX7662
Sulwath Brewery (01556) 504525
King Street; DG7 1DT Convivial bar
attached to this small brewery, six Sulwath
ales in top condition and their bottled beers,
Weston's cider, limited food (hot pies), stools
and barrel tables, off-sales and souvenirs,
brewery tours Mon and Fri at 1pm (unless by
prior arrangement); dogs welcome, disabled
access, open 10am-6pm Mon-Sat. *(Giles and
Annie Francis)*

GATEHOUSE OF FLEET NX6056
Masonic Arms (01557) 814335
Ann Street; off B727; DG7 2HU Spacious
dining pub with comfortable two-room pubby
bar, traditional seating, pictures on timbered
walls, plates on delft shelf, stuffed fish above
brick fireplace (open fire), a couple of real
ales and good choice of malts, enjoyable
food in bar and contemporary restaurant,
curry night Weds, attractive terracotta-tiled
conservatory with cane furniture; background
music (live Thurs), quiz Fri, free wi-fi;
children and dogs welcome, picnic-sets under
parasols in neatly kept sheltered garden,
more seats in front, open all day. *(Alan and
Alice Morgan)*

GATEHOUSE OF FLEET NX5956
Ship (01557) 814217
Fleet Street; DG7 2JT Late Victorian
village inn on the banks of the River Fleet,
popular food, Belhaven beers, 200 malt
whiskies and several local artisan gins,
neatly kept interior with woodburner,
restaurant, pleasant service; waterside
garden, comfortable bedrooms and good
breakfast; Dorothy Sayers wrote *Five
Red Herrings* while staying here in the
1930s. *(Mike Benton)*

KIPPFORD
NX8355

Anchor (01556) 620205
Off A710 S of Dalbeattie; DG5 4LN
Popular waterfront inn overlooking yachting estuary and peaceful hills, nautical theme décor and slightly old-fashioned feel, open fire in small traditional back bar with local photographs, more tables in area off, bright roomy dining room, good choice of generously served pubby food including local fish, two or three ales such as Harviestoun and Sulwath, lots of malts; background music, TV; children and dogs welcome, tables out at front, good walks and bird-watching, on Seven Stanes cycle route, seven bedrooms, open all day in summer. *(David and Betty Gittins)*

KIRKCUDBRIGHT
NX6850

Selkirk Arms (01557) 330402
High Street; DG6 4JG Comfortable well run 18th-c hotel in pleasant spot by mouth of the Dee, simple locals' front bar (own street entrance), partitioned high-ceilinged and tartan-carpeted lounge with upholstered armchairs, wall banquettes and paintings for sale, ales including a house beer from local Sulwath, enjoyable food in bistro and restaurant from pub standards up, efficient service; background music, TV; children (not in bar) and dogs welcome, smart wooden furniture under blue parasols in neat garden with 15th-c font, 16 comfortable bedrooms, open all day. *(R A and E J Harkness)*

LANARKSHIRE

BALMAHA
NS4290

Oak Tree (01360) 870357
B837; G63 0JQ Family-run slate-clad inn on Loch Lomond's quiet side; beams, timbers and panelling, pubby bar with lots of old photographs, farm tools and collection of grandfather clocks, log fire, good choice of enjoyable food from sandwiches and snacks up, own-brew scottish ales and good whisky selection, restaurant, coffee shop and ice-cream parlour, village shop; children welcome, plenty of tables out around ancient oak tree, popular with West Highland Way walkers, seven attractive bedrooms, two bunkhouses and four cottages. *(Sophia and Hamish Greenfield)*

BIGGAR
NT0437

Crown (01899) 220116
High Street (A702); ML12 6DL
Friendly old pub with enjoyable food all day including home-made burgers and pizzas, Sun carvery, two well kept changing ales, open fire in beamed front bar, panelled lounge with old local pictures, restaurant; fortnightly acoustic music, Thurs poker night; children welcome, open (and food) all day. *(Simon Sharpe)*

FINTRY
NS6186

Fintry (01360) 860224
Main Street; G63 0XA Recently refurbished village pub with enjoyable food and beers from on-site microbrewery, friendly relaxed atmosphere; live traditional music Weds evening and Sun afternoon, quiz last Mon of the month; children welcome, dogs in pool room or suntrap back garden, open all day. *(Martin Turner)*

GLASGOW
NS5767

Belle (0141) 339 2299
Great Western Road; G12 8HX Busy pub with wide mix of customers; leather-topped stools, modern and traditional chairs around all sorts of tables on polished wood floor, stags' heads and unusual mirrors on painted or exposed stone walls, open fire, american craft beers and European lagers; dogs welcome, tables and chairs on pavement and in tiny leafy back garden. *(Belinda May)*

GLASGOW
NS5965

Counting House (0141) 225 0160
St Vincent Place/George Square; G1 2DH Wetherspoons bank conversion, imposing interior rising into lofty richly decorated coffered ceiling culminating in great central dome, big windows, decorative glasswork, wall-safes, several areas with solidly comfortable seating, smaller rooms (former managers' offices) around perimeter, one like a well stocked library, a few themed with pictures and prints of historical characters, real ales from far and wide, bottled beers and lots of malt whiskies, usual good value food all day; children welcome if eating, open 8am-midnight. *(Nick Higgins)*

GLASGOW
NS5865

Drum & Monkey (0141) 221 6636
St Vincent Street; G2 5TF Lively and busy Nicholsons bank conversion with ornate ceiling, granite pillars and lots of carved mahogany, Caledonian and other beers from island bar, decent range of wines and good value food, pleasant staff, quieter back area; open all day. *(Nick Higgins)*

GLASGOW
NS5865

Pot Still (0141) 333 0980
Hope Street; G2 2TH Comfortable and welcoming little pub with hundreds of malt whiskies (good value whisky of the month), traditional bare-boards interior with raised back area, button-back leather bench seats, dark panelling, etched and stained glass, columns up to ornately corniced ceiling, four changing ales and interesting bottled beers from nice old-fashioned servery, knowledgeable friendly staff; silent fruit machine; open all day and can get packed. *(Dr J Barrie Jones)*

GLASGOW
NS5965
★**Sloans** (0141) 221 8886
Argyle Arcade; G2 8BG Restored Grade
A listed building over three floors, many
original features including fine mahogany
staircase, etched glass, ornate woodwork and
moulded ceilings, ales such as Caledonian
and Kelburn, enjoyable modern food
in ground-floor bar-bistro and upstairs
restaurant, friendly staff; Tues film night and
other events in impressive barrel-vaulted
parquet-floored ballroom; children welcome,
tables in courtyard, weekend market, open
all day (till late Fri, Sat). *(Nick Higgins)*

GLASGOW
NS5865
State (0141) 332 2159
Holland Street; G2 4NG High-ceilinged
bar with marble pillars, lots of carved wood
including handsome oak island servery, half a
dozen or so well kept changing ales, bargain
basic lunchtime food from sandwiches
up (not weekends), some areas set for
dining, good atmosphere and friendly staff,
armchairs among other comfortable seats,
coal-effect gas fire in big wooden fireplace,
old prints and theatrical posters; background
music (live weekends and comedy nights),
silent sports TVs, games machine; open
all day. *(Steve McGann)*

GLASGOW
NS5666
Tennents (0141) 339 7203
Byres Road; G12 8TN Big busy high-
ceilinged Victorian corner pub near
university, ornate plasterwork, panelling
and paintings, traditional tables and chairs,
stools and wall seating, a dozen well kept
ales and keenly priced wines, wide range of
good value food from sandwiches and baked
potatoes up including bargain offers and
Sunday breakfast, basement bar for weekend
DJs and disco; sports TVs; open all day.
(Dr J Barrie Jones)

GLASGOW
NS5666
Three Judges (0141) 337 3055
*Dumbarton Road, opposite Byres Road;
G11 6PR* Traditional corner bar with up
to nine quickly changing ales from small
breweries far and wide (they get through
several hundred a year), farm cider, pump
clips on walls, friendly staff and locals, no
food; live jazz Sun afternoons; dogs welcome,
open all day. *(Steve McGann)*

MIDLOTHIAN

EDINBURGH
NT2574
★**Abbotsford** (0131) 225 5276
*Rose Street; E end, beside South St David
Street; EH2 2PR* Busy city pub with
unchanging feel; hefty Victorian island
bar (ornately carved from dark spanish
mahogany and highly polished) serving ales
such as Atlas, Caledonian, Fyne, Harviestoun,

Orkney and Stewart, also selection of bottled
american beers and around 70 malt whiskies,
traditional food, long wooden tables and
leatherette benches, high panelled walls and
handsome green and gold moulded ceiling,
smarter upstairs restaurant where children
allowed; open all day, food all day Fri, Sat.
(Nick Higgins)

EDINBURGH
NT2473
Blue Blazer (0131) 229 5030
Spittal Street/Bread Street; EH3 9DX
Traditional two-room drinkers' pub with up
to eight interesting scottish ales and fine
selection of rums (home of the Edinburgh
Rum Club), plenty of whiskies and gins too,
helpful knowledgeable staff, bare boards
and high ceilings, lots of black and white
photos, cartoons and drawings on the walls,
open fire; background and some live acoustic
music, TV; dogs welcome, open all day.
(Jeremy King)

EDINBURGH
NT2574
★**Café Royal** (0131) 556 1884
West Register Street; EH2 2AA
A favourite with readers and maintaining
its high standards; wonderful Victorian
baroque interior – floors and stairway
laid with marble, chandeliers hanging
from magnificent plasterwork ceilings,
superb series of Doulton tilework portraits
of historical innovators (Watt, Faraday,
Stephenson, Caxton, Benjamin Franklin
and Robert Peel), substantial island bar
serving well kept Greene King IPA, Belhaven
80/-, Stewart Edinburgh Gold and four
guests, several wines by the glass and 40
malts, very well liked food with emphasis
on fresh seafood, good friendly service, the
restaurant's stained glass is also worth a look
(children welcome here); background music;
open all day (till 1am Fri, Sat); can get very
busy. *(The Dutchman, Pat and Stewart Gordon,
Barry Collett, Comus and Sarah Elliott, Anthony,
Roger and Donna Huggins)*

EDINBURGH
NT2471
★**Canny Man's** (0131) 447 1484
*Morningside Road; aka Volunteer
Arms; EH10 4QU* Utterly individual and
distinctive, and always busy; saloon, lounge
and snug with fascinating bric-a-brac, ceiling
papered with sheet music, huge range of
appetising open sandwiches, lots of whiskies,
good wines and well kept ales such as
Caledonian and Timothy Taylors Landlord,
efficient friendly service; no credit cards,
mobile phones or backpackers; children
welcome, courtyard tables. *(Pat and Stewart
Gordon)*

EDINBURGH
NT2573
Deacon Brodies (0131) 225 6531
Lawnmarket; EH1 2NT Commemorating
the notorious highwayman town councillor
who was eventually hanged on the scaffold
he'd designed; very busy city bar with

wonderfully ornate high ceiling, well kept ales such as Belhaven and Caledonian from long counter, decent whisky selection, good choice of reasonably priced food in upstairs dining lounge where children allowed; background music, TV; pavement seating. *(Tony Scott)*

EDINBURGH NT2573
Doric (0131) 225 1084
Market Street; EH1 1DE Welcoming 17th-c pub-restaurant with plenty of atmosphere, simple furnishings in small bar with wood floor and lots of pictures, good range of changing ales and bottled beers, 50 single malts, friendly young staff, interesting modern food (must book) in upstairs wine bar (children welcome) and bistro; handy for Waverley station, open all day. *(Steve McGann)*

EDINBURGH NT2573
Ensign Ewart (0131) 225 7440
Lawnmarket, Royal Mile; last pub on right before castle; EH1 2PE Charming dimly lit old-world pub handy for castle (so gets busy), beams peppered with brasses, huge painting of Ewart at Waterloo capturing french banner, assorted furniture including elbow tables, well kept Caledonian ales and lots of whiskies, straightforward bar food; background and regular live music (not Tues, Thurs), games machine, keypad entry to lavatories; open all day. *(Nick Higgins)*

EDINBURGH NT2574
★**Guildford Arms** (0131) 556 4312
West Register Street; EH2 2AA Busy place with splendid Victorian décor; ornate painted plasterwork on lofty ceiling, dark mahogany fittings, tables and stools lined along towering arched windows, heavy swagged velvet curtains and a busy patterned carpet, Belhaven, Fyne, Oakham, Orkney, Mordue, Stewart and guests, ten wines by the glass, 50 malt whiskies and good range of rums and gins, decent food in snug upstairs gallery restaurant with modern décor (children allowed here); background music (live during Edinburgh Festival), TV, free wi-fi; dogs welcome, open all day. *(Brian and Anna Marsden, Dr J Barrie Jones, Dr Matt Burleigh, Barry Collett, Roger and Donna Huggins)*

EDINBURGH NT2573
★**Halfway House** (0131) 225 7101
Fleshmarket Close (steps between Cockburn Street and Market Street, opposite Waverley station); EH1 1BX Tiny one-room pub off steep steps, part carpeted, part tiled, with a few small tables and high-backed settles, lots of prints (some golf and railway themes), four well kept scottish ales and good range of malt whiskies, short choice of decent cheap food, friendly staff; dogs welcome, open (and food) all day. *(Dr J Barrie Jones)*

EDINBURGH NT2473
Hanging Bat (0131) 229 0759
Lothian Road; EH3 9AB Modern bar on three levels with own microbrewery, six real ales, 14 craft kegs and 120 bottled beers, food such as ribs and hot dogs; children till 8pm, open (and food) all day. *(Laura Reid)*

EDINBURGH NT2573
Inn on the Mile (0131) 556 9940
High Street; EH1 1LL Centrally placed pub-restaurant-boutique hotel in former bank, long high-ceilinged bar with booth seating, good selection of beers such as BrewDog, Caledonian, Harviestoun and Innis & Gunn, also a house beer (Mile Ale), plenty of wines, whiskies and cocktails, well priced food from panini to hearty helpings of pubby food, good friendly service; live music and quiz nights, big screens for sport, free wi-fi; children welcome, a few seats outside, nine bedrooms, open all day (till 1am Fri, Sat when can be lively). *(Nigel and Jean Eames)*

EDINBURGH NT2573
Jolly Judge (0131) 225 2669
James Court, by 495 Lawnmarket; EH1 2PB Small comfortable basement of 16th-c tenement with interesting fruit- and flower-painted wooden ceiling, welcoming relaxed atmosphere, two changing ales and good range of malts, lunchtime bar meals, log fire; no children, open all day. *(Giles and Annie Francis, Tony Scott)*

EDINBURGH NT2676
Kings Wark (0131) 554 9260
The Shore, Leith; EH6 6QU Enjoyable old bare-boards pub on Leith's restored waterfront; plenty of atmosphere in stripped-stone candlelit interior, good selection of well kept ales, interesting modern cooking including popular Sunday breakfasts, helpful friendly service, good value wines; seats outside, open all day. *(Nick Higgins)*

EDINBURGH NT1968
Kinleith Mill (0131) 453 3214
Lanark Road (A70); EH14 5EN Newly refurbished pub (was Kinleith Arms) with contemporary bar, well kept ales and popular food including early-bird menu; sports TV, darts; suntrap back garden; open all day. *(Jimmy Lothian)*

EDINBURGH NT2473
Oxford (0131) 539 7119
Young Street; EH2 4JB Friendly no-frills backstreet local with links to Ian Rankin/Inspector Rebus and other scottish writers and artists; tiny bustling bar with a couple of built-in wall settles, steps up to quieter back room, four well kept scottish beers and good range of whiskies; TV; no food or children, dogs welcome, open all day. *(Comus and Sarah Elliott)*

EDINBURGH NT2573

Sandy Bells (0131) 225 1156

Forrest Road; EH1 2QH Small unpretentious place popular for its nightly folk music, eight scottish ales and wide choice of whiskies (including whisky of the month), simple food, good mix of customers and friendly atmosphere; open all day. *(Giles and Annie Francis)*

EDINBURGH NT2374

Scran & Scallie (0131) 332 6281

Comely Bank Road; EH4 1DT Good food but also a proper bar serving scottish ales, impressive range of whiskies and inventive house cocktails, simple modern furnishings with tweed and tartan fabrics and the odd fur throw, sizeable dining area (and smaller room off) with mismatched wooden chairs around medley of tables, bare and painted brick walls, contemporary wallpaper and cream-coloured woodburner, helpful friendly service; children and dogs welcome, open all day weekends. *(Nick Higgins)*

EDINBURGH NT2872

Sheep Heid (0131) 661 7974

The Causeway, Duddingston; EH15 3QA Comfortably updated former coaching inn (part of the Village Pub & Kitchen chain) in lovely spot near King Arthur's Seat, long history and some famous guests such as Mary, Queen of Scots, fine rounded servery in main room, well kept beers and good, enterprising food including children's menu, friendly young staff, attractive dining rooms, skittle alley; courtyard tables, open (and food) all day. *(Adrian Johnson)*

EDINBURGH NT2574

Standing Order (0131) 225 4460

George Street; EH2 2LR Grand Wetherspoons bank conversion in three elegant Georgian houses, enormous main room with elaborate colourful ceiling, lots of tables and smaller side booths, other rooms including two with floor-to-ceiling bookshelves, comfortable clubby seats, various portraits and an Adam fireplace, wide range of real ales from long counter, usual bar food, gets very busy (particularly Sat night) but obliging staff cope well; weekend live music, sports TV, free wi-fi; children welcome, disabled facilities, open 8am-1am. *(Roger and Donna Huggins)*

EDINBURGH NT2574

★ **Starbank** (0131) 552 4141

Laverockbank Road, off Starbank Road, just off A901 Granton–Leith; EH5 3BZ Cheerful pub in a fine spot with terrific views over the Firth of Forth, long airy bare-boards bar with leather bench and tub seats, up to eight well kept ales and good choice of malt whiskies, interesting food (and set menus) in conservatory restaurant; background and regular live music and quiz nights, sports TV, fruit machine; children welcome till 9pm if dining, dogs on leads, sheltered back terrace, parking on adjacent hilly street, open all day. *(Alan and Alice Morgan)*

EDINBURGH NT2574

Stockbridge Tap (0131) 343 3000

Raeburn Place, Stockbridge; EH4 1HN Welcoming corner pub with traditional L-shaped interior, seven interesting beers from Scotland and further afield, good reasonably priced food (not Sun evening, Mon or Tues), friendly helpful staff; no children, dogs welcome, open all day (till 1am Fri, Sat). *(Anthony)*

MORAYSHIRE

FINDHORN NJ0464

Crown & Anchor (01309) 690243

Off A96; IV36 3YF Nice village setting adjacent to small sheltered harbour, enjoyable food including good fish/seafood specials, a couple of real ales and plenty of whiskies, woodburner in cosy bar; sports TV; children welcome (under-14s in conservatory and restaurant till 8pm), outside seating and smokers' shelter 'the Smokooterie', seven bedrooms, sand dune walks and good boating in Findhorn Bay, open all day. *(Martin and Alison Stainsby)*

PEEBLESSHIRE

INNERLEITHEN NT3336

★ **Traquair Arms** (01896) 830229

B709, just off A72 Peebles–Galashiels; follow signs for Traquair House; EH44 6PD Modernised inn at heart of pretty borders village, one of the few places serving Traquair ale (produced in original oak vessels in 18th-c brewhouse at nearby Traquair House), also Caledonian Deuchars IPA and Timothy Taylors Landlord, 40 malt whiskies, enjoyable italian-influenced food (all day weekends), main bar with warm open fire, another in relaxed bistro-style restaurant, good mix of customers; background music, TV; children welcome, dogs in bar, picnic-sets on neat back lawn, 14 bedrooms and six self-catering cottages, open all day. *(Helena and Trevor Fraser)*

PERTHSHIRE

BANKFOOT NO0635

Bankfoot (01738) 787243

Main Street; PH1 4AB Traditional coaching inn dating from 1760, two bars and

---

If you know a pub is ever open all day, please tell us.

restaurant, well kept local ales and enjoyable food cooked by landlady, friendly helpful staff, open fires; live folk night Weds; dogs welcome, six comfortable bedrooms, open all day weekends, closed lunchtimes Mon, Tues (food for residents only on those days). *(Julie Braeburn)*

BLAIR ATHOLL   NN8765

★**Atholl Arms** (01796) 481205
B8079; PH18 5SG Sizeable hotel with two cosy bar rooms (one beamed and tartan-carpeted), open fires, armchairs, sofas and traditional tables, chairs and benches, grand dining room with suit of armour and stag's head, four local Moulin ales, good well priced food all day using local salmon and meat, quick friendly service; 31 good value bedrooms, self-catering cottage, lovely setting near the castle. *(Jimmy Lothian)*

BRIG O' TURK   NN5306

★**Byre** (01877) 376292
A821 Callander–Trossachs, just outside village; FK17 8HT Beautifully placed byre conversion with slate-floored log-fire bar and roomier high-raftered restaurant, good popular food (best to book) including local game and fish, a couple of changing scottish ales and nice wines, friendly helpful staff; children welcome, outside tables and boules piste, lovely walks, closed Mon, Tues during winter (and all Jan), otherwise open all day. *(Paul Baxter)*

CALLANDER   NN6208

Old Rectory (01877) 339215
Leny Road (A84); FK17 8AL Friendly 19th-c stone inn away from the town centre, cosy bar with fine range of whiskies, good reasonably priced traditional food in small restaurant, pleasant helpful staff; live folk music Weds and some weekends, Tues quiz, free wi-fi; dogs welcome, four bedrooms, handy for Trossachs National Park, open all day. *(John Evans)*

DUNBLANE   NN7801

Tappit Hen (01786) 825226
Kirk Street; FK15 0AL
Across close from cathedral, small drinkers' pub with five changing ales and good range of malt whiskies, friendly busy atmosphere; traditional music Tues; open all day (till 1am Fri, Sat). *(Les and Sandra Brown)*

DUNKELD   NO0243

Atholl Arms (01350) 727219
Atholl Street (A923); PH8 0AQ Sizeable Victorian hotel with comfortably furnished smallish bar and lounge, open fires, good choice of well kept ales such as Inveralmond, pleasing all-day food from varied menu including cullen skink and beef stovies, pleasant service; 17 bedrooms (some with views of River Tay). *(William Slade)*

DUNNING   NO0114

Kirkstyle (01764) 684248
B9141, off A9 S of Perth; Kirkstyle Square; PH2 0RR Unpretentious 18th-c streamside pub with chatty regulars, log fire in snug bar, up to three real ales and good choice of whiskies, enjoyable good value home-made food including some interesting specials (book in season), attentive friendly service, split-level stripped-stone back restaurant; background music; children welcome, dogs in garden only, open all day weekends, from 5pm Mon, Tues. *(William Slade)*

KENMORE   NN7745

★**Kenmore Hotel** (01887) 830205
A827 W of Aberfeldy; PH15 2NU Civilised small hotel dating from the 16th c in pretty Loch Tay village; comfortable traditional front lounge with warm log fire and poem pencilled by Burns himself on the chimney breast, dozens of malts helpfully arranged alphabetically, polite uniformed staff, modern restaurant with balcony; back bar and terrace overlooking River Tay with enjoyable food from lunchtime soup and sandwiches up (especially good grills), Inveralmond Ossian and decent wines by the glass; pool and winter darts, juke box, TV, fruit machine; children and dogs welcome, 40 good bedrooms plus luxury lodges, open all day. *(Lance and Sarah Milligan)*

KILMAHOG   NN6008

★**Lade** (01877) 330152
A84 just NW of Callander, by A821 junction; FK17 8HD Lively place with a strong scottish theme – traditional weekend music, real ale shop with over 190 bottled beers from regional microbreweries and their own-brewed WayLade ales; plenty of character in several cosy beamed areas with panelling and stripped stone, highland prints and works by local artists, 40 malt whiskies, enjoyable home-made food from bar snacks up, big-windowed restaurant, friendly staff; background music; children and dogs (in bar) welcome, disabled access, terrace tables, pleasant garden with fish ponds, open all day (till 1am Fri, Sat). *(Dave Sutton)*

KIRKTON OF GLENISLA   NO2160

Glenisla Hotel (01575) 582223
B951 N of Kirriemuir and Alyth; PH11 8PH Refurbished 17th-c coaching inn with good local atmosphere in traditional split-level bar, beams, flagstones and warm log fire, two well kept scottish ales and eight wines by the glass, popular home-made food using local produce from bar snacks up, good friendly service; children and dogs welcome, garden with play area, bedrooms, good walks from the door (on Cateran Trail), open all day in season. *(Lance and Sarah Milligan)*

PERTH NO1223
Greyfriars (01738) 633036
South Street; PH2 8PG Small comfortable local in old part of town, a couple of well kept changing ales and good whisky/gin range, enjoyable lunchtime food (not Sun) in bar or little upstairs dining room, friendly welcoming staff; live music Weds (open mike) and Sat; open all day. *(Tony Scott)*

PITLOCHRY NN9163
★ Killiecrankie Hotel (01796) 473220
Killiecrankie, off A9 N; PH16 5LG Comfortable splendidly placed country hotel with attractive panelled bar and airy conservatory, well kept ales, over 40 malt whiskies and well chosen wines, good imaginative food in bar or more formal evening restaurant, friendly efficient service; children in eating areas, dogs welcome, extensive peaceful grounds with dramatic views, ten pretty bedrooms.
(Mr and Mrs J Watkins)

PITLOCHRY NN9459
★ Moulin (01796) 472196
Kirkmichael Road, Moulin; A924 NE of Pitlochry centre; PH16 5EH Attractive much-extended inn brewing its own good beers in stables across the street, decent wines by the glass too and 45 malt whiskies, cheerfully busy down-to-earth bar in oldest part with traditional character, smaller bareboards room and bigger carpeted area with cushioned booths divided by stained-glass country scenes, well liked food, separate restaurant; bar billiards and 1960s one-arm bandit; children and dogs (in bar) welcome, picnic-sets on gravel looking across to village kirk, good nearby walks, 15 comfortable bedrooms and two self-catering cottages, open all day. *(Mr and Mrs J Watkins, Adrian Johnson, Barry Collett)*

PITLOCHRY NN9358
Old Mill (01796) 474020
Mill Lane; PH16 5BH Welcoming family-run inn (former 19th-c watermill), enjoyable food from sandwiches and sharing plates up, four real ales including Strathbraan and good wine and whisky choice, friendly staff; live music Fri, Sat, free wi-fi; courtyard tables by Moulin Burn, comfortable bedrooms, open all day. *(Susan Ingram)*

ROSS-SHIRE

BADACHRO NG7873
★ Badachro Inn (01445) 741255
2.5 miles S of Gairloch village turn off A832 on to B8056, then after another 3.25 miles turn right in Badachro to the quay and inn; IV21 2AA Superbly positioned by Loch Gairloch with terrific views from decking down to water's edge, popular (especially summer) with mix of sailing visitors (free moorings) and chatty locals; welcoming bar with interesting photographs, An Teallach, Caledonian and a guest ale, about 50 malt whiskies and eight wines by the glass, quieter eating area with big log fire, dining conservatory overlooking bay, fair-priced food including locally smoked fish and seafood; background music; children and dogs welcome, one bedroom, open all day. *(The Dutchman)*

FORTROSE NH7256
★ Anderson (01381) 620236
Union Street, off A832; IV10 8TD Friendly enthusiastic american licensees at this seaside hotel with vast selection of international beers (one of the largest collections of bottled belgians in the UK), also four well kept changing ales, Addlestone's cider and 250 malt whiskies, quite a few wines too, good food in homely bar and light airy dining room with open fire, board and puzzle-type games; background and live traditional music (every other Sun), knitting club Mon evening and monthly quiz; children welcome, dogs in bar (resident cat and cat), seats out behind on gravel, nine bedrooms, open from 4pm (3pm Sun). *(Melanie and David Lawson)*

GAIRLOCH NG8075
Old Inn (01445) 712006
Just off A832/B8021; IV21 2BD Quietly positioned old drovers' inn by stream, own-brew beers and guests, decent wines by the glass and 20 malt whiskies, food (not Sun evening) including local fish and game, own smokery, relaxed locals' bar with traditional décor and woodburner, bistro/restaurant; background music (live Fri), TV, fruit machine; children and dogs welcome, picnic-sets out by trees, bedrooms, open all day till 1am (11pm Sun). *(Dave Sutton)*

GLENELG NG8119
Glenelg Inn (01599) 522273
Unmarked road from Shiel Bridge (A87) towards Skye; IV40 8JR Unpretentious mountain cabin-like bar in small hotel reached by dramatic drive with spectacular views of Loch Duich to Skye, beams, wood-clad walls and big fireplace, a couple of real ales and good fresh local food including seafood from daily changing menu, friendly welcoming staff, dining room; regular live music; children and dogs welcome, lovely garden, views from some bedrooms, summer ferry to Skye, open all day. *(David Todd)*

PLOCKTON NG8033
★ Plockton Inn (01599) 544222
Innes Street; unconnected to Plockton Hotel (see Main Entries); IV52 8TW Close to the harbour in this lovely village, congenial bustling atmosphere even in winter, good well priced food with emphasis on local fish/seafood (some from own back smokery), friendly efficient service, well kept

changing beers and good range of malts, lively public bar with traditional music Thurs (also Tues in summer); seats out on decking, 14 bedrooms (seven in annexe over road), good breakfast. *(Melanie and David Lawson)*

SHIEL BRIDGE   NG9319
Kintail Lodge (01599) 511275
A87, N of Shiel Bridge; IV40 8HL Lots of varnished wood in large plain bar adjoining hotel, convivial bustle in season, Isle of Skye Red Cuillin and plenty of malt whiskies, particularly good food from same kitchen as attractive restaurant/conservatory with magnificent view down Loch Duich to Skye, friendly efficient service; 12 comfortable bedrooms, bunkhouse, good breakfast, dogs welcome. *(Dave Sutton)*

★ULLAPOOL   NH1293
Ceilidh Place (01854) 612103
West Argyle Street; IV26 2TY Pretty white house and more arty café-bar than pub with gallery, bookshop and coffee shop; conservatory-style main area with mix of dining chairs around dark wood tables, cosy bar and other rooms with armchairs, sofas and scatter-cushioned wall seats, rugs on floors, woodburner, a beer from An Teallach, lots of wines by the glass and 75 malt whiskies, tasty food (something available all day); regular jazz, folk and classical music; children welcome (but must leave bar by 7pm), tables on front terrace looking over houses to distant hills beyond natural harbour, comfortable bedrooms, open all day, closed Jan. *(Isobel Mackinlay, Mary Kirkwood)*

ULLAPOOL   NH1294
Morefield Motel (01854) 612161
A835 N edge of town; IV26 2TQ Modern family-run place, clean and bright, with cheerful L-shaped lounge bar, reliably good food including local fish and seafood, well kept changing ales, decent wines and over 50 malt whiskies, large conservatory; background music, pool and darts; children welcome, terrace tables, bike lock-up, bedrooms, open all day. *(Belinda May)*

ROXBURGHSHIRE

★KELSO   NT7234
Cobbles (01573) 223548
Bowmont Street; TD5 7JH Small comfortably refurbished 19th-c dining pub just off the main square, friendly and well run with good range of food from pub standards to more enterprising dishes, local Tempest beers and decent range of wines and malts, open fire and pubby furnishings in bar, elegantly furnished dining room with overspill room upstairs; folk music Fri evening; children welcome, disabled facilities, open all day (till late Fri, Sat). *(David Longhurst, Rona Mackinlay)*

KIRK YETHOLM   NT8328
★Border (01573) 420237
Village signposted off B6352/B6401 crossroads, SE of Kelso; The Green; TD5 8PQ Comfortable family-run inn facing village green, nice traditional bar with beams, flagstones and log fire, snug side rooms, two or three ales including Hadrian Border, decent wines and numerous whiskies, good home-made food from snacks and pub favourites up, friendly service, spacious dining room with fishing theme, lounge with another fire and neat conservatory; background music; children and dogs (in bar) welcome, sheltered back terrace, five bedrooms, good breakfast, at end of Pennine Way and start of Scottish National Trail, open all day. *(John and Sylvia Harrop, Sara Fulton, Roger Baker)*

ST BOSWELLS   NT5930
Buccleuch Arms (01835) 822243
A68 just S of Newtown St Boswells; TD6 0EW Civilised 19th-c sandstone hotel opposite village green; bar, comfortable lounge and bistro, good popular food from bar snacks up, prompt friendly service, two or three real ales such as Belhaven, open fires; children and dogs welcome, tables in attractive garden behind, 19 bedrooms, open (and food) all day. *(Martin Day)*

SELKIRKSHIRE

MOUNTBENGER   NT3324
Gordon Arms (01750) 82261
A708/B709; TD7 5LE Refurbishment as we went to press for this nice old pub – an oasis in these empty moorlands; a couple of real ales and enjoyable reasonably priced pubby food cooked by landlord, good regular traditional music (there's a recording studio on site); children and dogs welcome, comfortable bedrooms, good walking country, open all day in summer (shuts Mon-Weds winter – check website for details). *(Charles Mason)*

STIRLINGSHIRE

DRYMEN   NS4788
Winnock (01360) 660245
Just off A811; The Square; G63 0BL Big Best Western's modern split-level stripped-stone and beamed lounge bar, blazing log fires, leather sofas and easy chairs, well kept Caledonian Deuchars IPA and good range of malt whiskies, wide choice of well thought-of food (tasty steak pies), quick service from neat helpful young staff, steps down to restaurant area and airy conservatory; background and live music; large garden, 73 comfortable bedrooms. *(Lance and Sarah Milligan)*

KIPPEN
NS6594

★**Cross Keys** (01786) 870293

Main Street; village signposted off A811 W of Stirling; FK8 3DN Cosy and gently civilised 18th-c inn; log fires in two bars, exposed stonework, bare boards or carpeting, built-in wall seating, wooden dining chairs and stools against counter serving a couple of Fallen beers, 20 malt whiskies and a dozen wines by the glass, very good food including lighter lunch menu, friendly staff; background music, live folk first and third Sun of month, free wi-fi ; children (till 9pm) and dogs welcome, tables in garden looking across to the Ochil Hills, comfortable bedrooms, generous breakfast, open (and food) all day weekends, food all day Sun. *(Lindy Andrews, Iain Waterson, Sally Anne and Peter Goodale, Roy and Gill Payne, John Evans)*

STRATHCLYDE

CAIRNDOW
NN1810

Stagecoach (01499) 600286

Just off and signed from A83; PA26 8BN Modernised old inn run by same family for 45 years and in lovely setting overlooking Loch Fyne; good local fish and seasonal produce in bar and restaurant, Fyne ales and plenty of whiskies, efficient friendly service; live music and quiz nights; children welcome, garden picnic-sets, 19 bedrooms (some in separate building with balconies taking in the view), open (and food) all day. *(Darren and Jane Staniforth)*

SUTHERLAND

KYLESKU
NC2333

★**Kylesku Hotel** (01971) 502231

A894, S side of former ferry crossing; IV27 4HW Remote NW hotel on shores of Loch Glendhu, pleasant tartan-carpeted bar facing glorious mountain and loch view, with seals and red-throated divers often in sight (tables outside too); wonderfully fresh seafood along with other locally sourced food, friendly accommodating staff, well kept ales such as An Teallach, good wines by the glass and numerous malt whiskies, more expensive loch-view restaurant extension; children welcome, eight comfortable bedrooms, good boat trips from hotel slipway, closed in winter. *(Neil and Angela Huxter)*

LAIRG
NC5224

★**Crask Inn** (01549) 411241

A836 13 miles N towards Altnaharra; IV27 4AB Remote homely inn on single-track road through peaceful moorland, good simple food including own lamb (the friendly hard-working licensees keep sheep on this working croft), comfortably basic bar with large peat stove to dry the sheepdogs (other

dogs welcome), a summer real ale, Black Isle bottled beers in winter, interesting books, piano, pleasant separate dining room; three bedrooms (lights out when generator goes off), simple nearby bunkhouse; up for sale so things will change. *(Mike Benton)*

LOCHINVER
NC0922

★**Caberfeidh** (01571) 844321

Culag Road (A837); IV27 4JY Delightful lochside position and lovely views; cosy bar, conservatory and more formal evening restaurant, shortish changing menu with emphasis on local seafood (one or two large plates and a selection of smaller tapas-style dishes), well kept beers such as Isle of Skye and good choice of wines by the glass, very welcoming staff and cheerful atmosphere; children and dogs (in bar) allowed, small harbourside garden, open all day in summer (all day Sat, closed Sun evening, Mon and weekday lunchtimes in winter). *(Neil and Angela Huxter)*

WEST LOTHIAN

BO'NESS
NS9981

Corbie (01506) 825307

A904 Corbiehall; EH51 0AS Neatly furnished pub with up to six well kept local ales including own Kinneil brewed behind, 70 malt whiskies (tasting evenings) and enjoyable uncomplicated food at very reasonable prices, friendly staff; children welcome, garden with play area, open (and food) all day. *(Helena and Trevor Fraser)*

LINLITHGOW
NS0077

★**Four Marys** (01506) 842171

High Street; 2 miles from M9 junction 3 (and little further from junction 4) – town signposted; EH49 7ED Named after Mary, Queen of Scots' four ladies-in-waiting and filled with mementoes of the ill-fated queen including pictures and written records, pieces of bed curtain and clothing, even a facsimile of her death-mask; L-shaped room with traditional and more modern seating on wood-block floor, mainly stripped-stone walls (some remarkable masonry in the inner area), elaborate Victorian dresser serving as part of the bar, seven well kept ales (taster glasses available, May, Oct festivals), good range of malt whiskies and gins, enjoyable reasonably priced food, friendly staff, tartan carpeted dining area where children allowed (till 8pm); background and live music; enclosed terrace, open all day. *(Giles and Annie Francis, Paul Baxter)*

WIGTOWNSHIRE

BLADNOCH
NX4254

Bladnoch Inn (01988) 402200

Corner of A714 and B7005; DG8 9AB Cheerful neat bar with eating area and separate restaurant, enjoyable pubby food from sandwiches up, Sun carvery, a couple of changing real ales, friendly obliging service; background music; children and dogs welcome, picturesque riverside setting across from Bladnoch distillery (tours), four good value bedrooms, open all day. *(Sam Tyler)*

PORTPATRICK NW9954

Crown (01776) 810261

North Crescent; DG9 8SX Popular seafront hotel in delightful harbourside village, enjoyable reasonably priced food including notable seafood, friendly prompt service, several dozen malts and decent wines by the glass, warm fire in rambling traditional bar with cosy corners, sewing machine tables, old photographs and posters, attractively decorated early 20th-c dining room opening through conservatory into sheltered back garden; background music, TV; children and dogs welcome, tables out in front, open (and food) all day. *(Ruaraidh)*

STRANRAER NX0660

Grapes (01776) 703386

Bridge Street; DG9 7HY Popular and welcoming 19th-c local, simple and old-fashioned, with a couple of well kept ales and over 60 malts, regular traditional music in bar or upstairs room; dogs welcome, courtyard seating, open all day. *(Laura Reid)*

Scottish Islands

ARRAN

CATACOL NR9049

Catacol Bay (01770) 830231

A841; KA27 8HN Unpretentious hotel rather than pub run by same family for 37 years, wonderful setting just yards from the sea looking across to Kintyre; simple bar with log fire, Timothy Taylors Landlord and a guest, all-day food (Sunday buffet until 4pm) and hearty breakfasts; pool, TV; tables outside and children's play area, six simple bedrooms with washbasins (ones at front have the view), own mooring, open all day in summer, closed Mon, Tues winter. *(Alan and Alice Morgan)*

BARRA

CASTLEBAY NL6698

Castlebay Hotel (01871) 810223

By aeroplane from Glasgow or ferry from Oban; HS9 5XD Comfortable cheerful bar next to the hotel, popular food from sandwiches up, keg and bottled beers,

also two-level lounge/restaurant with great harbour view, pleasant young staff; regular live music; decent bedrooms. *(Iona)*

BUTE

PORT BANNATYNE NS0767

Port Royal (01700) 505073

Marine Road; PA20 0LW Cheerful stone-built place (more restaurant than pub) looking across the sea to Argyll, interior reworked as pre-revolution russian tavern with bare boards, painted timbers and tapestries, food including russian dishes and good seafood, choice of russian beers and vodkas too, open fire, candles and wild flowers; two annexe bedrooms, substantial breakfast, closed lunchtimes and all day Tues. *(Caro and Steve)*

ROTHESAY NS0864

Black Bull (01700) 502366

W Princes Street; PA20 9AF Traditional comfortably furnished pub with enjoyable reasonably priced food and two well kept ales, good attentive service, fine display of old Clyde steamers; opposite pier with its wonderfully restored Victorian gents', open all day. *(Alan and Alice Morgan)*

COLONSAY

SCALASAIG NR3893

★ **Colonsay** (01951) 200316

W on B8086; PA61 7YP Extended stylish 18th-c hotel, a haven for ramblers and birders; chatty bar is hub of the island and full of locals and visitors, comfortable sofas and armchairs on painted boards, pastel walls hung with interesting old islander pictures, log fires, Colonsay IPA, several wines by the glass and interesting selection of whiskies, relaxed informal restaurant overlooking the harbour, good food using home-grown produce (own oyster farm) including pre-ferry two-course offer, friendly efficient service; children and dogs (in bar) welcome, nice views from garden, ten comfortable pretty bedrooms, closed Nov-Feb except Christmas and New Year, otherwise open all day (till 1am Sat). *(Mary Kirkwood, Neil Allen)*

CUMBRAE

MILLPORT NS1554

Frasers (01475) 530518

Cardiff Street; KA28 0AS Small cheerful pub set just back from the harbour, bar and lounge with old paddle-steamer pictures, open fire, enjoyable very reasonably priced

---

There are report forms at the back of the book.

pubby food, a couple of beers from Houston, friendly staff; children welcome, no dogs, tables in yard behind, open all day. *(Dave Braisted)*

HARRIS

TARBERT   NB1500
★ **Harris Hotel** (01859) 502154
Scott Road; HS3 3DL Large hotel in same family for over a century; small welcoming panelled bar with Hebridean brewed ales and some rare malt whiskies, interesting food using local game and seafood from lunchtime baguettes and afternoon teas up, smart (but relaxed) airy restaurant; 23 comfortable sea-view bedrooms (some up narrow stairs). *(Alan and Alice Morgan)*

ISLAY

BOWMORE   NR3159
★ **Harbour Inn** (01496) 810330
The Square; PA43 7JR Fine inn with traditional bar and plenty of regulars, lovely harbour/loch views from attractive dining room and conservatory, good local fish and seafood, proper afternoon teas, nice choice of wines and plenty of Islay malts including some rarities, friendly welcoming staff; reasonably priced bedrooms with views. *(Ruaraidh)*

PORT ASKAIG   NR4369
Port Askaig (01496) 840245
A846, by port; PA46 7RD Family-run inn on shores of the Sound of Islay overlooking ferry pier; snug, tartan-carpeted bar with good range of malt whiskies, local bottled ales and popular all-day food, neat sea-view restaurant and traditional residents' lounge; dogs welcome in bar, plenty of picnic-sets on waterside grass, eight neat bedrooms and self-catering apartment, open all day. *(Jimmy Lothian)*

PORT CHARLOTTE   NR2558
★ **Port Charlotte Hotel**
(01496) 850360 *Main Street; PA48 7TU* Most beautiful of Islay's Georgian villages in lovely position with sweeping views over Loch Indaal, exceptional collection of around 150 Islay malts including rarities, two changing local ales and decent wines by the glass, good food using local meat, game and seafood, civilised bare-boards pubby bar with padded wall seats, open fire and modern artwork, second comfortable back bar, neatly kept restaurant and roomy conservatory (overlooking beach); regular traditional live music; children welcome, garden tables, near sandy beach, ten attractive bedrooms (nine with sea view), open all day till 1am. *(Caro and Steve)*

PORTNAHAVEN   NN1652
An Tighe Seinnse (01496) 860224
Queen Street; PA47 7SJ Friendly little end-of-terrace harbourside pub tucked away in this remote attractive fishing village, cosy bar with room off, open fire, fair-priced tasty food including local seafood, Belhaven keg beer and bottled Islay ales, good choice of malts; sports TV and occasional live music; can get crowded, open all day. *(Caro and Steve)*

JURA

CRAIGHOUSE   NR5266
Jura Hotel (01496) 820243
A846, opposite distillery; PA60 7XU Family-run and in superb setting with views over the Small Isles to the mainland; bar, two lounges and restaurant, good food; garden down to water's edge, 17 bedrooms (most with sea view), camping. *(Ruariadh)*

MULL

DERVAIG   NM4251
★ **Bellachroy** (01688) 400314
B8073; PA75 6QW Island's oldest inn dating from 1608; pub and restaurant food including local seafood, afternoon teas, local ales and good choice of whiskies and wine, traditional bar with darts, attractive dining area, comfortable residents' lounge with games and TV; children and dogs welcome, covered outside area plus plenty of picnic-sets, nice spot in sleepy lochside village, six comfortable bedrooms, open all year. *(Lance and Sarah Milligan)*

TOBERMORY   NM5055
Macdonald Arms (01688) 302011
Main Street; PA75 6NT Seafront hotel very popular locally for its tasty low-priced food, well kept Belhaven Best, basic décor and furnishings and winter fire. *(Isobel Mackinlay)*

TOBERMORY   NM5055
Mishnish (01688) 302500
Main Street – the yellow building; PA75 6NU Popular and lively place right on the bay, dimly lit two-room bar with cask tables, old photographs and nautical/fishing bric-a-brac, woodburner, little snugs, well kept Belhaven and Isle of Mull, enjoyable bar food, can also eat in next-door Mishdish or italian restaurant upstairs; background and live music, pool; beer garden behind, 14 refurbished bedrooms (some with sea view), good breakfast, open all day till late. *(Pat and Stewart Gordon, Dave Braisted)*

ORKNEY

DOUNBY
HY3001

Merkister (01856) 771366

Russland Road, by Harray Loch; KW17 2LF Fishing hotel in great location on the loch shore, bar dominated by prize catches, good food here and in evening restaurant including hand-dived scallops and local aberdeen angus steaks, local bottled beers, good friendly service; 16 bedrooms, open all day. *(Alf Wright)*

ST MARY'S
HY4700

Commodore (01856) 781788

A961; KW17 2RU Modern single-storey building with stunning views over Scapa Flow, bar with well kept Orkney beers, pool and darts, good food using local produce in contemporary restaurant; open all day. *(Gus Swan)*

WESTRAY
HY4348

Pierowall Hotel (01857) 677472

Centre of Pierowall village, B9066; KW17 2BZ Comfortable pub-hotel near ferry, friendly main bar largely given over to enjoyable food from sandwiches and snacks to good freshly landed fish, bottled Orkney beers and plenty of malts, lounge bar, pool room and separate dining area; six bedrooms with bay or hill views. *(Gus Swan)*

SKYE

ARDVASAR
NG6303

Ardvasar Hotel (01471) 844223

A851 at S of island, near Armadale pier; IV45 8RS Wonderful sea and mountain views from this comfortable peacefully placed white stone inn, charming owner (will pick you up from the ferry) and friendly efficient staff, good home-made food using local fish and meat, 32 malt whiskies, real ales including Isle of Skye, two bars and games room; background music, TV; children welcome in eating areas, tables outside, lovely walks, ten bedrooms (front ones overlook the sound), open all day. *(Dave Braisted)*

CARBOST
NG3731

★ Old Inn (01478) 640205

B8009; IV47 8SR Little-changed unpretentious waterside pub with stunning views, well positioned for walkers and climbers; simply furnished chatty bar with exposed stone walls, bare-board or tiled floors, open fire, Cuillin ales and a guest, traditional cider and quite a few malt whiskies, tasty fair priced food using local fish and highland meat; background music

(live Weds, Fri), darts and pool; children and dogs welcome, picnic-sets on terrace by the water, bedrooms and bunkhouse taking in the views, Talisker distillery nearby, closed afternoons in winter, otherwise open (and food) all day. *(Emma Scofield)*

DUNVEGAN
NG2547

Dunvegan (01470) 521497

A850/A863; IV55 8WA Early 19th-c inn on the Duirinish peninsula; good food from baguettes to local seafood in airy lounge bar or evening restaurant (open Easter-Oct), conservatory with superb loch and mountain views, friendly helpful service, cellar bar with live music (Thurs and Sat evenings in season) and games area; waterfront garden, six bedrooms and bunkhouse. *(Alf Wright)*

EDINBANE
NG3451

Edinbaine (01470) 582414

Just off A850, signed for Meadhan a Bhaile; IV51 9PW Friendly former farmhouse with simply furnished modernised bar, light wood flooring and woodburner in stone fireplace, well kept Isle of Skye beers, airy carpeted dining room serving good attractively presented food including local fish and seafood, friendly staff; live traditional music (Weds, Fri and Sun); children and dogs welcome, open all day (but best to check winter hours). *(James Darkins)*

ISLE ORNSAY
NG7012

★ Eilean Iarmain (01471) 833332

Off A851 Broadford–Armadale; IV43 8QR Smartly old-fashioned 19th-c hotel in beautiful location looking over the Sound of Sleat; small traditional bar with panelling and open fire, well kept Isle of Skye and good choice of vatted (blended) malt whiskies including their own Gaelic Whisky Collection, good food here or in charming sea-view restaurant, friendly efficient service; traditional background and live music; children welcome, outside tables with spectacular views, 16 comfortable bedrooms, open all day. *(Alf Wright)*

SOUTH UIST

LOCH CARNAN
NF8144

Orasay Inn (01870) 610298

Signed off A865 S of Creagorry; HS8 5PD Wonderful remote spot overlooking the sea (lovely sunsets), good local fish/seafood and beef from own herd in comfortable modern lounge or conservatory-style restaurant, friendly service, pleasant simply furnished public bar; seats outside on raised decked area, compact comfortable bedrooms (two with own terrace), open all day at least in summer. *(Gus Swan)*

WALES

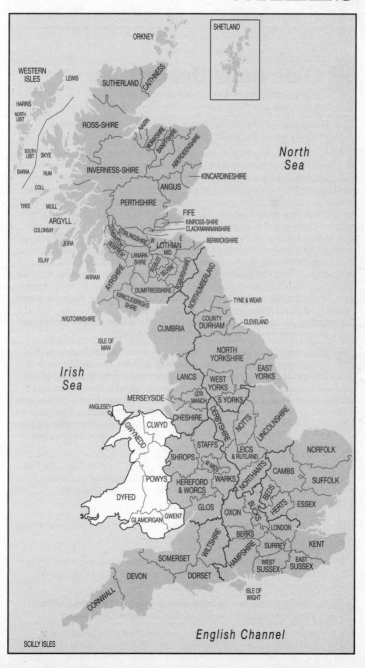

SHETLAND

ORKNEY

WESTERN
ISLES

LEWIS

HARRIS

NORTH
UIST

SOUTH
UIST

BARRA

SKYE

RUM

COLL

TIREE

MULL

COLONSAY

JURA

ISLAY

ARGYLL

ARRAN

SUTHERLAND

CAITHNESS

NAIRN

MORAYSHIRE

BANFFSHIRE

ROSS-SHIRE

INVERNESS-SHIRE

ABERDEENSHIRE

KINCARDINESHIRE

ANGUS

North
Sea

PERTHSHIRE

FIFE

KINROSS-SHIRE

CLACKMANNANSHIRE

STIRLINGSHIRE

DUNBARTON

RENFREW

W

LOTHIAN

E

MID

BERWICKSHIRE

LANARK-
SHIRE

PEEBLES

SELKIRK

AYRSHIRE

ROXBURGHSHIRE

DUMFRIESSHIRE

NORTHUMBERLAND

KIRKCUDBRIGHT-
SHIRE

TYNE & WEAR

WIGTOWNSHIRE

CUMBRIA

COUNTY
DURHAM

CLEVELAND

ISLE OF
MAN

NORTH
YORKSHIRE

Irish
Sea

LANCS

WEST
YORKS

EAST
YORKS

MERSEYSIDE

GTR
MANCH

S YORKS

ANGLESEY

CHESHIRE

DERBYSHIRE

NOTTS

LINCOLNSHIRE

GWYNEDD

CLWYD

STAFFS

LEICS
& RUTLAND

NORFOLK

SHROPS

W MIDS

POWYS

HEREFORD
& WORCS

WARKS

NORTHANTS

CAMBS

SUFFOLK

DYFED

BEDS

HERTS

ESSEX

GLOS

OXON

BUCKS

GLAMORGAN

GWENT

LONDON

WILTSHIRE

BERKS

SURREY

KENT

HAMPSHIRE

WEST
SUSSEX

EAST
SUSSEX

SOMERSET

DEVON

DORSET

ISLE OF
WIGHT

CORNWALL

SCILLY ISLES

English Channel

KEY ★ Star Pub 🍽 Top Quality Food 🍺 Great Beer

♀ Good Wines £ Bargain Meals 🛏 Good Bedrooms 🍴 Serves Food

 BEAUMARIS   SH6076 Map 6

Olde Bulls Head 🍽 ♀ 🛏

(01248) 810329 – www.bullsheadinn.co.uk

Castle Street; LL58 8AP

Interesting historic inn with plenty of interest, a rambling bar, stylish brasserie and restaurant; well equipped bedrooms

---

The bedrooms in this 15th-c inn are named after characters in Dickens' novels (Dickens himself popped in for a drink in 1859) and are very well equipped; some are traditional, others more contemporary in style. They also have bedrooms in the Townhouse, an adjacent property with disabled access. At the heart of the place is a delightful beamed and rambling bar with comfortable low-seated settles, leather-cushioned window seats and a good log fire – there are also plenty of interesting reminders of the town's past such as a rare 17th-c brass water clock, a bloodthirsty crew of cutlasses and even an oak ducking stool tucked among the snug alcove; lots of copper and china jugs too; board games. Kindly staff serve Bass, Hancocks HB and a guest such as Timothy Taylors Landlord on handpump. In contrast, the busy brasserie behind is lively and stylishly modern with around 14 wines by the glass, while the exceptionally good upstairs restaurant is an elegantly smart choice for a more formal meal and has a wine list that runs to 120 bottles. The entrance to the pretty courtyard is closed by a huge simple-hinged door that's an astonishing 3.3 metres wide and 4 metres high.

🍽 Highly thought-of contemporary food includes lunchtime sandwiches, devilled lamb kidneys on toasted sourdough, pickled artichoke, feta and fig salad with quinoa and wild black rice, spiced orange and ginger dressing, goats cheese, spinach and pine nut quiche with beetroot and apple coleslaw, spiced venison sausage and kidney bean stew with sticky red cabbage, lemon and dill creamy fish pie, braised lamb shank with rosemary mash, onion gravy and honey-glazed vegetables, and puddings such as apple, ginger and raisin custard and dark chocolate and mint mousse with chocolate ice-cream. *Benchmark main dish: burger with caramelised onion, toppings and chips £14.00. Two-course evening meal £21.00.*

Free house ~ Licensee David Robertson ~ Real ale ~ Open 11-11 (10.30 Sun) ~ Bar food 12-2 (3 Sun), 7-9; 12-9 ~ Restaurant ~ Children welcome ~ Dogs allowed in bar and bedrooms ~ Wi-fi ~ Bedrooms: £85/£110 *Recommended by Chris and Val Ramstedt, Andrew Vincent, Tim King*

 COLWYN BAY   SH8478 Map 6

Pen-y-Bryn 🍽 ♀ 🍺

(01492) 533360 – www.brunningandprice.co.uk/penybryn

B5113 Llanwrst Road, on southern outskirts; when you see the pub, turn off into Wentworth Avenue for the car park; LL29 6DD

Spacious open-plan modern bungalow overlooking the bay, with reliable food all day, good range of drinks and obliging staff

---

Don't be put off by the rather unprepossessing exterior of this pub because, once inside, it's charming. Extending around the three long sides of the bar counter, you'll find welcoming coal fires, oriental rugs on pale stripped boards, a mix of seating and well spaced tables, shelves of books, a profusion of pictures, big pot plants, careful lighting and dark green old-fashioned school radiators. A fine choice of drinks served by knowledgeable, perky young staff includes Phoenix Brunning & Price Original plus Adnams Ghost Ship, Heavy Industry Collaborator, Purple Moose Snowdonia Ale and Tomos Watkin Blodwens Beer on handpump, well chosen good value wines including 19 by the glass and 65 malt whiskies; board games and background music. The big windows at the back look over nicely weathered seats and tables on the terraces and in the sizeable garden surrounded by pine trees, and then out to the sea and the Great Orme. In summer, the award-winning flowering tubs and hanging baskets are lovely.

Tempting brasserie-style food includes sandwiches, air-dried beef and short rib fritters with roasted peach, basil and english mustard mayonnaise, tempura bass with shredded fennel and asparagus salad and saffron aioli, chargrilled harissa halloumi with toasted coconut, pineapple and mango salsa with hummus, hot smoked salmon salad with horseradish crème fraîche and pickled cucumber, steak and blue cheese pie, beer-battered haddock and chips, thai red fish curry with coconut rice, steak burger with toppings, coleslaw and chips, and puddings such as chocolate brownie with chocolate sauce and bread and butter pudding with apricot sauce. *Benchmark main dish: slow-braised lamb shoulder with red wine sauce £16.95. Two-course evening meal £25.00.*

Brunning & Price ~ Manager Andrew Grant ~ Real ale ~ Open 11.30-11; 11-11 Sat; 11-10.30 Sun ~ Bar food 12-9.30 (9 Sun) ~ Children welcome ~ Dogs allowed in bar ~ Wi-fi
Recommended by W K Wood, Tony Smaithe, Pauline and Mark Evans

CRICKHOWELL

SO2118   Map 6

Bear ★ ♗ 🛏

(01873) 810408 – www.bearhotel.co.uk
Brecon Road; A40; NP8 1BW

Convivial, interesting inn with a splendid, old-fashioned bar area, log fires and fresh flowers and rewarding food; comfortable bedrooms

'Such a shame this is not nearer home' and 'it doesn't matter what time of day we visit, it's always marvellous' are just two comments from our readers – who all remain delighted that the same warmly friendly family continue to run the place and that their high standards remain unchanged. The heavily beamed lounge is chatty and bustling, with lots of little plush-seated bentwood armchairs and handsome cushioned antique settles, fresh flowers on tables, and a window seat that looks down on the market square. Next to the great roaring log fire are a big sofa and leather easy chairs on oak parquet flooring with rugs. Other antiques include a fine oak dresser filled with pewter mugs and brassware, a longcase clock and interesting prints. Brains Rev James, Conwy Welsh Pride, Marstons Old Empire, Sharps Doom Bar and a frequently changing guest on handpump, alongside 32 malt whiskies, local ciders, vintage and late-bottled ports and unusual wines (with 14 by the glass); disabled lavatories. This is a particularly appealing place to stay: the older bedrooms in the main building have antiques, some of the refurbished ones are in a country style and the luxury ones have hot tubs and four-poster beds; breakfasts are excellent. Reception rooms, ably hosted by patient staff, are comfortably furnished, and there are seats in the small garden.

From a menu featuring much regional produce, the high quality food includes sandwiches (until 6pm), duck liver and Armagnac parfait with red onion marmalade, chicken satay with peanut sauce, faggots with onion gravy, lamb shank with spring onion mash and braising juices, potato gnocchi with garlic-sautéed mushrooms and parmesan, jamaican jerk flat rib of beef with sweet potato fries, whole plaice with parsley and caper butter, duck breast with red cabbage and sweet red wine sauce, and puddings such as chocolate and cherry roulade with honey ice-cream and almond and mascarpone sponge torte with strawberry sorbet. *Benchmark main dish: chicken supreme in madeira sauce £14.95. Two-course evening meal £21.00.*

Free house ~ Licensee Judy Hindmarsh ~ Real ale ~ Open 11-11 (10.30 Sun) ~ Bar food 12-10; 12-2.15, 3-9.30 Sun ~ Restaurant ~ Children welcome but no under-6s in restaurant areas ~ Dogs allowed in bar and bedrooms ~ Wi-fi ~ Bedrooms: £96/£115
Recommended by Tom and Ruth Rees, B and M Kendall, Mike Beach, Mike and Mary Carter

DALE
Griffin

SM8105 Map 6

(01646) 636227 ~ www.griffininndale.co.uk
B4327, by sea on one-way system; SA62 3RB

Friendly waterside pub with fresh fish and shellfish, local ales and two attractive upstairs rooms

Right by the water, this friendly old pub has picnic-sets on the front terrace that make the most of the lovely estuary view, and there's a pontoon and a seawall. Inside, you'll find a genuine welcome from the helpful licensees and two imaginatively decorated rooms with open fires, wood panelling, traditional red quarry tiles and an easy-going atmosphere. Brains Rev James, Cwrw lal Haf Gwyn and a guest from Tenby on handpump, six wines by the glass, local cider and malt whiskies – including a welsh one; background music and board games. There are lovely coastal walks to either side.

The pub co-owns a local fishing boat and the menu majors on fresh fish and shellfish – king prawns, razor clams, scallops, whole sea bream, hake, cod and haddock. They also offer vegetable lasagne, burger with relish, onion rings and chips, chicken and leek pie, gammon with free-range eggs or pineapple, local 10oz rump steak with creamy pepper sauce, and puddings such as sticky toffee pudding and fruit crumble. *Benchmark main dish: cod loin in creamy white wine sauce £21.95. Two-course evening meal £24.00.*

Free house ~ Licensees Sian Mathias and Simon Vickers ~ Real ale ~ Open 12-11 (10.30 Sun); check website for times in winter ~ Bar food 12-2.30, 6-8.30 ~ Restaurant ~ Children welcome ~ Wi-fi *Recommended by John and Enid, Harvey Brown, S and L McPhee, Simon Sharpe*

EAST ABERTHAW
Blue Anchor ◖ £

ST0366 Map 6

(01446) 750329 ~ www.blueanchoraberthaw.com
Village signed off B4265; CF62 3DD

Thatched character pub with cosy range of low-beamed little rooms, making a memorable spot for a drink

The snug low-beamed little rooms of this atmospheric place date back nearly 650 years, making it one of the oldest pubs in Wales. There's a central servery and the character rooms leading off have tiny doorways, open fires (including one in an inglenook with antique oak seats built into the stripped stonework) and other seats and tables worked into a series of chatty little alcoves. The more open front bar still has an ancient lime-ash floor and keeps Brains Bitter, Theakstons Old Peculier, Wadworths 6X, Wye Valley HPA and a guest from Tomos Watkin on handpump, as well as farm cider and eight wines by the glass. Rustic seats shelter peacefully among tubs and troughs of flowers outside, with stone tables on a newer terrace.

The pub can get very full in the evenings and on summer weekends. A path from here leads to the shingle flats of the estuary.

Tasty food includes sandwiches, confit duck leg samosa with barbecue sauce, twice-baked cheddar and chive soufflé with walnut, pear and leaf salad, spinach and ricotta ravioli topped with tomato coulis, thai green chicken curry, bass fillet with brown shrimp, mussel and saffron sauce, pheasant coq au vin, venison haunch with celeriac mash and wild mushroom and madeira sauce, and puddings such as sticky toffee pudding with toffee sauce and vanilla and honeycomb cheesecake with salted caramel sauce. *Benchmark main dish: slow-braised rib of beef £11.50. Two-course evening meal £15.00.*

Free house ~ Licensee Jeremy Coleman ~ Real ale ~ Open 11-11; 12-10.30 Sun ~ Bar food 12-2, 6-9; 12-3 Sun ~ Restaurant ~ Children welcome ~ Dogs allowed in bar ~ Wi-fi
Recommended by Alfie Bayliss, Harvey Brown, Melvyn Jones, Ian Duncan

FELINFACH
Griffin 🍴 ♀ 🍺 🛏   SO0933 Map 6

(01874) 620111 – www.eatdrinksleep.ltd.uk
A470 NE of Brecon; LD3 0UB

Wales Dining Pub of the Year

Highly thought-of dining pub with excellent food, a fine range of drinks and upbeat rustic décor; inviting bedrooms

Civilised but easy-going and genuinely friendly, this is a special place with every aspect carefully thought out. The back bar is quite pubby in an up-to-date way, with four leather sofas around a low table on pitted quarry tiles by a high slate hearth with a log fire. Behind them are mixed stripped seats around scrubbed kitchen tables on bare boards, and a bright blue and ochre colour scheme with some modern prints. The acoustics are pretty lively, due to so much bare flooring and uncurtained windows; background music, board games and plenty of books. Efficient staff serve interesting drinks, many from smaller independent suppliers, including well chosen wines (18 by the glass and carafe and they have a wine shop), welsh spirits, cocktails, local bottled cider, locally sourced apple juice, non-alcoholic cocktails made with produce from their garden, unusual continental and local bottled beers and a range of sherries. There's Coastal Drummer Boy, Montys Pale Ale and Wye Valley Butty Bach on handpump. The two smallish front dining rooms that link to the back bar are attractive. On the left: mixed dining chairs around mainly stripped tables on flagstones and white-painted rough stone walls, with a cream-coloured Aga in a big stripped-stone embrasure. On the right: similar furniture on bare boards, big modern prints on terracotta walls and smart dark curtains. Children can play with the landlady's dog and visit the chickens in the henhouse. Dogs may sit with owners at certain tables while dining. There are seats and tables outside. The inn makes a fine base for exploring the area, with comfortable, tastefully decorated bedrooms and hearty breakfasts that are nicely informal – you make your own toast and help yourself to home-made marmalade and jam. Good wheelchair access.

Exceptional food using home-grown and other local produce includes pig cheek with carrot and apple slaw and barbecue sauce, mackerel with celeriac, pear and air-dried ham, potato gnocchi with spring onion, goats curd, pine nuts and asparagus velouté, smoked local sausage with baby leeks, jerusalem artichoke and apple, coq au vin, duck leg with pomme purée, peas, asparagus and pancetta and gem lettuce fricassée, hake with celeriac, sesame, brown crab and soy butter, and puddings such as chocolate pave with redcurrants and mint and gooseberry and apple compote with sugar crumb and sorbet. *Benchmark main dish: venison haunch with beetroot, pickled red cabbage and cacao £21.00. Two-course evening meal £25.00.*

Free house ~ Licensees Charles and Edmund Inkin and Julie Bell ~ Real ale ~ Open 11-11 ~ Bar food 12-2.30, 6-9 (9.30 Fri, Sat) ~ Restaurant ~ Children welcome ~ Dogs allowed in bar and bedrooms ~ Bedrooms: £110/£130 *Recommended by John Jenkins, Mrs A W Johns, Miss B D Picton, Guy Vowles, Brian and Sally Wakeham*

GRESFORD
SJ3453   Map 6

Pant-yr-Ochain 🌟 ♟ 🍺

(01978) 853525 – www.brunningandprice.co.uk/pantyrochain

Off A483 on N edge of Wrexham: at roundabout take A5156 (A534) towards Nantwich, then first left towards the Flash; LL12 8TY

Particularly well run dining pub with good food all day, a very wide range of drinks and pretty lakeside garden

Surrounded by herbaceous borders, the tables and chairs on the terrace in front of this elaborately gabled 16th-c place look over a lake with waterfowl; there are more seats spread around the attractive grounds. The light and airy rooms inside are stylishly decorated with a wide range of interesting prints and bric-a-brac, and a good mix of individually chosen country furnishings, including comfortable seats for relaxing as well as more upright ones for eating. One area is set out as a library, with floor-to-ceiling bookshelves, there's a good open fire, and a popular dining conservatory overlooking the garden; board games. The impressive line-up of drinks served by well trained staff includes Phoenix Brunning & Price Original and guests such as Big Hand Havok, Hawkshead Brodies Prime Export, Purple Moose Snowdonia Ale, and Stonehouse Off the Rails on handpump, a farm cider, 17 wines by the glass, around 80 malt whiskies and a good choice of gins and vodkas. Good disabled access.

 Good, interesting food includes sandwiches, tempura calamari with pickled cucumber and roast garlic aioli, smoked salmon and crab parcel with basil mayonnaise, king prawn and chorizo pasta with tomato sauce, coq au vin, honey-roasted ham with free-range eggs, cauliflower, sweet potato and chickpea tagine with couscous, lamb and vegetable pudding with mint gravy, fish pie, duck breast with garlic and herb parmentier potatoes and redcurrant jus, and puddings such as eton mess and baked vanilla cheesecake with raspberry sorbet. *Benchmark main dish: beer-battered fish and chips £12.95. Two-course evening meal £20.00.*

Brunning & Price ~ Licensee James Meakin ~ Real ale ~ Open 11-11; 12-10.30 Sun ~ Bar food 12-9.30 (9 Sun) ~ Children welcome ~ Dogs allowed in bar ~ Wi-fi *Recommended by Clive Watkin, Miles Green, Sandra Morgan, Douglas Power*

LLANARMON DYFFRYN CEIRIOG
SJ1532   Map 6

Hand 🛏

(01691) 600666 – www.thehandhotel.co.uk

B4500 from Chirk; LL20 7LD

16th-c country inn with easy-going atmosphere in bar and dining room, friendly owners and enjoyable food and drinks; bedrooms

Our readers very much enjoy staying overnight in this remote, warmly welcoming former drovers' inn. The bedrooms are well equipped and spacious and the breakfasts splendid. A low-beamed bar has an inglenook log fire, sturdy tables and a mix of seating including settles, wheelbacks and mate's chairs on carpet, old prints on the walls and stools along the counter where they keep Big Hand Bastion and Weetwood Cheshire Cat Blonde Ale on handpump, seven wines by the glass and 17 malt whiskies. The largely stripped-stone dining room has a woodburning stove, and there's a quiet sitting room (ideal for planning excursions); the games room has darts and pool. Picnic-tables sit on the crazy-paved front terrace and the garden has more seats and tables. You can walk for hours from the door as the pub is at the heart of the Upper Ceiriog Valley and backdropped by the Berwyn Mountains; dogs are allowed in some bedrooms – best to ring in advance.

Good food includes sandwiches, venison carpaccio with yoghurt, cheese and onion seeds, spiced duck pakoras with cauliflower cheese purée, vegetable bhajis with cheese and leeks, smoked and fresh haddock fish pie topped with smoked paprika mash, cider-braised pork loin with cassis onions, pork and peanut crumbs and cider butter sauce, salmon fillet with a broth of bean sprouts, coriander, soy, fennel and fresh coconut, and puddings such as Valrhona dark chocolate délice and lemon curd and thyme crème brûlée. *Benchmark main dish: roast rump of lamb £16.50. Two-course evening meal £22.00.*

Free house ~ Licensees Jonathan and Jackie Greatorex ~ Real ale ~ Open 11-11 (1am Sat); 12-11.30 Sun ~ Bar food 12-2.30, 6-8.30 ~ Restaurant ~ Children welcome but not after 8pm in bar ~ Dogs allowed in bar and bedrooms ~ Wi-fi ~ Bedrooms: £55/£107.50
Recommended by Clive Watkin, Dennis and Doreen Haward, Julie Braeburn

LLANARMON DYFFRYN CEIRIOG SJ1532 Map 6

West Arms

(01691) 600665 – www.thewestarms.co.uk
End of B4500 W of Chirk; LL20 7LD

An inn since 1570 with fine walks all around, public bar, lounge and separate restaurant, excellent food and pretty gardens; bedrooms

The surroundings here are lovely and this former farm has been offering shelter and food to customers for around 500 years. There's a small back public bar plus a beamed and timbered smarter lounge with antique settles, sofas and even an elaborately carved confessional stall. The old-fashioned entrance hall has more sofas, and there are several log fires, horsebrasses and copper and brass items and an attractive, slightly more formal restaurant. Brains Rev James, Sharps Doom Bar and Wye Valley HPA on handpump served by friendly staff, six wines by the glass and six malt whiskies; background music, darts and board games. The garden has plenty of seats and a pretty lawn running down to River Ceiriog (fishing for residents). There's a choice of character bedrooms in the main building or contemporary ones at the back – all are well equipped and comfortable; marvellous walks are available all around.

From a well judged menu, the highly thought-of food includes sandwiches, king scallops with pancetta and cauliflower purée and white wine sauce, venison and prawn terrine wrapped in bacon with chutney, butternut squash, gruyère and spinach with white wine sauce, gammon with free-range eggs or pineapple, duck breast with oriental greens, croquette potato and port and damson sauce, guinea fowl with bacon and thyme, rösti potato and wild mushroom and madeira sauce, and puddings such as belgian waffle with butterscotch sauce and coconut, and strawberry and white chocolate cheesecake. *Benchmark main dish: local rib-eye steak with garlic mushrooms and chips £19.75. Two-course evening meal £22.75.*

Free house ~ Licensee Phillip Evoy ~ Real ale ~ Open 12-11 ~ Bar food 12-2, 6.30-9 ~ Restaurant ~ Children welcome ~ Dogs allowed in bar and bedrooms ~ Wi-fi ~ Bedrooms: £65/£115 *Recommended by Isobel Mackinlay, Belinda May, Sally and David Champion, Dave Sutton*

LLANBERIS
Pen-y-Gwryd 🛏

SH6655 Map 6

(01286) 870211 – www.pyg.co.uk

Nant Gwynant; at junction of A498 and A4086, ie across mountains from Llanberis –
OS Sheet 115 map reference 660558; LL55 4NT

Atmospheric and cheerfully unchanged mountaineers' haunt in the wilds of Snowdonia, run by the same family since 1947; bedrooms

Memorably placed beneath Snowdon and the Glyders, this family-run mountain inn is packed with items left by the climbing fraternity. You can still make out the fading signatures scrawled on the ceiling by the 1953 Everest team, who used this as a training base, and on display is the very rope that connected Hillary and Tenzing on top of the mountain. One snug little room in the homely slate-floored log cabin bar has built-in wall benches and sturdy country chairs. From here you can look out to precipitous Moel Siabod beyond the lake opposite. A smaller room has a worthy collection of illustrious boots from famous climbs, while a cosy panelled smoke room has more fascinating climbing mementoes and equipment; darts, pool, board games, skittles, bar billiards and table tennis. Purple Moose Glaslyn and Madogs are on handpump and they have several malts. Staying in the comfortable but basic bedrooms can be quite an experience, and there's an excellent traditional breakfast (served 8.30-9am, though they may serve earlier); dogs £5 a night. The inn has its own chapel (built for the millennium and dedicated by the Archbishop of Wales), sauna and outdoor natural pool, and the garden overlooks a lake.

The short choice of simple, good-value lunchtime food includes rolls, ploughman's, pies, salads, and quiche of the day as well as daily specials such as roast beef. The hearty three- or five-course set meal in the evening restaurant is signalled by a gong at 7.30pm (if you're late, you'll miss it): maybe chicken liver pâté or smoked salmon followed by loin of pork with leeks, cannellini beans and cream, beef in ale pie or salmon fillet with hollandaise, and puddings such as banoffi pie or chocolate bread and butter pudding. *Benchmark main dish: roast lamb £10.95. Two-course evening meal £25.00.*

Free house ~ Licensee Nicholas Pullee ~ Real ale ~ Open 11-11; closed weekdays Dec in winter; closed Jan, Feb ~ Bar food 12-2; evening meal 7.30pm ~ Restaurant evening ~ Children welcome ~ Dogs welcome ~ Wi-fi ~ Bedrooms: £45/£90 *Recommended by Isobel Mackinlay, Alison and Michael Harper, Peter and Emma Kelly, Helena and Trevor Fraser*

LLANDUDNO JUNCTION
Queens Head ⭐❂ 🍷

SH8180 Map 6

(01492) 546570 – www.queensheadglanwydden.co.uk

Glanwydden; heading towards Llandudno on B5115 from Colwyn Bay, turn left
into Llanrhos Road at roundabout as you enter the Penrhyn Bay speed limit;
Glanwydden is signed as the first left turn; LL31 9JP

Consistently good food served all day at comfortably modern dining pub

Although this looks like an unassuming village pub, don't be fooled. The main draw is the excellent food which customers travel many miles for – so you must book a table in advance. The spacious modern lounge bar – partly divided by a white wall of broad arches – has beams, beige plush wall banquettes, rush-seated wooden and high-backed black leather dining chairs around neat black tables on tartan carpeting, an open woodburning stove and fresh flowers. The little public bar keeps Adnams Best, Great Orme IPA and a guest beer on handpump, 12 decent wines by the glass, several malt whiskies and good coffee; background music. There's a pleasing mix of seats and tables under parasols outside. Northern Snowdonia is within easy reach, and the pretty stone cottage (which sleeps two) across the road is for rent.

 Tempting food using local ingredients includes sandwiches, crispy lamb and feta salad with mint and yoghurt dressing, avocado, prawns and smoked salmon, pea and asparagus risotto with truffle oil, moules marinière, burger with toppings and chips, thai-spiced salmon, lime and coriander fishcakes with chilli jam, steak in ale pie, chicken korma, calves liver and crispy bacon with onion gravy, seafood vol au vent, and puddings such as cherry bakewell tart and white chocolate tiramisu. *Benchmark main dish: braised lamb shoulder with mash and redcurrant and rosemary gravy £14.95. Two-course evening meal £19.00.*

Free house ~ Licensees Robert and Sally Cureton ~ Real ale ~ Open 12-11 ~ Bar food 12-9 ~ Restaurant ~ Children welcome ~ Wi-fi *Recommended by Barry and Daphne Gregson, Mike and Mary Carter, Graham Smart*

LLANELIAN-YN-RHOS SH8676 Map 6
White Lion
(01492) 515807 – www.whitelioninn.co.uk
Signed off A5830 (shown as B5383 on some maps) and B5381, S of Colwyn Bay; LL29 8YA

Bustling local with bar and spacious dining areas, tasty food, real ales and helpful staff

This picturesque old village pub is tucked away at a crossing of narrow lanes in quiet hilly countryside above Colwyn Bay. Each of the two distinct parts, linked by a broad flight of steps, has its own cheery personality. Up at the top is a very spacious and neat dining area, while at the other end is a traditional old bar with antique high-backed settles fitting snugly around a big fireplace, and flagstones by the counter; parts of the building are said to date back 1,200 years. Marstons Burton Bitter, Purple Moose Fleetwing and Spitting Feathers Thirst Quencher on handpump, 13 wines by the glass, farm cider and ten malt whiskies are served by helpful staff. Off to the left is another dining room with jugs hanging from beams and teapots above the windows; background music. There are tables in an attractive courtyard (also used for parking) next to the church.

Popular food includes sandwiches, deep-fried goats cheese with red onion chutney, prawn cocktail, steak and kidney pies, chicken curry, flat mushroom with garlic, pesto, basil and stilton on potato salad, barbecue spare ribs with chips, slow-cooked beef in Guinness with peppered red cabbage, chicken topped with bacon, cheese and mushrooms with rosemary and sage sauce, steaks with a choice of sauces, and puddings such as apple pie and chocolate fudge cake. *Benchmark main dish: roast beef with yorkshire pudding £10.95. Two-course evening meal £18.00.*

Free house ~ Licensee Simon Cole ~ Real ale ~ Open 12-3.30, 6 (5 Sat)-11; 12-10.30 Sun; closed Mon except school and bank holidays ~ Bar food 12-2, 6 (5 Fri, Sat)-9; 12-8.30 Sun ~ Restaurant ~ Children welcome ~ Wi-fi ~ Live jazz Tues evening, live music Weds evening, sing-along first Sun of month, welsh singing 3rd Sat evening of month
Recommended by Rob Anderson, Alison and Michael Harper, George Sanderson

---

Please tell us if the décor, atmosphere, food or drink at a pub is different from our description. We rely on readers' reports to keep us up to date: feedback@goodguides.com, or (no stamp needed) The Good Pub Guide, FREEPOST RTJR-ZCYZ-RJZT, Perrymans Lane, Etchingham TN19 7DN.

LLANFAETHLU
Black Lion 🌟 🛏

SH3286 Map 6

(01407) 730718 – www.blacklionanglesey.com

A5025; LL65 4NL

Friendly pub with enjoyable food and drink, a friendly welcome and fine views from terrace; comfortable bedrooms

Carefully renovated after seven years of dereliction, this 18th-c inn is now a bustling pub with hard-working licensees. It's been brought back to life with elegant simplicity and contemporary paintwork and the atmosphere throughout is easy-going and friendly. There's a cosy bar equipped with a woodburning stove, wooden tables and chairs on black slates and a few high-backed stools at the oak-topped counter where they keep Marstons Pedigree, Purple Moose Snowdonia Ale and a summer guest on handpump, seven wines by the glass and welsh whisky and gin; background music. A high-raftered, similarly furnished dining room with another woodburner has french doors leading out to the terrace where there are seats that look across the countryside to the magnificent Snowdonia mountains. The two spacious bedrooms are well appointed.

 Particularly good food using meat from the family farm and other local and foraged produce includes interesting nibbles, crispy poached egg with pressed tomato and garlic, black pudding purée and bacon bits, mini haddock goujons with pea purée, parmentier potatoes and tartare sauce, a pie of the day, vegetable and toasted nut baklava with braised red cabbage and creamed leeks, seared fish of the day with steamed mussels and creamy garlic butter, slow-roasted pork belly with chorizo, butter bean and spinach stew, two-way beef (braised ox cheek and brisket cottage pie), and puddings such as rhubarb and elderflower syrup sponge cake with vanilla crisp sticks and crushed meringue-coated vanilla ice-cream and salted caramel pannacotta with peanut brittle and peanut butter fudge. *Benchmark main dish: slow-braised lamb shoulder £16.95. Two-course evening meal £23.00.*

Free house ~ Licensees Leigh and Mari Faulkner ~ Real ale ~ Open 12-3, 5.30-11; 12-11 Sat, Sun; closed Mon, Tues, lunchtime Weds; check website for opening hours outside school holidays ~ Bar food 12-1.45, 6-8 (9 Fri, Sat); 12-1.45 Sun ~ Children welcome ~ Dogs welcome ~ Wi-fi ~ Bedrooms: £90/£115 *Recommended by Rob Anderson, Alison and Michael Harper, Pip White*

LLANFIHANGEL-Y-CREUDDYN
Y Ffarmers 🌟

SN6676 Map 6

(01974) 261275 – www.yffarmers.co.uk

Village signed off A4120 W of Pisgah; SY23 4LA

Welsh- and English-speaking pub with traditional furnishings in bar and dining areas, local ales and good food

The chef-landlord and his wife work hard to attract both drinkers and diners to their bilingual pub, which is very much the hub of the community. It's been carefully and simply refurbished, with high chairs and stools against the green-painted counter where they keep local ales on handpump such as Evan Evans Cwrw, Mantle Moho and maybe a guest from Montys, farm ciders and six wines by the glass; background music, TV and darts. There's a woodburning stove in a little fireplace, cushioned armed wheelback chairs, mate's chairs and a box settle around dark tables (each set with fresh flower arrangements), wooden floors and walls painted white or red. As well as a sunken terrace with seats, there's a lawn with picnic-sets under parasols. The 13th-c village church is opposite.

Food is especially good and uses trusted local producers: beetroot carpaccio with walnuts and goats cheese, mini fish pie with salmon, cod and crab, a pie of the day, courgette, chickpea and cashew nut curry with onion bhaji, beer-battered cod and chips, duck breast with sweet potato galette, charred asparagus and madiera, shallot and lemongrass sauce, guinea fowl with wild garlic sauce, honey-roast bacon steak with hash brown and pineapple salsa, and puddings such as gorse-flower crème brûlée with coconut sorbet and chocolate brownie with salted caramel ice-cream. *Benchmark main dish: local monkfish with samphire and Noilly Prat sauce £17.00. Two-course evening meal £19.00.*

Free house ~ Licensees Esther Prytherch and Rhodri Edwards ~ Real ale ~ Open 12-2, 6-11 (midnight Sat); 12-2, 7-11 Sun; closed Mon, winter Sun evening, first week Jan ~ Bar food 12-2, 6-9; not Sun evening, Mon, Tues lunchtime ~ Restaurant ~ Children welcome ~ Dogs allowed in bar ~ Wi-fi *Recommended by Andrew Stone, Toby Jones, B and M Kendall, Dr Simon Innes*

LLANGOLLEN
SJ2142 Map 6

Corn Mill 🌟 ♟ 🍺

(01978) 869555 – www.brunningandprice.co.uk/cornmill

Dee Lane, very narrow lane off Castle Street (A539) just S of bridge; nearby parking can be tricky, may be best to use public park on Parade Street/East Street and walk; LL20 8PN

Fascinating riverside building with fine views, personable young staff, super food all day and good beers

'Excellent in every aspect' is just one enthusiastic comment from our readers about this cleverly restored watermill. Inside, the interior has been interestingly refitted with pale pine flooring on stout beams, a striking open stairway with gleaming timber and tensioned steel rails, and mainly stripped-stone walls. Quite a lot of the old machinery is still in place, including the huge waterwheel (often turning) and there are good-sized dining tables, big rugs, thoughtfully chosen pictures (many to do with water) and several pot plants. One of the two serving bars, away from the water, has a much more local feel with regulars sitting on bar stools, pews on dark slate flagstones and daily papers. Helpful young staff serve Phoenix Brunning & Price Original and Facers DHB on handpump with a couple of guests such as Otter Summer Light and Phoenix Arizona; also, farm cider, around 50 sensibly priced malt whiskies and a decent wine choice with around a dozen by the glass. There are seats on a raised deck at the front that overlook the rushing millrace and rapids below; you can also watch steam trains arriving and leaving the station on the opposite riverbank.

Well presented and highly regarded food includes sandwiches, shredded duck, orange and pistachio nut salad with pomegranate dressing, devilled bass fillet with cucumber, mint and pink grapefruit salad with saffron mayonnaise, aubergine, red lentil and spinach curry with cauliflower pakora and raita, ham and free-range eggs, steak in ale pie, provençale fish stew with gruyère cheese croutons, pork and caramelised red onion sausages with mash and onion gravy, and puddings such as glazed lemon tart with raspberry sorbet and eton mess. *Benchmark main dish: slow-braised lamb shoulder with dauphinoise potatoes and red wine and rosemary sauce £16.95. Two-course evening meal £24.95.*

Brunning & Price ~ Manager Andrew Barker ~ Real ale ~ Open 11-11 (10.30 Sun) ~ Bar food 12-9.30 (9 Sun) ~ Restaurant ~ Children welcome ~ Dogs allowed in bar ~ Wi-fi *Recommended by Clive and Fran Dutson, Clive Watkin, John and Enid, Mike and Mary Carter, Helen McLagan*

LLANMADOC
SS4493 Map 6

Britannia

(01792) 386624 – www.britanniainngower.co.uk

The Gower, near Whiteford Burrows (NT); SA3 1DB

Fine views from seats behind this popular pub with more in the big garden, well liked food and ales and friendly staff

As this 18th-c dining pub is on the north coast of the Gower peninsula, there are lovely nearby walks. You can warm yourself afterwards by the newly installed woodburning stove in the refurbished beamed bar and enjoy a pint of Marstons Pedigree and Sharps Doom Bar on handpump and several wines by the glass; darts and TV. The beamed restaurant has attractive modern wooden tables and chairs on a striped carpet and paintings on bare stone walls. The picnic-sets on the raised decked area at the back of the building have marvellous views over the Loughor estuary and get snapped up quickly when the weather is warm; there are also tables out in front and in the spacious garden. They have a rabbit hutch and an aviary which houses budgies, cockatiels, quails and a parrot.

 Reliably good food includes sandwiches, chicken liver parfait, pigeon breast with black pudding, pea purée and wild mushroom fricassée and a quail egg, vegetable thai curry, steak in ale pie, pheasant breast and confit leg with caramelised red cabbage and mulled wine jus, beer-battered hake and chips, slow-braised rabbit casserole, bream fillet with saffron and mussel curry cream, and puddings such as profiteroles filled with white chocolate mousse and covered in hot chocolate sauce and sticky toffee pudding; they also offer a two- and three-course menu. *Benchmark main dish: trio of salt marsh lamb with dauphinoise potatoes, truffle celeriac purée and lamb gravy £25.00. Two-course evening meal £25.00.*

Enterprise ~ Tenants Martin and Lindsey Davies ~ Real ale ~ Open 12-11 ~ Bar food 12-2.30, 6.30-8.30; all day weekends ~ Restaurant ~ Children welcome ~ Dogs allowed in bar ~ Wi-fi *Recommended by Hugh Roberts, R T and J C Moggridge*

MOLD
SJ2465 Map 6

Glasfryn 🏵 ⚪ 🍺

(01352) 750500 – www.brunningandprice.co.uk/glasfryn

N of the centre on Raikes Lane (parallel to the A5119), just past the well signposted Theatr Clwyd; CH7 6LR

Lively open-plan bistro-style pub with inventive all-day food, nice décor and wide choice of drinks

There's a lively, cheerful atmosphere and wide mix of customers in this neat and rather unassuming-looking pub. The open-plan interior is cleverly laid out to create plenty of nice quiet corners with a mix of informal, attractive country furnishings, turkey-style rugs on bare boards, deep red ceilings (some high), a warming fire and plenty of close-hung homely pictures; background music. The fine selection of drinks includes Phoenix Brunning & Price Original plus guests such as Crouch Vale Brewers Gold, Hobsons Best, Roosters Yankee, Salopian Darwins Origin, Tatton Best and Timothy Taylors Boltmaker on handpump, 22 wines by the glass, 30 gins, 25 rums, 60 malt whiskies and farm cider. On warm days, the wooden tables on the large front terrace are a restful place to sit, providing sweeping views of the Clwydian Hills. Theatre Clwyd is just over the road.

Rewarding food includes sandwiches, satay king prawns with toasted cashew nuts, chicken liver pâté with fig chutney, pork and leek sausages with onion gravy, cheese, leek and potato pie with cranberry jus, chicken breast with haggis cake, neeps and tatties, smoked bacon and barley broth, steak in ale pudding, cod loin with saffron fondant and bisque sauce, seared duck with duck croquette, baby parsnips and clementine purée, and puddings such as hot waffle with caramelised banana and toffee sauce, and rhubarb trifle with orange cream. *Benchmark main dish: sicilian fish stew £15.95. Two-course evening meal £19.50.*

Brunning & Price ~ Manager Graham Arathoon ~ Real ale ~ Open 10.30am-11pm (10.30pm Sun) ~ Bar food 12-9.30 (9 Sun) ~ Children welcome ~ Dogs allowed in bar ~ Wi-fi *Recommended by Clive Watkin, Mike and Mary Carter, Stuart Paulley*

 MONKNASH   SS9170   Map 6

Plough & Harrow  £

(01656) 890209 ~ www.ploughandharrow.org
Signposted 'Marcross, Broughton' off B4265 St Brides Major–Llantwit Major – turn left at end of Water Street; OS Sheet 170 map reference 920706; CF71 7QQ

Old building full of history and character, with a huge log fire and a good choice of real ales

They keep a fine range of eight real ales on handpump or tapped from the cask in this historic pub, such as Bass, Cwrw lal Haf Gwyn, Purple Moose Glaslyn Ale, Sharps Atlantic, Valley Forge Vanilla Porter, Wye Valley HPA and a guest from Mumbles or Tomos Watkin; they usually hold beer festivals in June and September. Also, a good range of local farm cider and welsh and scottish malt whiskies. The unspoilt main bar with its massively thick stone walls used to be the scriptures room and mortuary (some of the building once formed part of a monastic grange); it has ancient ham hooks in the heavily beamed ceiling, an intriguing arched doorway at the back, broad flagstones and a comfortably informal mix of furnishings that includes three fine stripped-pine settles. There's a log fire in a huge fireplace with a side bread oven large enough to feed a village; background music in the left-hand room. The front garden has some picnic-sets. A path from the pub leads through the wooded valley of Cwm Nash to the coast, revealing a spectacular stretch of cliffs around Nash Point. Dogs are welcome in the bar, but are not allowed there while food is being served.

Changing food includes sandwiches, garlic mushrooms, squid and chorizo with chilli, spring onion, mushroom and garlic risotto, burgers with toppings and chips, a fresh fish dish of the day, cajun chicken with sautéed potatoes, lamb shank in red wine jus, and puddings such as apple crumble and sticky toffee pudding. *Benchmark main dish: swordfish with basil pesto £12.50. Two-course evening meal £18.00.*

Free house ~ Licensee Paula Jones ~ Real ale ~ Open 12-11 (10.30 Sun) ~ Bar food 12-2.30 (5 weekends), 6-9; not Sun evening ~ Restaurant ~ Children welcome ~ Dogs allowed in bar ~ Live music Sat evening *Recommended by Martin Jones, Andrew Stone, Alan and Alice Morgan, Sandra King*

 NEWPORT   SN0539   Map 6

Golden Lion 🛏

(01239) 820321 ~ www.goldenlionpembrokeshire.co.uk
East Street (A487); SA42 0SY

Nicely redone and friendly local, with tasty food and pleasant staff; well appointed bedrooms

Our readers love staying in the comfortable and fair value bedrooms in this lively local. But then they also like popping in for a drink and a chat and having a particularly good meal in the incredibly popular restaurant too; it really is a smashing all-rounder. As well as a genuinely pubby bar, there's a cosy series of beamed rooms with distinctive old settles, Sharps Doom Bar and a couple of guest ales from the nearby Bluestone Brewery on handpump, as well as several malt whiskies, wines by the glass and Gwynt y Ddraig cider; background music, pool, juke box, darts, board games, dominoes and games machine. The dining room has elegant blond oak furniture, whitewashed walls and potted plants; service is efficient and friendly. There are tables outside at the front and in a side garden; good disabled access and facilities. Pembrokeshire Coast Path is not far.

Extremely tasty food includes lunchtime sandwiches, smoked salmon, king prawns and lemon aioli, creamy garlic mushrooms, burger with toppings, mustard mayonnaise and chips, thai green vegetable curry, gammon steak with leek, mustard and melted cheese topping, lemon, garlic and chilli marinated chicken supreme, local lamb chops with rosemary and mint sauce, and puddings such as a crumble of the day with coconut and almond topping and dark chocolate and peanut brownie with vanilla ice-cream. *Benchmark main dish: beer-battered cod and chips £11.95. Two-course evening meal £18.00.*

Free house ~ Licensee Daron Paish ~ Real ale ~ Open 12pm-2am ~ Bar food 12-2.30, 6.30-9 ~ Restaurant ~ Children welcome ~ Dogs allowed in bar and bedrooms ~ Wi-fi ~ Bedrooms: £80/£100 *Recommended by Ron Corbett, R T and J C Moggridge, Colin and Daniel Gibbs, Mark Hamill*

OLD RADNOR
SO2459 Map 6

Harp 🌟 ⇖

(01544) 350655 – www.harpinnradnor.co.uk
Village signposted off A44 Kington–New Radnor in Walton; LD8 2RH

Delightful inn in beautiful spot, with cottagey bar, tasty food and well kept ales; comfortable bedrooms

You can be sure of a genuine welcome from the hands-on licensees in this charming place in its spectacular location on the top of a hill. The public bar has a great deal of character plus high-backed settles, an antique reader's chair and other venerable chairs around a log fire; board games, cribbage, darts and quoits. The snug slate-floored bar contains a handsome curved antique settle, a log fire in a fine inglenook and lots of local books, maps and guides for residents; a quieter dining area off to the right extends into another dining room with a woodburning stove. Hobsons Town Crier and Twisted Spire and Three Tuns XXX on handpump, as well as five wines by the glass, Dunkerton's cider and perry, local apple and pear juices, and several malt whiskies. Tables outside make the most of the view overlooking the heights of Radnor Forest. Our readers very much enjoy staying in the spic and span rooms here (no door keys) which share the same lovely views; enjoyable breakfasts too. The impressive village church is worth a look for its early organ case (Britain's oldest), fine rood screen and ancient font.

Appealing food using local produce includes sandwiches, chicken liver pâté with red onion jam, smoked salmon and caper butter roulade, crab-stuffed tomato, crayfish and sweet chilli cocktail, pickled cucumber and dill scone, home-cooked ham and eggs, celeriac and sweet potato dauphinoise with tofu, sesame-battered green beans and beetroot dressing, braised lamb shoulder with carrot purée, pickled red cabbage and jus, and puddings such as bitter chocolate parfait with poached pear, stem ginger ice-cream and ginger syrup and steamed toffee apple pudding with white chocolate ice-cream. *Benchmark main dish: 8oz rump steak with home-made chips £15.00. Two-course evening meal £21.00.*

Free house ~ Licensees Chris and Angela Ireland ~ Real ale ~ Open 6-11 Weds, Thurs; 12-3, 6-11 Fri-Sun; closed Mon, Tues ~ Bar food 12-2 Fri-Sun; 6-9 Weds-Sat ~ Children

welcome ~ Dogs allowed in bar and bedrooms ~ Wi-fi ~ Bedrooms: £75/£105
Recommended by Sara Fulton, Roger Baker, Anne and Ben Smith, Alison and Michael Harper

OVERTON BRIDGE

SJ3542   Map 6

Cross Foxes 🌟 ♀

(01978) 780380 – www.brunningandprice.co.uk/crossfoxes
A539 W of Overton, near Erbistock; LL13 0DR

**Terrific river views, contemporary food and an extensive range
of drinks in bustling, well run pub**

A fine range of drinks in this 18th-c coaching inn includes 40 malt
whiskies, 30 Armagnacs, 28 gins and lots of wines by the glass – plus
Phoenix Brunning & Price Original, Brakspears Bitter, Jennings Queen Bee,
Marstons EPA, Wychwood Jester Jack and a couple of guests on handpump
and a farm cider; service is friendly and efficient. The ancient low-beamed
bar, with its red tiled floor, dark timbers, warm fire in the big inglenook
and built-in old pews, is more traditional than most pubs in the Brunning
& Price group, though the characteristic turkey rugs, large pot plants and
frame-to-frame pictures are present, as they are in the dining areas; board
games and newspapers. Big windows all round the airy dining conservatory
provide views over the River Dee, as do seats and tables set out on the
raised terrace and picnic-sets on grass.

 A wide choice of well presented modern dishes includes sandwiches, duck
croquettes with asian noodles, pickled pak choi and hoisin dressing, scallops
with leeks and wild garlic, crispy cured ham and bloody mary sauce, spiced lamb kofta
kebab with tzatziki, mustard- and sugar-baked ham with free-range eggs, blue cheese
and walnut ravioli with garlic pesto and peppers, chicken breast stuffed with asparagus,
wrapped in bacon with lemon thyme risotto and salsa verde, beer-battered haddock and
chips, seared pigeon with peas, bacon and gem lettuce with a raspberry and balsamic
vinaigrette, and puddings such as rhubarb trifle and crème brûlée. *Benchmark main
dish: pork and chorizo meatballs with tomato sauce on linguine £12.95. Two-course
evening meal £20.00.*

Brunning & Price ~ Manager Ian Pritchard-Jones ~ Real ale ~ Open 11-11 (10.30 Sun) ~
Bar food 12-9.30 (9 Sun) ~ Children welcome ~ Dogs allowed in bar ~ Wi-fi
Recommended by David Longhurst, Julie Swift, Christopher Mannings

PANTYGELLI

SO3017   Map 6

Crown 🌟 ♀ 🍴

(01873) 853314 – www.thecrownatpantygelli.com
*Old Hereford Road N of Abergavenny; off A40 by war memorial via Pen Y Pound,
passing leisure centre; Pantygelli also signposted from A465; NP7 7HR*

**Country pub in fine scenery, attractive inside and out,
with good food and drinks**

On the edge of the Brecon Beacons National Park, this highly thought-
of pub is run by warmly friendly licensees. Wrought-iron and wicker
chairs on the flower-filled front terrace look up from the lush valley to
the hills and there's also a smaller back terrace surrounded by lavender.
Inside, the dark flagstoned bar, with sturdy timber props and beams, has
a log fire in a stone fireplace, a piano at the back with darts opposite,
Bass, Montys Pale Ale, Rhymney Best and Tomos Watkin Cwrw Haf on
handpump from the slate-roofed counter, Gwatkin's farm cider, seven good
wines by the glass, local organic apple juice and good coffees. On the left
are four smallish, linked, carpeted dining rooms, the front pair separated

by a massive stone chimneybreast; thoughtfully chosen individual furnishings and lots of attractive prints by local artists make it all thoroughly civilised. Also, background music, darts and board games.

 Popular, good food includes baguettes and ciabattas, prawn cocktail, pâté of the day with chutney, goats cheese tart, venison sausages with red onion gravy, lamb navarin with kale and roast sweet potatoes, chicken breast with leek and blue cheese-stuffed flat mushroom, potato rösti and red wine sauce, cod steak with sautéed peas, pancetta, artichoke heart, pimento peppers and pea purée, and puddings such as sticky toffee pudding with butterscotch sauce and Baileys and white chocolate cheesecake. *Benchmark main dish: steak in ale pie £11.00. Two-course evening meal £17.00.*

Free house ~ Licensees Steve and Cherrie Chadwick ~ Real ale ~ Open 12-2.30 (3 Sat), 6-11; 12-3, 6-10.30 Sun; closed Mon lunchtime ~ Bar food 12-2, 7-9; not Sun evening or Mon ~ Restaurant ~ Children welcome ~ Dogs allowed in bar ~ Wi-fi *Recommended by Christopher Mannings, Julian Richardson, Tim King*

PENNAL
Riverside 🍴
SH6900 Map 6

(01654) 791285 – www.riversidehotel-pennal.co.uk
A493; opposite church; SY20 9DW

Carefully refurbished pub with tasty food and local beers, and efficient young staff; bedrooms

This bustling pub is just inside the southern boundary of Snowdonia National Park, with plenty of fine surrounding walks. Most people are here to enjoy the wide choice of good quality food but there's quite a range of thoughtful drinks too. The neatly furnished rooms have green and white walls, slate tiles on the floor, a woodburning stove, modern light wood dining furniture and some funky fabrics. High-backed stools are lined up along the stone-fronted counter where they serve Purple Moose Glaslyn, Salopian Golden Thread and Tiny Rebel Cwtch with a guest from Vale of Glamorgan on handpump, 30 malt whiskies, 30 gins, 12 wines by the glass and farm cider; background music and dominoes. There are seats and tables in the garden, and they also run a Georgian guesthouse in the pretty village.

Interesting food includes baguettes, melon, prawn and crayfish with thai-spiced mayonnaise, crisp whitebait with tartare sauce, sharing boards, steak burger with toppings, chilli relish and skinny fries, mushroom risotto with a poached egg, chicken kiev with sweet potato fries and lemon mayonnaise, spiced mediterranean fish stew, gammon with free-range eggs, and puddings such as crème brûlée and a hot pudding of the day; they also offer a two- and three-course set menu (not weekend lunchtimes). *Benchmark main dish: local lamb steak with dauphinoise potatoes and red wine jus £17.50. Two-course evening meal £20.00.*

Free house ~ Licensees Glyn and Corina Davies ~ Real ale ~ Open 12-3, 6-11; 12-midnight Sat; 12-11 Sun; closed Mon; two weeks Jan ~ Bar food 12-2 (2.30 Sun), 6-9 ~ Restaurant ~ Children welcome ~ Dogs allowed in bar ~ Wi-fi ~ Bedrooms: £55/£75
Recommended by John Evans, Michael Butler, Mike and Mary Carter, Alf Wright

PENTYRCH
Kings Arms 🍴 ♀
ST1081 Map 6

(029) 2089 0202 – www.kingsarmspentyrch.co.uk
Church Road; CF15 9QF

Village pub very much part of the community with a perky bar, civilised lounge and top class food

Although many customers are here to enjoy the fantastic food, this 16th-c longhouse is not a straightforward dining place. It's very much a proper pub with plenty of regulars, and the cosy bar has a cheerful atmosphere, an open log fire in a sizeable brick fireplace and a mix of seats on flagstones. There's Brains Bitter and SA and guests from Grey Trees and Tiny Rebel on handpump, 14 wines by the glass and up to ten malt whiskies, all served by helpful, friendly staff. There's also a comfortable lounge and a cosy restaurant. If the weather is kind, there are plenty of seats on a terrace and picnic-sets under parasols in the garden.

 Cooked by the chef-patron, the highly rewarding food includes ham hock with crispy black pudding, apple, pickled shallot, honey-glazed bacon, crackling and poached egg, king scallops with crab bonbon and chilli jam, sharing boards, moroccan-style vegetable curry with pepper and chickpea couscous, flatbread and yoghurt, chicken kiev with aioli and chips, cod with sweetcorn purée, crab and spring onion croquette, chilli, spinach and sweetcorn chowder, a plate of pork (cider-braised cheek, pork belly, black pudding) with caramelised apple and cider jus, and puddings such as salted caramel chocolate tart with caramel parfait and lemon cheesecake with lemon curd. *Benchmark main dish: beer-battered fish and chips £11.00. Two-course evening meal £22.00.*

Free house ~ Licensee Andrew Aston ~ Real ale ~ Open 12-11; 12-midnight Sat; 12-8 Sun ~ Bar food 12-3, 5.30-9.30; 12-9.30 Sat; 12-4 Sun ~ Restaurant ~ Children welcome ~ Dogs allowed in bar ~ Wi-fi *Recommended by Martin Jones, Toby Jones, Patrick and Daphne Darley, Sally and David Champion*

PONTYPRIDD
Bunch of Grapes 🍴⭐ ♀ ◧

ST0790 Map 6

(01443) 402934 – www.bunchofgrapes.org.uk
Off A4054; Ynysangharad Road; CF37 4DA

Bustling pub with a fine choice of drinks in friendly, relaxed bar, delicious inventive food and a warm welcome for all

As well as exceptional food, this fine 18th-c pub offers a fantastic range of drinks too. Served by knowledgeable, friendly and efficient staff, these might include their own Otley O2 Croeso and three Otley guests plus other quickly changing guests such as Crouch Vale Amarillo, Dark Star Hophead and Salopian Hop Twister on handpump. They hold around six beer and music festivals each year, and also keep continental and american ales on draught or in bottles, a couple of local ciders or perrys, eight wines by the glass and good coffee. The cosy bar has an informal, relaxed atmosphere, comfortable leather sofas, wooden chairs and tables, a roaring log fire, newspapers to read and background music and board games. There's also a restaurant with elegant high-backed wooden dining chairs around a mix of tables and black and white local photo-prints taken by the landlord, who used to be a professional photographer. A deli offers home-baked bread and chutneys, home-cooked ham, local eggs and quite a choice of welsh cheeses and so forth, and they hold regular themed cookery evenings. There are seats outside on decking.

Accomplished cooking from a well judged menu includes sandwiches (until 6pm), scallops and cockles with laverbread crumb, leek purée and crispy pancetta, pork, raisin and sunflower seed terrine with white onion and fennel seed chutney, burgers with toppings and chips, pea, broad bean and spring onion risotto with leek and parsley purée and crisped banana shallot petals, slow-braised rabbit in cider with red chilli and garlic, black pudding and pomme gaufrette (very thinly sliced deep-fried potato), chicken with saffron aioli and dehydrated home-cured ham, sea trout with deep-fried wild garlic and lemon croquettes and burnt onion ketchup, and puddings such as lavender crème brûlée and white chocolate and raspberry cheesecake. *Benchmark main dish: slow-cooked shin of local beef with sun-dried tomato mash, breaded spring onion and red wine jus £15.50. Two-course evening meal £22.00.*

Free house ~ Licensee Nick Otley ~ Real ale ~ Open 11am-11.30pm; 12-11 Sun ~ Bar food 12-8.30 (7 Fri); 12-6.30 Sat ~ Restaurant ~ Children welcome ~ Dogs allowed in bar ~ Wi-fi
Recommended by Christopher Mannings, Edward Edmonton, Barry and Daphne Gregson, Elizabeth and Peter May

PUMSAINT   SN6540   Map 6

Dolaucothi Arms

(01558) 650237 ~ www.thedolaucothiarms.co.uk
A482 Lampeter–Llandovery; SA19 8UW

Friendly owners for much enjoyed little inn with simply furnished bar and dining room, local beers and riverside garden; bedrooms

This is a warm and cosy place to stay, with simply furnished bedrooms complete with a decanter of port and fresh biscuits. It's a genuinely welcoming National Trust-owned pub (and part of the Dolaucothi Estate). The chatty bar has a chesterfield and button-back armchair on red and black tiles to one side of the woodburning stove, stone bottles on the mantelpiece, some tables and chairs near the counter and Bluestone Rockhopper Pale Bitter and Evan Evans Cwrw on handpump, eight wines by the glass and farm cider; darts, background music and board games. The terracotta-painted dining room has another woodburning stove, heavy welsh dressers and all sorts of nice old dining chairs and tables on big flagstones; walls are hung with local art, maps and old photos of the pub, the village and the Estate. Outside, there are picnic-sets in a neat garden that overlooks the Cothi River where the pub has four miles of fishing rights.

As well as their popular pies and curries, the pleasing food (using produce from their new kitchen garden) includes sandwiches, black pudding scotch egg with pickled cabbage, roquefort soufflé, caramelised garlic and goats cheese tart, monkfish scampi with chips, beef cheeks braised in beer with swede and carrot mash and horseradish dumplings, 21-day-aged rump steak with garlic and thyme field mushrooms and onion rings, and puddings such as apple, rhubarb and almond crumble with custard and chocolate orange brownie with lemon curd and ice-cream. *Benchmark main dish: pie of the day £10.00. Two-course evening meal £15.00.*

Free house ~ Licensee David Joy ~ Real ale ~ Open 12-11; 4-11 Tues-Thurs; 12-8 Sun; closed Mon ~ Bar food 12.30-2.30, 6.30-8.30; not Tues lunchtime ~ Restaurant ~ Children welcome ~ Dogs allowed in bar and bedrooms ~ Wi-fi ~ Bedrooms: £60/£80 *Recommended by David Longhurst, Peter Barrett, James Allsopp*

RAGLAN   SO3609   Map 6

Clytha Arms 🎖 ♀ 🍷 🛏

(01873) 840206 ~ www.clytha-arms.com
Clytha, off Abergavenny road – former A40, now declassified; NP7 9BW

Fine setting in spacious grounds, a relaxing spot for enjoying good food and impressive range of drinks; comfortable bedrooms

This fine old country inn, with long heated verandahs and diamond-paned windows, stands in its own extensive well cared-for grounds on the edge of Clytha Park and a short stroll from the riverside path by the Usk. It's a great all-rounder that appeals to a wide mix of customers, and the bar and lounge are comfortable, light and airy, with a good mix of nice old furniture, pine settles, window seats with big cushions, scrubbed wood floors and a couple of open log fires; the contemporary restaurant is linen-set. The notable array of drinks includes Brecon Three Beacons, Untapped Sundown (from a little brewery just down the road) and Wye Valley Bitter and three swiftly changing guests on handpump, an extensive wine list with 11 by the glass, 20 malt whiskies, three farm ciders, their own perry and various continental beers; they hold a cider and beer festival over the late May Bank Holiday weekend. Darts, bar skittles, boules, board games and large-screen TV for rugby matches. The bedrooms are comfortable and the welsh breakfasts good. Dogs are welcome – the pub has its own labrador and collie.

 Reliably high standards of hearty modern cooking includes tapas such as potted crab with laverbread, teriyaki chicken with noodles, and walnut and cheese stuffed mushrooms, as well as sandwiches, shellfish bourride, pork and wild mushroom faggots with black pudding mash, lentil moussaka with greek salad, stuffed ham in cider sauce with garlic and rosemary potatoes, wild boar and german sausages with potato pancakes, steak and kidney pudding, chicken and lemongrass curry, and puddings such as treacle pudding with custard and a trio of chocolate. *Benchmark main dish: wild boar and duck cassoulet £15.00. Two-course evening meal £23.00.*

Free house ~ Licensees Andrew and Beverley Canning ~ Real ale ~ Open 12-3, 6-midnight; 12-midnight Fri, Sat; 12-10.30 Sun; closed Mon lunchtime ~ Bar food 12.30-2.15, 7-9.30; not Sun evening ~ Restaurant ~ Children welcome ~ Dogs allowed in bar and bedrooms ~ Wi-fi ~ Bedrooms: £60/£90 *Recommended by Andrew Stone, Heather and Richard Jones, Simon and Miranda Davies*

SKENFRITH
Bell 🏆 ♀ 🛏   SO4520   Map 6

(01600) 750235 – www.skenfrith.co.uk
Just off B4521, NE of Abergavenny and N of Monmouth; NP7 8UH

Elegant but relaxed inn much praised for classy food and thoughtful choice of drinks; excellent bedrooms

Being close to the impressive ruin of Skenfrith Castle (National Trust) and a pretty bridge over the River Monnow, this smart and civilised inn is just the place for lunch; they also have circular walks. The two bars have flagstoned floors and one welcomes dogs and walkers. The main bar has a big inglenook fireplace with comfortable sofas, a couple of pews and lots of tables and chairs. From the bleached oak counter they serve Bespoke Saved by the Bell, Wickwar BOB and Wye Valley Butty Bach on handpump, plus bottled local cider and perry, 12 wines by the glass from an impressive list, local sparkling wine, early-landed cognacs and a good range of malt whiskies; background music. There's a new sitting room for resident guests with more sofas and tables and stocked with plenty of books, magazines and board games. The terrace has good solid tables under parasols, with steps leading up to a sloping lawn and an orchard area (ideal for families and they'll make a picnic and provide a rug for you to sit on); the kitchen garden is immaculate. The individually decorated bedrooms (named after brown-trout fishing flies) make a fine base for exploring the area; dogs are welcome in some rooms. Good disabled access.

 Home-grown and local produce feature strongly on the menu and the fine food includes sandwiches, blue cheese brûlée with peached pear and candied walnut salad, duck, pheasant and chicken liver terrine with caramelised fennel marmalade, sharing platters, spiced lentil and goats cheese charlotte with spinach pesto, lamb and leek cawl, burger with dijon mustard mayonnaise and chips, beer-battered cod fillet with pea purée and chips, rib-eye steak with béarnaise sauce, and puddings such as dark chocolate and kirsch cherry brownie and blood orange cheesecake with raspberry and champagne sorbet. *Benchmark main dish: skate wing with roast salsify and lemon and herb butter £15.95. Two-course evening meal £24.50.*

Free house ~ Licensee Richard Ireton ~ Real ale ~ Open 10am-11pm (10.30pm Sun) ~ Bar food 12-2.30, 6-9; 12-8 Sun ~ Restaurant ~ Well behaved children welcome ~ Dogs allowed in bar and bedrooms ~ Wi-fi ~ Bedrooms: £90/£150 *Recommended by Miss B D Picton, Peter Harrison*

ST GEORGE
Kinmel Arms 🌟 🛏

SH9775 Map 6

(01745) 832207 – www.thekinmelarms.co.uk

Off A547 or B5381 SE of Abergele; LL22 9BP

Stylish food in bustling inn, a wide choice of drinks, courteous staff and lovely position; bedrooms

The countryside surrounding this 17th-c sandstone inn is stunning and there are good walks from the front door. It has mullioned windows and handsome carriage-lamps at the front, and also a bar with sofas on either side of a woodburning stove, an attractive mix of nice old wooden chairs and tables on the wooden floor and seats against the counter (with stained glass above) where they keep Great Orme Welsh Gold and Spitting Feathers Thirst Quencher on handpump, 21 wines by the glass and farm cider; service is helpful and friendly. The restaurant, with rattan chairs around marble-topped tables, has big house plants, contemporary art painted by Tim Watson (one of the owners) and evening candles and twinkling lights. To one side is a newly opened tea room with silver teapots and pretty bone china cups and saucers – it's here that you can buy their hampers, chutneys, port and cheese boxes and so forth. There are picnic-sets out in front. The bedrooms consist of comfortable contemporary suites, each with their own decked area.

 Championing local produce, the interesting modern food includes lunchtime sandwiches, white and brown crab with watermelon, pickled mooli and lemongrass, pressed pork belly with rhubarb, red wine salsify, black pudding purée and pearl barley, lunchtime eggs benedict, a pie of the day, braised fennel with herb gnocchi and vegetables, lamb rump with shepherd's pie and peas, duck breast with squash, choi sum (a chinese green leaf) and gabure (a rustic soup), sea trout with cucumber and horseradish, and puddings such as pistachio soufflé with pistachio ice-cream and chocolate tart with salted caramel and passion-fruit sorbet; they also offer a two- and three-course early-bird menu (6-7pm Tues-Thurs). *Benchmark main dish: beef fillet topped with duck liver and truffle foam £25.00. Two-course evening meal £27.00.*

Free house ~ Licensees Lynn Cunnah-Watson and Tim Watson ~ Real ale ~ Open 11-11 (11.30 Fri, Sat); closed Sun, Mon ~ Bar food 12-2, 6-9 (9.30 Fri, Sat); light meals all day; afternoon tea 2-4.30pm ~ Restaurant ~ Children welcome but not in bedrooms ~ Dogs allowed in bar ~ Wi-fi ~ Bedrooms: /£135 *Recommended by Pip White, Alison and Michael Harper, Geoff and Ann Marston, Brian and Sally Wakeham*

STACKPOLE
Stackpole Inn 🌟 🛏

SR9896 Map 6

(01646) 672324 – www.stackpoleinn.co.uk

Village signed off B4319 S of Pembroke; SA71 5DF

Busy pub, a good base for the area, with enjoyable food and friendly service; comfortable bedrooms

It's not surprising this pub is so popular with walkers since it's very near the Pembrokeshire Coast Path and the Bosherston Lily Ponds; they even have a walkers' lunch menu. There's an area around the bar with pine tables and chairs, but most of the pub, L-shaped on four different levels, is given over to diners, with neat light oak furnishings, ash beams and low ceilings to match; background music and board games. Brains Rev James, Felinfoel Best Bitter and Double Dragon and a changing guest ale on handpump, 14 wines by the glass, 15 malt whiskies and two farm ciders. Attractive gardens feature colourful flower beds and mature trees and there are plenty of picnic-sets at the front. The bedrooms are spotless and the breakfasts enjoyable.

As well as half a dozen or so daily fresh fish and shellfish dishes with a choice of sauces, the enjoyable food includes lunchtime rolls and ploughman's, duck confit terrine with red onion marmalade and parsley and apple dressing, hot smoked salmon with duo of beetroot, local sausages with cider gravy, wholegrain mustard mash and greens, roasted mushroom and onion tagliatelle in creamy madeira sauce, lamb rump with dauphinoise potatoes, butternut squash purée, kale and lamb jus, 10oz sirloin steak with garlic and herb butter and twice-cooked chips, and puddings such as vanilla pannacotta with rosewater poached rhubarb and crumble topping and belgian chocolate, cranberry and pecan with cherry yoghurt ice-cream. *Benchmark main dish: fresh fish dish of the day £15.00. Two-course evening meal £19.00.*

Free house ~ Licensees Gary and Becky Evans ~ Real ale ~ Open 12-3, 6-11; 12-11 Sat, Sun ~ Bar food 12-2.15, 6.30-9 ~ Restaurant ~ Children welcome ~ Dogs allowed in bar ~ Wi-fi ~ Bedrooms: £60/£90 *Recommended by M G Hart, Hugh Roberts, S and L McPhee, Mike Benton, Jamie Green*

TINTERN
Anchor

SO5300   Map 6

(01291) 689582 – www.theanchortintern.co.uk
Off A466 at brown Abbey sign; NP16 6TE

Wonderful setting for ancient inn next to Tintern Abbey ruins and river, historic features, plenty of space and good ales and food

The magnificent ruins of Tintern Abbey (Cadw), which are floodlit at night, are right next to this medieval building and can be enjoyed from picnic-sets on the terrace and in the front garden and from the Garden Room. The bar was originally a cider mill attached to the abbey's orchard and the horse-drawn cider press is the central feature; also, little plush stools around circular tables, heavy beams, flagstones, four real ales such as Otter Bitter, Wye Valley Butty Bach and a couple of guests on handpump and local ciders served by friendly, hard-working staff. The restaurant was once the ferryman's cottage and boat house and is connected to the abbey's north wall: bare stone walls, high-backed leather dining chairs around all sorts of tables and more flagstones. There's also an airy café (open 9am-5pm) with colourfully painted chairs and a 100-year-old olive tree. The River Wye is just behind and there are lots of walks surrounding the inn.

Popular food includes crayfish cocktail with apple slaw, pork rillettes with apricot and pistachio chutney, wild mushroom risotto, burger with toppings, coleslaw and french fries, smoked cod loin with crushed potatoes, spinach, poached egg and wholegrain mustard cream sauce, coq au vin, home-smoked lamb rump with pea purée, olives and red onion and pine nut salsa, duck breast with sweet potato mash and raspberry jus, and puddings such as cappuccino mousse with hazelnut cream and lavender and buttermilk pannacotta with blueberries. *Benchmark main dish: beef in ale pie £11.00. Two-course evening meal £19.00.*

Free house ~ Licensee Robert Parkin ~ Real ale ~ Open 11-11 (10.30 Sun) ~ Bar food 12-2.45, 6-9; 12-3.45, 5.30-7.30 Sun ~ Restaurant ~ Children welcome ~ Dogs allowed in bar ~ Wi-fi *Recommended by Ian and Rose Lock, Simon and Miranda Davies, Charles Todd, Julie Braeburn*

USK

SO3700 Map 6

Nags Head ♀

(01291) 672820

The Square; NP15 1BH

Spotlessly kept and traditional in style with a hearty welcome and good food and drinks

Standards here remain consistently high and our readers are full of praise for the way the long-serving and friendly Key family run this handsome coaching inn. The traditional main bar is cheerily chatty and cosy, with lots of well polished tables and chairs packed under its beams (some with farming tools, lanterns or horsebrasses and harness attached), as well as leatherette wall benches and various sets of sporting prints and local pictures – look out for the original deeds to the pub. Tucked away at the front is an intimate little corner with some african masks, while on the other side of the room a passageway leads to a dining area; background music. There may be prints for sale, and perhaps a group of sociable locals. They offer nine wines by the glass, along with Brains Rev James and SA and a guest such as Sharps Doom Bar on handpump. The church is well worth a look. The pub has no parking and nearby street parking can be limited.

Generous helpings of tasty food includes sandwiches, leek and welsh cheddar soup, faggots and gravy, steak pie, sausages and mash, pheasant in port, local steaks with trimmings, and puddings such as treacle and walnut tart and sticky toffee pudding. *Benchmark main dish: rabbit pie £10.50. Two-course evening meal £15.50.*

Free house ~ Licensee Key family ~ Real ale ~ Open 10.30-3, 5-11 ~ Bar food 12-2, 5.30-9 ~ Restaurant ~ Children welcome ~ Dogs welcome ~ Wi-fi *Recommended by Phil and Jane Hodson, Peter Barrett, Caroline Sullivan*

Also Worth a Visit in Wales

Besides the fully inspected pubs, you might like to try these pubs that have been recommended to us and described by readers. Do tell us what you think of them: feedback@goodguides.com

ANGLESEY

ABERFFRAW
SH3568

Crown (01407) 840222

Bodorgan Square; LL63 5BX Village-square pub with two well kept ales and enjoyable competitively priced home-made food including daily specials, quick friendly service; sports TV; well behaved children and dogs welcome, suntrap beer garden with sturdy furniture and views towards the dunes, open all day Sat, till 6pm Sun. *(Michael Butler)*

GAERWEN
SH4972

Gaerwen Arms (01248) 421906

Chapel Street; LL60 6DW Refurbished dining pub with good well presented food at sensible prices, local Coppertown beers, efficient friendly service; children welcome, seats outside with views over to Snowdonia, play area, useful stop before Holyhead for the Irish ferries, open (and food) all day weekends. *(Sandra King)*

MENAI BRIDGE
SH5773

Gazelle (01248) 713364

Glyngarth; A545, halfway towards Beaumaris; LL59 5PD Hotel and restaurant rather than pub in outstanding waterside position looking across to Snowdonia, main bar with smaller rooms off, up to three Robinsons ales kept well and seven wines by the glass, good reasonably priced food from bar snacks up; children and dogs (in bar) welcome, steep garden behind (and walk down from car park), 11 bedrooms, slipway and mooring for visiting boats, open all day summer, all day Fri-Sun winter. *(Edward Edmonton)*

MENAI BRIDGE
SH5572

Liverpool Arms (01248) 712453

St Georges Road/Water Street; LL59 5EY Refurbished pub close to the quay and not far from the famous suspension bridge; ales such as Bass, Facers and Greene King, enjoyable home-made food (all day Fri-Sun) including carve your own joint (advance booking) and daily specials, quick friendly service; quiz nights Weds and Sun; children welcome, part covered terrace, open all day (till 1am Fri, Sat). *(Dave Braisted)*

RED WHARF BAY   SH5281
Ship (01248) 852568
Village signed off A5025 N of Pentraeth; LL75 8RJ Whitewashed 18th-c pub right on Anglesey's east coast – fantastic views of miles of tidal sands; big old-fashioned rooms either side of bar counter, nautical bric-a-brac, long varnished wall pews, cast-iron-framed tables and open fires, three well kept ales including Adnams, 50 malt whiskies and decent choice of wines, enjoyable food; if you run a tab they lock your card in a numbered box, background music in lounge; children welcome in room on left, dogs in bar, limited disabled access, numerous outside tables, open all day. *(Michael Butler)*

RHOSCOLYN   SH2675
★ White Eagle (01407) 860267
Off B4545 S of Holyhead; LL65 2NJ Remote place rebuilt almost from scratch on site of an old pub; airy modern feel in neatly kept rooms, relaxed atmosphere and nice winter fire, Conwy, Weetwood and three guests from smart oak counter, several wines by the glass, extensive choice of good locally sourced food (all day weekends and school holidays, best to book), friendly helpful service, restaurant; children welcome, dogs in bar (biscuits for them), terrific sea views from decking and picnic-sets in good-sized garden, lane down to beach, open all day. *(Michael Butler, Roy and Gill Payne, Chris and Val Ramstedt)*

RHOSNEIGR   SH3272
Oystercatcher (01407) 812829
A4080; LL64 5JP Modern glass-fronted Huf Haus in dunes close to the sea – same owners as the White Eagle at Rhoscolyn but not really a pub (created as a restaurant/chefs' academy); great views from upstairs restaurant and bar with good range of enjoyable food, beers such as Great Orme and Weetwood, decent choice of wines by the glass, ground-floor coffee/wine bar serving lighter meals till 6pm; children welcome, upper terrace with rattan sofas and colourful beach huts, full wheelchair access, open all day. *(Chris and Val Ramstedt)*

CLWYD

CAERWYS   SJ1373
Piccadilly (01352) 720284
North Street; CH7 5AW Pleasantly modernised pub-restaurant; high-ceilinged bare-boards bar with raised central woodburner, dining room across corridor with white-painted beams and tartan carpet, spacious slate-floor restaurant behind has banquettes and light wood furniture, stairs

up to further eating area, enjoyable modern food, three real ales, good friendly service; background music, daily papers; children welcome, partly covered side terrace, open (and food) all day, till 7.30pm Sun. *(Robert Wivell)*

CARROG   SJ1143
Grouse (01490) 430272
B5436, signed off A5 Llangollen–Corwen; LL21 9AT Small unpretentious pub with superb views over River Dee and beyond from bay window and balcony, Lees ales, decent food from sandwiches up, reasonable prices, friendly helpful staff, local pictures, pool in games room; background music; children welcome, wheelchair access (side door a bit tight), tables in pretty walled garden, covered terrace for smokers, narrow turn into car park, handy for Llangollen steam railway; open (and food) all day. *(Elizabeth and Peter May)*

CWM   SJ0677
Blue Lion (01745) 289229
B5429, off A55 at Rhuallt S of Dyserth; LL18 5SG Newish friendly licensees and refurbishment for this 17th-c pub in lovely hill setting with views over Vale of Clwyd towards Snowdonia; various areas with beams and inglenook log fires, comfortable sofas, Marstons Burton Bitter and a guest, enjoyable reasonably priced home-made food in bar or restaurant, games room with pool and darts; Weds quiz, some live music, free wi-fi; children and dogs welcome, seats on raised terrace taking in the view, just off Offa's Dyke Path, closed Mon, Tues lunchtime, otherwise open all day from 1pm (midday Sun). *(James Allsopp)*

ERBISTOCK   SJ3542
Boat (01978) 780666
Village signed off A539 W of Overton, then pub signed; LL13 ODL Ancient stone coaching inn enchantingly placed on banks of the River Dee; split-level, beamed and flagstoned interior, woodburner and fire in old blackened range, three Weetwood ales, several wines by the glass and good choice of enjoyable sensibly priced food, friendly helpful service; children and dogs welcome, river views from picnic sets on terrace and well manicured lawn, bedrooms, open (and food) all day. *(Richard Stanfield)*

GRAIG FECHAN   SJ1454
Three Pigeons (01824) 703178
Signed off B5429 S of Ruthin; LL15 2EU Extended largely 18th-c pub with enjoyable inexpensive food (all day Sun) from sandwiches up, friendly licensees, good range of quickly changing real ales and plenty of wines by the glass, various nooks and corners, interesting mix of furniture and some old signs on the walls, great country views from restaurant; children allowed if eating, big garden with terrace and

same views, good walks, two self-catering apartments, closed Mon. *(James Allsopp)*

HAWARDEN   SJ3266
★**Glynne Arms** (01244) 569988
Glynne Way; CH5 3NS Nicely renovated early 19th-c stone coaching inn, good food (some prices on the high side) in bar and bistro-style restaurant using own locally farmed produce (they also have a farm shop nearby), six regional ales, good choice of wines and cocktails, efficient friendly service; daily papers, free wi-fi; children and dogs (in some areas) welcome, courtyard garden, open (and food) all day. *(Elizabeth and Peter May)*

LLANFERRES   SJ1860
Druid (01352) 810225
A494 Mold–Ruthin; CH7 5SN Extended 17th-c whitewashed inn set in fine walking country along the Alyn Valley towards Loggerheads Country Park, or up Offa's Dyke Path to Moel Famau; views from broad bay window in civilised plush lounge and from bigger beamed back bar with two handsome antique oak settles, pleasant mix of more modern furnishings and quarry-tiled area by log fire. Marstons-related ales, 30 malt whiskies, reasonably priced traditional food plus specials, games room with darts and pool, board games; background music, TV; children welcome, dogs in bar and bedrooms, stables outside at the front, open all day Fri-Sun. *(James Allsopp)*

MINERA   SJ2651
Tyn-y-Capel (01978) 269347
Church Road; LL11 3DA Community-owned pub run mainly by volunteers, good locally sourced food (not Mon or Tues lunchtime) including ramblers' menu, half a dozen changing ales (one badged for them from Big Hand), local cider; regular live music, Sun quiz; children and dogs (in bar) welcome, lovely hill views from terrace, park opposite with play area, open all day. *(Tim King)*

RUABON   SJ3043
Bridge End (01978) 810881
Bridge Street; LL14 6DA Proper old-fashioned pub serving own McGivern ales (brewed here) alongside several guests and ciders, friendly staff and cheerful local atmosphere, snacky food such as sandwiches and pies, black beams, open fires; Tues quiz, regular summer live music; children and dogs welcome, garden, open all day weekends, from 5pm weekdays (4pm Fri). *(Tim King)*

DYFED

ABERAERON   SN4562
Castle (01545) 570205
Market Street; SA46 0AU Red-painted early 19th-c corner building with popular boldly decorated café-bar and elegant wood-floored restaurant upstairs, friendly efficient service, good freshly cooked food and sensibly priced wine list, Evan Evans or Sharps Doom Bar, welsh whisky; background music, sports TV; six comfortable bedrooms and self-catering apartment, open all day. *(Francis)*

ABERAERON   SN4562
★**Harbourmaster** (01545) 570755
Quay Parade; SA46 0BA Handsome, well run and welcoming small hotel in prime spot by yacht-filled harbour; bar with assortment of leather sofas, zinc-clad counter and stuffed albatross (reputed to have collided with a ship belonging to owner's great-grandfather), well kept ales including a house beer from Purple Moose, traditional cider and 14 good wines by the glass, big minimalist dining area with modern light wood furniture on pale floorboards, good interesting food, there's also a four-seater cwtch (or snug) in former porch; TV for rugby, free wi-fi; children over 5 welcome if staying, disabled access, can sit on outside bench and enjoy the view, most bedrooms also overlook the harbour, good breakfast, self-catering cottage, open all day from 8am. *(Mr and Mrs P R Thomas, John and Enid, Michael Goodden, R T and J C Moggridge, Paul Baxter)*

ABERCYCH   SN2539
★**Nags Head** (01239) 841200
Off B4332 Cenarth–Boncath; SA37 0HJ Friendly tucked-away riverside pub with dimly lit beamed and flagstoned bar, stripped wood tables and woodburner in big fireplace, hundreds of beer bottles, clocks showing time around the world, photographs of locals on brick and stone walls, a coracle hanging from the ceiling in one part, even a large stuffed rat, Mantle Cwrw Teifi and two guests, pubby food and specials in two sizeable dining areas; background music, piano; children and dogs welcome, benches in garden overlooking river (fishing rights), play area with wooden castle, barbecues, three bedrooms, open all day Fri-Sun, closed Mon. *(R T and J C Moggridge, John and Enid)*

ABERGORLECH   SN5833
★**Black Lion** (01558) 685271
B4310; SA32 7SN Friendly old pub in fine rural position; traditional stripped-stone beamed bar, oak furniture and black settles on flagstones, old jugs and other bits and pieces on shelves, local paintings, woodburner, Rhymney and a guest beer, proper ciders and varied choice of fair-priced home-cooked food including good daily specials, dining extension with another woodburner; background music, free wi-fi; children and dogs welcome, lovely views of Cothi Valley from riverside garden, two self-catering cottages, good nearby mountain biking, open all day weekends, closed Mon, Tues-Weds lunchtimes. *(Caroline Sullivan)*

ABERYSTWYTH SN6777

Halfway Inn (01970) 880631

Pisgah – A4120 right out towards Devil's Bridge; SY23 4NE Panoramic views from this friendly roadside country pub, log fire, beams, stripped stone and flagstones, scrubbed tables and settles, well kept Sharps Doom Bar and enjoyable good value home-cooked food; background music, pool; children and dogs (in bar) welcome, picnic-sets outside, two comfortable bedrooms, free overnight camping if you buy a meal, closed Mon-Weds in winter. *(Sandra King)*

ANGLE SM8703

★ Old Point House (01646) 641205

Signed off B4320 in village, along long rough waterside track; SA71 5AS New owners for this quaint simple place in idyllic spot overlooking sheltered anchorage; snug bar with two settles and warming log fire in old range, small corner counter serving Worthingtons Cask and a guest, farm cider and several wines by the glass, enjoyable bar food in carpeted lounge; outside lavatories; children and dogs welcome, picnic-sets on grass with charming views across the water, lovely surrounding walks (on Pembrokeshire Coast Path), open (and food) all day in summer, check website for winter hours; note that the road from Angle is unmade and gets cut off by spring tides about four times a year for a couple of hours. *(Paul Baxter)*

BOSHERSTON SR9694

St Govans Country Inn

(01646) 661311 *Off B4319 S of Pembroke; SA71 5DN* Busy pub with big modernised open-plan bar, cheery and simple, with several changing ales and enjoyable well priced pubby food, good climbing photographs and murals of local beauty spots, log fire in large stone fireplace; background music, TV, games machine and pool (winter only); children and dogs welcome, picnic-sets on small front terrace, four good value bedrooms (residents' parking), handy for water-lily lakes, beach and cliff walks, open all day in season (all day weekends at other times). *(Mike Benton)*

BRECHFA SN5230

Forest Arms (01267) 202288

Opposite church (B4310); SA32 7RA Renovated stone-built village inn with well kept ales and enjoyable reasonably priced food from welsh tapas to daily specials, friendly helpful staff, two beamed bars, one with big inglenook and angling theme (pub can arrange fishing on River Cothi), the other in two sections, note Bob the stuffed raven, also pitched-ceilinged dining/function room with another log fire; children and dogs welcome, picnic-sets in back garden, good walks and mountain-bike trails, comfortable bedrooms, closed Mon. *(Charles Todd)*

BROAD HAVEN SM8614

★ Druidstone Hotel (01437) 781221

N on coast road, bear left for about 1.5 miles then follow sign left to Druidstone Haven; SA62 3NE Cheerfully informal country house hotel in grand spot above the sea, individual, relaxed and with terrific views; inventive cooking using fresh often organic ingredients (best to book) including good value themed 'feast evening' (Tues), helpful efficient service, cellar bar with local ale tapped from the cask, country wines and other drinks, ceilidhs and folk events, friendly pub dogs (others welcome); attractive high-walled garden, all sorts of sporting activities from boules to sand-yachting, spacious homely bedrooms and self-catering cottages, closed Jan, Nov, restaurant closed Sun evening. *(John and Enid)*

CAIO SN6739

Brunant Arms (01558) 650483

Off A482 Llanwrda–Lampeter; SA19 8RD Unpretentious village pub, comfortable and friendly with helpful staff, beams, old settles, china on delft shelving and nice log fire, a couple of ales such as Evan Evans, enjoyable regularly changing home-made food from baguettes up, stripped-stone public bar with games including pool; some live music, sports TV; children and dogs welcome, small Perspex-roofed verandah and lower terrace, two bedrooms, handy for Dolaucothi Gold Mines (NT), closed Sun evening to Tues lunchtime. *(Charles Todd)*

CAREW SN0403

★ Carew Inn (01646) 651267

A4075 off A477; SA70 8SL Stone-built pub with appealing cottagey atmosphere, unpretentious small panelled public bar, nice old bentwood stools and mix of tables and chairs on bare boards, small dining area, lounge bar with low tables, warm open fires, two changing beers and enjoyable generously served food (Tues curry, Thurs steak night), two upstairs dining rooms with leather chairs at black tables; background music, dominoes, darts; children and dogs (in bar) welcome, enclosed back garden with play equipment, view of imposing Carew Castle ruins and remarkable 9th-c celtic cross, open all day. *(Charles Todd)*

CILYCWM SN7540

Neuadd Fawr Arms (01550) 721644

By church entrance; SA20 0ST Nicely placed 18th-c drovers' inn above River Gwenlais among lanes to Llyn Brianne; eclectic mix of old furniture on huge slate flagstones, woodburners, good seasonal food with interesting specials in bar or smaller dining room, one or two changing local ales, friendly helpful service and chatty locals; children and dogs welcome, open all day weekends, may close weekday lunchtimes in winter. *(Charles Todd)*

COSHESTON   SN0003
Brewery Inn (01646) 686678
Signed E from village crossroads;
SA72 4UD Welcoming 17th-c village pub
with attractively furnished bar, flagstones
and exposed stone walls, enjoyable fairly
priced food including good pies and burgers,
a locally brewed house beer and guest,
helpful friendly service; quiz Weds, live
music last Sat of month; children and dogs
welcome, closed Sun evening, Mon.
(Sandra King)

CRESSWELL QUAY   SN0506
★Cresselly Arms (01646) 651210
Village signed from A4075; SA68 0TE
Simple unchanging alehouse overlooking
tidal creek; plenty of local customers in
two welcoming old-fashioned linked rooms,
built-in wall benches, kitchen chairs and plain
tables on red and black tiles, open fire in one
room, Aga in the other with lots of pictorial
china hanging from high beam-and-plank
ceiling, third more conventionally furnished
red-carpeted room, a house beer from Caffle
along with Sharps, Worthington and a guest
served from glass jugs; no children or dogs,
seats outside making most of view, you can
arrive by boat if tide is right, open all day in
summer. *(Daphne and Barry Gregson)*

CWM GWAUN   SN0333
★Dyffryn Arms (01348) 881305
Cwm Gwaun and Pontfaen signed off
B4313 E of Fishguard; SA65 9SE
Classic rural time warp know locally as
Bessie's after the much-loved veteran
landlady (her farming family have run it
since 1840 and she's been in charge for
well over a third of that time); basic 1920s
front parlour with plain deal furniture and
draughts boards inlaid into tables, red and
black quarry tiles, woodburner, well kept
Bass served by jug through sliding hatch,
low prices, World War I prints and posters,
a young portrait of the Queen and large
collection of banknotes, darts; may be duck
eggs for sale; lovely outside view and walks
in nearby Preseli Hills, open more or less
all day (may close if no customers).
(Giles and Annie Francis)

DINAS   SN0139
Old Sailors (01348) 811491
Pwllgwaelod; from A487 in Dinas Cross
follow Bryn-henllan signpost; SA42 0SE
Shack-like building in superb position,
snugged down into the sand by isolated cove
below Dinas Head with its bracing walks;
good local fish/seafood (often crab and
lobster), also snacks, coffee and summer
cream teas, well kept Felinfoel Double
Dragon and decent wine, maritime bric-
a-brac; children welcome, no dogs inside,
picnic-sets on grass overlooking beach with
views across to Fishguard, closed Sun and
Mon evenings. *(Simon Sharpe)*

FISHGUARD   SM9537
★Fishguard Arms (01348) 872763
Main Street (A487); SA65 9HJ Tiny
unspoilt bay-windowed terrace pub with
friendly community atmosphere and
character landlord, front bar with unusually
high counter serving well kept/priced Bass
direct from the cask, rugby photographs
and open fire, back snug with woodburner,
traditional games and sports TV, no food;
smokers' area out behind, open all day,
closed Weds evening. *(Giles and Annie Francis)*

FISHGUARD   SM9637
Ship (01348) 874033
Newport Road, Lower Town; SA65 9ND
Cheerful atmosphere and charming landlord
in softly lit 18th-c pub near old harbour,
well kept Felinfoel Double Dragon and
Theakstons tapped from the cask, coal fire,
lots of boat pictures, model ships and photos
of actors such as Richard Burton and Peter
O'Toole who drank here while filming locally,
no food, piano and occasional live music; TV
for rugby; children welcome (toys provided),
dogs on leads, open all day weekends, closed
Mon (also Tues in winter) and weekday
lunchtimes. *(Giles and Annie Francis)*

HERMON   SN2031
Lamb (01239) 831864
Taylors Row; SA36 0DS Friendly family-
run pub dating from the 17th c, homely
and comfortable, with generously served
food cooked by landlady; well behaved
dogs welcome, three good value bedrooms,
caravan pitches. *(Ron Corbett)*

JAMESTON   SS0699
Tudor Lodge (01834) 871212
A4139, E of Jameston; SA70 7SS
Friendly family-run inn close to the coast,
two character bars with open fire and
woodburner, Sharps Doom Bar and several
wines by the glass, airy carpeted dining
room with pale beams and high-backed
chairs around sturdy tables, second dining
room with modern artwork, well liked food
including Tues curries and Thurs steak
night, early-bird deal (4-6pm Mon-Fri);
children welcome, play area and plenty of
picnic-sets outside, five stylish comfortable
bedrooms, good breakfast, open (and food)
all day weekends, from 4pm weekdays.
(M G Hart)

LITTLE HAVEN   SM8512
Castle Inn (01437) 781445
Grove Place; SA62 3UF Welcoming pub
well placed by green looking over sandy bay
(lovely sunsets), popular generously served
food including pizzas and good local fish,
Marstons-related ales, decent choice of wines
by the glass, tea and cafetière coffee, bare-
boards bar and carpeted dining area with
big oak tables, beams, some stripped stone,
castle prints; children and dogs welcome,

picnic-sets out in front, New Year's Day charity swim, open all day. *(Norman Jones, John and Enid)*

LITTLE HAVEN   SM8512

St Brides Inn (01437) 781266

St Brides Road; SA62 3UN Just 20 metres from Pembrokeshire Coast Path; neat stripped-stone bar and linked carpeted dining area, traditional furnishings, log fire, interesting well in back corner grotto thought to be partly Roman, Banks's, Marstons and a guest, enjoyable bar food including fresh fish and local meat; background music and TV; children welcome, no dogs inside, seats in sheltered suntrap terrace garden across road, two bedrooms, open all day summer. *(Simon Sharpe)*

LITTLE HAVEN   SM8512

Swan (01437) 781880

Point Road; SA62 3UL Attractive old pub overlooking bay; traditional oak-floored bar with mix of furniture including cask tables, a couple of leather armchairs by open fire at one end, woodburner the other, snug with one large table suitable for ten diners, Bass, Brains Rev James and three pembrokeshire guests, ten wines by the glass from extensive list, blue-painted dining room and more contemporary upstairs restaurant, good locally sourced food including speciality fish/seafood, friendly helpful staff; background and some live music; children welcome, dogs in bar, sea views from raised heated terrace with rattan-style furniture, good coastal walks, open all day (from 9am in summer for breakfast). *(John and Enid, Hugh Roberts)*

LLANDDAROG   SN5016

★ **Butchers Arms** (01267) 275330

On back lane by church; SA32 8NS Ancient black-beamed local run by same owners for 30 years, three intimate eating areas off small central bar, popular generously served food, Felinfoel ales tapped from the cask and nice wines by the glass, friendly service, conventional pub furniture, gleaming brass, candles in bottles, open woodburner in biggish fireplace; background music; children welcome, tables outside and pretty window boxes, bedroom in converted stables, closed Sun and Mon. *(Simon Sharpe)*

LLANDDAROG   SN5016

White Hart (01267) 275395

Aka Yr Hydd Gwyn; off A48 E of Carmarthen, via B4310; SA32 8NT Ancient thatched pub brewing beers using water from 90-metre borehole, also own ciders and new distillery about to open as we went to press; comfortable lived-in beamed rooms with lots of engaging bric-a-brac and antiques including a suit of armour, 17th-c

carved settles by huge log fire, interestingly furnished high-raftered dining room, generous if not cheap food (surcharge if paying by credit card), home-made jams, chutneys and honey for sale; background music; children welcome, no dogs inside, disabled access (ramps provided), picnic-sets on front terrace and in back garden with play area, closed Weds. *(Mike and Mary Carter)*

LLANDOVERY   SN7634

Castle (01550) 720343

Kings Road; SA20 0AP Popular welcoming hotel next to castle ruins, good attractively presented food from sandwiches and deli boards to charcoal grills and fresh fish specials (breakfasts 8-11am, afternoon teas), courteous efficient service, well kept Gower and a couple of guests; children and dogs welcome, picnic-sets out in front under parasols, comfortable bedrooms, open (and food) all day. *(R T and J C Moggridge)*

LLANDOVERY   SN7634

Kings Head (01550) 720393

Market Square; SA20 0AB Early 18th-c beamed coaching inn, pattern-carpeted bar with exposed stonework and large woodburner, three well kept ales including Evan Evans, enjoyable food from snacks and bar meals up, friendly service; children and dogs welcome, nine bedrooms, open all day. *(R T and J C Moggridge)*

LLANGRANNOG   SN3154

Pentre Arms (01239) 654345

On the front; SA44 6SP Friendly old seafront pub beautifully placed in this pretty coastal village, magnificent sunset sea views from bar's picture window, well kept Gales, St Austell and a guest, usual food including good steaks and often fresh fish, separate restaurant, pool room with games machines and TV; regular live music; children and dogs (in bar) welcome, seven bedrooms (some directly overlooking the small bay), staff will advise on dolphin watching, handy for coast path, open all day. *(Mike and Eleanor Anderson)*

LLANGRANNOG   SN3154

Ship (01239) 654510

Near the front, by car park entrance; SA44 6SL Just back from the bay with tables out by beachside car park; good generous food including local fish/seafood (booking advised weekends), friendly accommodating staff, well kept ales such as Mantle and good selection of gins, refurbished bare-boards bar with burnt-orange walls and big woodburner, further spacious upstairs eating area, local artwork for sale, games room with pool; weekend live music; children and dogs welcome, can get

---

We say if we know a pub allows dogs.

busy in summer, car parking charge refunded against food, open all day. *(Mike and Eleanor Anderson)*

MARLOES SM7908
Lobster Pot (01646) 636233
Gay Lane; SA62 3AZ Village local handy for lovely beach and coast walk; enjoyable reasonably priced food from well filled baguettes up (fresh fish too), Felinfoel Double Dragon and Sharps Doom Bar, friendly staff, games area with darts; background music; children welcome, no dogs inside, tables out in front and in back garden with play area, open all day. *(Mike and Jayne Bastin)*

NEWCHAPEL SN2239
Ffynnone Arms (01239) 841800
B4332; SA37 0EH Welcoming 18th-c beamed pub with enjoyable traditional food including Sun carvery, special diets catered for and some produce home-grown, a couple of changing ales, local cider and afternoon teas in season, two woodburners; darts, pool and table skittles; disabled facilities, picnic-sets in small garden, open all day weekends (from 2pm Sat), closed weekday lunchtimes, food served Wed evening to Sun lunchtime. *(Sandra King)*

NEWPORT SN0539
Castle (01239) 820742
Bridge Street; SA42 0TB Welcoming old pub with bar, lounge, restaurant and new coffee shop (8.30am-2pm, not Sun), enjoyable reasonably priced home-made food including Sun carvery, ales from Mantle and Wye Valley, pleasant service; some live music; children and dogs welcome, three bedrooms, handy for Parrog estuary walk (especially for birdwatchers), open all day. *(Simon Sharpe)*

PEMBROKE DOCK SM9603
Shipwright (01646) 682090
Front Street; SA72 6JX Little blue-painted end-of-terrace pub on waterfront overlooking estuary, enjoyable home-made food and a couple of well kept ales, friendly efficient staff, bare-boards interior with nautical and other memorabilia, some booth seating; children welcome, five minutes from Ireland ferry terminal. *(D and M T Ayres-Regan)*

PENRHIWLLAN SN3641
Daffodil (01559) 370343
A475 Newcastle Emlyn–Lampeter; SA44 5NG Contemporary open-plan dining pub with comfortable welcoming bar (though most there to eat), sofas and leather tub chairs on pale limestone floor, woodburner, Greene King Abbot, Hancocks HB and maybe a guest from granite-panelled counter, two lower-ceilinged end rooms with big oriental rugs, steps down to a couple of airy dining rooms, one with picture windows by open kitchen, good locally sourced food including daily specials and two-course lunch menu;

background music; children welcome, nicely furnished decked area outside with valley views. *(Kristin Warry)*

PONTRHYDFENDIGAID SN7366
Black Lion (01974) 831624
Off B4343 Tregaron–Devil's Bridge; SY25 6BE Relaxed country inn under friendly landlord, smallish main bar with dark beams and floorboards, lots of stripped stone, old country furniture, woodburner and big pot-irons in vast fireplace, copper, brass and so forth on mantelpiece, historical photographs, Felinfoel Double Dragon and a local guest, seven wines by the glass and enjoyable good value home-cooked food, quarry-tiled back dining room, small games room with pool and darts; background music; children and dogs (away from diners) welcome, back courtyard and tree-shaded garden, seven bedrooms (five in converted stables), good walking/cycling country and not far from Strata Florida Abbey (Cadw), open all day. *(Taff Thomas)*

PORTHGAIN SM8132
★ Sloop (01348) 831449
Off A487 St Davids–Fishguard; SA62 5BN Busy tavern (especially holiday times) snuggled down in cove wedged tightly between headlands on Pembrokeshire Coast Path – fine walks in either direction; plank-ceilinged bar with lots of lobster pots and fishing nets, ship clocks, lanterns and some relics from local wrecks, decent-sized eating area with simple furnishings and freezer for kid's ice-creams, well liked bar food from sandwiches to good steaks, fresh fish (own fishing business) and all-day coffee and cake, Brains, Felinfoel and Greene King, separate games room with juke box; seats on heated terrace overlooking harbour, self-catering cottage in village, open all day from 9.30am for breakfast, till midnight Sat. *(Simon Watkins)*

RHANDIRMWYN SN7843
Royal Oak (01550) 760201
7 miles N of Llandovery; SA20 0NY Friendly 17th-c stone-built inn set in remote peaceful walking country, comfortable traditional bar with log fire, four well kept local ales, ciders and perries, good variety of popular sensibly priced food sourced locally, big dining area, pool room; children and dogs (on a lead) welcome, hill views from garden and cottagey bedrooms, handy for Brecon Beacons; closed Mon lunchtime. *(Mike Benton)*

ROSEBUSH SN0729
★ Tafarn Sinc (01437) 532214
B4329 Haverfordwest–Cardigan; SA66 7QU Former Victorian hotel on long-defunct railway (once served the nearby abandoned slate quarries); extraordinary maroon-painted corrugated structure; the halt itself has been more or less re-created, even down to life-size dummy passengers

on the platform, the sizeable garden is periodically enlivened by sounds of chuffing steam trains (actually broadcast from a replica signal box); interior reminiscent of a local history museum with sawdust floors, hams, washing and goodness knows what else hanging from the ceiling, bar has plank panelling, informal mix of old chairs and pews and a woodburner, Cwrw Tafarn Sinc (brewed locally for them) and Sharps Doom Bar, simple food, buoyant atmosphere with welsh spoken; background music, darts, games machine, board games and TV; children welcome, closed Mon (except Aug and bank holidays), otherwise open all day. *(Simon Watkins, John and Enid)*

ST DAVIDS
SM7525
Farmers Arms (01437) 721666
Goat Street; SA62 6RF Bustling old-fashioned low-ceilinged pub by cathedral gate, cheerful and unpretentiously pubby, mainly drinking on the left and eating on the right, central servery with three well kept ales including Felinfoel Double Dragon, tasty good value food from snacks up (not during the winter), friendly staff and atmosphere; TV for rugby, pool, free wi-fi; children and dogs welcome, cathedral view from large tables on big back suntrap terrace, open all day in summer, closed weekday lunchtimes winter. *(B and M Kendall)*

ST DOGMAELS
SN1646
Ferry (01239) 615172
B4546; SA43 3LF Old stone building with spectacular views of Teifi estuary and hills from attractively furnished picture-window dining extension, popular freshly made food, character bar with pine tables and interesting old photographs, Brains and summer guests, several wines by the glass, pleasant attentive staff; background music; children and dogs welcome, plenty of room outside on linked decked areas, open all day. *(Sandra King)*

TRESAITH
SN2751
Ship (01239) 811816
Off A487 E of Cardigan; bear right in village and keep on down – pub's car park fills quickly; SA43 2JL Excellent position beside broad sandy surfing beach (maybe dolphins), seats under canopy on heated deck and picnic-sets on two-level terrace; front dining area with same view, room behind with winter log fire and two further back rooms (one with stove), Brains Rev James and SA, food can be good; children and dogs welcome, four sea-view bedrooms

and lovely coastal walks from this steep little village, open all day. *(Simon Sharpe)*

GLAMORGAN

BISHOPSTON
SS5789
Joiners Arms (01792) 232658
Bishopston Road, just off B4436 SW of Swansea; SA3 3EJ Thriving 19th-c stone local brewing its own good value Swansea ales along with well kept guests such as Courage Best, ample helpings of enjoyable freshly made pub food (not Sun evening, Mon), friendly staff, unpretentious quarry-tiled bar with massive solid-fuel stove, comfortable lounge; TV for rugby; children and dogs welcome, open all day (from 3pm Mon and Tues). *(M G Hart)*

BISHOPSTON
SS5889
Plough & Harrow (01792) 234459
Off B4436 Bishopston–Swansea; SA3 3DJ Cleanly modernised old pub with L-shaped bar and restaurant, good imaginative food from chef-owner including good value two-course lunch deal and antipasto/pizza menu Sun evening, ales such as Brains, Fullers and St Austell, a dozen wines by the glass, helpful courteous service; open all day Sun, closed Mon. *(Mrs Julie Thomas)*

CARDIFF
ST1876
City Arms (029) 2064 1913
Quay Street; CF10 1EA City-centre alehouse with four Brains beers and ten regularly changing guests (some cask-tapped), tasting trays available, also plenty of draught/bottled continentals and real cider, friendly knowledgeable staff, no food; some live music, darts, free wi-fi; open all day (till 2am Fri, Sat), very busy on rugby match days. *(Charles Todd)*

CARDIFF
ST1776
Cricketers (029) 2034 5102
Cathedral Road; CF11 9LL Victorian townhouse in quiet residential area backing on to Glamorgan CC, well kept Evan Evans ales and enjoyable freshly made food (all day Fri, Sat, not Sun evening); children welcome, sunny back garden, open all day. *(Michael Butler)*

CARDIFF
ST1876
Zero Degrees (029) 2022 9494
Westgate Street; CF10 1DD Lively contemporary place on two levels visibly brewing its own interesting beers, good

---

A star symbol before the name of a pub shows exceptional character and appeal. It doesn't mean extra comfort. And it's nothing to do with exceptional food quality, for which there's a separate star-on-a-plate symbol. Even quite a basic pub can win a star, if it's individual enough.

selection of other drinks including cocktails and 'beertails', enjoyable italian-leaning food, friendly staff; background music, sports TVs, free wi-fi; open all day. *(Charles Todd)*

COWBRIDGE   SS9974
★**Bear** (01446) 774814
High Street, with car park behind off North Street; signed off A48; CF71 7AF Busy Georgian coaching inn in smart village, well kept Brains, Hancocks and guests, decent house wines, enjoyable food (including set menus) from good sandwiches and wraps up, friendly helpful service, three attractively furnished bars with flagstones, bare boards or carpet, some stripped stone and panelling, big hot open fires, barrel-vaulted cellar restaurant; children and dogs (in one bar) welcome, courtyard tables, comfortable quiet bedrooms, disabled parking, open all day. *(Julian Richardson)*

GWAELOD-Y-GARTH   ST1183
Gwaelod y Garth Inn
(029) 2081 0408 *Main Road; CF15 9HH* Meaning 'foot of the mountain', this stone-built village pub has wonderful valley views and is popular with walkers on the Taff Ely Ridgeway Path; highly thought-of well presented food (all day Fri and Sat, not Sun evening), friendly efficient service, own-brew beer along with Wye Valley and guests from pine-clad bar, log fires, upstairs restaurant (disabled access from back car park); table skittles, pool, juke box; children and dogs welcome, three bedrooms, open all day. *(Julian Richardson)*

KENFIG   SS8081
★**Prince of Wales** (01656) 740356
2.2 miles from M4 junction 37; A4229 towards Porthcawl, then right when dual carriageway narrows on bend, signed 'Maudlam, Kenfig'; CF33 4PR Ancient local with plenty of individuality by historic sand dunes, cheerful welcoming landlord, well kept ales tapped from the cask, decent wines and good choice of malts, enjoyable straightforward food at fair prices (not Sun evening, Mon), chatty panelled room off main bar (dogs allowed here), log fires, stripped stone and lots of wreck pictures, restaurant with upstairs overspill room; TV for special rugby events; children till 9pm, handy for nature reserve (June orchids), open all day. *(Julian Richardson)*

LISVANE   ST1883
Ty Mawr Arms (01222) 754456
From B4562 on E edge turn N into Church Road, bear left into Llwyn y Pia Road, keep on along Graig Road; CF14 0UF Large welcoming country pub with good choice of popular food, well kept Brains and guests, decent wines by the glass, teas and coffees, friendly service, great views over Cardiff from spacious bay-windowed dining area off traditional log-fire bar;

children welcome, disabled access with help to main bar area, attractive big garden with pond, open all day. *(Heather and Richard Jones)*

LLANBLETHIAN   SS9873
Cross (01446) 772995
Church Road; CF71 7JF Welcoming former staging inn, enjoyable freshly made food from pubby choices up in bar or airy split-level restaurant, reasonable prices and various deals, well kept Wye Valley and guests, good choice of wines, woodburner and open fire; children welcome, dogs in bar, tables out on decking, open all day. *(Julian Richardson)*

LLANCARFAN   ST0570
Fox & Hounds (01446) 781287
Signed off A4226; can also be reached from A48 from Bonvilston or B4265 via Llancadle; CF62 3AD Good attractively presented food using local ingredients and cooked by chef-patron in neat comfortably modernised village pub, local ales and nice choice of wines, friendly staff; unobtrusive background music; tables on covered terrace, charming streamside setting by interesting church, eight comfortable pretty bedrooms, good breakfast, closed Mon. *(Julian Richardson)*

LLANGENNITH   SS4291
Kings Head (01792) 386212
Clos St Cenydd, opposite church; SA3 1HX Extended 17th-c stone-built inn with wide choice of popular food including good curries, own Gower beers (brewed at sister pub, the Greyhound at Oldwalls), over 100 malt whiskies, friendly staff; pool and juke box in lively public bar – back bar quieter with dining areas; children and dogs welcome, large terrace with village views, good walks, not far from great surfing beach and large campsite, bedrooms in separate buildings to the side and rear, open (and food) all day, breakfast for non-residents (8.30-10.30am). *(David and Judy Robison)*

MUMBLES   SS6287
Pilot 07897 895511
Mumbles Road; SA3 4EL Friendly 19th-c seafront local with half a dozen well kept ales including some from own back microbrewery, slate-floored bar with boat suspended from planked ceiling, no food; daily newspapers, TV, free wi-fi; dogs welcome, open all day. *(Chris Marsh)*

OLDWALLS   SS4891
Greyhound (01792) 391027
W of Llanrhidian; SA3 1HA 19th-c pub with spacious beamed and dark-panelled carpeted lounge bar, well kept ales including own Gower brews, decent wine and coffee, wide choice of popular food from sandwiches, baguettes and wraps up, friendly staff, hot coal fires, back dining room and upstairs

overspill/function room; children and dogs welcome, picnic-sets in big garden with terrace, play area and good views, open all day. *(Heather and Richard Jones)*

PENARTH　　　　　　　　　ST1771
Pilot (029) 2071 0615
Queens Road; CF64 1DJ End-of-terrace pub set high in residential area overlooking Cardiff Bay; good often interesting food from changing menu, four well kept ales, friendly welcoming staff; regular live music, cocktail evenings and summer beer/cider festival; children and dogs allowed, tables out in narrow front area, open all day.
(John Jenkins)

PONTNEDDFECHAN　　　　SN8907
Angel (01639) 722013
Just off A465; Pontneathvaughan Road; SA11 5NR Friendly comfortably opened-up 16th-c pub, well kept ales such as Neath and Rhymney, wide choice of enjoyable fairly priced pub food, masses of jugs on beams, ancient houseware and old kitchen range, separate flagstoned bar; children welcome, terrace tables, good walks including the waterfalls, open all day in summer.
(Julian Richardson)

REYNOLDSTON　　　　　　SS4889
★ **King Arthur** (01792) 390775
Higher Green, off A4118; SA3 1AD Cheerful pub-hotel with timbered main bar, country-style restaurant and summer family dining area (games room with pool in winter), good fairly priced food from sandwiches and pub favourites up, afternoon teas, Felinfoel and guests kept well, log fires and country house bric-a-brac, buoyant local atmosphere in the evening; background music; tables out on green, play area, 18 bedrooms and self-catering apartments, open (and food) all day. *(M G Hart, Christian Mole)*

ST HILARY　　　　　　　　ST0173
Bush (01446) 776888
Off A48 E of Cowbridge; CF71 7DP Cosily restored 16th-c thatched and beamed pub, flagstoned main bar with inglenook, bare-boards lounge and snug, nice mix of old furniture, Bass, Greene King, Hancocks and a guest, Weston's cider and good wines by the glass, enjoyable food including home-made pies and wellingtons, gluten-free choices too, friendly service, restaurant; children and dogs (in bar) welcome, some picnic benches out at front, garden behind, open all day Fri-Sun. *(Andrew Vincent)*

SWANSEA　　　　　　　　　SS6492
Brunswick (01792) 465676
Duke Street; SA1 4HS Large rambling local with traditional pubby furnishings, lots of knick-knacks, artwork and prints for sale, bargain popular weekday food till 7.30pm (also Sun lunch), six well kept ales including Courage and Greene King plus local guests,

friendly helpful service, regular live music, quiz night Mon; no dogs, open all day.
(S and L McPhee)

TAFFS WELL　　　　　　　ST1283
Fagins (029) 2081 1800
Cardiff Road, Glan-y-Llyn; CF15 7QD Terrace-row pub with interesting range of cask-tapped ales, friendly olde-worlde atmosphere, benches, pine tables and other pubby furniture on flagstones, faux black beams, woodburner, good value straightforward food (not Sun evening, Mon) from filling lunchtime baguette up, restaurant; live music, sports TV; children and dogs welcome, open all day.
(R T and J C Moggridge)

GWENT

ABERGAVENNY　　　　　　SO2914
Angel (01873) 857121
Cross Street, by town hall; NP7 5EN Comfortable late Georgian coaching inn; good local atmosphere in two-level bar, rugs on flagstones, big sofas, armchairs and settles, some lovely bevelled glass behind counter serving Evan Evans, Hereford, Rhymney and Wye Valley, 11 wines by the glass, 15 malt whiskies and proper cider, well liked food, friendly helpful staff, attractive lounge (popular afternoon tea) and smart dining room; free wi-fi; children welcome, dogs in bar, pretty candlelit courtyard, 35 bedrooms (some in other buildings), open all day. *(Toby Jones)*

ABERGAVENNY　　　　　　SO3111
★ **Hardwick** (01873) 854220
Hardwick; B4598 SE, off A40 at A465/ A4042 exit – coming from E on A40, go right round the exit system, as B4598 is final road out; NP7 9AA Restaurant-with-rooms and you'll need to book for owner-chef's highly regarded imaginative food; drinkers welcome in simple bar with spindleback chairs around pub tables, stripped brickwork by fireplace and small corner counter serving Rhymney and Wye Valley, local perry and a dozen wines by the glass, two dining rooms, one with beams, bare boards and huge fireplace, the other in lighter carpeted extension, friendly service; background music; no under-8s in restaurant after 8pm, teak tables and chairs under umbrellas by car park, neat garden, bedrooms, open all day (till 10pm Sun), closed winter Mon and second week Jan. *(Mike and Mary Carter)*

CAERLEON　　　　　　　　ST3490
★ **Bell** (01633) 420613
Bulmore Road; off M4 junction 24 via B4237 and B4236; NP18 1QQ Nicely furnished linked beamed areas in old stone coaching inn, good imaginative food using local ingredients (should book weekends),

well kept Caledonian Deuchars IPA and a couple of guests, over 20 welsh ciders/perries, big open fireplace; unobtrusive background music (live Sun afternoon); children welcome, pretty back terrace with koi tank, open all day. *(Alf Wright)*

CHEPSTOW ST5394
Three Tuns (01291) 645797
Bridge Street; NP16 5EY Early 17th-c and a pub for much of that time; refurbished bare-boards interior with painted farmhouse pine furniture, a couple of mismatched sofas by woodburner, dresser with china plates, five local ales and ciders from nice wooden counter at unusual angle, very reasonably priced home-made bar food (not Mon or Tues); friendly staff; background music (live weekends); dogs welcome, disabled access (one bedroom suitable), open all day. *(Daphne and Barry Gregson)*

GROSMONT SO4024
Angel (01981) 240646
Corner of B4347 and Poorscript Lane; NP7 8EP Small welcoming 17th-c local, rustic interior with simple wooden furniture, Wye Valley Butty Bach, a couple of guests and local cider (regular summer beer/cider festivals), reasonably priced traditional food (not Sun, Mon or Weds), pool room with darts; TV for rugby, no lavatories – public ones close by; dogs welcome, seats out by ancient market cross on attractive steep street in sight of castle, back garden with boules, good local walks, open all day Sat, closed Sun evening and weekday lunchtimes. *(Andrew Vincent)*

LLANDENNY SO4103
★ Raglan Arms (01291) 690800
Centre of village; NP15 1DL Well run dining pub with interesting freshly cooked food including set menus Weds-Fri and brunch Sat, Wye Valley Butty Bach and good selection of wines, friendly welcoming young staff, big pine tables and a couple of leather sofas in linked dining rooms leading to conservatory, log fire in flagstoned bar's handsome stone fireplace, relaxed informal atmosphere; children welcome, garden tables, closed Mon. *(Andrew Vincent)*

LLANFIHANGEL
CRUCORNEY SO3220
Skirrid (01873) 890258
Signed off A465; NP7 8DH One of Britain's oldest pubs, dating partly from 1110 and a former courthouse – plenty of atmosphere and ghostly tales; ancient studded door to high-ceilinged main bar, exposed stone, flagstones and panelling, huge log fire, well kept ales and enjoyable range of pubby food, friendly service, separate dining room; children and dogs welcome, tables on terrace and small sloping back lawn, bedrooms, closed Sun evening, Mon lunchtime. *(R T and J C Moggridge)*

LLANGATTOCK LINGOED SO3620
Hunters Moon (01873) 821499
Off B4521 just E of Llanvetherine; NP7 8RR Attractive tucked-away pub dating from the 13th c, beams, dark stripped stone and flagstones, woodburner, friendly licensees and locals, welsh ales tapped from the cask and enjoyable straightforward food, separate dining room; children welcome, tables out on deck and in charming dell, waterfall, four comfortable bedrooms, glorious country on Offa's Dyke Path, open all day. *(Andrew Vincent)*

LLANGYBI ST3797
White Hart (01633) 450258
On main road; NP15 1NP Friendly village dining pub in delightful 12th-c monastery building (part of Jane Seymour's dowry); pubby bar with roaring log fire, steps up to pleasant light restaurant, good food from pub favourites up including two-course lunch menu, well kept mainly welsh ales and good choice of wines by the glass; children welcome, two nice bedrooms, closed Sun evening, Mon, otherwise open all day. *(Edward Edmonton)*

LLANOVER SO2907
★ Goose & Cuckoo (01873) 880277
Upper Llanover signed up track off A4042 S of Abergavenny; after 0.5 miles take first left; NP7 9ER Newish owner for this remote pub looking over picturesque valley just inside Brecon Beacons National Park; essentially one small rustically furnished room with woodburner in arched stone fireplace, small picture-window extension makes most of the view, well kept ales, 80 whiskies and generous helpings of simple tasty food; board games, cribbage and darts; children and dogs welcome, picnic-sets out on gravel below, ten rooms, open all day weekends. *(James Allsopp)*

LLANTHONY SO2827
★ Priory Hotel (01873) 890487
Aka Abbey Hotel, Llanthony Priory; off A465, back road Llanvihangel Crucorney–Hay; NP7 7NN Magical setting for plain bar in dimly lit vaulted crypt of graceful ruined Norman abbey, lovely in summer, with lawns around and the peaceful border hills beyond; well kept ales such as Brains and Felinfoel, summer farm cider, simple lunchtime bar food and evening restaurant, occasional live music; no dogs, children welcome but not in hotel part (four bedrooms in restored abbey walls), open all day weekends in summer (closed Mon-Thurs and Sun evening in winter). *(Helena and Trevor Fraser)*

LLANTRISANT FAWR ST3997
Greyhound (01291) 672505
Off A449 near Usk; NP15 1LE Prettily set 18th-c country inn with relaxed homely

feel in three linked beamed rooms, steps between two, nice mix of furnishings and rustic decorations, enjoyable home cooking at sensible prices, efficient service, two or more well kept ales, decent wines by the glass, log fires, pleasant panelled dining room; muddy boots/dogs welcome in stable bar, attractive garden with big fountain, hill views, comfortable bedrooms in converted stable block, closed Sun evening. *(Helena and Trevor Fraser)*

MAMHILAD   SO3004
Horseshoe (01873) 880542
Old Abergavenny Road; NP4 8QZ
Old beamed country pub with slate-floor bar, traditional pubby furniture and a couple of unusual posts acting as elbow tables, original Hancocks pub sign, ornate woodburner in stone fireplace, tasty fairly priced food (good pies) from lunchtime baguettes up, Great Orme and Wye Valley ales, Blaengawney cider; children welcome, dogs away from dining area, lovely views particularly from tables by car park over road, open all day Fri-Sun. *(Edward Edmonton)*

PENALLT   SO5209
★**Inn at Penallt** (01600) 772765
Village signed off B4293; at crossroads in village turn left; NP25 4SE 17th-c stone inn with good imaginative food using local produce, well priced wine list, welsh ales and cider, courteous efficient service, roaring woodburner in airy slate-floored bar, restaurant and small back conservatory with fine Forest of Dean views; children and dogs welcome, big garden with terrace and play area, four bedrooms, closed Mon (and from 5pm Sun in winter) otherwise open all day. *(Jim and Lynne Allen)*

RAGLAN   SO4107
Beaufort Arms (01291) 690412
High Street; NP15 2DY Pub-hotel (former 16th-c coaching inn) with two character beamed bars, one with big stone fireplace and comfortable seats on slate floor, well kept local ales, carefully sourced food (some home-grown produce) including good seafood and set lunch/early evening menu, light airy brasserie, friendly attentive service; background music; children welcome, terrace tables, 17 good bedrooms, open all day. *(Miles Green)*

REDBROOK   SO5309
★**Boat** (01600) 712615
Car park signed on A466 Chepstow–Monmouth, then 30-metre footbridge over Wye; or very narrow steep car access from Penallt in Wales; NP25 4AJ Beautifully set riverside pub with well kept Wye Valley and guests tapped from the cask, lots of ciders, perries and country

wines, enjoyable good value food (not Sun evening) from baguettes and baked potatoes up, helpful staff, unchanging interior with stripped-stone walls, flagstones and woodburner; live bands Thurs evening; children and dogs welcome, home-built rustic seats in informal tiered suntrap garden with stream spilling down into duck pond, open all day in summer, closed winter Tues, and from 9pm Sun, Mon. *(Miles Green)*

TALYCOED   SO4115
Warwicks (01600) 780227
B4233 Monmouth–Abergavenny; though its postal address is Llantilio Crossenny, the inn is actually in Talycoed, a mile or two E; NP7 8TL Pretty wisteria-clad 17th-c beamed pub under welcoming newish management; softly lit snug bar with good log fire in stone fireplace, settles and mix of other old furniture, horsebrasses and assorted memorabilia, well kept Otter Bitter, good range of food including daily specials, cosy little dining room; children welcome, dogs in bar, seats on front terrace and in neat garden, lovely countryside and surrounding walks, open all day weekends, closed Mon-Weds lunchtime. *(Derek Stafford)*

TRELLECK   SO5005
Lion (01600) 860322
B4293 6 miles S of Monmouth; NP25 4PA Open-plan bar with one or two low black beams, nice mix of old furniture and two log fires, ales such as Butcombe, Felinfoel and Wye Valley, wide range of fair-priced traditional food with specials such as ostrich and kangaroo (not Sun evening), takeaway pizzas, traditional games such as shove-ha'penny, ring the bull and table skittles; background music; children and dogs welcome, picnic-sets on grass, side courtyard overlooking church, self-catering cottage, open all day. *(Tim King)*

TRELLECK GRANGE   SO5001
Fountain (01291) 689303
Minor road Tintern–Llanishen, SE of village; NP16 6QW Traditional 17th-c country pub under friendly family management, enjoyable local food from pub favourites to game specials, three well kept welsh ales, farm cider and perry, roomy low-beamed flagstoned bar with log fire; dogs welcome, small walled garden, peaceful spot on small winding road, comfortable bedrooms (no children), camping, closed Mon and lunchtimes Tues-Thurs, otherwise open all day (till 9pm Tues, Sun). *(Miles Green)*

USK   SO3700
Kings Head (01291) 672963
Old Market Street; NP15 1AL Popular 16th-c family-run inn, chatty and relaxed, with generously served traditional food and

---

We say if we know a pub allows dogs.

well kept beers, friendly efficient staff, huge log fire in superb fireplace; sports TV; nine bedrooms, open all day. *(David Longhurst)*

GWYNEDD

ABERDOVEY   SN6196
Britannia (01654) 767426
Sea View Terrace; LL35 0EF Friendly busting harbourside inn; great estuary and distant mountain views from upstairs restaurant with balcony, good range of enjoyable well priced food including fresh crab and summer afternoon teas with home-made cakes, locals' bar downstairs with five real ales, darts and TV, woodburner in cosy back snug; children welcome (not in bar), three bedrooms, open all day. *(Miles Green)*

ABERDOVEY   SN6196
★Penhelig Arms (01654) 767215
Opposite Penhelig station; LL35 0LT Fine harbourside location for this popular 18th-c hotel; traditional bar with warm fire in central stone fireplace, some panelling, Brains ales and a guest, good choice of wines and malt whiskies, enjoyable food including good fish and chips; children welcome, dogs allowed in bar and comfortable bedrooms (some have balconies overlooking estuary, ones nearest road can be noisy), open (and food) all day. *(Christopher Mannings)*

BETWS-Y-COED   SH7955
★Ty Gwyn (01690) 710383
A5 just S of bridge to village; LL24 0SG Family-run restaurant-with-rooms rather than pub (you must eat or stay overnight to be served drinks), but pubby feel in character beamed lounge bar with ancient cooking range, easy chairs, antiques, old prints and bric-a-brac, highly regarded interesting food using local produce including own fruit and vegetables, beers such as Brains and Great Orme, friendly professional service; background music; children welcome, 12 comfortable bedrooms and holiday cottage, closed Mon-Weds in Jan. *(Mike and Mary Carter)*

BLAENAU FFESTINIOG   SH7041
Pengwern Arms (01766) 762200
Church Square, Ffestiniog; LL41 4PB Co-operative-owned village square pub with well kept/priced ales such as Cwrw Llyn and Purple Moose in panelled bar, dining area serving good value food evenings (not Sun) and weekend lunchtimes, friendly local atmosphere; games room, live music; dogs welcome in bar, fine views from back garden, eight bedrooms. *(Simon Sharpe)*

CAERNARFON   SH4762
★Black Boy (01286) 673604
Northgate Street; LL55 1RW Busy traditional 16th-c inn with cosy beamed lounge bar, sumptuously furnished and

packed with tables, additional dining room across corridor and dimly lit atmospheric public bar, well kept Bass, Cwrw Llyn, Purple Moose and two guests, several wines by the glass and good generous food from sandwiches up (try the traditional 'lobsgows' stew), lunchtime set deal, good friendly service and lots of welsh chat; background music, TV, free wi-fi; disabled access (ramps) and loos, a few pavement tables, 26 bedrooms, more in separate townhouse, open (and food) all day. *(Ian Herdman, Peter and Anne Hollindale)*

CAPEL CURIG   SH7257
★Bryn Tyrch (01690) 720223
A5 E; LL24 0EL Family-owned roadside inn perfectly placed for mountains of Snowdonia; bare-stone walkers' bar with big communal tables and amazing picture-windows views, Conwy Welsh Pride and a guest, quite a few malt whiskies, comprehensive choice of good well presented food including packed lunches and hampers, second bar with big menu boards, leather sofas and mix of tables on bare boards, coal fire; children and dogs welcome, steep little side garden, more seats on terrace and across road by stream, 11 bedrooms including two bunk rooms, open all day in summer. *(S and L McPhee)*

CAPEL CURIG   SH7357
Tyn y Coed (01690) 720331
A5 SE of village; LL24 0EE Bustling inn across road from River Llugwy with stage coach at entrance; enjoyable home-made food using local produce, well kept Purple Moose and two guests, pleasant quick service, log fires, pool room with juke box; nice side terrace, good surrounding walks, comfortable bedrooms, cycle storage and drying room, closed weekday lunchtimes out of season, otherwise open all day. *(Andrew Vincent)*

CONWY   SH7777
Albion (01492) 582484
Uppergate Street; LL32 8RF Interesting sensitively restored 1920s pub under collective ownership of four welsh brewers – Conwy, Great Orme, Nant and Purple Moose, their beers and guests kept well, friendly staff, some snacky food, three linked rooms with plenty of well preserved features including stained glass and huge baronial fireplace, back part with serving hatch is quieter; open all day. *(Simon Collett-Jones, Dr and Mrs A K Clarke)*

DOLGELLAU   SH7318
Royal Ship (01341) 4222209
Queens Square; LL40 1AR Small civilised central hotel (19th-c coaching inn) with good well priced food from sandwiches and sharing boards up, well kept Robinsons ales and decent choice of wines by the glass, friendly service; children welcome,

comfortable bedrooms, open (and food) all day. *(John Wooll)*

LLANDUDNO SH7882
Cottage Loaf (01492) 870762
Market Street; LL30 2SR Popular former bakery with three linked rooms, dark beams and timbers, rugs on pale flagstones or bare boards, good mix of tables, benches, cushioned settles and dining chairs, woodburners, decent brasserie-style food from sandwiches up, well kept Conwy, Courage, Brains and a couple of guests (often from local microbreweries), friendly attentive service, big garden room extension; teak furniture on front and back terraces, children welcome, open (and food) all day. *(Simon Collett-Jones)*

LLANDUDNO SH7882
Queen Victoria (01492) 860952
Church Walks; LL30 2HD Traditional Victorian pub away from the high-street bustle, five well kept Marstons-related beers, good choice of affordable pubby food in bar or upstairs restaurant, congenial atmosphere and good service; background music, free wi-fi; children and dogs welcome, a few seats out in front, not far from the Great Orme Tramway, open (and food) all day. *(Simon Collett-Jones)*

LLANFROTHEN SH6141
Brondanw Arms (01766) 770555
Aka Y Ring; A4085 just N of B4410; LL48 6AQ Welsh-speaking village pub at end of short whitewashed terrace, main bar with slate floor and woodburner in large fireplace, pews and window benches, old farm tools on the ceiling, snug with panelled booths and potbelly stove, long spacious dining room behind with contrasting red walls, good home-cooked food (all day Sun), Robinsons ales, friendly helpful staff; free wi-fi; children welcome, wheelchair access (two long shallow steps at front), Snowdonia National Park views from garden with play area, camping and good walks, handy for Plas Brondanw Gardens. *(Elizabeth and Peter May)*

LLANUWCHLLYN SH8730
Eagles (01678) 540278
Aka Eryrod; A494/B4403; LL23 7UB Family-run and welcoming with good reasonably priced food (not Mon lunchtime) using own farm produce, ales such as Purple Moose, limited wine choice in small bottles, opened-up slate-floor bar with log fire, beams and stripped stone, back picture-window view of mountains with Lake Bala in the distance; sports TV; children welcome, metal tables and chairs on flower-filled back

terrace, open all day summer (afternoon break Mon). *(Mike and Mary Carter)*

MAENTWROG SH6640
Grapes (01766) 590365
A496; village signed from A470; LL41 4HN Handsome 17th-c inn under new management, three bars and good-sized conservatory with views of steam trains on Ffestiniog Railway, enjoyable reasonably priced pubby food, ales such as Hancocks, Llyn and Purple Moose, friendly helpful staff; children welcome, seats on pleasant terrace, six refurbished bedrooms, open all day. *(Aiden)*

PORTH DINLLAEN SH2741
★ Ty Coch (01758) 720498
Beach car park signed from Morfa Nefyn, then 15-minute walk; LL53 6DB Former 19th-c vicarage in idyllic location right on the beach with wonderful views, far from roads and only reached on foot; bar crammed with nautical paraphernalia, pewter, old miners' and railway lamps and other memorabilia, simple furnishings, coal fire, up to three real ales and a craft beer (served in plastic as worried about glass on beach), short lunchtime bar menu; children and dogs welcome, open all day in season and school holidays (till 5pm Sun), 12-4pm weekends only during winter. *(Daphne and Trevor Gregson)*

PORTHMADOG SH5639
Australia (01766) 515957
High Street; LL49 9LR Recently taken over by a consortium of brewers – Conwy, Great Orme, Nant and Purple Moose, their ales in top condition.

PORTHMADOG SH5738
Spooners (01766) 516032
Harbour station; LL49 9NF Platform café-bar at steam line terminus, lots of railway memorabilia including a former working engine in one corner, four real ales such as Purple Moose, good value straightforward food from 9am breakfast on; children welcome, platform tables, open all day. *(Tony and Wendy Hobden)*

PWLLHELI SH3735
Whitehall (01758) 614091
Gaol Street; LL53 5RG Newly refurbished pub-bistro in centre of this market town, local ales such as Llyn and good choice of wines, popular freshly made food from shortish menu, early-bird weekday deal before 6.30pm, Fri steak night, friendly staff, spiral staircase to upstairs dining room; TV in bar; children welcome, open all day (till late Fri, Sat). *(Hefina Pritchard)*

Half pints: by law, a pub should not charge more for half a pint than half the price of a full pint, unless it shows that half-pint price on its price list.

RHYD DDU   SH5652
Cwellyn Arms (01766) 890321
A4085 N of Beddgelert; LL54 6TL Simple
18th-c village pub (same owners for over 30
years) not far below Welsh Highland Railway
top terminus, up to nine real ales and good
choice of popular seasonal food from home-
baked rolls to blackboard specials, friendly
helpful staff, two cosy bars and restaurant,
log fires; children, walkers and dogs
welcome, spectacular Snowdon views from
garden tables, babbling stream just over wall,
campsite, bedrooms and bunkhouses, open
all day. *(Paul Collins)*

TREFRIW   SH7863
Old Ship (01492) 640013
B5106; LL27 0JH Well run old pub with
nice staff and cheerful local atmosphere,
good home-made food from daily changing
blackboard menu, Marstons-related beers
and local guests in top condition, good
selection of wines/malt whiskies, log fire and
inglenook woodburner; garden with picnic-
sets by stream, children welcome, open
all day weekends, closed Mon except bank
holidays. *(Martin Cawley)*

TREMADOG   SH5640
Union (01766) 512748
Market Square; LL49 9RB Traditional
early 19th-c stone-built pub in terrace
overlooking square, cosy and comfortable,
with quiet panelled lounge on left, carpeted
public bar to the right with exposed stone
walls and woodburner, well kept ales such
as Great Orme and Purple Moose, enjoyable
pubby food from lunchtime sandwiches up,
friendly staff, back restaurant; darts and TV;
children and dogs welcome, paved terrace
behind. *(Tony and Wendy Hobden)*

TUDWEILIOG   SH2336
Lion (01758) 659724
*Nefyn Road (B4417), Llŷn Peninsula;
LL53 8ND* Cheerful village inn with
enjoyable sensibly priced food from
baguettes to blackboard specials, traditional
furnishings in lounge bar and two dining
rooms (one for families, other with
woodburner), quick friendly service, real
ales such as Purple Moose (up to three in
summer), dozens of malt whiskies and decent
wines; pool and board games in public bar;
pleasant front garden, four bedrooms, open
all day in season. *(Charles Todd)*

TY'N-Y-GROES   SH7773
★ Groes (01492) 650545
B5106 N of village; LL32 8TN Now run
by retired landlady's daughter, this 15th-c
inn is in a fine setting overlooking the Vale
of Conwy and peaks of Snowdonia; rambling
low-beamed, thick-walled rooms with
antique settles, clocks, portraits and other
bits and pieces, big fireplace in back bar,
an ale named for the pub from the family's

nearby Great Orme brewery, plus a guest and
several bottled Great Orme beers, 20 wines
by the glass and good range of malt whiskies,
enjoyable food in bar, airy conservatory or
smart restaurant; background music, free
wi-fi; children and dogs welcome, idyllic
back garden with flower-filled hayracks,
more seats on narrow flower-decked roadside
terrace, well equipped bedroom suites
(some with terraces/balconies taking in the
view). *(Mike and Mary Carter, Paul and Sonia
Broadgate)*

POWYS

BEGUILDY   SO1979
Radnorshire Arms (01547) 510634
B4355 Knighton–Newtown; LD7 1YE
17th-c black and white beamed country
pub with enjoyable good value food,
Ludlow, Stonehouse and a beer badged for
them, friendly helpful service inglenook
woodburner; pool; no dogs inside, beer
garden, closed Mon. *(Miles Green)*

BLEDDFA   SO2068
Hundred House (01547) 550441
A488 Knighton–Penybont; LD7 1PA
New owners and renovation for this 16th-c
pub (former courthouse) opposite village
green; bar with pitched ceiling, oak flooring
and double-sided woodburner, three
changing local ales and good selection of
home-made pies, dining room with new
slate floor; children welcome, tables in side
garden with play area, lovely countryside,
open all day weekends, closed Mon.
(Tim King)

CRICKHOWELL   SO2118
Dragon (01873) 810362
High Street; NP8 1BE Welcoming old
family-owned inn, more hotel-restaurant
than pub, but with neat small bar serving
Rhymney, stone and wood floors, sofas and
armchairs by open fire, enjoyable traditional
food including welsh choices in tidy dining
room, good friendly service; 15 bedrooms;
open (and food) all day. *(Andrew Vincent)*

CRICKHOWELL   SO1919
★ Nantyffin Cider Mill
(01873) 810775 *A40/A479 NW;
NP8 1SG* Former 16th-c drovers' inn
facing River Usk in lovely Black Mountains
countryside – charming views from tables
on lawn; bar with solid furniture on tiles
or carpet, woodburner in broad fireplace,
Felinfoel Double Dragon, proper ciders
and several wines by the glass, open-plan
main area with beams, standing timbers
and open fire in grey stonework wall,
striking high-raftered restaurant with old
cider press, good home-made food from
sandwiches to grills; background music;
children and dogs (in bar) welcome,
bedrooms, handy for Tretower Court (Cadw)

and Castle, closed lunchtimes Mon and Tues, otherwise open all day. *(Mike and Mary Carter, Taff Thomas)*

DERWENLAS   SN7299

★**Black Lion** (01654) 703913

A487 just S of Machynlleth; SY20 8TN
Cosy 16th-c country pub with extensive range of good well priced food including children's menu and daily specials, friendly staff coping well at busy times, Wye Valley Butty Bach and a guest, decent wines, heavy black beams, thick walls and black timbering, attractive pictures, brasses and lion models, carpet over big slate flagstones, good log fire; background music; garden behind with play area and steps up into woods, limited parking, bedrooms, closed Mon. *(John Evans)*

DINAS MAWDDWY   SH8514

Red Lion (01650) 531247

Dyfi Road; off A470 (N of A458 junction); SY20 9JA Two small traditional front bars and more modern back extension, changing ales and decent food including popular pies and Sunday carvery, friendly efficient service, open fire, beams and lots of brass; children welcome, six simple bedrooms (four ensuite), pub named in welsh (Llew Coch).
(Andrew Vincent)

GLADESTRY   SO2355

Royal Oak (01544) 370669

B4594; HR5 3NR Friendly old-fashioned village pub on Offa's Dyke Path, simple stripped-stone slate-floored walkers' bar, beams hung with tankards and lanterns, carpeted lounge, open fires, ales from Golden Valley and Wye Valley, uncomplicated home-made food from sandwiches up; no credit cards; children welcome, dogs in bar (and bedrooms by arrangement), sheltered sunny back garden, camping, closed Mon and Tues.
(Miles Green)

GLASBURY   SO1839

Harp (01497) 847373

B4350 towards Hay, just N of A438; HR3 5NR Welcoming homely old place with good value pubby food (not Mon) cooked by landlady including proper pies and take-away pizzas, log-fire lounge with eating areas, black beamed bar, well kept local ales, picture windows over wooded garden sloping to River Wye; some live folk music, darts; river views from picnic-sets on terrace and back bedrooms, good breakfast. *(Sandra King)*

HAY-ON-WYE   SO2242

★**Blue Boar** (01497) 820884

Castle Street/Oxford Road; HR3 5DF Medieval bar in character pub, cosy corners, dark panelling, pews and country chairs, open fire in Edwardian fireplace, four well kept local ales including a house beer from Hydes, organic bottled cider and decent wines by the glass, decent food (from breakfast on) in quite different long open café/dining room, bright light décor, local artwork for sale and another open fire, friendly efficient service; background music; children and dogs welcome, tables in tree-shaded garden, open all day from 9am.
(David Longhurst)

HAY-ON-WYE   SO2242

★**Three Tuns** (01497) 821855

Broad Street; HR3 5DB Sizeable old pub with low beams, exposed stone walls and woodburners in hefty fireplaces (one with a beautiful old curved settle beside it), upstairs summer restaurant, well kept ales and good wine choice, popular freshly prepared food from ciabattas, pizzas and pubby choices to pricier upscale dishes, prompt helpful service (they ask for a credit card if you run a tab); children welcome till 7pm, no dogs, disabled access/facilities, seats under big parasols in sheltered courtyard, open all day Sun, may close Mon and Tues out of season.
(Heather and Richard Jones)

KNIGHTON   SO2872

Horse & Jockey (01547) 520062

Wylcwm Place; LD7 1AE Popular old family-run pub with several cosy areas, one with log fire, enjoyable good value food cooked by owner from traditional choices and pizzas up in bar and adjoining restaurant, cheerful service, well kept beers; tables in pleasant medieval courtyard, six bedrooms, handy for Offa's Dyke Path. *(Charles Todd)*

LIBANUS   SN9926

Tai'r Bull (01874) 622600

A470 SW of Brecon; LD3 8EL Welcoming old roadside village pub with well kept ales such as Greene King and Wye Valley, enjoyable food from good sandwiches up, woodburner in large stone fireplace, light airy restaurant; great views of Pen-y-Fan from small front terrace, five bedrooms.
(Brian and Jacky Wilson)

LLANBEDR   SO2320

Red Lion (01873) 810754

Off A40 at Crickhowell; NP8 1SR Quaint old local in pretty village set in dell, heavy beams, antique settles in lounge and snug, log fires, well kept Rhymney, Wye Valley and a guest ale, front dining area with fair value home-made food; good walking country (porch for muddy boots), open all day weekends, closed Mon, and weekday lunchtimes. *(Charles Todd)*

LLANFIHANGEL-NANT-MELAN   SO1958

Red Lion (01544) 350220

A44 10 miles W of Kington; LD8 2TN Stripped-stone and beamed pub, roomy main bar with flagstones and woodburner, carpeted restaurant, front sun porch, good fair priced home-made food from shortish interesting menu, Brains and changing guests, friendly service, back bar with another woodburner; pool and darts; children and dogs welcome, country views from pleasant garden, seven bedrooms (three in annexe), handy for Radnor Forest walks and near impressive waterfall, open all day Sun till 9pm, closed Tues. *(Christopher Mannings)*

LLANGEDWYN SJ1924

Green Inn (01691) 828234

B4396 E of village; SY10 9JW Old country dining pub refurbished under current owners, various snug alcoves, nooks and crannies, good mix of furnishings including oak settles and leather sofas, woodburner, Stonehouse, Sharps Doom Bar and a guest, enjoyable food including Sun carvery served by friendly helpful staff; children and dogs welcome, attractive garden over road running down towards River Tanat, closed winter Mon and Tues, otherwise open all day. *(Charles Todd)*

LLANGURIG SN9079

Blue Bell (01686) 440254

A44 opposite church; SY18 6SG Friendly old-fashioned village inn with comfortable flagstoned bar, well kept Brains Rev James and Wye Valley Butty Bach, Thatcher's cider, ample helpings of enjoyable good value pubby food, small dining room, games room with darts, dominoes and pool; background music; children welcome, no dogs, nine simple inexpensive bedrooms, open all day. *(S and L McPhee)*

LLANIDLOES SN9584

Crown & Anchor (01686) 412398

Long Bridge Street; SY18 6EF Friendly unspoilt town-centre pub known locally as Rubys after landlady who has run it for over 50 years (been in her family for a lot longer), well kept Brains Rev James and Worthington Bitter, chatty locals' bar, lounge, snug and two other rooms, one with pool and games machine separated by central hallway; open all day. *(Christopher Mannings)*

LLANWRTYD WELLS SN8746

Neuadd Arms (01591) 610236

The Square; LD5 4RB Sizeable 19th-c hotel (friendly and by no means upmarket) brewing its own good value Heart of Wales beers in back stable block (ten on at once), enjoyable straightforward home-made food, log fires in lounge and small tiled public bar still with old service bells, restaurant, games room; well behaved dogs in bars, a few tables out at front, 21 bedrooms (front ones can be noisy), engaging very small town in good walking area, novel events such as bogsnorkelling and man v horse, open all day. *(James Allsopp)*

MALLWYD SH8612

Brigands (01650) 511999

A470 by roundabout in village; SY20 9HJ Sizeable 15th-c beamed coaching inn with

gently civilised atmosphere, enjoyable fairly priced food using local produce, popular afternoon teas, Cader ales and a summer guest, friendly efficient staff; children and dogs welcome, extensive lawns with lovely views, can arrange fishing on River Dovey, nine bedrooms, open (and some food) all day. *(Mike and Mary Carter)*

PAINSCASTLE SO1646

★ **Roast Ox** (01497) 851398

Off A470 Brecon–Builth Wells, or from A438 at Clyro; LD2 3JL Well restored pub with beams, flagstones, stripped stone, appropriate simple furnishings and some rustic bric-a-brac, huge antlers above open fire, ales tapped from the cask and good range of ciders, popular freshly made food, friendly quick service; children and dogs welcome, picnic-sets outside, attractive hill country, ten comfortable neat bedrooms. *(Taff Thomas)*

PENCELLI SO0925

Royal Oak (01874) 665396

B4558 SE of Brecon; LD3 7LX Unpretentious and friendly with two small bars, low beams and log fires, assorted pine furniture on flagstones, autographed sporting memorabilia, well kept Brains Rev James and a guest, small blackboard choice of enjoyable home-made food (standard times in summer, Thurs-Sat evenings and weekend lunchtimes in winter), simple modern candlelit dining room; children welcome and dogs (but do ask first), terraces backing on to Monmouth & Brecon Canal (nearby moorings), lovely canalside walks and well placed for Taff Trail, closed Mon-Weds out of season. *(James Allsopp)*

PENYCAE SN8313

Ancient Briton (01639) 730273

Brecon Road (A4067); SA9 1YY Friendly opened-up roadside pub, log fire in bar, seven or more well kept ales from far and wide, local cider and enjoyable reasonably priced home-made food; children and dogs welcome, seats outside and play area, four bedrooms, campsite (good facilities), handy for Dan-yr-Ogof caves, Henrhyd waterfall and Craig-y-Nos Country Park, open all day. *(Mike Benton)*

RHAYADER SN9668

★ **Triangle** (01597) 810537

Cwmdauddwr; B4518 by bridge over River Wye, SW of centre; LD6 5AR Interesting little 16th-c pub with buoyant local atmosphere, shortish choice of good value home-made pubby food (best to book evenings), well kept Brains Rev James, Hancocks HB and reasonably priced wines, friendly staff, dining area with nice view over park to River Wye; quiz nights and darts; self-catering cottage opposite, three tables on small front terrace, parking can be difficult. *(Taff Thomas)*

A little further afield

CHANNEL ISLANDS

GUERNSEY

FOREST

Deerhound (01481) 238585
Le Bourg; GY8 0AN Spacious roadside
dining pub with modern interior, popular well
priced food including summer seafood menu,
Liberation ales, friendly helpful service; free
wi-fi; children welcome, sunny, sheltered
terrace with parasols, handy for the airport,
open all day. *(John Harris)*

KING'S MILLS

★**Fleur du Jardin** (01481) 257996
King's Mills Road; GY5 7JT Lovely 15th-c
country hotel in attractive walled garden
with solar-heated swimming pool, relaxing
low-beamed flagstoned bar with good log
fire, old prints and subdued lighting, good
food strong on local produce and seafood,
afternoon tea, friendly helpful service,
Liberation ales plus guests, good choice of
wines by the glass, local cider, restaurant;
background music; children and small dogs
welcome, plenty of tables on back terrace,
15 clean comfortable bedrooms, open all day.
(John Harris, Alex Sumner)

ST PETER PORT

Ship & Crown (01481) 728994
*Opposite Crown Pier, Esplanade;
GY1 2NB* Bustling town pub with bay
windows overlooking harbour; interesting
photographs (especially of World War II
occupation, also boats and local shipwrecks),
decent all-day bar food from sandwiches
up, ales such as Fullers London Pride,
welcoming prompt service even when busy,
more modern-feel Crow's Nest brasserie
upstairs with good views; sports TVs in bar;
open all day from 10am till late. *(John and
Mary Warner)*

VALE

Houmet (01481) 242214
Grande Havre; GY6 8JR Modern
building overlooking Grande Havre Bay,
front restaurant/bar with conservatory,
good choice of reasonably priced popular
food (best to book) including fresh fish and
seafood, friendly service, a couple of real ales
and several wines by the glass, back public
bar with pool, darts and big-screen sports
TV (dogs allowed here); children welcome,
tables out on sheltered decking, open all day
(not Sun evening). *(John Harris)*

JERSEY

GRÈVE DE LECQ

★**Moulin de Lecq** (01534) 482818
Mont de la Grève de Lecq; JE3 2DT
Cheerful family-friendly mill conversion
dating from the 12th c with massive
waterwheel dominating the softly lit beamed
bar, good varied choice of enjoyable food,
four changing ales and a couple of real
ciders, prompt friendly service, restaurant
extension and upstairs games room with pool
and TV; dogs welcome in bar, terrace picnic-
sets and good adventure playground, quiet
streamside spot with nice walks, open all day
in summer. *(John and Mary Warner)*

ST AUBIN

Boat House (01534) 747141
North Quay; JE3 8BS Modern steel and
timber-clad harbourside building with great
views (window tables for diners), bar serving
well kept local ales and several wines by
the glass, good food ranging from tapas to

Josper-grilled steaks, airy upstairs restaurant (evenings, weekends); balcony and decked terrace overlooking harbour, open all day. *(Nick Sharpe)*

ST AUBIN
★ **Old Court House Inn**
(01534) 746433 *Harbour Boulevard; JE3 8AB* Bustling bar with low beams and open fire, other rambling areas including bistro, appetising food from snacks to good fresh fish, well kept ales and 15 wines by the glass, handsome upstairs restaurant with lovely views across the bay to St Helier; children welcome, front deck overlooking harbour, more seats in courtyard behind, ten comfortable well equipped bedrooms, open all day (food all day in summer). *(Paul and Sue Merrick)*

ST AUBIN
Tenby (01534) 741224
Le Boulevard, towards St Helier; JE3 8AB Randalls pub overlooking the harbour; large bar and several other rooms, good choice of pubby food from sandwiches and wraps up, a couple of real ales such as Skinners, helpful service; children welcome, disabled access/loos, seats out on small front deck under awning, more on paved side terrace, open all day. *(Paul and Sue Merrick, Paul Humphreys)*

ST BRELADE
Old Smugglers (01534) 741510
Ouaisne Bay; OS map reference 595476; JE3 8AW Unpretentious black-beamed pub just above Ouaisne beach, up to four well kept ales, proper cider and enjoyable traditional pubby food, friendly service, log fires, traditional built-in settles, darts, cribbage and dominoes, restaurant; occasional live music, sports TV; children and dogs welcome, sun porch with coast views, open all day in summer. *(Alison and Michael Harper)*

ST HELIER
Cock & Bottle (01534) 722184
Royal Square; JE2 4WA Big lively outside eating area in Royal Square with lovely big hanging baskets, rattan tables and chairs under parasols, heaters and blankets for cooler evenings; cosy inside with tartan-upholstered settles and small stools in front of large fireplace, wide choice of good food from sandwiches and baguettes through pubby and french choices to summer seafood menu, local ales; open all day, no food Fri-Sun evenings. *(Paul and Sue Merrick)*

ST HELIER
Halkett (01534) 732769
Halkett Place; JE2 4WG Modern pub-bar close to tree-lined square, mix of traditional and contemporary décor and furnishings, Liberation ale, 17 wines by the glass and wide choice of food from pubby and brasserie dishes to summer seafood menu; very busy with visitors and locals; weekend DJ; open all day, no food Sun evening. *(Paul and Sue Merrick)*

ST HELIER
★ **Lamplighter** (01534) 723119
Mulcaster Street; JE2 3NJ Small friendly pub with up to eight well kept ales, real ciders and over 150 malt whiskies from pewter-topped counter, low-priced pubby food including good crab sandwiches and popular steak nights (Tues and Thurs), traditional décor with lots of pump clips on heavy timbers and some old gas light fittings; sports TV, can get very busy; interesting patriotic façade (the only union flag visible during Nazi occupation), open all day, no evening food Fri-Sun. *(Paul and Sue Merrick, David Carr)*

ST HELIER
Post Horn (01534) 872853
Hue Street; JE2 3RE Popular centrally placed pub with modernised interior, four well kept ales including Liberation and eight wines by the glass, fair value pubby food (not Sun), open fire; sports TV; tables out in front, open all day. *(Paul and Sue Merrick)*

ST MARY
St Marys (01534) 482897
La Rue des Buttes; JE3 3DF Friendly old inn opposite attractive church, modern interior with bar and spacious dining area, good choice of popular reasonably priced food from lunchtime sandwiches up (summer seafood), Liberation and guests, plenty of wines by the glass; pool, darts, free wi-fi; children welcome, seats in front garden and back courtyard, bedrooms, open all day. *(Alison and Michael Harper)*

ISLE OF MAN

BALDRINE   SC4180
Liverpool Arms (01624) 674787
Main Road; IM4 6AE Former coaching inn with enjoyable choice of reasonably priced pubby food (all day Fri-Sun), Okells Bitter and a summer guest, friendly welcoming staff, open fires; sports TV, pool and darts; picnic-sets outside, children and dogs (in bar) allowed, open all day. *(Chris Webster)*

LAXEY   SC4382
Shore (01624) 861509
Old Laxey Hill; IM4 7DA Friendly nautically themed village pub brewing its own Old Laxey Bosun Bitter, good value wines by the glass and enjoyable pubby lunchtime food (may have Tues curry and Thurs steak nights); children welcome till 9pm, picnic-sets out by lovely stream, nice walk to Laxey waterwheel, open all day. *(Anne Taylor)*

PEEL   SC2484

Creek (01624) 842216

Station Place/North Quay; IM5 1AT
In lovely setting on the ancient quayside
opposite Manannan Heritage Centre,
welcoming relaxed atmosphere, wide choice
of highly thought-of food including fish, crab
and lobster fresh from the boats, good local
kippers too, ten well kept changing ales
(always some from Okells), nautical-themed
lounge bar with etched mirrors and mainly
old woodwork, public bar with TVs and
weekend live music; children welcome, tables
outside overlooking harbour, open (and food)
all day. *(Chris Webster)*

PORT ERIN   SC1969

Falcons Nest (01624) 834077

Station Road; IM9 6AF Friendly family-
run hotel overlooking the bay, enjoyable
food including local fish/seafood and Sun
carvery, up to five well kept ales and some
60 malt whiskies, two bars, one with open
fire, conservatory and restaurant; sports TV;
children welcome, 39 bedrooms many with
sea view, also eight self-catering apartments,
handy for steam rail terminus, open all day.
(Charlie Parker)

Pubs that serve food all day

We list here all the pubs (in the Main Entries) that have told us they plan to serve food all day, even if it's only one day of the week. The individual entries for the pubs themselves show the actual details.

Bedfordshire

Ireland, Black Horse
Oakley, Bedford Arms

Berkshire

Kintbury, Dundas Arms
Pangbourne, Elephant
Peasemore, Fox
Sonning, Bull
White Waltham, Beehive

Buckinghamshire

Forty Green, Royal Standard of England
Stoke Mandeville, Bell

Cambridgeshire

Cambridge, Punter
Peterborough, Brewery Tap
Stilton, Bell

Cheshire

Aldford, Grosvenor Arms
Allostock, Three Greyhounds Inn
Astbury, Egerton Arms
Aston, Bhurtpore
Bostock Green, Hayhurst Arms
Bunbury, Dysart Arms
Burleydam, Combermere Arms
Burwardsley, Pheasant
Chester, Architect
Chester, Mill
Chester, Old Harkers Arms
Cholmondeley, Cholmondeley Arms
Cotebrook, Fox & Barrel
Delamere, Fishpool
Eaton, Plough
Macclesfield, Sutton Hall
Marton, Davenport Arms
Mobberley, Bulls Head
Mobberley, Church Inn
Mottram St Andrew, Bulls Head
Nether Alderley, Wizard
Spurstow, Yew Tree
Thelwall, Little Manor
Warmingham, Bears Paw

Cornwall

Morwenstow, Bush
Mylor Bridge, Pandora
Porthtowan, Blue

Cumbria

Cartmel Fell, Masons Arms
Crosthwaite, Punch Bowl
Elterwater, Britannia
Ings, Watermill
Levens, Strickland Arms
Lupton, Plough
Ravenstonedale, Black Swan

Derbyshire

Chelmorton, Church Inn
Fenny Bentley, Coach & Horses
Hathersage, Plough
Hayfield, Lantern Pike
Hayfield, Royal
Ladybower Reservoir, Yorkshire
   Bridge

Devon

Cockwood, Anchor
Iddesleigh, Duke of York
Postbridge, Warren House
Sidbury, Hare & Hounds

Dorset

Tarrant Monkton, Langton Arms
Weymouth, Red Lion
Worth Matravers, Square &
   Compass

Essex

Feering, Sun
Fyfield, Queens Head
Little Walden, Crown
South Hanningfield,
   Old Windmill

Gloucestershire

Didmarton, Kings Arms
Ford, Plough
Nailsworth, Weighbridge
Sheepscombe, Butchers Arms

Hampshire

Bransgore, Three Tuns
Cadnam, White Hart
Littleton, Running Horse
Portsmouth, Old Customs House

Hertfordshire

Ashwell, Three Tuns
Barnet, Duke of York
Berkhamsted, Highwayman
Harpenden, White Horse

Isle of Wight

Hulverstone, Sun
Shorwell, Crown

Kent

Chiddingstone Causeway, Little
   Brown Jug
Langton Green, Hare
Penshurst, Bottle House
Sevenoaks, White Hart
Shipbourne, Chaser
Stalisfield Green, Plough

Lancashire

Bashall Eaves, Red Pump
Bispham Green, Eagle & Child
Formby, Sparrowhawk
Great Mitton, Aspinall Arms
Manchester, Wharf
Uppermill, Church Inn
Waddington, Lower Buck

Leicestershire

Coleorton, George
Lyddington, Marquess of Exeter
Swithland, Griffin

Lincolnshire

Kirkby la Thorpe, Queens Head
Stamford, George of Stamford

Norfolk

King's Lynn, Bank House
Larling, Angel
Morston, Anchor
Salthouse, Dun Cow
Thorpe Market, Gunton Arms
Woodbastwick, Fur & Feather

Northamptonshire

Ashby St Ledgers, Olde Coach
   House
Oundle, Ship

Northumbria

Blanchland, Lord Crewe Arms
Carterway Heads, Manor House Inn
Mickleton, Crown
Newton, Duke of Wellington
Stannington, St Marys Inn

Oxfordshire

Kingham, Plough
Oxford, Bear
Oxford, Punter
Sparsholt, Star
Wolvercote, Jacobs Inn

Shropshire

Chetwynd Aston, Fox
Shipley, Inn at Shipley
Shrewsbury, Armoury

Somerset

Bath, Marlborough
Dunster, Luttrell Arms
Hinton St George, Lord Poulett
   Arms

Stanton Wick, Carpenters Arms
Wedmore, Swan

Staffordshire

Brewood, Oakley
Longdon Green, Red Lion
Salt, Holly Bush
Wrinehill, Hand & Trumpet

Suffolk

Chelmondiston, Butt & Oyster
Southwold, Harbour Inn
Stoke-by-Nayland, Crown
Waldringfield, Maybush

Surrey

Buckland, Pheasant
Chiddingfold, Swan
Chobham, White Hart
Elstead, Mill at Elstead
Englefield Green, Bailiwick
Milford, Refectory

Sussex

Alfriston, George
Charlton, Fox Goes Free
Eridge Green, Nevill Crest & Gun
Friday Street, Farm at Friday Street
Horsham, Black Jug
Ringmer, Cock

Warwickshire

Birmingham, Old Joint Stock
Hunningham, Red Lion
Leamington Spa, Star & Garter
Long Compton, Red Lion
Shipston-on-Stour, Black Horse
Warmington, Falcon
Welford-on-Avon, Bell

Wiltshire

Bradford-on-Avon, Castle

Yorkshire

Beck Hole, Birch Hall

Blakey Ridge, Lion

Bradfield, Strines Inn

Elslack, Tempest Arms

Grinton, Bridge Inn

Halifax, Shibden Mill

Hartshead, Gray Ox

Hetton, Angel

Ledsham, Chequers

Linton in Craven, Fountaine

Welburn, Crown & Cushion

Widdop, Pack Horse

London

Central London, Old Bank of England, Olde Mitre, Seven Stars, Thomas Cubitt

North London, Hare, Holly Bush, Latchmere, Victoria

West London, Dove, Duke of Sussex, Mute Swan, Old Orchard, White Horse, Windsor Castle

Scotland

Applecross, Applecross Inn

Glasgow, Babbity Bowster

Glasgow, Bon Accord

Shieldaig, Tigh an Eilean Hotel

Thornhill, Lion & Unicorn

Sligachan, Sligachan Hotel

Wales

Colwyn Bay, Pen-y-Bryn

Gresford, Pant-yr-Ochain

Llandudno Junction, Queens Head

Llanelian-yn-Rhos, White Lion

Llangollen, Corn Mill

Mold, Glasfryn

Overton Bridge, Cross Foxes

Pontypridd, Bunch of Grapes

Pubs near motorway junctions

The number at the start of each line is the junction number.

Detailed directions are given in the Main Entry for each pub. In this section, to help you find the pubs quickly before you're past the junction, we give the name of the chapter where you'll find the text.

M1

9: Redbourn, Cricketers (Hertfordshire) 3.2 miles

13: Woburn, Birch (Bedfordshire) 3.5 miles

18: Ashby St Ledgers, Olde Coach House (Northamptonshire) 4 miles

M3

1: Sunbury, Flower Pot (Surrey) 1.6 miles

3: West End, The Inn West End (Surrey) 2.4 miles; Chobham, White Hart (Surrey) 4 miles

5: North Warnborough, Mill House (Hampshire) 1 mile; Hook, Hogget (Hampshire) 1.1 miles

7: North Waltham, Fox (Hampshire) 3 miles

9: Easton, Chestnut Horse (Hampshire) 3.6 miles

M4

9: Bray, Crown (Berkshire) 1.75 miles; Bray, Hinds Head (Berkshire) 1.75 miles

13: Chieveley, Crab & Boar (Berkshire) 3.5 miles; Peasemore, Fox (Berkshire) 4 miles

14: Shefford Woodlands, Pheasant (Berkshire) 0.3 miles

M5

4: Holy Cross, Bell & Cross (Worcestershire) 4 miles

10: Coombe Hill, Gloucester Old Spot (Gloucestershire) 1 mile

13: Eastington, Old Badger (Gloucestershire) 1 mile; Clapton-in-Gordano, Black Horse (Somerset) 4 miles

30: Woodbury Salterton, Diggers Rest (Devon) 3.5 miles

M6

16: Barthomley, White Lion (Cheshire) 1 mile

17: Sandbach, Old Hall (Cheshire) 1.2 miles

18: Allostock, Three Greyhounds Inn (Cheshire) 4.7 miles

19: Mobberley, Bulls Head (Cheshire) 4 miles

33: Bay Horse, Bay Horse (Lancashire) 1.2 miles

36: Lupton, Plough (Cumbria) 2 miles; Levens, Strickland Arms (Cumbria) 4 miles

40: Yanwath, Gate Inn (Cumbria) 2.25 miles; Tirril, Queens Head (Cumbria) 3.5 miles

M11

9: Hinxton, Red Lion (Cambridgeshire) 2 miles

10: Duxford, John Barleycorn (Cambridgeshire) 1.8 miles; Whittlesford, Tickell Arms (Cambridgeshire) 2.4 miles

M25

5: Chipstead, George & Dragon (Kent) 1.25 miles

8: Walton on the Hill, Blue Ball (Surrey) 3.7 miles

16: Denham, Swan (Buckinghamshire) 0.75 miles

18: Flaunden, Bricklayers Arms (Hertfordshire) 4 miles

21A: Potters Crouch, Holly Bush (Hertfordshire) 2.3 miles

M27

1: Cadnam, White Hart (Hampshire) 0.5 miles; Fritham, Royal Oak (Hampshire) 4 miles

M40

2: Hedgerley, White Horse (Buckinghamshire) 2.4 miles; Forty Green, Royal Standard of England (Buckinghamshire) 3.5 miles

12: Gaydon, Malt Shovel (Warwickshire) 0.9 miles

M42

5: Barston, Malt Shovel (Warwickshire) 3 miles

6: Hampton-in-Arden, White Lion (Warwickshire) 1.25 miles

M50

1: Baughton, Jockey (Worcestershire) 4 miles

3: Kilcot, Kilcot Inn (Gloucestershire) 2.3 miles

M60

13: Worsley, Worsley Old Hall (Lancashire) 1 mile

M62

25: Hartshead, Gray Ox (Yorkshire) 3.5 miles

MAPS

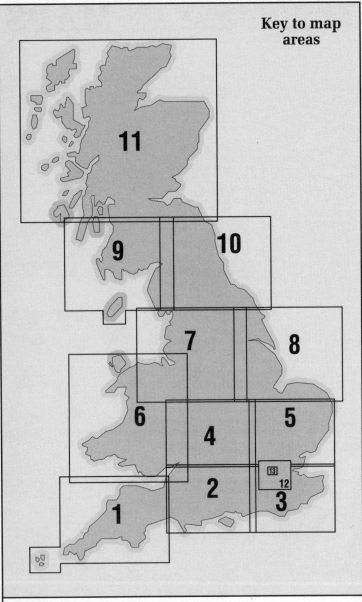

Key to map areas

Reference to sectional maps

▬▬▬ Motorway	● Main Entry
▬▬▬ Major road	◉ Main Entry with accommodation
----- County boundary	■ Place name to assist navigation

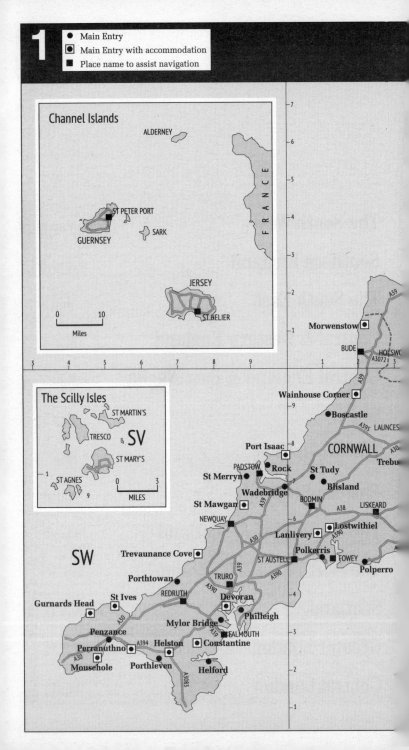

1

- ● Main Entry
- ◉ Main Entry with accommodation
- ■ Place name to assist navigation

Channel Islands

ALDERNEY

FRANCE

GUERNSEY ■ ST PETER PORT

SARK

JERSEY

■ ST HELIER

0   10
Miles

The Scilly Isles

ST MARTIN'S

TRESCO

SV

ST MARY'S

ST AGNES

0   3
MILES

Morwenstow ◉

BUDE ■   HOLSWO
A3072

Wainhouse Corner ◉

● Boscastle

A395 LAUNCES

Port Isaac ●   **CORNWALL**
A30
PADSTOW ■   Rock ●   St Tudy ●   Trebu

St Merryn ●   ● Blisland

Wadebridge ●   BODMIN ■
A38   LISKEARD ■
St Mawgan ◉

NEWQUAY ■   Lanlivery ◉   ◉ Lostwithiel
A30   A390

SW   Trevaunance Cove ◉   Polkerris ■   FOWEY ■
ST AUSTELL ■   ● Polperro

Porthtowan ●   TRURO ■   A390

REDRUTH ■   Devoran ●
● St Ives   Philleigh ●

Gurnards Head ◉   A30
Mylor Bridge ●
Penzance ●   FALMOUTH ■
Perranuthno ◉   A394   Helston ◉   ◉ Constantine
Mousehole ●   Porthleven ●   Helford ●
A3083

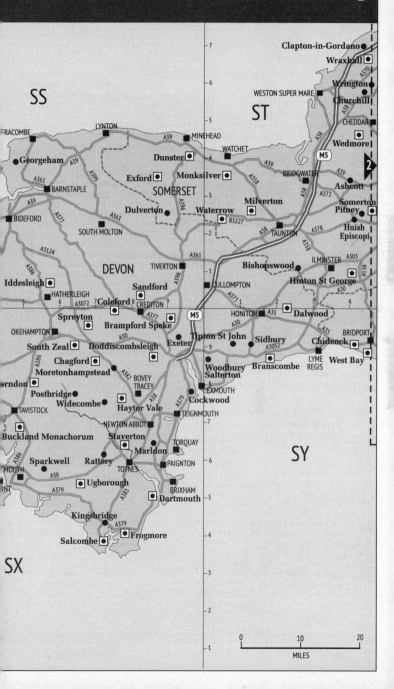

● Main Entry
◉ Main Entry with accommodation
■ Place name to assist navigation

4

Tetbury
Cricklade
Oldbury-on-Severn
Crudwell
GLOUCESTERSHIRE
Didmarton
Sherston
MALMESBURY
Swindon

M4
M5
M5
M4
CHIPPENHAM

Bristol
Corsham
CALNE
Marlborou
Monkton
Farleigh
South Wraxall
Manton
Stanton Wick
Bath
Holt
Rowde
Wrington
Monkton Combe
MELKSHAM
DEVIZES
WILTSHIRE
Midford
Bradford-on-Avon
Poulshot
Combe Hay
TROWBRIDGE
Edington
MIDSOMER NORTON
East Chisenbu
CHEDDAR
Holcombe
Mells
Upton Scudamore
Priddy
WELLS
Croscombe
Frome
WARMINSTER
SHEPTON
MALLET
SOMERSET
Newton
GLASTONBURY
WYLYE
AMERSBURY
ST
Bourton
Fonthill Gifford
Babcary
East Knoyle
Pitt
WINCANTON
SALISBURY
Kingsdon
Chicksgrove
Corton Denham
West Stour
Charlton
Horethorne
SHAFTESBURY
Tollard Royal
Rockbourne
Trent
FORDINGBRIDGE
YEOVIL
Odcombe
Sherborne
Shroton
Farnham
Fritha
Chetnole
Cranborne
DORSET
Eversdot
Middlemarsh
BLANDFORD
FORUM
Tarrant Monkton
RINGWC
Cerne Abbas
Plush
Wimborne
Minster
Nettlecombe
Bransgore
Askerswell
BRIDPORT
DORCHESTER
POOLE
CHRISTC
West Bay
BOURNEMOUTH
WAREHAM
Church Knowle
Weymouth
Kingston
SWANAGE
SY
Worth Matravers

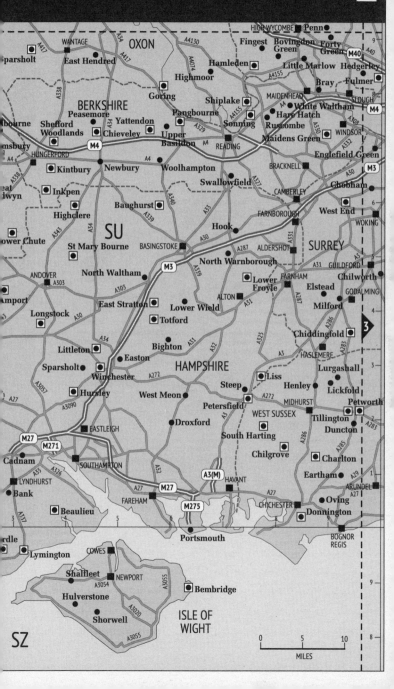

2

SZ

3
- ● Main Entry
- ◉ Main Entry with accommodation
- ■ Place name to assist navigation

BUCKS

M1 M11 **5** M25 A127

Harefield (see West London) GREATER LONDON

Hedgerley ● Denham ● Horndon-on-the-Hill ■ A128

M40 Fulmer ● UXBRIDGE M25

BERKS M4 A127

M25 A30 STAINES TILBURY ■ A128

Englefield Green ● DARTFORD GRAVESEND ■

M3 A30 Sunbury ◉ ROCHES A2

Chobham ● Esher ● Meopham ●

M25 M20 A227 A228

WOKING ■ A3 M25 MAIDS M

6 Walton on the Hill ● Chipstead ● Chipstead ● M26

SURREY A24 Ivy Hatch ● TQ

Mickleham ◉ A217 M25 WESTERHAM ■ Sevenoaks ● Shipbourne ●

GUILDFORD ■ A25 Buckland ● A25 A227 A26

Chilworth ● DORKING REIGATE Chiddingstone ● TONBRIDGE ■

A25 A217 A23 Penshurst ◉ Bidborough ● Matfie

Shamley Green ● A29 M23 A264 Speldhurst ● Goudh

A281 A24 Langton Green ● Tunbridge Wells ●

CRAWLEY Copthorne ● EAST GRINSTEAD ■ Eridge

Horsham ● A264 West Hoathly ◉ Withyham ● Green ● A21

2 Horsted Keynes ◉ CROWBOROUGH Mark Cross ●

Warninglid ◉ Danehill ◉ High Hurstwood ● A267 Ticehurst ◉

A272 HAYWARDS HEATH Fletching ◉ Heathfield ● A265 Sale

Petworth ◉ Dial Post ◉ A23 BURGESS HILL ■ Uckfield ● Robertsbridg

A283 WEST SUSSEX A273 A272 A26 A22 A367 EAST SUSSEX

A29 Ditchling ◉ Ringmer ● HAILSHAM ■ A271

1 A283 LEWES A259

ARUNDEL ■ A27 Firle ● A27

A259 WORTHING ■ A259 NEWHAVEN Alfriston ● Friday St ●

BRIGHTON A26 EASTBOURNE ■

East Dean ◉

9 TV

8

1 2 3 4 5 6 7

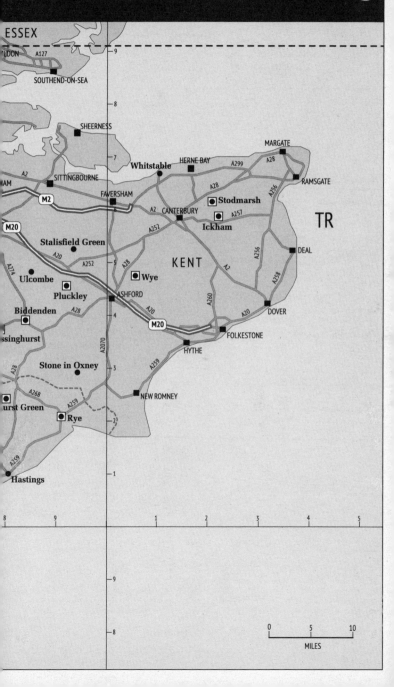

3

ESSEX

LDON
A127
SOUTHEND-ON-SEA

SHEERNESS

MARGATE

HERNE BAY
A299
A28
RAMSGATE

HAM
A2
SITTINGBOURNE
Whitstable
A28

FAVERSHAM
Stodmarsh

M2
A2
CANTERBURY
A257

M20
A252
Ickham

Stalisfield Green
A256
DEAL

A20
A252
A28
KENT
A2
A256

A174
Ulcombe
Wye
A359

Pluckley
ASHFORD
A260
DOVER

Biddenden
A28
A20
A20
FOLKESTONE

ssinghurst
M20
HYTHE

A28
Stone in Oxney
A259

A268
NEW ROMNEY
urst Green
A259
Rye

A259
Hastings

TR

0   5   10
MILES

- ● Main Entry
- ◉ Main Entry with accommodation
- ■ Place name to assist navigation

Shrewsbury

A5

TELFORD

● Breewood

CANNOCK

M6

LICHFIELD

M54

STAFFS

M6 Toll

TAMWC

0 5 10

◉ Ironbridge

A442

SJ

A5

M6

MILES

A41

A449

A449

5

A458 6 A4169

◉ Coalport

8

9

A38

2

● Cardington

● Shipley

A454

WOLVERHAMPTON

WALSALL

M4

SHROPSHIRE

Bridgnorth

WEST BROMWICH

A4123

A38(M)

M6

A458

STOURBRIDGE

◉ Birmingham

A442

M5

● Clent

8

◉ Hampton in Arden

A34

● Ba

LUDLOW

A4117

KIDDERMINSTER

A456

● Holy Cross

M42

M42

BEWDLEY

A456

A449

BROMSGROVE

A448

7

M40

◉ Tenbury Wells

A443

A451

A449

● Cutnall Green

REDDITCH

A4189

● Presto Bagot

A435

WORCESTERSHIRE

6

A3400

LEOMINSTER

A38

A422

STRATFORD-UPO

◉ Knightwick

WORCESTER

A46

A44

5

● Little Cowarne

◉ Bransford

A4103

● Newland

A44

A4104

● Welford-on-Avon B439

Alderm

HEREFORDSHIRE

◉ Malvern

A449

A46

● Bretforton

Arms

A417

SO

◉ Upper Colwall

● Baughton

4

◉ Ilmington

HEREFORD

A438

◉ Ledbury

● Welland

M5

Weston Subedge

EVESHAM ◉

Shi on

● Woolhope

A438

● Childswickham

◉ Chipping Campden

◉ Carey

A449

TEWKESBURY

A46

● Broadway

Bourton-on-the-Hill ◉

MORETON-IN-

M50

◉ Winchcombe

● Ford

U Odd

● Ross-on-Wye

● Coombe Hill

A435

◉ Lower Slaughter

● Walford

A38

Stow-on-the-Wold

A436

◉ Bledingto

Nether Westcote

● Symonds Yat

A40

Cheltenham

A46

● Brockhampton

A40

A429

Milton Wych

A4136

MONMOUTH

● Gloucester

● Cowley ◉

◉ Northleach

Burf

● Newland

GLOUCESTERSHIRE

● Sheepscombe

A417

1

S

Tintern

A48

STROUD

● Oakridge Lynch

◉ Barnsley

B4425

Filkin

A419

◉ Cirencester

A417

A466

● Eastington

8

9

● Nailsworth

A433

A419

2

● Dursley

A4135

Marston Meysey

Kel

◉ Oldbury-on-Severn

M5

Tetbury

A429

◉ Cricklade

CHEPSTOW

Crudwell

6

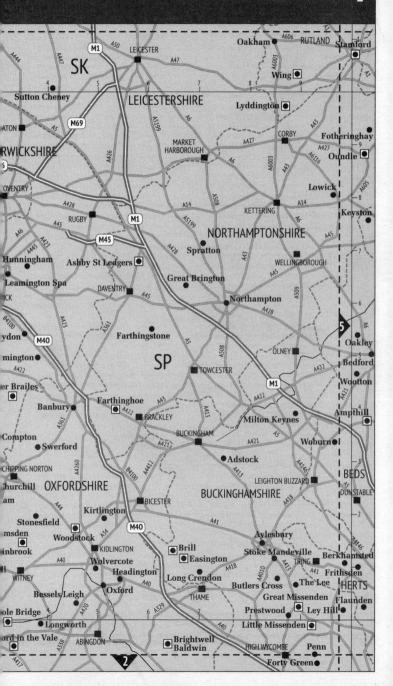

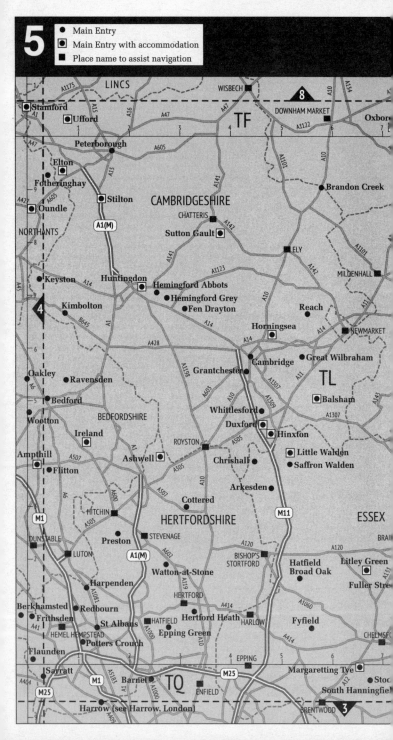

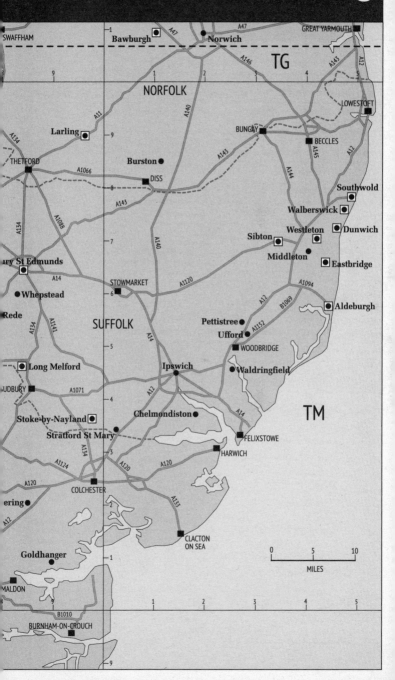

5

SWAFFHAM

Bawburgh

Norwich

GREAT YARMOUTH

A47

A47

A146

TG

A143

A12

9

LOWESTOFT

NORFOLK

A11

A140

Larling

9

BUNGAY

BECCLES

A145

A12

A134

THETFORD

A1066

Burston

A143

DISS

8

A144

Southwold

A143

Walberswick

Westleton

Dunwich

A140

7

Sibton

Middleton

Eastbridge

A1088

ury St Edmunds

A134

A14

Whepstead

STOWMARKET

6

A1120

A1094

A12

B1069

Aldeburgh

Rede

A134

A1141

SUFFOLK

A14

5

Pettistree

Ufford

A1152

WOODBRIDGE

Long Melford

Ipswich

Waldringfield

UDBURY

A1071

A12

4

Stoke-by-Nayland

Chelmondiston

A14

TM

Stratford St Mary

FELIXSTOWE

HARWICH

A1124

A134

A120

A120

3

ering

A120

COLCHESTER

A133

Goldhanger

CLACTON ON SEA

1

0   5   10

MILES

MALDON

B1010

BURNHAM-ON-CROUCH

9

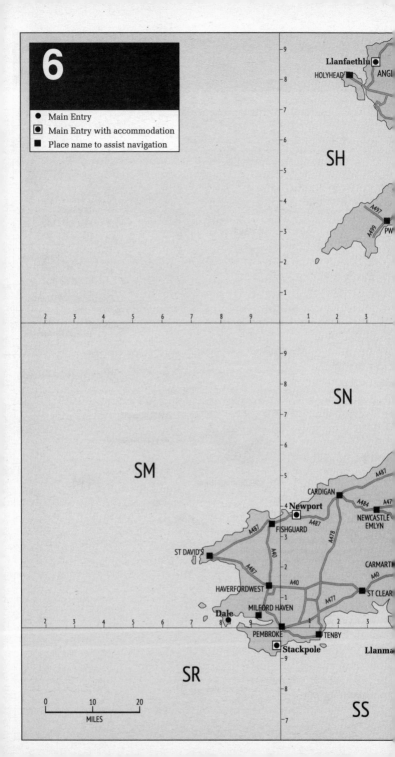

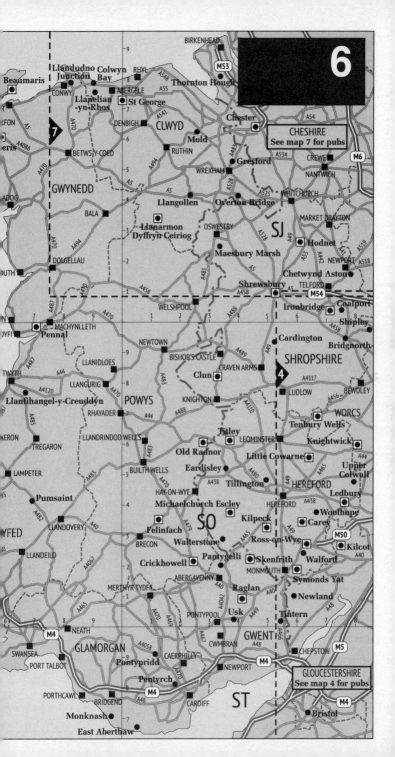

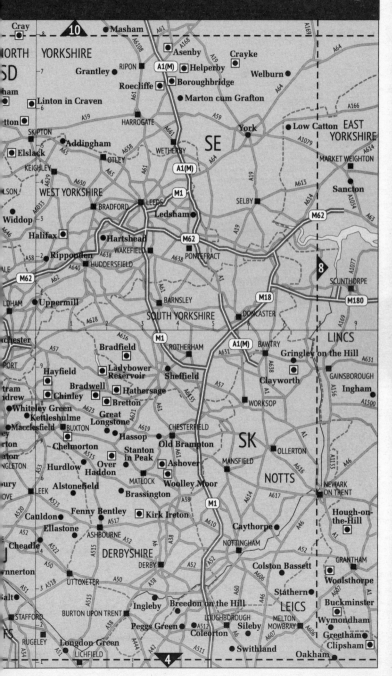

Cray
10
Masham
A61
NORTH YORKSHIRE
A6108
Asenby
A19
Crayke
A168
SD
-7
Grantley
RIPON
A1(M)
Helperby
Welburn
A64
ham
Linton in Craven
Roecliffe
Boroughbridge
6
Marton cum Grafton
A166
tton
HARROGATE
A59
A59
York
Low Catton
EAST YORKSHIRE
SKIPTON
A61
SE
A1079
Addingham
A59
WETHERBY
A64
MARKET WEIGHTON
Elslack
A65
OTLEY
A661
A1(M)
A613
Sancton
KEIGHLEY
A629
A650
A65
A61
M1
A19
A63
WEST YORKSHIRE
LSON
BRADFORD
LEEDS
SELBY
M62
Widdop
-3
Ledsham
A19
Halifax
Hartshead
M62
Ripponden
WAKEFIELD
A638
PONTEFRACT
A1077
ALE
M62
A62
A640
HUDDERSFIELD
A61
8
SCUNTHORPE
LDHAM
Uppermill
A628
BARNSLEY
M18
M180
SOUTH YORKSHIRE
DONCASTER
A159
chester
A57
M1
LINCS
PORT
9
Bradfield
ROTHERHAM
A1(M)
BAWTRY
Gringley on the Hill
A631
Hayfield
Ladybower Reservoir
Sheffield
A638
Clayworth
GAINSBOROUGH
tram
Bradwell
Hathersage
A57
A1
Ingham
ndrew
Chinley
Bretton
A635
WORKSOP
A1500
Whiteley Green
Great Longstone
A623
A621
CHESTERFIELD
SK
Kettleshulme
A619
Macclesfield
BUXTON
Hassop
Old Brampton
A61
OLLERTON
A1133
rton
Chelmorton
Stanton in Peak
MANSFIELD
A616
aton
A515
Ashover
NOTTS
NEWARK ON TRENT
NGLETON
Hurdlow
Over Haddon
MATLOCK
Woolley Moor
A617
ury
Alstonefield
Brassington
A38
M1
A614
Hough-on-the-Hill
LEEK
A523
Fenny Bentley
Kirk Ireton
A610
A46
A1
OVE
Cauldon
A517
Caythorpe
A520
Ellastone
ASHBOURNE
A52
NOTTINGHAM
A52
GRANTHAM
A52
Cheadle
A522
A515
DERBYSHIRE
Colston Bassett
Woolsthorpe
nnerton
A50
DERBY
A38
A52
A60
A607
salt
A518
UTTOXETER
A50
A38
Stathern
Buckminster
STAFFORD
A515
Ingleby
Breedon on the Hill
A46
LEICS
Wymondham
RS
BURTON UPON TRENT
A38
LOUGHBOROUGH
MELTON MOWBRAY
A606
Greetham
RUGELEY
Peggs Green
A512
Sileby
Clipsham
Longdop Green
A51
LICHFIELD
A42
Coleorton
Swithland
Oakham
A34
A444
A511
4

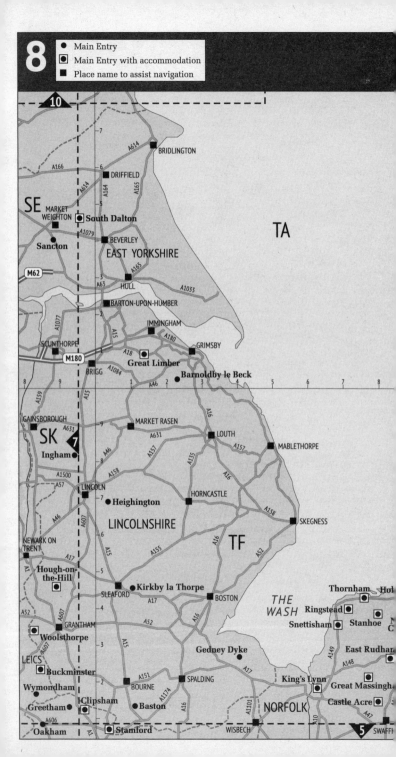

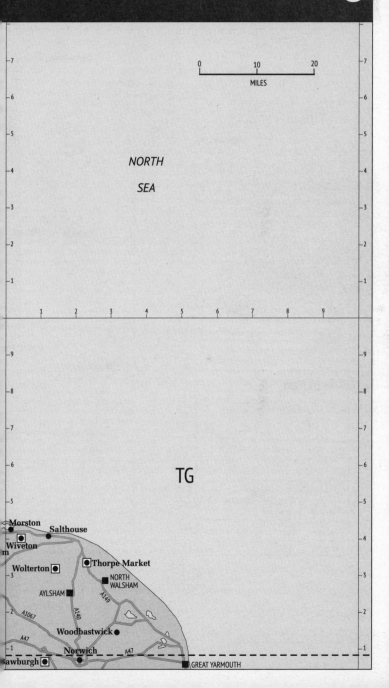

0   10   20
MILES

NORTH

SEA

7

6

5

4

3

2

1

1   2   3   4   5   6   7   8   9

9

8

7

6

TG

5

Morston

Salthouse

Wiveton
m

Wolterton   **Thorpe Market**

NORTH
WALSHAM

AYLSHAM

A149

A1067   A140

Woodbastwick

A47

Norwich   A47

awburgh   **GREAT YARMOUTH**

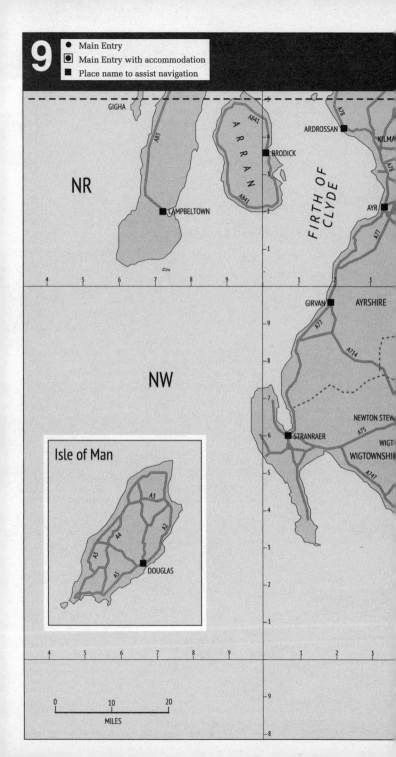

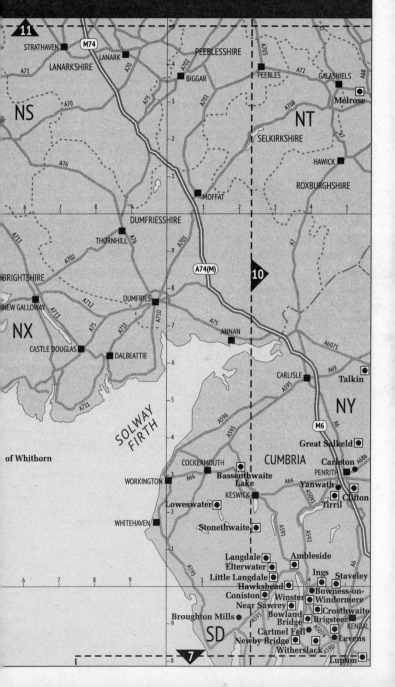

STRATHAVEN
M74
LANARK
LANARKSHIRE
A71
A70
A70
A73
A76
NS
PEEBLESSHIRE
A702
A701
BIGGAR
A703
PEEBLES
A72
GALASHIELS
A68
Melrose
NT
A708
A7
SELKIRKSHIRE
A7
HAWICK
ROXBURGHSHIRE
MOFFAT
A701
DUMFRIESSHIRE
THORNHILL
A76
A76
A702
A701
A74(M)
10
A7
BRIGHTSHIRE
NEW GALLOWAY
A712
DUMFRIES
A75
ANNAN
A75
A6071
NX
A713
A711
A710
CASTLE DOUGLAS
DALBEATTIE
CARLISLE
A595
A69
Talkin
A711
NY
SOLWAY
FIRTH
A596
M6
A6
Great Salkeld
of Whithorn
A595
CUMBRIA
Carleton
A686
PENRITH
COCKERMOUTH
A66
A66
Yanwath
WORKINGTON
Bassenthwaite
Lake
A5091
Clifton
Tirril
KESWICK
Loweswater
A591
WHITEHAVEN
Stonethwaite
A591
A592
Langdale
Ambleside
Elterwater
Ings
Staveley
Little Langdale
A595
Hawkshead
Bowness-on-
Coniston
Winster
Windermere
Near Sawrey
Crosthwaite
Broughton Mills
Bowland
Brigsteer
Bridge
A5074
KENDAL
Cartmel Fell
Levels
SD
Newby Bridge
A590
Witherslack
Lupton

11

6 7 8 9

6 7 8 9

6 7 8 9

9
1
2
3
4
5
6
7
8
9

1 2 3 4 5

10
● Main Entry
◉ Main Entry with accommodation
■ Place name to assist navigation

11

BERWICKSHIRE

Swinton

BERWICK-UPON-TWEED

PEEBLES

GALASHIELS

Melrose

KELSO

COLDSTREAM

NT

WOOLER

Seah

Ellingham

Newton-by-the-

SELKIRKSHIRE

Ancrum

JEDBURGH

ALNWICK

HAWICK

ROXBURGHSHIRE

NORTHUMBERLAND

DUMFRIESSHIRE

9

OTTERBURN

Stannersburn

MORPETH

Stannington

Wark

HAYDON BRIDGE

Gilsland

BRAMPTON

Newton

North Sh

CARLISLE

Talkin

HEXHAM

Diptonmill

CORBRIDGE

NEWCASTLE UPON

GATES

Hedley on the Hill

CONSETT

NY

ALSTON

Blanchland

Carterway Heads

Durham

DURHAM

Great Salkeld

PENRITH

Carleton

Yanwath

Clifton

Tirril

BISHOP AUCKLAND

KESWICK

Mickleton

Stonethwaite

Romaldkirk

Cotherstone

Winston

CUMBRIA

BROUGH

BARNARD CASTLE

DARLINGTON

Langdale

Elterwater

Ambleside

Little Langdale

Ings

Staveley

Ravenstonedale

SCOTCH CORNER

Mou

Hawkshead

Winster

Bowness-on-Windermere

Coniston

Crosthwaite

Grinton

Downholme

NOR

Near Sawrey

KENDAL

Bowland Bridge

Constable Burton

Cartmel Fell

Brigsteer

Levels

Witherslack

SD

SEDBERGH

East Witton

Thornton Watlass

Newby Bridge

Lupton

Masham

7

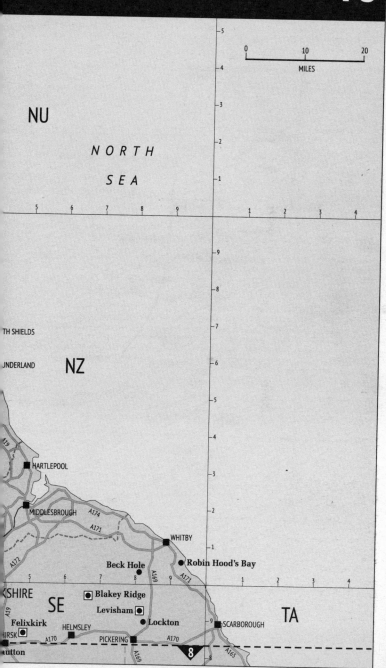

NU

N O R T H

S E A

0   10   20
MILES

TH SHIELDS

UNDERLAND

NZ

HARTLEPOOL

MIDDLESBROUGH   A174

A171

A172

WHITBY

Beck Hole   ● Robin Hood's Bay

◉ Blakey Ridge

Levisham ◉

● Lockton

SE

TA

Felixkirk

HELMSLEY

◉SCARBOROUGH

THIRSK◉

A170   PICKERING   A170

utton   A169   **8**

A165

KSHIRE

A19

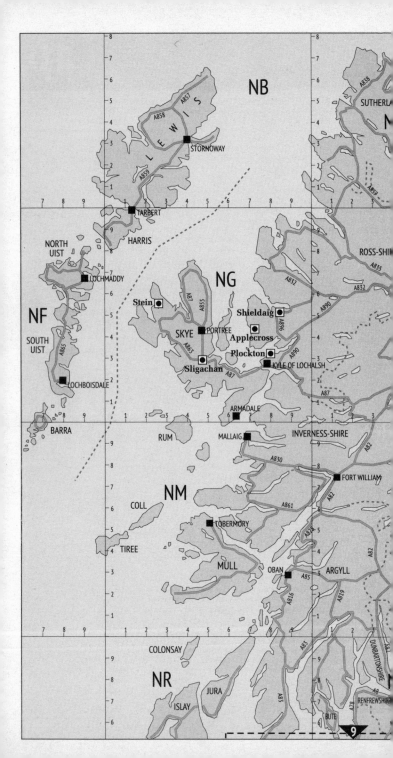

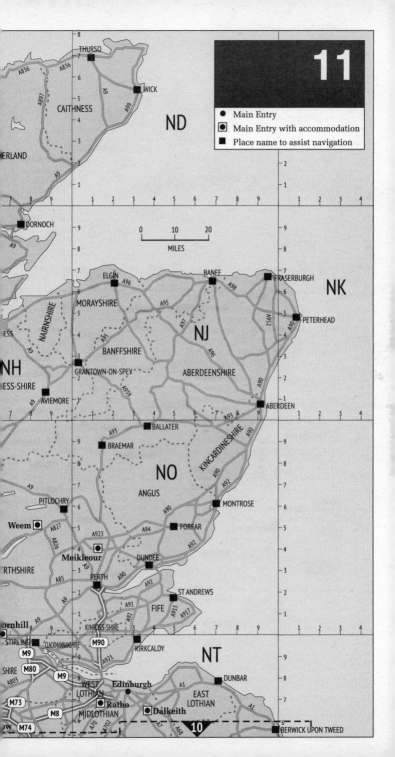

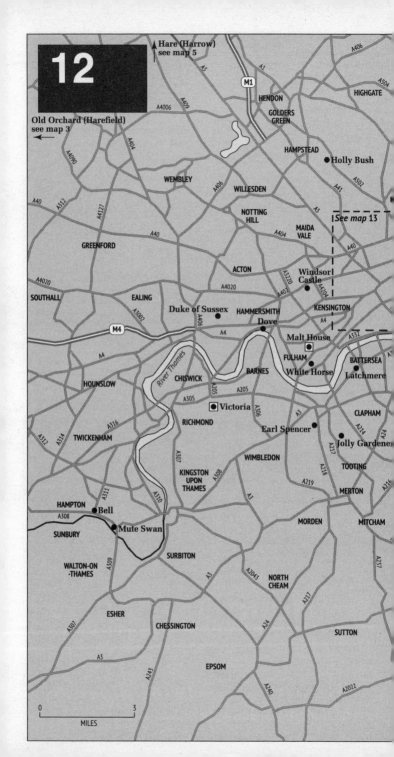

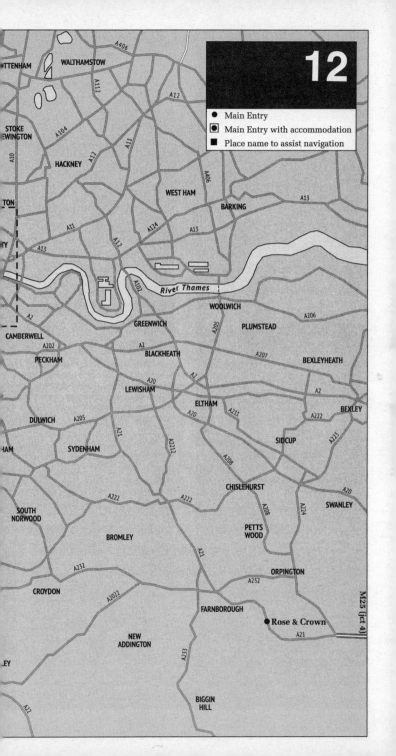

12

- ● Main Entry
- ◉ Main Entry with accommodation
- ■ Place name to assist navigation

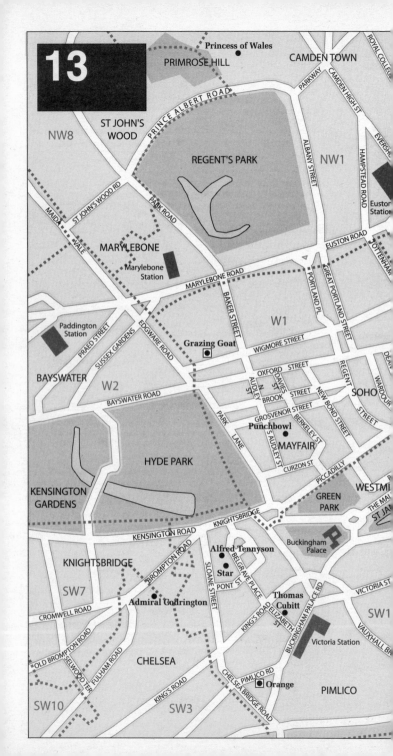

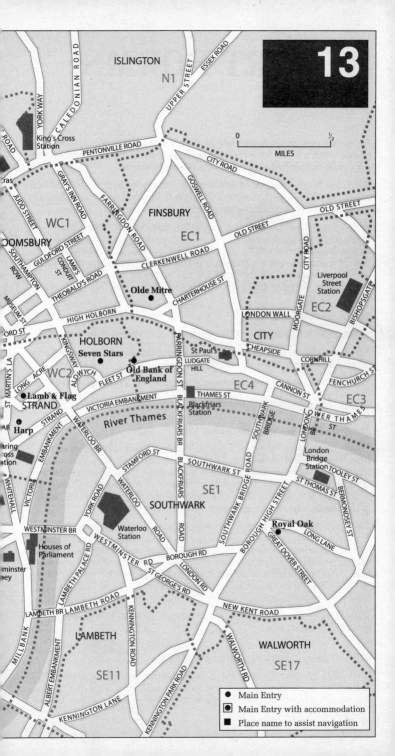

REPORT FORMS

We would very much appreciate hearing about your visits to pubs in this *Guide*, whether you have found them as described and recommend them for continued inclusion or noticed a fall in standards.

We'd also be glad to hear of any new pubs that you think we should know about. Readers' reports are very valuable to us, and sometimes pubs are dropped simply because we have had no up-to-date news on them.

You can use the tear-out forms on the following pages, email us at feedback@goodguides.co.uk or send us comments via our website (www.thegoodpubguide.co.uk) or app. We include two types of forms: one for you to simply list pubs you have visited and confirm that our review is accurate, and the other for you to give us more detailed information on individual pubs. If you would like more forms, please write to us at:

The Good Pub Guide

FREEPOST RTJR-ZCYZ-RJZT, Perrymans Lane, Etchingham TN19 7DN

Though we try to answer all letters, please understand if there's a delay (particularly in summer, our busiest period).

We'll assume we can print your name or initials as a recommender unless you tell us otherwise.

MAIN ENTRY OR 'ALSO WORTH A VISIT'?

Please try to gauge whether a pub should be a Main Entry or go in the Also Worth a Visit section (and tick the relevant box). Main Entries need to have qualities that would make it worth other readers' while to travel some distance to them. If a pub is an entirely new recommendation, the Also Worth a Visit section may be the best place for it to start its career in the *Guide* – to encourage other readers to report on it.

The more detail you can put into your description of a pub, the better. Any information on how good the landlord or landlady is, what it looks like inside, what you like about the atmosphere and character, the quality and type of food, which real ales are available and whether they're well kept, whether bedrooms are available, and how big/attractive the garden is. Other helpful information includes prices for food and bedrooms, food service and opening hours, and if children or dogs are welcome.

If the food or accommodation is outstanding, tick the FOOD AWARD or the STAY AWARD box.

If you're in a position to gauge a pub's suitability or otherwise for disabled people, do please tell us about that.

If you can, give the full address or directions for any pub not currently in the *Guide* – most of all, please give us its postcode. If we can't find a pub's postcode, we don't include it in the *Guide*.

I have been to the following pubs in *The Good Pub Guide 2017* in the last few months, found them as described, and confirm that they deserve continued inclusion:

continued overleaf

PLEASE GIVE YOUR NAME AND ADDRESS ON THE BACK OF THIS FORM

Pubs visited continued..........

By returning this form, you consent to the collection, recording and use of the information you submit, by The Random House Group Ltd. Any personal details which you provide from which we can identify you are held and processed in accordance with the Data Protection Act 1998 and will not be passed on to any third parties. The Random House Group Ltd may wish to send you further information on their associated products.

Please tick box if you do not wish to receive any such information. □

Your own name and address *(block capitals please)*

....

....

....

Postcode..

In returning this form I confirm my agreement that the information I provide may be used by The Random House Group Ltd, its assignees and/or licensees in any media or medium whatsoever.

Please return to

The Good Pub Guide
FREEPOST RTJR-ZCYZ-RJZT,
Perrymans Lane,
Etchingham
TN19 7DN

IF YOU PREFER, YOU CAN SEND
US REPORTS BY EMAIL:

feedback@goodguides.com

I have been to the following pubs in *The Good Pub Guide 2017* **in the last few months, found them as described, and confirm that they deserve continued inclusion:**

continued overleaf

PLEASE GIVE YOUR NAME AND ADDRESS ON THE BACK OF THIS FORM

Pubs visited continued..........

Your own name and address *(block capitals please)*

....

....

....

Postcode...

Please return to

The Good Pub Guide
FREEPOST RTJR-ZCYZ-RJZT,
Perrymans Lane,
Etchingham
TN19 7DN

IF YOU PREFER, YOU CAN SEND US REPORTS BY EMAIL:
feedback@goodguides.com

I have been to the following pubs in *The Good Pub Guide 2017* in the last few months, found them as described, and confirm that they deserve continued inclusion:

continued overleaf

PLEASE GIVE YOUR NAME AND ADDRESS ON THE BACK OF THIS FORM

Pubs visited continued..........

By returning this form, you consent to the collection, recording and use of the information you submit, by The Random House Group Ltd. Any personal details which you provide from which we can identify you are held and processed in accordance with the Data Protection Act 1998 and will not be passed on to any third parties. The Random House Group Ltd may wish to send you further information on their associated products.

Please tick box if you do not wish to receive any such information. ☐

Your own name and address *(block capitals please)*

....

....

....

Postcode...

In returning this form I confirm my agreement that the information I provide may be used by The Random House Group Ltd, its assignees and/or licensees in any media or medium whatsoever.

Please return to

The Good Pub Guide
FREEPOST RTJR-ZCYZ-RJZT,
Perrymans Lane,
Etchingham
TN19 7DN

IF YOU PREFER, YOU CAN SEND
US REPORTS BY EMAIL:

feedback@goodguides.com

I have been to the following pubs in *The Good Pub Guide 2017* **in the last few months, found them as described, and confirm that they deserve continued inclusion:**

continued overleaf

PLEASE GIVE YOUR NAME AND ADDRESS ON THE BACK OF THIS FORM

Pubs visited continued..........

Your own name and address *(block capitals please)*

....

....

....

Postcode...

Please return to

The Good Pub Guide
FREEPOST RTJR-ZCYZ-RJZT,
Perrymans Lane,
Etchingham
TN19 7DN

IF YOU PREFER, YOU CAN SEND
US REPORTS BY EMAIL:

feedback@goodguides.com

I have been to the following pubs in *The Good Pub Guide 2017* **in the last few months, found them as described, and confirm that they deserve continued inclusion:**

continued overleaf

PLEASE GIVE YOUR NAME AND ADDRESS ON THE BACK OF THIS FORM

Pubs visited continued..........

Your own name and address *(block capitals please)*

....

....

....

Postcode...

Please return to

The Good Pub Guide
FREEPOST RTJR-ZCYZ-RJZT,
Perrymans Lane,
Etchingham
TN19 7DN

IF YOU PREFER, YOU CAN SEND US REPORTS BY EMAIL:
feedback@goodguides.com

I have been to the following pubs in *The Good Pub Guide 2017* in the last few months, found them as described, and confirm that they deserve continued inclusion:

continued overleaf

PLEASE GIVE YOUR NAME AND ADDRESS ON THE BACK OF THIS FORM

Pubs visited continued..........

By returning this form, you consent to the collection, recording and use of the information you submit, by The Random House Group Ltd. Any personal details which you provide from which we can identify you are held and processed in accordance with the Data Protection Act 1998 and will not be passed on to any third parties. The Random House Group Ltd may wish to send you further information on their associated products.

Please tick box if you do not wish to receive any such information. ☐

Your own name and address *(block capitals please)*

....

....

....

Postcode..

In returning this form I confirm my agreement that the information I provide may be used by The Random House Group Ltd, its assignees and/or licensees in any media or medium whatsoever.

Please return to

The Good Pub Guide
FREEPOST RTJR-ZCYZ-RJZT,
Perrymans Lane,
Etchingham
TN19 7DN

IF YOU PREFER, YOU CAN SEND
US REPORTS BY EMAIL:

feedback@goodguides.com

I have been to the following pubs in *The Good Pub Guide 2017* in the last few months, found them as described, and confirm that they deserve continued inclusion:

continued overleaf

PLEASE GIVE YOUR NAME AND ADDRESS ON THE BACK OF THIS FORM

Pubs visited continued..........

_____

Your own name and address *(block capitals please)*

....

....

....

Postcode...

Please return to

The Good Pub Guide
FREEPOST RTJR-ZCYZ-RJZT,
Perrymans Lane,
Etchingham
TN19 7DN

IF YOU PREFER, YOU CAN SEND
US REPORTS BY EMAIL:

feedback@goodguides.com

I have been to the following pubs in *The Good Pub Guide 2017* in the last few months, found them as described, and confirm that they deserve continued inclusion:

continued overleaf

PLEASE GIVE YOUR NAME AND ADDRESS ON THE BACK OF THIS FORM

Pubs visited continued..........

Your own name and address *(block capitals please)*

....

....

....

Postcode..

Please return to

The Good Pub Guide
FREEPOST RTJR-ZCYZ-RJZT,
Perrymans Lane,
Etchingham
TN19 7DN

IF YOU PREFER, YOU CAN SEND
US REPORTS BY EMAIL:

feedback@goodguides.com

I have been to the following pubs in *The Good Pub Guide 2017* in the last few months, found them as described, and confirm that they deserve continued inclusion:

continued overleaf

PLEASE GIVE YOUR NAME AND ADDRESS ON THE BACK OF THIS FORM

Pubs visited continued..........

By returning this form, you consent to the collection, recording and use of the information you submit, by The Random House Group Ltd. Any personal details which you provide from which we can identify you are held and processed in accordance with the Data Protection Act 1998 and will not be passed on to any third parties. The Random House Group Ltd may wish to send you further information on their associated products.

Please tick box if you do not wish to receive any such information. ☐

Your own name and address *(block capitals please)*

....

....

....

Postcode..

In returning this form I confirm my agreement that the information I provide may be used by The Random House Group Ltd, its assignees and/or licensees in any media or medium whatsoever.

Please return to

The Good Pub Guide
FREEPOST RTJR-ZCYZ-RJZT,
Perrymans Lane,
Etchingham
TN19 7DN

IF YOU PREFER, YOU CAN SEND
US REPORTS BY EMAIL:

feedback@goodguides.com

Report on (pub's name)

....

Pub's address

....

☐ YES MAIN ENTRY   ☐ YES WORTH A VISIT   ☐ NO don't include

Please tick one of these boxes to show your verdict, and give reasons, descriptive comments, prices and the date of your visit

☐ Deserves **FOOD Award**   ☐ Deserves **STAY Award**   2017: 1

PLEASE GIVE YOUR NAME AND ADDRESS ON THE BACK OF THIS FORM

✂ ....

Report on (pub's name)

....

Pub's address

....

☐ YES MAIN ENTRY   ☐ YES WORTH A VISIT   ☐ NO don't include

Please tick one of these boxes to show your verdict, and give reasons, descriptive comments, prices and the date of your visit

☐ Deserves **FOOD Award**   ☐ Deserves **STAY Award**   2017: 2

PLEASE GIVE YOUR NAME AND ADDRESS ON THE BACK OF THIS FORM

Your own name and address *(block capitals please)*

In returning this form I confirm my agreement that the information I provide may be used by The Random House Group Ltd, its assignees and/or licensees in any media or medium whatsoever.

DO NOT USE THIS SIDE OF THE PAGE FOR WRITING ABOUT PUBS

✂ ....

Your own name and address *(block capitals please)*

In returning this form I confirm my agreement that the information I provide may be used by The Random House Group Ltd, its assignees and/or licensees in any media or medium whatsoever.

DO NOT USE THIS SIDE OF THE PAGE FOR WRITING ABOUT PUBS

Report on (pub's name)

....

Pub's address

....

☐ YES MAIN ENTRY ☐ YES WORTH A VISIT ☐ NO don't include

Please tick one of these boxes to show your verdict, and give reasons, descriptive comments, prices and the date of your visit

☐ Deserves **FOOD Award** ☐ Deserves **STAY Award** 2017: 3

PLEASE GIVE YOUR NAME AND ADDRESS ON THE BACK OF THIS FORM

✂ ....

Report on (pub's name)

....

Pub's address

....

☐ YES MAIN ENTRY ☐ YES WORTH A VISIT ☐ NO don't include

Please tick one of these boxes to show your verdict, and give reasons, descriptive comments, prices and the date of your visit

☐ Deserves **FOOD Award** ☐ Deserves **STAY Award** 2017: 4

PLEASE GIVE YOUR NAME AND ADDRESS ON THE BACK OF THIS FORM

Your own name and address *(block capitals please)*

In returning this form I confirm my agreement that the information I provide may be used by The Random House Group Ltd, its assignees and/or licensees in any media or medium whatsoever.

DO NOT USE THIS SIDE OF THE PAGE FOR WRITING ABOUT PUBS

By returning this form, you consent to the collection, recording and use of the information you submit, by The Random House Group Ltd. Any personal details which you provide from which we can identify you are held and processed in accordance with the Data Protection Act 1998 and will not be passed on to any third parties. The Random House Group Ltd may wish to send you further information on their associated products. Please tick box if you do not wish to receive any such information.

✂ ....

Your own name and address *(block capitals please)*

In returning this form I confirm my agreement that the information I provide may be used by The Random House Group Ltd, its assignees and/or licensees in any media or medium whatsoever.

DO NOT USE THIS SIDE OF THE PAGE FOR WRITING ABOUT PUBS

By returning this form, you consent to the collection, recording and use of the information you submit, by The Random House Group Ltd. Any personal details which you provide from which we can identify you are held and processed in accordance with the Data Protection Act 1998 and will not be passed on to any third parties. The Random House Group Ltd may wish to send you further information on their associated products. Please tick box if you do not wish to receive any such information.

Report on

(pub's name)

....

Pub's address

....

☐ YES MAIN ENTRY   ☐ YES WORTH A VISIT   ☐ NO don't include

Please tick one of these boxes to show your verdict, and give reasons,
descriptive comments, prices and the date of your visit

☐ Deserves **FOOD Award**   ☐ Deserves **STAY Award**   2017: 5

PLEASE GIVE YOUR NAME AND ADDRESS ON THE BACK OF THIS FORM

✂ ....

Report on

(pub's name)

....

Pub's address

....

☐ YES MAIN ENTRY   ☐ YES WORTH A VISIT   ☐ NO don't include

Please tick one of these boxes to show your verdict, and give reasons,
descriptive comments, prices and the date of your visit

☐ Deserves **FOOD Award**   ☐ Deserves **STAY Award**   2017: 6

PLEASE GIVE YOUR NAME AND ADDRESS ON THE BACK OF THIS FORM

Your own name and address *(block capitals please)*

In returning this form I confirm my agreement that the information I provide may be used by The Random House Group Ltd, its assignees and/or licensees in any media or medium whatsoever.

DO NOT USE THIS SIDE OF THE PAGE FOR WRITING ABOUT PUBS

By returning this form, you consent to the collection, recording and use of the information you submit, by The Random House Group Ltd. Any personal details which you provide from which we can identify you are held and processed in accordance with the Data Protection Act 1998 and will not be passed on to any third parties. The Random House Group Ltd may wish to send you further information on their associated products. Please tick box if you do not wish to receive any such information.

✂ ....

Your own name and address *(block capitals please)*

In returning this form I confirm my agreement that the information I provide may be used by The Random House Group Ltd, its assignees and/or licensees in any media or medium whatsoever.

DO NOT USE THIS SIDE OF THE PAGE FOR WRITING ABOUT PUBS

By returning this form, you consent to the collection, recording and use of the information you submit, by The Random House Group Ltd. Any personal details which you provide from which we can identify you are held and processed in accordance with the Data Protection Act 1998 and will not be passed on to any third parties. The Random House Group Ltd may wish to send you further information on their associated products. Please tick box if you do not wish to receive any such information.

Report on   (pub's name)

....

Pub's address

....

☐ YES MAIN ENTRY   ☐ YES WORTH A VISIT   ☐ NO don't include

Please tick one of these boxes to show your verdict, and give reasons,
descriptive comments, prices and the date of your visit

☐ Deserves **FOOD Award**   ☐ Deserves **STAY Award**   2017: 7

PLEASE GIVE YOUR NAME AND ADDRESS ON THE BACK OF THIS FORM

✂ ....

Report on   (pub's name)

....

Pub's address

....

☐ YES MAIN ENTRY   ☐ YES WORTH A VISIT   ☐ NO don't include

Please tick one of these boxes to show your verdict, and give reasons,
descriptive comments, prices and the date of your visit

☐ Deserves **FOOD Award**   ☐ Deserves **STAY Award**   2017: 8

PLEASE GIVE YOUR NAME AND ADDRESS ON THE BACK OF THIS FORM

Your own name and address *(block capitals please)*

In returning this form I confirm my agreement that the information I provide may be used by The Random House Group Ltd, its assignees and/or licensees in any media or medium whatsoever.

DO NOT USE THIS SIDE OF THE PAGE FOR WRITING ABOUT PUBS

✂ ....

Your own name and address *(block capitals please)*

In returning this form I confirm my agreement that the information I provide may be used by The Random House Group Ltd, its assignees and/or licensees in any media or medium whatsoever.

DO NOT USE THIS SIDE OF THE PAGE FOR WRITING ABOUT PUBS

Report on (pub's name)

....

Pub's address

....

☐ YES MAIN ENTRY   ☐ YES WORTH A VISIT   ☐ NO don't include

Please tick one of these boxes to show your verdict, and give reasons, descriptive comments, prices and the date of your visit

☐ Deserves **FOOD Award**   ☐ Deserves **STAY Award**   2017: 9

PLEASE GIVE YOUR NAME AND ADDRESS ON THE BACK OF THIS FORM

✂ ....

Report on (pub's name)

....

Pub's address

....

☐ YES MAIN ENTRY   ☐ YES WORTH A VISIT   ☐ NO don't include

Please tick one of these boxes to show your verdict, and give reasons, descriptive comments, prices and the date of your visit

☐ Deserves **FOOD Award**   ☐ Deserves **STAY Award**   2017: 10

PLEASE GIVE YOUR NAME AND ADDRESS ON THE BACK OF THIS FORM

Your own name and address *(block capitals please)*

In returning this form I confirm my agreement that the information I provide may be used by The Random House Group Ltd, its assignees and/or licensees in any media or medium whatsoever.

DO NOT USE THIS SIDE OF THE PAGE FOR WRITING ABOUT PUBS

By returning this form, you consent to the collection, recording and use of the information you submit, by The Random House Group Ltd. Any personal details which you provide from which we can identify you are held and processed in accordance with the Data Protection Act 1998 and will not be passed on to any third parties. The Random House Group Ltd may wish to send you further information on their associated products. Please tick box if you do not wish to receive any such information.

✂ ....

Your own name and address *(block capitals please)*

In returning this form I confirm my agreement that the information I provide may be used by The Random House Group Ltd, its assignees and/or licensees in any media or medium whatsoever.

DO NOT USE THIS SIDE OF THE PAGE FOR WRITING ABOUT PUBS

By returning this form, you consent to the collection, recording and use of the information you submit, by The Random House Group Ltd. Any personal details which you provide from which we can identify you are held and processed in accordance with the Data Protection Act 1998 and will not be passed on to any third parties. The Random House Group Ltd may wish to send you further information on their associated products. Please tick box if you do not wish to receive any such information.

Report on (pub's name)

....

Pub's address

....

☐ YES MAIN ENTRY   ☐ YES WORTH A VISIT   ☐ NO don't include

Please tick one of these boxes to show your verdict, and give reasons,
descriptive comments, prices and the date of your visit

☐ Deserves **FOOD Award**   ☐ Deserves **STAY Award**   2017: 11

PLEASE GIVE YOUR NAME AND ADDRESS ON THE BACK OF THIS FORM

✂ ....

Report on (pub's name)

....

Pub's address

....

☐ YES MAIN ENTRY   ☐ YES WORTH A VISIT   ☐ NO don't include

Please tick one of these boxes to show your verdict, and give reasons,
descriptive comments, prices and the date of your visit

☐ Deserves **FOOD Award**   ☐ Deserves **STAY Award**   2017: 12

PLEASE GIVE YOUR NAME AND ADDRESS ON THE BACK OF THIS FORM

Your own name and address *(block capitals please)*

In returning this form I confirm my agreement that the information I provide may be used by The Random House Group Ltd, its assignees and/or licensees in any media or medium whatsoever.

DO NOT USE THIS SIDE OF THE PAGE FOR WRITING ABOUT PUBS

By returning this form, you consent to the collection, recording and use of the information you submit, by The Random House Group Ltd. Any personal details which you provide from which we can identify you are held and processed in accordance with the Data Protection Act 1998 and will not be passed on to any third parties. The Random House Group Ltd may wish to send you further information on their associated products. Please tick box if you do not wish to receive any such information. □

✂ ....

Your own name and address *(block capitals please)*

In returning this form I confirm my agreement that the information I provide may be used by The Random House Group Ltd, its assignees and/or licensees in any media or medium whatsoever.

DO NOT USE THIS SIDE OF THE PAGE FOR WRITING ABOUT PUBS

By returning this form, you consent to the collection, recording and use of the information you submit, by The Random House Group Ltd. Any personal details which you provide from which we can identify you are held and processed in accordance with the Data Protection Act 1998 and will not be passed on to any third parties. The Random House Group Ltd may wish to send you further information on their associated products. Please tick box if you do not wish to receive any such information. □

Report on (pub's name)

....

Pub's address

....

☐ YES MAIN ENTRY ☐ YES WORTH A VISIT ☐ NO don't include

Please tick one of these boxes to show your verdict, and give reasons,
descriptive comments, prices and the date of your visit

☐ Deserves **FOOD Award** ☐ Deserves **STAY Award** 2017: 13

PLEASE GIVE YOUR NAME AND ADDRESS ON THE BACK OF THIS FORM

✂ ....

Report on (pub's name)

....

Pub's address

....

☐ YES MAIN ENTRY ☐ YES WORTH A VISIT ☐ NO don't include

Please tick one of these boxes to show your verdict, and give reasons,
descriptive comments, prices and the date of your visit

☐ Deserves **FOOD Award** ☐ Deserves **STAY Award** 2017: 14

PLEASE GIVE YOUR NAME AND ADDRESS ON THE BACK OF THIS FORM

Your own name and address *(block capitals please)*

In returning this form I confirm my agreement that the information I provide may be used by The Random House Group Ltd, its assignees and/or licensees in any media or medium whatsoever.

DO NOT USE THIS SIDE OF THE PAGE FOR WRITING ABOUT PUBS

✂ ....

Your own name and address *(block capitals please)*

In returning this form I confirm my agreement that the information I provide may be used by The Random House Group Ltd, its assignees and/or licensees in any media or medium whatsoever.

DO NOT USE THIS SIDE OF THE PAGE FOR WRITING ABOUT PUBS

Report on (pub's name)

....

Pub's address

....

☐ YES MAIN ENTRY   ☐ YES WORTH A VISIT   ☐ NO don't include

Please tick one of these boxes to show your verdict, and give reasons, descriptive comments, prices and the date of your visit

☐ Deserves **FOOD Award**   ☐ Deserves **STAY Award**   2017: 15

PLEASE GIVE YOUR NAME AND ADDRESS ON THE BACK OF THIS FORM

✂ ....

Report on (pub's name)

....

Pub's address

....

☐ YES MAIN ENTRY   ☐ YES WORTH A VISIT   ☐ NO don't include

Please tick one of these boxes to show your verdict, and give reasons, descriptive comments, prices and the date of your visit

☐ Deserves **FOOD Award**   ☐ Deserves **STAY Award**   2017: 16

PLEASE GIVE YOUR NAME AND ADDRESS ON THE BACK OF THIS FORM

Your own name and address *(block capitals please)*

In returning this form I confirm my agreement that the information I provide may be used by The Random House Group Ltd, its assignees and/or licensees in any media or medium whatsoever.

DO NOT USE THIS SIDE OF THE PAGE FOR WRITING ABOUT PUBS

✂ ....

Your own name and address *(block capitals please)*

In returning this form I confirm my agreement that the information I provide may be used by The Random House Group Ltd, its assignees and/or licensees in any media or medium whatsoever.

DO NOT USE THIS SIDE OF THE PAGE FOR WRITING ABOUT PUBS

By returning this form, you consent to the collection, recording and use of the information you submit, by The Random House Group Ltd. Any personal details which you provide from which we can identify you are held and processed in accordance with the Data Protection Act 1998 and will not be passed on to any third parties. The Random House Group Ltd may wish to send you further information on their associated products. Please tick box if you do not wish to receive any such information.